- "It took several dozen rejections to realize just how valuable writer's guidelines and careful study of editorial direction in market guides could be. When I finally sold that first piece, it was because I successfully married the work to the right publication and editor."
  —Kelly Milner Halls, nonfiction children's writer

- "I always supply sidebars and other little extras to complement the piece, and editors really like that. If you're going to deliver a product, that means you provide whatever is necessary for the piece, be it photos, sidebars, graphs or noteworthy quotes."
  —John Woram, monthly columnist and author of three books

- "I think it's best to become an expert in an area. Then it's just a matter of looking at a subject from different angles and finding the right publications. Angles are critical."
  —Karen Berger, contributing editor and author of two books

- "The most memorable aspects of writing magazine articles are all the people you talk to, all the research you put into a project and what you learn from it. It's great to get paid and recognized while at the same time you're growing and learning." **—Barry DiGregorio, entertainment and science writer**

There are many paths to becoming a professional writer. In *Writer to Writer: Emergency Roadside Service*, four writers share what they have learned on their road to success.

1997
WRITER'S
MARKET

WHERE & HOW TO SELL WHAT YOU WRITE

EDITOR
KIRSTEN C. HOLM

ASSISTANT EDITOR
DON PRUES

WRITER'S DIGEST BOOKS
CINCINNATI, OHIO

Managing Editor, Market Books Department: Constance J. Achabal
Supervisory Editor: Mark Garvey
Production Editor: Richard D. Muskopf

This edition of Writer's Market *features a "self-jacket" that eliminates the need for a separate dust jacket. It provides sturdy protection for your book while it saves paper, trees and energy.*

Library of Congress Catalog Number 31-20772
International Standard Serial Number 0084-2729
International Standard Book Number 0-89879-742-X

Cover illustration: Celia Johnson
U.S. Postage by the Page by Carolyn Lieberg
Canadian Postage by the Page by Barbara Murrin

Attention Booksellers: This is an annual directory of F&W Publications. Return deadline for this edition is December 31, 1997.

Contents

From Stickball to Screen: Using Networking and Ingenuity to Get to the Front of the Line, by Alan Steinberg **63**

A successful author traces his path from unpublished writer to fame and fortune in magazines, books and movies, and advises how you can cross formats and genres yourself.

Get Connected: An Overview of the Internet, by Richard Muskopf **66**

The Internet requires some specific equipment before you can access the exciting resources available on the World Wide Web. This article offers guidelines on what you need and where to get it to go online.

Important Listing Information and Key to Symbols and Abbreviations 70

The Markets

Book Publishers 71

From Abbott, Langer to Zondervan, hundreds of places to sell your book ideas. The introduction to this section helps you refine your approach to publishers and features an interview with Dan Simon, founder of Seven Stories Press, discussing the role of independent presses and the need for new voices in publishing on page 73.

Canadian and International Book Publishers 239

The introduction to this section covers how to submit your work to international markets.

Small Presses 263

Companies publishing three or fewer books per year are listed here. Small presses often have narrowly tailored subjects—be sure to read the listing closely.

Book Producers 285

Book producers, or packagers as they are sometimes called, assemble the elements of books (writers, editors, designers and illustrators) for publishers.

Consumer Magazines 293

This section offers plentiful opportunities for writers with hundreds of listings for magazines on nearly every subject under the sun. The introudction offers tips on approaching consumer magazine markets and includes an interview with freelance writer Sherry Von Ohlsen-Karasik, on page 295, sharing tips on building a freelance career.

Trade, Technical and Professional Journals 676

*Magazines listed in this section serve a wide variety of trades and professions. The
introduction tells how to break in and establish yourself in the trades, while electronics and
entertainment freelancer **Rebecca Day** discusses the benefits of trade magazine-writing on
page 677.*

Scriptwriting 807

*Markets for film and television scripts and stageplays are listed here. An interview with **Mike Sikowitz**, senior writer for "Friends," on **page 840**, offers insights on breaking into this specialized field.*

Syndicates 853

Newspaper syndicates distribute writers' works around the nation and the world. The introduction offers advice for breaking into this market.

Greeting Cards & Gift Ideas 863

Greeting card and gift markets provide outlets for a wide variety of writing styles. The introduction to this section tells you how to approach these companies professionally.

Contests and Awards 872

*Contests and awards offer many opportunities for writers, and can launch a successful writing career. **Sarah Heekin Redfield** discusses the support the Heekin Foundation offers to writers and the benefits of entering contests on **page 873**.*

Resources

Publications of Interest 932

Organizations of Interest 934

Websites of Interest 936

U.S. Postage by the Page 938

Canadian Postage by the Page 940

Glossary 942

Book Publishers Subject Index 946

General Index 971

From the Editors

At the risk of sounding too New Age-y, I've recently discovered the concept of *hormé*, the life force that impels us from one phase in life to another. Watching my little girl go from a blanketed bundle to a cooing, kicking baby eager to play and ready for teeth, I wonder what makes her want to sit up and then stand. Why does she want to change? How does she know the way from one stage to another?

Every one of us has our own hormé, that makes us want to stretch and grow. Evolving is not always easy, but we pursue it without necessarily knowing why we want what we want. You may know that you love to write, but why? What inside you makes you write? What pushes you to continue to write and revise, and then move on to write some more?

Some of you are unpublished and ready to make the transition to published writer. Others have had some success in placing work and want to discover new audiences. Others have published in one genre or format and are ready to advance into others. *Writer's Market* can not tell you why you want to do these things. But it can help you discover how.

Every writer in this book has made the leap from unpublished to published, but in his individual way or for her idiosyncratic reasons. Ernest Hill was impelled to write and self-publish a novel that communicates from one race to another. Alan Duncan Ross abandoned a medical career for the emotional honesty writing brings to his life. For Sherry Von Ohlsen-Karasik, writing was her "home," and offered opportunity to make a difference, while John Woram's career came about more from a need for his technical knowledge than a desire to be a writer.

In Writer to Writer: Emergency Roadside Service, you'll meet four writers who, using different roadmaps, found their way to successful freelance careers. In How Much Should I Charge?, our own Robin Gee, former editor of *Novel & Short Story Writer's Market* who has made the leap to a freelance career herself, reports back with insider information you can use about rates and fees for various writing services. In From Stickball to the Screen, writer Alan Steinberg recounts how he got started—and then kept going—from magazines to books to movies, with advice on how to make the transitions yourself.

Each editor interviewed offers insights into what spurs a writer on to success. Dan Simon, of Seven Stories Press, counsels writers to concentrate first and foremost on finding their subject and voice, and discussees the importance of independent presses in developing and publishing new writers. Celia Meadow, of *Troika* magazine, discusses how establishing a good working relationships can lead to multiple opportunities for writers. Stu Slayen, of the Canadian *What! A Magazine*, advises writers on locating the right tone in addressing teen markets. And Deborah Forte, senior vice president of Scholastic, Inc., presents her views on the need to take creative risks to realize the opportunities in multiple media publishing.

Even *Writer's Market* itself has a hormé. Changes this year range from the visual to the virtual. You'll notice a lighter, fresher look as you skim through the pages. To help you maximize your earnings, we've broken out information on selling article reprints with a separate heading in the magazine sections. Website addresses are included throughout the book, allowing immediate access to additional information directly from a market, from book publishers' catalogues, to online magazines, to contest entry forms and guidelines. A page of Websites of Interest is new to the Resources section.

In keeping with our mission to provide you information on "where and how to sell what you write," we have eliminated the section of subsidy/royalty book publishers, and only present those publishers that will pay you, not vice versa. If a publisher listed here asks you to pay all or a portion of the publishing costs, please let us know.

Perhaps the biggest change this year is an exciting metamorphosis. After 75 years of continued growth in size and scope, what started out as a brief, pamphlet-sized guide is going digital. As a CD-ROM, *Writer's Market—The Electronic Edition* represents a new and exciting phase in this long-lived book's development.

Whichever form of *Writer's Market* you are using to assist your writing hormé, we wish you the best of luck. The coming year will see many of you move from one phase to another in your development as writers. We hope to see you again next year—on the same page, but not in the same place.

Kirsten Campbell Holm

Kirsten Campbell Holm
Editor

Don Prues

Don Prues
Assistant Editor

How to Get the Most Out of *Writer's Market*

Writer's Market is here to help you decide where and how to submit your writing to appropriate markets. Each listing contains information about the editorial focus of the market, how they prefer material to be submitted, payment information and other helpful tips.

Where to Start

A quick look at the Table of Contents will familiarize you with the arrangement of *Writer's Market*. The three largest sections of the book are the market listings of Book Publishers; Consumer Magazines; and Trade, Technical and Professional Journals. You will also find sections for scriptwriting markets, syndicates, greeting card publishers and contests and awards. Be sure to read the introduction for each section before you turn to the listings. The section introductions contain specific information about trends, submission methods and other helpful resources for the material included in that section.

Narrowing Your Search

After you've identified the market categories you're interested in, you can begin researching specific markets within each section.

Publishers listed in the Book Publishers section are categorized, in the Book Publishers Subject Index, according to types of books they are interested in. If, for example, you plan to write a book on a religious topic, simply turn to the Book Publishers Subject Index and look under the Religion subhead in Nonfiction for the names and page numbers of companies that publish such books.

Consumer Magazines and Trade, Technical and Professional Journals are categorized by subject to make it easier for you to identify markets for your work. If you want to publish an article dealing with some aspect of retirement, you could look under the Retirement category of Consumer Magazines to find an appropriate market. You would want to keep in mind, however, that magazines in other categories might also be interested in your article (for example, women's magazines publish such material as well). Keep your antennae up while studying the markets: less obvious markets often offer the best opportunities.

Interpreting the Markets

Once you've identified companies or publications that cover the subjects you're interested in, you can begin evaluating specific listings to pinpoint the markets most receptive to your work and most beneficial to you.

In evaluating an individual listing, first check the location of the company, the types of material it is interested in seeing, submission requirements, and rights and payment policies. Depending upon your personal concerns, any of these items could be a deciding factor as you determine which markets you plan to approach. Many listings also include a reporting time, which lets you know how long it will typically take for the publisher to respond to your initial query or submission. (We suggest that you allow an additional month for a response, just in case your submission is under further review or the publisher is backlogged.)

Check the Glossary at the back of the book for unfamiliar words. Specific symbols and abbreviations are explained in the table on page 70. The most important abbreviation is SASE—self-addressed, stamped envelope. Always enclose one when you send unsolicited queries, proposals or manuscripts. This requirement is not included in most of the individual market listings because it is a "given" that you must follow if you expect to receive a reply.

A careful reading of the listings will reveal many editors are very specific about their needs. Your chances of success increase if you follow directions to the letter. Often companies do not accept unsolicited manuscripts and return them unread. Read each listing closely, heed the tips given, and follow the instructions. Work presented professionally will normally be given more serious consideration.

Whenever possible, obtain writer's guidelines before submitting material. You can usually obtain them by sending a SASE to the address in the listing. You should also familiarize yourself with the company's publications. Many of the listings contain instructions on how to obtain sample copies, catalogs or market lists. The more research you do upfront, the better your chances of acceptance, publication and payment.

Additional Help

This year's book contains articles on the Internet, current trends in book and magazine publishing and much more. "Insider Reports"—interviews with writers, editors and publishers—offer advice and an inside look at publishing. Some listings contain editorial comments, indicated by a bullet (●), that provide additional information discovered during our compilation of this year's *Writer's Market*. World Wide Websites have been included in many markets. A Websites of Interest page in the Resources section points writers in the direction of writing resources on the Web. A new "Reprints" heading provides information on approaching markets accepting previously published submissions.

Minding the Details offers valuable information about rights, taxes and other practical matters. New or unpublished writers should also read Before Your First Sale. There is also a helpful section titled How Much Should I Charge? that offers guidance for setting your freelance writing fees.

Getting Published

Before Your First Sale

Many writers new to the craft feel that achieving publication—and getting paid for their work—is an accomplishment so shrouded in mystery and magic that there can be little hope it will ever happen to *them*. Of course, that's nonsense. All writers were newcomers once. Getting paid for your writing is not a matter of insider information or being handed the one "key" to success. There's not even a secret handshake.

Making money from your writing will require three things of you:

- Good writing;
- Knowledge of writing markets (magazines and book publishers) and how to approach them professionally;
- Persistence.

Good writing without marketing know-how and persistence might be art, but who's going to know if it never sells? A knowledge of markets without writing ability or persistence is pointless. And persistence without talent and at least a hint of professionalism is simply irksome. But a writer who can combine the above-mentioned virtues stands a good chance of not only selling a piece occasionally, but enjoying a long and successful writing career.

You may think a previously unpublished writer has a difficult time breaking into the field. As with any profession, experience is valued, but that doesn't mean publishers are closed to new writers. While it is true some editors prefer working with established writers, most are open to professional submissions and good ideas from any writer, and quite a few magazine editors like to feature different styles and voices.

In nonfiction book publishing, experience in writing or in a particular subject area is valued by editors as an indicator of the author's ability and expertise in the subject. As with magazines, the idea is paramount, and new authors break in every year with good, timely ideas.

As you work in the writing field, you may read articles or talk to writers and editors who give conflicting advice. There are some norms in the business, but they are few. You'll probably hear as many different routes to publication as writers you talk to.

The following information on submissions has worked for many writers, but it's not the *only* method you can follow. It's easy to get wrapped up in the specifics of submitting (should my name go at the top left or right of the manuscript?) and fail to consider weightier matters (is this idea appropriate for this market?). Let common sense and courtesy be your guides as you work with editors, and eventually you'll develop your own most effective submission methods.

ETING YOUR IDEAS

often think of an interesting story, complete the manuscript and then begin for a suitable publisher or magazine. While this approach is common for poetry and screenwriting, it reduces your chances of success in many other writing areas. Instead, try choosing categories that interest you and study those sections in *Writer's Market*. Select several listings that you consider good prospects for your type of writing. Sometimes the individual listings will even help you generate ideas.

Next, make a list of the potential markets for each idea. Make the initial contact with markets using the method stated in the market listings. If you exhaust your list of possibilities, don't give up. Reevaluate the idea, revise it or try another angle. Continue developing ideas and approaching markets with them. Identify and rank potential markets for an idea and continue the process.

As you submit to the various periodicals listed in *Writer's Market*, it's important to remember that every magazine is published with a particular slant and audience in mind. Probably the number one complaint we hear from editors is that writers often send material and ideas that are completely wrong for their magazines. The first mark of professionalism is to know your market well. That knowledge starts here in *Writer's Market*, but you should also search out back issues of the magazines you wish to write for and learn what specific subjects they have published in past issues and how those subjects have been handled.

Prepare for rejection and the sometimes lengthy wait. When a submission is returned, check your file folder of potential markets for that idea. Cross off the market that rejected the idea and immediately mail an appropriate submission to the next market on your list. If the editor has given you suggestions or reasons as to why the manuscript was not accepted, you might want to incorporate these when revising your manuscript.

About rejection. Rejection is a way of life in the publishing world. It's inevitable in a business that deals with such an overwhelming number of applicants for such a limited number of positions. Anyone who has published has lived through many rejections, and writers with thin skin are at a distinct disadvantage. The key to surviving rejection is to remember that it is not a personal attack—it's merely a judgment about the appropriateness of your work for that particular market at that particular time. Writers who let rejection dissuade them from pursuing their dream or who react to each editor's "No" with indignation or fury do themselves a disservice. Writers who let rejection stop them do not publish. Resign yourself to facing rejection now. You will live through it, and you will eventually overcome it.

QUERY AND COVER LETTERS

A query letter is a brief but detailed letter written to interest an editor in your manuscript. It is a tool for selling both nonfiction magazine articles and nonfiction books. With a magazine query you are attempting to interest an editor in buying your article for her periodical. A book query's job is to get an editor interested enough to ask you for either a full proposal or the entire manuscript. (Note: Some book editors accept proposals on first contact. Refer to individual listings for contact guidelines.) Some beginners are hesitant to query, thinking an editor can more fairly judge an idea by seeing the entire manuscript. Actually, most nonfiction editors prefer to be queried.

There is no query formula that guarantees success, but there are some points to consider when you begin. Queries should:
- Be limited to one page, single-spaced, and address the editor by name (Mr. or Ms. and the surname).
- Grab the editor's interest with a strong opening. Some magazine queries begin with a paragraph meant to approximate the lead of the intended article.

- Indicate how you intend to develop the article or book. Give the editor some idea of the work's structure and contents.
- Let the editor know if you have photos available to accompany your magazine article (never send original photos—send duplicates).
- Mention any expertise or training that qualifies you to write the article or book. If you've published before, mention it; if not, don't.
- End with a direct request to write the article (or, if you're pitching a book, ask for the go-ahead to send in a full proposal or the entire manuscript). Give the editor an idea of the expected length and delivery date of your manuscript.

For more information about writing query letters, read *How To Write Attention-Grabbing Query & Cover Letters*, by John Wood (Writer's Digest Books).

Querying for Fiction

Fiction is sometimes queried, but most fiction editors don't like to make a final decision until they see the complete manuscript. Most editors will want to see a synopsis and sample chapters for a book, or a complete short story manuscript. Consult individual listings for specific fiction guidelines. If a fiction editor does request a query, briefly describe the main theme and story line, including the conflict and resolution.

Some writers state politely in their query letters that after a specified date (slightly beyond the listed reporting time), they will assume the editor is not currently interested in their topic and will submit the query elsewhere. It's a good idea to do this only if your topic is a timely one that will suffer if not considered quickly.

A brief single-spaced cover letter enclosed with your manuscript is helpful in personalizing a submission. If you have previously queried the editor on the article or book, the cover letter should be a brief reminder, not a sales pitch. "Here is the piece on goat herding, which we discussed previously. I look forward to hearing from you at your earliest convenience."

If you are submitting to a market that considers unsolicited complete manuscripts, your cover letter should tell the editor something about your manuscript and about you—your publishing history and any particular qualifications you have for writing the enclosed manuscript.

Once your manuscript has been accepted, you may offer to get involved in the editing process, but policy on this will vary from magazine to magazine. Most magazine editors don't send galleys to authors before publication, but if they do, you should review the galleys and return them as soon as possible. Book publishers will normally involve you in rewrites whether you like it or not.

BOOK PROPOSALS

Most nonfiction books are sold by book proposal, a package of materials that details what your book is about, who its intended audience is, and how you intend to write it. Most fiction is sold either by complete manuscript, especially for first-time authors, or by two or three sample chapters. Take a look at individual listings to see what submission method editors prefer.

The nonfiction book proposal includes some combination of a cover or query letter, an overview, an outline, author's information sheet and sample chapters. Editors also want to see information about the audience for your book and about titles that compete with your proposed book.

If a listing does not specify, send as much of the following information as you can.

- The cover or query letter should be a short introduction to the material you include in the proposal.
- An overview is a brief summary of your book. For nonfiction, it should detail

INSIDER REPORT

Writing to Answer Questions and Achieve an Understanding

"If you want to succeed you will succeed, not because others will let you, but because no one can stop you," says Ernest Hill, author of *Satisfied with Nothin'*, a book which he initially self-published that was later bought by Simon & Schuster. "There is a formula for success and the main ingredients are determination, being informed, and not only hard work, but smart work."

Hill's novel follows the character of Jamie Ray Griffin, a young black man, through the desegregation of Louisiana's public schools in the '70s, a football scholarship at the University of Louisiana, a failed attempt at the NFL, and his return to his hometown. It chronicles the influences of race, community expectations and individual choice in Jamie Ray's life and its tragic end.

Ernest Hill

Photograph by Gwendolyn King Perry

Satisfied with Nothin' was written while Hill was a graduate student at Cornell and UCLA, and examines some of the same issues of achievement and overcoming obstacles he confronted in self-publishing and distributing his work. "When I left Louisiana and went off to college, I began to reflect on my family and my upbringing. I grew up in a small, poor, strictly segregated farming town. Both my parents were teachers, but my mother retired to devote her energy to raising the kids. There were nine kids in our family and all turned out to be extremely successful people. Eight went to college, three to Yale. At some point I began to wonder why we succeeded and so many others that I knew fell into the trap of drugs, violence and crime. Trying to answer that basic question provided the impetus to write the book.

"The night I completed my Masters, a friend asked what my future plans were. I told her I was entering the doctoral program at UCLA. She asked what I wanted to do after that. Without hesitation I responded 'Write novels.' She asked 'Do you need a PhD to write a novel?' That night I started writing.

"Once I began my doctorate it took a great deal of discipline and determination to find the time to write. I would get up in the morning at 5 o'clock and write until I had to go to class. After studying in the evening I would write a few more hours before going to bed. It took about 2½ years to complete the novel. When I finished, I decided to get it published. I wasn't necessarily writing for publication, but I didn't doubt that it was publishable. I submitted it to a few places, but not many. I showed it to Henry Louis Gates, Jr., my former chairperson, who asked me to send it to his agent, which I did. There was a smaller publisher in

INSIDER REPORT, *Hill*

Northern California that wanted it. I spoke with a friend about this whoı
experience and the need for more publishing houses, especially those specializing
in African-American fiction. She asked, 'Why don't you do it yourself?' I thought
about it and decided I wanted to be a part of creating something like that. Maybe
publishing three or four of my own novels might launch something.

Having decided to self-publish, Hill focused considerable energy and attention
on the project. "I guess we were raised to be very competitive, and to do your
best and the best would return." He read every book on publishing and marketing
he could find, and networked with people he had met through his educational
career. He had a small run printed and began the work of selling. "I did
everything. I used a couple of different names, but it was all Ernest Hill. It was
a tremendous amount of work. But I learned a lot about the business and in the
end it paid off."

Hill kept his eye out for opportunities to publicize his book. "I carried the book
around with me—I always had a couple in my bookbag. Being in the educational
environment, I had the opportunity to go to several national conferences and was
invited to present at a few. I sent copies to scholars who taught classes pertaining
to race, the black male or the sociology of sports. If an interesting person came
to campus, I would give them a copy. I wouldn't ask them for anything; I'm a
firm believer that at some point the work has to speak for itself."

As a result of his efforts, the book started selling. "People really responded
to the book. I did TV and radio interviews, schools began adopting the book. It
began to grow, in fact it grew much larger much faster than I had anticipated."
Sales eventually reached 10,000 copies, and it was on the required reading list
for a number of college courses across the country.

Hill envisioned adapting the story for the screen, and when he saw the
chairperson of the UCLA Film and Television Department, Richard Walter, on
TV he placed a copy of the book in Walter's mailbox with a note introducing
himself. Walter wrote back praising the book and inviting Hill to an upcoming
seminar, which would also include prominent producers and agents. During the
course of his lecture Walter introduced Hill and made reference to the particular
strengths of *Satisfied with Nothin'* several times. Leslie Kallen, a literary agent
in attendance, approached Hill about the work, and he gave her a copy. Kallen
was enthusiastic about the possibilities, and Hill decided to let her shop it around.

"A year later I decided to return to Louisiana and take a position teaching
creative writing. I pulled it off as a graduate student, but I knew there was no
way I could continue to act as a publisher and lecturer and also teach. At that
point I decided to see if I could attract a larger trade publisher. I called Leslie,
who I knew only handled screenwriters, and she said she knew a literary agent
who might be interested. She spoke to Frank [Weimann, of The Literary Group]
and called me back. She asked if there was a paper trail, had it been rejected 500
times, and I told her I hadn't shopped it very much. By the end of the week Frank
called to say he was interested. By the end of the next week he had an offer. It
was unbelievable to me. I had anticipated the process taking weeks and weeks."
Hill was offered a two-book deal with Simon & Schuster.

"It's very difficult to separate myself, the writer, and the scholar, from the
upbringing I've had that enables me to achieve. One of my primary philosophies

education is something my grandmother told me when I came
ll. She said, 'Boy, now you have more degrees than a
vhen you get through with all of that I'm going to teach you
'e. Knowledge and wisdom are wonderful things to have, but
ou can get is an understanding.' One of the things I'm trying
ιυ υο with my writing is to create an understanding between people. The biggest
fear is being misunderstood. But that's going to happen anyway. Hopefully the
work will speak to people and they will come to an understanding."
—*Kirsten Holm*

your book's subject and give an idea of how that subject will be developed. If
you're sending a synopsis of a novel, cover the basic plot.

- An outline covers your book chapter by chapter. The outline should include all
  major points covered in each chapter. Some outlines are done in traditional outline
  form, but most are written in paragraph form.
- An author's information sheet should—as succinctly and clearly as possible—
  acquaint the editor with your writing background and convince her of your qualifications to write about the subject.
- Many editors like to see sample chapters, especially for a first book. In fiction
  it's essential. In nonfiction, sample chapters show the editor how well you write
  and develop the ideas from your outline.
- Marketing information—i.e., facts about how and to whom your book can be
  successfully marketed—is now expected to accompany every book proposal. If
  you can provide information about the audience for your book and suggest ways
  the book publisher can reach those people, you will increase your chances of
  acceptance.
- Competitive title analysis is an integral part of the marketing information. Check
  the *Subject Guide* to *Books in Print* for other titles on your topic. Write a one-
  or two-sentence synopsis of each. Point out how your book differs and improves
  upon existing titles.

A WORD ABOUT AGENTS

An agent represents a writer's work to publishers, negotiates publishing contracts,
follows up to see that contracts are fulfilled and generally handles a writer's business
affairs, leaving the writer free to write. Effective agents are valued for their contacts
in the publishing industry, their savvy about which publishers and editors to approach
with which ideas, their ability to guide an author's career and their business sense.

While most book publishers listed in *Writer's Market* publish books by unagented
writers, some of the larger ones are reluctant to consider submissions that have not
reached them through a literary agent. Companies with such a policy are so noted in
the listings.

For more information about finding and working with a literary agent, see *Guide to
Literary Agents* (Writer's Digest Books). The *Guide* offers listings of agents as well as
helpful articles written by professionals in the field.

PROFESSIONALISM AND COURTESY

Publishers are as crunched for time as any other business professional. Between struggling to meet deadlines without exceeding budgets and dealing with incoming submissions, most editors find that time is their most precious commodity. This state of affairs means an editor's communications with new writers, while necessarily a part of his job, have to be handled efficiently and with a certain amount of bluntness.

But writers work hard too. Shouldn't editors treat them nicely? Shouldn't an editor take the time to point out the *good* things about the manuscript he is rejecting? Is that too much to ask? Well, in a way, yes. It *is* too much to ask. Editors are not writing coaches; much less are they counselors or therapists. Editors are in the business of buying workable writing from people who produce it. This, of course, does not excuse editors from observing the conventions of common business courtesy. Good editors know how to be polite (or they hire an assistant who can be polite for them).

The best way for busy writers to get along with (and flourish among) busy editors is to develop professional business habits. Correspondence and phone calls should be kept short and to the point. Don't hound editors with unwanted calls or letters. Honor all agreements, and give every assignment your best effort. Pleasantness, good humor, honesty and reliability will serve you as well in publishing as they will in any other area of life.

You will occasionally run up against editors and publishers who don't share your standard of business etiquette. It is easy enough to withdraw your submissions from such people and avoid them in the future.

WRITING TOOLS

Typewriters and computers. For many years, *the* tool of the writer's trade was the typewriter. While many writers continue to produce perfectly acceptable material on their manual or electric typewriters, more and more writers have discovered the benefits of writing on a computer. Editors, too, have benefited from the change; documents produced on a computer are less likely to present to the editor such distractions as typos, eraser marks or globs of white correction fluid. That's because writing composed on a computer can be corrected before it is printed out.

If you think computers are not for you, you should reconsider. A desktop computer, running a good word processing program, can be the greatest boon to your writing career since the dictionary. For ease of manipulating text, formatting pages and correcting spelling errors, the computer handily outperforms the typewriter. Many word processing programs will count words for you, offer synonyms from a thesaurus, construct an index and give you a choice of typefaces to print out your material. Some will even correct your grammar (if you want them to). When you consider that the personal computer is also a great way of tracking your submissions and staying on top of all the other business details of a writing career—and a handy way to do research if you have a modem—it's hard to imagine how we ever got along without them.

Many people considering working with a computer for the first time are under the mistaken impression that they face an insurmountable learning curve. That's no longer true. While learning computer skills once may have been a daunting undertaking, today's personal computers are much more user-friendly than they once were.

Whether you're writing on a computer or typewriter, your goal should be to produce pages of clean, error-free copy. Stick to standard typefaces, avoiding such unusual styles as script or italic. Your work should reflect a professional approach and consideration for your reader. If you are printing from a computer, avoid sending material printed from a low-quality dot-matrix printer, with hard-to-read, poorly shaped characters. Many editors are unwilling to read these manuscripts. New laser and ink jet printers, however, produce high-quality pages that *are* acceptable to editors. Readability is the key.

Electronic submissions. Many publishers are accepting or even requesting that final manuscript submissions be made on computer disk. This saves the magazine or book publisher the expense of having your manuscript typeset, and can be helpful in the editing stage. The publisher will simply download your finished manuscript into the computer system they use to produce their product. Be sure to mention if you are able to submit the final manuscript on disk. The editors will let you know what computer format they use and how they would like to receive your material.

Some publishers who accept submissions on disk also will accept electronic submissions by modem. Modems are computer components that can use your phone line to send computerized files to other computers with modems. It is an extremely fast way to get your manuscript to the publisher. You'll need to work out submission information with the editor before you send something via modem.

Fax machines and e-mail. Fax machines transmit copy across phone lines. E-mail addresses are for receiving and sending electronic mail over a computer network, most commonly the Internet. Those publishers who wanted to list their fax machine numbers and e-mail addresses have done so.

Between businesses, the fax has come into standard daily use for materials that have to be sent quickly. In addition, some public fax machines are being installed in airports, hotels, libraries and even grocery stores. However, do not fax or e-mail queries or entire manscripts to editors unless they specifically request it. Writers should continue to use traditional means for sending manuscripts and queries and use the fax number or e-mail address we list only when an editor asks to receive correspondence by this method.

Letters and manuscripts sent to an editor for consideration should be neat, clean and legible. That means typed (or computer-printed), double spaced, on $8\frac{1}{2} \times 11$ inch paper. Handwritten materials will most often not be considered at all. The typing paper should be at least 16 lb. bond (20 lb. is preferred). Very thin papers and erasable bond papers are not recommended for manuscripts. A proposal on shiny fax paper curling into itself on the editor's desk makes an impression—but not the one you want. If your proposal is being considered, it will probably be routed to a number of people for their reactions. Fax paper won't stand up well to that amount of handling.

The first impression an editor has of your work is its appearance on the page. Why take the chance of blowing that impression with a manuscript or letter that's not as appealing as it could be?

You don't need fancy letterhead for your correspondence with editors. Plain bond paper is fine. Just type your name, address, phone number and the date at the top of the page—centered or in the right-hand corner. If you want letterhead, make it as simple and businesslike as possible. Many quick print shops have standard typefaces and can supply letterhead stationery at a relatively low cost. Never use letterhead for typing your manuscripts. Only the first page of queries, cover letters and other correspondence should be typed on letterhead.

MANUSCRIPT FORMAT

When submitting a manuscript for possible publication, you can increase its chances of making a favorable impression by adhering to some fairly standard matters of physical format. Many professional writers use the format described here. Of course, there are no "rules" about what a manuscript must look like. These are just guidelines— some based on common sense, others more a matter of convention—that are meant to help writers display their work to best advantage. Strive for easy readability in whatever method you choose and adapt your style to your own personal tastes and those of the editors to whom you submit. Complete information on formats for books, articles,

INSIDER REPORT

Forging Lasting Relationships With Editors

Troika magazine is a cutting-edge contemporary culture quarterly geared toward a young, educated, affluent audience. Says Editor Celia Meadow, "We are aimed at those who have given up the '80s lifestyle and are kicking back and trying to establish balance in their lives among three things: personal achievement, family commitment, and community involvement."

Created in 1994 by husband and publisher Eric Meadow, *Troika* has already garnered national recognition. It was named "one of the 50 most notable launches of 1994" by Samir Husni's *Guide To New Consumer Magazines*, and has earned a number of top design awards, including two Ozzies. "We're considered a thought-leader magazine. We

Celia Meadow

try to be visually appealing, provocative, insightful, analytical, investigative," says Ms. Meadow.

Troika's editorial staff relies heavily on a variety of freelance writers. "Probably 80% of our work comes from freelance sources. We've been using a lot of fresh, new voices. Of course, we certainly welcome established writers, but any writer who has something original to say, if it is well-written, beautifully expressed and in the scope of our editorial mission, will be considered."

A testimony to Meadow's commitment to publish unknown writers occurred in the Spring of 1996 when *Troika* printed an essay by an intern—a high school senior—about college application. Instead of enumerating statistics about the number of applicants and how hard it is to get in to Ivy League schools, *Troika* offered a unique angle by publishing a young woman's reflective perspective on the process—even though the magazine's readers are her parents' age.

Like all magazines, *Troika* is hungry for original, interesting stories. Meadow says one way to make yourself saleable is to stretch your boundaries. Write about unusual topics, or write an unusual take on a familiar topic, such as a witty piece *Troika* printed in its travel section in which the writer never left home. "Anything clever and unique that's not just different for different's sake is appealing," Meadow says. Take a recent article Meadow published on transvestism, written by the daughter of a practicing transvestite. "This was an interesting and well-written piece. How many pieces have been written in that kind of voice?"

Most publications nowadays want only a brief one-page query, but Meadow

INSIDER REPORT, *continued*

prefers either a complete manuscript or a lengthy query. "If I see the finished piece or a two- or three-page query then I can get a good sense of the writer, before I go ahead and engage their time. The more I know about a writer and the more of their writing I can see, the better it is for me." *Troika* buys only finished manuscripts and pays on publication, not acceptance. "I don't buy anything I haven't seen in completion, and I won't make firm assignments."

Such a policy holds true even for writers who have already published in *Troika*. That's not to say advantages do not exist for such writers; they do. "While I don't pay on assignment for any writer, I will say to writers I've used who have a particular niche: 'I have this idea. Can you pursue this and explore it?' But because we are a young magazine with an evolving voice, the understanding is that it's always on speculation, meaning they have to be willing to go out and research the material, write the piece, do whatever else I need, and then—like everybody else—submit it. If the submitted version meets our criteria, then we'll almost certainly take it."

Although Meadow often publishes unfamiliar writers, she values working with writers she's already published. "It's great to reuse writers. They've proven themselves; you know their style; you know they'll do rewrites; and you can ask something of them in a crunch. Working with someone over and over makes the exchange so easy. There definitely are many benefits to working with the same writers over and over again."

So what's a writer's ticket for increasing chances of landing repeat projects? "Good writers won't burn bridges," says Meadow. Even if a project goes awry and falls through, she emphasizes, a writer shouldn't get too antagonistic with the editor, because there might be future articles for which the magazine will need that writer's work. In addition, establishing a solid relationship with an editor at one magazine can often lead to opportunities at other publications. "With writers who repeatedly work well with us, I try to steer other opportunities their way. I'll pass names on. I'll permit our articles to be reprinted in other magazines. All this helps the writer, both in getting more money and exposure."

Like all editors, Meadow seeks writers with professionalism as well as strong writing. "I want professional writers who aren't going to badger me about the exact publication date when their article will appear. I also want writers who will write on speculation, will rewrite if needed, will take constructive criticism and editorial input professionally, and will understand that once in a while manuscripts that were intended for publication get bumped. I also expect writers to do their own fact-checking, their own proofreading."

Meadow's expectations do not differ from expectations of editors at other magazines. "As an editor, I know writers are creative beings, but they have to balance their creativity with professionalism. My writer from hell is a creative prima donna who demands payment on acceptance, who hounds my editorial team about publication date and payment, and who has trouble with editorial rewrites and comments."

Meadow stresses that another way to appeal to editors, and to possibly get repeat writing assignments, is to include a strong biography with your submissions. "Writers should include a detailed bio when they make their scripts, proposals and cover letters, with illustrated examples, is available in *The Writer's Digest Guide to Manuscript Formats*, by Dian Dincin Buchman and Seli Groves (Writer's Digest Books).

Most manuscripts do not use a cover sheet or title page. Use a paper clip to hold pages together, not staples. This allows editors to separate the pages easily for editing. Scripts should be submitted with plain cardstock covers front and back, held together by Chicago or Revere screws.

The upper corners of the first page of an article manuscript contain important information about you and your manuscript. This information should be single-spaced. In the upper *left* corner list your name, address and phone number. If you are using a pseudonym for your byline, your legal name still must appear in this space. In the upper *right* corner, indicate the approximate word count of the manuscript, the rights you are offering for sale and your copyright notice (© 1997 Ralph Anderson). A handwritten copyright symbol is acceptable. (For more information about rights and copyright, see Minding the Details on page 37) For a book manuscript include the same information with the exception of rights. Do not number the first page of your manuscript.

Center the title in capital letters one-third of the way down the page. Set your typewriter to double-space. Type "by" and your name or pseudonym centered one double-space beneath that.

After the title and byline, drop down two double-spaces, paragraph indent, and begin the body of your manuscript. Always double-space your manuscript and use standard paragraph indentations of five spaces. Margins should be about 1½ inches on all sides of each full page of typewritten manuscript.

On every page after the first, type your last name, a dash and the page number in either the upper left or right corner. The title of your manuscript may, but need not, be typed on this line or beneath it. Page number two would read: Anderson—2. Follow this format throughout your manuscript.

If you are submitting novel chapters, leave the top one-third of the first page of each chapter blank before typing the chapter title. Subsequent pages should include the author's last name, the page number, and a shortened form of the book's title: Anderson—2—Skating. (In a variation on this, some authors place the title before the name on the left side and put the page number on the right-hand margin.)

When submitting poetry, the poems should be typed single-spaced (double-space between stanzas), one poem per page. For a long poem requiring more than one page, paper clip the pages together. You may want to write "continued" at the bottom of the page, so if the pages are separated, editors, typesetters and proofreaders won't assume your poem ends at the bottom of the first page.

ESTIMATING WORD COUNT

Many computers will provide you with a word count of your manuscript. Your editor will count again after editing the manuscript. Although your computer is counting characters, an editor or production editor is more concerned with the amount of space the text will occupy on a page. Several small headlines, or subheads, for instance, will be counted the same by your computer as any other word of text. An editor may count them differently to be sure enough space has been estimated for larger type.

For short manuscripts, it's often quickest to count each word on a representative page and multiply by the number of pages. You can get a very rough count by multiplying the number of pages in your manuscript by 250 (the average number of words on a double-spaced typewritten page). Do not count words for a poetry manuscript or put the word count at the top of the manuscript.

To get a more precise count, add the number of characters and spaces in an average line and divide by six for the average words per line. Then count the number of lines of type on a representative page. Multiply the words per line by the lines per page to find the average number of words per page. Then count the number of manuscript pages (fractions should be counted as fractions, except in book manuscript chapter headings, which are counted as a full page). Multiply the number of pages by the number of words per page you already determined. This will give you the approximate number of words in the manuscript.

PHOTOGRAPHS AND SLIDES

The availability of good quality photos can be a deciding factor when an editor is considering a manuscript. Many publications also offer additional pay for photos accepted with a manuscript. Check the magazine's listing when submitting black & white prints for the size an editor prefers to review. The universally accepted format for transparencies is 35mm; few buyers will look at color prints. Don't send any transparencies or prints with a query; wait until an editor indicates interest in seeing your photos.

On all your photos and slides, you should stamp or print your copyright notice and "Return to:" followed by your name, address and phone number. Rubber stamps are preferred for labeling photos since they are less likely to cause damage. You can order them from many stationery or office supply stores. If you use a pen to write this information on the back of your photos, be careful not to damage the print by pressing too hard or by allowing ink to bleed through the paper. A felt tip pen is best, but you should take care not to put photos or copy together before the ink dries.

Captions can be typed on a sheet of paper and taped to the back of the prints. Some writers, when submitting several transparencies or photos, number the photos and type captions (numbered accordingly) on a separate 8½×11 sheet of paper.

Submit prints rather than negatives or consider having duplicates made of your slides or transparencies. Don't risk having your original negative or slide lost or damaged when you submit it.

PHOTOCOPIES

Make copies of your manuscripts and correspondence before putting them in the mail. Don't learn the hard way, as many writers have, that manuscripts get lost in the mail and that publishers sometimes go out of business without returning submissions.

You might want to make several good quality copies of your manuscript while it is still clean and submit them while keeping the original manuscript as a file copy.

Some writers include a self-addressed postcard with a photocopied submission and suggest in the cover letter that if the editor is not interested in the manuscript, it may be tossed out and a reply returned on the postcard. This practice is recommended when dealing with international markets. If you find that your personal computer generates copies more cheaply than you can pay to have them returned, you might choose to send disposable manuscripts. Submitting a disposable manuscript costs the writer some photocopy or computer printer expense, but it can save on large postage bills.

MAILING SUBMISSIONS

No matter what size manuscript you're mailing, always include a self-addressed, stamped envelope (SASE) with sufficient return postage that is large enough to contain your manuscript if it is returned.

A manuscript of fewer than six pages may be folded in thirds and mailed as if it were a letter using a #10 (business-size) envelope. The enclosed SASE can be a #10 folded in thirds or a #9 envelope which will slip into the mailing envelope without being folded. Some editors also appreciate the convenience of having a manuscript folded into halves in a 6×9 envelope. For manuscripts of six pages or longer, use 9×12 envelopes for both mailing and return. The return SASE may be folded in half.

A book manuscript should be mailed in a sturdy, well-wrapped box. Enclose a self-addressed mailing label and paper clip your return postage stamps or International Reply Coupons to the label.

Always mail photos and slides First Class. The rougher handling received by standard mail could damage them. If you are concerned about losing prints or slides, send them certified or registered mail. For any photo submission that is mailed separately from a manuscript, enclose a short cover letter of explanation, separate self-addressed label, adequate return postage and an envelope. Never submit photos or slides mounted in glass.

To mail up to 20 prints, you can buy photo mailers that are stamped "Photos—Do Not Bend" and contain two cardboard inserts to sandwich your prints. Or use a 9×12 manila envelope, write "Photos—Do Not Bend" and make your own cardboard inserts. Some photography supply shops also carry heavy cardboard envelopes that are reusable.

When mailing a number of prints, say 25-50 for a book with illustrations, pack them in a sturdy cardboard box. A box for typing paper or photo paper is an adequate mailer. If, after packing both manuscript and photos, there's empty space in the box, slip in enough cardboard inserts to fill the box. Wrap the box securely.

To mail transparencies, first slip them into protective vinyl sleeves, then mail as you would prints. If you're mailing a number of sheets, use a cardboard box as for photos.

Types of Mail Service

- First Class is an expensive way to mail a manuscript, but many writers prefer it. First Class mail generally receives better handling and is delivered more quickly. Mail sent First Class is also forwarded for one year if the addressee has moved, and is returned automatically if it is undeliverable.
- Priority mail reaches its destination within 2-3 days. To mail a package of up to 2 pounds costs $3, less than either United Parcel Service or Federal Express. First Class mail over 11 ounces is classified Priority.
- Standard mail rates are available for packages, but be sure to pack your materials carefully because they will be handled roughly. To make sure your package will be returned to you if it is undeliverable, print "Return Postage Guaranteed" under your address.

- Certified Mail must be signed for when it reaches its destination. If requested, a signed receipt is returned to the sender. There is a $1.10 charge for this service, in addition to the required postage, and a $1.10 charge for a return receipt.
- Registered Mail is a high-security method of mailing where the contents are insured. The package is signed in and out of every office it passes through, and a receipt is returned to the sender when the package reaches its destination. The cost depends on the weight, destination and whether you obtain insurance.
- If you're in a hurry to get your material to your editor, you have a lot of choices these days. In addition to fax and computer technologies mentioned earlier, overnight and two-day mail services are provided by both the U.S. Postal Service and several private firms. More information on next day service is available from the U.S. Post Office in your area, or check your Yellow Pages under "Delivery Services."

Other Correspondence Details

Use money orders if you are ordering sample copies or supplies and do not have checking services. You'll have a receipt, and money orders are traceable. Money orders for up to $700 can be purchased from the U.S. Postal Service for an 85 cents service charge. Banks, savings and loans, and some commercial businesses also carry money orders; their fees vary. *Never* send cash through the mail for sample copies.

Insurance is available for items handled by the U.S. Postal Service but is payable only on typing fees or the tangible value of the item in the package—such as typing paper—so your best insurance when mailing manuscripts is to keep a copy of what you send. Insurance is 75 cents for $50 or less and goes up to a $6 plus postage maximum charge.

When corresponding with publishers in other countries, International Reply Coupons (IRCs) must be used for return postage. Surface rates in other countries differ from those in the U.S., and U.S. postage stamps are of use only within the U.S. Currently, one IRC costs $1.05 and is sufficient for one ounce traveling at surface rate; two must be used for airmail return. Canadian writers pay $3.50 for an IRC which is redeemable for 45 cents in postage.

Because some post offices don't carry IRCs (or because of the added expense), many writers dealing with international mail send photocopies and tell the publisher to dispose of them if the manuscript is not appropriate. When you use this method, it's best to set a deadline for withdrawing your manuscript from consideration, so you can market it elsewhere.

International money orders are also available from the post office for a $3 charge. See U.S. and Canadian Postage by the Page on page 938-941 for specific mailing costs. All charges were current at press time but are subject to change during the year.

RECORDING SUBMISSIONS

Once you begin submitting manuscripts, you'll need to manage your writing business by keeping copies of all manuscripts and correspondence, and by recording the dates of submissions.

One way to keep track of your manuscripts is to use a record of submissions that includes the date sent, title, market, editor and enclosures (such as photos). You should also note the date of the editor's response, any rewrites that were done, and, if the manuscript was accepted, the deadline, publication date and payment information. You might want to keep a similar record just for queries.

Also remember to keep a separate file for each manuscript or idea along with its list

Maintaining the Balance Between Cool and Responsible

Your assignment: Write an article for a teen magazine. Sound easy? Okay, here's a pop quiz: What's hip with today's teens? What are they into? What's important to them? What are they talking about? You can't find answers by paging through a few issues of *Seventeen* or watching reruns of "My So-Called Life." Try following the advice of Stu Slayen, editor of the cool Canadian teen mag *What! A Magazine*: Talk to teenagers.

Slayen not only preaches but practices this advice. He and the staff of *What!* annually assemble what's called the National Editorial Advisory Committee, made up of 10-13 teens from across Canada, chosen through an application process to represent the diversity of the country's teen population. The committee provides feedback and opinion on story ideas.

Stu Slayen

"There are a lot of intelligent teens out there, and I don't think the adult media portray teens in a positive or objective light. It's really good for us to hear what they're saying because we think we get a more accurate snapshot than a large TV network or a daily newspaper would."

Slayen's second piece of advice is "Talk to teachers. Teachers see teens in their very real light. At least they have the opportunity to, whether or not they choose to take advantage of it. And I think they can provide an objective opinion," he says.

Though he also recommends writers read teen magazines, Slayen cautions against using them as a research tool and getting caught up in the clichés of what adults think teen magazines are all about—fashion, makeup and what to wear to the prom. "I think there's a lot of room for improvement in youth media. I was interviewed recently by a Canadian youth cable channel, and the reporter asked me to describe the typical teen. To me, that is the most inane question, because there's no such thing. And I think that a lot of mainstream media assume there is."

Slayen feels that teens are interested in many of the same things adults are, but from a perspective relevant to them. "If you want to talk about something as obscure as the International Monetary Fund, I think you can do that as long as you write about it in such a way that there are applications to what it means to a teenager," he says.

For example, *What!* did an article on problem gambling. "That story's been done a thousand times, but we did it from the perspective of teens who have

INSIDER REPORT, *continued*

problems. That's not cliché teen journalism—that's what they want to read," he says. "My recommendation to writers is whatever you think teen writing should be, stop and start again."

What! often addresses topics which you may be surprised to find in a teen magazine. They kept readers up-to-date on the Quebec Referendum. They put together a piece on starting your own business. They ran an article on buying your first car. They even tackled the search for spiritual fulfillment (for which they received great response from their young readership). Slayen feels this type of intelligent journalism is important for teen publications. "We try to be interactive, empowering and entertaining. I know these are all buzzwords, but we really try to do that in every issue."

Recurring entertainment features in *What!* include music and movie reviews; sports news; and interviews with celebrities in music, movies and TV (such as Alanis Morissette, Tori Amos, Stone Temple Pilots, the Kids in the Hall, Scott Wolf and Johnny Depp). But *What!* mainly uses freelancers for feature articles.

There is something special about *What! A Magazine* that writers should keep in mind—it's distributed almost solely through Canadian high schools (about 1,000, who must request the free magazine). That means the editorial staff has two masters: "the readers and the environment in which we distribute." So Slayen and his staff strive to produce a "cool yet responsible" publication. Maintaining that balance is a bit instinctive, says Slayen. It's having the right story idea combined with common sense, and it's providing editorial that excites the readers, that is in keeping with societal and entertainment trends but is still sensitive to the school environment.

"We did a story on body piercing last year, and we had a couple of photos that were graphic, and we had a few schools cancel because of the shocking nature of seeing someone with a pierced neck or navel." But cases like this, says Slayen, are few and far between. "Canadian educators are very hip, very modern, very progressive, very respectful of what their students are reading, and still happy to distribute the magazine."

Audience gender is a consideration when working for teen publications. *What!*'s editors try to achieve gender balance. "We're in schools. It would be a huge error to target one gender," says Slayen. "If we feel an issue is leaning a little feminine, we try to put something in that might be a little more male-oriented, and vice versa. But a lot of things could appeal to either."

In terms of writing style, Slayen urges freelancers writing for teens not to change how they write. "Just be conversational, chatty, use humor when appropriate. The basic tenets of journalism still apply—accuracy and balance are absolutely crucial." But most importantly, don't talk down to the readers. "If you use a condescending lead in a story, [teenagers] probably won't read the rest of the story. They might not read the rest of the issue."

—*Alice P. Buening*

of potential markets. You may want to keep track of expected reporting times on a calendar, too. Then you'll know if a market has been slow to respond and you can follow up on your query or submission. It will also provide you with a detailed picture of your sales over time.

Current Trends in Publishing

BY KIRSTEN HOLM

BOOK PUBLISHING

Compared to the upheavals in the publishing industry in the recent past, last year was relatively calm. Growth in book sales was slow but steady, ending the year 3 percent over the previous year. However, sales had been predicted to grow 7.2 percent, and figures for the first few months of 1996 show this disappointing pattern continuing.

The trend in publishing in general is toward consolidation. More books sold 100,000 copies, and 11 books sold over one million copies (seven of those were fiction), but the seven largest conglomerate publishers produced 85 percent of the year's bestsellers. This doesn't leave a lot of room at the top for midsize and smaller publishers. Most authors on last year's bestseller list were already well-established. Of the top 15 novels, 11 were penned by a previously bestselling author. This doesn't leave a lot of room for newer writers. The four largest book chains account for almost 45 percent of all bookstore sales. While small independent bookstores are struggling, the chains are closing their mall stores and opening "superstores" at a brisk rate.

The growth of these superstores can benefit the smaller publishers and their authors. With increased shelf space to fill, the Barnes & Nobles and Books-a-Millions are placing smaller books within the reach of more readers. "All-media" outlets such as Media Play, featuring books, music and video, have grown impressively, and nonbookstore outlets are expanding a publisher's reach into new markets. The home shopping network QVC alone sold 2.3 million books last year.

An area of concern to both large and small publishers is the cost of physically producing a book. The past few years have seen paper prices increase exponentially. However, this situation is beginning to stabilize somewhat. Supply is predicted to grow a small amount each year for the next several years, and publishers have instituted various cost-cutting and paper-saving changes in production. Paper prices are anticipated to remain high, or decrease slightly, but most publishers feel they are in a position to absorb any future increases without raising book prices.

CD-ROM and the Internet: Investments Not Paying Off . . . Yet

The upswing in paper prices coincides with publishers' exploration of alternative ways of delivering their products. Chief among the options is electronic publishing, which usually means CD-ROM, but there is increasing interest in online publishing.

The potential market for CD-ROM is amazing. It is estimated that by 1998 40 million multimedia PCs will be in place. Tapping into this market is almost every publisher's dream, and there are many exciting products out there, but publishing successfully *and* profitably is a challenge. While many publishers are creating multimedia products, most are losing money. Not many CD-ROMs are profitable yet, largely due to intensive development costs. Two types doing well now are reference works and games. Some publishers are pulling out entirely, but for the most part, publishers who have already invested in exploring multimedia take the long view, looking at current efforts as acquiring skills and expertise to be able to respond to whatever new media applications and ventures arise in the future.

The latest news in electronic publishing is the Internet and online publishing. Issues of authorship, copyright and payment must all be sorted out before any serious movement in this direction occurs, but a number of industry experts are predicting that online will replace CD-ROM, already considered outmoded technology in some circles. While commercially successful publishing on the Internet may not be a reality for quite awhile, websites have become quite common and online bookstores a reality.

The battleground for writers here is the disposition of rights to their work appearing in an electronic format. The extent to which these electronic rights are treated like any other is a strongly contested area between publishers and authors and their representatives. *The New York Times* initiated a new standard contract policy in which the paper retains all rights, including electronic, in perpetuity without additional payment. This was met with howls of outrage from all sides, including the Authors Guild, the American Society of Journalists and Authors, the National Writers Union and the Association of Authors Representatives. Last year this same group of organizations joined forces to form the Authors Registry, Inc., an "ASCAP"-style agency providing an accounting system to pay royalties to registered authors when their work is accessed. The National Writers Union calls for a 15% increase in payment when selling all rights. A few magazines, notably *Harper's*, recognize and pay for electronic rights.

What Do These Trends Mean For Writers?

With book sales not growing as much as expected, publishers are looking more closely at decisions to publish. For larger publishers to accept a manuscript, there has to be a demonstrable need for a book of broad enough interest to sell a significant number of copies. And there usually isn't much time to develop authors. While mid-size and smaller publishers often have the patience and perseverance to help develop new authors, cuts in NEA funding, distribution difficulties, and the loss of independent bookstores all combine to keep publishing lists small and sales low.

One solution that has become more popular in the last few years is self-publishing. While the challenges of successfully marketing a self-published book remain significant, an increasing number of these books are picked up by larger houses after posting attention-getting sales figures. Books such as *The Celestine Prophecy* and *The Christmas Box* enjoyed large sales before Warner and Simon & Schuster bought the rights. Book reps from larger houses have started making a practice of asking after local books. These success stories, however, are still the exception rather than the rule.

With all that said, all is not gloom and doom in the publishing world. Good books and good writers are being published. Regardless of the subject or format, successful books are a combination of content and marketing. Publishers are placing increasing emphasis on market analysis in book proposals. One successful agent tells her clients they must have "the Martha Stewart attitude" of willingness to do anything and everything it takes to sell their book.

But first you have to write something people want to read. Figuring out what is selling now offers some indication of what the public will be reading in the future. The one caveat is that the time between acceptance and publication can often be 12-18 months. What are white hot topics now will be as cold and stale as yesterday's toast if simply repeated. Success lies in finding new attitudes and approaches.

Three Major Nonfiction Trends

Three major trends in popular adult nonfiction have arisen in the past few years: spiritual health, physical health, and a host of topics that fall under the rough category of "lifestyle," such as cooking and gardening. The influence of the baby boomer generation's interests can be felt throughout, as publishers seek to respond to the needs and interests of such a large population of book readers and book buyers.

Spirituality

Perhaps the biggest theme in adult nonfiction has been a loosely knit blend of religion and psychology, often with a dash of New Age thinking, that is termed "spirituality." Publishers such as Thomas Nelson/Word, Crossroad and Zondervan are finding new mainstream audiences and wider distribution. Books dealing with inspirational themes, finding meaning in life and developing morality and values are extremely popular with baby boomers in particular, trying to find answers to life's problems. Divorce, raising children, aging parents, uncertain employment and financial problems all contribute to a sense of impermanence in this world. The market for spiritual books reflects a desire to uncover inner resources as well as external resources of purpose and meaning.

Devotional materials, guiding the reader in prayer, are extremely popular. There are books about how to pray, the history of prayer, prayers for women, for men, for children, for cancer survivors and so on. While many religious traditions are represented, the majority are Christian in orientation. Celebrity prayerbooks exist right alongside a number of prayer journals wherein readers chronicle their own prayer life. Finding time to incorporate spiritual development within the confines of a busy life is important, and these prayer journals, diaries and calendars help to keep their audience focused.

Since women buy nearly twice as many books as men, it's no surprise that books treating their unique spiritual sensibilities and experiences are popular. The overwhelming success of Clarissa Pinkola Estes and Marianne Williamson signals an interest in the strength and creative power of women and their spirituality. Several books set out prayers and rituals for women of specific faiths as well as less-well-defined movements such as Goddess worship or Wiccan beliefs.

The men's movement has also created a market for books on their spiritual side. This trend stretches to include several diverse groups, from the Promise Keepers, the men of the Million Man March, and gay men. The Promise Keepers, an initially evangelical group, holds individual prayer meetings and mass rallies of men looking for spiritual renewal. A number of books for men seeking spiritual direction in their lives emphasize responsibility in family and community relationships.

As an aside, religious fiction is developing into a healthy sector. Genres such as mysteries, thrillers and romances with religious underpinnings are enjoying considerable success. Janet Oke's romances and Frank Peretti's thrillers command a large number of mainstream readers who might not normally read "religious" books.

The development of a moral center, both in themselves and in their children, is a concern that parents of all denomiations share. A large number of books with the word "virtue" in the title offer short stories, poems and essays illustrating positive character traits such as honesty and courage that help the reader navigate through daily life.

Spiritual comfort books are also big. So far we've had three helpings of *Chicken Soup for the Soul*. There's a terrible pun in here about America's increasing taste for "soul food," but we'll let it go at saying that books offering insight and inspiration offer moral nourishment for a spiritual hunger.

Health and Fitness: A Variety of Approaches

Which brings us to the second major trend, physical health. Again, baby boomers are a major impetus in the surge of diet and fitness books. Titles such as *Fit Over Forty* and *Fitness After Fifty* are designed with this audience in mind, as they attempt to stave off the effects of aging.

A unified, holistic approach in which diet, exercise and mental health work together is enjoying a large degree of success. Many of these books emphasize not only losing weight but gaining self-esteem; slimming down while modifying behaviors such as food choice and physical activity. Many diet books feature exercise sections, and fitness books feature diet plans, but the emphasis is more on personal choice and empowering oneself to take control of one's life. Self-published titles such as *Butterbusters* and *Healthy Exchanges* from women who have walked the walk and lost the weight have had such phenomenal sales that publishers such as Warner and Putnam have picked them up for mass distribution. Celebrity cookbooks are popular.

Mixing spirituality and health is a winning combination. Holistic approaches to spiritual, mental and physical health have proven extremely popular. Thanks in large part to the works of Dr. Deepak Chopra, pathways to a mind/body approach to healing have become an increasingly accepted method of dealing with disease. With publishers such as Reader's Digest publishing books on aromatherapy and homeopathic medicine, what was considered alternative is now definitely mainstream.

Lifestyle Issues

It's the enhancement of well-being that forms the core of the third trend—lifestyle topics. And again, the baby boomer generation is at the fore of the demand for books on topics such as cooking, gardening and decorating. The trend of "cocooning," of staying home, spending more time with family and developing interests and activities, along with more discretionary time and income, contributes to the increasing market for these books.

One response to this trend of slowing down and turning inward is the elimination of stressful elements. Books emphasizing simplicity, with suggestions ranging from housing options to clothing selections, focus on stripping life of unnecessary clutter to get to the things that really matter.

In the cookbook category, more entries are taking health concerns into account, providing a low-fat high-flavor approach to eating that often emphasizes fresh seasonal ingredients and vegetarian principles. Cookbooks such as *Big Flavors* or *Roasting* emphasize robust ingredients and methods of cooking that create intense flavor. Even general cookbooks are including more recipes using grains and vegetables. Books exploring ethnic cuisines are also a part of this movement.

On one end of the spectrum, books that celebrate the complexity of food are successfully finding a niche. For many people, cooking is becoming a leisure activity, a skill they develop to enrich their lives. These books are written for readers who appreciate good food in all its various forms. On the other end are cookbooks emphasizing speed and simplicity. Titles such as *Low Fat in Nothing Flat* offer short cuts to healthy eating. A subcategory in this area is "minimalist" cookbooks such as *Cooking with Three Ingredients*.

Gardening is another burgeoning leisure time activity that publishers are tapping into in a big way. Getting back to nature and the emotional aspects of enriching life with beautiful things has a strong appeal. Many people are finding that gardening can be a calming, even healing experience. Basic books for beginning gardeners are popular, appealing to readers looking for solid startup information. Books from familiar institutions offer advice with the ring of authority. Subject-specific books, with a depth of information on specialty topics, are also finding an eager market. A surprising number of books are being published for the cook who gardens and the gardener who cooks.

CONSUMER MAGAZINES

It was a challenging year for magazines as well. Increases in paper prices as much as 40% hit magazines hard, as did increases in postal rates. Despite these difficulties, the publishing divisions of larger companies such as Time Warner, K-III and Meredith had good years. Their success is attributed to a number of factors, including a booming advertising market and higher subscription and newsstand prices.

Other companies, such as the magazine components of Reader's Digest and The New York Times, weren't as able to overcome these hurdles. The Reader's Digest Association announced the layoff of 1,000 employees and sold *Travel Holiday* to Hachette Fillipacchi. In general, the majority of companies that were hardest hit last year were those publishers relying more on circulation than advertising income.

As with book publishing, more and more magazines are entering the world of electronic publishing. Magazine publishers are mixing and matching multiple media elements, such as CD-ROM, online and cable TV, to create their own electronic presence.

Almost all larger magazines exist in some form online. Many are represented on services. This year *Writer's Market* asked magazines to include a World Wide Web address, if they had one, and discovered that an astounding number of magazines have leapt into cyberspace. While many magazines create their own sites, Condé Nast Publications' electronic division takes a different approach. Their strategy is to create a site based on a category of interest. Last year it rolled out Epicurious, which offered more than typical online magazine fare. While *Gourmet* and *Bon Appetit* are a part of the site, users can also access a number of related services, such as restaurant reviews, a food and wine guide, a recipe database and even a section on food etiquette.

Magazines For Every Reader

In terms of subject matter, you will find magazines of varying sizes all over the map of readers' interests. With the advent of desktop publishing, the 'zine has come into its own. Anyone with a computer and something to say can self-publish. Magazine publishers search out specific niche markets and tailor editorial content to their needs.

There has been a spate of twenty-something magazines, ranging from the well-funded to the one-person operation. Magazines such as *Might*, *Swing* and *KGB* offer stories on music, movies, celebrities and current events geared to a younger sensibility.

Last edition saw a surge in magazines with religious subjects—over 30 such magazines new to that edition. Many are published by specific denominations for their pastorate, others approach current events from a non-sectarian view.

The nesting trend is influential in magazines as well as books. Home and shelter topics are doing very well. New magazines such as *Classic Home* join popular magazines such as *Metropolitan Home* and *House Beautiful*.

Gardening magazines are blooming. *American Homestyle* added "*& Gardening*" to its title and newer magazines such as *Garden Design* and *Organic Flower Gardening* have hit the stands, joining *Horticulture* and *Fine Gardening*. With kitchen gardens such a hot topic in books, Taunton Press has launched *Kitchen Garden* magazine.

The epicurean category is expanding as well. *Fine Cooking* and *Saveur* are for readers interested in "the art and craft of food." *Gourmet*, *Bon Appetit* and *Food & Wine* address a similar audience of food enthusiasts. Healthy food is emphasized in *Cooking Light* and *Eating Well*, while *Fast and Healthy* aims for the market of busy people who still want to eat right.

Health and fitness is an important area for magazines, with an emphasis on well-being and strength over past obsessions with muscle mass. Magazines such as *Men's Fitness* and *Men's Health* answer their health concerns, while *Fitness*, *Shape* and *Health* answer the concerns of women. *Heart and Soul* targets the health of African-American women. Magazines such as *New Choices*, *50 and Forward* and *Fifty-Something* cover issues of interest to older Americans.

Magazines covering child care and parental guidance are holding their own. Niche magazines such as *Successful Black Parenting* and *Catholic Parent* answer the specific questions of a smaller group of readers, while *American Baby* and *Child* address their articles to the wider concerns of a general audience.

KEEPING UP WITH THE TRENDS

Trends aren't static. They grow and develop, changing as our world and interests change. Stack the hard-edged, cutthroat business books of the '80s against a book such as Stephen Covey's *7 Habits of Highly Effective People* and you'll see the difference. Often one trend will combine with another and produce a third direction. Gardening plus multimedia equals *The American Garden Guides*, published by Pantheon, Microsoft and online with the Microsoft Network. Gardening plus spirituality has produced titles such as *Growing Myself: A Spiritual Journey Through Gardening*. Gardening combined with health results in books such as *Herbal Remedies in Pots*.

With stiff competition, marketing information becomes paramount. How many other books are being published on this topic? What makes your take on the subject different (and better) than these others? Who *will* buy (not who *ought* to buy) this book? Publishers must answer these questions before they offer you a contract.

To keep up with book publishing trends you can turn to several sources. One invaluable resource is your local bookseller, who is keenly aware of which subjects are selling and which are not. *Publishers Weekly*, *Library Journal* and *American Bookseller* feature up-to-date news on publishing and bookselling, as well as chart book sales and trends. *Book Industry Trends*, published by the Book Industry Study Group, analyzes the past year in publishing and predicts how the industry will perform in the years ahead. Almost all writers' organizations offer newsletters with market information. Check into groups in your area, or contact national groups such as the American Society of Journalists and Authors or the National Writers Union. All offer invaluable market direction insights that can help you present your proposal in its most favorable light.

With magazines starting up and shutting down so rapidly, it's important for writers to stay on top of changes in specific markets as well as in the industry. Libraries, bookstores and newsstands are all good sources of field research. Trade magazines such as *Folio*, *Advertising Age* and *Writer's Digest* offer information and analysis of trends in subject matter as well as business aspects such as advertising and circulation. Newsletters such as *Writing for Money*, *Travelwriter Marketletter* and *Gila Queen's Guide to the Markets* offer specific market information.

Perhaps the most important step in building a career in magazine writing is magazine reading. Check your local library's holdings or order a few sample copies for a market in which you are particularly interested. Peruse a few issues to get a flavor and perspective of a magazine, and gather a list of article ideas the editors might be interested in. Request a copy of the writer's guidelines and editorial calendar. Study the listing information closely and construct your query letter with care. Impress the editor with your knowledge of the magazine's editorial mission and understanding of its audience.

Whether you're writing books or for magazines, one thing to remember is that, ultimately, editors and publishers are looking for new voices. It's the fresh attitudes and approaches with new ideas that keep readers reading—and buying.

Writer to Writer:
Emergency Roadside Service

BY DON PRUES

Anyone who's taken I-70 through Kansas on a clear summer's day knows the smooth drive requires almost no tilting of the wheel. With few twists and turns, plenty of signs and mileage markers, and close to no major stumbling blocks or surprises (save the Kansas State Highway Patrol), it's an easy road to travel. Unlike the road to publication. Chances are Publication Road is more of a dark, ridge-hugging gravel stretch you're trying to traverse in the midst of a Rocky Mountain blizzard. Visibility is poor; road signs are buried; and you're not sure where the road is going—or if you're even on the right road. Plus your gas gauge is teetering on empty. Quite a stress-inducing drive.

Undaunted, you refuse to turn back, however irrational. But before you know it you're stuck in a ditch, wheels spitting snow. You just know you're going to die on Publication Road. Wait! Headlights are coming your way. So you open your door and flag the oncoming car, staggering to the driver's window.

Inside the well-equipped 4×4 you find four experienced Publication Road drivers: Karen Berger, Barry DiGregorio, Kelly Milner Halls and John Woram.

Karen Berger is a contributing editor for *Backpacker Magazine* and author of two books, *Where the Waters Divide: A Walk Across America Along the Continental Divide* (Harmony, 1993) and *Hiking and Backpacking: A Complete Guide* (Norton, 1995). She is currently completing two more books on backpacking for W.W. Norton and The Mountaineers Books.

Photograph by Dennis Stierer

Barry DiGregorio is an entertainment and science specialist, whose first book, *Mars the Living Planet* (North Atlantic Books/Frog Limited), has a publication date of April, 1997. He is also an exhibit developer for the Buffalo Museum of Science.

Kelly Milner Halls is a nonfiction children's writer. She recently published her first book, *Dino Trekking* (Wiley, 1996), and is working on her second, *Kids Go Denver*, due out in June, 1997.

John Woram is a senior contributing editor and monthly columnist for *Windows Magazine* and author of three books: *Sound Recording Handbook* (H.W. Sams & Co., 1989), *PC Configuration Handbook, 2nd Edition* (Random House, 1990) and *Windows Configuration Handbook, 1st Edition* (Random House, 1993).

Although these writers haven't fully mastered the road—they slip and slide on occasion—they do travel it often and successfully. Lucky you, no longer stranded. The veterans offer to help guide you to your destination. You eagerly hop in the back seat and begin asking questions:

When did you begin writing seriously as a freelancer, and how long did it take you to get to this point?

Berger: I started writing when I got a college internship in 1980. I was a classical music major and upon graduation I became assistant editor at a music magazine, which gave me the opportunity to write a lot of feature stories and interviews. I decided to try selling articles to other places, specializing in classical music. It wasn't too difficult, I think, because I had the technical background. Then I got my first major byline in *The New York Times* in 1982. It was a blind query. I wrote that I wanted to do a descriptive, slice-of-life piece about this local beach community near my parents' house that had an interesting winter communal life. The editor thought the idea was unique. What mattered after that was if I could write a good descriptive piece, which I guess I did. I got a whopping $150 dollars for a 1,200 word piece.

Milner Halls: About five years ago, I was discussing my writing with an associate. I'd worked briefly for a newspaper before I got pregnant with my first child. He asked me why I hadn't resumed my writing career and I said something about knowing I was good and not having to prove it by being published. He countered by saying most people who make that claim are more afraid of failure than reluctant to succeed. I knew he was right. I was afraid I wasn't good enough. The next day, I moved my desk into the living room and started work on my book *Dino Trekking*. I had toyed with the idea of writing professionally and it was time to see if I really had what it took to succeed.

When I found Vince Santucci, a pistol-packing paleontologist who fought against fossil thieves at Arizona's Petrified Forest National Park, I couldn't resist writing it up for the children's magazine market. I'd never before submitted to a magazine editor, but I figured it was time to try.

Woram: Actually, I had no intentions of becoming a writer. I wrote a few pieces in the audio business. Then, back in the '60s, I went to the Soviet Union and I was asked to write a piece on audio in the Soviet Union, not because I was a great writer but because I knew audio and was one of the few people to go to the Soviet Union at the time. So I didn't pursue a writing career. It more came about out of other people's need.

DiGregorio: I started writing in 1988. Because I had been involved in the local music scene for over 20 years, I built up many professional music contacts. I wrote for local papers and progressed to submitting to magazines like *DISCoveries* and *Creem*. Since I didn't make much money at first, I found lots of work doing concert reviews and interviews. Working for these small entertainment papers taught me how to work alone and professionally.

How long did it take you to establish a reputation as a solid writer?

Milner Halls: It took me two years to place that first article. I realize now it wasn't the quality of the writing that held me back as much as it was my ability (or lack of ability) to read the market. I had my writer's guide, I had my sample issues. But somehow I was not connecting on just what each editor was after. It took several dozen rejections for me to realize just how valuable writer's guidelines and careful study of editorial direction within the market guides could be. When I finally sold that first piece, it was because I successfully married the work to the right publication and editor. Eventually, more and more editors decided to give me a shot. By the time I'd submitted for three years, I had a pretty solid reputation.

DiGregorio: It took me three years to become established and build a good résumé. That's what aspiring writers should shoot for: building credible résumés and adding to their credentials every time they do some work. It doesn't matter whether you work for small local presses or local newspapers, include everything in chronological order in your résumé.

Woram: I wrote for a few engineering magazines in the audio field. Then I wrote a monthly column. Then I wrote for *Billboard* magazine. It was really a matter of one thing leading to another. I was also a recording engineer at RCA records, during the beginning of the so called multi-track era. There was a big interest in it, so I began writing about it, again, not because I was a writer but because I was in the middle of the new technology. I wrote *Sound Recording Handbook* which covered recording studio technology. Eventually I just wandered into fulltime writing.

Berger: It wasn't until I got my first book published (*Where the Waters Divide: A Walk Across America Along the Continental Divide*) that I became confident I was a legitimate writer. Even though I had a big stack of clips before that, the book was the clincher. But that took 13 years. I think my proposals started getting put into a different file once I had a book in print. Nowadays, I don't send out many blind queries. Sending them worked okay for me when I was starting out, but it can be very time-consuming, inefficient and discouraging.

What strategy did you use to land your first assignment? How do you approach editors now? Do you send queries to new magazine markets or are you more aggressive?

Berger: I really believe in networking and meeting editors. Once I've got a contact, I hammer it and hammer it and hammer it. Writing for the same places and people is very time efficient. Once you've got a client try to make them a repeat client. Now, I look for an angle. For instance, if I were going to write for a western magazine, what I'd do is send them copies of the local reviews of *Where the Waters Divide* to establish a connection. I could say, "Here's what your editors/reviewers had to say about my book. I'd like to write for you." Essentially, a writer has to say, "Here's why you should choose me above everyone else."

Milner Halls: For me, it was easier at first to submit complete manuscripts. I figured if they could see at least one finished slant on a story idea complete with details, they could see my style as a writer. Now I'm relatively sure most stories will find an editorial home. So while I do send queries to the editors I've worked for, when I'm fairly sure it's something they'll want I start to work on the piece right away. I try to anticipate my editors' needs in advance, based on a careful study of their magazines. I submit with photo research complete, or at least a local photographer in mind. And I try to submit a day ahead of the deadline assigned. If you get a nibble on a query, follow through. If an editor likes your idea but not the approach, willingly offer a rewrite. Realize writing is a business.

DiGregorio: My strategy is that I'm a readaholic. Constant reading and keeping up to date on subjects you want to write about is your best strategy. I look for stories that have not been completely worn out. That involves staying in touch with people who are around ground-breaking news. It's hard for a magazine editor to turn down a brand new idea that has been well-researched. I always send a one- or two-page query describing what I have to offer the editor. I take the time to read the magazine and analyze the content. The best way to get into a new magazine is to try the smaller monthly columns. And I never forget a SASE. If a submission doesn't have one, editors will immediately throw away the query. I always present a neat proposal package.

Woram: After I had a couple of computer books out, I approached *Windows Magazine* and wanted them to do a few reviews of my latest book. I also told them—and I thought this was a fat chance—that they might consider printing a few excerpts from the book. Well, they apparently liked my stuff because they came to me with an offer to write a monthly column.

Is it possible these days for a writer to sustain a living by freelancing?

Woram: If you find the right niche it's possible. I remember when I was writing one of my first audio books I was chatting with Dr. Ray Dolby about his noise reduction system. I said, "Did you mean so and so when you were saying so and so" referring to this piece he'd written. He said, "Of course I did, didn't you read my paper?" I said, "Yes. That's why I'm asking." He said, "Well it's right there." I said, "I know it's right there, Ray, but that's incomprehensible for us mortals." I knew him, knew the system, but I still didn't get it. And I thought I wasn't alone in my confusion. That's when I figured there was a strong market for translating technical language for the regular person who just wants to use the stuff. I never thought of myself as an expert in any area. I was more of an intelligent layman who couldn't comprehend the experts because they had their own language. Sometimes experts need a translator.

Milner Halls: It isn't easy. But yes, I believe it's possible. Dozens of new publications pop up every year. If a writer works hard, really pours on the steam, and networks effectively, I think it is possible to make a reasonable living freelancing. Will you get rich? Probably not writing for children. But it's as much a lifestyle as it's a career choice. I enjoy the quick turnaround of freelancing, the change in subject matter. I like meeting and interviewing a diverse population, and freelancing feeds those preferences. The payoff is more than simple financial gain.

DiGregorio: It is both tougher and easier to make money in the freelance writing market. It's easier because there are thousands of magazines to work for and all require a steady flux of good reading material. It's tougher, however, because of the enormous crowd of established writers who get the feature articles. I have been freelancing since 1988, and if I did not do several other jobs I wouldn't be able to support myself. Not on magazines anyway! It's too competitive. The best thing a freelancer can hope for is to gain enough writing experience to become a staff writer for a major publication. To get there is a challenge, though. Most freelancers I know have other jobs. The trick is to remain flexible and have several opportunities going at once. Always keep thinking of new ideas and approaches. Ask yourself: Do I have enough experience to start submitting book proposals? Can I write for TV? Are there any radio stations in my area looking for a freelance writer?

Berger: Absolutely. But it takes commitment, hustle and endurance. I had my first byline in 1980. So it's taken me sixteen years to get this far. Also, I've done a lot of sacrificing to get where I am. You have to write about what you're not that interested in sometimes. I spent two years studying and writing about financial management because that's the job I could get. My heart wasn't in that, but you take whatever opportunity you've got and do it as best you can. A lot of people only see the perks of being a freelancer: you're independent; you create something; you get to see your name in print; you get to follow subjects that interest you. But people don't realize all the scut work. I don't have a secretary. I do all my typing, all my mailing, all my bookkeeping, all my follow-up calls. I do all this work that the office manager would be taking care of. Add to those things all the expenses. You can't think that because you're getting $1,500 for a 1,500 word piece that you're making all this great money, because you've also got to factor in all those queries that didn't pan out, the revisions that always come, the calls you're going to make to chase down an extra fact. It's simply not as easy and as glamorous as people think.

How do you generate ideas?

Woram: Sometimes you look at that blank screen and say, "C'mon baby, talk to me." And it is nice when every once in a while the editors come to you and say, "Hey, we're getting a lot of mail about a certain item, could you cover this in your column?" Writers never really know what other writers are working on, so there's always a chance for overlap. You might come up with a great idea for a piece and then get upset when your proposal is rejected only to find the magazine just bought a similar piece the day before. I did an article on a specific software product and had it almost finished only to find another columnist for *Windows* did a piece on that same software just three months before, so I had to change gears.

DiGregorio: My method is to thoroughly study the subject I wish to write about and then tell the story from a new perspective. It sounds easy but it is not. Only by becoming an expert in a particular subject can you then expect to write a new perspective on it.

Milner Halls: I read. I read newspapers; I read magazines; I read fliers; I read brochures. If I'm sitting in a car repair shop, I'll leaf through the auto mechanic trades. If I'm at the pediatrician's, I'll read up on medical health issues. If I'm watching TV, a part of my brain is taking notes, collecting story ideas. I keep my eyes open virtually every waking minute. And I am never lacking for story ideas as a result.

Berger: Notice what moves you—read everything. And listen to your friends. I'm serious. Sometimes they have great ideas for you, even if they're wrong about where these ideas should be published. I was telling a story once and my friends thought it was hilarious. One of them said, "You should write a story about this for *Reader's Digest.*" He was completely off base on where the piece should be sold, but the idea of writing it and publishing it was a good one. So I found a more suitable magazine and sold the story.

How do you recycle or rework ideas to get a few articles out of one topic? Could you give me an example?

DiGregorio: If I do an interview with a famous person and retain publishing rights, I can later break the interview down, paraphrasing and combining it with new information to make it look like a completely new story and resell it. But to do this I have to retain republishing rights; otherwise it's back to the drawing board. If I retain all rights, I can publish the story as many times as I can find a magazine for it.

Woram: I just stay up with the industry, and I of course borrow material from my books to put into my columns. I also search message boards on online services and the Internet to see what people are talking about. If a few related issues keep getting attention then I'll do my research on the whole lot and see what I come up with after that.

Milner Halls: I did an interview with natural science artist John Gurche about two years ago. It was a fascinating interview, and I initially sought him to create an article for *Highlights for Children* about his work reconstructing the face of a 5,000 year old mummy found in the Italian Alps. But before the interview I did my homework. By the time I met with him, I knew he had also illustrated a number of dinosaur projects including stamps for the United States Post Office. My ongoing market research told me *Crayola Kids* was planning a dinosaur issue. So after I collected anthropological details about the mummy, I asked him if he'd mind talking about his dinosaur illustrations. He agreed, so I created a straight question and answer piece about his work as a dinosaur illustrator for *Crayola Kids*. But, as we talked about that part of his work, he mentioned he had done pre-production sketches for the film *Jurassic Park*. I took careful notes, and eventually sold a story based on that part of my interview to the Dinosaur Society's *Dino Times*. By keeping several publications with special needs in mind, I was able to sell three stories without compromising any of my editor's needs.

Berger: I think it's best to become an expert in an area, that way you can write about all that subject's aspects for a variety of publications without wasting too much time doing individual research—you already know the material like the back of your hand. Then it's just a matter of looking at a subject from a lot of different angles and finding the right publications. Angles are critical—you have to understand what subtle differences make a subject and approach right for one publication and not the other.

How do you negotiate a higher rate or increase your fee? Do you offer to supply photos, sidebars and other extras?

DiGregorio: There is no way to negotiate for a higher rate or fee unless you have a story that is hot and the editors need to have it at any cost. This rarely occurs for the magazines I write for, but tabloids are willing to pay seemingly any amount for the right gossip. Some magazine editors expect you to supply photos with your article at no extra fee. Those writers who can and do get paying jobs more often. Always request the prompt return of photographs you send with your articles. Get it in writing that they will be returned. Otherwise, if you borrow photographs like I do and don't get them back, you can be held accountable for them.

Berger: I have no problem telling editors I want more money than what they're offering if it's appropriate. I'll say, "I think that such and so would be a better fee for this article because I'm going to have to do x, y, and z for it." Photos and sidebars are extra work. I want to be compensated for adding those elements. It depends on the magazine, too: what it can afford to pay, how much you want to write for them, and whether they are a regular client. I have recently set a minimum rate, and I'm very upfront about it if someone asks me to write for less. I don't write for the same amount for every magazine. I'll get $1 a word for some publications, but others can't pay that. It's also a good idea to learn to take decent photographs. Sometimes you get more for the pictures than you do for the article. At most of the magazines I write for, the going rate for color transparencies is somewhere between $75 and $150 for a small picture. And it can be more.

Milner Halls: I don't usually expect fees for photo research. I consider that part of my job, although I certainly wouldn't turn down additional pay. But I try to create sidebars to go with my articles wherever possible. They are almost always welcome and generate additional income.

Woram: Most magazines have a certain range. The magazines who are paying some writers $1 a word are not paying others 10¢ a word. There's a consistency, I think, for each magazine. The pay proposed is usually in the ball park, although there are times when a little negotiation is necessary. It's much harder to negotiate book deals than article deals. But for magazines I always supply sidebars and other little extras to complement the piece, and editors tend to really like that. If you're going to deliver a product you're going to deliver a product, and that means you provide whatever is necessary for the piece, be it photos, sidebars, graphs or noteworthy quotes. Some of these extras can easily be cut, of course, but it's nice to give editors as much as possible to work with and let them decide what they want to do with the article.

What, in your opinion, is the most difficult task for writers trying to break into freelancing, especially if they want to try to sustain a living just by writing?

Milner Halls: Multi-tasking is always a challenge. To even attempt making a living at freelancing, you almost have to have half a dozen stories floating around your head at one time. If a writer isn't organized, the waters will cloud—you won't stay on top of your obligations. That is the most difficult part, once you get started. It's not easy going through the ranks. Everyone is tempted to start at the top. But the lessons you learn as you climb the freelancing ladder are invaluable. Consider the lean times a freelance education. And know for every low budget piece you publish you are that much closer to the brass ring.

DiGregorio: Owning up to the reality that you must keep a second job in the event you are out of work for long periods is tough. Most magazines pay upon publication and that translates into getting paid sometimes six months after you submitted the article. Even if you have 10 or 12 very good paying feature articles, which is certainly rare, in one year, your checks will come in at different times. Magazine writing should not be thought of as the final destination of the writer. Instead, after gaining experience in this field and establishing a name for yourself, you will have to consider writing books if you really want to make a living at writing.

Berger: I think many writers are so grateful to be published, they'll take anything—or write for free! I never write for no pay and I won't volunteer as a writer. I don't believe in it. I think volunteering as a writer is taking away work from people who are at the lower rungs of the ladder who need those jobs. Why are writers asked so frequently to do volunteer work? Why is our work so frequently thought of as something that can be given away? I mean would you ask a doctor or a lawyer to give away their work? If you need to get started and haven't got a clip in the world, then maybe you could consider writing for free, if you're absolutely convinced that it's something you want to do. I don't think it's that difficult to get published by local publications. If you can't get published for pay, even a little bit of pay, then you really need to reevaluate whether you're in the right field, because you may lack either the business savvy to get the work or you may not be able to write well.

Woram: Writers really need to do their jobs thoroughly. One of my bugaboos is research, which is a really tough call. I'll be reading historical accounts of something and those accounts have nothing to do with what actually happened. The author failed to check facts or even made up facts. Some writers just invent stories just to have a story. Often, one writer will swipe something from another and none of them go back to the original source so the wrong information keeps getting printed and what really happened gets lost. It's amazing what goes past editors; either because of deadlines or they assume the writer is the authority, they don't check on or challenge the writer. So make sure you know the facts before you put something into print.

Do you have any other advice for writers eager to launch a freelance career in magazines?

Woram: Since I never had the intent to become a writer it's difficult to say. I think it's important to keep challenging yourself and to feel what you do is worthwhile. I'm challenged by writing. Especially now that I'm in the computer business where nobody speaks English. I read the words and I recognize the words but I often find I have no idea what this person is talking about. I'm intrigued at the difficulty of expressing something in clear English so that somebody who is not super-technical can understand it. That's part of the draw, to make a connection between these two different languages.

Milner Halls: Try not to take rejection personally. If you approach rejections the right way, they are very helpful. One, they help you understand what an editor wants or doesn't want. Two, if critical comments are offered, they help you improve your work. And three, even rejections help make your work known at various editorial offices. If you are persistent in submitting various ideas at the same publication, the editors might eventually start taking the time to give you a little guidance. Take it with a joyous and thankful heart. It's a gift. If you are rejected, remember, it happens to the best writers. Take it in stride. Look over your work carefully. Try to decide if it's the best you can do. You will usually see some place for improvement, regardless of your level of expertise. I read my published work and see room for improvement, almost every time. Once you assess the submission, rewrite it and submit it again and again and again to new markets. Remember: it took me two years and a dozen rejections slips to sell my first article. But I didn't give up. And if you really want to write for a living, you shouldn't either.

Berger: First, I don't believe in writer's block. I don't think plumbers have plumber's block and I don't think teachers have teacher's block. I think if you're stuck on something you should go write something else. If you can't do that then you're probably not a professional writer. Not everything you write is going to be perfect the first time but that's what computers are for. I revise and revise and revise until I'm blue in the face and then I come back a week later and revise even more. Writing doesn't come easily for me, but it does come. If I'm inspired by something it comes much easier, of course, but writers, like all people, aren't always that inspired. Second, do anything you can to get yourself out of the slush pile. I go to writer's conferences. I go to meetings in my field. I give lectures, meet editors, make contacts. Being a writer is not just stringing words together. Only half of the job is sitting around thinking how to craft beautiful sentences. The other half is plain old unglamourous work: research, getting quotes, calling people, bills. Third, you also need to have a passion for writing, not for becoming a writer. A lot of people are really in love with the idea of being a writer but not in love with writing. And, finally, remember that all editors ask the same questions: Have we worked with this person before? How do we know she will produce? Can we count on strong writing, turned in on time? The first question you've got to answer, almost before you even propose your topic, is: Can they count on you? Reputation is so important as a writer. It's really all you have to sell, because there are thousands of writers out there to take your place if you slip. You get a solid reputation by getting things done on time and doing them right.

DiGregorio: Launch yourself with the idea that you want to be hired as a permanent staff writer or assistant editor one day. Do not disillusion yourself by thinking a freelance magazine career is a stable profession. Magazines go out of business every day and new ones are formed, but to expect to support yourself or an entire family on just magazines is unrealistic. I'm sure there are probably some writers out there who are doing it, but I imagine they must be on the hustle 24 hours a day submitting hundreds of queries per month just to make ends meet. Remember, writing for today's widely-read magazines is an opportunity few authors knew just 20 years ago. The most memorable aspects of writing magazine articles are all the people you talk to, all the research you put into a project and what you learn from it. It's great to get paid and recognized while at the same time you're growing and learning. What could be better?

Probably not much. Why else would you be reading this book? And look, you've returned to the spot on Publication Road where your life was so graciously salvaged. But the snow has miraculously stopped, your car has 4-wheel drive, plus it's back on the road and full of gas. You're in the driver's seat, ready to go. How did that happen? Why do you have a renewed sense of where you're going and what obstacles await you? From where did this sudden clarity and readiness come? Oh the magic of posing a few pointed questions to just the right people.

The Business of Writing

Minding the Details

Writers who have had some success in placing their work know that the effort to publish requires an entirely different set of skills than does the act of writing. A shift in perspective is required when you move from creating your work to selling it. Like it or not, successful writers—*career* writers—have to keep the business side of the writing business in mind as they work.

Each of the following sections discusses a writing business topic that affects anyone selling his writing. We'll take a look at contracts and agreements—the documents that license a publisher to use your work. We'll consider your rights as a writer and sort out some potentially confusing terminology. We'll cover the basics of copyright protection—a topic of perennial concern for writers. And for those of you who are already making money with your writing, we'll offer some tips for keeping track of financial matters and staying on top of your tax liabilities.

Our treatment of the business topics that follow is necessarily limited. Look for complete information on each subject at your local bookstore or library—both in books (some of which we mention) and periodicals aimed at writers. Information is also available from the federal government, as indicated later in this article.

CONTRACTS AND AGREEMENTS

If you've been freelancing even a short time, you know that contracts and agreements vary considerably from one publisher to another. Some magazine editors work only by verbal agreement; others have elaborate documents you must sign in triplicate and return before you begin the assignment. As you evaluate any contract or agreement, consider carefully what you stand to gain and lose by signing. Did you have another sale in mind that selling all rights the first time will negate? Does the agreement provide the publisher with a number of add-ons (advertising rights, reprint rights, etc.) for which they won't have to pay you again?

In contract negotiations, the writer is usually interested in licensing the work for a particular use but limiting the publisher's ability to make other uses of the work in the future. It's in the publisher's best interest, however, to secure rights to use the work in as many ways as possible, both now and later on. Those are the basic positions of each party. The negotiation is a process of compromise and capitulation on questions relating to those basic points—and the amount of compensation to be given the writer for his work.

A contract is rarely a take-it-or-leave-it proposition. If an editor tells you that his company will allow *no* changes on the contract, you will then have to decide how important the assignment is to you. But most editors are open to negotiation, and you

INSIDER REPORT

Suture Self: From a Career in Medicine to a Career in Writing

A former hospital administrator, Alan Duncan Ross has a clear rationale for committing himself to writing instead of medicine: Writing forces you to explore emotion, whereas medicine forces you to suppress it. Thus his chief reason for leaving the hospital was that he did not want to anaesthetize himself to basic feelings. "To do an efficient job in medicine, you can't be consumed by the emotional toll of patients. I want things to affect me in a very full way. Going into writing was a matter of following what I've always felt I should be doing."

Ross's now impressive writing career began in college when he published an article with a small-circulation educational newsletter about his experiences teaching creative writing in a Boston prison. "They only gave me $50, but it proved to me that if it happened once, it could happen again."

Soon after publishing that article, Ross had several "near misses" in getting a few book manuscripts published. "When you get that close and things don't come through, you either quit or you believe you can go over the finish line," he says. "Sometimes publishing a book is less a matter of talent than endurance and perseverance. He who stands last will go over the finish line. That's what I've learned and continue to pursue endlessly."

But make sure you know your motivations for writing, for wanting to go over that finish line. "If your writing is compelling or finds a niche or market, that's great, but that should not, especially in the beginning, be the spirit in which one pursues a writing career. You must have something to say and be patient enough to wait for people to hear it."

Not surprisingly, Ross's successful transition from medicine to writing has been a matter of attrition and practicality. "I always kept writing no matter what else I was doing, which is what you've got to do if you're a writer at heart. And, more importantly, I knew the medical field was not where I wanted to go with my life. I was practical enough to hold down a job and write on the side. But I did enjoy studying medicine. I'm still fascinated by it."

Learning so much about medicine certainly hasn't hurt Ross's writing. Co-authored with Harlan Gibbs, his latest endeavor, *The Medicine of ER* (Basic Books, October 1996), is an informative nonfiction book that explains the facts behind the fiction in television's favorite emergency room. "When they scream out PTIV, 2ccs, you not only know what it means," says Ross, "but as they do a procedure you figure out why they're doing it, when they're doing it, what they're going to do next, what it leads them to. I'm kind of like a commentator at a football game who's making comments on the plays and why the players and coaches make the decisions they make."

INSIDER REPORT, *Ross*

Having areas of interest and expertise can only help a writer's career, says Ross. When still an unpublished author, Ross decided to put together a "photographic travelogue," as he calls it, about some of his travels. Random House almost published the book, but the deal collapsed. Yet that "near miss" was enough to whet Ross's appetite.

He kept writing and eventually landed a four-book contract with Warner Books. "That was the first book deal in which I actually received an advance. Warner bought four finished manuscripts for $50,000." As grand as that might sound, none of those four books ever made it into print. Soon after the contract was signed, Warner changed their publishing mission, which meant not publishing Ross's books. But he got to keep the advance.

Ross decided to write about another interest: games kids can play without spending lots of money, such as marbles. Just before the manuscript of *Street Games* was given up for dead, Ross got word that McGraw-Hill would publish it. Although Ross earned little financially from that first book, its publication did lead to many other opportunities, particularly in the film industry.

Ross's first script deal came when he was flown to California to promote *Street Games*. While there, he was asked to write a few comedy sketches. Writing these sketches led to payment for his first teleplay for ABC, *How the West Was Fun*. "Somebody involved with *Street Games* heard I could write fast and well, so they called me on a Thursday and said, 'We need a polished script for this television special by Monday, can you do it?' " Needless to say, Ross delivered.

Meanwhile, *Street Games* attracted the attention of writer Anita Loos (*San Francisco, Gentlemen Prefer Blondes*), who read the book and called him. Says Ross, "I'd never spoken to this woman in my life and she called and said, 'I'd like to meet you, young man. You're a good writer, but you shouldn't write books, you should write screenplays.' " They met, and Loos kept encouraging Ross to pursue the creative route through scripts. "So I listened to her," says Ross. "She was an important force in my transition into screenplays."

Since that first script sale of *How the West Was Fun*, Ross has written scripts for *California Dreaming*, *Psycho 4*, and other films and documentaries. Recently, he was co-writer and executive producer of the Warner Brothers/NBC science fiction movie *The Seekers*, and he's working with producer Gale Anne Hurd (*Terminator* and *The Abyss*) on an historical romance, *Dominion*.

Who would have thought the publication of a small book on games would become the catalyst not only for Ross to make the transition from hospital administrator to published author, but from books to comedy to screenplays as well? In this business you just never know in what direction one piece of writing will take you.

—*Don Prues*

should learn to compromise on points that don't matter to you while maintaining your stand on things that do.

When it's not specified, most writers assume that a magazine publisher is buying first rights. Some writers' groups can supply you with a sample magazine contract to use when the publisher doesn't supply one, so you can document your agreement in writing. Members of The Authors Guild are given a sample book contract and information about negotiating when they join. For more information about contracts and agreements, see *Business and Legal Forms for Authors & Self-Publishers*, by Tad Crawford (Allworth Press, 1990); *From Printout to Published*, by Michael Seidman (Carroll & Graf, 1992) or *The Writer's Guide to Contract Negotiations*, by Richard Balkin (Writer's Digest Books, 1985), which is out of print but should be available in libraries.

RIGHTS AND THE WRITER

A creative work can be used in many different ways. As the originator of written works, you enjoy full control over how those works are used; you are in charge of the rights that your creative works are "born" with. When you agree to have your work published, you are giving the publisher the right to use your work in one or more ways. Whether that right is simply to publish the work for the first time in a periodical or to publish it as many times as he likes and in whatever form he likes is up to you—it all depends on the terms of the contract or agreement the two of you arrive at. As a general rule, the more rights you license away, the less control you have over your work and the more money you should be paid for the license. We find that writers and editors sometimes define rights in different ways. For a classification of terms, read Types of Rights, below.

Sometimes editors don't take the time to specify the rights they are buying. If you sense that an editor is interested in getting stories but doesn't seem to know what his and the writer's responsibilities are regarding rights, be wary. In such a case, you'll want to explain what rights you're offering (preferably one-time or first serial rights only) and that you expect additional payment for subsequent use of your work.

You should strive to keep as many rights to your work as you can from the outset, otherwise, your attempts to resell your writing may be seriously hampered.

The Copyright Law that went into effect January 1, 1978, said writers were primarily selling one-time rights to their work unless they—and the publisher—agreed otherwise in writing. Book rights are covered fully by the contract between the writer and the book publisher.

TYPES OF RIGHTS

- First Serial Rights—First serial rights means the writer offers a newspaper or magazine the right to publish the article, story or poem for the first time in any periodical. All other rights to the material remain with the writer. The qualifier "North American" is often added to this phrase to specify a geographical limit to the license.

  When material is excerpted from a book scheduled to be published and it appears in a magazine or newspaper prior to book publication, this is also called first serial rights.
- One-Time Rights—A periodical that licenses one-time rights to a work (also known as simultaneous rights) buys the *nonexclusive* right to publish the work once. That is, there is nothing to stop the author from selling the work to other publications at the same time. Simultaneous sales would typically be to periodicals without overlapping audiences.
- Second Serial (Reprint) Rights—This gives a newspaper or magazine the opportunity to print an article, poem or story after it has already appeared in another newspaper or magazine. Second serial rights are nonexclusive—that is, they can be licensed to more than one market.
- All Rights—This is just what it sounds like. If you license away all rights to your

work, you forfeit the right to ever use it again. If you think you'll want to use the material later, you must avoid submitting to such markets or refuse payment and withdraw your material. Ask the editor whether he is willing to buy first rights instead of all rights before you agree to an assignment or sale. Some editors will reassign rights to a writer after a given period, such as one year. It's worth an inquiry in writing.

- Subsidiary Rights—These are the rights, other than book publication rights, that should be covered in a book contract. These may include various serial rights; movie, television, audiotape and other electronic rights; translation rights, etc. The book contract should specify who controls these rights (author or publisher) and what percentage of sales from the licensing of these sub rights goes to the author.
- Dramatic, Television and Motion Picture Rights—This means the writer is selling his material for use on the stage, in television or in the movies. Often a one-year option to buy such rights is offered (generally for 10% of the total price). The interested party then tries to sell the idea to other people—actors, directors, studios or television networks, etc. Some properties are optioned over and over again, but most fail to become dramatic productions. In such cases, the writer can sell his rights again and again—as long as there is interest in the material. Though dramatic, TV and motion picture rights are more important to the fiction writer than the nonfiction writer, producers today are increasingly interested in nonfiction material; many biographies, topical books and true stories are being dramatized.

SELLING SUBSIDIARY RIGHTS

The primary right in the world of book publishing is the right to publish the book itself. All other rights (such as movie rights, audio rights, book club rights, electronic rights and foreign rights) are considered secondary, or subsidiary, to the right to print publication. In contract negotiations, authors and their agents traditionally try to avoid granting the publisher subsidiary rights that they feel capable of marketing themselves. Publishers, on the other hand, typically hope to obtain control over as many of the sub rights as they can. Philosophically speaking, subsidiary rights will be best served by being left in the hands of the person or organization most capable of—and interested in—exploiting them profitably. Sometimes that will be the author and her agent, and sometimes that will be the publisher.

Larger agencies have experience selling foreign rights, movie rights and the like, and many authors represented by such agents prefer to retain those rights and let their agents do the selling. Book publishers, on the other hand, have subsidiary rights departments, which are responsible for exploiting all sub rights the publisher was able to retain during the contract negotiation.

That job might begin with a push to sell foreign rights, which normally bring in advance money which is divided among author, agent and publisher. Further efforts then might be made to sell the right to publish the book as a paperback (although many book contracts now call for hard/soft deals, in which the original hardcover publisher buys the right to also publish the paperback version).

Any other rights which the publisher controls will be pursued, such as book clubs and magazines. Publishers usually don't control movie rights to a work, as those are most often retained by author and agent.

The marketing of electronic rights to a work, in this era of rapidly expanding capabilities and markets for electronic material, can be tricky. With the proliferation of electronic and multimedia formats, publishers, agents and authors are going to great pains

INSIDER REPORT

Taking Risks in a World of Multiple Media

Deborah Forte rejects the term "multimedia." As Senior Vice President of Scholastic Inc. and head of Scholastic Productions, the branch of the company responsible for expanding Scholastic's book offerings into the realms of video, television and CD-ROM, she considers herself simply "a media person. I think media in general is in a state of transition and I think new media, multimedia—people don't even really know what that means."

As consumers begin to sort out the expanding universe of media available for their entertainment and education, Forte feels writers must be open to the various platforms as well. "I think one of the things that will be important for the creative com-

Deborah Forte

munity's move forward is the ability to visualize and work across multiple media platforms. People are going to depend on their success from multiple markets rather than a single marketplace," she says. "And the better projects will be those that maintain their integrity across each media platform or across all media platforms. Writers must be creative, take risks and not think in terms of a single media platform."

Taking creative risks is not merely Forte's advice—it seems to be her job description. In 1984, she began at Scholastic working in what was then a new format, home video. From there Scholastic Productions developed into a producer of multiple media projects for kids, such as the successful public television series "The Magic School Bus" and a number of *Goosebumps*-related projects, which evolved from the phenomenally successful line of creepy tales for kids by R.L. Stine. The company is also developing original alternative media projects (work that was not first published in book form).

When she took on production of "Goosebumps" as a weekly anthology TV series, Forte says everyone in the television business told her such series don't work, that kids don't like them. "They said if there are not repeating characters and locations that are continually familiar to the audience, your audience won't stick with your show. Everyone told me that."

But since its debut in November of 1995, "Goosebumps" has consistently been the top-rated kids show on TV. "To be good in this business you must take creative risks. You must be willing to do things differently."

Whether someone likes Power Rangers or Barney, says Forte, they weren't like anything else on television when they started. "And they broke the mold. A

INSIDER REPORT, *Forte*

lot of the media marketplace is characterized by imitation. People want to develop and produce things that are like other things that have been successful. I would not spend my time imitating successful things," she says. "The real challenge and the real excitement about being in this business is the opportunity to make something new that is unique that people will respond to."

The success of "Goosebumps" on television led to a partnership with Steven Spielberg's Dreamworks SKG to develop a "Goosebumps" CD-ROM. (Microsoft also produces CD-ROMs for Scholastic.) In its early development, Dreamworks interviewed interactive writers to script the CD-ROM. "But our inclination was to go with a writer of filmed entertainment because we felt that although the interactivity in the CD-ROM would be very different from the linear characteristics of television, we still wanted there to be story and characters," says Forte. "We all conferred and agreed to hire a feature film writer for the CD-ROM. That was a risk." But it was a way to combine the best of filmed entertainment with the best of interactivity.

Story and characters are indeed important factors in deciding which books will translate well into alternative media. Uniqueness is another. "I don't think 'Goosebumps' would have been successful if there were four other things out there that were scary, funny series. And I don't think I would have done it. But it's unique and had a reason to be. 'Magic School Bus' is the same way."

"Magic School Bus," like "Goosebumps," is an example of an idea that worked in multiple media platforms. The successful book series spawned the PBS series. Traveling "Magic School Bus" exhibits are seen by young museum-goers throughout the U.S. as well as "Magic School Bus" science activity trunks, CD-ROMs, videos and magazine tie-ins.

"The whole idea is that when you have a franchise, you can develop it so that it works across all media platforms as an interactive experience. The CD-ROMs we do with Microsoft and Dreamworks are electronic interactive experiences. The television is a different kind of experience. They all complement each other. And that's what more and more in the world of media will be about."

But, Forte points out, each medium cannibalizes the others to some extent in terms of audience. "There are fewer people doing any one thing at one time because there are so many new media platforms. People only have a specific amount of leisure time to do all these things. Even children. Especially children."
—*Alice P. Buening*

these days to make sure contracts specify exactly *which* electronic rights are being conveyed (or retained).

Compensation for these rights is a major source of conflict between writers and publishers, as many book publishers seek control of them and many magazines routinely include electronic rights in the purchase of all rights, often with no additional payment. Alternative ways of handling this issue include an additional 15% added to the amount to purchase first rights to a royalty system based on the number of times an article is accessed from an electronic database.

COPYRIGHT

Copyright law exists to protect creators of original works. It is engineered to encourage creative expression and aid in the progress of the arts and sciences by ensuring that artists and authors hold the rights by which they can profit from their labors.

Copyright protects your writing, unequivocally recognizes you (its creator) as its owner, and grants you all the rights, benefits and privileges that come with ownership. The moment you finish a piece of writing—whether it is a short story, article, novel or poem—the law recognizes that only you can decide how it is to be used.

The basics of copyright law are discussed here. More detailed information can be obtained from the Copyright Office and in the books mentioned at the end of this section.

Copyright law gives you the right to make and distribute copies of your written works, the right to prepare derivative works (dramatizations, translations, musical arrangements, etc.—any work based on the original) and the right to perform or publicly display your work. With very few exceptions, anything you write today will enjoy copyright protection for your lifetime plus 50 years. Copyright protects "original works of authorship" that are fixed in a tangible form of expression. Titles, ideas and facts can *not* be copyrighted.

Some people are under the mistaken impression that copyright is something they have to send away for, and that their writing is not properly protected until they have "received" their copyright from the government. The fact is, you don't have to register your work with the Copyright Office in order for your work to be copyrighted; any piece of writing is copyrighted the moment it is put to paper. Registration of your work does, however, offer some additional protection (specifically, the possibility of recovering punitive damages in an infringement suit) as well as legal proof of the date of copyright.

Registration is a matter of filling out a form (for writers, that's generally form TX) and sending the completed form, a copy of the work in question and a check for $20 to the Register of Copyrights, Library of Congress, Washington DC 20559. If the thought of paying $20 each to register every piece you write does not appeal to you, you can cut costs by registering a group of your works with one form, under one title for one $20 fee.

Most magazines are registered with the Copyright Office as single collective entities themselves; that is, the individual works that make up the magazine are *not* copyrighted individually in the names of the authors. You'll need to register your article yourself if you wish to have the additional protection of copyright registration. It's always a good idea to ask that your notice of copyright (your name, the year of first publication, and the copyright symbol ©) be appended to any published version of your work. You may use the copyright notice regardless of whether or not your work has been registered.

One thing writers need to be wary of is "work for hire" arrangements. If you sign an agreement stipulating that your writing will be done as work for hire, you will not control the copyright of the completed work—the person or organization who hired you will be the copyright owner. Work for hire arrangements and transfers of exclusive rights must be in writing to be legal, but it's a good idea to get every publishing agreement in writing before the sale.

You can obtain more information about copyright from the Copyright Office, Library of Congress, Washington DC 20559. To get answers to specific questions about copyright, call the Copyright Public Information Office at (202)707-3000 weekdays between 8:30 a.m. and 5 p.m. eastern standard time. To order copyright forms by phone, call (202)707-9100. Forms can also be downloaded from the Library of Congress website at http://lcweb. loc.gov/copyright. The website also includes information on filling out the forms, general copyright information and links to other websites related to copyright issues. A thorough (and thoroughly enjoyable) discussion of the subject of copyright law as it applies to writers can be found in Stephen Fishman's *The Copyright Handbook: How to Protect and Use Written Works* (Nolo Press, 1994). A shorter but no less enlightening treatment is Ellen Kozak's *Every Writer's Guide to Copyright & Publishing Law* (Henry Holt, 1990).

FINANCES AND TAXES

As your writing business grows, so will your obligation to keep track of your writing-related finances and taxes. Keeping a close eye on these details will help you pay as little tax as possible and keep you apprised of the state of your freelance business. A writing business with no systematic way of tracking expenses and income will soon be no writing business at all. If you dislike handling finance-related tasks, you can always hire someone else to handle them for a fee. If you do employ a professional, you must still keep the original records with an eye to providing the professional with the appropriate information.

If you decide to handle these tasks yourself—or if you just want to know what to expect of the person you employ—consider these tips:

Accurate records are essential, and the easiest way to keep them is to separate your writing income and expenses from your personal ones. Most professionals find that separate checking accounts and credit cards help them provide the best and easiest records.

Get in the habit of recording every transaction (both expenses and earnings) related to your writing. You can start at any time; you don't need to begin on January 1. Because you're likely to have expenses before you have income, start keeping your records whenever you make your first purchase related to writing—such as this copy of *Writer's Market*.

Any system of tracking expenses and income will suffice, but the more detailed it is, the better. Be sure to describe each transaction clearly—including the date; the source of the income (or the vendor of your purchase); a description of what was sold or bought; whether the payment was by cash, check or credit card; and the amount of the transaction.

The other necessary component of your financial record-keeping system is an orderly way to store receipts related to your writing. Check stubs, receipts for cash purchases, credit card receipts and similar paperwork should all be kept as well as recorded in your ledger. Any good book about accounting for small business will offer specific suggestions for ways to track your finances.

Freelance writers, artists and photographers have a variety of concerns about taxes that employees don't have, including deductions, self-employment tax and home office credits. Many freelance expenses can be deducted in the year in which they are incurred (rather than having to be capitalized, or depreciated, over a period of years). For details, consult the IRS publications mentioned later. Keep in mind that to be considered a business (and not a hobby) by the IRS you need to show a profit in three of the past five years. Hobby losses are deductible only to the extent of income produced by the activity.

There also is a home office deduction that can be claimed if an area in your home is used *exclusively* and *regularly* for business. Contact the IRS for information on requirements and limitations for this deduction. If your freelance income exceeds your expenses, regardless of the amount, you must declare that profit. If you make $400 or more after deductions, you must pay Social Security tax and file Schedule SE, a self-

INSIDER REPORT

Writing About Science, Sex and Almost Anything in Between

"Writing is a great way not to make a living," teases Hannah Holmes, who has been freelancing from her native Maine home for about four years. After stints at local Portland news weeklies, Holmes left the Pine Tree State for New York City, where she landed a job as an editor at environmentally-driven *Garbage* magazine. "I lived in the city a few years but couldn't stand it, so I moved back to Maine. Fortunately, *Garbage* let me keep my staff position while working from home." Laboring from her house proved invaluable for Holmes, allowing her to experience a quasi-freelance writing lifestyle while also putting her in the habit of planting herself at her desk every day from nine to five. She still enforces such rigorous self-discipline.

Hannah Holmes

Photograph by Herb Swanson

Now, however, Holmes is doing a lot more than sitting in Maine writing for only one magazine. Recently she's landed assignments that have taken her to places as exotic as Panama and Madagascar. "I write about everything from composting toilets to sex to rainforest biology, and I just think that's a writer's job description, to write about almost anything." She's not stretching the truth, either, evident in the eclectic assortment of magazines in which she's published: *Backpacker, EcoTraveler, Healthy Woman, Modern Maturity, Old House Journal, Self, Sierra Magazine* and *The Utne Reader.*

How does Holmes manage to write about so many varied subjects? "If I select my clips carefully, I can appear to be a specialized writer in a particular field, whether it's science writing or sex writing or whatever kind of writing." Holmes can also write for such a broad variety of magazines because she excels at maximizing the number of articles she gets out of one topic, mostly by making unconventional associations. Here's how she does it: She'll research a story, write it, then put a different spin on that already well-researched piece, and, voila!, she's sold two or three additional articles. Take, for instance, related articles Holmes sold to *Modern Maturity* and *Ms.* about this new, empowering ritual post-menopausal women are discovering and sharing, called "croning." One piece was "recycled" from the other. Holmes made a brilliant connection as she selected her markets: The piece was perfect for *Ms.* because it celebrated womanhood, and its focus on aging adults inevitably attracted editors at *Modern Maturity.* Her plan worked.

Having a plan is paramount for Holmes because it puts her in the position to dictate what she'll write. "I often decide what I want to write about, then seek an assignment," says Holmes, whose projects are often grand in scope and execution (like going to Panama and Madagascar). Such projects are not easy for a writer to finagle, though. Why, then, does Holmes insist on pursuing them? "I can spend the rest of my life writing hundred dollar stories and I'll never find time to write anything more. There's an endless demand for hundred dollar stories, and I don't want to spend my time writing them." So she doesn't. Instead, she invests lots of time researching and chasing larger projects. "I spent 18 months trying to put together that Madagascar trip. I was rejected 14 times trying to sell it, and on my fifteenth I was finally accepted." Her persistence obviously paid off; she left for Madagascar with not one but three story assignments. She's optimistic she'll land more assignments from that trip, too—and you can bet she's making more than a hundred dollars for each piece.

As far as querying is concerned, Holmes practices but doesn't endorse the quantity over quality strategy. "Some of my friends who are freelancers spend lots of time on their proposals, but I generally don't. I do a lot of bulk mailing. There have been weeks when I send out at least 25 proposals. I'm not sure that's a method to be imitated, but that's how I work." And her rejection rate is pretty estimable. "For a good month my rejection rate is 90 percent, which isn't bad. I'm more than happy to sell one out of ten proposals. But that's tough to do month after month."

All isn't as rosy as it seems for Holmes: Every day she must seek new markets for her work. "It's not easy living with the financial uncertainty. Some months I'll make $5,000 and others I'll be lucky to make $500." Although she's established some solid relationships with editors over the years, Holmes emphasizes that having regular contacts is no guarantee of survival in the freelancing jungle. "Contacts aren't enough in this business. The magazine could fold or the editor could get hit by a truck." She's not embellishing, either. "Contact disasters have been an unpleasant theme in my life. Last year, for example, I did $8,000 worth of work for *Healthy Woman Magazine*. This year they're out of business. So that's $8,000 I have to pick up elsewhere this year."

Still, part of Holmes's success is her tactful approach in dealing with editors. "I almost never call editors, no matter how many previous assignments I've gotten from them. My other writer friends will call, but what I tend to do is write these really silly harassment faxes: Have you lost my number? Did the dog eat my proposal? I don't call because I don't like to feel pushy." One other benefit of this method is that Holmes, like most of us, writes better than she speaks. By writing a letter she can showcase her writing, whereas over the phone she might sound like a fool and thus blow a potential assignment. Plus editors can read letters at their convenience, which minimizes the chances of being deemed a nuisance. "Having been an editor I know how unbelievably busy that job can be, and the last thing a busy editor wants is a pesty writer calling."

For Holmes, the best writing both piques a reader's interest and makes the reading process fun. "When I read I want to be entertained. And I think I'm pretty typical. So that's what I strive for in my writing. There should be a reward for reading; it needs to feel good. Even in science writing, you can inject some humor and levity in the material." This is Holmes's strongest asset: her spirited personality emanates from even the driest topic. "Anybody can put words

---

INSIDER REPORT, *Holmes*

on a page, but not everyone does it well and interestingly. Anybody can point a camera at something and push the button and a picture comes out, but it's only talented photographers who capture images people really want to look at."
—*Don Prues*

---

employment form, along with your Form 1040 and Schedule C tax forms.

While we cannot offer you tax advice or interpretations, we can suggest several sources for the most current information.

- Call your local IRS office. Look in the white pages of the telephone directory under U.S. Government—Internal Revenue Service. Someone will be able to respond to your request for IRS publications and tax forms or other information. Ask about the IRS Tele-tax service, a series of recorded messages you can hear by dialing on a touch-tone phone. If you need answers to complicated questions, ask to speak with a Taxpayer Service Specialist.
- Obtain the basic IRS publications. You can order them by phone or mail from any IRS office; most are available at libraries and some post offices. Start with *Your Federal Income Tax* (Publication 17) and *Tax Guide for Small Business* (Publication 334). These are both comprehensive, detailed guides—you'll need to find the regulations that apply to you and ignore the rest. There are many IRS publications relating to self-employment and taxes; Publication 334 lists many of these publications—such as *Business Use of Your Home* (Publication 587) and *Self-Employment Tax* (Publication 533).
- Consider other information sources. Many public libraries have detailed tax instructions available on tape. Some colleges and universities offer free assistance in preparing tax returns. And if you decide to consult a professional tax preparer, the fee is a deductible business expense on your tax return.

How Much Should I Charge?

BY ROBIN GEE

More and more writers are making the switch from a fulltime job to a combination of a part-time job and freelance work or a fulltime freelance career. Economic factors play a part, of course, as employers continue to downsize, but many choose the freelance life for a variety of reasons—for more freedom, to have more time with their families, to have more control over their careers, and, simply, because they want to make a living doing what they love.

One of the first questions new freelancers ask is, "How much should I charge?" Unfortunately, there is not one set of standard, agreed upon rates. Many factors play a part in how fees are set. Freelancers must take into account their overhead and the costs of doing business, their level of experience, area of expertise and the kind of work they do. Sometimes location plays a part, as does the nature and size of a client's business.

PRICING IN THE FREELANCE MARKET

The information supplied in this section is designed to give new freelancers and those interested in trying other areas of freelance an idea of what other freelancers are charging. Based on research—surveys and interviews with freelancers, clients and writers' organizations in the U.S. and Canada—we've compiled a list of typical freelance projects or services and typical ranges. Some of the ranges are quite broad because fees vary widely depending on location (generally more on either coast), the nature of the client (nonprofits and small businesses pay less than large corporations) and the size or complexity of the job (highly skilled or technical tasks pay more than more generalized work).

Knowing what the market will bear is an important part of establishing a viable fee schedule. The most common mistake freelancers make is selling themselves short, underestimating the value of good writing and editing skills to business and others in need of such services. On the other hand, you don't want to price yourself out of the market.

Networking with other writers in your area is the best way to learn how much to charge for your level of expertise and location. Not only can talking to other writers help you determine how much you can charge for a particular service, it can also help you learn of new opportunities as well as combat the isolation that can come from working alone. The grapevine is also very useful in identifying problem clients and areas of concern.

FREELANCERS' ORGANIZATIONS

Most freelancers belong to at least one writers' or freelancers' organization. The National Writers Association and the Freelance Editorial Association are two national groups working for the best interests of freelance writers and editors. If you specialize in a particular area such as translation or indexing there are a number of professional organizations for those working in these areas. Check the Organizations of Interest

---

ROBIN GEE *is former editor of* Novel & Short Story Writer's Market *and is currently a freelance writer and editor in Madison, Wisconsin.*

section in *Writer's Market* or in the *Literary Market Place* publishing trade directory for names and addresses of writers' organizations. Just as important are regional and local associations—not just for writers and editors—but also chambers of commerce and business groups in which you are likely to meet potential contacts.

"At least 25 percent of my new business comes from networking," says Colorado-based freelancer Carole Williams, who went from a full-time career as the director of information for a nonprofit organization to freelancing. Williams is a member of the National Writers Association, her local Chamber of Commerce, the Denver Women's Press Club and the Colorado Independent Publishers Association, where she meets many self-publishers looking for help with promotion.

"I've also received many wonderful referrals from graphic designers and other writers," she says. In fact, she and other writers sometimes subcontract work on large jobs to each other. "In this business it's better to be open to working with and referring others rather than to be highly competitive."

SETTING YOUR FEES

Take what you've learned from others in the field and the ranges provided here as starting points for establishing your own fees. You must also assess how much your particular client is willing or able to pay. In general, working in advertising or for businesses pays better than writing for magazines or editing books. Yet many freelancers prefer to work in the publishing industry because it can be steady and interesting. If, after you've studied the market, you are still unsure about a particular client, try to find out what the budget is for a project and work from there.

Location used to play a larger part in influencing fees. Although, East and West Coast clients still tend to pay more, the rest of the country is catching up. Thanks to fax machines, e-mail and other technology, where you live is less important for many businesses. You may live in the South or Midwest and end up working for an East Coast publisher accustomed to paying higher rates. On the other hand, living near a small business or publisher may give you the edge and create a steady income even though your clients may not pay as much as those far away.

While you can quote flat fees for various projects, experienced freelancers say the best way to start out is to charge hourly rates until you are certain how long a particular type of job should take. Still, there are surprises. Before taking on any new project, it's best to take a good look at it first. Ask if you can do a sample—a few pages—so you and the client can be certain you understand exactly what the job entails, and you can get a feel for how long it is likely to take.

One way to determine an hourly fee is to determine how much a company might pay per hour for someone on staff to do the same job. If, for example, you think a client would have to pay a staff person $26,000/year, divide that by 2,000 (approximately 40 hours a week for 50 weeks) and you would get $13/hour.

Next, add another 33 percent to cover the cost of fringe benefits that an employer would normally pay in Social Security, unemployment insurance, hospitalization, retirement funds, etc. This figure varies from employer to employer but the U.S. Chamber of Commerce reports that the U.S. average paid by employers is 37.6 percent of an employee's salary.

Then add a dollars-per-hour figure to cover your actual overhead expenses for office space, equipment, supplies plus time spent for professional meetings, research and soliciting new business. (To get this figure, add one year's expenses and divide by the number of hours per year you have been freelancing.) In the beginning (when you have large investments such as a computer) you may have to adjust this amount to avoid pricing yourself out of the market. Finally, you may wish to figure in a profit percentage to be useful for capital investments or future growth.

Here's an example:
$26,000 (salary) ÷ 2,000 (hours) = $13.00 per hour
+ 4.29 (33% to cover fringe benefits, taxes, etc.)
+ 2.50 (overhead based on annual expenses of $5,000)
+ 1.30 (10% profit margin)
$21.09 per hour charge

It's useful to take this figure and compare it to the ranges provided here or those suggested by the different freelance organizations. Many freelancers temper the figure from the above formula with what they've learned from suggested ranges and networking. Keep in mind, too, that few fulltime freelancers bill 2,000 hours per year. Most who consider themselves fulltime bill about half that many hours. Some freelancers start with the amount they'd like to make in a year and work down to determine how many projects they need to do and what rate to charge. No matter how you determine your fees initially, you will need to consider your experience, your client's budget and the current market value of your service.

Once you and your client have come to an agreement on how much to charge and the details of your assignment, make sure you follow up with a written contract or letter of agreement signed by both parties outlining exactly what is to be done. Experienced freelancers say this is the best way to avoid misunderstandings down the line. If there is any question about how long a job should take, be sure the agreement indicates that you are estimating the time and that your project fee is based on a certain number of hours. If you quote a flat fee, you should stipulate in the agreement that a higher rate might be charged for overtime hours or late changes in the project.

Communication is important in dealing with clients. Make sure they know right away if you find the project is more complex and will take more time than you anticipated. Leave yourself open to renegotiation and, again, be sure to put any renegotiated fees in writing. On big jobs, some freelancers ask for partial payment at different stages of the project.

Freelancers who deal with businesses (especially those working in public relations and advertising) are careful to outline additional expenses that might be charged. Some figure this into their flat fees, but if you require reimbursement for extensive photocopying, postage, gas mileage, etc., it's best to make sure your client knows upfront and that you get it in writing that these expenses will be paid. The bottom line: clear communication and mutual respect between you and your client is an important factor in building your credibility and your business.

FREELANCE TRENDS

"How Much Should I Charge" has become a regular feature in this book and you will notice this year we've streamlined and reorganized some of the categories to better reflect changes in the field. We've noticed a few trends worth mentioning, too. Several freelance writers and editors have come to think of themselves as consultants. Writing consultants used to deal mostly with training others to improve their writing and editing skills. This is still a primary focus of many consultants, but others have added editing, manuscript evaluation and various writing projects to their list of services. In fact, the Professional Writing Consultants organization recently changed its name to the Association of Professional Communications Consultants to better reflect the growing diversity in their field.

Consultant Dan Deiterich says consulting is well suited to writers or editors who are comfortable working in front of a group and who enjoy teaching others how to improve their writing skills. Some beginning consultants fear selling themselves as trainers. Yet, he says, keep in mind that if you develop a good program you will be benefiting a large group of people as well as yourself.

"Many consultants get into the business through academia, a place where we teach for the love of learning, so we tend to undercharge for our services. Good communication skills can make the difference between success and failure in business and many organizations are willing to pay for help in these areas accordingly," he says. Deiterich has done a variety of work for various businesses including business communication development and proposal evaluation, but he enjoys teaching others best. Some of the training he's done includes helping school teachers eliminate sexist language from their communications, assisting business people assess their needs in order to write better proposals, and helping businesses develop their own inhouse training programs.

Another growing area is technical writing. Ever since computers became commonplace there has been a need for writers and editors who can help develop clear training manuals and documentation, but the World Wide Web and an explosion in software has added even more opportunities for those with computer savvy. Indexing skills are needed for computer database archiving, and editors or writers who can identify key words and write clearly may find a number of projects developing online help programs for various software.

Writers and designers are needed for webpage development and editing for almost every type of business. Since this is such a new area, we took the average rate range, but have heard of freelancers receiving everything from $10-12/hour for a small organization's webpage to charging more than $10,000 for a large corporate site.

This type of work, however, usually requires expertise in writing in the HTML computer language and often jobs include graphic-design skills. Training in this area is becoming more available. Kurt Foss, professor of journalism at the University of Wisconsin, teaches a multimedia publishing course designed to prepare students for changes in technology. He says businesses are beginning to understand that they may need to hire writers and designers separately for webpage jobs. Yet, even if design is not included, writers will have to learn new skills to write effectively for webpages and software programs.

"There's a whole new area called multimedia reporting. Writers need to write in a nonlinear fashion," says Foss. People using websites and CD-ROM programs can start at different places and move about at random within the program so writing must be self-contained on each subject. Also writers need to think in terms of a variety of media. When interviewing, Foss thinks of sound clips from his taped interviews and possibilities for visuals.

Even in established areas of freelancing there have been some changes. In the public relations field more and more companies are outsourcing all their PR services. They may hire on an as-needed basis or hire someone who works on a retainer. Many former public relations employees are taking their skills into the freelance marketplace.

Again, keep in mind that reading the ranges in this book or looking at those provided by some of the professional organizations is only a first step in determining how much you should charge. Networking and studying the ever-changing market will help you remain competitive and motivated.

ADVERTISING, COPYWRITING & PR

Advertising copywriting: $35-100/hour; $250 and up per day; $500 and up per week; $1,000-$2,000 as a monthly retainer. Flat-fee-per-ad rates could range from $100 and up per page depending on the size and kind of client. In Canada rates range from $40-80/hour.

Advertorials: $25-35/hour; up to $1/word or by flat fee ($300 for about 700 words is typical). In Canada, 40-80¢/word; $35-75/hour.

Book jacket copywriting: $100-600 for front cover jacket plus flaps and back jacket copy summarizing content and tone of the book.

Catalog copywriting: $25-$45/hour or $85 and up per project.

Copyediting for advertising: $25-35/hour.

Direct-mail copywriting: $25-45/hour; $75 and up per item or $60-1,000/page.

Direct-mail packages: This includes copywriting direct mail letter, response card and advertising materials. Up to $85/hour or $500-3,000/project, depending on complexity of the project. Additional charges for production such as desktop publishing, addressing, etc.

Direct mail response card for a product: $250-500/project.

Fundraising campaign brochure: $50-75 for research (20 hours) and copywriting (30 hours); up to $5,000 for major campaign brochure, including research, writing and production (about 50 hours of work).

New product release: $20-35/hour or $300-500/release.

News release: *See Press release.*

Political campaigns, public relations: Small town or state campaigns, $10-50/hour; congressional, gubernatorial or other national campaigns, $25-100/hour or up to 10 percent of campaign budget.

Promotion for events: $20-30/hour. For conventions and longer events, payment may be per diem or a flat fee of $500-2,500. *See also Press release.*

Press kits: $500-3,000/project.

Press release: $20-30/hour or $200-500/release.

Print advertisement: $200-500/project. In Canada, $100-200/concept. *See also Advertising copywriting*

Product information: $30-60/hour; $400-500/day or $100-300/page. *See also Sales and services brochures and fliers for smaller projects.*

Promotion for tourism, museums, art shows, etc.: $20-$50 and up per hour for writing or editing promotion copy. Additional charges for production, mailings, etc.

Public relations for businesses: $250-600/day plus expenses average—more for large corporations.

Public relations for government: $25-50/hour or a monthly retainer based on number of hours per period. Lower fees for local government agencies, higher for state-level and above.

Public relations for organizations or nonprofits: $15-35/hour. If working on a monthly retainer, $100-500/month.

Public relations for schools or libraries: $15-20/hour for small districts or libraries; up to $35 for larger districts.

Radio advertisement: $50-100/script; $200-400/week for part-time positions writing radio ads, depending on the size of the city (and market).

Sales and services brochures and fliers: $20-$600/published page or from $100 to $7,500/project depending on size and type of business (small nonprofit organization to a large corporation) and on the number of pages (usually from 1-16) and complexity of the job.

Sales letters: $350-1,000 for 1-2 pages.

Speech editing or evaluation: $20/hour and up.

Speechwriting (general): $30-85/hour. In Canada, $75-125/hour or $70-100/minute of speech.

Speechwriting for business owners or executives: Up to $80/hour or a flat fee of about $100 for a short (6- or 7- minute speech); $500-3,000 for up to 30 minutes. Rates also depend on size of the company and the event.

Speechwriting for government officials: $4,000 for 20 minutes plus up to $1,000 for travel and expenses.

Speechwriting for political candidates: $250 and up for local candidates (about 15 minutes); $375-800 for statewide candidates and $1,000 or more for national congressional candidates.

TV commercial: $60-375/finished minute; $1,000-2,000/finished project. In Canada, $60-130/minute of script (CBC pays Writers Guild rates, CTV pays close to that and others pay less. For example, TV Ontario pays $70-100/script minute).

AUDIOVISUALS & ELECTRONIC COMMUNICATIONS

Audiocassette scripts: $10-50/scripted minute, assuming written from existing client materials, with no additional research or meetings; otherwise $75-100/minute, $750 minimum.

Audiovisuals: For writing, $250-350/requested scripted minute; includes rough draft, editing conference with client, and final shooting script. For consulting, research, producing, directing, soundtrack oversight, etc. $400-600/day plus travel and expenses. Writing fee is sometimes 10% of gross production price as billed to client. Some charge flat fee of $1,500-2,100/package.

Book summaries for film producers: $50-100/book. *Note: You must live in the area where the business is located to get this kind of work.*

Business film scripts (training and information): $200-250/day.

Copyediting audiovisuals: $20-25/hour.

Industrial product film: $125-150/minute; $500 minimum flat fee.

Novel synopsis for film producer: $150 for 5-10 pages typed, single spaced.

Radio continuity writing: $5/page to $150/week, part-time. In Canada, $40-80/minute of script; $640/show for a multi-part series.

Radio copywriting: *See Advertising, Copywriting & PR.*

Radio documentaries: $258 for 60 minutes, local station.

Radio editorials: $10-30 for 90-second to two-minute spots.

Radio interviews: For National Public Radio, up to 3 minutes, $25; 3-10 minutes, $40-75; 10-60 minutes, $125 to negotiable fees. Small radio stations would pay approximately 50% of the NPR rate; large stations, double the NPR rate.

Script synopsis for business: $40/hour.

Script synopsis for agent or film producer: $75 for 2-3 typed pages, single-spaced.

Scripts for nontheatrical films for education, business, industry: Prices vary among producers, clients, and sponsors and there is no standardization of rates in the field. Fees include $75-120/minute for one reel (10 minutes) and corresponding increases with each successive reel; approximately 10% of the production cost of films that cost the producer more than $1,500/release minute.

Screenwriting: $6,000 and up per project.

Slide presentation: Including visual formats plus audio, $150-600 for 10-15 minutes.

Slide/single image photos: $75 flat fee.

Slide/tape script: $75-100/minute, $750 minimum.

TV commercial: *See Advertising, Copywriting & PR.*

TV documentary: 30-minute 5-6 page proposal outline, $1,839 and up; 15-17 page treatment, $1,839 and up; less in smaller cities. In Canada research for a documentary runs about $6,500.

TV editorials: $35 and up for 1-minute, 45 seconds (250-300 words).

TV filmed news and features: From $10-20/clip for 30-second spot; $15-25 for 60-second clip; more for special events.

TV information scripts: Short 5- to 10-minute scripts for local cable TV stations, $10-15/hour.

TV news film still photo: $3-6 flat fee.

TV news story: $16-25 flat fee.

TV, national and local public stations: For programs, $35-100/minute down to a flat fee of $5,000 and up for a 30- to 60-minute script.

TV scripts: (Teleplay only), 60 minutes; network prime time, Writers Guild rates: $14,048; 30 minutes, $10,414. In Canada, $60-130/minute of script.

BOOK PUBLISHING

Abstracting and abridging: Up to $75/hour for nonfiction; $30-35/hour for reference and professional journals.

Anthology editing: Variable advance plus 3-15 percent of royalties. Advance should cover reprint fees or fees are handled by the publisher. Flat-fee-per-manuscript rates range from $500-5,000 and up.

Book proposal consultation: $20-75/hour or a flat rate of $100-250.

Book proposal writing: Up to $150/page or a flat rate of $175-3,000 depending on length and whether the client provides full information or the writer must do research, and whether a sample chapter is required.

Book query critique: $50 for critique of letter to the publisher and outline.

Book summaries for book clubs: $50-100/book.

Content editing: $20-50/hour or $600-5,000/manuscript, based on the size and complexity of the project.

Copyediting: $16-40/hour or $2-4/page. Lower-end rates charged for light copyedit (3-10 pages per hour) of general, trade material. Higher-end rates charged for substantive copyediting or for textbooks and technical material (2-5 pages per hour).

Ghostwriting, as told to: This is writing for a celebrity or expert either for a self-published book or for a publisher. Author gets full advance plus 50 percent of royalties. Hourly rates for subjects who are self-publishing are $25-80/hour. In Canada, author also gets full advance and 50 percent of royalties or $10,000-20,000 flat fee per project. Research time is charged extra.

Ghostwriting, no credit: Projects may include writing for an individual planning to self publish or for a book packager, book producer, publisher, agent or corporation. Rates range from $5,000-35,000 and up (plus expenses) per project; packagers pay flat fee or combination of advance plus royalties. For self-published clients, ask for one-fourth down payment, one-fourth when book is half-finished, one-fourth at the three-quarters mark and one-fourth upon completion.

Indexing: $20-40/hour; charge higher hourly rate if using a computer index program that takes fewer hours. Also can charge $2-6/indexable page; 40-70 cents per line of index or a flat fee of $250-500 depending on length.

Jacket copywriting: *See Advertising, Copywriting & PR.*

Manuscript evaluation and critique: $150-200 for outline and first 20,000 words; $300-500 for up to 100,000 words. Also $15-35/hour for trade books, slightly less for nonprofits. Page rates run from $1.50-2.50/page.

Movie novelization: $3,500-15,000, depending on writer's reputation, amount of work to be done and amount of time writer is given.

Novel synopsis for a literary agent: $150 for 5-10 pages typed, single-spaced.

Page layout (desktop publishing): $20-35/hour or $5-15/page. Higher per page rates may be charged if material involves complex technical material and graphics.

Production editing/project management: This is overseeing the production of a project, coordinating editing and production stages, etc. $25-50/hour.

Proofreading: $12-30/hour or $1.50-3.50/page. High-end rates are charged for technical, scientific and reference material.

Research for writers or book publishers: $20-40/hour and up; $150 and up per day plus expenses. A flat rate of $300-500 may be charged, depending on complexity of the job.

Rewriting: $18-50/hour; $5-7/page. Some writers receive royalties on book projects.

Translation (literary): $30-35/hour; also $95-125 per 1,000 English words.

Typesetting: $20-35/hour or $4-7/page.

BUSINESS

Annual reports: A brief report with some economic information and an explanation of figures, $25-60/hour; 12- to 16-page report, $600-1,500 flat fees for editing. If extensive research and/or writing is involved in a large project, rates could go as high as $5,000-10,000/project. A report that must meet Securities and Exchange Commission (SEC) standards and reports requiring legal language could bill $40-85/hour. Bill separately if desktop publication (typesetting, page layout, etc.) is involved (some smaller firms and nonprofits may ask for writing/production packages).

Associations and organizations (writing for): $15-25/hour for small organizations; up to $50/hour for larger associations or a flat fee depending on the length and complexity of the project. For example, $500-1,000 for association magazine article (2,000 words) or $1,000-1,800 for a 10-page informational booklet.

Audiovisuals/audiocassette scripts: *See Audiovisuals & Electronic Communications.*

Book summaries for businesses: $25-50/page or $20-35/hour.

Brochures, fliers, booklets for business: $25-40/hour for writing or from $500-$4,000 and up per project (12-16 pages and more). Additional charges for desktop publishing, usually $20-40/hour; $20-30/page or a flat fee per project. *See also Copyediting for business or Manuscript editing/evaluation for business in this section.*

Business editing (general): $25-50/hour.

Business letters: For letters such as form letters designed to improve customer relations or interoffice communications, $100-500/letter depending on the size of the business and the length/complexity of the material.

Business plan: $1/word; $200/manuscript page or up to $1,500/project. High-end rates are charged if extensive research is involved. Sometimes research is charged separately per hour or per day.

Business writing (general): $30-80/hour. In Canada, $1-2/word or $50-100/hour. *See other entries in this section and in Advertising, Copywriting & PR for specific projects such as brochures, copywriting, speechwriting, brochures or business letters. For business film scriptwriting see Audiovisuals & Electronic Communications.*

Business writing seminars: $500 for a half-day seminar, plus travel expenses or $1,000-5,000/day. Rates depend on number of participants as well as duration. Average per-person rate is $50/person for a half-day seminar. *See also Educational and Literary Services.*

Catalogs for business: $25-40/hour or $25-600/printed page; more if tables or charts must be reworked for readability or consistency. Additional charges for desktop publishing ($20-40/hour is average).

Collateral materials for business: *See individual pieces (brochures, catalogs, etc.) in this section and in Advertising, Copywriting & PR.*

Commercial reports for business, insurance companies, credit agencies: $6-15/page.

Consultation on communications: $300-2,000/day. Lower-end fees charged to nonprofits and small businesses.

Consumer complaint letters (answering): $25-30/letter.

Copyediting for business: $20-40/hour or $20-50/manuscript page, up to $40/hour for business proposals. Charge lower-end fees ($15-25/hour) to nonprofits and very small businesses.

Corporate histories: $1,000-2,000 flat fee.

Corporate periodicals, editing: $30-75/hour.

Corporate periodicals, writing: $30-100/hour, depending on size and nature of the corporation. Also 50¢ to $1/word. In Canada, $1-2/word or $40-90/hour.

Corporate profile: $1,250-2,500 flat fee for up to 3,000 words or charge on a per word basis, up to $1/word.

Financial presentation: $1,500-4,500 for a 20-30 minute presentation.

Fundraising campaign brochure: *See Advertising, Copywriting & PR.*

Ghostwriting for business (usually trade magazine articles or business columns): $25-100/hour; $200 or more per day plus expenses (depending on amount of research involved, length of project).

Government research: $35-50/hour.

Government writing: $30-50/hour. In Canada, $50-80/hour.

Grant proposal writing for nonprofits: $30-100/hour or flat fee.

Indexing for professional journals: $20-40/hour.

Industrial/service business training manual: $25-40/hour; $50-100/manuscript page or a flat fee, $1,000-4,000, depending on number of pages and complexity of the job.

Industry training film scripts: *See Business film scripts in Audiovisuals & Electronic Communications.*

Industrial product film script: *See Audiovisuals & Electronic Communications.*

Job application letters: $20-40/letter.

Manuals/documentation: $25-60/hour. *See also Computers, Science and Technical Writing.*

Manuscript editing/evaluation for trade journals: $20-40/hour.

Market research survey reports: $25-50/hour or $500-1,500/day; also flat rates of $500-2,000/project.

Newsletters, abstracting: $30/hour.

Newsletters, desktop publishing/production: $20-60/hour. Higher-end rates for scanning photographs, advertising layout, illustration or design. Editing charged extra.

Newsletters, editing: $25-45/hour; $50-500/issue. Higher-end fees charged if writing or production is included. Editors who produce a regular newsletter on a monthly or quarterly basis tend to charge per month or per issue—and find them easier to do after initial set up.

Newsletters, writing: $25-45/hour; 25¢ to $1/word; $25-300/page; $35-2,500/story or $375-2,500/issue. In Canada, $45-70/hour.

Programmed instruction consultation fees: *See Educational & Literary Services.*

Programmed instruction materials for business: *See Educational & Literary Services.*

Proofreading for business: $15-50/hour; low-end fees for nonprofits.

Public relations: *See Advertising, Copywriting and PR.*

Retail newsletters for customers: Charge regular newsletter rates or $175-300 per 4-page project. Additional charges for desktop publishing.

Sales brochures, fliers, letters, other advertising materials: *See Advertising, Copywriting & PR.*

Scripts for business/training films: *See Audiovisuals & Electronic Communications.*

Translation, commercial: $30-45/hour; $115-125 per 1,000 words. Higher-end fees for non-European languages into English.

Translation for government agencies: $30-45; up to $125 per 1,000 words. Higher-end fees for non-European languages into English.

Translation through translation agencies: Agencies by 33⅓ percent average less than end-user clients and mark up translator's prices by as much as 100 percent or more.

Translation, technical: $30-45/hour; $125 and up per 1,000 words, depending on complexity of the material.

COMPUTER, SCIENTIFIC & TECHNICAL

Computer documentation, general (hard copy): $30-75/hour; $20-30/page. *See also Software manual writing in this section.*

Computer documentation (on line): $30-35/hour; $15-25/screen.

Demonstration software: $70 and up per hour.

Legal/government editing: $20-65/hour.

Legal/government writing: $30-65/hour.

Medical and science editing: $20-65/hour, depending on the complexity of the material and the expertise of the editor.

Medical and science proofreading: $15-30/hour.

Medical and science writing: $30-65/hour; $20-30/page, depending on the complexity of the project and the writer's expertise.

Online editing: $30-35/hour.

Software manual writing: $35-50/hour for research and writing.

Technical editing: $20-60/hour or $150-1,000/day.

Technical typesetting: $4-7/page; $25-35/hour; more for inputting of complex material.

Technical writing: $30-75/hour; $20-30/page. *See Computer documentation and Software manual writing in this section.*

Technical translation: *See item in Business section.*

Webpage design: $50-100/page.

Webpage editing: $30/page and up.

EDITORIAL/DESIGN PACKAGES

Business catalogs: *See Business.*

Desktop publishing: For 1,000 dots-per-inch type, $5-15/camera-ready page of straight type; $30/camera-ready page with illustrations, maps, tables, charts, photos; $100-150/camera-ready page for oversize pages with art. Also $20-40/hour depending on graphics, number of photos, and amount of copy to be typeset. Packages often include writing, layout/design, and typesetting services.

Greeting cards ideas (with art included): Anywhere from $30-300, depending on size of company.

Newsletters: *See Desktop Publishing (this section) and Newsletters (Business).*

Picture editing: $20-40.

Photo brochures: $700-15,000 flat fee for photos and writing.
Photo research: $15-30/hour.
Photography: $10-150/b&w photo; $25-300/color photo; also $800/day.

EDUCATIONAL & LITERARY SERVICES

Business writing seminars: *See Business.*
Consultation for individuals (in business): $250-1,000/day.
Consultation on communications: *See Business.*
Developing and designing courses for business or adult education: $250-$1,500day or flat fee.
Editing for individual clients: $10-50/hour or $2-7/page.
Educational consulting and educational grant and proposal writing: $250-750/day or $30-75/hour.
Lectures at national conventions by well-known authors: $2,500-20,000 and up, plus expenses; less for panel discussions.
Lectures at regional writers' conferences: $300 and up, plus expenses.
Lectures to local groups, librarians or teachers: $50-150.
Lectures to school classes: $25-75; $150/day; $250/day if farther than 100 miles.
Manuscript evaluation for theses/dissertations: $15-30/hour.
Poetry manuscript critique: $25 per 16-line poem.
Programmed instruction consultant fees: $300-1,000/day, $50-75/hour.
Programmed instruction materials for business: $50/hour for inhouse writing and editing; $500-1,000/day plus expenses for outside research and writing. Alternate method: $2,000-5,000/hour of programmed training provided depending on technicality of subject.
Public relations for schools: *See Advertising, Copywriting & PR.*
Readings by poets, fiction writers: $25-600 depending on author.
Scripts for nontheatrical films for education: *See Audiovisuals & Electronic Communications.*
Short story manuscript critique: 3,000 words, $40-60.
Teaching adult education course: $10-60/class hour; fee usually set by school, not negotiated by teachers.
Teaching adult seminar: $400 plus mileage and per diem for a 6- or 7-hour day; plus 40% of the tuition fee beyond the sponsor's break-even point. In Canada, $35-50/hour.
Teaching Business writing to company employees: *See Consultation on communications in Business section.*
Teaching college course or seminar: $15-70/class hour.
Teaching creative writing in school: $15-70/hour of instruction, or $1,500-2,000 per 12-15 week semester; less in recessionary times.
Teaching elementary and middle school teachers how to teach writing to students: $75-150 for a 1- to 1½ hour session.
Teaching home-bound students: $5-15/hour.
Tutoring: $25 per 1- to 1½ hour private session.
TV instruction taping: $150 per 30-minute tape; $25 residual each time tape is sold.
Writer-in-schools: Arts council program, $130/day; $650/week. Personal charges plus expenses vary from $25/day to $100/hour depending on school's ability to pay.
Writer's workshop: Lecturing and seminar conducting, $50-150/hour to $750/day plus expenses; local classes, $35-50/student for 10 sessions.
Writing for individual clients: $25-100/hour, depending on the situation. *See also Business writing in Business section.*

Writing for scholarly journals: $75/hour.

MAGAZINES & TRADE JOURNALS

Abstracting: $20-30/hour for trade and professional journals; $8 per abstract for scholarly journals.

Article manuscript critique: 3,000 words, $40.

Arts reviewing: $35-100 flat fee or 20-30¢/word, plus admission to events or copy of CD (for music).

Book reviews: $50-300 flat fee and copy of book.

Consultation on magazine editorial: $1,000-1,500/day plus expenses.

Copyediting magazines: $16-30/hour.

Editing: General, $25-500/day or $250-2,000/issue; Religious publications, $200-500/month or $15-30/hour.

Fact checking: $17-25/hour or 75¢ to $1/item.

Feature articles: Anywhere from 20¢ to $4/word; or $200-2,000 per 2,000 word article, depending on size (circulation) and reputation of magazine.

Ghostwriting articles (general): Up to $2/word; or $300-3,000/project.

Indexing: $15-40/hour.

Magazine, city, calendar of events column: $50-150/column.

Magazine column: 200 words, $40; 800 words, $400. Also $1/word. Larger circulation publications pay fees related to their regular word rate.

Manuscript consultation: $25-50/hour.

Manuscript criticism: $40-60 per article or short story of up to 3,000 words. Also $20-25/hour.

Picture editing: *See Editorial/Design Packages.*

Permission fees to publishers to reprint article or story: $75-500; 10-15¢/word; less for charitable organizations.

Production editing: $15-30/hour.

Proofreading: $12-25/hour.

Research: $20-25/hour.

Rewriting: Up to $80/manuscript page; also $100/published page.

Science writing for magazines: $2,000-5,000/article. *See also Computer, Scientific & Technical Writing.*

Special news article: For a business's submission to trade publication, $250-500 for 1,000 words. In Canada, 25-45¢/word.

Stringing: 20¢ to $1/word based on circulation. Daily rate: $150-250 plus expenses; weekly rate: $900 plus expenses. Also $10-35/hour plus expenses; $1/column inch.

Trade journal ad copywriting: *See Advertising, Copywriting & PR.*

Trade journal feature article: For business client, $400-1,000. Also $1-2/word.

NEWSPAPERS

Ads for small business: $25 for a small, one-column ad, or $10/hour and up. *See also Advertising, Copywriting & PR.*

Arts reviewing: For weekly newspapers, $15-35 flat fee; for dailies, $45 and up; for Sunday supplements, $100-400. Also admission to event or copy of CD (for music).

Book reviews: For small newspapers, byline and the book only; for larger publications, $35-200. Also copy of the book.

Column, local: $10-20 for a weekly; $15-30 for dailies of 4,000-6,000 circulation; $35-50 for 7,000-10,000 dailies; $40-75 for 11,000-25,000 dailies; and $100 and up for larger dailies. Also 15-80¢/word depending on circulation.

Copyediting: $10-30/hour; up to $40/hour for large daily paper.

Copywriting: *See Advertising, Copywriting & PR.*

Dance criticism: $25-400/article.

Drama criticism: Local, newspaper rates; non-local, $50 and up per review.

Editing/manuscript evaluation: $25/hour.

Fact checking: *See Magazines & Trade Journals.*

Feature: $25-35/article plus mileage for a weekly; $40-500 for a daily (depending on size of paper). Also 10-30¢/word. In Canada $15-40/word, but rates vary widely.

Obituary copy: Where local newspapers permit lengthier than normal notices paid for by the funeral home (and charged to the family), $15-25. Writers are engaged by funeral homes.

Picture editing: *See Editorial/Design Packages.*

Proofreading: $16-20/hour.

Science writing for newspapers: *See Computer, Scientific & Technical Writing.*

Stringing: Sometimes flat rate of $20-35 to cover meeting and write article; sometimes additional mileage payment.

Syndicted column, self-promoted: $5-10 each for weeklies; $10-25/week for dailies, based on circulation.

MISCELLANEOUS

Comedy writing for night club entertainers: Gags only, $5-25 each. Routines, $100-1,000 per minute. Some new comics may try to get a 5-minute routine for $150; others will pay $2,500 for a 5-minute bit from a top writer.

Comics writing: $35-50/page and up for established comics writers.

Contest judging: Short manuscripts, $10/entry; with one-page critique, $15-25. Overall contest judging: $100-500.

Corporate comedy skits: $300-800 for half-hour skit (used at meetings, conventions).

Craft ideas with instructions: $50-200/project.

Encyclopedia articles: Entries in some reference books, such as biographical encyclopedias, 500-2,000 words; pay ranges from $60-80 per 1,000 words. Specialists' fees vary.

Family histories: Fees depend on whether the writer edits already prepared notes or does extensive research and writing; and the length of the work, $500-15,000.

Institutional (church, school) history: $200-1,000 for 15-50 pages, or $20-35/hour.

Manuscript typing: Depending on manuscript length and delivery schedule, $1.25-2/page with one copy; $15/hour.

Party toasts, limericks, place card verses: $1.50/line.

Research for individuals: $5-30/hour, depending on experience, geographic area and nature of work.

Special occasion booklet: Family keepsake of a wedding, anniversary, Bar Mitzvah, etc., $120 and up.

From Stickball to the Screen: Using Networking and Ingenuity to Get to the Front of the Line

BY ALAN STEINBERG

My idea of becoming a writer wasn't just to sell something. It was to sell *everything*. Let me explain.

When I was a kid in New York, I learned to look for openings, options, angles. I had to; there was competition in everything, from getting a seat on the bus to making the high school baseball team. There were always those better, smarter, quicker. So if I wanted something *they* wanted, I had to find creative ways to get it. In this process, I picked up three guiding principles of success, which still apply today to my life and career: *versatility*, *networking*, *ingenuity*.

VERSATILITY: IF YOU AIN'T HITTING LEFTY, BAT RIGHTY

At age four, my father taught me valuable life lessons. The key one for my future writing career was how to get an advantage on the other guy. Pop's baseball version was to make me a switch-hitter, which proved invaluable; I had a permanent advantage on my non-switch-hitting teammates.

One mistake amateur writers make is to pigeon-hole their talents. Like actors repeatedly cast in similar roles, writers let editors typecast them. To avoid this problem you must make yourself versatile by writing in *several* genres. Versatility makes you stand out *and* it's practical. If you aren't selling articles, you can switch to essays or novels or nonfiction books or screenplays. Even industrial films. Whatever *pays*.

When I wasn't selling enough magazine articles, I tried to write a book. First, I selected a topic that fascinated me: true crime. Then, looking for a scoop, I read newspapers and magazines. When nothing materialized, I scanned the "Co-Author Wanted" ads in *Writer's Digest*. Finally, I answered one by mail and ended up auditioning for the woman who placed the ad. When she hired me, I had never written a book, so it was on-the-job training. Which was exactly why I did it: to *learn* how to write a book. Making the transition from magazine writing to writing books isn't that daunting. It's not like switching from lawyer to doctor; it's more like switching from lefty to righty. Remember: you're still using words.

After writing that book I turned to screenwriting, which required a bit of inventive networking. I read in the *Lansing State Journal* that my college friend Jack Epps, and his partner, Jim Cash, had just sold their first script for $125,000 to producer Bud Yorkin. I was impressed, so I called Jack and asked him to introduce me to Cash. He did that by phone, and Cash and I met for lunch and got acquainted. A frustrated

---

ALAN STEINBERG *writes magazine articles, nonfiction books, novels, and screenplays. His latest book,* Black Profiles in Courage, *with Kareem Abdul-Jabbar, was published by William Morrow in October 1996. He lives in Chicago.*

novelist, Cash was impressed that I had gone away for a year to write a book. That opened him up to talking about screenwriting with me.

He inspired me so much that I co-wrote my first script, "Hourglass," and asked Cash to critique it. He thoughtfully mailed me a half-dozen tapes that are probably teaching classics. He reads the script sentence-by-sentence, offering analysis and tips. Even producers aren't this thorough. Oh, did I mention that Cash and Epps got pretty successful after this? They wrote "Top Gun" and "Dick Tracy," and script-doctored "Turner and Hooch" and "Sister Act." We revised according to Cash's suggestions, and actor Ron Silver optioned "Hourglass."

I taught myself the scriptwriting format by sending away for Hollywood scripts, studying them, and writing. Eventually, I was hired to write a script which is now in development with Neil Machlis, producer of "Birdcage." I also have another script in the pipeline called "Latchkey," co-written with renowned forensic detective Dr. Thomas Streed, a man who has interviewed most of the worst serial killers from Charlie Manson to Ted Bundy.

If you don't have access to a Jim Cash, you can buy screenwriting books and scripts of successful films; attend screenwriting seminars and talk to the instructors after class; and write scripts till they come out your ears. After perfecting your work, you go after an agent and let the *agent* worry about selling you. It is no accident that, today, I can't be labeled a sports writer, novelist or screenwriter. I do them all. And I do them all because if one isn't paying at the time, another one can. So remember to concentrate on becoming versatile. Try *everything*. The more aces you hold, the higher your odds at winning a hand.

INGENUITY: IF YOU CAN'T FIND THE ROAD, INVENT ONE

My grandfather used to say: "Don't look for answers. Only God has all the answers, and He's not talking." In other words: Make your own way by being constantly alert for opportunities. To wit: While I was teaching English at Michigan State, Jack Epps cooked up a project for his film class: a documentary on the Bull Bowl, a charity football game between local street people and cops. I realized: *Magazine article*.

Epps needed me and my brother Mike to do on-camera interviews. We did well: The movie won the Midwest Film Festival—and Mike and I earned our first-paying magazine article. We'd been reading articles in *Detroit*, the Sunday magazine of the *Detroit Free Press*, and felt we were better than anyone they published. We had no idea how to approach the magazine, so we wrote up our satiric take on the game and sent it to the editor in a 12-cent envelope. Nobody said to *query first*. (I told you we had no clue).

Sometimes naivete—or doing the unexpected—can be a plus. The editor called and said, "You guys can write. You got a sale." He didn't say, "This isn't a query." And he didn't ask: "What else have you published?" I filed that: *They do not ask what you expect them to ask*. If you can slip by *acting* like a pro until you are one, slip on by.

So if you're a fledgling writer, I suggest you begin by trying local major markets, like Sunday magazines. Every big city has one; some have two. Read the fare, query for assignments. Invent ideas in your fields of interest. But: *do not limit yourself to what you know or even like*. Something an actor-friend once taught me applies here. He said that whenever he wanted to accomplish something, despite his lack of experience at it, he always told himself, "I *invented* it." *If you can't find the road, invent one*. You do not need to be an expert in something to write about it. You need ingenuity and guts.

By focusing on versatility and ingenuity, I learned you could forge your own path in the business without following specific rules. In fact, my first rule became: *If you break the rules, you will probably have an edge.* After all, Mike and I knew zilch about the business, had never published, and couldn't have written a professional query if our bar mitzvah checks depended on it. Yet we landed a major market, a byline, cover hype, a bio blurb, and $125—a lot in 1972.

Here's the approach I took to land my first sale to a major-market *national* magazine. In 1977, I read that Karl Thomas, a steel salesman from Troy, Michigan, who a year earlier failed spectacularly to become the first person to cross the Atlantic alone in a helium balloon, was set for another adventure: crossing America in a hot-air balloon. Great story. I had heard his name on TV and read that he'd done 10,000 newspaper interviews worldwide—so how could *I* get to him? I was nobody.

Ingenuity. I knew that most professional writers would contact him at his office, where a secretary would screen his calls. His home number was unlisted, so I went to the library which was still using last year's phone book. I figured he just got famous *this* year, so he was probably listed. Bingo. I got his number and called. He thought I was clever enough to talk to and granted me fifteen minutes in person. I turned the fifteen minutes into three hours. That interview was the first of at least a half-dozen that landed me on Thomas's transcontinental balloon trip team. For three weeks, I was part of the chase team that crossed America (we were featured in media reports daily around the world) and my interviews along the way netted six magazine articles. The biggest was a *People* bio, my first big national score (They paid $1,000 plus $600 for my photos). I was now a "pro"—my price doubled "overnight."

Another example that anyone can apply. When I wanted to become a contributing writer at a national magazine, but had no clue how to do it, I found a way. While living in Chicago, I saw an ad in the *Tribune* for editors for *Inside Sports*, a magazine based in nearby Evanston. I arranged a meeting with the editor. When I entered his office, I saw dozens of résumé folders from people who applied by mail. Apparently, I was the only one who bothered to go in person—I was banking on that. I dropped as many names as I knew in the business; showed him my best articles (like the *People* bio); and walked out with an assignment for $1,500. It ran in the inaugural issue in 1983. Soon, I was listed in the masthead and earning up to $2,500 per assignment, plus travel, all expenses paid. Eight years later, I'd published pieces with, among others: Michael Jordan, Joe Montana, Reggie Jackson, Andrea Jaeger, Don "Murder" Murdoch, Mickey Mantle, NFL referee Jerry Markbreit (subject of my first published book), and Dennis Rodman (subject of my 1994 book, *Rebound*). All this from showing up in person, deliberately, for the wrong job, figuring I might talk them into creating the right job.

Okay, that's what *I* did; what can *you* do? It's not that hard. Simply remind yourself that the squeaky wheel gets the grease. Find a path to your subject; nobody's going to lead you by the hand. Identify the expected approach, assume that 99% of writers will take it, then take a *different* path.

NETWORKING: WHOEVER THEY KNOW, YOU WANNA KNOW TOO

Remember Ron Silver optioning my first script? You thought that was talent? Accident? Luck? Mostly, it was networking. When I was in college at Buffalo, I auditioned for the play "Stalag 17." The student-director was Ron. He cast me and we became friends. The last time I saw him was in the early 70s, when he was doing Charmin commercials and the TV show "Rhoda." I called him in the early 80s, when he was an established actor. He read my script, liked it, and wanted to play the lead. So he optioned it. Hollywood didn't know I was alive. Ron never got the movie made, but by calling him and piquing his interest, it introduced me to the business.

If you know anyone in show business, ask for help. If you know another writer, ask for his help. If someone you know knows a celebrity, ask for an introduction. Network wherever you can. Failing that, if you know a particular celebrity is coming to town, call the Actor's Guild in L.A. and get the name of the actor's agent. Call the agent and say you're writing a magazine piece and need an interview. Your attitude must be: *I do this for a living. I do it all the time.* If you get an interview, query an editor with the same attitude: *Dear Editor: I just did an exclusive interview with—.* Talent means zero if no one knows you've got it.

The same applies, of course, to magazine networking. After you publish somewhere, network the editor. Who else does she know who might like your work? What agents does she know? What publishers? Also, if you keep schmoozing an editor about new ideas, you will end up with assignments. By calling the editor incessantly after our first piece ran in *Detroit*, my brother Mike and I developed a steady market. When we ran low on feature ideas, we invented a column about how professionals played their sports. The editors liked it and kept paying us.

That little column laid future groundwork. I learned how to control a Q & A. It forced me to handle awkward situations with celebrities who rarely let their guard down and routinely duck tough questions. If it worked for me, it can work for anyone. Suggest column ideas to Sunday magazine editors. Do one on spec. Try unique angles. Keep calling, querying, writing. Visit editors in person when it's practical; talent being equal, if they can put a face on a call or query, it results in a sale.

My best advice for positioning yourself to sell what you write, even if you're not established, is to remember: *VERSATILITY, INGENUITY, NETWORKING.* When you get discouraged, recall this Irish folksaying Jim Cash told me: "Don't tell me the seas were rough, tell me you brought the boat home safe."

If you don't know how to do that, hey, *invent* a way.

Get Connected: An Overview of the Internet

BY RICHARD MUSKOPF

They're everywhere: on television, in magazines, even on billboards along the express-way. If you don't know anything about them, they're a meaningless string of letters, numbers, slashes and squiggles. But even if you do know what they are, you may not know what they can do for you. They are "addresses" on the Internet and they can provide writers with invaluable information.

What is the Internet, anyway? Basically, it is a giant network of computers linked together via various electronic means. Universities, corporations and scientific and gov-ernment organizations make up a large part of the Internet. The rest is composed of computer online services (America Online, CompuServe, etc.), nonprofit organizations, and anyone who wants to be connected. As you might expect, such a large pool of resources can be quite useful to those linked to it.

Resources provided by the Internet are wide-ranging, but there are three that can be most useful to writers. They are electronic mail, newsgroups and the World Wide Web.

• Electronic mail, more commonly known as "e-mail," is mail composed and deliv-ered over the Internet. The primary advantage of e-mail is its speed. Usually e-mail is delivered to its recipient within a matter of minutes. A handy feature is the ability to attach computer files (such as a word processor document) to your message.

Example of an e-mail address: wdigest@aol.com

• Newsgroups are worldwide discussion groups on subjects too numerous to count. A newsgroup is similar to e-mail, except you go to the newsgroup to post and read messages, the messages don't come to you. Also, all postings are available for everyone to read. There are groups on writing, literature, specific genres, poetry, etc. If you are interested in a certain topic, chances are there is a newsgroup for it.

Example of a newsgroup: misc.writing (discussion of writing in all its forms)

• The World Wide Web (WWW) is the fastest growing part of the Internet, and for good reason. Assuming you have the right computer hardware and software (discussed later), a connection to the web displays formatted text, color graphics, sounds and animation on your computer. Of course, bunches of pretty colors and noises aren't much good to you without content to go with them, and there is a lot of fluff on the web. However, there is much that's worthwhile on it, too. The Library of Congress is on the WWW, as are writers' organizations like the National Writers Union. As with newsgroups, if you have an interest, you can probably find something about it on the World Wide Web. Those funny strings of characters you see in television and magazine advertisements are addresses for websites, also known as "homepages."

Example of a website: http://www.loc.gov (Library of Congress)

A list of websites useful to writers appears in Websites of Interest on page 936.

The World Wide Web is based on hypertext, which is highlighted text or graphics linked to additional information. Clicking on the text might display further information about the clicked word, or a graphic, or it may transport you to another website.

If you don't know what you are looking for, you could find yourself bouncing from website to website. Before you know it, you will have wasted hours. To streamline the process, you can access what is known as a "search engine." After you have called up a search engine, you type in the subject or phrase you are looking for and set parameters for the search. The results you get will be hypertext links to websites meeting the criteria you set for the search. Not every link will be useful, though, since the searches will pick up even passing references to your criteria. If you are more focused in your search criteria, you will pick up less "noise."

GETTING CONNECTED

Before you can hook up to the Internet, you must have four things: a computer, a modem, a telephone line and an Internet account. Of these, selecting a computer is the most difficult task; you must decide whether you want an IBM-compatible computer or an Apple Macintosh. Check out each type in a store and see which one is best suited to you. Here are some basic specifications for each if you want to get on the Internet.

IBM-compatible:

- Microsoft Windows 3.1 or higher or IBM OS/2 (such as Warp)
- 486 or higher processor is highly recommended
- super VGA (SVGA) color monitor
- 20-30 megabytes available hard disk space
- 8 megabytes of RAM (memory)
- mouse
- optional 16-bit sound card (Sound Blaster-compatible). Most computers sold these days come with a sound card.

Apple Macintosh:

- System 7 or higher
- 68030 processor or higher
- color monitor
- 20-30 megabytes hard disk space
- 8 megabytes RAM
- mouse

Modem

Purchase at least a 14,400 bits per second (14.4 Kbps) modem (28.8 Kbps with V.34 *strongly* recommended)—anything slower is worthless. Most computers these days are sold with a modem; make sure it has one of these speeds.

Modems come in two configurations: internal or external. An internal modem is installed inside the computer case. An external sits outside a computer and is plugged into a port on the back of the computer case. If you get an external unit for an IBM-compatible, make sure your computer has a 16550 UART communications port. Check the computer's specifications. If you don't have one, an inexpensive upgrade is available at many computer stores. You don't have to worry about this for an internal modem. Ensure the modem you buy is designed for your computer (IBM-compatible or Macintosh).

Internet Accounts

There are a number of ways to access the Internet. If you are a student or educator, you can probably obtain a free account through your school. Talk to someone in the computer department. If you don't have access through a school, your employer may

TACKLING THE TERMINOLOGY

CD-ROM—Compact Disc-Read Only Memory. A computer information storage medium capable of holding enormous amounts of data. Information on a CD-ROM cannot be deleted. A computer user must have a CD-ROM drive to access a CD-ROM.

E-mail—Electronic mail. Mail generated on a computer and delivered over a computer network to a specific individual or group of individuals. To send or receive e-mail, a user must have an account, which provides an e-mail address and electronic mailbox. Such accounts can be set up through online and Internet service providers.

Hardware—The actual computer equipment, as opposed to software, used by a computer operator. The monitor, keyboard, disk drive and printer are all examples of hardware.

Hypertext—Words or groups of words in an electronic document that are linked to other text, such as a definition or a related document. Hypertext can also be linked to illustrations.

Interactive—A type of computer interface that takes user input, such as answers to computer-generated questions, and then acts upon that input.

Internet— A worldwide network of computers that offers access to a wide variety of electronic resources.

Modem—MOdulator/DEModulator. A computer device used to send data from one computer to another via telephone line.

Multimedia—Computers and software capable of integrating text, sound, photographic-quality images, animation and video.

Network—A group of computers electronically linked to share information and resources.

Software—The computer programs that control computer hardware, usually run from a disk drive of some sort. Computers need software in order to run. These can be word processors, games, spreadsheets, etc.

World Wide Web (WWW)—An Internet resource that utilizes hypertext to access information. It also supports formatted text, illustrations and sounds, depending on the user's computer capabilities.

have access to the Internet, although many companies regulate usage. Ask the company network administrator.

If you have neither student nor employee access to the Internet, you have two options: going with an Online Service Provider (OSP) or using an Internet Service Provider (ISP). Each has its benefits and drawbacks, so you must decide which is the most suitable for you.

An online service provider develops its own content. Most OSPs developed outside the Internet, but added access later when they saw the demand. America Online and CompuServe are the two largest online service providers. An OSP usually develops its own areas of interest, such as writers' areas, reference, computer software and hardware support, etc. For those needing a little hand holding around computer technology, an OSP is probably the way to go. Internet service is usually integrated with the main service, so you don't have to worry about setting up all the software. Two drawbacks: these services are expensive, since they charge by the hour, and they are somewhat slower than direct access through an Internet service provider. This may be worth it if you are not computer savvy or don't want any hassles. Names and phone numbers for the more prominent services appear at the end of this article.

Internet service providers do not develop their own content, but merely provide access to the Internet. If you know your way around computers and want to save some money, then an ISP is the way to go. Many services provide a flat rate for access (unlimited access for one price). If this is the route you want to take, here is what you will need:

- Internet dialup software to make the connection. Some standard modem communications programs have this ability. Microsoft Windows 95 comes with this feature built in.
- a World Wide Web browser (also known as a client), such as Netscape Navigator or Microsoft Internet Explorer.
- an electronic mail client, such as Eudora. Some web browsers have this feature built in, Netscape Navigator for one.

All items can be found at a computer software retailer. Some Internet service providers have simplified the process for new members and provide everything you need in one package. There is a list of such ISPs at the end of the article. You can also purchase Internet starter kits in computer stores (Internet in a Box). Microsoft Windows 95, IBM OS/2 Warp Connect and most Macintoshes provide Internet support out of the box; check your manuals.

Once you have installed your hardware and software, start exploring the Internet. If you want to learn more about the Internet, including features not mentioned here, check your local bookstore or library. See the brief book list provided.

RESOURCES

Online Service Providers

America Online—(800)827-6364
CompuServe Information Service—(800)848-8199
The Microsoft Network—(206)882-8080
Prodigy—(914)448-8000

National Internet Service Providers

AT&T Worldnet—(800)WORLDNET
Global Network Navigator (GNN)—(800)819-6112
IBM Global Network—(800)455-5056
NetCom Internet Services—(800)353-5600
Pipeline USA—(703)904-4100

Search Engines

Alta Vista—http://www.altavista.digital.com/
Excite—http://www.excite.com/
Lycos—http://www.lycos.com/
Webcrawler—http://www.webcrawler.com/
Yahoo!—http://www.yahoo.com/

Further Reading

Internet and World Wide Web Simplified, by Ruth Maran (IDG Books)
Internet Complete Reference, by Hahn (Osborne)
The Internet for Dummies, by John Levine (IDG Books)
The Whole Internet User's Guide, by Ed Krol (O'Reilly & Associates)
Zen And The Art Of The Internet, by Brendan Kehoe (Prentice Hall)

IMPORTANT LISTING INFORMATION

• Listings are based on editorial questionnaires and interviews. They are not advertisements; publishers do not pay for their listings. The markets are not endorsed by *Writer's Market* editors.

• All listings have been verified before publication of this book. If a listing has not changed from last year, then the editor told us the market's needs have not changed and the previous listing continues to accurately reflect its policies. We require documentation in our files for each listing and never run a listing without its editorial office's approval.

• *Writer's Market* reserves the right to exclude any listing.

• When looking for a specific market, check the index. A market may not be listed for one of these reasons.

1. It doesn't solicit freelance material.
2. It doesn't pay for material.
3. It has gone out of business.
4. It has failed to verify or update its listing for the 1997 edition.
5. It was in the middle of being sold at press time, and rather than disclose premature details, we chose not to list it.
6. It hasn't answered *Writer's Market* inquiries satisfactorily. (To the best of our ability, and with our readers' help, we try to screen out fraudulent listings.)
7. It buys few manuscripts, constituting a very small market for freelancers.

• Individual markets that appeared in last year's edition but are not listed in this edition are included in the general index, with a notation giving the basis for their exclusion.

KEY TO SYMBOLS AND ABBREVIATIONS

●—Editorial comment offering additional market information from the editors of *Writer's Market*

‡—New listing in all sections

□—Cable TV market in Scriptwriting section

ms—manuscript; **mss**-manuscripts

b&w—black and white (photo)

SASE—self-addressed, stamped envelope

SAE—self-addressed envelope

IRC—International Reply Coupon, for use on reply mail in countries other than your own.

See Glossary for definitions of words and expressions used in writing and publishing.

The Markets
Book Publishers

The book business, for the most part, runs on hunches. Whether the idea for a book comes from a writer, an agent or the imagination of an acquiring editor, it is generally expressed in these terms: "This is a book that I *think* people will like. People will *probably* want to buy it." The decision to publish is mainly a matter of the right person, or persons, agreeing that those hunches are sound.

THE PATH TO PUBLICATION

Ideas reach editors in a variety of ways. They arrive unsolicited every day through the mail. They come by phone, sometimes from writers but most often from agents. They arise in the editor's mind because of his daily traffic with the culture in which he lives. The acquiring editor, so named because he is responsible for securing manuscripts for his company to publish, sifts through the deluge of possibilities, waiting for a book idea to strike him as extraordinary, inevitable, profitable.

In some companies, acquiring editors possess the authority required to say, "Yes, we will publish this book." In most publishing houses, though, the acquiring editor must prepare and present the idea to a proposal committee made up of marketing and administrative personnel. Proposal committees are usually less interested in questions of extraordinariness and inevitability than they are in profitability. The editor has to convince them that it makes good business sense to publish this book.

Once a contract is signed, several different wheels are set in motion. The author, of course, writes the book if he hasn't done so already. While the editor is helping to assure that the author is making the book the best it can be, promotion and publicity people are planning mailings of review copies to influential newspapers and review periodicals, writing catalog copy that will help sales representatives push the book to bookstores, and plotting a multitude of other promotional efforts (including interview tours and bookstore signings by the author) designed to dangle the book attractively before the reading public's eye.

When the book is published, it usually receives a concerted promotional push for a month or two. After that, the fate of the book—whether it will "grow legs" and set sales records or sit untouched on bookstore shelves—rests in the hands of the public. Publishers have to compete with all of the other entertainment industries vying for the consumer's money and limited leisure time. Successful books are reprinted to meet the demand. Unsuccessful books are returned from bookstores to publishers and are sold off cheaply as "remainders" or are otherwise disposed of.

THE STATE OF THE BUSINESS

The book publishing business, while not growing by leaps and bounds, remained healthy over the past year. Much of publishing's success in recent years has been traceable to the continuing growth of book superstores. Hundreds of the giant stores are now up and running all over the country, and many more are slated to be in place by the end of 1997. The superstore phenomenon—and the increased shelf space such stores offer—has allowed publishers to reach more customers with more books on a wider range of topics than ever before.

But that's not to say publishers are rushing to bring esoteric or highly experimental material to the marketplace. The blockbuster mentality—publishing's penchant for sticking with "name brand" novelists—still drives most large publishers. Of the top 11 bestselling novels last year, 9 of the authors had bestsellers the previous year. It's simply a less risky venture to continue publishing authors whom they know readers like. On the other hand, the prospects for nonfiction authors are perhaps better than they have been for years. The boom in available shelf space has provided entree to the marketplace for books on niche topics that heretofore would not have seen the light of day in most bookstores. The superstores position themselves as one-stop shopping centers for readers of every stripe. As such, they must carry books on a wide range of subjects.

Paper costs continue to be an area of concern for publishers, although prices are predicted to remain relatively stable and supply is estimated to grow slightly yet steadily over the next several years. Most publishers have laid in a supply that would get them through any price increases without upsetting their budgets.

The publishing community as a whole seems to be stepping back from the multimedia "hysteria" of the past few years, and approaching the market a little more cautiously. While the possibilities of CD-ROM are still being explored vigorously, the number of unsuccessful products in this area is a warning that the content must fit the format in order to sell.

WHAT IS EVERYBODY READING?

The list of authors penning bestselling fiction over the past year includes few unfamiliar names. Of the bestselling novels on *Publishers Weekly*'s Top 15 list, 11 were penned by authors from 1994's list as well. Blockbusters from John Grisham, Michael Crichton, Danielle Steel, Mary Higgins Clark and Anne Rice leave little room at the top for new blood.

Bestselling nonfiction continued many trends set earlier. Relationships, spirituality, healing and the mind, the development of values and morality, biography, cooking (often with celebrities) and celebrity-penned humor. Again, nearly all the bestsellers were by well-known personalities or writers with previous books to their credit. The relationship of Mars and Venus spawned two bestsellers, while the "Oprah cookbook" sold nearly 500,000 more copies in 1995, to add to the 5.6 million copies in print at the end of 1994. Mother Theresa hit the Top 20 for the year, while William Bennett's *The Moral Compass* and *The Book of Virtues* occupied two slots in the Top 15. Deepak Chopra continued to add to his considerable list with *The Seven Spiritual Laws of Success*, while Andrew Weil took up the mind/body torch with *Spontaneous Healing*. More information on trends can be found in Current Trends in Publishing on page 22.

HOW TO PUBLISH YOUR BOOK

The markets in this year's Book Publishers section offer opportunities in nearly every area of publishing. Large, commercial houses are here as are their smaller counterparts; large and small "literary" houses are represented as well. In addition, you'll find university presses, industry-related publishers, textbook houses and more.

The Book Publishers Subject Index is the place to start. You'll find it in the back of the book, before the General Index. Subject areas for both fiction and nonfiction are broken out for the more than over 1,000 total book publisher listings. Not all of them buy the kind of book you've written, but this Index will tell you which ones do.

Seven Stories Press: A Home for New Voices

Daniel Simon, founder of Four Walls Eight Windows Press and, more recently, Seven Stories Press, notes proudly that he "started at the bottom." Simon's first publishing job was entry-level permissions assistant for Harper and Row. Several publishing jobs later, while editing for Writers and Readers Publishing Cooperative, Simon happened upon an out-of-print volume of Nelson Algren short stories that inspired him to begin his own small press.

Photography by Miriam Berkley

Daniel Simon

"Nelson Algren was the most wonderful user of the language I'd ever come across," says Simon. "Then I did a little research and found out that all his books were out of print." In 1984, after a year of waiting to get permission from Algren's estate, Simon published Algren's *The Neon Wilderness* as the first title under his Four Walls Eight Windows imprint. In 1986, he formed a partnership with John Oakes and for the next ten years the two built Four Walls into "something which was still small but made a name for doing some interesting things."

In 1995, Simon left Four Walls to form Seven Stories Press which he describes as "a continuation of what I was doing at Four Walls." With a fulltime staff of two editors and one part-time person, Seven Stories will release 15 titles this year. Among those will be books by Octavia Butler, Annie Ernaux and health and nutrition author Gary Null. Simon will also continue publishing works from the estate of Nelson Algren and the annual *Censored: The News That Didn't Make the News—And Why*, edited by Carl Jensen. Newly signed writers to Seven Stories include Cynthia Voight, National Book Award finalist Charles Rosen, and Greek author Vassilis Vassilikos.

Simon sees his job as that of shaping the books he publishes. "If all, or any, of the books came into us with anything approaching the quality that we expect them to have when they go to the printer, they wouldn't be available to us. They would be going to bigger houses for more money than we could afford to pay. So, because we're independent, because we're small, our method of operation has to be a rigorous, opinionated and powerful editorial shaping process. Typically, a manuscript will come into us and we will say this has problems but there's a fire, there's an excitement to it—this writer is saying something important that needs to be said because there's nothing else out there like it; this is an important voice of someone who needs to be heard."

INSIDER REPORT, *continued*

Simon stresses, however, that ultimately the writer makes a manuscript publishable. "It's almost impossible to take an unpublishable book and make it better inhouse. Editing can do important things, but it's not the same as what a writer can do. We hold up a certain standard, put some demands on the writer. If what we're saying makes sense, the writer will, with some specific context and some specific input and direction, bring the book along in a second or third draft."

The close, ongoing, multibook working relationship between writers and editors is something Simon values. "The quality of relationships is the most important asset in my publishing company. To do my job well I need a writer I can help build over time, one who will keep an ongoing body of work coming to me. That way, I can really develop a look for the books, and can basically, over time, even create a readership for that writer."

Simon also emphasizes the importance of the relationship between writers and their work. "The biggest problem for a writer is not how to get a publisher to read your work or how to get the right agent. The problem is finding your subject and getting to the point where you're listening to yourself and listening to the world around you. Annie Ernaux and Octavia Butler are very clear about what their subjects are. They're committed to their work, they listen to their own voices and rhythms, and they listen to what's going on in the world. With writers like these, marvelous things happen. Instead of having to knock down doors that won't open, the booksellers get very excited and people buy the books and the media people are figuring out ways to feature that author—it's wonderful."

Finding new voices, says Simon, is perhaps the most important function of today's independent small press. "The more the big publishers shy away from developing writers and become more concerned with the commercial side of publishing, the more room there is for independent publishers to find those voices. There is a trend among larger publishers to think of the writer as playing a smaller part in the production of a successful book. The big publishers are becoming more driven by marketing, by sales, by bottom-line businessmen, and so the gulf between those people and the people actually writing the books keeps getting larger."

Referring to the need for small presses to remain strong in the current publishing climate, Simon says, "this is a time of strategic alliances. The trick is to make these alliances, but also to hold onto our independence." Although Simon points out that some small presses are surviving by simply cutting back on the number of titles they publish, he sees great advantage in sublicensing paperback editions of original hardback titles to big presses. "We benefit substantially from sublicensing, and the author has the best of both worlds—the special handling we provide when the hardcover edition is being created and the larger reach of the big press for the mass market editions."

Simon's advice for writers wishing to survive in today's publishing world is to "not be distracted by the difficulties in getting published. Instead, keep your primary objective of writing in mind which is to keep searching for your subject and voice. Editors and publishers are looking for strong writers whose voices are clear, who are saying things that are exciting, who are speaking to the moment. When we see that work, we want it. It's important for writers to remember that."

—*Barbara Kuroff*

When you have compiled a list of publishers interested in books in your subject area, read the detailed listings. Pare down your list by cross-referencing two or three subject areas and eliminating the listings only marginally suited to your book. When you have a good list, send for those publishers' catalogs and any manuscript guidelines available. You want to make sure your book idea is not a duplicate of something they've already published. Visit bookstores and libraries to see if their books are well represented. When you find a couple of books they have published that are similar to yours, write or call the company to find out who edited these books. This last, extra bit of research could be the key to getting your proposal to precisely the right editor.

Publishers prefer different kinds of submissions on first contact. Most like to see a one-page query with SASE, especially for nonfiction. Others will accept a brief proposal package that might include an outline and/or a sample chapter. Some publishers will accept submissions from agents only. Virtually no publisher wants to see a complete manuscript on initial contact, and sending one when they prefer another method will signal to the publisher "this is an amateur's submission." Editors do not have the time to read an entire manuscript, even editors at small presses who receive fewer submissions. Perhaps the only exceptions to this rule are children's book manuscripts and poetry manuscripts, which take only as much time to read as an outline and sample chapter anyway.

In your one-page query, give an overview of your book, mention the intended audience, the competition (check *Books in Print* and local bookstore shelves), and what sets your book apart. Detail any previous publishing experience or special training relevant to the subject of your book. All of this information will help your cause; it is the professional approach.

Only one in a thousand writers will sell a book to the first publisher they query, especially if the book is the writer's first effort. Make a list of a dozen or so publishers that might be interested in your book. Try to learn as much about the books they publish and their editors as you can. Research, knowing the specifics of your subject area, and a professional approach are often the difference between acceptance and rejection. You are likely to receive at least a few rejections, however, and when that happens, don't give up. Rejection is as much a part of publishing, if not more, than signing royalty checks. Send your query to the next publisher on your list. Multiple queries can speed up the process at this early stage.

Personalize your queries by addressing them individually and mentioning what you know about a company from its catalog or books you've seen. Never send a form letter as a query. Envelopes addressed to "Editor" or "Editorial Department" end up in the dreaded slush pile.

If a publisher offers you a contract, you may want to seek advice before signing and returning it. An author's agent will very likely take 15% if you employ one, but you could be making 85% of a larger amount. Some literary agents are available on an hourly basis for contract negotiations only. For more information on literary agents, contact the Association of Author's Representatives, 10 Astor Place, 3rd Floor, New York NY 10003, (212)353-3709. Also check the current edition of *Guide to Literary Agents* (Writer's Digest Books). Attorneys will only be able to tell you if everything is legal, not if you are getting a good deal, unless they have prior experience with literary contracts. If you have a legal problem, you might consider contacting Volunteer Lawyers for the Arts, 1 E. 53rd St., 6th Floor, New York NY 10022, (212)319-2787.

AUTHOR-SUBSIDY PUBLISHER'S LISTINGS ELIMINATED

In previous editions a section of Subsidy/Royalty publishers was included in *Writer's Market*. Subsidy publishing involves paying money to a publishing house to publish a book. The source of the money could be a government, foundation or university grant, or it could be the author of the book. Beginning with this edition, listings for book publishers offering author-subsidy arrangements are eliminated. Publishers offering nonauthor-subsidized arrangements have been included in the appropriate section.

Writer's Market is a reference tool to help you sell your writing, and we encourage you to work with publishers that pay a royalty. If one of the publishers listed here offers you an author-subsidy arrangement (sometimes called "cooperative publishing," "co-publishing" or "joint venture"), asks you to pay for all or part of the cost of any aspect of publishing (printing, advertising, etc.) or to guarantee the purchase of any number of the books yourself, we would like you to let us know about that company immediately.

Publishers are offering more author-subsidy arrangements than ever before. Some publishers feel they must seek them to expand their lists beyond the capabilities of their limited resources. This may be true, and you may be willing to agree to it, but we choose to list only those publishers paying a royalty without requiring a financial investment from the author.

For a list of publishers according to their subjects of interest, see the nonfiction and fiction sections of the Book Publishers Subject Index. Information on some book publishers and producers not included in this edition of *Writer's Market* can be found in the General Index.

ABBOTT, LANGER & ASSOCIATES, 548 First St., Crete IL 60417-2199. (708)672-4200. President: Dr. Steven Langer. Estab. 1967. Publishes trade paperback originals, loose-leaf books. Publishes 25 titles/year, mostly prepared inhouse. Receives 25 submissions/year. 10% of books from first-time authors; 90% of books from unagented writers. Pays 10-15% royalty. Offers advance. Publishes book 18 months after acceptance. Book catalog for 6×9 SAE with 2 first-class stamps. Reports in 1 month on queries, 3 months on mss.
Nonfiction: How-to, reference, technical on some phase of human resources management, security, sales management, etc. Especially needs "a very limited number (3-5) of books dealing with very specialized topics in the field of human resource management, wage and salary administration, sales compensation, recruitment, selection, etc." Publishes for human resources directors, wage and salary administrators, sales/marketing managers, security directors, etc. Query with outline. Reviews artwork/photos.
Tips: "A writer has the best chance selling our firm a how-to book in human resources management, sales/marketing management or security management."

ABC-CLIO, INC., 501 S. Cherry St., Suite 350, Denver CO 80222. (303)333-3003. Fax: (303)333-4037. Subsidiaries include ABC-CLIO Ltd. President: Heather Cameron. Editorial Director: Jeffrey Serena. Estab. 1955. Publishes hardcover originals. Publishes 35 titles/year. Receives 500 submissions/year. 20% of books from first-time authors; 95% from unagented writers. Pays royalty on net receipts. Offers advance. Publishes ms 10 months after acceptance. Reports in 2 months on queries. Book catalog and ms guidelines free.
Nonfiction: Reference. Subjects include art/architecture, education, environmental issues, government/politics, history, literary studies, multicultural studies, mythology, science, women's issues/studies. "Looking for reference books on current world issues, women's issues, and for subjects compatible with high school curriculum. No monographs or textbooks." Query or submit outline and sample chapters.
Recent Nonfiction Title: *Encyclopedia of the Persian Gulf War.*

THE ABERDEEN GROUP, 426 S. Westgate St., Addison IL 60101. (630)543-0870. Fax: (630)543-3112. Acquisitions: Mark D. Cicco. Publishes trade paperback originals. Publishes 6 titles/year. Receives 75 queries and 12 mss/year. 10% of books from first-time authors; 100% from unagented writers. Pays 6-18% royalty on retail price. Offers $1,000-2,000 advance. Publishes book 6 months after acceptance of ms. Accepts simultaneous submissions. Reports in 1 month on queries and proposals, 2 months on mss. Book catalog free on request.
Nonfiction: How-to, technical. Subjects include architecture, construction, general engineering and construction business. Query with outline, 2-3 sample chapters, definition of topic, features, market.
Recent Nonfiction Title: *Designing Floor Slabs On Grade*, by Ringo/Anderson (how-to/technical).

ABINGDON PRESS, Imprint of The United Methodist Publishing House, P.O. Box 801, Nashville TN 37202-0801. (615)749-6301. Fax: (615)748-6512. President/Publisher: Neil M. Alexander. Contact: Michael E. Lawrence, managing director/assistant editorial director. Senior Editor, General Interest Books: Mary

Catherine Dean. Senior Editor, Academic Books: Rex Mathews. Senior Editor, United Methodist Newscope: J. Richard Peck. Senior Editor, Professional Products: Paul Franklyn. Senior Editor, Reference Books: Jack Keller. Senior Editor, Music: Gary A. Smith. Estab. 1789. Publishes hardcover and paperback originals and reprints; church supplies. Publishes 130 titles/year. Receives approximately 2,500 submissions/year. Few books from first-time authors; 90-95% of books from unagented writers. Average print order for a first book is 4,000-5,000. Pays royalty. Publishes book 2 years after acceptance. Manuscript guidelines for SASE. Reports in 3 months.

Nonfiction: Religious-lay and professional, children's religious books, academic texts. Length: 32-300 pages. Query with outline and samples only.

Recent Nonfiction Title: *The New Interpreter's Bible: A Commentary in Twelve Volumes.*

‡HARRY N. ABRAMS, INC., Subsidiary of Times Mirror Co., 100 Fifth Ave., New York NY 10011. (212)206-7715. President/Publisher/Editor-in-Chief: Paul Gottlieb. Estab. 1949. Publishes hardcover and "a few" paperback originals. Publishes 100 titles/year. "We are one of the few publishers who publish almost exclusively illustrated books. We consider ourselves the leading publishers of art books and high-quality artwork in the U.S." Offers variable advance. Publishes book 2 years after acceptance. Reports in 3 months. Book catalog for $5.

Nonfiction: Art, nature and science, outdoor recreation. Requires illustrated material for art and art history, museums. Submit outline, sample chapters and illustrations. Reviews artwork/photos as part of ms package.

Tips: "We publish *only* high-quality illustrated art books, i.e., art, art history, museum exhibition catalogs, written by specialists and scholars in the field. Once the author has signed a contract to write a book for our firm the author must finish the manuscript to agreed-upon high standards within the schedule agreed upon in the contract."

ACA BOOKS, American Council for the Arts, 1 E. 53rd St., 3rd Floor, New York NY 10022. (212)223-2787. E-mail: djones@artsusa.org. Website: http://www.artsusa.org. Publications Editor: Daniel Jones. Publishes trade paperback originals and reprints. Publishes 4 titles/year. Receives 60 queries and 30 mss/year. 100% of mss from unagented writers. Publishes book 1 year after acceptance of ms. Accepts simultaneous submissions. Reports in 3 months on queries. Book catalog free on request.

Nonfiction: Reference, textbook. Subjects include art, education and government/politics. "We do *not* publish art books (i.e. studies of artwork, coffee table books). We are most interested in books on careers in the arts, arts policy, arts education, arts fundraising and management. Query.

Recent Nonfiction Title: *Beyond Enrichment: Building Effective Arts Partnerships with Schools and Your Community*, by Jane Remer (arts education policy).

ACADEMY CHICAGO, 363 W. Erie St., Chicago IL 60610-3125. (312)751-7300. Fax: (312)751-7306. Editorial Director/Senior Editor: Anita Miller. Assistant Editor: Catherine Prendergast. Estab. 1975. Publishes hardcover and paperback originals and reprints. Publishes 20 titles/year. Receives approximately 2,000 submissions/year. Average print order for a first book is 1,500-5,000. Pays 7-10% royalty. Modest advances. Publishes book 18 months after acceptance. Book catalog for 9 × 12 SAE with 5 first-class stamps. Manuscript guidelines for #10 SASE. Query with first 4 chapters and SASE. Reports in 2 months.

Nonfiction: Adult, biography, historical, travel, true crime, reprints. No how-to, cookbooks, self-help, etc. Query and submit first 4 consecutive chapters.

Recent Nonfiction Title: *Chicago By Gaslight*, by Richard Lindberg (history).

Fiction: Mainstream novels, mysteries. No romantic, children's, young adult, religious or sexist fiction; nothing avant-garde. Query with first 3 chapters.

Recent Fiction Title: *Circling Eden*, by Carol Magun.

Tips: "At the moment, we are looking for good nonfiction; we certainly want excellent original fiction, but we are swamped. No fax queries, no disks. We are always interested in reprinting good out-of-print books."

ACCENT ON LIVING, Subsidiary of Cheever Publishing, Inc., P.O. Box 700, Bloomington IL 61702. (309)378-2961. Fax: (309)378-4420. Editor: Betty Garee. Publishes 4 titles/year. Receives 300 queries and 150 mss/year. 70% of books from first-time authors; 100% from unagented writers. Pays 6% royalty or makes outright purchase. Publishes book 3 months after acceptance of ms. Accepts simultaneous submissions. Reports on queries in 1 month. *Writer's Market* recommends allowing 2 months for reply. Book catalog for 8 × 10 SAE with 2 first-class stamps. Manuscript guidelines for #10 SASE.

Nonfiction: How-to. Anything pertaining to physically disabled. Query. Reviews artwork/photos as part of ms package. Send snapshots or slides.

Recent Nonfiction Title: *If It Weren't for the Honor, I'd Rather Have Walked*, by Jan Little.

ACCENT PUBLICATIONS, Cook Communications Ministries, P.O. Box 36640, Colorado Springs CO 80936-3664. (719)536-0100 ext. 3337. Managing Editor: Mary B. Nelson. Estab. 1947. Publishes evangelical Christian education and church resource products. Publishes 6-8 titles/year. 100% of books from unagented writers. Pays royalty on retail price or makes outright purchase. Publishes book 1 year after acceptance. Query with 3 sample chapters, brief synopsis and chapter outline. Do not submit full ms unless requested.

No phone calls, please. Reports in 4 months. Manuscript guidelines for #10 SASE.
Nonfiction: "We are currently soliciting only nonfiction proposals in the areas of Christian education and Church Resources. C.E. products are teaching tools designed for the volunteer or professional Christian leadership to use in the church's education process. Church Resources are products that can be used in any aspect of the local church ministry. We would consider Bible studies, study guides, teacher helps, ministry aids, and other C.E. products. We do not consider games, puzzles, puppet books, fiction for children, youth, or adults. We do not consider devotionals, poetry, biographies, autobiographies, personal experience stories, manuscripts with a charismatic emphasis, or general Christian living books."
Nonfiction Title: *Celebrating the Heart of Marriage*, by Kathy Collard Miller (Women's Bible study).

ACE SCIENCE FICTION, Imprint of The Berkley Publishing Group, 200 Madison Ave., New York NY 10016. (212)686-9820. E-mail: acebooks@genie.com. Website: http://www.berkly.com. Editor: Laura Anne Gilman. Estab. 1953. Publishes paperback originals and reprints. Publishes 96 titles/year. Reports in 6 months. Manuscript guidelines for #10 SASE.
Fiction: Science fiction, fantasy. Query first with SASE.
Recent Fiction Title: *Branch Point*, by Mona Clee.

ACTA PUBLICATIONS, 4848 N. Clark St., Chicago IL 60640-4711. Copublishers: Gregory F. Augustine Pierce, Thomas R. Artz. Estab. 1958. Publishes trade paperback originals. Publishes 10 titles/year. Receives 50 queries and 15 mss/year. 50% of books from first-time authors; 90% from unagented writers. Pays 7½-12½% royalty on wholesale price. Publishes book 1 year after acceptance of ms. Reports in 2 months on proposals. Book catalog and author guidelines for SASE.
Nonfiction: Religion. "We publish non-academic, practical books aimed at the mainline religious market." Submit outline and 1 sample chapter. Reviews artwork/photos as part of ms package. Send photocopies.
Tips: "Don't send a submission unless you have read our catalog or one of our books."

ACTIVE PARENTING PUBLISHERS, INC., 810-B Franklin Court, Marietta GA 30067. Fax: (770)429-0334. E-mail: cservice@activeparenting.com. Website: http://www.activeparenting.com. Editorial Manager: Shelly Cox. Publishes 4 titles/year.
Nonfiction: Self-help, textbook, educational. Subjects include child guidance/parenting, psychology, loss, self-esteem. Nonfiction work; mainly parent education and family issues. Does not accept unsolicited mss.
Recent Nonfiction Title: *How to Help Your Child Succeed in School*, by Michael H. Popkin, Ph.D., Betty B. Youngs, Ph.D. and Jane M. Healy, Ph.D. (self-help).

ADAMS MEDIA CORPORATION, (formerly Adams Publishing), 260 Center St., Holbrook MA 02343. (617)767-8100. Fax: (617)767-0994. Website: http://www.adamsonline.com. Editor-in-Chief: Edward Walters. Publishes hardcover originals, trade paperback originals and reprints. Publishes 100 titles/year. Receives 1,500 queries and 500 mss/year. 25% of books from first-time authors; 25% from unagented writers. Pays standard royalty or makes outright purchase. Offers variable advance. Publishes book 1 year after acceptance of ms. Accepts simultaneous submissions. Reports in 3 months. Book catalog for SAE with 4 first-class stamps.
Nonfiction: Biography, children's/juvenile, cookbook, gift book, how-to, humor, illustrated book, reference, self-help. Subjects include Americana, animals, business and economics, child guidance/parenting, cooking/foods/nutrition, gardening, government/politics, health/medicine, history, hobbies, language/literature, military/war, money/finance, nature/environment, psychology, regional, science, sports, women's issues/studies. "We publish commercial nonfiction, not scholarly or literary material." Submit outline.
Recent Nonfiction Title: *Wake Me When It's Funny*, by Garry Marshall (memoir).

ADAMS-BLAKE PUBLISHING, 8041 Sierra St., Fair Oaks CA 95628. (916)962-9296. Vice President: Paul Raymond. Senior Editor: Monica Blane. Publishes trade paperback originals and reprints. Publishes 10-15 titles/year. Receives 150 queries and 90 mss/year. 90% of books from first-time authors; 90% from unagented writers. Pays 10% royalty on wholesale price. Publishes book 6 months after acceptance of ms. Accepts simultaneous submissions. Reports in 1 month on mss. *Writer's Market* recommends allowing 2 months for reply.
Nonfiction: How-to, technical. Subjects include business and economics, computers and electronics, health/medicine, money/finance, software. "We are looking for business, technology and finance titles that can be targeted to older or retired members of the workforce. We also seek information on data that can be bound/packaged and sold to specific industry groups at high margins." Query with sample chapters or complete ms. Reviews artwork/photos as part of ms package. Send photocopies.
Recent Nonfiction Title: *Tears and Rage: The Nursing Crisis in America*, by Jane Schweitzer (nursing).
Tips: "We will take a chance on material the big houses reject. Since we sell the majority of our material directly, we can publish material for a very select market. Author should include a marketing plan. Sell us on the project!"

ADDICUS BOOKS, INC., P.O. Box 37327, Omaha NE 68137. President: Rod Colvin. Publishes trade paperback originals. Publishes 8-10 titles/year. 70% of books from first-time authors; 60% from unagented writers. Pays royalty on retail price. Publishes book 9 months after acceptance of ms. Accepts simultaneous submissions. Reports in 1 month on proposals. *Writer's Market* recommends allowing 2 months for reply. Book catalog and ms guidelines for #10 SASE.

Nonfiction: How-to, self-help. Subjects include Americana, business and economics, health/medicine, psychology, regional, true-crime. Query with outline and 3-4 sample chapters.

Recent Nonfiction Title: *Not the Way It's Supposed to Be: A Breviary of Sin*, by Cornelius Plantinga (awarded *Christianity Today's* 1996 book of the year).

Tips: "With health titles, we're looking for high-quality manuscripts from authors who have done their market research. In addition to books with national appeal, we will consider titles with strong regional appeal, such as true-crime. Here, we're looking for well-written, well-researched manuscripts with interesting stories behind the crimes."

‡ADDISON-WESLEY LONGMAN, INC., (formerly Addison-Wesley Publishing Co., Inc.), General Publishing Group, One Jacob Way, Reading MA 01867. (617)944-3700. Fax: (617)944-8243. Publisher: David Goehring. Contact: Editorial Department. Estab. 1942. Publishes hardcover and paperback originals. Publishes 125 titles/year. Pays royalty.

Nonfiction: Publishes general nonfiction, business, science, health, parenting/child care, psychology, current affairs, biography/memoir, social science/history/politics, narrative nonfiction, children's multimedia. No fiction. Query by letter or phone, then submit synopsis and 1 sample chapter.

AFRICAN AMERICAN IMAGES, 1909 W. 95th St., Chicago IL 60643. (312)445-0322. Publisher: Dr. Jawanza Kunjufu. Publishes trade paperback originals. Publishes 10 titles/year. Receives 520 queries and 520 mss/year. 90% of books from first-time authors; 95% from unagented writers. Pays 10% royalty on wholesale price. Publishes book 6 months after acceptance of ms. Accepts simultaneous submissions. Reports in 1 month on queries, 2 months on mss. Book catalog and ms guidelines free on request.

Nonfiction: Children's/juvenile. Subjects include education, ethnic, history, psychology. Submit complete ms. *Writer's Market* recommends sending a query with SASE first. Must be Africentric.

Fiction: Juvenile. Must be Africentric.

‡AKTRIN FURNITURE RESEARCH, 164 S. Main St., P.O. Box 898, High Point NC 27261. (910)841-8535. Fax: (910)841-5435. Director of Operations: Carlene Damba. Imprint is AKTRIN Furniture Research-Canada (151 Randall St., Oakville, Ontario L6J 1P5 Canada. (905)845-3474. Contact: Stefan Wille). Publishes trade paperback originals. Publishes 8 titles/year. Receives 5 queries/year. 20% of books from first-time authors; 20% from unagented writers. Makes outright purchase of $1,500 minimum. Offers $300-600 advance. Publishes book 2 months after acceptance. Accepts simultaneous submissions. Reports in 1 month. *Writer's Market* recommends allowing 2 months for reply. Book catalog free on request.

Nonfiction: Reference. Subjects include business and economics. "Have an understanding of business and economics. We are writing only about the furniture industry." Query.

Recent Nonfiction Title: *Standards in the Furniture Industry*, by Sean Fegan (business).

Tips: Audience is executives of furniture companies (manufacturers and retailers) and suppliers to the furniture industry.

ALASKA NORTHWEST BOOKS, Imprint of Graphic Arts Center Publishing. Editorial offices: Suite 300, 2208 NW Market St., Seattle WA 98107. (206)784-5071. Fax: (206)784-5316. Contact: Marlene Blessing. Estab. 1959. Publishes hardcover and trade paperback originals and reprints. Publishes 12 titles/year. Receives hundreds of submissions/year. 10% of books from first-time authors; 90% from unagented writers. Pays 10-15% royalty on wholesale price. Buys mss outright (rarely). Offers advance. Publishes book an average of 1 year after acceptance. Accepts simultaneous submissions. Reports in 6 months on queries. Book catalog and ms guidelines for 9×12 SAE with 6 first-class stamps.

● Editor reports this house is initating more of their own projects and publishing fewer unsolicited manuscripts.

Nonfiction: "All written for a general readership, not for experts in the subject." Subjects include nature and environment, travel, cookbooks, Native American culture, adventure, outdoor recreation and sports, the arts, children's books. "Our book needs are as follows: one-half Alaskan focus, one-quarter Northwest, one-eighth Pacific coast, one-eighth national (looking for logical extensions of current subjects)." Submit outline/synopsis and sample chapters.

Recent Nonfiction Title: *Place of Pretend People*, by Carolyn Kramers.

Tips: "Book proposals that are professionally written and polished, with a clear market receive our most careful consideration. We are looking for originality. We publish a wide range of books for a wide audience. Some of our books are clearly for travelers, others for those interested in outdoor recreation or various regional subjects. If I were a writer trying to market a book today, I would research the competition (existing books) for what I have in mind, and clearly (and concisely) express why my idea is different and better. I would describe the bookbuyers (and readers)—where they are, how many of them are there, how they can be reached (organizations, publications), why they would want or need my book."

THE ALBAN INSTITUTE, 4550 Montgomery Ave., Suite 433 North, Bethesda MD 20814-3341. (301)718-4407. Fax: (301)718-1958. Editor-in-Chief: Celia A. Hahn. Publishes trade paperback originals. Publishes 10 titles/year. Receives 100 submissions/year. 100% of books from unagented writers. Pays 7-10% royalty on books; makes outright purchase of $50-100 on publication for 450-2,000 word articles relevant to congregational life—practical—ecumenical. Publishes book 1 year after acceptance. Reports in 4 months. Proposals only, no unsolicited mss. Book catalog and ms guidelines for 9 × 12 SAE with 3 first-class stamps.
Nonfiction: Religious—focus on local congregation—ecumenical. Must be accessible to general reader. Research preferred. Needs mss on the task of the ordained leader in the congregation, the career path of the ordained leader in the congregation, problems and opportunities in congregational life, and ministry of the laity in the world and in the church. No sermons, devotional, children's titles, novels, inspirational or prayers. Query for guidelines.
Tips: "Our audience is comprised of intelligent, probably liberal mainline Protestant and Catholic clergy and lay leaders, executives and seminary administration/faculty—people who are concerned with the local church at a practical level and new approaches to its ministry. We are looking for titles on congregations, the clergy role, calling and career; visions, challenges, how-to's; and the ministry of the laity in the church and in the world."

ALLEN PUBLISHING CO., 7324 Reseda Blvd., Reseda CA 91335. (818)344-6788. Owner/Publisher: Michael Wiener. Estab. 1979. Publishes mass market paperback originals. Publishes 4 titles/year. Receives 50-100 submissions/year. 50% of books from first-time authors; 90% from unagented writers. Makes outright purchase for negotiable sum. Publishes book 6 months after acceptance. Accepts simultaneous submissions. Reports in 2 weeks. *Writer's Market* recommends allowing 2 months for reply. Book catalog and writer's guidelines for #10 SASE.
   ● This publisher reports having received many manuscripts outside its area of interest. Writers are encouraged to follow the publisher's subject matter guidelines.
Nonfiction: How-to, self-help. Subjects include how to start various businesses and how to improve your financial condition. "We want self-help material, 25,000 words approximately, aimed at wealth-builders, opportunity seekers, aspiring entrepreneurs. We specialize in material for people who are relatively inexperienced in the world of business and have little or no capital to invest. Material must be original and authoritative, not rehashed from other sources. All our books are marketed exclusively by mail, in soft-cover, 8½ × 11 format. We are a specialty publisher and will not consider anything that does not exactly meet our needs." Query. Reviews artwork/photos as part of ms package.
Recent Nonfiction Title: *How To Find The One Opportunity Ad That Can Make You Rich*, by Mike Wiener (exposé of various get-rich-quick scams).
Tips: "We are a specialty publisher, as noted above. If your subject does not match our specialty, do not waste your time and ours by submitting a query we cannot possibly consider."

ALLWORTH PRESS, 10 E. 23rd St., New York NY 10010-4402. Website: http://www.arts-online.com/allworth/home.html. Editor: Ted Gachot. Publisher: Tad Crawford. Estab. 1989. Publishes trade paperback originals. Publishes 10 titles/year. Pays 6-7½% royalty (for paperback) on retail price. Reports in 1 month on queries and proposals. *Writer's Market* recommends allowing 2 months for reply. Book catalog and ms guidelines free on request.
Nonfiction: How-to, reference. Subjects include the business aspects of art, design, photography, performing arts, writing, as well as legal guides for the public. "We are trying to give ordinary people advice to better themselves in practical ways—as well as helping creative people in the fine and commercial arts." Query.
Recent Nonfiction Title: *Immigration Questions and Answers*, by Carl Baldwin (legal self-help).

ALMAR PRESS, 4105 Marietta Dr., Vestal NY 13850-4032. (607)722-0265. Fax: (607)722-3545. Editor-in-Chief: A.N. Weiner. Managing Editor: M.F. Weiner. Estab. 1977. Publishes hardcover and paperback originals and reprints. Publishes 8 titles/year. Receives 200 submissions/year. 75% of books from first-time authors; 100% from unagented writers. Average print order for a first book is 2,000. Pays 10% royalty. No advance. Publishes book 6 months after acceptance. Prefers exclusive submissions; however, accepts simultaneous submissions, if so noted. Reports within 2 months. Book catalog for #10 SAE with 2 first-class stamps. Submissions *must* include SASE for reply.
Nonfiction: Publishes business, technical, regional, consumer books and reports. "These main subjects include general business, financial, travel, career, technology, personal help, Northeast regional, hobbies, general medical, general legal, how-to. *Almar Reports* are business and technology subjects published for management use and prepared in 8½ × 11 book format. Reprint publications represent a new aspect of our business." Submit outline and sample chapters. Reviews artwork/photos as part of ms package.
Tips: We would like to expand our books on avoiding crime problems in business and personal life. Also, books covering unusual business topics—*not* the usual "How to succeed in business," or "How I made a fortune in business." We are open to any suggested topic. This type of book will be important to us. We look for timely subjects. The type of book the writer has the best chance of selling to our firm is something different or unusual—*no* poetry or fiction, also *no* first-person travel or family history. The book must be complete and of good quality."

ALPINE PUBLICATIONS, 225 S. Madison Ave., Loveland CO 80537. Publisher: Ms. B.J. McKinney. Imprint is Blue Ribbon Books. Publishes hardcover and trade paperback originals and reprints. Publishes 6-10 titles/year. 30% of books from first-time authors; 95% from unagented writers. Pays 7-15% royalty on wholesale price or occasionally makes outright purchase. Publishes book 18 months after acceptance. Accepts simultaneous submissions. Reports in 1 month on queries; 3 months on mss. Book catalog free on request. Manuscript guidelines for #10 SASE.

Nonfiction: Animal subjects. "Alpine specializes in books that promote the enjoyment of and responsibility for companion animals with emphasis on dogs, cats and horses." Submit 2-3 sample chapters, summary, outline with SASE. Reviews artwork/photos as part of ms package. Send photocopies.

Recent Nonfiction Title: *The Mentally Sound Dog*, by Clark (dog behavior modification).

Fiction: "We publish fiction only occasionally. Must fit our established audience and markets."

Tips: Audience is pet owners, breeders and exhibitors, veterinarians, animal trainers, animal care specialists, judges. "We prefer to work directly with authors, not through agents. Look up some of our titles before you submit. See what is unique about our books. Write your proposal to suit our guidelines."

ALYSON PUBLICATIONS, INC., P.O. Box 4371, Los Angeles CA 90078. (213)871-1225. Fax: (213)467-6805. Publisher: Tom Radko. Estab. 1979. Imprint is Alyson Wonderland. Publishes trade paperback originals and reprints. Publishes 40 titles/year. Receives 1,500 submissions/year. 40% of books from first-time authors; 80% from unagented writers. Average print order for a first book is 6,000. Pays 8-15% royalty on net price. Offers $1,500-15,000 advance. Publishes book 15 months after acceptance. Reports in 1 month. *Writer's Market* recommends allowing 2 months for reply. Book catalog and ms guidelines for 6×9 SAE with 3 first-class stamps.

Nonfiction: Gay/lesbian subjects. "We are especially interested in nonfiction providing a positive approach to gay/lesbian issues." Accepts nonfiction translations. Submit 2-page outline. Reviews artwork/photos as part of ms package with SASE.

Recent Nonfiction Title: *Out in the Workplace*, by Richard A. Rasi and Lourdes Rodriguez-Nogués.

Fiction: Gay novels. Accepts fiction translations. Submit 1-2 page synopsis with SASE.

Recent Fiction Title: *Does Freddy Dance*, by Dick Scanlan.

Tips: "We publish many books by new authors. The writer has the best chance of selling to our firm well-researched, popularly written nonfiction on a subject (e.g., some aspect of gay history) that has not yet been written about much. With fiction, create a strong storyline that makes the reader want to find out what happens. With nonfiction, write in a popular style for a non-academic audience. Actively soliciting manuscripts aimed at kids of lesbian and gay parents."

AMACOM BOOKS, Imprint of American Management Association, 1601 Broadway, New York NY 10019-7406. (212)903-8081. Managing Director: Weldon P. Rackley. Estab. 1923. Publishes hardcover and trade paperback originals and trade paperback reprints. Publishes 68 titles/year. Receives 200 submissions/year. 50% of books from first-time authors; 90% from unagented writers. Pays 10-15% royalty on net receipts by the publisher. Publishes book 9 months after acceptance. Reports in 2 months. Free book catalog and proposal guidelines.

Nonfiction: Publishes business books of all types, including management, marketing, technology (computers), career, professional skills, small business. Retail, direct mail, college, corporate markets. Query. Submit outline/synopsis, sample chapters, résumé/vita.

Tips: "Our audience consists of people in the business sector looking for practical books on business issues, strategies, and tasks."

AMERICA WEST PUBLISHERS, P.O. Box 3300, Bozeman MT 59772-3300. (406)585-0700. Fax: (406)585-0703. Review Editor: George Green. Estab. 1985. Publishes hardcover and trade paperback originals and reprints. Publishes 20 titles/year. Receives 150 submissions/year. 90% of books from first-time authors; 90% from unagented writers. Pays 10% on wholesale price. Offers $300 average advance. Publishes book 6 months after acceptance. Accepts simultaneous submissions. Reports in 1 month. *Writer's Market* recommends allowing 2 months for reply. Book catalog and ms guidelines free.

Nonfiction: UFO—metaphysical. Subjects include health/medicine (holistic self-help), political (including cover-up), economic. Submit outline/synopsis and sample chapters. Reviews artwork/photos as part of ms package.

Recent Nonfiction Title: *Chaos In America*, by John King.

Tips: "We currently have materials in all bookstores that have areas of UFOs and also political and economic nonfiction."

AMERICAN & WORLD GEOGRAPHIC PUBLISHING, P.O. Box 5630, Helena MT 59604. (406)443-2842. General Manager: Brad Hurd. Publications Director: Barbara Fifer. Publishes trade paperback originals. Publishes 12-15 titles/year. Receives 40 queries and 8 mss/year. 10% of books from first-time authors; 100% from unagented writers. No advance. Makes outright purchase of $7,000-8,000. Publishes book 18 months after acceptance of ms. Accepts simultaneous submissions. Reports in 4 months on proposals. Book catalog and ms guidelines free on request.

Nonfiction: Coffee table book, gift book, illustrated book. Subjects include recreation, regional. "Most of our titles are commissioned." Query with proposal package, including outline, sample chapter, photography with SASE. Reviews artwork/photos as part of ms package. Send transparencies; dupes acceptable.
Recent Nonfiction Titles: *Natchez Trace: Two Centuries of Travel*, text and photos by Bert Gildart.

AMERICAN ASTRONAUTICAL SOCIETY, Univelt, Inc., Publisher, P.O. Box 28130, San Diego CA 92198. (619)746-4005. Fax: (619)746-3139. Editorial Director: Robert H. Jacobs. Estab. 1970. Publishes hardcover originals. Publishes 8 titles/year. Receives 12-15 submissions/year. 5% of books from first-time authors; 5% from unagented writers. Average print order for a first book is 300-1,500. Pays 10% royalty on actual sales. Publishes book 4 months after acceptance. Accepts simultaneous submissions. Reports in 1 month. *Writer's Market* recommends allowing 2 months for reply. Book catalog and ms guidelines for 9 × 12 SAE with 3 first-class stamps.
Nonfiction: Proceedings or monographs in the field of astronautics, including applications of aerospace technology to Earth's problems. "Our books must be space-oriented or space-related. They are meant for technical libraries, research establishments and the aerospace industry worldwide." Call first, then submit outline and 1-2 sample chapters. Reviews artwork/photos as part of ms package.
Recent Nonfiction Title: *Strategies for Mars: A Guide to Human Exploration*, edited by Carol R. Stoker, Carter Emmart.

AMERICAN ATHEIST PRESS, P.O. Box 140195, Austin TX 78714-0195. (512)458-1244. Fax: (512)467-9525 Editor: Frank Zindler. Estab. 1959. Imprints include Gusttav Broukal Press. Publishes trade paperback originals and reprints. Publishes 12 titles/year. Receives 200 submissions/year. 40-50% of books from first-time authors; 100% from unagented writers. Pays 5-10% royalty on retail price. Publishes book 2 years after acceptance. Accepts simultaneous submissions. Reports in 4 months on queries. Book catalog for 6½ × 9½ SAE. Writer's guidelines for 9 × 12 SAE.
Nonfiction: Biography, reference, general. Subjects include history (of religion and atheism, of the effects of religion historically); philosophy and religion (from an atheist perspective, particularly criticism of religion); politics (separation of state and church, religion and politics); atheism (particularly the lifestyle of atheism; the history of atheism; applications of atheism). "We are interested in hard-hitting and original books expounding the lifestyle of atheism and criticizing religion. We would like to see more submissions dealing with the histories of specific religious sects, such as the L.D.S., the Worldwide Church of God, etc. We are generally not interested in biblical criticism." Submit outline and sample chapters. Reviews artwork/photos.
Recent Nonfiction Title: *Manual of a Perfect Atheist*, by Rios.
Fiction: Humor (satire of religion or of current religious leaders); anything of particular interest to atheists. "We rarely publish any fiction. But we have occasionally released a humorous book. No mainstream. For our press to consider fiction, it would have to tie in with the general focus of our press, which is the promotion of atheism and free thought." Submit outline/synopsis and sample chapters.
Tips: "We will need more how-to types of material—how to argue with creationists, how to fight for state/church separation, etc. We have an urgent need for literature for young atheists."

AMERICAN CORRECTIONAL ASSOCIATION, 4380 Forbes Blvd., Lanham, MD 20706. (301)918-1800. Fax: (301)918-1900. Managing Editor: Alice Fins. Estab. 1870. Publishes hardcover and trade paperback originals. Publishes 18 titles/year. Receives 40 submissions/year. 90% of books from first-time authors; 100% from unagented writers. Pays 10% royalty on net sales. Publishes book 6 months to 1 year after acceptance. Reports in 4 months. Book catalog and ms guidelines free.
- This publisher advises out-of-town freelance editors, indexers and proofreaders to refrain from requesting work from them.
Nonfiction: How-to, reference, technical, textbook, correspondence courses. "We are looking for practical, how-to texts or training materials written for the corrections profession. No true-life accounts by current or former inmates or correctional officers, theses, or dissertations." Query. Reviews artwork/photos as part of ms package.
Tips: "Our niche is in providing practical information on jails, prisons, boot camps, probation, parole, community corrections, juvenile facilities and programs rehabilitation, substance abuse programs and other areas of corrections. Our audience is made up of corrections professionals and criminal justice students."

AMERICAN COUNSELING ASSOCIATION, 5999 Stevenson Ave., Alexandria VA 22304-3300. (703)823-9800. Acquisitions and Development Editor: Carolyn C. Baker. Scholarly paperback originals. Publishes 10-15 titles/year. Receives 200 queries and 125 mss/year. 5% of books from first-time authors; 90% from unagented writers. Pays 10-15% royalty on wholesale price. Publishes book within 7 months after acceptance. Accepts simultaneous submissions. Reports in 2 months on queries and proposals, 4 months on mss. Manuscript guidelines free on request.
Nonfiction: Reference, textbooks for professional counselors. Subjects include education, gay/lesbian, health/medicine, psychology, religion, sociology, women's issues/studies. ACA does not publish self-help books or autobiographies. Query with proposal package, including outline, 2 sample chapters and vitae.

Recent Nonfiction Title: *Counseling Interracial Individuals and Families*, by Bea Wehrly.
Tips: "Target your market. Your books will not be appropriate for everyone across all disciplines."

‡**AMERICAN DIABETES ASSOCIATION**, 1660 Duke St., Alexandria VA 22314. (703)549-1500. Acquisitions Editor: Susan Reynolds. Publishes hardcover originals and trade and mass market paperback originals. Publishes 15 titles/year. Publishes 15 titles/year. Receives 60 queries and 20 mss/year. 10% of books from first-time authors; 80% from unagented writers. Pays 7-10% royalty on retail price. Offers $0-2,000 advance. Publishes book 8 months after acceptance of ms. Reports in 2 months. Book catalog free on request.
Nonfiction: Children's/juvenile, cookbook, how-to, reference, self-help. Subjects include child guidance/parenting, cooking/foods/nutrition, health/medicine, psychology. "Our books are written for readers with diabetes. We are interested in the medical, nutritional and psychosocial aspects of living with diabetes." Query with outline and 2 sample chapters. Reviews artwork/photos as part of ms package. Send photocopies.
Recent Nonfiction Title: *Raising a Child with Diabetes*, by Linda Siminerio and Jean Betschart (information).
Fiction: Juvenile. "We publish very little fiction—all for juveniles with diabetes." Query with synopsis and 2 sample chapters.
Recent Fiction Title: *The Dinosaur Tamer*, by Marcia Levine Mazur (juvenile fiction).
Tips: "Our audience consists primarily of consumers with diabetes who want to better manage their illness. Obtain a few of our books to better understand our target audience and appropriate reading level."

AMERICAN EAGLE PUBLICATIONS INC., P.O. Box 1507, Show Low AZ 85901. Phone/fax: (520)367-1621. Publisher: Mark Ludwig. Estab. 1988. Publishes hardcover and trade paperback originals and reprints. Publishes 8 titles/year. 50% of books from first-time authors; 100% from unagented writers. Pays 5-12% royalty on retail price. Offers $1,000 average advance. Publishes book 6 months after acceptance of ms. Accepts simultaneous submissions. Reports in 2 months. Catalog for #10 SASE.
● Publisher reports no interest in seeing military or other autobiographies.
Nonfiction: Historical biography, technical. Subjects include computers and electronics (security), military/war and science (computers and artificial intelligence). "We are highly specialized in nonfiction. Writers should call and discuss what they have first." Query. Reviews artwork/photos as part of freelance ms package. Send photocopies.
Recent Nonfiction Title: *The Quest for Water Planets*, by Ray Halyard (science).
Tips: Audience is "scholarly, university profs, (some used as textbooks), very technical programmers and researchers, military, very international. No autobiographies."

AMERICAN FEDERATION OF ASTROLOGERS, P.O. Box 22040, Tempe AZ 85285. Fax: (602)838-8293. Publications Manager: Kris Brandt Riske. Publishes trade paperback originals and reprints. Publishes 15-20 titles/year. Receives 10 queries and 20 mss/year. 30% of books from first-time authors; 100% from unagented writers. Pays 10% royalty. Publishes book 10 months after acceptance of ms. Accepts simultaneous submissions. Reports in 6 months on mss. Book catalog for $2. Manuscript guidelines free on request.
Nonfiction: Astrology. Submit complete ms. *Writer's Market* recommends sending a query with SASE first.
Recent Nonfiction Title: *The Astrologer's Forecasting Workbook*, by Lloyd Cope.

AMERICAN HOSPITAL PUBLISHING, INC., American Hospital Association, 737 N. Michigan Ave., Chicago IL 60611-2615. (312)440-6800. Fax: (312)951-8491. Vice President, Books: Marcia Bottoms. Estab. 1979. Publishes trade paperback originals. Publishes 20-30 titles/year. Receives 75-100 submissions/year. 20% of books from first-time authors; 100% from unagented writers. Pays 10-12% royalty on retail price. Offers $1,000 average advance. Publishes book 1 year after acceptance. Reports in 3 months. Book catalog and ms guidelines for 9×12 SAE with 7 first-class stamps.
Nonfiction: Reference, technical, textbook. Subjects include business and economics (specific to health care institutions); health/medicine (never consumer oriented). Need field-based, reality-tested responses to changes in the health care field directed to hospital CEO's, planners, boards of directors, or other senior management. No personal histories, untested health care programs or clinical texts. Query.
Tips: "The successful proposal demonstrates a clear understanding of the needs of the market and the writer's ability to succinctly present practical knowledge of demonstrable benefit that comes from genuine experience that readers will recognize, trust and accept. The audience is senior and middle management of health care institutions."

‡**AMERICAN NURSES PUBLISHING**, American Nurses Foundation, #100 W. 600 Maryland Ave., Washington DC 20024. (202)651-7213. Publishing Manager: Mandy Mikulencak. Publishes trade paperback originals and reprints. Publishes 20 titles/year. Receives 20 queries and 10 mss/year. 75% of books from first-time authors; 100% from unagented writers. Pays 10% royalty on retail price. Publishes book 16 months after acceptance of ms. Reports in 6 months on proposals and mss. Free catalog and ms guidelines.
Nonfiction: How-to, illustrated book, reference, technical and textbook. Subjects include business and economics, education, health/medicine, money/finance, psychology, science, women's issues/studies and

nursing. Submit outline and 1 sample chapter. Reviews artwork/photos as part of ms package. Send photocopies.

Recent Nonfiction Title: *Innovation at the Work Site*, by Barbara Burges (reference/text).

Tips: Audience is nurses.

‡**AMERICAN PRESS**, 520 Commonwealth Ave., Boston MA 02215-2605. Editor: Marcy Taylor. Publishes college textbooks. Publishes 25 titles/year. Receives 350 queries and 100 mss/year. 50% of books from first-time authors; 90% from unagented writers. Pays 5-15% royalty on wholesale price. Publishes book 9 months after acceptance of ms. Reports in 3 months. Book catalog free on request.

Nonfiction: Technical, textbook. Subjects include agriculture/horticulture, anthropology/archaeology, art/architecture, business and economics, education, government/politics, health/medicine, history, music/dance, psychology, science, sociology, sports. "We prefer that our authors actually teach courses for which the manuscripts are designed." Query or submit outline with tentative table of contents. No complete mss.

AMERICAN SOCIETY OF CIVIL ENGINEERS, ASCE Press, 345 E. 47th St., New York NY 10017-2398. (212)705-7689. Fax: (212)705-7712. E-mail: mluke@ny.asce.org. Website: http://www.asce.org. Book Acquisitions Editor: Mary Grace Luke. Estab. 1988. Publishes 10 titles/year. 50% of books from first-time authors; 100% from unagented writers. Pays 10% royalty. No advance. Accepts simultaneous submissions. Request proposal guidelines.

Nonfiction: Civil engineering. "We are looking for topics that are useful and instructive to the engineering practitioner." Query with outline, sample chapters and cv.

Recent Nonfiction Title: *Cable Corrosion in Bridges*, by Stahl and Gagnon (engineering practice).

Tips: "ASCE is a not-for-profit organization, so we've always been cost conscious. The recession made us *more* conscious and much more cautious about our spending habits. We have increased the number of new books that we are producing by about 50-100%."

AMHERST MEDIA, INC., 418 Homecrest Dr., Amherst NY 14226-1219. (716)874-4450. Fax: (716)874-4508. Publisher: Craig Alesse. Estab. 1974. Publishes trade paperback originals and reprints. Publishes 10 titles/year. Receives 50 submissions/year. 80% of books from first-time authors; 100% from unagented writers. Pays 8% royalty on retail price. Publishes book 1 year after acceptance. Accepts simultaneous submissions. Reports in 2 months. Book catalog and ms guidelines free on request.

Nonfiction: How-to. Subjects include photography, astronomy, video. Looking for well-written and illustrated photo, video and astronomy books. Query with outline, 2 sample chapters and SASE. Reviews artwork/photos as part of ms package.

Recent Nonfiction Title: *Wide-Angle Photography*, by Joseph Paduano.

Tips: "Our audience is made up of beginning to advanced photographers and videographers. If I were a writer trying to market a book today, I would fill the need of a specific audience and self-edit in a tight manner."

THE AMWELL PRESS, P.O. Box 5385, Clinton NJ 08809-0385. (908)537-6888. President: James Rikhoff. Vice President: Monica Sullivan. Corporate Secretary: Genevieve Symonds. Estab. 1976. Publishes hardcover originals. Publishes 6 titles/year. Publishes book 18 months after acceptance. Reports in 2 months on queries.

● No fiction.

Nonfiction: Hunting and fishing stories/literature (not how-to). Mostly limited editions. Query.

Recent Nonfiction Title: *Taking Your Chances in the High Country*, anthology compiled by Jim Rikhoff.

ANCHORAGE PRESS, INC., P.O. Box 8067, New Orleans LA 70182-8067. (504)283-8868. Fax: (504)866-0502. Editor: Orlin Corey. Publishes hardcover originals. Estab. 1935. Publishes 10 titles/year. Receives 450-900 submissions/year. 50% of books from first-time authors; 80% from unagented writers. Pays 10-15% royalty on retail price. Playwrights also receive 50-75% royalties. Publishes book 1 year after acceptance. Reports in 1 month on queries, 4 months on mss. Book catalog and ms guidelines free.

Nonfiction: Textbook, plays. Subjects include education, language/literature, plays. "We are looking for play anthologies; and texts for teachers of drama/theater (middle school and high school.)" Query. Reviews artwork/photos as part of ms package.

Recent Title: *Ugly Duck*, by Jas Still (play).

Fiction: Plays of juvenile/young people's interest. Query.

‡**AND BOOKS**, 702 S. Michigan, South Bend IN 46601. (219)232-3134. E-mail: andbooks@ripco.com. Editor: Janos Szebedinsky. Estab. 1980. Publishes trade paperback originals. Publishes 10 titles/year. Receives 1,000 submissions/year. 50% of books from first-time authors; 90% from unagented writers. Pays 6-10% royalty on retail price. Accepts simultaneous submissions. Publishes books 1 year after acceptance. Reports in up to 3 months. Book catalog for #10 SASE.

Nonfiction: Subjects include computers (consumer-level), current affairs, social justice, psychology, religion, music: blues, classical. Especially needs books on computers and electronic publishing. No biography, humor or diet books. *Writer's Market* recommends sending a query with SASE first.

Tips: "Attempt to get an intro or foreword by a respected authority on your subject. Include comments by others who have reviewed your material. Research the potential market and include the results with your proposal. In other words, make every effort to communicate your knowledge of the publishing process. A little preliminary legwork and market investigation can go a long way to influence a potential publisher. No longer interested in books on sports or law."

ANDREWS AND McMEEL, 4520 Main St., Kansas City MO 64111-7701. Vice President/Editorial Director: Christine Schillig. (816)932-6700. Publishes hardcover and paperback originals. Publishes 300 titles/ year. Pays royalty on retail price. Offers advance. Query only. Accepts only agented material. Areas of specialization include general trade, humor, how-to, journalism, juvenile, consumer reference books. Also produces gift books, posters and kits. *Writer's Market* recommends allowing 2 months for reply.
Recent Nonfiction Title: *Dating Is About Finding Someone So You Never Have to Date Again*, by Nancy Davidoff Kelton.

‡APOLLO BOOKS, 124 Beacon St., Boston MA 02116. (617)536-3720. Fax: (617)536-3721. Owner: Gregory Morson. Estab. 1994. Publishes 4-6 titles/year. Receives 12 submissions/year. Pays royalty or makes outright purchase. Publishes book 6 months after acceptance. Simultaneous submissions OK. Reports in 2 months. Book catalog for 9×12 SAE with 4 first-class stamps.
Nonfiction: Biography, coffee table book and reference. Subjects include art/architecture and gardening. Query. Reviews artwork as part of ms package.
Recent Nonfiction Title: *Chinese and Other Far Eastern Art.*

APPALACHIAN MOUNTAIN CLUB BOOKS, 5 Joy St., Boston MA 02108. Editor: Gordon Hardy. Publishes trade paperback originals. Publishes 6-10 titles/year. Receives 200 submissions/year. Receives 200 queries and 20 mss/year. 30% of books from first-time authors; 90% from unagented writers. Pays 6-10% royalty on retail price. Offers modest advance. Publishes book 10 months after acceptance of ms. Accepts simultaneous submissions. Reports in 2-3 months on proposals. Book catalog for $8\frac{1}{2} \times 11$ SAE with 4 first-class stamps. Manuscript guidelines for #10 SASE.
Nonfiction: How-to, guidebooks. Subjects include history (mountains, Northeast), nature/environment, recreation, regional (Northeast outdoor recreation). "We publish hiking guides, water-recreation guides (non-motorized), nature, conservation and mountain-subject guides for America's Northeast. Writers should avoid submitting: proposals on Appalachia (rural southern mountains); not enough market research; too much personal experience—autobiography." Query. Reviews artwork/photos as part of ms package. Send photocopies and transparencies "at your own risk."
Recent Nonfiction Title: *Nature Hikes in the White Mountains*, by Robert Buchsbaum (family hiking guidebook).
Tips: "Our audience is outdoor recreationalists, conservation—minded hikers and canoeists, family outdoor lovers, armchair enthusiasts. We connect recreation to conservation—our guidebooks have a strong conservation message."

ARCADE PUBLISHING, 141 Fifth Ave., New York NY 10010. (212)475-2633. Publisher: Richard Seaver. Associate Publisher: Jeanette Seaver; General Manager: Cal Barksdale. Publishes hardcover originals, trade paperback originals and reprints. Publishes 40 titles/year. 5% of books from first-time authors. Pays royalty on retail price. Offers $1,000-100,000 advance. Publishes book 18 months after acceptance of ms. *Agented submissions only.* Reports in 3 months on queries.
Nonfiction: Biography, cookbook, general nonfiction. Subjects include cooking/foods/nutrition, government/politics, history, nature/environment and travel. Query. Reviews artwork/photos as part of ms package. Send photocopies.
Recent Nonfiction Title: *Dragon Ascending: Vietnam and the Vietnamese*, by Henry Kamm.
Fiction: Ethnic, historical, humor, literary, mainstream/contemporary, mystery, short story collections, suspense. Query. *Agented submissions only.*
Recent Fiction Title: *Trying to Save Piggy Sneed*, by John Irving.
Poetry: "We do not publish poetry as a rule; since our inception we have published only a few volumes of poetry." Query.

ARCHWAY PAPERBACKS/MINSTREL BOOKS, Imprint of Pocket Books, 1230 Avenue of the Americas, New York NY 10020. (212)698-7669. Vice President/Editorial Director: Patricia MacDonald. Send all submissions Attn: Manuscript Proposals. Publishes mass market paperback originals and reprints. Publishes 80 titles/year. Receives over 1,000 submissions/year. Pays royalty. Publishes book 2 years after acceptance. Reports in 3 months. SASE for all material necessary or query not answered.
Nonfiction: Middle grade, young adult. Subjects include current popular subjects or people, sports. Query with SASE. Submit outline/synopsis and 2 sample chapters. Reviews artwork/photos as part of ms package.
Fiction: Middle grade (6 to 11), young adult. Suspense thrillers and soap-opera romances for YA; mysteries, school stories, funny/scary stories, animal fantasy stories for middle grade readers. No picture books. Query with SASE. Submit outline/synopsis and sample chapters.

Recent Fiction Title: *I Left My Sneakers in Dimension X.*

ARDEN PRESS INC., P.O. Box 418, Denver CO 80201-0418. (303)697-6766. Publisher: Susan Conley. Estab. 1980. Publishes hardcover and trade paperback originals and reprints. 95% of books are originals; 5% are reprints. Publishes 4-6 titles/year. Receives 600 submissions/year. 20% of books from first-time authors; 80% from unagented writers. Pays 8-15% royalty on wholesale price. Offers $2,000 average advance. Publishes book 6 months after acceptance. Accepts simultaneous submissions. Reports in 2 months on queries. Manuscript guidelines free on request.

Nonfiction: Practical guides in many subjects, biography, reference, textbooks. Subjects include women's issues/studies (history, biography, practical guides). No personal memoirs or autobiographies. Query with outline/synopsis and sample chapters.

Recent Nonfiction Title: *Defying Male Civilization: Women in the Spanish Civil War*, by Mary Nash (women's history).

Tips: "Writers have the best chance selling us nonfiction on women's subjects. We sell to general and women's bookstores and public and academic libraries. Many of our titles are adopted as texts for college courses. If I were a writer trying to market a book today, I would learn as much as I could about publishers' profiles *then* contact those who publish similar works."

ARDSLEY HOUSE PUBLISHERS, INC., 320 Central Park West, New York NY 10025. (212)496-7040. Contact: Christopher Miragliotta. Publishes hardcover and trade paperback originals and reprints. Publishes 5-8 titles/year. 25% of books from first-time authors; 100% from unagented writers (all are college professors). Pays generally by royalty. No advance. Publishes book 15 months after acceptance of ms. Reports in 1 month on queries, 2 months on proposals, 3 months on mss. Book catalog free on request.

Nonfiction: Textbook (college). Subjects include Americana, history, music/dance, philosophy, film. "We publish only college-level textbooks—particularly in the areas of music, philosophy, history, and film. We don't accept any other type of manuscript." Query with proposal package, including outline, 2-3 sample chapters, prospectus, author's résumé and SASE. Reviews artwork/photos as part of ms package. Send photocopies.

Recent Nonfiction Title: *A Mathematics Sampler: Topics for the Liberal Arts*, 4th ed., by Birlinghoff, Grant & Skrien.

JASON ARONSON, INC., 230 Livingston St., Northvale NJ 07647-1726. (201)767-4093. Fax: (201)767-4330. Website: http://www.aronson.com. Editor-in-chief: Arthur Kurzweil. Estab. 1967. Publishes hardcover and trade paperback originals and reprints. Publishes 250 titles/year. 50% of books from first-time authors; 95% from unagented writers. Pays 10-15% royalty on retail price. Offers $250-$2500 advance. Publishes book an average of 1 year after acceptance. Reports in 1 month. *Writer's Market* recommends allowing 2 months for reply. Catalog and ms guidelines free on request.

Nonfiction: Subjects include history, philosophy, psychology, religion translation. "We publish in two fields: psychotherapy and Judaica. We are looking for high quality books in both fields." Query or submit outline and sample chapters. Reviews artwork/photos as part of ms packages. Send photocopies.

Recent Nonfiction Title: *Borderline Conditions*, by Otto Kernberg (psychotherapy).

‡ART DIRECTION BOOK COMPANY, INC., 456 Glenbrook Rd., Glenbrook CT 06096-1800. (203)353-1441. Fax: (203) 353-1371. Editorial Director: Don Barron. Imprint is Infosource Publications. Publishes hardcover and paperback originals. Publishes 6 titles/year. Pays 10% royalty on retail price. Offers average $1,000 advance. Publishes book 1 year after acceptance. Reports in 3 months. Book catalog for 6×9 SASE.

Nonfiction: Commercial art, ad art how-to and textbooks. "We are interested in books for the professional advertising art field—books for art directors, designers, etc.; also entry level books for commercial and advertising art students in such fields as typography, photography, paste-up, illustration, clip-art, design, layout and graphic arts." Query with outline and 1 sample chapter. Reviews artwork/photos as part of ms package.

‡ASA, AVIATION SUPPLIES & ACADEMICS, 7005 132nd Place SE, Newcastle WA 98059. (206)235-1500. Director of Operations: Mike Lorden. Editor: Jennifer Trerise. Publishes 25-40 titles/year. 100% of books from unagented writers. Publishes book 9 months after acceptance. Reports in 3 months on proposals. Book catalog free on request.

MARKET CONDITIONS are constantly changing! If this is 1998 or later, buy the newest edition of *Writer's Market* at your favorite bookstore or order directly from Writer's Digest Books.

Nonfiction: How-to, humor, technical, education. All subjects must be related to aviation. "We are primarily an aviation publisher. Educational books in this area are great; other aviation books will be considered." Query with outline. Send photocopies.
Recent Nonfiction Title: *Say Again, Please*, by Bob Gardner (guide to aviation radio communications).
Fiction: Aviation. *Writer's Market* recommends sending a query with SASE first.
Tips: "We have a new series that we are looking for titles to include: ASA's *Focus Series*. These will be books on *specific* aviation topics, which we decide need their own, more detailed and *focused* approach."

ASIAN HUMANITIES PRESS, Imprint of Jain Publishing Co., P.O. Box 3523, Fremont CA 94539. (510)659-8272. Fax: (510)659-0501. Website: http://www.jainpub.com. Editor: M.K. Jain. Estab. 1976. Publishes hardcover and trade paperback originals and reprints. Publishes 10 titles/year. Receives 200 submissions/year. 90% of books from unagented authors. Pays up to 10% royalty on net sales. Publishes book 1 year after acceptance. Reports in 3 months on mss. Book catalog for 6×9 SAE with 2 first-class stamps. Manuscript guidelines for #10 SASE.
  • Publisher reports an increased emphasis on undergraduate level textbooks.
Nonfiction: Reference, textbooks, general trade books. Subjects include Asian classics, language/literature (Asian), philosophy/religion (Asian and East-West), psychology/spirituality (Asian and East-West), art/culture (Asian and East-West). Submit proposal package, including vita, list of prior publications and SASE. Reviews artwork/photos as part of ms package. Send photocopies.
Recent Nonfiction Title: *Buddhism: A History*, by Noble Ross Reat (textbook).

ASTRO COMMUNICATIONS SERVICES, INC., P.O. Box 34487, San Diego CA 92163-4487. (619)492-9919. Fax: (619)492-9917. E-mail: maritha@astrocom.com. Website: http://www.astrocom.com. Editorial Director: Maritha Pottenger. Estab. 1973. Publishes trade paperback originals and reprints. Publishes 4-6 titles/year. Receives 400 submissions/year. 50% of books from first-time authors; 95% from unagented writers. Average print order for a first book is 3,000. Pays 10-12% royalty "on monies received through wholesale and retail sales." No advance. Publishes book 1 year after acceptance. Reports in 3 months. Book catalog and ms guidelines for 9×12 SAE with 2 first-class stamps.
Nonfiction: Astrology. "Our market is astrology. We are seeking pragmatic, useful, immediate applicable contributions to field; prefer psychological approach. Specific ideas and topics should enhance people's lives. Research also valued. No determinism ('Saturn made me do it.'). No autobiographies. No airy-fairy 'space cadet' philosophizing. Keep it grounded, useful, opening options (not closing doors) for readers." Query with outline and 3 sample chapters.
Recent Nonfiction Title: *Astrology for the Light Side of the Brain*, by Kim Roger-Gallagher.
Tips: "The most common mistake writers make when trying to get their work published is to send works to inappropriate publishers. We get too many submissions outside our field or contrary to our world view."

ATHENEUM BOOKS FOR YOUNG READERS, Imprint of Simon & Schuster, 1230 Avenue of the Americas, New York NY 10020. (212)702-7894. Associate Publisher, Vice President/Editorial Director: Jonathan J. Lanman. Editors: Marcia Marshall, Sarah Caguiat, Ana Cerro and Jean Karl. Anne Schwartz, director of Anne Schwartz books. Estab. 1960. Publishes hardcover originals. Publishes 70 titles/year. Receives 15,000 submissions/year. 8-12% of books from first-time authors; 50% from unagented writers. Pays 10% royalty on retail price. Offers $2,000-3,000 average advance. Publishes book 18 months after acceptance. Reports within 3 months. Manuscript guidelines for #10 SASE.
Nonfiction: Biography, history, science, how-to, humor, self-help, all for juveniles. Subjects include: Americana, animals, art, business and economics, health, music, nature, photography, politics, psychology, recreation, religion, sociology, sports and travel. "Do remember, most publishers plan their lists as much as two years in advance. So if a topic is 'hot' right now, it may be 'old hat' by the time we could bring it out. It's better to steer clear of fads. Some writers assume juvenile books are for 'practice' until you get good enough to write adult books. Not so. Books for young readers demand just as much 'professionalism' in writing as adult books. So save those 'practice' manuscripts for class, or polish them before sending them." Query only.
Fiction: Adventure, ethnic, experimental, fantasy, gothic, historical, horror, humor, mainstream, mystery, science fiction, suspense, western, all in juvenile versions. "We have few specific needs except for books that are fresh, interesting and well written. Again, fad topics are dangerous, as are works you haven't polished to the best of your ability. (The competition is fierce.) We've been inundated with dragon stories (misunderstood dragon befriends understanding child), unicorn stories (misunderstood child befriends understanding unicorn), and variations of 'Ignatz the Egg' (Everyone laughs at Ignatz the egg [giraffe/airplane/accountant] because he's square [short/purple/stupid] until he saves them from the eggbeater [lion/storm/I.R.S. man] and becomes a hero). Other things we don't need at this time are safety pamphlets, ABC books, coloring books, board books, and rhymed narratives. In writing picture book texts, avoid the coy and 'cutesy.' " Query only for all submissions. Reviews artwork as part of ms package. Send photocopies.
Recent Fiction Title: *Alice in Lace*, by Phyllis Reynolds Naylor.
Poetry: "At this time there is a growing market for children's poetry. However, we don't anticipate needing any for the next year or two, especially rhymed narratives."

Tips: "Our books are aimed at children from pre-school age, up through high school. We no longer publish Argo Books."

‡**AUGSBURG BOOKS,** Imprint of Augsburg Fortress, Publishers, P.O. Box 1209, 426 S. Fifth St., Minneapolis MN 55440. Contact: Children's Editor. Publishes trade and mass market paperback originals and reprints. Publishes 37 titles/year. 2-3% of books from first-time authors. Pays royalty. Publishes book 18 months after acceptance of ms. Accepts queries only; *no unsolicited mss.* Reports in 3 months. Book catalog for 8½×11 SAE with 3 first-class stamps. Manuscript guidelines for #10 SASE.
Nonfiction: Children's/juvenile, self-help. Subjects include religion, adult spirituality, life issues, devotions, "over 50" titles, men's and women's books, family, Christmas, Lent/Easter. "We publish for the mainline Christian market." Submit outline and 1-2 sample chapters if requested. Overstocked in children's book mss.

‡**AUTONOMEDIA,** P.O. Box 568, Williamsburgh Station, Brooklyn NY 11211. (718)963-2603. Editor: Jim Fleming. Imprints are Semiotext(e) (contact Jim Fleming); New Autonomy (contact Peter Lamborn Wilson). Publishes trade paperback originals and reprints. Publishes 25 titles/year. Receives 350 queries/year. 30% of books from first-time authors; 90% from unagented writers. Pays variable royalty. Offers $100 advance. Publishes book 6 months after acceptance of ms. Accepts simultaneous submissions. Reports in 2 months. Book catalog for $1.
Nonfiction: Subjects include anthropology/archaeology, art/architecture, business and economics, gay/lesbian, government/politics, history, nature/environment, philosophy, religion, translation, women's issues/studies. Submit outline with SASE. Reviews artwork/photos as part of ms package. Send photocopies.
Recent Nonfiction Title: *Foucault Live,* by Michel Foucault (interviews).
Fiction: Erotica, experimental, feminist, gay/lesbian, literary, mainstream/contemporary, occult, science fiction, short story collections. Submit synopsis with SASE.
Recent Fiction Title: *Cutmouth Lady,* by Romy Ashby (contemporary).
Poetry: Submit sample poems.
Recent Poetry Title: *Not Me,* by Eileen Myles (lesbian).

AVALON BOOKS, Imprint of Thomas Bouregy & Co., Inc., 401 Lafayette St., New York NY 10003-7014. Vice President/Publisher: Marcia Markland. Estab. 1950. Publishes 60 titles/year. Reports in 6 months.
Fiction: "We publish wholesome romances, mysteries, westerns. Our books are read by adults as well as teenagers, and their characters are all adults. All the romances and mysteries are contemporary; all the westerns are historical." Length: 40,000-50,000 words. Submit first chapter, a brief, but complete summary of the book and SASE with sufficient postage.
Recent Fiction Title: *The Curious Cape Cod Skull,* by Marie Lee (mystery).
Tips: "We are looking for love stories, heroines who have interesting professions, and we are actively seeking ethnic fiction. We do accept unagented manuscripts, and we do publish first novels. Right now we are concentrating on finding talented new mystery and romantic suspense writers."

AVANYU PUBLISHING INC., P.O. Box 27134, Albuquerque NM 87125. (505)266-6128. Fax: (505)821-8864. President: J. Brent Ricks. Estab. 1984. Publishes hardcover and trade paperback originals and reprints. Publishes 4 titles/year. Receives 40 submissions/year. 30% of books from first-time authors; 90% from unagented writers. Pays 8% maximum royalty on wholesale price. No advance. Publishes book 1 year after acceptance. Reports in 6 weeks. *Writer's Market* recommends allowing 2 months for reply. Book catalog for #10 SASE.
Nonfiction: Biography, illustrated book, reference, Southwest Americana. Subjects include Americana, anthropology/archaeology, art/architecture, ethnic, history, photography, regional, sociology. Query. Reviews artwork/photos as part of ms package.
Fiction: Adventure, historical, western. Query.
Tips: "Writers have the best chance selling us history-oriented books with lots of pictures, or contemporary Indian/Western art. Our audience consists of libraries, art collectors and history students."

AVON BOOKS, Division of the Hearst Corp., 1350 Avenue of the Americas, New York NY 10019. Send queries to Alice Webster-Williams. Estab. 1941. Publishes trade and mass market paperback originals and reprints. Publishes 400 titles/year. Royalty and advance negotiable. Publishes ms 2 years after acceptance. Accepts simultaneous submissions. Reports in 3 months. Guidelines for SASE.
Nonfiction: How-to, popular psychology, self-help, health, history, war, sports, business/economics, biography, politics. No textbooks. Query only with SASE.
Recent Nonfiction Title: *Don't Know Much About Geography* (trade).
Fiction: Romance (contemporary, historical), science fiction, fantasy, men's adventure, suspense/thriller, mystery, western. Query only with SASE.
Recent Fiction Title: *Memoir from Antproof Case,* by Mark Haelprin.

AVON FLARE BOOKS, Young Adult Imprint of Avon Books, Division of the Hearst Corp., 1350 Avenue of the Americas, New York NY 10019. (212)261-6817. Fax: (212)261-6895. Editorial Director: Gwen Montgomery. Publishes mass market paperback originals and reprints. Imprint publishes 20-24 new titles/year. 25% of books from first-time authors; 15% from unagented writers. Pays 6-8% royalty. Offers $2,500 minimum advance. Publishes book 2 years after acceptance. Accepts simultaneous submissions. Reports in 4 months. Book catalog and ms guidelines for 8×10 SAE with 5 first-class stamps.

Nonfiction: General. Submit outline/synopsis and sample chapters. "*Very* selective with young adult nonfiction."

Recent Nonfiction Title: *Ask Me Anything About Monsters*, by Louis Phillips.

Fiction: Adventure, ethnic, humor, mainstream, mystery, romance, suspense, contemporary. "Very selective with mystery." Manuscripts appropriate to ages 12-18. Query with sample chapters and synopsis.

Recent Fiction Title: *Christie & Company*, by Kathryn Hall Page.

Tips: "The YA market is not as strong as it was five years ago. We are very selective with young adult fiction. *Avon does not publish picture books,* nor do we use freelance readers."

AZTEX CORP., P.O. 50046, Tucson AZ 85703-1046. (520)882-4656. Estab. 1976. Publishes hardcover and paperback originals. Publishes 10 titles/year. Receives 250 submissions/year. 100% of books from unagented writers. Average print order for a first book is 3,500. Pays 10% royalty. Publishes book 18 months after acceptance. Reports in 3 months. "Queries without return envelopes or postage are not responded to."

 • This company received the Thomas McKean Award from the Antique Automobile Club of America for outstanding research for *Tire Wars: Racing With Goodyear.*

Nonfiction: "We specialize in transportation subjects (how-to and history)." Accepts nonfiction translations. Submit outline and 2 sample chapters. Reviews artwork/photos as part of ms package.

Tips: "We look for accuracy, thoroughness and interesting presentation."

BAEN PUBLISHING ENTERPRISES, P.O. Box 1403, Riverdale NY 10471-0671. (718)548-3100. Website: http://baen.com. Executive Editor: Toni Weisskopf. Estab. 1983. Publishes hardcover, trade paperback and mass market paperback originals and reprints. Publishes 120 titles/year. Receives 8,000 submissions/year. 5% of books from first-time authors; 50% from unagented writers. Pays royalty on retail price. Reports in 1 month on queries and proposals, 1-6 months on complete mss. Queries not necessary. *Writer's Market* recommends sending a query with SASE first. Book catalog free on request. Manuscript guidelines for #10 SASE.

Fiction: Fantasy, science fiction. Submit outline/synopsis and sample chapters or complete ms.

Recent Fiction Title: *Cetaganda*, by Lois McMaster Bujold.

Tips: "See our books before submitting. Send for our writers' guidelines."

BAKER BOOKS, Division of Baker Book House Company, P.O. Box 6287, Grand Rapids MI 49516-6287. Director of Publications: Allan Fisher. Assistant to the Director of Publications: Jane Schrier. Estab. 1939. Publishes hardcover and trade paperback originals. Publishes 120 titles/year. 10% of books from first-time authors; 85% from unagented writers. Queries and proposals only. No unsolicited mss. Pays 14% royalty on net receipts. Publishes book within 1 year after acceptance. Accepts simultaneous submissions (if so identified). Reports in 3 months. Book catalog for 9×12 SAE with 6 first-class stamps.

Nonfiction: Contemporary issues, women's concerns, parenting, singleness, seniors' concerns, self-help, children's books, Bible study, Christian doctrine, reference books, books for pastors and church leaders, textbooks for Christian colleges and seminaries. Query with proposal.

Fiction: Literary novels focusing on women's concerns, mysteries. Query.

Tips: "Most of our authors and readers are evangelical Christians, and our books are purchased from Christian bookstores, mail-order retailers, and school bookstores."

BALE BOOKS, Division of Bale Publications, P.O. Box 2727, New Orleans LA 70176. Editor-in-Chief: Don Bale, Jr. Estab. 1963. Publishes hardcover and paperback originals and reprints. Publishes 10 titles/year. Receives 25 submissions/year. 50% of books from first-time authors; 90% from unagented writers. Average print order for a first book is 1,000. Offers standard 10-12½-15% royalty contract on wholesale or retail price; sometimes makes outright purchases of $500. No advance. Publishes book 3 years after acceptance. Reports in 3 months. Book catalog for #10 SAE with 2 first-class stamps.

Nonfiction: Numismatics. "Our specialties are coin and stock market investment books; especially coin investment books and coin price guides. Most of our books are sold through publicity and ads in the coin newspapers. We are open to any new ideas in the area of numismatics. The writer should write for a teenage through adult level. Lead the reader by the hand like a teacher, building chapter by chapter. Our books sometimes have a light, humorous treatment, but not necessarily. We look for good English, construction and content, and sales potential." Submit outline and 3 sample chapters.

Recent Nonfiction Title: *Gold Mine in Your Pocket.*

BALLANTINE BOOKS, Subsidiary of Random House, Inc., 201 E. 50th St., New York NY 10022. (212)572-4910. Contact: Louis Mendez, executive administrative assistant.

 • Also see the listing for Random House, Inc.

Nonfiction: How-to, humor, illustrated book (cartoons), reference, self-help. Subjects include animals, child guidance/parenting, cooking/foods/nutrition, health/medicine. Submit proposal and 100 ms pages with SASE. Reviews artwork/photos as part of ms package. Send photocopies.

Recent Nonfiction Title: *How to Get Your Cat to Do What you Want Him to Do,* by Warren Eckstein.

Fiction: Publishes originals (general fiction, mass market, trade paperback and hardcover). Needs: Historical fiction, women's mainstream, multicultural and general fiction. Submit query letter or brief synopsis, first 100 pages of ms and SASE of proper size to Louis Mendez. Responds promptly to queries; 5 months on mss.

Recent Fiction Title: *Weighed in the Balance,* by Anne Perry.

B&B PUBLISHING, INC., P.O. Box 96, Walworth WI 53184. Fax: (414)275-9530. Contact: Katy O'Shea. Publishes hardcover and trade paperback originals. Publishes 5-10 titles/year. Receives 1,000 queries and 100 mss/year. 10% of books from first-time authors; 90% from unagented writers. Usually contracts authors as "Work For Hires." Publishes book 1 year after acceptance. Accepts simultaneous submissions. "Do not send entire manuscript unless requested to do so. Any submission or query without SASE will not be acknowledged." Reports in 2-3 months. Book catalog and ms guidelines free on request.

● Publisher would like to hear from journalists interested in writing/researching state trivia almanacs.

Nonfiction: Children's/juvenile, reference, Americana, trivia. "We are seeking innovative supplementary educational materials for grades K-12." Query with SASE. Reviews artwork/photos as part of ms package. Send photocopies.

Recent Nonfiction Title: *Serengeti Plain,* by Terri Wills.

Tips: Audience is interested in supplementary educational material.

BANKS-BALDWIN LAW PUBLISHING CO., 6111 Oak Tree Blvd., Cleveland OH 44131. (216)520-5600. Fax: (216)520-5656. Affiliate of West Publishing of Eagan, Minnesota. Editor-in-Chief: P.J. Lucier. Managing Editor: Fred K. Gordon. Estab. 1804. Publishes law books and services in a variety of formats. Publishes 10 new titles/year. Receives 10-15 submissions/year. 5% of books from first-time authors; 90% from unagented writers. "Most titles include material submitted by outside authors." Pays 8-16% royalty on net revenue, or fee. Offers advance not to exceed 25% of anticipated royalty or fee. Publishes book 18 months after acceptance, 3 months after receipt of ms. Reports in 3 weeks on queries. *Writer's Market* recommends allowing 2 months for reply. Book catalog and ms guidelines for SASE.

Nonfiction: Reference, law/legal. Query.

Recent Nonfiction Title: *Ohio Planning & Zoning Law,* by Meck & Pearlman (treatise).

Tips: "We publish books for attorneys, government officials and professionals in allied fields. Trends in our field include more interest in handbooks, less in costly multi-volume sets; electronic publishing. A writer has the best chance of selling us a book on a hot new topic of law. Check citations and quotations carefully."

BANTAM BOOKS, Subsidiary of Bantam Doubleday Dell, Dept. WM, 1540 Broadway, New York NY 10036. (212)354-6500. Imprints are Bantam Classics, Crime Line, Golden Apple, Love Swept, New Age Books, New Fiction, New Sciences, Peacock Press, Perigord Press, Spectra, Sweet Dreams. Publishes hardcover, trade paperback and mass market paperback originals, trade paperback, mass market paperback reprints and audio. Publishes 350 titles/year. Publishes book an average of 8 months after ms is accepted. Accepts simultaneous submissions from agents.

Nonfiction: Biography, how-to, cookbook, humor, illustrated book, self-help. Subjects include Americana, business/economics, child care/parenting, diet/fitness, education, cooking/foods/nutrition, gay/lesbian, government/politics, health/medicine, history, language/literature, military/war, mysticism/astrology, nature, philosophy/mythology, psychology, religion/inspiration, science, sociology, spirituality, sports, true crime, women's studies.

Fiction: Adventure, fantasy, feminist, gay/lesbian, historical, horror, juvenile, literary, mainstream/contemporary, mystery, romance, science fiction, suspense, western. Query or submit outline/synopsis. All unsolicited mss returned unopened.

BANTAM DOUBLEDAY DELL, 1540 Broadway, New York NY 10036.

● See separate listings for Bantam Books, Doubleday, Dell Publishing and Broadway Books.

BARBOUR AND COMPANY, INC., P.O. Box 719, Uhrichsville OH 44683. Vice President Editorial: Stephen Reginald. Imprints are Barbour Books, managing editor Rebecca Germany; and Heartsong Presents, managing editor Susan Johnson (fiction). Publishes hardcover, trade paperback and mass market paperback originals and reprints. Publishes 75 titles/year. Receives 300 queries and 150 mss/year. 40% of books from first-time authors; 99% from unagented writers. Subsidy publishes .5% of books. Pays royalty on wholesale price or makes outright purchase of $1,000-2,500. Offers $250-500 advance. Publishes book 6 months after acceptance of ms. Accepts simultaneous submissions. Reports in 1 month on queries, 3 months on proposals and mss. Book catalog for $2. Manuscript guidelines for #10 SASE.

Nonfiction: Biography, humor, children's/juvenile. Religious subjects. "We're a Christian evangelical publisher." Query.

Recent Nonfiction Title: *Corrie ten Boom*, by Sam Wellman (biography).
Fiction: Historical, religious, romance "All these elements combined. We publish four inspirational romance titles every four weeks. Two historical and two contemporary romances." Submit synopsis and 3 sample chapters.
Recent Fiction Title: *Callie's Challenge*, by Veda Boyd Jones (contemporary romance, Heartsong).
Tips: "Having a great agent won't help here. A great idea or book will catch our attention."

‡**BARRICADE BOOKS INC.**, 150 Fifth Ave., Suite 700, New York NY 10011-4311. Publisher: Carole Stuart. Publishes hardcover and trade paperback originals and trade paperback reprints. Publishes 30 titles/year. Receives 200 queries and 100 mss/year. 80% of books from first-time authors; 50% from unagented writers. Pays 10-12% royalty on retail price for hardcover. Advance varies. Publishes book 18 months after acceptance of ms. Simultaneous submissions not encouraged. Reports in 1 month on queries. Book catalog for $1.
Nonfiction: Biography, how-to, reference, self-help. Subjects include business and economics, child guidance/parenting, ethnic, gay/lesbian, government/politics, health/medicine, history, nature/environment, psychology, sociology, women's issues/studies. Query with outline and 1-2 sample chapters. Reviews artwork/photos as part of ms package. Writers should send photocopies.
Recent Nonfiction Title: *The Secret Life of Bob Hope*, by Arthur Marx (biography).
Tips: "Do your homework. Visit bookshops to find publishers who are doing the kinds of books you want to write. Always submit to a *person*—not just 'editor.' Always enclose SASE."

BARRON'S EDUCATIONAL SERIES, INC., 250 Wireless Blvd., Hauppauge NY 11788. Fax: (516)434-3217. Director of Acquisitions: Grace Freedson. Publishes hardcover and paperback originals and software. Publishes 170 titles/year. 10% of books from first-time authors; 90% from unagented writers. Pays royalty based on both wholesale and retail price. Publishes book 1 year after acceptance. Accepts simultaneous submissions. Reports in 8 months. Book catalog free.
Nonfiction: Adult education, art, business, cookbooks, crafts, foreign language, review books, guidance, pet books, travel, literary guides, parenting, health, juvenile, young adult sports, test preparation materials and textbooks. Reviews artwork/photos as part of ms package. Query or submit outline/synopsis and 2-3 sample chapters. Accepts nonfiction translations.
Recent Nonfiction Title: *Barron's Business Thesaurus*, by Mary A. Derries.
Tips: "The writer has the best chance of selling us a book that will fit into one of our series."

BEACON HILL PRESS OF KANSAS CITY, Book Division of Nazarene Publishing House, 6401 The Paseo, Kansas City MO 64131. Fax: (816)363-5191. E-mail: bhp@nazarene.org. Editorial Coordinator: Shona Fisher. Estab. 1912. Publishes hardcover and paperback originals. Publishes 30 titles/year. Standard contract is 12% royalty on net sales for first 10,000 copies and 14% on subsequent copies. (Sometimes makes flat rate purchase.) Publishes book within 1 year after acceptance. Reports within 3 months. Accent on holy living; encouragement in daily Christian life. Query or proposal preferred. Average ms length: 30,000-60,000 words.
Nonfiction: Inspirational, Bible-based. Doctrinally must conform to the evangelical, Wesleyan tradition. No autobiography, poetry, short stories or children's picture books. Contemporary issues acceptable.
Recent Nonfiction Title: *Second Row, Piano Side*, by Chonda Pierce (biography).
Fiction: Wholesome, inspirational. Considers historical and Biblical fiction, Christian romance, but no teen or children's.
Recent Fiction Title: *The Lord is My Song*, by Lynn Auston (biblical fiction).

BEACON PRESS, 25 Beacon St., Boston MA 02108-2892. (617)742-2110. Fax: (617)723-3097. E-mail: hbordas@beacon.org. Website: http://www.beacon.org/beacon/homepage.html. Director: Helene Atwan. Estab. 1854. Publishes hardcover originals and paperback reprints. Publishes 60 titles/year. Receives 4,000 submissions/year. 10% of books from first-time authors; 70% from unagented writers. Average print order for a first book is 3,000. Pays royalty on net retail price. Advance varies. Publishes book 1 year after acceptance. Accepts simultaneous submissions. Reports in 3 months.
Nonfiction: General nonfiction including works of original scholarship, religion, women's studies, philosophy, current affairs, anthropology, environmental concerns, African-American studies, gay and lesbian studies. Query with outline/synopsis and sample chapters with SASE.
Recent Nonfiction Title: *Principal Products of Portugal*, by Donald Hall (literature).
Tips: "We probably accept only one or two manuscripts from an unpublished pool of 4,000 submissions per year. No fiction, children's book, or poetry submissions invited. Authors should have academic affiliation."

BEAR AND CO., INC., Aquisitions Dept., P.O. Box 600E, Lakeville CT 06039. (505)983-5968. Fax: (505)989-8386. Vice President, Editorial: Barbara Clow. Estab. 1978. Publishes trade paperback originals. Publishes 12 titles/year. Receives 6,000 submissions/year. 20% of books from first-time authors; 90% from unagented writers. Pays 10% royalty on net. Publishes book 18 months after acceptance. Reports in 1 month on queries. *Writer's Market* recommends allowing 2 months for reply. "No response without SASE." Book catalog for 9×12 SAE with 3 first-class stamps.

Nonfiction: Illustrated books, science, theology, mysticism, religion, ecology. "We publish books to 'heal and celebrate the earth.' Our interest is in New Age, western mystics, new science, ecology. Our readers are people who are open to new ways of looking at the world. They are spiritually oriented but not necessarily religious; interested in healing of the earth, peace issues, and receptive to New Age ideas." Query or submit outline and sample chapters. Reviews artwork/photos as part of ms package.

Tips: "We have continued to publish 12 titles/year, instead of going to 15-20 at this point. We have *increased* publicity and marketing work, and our sales have not dropped."

BEHRMAN HOUSE INC., 235 Watchung Ave., West Orange NJ 07052-9827. (201)669-0447. Fax: (201)669-9769. Projects Editor: Adam Siegel. Managing Editor: Adam Bengal. Estab. 1921. Publishes Jewish nonfiction— history, Bible, philosophy, holidays, ethics—for children and adults. Publishes 20 titles/year. Receives 200 submissions/year. 20% of books from first-time authors; 95% from unagented writers. Pays 2-10% on wholesale price or retail price or makes outright purchase of $500-10,000. Offers $1,000 average advance. Publishes book 18 months after acceptance. Accepts simultaneous submissions. Reports in 2 months. Book catalog free.

Nonfiction: Juvenile (1-18), reference, textbook. Subjects include religion. "We want Jewish textbooks for the el-hi market." Query with outline and sample chapters.

Recent Nonfiction Title: *It's a Mitzvah!*, by Bradley Artson (step-by-step guide to Jewish living).

FREDERIC C. BEIL, PUBLISHER, INC., 609 Whitaker St., Savannah GA 31401. Phone/fax: (912)233-2446. E-mail: beilbook@beil.com. Website: http://www.beil.com. Editor: Mary Ann Bowman. Publishes hardcover originals and reprints. Publishes 7 titles/year. Receives 700 queries and 9 mss/year. 15% of books from first-time authors; 80% from unagented writers. Pays 7½% royalty on retail price. Publishes book 20 months after acceptance. Accepts simultaneous submissions. Reports in 1 month on queries. Book catalog free on request.

Nonfiction: Biography, general trade, illustrated book, juvenile, reference. Subjects include art/architecture, history, language/literature, book arts. Query. Reviews artwork/photos as part of ms package. Send photocopies.

Recent Nonfiction Title: *Savannah: A History of Her People Since 1733*, by Preston and Barbara Russell.

Fiction: Historical and literary. Query.

Recent Fiction Title: *A Woman of Means*, by Peter Taylor.

ROBERT BENTLEY, INC., Automotive Publishers, 1033 Massachusetts Ave., Cambridge MA 02138. (617)547-4170. Publisher: Michael Bentley. Estab. 1949. Publishes hardcover and trade paperback originals and reprints. Publishes 15-20 titles/year. 20% of books are from first-time authors; 95% from unagented writers. Pays 10-15% royalty on net price or makes outright purchase. Advance negotiable. Publishes book 1 year after acceptance. Reports in 6 weeks. Book catalog and ms guidelines for 9×12 SAE with 4 first-class stamps.

Nonfiction: How-to, technical, theory of operation, coffee table. Automotive subjects only; this includes motor sports. Query or submit outline and sample chapters. Reviews artwork/photos as part of ms package.

Recent Nonfiction Title: *Think to Win: The New Approach to Fast Driving.*

Tips: "We are excited about the possibilities and growth in the automobile enthusiast book market. Our audience is composed of serious, intelligent automobile, sports car, and racing enthusiasts, automotive technicians and high-performance tuners."

THE BERKLEY PUBLISHING GROUP, Publishers of Berkley/Berkley Trade Paperbacks/Jove/Boulevard/Ace Science Fiction, Division of the Putnam Berkeley Group, 200 Madison Ave., New York NY 10016. (212)951-8800. Editor-in-Chief: Leslie Gelbman. Publishes paperback originals and reprints. Publishes approximately 800 titles/year. Pays 4-10% royalty on retail price. Offers advance. Publishes book 2 years after acceptance.

Nonfiction: How-to, family life, business, health, nutrition, true crime.

Fiction: Historical, mainstream, mystery, suspense, romance, science fiction, western. Submit outline/synopsis and first 3 chapters for Ace Science Fiction *only*. No other unagented mss accepted.

Tips: No longer seeking adventure or occult fiction. Does not publish memoirs or personal stories.

BERKSHIRE HOUSE PUBLISHERS, INC., 480 Pleasant St., Suite #5, Lee MA 01238. (413)243-0303 or (800)321-8526. Fax: (413)243-4737. President: Jean J. Rousseau. Estab. 1989. Publishes 12-15 titles/year. Receives 100 queries and 6 mss/year. 50% of books from first-time authors; 80% from unagented writers. Pays 5-10% royalty on retail price. Offers $500-5,000 advance. Publishes book 18 months after acceptance. Accepts simultaneous submissions. Reports in 1 month on proposals. Book catalog free on request.

Nonfiction: Biography, cookbook. Subjects include Americana, history, nature/environment, recreation (outdoors), wood crafts, regional. "All our books have a strong Berkshires or New England orientation—no others, please. To a great extent, we choose our topics then commission the authors, but we don't discourage

speculative submissions. We just don't accept many. Don't overdo it; a well-written outline/proposal is more useable than a full manuscript. Also, include a cv with writing credits."
Recent Nonfiction Title: *Country Inns & Back Roads Cookbook*, by Linda Glick Conway.
Tips: "Our readers are literate, active, prosperous, interested in travel, especially in selected 'Great Destinations' areas and outdoor activities and cooking."

BETHEL PUBLISHING, Subsidiary of Missionary Church, Inc., 1819 S. Main St., Elkhart IN 46516-4299. (219)293-8585. Fax: (219)522-5670. Executive Director: Rev. Richard Oltz. Estab. 1903. Publishes trade paperback originals and reprints. Publishes 5 titles/year. Receives 250 submissions/year. 80% of books from first-time authors; 90% from unagented writers. Pays 5-10% royalties. Publishes book 1 year after acceptance. Accepts simultaneous submissions. Reports in 2 months. Book catalog for 9×12 SAE with 3 first-class stamps.
Nonfiction: Reference. Religious subjects. Query. Reviews artwork/photos as part of ms package.
Fiction: Adventure, religious, suspense, young adult. Books must be evangelical in approach. No occult, gay/lesbian or erotica. Query.
Recent Fiction Title: *August Gamble*, by Linda Hall (adult).
Tips: "Our audience is made up of Christian families with children. If I were a writer trying to market a book today, I would find out what publisher specializes in the type of book I have written."

BETTERWAY BOOKS, Imprint of F&W Publications, 1507 Dana Ave., Cincinnati OH 45207. (513)531-2690. Editors: David Lewis, William Brohaugh. Estab. 1982. Publishes hardcover and trade paperback originals, trade paperback reprints. Publishes 30 titles/year. Pays 10-20% royalty on net receipts. Offers $3,000-5,000 advance. Accepts simultaneous submissions, if so noted. Publishes book 18 months after acceptance. Reports in 1 month. Book catalog for 9×12 SAE with 6 first-class stamps.
Nonfiction: How-to, illustrated book, reference and self-help in eight categories. Direct queries for these categories to David Lewis: home building and remodeling, woodworking, small business and personal finance, hobbies and collectibles. Direct queries for these categories to William Brohaugh: sports and recreation, reference books and handbooks (including genealogy), lifestyle (including home organization), theater and the performing arts. "Betterway books are instructional books that are to be *used*. We like specific step-by-step advice, charts, illustrations, and clear explanations of the activities and projects the books describe. We are interested mostly in original material, but we will consider republishing self-published nonfiction books and good instructional or reference books that have gone out of print before their time. Send a sample copy, sales information, and reviews, if available. If you have a good idea for a reference book that can be updated annually, try us. We're willing to consider freelance compilers of such works." No cookbooks, diet/exercise, psychology self-help, health or parenting books. Query with outline and sample chapters. Reviews artwork/photos as part of ms package.
Recent Nonfiction Title: *Kids, Money & Values*, by Patricia Schoff Estes and Irving Barocas.
Tips: "Keep the imprint name well in mind when submitting ideas to us. What is the 'better way' you're proposing? How will readers benefit *immediately* from the instruction and information you're giving them?"

BLACK HERON PRESS, P.O. Box 95676, Seattle WA 98145. Publisher: Jerry Gold. Publishes hardcover and trade paperback originals. Publishes 4 titles/year. Pays 8-10% royalty on retail price. Reports in 3 months on queries, 6 months on proposals and mss.
Fiction: High quality, innovative fiction. Query with outline, 3 sample chapters and SASE.
Recent Fiction Title: *Terminal Weird*, by Jack Remick (surrealistic short stories).

BLACKBIRCH PRESS, INC., 260 Amity Rd., Woodbridge CT 06525. Editorial Director: Bruce Glassman. Publishes hardcover and trade paperback originals. Publishes 30 titles/year. Receives 400 queries and 75 mss/year. 100% of books from unagented writers. Pays 4-8% royalty on wholesale price or makes outright purchase. Offers $1,000-5,000 advance. Publishes book 1 year after acceptance of ms. Accepts simultaneous submissions. Reports in 2 months.
Nonfiction: Biography, illustrated books, children's/juvenile, reference. Subjects include animals, anthropology/archeology, health/medicine, history, nature/environment, science, sports, women's issues/studies. Query. No unsolicited mss or proposals. Cover letters and résumés are useful for identifying new authors. Reviews artwork/photos as part of ms package. Send photocopies. No fiction or adult proposals, please.

JOHN F. BLAIR, PUBLISHER, 1406 Plaza Dr., Winston-Salem NC 27103-1470. (910)768-1374. Fax: (910)768-9194. Editor: Carolyn Sakowski. Estab. 1954. Publishes hardcover originals and trade paperbacks. Publishes 15 titles/year. Receives 5,000 submissions/year. 20-30% of books from first-time authors; 90% from unagented writers. Average print order for a first book is 5,000. Royalty negotiable. Publishes book 18 months after acceptance. Reports in 3 months. Book catalog and ms guidelines for 9×12 SAE with 5 first-class stamps.
Nonfiction: Especially interested in travel guides dealing with the Southeastern US. Also interested in Civil War, outdoors, travel and Americana; query on other nonfiction topics. Looks for utility and significance. Submit outline and first 3 chapters. Reviews artwork/photos as part of ms package.

Fiction: "We are interested only in material related to the Southeastern US." No category fiction, juvenile fiction, picture books or poetry. *Writer's Market* recommends sending a query with SASE first.

‡BLOOMBERG PRESS, Imprint of Bloomberg L.P., 100 Business Park Dr., P.O. Box 888, Princeton NJ 08542-0888. Editorial Director: Jared Kieling. Imprints are Bloomberg Personal Bookshelf, Bloomberg Professional Library. Publishes hardcover and trade paperback originals. Publishes 12 titles/year. Receives 35 queries and 10 mss/year. 5% of books from first-time authors; 45% from unagented writers. Pays royalty on net receipts. Offers negotiable advance. Publishes book 9 months after acceptance of ms. Accepts simultaneous submissions. Reports in 1 month on queries. Book catalog for 10×13 SAE with 5 first-class stamps.
Nonfiction: How-to, reference, technical. Subjects include business and economics, money/finance, personal finance for consumers, professional books on finance, investment and business. "Almost all of Bloomberg Press's books originate within Bloomberg L.P. or are being written by authors and journalists who write for our two magazines, *Bloomberg* magazine and *Bloomberg Personal*. Books must fit the standards of Bloomberg L.P., a global multimedia information provider. All our authors are experienced business and financial journalists and/or financial professionals prominent in their specialty for some time. Our books are distributed by Irwin Professional Publishing." Submit outline, sample chapter with SASE.
Recent Nonfiction Title: *A Commonsense Guide to Mutual Funds*, by Mary Rowland (personal finance).
Tips: *Bloomberg Professional Library*: Audience is upscale financial professionals—traders, dealers, brokers, company executives, sophisticated investors, such as people who lease a Bloomberg terminal system. *Bloomberg Personal Bookshelf*: Audience is upscale consumers and individual investors, as well as all categories listed for the Professional Library—readers of our magazine *Bloomberg Personal*. "Do research on Bloomberg L.P., and look at our specially formatted books in a library or bookstore, and read *Bloomberg Personal* and *Bloomberg* magazines before proposing a book to Bloomberg Press."

BLUE BIRD PUBLISHING, 2266 S. Dobson, Suite 275, Mesa AZ 85202. (602)831-6063. Fax: (602)831-1829. Publisher: Cheryl Gorder. Estab. 1985. Publishes trade paperback originals. Publishes 10 titles/year. 50% of books from first-time authors; 100% from unagented writers. Pays 10% royalty on wholesale price; 15% on retail price. Publishes book 9 months after acceptance. Accepts simultaneous submissions. Reports in 3 months. Book catalog and ms guidelines for #10 SASE.
Nonfiction: How-to, reference. Subjects include child guidance/parenting, education (especially home education), sociology (current social issues). "The homeschooling population in the US is exploding. We have a strong market for anything that can be targeted to this group: home education manuscripts, parenting guides, curriculum ideas. We would also like to see complete nonfiction manuscripts in current issues, how-to topics." Submit complete ms. *Writer's Market* recommends sending a query with SASE first. Reviews artwork/photos as part of ms package.
Recent Nonfiction Title: *Multicultural Education Resource Guide; Home Education Resource Guide* (4th edition).
Tips: "We are interested if we see a complete manuscript that is aimed toward a general adult nonfiction audience. We are impressed if the writer has really done his homework and the manuscript includes photos, artwork, graphs, charts, and other graphics. Please do not send fiction or short stories."

BLUE DOLPHIN PUBLISHING, INC., P.O. Box 8, Nevada City CA 95959-0008. (916)265-6925. Fax: (916)265-0787. E-mail: bdolphin@netshel.net. Imprint is Pelican Pond Publishing (mass market, contact Christopher Comins). Publisher: Paul M. Clemens. Estab. 1985. Publishes hardcover, trade and mass market paperback originals. Publishes 12-15 titles/year. Receives over 3,000 submissions/year. 65% of books from first-time authors; 90% from unagented writers. Pays 10-15% royalty on wholesale price. Publishes book 8 months after acceptance. Accepts simultaneous submissions. Reports in 3 months on queries; "longer with books we're considering more closely." Query with SASE. Book catalog and ms guidelines free.
Nonfiction: Biography, gift book, how-to, nature/environment, self-help. Subjects include anthropology/archaeology, foods/nutrition, ecology, education, health/medicine, psychology, comparative religion, women's issues/studies. "Blue Dolphin specializes in publishing books on comparative spiritual traditions, lay and transpersonal psychology, self-help, health, healing, ecology and whatever helps people grow in their social awareness and conscious evolution." Submit outline, 3 sample chapters, synopsis, table of contents, author bio, with SASE. Reviews artwork as part of ms package. Send photocopies.
Recent Nonfiction Title: *The Way It Is: One Water, One Air, One Mother Earth*, by Corbin Harney.
Fiction: Ethnic, literary, mainstream/contemporary, religious. "Note: We are *not* fiction-based, but are publishing 1-2 year." Query with 2-page synopsis.
Recent Fiction Title: *Billabong Dreaming: An Australian Adventure*, by Brian Jones.
Poetry: "We will only consider previously published authors of some merit or translations of noted works. Interested primarily in classical poetry or translations." Submit complete ms.
Tips: "Our audience is the concerned person interested in self-growth and awareness for oneself and the planet. We are looking for well-prepared query letters and manuscripts with adequate return postage. We will consider publishing Metaphysical/New Age Romance Fiction—1-2 titles per year. *Stories must be innovative*, have an overall theme of spiritual growth and be uplifting. Do not send entire manuscript. Send query letter and synopsis of story and one sample chapter along with a SASE. We are only interested in highly

polished works that demonstrate a thorough awareness of good literature techniques."

BLUE MOON BOOKS, INC., North Star Line, 61 Fourth Ave., New York NY 10003. Publisher/Editor: Barney Rosset. Publishes trade paperback and mass market paperback originals. Publishes 24-40 titles/year. Receives 700 queries and 500 mss/year. Pays 7½-10% royalty on retail price. Offers $500 and up advance. Publishes book 1 year after acceptance of ms. Accepts simultaneous submissions. Reports in 2 months. Book catalog free on request. Manuscript guidelines for #10 SASE.
Nonfiction: General nonfiction. Query with outline and 3-6 sample chapters. Reviews artwork/photos as part of ms package if part of story. Color photocopies best but not necessary.
Recent Nonfiction Title: *Patrong Sisters: An American Woman's View of the Bangkok Sex World*, by Cleo Odzer.
Fiction: Erotica. Query with synopsis and 3-6 sample chapters.

BLUE POPPY PRESS, 1775 Linden Ave., Boulder CO 80304-1537. (303)442-0796. Fax: (303)447-8372. E-mail: 102151.1614@compuserve.com. Editor-in-Chief: Bob Flaws. Publishes hardcover and trade paperback originals. Publishes 9-12 titles/year. Receives 50-100 queries and 20 mss/year. 40-50% of books from first-time authors; 100% from unagented writers. Pays 10-15% royalty "of sales price at all discount levels." Publishes book 6-12 months after acceptance. Reports in 1 month. Book catalog and ms guidelines free on request.
Nonfiction: Self-help, technical, textbook related to acupuncture and Oriental medicine. "We only publish books on acupuncture and Oriental medicine by authors who can read Chinese and have a minimum of five years clinical experience. We also require all our authors to use Wiseman's *Glossary of Chinese Medical Terminology* as their standard for technical terms." Query or submit outline, 1 sample chapter and SASE.
Recent Nonfiction Title: *The Secret of Chinese Diagnosis*, by Bob Flaws.
Tips: Audience is "practicing accupuncturists, interested in alternatives in healthcare, preventive medicine, Chinese philosophy and medicine."

BLUE STAR PRODUCTIONS, a Division of Bookworld, Inc., 9666 E. Riggs Rd., #194, Sun Lakes AZ 85248. (602)895-7995. Editor: Barbara DeBolt. Publishes trade and mass market paperback originals. Publishes 10-12 titles/year. Receives 500 queries and 400-500 mss/year. 75% of books from first-time authors; 99% from unagented writers. Pays 10% royalty on wholesale or retail price. Reports in 1 month on queries, 2 months on proposals, 6 months on mss. Book catalog free on request. Manuscript guidelines for #10 SASE.
Nonfiction: Subjects include philosophy, ufology, spiritual (metaphysical), self-help. Reviews artwork/photos as part of the ms package. Send photocopies.
Recent Nonfiction Title: *Cataclysms: A New Look at Earth Changes*, by Norma Hickox.
Fiction: Fantasy, spiritual (metaphysical), UFO's. Query or submit synopsis and the first 3 chapters. SASE a must.
Recent Fiction Title: *Dance on the Water*, by Laura Leffers (Native American mysticism).
Tips: "Know our no-advance policy beforehand and know our guidelines. No response ever without a SASE. Absolutely no phone queries. We have temporarily restricted our needs to those manuscripts whose focus is metaphysical, ufology, time travel and Native American. Query to see if this restriction has been lifted before submitting other material."

BNA BOOKS, Division of The Bureau of National Affairs, Inc., 1250 23rd St. NW, Washington DC 20037-1165. (202)833-7470. Fax: (202)833-7490. E-mail: books@bna.com. Website: http://www.bna.com. Administrative Assistant: Esther H. Marshall. Estab. 1929. Publishes hardcover and softcover originals. Publishes 35 titles/year. Receives 200 submissions/year. 20% of books from first-time authors; 95% from unagented writers. Pays 5-15% royalty on net cash receipts. Offers $500 average advance. Publishes book 1 year after acceptance. Accepts simultaneous submissions. Reports in 3 months on queries. Book catalog and ms guidelines free.
Nonfiction: Reference, professional/scholarly. Subjects include labor and unemployment law, environmental law, legal practice, labor relations and intellectual property law. No biographies, bibliographies, cookbooks, religion books, humor or trade books. Submit detailed table of contents or outline.
Recent Nonfiction Title: *Biotechnology & the Federal Circuit*, by Kenneth Burchfiel (environmental).
Tips: "Our audience is made up of practicing lawyers and business executives; managers, federal, state, and local government administrators; unions; and law libraries. We look for authoritative and comprehensive works that can be supplemented or revised every year or two on subjects of interest to those audiences."

BONUS BOOKS, INC., Parent of Precept Press, 160 E. Illinois St., Chicago IL 60611. (312)467-0580. Website: http://www.bonus-books.com. Managing Editor: Deborah Flapan. Estab. 1985. Publishes hardcover and trade paperback originals and reprints. Publishes 30 titles/year. Receives 400-500 submissions/year. 40% of books from first-time authors; 60% from unagented writers. Royalties vary. Advances are not frequent. Publishes book 8 months after acceptance. Accepts simultaneous submissions, if so noted. Reports in 2 months on queries. Book catalog for 9×11 SASE. Manuscript guidelines for #10 SASE. All submissions and queries must include SASE.

Nonfiction: Subjects include automotive/self-help, biography/current affairs, broadcasting, business/self-help, Chicago people and places, collectibles, cookbooks, education/self-help, fund raising, handicapping winners, home and health, humor, entertainment, regional, sports and women's issues/studies. Query with outline, sample chapters and SASE. Reviews artwork/photos as part of ms package.
Recent Nonfiction Title: *What Will My Mother Say*, by Dympna Ugwu-Oju (women's studies).

BOOKCRAFT, INC., 1848 West 2300 South, Salt Lake City UT 84119. (801)972-6180. Editorial Manager: Cory H. Maxwell. Estab. 1942. Imprint is Parliament. Publishes mainly hardcover and trade paperback originals. Publishes 40-45 titles/year. Receives 500-600 submissions/year. 20% of books from first-time authors; virtually 100% from unagented writers. Pays standard 7½-10-12½-15% royalty on retail price. Rarely gives advance. Publishes book 6 months after acceptance. Accepts simultaneous submissions. Reports in about 2 months. Book catalog and ms guidelines for #10 SASE.
Nonfiction: "We publish for members of The Church of Jesus Christ of Latter-Day Saints (Mormons) and our books are closely oriented to the faith and practices of the LDS church, and we will be glad to review such mss. Those which have merely a general religious appeal are not acceptable. Ideal book lengths range from about 100-300 pages or so, depending on subject, presentation, and age level. We look for a fresh approach—rehashes of well-known concepts or doctrines not acceptable. Manuscripts should be anecdotal unless truly scholarly or on a specialized subject. We do not publish anti-Mormon works. We also publish short and moderate length books for children and young adults, and fiction as well as nonfiction. These reflect LDS principles without being 'preachy'; must be motivational. 30,000-45,000 words is about the right length, though good, longer manuscripts are not ruled out. We publish only 5 or 6 new juvenile titles annually. No poetry, plays, personal philosophizings, or family histories." Biography, childrens/juvenile, coffee table book, how-to, humor, reference, self-help. Subjects include: child guidance/parenting, history, religion. Query with full ms and SASE. *Writer's Market* recommends sending a query with SASE first. Reviews artwork/photos as part of ms package. Send photocopies.
Recent Nonfiction Title: *Sunshine* by Elaine Cannon (inspirational).
Fiction: Should be oriented to LDS faith and practices. Adventure, historical, juvenile, literary, mainstream/contemporary, mystery, religious, romance, short story collections, suspense, western, young adult. Submit full ms with SASE. *Writer's Market* recommends sending a query with SASE first.
Recent Fiction Title: *The Work and the Glory: Praise to the Man*, volume 6, by Gerald N. Lund.
Tips: "The competition in the area of fiction is much more intense than it has ever been before. We receive two or three times as many quality fiction manuscripts as we did even as recently as five years ago."

‡BOOKHAVEN PRESS, P.O. Box 1243, 401 Amherst Ave., Moon Township PA 15108. (412)262-5578. Publisher: Victor Richards. Publishes trade paperback originals. Publishes 8 titles/year. Receives 12 queries and 5 mss/year. 100% of books from first-time authors; 100% from unagented writers. Pays 7-12% royalty on wholesale price. No advance. Publishes book 6 months after acceptance of ms. Accepts simultaneous submissions. Does not return submissions. Form letter for rejection, destroys originals. Reports in 3 months on queries, 1 month on proposals, 2 months on mss. Book catalog free on request.
Nonfiction: How-to, reference. Subjects include business and economics, education, money/finance and careers. "We look for well developed manuscripts from computer literate writers. All manuscripts must be available in IBM computer format (Word Perfect Preferred)." Submit outline and 2 sample chapters. Reviews artwork/photos as part of ms package. Send photocopies.
Recent Nonfiction Title: *Post Office Jobs*, by Dennis V. Damp (career guide).

THE BORGO PRESS, P.O. Box 2845, San Bernardino CA 92406-2845. (909)884-5813. Fax: (909)888-4942. Website: http://www.bville.com/mall/borgopress. Publishers: Robert Reginald, Mary A. Burgess. Estab. 1975. Publishes hardcover and paperback originals. Publishes 50 new titles/year, plus 150 new distributed books. Receives 500 submissions/year. 90% of books from first-time authors; 100% of books from unagented writers. Pays 10% royalty on retail price. No advance. Publishes book 3 years after acceptance. "99% of our sales go to the academic library market; we do not sell to the trade (i.e., bookstores)." Reports in 3 months. Book catalog for 9 × 12 SAE with 6 first-class stamps.
Nonfiction: Publishes literary critiques, bibliographies, historical research, film critiques, theatrical research, interview volumes, scholarly biographies, social studies, political science, and reference works for the academic library market only. Query with letter or outline/synopsis and 1 sample chapter. "All of our proprietary books, without exception, are published in open-ended, numbered, monographic series. Do not submit proposals until you have looked at actual copies of recent Borgo Press publications (*not our catalog*). We are *not* a market for fiction, poetry, popular nonfiction, artwork, or anything else except scholarly monographs in the humanities and social sciences. We discard unsolicited manuscripts from outside of our subject fields that are not accompanied by SASE. The vast majority of proposals we receive are clearly unsuitable and are a waste of both our time and the prospective author's."
Recent Nonfiction Title: *The Work of Stephen King*, by Collings (bibliography).

BOWLING GREEN STATE UNIVERSITY POPULAR PRESS, Bowling Green State University, Bowling Green OH 43403-1000. (419)372-7866. Fax: (419)372-8095. Editor: Ms. Pat Browne. Estab. 1967.

Publishes hardcover originals and trade paperback originals and reprints. Publishes 25 titles/year. Receives 400 submissions/year. 50% of books from first-time authors; 100% from unagented writers. Pays 5-12% royalty on wholesale price or makes outright purchase. Publishes book 9 months after acceptance. Reports in 3 months. Book catalog and ms guidelines free on request.

Nonfiction: Biography, reference, textbook. Subjects include Americana, art/architecture, ethnic, history, language/literature, regional, sports, women's issues/studies. Submit outline and 3 sample chapters.

Recent Nonfiction Titles: *Stephen King's America*, by Jonathan Davis.

Tips: "Our audience includes university professors, students, and libraries."

BOYDS MILLS PRESS, Subsidiary of *Highlights for Children*, 815 Church St., Honesdale PA 18431-1895. (717)253-1164. Imprint is Wordsong—publishes works of poetry. Manuscript Coordinator: Beth Troop. Estab. 1990. Publishes hardcover originals. Publishes 50 titles/year. Receives 10,000 queries and mss/year. 20% of books are from first-time authors; 75% from unagented writers. Pays varying royalty on retail price. Offers varying advance. Accepts simultaneous submissions. Reports in 1 month. *Writer's Market* recommends allowing 2 months for reply. Manuscript guidelines free. Book catalog for 9×12 SASE with 7 first-class stamps.

• Boyds Mills Press published two 1995 Junior Library Guild Selections, *The Long Silk Strand* and *The Case of the Mummified Pig*.

Nonfiction: Juvenile on all subjects. "Boyds Mills Press is not interested in manuscripts depicting violence, explicit sexuality, racism of any kind or which promotes hatred. We also are not the right market for self-help books." Submit outline and sample chapters. Reviews artwork/photos as part of ms package.

Recent Nonfiction Title: *Faces Only a Mother Could Love*, by Jennifer Owings Dewey.

Fiction: Juvenile—picture book, middle grade, young adult, poetry. Submit outline/synopsis and sample chapters for novel or complete ms for picture book.

Recent Fiction Title: *Leah's Pony*, by Elizabeth Friedrich.

Tips: "Our audience is pre-school to young adult. Concentrate first on your writing. Polish it. Then—and only then—select a market. We need primarily picture books with fresh ideas and characters—avoid worn themes of 'coming-of-age,' 'new sibling,' and self-help ideas. We are always interested in multicultural settings. Please—no anthropomorphic characters."

BRANDEN PUBLISHING CO., INC., 17 Station St., Box 843, Brookline Village MA 02147. Fax: (617)734-2046. E-mail: branden@usa1.com. Website: http://www1.usa1.com/~branden/. Editor: Adolph Caso. Estab. 1965. Subsidiaries include International Pocket Library and Popular Technology, Four Seas and Brashear. Publishes hardcover and trade paperback originals, reprints and software. Publishes 15 titles/year. Receives 1,000 submissions/year. 80% of books from first-time authors; 90% from unagented writers. Average print order for a first book is 3,000. Pays 5-10% royalty on net. Offers $1,000 maximum advance. Publishes book 10 months after acceptance. Reports in 1 month. *Writer's Market* recommends allowing 2 months for reply.

Nonfiction: Biography, illustrated book, juvenile, reference, technical, textbook. Subjects include Americana, art, computers, health, history, music, photography, politics, sociology, software, classics. Especially looking for "about 10 manuscripts on national and international subjects, including biographies of well-known individuals." No religion or philosophy. Paragraph query with author's vita and SASE. No unsolicited mss. No telephone inquiries. Reviews artwork/photos as part of ms package.

Recent Nonfiction Title: *From Trial Court*, by Walkowski (freedom of speech).

Fiction: Ethnic (histories, integration); religious (historical-reconstructive). No science, mystery or pornography. Paragraph query with author's vita and SASE. No unsolicited mss. No telephone inquiries.

Recent Fiction Title: *The Straw Obelisk*, by Caso (World War II).

Tips: "Branden publishes only manuscripts determined to have a significant impact on modern society. Our audience is a well-read general public, professionals, college students, and some high school students. If I were a writer trying to market a book today, I would thoroughly investigate the number of potential readers interested in the content of my book. We like books by or about women."

BRASSEY'S, INC., Division of Brassey's Ltd. (London), 1313 Dolley Madison Blvd., Suite #401, McLean VA 22101. (703)442-4535. Fax: (703)442-9848. Editorial Director: Don McKeon. Publishes hardcover and trade paperback originals and reprints. Publishes 30 titles/year. Receives 900 queries/year. 30% of books from first-time authors; 80% from unagented writers. Pays 6-12% royalty on wholesale price. Offers $50,000 maximum advance. Publishes book 1 year after acceptance of ms. Accepts simultaneous submissions. Reports in 2 months on proposals. Book catalog and ms guidelines for 9×12 SASE.

Nonfiction: Biography, coffee-table book, reference, textbook. Subjects include government/politics, national and international affairs, history, military/war, intelligence studies and sports. "We are seeking to build our biography, military history and national affairs lists and have also created a new imprint, Brassey's Sports." When submitting nonfiction, be sure to include sufficient biographical information (e.g., track records of previous publications), and "make clear in proposal how your work might differ from other such works already published and with which yours might compete." Submit proposal package, including outline,

1 sample chapter, bio, analysis of book's competition, return postage and SASE. Reviews artwork/photos as part of ms package. Send photocopies.

Recent Nonfiction Title: *Official Companion to the Olympic Games: Atlanta Edition*, The International Olympic Committee (sports/reference).

Fiction: "Submissions must be related to history, military, or intelligence topics, and authors must have previously published novels or have some special qualifications relevant to the topic." Submit synopsis, 1 sample chapter and SASE.

Tips: "Our audience consists of military personnel, government policymakers, and general readers with an interest in military history, biography, national and international affairs, defense issues, intelligence studies and sports."

BREVET PRESS, INC., P.O. Box 1404, Sioux Falls SD 57101. Publisher: Donald P. Mackintosh. Managing Editor: Peter E. Reid. Estab. 1972. Publishes hardcover and paperback originals and reprints. Publishes 15 titles/year. Receives 40 submissions/year. 50% of books from first-time authors; 100% from unagented writers. Average print order for a first book is 5,000. Pays 5% royalty. Offers $1,000 average advance. Publishes book 1 year after acceptance. Accepts simultaneous submissions. Reports in 2 months. Book catalog free.

Nonfiction: Specializes in business management, history, place names, and historical marker series. Americana (A. Melton, editor); business (D.P. Mackintosh, editor); history (B. Mackintosh, editor); technical books (Peter Reid, editor). Query. "After query, detailed instructions will follow if we are interested." Reviews artwork/photos as part of ms package. Send photocopies.

Tips: "Write with market potential and literary excellence. Keep sexism out of the manuscripts."

BREWERS PUBLICATIONS, Division of Association of Brewers, 736 Pearl St., Boulder CO 80302. (303)447-0816. Fax: (303)447-2825. Website: http://www.aob/aob. Publisher: Elizabeth Gold. Publishes trade paperback and mass market paperback originals. Publishes 8-10 titles/year. Receives 50 queries and 6 mss/year. 25% of books from first-time authors; 100% from unagented writers. Pays 2-15% royalty on net receipts. Offers $500 maximum advance. Publishes book within 18 months of acceptance of ms. Accepts simultaneous submissions. Reports in 3 months. Book catalog free on request.

Nonfiction: "We only publish books about beer and brewing—for professional brewers, homebrewers and beer enthusiasts." Query first, then submit outline if requested. Reviews artwork/photos only after a ms is accepted.

Recent Nonfiction Title: *The Art of Cidermaking*, by Paul Correnty.

BRIGHTON PUBLICATIONS, INC., P.O. Box 120706, St. Paul MN 55112-0706. (612)636-2220. Editor: Sharon E. Dlugosch. Publishes trade paperback originals. Publishes 4 titles/year. Receives 100 queries and 100 mss/year. 50% of books from first-time authors; 100% from unagented writers. Pays 10% royalty on wholesale price. Publishes book 6 months after acceptance. Accepts simultaneous submissions. Reports in 3 months. Book catalog and ms guidelines for #10 SASE.

Nonfiction: How-to, business, tabletop, party themes, home making. "We're interested in topics telling how to live any part of life well. Specifically, we're developing business games for meetings, annual parties, picnics, etc., celebration themes, and party/special event planning." Query. Submit outline and 2 sample chapters.

BRISTOL PUBLISHING ENTERPRISES, INC., P.O. Box 1737, San Leandro CA 94577. (510)895-4461. Imprints include Nitty Gritty Cookbooks. Chairman: Patricia J. Hall. President: Brian Hall. Estab. 1988. Publishes 12-14 titles/year. Receives 750 proposals/year. 10% of books from first-time authors; 100% from unagented writers. Publishes within 1 year of acceptance. Reports in 4 months. Book catalog for SAE with 2 first-class stamps.

Nonfiction: Cookbooks. Submit theme, outline and author's background.

BROADMAN & HOLMAN PUBLISHERS, (formerly Broadman & Holman Press) 127 Ninth Ave. N, Nashville TN 37234. Contact: Ken Stephens. Assistant: Sandra Corbin. Publishes hardcover and paperback originals. Publishes 48 titles/year. Pays negotiable royalty. Reports in 2 months. Writer's guidelines for #10 SAE with 2 first-class stamps.

Nonfiction: Religion. "We are open to freelance submissions in all areas. Materials in these areas must be suited for an evangelical Christian readership. No poetry, biography, sermons, or art/gift books. Query with outline/synopsis and sample chapters.

---

‡ THE DOUBLE DAGGER before a listing indicates that the listing is new in this edition. New markets are often more receptive to freelance submissions.

Fiction: Religious. "We publish almost no fiction. For our occasional publication we want not only a very good story, but also one that sets forth Christian values. Nothing that lacks a positive Christian emphasis; nothing that fails to sustain reader interest."

Tips: "Textbook and family material are becoming an important forum for us—Bible study is very good for us. Preparation for the future and living with life's stresses and complexities are trends in the subject area."

BROADWAY BOOKS, Division of Bantam Books, 1540 Broadway, New York NY 10036. (212)234-6500. Publisher: William Shinker. Editor-in-Chief: John Sterling. Publishes hardcover and trade paperback originals.

Nonfiction: General interest adult books. Subjects include autobiography/memoirs, business, child care/parenting, cookbooks, current affairs, diet/nutrition, ecology, education, health, history, illustrated books, New Age/spirituality, money/finance, politics, popular culture, psychology, women's issues/studies.

Recent Nonfiction Title: *Life Preservers: Staying Afloat in All Your Relationships*, by Harriet Lerner, Ph.D.

Fiction: Publishes commercial literary fiction.

Recent Fiction Title: *A Face at the Window*, by Denis McFarland (literary ghost story).

‡BROOKLINE BOOKS, P.O. Box 1047, Cambridge MA 02238. (617)868-0360. Fax: (617)868-1772. E-mail: brooklinebks@delphi.com. Editor: Theodore Knight. Publishes trade and professional paperback originals and reprints. Publishes 8-12 titles/year. Receives 50-100 queries and 30-50 mss/year. 30% of books from first-time authors; majority from unagented writers. Pays 10-15% royalty on wholesale price. Publishes book 8 months after acceptance of ms. Accepts simultaneous submissions. Reports in 1 month on queries, 2 months on proposals and mss. Book catalog and ms guidelines free on request.

Nonfiction: Reference, technical, textbook, professional. Subjects include child guidance/parenting, education, health/medicine, language/literature, psychology, translation, special needs/disabilities. Query or submit outline, 3 sample chapters and SASE. Reviews artwork/photos as part of ms package. Send photocopies.

Recent Nonfiction Title: *Raising Your Child to be Gifted*, by James Campbell (parenting/education).

Fiction: First time translations of Latin American, European and Asian literary fiction and nonfiction. Query or submit synopsis, 3 sample chapters and SASE.

Recent Fiction Title: *Memoirs of a Dissolute Gentleman*, by Hector Abad (novel).

‡BRYANT & DILLON PUBLISHERS, INC., P.O. Box 39, Orange NJ 07050. (201)675-5668. Fax: (201)675-8443). Contact: Gerri Dillon. Publishes hardcover and trade paperback originals. Publishes 8-10 titles/year. Receives 30 queries and 20-30 mss/year. 100% of books from first-time authors; 90% from unagented writers. Pays 6-10% royalty on retail price. Publishes book 1 year after acceptance of ms. Accepts simultaneous submissions. Reports in 2 months on proposals.

Nonfiction: Biography, gift book, how-to, self-help. Subjects include business and economics, education, ethnic, government/politics, history, language/literature, money/finance, women's issues/studies. Submit outline and 3 sample chapters with SASE.

Recent Nonfiction Title: *Black Survival in White America*, by Jeanette Davis-Adeshote (Black studies).

Fiction: Ethnic, mystery, romance, short story collections, suspense. Submit synopsis and 3 sample chapters with SASE.

Recent Fiction Title: *You Can Get There From Here*, by D. Anne Browne (self help).

Tips: Audience is all ethnic groups who would like a better understanding about each other.

BUCKNELL UNIVERSITY PRESS, Lewisburg PA 17837. (717)524-3674. Fax: (717)524-3797. E-mail: medgertn@bucknell.edu. Director: Mills F. Edgerton, Jr. Estab. 1969. Publishes hardcover originals. Publishes 25 titles/year. Receives 150 inquiries and submissions/year. 20% of books from first-time authors; 99% from unagented writers. Pays royalty. Publishes book 2 years after acceptance. Reports in 1 month on queries. *Writer's Market* recommends allowing 2 months for reply. Book catalog free.

Nonfiction: Subjects include scholarly art history, history, literary criticism, music, philosophy, political science, psychology, religion, sociology. "In all fields, our criterion is scholarly presentation; manuscripts must be addressed to the scholarly community." Query.

Recent Nonfiction Title: *The Play in the Mirror: Lacanian Perspectives on Spanish Baroque Theater*, by Matthew D. Stroud.

Tips: "An original work of high-quality scholarship has the best chance with us. We publish for the scholarly community."

‡BULL PUBLISHING CO., 110 Gilbert, Menlo Park CA 94025-2833. (415)332-2855. Fax: (415)327-3300. Publisher: James Bull. Estab. 1974. Publishes hardcover and trade paperback originals. Publishes 2-4 titles/year. Receives 100 submissions/year. 40-50% of books from first-time authors; 99% from unagented writers. Pays 14-16% royalty on wholesale price (net to publisher). Publishes ms an average of 6 months after acceptance. Book catalog free on request.

Nonfiction: How-to, self-help. Subjects include foods and nutrition, fitness, child health and nutrition, health education, sports medicine. "We look for books that fit our area of strength: responsible books on health that fill a substantial public need, and that we can market primarily through professionals." Submit outline and sample chapters. Reviews artwork/photos as part of ms package.

Recent Nonfiction Title: *Living A Healthy Life With Chronic Conditions: Self-Management of Heart Disease, Arthritis, Stroke, Diabetes, Asthma, Bronchitis, Emphysema & Others* by Kate Lorig, RN DrPH et al.

‡THE BUREAU FOR AT-RISK YOUTH, 645 New York Ave., Huntington NY 11743. Editor-in-Chief: Sally Germain. Publishes booklets, pamphlets, curriculum and other educational materials. Publishes 25-50 titles/year. Receives 50-100 queries and 30-50 mss/year. Most books from first-time authors; 100% from unagented writers. Pays royalty of 10% maximum on selling price. Advance varies. Publication 6 months after acceptance of ms. Accepts simultaneous submissions. Reports on queries, proposals, mss in 1-8 months. Book catalog free if appropriate after communication with author.

Nonfiction: Educational materials for parents, educators and other professionals who work with youth. Subjects include child guidance/parenting, education. "The materials we publish are curriculum, book series or how-to oriented pieces tailored to our audience. They are generally not single book titles and are rarely book length." Query.

Recent Nonfiction Title: *Peace by Peace. Conflict Resolution Through Peer Mediation* (Middle and High School Peer Mediation Program).

Tips: "Publications are sold exclusively through direct mail catalog to educators, parents, mental health and juvenile justice professionals. We do not publish book-length pieces. Writers whose expertise is appropriate to our customers should send query or proposal since we tailor everything very specifically to meet our audience's needs."

BUSINESS McGRAW-HILL, The McGraw Hill Companies, 11 W. 19th St., New York NY 10011. (212)337-4098. Fax: (212)337-5999. Publisher: Philip Ruppel. Publishes hardcover and trade paperback originals. Publishes 100 titles/year. Receives 1,200 queries and 1,200 mss/year. 30% of books from first-time authors; 60% from unagented writers. Pays 5-17% royalty on net price. Offers $1,000-100,000 advance. Publishes book 6 months after acceptance of ms. Accepts simultaneous submissions. Reports in 3 months. Book catalog and ms guidelines free on request with SASE.

Nonfiction: How-to, reference, self-help, technical. Subjects include business and economics, government/politics, money/finance. "Current, up-to-date, original ideas are needed. Good self-promotion is key. We publish in a broad area of business." Submit proposal package, including outline, table of contents, concept.

Recent Nonfiction Title: *Informed Consent*, by John Byrne (general interest).

BUTTERWORTH-HEINEMANN, Division of Reed-Elsevier, 313 Washington St., Newton MA 02158-1626. Publishing Director: Karen Speerstra. Imprints are Focal Press (Marie Lee, senior editor); International Digital Press (Mike Cash, publisher); Butterworth-Heinemann (Karen Speerstra, publishing director); Medical (Susan Poli, publishing director). Publishes hardcover and trade paperback originals. Publishes 100 titles/year. Each imprint publishes 25-30 titles/year. 25% of books from first-time authors; 95% from unagented writers. Pays 10-12% royalty on wholesale price. Offers modest advance. Publishes book 9 months after acceptance of ms. Reports in 1 month on proposals. Book catalog and ms guidelines free on request.

Nonfiction: How-to (in our selected areas), reference, technical, textbook. Subjects include business, computers and electronics, health/medicine, photography, security/criminal justice, audio-video broadcast, communication technology. "We publish technical professional and academic books; no fiction." Submit outline, 1-2 sample chapters, competing books and how yours is different/better with SASE. Reviews artwork/photos as part of ms package. Send photocopies.

C Q INC., Imprint of Congressional Quarterly, Inc., 1414 22nd St. NW, Washington DC 20037. (202)887-8640 or 8645. Fax: (202)822-6583. E-mail: swagger@cqalert.com or dtarr@cqalert.com. Acquisitions Editors: David Tarr, Shana Wagger. Publishes 30-40 hardcover and paperback titles/year. 95% of books from unagented writers. Pays royalties on net receipts. Sometimes offers advance. Publishes book an average of 1 year after acceptance. Accepts simultaneous submissions. Reports in 3 months. Book catalog free.

Nonfiction: Reference books, information directories on federal and state governments, national elections, international/state politics and governmental issues. Submit prospectus, writing sample and cv.

Tips: "Our books present important information on American government and politics, and related issues, with careful attention to accuracy, thoroughness and readability."

C Q PRESS, Imprint of Congressional Quarterly, Inc., 1414 22nd St. NW, Washington DC 20037. (202)887-8641. Website: http://www.voter96.cqalert.com/cq-mall/htm. Acquisitions Editor: Brenda Carter. Publishes 20-30 hardcover and paperback titles/year. 95% of books from unagented writers. Pays standard college royalty on wholesale price. Offers college text advance. Publishes book 6 months after acceptance of final ms. Accepts simultaneous submissions. Reports in 3 months. Book catalog free.

Nonfiction: All levels of college political science texts. "We are interested in American government, public administration, comparative government, and international relations." Submit proposal, outline and bio.

CADDO GAP PRESS, 3145 Geary Blvd., Suite 275, San Francisco CA 94118-3300. (415)750-9978. Fax: (415)668-5450. E-mail: caddogap@aol.com. Publisher: Alan H. Jones. Estab. 1989. Publishes trade paperback originals and educational journals and newsletters. Publishes 4 titles/year. Receives 20 queries and 10 mss/year. 50% of books from first-time authors; 100% from unagented writers. Pays 10% royalty on wholesale price. Publishes book 1 year after acceptance of ms. Accepts simultaneous submissions. Reports in 2 months on proposals.
Nonfiction: Subjects limited to teacher education, social foundations of education, and multicultural education. Query.
Recent Nonfiction Title: *Schoolmarms: Women in America's Schools*, by Edwina Walsh.

CAMBRIDGE EDUCATIONAL, P.O. Box 2153, Charleston WV 25328-2153. (800)468-4227. Fax: (304)744-9351. Subsidiaries include: Cambridge Parenting and Cambridge Job Search. President: Edward T. Gardner, Ph.D. Estab. 1980. Publishes hardcover and trade paperback originals. Publishes 12 titles/year. Receives 200 submissions/year. 20% of books from first-time authors; 90% from unagented writers. Makes outright purchase of $1,500-4,000. Occasional royalty arrangement. Publishes book 8 months after acceptance. Accepts simultaneous submissions. "No report unless interested."
 ● Publisher reports a greater focus on social studies and science.
Nonfiction: Subjects include child guidance/parenting, cooking/foods/nutrition, education, health/medicine, money/finance, career guidance, social studies and science. "We are looking for scriptwriters in the same subject areas and age group. We only publish books written for young adults and primarily sold to libraries, schools, etc. We do not seek books targeted to adults or written at high readability levels." Query or submit outline/synopsis and sample chapters. Reviews artwork/photos as part of ms package. No response unless interested.
Tips: "We encourage the submission of high-quality books on timely topics written for young adult audiences at moderate to low readability levels. Call and request a copy of all our current catalogs, talk to the management about what is timely in the areas you wish to write on, thoroughly research the topic, and write a manuscript that will be read by young adults without being overly technical. Low to moderate readability yet entertaining, informative and accurate."

CAMBRIDGE UNIVERSITY PRESS, 40 W. 20th St., New York NY 10011-4211. Editorial Director: Sidney Landau. Estab. 1534. Publishes hardcover and paperback originals. Publishes 1,300 titles/year. Receives 1,000 submissions annually. 50% of books from first-time authors; 99% from unagented writers. Pays 10% royalty on receipts; 8% on paperbacks. Publishes book an average of 1 year after acceptance. Query for electronic submissions. Reports in 4 months.
Nonfiction: Anthropology, archeology, economics, life sciences, medicine, mathematics, psychology, physics, art history, upper-level textbooks, academic trade, scholarly monographs, biography, history, and music. Looking for academic excellence in all work submitted. Department Editors: Frank Smith (history, social sciences); Mary Vaughn (English as second language); Deborah Goldblatt (English as a second language); Sidney Landau (reference); Lauren Cowles (mathematics, computer science); Scott Parris (economics); Julia Hough (developmental and social psychology, cognitive science); Alex Holzman (politics, history of science); Beatrice Rehl (fine arts, film studies); Richard Barling (medicine); Robin Smith (life sciences); Catherine Flack (earth sciences); Alan Harvey, (applied mathematics); Florence Padgett, (engineering, materials science); Terence Moore (philosophy); Susan Chang (American literature, Latin American literature); Elizabeth Neal (sociology, East Asian studies). Query. Reviews artwork/photos.

CAMELOT BOOKS, Children's Book Imprint of Avon Books, Division of the Hearst Corp., 1350 Avenue of the Americas, New York NY 10019. (212)261-6817. Fax: (212)261-6895. Editorial Director: Gwen Montgomery. Publishes paperback originals and reprints. Publishes 60-70 titles/year. Receives 1,000-1,500 submissions/year. 10-15% of books from first-time authors; 50% from unagented writers. Pays 6-8% royalty on retail price. Offers $2,000 minimum advance. Publishes book 2 years after acceptance. Accepts simultaneous submissions. Reports in 3 months. Book catalog and ms guidelines for 8 × 10 SAE with 5 first-class stamps.
Fiction: Subjects include adventure, humor, juvenile (Camelot, 8-12 and Young Camelot, 7-10) mainstream, mystery, ("very selective with mystery"), suspense. Avon does not publish picture books. Submit entire ms or 3 sample chapters and a brief, general summary of the story, chapter by chapter.
Recent Fiction Title: *Night of the Living Yogurt*, by William and Matthew DeAndrea.

CAMINO BOOKS, INC., P.O. Box 59026, Philadelphia PA 19102. (215)732-2491. Publisher: E. Jutkowitz. Estab. 1987. Publishes hardcover and trade paperback originals. Publishes 8 titles/year. Receives 500 submissions/year. 20% of books from first-time authors. Pays 6-12% royalty on net price. Offers $1,000 average advance. Publishes book 1 year after acceptance. Reports in 2 weeks on queries. *Writer's Market* recommends allowing 2 months for reply.

Nonfiction: Biography, cookbook, how-to, juvenile. Subjects include agriculture/horticulture, Americana, art/architecture, child guidance/parenting, cooking/foods/nutrition, ethnic, gardening, government/politics, history, regional, travel. Query with outline/synopsis and sample chapters with SASE.
Tips: "The books must be of interest to readers in the Middle Atlantic states, or they should have a clearly defined niche, such as cookbooks."

‡C&T PUBLISHING, 5021 Blum Rd., #1, Martinez CA 94553. (510)370-9600. Fax: (510)370-1576. E-mail: ctinfo@ctpub.com. Website: http://www.ctpub.com. Editorial Directors: Diane Pedersen, Liz Aneloski. Estab. 1983. Publishes hardcover and trade paperback originals. Publishes 12-14 titles/year. Receives 48 submissions/year. 10% of books from first-time authors; 100% from unagented writers. Pays 5-10% royalty on retail price. Offers $1,000 average advance. Publishes book 9 months after acceptance. Simultaneous submissions OK. Reports in 1 month. *Writer's Market* recommends allowing 2 months for reply. Free book catalog and ms guidelines.
Nonfiction: Quilting books, primarily how-to, occasional quilt picture books, children's books relating to quilting, quilt-related crafts, wearable art, needlework, fiber and surface embellishments, other books relating to fabric crafting. "Please submit ms with color photos of your work." *Writer's Market* recommends sending a query with SASE first.
Recent Nonfiction Title: *Elegant Stitches*, by Judith Baker Montano.
Tips: "In our industry, we find that how-to books have the longest selling life. Quiltmakers, sewing enthusiasts, needle artists and fiber artists are our audience."

CARADIUM PUBLISHING, 2503 Del Prado Blvd S., #435, Cape Coral FL 33904. Product Evaluation: Troy Dunn. Estab. 1989. Publishes hardcover, trade and mass market paperback originals. Publishes 15-20 titles/year. Receives 300 queries and 250 mss/year. 50% of books from first-time authors; 90% from unagented writers. Pays 15-20% royalty on retail price or makes outright purchase of $100 minimum. Offers $0-5,000 advance. Publishes book 6 months after acceptance of ms. Accepts simultaneous submissions. Does not return submissions; mss remain on file or destroyed. Reports on queries in 2 months.
Nonfiction: Business related: how-to, reference, self-help. Subjects include business and economics (motivation and how-to), money/finance. "We specialize in infomercials for our products." Query with outline and 3 sample chapters. Reviews artwork/photos as part of ms package. Send photocopies.
Recent Nonfiction Title: *The Locator*, by Klunder (self-help).
Tips: "Know the market you want to reach statistically and be creative in your submissions. We are seeking self-help books with action plans in them, not theory or story telling."

CARDOZA PUBLISHING, 132 Hastings St., Brooklyn NY 11235. (718)743-5229. Acquisitions Editor: Rose Swann. Imprints are Gambling Research Institute and Word Reference Library. Publishes trade paperback originals, mass market paperback originals and reprints. Publishes 175 titles/year. Receives 175 queries and 70 mss/year. 50% of books from first-time authors; 90% from unagented writers. Pays 5% royalty on retail price. Offers $500-2,000 advance. Publishes book 6 months after acceptance of ms. Accepts simultaneous submissions. Reports in 2 months on queries.
Nonfiction: How-to, reference. Subjects include gaming, gambling, health/fitness, publishing, reference/word, travel. "The world's foremost publisher of gaming and gambling books is expanding into how-to books by qualified and knowledgeable writers. We're also actively seeking travel guides for our sister company Open Road Publishing and multimedia and software titles on all subjects for our sister company, Cardoza Entertainment." Submit outline, table of contents and 2 sample chapters.
Recent Nonfiction Title: *Silberstang's Encyclopedia of Games & Gambling*, by Edwin Silberstang.
Tips: "The best manuscripts target the audience and appeal to readers in clear, easy-to-read writing."

CAREER PUBLISHING, INC., P.O. Box 5486, Orange CA 92613-5486. (714)771-5155. Fax: (714)532-0180. Editor-in-Chief: Marilyn M. Martin. Publishes paperback originals and software. Publishes 6-20 titles/year. Receives 300 submissions/year. 80% of books from first-time authors; 90% of books from unagented writers. Average print order for a first book is 3,000-10,000. Pays 10% royalty on actual amount received. No advance. Publishes book 1 year after acceptance. Accepts simultaneous submissions (if informed of names of others to whom submissions have been sent). Reports in 2 months. Book catalog and ms guidelines for 9×12 SAE with 2 first-class stamps.
Nonfiction: Software related to work experience, allied health and medical, and transportation (trucking business, etc.) "Textbooks should provide core upon which class curriculum can be based: textbook, workbook or kit with 'hands-on' activities and exercises, and teacher's guide. Should incorporate modern and effective teaching techniques. Should lead to a job objective. We also publish support materials for existing courses and are open to unique, marketable ideas with schools (secondary and post secondary) in mind. Reading level should be controlled appropriately—usually 7th-10th grade equivalent for vocational school and community college level courses. Any sign of sexism or racism will disqualify the work. No career awareness masquerading as career training." Submit outline, 2 sample chapters and table of contents. Reviews artwork/photos as part of ms package. If material is to be returned, enclose SAE and return postage.

Recent Nonfiction Title: *Become a 911 Dispatcher: Your Personal Career Guide*, by Capt. Richard Callen. **Tips:** "Authors should be aware of vocational/career areas with inadequate or no training textbooks and submit ideas and samples to fill the gap. Trends in book publishing that freelance writers should be aware of include education—especially for microcomputers."

CAROL PUBLISHING, 120 Enterprise Ave., Secaucus NJ 07094. (201)866-0490. Fax: (201)866-8159. Publisher: Steven Schragis. Imprints include Birch Lane Press (contact Hillel Black), Citadel Press (contact Kevin McDonough), University Books (contact Jim Ellison), Lyle Stuart (contact Allen Wilson). Publishes hardcover originals, trade paperback originals and reprints. Publishes 180 titles/year. Receives 2,000 submissions/year. 10% of books from first-time authors; 10% from unagented writers. Pays 5-15% royalty on retail price. Offers $5,000-10,000 advance. Publishes book 1 year after acceptance. Accepts simultaneous submissions. Reports in 2 months.
Nonfiction: Biography, cookbook, gift book, cookbook, gift book, how-to, humor, self-help. Subjects include Americana, animals, art/architecture, business and economics, computers and electronics, cooking/foods/nutrition, education ethnic, gay/lesbian, government/politics, health/medicine, history, hobbies, language/literature, military/war, money/finance, music/dance, nature/environment, philosophy, psychology, recreation, regional, science, sports, travel, women's issues/studies. Submit outline/synopsis, sample chapters and SASE. Reviews artwork as part of ms package. Send photocopies.
Fiction: Very infrequently.

CAROLRHODA BOOKS, INC., 241 First Ave. N., Minneapolis MN 55401. (612)332-3344. Submissions Editor: Rebecca Poole. Estab. 1969. Publishes hardcover originals. Publishes 50-60 titles/year. Receives 1,500 submissions/year. 15% of books from first-time authors; 95% from unagented writers. Makes outright purchase or negotiates payments of cents per printed copy. Publishes book 18 months after acceptance. Accepts simultaneous submissions. Include SASE for return of ms. Book catalog and ms guidelines for 9×12 SASE with 6 first-class stamps. No phone calls.
Nonfiction: Publishes only children's books. Subjects include biography, animals, art, history, music, nature. Needs "biographies in story form on truly creative individuals—25 manuscript pages in length." Send full ms. *Writer's Market* recommends sending a query with SASE first. Reviews artwork/photos separate from ms. Send color copies, no originals.
Recent Nonfiction Title: *Say It With Music: A Story About Irving Berlin*, by Tom Streissguth, illustrated by Karen Ritz.
Fiction: Children's historical. No anthropomorphized animal stories. Submit complete ms. *Writer's Market* recommends sending a query with SASE first.
Recent Fiction Title: *Jennifer Jean, the Cross-Eyed Queen*, by Phyllis Reynolds Naylor, illustrated by Karen Ritz.
Tips: "Our audience consists of children ages four to eleven. We publish very few picture books. Nonfiction science topics, particularly nature, do well for us, as do biographies, photo essays, and easy readers. We prefer manuscripts that can fit into one of our series. Spend time developing your idea in a unique way or from a unique angle; avoid trite, hackneyed plots and ideas."

CASSANDRA PRESS, P.O. Box 868, San Rafael CA 94915. (415)382-8507. President: Gurudas. Estab. 1985. Publishes trade paperback originals. Publishes 6 titles/year. Receives 200 submissions/year. 50% of books from first-time authors; 50% from unagented writers. Pays 6-8% maximum royalty on retail price. Advance rarely offered. Publishes book 1 year after acceptance. Accepts simultaneous submissions. Reports in 3 weeks on queries, 3 months on mss. Book catalog and ms guidelines free.
Nonfiction: New Age, how-to, self-help. Subjects include cooking/foods/nutrition, health/medicine (holistic health), philosophy, psychology, religion (New Age), metaphysical. "We like to do around six titles a year in the general New Age, metaphysical and holistic health fields so we continue to look for good material. No children's books." Submit outline and sample chapters. Reviews artwork/photos as part of ms package.
Recent Nonfiction Title: *Treason the New World Order*, by Gurudas (political).
Tips: "Not accepting fiction or children's book submissions."

CATBIRD PRESS, 16 Windsor Rd., North Haven CT 06473-3015. (203)230-2391. E-mail: catbird@pipelin e.com. Publisher: Robert Wechsler. Estab. 1987. Publishes hardcover and trade paperback originals and trade paperback reprints. Publishes 4-5 titles/year. Receives 1,000 submissions/year. 10% of books from first-time authors. 100% from unagented writers. Pays 2½-10% royalty on retail price. Offers $2,000 average advance. Publishes book 1 year after acceptance. Accepts simultaneous submissions, if so noted. Reports in 1 month on queries if SASE is included. *Writer's Market* recommends allowing 2 months for reply. Book catalog free on request. Manuscript guidelines for #10 SASE.
Nonfiction: Humor, reference. "We are looking for up-market prose humor and legal humor books. No joke or other small gift books." Submit outline, sample chapters and SASE.

Recent Nonfiction Title: *Was That a Tax Lawyer Who Just Flew Over*, by Arnold B. Kanter (humor).
Fiction: Humor, literary. "We are looking for well-written literature with a comic vision or style that takes a fresh approach and has a fresh, sophisticated style. No genre, wacky, or derivative mainstream fiction." Submit outline/synopsis, sample chapter and SASE.
Recent Fiction Title: *Human Resources*, by Floyd Kemske (novel).
Tips: "Our audience is generally up-market. If I were a writer trying to market a book today, I would learn about the publishing industry just as a musician learns about night clubs. If you play jazz, you should know the jazz clubs. If you write children's books, you should learn the children's book publishers. Writing is just as much an art and a business as jazz."

CATHOLIC UNIVERSITY OF AMERICA PRESS, 620 Michigan Ave. NE, Washington DC 20064. (202)319-5052. Fax: (202)319-4985. E-mail: mcgonagle@cua.edu. Director: Dr. David J. McGonagle. Estab. 1939. Marketing Manager: Val Poletto. Publishes 15-20 titles/year. Receives 100 submissions/year. 50% of books from first-time authors; 100% from unagented writers. Average print order for a first book is 750. Pays variable royalty on net receipts. Publishes book 1 year after acceptance. Query for electronic submissions. Reports in 3 months. Book catalog for SASE.
Nonfiction: Publishes history, languages and literature, philosophy, religion, church-state relations, political theory. No unrevised doctoral dissertations. Length: 80,000-200,000 words. Query with outline, sample chapter, cv and list of previous publications.
Tips: "Freelancer has best chance of selling us scholarly monographs and works suitable for adoption as supplementary reading material in courses."

CATO INSTITUTE, 1000 Massachusetts Ave. NW, Washington DC 20001. (202)842-0200. Executive Vice President: David Boaz. Director of Special Projects: Tom Palmer. Estab. 1977. Publishes hardcover originals, trade paperback originals and reprints. Publishes 12 titles/year. Receives 50 submissions/year. 25% of books from first-time authors; 90% from unagented writers. Makes outright purchase of $1,000-10,000. Publishes book 9 months after acceptance. Accepts simultaneous submissions. Reports in 3 months. Book catalog free on request.
Nonfiction: Public policy *only*. Subjects include foreign policy, economics, education, government/politics, health/medicine, monetary policy, sociology. "We want books on public policy issues from a free-market or libertarian perspective." Query.

CAVE BOOKS, 756 Harvard Ave., St. Louis MO 63130-3134. (314)862-7646. Editor: Richard Watson. Estab. 1980. Publishes hardcover and trade paperback originals and reprints. Publishes 4 titles/year. Receives 20 queries and 10 mss/year. 75% of books from first-time authors; 100% from unagented writers. Pays 10% royalty on retail price. Publishes book 18 months after acceptance. Accepts simultaneous submissions. Reports in 3 months on mss.
Nonfiction: Biography, technical (science), adventure. Subjects are Americana, animals, anthropology/archaeology, history, nature/environment, photography, recreation, regional, science, sports (cave exploration), travel. "We publish only books on caves, karst, and speleology." Send complete ms. *Writer's Market* recommends sending a query with SASE first. Reviews artwork/photos as part of ms package. Send photocopies.
Recent Nonfiction Title: *The Art of Caving*, by Linda Heslop (drawings).
Fiction: Adventure, historical, literary. "All must be realistic and centrally concerned with cave exploration. No gothic, science fiction, fantasy, romance, mystery, poetry or novels that are not entirely about caves. The cave and action in the cave must be central, authentic, and realistic." Send complete ms.
Tips: "Our readers are interested only in caves, karst, and speleology. Please do not send manuscripts on other subjects. Query with outline and SAE first."

THE CAXTON PRINTERS, LTD., 312 Main St., Caldwell ID 83605-3299. (208)459-7421. Fax: (208)459-7450. President: Gordon Gipson. General Editor: Pam Hardenbrook. Estab. 1907. Publishes hardcover and trade paperback originals. Publishes 6-10 titles/year. Receives 250 submissions/year. 50% of books from first-time authors; 60% from unagented writers. Pays royalty. Offers $500-2,000 advance. Publishes book 18 months after acceptance. Accepts simultaneous submissions. Reports in 3 months. Book catalog for 9×12 SASE.
Nonfiction: Coffee table, Americana, Western Americana. "We need good Western Americana, especially the Northwest, preferably copiously illustrated with unpublished photos." Query. Reviews artwork/photos as part of ms package.
Recent Nonfiction Title: *Lora Webb Nichols*, by Nancy Anderson (historical, Wyoming).
Tips: "Audience includes Westerners, students, historians and researchers."

CCC PUBLICATIONS, 20306 Tau Place, Chatsworth CA 91311. (805)375-7700. Contact: Editorial Director: Cliff Carle. Estab. 1983. Publishes trade paperback and mass market paperback originals. Publishes 25-30 titles/year. Receives 400-600 mss/year. 50% of books from first-time authors; 50% of books from unagented writers. Pays 7-12% royalty on wholesale price. Publishes book 6 months after acceptance. Accepts

simultaneous submissions. Reports in 3 months. Catalog for 10×13 SAE with 2 first-class stamps.
- CCC is looking for short, punchy pieces with *lots* of cartoon illustrations.

Nonfiction: Humorous how-to/self-help. "We are looking for *original, clever* and *current* humor that is not too limited in audience appeal or that will have a limited shelf life. All of our titles are as marketable five years from now as they are today. No rip-offs of previously published books, or too special interest manuscripts." Query or complete manuscript with SASE. Reviews artwork/photos as part of ms package.
Tips: "Humor—we specialize in the subject and have a good reputation with retailers and wholesalers for publishing super-impulse titles. SASE is a must!"

‡CELESTIAL ARTS, Division of Ten Speed Press, P.O. Box 7327, Berkeley CA 94707. (510)559-1600. Managing Editor: Veronica Randall. Publishes hardcover and trade paperback originals and reprints. Publishes 40 titles/year. Receives 500 queries and 200 mss/year. 30% of books from first-time authors; 10% from unagented writers. Pays royalty on wholesale or retail price. No advance. Publishes book 6 months after acceptance of ms. Accepts simultaneous submissions. Reports in 6 weeks on queries, 3 months on proposals and mss. Book catalog and ms guidelines free on request.
Nonfiction: Biography, coffee table book, cookbook, gift book, how-to, illustrated book, reference, self-help. Subjects include animals (care of), art/architecture, child guidance/parenting, cooking/foods/nutrition, education, gay/lesbian, government/politics, health/medicine, music/dance, philosophy, photography, psychology, religion (spirituality), sociology, women's issues/studies. "We are interested in any work that offers useful information, on a unique perspective on a subject." Submit proposal package, including: outline, 1-2 sample chapters, author background and SASE. Reviews artwork/photos as part of ms package. Send photocopies.
Recent Nonfiction Title: *Blessings in Disguise*, by Carolyn Ball, M.A. (spirituality).
Tips: Audience is fairly well-informed, interested in psychology and sociology related topics, open-minded, innovative, forward-thinking. "The most completely thought-out (developed) proposals earn the most consideration."

CENTER PRESS, P.O. Box 16452, Encino CA 91416-6452. Managing Editor: Gabriella Stone. Publishes hardcover and trade paperback originals. Publishes 4-6 titles/year. Receives 600 queries and 300 mss/year. "We are no longer accepting unsolicited manuscripts. Only manuscripts received from agents, direct solicitation and through our sponsored literary contest will be read through 01/01/98." 25% of books from first-time authors. Pays 10-30% royalty on wholesale price or makes outright purchase of $500-5,000. "This depends largely on estimated sales." Offers $200-2,000 advance. Publishes book 10 months after acceptance. Accepts simultaneous submissions. Reports in 3 months on mss. Manuscript guidelines for #10 SASE.
Nonfiction: How-to, humor. Subjects include art/architecture, literature, money/finance, philosophy, photography. "We publish calendars and 'daily minders' that use photographs. We won't consider work which isn't *top* quality." Submit 1 sample chapter (maximum of 20 pages). Reviews artwork/photos as part of ms package. Send 3×5, 5×7 or 8×10 prints.
Fiction: Humor, literary, picture books. "We will soon publish a collection of the winners of the "Masters Literary Award." Submit 1 sample chapter (up to 20 pages). "Will soon be joint venturing for an American version of an eastern European magazine similar to *Vanity Fair* with a tinge of *Playboy*."
Poetry: Contemporary only, *very* professional, nothing saccharine, silly or sloppy. Don't confuse rhyming, metered jingles w/poetry. Submit 4-6 sample poems.
Tips: "Our readers are typically well-educated, tending to urbane, creative, middle income (mostly), eclectic and well-intended. *Read! Read! Read!* Then either have a list of sound publishing credits, or have taken several quality writing workshops from competent professionals."

CENTERSTREAM PUBLICATIONS, P.O. Box 17878, Anaheim Hills CA 92807. (714)779-9390. Owner: Ron Middlebrook. Estab. 1980. Publishes hardcover and mass market paperback originals, trade paperback and mass market paperback reprints. Publishes 12 titles/year. Receives 15 queries and 15 mss/year. 80% of books from first-time authors; 100% from unagented writers. Pays royalty on wholesale price. Publishes book 8 months after acceptance of ms. Accepts simultaneous submissions. Reports in 3 months on queries. Book catalog free on request.
Nonfiction: Currently publishing only music history and music instructional book. *Writer's Market* recommends sending a query with SASE first.
Recent Nonfiction Title: *Making an Archtop Guitar*, by Bob Benadentto.

CHAMPION BOOKS INC., P.O. Box 636, Lemont IL 60439. (800)230-1135. President: Rebecca Rush. Imprint is New Shoes Series. Publishes trade paperback originals. Publishes 5 titles/year. 100% of books from first-time authors; 100% from unagented writers. Pays 8-10% royalty on retail price. Publishes book 5 months after acceptance of ms. Accepts simultaneous submissions. Reports in 4 months on mss. Book catalog and ms guidelines for SASE.
Fiction: Ethnic, feminist, gay/lesbian, literary, poetry, short story collections. Any finished/unfinished fiction works will be considered. *Writer's Market* recommends sending a query with SASE first.

Recent Fiction Title: *Warning This is Not a Book*, by Pete Babones.
Recent Poetry Title: *Simple Shrine*, by Jim Vetter.
Tips: "We are seeking works that apply to or deal with contemporary American Society with an emphasis on counterculture and alternative lifestyles."

‡**CHATHAM PRESS**, Box A, Old Greenwich CT 06870. Fax: (203)531-7755. Contact: Editor. Estab. 1971. Publishes hardcover and paperback originals, reprints and anthologies. Publishes 10 titles/year. Receives 50 submissions annually. 25% of books from first-time authors; 75% from unagented writers. Subsidy publishes mainly poetry or ecological topics (nonauthor) 10% of books. "Standard book contract does not always apply if the book is heavily illustrated. Average advance is low." Publishes book 6 months after acceptance. Reports in 1 month. *Writer's Market* recommends allowing 2 months for reply. Book catalog and ms guidelines for 6×9 SAE with 6 first-class stamps.
  • Due to the current economy this press indicates their need for freelance material has lessened.
Nonfiction: "Publishes mostly regional history and natural history, involving mainly Northeast seaboard to the Carolinas, mostly illustrated, with emphasis on conservation and outdoor recreation." Accepts nonfiction translations from French and German. Query with outline and 3 sample chapters. Reviews artwork/photos as part of ms package.
Tips: "Illustrated New England-relevant titles have the best chance of being sold to our firm. We have a slightly greater (15%) skew towards cooking and travel titles."

CHESS ENTERPRISES, 107 Crosstree Rd., Caraopolis PA 15108-2607. Fax: (412)262-2138. Owner: Bob Dudley. Estab. 1981. Publishes trade paperback originals. Publishes 10 titles/year. Receives 20 queries and 12 mss/year. 10% of books from first-time authors; 100% from unagented writers. No advance. Makes outright purchase of $500-3,000. Publishes book 4 months after acceptance of ms. Accepts simultaneous submissions. Reports in 1 month.
Nonfiction: Game of chess only. Query.
Recent Nonfiction Title: *Learn to Attack with Rudolf Spielman*, by Eric Schiller (collection of chess games).
Tips: "Books are targeted to chess tournament players, book collectors."

CHICAGO REVIEW PRESS, 814 N. Franklin, Chicago IL 60610-3109. Editorial Director: Cynthia Sherry. Estab. 1973. Publishes hardcover and trade paperback originals and trade paperback reprints. Publishes 25 titles/year. Receives 300 queries and 300 manuscripts/year. 30% of books from first-time authors; 50% from unagented writers. Pays 7½-12½% royalty. Offers $1,000 average advance. Publishes book 15 months after acceptance. Accepts simultaneous submissions. Reports in 2 months. Book catalog for 9×12 SAE with 10 first-class stamps. Manuscript guidelines for #10 SASE.
Nonfiction: Children's/juvenile (activity books only), cookbooks (specialty only), how-to, child guidance/parenting/pregnancy, education, gardening (regional), history, hobbies, regional. "We're looking for intelligent nonfiction for educated readers (books for people with special interests in timely subjects). Submit outline and 1-2 sample chapters or proposal package (see our guidelines). Reviews artwork/photos.
Recent Nonfiction Title: *Westward Ho: An Activity Guide to the Wild West*, by Laurie Carlson.
Tips: "Please send for our guidelines and read them carefully."

CHILD WELFARE LEAGUE OF AMERICA, 440 First St. NW, Suite 310, Washington DC 20001. (202)638-2952. Fax: (202)638-4004. Director, Publications: Susan Brite. Publishes hardcover and trade paperback originals. Publishes 10-12 titles/year. Receives 60-100 submissions/year. 95% of books from unagented writers. 50% of books are nonauthor-subsidy published. Pays 0-10% royalty on net domestic sales. Publishes book 1 year after acceptance. Reports on queries in 3 months. Book catalog and ms guidelines free.
Nonfiction: Child welfare. Subjects include child guidance/parenting, sociology. Submit outline and sample chapters.
Recent Nonfiction Title: *That's My Child: Strategies for Parents of Children with Disabilities*, by Lizanne Capper.
Tips: "Our audience is child welfare workers, administrators, agency executives, parents, etc. We also publish training curricula, including videos."

‡**CHILDREN'S PRESS**, Sherman Turnpike, Danbury CT 06813. (203)797-6802. Fax: (203)797-6986. E-mail: eddirector@aol.com. Website: http://www.grolier.com. Publishes nonfiction hardcover originals. Publishes 120-140 titles/year. Not accepting unsolicited mss. No advance. Makes outright purchase for $500-1,000. Publishes book 20 months after acceptance. Book catalog available.
Nonfiction: Children's/juvenile. Subjects include animals, anthropology/archaeology, art/architecture, ethnic, health/medicine, history, hobbies, music/dance, nature/environment, science and sports. "We publish nonfiction books that supplement the elementary school curriculum."
Recent Nonfiction Title: *Duke Ellington*, by Mike Venezia.

CHOSEN BOOKS PUBLISHING CO., LTD., Division of Baker Book House Company, 3985 Bradwater St., Fairfax VA 22031-3702. (703)764-8250. Fax: (703)764-3995. Editor: Jane Campbell. Estab. 1971. Publishes hardcover and trade paperback originals. Publishes 8 titles/year. Receives 600 submissions/year. 15% of books from first-time authors; 99% from unagented writers. Pays royalty on net receipts. Publishes book 2 years after acceptance. Accepts simultaneous submissions. Reports in 3 months. Manuscript guidelines for #10 SASE.

Nonfiction: Expositional books on narrowly focused themes. "We publish books reflecting the current acts of the Holy Spirit in the world, books with a charismatic Christian orientation." No New Age, poetry, fiction, autobiographies, academic or children's books. Submit synopsis, chapter outline, résumé, 2 sample chapters and SASE. No complete mss. No response without SASE.

Recent Nonfiction Title: *Deliverance from Evil Spirits*, by Francis MacNutt (expositional nonfiction).

Tips: "We look for solid, practical advice for the growing and maturing Christian from authors with professional or personal experience platforms. No conversion accounts or chronicling of life events, please. State the topic or theme of your book clearly in your cover letter."

CHRISTIAN PUBLICATIONS, INC., 3825 Hartzdale Dr., Camp Hill PA 17011. (717)761-7044. Interim Managing Editor: David E. Fessenden. Imprints are Christian Publications, Inc., Horizon Books. Publishes hardcover originals and trade paperback originals and reprints. Publishes 48 titles/year (about 50% are reprints of classic authors). Receives 300 queries and 900 mss/year. 25% of books from first-time authors; 80% from unagented writers. Pays variable royalty or makes outright purchase. Publishes book 18 months after acceptance of ms. Accepts simultaneous submissions. Book catalog for 9×12 SAE with 7 first-class stamps. Manuscript guidelines for #10 SASE.

Nonfiction: Biography (missions-related preferred), how-to, reference (reprints *only*), self-help. Subjects include religion (Evangelical Christian perspective). "We are owned by The Christian and Missionary Alliance denomination; while we welcome and publish authors from various denominations, their theological perspective must be compatible with The Christian and Missionary Alliance. We are especially interested in fresh, practical approaches to deeper life—sanctification with running shoes on." Submit proposal package, including chapter synopsis, 2 sample chapters (including chapter 1), audience and market ideas, author bio.

Recent Nonfiction Title: *Lambs on the Ledge*, by Joyce Strong (church life/ministry).

Fiction: "At the present time, we are not accepting unsolicited fiction, poetry or children's books."

Tips: "Take time with your proposal—make it thorough, concise, complete. Authors who have done their homework regarding our message and approach have a much better chance of being accepted."

CHRONICLE BOOKS, Chronicle Publishing Co., 85 Second St., San Francisco CA 94105. (415)777-7240. Fax: (415)777-8887. E-mail: frontdesk@chronbooks.com. Website: http://www.chronbooks.com. Publisher: Jack Jensen. Associate Publishers: Nion McEvoy, Caroline Herter, Victoria Rock. Editor, fiction: Jay Schaefer. Editor, cookbooks: Bill LeBlond. Editor, general: Annie Barrows. Editor, children's: Victoria Rock. Editor, ancillary products: Debra Lande. Editor, multimedia: Nion McEvoy. Editor, gardening: Leslie Jonath. Editor, regional: Karen Silver. Editor, art: Annie Barrows. Publishes hardcover and trade paperback originals. Publishes 200 titles/year. Receives 22,500 submissions/year. 20% of books from first-time authors. 15% from unagented writers. Publishes book 18 months after acceptance. Accepts simultaneous submissions. Reports in 3 months on queries. Book catalog for 11×14 SAE with 5 first-class stamps.

Nonfiction: Coffee table book, cookbook, regional California, architecture, art, design, gardening, gift, health, nature, nostalgia, photography, recreation, travel. Query or submit outline/synopsis with artwork and sample chapters.

Recent Nonfiction Title: *LaParilla: The Mexican Grill*, by Reed Hearon (cookbook).

Fiction: Novels, novellas, short story collections. Submit complete ms and synopsis; do not query.

Recent Fiction Title: *Lies of the Saints*, by Erin McGraw (short story collection).

CHURCH GROWTH INSTITUTE, P.O. Box 7000, Forest VA 24551. (804)525-0022. Fax: (804)525-0608. Director of Resource Development: Cindy Spear. Estab. 1984. Publishes trade paperback originals. Publishes 10 titles/year. Pays 5% royalty on retail price or makes outright purchase. Publishes book 1 year after acceptance of ms. Accepts simultaneous submissions. Reports in 2 months on queries. Resource catalog for 9×12 SAE with 4 first-class stamps. Manuscript guidelines given after query and outline is received.

Nonfiction: How-to, manuals. Subjects include religious education (church-growth related). "Material should originate from a conservative Christian view and cover topics that will help churches grow, through leadership training, new attendance or stewardship programs, and new or unique ministries. Accepted manuscripts will be adapted to our resource packet format. All material must be practical and easy for the *average* Christian to understand." Query or submit outline and brief explanation of what the packet will accomplish in the local church and whether it is leadership or lay-oriented. Reviews artwork/photos as part of ms package. Send photocopies or transparencies.

Recent Nonfiction Title: *Designing a Worship Service to Reach the Unchurched*, by Dr. Glen Martin (resource packet with loose-leaf text and video).

Tips: "We are not publishing many *textbooks*. Concentrate on how-to manuals, video curriculum for small group studies and complete resource packets (planning a campaign, program or ministry, step-by-step agenda, resource list, etc., plus audio- or video-cassettes)."

CIRCLET PRESS INC., P.O. Box 15143, Boston MA 02215-0143. E-mail: circlet-info@circlet.com. Publisher/Editor: Cecilia Tan. Publishes hardcover and trade paperback originals. Publishes 6-10 titles/year. Receives 50-100 queries and 200-300 mss/year. 50% of stories from first-time authors; 90% from unagented writers. Pays 4-12% royalty on retail price or makes outright purchase (depending on rights); also pays in books if author prefers. Publishes stories 1 year after acceptance. Accepts simultaneous submissions. Reports in 1 month on queries, 6 months on mss. Book catalog and ms guidelines for #10 SASE.
  • Circlet Press currently accepts manuscripts between April 15 and August 31. Manuscripts received outside this reading period are held until next reading period.
Fiction: Erotic science fiction and fantasy short stories only. Gay/lesbian stories needed but all persuasions welcome. "Fiction must combine both the erotic and the fantastic. The erotic content needs to be an integral part of a science fiction story, and vice versa. Writers should not assume that any sex is the same as erotica." Submit full short stories up to 10,000 words. *Writer's Market* recommends sending a query with SASE first. Queries only via e-mail.
Recent Fiction Title: *Earthly Pleasures*, by Reed Manning.
Tips: "Our audience is adults who enjoy science fiction and fantasy, especially the works of Anne Rice, Storm Constantine, Samuel Delany, who enjoy vivid storytelling and erotic content. Seize your most vivid fantasy, your deepest dream and set it free onto paper. That is at the heart of all good speculative fiction. Then if it has an erotic theme as well as a science fictional one, send it to me. No horror, rape, death or mutilation! I want to see stories that *celebrate* sex and sexuality in a positive manner. Please write for our guidelines as each year we have a specific list of topics we look for."

CITADEL PRESS, Imprint of Carol Publishing Group, 120 Enterprise, Secaucus NJ 07094. Fax: (201)866-8159. Editorial Director: Allan J. Wilson. Estab. 1945. Other imprints are Lyle Stuart, Birch Lane Press and University Books. Publishes hardcover originals and paperback reprints. Publishes 60-80 titles/year. Receives 800-1,000 submissions/year. 7% of books from first-time authors; 50% from unagented writers. Average print order for a first book is 5,000. Pays 10% royalty on hardcover, 5-7% on paperback. Offers average $7,000 advance. Publishes book 1 year after acceptance. Accepts simultaneous submissions. Reports in 2 months. Book catalog for $1.
  • Citadel Press also publishes books in conjunction with the Learning Annex, a popular adult education and self-improvement school in New York City.
Nonfiction: Biography, film, psychology, humor, history. Also seeks "off-beat material, but no fiction, poetry, religion, politics." Accepts nonfiction translations. Query or submit outline/synopsis and 3 sample chapters. Reviews artwork/photos as part of ms package. Send photocopies with SASE.
Tips: "We concentrate on biography, popular interest, and film, with limited fiction (no romance, religion, poetry, music)."

CLARION BOOKS, Imprint of Houghton Mifflin Company, 215 Park Ave. S., New York NY 10003. Editor/Publisher: Dorothy Briley. Executive Editor: Dinah Stevenson. Senior Editor: Nina Ignatowicz. Estab. 1965. Publishes hardcover originals. Publishes 50 titles/year. Pays 5-10% royalty on retail price. Advances from $4,000. Prefers no multiple submissions. Reports in 2 months. Publishes book 2 years after acceptance. Manuscript guidelines for #10 SASE.
Nonfiction: Americana, biography, history, holiday, humor, nature, photo essays, word play. Prefers books for younger children. Query. Reviews artwork/photos as part of ms package. Send photocopies.
Fiction: Adventure, humor, mystery, strong character studies, suspense. "We would like to see more distinguished short fiction for readers seven to ten." Accepts fiction translations. Send complete ms.
Tips: Looks for "freshness, enthusiasm—in short, life" (fiction and nonfiction).

‡CLARKSON POTTER, Imprint of The Crown Publishing Group, Division of Random House, 201 E. 50th St., New York NY 10022. Editorial Director: Lauren Shakely. Publishes hardcover and trade paperback originals. Publishes 55 titles/year. 15% of books from first-time authors. Reports in 2-3 months on queries and proposals.
Nonfiction: Publishes art/architecture, biography, child guidance/parenting, crafts, cooking and foods, decorating, design gardening, how-to, humor, photography, and popular psychology. Query or submit outline and sample chapter with tearsheets from magazines and artwork copies (e.g.—color photocopies or duplicate transparencies).

CLEAR LIGHT PUBLISHERS, 823 Don Diego, Santa Fe NM 87501-4224. (505)989-9590. E-mail: clpublish@aol.com. Publisher: Harmon Houghton. Estab. 1981. Publishes hardcover and trade paperback originals. Publishes 12 titles/year. Receives 100 queries/year. 10% of books from first-time authors; 50% from unagented writers. Pays 10% royalty on wholesale price. Offers advance: as percent of gross potential.

Publishes book 1 year after acceptance of ms. Accepts simultaneous submissions. Reports in 3 months on queries. Book catalog free on request.

Nonfiction: Biography, coffee table book, cookbook, humor. Subjects include Americana, anthropology/ archaelogy, art/architecture, cooking/foods/nutrition, ethnic, history, nature/environment, philosophy, photography, regional (Southwest). Query with SASE. Reviews artwork/photos as part of ms package. Send photocopies (no originals).

Recent Nonfiction Title: *One Nation Under God*, by Huston Smith (Native American Church).

CLEIS PRESS, P.O. Box 14684, San Francisco CA 94114-0684. Fax: (415)864-3385. Acquisitions Coordinator: Frederique Delacoste. Estab. 1980. Publishes trade paperback originals and reprints. Publishes 12 titles/year. 20% of books are from first-time authors; 75% from unagented writers. Pays variable royalty on retail price. Publishes book 1 year after acceptance. Accepts simultaneous submissions "only if accompanied by an original letter stating where and when ms was sent." Reports in 2 months. Book catalog for #10 SAE with 2 first-class stamps.

Nonfiction: Subjects include feminist, gay/lesbian, queer human rights. "We are interested in books that: will sell in feminist and progressive bookstores, and will sell in Europe (translation rights). We are interested in books by and about women in Latin America; on lesbian and gay rights; on sexuality; and other feminist topics which have not already been widely documented. We do not want religious/spiritual tracts; we are not interested in books on topics which have been documented over and over, unless the author is approaching the topic from a new viewpoint." Query or submit outline and sample chapters.

Recent Nonfiction Title: *The Good Vibrations Guide to Sex*, edited by Anne Semens and Cathy Winks.

Fiction: Feminist, gay/lesbian, literary. "We are looking for high quality fiction by women. We are especially interested in translations of Latin American women's fiction. No romances!" Submit complete ms. *Writer's Market* recommends sending a query with SASE first.

Recent Fiction Title: *Memory Mambo*, a novel by Achy Obejas.

Tips: "If I were trying to market a book today, I would become very familiar with the presses serving my market. More than reading publishers' catalogs, I think an author should spend time in a bookstore whose clientele closely resembles her intended audience; be absolutely aware of her audience; have researched potential market; present fresh new ways of looking at her topic; avoid 'PR' language in query letter."

CLIFFS NOTES, INC., P.O. Box 80728, Lincoln NE 68501. (402)423-5050. General Editor: Michele Spence. Notes Editor: Gary Carey. Studyware Editor: Chrissy Frye. Imprint is Centennial Press. Estab. 1958. Publishes trade paperback originals and educational software. Averages 20 titles/year. 100% of books from unagented writers. Pays royalty on wholesale price. Buys majority of mss outright; "full payment on acceptance of ms." Publishes book 1 year after acceptance. Reports in 1 month. *Writer's Market* recommends allowing 2 months for reply. "We provide specific guidelines when a project is assigned."

Nonfiction: Self-help, textbook. "We publish self-help study aids directed to junior high through graduate school audience. Publications include *Cliffs Notes*, *Cliffs Test Preparation Guides*, *Cliffs Quick Reviews*, *Cliffs StudyWare*, and other study guides. Most authors are experienced teachers, usually with advanced degrees. Some books also appeal to a general lay audience. Query.

Recent Nonfiction Title: Cliffs *Quick Review Chemistry*.

COBBLEHILL BOOKS, Imprint of Dutton Children's Books, 375 Hudson St., New York NY 10014. (212)366-2000. Editorial Director: Joe Ann Daly. Executive Editor: Rosanne Lauer. Pays royalty. Publishes fiction and nonfiction for young readers, middle readers and young adults, and picture books. Query for mss longer than picture book length; submit complete ms for picture books. Reports in 1 month. *Writer's Market* recommends allowing 2 months for reply. Accepts simultaneous submissions, if so noted.

Recent Nonfiction Title: *The Storm*, by Marc Harshman, illustrated by Mark Mohr (picture book).

COFFEE HOUSE PRESS, 27 N. Fourth St., Suite 400, Minneapolis MN 55401. Editorial Assistant: Chris Fischbach. Estab. 1984. Publishes trade paperback originals. Publishes 15 titles/year. Receives 4,500 queries and mss/year. 95% of books are from unagented writers. Pays 8% royalty on retail price. Offers average $750 advance. Publishes book 18 months after acceptance. Reports in 2 months on queries, 6 months on mss. Book catalog and ms guidelines for #10 SAE with 2 first-class stamps.

Fiction: Literary novels, short story collections, and short-short story collections. No genre. Looking for prose by women and writers of color. Query first with samples and SASE.

ALWAYS SUBMIT unsolicited manuscripts or queries with a self-addressed, stamped envelope (SASE) within your country or a self-addressed envelope with International Reply Coupons (IRC) purchased from the post office for other countries.

Recent Fiction Title: *Ex Utero*, by Laurie Foos (novel).
Tips: Look for our books at stores and libraries to get a feel for what we like to publish. Please, no phone calls or faxes.

‡**COLLECTOR BOOKS**, Division of Schroeder Publishing Co., Inc., 5801 Kentucky Dam Rd., P.O. Box 3009, Paducah KY 42002-3009. Editor: Lisa Stroup. Estab. 1974. Publishes hardcover and paperback originals. Publishes 35 titles/year. 50% of books from first-time authors; 100% of books from unagented writers. Average print order for a first book is 5,000-10,000. Pays 5% royalty on retail price. No advance. Publishes book 9 months after acceptance. Reports in 1 month. *Writer's Market* recommends allowing 2 months for reply. Book catalog for 9 × 12 SAE with 4 first-class stamps. Manuscript guidelines for #10 SASE.
Nonfiction: "We *only* publish books on antiques and collectibles. We require our authors to be very knowledgeable in their respective fields and have access to a large representative sampling of the particular subject concerned." Query with outline and 2-3 sample chapters. Reviews artwork/photos as part of ms package.
Tips: "Common mistakes writers make include making phone contact instead of written contact and assuming an accurate market evaluation."

THE COLLEGE BOARD, Imprint of College Entrance Examination Board, 45 Columbus Ave., New York NY 10023-6992. (212)713-8000. Website: http://www.collegeboard.org. Director of Publications: Carolyn Trager. Publishes trade paperback originals. Publishes 30 titles/year; imprint publishes 12 titles/year. Receives 50-60 submissions/year. 25% of books from first-time authors; 50% from unagented writers. Pays royalty on retail price of books sold through bookstores. Offers advance based on anticipated first year's earnings. Publishes book 9 months after acceptance. Reports in 1 month on queries. *Writer's Market* recommends allowing 2 months for reply. Book catalog free on request.
Nonfiction: Education-related how-to, reference, self-help. Subjects include college guidance, education, language/literature, science. "We want books to help students make a successful transition from high school to college." Query or send outline and sample chapters.
Recent Nonfiction Title: *Summer on Campus*, by Shirley Levin (guide to summer college programs).
Tips: "Our audience consists of college-bound high school students, beginning college students and/or their parents."

COMBINED BOOKS, INC., 151 E. Tenth Ave., Conshohocken PA 19428. (610)828-2595. Fax: (610)828-2603. Senior Editor: Kenneth S. Gallagher. Publishes hardcover originals and trade paperback reprints. Publishes 12-14 titles/year. 30% of books from first-time authors; 100% from unagented writers. Pays 8-10% royalty on wholesale price. Offers $1,000-1,500 advance. Publishes book 1 year after acceptance of ms. Reports in 4 months. Book catalog free on request.
Nonfiction: Military history. "We publish a series called Great Campaigns. Authors should be aware of the editorial formula of this series." Submit outline, 1 sample chapter and SASE. Reviews artwork/photos as part of ms package. Send photocopies only.
Recent Nonfiction Title: *Gettysburg July 1*, by David G. Martin (trade military).

COMIC ART PUBLISHING CO., Imprint of Adventure Feature Syndicate, 329 Harvey Dr., Glendale CA 91206. (818)551-0077. Editor: Jo Bustamante. Publishes trade paperback originals and reprints. Publishes 6 titles/year. Receives 200 queries and 100 mss/year. 100% of books from first-time authors; 100% from unagented writers. Pays 30% royalty. Offers $1,500 advance. Publishes books 6 months after acceptance of ms. Accepts simultaneous submissions. Reports in 2 months on queries. Book catalog for #10 SASE. Guidelines for $2 and 2 first-class stamps.
Nonfiction: Children's/juvenile, how-to, illustrated book, textbook, art. Subjects include education, hobbies. Query. Reviews artwork/photos as part of ms package. Send photocopies.
Fiction: Adventure, fantasy, mystery, suspense, western. Submit synopsis and sample chapters.

COMMUNE-A-KEY PUBLISHING, P.O. Box 58637, Salt Lake City UT 84158. (801)581-9191. Fax: (801)581-9196). E-mail: cakpublish@aol.com. Editor-in-Chief: Caryn Summers. Publishes trade paperback originals and reprints and audiotapes. Publishes 4-6 titles/year. 40% of books from first-time authors; 75% from unagented writers. Pays 7-8% royalty on retail price. Publishes book 1 year after acceptance of ms. Accepts simultaneous submissions. Reports in 1 month on queries and proposals, 2 months on mss. Book catalog and ms guidelines free on request.
Nonfiction: Gift book/inspirational, humor, self-help/psychology, spiritual. Subjects include health/medicine, psychology, men's or women's issues/studies, recovery, Native American. "Commune-A-Key's mission statement is: 'Communicating Keys to Growth and Empowerment.' " Query. Reviews artwork/photos as part of ms package. Send photocopies.

‡**COMPANION PRESS**, P.O. Box 2575, Laguna Hills CA 92654. Publisher: Steve Stewart. Publishes trade paperback originals. Publishes 6 titles/year. Receives 50 queries and 25 mss/year. 50% of books from first-time authors; 100% from unagented writers. Pays 7-9% royalty on retail price or makes outright purchase. Offers $500-1,000 advance. Publishes book 6 months after acceptance of ms. Reports in 1 month. *Writer's*

Market recommends allowing 2 months for reply. Book catalog and manuscript guidelines for #10 SASE.
Nonfiction: Movie and video guides. "We are interested in cinema books written for the general reader, rather than the academic. Categories, adult, bisexuality, erotic, fetishes, homosexuality, nudity and sex in the movies." Query. Reviews artwork/photos as part of ms package. Send photocopies.
Recent Nonfiction Title: *Gay Hollywood Film & Video Guide*, by Steve Stewart (cinema).

COMPUTER SCIENCE PRESS, Imprint of W.H. Freeman and Company, 41 Madison Ave., New York NY 10010. (212)576-9451. Fax: (212)689-2383. E-mail: rjbonacci@whfreeman.com. Website: http://www.whfreeman.com. Publisher: Richard T. Bonacci. Estab. 1974. Publishes hardcover and paperback originals. Publishes 5 titles/year. 25% of books from first-time authors; 98% of books from unagented writers. All authors are recognized subject area experts. Pays royalty on net price. Publishes book 6-9 months after acceptance. Reports ASAP.
Nonfiction: "Technical books in all aspects of computer science, computer engineering, information systems and telecommunications. Primarily textbooks. Also considers public appeal 'trade' books in computer science, manuscripts and diskettes." Query or submit sample chapters of ms. Looks for "technical accuracy of the material and an explanation of why this approach was taken. We would also like a covering letter stating what the author sees as the competition for this work and why this work is superior or an improvement on previous available material."
Recent Nonfiction Title: *Programming Visual Basic*, by Gersting (textbook).
Tips: "We are looking for more trade titles on technology's effect on society, politics or business."

CONARI PRESS, 2550 Ninth St., Suite 101, Berkeley CA 94710. (510)649-7175. Website: http://www.conan.com. Executive Editor: Mary Jane Ryan. Editorial Associate: Claudia Schaab. Estab. 1987. Publishes hardcover and trade paperback originals. Publishes 23 titles/year. Receives 1,000 submissions/year. 50% of books from first-time authors; 50% from unagented writers. Pays 8-12% royalty on list price. Offers $1,500 average advance. Publishes book 1 year after acceptance. Accepts simultaneous submissions. Reports in 3 months. Manuscript guidelines for #10 SASE.
Nonfiction: Psychology, spirituality, women's issues. Submit outline and sample chapters, attn: Claudia Schaab. Reviews artwork/photos as part of ms package.
Recent Nonfiction Title: *House as a Mirror of Self*, by Clare Cooper Marcus.
Tips: "Writers should send us well-targeted, specific and focused manuscripts. No recovery issues."

CONCORDIA PUBLISHING HOUSE, 3558 S. Jefferson Ave., St. Louis MO 63118-3968. (314)268-1000. Fax: (314)268-1329. Family and Children's Editor: Ruth Geisler. Church Resources Director: Barry Bobb. Editorial Associate: Doris M. Schraer. Estab. 1869. Publishes hardcover and trade paperback originals. Publishes 60 titles/year. Receives 2,000 submissions/year. 10% of books from first-time authors; 95% from unagented writers. Pays royalty or makes outright purchase. Publishes book 1 year after acceptance. Simultaneous submissions discouraged. Reports in 2 months on queries. Manuscript guidelines for #10 SASE.
Nonfiction: Juvenile, adult. Subjects include child guidance/parenting (in Christian context), inspirational, how-to, religion. "We publish Protestant, inspirational, theological, family and juveniles. All manuscripts must conform to the doctrinal tenets of The Lutheran Church—Missouri Synod." *Writer's Market* recommends sending a query with SASE first.
Recent Nonfiction Title: *Real Men Pray*, by Tom Couser (devotional for men).
Fiction: Juvenile. "We will consider preteen and children's fiction and picture books. All books must contain Christian content. No adult Christian fiction." *Writer's Market* recommends sending a query with SASE first.
Recent Fiction Title: *The Disappearing Card Trick*, by Vicki Berger Erwin.
Tips: "Our needs have broadened to include writers of books for lay adult Christians and of Christian novels (low-key, soft-sell) for pre-teens and teenagers."

CONFLUENCE PRESS, INC., Lewis-Clark State College, 500 Eighth Ave., Lewiston ID 83501-1698. (208)799-2336. Fax: (208)799-2324. Publisher/Director: James R. Hepworth. Publishes hardcover originals and trade paperback originals and reprints. Publishes 4-5 titles/year. Receives 500 queries and 150 mss/year. 50% of books from first-time authors; 50% from unagented writers. Pays 10-15% royalty on net sales price. Offers $100-2,000 advance. Publishes book 18 months after acceptance of ms. Accepts simultaneous submissions. Reports in 2 months on queries, 1 month on proposals, 3 months on mss. Book catalog and ms guidelines free on request.
Nonfiction: Reference, bibliographies. Subjects include Americana, ethnic, history, language/literature, nature/environment, regional, translation. Query.
Recent Nonfiction Title: *River of Life, Channel of Death: Fish and Dams on the Lower Snake*, by Keith C. Petersen.
Fiction: Ethnic, literary, mainstream/contemporary, short story collections. Query.
Recent Fiction Title: *Cheerleaders From Gomorrah*, by John Rember.
Poetry: Submit 6 sample poems.
Recent Poetry Title: *Even in Quiet Places*, by William Stafford.

THE CONSULTANT PRESS, 163 Amsterdam Ave., #201, New York NY 10023-5001. (212)838-8640. Fax: (212)873-7065. Publisher: Bob Persky. Imprint is The Photographic Arts Center. Estab. 1980. Publishes trade paperback originals. Publishes 7 titles/year. Receives 25 submissions/year. 20% of books from first-time authors; 75% from unagented writers. Pays 7-12% royalty on receipts. Offers $500 average advance. Publishes book 6 months after acceptance. Reports in 3 weeks. *Writer's Market* recommends allowing 2 months for reply. Book catalog free.

Nonfiction: How-to, reference, art/architecture, business and economics of the art world and photography. "Our prime areas of interest are books on the business of art and photography. Writers should check *Books In Print* for competing titles." Submit outline and 2 sample chapters.

Recent Nonfiction Title: *Creating Effective Advertising Using Semiotics*, by Mihal Nadin.

Tips: "Artists, photographers, galleries, museums, curators and art consultants are our audience."

‡CONSUMER PRESS, 13326 SW 28 St., Suite 102, Ft. Lauderdale FL 33330. Editorial Director: Joseph Pappas. Imprint is Women's Publications. Publishes trade paperback originals. Publishes 2-5 titles/year. Receives 500 queries and 250 mss/year. 50% of books from first-time authors; 70% from unagented writers. Pays royalty on wholesale price or on retail price, as per agreement. Publishes book 6 months after acceptance of ms. Accepts simultaneous submissions. Book catalog free on request.

Nonfiction: How-to, self-help. Subjects include child guidance/parenting, health/medicine, money/finance, women's issues/studies. Query with outline, 3 sample chapters and SASE. Reviews artwork/photos as part of ms package. Send photocopies.

Recent Nonfiction Title: *The Ritalin Free Child*, by Diana Hunter.

CONSUMER REPORTS BOOKS, Subsidiary of Consumers Union, 101 Truman Ave., Yonkers NY 10703-1057. Fax: (914)378-2904. Contact: Mark Hoffman. Estab. 1936. Publishes hardcover and trade paperback originals and reprints. Publishes 15-20 titles/year. Receives 500 submissions/year. Pays variable royalty on retail price or makes outright purchase. Publishes book 18 months after acceptance. Accepts simultaneous submissions. Reports in 1 month on queries, 2 months on mss. Book catalog free on request.

Nonfiction: How-to, reference, self-help, automotive. Subjects include health and medicine, automotive, consumer guidance, home owners reference, money and finance. Submit outline/synopsis and 1-2 sample chapters.

Recent Nonfiction Title: *Investing on Your Own*, by Deborah Rankin (personal finance).

CONTEMPORARY BOOKS, INC., Two Prudential Plaza, Suite 1200, Chicago IL 60601. (312)540-4500. Fax: (312)540-4657. Editorial Director: Nancy J. Crossman. Estab. 1947. Publishes hardcover originals and trade paperback originals and reprints. Publishes 75 titles/year. Receives 2,500 submissions/year. 10% of books from first-time authors; 25% of books from unagented writers. Pays 6-15% royalty on retail price. Publishes book 10 months after acceptance. Accepts simultaneous submissions. Reports in 2 months. Manuscript guidelines for SASE.

Nonfiction: Biography, cookbook, how-to, humor, reference, self-help. Subjects include business, finance, cooking, health/fitness, psychology, sports, real estate, nutrition, popular culture, women's studies. Submit outline, sample chapters and SASE. Reviews artwork/photos as part of ms package.

Recent Nonfiction Title: *Golf Shorts*, by Glenn Liebman (quotation book).

COPPER CANYON PRESS, P.O. Box 271, Port Townsend WA 98368. (360)385-4925. Editor: Sam Hamill. Publishes trade paperback originals and occasional clothbound editions. Publishes 8 titles/year. Receives 1,500 queries/year and 500 mss/year. 10% of books from first-time authors; 95% from unagented writers. Pays 7-10% royalty on retail price. Publishes book 18 months after acceptance of ms. Reports in 1 month. Book catalog and ms guidelines free on request.

Poetry: Query with 5-7 sample poems.

Recent Poetry Titles: *Collected Poems*, by Hayden Carruth.

CORNELL MARITIME PRESS, INC., P.O. Box 456, Centreville MD 21617-0456. (410)758-1075. Fax: (410)758-6849. Managing Editor: Charlotte Kurst. Estab. 1938. Publishes hardcover originals and quality paperbacks for professional mariners and yachtsmen. Publishes 7-9 titles/year. Receives 150 submissions/year. 41% of books from first-time authors; 99% from unagented writers. "Payment is negotiable but royalties do not exceed 10% for first 5,000 copies, 12½% for second 5,000 copies, 15% on all additional. Royalties for original paperbacks are invariably lower. Revised editions revert to original royalty schedule." Publishes book 1 year after acceptance. Query first, with writing samples and outlines of book ideas. Reports in 2 months. Book catalog for 10×13 SAE with 5 first-class stamps.

Nonfiction: Marine subjects (highly technical), manuals, how-to books on maritime subjects. Tidewater imprint publishes books on regional history, folklore and wildlife of the Chesapeake Bay and the Delmarva Peninsula.

Recent Nonfiction Title: *U.S. Regulation of Ocean Transportation*, by Gerald Ullman..

CORWIN PRESS, INC., 2455 Teller Rd., Thousand Oaks CA 91320. (805)499-9734. Editor: Ann McMartin. Publishes hardcover and paperback originals. Publishes 70 titles/year. Pays 10% royalty on net sales.

Publishes book 7 months after acceptance of ms. Reports on queries in 1 month. *Writer's Market* recommends allowing 2 months for reply. Manuscript guidelines for #10 SASE.

Nonfiction: Professional-level publications for administrators, teachers, school specialists, policymakers, researchers and others involved with K-12 education. Seeking leading-edge books that offer fresh insights, conclusions and recommendations for action. Prefer user-friendly, authored books that are theory or research based and that provide real-world examples and practical, hands-on strategies to help busy educators be successful. No textbooks that simply summarize existing knowledge or mass-market books. Query.

COTTONWOOD PRESS, INC., 305 W. Magnolia, Suite 398, Fort Collins CO 80521. Editor: Cheryl Thurston. Publishes trade paperback originals. Publishes 2-8 titles/year. Receives 50 queries and 400 mss/year. 50% of books from first-time authors; 100% from unagented writers. Pays 10-12% royalty on net sales. Publishes book 1 year after acceptance. Accepts simultaneous submissions, if so noted. Reports in 1 month on queries and proposals, 3 months on mss. Book catalog for 6×9 SAE with 2 first-class stamps. Manuscript guidelines for #10 SASE.

Nonfiction: Textbook. Subjects include education, language/literature. "We publish *only* supplemental textbooks for English/language arts teachers, grades 5-12, with an emphasis upon middle school and junior high materials. Don't assume we publish educational materials for all subject areas. We do not. Never submit anything to us before looking at our catalog. We have a very narrow focus and a distinctive style. Writers who don't understand that are wasting their time." Query with outline and 1-3 sample chapters.

Recent Nonfiction Title: *Hot Fudge Monday—Tasty Ways to Teach Parts of Speech to Students Who Have a Hard Time Swallowing Anything to Do With Grammar*, by Randy Larson (resource book for teachers).

‡COUNTERPOINT, 1627 I St. NW, Suite 850, Washington DC 20006. Fax: (202)887-0562. Editor-in-Chief: Jack Shoemaker. Publishes hardcover and trade paperback originals and reprints. Publishes 20-25 titles/year. Receives 10 queries/week, 250 mss/year. 2% of books from first-time authors; 2% from unagented writers. Pays 7.5-15% royalty on retail price. Publishes book 18 months after acceptance of ms. Accepts simultaneous submissions. Reports in 2 months.

Nonfiction: Biography, coffee table book, gift book. Subjects include agriculture/horticulture, art/architecture, history, language/literature, nature/environment, philosophy, religion, science, translation. Agented submissions only. Reviews artwork/photos as part of ms package. Send photocopies.

Recent Nonfiction Title: *Tube: The Invention of Television*, by David E. Fisher and Marshall John Fisher (history of science).

Fiction: Historical, humor, literary, mainstream/contemporary, religious, short story collections. Agented submissions only.

Recent Fiction Title: *Women in Their Beds*, by Gina Berriault (short stories).

COUNTRYSPORT PRESS, 1515 Cass, P.O. Box 1856, Traverse City MI 49685. Editorial Director: Art DeLaurier Jr.. Publishes hardcover originals and reprints. Publishes 12 titles/year. 20% of books from first-time authors; 90% from unagented writers. Pays royalty on wholesale price. Advance varies by title. Publishes book 1 year after acceptance of ms. Accepts simultaneous submissions. Reports in 1 month on queries; 3 months on proposals and mss. Book catalog free.

Nonfiction: Coffee table book, illustrated book, other. Subjects include animals, hobbies, nature/environment, wingshooting, fly fishing, outdoor-related subjects. "We are looking for high-quality writing that is often reflective, anecdotal, and that offers a complete picture of an outdoor experience. Less interested in how-to." Query with outline and 3 sample chapters.

Recent Nonfiction Title: *Field Days*, by Charley Waterman (outdoor stories).

Tips: "Our audience is upscale sportsmen with interests in wingshooting, fly fishing, and other outdoor activities."

CRAFTSMAN BOOK COMPANY, 6058 Corte Del Cedro, Carlsbad CA 92009-9974. (619)438-7828 or (800)829-8123. Fax: (619)438-0398. Website: http://www.win.net/~contractor. Editorial Manager: Laurence D. Jacobs. Estab. 1957. Publishes paperback originals. Publishes 12 titles/year. Receives 50 submissions/year. 85% of books from first-time authors; 98% from unagented writers. Pays 7½-12½% royalty on wholesale price or retail price. Publishes book 18 months after acceptance. Accepts simultaneous submissions. Reports in 1 month on queries. *Writer's Market* recommends allowing 2 months for reply. Book catalog and ms guidelines free.

Nonfiction: How-to, technical. All titles are related to construction for professional builders. Query. Reviews artwork/photos as part of ms package.

Recent Nonfiction Title: *Professional Kitchen Design*, by Murray Shaw (how-to manual).

Tips: "The book should be loaded with step-by-step instructions, illustrations, charts, reference data, forms, samples, cost estimates, rules of thumb, and examples that solve actual problems in the builder's office and in the field. The book must cover the subject completely, become the owner's primary reference on the subject, have a high utility-to-cost ratio, and help the owner make a better living in his chosen field."

CREATION HOUSE, Strang Communications, 600 Rinehart Rd., Lake Mary FL 32746. (407)333-3132. Contact: Submissions Coordinator. Publishes hardcover and trade paperback originals. Publishes 18 titles/year. Receives 100 queries and 600 mss/year. 2% of books from first-time authors; 95% from unagented writers. Pays 5-20% royalty on wholesale price. Offers $500-3,000 advance. Publishes book 9 months after acceptance of ms. Accepts simultaneous submissions. Reports in 2 months on proposals. Manuscript guidelines for #10 SASE.
Nonfiction: Christian. "Our target market is Pentecostal/charismatic Christians." Submit outline, 3 sample chapters and author bio. Reviews artwork/photos as part of ms package. Send photocopies.
Recent Nonfiction Title: *The Father's Blessing*, by John Arnott.

‡**CREATIVE BOOK COMPANY**, 13920 Roscoe Blvd., Panorama City CA 91402-4213. (818)893-3565. Fax: (818)894-5282. President: Sol H. Marshall. Imprints are Edinburgh Castle Books, Ranchito del Sol Publications. Publishes trade and mass market paperback originals. Publishes 4-6 titles/year. 100% of books from first-time authors; 100% from unagented writers. Pays $100-500. Publishes book 8 months after acceptance of ms. Accepts simultaneous submissions. Reports in 2 months. Book catalog and ms guidelines for 9 × 12 SAE with 3 first-class stamps.
Nonfiction: Cookbooks, humor, Jewish interest. Subjects include Judaism, gerontology, public relations. "Writers should know accepted procedures for submitting queries or proposals." Query with SASE. Reviews artwork/photos as part of ms package. Send photocopies.
Recent Nonfiction Title: *Recipes in Rhyme*, by Sol H. Marshall (cookbook).
Tips: Audience is beginning writers, publicists, cookbook collectors, gerontologists, educators and others interested in Judaica.

CREATIVE PUBLISHING CO., The Early West, Box 9292, College Station TX 77842-0292. (409)775-6047. Fax: (409)764-7758. Contact: Theresa Earle. Estab. 1978. Publishes hardcover originals. Receives 20-40 submissions/year. 50% of books from first-time authors; 100% from unagented writers. Royalty varies on wholesale price. Publishes book 8 months after acceptance. *Writer's Market* recommends allowing 2 months for reply. Free book catalog.
Nonfiction: Biography. Subjects include Americana (western), history. No mss other than 19th century Western America. Query. Reviews artwork/photos as part of ms package.
Recent Nonfiction Title: *Goodbye Billy the Kid*, by Harold Edwards.

CROSS CULTURAL PUBLICATIONS, INC., P.O. Box 506, Notre Dame IN 46556. Fax: (219)273-5973. General Editor: Cyriac Pullapilly. Publishes hardcover and software originals. Publishes 15-20 titles/year. Receives 3,000 queries and 1,000 mss/year. 25% of books from first-time authors; 99% from unagented writers. Pays 10% royalty on wholesale price. Publishes book 6 months after acceptance of ms. Accepts simultaneous submissions. Reports in 1 month on queries. *Writer's Market* recommends allowing 2 months for reply. Book catalog free on request.
Nonfiction: Biography. Subjects include government/politics, history, philosophy, religion, sociology, scholarly. "We publish scholarly books that deal with intercultural topics—regardless of discipline. Books pushing into new horizons are welcome, but they have to be intellually sound and balanced in judgement." Query.
Recent Nonfiction Title: *Mysteries of Purity*, by Ibn Al-Arabis Asrar, translated by Eric Winkel (religion).

THE CROSSING PRESS, 97 Hangar Way, Watsonville CA 95019. Publisher: Elaine Goldman Gill. Editor: Linda Gunnarson. Publishes hardcover and trade paperback originals. Publishes 50 titles/year. Receives 1,600 submissions/year. 10% of books from first-time authors; 75% from unagented writers. Pays royalty. Publishes book 18 months after acceptance. Accepts simultaneous submissions. Reports in 2 months on queries. Book catalog free.
Nonfiction: Cookbook, women's interest. Subjects include alternative health, New Age (astrology, magic, psychic healing, spiritual growth), gender issues, gay and lesbian, extended family and community. Submit outline and sample chapter.
Recent Nonfiction Title: *Sacrificing Our Selves for Love*, by Jane Hyman and Esther Rome.
Tips: "Simple intelligent query letters do best. No come-ons, no cutes. It helps if there are credentials. Authors should research the press first to see what sort of books it publishes."

CROSSWAY BOOKS, Division of Good News Publishers, 1300 Crescent St., Wheaton IL 60187-5800. Fax: (708)682-4785. Vice President, Editorial and Editor-in-Chief: Leonard G. Goss. Contact: Jill Carter. Estab. 1938. Publishes hardcover and trade paperback originals. Publishes 50 titles/year. Receives 3,000 submissions/year. 5% of books from first-time authors; 75% from unagented writers. Average print order for a first book is 5,000-10,000. Pays negotiable royalty. Offers negotiable advance. Publishes book 1 year after acceptance. No phone queries. Reports in up to 9 months. Book catalog and ms guidelines for 9 × 12 SAE with 6 first-class stamps.
Nonfiction: "Books that provide fresh understanding and a distinctively Christian examination of questions confronting Christians and non-Christians in their personal lives, families, churches, communities and the wider culture. The main types include: (1) Issues books that typically address critical issues facing Christians

today; (2) Books on the deeper Christian life that provide a deeper understanding of Christianity and its application to daily life; and, (3) Christian academic and professional books directed at an audience of religious professionals." *Writer's Market* recommends sending a query with SASE first.

Recent Nonfiction Title: *No More Excuses*, by Tony Evans.

Fiction: "We publish fiction that falls into these categories: (1) Christian realism, or novels set in modern, true-to-life settings as a means of telling stories about Christians today in an increasingly post-Christian era; (2) Supernatural fiction, or stories typically set in the "real world" but that bring supernatural reality into it in a way that heightens our spiritual dimension; (3) Historical fiction, using historical characters, times and places of interest as a mirror for our own times; (4) Some genre-technique fiction (mystery, western); and (5) Children's fiction." *Writer's Market* recommends sending a query with SASE first.

Recent Fiction Title: *Fated Genes*, by Harry Lee Kraus.

Tips: "We are not interested in romance novels, horror novels, biblical novels (i.e., stories set in Bible times that fictionalize events in the lives of prominent biblical characters), issues novels (i.e., fictionalized treatments of contemporary issues), and end times/prophecy novels."

CROWN PUBLISHING GROUP, Division of Random House, 201 E. 50th St., New York NY 10022. General interest publisher of hardcover and trade paperback originals. Publishes 277 titles. Imprints include Bell Tower, Clarkson Potter, Crown Arts & Letters, Harmony Books, Living Language, Prince Paperbacks, Carol Southern Books. *Writer's Market* recommends sending a query with SASE first. *Writer's Market* recommends allowing 2 months for reply.

‡CURRENT CLINICAL STRATEGIES PUBLISHING, 27071 Cabot Rd., Suite 126, Laguna Hills CA 92653. Editor: Camille Chan. Publishes trade paperback originals. Publishes 20 titles/year. Receives 10 queries and 10 mss/year. 90% of books from first-time authors; 90% from unagented writers. Pays royalty. Publishes book 6 months after acceptance of ms. Accepts simultaneous submissions. Book catalog and ms guidelines free on request.

Nonfiction: Technical. Subjects include health/medicine. Submit 4 sample chapters. Reviews artwork/photos as part of ms package. Send photocopies.

Recent Nonfiction Title: *Current Clinical Strategies, Gynecology and Obstetrics, 3rd ed.*, by Paul D. Chan and Christopher R. Winkle (medical reference).

CYPRESS PUBLISHING GROUP, 11835 ROE #187, Leawood KS 66211. (913)681-9875. Vice President Marketing: Carl Heintz. Publishes hardcover and trade paperback originals. Publishes 10 titles/year. 80% of books from first-time authors; 90% from unagented writers. Pays 10-15% royalty on wholesale price. Publishes book 8 months after acceptance of ms. Reports in 2 weeks on queries, 1 month on proposals and mss. *Writer's Market* recommends allowing 2 months for reply. Book catalog free on request. Manuscript guidelines for #10 SASE.

Nonfiction: How-to, illustrated book, self-help, technical, textbook. Subjects include business and economics, computers and electronics (business related), hobbies (amateur radio, antique radio), money/finance, psychology (business related), software (business related). "We use America Online and CompuServe extensively. Our editorial plans change—we are always looking for outstanding submissions. Many writers fail to consider what other books on the topics are available. The writer must think about the fundamental book marketing question: Why will a customer *buy* the book?" Query with proposal package, including outline, 1-3 sample chapters, overview of book. Send photocopies.

Recent Nonfiction Title: *The Edison Effect*, by Ron Ploof (adapting to technological change).

DANCE HORIZONS, Imprint of Princeton Book Co., Publishers, P.O. Box 57, 12 W. Delaware Ave., Pennington NJ 08534. (609)737-8177. Fax: (609)737-1869. Publicity Manager: Frank Bridges. Estab. 1976. Publishes hardcover and paperback originals, paperback reprints. Publishes 10 titles/year. Receives 25-30 submissions/year. 50% of books from first-time authors; 98% of books from unagented writers. Pays 10% royalty on net receipts. No advance. Publishes book 10 months after acceptance. Accepts simultaneous submissions. Reports in 3 months. Book catalog free.

Nonfiction: Dance and children's movement subjects only. *Writer's Market* recommends sending a query with SASE first.

Recent Nonfiction Title: *Inside Tap*, by Anita Feldman (tap dancing instruction).

Tips: "We're very careful about the projects we take on. They have to be, at the outset, polished, original and cross-marketable."

DANCING JESTER PRESS, 3411 Garth Rd., Suite 208, Baytown TX 77521. (713)427-9560. E-mail: djpress@aol.com. Publisher/Editor: Glenda Daniel. Dancing Dagger Publications (Dan L. Gilbert, mystery); Dancing Jester Poetry (Dorothy Lawson, poetry editor); Dancing Jester Fiction (Shiloh Daniel, fiction). Publishes hardcover and trade paperback originals and reprints. Publishes 16 titles/year. Imprints publish 4 titles/year. 15% of books from first-time authors; 100% from unagented writers. Pays 4-12% royalty on retail price or makes outright purchase. No advance. Publishes book 18 months after acceptance of ms. Accepts

simultaneous submissions. Reports in 3 months on proposals, 6 months on mss. Book catalog for $2. Manuscript guidelines for #10 SASE and $1.
* Dancing Jester Press also sponsors the "One Night in Paris Should Be Enough" prize. See the Contests and Awards section for more information.

Nonfiction: Autobiography, children's/juvenile, coffee table book, cookbook, how-to, humor, illustrated book, multimedia (CD-ROM), reference, self-help, textbook. Subjects include animals (rights), anthropology/archaeology, art/architecture, cooking/foods/nutrition (vegan/low-fat only), ethnic, lesbian, government/politics, health/medicine, history (of censorship), language/literature/criticism/theory, music/dance, nature/environment, philosophy, photography, psychology, recreation, religion, science, sociology, software, translation, women's issues/studies. Query with outline and SASE. Reviews artwork/photos as part of ms package. Send photocopies or transparencies.

Recent Nonfiction Title: *Low-fat Back Packing*, by Alex Roman (low-fat vegan cookbook).

Fiction: Adventure, erotica, ethnic, experimental, feminist, gay/lesbian, historical, humor, juvenile, literary, mainstream/contemporary, mystery, picture books, plays, short story collections, suspense, western, young adult. For children's mystery imprint we will consider 100-page manuscripts of books easily expandable into series." Query with synopsis, 3 sample chapters and SASE.

Recent Fiction Title: *Twin Blue Slipper Mystery of Swan Lake*, by Lillian Cagle (children's mystery series).

Poetry: "If you wake up one day and realize you can write like a 1990's Robinson Jeffers—"Vultures", contact me immediately. We can do business. Submit complete ms, e-mail address for a prompt response. *Writer's Market* recommends sending a query with SASE first.

Recent Poetry Title: *Sex Lives of Animals*, by Jason Love (annotated limericks).

Tips: "In order to book together a gestalt of common purpose must form. For the Dancing Jester Press such an enterprise must be grounded upon understanding, cooperation and tolerance. I envision an audience tolerant enough to consider diverse viewpoints by listening to the symphony of human voices: quartets, trios, duets and solos."

DANTE UNIVERSITY OF AMERICA PRESS, INC., P.O. Box 843, Brookline Village MA 02147-0843. Fax: (617)734-2046. E-mail: danteu@usa1.com. Website: http://www1.usa1.com/~danteu/. President: Adolph Caso. Estab. 1975. Publishes hardcover and trade paperback originals and reprints. Publishes 5 titles/year. Receives 50 submissions/year. 50% of books from first-time authors; 50% from unagented writers. Average print order for a first book is 3,000. Pays royalty. Negotiable advance. Publishes book 10 months after acceptance. Query with SASE. Reports in 2 months.

Nonfiction: Biography, reference, reprints, translations from Italian and Latin. Subjects include general scholarly nonfiction, Renaissance thought and letter, Italian language and linguistics, Italian-American history and culture, bilingual education. Query first with SASE. Reviews artwork/photos as part of ms package.

Fiction: Translations from Italian and Latin. Query first with SASE.

Recent Fiction Title: *Rogue Angel*, by Carol Damioli.

Poetry: "There is a chance that we would use Renaissance poetry translations."

Recent Poetry Title: *Italian Poetry 1950-1990*.

‡**DARLINGTON PRODUCTIONS, INC.**, P.O. Box 5884, Darlington MD 21034. (410)457-5400. President: Jeffrey D. McKaughan. Publishes hardcover originals, trade paperback originals and reprints. Publishes 9 titles/year. Receives 20 queries/year. 75% of books published are from first-time writers; 100% from unagented writers. Pays 10% royalty on retail price and small bulk fee at time of release. No advance. Publishes book 6 months after acceptance. Accepts simultaneous submissions. Reports in 1 month on queries and proposals, 3 months on mss. Book catalog and ms guidelines free on request.

Nonfiction: Illustrated book, reference, technical. Subjects include: history, hobbies, military/war. Query with outline. Reviews artwork/photos as part of ms package. Send photocopies.

Recent Nonfiction Title: *Tech Intell*, Vols. 1 and 2, compiled by J. McKaughan (military history).

‡**DATABOOKS**, Subsidiary of Rainbow New England Corp., 335 Chandler St., Worcester MA 01602. (508)756-7644. Fax: (508)756-9425. E-mail: databooks@delphi.com. Publisher: Lawrence J. Abramoff. Publishes hardcover and trade paperback originals and reprints. Publishes 12-15 titles/year. Receives 200 queries and 50 mss/year. 50% of books from first-time authors; 70% from unagented writers. Pays royalty on retail price or makes outright purchase. Publishes book 1 year after acceptance of ms. Accepts simultaneous submissions. Reports in 1 month. *Writer's Market* recommends allowing 2 months for reply. Book catalog and manuscript guidelines free on request.

Nonfiction: Biography, cookbook, gift book, how-to, illustrated book, reference, self-help, technical. Subjects include Americana, cooking/foods/nutrition, history, military/war, recreation, regional, science, sports, travel. Submit outline, 1-3 sample chapters and SASE. Reviews artwork/photos as part of ms package. Send photocopies.

Recent Nonfiction Title: *More Once Told Tales*, by Albert Southwick (regional history).

Fiction: Historical.

MAY DAVENPORT, PUBLISHERS, 26313 Purissima Rd., Los Altos Hills CA 94022. (415)948-6499. Editor/Publisher: May Davenport. Estab. 1976. Imprint is md Books (nonfiction and fiction). Publishes hardcover and trade paperback originals. Publishes 4 titles/year. Receives 1,500 submissions/year. 95% of books from first-time authors; 100% from unagented writers. Pays 15% royalty on retail price. No advance. Publishes book 1 year after acceptance. Reports in 1 month. *Writer's Market* recommends allowing 2 months for reply. Book catalog and ms guidelines for #10 SASE.
Nonfiction: Juvenile (13-17). Subjects include: Americana, language/literature, humorous memoirs for children/young adults. "For children. Stories to read with pictures to color. Either the writer can express himself in 500 words to make children laugh (and learn) or he can't. For young adults: humorous memoirs. Forget the Depression, WWII. Entertain an unseen audience with words." Query with SASE. Reviews artwork/photos as part of ms package. Send thumbnail sketches.
Fiction: Humor, literary. "We want to focus on novels written by junior and senior high school teachers."
Recent Fiction Title: *Mickey Steals the Show*, by Diane Harris-Filderman.
Tips: "Since the TV-oriented youth in schools today do not like to read or write, why not create books for that impressionable and captive audience. And if we can be successful with *Tug of War* as a textbook in Missouri middle schools, why not try to get it in the schools nationally? Great to work with talented writers. Perhaps we might motivate some youthful persons to become writers, to value the print media."

JONATHAN DAVID PUBLISHERS, INC., 68-22 Eliot Ave., Middle Village NY 11379-1194. Fax: (718)894-2818. Editor-in-Chief: Alfred J. Kolatch. Estab. 1948. Publishes hardcover and trade paperback originals and reprints. Publishes 20-25 titles/year. 50% of books from first-time authors; 90% from unagented writers. Pays royalty or makes outright purchase. Offers $1,000-5,000 advance. Publishes book 18 months after acceptance of ms. Reports in 2 months on queries. Book catalog for 6×9 SAE with 4 first-class stamps.
● This publisher has expressed an interest in seeing more projects geared toward children.
Nonfiction: Cookbook, how-to, reference, self-help. "We specialize in Judaica." Submit outline, 1 sample chapter and SASE.
Recent Nonfiction Title: *Jewish Folklore in America*, by Eichhorr (compilation of folklore from different regions of the US).
Tips: "We'd like books re: Judaica, sports and perhaps cooking geared towards children."

HARLAN DAVIDSON, INC., 773 Glenn Ave., Wheeling IL 60090-6000. (847)541-9720. Fax: (847)541-9830. Vice President: Andrew J. Davidson. Estab. 1972. Additional Imprint is Forum Press, Inc. Publishes college texts, both hardcover and paperback. Publishes 10 titles/year. Receives 200 queries and 25 mss/year. 100% of books from unagented writers. Manuscripts contracted as work for hire. Pays royalty on net. Publishes book 10 months after acceptance of ms. Accepts simultaneous submissions. Reports in 3 months on proposals. Book catalog free on request.
Nonfiction: Subjects include business, education, ethnic history, government, history (main list), biographical history, literature, philosophy, regional and state histories, women's issues/studies. "Because we are a college textbook publisher, academic credentials are extremely important. We usually find our own authors for a need in the field that we identify, but we are also receptive to ideas brought to us by qualified professionals, in history, especially." Submit proposal package, including outline, brief description of proposed book, its market and competition and a recent vita.
Recent Nonfiction Title: *America's Civil War*, by Brooks D. Simpson (history).

DAVIS PUBLICATIONS, INC., 50 Portland St., Worcester MA 01608. (508)754-7201. Fax: (508)753-3834. Acquisitions Editors: Claire M. Golding, Helen Ronan. Estab. 1901. Publishes 5-10 titles/year. Pays 10-12% royalty. Publishes book 1 year after acceptance. Book catalog for 9×12 SAE with 2 first-class stamps. Authors guidelines for SASE.
Nonfiction: Publishes technique-oriented art, design and craft books for the educational market. Accepts nonfiction translations. "Keep in mind the intended audience. Our readers are visually oriented. All illustrations should be collated separately from the text, but keyed to the text. Photos should be good quality transparencies and black and white photographs. Well-selected illustrations should explain, amplify, and enhance the text. We average 2-4 photos/page. We like to see technique photos as well as illustrations of finished artwork, by a variety of artists, including students. Recent books have been on printmaking, clay sculpture, design, jewelry, drawing and watercolor painting." Submit outline, sample chapters and illustrations. Reviews artwork/photos as part of ms package.
Recent Nonfiction Title: *3-D Wizardry: Design in Papier-Mâché, Plaster and Foam*, by George Wolfe.

DAW BOOKS, INC., 375 Hudson St., 3rd Floor, New York NY 10014-3658. Submissions Editor: Peter Stampfel. Estab. 1971. Publishes science fiction and fantasy hardcover and paperback originals and reprints. Publishes 60-80 titles/year. Pays in royalties with an advance negotiable on a book-by-book basis. Sends galleys to author. Simultaneous submissions "returned unread at once, unless prior arrangements are made by agent." Reports in 6 weeks "or longer, if a second reading is required." Book catalog free.
Fiction: "We are interested in science fiction and fantasy novels. We need science fiction more than fantasy right now, but we're still looking for both. We're not looking for horror novels, but we are looking for

mainstream suspense thrillers. We accept both agented and unagented manuscripts. We are not seeking collections of short stories or ideas for anthologies. We do not want any nonfiction manuscripts." Submit complete ms. *Writer's Market* recommends sending a query with SASE first.
Recent Fiction Title: *Crown of Shadows*, by C.S. Friedman.

DAWN PUBLICATIONS, 14618 Tyler Foote Rd., Nevada City CA 95959. (800)545-7475. Editor: Glenn J. Hovemann. Publishes hardcover and trade paperback originals. Publishes 6 titles/year. Receives 250 queries and 1,500 mss/year. 35% of books from first-time authors; 100% from unagented writers. Pays royalty on wholesale price. Publishes book 1 year after acceptance of ms. Accepts simultaneous submissions. Reports in 2 months. Book catalog and ms guidelines for #10 SASE.
Nonfiction: Children's/juvenile. Nature awareness and inspiration. Query with SASE.
Recent Nonfiction Title: *A Fly in the Sky*, by Kristin Joy Pratt (children's nature awareness).
Fiction: Children's juvenile. Nature awareness and inspiration. *Writer's Market* recommends sending a query with SASE first.
Recent Fiction Title: *Grandpa's Garden*, by Shea Darian (children's inspiration).

DEARBORN FINANCIAL PUBLISHING, INC., 155 N. Wacker Dr., Chicago IL 60606-1719. (312)836-4400. Fax: (312)836-1021. Senior Vice President: Anita Constant. Estab. 1959. Imprints are Dearborn/R&R Newkirk (contact: Anne Shropshire), Enterprise/Dearborn (contact: Anita Constant), Real Estate Education Co. (contact: Carol Luitjens), and Upstart Publishing Co. (contact: Mr. Jere Calmes). Publishes hardcover and paperback originals. Publishes 200 titles/year. Receives 200 submissions/year. 50% of books from first-time authors; 50% from unagented writers. Pays 1-15% royalty on wholesale price. Publishes book 6 months after acceptance. Accepts simultaneous submissions. Reports in 1 month. *Writer's Market* recommends allowing 2 months for reply. Book catalog and ms guidelines free.
Nonfiction: How-to, reference, textbooks. Subjects include small business, real estate, insurance, banking, securities, money/finance. Query.
Tips: "People seeking real estate, insurance, broker's licenses are our audience; also professionals in these areas. Additionally, we publish for consumers who are interested in buying homes, managing their finances; and people interested in starting and running a small business."

IVAN R. DEE, INC., 1332 N. Halsted St., Chicago IL 60622-2637. (312)787-6262. Fax: (312)787-6269. President: Ivan R. Dee. Estab. 1988. Imprint is Elephant Paperbacks. Publishes hardcover originals and trade paperback originals and reprints. Publishes 25 titles/year. 10% of books from first-time authors; 75% from unagented writers. Pays royalty. Publishes book 9 months after acceptance. Reports in 1 month on queries. *Writer's Market* recommends allowing 2 months for reply. Book catalog free on request.
Nonfiction: History, literature and letters, biography, politics, contemporary affairs, theater. Submit outline and sample chapters. Reviews artwork/photos as part of ms package.
Recent Nonfiction Title: *Ideology of Death: Why the Holocaust Happened in Germany*, by John Weiss.
Tips: "We publish for an intelligent lay audience and college course adoptions."

DEL REY BOOKS, Imprint of Ballantine Books, Division of Random House, 201 E. 50th St., New York NY 10022-7703. (212)572-2677. Executive Editor: Shelly Shapiro. Senior Editor: Veronica Chapman. Contact: Jill Benjamin. Estab. 1977. Publishes hardcover, trade paperback, and mass market originals and mass market paperback reprints. Publishes 60 titles/year. Receives 1,900 submissions/year. 10% of books from first-time authors; 40% from unagented writers. Pays royalty on retail price. Offers competitive advance. Publishes book 1 year after acceptance. Reports in 6 months, occasionally longer. Writer's guidelines for #10 SASE.
Fiction: Fantasy ("should have the practice of magic as an essential element of the plot"), science fiction ("well-plotted novels with good characterization, exotic locales, and detailed alien cultures"). Query first to Jill Benjamin with detailed outline and synopsis of story from beginning to end. *Does not accept unsolicited mss.*
Recent Fiction Title: *First King of Shamara*, by Terry Brooks.
Tips: "Del Rey is a reader's house. Our audience is anyone who wants to be pleased by a good, entertaining novel. Pay particular attention to plotting and a satisfactory conclusion. It must be/feel believable. That's what the readers like."

DELACORTE PRESS, Imprint of Dell Publishers, Division of Bantam Doubleday Dell, 1540 Broadway, New York NY 10036. (212)354-6500. Editor-in-Chief: Leslie Schnur. Publishes hardcover originals. Publishes 36 titles/year. Royalty and advance vary. Publishes book 2 years after acceptance, but varies. Accepts simultaneous submissions. Reports in 3-4 months. Guidelines for 9×12 SASE.
Nonfiction and Fiction: Query with outline, first 3 chapters or brief proposal. No mss for children's or young adult books accepted in this division. No poetry accepted.

DELL PUBLISHERS, Division of Bantam Doubleday Dell, Inc., 1540 Broadway, New York NY 10036. Imprints include DTP, Delacorte, Dell Books, Dell Abyss, Delta Books, Dial Press, Bland Books and Laurel

Books. General interest publisher of all categories of fiction and nonfiction. Publishes approximately 40 books/month. Query Editorial Department before submitting. Unsolicited and unagented mss will not receive a response for 4 months.

THE DENALI PRESS, P.O. Box 021535, Juneau AK 99802-1535. (907)586-6014. Fax: (907)463-6780. E-mail: denalipr@alaska.net. Website: http://www.alaska.net/~denalipr/index.html. Editorial Director: Alan Schorr. Editorial Associate: Sally Silvas-Ottumwa. Estab. 1986. Publishes trade paperback originals. Publishes 5 titles/year. Receives 120 submissions/year. 50% of books from first-time authors; 80% from unagented writers. Pays 10% royalty on wholesale price or makes outright purchase. Publishes book 1 year after acceptance. Accepts simultaneous submissions. Reports in 1 month. *Writer's Market* recommends allowing 2 months for reply. Prefers letter of inquiry. Book catalog free on request.
Nonfiction: Reference. Subjects include Americana, Alaskana, anthropology, ethnic, government/politics, history, recreation. "We need reference books—ethnic, refugee and minority concerns." Query with outline and sample chapters. All unsolicited mss are tossed. Author must contact prior to sending ms.
Recent Nonfiction Title: *Hispanic Resource Directory*, 3rd ed.
Tips: "We are looking for reference works suitable for the educational, professional and library market."

T.S. DENISON & CO., INC., 9601 Newton Ave. S., Minneapolis MN 55431-2590. (612)888-6404. Fax: (612)888-6318. Director of Product Development: Sherrill B. Flora. Acquisitions Editor: Danielle de Gregory. Estab. 1876. Publishes teacher aid materials. Receives 1,500 submissions/year. 20% of books from first-time authors; 100% from unagented writers. Average print order for a first book is 3,000. No advance. Makes outright purchase. Publishes book 2 years after acceptance. Reports in 2 months. Book catalog and ms guidelines for 9×12 SAE with 3 first-class stamps.
Nonfiction: Specializes in early childhood and elementary school teaching aids. Submit complete ms. *Writer's Market* recommends query with SASE first. Reviews artwork/photos as part of ms package. Send prints if photos are to accompany ms.

‡DENLINGERS PUBLISHERS, LTD., P.O. Box 2300, Centreville VA 22020-2300. (703)830-4646. Fax: (703)830-5303. Publisher: William W. Denlinger. Estab. 1926. Publishes hardcover and trade paperback originals and reprints. Publishes 12 titles/year. Receives 250 submissions/year. 10% of books from first-time authors; 85% of books from unagented writers. Average print order for a writer's first book is 3,000. Pays variable royalty. No advance. Publishes book 1 year after acceptance. Accepts simultaneous submissions. Reports in 1 week on queries. *Writer's Market* recommends allowing 2 months for reply. Book catalog for SASE.
Nonfiction: How-to and technical books; dog-breed books only. Query. Reviews artwork/photos as part of ms package.
Recent Nonfiction Title: *Proction Dogs*, by Weiss and Rose.

DEVYN PRESS, Subsidiary of Baron Barclay Bridge Supplies, 3600 Chamberlain Lane, Suite 230, Louisville KY 40241. (502)426-0410. President: Randy Baron. Publishes hardcover and trade paperback originals and reprints. Publishes 10 titles/year. Receives 40 queries and 20 mss/year. 50% of books from first-time authors; 90% from unagented writers. Pays 5-10% royalty on wholesale price. Offers $500-1,000 advance. Publishes book 6 months after acceptance of ms. Accepts simultaneous submissions. Reports in 2 months on queries. Book catalog and ms guidelines free on request.
Nonfiction: How-to, self-help. Subjects include sports and games/bridge. "We are the world's largest publisher of books on the game of bridge." Query. Reviews artwork/photos as part of ms package. Send photocopies.

DIAL BOOKS FOR YOUNG READERS, Division of Penguin USA Inc., 375 Hudson St., 3rd Floor, New York NY 10014. (212)366-2800. Editorial Assistant: Victoria Wells. Imprints include Dial Easy-to-Read Books, Dial Very First Books. Publishes hardcover originals. Publishes 80 titles/year. Receives 8,000 submissions/year. 10% of books from first-time authors. Pays variable royalty and advance. Reports in 4 months.
Nonfiction: Juvenile picture books, young adult books. Especially looking for "quality picture books and well-researched young adult and middle-reader manuscripts." Not interested in alphabet books, riddle and game books, and early concept books. Agented mss only. No unsolicited mss.
Fiction: Juvenile picture books, young adult books. Adventure, fantasy, historical, humor, mystery, romance (appropriate for young adults), suspense. Especially looking for "lively and well written novels for middle grade and young adult children involving a convincing plot and believable characters. The subject matter or theme should not already be overworked in previously published books. The approach must not be demeaning to any minority group, nor should the roles of female characters (or others) be stereotyped, though we don't think books should be didactic, or in any way message-y. No topics inappropriate for the juvenile, young adult, and middle grade audiences. No plays." Also publishes Pied Piper Books (paperback Dial reprints) and Pied Piper Giants (1½ feet tall reprints). Agented mss only.

Tips: "Our readers are anywhere from preschool age to teenage. Picture books must have strong plots, lots of action, unusual premises, or universal themes treated with freshness and originality. Humor works well in these books. A very well thought out and intelligently presented book has the best chance of being taken on. Genre isn't as much of a factor as presentation."

‡**DIMI PRESS**, 3820 Oak Hollow Lane, SE, Salem OR 97302-4774. (503)364-7698. Fax: (503)364-9727. E-mail: dickbook@aol.com. President: Dick Lutz. Publishes trade paperback originals. Publishes 5 titles/year. Receives 100-150 queries and 20-25 mss/year. 80% of books from first-time authors; 100% from unagented writers. Pays 10% royalty on net receipts. No advance. Publishes book 9 months after acceptance of ms. Accepts simultaneous submissions. Reports in 2 weeks on queries and proposals, 1 month on mss. *Writer's Market* recommends allowing 2 months for reply. Book catalog and ms guidelines for #10 SASE.
Nonfiction: How-to, self-help. Subjects include child guidance/parenting, health/medicine, hobbies, money/finance, nature/environment, psychology, travel. "We are interested in practical, hands-on material." Query with outline and 1 sample chapter and SASE, if answer is desired. Reviews artwork/photos as part of ms package. Send photocopies.
Recent Nonfiction Title: *Drugs and Kids, How Parents Can Keep Them Apart*, by Gary Somdahl (how-to).
Tips: "Audience is adults who wish to learn something, save money, solve a problem, etc. Please send for guidelines before submitting."

DISCIPLESHIP RESOURCES, 1908 Grand Ave., Box 840, Nashville TN 37202-0840. (615)340-7068. Fax: (615)340-7006. Publisher: David Hazlewood. Publishes trade paperback originals and reprints. Publishes 15 titles/year. Receives 300 queries and 150 mss/year. 20% of books from first-time authors; 40% from unagented writers. Pays 5-10% royalty on net sales. Publishes book 6 months after acceptance of ms. Reports in 2 months on queries. Book catalog and ms guidelines for #10 SASE.
Nonfiction: Subjects include theology of ministry, evangelism, worship, stewardship, ministry of laity, family ministry, Christian education, ethnic (church), history (Methodist/church), music/dance (religious), nature/environment (ecology), recreation (leisure ministry), Christian biography (ecclesiastical). "Materials must be focused on specific ministries of the church, in particular the United Methodist Church, but we also work with ecumenical resources." Query with proposal package, including outline, sample chapter, description of audience. Reviews artwork/photos as part of ms package. Send photocopies.
Tips: "Focus on ministry, write simply, and do more research."

‡**DO-IT-YOURSELF LEGAL PUBLISHERS**, 24 Commerce St., Suite 1732, Newark NJ 07102. (201)242-0282. Associate Editor: Dan Benjamin. Imprint is Selfhelper Law Press of America. Publishes trade paperback originals. Publishes 6 titles/year. Imprint publishes 2 titles/year. Receives 25 queries/year. Pays 15-20% royalty on wholesale price. No advance. Publishes book 1 year after acceptance of ms. Accepts simultaneous submissions. Reports in 1 month on queries and proposals, 3 months on mss.
Nonfiction: How-to (law topics), self-help (law topics). Subject matter should deal with self-help law topics that instruct the lay person on how to undertake legal tasks without the use of attorney or other high cost experts. Query.
Recent Nonfiction Title: *How to Form Your Own Profit or Non-Profit Corporation without a Lawyer*, by Benji O. Anosike (paperback).

DORAL PUBLISHING, INC., 8560 SW Salish Lane, #300, Wilsonville OR 97070-9625. (503)682-3307. Fax: (503)682-2648. Editor-in-Chief: Luana Luther. Imprints are Golden Boy Press (Lynn Grey, marketing coordinator); Swan Valley Press (Joan Bailey, editor); Adele Publications (William Cusick, publisher). Publishes hardcover and trade paperback originals. Publishes 7 titles/year. Receives 16 queries and 12 mss/year. 60% of mss from first-time authors, 85% from unagented writers. Pays 10-17% royalty on wholesale price. Publishes book 4 months after acceptance of ms. *Writer's Market* recommends allowing 2 months for reply. Book catalog free on request. Manuscript guidelines for #10 SASE.
Nonfiction: How-to, children's/juvenile, reference. Subjects include animals (dogs). "We publish only books about Pure Bred Dogs. No flowery prose." Submit outline and 2 sample chapters. Reviews artwork/photos as part of the ms package. Send photocopies.

DOUBLEDAY, Division of Bantam Doubleday Dell, Inc., 1540 Broadway, New York NY 10036. (212)354-6500. Imprints are Anchor Books, Currency, DD Equestrian Library, Dolphin Books, Double D Western, Doubleday Activity Books, Foundation Books, Galilee Books, Image Books, Jerusalem Bible, Loveswept, Made Simple Books, Main Street/Backlist, New Jerusalem Bible, Nan A. Talese Books, Outdoor Bible series, Perfect Crime, Spy Books. General interest publisher of both fiction and nonfiction, including mysteries, romance, westerns, science, science fiction, religion, Bibles, biography, business, history, reference. Accepts only agented material. No unsolicited mss. Publishes everything but poetry and coffee table books.
Recent Nonfiction Title: *Schoolgirls*, by Peggy Orenstein.
Recent Fiction Title: *The Rainmaker*, by John Grisham.

DOWN EAST BOOKS, Division of Down East Enterprise, Inc., P.O. Box 679, Camden ME 04843-0679. Fax: (207)594-7215. Managing Editor: Karin Womer. Estab. 1954. Publishes hardcover and trade paperback originals, trade paperback reprints. Publishes 10-14 titles/year. Receives 300 submissions/year. 50% of books from first-time authors; 90% from unagented writers. Average print order for a first book is 3,000. Pays 10-15% on receipts. Offers $200 average advance. Publishes book 1 year after acceptance. Accepts simultaneous submissions. Reports in 2 months. Manuscript guidelines for 9×12 SAE with 3 first-class stamps.
Nonfiction: Books about the New England region, Maine in particular. Subjects include Americana, history, nature, guide books, crafts, recreation. "All of our books must have a Maine or New England emphasis." Query. Reviews artwork/photos as part of ms package.
Recent Nonfiction Title: *Neil Welliver Prints*, by N. Welliver (catalog raisonné of Maine artist).
Fiction: "We publish 1-2 juvenile titles/year (fiction and non-fiction), and 1-2 adult fiction titles/year." *Writer's Market* recommends sending a query with SASE first.
Recent Fiction Title: *Murder on Mount Desert*, by D. Rawson (regional mystery).

‡**DOWN HOME PRESS**, P.O. Box 4126, Asheboro NC 27204. (910)672-6889. Fax: (910)672-2003. E-mail: jbleddhome@aol.com. Editor: Jerry Bledsoe. Imprint is Imprimatur Books. Publishes hardcover originals and trade paperback originals and reprints. Publishes 8-10 titles/year. Receives 250 queries and 100 mss/year. 95% of books from unagented writers. Pays 8-15% royalty on wholesale price. Offers $500 advance. Publishes book 1 year after acceptance of ms. Reports in 3 months on queries, 6 months on proposals and mss. Book catalog for 9×12 SAE with 5 first-class stamps. Manuscript guidelines for #10 SASE.
Nonfiction: Biography, cookbook, how-to, humor, illustrated book. Subjects include agriculture/horticulture, cooking/foods/nutrition, gardening, government/politics, history, hobbies, language/literature, nature/environment, photography, recreation, regional, sports, travel, Carolinas and South. Query. Submit outline and 1 sample chapter with SASE. Reviews artwork/photos as part of ms package. Send photocopies.
Recent Nonfiction Title: *Ocracoke Wild*, by Pat Garber (nature/travel).
Tips: Audience is mostly Southerners and Carolinians.

DRAMA PUBLISHERS, 260 Fifth Ave., New York NY 10001. (212)725-5377. Fax: (212)725-8506. E-mail: dramapub@interport.net. Website: http://www.interport.net/~dramapub/. Managing Editor: Ina Kohler. Estab. 1967. Publishes hardcover and paperback originals and reprints. Publishes 4-15 titles/year. Receives 420 submissions/year. 70% of books from first-time authors; 90% from unagented writers. Royalty varies. Advance negotiable. Publishes book 18 months after acceptance. Reports in 2 months.
Nonfiction: Texts, guides, manuals, directories, reference and multimedia—for and about performing arts theory and practice: acting, directing; voice, speech, movement, music, dance, mime; makeup, masks, wigs; costumes, sets, lighting, sound; design and execution; technical theatre, stagecraft, equipment; stage management; producing; arts management, all varieties; business and legal aspects; film, radio, television, cable, video; theory, criticism, reference; playwriting; theatre and performance history. Accepts nonfiction and technical works in translations also. Query with 1-3 sample chapters. No complete mss. Reviews artwork/photos as part of ms package.
Recent Nonfiction Title: *Wearing of Costume*, by Green.

DUKE PRESS, Subsidiary of Duke Communications International, 221 E. 29th St., Loveland CO 80538. (970)663-4700. Fax: (970)667-2321. E-mail: dbernard@duke.com. Publisher: David R. Bernard. Publishes trade paperback originals. Publishes 10-15 titles/year. Receives 12 queries and 8 mss/year. Pays 8-12% royalty on retail price. Offers $500-2,000 advance. Publishes book 9 months after acceptance. Query with SASE. Reports in 1 month on proposals. Book catalog and ms guidelines free on request.
Nonfiction: How-to, technical, textbook. Subjects include IBM AS/400 midrange computer and Windows NT operating system. Submit outline and 2 sample chapters.
Recent Nonfiction Title: *Inside the AS/400*, by Frank Soltis (computer/technical).
Tips: "Readers are MIS managers, programmers, and system operators working on an IBM AS/400 midrange computer or a Windows NT platform. Authors must have technical knowledge and experience on an IBM AS/400 or Windows NT."

‡**DUNCAN & DUNCAN, INC. PUBLISHERS**, 2809 Pulaski Hwy. P.O. Box 1137, Edgewood MD 21040. (410)538-5580. Fax: (410)538-5584. Publisher: Mike Duncan. Vice President: Shirley Duncan. Imprint is WriteMore Publications. Publishes hardcover and trade paperback originals. Publishes 8-10 titles/year. Imprint publishes 4 titles/year. Receives 60 queries and 50 mss/year. 100% of books from first-time authors; 100% from unagented writers. Pays 8-12% royalty on wholesale price. No advance. Publishes book 5 months after acceptance of ms. Accepts simultaneous submissions. Reports in 1 month. *Writer's Market* recommends allowing 2 months for reply. Book catalog and ms guidelines free on request.
Nonfiction: Autobiography, how-to, reference, self-help, technical. Subjects include business and economics, child guidance/parenting, education, ethnic, government/politics, history, money/finance, psychology, religion, sociology, sports, women's issues/studies. Submit outline, 4 sample chapters and SASE. Reviews artwork/photos as part of ms package. Send photocopies.

Recent Nonfiction Title: *The Black Entrepreneur's Guide to Success,* by Melvin J. Gravely, II (business).
Fiction: Ethnic, mainstream/contemporary, mystery, romance, suspense. Submit synopsis, 4 sample chapters and SASE.

DUSTBOOKS, Box 100, Paradise CA 95967. (916)877-6110. Publisher: Len Fulton. Publishes hardcover and paperback originals. Publishes 7 titles/year. Offers 15% royalty. Accepts simultaneous submissions, if so noted. Reports in 2 months. Book catalog free.
Nonfiction: "Our specialty is directories of small presses, poetry publishers, and a monthly newsletter on small publishers (*Small Press Review*)." Publishes annual *International Directory of Little Magazines & Small Presses. Writer's Market* recommends sending a query with SASE first.

DUTTON, Division of Penguin USA, 375 Hudson St., New York NY 10014. (212)366-2000. Publisher: Elaine Koster. Estab. 1852. Imprints are Signet, Onyx, Topaz, NAL, Plume. Publishes hardcover originals. No unsolicited mss.
Nonfiction: Biography, self-help, serious nonfiction, politics, psychology, science.
Fiction: Mainstream/contemporary. "We don't publish genre romances or westerns."

DUTTON CHILDREN'S BOOKS, Division of Penguin USA, 375 Hudson St., New York NY 10014. (212)366-2000. Editor-in-Chief: Lucia Monfried. Estab. 1852. Publishes hardcover originals. Publishes 70 titles/year. 15% from first-time authors. Pays royalty on retail price.
Nonfiction: For preschoolers to middle-graders; including animals/nature, US history, general biography, science and photo essays. Query with SASE.
Recent Nonfiction Title: *Tundra Swans,* by Bianca Lavies.
Fiction: Dutton Children's Books has a complete publishing program that includes picture books; easy-to-read books; and fiction for all ages, from "first-chapter" books to young adult readers. Query with SASE.
Recent Fiction Title: *The Arkadians,* by Lloyd Alexander.

E.M. PRESS, INC., Box 4057, Manassas VA 20108. (540)439-0304. Editor/Publisher: Beth Miller. Estab. 1991. "We are looking for quality mainstream literature (biographies, historical events, life-experience, literary fiction) from first-time writers and veterans alike. We will consider how-to, hobby and sports material. No textbooks." "We are interested in children's books and in area fiction (limited) and nonfiction. We find it easier to promote local authors and/or local (UA, Maryland, D.C.) material. Because of a more focused approach, our capabilities are on the rise."

EAGLE'S VIEW PUBLISHING, 6756 N. Fork Rd., Liberty UT 84310. Fax: (801)745-0903. Editor-in-Chief: Denise Knight. Estab. 1982. Publishes trade paperback originals. Publishes 4-6 titles/year. Receives 40 queries and 20 mss/year. 90% of books from first-time authors; 100% from unagented writers. Pays 8-10% royalty on wholesale price. Publishes book 1 year or more after acceptance of ms. Accepts simultaneous submissions. Reports in 18 months on proposals. Book catalog and ms guidelines for $1.50.
Nonfiction: How-to, Indian, mountain man and American frontier (history and craft). Subjects include anthropology/archaeology (Native American crafts), ethnic (Native American), history (American frontier), hobbies (crafts, especially beadwork, earrings). "We are expanding from our Indian craft base to more general crafts." Submit outline and 1-2 sample chapters. Reviews artwork/photos as part of ms package. Send photocopies or sample illustrations. "We prefer to do photography in house."
Recent Nonfiction Title: *Plains Indian and Mountain Man Arts & Crafts, vols. I & II,* by Charles Overstreet (how-to craft projects).
Tips: "We will not be publishing any new beaded earrings books for 1 to 2 years. We are interested in other craft projects using seed beads, especially books that feature a variety of items, not just different designs for one type of item."

EAKIN PRESS/SUNBELT MEDIA, INC., P.O. Box 90159, Austin TX 78709-0159. (512)288-1771. Fax: (512)288-1813. Imprints are Eakin Press and Nortex Press. Editorial Director: Edwin M. Eakin. Estab. 1978. Publishes hardcover and paperback originals and reprints. Publishes 35 titles/year. Receives 1,500 submissions/year. 50% of books from first-time authors; 90% from unagented writers. Average print order for a first book is 2,000-5,000. Pays 10-12-15% royalty on net sales. Publishes book 18 months after acceptance. Accepts simultaneous submissions. Reports in 3 months. Book catalog for $1.25. Manuscript guidelines for #10 SASE.
Nonfiction: Adult nonfiction categories include Western Americana, African American studies, business, sports, biographies, Civil War, regional cookbooks, Texas history. Juvenile nonfiction includes biographies of historic personalities, prefer with Texas or regional interest, or nature studies. Easy-read illustrated books for grades 1-3. Query with SASE.
Recent Nonfiction Title: *The Fall of the Duke of Duval,* by John Clark.
Fiction: No longer publishes adult fiction. Juvenile fiction for grades 4-7, preferably relating to Texas and the southwest or contemporary. Query or submit outline/synopsis and sample chapters.

‡**EASTERN NATIONAL PARK & MONUMENT ASSOCIATION**, 446 North Lane, Conshohocken PA 19428. (610)832-0555. Production Coordinator: Patti Plummer. Estab. 1948. Imprint is Eastern Acorn Press. Publishes trade paperback originals and reprints. Publishes 50-60 titles/year. Receives 20 queries and 10 mss/year. 5% of books from first-time authors; 50% from unagented writers. Pays 1-10% royalty on retail price or makes outright purchase of $6,000 maximum. Publishes book 2 years after acceptance of ms. Reports in 1 month on queries. *Writer's Market* recommends allowing 2 months for reply. Book catalog free on request.

Nonfiction: Biography, children's/juvenile. Subjects include Americana, history, military/war and nature/environment. "Requests for editorial plans are only accepted from member agencies." Query. All unsolicited mss are returned unopened.

Recent Nonfiction Title: *Siege of Petersburg*, by Andre Trudeau (Civil War history).

EASTLAND PRESS, P.O. Box 99749, Seattle WA 98199. (206)217-0204. Fax: (206)217-0205. Managing Editor: John O'Connor. Publishes hardcover and trade paperback originals. Publishes 4-6 titles/year. Receives 25 queries/year. 50% of books from first-time authors; 90% from unagented writers. Pays 8-15% royalty based on receipts. Offers $500-1,500 advance. Publishes book 18 months after acceptance of ms. Accepts simultaneous submissions. Reports in 2 months. Book catalog free on request.

Nonfiction: Reference, textbook, alternative medicine (Chinese and physical). Health/medicine subjects (alternative: Chinese & physical). "We are primarily interested in textbooks for practitioners of alternative medical therapies. We prefer that a manuscript be completed or close to completion before we will consider publication. Proposals are rarely considered, unless submitted by a published author or teaching institution." Submit outline and 2-3 sample chapters. Reviews artwork/photos as part of ms package. Send photocopies.

Recent Nonfiction Title: *Mind Matters: Psychological Medicine in Holistic Practice*, by J.R. Millenson.

THE ECCO PRESS, 100 W. Broad St., Hopewell NJ 08525. (609)466-4748. Editor-in-Chief: Daniel Halpern. Publishes hardcover and mass market paperback originals and reprints and trade paperback reprints. Publishes 60 titles/year. Receives 1,200 queries/year. Pays 7½-15% royalty. Offers $250-5,000 advance. Publishes book 1 year after acceptance of ms. Reports in 2 months on queries. Book catalog and ms guidelines free on request.

Nonfiction: Biography, coffee table book, cookbook. Subjects include Americana, art/architecture, cooking/foods/nutrition, government/politics, history, language/literature, music/dance, regional, translation, travel. Query. Reviews artwork/photos as part of ms package. Send transparencies.

Recent Nonfiction Title: *On Water*, by Thomas Farber (short essays).

Fiction: Ethnic, historical, literary, plays, short story collections.

Recent Fiction Title: *The American Story*, edited by Michael Rea (short story anthology).

Poetry: Submit 10 sample poems.

Recent Poetry Title: *Essential Haiku*, edited by Robert Hass (haiku anthology).

THE EDUCATION CENTER, INC., 1607 Battleground Ave., Greensboro NC 27408. Fax: (910)274-4574. Contact: Julie Deck, editorial business manager. Estab. 1973. Publishes supplementary resource books for elementary teachers: preschool/grade 6. Publishes 40 titles/year. Receives 300 queries and 100 mss/year. Under 5% of books from first-time authors; 100% from unagented writers. Pays 2-6% royalty on wholesale price (on books sold through dealers); 2-6% royalty on retail price (on books sold through direct mail). "Payment schedule and amount negotiated when contract signed." Publishes book 1 year after acceptance of ms (depending on condition of ms). Reports in 2 months on proposals. Book catalog and ms guidelines for 9 × 12 SASE.

● The Education Center is looking for seasonal/holiday and monthly teaching ideas as well as more preschool books in a series.

Nonfiction: Teacher resource/supplementary materials. Subjects include education P/K-6, language/literature. "We place a strong emphasis on materials that teach the basic language arts and math skills. We are also seeking materials for teaching science and geography, literature-based activities for the whole language classroom, cooperative learning ideas and multicultural materials. Technical, complex or comprehensive manuscripts (such as textbooks and theory/practice articles) are not accepted." Submit outline and 1 sample chapter.

Recent Nonfiction Title: *Arts & Crafts for Little Hands*, by Jennifer Overend.

‡**EDUCATIONAL TECHNOLOGY PUBLICATIONS**, 700 Palisade Ave., Englewood Cliffs NJ 07632. (201)871-4007. Publisher: Lawrence Lipsitz. Publishes hardcover and trade paperback originals.

FOR INFORMATION on book publishers' areas of interest, see the nonfiction and fiction sections in the Book Publishers Subject Index.

Publishes 12-15 titles/year. Receives 100 queries and 50 mss/year. 33% of books from first-time authors; 100% from unagented writers. Pays 10-15% royalty on wholesale or retail price, "depends." No advance. Publishes book 1 year after acceptance of ms. Reports in 1 month.
Nonfiction: Technical, textbook, professional books. Subjects include education. Query with outline and SASE. Reviews artwork/photos as part of ms package.
Recent Nonfiction Title: *Designing Communication and Learning Environments*, by Diane M. Gayeski (educational strategies).
Tips: "Audience is sophisticated educators interested in all areas of technology in education. We desire only very expert authors, able to do high-level work—not P.R. "flacks." Only leading-edge, up-to-date material will be considered."

WILLIAM B. EERDMANS PUBLISHING CO., 255 Jefferson Ave. SE, Grand Rapids MI 49503. (616)459-4591. Fax: (616)459-6540. Editor-in-Chief: Jon Pott. Assistant to the Editor: Anne Salsich. Managing Editor: Charles Van Hof. Children's Book Editor: Amy Eerdmans. Estab. 1911. Publishes hardcover and paperback originals and reprints. Publishes 120-130 titles/year. Receives 1,500-2,000 submissions/year. 10% from first-time authors; 95% from unagented writers. Average print order for a first book is 4,000. Pays 7½-10% royalty on retail price. Publishes book 1 year after acceptance. Accepts simultaneous submissions if noted. Reports in 6 weeks on queries. *Writer's Market* recommends allowing 2 months for reply. Book catalog free.
Nonfiction: Religious, reference, textbooks, monographs, children's books. Subjects include ethics, religious literature, history, philosophy, psychology, religion, sociology, regional history. "Approximately 80% of our publications are religious and largely of the more academic or theological variety (as opposed to the devotional, inspirational or celebrity-conversion books). Our history and social issues titles aim, similarly, at an educated audience. We prefer that writers take the time to notice if we have published anything at all in the same category as their manuscript before sending it to us." Accepts nonfiction translations. Query with outline, 2-3 sample chapters and SASE for return of ms. Reviews artwork/photos.
Recent Nonfiction Title: *The Sword of Imagination: Memoirs of a Half-Century of Literary Conflict*, by Russell Kirk.
Tips: "We look for quality and relevance."

ELDER BOOKS, P.O. Box 490, Forest Knolls CA 94933. (415)488-9002. Director: Carmel Sheridan. Publishes trade paperback originals. Publishes 6-10 titles/year. Receives 200 queries and 50 mss/year. 50% of books from first-time authors; 50% from unagented writers. Pays .7% royalty on retail price. No advance. Publishes book 9 months after acceptance of ms. Reports in 3 months on queries. Book catalog free on request.
Nonfiction: Gift book, how-to, multimedia, self-help. Subjects include child guidance/parenting, education, health/medicine, money/finance, psychology, religion, senior issues, Alzheimer's disease, women's issues/studies. Submit outline, 2 sample chapters. Reviews artwork/photos as part of ms package. Send photocopies.
Recent Nonfiction Title: *Living in the Labyrinth*, by Diana Gowin.

ELLIOTT & CLARK PUBLISHING, INC., P.O. Box 21038, Washington DC 20009. (202)387-9805. Fax: (202)483-0355. E-mail: ecp@dgsys.com. Publisher: Carolyn M. Clark. Publishes hardcover and trade paperback originals. Publishes 7 titles/year. 50% of books from first-time authors; 90% from unagented writers. Pays royalty on wholesale price. Offers $1,000-7,500 advance. Publishes book 15 months after acceptance. Accepts simultaneous submissions. Reports in 2 months on proposals. Book catalog and ms guidelines free on request.
Nonfiction: Subjects include Americana, art/architecture, biography, gardening, history, nature/environment, photography. "We specialize in illustrated histories—need to think of possible photography/illustration sources to accompany manuscript. Submit an analysis of audience or a discussion of possible sales avenues beyond traditional book stores (such as interest groups, magazines, associations, etc.)." Submit proposal package, including possible illustrations (if applicable), outline, sales avenues. Reviews artwork/photos as part of ms package. Send transparencies. SASE must be included for response and returned materials.
Recent Nonfiction Title: *Dorothea Lange's Ireland*, by Gerry Mullins (photo essay).
Tips: "We prefer proactive authors who are interested in providing marketing and the right leads."

‡ENGINEERING & MANAGEMENT PRESS, 25 Technology Park, Norcross GA 30092. (770)449-0461. Acquisitions Administrator: Eric Torrey. Publishes hardcover and trade paperback originals. Publishes 6-10 titles/year. Receives 60-80 queries and 40-50 mss/year. 75% of books from first-time authors; 100% from unagented writers. Pays 10-15% royalty. Offers up to $1,000 advance. Publishes book 1 year after acceptance of ms. Accepts simultaneous submissions. Reports in 3 months on mss. Book catalog and ms guidelines free on reqeust.
Nonfiction: Reference, technical, textbook. Subjects include business, computers and electronics, health/medicine (healthcare administration), industrial engineering and related topics. All books relate to industrial engineering disciplines. Submit proposal package, including outline, 2 sample chapters, competitive analysis and what makes your book unique. Reviews artwork/photos as part of ms package. Send photocopies.

Recent Nonfiction Title: *By What Method?*, by D. Scott Sink, Ph.D. (management).
Tips: Audience is professionals working in the field of industrial engineering.

ENSLOW PUBLISHERS INC., 44 Fadem Rd., P.O. Box 699, Springfield NJ 07081. (201)379-8890. Editor: Brian D. Enslow. Estab. 1977. Publishes hardcover and paperback originals. Publishes 90 titles/year. 30% require freelance illustration. Pays royalty on net price. Offers advance. Publishes book 1 year after acceptance. Reports in 1 month. *Writer's Market* recommends allowing 2 months for reply. Book catalog for $2 and 9×12 SAE with 3 first-class stamps. Writer's guidelines for SASE.
  • This publisher is especially interested in ideas for series. It does not publish fiction, fictionalized history or educational materials.
Nonfiction: Interested in nonfiction mss for young adults and children. Some areas of special interest are science, social issues, biography, reference topics, recreation. Query with information on competing titles and writer's résumé.

EPICENTER PRESS INC., P.O. Box 82368, Kenmore WA 98028. (206)485-6822. Fax: (206)481-8253. E-mail: epibooks@aol.com. Publisher: Kent Sturgis. Associate Editor: Christine Ummel. Imprint is Umbrella Books. Publishes hardcover and trade paperback originals. Publishes 10 titles/year. Receives 200 queries and 100 mss/year. 90% of books from first-time authors; 90% from unagented writers. Advance negotiable. Publishes book 2 years after acceptance of ms. Reports in 2 months on queries. Book catalog and ms guidelines free on request.
Nonfiction: Biography, coffee table book, gift books, humor. Subjects include animals, art/architecture, ethnic, history, nature/environment, photography, recreation, regional, travel, women's issues/studies. "Our focus is the Pacific Northwest and Alaska. We do not encourage nonfiction titles from outside Alaska and the Pacific Northwest, nor travel from beyond Alaska, Washington, Oregon and California." Submit outline and 3 sample chapters. Reviews artwork/photos as part of ms package. Send photocopies.
Recent Nonfiction Title: *Dog Heroes*, by Tim Jones, illustrated by Jon Van Zyle.

PAUL S. ERIKSSON, PUBLISHER, P.O. Box 62, Forest Dale VT 05745-4210. (802)247-4210. Publisher/ Editor: Paul S. Eriksson. Associate Publisher/Co-Editor: Peggy Eriksson. Estab. 1960. Publishes hardcover and paperback trade originals, paperback trade reprints. Publishes 5 titles/year. Receives 1,500 submissions/ year. 25% of books from first-time authors; 95% from unagented writers. Average print order for a first book is 3,000-5,000. Pays 10-15% royalty on retail price. Offers advance if necessary. Publishes book 6 months after acceptance. *Writer's Market* recommends allowing 2 months for reply. Catalog for #10 SASE.
Nonfiction: Americana, birds (ornithology), art, biography, business/economics, cooking/foods/nutrition, health, history, hobbies, how-to, humor, nature, politics, psychology, recreation, self-help, sociology, sports, travel. Query with SASE.
Recent Nonfiction Title: *Oskar Schindler And His List*, by Thomas Fensch.
Fiction: Serious, literary. Query with SASE. No simultaneous submissions.
Tips: "We look for intelligence, excitement and saleability."

ETC PUBLICATIONS, 700 E. Vereda Sur, Palm Springs CA 92262-4816. (619)325-5352. Editorial Director: LeeOna S. Hostrop. Senior Editor: Dr. Richard W. Hostrop. Estab. 1972. Publishes hardcover and paperback originals. Publishes 6-12 titles/year. Receives 100 submissions/year. 75% of books from first-time authors; 90% from unagented writers. Average print order for a first book is 2,500. Offers 5-15% royalty, based on wholesale and retail price. No advance. Publishes book 9 months after acceptance. *Writer's Market* recommends allowing 2 months for reply.
Nonfiction: Educational management, gifted education, futuristics, textbooks. Accepts nonfiction translations in above areas. Submit complete ms with SASE. *Writer's Market* recommends query first with SASE. Reviews artwork/photos as part of ms package.
Recent Nonfiction Title: *The Magic of Matsumoto: The Suzuki Method of Education*, by Carolyn M. Barrett, Ph.D (education).
Tips: "ETC will seriously consider textbook manuscripts in any knowledge area in which the author can guarantee a first-year adoption of not less than 500 copies. Special consideration is given to those authors who are capable and willing to submit their completed work in camera-ready, typeset form."

M. EVANS AND CO., INC., 216 E. 49th St., New York NY 10017-1502. Fax: (212)486-4544. Editor-in-Chief: George C. deKay. Contact: Betty Ann Crawford, senior editor. Estab. 1960. Publishes hardcover originals. Pays negotiable royalty. Publishes 30-40 titles/year. 5% of books from unagented writers. Publishes book 8 months after acceptance. Query. No unsolicited mss. Reports in 2 months. Book catalog for 9×12 SAE with 3 first-class stamps.
Nonfiction: "Our most successful nonfiction titles have been related to health and the behavioral sciences." No limitation on subject.
Recent Nonfiction Title: *An Inquiry Into the Existence of Guardian Angels*, by Pierre Jovanovic (general nonfiction).

Fiction: "Our general fiction list, which is very small, represents an attempt to combine quality with commercial potential."

Recent Fiction Title: *A Fine Italian Hand*, by William Murray (mystery).

Tips: "We publish a general trade list of adult fiction and nonfiction, cookbooks and semi-reference works. The emphasis is on selectivity. A writer should clearly indicate what his book is all about, frequently the task the writer performs least well. His credentials, although important, mean less than his ability to convince this company that he understands his subject and that he has the ability to communicate a message worth hearing. Writers should review our book catalog before making submissions."

EXCALIBUR PUBLICATIONS, P.O. Box 36, Latham NY 12110-0036. Editor: Alan M. Petrillo. Publishes trade paperback originals. Publishes 6-8 titles/year. Pays royalty or makes outright purchase. Reports in 2 months on mss.

Nonfiction "We publish works on military history, strategy and tactics, as well as the history of battles, firearms, arms and armour. We are seeking well-researched and documented works. Unpublished writers are welcome." Query with outline, 1st and any 2 additional consecutive chapters with SASE. Include notes on photos, illustrations and maps.

Recent Nonfiction Title: *Japanese Rifles of World War II*, by Duncan O. McCollum (historical/technical).

FABER & FABER, INC., Division of Faber & Faber, Ltd., London, England; 53 Shore Rd., Winchester MA 01890. (617)721-1427. Fax: (617)729-2783. Contact: Publishing Assistant. Estab. 1976. Publishes hardcover and trade paperback originals. Publishes 30 titles/year. Receives 1,200 submissions/year. 10% of books from first-time authors; 25% from unagented writers. Pays royalty on retail price. Advance varies. Publishes book 1 year after acceptance. Accepts simultaneous submissions. Reports in 3 months on queries. Book catalog for 9×12 SAE with 4 first-class stamps. Writer's guidelines for #10 SASE.

Nonfiction: Anthologies, biography, contemporary culture, film and screenplays, history and natural history, cooking, popular science. Query with synopsis, outline and SASE. Reviews artwork/photos as part of ms package.

Recent Nonfiction Title: *Uncommon Voyage: Parenting a Special Needs Child in the World of Alternative Medicine*, by Laura Shapiro Kramer.

Fiction: No mysteries or thrillers, no children's. Query with synopsis, outline and SASE.

Recent Fiction Title: *Empire Under Glass*, by Julian Anderson.

Tips: "Subjects that have consistently done well for us include popular culture; serious, intelligent rock and roll books; and literary, somewhat quirky fiction. Please do not send entire manuscript; include SASE for reply."

FACTS ON FILE, INC., 11 Penn Plaza, New York NY 10001. (212)967-8800. Contact: Editor. Estab. 1941. Publishes hardcover originals and reprints. Publishes 135 titles/year. Receives approximately 2,000 submissions/year. 25% of books from unagented writers. Pays 10-15% royalty on retail price. Offers $10,000 average advance. Accepts simultaneous submissions. Reports in 2 months on queries. Book catalog free.

Nonfiction: Reference. Informational books on health, history, entertainment, natural history, philosophy, psychology, recreation, religion, language, sports, multicultural studies, science, popular culture. "We need serious, informational books for a targeted audience. All our books must have strong library interest, but we also distribute books effectively to the book trade. Our books fit the junior and senior high school curriculum." No computer books, technical books, cookbooks, biographies (except YA), pop psychology, humor, do-it-yourself crafts, fiction or poetry. Query or submit outline and sample chapter with SASE. No submissions returned without SASE.

Tips: "Our audience is school and public libraries for our more reference-oriented books and libraries, schools and bookstores for our less reference-oriented informational titles."

FAIRLEIGH DICKINSON UNIVERSITY PRESS, 285 Madison Ave., Madison NJ 07940. Phone/fax: (201)443-8564. E-mail: fdupress@fdu.edu. Director: Harry Keyishian. Estab. 1967. Publishes hardcover originals. Publishes 45 titles/year. Receives 300 submissions/year. 33% of books from first-time authors; 95% from unagented writers. Average print order for a first book is 1,000. "Contract is arranged through Associated University Presses of Cranbury, New Jersey. We are a *selection* committee only." Nonauthor subsidy publishes 2% of books. Publishes book 1 year after acceptance. Reports in 2 weeks on queries. *Writer's Market* recommends allowing 2 months for reply.

Nonfiction: Reference, scholarly books. Subjects include art, business and economics, Civil War, film, history, Jewish studies, literary criticism, music, philosophy, politics, psychology, sociology, women's studies. Looking for scholarly books in all fields; no nonscholarly books. Query with outline and sample chapters. Reviews artwork/photos as part of ms package.

Recent Nonfiction Title: *Mary Wollstonecraft and the Language of Sensibility*, by Syndy McMillen Conger.

Tips: "Research must be up to date. Poor reviews result when authors' bibliographies and notes don't reflect current research. We follow *Chicago Manual of Style* (14th edition) style in scholarly citations."

‡**FAIRVIEW PRESS**, (formerly Deaconess Press), 2450 Riverside Ave. S., Minneapolis MN 55454. (800)544-8207. Website: http://www.press.fairview.org. Senior Editor: Julie Smith. Imprint is Growing & Reading with Bob Keeshan (Robyn Hansen, children's book editor). Publishes hardcover and trade paperback originals and reprints. Publishes 24-30 titles/year. Imprint publishes 8-10 titles/year. Receives 500 queries and 200 mss/year. 40% of books from first-time authors; 65% from unagented writers. Pays 16-22% royalty on wholesale price. Offers $500-2,500 advance. Publishes book 1 year after acceptance of ms. Accepts simultaneous submissions. Reports in 4 months on proposals. Book catalog and manuscript guidelines free on request.

Nonfiction: Children's/juvenile, how-to, reference, self-help. Subjects include child guidance/parenting, psychology, sociology, social and family issues. "We publish books on issues that impact families and the communities in which they live. Manuscripts are essentially one person's story are rarely saleable." Submit proposal package, including outline, 2 sample chapters, author information, marketing ideas and SASE. Reviews artwork/photos as part of ms package. Send photocopies.

Recent Nonfiction Title: *Family-by-Choice*, by Susan Ahern (lifestyles/social issues).

Tips: Audience is general reader, especially families. "Tell us what void your book fills in the market; give us an angle. Tell us who will buy your book. We have moved away from recovery books and have focused on social, community and family issues."

FARRAR, STRAUS AND GIROUX, INC., 19 Union Square West, New York NY 10003. *(212)741-6900* Fax: (212)633-2427. Imprints are Noonday Press, Hill and Wang, Sunburst Books, Aerial Fiction, Mirasol and North Point Press. Editor-in-Chief, Books for Young Readers: Margaret Ferguson. Publishes hardcover originals. Publishes 120 titles/year. Receives 5,000 submissions/year. Pays royalty. Offers advance. Publishes book 18 months after acceptance. Reports in 3 months. Catalog for 9×12 SAE with 3 first-class stamps.

Nonfiction and Fiction: "We are primarily interested in fiction picture books and novels for children and middle readers, but do some nonfiction—both picture book and longer formats." Submit outline/synopsis and sample chapters. Reviews copies of artwork/photos as part of ms package.

Recent Nonfiction Title: *Television*, by Carter Merbreier (behind-the-scenes, illustrated).

Recent Fiction Title: *Dove and Sword*, by Nancy Garden (historical fiction).

Recent Picture Book Title: *Carl Makes a Scrapbook*, by Alexandra Day.

Tips: "Study our style and our list."

FAWCETT JUNIPER, Imprint of Ballantine/Del Rey/Fawcett/Ivy, Division of Random House, 201 E. 50th St., New York NY 10022. (212)751-2600. Editor-in-Chief/Vice President: Leona Nevler. Publishes 24 titles/year. Pays royalty. Offers advance. Publishes book 1 year after acceptance. Accepts simultaneous submissions. Reports in 6 months on queries.

Nonfiction: Adult books.

Recent Nonfiction Title: *My Life: Magic Johnson*, by Magic Johnson.

Fiction: Mainstream/contemporary, young adult (12-18). No children's books. Query.

Recent Fiction Title: *The Secret History*, by Donna Tartt.

THE FEMINIST PRESS AT THE CITY UNIVERSITY OF NEW YORK, 311 E. 94th St., 2nd Floor, New York NY 10128. (212)360-5790. Fax: (212)348-1241. Senior Editor: Jean Casella. Estab. 1970. Publishes hardcover and trade paperback originals and reprints. Publishes 10-12 titles/year. Receives 500 submissions/year. 20% of books from first-time authors; 90% from unagented writers. Pays royalty on net price. Offers $100 average advance. Accepts simultaneous submissions. Reports in 4 months on proposals. Book catalog and ms guidelines free on request.

Nonfiction: "The Feminist Press's primary mission is to publish works committed to the eradication of gender-role stereotyping that are multicultural in focus. Persons should write for our guidelines for submission and catalog; note that we generally publish for the college classroom." Children's (ages 8 and up)/juvenile, primary materials for the humanities and social science classroom and general readers. Subjects include ethnic, gay/lesbian, government/politics, health/medicine, history, language/literature, music, sociology, translation, women's issues/studies and peace, memoir, international. Send proposal package, including materials requested in guidelines. Reviews artwork/photos as part of ms package. Send photocopies and SASE.

Recent Nonfiction Title: *Among the White Moon Faces: An Asian-American Memoir*, by Shirley Geok-lin Lim (memoir).

Fiction: "The Feminist Press publishes fiction reprints only. No original fiction is considered."

Tips: "Our audience consists of college students, professors, general readers."

J.G. FERGUSON PUBLISHING COMPANY, 200 W. Madison, Suite 300, Chicago IL 60606. Editorial Director: Holli Cosgrove. Estab. 1940. Publishes hardcover originals. Publishes 5 titles/year. Reports in 3 months on queries. Pays by project.

Nonfiction: Reference. "We publish work specifically for the junior high/high school/college library reference market. Works are generally encyclopedic in nature. Our current focus is career encyclopedias. No mass market, scholarly, or juvenile books, please." Query or submit outline and 1 sample chapter.

Recent Nonfiction Title: *Exploring Tech Careers* (career reference book).

Tips: "We like writers who know the market—former or current librarians or teachers or guidance counselors."

DONALD I. FINE BOOKS, Division of Penguin USA, 375 Hudson St., New York NY 10014. (212)366-2570. Fax: (212)366-2933. Imprints include Primus Library of Contemporary Americana. Publishes hardcover originals and trade paperback originals and reprints. Publishes 20 titles/year. Receives 1,000 submissions/year. 30% of books from first-time authors. Pays royalty on retail price. Advance varies. Publishes book 1 year after acceptance.

Nonfiction: Biography, cookbook, self-help. Subjects include history, military/war, sports. All unsolicited mss returned unopened. Reviews artwork/photos as part of ms package.

Recent Nonfiction Title: *Miss Rhythm: The Autobiography of Ruth Brown, Rhythm and Blues Legend*, by Ruth Brown with Andrew Yule.

Fiction: Adventure, ethnic, historical, horror, literary, mainstream/contemporary, mystery, suspense, Western. All unsolicited mss returned unopened.

Recent Fiction Title: *Grand Jury*, by Philip Friedman (thriller).

FIREBRAND BOOKS, 141 The Commons, Ithaca NY 14850. (607)272-0000. Publisher: Nancy K. Bereano. Estab. 1985. Publishes hardcover and trade paperback originals. Publishes 8-10 titles/year. Receives 400-500 submissions/year. 50% of books from first-time authors; 90% from unagented writers. Pays 7-9% royalty on retail price, or makes outright purchase. Publishes book 18 months after acceptance. Accepts simultaneous submissions, if so noted. Reports in 1 month on queries. *Writer's Market* recommends allowing 2 months for reply. Book catalog free.

Nonfiction: Personal narratives, essays. Subjects include feminism, lesbianism. Submit complete ms.

Fiction: Considers all types of feminist and lesbian fiction.

Tips: "Our audience includes feminists, lesbians, ethnic audiences, and other progressive people."

FISHER BOOKS, 4239 W. Ina Road, Suite 101, Tucson AZ 85741. (520)744-6110. Fax: (520)744-0944. Contact: Editorial Submissions Director. Estab. 1987. Publishes trade paperback originals and reprints. Publishes 16 titles/year. 25% of books from first-time authors; 75% from unagented writers. Pays 10-15% royalty on wholesale price. Accepts simultaneous submissions. Reports in 2 months. Book catalog for 8½×11 SAE with 3 first-class stamps.

Nonfiction: Subjects include automotive, business, cooking/foods/nutrition, regional gardening, family health, self-help. Submit outline and sample chapter, not complete ms. Include SAE and return postage.

Recent Nonfiction Title: *Your Pregnancy Questions & Answers*, by Glade B. Curtis (health).

‡FJORD PRESS, P.O. Box 16349, Seattle WA 98116. (206)935-7376. Fax: (206)938-1991. E-mail: fjord@h alcyon.com. Editor-in-Chief: Steven T. Murray. Publishes hardcover originals, trade paperback originals and reprints. Publishes 4-8 titles/year. Receives 100 queries and 40 mss/year. .01% of books from first-time authors; 80% from unagented writers. Pays 10-15% royalty on retail price or small advance and royalty. Offers $100-1,000 advance. Publishes book 2 years after acceptance of ms. Accepts simultaneous submissions. Reports in 1 month on queries. *Writer's Market* recommends allowing 2 months for reply. Book catalog for #10 SASE.

Fiction: Ethnic, feminist (but not anti-male), literary, mainstream/contemporary, mystery (no cozies), suspense (international thrillers), literature in translation. "We publish only literary fiction of the highest quality, including thrillers and mysteries. No supermarket genre fiction please." Query or submit synopsis, 1 sample chapter (not over 20 pages) and SASE.

Recent Fiction Title: *Maija*, by Tiina Nunnally (mainstream ethnic novel).

Tips: Audience is literate readers looking for something different from what normally comes out of New York, and willing to take a chance on an unfamiliar author. "If your fiction isn't as good as what's out there on the market, save your postage and keep practicing."

FOCAL PRESS, Subsidiary of Butterworth Heinemann, Division of Reed Elsevier (USA) Inc., 313 Washington St., Newton MA 02158-1630. Senior Editor: Marie Lee. Estab. US, 1981; UK, 1938. Imprint publishes hardcover and paperback originals and reprints. Publishes 30-35 UK-US titles/year; entire firm publishes 100 titles/year. Receives 500-700 submissions/year. 25% of books from first-time authors; 90% from unagented writers. Pays 10-12% royalty on wholesale price. Offers modest advance. Publishes book 9 months after acceptance. Accepts simultaneous submissions. Reports in 2 months. Book catalog and ms guidelines for SASE.

Nonfiction: How-to, reference, technical and textbooks in media arts: photography, film and cinematography, broadcasting, theater and performing arts. High-level scientific/technical monographs are also considered. "We do not publish collections of photographs or books composed primarily of photographs. Our books are text-oriented, with artwork serving to illustrate and expand on points in the text." Query preferred, or submit outline and sample chapters. Reviews artwork/photos as part of ms package.

Recent Nonfiction Title: *The Darkroom Cookbook* by Steve Ahchell.
Tips: "We are publishing fewer photography books. Our advances and royalties are more carefully determined with an eye toward greater profitability for all our publications."

FOCUS ON THE FAMILY BOOK PUBLISHING, 8605 Explorer Dr., Colorado Springs CO 80920. Contact: Editor. Publishes hardcover and trade paperback originals. Publishes 15-20 titles/year. 25% of books from first-time authors; 25% from unagented writers. Pays royalty. Offers advance. Publishes book 1 year after acceptance of ms. Accepts simultaneous submissions. Reports in 1 month on queries, 2 months on proposals. Book catalog free on request. Manuscript guidelines for #10 SASE.
Nonfiction: How-to, juvenile, self-help. Subjects include child guidance/parenting, money/finance, women's issues/studies. "We are the publishing arm of Focus on the Family, an evangelical Christian organization. Authors need to be aware that our book publishing is closely related to the focus of the organization, which is the strengthening and preservation of family and marriages." Query before submitting ms.
Tips: Our audience is "families and the people who make up families. Know what we publish before submitting query."

FOGHORN PRESS, 555 De Haro St., #220, San Francisco CA 94107. (415)241-9550. Fax: (415)241-9648. Website: http://www.foghorn.com. Acquisitions Editor: Judith Pynn. Publishes trade paperback originals and reprints. Publishes 35 titles/year. Receives 500 queries and 200 mss/year. 50% of books from first-time authors; 98% from unagented writers. Pays 12% royalty on wholesale price; occasional work-for-hire. Publishes book 1 year after acceptance of ms. Accepts simultaneous submissions. Reports in 1 month on queries, 2 months on proposals and mss. Book catalog and ms guidelines free on request.
   • *California Dog Lover's Companion* was voted best book for 1995 by the Outdoor Writers Association.
Nonfiction: Guidebooks. Subjects include nature/environment, recreation, sports, outdoors, leisure. Submit proposal package, including outline or chapter headings, résumé, 2 or more sample chapters, marketing plan.
Recent Nonfiction Title: *California Beaches*, by Parke Puterbaugh and Alan Bisbort (guide to what to do on and near all the beaches in the state).
Tips: "We're searching for writers throughout the U.S. and Canada to write our format guidebooks in several series."

‡FOREIGN POLICY ASSOCIATION, 470 Park Ave. S., New York NY 10016. (212)481-8100. Editor-in-Chief: Nancy Hoepli-Phalon. Imprints are Headline Series, Great Decisions. Publishes hardcover and trade paperback originals. Publishes 5-6 titles/year. Receives 12 queries and 6 mss/year, 99% from unagented writers. No advance. Pays outright purchase of $2,000-4,000. Publishes book 9 months after acceptance. Accepts simultaneous submissions. Reports in 2 months. Publications catalog free on request.
Nonfiction: Reference and textbook. Subjects include foreign policy, government/politics, history and social studies. "We are a nonpartisan educational organization. Audience: students, educators, general public with an interest in international relations." Query. Submit outline.
Recent Nonfiction Title: *U.S. Information Policy and Cultural Diplomacy*, by Frank Ninkovich (Headline Series quarterly).
Tips: Audience is students and people with an interest in but not necessarily any expertise in foreign policy and international relations.

FORUM PUBLISHING COMPANY, 383 E. Main St., Centerport NY 11721. (516) 754-5000. Contact: Martin Stevens. Publishes trade paperback originals. Publishes 12 titles/year. Receives 200 queries and 25 mss/year. 75% of books from first-time authors; 75% from unagented writers. No advance. Makes outright purchase of $250-750. Publishes book 4 months after acceptance. Accepts simultaneous submissions. Reports in 1 month on mss. *Writer's Market* recommends allowing 2 months for reply. Book catalog free on request.
Nonfiction: Subjects include business and economics, money/finance. "We only publish business titles." Submit outline. Reviews artwork/photos as part of ms package. Send photocopies.
Recent Nonfiction Title: *Selling Information By Mail*, by Glen Gilcrest.

FORWARD MOVEMENT PUBLICATIONS, 412 Sycamore St., Cincinnati OH 45202. E-mail: forward movement@ecunet.org. Editor and Director: Edward S. Gleason. Publishes trade paperback originals. Publishes 12 titles/year. 50% of books from first-time authors; 100% from unagented writers. Pays one-time honorarium. Reports in 2 months on queries and proposals, 3 months on mss. Book catalog for #10 SAE with 3 first-class stamps.
Nonfiction: Essays. Religious subjects. "We publish a variety of types of books, but they all relate to the lives of Christians. We are an agency of the Episcopal Church." Query with SASE.
Recent Nonfiction Title: *Smoke and Mirrors*, by Dorothy Marie England (addiction).
Tips: Audience is primarily members of mainline Protestant churches.

FOUR WALLS EIGHT WINDOWS, 39 W. 14th St., Room 503, New York NY 10011. Estab. 1987. Publishes hardcover originals, trade paperback originals and reprints. Publishes 20 titles/year. Receives 2,000 submissions/year. 15% of books from first-time authors; 50% from unagented writers. Pays royalty on retail price. Offers $1,500 average advance. Publishes book 1 year after acceptance. Reports in 2 months on queries. Book catalog for 6×9 SAE with 3 first-class stamps.

Nonfiction: Political, investigative. Subjects include art/architecture, government/politics, history, language/literature, nature/environment, science, travel. "We do not want New Age works." Query first with outline and SASE. All sent without SASE discarded.

Recent Nonfiction Title: *Bike Cult*, by David Perry.

Fiction: Ethnic, feminist, literary. "No romance, popular." Query first with outline/synopsis and SASE.

Recent Fiction Title: *Ribofunk*, by Paul DiFilippo.

Tips: No longer accepts unsolicited submissions.

‡**FOX CHAPEL PUBLISHING**, P.O. Box 7948, Lancaster PA 17604. Acquisitions: John Alan. Publishes hardcover and trade paperback originals and trade paperback reprints. Publishes 12 titles/year. 80% of books from first-time authors; 100% from unagented writers. Pays royalty or makes outright purchase. No advance. Publishes book 6 months after acceptance of ms. Accepts simultaneous submissions. Reports in 2 months on queries.

Nonfiction: Woodworking, woodcarving and related titles. Query. Reviews artwork/photos as part of ms package. Send photocopies.

Tips: "We're looking for knowledgeable artists, woodworkers first, writers second in our how-to line."

FRANCISCAN UNIVERSITY PRESS, University Blvd., Steubenville OH 43952. Fax: (614)283-6427. Website: http://esoptron.umd.edu/fusfolder/press.html. Editor: Celeste Gregory. Publishes trade paperback originals and reprints. Publishes 7 titles/year. 5% of books from first-time authors; 100% from unagented writers. Pays 5-15% royalty on retail price. Publishes book 1 year after acceptance of ms. Reports in 3 months on proposals. Book catalog and ms guidelines free on request.

Nonfiction: Popular level Catholic theology. Subjects include catechetics, scripture, Catholic apologetics. Submit proposal package, including outline, 3 sample chapters, author cv.

Recent Nonfiction Title: *If Your Mind Wanders at Mass*, by Thomas Howard (religion/liturgy).

Tips: "We seek to further the Catholic and Franciscan mission of Franciscan University of Steubenville by publishing quality popular-level Catholic apologetics and biblical studies. In this manner we hope to serve Pope John Paul II's call for a new evangelization of today's Catholics. 95% of our publications are solicited."

‡**THE FREE PRESS**, Imprint of Simon & Schuster, 1230 Avenue of the Americas, New York NY 10020. (212)698-7000. Publisher: Michael Jacobs. Estab. 1947. Publishes 120 titles/year. Receives 3,000 submissions/year. 15% of books from first-time authors; 50% of books from unagented writers. Pays variable royalty. Publishes book 1 year after acceptance of ms. Reports in 2 months.

Nonfiction: Publishes adult nonfiction, professional books and college texts in the social sciences, humanities and business. Reviews artwork/photos as part of ms package "but we can accept no responsibility for photos or art. Looks for identifiable target audience, evidence of writing ability." Accepts nonfiction translations. Send 1-3 sample chapters, outline, and query letter before submitting mss.

FREE SPIRIT PUBLISHING INC., 400 First Ave. N., Suite 616, Minneapolis MN 55401-1730. (612)338-2068. Acquisitions Editor: Elizabeth H. Verdick. Publishes trade paperback originals and reprints. Publishes 20 titles/year. 10% of books from first-time authors; 90% from unagented writers. Offers advance. Book catalog and ms guidelines free on request.

Nonfiction: Children's/juvenile, self-help (children's only). Subjects include child guidance/parenting, education (pre-K-12, but not textbooks or basic skills books like reading, counting, etc.), health (mental/emotional health—*not* physical health—for/about children), psychology (for/about children), sociology (for/about children). Query with outline, 2 sample chapters and SASE. Send photocopies. "Many of our authors are teachers, counselors or others involved in helping kids."

Recent Nonfiction Title: *What Kids Need To Succeed*, by Benson, Galbraith & Espeland (parenting/child rearing).

Tips: "Our audience is children, teens, teachers, parents and youth counselors. We are concerned with kids' well-being. We are not looking for academic or religious materials, nor books that analyze problems with the nation's school systems. Instead we want books that offer practical, positive advice so kids can help themselves."

FRIENDS UNITED PRESS, 101 Quaker Hill, Richmond IN 47374. (317)962-7573. Fax: (317)966-1293. Editor/Manager: Ardith Talbot. Estab. 1968. Publishes 5 titles/year. Receives 100 queries and 80 mss/year. 50% of books from first-time authors; 99% from unagented writers. Pays 7½% royalty. Publishes ms 1 year after acceptance of ms. Accepts simultaneous submissions. Reports in 16 months. Book catalog and ms guidelines free on request.

Nonfiction: Biography, humor, children's/juvenile, reference, textbook. Religious subjects. "Authors should be Quaker and should be familiar with Quaker history, spirituality and doctrine." Submit proposal package. Reviews artwork/photos as part of ms package. Send photocopies.

Fiction: Historical, juvenile, religious. "Must be Quaker-related." Query.

Tips: "Spirituality manuscripts must be in agreement with Quaker spirituality."

GASLIGHT PUBLICATIONS, 2809 Wilmington Way, Las Vegas NV 89102-5989. (702)221-8495. Fax: (702)221-8297. E-mail: 71604.511@compuserve.com. Publisher: Jack Tracy. Estab. 1979. Imprints include McGuffin Books. Publishes hardcover and paperback originals. Publishes 6 titles/year. Receives 15-20 submissions/year. 75% of books from first-time authors; 90% from unagented writers. Pays 10% royalty. Publishes book 1 year after acceptance. Accepts simultaneous submissions. Reports in 1 month. *Writer's Market* recommends allowing 2 months for reply. Book catalog free.

Nonfiction: "We publish specialized studies of the mystery genre and related fields: biography, criticism, analysis, reference, film, true crime. Submissions should be serious, well-researched, not necessarily for the scholar, but for readers who are already experts in their own right. 12,000 words minimum." Query with outline/synopsis and sample chapters or send complete ms. Reviews artwork/photos as part of ms package. "Please—we do *not* publish unsolicited fiction."

Recent Nonfiction Title: *Myth and Modern Man in Sherlock Holmes: Sir Arthur Conan Doyle and the Uses of Nostalgia.*

Tips: "Our purchasers tend to be public libraries and knowledgeable mystery aficionados."

GAY SUNSHINE PRESS and LEYLAND PUBLICATIONS, P.O. Box 410690, San Francisco CA 94141-0690. Editor: Winston Leyland. Estab. 1970. Publishes hardcover originals, trade paperback originals and reprints. Publishes 6-8 titles/year. Pays royalty or makes outright purchase. Reports in 6 weeks on queries. Book catalog for $1.

Nonfiction: How-to and gay lifestyle topics. "We're interested in innovative literary nonfiction which deals with gay lifestyles." No long personal accounts, academic or overly formal titles. Query. "After query is returned by us, submit outline and sample chapters with SASE. All unsolicited manuscripts are returned unopened."

Fiction: Erotica, ethnic, experimental, historical, mystery, science fiction, gay fiction in translation. "Interested in well-written novels on gay themes; also short story collections. We have a high literary standard for fiction." Query. "After query is returned by us, submit outline/synopsis and sample chapters with SASE. All unsolicited manuscripts are returned unopened."

GEM GUIDES BOOK COMPANY, 315 Cloverleaf Dr., Suite F, Baldwin Park CA 91706-6510. (818)855-1611. Fax: (818)855-1610. Imprints include Gembooks. Editor: Robin Nordhues. Publishes trade paperback originals. Publishes 6-8 titles/year. Receives 40 submissions/year. 30% of books from first-time authors; 100% from unagented writers. Pays 6-10% royalty on retail price. Offers $1,000 average advance. Publishes book 8 months after acceptance. Accepts simultaneous submissions. Reports in 1 month. *Writer's Market* recommends allowing 2 months for reply.

Nonfiction: Regional books for the Western US. Subjects include hobbies, Western history, nature/environment, recreation, travel. "We are looking for books on earth sciences, nature books, also travel/local interest titles for the Western US." Query with outline/synopsis and sample chapters. Reviews artwork/photos as part of ms package.

Recent Nonfiction Title: *1995 The Nevada Trivia Book*, by Moreno (local interest).

Tips: "Authors have the best chance selling us books about rocks, minerals, and recreational opportunities in the Western US. We have a general audience of people interested in recreational activities. Publishers plan and have specific book lines in which they specialize. Learn about the publisher and submit materials compatible with that publisher's product line."

‡GENERAL PUBLISHING GROUP, 2701 Ocean Park Blvd., Suite 140, Santa Monica CA 90405. (310)314-4000. Managing Editor: Peter Hoffman. Publishes hardcover and trade paperback originals. Publishes 30 titles/year. Recives 100 queries/year; receives 250 mss/year. 25% of books from first-time authors; 50% from unagented writers. Pays royalty. Offers $5,000-10,000 advance. Publishes ms 8 months after acceptance. Accepts simultaneous submissions. Reports in 4 months on queries. Book catalog free on request.

Nonfiction: Biography, children's/juvenile, coffee table book, gift book, humor, illustrated book. Subjects include Americana, art/architecture, music/dance, photography, entertainment/media. Query with proposal package, including sample chapters, toc and SASE. Reviews artwork as part of ms package. Send photocopies.

Recent Nonfiction Title: *Frank Sinatra: An American Legend*, by Nancy Sinatra (biography/tribute).

GLENBRIDGE PUBLISHING LTD., 6010 W. Jewell Ave., Denver CO 80232-7106. Fax: (303)987-9037. Editor: James A. Keene. Estab. 1986. Publishes hardcover originals and reprints, trade paperback originals. Publishes 6-8 titles/year. Pays 10% royalty. Publishes book 1 year after acceptance. Accepts simultaneous submissions. Reports in 2 months on queries. Book catalog for 6×9 SASE. Manuscript guidelines for #10 SASE.

Nonfiction: General. Subjects include Americana, business and economics, history, music, philosophy, politics, psychology, sociology, cookbooks. Query with outline/synopsis, sample chapters and SASE.

Recent Nonfiction Title: *Till Divorce Do Us Part*, by Grottkau and Rumpf (problems of women in divorce).

THE GLOBE PEQUOT PRESS, INC., P.O. Box 833, Old Saybrook CT 06475-0833. (203)395-0440. Fax: (203)395-1418. Submissions Editor: Laura Strom. Estab. 1947. Imprints are Voyager Books and East Woods Books. Publishes hardcover originals, paperback originals and reprints. Publishes 80 titles/year. Receives 1,500 submissions/year. 30% of books from first-time authors; 60% from unagented writers. Average print order for a first book is 4,000-7,500. Makes outright purchase or pays 7½-10% royalty on net price. Offers advance. Publishes book 1 year after acceptance. Accepts simultaneous submissions. Reports in 3 months. Book catalog for 9×12 SASE.
Nonfiction: Travel guidebooks (regional OK), outdoor recreation, home-based business, personal finance, how-to, cookbooks. No doctoral theses, fiction, genealogies, memoirs, poetry or textbooks. Submit outline, table of contents, sample chapter and résumé/vita. Reviews artwork/photos.

DAVID R. GODINE, PUBLISHER, INC., P.O. Box 9103, Lincoln MA 01773. President: David Godine. Editorial Director: Mark Polizzotti. Estab. 1970. Publishes hardcover and trade paperback originals and reprints. Publishes 30 titles/year. Pays royalty on retail price. Publishes book 3 years after acceptance of ms. Book catalog for 5×8 SAE with 3 first-class stamps.
Nonfiction: Biography, coffee table book, cookbook, illustrated book, children's/juvenile. Subjects include Americana, art/architecture, gardening, nature/environment, photography, literary criticism and current affairs. *Writer's Market* recommends sending a query with SASE first.
Recent Nonfiction Title: *Grass Soup*, by Zhang Xianliang.
Fiction: Literary, mystery, short story collection, children's/juvenile. "We are not currently considering unsolicited manuscripts."
Recent Fiction Title: *Little Jordan*, by Marly Youmans.
Poetry: "Our poetry list is filled through 1997."
Recent Poetry Title: *New and Selected Poems*, by Ron Padgett.

GOLDEN WEST PUBLISHERS, 4113 N. Longview, Phoenix AZ 85014. (602)265-4392. Editor: Hal Mitchell. Estab. 1973. Publishes trade paperback originals. Publishes 5-6 titles/year. Receives 200 submissions/year. 50% of books from first-time authors; 100% from unagented writers. Average print order for a first book is 5,000. Prefers mss on work-for-hire basis. No advance. Publishes book an average of 6 months after acceptance. Accepts simultaneous submissions. Reports in 1 month on queries, 2 months on mss.
Nonfiction: Cookbooks, books on the Southwest and West. Subjects include cooking/foods, Southwest history and outdoors, travel. Query. Reviews artwork/photos as part of ms package.
Tips: "We are interested in Arizona and Southwest material, and cookbooks, and welcome material in these areas."

THE GRADUATE GROUP, P.O. Box 370351, West Hartford CT 06137-0351. Vice President: Robert Whitman. Publishes trade paperback originals. Publishes 25 titles/year. Receives 100 queries and 70 mss/year. 60% of books from first-time authors; 90% from unagented writers. Pays 20% royalty on retail price. Publishes book 3 months after acceptance of ms. Accepts simultaneous submissions. Reports in 1 month. *Writer's Market* recommends allowing 2 months for reply. Book catalog and ms guidelines free on request.
Nonfiction: Reference. Subjects include career/internships/law/medicine.
Recent Nonfiction Title: *Outstanding Résumés for College, Business And Law Graduate*, by Robert Whitman (reference).
Tips: Audience is career planning offices, college and graduate school libraries and public libraries. "We are very open to all submittals, especially those involving career planning, internships and other nonfiction titles." Looking for books on law enforcement, books for prisoners and reference books.

GRAPEVINE PUBLICATIONS, INC., P.O. Box 2449, Corvallis OR 97339-2449. (541)754-0583. Fax: (541)754-6508. Managing Editor: Christopher M. Coffin. Estab. 1983. Publishes trade paperback originals. Publishes 2-4 titles/year. Receives 200-300 submissions/year. 20% of books from first-time authors; 100% from unagented writers. Pays 6-9% royalty on net sales. Publishes book 6 months after acceptance. Accepts simultaneous submissions. "Due to volume, we respond only if interested."
Nonfiction: Tutorials on technical subjects written for the layperson, innovative curricula or resources for math and science teachers. Subjects include math, science, computers, calculators, software, video, audio and other technical tools. Submit complete ms. *Writer's Market* recommends sending a query with SASE first.
Recent Nonfiction Title: *Calculus on the HP48G/GX*, by D. Coffin (instructional).
Fiction: Children's picture books, juvenile fiction. Submit complete ms.

GRAPHIC ARTS TECHNICAL FOUNDATION, 4615 Forbes Ave., Pittsburgh PA 15213-3796. (412)621-6941. Fax: (412)621-3049. E-mail: info@gatf.lm.com. Website: http://www.gatf.lm.com. Editor-in-Chief: Thomas M. Destree. Technical Editor: Pamela J. Groff. Estab. 1924. Publishes trade paperback originals and hardcover reference texts. Publishes 10 titles/year. Receives 15 submissions/year. 50% of books from first-time authors; 100% from unagented writers. Pays 5-15% royalty on average price. Publishes book 1 year after acceptance. Reports in 1 month on queries. *Writer's Market* recommends allowing 2 months for reply. Book catalog for 9×12 SAE with 2 first-class stamps. Manuscript guidelines for #10 SASE.

Nonfiction: How-to, reference, technical, textbook. Subjects include printing/graphic arts. "We want textbook/reference books about printing and related technologies, providing that the content does not overlap appreciably with any other GATF books in print or in production. Although original photography is related to printing, we do not anticipate publishing any books on that topic." Query with SASE or submit outline, sample chapters and SASE. Reviews artwork/photos as part of ms package.

Recent Nonfiction Title: *Guide to Desktop Publishing*, by Jim Cavuto and Stephen Beale (2nd ed.).

Tips: "We are looking toward adapting more of our titles for alternative media—CD and online publishing. We are also publishing shorter titles that are updated more frequently, such as our Prepress Essentials series. Recently, we had an author prepare the entire manuscript for us—all the way up to plate-ready films. The idea is to get it in and out as a marketable product as quickly as we can. We are more likely to work with authors who can bring a manuscript in quickly with a minimum of editing required."

GREAT QUOTATIONS PUBLISHING, 1967 Quincy Ct., Glendale Heights IL 60139. (708)582-2800. Fax: (708)582-2813. Editor/Publisher: Ringo Suek. Publishes 40 titles/year. Receives 400 queries and 300 mss/year. 50% of books from first-time authors; 80% from unagented writers. Pays 3-10% royalty on net sales or makes outright purchase of $300-3,000. Offers $200-1,200 advance. Publishes book 6 months after acceptance of ms. Accepts simultaneous submissions. "Usually we return submissions, but we do not guarantee 100% that they will be returned." Reports in 2 months. Book catalog for $1.50. Manuscript guidelines for #10 SASE.

Nonfiction: Humor, illustrated book, self-help, quotes. Subjects include business and economics, child guidance/parenting, nature/environment, religion, sports, women's issues/studies. "We look for subjects with identifiable markets, appeal to the general public." Submit outline and 2 sample chapters. Reviews artwork/photos as part of ms package. Send photocopies, transparencies.

Recent Nonfiction Title: *Secret Language of Men*, by Shearer Weaver (gift book).

Poetry: "Presently, we would be most interested in upbeat and juvenile poetry."

Tips: "Our books are physically small, and generally a very quick read. These books are available at gift shops and book shops throughout the country. We are very aware that most of our books are bought on impulse and given as gifts. We need very strong, clever, descriptive titles; beautiful cover art, and brief, positive, upbeat text. Be prepared to submit final manuscript on computer disk, according to our specifications. (It is not necessary to try to format the typesetting of your manuscript to look like a finished book.)"

‡**GREENE BARK PRESS**, P.O. Box 1108, Bridgeport CT 06601. (203)372-4861. Publisher: Thomas J. Greene. Publishes hardcover originals. Publishes 5 titles/year. Receives 100 queries and 3,000 mss/year. 60% of books from first-time authors; 100% from unagented writers. Pays 10-15% royalty on wholesale price. Offers $200-300 advance. Publishes book 1 year after acceptance of ms. Accepts simultaneous submissions. Reports in 3 months on mss. Book catalog and ms guidelines free on request.

Fiction: Juvenile. "We only publish children's fiction—all subjects, but in reading picture book format appealing to ages 3-9 or all ages." Submit entire ms with SASE.

Recent Fiction Title: *The Butterfly Bandit*, by Ester Hauser Laurence (hardcover picture book).

Tips: Audience is "children who read to themselves and others. Mothers, fathers, grandparents, God-parents who read to their respective children; grandchildren. Include SASE, be prepared to wait, do not inquire by telephone."

GREENHAVEN PRESS, INC., P.O. Box 289009, San Diego CA 92198-9009. Managing Editor: Scott Barbour. Estab. 1970. Publishes hard and softcover educational supplementary materials and (nontrade) nonfiction on contemporary issues for high school and college readers. Publishes 8 mss/year; all anthologies are works for hire; 1-4 single titles are royalty contracts. Receives 100 submissions/year. 25% of books from first-time authors; 100% of books from unagented writers. Makes outright purchase of $1,000-3,000. Publishes ms 1 year after acceptance. Book catalog for 9×12 SAE with 3 first-class stamps.

Nonfiction: "We produce tightly formatted anthologies on contemporary controversial issues for high school- and college-level readers. Each series has specific requirements. Potential writers should familiarize themselves with our catalog and senior high and college material." Query. No unsolicited mss.

GROSSET & DUNLAP PUBLISHERS, Imprint of the Putnam Berkley Publishing Group, 200 Madison Ave., New York NY 10016. President: Jane O'Connor. Editor-in-Chief: Judy Donnelly. VP/Art Director:

FOR EXPLANATION of symbols, see the Key to Symbols and Abbreviations. For unfamiliar words, see the Glossary.

Ronnie Ann Herman. Estab. 1898. Imprints are Tuffy Books and Platt & Munk. Publishes hardcover and paperback originals. Publishes 75 titles/year. Receives more than 3,000 submissions/year. Publishes book 18 months after acceptance. Accepts simultaneous submissions. Reports in 2 months.

Nonfiction: Juveniles. Submit proposal or query first. Nature and science are of interest. Looks for new ways of looking at the world of a child.

Fiction: Juveniles. Submit proposal or query first.

Tips: "Nonfiction that is particularly topical or of wide interest in the mass market; new concepts for novelty format for preschoolers; and very well-written easy readers on topics that appeal to primary graders have the best chance of selling to our firm."

GROUP PUBLISHING, INC., 2890 N. Monroe Ave., Box 481, Loveland CO 80539. Fax: (303)669-3269. E-mail: greditor@aol.com. Website: http://www.grouppublishing.com. Book Acquisitions Editorial Assistant: Kerri Nance. Publishes trade paperback originals. Publishes 20-30 titles/year. Receives 200-400 queries and 300-500 mss/year. 30% of books from first-time authors; 95% from unagented writers. Pays up to 10% royalty on wholesale price or makes outright purchase. Offers up to $1,000 advance. Publishes 18 months after acceptance of ms. Accepts simultaneous submissions. Reports in 2 months on queries, 6 months on proposals. Book catalog for 9×12 SAE with 2 first-class stamps. Manuscript guidelines for #10 SASE.

Nonfiction: How-to, adult, youth and children's ministry resources. Subjects include education, religion and any subjects pertinent to adult, youth or children's ministry in a church setting. "We're an interdenominational publisher of resource materials for people who work with adults, youth or children in a Christian church setting. We also publish materials for use directly by youth or children (such as devotional books, workbooks or stories). Everything we do is based on concepts of active and interactive learning as described in *Why Nobody Learns Much of Anything at Church: And How to Fix It* by Thom and Joani Schultz. We need new, practical, hands-on, innovative, out-of-the-box ideas—things that no one's doing . . . yet." Submit proposal package, including outline, 2 sample chapters, introduction to the book (written as if the reader will read it), and sample activities if appropriate.

Recent Nonfiction Title: *Children's Ministry Guide for Smaller Churches*, by Rick Chromey (how-to).

Tips: "We're seeking proposals for CD-ROM projects."

GROVE/ATLANTIC, INC., 841 Broadway, New York NY 10003. Publishes 70 titles/year. General interest publisher of literary fiction and nonfiction. Query before submitting. No unsolicited mss.

Nonfiction: Subjects include current events, film, drama, social issues, arts.

GRYPHON HOUSE, INC., P.O. Box 207, Beltsville MD 20704. (301)595-9500. Fax: (301)595-0051. Editor-in-Chief: Kathy Charner. Publishes trade paperback originals. Publishes 6 titles/year. Pays royalty on wholesale price. Reports in 3 months.

Nonfiction: How-to and creative educational activities for teachers to do with preschool children ages 1-5. Submit outline, 2-3 sample chapters and SASE.

Recent Nonfiction Title: *Preschool Art*, by Maryann Kohl (open-ended art activities for young children).

GRYPHON PUBLICATIONS, P.O. Box 209, Brooklyn NY 11228. Owner/Publisher: Gary Lovisi. Imprints are Paperback Parade Magazine, Hardboiled Magazine, Other Worlds Magazine, Gryphon Books, Gryphon Doubles. Publishes hardcover originals and trade paperback originals and reprints. Publishes 10 titles/year. Receives 500 queries and 1,000 mss/year. 60% of books from first-time authors; 90% from unagented writers. No advance. Makes outright purchase by contract, price varies. Publishes book 2 years after acceptance of ms. Reports in 1 month on queries. *Writer's Market* recommends allowing 2 months for reply. Book catalog and ms guidelines for #10 SASE.

Nonfiction: Reference, bibliography. Subjects include hobbies, literature and book collecting. "We need well-written, well-researched articles, but query first on topic and length. Mistakes writers often make when submitting nonfiction are submitting not fully developed/researched material." Query. Reviews artwork/photos as part of ms package. Send photocopies (slides, transparencies may be necessary later).

Fiction: Mystery, science fiction, suspense, urban horror, hardboiled fiction. "We want cutting-edge fiction, under 3,000 words with impact!" Query or submit complete ms. on short stories only. *No novels.*

Tips: "We are very particular about novels and book-length work. A first-timer has a better chance with a short story or article. On anything over 6,000 words *do not* send manuscript, send *only* query letter about the piece with SASE."

HALF HALT PRESS, INC., P.O. Box 67, Boonsboro MD 21713. (301)733-7119. Fax: (301)733-7408. Publisher: Elizabeth Carnes. Estab. 1986. Publishes 90% hardcover and trade paperback originals and 10% reprints. Publishes 15 titles/year. Receives 150 submissions/year. 25% of books from first-time authors; 50% from unagented authors. Pays 10-12½% royalty on retail price. Offers advance by agreement. Publishes book 1 year after acceptance. Reports in 1 month on queries. *Writer's Market* recommends allowing 2 months for reply. Book catalog for 6×9 SAE with 2 first-class stamps.

Nonfiction: Instructional: horse and equestrian related subjects only. "We need serious instructional works by authorities in the field on horse-related topics, broadly defined." Query. Reviews artwork/photos as part of ms package.

Recent Nonfiction Title: *Emergency! The Active Horseman's Guide to Emergency Care*, by Dr. Karen Hayes.

Recent Fiction Title: *A New Horse for Marny*, by Libby Anderson.

Tips: "Writers have the best chance selling us well-written, unique works that teach serious horse people how to do something better. If I were a writer trying to market a book today, I would offer a straightforward presentation, letting work speak for itself, without hype or hard sell. Allow publisher to contact writer, without frequent calling to check status. They haven't forgotten the writer but may have many different proposals at hand; frequent calls to 'touch base,' multiplied by the number of submissions, become an annoyance. As the publisher/author relationship becomes close and is based on working well together, early impressions may be important, even to the point of being a consideration in acceptance for publication."

ALEXANDER HAMILTON INSTITUTE, 70 Hilltop Rd., Ramsey NJ 07446-1119. (201)825-3377. Fax: (201)825-8696. Editor-in-Chief: Brian L.P. Zevnik. Estab. 1909. Publishes 3-ring binder and paperback originals. Publishes 10-15 titles/year. Receives 50 queries and 10 mss/year. 25% of books from first-time authors; 95% from unagented writers. Pays 5-8% royalty on retail price or makes outright purchase ($3,500-7,000). Offers $3,500-7,000 advance. Publishes book 10 months after acceptance. Accepts simultaneous submissions. Reports in 1 month on queries, 2 months on mss.

Nonfiction: Executive/management books for 2 audiences. The first is overseas, upper-level manager. "We need how-to and skills building books. *No* traditional management texts or academic treatises." The second audience is US personnel executives and high-level management. Subject is legal personnel matters. "These books combine court case research and practical application of defensible programs." Submit outline, 3 paragraphs on each chapter, examples of lists, graphics, cases.

Tips: "We sell exclusively by direct mail to managers and executives around the world. A writer must know his/her field and be able to communicate practical systems and programs."

HANCOCK HOUSE PUBLISHERS LTD., 1431 Harrison Ave., Blaine WA 98230-5005. (604)538-1114. Fax: (604)538-2262. E-mail: hancock@uniserve.com. Publisher: David Hancock. Estab. 1971. Publishes hardcover and trade paperback originals and reprints. Publishes 12 titles/year. Receives 400 submissions/year. 50% of books from first-time authors; 100% from unagented writers. Pays 10% royalty. Accepts simultaneous submissions. Publishes book 6 months after acceptance. Reports in 6 months. Book catalog free on request.

Nonfiction: Pacific Northwest history and biography, nature guides, native culture, and natural history.

Recent Nonfiction Title: *Fatal Prescription*, by John Griffiths (true crime).

‡**HANSER GARDNER PUBLICATIONS**, 6600 Clough Pike, Cincinnati OH 45244-4090. (513)527-8977. Fax: (513)527-8950. Website: http://www.gardnerweb.com. Development Editor: Jennifer King. Publishes hardcover originals and reprints. Publishes 5-10 titles/year. Receives 40-50 queries and 5-10 mss/year. 75% of books from first-time authors; 100% from unagented writers. Pays 6-12% royalty on net receipts. No advance. Publishes book 4-6 months after acceptance of ms. Accepts simultaneous submissions. Reports in 2 weeks on queries, 2 months on proposals and mss. Book catalog and ms guidelines free on request.

Nonfiction: How-to, technical, textbook. Subjects include metalworking and finishing processes, and related management topics. "Our books are primarily basic introductory-level training books, and books that emphasize practical applications. Strictly deal with subjects shown above." Query with proposal package, including résumé, preface, outline, sample chapter, comparison to competing or similar titles. Reviews artwork/photos as part of ms package. Send photocopies.

Recent Nonfiction Title: *Industrial Painting*, by Norman R. Roobol (industrial reference).

Tips: "Our readers and authors occupy various positions within small and large metalworking, machining and finishing shops/plants. We prefer that interested individuals write, call, or fax us with their queries first, so we can send them our proposal guideline form."

‡**HARBOR PRESS**, 5713 Wollochet Dr. NW, Gig Harbor WA 98335. Fax: (206)851-5191. E-mail: skyblue688@aol.com. President/Publisher: Harry R. Lynn. Acquisitions Editor: Deborah Young. Publishes hardcover and trade paperback originals and reprints. Publishes 8-10 titles/year. Negotiates competitive royalties on wholesale price or makes outright purchase.

Nonfiction: Cookbook, gift book, self-help. Subjects include cooking/foods/nutrition, health/medicine, money/finance. Publication plans include consumer-oriented, self-help and health books that have potential for both trade and mail order markets. Query with proposal package, including outline, 3 sample chapters, synopsis and SASE. Reviews artwork/photos as part of ms package. Send photocopies.

Recent Nonfiction Title: *How to Fix Your Aching Back*, by Dr. Arthur Brownstein (health).

‡**HARCOURT BRACE & COMPANY**, Children's Books Division, 525 B St., #1900, San Diego CA 92101. (619)699-6810. Contact: Manuscript Submissions. Imprints include Harcourt Brace Children's Books,

Gulliver Books, Browndeer Press, Red Wagon, Voyager and Odyssey Paperbacks, Jane Yolen Books and Magic Carpet. Publishes hardcover originals and trade paperback reprints. Considers only query letters and agented mss.

Recent Nonfiction Title: *Wilma Unlimited*, by Kathleen Krull (nonfiction picture book).

Recent Fiction Title: *The Bomb*, by Theodore Taylor (young adult fiction).

Recent Poetry Title: *Sawgrass Poems*, by Frank Arch (poetry/photo essay).

HARCOURT BRACE & COMPANY, Trade Division, 525 B St., Suite 1900, San Diego, CA 92101. (619)699-6560. Contact: Marsha Brubaker.

Nonfiction: Publishes all categories except business/finance (university texts), cookbooks, self-help, sex.

Recent Nonfiction Title: *The Western Canon*, by Harold Bloom.

Recent Fiction Title: *Snow Falling on Cedars*, by David Guterson.

HARPER SAN FRANCISCO, Division of HarperCollins, 1160 Battery St., 3rd Floor, San Francisco CA 94111-1213. (415)477-4400. Fax: (415)477-4444. Publisher: Thomas Grady. Estab. 1817. Publishes hardcover originals, trade paperback originals and reprints. Publishes 125 titles/year. Receives about 10,000 submissions/year. 5% of books from first-time authors; 30% from unagented writers. Pays royalty. Publishes book 18 months after acceptance. Accepts simultaneous submissions, if so noted. Reports in 3 months on queries. Manuscript guidelines free.

Nonfiction: Biography, how-to, reference, self-help. Subjects include psychology, religion, self-help, spirituality. Query or submit outline and sample chapters with SASE.

Recent Nonfiction Title: *Honest Jesus*, by Robert Funk.

HARPERCOLLINS PUBLISHERS, 10 E. 53rd St., New York NY 10022. (212)207-7000. Executive Managing Editor: Kim Lewis. Imprints include Harper Adult Trade; Harper San Francisco (religious/New Age books only); Harper Perennial; Harper Reference; Harper Interactive; Basic Books; Harper Business; Harper Torchbooks; Harper Paperbacks; Harper Audio. Publishes hardcover and paperback originals and paperback reprints. Trade publishes more than 500 titles/year. Pays standard royalties. Advance negotiable. *No unsolicited queries or mss.* Reports on solicited queries in 6 weeks. *Writer's Market* recommends allowing 2 months for reply.

Nonfiction: Americana, animals, art, biography, business/economics, current affairs, cookbooks, health, history, how-to, humor, music, nature, philosophy, politics, psychology, reference, religion, science, self-help, sociology, sports, travel.

Recent Nonfiction Title: *Dolly*.

Fiction: Adventure, fantasy, gothic, historical, mystery, science fiction, suspense, western, literary. "We look for a strong story line and exceptional literary talent."

Recent Fiction Title: *Hostile Witness*.

Tips: "We do not accept any unsolicited material."

HARTLEY & MARKS, P.O. Box 147, Point Roberts WA 98281. (360)945-2017. Editorial Director: Vic Marks. Estab. 1973. Publishes hardcover and trade paperback originals. Publishes 8-10 titles/year. Receives 700 submissions/year. 80% of books from first-time authors; 95% from unagented writers. Pays 7-10% royalty on retail price. Reports in 2 months. Book catalog for SASE.

Nonfiction: How-to, self-help, technical. Subjects include agriculture/gardening (organic), building, healthy lifestyles, preventive and holistic medicine, useful crafts, nature/environment (practical how-to), psychology self-help, typography, translations of aforementioned subjects. No metaphysical books, autobiography or recipe books. Query or submit outline and sample chapters.

THE HARVARD COMMON PRESS, 535 Albany St., Boston MA 02118-2500. (617)423-5803. Fax: (617)423-0679 or (617)695-9794. President/Publisher: Bruce P. Shaw. Associate Publisher: Dan Rosenberg. Imprint is Gambit Books. Estab. 1976. Publishes hardcover and trade paperback originals and reprints. Publishes 8 titles/year. Receives 1,000 submissions/year. 50% of books from first-time authors; 75% of books from unagented writers. Average print order for a first book is 10,000-20,000 copies. Pays royalty. Offers average $4,000 advance. Publishes book 1 year after acceptance. Accepts simultaneous submissions. Reports in 2 months. Book catalog for 9×12 SAE with 3 first-class stamps. Manuscript guidelines for SASE.

• Harvard Common Press has changed subject focus from family matters to childcare.

Nonfiction: Cooking, childcare and parenting, travel. "We want strong, practical books that help people gain control over a particular area of their lives. An increasing percentage of our list is made up of books about cooking, child care and parenting; in these areas we are looking for authors who are knowledgeable, if not experts, and who can offer a different approach to the subject. We are open to good nonfiction proposals that show evidence of strong organization and writing, and clearly demonstrate a need in the marketplace. First-time authors are welcome." Accepts nonfiction translations. Submit outline and 1-3 sample chapters. Reviews artwork/photos.

Recent Nonfiction Title: *The Nursing Mother's Companion*, (3rd ed.), by Huggins (childcare).
Tips: "We are much more demanding about the quality of proposals; in addition to strong writing skills and thorough knowledge of the subject matter, we require a detailed analysis of the competition."

HARVEST HOUSE PUBLISHERS, 1075 Arrowsmith, Eugene OR 97402-9197. (541)343-0123. Manager: LaRae Weikert. Estab. 1974. Publishes hardcover, trade paperback and mass market originals and reprints. Publishes 70-80 titles/year. Receives 3,500 submissions/year. 10% of books from first-time authors; 90% from unagented writers. Pays 14-18% royalty on wholesale price. Publishes book 1 year after acceptance. Accepts simultaneous submissions. Reports in 10 weeks. Book catalog for 9×12 SAE with 2 first-class stamps. Manuscript guidelines for SASE.
  ● Harvest House is no longer interested in manuscripts dealing with counseling, children's books or juvenile fiction.
Nonfiction: Self-help, current issues, women's and family on Evangelical Christian religion. No cookbooks, theses, dissertations, music, or poetry. Query or submit outline and sample chapters.
Recent Nonfiction Title: *Fill My Cup, Lord*, by Emilie Barnes (devotional).
Fiction: Historical, mystery, religious. No short stories. Query or submit outline/synopsis and sample chapters.
Recent Fiction Title: *Where the Wild Rose Blooms*, by Lori Wick (romance).
Tips: "Audience is primarily women ages 25-40—evangelical Christians of all denominations."

HASTINGS HOUSE, Eagle Publishing Corp., 141 Halstead Ave., Mamaroneck NY 10543-2652. (914)835-4005. Fax: (914)835-1037. Editor/Publisher: Hy Steirman. Publishes hardcover and trade paperback originals and reprints. Publishes 12 titles/year. Receives 350 queries and 125 mss/year. 5% of books from first-time authors; 40% from unagented writers. Pays 8-10% royalty on retail price on trade paperbacks. Offers $1,000-10,000 advance. Publishes book 10 months after acceptance of ms. Reports in 1 month. *Writer's Market* recommends allowing 2 months for reply.
Nonfiction: Biography, coffee table book, cookbook, how-to, humor, reference, self-help, consumer. Subjects include business and economics, cooking/foods/nutrition, health/medicine, psychology, travel, writing. "We are looking for books that address consumer needs." Query or submit outline.
Recent Nonfiction Title: *Lincoln's Unknown Private Life*.

‡HATHERLEIGH PRESS, 420 E. 51st St., New York NY 10022. (212)355-0882. Fax: (212)308-7930. Editor-In-Chief: Frederic Flach. Publishes hardcover originals, trade paperback originals and reprints. Publishes 10-12 titles/year. Receives 20 queries and 20 mss/year. Pays 5-15% royalty on retail price or makes outright purchase. Offers $500-5,000 advance. Publishes book 6 months after acceptance of ms. Reports in 2 months on queries. Book catalog free on request.
Nonfiction: Reference, self-help, technical. Subjects include health/medicine, psychology. Submit outline and 1 sample chapter with SASE. Reviews artwork/photos as part of ms package. Send photocopies.
Recent Nonfiction Title: *The Second Decade of AIDS*, Ed. Michael Shernoff/Walt Odets (hardcover and trade paper).
Tips: Audience is mental health professionals, general (self-help, etc.). Submit a clear outline that includes what the market and audience for your book is.

HAY HOUSE, INC., P.O. Box 5100, Carlsbad CA 92018-5100. (619)431-7695. Fax: (619)431-6948. Editorial Director: Jill Kramer. Estab. 1985. Publishes hardcover originals, trade paperback originals and reprints. Publishes 15 titles/year. Receives 1,200 submissions/year. 10% of books are from first-time authors; 25% from unagented writers. Pays standard royalty. Publishes book 15 months after acceptance. Accepts simultaneous submissions. Reports in 2 months. Book catalog free on request. Does not respond or return mss without SASE.
Nonfiction: Self-help, primarily. Subjects include relationships, ecology, nutrition, education, astrology, environment, health/medicine, money/finance, nature, philosophy/New Age, psychology, recreation, religion, science, sociology, women's issues/studies. "Hay House is interested in a variety of subjects so long as they have a positive self-help slant to them. No poetry, children's books, or negative concepts that are not conducive to helping/healing ourselves or our planet." Query or submit outline, sample chapters and SASE.
Recent Nonfiction Title: *Silent Power*, by Stuart Wilde (self-help).
Recent Fiction Title: *Big George: The Autobiography of an Angel* (spiritual fiction).
Tips: "Our audience is concerned with our planet, the healing properties of love, and general self-help principles. Hay House has noticed that our reader is interested in taking more control of his/her life. A writer has a good chance of selling us a book with a unique, positive message. If I were a writer trying to market a book today, I would research the market thoroughly to make sure that there weren't already too many books on the subject I was interested in writing about. Then I would make sure that I had a unique slant on my idea. SASE a must!"

HEALTH COMMUNICATIONS, INC., 3201 SW 15th St., Deerfield Beach FL 33442. Fax: (954)360-0909. E-mail: 102450.722@compuserve.com. Website: http://www.pwr.com/hci/. Editorial Director: Christine Belleris. Publishes hardcover and trade paperback originals. Publishes 40 titles/year. 20% of books from first-time authors; 90% from unagented writers. Pays 15-20% royalty on retail price. Publishes book 9 months after acceptance of ms. Accepts simultaneous submissions. Reports in 1 month on queries, 3 months on proposals and mss. Book catalog for 8½ × 11 SASE. Manuscript guidelines for #10 SASE.

Nonfiction: Gift book, self-help. Subjects include child guidance/parenting, inspiration, psychology, spirituality, women's issues/studies, recovery. "We publish general self-help books, and are expanding to include new subjects such as business self-help and possibly alternative healing." Submit proposal package, including outline, 2 sample chapters, vitae, marketing study and SASE. Reviews artwork/photos as part of ms package. Send photocopies. No phone calls.

Recent Nonfiction Title: *Chicken Soup for the Soul*, by Jack Canfield and Mark Victor Hansen (self-help/inspiration).

Tips: Audience is composed primarily of women, aged 25-60, interested in personal growth and self-improvement. "Please do your research in your subject area. We need to know why there is a need for your book, how it might differ from other books on the market and what you have to offer in the way of promoting your work."

HEALTH PRESS, P.O. Box 1388, Santa Fe NM 87504. (505)982-9373. Fax: (505)983-1733. Editor: K. Schwartz. Publishes hardcover and trade paperback originals. Publishes 4 titles/year. 90% of books from first-time authors; 90% from unagented writers. Pays standard royalty on wholesale price. Publishes book 1 year after acceptance of ms. Accepts simultaneous submissions. Reports in 2 months on proposals. Book catalog and ms guidelines free on request.

Nonfiction: Subjects include health/medicine, patient education. "We want books by health care professionals on cutting-edge patient education topics." Submit proposal package, including résumé, outline and 3 complete chapters. Reviews artwork/photos as part of ms package. Send photocopies.

Recent Nonfiction Title: *Addiction: The High-Low Trap*, by Irving Cohen, M.D.

‡HEINEMANN, 361 Hanover St., Portsmouth NH 03801. Publisher, Trade Division: Cheryl Kimball. Publishes hardcover and trade paperback originals. Publishes 80-100 titles/year. 50% of books from first-time authors; 75% from unagented writers. Pays royalty on wholesale price. Advance varies widely. Publishes book 9 months after acceptance of ms. Accepts simultaneous submissions. Reports in 3 months on proposals. Book catalog free on request. Manuscript guidelines for #10 SASE.

Nonfiction: How-to, reference. Subjects include parenting as it relates to school education, education, gay/lesbian issues, language arts, women's issues/studies, African studies, drama. "We publish very strictly within our categories. We do not publish classroom textbooks." Query. Submit proposal package, including table of contents, outline, 1-2 sample chapters.

Recent Nonfiction Title: *My Name's Not Susie*, by Sharon Jean Hamilton (biographical treatment of how literacy changed author's life).

Tips: "Keep your queries (and manuscripts!) short, study the market, be realistic, and be prepared to promote your book!"

HENDRICK-LONG PUBLISHING CO., INC., P.O. Box 25123, Dallas TX 75225-1123. (214)358-4677. Contact: Joann Long. Estab. 1969. Publishes hardcover and trade paperback originals and hardcover reprints. Publishes 8 titles/year. Receives 500 submissions/year. 90% of books from unagented writers. Pays royalty on selling price. Publishes book 18 months after acceptance. Reports in 1 month on queries, 2 months if more than query sent. *Writer's Market* recommends allowing 2 months for reply. Book catalog for 8½ × 11 or 9 × 12 SAE with 4 first-class stamps. Manuscript guidelines for #10 SASE.

Nonfiction: Biography, history. Needs Texas and Southwest focused material for children and young adults. Query or submit outline and 2 sample chapters. Reviews artwork/photos as part of ms package; copies of material are acceptable. Do not send original art.

Recent Nonfiction Title: *Life in a Rock Shelter: Prehistoric Indians of the Lower Pecos*, by Elaine Acker.

Fiction: Texas and the Southwest for kindergarten through young adult. Query or submit outline/synopsis and 2 sample chapters.

Recent Fiction Title: *Race to Velasco*, by Paul Spellman.

‡HENDRICKSON PUBLISHERS, INC., 137 Summit St., P.O. Box 3473, Peabody MA 01961-3473. Acquisitions Editor: Phil Anderson. Estab. 1983. Publishes hardcover and trade paperback originals and reprints. Publishes 25 titles/year. Receives 200 submissions/year. 3% of books from first-time authors; 100% from unagented writers. Publishes book an average of 1 year after acceptance. Simultaneous submissions OK (if so notified). Reports in 2 months. Book catalog and ms guidelines for SASE.

Nonfiction: Religious, principally academic. "We will consider any quality manuscript within the area of religion specifically related to biblical studies and related fields. Popularly written manuscripts, poetry, plays or fiction are not acceptable." Submit outline and sample chapters.

Recent Nonfiction Title: *Speaking of God*, by Jerry Camery-Hoggatt (biblical studies/pastoral helps).

VIRGIL HENSLEY PUBLISHING, 6116 E. 32nd St., Tulsa OK 74135-5494. (918)664-8520. Editor: Terri Kalfas. Estab. 1965. Publishes hardcover and paperback originals. Publishes 5-10 titles/year. Receives 800 submissions/year. 50% of books from first-time authors; 50% from unagented writers. Pays 5% minimum royalty on gross sales or makes outright purchase of $250 minimum for study aids. Publishes ms 18 months after acceptance. Reports in 2 months on queries. Manuscript guidelines for #10 SASE.
Nonfiction: Bible study curriculum. Subjects include child guidance, parenting, money/finance, men's and women's Christian education, prayer, prophecy, Christian living, large and small group studies, discipleship, adult development, parenting, personal growth, pastoral aids, church growth, family. "We do not want to see anything non-Christian." Actively seeking nonfiction other than Bible studies. No New Age, poetry, plays, sermon collections. Query with synopsis and sample chapters.
Recent Nonfiction Title: *Holy Burnout*, by Steve Roll.
Tips: "Submit something that crosses denominational lines directed toward the large Christian market, not small specialized groups. We serve an interdenominational market—all Christian persuasions."

HERALD PRESS, Imprint of Mennonite Publishing House, 616 Walnut Ave., Scottdale PA 15683-1999. (412)887-8500. Fax: (412)887-3111. Senior Editor: David Garber. Estab. 1908. Publishes hardcover and trade paperback originals and reprints. Publishes 30 titles/year. Receives 1,000 submissions/year. 15% of books from first-time authors; 95% from unagented writers. Pays royalty of 10-12% retail. Advance seldom given. Publishes book 1 year after acceptance. Reports in 3 months. Book catalog for 75¢.
Nonfiction: Christian inspiration, Bible study, current issues, missions and evangelism, peace and justice, family life, Christian ethics and theology, ethnic (Amish, Mennonite), self-help, juvenile (mostly ages 8-14). No drama or poetry. Query or submit outline and 2 sample chapters. Reviews artwork/photos as part of ms package.
Recent Nonfiction Title: *Words for Worship*, by Arlene M. Mark (prayers and litanies, worship/aids).
Fiction: Religious. Needs some fiction for youth and adults reflecting themes similar to those listed in nonfiction, also "compelling stories that treat social and Christian issues in a believable manner." No fantasy. Query or submit outline/synopsis and sample chapters.
Recent Fiction Title: *Abigail*, by James R. Shott (Bible fiction).
Tips: "We currently have a surplus of juvenile book proposals. We have been more selective to make sure of market for proposed book."

HERITAGE BOOKS, INC., 1540-E Pointer Ridge Place, Bowie MD 20716-1859. (301)390-7708. Fax: (301)390-7193. Editorial Director: Karen Ackermann. Estab. 1978. Publishes hardcover and paperback originals and reprints. Publishes 100 titles/year. Receives 300 submissions/year. 25% of books from first-time authors; 100% from unagented writers. Pays 10% royalty on list price. No advance. Accepts simultaneous submissions. Reports in 1 month. *Writer's Market* recommends allowing 2 months for reply. Book catalog for SAE.
Nonfiction: "We particularly desire nonfiction titles dealing with history and genealogy including how-to and reference works, as well as conventional histories and genealogies. Ancestries of contemporary people are not of interest. The titles should be either of general interest or restricted to Eastern US and Midwest, United Kingdom, Germany. Material dealing with the present century is usually not of interest." Query or submit outline. Reviews artwork/photos.
Tips: "The quality of the book is of prime importance; next is its relevance to our fields of interest."

HEYDAY BOOKS, Box 9145, Berkeley CA 94709-9145. (415)549-3564. Publisher: Malcolm Margolin. Estab. 1974. Publishes hardcover originals, trade paperback originals and reprints. Publishes 8-10 titles/year. Receives 200 submissions/year. 50% of books from first-time authors; 90% of books from unagented writers. Pays 8-15% royalty on net price. Publishes book 8 months after acceptance. Reports in 1 week on queries, 5 weeks on mss. *Writer's Market* recommends sending a query with SASE first. Book catalog for 7×9 SAE with 2 first-class stamps.
Nonfiction: Books about California only: how-to, reference. Subjects include Americana, history, nature, travel. "We publish books about native Americans, natural history, history, and recreation, with a strong California focus." Query with outline and synopsis. Reviews artwork/photos.
Tips: "Give good value, and avoid gimmicks. We are accepting *only* nonfiction books with a California focus."

HIGH PLAINS PRESS, P.O. Box 123, 539 Cassa Rd., Glendo WY 82213. Fax: (307)735-4590. Publisher: Nancy Curtis. Publishes hardcover and trade paperback originals. Publishes 4 titles/year. Receives 300 queries and 200 mss/year. 80% of books from first-time authors; 95% from unagented writers. Pays 10% royalty on wholesale price. Offers $100-600 advance. Publishes book 2 years after acceptance. Accepts simultaneous submissions. Reports in 1 month on queries and proposals, 3 months on mss. Book catalog and ms guidelines for 8½×10 SASE.
Nonfiction: Biography, Western Americana, Americana, art/architecture, history, nature/environment, regional. "We focus on books of the American West, particularly history." Submit outline. Reviews artwork/photos as part of ms package. Send photocopies.

Recent Nonfiction Title: *I See By Your Outfit: Historic Cowboy Gear of the Northern Plains*, by Tom Lindmier and Steve Mount (western historical with many photos).

Poetry: "We only seek poetry closely tied to the Rockies. Poets should not submit single poems." Query with complete ms.

Recent Poetry Title: *Circle of Light*, by Charles Levendosky.

HIGHSMITH PRESS, P.O. Box 800, Fort Atkinson WI 53538-0800. (414)563-9571. E-mail: hpress@highs mith.com. Website: http://www.hpress.highsmith.com. Publisher: Donald J. Sager. Publishes hardcover and paperback originals. Publishes 20 titles/year. Receives 500-600 queries and 400-500 mss/year. 30% of books from first-time authors; 100% from unagented writers. Pays 10-12% royalty on net sales price. Offers $250-2,000 advance. Publishes book 6 months after acceptance of ms. Accepts simultaneous submissions. Reports in 1 month on queries, 2 months on proposals, 3 months on mss. Book catalog and ms guidelines free on request.

Nonfiction: Reference and professional. Subjects include education, language/literature, multicultural, professional (library science), teacher activity. "We are primarily interested in reference and library professional books, multicultural resources for youth, library and study skills, curricular and activity books for teachers and others who work with preschool through high school youth." Query with outline and 1-2 sample chapters. Reviews artwork/photos as part of ms package. Send transparencies.

Recent Nonfiction Title: *Customer Service & Innovation*, by Glenn Miller (professional).

Fiction: No longer accepting children's picture book ms. "Our current emphasis is on storytelling collections for children, preschool-grade 6. We prefer stories that can be easily used by teachers and children's librarians, multicultural topics, and manuscripts that feature fold and cut, flannelboard, tangram, or similar simple patterns that can be reproduced."

Recent Fiction Title: *Storyteller's Sampler*, by Valerie Marsh.

HIPPOCRENE BOOKS INC., 171 Madison Ave., New York NY 10016. (212)685-4371. President: George Blagowidow. Contact: Jacek Galazka, publisher. Estab. 1971. Publishes hardcover and trade paperback originals. Publishes 100 titles/year. Receives 250 submissions/year. 10% of books from first-time authors; 95% from unagented writers. Pays 6-10% royalty on retail price. Offers $2,000 advance. Publishes book 16 months after acceptance. Accepts simultaneous submissions. Reports in 2 months. Book catalog for 9×12 SAE with 5 first-class stamps. Manuscript guidelines for #10 SASE.

Nonfiction: Reference. Subjects include foreign language, Judaic reference, ethnic and special interest travel, military history, bilingual love poetry, bilingual proverbs, international cookbooks, Polish interest, foreign language, dictionaries and instruction. Submit outline, 2 sample chapters, toc.

Recent Nonfiction Title: *The Best of Czech Cooking*, by Peter Trinka.

Tips: "Our recent successes in publishing general books considered midlist by larger publishers is making us more of a general trade publisher. We continue to do well with reference books like dictionaries, atlases and language studies. We ask for proposal, sample chapter, and table of contents. We then ask for material if we are interested."

HOLIDAY HOUSE, 425 Madison Ave., New York NY 10017. (212)688-0085. Editor-in-Chief: Regina Griffin. Estab. 1935. Publishes hardcover originals, hardcover and trade paperback reprints. Publishes 50 titles/year. Receives 3,000 submissions/year. 20% of books from first-time authors; 50% from unagented writers. Pays royalty. Publishes book 1 year after acceptance. Accepts simultaneous submissions. Reports in 2 weeks on queries. *Writer's Market* recommends allowing 2 months for reply. Book catalog for 9×12 SAE with 7 first-class stamps. Manuscript guidelines for #10 SASE.

Nonfiction: Illustrated book, juvenile. Submit outline and sample chapters; submit complete ms for picture books only. Reviews artwork/photos as part of ms package.

Fiction: "We are interested in a wide range of fiction for readers 8-12, but don't think of us for paperback series. We do publish some YA novels, but not many. Please submit outline/synopsis and 3 sample chapters; submit complete ms only for picturebooks."

Recent Fiction Title: *The Hanukkah Ghosts*, by Malka Penn.

Tips: "We need picturebook texts with strong stories and writing. We are not interested in folktales or short chapter books. We do not publish board books, or books for toddlers."

HOLLOW EARTH PUBLISHING, P.O. Box 1355, Boston MA 02205-1355. (617)746-3130. E-mail: hep2@aol.com. Editor/Publisher: Helian Yvette Grimes. Publishes hardcover, trade and mass market paperback originals and reprints. Publishes 6 titles/year. Receives 250 submissions/year. 30% of books from first-time authors. Pays 5-15% royalty on wholesale price. Publishes book 6 months after acceptance. Reports in 3 weeks on queries . *Writer's Market* recommends allowing 2 months for reply. Book catalog for 9×12 SAE with 3 first-class stamps. Manuscript guidelines for #10 SASE.

Nonfiction: How-to, reference, technical (computer), mythology. Subjects include architecture, computers and electronics, photography, religion/mythology and travel. "We are currently interested in books on technical aspects of photography and computer books on object-oriented programming." Query. All unsolicited mss are returned unopened. Reviews artwork/photos as part of ms package.

Fiction: Fantasy, literary, mystery, science fiction. Submit outline/synopsis and sa~~mple~~ ited mss are returned unopened.
Tips: "Computer books are fairly easy to publish because they can be marketed ~~...~~

HOLMES & MEIER PUBLISHERS, INC., East Building, 160 Broadway, New ~~York~~ 0100. Fax: (212)374-1313. Publisher: Miriam H. Holmes. Executive Editor: Ka~~...~~ Imprint is Africana Publishing Co. Publishes hardcover and paperback origin~~als~~. Pays royalty. Publishes book an average of 18 months after acceptance. Repor~~ts...~~ with SASE. Book catalog free.
Nonfiction: Africana, art, biography, business/economics, history, Judaica, La~~tin...~~ criticism, politics, reference and women's studies. Accepts translations. "We are noted as an academic publishing house and are pleased with our reputation for excellence in the field. However, we are also expanding our list to include books of more general interest." Query first with outline, sample chapters, cv and idea of intended market/audience.

‡HOLMES PUBLISHING GROUP, P.O. Box 623, Edmonds WA 98020. E-mail: jdh@jdh.seanet.com. CEO: J.D. Holmes. Imprints are Alchemical Press, Sure Fire Press and Contra/Thought (contact L.Y. Fitzgerald). Publishes hardcover and trade paperback originals and reprints. Publishes 40 titles/year. Receives 120 queries and 80 mss/year. 20% of books from first-time authors; 20% from unagented writers. Pays 10% royalty on wholesale price. Publishes book 4 months after acceptance of ms. Reports in 2 months. Book catalog for $3.
Nonfiction: Self-help. Subjects include health/medicine, occult, philosophy, religion, metaphysical. "We do not publish titles that are more inspirational than informative." Query or submit complete ms with SASE. Reviews artwork/photos as part of ms package. Send photocopies.
Recent Nonfiction Title: *Secrets of Dr. John Dee*, by Gordon James (alchemy, occult).
Fiction: Erotica, occult. Query.

HENRY HOLT & COMPANY, INC., 115 W. 18th St., New York NY 10011. Imprints are Owl Books, MIS: Press Inc., Metropolitan Books, Edge Books, M&T Books, Red Feather Books, John Macrae Books, Bill Martin Jr. Books, Marian Wood Books. General interest publisher of both fiction and nonfiction. Query before submitting.

HOME EDUCATION PRESS, P.O. Box 1083, Tonasket WA 98855. (509)486-1351. Fax: (509)486-2628. E-mail: hegener@aol.com. Website: http://www.home-ed-press.com. Publisher: Helen Hegener. Publishes trade paperback originals. Publishes 6-8 titles/year. Receives 20-40 queries and 10-12 mss/year. 95% of books from first-time authors; 95% from unagented writers. Pays 10% royalty on retail price. Publishes book 1 year after acceptance of ms. Reports in 1 month on queries. *Writer's Market* recommends allowing 2 months for reply. Book catalog free on request. Manuscript guidelines for #10 SASE.
Nonfiction: How-to, education; specifically homeschooling. Subjects include child guidance/parenting, education and homeschooling. Query. Reviews artwork/photos as part of ms package as appropriate. Send photocopies.
Tips: "We are not interested in any books not directly relating to homeschooling." Mistake writers often make when submitting nonfiction is "submitting curriculum or 'how to teach. . .' books. We are *not* interested in new ideas for teaching kids to read or write. We're more interested in real life experiences than academic expertise."

HOUGHTON MIFFLIN CO., Adult Trade Division, 222 Berkeley St., Boston MA 02116-3764. (617)351-5000. Contact: Submissions Editor. General interest publisher of both fiction and nonfiction.
Nonfiction: Current affairs, general nonfiction, juvenile, nature, popular science, reference.
Recent Nonfiction Title: *The Good Marriage: How and Why Love Lasts*, by Judith S. Wallerstein and Sandra Blakeslee.
Recent Fiction Title: *In the Loyal Mountains: Stories*, by Rick Bass.

HOUGHTON MIFFLIN CO., Children's Books, 222 Berkeley St., Boston MA 02116-3764. Website: http://www.hmco.com/trade/. Submissions Coordinator: Sarah Hines-Stephens. Estab. 1864. Publishes hardcover originals and trade paperback reprints (picture books and novels). Publishes 50 titles/year. Pays standard royalty. Offers advance. Reports in 2 months. Enclose SASE to fit ms.
Nonfiction: Submit outline/synopsis and sample chapters. Reviews artwork/photos as part of ms package.
Recent Nonfiction Title: *Painting Dreams*, by Mary Lyons (48 pg., full color illus. bio of folk artist).
Fiction: Submit complete ms.
Recent Fiction Title: *Mrs. Brown Went to Town*, by Herb Yee (picture book).

HOWELL PRESS, INC., 1147 River Rd., Suite 2, Charlottesville VA 22901-4172. (804)977-4006. Fax: (804)971-7204. President: Ross A. Howell Jr. Estab. 1985. Publishes 6 titles/year. Receives 500 submissions/year. 10% of books from first-time authors; 80% from unagented writers. Pays 5-7% on net retail price. "We

an advance, but amount differs with each project and is generally negotiated with authors on
ase basis." Publishes book 18 months after acceptance. Reports in 2 months. Book catalog for
E with 4 first-class stamps. Manuscript guidelines for #10 SASE.
tion: Illustrated books, historical texts. Subjects include aviation, military history, cooking, maritime
ry, motorsports, gardening. "Generally open to most ideas, as long as writing is accessible to average
dult reader. Our line is targeted, so it would be advisable to look over our catalog before querying to better
understand what Howell Press does." Query with outline and sample chapters. Reviews artwork/photos as
part of ms package. Does not return mss without SASE.
Recent Nonfiction Title: *Cooking in the Nude: Quickies*, by Debbie Cornwell (gift book).
Tips: "Focus of our program has been illustrated books, but we will also consider nonfiction manuscripts
that would not be illustrated. Selections limited to history, transportation, cooking and gardening."

HOWELLS HOUSE, P.O. Box 9546, Washington DC 20016-9546. (202)333-2182. Publisher: W.D. Howells. Estab. 1988. Imprints are The Compass Press, Whalesback Books. Publishes hardcover and trade paperback originals and reprints. Publishes 4 titles/year; each imprint publishes 2-3 titles/year. Receives 2,000
queries and 300 mss/year. 50% of books from first-time authors; 60% from unagented writers. Pays 15%
net royalty or makes outright purchase. May offer advance. Publishes book 8 months after ms development
completed. Reports in 2 months on proposals.
Nonfiction: Biography, illustrated book, textbook. Subjects include Americana, anthropology/archaeology,
art/architecture, business and economics, education, government/politics, history, military/war, photography,
science, sociology, translation. Query.
Fiction: Historical, literary, mainstream/contemporary. Query.
Tips: "Our interests will focus on institutions and institutional change."

HUDSON HILLS PRESS, INC., 230 Fifth Ave., Suite 1308, New York NY 10001-7704. (212)889-
3090. Fax: (212)889-3091. President/Editorial Director: Paul Anbinder. Estab. 1978. Publishes hardcover
and paperback originals. Publishes 10 titles/year. Receives 50-100 submissions/year. 15% of books from
first-time authors; 90% from unagented writers. Average print order for a first book is 3,000. Pays 4-6%
royalty on retail price. Offers $3,500 average advance. Publishes book 1 year after acceptance. Accepts
simultaneous submissions. Reports in 2 months. Book catalog for 6×9 SAE with 2 first-class stamps.
Nonfiction: Art, photography. "We are only interested in publishing books about art and photography,
including monographs." Query first, then submit outline and sample chapters. Reviews artwork/photos as
part of ms package.

‡**HUMAN KINETICS PUBLISHERS, INC.**, P.O. Box 5076, Champaign IL 61825-5076. (217)351-5076.
Fax: (217)351-2674. Publisher: Rainer Martens. Director, Trade: Ted Miller. Director, Academic: Rick Frey.
Imprints are HK Trade, HK Academic. Estab. 1974. Publishes hardcover and paperback text and reference
books and trade paperback originals. Publishes 100 titles/year. Receives 300 submissions/year. 50% of books
from first-time authors; 97% of books from unagented writers. Pays 10-15% royalty on net income. Publishes
book an average of 18 months after acceptance. Accepts simultaneous submissions. Reports in 2 months.
Book catalog free.
Nonfiction: How-to, reference, self-help, technical and textbook. Subjects include health, recreation, sports,
sport sciences and sports medicine, and physical education. Especially interested in books on fitness; books
on all aspects of sports technique or how-to books and coaching books; books which interpret the sport
sciences and sports medicine, including sport physiology, sport psychology, sport pedagogy and sport bio-
mechanics. No sport biographies, sport record or statistics books or regional books. Submit outline and
sample chapters. Reviews artwork/photos as part of ms package.
Recent Nonfiction Title: *Complete Home Fitness Handbook*, by Edmund R. Burke.
Tips: "Books which accurately interpret sport sciences and health research to coaches, athletes and fitness
enthusiasts have the best chance of selling to us."

HUMAN SERVICES INSTITUTE, INC., 165 W. 91st St, Suite 7-H, New York NY 10024-1357.
(212)769-9738. Senior Editor: Dr. Lee Marvin Joiner. Estab. 1988. Publishes hardcover and trade paperback
originals. Publishes 10-12 titles/year. Receives 100 submissions/year. 95% of books are from first-time
authors; 100% from unagented writers. Pays 7-15% royalty on wholesale price. Publishes book 9 months
after acceptance. Reports in 1 month on queries, 2 months on mss. Book catalog and ms guidelines free.
Nonfiction: Self-help. Subjects include child guidance/parenting, psychology, women's issues/studies. "We
are looking for books on divorce, cocaine, cults, sexual victimization, alternative medicine, mental health,
secular recovery and violence. No autobiographical accounts." Query or submit outline/synopsis and sample
chapters.
Tips: "Our audience is made up of clinics, hospitals, prisons, mental health centers, human service professionals and general readers."

HUMANICS PUBLISHING GROUP, 1482 Mecaslin St. NW, Atlanta GA 30309. (404)874-2176. Fax:
(404)874-1976. Acquisitions Editor: W. Arthur Bligh. Imprints are Humanics Trade, Humanics Learning,

Humanics Children's House. Publishes hardcover and trade paperback originals. Publishes 12 titles/year; each imprint publishes 4 titles/year. Receives 2,000 queries and 800 mss/year. 90% of books from first-time authors; 75% from unagented writers. Pays 10-20% royalty on wholesale price. Advance varies. Publishes book 5 months after acceptance of ms. Accepts simultaneous submissions, if so noted. Reports in 1 month on queries and proposals, 3 months on mss. Book catalog for #10 SASE. Manuscript guidelines for 4×9 SASE.

Nonfiction: Children's/juvenile, cookbook, how-to, illustrated book (4-color for children only), self-help, activity books for parents and educators of young children. Subjects include anthropology, child guidance/parenting, cooking/foods/nutrition, education (for young children, elementary and before), ethnic (multicultural children's books), health/medicine, music/dance, philosophy, psychology, sociology, spirituality, women's issues/studies. "We are interested in books about growth—spiritual, emotional and physical. Submitting an entire manuscript is a mistake; query letters save time, energy and frustration." Query with SASE. Reviews artwork/photos as part of ms package. Send photocopies.

Recent Nonfiction Title: *The Tao of Women*, by Pamela K. Metz amd Jacqueline L. Tobin.

Tips: "For our activity books, audience is parents and educators looking for books which will enrich their children's lives. For our trade books, audience is anyone interested in positive, healthy self-development. We are looking for quality and creativity. As a small publisher, we don't waste our time or an author's time on books that are not of lasting importance or value."

HUNTER HOUSE, P.O. Box 2914, Alameda CA 94501. Website: http://www.hunterhouse.com. Editor: Lisa E. Lee. Publishes hardcover and trade paperback originals and reprints. Publishes 10 titles/year. Receives 200-300 queries and 100 mss/year. 50% of books from first-time authors; 80% from unagented writers. Pays 12% royalty on net receipts, defined as selling price. Offers $0-2,000 advance. Publishes book 2 years after acceptance of final ms. Accepts simultaneous submissions. Reports in 2 months on queries, 3 months on proposals, 6 months on mss. Book catalog and ms guidelines for 8½×11 SAE with 3 first-class stamps.

Nonfiction: Reference, (only health reference); self-help, social issues. Subjects include education, health/medicine, women's issues/studies, sexuality, aging, family. "We are looking for manuscripts that will flesh out our three specific lines—health, family, community." Query with proposal package, including outline, 1 sample chapter, target audience info, relevant statistics, competition. Reviews artwork/photos as part of ms package. Send photocopies.

Recent Nonfiction Title: *Menopause Without Medicine*, by Linda Ojeda, Ph.D. (health).

Tips: Audience is "relatively savvy, concerned and sensitive people who are looking to educate themselves and their community about real-life issues that affect them. Please send as much information as possible about *who* your audience is, *how* your book addresses their needs, and *how* a publisher can reach that audience."

HUNTER PUBLISHING, INC., 300 Raritan Center Pkwy., Edison NJ 08818. President: Michael Hunter. Editor: Kim André. Estab. 1985. Publishes 100 titles/year. Receives 300 submissions/year. 10% of books from first-time authors; 75% from unagented writers. Pays royalty. Offers $0-2,000 average advance. Publishes book 5 months after acceptance. Accepts simultaneous submissions. Reports in 3 weeks on queries, 1 month on ms. *Writer's Market* recommends allowing 2 months for reply. Book catalog for #10 SAE with 4 first-class stamps.

Nonfiction: Reference. Subjects include travel. "We need travel guides to areas covered by few competitors: Caribbean Islands, South and Central America, Mexico, regional US from an active 'adventure' perspective." No personal travel stories or books not directed to travelers. Query or submit outline/synopsis and sample chapters. Reviews artwork/photos as part of ms package.

Tips: "Study what's out there, pick some successful models, and identify ways they can be made more appealing. We need active adventure-oriented guides and more specialized guides for travelers in search of the unusual."

HUNTINGTON HOUSE PUBLISHERS, P.O. Box 53788, Lafayette LA 70505-3788.(318)237-7049. Editor-in-Chief: Mark Anthony. Estab. 1982. Publishes hardcover, trade paperback and mass market paperback originals, trade paperback reprints. Publishes 5 titles/year. Receives 1,500 submissions/year. 25% of books from first-time authors; 90% from unagented writers. Average print order for a first book is 5,000-10,000. Pays up to 10% royalty on sale price. Publishes book 1 year after acceptance. Accepts simultaneous submissions. Reports in 4 months. Manuscript guidelines free.

MARKET CONDITIONS are constantly changing! If this is 1998 or later, buy the newest edition of *Writer's Market* at your favorite bookstore or order directly from Writer's Digest Books.

Nonfiction: Current social and political issues, especially the globalist movement, conspiracy theories and New Age topics. Query with descriptive outline.

Tips: "Write clear, crisp and exciting manuscripts that grab the reader. The company's goal is to educate and keep readers abreast of critical current events. Published authors should expect a heavy publicity schedule."

HYPERION, Division of Disney Book Publishing, Inc., 114 Fifth Ave., New York NY 10011. General interest publisher of both fiction and nonfiction. Imprint is Miramax Books. Also Hyperion Books for Children, and Disney Press. Publishes hardcover and trade paperback originals.

Nonfiction: Current events, humor, international affairs, popular culture, psychology, self-help. Query before submitting; no unsolicited mss.

Recent Nonfiction Title: *Catching Kevin: The Pursuit and Capture of America's Most Wanted Computer Criminal*, by Tsutumo Shinomura and John Markoff.

Fiction: Mainstream, literary, juvenile, young adult. Query before submitting; no unsolicited mss.

Recent Fiction Title: *Burning Angel*, by James Lee Burke.

ICS BOOKS, INC., 1370 E. 86th Place, Merrillville IN 46410. (219)769-0585. Publisher/Editor: Thomas A. Todd. Publishes trade paperback originals. Publishes 8-10 titles/year. 40% of books from first-time authors; 95% from unagented writers. Pays 10% royalty on wholesale price. Publishes book 9 months after acceptance of ms. Accepts simultaneous submissions. Reports in 3 months on mss. Book catalog and ms guidelines free on request.

Nonfiction: Children's/juvenile, coffee table book, cookbook, gift book, how-to, humor, illustrated book. Subjects include animals, cooking/foods/nutrition, government/politics, health/medicine, nature/environment, photography, recreation, sports, travel, women's issues/studies. Send proposal package, including cover letter, outline, 3-5 sample chapters and SASE. Reviews artwork/photos as part of ms package.

Fiction: Adventure, humor.

Tips: "Send a thoughtful proposal with cover letter, table of contents and synopsis. Include number of words, submission date and retail preference. We are looking for 15,000- to 18,000-word manuscripts on team sports and components of each sport (i.e., base stealing, hitting, passing, pitching, darts and billiards)." Query with SASE.

ICS PUBLICATIONS, Institute of Carmelite Studies, 2131 Lincoln Rd. NE, Washington DC 20002. (202)832-8489. Fax: (202)832-8967. Website: http://www.ocd.or.at/ics. Editorial Director: Steven Payne, O.C.D. Publishes hardcover and trade paperback originals and reprints. Publishes 8 titles/year. Receives 10-20 queries and 10 mss/year. 10% of books from first-time authors; 90-100% from unagented writers. Pays 2-6% royalty on retail price or makes outright purchase. Offers $500 advance. Publishes book 2 years after acceptance. Accepts simultaneous submissions, if so noted. Reports in 2 months on proposals. Book catalog for 7 × 10 SAE with 2 first-class stamps. Writer's guidelines for #10 SASE.

Nonfiction: Religious (should relate to Carmelite spirituality and prayer). "We are looking for significant works on Carmelite history, spirituality, and main figures (Saints Theresa, John of the Cross, Therese of Lisieux, etc.). Also open to more general works on prayer, spiritual direction, etc. Too often we receive proposals for works that merely repeat what has already been done, or are too technical for a general audience, or have little to do with the Carmelite tradition and spirit." Query or submit outline and 1 sample chapter.

Recent Nonfiction Title: *Letters from Carmel*, by Bl. Elizabeth of the Trinity (spirituality).

Tips: "Our audience consists of those interested in the Carmelite tradition or in developing their life of prayer and spirituality."

IDE HOUSE PUBLISHERS, 4631 Harvey Dr., Mesquite TX 75150-1609. (214)686-5332. Senior Executive Vice President: Ryan Idol. Publishes hardcover and trade paperback originals. Publishes 10 titles/year. Receives 300 queries and 500 mss/year. 70% of books from first-time authors; 100% from unagented writers. Pays 4-7% royalty on retail price. Publishes book 1 year after acceptance of ms. Reports in 1 month on queries and proposals, 4 months on mss. Book catalog for 6 × 9 SAE with 5 first-class stamps. Manuscript guidelines for #10 SASE.

Nonfiction: Women's history. Subjects include gay/lesbian, government/politics (liberal only), history, women's issues/studies. "We accept only nonsexist/nonhomophobic scholarly works." Query with outline and 2 sample chapters. All unsolicited mss returned unopened.

Recent Nonfiction Title: *Socks & Cretin*, by Lyle Shannon (politics).

Tips: "Inaugerating poetry branch. We are emphasizing a quest for liberal politics and have budgeted for 100 titles in 1996-1997."

IDEALS CHILDREN'S BOOKS, Imprint of Hambleton-Hill Publishing, Inc., 1501 County Hospital Rd., Nashville TN 37218. Contact: Suzanne Smith, copy editor. Publishes children's hardcover and trade paperback originals. Publishes 40 titles/year. Receives 200 queries and 2,000-2,500 mss/year. 10% of books from first-time authors; 50% from unagented writers. Pay determined by individual contract. Publishes book 18 months after acceptance of ms. Reports in 2 months on queries, 6 months on proposals and mss. Book catalog for 9×12 SASE with 11 first-class stamps. Manuscript guidelines for #10 SASE.

● This publisher only accepts unsolicited mss from agents and members of the Society of Children's Bookwriters & Illustrators.

Nonfiction: Children's. Subjects include Americana, animals, art/architecture, nature/environment, science, sports. No middle-grade or young adult novels. Submit proposal package. Reviews artwork/photos as part of ms package. Send photocopies.

Recent Nonfiction Title: *What Do Animals Do in Winter?*, by Melvin and Gilda Berger (easy reader).

Fiction: Query with SASE.

Recent Fiction Title: *Wish You Were Here*, by Martina Selway (children's picture book).

Poetry: Query with SASE.

Recent Poetry Title: *I Wish I Was the Baby*, by DJ Long (children's rhymed picture book).

Tips: Audience is children in the toddler to 10-year-old range. "We are seeking original, child-centered fiction for the picture book format. Innovative nonfiction ideas for easy readers are also being sought."

‡IDEALS PUBLICATIONS INC., 535 Metroplex Dr., Suite 250, Nashville TN 37211. (615)333-0478. Publisher: Patricia Pingry. Editor: Lisa Ragan. Contact: Michelle Burke, copy editor. Estab. 1944. Publishes highly-illustrated seasonal and nostalgic hardbound books. Uses short prose and poetry. Also publishes *Ideals* magazine. Publishes 4 hardbound books, 6 *Ideals*, 1-2 others titles/year. Payment varies. Accepts simultaneous submissions. Accepts previously published material. Send information about when and where the piece previously appeared. Reports in 2 months. Manuscript guidelines free with SASE.

● No longer publishing children's titles.

IDYLL ARBOR, INC., P.O. Box 720, Ravensdale WA 98051. (206)432-3231. E-mail: idyarbor@ix.netcom. com. Contact: Tom Blaschko. Publishes hardcover and trade paperback originals and trade paperback reprints. Publishes 6 titles/year. 50% of books from first-time authors; 100% from unagented writers. Pays 8-20% royalty on wholesale price or retail price. Publishes book 6 months after acceptance of ms. Accepts simultaneous submissions. Reports in 1 month on queries, 2 months on proposals, 4 months on mss. Book catalog and ms guidelines free.

Nonfiction: Technical, textbook. Subjects include agriculture/horticulture (used in long term care activities or health care—therapy), health/medicine (for therapists, social service providers and activity directors), recreation (as therapy). "We look for manuscripts from authors with recent clinical experience. Good grounding in theory is required, but practical experience is more important." Query preferred with outline and 1 sample chapter. Reviews artwork/photos as part of ms package. Send photocopies.

Recent Nonfiction Title: *Quality Assurance*, by Cunningham and Martini (health care text).

Tips: "Our books provide practical information on the current state and art of health care practice. We currently emphasize therapies (recreational, occupational, music, horticultural), activity directors in long term care facilities, and social service professionals. The books must be useful for the health practitioner who meets face to face with patients *or* the books must be useful for teaching undergraduate and graduate level classes. We are especially looking for therapists with a solid clinical background to write on their area of expertise."

‡INCENTIVE PUBLICATIONS, INC., 3835 Cleghorn Ave., Nashville TN 37215-2532. (615)385-2934. Editor: Anna Quinn. Contact: Catherine Aldy. Estab. 1970. Publishes paperback originals. Publishes 25-30 titles/year. Receives 350 submissions/year. 25% of books from first-time authors; 95% from unagented writers. Pays royalty or makes outright purchase. Publishes book an average of 1 year after acceptance. Reports in 1 month on queries. *Writer's Market* recommends allowing 2 months for reply.

Nonfiction: Teacher resources and books in pre-K through 8th grade educational areas. Query with synopsis and detailed outline.

Recent Nonfiction Title: *Preparing Students to Raise Achievement Scores* (4-book series covering grades 1-8).

INDEX PUBLISHING GROUP, INC., 3368 Governor Dr., Suite 273, San Diego CA 92122. (619)281-2957. Fax: (619)281-0547. E-mail: indexboox@aol.com. Website: http://www.electriciti.com/~ipgbooks. Publisher: Linton M. Vandiver. Publishes hardcover and trade paperback originals. Publishes 25 titles/year. Receives 100 queries and 40 mss/year. 40% of books from first-time authors; 100% from unagented writers. Pays 6-20% royalty on price. Publishes book 4 months after acceptance. Accepts simultaneous submissions. Query for electronic submissions. Reports in 1 week on queries, 2 weeks on proposals. *Writer's Market* recommends allowing 2 months for reply. Book catalog and ms guidelines free on request.

Nonfiction: Reference, technical, trade nonfiction. Subjects include gambling, computers and electronics, hobbies (consumer electronics: ham radio, scanners), electronic crime: cellular telephones, computer hacking, etc. "Index Publishing specializes in trade nonfiction (paper and hardcover) in three broad areas: (1) communication electronics, especially ham radio, scanning and radio monitoring, cellular telephones, computer hacking, etc.; (2) controversial topics such as eavesdropping, cable and satellite TV signal piracy, identity changes, electonic crime prevention; (3) gambling, especially casino gambling and gaming theory." Query.

Recent Nonfiction Title: *Smart Casino Gambling*, by Olaf Vancura, Ph.D.

INDIANA UNIVERSITY PRESS, 601 N. Morton St., Bloomington IN 47404-3797. (812)337-4203. Fax: (812)855-7931. E-mail: jgallman@indiana.edu. Director: John Gallman. Estab. 1951. Publishes hardcover originals, paperback originals and reprints. Publishes 175 titles/year. 30% of books from first-time authors; 98% from unagented writers. Average print order for a first book varies depending on subject. Nonauthor subsidy publishes 9% of books. Pays maximum 10% royalty on retail price. Offers occasional advance. Publishes book 1 year after acceptance. Reports in 2 months. Book catalog and ms guidelines free.

Nonfiction: Scholarly books on humanities, history, philosophy, religion, Jewish studies, Black studies, criminal justice, translations, semiotics, public policy, film, music, philanthropy, social sciences, regional materials, African studies, Russian Studies, women's studies, and serious nonfiction for the general reader. Also interested in textbooks and works with course appeal in designated subject areas. Query with outline and sample chapters. "Queries should include as much descriptive material as is necessary to convey scope and market appeal to us." Reviews artwork/photos.

Recent Nonfiction Title: *The Making of a Conservative Environmentalist*, by Gordon Durnil.

Tips: Looking for fewer, better-selling books. "We have been a bit more cautious about specialized monographs."

‡INITIATIVES PUBLISHING CO., 1444 Indian Way NW, Lilburn GA 30247-3761. Publisher: Jason Harriman. Estab. 1988. Publishes hardcover originals, trade paperback originals and reprints. Publishes 6-10 titles/year. Receives 350 queries and 50 mss/year. 80% of mss from first-time authors, 90% from unagented writers. Pays 4-12% royalty on wholesale price or makes outright purchase for $2,500-5,000. Publishes book 10 months after acceptance. Reports in 2 months on proposals. Book catalog and ms guidelines free on request.

Nonfiction: How-to, reference and technical. Subjects include business and money/finance (primary focus), digital publishing, graphics management. Submit outline and 1 sample chapter or proposal package, including proposed market. Reviews artwork/photos as part of ms package. Writers should send photocopies.

Recent Nonfiction Title: *A Designer's Guide to Digital File Preparation*, by Gary "Zack" Smith.

Tips: "We have a strong advocacy position in favor of those wishing to improve the prosperity of their lives, through planning, education, working smarter (no self-help or financial fads). The biggest mistake that writers often make is failure to consider a broad enough market to warrant investment necessary to produce and market a book. We have a stronger emphasis on niche publishing (graphic arts, electronic prepress, digital publishing)."

INNER TRADITIONS INTERNATIONAL, P.O. Box 388, 1 Park St., Rochester VT 05767. (802)767-3174. Fax: (802)767-3726. Acquisitions Editor: (Ms.) Lee Wood. Estab. 1975. Imprints are Inner Traditions, Destiny Books, Healing Arts Press, Park Street Press. Publishes hardcover and trade paperback originals and reprints. Publishes 40 titles/year. Receives 2,000 submissions/year. 5% of books from first-time authors; 5% from unagented writers. Pays 8-10% royalty on net receipts. Offers $1,000 average advance. Publishes book 1 year after acceptance. Reports in 3 months on queries, 6 months on mss. Book catalog and ms guidelines free.

Nonfiction: Subjects include anthropology/archaeology, natural foods, cooking, nutrition, health/alternative medicine, history and mythology, indigenous cultures, music/dance, nature/environment, esoteric philosophy, psychology, world religions, women's issues/studies, New Age. Query or submit outline and sample chapters with SASE. Does not return mss without SASE. Reviews artwork/photos as part of ms package.

Recent Nonfiction Title: *The Great Book of Hemp*, by Rowan Robinson (current affairs).

Tips: "We are interested in the spiritual and transformative aspects of the above subjects, especially as they relate to world cultures. We are not interested in autobiographical stories of self-transformation. We do not accept any electronic submissions (via e-mail)."

INSIGHT BOOKS, Imprint of Plenum Publishing Corp., 233 Spring St., New York NY 10013-1578. (212)620-8000. Fax: (212)463-0742. Editor: Frank K. Darmstadt. Plenum estab. 1946. Publishes trade nonfiction hardcover and paperback originals. Publishes 12 titles/year. Receives 1,000 submissions/year. 50% of books from first-time authors; 75% from unagented writers. Prefers proposals from agents. Pays royalty. Advance varies. Publishes book 2 years after acceptance. Accepts simultaneous submissions. Reports in 2 months. Book catalog free.

Nonfiction: Self-help, how-to, treatises. Subjects include anthropology, art/architecture, business and economics, education, ethnic, gay and lesbian studies, government/politics, health/medicine, language/literature, money/finance, nature/environment, psychology, science, sociology, women's issues/studies. Submit outline, sample chapters and résumé.

Recent Nonfiction Title: *Racism or Attitude?*, by J. Robinson (social commentary).

Tips: "Writers have the best chance selling authoritative, well-written, serious information in areas of health, mental health, social sciences, education and contemporary issues. Our audience consists of informed general readers as well as professionals and students in human, life and social sciences. If I were a writer trying to market a book today, I would say something interesting, important and useful, and say it well."

‡**INSTITUTE OF POLICE TECHNOLOGY AND MANAGEMENT**, University of North Florida, 4567 St. Johns Bluff Rd., S., Jacksonville FL 32224-2645. (904)646-2722. Editor: Richard C. Hodge. Publishes trade paperback originals. Publishes 8 titles/year. Receives 30 queries and 12 mss/year. 50% of books from first-time authors; 100% from unagented writers. Pays 25% royalty on retail price or makes outright purchase of $300-2,000 (may be some combination of above). No advance. Publishes book 2 months after acceptance of ms. Accepts simultaneous submissions. Reports in 1 month. *Writer's Market* recommends allowing 2 months for reply.

Nonfiction: Illustrated book, reference, technical, textbook. Subjects include law enforcement. "Our publications are principally for law enforcement. Our authors are almost all present or retired law enforcement officers with an excellent up-to-date knowledge of a particular field; they are not necessarily persons whose works have been published. Manuscripts should *not* be submitted until the author has talked with the editor on the telephone. The best procedure is to have this talk before beginning to write. Articles and short handbooks are acceptable as well as longer manuals." Query by phone first. Reviews artwork/photos as part of ms package. Send photocopies.

Recent Nonfiction Title: *Training and Reference Manual for Traffic Accident Investigation*, by R.W. Rivers (law enforcement).

Tips: Audience is law enforcement, private investigators, personal injury attorneys, insurance investigators and adjustors.

INTERCULTURAL PRESS, INC., P.O. Box 700, Yarmouth ME 04096. (207)846-5168. Fax: (207)846-5168. E-mail: interculturalpress@mcimail.com. Contact: Judy Carl-Hendrick, managing editor. Estab. 1980. Publishes hardcover and trade paperback originals. Publishes 10-15 titles/year. Receives 50-80 submissions/year. 50% of books from first-time authors; 95% of books from unagented writers. Pays royalty. Offers small advance occasionally. Publishes book 2 years after acceptance. Accepts simultaneous submissions. Reports in 2 months. Book catalog and ms guidelines free.

Nonfiction: How-to, reference, self-help, textbook and theory. "We want books with an international or domestic intercultural or multicultural focus, especially those on business operations (how to be effective in intercultural business activities), education (textbooks for teaching intercultural subjects, for instance) and training (for Americans going abroad or foreign nationals coming to the United States). Our books are published for educators in the intercultural field, business people who are engaged in international business, managers concerned with cultural diversity in the workplace, and anyone else who works in an occupation where cross-cultural communication and adaptation are important skills. No manuscripts that don't have an intercultural focus." Accepts nonfiction translations. Query with outline or proposal. Do not submit mss unless invited.

Recent Nonfiction Title: *Experimental Activities for Intercultural Learning*, by Ned Seelye (cross-cultural training and education).

INTERLINK PUBLISHING GROUP, INC., 46 Crosby St., Northampton MA 01060. (413)582-7054. Fax: (413)582-7057. E-mail: interpg@aol.com. Publisher: Michel Moushabeck. Imprints are Interlink Books, Crocodile Books, USA, Olive Branch Press. Publishes hardcover and trade paperback originals. Publishes 30 titles/year. Receives 200 submissions/year. 30% of books from first-time authors; 50% from unagented writers. Pays 5-7% royalty on retail price. Publishes book 18 months after acceptance. Accepts simultaneous submissions. Reports in 1 month on queries. *Writer's Market* recommends allowing 2 months for reply. Book catalog and ms guidelines free.

● This publisher is looking for folktale collections to add to its International Folk Tale series; also political/current affairs titles for new Voices & Visions series as well as titles on world travel.

Nonfiction: World travel, world history and politics, ethnic cooking. Submit outline and sample chapters for adult nonfiction; complete ms for juvenile titles. Reviews artwork/photos as part of ms package.

Recent Nonfiction Title: *A Traveller's History of China*, by Stephen Haw (travel/history).

Fiction: Ethnic, international feminist, juvenile, picture books, short story collections (only third world). "Adult fiction—We are looking for translated works relating to the Middle East, Africa or Latin America. Juvenile/Picture Books—Our list is full for the next two years. No science fiction, romance, plays, erotica, fantasy, horror. Submit outline/synopsis and sample chapters.

Recent Fiction Title: *Samarkind*, by Amin Maalouf (translated fiction).

Recent Poetry Title: *On Entering the Sea*, by Nizar Qabbani (translated poetry).

Tips: "Any submissions that fit well in our International Folktale, Emerging Voices: New International Fiction Series or The Independent Walker Series will receive careful attention."

‡**INTERNATIONAL CITY/COUNTY MANAGEMENT ASSOCIATION**, 777 N. Capitol St., NE, Suite 500, Washington DC 20002. (202)962-3648. Director of Publishing: Barbara Moore. Publishes hardcover and paperback originals. Publishes 10-15 titles/year. Receives 50 queries and 20 mss/year. 20% of books from first-time authors; 100% from unagented writers. Makes negotiable outright purchase. No advance. Publishes book 18 months after acceptance of ms. Reports in 1 month. *Writer's Market* recommends allowing 2 months for reply. Book catalog and ms guidelines free on request.

Nonfiction: Reference, textbook, training manuals. Subjects include government/politics. Query with outline and 1 sample chapter. Reviews artwork/photos as part of ms package. Send photocopies.
Recent Nonfiction Title: *Family & Medical Leave: The Public Employer's Guide*, by Katherine Gustafson (reference).

INTERNATIONAL FOUNDATION OF EMPLOYEE BENEFIT PLANS, P.O. Box 69, Brookfield WI 53008-0069. (414)786-6700. Fax: (414)786-8670. E-mail: books@ifebp.org. Website: http://www.ifebp.o rg. Senior Director of Publications: Dee Birschel. Estab. 1954. Publishes hardcover and trade paperback originals. Publishes 10 titles/year. Receives 20 submissions/year. 15% of books from first-time authors; 80% from unagented writers. Pays 5-15% royalty on wholesale and retail price. Publishes book 1 year after acceptance. Reports in 3 months on queries. Book catalog free on request. Manuscript guidelines for SASE.
Nonfiction: Reference, technical, consumer information, textbook. Subjects limited to health care, pensions, retirement planning, and employee benefits. "We publish general and technical monographs on all aspects of employee benefits—pension plans, health insurance, etc." Query with outline.
Recent Nonfiction Title: *Managed Vision Benefits*, by Jessie Rosenthal.
Tips: "Be aware of interests of employers and the marketplace in benefits topics, for example, how AIDS affects employers, health care cost containment."

INTERNATIONAL MARINE, Division of the McGraw-Hill Companies, P.O. Box 220, Camden ME 04843-0220. Fax: (207)236-6314. Imprints are International Marine, Ragged Mountain Press. Acquisitions Editor: John J. Kettlewell. Editorial Director: Jonathan Eaton. Estab. 1969. Publishes hardcover and paperback originals. Publishes 40 titles/year. Receives 500-700 mss/year. 30% of books from first-time authors; 80% from unagented writers. Pays standard royalties based on net price. Offers advance. Publishes book 1 year after acceptance. Reports in 2 months. Book catalog and ms guidelines for SASE.
Nonfiction: "Marine nonfiction. A wide range of subjects include: boatbuilding, boat design, yachting, seamanship, boat maintenance, maritime history, etc." All books are illustrated. "Material in all stages welcome." Query first with outline and 2-3 sample chapters. Reviews artwork/photos as part of ms package.
Recent Nonfiction Title: *Sailboat Refinishing*, by Don Casey (how-to).
Tips: "Freelance writers should be aware of the need for clarity, accuracy and interest. Many progress too far in the actual writing, with an unsaleable topic."

INTERNATIONAL MEDICAL PUBLISHING, 1516 Mintwood Dr., McLean VA 22101. (703)519-0807. Fax: (703)519-0806. Editor: Thomas Masterson, MD. Publishes mass market paperback originals. Publishes 11 titles/year. Receives 20 queries and 2 mss/year. 5% of books from first-time authors; 100% from unagented writers. Pays royalty on gross receipts. Publishes book 8 months after acceptance. Reports in 2 months on queries. Book catalog free on request.
Nonfiction: Reference, textbook. Health/medicine subjects. "We distribute only through medical and scientific bookstores. Look at our books. Think about practical material for doctors-in-training. We are interested in handbooks. Keep prose simple when dealing with very technical subjects." Query with outline. Reviews artwork/photos as part of ms package. Send photocopies.
Recent Nonfiction Title: *How to be a Truly Excellent Medical Student*, by Robert Lederman (medical).
Tips: Audience is medical students and physicians.

INTERNATIONAL PUBLISHERS CO., INC., P.O. Box 3042, New York NY 10116-3042. (212)366-9816. Fax: (212)366-9820. President: Betty Smith. Estab. 1924. Publishes hardcover originals, trade paperback originals and reprints. Publishes 10-15 titles/year. Receives 50-100 mss/year. 10% of books from first-time authors. Pays 5-7½% royalty on paperbacks; 10% royalty on cloth. No advance. Publishes book 6 months after acceptance. Accepts simultaneous submissions. Reports in 1 month on queries with SASE, 6 months on mss. Book catalog and ms guidelines for SAE with 2 first-class stamps.
Nonfiction: Biography, reference, textbook. Subjects include Americana, economics, history, philosophy, politics, social sciences, Marxist-Leninist classics. "Books on labor, black studies and women's studies based on Marxist science have high priority." Query or submit outline, sample chapters and SASE. Reviews artwork/photos as part of ms package.
Recent Nonfiction Title: *Economics of Racism, II*, by Victor Penlo and others.
Tips: No fiction or poetry.

‡**INTERNATIONAL SCHOLARS PUBLICATIONS**, 7831 Woodmont Ave., #345, Bethesda MD 20814. (800)55-PUBLISH. Fax: (301)654-7336. Editor-in-Chief: Robert West. Imprints(s) are Catholic Scholars Press, Christian Universities Press, Jewish Scholars Press. Publishes hardcover originals and reprints. Publishes 36 titles/year. Receives 140 queries and 150 mss/year. 20% of books from first-time authors; 100% from unagented writers. Pays 8-10% royalty. Publishes book 9 months after acceptance of ms. Accepts simultaneous submissions. Reports in 2 months on queries, 1 month on proposals and mss. *Writer's Market* recommends allowing 2 months for reply. Book catalog and ms guidelines free on request.
Nonfiction: Scholarly. Subjects include history, philosophy, religion. "We need scholarly research material, the core of our list. We are a major dissertation publisher." Writers must clearly define topic, length and

time period involved in preparation on their part. Submit proposal package, including cv, outline, table of contents, sample chapters.

Recent Nonfiction Title: *Aquinas on the Nature and Treatment of Animals*, by Judith Barad (religion/philosophy).

Tips: Audience is academic libraries, universities and colleges.

INTERNATIONAL WEALTH SUCCESS, P.O. Box 186, Merrick NY 11570-0186. (516)766-5850. Fax: (516)766-5919. Editor: Tyler G. Hicks. Estab. 1967. Publishes 10 titles/year. Receives 100 submissions/year. 100% of books from first-time authors; 100% from unagented writers. Average print order for a first book "varies from 500 and up, depending on the book." Pays 10% royalty on wholesale or retail price. Buys all rights. Offers usual advance of $1,000, but this varies depending on author's reputation and nature of book. Publishes book 4 months after acceptance. Reports in 1 month. *Writer's Market* recommends allowing 2 months for reply. Book catalog and ms guidelines for 9×12 SAE with 3 first-class stamps.

Nonfiction: Self-help, how-to. "Techniques, methods, sources for building wealth. Highly personal, how-to-do-it with plenty of case histories. Books are aimed at the wealth builder and are highly sympathetic to his and her problems." Financing, business success, venture capital, etc. Length: 60,000-70,000 words. Query. Reviews artwork/photos as part of ms package.

Recent Nonfiction Title: *How To Be A Second Mortgage Loan Broker*, by R. Brisky (self-help).

Tips: "With the mass layoffs in large and medium-size companies there is an increasing interest in owning your own business. So we will focus on more how-to hands-on material on owning—and becoming successful in—one's own business of any kind. Our market is the BWB—Beginning Wealth Builder. This person has so little money that financial planning is something they never think of. Instead, they want to know what kind of a business they can get into to make some money without a large investment. Write for this market and you have millions of potential readers. Remember—there are a lot more people *without* money than *with* money."

INTERWEAVE PRESS, 201 E. Fourth St., Loveland CO 80537. (667)669-7672. Fax: (970)669-8317. Book Editor: Judith Durant. Estab. 1975. Publishes hardcover and trade paperback originals. Publishes 8-12 titles/year. Receives 50 submissions/year. 60% of books from first-time authors; 98% from unagented writers. Pays 10% royalty on net receipts. Offers $500 average advance. Publishes book 1 year after acceptance. Accepts simultaneous submissions, if so noted. Reports in 2 months. Book catalog and ms guidelines free.

Nonfiction: How-to, technical. Subjects limited to fiber arts—basketry, spinning, knitting, dyeing and weaving, and hebal topics—gardening, cooking, and lore. Submit outline/synopsis and sample chapters. Reviews artwork/photos as part of ms package.

Tips: "We are looking for very clear, informally written, technically correct manuscripts, generally of a how-to nature, in our specific fiber and herb fields only. Our audience includes a variety of creative self-starters who appreciate inspiration and clear instruction. They are often well educated and skillful in many areas."

IOWA STATE UNIVERSITY PRESS, 2121 S. State Ave., Ames IA 50014-8300. (515)292-0140. Fax: (515)292-3348. E-mail: acqisup@metins.met. Acquisitions Editor: Laura Moran. Editor-in-Chief: Gretchen Van Houten. Estab. 1924. Publishes hardcover and paperback originals. Publishes 55 titles/year. Receives 450 submissions/year. 98% of books from unagented writers. Average print order for a first book is 1,000. Nonauthor-subsidy publishes some titles, based on sales potential of book and contribution to scholarship on trade books. Pays 10% royalty for trade books on wholesale price. No advance. Publishes book 1 year after acceptance. Accepts simultaneous submissions, if so noted. Reports in up to 6 months. Book catalog free. Manuscript guidelines for SASE.

Nonfiction: Publishes agriculture, food and nutrition, economics, aviation, journalism, veterinary sciences. Accepts nonfiction translations. Submit outline and several sample chapters, preferably not in sequence. Looks for "unique approach to subject."

Recent Nonfiction Title: *Equine Color Genetics*, by D. Philip Sponenberg (veterinary medicine).

Tips: "Editorial program is becoming increasingly focused in the areas of agriculture, aviation, journalism and mass communications, veterinary medicine and to a limited extent Iowa Trade books. We are also increasing and strenghtening our agriculture-related holdings."

‡IRI/SKYLIGHT TRAINING AND PUBLISHING, INC., 2626 Clearbrook Dr., Arlington Heights IL 60005. (800)348-4474. E-mail: irisky@xnet.com. Website: http://www.business1.com/iri_sky/. Managing/Acquisitions Editor: Julia E. Noblitt. Publishes 20-25 titles/year. Receives 100 queries and 60 mss/year. 40% of books from first-time authors; 100% from unagented writers. Pays 5-10% royalty on retail price. No advance. Publishes book 9 months after acceptance of ms. Accepts simultaneous submissions. Reports in 1 month on queries, 4 months on proposals and mss. Book catalog and ms guidelines free on request.

Nonfiction: Educational how-to for K-12 classroom practitioners. "We seek books that provide a bridge from the theory to practice in the classroom. Multiple intelligences, integrated curriculum, year-round education, multi-age classroom, diversity, inclusion, cooperative learning, higher-level thinking and technology in the classroom. Submit outline and 1 sample chapter. Reviews artwork/photos as part of ms package. Send photocopies.

Recent Nonfiction Title: *A Multiple Intelligences Road to a Quality Classroom*, by Sally Berman (activity-based classroom lessons).

Tips: "Target K-12 classroom practitioners, staff developers, school administrators, education students. We are interested in research-based books that tell teachers in a clear, friendly, direct manner how to apply educational best practices to their classrooms. We are especially interested in books that give teachers the tools to create lessons on their own, no matter what subject area they teach."

ITALICA PRESS, 595 Main St., Suite 605, New York NY 10044-0047. (212)935-4230. Fax: (212)838-7812. E-mail: italica@aol.com. Publisher: Eileen Gardiner. Estab. 1985. Publishes trade paperback originals. Publishes 6 titles/year. Receives 75 queries and 20 mss/year. 50% of books from first-time authors; 100% from unagented writers. Pays 7-15% royalty on wholesale price. Publishes book 1 year after acceptance of ms. Accepts simultaneous submissions. Reports in 1 month on queries. *Writer's Market* recommends allowing 2 months for reply. Book catalog free.

Nonfiction: "We publish *only* English translations of medieval and Renaissance source materials and English translations of modern Italian fiction." Query. Reviews artwork/photos as part of ms package. Send photocopies.

Tips: "We are interested in considering a wide variety of medieval and Renaissance topics (not historical fiction), and for modern works we are only interested in translations from Italian fiction."

‡IVORY TOWER BOOKS, 111 Bauer Dr., Oakland NJ 07436. Contact: Angelica Berrie. Publishes trade paperback originals. Publishes 30 titles/year. 5% of books from first-time authors. Sometimes pays in royalties, sometimes advance against royalties. Publishes book 3 months after acceptance of ms. Accepts simultaneous submissions. Reports in 3 months on queries.

Nonfiction: Children's/juvenile, gift book, humor. Subjects include child guidance/parenting, cooking/foods/nutrition, gardening, hobbies, music/dance, sports, women's issues/studies. "Looking for books that can sell in gift and card shops geared to occasions. Light, humorous or inspirational treatments. Nothing heavy. Fun books that can be read in an hour or so. Query with outline, representative sampling of content and SASE.

‡J & L LEE CO., P.O. Box 5575, Lincoln NE 68505. Publisher: James L. McKee. Imprints are Salt Creek Press, Young Hearts, J & L Lee Co. Publishes trade paperback originals and reprints. Publishes 5 titles/year. Receives 25 queries and 5-10 mss/year. 20% of books from first-time authors; 60% from unagented writers. Pays 10% royalty on retail price or makes outright purchase of $100 minimum. Rarely offers advance. Publishes book 10 months after acceptance of ms. Accepts simultaneous submissions. Reports in 6 months on queries and mss, 1 month on proposals. Book catalog free on request.

Nonfiction: Biography, reference. Subjects include Americana, history, regional. "Virtually everything we publish is of a Great Plains nature." Query.

Recent Nonfiction Title: *Oh, Grandma, You're Kidding*, by Gladyss Douglass (regional history).

JAIN PUBLISHING CO., P.O. Box 3523, Fremont CA 94539. (510)659-8272. Fax: (510)659-0501. Website: http://www.jainpub.com. Editor-in-chief: M.K. Jain. Estab. 1987. Imprint is Asian Humanities Press. Publishes hardcover and trade paperback originals and reprints. Publishes 15 titles/year. Receives 500 queries/year. 20% of books from first-time authors; 100% from unagented writers. Pays up to 10% royalty on net sales or makes outright purchase of $500-2,000. Offers occasional $1,000-2,000 advance. Publishes book 1 year after acceptance. Reports in 3 months on mss. Book catalog for 6×9 SAE with 2 first-class stamps. Manuscript guidelines for #10 SASE.

• Jain is putting more emphasis on general purpose computer books and books dealing with health/fitness and business/management. Continued emphasis on undergraduate textbooks.

Nonfiction: Self-help, motivational/inspirational, how-to, cooking/foods/nutrition (vegetarian), health/fitness, gift books, guides and handbooks, personal finance, computer books (general purpose), business/management, children's, reference, textbooks. "Manuscripts should be related to our subjects and written in an 'easy to read' and understandable format. Preferably between 40,000-80,000 words." Submit proposal package, including cv and list of prior publications with SASE. Reviews artwork/photos as part of ms package. Send photocopies.

Recent Nonfiction Title: *Internet: A Comprehensive Guide*, by Holly Taylor (computers).

Tips: "We're interested more in user-oriented books than general treatises."

THOMAS JEFFERSON UNIVERSITY PRESS, NMSU MC111L, Kirksville MO 63501. (816)785-4665. Director: Robert V. Schnucker. Publishes 4-6 titles/year. Pays 25% maximum royalty on net sales.

Nonfiction: Biography, illustrated book, textbook and monographs on Americana, anthropology/archaeology, art/architecture, government/politics, history, language/literature, military/war, philosophy, religion, sociology and translation.

Recent Nonfiction Title: *In Footsteps of Dvorak*, by Ivonin (biography).

JEWISH LIGHTS PUBLISHING, Division of Long Hill Partners Inc., P.O. Box 237, Sunset Farm Offices, Rte. 4, Woodstock VT 05091. Publishes hardcover originals, trade paperback originals and reprints. Publishes 12 titles/year. Receives 1,000 queries and 500 mss/year. Pays royalty of net sales, 10% on first printing, then increases. Offers advance. Publishes book 6 months after acceptance of ms. Accepts simultaneous submissions. Reports in 4 months. Book catalog free on request. Manuscript guidelines for #10 SASE.

Nonfiction: Children's/juvenile, self-help, spirituality. Subjects include philosophy, religion, women's issues/studies, spirituality. "We publish a particular style of books. Find out about our books by looking at them or a catalog, before submitting. We don't publish 'Judaica' as it's typically defined. No biography or autobiography." Query with outline, sample chapter and SASE.

Tips: "Our audience includes people of all faiths, all backgrounds who yearn for books that attract, engage, educate and spiritually inspire."

JEWISH PUBLICATION SOCIETY, 1930 Chestnut St., Philadelphia PA 19103. (215)564-5925. Editor-in-Chief: Dr. Ellen Frankel. Publishes hardcover and trade paperback originals, trade paperback reprints. Publishes 12 titles/year. 20% of books from first-time authors; 75% from unagented writers. Pays 10-15% royalty on wholesale price. Offers $1,000-4,000 advance. Publishes book 18 months after acceptance. Accepts simultaneous submissions. Reports in 3 months on proposals. Book catalog free on request.

Nonfiction: Children's/juvenile, reference, trade books. Subjects include history, language/literature, religion, women's issues/studies. "We are interested in books of Judaica for a college-educated readership. No monographs or textbooks. We do not accept memoirs, biographies, art books, coffee-table books." Query with proposal package including outline, description and proposed table of contents, curriculum vitae with SASE.

Recent Nonfiction Title: *Reclaiming the Dead Sea Scrolls*, by Lawrence Schiffman (Jewish history).

Poetry: "We publish no original poetry in English. We would consider a topical anthology on a Jewish theme." Query.

Recent Poetry Title: *Modern Poems on the Bible*, edited by David Curzon (responses to biblical texts - 20 C.).

Tips: "Our audience is college-educated Jewish readers interested in Bible, Jewish history or Jewish practice."

JIST WORKS, INC., 720 N. Park Ave., Indianapolis IN 46202-3431. (317)264-3720. Fax: (317)264-3709. E-mail: jistworks@aol.com. Managing Editor: Sara Hall. Estab. 1981. Publishes trade paperback originals and reprints. Publishes 40 titles/year. Receives 300 submissions/year. 60% of books from first time authors; 100% from unagented writers. Pays 5-12% royalty on wholesale price or makes outright purchase (negotiable). Publishes book 1 year after acceptance. Accepts simultaneous submissions. Query with SASE. Reports in 3 months on queries. Book catalog and ms guidelines for 9×12 SAE with 6 first-class stamps.

● JIST Works has adopted a new imprint, Park Avenue Publications, to publish business and self-help manuscripts that fall outside of the JIST topical parameters.

Nonfiction: How-to, career, reference, self-help, software, video, textbook. Specializes in job search, self-help and career related topics. "We want text/workbook formats that would be useful in a school or other institutional setting. We also publish trade titles, all reading levels. Will consider books for professional staff and educators, appropriate software and videos." Reviews artwork/photos as part of ms package.

Recent Nonfiction Title: *The Quick Interview & Salary Negotiation Book*, by J. Michael Farr (career/reference).

Tips: "Institutions and staff who work with people of all reading and academic skill levels, making career and life decisions or people who are looking for jobs are our primary audience, but we're focusing more on business and trade topics for consumers."

JOHNSON BOOKS, Johnson Publishing Co., 1880 S. 57th Court., Boulder CO 80301. (303)443-9766. Fax: (303)443-1679. Editorial Director: Stephen Topping. Estab. 1979. Imprints are Spring Creek Press and Cordillera Press. Publishes hardcover and paperback originals and reprints. Publishes 10-12 titles/year. Receives 500 submissions/year. 30% of books from first-time authors; 90% from unagented writers. Average print order for a first book is 5,000. Royalties vary. Publishes book 1 year after acceptance. Reports in 3 months. Book catalog and ms guidelines for 9×12 SAE with 5 first-class stamps.

Nonfiction: General nonfiction, books on the West, environmental subjects, natural history, paleontology, geology, archaeology, travel, guidebooks, outdoor recreation. Accepts nonfiction translations. "We are primarily interested in books for the informed popular market, though we will consider vividly written scholarly works. As a small publisher, we are able to give every submission close personal attention." Submit outline/synopsis and 3 sample chapters. Looks for "good writing, thorough research, professional presentation and appropriate style. Marketing suggestions from writers are helpful." Reviews artwork/photos.

Recent Nonfiction Title: *Squirrels*, by Kim Long (fact book).

Tips: "We are looking for titles with broad national, not just regional, appeal. We are especially interested in 'useful' books with strong backlist potential."

BOB JONES UNIVERSITY PRESS, Greenville SC 29614-0001. Acquisitions Editor: Ms. Gloria Repp. Estab. 1974. Publishes trade paperback originals and reprints. Publishes 10 titles/year. Receives 50 queries and 300 mss/year. 40% of books from first-time authors; 100% from unagented writers. Makes outright purchase of $500-1,250; royalties to established authors. Publishes book 18 months after acceptance. Accepts simultaneous submissions. Reports in 2 months on mss. Book catalog and ms guidelines free on request.
Nonfiction: Biography (for teens), children's/juvenile. Subjects include animals, gardening, health/medicine, history, nature/environment, sports. "We're looking for concept books on almost any subject suitable for children. We also like biographies." Submit outline and 3 sample chapters.
Fiction: Juvenile, young adult. "We're looking for well-rounded characters and plots with plenty of action suitable for a Christian audience. Avoid being preachy." Submit synopsis and 5 sample chapters or complete ms.
Recent Nonfiction Title: *Dust of the Earth*, by Donna Hess (biographical fiction ages 12+).
Tips: "Our readers are children ages two and up, teens and young adults. We're looking for high-quality writing that reflects a Christian perspective and features well-developed characters in a convincing plot. Most open to: first chapter books; adventure; biography."

JUDSON PRESS, P.O. Box 851, Valley Forge PA 19482-0851. (610)768-2118. Fax: (610)768-2441. Publisher: Harold W. Rast. Acquisitions: Kristy Pullen. Editorial Manager: Mary Nicol. Estab. 1824. Publishes hardcover and paperback originals. Publishes 15-20 titles/year. Receives 750 queries/year. Average print order for a first book is 5,000. Pays royalty or makes outright purchase. Publishes book 15 months after acceptance. Accepts simultaneous submissions. Reports in 6 months. Enclose return postage. Book catalog for 9×12 SAE with 4 first-class stamps. Manuscript guidelines for #10 SASE.
Nonfiction: Adult religious nonfiction of 30,000-80,000 words. "Our audience is mostly church members who seek to have a more fulfilling personal spiritual life and want to serve Christ in their churches and other relationships." Query with outline and sample chapter.
Tips: "Writers have the best chance selling us practical books assisting clergy or laypersons in their ministry and personal lives. Our audience consists of Protestant church leaders and members. Be sensitive to our workload and adapt to the market's needs. Books on multicultural issues are very welcome."

JUST US BOOKS, INC., 356 Glenwood Ave., 3rd Floor, East Orange NJ 07017. Fax: (201)677-7570. Website: http://www.quiknet.com/mbt/justus.html. Submissions Manager: Allyson Sherwood. Imprint is Afro-Bets® (Cheryl Willis Hudson, publisher). Publishes hardcover and trade paperback and mass market paperback originals. Publishes 3-5 titles/year. Receives 300 queries and 500 mss/year. 33% of books from first-time authors; 33% from unagented writers. Pays royalty or makes outright purchase. Offers variable advance. Publishes book 18 months after acceptance of ms. Accepts simultaneous submissions. Reports in 1 month on queries and proposals, 3 months on mss. Book catalog and ms guidelines for 6×9 SAE with 2 first-class stamps.
Nonfiction: Biography, children's/juvenile, illustrated books, middle readers and young adult. Emphasis on African-American subjects. Concentrate on young adult readers—no picture books. Query with SASE. Reviews artwork/photos as part of ms package. Send photocopies, transparencies or color or b&w sketches.
Recent Nonfiction Title: *Book of Black Heroes, Vol. 2 Great Women in the Struggle*, by Toyomi Igus et. al. (biographical).
Fiction: Adventure, fantasy, historical, humor, multicultural, science fiction, suspense, young adult. Looking for "contemporary, realistic, appealing fiction for readers aged 9-12, especially stories involving boys. Stories may take the form of chapter books with a range of 5,000-20,000 words." Query with SASE. Unsolicited mss will be returned unread.
Recent Fiction Title: *Ziggy and the Black Dinosaurs: Lost in the Tunnel of Time*, by Sharon M. Draper (mystery).
Poetry: Not considering poetry at this time.
Tips: "We want stories for middle readers that appeal to both girls and boys (ages 9-12). This group still has higher priority for us than acquiring picture books."

KALMBACH PUBLISHING CO., 21027 Crossroads Circle, P.O. Box 1612, Waukesha WI 53187-1612. Fax: (414)796-1142. E-mail: tspohn@kalmbach.com. Senior Acquisitions Editor: Terry Spohn. Estab. 1934. Publishes hardcover and paperback originals, paperback reprints. Publishes 15-20 titles/year. Receives 100 submissions/year. 85% of books from first-time authors; 100% from unagented writers. Pays 10% royalty on net. Offers $1,500 average advance. Publishes book 18 months after acceptance. Reports in 2 months.
Nonfiction: Hobbies, how-to, amateur astronomy, railroading. "Our book publishing effort is in amateur astronomy, railroading and hobby how-to-do-it titles *only*." Query first. "I welcome telephone inquiries. They save me a lot of time, and they can save an author a lot of misconceptions and wasted work." In written query, wants detailed outline of 2-3 pages and a complete sample chapter with photos, drawings, and how-to text. Reviews artwork/photos as part of ms package.
Recent Nonfiction Title: *Beginner's Guide to the Sun*, by Taylor and Hendrickson (astronomy).
Tips: "Our books are about half text and half illustrations. Any author who wants to publish with us must be able to furnish good photographs and rough drawings before we'll consider contracting for his book."

KAR-BEN COPIES INC., 6800 Tildenwood Lane, Rockville MD 20852-4371. (301)984-8733 or 1-800-4KARBEN. Fax: (301)881-9195. President: Judye Groner. Contact: Madeline Wikler. Estab. 1975. Publishes hardcover and trade paperback originals on Jewish themes for young children. Publishes 8-10 titles/year. Receives 150 submissions/year. 25% of books from first-time authors; 100% from unagented writers. Average print order for a first book is 10,000. Pays 6-8% royalty on net receipts or makes negotiable outright purchase. Offers $1,000 average advance. Publishes book 1 year after acceptance. Reports in 2 months. Book catalog and ms guidelines for 9×12 SAE with 2 first-class stamps.
Nonfiction: Jewish juvenile (ages 1-9). Especially looking for books on Jewish life-cycle, holidays, and customs for children—"early childhood and elementary." Send only mss with Jewish content. Query with outline and sample chapters. Reviews artwork/photos as part of ms package.
Fiction: Adventure, fantasy, historical, religious (all Jewish juvenile). Especially looking for Jewish holiday and history-related fiction for young children. Submit outline/synopsis and sample chapters or complete ms.
Tips: "We envision Jewish children and their families, and juveniles interested in learning about Jewish subjects, as our audience."

‡KAYA PRODUCTION, 8 Harrison St., New York NY 10013. (212)966-4798. Fax: (212)966-3987. E-mail: kaya@panix.com. Associate Editor: Sunyoung Lee. Publishes hardcover originals and trade paperback originals and reprints. Publishes 4 titles/year. Receives 50 queries/year. 25% of books from first-time authors. Pays 7-15% royalty on retail price. Offers $500-1,000 advance. Publishes book 2 years after acceptance of ms. Accepts simultaneous submissions. Reports in 6 months on mss. Book catalog free on request. Manuscript guidelines for #10 SASE.
  ● Kaya is a 1995 recipient of the Gregory Kolovakos Seed Grant Award given by the CLMP.
Nonfiction: Biography. Subjects include anthropology/archaeology, art/architecture, ethnic (Asian, Asian-American), gay/lesbian, language/literature, philosophy, photography, regional, sociology, translation, women's issues/studies. Submit proposal package, including outline, sample chapters, previous publications with SASE. Reviews artwork/photos as part of ms package. Send photocopies.
Recent Nonfiction Title: *Muae: A Journal of Transcultural Production*, edited by Walter K. Lew (journal).
Fiction: Ethnic, experimental, feminist, gay/lesbian, historical, literary, mystery, picture books, plays, science fiction, short story collections, suspense. "Kaya publishes Asian, Asian-American and Asian diasporic materials. We are looking for innovative writers with a commitment to quality literature." Submit synopsis and 2-4 sample chapters with SASE.
Recent Fiction Title: *Rolling the R's*, by R. Zamora Linmark (novel).
Poetry: Submit complete ms.
Recent Poetry Title: *The Unbearable Heart*, by Kimiko Hahn (poetry collection).
Tips: Audience is people interested in a high standard of literature and who are interested in breaking down easy approaches to multicultural literature.

KENT STATE UNIVERSITY PRESS, P.O. Box 5190, Kent OH 44242-0001. (330)672-7913. Fax: (330)672-3104. Director: John T. Hubbell. Senior Editor: Julia Morton. Estab. 1965. Publishes hardcover and paperback originals and some reprints. Publishes 20-25 titles/year. Nonauthor subsidy publishes 20% of books. Standard minimum book contract on net sales. Offers advance rarely. "Always write a letter of inquiry before submitting manuscripts. We can publish only a limited number of titles each year and can frequently tell in advance whether or not we would be interested in a particular manuscript. This practice saves both our time and that of the author, not to mention postage costs. If interested we will ask for complete manuscript. Decisions based on inhouse readings and two by outside scholars in the field of study." Reports in 3 months. Enclose return postage. Book catalog free.
Nonfiction: Especially interested in "scholarly works in history and literary studies of high quality, any titles of regional interest for Ohio, scholarly biographies, archaeological research, the arts, and general nonfiction."
Recent Nonfiction Title: *April '65*, by William A. Tidwell (US history).
Recent Fiction Title: *Tales from the Irish Club*, by Lester Goran (original short stories).
Recent Poetry Title: *Already the World*, by Victoria Redel.
Tips: "We are cautious about publishing heavily-illustrated manuscripts."

MICHAEL KESEND PUBLISHING, LTD., 1025 Fifth Ave., New York NY 10028. (212)249-5150. Director: Michael Kesend. Editor: Judy Wilder. Estab. 1979. Publishes hardcover and trade paperback originals and reprints. Publishes 4-6 titles/year. Receives 300 submissions/year. 20% of books from first-time authors; 40% from unagented writers. Pays 6% royalty on wholesale price. Advance varies. Publishes book 18 months after acceptance. Reports in 2 months on queries. Guidelines for #10 SASE.
Nonfiction: Biography, how-to, illustrated book, self-help, sports. Subjects include animals, health, history, hobbies, nature, sports, travel, the environment, guides to several subjects. Needs sports, health self-help and environmental awareness guides. No photography mss. Submit outline and sample chapters. Reviews artwork/photos as part of ms package.
Recent Nonfiction Title: *Walks in Welcoming Place*, by Harrison (regional guide for seniors and disabled).
Tips: "Looking for national guides, outdoor travel guides and sports nonfiction."

KINSEEKER PUBLICATIONS, P.O. Box 184, Grawn MI 49637-0184. (616)276-6745. E-mail: ab∅64@t raverse.lib.mi.us. Editor: Victoria Wilson. Estab. 1986. Publishes trade paperback originals. Publishes 6 titles/ year. 100% of books from unagented writers. Pays 10-25% royalty on retail price. Publishes book 8 months after acceptance. Accepts simultaneous submissions. Reports in 3 months. Book catalog and ms guidelines for #10 SASE.
Nonfiction: Reference books. Subjects are local history and genealogy. Query or submit outline and sample chapters. Reviews artwork/photos as part of ms package.

B. KLEIN PUBLICATIONS, P.O. Box 6578, Delray Beach FL 33482. (407)496-3316. Fax: (407)496-5546. Editor-in-Chief: Bernard Klein. Estab. 1946. Publishes hardcover and paperback originals. Specializes in directories, annuals, who's who books, bibliography, business opportunity, reference books. Publishes 5 titles/year. Pays 10% royalty on wholesale price, "but we're negotiable. Advance depends on many factors." Markets books by direct mail and mail order. Accepts simultaneous submissions. Reports in 2 months. Book catalog for #10 SASE.
Nonfiction: Business, hobbies, how-to, reference, self-help, directories and bibliographies. Query or submit outline and sample chapters.
Recent Nonfiction Title: *Guide to American Directories*, by Bernard Klein.

ALFRED A. KNOPF, INC., Division of Random House, 201 E. 50th St., New York NY 10022. (212)751-2600. Submit mss to Senior Editor or Children's Book Editor. Publishes hardcover and paperback originals. Averages 200 titles/yearly. 15% of books from first-time authors; 30% from unagented writers. Royalty and advance vary. Publishes book 1 year after acceptance. Accepts simultaneous submissions if so informed. Reports in 3 months. Book catalog for 7½ × 10½ SAE with 5 first-class stamps.
• Knopf books won three Pulitzer Prizes in 1995.
Nonfiction: Book-length nonfiction, including books of scholarly merit. Preferred length: 50,000-150,000 words. "A good nonfiction writer should be able to follow the latest scholarship in any field of human knowledge, and fill in the abstractions of scholarship for the benefit of the general reader by means of good, concrete, sensory reporting." Query. Reviews artwork/photos as part of ms package.
Recent Nonfiction Title: *Hitler's Willing Executioners*, by Daniel Jonah Goldhagen.
Fiction: Publishes book-length fiction of literary merit by known or unknown writers. Length: 40,000-150,000 words. *Writer's Market* recommends writers query with sample chapters.
Recent Fiction Title: *I Was Amelia Earhart*, by Jane Mendelsohn.

KNOWLEDGE, IDEAS & TRENDS, INC. (KIT), 1131-0 Tolland Turnpike, Suite 175, Manchester CT 06040. (203)646-0745. Publishes hardcover and trade paperback originals. Publishes 4-5 titles/year. 80% of books from first-time authors; 100% from unagented writers. Pays royalty on wholesale price or advance against royalty. Advance varies. Publishes book 18 months after acceptance. Accepts simultaneous submissions. Reports in 3 months on mss. Book catalog and ms guidelines free on request.
Nonfiction: Biography, how-to, humor, reference, self-help. Subjects include anthropology/archaeology, business and economics, ethnic, history, psychology, sociology, women's issues/studies. Send outline and 3 sample chapters to Editor. Reviews artwork/photos as part of ms package. Send photocopies.
Recent Nonfiction Title: *The Negativity Trap*, by Lois Wolfe-Mozgar.
Tips: "Audience is general readers, academics, older women, sociologists."

KODANSHA AMERICA, INC., 114 Fifth Ave., New York NY 10011. (212)727-6460. Fax: (212)727-9177. Contact: Editorial Department. Estab. 1989 (in US). Publishes 50% hardcover and trade paperback originals; 50% trade paperback originals and reprints in Kodansha Globe series. Publishes 35-40 titles/year. Receives 3,000 submissions/year. 10% of books from first-time authors; 30% from unagented writers. Pays 6-15% royalty on retail price. Offers $2,000 (reprints), $10,000 (original) average advances. Publishes book 9 months after acceptance. Accepts simultaneous submissions. Reports in up to 3 months. Book catalog for 9 × 12 SAE with 6 first-class stamps.
• In 1995, Kodansha America published the critically acclaimed and commercially successful, *A Diary of the Century: Tales from America's Greatest Diarist*, by Edward Robb Ellis.
Nonfiction: Biography, anthropology/archaeology, business and economics, cooking, gardening, history, crafts, language, nature/environment, philosophy, psychology, religion, science, sociology, translation, travel, Asian subjects. Looking for distinguished critical books on international subjects. No fiction. Query with sample chapters and SASE. Reviews artwork/photos as part of ms package.

● **A BULLET** introduces comments by the editors of *Writer's Market* indicating special information about the listing.

Recent Nonfiction Title: *A Diary of the Century.*
Tips: "Our focus is on nonfiction titles of an international and cross-cultural nature, well-researched, written with authority, bringing something of a world view to the general reading public. We are especially interested in titles with staying power, which will sell as well in five years' time as now. Potential authors should be aware of what comparable titles are on the market, and from whom."

KREGEL PUBICATIONS, Kregel, Inc., P.O. Box 2607, Grand Rapids MI 49501. E-mail: kregelpub@aol.com. Senior Editor: Dennis R. Hillman. Imprints are Kregel Publications, Kregel Resources, Kregel Classics. Publishes hardcover and trade paperback originals and reprints. Publishes 80 titles/year. Receives 150 queries and 100 mss/year. 5% of books from first-time authors; 100% from unagented writers. Pays 8-14% royalty on wholesale price or makes outright purchase of $500-1,000. Offers negotiated advance. Publishes book 1 year after acceptance of ms. Accepts simultaneous submissions. Reports in 1 month on queries and proposals, 3 months on mss. Book catalog for 9×12 SAE with 3 first-class stamps. Manuscript guidelines for #10 SASE.
Nonfiction: Biography (Christian), reference, textbook. Subjects include religion. "We serve evangelical Christian readers and those in career Christian service." Query with outline, 2 sample chapters, bio and market comparison.
Recent Nonfiction Title: *52 Ways to Keep Your Promises*, by Wayne and Judith Rolfs.
Tips: "Looking for titles with broad appeal in the area of biblical studies and spiritual living."

‡KRIEGER PUBLISHING CO., P.O. Box 9542, Melbourne FL 32902-9542. (407)724-9542. Fax: (407)951-3671. Production Manager: Marie Bowles. Imprints are Orbit Series, Anvil Series and Public History. Publishes hardcover and paperback originals and reprints. Publishes 60 titles/year. Receives 50-60 submissions/year. 30% of books from first-time authors; 100% from unagented writers. Pays royalty on net realized price. Publishes book 8 months after acceptance. Reports in 1 month. *Writer's Market* recommends allowing 2 months for reply. Book catalog free.
Nonfiction: College reference, technical, textbook. Subjects include history, music, philosophy, psychology, space science, herpetology, chemistry, physics, engineering, medical. Query. Reviews artwork/photos as part of ms package.
Recent Nonfiction Title: *Reptile Clinician's Handbook: A Compact Clinical and Surgical Reference*, by Fredric L. Frye.

LAKE VIEW PRESS, P.O. Box 578279, Chicago IL 60657. Director: Paul Elitzik. Publishes hardcover and trade paperback originals. Publishes 5 titles/year. Receives 100 queries and 10 mss/year. 100% of books from unagented writers. Pays 6-10% royalty on wholesale price. Publishes book 1 year after acceptance of ms. Reports in 1 month on queries. *Writer's Market* recommends allowing 2 months for reply. Query with toc, c.v. and SASE. No sample chapters. Book catalog for #10 SASE.
Nonfiction: Biography, reference, technical. Subjects include government/politics, history, language/literature, sociology, women's issues/studies. Query.
Recent Nonfiction Title: *Forsaking our Children: Bureaucracy & Reform in the Child Welfare System*, by John M. Hagedorn (scholarly).
Tips: "We are interested mainly in scholarly nonfiction which is written in a manner accessible to a nonprofessional reader."

PETER LANG PUBLISHING, Subsidiary of Peter Lang AG, Bern, Switzerland, 275 Seventh Ave., New York NY 10001. (212)647-7700. Fax: (212)647-7707. Website: http://www.peterlang.com. Managing Director: Christopher S. Myers. Acquisitions Editor: Owen Lancer. Estab. 1952. Publishes mostly hardcover originals. Publishes 300 titles/year. 75% of books from first-time authors; 98% from unagented writers. Publishes scholarly monographs in the Humanities and Social Sciences, as well as textbooks in selected fields of the Humanities and Social Sciences. Write or call for submission requirements. Pays 10-20% royalty on net price. Translators get flat fee plus percentage of royalties. No advance. Publishes book 1 year after acceptance. Reports in 2 months. Book catalog free.
Nonfiction: General nonfiction, reference works, scholarly monographs. Subjects include literary criticism, Germanic and Romance languages, art history, business and economics, American and European political science, history, music, philosophy, psychology, religion, sociology, biography. All books are scholarly monographs, textbooks, reference books, reprints of historic texts, critical editions or translations. No mss shorter than 200 pages. Submit complete ms. *Writer's Market* recommends sending a query with SASE first. Fully refereed review process.
Recent Nonfiction Title: *American Women Playwrights, 1900-1950*, by Yvonne Shafer (survey of playwrights).
Fiction and Poetry: "We do not publish original fiction or poetry. We seek scholarly and critical editions only. Submit complete manuscript." *Writer's Market* recommends sending a query with SASE first.
Tips: "Besides our commitment to specialist academic monographs, we are one of the few US publishers who publish books in most of the modern languages. A major advantage for Lang authors is international marketing and distribution of all titles. Translation rights sold for many titles."

LANGENSCHEIDT PUBLISHING GROUP, 46-35 54th Rd., Maspeth NY 11378. (800)432-MAPS. Fax: (718)784-0640. Acquisitions Editor: Christine Cardone. Imprints are Hagstrom Map, American Map, Trakker Map, Arrow Map, Creative Sales. Publishes hardcover, trade paperback and mass market paperback originals. Publishes over 100 titles/year; each imprint publishes 20 titles/year. Receives 25 queries and 15 mss/year. 100% of books from unagented writers. Pays royalty or makes outright purchase. Publishes book 6 months after acceptance of ms. Accepts simultaneous submissions. Reports in 2 months on proposals. Book catalog free on request.
Nonfiction: Reference. Subjects include foreign language. "Any foreign language that fills a gap in our line is welcome." Submit outline and 2 sample chapters (complete ms preferred.)
Recent Nonfiction Title: Notebook Dictionary Series (students' dictionary).

LARK BOOKS, Altamont Press, 50 College St., Asheville NC 28801. Publisher: Rob Pulleyn. Estab. 1976. Imprints are: Lark Books; Sterling/Lark Books. Publishes hardcover and trade paperback originals and reprints. Publishes 40 titles/year. Sterling publishes 25; Lark publishes 15. Receives 300 queries and 100 mss/year. 80% of books from first-time authors; 100% from unagented writers. Pays 10% royalty on gross income or makes outright purchase. Offers up to $2,500 advance. Publishes book 1 year after acceptance of ms. Accepts simultaneous submissions. Reports in 2 months.
Nonfiction: Coffee table book, cookbook, how-to, illustrated book, nonfiction children's/juvenile. Subjects include cooking, gardening, hobbies, nature/environment, crafts. "We publish high quality, highly illustrated books, primarily in the crafts/leisure markets. We work closely with bookclubs. Our books are either how-to, 'gallery' or combination books." Submit outline and 1 sample chapter, sample projects, table of contents. Reviews artwork/photos as part of ms package. Send transparencies if possible.
Recent Nonfiction Title: *Handmade Tiles*, by Frank Giorgini (how-to and gallery book, all color, technique, projects, portfolio).

LARSON PUBLICATIONS/PBPF, 4936 Rt. 414, Burdett NY 14818-9729. (607)546-9342. Director: Paul Cash. Estab. 1982. Publishes hardcover and trade paperback originals. Publishes 4-5 titles/year. Receives 1,000 submissions/year. 5% of books from first-time authors. Pays 7½% royalty on retail price or 10% cash received. Rarely offers advance. Publishes book 1 year after acceptance. Accepts simultaneous submissions. Reports in 4 months on queries. Unsolicited mss not accepted; queries only. Book catalog for 9×12 SAE with 3 first-class stamps.
Nonfiction: Spiritual philosophy. Subjects include philosophy, psychology and religion. "We are looking for studies of comparative spiritual philosophy or personal fruits of independent (transsectarian viewpoint) spiritual research/practice." Query or submit outline and sample chapters. Reviews artwork/photos as part of ms package.
Recent Nonfiction Title: *Love is the Link*, by Pam Kircher, M.D. (near-death/hospice work).

LAUREATE PRESS, P.O. Box 96, Milbridge ME 04658. Editor/Publisher: Lance C. Lobo. Publishes trade paperback originals and reprints. Publishes 3 titles/year. Pays 6-10% royalty on wholesale price. Offers $100 advance. Reports in 2 months on queries.
Nonfiction: Fencing subjects only—how-to, technical. Fencing books must be authored by diplomaed fencing masters. Query with outline and SASE.
Recent Nonfiction Title: *On Fencing*, by Aldo Nadi (fencing-technical).
Tips: Audience is recreational and competitive fencers worldwide.

MERLOYD LAWRENCE BOOKS, Imprint of Addison Wesley, 102 Chestnut St., Boston MA 02108. President: Merloyd Lawrence. Estab. 1982. Publishes hardcover and trade paperback originals. Publishes 7-8 titles/year. Receives 400 submissions/year. 25% of books from first-time authors; 20% from unagented writers. Pays royalty on retail price. Publishes book 1 year after acceptance. Accepts simultaneous submissions. Reports in 3 weeks on queries; no unsolicited mss read. Book catalog available from Addison Wesley.
Nonfiction: Biography. Subjects include child development/parenting, health/medicine, nature/environment, psychology. Query with SASE. *All queries with SASE read and answered.*

LAWYERS & JUDGES PUBLISHING CO., P.O. Box 30040, Tucson AZ 85751-0040. (520)323-1500. Fax: (520)323-0055. President: Steve Weintraub. Publishes professional hardcover originals. Publishes 15 titles/year. Receives 200 queries and 30 mss/year. 5% of books from first-time authors; 100% from unagented writers. Pays 7-10% royalty on retail price. Publishes book 5 months after acceptance of ms. Accepts simultaneous submissions. Reports in 2 months. Book catalog free.
Nonfiction: Reference. Legal/insurance subjects. "We are a highly specific publishing company, reaching the legal and insurance fields and accident reconstruction. Unless a writer is an expert in these areas, we are not interested." Submit proposal package, including full or *very* representative portion of ms. *Writer's Market* recommends query with SASE first.
Recent Nonfiction Title: *Aircraft Accident Reconstruction & Litigation*, by Dr. Barnes McCormick and Myron P. Papadakis, Esq.

LEADERSHIP PUBLISHERS, INC., Talented and Gifted Education, P.O. Box 8358, Des Moines IA 50301-8358. (515)278-4765. Fax: (515)270-8303. Editorial Director: Lois F. Roets. Estab. 1982. Publishes trade paperback originals. Publishes 5 titles/year. Receives 25 queries and 10 mss/year. Pays 10% royalty of sales. Publishes book 1 year after acceptance of ms. Reports in 3 months. Book catalog and ms guidelines for 9 × 12 SAE with 2 first-class stamps.
Nonfiction: Textbook. Education subjects. "We publish enrichment/supplementary educational programs and teacher reference books; our specialty is education of the talented and gifted." Submit outline and 2 sample chapters. Reviews artwork/photos as part of ms package. Send photocopies.

THE LEARNING WORKS, INC., P.O. Box 6187, Santa Barbara CA 93160. (805)964-4220. Fax: (805)964-1466. President: Linda Schwartz. Publishes trade paperback originals. Publishes 10 titles/year. Receives 75 queries and 50 mss/year. 5% of books from first-time authors; 95% from unagented writers. Makes outright purchase, amount varies according to author's experience. Publishes book within 1 year of acceptance of ms. Reports in 1 month. *Writer's Market* recommends allowing 2 months for reply. Book catalog and ms guidelines free on request.
Nonfiction: Children's/juvenile. Subjects include animals, anthropology/archaeology, art/architecture, child guidance/parenting, education, ethnic, health/medicine, history, language/literature, nature/environment, science, sports, travel, safety, arts/crafts, self-esteem, values clarification. "The Learning Works specializes in educational activity books for children, parents, and teachers. Subject matter ranges across the curriculum. Many are supplementary educational materials for ages preschool to 18. We do not publish story books or music." Query with outline, 10 sample activities and SASE.
Recent Nonfiction Title: *Create A Culture*, by Carol Nordgaarden (multicultural).

LEE & LOW BOOKS, 95 Madison Ave., New York NY 10016. (212)779-4400. Publisher: Philip Lee. Editor-in-Chief: Elizabeth Szabla. Estab. 1991. "We focus on multicultural children's picture books. Of special interest are stories set in contemporary America. We are interested in fiction as well as nonfiction." Publishes 13 titles/year.
Recent Fiction Title: *Sam and the Lucky Money*, by Karen Chinn (children's picture book).

LEHIGH UNIVERSITY PRESS, Linderman Library, 30 Library Dr., Lehigh University, Bethlehem PA 18015-3067. (610)758-3933. Fax: (610)974-2823. E-mail: inlup@lehigh.edu. Director: Philip A. Metzger. Estab. 1985. Publishes hardcover originals. Publishes 10 titles/year. Receives 30 queries and 25 mss/year. 70% of books from first-time authors; 100% from unagented writers. Pays royalty. Publishes book 18 months after acceptance of ms. Accepts simultaneous submissions. Reports in 3 months. Book catalog and ms guidelines free.
Nonfiction: Biography, reference, academic. Subjects include Americana, art/architecture, history, language/literature, science. "We are an academic press publishing scholarly monographs. We are especially interested in works on 18th century studies and the history of technology, but consider works of quality on a variety of subjects." Submit 1 sample chapter and proposal package.

LEISURE BOOKS, Division of Dorchester Publishing Co., Inc., 276 Fifth Ave., Suite 1008, New York NY 10001-0112. (212)725-8811. Editorial Assistant: Jennifer Eaton. Estab. 1970. Publishes mass market paperback originals and reprints. Publishes 160 titles/year. Receives thousands of submissions/year. 20% of books from first-time authors; 20% from unagented writers. Pays royalty on retail price. Advance negotiable. Publishes book 18 months after acceptance. Reports in 4 months on queries. Book catalog and ms guidelines for #10 SASE.
  ● Love Spell, an imprint, publishes only romance titles.
Nonfiction: "Our needs are minimal as we publish perhaps two nonfiction titles a year." Query.
Fiction: Historical romance (115,000 words); time-travel romance (90,000 words); futuristic romance (90,000 words); westerns (75,000-115,000 words); horror (90,000 words); techno-thrillers (90,000 words). "We are strongly backing historical romance. No sweet romance, gothic, science fiction, erotica, contemporary women's fiction, mainstream or action/adventure." Query or submit outline/synopsis and sample chapters. "No material will be returned without SASE."
Recent Fiction Title: *Angel & the Outlaw*, by Madeline Baker (romance).
Tips: "Historical romance is our strongest category. We are also seeking time-travel and futuristic romances, westerns, horror and techno-thrillers."

LERNER PUBLICATIONS COMPANY, 241 First Ave. N., Minneapolis MN 55401. (612)332-3344. Submissions Editor: Jennifer Martin. Estab. 1959. Imprints are Runestone Press, First Avenue Editions. Publishes hardcover originals. Publishes 75-100 titles/year. Receives 1,000 queries and 300 mss/year. 50% of books from first-time authors; 90% from unagented writers. Pays negotiable royalty or makes outright purchase. Publishes book 2 years after acceptance of ms. Accepts simultaneous submissions. Reports in 4 months on proposals. Catalog for 9 × 12 SAE with 6 first-class stamps. Manuscript guidelines for #10 SAE.
Nonfiction: Children's/juvenile. Subjects include animals, anthropology/archaeology, art/architecture, business and economics, computers and electronics, cooking/foods/nutrition, ethnic, government/politics, health/

medicine, history, language/literature, money/finance, multicultural, music/dance, nature/environment, recreation, science, sports, biography and geography. "We are interested in multicultural work by authors of the focus ethnic groups. Picture books or any work clearly intended for adults (parents and teachers) are not of interest to us. We also do not publish video or audio cassettes. Our main audience consists of children in grades 3-9." Submit proposal package, including introductory letter, outline, 1-2 sample chapters, résumé and SASE.

Fiction: Young adult, middle grade. "We publish very little fiction—usually only one or two titles per year—mainly in the mystery and/or multicultural issues areas. We do not publish adult fiction, picture books, 'Babysitters Club'-type series." Query.

Recent Fiction Title: *Jaws of the Dragon*, by Alan Gibbons.

‡**LEXIKOS**, P.O. Box 296, Lagunitas CA 94938. (415)488-0401. Fax: (415)488-0401. Editor: Mike Witter. Estab. 1981. Imprint is Don't Call It Frisco Press. Publishes hardcover and trade paperback originals and trade paperback reprints. Publishes 8 titles/year. Receives 200 submissions/year. 50% of books from first-time authors; 90% from unagented writers. Average print order for a first book is 5,000. Royalties vary from 8-12½% according to books sold. "Authors asked to accept lower royalty on high discount (50% plus) sales." Offers $1,000 average advance. Publishes book 10 months after acceptance. Accepts simultaneous submissions. Reports in 1 month. *Writer's Market* recommends allowing 2 months for reply. Book catalog and ms guidelines for 6×9 SAE with 2 first-class stamps.

Nonfiction: Coffee table book, illustrated book. Subjects include regional, outdoors, oral histories, Americana, history, nature. Especially looking for 50,000-word "city and regional histories, anecdotal in style for a general audience; books of regional interest about *places*; adventure and wilderness books; annotated reprints of books of Americana; Americana in general." No health, sex, European travel, diet, broad humor, fiction, quickie books ("we stress backlist vitality"), religion, children's or nutrition. Submit outline and sample chapters. Reviews artwork/photos as part of ms package.

Recent Nonfiction Title: *Confessions of a Fundraiser*, by Scottow (memoir).

Tips: "A regional interest or history book has the best chance of selling to Lexikos. Submit a short, cogent proposal; follow up with letter queries. Give the publisher reason to believe you will help him *sell* the book (identify the market, point out the availability of mailing lists, distinguish your book from the competition). Avoid grandiose claims."

THE LIBERAL PRESS, P.O. Box 140361, Las Colinas TX 75014. (214)686-5332. Executive Vice President: Rick Donovon. Publishes trade paperback originals. Publishes 4 titles/year. Receives 250 queries and 100 mss/year. 50% of books from first-time authors; 100% from unagented writers. Pays 4% royalty on retail price. Publishes book 1 year after acceptance of ms. Reports in 1 month on queries, 4 months on mss. Book catalog for 6×9 SAE with 5 first-class stamps. Manuscript guidelines for #10 SASE.

Nonfiction: Textbook. Subjects include gay/lesbian, government/politics (liberal only), history, women's issues/studies. "Work must be gender-free nonsexist, historical/factual with necessary bibliographic material (footnote/bibliography)." Query with outline and 2 sample chapters. All unsolicited mss returned unopened.

Recent Nonfiction Title: *An Ambitious Sort of Grief*, by Marion Cohen (neo-natal loss).

‡**LIBRARIES UNLIMITED**, P.O. Box 6633, Englewood CO 80155. (303)770-1220. Fax: (303)220-8843. E-mail: lu-editorial@lu.com. Managing Editor: Kim Dority. Imprints are Teacher Ideas Press (Susan Zernial, acquisitions editor); Ukranian Academic Press. Publishes hardcover originals. Publishes 75 titles/year. Receives 100 queries and 75 mss/year. 75% of books from first-time authors; 100% from unagented writers. Pays 8-15% royalty on wholesale price. Publishes book 1 year after acceptance of ms. Accepts simultaneous submissions. Reports in 1 month on queries, 2 months on proposals and mss. Book catalog and manuscript guidelines free on request.

Nonfiction: Reference, textbook, teacher resource and activity books. Reference books on these topics for libraries: agriculture/horticulture, anthropology/archaeology, art/architecture, business and economics, education, ethnic, health/medicine, history, language/literature, military/war, music/dance, philosophy, psychology, religion, science, sociology, women's issues/studies. Interested in reference books of all types (annotated bibliographies, sourcebooks and handbooks, dictionaries and encyclopedias) as well as curriculum enrichment/support books for teachers K-12 and school librarians. Submit proposal package, including brief description of book, outline, 1 sample chapter, author credentials, comparison with competing titles, audience and market. Reviews artwork/photos as part of ms package. Send photocopies.

Recent Nonfiction Title: *Video Projects for Elementary and Middle Schools*, by Keith Kyker and Christopher Curchy (how-to).

Tips: Audience is librarians (school, public, academic and special) and teachers (K-12). "We welcome any ideas that combine professional expertise, writing ability, and innovative thinking."

LIFETIME BOOKS, INC., 2131 Hollywood Blvd., Hollywood FL 33020. (954)925-5242. Fax: (954)925-5244. E-mail: lifetime@shadow.net. Website: http://www.lifetimebooks.com. Senior Editor: Brian Feinblum. Imprints are Fell Publishers, Compact Books, Lifetime Periodicals. Publishes hardcover and trade paperback originals and reprints. Publishes 25 titles/year. Receives 3,000 queries and 1,500 mss/year. 60% of books

from first-time authors; 90% from unagented writers. Pays 6-10% royalty on retail price. Offers advance of $500-5,000 on rare occasions. Publishes book 9 months after acceptance. Accepts simultaneous submissions. Reports in 1 month on mss. *Writer's Market* recommends allowing 2 months for reply. Book catalog and ms guidelines for 9×12 SAE with 5 first-class stamps.
Nonfiction: How-to, self-help. Subjects include business and sales, child guidance/parenting, foods/nutrition, education, hobbies, Hollywood bio/exposé, money/finance, true crime. "We are interested in material on business, health and fitness, self-improvement and reference. We will not consider topics that only appeal to a small, select audience." Submit outline and 2 sample chapters. Reviews artwork as part of ms package. Send photocopies.
Recent Nonfiction Title: *100 Ways To Make Sex Sensational—And 100% Safe!*, by Rachel Copelan.
Fiction: "We are currently publishing very little fiction." Submit outline/synopsis and sample chapters. No poetry.
Tips: "We are most interested in well-written, timely nonfiction with strong sales potential. Our audience is very general. Learn markets and be prepared to help with sales and promotion. Show us how your book is unique, different or better than the competition."

LIGUORI PUBLICATIONS, One Liguori Dr., Liguori MO 63057. (314)464-2500. Fax: (314)464-8449. Publisher: Thomas M. Santa, C.SS.R. Imprints are Liguori Books and Triumph Books™ (contact Robert Pagliari, editor-in-chief or Patricia Kossman, executive editor). Publishes hardcover originals and trade paperback originals and reprints. Publishes 20 titles/year; each imprint publishes 10 titles/year. Pays 9% royalty on retail price or makes outright purchase. Advance varies. Publishes book 2 years after acceptance of ms. No simultaneous submissions. Query for disk, CD ROM and Internet publishing. Reports in 2 months on queries and proposals, 3 months on mss. Author guidelines free on request.
Nonfiction: Children's/juvenile, self-help, devotional disk, CD ROM, Internet. Religious subjects. Query with outline, 1 sample chapter and SASE.
Recent Nonfiction Title: *To Hell and Back with Dante*, by Joseph Gallagher.

LIMELIGHT EDITIONS, Imprint of Proscenium Publishers Inc., 118 E. 30th St., New York NY 10016. Fax: (212)532-5526. E-mail: jjlmlt@haven.ios.com. President: Melvyn B. Zerman. Administrative Assistant: Jenna Johnson. Publishes hardcover and trade paperback originals, trade paperback reprints. Publishes 14 titles/year. Receives 150 queries and 40 mss/year. 15% of books from first-time authors; 20% from unagented writers. Pays 7½ (paperback)-10% (hardcover) royalty on retail price. Offers $500-2,000 advance. Publishes book 10 months after acceptance of ms. Reports in 1 month on queries and proposals, 3 months on mss. Book catalog and ms guidelines free on request.
Nonfiction: Biography, humor, illustrated book, music/dance, self-help, theater/film. "All books are on the performing arts *exclusively.*" Query with proposal package, including 2-3 sample chapters, outline. Reviews artwork/photos as part of ms package. Send photocopies.
Recent Nonfiction Title: *Orson Welles*, by Barbara Leaming (biography).

LION BOOKS, Subsidiary of Sayre Ross Co., 210 Melson Rd., Scarsdale NY 10583. (914)725-3372. Editor: Harriet Ross. Publishes hardcover originals and reprints, trade paperback reprints. Publishes 14 titles/year. Receives 60-150 queries and 50 mss/year. 60% of books from first-time authors. Pays 7-15% royalty on wholesale price or makes outright purchase of $500-5,000. Publishes book 5 months after acceptance of ms. Reports in 1 week on queries, 1 month on mss.
Nonfiction: Biography, how-to. Subjects include Americana, ethnic, government/politics, history, recreation, sports. Submit complete mss with SASE. *Writer's Market* recommends sending a query with SASE first.

‡**LION PUBLISHING**, 4050 Lee Vance VW, Colorado Springs CO 80918-7102. (719)536-3271. Assistant Editor: Elisabeth Brown. Estab. 1971. Publishes hardcover and trade paperback originals. Publishes 15 titles/year. Pays royalty. Publishes book 18 months after acceptance. Reports in 3 months.
Nonfiction: Subjects include child guidance/parenting, social concerns, biography and religion. "We are especially interested in manuscripts on relationships and on spirituality. We do not want Bible studies or sermons." Query or submit outline and sample chapters.
Recent Nonfiction Title: *The Lion Storyteller Bible*, by Bob Hartman (storybook for children).
Fiction: Fantasy, literary historical and juvenile. "Give us a story that anyone would be intrigued with—and write it from a Christian perspective." Submit complete ms. *Writer's Market* recommends query with SASE first.
Recent Fiction Title: *At Home in Mitford*, by Jan Karon.
Tips: "All Lion books are written from a Christian perspective. However, they must speak primarily to a general audience. Half of our titles are children's books, yet we receive few manuscripts of publishable quality and almost no nonfiction (say, for 8-12 year olds) of *any* kind. In short, we need high-quality nonfiction of all types that fit our guidelines."

LITTLE, BROWN AND CO., INC., Division of Time Warner Inc., 1271 Avenue of the Americas, New York NY 10020. (212)522-8700. Contact: Editorial Department, Trade Division. Estab. 1837. Imprints are Bulfinch Press and Back Bay Books. Publishes hardcover originals and paperback originals and reprints. Publishes 100 titles/year. "Royalty and advance agreements vary from book to book and are discussed with the author at the time an offer is made. Submissions from literary agents only. No unsolicited mss or proposals."

Nonfiction: "Some how-to books, distinctive cookbooks, biographies, history, popular science and nature, and sports." Query *only*. No unsolicited mss or proposals.

Fiction: Contemporary popular fiction as well as fiction of literary distinction. Query *only*. No unsolicited mss or proposals.

LITTLE, BROWN AND CO., INC., CHILDREN'S BOOK DIVISION, 34 Beacon St., Boston MA 02108. (617)227-0730. Editorial Assistant: Erica Stahler. Only accepting submissions through literary agents and from authors with previous credits in children's book or magazine publishing. List of writing credits *must* accompany all submissions. Pays royalty on retail price. Offers advance to be negotiated individually. Publishes book 2 years after acceptance of ms. Accepts simultaneous submissions, if so noted. Reports in 1 month on queries, 3 months on proposals and mss. Book catalog for 8×10 SAE with 3 first-class stamps. Manuscript guidelines free on request.

Nonfiction: Children's/juvenile. Subjects include animals, art/architecture, cooking/foods/nutrition, ethnic, gay/lesbian, history, hobbies, nature/environment, recreation, science, sports. "We publish books on a wide variety of nonfiction topics which may be of interest to children and are looking for strong writing and presentation, but no predetermined topics." Writers should avoid "looking for the 'issue' they think publishers want to see, choosing instead topics they know best and are most enthusiastic about/inspired by." Submit outline and 3 sample chapters or proposal package, including "most complete outline, possible samples and background info (if project is not complete due to necessary research)." Reviews artwork/photos as part of package. Send photocopies (color if possible).

Recent Nonfiction Title: *The Bone Detectives*, by Donna Jackson (middle reader nonfiction).

Fiction: All juvenile/young adult. Categories include adventure, ethnic, fantasy, feminist, gay/lesbian, historical, humor, mystery, picture books, science fiction and suspense. "We are looking for strong fiction for children of all ages in any area, including multicultural. We always prefer full manuscripts for fiction."

Recent Fiction Title: *Step By Wicked Step*, by Anne Fine (young adult fiction).

Tips: "Our audience is children of all ages, from preschool through young adult. We are looking for quality material that will work in hardcover—send us your best."

‡LIVING THE GOOD NEWS, Division of The Morehouse Group, 600 Grant St., Suite #400, Denver CO 80203. Fax: (303)832-4971. Editorial Administrator: Liz Riggleman. Publishes hardcover and trade paperback originals. Publishes 15 titles/year. Pays royalty. Publishes book 1 year after acceptance of ms. Accepts simultaneous submissions. Reports in 2 months on proposals. Book catalog for 9×12 SAE and 4 first-class stamps. Manuscript guidelines for #10 SASE.

Nonfiction: Children's/juvenile, gift book, how-to, illustrated book, self-help. Subjects include child guidance/parenting, grandparenting, education, religion (prayer, scripture, saints, ritual and celebration), storytelling, contemporary issues. No poetry or drama. "Looking for books on practical, personal, spiritual growth for children, teens, families and faith communities." Query. Submit proposal package, including cover letter, chapter outline, sample chapter, author information and SASE. Reviews artwork/photos as part of ms package. Send photocopies.

Recent Nonfiction Title: *Children and Christian Initiation: A Practical Guide*, by Kathy Coffey (leader's guide).

Fiction: Juvenile, picture books, religious, young adult. Query. Submit synopsis with SASE.

Tips: Audience is those seeking to enrich their spiritual journey, typically from mainline and liturgical church backgrounds. "We look for original, creative ways to build connectedness with self, others, God and the earth."

LIVINGSTON PRESS, Station 22, University of West Alabama, Livingston AL 35470. Director: Joe Taylor. Imprint is Swallow's Tale Press. Publishes hardcover and trade paperback originals. Publishes 4-6 titles/year; imprint publishes 1 title/year. 20% of books from first-time authors; 90% from unagented writers. Pays 7½% royalty on retail price or 12½% of book run. Publishes book 15 months after acceptance of ms. Accepts simultaneous submissions. Reports in 1 month on queries; 1 year on mss.

Nonfiction: Local history, folklore only. All unsolicited mss returned.

Fiction: Experimental, literary, short story collections. Query with SASE.

Recent Fiction Title: *Alabama Bound*, by James Colquitt (story anthology).

Poetry: "We publish very little poetry, mostly books we have asked to see." Query.

Recent Poetry Title: *Flight From Valhalla*, by Michael Bugeja (poetry).

Tips: "Our readers are interested in literature, often quirky literature."

LLEWELLYN PUBLICATIONS, Subsidiary of Llewellyn Worldwide, Ltd., P.O. Box 64383, St. Paul MN 55164-0383. (612)291-1970. Fax: (612)291-1908. Acquisitions Manager: Nancy J. Mostad. Estab. 1901. Publishes trade and mass market paperback originals. Publishes 72 titles/year. Receives 500 submissions/ year. 30% of books from first-time authors; 90% from unagented writers. Pays 10% royalty on moneys received both wholesale and retail. Accepts simultaneous submissions. Reports in 3 months. Book catalog for 9×12 SAE with 4 first-class stamps. Manuscript guidelines for SASE.
  • Llewellyn has had a 20% growth rate in sales each year for the past six years.
Nonfiction: How-to, self-help. Subjects include nature/environment, health and nutrition, metaphysical/ magic, psychology, women's issues/studies. Submit outline and sample chapters. Reviews artwork/photos as part of ms package.
Recent Nonfiction Title: *Yoga for Every Day Athletes*, by Aladar Koglar Ph.D.
Fiction: Metaphysical/occult, which is authentic and educational, yet entertaining.

LOCUST HILL PRESS, P.O. Box 260, West Cornwall CT 06796-0260. (860)672-0060. Fax: (860)672-4968. Publisher: Thomas C. Bechtle. Publishes hardcover originals. Publishes 12 titles/year. Receives 150 queries and 20 mss/year. 100% of books from unagented writers. Pays 12-18% royalty on retail price. Publishes book 6 months after acceptance of ms. Accepts simultaneous submissions. Reports in 1 month on queries. *Writer's Market* recommends allowing 2 months for reply. Book catalog free.
Nonfiction: Reference. Subjects include ethnic, language/literature, women's issues/studies. "Since our audience is exclusively college and university libraries (and the occasional specialist), we are less inclined to accept manuscripts in 'popular' (i.e., public library) fields. While bibliography has been and will continue to be a specialty, our Locust Hill Literary Studies is gaining popularity as a series of essay collections and monographs in a wide variety of literary topics." Query.
Recent Nonfiction Title: *Words Like Freedom: Essays in African-American Culture and History*, by Richard Newman.
Tips: "Remember that this is a small, very specialized academic publisher with no distribution network other than mail contact with most academic libraries worldwide. Please shape your expectations accordingly. If your aim is to reach the world's scholarly community by way of its libraries, we are the correct firm to contact. But *please*: no fiction, poetry, popular religion, or personal memoirs."

LODESTAR BOOKS, Affiliate of Dutton Children's Books, Division of Penguin Books USA, 375 Hudson St., New York NY 10014. (212)366-2627. Fax: (212)366-2011. Editorial Director: Virginia Buckley. Executive Editor: Rosemary Brosnan. Publishes hardcover originals: juveniles, young adults, fiction, nonfiction and picture books. Publishes 20-25 titles/year. Receives 1,000 submissions/year. 10-20% of books from first-time authors; 25-30% from unagented writers. Average print order for a first novel or nonfiction is 4,000-5,000; picture book print runs are higher. Pays royalty on invoice list price. Offers advance. Publishes book 18 months after acceptance. Reports in 3 months. Manuscript guidelines for SASE.
Nonfiction: Query letters only. State availability of photos and/or illustrations. Reviews artwork/photos as part of ms package.
Recent Nonfiction Title: *Bound for the Promised Land*, by Michael Cooper.
Fiction: Publishes for young adults (middle grade) and juveniles (ages 5-17). Subjects include adventure, contemporary, fantasy, historical, humorous, multicultural, mystery, science fiction, suspense, western books, also picture books. Query only.
Recent Fiction Title: *Like Sisters on the Homefront*, by Rita Williams-Garcia.
Tips: "A young adult or middle-grade novel that is literary, fast-paced, well-constructed (as opposed to a commercial novel); well-written nonfiction on contemporary issues, photographic essays, and nonfiction picture books have been our staples. We do only a select number of picture books, which are very carefully chosen."

LONE EAGLE PUBLISHING CO., 2337 Roscomare Rd., Suite 9, Los Angeles CA 90077-1851. (310)471-8066. Toll Free: 1-800-FILMBKS. Fax: (310)471-4969. E-mail: info-le@loneeagle.com. President: Joan V. Singleton. VP/Editorial: Beth Ann Wetzel. Estab. 1982. Publishes perfectbound and trade paperback originals. Publishes 15 titles/year. Receives 100 submissions/year. 80% of books from unagented writers. Pays 10% royalty minimum on net income wholesale and retail. Offers $500-1,000 average advance. Publishes book 1 year after acceptance. Accepts simultaneous submissions. Reports quarterly on queries. Book catalog free on request.
Nonfiction: Technical, how-to, reference. Film and television subjects. "We are looking for technical books in film and television. No unrelated topics or biographies." Submit outline and sample chapters. Reviews artwork/photos as part of ms package.
Tips: "A well-written, well-thought-out book on some technical aspect of the motion picture (or video) industry has the best chance: for example, script supervising, editing, special effects, costume design, production design. Pick a subject that has not been done to death, make sure you know what you're talking about, get someone well-known in that area to endorse the book and prepare to spend a lot of time publicizing the book."

ELY PLANET PUBLICATIONS, 155 Filbert St., Suite 251, Oakland CA 94607-2538. Fax: (510)893-8563. E-mail: info@lonelyplanet.com. Website: http://www.lonelyplanet.com. Publishing Manager: Caroline Liou. Estab. 1973. Publishes trade paperback originals. Publishes 30 titles/year. Receives 500 queries and 100 mss/year. 5% of books from first-time authors; 50% from unagented writers. Makes outright purchase or negotiated fee—⅓ on contract, ⅓ on submission, ⅓ on approval. Publishes book 2 years after acceptance of ms. Accepts simultaneous submissions. Reports in 3 months on queries. Book catalog free.

Nonfiction: Travel guides, phrasebooks atlases and travel literature exclusively. "Writers should request our catalog first to make sure we don't already have a book similar to what they have written or would like to write. Also they should call and see if a similar book is on our production schedule." Submit outline or proposal package. Reviews artwork/photos as part of ms package. Send photocopies. "Don't send unsolicited transparencies!"

Recent Nonfiction Title: *Pacific Northwest USA*, by Bill McRae (travel guide).
Recent Fiction Title: *The Gates of Damascus*, by Lieve Joris.

LONGSTREET PRESS, INC., 2140 Newmarket Parkway, Suite 118, Marietta GA 30067. (404)980-1488. Fax: (404)859-9894. Associate Editor: Suzanne Bell. Estab. 1988. Publishes hardcover and trade paperback originals. Publishes 40 titles/year. Receives 2,500 submissions/year. 25-30% of books from first-time authors. Pays royalty. Publishes book 1 year after acceptance. Accepts simultaneous submissions. Reports in 3 months. Book catalog for 9×12 SAE with 4 first-class stamps. Manuscript guidelines for #10 SASE.

Nonfiction: Biography, coffee table book, cookbook, humor, illustrated book, reference. Subjects include Americana, cooking/foods/nutrition, gardening, history, language/literature, nature/environment, photography, regional, sports, women's issues/studies. "We want serious journalism-oriented nonfiction on subjects appealing to a broad, various audience. No poetry, how-to, religious or inspirational, scientific or highly technical, textbooks of any kind, erotica." Query or submit outline and sample chapters. Reviews artwork as part of ms package.

Fiction: Literary, mainstream/contemporary. Agented fiction only. "We are not interested in formula/genre novels, but we're open to popular fiction that's exceptionally well done."

Tips: "Midlist books have a harder time making it. The nonfiction book, serious or humorous, with a clearly defined audience has the best chance. The audience for our books has a strong sense of intellectual curiosity and a functioning sense of humor. If I were a writer trying to market a book today, I would do thorough, professional work aimed at a clearly defined and reachable audience."

LOOMPANICS UNLIMITED, P.O. Box 1197, Port Townsend WA 98368-0997. Fax: (360)385-7785. E-mail: loompanx@well.com. Website: gophergopher.well.com"business in cyberspace". President: Michael Hoy. Editorial Director: Dennis P. Eichhorn. Estab. 1975. Publishes trade paperback originals. Publishes 15 titles/year. Receives 500 submissions/year. 40% of books from first-time authors; 100% from unagented writers. Average print order for a first book is 2,000. Pays 10-15% royalty on wholesale or retail price or makes outright purchase of $100-1,200. Offers $500 average advance. Publishes book 1 year after acceptance. Accepts simultaneous submissions. Reports in 2 months. Author guidelines free. Book catalog for $5, postpaid.

Nonfiction: How-to, reference, self-help. "In general, works about outrageous topics or obscure-but-useful technology written authoritatively in a matter-of-fact way." Subjects include the underground economy, crime, drugs, privacy, self-sufficiency, anarchism and "beat the system" books. "We are looking for how-to books in the fields of espionage, investigation, the underground economy, police methods, how to beat the system, crime and criminal techniques. We are also looking for similarly-written articles for our catalog and its supplements. No cookbooks, inspirational, travel, management or cutesy-wutesy stuff." Query or submit outline/synopsis and sample chapters. Reviews artwork/photos.

Recent Nonfiction Title: *Politics of Consciousness*, by Steve Kubby (philosophy of drug use).

Tips: "Our audience is young males looking for hard-to-find information on alternatives to 'The System.' Your chances for success are greatly improved if you can show us how your proposal fits in with our catalog."

LOTHROP, LEE & SHEPARD BOOKS, Imprint of William Morrow & Company, 1350 Avenue of the Americas, New York NY 10019. (212)261-6500. Fax: (212)261-6648. Editor-in-Chief: Susan Pearson. Estab. 1859. Other children's imprints are Morrow Junior Books, Greenwillow Books and Tambourine Books. Publishes hardcover original children's books only. Royalty and advance vary according to type of book. Publishes 30 titles/year. Fewer than 2% of books from first-time authors; 25% of books from unagented writers. Average print order for a first book is 6,000-10,000. Publishes book 2 years after acceptance. *No unsolicited mss.* Reports in 3 months.

Fiction and Nonfiction: Publishes picture books, general nonfiction, and novels. Juvenile fiction emphasis is on picture books for the 8-12 age group. Looks for "organization, clarity, creativity, literary style." Query *only.* No unsolicited mss.

Recent Nonfiction Title: *Free To Dream*, by Audrey Osofsky.

Tips: "Trends in book publishing that freelance writers should be aware of include the demand for books for children under age three and the shrinking market for young adult books, especially novels."

LOUISIANA STATE UNIVERSITY PRESS, Baton Rouge LA 70894-5053. (504)388-6294. Fax: (504)388-6461. Director: L.E. Phillabaum. Estab. 1935. Publishes hardcover originals, hardcover and trade paperback reprints. Publishes 60-70 titles/year. Receives 800 submissions/year. 33% of books from first-time authors. 90% from unagented writers. Pays royalty on wholesale price. Publishes book 1 year after acceptance. Reports in 3 weeks on queries. *Writer's Market* recommends allowing 2 months for reply. Book catalog and ms guidelines free.

Nonfiction: Biography and literary poetry collections. Subjects include anthropology/archaeology, art/architecture, ethnic, government/politics, history, language/literature, military/war, music/dance, philosophy, photography, regional, sociology, women's issues/studies. Query or submit outline and sample chapters/poems.

Recent Nonfiction Title: *The New South*, by Numan V. Bartley (history).

Recent Poetry Title: *Fate's Kite*, by Dave Smith.

Tips: "Our audience includes scholars, intelligent laymen, general audience."

THE LOVE AND LOGIC PRESS, INC., Imprint of Cline/Fay Institute, Inc. 2207 Jackson St., Golden CO 80401. Executive Vice President/Publisher: Nancy Henry. Publishes hardcover and trade paperback originals. Publishes 5-12 titles/year. 10% of books from first-time authors; 100% from unagented writers. Pays 7½-12% royalty on wholesale price. Offers $500-5,000 advance. Publishes book 18 months after acceptance of ms. Accepts simultaneous submissions. Reports in 1 month on queries and proposals; 3 months on mss. Book catalog free on request.

Nonfiction: Self-help. Subjects include child guidance/parenting, education, health/medicine, psychology, sociology, current social issue trends. "We will consider any queries/proposals falling into the above categories (with the exception of parenting) but especially psychology/sociology and current social issues and trends." Please do not submit mss or proposal in New Age category, personal recovery stories, i.e., experiences with attempted suicide, drug/alcohol abuse, institutionalization or medical experiences. Query. Reviews artwork/photos as part of ms package. Send photocopies.

Recent Nonfiction Title: *Soul Medicine*, by John E. Postley, MD (self-help/medical, paper).

LOYOLA PRESS, (formerly Loyola University Press), 3441 N. Ashland Ave., Chicago IL 60657-1397. (312)281-1818 ext. 240. Fax: (312)281-0885. Editorial Director: Rev. Joseph F. Downey. Estab. 1912. Imprints are Jesuit Way Books, and Wild Onion (Chicago regional) Books. Publishes hardcover and trade paperback originals and reprints. Publishes 14 titles/year. Receives 150 submissions/year. 60% of books from first-time authors; 95% from unagented writers. Pays 10% royalty on net price, retail and wholesale. No advance. Publishes book 1 year after acceptance. Accepts simultaneous submissions. Reports in 2 months. Book catalog for 6×9 SASE.

Nonfiction: Biography, textbook. Subjects include art (religious), history (church), religion. Jesuit Way Books include Jesuitica (Jesuit history, biography and spirituality). Loyola Press Books feature books dealing with theological or religious aspects of literary works or authors; contemporary Christian concerns such as books on morality, spirituality, family life, pastoral ministry, prayer, worship, etc. Wild Onion Books deal with the city of Chicago from historical, artistic, architectural, or ethnic perspectives, but with religious emphases. Query before submitting ms. Reviews artwork/photos.

Recent Nonfiction Title: *Chicago Sketches: Urban Tales, Stories and Legends from Chicago History*, by June Skinner Sawyers.

Tips: "Our audience is principally the college-educated reader with a religious, theological interest."

‡LRP PUBLICATIONS, INC., P.O. Box 980, Horsham PA 19044-0980. Director of Publishing: Gail M. Richman. Publishes hardcover and trade paperback originals. Publishes 10 titles/year. Receives 15 queries and 12 mss/year. 95% of books from first-time authors; 100% from unagented writers. Royalties vary. Offers $0-1,000 advance. Publishes book 9 months after acceptance of ms. Reports in 1 month on queries, 2 months on proposals, 3 months on mss. Book catalog and manuscript guidelines free on request.

Nonfiction: Reference. Subjects include business and economics, law. Submit proposal package, including outline, cv, market analysis, competition.

Recent Nonfiction Title: *Workplace Drug Testing*, by Kevin L. McCloskey.

Tips: Audience is professionals such as human resource managers, attorneys, risk managers, school administrators, consulting experts in litigation.

LUCENT BOOKS, P.O. Box 289011, San Diego CA 92198-9011. (619)485-7424. Fax: (619)485-9549. Managing Editor: Bonnie Szumski. Contact: Lori Shein, editor. Estab. 1988. Publishes hardcover educational supplementary materials and (nontrade) juvenile nonfiction. Publishes 75 books/year. All are works for hire, done by assignment only. 5% of books from first-time authors; 95% from unagented writers. Makes outright purchase of $2,500-3,000. No unsolicited mss. Query for book catalog and ms guidelines; send 9×12 SAE with 3 first-class stamps.

Nonfiction: Juvenile. "We produce tightly formatted books for middle grade readers. Each series has specific requirements. Potential writers should familiarize themselves with our material." Series deal with history, current events, social issues.

Recent Nonfiction Title: *The Battle of Midway*, by Earle Rice Jr. (military history).
Tips: "We expect writers to do thorough research using books, magazines and newspapers. Biased writing—whether liberal or conservative—have no place in our books. We prefer to work with writers who have experience writing nonfiction for middle grade students."

LYONS & BURFORD, PUBLISHERS, INC., 31 W. 21st St., New York NY 10010. (212)620-9580. Fax: (212)929-1836. Publisher: Peter Burford. Estab. 1984. Publishes hardcover and trade paperback originals and reprints. Publishes 40-50 titles/year. 50% of books from first-time authors; 75% from unagented writers. Pays varied royalty on retail price. Publishes book 1 year after acceptance. Accepts simultaneous submissions. Reports in 2 weeks on queries. *Writer's Market* recommends allowing 2 months for reply. Book catalog free.
Nonfiction: Subjects include agriculture/horticulture, Americana, animals, art/architecture, cooking/foods/nutrition, gardening, hobbies, nature/environment, science, sports, travel. Query.
Recent Nonfiction Title: *The Wold Almanac*, by Robert Busch.
Tips: "We want practical, well-written books on any aspect of the outdoors."

McDONALD & WOODWARD PUBLISHING CO., 6414 Riverland Dr., Fort Pierce FL 34982-7644. (407)468-6361. Fax: (407)468-6571. Managing Partner: Jerry N. McDonald. Estab. 1986. Publishes hardcover and trade paperback originals. Publishes 8 titles/year. Receives 100 queries and 20 mss/year. 50% of books from first-time authors; 100% from unagented writers. Pays 10% royalty on net receipts. Publishes book 1 year after acceptance of ms. Accepts simultaneous submissions. Reports in 2 months. Book catalog free.
Nonfiction: Biography, coffee table book, how-to, illustrated book, self-help. Subjects include Americana, animals, anthropology, ethnic, history, nature/environment, science, travel. Query or submit outline and sample chapters. Reviews artwork/photos as part of ms package. Send photocopies.
Recent Nonfiction Title: *Old Southern Apples*, by Lee Calhoun (agricultural history).
Tips: "We are especially interested in additional titles in our 'Guides to the American Landscape' series. Should consult titles in print for guidance. We want well organized, clearly written, substantive material."

MARGARET K. McELDERRY BOOKS, Imprint of Simon & Schusters Children's Publishing Division, 1230 Sixth Ave., New York NY 10020. Fax: (212)698-2796. Vice President/Publisher: Margaret K. McElderry. Editor: Emma D. Dryden. Estab. 1971. Publishes hardcover originals. Publishes 25 titles/year. Average print order is 6,000-7,500 for a first teen book; 10,000-15,000 for a first picture book. Pays royalty on retail price. Publishes book 18 months after acceptance. Catalog for 9 × 12 SAE with 4 first-class stamps. Manuscript guidelines for #10 SASE.
Nonfiction and Fiction: Quality material for preschoolers to 16-year-olds, but publishes only a few YAs. Looks for originality of ideas, clarity and felicity of expression, well-organized plot and strong characterization (fiction) or clear exposition (nonfiction); quality. "We do not accept any unsolicited manuscripts. We will accept one-page query letters for picture books or novels."
Recent Titles: *Scaredy Cat*, by Joan Rankin (picture book); *Moon Window*, by Jane Louise Curry (young adult fiction).
Tips: "There is not a particular 'type' of book that we are interested in above others. Rather, we look for superior quality in both writing and illustration. Freelance writers should be aware of the swing away from teen-age novels to books for younger readers and of the growing need for beginning chapter books for children just learning to read on their own."

McFARLAND & COMPANY, INC., PUBLISHERS, P.O. Box 611, Jefferson NC 28640. (910)246-4460. Fax: (910)246-5018. President and Editor-in-Chief: Robert Franklin. Vice President: Rhonda Herman. Editors: Lisa Camp, Steve Wilson, Barry Greene. Estab. 1979. Publishes mostly hardcover and a few "quality" paperback originals; a non-"trade" publisher. Publishes 125 titles/year. Receives 1,000 submissions/year. 70% of books from first-time authors; 95% from unagented writers. Average first printing for a book is 750. Pays 10-12½% royalty on net receipts. No advance. Publishes book 10 months after acceptance. Reports in 2 weeks. *Writer's Market* recommends allowing 2 months for reply.
Nonfiction: Reference books and scholarly, technical and professional monographs. Subjects include African American studies (very strong), art, business, chess, drama/theatre, cinema/radio/TV (very strong), health, history, librarianship (very strong), music, pop culture, sociology, sports/recreation (very strong), women's studies (very strong), world affairs (very strong). "We will consider *any* scholarly book—with authorial maturity and competent grasp of subject." Reference books are particularly wanted—fresh material (i.e., not in head-to-head competition with an established title). "We don't like manuscripts of fewer than 225 double-spaced pages. Our market consists mainly of libraries." No New Age material, exposés, poetry, children's books, devotional/inspirational works or personal essays. Query with outline and sample chapters. Reviews artwork/photos as part of ms package.
Recent Nonfiction Title: *African Placenames: Origins and Meanings of the Names for Over 2000 Natural Features, Towns, Cities, Provinces and Countries*, by Adrian Room.

Tips: "We do *not* accept novels or fiction of any kind or personal Bible studies. What we want is well-organized *knowledge* of an area in which there is not good information coverage at present, plus reliability so we don't feel we have to check absolutely everything."

McGRAW-HILL COMPANIES, 1221 Avenue of the Americas, New York NY 10020. Divisions include Business McGraw Hill; Computing McGraw Hill; McGraw Hill Inc./TAB Books; McGraw-Hill Ryerson (Canada), Osborne/McGraw-Hill, Professional Book Group. General interest publisher of both fiction and nonfiction. Query before submitting.

THE McGRAW-HILL COMPANIES, Professional Book Group Division, 11 W. 19th St., New York NY 10011. Imprints are Engineering & Science (contact Sybil Parker); Business (contact Philip Ruppel); Computing (contact Mike Hayes); International Marine and Ragged Mountain Press (contact John Eaton). Publishes hardcover and trade paperback originals and reprints. Publishes 800 titles/year. 30% of books from first-time authors; 70% from unagented writers. Pays royalty. Offers $3,000 and up advance. Publishes book 10 months after acceptance of ms. Accepts simultaneous submissions. Reports in 1 month on queries. Book catalog and ms guidelines free on request.
Nonfiction: How-to, multimedia (disk and CD ROM), reference, self-help, technical, professional. Subjects include art/architecture, business and economics, computers and electronics, money/finance, science, software, sports, technical engineering, boating. Query with proposal package, including outline, sample chapters, author bio, marketing information. Reviews artwork/photos as part of ms package.
Recent Nonfiction Title: *Heart at Work*, by Jack Canfield.

McGUINN & McGUIRE PUBLISHING INC., P.O. Box 20603, Bradenton FL 34203-0603. Managing Editor: Christopher Carroll. Estab. 1991. Publishes hardcover and trade paperback originals. Publishes 6 titles/year. Receives 500 queries and 75 mss/year. 50% of books from first-time authors; 100% from unagented writers. Pays 10-15% royalty on net receipts. Offers $250 advance. Publishes book 1 year after acceptance of ms. Accepts simultaneous submissions. Reports in 1 month on queries and proposals, 2 months on mss. Book catalog and ms guidelines for #10 SASE. Will not return submissions without SASE.
Nonfiction: Biography. Subjects include business, history. "We are not interested in religious materials, memoirs, books relating a personal philosophy, diet books, or investment books. Author should be able to demonstrate how his/her book fills a void in the market." Query or submit outline and 3 sample chapters. Reviews artwork/photos as part of the ms package. Send photocopies.
Recent Nonfiction Title: *Buster: A Legend in Laughter*, by Larry Edwards (biography).
Tips: "Always include a word count with queries and proposals. We will only consider books which are at least 50,000 words. Our audience consists of college-educated adults who look for books written by experts in their field. We are particularly interested in reviewing business books which help managers improve their business skills."

MADISON BOOKS, 4720 Boston Way, Lanham MD 20706. (301)459-3366. Fax: (301)459-2118. Publisher: James E. Lyons. Managing Editor: Julie Kirsch. Estab. 1984. Publishes hardcover originals, trade paperback originals and reprints. Publishes 40 titles/year. Receives 1,200 submissions/year. 15% of books from first-time authors; 65% from unagented writers. Pays 10-15% royalty on net price. Publishes ms 1 year after acceptance. *Writer's Market* recommends allowing 2 months for reply. Book catalog and ms guidelines for 9 × 12 SAE with 4 first-class stamps.
Nonfiction: History, biography, contemporary affairs, trade reference. Query or submit outline and sample chapter. No complete mss.

‡MAGE PUBLISHERS INC., 1032 29th St. NW, Washington DC 20007. E-mail: mage1@access.digex.c om. Website: http://www.mage-com. Assistant to Publisher: Amin Sepehri. Publishes hardcover originals and reprints, trade paperback originals. Publishes 4 titles/year. Receives 40 queries and 20 mss/year. 10% of books from first-time authors; 95% from unagented writers. Pays variable royalty. Offers $250-1,500 advance. Publishes book 10 months after acceptance of ms. Accepts simultaneous submissions. Reports in 1 month on queries and proposals, 3 months on mss. Book catalog free on request.
Nonfiction: Biography, children's/juvenile, coffee table book, cookbook, gift book, illustrated book. Subjects include anthropology/archaeology, art/architecture, cooking/foods/nutrition, ethnic, history, language/literature, music/dance, sociology, translation. "We only publish books which relate to Persian/Iranian culture." Query. Reviews artwork/photos as part of ms package. Send photocopies.
Recent Nonfiction Title: *Persian Cooking for a Healthy Kitchen*, by N. Batmanglij (cookbook).
Fiction: Ethnic, feminist, historical, literary, mainstream/contemporary, short story collections. Must relate to Persian/Iranian culture. Query.
Recent Fiction Title: *King of the Benighted*, by Manuchehr Irani (novella).
Poetry: Must relate to Persian/Iranian culture. Query.
Recent Poetry Title: *Hafez: Dance of Life*, by Hafez.
Tips: Audience is the Iranian-American community in America interested in the Middle East.

MAISONNEUVE PRESS, P.O. Box 2980, Washington DC 20013-2980. (301)277-7505. Fax: (301)277-2467. E-mail: rmerrill@mica.edu. Editor: Robert Merrill. Publishes hardcover and trade paperback originals. Publishes 4 titles/year. 5% of books from first-time authors; 100% from unagented writers. Pays 2-9% royalty on wholesale price or $2,000 maximum outright purchase. Publishes book 1 year after acceptance. Accepts simultaneous submissions. Reports in 1 month on queries; 2 months on proposals; 5 months on mss. Book catalog free on request. Send letter for guidelines; individual response.

Nonfiction: Biography, philosophy, literary criticism, social theory. Subjects include education, ethnic, gay/lesbian, government/politics, history, language/literature, military/war, philosophy, psychology, sociology, translation, women's issues/studies, politics, economics, essay collections. "We make decisions on completed mss only. Will correspond on work in progress. Some books submitted are too narrowly focused; not marketable enough." Query; then send completed ms. Reviews artwork/photos as part of ms package. Send photocopies.

Recent Nonfiction Title: *Positively Postmodern: The Multi-Media Muse in America*, ed. by Nicholas Zurburgg.

Tips: Audience is serious adult readers: academics, political activists. "Need solid, first-hand information in the book."

‡**M&T BOOKS**, Division of MIS: Press, subsidiary of Henry Holt, 115 W. 18th St., New York NY 10011. (212)886-9355. Fax: (212)807-6654. Website: http://www.mispress.com. Associate Publisher: Paul Farrell. Publishes trade paperback computer books for the higher level user. Publishes 40 titles/year. Receives 200 queries/year. 20% of books from first-time authors. Pays 5-15% royalty on net receipts. Offers $8,000 average advance. Publishes book 4 months after contract.

Nonfiction: Networking, programming, databases, operating systems.

Recent Nonfiction Title: *Windows 95: A Developer's Guide*, by Jeffrey Richter and Jonathan Locke.

‡**MARCH STREET PRESS**, 3413 Wilshire, Greensboro NC 27408. Website: http://users.aol.com/marchst/msp.html. Editor/Publisher: Robert Bixby. Publishes literary chapbooks. Publishes 6-10 titles/year. Receives 12 queries and 30 mss/year. 50% of books from first-time authors; 100% from unagented writers. Pays 15% on royalty. Offers advance of 10 copies. Publishes book 6 months after acceptance of ms. Accepts simultaneous submissions. Reports in 3 months on mss. Book catalog and ms guidelines for #10 SASE.

Poetry: "My plans are based on the submissions I receive, not vice versa." Submit complete ms.

Recent Poetry Title: *The Mad Painter Poems*, by Judith Minty.

Tips: "Audience is extremely sophisticated, widely read graduates of MA, MFA and PhD programs in English and fine arts. Also lovers of significant, vibrant and enriching verse regardless of field of study or endeavor. Most beginning poets, I have found, think it beneath them to read other poets. This is the most glaring flaw in their work. My advice is to read ceaselessly. Otherwise, you may be published, but you will never be accomplished."

MARKETSCOPE BOOKS, 119 Richard Court, Aptos CA 95003. (408)688-7535. Editor-in-Chief: Ken Albert. Estab. 1985. Publishes hardcover and trade paperback originals. Publishes 10 titles/year. 50% of books from first-time authors; 50% from unagented writers. Pays 10-15% royalty on wholesale price. Publishes book 1 year after acceptance. Accepts simultaneous submissions. Reports in 1 week on queries. *Writer's Market* recommends allowing 2 months for reply.

Nonfiction: Biography, how-to, humor, self-help. Subjects include sexuality, health/medicine, hobbies, money/finance, nature/environment, recreation, regional. Query. Reviews artwork/photos as part of the ms package.

MARKOWSKI INTERNATIONAL PUBLISHERS, One Oakglade Circle, Hummelstown PA 17036-9525. (717)566-0468. Fax: (717)566-6423. Imprints are Success Publishers, Aviation Publishers and Markowski International Publishers. Editor-in-Chief: Marjorie L. Markowski. Estab. 1981. Publishes hardcover and trade paperback originals. Publishes 12 titles/year. Receives 1,000 submissions/year. 90% of books from first-time authors; 100% from unagented writers. Average print order for a first book is 5,000-50,000. Royalty agreements vary or makes outright purchase. Publishes book 1 year after acceptance. Accepts simultaneous submissions. Reports in 2 months. Book catalog and ms guidelines for #10 SAE with 2 first-class stamps.

Nonfiction: Primary focus on popular health and fitness, marriage and human relations, career, personal development, self-help, personal growth, sales and marketing, leadership training, network marketing, motivation and success and Christian topics. Also publishes books on various aviation and model aviation topics. We are interested in how-to, motivational and instructional books of short to medium length that will serve recognized and emerging needs of society." Query or submit outline and entire ms. Reviews artwork/photos as part of ms package.

Recent Nonfiction Title: *No Excuse!, A New Philosophy for Overcoming Obstacles and Achieving Excellence*, by Jay Rifenbary.

Tips: "We're intensifying our search for bestseller manuscripts. We're looking for authors who are dedicated to their message and want to make a difference in the world. We especially like to work with authors who speak and consult."

MARLOR PRESS, INC., 4304 Brigadoon Dr., St. Paul MN 55126. (612)484-4600. Publisher: Marlin Bree. Estab. 1981. Publishes trade paperback originals. Publishes 6 titles/year. Receives 100 queries and 25 mss/ year. Pays 10% royalty on wholesale price. Publishes book 8 months after final acceptance. Reports in 2 months on queries and proposals, 3 months on mss. Book catalog for 6×9 SAE with 2 first-class stamps. Manuscript guidelines for #10 SASE.
Nonfiction: Travel, boating, children's, pet and gift books. Query first; submit outline with sample chapters only when requested. Do not send full ms. Reviews artwork/photos as part of ms package.
Recent Nonfiction Title: *The Other Side of Sydney*, by Zena L. Polin and Stephen G. Gatward.
Tips: "We only look for nonfiction titles and want more sailing and travel books. One new category, with publication of *Tale of a Cat* is nonfiction pet books."

MASTERS PRESS, 2647 Waterfront Pkwy., Suite 300, Indianapolis IN 46214-2041. (317)298-5706. Fax: (317)298-5604. Managing Editor: Holly Kondras. Estab. 1986. Imprint is Spalding Sports Library. Publishes hardcover and trade paperback originals. Publishes 30-40 titles/year; imprint publishes 20 titles/year. Receives 60 queries and 50 mss/year. 25% of books from first-time authors; 75% from unagented writers. Pays 10-15% royalty. Offers $1,000-5,000 advance. Publishes book 1 year after acceptance. Accepts simultaneous submissions. Reports in 2 months on proposals. Book catalog free on request.
Nonfiction: Biography, how-to, reference, self-help. Subjects include recreation, sports, fitness. Submit outline, 2 sample chapters, author bio and marketing ideas.
Recent Nonfiction Title: *Ted Williams' Hit List*, by Ted Williams and Jim Prime.
Tips: "Our audience is sports enthusiasts and participants, people interested in fitness."

MAVERICK PUBLICATIONS, P.O. Box 5007, Bend OR 97708. (541)382-6978. Fax: (541)382-4831. E-mail: gmasher@mavbooks.com. Website: http://www.mavbooks.com. Publisher: Gary Asher. Estab. 1968. Publishes trade paperback originals and reprints. Publishes 10 titles/year. Receives 100 submissions/year. Pays 15% royalty on wholesale price. Publishes book 1 year after acceptance. Accepts simultaneous submissions. Reports 2 months.
Nonfiction: Pacific Northwest only: aviation, cooking, history, hobby, how-to, marine, Native American, nature and environment, recreation, reference, sports, travel. Submit proposal.
Recent Nonfiction Title: *Recipes from the Vineyards of Oregon*.

‡MAXIMUM PRESS, 605 Silverthorn Rd., Gulf Breeze FL 32561. (904)934-0819. Publisher: Jim Hoskins. Publishes trade paperback originals. Publishes 10-12 titles/year. Receives 10 queries and 10 mss/year. 40% of books from first-time authors; 100% from unagented writers. Pays 7½-15% royalty on wholesale price. Offers $1,000-2,500 advance. Publishes book 3 months after acceptance of ms. Reports in 1 month. *Writer's Market* recommends allowing 2 months for reply. Book catalog free on request.
Nonfiction: How-to, technical. Subjects include business, computers and Internet. Query with proposal package, including credentials.
Recent Nonfiction Title: *Marketing on the Internet*, by Michael Mathiesen (computer/Internet).

MAYFIELD PUBLISHING COMPANY, 1280 Villa St., Mountain View CA 94041. President: Richard Greenberg. Publishes 40-50 titles/year. Accepts simultaneous submissions. Reports in 2 months. Manuscript guidelines free on request.
Nonfiction: Textbook (college only). Subjects include anthropology/archaeology, art, child guidance/parenting, communications/theater, ethnic, health/physical education, language/literature, music/dance, philosophy, psychology, religion, sociology, women's studies. Submit proposal package including outline, table of contents, sample chapter, description of proposed market.

MEADOWBROOK PRESS, 18318 Minnetonka Blvd., Deephaven MN 55391. (612)473-5400. Fax: (612)475-0736. Contact: Submissions Editor. Estab. 1975. Publishes trade paperback originals and reprints. Publishes 12 titles/year. Receives 1,500 queries/year. 15% of books from first-time authors. Publishes book 1 year after acceptance. Accepts simultaneous submissions. Reports in 5 months on queries. Book catalog and ms guidelines for #10 SASE.

ALWAYS ENCLOSE a self-addressed, stamped envelope (SASE) with all your queries and correspondence.

● Meadowbrook has a need for parenting titles, humorous children's poetry and juvenile fiction (send for guidelines).

Nonfiction: How-to, humor, reference. Subjects include baby and childcare, senior citizens, children's activities, relationships. No academic or autobiography. Query with outline and sample chapters. "We prefer a query first; then we will request an outline and/or sample material."

Recent Nonfiction Title: *Age Happens: The Best Quotes About Growing Older*, selected by Bruce Lansky.

Tips: "We like how-to books in a simple, accessible format and any new advice on parenting. We look for a fresh approach to overcoming traditional problems (e.g. potty training)."

MEDIA BRIDGE, 2280 Grass Valley Hwy., #181, Auburn CA 95603. (916)889-4438. Fax: (916)888-0690. E-mail: mbt@quickcnet.com. Website: http://www.quiknet.com/mbt/media and http://www.gamekids.com. Publisher: Rennie Mau. Imprints are Videobridge, Audiobridge, Family Media. Publishes trade paperback and mass market paperback originals. Publishes 6-10 titles/year. Each imprint publishes 4 titles/year. 50% of books from first-time authors; 75% from unagented writers. Pays 7-12% royalty on wholesale price. Publishes book 6 months after acceptance. Reports in 1 month on queries, 2 months on proposals, 3 months on mss.

Nonfiction: Children's/juvenile, cookbook, how-to, multimedia (CD ROM), self-help, textbook. Subjects include education, ethnic, music/dance, religion, multicultural. Submit outline, 2 sample chapters and SASE. Reviews artwork/photos as part of ms package. Send photocopies.

Recent Nonfiction Title: *Talking Story*, by Grant Lee (religious).

Fiction: Ethnic, juvenile, picture books, plays, religious, young adult. Submit synopsis, 2 sample chapters and SASE.

Recent Fiction Title: *Telling*, by Marilyn Reynolds (children).

Tips: "We need games (non-computer) and activities for our internet web site, Game Kids Club."

MERCURY HOUSE, INC., 785 Market St., Suite 1500, San Francisco CA 94103. (415)974-0729. Fax: (415)974-0832. Managing Editor: K. Janene-Nelson. Publishes hardcover originals and trade paperbacks originals and reprints. Averages 10 titles/year. Pays 10-20% royalty on retail price. Offers $3,000-6,000 advance. Publishes book 1 year after acceptance of ms. Reports in 3 months. Catalog for 55¢ postage. "We no longer accept unsolicited manuscripts."

Nonfiction: Biography, essays, memoirs. Subjects include anthropology, ethnic gay/lesbian, politics/current affairs, language/literature, literary current affairs, nature/environment, philosophy, translation, literary travel, women's issues/studies, human rights/indigenous peoples. "Within the subjects we publish, we are above all a literary publisher looking for a high quality of writing and innovative approach to book structure, research approach, etc." Query.

Recent Nonfiction Title: *Shell Game*, by Martien.

Fiction: Ethnic, experimental, feminist, gay/lesbian, historical, literary, short story collections, literature in translation. "Very limited spots. We prefer sample chapters to determine writing style. It's very important to submit only if the subject is appropriate (as listed), though we do enjoy mutations/blending of genres (high quality, thoughtful work!). We do not publish mainstream, thrillers, sexy books. We look for a well-written cover letter.

Recent Fiction Title: *Ledoyt*, by Emshwiller.

Tips: "Our reader is a person who is discriminating about his/her reading material, someone who appreciates the extra care we devote to design, paper, cover, and exterior excellence to go along with the high quality of the writing itself. Be patient with us concerning responses: it's easier to reject the manuscript of a nagging author than it is to decide upon it. The manner in which an author deals with us (via letter or phone) gives us a sense of how it would be to work with this person for a whole project; good books with troublesome authors are to be avoided."

MERIWETHER PUBLISHING LTD., 885 Elkton Dr., Colorado Springs CO 80907-3557. (719)594-4422. Editors: Arthur or Theodore Zapel. Estab. 1969. Publishes trade paperback originals and reprints. Publishes 10-12 books/year; 35-50 plays/year. Receives 1,200 submissions/year. 50% of books from first-time authors; 90% from unagented writers. Pays 10% royalty on retail price or makes outright purchase. Publishes book 6 months after acceptance. Accepts simultaneous submissions. Reports in 2 months. Book catalog and ms guidelines for $2.

● Meriwether is looking for more books of short scenes and textbooks on directing, staging, make-up, lighting etc.

Nonfiction: How-to, reference, educational, humor, inspirational. Also textbooks. Subjects include art/theatre/drama, music/dance, recreation, religion. "We're looking for unusual textbooks or trade books related to the communication or performing arts and "how-to" books on staging, costuming, lighting, etc. We are not interested in religious titles with fundamentalist themes or approaches—we prefer mainstream religion titles." Query or submit outline/synopsis and sample chapters.

Fiction: Plays. "Plays only—humorous, mainstream, mystery, religious, suspense."

Tips: "Our educational books are sold to teachers and students at college and high school levels. Our religious books are sold to youth activity directors, pastors and choir directors. Our trade books are directed at the public with a sense of humor. Another group of buyers is the professional theatre, radio and TV category. We will focus more on books of plays and theater texts."

‡**THE MESSAGE COMPANY**, 4 Camino Azul, Sante Fe NM 87505. (505)474-0998. President: James Berry. Publishes trade paperback originals and reprints. Publishes 6-8 titles/year. Receives 20 queries and 12 mss/year. 80% of books from first-time authors; 100% from unagented writers. Pays 6-10% royalty on retail price or makes outright purchase of $500-2,000. No advance. Publishes book 3 months after acceptance of ms. Accepts simultaneous submissions. Reports in 1 month on mss. *Writer's Market* recommends allowing 2 months for reply. Book catalog for 6×9 SAE with 2 first-class stamps.
Nonfiction: How-to. Subjects include business and economics (spirituality in business-related only), government/politics (freedom/privacy issues only), science (new energy/new science only). Submit proposal package, including outline and sample chapters. Reviews artwork/photos as part of ms package. Send photocopies.
Recent Nonfiction Title: *Spiritual Vampires*, by Marty Raphael (trade paperback).
Tips: Alternative topics packaged for mainstream market.

METAL POWDER INDUSTRIES FEDERATION, 105 College Rd. E., Princeton NJ 08540. (609)452-7700. Fax: (609)987-8523. Publications Manager: Cindy Jablonowski. Estab. 1946. Publishes hardcover originals. Publishes 10 titles/year. Pays 3-12½% royalty on wholesale or retail price. Offers $3,000-5,000 advance. Reports in 1 month. *Writer's Market* recommends allowing 2 months for reply.
Nonfiction: Work must relate to powder metallurgy or particulate materials.
Recent Nonfiction Title: *Advances in Powder Metallurgy and Particulate Materials* (conference proceeding).
Tips: "We publish monographs, textbooks, handbooks, design guides, conference proceedings, standards, and general titles in this field."

METAMORPHOUS PRESS, P.O. Box 10616, Portland OR 97210-0616. (503)228-4972. Fax: (503)223-9117. Publisher: David Balding. Editorial Director: Lori Stephens. Acquisitions Editor: Nancy Wyatt-Kelsey. Estab. 1982. Publishes trade paperback originals and reprints. Publishes 4-5 titles/year. Receives 2,500 submissions/year. 90% of books from first-time authors; 90% from unagented writers. Average print order for a first book is 2,000-5,000. Pays minimum 10% profit split on wholesale prices. No advance. Publishes book 1 year after acceptance. Accepts simultaneous submissions. Reports in 3 months. Book catalog and ms guidelines for 9×12 SAE with 3 first-class stamps.
Nonfiction: How-to, reference, self-help, technical, textbook—all related to behavioral science and personal growth. Subjects include business and sales, health, psychology, sociology, education, science and new ideas in behavioral science. "We are interested in any well-proven new idea or philosophy in the behavioral science areas. Our primary editorial screen is 'will this book further define, explain or support the concept that we are responsible for our reality or assist people in gaining control of their lives.' " Submit idea, outline, and table of contents only. Reviews artwork/photos as part of ms package.
Recent Nonfiction Title: *Training Trances*, by Silverthorn/Overdurf (hypnotherapy).

MICHIGAN STATE UNIVERSITY PRESS, 1405 S. Harrison Rd., Suite 25, East Lansing MI 48823-5202. (517)355-9543. Fax: (800)678-2120; local/international (517)432-2611. E-mail: msp08@msu.edu Website: http://web.msu.edu/press. Director: Fred Bohm. Editor-in-Chief: Julie Loehr. Contact: Martha Bates, acquisitions editor. Estab. 1947. Publishes hardcover and softcover originals. Publishes 30 titles/year. Receives 400 submissions/year. 75% of books from first-time writers; 100% from unagented writers. Pays 10% royalty on net sales. Publishes ms 18 months after acceptance. Book catalog and ms guidelines for 9×12 SASE.
Nonfiction: Reference, technical, scholarly. Subjects include Afro-American Studies, American history, American Studies, business and economics, Canadian Studies, Civil War history, communication and speech, Great Lakes Regional Studies, literature, Native American Studies, philosophy, politics, Women's Studies. Looking for "scholarship that addresses the social and political concerns of the late 20th century." Query with outline and sample chapters. Reviews artwork/photos.
Recent Nonfiction Title: *No Time for Fear: Voices of American Military Nurses in World War II*, by Diane Burke Fessler.

MID-LIST PRESS, Imprint of Jackson, Hart & Leslie, 4324 12th Ave S., Minneapolis MN 55407-3218. Contact: Lane Stiles. Estab. 1989. Publishes hardcover originals and reprints, trade paperback originals. Publishes minimum 4 titles/year. Pays 40-50% royalty of profits. Offers $500-1,000 advance. Mid-List Press is an independent press. In addition to publishing the annual winners of the Mid-List Press First Series Awards, Mid-List Press publishes general interest fiction and nonfiction by first-time and established writers. Send SASE for First Series guidelines and/or general submission guidelines.
Recent Fiction Title: *The Hemingway Sabbatical*, by Allan Conan (novel).
Tips: "We are now considering books of poetry and short fiction by writers who have previously published books in these categories."

MILKWEED EDITIONS, 430 First Ave. N, Suite 400, Minneapolis MN 55401-1743. (612)332-3192. Publisher: Emilie Buchwald. Contact: Elisabeth Fitz. Estab. 1980. Publishes hardcover originals and paperback originals and reprints. Publishes 20 titles/year. Receives 1,560 submissions/year. 30% of books from first-time authors; 70% from unagented writers. Pays 7½% royalty on list price. Advance varies. Publishes work 1 year after acceptance. Accepts simultaneous submissions. Reports in 6 months. Book catalog for $1. Manuscript guidelines for SASE. Returns unsolicited mss if SASE provided.
Nonfiction: Literary. Subjects include government/politics, history, language/literature, nature/environment, women's issues/studies, education. Query.
Recent Nonfiction Title: *Grass Roots: The Universe of Home*, by Paul Gruchow.
Fiction: Literary. Novels for readers aged 8-14. High literary quality. Query.
Recent Fiction Title: *Live at Five*, by David Haynes.
Tips: "We are looking for excellent writing in fiction, nonfiction, poetry and children's novels, with the intent of making a humane impact on society. Send for guidelines. Acquaint yourself with our books in terms of style and quality before submitting. Many factors influence our selection process, so don't get discouraged. Nonfiction is taking a predominantly environmental as well as educational focus. We no longer publish children's biographies."

MINNESOTA HISTORICAL SOCIETY PRESS, Minnesota Historical Society, 345 Kellogg Blvd. W., St. Paul MN 55102-1906. (612)297-4457. Managing Editor: Ann Regan. Imprint is Borealis Books (reprints only). Publishes hardcover and trade paperback originals, trade paperback reprints. Publishes 10 titles/year (5 for each imprint). Receives 100 queries and 25 mss/year. 8% of books from first-time authors; 100% from unagented writers. Pays 5% royalty on net income. Publishes book 14 months after acceptance. Reports in 1 month on queries. *Writer's Market* recommends allowing 2 months for reply. Book catalog free on request.
● Minnesota Historical Society Press is getting many inappropriate submissions from their listing. A regional connection is required.
Nonfiction: Regional works only: biography, coffee table book, cookbook, illustrated book, reference. Subjects include anthropology/archaeology, art/architecture, history, memoir, photography, regional, women's issues/studies, Native American studies. Query with proposal package including letter, outline, vita, sample chapter. Reviews artwork/photos as part of ms package. Send photocopies.
Recent Nonfiction Title: *John Dillinger Slept Here: A Crooks' Tour of Crime and Corruption in St. Paul 1920-1936*, by Paul Maccabee.

MIS PRESS, Subsidiary of Henry Holt & Co., 115 W. 18th St., New York NY 10011. (212)886-9210. Fax: (212)807-6654. Website: http://www.mispress.com. Associate Publisher: Paul Farrell. Publishes trade paperback originals. Publishes 60 titles/year. Receives 250 queries/year. 20% of books from first-time authors; 50% from unagented writers. Pays 5-15% royalty on net price received (receipts), or makes outright purchase of $5,000-20,000. Offers $5,000-10,000 advance. Publishes book 4 months after acceptance. Accepts simultaneous submissions. Book catalog and ms guidelines free on request.
Nonfiction: Technical, computer, electronic, internet, world wide web. "Submissions should be about or related to computer software or hardware." Submit outline and proposal package.
Recent Nonfiction Title: *The Doom Hacker's Guide*, by Hank Leukart.

‡MITCHELL LANE PUBLISHERS, P.O. Box 200, Childs MD 21916. Fax: (410)392-4781. Publisher: Barbara Mitchell. Publishes hardcover and trade paperback originals. Publishes 4-6 titles/year. Receives 2 queries and 5 mss/year. 10% of books from first-time authors; 100% from unagented writers. Pays 3-7% royalty on wholesale price or makes outright purchase work-for-hire. No advance. Publishes book 1 year after acceptance of ms. Reports in 1 month. *Writer's Market* recommends allowing 2 months for reply. Book catalog free on request.
Nonfiction: Biography, multicultural. Subjects include ethnic. "As of now, we only publish multicultural biographies and use writers on 'work-for-hire' basis." Query with SASE.
Recent Nonfiction Title: *Tommy Nuñez*, by B. Marvis (young adult biography).

MODERN LANGUAGE ASSOCIATION OF AMERICA, Dept. WM, 10 Astor Pl., New York NY 10003. (212)475-9500. Fax: (212)477-9863. Director of Book Acquisitions and Development: Joseph Gibaldi. Director of MLA Book Publications: Martha Evans. Estab. 1883. Publishes hardcover and paperback originals. Publishes 15 titles/year. Receives 125 submissions/year. 100% of books from unagented writers. Pays 5-10% royalty on net proceeds. Publishes book 1 year after acceptance. Reports in 2 months on mss. Book catalog free on request.
Nonfiction: Scholarly, professional. Subjects include language and literature. Publishes on current issues in literary and linguistic research and teaching of language and literature at postsecondary level. No critical monographs. Query with outline/synopsis.

MONUMENT PRESS, P.O. Box 140361, Las Colinas TX. 75014-0361. (214)686-5332. Contact: Mary Markal. Publishes trade paperback originals. Publishes 15 titles/year. Receives 100 queries and 50 mss/year. 100% of books from first-time authors; 100% from unagented writers. Pays 4% minimum royalty on retail

price. Publishes book 1 year after acceptance of ms. Reports in 4 months. Book catalog for 6×9 SA
6 first-class stamps. Manuscript guidelines for #10 SASE.

Nonfiction: Textbook. Subjects include gay/lesbian, government/politics, health/medicine, military
religion, women's issues/studies. Query with outline and 2 sample chapters. All unsolicited mss returned
unopened.

Recent Nonfiction Title: *Military Secret*, by Robert Graham (homosexuality in Navy).

MOON PUBLICATIONS, INC., P.O. Box 3040, Chico CA 95927-3040. (916)345-3778. Fax: (916)345-6751. Executive Editor: Taran March. Senior Editor: Kevin Jeys. Estab. 1973. Publishes trade paperback originals. Publishes 15 titles/year. Receives 100-200 submissions/year. 50% from first-time authors; 95% from unagented writers. Pays royalty on net price. Offers advance of up to $10,000. Publishes book an average of 9 months after acceptance. Accepts simultaneous submissions. Reports in 2 months. Book catalog and proposal guidelines for 7½×10½ SAE with 2 first-class stamps.

• Moon is putting increased emphasis on acquiring writers who are experts in a given destination
   and demonstrate above-average writing ability.

Nonfiction: "We specialize in travel guides to Asia and the Pacific Basin, the United States, Canada, the Caribbean, Latin America and South America, but are open to new ideas. Our guides include in-depth cultural and historical background, as well as recreational and practical travel information. We prefer comprehensive guides to entire countries, states, and regions over more narrowly defined areas such as cities, museums, etc. Writers should write first for a copy of our guidelines. Proposal required with outline, table of contents, and writing sample. Author should also be prepared to provide photos, artwork and base maps. No fictional or strictly narrative travel writing; no how-to guides." Reviews artwork/photos as part of ms package.

Recent Nonfiction Title: *Road Trip, U.S.A.*, by Jamie Jensen.

Tips: "Moon Travel Handbooks are designed by and for independent travelers seeking the most rewarding travel experience possible. Our Handbooks appeal to all travelers because they are the most comprehensive and honest guides available."

MOREHOUSE PUBLISHING CO., 871 Ethan Allen Hwy., Ridgefield CT 06877-2801. Fax: (203)431-3964. E-mail: eakelley@aol.com. Publisher: E. Allen Kelley. Senior Editor: Deborah Grahame-Smith. Estab. 1884. Publishes hardcover and paperback originals. Publishes 15 titles/year. Receives 500 submissions/year. 40% of books from first-time authors; 75% from unagented writers. Pays 7-10% royalty. Offers $500-1,000 advance. Publishes book 8 months after acceptance. Accepts simultaneous submissions. Reports in 4 months. Book catalog for 9×12 SAE with $1.01 in postage stamps.

Nonfiction: Specializes in Christian publishing (with an Anglican emphasis). Theology, spirituality, ethics, church history, pastoral counseling, liturgy, religious education activity and gift books, and children's books (preschool-teen). No poetry or drama. Submit outline/synopsis and 1-2 sample chapters. Reviews artwork/photos as part of ms package. Send photocopies, color for color photos.

Recent Nonfiction Title: *Scared: Growing Up in America*, by George H. Gallup, Jr. with Wendy Plump.

Fiction: Juvenile, picture books, religious, young adult. Small children's list. Artwork essential. Query with synopsis, 2 chapters, intro and SASE.

Recent Fiction Title: *A Good Day for Listening*, Maryellen King.

WILLIAM MORROW AND CO., 1350 Avenue of the Americas, New York NY 10019. (212)261-6500. Fax: (212)261-6595. Editorial Director: Will Schwalbe. Managing Editor: Michael Beacon. Imprints include Beech Tree Books, Mulberry Books, Tambourine Books (juvenile), Paulette Kaufmann, editor-in-chief. Greenwillow Books (juvenile), Susan Hirschman, editor-in-chief. Hearst Books (trade), Ann Bramson, editorial director. Hearst Marine Books (nautical), Ann Bramson, editor. Lothrop, Lee & Shepard (juvenile), Susan Pearson, editor-in-chief. Morrow Junior Books (juvenile), David Reuther, editor-in-chief. Quill Trade Paperbacks, Toni Sciarra, editor. Estab. 1926. Publishes 200 titles/year. Receives 10,000 submissions/year. 30% of books from first-time authors; 5% from unagented writers. Pays standard royalty on retail price. Advance varies. Publishes book 2 years after acceptance. Reports in 3 months. Query letter on all books. *No unsolicited mss or proposals.*

Nonfiction and Fiction: Publishes adult fiction, nonfiction, history, biography, arts, religion, poetry, how-to books, cookbooks. Length: 50,000-100,000 words. Query only; mss and proposals should be submitted only through an agent.

MORROW JUNIOR BOOKS, Division of William Morrow and Co., 1350 Avenue of the Americas, New York NY 10019. (212)261-6691. Editor-in-Chief: David L. Reuther. Executive Editor: Meredith Charpentier. Senior Editor: Andrea Curley. Publishes hardcover originals. Publishes 50 titles/year. All contracts negotiated individually. Offers variable advance. Book catalog and guidelines for 9×12 SAE with 3 first-class stamps.

Nonfiction: Juveniles (trade books). No textbooks.

Fiction: Juveniles (trade books).

Tips: "We are no longer accepting unsolicited manuscripts."

‡**MOTORBOOKS INTERNATIONAL**, 729 Prospect Ave., Osceola WI 54020. Fax: (715)294-4448. E-mail: mbibks@win.bright.net. Publishing Director: Jack Savage. Senior Editor: Zack Miller. Estab. 1973. Publishes hardcover and paperback originals. Publishes 100 titles/year. 95% of books from unagented writers. Pays 12% royalty on net receipts. Offers $3,000 average advance. Publishes book 1 year after acceptance. Accepts simultaneous submissions. Reports in 3 months. Free book catalog. Manuscript guidelines for #10 SASE.
Nonfiction: History, how-to, photography (as they relate to cars, trucks, motorcycles, motor sports, aviation—domestic, foreign and military). Accepts nonfiction translations. Submit outline, 1-2 sample chapters and sample of illustrations. "State qualifications for doing book." Reviews artwork/photos as part of ms package.
Recent Nonfiction Title: *Route 66 Remembered*, by Michael Karl Witzel.

THE MOUNTAINEERS BOOKS, 1001 SW Klickitat Way, Suite 201, Seattle WA 98134-1162. (206)223-6303. Director: Donna DeShazo. Editor-in-Chief: Margaret Foster. Estab. 1961. Publishes 95% hardcover and trade paperback originals and 5% reprints. Publishes 40 titles/year. Receives 150-250 submissions/year. 25% of books from first-time authors; 98% from unagented writers. Average print order for a first book is 5,000-7,000. Pays royalty based on net sales. Offers advance. Publishes book 1 year after acceptance. Reports in 3 months. Book catalog and ms guidelines for 9 × 12 SAE with 3 first-class stamps.
 • Mountain Books is looking for manuscripts with more emphasis on regional conservation and natural history. See the Contests and Awards section for information on the Barbara Savage/"Miles From Nowhere" Memorial Award offered by Mountain Books.
Nonfiction: Guidebooks for national and international adventure travel, recreation, natural history, conservation/environment, non-competitive self-propelled sports, outdoor how-to, and some children's books. "We specialize in books dealing with mountaineering, hiking, backpacking, skiing, snowshoeing, canoeing, bicycling, etc. These can be either how-to-do-it or where-to-do-it (guidebooks)." Does *not* want to see "anything dealing with hunting, fishing or motorized travel." Submit author bio, outline and minimum of 2 sample chapters. Accepts nonfiction translations. Looks for "expert knowledge, good organization." Also interested in nonfiction adventure narratives. Ongoing award—The Barbara Savage/"Miles from Nowhere" Memorial Award for outstanding adventure narratives is offered.
Fiction: "We might consider an exceptionally well-done book-length manuscript on mountaineering." Does *not* want poetry or mystery. Query first.
Tips: "The type of book the writer has the best chance of selling our firm is an authoritative guidebook (*in our field*) to a specific area not otherwise covered; or a how-to that is better than existing competition (again, *in our field*)."

MUSTANG PUBLISHING CO., P.O. Box 3004, Memphis TN 38173-0004. (901)521-1406. Editor: Rollin Riggs. Estab. 1983. Publishes hardcover and trade paperback originals. Publishes 10 titles/year. Receives 1,000 submissions/year. 50% of books from first-time authors; 90% of books from unagented writers. Pays 6-8% royalty on retail price. Publishes book 1 year after acceptance. Accepts simultaneous submissions. Address proposals to Rollin Riggs. No phone calls, please. Reports in 1 month. *Writer's Market* recommends allowing 2 months for reply. Book catalog for $1 and #10 SASE.
Nonfiction: How-to, humor, self-help. Subjects include Americana, hobbies, recreation, sports, travel. "Our needs are very general—humor, travel, how-to, etc.—for the 18-to 40-year-old market." Query or submit outline and sample chapters with SASE.
Recent Nonfiction Title: *How to Be a Way Cool Grandfather*, by Verne Steen.
Tips: "From the proposals we receive, it seems that many writers never go to bookstores and have no idea what sells. Before you waste a lot of time on a nonfiction book idea, ask yourself, 'How often have my friends and I actually *bought* a book like this?' Know the market, and know the audience you're trying to reach."

THE MYSTERIOUS PRESS, Subsidiary of Warner Books, 1271 Avenue of the Americas, New York NY 10020. (212)522-5144. Fax: (212)522-7990. Editor-in-Chief: William Malloy. Executive Editor: Sara Ann Freed. Editorial Assistant: Theresa Loong. Estab. 1976. Publishes hardcover and mass market editions. Averages 70-90 titles/year. Accepts no unagented mss. Pays standard, but negotiable, royalty on retail price. Amount of advance varies widely. Publishes book an average of 1 year after acceptance. Reports in 2 months.
Fiction: Mystery, suspense. "We will consider publishing any outstanding crime/suspense/detective novel that comes our way. No short stories." Query with SASE.
Recent Fiction Title: *Fugitive Colors*, by Margaret Maron.
Tips: "We do not read unagented material. Agents only, please."

THE NAIAD PRESS, INC., P.O. Box 10543, Tallahassee FL 32302. (904)539-5965. Fax: (904)539-9731. Editorial Director: Barbara Grier. Estab. 1973. Publishes paperback originals. Publishes 28 titles/year. Receives over 1,500 submissions/year. 20% of books from first-time authors; 99% from unagented writers. Average print order for a first book is 8,000. Pays 15% royalty on wholesale or retail price. No advance.

Publishes book 2 years after acceptance. Reports in 4 months. Book catalog and ms guidelines for 6×9 SAE and $1.50 postage and handling

Recent Nonfiction Title: *Lesbian Sex: An Oral History*, by Susan Johnson.

Fiction: "We publish lesbian fiction, preferably lesbian/feminist fiction. We are not impressed with the 'oh woe' school and prefer realistic (i.e., happy) novels. We emphasize fiction and are now heavily reading manuscripts in that area. We are working in a lot of genre fiction—mysteries, short stories, fantasy—all with lesbian themes, of course. We have instituted an inhouse anthology series, featuring short stories only by our own authors (i.e. authors who have published full length fiction with us or those signed to do so)." Query.

Recent Fiction Title: *Forbidden Fires*, by Margaret Anderson.

Tips: "There is tremendous world-wide demand for lesbian mysteries from lesbian authors published by lesbian presses, and we are doing several such series. We are no longer seeking science fiction. Manuscripts under 50,000 words have twice as good a chance as over 50,000."

NASW PRESS, Division of National Association of Social Workers, 750 First St. NE, Suite 700, Washington DC 20002-4241. Fax: (202)336-8312. E-mail: press@naswdc.org. Executive Editor: Linda Beebe. Estab. 1956. Publishes 10-12 titles/year. Receives 100 submissions/year. 20% of books from first-time authors; 100% from unagented writers. Pays 10-15% royalty on net prices. Publishes book 8 months after acceptance of ms. Reports within 4 months on submissions. Book catalog and ms guidelines free.

• NASW will be putting more emphasis on publishing health, policy and substance abuse books.

Nonfiction: Textbooks of interest to professional social workers. "We're looking for books on social work in health care, mental health, multicultural competence and substance abuse. Books must be directed to the professional social worker and build on the current literature." Submit outline and sample chapters. Rarely reviews artwork/photos as part of ms package.

Tips: "Our audience includes social work practitioners, educators, students and policy makers. They are looking for practice-related books that are well grounded in theory. The books that do well are those that have direct application to the work our audience does. New technology, AIDS, welfare reform, and health policy will be of increasing interest to our readers. We are particularly interested in manuscripts for fact-based practice manuals that will be very user-friendly."

NATIONAL PRESS BOOKS, INC., 1925 K St., Suite 100, Washington DC 20006. (202)833-2021. Fax: (202)822-6062. Editorial Director: G. Edward Smith. Estab. 1984. Publishes hardcover and trade paperback originals. Publishes 23 titles/year. Receives 1,500 submissions/year. 20% of books are from first-time authors; 80% from unagented writers. Pays 5-10% royalty on wholesale or retail price or makes outright purchases. Offers variable advance. Publishes book 8 months after acceptance. Accepts simultaneous submissions. Reports in 4 months. Book catalog and ms guidelines for 7½×10½ SAE with 4 first-class stamps.

Nonfiction: Biography, cookbook, self-help. Subjects include business and economics, child guidance/parenting, government/politics, health/medicine, history, money/finance, psychology. Query or submit outline and sample chapters. Reviews artwork/photos as part of ms package.

NATIONAL TEXTBOOK CO., Imprint of NTC Publishing Group, 4255 W. Touhy Ave., Lincolnwood IL 60646. (847)679-5500. Fax: (847)679-2494. President/CEO: Mark R. Pattis. Publishes originals for education and trade market, and software. Publishes 100-150 titles/year. Receives 1,000 submissions annually. 10% of books from first-time authors. 75% from unagented writers. Manuscripts purchased on either royalty or fee basis. Publishes book 1 year after acceptance. Reports in 3 months. Book catalog and ms guidelines for 6×9 SAE and 2 first-class stamps.

Nonfiction: Textbooks. Major emphasis being given to foreign language and language arts classroom texts, especially secondary level material, and business and career subjects (marketing, advertising, sales, etc.). John T. Nolan, editorial group director; N. Keith Fry, executive editor/Foreign Language and ESL; Anne Knudsen, executive editor/Quilt Digest Press (nonfiction books on quilting, 5 titles/year); Betsy Lancefield, executive editor/VGM Career Horizons. Send sample chapter and outline or table of contents.

THE NAUTICAL & AVIATION PUBLISHING CO., 8 W. Madison St., Baltimore MD 21201. (410)659-0220. Fax: (410)539-8832. President/Publisher: Jan Snouck-Hurgronje. Editor: Rebecca Irish. Estab. 1979. Publishes hardcover originals and reprints. Publishes 10-12 titles/year. Receives 125 submissions/year. Pays 10-15% royalty on net selling price. Rarely offers advance. Accepts simultaneous submissions. Book catalog free.

Nonfiction: Reference. Subjects include history, military/war. Query with synopsis and 3 sample chapters. Reviews artwork/photo as part of package.

Recent Nonfiction Title: *The Battle of Tassafaronga*, by Captain Russell.

Fiction: Historical. Submit outline/synopsis and sample chapters.

Recent Fiction Title: *Normandy*, by VAdm. William P. Mack and S. Crenshaw, Jr. USN (Ret.).

Tips: "Please note that we are publishers of *military* history only—our name is misleading, and we often get inquiries on general nautical or aviation books. We generally do not publish fiction titles. We are primarily and increasingly a nonfiction publishing house."

NAVAL INSTITUTE PRESS, Imprint of U.S. Naval Institute, 118 Maryland Ave., Annapolis MD 21402-5035. Executive Editor: Paul Wilderson. Press Director: Ronald Chambers. Contact: Jean Tyson, acquisitions coordinator. Estab. 1873. Publishes 65 titles/year. Receives 400-500 submissions/year. 60% of books from first-time authors; 85% from unagented writers. Average print order for a first book is 2,000. Pays 5-10% royalty based on net sales. Publishes book 1 year after acceptance. Query letter strongly recommended. *Writer's Market* recommends allowing 2 months for reply. Book catalog free with 9 × 12 SASE. Manuscript guidelines for #10 SASE.
Nonfiction: "We are interested in naval and maritime subjects and in broad military topics, including government policy and funding. Specific subjects include: tactics, strategy, navigation, history, biographies, aviation, technology and others."
Recent Nonfiction Title: *Spy Sub: A Top Secret Mission to the Bottom of the Pacific*, by Roger Dunham (Cold War history).
Fiction: Limited fiction on military and naval themes.

NEAL-SCHUMAN PUBLISHERS, INC., 100 Varick St., New York NY 10013. (212)925-8650. Fax: (212)219-8916. Editorial Director: Charles Harmon. Publishes hardcover and trade paperback originals. Publishes 30 titles/year. Receives 80 submissions/year. 75% of books from first-time authors; 80% from unagented writers. Pays 10% royalty on net sales. Offers advances infrequently. Publishes book 1 year after acceptance. Reports in 1 month on proposals. *Writer's Market* recommends allowing 2 months for reply. Book catalog and ms guidelines free.
Nonfiction: How-to, reference, software, technical, textbook, texts and professional books in library and information science. Subjects include business and economics, child guidance/parenting, computers/electronics and the Internet, education, gay/lesbian, government/politics, health/medicine, language/literature, money/finance, recreation, software, travel. "We are looking for reference books in business and health-related sciences." Submit proposal package, including vita, outline, preface and sample chapters.
Recent Nonfiction Title: *The Complete Internet Companion for Librarians*, by Allen Benson.

NEGATIVE CAPABILITY, 62 Ridgelawn Dr. E., Mobile AL 36608. Fax: (334)344-8478. Editor/Publisher: Sue Walker. Publishes hardcover and trade paperback originals. Publishes 4 titles/year. Negotiates royalty. Publishes book 10 months after acceptance of ms. Reports in 2 months. Manuscript guidelines free.
Nonfiction: Self-help. Subjects include education, health/medicine, language/literature, women's issues/studies.
Recent Nonfiction Title: *Deeper Than Monday Night Football: Thoughts On High School & Beyond*, by James Brannan Walker (self-help advice for students).
Fiction: Feminist, historical, literary, short story collections. Query with SASE.
Recent Fiction Title: *Little Dragons*, by Michael Bugeja (short story collection).
Poetry: Submit 5 sample poems.
Recent Poetry Title: *The Mouse Whole*, by Richard Moore (poetry).

THOMAS NELSON PUBLISHERS, Nashville TN. Corporate address does not accept unsolicited manuscripts. No phone queries. Send brief prosaic résumé, 1 page synopsis, and 1 sample chapter to one of the Acquisitions Editors at the following locations: Janet Thoma, Janet Thoma Books, 1157 Molokai, Tega Cay SC 29715. Fax: (803)548-2684. Victor Oliver, Oliver-Nelson Books, 1360 Center Dr., Suite 102-B, Atlanta GA 30338. Fax: (770)391-9784. Rick Nash, Thomas Nelson Trade Book Division, P.O. Box 141000, Nashville TN 37214-1000. Fax: (615)391-5225. For Biblical/Religious Reference Books: Contact: Mark Roberts, Nelson Reference Publishing, P.O. Box 1410000, Nashville TN 37214. Fax: (615)391-5225. Publishes 150-200 titles/year. Books published 1-2 years after acceptance. Send proposals as described above with SASE. Reports in 3 months. Accepts simultaneous submissions if so stated in your cover letter.
Nonfiction: Adult inspirational, motivational, devotional, self-help, Christian living, prayer and evangelism, reference/Bible study.
Fiction: Seeking successfully published commercial fiction authors who write for adults from a Christian perspective.

NELSON-HALL PUBLISHERS, 111 N. Canal St., Chicago IL 60606. (312)930-9446. General Manager: Richard O. Meade. Estab. 1909. Publishes hardcover and paperback originals. Publishes 30 titles/year. Receives 200 queries and 20 mss/year. 90% of books submitted by unagented writers. Pays 5-15% royalty on wholesale price. Publishes book 1 year after acceptance. Accepts simultaneous submissions. Reports in 1 month on queries. *Writer's Market* recommends allowing 2 months for reply.
Nonfiction: College textbooks and general scholarly books in the social sciences. Subjects include anthropology/archaeology, government/politics, music/dance, psychology, sociology. Query with outline, 2 sample chapters, cv.
Recent Nonfiction Title: *The Rich Get Richer*, by Denny Braun, Ph.D.

NEW HARBINGER PUBLICATIONS, 5674 Shattuck Ave., Oakland CA 94609. Fax: (510)652-5472. E-mail: newharbpub@aol.com. Website: http://www.newharbinger.com. Aquisition Editor: Kristin Beck.

Publishes 22 titles/year. Receives 750 queries and 200 mss/year. 60% of books from first-time authors; 95% from unagented writers. Pays 12% royalty on wholesale price. Offers $0-3,000 advance. Publishes book 1 year after acceptance of ms. Accepts simultaneous submissions. Reports in 1 month on queries and proposals, 2 months on mss. Book catalog and ms guidelines free on request.
Nonfiction: Self-help (psychology/health), textbooks. Subjects include child guidance/parenting, health/medicine, psychology. "Authors need to be a qualified psychotherapist or health practitioner to publish with us." Submit proposal package, including outline, 3 sample chapters, competing titles and why this one is special.
Recent Nonfiction Title: *The Stop Smoking Workbook*, by Steric-Rust/Maximin (psychology/medical self-help).
Tips: Audience includes psychotherapists and lay readers wanting step-by-step strategies to solve specific problems.

NEW HOPE, Woman's Missionary Union, P.O. Box 12065, Birmingham AL 35202-2065. (205)991-8100. Website: http://www.wmu.com/wmu. Editorial Director: Cindy McClain. Imprints are New Hope, Woman's Missionary Union. Publishes 15 titles/year. Receives 100 queries and 60 mss/year. 50% of books from first-time authors; 98% from unagented writers. Pays 7-10% royalty on retail price or makes outright purchase. Publishes book 2 years after acceptance of ms. No simultaneous submissions. Reports in 6 months on mss. Book catalog for 9×12 SAE with 3 first-class stamps. Manuscript guidelines for 10 SASE.
Nonfiction: How-to, children's/juvenile (religion), personal spiritual growth. Subjects include child guidance/parenting (from Christian perspective), education (Christian church), religion (Christian faith—must relate to missions work, culture, Christian concerns, Christian ethical issues, spiritual growth, etc.), women's issues/studies from Christian perspective. "We publish Christian education materials that focus on missions work or educational work in some way. Teaching helps, spiritual growth material, ideas for working with different audiences in a church, etc.—missions work overseas or church work in the US, women's spiritual issues, guiding children in Christian faith." Submit outline and 3 sample chapters for review. Submit complete ms for acceptance decision.
Recent Nonfiction Title: *Broken Dreams*, by Karen Linamen and Keith Wall (AIDS account).
Recent Fiction Title: *The Elephant Path*, by Judy Langley (children's story/picture book).

‡NEW LEAF PRESS, INC., P.O. Box 726, Green Forest AR 72638-0726. Fax: (501)438-5120. Contact: Editorial Board. Estab. 1975. Publishes hardcover and paperback originals. Publishes 15-20 titles/year. Receives 400 submissions/year. 15% of books from first-time authors; 90% from unagented writers. Average print order for a first book is 10,000. Pays 10% royalty once per year. No advance. Send photos and illustrations to accompany ms. Publishes book 10 months after acceptance. Accepts simultaneous submissions. Reports in 3 months. Book catalog and ms guidelines for 9×12 SAE with 5 first-class stamps.
Nonfiction: How to live the Christian life, humor, self-help. Length: 100-400 pages. Submit complete ms. *Writer's Market* recommends sending a query with SASE first. Reviews artwork/photos as part of ms package.
Tips: "Self-help and Christian living guides, devotionals, relevant nonfiction and humor are areas our firm is looking at. Quality Christian writing is still the measuring stick, so writers should submit accordingly."

THE NEW LEXINGTON PRESS, (formerly Lexington Books), Imprint of Jossey-Bass Publishers, Inc., 350 Sansome St., Fifth Floor, San Francisco CA 94104-1342. (415)433-1740. Publisher: William H. Hicks. Imprint publishes 40 titles/year. Receive 500 queries and 100 mss/year. 80% from unagented writers. Pays 7½-15% royalty on wholesale price. Publishes book within 6 months after acceptance of ms. Accepts simultaneous submissions. Reports in 1 month on proposals. *Writer's Market* recommends allowing 2 months for reply. Manuscript guidelines available on request.
Nonfiction: Scholarly/academic. Subjects include business and management theory, psychology, research methods, environmental issues. "We publish cutting-edge scholarly books for researchers, academics, advanced graduate students and thinking professionals."

NEW RIVERS PRESS, 420 N. Fifth St., Suite 910, Minneapolis MN 55401. Editor: Edward Dingle. Publishes trade paperback originals. Publishes 8-10 titles/year. Receives 500 queries and 1,000 mss/year. 95% of books from first-time authors; 99.9% from unagented writers. Pays 12-15% royalty or makes outright purchase. Publishes book 14 months after acceptance. Query first with a synopsis or proposal. Reports in 6 months. Book catalog free on request. Manuscript guidelines for 10 SASE.
Nonfiction: Creative prose. "We publish memoirs, essay collections, and other forms of creative nonfiction." Query.
Recent Nonfiction Title: *Mykonos*, by Nancy Raeburn (memoir).
Fiction: Literary and short story collections. Query with synopsis and 2 sample chapters.
Poetry: Submit 10-15 sample poems.

NEW VICTORIA PUBLISHERS, P.O. Box 27, Norwich VT 05055-0027. Phone/fax: (802)649-5297. E-mail: newvic@valley.net. Editor: Claudia Lamperti. Estab. 1976. Publishes trade paperback originals. Publishes 8-10 titles/year. Receives 100 submissions/year. 50% of books from first-time authors; most books from unagented writers. Pays 10% royalty. Publishes book 1 year after acceptance. Reports on queries in 1 month. *Writer's Market* recommends allowing 2 months for reply. Book catalog free.

Nonfiction: History. "We are interested in feminist history or biography and interviews with or topics relating to lesbians. No poetry." Submit outline and sample chapters.

Fiction: Adventure, erotica, fantasy, historical, humor, mystery, romance, science fiction, western. "We will consider most anything if it is well written and appeals to lesbian/feminist audience." Submit outline/synopsis and sample chapters. Hard copy only—no discs.

Recent Fiction Title: *I Knew You'd Call*, by Kate Allen (mystery).

Recent Poetry Title: *I Change, I Change*, by Barbara Deming (poetry).

Tips: "Try to appeal to a specific audience and not write for the general market. We're still looking for well-written, hopefully humorous, lesbian fiction and well-researched biography or nonfiction."

NEW WORLD LIBRARY, Subsidiary of Whatever Publishing, Inc., 14 Pamaron Way, Novato CA 94949. (415)884-2100. Fax: (415)884-2199. E-mail: beckynwlib.com. Publisher: Marc Allen. Contact: Becky Benenate, editor. Imprint is Amber Allen Publishing (contact Janet Mills). Publishes hardcover and trade paperback originals and reprints. Publishes 25 titles/year. 10% of books from first-time authors; 50% from unagented writers. Pays 12-16% royalty on wholesale price. Offers $0-200,000 advance. Publishes book 1 year after acceptance of ms. Accepts simultaneous submissions. Reports in 2 months. Book catalog and ms guidelines free on request.

• New World Library also has an extensive audio program.

Nonfiction: Gift book, self-help. Subjects include business/prosperity, cooking/foods/nutrition, ethnic (African-American, Native American), money/finance, nature/environment, personal growth, psychology, religion, women's issues/studies. Query or submit outline, 1 sample chapter and author bio with SASE. Reviews artwork/photos as part of ms package. Send photocopies.

Recent Nonfiction Title: *Visionary Business*, by Marc Allen (business).

NEW YORK NICHE PRESS, 175 Fifth Ave., Suite 2646, New York NY 10010. (718)779-1754. Publisher: Michael Danowski. Publishes trade paperback originals and newsletters. Publishes 4 titles/year. Receives 4 queries/year. 50% of books from first-time authors; 100% from unagented writers. Accepts simultaneous submissions.

Nonfiction: Regional, travel. Subjects include New York City recreation and travel. "Timely information should be balanced with useful material that will not date the work. Should be street-smart in style." Submit outline with 1 sample chapter. Reviews artwork/photos as part of ms package. Send photocopies.

Recent Nonfiction Title: *Dim Sum: How About Some? A Guide to NYC's Liveliest Chinese Dining & How To Make A Day of It*, by Wanda Chin and Michael P. Danowski (New York restaurant/travel guide).

Tips: "Our readers are New York residents and enthusiastic visitors to NYC. We use material with the 'New York attitude.' We are considering children's fiction about and for New York."

‡NEWCASTLE PUBLISHING CO., INC., 13419 Saticoy, N. Hollywood CA 91605. (213)873-3191. Fax: (213)780-2007. Editor-in-Chief: Alfred Saunders. Contact: Daryl Jacoby, editor. Estab. 1970. Publishes trade paperback originals and reprints. Publishes 10 titles/year. Receives 300 submissions/year. 70% of books from first-time authors; 95% of books from unagented writers. Average print order for a first book is 3,000-5,000. Pays 5-10% royalty on retail price. No advance. Publishes book an average of 8 months after acceptance. Accepts simultaneous submissions. Reports in 1 month. *Writer's Market* recommends allowing 2 months for reply. Free book catalog; ms guidelines for SASE.

Nonfiction: How-to, self-help, metaphysical, New Age and practical advice for older adults. Subjects include health (physical fitness, diet and nutrition), psychology and religion. "Our audience is made up of college students and college-age nonstudents; also, adults ages 25 and up and older adults of above average education. They are of above average intelligence and are fully aware of what is available in the bookstores." No biography, travel, children's books, poetry, cookbooks or fiction. Query or submit outline and sample chapters. Looks for "something to grab the reader so that he/she will readily remember that passage."

Recent Nonfiction Title: *Schemes & Scams*, by John T. (consumer affairs).

Tips: "Check the shelves in the larger bookstores on the subject of the manuscript being submitted. A book on life extension, holistic health, or stress management has the best chance of selling to our firm along with books geared for older adults on personal health issues, etc."

‡NICHOLS PUBLISHING, P.O. Box 6036, E. Brunswick NJ 08816. (908)297-2862. Fax: (908)940-0549. Vice President and Publisher: Fran Van Dalen. Contact: Fran Lubrano, editorial director. Estab. 1979. Publishes hardcover and paperback originals. Publishes 50 titles/year. 15% of books from first-time authors; 98% from unagented writers. Pays 5-15% royalty on wholesale price. Offers $300-500 average advance. Publishes book 9 months after acceptance. Simultaneous submissions OK. Reports on queries in 1 month. *Writer's Market* recommends allowing 2 months for reply. Book catalog and ms guidelines free on request.

Nonfiction: Reference, technical. Subjects include management, education, training. Submit outline and sample chapters.

Recent Nonfiction Title: *Assembling Course Materials*, by Nicolay and Barrett.
Tips: "We need more books on training. No longer seeking books on architecture, computers and electronics, or engineering."

‡**NO STARCH PRESS**, 401 China Basin St., Suite 108, San Francisco CA 94107. (415)284-9900. Publisher: William Pollock. Imprint is No Starch Comix. Publishes trade paperback originals. Publishes 6-10 titles/year. Receives 10 queries and 5 mss/year. 80% of books from first-time authors; 90% from unagented writers. Pays 10-15% royalty on wholesale price. Offers negotiable advance. Publishes book 8 months after acceptance of ms. Accepts simultaneous submissions. Book catalog free on request.
Nonfiction: How-to, reference, technical. Subjects include computers and electronics, hobbies, software. Only consider computer-related books or underground comics. Submit outline, 1 sample chapter, bio, market rationale. Reviews artwork/photos as part of ms package. Send photocopies.
Recent Nonfiction Title: *Internet for Cats*, by Judy Heim (humor/computer).
Tips: Audience is non-computer people. "Understand how your book fits into the market. Tell us why someone, anyone, will buy your book. Be enthusiastic."

THE NOBLE PRESS, INC., 213 W. Institute Place, Suite 508, Chicago IL 60610. (312)642-1168. Fax: (312)642-7682. Executive Editor: Janet Bell. Estab. 1988. Publishes hardcover and trade paperback originals. Publishes 8-12 titles/year. Receives 1,500 submissions/year. 50% of books from first-time authors; 70% from unagented writers; 30% agented. Pays 5-15% royalty on retail price. Offers variable advance. Publishes book an average of 8 months after acceptance. Accepts simultaneous submissions. Reports in 10 weeks. Manuscript guidelines for SASE.
Nonfiction: Subjects should be multi-cultural. No cookbooks, technical manuals, or texts in full. Query or submit outline and 1 sample chapter.
Recent Nonfiction Title: *Spirit Speaks to Sisters*, by June Gatlin.
Recent Fiction Title: *Urban Romance*, by Nelson George.
Tips: "The writer has the best chance of selling us a nonfiction or fiction book that concerns African-Americans and would be of interest to multi-cultural readers."

NODIN PRESS, Imprint of Micawber's Inc., 525 N. Third St., Minneapolis MN 55401. (612)333-6300. President: Norton Stillman. Publishes hardcover and trade paperback originals. Publishes 4 titles/year. Receives 20 queries and 20 mss/year. 75% of books from first-time authors; 100% from unagented writers. Pays 10% royalty. Offers $250-1,000 advance. Publishes book 20 months after acceptance of ms. Accepts simultaneous submissions. Reports in 6 months on queries. Book catalog or ms guidelines free on request.
Nonfiction: Biography, regional guide book. Subjects include ethnic, history, sports, travel. Query.
Recent Nonfiction Title: *Golden Memories*, by Christensen (autobiography).

NORTH LIGHT BOOKS, Imprint of F&W Publications, 1507 Dana Ave., Cincinnati OH 45207. Editorial Director: David Lewis. Publishes hardcover and trade paperback originals. Publishes 30-35 titles/year. Pays 10-20% royalty on net receipts. Offers $4,000 advance. Accepts simultaneous submissions. Reports in 1 month. Book catalog for 9×12 SAE with 6 first-class stamps.
Nonfiction: Art, decorative painting, craft and graphic design instruction books. Interested in books on watercolor painting, oil painting, pastel, basic drawing, pen and ink, airbrush, crafts, decorative painting, basic design, computer graphics, desktop design, layout and typography. Do not submit coffee table art books without how-to art instruction. Query or submit outline and examples of artwork (transparencies and photographs).
Recent Nonfiction Title: *Timeless Techniques for Better Oil Paintings*.

NORTHLAND PUBLISHING CO., INC., P.O. Box 1389, Flagstaff AZ 86002-1389. (602)774-5251. Fax: (602)774-0592. Editor: Erin Murphy. Estab. 1958. Publishes hardcover and trade paperback originals. Publishes 25 titles/year. Receives 4,000 submissions/year. 30% of books from first-time authors; 95% from unagented writers. Pays 8-12% royalty on net receipts, depending upon terms. Offers $1,000-3,000 average advance. Publishes book 2 years after acceptance. Accepts simultaneous submissions if so noted. Reports in 1 month on queries, 2 months on mss. Book catalog and ms guidelines for 9×12 SAE with $1.50 in postage.
● This publisher has received the following awards in the past year: National Cowboy Hall of Fame Western Heritage Award for Outstanding Juvenile Book (*The Night the Grandfathers Danced*); Colo-

FOR INFORMATION on book publishers' areas of interest, see the nonfiction and fiction sections in the Book Publishers Subject Index.

rado Book Awards—Best Children's Book (*Goose and the Mountain Lion*); Reading Rainbow Book (*It Rained on the Desert Today*).

Nonfiction: Subjects include animals, anthropology/archaeology, art/architecture, cooking, history, nature/environment, photography and regional (American West/Southwest). "We are seeking authoritative, well-written manuscripts on natural history subjects. We do not want to see poetry; general fiction; mainstream, or New Age or science fiction material." Query or submit outline/synopsis and sample chapters. Reviews manuscripts and artwork/photos separately.

Recent Nonfiction Title: *Following the Sun and Moon: Hopi Kachina Tradition*, by Alph H. Secakuku, in cooperation with the Heard Museum.

Fiction: Unique children's picture book and middle reader chapter book stories, especially those with Southwest/West regional theme; Native American folktales (retold by Native Americans only, please). Picture book mss should be 350-1,500 words; chapter book mss should be approximately 20,000 words. Does not want to see "mainstream" stories. Northland does not publish general trade fiction.

Recent Fiction Title: *The Night the Grandfathers Danced*, by Linda Theresa Raczek, illustrated by Katalin Ohla Ehling.

Tips: "Our audience is composed of general interest readers and those interested in specialty subjects such as Native American culture and crafts. It is not necessarily a scholarly market, but is sophisticated."

NORTHWORD PRESS, INC., P.O. Box 1360, Minocqua WI 54548. (715)356-7644. Managing Editor: Barbara K. Harold. Publishes hardcover and trade paperback originals for adults, teens, and children. Publishes 30 titles/year. Estab. 1984. Receives 600 submissions/year. 50% of books are from first-time authors; 90% are from unagented writers. Pays 10-15% royalty on wholesale price. Offers $2,000-20,000 advance. Publishes book 1 year after acceptance. Accepts simultaneous submissions. Reports in 2 months on queries. Book catalog for 9 × 12 SASE with 7 first-class stamps. Manuscript guidelines for SASE.

● The editor reports rapid growth for this company.

Nonfiction: Coffee table books, introductions to wildlife and natural history, guidebooks, children's illustrated books, juvenile adventure; nature and wildlife subjects exclusively. Query with outline, sample chapters and SASE.

Recent Nonfiction Title: *Grizzlies in the Wild*, by Kennan Ward.

Tips: "We do not publish poetry, fiction or memoirs. Think nature and wildlife. That's exclusively what we publish. We have expanded our wildlife/natural history topics to include exotic and non-North American species."

W.W. NORTON CO., INC., 500 Fifth Ave., New York NY 10110. General trade publisher of fiction and nonfiction, educational and professional books. Subjects include biography, history, music, psychology, and literary fiction. Do not submit juvenile or young adult, religious, occult or paranormal, genre fiction (formula romances, science fiction or westerns), or arts and crafts. Query with outline, first 3 chapters and SASE.

NOVA PRESS, 11659 Mayfield Ave., Suite 1, Los Angeles CA 90049. (310)207-4078. Fax: (310)207-4078. E-mail: novapress@aol.com. President: Jeff Kolby. Publishes trade paperback originals. Publishes 10 titles/year. Pays 10-22½% royalty on net price. Publishes book 6 months after acceptance of ms. Book catalog free on request.

Nonfiction: How-to, self-help, technical. Subjects include education, software.

Recent Nonfiction Title: *Law School Basics*, by David Hricik.

Tips: "All our books relate to academics: mainly college level, but also high school and adult."

NOVA SCIENCE PUBLISHERS INC., 6080 Jericho Turnpike, Suite 207, Commack NY 11725-2808. (516)499-3103. Fax: (516)499-3146. E-mail: novasci1@aol.com. Subsidiary is Kroshka Books. Editor-in-Chief: Frank Columbus. Publishes hardcover and paperback originals. Publishes 150 titles/year. Receives 1,000 queries/year. Pays royalty. Publishes book 1 year after acceptance. Accepts simultaneous submissions. Reports in 1 month. *Writer's Market* recommends allowing 2 months for reply.

Nonfiction: Biography, novels, self-help, technical, textbook. Subjects include Americana, anthropology, business and economics, computers and electronics, nutrition, education, government/politics, health/medicine, history, money/finance, nature/environment, philosophy, poetry, psychology, recreation, religion, science, sociology, software, sports, childhood development. Query. Reviews artwork/photos as part of ms package. Send photocopies.

Recent Nonfiction Title: *Understanding Suicide*, by D. Lester.

NOYES DATA CORP., 120 Mill Rd., Park Ridge NJ 07656. Fax: (201)391-6833. Contact: George Narita. Estab. 1959. Publishes hardcover originals. Publishes 30 titles/year. Pays 12% royalty on net proceeds. Advance varies, depending on author's reputation and nature of book. Reports in 2 weeks. Book catalog free.

Nonfiction: Noyes Publications and Noyes Data Corp. publish technical books on practical industrial processing, science, economic books pertaining to chemistry, chemical engineering, food, textiles, energy, electronics, pollution control, material science, semi-conductor material and process technology—primarily of interest to the business executive and practicing research scientists and research engineers. Length: 50,000-250,000 words. Query the Editorial Department.

NTC PUBLISHING GROUP, 4255 W. Touhy Ave., Lincolnwood IL 60646-1975. (847)679-5500. Fax: (847)679-2494. Imprints include National Textbook Company, Passport Books, NTC Business Books, VGM Career Books, The Quilt Digest Press. Foreign Language and English as a Second Language Executive Editor: Keith Fry. Language Arts Editorial Group Director: John Nolan. NTC Business Books Editor: Richard Hagle. VGM Career Books: Betsy Lancefield. Executive Editor, The Quilt Digest Press: Anne Knudsen. Director of Dictionaries: Richard Spears. Estab. 1960. Publishes hardcover and trade paperback originals and reprints. Publishes 150 titles/year. Receives 1,000 submissions/year. 90% of books from unagented writers. Pays royalty or makes outright purchase. Offers varying advance. Publishes book 8 months after acceptance. Accepts simultaneous submissions. Reports in 2 months. Book catalog free on request.
Nonfiction: Textbook, travel, foreign language, reference, advertising and marketing business books. Subjects include business, education, language/literature, photography, travel, quilts and books related to the fiber arts. Query. Reviews artwork/photos as part of ms package.
Recent Nonfiction Title: *Everyday Creative Writing: Panning for Gold in the Kitchen Sink*, by Michael Smith and Suzanne Greenberg.

OAK KNOLL PRESS, 414 Delaware St., New Castle DE 19720. (302)328-7232. Fax: (302)328-7274. E-mail: oakknoll@ssnet.com. Website: http://www.oakknoll.com. Publishes hardcover and trade paperback originals and reprints. Publishes 12 titles/year. Receives 25 queries and 5 mss/year. 5% of books from first-time authors; 100% from unagented writers. Pays 7-10% royalty on income. Publishes book 18 months after acceptance of ms. Accepts simultaneous submissions. Reports in 1 month on queries. *Writer's Market* recommends allowing 2 months for reply. Book catalog free on request.
Nonfiction: Book arts. Subjects include printing, papermaking, bookbinding, book collecting, etc. "We only specialize in books about books." Query. Reviews artwork/photos as part of ms package. Send photocopies.
Recent Nonfiction Title: *Bookbinding & Conservation by Hand*, by Laura Young.

OCTAMERON ASSOCIATES, 1900 Mt. Vernon Ave., Alexandria VA 22301. (703)836-5480. Editorial Director: Karen Stokstad. Estab. 1976. Publishes trade paperback originals. Publishes 15 titles/year. Receives 100 submissions/year. 10% of books from first-time authors; 100% from unagented writers. Average print order for a first book is 8,000-10,000. Pays 7½% royalty on retail price. Publishes book 6 months after acceptance. Accepts simultaneous submissions. Reports in 2 months. Book catalog for #10 SAE with 2 first-class stamps.
Nonfiction: Reference, career, post-secondary education subjects. Especially interested in "paying-for-college and college admission guides." Query with outline and 2 sample chapters. Reviews artwork/photos as part of ms package.
Recent Nonfiction Title: *SAT Savvy: Last Minute Tips and Strategies*, by Marian Martin.

‡OHIO STATE UNIVERSITY PRESS, 1070 Carmack Rd., Columbus OH 43210. (614)292-6930. Acquisitions Editor: Charlotte Dihoff. Pays royalty on wholesale or retail price. Publishes 30 titles/year. Reports in 3 months; ms held longer with author's permission.
Nonfiction: History, political science, literature, criminology, education, sociology, urban studies, regional titles and general scholarly nonfiction. Query with outline and sample chapters.
Recent Nonfiction Title: *Welcome to Heights High: The Crippling Politics of Restructuring America's Public Schools*, by Diana Tittle.
Recent Poetry Title: *Crossing the Snow Bridge*, by Fatima Lim-Wilson.
Tips: "Publishes some poetry and fiction. Query first."

‡OHIO UNIVERSITY PRESS, Scott Quadrangel, Athens OH 45701. (614)593-1155. Associate Director: Holly Panich. Imprints are Swallow Press (David Sanders, director); Ohio University Monographs in International Studies (Gillian Berchowitz, executive editor). Publishes hardcover and trade paperback originals and reprints. Publishes 42 titles/year. Receives 500 queries and 50 mss/year. 60% of books from first-time authors; 85% from unagented writers. Pays royalty on net sales. No advance. Publishes book 1 year after acceptance of ms. Accepts simultaneous submissions. Reports in 1 month on queries and proposals, 2 months on mss. Book catalog and manuscript guidelines free on request.
Nonfiction: Biography, cookbook, how-to, illustrated book, reference, self-help. Subjects include African studies, agriculture/horticulture, Americana, animals, anthropology/archaeology, art/architecture, business and economics, cooking/foods/nutrition, education, ethnic, gardening, government/politics, health/medicine, history, language/literature, music/dance, nature/environment, philosophy, psychology, recreation, regional, religion, sociology, translation, travel, women's issues/studies. Query with proposal package, including outline, 1-2 sample chapters. "We require a completed manuscript before accepting a proposal for consideration." Reviews artwork/photos as part of ms package. Send photocopies.
Recent Nonfiction Title: *Trollope and Victorian Moral Philosophy*, by Jane Nardin (literary criticism).

ONE ON ONE COMPUTER TRAINING, Subsidiary of Mosaic Media, Suite 100, 2055 Army Trail Rd., Addison IL 60101. Manager Product Development: N.B. Young. Imprints are FlipTrack Learning Systems, OneOnOne Computer Training, Math House. Publishes 5-10 titles/year. 100% of books from unagented writers. Makes outright purchase of $2,000-12,000. Advance depends on purchase contract. Publishes book 4 months after acceptance of ms. Accepts simultaneous submissions. Reports in 2 months on proposals. Book catalog free on request.

Nonfiction: How-to, self-help, technical. Subjects include computers, software. Query. All unsolicited mss returned unopened.

Recent Nonfiction Title: *How to Use Microsoft Access for Windows 95.*

OPEN ROAD PUBLISHING, P.O. Box 20226, Columbus Circle Station, New York NY 10023. Fax: (212)974-2108. E-mail: jopenroad@aol.com. Contact: B. Borden. Publishes trade and mass market paperback originals. Publishes 15-17 titles/year. Receives 80 queries and 60 mss/year. 40% of books from first-time authors; 95% from unagented writers. Pays 5-6% royalty on retail price. Offers $500-4,000 advance. Publishes book 6 months after acceptance of ms. Accepts simultaneous submissions. Reports in 1 month on proposals. *Writer's Market* recommends allowing 2 months for reply. Book catalog free on request. Manuscript guidelines for #10 SASE.

Nonfiction: Travel guides. Subjects include sports, especially running and fitness guides. "We're looking for opinionated, selective travel guides that appeal to mainstream travelers in their mid-20s to early 50s. Our guides are fun, literate, and have a sense of adventure, offering readers solid cultural background and the opportunity to experience the country or city—not just visit it." Submit cover letter, outline and 2 sample chapters.

Recent Nonfiction Title: *Italy Guide*, by Doug Morris (travel guide).

‡OPTIMA BOOKS, 2820 Eighth St., Berkeley CA 94710. (510)848-8708. Editor: Dan Connell. Publishes trade paperback originals and reprints. Publishes 4 titles/year. Receives 8 queries and 5 mss/year. 0% of books from first-time authors; 100% from unagented writers. Makes outright purchase. No advance. Publishes book 8 months after acceptance of ms. Accepts simultaneous submissions. Reports in 2 months on mss.

Nonfiction: Textbook, self teaching. Subjects include languag/literature, ESL (English as a second language). "Books should be usable in the classroom—or by the individual in a self teaching capacity. Should be written for the non-native speaker desiring knowledge of American slang and jargon." Query with SASE. Reviews artwork/photos as part of ms package. Send photocopies.

Recent Nonfiction Title: *Street Talk-3*, by David Burke (guide to American slang, self teaching).

ORCHISES PRESS. P.O. Box 20602, Alexandria VA 22320-1602. (703)683-1243. E-mail: rlathbur@osfl.g mu.edu. Editor-in-Chief: Roger Lathbury. Estab. 1983. Publishes hardcover and trade paperback originals and reprints. Publishes 4-5 titles/year. Receives 600 queries and 200 mss/year. 1% of books from first-time authors; 95% from unagented writers. Pays 36% of receipts after Orchises has recouped its costs. Publishes book 1 year after acceptance. Accepts simultaneous submissions. Reports in 3 months. Book catalog for #10 SASE.

Nonfiction: Biography, how-to, humor, reference, technical, textbook. No real restrictions on subject matter. Query. Reviews artwork/photos as part of the ms package. Send photocopies.

Recent Nonfiction Title: *College*, by Stephen Akey (memoir).

Poetry: Poetry must have been published in respected literary journals. Although publishes free verse, has strong formalist preferences. Query or submit 5 sample poems.

Recent Poetry Title: *Big-Leg Music*, by David Kirby (poetry).

Tips: "Audience is professional, literate and academic. Show some evidence of appealing to a wider audience than simply people you know."

OREGON STATE UNIVERSITY PRESS, 101 Waldo Hall, Corvallis OR 97331-6407. (541)737-3166. Fax: (541)737-3170. Managing Editor: Jo Alexander. Contact: Tom Booth, acquisitions editor. Estab. 1965. Publishes hardcover and paperback originals. Publishes 9 titles/year. Receives 100 submissions/year. 75% of books from first-time authors; 100% of books from unagented writers. Average print order for a first book is 1,500. Pays royalty on net receipts. No advance. Publishes book 1 year after acceptance. Reports in 3 months. Book catalog for 6×9 SAE with 2 first-class stamps.

● This publisher recently won the Oregon Book Award for its Oregon Literature series.

Nonfiction: Publishes scholarly books in history, biography, geography, literature, life sciences and natural resource management, with strong emphasis on Pacific or Northwestern topics. Submit outline and sample chapters.

Recent Nonfiction Title: *Fool's Hill*, by John Quick (creative nonfiction).

Tips: "Over the next few years we will increase the number of books we publish from approximately 9/year to 20. We have launched two new series: Culture & Environment in the Pacific West and Northwest Readers."

‡**ORLOFF PRESS**, P.O. Box 8536, Berkeley CA 94707-8536. (510)524-9121. Editor: John Spencer. Publishes hardcover originals and reprints. Publishes 4-6 titles/year. Receives 100 queries and 200 mss/year. 50% of books from first-time authors; 50% from unagented writers. Pays 10% royalty on wholesale price. No advance. Publishes book 9 months after acceptance. Accepts simultaneous submissions. Reports in 1 month on queries, 2 months on mss. Book catalog free on request.
Fiction: Erotica, historical, humor, literary, mainstream/contemporary, mystery, short story collections. Submit synopsis, 3 sample chapters and SASE.
Recent Fiction Title: *Superstoe*, by William Borden (novel).

ORTHO INFORMATION SERVICES, The Solaris Group/Monsanto, P.O. Box 5006, San Ramon CA 94583. Editorial Director: Christine Jordan. Publishes 10 titles/year. Makes outright purchase.
Nonfiction: How-to. Subjects include gardening and home improvement. Query. All unsolicited mss returned unopened.

ORYX PRESS, 4041 N. Central Ave., Suite 700, Phoenix AZ 85012. (602)265-2651. Fax: (602)265-6250. E-mail: info@oryxpress.com. Website: http://www.oryxpress.com/. President: Phyllis B. Steckler. Acquisitions Editors: Art Stickney (reference); Robert Clarfield (electronic); Martha Wilke Montz (submissions). Estab. 1975. Publishes 50 titles/year. Receives 500-1,000 submissions/year. 40% of books from first-time authors; 80% from unagented writers. Average print order for a first book is 1,500. Pays 10% royalty on net receipts. No advance. Publishes book 9 months after acceptance. Proposals via Internet welcomed. Reports in 3 months. Book catalog and author guidelines free.
Nonfiction: Directories, dictionaries, encyclopedias, other general reference works; special subjects: business, education, consumer health care, government information, gerontology, social sciences. Publishes print and/or electronic reference sources for public, college, K-12 school, business and medical libraries, and multicultural/literature-based/social studies resource materials for K-12 classroom use. Query or submit outline/rationale and samples. Queries/mss may be routed to other editors in the publishing group.
Recent Nonfiction Title: *Distinguished African American Scientists in the 20th Century*, by Kate Morin, James H. Kessler, Jerry S. Kidd, Renée Kidd (reference).
Tips: "We are accepting and promoting more titles over the internet. We are also looking for up-to-date, relevant ideas to add to our established line of print and electronic works."

‡**OSBORNE/MCGRAW-HILL**, Subsidiary of The McGraw-Hill Companies, Dept. WM, 2600 10th St., Berkeley CA 94710. (510)548-2805. (800)227-0900. Executive Editor: Scott Rogers. Estab. 1979. Publishes trade paperback originals. Averages 65 titles/year. Receives 120 submissions/year. 30% of books from first-time authors; 95% from unagented writers. Pays 8-15% royalty on wholesale price. Offers $5,000 average advance. Publishes book an average of 6 months after acceptance. Accepts simultaneous submissions. Reports in 2 months. Book catalog free on request.
Nonfiction: Software, technical. Subjects include computers. Query with outline and sample chapters. Reviews artwork/photos as part of ms package.

OUR SUNDAY VISITOR, INC., 200 Noll Plaza, Huntington IN 46750-4303. (219)356-8400. Fax: (219)359-9117. President/Publisher: Robert Lockwood. Editor-in-Chief: Greg Erlandson. Acquistions Editor: James Manney. Estab. 1912. Publishes paperback and hardbound originals. Averages 20-30 titles/year. Receives over 100 submissions/year. 10% of books from first-time authors; 90% from unagented writers. Pays variable royalty on net receipts. Offers $1,000 average advance. Publishes book 1 year after acceptance. Query for electronic submissions. Reports in 3 months on most queries and submissions. Author's guide and catalog for SASE.
Nonfiction: Catholic viewpoints on current issues, reference and guidance, Bibles and devotional books, and Catholic heritage books. Prefers to see well-developed proposals as first submission with annotated outline, 3 sample chapters and definition of intended market. Reviews artwork/photos as part of ms package.
Tips: "Solid devotional books that are not first person, well-researched church histories or lives of the saints and catechetical books have the best chance of selling to our firm. Make it solidly Catholic, unique, without pious platitudes."

THE OVERLOOK PRESS, Distributed by Viking/Penguin, 149 Wooster St., New York NY 10012. Contact: Editorial Department. Imprint is Tusk Books. Publishes hardcover and trade paperback originals and hardcover reprints. Publishes 40 titles/year. Receives 300 submissions/year. Pays 3-15% royalty on wholesale or retail price. Agented submissions only. Reports in 5 months. Book catalog free.
Nonfiction: Art, architecture, design, film, history, biography, current events, popular culture, New York State regional. No pornography.
Fiction: Literary fiction, fantasy, foreign literature in translation. "We tend not to publish commercial fiction."

RICHARD C. OWEN PUBLISHERS INC., P.O. Box 585, Katonah NY 10536. Contact: Janice Boland. Publishes hardcover and paperback originals. Publishes 3-12 titles/year. Receives 25 queries and 1,000 mss/

year. 99% of books from first-time authors; 100% from unagented writers. Pays 5-8% royalty on wholesale price. Publishes book 3 years after acceptance of ms. Accepts simultaneous submissions, if so noted. Reports in 6 months on mss. Manuscript guidelines for #10 SASE.

Nonfiction: Children's/juvenile. Subjects include animals, nature/environment. "Our books are for 5-7-year-olds. The stories are very brief—under 100 words—yet well structured and crafted with memorable characters, language and plots." Send for ms guidelines, then submit complete ms. *Writer's Market* recommends sending a query with SASE first.

Fiction: Picture books. "Brief, strong story line, real characters, natural language, exciting—child-appealing stories with a twist. No lists, alphabet or counting books." Submit full ms with SASE. *Writer's Market* recommends sending a query with SASE first.

Poetry: Poems that excite children, fun, humorous, fresh. No jingles. Must rhyme without force or contrivance. Send for ms guidelines, then submit complete ms.

OWL CREEK PRESS, 1620 N. 45th St., #205, Seattle WA 98103. Editor: Rich Ives. Publishes hardcover originals, trade paperback originals and reprints. Publishes 4-6 titles/year. 50% of books from first time authors; 95% from unagented writers. Pays 10-15% royalty, makes outright purchase or with a percentage of print run. Publishes book 2 years after acceptance. Reports in 3 months. Book catalog for #10 SASE.

Fiction: Literary, short story collections. Submit 1 sample chapter.

Recent Fiction Title: *For Her Dark Skin*, by Percival Everett.

• Owl Creek Press holds two contests, the Owl Creek Poetry Prize and the Green Lake Chapbook Prize, and publishes the winners. See the Contests and Awards section for details.

Recent Poetry Title: *Children of Gravity*, by Laurie Blauner.

OXFORD UNIVERSITY PRESS, 198 Madison Ave., New York NY 10016. (212)679-7300. Website: http://www.oup-usa.org/. Contact: Humanities and Science (Helen McInnis, editorial director); Trade (Laura Brown, director, trade publishing). Publishes hardcover and trade paperback originals and reprints. Publishes 1,500 titles/year. 40% of books from first-time authors; 80% from unagented writers. Pays 0-15% royalty on wholesale price or retail price. Offers $0-40,000 advance. Publishes book 10 months after acceptance of ms. Accepts simultaneous submissions. Reports in 3 months on proposals. Book catalog free on request.

Nonfiction: Biography, children's/juvenile, reference, technical, textbook. Subjects include anthropology/archaeology, art/architecture, business and economics, computers and electronics, gay/lesbian, government/politics, health/medicine, history, language/literature, law, military/war, music/dance, nature/environment, philosophy, psychology, religion, science, sociology, women's issues/studies. Oxford is an academic, scholarly press. Submit outline and sample chapters. Reviews artwork/photos as part of ms package (but not necessary).

Recent Nonfiction Title: *At Home in the Universe*, by Stuart Kauffman.

‡**PACIFIC BOOKS, PUBLISHERS**, P.O. Box 558, Palo Alto CA 94302-0558. (415)965-1980. Editor: Henry Ponleithner. Estab. 1945. Publishes 6-12 titles/year. Pays variable royalty. No advance. Reports in 1 month. *Writer's Market* recommends allowing 2 months for reply. Book catalog and guidelines for 9×12 SASE.

Nonfiction: General interest, professional, technical and scholarly nonfiction trade books. Specialties include western Americana and Hawaiiana. Looks for "well-written, documented material of interest to a significant audience." Also considers text and reference books for high school and college. Accepts artwork/photos and translations. Query with outline and SASE.

Recent Nonfiction Title: *The Persistence of Economic Discrimination: Race, Ethnicity, Gender*, by Elias H. Tuma (economics).

‡**PACIFIC PRESS PUBLISHING ASSOCIATION**, Book Division, Seventh-day Adventist Church, P.O. Box 5353, Nampa ID 83653-5353. (208)465-2570. Fax: (208)465-2531. E-mail: kenwad@rmci.net. Website: http://www.pacificpress.com. Acquisitions Editor: Kenneth Wade. Estab. 1874. Publishes hardcover and trade paperback originals and reprints. Publishes 35 titles/year. Receives 600 submissions and proposals/year. Up to 35% of books from first-time authors; 100% from unagented writers. Pays 8-16% royalty on wholesale price. Offers $300-1,500 average advance depending on length. Publishes book 10 months after acceptance. Query for electronic submissions. Reports in 3 months. Manuscript guidelines for #10 SASE.

Nonfiction: Biography, cookbook (vegetarian), how-to, juvenile, self-help, textbook. Subjects include cooking and foods (vegetarian only), health, nature, religion, family living. "We are an exclusively religious publisher. We are looking for practical, how-to oriented manuscripts on religion, health, and family life that speak to human needs, interests and problems from a Biblical perspective. We can't use anything totally secular or written from other than a Christian perspective." Query or request information on how to submit a proposal. Reviews artwork/photos as part of ms package.

Recent Nonfiction Title *One Nation Under God?*, by Clifford Goldstein (politics, religious liberty).

Tips: "Our primary audiences are members of our own denomination (Seventh-day Adventist), the general Christian reading market, and the secular or nonreligious reader. Books that are doing well for us are those that relate the Biblical message to practical human concerns and those that focus more on the experiential rather than theoretical aspects of Christianity. We are assigning more titles, using less unsolicited material—although we still publish manuscripts from freelance submissions and proposals."

PACIFIC VIEW PRESS, P.O. Box 2657, Berkeley CA 94702. Acquisitions Editor: Pam Zumwalt. Publishes hardcover and trade paperback originals. Publishes 4-6 titles/year. 50% of books from first-time authors; 100% from unagented writers. Pays 10% maximum royalty on retail price. Offers $1,000-5,000 advance. Publishes book 1 year after acceptance. Accepts simultaneous submissions. Reports in 2 months on queries and proposals. Book catalog free on request. Writer's guidelines for #10 SASE.
Nonfiction: Children's/juvenile (Asia/multicultural only), reference, textbook (Chinese medicine only), contemporary Pacific Rim affairs. Subjects include business/economics (Asia and Pacific Rim only), health/medicine (Chinese medicine), history (Asia), regional (Pacific Rim), travel (related to Pacific Rim). Query with proposal package including outline, 1-2 chapters, target audience and SASE.
Recent Nonfiction Title: *Fighting Drug Abuse with Acupuncture: The Treatment that Works*, Ellinor Mitchell.
Tips: Audience is "persons professionally/personally aware of growing importance of Pacific Rim and/or modern culture of these countries, especially China. Business people, academics, travelers, etc."

PALADIN PRESS, P.O. Box 1307, Boulder CO 80306-1307. (303)443-7250. Fax: (303)442-8741. E-mail: clubed@rmii.com. President/Publisher: Peder C. Lund. Editorial Director: Jon Ford. Estab. 1970. Publishes hardcover and paperback originals and paperback reprints. Publishes 36 titles/year. 50% of books from first-time authors; 100% from unagented writers. Pays 10-12-15% royalty on net sales. Publishes book 1 year after acceptance. Accepts simultaneous submissions. Reports in 2 months. Book catalog free.
Nonfiction: "Paladin Press primarily publishes original manuscripts on military science, weaponry, self-defense, personal privacy, financial freedom, espionage, police science, action careers, guerrilla warfare, fieldcraft and 'creative revenge' humor. How-to manuscripts are given priority. If applicable, send sample photographs and line drawings with complete outline and sample chapters." Query with outline and sample chapters.
Recent Nonfiction Title: *The Tactical Pistol*, by Gabriel Suarez (training reference).
Tips: "We need lucid, instructive material aimed at our market and accompanied by sharp, relevant illustrations and photos. As we are primarily a publisher of 'how-to' books, a manuscript that has step-by-step instructions, written in a clear and concise manner (but not strictly outline form) is desirable. No fiction, first-person accounts, children's, religious or joke books. We are also interested in serious, professional videos and video ideas (contact Michael Janich)."

‡PANSOPHIC PUBLISHING, 2308 S. 18th, St. Joseph MO 64503. (816)364-1623. Publisher: Christina Shellhorn. Publishes hardcover and trade paperback originals. Publishes 4 titles/year. Receives 10 queries and 10 mss/year. 90% of books from first-time authors; 90% from unagented writers. Pays 8-15% royalty. No advance. Publishes book 2 years after acceptance of ms. Accepts simultaneous submissions. Reports in 4 months on mss. Manuscript guidelines free on request.
Nonfiction: How-to, self-help, history. Subjects include history, hobbies, philosophy, psychology, regional, religion, sociology, travel. Query. Submit outline with SASE. Reviews artwork/photos as part of ms package. Send photocopies.
Recent Nonfiction Title: *This Is St. Joseph*, by Christina Schellhorn (historical).
Fiction: Historical, juvenile, picture books, plays, religious.
Tips: "Remember we want books to enlighten our readers."

PANTHEON BOOKS, Division of Random House, Inc., 201 E. 50th St., 25th Floor, New York NY 10022. Managing Editor: Altie Karper. Publishes quality fiction and nonfiction. Offers advance. Send query letter first, addressed to Adult Editorial Department.
Nonfiction: History, politics, autobiography, biography, interior design.
Recent Nonfiction Title: *First Comes Love*, by Marion Winik.
Recent Fiction Title: *The Moor's Last Sigh*, by Salman Rushdie.

PAPER CHASE PRESS, 5721 Magazine St., #152, New Orleans LA 70115. (504)522-2025. Editor: Jennifer Osborn. Publishes hardcover and trade paperback originals and reprints. Publishes 5 titles/year. 90% of books from first-time authors; 100% from unagented writers. Pays royalty on retail price; varies from hardcover to trade. Publishes book 18 months after acceptance of ms. Accepts simultaneous submissions. Manuscripts will not be returned. Reports in 2 months on queries.
Nonfiction: How-to, self-help. Subjects include business and economics, hobbies, psychology, recreation, sports, women's issues/studies. "We look for enthusiasm about subject matter, fresh ideas, willingness of author to be involved in promotion of book (good speaking ability, willing to travel, etc.)." Send 1-page query letter only.
Recent Nonfiction Title: *The Art of Talk*, by Art Bell (autobiography).
Fiction: Mainstream/contemporary. "We don't want to see someone's first draft. Stay in tune with current trends in fiction. The beginning of the story should be strong enough to *immediately* generate interest in the

whole book—sympathetic characters with depth and variety." Query; submit synopsis and first 2 chapters only.

Tips: Audience is "mainstream—people who read a lot and are open to all kinds of fiction, literary or otherwise. Relationship issues are particularly interesting to us, i.e., family relationhips, personal relationships. Make your characters and your story believable!"

PAPIER-MACHE PRESS, 135 Aviation Way, #14, Watsonville CA 95076. (408)763-1420. Acquisitions Editor: Shirley Coe. Publishes 6-8 titles/year. 90% of books from first-time authors; 95% from unagented writers. Pays royalty. Offers $500-1,000 advance. Publishes book 18 months after acceptance. Accepts simultaneous submissions. Reports in 2 months on queries, 4 months on mss. Book catalog and ms guidelines free on request.
Nonfiction: Women's stories, essays, interviews, biography, gift book. Subjects include women's issues/ studies, aging. Focus on women's issues; no technical or how-to books—creative nonfiction. Query with proposal package, including outline, 3-4 sample chapters, target audience, author's qualifications, similar books in marketplace and SASE.
Recent Nonfiction Title: *A Question of Balance: Artists and Writers on Motherhood*, by Judith Pierce Rosenberg.
Fiction: Feminist, mainstream/contemporary (women), short story collections (women), aging. "We publish books about women's lives—primarily midlife women. We don't consider books with graphic sex or violence." Query with synopsis, 3-4 sample chapters and SASE.
Recent Fiction Title: *Late Summer Break*, by Ann B. Knox (short stories).
Poetry: Manuscripts must be 100-120 pages long. Prefers collections centered around 1 or 2 major themes. Accepts poetry in July and August only. Submit complete ms.
Recent Poetry Title: *Washing the Stones: Selected Poems 1975-1995*, by Maude Meehan.
Tips: Audience is women, 35-55 years old. Always request submission guidelines before submitting a ms.

PARADIGM PUBLISHING INC., Subsidiary of EMC Corporation, 300 York Ave., St. Paul MN 55101. (612)771-1555. Fax: (612)772-5196. E-mail: publish@emcp.com. Website: http://www.emcp.com. Publisher: Mel Hecker. Publishes 50 titles/year. Receives 60 queries and 35 mss/year. 20% of books from first-time authors; 100% from unagented writers. Pays 6-10% royalty on net. Offers $1,000-2,500 advance. Publishes book 1 year after acceptance of ms. Accepts simultaneous submissions. Reports in 2 months on proposals. Book catalog for 8×12 SAE with 4 first-class stamps. Manuscript guidelines free on request.
Nonfiction: Textbook. Subjects include business and office, communications, computers, psychology and software. "We focus on textbooks for business and office and computer information systems education marketed to proprietary business schools and community colleges." Submit outline and 2 sample chapters.
Recent Nonfiction Title: *Business Math*, by Lloyd Brooks (textbook).
Tips: "With the cost of paper escalating, multimedia is a sure winner in educational publishing."

‡PARKWAY PUBLISHERS, INC., Box 3678, Boone NC 28607. Phone/fax: (704)265-3993. E-mail: aluri@netins.net. Website: http://www.netins.net/showcase/alurir. President: Rao Aluri. Publishes hardcover and trade paperback originals. Publishes 4-6 titles/year. Receives 15-20 queries and 10 mss/year. 75% of books from first-time authors; 100% from unagented writers. Pays 10-15% royalty on retail price. No advance. Publishes book 8 months after acceptance. Reports in 1 month on queries, 2 months on mss. Book catalog on world wide web.
Nonfiction: Reference, technical. Subjects include agriculture/horticulture, computers and electronics, science. "Interested in scholarly publications with good market potential." Prefer complete ms with SASE. *Writer's Market* recommends sending a query with SASE first.
Recent Nonfiction Title: *Living with Autism: The Parents' Stories*, by Kathleen Dillon (psychology).
Recent Poetry Title: *Ransom Street Quartet*, by Juanita Tobin (poems and stories).
Tips: Audience is academic and research libraries, scholars and researchers.

‡PARNASSUS IMPRINTS, 30 Perseverance Way, Suite 7, Hyannis MA 02601. (508)790-1175. Publisher: Wallace Exman. Publishes hardcover originals, trade paperback originals and reprints. Publishes 6-8 titles/ year. Receives 25-35 queries and 15-20 mss/year. 25% of books from first-time authors; 50% from unagented writers. Pays 7½-15% royalty on retail price. Offers variable advance. Publishes book 1 year after acceptance of ms. Accepts simultaneous submissions. Reports in 1 month on queries, 2 months on proposals and mss. Book catalog for $1 postage.
Nonfiction: Subjects include regional Americana, anthropology/archaeology, art/architecture, cooking/food/ nutrition, gardening, history, hobbies, nature/environment, recreation, sports, travel. "Parnassus Imprints focuses on publishing nonfiction works relating to Cape Cod and regional (New England) interests. One or more books per list will be of national interest." Query with outline, proposal, 3 sample chapters and SASE. Reviews artwork/photos as part of ms package. Send photocopies.
Recent Nonfiction Title: *The Cape Cod Garden*, by C.L. Fornari (gardening/horticulture).
Tips: Audience is readers interested in Cape Cod/New England subjects.

PASSPORT PRESS, P.O. Box 1346, Champlain NY 12919-1346. Publisher: Jack Levesque. Estab. 1975. Publishes trade paperback originals. Publishes 4 titles/year. 25% of books from first-time authors; 100% from unagented writers. Pays 6% royalty on retail price. Publishes book 9 months after acceptance. Send 1-page query only. Does not return submissions.
Nonfiction: Travel books only, not travelogues. Especially looking for mss on practical travel subjects and travel guides on specific countries. Query. Reviews artwork/photos as part of ms package.
Recent Nonfiction Title: *Montreal and The Casino*, by Zach Lewis (travel-gambling).

PAULINE BOOKS & MEDIA, Daughters of St. Paul, 50 St. Paul's Ave., Boston MA 02130. (617)522-8911. Fax: (617)541-9805. Website: http://www.pauline.org. Director, Editorial Department: Sister Mary Mark, FSP. Estab. 1948. Publishes hardcover and trade paperback originals and reprints. Publishes 35 titles/year. Receives approximately 1,300 proposals/year. Pays authors 8-12% royalty on net sales. Publishes ms 2 years after acceptance. Reports in 3 months. Book catalog for 9 × 12 SAE with 4 first-class stamps.
Nonfiction: Biography, juvenile, spiritual growth and development. Subjects include child guidance/parenting, psychology, religion. "No strictly secular manuscripts." Query only. No unsolicited mss without prior query.
Recent Nonfiction Title: *God and Your Personality*, by Dr. Dan Montgomery.
Fiction: Juvenile. Query only. No unsolicited mss without prior query.
Recent Fiction Title: *Marie of Bayou Teche*, by Billie Touchstone Signer (adolescent fiction).
Tips: "We are more interested in books concerning faith and moral values, as well as in works on spiritual growth and development. Always interested in books of Christian formation for families. No New Age books, poetry or autobiographies please."

PAULIST PRESS, 997 Macarthur Blvd., Mahwah NJ 07430. (201)825-7300. Fax: (201)825-8345. Editor: Rev. Kevin A. Lynch. Managing Editor: Donald Brophy. Children's and Juvenile Books: Karen Schilabba. Estab. 1865. Publishes hardcover and paperback originals and paperback reprints. Publishes 90-100 titles/year. Receives 500 submissions/year. 5-8% of books from first-time authors; 95% from unagented writers. Nonauthor subsidy publishes 1-2% of books. Pays royalty on retail price. Usually offers advance. Publishes book 10 months after acceptance. Reports in 2 months.
Nonfiction: Philosophy, religion, self-help, textbooks (religious). Accepts nonfiction translations from German, French and Spanish. "We would like to see theology (Catholic and ecumenical Christian), popular spirituality, liturgy, and religious education texts." Submit outline and 2 sample chapters. Reviews artwork/photos as part of ms package.
Recent Nonfiction Title: *Ethics in Pastoral Ministry*, by Richard Gula.

PBC INTERNATIONAL INC., 1 School St., Glen Cove NY 11542. (516)676-2727. Fax: (516)676-2738. Publisher: Mark Serchuck. Managing Editor: Susan Kapsis. Estab. 1980. Imprints are Library of Applied Design, Architecture & Interior Design Library, Great Graphics Series, Design In Motion Series, Showcase Edition. Publishes hardcover and paperback originals. Publishes 18 titles/year. Receives 100-200 submissions/year. Most of books from first-time authors and unagented writers done on assignment. Pays royalty and/or flat fees. Accepts simultaneous submissions. Reports in 2 months. Book catalog for 9 × 12 SASE.
Nonfiction: Subjects include design, graphic art, architecture/interior design, packaging design, marketing design, product design. No submissions not covered in the above listed topics. Query with outline and sample chapters. Reviews artwork/photos as part of ms package.
Recent Nonfiction Title: *Designing With Wood: The Creative Touch*, by Carol Soucek King, Ph.D. (interior design).
Tips: "PBC International is the publisher of full-color visual idea books for the design, marketing and graphic arts professional."

PEACHPIT PRESS, 2414 Sixth St., Berkeley CA 94710. (510)548-4393. Fax: (510)548-8192. E-mail: roslyn@peachpit.com. Contact: Roslyn Bullas. Estab. 1986. Publishes trade paperback originals. Publishes over 30 titles/year. Receives 250 queries and 6 mss/year. 10% of books from first-time authors; 80% from unagented writers. Pays 12-20% royalty on wholesale price. Offers $2,000-15,000 advance. Publishes book 6 months after acceptance of ms. Accepts simultaneous submissions. Reports in 3 months on proposals. Book catalog free on request.
Nonfiction: How-to, reference, technical. Subjects include computers and electronics. "We prefer no phone calls." Submit short, 1-page proposal (preferred) or outline. Reviews artwork/photos as part of ms package. Send photocopies.
Recent Nonfiction Title: *The Photoshop 3 Wow! Book*, by Linnea Dayton and Jack Davis.

PEACHTREE PUBLISHERS, LTD., 494 Armour Circle NE, Atlanta GA 30324-4888. (404)876-8761. Contact: Managing Editor. Estab. 1977. Publishes hardcover and trade paperback originals. Publishes 15-20 titles/year; 1 fiction book/year. Approximately 33% of Peachtree's list consists of children's books. Receives up to 18,000 submissions/year. 25% of books from first-time authors; 75% from unagented writers. Average print order for a first book is 5,000-10,000. Publishes book 2 years after acceptance. Reports in 6 months on queries. Book catalog for 9×12 SAE with 3 first-class stamps.

Nonfiction: General and humor. Subjects include animals, children's titles and juvenile chapter books, cooking/foods, history, self-help, gardening, biography, general gift, recreation. No technical or reference. Submit outline and sample chapters. Reviews artwork/photos as part of ms package. No originals, please.

Recent Nonfiction Title: *Teaching Your Child the Language of Social Success*, by Marshall R. Duke, Ph.D.; Stephen Nowicki, Jr., Ph.D.; Elisabeth A. Martin, M.Ed. (self-help/parenting).

Fiction: Literary, juvenile, mainstream. No fantasy, science fiction, mystery or romance. Submit sample chapters.

Recent Fiction Title: *Out to Pasture (But Not Over the Hill)*, by Effie Leland Wilder.

Tips: "Peachtree Publishers prefers to work with Southern writers, professional storytellers, and previously published authors."

PELICAN PUBLISHING COMPANY, 1101 Monroe St., P.O. Box 3110, Gretna LA 70053. (504)368-1175. Editor-in-Chief: Nina Kooij. Estab. 1926. Publishes hardcover, trade paperback and mass market paperback originals and reprints. Publishes 70 titles/year. Receives 4,000 submissions/year. 20% of books from first-time authors; 80% from unagented writers. Pays royalty on actual receipts. Publishes book 18 months after acceptance. Reports in 1 month on queries. *Writer's Market* recommends allowing 2 months for reply. Writer's guidelines for SASE.

Nonfiction: Biography, coffee table book (limited), humor, illustrated book, juvenile, motivational, inspirational, Scottish. Subjects include Americana (especially Southern regional, Ozarks, Texas, Florida and Southwest); business (popular motivational, if author is a speaker); health; history; music (American artforms: jazz, blues, Cajun, R&B); politics (special interest in conservative viewpoint); recreation; religion (for popular audience mostly, but will consider others). *Travel*: Regional and international (especially areas in Pacific). *Motivational*: with business slant. *Inspirational*: author must be someone with potential for large audience. *Cookbooks*: "We look for authors with strong connection to restaurant industry or cooking circles, i.e. someone who can promote successfully." Query with SASE. "We require that a query be made first. This greatly expedites the review process and can save the writer additional postage expenses." No multiple queries or submissions. Reviews artwork/photos as part of ms package. Send photocopies only.

Recent Nonfiction Title: *Oswald Talked: The New Evidence in the JFK Assassination*, by Ray and Mary LaFontaine.

Fiction: Historical, humor, Southern, juvenile. "We publish maybe one novel a year, ususally by an author we already have. Almost all proposals are returned. We are most interested in Southern novels." No young adult, romance, science fiction, fantasy, gothic, mystery, erotica, confession, horror, sex or violence. Submit outline/synopsis and 2 sample chapters with SASE.

Recent Fiction Title: *Mimi and Jean-Paul's Cajun Mardi Gras*, by Alice Couvillon and Elizabeth Moore.

Tips: "We do extremely well with cookbooks, travel and popular histories. We will continue to build in these areas. The writer must have a clear sense of the market and this includes knowledge of the competition. A query letter should describe the project briefly, give the author's writing and professional credentials, and promotional ideas."

‡PENCIL POINT PRESS, INC., 277 Fairfield Rd., Fairfield NJ 07004. Publisher: Gene Garone. Publishes 12 titles/year. Receives 4 queries and 4 mss/year. 100% of books from first-time authors. Pays 5-16% royalty on retail price or makes outright purchase of $25-50/page. No advance. Publishes book 4 months after acceptance. Accepts simultaneous submissions. Reports in 2 months on proposals. Book catalog free on request.

Nonfiction: Reference, technical, textbook. Subjects include education, music, science, mathematics, language arts, ESL and special needs. Prefers supplemental resource materials for teachers grades K-12 and college (especially mathematics). Submit proposal package, including outline, 2 sample chapters and memo stating rationale and markets.

Tips: Audience is K-8 teachers, 9-12 teachers and college-level supplements. No children's trade books or poetry.

PENGUIN STUDIO, (formerly Viking Studio Books), Imprint of Penguin USA, 375 Hudson St., New York NY 10014. (212)366-2191. Contact: Michael Fragnito, publisher. Publishes hardcover originals. Publishes 35-40 titles/year. Receives 300 submissions/year. Less than 10% of books are from first-time authors; less than 5% from unagented writers. Publishes book 1 year after acceptance. Accepts simultaneous submissions. Reports in 2 months.

Nonfiction: Coffee table book, cookbook, gift book, illustrated book. Subjects include Americana, cooking/foods/nutrition, gardening, gay/lesbian, health/medicine, military/war, music/dance, photography, science, women's issues/studies, New Age/metaphysics. "We do not accept unsolicited material. We publish high-quality hardcover/trade books." Query. Agented submissions only. Reviews artwork as part of ms package. Send photocopies.

Recent Nonfiction Title: *Vision: The Life and Music of Hildegard von Bingen*, by Jane Bobko, with commentary by Matthew Fox and Barbara Newman.

Tips: "Often writers/agents misspell the publisher's name—be careful. It's hard to take someone seriously when those kinds of mistakes are the first thing the editor or publisher sees on a query letter or manuscript."

PENGUIN USA, 375 Hudson St., New York NY 10014. President: Peter Mayer. Imprints include Viking, Penguin, Viking Studio, Dutton, New American Library, Obelisk, Onyx, Plume, Roc, Signet, Topaz. Children's division: Cobblehill Books, Dial Books for Young Readers, Dutton's Children's Books, Lodestar Books, Puffin Books, Viking Children's Books. General interest publisher of both fiction and nonfiction. Query before submitting.
Recent Fiction: Stephen King.

PENNSYLVANIA HISTORICAL AND MUSEUM COMMISSION, Imprint of the Commonwealth of Pennsylvania, P.O. Box 1026, Harrisburg PA 17108-1026. (717)787-8099. Fax: (717)787-8312. Website: http://www.state.pa.us. Chief, Publications and Sales Division: Diane B. Reed. Estab. 1913. Publishes hardcover and paperback originals and reprints. Publishes 6-8 titles/year. Receives 25 submissions/year. Pays 5-10% royalty on retail price. Makes outright purchase or sometimes makes special assignments. Publishes book 18 months after acceptance. Accepts simultaneous submissions. Reports in 4 months. Prepare mss according to the *Chicago Manual of Style*.
Nonfiction: All books must be related to Pennsylvania, its history or culture: biography, illustrated books, reference, technical and historic travel. "The Commission seeks manuscripts on Pennsylvania, specifically on archaeology, history, art (decorative and fine), politics, and biography." Query or submit outline and sample chapters. Guidelines and proposal forms available.
Recent Nonfiction Title: *Prehistoric Cultures of Eastern Pennsylvania*, by Jay Custer (archaeology).
Tips: "Our audience is diverse—students, specialists and generalists—all of them interested in one or more aspects of Pennsylvania's history and culture. Manuscripts must be well researched and documented (footnotes not necessarily required depending on the nature of the manuscript) and interestingly written. Manuscripts must be factually accurate, but in being so, writers must not sacrifice style. We have a tradition of publishing scholarly and reference works, as well as more popularly styled books that reach an even broader audience."

PENNWELL BOOKS, PennWell Publishing, P.O. Box 1260, 1421 S. Sheridan Rd., Tulsa OK 74101-6619. Fax: (918)832-9319. Acquisitions Manager: Sue Rhodes Sesso. Estab. 1910. Publishes hardcover originals. Publishes 50 titles/year. Receives 200 queries and 75 mss/year. 25% of books from first-time authors; 99% from unagented writers. Pays 5-15% royalty on net receipts. Publishes book 9 months after acceptance of ms. Query with SASE, "but we expect all authors to keep their originals, and we cannot be held responsible for any submissions." Reports in 6 months on proposals. Book catalogs free on request; call 1-800-752-9764.
Nonfiction: Technical. Subjects include petroleum, dental, environmental, electric utility and municipal water. "Texts must have practical application for professionals in the markets we serve. Study our catalogs first before submitting anything. Your expertise as a practitioner within the specific industry is an essential component. We do *not* publish theory or philosophy, nor do we publish texts for the general public. We *do* publish practical, how-to, reference-type books only for the industries we serve." Submit proposal package, including table of contents, chapter-by-chapter synopsis, résumé and sample chapter(s). Reviews artwork/photos as part of ms package. Send photocopies.
Recent Nonfiction Titles: *Financing Energy Projects in Emerging Economics*, by Hossein Razair, Ph.D.
Tips: Audiences include: Petroleum—engineers, geologists, chemists, geophysicists, economists, managers. Environmental—petroleum industry people needing information on hazardous materials, safety and crisis management. Electric utility—managers and engineers in the power industry. Dental—practicing dentists and hygienists and their staffs. Water—municipal water practitioners in water and wastewater facilities.

‡PENNYWHISTLE PRESS, P.O. Box 734, Tesuque NM 87574. (505)982-0000. Fax: (505)982-0066. E-mail: poemsrus@aol.com. Managing Editor: Jeanie C. Williams. Publishes 6 titles/year. Receives 400 queries and 500 mss/year. 50% of books from first-time authors; 100% from unagented writers. Pays $100, chapbook plus 50 copies of book to author. Publishes book 1 year after acceptance. Accepts simultaneous submissions. Reports in 1 month on queries, 2 months on proposals, 3 months on mss. Book catalog for 9 × 12 SAE with 98¢ postage. Manuscript guidelines free on request.
• Pennywhistle publishes only poetry chapbooks.

MARKET CONDITIONS are constantly changing! If this is 1998 or later, buy the newest edition of *Writer's Market* at your favorite bookstore or order directly from Writer's Digest Books.

Poetry: Submit 30 sample poems.
Recent Poetry Title: *i saludos! Poems of New Mexico.*

THE PERMANENT PRESS/SECOND CHANCE PRESS, 4170 Noyac Rd., Sag Harbor NY 11963. (516)725-1101. Editor: Judith Shepard. Estab. 1978. Publishes hardcover originals. Permanent Press publishes literary fiction. Second Chance Press devotes itself exclusively to re-publishing fine books that are out of print and deserve continued recognition. Publishes 12 titles/year. Receives 7,000 submissions/year. 60% of books from first-time authors; 60% from unagented writers. Average print order for a first book is 2,000. Pays 10-20% royalty on wholesale price. Offers $1,000 advance for Permanent Press books; royalty only on Second Chance Press titles. Publishes book 18 months after acceptance. Accepts simultaneous submissions. Reports in 6 months on queries. Book catalog for 8×10 SAE with 7 first-class stamps. Manuscript guidelines for #10 SASE.
   ● Permanent Press does not employ readers and the number of submissions it receives has grown. If the writer sends a query or manuscript that the press is not interested in, we may reply in two or three weeks. But if there is interest, it may take 3 to 6 months.
Nonfiction: Biography, autobiography, historical. No scientific and technical material, academic studies. Query.
Fiction: Literary, mainstream, mystery. Especially looking for high line literary fiction, "original and arresting." No genre fiction. Query with first 20 pages.
Recent Fiction Title: *Castle Garden*, by Bill Alber (literary fiction).
Tips: "We are interested in the writing more than anything and long outlines are a turn-off. The SASE is vital to keep track of things, as we are receiving ever more submissions. We aren't looking for genre fiction but a compelling, well-written story."

PERMEABLE PRESS, 47 Noe St., #4, San Francisco CA 94114-1017. (415)255-9765. Publisher: Brian Clark. E-mail: bcclark@igc.apc.org. Website: http://www.armory.com/~jay/permeable.html. Publishes hardcover and trade paperback originals. Publishes 4-6 titles/year. Pays 10-20% royalty on wholesale price. Offers advance of $100 or more. Reports in 1 month. *Writer's Market* recommends allowing 2 months for reply.
Fiction: "Permeable publishes 'high risk' fiction that other publishers cannot stomach, but which is too good to go unpublished. Become familiar with the books we publish and the alternative fiction market in general. Read one of our magazines." Query with SASE.
Recent Fiction Title: *The Elements of Style*, by Sarah Hafner (adult fiction).
Tips: "Writers are encouraged to sample published work of our website to get a better feel of what we like."

PETER PAUPER PRESS, INC., 202 Mamaroneck Ave., White Plains NY 10601-5376. Fax: (914)681-0389. Creative Director: Solomon M. Skolnick. Estab. 1928. Publishes hardcover originals. Publishes 36-50 titles/year. Receives 450-500 queries and 150-200 mss/year. 2% of books from first-time authors; 99% from unagented writers. Publishes ms 9-15 months after acceptance. Reports in 1 month. *Writer's Market* recommends allowing 2 months for reply. Book catalog for $1. Manuscript guidelines for #10 SASE.
Nonfiction: Subjects include gardening, friendship, illustrated small-format gift books for special events and occasions (Valentines Day, Mother's Day, Christmas, etc.). "We do not publish narrative works. We publish collections of brief quotes, aphorisms, and wise sayings. Do not send us prescriptive material, how-to, or practical material." Submit outline with SASE. Reviews artwork as part of ms package. Send color photocopies or transparencies, not original art.
Recent Nonfiction Title: *Angels In Our Midst*, by Suzanne Siegel (with compact disc).
Tips: "Our readers are primarily female, 35 and over, who are likely to buy a 'gift' book in a stationery, gift or boutique store. Writers should become familiar with our previously published work. We publish hardcovers only—56-80 pages depending upon format."

PETERSON'S, P.O. Box 2123, Princeton NJ 08543-2123. (800)338-3282. Chief Executive Officer: Peter W. Hegener. President, Publishing: Carole Cushmore. Estab. 1966. Publishes trade and reference books. Publishes 55-75 titles/year. Receives 200-250 submissions/year. 10% of books from first-time authors; 20% from unagented writers. Average print order for a first book is 10,000-15,000. Pays 10-12% royalty on net sales. Offers advance. Publishes book 1 year after acceptance. Reports in 2 months. Book catalog free.
Nonfiction: Business, careers, education, parenting and family books, as well as educational and career directories. Submit complete ms or detailed outline and sample chapters. *Writer's Market* recommends query with SASE first. Looks for "appropriateness of contents to our markets, author's credentials, and writing style suitable for audience." Reviews artwork/photos as part of ms package.
Recent Nonfiction Title: *Conservative Innovation.*

PHI DELTA KAPPA EDUCATIONAL FOUNDATION, P.O. Box 789, Bloomington IN 47402. (812)339-1156. Fax: (812)339-0018. E-mail: special.pubs@pdkintl.org. Website: http://www.pdkintl.org. Editor of Special Publications: Donovan R. Walling. Publishes hardcover and trade paperback originals. Publishes 24-30 titles/year. Receives 100 queries and 50-60 mss/year. 50% of books from first-time authors; 100% from unagented writers. Pays honorarium of $500-5,000. Publishes book 6-9 months after acceptance of ms. Reports in 3 months on proposals. Book catalog and ms guidelines free on request.

Nonfiction: How-to, reference, essay collections. Subjects include child guidance/parenting, education, and legal issues. "We publish books for educators—K-12 and higher ed. Our professional books are often used in college courses but are never specifically designed as textbooks." Query with outline and 1 sample chapter. Reviews artwork/photos as part of ms package.

Recent Nonfiction Title: *When Learned Men Murder*, by David Patterson (essays).

PHILOMEL BOOKS, Division of The Putnam Publishing Group, 200 Madison Ave., New York NY 10016. (212)951-8700. Editorial Director: Patricia Lee Gauch. Associate Editor: Michael Green. Assistant Editor: David Briggs. Estab. 1980. Publishes hardcover originals. Publishes 25-30 titles/year. Receives 2,600 submissions/year. 15% of books from first-time authors; 30% from unagented writers. Pays standard royalty. Advance negotiable. Publishes book 2 years after acceptance. Reports in 1 month on queries, 3 months on unsolicited mss. Book catalog for 9 × 12 SAE with 4 first-class stamps. Request book catalog from marketing department of Putnam Publishing Group.

Fiction: Children's picture books (ages 3-8); middle-grade fiction and illustrated chapter books (ages 7-10); and young adult novels (ages 10-15). Particularly interested in picture book mss with original stories and regional fiction with a distinct voice. Historical fiction OK. Unsolicited mss accepted for picture books only; query first for long fiction. Always include SASE. No series or activity books.

Tips: "We prefer a very brief synopsis that states the basic premise of the story. This will help us determine whether or not the manuscript is suited to our list. If applicable, we'd be interested in knowing the author's writing experience or background knowledge. We are always looking for beautifully written manuscripts with stories that engage. We try to be less influenced by the swings of the market than in the power, value, essence of the manuscript itself."

‡PHILOSOPHY DOCUMENTATION CENTER, Bowling Green State University, Bowling Green OH 43403-0189. (419)372-2419, (800)444-2419. Fax: (419)372-6987. Director: Dr. George Leaman. Publishes 4 titles/year. Receives 4-6 queries and 4-6 mss/year. 50% of books from first-time authors. Pays 2½-10% royalty. Publishes book 6 months after acceptance. Reports in 2 months. Book catalog free on request.

Nonfiction: Textbook, software, guidebooks, directories. "We want to increase our range of philosophical titles and are especially interested in electronic publishing." Query with outline.

Recent Nonfiction Title: *Philosophy in Cyberspace*, by Dey Alexander (reference).

PICCADILLY BOOKS, P.O. Box 25203, Colorado Springs CO 80936-5203. (719)548-1844. Publisher: Bruce Fife. Estab. 1985. Publishes hardcover and trade paperback originals and trade paperback reprints. Publishes 3-8 titles/year. Receives 300 submissions/year. 70% of books from first-time authors; 95% from unagented writers. Pays 5-10% royalty on retail price. Publishes book 1 year after acceptance. Accepts simultaneous submissions. Responds only if interested.

Nonfiction: How-to books on entertainment, humor and performing arts. "We have a strong interest in subjects on clowning, magic, puppetry and related arts, including comedy skits and dialogs." Query with sample chapters.

Recent Nonfiction Title: *The World's Funniest Clown Skits*, by Barry DeChant.

PICTON PRESS, Imprint of Picton Corp., P.O. Box 250, Rockport ME 04856-0250. (207)236-6565. Fax: (207)236-6713. E-mail: picton@midcoast.com. Website: http://www.midcoast.com/~picton. Imprints are Picton Press, Penobscot Press (contact Lew Rohrbach), Cricketfield Press. Publishes hardcover and mass market paperback originals and reprints. Publishes 30 titles/year. Receives 30 queries and 15 mss/year. 50% of books from first-time authors; 100% from unagented writers. Pays 0-10% royalty on wholesale price or makes outright purchase. Publishes book 6 months after acceptance of ms. Reports in 2 months on queries and proposals, 3 months on mss. Book catalog free on request.

Nonfiction: Reference, textbook. Subjects include Americana, genealogy, history, vital records. Query with outline.

Recent Nonfiction Title: *Bibliography of Swiss Genealogies*, by Mario von Moos.

‡PIERIAN PRESS, P.O. Box 1808, Ann Arbor MI 48108. (313)434-5530. Publisher: C. Edward Wall. Publishes hardcover and trade paperback originals, hardcover reprints. Publishes 10 titles/year. Pays 10-15% royalty on wholesale price. No advance. Book catalog and ms guidelines free on request.

Nonfiction: Reference, textbook. Subjects include agriculture/horticulture, business and economics, education, government/politics, health/medicine, history, music/dance, nature/environment, philosophy, psychology, religion, sociology, library and information science. Query.

‡THE PILGRIM PRESS, United Church Board for Homeland Ministries, 700 Prospect Ave. E., Cleveland OH 44115-1100. (216)736-3700. Fax: (216)736-3703. E-mail: brownr@ucc.org. Editorial Director: Richard E. Brown. Publishes hardcover and trade paperback originals. Publishes 20 titles/year. 20% of books from first-time authors; 100% from unagented writers. Pays standard royalties and advances where appropriate.

Publishes book an average of 18 months after acceptance. Reports in 3 months on queries. Book catalog and ms guidelines free on request.

Nonfiction: Ethics, social issues with a strong commitment to justice—addressing such topics as public policy, sexuality and gender, economics, medicine, gay and lesbian concerns, human rights, minority liberation and the environment—primarily in a Christian context, but not exclusively.

Recent Nonfiction Title: *Toward the Beloved Community: Martin Luther King Jr. and South Africa.*

Tips: "We are concentrating more on academic and trade submissions. Writers should send books about contemporary social issues. Our audience is liberal, open-minded, socially aware, feminist, church members and clergy, teachers and seminary professors."

PILOT BOOKS, 103 Cooper St., Babylon NY 11702-2319. (516)422-2225. Fax: (516)422-2227. President: Sam Small. Estab. 1959. Publishes paperback originals. Publishes 20-30 titles/year. Receives 100-200 submissions/year. 20% of books from first-time authors; 90% from unagented writers. Average print order for a first book is 3,000. Offers standard royalty contract based on wholesale or retail price. Offers $250 usual advance, but this varies, depending on author's reputation and nature of book. Publishes book an average of 8 months after acceptance. Reports in 1 month. *Writer's Market* recommends allowing 2 months for reply. Book catalog and guidelines for #10 SASE.

Nonfiction: Financial, business, travel, career, personal guides and training manuals. "Our training manuals are utilized by America's major corporations, as well as the government. Directories and books on travel and moneymaking opportunities. Wants clear, concise treatment of subject matter." Length: 8,000-30,000 words. Send outline. Reviews artwork/photos as part of ms package.

Recent Nonfiction Title: *The Hotel/Motel Special Program and Discount Guide*, by Boe and Philcox.

PINEAPPLE PRESS, INC., P.O. Box 3899, Sarasota FL 34230. (813)952-1085. Editor: June Cussen. Estab. 1982. Publishes hardcover and trade paperback originals. Publishes 20 titles/year. Receives 1,500 submissions/year. 20% of books from first-time authors; 80% from unagented writers. Pays 6½-15% royalty on retail price. Seldom offers advance. Publishes book 18 months after acceptance. Accepts simultaneous submissions. Reports in 3 months. Book catalog for 9×12 SAE with $1.05 postage.

Nonfiction: Biography, how-to, reference, regional (Florida), nature. Subjects include animals, history, gardening, nature. "We will consider most nonfiction topics. We are seeking quality nonfiction on diverse topics for the library and book trade markets. Most, though not all, of our fiction and nonfiction deals with Florida." No pop psychology or autobiographies. Query or submit outline/brief synopsis, sample chapters and SASE.

Recent Nonfiction Title: *Tellable Cracker Tales*, by Annette Bruce (folktales).

Fiction: Literary, historical, mainstream, regional (Florida). No romance, science fiction, children's. Submit outline/brief synopsis and sample chapters.

Recent Fiction Title: *Death in Bloodhound Red*, by Virginia Lanier.

Tips: "If I were a writer trying to market a book today, I would learn everything I could about book publishing and book publicity and agree to actively participate in promoting my book. A query on a novel without a brief sample seems useless."

PIPPIN PRESS, 229 E. 85th St., P.O. Box 1347, Gracie Station, New York NY 10028. (212)288-4920. Fax: (908)225-1562. Publisher/President: Barbara Francis. Estab. 1987. Publishes hardcover originals. Publishes 4-6 titles/year. Receives 4,500 queries/year. 80% of queries from unagented writers. Pays royalty. Publishes book 2 years after acceptance. Query with SASE. Do *not* send mss. Reports in 3 weeks on queries. *Writer's Market* recommends allowing 2 months for reply. Book catalog for 6×9 SASE. Manuscript guidelines for #10 SASE.

Nonfiction: Children's books: biography, humor, picture books. Subjects include animals, history, language/literature, nature, science. General nonfiction for children ages 4-10. Query with SASE only. Reviews artwork/photos as part of ms package. Send photocopies.

Fiction: Adventure, fantasy, historical, humor, mystery, picture books, suspense. "We're looking for small chapter books with animal-fantasy themes, stories for 7-11 year olds, by people of many cultures." Wants humorous fiction for ages 7-11. Query with SASE only.

Recent Fiction Title: *Abigail's Drum*, by John A. Minahan, illustrated by Robert Quackenbush.

Tips: "Read as many of the best children's books published in the last five years as you can. We are looking for multi-ethnic fiction and nonfiction for ages 7-10, as well as general fiction for this age group. I would pay particular attention to children's books favorably reviewed in *School Library Journal, The Booklist, The New York Times Book Review*, and *Publishers Weekly*."

PLANNERS PRESS, Imprint of American Planning Association, 122 S. Michigan Ave., Chicago IL 60603. Acting Executive Director: Frank So. Publishes hardcover and trade paperback originals. Publishes 4-6 titles/year. Receives 20 queries and 6-8 mss/year. 50% of books from first-time authors; 100% from unagented writers. Pays 7½-12% royalty on retail price. Publishes book 1 year after acceptance. Reports in 1 month on queries, 2 months on proposals and mss. Book catalog and ms guidelines free on request.

Nonfiction: Technical (specialty-public policy and city planning). Subjects include government/politics. "Our books have a narrow audience of city planners and often focus on the tools of city planning." Submit 2 sample chapters and table of contents. Reviews artwork/photos as part of ms package. Send photocopies.
Recent Nonfiction Title: *What Planners Do*, by Charles Hoch (essay).

PLANNING/COMMUNICATIONS, 7215 Oak Ave., River Forest IL 60305. (708)366-5200. President: Daniel Lauber. Publishes hardcover, trade and mass market paperback originals, trade paperback reprints. Publishes 3-8 titles/year. Receives 10 queries and 3 mss/year. 50% of books from first-time authors; 100% from unagented writers. Pays 15-20% royalty on net sales. Publishes book 6 months after acceptance of ms. Accepts simultaneous submissions. Reports in 2 months on queries, 3 months on proposals and mss. Book catalog for $1.95. Manuscript guidelines for #10 SASE.
 ● Planning/Communications no longer seeks mysteries.
Nonfiction: Self-help, careers. Subjects include business and economics (careers), education, government/politics, money/finance, sociology, software. Submit outline and 3 sample chapters with SASE. Reviews artwork/photos as part of ms package. Send photocopies.
Recent Nonfiction Title: *Professional's Job Finder*, D. Lauber (trade).

PLAYERS PRESS, INC., P.O. Box 1132, Studio City CA 91614-0132. (818)789-4980. Vice President, Editorial: Robert W. Gordon. Estab. 1965. Publishes hardcover and trade paperback originals, and trade paperback reprints. Publishes 25-35 titles/year. Receives 200-1,000 submissions/year. 10% of books from first-time authors; 80% from unagented writers. Pays royalty on wholesale price. Publishes book 20 months after acceptance. Reports on queries in 1 month, up to 1 year on mss. Book catalog and guidelines for 9 × 12 SAE with 4 first-class stamps.
Nonfiction: Juvenile and theatrical drama/entertainment industry. Subjects include the performing arts, costume, theater and film crafts. Needs quality plays and musicals, adult or juvenile. Query. Reviews artwork/photos as part of package.
Fiction: Subject matter of plays include adventure, confession, ethnic, experimental, fantasy, historical, horror, humor, mainstream, mystery, religious, romance, science fiction, suspense, western. Submit complete ms for theatrical plays only. "No novels or story books are accepted. We publish plays, musicals and books on theatre, film and television, only."
Tips: "Plays, entertainment industry texts, theater, film and television books have the only chances of selling to our firm."

‡**PLEASANT COMPANY PUBLICATIONS**, Imprint of American Girls Collection®. 8400 Fairway Pl., Middleton WI 53562. Fax: (608)836-1999. Submissions Editor: Jennifer Hirsch. Publishes hardcover and trade paperback originals. Publishes 3-25 title/year. Receives 100 queries and 75 mss/year. 50% of books from unagented writers. Pays royalty. Advance varies. Accepts simultaneous submissions. Reports in 2 months. Book catalog free on request.
Nonfiction: Children's/juvenile. Subjects include Americana. "Our audience is girls ages 7-12. We also publish for the education market." Query.
Recent Nonfiction Title: *Help! An Absolutely Indispensible Guide to Life for Girls*, by Nancy Molyoke.
Fiction: Juvenile. Query.

PLENUM PUBLISHING, 233 Spring St., New York NY 10013-1578. (212)620-8000. Executive Editor, Trade Books: Linda Greenspan Regan. Estab. 1946. Publishes hardcover originals. Publishes 350 titles/year; Plenum Trade publishes 12. Receives 1,000 submissions/year. 20% of books from first-time authors; 20% from unagented writers. Publishes book 8-16 months after acceptance. Accepts simultaneous submissions. Reports in 6-8 months.
Nonfiction: Subjects include trade science, criminology, anthropology, mathematics, sociology, psychology, health. "We are seeking high quality, popular books in the sciences and social sciences." Query only.
Tips: "Our audience consists of intelligent laymen and professionals. Authors should be experts on subject matter of book. They must compare their books with competitive works, explain how theirs differs, and define the market for their books."

POCKET BOOKS, Division of Simon & Schuster, Dept. WM, 1230 Avenue of the Americas, New York NY 10020. Imprints include Pocket Books, Washington Square Press (high-quality mass market), Archway and Minstrel (juvenile/YA imprints), Folger Shakespeare Library, Star Trek. Publishes paperback originals and reprints, mass market and trade paperbacks and hardcovers. Publishes 450 titles/year. Receives 5,000 submissions/year. 15% of books from first-time authors; 100% from agented writers. Pays royalty on retail price. Publishes book an average of 1 year after acceptance. *No unsolicited mss or queries.* "All submissions must go through a literary agent."
Nonfiction: History, biography, reference and general nonfiction, humor, calendars.
Fiction: Adult (mysteries, thriller, psychological suspense, Star Trek ® novels, romance, westerns).

POLYCHROME PUBLISHING CORPORATION, 4509 N. Francisco, Chicago IL 60625. (312)478-4455. Contact: Editorial Board. Publishes hardcover originals and reprints. Publishes 4 titles/year. Receives

3,000 queries and 7,500-8,000 mss/year. 50% of books from first-time authors; 100% from unagented writers. Pays royalty, "usually a combination of fee plus royalties." Advance "depends upon amount of editorial work necessary." Publishes book 2 years after acceptance. Accepts simultaneous submissions. Reports in 8 months on mss. Book catalog and ms guidelines for #10 SASE.

Nonfiction: Children's/juvenile. Subjects emphasize ethnic, particularly multicultural/Asian-American. Submit outline and 3 sample chapters. Reviews artwork/photos as part of ms package, but not necessary. Send photocopies.

Fiction: Multicultural, particularly Asian-American. Ethnic, juvenile, picture books, young adult. "We do not publish fables, folktales, fairytales or anthropomorphic animal stories." Submit synopsis and 3 sample chapters; for picture books, submit whole ms.

Recent Fiction Title: *Thanksgiving at Obachan's*, by Janet Mitsui Brown (picture).

‡POPULAR CULTURE INK, P.O. Box 1839, Ann Arbor MI 48106. (313)761-4300. Publisher: Tom Schultheiss. Publishes hardcover originals and reprints. Publishes 4-6 titles/year. Receives 50 queries and 20 mss/year. 100% of books from first-time authors; 100% from unagented writers. Pays variable royalty on wholesale price. Offers variable advance. Publishes book 2 years after acceptance. Accepts simultaneous submissions. Reports in 1 month. *Writer's Market* recommends allowing 2 months for reply. Book catalog and ms guidelines free on request.

Nonfiction: Reference. Subjects include music/dance, popular entertainment. Query.

Recent Nonfiction Title: *Reelin' & Rockin'*, by Lee Colter (music history).

Tips: Audience is libraries, avid collectors. "Know your subject backwards. Make sure your book is unique."

‡PRAEGER PUBLISHERS, Imprint of the Greenwood Publishing Group, Inc., 88 Post Road W., Westport CT 06881. (203)226-3571. Fax: (203)226-6009. General Manager: Jim Dunton. Estab. 1950. Publishes hardcover originals and reprints and trade paperback originals. Publishes 280 titles/year. Receives 1,200 submissions/year. 5% of books from first-time authors; 90% from unagented writers. Pays 6½-15% royalty on net sales. Advance offered varies. Publishes book an average of 9 months after acceptance. Accepts simultaneous submissions. Reports in 1 month. *Writer's Market* recommends allowing 2 months for reply. Book catalog and manuscript guidelines free on request.

Nonfiction: "We are looking for women's studies, sociology, psychology, education, contemporary history, military studies, political science, business, economics, international relations, philosophy. No language and literature." Query or submit outline and sample chapters.

Recent Nonfiction Title: *An American Paradox: Censorship in a Nation of Free Speech*, by Patrick Garry.

PRAKKEN PUBLICATIONS, INC., P.O. Box 8623, Ann Arbor MI 48107-8623. (313)769-1211. Fax: (313)769-8383. Publisher: George Kennedy. Managing Editor: Susanne Peckham. Estab. 1934. Publishes educational hardcover and paperback originals as well as educational magazines. Publishes 4 book titles/year. Receives 50 submissions/year. 20% of books from first-time authors; 95% from unagented writers. Pays 10% royalty on net sales (negotiable, with production costs). Publishes book 1 year after acceptance. Accepts simultaneous submissions. Reports in 2 months if reply requested and SASE furnished. Book catalog for #10 SASE.

Nonfiction: Industrial, vocational and technology education and related areas; general educational reference. "We are interested in manuscripts with broad appeal in any of the specific subject areas of industrial arts, vocational-technical education, and reference for the general education field." Submit outline and sample chapters. Reviews artwork/photos as part of ms package.

Recent Nonfiction Title: *Technology's Past*, by D. Karwatka.

Tips: "We have a continuing interest in magazine and book manuscripts which reflect emerging issues and trends in education, especially vocational, industrial, and technological education."

PRECEPT PRESS, Subsidiary of Bonus Books, 160 E. Illinois St., Chicago IL 60611. (312)467-0424. Website: www.bonus-books.com. Managing Editor: Deborah Flapan. Publishes hardcover and trade paperback originals. Publishes 20 titles/year. Receives 300 queries and 100 mss/year. 25% of books from first-time authors; 90% from unagented writers. Pays royalty. Publishes book 8 months after acceptance. Accepts simultaneous submissions if so noted. Reports in 3 months on proposals. Manuscript guidelines for #10 SASE.

Nonfiction: Including reference, technical, clinical, textbook. Subjects include business, CD-Rom, medical and oncology texts. Query with SASE.

Recent Nonfiction Title: *Nutritional Care for High-Risk Newborns*, by Sharon Groh-Wargo, Melody Thompson and Janice Hovasi Cox (neonatal nutrition).

PREP PUBLISHING, Subsidiary of PREP, Inc., 1110½ Hay St., Fayetteville NC 28305. (910)483-6611. Managing Editor: Anne McKinney. Imprints are Mysterious PREP (contact Anne McKinney); Religious/spiritual PREP (contact Pat Mack); Young Adult (YA) PREP (contact Louise Jarvis); Nonfiction PREP (contact Anne McKinney). Publishes hardcover and trade paperback originals. Publishes 10 titles/year. Receives 3000 queries/year. 30% of books from first-time authors; 90% from unagented writers. Pays 6-17%

royalty on retail price. Publishes book 18 months after acceptance of ms. Accepts simultaneous submissions. Reports in 3 months on mss. Manuscript guidelines for SASE.

Nonfiction: Biography, children's/juvenile, how-to, humor, self-help, career advice. Subjects include Americana, business and economics, money/finance (self-help, how-to), philosophy, psychology, regional (especially the South), religion, women's issues/studies. Query with SASE. Reviews artwork/photos as part of ms package. Send photocopies.

Recent Nonfiction Title: *Résumés & Cover Letters That Have Worked*, edited by Anne McKinney (self-help for people changing fields/jobs).

Fiction: Adventure, historical, horror, humor, juvenile, literary, mainstream/contemporary, mystery, religious, romance, science fiction, suspense, western, young adult. "We seek fiction for a wide general audience." Query with SASE.

Recent Fiction Title: *Second Time Around*, by Patty Sleem (Christian fiction presented as a murder mystery/psychological thriller).

Poetry: Query with SASE.

Tips: "Wide general audience of adults for most of our books. We have a strong interest in biographies of interesting people—entrepreneurs, leaders in all fields, and others."

PRICE STERN SLOAN, INC., Member of the Putnam & Grosset Group, New York, 11835 Olympic Blvd., 5th Floor, Los Angeles CA 90064-5006. Fax: (310)445-3933. Juvenile submissions to Submissions Editor. Adult calendar submissions to Bob Lovka. Estab. 1963. Imprints are Troubador Press, Wee Sing®, Doodle Art®, Mad Libs®, Mad Mysteries®, Serendipity®. Publishes trade paperback originals. Publishes 80 titles/year (95% children's). Receives 3,000 submissions/year. 20% of books from first-time authors; 20% from unagented writers. Pays royalty on net retail or makes outright purchase. Offers advance. Publishes book 1 year after acceptance. Reports in 3 months. Catalog for 9×12 SAE with 5 first-class stamps. Manuscript guidelines for SASE.

● Price Stern Sloan currently has smaller print runs and fewer titles per list.

Nonfiction: Subjects include humor, calendars and satire (limited). Juvenile fiction and nonfiction (all ages). Query *only*. Reviews artwork/photos as part of ms package. Do not send *original* artwork or ms. "Most of our titles are unique in concept as well as execution."

Tips: "We have been assigning a lot of work-for-hires for ongoing series. But writers must have a proven track record in those formats. As electronic technology flourishes, the lines between traditional publishing and new media blur. As our books tie in with movies, TV, toys, games, animated characters and more, I imagine our products will expand as the new media grows. We think our edginess makes us quite distinct in the children's publishing arena."

PRIMA PUBLISHING, P.O. Box 1260, Rocklin CA 95677-1260. (916)768-0426. Publisher: Ben Dominitz, Lifestyles Division: Senior Acquisitions Editor, Jennifer Bayse-Sander. Computer Professional Reference Division: Senior Acquisitions Editor, Sherri Morningstar. Entertainment Division: Senior Acquisitions Editor, Hartley Lesser. Publishes hardcover originals and trade paperback originals and reprints. Publishes 300 titles/year. Receives 750 queries/year. 10% of books from first-time authors; 30% from unagented writers. Pays 15-20% royalty on wholesale price. Advance varies. Publishes book 12 months after acceptance. Accepts simultaneous submissions. Query for electronic submissions. Reports in 3 months. Catalog for 9×12 SAE with 8 first-class stamps. Writer's guidelines for #10 SASE.

Nonfiction: Biography, cookbook, how-to, self-help, travel. Subjects include business and economics, cooking/foods, health, music, politics, psychology. "We want books with originality, written by highly qualified individuals. No fiction at this time." Query with SASE.

Recent Nonfiction Title: *Gooey Desserts*, by Elaine Corn (cookbook).

Tips: "Prima strives to reach the primary and secondary markets for each of its books. We are known for promoting our books aggressively. Books that genuinely solve problems for people will always do well if properly promoted. Try to picture the intended audience while writing the book. Too many books are written to an audience that doesn't exist."

PROFESSIONAL PUBLICATIONS, INC., 1250 Fifth Ave., Belmont CA 94002-3863. (415)593-9119. Fax: (415)592-4519. Acquisitions Editor: Gerald Galbo. Estab. 1975. Publishes hardcover and paperback originals. Publishes 12 titles/year. Receives 100-200 submissions/year. Publishes book 18 months after acceptance. Accepts simultaneous submissions. Reports in 2 weeks on queries. *Writer's Market* recommends allowing 2 months for reply. Book catalog and ms guidelines free.

● Professional Publications wants only professionals practicing in the field to submit material.

Nonfiction: Reference, technical, textbook. Subjects include mathematics, engineering, architecture, interior design. Especially needs "review books for all professional licensing examinations." Query or submit outline and sample chapters. Reviews artwork/photos as part of ms package.

Tips: "We specialize in books for working professionals: engineers, architects, contractors, interior designing, etc. The more technically complex the manuscript is the happier we are. We love equations, tables of data, complex illustrations, mathematics, etc. In technical/professional book publishing, it isn't always obvious to us if a market exists. We can judge the quality of a manuscript, but the author should make some effort to convince us that a market exists. Facts, figures, and estimates about the market—and marketing ideas from the author—will help sell us on the work. Besides our interest in highly technical materials, we will be trying to broaden our range of titles in each discipline. Specifically, we will be looking for career guides for interior designers and architects, as well as for engineers."

PROFESSIONAL RESOURCE PRESS, Imprint of Professional Resource Exchange, Inc., 2033 Wood St., Suite 215, Sarasota FL 34237. (941)366-7913. Managing Editor: Debra Fink. Publishes trade paperback originals. Publishes 15 titles/year. Receives 100 queries and 80 mss/year. 50% of books from first-time authors; 100% from unagented writers. Pays 6-10% royalty on wholesale price. Publishes book 1 year after acceptance of ms. No simultaneous submissions. Reports in 6 months. Book catalog and ms guidelines free on request.
Nonfiction: Reference, textbook; books for mental health professionals. "Authors must be mental health professionals and works must be highly applied and focused." Submit outline, professional résumé/cv and 2-4 sample chapters.
Recent Nonfiction Title: *Assessing Allegations of Child Sexual Abuse*, by Kathryn Kuehnle.

‡PROLINGUA ASSOCIATES, 15 Elm St., Brattleboro VT 05301. (802)207-7779. Senior Editor: Raymond C. Clark. Publisher: Arthur A. Burrows. Estab. 1980. Publishes paperback originals. Publishes 6 titles/year. Receives 30-50 submissions/year. 25% of books from first-time authors; 100% from unagented writers. Pays 5-10% royalty on net sales. Publishes book 1 year after acceptance. Accepts simultaneous submissions. Reports in 2 weeks on queries. *Writer's Market* recommends allowing 2 months for reply. Book catalog for 9 × 12 SAE with 4 first-class stamps.
Nonfiction: Reference, textbook. Subjects include English as a second language, French and Spanish. "We are always willing to consider innovative language texts and language teacher resources which fit with our approach to language teaching. Also interested in intercultural training." Query or submit outline and sample chapters.
Tips: "Get a catalog of our books, take a couple of books by ProLingua out of the library or from a nearby language department, ask about ProLingua, and in general try to determine whether your book would fit into ProLingua's list."

PROMPT PUBLICATIONS, Imprint of Howard W. Sams & Co., A Bell Atlantic Company, 2647 Waterfront Parkway E. Dr., Suite 300, Indianapolis IN 46214-2041. Fax: (317)298-5604. Contact: Candace Lake. Publishes trade paperback originals and reprints. Publishes 20 titles/year. Receives 30-40 queries and 25 mss/year. 60% of books from first-time authors; 90% from unagented writers. Pays negotiable royalty on wholesale price. Publishes book 1 year after acceptance of ms. Reports in 1 month on queries, 2 months on proposals, 4 months or more on mss. Book catalog free on request.
Nonfiction: How-to, reference, technical. Subjects include audio/visual, computers and electronics, electronics repair, science (electricity). "Books should be written for beginners *and* experts, hobbyists *and* professionals. Books on home electronics (stereos, etc.,) are a plus." Query with proposal package, including author bio, outline, 3 sample chapters and SASE. Reviews artwork/photos as part of ms package. Send photocopies or sketches ("we have technicians to produce illustrations if necessary").
Recent Nonfiction Title: *Electrical Wiring*, by Arthur C. Seale, Jr. (technical).
Tips: Audience is electronics/technical hobbyists, professionals needing reference books, and technical schools. "Please keep in mind that most technical books have a short shelf life, and write accordingly. Remember, also, that it takes a while for a book to be published, so keep notes on updating some of your material when the book is ready to go to print. *When submitting:* Above all, *Be patient.* It can take up to a year for a publisher to decide whether or not to publish your book."

PRUETT PUBLISHING, 2928 Pearl St., Boulder CO 80301. (303)449-4919. Fax: (303)443-9019. Publisher: Jim Pruett. Editor: Mary Kay Scott. Estab. 1959. Publishes hardcover paperback and trade paperback originals and reprints. Publishes 10-15 titles/year. 60% of books are from first-time authors; 100% from unagented writers. Pays 10-12% royalty on net income. Publishes book 18 months after acceptance. Accepts simultaneous submissions. Reports in 2 months on queries. Book catalog and ms guidelines free.
• Pruett Publishing is no longer seeking coffee table books, child guidance/parenting books or railroad histories.
Nonfiction: Regional history, guidebooks, nature, biography. Subjects include Americana (Western), archaeology (Native American), history (Western), nature/environment, recreation (outdoor), regional/ethnic cooking/foods (Native American, Mexican, Spanish), regional travel, regional sports (cycling, hiking, fishing). "We are looking for nonfiction manuscripts and guides that focus on the Rocky Mountain West." Reviews artwork/photos and formal proposal as part of ms package.
Recent Nonfiction Title: *Flyfishing the Yellowstone River: An Angler's Guide*, by Rod Walinehus (flyfishing guide book).
Tips: "There has been a movement away from large publisher's mass market books and towards small publisher's regional interest books, and in turn distributors and retail outlets are more interested in small publishers. Authors don't need to have a big-name to have a good publisher. Look for similar books that

you feel are well produced—consider design, editing, overall quality and contact those publishers. Get to know several publishers, and find the one that feels right—trust your instincts."

‡PRUFROCK PRESS, P.O. Box 8813, Waco TX 76714. (817)756-3337. Website: http://www.prufrock.c om. Publisher: Joel McIntosh. Publishes trade paperback originals and reprints. Publishes 15 titles/year. Receives 150 queries and 50 mss/year. 50% of books from first-time authors; 100% from unagented writers. Pays 10% royalty on wholesale price. Publishes book 9 months after acceptance of ms. Reports in 2 months. Book catalog and manuscript guidelines free on request.
Nonfiction: Children's/juvenile, how-to, textbook. Subjects include child guidance/parenting, education. "We publish for the education market. Our readers are typically teachers or parents of gifted and talented children. Many authors send us classroom activity books. Our product line is built around professional development books for teachers. While some of our books may include activities, many are included to illustrate a teaching concept on strategies, or strategy in use at an application level." Submit proposal package, including outline, 2 sample chapters, statement of purpose, audience and need. Reviews artwork/photos as part of ms package. Send photocopies.
Recent Nonfiction Title: *Coping for Capable Kids*, by Dr. Leonora M. Cohen and Dr. Erica Frydenberg.
Tips: Audience is teachers and parents of gifted and talented children. "We are one of the larger independent education publishers; however, we have worked hard to offer authors a friendly, informal atmosphere. Authors should feel comfortable calling up and bouncing an idea off of us or writing us to get our opinion of a new project idea."

PSI RESEARCH, 300 N. Valley Dr., Grants Pass OR 97526. (503)479-9464. Fax: (503)476-1479. Contact: Emmett Ramey. Estab. 1975. Imprint is Oasis Press. Publishes hardcover, trade paperback and binder origi- nals. Publishes 20-30 books/year. Receives 90 submissions/year. 60% of books from first-time authors; 90% from unagented writers. Pays royalty. Publishes book 1 year after acceptance. Accepts simultaneous submissions. Reports in 2 months (initial feedback) on queries. Book catalog and ms guidelines free.
Nonfiction: How-to, reference, textbook. Subjects include business and economics, computers, education, money/finance, retirement, exporting, franchise, finance, marketing and public relations, relocations, environ- ment, taxes, business start up and operation. Needs information-heavy, readable mss written by professionals in their subject fields. Interactive where appropriate. Authorship credentials less important than hands-on experience qualifications. Must relate to either small business or to individuals who are entrepreneurs, owners or managers of small business (1-300 employees). Query for unwritten material or to check current interest in topic and orientation. Submit outline/synopsis and sample chapters. Reviews artwork/photos as part of ms package.
Recent Nonfiction Title: *Successful Network Marketing for the 21st Century*, by Rod Nichols.
Tips: "Best chance is with practical, step-by-step manuals for operating a business, with worksheets, check- lists. The audience is made up of entrepreneurs of all types: small businesses and those who would like to be; attorneys, accountants and consultants who work with small businesses; college students; dreamers. Make sure your information is valid and timely for its audience, also that by virtue of either its content quality or viewpoint, it distinguishes itself from other books on the market."

PUBLISHERS ASSOCIATES, P.O. Box 140361, Las Colinas TX 75014-0361. (214)686-5332. Senior Editor: Belinda Buxjom. Manuscript Coordinator: Mary Markal. Estab. 1974. Imprints are Hercules Press, The Liberal Press, Liberal Arts Press, Minuteman Press, Monument Press, Nichole Graphics, Scholars Books, Tagelwüld. Publishes trade paperback originals. Publishes 20 titles/year. Receives 1,500 submissions/year. 60% of books from first-time authors; 100% from unagented writers. Pays 4% and up royalty on retail price. Publishes book 1 year after acceptance. Reports in 4 months. Book catalog for 6×9 SAE with 4 first-class stamps. Manuscript guidelines for #10 SAE with 2 first-class stamps.
Nonfiction: Textbook (scholarly). Subjects include gay/lesbian, government politics (liberal), history, reli- gion (liberation/liberal), women's issues/studies. "We are looking for gay/lesbian history, pro-choice/feminist studies and liberal politics. Quality researched gay/lesbian history will pay beginning royalty of 7% and up. Academics are encouraged to submit. No biographies, evangelical fundamentalism/bible, conservative poli- tics, New Age studies or homophobic. No fiction or poetry." Query. Reviews artwork/photos as part of ms package.
Recent Nonfiction Title: *Harvest of Contempt*, by Joe Armey (liberal politics).
Tips: "Writers have the best chance with gender-free/nonsexist, liberal academic studies. We sell primarily to libraries and to scholars. Our audience is highly educated, politically and socially liberal, if religious they are liberational. If I were a writer trying to market a book today, I would compare my manuscript with books already published by the press I am seeking to submit to."

THE PUTNAM BERKLEY GROUP, 200 Madison Ave., New York NY 10016. Divisions and imprints include the Berkley Publishing Group (including Ace Science Fiction & Fantasy), G.P. Putnam's Sons, Perigee Books, Grosset & Dunlap, Philomel Books and Price Stern Sloan. Putnam did not respond to our request for information. Query before submitting.

QED PRESS, Subsidiary of Comp-Type, Inc., 155 Cypress St., Fort Bragg CA 95437. (707)964-9520. E-mail: qedpress@mcn.org. Senior Editor: John Fremont. Publishes hardcover and trade paperback originals. Publishes 10 titles/year. Receives 3,000 queries and 2,000 mss/year. 75% of books from first-time authors; 75% from unagented writers. Pays 7-15% royalty on retail price. Publishes book 16 months after acceptance of ms. Accepts simultaneous submissions. Reports in 1 month on queries, 3 months on mss. Book catalog for 9×12 SAE with 2 first-class stamps. Manuscript guidelines for #10 SASE.

Nonfiction: Biography, how-to, self-help. Subjects include health/medicine, history, language/literature, psychology, translation. "We seek books on the aging process and health, coping with aging, careers for older people, investments, etc. No juvenile, illustrated, photography or travel or cookbooks." Query with outline, 3 sample chapters and SASE. Reviews artwork/photos as part of ms package. Send photocopies.

Recent Nonfiction Title: *Finding the Way Home: A Compassionate Approach to Chronic Illness*, by Gayle Heiss (health/healing).

Fiction: Ethnic, literary, mystery, suspense. "Our thrust will be the acquisition of translated fiction by contemporary European, African and South American authors." Query with synopsis, 3 sample chapters and SASE.

Recent Fiction Title: *Tales From the Mountain*, by Miguel Torga, tr. by Ivana Carlsen (short stories [Portugese]).

Poetry: "We have minimal needs for poetry. No traditional, religious, rhymed, or derivative poetry." Query with sample poems and author bio.

Recent Poetry Title: *Solar Matter/Materia Solar*, by Eugenio de Andrade, translated by Alexis Levitin.

Tips: "Our audience is older, literary, literate, involved and politically aware. Study the market, and think before you send."

QUEST BOOKS, Theosophical Publishing House, P.O. Box 270, Wheaton IL 60189. (708)665-0130. Fax: (708)665-8791. E-mail: questbooks@aol.com. Executive Editor: Brenda Rosen. Publishes hardcover originals and trade paperback originals and reprints. Publishes 12-15 titles/year. Receives 400 queries and 150 mss/year. 25% of books from first-time authors; 50% from unagented writers. Pays 10% royalty on net minimum or 12% royalty on gross maximum. Offers $2,000-10,000 advance. Publishes book 20 months after acceptance of ms. Accepts simultaneous submissions. Reports in 1 month on queries and proposals, 3 months on mss. Book catalog and ms guidelines free on request.

● Quest gives preference to writers with established reputations/successful publications. Manuscript required on disk if accepted for publication.

Nonfiction: Subjects include self-development, self-help, philosophy (holistic), psychology (transpersonal), Eastern and Western religions, theosophy, comparative religion, men's and women's spirituality, Native American spirituality, holistic implications in science, health and healing, yoga, meditation, astrology. "TPH seeks works that are compatible with the theosophical philosophy. Our audience includes the 'New Age' community, seekers in all religions, general public, professors, and health professionals. No submissions that do not fit the needs outlined above." Accepts nonfiction translations. Query or submit outline and sample chapters. Reviews artwork/photos as part of ms package.

Recent Nonfiction Title: *Tying Rocks to Clouds: Meetings and Conversations with Wise and Spiritual People*, by William Elliott.

Tips: "The writer has the best chance of selling our firm a book that illustrates a connection between spiritually-oriented philosophy or viewpoint and some field of current interest."

QUILL DRIVER BOOKS/WORD DANCER PRESS, 950 N. Van Ness, Fresno CA 93728. (209)497-0809. Publisher: Stephen Blake Mettee. Imprints are Quill Driver Books, Word Dancer Press. Publishes hardcover and trade paperback originals and reprints. Publishes 10-12 titles/year. (Quill Driver Books: 4/year, Word Dancer Press: 6-8/year). 20% of books from first-time authors; 95% from unagented writers. Pays 6-10% royalty on retail price. Offers $500-10,000 advance. Publishes book 9 months after acceptance. Accepts simultaneous submissions. Reports in 1 month on queries and proposals, 3 months on mss. Book catalog and ms guidelines for #10 SASE.

Nonfiction: Biography, how-to, reference, general nonfiction. Subjects include Americana, regional, fund-raising, writing. "We are interested in any well-written, well-researched nonfiction book with a large identifiable market." Query with proposal package. Reviews artwork/photos as part of ms package. Send photocopies.

Recent Nonfiction Title: *Three Strikes and You're Out! . . . A Promise to Kimber: The Chronicle of America's Toughest Anti-Crime Law*, by Mike Renolds, Bill Jones and Dan Evans (politics, current events).

‡QUIXOTE PRESS, 615 Ave. H, Fort Madison IA 52627. (319)372-7480. Fax: (319)372-7480. President: Bruce Carlson. Imprints are Hearts & Tummies Cookbooks, Quixote Press. Publishes trade paperback originals and reprints. Publishes 20 titles/year. Receives 50-75 queries and 25-50 mss/year. 90% of books from first-time authors; 100% from unagented writers. Pays 10% royalty on wholesale price. No advance. Publishes book 1 year after acceptance. Accepts simultaneous submissions. Reports in 2 weeks. *Writer's Market* recommends allowing 2 months for reply. Book catalog and manuscript guidelines for #10 SASE.

Nonfiction: Children's/juvenile, cookbook, humor, self-help. Subjects include agriculture/horticulture, Americana, cooking/foods/nutrition, regional, travel, folklore. "We must be in on ground floor of the product design." Submit outline, 2 sample chapters and SASE. Reviews artwork/photos as part of ms package. Send photocopies.
Recent Nonfiction Title: *Kansas Roadkill Cookbook*, by B. Carlson.
Fiction: Adventure, ethnic, experimental, humor, short story collections, children's. Query with synopsis and SASE.
Recent Fiction Title: *Tall Tales of the Mississippi River*, by Dan Titus.
Tips: Audience is women in gift shops. Carefully consider marketing considerations.

RAGGED MOUNTAIN PRESS, Imprint of International Marine/The McGraw-Hill Companies, P.O. Box 220, Camden ME 04843-0220. (207)236-4837. Fax: (207)236-6314. Acquisitions Editor: John J. Kettlewell. Editorial Director: Jonathan Eaton. Estab. 1969. Publishes hardcover and trade paperback originals and reprints. Publishes 40 titles/year; imprint publishes 12, remainder are International Marine. Receives 200 queries and 100 mss/year. 30% of books from first-time authors; 90% from unagented writers. Pays 10-15% royalty on wholesale price. Offers advance. Publishes book 1 year after acceptance of ms. Accepts simultaneous submissions. Reports in 1 month on queries. *Writer's Market* recommends allowing 2 months for reply. Book catalog for 9×12 SAE with 10 first-class stamps. Manuscript guidelines for #10 SASE.
Nonfiction: Outdoor-related how-to, humor, essays. Subjects include outdoor cooking, fishing, camping, climbing and kayaking. "Ragged Mountain publishes nonconsumptive outdoor and environmental issues books of literary merit or unique appeal. Be familiar with the existing literature. Find a subject that hasn't been done, or has been done poorly, then explore it in detail and from all angles." Query with outline and 3 sample chapters. Reviews artwork/photos as part of ms package. Send photocopies.
Recent Nonfiction Title: *The Essential Outdoor Gear Manual*, by Annie Getchell.

RAINBOW PUBLISHERS, P.O. Box 261129, San Diego CA 92196. (619)271-7600. Editor: Christy Allen. Publishes 12 titles/year. Receives 250 queries and 100 mss/year. 50% of books from first-time authors. Publishes book 18 months after acceptance of ms. Accepts simultaneous submissions. Reports in 3 months on queries and proposals, 6 months on mss. Book catalog for 9×12 SAE with 2 first-class stamps. Manuscript guidelines for #10 SASE.
Nonfiction: How-to, textbook. Subjects include religion and reproducible activity books for Sunday school teachers. "We publish 64-page reproducible activity books for teachers to use in teaching the Bible to children ages 2-12." Query with outline, sample pages, age level, introduction. "We do use freelance artists. Send a query and photocopies of art samples." Will also be creating a line of Christian education books for the adult market this year.
Recent Nonfiction Title: *Bible Activities for Class and Home*, by Mark Rasche (children's activities).
Tips: "We are seeking manuscripts for *both* the children's and adult Christian book market, focusing on Christian education. We plan a much more aggressive publishing schedule than in the past."

RANDOM HOUSE, INC., Subsidary of Advance Publications, 201 E. 50th St., 11th Floor, New York NY 10022. (212)751-2600. Random House Trade Division publishes 120 titles/year. Receives 3,000 submissions/year. Imprints include Random House, Alfred A. Knopf, Ballantine, Crown, Del Rey, Fawcett, Harmony, Modern Library, Pantheon, Clarkson N. Potter, Villard, and Vintage. Pays royalty on retail price. Accepts simultaneous submissions. Reports in 2 months. Book catalog free. Manuscript guidelines for #10 SASE.
Nonfiction: Biography, cookbook, humor, illustrated book, self-help. Subjects include Americana, art, business and economics, classics, cooking and foods, health, history, music, nature, politics, psychology, religion, sociology and sports. No juveniles or textbooks (separate division). Query with outline, at least 3 sample chapters and SASE.
Fiction: Adventure, confession, experimental, fantasy, historical, horror, humor, mainstream, mystery, and suspense. Submit outline/synopsis, at least 3 sample chapters and SASE.

RANDOM HOUSE, INC. JUVENILE BOOKS, 201 E. 50th St., New York NY 10022. (212)572-2600. Subsidiaries include Random House Children's Books, Crown and Knopf Children's Books and Dragonfly paperbacks. Juvenile Division: Kate Klimo, publishing director, Random House. Simon Boughton, publishing director, Arthur Levine, editor-in-chief, Crown/Knopf. Managing Editor (all imprints): Amy Nathanson. Publishes hardcover, trade paperback and mass market paperback originals, mass market paperback reprints. Publishes 300 titles/year. *Unsolicited material no longer accepted by any imprint.*
Nonfiction: Biography, humor, illustrated books, juvenile. Subjects include animals, nature/environment, recreation, science, sports.
Fiction: Adventure, confession (young adult), fantasy, historical, horror, humor, juvenile, mystery, picture books, science fiction (juvenile/young adult), suspense, young adult.

RAWHIDE WESTERN PUBLISHING, P.O. Box 327, Safford AZ 85548. (520)428-5956. Publisher/ Senior Editor: Tim R. Walters. Publishes trade paperback originals and reprints. Publishes 4-6 titles/year.

50% of books from first-time authors; 100% from unagented writers. Pays 10-15% royalty on wholesale price. Publishes book 6 months after acceptance. Accepts simultaneous submissions. Reports in 1 month on queries and mss. *Writer's Market* recommends allowing 2 months for reply. Book catalog and ms guidelines for #10 SASE.

Nonfiction: Grassroots informational. Subjects include Americana, government/politics, history, nature/environment, religion, sociology, constitutional rights/issues. "Books 50,000-80,000 words only." Query with 3 sample chapters and SASE. Reviews artwork/photos as part of ms package. Send photocopies.

Recent Nonfiction Title: *From My Cold Dead Fingers: Why America Needs Guns*, by Richard I. Mack and Timothy Robert Walters (political/constitution).

Tips: "Don't hesitate to query about 'politically incorrect' material and ideas—intelligent, sound presentation valued over radical."

‡**REFERENCE PRESS INTERNATIONAL**, P.O. Box 812726, Boca Raton FL 33481-2726. (407)994-3499. Fax: (407)994-1255. Senior Editor: Cheryl Lacoff. Publishes hardcover and trade paperback originals. Publishes 6 titles/year. Receives 50 queries and 20 mss/year. 75% of books from first-time authors; 100% from unagented writers. Pays royalty or makes outright purchase. Advance determined by project. Publishes book 6 months after acceptance. Accepts simultaneous submissions. Reports in 3 months. Book catalog for #10 SASE.

Nonfiction: How-to, illustrated book, multimedia (audio, video, CD-ROM), reference, technical, educational, instructional. Subjects include Americana, art/architecture, business and economics, hobbies, money/finance, gardening, photography, anything related to the arts or crafts field. "Follow the guidelines as stated concerning subjects and type of books we're looking for." Query with outline, 1-3 sample chapters and SASE. Reviews artwork/photos as part of ms package. Send photocopies.

Recent Nonfiction Title: *Developing Your Artistic Creativity*, by Cheryl Klein Lacoff (how-to).

Tips: "We are interested in both first-time and published authors."

REFERENCE SERVICE PRESS, 1100 Industrial Rd., Suite 9, San Carlos CA 94070-4131. (415)594-0743. Fax: (415)594-0411. E-mail: rspstaff@aol.com. Website: http://www.rspfunding.com. Acquisitions Editor: Stuart Hauser. Estab. 1977. Publishes hardcover originals. Publishes 5-10 titles/year. 100% of books from unagented writers. Pays 10% or higher royalty. Publishes book 6 months after acceptance. Accepts simultaneous submissions. Reports in 2 months. Book catalog for #10 SASE.

● This publisher maintains databases on America Online.

Nonfiction: Reference. Subjects include education, ethnic, military/war, women's issues/studies, disabled. "We are interested only in directories and monographs dealing with financial aid." Submit outline and sample chapters.

Recent Nonfiction Title: *College Student Guide to Merit Funding.*

Tips: "Our audience consists of librarians, counselors, researchers, students, reentry women, scholars and other fundseekers."

REGNERY PUBLISHING, INC., 422 First St. SE, Suite 300, Washington DC 20003. Publisher: Alfred S. Regnery. Executive Editor: Richard Vigilante. Managing Editor: Jamila S. Abdelghani. Direct submissions to Submissions Editor. Estab. 1947. Imprints are Gateway Editions and Tumbleweed Press. Publishes hardcover originals and paperback originals and reprints. Publishes 30 titles/year. Pays 8-15% royalty on retail price. Offers $0-50,000 advance. Publishes book 1 year after acceptance. Accepts simultaneous submissions. Reports in 6 months on proposals.

Nonfiction: Biography, business and economics, education, government/politics, health/medicine, history, military/war, nature/environment, philosophy, religion, science, sociology. Query with outline and 2-3 sample chapters. Reviews artwork/photos as part of ms package. Send photocopies.

Recent Nonfiction Title: *Inventing the Aids Virus*, by Dr. Peter H. Duesberg.

RELIGIOUS EDUCATION PRESS, 5316 Meadow Brook Rd., Birmingham AL 35242-3315. (205)991-1000. Fax: (205)991-9669. Vice President, Operations: Dr. Nancy J. Vickers. Estab. 1974. Publishes trade paperback and hardback originals. Publishes 5 titles/year. Receives 350 submissions/year. 40% of books from first-time authors; 100% of books from unagented writers. Pays 10% royalty on net price. No advance. Reports in 2 months. Book catalog free.

MARKET CONDITIONS are constantly changing! If this is 1998 or later, buy the newest edition of *Writer's Market* at your favorite bookstore or order directly from Writer's Digest Books.

Nonfiction: Technical and textbook. Scholarly subjects in religion and religious education. "We publish serious, significant and scholarly books on religious education and pastoral ministry." Query with outline, 1 sample chapter and SASE.

Recent Nonfiction Title: *Handbook of Family Religious Education*, edited by Blake J. Neff and Donald Ratcliff (religious education).

Tips: "Our books are written for an ecumenical audience, for pastors, religious educators, and persons interested in the field of religious education, on a serious, scholarly level."

RENAISSANCE HOUSE PUBLISHERS, Subsidiary of Jende-Hagan, Inc., 541 Oak St., P.O. Box 177, Frederick CO 80530-0177. (303)833-2030. Fax: (303)833-2030. Editor: Eleanor Ayer. Publishes an ongoing series of 48-page guidebooks of travel-related interest. Publishes 8 titles/year. Receives 125 submissions/ year. 60% of books from first-time authors; 75% of books from unagented writers. Pays 8-10% royalty on net receipts. Offers 10% average advance on anticipated first printing royalties. May consider work for hire by experts in specific fields of interest. Publishes book 18 months after acceptance. Reports in 1 month on queries. *Writer's Market* recommends allowing 2 months for reply.

Nonfiction: Regional guidebooks. No fiction, personal reminiscences, general traditional philosophy, books on topics totally unrelated to subject areas specified above. "Please—no inquiries outside the topic of regional guidebooks! We publish to a very specific formula." *Writer's Market* recommends query with SASE first.

Tips: "We rely exclusively on inhouse generation of book concepts and then find authors who will write for hire to our specifications."

REPUBLIC OF TEXAS PRESS, Imprint of Wordware Publishing, Inc., 1506 Capitol Ave., Plano TX 75074. (214)423-0090. Editor: Mary Goldman. Publishes trade and mass market paperback originals. Publishes 25-30 titles/year. Receives 400 queries and 300 mss/year. 80% of books from unagented writers. Pays 8-12% royalty on wholesale price. Publishes book 9 months after acceptance of ms. Reports in 2 months. Book catalog and ms guidelines for SASE.

Nonfiction: History, Texana material, general interest. Subjects include Old West, Southwest, Military, Women of the West, government/politics, recreation and biography. Submit table of contents, 2 sample chapters, target audience and author experience.

Recent Nonfiction Title: *Cripple Creek Bonanza*, by Chet Cunningham (historical nonfiction).

RESURRECTION PRESS, LTD., P.O. Box 248, Williston Park NY 11596. (516)742-5686. Fax: (516)746-6872. Publisher: Emilie Cerar. Imprint is Spirit Life Series. Publishes trade paperback originals and reprints. Publishes 8-10 titles/year; imprint publishes 4 titles/year. Receives 100 queries and 100 mss/year. 50% of books from first-time authors; 100% from unagented writers. Pays 5-10% royalty on retail price. Offers $250-2,000 advance. Publishes book 1 year after acceptance of ms. Accepts simultaneous submissions. Reports in 1 month on queries and proposals, 2 months on mss. Book catalog and ms guidelines free on request.

Nonfiction: Self-help. Religious subjects. Wants mss of no more than 200 double-spaced typewritten pages. Query with outline and 2 sample chapters. Reviews artwork/photos as part of ms package. Send photocopies.

FLEMING H. REVELL PUBLISHING, Subsidiary of Baker Book House, P.O. Box 6287, Grand Rapids MI 49516. Editorial Director: William J. Petersen. Imprint is Spire Books. Publishes hardcover, trade paperback and mass market paperback originals and reprints. Publishes 50 titles/year; imprint publishes 10 titles/ year. Receives 750 queries and 1,000 mss/year. 10% of books from first-time authors; 75% from unagented writers. Pays royalty on wholesale price. Publishes book 1 year after acceptance of ms. Accepts simultaneous submissions. Reports in 2 months. Manuscript guidelines for #10 SASE.

Nonfiction: Biography, coffee table book, how-to, self-help. Subjects include child guidance/parenting, religion. Query with outline and 2 sample chapters.

Recent Nonfiction Title: *Coming Home to Raise Your Children*, by Christine Feld.

Fiction: Religious. Submit synopsis and 2 sample chapters.

Recent Fiction Title: *Web of Deception*, by Jane Peart (Victorian romance-suspense).

‡RICHBORO PRESS, P.O. Box 947, Southampton PA 18966-0947. (215)364-2212. Fax: (215)364-2212. Editor: George Moore. Estab. 1979. Publishes hardcover, trade paperback originals and software. Publishes 4 titles/year. Receives 500 submissions/year. 90% of books from unagented writers. Pays 10% royalty on retail price. Publishes book 1 year after acceptance. Electronic submissions preferred. Reports in 2 months on queries. Free book catalog. Manuscript guidelines for $1 and #10 SASE.

Nonfiction: Cookbook, how-to, gardening. Subjects include cooking/foods. Query.

RISING TIDE PRESS, 5 Kivy St., Huntington Station NY 11746-2020. (516)427-1289. E-mail: rtpress@ao l.com. Editor/Publisher: Lee Boojamra. Senior Editor: Alice Frier. Estab. 1991. Publishes trade paperback originals. Publishes 10-20 titles/year. Receives 500 queries and 150 mss/year. 75% of books from first-time authors; 100% from unagented writers. Pays 10-15% royalty on wholesale price. Publishes book 15 months after acceptance. Reports in 1 week on queries, 1 months on proposals, 2 months on mss. Book catalog for $1. Writer's guidelines for #10 SASE.

Nonfiction: Lesbian nonfiction. Query with outline, entire ms and *large* SASE. *Writer's Market* recommends sending a query with SASE first. Reviews artwork/photos as part of ms package. Send photocopies.

Fiction: "Lesbian fiction only." Adventure, erotica, fantasy, historical, horror, humor, literary, mainstream/contemporary, mystery, occult, romance, science fiction, suspense, mixed genres. "Major characters must be lesbian. Primary plot must have lesbian focus and sensibility." Query with synopsis or entire ms and SASE. *Writer's Market* recommends sending a query with SASE first.

Recent Fiction Title: *No Witness* (mystery).

Tips: "Our books are for, by and about lesbian lives. We welcome unpublished authors. We do *not* consider agented authors. Any material submitted should be proofed."

‡**RIVERRUN PRESS**, 1170 Broadway, Suite 807, New York NY 10001. President: John M. Calder. Publishes hardcover originals and trade paperback originals and reprints. Publishes 24 titles/year. Receives 2,500 queries and 1,000 mss/year. 50% of books from first-time authors; 50% from unagented writers. Pays royalty on retail price (contributions to anthologies, etc., are sometimes commissioned as works-for-hire). Offers $500 and up advance. Publishes book 3 years after acceptance. Accepts simultaneous submissions. "We never, ever, under any circumstances, return mss not accompanied by postage." Reports in 1 month on queries, 8 months on mss. Book catalog free on request.

Nonfiction: Biography, illustrated book, reference. Subjects include business and economics, education, gay/lesbian, government/politics, history, language/literature, music, philosophy, translation, travel. "Our focus is on non-traditional viewpoints, controversial topics, and conservative-bashing. Mistake writers make is not including information on competing works—and yes, there are always competing works—and not including an annotated table of contents for the entire work." Submit proposal package, including annotated table of contents, market research, one chapter and SASE. Reviews artwork/photos as part of ms package. Send photocopies if of good quality.

Recent Nonfiction Title: *Alexander I, Emperor of Russia*, by Ludmila Eureinov (biography).

Fiction: Ethnic, experimental, gay/lesbian, historical, humor, literary, plays, short story collections, translations. "Mainstream fiction doesn't do it for us at all. Mistake writers make is sending genre fiction and saying 'it transcends the boundaries of the genre.' No, it doesn't." Submit synopsis, 2 sample chapters and SASE. Do not send entire ms!

Recent Fiction Title: *Blight*, by D.H. Mechem (eco-fable).

Tips: Audience is sophisticated, culturally literate iconoclasts. "Writing must be as important to you as breathing. Don't expect to make a living at it. We don't. Tell stories, don't make points—even (or especially) in nonfiction—if you tell the story well, the point is made."

ROUTLEDGE, INC., Subsidiary of International Thompson Publishing, 29 W. 35th St., New York NY 10001-2299. (212)244-3336. Editorial Director (New York): William P. Germano. Imprint is Theatre Arts Books. Routledge list includes humanities, social sciences, business and economics, reference. Monographs, reference works, hardback and paperback upper-level texts, academic general interest. Publishes 100 titles/year in New York. 10% of books from first-time authors; 95% of books from unagented authors. Pays royalty. Publishes book 1 year after acceptance. Accepts simultaneous submissions. Reports in 3 months on queries. Query with proposal package, including toc, intro, sample chapter, overall prospectus, cv and SASE.

Nonfiction: Academic subjects include philosophy, literary criticism, psychoanalysis, social sciences, business and economics, history, psychology, women's studies, lesbian and gay studies, race and ethnicity, political science, anthropology, geography development, education, reference.

Recent Nonfiction Title: *Unequal Sisters*, by Vicki L. Ruiz and Ellen Carol DuBois, eds. (women's studies/race and ethnicity).

Tips: "Audience is professors, graduates and undergratuate students and trade."

ROXBURY PUBLISHING CO., P.O. Box 491044, Los Angeles CA 90049. (213)653-1068. Executive Editor: Claude Teweles. Publishes hardcover and paperback originals and reprints. Publishes 10 titles/year. Pays royalty. Accepts simultaneous submissions. Reports in 2 months.

Nonfiction: College-level textbooks *only*. Subjects include humanities, speech, developmental studies, social sciences, sociology, criminology. Query, submit outline/synopsis and sample chapters, or submit complete ms. *Writer's Market* recommends sending a query with SASE first.

ROYAL FIREWORKS PRESS, 1 First Ave., Unionville NY 10988. (914)726-3333. Editor: Charles Morgan. Publishes hardcover originals and reprints, trade paperback originals. Publishes 125 titles/year. 75% of books from first-time authors; 90% from unagented writers. Pays royalty. Publishes book 6 months after acceptance. Reports in 3 months on mss. Book catalog for SAE with 4 first-class stamps. Manuscript guidelines for #10 SASE.

Nonfiction: Biography, children's/juvenile, how-to, humor, illustrated book, self-help, technical, textbook. Subjects include Americana, business and economics, child guidance/parenting, computers and electronics, education, ethnic, history, language/literature, software, women's issues/studies. Submit proposal package,

including entire ms with SASE. *Writer's Market* recommends sending a query with SASE first. Reviews artwork/photos as part of ms package. Send photocopies.
Recent Nonfiction Title: *Prairie Adventures of Turk and His Gobblers.*
Fiction: Ethnic, juvenile, mystery, science fiction. "Most of our concentration will be on novels for middle school and young adult readers." Submit entire ms with SASE. *Writer's Market* recommends sending a query with SASE first.
Recent Fiction Title: *Kipton in Wonderland*, by Chris L. Fontenay.
Recent Poetry Title: *The Poetry Pad*, by Sue Thomas.

RUSSIAN INFORMATION SERVICES, 89 Main St., Suite 2, Montpelier VT 05602. (802)223-4955. Vice President: Stephanie Ratmeyer. Publishes trade paperback originals and reprints. Publishes 5-10 titles/year. Receives 20-30 queries and 10 mss/year. 50% of books from first-time authors; 100% from unagented writers. Pays 8-12% royalty on retail price. Publishes book 8 months after acceptance of ms. Accepts simultaneous submissions. Reports in 2 months on mss. Book catalog free on request.
Nonfiction: Reference, travel, business. Subjects include business and economics, language/literature, travel. "Our editorial focus is on (1) Russia and the NIS, and (2) newly emerging economies, ripe for foreign investment (China, Latin America, SE Asia). We currently are seeking authors for these latter regions." Submit proposal package, including ms, summary and cv. *Writer's Market* recommends sending a query with SASE first. Reviews artwork/photos as part of ms package. Send photocopies.
Recent Nonfiction Title: *Russia Survival Guide: Business & Travel*, by Richardson (travel/business).
Tips: Audience is business people and independent travelers to Russia, NIS, China, SE Asia, Latin America.

RUTLEDGE HILL PRESS, 211 Seventh Ave. N., Nashville TN 37219-1823. (615)244-2700. Fax: (615)244-2978. Editorial Secretary: Kirsten Hansen. Estab. 1982. Publishes hardcover and trade paperback originals and reprints. Publishes 35 titles/year. Receives 1,000 submissions/year. 40% of books from first-time authors; 90% from unagented writers. Pays 10-20% royalty on wholesale price. Publishes book 1 year after acceptance. Reports in 3 months. Book catalog for 9 × 12 SAE with 4 first-class stamps.
Nonfiction: Biography, cookbook, humor, reference, self-help, travel, Civil War history, quilt books. "The book must have an identifiable market, preferably one that is geographically limited." Submit outline and sample chapters. Reviews artwork/photos as part of ms package.

‡SAFER SOCIETY PRESS, Safer Society Foundation, Inc., P.O. Box 340, Brandon VT 05733. (802)247-3132. Fax: (802)247-4233. Director: Rob Freeman-Longo. Publishes trade paperback originals. Publishes 6-8 titles/year. Receives 15-20 queries and 10-15 mss/year. 90% of books from first-time authors; 100% from unagented writers. Pays 5% maximum royalty on retail price. No advance. Publishes book 1 year after acceptance. Accepts simultaneous submissions. Reports in 1 month on queries, 2 months on proposals, 6 months on mss. Book catalog free on request.
Nonfiction: Self-help (sex abuse prevention and treatment). Subjects include psychology (sexual abuse). Query with proposal package, including complete ms with SASE. *Writer's Market* recommends sending a query with SASE first. Reviews artwork/photos as part of ms package. Send photocopies. We are a small nonprofit nitch press.
Recent Nonfiction Title: *When Children Abuse*, by Cunningham (psychology/health).
Tips: Audience is persons working in mental health/persons needing self-help books. Pays small fees or low royalties.

ST. ANTHONY MESSENGER PRESS, 1615 Republic St., Cincinnati OH 45210-1298. (513)241-5615. Fax: (513)241-0399. E-mail: saintanth@aol.com. Publisher: The Rev. Jeremy Harrington, O.F.M. Managing Editor: Lisa Biedenbach. Estab. 1970. Publishes trade paperback originals. Publishes 12-16 titles/year. Receives 200 queries and 50 mss/year. 5% of books from first-time authors; 100% from unagented writers. Pays 10-12% royalty on net receipts of sales. Offers $600 average advance. Publishes book 18 months after acceptance. Reports in 1 month on queries, 2 months on proposals and mss. Book catalog for 9 × 12 SAE with 4 first-class stamps. Manuscript guidelines free on request.
Nonfiction: History, religion, Catholic identity and teaching, prayer and spirituality resources, scripture study. Query with outline and SASE. Reviews artwork/photos as part of ms package.
  • St. Anthony Messenger Press especially seeks books which will sell in bulk quantities to parishes, teachers, pastoral ministers, etc. They expect to sell at least 5,000 to 7,000 copies of a book.
Recent Nonfiction Title: *Jesus' Plan for a New World: The Sermon on the Mount*, by Richard Rohr with John Bookser Feister.
Tips: "Our readers are ordinary 'folks in the pews' and those who minister to and educate these folks. Writers need to know the audience and the kind of books we publish. Manuscripts should reflect best and current Catholic theology and doctrine."

ST. BEDE'S PUBLICATIONS, Subsidiary of St. Scholastica Priory, P.O. Box 545, Petersham MA 01366-0545. (508)724-3407. Fax: (508)724-3574. Website: http://www.stbedes.org. Editorial Director: Sr. Scholastica Crilly, OSB. Estab. 1978. Publishes hardcover originals, trade paperback originals and reprints. Publishes

8-12 titles/year. Receives 100 submissions/year. 30-40% of books from first-time authors; 90% from un-agented writers. Nonauthor subsidy publishes 10% of books. Pays 5-10% royalty on wholesale price or retail price. No advance. Publishes book 2 years after acceptance. Accepts simultaneous submissions. Unsolicited mss not returned unless accompanied by sufficient return postage. Reports in 2 months. Book catalog and ms guidelines for 9×12 SAE and 2 first-class stamps.

Nonfiction: Textbook (theology), religion, prayer, spirituality, hagiography, theology, philosophy, church history, related lives of saints. "We are always looking for excellent books on prayer, spirituality, liturgy, church or monastic history. Theology and philosophy are important also. We publish English translations of foreign works in these fields if we think they are excellent and worth translating." No submissions unrelated to religion, theology, spirituality, etc. Query or submit outline and sample chapters.

Recent Nonfiction Title: *The Christian Mystery*, by Louis Bouger (theology).

Tips: "There seems to be a growing interest in monasticism among lay people and we will be publishing more books in this area. For our theology/philosophy titles our audience is scholars, colleges and universities, seminaries, etc. For our other titles (i.e. prayer, spirituality, lives of saints, etc.) the audience is above-average readers interested in furthering their knowledge in these areas."

ST. MARTIN'S PRESS, 175 Fifth Ave., New York NY 10010. Imprints include Bedford Books, Picador USA, Stonewall Inn Editions, and Tor Books. Publishes hardcover, trade paperback and mass market origi-nals. Publishes 1,500 titles/year. General interest publisher of both fiction and nonfiction. The company did not respond to our request for information. Query before submitting.

Nonfiction: General nonfiction, reference, scholarly, textbook. Biography, business/economics, contempo-rary culture, cookbooks, self-help, sports, true crime.

Recent Nonfiction Title: *The Girls in the Back of the Class*, by LouAnn Johnson.

Fiction: General fiction. Fantasy, historical, horror, literary, mainstream, mystery, science fiction, suspense, thriller, western (contemporary).

Recent Fiction Title: *Passover*, by David Mamet.

SALINA BOOKSHELF, 10250 Palomino Rd., Flagstaff AZ 86004. (602)527-0070. Publisher: Louise Lockard. Publishes trade paperback originals and reprints. No books from first-time authors; 100% from unagented writers. Pays 20% minimum royalty. Publishes book 6 months after acceptance. Accepts simultane-ous submissions. Reports in 3 months.

Nonfiction: Children's/juvenile, textbook (Navajo language). Ethnic subjects. "We publish childrens' bilin-gual readers. Nonfiction should be appropriate to science and social studies curriculum grades 3-8." Query. Reviews artwork/photos as part of ms package. Send photocopies.

Fiction: Juvenile. "Submissions should be in English/a language taught in Southwest classrooms." Query.

Recent Fiction Title: *Who Wants to be a Prairie Dog?*, by Ann Nolan Clark (children's picture book).

Poetry: "We accept poetry in English/Southwest language for children." Submit 3 sample poems.

‡SANDHILL CRANE PRESS, PUBLISHERS, 2406 NW 47th Terrace, Gainesville FL 32606-6583. (352)371-9858. Fax: (352)371-0962. Publisher: Dr. Ross H. Arnett, Jr. Estab. 1947. Imprint is Flora & Fauna Publications. Publishes hardcover and trade paperback originals. Publishes 10-12 titles/year. Receives 70 submissions/year. 50% of books from first-time authors; 100% from unagented writers. Average print order for a first book is 1,500. Pays 10% royalty on list price. Advance negotiable. Publishes book 1 year after acceptance. Reports in 2 months on queries.

Nonfiction: Reference, technical, textbook, directories. Subjects include plants and animals (for amateur and professional biologists), natural history and environment. Looking for "books dealing with kinds of plants and animals; nature guide series. No nature stories or 'Oh My' nature books." Query with outline and 2 sample chapters. Reviews artwork/photos as part of ms package.

Tips: "Well-documented books, especially those that fit into one of our series, have the best chance of selling to our firm—biology, natural history, environment, usually no garden books."

‡SANDLAPPER PUBLISHING, INC., P.O. Box 730, Orangeburg SC 29116-0730. (803)531-1658. Fax: (803)534-5223. Managing Editor: Amanda Gallman. Estab. 1982. Publishes hardcover and trade paperback originals and reprints. Publishes 6 titles/year. Receives 200 submissions/year. 80% of books from first-time authors; 95% from unagented writers. Pays 15% maximum royalty on net receipts. Publishes book 20 months after acceptance. Accepts simultaneous submissions, if so noted. Reports in 3 months. Book catalog and ms guidelines for 9×12 SAE with 4 first-class stamps.

Nonfiction: History, biography, illustrated books, humor, cookbook, juvenile (ages 9-14), reference, text-book. Subjects are limited to history, culture and cuisine of the Southeast and especially South Carolina. "We are looking for manuscripts that reveal under-appreciated or undiscovered facets of the rich heritage of our region. If a manuscript doesn't deal with South Carolina or the Southeast, the work is probably not appropriate for us. We don't do self-help books, children's books about divorce, kidnapping, etc., and abso-lutely no religious manuscripts." Query or submit outline and sample chapters "if you're not sure it's what we're looking for, otherwise complete ms." *Writer's Market* recommends query with SASE first. Reviews artwork/photos as part of ms package.

Recent Nonfiction Title: *A Sweet, Sweet Basket*, by M. Clary (children's).
Fiction: "We do not need fiction submissions at present, and will not consider any horror, romance or religious fiction." Query or submit outline/synopsis and sample chapters. "Do check with us on books dealing with regional nature, science and outdoor subjects."
Tips: "Our readers are South Carolinians, visitors to the region's tourist spots, and friends and family that live out-of-state. We are striving to be a leading regional publisher for South Carolina. We will be looking for more history and biography."

‡SAS INSTITUTE INC., SAS Campus Dr., Cary NC 27513-2414. (919)677-8000. Fax: (919)677-4444. E-mail: sasbbu@unk.sas.com. Website: http://www.sas.com. Editor-in-Chief: David D. Baggett. Estab. 1976. Publishes hardcover and trade paperback originals. Publishes 40 titles/year. Receives 10 submissions/year. 50% of books from first-time authors; 100% from unagented writers. Payment negotiable. Offers negotiable advance. Reports in 2 weeks on queries. *Writer's Market* recommends allowing 2 months for reply. Book catalog and ms guidelines free.
Nonfiction: Software, technical, textbook, statistics. "SAS Institute's Publications Division publishes books developed and written inhouse. Through the Books by Users program, we also publish books by SAS users on a variety of topics relating to SAS software. We want to provide our users with additional titles to supplement our primary documentation and to enhance the users' ability to use the SAS System effectively. We're interested in publishing manuscripts that describe or illustrate using any of SAS Institute's software products. Books must be aimed at SAS software users, either new or experienced. Tutorials are particularly attractive, as are descriptions of user-written applications for solving real-life business, industry, or academic problems. Books on programming techniques using the SAS language are also desirable. Manuscripts must reflect current or upcoming software releases, and the author's writing should indicate an understanding of the SAS System and the technical aspects covered in the manuscript." Query. Submit outline/synopsis and sample chapters. Reviews artwork/photos as part of ms package.
Recent Nonfiction Title: *The Little SAS Book: A Primer*, by Lora D. Delwiche and Susan J. Slaughter (computer software guide).
Tips: "Our readers are SAS software users, both new and experienced. If I were a writer trying to market a book today, I would concentrate on developing a manuscript that teaches or illustrates a specific concept or application that SAS software users will find beneficial in their own environments or can adapt to their own needs."

SASQUATCH BOOKS, 1008 Western Ave., #300, Seattle WA 98104. (206)467-4300. Fax: (206)467-4301. E-mail: books@sasquatchbooks.com. Contact: Stephanie Irving, acquisition editor. Estab. 1975. Publishes regional hardcover and trade paperback originals. Publishes 30-40 titles/year. 20% of books from first-time authors; 85% from unagented writers. Pays authors royalty on cover price. Offers wide range of advances. Publishes ms 6 months after acceptance. Query first. Reports in 3 months. Book catalog for 9 × 12 SAE with 2 first-class stamps.
Nonfiction: Subjects include regional art/architecture, children's books, cooking, foods, gardening, history, nature/environment, recreation, sports, travel and outdoors. "We are seeking quality nonfiction works about the Pacific Northwest and West Coast regions (including Alaska to California). In this sense we are a regional publisher, but we do distribute our books nationally." Submit outline and sample chapters.
Recent Nonfiction Title: *Native Peoples of the Northwest*, by Jan Halliday and Gail Chehak.
Tips: "We sell books through a range of channels in addition to the book trade. Our primary audience consists of active, literate residents of the West Coast."

SCARECROW PRESS, INC., Division of University Press of America, 4720 Boston Way, Lanhau MD 20706. (301)459-3366. Fax: (301)459-2118. Contact: Editorial Dept. Estab. 1950. Publishes hardcover originals. Publishes 150 titles/year. Receives 600-700 submissions/year. 70% of books from first-time authors; 100% from unagented writers. Average print order for a first book is 1,000. Pays 10% royalty on net of first 1,000 copies; 15% of net price thereafter. 15% initial royalty on camera-ready copy. Offers no advance. Publishes book 18 months after receipt of ms. Reports in 1 month. *Writer's Market* recommends allowing 2 months for reply. Book catalog for 9 × 12 SAE and 4 first-class stamps.
Nonfiction: Needs reference books and meticulously prepared annotated bibliographies, indexes and books on women's studies, music, movies and stage. Query. Occasionally reviews artwork/photos as part of ms package.
Recent Nonfiction Title: *Library Lessons Grades 7-9*, by Druce (resource).
Tips: "Essentially we consider any scholarly title likely to appeal to libraries. Emphasis is on reference material, but this can be interpreted broadly, provided author is knowledgeable in the subject field."

SCHIRMER BOOKS, Imprint of Simon & Schuster, 1633 Broadway, New York NY 10016-6785. (212)654-8464. Fax: (212)654-4745. Senior Editor: Richard Carlin. Acquisitions Editor: Jill Lectka. Editor: Jonathan Wiener. Publisher: William P. Boger, Jr. Publishes hardcover and paperback originals, related audio recordings, paperback reprints and some software. Publishes 30 books/year. Receives 250 submissions/year. 25% of books from first-time authors; 75% of books from unagented writers. Submit photos and/or illustrations

only "if central to the book, not if decorative or tangential." Publishes book 1 year after acceptance. Reports in 4 months. Book catalog and ms guidelines for SASE.
- Schirmer Books reports more interest in popular music, including rock and jazz.

Nonfiction: Publishes college texts, biographies, scholarly, reference, and trade on the performing arts specializing in music, film and theatre. Submit outline/synopsis, sample chapters and current vita. Reviews artwork/photos as part of ms package.

Recent Nonfiction Title: *Tattooed on Their Tongues: A Journey Through the Backrooms of American Music*, by Colin Escott.

Tips: "The writer has the best chance of selling our firm a music book with a clearly defined, reachable audience, either scholarly or trade. Must be an exceptionally well-written work of original scholarship prepared by an expert in the field who has a thorough understanding of correct manuscript style and attention to detail (see the *Chicago Manual of Style*)."

SCHOLASTIC INC., 555 Broadway, New York NY 10012. (212)343-6100. Divisions: Scholastic Inc. Editorial Director: Craig Walker. Estab. 1920. Publishes juvenile trade paperback originals. Scholastic Press. Editorial Director: Brenda Bowen. Publishes juvenile hardcover picture books, novels and nonfiction. The Blue Sky Press. Editorial Director: Bonnie Verburg. Publishes juvenile hardcover picture books, novels and nonfiction. All divisions: Pays advance and royalty on retail price. Reports in 6 months. Manuscript guidelines for #10 SASE.

Nonfiction: Publishes nonfiction for children ages 4 to teen. Query.

Recent Nonfiction Title: *The Great Fire*, by Jim Murphy (Newbery Medal Book).

Fiction: Hardcover—open to all subjects suitable for children. Paperback—family stories, mysteries, school, friendships for ages 8-12, 35,000 words. YA fiction, romance, family and mystery for ages 12-15, 40,000-45,000 words for average to good readers. Queries welcome; unsolicited manuscripts discouraged.

Recent Fiction Titles: *Her Stories: African American Folktales, Fairy Tales and True Tales*, by Virginia Hamilton, illustrated by Leo and Diane Dillon.

Tips: New writers for children should study the children's book field before submitting.

SCHOLASTIC PROFESSIONAL BOOKS, 411 Lafayette, New York NY 10003. Publishing Director: Claudia Cohl. Editor-in-Chief: Terry Cooper. Assistant Managing Editor: Shawn Richardson. Publishes 45-50 books/year. "Writer should have background working in the classroom with elementary or middle school children teaching pre-service students and developing quality, appropriate, and innovative learning experiences and/or solid background in developing supplementary educational materials for these markets." Offers standard contract. Reports in 2 months. Book catalog for 9 × 12 SAE.

Nonfiction: Elementary and middle-school level enrichment—all subject areas, whole language, theme units, integrated materials, writing process, management techniques, teaching strategies based on personal/professional experience in the classroom. Production is limited to printed matter: resource and activity books, professional development materials, reference titles. Length: 6,000-12,000 words. Query with table of contents.

‡SEASIDE PRESS, Imprint of Wordware Publishing, Inc., 1506 Capitol Ave., Plano TX 75074. (214)423-0090. President: Russell A. Stultz. Publishes trade paperback originals and reprints and mass market paperback originals. Publishes 50-70 titles/year. Receives 50-60 queries and 10-15 mss/year. 40% of books from first-time authors; 95% from unagented writers. Pays 8-12% royalty on wholesale price. Publishes book 6 months after acceptance of ms. Accepts simultaneous submissions. Reports in 2 months. Book catalog and ms guidelines with SASE.

Nonfiction: How-to, pet care, humor, self-help. Subjects include travel/history (Cities Uncovered series), philosophy, religion. Submit proposal package, including table of contents, 2 sample chapters, target audience summation, competing products.

Recent Nonfiction Title: *Seattle Uncovered*, by Joann Roe (travel/history).

Tips: "We have expanded the Cities Uncovered series, and are not currently taking submissions for children's books. We are also doing a bit more about pet care and less about self-help subjects."

SERENDIPITY SYSTEMS, P.O. Box 140, San Simeon CA 93452. (805)927-5259. E-mail: j.galuszka@gen ie.geis.com. Publisher: John Galuszka. Imprints are Books-on-Disks, Eco-Books. Publishes electronic books for IBM-PC compatible computers. Publishes 6-12 titles/year; each imprint publishes 0-6 titles/year. Receives 600 queries and 150 mss/year. 100% of books from unagented writers. Pays 25-33% royalty on wholesale price or on retail price, "depending on how the book goes out." Publishes book 2 months after acceptance of ms. Accepts simultaneous submissions. Electronic submissions required. Queries by e-mail; mss, summaries with sample chapters, and long documents should be sent by postal mail. Reports in 1 month on mss. *Writer's Market* recommends allowing 2 months for reply. Book catalog on IBM-PC disk and in hypertext available for $1 (indicate 3½" or 5¼" disk). Manuscript guidelines for #10 SASE.

Nonfiction: Reference on literature, writing, publishing. Subjects include computers and electronics, language/literature, software. "We only publish nonfiction books on literature, writing and electronic publishing." Submit entire ms on disk in ASCII files. *Writer's Market* recommends sending a query first.

Recent Nonfiction Title: *Diskbook—An Introduction to Electronic Publishing for Writers*, J. Galuszka (reference).
Fiction: We want to see *only* works which use (or have a high potential to use) hypertext, multimedia, interactivity, or other computer-enhanced features. Submit entire ms on disk in ASCII files (unless author has already added hypertext, etc.). *Writer's Market* recommends sending a query first.
Recent Fiction Title: *Say Goodbye to Midnight*, by C.J. Newton (mystery novel).

SERGEANT KIRKLAND'S, Imprint of Sergeant Kirkland's Museum and Historical Society, Inc., 912 Lafayette Blvd., Fredericksburg VA 22401-5617. (540)899-5565. Fax: (540)899-7643. E-mail: civil-war@msn.com. Editor: Ronald Seagrave. Publishes hardcover originals and reprints. Publishes 12-14 titles/year. Receives 20 queries and 15 mss/year. 60% of books from first-time authors; 100% from unagented writers. Pays 25% royalty on wholesale price. Publishes book 3 months after acceptance. Accepts simultaneous submissions. Reports in 1 month. *Writer's Market* recommends allowing 2 months for reply. Book catalog and ms guidelines free on request.
Nonfiction: Subjects include Americana, archaeology, history, military/war (American Civil War). Mistake writers most often make is not including biography, index, footnotes and table of contents. Query with outline and 2-3 sample chapters. Reviews artwork as part of ms package. Send photocopies.
Recent Nonfiction Title: *A Bridge of No Return*, by Dr. Phillip T. Tucker.

SERVANT PUBLICATIONS, 840 Airport Blvd., P.O. Box 8617, Ann Arbor MI 48107. (313)761-8505. Editorial Director: Bert Ghezzi. Estab. 1972. Imprints are Vine Books, "especially for evanglical Protestant readers"; and Charis Books, "especially for Roman Catholic readers." Publishes hardcover, trade and mass market paperback originals and trade paperback reprints. Publishes 40 titles/year. 5% of books from first-time authors; 85% from unagented writers. Publishes book 1 year after acceptance. Reports in 2 months. Book catalog for 9 × 12 SASE.
Nonfiction: "We're looking for practical Christian teaching, self-help, scripture, current problems facing the Christian church, and inspiration." No heterodox or non-Christian approaches. Submit query letter only. All unsolicited mss returned unopened.
Recent Nonfiction Title: *The Search for Peace*, by Robert McGee.
Fiction: Accepts unsolicited queries only, from published authors or agents. All unsolicited mss returned unopened.
Recent Fiction Title: *Behind the Glittering Mask*, by Mark Rutland.

‡**SEVEN STORIES PRESS**, 632 Broadway, 7th Floor, New York NY 10012. (212)995-0908. Publisher: Daniel Simon. Publishes hardcover and trade paperback originals. Publishes 15 titles/year. 15% of books from first-time authors; 15% from unagented writers. Pays 7-15% royalty on retail price. Publishes book 1-3 years after acceptance. Accepts simultaneous submissions. Reports in 3 months. Book catalog and manuscript guidelines free on request.
  • See the interview with Daniel Simon in this edition of *Writer's Market*.
Nonfiction: Biography. Subjects include general nonfiction. Submit proposal package, including outline, 1-2 sample chapters and SASE.
Recent Nonfiction Title: *Censored: The News That Didn't Make The News*, by Carl Jensen (media/contemporary affairs).
Fiction: Contemporary). Submit 1-2 sample chapters and SASE.
Recent Fiction Title: *Parable of the Sower*, by Octavia E. Butler (feminist fiction).
Tips: Audience is well-educated, progressive and mainstream.

HAROLD SHAW PUBLISHERS, 388 Gundersen Dr., P.O. Box 567, Wheaton IL 60189. (708)665-6700. Managing Editor: Joan Guest. Bible Study Editor: Mary Horner Collins. Literary Editor: Lil Copan. Estab. 1967. Publishes mostly trade paperback originals and reprints. Publishes 38 titles/year. Receives 1,000 submissions/year. 10-20% of books from first-time authors; 90% from unagented writers. Offers 5-10% royalty on retail price. Sometimes makes outright purchase of $375-2,500 for Bible studies and compilations. Publishes book 18 months after acceptance. Reports in 3 months on queries. Request ms guidelines with SASE. Catalog for 9 × 12 SAE with 5 first-class stamps.
Nonfiction: Subjects include marriage, family and parenting, self-help, mental health, spiritual growth, Bible study and literary topics. "We are looking for adult general nonfiction, with different twists—self-help manuscripts with fresh insight and colorful, vibrant writing style. No autobiographies or biographies accepted. Must have an evangelical Christian perspective for us even to review the manuscript." Query.
Recent Nonfiction Title: *Knowing Christianity*, by J.I. Packer (Christian doctrine).
Tips: "Get an editor who is not a friend or a spouse who will tell you honestly whether your book is marketable. It will save a lot of your time and money and effort. Then do an honest evaluation. Who would actually read the book other than yourself? If it won't sell at least 5,000 copies, it's not very marketable and most publishers wouldn't be interested."

SIBYL PUBLICATIONS, Subsidiary of Micro One, Inc., 600 SE Powell Blvd., Portland OR 97202. (503)231-6519. Fax: (503)231-7492. Publisher: Miriam Selby. Publishes trade paperback originals. Publishes 4-6 titles/year. 75% of books from first-time authors; 100% from unagented writers. Pays 10-15% royalty on wholesale price. Publishes book 9 months after acceptance of ms. Accepts simultaneous submissions. Reports in 1 month on queries, 2 months on proposals and mss. Book catalog and ms guidelines for #10 SASE.
Nonfiction: Biography, gift book, self-help, textbook, book and card set. Subjects include psychology, women's issues/studies, women's spirituality. "We publish nonfiction positive books by and about women." Query with outline, 3 sample chapters and SASE.
Recent Nonfiction Title: *Redefining Success: Women's Unique Paths*, by Nancy Johnson.
Tips: Audience is women in midlife, ages 36-60, who are interested in spirituality, mythology, psychology, women's studies, women's issues. "Make your writing unique and compelling. Give the reader a reason to buy your book; something new, different, better. Characters who are positive women who can be role models."

THE SIDRAN PRESS, Imprint of The Sidran Foundation, 2328 W. Joppa Rd., Suite 15, Lutherville MD 21093. (410)825-8888. Fax: (410)337-0747. E-mail: sidran@access.digex.net. Website: http://www.access.di gex.net/~sidran. President: Esther Giller. Publishes hardcover originals and trade paperback originals and reprints. Publishes 5-6 titles/year. Receives 75 queries and 40 mss/year. 20% of books from first-time authors; 95% from unagented writers. Pays 8-10% royalty on wholesale price. Publishes book 1 year after acceptance of ms. No simultaneous submissions. Reports in 1 month on queries, 3 months on proposals, 6 months on mss. Book catalog and ms guidelines free on request.
Nonfiction: Reference, self-help, textbook, professional. Subjects include psychiatry, expressive therapies, psychology. Specializes in trauma/abuse/domestic violence and mental health issues. Query with proposal package including outline, 2-3 sample chapters, introduction, competing titles, market information.
Recent Nonfiction Title: *Vietnam Wives*, by Matsakis (self-help, psychology).

SIERRA CLUB BOOKS, Dept. WM, 100 Bush St., San Francisco CA 94104. (415)291-1600. Fax: (415)291-1602. Senior Editor: James Cohee. Estab. 1962. Publishes hardcover and paperback originals and reprints. Publishes 30 titles/year. Receives 1,000 submissions/year. 50% of books from unagented writers. Royalties vary by project. Offers $3,000-15,000 average advance. Publishes book 18 months after acceptance. Reports in 2 months. Book catalog free.
Nonfiction: A broad range of environmental subjects: outdoor adventure, descriptive and how-to, women in the outdoors; landscape and wildlife pictorials; literature, including travel and works on the spiritual aspects of the natural world; travel and trail guides; natural history and current environmental issues, including public health and uses of appropriate technology; gardening; general interest; and children's books. "The Sierra Club was founded to help people to explore, enjoy and preserve the nation's forests, waters, wildlife and wilderness. The books program looks to publish quality trade books about the outdoors and the protection of natural resources. Specifically, we are interested in literary natural history, environmental issues such as nuclear power, self-sufficiency, politics and travel, and juvenile books with an ecological theme." Does *not* want "proposals for large color photographic books without substantial text; how-to books on building things outdoors; books on motorized travel; or any but the most professional studies of animals." Query first, then submit outline and sample chapters. Reviews artwork/photos as part of ms package. Send photocopies.
Recent Nonfiction Title: *The World of the Fox* (literary natural history).
Fiction: Adventure, historical, mainstream and ecological fiction. "We do very little fiction, but will consider a fiction manuscript if its theme fits our philosophical aims: the enjoyment and protection of the environment." Query first, then submit outline/synopsis and sample chapters.
Recent Fiction Title: *The Condor Brings the Sun*.
Recent Poetry Title: *News of the Universe* (poetry anthology).

SIGNATURE BOOKS, 564 West 400 North, Salt Lake City UT 84116-3411. (801)531-1483. Fax: (801)531-1488. Director of Publishing: Gary Bergera. Estab. 1981. Publishes hardcover, trade and mass market paperback originals. Publishes 12 titles/year. Receives 100 queries and 100 mss/year. 10% of books from first-time authors; 100% from unagented writers. Pays royalty. Publishes book 1 year after acceptance of ms. Accepts simultaneous submissions. "Submit proposal or outline with autobiographical info, and maybe sample chapter or poem." Reports in 6 months on proposals. Book catalog and ms guidelines free on request.
Nonfiction: Western Americana, biography, humor, essays. Subjects include history, religion (predominantly Mormon), women's issues/studies. "We prefer manuscripts in Utah/Western studies. Familiarize yourself with our backlist before submitting a proposal." Submit proposal package, including 2-3 sample chapters. Reviews artwork/photos as part of ms package. Send photocopies.
Recent Nonfiction Title: *History of San Bernardino*, by Leo Lyman (history).
Fiction: Western Americana: historical, humor, religious. Query or submit synopsis.
Recent Fiction Title: *Secrets Keep*, by Linda Sillitoe (novel).
Poetry: Submit complete ms. *Writer's Market* recommends sending a query with SASE first.
Recent Poetry Title: *On Keeping Things Small*, by Marilyn Bushman-Carlton (poetry).
Tips: "We have a general adult audience that is somewhat Mormon-oriented."

SILHOUETTE BOOKS, 300 E. 42nd St., New York NY 10017. (212)682-6080. Fax: (212)682-4539. Website: http://www.romance.net. Editorial Director, Silhouette Books, Harlequin historicals: Isabel Swift. Estab. 1979. Publishes mass market paperback originals. Publishes 350 titles/year. Receives 4,000 submissions/year. 10% of books from first-time authors; 50% from unagented writers. Pays royalty. Publishes book 3 years after acceptance. No unsolicited mss. Send query letter, 2 page synopsis and SASE to head of imprint. Manuscript guidelines for #10 SASE.

Imprints: Silhouette Romances (contemporary adult romances, 53,000-58,000 words), Melissa Senate, senior editor. Silhouette Special Editions (contemporary adult romances, 75,000-80,000 words), Tara Gavin, senior editor. Silhouette Desires (contemporary adult romances, 55,000-60,000 words), Lucia Macro, senior editor. Silhouette Intimate Moments (contemporary adult romances, 80,000-85,000 words). Silhouette Yours Truly (contemporary adult romances, 53,000-58,000 words), Leslie Wainger, senior editor and editorial coordinator. Harlequin Historicals (adult historical romances, 95,000-105,000 words), Tracy Farrell, senior editor.

Recent Nonfiction Title: *How To Talk To A Naked Man*, by Melanie Mills (advice).

Fiction: Romance (contemporary and historical romance for adults). "We are interested in seeing submissions for all our lines. No manuscripts other than the types outlined above. Manuscript should follow our general format, yet have an individuality and life of its own that will make it stand out in the readers' minds."

Recent Fiction Title: *Tallchief For Keeps*, by Cait London.

Tips: "The romance market is constantly changing, so when you read for research, read the latest books and those that have been recommended to you by people knowledgeable in the genre. We are actively seeking new authors for all our lines, contemporary and historical."

SILVER BURDETT PRESS, Imprint of Simon & Schuster, 299 Jefferson Rd., Parsippany NJ 07054. (201)739-8000. Manager: David Vissoe. Imprints are Julian Messner, Silver Press (preschool and primary fiction and nonfiction), Crestwood House, Dillon Press and New Discovery. Publishes hardcover and paperback originals. Publishes 65-80 titles/year. No unsolicited mss. Publishes book 1 year after acceptance. Offers variable advance. Book catalog free.

Nonfiction: Juvenile and young adult reference. Subjects include Americana, science, history, nature, and geography. "We're primarily interested in nonfiction for students on subjects which supplement the classroom curricula, but are graphically appealing and, in some instances, have commercial as well as institutional appeal." Query.

Recent Nonfiction Title: *History of the Civil Rights Movement*, introduction by Andrew Young.

Tips: "Our books are primarily bought by school and public librarians for use by students and young readers. Virtually all our nonfiction and done as part of a series."

SIMON & SCHUSTER, 1230 Avenue of the Americas, New York NY 10020. Imprints include Fireside, Touchstone, Simon & Schuster, Scribner (Lisa Drew), Scribner Paperback Fiction, Free Press/Lexington Books, Pocket Books, Simon & Schuster Children's Publishing and New Media Division includes these imprints: Atheneum Books for Young Readers, Rawson Associates, Simon & Schuster Aguilar Libros en Español, Margaret K. McElderry Books, Simon & Schuster Books for Young Readers, Aladdin Paperbacks, Little Simon, Rabbit Ears Book and Audio. General interest publisher of both fiction and nonfiction. Query before submitting to attn: Wendy Nicholson.

SJL PUBLISHING COMPANY, P.O. Box 152, Hanna IN 46340. (219)324-9678. Publisher/Editor: Sandra J. Cassady. Publishes hardcover and trade paperback originals. Publishes 8-10 titles/year. Receives 1,000 queries and 100 mss/year. 40% of books from first-time authors; 100% from unagented writers. Pays 10% royalty. Publishes book 1 year after acceptance of ms. Accepts simultaneous submissions. Reports in 1 month on queries and proposals, 2 months on mss. Manuscript guidelines for #10 SASE.

Nonfiction: Cookbook, children's/juvenile, reference, self-help, technical. Subjects include business and economics, computers and electronics, cooking/foods/nutrition, gardening, government/politics, science, sports. "Looking for good scientific publications." Query with synopsis and SASE. Reviews artwork/photos as part of ms package. Send photocopies.

Recent Nonfiction Title: *In Search of the Circle—The Rotary Engine*, by Wolf Brinsbury (science).

Fiction: Humor, juvenile, science fiction. Query with synopsis and SASE.

SKY PUBLISHING CORP., P.O. Box 9111, Belmont MA 02178-9111. (617)864-7360. Fax: (617)864-6117. E-mail: postmaster@skypub.com. Website: http://www.skypub.com. President/Publisher: Richard Tresch Fienberg. Estab. 1941. Publishes 6 titles/year. Publishes hardcover and trade paperback originals on topics of interest to serious amateur astronmers as well as *Sky & Telescope*, the Essential Magazine of Astronomy; *CCD Astronomy*, the Magazine of Electronic Imaging. Nonfiction only. Magazine articles: pays $0.20/word. Books: pays 10% royalty on net sales. Magazine author and book proposal guidelines available on request. Sky Publishing catalog free on request.

Recent Nonfiction Title: *Astrophotography*, by H.J.P. Arnold (observer's guide).

SLACK INC., 6900 Grove Rd., Thorofare NJ 08086. (609)848-1000. Fax: (609)845-9230. E-mail: adrummond@slackinc.com. Website: http://www.slackinc.com. Acquisitions Editor: Amy E. Drummond. Publishes hardcover and softcover originals. Publishes 15 titles/year. Receives 60 queries and 20 mss/year. 75% of books from first-time authors; 100% from unagented writers. Pays 10% royalty. Publishes book 6 months after acceptance. Accepts simultaneous submissions. Reports in 4 months on queries, 1 month on proposals, 3 months on mss. Book catalog and ms guidelines free on request.

Nonfiction: Textbook (medical). Subjects include ophthalmology, athletic training, optometry, physical therapy, occupational therapy. Submit proposal package, including outline, 2 sample chapters, market profile and cv. Reviews artwork/photos as part of ms package. Send photocopies.

Recent Nonfiction Title: *Corneal Topography*, by Donald Sanders, MD (opthalmology).

‡SLIGO PRESS, P.O. Box 523, Bend OR 97709. (541)317-9402. Publisher: Eric G. Bollinger. Publishes hardcover originals. Publishes 12 titles/year. Receives 500 queries/year; 200 mss/year. 90% of books are from first-time authors; 90% from unagented writers. Pays 10-15% royalty on wholesale price. Offers $1,000-5,000 advance. Publishes book 8 months after acceptance. Accepts simultaneous submissions. Reports in 1 month on queries and proposals, 3 months on mss. Writer's guidelines for #10 SASE.

Nonfiction: Biography, cookbook, how-to, self-help. Subjects include gay/lesbian, government/politics, history, hobbies, military/war, regional, travel, women's issues/studies. Query with SASE.

Fiction: Adventure, feminist, gay/lesbian, historical, humor, literary, mainstream/contemporary, mystery, suspense. No children's. Query with SASE.

Tips: "We work with new, unagented authors. We are new, but well capitalized with excellent editors. We target the book's market, then aggressively go after it."

THE SMITH, The Generalist Association, Inc., 69 Joralemon St., Brooklyn NY 11201-4003. (718)834-1212. Publisher: Harry Smith. Estab. 1964. Publishes hardcover and trade paperback originals. Publishes 5 titles/year. Receives 2,500 queries/year. 50% of books from first-time authors; more than 90% from unagented writers. Pays royalty. Offers $500 advance. Publishes book 9 months after acceptance. Accepts simultaneous submissions. Reports in 3 months. Book catalog and guidelines on request for SASE.

Nonfiction: Literary essays, language and literature. "The 'how' is as important as the 'what' to us. Don't bother to send anything if the prose is not outstanding itself. We don't publish anything about how to fix your car or your soul." Query with proposal package including outline and sample chapter. Reviews artwork/photos as part of ms package. Send photocopies.

Fiction: Experimental, feminist, literary. "Emphasis is always on artistic quality. A synopsis of almost any novel sounds stupid." Query with 1 sample chapter. Do not send complete ms. Irregular hours preclude acceptance of registered mail.

Recent Fiction Title: *Bodo*, by John Bennett (novel).

Poetry: "No greeting card sentiments, no casual jottings." Do not send complete ms. Do not send registered mail. Submit 7-10 sample poems.

‡SMITH AND KRAUS PUBLISHERS, INC., One Main St., P.O. Box 127, Lyme NH 03768. (603)795-4331. President/Publisher: Marisa Smith. Publishes hardcover and trade paperback originals. Publishes 35-40 books/year. 10% of books from first-time authors; 10-20% from unagented writers. Pays 10% royalty of net on retail price. Offers $500-2,000 advance. Publishes book 1 year after acceptance. Does not return submissions. Reports in 1 month on queries, 2 months on proposals, 4 months on mss. Book catalog free on request.

Nonfiction: Drama, theater. Query.

Recent Nonfiction Title: *Plays of America from American Folklore for Children*, by L.E. McCullough.

SOCIAL SCIENCE EDUCATION CONSORTIUM, P.O. Box 21270, Boulder CO 80308-4270. (303)492-8154. Fax: (303)449-3925. E-mail: singletl@ucsu.colorado.edu. Managing Editor: Laurel R. Singleton. Estab. 1963. Publishes trade paperback originals. Publishes 8 titles/year. 25% of books from first-time authors; 100% from unagented writers. Pays 8-12% royalty on net sales (retail price minus average discount). Publishes book 6 months after acceptance. Accepts simultaneous submissions. Reports in 1 month on proposals. *Writer's Market* recommends allowing 2 months for reply.

Nonfiction: Teacher resources. Subjects include education, government/politics, history; must include teaching applications. "We publish titles of interest to social studies teachers particularly; we do not generally publish on such broad educational topics as discipline, unless there is a specific relationship to the social studies/social sciences." Submit outline and 1-2 sample chapters.

Recent Nonfiction Title: *H Is for History: Using Children's Literature to Develop Historical Understandings*, by Laurel R. Singleton (teacher resource).

SOCIETY PUBLISHING, P.O. Box 66271, Auburndale Branch, Boston MA 02165. (617)965-7129. Contact: Editor. Publishes hardcover and trade paperback originals. Publishes 4 titles/year. Receives 60 queries/year. 50% of books from first-time authors; 100% from unagented writers. Pays on contract basis. Publishes book 1 year after acceptance of ms. No simultaneous submissions. Reports in 2 months on queries.

Nonfiction: Self-help. Subjects include health/medicine, psychology, spiritual. Query.

SOHO PRESS, INC., 853 Broadway, New York NY 10003. (212)260-1900. Editor-in-Chief: Juris Jurjevics. Estab. 1986. Publishes hardcover and trade paperback originals. Publishes 25 titles/year. Receives 5,000 submissions/year. 75% of books from first-time authors; 50% from unagented writers. Pays 7½-15% royalty on retail price. Offers advance. Publishes book within 1 year after acceptance. Accepts simultaneous submissions. Reports in 1 month. Book catalog for 6×9 SAE with 2 first-class stamps.
Nonfiction: Literary nonfiction: travel, autobiography, biography, etc. "No self-help." Submit outline and sample chapters.
Recent Nonfiction Title: *Vietnamerica: The War Comes Home*, by Thomas Bass.
Fiction: Adventure, ethnic, feminist, historical, literary, mainstream/contemporary, mystery, suspense. Submit complete ms with SASE. *Writer's Market* recommends query with SASE first.
Recent Fiction Title: *Krik Krak*, by Edwidge Danticat.

SOUNDPRINTS, Division of Trudy Corporation, 165 Water St., Norwalk CT 06856. Fax: (203)866-9944. Assistant Editor: Deirdre Langeland. Publishes hardcover originals. Publishes 10-14 titles/year. Receives 200 queries/year. 20% of books from first-time authors; 90% of books from unagented writers. No advance. Makes outright purchase. Publishes book 2 years after acceptance. Accepts simultaneous submissions. Reports on queries in 3 months. Book catalog for 9×12 SAE with $1.05 postage. Manuscript guidelines for #10 SASE.
   ● This publisher creates multimedia sets for the Smithsonian Wild Heritage Collection, the Smithsonian Oceanic Collection and Smithsonian's Backyard. Sets include a book, read-a-long audiotape and realistic stuffed animal, combining facts about North American wildlife with stories about each animal's habits and habitats. They have received the Parent's Choice Award for 1993, 1994 and 1995.
Nonfiction: Children's/juvenile, animals. "We focus on North American wildlife and ecology. Subject animals must be portrayed realistically and must not be anthropomorphic. Meticulous research is required." Query with SASE. Does not review artwork/photos as part of ms package. (All books are now illustrated in full color.)
Recent Nonfiction Title: *Chipmunk on Hollow Tree Lane* (winner of the 1994 Parent's Choice Award).
Fiction: Juvenile. "When we publish juvenile fiction, it will be about wildlife and all information in the book *must* be accurate." Query.
Tips: "Our books are written for children from ages 4-8. Our most successful authors can craft a wonderful story which is derived from authentic wildlife facts. First inquiry to us should ask about our interest in publishing a book about a specific animal or habitat. We launched a new series in fall of 1996. Stories are about historical events that are represented by exhibits in the Smithsonian Institution's museums."

SOURCEBOOKS, INC., P.O. Box 372, Naperville IL 60566. (708)961-3900. Fax: (708)961-2168. Publisher: Dominique Raccah. Editor: Todd Stocke. Estab. 1987. Publishes hardcover and trade paperback originals. Publishes 35 titles/year. 50% of books from first-time authors; 100% from unagented writers. Pays 6-15% royalty on wholesale price. Publishes book 6 months after acceptance. Accepts simultaneous submissions. Reports in 3 months on queries. No complete mss. Book catalog and ms guidelines for 9×12 SASE.
Nonfiction: *Small Business Sourcebooks:* books for small business owners, entrepreneurs and students. "A key to submitting books to us is to explain *how* your book helps the reader, *why* it is different from the books already out there (please do your homework) and the *author's credentials* for writing this book." *Sourcebooks Trade:* gift books, self-help, general business, and how to. "Books likely to succeed with us are self-help, art books, parenting and childcare, psychology, women's issues, how-to, house and home, gift books or books with strong artwork." Query or submit outline and 2-3 sample chapters (not the first). Reviews artwork/photos as part of ms package.
Recent Nonfiction Title: *365 Days of Creative Play*, by Sheila Ellison and Judith Gray (children/parenting).
Tips: "We love to develop books in new areas or develop strong titles in areas that are already well developed. Our goal is to provide customers with terrific innovative books at reasonable prices."

‡**SOUTH END PRESS**, 116 Saint Botolph St., Boston MA 02115. (617)266-0629. Fax: (617)266-1595. Contact: Dionne Brooks. Publishes hardcover and trade paperback originals and reprints. Publishes 15 titles/year. Receives 400 queries and 100 mss/year. 50% of books from first-time authors; 95% from unagented writers. Pays 10% royalty on wholesale price. Occasionally offers $500-2,500 advance. Publishes book 9 months after acceptance. Accepts simultaneous submissions. Reports in up to 3 months on queries and proposals. Book catalog and ms guidelines free on request.

   ● **A BULLET** introduces comments by the editors of *Writer's Market* indicating special information about the listing.

Nonfiction: Subjects include economics, education, ethnic, gay/lesbian, government/politics, health/medicine, history, nature/environment, philosophy, science, sociology, women's issues/studies, political. "We publish books with a new left/feminist multi-cultural perspective." Query or submit 2 sample chapters including intro or conclusion. Reviews artwork/photos as part of ms package. Send photocopies.
Recent Nonfiction Title: *Eyes Right*, edited by Chip Berlet (political).

SOUTHERN METHODIST UNIVERSITY PRESS, P.O. Box 415, Dallas TX 75275. Fax: (214)768-1428. Senior Editor: Kathryn Lang. Establ. 1937. Publishes hardcover and trade paperback originals and reprints. Publishes 10-15 titles/year. Receives 500 queries and 500 mss/year. 75% of books from first-time authors; 95% from unagented writers. Pays up to 10% royalty on wholesale price. Offers $500 advance. Publishes book 1 year after acceptance. Reports in 1 month on queries and proposals, 6 months on mss.
   • Southern Methodist University Press has been accepting fewer manuscripts.
Nonfiction: Subjects include medical ethics/human values and history (regional). "We are seeking works in the following areas: theology; film/theater; medical ethics/human values." Query with outline, 3 sample chapters, table of contents and author bio. Reviews artwork/photos as part of the ms package. Send photocopies.
Fiction: Literary novels and short story collections. Query.
Tips: Audience is general educated readers of quality fiction and nonfiction.

SOUTHFARM PRESS, Haan Graphic Publishing Services, Ltd., P.O. Box 1296, Middletown CT 06457. (860)346-8798. Publisher: Walter J. Haan. Estab. 1983. Publishes trade paperback originals. Publishes 5 titles/year. 50% from first-time authors; 100% from unagented writers. Pays 5-10% royalty on retail price. No advance. Publishes book 1 year after acceptance. Accepts simultaneous submissions. Reports in 1 month. *Writer's Market* recommends allowing 2 months for reply.
Nonfiction: Subjects include history, military/war and dog breeds. Submit outline/synopsis and sample chapters.
Recent Nonfiction Title: *Reflections on the Tibetan Terrier*, by Jane Reif (readings about the breed).

SPAN PRESS INC., 5722 S. Flamingo Rd., #277, Cooper City FL 33330. (305)434-4991. Fax: (305)477-5632. E-mail: justor@aol.com. Director, Editorial Services: Barbara Teuten. Publishes trade paperback originals. Publishes 100 titles/year. Receives 75-80 queries and 50 mss/year. 75% of books from first-time authors; 100% from unagented writers. Pays 4-10% royalty on wholesale price. Publishes book 18 months after acceptance of ms. Reports in 3 months on mss. Manuscript guidelines free on request.
Nonfiction: Spanish. Subjects include education, life of Hispanics in US. Submit 2 sample chapters. Reviews artwork/photos as part of ms package. Send photocopies.
Recent Nonfiction Title: *Lalo*, by Elizabeth Jimenez (education).
Fiction: Spanish. *Writer's Market* recommends sending a query with SASE first.
Tips: Looking for more authentic Hispanic culture stories appropriate for kindergarten, 1st and 2nd grades.

SPECTRUM PRESS INC., 3023 N. Clark St., #109, Chicago IL 60657. (312)281-1419. E-mail: chspecpres s@aol.com. Website: http://www.usere.aol.com/specpress/index.utml. Editor-in-Chief: Dan Agin. Publishes floppy disk books. Publishes 50 titles/year. Receives 1,000 queries and 300 mss/year. 75% of books from first-time authors; 90% from unagented writers. Pays 10-15% royalty on retail price. Publishes book 3 months after acceptance of ms. Accepts simultaneous submissions. Electronic submissions preferred. Reports in 1 month. *Writer's Market* recommends allowing 2 months for reply. Book catalog and ms guidelines for #10 SASE.
Nonfiction: Biography, reference. Subjects include Americana, anthropology/archaeology, art/architecture, ethnic, gay/lesbian, government/politics, history, language/literature, philosophy, sociology, translation, women's issues/studies. Query.
Recent Nonfiction Title: *Mirrors*, by Beth Elliott (biography).
Fiction: Erotica, ethnic, experimental, feminist, gay/lesbian, literary, mainstream/contemporary, plays, short story collections. Submit complete work on floppy disk. *Writer's Market* recommends sending a query with SASE first.
Recent Fiction Title: *Case Closed*, by Daniel Vian (novel).
Poetry: "Interested in new strong poetry." Submit 10 sample poems or complete ms.
Recent Poetry Title: *Souvenirs From the Bog*, by Christina Starobin.

THE SPEECH BIN, INC., 1965 25th Ave., Vero Beach FL 32960-3062. (407)770-0007. Senior Editor: Jan Binney. Estab. 1984. Publishes trade paperback originals. Publishes 10-20 titles/year. Receives 500 mss/year. 50% of books from first-time authors; 90% from unagented writers. Pays negotiable royalty on wholesale price. Publishes ms 6 months after acceptance. Reports in up to 3 months. Book catalog for 9×12 SASE and $1.48 postage.
   • The Speech Bin is increasing the number of books published per year and is especially interested in reviewing treatment materials for adults and adolescents.

Nonfiction: How-to, illustrated book, juvenile (preschool-teen), reference, textbook, educational material and games for both children and adults. Subjects include health, communication disorders and education for handicapped persons. Query or submit outline and sample chapters. Reviews artwork/photos as part of ms package. Send photocopies only, no original artwork.

Recent Nonfiction Title: *Techniques for Aphasia Rehabilitation*, by Mary Jo Santo Pietro and Robert Goldfarb.

Fiction: "Booklets or books for children and adults about handicapped persons, especially with communication disorders." Query or submit outline/synopsis and sample chapters. "This is a potentially new market for The Speech Bin."

Tips: "Our audience is made up of special educators, speech-language pathologists and audiologists, occupational and physical therapists, parents, caregivers, and teachers of children and adults with developmental and post-trauma disabilities. Books and materials must be research-based, clearly presented, well written, competently illustrated, and unique. We'll be adding books and materials for use by other allied health professionals. We are also looking for more materials for use in treating adults and very young children with communication disorders. Please do not fax manuscripts to us."

SPINSTERS INK, 32 E. First St., #330, Duluth, MN 55802. (218)727-3222. Fax: (218)727-3119. E-mail: spinsters@aol.com. Website: http://www.lesbian.org/spinsters-ink. Acquisitions: Jami Snyder. Estab. 1978. Publishes trade paperback originals and reprints. Publishes 6 titles/year. Receives 300 submissions/year. 50% of books from first-time authors; 95% from unagented writers. Pays 7-11% royalty on retail price. Publishes book 18 months after acceptance. Reports in 4 months. Book catalog free. Manuscript guidelines for SASE.

Nonfiction: Feminist analysis for positive change. Subjects include women's issues. "We are interested in books that not only name the crucial issues in women's lives, but show and encourage change and growth. We do not want to see work by men, or anything that is not specific to women's lives (humor, children's books, etc.)." Query. Reviews artwork/photos as part of ms package.

Fiction: Ethnic, women's, lesbian. "We do not publish poetry or short fiction. We are interested in fiction that challenges, women's language that is feminist, stories that treat lifestyles with the diversity and complexity they deserve. We are also interested in genre fiction, especially mysteries." Submit outline/synopsis and sample chapters.

Recent Fiction Title: *Martha Moody*, by Susan Stinson.

STACKPOLE BOOKS, 5067 Ritter Rd., Mechanicsburg PA 17055. Fax: (717)796-0412. Editorial Director: Judith Schnell. Estab. 1935. Publishes hardcover and paperback originals and reprints. Publishes 75 titles/year. Publishes book 1 year after acceptance. Reports in 1 month. *Writer's Market* recommends allowing 2 months for reply.

Nonfiction: Outdoor-related subject areas—nature, wildlife, outdoor skills, outdoor sports, fly fishing, paddling, climbing, crafts and hobbies, gardening, decoy carving, woodworkng, history especially Civil War and military guides. Query. Unsolicited mss and materials will not be returned. Reviews artwork/photos as part of ms package.

Recent Nonfiction Title: *Canoeing*, by Dave Harrison.

Tips: "Stackpole seeks well-written, authoritative manuscripts for specialized and general trade markets. Proposals should include chapter outline, sample chapter and illustrations and author's credentials."

STANDARD PUBLISHING, Division of Standex International Corp., 8121 Hamilton Ave., Cincinnati OH 45231. (513)931-4050. Publisher/President: Eugene H. Wigginton. Contact: Theresa Hayes, acquisitions coordinator. Estab. 1866. Publishes hardcover and paperback originals and reprints. Specializes in religious books for children. Publishes book 18 months after acceptance. Reports in 3 months. Manuscript guidelines for #10 SASE; send request to Acquisitions Coordinator.

Nonfiction: Publishes crafts (to be used in Christian education), children's picture books, Christian education (teacher training, working with volunteers), quiz, puzzle. All mss must pertain to religion. *Writer's Market* recommends sending a query with SASE first.

Recent Nonfiction Title: *The 21st Century Sunday School*, by Wes Haystead.

STANFORD UNIVERSITY PRESS, Stanford CA 94305-2235. (415)723-9598. Editor-in-Chief: Norris Pope. Estab. 1925. Publishes 100 titles/year. Receives 1,500 submissions/year. 40% of books from first-time authors; 95% from unagented writers. Nonauthor-subsidy publishes 65% of books. Pays up to 15% royalty ("typically 10%, often none"). Sometimes offers advance. Publishes book 16 months after receipt of final ms. Reports in 6 weeks.

Nonfiction: Scholarly books in the humanities, social sciences, and natural sciences: history and culture of China, Japan, and Latin America; European history; literature, criticism, and literary theory; political science and sociology; biology, natural history, and taxonomy; anthropology, linguistics, and psychology; archaeology and geology; and medieval and classical studies. Also high-level textbooks and books for a more general audience. Query. "We like to see a prospectus and an outline." Reviews artwork/photos as part of ms package.

Tips: "The writer's best chance is a work of original scholarship with an argument of some importance."

STERLING PUBLISHING, 387 Park Ave. S., New York NY 10016. (212)532-7160. Fax: (212)213-2495. Acquisitions Manager: Sheila Anne Barry. Estab. 1949. Publishes hardcover and paperback originals and reprints. Publishes 200 titles/year. Pays royalty. Offers advance. Publishes book 8 months after acceptance. Reports in 2 months. Guidelines for SASE.

Nonfiction: Alternative lifestyle, fiber arts, games and puzzles, health, how-to, hobbies, children's humor, children's science, nature and activities, pets, recreation, reference, sports, technical, wine, gardening, art, home decorating, dolls and puppets, ghosts, UFOs, woodworking, crafts, history, medieval, Celtic subjects, alternative health and healing, new consciousness. Query or submit complete chapter list, detailed outline and 2 sample chapters with photos if applicable. Reviews artwork/photos as part of ms package.

Recent Nonfiction Title: *Intriguing Lateral Thinking Puzzles*, by Paul Sloane and Des MacHale.

STILLPOINT PUBLISHING, Division of Stillpoint International, Inc., P.O. Box 640, Walpole NH 03608. (603)756-9281. Fax: (603)756-9282. Editor-in-Chief: Claire Gerus. Publishes hardcover originals and trade paperback originals and reprints that awaken the human spirit. Publishes 8-10 titles/year. Receives 500 submissions/year. 50% of books from first-time authors; 90% from unagented writers. Pays royalty. Publishes book 15 months after acceptance. Accepts simultaneous submissions. Response in 10 weeks. Manuscript guidelines for SASE.

Nonfiction: Topics include personal growth and spiritual development; holistic health and healing for individual and global well-being; spirituality in business, work and community; inspirational; psychology/self-help. Submit complete ms or query with table of contents and sample chapters. *Writer's Market* recommends sending a query with SASE first.

Recent Nonfiction Title: *Anyone Can See the Light*, by Dianne Morrissey, Ph.D.

Tips: "We are looking for manuscripts with a unique, clearly-stated theme supported by persuasive evidence. We publish nonfiction based on experience and/or research that illuminates an area of personal growth or spiritual development. The work needs to be insightful and practical. We're now looking for books with mass-market appeal in the spiritual/new thought/inspirational categories."

STIPES PUBLISHING CO., 10-12 Chester St., Champaign IL 61824-9933. (217)356-8391. Fax: (217)356-5753. Contact: Robert Watts. Estab. 1925. Publishes hardcover and paperback originals. Publishes 15-30 titles/year. Receives 150 submissions/year. 50% of books from first-time authors; 95% from unagented writers. Pays 15% maximum royalty on retail price. Publishes book 4 months after acceptance. Reports in 2 months.

Nonfiction: Technical (some areas), textbooks on business and economics, music, chemistry, agriculture/horticulture, environmental education, and recreation and physical education. "All of our books in the trade area are books that also have a college text market. No books unrelated to educational fields taught at the college level." Submit outline and 1 sample chapter.

Recent Nonfiction Title: *Manual of Woody Landscape Plants*, by Michael Dirr (text and professional reference).

STOEGER PUBLISHING COMPANY, 5 Mansard Court, Wayne NJ 07470. (201)872-9500. Fax: (201)872-2230. Vice President: David Perkins. Estab. 1925. Publishes trade paperback originals. Publishes 12-15 titles/year. Royalty varies, depending on ms. Accepts simultaneous submissions. Reports in 1 month on queries. *Writer's Market* recommends allowing 2 months for reply. Book catalog for #10 SAE with 2 first-class stamps.

Nonfiction: Specializing in reference and how-to books that pertain to hunting, fishing and appeal to gun enthusiasts. Submit outline and sample chapters.

Recent Nonfiction Title: *Gunsmithing at Home*, by John Traister (sporting).

STONE BRIDGE PRESS, P.O. Box 8208, Berkeley CA 94707. (510)524-8732. Fax: (510)524-8711. E-mail: sbp@netcom.com. Website: http://www.stonebridge.com/~sbp/. Publisher: Peter Goodman. Imprint is The Rock Spring Collection of Japanese Literature. Publishes hardcover and trade paperback originals. Publishes 6 titles/year; imprint publishes 2 titles/year. Receives 100 queries and 75 mss/year. 15-20% of books from first-time authors; 90% from unagented writers. Pays royalty on wholesale price. Advance varies. Publishes book 2 years after acceptance. Accepts simultaneous submissions. Reports in 1 month on queries and proposals, 4 months on mss. Book catalog free on request.

Nonfiction: How-to, reference. Subjects include art/architecture, business and economics, government/politics, language/literature, philosophy, translation, travel, women's issues/studies. "We publish Japan- (and some Asia-) related books only." Query with SASE. Reviews artwork/photos as part of ms package. Send photocopies.

Fiction: Experimental, fantasy, feminist, gay/lesbian, literary, mystery, science fiction, short story collections, translation. "Japan-related only based on author's first-hand experience, not Western exotic recreations." Query with SASE.

Poetry: Translations from Japanese only. Query.

Tips: Audience is "intelligent, worldly readers with an interest in Japan based on personal need or experience. No children's books. No commercial or genre fiction. Realize that interest in Japan is a moving target. Please don't submit yesterday's trends or rely on a view of Japan that is outmoded. Stay current!"

STOREY COMMUNICATIONS/GARDEN WAY PUBLISHING, Schoolhouse Rd., Pownal VT 05261. (802)823-5200. Fax: (802)823-5819. Editorial Director: Gwen Steege. Estab. 1983. Publishes hardcover and trade paperback originals and reprints. Publishes 45 titles/year. Receives 350 queries and 150 mss/year. 25% of books from first-time authors; 80% from unagented writers. Pays royalty or makes outright purchase. Publishes book within 2 years of acceptance. Accepts simultaneous submissions. Reports in 1 month on queries, 3 months on proposals and mss. Book catalog and ms guidelines free on request.
Nonfiction: Cookbook, how-to, children's/juvenile. Subjects include agriculture/horticulture, animals, building, beer, cooking/foods/nutrition, crafts, gardening, hobbies, nature/environment. Submit proposal package, including outline, sample chapter, competitive books, author résumé. Occasionally reviews artwork/photos as part of the ms package.
Recent Nonfiction Title: *The Herb Gardener*, by Susan McClure (4-color, how-to gardening book).

‡**STORY LINE PRESS**, Three Oaks Farm, Brownsville OR 97327. (541)466-5352. Executive Director: Robert McDowell. Publishes hardcover and trade paperback originals. Publishes 10-12 titles/year. Receives 100 queries and 100 mss/year. 10% of books from first-time authors; most from unagented writers. Pays 10-15% royalty on retail price or makes outright purchase of $250-1,000. Offers $0-1,000 advance. Publishes book 1 year after acceptance of ms. Accepts simultaneous submissions. Reports in 1 month on queries, 2 months on mss. Book catalog free on request. Manuscript guidelines for #10 SASE.
Nonfiction: Literary. Subjects include authors/literature. Query with SASE.
Recent Nonfiction Title: *The Wilderness of Vision*, by Kevin Walzer, Kevin Bezner (essays on John Haines).
Fiction: Literary. "We currently have a backlist through the year 2000. Please send query letter first." Query with SASE.
Recent Fiction Title: *Summer Blue*, by Floyd Skloot (literary novel).
Poetry: "Backlist for publication is through the year 2000. Please send query letter first. Consider our Nicholas Roerich Poetry Prize for previously unpublished poetry book authors of book-length mss." Query.
Recent Poetry Title: *There You Are*, by Louis Simpson (narrative).
Tips: Audience is "the interested literary reader who displays alignment with the principles of New Formalism and New Narrative poetry and with the story line in every book. We have a long list to publish already and it keeps growing, so save postage and send a query letter first with a SASE."

SUCCESS PUBLISHING, 3419 Dunham Rd., Warsaw NY 14569-9735. (800)330-4643. President: Allan H. Smith. Submission Manager: Robin Garretson. Estab. 1982. Publishes trade paperback originals. Publishes 6 titles/year. Receives 200 submissions/year. 75% of books from first-time authors; 100% from unagented writers. Pays 7% royalty. Publishes book 3 months after acceptance. Accepts simultaneous submissions. Reports in 2 months on queries. Book catalog and ms guidelines for #10 SAE with 2 first-class stamps.
• Success Publishing is looking for ghostwriters.
Nonfiction: How-to, humor, self-help. Subjects include business and economics, hobbies, money/finance. "We are looking for books on how-to subjects such as home business and sewing." Query.
Recent Nonfiction Title: *How To Write A "How To" Book*, by Smith (how-to).
Tips: "Our audience is made up of housewives, hobbyists and owners of home-based businesses. If I were a writer trying to market a book today, I would read books about how to market a self-written book."

‡**SUDBURY PRESS**, Profitable Technology, Inc., 40 Maclean Dr., Sudbury MA 01776. Fax: (508)443-0734. E-mail: press@intertain.com. Website: http://www.intertain.com. Publisher: Susan Gray. Publishes hardcover and mass market paperback originals. Publishes 8 titles/year. Receives 100 queries and 20 mss/year. 100% of books from first-time authors; 100% from unagented writers. Pays 5-15% royalty on wholesale price. Offers $0-3,000 advance. Publishes book 6 months after acceptance. Reports in 1 month. *Writer's Market* recommends allowing 2 months for reply. Book catalog on Internet.
Fiction: "We look for cozy mysteries in the style of Agatha Christie." Submit synopsis, 2 sample chapters and SASE. Prefers complete ms.

SULZBURGER & GRAHAM PUBLISHING, LTD., 505 Eighth Ave., New York NY 10018. Publisher: Neil Blond. Imprints are Human Services Institute, Blond's Law Guides, Carroll Press. Publishes hardcover and trade paperback originals and reprints. Publishes 35 titles/year. Publishes 10-15 imprint titles/year. Receives 400 queries and 100 mss/year. 80% of books from first-time authors; 95% from unagented writers. Pays 0-15% royalty on wholesale price. Offers $100-2,000 advance. Publishes book 6 months after acceptance of ms. Accepts simultaneous submissions. Reports in 2 months on queries and proposals, 4 months on mss. Book catalog for 8×11 SAE with 4 first-class stamps. Manuscript guidelines for #10 SASE.
Nonfiction: How-to, reference, self-help, technical, textbook. Subjects include business and economics, child guidance/parenting, computers and electronics, education, health/medicine, hobbies, money/finance, psychology, recreation, science, software, travel, women's issues/studies. Query with outline and 1 sample chapter. Reviews artwork/photos as part of ms package. Send photocopies.

Recent Nonfiction Title: *Scoring High on Bar Exams*, by Mary Gallagher (test preparation).

SUMMERS PRESS, INC., also known as Business Publishing, 7035 Bee Caves Rd., Suite 203, Austin TX 78746. Editor: Mark Summers. Publishes hardcover originals. Publishes 5 titles/year. Some books from first-time authors. Pays 2-5% royalty on retail price or makes outright purchase. Offers $1,000-2,500 advance. Also purchases completed mss. Accepts simultaneous submissions.
Nonfiction: Reference, technical, legal references for businesses. Subjects include employment, health, and safety law. Includes software. "Manuscript should be easily accessible, use short sentences, and attempt to convey complex information on a 10-12th grade reading level." Query with outline, 1 chapter and SASE.
Recent Nonfiction Title: *OSHA Compliance Guide*, (reference book for businesses).

THE SUMMIT PUBLISHING GROUP, One Arlington Center, 112 E. Copeland, 5th Floor, Arlington TX 76112. Managing Editor: Mark Murphy. Publishes hardcover originals, trade paperback originals and reprints. Publishes 35 titles/year. 40% of books from first-time authors; 80% from unagented writers. Pays 5-20% royalty on wholesale price. Offers $2,000 and up advance. Publishes book 6 months after acceptance of ms. Accepts simultaneous submissions. Reports in 1 month on queries and proposals, 3 months on mss.
Nonfiction: Biography, children's/juvenile, coffee table book, cookbook, gift book, how-to, humor, self-help. Subjects include art/architecture, business/economics, cooking, ethnic, gardening, government/politics, health/medicine, history, hobbies, military/war, money/finance, nature/environment, recreation, regional, religion, science, sociology, sports, women's issues/studies. "Books should have obvious national-distribution appeal, be of a contemporary nature and be marketing-driven: author's media experience and contacts a strong plus. Submit proposal package including outline, 2 sample chapters, table of contents, proposal marketing letter and résumé with SASE. Reviews artwork/photos as part of ms package. Send photocopies.
Recent Nonfiction Title: *On the Brink: The Life and Leadership of Norman Brinker*, by Norman Brinker and Donald T. Phillips (business biography).
Fiction: Literary, religious. Submit synopsis, 2 sample chapters and SASE.
Recent Fiction Title: *The Gospel of Elvis*, by Louie Ludwig (humor).

SUNSTONE PRESS, Imprint of Sunstone Corp., P.O. Box 2321, Santa Fe NM 87504-2321. (505)988-4418. President: James C. Smith Jr. Estab. 1971. Other imprint is Sundial Publications. Publishes paperback and hardcover originals. Publishes 25 titles/year. Receives 400 submissions/year. 70% of books from first-time authors; 100% from unagented writers. Average print order for a first book is 2,000-5,000. Pays royalty on wholesale price. Publishes book 18 months after acceptance. Reports in 1 month.
• The focus of this publisher is still the Southwestern U.S. but it receives many, many submissions outside this subject. It does not publish poetry.
Nonfiction: How-to series craft books. Books on the history and architecture of the Southwest. "Looks for strong regional appeal (Southwestern)." Query with SASE. Reviews artwork/photos as part of ms package.
Recent Nonfiction Title: *Dinetah: An Early History of the Navajo People*, by Dean Sundberg.
Fiction: Publishes material with Southwestern theme. Query with SASE.
Recent Fiction Title: *Heart of Stone*, by Anne Denton.

SWAN-RAVEN & CO., Imprint of Blue Water Publishing, Inc., P.O. Box 726, Newberg OR 97132. (503)538-0264. Fax: (503)538-8485. President: Pam Meyer. Contact: David Kyle. Publishes trade paperback originals. Publishes 6 titles/year. Receives 25 queries and 15 mss/month. 80% of books from first-time authors; 90% from unagented writers. Pays 5-12% royalty on wholesale price. Publishes book 16 months after acceptance of ms. Accepts simultaneous submissions. Reports in 1 month on mss. *Writer's Market* recommends allowing 2 months for reply. Book catalog free on request. Manuscript guidelines for #10 SASE.
Nonfiction: Subjects include health, philosophy, women's issues/studies, spiritual, future speculation. Query with outline. Reviews artwork/photos as part of ms package. Send photocopies.
Recent Nonfiction Title: *Calling the Circle: The First and Future Culture*, by Christina Baldwin.

SWEDENBORG FOUNDATION, P.O. Box 549, West Chester PA 19381-0549. (610)430-3222. Fax: (610)430-7982. Imprints are Chrysalis Books, Swedenborg Foundation, Chrysalis Reader. Publishes hardcover and trade paperback originals and reprints. Publishes 6-10 titles/year; imprints publish 2-4 titles/year. Pays 5-10% royalty on net receipts or makes outright purchase. Offers $500 minimum advance. Reports in 3 months on queries, 6 months on proposals, 9 months on mss. Book catalog and ms guidelines free on request.
• See also Chrysalis Reader under Consumer Magazines/Religious.
Nonfiction: Biography, spiritual growth, self-transformation, writings of Emanuel Swedenborg. Subjects include philosophy, psychology, religion. Query with proposal package, including synopsis, outline, sample chapter and SASE. Reviews artwork/photos as part of ms package. Send photocopies.
Recent Nonfiction Title: *Angels in Action*, by Robert Kirven (religion).
Tips: "The Swedenborg Foundation publishes books by and about Emanuel Swedenborg (1688-1772), his ideas, how his ideas have influenced others, and related topics. Most readers of our books are thoughtful, well-read individuals seeking resources for their philosophical, spiritual, or religious growth. Especially

sought are nonfiction works that bridge contemporary issues to spiritual insights."

SYBEX, INC., 2021 Challenger Dr., Alameda CA 94501. (510)523-8233. Fax: (510)523-2373. E-mail: kplachy@sybex.com. Website: http://www.sybex.com. Editor-in-Chief: Bruce M. Spatz. Acquisitions Editor and Manager: Kristine Plachy. Estab. 1976. Publishes paperback originals. Publishes 120 titles/year. Royalty rates vary. Offers competitive average advance. Publishes book 3 months after acceptance. Accepts simultaneous submissions. Reports in up to 6 months. Free book catalog.
Nonfiction: Computers, computer software. "Manuscripts most publishable in the field of database development, word processing, programming languages, suites, computer games, Internet/Web and networking." Submit outline and 2-3 sample chapters. Looks for "clear writing, logical presentation of material; and good selection of material such that the most important aspects of the subject matter are thoroughly covered; well-focused subject matter; clear understanding of target audience; and well-thought-out organization that helps the reader understand the material." Reviews artwork/photos, disk/CD as part of ms package.
Recent Nonfiction Title: *Mastering Windows 95*, by Robert Cowart.
Tips: Queries/mss may be routed to other editors in the publishing group. Also seeking freelance writers for revising existing works and as contributors in multi-author projects.

SYSTEMS CO. INC., P.O. Box 339, Carlsborg WA 98324. (360)683-6860. President: Richard H. Peetz, Ph.D. Publishes hardcover and trade paperback originals. Publishes 3-5 titles/year. 50% of books from first-time authors; 100% from unagented writers. Pays 20% royalty on wholesale price after costs. Publishes book 6 months after acceptance of ms. Accepts simultaneous submissions. Reports in 2 months. Book catalog free on request. Manuscript guidelines for $1.
Nonfiction: How-to, self-help, technical, textbook. Subjects include business and economics, automotive, health/medicine, money/finance, nature/environment, science/engineering. "In submitting nonfiction, writers often make the mistake of picking a common topic with lots of published books in print." Submit outline, 2 sample chapters and SASE. Reviews artwork/photos as part of ms package. Send photocopies.
Recent Nonfiction Title: *Radiation Effects on Electronics-5th Ed.*, by F.L. Bouquet (technical).
Tips: "Our audience consists of people in technical occupations, people interested in doing things themselves."

TAMBOURINE BOOKS, Imprint of William Morrow & Co., Inc., 1350 Avenue of the Americas, New York NY 10019. (212)261-6661. Editorial Assistant: Ben Schafer. Estab. 1989. Publishes hardcover originals. Publishes 20 titles/year. Receives 120 queries and 2,000 mss/year. Accepts simultaneous submissions. Reports in 2 months on queries. Book catalog for 9×12 SASE. Manuscript guidelines for #10 SASE.
Nonfiction: Children's/juvenile. Subjects include history, hobbies, money/finance, science. Query with SASE. Reviews artwork/photos as part of ms package. Send color photocopies.
Recent Nonfiction Title: *First Children Growing Up in the White House*, by Katherine Leiner, illustrated by Katie Keller (history/biography/middle media).
Fiction: Juvenile, young adult. Primary emphasis on picture books and fiction. Query for novels, chapter books. For picture books send ms with SASE.
Recent Fiction Title: *When the Whippoorwill Calls*, by Candace F. Ransom, illustrated by Kimberly Bulcken Root (picture book).

TAYLOR PUBLISHING COMPANY, 1550 W. Mockingbird Lane, Dallas TX 75235. (214)819-8560. Fax: (214)819-8580. Website: http://www.taylorpub.com. Contact: Crystal Blackburn, editorial assistant, Trade Books Division. Estab. 1981. Publishes hardcover and softcover originals. Publishes 35 titles/year. Receives 1,000 submissions/year. 25% of books from first-time authors; 25% from unagented writers. Publishes book 18 months after acceptance. Accepts simultaneous submissions. Reports in 2 months. Book catalog and ms guidelines for 10×13 SASE.
Nonfiction: Gardening, sports, popular culture, parenting, health, home improvement, how-to, celebrity biography, miscellaneous nonfiction. Submit outline, sample chapter, an overview of the market and competition and an author bio as it pertains to proposed subject matter. Reviews artwork/photos as part of ms package.
  ● No longer seeking true crime, cookbooks, humor, self-help or trivia.
Recent Nonfiction Title: *Cruise: The Unauthorized Biography*, by Frank Sanello.

TEACHERS COLLEGE PRESS, 1234 Amsterdam Ave., New York NY 10027. (212)678-3929. Fax: (212)678-4149. Director: Carole P. Saltz. Executive Acquisitions Editor: Faye Zucker. Estab. 1904. Publishes hardcover and paperback originals and reprints. Publishes 40 titles/year. Pays royalty. Publishes book 1 year after acceptance. Reports in 2 months. Book catalog free.
Nonfiction: "This university press concentrates on books in the field of education in the broadest sense, from early childhood to higher education: good classroom practices, teacher training, special education, innovative trends and issues, administration and supervision, film, continuing and adult education, all areas of the curriculum, computers, guidance and counseling and the politics, economics, philosophy, sociology and history of education. We have recently added women's studies to our list. The Press also issues classroom

materials for students at all levels, with a strong emphasis on reading and writing and social studies." Submit outline and sample chapters.

Recent Nonfiction Title: *Reframing Educational Policy*, by Kahne (professional).

TEMPLE UNIVERSITY PRESS, Broad and Oxford Sts., Philadelphia PA 19122. (215)204-8787. Fax: (215)204-4719. Editor-in-Chief: Michael Ames. Publishes 70 titles/year. Pays royalty of up to 10% on wholesale price. Publishes book 1 year after acceptance. Reports in 2 months. Book catalog free.

Nonfiction: American history, sociology, women's studies, health care, ethics, labor studies, photography, urban studies, law, Latin American studies, Afro-American studies, Asian-American studies, public policy and regional (Philadelphia area). "No memoirs, fiction or poetry." Uses *Chicago Manual of Style*. Reviews artwork/photos as part of ms package. Query.

TEN SPEED PRESS, P.O. Box 7123, Berkeley CA 94707. (510)559-1600. Address submissions to "Acquisitions Department." Contact: Phillip Wood. Estab. 1971. Imprints are Celestial Arts and Tricycle Press. Publishes trade paperback originals and reprints. Firm publishes 60 titles/year; imprint averages 20 titles/year. 25% of books from first-time authors; 50% from unagented writers. Pays 8-12% royalty on retail price. Offers $2,500 average advance. Publishes book 1 year after acceptance. Accepts simultaneous submissions. Reports in 3 months on queries. Book catalog for 9 × 12 SAE with 6 first-class stamps. Manuscript guidelines for #10 SASE.

Nonfiction: Cookbook, how-to, reference, self-help. Subjects include business and career, child guidance/parenting, cooking/foods/nutrition, gardening, health/medicine, money/finance, nature/environment, recreation, science. "We mainly publish innovative how-to books. We are always looking for cookbooks from proven, tested sources—successful restaurants, etc. *Not* 'grandma's favorite recipes.' Books about the 'new science' interest us. No biographies or autobiographies, first-person travel narratives, fiction or humorous treatments of just about anything." Query or submit outline and sample chapters.

Recent Nonfiction Title: *The Packing Book*, by Judith Gilford.

Tips: "We like books from people who really know their subject, rather than people who think they've spotted a trend to capitalize on. We like books that will sell for a long time, rather than nine-day wonders. Our audience consists of a well-educated, slightly weird group of people who like food, the outdoors and take a light but serious approach to business and careers. If I were a writer trying to market a book today, I would study the backlist of each publisher I was submitting to, and tailor my proposal to what I perceive as their needs. Nothing gets a publisher's attention like someone who knows what he or she is talking about, and nothing falls flat like someone who obviously has no idea who he or she is submitting to."

TEXAS A&M UNIVERSITY PRESS, Drawer C, College Station TX 77843-4354. (409)845-1436. Fax: (409)847-8752. E-mail: fdl@tampress.tamu.edu. Website: http://www.tamu.edu/upress. Editor-in-Chief: Noel Parsons. Managing Editor: Mary Lenn Dixon. Editorial Assistant: Diana Vance. Estab. 1974. Publishes 40 titles/year. Nonauthor-subsidy publishes 25% of books. Pays in royalties. Publishes book 1 year after acceptance. Reports in 1 month on queries. *Writer's Market* recommends allowing 2 months for reply. Book catalog free.

Nonfiction: Natural history, American history, environmental history, business history, military history, women's studies, economics, Eastern European studies, regional studies. *Writer's Market* recommends query with SASE first.

Recent Nonfiction Title: *Serbia's Secret War*, by Philip J. Cohen (Eastern European history).

Tips: New publishing fields of Eastern European studies and U.S.-Mexican Borderlands studies.

TEXAS CHRISTIAN UNIVERSITY PRESS, P.O. Box 298300, TCU, Fort Worth TX 76129. (817)921-7822. Fax: (817)921-7333. Director: Judy Alter. Editor: A.T. Row. Estab. 1966. Publishes hardcover originals, some reprints. Publishes 10 titles/year. Receives 100 submissions/year. 10% of books from first-time authors; 75% from unagented writers. Nonauthor-subsidy publishes 10% of books. Pays royalty. Publishes book 16 months after acceptance. Reports in 3 months on queries.

Nonfiction: American studies, juvenile (Chaparral Books, 10 and up), Texana, literature and criticism. "We are looking for good scholarly monographs, other serious scholarly work and regional titles of significance." Query. Reviews artwork/photos as part of ms package.

Recent Nonfiction Title: *Fort Worth's Legendary Landmarks*, by Roark (coffee table historical).

Fiction: Regional fiction. Considers mss by invitation only. Please do not query.

Recent Fiction Title: *Living with the Hyenas*, by Flynn (short stories).

Tips: "Regional and/or Texana nonfiction or fiction have best chance of breaking into our firm."

TEXAS STATE HISTORICAL ASSOCIATION, 2.306 Richardson Hall, University Station, Austin TX 78712. (512)471-1525. Assistant Director: George Ward. Publishes hardcover and trade paperback originals and reprints. Publishes 8 titles/year. Receives 50 queries and 50 mss/year. 10% of books from first-time authors; 95% from unagented writers. Pays 10% royalty on net cash proceeds. Publishes book 1 year after acceptance. Reports in 2 months on mss. Book catalog and ms guidelines free on request.

Nonfiction: Biography, coffee table book, illustrated book, reference. Historical subjects. "We are interested primarily in scholarly historical articles and books." Query. Reviews artwork/photos as part of ms package. Send photocopies.

TEXAS WESTERN PRESS, Imprint of The University of Texas at El Paso, El Paso TX 79968-0633. (915)747-5688. Fax: (915)747-5111. Director: John Bristol. Estab. 1952. Imprint is Southwestern Studies. Publishes hardcover and paperback originals. Publishes 7-8 titles/year. "This is a university press, 45 years old; we offer a standard 10% royalty contract on our hardcover books and on our paperbacks as well. We try to treat our authors professionally, produce handsome, long-lived books and aim for quality, rather than quantity of titles carrying our imprint." Reports in 2 months. Book catalog and ms guidelines free.
  • This publisher has launched a new numbered series—*The Border/La Frontera*, which deals with current border related issues. Interdisciplinary in scope and will include research from the fields of biology, public health, demography, applied environmental sciences, education, research in literature, history and social sciences, among others. Volumes will be published in English, Spanish or a bilingual format as warranted by the subject matter. Up to 300 book pages or 75,000 words.
Nonfiction: Scholarly books. Historic and cultural accounts of the Southwest (West Texas, New Mexico, northern Mexico and Arizona). Occasional technical titles. "Our *Southwestern Studies* use manuscripts of up to 30,000 words. Our hardback books range from 30,000 words up. The writer should use good exposition in his work. Most of our work requires documentation. We favor a scholarly, but not overly pedantic, style. We specialize in superior book design." Query with outline. Follow *Chicago Manual of Style*.
Tips: "Texas Western Press is interested in books relating to the history of Hispanics in the U.S., will experiment with photo-documentary books, and is interested in seeing more 'popular' history and books on Southwestern culture/life."

THIRD SIDE PRESS, INC., 2250 W. Farragut, Chicago IL 60625. Website: http://www.smallmedia.com. Editor/Publisher: Midge Stocker. Publishes 4-5 titles/year. 30% of books from first-time authors; 100% from unagented writers. Pays 6% royalty and up on wholesale price. Publishes book 18 months after acceptance of ms. Accepts simultaneous submissions (with nonfiction). Reports in 1 month on queries, 6 months on mss. Book catalog for 9 × 12 SAE with 2 first-class stamps. Manuscript guidelines for #10 SASE.
Nonfiction: Self-help. Subjects include business and economics (relating to women), health/medicine (women's only), language/literature, lesbian, psychology, women's issues/studies. "We are looking for manuscripts that approach women's health issues from a feminist perspective." Query with SASE.
Recent Nonfiction Title: *The Woman-Centered Economy*, edited by Loraine Edwalds and Midge Stocker.
Fiction: Contemporary, experimental, feminist, lesbian, literary. "We are not seeking collections of short stories by individual authors. We are actively seeking quality novels with lesbian main characters." Query with complete ms and SASE.
Recent Fiction Title: *Entwined*, by Beatrice Stone (lesbian novel).

THIRD WORLD PRESS, P.O. Box 19730, Chicago IL 60619. (312)651-0700. Publisher: Haki R. Madhubuti. Publishes hardcover and trade paperback originals and reprints. Publishes 20 titles/year. Receives 200-300 queries and 200 mss/year. 20% of books from first-time authors; 80% from unagented writers. Pays 7% royalty on retail price. Publishes book 18 months after acceptance of ms. Open submissions each January and July. Accepts simultaneous submissions. Reports in 6 months. Book catalog and ms guidelines free on request.
Nonfiction: African-centered and African American materials: illustrated book, children's/juvenile, reference, self-help, textbook. Subjects include anthropology/archaeology, Black studies, education, ethnic, government/politics, health/medicine, history, language/literature, literary criticism, philosophy, psychology, regional, religion, sociology, women's issues/studies. Query with outline and 5 sample chapters. Reviews artwork/photos as part of ms package. Send photocopies.
Recent Nonfiction Title: *Report From Part Two*, Gwendolyn Brooks (autobiography).
Fiction: African-centered and African American materials: Ethnic, feminist, historical, juvenile, literary, mainstream/contemporary, picture books, plays, short story collections, young adult. Query with synopsis and 5 sample chapters.
Recent Fiction Title: *The Sweetest Berry On The Bush*, Nubia Kai (folktales).
Poetry: Submit 5 pages.
Recent Poetry Title: *Wise, Why's, Y's*, by Amiri Baraka.

THREE CONTINENTS PRESS, P.O. Box 38009, Colorado Springs CO 80937-8009. Fax: (719)576-4689. E-mail: threecp@aol.com. Website: http://members.aol.com/Three CP/3CP—home.htm. Publisher/Editor-in-Chief: Donald E. Herdeck. General Editor: Harold Ames, Jr. Estab. 1973. Publishes hardcover and paperback originals and reprints. Publishes 20-30 titles/year. Receives 200 submissions/year. 15% of books from first-time authors; 99% from unagented writers. Average print order for a first book is 1,000. Length: 50,000-125,000 words. Nonauthor-subsidy publishes 5% of books. Pays 10% royalty. Offers advance "only on delivery of complete manuscript which is found acceptable; usually $300." Accepts simultaneous submis-

sions. Reviews artwork/photos as part of ms package. State availability of photos/illustrations. Reports in 2 months.
Nonfiction: Query with outline, table of contents.
Recent Nonfiction Title: *Child of Two Worlds: An Autobiography of a Filipino-American or Vice Versa*, by Norman Reyes (autobiography).
Fiction: Query with synopsis, plot summary (1-3 pages).
Recent Fiction Title: *Inspector Ali*, by Driss Chraibi (novel).
Poetry: Submit 5-10 sample poems.
Recent Poetry Title: *The Right to Err*, by Nina Istrenko (poetry-bilingual English and Russian).
Tips: Specializes in African, Caribbean, Middle Eastern (Arabic and Persian) and Asian-Pacific literature, criticism and translation, Third World literature and history. Scholarly, well-prepared mss; creative writing. Fiction, poetry, criticism, history and translations of creative writing. "We search for books that will make clear the complexity and value of non-Western literature and culture, including bilingual texts (Arabic language/English translations). We are always interested in genuine contributions to understanding non-Western culture. We need a *polished* translation, or original prose or poetry by non-Western authors *only*. Critical and cross-cultural studies are accepted from any scholar from anywhere."

THUNDER'S MOUTH PRESS, 632 Broadway, 7th Floor, New York NY 10012. (212)780-0380. Publisher: Neil Ortenberg. Estab. 1982. Publishes hardcover and trade paperback originals and reprints, almost exclusively nonfiction. Publishes 15-20 titles/year. Receives 1,000 submissions/year. 10% of books from unagented writers. Average print order for a first book is 7,500. Pays 5-10% royalty on retail price. Offers $15,000 average advance. Publishes book 8 months after acceptance. Reports in 3 months on queries.
Nonfiction: Biography, politics, popular culture. Query with SASE; no unsolicited mss.
Fiction: Query only.

TIARE PUBLICATIONS, P.O. Box 493, Lake Geneva WI 53147-0493. Fax: (414)248-8927. President: Gerry L. Dexter. Estab. 1986. Imprints are Limelight Books and Balboa Books. Publishes trade paperback originals. Publishes 6-12 titles/year. Receives 25 queries and 10 mss/year. 40% of books from first-time authors; 100% from unagented writers. Pays 15% royalty on retail/wholesale price. Publishes book 3 months after acceptance. Reports in 1 month on queries. *Writer's Market* recommends allowing 2 months for reply. Book catalog for $1.
Nonfiction: Technical, general nonfiction, mostly how-to, (Limelight); jazz/big bands (Balboa). "We are always looking for new ideas in the areas of amateur radio, shortwave listening, scanner radio monitoring, monitoring satellite transmissions—how to, equipment, techniques, etc." Query.
Recent Nonfiction Title: *Now You Know—The Story of the Four Freshmen*, by Ross Barbour.

TIDEWATER PUBLISHERS, Imprint of Cornell Maritime Press, Inc., P.O. Box 456, Centreville MD 21617-0456. (410)758-1075. Fax: (410)758-6849. Managing Editor: Charlotte Kurst. Estab. 1938. Publishes hardcover and paperback originals. Publishes 7-9 titles/year. Receives 150 submissions/year. 41% of books from first-time authors; 99% from unagented writers. Pays 7½-15% royalty on retail price. Publishes book 1 year after acceptance. Reports in 2 months. Book catalog for 10×13 SAE with 5 first-class stamps.
Nonfiction: Cookbook, history, illustrated book, juvenile, reference. Regional subjects. Query or submit outline and sample chapters. Reviews artwork/photos as part of ms package.
Recent Nonfiction Title: *Chesapeake Bay in the Civil War*, by Eric Mills.
Fiction: Regional juvenile fiction only. Query or submit outline/synopsis and sample chapters.
Recent Fiction Title: *Toulouse: The Story of a Canada Goose*, by Priscilla Cummings, illus. by A.R. Cohen.
Tips: "Our audience is made up of readers interested in works that are specific to the Chesapeake Bay and Delmarva Peninsula area."

TIME-LIFE BOOKS INC., Division of Time Warner Inc., 777 Duke St., Alexandria VA 22314. (703)838-7000. Fax: (703)838-6946. Managing Editor: Neil Kagan. Estab. 1960. Publishes hardcover originals. Publishes 40 titles/year. Books are almost entirely staff-generated and staff-produced, and distribution is primarily through mail order sale. TLB is always interested in freelance narrative and how-to writers. Submit résumé and clips to Managing Editor. No unpublished mss or book proposals.
Recent Nonfiction Title: *Perennials* (*The Complete Gardener* series).

TIMES BOOKS, Imprint of Random House, Inc., 201 E. 50th St., New York NY 10022. (212)872-8110. Vice President and Publisher: Peter Osnos. Vice President and Associate Publisher: Carie Freimuth. Editorial Director: Steve Wasserman. Publishes hardcover and paperback originals and reprints. Publishes 50-60 titles/year. Pays royalty. Offers average advance. Publishes book 1 year after acceptance. *Writer's Market* recommends allowing 2 months for reply.
Nonfiction: Business/economics, science and medicine, history, biography, women's issues, the family, cookbooks, current affairs. Accepts only solicited mss. Reviews artwork/photos as part of ms package.
Recent Nonfiction Title: *In Retrospect: The Tragedy and Lessons of Vietnam*, by Robert S. McNamara.

TODD PUBLICATIONS, 18 N. Greenbush Rd., West Nyack NY 10994. (914)358-6213. E-mail: toddpub @aol.com. President: Barry Klein. Publishes hardcover and trade paperback originals. Publishes 5 titles/year. 1% of books from first-time authors. Pays 5-15% royalty on wholesale price. Publishes book 6 months after acceptance. Accepts simultaneous submissions. Reports in 2 months on proposals. Book catalog free. Manuscript guidelines for #10 SASE.
Nonfiction: How-to, reference, self-help. Subjects include business and economics, ethnic, health/medicine, money/finance, travel. Submit 2 sample chapters.
Recent Nonfiction Title: *Insider's Guide to Credit Cards.*

TOR BOOKS, Subsidiary of St. Martin's Press, 14th Floor, 175 Fifth Ave., New York NY 10010. (212)388-0100. Fax: (212)388-0191. Publisher: Tom Doherty. Associate Publisher: Linda Quinton. Estab. 1980. Publishes mass market, hardcover and trade paperback originals and reprints. Publishes 250 books/year. Pays 6-8% royalty to unpublished authors (paperback); 8-10% to established authors (paperback). Hardcover: 10% on first 5,000; 12½% on second 5,000; 15% thereafter. Offers negotiable advance. Reports in 4 months. Book catalog for 9×12 SAE with 2 first-class stamps.
   ● TOR publishes selected nonfiction. Query first.
Fiction: Science fiction, fantasy, horror, techno-thrillers, "women's" suspense, American historicals, westerns. "We prefer an extensive chapter-by-chapter synopsis and the first three chapters complete." Prefers agented mss or proposals.
Recent Fiction Title: *Mount Dragon,* by Douglas Preston and Lincoln Child.
Tips: "We're never short of good sci fi or fantasy, but we're always open to solid, technologically knowledgeable hard science fiction or thrillers by writers with solid expertise."

‡TOWER PUBLISHING, 588 Saco Rd., Standish ME 04084. (207)642-5400. Fax: (207)642-5463. E-mail: tower@mainelink.net. Website: http://www.mainelink.net/tower. President: Michael Lyons. Imprints are ME/NH Register, ME/NH Manufacturing Directory, ME/NH Business Professional Directory. Publishes hardcover originals and reprints, trade paperback originals. Publishes 10 titles/year. Receives 60 queries and 30 mss/year. 10% of books from first-time authors; 90% from unagented writers. Pays royalty on net receipts. No advance. Publishes book 6 months after acceptance of ms. Accepts simultaneous submissions. Reports in 1 month on queries, 2 months on proposals and mss. Book catalog and manuscript guidelines free on request.
Nonfiction: Reference. Subjects include business and economics. Looking for legal books of a national stature. Query with outline.
Recent Nonfiction Title: *Maine Manufacturing Directory* (business directory).

TRAFALGAR SQUARE PUBLISHING, P.O. Box 257, N. Pomfret VT 05053-0257. (802)457-1911. Publisher: Caroline Robbins. Contact: Martha Cook, managing editor. Publishes hardcover and trade paperback originals and reprints. Publishes 6 titles/year. Pays royalty. No advance. Reports in 1 month on queries and proposals, 2 months on mss.
Nonfiction: Books about horses. "We publish books for intermediate to advanced riders and horsemen. No stories, children's books or horse biographies." Query with proposal package, including outline, 1-2 sample chapters, letter of writer's qualifications and audience for book's subject.
Recent Nonfiction Title: *Getting in Touch,* by Linda Tellington-Jones (horse book).

TRANSPORTATION TRAILS, Imprint of National Bus Trader, Inc., 9698 W. Judson Rd., Polo IL 61064-9015. (815)946-2341. Fax: (815)946-2347. Editor: Larry Plachno. Estab. 1977. Publishes hardcover, trade paperback and mass market paperback originals. Publishes 8 titles/year. Receives 10 submissions/year. 50% of books from first-time authors; 100% from unagented writers. Pays 10-15% on retail price. Publishes book 1 year after acceptance. Accepts simultaneous submissions. Reports in 1 month. *Writer's Market* recommends allowing 2 months for reply. Book catalog and ms guidelines free.
Nonfiction: "We are interested in transportation history—prefer electric interurban railroads or trolley lines but will consider steam locomotives, horsecars, buses, aviation and maritime." Query. Reviews artwork/photos as part of ms package.
Tips: "We are not interested in travel nonfiction."

TRILOGY BOOKS, 50 S. DeLacey Ave., Suite 201, Pasadena CA 91105. (818)440-0669. Fax: (818)585-9441. E-mail: 72274,44@compuserve.com. Publisher: Marge Wood. Publishes trade paperback originals. Publishes 4 titles/year. Pays 6-10% royalty on retail price. Advance varies. Publishes book 1 year after

---

FOR INFORMATION on book publishers' areas of interest, see the nonfiction and fiction sections in the Book Publishers Subject Index.

acceptance of ms. Accepts simultaneous submissions. Reports in 1 month on queries. *Writer's Market* recommends allowing 2 months for reply. Book catalog and ms guidelines free on request.

Nonfiction: Biography and autobiography, self-help. Subjects include (women's) history, women's issues/studies. "We are seeking manuscripts that have mainstream as well as scholarly or academic appeal, and that focus on women's lives." Query.

Recent Nonfiction Title: *Sisters of the Wind: Voices of Early Women Aviators*, by Elizabeth S. Bell (women's history).

Tips: Audience is academic and well-educated mainstream women.

TRIUMPH BOOKS, Imprint of Liguori Publications, 333 Glen Head Rd., Old Brookville NY 11545. Executive Editor: Patricia A. Kossmann. Publishes hardcover originals and trade paperback originals and reprints. Publishes 75 titles/year; imprint publishes 20 titles/year. 10% of books from first-time authors; 75% from unagented writers. Pays 7-15% royalty on retail price. Offers $2,500-7,500 advance. Publishes book 10 months after acceptance of ms. Accepts simultaneous submissions. Reports in 1 month on queries and proposals, 3 months on mss if SASE included. Book catalog free to agents and published authors.

Nonfiction: Self-help, spirituality/inspiration. Subjects include religion (Catholic; mainline Protestant; interreligious; some theology), women's issues/studies (from a religious or spiritual perspective). Serious, upscale, "thinking" books—well-grounded and well-written. Submit outline and 2 sample chapters with SASE. Reviews artwork/photos as part of ms package.

Recent Nonfiction Title: *Toward God*, by Michael Casey (prayer/spiritual life).

Tips: Audience is spiritual seekers (especially babyboomers) and the educated adult open to new thought and guidance. "Do *not* welcome telephone inquiries from unpublished authors. All submissions *must* be accompanied by return postage. No interest in evangelical Christian works."

TSR, INC., 201 Sheridan Spring Rd., Lake Geneva WI 53147. (414)248-3625. Estab. 1975. Executive Editor: Brian Thomsen. Contact: Submissions Editor. Imprints are TSR™ Books, Dungeons & Dragons Books, Dragonlance® Books, Forgotten Realms™ Books, Ravenloft™ Books, Dark Sun™ Books, Planescape℠ Books, Birthright℠ Books. Publishes hardcover and trade paperback originals and trade paperback reprints. Publishes 40-50 titles/year. Receives 600 queries and 300 mss/year. 10% of books from first-time authors; 20% from unagented authors. Pays 4-8% royalty on retail price. Offers $4,000-6,000 average advance. Publishes book 1 year after acceptance. Accepts simultaneous submissions. Reports in 2 months on queries.

Nonfiction: "All of our nonfiction books are generated inhouse."

Fiction: Fantasy, gothic, humor, science fiction short story collections, young adult. "We have a very small market for good science fiction and fantasy for the TSR Book line, but also need samples from writers willing to do work-for-hire for our other lines. No excessively violent or gory fantasy or science fiction." Query with outline/synopsis and 3 sample chapters.

Recent Fiction Title: *Masquerades*, by Kate Novak and Jeff Grudd.

Tips: "Our audience is comprised of highly imaginative 12-40 year-old males."

TUDOR PUBLISHERS, P.O. Box 38366, Greensboro NC 27438. (910)282-5907. Senior Editor: Pam Cox. Publishes hardcover and trade paperback originals. Publishes 4-6 titles/year. Receives 400 queries and 200 mss/year. 80% of books from first-time authors; 90% from unagented writers. Pays 10% royalty on wholesale price. No advance. Publishes book 9 months after acceptance of ms. Accepts simultaneous submissions. Reports in 1 month on queries and proposals, 3 months on mss. Book catalog and ms guidelines for #10 SASE.

Nonfiction: Biography, juvenile, cookbook, how-to, reference, self-help, technical, textbook. Subjects include Americana, child guidance/parenting, cooking/foods/nutrition, education, history, hobbies, military/war, psychology, regional, science, sports, women's issues/studies. Query with outline. "Writers should have a concise proposal statement on initial inquiry, author bio and publication credits with SASE. Upon request for outline, it should be detailed chapter by chapter, with SASE. Request for complete ms should result in accompanying SASE or postage." Reviews artwork as part of ms package.

Recent Nonfiction Title: *Who's Who on the Moon*, by Elijah E. Cocks and Josiah C. Cocks (astronomy/reference/biography).

Fiction: Adventure, ethnic, historical, humor, juvenile, mainstream/contemporary, mystery, romance, science fiction, short story collections, suspense, western, young adult. Query with synopsis.

Recent Fiction Title: *The Sweet Revenge of Melissa Chavez*, by Niel Davidson (young adult fiction).

TURTLE PRESS, Subsidiary of S.K. Productions Inc., P.O. Box 290206, Wethersfield CT 06129-0206. (860)529-7770. Fax: (860)529-7775. E-mail: jcjv99a@prodigy.com. Editor: Cynthia Kim. Publishes hardcover originals, trade paperback originals and reprints. Publishes 4-6 titles/year. Pays 8-10% royalty. Offers $500-1,000 advance. Reports in 1 month on queries. *Writer's Market* recommends allowing 2 months for reply.

Nonfiction: How-to, martial arts, philosophy, self-help, sports. "We prefer tightly targeted topics on which there is little or no information currently available in the market, particularly for our sports and martial arts titles." Query with SASE

Recent Nonfiction Title: *Maximize Your Martial Arts Training*, by Dr. Art Brisacher (martial arts training diary).

Fiction: "We have just begun a line of children's martial arts adventure stories and are very much interested in submissions to expand this line." Query with SASE.

Recent Fiction Title: *A Part of the Ribbon*, by Ruth Hunter and Debra Fritsch (children's chapter book).

‡**CHARLES E. TUTTLE CO.**, 153 Milk St., 5th Floor, Boston MA 02109. Acquisitions Editor: Michael Lewis. Publishes hardcover and trade paperback originals and reprints. Publishes 60 titles/year. Receives 200 queries/year. 20% of books from first-time authors; 60% from unagented writers. Pays 5-8% royalty on retail price. Offers $1,000 average advance. Publishes book 18 months after acceptance of ms. Accepts simultaneous submissions. Reports in 6 weeks on proposals. Book catalog free on request.

Nonfiction: Self-help, Eastern philosophy, alternative health. Subjects include cooking/foods/nutrition (Asian related), philosophy, Eastern, Buddhist, Taoist), religion (Eastern). Submit query, outline and SASE. Cannot guarantee return of ms.

Recent Nonfiction Title: *Taoist Cookbook*, by Michael Saso.

TWENTY-FIRST CENTURY BOOKS, Imprint of Henry Holt and Company, Inc., 115 W. 18th St., New York NY 10011. Editorial Assistant: Sydra Mallery. Publishes hardcover originals. Publishes 50 titles/year. Receives 200 queries and 50 mss/year. 20% of books from first-time writers; 75% from unagented writers. Pays 5-8% royalty on net price. Offers $2,000 advance. Publishes book 10 months after acceptance of ms. Accepts simultaneous submissions. Reports in 3 months on proposals.

Nonfiction: Children's nonfiction. Subjects include government/politics, health/medicine, history, military/ war, nature/environment, science, current events and social issues. "We publish primarily in series of four or more titles, for ages 10 and up, grades 5 and up (middle grade). No picture books or adult books." Submit proposal package including outline, sample chapter and SASE. Does not review artwork.

Recent Nonfiction Title: The *Exploring Earth's Biomes* series.

Tips: "We are now accepting single titles for both middle grade and young adult readers."

TYNDALE HOUSE PUBLISHERS, INC., 351 Executive Dr., P.O. Box 80, Wheaton IL 60189-0080. (708)668-8300. Vice President, Editorial: Ronald Beers. Contact: Manuscript Review Committee. Estab. 1962. Publishes hardcover and trade paperback originals and mass paperback reprints. Publishes 100 titles/ year. 5-10% of books from first-time authors. Average first print order for a first book is 5,000-10,000. Royalty and advance negotiable. Publishes book 18 months after acceptance. Send query and synopsis, not whole ms. Reviews solicited mss only. Reports in up to 2 months. Book catalog and ms guidelines for 9 × 12 SAE with 9 first-class stamps.

● This publisher has received Book of the Year Award (CBA) and the *Campus Life* Book of the Year Award (2 titles).

Nonfiction: "Practical, user-friendly Christian books: home and family, Christian growth/self-help, devotional/inspirational, theology/Bible doctrine, children's nonfiction, contemporary/critical issues." Query.

Fiction: "Biblical, historical and other Christian themes. No short story collections. Youth books: character building stories with Christian perspective. Especially interested in ages 10-14." Query.

ULYSSES PRESS, P.O. Box 3440, Berkeley CA 94703. (510)601-8301. Fax: (510)601-8307. Editorial Director: Leslie Henriques. Estab. 1982. Publishes trade paperback originals. Publishes 20 titles/year. 25% of books from first-time authors; 75% from unagented writers. Pays 12-16% royalty on wholesale price. Offers $2,000-8,000 advance. Publishes book 6 months after acceptance. Accepts simultaneous submissions. Reports in 2 months on proposals. Book catalog free on request.

● Ulysses is rapidly expanding its lines of travel and health books and is very interested in looking at proposals in these areas.

Nonfiction: Travel, health. Submit proposal package including outline, 2 sample chapters, and market analysis. Reviews artwork/photos as part of freelance ms package. Send photocopies.

Recent Nonfiction Title: *Panic Attacks: A Natural Approach* (health).

Tips: Publishes two series of travel guidebooks—*Hidden* and the *The New Key to* . . . .

UNITY BOOKS, Unity School of Christianity, 1901 NW Blue Parkway, Unity Village MO 64065-0001. (816)524-3550 ext. 3190. Associate Editor: Brenda Markle. Publishes hardcover and trade paperback originals and reprints. Publishes 16 titles/year. Receives 100 queries and 300 mss/year. 30% of books from first-time authors; 95% from unagented writers. Pays 10-11½% royalty on retail price. Publishes book 11 months after acceptance of ms. Accepts simultaneous submissions. Reports in 1 month on queries and proposals, 2 months on mss. *Writer's Market* recommends allowing 2 months for reply. Book catalog and ms guidelines free on request.

Nonfiction: Inspirational, self-help, reference (spiritual/metaphysical). Subjects include health (nutrition/holistic), philosophy (perennial/New Thought), psychology (transpersonal), religion (spiritual/metaphysical Bible interpretation/modern Biblical studies). "Writers should be familiar with principles of metaphysical Christianity but not feel bound by them. We are interested in works in the related fields of holistic health, spiritual psychology as well as the philosophy of other world religions." Book proposal and/or query with outline and sample chapter. Reviews artwork/photos as part of ms package. Send photocopies.

Recent Nonfiction Title: *Finding Yourself in Transition*, by Robert Brumet (using life's changes for spiritual awakening).

Fiction: Spiritual, inspirational, metaphysical. Query with synopsis and sample chapter.

Recent Fiction Title: *The Adventures of the Little Green Dragon*, by Mari Prisette Ulmer.

UNIVELT, INC., P.O. Box 28130, San Diego CA 92198. (619)746-4005. Fax: (619)746-3139. Publisher: Robert H. Jacobs. Estab. 1970. Imprints are American Astronautical Society, National Space Society. Publishes hardcover originals. Publishes 8 titles/year. Receives 20 submissions/year. 5% of books from first-time authors; 5% from unagented writers. Nonauthor-subsidy publishes 10% of books. Average print order for a first book is 400-1,500. Pays 10% royalty on actual sales. No advance. Publishes book 4 months after acceptance. Reports in 1 month. *Writer's Market* recommends allowing 2 months for reply. Book catalog and ms guidelines for SASE.

Nonfiction: Publishes in the field of aerospace, especially astronautics, but including application of aerospace technology to Earth's problems. Call first, then submit outline and 1-2 sample chapters. Reviews artwork/photos as part of ms package.

Tips: "Writers have the best chance of selling manuscripts on the history of astronautics (we have a history series) and astronautics/spaceflight subjects. We publish for the American Astronautical Society."

UNIVERSITY OF ALASKA PRESS, P.O. Box 756240, 1st Floor Gruening Bldg., UAF, Fairbanks AK 99775-6240. (907)474-6389. Fax: (907)474-5502. Manager: Debbie Van Stone. Acquisitions: Pam Odom. Estab. 1967. Imprints are Ramuson Library Historical Translation Series, LanternLight Library, Oral Biographies, and Classic Reprints. Publishes hardcover originals, trade paperback originals and reprints. Publishes 5-10 titles/year. Receives 100 submissions/year. Pays 7½-10% royalty on net sales. Publishes book 2 years after acceptance. Reports in 2 months. Book catalog free on request.

Nonfiction: Biography, reference, technical, textbook, scholarly nonfiction relating to Alaska-circumpolar regions. Subjects include agriculture/horticulture, Americana (Alaskana), animals, anthropology/archaeology, art/architecture, education, ethnic, government/politics, health/medicine, history, language, military/war, nature/environment, regional, science, translation. Nothing that isn't northern or circumpolar. Query or submit outline. Reviews copies of artwork/photos as part of ms package.

Recent Nonfiction Title: *The Thousand-Mile War, World War II in Alaska and the Aleutians*, by Brian Garfield (historical narrative).

Tips: "Writers have the best chance with scholarly nonfiction relating to Alaska, the circumpolar regions and North Pacific Rim. Our audience is made up of scholars, historians, students, libraries, universities, individuals."

UNIVERSITY OF ARIZONA PRESS, 1230 N. Park Ave., #102, Tucson AZ 85719-4140. (520)621-1441. Fax: (520)621-8899. E-mail: dmcclellan@uapress.arizona.edu. Website: http://www.uapress.arizona.edu. Director: Stephen Cox. Senior Editor: Joanne O'Hare. Estab. 1959. Publishes hardcover and paperback originals and reprints. Publishes 50 titles/year. Receives 300-400 submissions/year. 30% of books from first-time authors; 95% from unagented writers. Average print order is 1,500. Royalty terms vary; usual starting point for scholarly monograph is after sale of first 1,000 copies. Publishes book 1 year after acceptance. Reports in 3 months. Book catalog for 9×12 SASE. Manuscript guidelines for #10 SASE.

● *Downcanyon: A Naturalist Explores the Colorado River Through the Grand Canyon*, by Ann Zwinger, was awarded the 1995 Book Award by the Western States Art Federation.

Nonfiction: Scholarly books about anthropology, Arizona, American West, archaeology, environmental science, global change, Latin America, Native Americans, natural history, space sciences and women's studies. Query with outline, list of illustrations and sample chapters. Reviews artwork/photos as part of ms package.

Tips: "Perhaps the most common mistake a writer might make is to offer a book manuscript or proposal to a house whose list he or she has not studied carefully. Editors rejoice in receiving material that is clearly targeted to the house's list, 'I have approached your firm because my books complement your past publications in . . .,' presented in a straightforward, businesslike manner."

THE UNIVERSITY OF ARKANSAS PRESS, 201 Ozark Ave., Fayetteville AR 72701-1201. (501)575-3246. Fax: (501)575-6044. Director: Miller Williams. Acquisitions Editor: Kevin Brock. Estab. 1980. Publishes hardcover and trade paperback originals and reprints. Publishes 32 titles/year. Receives 4,000 submissions/year. 30% of books from first-time authors; 90% from unagented writers. Pays 10% royalty on net receipts from hardcover; 6% on paper. Publishes book 1 year after acceptance. Accepted mss must be submitted on disk. Reports in up to 3 months. Book catalog for 9×12 SAE with 5 first-class stamps. Manuscript guidelines for #10 SASE.

Nonfiction: Americana, history, humanities, nature, general politics and history of politics, sociology. "Our current needs include literary criticism, history and biography. We won't consider manuscripts for texts, juvenile or religious studies, or anything requiring a specialized or exotic vocabulary." Query or submit outline and sample chapters.

Recent Nonfiction Title: *Black Savannah, 1788-1864*, by Whittington B. Johnson.

Poetry: Arkansas Poetry Award offered for publication of first book. Write for contest rules.

UNIVERSITY OF CALIFORNIA PRESS, 2120 Berkeley Way, Berkeley CA 94720. Director: James H. Clark. Associate Director: Lynne E. Withey. Estab. 1893. Los Angeles office: 405 Hilgard Ave., Los Angeles CA 90024-1373. UK office: University Presses of California, Columbia, and Princeton, 1 Oldlands Way, Bognor Regis, W. Sussex PO22 9SA England. Publishes hardcover and paperback originals and reprints. "On books likely to do more than return their costs, a standard royalty contract beginning at 7% on net receipts is paid; on paperbacks it is less." Publishes 180 titles/year. Queries are always advisable, accompanied by outlines or sample material. Accepts nonfiction translations. Send to Berkeley address. Reports vary, depending on the subject. *Writer's Market* recommends allowing 2 months for reply. Enclose return postage.

Nonfiction: "Most of our publications are hardcover nonfiction written by scholars." Publishes scholarly books including history, art, literary studies, social sciences, natural sciences and some high-level popularizations. No length preferences. *Writer's Market* recommends query with SASE first.

Fiction and Poetry: Publishes fiction and poetry only in translation.

UNIVERSITY OF IDAHO PRESS, 16 Brink Hall, Moscow ID 83844-1107. (208)885-5939. Fax: (208)885-9059. E-mail: uipress@raven.csrv.uidaho.edu. Imprints are: Northwest Folklife; Idaho Yesterdays; Northwest Naturalist Books; Living the West. Director: Peggy Pace. Estab. 1972. Publishes hardcover and trade paperback originals and reprints. Publishes 8-10 titles/year. Receives 150-250 queries and 25-50 mss/year. 100% of books from unagented writers. Pays up to 10% royalty on net sales. Publishes book 1 year after acceptance of ms. Reports in 6 months. Book catalog and ms guidelines free on request.

Nonfiction: Biography, reference, technical, textbook. Subjects include agriculture/horticulture, Americana, anthropology/archaeology, ethnic, folklore, history, language/literature, nature/environment, recreation, regional, women's issues/studies. "Writers should contact us to discuss projects in advance and refer to our catalog to become familiar with the types of projects the press publishes. Avoid being unaware of the constraints of scholarly publishing, and avoid submitting queries and manuscripts in areas we don't publish in." Query or submit proposal package, including sample chapter, contents, vita. Reviews artwork/photos as part of ms package. Writers should send photocopies.

Recent Nonfiction Title: *Arams of Idaho*, by Kristi Youngdahl (history).

Tips: Audience is educated readers, scholars.

UNIVERSITY OF ILLINOIS PRESS, 1325 S. Oak St., Champaign IL 61820-6903. (217)333-0950. Fax: (217)244-8082. Director/Editor-in-Chief: Richard L. Wentworth. Contact: Janice Roney. Estab. 1918. Publishes hardcover and trade paperback originals and reprints. Publishes 100-110 titles/year. 50% of books from first-time authors; 95% from unagented writers. Nonauthor-subsidy publishes 10% of books. Pays 0-10% royalty on net sales; offers $1,000-1,500 average advance (rarely). Publishes book 1 year after acceptance. Reports in 1 month. *Writer's Market* recommends allowing 2 months for reply. Book catalog for 9×12 SAE with 2 first-class stamps.

Nonfiction: Biography, reference, scholarly books. Subjects include Americana, history (especially American history), music (especially American music), politics, sociology, philosophy, sports, literature. Always looking for "solid scholarly books in American history, especially social history; books on American popular music, and books in the broad area of American studies." Query with outline.

Recent Nonfiction Title: *Muhammad Ali, the People's Champ*, edited by Elliott J. Gorn.

Fiction: Ethnic, experimental, mainstream. "We are not presently looking at unsolicited collections of stories. We do not publish novels." Query.

Recent Fiction Title: *Taking It Home: Stories from the Neighborhood*, by Tony Ardizzone.

Tips: "Serious scholarly books that are broad enough and well-written enough to appeal to non-specialists are doing well for us in today's market."

UNIVERSITY OF IOWA PRESS, 119 W. Park Rd., Iowa City IA 52242-1000. (319)335-2000. Fax: (319)335-2055. Website: http://www.uiowa.edu/~uipress. Director: Paul Zimmer. Estab. 1969. Publishes hardcover and paperback originals. Publishes 35 titles/year. Receives 300-400 submissions/year. 30% of books from first-time authors; 95% from unagented writers. Average print order for a first book is 1,000-1,200. Pays 7-10% royalty on net price. "We market mostly by direct mailing of fliers to groups with special interests in our titles and by advertising in trade and scholarly publications." Publishes book 1 year after acceptance. Reports within 4 months. Book catalog and ms guidelines free.

Nonfiction: Publishes anthropology, archaeology, British and American literary studies, history (Victorian, US, regional Latin American), jazz studies, history of photography and natural history. Looks for evidence of original research; reliable sources; clarity of organization, complete development of theme with documentation and supportive footnotes and/or bibliography; and a substantive contribution to knowledge in the field treated. Query or submit outline. Use *Chicago Manual of Style*. Reviews artwork/photos as part of ms package.

Recent Nonfiction Title: *The Guide to Classic Recorded Jazz*, by Tom Piazza.

Fiction and Poetry: Currently publishes the Iowa Short Fiction Award selections and winners of the Iowa Poetry Prize Competition. Query regarding poetry or fiction before sending ms.

Tips: "Developing a list of books on baseball history."

UNIVERSITY OF MAINE PRESS, 5717 Corbett Hall, Orono ME 04469-5717. (207)581-1408. Contact: Director. Publishes hardcover and trade paperback originals and reprints. Publishes 4 titles/year. Receives 50 queries and 25 mss/year. 10% of mss from first-time authors; 90% from unagented writers. Publishes book 1 year after acceptance of ms. Accepts simultaneous submissions. *Writer's Market* recommends allowing 2 months for reply.

Nonfiction: "We are an academic book publisher, interested in scholarly works on regional history, regional life sciences, Franco-American studies. Authors should be able to articulate their ideas on the potential market for their work." Query.

Recent Nonfiction Title: *Maine: The Pine Tree State*, by Judd, et.al. (history of Maine).

Fiction: Rarely. "The University of Maine Press publishes primarily regional fiction: Maine, New England, Canadian Maritimes." Query.

UNIVERSITY OF MASSACHUSETTS PRESS, P.O. Box 429, Amherst MA 01004-0429. (413)545-2217. Fax: (413)545-1226. Director: Bruce Wilcox. Senior Editor: Clark Dougan. Assistant Editor: Chris Hammel. Estab. 1963. Publishes hardcover and paperback originals, reprints and imports. Publishes 30 titles/year. Receives 600 submissions/year. 20% of books from first-time authors; 90% from unagented writers. Average print order for a first book is 1,500. Royalties generally 10% of net income. Advance rarely offered. No author subsidies accepted. Publishes book 1 year after acceptance. Preliminary report in 1 month. *Writer's Market* recommends allowing 2 months for reply. Book catalog free.

Nonfiction: Publishes African-American studies, art and architecture, biography, criticism, history, natural history, philosophy, poetry, public policy, sociology and women's studies in original and reprint editions. Accepts nonfiction translations. Submit outline and 1-2 sample chapters. Reviews artwork/photos as part of ms package.

Recent Nonfiction Title: *Black Legacy: America's Hidden Heritage*, by William D. Piersen.

UNIVERSITY OF MISSOURI PRESS, 2910 LeMone Blvd., Columbia MO 65201. (573)882-7641. Director: Beverly Jarrett. Publishes hardcover and paperback originals and paperback reprints. Publishes 50 titles/year. Receives 500 submissions/year. 25-30% of books from first-time authors; 90% from unagented writers. Average print order for a first book is 1,000-1,500. Pays up to 10% royalty on net receipts. No advance. Publishes book 1 year after acceptance. Reports in 6 months. Book catalog free.

Nonfiction: Scholarly publisher interested in history, literary criticism, political science, journalism, social science, some art history. Also regional books about Missouri and the Midwest. No mathematics or hard sciences. Query or submit outline and sample chapters. Consult *Chicago Manual of Style*.

Fiction: "Collections of short fiction are considered throughout the year; the press does not publish novels. Inquiries should be directed to Clair Willcox, acquisitions editor, and should include sample story, a table of contents, and a brief description of the manuscript that notes its length."

UNIVERSITY OF NEBRASKA PRESS, 312 N. 14th St., P.O. Box 880484, Lincoln NE 68588-0484. (402)472-3581. Editor-in-Chief: Douglas Clayton. Estab. 1941. Publishes hardcover and paperback originals and reprints. Specializes in scholarly nonfiction, some regional books; reprints of Western Americana; American history and culture. Publishes 75 new titles, 75 paperback reprints (*Bison Books*)/year. Receives more than 1,000 submissions/year. 25% of books from first-time authors; 95% from unagented writers. Average print order for a first book is 1,000. Pays graduated royalty from 10% on wholesale price for original books. Occasional advance. Reports in 4 months. Book catalog and guidelines for 9×12 SAE with 5 first-class stamps.

Nonfiction: Publishes Americana, biography, history, military, nature, photography, psychology, sports, literature, agriculture, American Indian themes. Accepts nonfiction translations. Query with outline/synopsis, 2 sample chapters and introduction. Looks for "an indication that the author knows his/her subject thoroughly and interprets it intelligently." Reviews artwork/photos as part of ms package.

Recent Nonfiction Title: *Lee the Soldier*, edited by Gary Gallagher (history).

Fiction: Accepts fiction translations but no original fiction.

Recent Fiction Title: *Candy Story*, by Marie Redonnet (translated fiction).

UNIVERSITY OF NEVADA PRESS, Reno NV 89557-0076. (702)784-6573. Fax: (702)784-6200. E-mail: dalrympl@scs.unr.edu. Director: to be announced. Editor-in-Chief: Margaret F. Dalrymple. Estab. 1961. Publishes hardcover and paperback originals and reprints. Publishes 35 titles/year. 20% of books from first-time authors; 99% from unagented writers. Average print order for a first book is 2,000. Pays average of 10% royalty on net price. Publishes book 1 year after acceptance. Preliminary report in 2 months. Book catalog and ms guidelines free.

Nonfiction: Specifically needs regional history and natural history, literature, current affairs, ethnonationalism, gambling and gaming, anthropology, biographies, Basque studies. "We are the first university press to sustain a sound series on Basque studies—New World and Old World." No juvenile books. Submit complete ms. *Writer's Market* recommends query with SASE first. Reviews photocopies of artwork/photos as part of ms package.

Recent Nonfiction Title: *Atlas of Nevada Conifers: A Phytogeographic Reference*, by David Alan Charlet.
Recent Fiction Title: *The Measurable World*, by Katharine Coles (novel).
Recent Poetry Title: *From the Still Empty Grave*, by A. Wilber Stevens (collected poems).

UNIVERSITY OF NEW MEXICO PRESS, 1720 Lomas Blvd. NE, Albuquerque NM 87131-1591. (505)277-2346. Contact: Editor. Estab. 1929. Publishes hardcover originals and trade paperback originals and reprints. Publishes 50 titles/year. Receives 500 submissions/year. 12% of books from first-time authors; 90% from unagented writers. Pays up to 15% royalty on wholesale price. Publishes book 1 year after acceptance. Reports in 2 weeks on queries. *Writer's Market* recommends allowing 2 months for reply. Book catalog free.

Nonfiction: Biography, illustrated book, scholarly books. Subjects include anthropology/archaeology, art/architecture, ethnic, history, photography. "No how-to, humor, juvenile, self-help, software, technical or textbooks." Query. Reviews artwork/photos as part of ms package. Prefers to see photocopies first.

Tips: "Most of our authors are academics. A scholarly monograph by an academic has a better chance than anything else. Our audience is a combination of academics and interested lay readers."

THE UNIVERSITY OF NORTH CAROLINA PRESS, P.O. Box 2288, Chapel Hill NC 27515-2288. (919)966-3561. Fax: (919)966-3829. E-mail: uncpress@unc.edu. Website: http://www.sunsite.unc.edu/uncpress. Director: Kate Douglas Torrey. Publishes hardcover and paperback originals and occasionally, paperback reprints. Specializes in scholarly books and regional trade books. Publishes 80 titles/year, 90% from unagented writers. Royalty schedule "varies." Occasional advances. Publishes book 1 year after acceptance. Reports in 5 months. Free book catalog. Manuscript guidelines for SASE.

Nonfiction: "Special focus on general interest books on the lore, crafts, cooking, gardening and natural history of the Southeast. Also, scholarly books in legal history, Civil War history, literary studies, classics, gender studies, oral history, folklore, political science, religious studies, historical sociology, Latin American studies. In European studies, focus is on history of the Third Reich, 20th-century Europe, and Holocaust history. Submit outline/synopsis and sample chapters; must follow *Chicago Manual of Style*. Looks for "intellectual excellence and clear writing. We do *not* publish poetry or original fiction." Reviews artwork/photos as part of ms package.

Recent Nonfiction Title: *Passalong Plants*, by Steve Bender and Felder Rushing.

UNIVERSITY OF NORTH TEXAS PRESS, P.O. Box 13856, Denton TX 76203-3856. Fax: (817)565-4590. E-mail: untpress@abn.unt.edu. Director: Frances B. Vick. Editor: Charlotte Wright. Estab. 1987. Publishes hardcover and trade paperback originals and reprints. Publishes 15-20 titles/year. Receives 400 queries and mss/year. 95% of books from unagented writers. Pays 7½-10% royalty of net. Publishes book 2 years after acceptance of ms. Reports in 3 months on queries. Book catalog for 8½×11 SASE.

Nonfiction: Biography, reference. Subjects include agriculture/horticulture, Americana, ethnic, government/politics, history, language/literature, military/war, nature/environment, regional. "We have series called War and the Southwest; Environmental Philosophy Series; Practical Guide Series; Texas Folklore Society Publications series; the Western Life Series; Literary biographies of Texas writers series." Query. Reviews artwork/photos as part of ms package. Send photocopies.

Poetry: Offers the Vassar Miller Prize in Poetry, an annual, national competition resulting in the publication of a winning manuscript each fall. Query first.

Tips: Books distributed by Texas A&M University Consortium.

UNIVERSITY OF OKLAHOMA PRESS, 1005 Asp Ave., Norman OK 73019-0445. (405)325-5111. Fax: (405)325-4000. E-mail: jdrayton@uoknor.edu. Editor-in-Chief: John Drayton. Estab. 1928. Imprint is Oklahoma Paperbacks. Publishes hardcover and paperback originals and reprints. Publishes 90 titles/year. Pays royalty comparable to those paid by other publishers for comparable books. Publishes book 18 months after acceptance. Reports in 3 months. Book catalog for $1 and 9×12 SAE with 6 first-class stamps.

Nonfiction: Publishes American Indian studies, Western US history, political science, literary theory, natural history, women's studies, classical studies. No unsolicited poetry and fiction. Query with outline, 1-2 sample chapters and author résumé. Use *Chicago Manual of Style* for ms guidelines. Reviews artwork/photos as part of ms package.

Recent Nonfiction Title: *International Encyclopedia of Horse Breeds*, by Bonnie L. Hendricks (reference).
Recent Fiction Title: *Eye Killers*, by A.A. Carr (novel).

UNIVERSITY OF PENNSYLVANIA PRESS, 423 Service Dr., Philadelphia PA 19104-6097. (215)898-6261. Fax: (215)898-0404. Editorial Director: Timothy Clancy. Estab. 1860. Publishes hardcover and paperback originals and reprints. Publishes 70 titles/year. Receives 650 submissions/year. 10-20% of books from first-time authors; 99% from unagented writers. Decision to publish determined by evaluation obtained by the press from outside specialists and approval by Faculty Editorial Board. Royalty determined on book-by-book basis. Publishes book 10 months after delivery of final ms. Reports in 3 months or less. Book catalog for 9×12 SAE with 6 first-class stamps. No unsolicited mss.

Nonfiction: Publishes literary criticism, women's studies, cultural studies, ancient studies, medieval studies, business, economics, history, law, anthropology, folklore, art history, architecture. "Serious books that serve the scholar and the professional." Follow the *Chicago Manual of Style*. Query with outline, résumé or vita. Reviews artwork as part of ms package. Send photocopies. Do not send ms.

Recent Nonfiction Title: *Bendectin and Birth Defects: The Challenges of Mass Toxic Substances Litigation*, by Michael D. Green.

Tips: "Queries/manuscripts may be routed to other editors in the publishing group."

UNIVERSITY OF SCRANTON PRESS, University of Scranton, Scranton PA 18510-4660. (717)941-4228. Fax: (717)941-4309. E-mail: rousseaur1@uofs.edu. Website: http://www.uofs.edu/admin/unpresshp.html. Director: Richard Rousseau. Estab. 1981. Imprint is Ridge Row Press. Publishes hardcover paperbacks and originals. Publishes 5 titles/year. Receives 200 queries and 45 mss/year. 60% of books from first-time authors; 100% from unagented writers. Pays 10% royalty. Publishes book 1 year after acceptance. Reports in 1 month on queries. *Writer's Market* recommends allowing 2 months for reply. Book catalog and ms guidelines free on request. Member of the Association of Jesuit University Presses.

Nonfiction: Scholarly monographs. Subjects include art/architecture, language/literature, philosophy, religion, sociology. Looking for clear editorial focus: theology/religious studies; philosophy/philosophy of religion; scholarly treatments; the culture of northeastern Pennsylvania. Query or submit outline and 2 sample chapters.

Recent Nonfiction Title: *Dhuoda: Ninth Century Mother & Theologian*, by Marie Anne Mayeski.

Poetry: Only poetry related to northeastern Pennsylvania.

Recent Poetry Title: *Coalseam*, edited by K. Blomain, 2nd ed.

THE UNIVERSITY OF TENNESSEE PRESS, 293 Communications Bldg., Knoxville TN 37996-0325. Fax: (423)974-3724. Website: http://www.lib.utk.edu/UTKgophers/UT-PRESS. Acquisitions Editor: Meredith Morris-Babb. Estab. 1940. Publishes 30 titles/year. Receives 450 submissions/year. 35% of books from first-time authors; 99% from unagented writers. Average print order for a first book is 1,000. Nonauthor-subsidy publishes 10% of books. Pays negotiable royalty on net receipts. Publishes book 1 year after acceptance. Reports in 2 months. Book catalog for 12×16 SAE with 2 first-class stamps. Manuscript guidelines for SASE.

● The University of Tennessee Press now accepts submissions of *regional* fiction.

Nonfiction: American history, cultural studies, religious studies, vernacular architecture and material culture, literary criticism, African-American studies, women's studies, Caribbean, anthropology, folklore and regional studies. Prefers "scholarly treatment and a readable style. Authors usually have Ph.D.s." Submit outline, author vita and 2 sample chapters. No poetry or plays. Reviews artwork/photos as part of ms package.

Recent Nonfiction Title: *Tennessee's Historic Landscape*, by C. Van West (travel).

Fiction: *Writer's Market* recommends sending a query with SASE first.

Recent Fiction Title: *Sharpshooter*, by David Madden (novel).

Tips: "Our market is in several groups: scholars; educated readers with special interests in given scholarly subjects; and the general educated public interested in Tennessee, Appalachia and the South. Not all our books appeal to all these groups, of course, but any given book must appeal to at least one of them."

UNIVERSITY OF TEXAS PRESS, P.O. Box 7819, Austin TX 78713-7819. Fax: (512)320-0668. E-mail: castiron@mail.utexas.edu. Website: http://www.utexas.edu/depts/utpress/. Executive Editor: Theresa May. Estab. 1952. Publishes 80 titles/year. Receives 1,000 submissions/year. 50% of books from first-time authors; 99% from unagented writers. Average print order for a first book is 1,000. Pays royalty usually based on net income. Offers advance occasionally. Publishes book 18 months after acceptance. Reports in up to 3 months. Book catalog and ms guidelines free.

Nonfiction: General scholarly subjects: natural history, American, Latin American, Native American, Chicano and Middle Eastern studies, classics and the ancient world, film, contemporary regional architecture, archeology, anthropology, geography, ornithology, environmental studies, biology, linguistics, women's literature, literary biography (Modernist period). Also uses specialty titles related to Texas and the Southwest, national trade titles, and regional trade titles. Accepts nonfiction translations related to above areas. Query or submit outline and 2 sample chapters. Reviews artwork/photos as part of ms package.

Recent Nonfiction Title: *Rereading the Spanish American Essay*, edited by Doris Meyer (essay collection).
Fiction: Latin American and Middle Eastern fiction only in translation.
Recent Fiction Title: *House of Mist & The Shrouded Woman*, by Maria Bombal (novel).
Recent Poetry Title: *Song of the Heart*, by Ramon Lopez Velarde.
Tips: "It's difficult to make a manuscript over 400 double-spaced pages into a feasible book. Authors should take special care to edit out extraneous material. Looks for sharply focused, in-depth treatments of important topics."

UNIVERSITY PRESS OF COLORADO, P.O. Box 849, Niwot CO 80544-0849. (303)530-5337. Fax: (303)530-5306. Director: Luther Wilson. Acquisitions Editor: Laura Furney. Estab. 1965. Publishes hardcover and paperback originals. Publishes 40 titles/year. Receives 1,000 submissions/year. 50% of books from first-time authors; 99% from unagented writers. Average print order for a first book is 1,500-2,000. Pays 7½-10-12½-15% royalty contract on net price. No advance. Publishes book 2 years after acceptance. Reports in 6 months. Book catalog free.
Nonfiction: Scholarly, regional and environmental subjects. Length: 250-500 pages. Query first with table of contents, preface or opening chapter. Reviews artwork/photos as part of ms package.
Recent Nonfiction Title: *John Otto*, by Alan Kania (western history).
Fiction: Limited fiction series; works of fiction on the trans-Mississippi West, by authors residing in the region. *Writer's Market* recommends sending a query with SASE first.
Recent Fiction Title: *The Eagle Catcher*, by Margaret Coel (mystery).
Tips: "Books should be solidly researched and from a reputable scholar, because we are a university press. We have new series on the Women's West and on Mesoamerican worlds."

UNIVERSITY PRESS OF KENTUCKY, 663 S. Limestone, Lexington KY 40508-4008. (606)257-2951. Fax: (606)257-2984. Website: http://www.uky.edu/UniversityPress/. Editor-in-Chief: Nancy Grayson Holmes. Estab. 1951. Publishes hardcover and paperback originals and reprints. Publishes 60 titles/year. Payment varies. No advance. Publishes ms 1 year after acceptance. Reports in 2 months on queries. Book catalog free.
Nonfiction: Biography, reference, monographs. "We are a scholarly publisher, publishing chiefly for an academic and professional audience. Strong areas are American history, literature, women's studies, American studies, folklore and ethnomusicology, Appalachian studies, Irish studies and military history. No textbooks, genealogical material, lightweight popular treatments, how-to books or books unrelated to our major areas of interest." The Press does not consider original works of fiction or poetry. Query.
Recent Nonfiction Title: *Women Politicians and the Media*, by Maria Braden.
Tips: "Most of our authors are drawn from our primary academic and professional audience. We are probably not a good market for the usual freelance writer."

UNIVERSITY PRESS OF MISSISSIPPI, 3825 Ridgewood Rd., Jackson MS 39211-6492. (601)982-6205. Fax: (601)982-6217. E-mail: press@ihl.state.ms.us. Director: Richard Abel. Associate Director and Editor-in-Chief: Seetha Srinivasan. Estab. 1970. Imprints are Muscadine Books (regional trade) and Banner Books (literary reprints). Publishes hardcover and paperback originals and reprints. Publishes 55 titles/year. Receives 750 submissions/year. 20% of books from first-time authors; 90% from unagented writers. "Competitive royalties and terms." Publishes book 1 year after acceptance. Reports in up to 3 months. Book catalog for 9×12 SAE with 3 first-class stamps.
Nonfiction: Americana, biography, history, politics, folklife, literary criticism, ethnic/minority studies, art, photography, music, health, popular culture with scholarly emphasis. Interested in southern regional studies and literary studies. Submit outline and sample chapters and curriculum vita to Acquisitions Editor. "We prefer a proposal that describes the significance of the work and a chapter outline." Reviews artwork/photos as part of ms package.
Fiction: Commissioned trade editions by prominent writers.

UNIVERSITY PRESS OF NEW ENGLAND, (includes Wesleyan University Press), 23 S. Main St., Hanover NH 03755-2048. (603)643-7100. Fax: (603)643-1540. E-mail: university.press@dartmouth.edu. Director: Thomas L. McFarland. Editorial Director: Phil Pochoda. Acquisitions Editor: TBA. Editor: Paul Schnee. Estab. 1970. "University Press of New England is a consortium of university presses. Some books—those published for one of the consortium members—carry the joint imprint of New England and the member: Wesleyan, Dartmouth, Brandeis, Tufts, University of New Hampshire and Middlebury College. Associate member: Salzburg seminar." Publishes hardcover and trade paperback originals, trade paperback reprints. Publishes 70 titles/year. Nonauthor-subsidy publishes 80% of books. Pays standard royalty. Offers advance occasionally. Reports in 2 months. Book catalog and guidelines for 9×12 SAE with 5 first-class stamps.
Nonfiction: Americana (New England), art, biography, history, music, nature, politics, reference, sociology, regional (New England). No festschriften, memoirs, unrevised doctoral dissertations, or symposium collections. Submit outline, 1-2 sample chapters with SASE.

Recent Nonfiction Title: *Winter's Light*, by John Preston (memoir/gay studies).
Fiction: Regional (New England) novels and reprints.
Recent Fiction Title: *Water Witches*, by Chris Bohjalian (novel).

UTAH STATE UNIVERSITY PRESS, Logan UT 84322-7800. (801)797-1362. Fax: (801)797-0313. Director: Michael Spooner. Estab. 1972. Publishes hardcover and trade paperback originals and reprints. Publishes 15 titles/year. Receives 170 submissions/year. 8% of books from first-time authors. Pays royalty on net price. No advance. Publishes book 18 months after acceptance. Reports in 1 month on queries. *Writer's Market* recommends allowing 2 months for reply. Book catalog free. Manuscript guidelines for SASE.
• Utah State University Press is especially interested in supporting Native American writers with scholarly or creative manuscripts.
Nonfiction: Biography, reference and textbook on folklore, Americana (history and politics). "Particularly interested in book-length scholarly manuscripts dealing with folklore, Western history, Western literature. *Writer's Market* recommends query with SASE first. Reviews artwork/photos as part of ms package.
Poetry: "Accepting very few creative works at present. Query before sending manuscript."
Tips: "Marketability of work is more important than ever."

VALLEY OF THE SUN PUBLISHING, P.O. Box 38, Malibu CA 90265. President: Richard Sutphen. Publishes hardcover and trade paperback originals and trade paperback reprints. Publishes 12 titles/year. 20% of books from first-time authors; 100% from unagented writers. Pays 8-10% royalty on net price. "We have a large-circulation magalog and it's not unusual to sell half our books directly at full price. The 8-10% is based upon what we sell them for." Offers $1,500-2,000 advance. Publishes book 9 months after acceptance of ms. Accepts simultaneous submissions. Reports in 2 months. Book catalog free. Manuscript guidelines for #10 SASE.
Nonfiction: Self-help, New Age metaphysical. Submit outline with 2 sample chapters or complete ms. *Writer's Market* recommends allowing 2 months for reply. Reviews artwork/photos as part of ms package. Send photocopies.
Recent Nonfiction Title: *Metaphysical Techniques That Really Work*, by Audrey Davis (New Age).

VANDAMERE PRESS, Imprint of ABI Associates, Inc., P.O. Box 5243, Arlington VA 22205. Acquisitions Editor: Jerry Frank. Publishes hardcover and trade paperback originals and reprints. Publishes 8 titles/year. Receives 750 queries and 2,000 mss/year. 50% of books from first-time authors; 90% from unagented writers. Pays royalty on revenues generated. Publishes book 2 years after acceptance. Accepts simultaneous submissions. Reports in 6 months.
• Vandamere Press is looking for more history and biography manuscripts.
Nonfiction: Subjects include Americana, biography, child guidance/parenting, education, history, military/war, regional, career guide. Submit outline and 2-3 sample chapters. Reviews artwork/photos as part of ms package. Send photocopies.
Recent Nonfiction Title: *By Trust Betrayed*, by Hugh G. Gallagher (history).
Fiction: General fiction including adventure, erotica, humor, mystery, suspense. Submit synopsis and 5-10 sample chapters. *Writer's Market* recommends sending a query with SASE first.
Recent Fiction Title: *Ancestral Voices*, by Hugh F. Ryan (Irish literary).
Tips: "Authors who can provide endorsements from significant published writers, celebrities, etc. will *always* be given serious consideration. Clean, easy-to-read, *dark* copy is essential. Patience in waiting for replies is essential. All unsolicited work is looked at but at certain times of the year our review schedule will stop." No response without SASE.

VANDERBILT UNIVERSITY PRESS, Box 1813, Station B, Nashville TN 37235. (615)322-3585. Fax: (615)343-8823. E-mail: vupress@vanderbilt.edu. Website: http://www.vanderbilt.edu/Publications/VUPress/welcome. Director: Charles Backus. Among other titles, publishes Vanderbilt Library of American Philosophy (Herman J. Saatkamp, editor). Also distributes for and co-publishes with the Country Music Foundation. Publishes hardcover originals and trade paperback originals and reprints. Publishes 12-15 titles/year. Receives 200-250 queries/year. 25% of books from first-time authors; 90% from unagented writers. Pays 15% maximum royalty on net income. Sometimes offers advance. Publishes book 10 months after acceptance. Accepts simultaneous submissions but prefers first option. Reports in 3 months on proposals. Book catalog and ms guidelines free on request.
• Vanderbilt University Press is not currently accepting poetry or fiction.
Nonfiction: Biography, illustrated book, reference, textbook, scholarly. Subjects include Americana, anthropology/archaeology, art/architecture/ education, government/politics, health/medicine, history, language/literature, music and popular culture, nature/environment, philosophy, regional, religion, translation, women's issues/studies. Submit outline, 1 sample chapter and cv. Reviews artwork/photos as part of ms package. Send photocopies.
Recent Nonfiction Title: *Glorious Battle: The Cultural Politics of Victorian Anglo-Catholicism*, by John Shelton Reed (social science).
Tips: "Our audience consists of scholars and educated general readers."

‡**VERSO**, 180 Varick St., 10th Fl., New York NY 10014. Managing Director: Colin Robinson. Publishes hardcover and trade paperback originals. Publishes 40-60 titles/year. Receives 300 queries and 150 mss/year. 10% of mss from first-time authors, 95% from unagented writers. Pays royalty. Publishes book 1 year after acceptance of ms. Accepts simultaneous submissions. Reports in 5 months. Book catalog free on request.
Nonfiction: Illustrated book. Subjects include economics, government/politics, history, philosophy, sociology and women's issues/studies. "We are loosely affiliated with *New Left Review* (London); Our books cover politics, culture, and history (among other topics), but all come from a critical, Leftist viewpoint, on the border between trade and academic. We are not interested in academic monographs." Submit proposal package, including at least one sample chapter.
Recent Nonfiction Title: *The Golden Age is In Us*, by Alexander Cockburn.

‡**VGM CAREER HORIZONS**, Imprint of NTC Publishing Group, 4255 W. Touhy Ave., Lincolnwood IL 60646-1975. (708)679-5500. Fax: (708)679-2494. Editorial Group Director: John Nolan. Editor: Betsy Lancefield. Estab. 1963. Publishes hardcover and paperback originals. Publishes 70-75 titles/year. Receives 200-250 submissions/year. 15% of books from first-time authors; 95% from unagented writers. Pays royalty or makes outright purchase. Advance varies. Publishes book 1 year after acceptance. Accepts simultaneous submissions. Reports in 3 months. Book catalog and ms guidelines for 9×12 SAE with 5 first-class stamps.
• VGM is looking for more revision authors to handle rewrites and new editions of existing titles.
Nonfiction: Textbook and general trade on careers in medicine, business, environment, etc. Query or submit outline and sample chapters. Reviews artwork/photos as part of ms package.
Recent Nonfiction Title: *Joyce Lain Kennedy's Career Book.*
Tips: "Our audience is made up of job seekers, career planners, job changers, and students and adults in education and trade markets. Study our existing line of books before sending proposals."

VILLARD BOOKS, Random House, 201 E. 50th St., New York NY 10022. (212)572-2878. Publisher: David Rosenthal. Executive Editor-in-Chief: Craig Nelson. Director of Publicity: Adam Rothberg. Estab. 1983. Publishes hardcover and trade paperback originals. Publishes 55-60 titles/year. 95% of books are agented submissions. Pays varying advances and royalties; negotiated separately. Accepts simultaneous submissions. *Writer's Market* recommends allowing 2 months for reply.
Nonfiction and Fiction: Looks for commercial nonfiction and fiction. Submit outline/synopsis and up to 50 pages in sample chapters. No unsolicited submissions.

‡**VITAL ISSUES PRESS**, P.O. Box 53788, Lafayette LA 70505-3788. (319)237-7049. Editor-in-Chief: Mark Anthony. Publishes hardcover, trade paperback and mass market paperback originals, trade paperback reprints. Publishes 25-30 titles/year. Receives 1,500 submissions/year. 25% of books from first-time authors; 90% from unagented writers. Average print order for a first book is 5,000-10,000. Pays up to 10% royalty on sale price. Pubilshes book 1 year after acceptance. Reports in 4 months. Manuscript guidelines free with SASE.
Nonfiction: Christian perspective on current political and social issues, biography, self-help, inspirational, children's books. Query with descriptive outline.
Tips: "The company's goal is to have a positive impact on our nation's culture. Write clear, crisp and exciting manuscripts that excite the reader. Published authors should expect a heavy publicity schedule."

VOLCANO PRESS, INC., P.O. Box 270, Volcano CA 95689-0270. (209)296-3445. Fax: (209)296-4515. E-mail: sales@volcanopress.com. Website: http://www.volcanopress.com. Publisher: Ruth Gottstein. Publishes trade paperback originals. Publishes 4-6 titles/year. Pays royalties based on monies received from sales. Offers $1,000 advance. Reports in 1 month on queries.
Nonfiction: "We publish women's health and social issues, particularly in the field of domestic violence, and multicultural books for children that are non-racist and non-sexist." Query with brief outline and SASE.
Recent Nonfiction Title: *Walking on Eggshells: Practical Counseling for Women in or Leaving a Violent Relationship*, by Ogawa (domestic violence).
Tips: "Obtain a free catalog from us, or look at our titles on the Web, and then submit materials that are consistent with what we already publish."

VOYAGEUR PRESS, 123 N. Second St., Stillwater MN 55082. (612)430-2210. Fax: (612)430-2211. Editorial Director: Michael Dregni. Publishes hardcover and trade paperback originals. Publishes 30 titles/year. Receives 1,200 queries and 500 mss/year. 10% of books from first-time authors; 90% from unagented writers. Pays royalty. Publishes book 1 year after acceptance of ms. Accepts simultaneous submissions. Reports in 3 months. Book catalog and ms guidelines free on request.
Nonfiction: Coffee table book (and smaller format photographic essay books), cookbook. Subjects include natural history, nature/environment, Americana, collectibles, history, outdoor recreation, regional, travel. Query or submit outline and proposal package. Reviews artwork/photos as part of ms package. Send transparencies—duplicates only and tearsheets.
Tips: "We publish books for a sophisticated audience interested in natural history and cultural history of a variety of subjects. Please present as focused an idea as possible in a brief submission (one page cover letter;

two page outline or proposal). Note your credentials for writing the book. Tell all you know about the market niche and marketing possibilities for proposed book."

WADSWORTH PUBLISHING COMPANY, Division of International Thomson Publishing Inc., 10 Davis Dr., Belmont CA 94002. (415)595-2350. Fax: (415)637-7544. Website: http://www.thomson.com/ wadsworth.html. Editorial Director: Gary Carlson. Estab. 1956. Other ITP Education Group divisions include Brooks/Cole Pub. Co., Heinle & Heinle Publishing Co., Delmar Publishing Company, South-Western Publishing Company, Course Technologies Inc. Publishes hardcover and paperback originals and software. Publishes 240 titles/year. 35% of books from first-time authors; 99% of books from unagented writers. Pays 5-15% royalty on net price. Advances not automatic policy. Publishes ms 1 year after acceptance. Accepts simultaneous submissions. Book catalog (by subject area) and ms guidelines available.
Nonfiction: Textbooks and multimedia products: higher education only. Subjects include statistics, biology, astronomy, earth science, music, social sciences, philosophy, religious studies, speech and mass communications, broadcasting, TV and film productions, English and multimedia. "We need books and media products that use fresh teaching approaches to all courses taught at schools of higher education throughout the US and Canada. We specifically do not publish textbooks in art." Query or submit outline/synopsis and sample chapters.
Recent Nonfiction Title: *Everyday Encounters*, by Julia Wood (interpersonal communication).

‡WAKE FOREST UNIVERSITY PRESS, P.O. Box 7333, Winston-Salem NC 27109. (910)759-5448. Director: Dillon Johnston. Manager: Candide Jones. Estab. 1976. Publishes hardcover and trade paperback originals. Publishes 5 titles/year. Receives 80 submissions/year. Pays 10% on retail price. Offers $500 average advance. Publishes book 6 months after acceptance. Reports in 2 months on queries. Book catalog free.
Nonfiction: Subjects include language/literature. "We publish exclusively poetry and criticism of the poetry of Ireland and bilingual editions of contemporary French poetry." Query.
Recent Poetry Title: *Collected Poems*, by John Montague.
Tips: "Readers of contemporary poetry and of books of Irish interest or French interest are our audience. We are no longer considering books on or about photography."

J. WESTON WALCH, PUBLISHER, P.O. Box 658, Portland ME 04104-0658. (207)772-2846. Fax: (207)772-3105. Editor-in-Chief: Joan E. Whitney. Editor: Elizabeth Isele. Math/Science Editor: Tom Cohn. Computer Editor: Robert Crepeau. Assistant Editors: Kate O'Halloran and Elaine Kerachsky. Estab. 1927. Publishes educational paperback originals and software. Publishes 75 titles/year. Receives 300 submissions/ year. 10% of books from first-time authors; 95% from unagented writers. Average print order for a first book is 700. Offers 10-15% royalty on gross receipts or makes outright purchase of $100-2,500. No advance. Publishes book 18 months after acceptance. Reports in 4 months. Book catalog for 9×12 SAE with 5 first-class stamps. Manuscript guidelines for #10 SASE.
Nonfiction: Subjects include art, business, computer education, economics, English, foreign language, geography, government, health, history, literacy, mathematics, middle school, music, psychology, science, social studies, sociology, special education. "We publish only supplementary educational material for grades six to twelve in the US and Canada. Formats include books, posters, blackline masters, card sets, cassettes, microcomputer courseware, video and mixed packages. Most titles are assigned by us, though we occasionally accept an author's unsolicited submission. We have a great need for author/artist teams and for authors who can write at third- to tenth-grade levels. We do *not* want basic texts, anthologies or industrial arts titles. Most of our authors—but not all—have secondary teaching experience. *Query first.* Looks for sense of organization, writing ability, knowledge of subject, skill of communicating with intended audience." Reviews artwork/ photos as part of ms package.
Recent Nonfiction Title: *Ellis Island and Beyond*, by Wendy Wilson and Jack Papadonis (reproducible teaching book).

WALKER AND CO., Division of Walker Publishing Co., 435 Hudson St., New York NY 10014. Fax: (212)727-0984. Contact: Submissions Editor. Estab. 1959. Publishes hardcover and trade paperback originals and a few reprints of British books. Publishes 100 titles/year. Receives 4,500 submissions/year. 30% of books from first-time authors; 30% from unagented writers. Pays varying royalty or makes outright purchase. Offers $1,000-3,000 average advance, "but could be higher or lower." Material without SASE will not be returned. Responds in 3 months. Book catalog and guidelines for 9×12 SAE with 3 first-class stamps.
Nonfiction: Biography, business, science and natural history, health, music, nature and environment, parenting, reference, popular science, sports/baseball, personal finance, some regional titles and self-help books. Query or submit outline and sample chapter. No phone calls. Reviews photos as part of ms package. Do not send originals.
Fiction: Mystery/suspense, western juvenile (ages 5 and up).
Tips: "We also need preschool to young adult nonfiction, biographies and middle-grade novels. Query."

WARD HILL PRESS, P.O. Box 04-0424, Staten Island NY 10304-0008. Editorial Director: Elizabeth Davis. Estab. 1989. Publishes hardcover and paperback originals for middle readers and young adults (ages

10+). Publishes 4-6 titles/year. Receives several hundred queries and mss/year. 75% of books from first-time authors; 90% from unagented writers. Pays 6-12% royalty on retail price. Offers advance. Publishes book 1 year after acceptance. Reports in 2 months on queries. Manuscript guidelines for #10 SASE.

Nonfiction and Fiction: Fiction and nonfiction for middle readers and young adults (ages 10 and up), with a special focus on American history since 1860, as well as multiculturalism. Query. Reviews artwork/photos as part of ms package. Send photocopies. "Query first. No phone calls please."

Recent Nonfiction Title: *Flatboating on the Yellowstone 1877*, by Fred G. Bond (historical narrative).

Recent Fiction Title: *My Best Defense*, by Bob Riggs (novel, ages 9-14).

Tips: "Looking for multiple biographies (biographies of six or more people in one manuscript), particularly those profiling minority women; first-person accounts of noteworthy events in history; and young adult fiction, set in a contemporary, urban environment, that deals with issues of race or culture."

‡**WARNER ASPECT**, 1271 Avenue of the Americas, New York NY 10020. Editor-in-Chief: Betsy Mitchell. Imprint of Warner Books. Publishes hardcover, trade paperback, mass market paperback originals and mass market paperback reprints. Imprint publishes 30 titles/year. Receives 500 queries and 350 mss/year. 5-10% of books from first-time authors; 1% from unagented writers. Pays royalty on retail price. Offers $5,000-up advance. Publishes book 10 weeks after acceptance of ms. Reports in 10 weeks on mss. Manuscript guidelines for #10 SASE.

Fiction: Fantasy, science fiction. "Sample our existing titles—we're a fairly new list and pretty strongly focused." Mistake writers often make is "hoping against hope that being unagented won't make a difference. We simply don't have the staff to look at unagented projects." Agented submissions only.

Recent Fiction Title: *Fisherman's Hope*, by David Feintuch (science fiction).

Tips: "Think big. We're looking for 'epic' stories in both fantasy and science fiction."

‡**WARNER BOOKS**, Time & Life Building, 1271 Avenue of the Americas, New York NY 10020. (212)522-7200. Publishes hardcover, trade paperback and mass market paperback originals and reprints. Publishes 350 titles/year. Imprints are Warner Aspect, Warner Vision.

Nonfiction: Biography, business, cooking, current affairs, history, home, humor, popular culture, psychology, reference, self-help, sports.

Recent Nonfiction Title: *Swim with the Dolphins*, by Connie Glaser.

Fiction: Fantasy, horror, mainsteam, mystery, romance (historical), science fiction, suspense, thriller.

Recent Fiction Title: *The Celestine Prophecy*, by James Redfield.

WARREN PUBLISHING HOUSE, INC., P.O. Box 2250, Everett WA 98203-0250. (206)353-3100. Managing Editor: Kathleen Cubley. Estab. 1975. Publishes educational activity books and parenting books for teachers and parents of 2-6-year-olds. Publishes 20-30 titles/year. Considers activity book mss from early childhood education professionals. Considers single activity submissions from early childhood professionals. Considers parenting activity mss from parenting experts. 100% from unagented writers. Makes outright purchase plus copy of book/newsletter author's material appears in. Book catalog and ms guidelines free upon written request.

Nonfiction: Illustrated activity book for parents and teachers of 2-6-year olds. Subjects include animals, art, child guidance/parenting, cooking with kids, foods and nutrition, education, ethnic, gardening, hobbies, language/literature, music, nature/environment, science. "We consider activity ideas submitted by early childhood professionals. Manuscript and ideas must be appropriate for people (teacher/parents) who work with children two to six years old." Query. No children's storybooks, fiction or poetry.

Recent Nonfiction Title: *A Year of Fun Just for Three's*, by Theodosia Spewock.

Tips: "Our audience is teachers and parents who work with children ages two to six. Write for submission requirements."

WASHINGTON STATE UNIVERSITY PRESS, Pullman WA 99164-5910. (800)354-7360. Fax: (509)335-8568. Director: Thomas H. Sanders. Editors: Keith Petersen (Acquisitions) and Glen Lindeman. Estab. 1928. Publishes hardcover originals, trade paperback originals and reprints. Publishes 10 titles/year. Receives 300-400 submissions/year. 50% of books from first-time writers; mostly unagented authors. Pays 5% minimum royalty, graduated according to sales. Publishes book 18 months after acceptance. Reports on queries in 2 months.

Nonfiction: Subjects include Americana, art, biography, economics, environment, ethnic studies, history (especially of the American West and the Pacific Northwest), politics, essays. "We seek manuscripts that focus on the Pacific Northwest as a region. No romance novels, how-to books, gardening books or books

---

✝ **THE DOUBLE DAGGER** before a listing indicates that the listing is new in this edition. New markets are often more receptive to freelance submissions.

specifically as classroom texts. We welcome innovative and thought-provoking titles in a wide diversity of genres, from essays and memoirs to history, anthropology and political science." Submit outline and sample chapters. Reviews artwork/photos as part of ms package.

Tips: "Our audience consists of specialists and general readers who are interested in well-documented research presented in an attractive well-written format. We have developed our marketing in the direction of regional and local history and have attempted to use this as the base around which we are expanding our publishing program. In regional history, the secret is to write a good narrative—a good story—that is substantiated factually. It should be told in an imaginative, clever way. Have visuals (photos, maps, etc) available to help the reader envision what has happened. Tell the regional history story in a way that ties it to larger, national, and even international events. Weave it into the large pattern of history. We have published our first books of essays and a regional cookbook, and will do more in these and other fields if we get the right manuscript."

FRANKLIN WATTS, INC., Division of Grolier, Inc., Sherman Turnpike, Danbury CT 06813. (203)797-6802. Fax: (203)797-6986. E-mail: erp3@aol.com. Publisher: John Selfridge. Contact: Submissions. Publishes both hardcover and softcover originals for middle schoolers and young adults. Publishes 150 titles/year. 10% of books from first-time authors; 90% from unagented writers. Reports in 2 months on queries with SASE. Book catalog for $3 postage.

Nonfiction: History, science, social issues, biography. Subjects include American and world history, politics, natural and physical sciences. Multicultural, curriculum-based nonfiction lists published twice a year. Strong also in the area of contemporary problems and issues facing young people. No humor, coffee table books, fiction, poetry, picture books, cookbooks or gardening books. Query. No calls or unsolicited mss.

WEIDNER & SONS PUBLISHING, P.O. Box 2178, Riverton NJ 08077. (609)486-1755. Fax: (609)486-7583. E-mail: weidner@waterw.com. Website: http://www.waterw.com/~weidner. President: James H. Weidner. Estab. 1967. Publishes hardcover and trade paperback originals and reprints. Imprints are Hazlaw Books, Medlaw Books, Bird Sci Books, Delaware Estuary Press, Tycooly Publishing USA and Pulse Publications. Publishes 10-20 titles/year; imprint publishes 10 titles/year. Receives 50 queries and 3 mss/year. 100% of books from first-time authors; 100% from unagented writers. Pays 10% maximum royalty on wholesale price. Average time between acceptance and publication varies with subject matter. Accepts simultaneous submissions. Reports in 1 month on queries. *Writer's Market* recommends allowing 2 months for reply. Book catalog for $1 (refundable with order).

Nonfiction: Reference, technical, textbook. Subjects include agriculture/horticulture, animals, business and economics, child guidance/parenting, computers and electronics, education, gardening, health/medicine, hobbies (electronic), language/literature, nature/environment, psychology, science and ecology/environment. "We are primarily science, text and reference books. Rarely fiction; never poetry. No topics in the 'pseudosciences': occult, astrology, New Age and metaphysics, etc." Query or submit outline and sample chapters. Reviews artwork/photos as part of ms package. Send photocopies.

Recent Nonfiction Title: *Chiropractic Practical Guide to Cranial Adjusting.*

Tips: "Our audience consists of scholars, college students and researchers."

SAMUEL WEISER, INC., P.O. Box 612, York Beach ME 03910-0612. (207)363-4393. Fax: (207)363-5799. Editor: Eliot Stearns. Estab. 1956. Publishes hardcover originals and trade paperback originals and reprints. Publishes 18-20 titles/year. Receives 200 submissions/year. 50% of books from first-time authors; 98% from unagented writers. Pays 10% royalty on wholesale and retail price. Offers $500 average advance. Publishes book 18 months after acceptance. Reports in 3 months. Book catalog free.

Nonfiction: How-to, self-help. Subjects include health, music, philosophy, psychology, religion. "We look for strong books in our specialty field—written by teachers and people who know the subject. Don't want a writer's rehash of all the astrology books in the library, only texts written by people with strong background in field. No poetry or novels." Submit complete ms. *Writer's Market* recommends query with SASE first. Reviews artwork/photos as part of ms package.

Recent Nonfiction Title: *Ayurveda: A Way of Life*, by Dr. Vinod Verma.

Tips: "Most new authors do not check permissions, nor do they provide proper footnotes. If they did, it would help. We specialize in oriental philosophy, metaphysics, esoterica of all kinds (tarot, astrology, qabalah, magic, etc.). We look at all manuscripts submitted to us. We are interested in seeing freelance art for book covers."

‡WEKA PUBLISHING, INC., 1077 Bridgeport Ave., Shelton CT 06484. Product Manager: Dawn M. Lombard. Publishes 8 titles/year. Receives 5-10 queries and 2-5 mss/year. 100% of books from first-time authors. Publishes book 6 months after acceptance of ms. Accepts simultaneous submissions. Reports in 2 months on queries, 1 month on proposals and mss. *Writer's Market* recommends allowing 2 months for reply. Book catalog and ms guidelines free on request.

Nonfiction: How-to, reference, technical, OSHA, electronics, quality topics. Subjects include computers and electronics, hobbies. "We look for how-to articles. These articles go into our title. Can be a part of more than one title." Submit proposal package, including table of contents, target market, benefits of chapters,

unique selling point. Reviews artwork/photos as part of ms package. Send photocopies.
Recent Nonfiction Title: *OSHA in the Construction Industry.*
Tips: "Our markets are manufacturing, health care, mining, transportation and construction. Prefer legal topics."

‡WESCOTT COVE PUBLISHING CO., P.O. Box 130, Stamford CT 06904. (203)322-0998. President: Julius M. Wilensky. Estab. 1968. Publishes trade paperback originals and reprints. Publishes 4 new titles/year. Receives 15 queries and 10 mss/year. 25% of books from first-time authors; 95% from unagented writers. Pays 5-10% royalty on retail price. Offers $1,000-1,500 advance. Publishes book 1 year after acceptance of ms. Accepts simultaneous submissions. Reports in 1 month on queries. *Writer's Market* recommends allowing 2 months for reply. Book catalog free on request.
Nonfiction: How-to, humor, illustrated book, reference, nautical books. Subjects include history, hobbies, regional, travel. "Mostly we seek out authors knowledgeable in sailing, navigation and cartography, and the area we want covered. Then we commission them to write the book." Query with outline, 1-2 sample chapters, author's credentials and SASE.
Recent Nonfiction Title: *Cruising Guide to Maine*, Vol. II, 2nd ed., by Don Johnson.

WESTERNLORE PRESS, P.O. Box 35305, Tucson AZ 85740. Fax: (520)624-9951. Editor: Lynn R. Bailey. Publishes 6-12 titles/year. Pays standard royalties on retail price "except in special cases." Query with SASE. Reports in 2 months.
Nonfiction: Publishes Western Americana of a scholarly and semischolarly nature: anthropology, history, biography, historic sites, restoration, and ethnohistory pertaining to the greater American West. Re-publication of rare and out-of-print books. Length: 25,000-100,000 words.
Recent Nonfiction Title: *The Apache Kid*, by de la Gaza (western history).

WHISPERING COYOTE PRESS, INC., 300 Crescent Court, Suite 860, Dallas TX 75201. Publisher: Mrs. Lou Alpert. Publishes children's picture books. Publishes 6 titles/year. 20% of books from first-time authors; 90% from unagented writers. Pays 8% royalty on retail price of first 10,000 copies, 10% after (combined author and illustrator). Offers $2,000-8,000 advance (combined author, illustrator). Publishes book 2 years after acceptance of ms. Accepts simultaneous submissions. Reports in 3 months. Book catalog and ms guidelines for #10 SASE.
Fiction: Adventure, fantasy, juvenile picture books. "We only do picture books." Submit complete ms. *Writer's Market* recommends sending a query with SASE first. If author is illustrator also, submit sample art. Send photocopies, no original art.
Recent Fiction Title: *Tracy's Mess*, by Elise Peterson, illustrated by Iza Trapani.
Poetry: "We like poetry—if it works in a picture book format. We are not looking for poetry collections." *Writer's Market* recommends sending a query with SASE first.
Recent Poetry Title: *Itsy Bitsy Spider*, by Iza Trapani (extended rhyme picture book).
Tips: Audience is children, 2-12.

WHITE CLIFFS MEDIA, INC., P.O. Box 433, Tempe AZ 85280-0433. (602)834-1444. Owner: Lawrence Aynesmith. Estab. 1985. Publishes hardcover and trade paperback originals. Publishes 5-10 titles/year. 50% of books from first-time authors; 50% from unagented writers. Pays 5-12% royalty or makes outright purchase. Publishes book 1 year after acceptance. No simultaneous submissions. Reports in 2 months on queries, 4 months on proposals, 6 months on mss. Book catalog for #10 SASE.
Nonfiction: Biography, textbook. Subjects include anthropology, education, ethnic, music/dance, sociology. Query. Reviews artwork/photos as part of ms package. Send photocopies.
Recent Nonfiction Title: *Drum Damba: Talking Drum Lessons*, by Locke (musical instruction).
Tips: "Distribution is more difficult due to the large number of publishers. Writers should send proposals that have potential for mass markets as well as college texts, and that will be submitted and completed on schedule. Our audience reads college texts, general interest trade publications. If I were a writer trying to market a book today, I would send a book on music comparable in quality and mass appeal to a book like Stephen Hawking's *A Brief History of Time*."

‡WHITE MANE PUBLISHING CO., INC., 63 W. Burd St., P.O. Box 152, Shippensburg PA 17257. (717)532-2237. Fax: (717)532-7704. Editor: Martin K. Gordon. Imprint is White Mane Publishing Company, Inc. Publishes hardcover originals and reprints, trade paperback originals. Publishes 50 titles/year. Receives 200 queries and 40 mss/year. 60% of books from first-time authors; 70% from unagented writers. Pays 7-12% royalty. No advance. Publishes book 18 months after acceptance of ms. Accepts simultaneous submissions. Reports in 1 month on queries, 2 months on proposals and mss. Book catalog and ms guidelines free on request.
Nonfiction: Biography, technical. Subjects include history, military/war. Query. Reviews artwork/photos as part of ms package.
Recent Nonfiction Title: *Nowhere to Run*, by John M. Priest (Civil War military history).

WHITE PINE PRESS, 10 Village Square, Fredonia NY 14063. (716)672-5743. Fax: (716)672-4724. Director: Dennis Maloney. Imprint is Springhouse Editions. Publishes hardcover and trade paperback originals. Publishes 10 titles/year. Receives 200 queries and 150 mss/year. 20% of books from first-time authors; 99% from unagented writers. Pays 5-10% royalty on wholesale price. Offers $250 and up advance. Publishes book 18 months after acceptance of ms. Accepts simultaneous submissions. Reports in 2 months on queries. Book catalog free on request.
Nonfiction: Subjects include ethnic, language/literature, translation, women's issues/studies. Query.
Recent Nonfiction Title: *Where the Angels Come Toward Us*, by David St. John.
Fiction: Ethnic, literary, short story collections. Very interested in strong novels. Query with synopsis and 2 sample chapters.
Recent Fiction Title: *Goldsmith's Return*, by Terry R. Bazes.
Poetry: "We do a large amount of poetry in translation. We award the White Pine Press Poetry Prize annually. Write for details. We read mss of American poetry only as part of our annual competition." Query.
Recent Poetry Title: *Destination Zero*, by Sam Hamill.

MARKUS WIENER PUBLISHERS INC., 114 Jefferson Rd., Princeton, NJ 08540. (609)971-1141. Editor-in-Chief: Shelley Frisch. Imprint is Topics in World History. Publishes hardcover originals and trade paperback originals and reprints. Publishes 20-25 titles/year; imprint publishes 5 titles/year. Receives 50-150 queries and 50 mss/year. Pays 10% royalty on net sales. Publishes book 1 year after acceptance. Reports in 2 months on queries and proposals. Book catalog free on request.
Nonfiction: Textbook. History subjects.
Recent Nonfiction Title: *Faces of Lebanon*, by William Harris.

WILD FLOWER PRESS, Imprint of Blue Water Publishing, P.O. Box 726, Newberg OR 97132. (503)538-0264. Fax: (503)538-8485. President: Pam Meyer. Contact: Brian Crissey. Publishes hardcover originals and trade paperback originals and reprints. Publishes 6 titles/year. Receives 30 queries and 15 mss/month. 80% of books from first-time authors; 90% from unagented writers. Pays royalty. Publishes book 16 months after acceptance of ms. Accepts simultaneous submissions. Reports in 2 months on mss. Manuscript guidelines for #10 SASE.
Nonfiction: Books about extraterrestrial research and experiences. Submit outline. Reviews artwork/photos as part of ms package. Send photocopies.
Recent Nonfiction Title: *The Watchers II*, by Raymond E. Fowler.

‡**WILDER PUBLISHING CENTER**, 919 Lafond Ave., St. Paul MN 55104. (612)659-6013. Managing Editor: Vincent Hyman. Publishes trade paperback originals. Publishes 4-6 titles/year. Receives 30 queries and 15 mss/year. 75% of books from first-time authors; 100% from unagented writers. Pays 10% royalty on net. Books are sold through direct mail; average discount is 15%. Offers $1,000-3,000 advance. Publishes book 1 year after acceptance of ms. Accepts simultaneous submissions, if so noted. Reports in 1 month on queries and proposals, 3 months on mss. Book catalog and ms guidelines free on request.
Nonfiction: Nonprofit management, organizational development, community organizing, violence prevention. Subjects include government/politics, sociology. "We are in a growth mode and welcome proposals in these areas. We are seeking manuscripts that report best practice methods using handbook or workbook formats." Phone query OK before submitting proposal with detailed chapter ouline, 1 sample chapter and SASE.
Recent Nonfiction Title: *Foundations for Violence Free Living*, by Dave Mathews (sociology/domestic abuse treatment package).
Tips: "Writers must be practitioners with a passion for their work and experience presenting their techniques at conferences. Freelance writers with an interest in our niches could do well searching out and teaming up with such practitioners as our books sell very well to a tightly targeted market."

WILDERNESS ADVENTURE BOOKS, P.O. Box 217, Davisburg MI 48350-0217. Fax: (810)634-0946. Editor: Erin Sims Howarth. Estab. 1983. Publishes hardcover and trade paperback originals and reprints. Publishes 6 titles/year. Receives 250 submissions/year. 90% of books from first-time authors; 90% from unagented writers. Pays 5-10% royalty on retail price. Offers $100 average advance. Publishes book 16 months after acceptance. Accepts simultaneous submissions. Reports in 2 months.
Nonfiction: How-to, illustrated book. Subjects include Americana, animals, history, nature/environment, regional, non-competitive sports, travel. Query. Reviews artwork/photos as part of ms package.
Recent Nonfiction Title: *Cadillac and the Dawn of Detroit*, by A. Hivert-Garthew (Michigan history).

WILDERNESS PRESS, 2440 Bancroft Way, Berkeley CA 94704-1676. (510)843-8080. Fax: (510)548-1355. E-mail: 74642.1147@compuserve.com. Editorial Director: Thomas Winnett. Assistant Publisher: Caroline Winnett. Estab. 1967. Publishes paperback originals. Publishes 6 titles/year. Receives 150 submissions/year. 20% of books from first-time authors; 95% from unagented writers. Average print order for a first book is 5,000. Pays 8-10% royalty on retail price. Offers $1,000 average advance. Publishes book 8 months after acceptance. Reports in 1 month. *Writer's Market* recommends allowing 2 months for reply. Book catalog for 9×12 SASE.

Nonfiction: "We publish books about the outdoors. Most of our books are trail guides for hikers and backpackers, but we also publish how-to books about the outdoors. The manuscript must be accurate. The author must thoroughly research an area in person. If he is writing a trail guide, he must walk all the trails in the area his book is about. The outlook must be strongly conservationist. The style must be appropriate for a highly literate audience." Request guidelines for proposals.

Recent Nonfiction Title: *The Bay Area Ridge Trail*, by Jean Rusmore.

JOHN WILEY & SONS, INC., 605 Third Ave., New York NY 10158. Associate Publisher/Editor-in-Chief of General Interest Publishing: Carole Hall. Publishes hardcover originals, trade paperback originals and reprints. Publishes 100 titles/year. Pays 10% royalty on wholesale price. Publishes book 1 year after acceptance. Accepts simultaneous submissions. Book catalog free on request.

Nonfiction: Biography, how-to, children's/juvenile, reference, self-help, technical, textbook. Subjects include business and economics, child guidance/parenting, gay/lesbian, government/politics, health/medicine, history, language/communications, military/war, psychology, science, sociology, software, women's issues/studies. Query.

Recent Nonfiction Title: *Weigh Less, Live Longer*, by Louis J. Aronne, M.D. (health).

WILLIAMSON PUBLISHING CO., P.O. Box 185, Church Hill Rd., Charlotte VT 05445. Website: http://www.williamsonbooks.com/publishing/. Editorial Director: Susan Williamson. Estab. 1983. Publishes trade paperback originals. Publishes 15 titles/year. Receives 1,500 queries and 800 mss/year. 75% of books from first-time authors; 90% from unagented writers. Pays royalty on wholesale price. Advance negotiable. Publishes book 1 year after acceptance. Accepts simultaneous submissions, but prefers 1 month exclusivity. Reports in 4 months with SASE. Book catalog for 8½×11 SAE with 4 first-class stamps.

● Williamson's biggest success is their *Kids Can!* series with books like *The Kids' Science Book* and *Hands Around the World. The Kids' Multicultural Art Book* won the Parents' Choice Gold Award; *Tales Alive* won Benjamin Franklin best juvenile fiction.

Nonfiction: Children's/juvenile, children's creative learning books on subjects ranging from science, art, to early learning skills. Adult books include psychology, cookbook, how-to, self-help. "Williamson has four very successful children's book series: *Kids Can!*® (ages 4-10), *Little Hands*® (ages 2-6), *Tales Alive*® (folktales plus activities, age 4-10) and *Kids Quest* (48-page, single subject, ages 4-10). They must incorporate learning through doing. No picture books please! Please don't call concerning your submission. It never helps your review, and it takes too much of our time. With an SASE, you'll hear from us." Submit outline, 2-3 sample chapters and SASE.

Recent Nonfiction Title: *Shapes, Sizes & More Surprises*, by Mary Tomczyk.

Tips: "Our children's books are used by kids, their parents, and educators. They encourage self-discovery, creativity and personal growth."

WILSHIRE BOOK CO., 12015 Sherman Rd., North Hollywood CA 91605-3781. (818)765-8579. Publisher: Melvin Powers. Senior Editor: Marcia Grad. Estab. 1947. Publishes trade paperback originals and reprints. Publishes 25 titles/year. Receives 3,000 submissions/year. 80% of books from first-time authors; 75% from unagented writers. Pays standard royalty. Publishes book 6 months after acceptance. Reports in 2 months. Welcomes telephone calls to discuss mss or book concepts.

Nonfiction: Self-help, motivation/inspiration/spirituality, psychology, recovery, how-to. Subjects include personal success, entrepreneurship, making money on the Internet, mail order, horsemanship. Examples: *Psycho-Cybernetics, The Magic of Thinking Big, New Guide to Rational Living, Three Magic Words, Think and Grow Rich, How to Get Rich in Mail Order, Making Money with Classified Ads* and *Marketing on the Internet*. Min. 60,000 words. Requires detailed chapter outline, 3 sample chapters and SASE. Accepts queries and complete mss. Reviews artwork/photos as part of ms package. Send photocopies.

Fiction: Allegories that teach principles of psychological/spiritual growth or offer guidance in living. Min. 30,000 words. Examples: *Illusions, The Little Prince, Greatest Salesman in the World, The Knight in Rusty Armor* and *The Princess Who Believed in Fairy Tales*. Requires synopsis, 3 sample chapters and SASE. Accepts complete mss.

Tips: "We are vitally interested in all new material we receive. Just as you hopefully submit your manuscript for publication, we hopefully read every one submitted, searching for those that we believe will be successful in the marketplace. Writing and publishing must be a team effort. We need you to write what we can sell. We suggest that you read the successful books mentioned above or others that are similar to the manuscript you want to write. Analyze them to discover what elements make them winners. Duplicate those elements in your own style, using a creative new approach and fresh material, and you will have written a book we can catapult onto the bestseller list."

WINDWARD PUBLISHING, INC., P.O. Box 371005, Miami FL 33137-1005. (305)576-6232. Vice President: Jack Zinzow. Estab. 1973. Publishes trade paperback originals. Publishes 6 titles/year. Receives 50 queries and 10 mss/year. 35% of books from first-time authors; 100% from unagented writers. Pays

10% royalty on wholesale price. Publishes book 14 months after acceptance of ms. Accepts simultaneous submissions. Reports in 2 weeks on queries. *Writer's Market* recommends allowing 2 months for reply.
Nonfiction: Illustrated books, children's/juvenile natural history, handbooks. Subjects include agriculture/horticulture, animals, gardening, nature/environment, recreation (fishing, boating, diving, camping), science. Query. Reviews artwork/photos as part of the ms package.
Recent Nonfiction Title: *Maybe I'll Grow Up to Be A Bullfrog* (children's).

WISDOM PUBLICATIONS, 361 Newbury St., 4th Floor, Boston MA 02115. (617)536-3358. Editorial Project Manager: Constance Miller. Publishes hardcover originals, trade paperback originals and reprints. Publishes 12-15 titles/year. Receives 150 queries and 50 mss/year. 50% of books from first-time authors; 95% from unagented writers. Pays 4-8% royalty on wholesale price (net). Publishes book 2 years after acceptance. Reports in 6 months on mss. Book catalog and ms guidelines free on request.
Nonfiction: Inspiration, reference, self-help, textbook. Subjects include philosophy (Buddhist or Comparative Buddhist/Western), East-West, Buddhism, Buddhist texts and Tibet, psychology, meditation. Submit proposal package, including hard copy of ms. *Writer's Market* recommends sending a query with SASE first. Reviews artwork/photos as part of ms package. Send photocopies.
Recent Nonfiction Title: *Meditation on Emptiness*, by Jeffrey Hopkins (Buddhism, Eastern philosophy).
Fiction: Children's books with spiritual themes.
Poetry: Buddhist, contemplative.
Recent Poetry Title: *Drinking the Mountain Stream*, by Lana Kinja and Brian Cutillo, translators (sacred Tibetan poetry by Milarepa).
Tips: "We are now publishing children's books with spiritual themes and contemplative/Buddhist poetry."

WOODLAND PUBLISHING INC., P.O. Box 160, Pleasant Grove UT 84062. Fax: (801)785-8511. Publisher: Mark Lisonbee. Publishes perfect bound and trade paperback originals. Publishes 20 titles/year. Receives 100 queries and 60 mss/year. 50% of books from first-time authors; 100% from unagented writers. Publishes book 6 months after acceptance of ms. Accepts simultaneous submissions. Reports in 1 month on proposals. *Writer's Market* recommends allowing 2 months for reply. Book catalog free on request.
Nonfiction: Health/alternative medicine subjects. "Our readers are interested in herbs and other natural health topics. Most of our books are sold through health food stores." Query.
Recent Nonfiction Title: *Today's Herbal Health for Children*, by Louise Tenney.

‡WORDWARE PUBLISHING, INC., 1506 Capitol Ave., Plano TX 75074. (214)423-0090. Fax: (214)881-9147. E-mail: 75031.2001@compuserve.com. Website: http://www.gunnyragg.com~wordware. President: Russell A. Stultz. Publishes trade paperback and mass market paperback originals. Publishes 50-70 titles/year. Receives 100-150 queries and 50-75 mss/year. 40% of books from first-time authors; 95% from unagented writers. Pays 8-12% royalty on wholesale price. Publishes book 6 months after acceptance of ms. Accepts simultaneous submissions. Reports in 2 months. Book catalog and ms guidelines free on request.
Nonfiction: Reference, technical, textbook. Subjects include computers, electronics. Submit proposal package, including table of contents, 2 sample chapters, target audience summation, competing books.
Recent Nonfiction Title: *The Visual Basic Example Book*, by Smith/Campbell/Vihlen (reference).

WORLD LEISURE, 177 Paris St., Boston MA 02128-3058. (617)569-1966. Fax: (617)561-7654. E-mail: wleisure@aol.com. President: Charles Leocha. Publishes trade paperback originals. Publishes 6-8 titles/year. Pays royalty or makes outright purchase. No advance. Reports in 2 months on proposals.
Nonfiction "We will be publishing annual updates to *Ski Europe* and *Skiing America*. Writers planning any ski stories should contact us for possible add-on assignments at areas not covered by our staff. We also will publish general travel titles such as Travelers' Rights, Family travel guides, guidebooks about myths and legends, the *Cheap Dates* (affordable activity guidebooks) series and self/help books such as *Getting To Know You*, and *A Woman's ABCs of Life*. Submit outline, intro chapter and annotated table of contents with SASE.

WRITE WAY PUBLISHING, 10555 E. Darmouth, Suite 210, Aurora CO 80014 Owner/Editor: Dorrie O'Brien. Publishes hardcover and trade paperback originals. Publishes 10 titles/year. Receives 300 queries and 600 mss/year. 50% of books from first-time authors; 95% from unagented writers. Pays 8-10% royalty on wholesale price. No advance. Publishes book 3 years after acceptance. Accepts simultaneous submissions. Reports in 1 month on queries and proposals; 6 months on mss. "We only consider completed works." Book brochure and ms guidelines free on request.
Nonfiction: Biography (of notable personages only). Subjects include government/politics (American or British only), history (American or British only), military, war (American or British only). No biographies of "unknowns." Query with short synopsis, 1-2 sample chapters and postage with proper-sized box or envelope. "Wait with material until we've determined if the manuscript is accepted for reading."
Fiction: Adventure, fantasy, historical, horror, mystery, occult, science fiction, suspense. Query with short synopsis, 1-2 sample chapters and postage with proper-sized box or envelope.

Recent Fiction Title: *Death of A DJ*, by Jane Rubino.

Tips: "We find that lengthy outlines and/or synopsis are unnecessary and much too time-consuming for our editors to read. We prefer a very short plot review and 1-2 chapters to get a feel for the writer's style. If we like what we read, then we'll ask for the whole manuscript."

WRITER'S DIGEST BOOKS, Imprint of F&W Publications, 1507 Dana Ave., Cincinnati OH 45207. Editor: Jack Heffron. Estab. 1920. Publishes hardcover and paperback originals. Publishes 24 titles/year. Pays 10-20% royalty on net receipts. Accepts simultaneous submissions, if so noted. Publishes book 18 months after acceptance. *Writer's Market* recommends allowing 2 months for reply. Book catalog for 9 × 12 SAE with 6 first-class stamps.

Nonfiction: Instructional and reference books for writers. "Our instruction books stress results and how specifically to achieve them. Should be well-researched, yet lively and readable. Our books concentrate on writing techniques over marketing techniques. We do *not* want to see books telling readers how to crack specific nonfiction markets: *Writing for the Computer Market* or *Writing for Trade Publications*, for instance. Concentrate on broader writing topics. In the offices here we refer to a manuscript's 4T value—manuscripts must have information writers can Take To The Typewriter. We are continuing to grow our line of reference books for writers, such as *Modus Operandi* and *Malicious Intent* in our Howdunit series, and *A Writer's Guide to Everyday Life in the Middle Ages*. References must be usable, accessible, and, of course, accurate." Query or submit outline and sample chapters with SASE. "Be prepared to explain how the proposed book differs from existing books on the subject." No fiction or poetry. "Writer's Digest Books also publishes instructional books for photographers and songwriters but the main thrust is on writing books. The same philosophy applies to songwriting and photography books: they must instruct about the creative craft, as opposed to instructing about marketing."

Recent Nonfiction Title: *Get That Novel Written*, by Donna Levin.

WRS PUBLISHING, P.O. Box 21207, Waco TX 76702. (817)776-6461. Fax: (817)757-1454. Acquisitions Director: Thomas Spence. Estab. 1967. Publishes hardcover, trade and mass market paperback originals. Publishes 6-10 titles/year. Receives 600 submissions/year. 20% of books from first-time authors; 50% from unagented writers. Pays 15% royalty on wholesale price. Advance negotiable. Publishes book 1 year after acceptance. Accepts simultaneous submissions, if so noted. Reports in 1 month on queries. *Writer's Market* recommends allowing 2 months for reply. Book catalog and ms guidelines for SASE.

Nonfiction: Practical books on family life, marriage, child-rearing, education and character-building. Books of social or cultural criticism, especially those relating to marriage and the family.

Recent Nonfiction Title: *Killing the Culture Softly*, by Robert H. Knight.

Tips: "We are primarily a secular publisher, but we welcome proposals for books having a spiritual element as well as those for purely secular works. No New Age books please. We have narrowed our focus to nonfiction titles relating to the family. We are interested in both practical books on parenting and marriage and books of social/cultural/criticism/commentary."

ZEBRA and PINNACLE BOOKS, 850 Third Ave., New York NY 10022. (212)407-1500. Publisher: Lynn Brown. Publishes hardcover, trade paperback and mass market paperback originals, trade paperback and mass market paperback reprints. Zebra publishes 360 titles/year; Pinnacle publishes 120 titles/year. Pays royalty. Rarely makes outright purchase. Publishes book 2 years after acceptance of ms. Accepts simultaneous submissions. Reports in 3 months on proposals. Manuscript guidelines for #10 SASE.

Nonfiction: Biography, how-to, humor, self-help. Subjects include business and economics, health/medicine, military/war, money/finance. Submit outline with 3-5 sample chapters.

Fiction: Adventure, erotica, fantasy, gothic, historical, horror, humor, literary, mainstream/contemporary, mystery, occult, romance, short story collections, suspense, western, young adult. Submit synopsis with 3-5 sample chapters.

ZOLAND BOOKS, INC., 384 Huron Ave., Cambridge MA 02138. (617)864-6252. Fax: (617)661-4998. Publisher/Editor: Roland Pease, Jr. Estab. 1987. Publishes hardcover and trade paperback originals. Publishes 8-12 titles/year. Receives 400 submissions/year. 15% of books from first-time authors; 60% from unagented writers. Pays 7% royalty on retail price. Publishes book 18 months after acceptance. Reports in 4 months. Book catalog for 6½ × 9½ SAE with 2 first-class stamps.

Nonfiction: Biography, art book. Subjects include art/architecture, language/literature, nature/environment, photography, regional, translation, travel, women's issues/studies. Query. Reviews artwork/photos as part of ms package.

Recent Nonfiction Title: *Talking Pictures*, by Rudy Burckhardt (photography).

Fiction: Literary and short story collections. Submit complete ms. *Writer's Market* recommends sending a query with SASE first.

Recent Fiction Title: *The Country Road*, by James Loughlin (lyric).
Tips: "We are most likely to publish books which provide original, thought-provoking ideas, books which will captivate the reader, and are evocative."

ZONDERVAN PUBLISHING HOUSE, 5300 Patterson Ave. SE, Grand Rapids MI 49530-0002. (616)698-6900. Contact: Editorial Coordinator. Estab. 1931. Publishes hardcover and trade paperback originals and reprints. Publishes 120 titles/year. Receives 3,000 submissions/year. 20% of books from first-time authors; 80% from unagented writers. Average print order for a first book is 5,000. Pays royalty of 14% of the net amount received on sales of cloth and softcover trade editions and 12% of net amount received on sales of mass market paperbacks. Offers variable advance. Reports in 3 months on proposals. SASE required. Recommend ms guidelines for #10 SASE. To receive a recording about submission call (616)698-6900.
Nonfiction and Fiction: Biography, autobiography, self-help, devotional, contemporary issues, Christian living, Bible study resources, references for lay audience; some adult fiction; youth and children's ministry, teens and children. Academic and Professional Books: college and seminary textbooks (biblical studies, theology, church history); preaching, counseling, discipleship, worship, and church renewal for pastors, professionals, and lay leaders in ministry; theological and biblical reference books. All from religious perspective (evangelical). Immediate needs listed in guidelines. Submit outline/synopsis, 1 sample chapter, and SASE for return of materials.
Recent Nonfiction Title: *The Jesus I Never Knew*, by Philip Yancey.
Recent Fiction Title: *The Campaign*, by Marilyn Tucker Quayle and Nancy Tucker Northcott.

PUBLISHERS THAT APPEARED in the 1996 edition of *Writer's Market* but are not included this year are listed in the General Index with a notation explaining their absence.

Canadian and International Book Publishers

Canadian book publishers share the same mission as their U.S. counterparts—publishing timely books on subjects of concern and interest to a targetable audience. Most of the publishers listed in this section, however, differ from U.S. publishers in that their needs tend toward subjects that are specifically Canadian or intended for a Canadian audience. Some are interested in submissions only from Canadian writers. There are many regional Canadian publishers that concentrate on region-specific subjects, and many Quebec publishers will consider only works in French.

U.S. writers hoping to do business with Canadian publishers should take pains to find out as much about their intended markets as possible. The listings will inform you about what kinds of books the companies publish and tell you whether they are open to receiving submissions from non-Canadians. To further target your markets and see very specific examples of the books they are publishing, send for catalogs from the publishers you are interested in.

There has always been more government subsidy of publishing in Canada than in the U.S. However, with continued cuts in such subsidies, government support appears to be on the decline. There still are a few author-subsidy publishers in Canada and writers should proceed with caution when they are made this offer.

Publishers offering author subsidy arrangements (sometimes referred to as "joint venture," "co-publishing" or "cooperative publishing") are not listed in *Writer's Market*. If one of the publishers in this section offers you an author-subsidy arrangement or asks you to pay for all or part of the cost of any aspect of publishing (printing, marketing, etc.) or asks you to guarantee the purchase of a number of books yourself, we would like you to let us know about that company immediately.

Despite a healthy book publishing industry, Canada is still dominated by publishers from the United States. Two out of every three books found in Canadian bookstores are published in the U.S. These odds have made some Canadian publishers even more determined to concentrate on Canadian authors and subjects. Writers interested in additional Canadian book publishing markets should consult *Literary Market Place* (R.R. Bowker & Co.), *The Canadian Writer's Guide* (Fitzhenry & Whiteside) and *The Canadian Writer's Market* (McClelland & Stewart).

INTERNATIONAL MAIL

U.S. postage stamps are useless on mailings originating outside of the U.S. When enclosing a self-addressed envelope for return of your query or manuscript from a publisher outside the U.S., you must include International Reply Coupons (IRCs). IRCs are available at your local post office and can be redeemed for stamps of any country. You can cut a substantial portion of your international mailing expenses by sending disposable proposals and manuscripts (i.e., photocopies or computer printouts which the recipient can recycle if she is not interested), instead of paying postage for the return of rejected material. Please note that the cost for items such as catalogs is expressed in the currency of the country in which the publisher is located.

For a list of publishers according to their subjects of interest, see the nonfiction and fiction sections of the Book Publishers Subject Index. Information on some book publishers and producers not included in this edition of *Writer's Market* can be found in the General Index.

‡**THE ALTHOUSE PRESS**, U.W.O., Faculty of Education, 1137 Western Rd., London, Ontario N6G 1G7 Canada. (519)661-2096. Fax: (519)661-3833. E-mail: press@edu.uwo.ca. Editorial Assistant: Katherine Butson. Publishes trade paperback originals and reprints. Publishes 1-5 titles/year. Receives 30 queries and 19 mss/year. 100% from unagented writers. Pays 10% royalty on retail price. Offers $300 advance. Accepts simultaneous submissions. Reports in 2 weeks on queries, 4 months on mss. Book catalog and manuscript guidelines free on request.
Nonfiction: Education subjects. Query. Reviews artwork/photos as part of ms package. Send photocopies.
Recent Nonfiction Title: *What Makes a Good Teacher*, by William Hare (education).
Tips: Audience is practicing teachers and graduate education students.

‡**ARSENAL PULP PRESS**, 100-1062 Homer St., Vancouver, British Columbia V6B 2W9 Canada. (604)687-4233. Editor: Linda Field. Estab. 1980. Imprint is Tillacum Library. Publishes hardcover and trade paperback originals. Publishes 12-15 titles/year. Receives 400 queries and 200 mss/year. 25% of books from first-time authors; 100% from unagented writers. Pays 15% royalty on wholesale price. Advance varies. Publishes book 1 year after acceptance of ms. Accepts simultaneous submissions. Reports in 4 months on queries, with exceptions. Book catalog and ms guidelines free on request.
Nonfiction: Humor. Subjects include ethnic (Canadian, aboriginal issues), gay/lesbian, popular music, history (cultural), literature, regional (British Columbia), women's issues/studies. Submit outline and 2-3 sample chapters.
Recent Nonfiction Title: *The Imaginary Indian*, by Daniel Francis (cultural studies).
Fiction: Experimental, feminist, gay/lesbian, literary and short story collections. "We only publish Canadian authors." Submit synopsis and 2-3 sample chapters.
Recent Fiction Title: *Eggplant Wife*, by J. Jill Robinson (short stories).
Recent Poetry Title: *Swerve*, by Sheri D. Wilson (poetry).

AURORA EDITIONS, 1184 Garfield St. N, Winnipeg, Manitoba R3E 2P1 Canada. Editor/Publisher: Roma Quapp. Publishes trade paperback originals. Publishes 5 titles/year. 20% of books from first-time authors; 100% from unagented writers. Pays 8-10% royalty and copies of work. Offers $50 advance. Publishes book 2 years after acceptance of ms. Accepts simultaneous submissions. Reports in 6 months on mss. Book catalog and ms guidelines for #10 SAE and IRC.
Nonfiction: Biography. Women's issues/studies subjects. "We are interested in short (maximum 15,000 words) literary biographies of Canadian women." Submit proposal package with 2 sample chapters or full ms and SAE and IRCs.
Recent Nonfiction Title: *A Slice of Life*, by Marie Barton (biography).
Fiction: Ethnic, experimental, feminist, literary, short story collections. "We publish very few titles, so chances are slim. But we do attempt to provide comments on all submissions." Submit full ms with SAE and IRCs. *Writer's Market* recommends sending a query with SAE and IRCs first.
Recent Fiction Title: *Tales of the Ex-Fire Eater*, by Sheila Dalton (literary).
Poetry: Publishes chapbooks of poetry by invitation only.
Recent Poetry Title: *Heartbeats*, by Joan McKay (modern).
Tips: "Audience is women and 'liberated men' (!), age 18-80; urban, professional."

BALLANTINE BOOKS OF CANADA, Division of Random House of Canada, Ltd., 1265 Aerowood Dr., Mississauga, Ontario L4W 1B9, Canada. General interest publisher of nonfiction and fiction. This publisher prefers not to share information. Query before submitting.

BANTAM BOOKS CANADA, INC., Subsidiary of Bantam Doubleday Dell Publishing Group, 105 Bond St., Toronto, Ontario M5B 1Y3, Canada. Query with proposal letter and résumé to Submissions Editor. No unsolicited mss. Reports in 3 months.

‡**BEACH HOLME PUBLISHERS LTD.**, 4252 Commerce Circle, Victoria, British Columbia V8Z 4M2 Canada. (604)727-6514. Managing Editor: Joy Gugeler. Editor: Antonia Banyard. Estab. 1971. Publishes trade paperback originals. Publishes 10 titles/year. Receives 1,000 submissions/year. "Accepting only Canadian submissions." 40% of books from first-time authors; 90% from unagented writers. Pays 10% royalty on retail price. Offers $500 average advance. Publishes ms 1 year after acceptance. Accepts simultaneous submissions (if so advised). Reports in 2 months.
Nonfiction: Wicca. "Interested in serious, well-written, marketable work." Submit outline and sample chapters.

Recent Nonfiction Title: *The Witch's Book of Days*, by Jean Kozocari.
Fiction: Adult literary fiction and poetry from authors published in Canadian literary magazines. Young adult (Canada historical/regional). "Interested in excellent quality, imaginative writing."
Recent Fiction Title: *Repeat This And You're Dead*, by Lawrence Russell.
Tips: "Make sure the manuscript is well written. We see so many that only the unique and excellent can't be put down. Send cover letter, SASE, outline and two chapters. Guidelines available."

‡**BLIZZARD PUBLISHING**, 73 Furby St., Winnipeg, Manitoba R3C 2A2 Canada. (204)775-2923. E-mail: atwood@blizzard.mb.ca. Managing Editor: Anna Synenko. Imprint is Bain & Cox, Publishers. Publishes hardcover and trade paperback originals. Averages 12-15 titles/year. Imprint publishes 4 titles/year. Receives 200 queries and 400 mss/year. 10% of books from first-time authors; 10% from unagented writers. Pays variable royalty on retail price. Offers $200-500 advance. Publishes book 1 year after acceptance of ms. Accepts simultaneous submissions. Reports in 3 months on queries; 10 months on mss. Book catalog for 9×12 SAE and 1 IRC. Manuscript guidelines free on request.
Nonfiction: Children's/juvenile, multimedia (CD-ROM). Subjects include art/architecture, ethnic, gay/lesbian, government/politics, history, language/literature, sociology, sports, women's issues/studies. Query with outline, sample chapter and SASE.
Recent Nonfiction Title: *A Passing Game: A History of the CFL*, by Frank Cosentino (sports history).
Fiction: Feminist, gay/lesbian, literary, plays, young adult. Query with synopsis, sample chapter and SASE.
Recent Fiction Title: *The Trials of Ezra Pound*, by Timothy Findley (drama).

BOREALIS PRESS, LTD., 9 Ashburn Dr., Nepean, Ontario K2E 6N4 Canada. Editorial Director: Frank Tierney. Senior Editor: Glenn Clever. Estab. 1972. Publishes hardcover and paperback originals. Publishes 10-12 titles/year. Receives 400-500 submissions/year. 80% of books from first-time authors; 95% from unagented writers. Pays 10% royalty on retail price. No advance. Publishes book 18 months after acceptance. "No multiple submissions or electronic printouts on paper more than 8½ inches wide." Reports in 2 months. Book catalog for $3 and SASE.
Nonfiction: "Only material Canadian in content." Biography, children's/juvenile, reference. Subjects include government/politics, history, language/literature. Query with outline, 2 sample chapters and SASE. No unsolicited mss. Reviews artwork/photos as part of ms package. Looks for "style in tone and language, reader interest, and maturity of outlook."
Recent Nonfiction Title: *All My Sisters*, by Clara Thomas (selected essays on Canadian women's writing).
Fiction: "Only material Canadian in content and dealing with significant aspects of the human situation." Adventure, ethnic, historical, juvenile, literary, romance, short story collections, young adult. Query with synopsis, 1-2 sample chapters and SASE. No unsolicited mss.
Recent Fiction Title: *Josie's Song*, by Kerry Rauch (young adult).
Recent Poetry Title: *As I See It*, by Fred Cogswell (poetry).

THE BOSTON MILLS PRESS, 132 Main St., Erin, Ontario N0B 1T0 Canada. (519)833-2407. Fax: (519)833-2195. President: John Denison. Estab. 1974. Publishes hardcover and trade paperback originals. Publishes 20 titles/year. Receives 200 submissions/year. 75% of books from first-time authors; 90% from unagented writers. Pays 10% royalty on retail price. Offers small advance. Publishes book 1 year after acceptance. Accepts simultaneous submissions. Reports in 2 months. Book catalog free.
Nonfiction: Illustrated book. Subjects include history. "We're interested in anything to do with Canadian or American history—especially transportation. We like books with a specific market." No autobiographies. Query. Reviews artwork/photos as part of ms package.
Recent Nonfiction Title: *Heartland*, by Greg McDonnell.
Tips: "We can't compete with the big boys so we stay with short-run specific market books that bigger firms can't handle. We've done well this way so we'll continue in the same vein."

‡**BROADVIEW PRESS LTD.**, P.O. Box 1243, Peterborough, Ontario K9J 7H5 Canada. (705)743-8990. Fax: (705)743-8353. President: Don LePan. Estab. 1985. Publishes paperback originals. Publishes 20-25 titles/year. Receives 250 submissions/year. 5-10% of books from first-time authors; 95% from unagented writers. Pays 4-10% royalty on retail price. Publishes book 18 months after acceptance. Accepts simultaneous submissions. Reports in 4 months on proposals.
Nonfiction: Textbook, general nonfiction. Subjects include anthropology, art/architecture, government/politics, history, language/literature, philosophy, women's issues/studies. "We specialize in university/college

ALWAYS SUBMIT unsolicited manuscripts or queries with a self-addressed, stamped envelope (SASE) within your country or a self-addressed envelope with International Reply Coupons (IRC) purchased from the post office for other countries.

supplementary textbooks which often have both a trade and academic market." Submit outline and sample chapters and proposal package, including quick description of intended market, table of contents and cv. Sometimes reviews artwork/photos as part of ms package.

Recent Nonfiction Title: *In Search of Authority: An Introduction to Literary Theory*, by Stephen Bunnycastle.

Tips: "We now consider *only* works aimed at least in *part* at a university textbook market in the arts or social sciences."

‡**BROKEN JAW PRESS**, Box 596 Station A, Fredericton, New Brunswick E3B 5A6 Canada. Publisher: Joe Blades. Imprints are Broken Jaw Press, SpareTime Editions, Book Rat, Dead Sea Physh Products. Publishes trade paperback originals and reprints. Publishes 16 titles/year. Receives 200 queries and 150 mss/ year. 25% of books from first-time authors; 100% from unagented writers. Pays 10-15% royalty on retail price or 10% of print run. No advance. Publishes book 1 year after acceptance of ms. Reports in 6 months. Book catalog and manuscript guidelines for #10 SASE (Canadian postage or IRC).
Nonfiction: Subjects include gay/lesbian, history, language/literature, nature/environment, regional (Canadian), women's issues/studies. Canadian writers only at this time. All unsolicited mss returned. Reviews artwork/photos as part of ms package.
Recent Nonfiction Title: *Under The Watchful Eye*, by James Deahl (literature/memoir).
Fiction: Literary, plays, short story collections. Only considers Canadian writers. All unsolicited mss returned unopened
Poetry: "We run an annual New Muse Award for poets without a first book. Send SASE for guidelines." Manuscripts of 50-60 pages and $15 fee. Deadline: March 31.
Recent Poetry Title: *The Best Lack All*, by Tom Schmidt.

‡**BROWN BEAR PRESS**, P.O. Box 325 Station P, Toronto, Ontario M5S 2S8 Canada. Publisher: Ruth Bradley-St-Cyr. Estab. 1995. Publishes trade paperback originals from Canadian authors only and reprints of Canadian classics. Publishes 4 titles/year. Pays 8-10% royalty on retail price. Offers $100-300 advance. Publishes books 1 year after acceptance of ms. Reports in 2 months on proposals. Submission guidelines free with Canadian SASE.
Nonfiction: Canadian social, political and family issues.
Fiction: Canadian literature for adults and children.

CAITLIN PRESS, INC., P.O. Box 2387 Station B, Prince George, British Columbia V2N 2S6 Canada. (604)964-4953. Fax: (604)964-4970. Contact: Cynthia Wilson. Estab. 1978. Publishes trade paperback and soft cover originals. Publishes 6-7 titles/year. Receives 105-120 queries and 50 mss/year. 100% of books from unagented writers. Pays 15% royalty on wholesale price. Publishes book 18 months after acceptance of ms. Accepts simultaneous submissions. Reports in 3 months on queries. Book catalog for #10 SASE.
Nonfiction: Biography, cookbook. Subjects include history, photography, regional. "We publish books about the British Columbia interior or by people from the interior. We are not interested in manuscripts that do not reflect a British Columbia influence." Submit outline and proposal package. Reviews artwork/photos as part of ms package. Send photocopies.
Recent Nonfiction Title: *Atlin's Gold*, by Peter Steele (autobiography/history/adventures).
Fiction: Adventure, historical, humor, mainstream/contemporary, short story collections, young adult. Submit ms only. *Writer's Market* recommends query with SASE first.
Poetry: Submit sample poems or complete ms.
Recent Poetry Title: *The Centre*, by Barry McKinnon.
Tips: "Our area of interest is British Columbia and northern Canada. Submitted manuscripts should reflect our interest area."

‡**THE CANADIAN INSTITUTE OF STRATEGIC STUDIES**, 76 St. Clair Ave. W., Suite 502, Toronto, Ontario M4V 1N2 Canada. (416)964-6632. Director of Publications: Susan McNish. Publishes hardcover and trade paperback originals. Publishes 3-4 books/year. Receives 10 queries and 10 mss/year. 50% of books from first-time authors; 100% of books from unagented writers. Negotiated payment and advance. Publishes book 6 months after acceptance of ms. Accepts simultaneous submissions.
Nonfiction: "The subject should fall within the area of national security of Canada." *Writer's Market* recommends sending a query with SASE first.
Recent Nonfiction Title: *The Persian Excursion: The Canadian Navy in the Gulf War*, by Sharon Hobson and Commodore Duncan (Dusty) E. Miller.

CANADIAN INSTITUTE OF UKRAINIAN STUDIES PRESS, CIUS Toronto Publications Office, University of Toronto, Dept. of Slavic Languages and Literatures, 21 Sussex Ave., Toronto, Ontario M5S 1A1 Canada. (416)978-8240. Fax: (416)978-2672. E-mail: tarn@epas.utoronto.ca. Director: Maxim Tarnawsky. Estab. 1976. Publishes hardcover and trade paperback originals and reprints. Publishes 5-10 titles/year. Receives 10 submissions/year. Nonauthor-subsidy publishes 20-30% of books. Pays 0-2% royalty on retail price. Publishes book 2 years after acceptance. Reports in 1 month on queries, 3 months on mss. Book catalog and ms guidelines free.

Nonfiction: Scholarly. Subjects include education, ethnic, government/politics, history, language/literature, religion, sociology, translation. "We publish scholarly works in the humanities and social sciences dealing with the Ukraine or Ukrainians in Canada." Query or submit complete ms. *Writer's Market* recommends sending a query with SASE first. Reviews artwork/photos as part of ms package.

Recent Nonfiction Title: *Ukraine And Russia in Their Historical Encounter*, edited by Peter J. Potichny; Marc Raeff, Jaroslaw Pelenski, Gleb Žekulin.

Fiction: Ukrainian literary works. "We do not publish fiction that does not have scholarly value."

Recent Fiction Title: *Yellow Boots*, by Vera Lysenko.

Tips: "We are a scholarly press and do not normally pay our authors. Our audience consists of university students and teachers and the general public interested in Ukrainian and Ukrainian-Canadian affairs."

‡CANADIAN LIBRARY ASSOCIATION, 200 Elgin St., Suite 602, Ottawa, Ontario K2P 1L5 Canada. (613)232-9625. Fax: (613)563-9895. E-mail: bj491@freenet.carleton.ca. Editor, Monographs: Elizabeth Morton. Publishes trade paperback originals. Publishes 4 titles/year. Receives 10 queries and 5 mss/year. 50% of books from first-time authors; 100% from unagented writers. Pays 10% minimum royalty on wholesale price. No advance. Publishes book 6 months after acceptance of ms. Reports in 1 month on queries, 3 months on proposals and mss. Book catalog and manuscript guidelines free on request.

Nonfiction: Reference, professional, academic. Subjects include history, library science. Query with outline. Reviews artwork/photos as part of ms package. Send photocopies.

Recent Nonfiction Title: *Fear of Words: Censorship and the Public Libraries of Canada*, by Alvin M. Schrader.

Tips: Audience is library and information scientists.

CANADIAN PLAINS RESEARCH CENTER, University of Regina, Regina, Saskatchewan S4S 0A2 Canada. (306)585-4795. Fax: (306)585-4699. Coordinator: Brian Mlazgar. Estab. 1973. Publishes scholarly paperback originals and some casebound originals. Publishes 5-6 titles/year. Receives 10-15 submissions/year. 35% of books from first-time authors. Nonauthor-subsidy publishes 80% of books. Publishes book 2 years after acceptance. Reports in 2 months. Book catalog and ms guidelines free. Also publishes *Prairie Forum*, a scholarly journal.

Nonfiction: Biography, illustrated book, technical, textbook, scholarly. Subjects include business and economics, history, nature, politics, sociology. "The Canadian Plains Research Center publishes the results of research on topics relating to the Canadian Plains region, although manuscripts relating to the Great Plains region will be considered. Material *must* be scholarly. Do not submit health, self-help, hobbies, music, sports, psychology, recreation or cookbooks unless they have a scholarly approach. For example, we would be interested in acquiring a pioneer manuscript cookbook, with modern ingredient equivalents, if the material relates to the Canadian Plains/Great Plains region." Submit complete ms. *Writer's Market* recommends query with SASE first. Reviews artwork/photos as part of ms package.

Recent Nonfiction Title: *The Records of the Department of the Interior and Research Concerning Canada's Western Frontier of Settlement*, by Irene M. Spry and Bennett McCardle.

Tips: "Pay great attention to manuscript preparation and accurate footnoting, according to the *Chicago Manual of Style*."

CARSWELL THOMSON PROFESSIONAL PUBLISHING, Imprint of the Thomson Corp., One Corporate Plaza, 2075 Kennedy Rd., Scarborough, Ontario M1T 3V4 Canada. (416)298-5024. Fax: (416)298-5094. E-mail: grodrigues@carswell.com. Website: http://www.carswell.com. Senior Vice President, Publishing: Gary P. Rodrigues. Publishes hardcover originals. Publishes 150-200 titles/year. 30-50% of books from first-time authors. Pays 5-15% royalty on wholesale price. Offers $1,000-5,000 advance. Publishes book 6 months after acceptance. Accepts simultaneous submissions. Reports in 3 months. Book catalog and ms guidelines free on request.

Nonfiction: Legal, tax and business reference. "Canadian information of a regulatory nature is our mandate." Submit proposal package, including résumé and outline.

Recent Nonfiction Title: *The Dictionary of Canadian Law*, by Daphne Dukalow and Betsy Nase (1,400-page dictionary).

Tips: Audience is Canada and persons interested in Canadian information; professionals in law, tax, accounting fields; business people interested in regulatory material.

‡CHARLTON PRESS, 2010 Yonge St., Toronto, Ontario M4S 1Z9 Canada. Fax: (416)488-4656. Managing Editor: Nicola Leedham. Publishes trade paperback originals and reprints. Publishes 15 titles/year. Receives 30 queries and 5 mss/year. 10% of books from first-time authors; 100% from unagented writers. Pays 10% minimum royalty on wholesale price or makes variable outright purchase. Offers $1,000 advance. Publishes book 6 months after acceptance of ms. Accepts simultaneous submissions. Reports in 1 month on queries and proposals, 2 months on mss. Book catalog free on request.

Nonfiction: Reference (price guides on collectibles). Subjects include art/architecture, hobbies, military/war, money/finance, sports. Submit outline. Reviews artwork/photos as part of ms package. Send photocopies.
Recent Nonfiction Title: *Royal Doulton Figurines,* by J. Dale (reference guide).

CHEMTEC PUBLISHING, 38 Earswick Dr., Toronto-Scarborough, Ontario M1E 1C6 Canada. (416)265-2603. Fax: (416)265-1399. E-mail: chemtec@io.org. Website: http://www.io.org/~chemtec. President: Anna Wypych. Publishes hardcover originals. Publishes 5 titles/year. Receives 10 queries and 7 mss/year. 20% of books from first-time authors. Pays 5-15% royalty on retail price. Publishes book 6 months after acceptance of ms. Accepts simultaneous submissions. Reports in 2 months on queries, 4 months on mss. Book catalog and ms guidelines free on request.
Nonfiction: Technical, textbook. Subjects include nature/environment, science, chemistry, polymers. Submit outline or sample chapter(s).
Recent Nonfiction Title: *Recycling of PVC and Mixed Waste,* by F.P. LaMantia (technical book).
Tips: Audience is industrial research and universities.

COTEAU BOOKS, 2206 Dewdney Ave., Suite 401, Regina, Saskatchewan S4R 1H3 Canada. (306)777-0170. Fax: (306)522-5152. E-mail: coteau@coteau.unibase.com. Website: http://www.coteau.unibase.com. Publisher: Geoffrey Ursell. Estab. 1975. Publishes fiction, poetry, drama, anthologies, young adult novels—only by Canadian writers. Publishes 12 titles/year. Receives approximately 1,000 queries and mss/year. 10% of books from first-time authors; 95% from unagented writers. Pays 12½% royalty on retail price or makes outright purchase of $50-200 for anthology contributors. Publishes book 18 months after acceptance. Reports in 1 month on queries, 4 months on mss. Book catalog free with SASE.
  ● Coteau Books published *Voice,* by Anne Szumigalski, winner of the 1995 Governor General's Award for Poetry.
Nonfiction: Reference, desk calendars. Subjects include language/literature, regional studies. "We publish only Canadian authors." *Writer's Market* recommends sending a query with SASE first.
Recent Nonfiction Title: *Many Patrols: Reminiscences of a Game Officer,* by R.D. Symons.
Fiction: Ethnic, feminist, humor, juvenile, literary, mainstream/contemporary, plays, short story collections. "No popular, mass market sort of stuff. We are a literary press." Submit complete ms. *Writer's Market* recommends sending a query with SASE first. "We publish fiction and poetry only from Canadian authors."
Recent Fiction Title: *Inspection of a Small Village,* by Connie Gault.
Tips: "We are not publishing children's picture books, but are still interested in juvenile and YA fiction from Canadian authors."

‡ROBERT DAVIES PUBLISHING, 4999 St. Catherine St. W, #311, Montreal, Quebec H3Z 1T3 Canada. Fax: (514)481-9973. E-mail: rdppub@vir.com. Website: http://www.rdppub.com. Publishes trade paperback originals and reprints. Publishes 32 titles/year. Receives 500 queries and 200 mss/year. 20% of books from first-time authors; 80% from unagented writers. Pays 10-15% royalty on wholesale price. Offers $2,000 advance. Publishes book 1 year after acceptance of ms. Accepts simultaneous submissions. Reports in 6 months. Book catalog for 9 × 12 SAE with 2 first-class Canadian stamps.
Nonfiction: Biography, children's/juvenile, coffee table book, cookbook, gift book, how-to, humor, illustrated book, self-help. Subjects include Art/architecture, business and economics, child guidance/parenting, cooking/foods/nutrition, gay/lesbian, health/medicine, history, hobbies, language/literature, money/finance, philosophy, psychology, religion, sociology, translation, women's issues/studies. Query with SASE.
Recent Nonfiction Title: *Dead Sea Scroll Palindromes,* by Howard Richter (humor).
Fiction: Adventure, fantasy, gay/lesbian, historical, juvenile, literary, mainstream/contemporary, mystery. Query with SASE.
Tips: Audience is general to university. "Don't oversell your idea. Present it rationally and neatly."

‡DETSELIG ENTERPRISES LTD., 1220 Kensington Rd. NW, 210, Calgary, Alberta T2H 3P5 Canada. President: T.E. Giles. Imprint is Temeron Books, Inc. Publishes hardcover and trade paperback originals. Publishes 20 titles/year. Receives 500 queries and 200 mss/year. 75% of books from first-time authors; 95% from unagented writers. Pays 8-13% royalty on wholesale price. No advance usually. Publishes book 10 months after acceptance of ms. Accepts simultaneous submissions. Reports in 3 months on queries, 4 months on proposals, 6 months on mss. Book catalog free on request.
Nonfiction: Biography, coffee table book, gift book, how-to, humor, illustrated book, reference, self-help, textbook. Subjects include animals, art/architecture, business and economics, child guidance/parenting, education, ethnic, government/politics, health/medicine, history, military/war, money/finance, nature/environment, philosophy, psychology, recreation, religion, sociology, women's issues/studies. Submit outline and 2 sample chapters. Reviews artwork/photos as part of ms package. Send photocopies.
Recent Nonfiction Title: *Adolescent Vulnerability,* by J. Mitchell (psychology).

DOUBLEDAY CANADA LIMITED, 105 Bond St., Toronto, Ontario M5B 1Y3, Canada. This publisher did not respond to our request for information. Query with proposal letter and résumé to Submissions Editor. No unsolicited mss.

DUNDURN PRESS LTD., 2181 Queen St. E., Toronto, Ontario M4E 1E5 Canada. (416)698-0454. Fax: (416)698-1102. Publisher: Kirk Howard. Senior Editor: Judith Turnbull. Estab. 1972. Publishes hardcover and trade paperback originals and reprints. Publishes 35 titles/year. Receives 500 submissions/year. 45% of books from first-time authors; 90% from unagented writers. Average print order for a first book is 2,000. Pays 10% royalty on retail price; 8% royalty on some paperback children's books. Publishes book 1 year after acceptance. Reports in 3 months.
Nonfiction: Biography, coffee table books, juvenile (12 and up), literary, reference. Subjects include Canadiana, art, history, hobbies, Canadian history, literary criticism. Especially looking for Canadian biographies. No religious or soft science topics. Query with outline and sample chapters. Reviews artwork/photos as part of ms package.
Tips: "Publishers want more books written in better prose styles. If I were a writer trying to market a book today, I would visit bookstores and watch what readers buy and what company publishes that type of book 'close' to my manuscript."

ECRITS DES FORGES, C.P. 335, 1497 Laviolette, Trois-Rivières, Quebec G9A 5G4 Canada. (819)379-9813. Fax: (819)376-0774. President: Gaston Bellemare. Publishes hardcover originals. Publishes 40 titles/year. Receives 30 queries and 1,000 mss/year. 10% of books from first-time authors; 90% from unagented writers. Pays 10-30% royalty. Offers 50% advance. Publishes book 9 months after acceptance of ms. Accepts simultaneous submissions. Reports in 9 months. Book catalog free on request.
Poetry: Poetry only and written in *French*. Submit 20 sample poems.
Recent Poetry Title: *Nous, l'étranger*, by Serge-Patrice Thibodeau.

ECW PRESS, 2120 Queen St. E., Suite 200, Toronto, Ontario M4E 1E2 Canada. (416)694-3348. Fax: (416)698-9906. E-mail: ecw@sympatico.ca. President: Jack David. Estab. 1979. Publishes hardcover and trade paperback originals. Publishes 20 titles/year. Receives 120 submissions/year. 50% of books from first-time authors; 80% from unagented writers. Nonauthor-subsidy publishes up to 5% of books. Pays 10% royalty on retail price. Accepts simultaneous submissions. Reports in 2 months. Book catalog free.
Nonfiction: Biography, directories, reference, Canadian literary criticism. "ECW is particularly interested in popular biography and all Canadian literary criticism aimed at the undergraduate and graduate university market." Query. Reviews artwork/photos as part of ms package.
Recent Nonfiction Title: *Paul Molitor*, by S. Broomer (biography).
Tips: "The writer has the best chance of selling reference works, biography, or literary criticism to our firm. ECW does not accept unsolicited fiction or poetry manuscripts. We are also looking for sports books and guidebooks."

‡EDITIONS DU NOROÎT, 1835 Les Hauteurs, St. Hippolyte, Quebec J0R 1P0 Canada. (514)563-1644. Directors: Claude Prud-Homme, Helene Dorion, Paul Belanger. Publishes trade paperback originals and reprints. Publishes 22 titles/year. Receives 500 queries and 500 mss/year. 50% of books from first-time authors; 95% from unagented writers. Pays 10% royalty on retail price. Publishes book 1 year after acceptance. Accepts simultaneous submissions. Reports in 3 months on mss. Book catalog free for SASE.
Poetry: Submit 40 sample poems.
Recent Poetry Title: *Saint Denys Garneau, Poemes choisis*.

ÉDITIONS LA LIBERTÉ INC., 3020 Chemin Ste-Foy, Ste-Foy, Quebec G1X 3V6 Canada. Phone/fax: (418)658-3763. Director of Operations: Pierre Reid. Publishes trade paperback originals. Publishes 4-5 titles/year. Receives 125 queries and 100 mss/year. 75% of books from first-time authors; 90% from unagented writers. Pays 10% royalty on retail price. Accepts only mss written in French. Publishes book 4 months after acceptance of ms. Accepts simultaneous submissions. Reports in 1 month on queries, 2 months on proposals, 3 months on mss. Book catalog free on request.
Nonfiction: Biography, children's/juvenile. Subjects include Americana, animals, anthropology/archaeology, child guidance/parenting, cooking/foods/nutrition, education, government/politics, history, hobbies, language/literature, music/dance, nature/environment, psychology, science, sociology. Submit proposal package, including complete ms. *Writer's Market* recommends sending a query with SASE first.
Recent Nonfiction Title: *Cahiers Des Dix #49*, collective (history).
Fiction: Historical, juvenile, literary, mainstream/contemporary, short story collections, young adult. Query with synopsis.
Recent Fiction Title: *Basse-ville*, by Robert Fleury.

‡EDITIONS PHIDAL, 5740 Ferrier, Mont-Royal, Quebec H4P 1M7 Canada. (514) 738-0202. Chief Editor: Lionel Soussan. Publishes hardcover and mass market paperback originals. Publishes 50-70 titles/year. Receives 50 queries and 20 mss/year. 5% of books from first-time authors; 5% from unagented writers. Pays 10% royalty on retail price. Publishes book 6 months after acceptance. Accepts simultaneous submissions. Reports in 2 months on mss.
Fiction: Juvenile. "We specialize in children's books ages three and up. Illustrations are very helpful." Submit synopsis and 3-5 sample chapters.

Recent Fiction Title: *Les Voyelles*, by Nicole Sallenave (children's).
Tips: Audience is children, both in English and French languages. Ages 3 and up.

EKSTASIS EDITIONS, P.O. Box 8474, Main Post Office, Victoria, British Columbia V8W 3S1 Canada. Phone/fax: (604)385-3378. Publisher: Richard Olafson. Publishes hardcover and trade paperback originals and reprints. Publishes 8-12 titles/year. Receives 85 queries and 100 mss/year. 65% of books from first-time authors; 100% from unagented writers. Pays 10% royalty on wholesale price. Publishes book 6 months after acceptance of ms. Accepts simultaneous submissions. Reports in 5 months on mss. Book catalog free on request.
Nonfiction: Biography. Subjects include government/politics, nature/environment, psychology, translation. Query. Reviews artwork/photos as part of ms package. Send photocopies.
Recent Nonfiction Title: *Eternal Lake O'Hara*, by Carol Ann Sokoloff (history).
Fiction: Erotica, experimental, gothic, juvenile, literary, mainstream/contemporary, plays, science fiction, short story collections. Query with synopsis and 3 sample chapters.
Recent Fiction Title: *Cities of India*, by Steve Noyes (short stories).
Poetry: "Ekstasis is a literary press, and is interested in the best of modern poetry and fiction." Submit 20 sample poems.
Recent Poetry Title: *From the Mouths of Angels*, by Richard Stevenson (lyric poetry).

EMPYREAL PRESS, P.O. Box 1746, Place Du Parc, Montreal, Quebec HZW 2R7 Canada. Publisher: Sonja Skarstedt. Publishes trade paperback originals. Publishes 1-4 titles/year. 50% of books from first-time authors; 90% from unagented writers. Pays 10% royalty on wholesale price. Offers $300 (Canadian) advance. Reports in 2 months. Book catalog for #10 SASE.
Fiction: Experimental, feminist, gay/lesbian, literary, short story collections. Query with SASE.
Recent Fiction Title: *The Space*, by Patrick Borden.

‡ESCART PRESS, Dept. ES2, University of Waterloo, Waterloo, Ontario N2L 3G1 Canada. (519)885-1211, ext. 3110. Managing Editor: Gary Brannon. Publishes trade paperback originals. Publishes 3 titles/year. 33% of books from first-time authors; 100% from unagented writers. Pays 10-15% royalty on wholesale price. No advance. Publishes book 6 months after acceptance. Accepts simultaneous submissions. Reports in 1 month. *Writer's Market* recommends allowing 2 months for reply. Book catalog free on request.
Nonfiction: Biography, reference. Subjects include Americana, art/architecture, history, nature/environment, regional, travel. "We will consider travel books—Europe, North America—Our North American Heritage Series documents history that involves Canada and US—100-175 pages softcover." Query with outline, 2 sample chapters and SASE for Canada. "We prefer to see manuscripts well thought out chapter by chapter, not just a first chapter and a vague idea of the rest." Reviews artwork/photos as part of ms package. Send photocopies.
Recent Nonfiction Title: *The Journeys of Remarkable Women*, by Les Harding (biography/travel).
Tips: "Electronic, preformatted submissions on disk are preferred—we are a MAC environment."

FITZHENRY & WHITESIDE, LTD., 195 Allstate Parkway, Markham, Ontario L3R 4T8 Canada. (905)477-9700. Fax: (905)477-9179. Senior Vice President: Robert Read. Estab. 1966. Publishes hardcover and paperback originals and reprints. Publishes 25 titles/year, text and trade. Royalty contract varies. Advance negotiable. Reports in 3 months. Enclose return postage.
Nonfiction: "Especially interested in topics of interest to Canadians, and by Canadians." Textbooks for elementary and secondary schools, also biography, history, nature, fine arts, Native studies, and children's books. Submit outline and 1 sample chapter. Length: open.
Recent Nonfiction Title: *Trees of Canada*.

GOOSE LANE EDITIONS, 469 King St., Fredericton, New Brunswick E3B 1E5 Canada. Acquisitions Editor: Laurel Boone. Estab. 1956. Publishes 12-14 titles/year. Receives 500 submissions/year. 20% of books from first-time authors; 75-100% from unagented writers. Pays royalty on retail price. Reports in 6 months. Manuscript guidelines for SASE (Canadian stamps or IRCs).
Nonfiction: Biography, illustrated book, literary history (Canadian). Subjects include art/architecture, history, language/literature, nature/environment, translation, women's issues/studies. No crime, confessional, how-to, self-help or cookbooks. Query first.
Fiction: Experimental, feminist, historical, literary, short story collections. "Our needs in fiction never change: substantial, character-centred literary fiction which shows more interest in the craft of writing (i.e. use of language, credible but clever plotting, shrewd characterization) than in cleaving to mainstream genre-conventions. No children's, YA, mainstream, mass market, genre, mystery, thriller, confessional or sci-fi fiction." Query or submit complete ms. *Writer's Market* recommends sending a query with SASE first.
Tips: "Writers should send us outlines and samples of books that show a very well-read author who has thought long and deeply about the art of writing and, in either fiction or nonfiction, has something of Canadian relevance to offer. We almost never publish books by non-Canadian authors. Our audience is literate, thoughtful and well-read. If I were a writer trying to market a book today, I would contact the

targeted publisher with a query letter and synopsis, and request manuscript guidelines. Purchase a recent book from the publisher in a relevant area, if possible. Never send a complete manuscript blindly to a publisher. **Never** send a manuscript or sample without IRC's or sufficient return postage in Canadian stamps."

GUERNICA EDITIONS, Box 117, Station P, Toronto, Ontario M5S 2S6 Canada. (416)658-9888. Fax: (416)657-8885. Editor/Publisher: Antonio D'Alfonso. Estab. 1978. Publishes trade paperback originals, reprints and software. Publishes 20 titles/year. Receives 1,000 submissions/year. 5% of books from first-time authors. Average print order for a first book is 1,000. Nonauthor-subsidy publishes 50% of titles. "Subsidy in Canada is received only when the author is established, Canadian-born and active in the country's cultural world. The others we subsidize ourselves." Pays 3-10% royalty on retail price or makes outright purchase of $200-5,000. Offers 10¢/word advance for translators. IRCs required. "American stamps are of no use to us in Canada." Reports in 3 months. Book catalog for SASE.
  ● Guernica Editions published *Aknos*, by Fulvio Caccia, winner of the Governor General Award.
Nonfiction: Biography, art, film, history, music, philosophy, politics, psychology, religion, literary criticism, ethnic history, multicultural comparative literature.
Fiction: Original works and translations. "We wish to open up into the fiction world and focus less on poetry. Also specialize in European, especially Italian, translations." Query.
Poetry: "We wish to have writers in translation. Any writer who has translated Italian poetry is welcomed. Full books only. Not single poems by different authors, unless modern, and used as an anthology. First books will have no place in the next couple of years." Submit samples.
Recent Poetry Title: *Where I Come From (New and Selected Poems)*, by Maria Mazziotti Gillan.
Tips: "We are seeking less poetry, more prose, essays, novels, and translations into English."

GUTTER PRESS, 109 Manning Ave., Suite 100, Toronto, Ontario M6J 2K6 Canada. (416)603-3181. E-mail: gutter@io.org. Website: http://www.io.org/~gutter/. Publisher: Sam Hiyate. Imprints are Ken Sparling Books, Eye Press, Kaleyard. Publishes trade paperback originals and reprints. Publishes 6 titles/year. Each imprint publishes 2 titles/year. 50% of books from first-time authors; 100% from unagented writers. Pays 10-15% royalty on retail price. Offers $500-1,500 (Canadian) advance. Publishes book 2 years after acceptance of ms. Accepts simultaneous submissions. Reports in 6 months. Manuscript guidelines for SAE and IRC.
Nonfiction: Biography, humor, literary theory. Subjects include art/architecture, education (theoretical), gay/lesbian, government/politics, history, language/literature, philosophy. Query.
Recent Nonfiction Title: *Fringe Film*, by Mike Hoolboom (pop. culture).
Fiction: Literary. "Ultimately, language is what has to be at issue, the issue you address with all your heart. Give us your heart and we'll give you ours back." Submit 3 sample chapters with SAE and IRC.
Recent Fiction Title: *Dark Rides*, by Derek McCormack.
Tips: "Our audience is people who care about language and what it can accomplish beyond what has already been accomplished."

HARCOURT BRACE CANADA, INC., Subsidiary of Harcourt Brace & Company Canada, Ltd., 55 Horner Ave., Toronto, Ontario M8Z 4X6 Canada. Editorial Directors (School Division): Hans Mills and Wendy Cochran. Publishes educational material K-12.

‡HARLEQUIN ENTERPRISES, LTD., Subsidiary of Torstar Corporation, Home Office: 225 Duncan Mill Rd., Don Mills, Ontario M3B 3K9 Canada. (416)445-5860. President and Chief Executive Officer: Brian E. Hickey. Editorial divisions: Harlequin Books (Randall Toye, editorial director); Silhouette Books (Isabel Swift, editorial director; for editorial requirements, see separate listing, under Silhouette Books); and Worldwide Library/Gold Eagle Books (Randall Toye, editorial director; see separate listing under Worldwide Library). Imprints: Harlequin Romance and Harlequin Presents (Karin Stoecker, director UK); Harlequin Superromance (Paula Eykelhof, senior editor); Harlequin Temptation (Birgit Davis-Todd, senior editor); Harlequin Intrigue and Harlequin American Romance (Debra Matteucci, senior editor and editorial coordinator); Harlequin Historicals (Tracy Farrell, senior editor). Estab. 1949. Submissions for Harlequin Intrigue, Harlequin American Romance and Harlequin Historicals should be directed to the designated editor and sent to Harlequin Books, 300 E. 42nd St., New York NY 10017. (212)682-6080. Romance and Presents submissions should be sent to Harlequin Mills and Books, Eton House, 18-24 Paradise Rd., Richmond Surey TW9 1SR United Kingdom. All other submissions should be directed to the Canadian address. Publishes mass market paperback originals. Publishes 780 titles/year; receives 10,000 submissions annually. 10% of books from first-time authors; 20% from unagented writers. Pays royalty. Offers advance. Publishes book 1 year after acceptance. Reports in 6 weeks on queries. *Writer's Market* recommends allowing 2 months for reply. Free writer's guidelines.
Fiction: Adult contemporary and historical romance, including novels of romantic suspense (Intrigue), short contemporary romance (Presents and Romance), long contemporary romance (Superromance), short contemporary sensuals (Temptation) and adult historical romance (Historicals). "We welcome submissions to all of our lines. Know our guidelines and be familiar with the style and format of the line you are submitting to. Stories should possess a life and vitality that makes them memorable for the reader." *Writer's Market* recommends sending a query with SASE first.

Tips: "Harlequin's readership comprises a wide variety of ages, backgrounds, income and education levels. The audience is predominantly female. Because of the high competition in women's fiction, readers are becoming very discriminating. They look for a quality read. Read as many recent romance books as possible in all series to get a feel for the scope, new trends, acceptable levels of sensuality, etc."

HARPERCOLLINS PUBLISHERS LTD., 55 Avenue Rd., Suite 2900, Toronto, Ontario M5R 3L2 Canada. (416) 975-9334. Publisher/Editor-in-Chief: Iris Tupholme. Imprint is Phyllis Bruce Books (contact Publisher: Phyllis Bruce). Publishes hardcover originals and reprints, trade paperback originals and reprints, mass market paperback reprints. Publishes 100 titles/year. Receives 350-400 queries and 250 mss/year. 1% of books from first-time authors; 50% from unagented writers. Pays 5-15% royalty on retail price. Offers from $500 to over six figures advance. Publishes book 18 months after acceptance. Reports in 1 month on queries and proposals. *Writer's Market* recommends allowing 2 months for reply. Book catalog free on request.
Nonfiction: Biography, coffee table book, cookbook, humor, illustrated book, children's/juvenile, self-help. Subjects include Art/architecture, business and economics, child guidance/parenting, cooking/foods/nutrition, ethnic, gardening, gay/lesbian, government/politics, health/medicine, history, language/literature, military/war, money/finance, nature/environment, photography, religion, sports, travel, women's issues/studies. Query.
Recent Nonfiction Title: *The Gift of Death: Confronting Canada's Tainted Blood Tragedy*, by André Picard (exposé).
Fiction: Ethnic, experimental, fantasy, feminist, gothic, historical, horror, humor, juvenile, literary, mainstream/contemporary, mystery, picture books, religious, short story collections, young adult. Query.
Recent Fiction Title: *Finding Moon*, by Tony Hillerman (mystery/suspense).

HERALD PRESS CANADA, Subsidiary of Mennonite Publishing House, 490 Dutton Dr., Waterloo, Ontario N2L 6H7 Canada. (412)887-8500. Fax: (412)887-3111. E-mail: garber%mph@mcimail.com. Website: http://www.mph.lm.com. Senior Editor: S. David Garber. Estab. 1908. Publishes hardcover and trade paperback originals and reprints. Publishes 30 titles/year. Receives 1,200 submissions/year. 15% of books are from first-time authors; 95% from unagented writers. Pays 10-12% royalty on retail price. Publishes book 1 year after acceptance. Reports in 1 month on queries. *Writer's Market* recommends allowing 2 months for reply. Book catalog for 60¢. Manuscript guidelines free on request.
Nonfiction: Coffee table book, cookbook, illustrated book, juvenile, reference, self-help, textbook. Subjects include child guidance/parenting, cooking/foods/nutrition, education, ethnic, Christian, Mennonite, Amish, history, language/literature, money/finance, stewardship, nature/environment, psychology, counseling, self-help, recreation, lifestyle, missions, justice, peace. "We will be seeking books on Christian inspiration, medium-level Bible study, current issues of peace and justice, family life, Christian ethics and lifestyle, and earth stewardship." Does not want to see war, politics, or scare predictions. Query with SASE. Reviews artwork/photos as part of ms package.
Recent Nonfiction Title: *Through Fire and Water*, by Harry Loewen et al.
Fiction: Ethnic (Mennonite/Amish), historical (Mennonite/Amish), humor, juvenile (Christian orientation), literary, picture books, religious, romance (Christian orientation), short story collections, young adult. Does not want to see war, gangs, drugs, explicit sex, or cops and robbers. Query or submit outline/synopsis and sample chapters.
Recent Fiction Title: *No Strange Fire*, by Ted Wojtasik.

‡HERITAGE HOUSE PUBLISHING CO. LTD., 17921 55th Ave., #8, Surrey, British Columbia V3S 6C4 Canada. Publisher/President: Rodger Touchie. Publishes trade paperback originals. Publishes 8 titles/year. Receives 50 queries and 30 mss/year. 50% of books from first-time authors; 100% from unagented writers. Pays 10-12% royalty. Publishes book 1 year after acceptance. Reports in 2 months. Book catalog for SASE.
Nonfiction: Biography, cookbook, how-to, illustrated book. Subjects include animals, anthropology/archaeology, cooking/foods/nutrition, history, nature/environment, recreation, regional, sports, western Canadiana. "Heritage emphasizes books with a Pacific Northwest focus. Writers should include a sample of their writing, an overview sample of photos or illustrations to support the text and a brief letter describing who they are writing for." Query with outline, 2-3 sample chapters and SASE. Reviews artwork/photos as part of ms package. Send photocopies.
Recent Nonfiction Title: *101 Dives in Washington & British Columbia*, by Betty Pratt Johnson (guidebook).
Fiction: Juvenile. Query with synopsis and SASE.
Recent Fiction Title: *Eagle's Reflection*, by Jim Challenger (children's).
Tips: "Our books appeal to residents and visitors to the northwest quadrant of the continent. Present your material after you have done your best. Double space. Don't worry about getting an agent if yours is a one-shot book. Write for the love it. The rest will take care of itself."

HIPPOPOTAMUS PRESS, 22 Whitewell Rd., Frome, Somerset BA11 4EL United Kingdom. 0173-466653. Editor: R. John. Imprints Hippopotamus Press, *Outposts* Poetry Quarterly; distributor for University

of Salzburg Press. Publishes hardcover and trade paperback originals. Publishes 6-12 titles/year. 90% of books from first-time authors; 90% from unagented writers. Pays 7½-10% royalty on retail price. Rarely offers advance. Publishes book 10 months after acceptance of ms. Accepts simultaneous submissions. Reports in 1 month. *Writer's Market* recommends allowing 2 months for reply. Book catalog free on request.
Nonfiction: Essays, literary criticism. Subjects include language/literature, translation. Submit ms. *Writer's Market* recommends sending a query with SASE first.
Recent Nonfiction Title: *Immigrants of Loss*, by G.S.Sharat Chandra (selected poems).
Poetry: "Read one of our authors! Poets often make the mistake of submitting poetry not knowing the type of verse we publish." Submit complete ms.
Recent Poetry Title: *Jewry*, by Chris Bendon (fifth collection).
Tips: "We publish books for a literate audience. Read what we publish."

HORSDAL & SCHUBART PUBLISHERS LTD., 623-425 Simcoe St., Victoria, British Columbia V8V 4T3 Canada. (604)360-0829. Editor: Marlyn Horsdal. Publishes hardcover originals and trade paperback originals and reprints. Publishes 8-10 titles/year. 50% of books from first-time authors; 100% from unagented writers. Pays 15% royalty on wholesale price. Negotiates advance. Publishes books 6 months after acceptance of ms. Accepts simultaneous submissions. Reports in 1 month on queries. *Writer's Market* recommends allowing 2 months for reply. Book catalog free on request.
Nonfiction: Biography. Subjects include anthropology/archaeology, art/architecture, government/politics, history, nature/environment, recreation, regional. Query with outline, 2-3 sample chapters and SASE or SAE with IRCs. Reviews artwork/photos as part of ms package. Send photocopies.
Recent Nonfiction Title: *The Spell of the Midnight Sun*, by Maurice Cloughley (regional/Arctic, travel, biography, art).

HOUNSLOW PRESS, Subsidiary of Dundurn Press Limited, 2181 Queen St., Suite 301, Toronto, Ontario M4E 1E5 Canada. Fax: (416)698-1102. General Manager: Tony Hawke. Estab. 1972. Publishes hardcover and trade paperback originals. Publishes 8 titles/year. Receives 250 submissions/year. 10% of books from first-time authors; 95% from unagented writers. Pays 10-12½% royalty on retail price. Offers $500 average advance. Publishes book 1 year after acceptance. Reports in 2 months on queries. Book catalog free.
Nonfiction: Biography, coffee-table book, cookbook, how-to, humor, illustrated book, self-help. Subjects include animals, art/architecture, business and economics, child guidance/parenting, cooking/foods/nutrition, health/medicine, history, money/finance, photography, translation, travel. "We are looking for controversial manuscripts and business books." Query.
Fiction: Literary and suspense. "We really don't need any fiction for the next year or so." Query.
Tips: "If I were a writer trying to market a book today, I would try to get a good literary agent to handle it."

‡HUMANITAS, 5780 Avenue Decelles, #301, Montreal, Quebec H3S 2C7. (514)737-1332. Fax: (514)737-1332. President: Constantin Stoiciu. Publishes hardcover originals. Publishes 20 titles/year. Receives 200 queries and 200 mss/year. 20% of books from first-time authors. Pays 10-12% royalty on wholesale price. Publishes book 2 months after acceptance of ms. Accepts simultaneous submissions. Book catalog and mss guidelines free on request.
Nonfiction: Biography. Subjects include history, language/literature, philosophy, photography, science. Query. Reviews artwork/photos as part of ms package. Send photocopies.
Recent Nonfiction Title: *Réalité et Fiction Identitaire*, by Andrei Stoiciu (essai).
Fiction: Fantasy, romance, short story collections. Query.
Recent Fiction Title: *L'etrange maison d'Elseva*, by Andrée Laurier (novel).
Poetry: Query.
Recent Poetry Title: *Moi Natif Natal*, by Gary Klang.

HYPERION PRESS, LTD., 300 Wales Ave., Winnipeg, Manitoba R2M 2S9 Canada. (204)256-9204. Fax: (204)255-7845. Publishes hardcover and trade paperback originals and reprints of children's picture books and how-to craft books for all ages. Publishes 8 titles/year. Receives 500 queries and 1,000 mss/year. 30% of books from first-time authors; 100% from unagented writers. Pays royalty. Publishes book 1 year after acceptance of ms. Accepts simultaneous submissions. Reports in 6 months on mss. Book catalog free on request.
Nonfiction: How-to, children's/juvenile. Ethnic subjects. Reviews artwork/photos as part of ms package. Send photocopies.
Recent Nonfiction Title: *Best Ever Paper Airplanes*, by Norman Schmidt.

INSTITUTE OF PSYCHOLOGICAL RESEARCH, INC./INSTITUT DE RECHERCHES PSY-CHOLOGIQUES, INC., 34 Fleury St. W., Montréal, Québec H3L 1S9 Canada. (514)382-3000. Fax: (514)382-3007. President and General Director: Jean-Marc Chevrier. Estab. 1958. Publishes hardcover and trade paperback originals and reprints. Publishes 12 titles/year. Receives 15 submissions/year. 10% of books from first-time authors, 100% from unagented writers. Pays 10-12% royalty. Publishes book 6 months after acceptance. Reports in 2 months.

Nonfiction: Textbooks, psychological tests. Subjects include philosophy, psychology, science, translation. "We are looking for psychological tests in French or English." Submit complete ms. *Writer's Market* recommends query with SASE first.

Recent Nonfiction Title: *Épreuve individuelle d'habileté mentale*, by Jean-Marc Chevrier (intelligence test).

Tips: "Psychologists, guidance counsellors, professionals, schools, school boards, hospitals, teachers, government agencies and industries comprise our audience."

KEY PORTER BOOKS LTD., 70 The Esplanade, Toronto, Ontario M5E 1R2 Canada. (416)862-7777. Editor-in-Chief: Susan Renou. Publishes hardcover originals and trade paperback originals and reprints. Publishes 50-60 titles/year. Receives 1,000 queries and 600 mss/year. 10% of books from first-time authors; 5% from unagented writers. Pays 4-15% royalty on retail price. Offers $1,000-10,000 advance. Publishes book 1 year after acceptance of ms.

Nonfiction: Biography, coffee table book, cookbook, humor, illustrated book, children's/juvenile, self-help. Subjects include agriculture/horticulture, animals, business and economics, cooking/foods/nutrition, government/politics, health/medicine, military/war, money/finance, nature/environment, photography, sports, women's issues/studies. Submit outline and 2 sample chapters. Reviews artwork/photos as part of ms package. Send transparencies.

Recent Nonfiction Title: *Elizabeth: A Biography of the Queen*, by Sarah Brad.

Fiction: Humor, mainstream/contemporary, picture books. Submit synopsis and 2 sample chapters.

Recent Fiction Title: *Ancestral Suitcase*, by Sylvia Fraser.

KINDRED PRODUCTIONS, 4-169 Riverton Ave., Winnipeg, Manitoba R2L 2E5 Canada. (204)669-6575. Fax: (204)654-1865. E-mail: kindred@cdnmbconf.ca. Manager: Marilyn Hudson. Publishes trade paperback originals and reprints. Publishes 3 titles/year. 1% of books from first-time authors; 100% from unagented writers. Subsidy publishes 20% of books, "largely determined by the perceived general interest in the material." Pays 10-15% royalty on retail price. Publishes book 18 months after acceptance of ms. Accepts simultaneous submissions. Reports in 2 months on queries, 3 months on proposals. Book catalog and ms guidelines free on request.

Nonfiction: Biography (select) and Bible study. Religious subjects. "Our books cater primarily to our Mennonite Brethren denomination readers." Query with outline, 2-3 sample chapters and SASE.

Recent Nonfiction Title: *A Time for Training Wheels*, by Mary-Lynn Chambers (family devotional).

Fiction: Historical (religious), juvenile, religious. "All our publications are of a religious nature with a high moral content." Submit synopsis, 2-3 sample chapters and SASE.

Tips: "Most of our books are sold to churches, religious bookstores and schools. We are concentrating on devotional and inspirational books. We are accepting *very* few children's manuscripts."

LONE PINE PUBLISHING, 10426 81st Ave., #206, Edmonton, Alberta T6E 1X5 Canada. (403)433-9333. Fax: (403)433-9646. Senior Editor: Nancy Foulds. Estab. 1980. Imprints are Lone Pine, Home World, Pine Candle and Pine Cone. Publishes hardcover and trade paperback originals and reprints. Publishes 12-20 titles/year. Receives 200 submissions/year. 45% of books from first-time authors; 95% from unagented writers. Pays royalty. Accepts simultaneous submissions. Reports in 2 months on queries. Book catalog free.

• Lone Pine published *Lois Hole's Perennial Favorites*, which, as part of their gardening series, received the 1995 Professional Plant Growers Association of America Educational Media Award.

Nonfiction: Biography, how-to, juvenile, nature/recreation guide books. Subjects include animals, anthropology/archaeology, gardening, history, nature/environment ("this is where most of our books fall"), photography, sports, travel ("another major category for us"). We publish recreational and natural history titles, and some historical biographies. The list is set for the next year and a half, but we are interested in seeing new material. Submit outline and sample chapters. Reviews artwork/photos as part of ms package.

Recent Nonfiction Title: *Lois Hole's Tomato Favorites*, by Lois Hole (gardening).

Tips: "Writers have their best chance with recreational or nature guidebooks and popular history. Most of our books are strongly regional in nature. We are mostly interested in books for Western Canada, Ontario and the U.S. Pacific Northwest."

JAMES LORIMER & CO., PUBLISHERS, 35 Britain St., Toronto, Ontario M5A 1R7 Canada. (416)362-4762. Publishing Assistant: Laura Ellis. Publishes trade paperback originals. Publishes 20 titles/year. Receives 150 queries and 50 mss/year. 10% of books from first-time authors; 100% from unagented writers. Pays 5-10% royalty on retail price. Offers negotiable advance. Publishes book 6 months after acceptance of ms. Reports in 4 months on proposals. Book catalog and ms guidelines for #10 SASE.

Nonfiction: Children's/juvenile. Subjects include business and economics, government/politics, history, sociology, women's issues/studies. "We publish Canadian authors only and Canadian issues/topics only." Submit outline, 2 sample chapters and résumé.

Recent Nonfiction Title: *Unnecessary Debts*, edited by Lars Osberg and Pierre Fortin.
Fiction: Juvenile, young adult. "No fantasy, science fiction, talking animals; realistic themes only. Currently seeking chapter books for ages 7-11 and sports novels for ages 9-13 (Canadian writers only)." Submit synopsis and 2 sample chapters.
Recent Fiction Title: *Hockey Night in Transcona*, by John Danakas.

M.A.P. PRODUCTIONS, Box 596, Station A, Fredericton, New Brunswick E3B 5A6 Canada. (506)454-5127. Publisher: Joe Blades. Imprints are Broken Jaw Press, Book Rat, SpareTime Editions. Publishes trade paperback originals and reprints. Publishes 8-12 titles/year. 50-75% of books from first-time authors; 100% from unagented writers. Pays 10% royalty on retail price or 10% of print run. Offers $0-100 advance. Publishes book 1 year after acceptance of ms. Reports in 6 months on mss. Book catalog for 6½ × 9½ SAE with 2 first-class Canadian stamps. Manuscript guidelines for #10 SASE (Canadian postage or IRC).
Nonfiction: Illustrated book. Subjects include history, language/literature, nature/environment, regional, translation, women's issues/studies, criticism, culture. Query with SASE (Canadian postage or IRC). Reviews artwork/photos as part of ms package. Send photocopies, transparencies.
Recent Nonfiction Title: *A Lad From Brantford*, by David Adams Richards (essays).
Fiction: Fantasy, literary. Query with bio and SASE.
Poetry: Submit complete ms for annual New Muse Award with $15 fee. Send SASE for guidelines. Deadline: March 31.
Recent Poetry Title: *The Best Lack All*, by Tom Schmidt.

McCLELLAND & STEWART INC., 481 University Ave., Suite 900, Toronto, Ontario M5G 2E9 Canada. (416)598-1114. Imprints are McClelland & Stewart, Stewart House, New Canadian Library. Publishes hardcover, trade paperback and mass market paperback originals and reprints. Publishes 80 titles/year. Receives thousands of queries/year. No unsolicited mss. 10% of books from first-time authors; 30% from unagented writers. Pays 10-15% royalty on wholesale price (hardcover rates). Offers advance. Publishes book 1 year after acceptance of ms. Reports in 3 months on proposals.
Nonfiction: Biography, coffee table book, how-to, humor, illustrated book, children's/juvenile, reference, self-help, textbook. Subjects include agriculture/horticulture, animals, art/architecture, business and economics, Canadiana, child guidance/parenting, cooking/foods/nutrition, education, gardening, gay/lesbian, government/politics, health/medicine, history, hobbies, language/literature, military/war, money/finance, music/dance, nature/environment, philosophy, photography, psychology, recreation, religion, science, sociology, sports, translation, travel, women's issues/studies. "We publish books by Canadian authors or on Canadian subjects." Submit outline; all unsolicited mss returned unopened.
Recent Nonfiction Title: *Memoirs*, by Pierre Trudeau (political memoirs).
Fiction: Experimental, historical, humor, literary, mainstream/contemporary, mystery, short story collections. "We publish quality fiction by prize-winning authors." Query. All unsolicited mss returned unopened.
Recent Fiction Title: *Away*, by Jane Urquhart.
Poetry: "Only Canadian poets should apply. We publish only 4 titles each year." Query.
Recent Poetry Title: *Stranger Music*, by Leonard Cohen.

‡McGRAW-HILL RYERSON LIMITED, Trade & Professional division of The McGraw-Hill Companies, 300 Water St., Whitby, Ontario L1N 9B6 Canada. Fax: (416)430-5020. Website: http://www.mghr.com. Publisher: Joan Homewood. Publishes hardcover and trade paperback originals and reprints. Publishes 20 new titles/year. 75% of books are originals; 25% are reprints. 15% of books from first-time authors; 85% from unagented writers. Pays 7½-15% royalty on retail price. Offers $2,000 average advance. Publishes book 1 year after acceptance. Accepts simultaneous submissions. Reports in 3 months on queries.
Nonfiction: How-to, reference, self-help, professional. Subjects include Canadiana, business, management and economics, military/war, money/finance, sports, training for business skills. "We are looking for books on Canadian small business and personal finance. No books and proposals that are American in focus. We publish primarily for the Canadian market, but work with McGraw-Hill U.S. on business and training titles." Query. Submit outline and sample chapters.
Recent Nonfiction Title: *The Canadian Snowbird Guide: Everything You Need to Know About Living Part-time in the USA*, by Doug Gray (personal finance).
Tips: "Writers have the best chance of selling us well-priced nonfiction, usually trade paper format. Proposal guidelines are available. Thorough market research on competitive titles increases chances of your proposal getting serious consideration, as does endorsement by or references from relevant professionals."

MACMILLAN CANADA, Division of Canada Publishing Corporation, 29 Birch Ave., Toronto, Ontario M4V 1E2 Canada. (416)963-8830. Vice President/Publisher: Denise Schon. Publishes hardcover and trade paperback originals. Publishes 30-35 titles/year. Receives 100-200 queries/year. 30% of books from first-time authors; 90% from unagented writers. Pays royalty. Publishes book 1 year aftr acceptance of ms. Accepts simultaneous submissions. Reports in 2 months. Book catalog free on request.
Nonfiction: Biography, cookbook, humor, reference, self-help. Subjects include business and economics, Canadiana, cooking/foods/nutrition, health/medicine, history, military/war, money/finance, recreation, sports.

Submit outline with 1-3 sample chapters, author bio, letter explaining rationale for book and SASE. Reviews artwork/photos as part of ms package. Writers should send photocopies.

NATURAL HERITAGE/NATURAL HERITAGE INC., P.O. Box 95, Station O, Toronto, Ontario M4A 2M8 Canada. (416)694-7907. Editor-in-Chief: Jane Gibson. Imprint is Natural Heritage. Publishes hardcover and trade paperback originals. Publishes 10-12 titles/year. 50% of books from first-time authors; 85% from unagented writers. Pays 8-10% royalty on retail price. Publishes book 2 years after acceptance of ms. Reports in 4 months on queries; 6 months on proposals and mss. Book catalog free. Manuscript guidelines for #10 SAE and IRC.
Nonfiction: Subjects include anthropology/archaeology, art/architecture, ethnic, history, military/war, nature/environment, photography, recreation, regional. "We are a Canadian publisher in the natural heritage and history fields." Submit outline with *details* of visuals.
Recent Nonfiction Title: *A Mill Should Be Built Thereon*, by Eleanor Darke (Toronto history).
Fiction: Historical, short story collections. Query.
Recent Poetry Title: *The Year Is A Circle: A Celebration of Henry David Thoreau*, by Victor Carl Friesen (poetry and nature photography).

NEWEST PUBLISHERS LTD., 10359 Whyte Ave., #310, Edmonton, Alberta T6E 1Z9 Canada. (403)432-9427. Fax: (403)432-9429. General Manager: Liz Grieve. Editorial Coordinator: Eva Radford. Estab. 1977. Publishes trade paperback originals. Publishes 8 titles/year. Receives 200 submissions/year. 40% of books from first-time authors; 90% from unagented writers. Pays 10% royalty. Publishes book 2 years after acceptance. Accepts simultaneous submissions. "We only publish Western Canadian authors." Reports in 2 months on queries. Book catalog for 9 × 12 SAE with 4 first-class Canadian stamps or US postal forms.
Nonfiction: Literary/essays (Western Canadian authors). Subjects include ethnic, government/politics (Western Canada), history (Western Canada), Canadiana. Query.
Fiction: Literary. Submit outline/synopsis and sample chapters.
Recent Fiction Title: *Icefields*, by Thomas Wharton.
Tips: "Our audience consists of people interested in the west and north of Canada; teachers, professors. Trend is towards more nonfiction submissions. Would like to see more full-length literary fiction."

‡NINE PINES PUBLISHING, Unity Arts Inc., 1128 Church St., P.O. Box 760, Manotick, Ontario K4M 1A7 Canada. (613)692-1601. Publishing Director: Bruce K. Filson. Publishes hardcover originals, trade paperback originals and reprints. Publishes 4 titles/year. Receives 100 queries and 40 mss/year. 50% of books from first-time authors; 100% from unagented writers. Pays 5-9% royalty on retail price. Publishes book 1 year after acceptance of ms. Accepts simultaneous submissions. Reports in 2 months on queries and proposals, 4 months on mss. Book catalog for $4.
Nonfiction: Biography, children's/juvenile, self-help. Subjects include child guidance/parenting, psychology, religion (Bahá'í religion). Writers must be intimately familiar with the Bahá'í Faith. Query with outline, 1 sample chapter and SASE.
Recent Nonfiction Title: *The Great Adventure*, by Florence Mayberry (autobiography).

ORCA BOOK PUBLISHERS LTD., P.O. Box 5626 Station B, Victoria, British Columbia V8R 6S4 Canada. (604)380-1229. Fax: (604)380-1892. E-mail: orca@pinc.com. Website: http://www.swiftly.com/orca. Publisher: R. Tyrrell. Children's Book Editor: Ann Featherstone. Estab. 1984. Publishes hardcover and trade paperback originals. Publishes 20-25 titles/year. Receives 500-600 submissions/year. 50% of books from first-time authors; 80% from unagented writers. Pays 10-12½% royalty on retail price. Offers $1,000 average advance. Publishes book 1 year after acceptance. Reports in 6 weeks on queries. Book catalog for 9 × 12 SAE and $2 postage (Canadian). Manuscript guidelines for SASE or IRCs.
Nonfiction: Biography, illustrated book, travel guides, children's. Subjects include history, nature/environment, recreation, sports, travel. Needs history (*West Coast Canadian*) and young children's book. Query or submit outline and sample chapters. Reviews artwork/photos as part of ms package. *Publishes Canadian material only.*
Fiction: Juvenile, illustrated children's books, 4-8-year-old range older juvenile and YA. Query or submit outline/synopsis and sample chapters.
Recent Nonfiction Title: *S.O.S. Guide to Essay Writing*, by Steve Good and Bill Jensen (essay writing guide).
Recent Fiction Title: *Moccasin Goalie*, by William Ray Brownridge.

SOME CANADIAN publishers will consider book proposals by Canadian authors only. Please check each listing carefully for this restriction.

PACIFIC EDUCATIONAL PRESS, Faculty of Education, University of British Columbia, Vancouver, British Columbia V6T 1Z4 Canada. Fax: (604)822-6603. E-mail: cedwards@unixg.ubc.ca. Director: Catherine Edwards. Publishes trade paperback originals. Publishes 6-8 titles/year. Receives 200 submissions/year. 15% of books from first-time authors; 100% from unagented writers. Accepts simultaneous submissions, if so noted. Reports in 6 months on mss. Book catalog free on request.
Nonfiction: Children's/juvenile, reference for teacher, textbook. Subjects for children: animals, Canadiana, history, language/literature. Subjects for children and teachers: art/architecture, education, ethnic (for children or professional resources for teachers), music/dance, nature/environment, regional (Pacific Northwest), science. "Our books often straddle the trade/educational line, but we make our selections based on educational potential (in classrooms or school libraries)." Submit outline and 3 sample chapters. Reviews artwork/photos as part of ms package. Send photocopies (color, if possible).
Recent Nonfiction Title: *In the Street of the Temple Cloth Printers*, by Dorothy Field (nonfiction picture book about traditional Hindu craftpeople for readers aged 11+).
Fiction: For children: ethnic, historical, juvenile, mystery, science fiction, young adult. For children or teachers: plays. "We select fiction based on its potential for use in language arts classes as well as its literary merit." Submit synopsis and 5 sample chapters; whole ms is best.
Recent Fiction Title: *The Reluctant Deckhand*, by Jan Padgett (juvenile novel about a young girl's summer aboard her mother's fishing boat).

PANDORA PRESS, Imprint of HarperCollins, 77-85 Fulham Palace Rd., Hammersmith, London W6 8JB England. Fax: 081-307-4440. Managing Director: Eileen Campbell. Commissioning Editor: Belinda Budge. Publishes hardcover and paperback originals. Publishes 30 titles/year. Pays 7½-10% royalty. Reports in 2 months. Book catalog free.
• No longer publishes fiction.
Nonfiction: Wide-ranging list of feminist writing includes subjects on culture and media, health, lifestyle and sexuality, biography and reference, and women's issues/studies.

PEGUIS PUBLISHERS LIMITED, 318 McDermot Ave., Winnipeg, Manitoba R3A OA2 Canada. (204)987-3500. Fax: (204)947-0080. Acquisitions: Mary Dixon. Estab. 1967. Educational paperback originals. Publishes 8 titles/year. Receives 150 submissions/year. 50% of books from first-time authors; 100% from unagented writers. Pays 10% average royalty on educational net (trade less 20%). Publishes book 2 years after acceptance. Accepts simultaneous submissions. Reports in 3 months on queries, 1 month on mss if quick rejection, up to 1 year if serious consideration. Book catalog free.
Nonfiction: Educational (focusing on teachers' resource material for primary education, integrated whole language). Submit outline/synopsis and sample chapters or complete ms.
Recent Nonfiction Title: *A Stone in My Shoe: Teaching Literacy in Times of Change*, by Lorri Neilsen.
Tips: "Writers have the best chance selling us quality professional materials for teachers that help them turn new research and findings into classroom practice."

PENGUIN BOOKS CANADA LTD., Subsidiary of The Penguin Publishing Co., Ltd., Suite 300, 10 Alcorn Ave., Toronto, Ontario M4V 3B2 Canada.
Nonfiction: Sports, true crime and any Canadian subject by Canadian authors. No unsolicited mss.
Recent Nonfiction Title: *The Canadian Revolution*, by Peter C. Newman (politics/history).
Recent Fiction Title: *The Saxon Shore*, by Jack Whyte.

‡**PINTER PUBLISHERS LTD.**, Cassell plc, Wellington House, 125 Strand, London WC2R OBB England. (71)420-5555. Potential authors in North America should contact: Pinter Cassell Academic, 215 Park Ave., S., New York NY 10003. (212)598-5717. Fax: (212)598-5740. Managing Director: Stephen Butcher. Publishes hardcover originals and paperback textbooks. Publishes 100 titles/year. Receives 1,000 queries and 100 mss/year. 10% of books from first-time authors; 99% from unagented writers. Pays 0-10% royalty. Publishes books 9 months after acceptance of ms. No simultaneous submissions. Reports in 1 month on proposals. *Writer's Market* recommends allowing 2 months for reply. Book catalog and ms guidelines free on request.
Nonfiction: Reference, technical, textbook. Subjects include anthropology/archaeology, business and economics, government/politics, history, sociology, linguistics. Submit outline.

PLAYWRIGHTS CANADA PRESS, Imprint of Playwrights Union of Canada, 54 Wolseley St., 2nd Floor, Toronto, Ontario M5T 1A5 Canada. (416)703-0201. Fax: (416)703-0059. E-mail: cdplays@interlog.com. Website: http://www.puc.ca. Managing Editor: Tony Hamill. Estab. 1972. Publishes paperback originals and reprints of plays by Canadian citizens or landed immigrants, whose plays have been professionally produced on stage. Receives 100 member submissions/year. 50% of plays from first-time authors; 50% from unagented authors. Pays 10% royalty on list price. Publishes 1 year after acceptance. No more than 2 simultaneous submissions. Reports in up to 1 year. Play catalog and ms guidelines free. Non-members should query. Accepts children's plays.

PRENTICE-HALL CANADA INC., Trade Division, Subsidiary of Simon & Schuster, 1870 Birchmount Rd., Scarborough, Ontario M1P 2J7 Canada. (416)293-3621. Fax: (416)293-3625. Acquisitions Editor: Sara

Borins. Estab. 1960. Publishes hardcover and trade paperback originals. Publishes about 25 titles/year. Receives 750-900 submissions/year. 30% of books from first-time authors; 40% from unagented writers. Pays negotiable royalty and advance. Publishes book 9 months after acceptance. Reports in 3 months. Manuscript guidelines for #10 SAE with 1 IRC.

Nonfiction: Subjects of Canadian and international interest: politics and current affairs, sports, business, finance, health, food. Submit outline and sample chapters. Reviews artwork/photos as part of ms package.

Recent Nonfiction Title: *Canadian Family On-Line: Every Parents Guide to the Internet*, by Wallace Whistance-Smith.

Tips: "Present a clear, concise thesis, well-argued with a thorough knowledge of existing works with strong Canadian orientation. Need general interest nonfiction books on topical subjects."

PRODUCTIVE PUBLICATIONS, P.O. Box 7200 Station A, Toronto, Ontario M5W 1X8 Canada. E-mail: iain.williamson@canrem.com. Owner: Iain Williamson. Estab. 1985. Publishes trade paperback originals. Publishes 21 titles/year. Receives 30 queries and 20 mss/year. 80% of books from first-time authors; 100% from unagented writers. Pays 5-18% royalty on wholesale price. Publishes book 3 months after acceptance of ms. Reports in 1 month on queries and proposals, 3 months on mss. Book catalog free on request.

● Productive Publications is also interested in books on business computer software, the Internet for business purposes, investment, stock market and mutual funds, etc.

Nonfiction: How-to, reference, self-help, technical. Subjects include business and economics, health/medicine, hobbies, software (business). "We are interested in small business/entrepreneurship/employment/self-help (business)/how-to/health and wellness—100 pages." Submit outline. Reviews artwork as part of ms package. Send photocopies.

Recent Nonfiction Title: *Tax Havens for Canadians*, by Adam Starchild.

Tips: "We are looking for books written by *knowledgeable, experienced experts* who can express their ideas *clearly* and *simply.*"

PURICH PUBLISHING, Box 23032, Market Mall Post Office, Saskatoon, Saskatchewan S7J 5H3 Canada. (306)373-5311. Publisher: Donald Purich. Publishes trade paperback originals. Publishes 3-5 titles/year. 20% of books from first-time authors. Pays 8-12% royalty on retail price or makes outright purchase. Offers $100-1,500 advance. Publishes book 4 months after acceptance of ms. Accepts simultaneous submissions. Reports in 1 month on queries, 3 months on mss. Book catalog free on request.

Nonfiction: Reference, technical, textbook. Subjects include agriculture/horticulture, government/politics, history, law, Aboriginal issues. "We are a specialized publisher and only consider work in our subject areas." Query.

Recent Nonfiction Title: *In Palliser's Triangle*, by Barry Potyondi (history).

QUARRY PRESS, P.O. Box 1061, Kingston, Ontario K7L-4Y5 Canada. Publisher: Bob Hilderley. Publishes hardcover originals, trade paperback originals and reprints. Publishes 30-40 titles/year. 10% of books from first-time authors; 90% from unagented writers. Pays 10% royalty on retail price. Publishes book 1 year after acceptance. Reports in 7 months. Book catalog for 9 × 12 SAE. Manuscript guidelines for #10 SASE.

Nonfiction: Biography, children's/juvenile (only by Canadians), gift book, humor. Subjects include art/architecture, education, gay/lesbian, history, language/literature, music/dance, photography, regional, religion, travel. "Our authors are generally Canadian." Query with SASE. Reviews artwork/photos as part of ms package. Send photocopies.

Recent Nonfiction Title: *Superman's Song: The Story of the Crash Test Dummies*, by Stephen Ostick (music/rock).

Fiction: Experimental, feminist, gay/lesbian, literary, mainstream/contemporary, science fiction, short story collections. Query with SASE.

Recent Fiction Title: *Under My Skin*, by Mary di Michele (fiction).

Poetry: "We publish Canadian poets only." Submit complete ms.

Recent Poetry Title: *Slow Reign of Calamity Jane*, by Gillian Robinson.

‡**QUINTET PUBLISHING LIMITED**, Quarto PLC, The Fitzpatrick Bldg., 188-195 York Way, London, England N7 9QR. 011.44.171.2001. New Titles Commissioning Editor: Stefanie Foster. Publishes hardcover and trade paperback originals and reprints. Publishes 80-100 titles/year. 50% of books from first-time authors; 100% from unagented writers. Makes outright purchase of $1,000-8,000 (US). Offers 33% advance. Publishes book 9 months after acceptance. Reports in 1 month.

Nonfiction: Coffee table book, cookbook, gift book, how-to, reference, technical. Subjects include: Americana, animals, anthropology/archaeology, art/architecture, child guidance/parenting, cooking/foods/nutrition, gardening, history, hobbies, military/war, music/dance, nature/environment, photography, recreation, sports. Writers should show a thorough awareness, reflected in their market analysis, of previously published titles in the subject area for which they are making a proposal. Query with proposal package including 1 sample chapter, marketing analysis and SASE. "Include a synopsis of all the elements of the book, so that we can consider how to make a flat-plan for an illustrated title." Reviews artwork/photos as part of ms package. Send transparencies.

Recent Nonfiction Title: *The Cigar Companion*, by Simon Chase and Anwar Bati (illustrated connoiseur/reference).

Fiction: Adventure, erotica, ethnic, historical, juvenile, mainstream/contemporary, occult, picture books, religious.

Tips: "We are a distinguished international illustrated book packager, and proposals must show the promise of broad appeal in many countries on all continents."

RAINCOAST BOOK DISTRIBUTION LIMITED, 8680 Cambie St., Vancouver, British Columbia V6P 6M9 Canada. Imprint is Raincoast Books. Managing Editor: Michael Carroll. Publishes hardcover and trade paperback originals and reprints. Publishes 15-20 titles/year. Receives 800 queries and 500 mss/year. 1% of books from first-time authors; 80% from unagented writers. Pays 8-12% royalty on retail price. Offers $1,000-6,000 advance. Publishes book within 2 years after acceptance of ms. Reports in 1 month on queries, 2 months on proposals, 3 months on mss. Book catalog and ms guidelines for #10 SASE.

Nonfiction: Children's, coffee table book, cookbook, gift book, humor, illustrated book. Subjects include animals, art/architecture, cooking/foods/nutrition, history, nature/environment, photography, recreation, regional, sports, travel, Canadian subjects and native studies/issues. "We are expanding rapidly and plan on publishing a great deal more over the next two or three years, particularly nonfiction. Proposals should be focused and include background information on the author. Include a market study or examination of competition. We like to see proposals that cover all the bases and offer a new approach to the subjects we're interested in. Query first. If we're interested, we will then ask for an outline, 3 sample chapters, author/artist bios, outline, sample chapters, market study with SASE." Reviews artwork/photos as part of ms package. Send color photocopies. Will request transparencies if interested.

Recent Nonfiction Title: *Fragments of Paradise*, by Paul and Audrey Grescoe (nature/wildlife).

Fiction: Literary, mystery, picture books. "Raincoast hopes to publish literary novels that have commercial appeal. Our interest is Canadian literary fiction or high-quality international literary fiction. Query first. If we're interested, we will then ask for a synopsis with SASE."

Recent Fiction Title: *If You're Not from the Prairie*, by Dave Bouchard, illustrated by Henry Ripplinger (children's).

Tips: "We have very high standards. Our books are extremely well designed and the texts reflect that quality. Be focused in your submission. Know what you are trying to do and be able to communicate it. Make sure the submission is well organized, thorough, and original. We like to see that the author has done some homework on markets and competition, particularly for nonfiction."

RANDOM HOUSE OF CANADA, Subsidiary of Random House, Inc., Suite 210, 33 Yonge St., Toronto, Ontario M5E 1G4 Canada. Imprint is Vintage Imprints. Publishes hardcover and trade paperback originals. Publishes 56 titles/year. No unsolicited mss. Agented submissions only. All unsolicited mss returned unopened. "We are NOT a mass market publisher."

‡RED DEER COLLEGE PRESS, Box 5005, 56th Ave. and 32nd St., Red Deer, Alberta T4N 5H5 Canada. (403)342-3321. Managing Editor: Dennis Johnson. Imprints are Northern Lights Books for Children, Northern Lights Young Novels, Discovery Books, Roundup Books, Writing West. Publishes trade paperback originals and occasionally reprints. Publishes 14-17 titles/year. Receives 1,400 queries and 1,000 mss/year. 20% of books from first-time authors; 90% from unagented writers. Pays 8-10% royalty on retail price. Publishes book 1 year after acceptance of ms. Accepts simultaneous submissions. Reports in 6 months. Book catalog free on request.

Nonfiction: Children's/juvenile, cookbook, humor, illustrated book. Subjects include anthropology/archaeology/paleontology, cooking/foods/nutrition, gardening, history (local/regional), nature/environment (local/regional), regional, travel. Nonfiction list focuses on regional history, paleontology, and some true crime, travel, gardening—much with a regional (Canadian) emphasis. "Writers should assess their competition in the marketplace and have a clear understanding of their potential readership." Query with SASE. Reviews artwork/photos as part of ms package. Send photocopies.

Recent Nonfiction Title: *The Third Suspect*, by David Staples and Greg Owens (true crime).

Fiction: Adventure, ethnic, experimental, fantasy, historical, humor, juvenile, literary, mainstream/contemporary, picture books, plays (occasionally), short story collections (occasionally), western, young adult. Adult fiction list includes well-established Canadian writers writing literary fiction, though the press is open to accepting other forms if tastefully and skillfully done. Query.

Recent Fiction Title: *Josepha: A Prairie Boy's Story*, by Jim McGugan/illustrated by Murray Kimber (children's illustrated).

Poetry: Query.

Recent Poetry Title: *Riding the Northern Range: Poems from the Last Best-West*, edited by Ted Stone (cowboy).

Tips: Audience varies from imprint to imprint. "Know as much as you can about the potential market/readership for your book and indicate clearly how your book is different from or better than others in the same genre."

REIDMORE BOOKS INC., 1200 Energy Square, 10109-106 Street, Edmonton, Alberta T5J 3L7 Canada. (403)424-4420. Fax: (403)441-9919. E-mail: reidmore@compusmart.ab.ca. Website: http://www.reidmore.c om. Director of Marketing/Sales: Cathie Crooks. Estab. 1979. Publishes hardcover originals and modular materials for elementary mathematics (grades 4, 5, 6). Publishes 10-12 titles/year. Receives 18-20 submissions/year. 60% of books from first-time authors; 100% from unagented writers. Subsidy publishes 5% of books. Pays royalty. Offers $1,500 average advance. Publishes book 1 year after acceptance. Reports in 3 months on queries. Book catalog free.
Nonfiction: Textbook. Subjects include ethnic, government/politics, history, elementary mathematics. Query. Most manuscripts are solicited by publisher from specific authors.
Recent Nonfiction Title: *Canada: Its Land and People*, by Massey (educational).

ROCKY MOUNTAIN BOOKS, #4 Spruce Centre SW, Calgary, Alberta T3C 3B3 Canada. Fax: (403)249-2968. E-mail: tonyd@cadvision.com. Website: http://www.ffa.ucalgary.ca/tmb/. Publisher: Tony Daffern. Publishes trade paperback originals. Publishes 5 titles/year. Receives 30 queries/year. 75% of books from first-time authors; 100% from unagented writers. Pays 10% royalty. Offers $1,000-2,000 advance. Publishes book 1 year after acceptance. Reports in 1 month on queries. *Writer's Market* recommends allowing 2 months for reply. Manuscript guidelines free on request.
Nonfiction: How-to. Subjects include nature/environment, recreation, travel. "Our main area of publishing is outdoor recreation guides to Western and Northern Canada." Query.
Recent Nonfiction Title: *Commuting by Bike*, by Will Orobko (recreation).

RONSDALE PRESS, 3350 W. 21st Ave., Vancouver, British Columbia V6S 1G7 Canada. Director: Ronald B. Hatch. Publishes trade paperback originals. Publishes 6 titles/year. Receives 100 queries and 200 mss/year. 60% of books from first time authors; 95% from unagented writers. Pays 10% royalty on retail price. Publishes book 1 year after acceptance of ms. Accepts simultaneous submissions. Reports in 1 week on queries, 1 month on proposals, 3 months on mss. Book catalog for #10 SASE. Writers *must* be Canadian citizens or landed immigrants.
Nonfiction: Biography, children's/juvenile. Subjects include history, language/literature, nature/environment, regional.
Recent Nonfiction Title: *Blackouts to Bright Lights: Canadian War Bride Stories*, ed. Ladouceur (oral histories).
Fiction: Experimental, novels, short story collections, children's literature. Query with at least 80 pages.
Recent Fiction Title: *The Seventh Circle*, by Benet Davetian (short stories).
Poetry: "Poets should have published some poems in magazines/journals." Submit complete ms.
Recent Poetry Title: *Burning Stone*, by Zoe Landale.

ROUSSAN PUBLISHERS INC., Roussan Editeur Inc., 2110 Decarie Blvd., Suite 100, Montreal, Quebec H4A 3J3 Canada. (514)481-2895. Editors: Kathryn Rhoades, Jane Frydenlund. Publishes trade paperback originals. Publishes 12 titles/year; each division publishes 6 titles/year. Receives 75 queries and 75 mss/year. 40% of books from first-time authors; 100% from unagented writers. Pays 8-10% royalty on retail price. Publishes book 8 months after acceptance of ms. Accepts simultaneous submissions. Reports in 3 months on proposals.
Fiction: Young adult and junior readers only—adventure, fantasy, feminist, historical, juvenile, mystery, science fiction. No picture books. Submit synopsis and 3 sample chapters.
Recent Fiction Title: *The Three Wishbells*, by Barbara Haworth-Attard (YA fantasy).

SCHOLASTIC CANADA LTD., 123 Newkirk Rd., Richmond Hill, Ontario L4C 3G5 Canada. Editor, Children's Books: Diane Kerner. Imprints are: North Winds Press (contact Joanne Richter); Les Éditions Scholastic (contact Sylvie Andrews, French editor). Publishes hardcover and trade paperback originals. Publishes 30 titles/year; imprint publishes 4 titles/year. 3% of books from first-time authors; 50% from unagented writers. Pays 5-10% royalty on retail price. Offers $1,000-5,000 (Canadian) advance. Publishes book 1 year after acceptance of ms. Accepts simultaneous submissions. Reports in 1 month on queries, 3 months on proposals. Book catalog for 8½×11 SAE with 2 first-class stamps (IRC or Canadian stamps only).
Nonfiction: Children's/juvenile. Subjects include animals, history, hobbies, nature/environment, recreation, science, sports. Query with outline, 1-2 sample chapters and SASE. No unsolicited mss. Reviews artwork/photos as part of ms package. Send photocopies.
Recent Nonfiction Title: *Take a Hike*, by Sharon Mackay and David Macleod (informal guide to hiking for kids).
Fiction: Children's/juvenile, young adult. Query with synopsis, 3 sample chapters and SASE.
Recent Fiction Title: *After the War*, by Carol Matas (juvenile novel).

SELF-COUNSEL PRESS, 1481 Charlotte Rd., North Vancouver, British Columbia V7J 1H1 Canada. (604)986-3366. Also 1704 N. State Street, Bellingham, WA 98225. (360)676-4530. Managing Editor: Ruth Wilson. Estab. 1970. Publishes trade paperback originals. Publishes 15-20 titles/year. Receives 1,000 submissions/year. 80% of books from first-time authors; 95% from unagented writers. Average print run for first book is 6,000. Pays 10% royalty on net receipts. Publishes book 9 months after acceptance. Accepts simultaneous submissions. Reports in 2 months. Book catalog and ms guidelines for 9 × 12 SAE.

Nonfiction: How-to, self-help. Subjects include business, law, reference. Query or submit outline and sample chapters.

Recent Nonfiction Title: *Small Business Guide to Doing Big Business on the Internet*, by Brian Hurley and Peter Birkwood (business).

Tips: "The self-counsel author is an expert in his or her field and capable of conveying practical, specific information to those who are not. We look for manuscripts full of useful information that will allow readers to take the solution to their needs or problems into their own hands and succeed. We do not want personal self-help accounts, however."

SHORELINE, 23 Ste.-Anne, Ste.-Anne-de-Bellevue, Quebec H9X 1L1 Canada. Fax: (514)457-5733. Editor: Judy Isherwood. Publishes trade paperback originals. Publishes 3 titles/year. Pays 10% royalty on retail price. Publishes book 1 year after acceptance. Reports in 1 month on queries, 4 month on ms. Book catalog for 50¢ postage.

Nonfiction: Biography, essays, humour, illustrated book, reference. Subjects include: America, art, Canada, education, ethnic, history, mediation, regional, religion, Mexico, Spain, travel, women's studies.

Recent Nonfiction Title: *Healing Waters, The Mayan Series*, by Anna Woods (paintings and stories).

Tips: Audience is "adults and young adults who like their nonfiction personal, different and special. Beginning writers welcome, agents unnecessary. Send your best draft (not the first!), make sure your heart is in it."

‡SNOWAPPLE PRESS, Box 66024, Heritage Postal Outlet, Edmonton, Alberta T6J 6T4 Canada. Editor: Vanna Tessier. Publishes hardcover originals, trade paperback originals and reprints, mass market paperback originals and reprints. Publishes 5-6 titles/year. Receives 25 queries/year. 50% of books from first-time authors; 100% from unagented writers. Pays 10-50% royalty on retail price or makes outright purchase of $100 or pays in copies. Offers $100-200 advance. Publishes book 2 years after acceptance. Accepts simultaneous submissions. Reports in 1 month on queries, 3 months on proposals and mss.

Fiction: Adventure, ethnic, experimental, fantasy, feminist, historical, literary, mainstream/contemporary, mystery, picture books, short story collections, young adult. Query with SASE.

Recent Fiction Title: *Missing Bones*, by Vanna Tessier (young adult mystery).

Poetry: Query with SASE.

Recent Poetry Title: *At This Time of Day*, by Peter Prest (new poetry).

Tips: Audience is educated readers. "We are a small press that will publish original, interesting and entertaining fiction and poetry."

SONO NIS PRESS, 1725 Blanshard St., Victoria, British Columbia V8W 2J8 Canada. (604)382-1024. Fax: (604)382-0775. Editor: A. West. Estab. 1968. Publishes hardcover and trade paperback originals and reprints. Receives hundreds of queries/year. 5-10% of books from first-time authors; 80% from unagented writers. Pays 10-12% royalty on retail price. Publishes book 14 months after acceptance. Accepts simultaneous submissions. Reports in 2 months on queries. Book catalog for 9 × 12 SAE with 3 IRCs.

Nonfiction: Biography, reference. Subjects include history (British Columbia), hobbies (trains), regional (British Columbia), maritime (British Columbia), transportation (Western Canada). Query or submit outline and 3 sample chapters. Reviews artwork/photos as part of ms package. Send photocopies.

Recent Nonfiction Title: *The Wilderness Profound*, by Richard Mackie.

Poetry: Query.

Recent Poetry Title: *Dream Museum*, by Liliane Welch.

‡SOUND AND VISION PUBLISHING LIMITED, 359 Riverdale Ave., Toronto, Ontario M4J 1A4 Canada. (416)465-8184. Fax: (416)465-4163. Contact: Geoff Sanace. Publishes trade paperback originals. Publishes 2 titles/year. Reports in 3 months on proposals.

Nonfiction: Humor. Music/dance subjects. Submit outline and SASE. Recent nonfiction title: *I Wanna Be Sedated: Pop Music of the 70s*, Dellio/Woods (music history).

‡SUNSHINE PUBLISHING, Box 29062, 125 Carlton St., St. Catharines, Ontario L2R 7P9 Canada. (905)685-8726. Ext. 2. Fax: (905)685-3829. E-mail: wstarchi@freenet.npiec.on.ca. Assistant Editor: Wolfgang Starchild. Publishes hardcover, trade paperback and mass market paperback originals. Publishes 10-20 titles/year. 50% of books from first-time authors; 75% from unagented writers. Pays 8-20% royalty on retail price. Publishes book 8 months after acceptance. Accepts simultaneous submissions. Reports in 2 months on queries, 4 months on proposals, 6 months on mss. Book catalog for SASE. Manuscript guidelines for #10 SASE.

Nonfiction: Children's/juvenile, cookbook, gift book, how-to, humor, illustrated book, multimedia (CD-ROM), self-help, technical, textbook. Subjects include agriculture/horticulture, alternative lifestyles, animals, business and economics, child guidance/parenting, computers and electronics, cooking/foods/nutrition, education, gardening, gay/lesbian, health/medicine, hobbies, language/literature, money/finance, nature/environment, occult, philosophy, psychology, software, women's issues/studies. Query with outline, 3 sample chapters and SASE. Reviews artwork/photos as part of ms package. Send photocopies.

Recent Nonfiction Title: *The 1996 Guide to Great Beer in Ontario*, by Roger Tottman.

Fiction: Adventure, confession, erotica, experimental, fantasy, feminist, gay/lesbian, horror, humor, juvenile, literary, mainstream/contemporary, mystery, occult, romance, science fiction, short story collections, suspense, young adult. Query with synopsis, 3 sample chapters and SASE.

THISTLEDOWN PRESS, 633 Main St., Saskatoon, Saskatchewan S7H 0J8 Canada. (306)244-1722. Fax: (306)244-1762. Editor-in-Chief: Patrick O'Rourke. Contact: Jesse Strothers. Estab. 1975. Publishes trade paperback originals by resident Canadian authors *only*. Publishes 10-12 titles/year. Receives 350 submissions/year. 10% of books from first-time authors; 90% from unagented writers. Average print order for a first poetry book is 500; fiction is 1,000. Pays standard royalty on retail price. Publishes book 2 years after acceptance. Reports in 2 months. Book catalog and guidelines for #10 SASE.

Fiction: Juvenile (ages 8 and up), literary. Interested in fiction mss from resident Canadian authors only. Minimum of 30,000 words. Accepts no unsolicited work. Query first.

Recent Fiction Title: *What Is Already Known*, edited by Séan Virgo (20th anniversary anthology).

Poetry: "The author should make him/herself familiar with our publishing program before deciding whether or not his/her work is appropriate." No poetry by people *not* citizens and residents of Canada. Prefers poetry mss that have had some previous exposure in literary magazines. Accepts no unsolicited work. Query first.

Recent Poetry Title: *Saved By the Telling*, by Eva Tihanyi.

Tips: "We prefer to receive a query letter first before a submission. We're looking for quality, well-written literary fiction—for children and young adults and for our adult fiction list as well. Increased emphasis on fiction (short story collections and novels) for young adults, aged 12-18 years."

THOMPSON EDUCATIONAL PUBLISHING INC., 14 Ripley Ave., Suite 105, Toronto, Ontario M6S 3N9 Canada. (416)766-2763. Fax: (416)766-0398. E-mail: thompson@canadabooks.ingenia.com. President: Keith Thompson. Publishes textbooks. Publishes 10 titles/year. Receives 15 queries and 10 mss/year. 80% of books from first-time authors; 100% from unagented writers. Pays 10% royalty on net price. Publishes book 1 year after acceptance. Reports in 1 month on proposals. *Writer's Market* recommends allowing 2 months for reply. Book catalog free on request.

Nonfiction: Textbook. Subjects include business and economics, education, government/politics, sociology, women's issues/studies. Submit outline and 1 sample chapter.

THORSONS, Imprint of HarperCollins, 77-85 Fulham Palace Rd., Hammersmith, London W6 8JB England. Fax: 081-307-4440. Managing Director: Eileen Campbell. Estab. 1930. Other imprint is Pandora. Publishes paperback originals. Publishes 150 titles/year. Pays 7½-10% royalty. Reports in 2 months. Book catalog free.

Nonfiction: Publishes books on health and lifestyle, environmental issues, business, popular psychology, self-help and positive thinking, therapy, religion and spirituality, philosophy, new science, psychic awareness, astrology, divination, and Western tradition.

TITAN BOOKS LTD., 42-44 Dolben St., London SE1 OUP England. Fax: (0171)620-0200. Senior Editor: D. Barraclough. Publishes trade and mass market paperback originals and reprints. Publishes 60-90 titles/year. Receives 1,000 queries and 500 mss/year. Less than 1% of books from first-time authors; 50% from unagented writers. Pays royalty of 6-8% on retail price. Advance varies. Publishes books 1 year after acceptance of ms. Accepts simultaneous submissions. Reports in 1 month on queries, 3 months on proposals, 6 months on mss. Manuscript guidelines for SASE with IRC.

Nonfiction: Biography, how-to, humor, illustrated book. Subjects include music, film and TV, erotica, comics. Query. Reviews artwork/photos as part of ms package. Send photocopies.

Recent Nonfiction Title: *Hong Kong Action Cinema*, by Bev Logan (cinema).

Recent Fiction Title: *The Watcher and the Watched*, by Michael Crawley (erotica).

‡TRILOBYTE PRESS, 1486 Willowdown Rd., Oakville, Ontario L6L 1X3 Canada. Fax: (905)847-7366. E-mail: doday@tuzo.erin. Publisher: Danton H. O'Day, Ph.D. Publishes trade paperback originals. Publishes 7-10 titles/year. Receives 12 queries and 6 mss/year. 50% of books from first-time authors; 100% from unagented writers. Pays 10% royalty on wholesale price. No advance. Publishes book 8 months after acceptance of ms. Accepts simultaneous submissions. Reports in 1 month on queries, 2 months on proposals. Book catalog and manuscript guidelines free on request.

Nonfiction: How-to, multimedia (IBM Windows®), reference, self-help, textbook. Subjects include child guidance/parenting, education, health/medicine, science. "We are continually looking for guides to help students succeed in school and in their careers." Query with proposal package, including outline, 2 sample chapters, qualifications of author and SASE. Reviews artwork/photos as part of ms package. Send photocopies.

Recent Nonfiction Title: *Stressed Out! Taking Control of Student Stress*, by David C. Rainham, M.D. (self-help).

Tips: Audience is "young people from high school through college age who want to do their best and get the job they want. Think about your submission—why us and why is your book worth publishing. Finally, who will read it and why."

TURNSTONE PRESS, 607-100 Arthur St., Winnipeg, Manitoba R3B 1H3 Canada. (204)947-1555. Fax: (204)942-1555. E-mail: editor@turnstonepress.mb.ca. Managing Editor: James Hutchison. Estab. 1971. Publishes trade paperback originals. Publishes 10-12 titles/year. Receives 1,000 mss/year. Publishes Canadians and permanent residents only. 25% of books from first-time authors; 75% from unagented writers. Pays 10% royalty on retail price. Offers $100-500 advance. Publishes book 1 year after acceptance of ms. Reports in 4 months. Book catalog free on request.

● Turnstone Press would like to see more novels and nonfiction books, particularly travel, memoir.

Recent Nonfiction Title: *One Room in a Castle*, by Karen Connelly.

Fiction: Adventure, ethnic, experimental, feminist, humor, literary, mainstream/contemporary, short story collections. Submit full ms. *Writer's Market* recommends query with SASE (Canadian postage) first.

Recent Fiction Title: *If Pigs Could Fly*, by David Arnason.

Poetry: Submit complete ms.

Recent Poetry Title: *Jesusalem Beloved*, by Di Brandt.

Tips: "We also publish one literary critical study per year and one general interest nonfiction book per year. Would like to see more ethnic writing, women's writing, gay and lesbian writing, as well as more travel, memoir, life-writing as well as eclectic novels. There is more than one way to tell a story."

CHARLES E. TUTTLE PUBLISHING COMPANY, INC., 2-6 Suido 1-Chome, Tokyo 112, Japan. Fax: 03-5689-4926. President: Nicholas Ingleton. Imprint is Yenbooks (less serious Asia-related books). Publishes hardcover and trade paperback originals and reprints. Publishes 36 titles/year. Receives 750 submissions/year. 10% of books from first-time authors; 80% from unagented writers. Subsidy publishes 5% of books. Pays 6-10% on wholesale price. Offers $1,000 average advance. Publishes book 8-12 months after acceptance. Accepts simultaneous submissions. Query for electronic submissions. Reports in 1 month. *Writer's Market* recommends allowing 2 months for reply. Book catalog and manuscript guidelines free.

Nonfiction: Cookbook, how-to, humor, illustrated book, reference. Subjects include art/architecture, business and economics, cooking/foods/nutrition, government/politics, history, language/literature, money/finance, philosophy, regional, religion, sports and travel. "We want Asia-related, but specifically Japan-related manuscripts on various topics, particularly business, martial arts, language, etc." Query with outline and sample chapters. Reviews artwork as part of ms package.

Recent Nonfiction Title: *Swimming Underground: My Years in the Warhol Factory*, by Mary Woronov.

Fiction: Literature of Japan or Asia in English translation. Query with outline/synopsis and sample chapters.

Poetry: Submit samples.

Tips: "Readers with an interest in Japan and Asia—culture, language, business, foods, travel, etc.—are our audience."

‡UNFINISHED MONUMENT PRESS, Mekler & Deahl, Publishers, 237 Prospect St. S., Hamilton, Ontario L8M 2Z6 Canada. Fax: (905)312-1779. E-mail: ad507@freenet.hamilton.on.ca. Managing Partner: James Deahl. Imprints are Unfinished Monument Northland (James Deahl, manager); Unfinished Monument America (Michael Wurster, manager). Publishes trade paperback originals and reprints. Publishes 4-6 titles/year. No books from first-time authors; 100% from unagented writers. Pays 10-12% royalty on retail price. Publishes book 10 months after acceptance. Accepts simultaneous submissions. Reports in 1 month on queries. *Writer's Market* recommends allowing 2 months for reply. Book catalog and ms guidelines free on request.

Nonfiction: Language/literature subjects. "We hope to move beyond literary criticism/literature soon." Query with SASE.

Recent Nonfiction Title: The Script of *Under The Watchful Eye*, by David Greene (TV script).

Fiction: Plays. "We hope to get into short stories soon." Query with SASE.

Poetry: We have a special interest in people's poetry. Query.

Recent Poetry Title: *Not To Rest In Silence*, edited by Ted Plantos (poetry anthology).

Tips: American authors can use our US address: P.O. Box 4279, Pittsburgh PA 15203, %Michael Wurster, Manager.

THE UNITED CHURCH PUBLISHING HOUSE (UCPH), 3250 Bloor St. W., 4th Floor, Etobicoke, Ontario M8X 2Y4 Canada. (416)231-5931. Managing Editor: Ruth Bradley-St-Cyr. Publishes trade paperback originals from Canadian authors only. Publishes 13 titles/year. Receives 30 queries and 20 mss/year. 80% of books from first-time authors; 99% from unagented writers. Pays 8-10% royalty on retail price. Offers $100-300 advance. Publishes book 1 year after acceptance. No simultaneous submissions. Reports in 2 months on proposals. Book catalog and ms guidelines free with SASE.

Nonfiction: Subjects include United Church of Canada, history, religion, sociology, women's issues/studies, theology and biblical studies. Submit outline and 1 sample chapter.
Recent Nonfiction Title: *God Hates Religion*, by Chris Levan (essay).

THE UNIVERSITY OF ALBERTA PRESS, 141 Athabasca Hall, Edmonton, Alberta T6G 2E8 Canada. (403)492-3662. Fax: (403)492-0719. Director: Glenn Rollans. Estab. 1969. Publishes hardcover and trade paperback originals and trade paperback reprints. Publishes 10 titles/year. Receives 100 submissions/year. 60% of books from first-time authors; majority from unagented writers. Average print order for a first book is 1,000. Pays 10% royalty on net price. Publishes book 1 year after acceptance. Reports in 3 months. Book catalog and ms guidelines free.
  • University of Alberta Press is looking for shorter works with minimum illustration.
Nonfiction: Scholarly or university textbook market. Preference given to Canadian authors or authors writing on Canadian topics. Subjects include art, history, nature, philosophy, politics, sociology. Submit table of contents and first chapter. No unrevised theses.
Tips: "We are interested in original research making a significant contribution to knowledge in the subject."

UNIVERSITY OF CALGARY PRESS, 2500 University Dr. NW, Calgary, Alberta T2N 1N4 Canada. (403)220-7578. Fax: (403)282-0085. Director: Shirley A. Onn. Estab. 1981. Publishes scholarly hardcover and paperback originals. Publishes 12-15 titles/year. Receives 175 submissions/year. Less than 5% of books from first-time authors; 99% from unagented authors. "As with all Canadian University Presses, UC Press does not have publication funds of its own. Money must be found to subsidize each project." Publishes book 1 year after acceptance. Pays negotiable royalties. "Manuscript must pass a two tier review system before acceptance." *Writer's Market* recommends allowing 2 months for reply. Book catalog and guidelines for 9×12 SAE with 2 IRCs.
Nonfiction: "UC Press has developed an active publishing program that includes up to 15 new scholarly and trade-based-on-scholarship titles each year and 6 scholarly journals. UC Press publishes in a wide variety of subject areas and is willing to consider any innovative scholarly manuscript. Particular areas of interest are Environmental Studies, International Relations and Northern Studies."
Recent Nonfiction Title: *A Baltic Odyssey: War and Survival*, by Jürgen and Martha von Rosen, edited by E. Whittaker (WWII autobiography).
Tips: "If I were trying to interest a scholarly publisher, I would prepare my manuscript on a word processor and submit a completed prospectus, including projected market, to the publisher."

UNIVERSITY OF MANITOBA PRESS, 15 Gillson St., University of Manitoba, Winnipeg, Manitoba R3T 5V6 Canada. Director: David Carr. Estab. 1967. Publishes hardcover and trade paperback originals. Publishes 4-6 titles/year. Pays 5-15% royalty on wholesale price. Reports in 3 months.
Nonfiction: Scholarly. Subjects include history, regional, religion, women's issues/studies, native. Query.
Recent Nonfiction Title: *The Geography of Manitoba: Its Land and Its People*, edited by J. Welsted, J. Everitt and C. Stadel.

UNIVERSITY OF MONTREAL PRESS, P.O. Box 6128, Station Downtown, Montreal H3C 3J7 Canada. (514)343-6929. Fax: (514)343-2232. Editor-in-Chief: Marise Labrecque. Publishes hardcover and trade paperback originals. Publishes 20-25 titles/year. Nonauthor-subsidy publishes 25% of books. Pays 8-12 % royalty on net price. Publishes book 6 months after acceptance of ms. Reports in 1 month on queries and proposals, 3 months on mss. Book catalog and ms guidelines free on request.
Nonfiction: Reference, textbook. Subjects include anthropology/archaeology, education, health/medicine, history, language/literature, philosophy, psychology, religion, sociology, translation. Submit outline and 2 sample chapters.

UNIVERSITY OF OTTAWA PRESS, 542 King Edward, Ottawa, Ontario K1N 6N5 Canada. (613)562-5246. Fax: (613)562-5247. Editor, English Publications: Suzanne Bossé. Estab. 1936. Publishes 22 titles/year; 10 titles/year in English. Receives 140 submissions/year. 20% of books from first-time authors; 95% from unagented writers. Determines nonauthor subsidy by preliminary budget. Pays 5-10% royalty on net price. Publishes book 4 months after acceptance. Reports in 2 months on queries, 4 months on mss. Book catalog and author's guide free.
Nonfiction: Reference, textbook, scholarly. Subjects include criminology, education, Canadian government/politics, Canadian history, language/literature, nature/environment, philosophy, religion, sociology, translation, women's issues/studies. Submit outline/synopsis and sample chapters.
Recent Nonfiction Title: *When Science Becomes Culture: World Survey of Scientific Culture*, edited by Bernard Schiele.
Tips: "Envision audience of academic specialists and (for some books) educated public."

VANWELL PUBLISHING LIMITED, 1 Northrup Crescent, P.O. Box 2131, St. Catharines, Ontario L2M 6P5 Canada. (905)937-3100. Fax: (905)937-1760. General Editor: Angela Dobler. Estab. 1983. Publishes trade originals and reprints. Publishes 5-7 titles/year. Receives 100 submissions/year. Publishes Canadian authors only. 85% of books from first-time authors; 100% from unagented writers. Pays 8-15% royalty on wholesale price. Offers $200 average advance. Publishes book 1 year after acceptance. Reports in 1 month on queries. *Writer's Market* recommends allowing 2 months for reply. Book catalog free.

● Vanwell Publishing Ltd. has received awards from Education Children's Book Centre and Notable Education Libraries Association. It is seeing increased demand for biographical nonfiction for ages 10-14.

Nonfiction: Biography. Subjects include military/war. All military/history related. *Writer's Market* recommends query with SASE first. Reviews artwork/photos as part of ms package.

Recent Nonfiction Title: *Our Little Army*, by Brian Reid (military history).

Tips: "The writer has the best chance of selling a manuscript to our firm which is in keeping with our publishing program, well written and organized. Our audience: older male, history buff, war veteran; regional tourist; students. *Canadian* only military/aviation, military/history and children's nonfiction have the best chance with us."

VEHICULE PRESS, Box 125, Place du Parc Station, Montreal, Quebec H2W 2M9 Canada. (514)844-6073. Fax: (514)844-7543. President/Publisher: Simon Dardick. Estab. 1973. Imprints include Signal Editions (poetry) and Dossier Quebec (history, memoirs). Publishes trade paperback originals by Canadian authors *only*. Publishes 13 titles/year. Receives 250 submissions/year. 20% of books from first-time authors; 95% from unagented writers. Pays 10-15% royalty on retail price. Offers $200-500 advance. Publishes book 1 year after acceptance. Reports in 4 months on queries. Book catalog for 9 × 12 SAE with IRCs.

Nonfiction: Biography, memoir. Subjects include Canadiana, feminism, history, politics, social history, literature. Especially looking for Canadian social history. Query. Reviews artwork/photos as part of ms package.

Recent Nonfiction Title: *Russia Between Yesterday & Tomorrow*, by Marika Prúska-Carroll.

Poetry: Contact: Michael Harris. Canadian authors *only*. Not accepting new material before 1997.

Recent Poetry Title: *The Signal Anthology*, edited by Michael Harris.

Tips: "We are only interested in Canadian authors."

VERSO, 6 Meard St., London WIV 3HR England. Fax: (171)734-0059. Commisioning Editor: Malcolm Imrie. Estab. 1970. Publishes hardcover and tradepaper originals. Publishes 60 titles/year. Receives 500 submissions/year. 15% of books from first-time authors; 80% from unagented writers. Pays 7-10% royalty on retail price. Offers $2,000 average advance. Publishes book 15 months after acceptance. Reports in 2 months.

Nonfiction: Academic, general. Subjects include economics, education, government/politics/social sciences, language/literature, nature/environment, philosophy, science, cultural and media studies, sociology, travel, women's issues/studies. Submit outline and sample chapters. Unsolicited mss not accepted.

Recent Nonfiction Title: *The Motorcycle Diaries: A Journey Around South America*, by Ernesto "Che" Guerara (hardback).

WALL & EMERSON, INC., 6 O'Connor Dr., Toronto, Ontario M4K 2K1 Canada. (416)467-8685. Fax: (416)696-2460. President: Byron E. Wall. Vice President: Martha Wall. Estab. 1987. Imprints are Wall & Thompson and Wall & Emerson. Publishes hardcover and trade paperback originals and reprints. Publishes 5 titles/year. 50% of books from first-time authors; 100% from unagented writers. Nonauthor-subsidy publishes 10% of books. (Only subsidies provided by external granting agencies accepted. Generally these are for scholarly books with a small market.) Pays royalty of 8-15% on wholesale price. Publishes book 1 year after acceptance. Accepts simultaneous submissions. Reports in 2 months on queries.

Nonfiction: Reference, textbook. Subjects include adult education, health/medicine, philosophy, science, mathematics. "We are looking for any undergraduate college text that meets the needs of a well-defined course in colleges in the US and Canada." Submit outline and sample chapters.

Recent Nonfiction Title: *Introduction to Industrial Ergonomics*, by T.M. Fraser.

Tips: "We are most interested in textbooks for college courses; books that meet well-defined needs and are targeted to their audiences are best. Our audience consists of college undergraduate students and college libraries. Our ideal writer is a college professor writing a text for a course he or she teaches regularly. If I were a writer trying to market a book today, I would identify the audience for the book and write directly to the audience throughout the book. I would then approach a publisher that publishes books specifically for that audience."

‡**WARWICK PUBLISHING INC.**, 24 Mercer St., #200, Toronto, Ontario M5V 1H3 Canada. Publisher: Nick Pitt. Publishes hardcover and trade paperback originals and reprints. Publishes 15-20 titles/year. Receives 30 queries and 20 mss/year. 40% of books from first-time authors; 90% from unagented writers. Pays 7-15% royalty on retail price or makes outright purchase of $1,500-7,500. Offers $1,000-10,000 advance. Publishes book 18 months after acceptance. Accepts simultaneous submissions. Reports in 2 months.

Nonfiction: Biography, coffee table book, cookbook, how-to, multimedia (CD-ROM). Subjects include business and economics, cooking/foods/nutrition, education, history, money/finance, photography, recreation, sports, travel. Send a strong query first. "We often receive manuscripts on topics we wouldn't pursue."

Query with SASE. Reviews artwork/photos as part of ms package. Send photocopies.
Recent Nonfiction Title: *Winetaster's Secrets*, by Andrew Sharp (how-to/reference).
Tips: Mainstream audience.

WHITECAP BOOKS LTD., 351 Lynn Ave., North Vancouver, British Columbia V7J 2C4 Canada. (604)980-9852. Publisher: Colleen MacMillan. Publishes hardcover and trade paperback originals. Publishes 24 titles/year. Receives 150 queries and 200 mss/year. 20% of books from first-time authors; 90% from unagented writers. Royalty and advance negotiated for each project. Publishes book 8 months after acceptance. Accepts simultaneous submissions. Reports in 2 months on proposals.
Nonfiction: Biography, coffee table book, cookbook, children's/juvenile. Subjects include animals, gardening, history, nature/environment, recreation, regional, travel. "We require an annotated outline. Writers should also take the time to research our list." Submit outline, 1 sample chapter, table of contents and SASE. Send photocopies, not original material.
Recent Nonfiction Title: *The Cycling Adventures of Coconut Head: A North American Odyssey*, by Ted Schredd (travel/adventure).
Tips: "We want well-written, well-researched material that presents a fresh approach to a particular topic."

WORDSTORM PRODUCTIONS INC., Box 49132, 7740 18th St. SE, Calgary, Alberta T2C 3W5 Canada. Phone/fax: (403)236-1275. E-mail: wordstrm@cadvision.com. Editor: Perry P. Rose. Publishes trade and mass market paperback originals. Publishes 3-5 titles/year. 90% of books from first-time authors; 100% from unagented writers. Pays 10-12% royalty on retail price. (Canadian works released in USA paid 66% of above.) Publishes book 1 year after acceptance of ms. Reports in 2 months on queries, 4 months on proposals, 6 months on mss. Manuscript guidelines for #10 SASE.
Nonfiction: Humor. Query with outline, 3 sample chapters and SASE or SAE and IRCs. Reviews artwork/photos as part of ms package. Send photocopies.
Fiction: Adventure, humor, mainstream/contemporary, mystery, suspense, children's books. Query with synopsis, 3 sample chapters and SASE or SAE and IRCs. All unsolicited mss returned unopened.
Recent Fiction Title: *Blue-Pers-(More) Tales from the Police Locker Room*, by Perry P. Rose (humor).
Tips: When sending self-addressed return envelope, please remember to use an international postal coupon if mailing is originating outside Canada.

YORK PRESS LTD., P.O. Box 1172, Fredericton, New Brunswick E3B 5C8 Canada. (506)458-8748. Fax: (506)458-8748. General Manager/Editor: Dr. S. Elkhadem. Estab. 1975. Publishes trade paperback originals. Publishes 10 titles/year. Receives 50 submissions/year. 10% of books from first-time authors; 100% from unagented writers. Pays 10-20% royalty on wholesale price. Publishes book 6 months after acceptance. Reports in 2 weeks. *Writer's Market* recommends allowing 2 months for reply.
Nonfiction and Fiction: Reference, textbook, scholarly. Especially needs literary criticism, comparative literature and linguistics and fiction of an experimental nature by well-established writers. Query.
Recent Nonfiction Title: *Herman Melville: Romantic & Prophet*, by C.S. Durer (scholarly literary criticism).
Recent Fiction Title: *The Moonhare*, by Kirk Hampton (experimental novel).
Tips: "If I were a writer trying to market a book today, I would spend a considerable amount of time examining the needs of a publisher *before* sending my manuscript to him. Scholarly books and creative writing of an experimental nature are the only kinds we publish. The writer must adhere to our style manual and follow our guidelines exactly."

PUBLISHERS THAT APPEARED in the 1996 edition of *Writer's Market* but are not included this year are listed in the General Index with a notation explaining their absence.

Small Presses

"Small press" is a relative term. Compared to the dozen or so conglomerates, the rest of the book publishing world may seem to be comprised of small presses. A number of the publishers listed in the Book Publishers section consider themselves small presses and cultivate the image. For our purpose of classification, the publishers listed in this section are called small presses because they publish three or fewer books per year.

The publishing opportunities are slightly more limited with the companies listed here than with those in the Book Publishers section. Not only are they publishing fewer books, but small presses are usually not able to market their books as effectively as larger publishers. Their print runs and royalty arrangements are usually smaller. It boils down to money, what a publisher can afford, and in that area, small presses simply can't compete with conglomerates.

However, realistic small press publishers don't try to compete with Bantam or Random House. They realize everything about their efforts operates on a smaller scale. Most small press publishers get into book publishing for the love of it, not solely for the profit. Of course, every publisher, small or large, wants successful books. But small press publishers often measure success in different ways.

Many writers actually prefer to work with small presses. Since small publishing houses are usually based on the publisher's commitment to the subject matter, and since they necessarily work with far fewer authors than the conglomerates, small press authors and their books usually receive more personal attention than the larger publishers can afford to give them. Promotional dollars at the big houses tend to be siphoned toward a few books each season that they have decided are likely to succeed, leaving hundreds of "midlist" books underpromoted, and, more likely than not, destined for failure. Since small presses only commit to a very small number of books every year, they are vitally interested in the promotion and distribution of each title they publish.

Just because they publish three or fewer titles per year does not mean small press editors have the time to look at complete manuscripts. In fact, the editors with smaller staffs often have even less time for submissions. The procedure for contacting a small press with your book idea is exactly the same as it is for a larger publisher. Send a one-page query with SASE first. If the press is interested in your proposal, be ready to send an outline or synopsis, and/or a sample chapter or two. Be patient with their reporting times; small presses can be slower to respond than larger companies. You might consider simultaneous queries, as long as you note them, to compensate for the waiting game.

For more information on small presses, see *Novel & Short Story Writer's Market* and *Poet's Market* (Writer's Digest Books), and *Small Press Review* and *The International Directory of Little Magazines and Small Presses* (Dustbooks).

For a list of publishers according to their subjects of interest, see the nonfiction and fiction sections of the Book Publishers Subject Index. Information on some book publishers and producers not included in this edition of *Writer's Market* can be found in the General Index.

ACME PRESS, P.O. Box 1702, Westminster MD 21158-1702. (410)848-7577. Managing Editor: Ms. E.G. Johnston. Estab. 1991. Publishes hardcover and trade paperback originals. Publishes 1-2 titles/year. Pays 50% of profits. No advance. Reports in 2 months on mss.

Fiction: Humor. "We accept submissions on any subject as long as the material is humorous; prefer full-length novels. No cartoons or art (text only). No pornography, poetry, short stories or children's material." Submit outline, first 50-75 pages and SASE. Recent fiction title: *Hearts of Gold*, by James Magorian (comic mystery).

Tips: "We are always looking for the great comic novel."

‡ACORN PUBLISHING, 1063 S. Talmadge, Waverly NY 14892-9514. (607)565-2536. Fax: (607)565-2560. Editor: Richard H. Mansfield. Estab. 1985. Publishes trade paperback originals. Publishes 2 titles/year. Pays 7-10% royalty. No advance. Reports in 1 month on queries. *Writer's Market* recommends allowing 2 months for reply.

Nonfiction: Regional mountain biking guides (Eastern), outdoor recreation books. Especially interested in regional mountain biking guides for eastern US. Submit outline. Recent nonfiction title: *Fit and Pregnant*, by Joan M. Butler (self-help/fitness).

‡ADAMS-HALL PUBLISHING, INC., 11661 San Vicente Blvd., Suite 210, Los Angeles CA 90049. (800)888-4452. Editorial Director: Sue Ann Bacon. Publishes hardcover and trade paperback originals and reprints. Publishes 3-4 titles/year. Pays 10% royalty on net receipts to publisher; advances negotiable. Reports in 1 month on queries. *Writer's Market* recommends allowing 2 months for reply. Accepts simultaneous submissions if so advised.

Nonfiction: Publishes quality business and personal finance books. Small, successful house that aggressively promotes select titles. Only interested in business or personal finance titles with broad appeal. Send query letter first with proposed book idea, a listing of current, competitive books, author qualifications, how book is unique and the market(s) for book. Query. Submit outline and 2 sample chapters with SASE. Recent nonfiction title: *Organized To Be The Best! New Timesaving Ways to Simplify and Improve How You Work* (third edition), by Susan Silver.

AEGIS PUBLISHING GROUP, 796 Aquidneck Ave., Newport RI 02842-7202. (401)849-4200. Publisher: Robert Mastin. Estab. 1992. Publishes trade paperback originals and reprints. Publishes 3 titles/year. Pays 12% royalty on net sales. Offers $1,000-4,000 advance. Reports in 2 months on queries.

Nonfiction: "Our specialty is telecommunications books targeted to small businesses, entrepreneurs and telecommuters—how they can benefit from the latest telecom products and services. Author must be an experienced authority in the subject, and the material must be very specific with helpful step-by-step advice." Query with SASE. Recent nonfiction title: *The Telecommuter's Advisor*, by June Langhoff.

‡ALASKA PRESS, P.O. Box 90565, Anchorage AK 99509-0565. Fax: (907)272-1302. Editor: Diane Ford Wood. Publishes trade paperback originals. Publishes 3-4 titles/year. 75% of books from first-time authors. Pays 10% royalty on net price. Reports in 1 month. *Writer's Market* recommends allowing 2 months for reply. Book catalog free on request. Manuscript guidelines for #10 SASE.

Nonfiction: Alaska pioneer memoirs and the histories of special Alaska places only. Query. Send outline, 3 sample chapters and SASE. Recent nonfiction title: *Home Sweet Homestead*, by Joy Griffin.

Tips: "Become familiar with the type and style of books published by publishers *before* making contact."

AMERICAN CATHOLIC PRESS, 16565 S. State St., South Holland IL 60473. (312)331-5845. Editorial Director: Rev. Michael Gilligan, Ph.D. Estab. 1967. Publishes hardcover originals and hardcover and paperback reprints. "Most of our sales are by direct mail, although we do work through retail outlets." Publishes 4 titles/year. Pays by outright purchase of $25-100. No advance.

Nonfiction: "We publish books on the Roman Catholic liturgy—for the most part, books on religious music and educational books and pamphlets. We also publish religious songs for church use, including Psalms, as well as choral and instrumental arrangements. We are interested in new music, meant for use in church services. Books, or even pamphlets, on the Roman Catholic Mass are especially welcome. We have no interest in secular topics and are not interested in religious poetry of any kind."

‡AMERICAN MEDICAL PUBLISHING COMPANY, INC., P.O. Box 604885, Bayside NY 11360-4885. (800)263-3782. Publisher: Charles Michaelson. Publishes trade paperback originals. Publishes 2-4 titles/year. Pays royalty or makes outright purchase. Offers $100 advance. Book catalog and manuscript guidelines free on request.

Nonfiction: Medical and health care booklets. "We are interested in social aspects of medical and health care issues." Query or submit outline with one page of copy. Recent nonfiction title: *Early Recognition of Elder Abuse*, by Andrew Weinberg, MD and Jeanne Wei, MD, PhD (reference).

Tips: Audience is medical and healthcare professionals, including physicians, nurses, pharmacologists, social workers, and teachers and lawyers.

AMIGADGET PUBLISHING COMPANY, P.O. Box 1696, Lexington SC 29071. (803)957-1106. Fax: (803)957-7495. E-mail: amigadget@cup.portal.com. Editor-in-Chief: Jay Gross. Publishes trade paperback originals. Publishes 2 titles/year. Pays royalty or makes outright purchase. Advance negotiable. Reports in 6 months.

Nonfiction: "Do not send manuscript. Queries only. No books on Windows." Recent title: *How to Start Your Own Underground Newspaper*, by J. Gross (how-to).

ANIMA PUBLICATIONS, Imprint of Anima Books, 1053 Wilson Ave., Chambersburg PA 17201-1247. (717)267-0087. Managing Editor: Barbara D. Rotz. Estab. 1974. "Our books are read at the undergraduate level as texts in religious studies programs and by the general reading audience with an interest in Asian religions."

ARIADNE PRESS, 4817 Tallahassee Ave., Rockville MD 20853-3144. (301)949-2514. President: Carol Hoover. Estab. 1976. Publishes hardcover and trade paperback originals. Pays 10% royalty on retail price. No advance. Reports in 1 month on queries, 3 months on mss.

Fiction: Adventure, feminist, historical, humor, literary, mainstream/contemporary. "We look for exciting and believable plots, strong themes, and non-stereotypical characters who develop in fascinating and often unpredictable directions." Query with 1-2 page plot summary, bio and SASE. Recent fiction title: *Cross a Dark Bridge*, by Deborah Churchman.

‡ASTARTE SHELL PRESS, P.O. Box 3648, Portland ME 04104. (207)828-1992. Contact: Sapphire. Publishes trade paperback originals. Publishes 2-3 titles/year. Pays 7% royalty on wholesale price. No advance. Reports in 2 months.

Nonfiction: "We focus on feminist spirituality and politics, including peace and social justice issues." Query with outline, 2-3 sample chapters or first 50 pages (approx.) with SASE. Recent nonfiction title: *Women & Worship at Philippi*, by Valerie A. Abrahamsen (religious studies/women's studies).

Fiction: "Seeking manuscripts that are multicultural in nature." Query with outline, 2-3 sample chapters or first 50 pages (approx.) with SASE. Recent fiction title: *The Eighth of September*, by Barbara Stevens Sullivan (social justice/family issues/ethics).

Tips: "Please be aware of our definition of feminism as seeking to eliminate oppression in all its forms and being committed to justice for women and all of life."

‡AUSTEN SHARP, P.O. Box 12, Newport RI 02840. (401)846-9884. E-mail: ascreengem@aol.com. President: Eleyne Austen Sharp. Estab. 1996. Children's imprint is Blue Villa. Publishes 1-2 titles/year. Pays 10% royalty on retail price.

Nonfiction: Children's, cookbooks, crafts, New Age, regional, seasonal, self-help and travel. Query only. Recent nonfiction title: *Haunted Newport*, by Eleyne Austen Sharp.

AUTO BOOK PRESS, P.O. Bin 711, San Marcos CA 92079-0711. (619)744-3582. Editorial Director: William Carroll. Estab. 1955. Publishes hardcover and paperback originals. Publishes 3 titles/year. Pays negotiated royalty on wholesale price. Advance varies. Reports in 1 month on queries. *Writer's Market* recommends allowing 2 months for reply.

Nonfiction: Automotive material only: technical or definitive how-to. Query with SASE. Recent nonfiction title: *Two Wheels to Panama*.

AVIATION BOOK COMPANY, 7201 Perimeter Rd. S., Seattle WA 98108. (800)423-2708. Fax: (206)767-5232. Editor: Nancy Griffith. Publishes hardcover and trade paperback originals and reprints. Publishes 2 titles/year. Pays 10% minimum royalty on retail price. Reports in 2 months on queries.

Nonfiction: Aviation titles, pilot manuals. Specializes in all nonfiction civil and military aviation books. Query. Recent nonfiction title: *Instrument Flight Training Manual*, by P. Dogan (training).

‡BALCONY PRESS, 2690 Locksley Place, Los Angeles CA 90039. (213)644-0741. Publisher: Ann Gray. Publishes hardcover and trade paperback originals. Publishes 2-4 titles/year. Pays 10% royalty on wholesale price. No advance. Reports in 1 month on queries and proposals; 3 months on mss. Book information free on request.

Nonfiction: Biography, coffee table books and illustrated books. Subjects include art/architecture, ethnic, gardening, history (relative to design, art and architecture) and regional. "We are interested in the human side of design as opposed to technical or how-to. We like to think our books will be interesting to the general public who might not otherwise select an architecture or design book." Query by telephone or letter. Submit

MARKET CONDITIONS are constantly changing! If this is 1998 or later, buy the newest edition of *Writer's Market* at your favorite bookstore or order directly from Writer's Digest Books.

outline and 2 sample chapters with introduction if applicable. Recent nonfiction title: *Images of the Gamble House*, by Jeannette Thomas (photography).

Tips: Audience consists of architects, designers and the general public who enjoy those fields. "Our books typically cover California subjects but that is not a restriction. It's always a nice surprise when an author has strong ideas about their audience and how the book can be effectively marketed. We are not afraid of small niches if a good sales plan can be devised."

BANDANNA BOOKS, 319-B Anacapa St., Santa Barbara CA 93101. (805)962-9915. Fax: (805)504-3278. Publisher: Sasha Newborn. Manuscript Editor: Joan Blake. Publishes trade paperback originals and reprints. Publishes 3 titles/year. Receives 300 queries and 100 mss/year. 50% of books from first-time authors; 95% from unagented writers. Pays 5-10% royalty on retail price (a few books gratis). Offers $50-200 advance. Publishes book 1 year after acceptance. Accepts simultaneous submissions. Reports in 2 months on proposals.

Nonfiction: Textbooks, some illustrated. Subjects include history, literature, language. "Bandanna Books seeks to humanize the classics, history, language in non-sexist, modernized translations, using direct and plain language. Suitable for advanced high school, college classes, and general audiences. For 1996 we are preparing materials for teachers as well as for students. Submit outline and 1-2 sample chapters. Reviews artwork/photos as part of ms package. Send photocopies. Recent nonfiction title: *Italian for Opera Lovers*, by Hassam W. Ebron (dictionary).

Tips: "Our readers are age 16-22 and up, high school or college age, liberal arts orientation. A well-thought-out proposal is important, even if unconventional. We are not interested in juvenile or young adult material."

BAY PRESS, INC., 115 W. Denny Way, Seattle WA 98119. Editor-in-Chief: Kimberly Barnett. Publishes trade paperback critical nonfiction originals on contemporary culture. Publishes 2-4 titles/year. Pays royalty on net receipts. Reports in 3 months on proposals.

Nonfiction: Our books are primarily anthologies. Submit proposal package including outline, intro, sample chapter and market analysis with SASE. Recent nonfiction title: *Let's Get It On: The Politics of Black Performance*, by Catherine Uguou (anthology).

BEACHWAY PRESS, 9201 Beachway Lane, Springfield VA 22153. Publisher: Scott Adams. Publishes 2-3 titles/year. Pays 10-15% royalty on wholesale price. Publishes book 1 year after acceptance of ms. Reports in 2 months on queries and proposals. Manuscript guidelines for #10 SASE.

Nonfiction: Innovative outdoor adventure and travel guidebooks. "We welcome ideas that explore the world of adventure and wonder; from day hikes to mountain bikes, from surf to skis. Our books are designed to open up new worlds of experiences for those anxious to explore, and to provide the detailed information necessary to get them started." Query with outline, methods of research and SASE. Reviews artwork/photos as part of ms package. Send proof prints. Recent nonfiction title: *Mountain Bike Indiana*, by Layne Cameron (guidebook).

Tips: "Someone interested in writing for us should be both an avid outdoors person and an expert in their area of interest. This person should have a clear understanding of maps and terrain and should enjoy sharing their adventurous spirit and enthusiasm with others."

BLACK TOOTH PRESS, 768 N. 26th St., Philadelphia PA 19130. (215)232-6611. Contact: Jim Anderson. Publishes trade paperback originals. Publishes 2 titles/year. Pays royalty by arrangement. Offers $500 advance. Reports in 2 months.

Nonfiction: Accepts only material of local interest to Philadelphia or nonfiction material related to beer. Query with SASE. Recent nonfiction title: *Stu Bykofsky's Little Black Book—A Gentleman's Guide to Philadelphia*. "We're looking for work which conforms to our slogan: 'Quick reading for the short-attention-span 90s!' "

BLISS PUBLISHING CO., P.O. Box 920, Marlborough MA 01752. (508)779-2827. Publisher: Stephen H. Clouter. Publishes hardcover and trade paperback originals. Publishes 2-4 titles/year. Pays 10-15% royalty on wholesale price. No advance. Reports in 2 months.

Nonfiction: Biography, illustrated book, reference, textbook. Subjects include government/politics, history, music/dance, nature/environment, recreation, regional. Submit proposal package, including outline, table of contents, bio, 2 sample chapters and SASE. Recent nonfiction title: *Ninnuock, The Algonkian People of New England*, by Steven F. Johnson.

‡BLUE SKY MARKETING, INC., P.O. Box 21583, St. Paul MN 55121. (612)456-5602. President: Vic Spadaccini. Publishes hardcover and trade paperback originals. Publishes 3 titles/year. Pays royalty on wholesale price. Reports in 3 months. Manuscript guidelines for 6×9 SAE with 4 first-class stamps.

Nonfiction: Gift book, how-to. Subjects include gardening, hobbies, regional, travel, house and home. We prefer proposals to mss. Submit proposal package, including outline, 1 sample chapter, author bio, intended market, analysis comparison to competing books with SASE. Recent nonfiction title: *Twin Cities Family Fun Spots*, by Lisa Sabroski (regional).

Fiction: Fantasy (children's fairy tales), juvenile, picture books. No adult poetry or literary. Query with synopsis, 1 sample chapter and SASE.
Tips: "Our books are primarily 'giftbooks.' They are sold to women primarily. They are sold in specialty stores/gift shops as well as bookstores."

‡**BOOKS BEYOND BORDERS LLC**, 3640 Walnut St., Suite A, Boulder CO 80301. (303)449-6440. Managing Editor: Judith Rydlun. Publishes 3 titles/year. Pays 8-10% royalty on wholesale price. Reports in 1 month on proposals. *Writer's Market* recommends allowing 2 months for reply. Book catalog and ms guidelines free on request.
Nonfiction: Biography, self-help. Subjects include ethnic, gay/lesbian, health/medicine, history, philosophy, psychology, women's issues/studies, spirituality. "Material should honor the persistence and power of life. We are looking for material that will affect change." Query. Submit proposal package, including outline, 2 sample chapters and anticipated markets/author biography. Recent nonfiction title: *Until Darkness Hold No Fear*, by Elizabeth Julie Mikal (psychology/MPD).

BRETT BOOKS, INC., P.O. Box 290-637, Brooklyn NY 11229-0011. Publisher: Barbara J. Brett. Estab. 1993. Publishes hardcover originals. Publishes 2 titles/year. Pays 5-15% royalty on retail price. Offers advance beginning at $1,500. Reports in 2 months on queries.
Nonfiction: General interest nonfiction books on timely subjects. Uplifting, inspirational nonfiction. Query with SASE. Recent nonfiction title: *Where Miracles Happen: True Stories of Heavenly Encounters*, by Joan Wester Anderson (inspirational).

BRIGHT MOUNTAIN BOOKS, INC., 138 Springside Rd., Asheville NC 28803. (704)684-8840. Editor: Cynthia F. Bright. Imprint is Historical Images. Publishes hardcover and trade paperback originals and reprints. Publishes 3 titles/year. Pays 5-10% royalty on retail price. No advance. Reports in 1 month on queries. *Writer's Market* recommends allowing 2 months for reply.
Nonfiction: "Our current emphasis is on regional titles, which can include nonfiction by local writers." Query with SASE. Recent nonfiction title: *Mountain Fever*, by Tom Alexander (regional autobiography).

BRIGHT RING PUBLISHING, INC., P.O. Box 31338, Bellingham WA 98228-3338. (360)734-1601. Owner: Mary Ann Kohl. Publishes trade paperback originals on creative ideas for children. No crafts, fiction, poetry or picture books. Publishes 1 title/year. Pays 3-5% royalty on net price. Offers $500 advance. Reports in 2 months. Manuscript guidelines for SASE.
Nonfiction: "Only books which specifically fit our format will be considered: art or creative activities with 1) materials 2) procedure 3) variations/extensions. One idea per page, about 150 ideas total. No crafts, stories or poetry." Query with 1-2 sample chapters or submit proposal package, including complete book, with SASE. *Writer's Market* recommends sending a query with SASE first. Recent nonfiction title: *Science Arts*, by Kohl & Potter (science experiments that are also art projects).
Tips: "Send for guidelines first. Check out books at the library or bookstore to see what style the publisher likes. Submit only ideas that specifically relate to the company's list."

BROADWAY PRESS, P.O. Box 1037, Shelter Island NY 11964-1037. (516)749-3266. Fax: (516)749-3267. Publisher: David Rodger. Estab. 1985. E-mail: drodger_broadwaypress@esta.org. Website: http://www.esta.org/homepages/broadwaypress. Publishes trade paperback originals. Publishes 2-3 titles/year. Receives 50-75 submissions/year. 50% of books from first-time authors; 75% from unagented writers. Pays negotiable royalty. Publishes book 18 months after acceptance. Accepts simultaneous submissions. Reports in 3 months on queries.
Nonfiction: Reference, technical. Subjects include theatre, film, television, performing arts. "We're looking for professionally-oriented and authored books." Submit outline and sample chapters. Recent nonfiction title: *Arena Rigging*, by Steve Nelson (field guide).
Tips: "Our readers are primarily professionals in the entertainment industries. Submissions that really grab our attention are aimed at that market."

CADMUS EDITIONS, P.O. Box 126, Tiburon CA 94920. Director: Jeffrey Miller. Publishes hardcover and trade paperback originals. Publishes 3-4 titles/year. Pays negotiated royalty. No advance. Reports in 1 month. *Writer's Market* recommends allowing 2 months for reply.
Fiction: Literary fiction. "We publish only 3-4 titles per year and are thus seeking only truly distinguished work." Query with SASE. Recent fiction title: *The Pelcari Project*, by R. Rey Rusa (novel about Guatemalan abuse of human rights).
Poetry: Query with SASE. Recent poetry title: *Wandering into the Wind*, by Sāntoka, translated by Cid Corman (Haiku poetry of last wandering itinerant monk in Japan).
Tips: "Do not submit unless work is truly distinguished and will fit well in our short but carefully selected and produced title list."

CALYX BOOKS, P.O. Box B, Corvallis OR 97339-0539. (541)753-9384. Also publishes *Calyx, A Journal of Art & Literature by Women*. Managing Editor: Margarita Donnelly. Estab. 1986 for Calyx Books; 1976 for Calyx, Inc. Publishes fine literature by women, fiction, nonfiction and poetry. Publishes 3 titles/year. Pays 10% royalty on net price. Offers $200-$800 advance. Reports in 6 months on queries.
  • Calyx Books is open for nonfiction queries only in 1996. Query with SASE for guidelines and deadlines on fiction and poetry books in 1997.
Nonfiction: Query with outline, 1 sample chapter and SASE. Recent nonfiction title: *The Violet Shyness of Their Eyes: Notes from Nepal*, by Barbara Scot (teaching/travel memoir).
Tips: "Please be familiar with our publications."

‡**CAROLINA WREN PRESS**, 120 Morris St., Durham NC 27701. (919)560-2738. "We are interested in poetry, fiction, nonfiction, biography, autobiography, literary nonfiction work by and/or about people of color, women, gay/lesbian issues."

CAROUSEL PRESS, P.O. Box 6061, Albany CA 94706-0061. (510)527-5849. Editor and Publisher: Carole T. Meyers. Estab. 1976. Publishes trade paperback originals and reprints. Publishes 1-2 titles/year. Pays 10-15% royalty on wholesale price. Offers $1,000 advance. Reports in 1 month on queries. *Writer's Market* recommends allowing 2 months for reply.
Nonfiction: Family-oriented travel and other travel books. Query with outline, 1 sample chapter and SASE. Recent nonfiction title: *The Zoo Book: A Guide to America's Best*, by A. Nyhius (guide).

CARTER PRESS, P.O. Box 1136, Oakland CA 94604. (510)208-3654. Publisher: David Carter. Publishes 2-3 titles/year. "Carter Press specializes in creative fiction, usually character-driven works. We are not interested in genre pieces (i.e., mystery, suspense, detective, etc.)." Recent fiction title: *The Ballad of Nonose Valley*, by J.P. Bernhard (outdoor fiction).

CENTER FOR AFRICAN-AMERICAN STUDIES PUBLICATIONS, University of California at Los Angeles, 160 Haines Hall, 405 Hilgard Ave., Los Angeles CA 90095-1545. (310)206-6340. Managing Editor: Toyomi Igus. Publishes hardcover and trade paperback originals. "All manuscripts should be scholarly works about the African-American experience. Authors should be able to demonstrate a thorough knowledge of the subject matter. Not interested in autobiographies, poetry or fiction." Recent title: *Residential Apartheid: The American Legacy*, edited by Robert Bullard, J. Eugene Grigsby III and Charles Lee.

CHARLES RIVER PRESS, 427 Old Town Court, Alexandria VA 22314-3544. (703)519-9197. Editor-in-Chief: Lynn Page Whittaker. Publishes trade paperback originals and reprints. Publishes 5 titles/year. Pays 5-15% royalty on wholesale price. Offers $0-1,000 advance. Reports in 1 month on proposals. *Writer's Market* recommends allowing 2 months for reply.
Nonfiction: Biography and general nonfiction. Subjects include Americana, ethnic, history (especially African-American), women's issues/studies (especially women's stories), travel memoirs, race relations. Submit proposal package, including outline, 1 sample chapter, letter saying why you have written the book, audience for it, bio and SASE. No phone calls, please. Recent nonfiction title: *Wave-Rings in the Water: My Years with the Women of Postwar Japan*, by Carmen Johnson (history/memoir).
Tips: "While I'm interested in personal stories and will consider first-time authors, writers should keep in mind that simply writing down their or other family's stories does not justify publication. I'm looking for writers who have achieved deep understanding and insights into those stories and their meaning. I am especially interested in stories of individuals that illustrate historical events and social issues and in academic work that can be adapted to a general audience."

CHRISTIAN MEDIA, Box 448, Jacksonville OR 97530. (541)899-8888. E-mail: cmedia@cosnet.net. Sole Proprietor: James Lloyd. Publishes trade paperback originals. Also publishes a bimonthly newsletter, particularly interested in exposés of Christian organizations, ministries or artists (musicians, writers, etc.) that are behaving in a manner that brings the cause of Christ into disrepute.

CLARITY PRESS INC., 3277 Roswell Rd. NE, #469, Atlanta GA 30305. (404)231-0649. Fax: (404)231-3899. E-mail: clarity@islandnet.com. Website: http://www.bookmasters.com/clarity. Editorial Committee Contact: Annette Gordon. Estab. 1984. Publishes mss on minorities, human rights in US, Middle East and Africa. No fiction. Responds *only* if interested, so do *not* enclose SASE.
Nonfiction: Human rights/minority issues. Query. Recent nonfiction title: *American Indians: Myths & Realities*, by Devon A. Mihesuah (trade/university level text).
Tips: "Check our titles on website."

CLEVELAND STATE UNIVERSITY POETRY CENTER, R.T. 1815, Cleveland State University, Cleveland OH 44115. (216)687-3986. Fax: (216)687-6943. Editor: Leonard M. Trawick. Estab. 1962. Publishes trade paperback and hardcover originals. Publishes 3 titles/year. Receives 400 queries and 900 mss/year. 60% of books from first-time authors; 100% from unagented writers. 30% of titles subsidized by CSU,

20% by government subsidy. CSU Poetry Series pays one-time, lump-sum royalty of $200-400 plus 50 copies; Cleveland Poetry Series (Ohio poets only) pays 100 copies. $1,000 prize for best ms each year. No advance. Publishes book 1 year after acceptance. Accepts simultaneous submissions. Reports in 2 weeks on queries, 8 months on mss. Book catalog for 6×9 SAE with 2 first-class stamps. Manuscript guidelines for SASE.

Poetry: No light verse, "inspirational," or greeting card verse. ("This does not mean that we do not consider poetry with humor or philosophical/religious import.") Query—ask for guidelines. Submit only December-February. $15 reading fee. Reviews artwork/photos if applicable (e.g., concrete poetry). Recent poetry title: *Improvising Rivers*, by David Jauss.

Tips: "Our books are for serious readers of poetry, i.e. poets, critics, academics, students, people who read *Poetry, Field, American Poetry Review*, etc. Trends include movement away from 'confessional' poetry; greater attention to form and craftsmanship. Try to project an interesting, coherent personality; link poems so as to make coherent unity, not just a miscellaneous collection. Especially needs poems with *mystery*, i.e., poems that suggest much, but do not tell all."

CORKSCREW PRESS, INC., 2300 W. Victory, Suite C-313, Burbank CA 91506. Editorial Director: J. Croker Norge. Estab. 1988. Reports in 6 months.
Nonfiction: Publishes trade humor and humorous how-to books.

DELANCEY PRESS, P.O. Box 40285, Philadelphia PA 19106. (215)238-9103. E-mail: morrcomm@aol.com. Editorial Director: Wesley Morrison. Estab. 1990. "We are open to reviewing all types of nonfiction. Queries by *letter* only; *no initial contact by phone.*"

‡DICKENS PRESS, P.O. Box 4289, Irvine CA 92716. (714)725-0788. Editorial Director: Diane Dennis. Publishes hardcover and trade paperback originals. Publishes 2-3 titles/year. Pays 12-16% royalty on wholesale price or offers work-for-hire. Offers up to $7,500 advance. Reports in 1 month on queries and proposals; 2 months on mss. Manuscript guidelines free on request.
Nonfiction: Coffee table book, gift book, how-to, humor, reference and self-help. Subjects include child guidance/parenting, education, government/politics, history and psychology. Query. Submit proposal package, including: outline, sample chapters, author bio, market analysis and SASE. Recent nonfiction title: *Ambush at Ruby Ridge*, by Alan Bock.
Fiction: Humor, mainstream/contemporary, picture books and suspense. Query with synopsis and 3 sample chapters. All unsolicited mss returned unopened.
Tips: "Audience consists of people who want to have more control over their lives by being better informed."

DISKOTECH, INC., 7930 State Line, Suite 210, Prairie Village KS 66208. (913)432-8606. Fax: (913)432-8606*51. E-mail: 74472.2263@compuserve.com. Submissions Editor: Jane Locke. Estab. 1989. Publishes multimedia nonfiction and fiction for PC's on CD-ROM. Publishes 2 titles/year. Pays 10-15% royalty on wholesale price. Reports in 2 months on queries, 4 months on proposals.
   ● Diskotech, Inc. is publishing a new form of the novel, a CVN® (computerized video novel), that combines print, software and video for CD-ROM.
Nonfiction: Considers most nonfiction subjects. Query first with SASE. Recent nonfiction title: *The Martensville Nighmare CVN®*, by Karen Smith (true crime story on CD-ROM text).
Fiction: Considers all fiction genres. Recent fiction title: *Negative Space CVN®*, (computerized video novel) by Holly Franking.

‡DOWLING PRESS, INC., 3200 West End Ave., Suite 500, Nashville TN 37203. (615)783-1668. President: M. McCombs. Publishes hardcover, trade paperback and mass market paperback originals. Publishes 5 titles/year. Receives 150 queries and 100 mss/year. Pays royalty on wholesale price. No advance. Reports in 4 months on queries, 6 months on proposals and mss. Manuscript guidelines free on request.
Nonfiction: Biography, cookbook, gift book, how-to, humor, self-help. Subjects include Americana, cooking/foods/nutrition, gardening, gay/lesbian, hobbies, music/dance, women's issues/studies. Query with outline, 3 sample chapters and SASE. Recent nonfiction title: *The Good Girls' Guide to Great Sex*, by Thom W. King and Debora Peterson (sexuality).
Tips: Audience is 18-40 year olds, middle class. "Please proofread! There is nothing worse than carelessness (especially in a cover letter). Don't call us a day after we've received the manuscript to ask what we think! Be patient."

DOWN THE SHORE PUBLISHING, Imprint of Cormorant Books & Calendars, 534 Cedar Run Dock Rd., Cedar Run NJ 08092. Publisher: Raymond G. Fisk. Publishes hardcover originals and trade paperback originals and reprints. "As a small regional publisher, we must limit our efforts and resources to our established market: New Jersey shore and mid-Atlantic. We specialize in regional histories and pictorial, coffee table books." Query with synopsis.

EARTH-LOVE PUBLISHING HOUSE LTD., 3440 Youngfield St., Suite 353, Wheat Ridge CO 80033. (303)233-9660. Fax: (303)233-9354. Director: Laodeciae Augustine. Publishes trade paperback originals and reprints. Publishes 1-2 books/year. Pays 6-10% royalty on wholesale price. No advance. Reports in 1 month on queries and proporals, 4 months on mss.
Nonfiction: Metaphysics and minerals. Query with SASE. Recent nonfiction title: *Love Is In The Earth— A Kaleidoscope of Crystals Update*, by Melody (metaphysical reference).

EASTERN PRESS, P.O. Box 881, Bloomington IN 47402-0881. Publisher: Don Lee. Estab. 1981. Publishes hardcover originals and reprints, trade paperback originals. Publishes 3 title/year. Pays by arrangement with author. No advance. Reports in 1 month on queries. *Writer's Market* recommends allowing 2 months for reply.
Nonfiction: Academic books on Asian subjects and pedagogy on languages. Query with outline, sample chapter and SASE. Recent nonfiction title: *An Annotated Prehistoric Bibliography on S. Asia.*

‡**ECOPRESS**, 1029 NE Kirsten Place, Corvallis OR 97330. (541)758-7545. Editor-in-Chief: Christopher Beatty. Publishes hardcover originals, trade paperback originals and reprints. Publishes 2-4 titles/year. Pays 6-15% royalty on retail price. Offers $0-5,000 advance. Reports in 1 month on queries and proposals, 3 months on mss. Manuscript guidelines for #10 SASE.
Nonfiction: Coffee table book, how-to, multimedia (CD or electronic). Subjects include agriculture/horticulture, animals, art/architecture, education, gardening, nature/environment, recreation (outdoor, hiking), science, sports (outdoor, fishing). "The work must have some aspect that enhances environmental awareness." Submit proposal package, including outline, 3 sample chapters and how the author would participate in marketing the work. Recent nonfiction title: *Two Wheels Around New Zealand*, by S. Bischke.
Fiction: Mainstream/contemporary. "There must be some aspect of the work that deals with nature or the environment." Query with synopsis. Recent fiction title: *Journey of the Tern*, by R. Beatty (novel).
Tips: Audience is "nature-oriented people and those who could be after reading our books!" Nonfiction: 1) Pick an issue you care about; 2) Make a proposal; 3) Do research; 4) Write and submit a manuscript.

‡**ESSENTIAL MEDICAL INFORMATION SYSTEMS, INC.**, P.O. Box 1607, Durant OK 74702. Vice President-Operations: Mark Gibson. Publishes trade paperback originals. Publishes 2 titles/year. Pays 12-17% royalty. Reports in 1 month on queries, 2 months on proposals and mss. Book catalog and manuscript guidelines free on request.
Nonfiction: Reference. Subjects include health/medicine and psychology. Submit proposal package, including outline, 2 sample chapters and estimated mass market potential. Recent nonfiction title: *Managing Contraceptive Pill Patients*, by Richard P. Dickey, M.D. (medical reference).
Tips: Audience is medical professionals and medical product manufacturers and distributors.

EVRAS PRESS, P.O. Box 5692, Hercules CA 94547. Managing Editor: Tony Sakkis. Publishes mass market paperback originals. Publishes 1-2 titles/year. Pays 10-25% royalty on wholesale price. Offers $1,000-10,000 advance. Manuscript guidelines for SASE.
Nonfiction: Reference, technical. Subjects include ethnic, sports, translation, travel. "We are looking for work that can fill out our universal guide series as well as automotive- and motorsports-related works. Recent nonfiction title: *Indy Championship Racing Guide: 1909-1996.*

EXCALIBUR PUBLISHING, 434 Avenue of Americas, #790, New York NY 10011. (212)777-1790. Publisher: Sharon Good. "We are interested in business, parenting and performing arts titles."

‡**FALLEN LEAF PRESS**, P.O. Box 10034, Berkeley CA 94709-5034. Phone/fax: (510)848-7805. E-mail: abasart@uclink.berkeley.edu. Owner: Ann Basart. Estab. 1984. Publishes reference books on music, books on contemporary composers and scores of contemporary American chamber music. "We publish three series: Fallen Leaf Reference Books in Music; Fallen Leaf Monographs in Contemporary Composers; and a series of musical scores, Fallen Leaf Publications in Contemporary Music." Publishes 2-5 books/year. Pays 10-15% royalty on wholesale price. Offers $250-500 advance. Reports in 2 months.
Nonfiction: "Reference books are scholarly, aimed at music librarians and/or performers; authors/compilers should be experienced bibliography, if possible. Monographs on 20th-century composers are aimed at general music-loving audiences, not for specialists." Submit proposal package, including outline, sample entries (for reference books) or outline and sample chapters for books on composers. Recent nonfiction title: *Confronting Silence*, by Toru Takemitsu (essays).

THE FAMILY ALBUM, Rt. 1, Box 42, Glen Rock PA 17327. (717)235-2134. Fax: (717)235-8765. E-mail: ronbiblio@delphi.com. Contact: Ron Lieberman. Estab. 1969. Publishes hardcover originals and reprints and software. Publishes 2 titles/year. Average print order for a first book is 1,000. Pays royalty on wholesale price. "Significant works in the field of (nonfiction) bibliography. Worthy submissions in the field of Pennsylvania history, folk art and lore. We are also seeking materials relating to books, literacy, and national development. Special emphasis on Third World countries, and the role of printing in international development." No religious material. Submit outline and sample chapters.

FATHOM PUBLISHING COMPANY, P.O. Box 200448, Anchorage AK 99520-0448. (907)272-3305. E-mail: fathompub@aol.com. Publisher: Constance Taylor. Publishes 1-2 trade paperback originals/year on Alaskana history, legal issues and reference. Prefers author participation in marketing efforts. Pays 10-15% royalty on retail price. No advance. Reports in 1 month. *Writer's Market* recommends allowing 2 months for reply.
Nonfiction: Wants Alaska legal issues or related texts. Submit outline, 1 sample chapter. Recent nonfiction title: *Valley of the Eagles*, by Cary Anderson (natural history).
Fiction: Wants Alaska related fiction. Query with outline, 1 sample chapter.

FIESTA CITY PUBLISHERS, ASCAP, P.O. Box 5861, Santa Barbara CA 93150. (805)733-1984. Publishes hardcover, trade paperback and mass market paperback originals. Publishes 2-3 titles/year. Pays 5-20% royalty on wholesale price. No advance. Reports in 1 month on queries and proposals, 3 months on mss. Book catalog and ms guidelines for #10 SASE.
Nonfiction: Children's/juvenile, cookbook, how-to, humor nonfiction and musical plays. "Prefers material appealing to young readers, especially related to music: composing, performing, etc." Query with outline and SASE. Recent nonfiction title: *Anything I Can Play, You Can Play Better* (self-teaching guitar method).
Fiction: Musical plays only. Query with SASE. Recent fiction title: *Break Point*, by Eddie Franck (juvenile musical play).

FILTER PRESS, P.O. Box 95, Palmer Lake CO 80133-0095. (719)481-2420. President: Doris Baker. Estab. 1956. Publishes trade paperback originals and reprints. Publishes 2-3 titles/year. Pays 10% royalty on wholesale price. Publishes ms an average of 8 months after acceptance.
Nonfiction: Subjects include Americana, anthropology/archaeology, cooking/foods/nutrition, ethnic, hobbies, regional, travel. "We're interested in the history of the American West, the natural history of the West, history of place names, etc. We will consider some Western Americana, up to 72 pages. We do not want family diaries. Most of our works are reprints of 19th century published things on Indians, Gold rushes, western exploration, etc. Very rarely do we use unsolicited material. I dream up a project, find an author in 90% of them." Query with SASE. Reviews artwork/photos as part of ms package.

FLOWER VALLEY PRESS, INC., 7851-C Beechcraft Ave., Gaithersburg MD 20879. (301)990-6405. Editor: Seymour Bress. Publishes hardcover and trade paperback originals and reprints. Publishes 3 titles/year. Book catalog for #10 SASE.
Nonfiction: Coffee table book, how-to nonfiction. Subjects include art, crafts and jewelry made with Polymer clay. "We look particularly for new and unique work of high quality (all of our recent books have been completely illustrated in color) and where the market for the book is relatively easy to identify and reach. Query. Reviews artwork/photos as part of ms package. Send transparencies. Recent nonfiction title: *The New Clay*, by Nan Roche (how-to).
Fiction: "Must catch us in the opening chapter or we'll never read beyond it." Submit synopsis and 1 sample chapter.

FRONT ROW EXPERIENCE, 540 Discovery Bay Blvd., Byron CA 94514-9454. Phone/fax: (510)634-5710. Contact: Frank Alexander. Estab. 1974. Imprint is Kokono. Publishes trade paperback originals and reprints. Publishes 1-2 titles/year. Pays 10% royalty on income received. No advance. Reports in 1 month. *Writer's Market* recommends allowing 2 months for reply.
Nonfiction: Teacher/educator edition paperback originals. Only wants submissions for "Movement Education," special education and related areas. Will accept submissions for parenting type books only from those people who are active in the field and can promote it through their activities. Query with SASE. Recent nonfiction title: *Funsical Fitness*, by Scott Liebler (movement education lesson plans for pre-k and early elementary).

GAFF PRESS, P.O. Box 1024, Astoria OR 97103-3051. (503)325-8288. Publisher: Paul Barrett. Publishes hardcover and trade paperback originals, poetry chapbooks. Publishes 1-2 titles/year. Payment varies with individual. Reports in 1 month. *Writer's Market* recommends allowing 2 months for reply.
Nonfiction: "Particularly interested in extraordinary ocean tales for next (third) book of sea stories and wondrous irresistible poems." Query with sample chapter and SASE. Recent nonfiction title: *How to Make a Book*, by John Paul Barrett.
Poetry: "I want to see only the absolute best the poet can offer." Submit 10 sample poems or complete ms with SASE. Recent poetry title: *The Bearheart Chronicles*, by L.B. Doran-Maurer.

GAMBLING TIMES INCORPORATED, 16140 Valerio St., Suite B, Van Nuys CA 91406-2916. (818)781-9355. Fax: (818)781-3125. Publisher: Stanley R. Suudikoff. Publishes hardcover and trade paperback originals. Publishes 2-4 titles/year. Pays royalty. No advance. Reports in 2 months on queries, 3 months on proposals, 6 months on mss.

Nonfiction: How-to and reference books on gambling. Submit proposal package, including ms and SASE. *Writer's Market* recommends sending a query with SASE first. Recent nonfiction title: *Book of Tells*, by Caro (poker).

GOOD BOOK PUBLISHING COMPANY, 2747 S. Kihei Rd., G102, Kihei HI 96753. Phone/fax: (808)874-4876. Publisher: Richard G. Burns. Publishes trade paperback originals and reprints. Publishes 5 titles/year. Pay 10% royalty. No advance. Reports in 1 month. *Writer's Market* recommends allowing 2 months for reply.

Nonfiction: Spiritual roots of Alcoholics Anonymous. Query with SASE. Recent nonfiction title: *New Light on Alcoholism*, by Dick B. (history of early AAs spiritual roots).

GREAT OCEAN PUBLISHERS, 1823 N. Lincoln St., Arlington VA 22207-3746. President: Mark Esterman. Estab. 1975. Publishes hardcover and trade paperback originals. Publishes 3-5 titles/year. Pays 10-15% royalty on wholesale price. Offers $1,000-3,000 advance. Reports in 1 month on queries and proposals, 3 months on mss.

Nonfiction: Biography, how-to, illustrated book, reference, self-help technical and educational. Submit outline, 3 sample chapters and SASE. Recent nonfiction title: *Smart Moves: Why Learning Is Not All in Your Head*, by Carla Hannoford.

Tips: "Main interest and focus is in area of *learning* as applied to school, home, workplace. We're interested in new ideas and new approaches to problems or issues."

GREENLAWN PRESS, 107 S. Greenlawn Ave., South Bend IN 46617. (219)234-5088. Publishes trade paperback originals and reprints. Publishes 1 title/year. Receives 10 queries and 5 mss/year. 50% of books from first-time authors; 100% from unagented writers. Pays royalty. Reports in 2 months.

Nonfiction: Christian. "We publish Christian books only, including books on prayer, personal relationships, family life, testimonies." Submit outline. Recent nonfiction title: *Into the Lion's Den*, by Tom Noe.

HEMINGWAY WESTERN STUDIES SERIES, Boise State University, 1910 University Dr., Boise ID 83725. (208)385-1999. Fax: (208)385-4373. E-mail: rentrusk@idbsu.idbsu.edu. Editor: Tom Trusky. Publishes multiple edition artist's books which deal with Rocky Mountain political, social and environmental issues. Write for author's guidelines and catalog.

HERBAL STUDIES LIBRARY, 219 Carl St., San Francisco CA 94117. (415)564-6785. Fax: (415)564-6799. Owner: J. Rose. Publishes trade paperback originals. Publishes 3 titles/year. Pays 5-10% royalty on retail price. Offers $500 advance. Reports in 1 month on mss with SASE. *Writer's Market* recommends allowing 2 months for reply.

Nonfiction: How-to, reference, self-help. Subjects include gardening, health/medicine, herbs and aromatherapy. No New Age. Query with sample chapter and SASE. Recent nonfiction title: *Guide to Essential Oils*, by Jeanne Rose (scientific information about essential oils).

‡HI-TIME PUBLISHING CORP., P.O. Box 33337-0337, Milwaukee WI 53213. (414)466-2420. Senior Editor: Lorraine M. Kukulski. Publishes 3 titles/year. Payment method may be outright purchase, royalty or down payment plus royalty. Book catalog and ms guidelines free on request.

Nonfiction: "We publish religious education material for Catholic junior high through adult programs. Most of our material is contracted in advance and written by persons with theology or religious education backgrounds. Query with SASE. Recent nonfiction title: *Family Faith & Fun Activities, Games & Prayer for Sharing Faith at Home*, by Gary Boelhower, Ph.D.

W.D. HOARD & SONS CO., Imprint of Hoard's Dairyman, 28 Milwaukee Ave. W., Fort Atkinson WI 53538-0801. Editor: Elvira Kau. Estab. 1870. Publishes trade paperback originals. Publishes 3-4 titles/year. Pays 8-15% royalty on wholesale or retail price. No advance. Reports in 2½ weeks on queries and mss. *Writer's Market* recommends allowing 2 months for reply.

Nonfiction: "We primarily are a dairy publishing company, but we have had success with a veterinarian who authored two James Herriott-type humor books for us, and we would consider regional (Wisconsin) titles as well. We also have published and would like to see submissions for agricultural science texts." Query with SASE. Recent nonfiction title: *The Dairy Cow Today*, by S. Spahr and G. Opperman (dairy, agscience).

THE HOFFMAN PRESS, P.O. Box 2996, Santa Rosa CA 95405. Publisher: R.P. Hoffman. Publishes mass market paperback originals. Publishes 2-4 titles/year. Pays 5-10% royalty on retail price or makes outright purchase of $0-3,000. No advance. Publishes book 2 years after acceptance of ms. Reports in 2 months.

Nonfiction: "We publish cookbooks only." Query with 3 sample chapters and SASE. Reviews artwork/photos as part of ms package. Send photocopies. Recent nonfiction title: *The California Wine Country Herbs & Spices Cookbook.*

I.A.A.S. PUBLISHERS, 7676 New Hampshire Ave., Langley Park MD 20783. (301)499-6308. Senior Editor, New Manuscripts: Anthony Green. Publishes hardcover, trade paperback and mass market paperback originals. Manuscript guidelines on request.
Nonfiction: Biography, children's/juvenile, how-to, illustrated book, textbook, Afro-America. Subjects include business and economics, child guidance/parenting, education, government/politics, health/medicine, history, military/war, money/finance, philosophy, psychology, sociology, Afro-American/African issues. Request "Guidelines for Authors" in advance of submission. Submit proposal package. Recent nonfiction title: *Cultural and Demographic Aspects of Health Care in Contemporary Sub-Saharan Africa,* edited by Ezekiel Kalipeni and Philip Thiuri.

IN PRINT PUBLISHING, 6770 W. State Route 89A, 346, Sedona AZ 86336-9758. (520)282-4589. Fax: (520)282-4631. Publisher/Editor: Tomi Keitlen. Estab. 1991. Publishes trade paperback originals. Publishes 2-5 titles/year. Pays 6-8% royalty on retail price. Offers $500 advance. Reports in 2 months.
Nonfiction: "We are interested in books that will leave a reader with hope. We are also interested in books that are metaphysical, books that give ideas and help for small business management and books that have impact in all general subjects. No violence, sex or poetry." Query with SASE. Recent nonfiction title: *Time for Truth,* by Princess Ashraf Pahlavi (political/history).
Tips: "We are interested in books about Angels. We are also interested in short books that will be part of a Living Wisdom Series™. These books must be no more than 18,000-20,000 words. We are not interested in any books that are over 300 pages—and are more likely interested in 75,000 words or less."

INDIANA HISTORICAL SOCIETY, 315 W. Ohio St., Indianapolis IN 46202-3299. (317)232-1882. Fax: (317)233-3109. Director of Publications: Thomas A. Mason. Estab. 1830. Publishes hardcover originals. Publishes 3 titles/year. Pays 6% royalty on retail price. Reports in 1 month on queries. *Writer's Market* recommends allowing 2 months for reply.
Nonfiction: "We seek book-length manuscripts that are solidly researched and engagingly written on topics related to the history of Indiana." Query with SASE. Recent nonfiction title: *The Miami Indians of Indiana: A Persistent People, 1654-1994,* by Stewart Rafert.

INTERTEXT, 2633 East 17th Ave., Anchorage AK 99508-3207. Editor: Sharon Ann Jaeger. Estab. 1982. Publishes trade paperback originals. Publishes 1-2 titles/year. Pays 10% or print run and 10% of profits. No advance. Reports in 1 month on samples. *Writer's Market* recommends allowing 2 months for reply.
Poetry: "We look for poetry that is rich in imagery, is skillfully crafted, is powerful and compelling and avails itself of the varied resonance and melody of the language. Cannot use religious verse. We expect book manuscripts to run 48-96 pages. (Please do *not* send an entire manuscript unless we specifically ask to see it.") Submit 3-5 sample poems by first-class mail with SASE. Recent poetry title: *Pelted with Petals: The Burmese Poems,* by Ky: May Kaung.
Tips: "Intertext is extremely selective; thus beginners should submit elsewhere. We regret that we cannot offer critiques of rejected work. Queries and samples lacking SASE cannot be returned. Cover letters need not be elaborate; fine poems (your sample) speak for themselves. Poets we admire include William Stafford, Gary Snyder, W.S. Merwin, A.R. Ammons, Robert Morgan, Charles Wright, Sarah Kirsch, António Ramos Rosa, Rainer Maria Rilke, Louis Hammer, Tomas Tranströmer and Bob Perelman."

INVERTED-A, INC., 401 Forrest Hill, Grand Prairie TX 75052. (214)264-0066. Editors: Amnon Katz and Aya Katz. Estab. 1977. Publishes nonfiction books on a range of subjects, novellas, short story collections and poetry. Reports in 1 month. Query with SASE.

ITHACA PRESS, P.O. Box 853, Lowell MA 01853. General Editor: Charles E. Ziavras. Publishes mass market paperback originals. Pays royalty on retail price. No advance. Reports in 1 month on queries. *Writer's Market* recommends allowing 2 months for reply.
Fiction: Publishes historical and mainstream/contemporary fiction. Query with SASE. Recent fiction title: *The Hero,* by Charles E. Ziavras (popular novel).

IVY LEAGUE PRESS, INC., P.O. Box 3326, San Ramon CA 94583-8326. 1-(800)IVY-PRESS or (510)736-0601. Fax: (510)736-0602. Editor: Maria Thomas. Publishes hardcover, trade paperback and mass market paperback originals. Reports in 3 months.
Nonfiction: Subjects include health/medicine, Judaica and self-help nonfiction. Query with SASE. Recent nonfiction title: *Jewish Divorce Ethics,* by Bulka.
Fiction: Medical suspense. Query with SASE. Recent fiction title: *Allergy Shots,* by Litman.
● Ivy League is focusing more on medical thrillers, although it still welcomes Judaica and other submissions.

JELMAR PUBLISHING CO., INC., P.O. Box 488, Plainview NY 11803. (516)822-6861. President: Joel J. Shulman. Publishes hardcover and trade paperback originals. Publishes 2-5 titles/year. Pays 25% royalty after initial production and promotion expenses of first printing.
Nonfiction: How-to and technical subjects on the packaging, package printing and printing fields. "The writer must be a specialist and recognized expert in the field." Query. Recent nonfiction title: *Graphic Design for Corrugated Packaging*, by Donald G. McCaughey Jr. (graphic design).

JOHNSTON ASSOCIATES, INTERNATIONAL (JASI), P.O. Box 313, Medina WA 98039. (206)454-3490. Publisher: Ann Schuessler. Publishes trade paperback originals. Publishes 3-5 titles/year. Pays 12-17% royalty on wholesale price. Offers $1,000-1,500 advance. Reports in 1 month. *Writer's Market* recommends allowing 2 months for reply.
Nonfiction: Travel and other nonfiction. Query with proposal package, including outline, sample chapter, target market, competition, reason why the book is different and SASE. Recent nonfiction title: *Microbreweries and Brewpubs of the Pacific Northwest*, by Dodd, Latterell, MacCormack and Zucker (regional guidebook).

KALI PRESS, P.O. Box 2169, Pagosa Springs CO 81147. (970)264-5200. Contact: Cynthia Olsen. Publishes trade paperback originals. Publishes 5 titles/year. Pays 8-12% royalty on retail price. No advance. Reports in 1 month on queries, 6 weeks on proposals, 2 months on mss.
Nonfiction: Children's/juvenile, natural health and spiritual nonfiction. Subjects include education (on natural health issues). Children's books with a lesson and natural health (international topics also). Query with 2 sample chapters and SASE. Reviews artwork/photos as part of ms package. Send photocopies. Recent nonfiction title: *Don't Drink the Water*, by Lono Kapua A'O (health/environmental).

LAHONTAN IMAGES, 210 S. Pine St., Susanville CA 96130. (916)257-6747. Fax: (916)251-4801. Owner: Tim I. Purdy. Estab. 1986. Publishes hardcover and trade paperback originals. Publishes 2 titles/year. Pays 10-15% royalty on wholesale or retail price. No advance. Reports in 2 months.
Nonfiction: Publishes nonfiction books pertaining to northeastern California and western Nevada. Query with outline and SASE. Recent nonfiction title: *Maggie Greeno*, by George McDow Jr. (biography).

‡LANDMINE BOOKS, P.O. Box 250702, Glendale CA 91225-0702. (213)860-9897. Editor: Jack Russell. Publishes trade paperback originals. Publishes 3 titles/year. Pays 5-7% royalty on retail price.
Nonfiction: Biography, how-to, reference, self-help. Subjects include Americana, cooking/foods/nutrition, education, health/medicine, history, language/literature, military/war, regional, translation. Query with SASE. All unsolicited mss returned unopened.
Fiction: Adventure, gothic, horror, literary, mainstream/contemporary, mystery, science fiction, suspense. Query with SASE. All unsolicited mss returned unopened. Recent fiction title: *Stripmall Bohemia*, by Jethro Paris (crime).

LAWCO LTD., P.O. Box 2009, Manteca CA 95336-1209. (209)239-6006. Imprints are Money Tree and Que House. Senior Editor: Bill Thompson. Publishes 1-6 titles/year. Pays 3-12% royalty on wholesale price or makes outright purchase of 2-4½¢/word. No advance. Reports in 1 month on queries. *Writer's Market* recommends allowing 2 months for reply.
Nonfiction: Books on billiards industry. "We are looking for business books targeting the small business. We will also consider sports-related books." Query with SASE. Recent nonfiction title: *The Backyard Cattle Ranch* (business-agriculture).
Tips: "Know the market, what the sales potential is, why the book is needed, who will buy it and why they will buy it."

‡LIBRARY OF VIRGINIA, 11th St. at Capitol Square, Richmond VA 23229. (804)786-2311. Director: of Publications: Sandra G. Treadway. Publishes hardcover and trade paperback originals. Publishes 3 titles/year. Payment varies. Reports in 1 month on queries and proposals, 3 months on mss. Book catalog and ms guidelines free on request.
Nonfiction: Biography, illustrated book, reference and monographs (documentary editions). Subjects include history and regional (Virginia). "We publish only in the field of Virginia history and culture." Query. Recent nonfiction title: *Women of Mark: History of the Woman's Club of Richmond*, by Sandra G. Treadway (history).
Tips: Audience is the general public interested in Virginia or Southern history, especially scholars and researchers.

LINCOLN SPRINGS PRESS, 32 Oak Place, Hawthorne NJ 07506. Contact: M. Gabrielle. Estab. 1987.
Nonfiction: Americana, ethnic, government/politics, history, language/literature, military/war, sociology, women's issues/studies. *Writer's Market* recommends sending a query with SASE first. Include SASE for reply or return.

Fiction: Ethnic, feminist, gothic, historical, literary, mainstream/contemporary, mystery, romance, short story collections. *Writer's Market* recommends sending a query with SASE first. Include SASE for reply or return of submission.

‡**LOLLIPOP POWER BOOKS**, 120 Morris St., Durham NC 27701. (919)560-2738. Editor: Ruth A. Smullin. Imprint of Carolina Wren Press. Imprint publishes trade paperback originals.
Fiction: "Current publishing pointers are 1) Books with African-American, Latino or native American charcaters 2) Bilingual Books (English/Spanish) 3) Books that show gay men or lesbian women as ordinary people who can raise children."

LORIEN HOUSE, P.O. Box 1112, Black Mountain NC 28711-1112. (704)669-6211. Owner/Editor: David A. Wilson. Estab. 1969. Publishes nonfiction. Subjects include Americana, history, nature/environment, philosophy, science. "I need only a few manuscripts at any time and therefore am very selective. I would like to see queries on the Appalachian region—nonfiction which can be technical or personal experience. I am 'fishing' for good material in what will be a new area for Lorien House."

McBOOKS PRESS, 908 Steam Mill Rd., Ithaca NY 14850. (607)272-2114. Publisher: Alexander G. Skutt. Publishes trade paperback originals and reprints. Pays 5-10% royalty on retail price. Offers $1,000-5,000 advance.
Nonfiction: Coffee table book, how-to, illustrated book, reference. Subjects include child guidance/parenting, cooking, regional, sports. "We are a small publishing house and we are only interested in queries within our narrow areas of interest: vegetarianism, parenting, regional books about upstate New York and (for a new imprint) sports history, records, and statistics." Query or submit outline and 2 sample chapters with SASE. Reports in 1 month. *Writer's Market* recommends allowing 2 months for reply. Recent nonfiction title: *Vegetarian Pregnancy*, by Sharon Yntema (nutrition/parenting).
Tips: Queries and proposals should be addressed to: Ms. S.K. List, Editorial Director.

MADWOMAN PRESS, P.O. Box 690, Northboro MA 01532-0690. (508)393-3447. E-mail: 76620.460@compuserve.com. Editor/Publisher: Diane Benison. Estab. 1991. Publishes 1-2 titles/year. Pays 15% royalty on revenues collected after production costs are recovered. No advance. Reports in 2 months.
Nonfiction: Lesbian fiction and nonfiction. Query with SASE a must. Recent nonfiction title: *Lesbians in the Military Speak Out*, by Winni S. Webber.
Fiction: We are primarily interested in mysteries. Query with SASE a must. Recent fiction title: *Fertile Betrayal*, by Becky Bohan (mystery).
Tips: "We hold ourselves out as a press that publishes *only* works by lesbian women. Please don't query if you don't meet the qualification. We make no exceptions to that policy."
 • Madwoman Press is looking for more mystery novels.

‡**MANGAJIN, INC.**, P.O. Box 7119, Marietta GA 30065. Publisher: V.P. Simmons. Publishes trade paperback originals. Publishes 2 titles/year. Pays 5-15% royalty on wholesale price. Reports in 2 months.
Nonfiction: Reference, textbook. Subjects include business and economics, government/politics, language/literature, religion, sociology, translation, travel. Mangajin publishes books about Japanese language and culture. Query. Recent nonfiction title: *Bringing Home the Sushi: Japanese Business Comics* (business).
Tips: Audience is "People interested in Japanese language and culture."

‡**MAUPIN HOUSE PUBLISHING**, P.O. Box 90148, Gainesville FL 32607-0148. Fax: (904)373-5588. Co-Publisher: Julia Graddy. Publishes trade paperback originals and reprints. Publishes 3 titles/year. Pays 5-10% royalty on retail price. Reports in 1 month on queries. *Writer's Market* recommends allowing 2 months for reply.
Nonfiction: Publishes nonfiction books on education, regional (Florida). "We are focusing on teacher resource books for language arts teachers K-12. We are looking for practical, in-classroom resource materials. Classroom teachers are our top choice as authors." Query with SASE. Recent nonfiction title: *Building a Writing Community*, by Marci Freemar (teacher resource for K-6).

‡**MEDIA FORUM INTERNATIONAL, LTD.**, RFD 1, P.O. Box 107, W. Danville VT 05873. (802)592-3444. or P.O. Box 265, Peacham VT 05862-0265. (802)592-3310. Managing Director: D.K. Bognár. Estab. 1969. Imprints are: Media Forum Books, Division, Ha' Penny Gourmet. Publishes hardcover and trade paperback originals. Publishes 2 titles/year. Pays 10% minimum royalty. "We are consultants primarily."
Nonfiction: Biography, humor, reference. Subjects include ethnic, broadcast/film. "All mss are assigned." Recent nonfiction title: *Ad Honorem/HIA*, projected for 1996/97.

MEYERBOOKS, PUBLISHER, P.O. Box 427, Glenwood IL 60425-0427. (708)757-4950. Publisher: David Meyer. Estab. 1976. Imprint is David Meyer Magic Books. Publishes hardcover and trade paperback originals and reprints. Publishes 5 titles/year. Pays 10-15% royalty on wholesale or retail price. No advance. Reports in 3 months on queries.

Nonfiction: History, reference and self-help works published on subjects of Americana, health and herbal studies, history of stage magic. Query with SASE. Recent nonfiction title: *Stage Flying: 431 B.C. to Modern Times*, by McKinven (theatrical history).

MIDDLE PASSAGE PRESS, 5517 Secrest Dr., Los Angeles CA 90043. (213)298-0266. Publisher: Barbara Bramwell. Estab. 1992. Publishes trade and mass market paperback and hardcover originals. Publishes 1 title/year. Pays 3-10% royalty on wholesale price. Offers $500-1,500 advance. Reports in 2 months.
Nonfiction: "The emphasis is on contemporary issues that deal directly with the African-American Experience. No fiction, no poetry." Query with SASE. Recent nonfiction title: *Beyond O.J.: Race, Sex & Class Lessons for America*, by Earl Ofari Hutchinson, Ph.D.
Tips: "Don't include scripts in place of manuscripts. I prefer query with 2 written chapters as opposed to a proposal. I want to see how someone writes."

MORTAL PRESS, 2315 N. Alpine Rd., Rockford IL 61107-1422. (815)399-8432. Editor/Publisher: Terry James Mohaupt. Publishes hardcover originals. Publishes 1 title/year. Royalty negotiable. No advance. "We will consider only works related to the fine arts, specifically literary and graphic arts, poetry or words and pictures."
Fiction: Query with SASE.
Poetry: Query with SASE.

MOSAIC PRESS MINIATURE BOOKS, 358 Oliver Rd., Cincinnati OH 45215-2615. (513)761-5977. Publisher: Miriam Irwin. Estab. 1977. Publishes 1 nonfiction book/year. "Subjects range widely. Please query."

MOUNTAIN AUTOMATION CORPORATION, P.O. Box 6020, Woodland Park CO 80866-6020. (719)687-6647. President: Claude Wiatrowski. Estab. 1976. Publishes trade paperback originals. Publishes 2 titles/year. Pays 10% royalty on wholesale price. No advance. Reports in 1 month. *Writer's Market* recommends allowing 2 months for reply.
Nonfiction: Illustrated souvenir books and videos for specific tourist attractions. Query with SASE. Recent nonfiction title: *German Village*, by Jean Conte (illustrated souvenir paperback).
Tips: "We are emphasizing videos more and books less."

‡**MOUNTAIN HOUSE PRESS**, Box 353, Philo CA 95466. (707)895-3241. Publisher: J.D. Colfax. Estab. 1988. Publishes trade paperback originals and reprints. Publishes 3 titles/year. Pays 10-15% royalty on wholesale or retail price. No advance. Reports in 1 month. *Writer's Market* recommends allowing 2 months for reply.
Nonfiction: Publishes books on education, politics, folklore and alternative agriculture. Query with 1 sample chapter and SASE. Recent nonfiction title: *Boontling*, by C. Adams (paperback, folklore/linguistics).

MYSTIC SEAPORT MUSEUM, 75 Greenmanville Ave., Mystic CT 06355-0990. (203)572-0711. Fax: (203)572-5326. Imprint is American Maritime Library. Publications Director: Joseph Gribbins. Estab. 1970. Publishes hardcover and trade paperback originals and reprints. Publishes 4-6 titles/year. Pays 15% royalty on wholesale price. Offers up to $10,000 advance. Reports in 3 months.
Nonfiction: "We need serious, well-documented biographies, studies of economic, social, artistic, or musical elements of American maritime (not naval) history; books on traditional boat and ship types and construction (how-to). We are now interested in all North American maritime history—not, as in the past, principally New England. We like to see anything and everything, from queries to finished work." Query with 3 sample chapters and SASE. Recent nonfiction title: *Saltwater Foodways*, by Sandra Oliver (nineteenth-century New England food history).

NATUREGRAPH PUBLISHERS, INC., P.O. Box 1075, Happy Camp CA 96039. (916)493-5353. Fax: (916)493-5240. Editor: Barbara Brown. Estab. 1946. Publishes trade paperback originals. Publishes 4 titles/year. Pays 8-10% royalty on wholesale price. No advance. Reports in 1 month on queries and proposals, 3 months on mss.
Nonfiction: Primarily publishes nonfiction for the layman in 6 general areas: natural history (biology, geology, ecology, astronomy); American Indian (historical and contemporary); outdoor living (backpacking, wild edibles, etc.); land and gardening (modern homesteading); crafts and how-to; holistic health (natural

---

‡ THE DOUBLE DAGGER before a listing indicates that the listing is new in this edition. New markets are often more receptive to freelance submissions.

foods and healing arts). Query with outline, 1 sample chapter and SASE. Recent nonfiction title: *Medicine Wheel Ceremonies*, by Vickie May and C.V. Nodberg (Native American).
Tips: "Write in easily understood language for the layperson. We do not publish highly technical jargon—but needs to be scientifically accurate."

NEW ENGLAND CARTOGRAPHICS, INC., P.O. Box 9369, North Amherst MA 01059. (413)549-4124. President: Chris Ryan. Publishes trade paperback originals. Publishes 3-4 titles/year. Pays 10-15% royalty on retail price. No advance. Reports in 1 month. *Writer's Market* recommends allowing 2 months for reply.
Nonfiction: Outdoor recreation nonfiction subjects include nature/environment, recreation, regional. "We are interested in specific "where to" in the area of outdoor recreation guidebooks of the northeast US. Topics of interest are hiking/backpacking, skiing, canoeing etc. Query with outline and SASE. Reviews artwork/photos as part of ms package. Send photocopies. Recent nonfiction title: *Great Rail-Trails of the Northeast*, by Craig Della Penna.

NEWJOY PRESS, P.O. Box 3437, Ventura CA 93006. (805)984-7371. Fax: (805)984-0503. E-mail: njpubli sh@aol.com. Publisher: Joy Nyquist. Publishes 3-5 titles/year. Pays 10-15% royalty on retail price.
Nonfiction: Publishes self-help, travel. Subjects include travel health, assertiveness/self-esteem, travelers' aid (not guidebooks), substance abuse treatment and self-help. "Our plan is to focus on traveler's aid books and substance abuse treatment for therapists and lay people. We will also consider self-help books in the categories of assertiveness, personal responsibility." Submit proposal package including outline, 1 sample chapter, marketing plans and author's qualifications with SASE. Recent nonfiction title: *Trust the Process: How to Enhance Recovery & Prevent Relapse*, by Linda Free-Gardiner.

NICOLAS-HAYS, Box 612, York Beach ME 03910. (207)363-4393. Publisher: B. Lundsted. Publishes trade paperback originals. Publishes 2-4 titles/year. Pays 15% royalty on wholesale price. Offers $200-500 advance. Reports in 2 months on mss.
Nonfiction: Publishes self-help; nonfiction. Subjects include philosophy (oriental), psychology (Jungian), religion (alternative), women's issues/studies. Query with 3 sample chapters and SASE. Recent nonfiction title; *Jungian Archetypes*, by Robin Robertson (Jungian psychology).
Tips: "We only publish books that are the lifework of authors—our editorial plans change based on what the author writes."

NORTHERN ILLINOIS UNIVERSITY PRESS, DeKalb IL 60115-2854. (815)753-1826/753-1075. Fax: (815)753-1845. Director/Editor-in-Chief: Mary L. Lincoln. Estab. 1965. Publishes 3 titles/year. Pays 10-15% royalty on wholesale price. Book catalog free.
Nonfiction: "The NIU Press publishes mainly history, political science, social sciences, philosophy, literary criticism and regional studies. We do not consider collections of previously published articles, essays, etc., nor do we consider unsolicited poetry." Accepts nonfiction translations. Query with outline and 1-3 sample chapters.

NORTHWOODS PRESS, Conservatory of American Letters, P.O. Box 298, Thomaston MA 04861. (207)354-0998. Fax: (207)354-8953. Editor: Robert W. Olmsted. Imprints are Northwoods Press, American History Press (division of Northwoods Press). Publishes hardcover and trade paperback originals. Publishes 2-3 titles/year. Pays 10-15% royalty on "amount received by us." Offers $250-500 advance. Publishes book 1 year after acceptance. Accepts simultaneous submissions, if so noted. Book catalog for 6×9 SAE with 2 first-class stamps. Manuscript guidelines for #10 SASE. Must request guidelines before submitting ms.
   • Northwoods Press requests a reading donation to read manuscripts.
Poetry: Request guidelines with #10 SASE. Then submit complete ms. Recent poetry title: *Pinwheels In a Hurricane*, by Melody Ziff.

OBERLIN COLLEGE PRESS, Rice Hall, Oberlin College, Oberlin OH 44074. (216)775-8407. Editors: Stuart Friebert, David Young, Alberta Turner, David Walker. Imprints are Field Magazine: Contemporary Poetry & Poetics, Field Translation Series, Field Poetry Series. Publishes hardcover and trade paperback originals. Publishes 2-3 titles/year. Pays 7½-10% royalty on retail price. Offers $500 advance. Reports in 1 month on queries and proposals, 2 months on mss. Query.
Poetry: Query with SASE. Recent poetry title; *By Common Salt*, by Killarney Clary.
Tips: "Make it look fresh, as if we were first in universe to lay eyes on it!"

OHIO BIOLOGICAL SURVEY, Subsidiary of The Ohio State University College of Biosciences, Museum of Biological Diversity, 1315 Kinnear Rd., Columbus OH 43212-1192. (614)292-9645. Fax: (614)292-7774. Editor: Veda M. Cafazzo. Director: Dr. Brian J. Armitage. Estab. 1912. "Subjects stress, but *not* limited to, information about Ohio's biota."

C. OLSON & CO., P.O. Box 100-WM, Santa Cruz CA 95063-0100. (408)458-9004. E-mail: clayolson@aol .com. Owner: C. Olson. Estab. 1981. Publishes trade paperback and mass market paperback originals and reprints. Publishes 1-2 titles/year. Royalty negotiable. Reports in 2 months on queries.
Nonfiction: "We are looking for nonfiction manuscripts or books that can be sold at natural food stores and small independent bookstores on health and on how to live a life which improves the earth's environment." Query first with SASE. Recent nonfiction title: *World Health, Carbon Dioxide & The Weather*, by J. Resclaw (ecology).

OMEGA PUBLICATIONS, 256 Darrow Rd., New Lebanon NY 12125-9801. (518)794-8181. Fax: (518)794-8187. E-mail: omegapub@taconic.net. Contact: Abi'l-Khayr. Estab. 1977. Publishes hardcover and trade paperback originals and reprints. Publishes 2-3 titles/year. Pays 6-12% royalty on wholesale price. Offers $500-1,000 advance. Reports in 3 months on mss.
Nonfiction: "We are interested in any material related to Sufism, and only that." Query with 2 sample chapters. Recent nonfiction title: *Creating the Person*, by Khan (spirituality).

OREGON HISTORICAL SOCIETY PRESS, Oregon Historical Society, 1200 SW Park, Portland OR 97205-2483. (503)222-1741. Fax: (503)221-2035. Managing Editor, Adair Law. Estab. 1873. Publishes hardcover originals, trade paperback originals and reprints and a quarterly historical journal, *Oregon Historical Quarterly*. Publishes 2-4 titles/year. Receives 150 submissions/year. 75% of books from first-time authors; 100% from unagented writers. Pays royalty on wholesale price or makes outright purchase. Publishes book 18 months after acceptance. Accepts simultaneous submissions. Reports in 6 months.
Nonfiction: Subjects include Northwestern Americana, art/architecture, biography, business history, ethnic, government/politics, history, nature/environment, North Pacific Studies, photography, reference, regional juvenile, women's. Query with outline/synopsis and sample chapters. Reviews artwork/photos as part of ms package. Recent nonfiction title: *Seeking Western Waters: The Lewis and Clark Trail From the Rockies to the Pacific*, by Ruth and Emory Strong (history and archaeology).

PACE UNIVERSITY PRESS, One Pace Plaza, New York NY 10038. (212)346-1405. Contact: Mark Hussey. Publishes hardcover originals. Publishes 2-3 titles/year. Pays 5-10% royalty on retail price. No advance. Reports in 1 month on queries and proposals, 6 months on mss.
Nonfiction: "We publish scholarly work in the humanities, business, and social science fields." Query with outline, 1 sample chapter and SASE. Recent nonfiction title: *My Cow Comes To Haunt Me*, by Norman Simms (cultural theory).

PACIFIC VIEW PRESS, P.O. Box 2657, Berkeley CA 94702. (510)849-4213. President: Pam Zumwalt. Publishes hardcover and trade paperback originals. Publishes 2-3 titles/year. Pays 5-10% royalty on wholesale or retail price. Offers $500-2,000 advance. Reports in 2 months. Book catalog free on request.
Nonfiction: Subjects include business and economics, current affairs, Chinese medicine, nonfiction multicultural children's books. "We are interested in Pacific Rim related issues." Query with proposal package, including outline, 1 sample chapter, author background, audience info and SASE. Recent nonfiction title: *Fighting Drug Abuse with Acupuncture: The Treatment That Works*, by Ellinor Mitchell.

PAIDEIA PRESS, P.O. Box 121303, Arlington TX 76012. (817)294-6072. E-mail: pdpress@globallink.c om. Website: http://www.paideiapress.com. Managing Editor: F.A. Nance. Publishes hardcover and trade paperback originals. Publishes 5-6 titles/year. 80% of books from first-time authors; 100% from unagented writers. Pays 5-15% royalty on retail price or makes outright purchase of $500. No advance. Publishes book 8 months after acceptance of ms. Accepts simultaneous submissions. Reports in 2 months on mss. Manuscript guidelines for #10 SASE.
Nonfiction: How-to, multimedia (CD-ROM, software), textbook. Subjects include education, philosophy, supplementary texts for education market (grades 5-college), women's issues/studies. "We are particularly interested in women's issues/studies and education texts and software dealing with the development of critical thinking skills." Submit proposal package, including full ms with SASE. *Writer's Market* recommends sending a query with SASE first. Reviews artwork/photos as part of ms package. Send photocopies. Recent nonfiction title: *The Critical i: Thinking & Writing*, by F. Andrew Wolf, Jr. (education/writing).
Tips: Audience is education/school market; retail and specialty store (e.g., teacher supply); library. "Do not be discouraged if you are told your book's market is too narrow. Properly marketed texts to niche markets are profitable if the marketer knows what he/she is doing. We are especially interested in education works that lend themselves to development of companion software. Do not only think in terms of printed text about your work. Consider your work in terms of software development as well."

‡PANSOPHIC PUBLISHING, 2308 S. 18th, St. Joseph MO 64503. (816)364-1623. Editor-in-Chief: Christina Schellhorn. Publishes hardcover, trade paperback originals. Publishes 4 titles/year. Pays 10-15% royalty on wholesale price. No advance. Reports in 4 months. Manuscript guidelines for #10 SASE with 2 first-class stamps.

Nonfiction: Children's/juvenile, gift book, how-to, self-help. Subjects include education (personal), history, philosophy, psychology, regional, religion, sociology, travel, women's issues/studies. "We want our books to enlighten our readers." Query with proposal package, including outline and SASE. Recent nonfiction title: *Children's Guide to Las Vegas,* by Christina Schellborn (travel).

PARROT PRESS, 42307 Osgood Rd., Unit N, Fremont CA 94539. (510)659-1030. Editor: Jennifer Warshaw. Publishes 3 titles/year. Pays 10-15% royalty on gross sales (wholesale, retail price).
Nonfiction: How-to, reference, self-help. Pet birds only. "We publish nonfiction books written for pet bird owners. We are most interested in well-researched books on pet bird husbandry, health care, diet and species profiles. Good, clear, accessible writing is a requirement." Submit outline and 1-3 sample chapters with SASE.

PARTNERS IN PUBLISHING, P.O. Box 50374, Tulsa OK 74150-0374. Phone/fax: (918)835-8258. Editor: P.M. Fielding. Estab. 1976. Publishes trade paperback originals. Publishes 1-2 titles/year. Pays royalty on wholesale price. No advance. Reports in 2 months on queries.
Nonfiction: Biography, how-to, reference, self-help, technical and textbooks on learning disabilities, special education for youth and young adults. Query with SASE. Recent nonfiction title: *Enhancing Self-Esteem for Exceptional Learners,* by John R. Moss and Elizabeth Ragsdale (for parents and teachers who deal with exceptional youth and young adults).
● This press reports being deluged with submissions having nothing to do with learning disabilities.

PERFECTION LEARNING CORP., 10520 New York Ave., Des Moines IA 50322-3775. (515)278-0133. Senior Editor: Marsha James. Estab. 1926. Imprint is Magic Key. Publishes hardcover and trade paperback originals. Publishes 10-20 fiction and informational; 50 teacher's resources titles/year. Payment varies greatly. Reports in 2 months.
Nonfiction: Publishes supplemental educational material grades K-12. Query. Recent nonfiction title: *Retold African-American Folktalks,* by David Haynes (classroom resource for high/low market).

POGO PRESS, INCORPORATED, 4 Cardinal Lane, St. Paul MN 55127-6406. E-mail: pogopres@minn. net. Vice President: Leo J. Harris. Publishes trade paperback originals. Publishes 3 titles/year. Receives 20 queries and 20 mss/year. 100% of books from unagented writers. Pays royalty on wholesale price. Publishes book 6 months after acceptance. Reports in 2 months. Book catalog free on request.
Nonfiction: "We limit our publishing to Breweriana, history, art and popular culture. Our books are heavily illustrated." Query. Reviews artwork/photos as part of ms package. Send photocopies. Recent nonfiction title: *Songs of Life—The Meaning of Country Music,* by Jennifer Lawler.

POPULAR MEDICINE PRESS, P.O. Box 1212, San Carlos CA 94070-1212. (415)593-3072. Fax: (415)594-1855. Vice President: John Bliss. Estab. 1986. Publishes hardcover and trade paperback originals. Publishes 1 title/year. Pays variable amount. No advance. Reports in 1 month on queries. *Writer's Market* recommends allowing 2 months for reply.
Nonfiction: Publishes books on nutrition, health and medicine. Query with SASE. "We're less active this year and expect minimal activity in 1997." Recent nonfiction title: *Popular Nutritional Practices: A Scientific Appraisal,* by Yetiv.
Tips: Material must be scientifically-based, not belief-based.

‡THE POST-APOLLO PRESS, 35 Marie St., Sausalito CA 94965. Publisher: Simone Fattal. Editorial Assistant: Margaret Butterfield. Publishes trade paperback originals and reprints. Publishes 2-3 titles/year. Pays 5-7% royalty on wholesale price. No advance. Reports in 3 months. Book catalog and ms guidelines for #10 SASE.
Nonfiction: Essay, letters. Subjects include art/architecture, language/literature, translation, women's issues/ studies. Query. Recent nonfiction title: *Rumi & Sufism,* Eva de Vitray-Meyerovitch (religion/philosophy).
Fiction: Ethnic, experimental, feminist, gay/lesbian, humor, literary, plays. Submit 1 sample chapter and SASE. Recent fiction title: *A Beggar At Damascus Gate,* by Yasmine Zahran (novel).
Poetry: Experimental/translations. Submit 1-5 sample poems and SASE. Recent poetry title: *A Descriptive Method,* by Claude Royet-Journoud (experimental/contemporary).
Tips: "We are interested in writers with a fresh and original vision. We often publish women who are well-known in their country, but new to the American reader."

POTENTIALS DEVELOPMENT, INC., 40 Hazelwood Dr., Suite 101, Amherst NY 14228. (716)691-6601. Fax: (716)691-6620. President: C.B. Seide. Estab. 1978. Publishes paperback originals. Averages 1 title/year. Average print order for a first book is 500. Pays at least 5% royalty on sales of first 3,000 copies; 8% thereafter. No advance. Reports in 2 months. Book catalog and ms guidelines for 9 × 12 SASE.
Nonfiction: Submit outline and/or 1-3 sample chapters with SASE. Recent nonfiction title: *How To Make Your Local Newspaper Work For You,* by Janette Martin (how-to manual/resource).

PRAIRIE OAK PRESS, 821 Prospect Place, Madison WI 53703. (608)255-2288. Vice President: Kristin Visser. Estab. 1991. Imprint is Prairie Classics. Publishes hardcover originals, trade paperback originals and reprints. Publishes 3-6 titles/year. Pays royalty. Offers $500-1,000 advance. Reports in 3 months on proposals.
Nonfiction: History and travel books about the Upper Great Lakes region, especially Wisconsin, Michigan, Illinois, Minnesota. Submit outline, 2-3 sample chapters and SASE. Recent nonfiction title: *Heart of John Muir's World*, by Millie Stanley (history/biography).
Fiction: "We publish very little fiction. Story must relate to upper Great Lakes—locale, characters." Submit outline, 3-4 sample chapters and SASE. Recent fiction title: *The Baraboo Guards*, by John Driscoll (novel about Wisconsin company in Civil War).
Tips: "Be sure your material is focused on Upper Great Lakes. If you aren't sure your title would be appropriate, send us a query letter."

PRIMER PUBLISHERS, 5738 N. Central Ave., Phoenix AZ 85012. (602)234-1574. Publishes trade paperback originals. Publishes 4-5 titles/year. Pays royalty. No advance. Reports in 1 month on queries. *Writer's Market* recommends allowing 2 months for reply.
Nonfiction: Mostly regional subjects; travel, outdoor recreation, history, etc. "We target Southwestern US parks, museum gift shops. We want to know how your book will sell in these retailers." Query first.

PUCKERBRUSH PRESS, 76 Main St., Orono ME 04473-1430. (207)581-3832 or 866-4808. Publisher/Editor: Constance Hunting. Estab. 1971. Publishes trade paperback originals and reprints of literary fiction and poetry. Publishes 3-4 titles/year. Pays 10-15% royalty on wholesale price or makes outright purchase. Reports in 2 months on queries and proposals, 3 months on mss.
Nonfiction: Belles lettres, translations. Query with SASE. Recent nonfiction title: *Welcome To A New World*, by Ernest Saunders (analysis of Gospel of John).
Fiction: Literary and short story collections. Recent fiction title: *Claiming*, Maine poems by Downeast Pat Ranzoni.

‡**RED EYE PRESS, INC.**, P.O. Box 65751, Los Angeles CA 90065. Publisher: James Goodwin. Publishes trade paperback originals and reprints. Publishes 1-2 titles/year. Pays 8-12% royalty on retail price or makes outright purchase of $1,000-10,000. Offers $1-2,000 advance. Reports in 1 month on queries and proposals, 2 months on mss.
Nonfiction: How-to, gardening, reference books. Query with outline and 2 sample chapters. Recent nonfiction title: *Marijuana Grower's Guide*, by Mel Frank (how-to).

REDBRICK PRESS, P.O. Box 1895, Sonoma CA 95476-1895. 707-996-2774. E-mail: jeredbrick@aol.com. Publisher: Jack Erickson. Estab. 1987. "RedBrick Press currently is publishing only books on microbreweries and specialty beers. We are expanding in 1997 to include food and travel related titles."

‡**REFERENCE PUBLICATIONS, INC.**, P.O. Box 344, Algonac MI 48001. (810)794-5722. Fax: (810)794-7463. Estab. 1975. Publishes hardcover originals. Pays 10% royalty on wholesale price. No advance. Reports in 1 month. *Writer's Market* recommends allowing 2 months for reply.
Nonfiction: Publishes Africana, Americana, and botany reference books. Query. Recent nonfiction title: *Dictionary of African Biography* (vol. 3-Southern Africa).

RESOLUTION BUSINESS PRESS, 11101 NE Eighth St., Suite 208, Bellevue WA 98004. (206)455-4611. Fax: (206)455-9143. E-mail: rbpress@halcyon.com. Editor: Karen Strudwick. Estab. 1987.
Nonfiction: "We publish computer-related books, including *Northwest High Tech*, a periodic guide to the computer industry of the Pacific Northwest and Western Canada, and *UNIX: An Open Systems Dictionary*, by William H. Holt and Rockie J. Morgan. We also publish a line of books that focus on the use of the Internet in education, including *Internet for Parents* (Karen Struwick et al) and *Teaching with the Internet: Putting Teachers Before Technology* (Douglas R. Steer et al)." Reports in 1 month on queries and 2 months on proposals and mss. Query with SASE.
Tips: "If possible, take a look at the information about our books at our home page on the World Wide Web (http://www.halcyon.com/ResPress) before you submit anything. This will give you details about our interests and direction."

ROCKBRIDGE PUBLISHING CO., P.O. Box 351, Berryville VA 22611-0351. (540)955-3980. Fax: (540)955-4126. E-mail: cwpub@aol.com. Publisher: Katherine Tennery. Estab. 1989. Publishes hardcover and trade paperback originals. Publishes 2-6 titles/year. Pays royalty on wholesale price. No advance. Reports in 3 months on proposals.
Nonfiction: "We are developing a series of travel guides to the country roads in various Virginia counties. The self-guided tours include local history, identify geographic features, etc. We are also looking for material about the Civil War, especially biographies, and expanding interests from Virginia to other southern states, notably Georgia." Query with outline, 3 sample chapters, author credentials and SASE. Recent nonfiction

title: *The Dulanys of Wellbourne: A Family in Mosby's Confederacy*, by Margaret Vogtsberge (Civil War letters and journals).

ST. JOHN'S PUBLISHING, INC., 6824 Oaklawn Ave., Edina MN 55435. (612)920-9044. President: Donna Montgomery. Estab. 1986. Publishes nonfiction books on parenting.

SAND RIVER PRESS, 1319 14th St., Los Osos CA 93402. (805)528-7347. Publisher: Bruce Miller. Estab. 1987. Publishes mostly nonfiction titles on literature, Native Americans, regional (California) and some literary fiction.

SCOTS PLAID PRESS, 53 Pine Lake Dr., Whispering Pines NC 28327-9388. Editor/Publisher: MaryBelle Campbell. Perfectbound, aesthetic paperback books, archival limited editions, library-quality hardbacks. **Nonfiction:** Publishes memoirs and academic books. Nonfiction only. Subjects include anthropology/archaeology, philosophy, psychology. No unsolicited mss. Query with bio, vita, PC disc information and cover letter with concept and purposed use for book. Send opening page and contents page only. Enclose SASE.
  ● This press reports being inundated with queries, but accepts only one in over 200 queries received per year.

‡SCOTTWALL ASSOCIATES, 95 Scott St., San Francisco CA 94117. (415)861-1956. Contact: James Heig. Publishes hardcover and trade paperback originals. Publishes 2-3 titles/year. Pays 6-10% royalty on retail price. No advance. Reports in 1 month on queries and proposals, 2 months on mss. Book catalog and ms guidelines free on request.
Nonfiction: Biography, illustrated book. Subjects include art/architecture, history, California history/biography. Submit 1-2 sample chapters and SASE. Reviews artwork/photos as part of the ms package. Send photocopies.

SILVERCAT PUBLICATIONS, 4070 Goldfinch St., Suite C, San Diego CA 92103-1865. (619)299-6774. Fax: (619)299-9119. E-mail: 74230.2735@compuserve.com. Editor: Robert Outlaw. Estab. 1988. Publishes trade paperback originals. Publishes 2-4 titles/year. Pays 12-17½% royalty on net receipts. Offers $0-1,000 advance. Reports in 2 months on queries.
Nonfiction: Consumer and quality-of-life issues, with an emphasis on the practical and constructive. "We prefer nuts-and-bolts, feet-on-the-ground material. Please do not send thought pieces, diatribes or minimally researched material." Query with SASE. Recent nonfiction title: *Teenagers! A Bewildered Parent's Guide*, by Elizabeth Caldwell.
Tips: "Silvercat books emphasize the constructive and the practical. We look for material that allows readers to participate actively in their own lives. We have no plans or desire to publish books that vent private anger, discuss personal misfortunes or exotic illnesses, or translate talk-radio venom into print."

‡STA-KRIS, INC., 107 N. Center, Marshalltown IA 50158. (515)753-4139. President: Kathy Wagoner. Publishes hardcover and trade paperback originals. Publishes 4 titles/year. Pays negotiated royalty on wholesale price or makes outright purchase. Advance negotiable. Publishes book 1 year after acceptance. Accepts simultaneous submissions. Reports in 2 months on queries and proposals, 4 months on mss. Book catalog free.
Nonfiction: Coffee table book, gift book, illustrated book, self-help. "We publish nonfiction gift books that: portray universal feelings, truths and values or have a special occasion theme plus small format compilations of statements about professions, issues, attitudes, etc." Query with proposal package including synopsis, bio, published credits.
Tips: "Our audience tends to be women ranging in age from 20s up. We are an independent publisher who supports the marketing of their books with great energy and knowledge."

‡STEEL BALLS PRESS, P.O. Box 807, Whittier CA 90608. Owner: R. Don Steele. Publishes hardcover and trade paperback originals. Publishes 2-4 titles/year. Pays 10% royalty on retail price or $2,000-10,000. Reports in 1 week on queries and proposals, 1 month on mss. *Writer's Market* recommends allowing 2 months for reply. Book catalog for #10 SASE.
Nonfiction: How-to, humor, self-help. Subjects include business and economics, money/finance, psychology, sociology, women's issues/studies. "We publish only controversial nonfiction." Query only with SASE. Recent nonfiction title: *Office Politics: The Woman's Guide to Beat the System.*
Tips: "Audience has an IQ above 110, is usually a single, mail-order buyer or Internet buyer. Write a persuasive query letter."

STORM PEAK PRESS, 157 Yesler Way, Suite 413, Seattle WA 98104. (206)223-0162. Publishes trade paperback originals and reprints. Publishes 3 books/year. Pays royalty on retail price or net revenues. Reports in 2 months.

Nonfiction: Biography, children's/juvenile. Subjects include Americana, health/medicine, history, travel. "We only consider high-quality, unique manuscripts." Query with SASE. Recent nonfiction title: *Catch A Falling Star*, by Betty Baker Spohr (autobiography).
Tips: "Get editorial help before sending a manuscript. Be confident the material is well-written."

STORMLINE PRESS, P.O. Box 593, Urbana IL 61801. (217)328-2665. Publisher: Raymond Bial. Estab. 1985. "Publishes fiction and nonfiction, generally with a Midwest connection. Needs photography and regional works of the highest literary quality, especially those having to do with rural and small town themes. Stormline prefers works which are rooted in a specific place and time, such as *Silent Friends: A Quaker Quilt*, by Margaret Lacey. The Press considers queries (with SASE only) during November and December. We do not consider unsolicited manuscripts."

STUDENT COLLEGE AID PUBLISHING DIVISION, 7950 N. Stadium Dr. #229, Houston TX 77030. Fax: (713)796-9963. Owner: Edward Rosenwasser. "We publish books about college financial aid and careers. Any book that is informative and interesting will be considered."

STUDIO 4 PRODUCTIONS, P.O. Box 280400, Northridge CA 91328. (818)700-2522. Editor-in-Chief: Charlie Matthews. Publishes trade paperback originals. Publishes 2-5 titles/year. Pays 10% royalty on retail price. Offers $500-1,000 advance. Reports in 1 month on queries, 2 months on proposals and mss.
Nonfiction: Subjects include character education (values, ethics and morals), child guidance, parenting, self-help. Query with SASE. Recent nonfiction title: *Grandma Was Right*, by Anne McKay Garris (parenting).

THE SUGAR HILL PRESS, 129 Beech Hill Rd., Weare NH 03281-4327. Publisher: L. Bickford. Estab. 1990. Publishes trade paperback originals. Publishes 1 title/year. Pays 15-20% royalty on publisher's revenues. No advance. Reports in 2 months on proposals.
Nonfiction: "We publish technical manuals for users of school administrative software *only*. (These are supplemental materials, not the manuals which come in the box.) A successful writer will combine technical expertise with crystal-clear prose." Query with outline and 2 sample chapters. Recent nonfiction title: *A Report Cards Handbook*, by Geoffrey Hirsch (technical manual).

THE SYSTEMSWARE CORPORATION, 973C Russell Ave., Gaithersburg MD 20879. (301)948-4890. Fax: (301)926-4243. Editor: Pat White. Estab. 1987.
Nonfiction: "We specialize in innovative books and periodicals on Knowledge Engineering or Applied Artificial Intelligence and Knowledge Based Systems. We also develop intelligent procurement-related software packages for large procurement systems." *Writer's Market* recommends sending a query with SASE first.

TAMARACK BOOKS, INC., P.O. Box 190313, Boise ID 83719-0313. (800)962-6657. (208)387-2656. Fax: (208)387-2650. President/Owner: Kathy Gaudry. Publishes trade paperback originals and reprints. Publishes 4-5 titles/year. Pays 10-15% royalty on retail price. Reports in 4 months on queries.
Nonfiction: Cookbooks, illustrated books and nonfiction on the West for people living in the American West or interested in the West. "We are looking for manuscripts for popular audience, but based on solid research. Can be travel, history, cookbook, but based in West." Query with SASE. Recent nonfiction title: *Women's Voices from the Western Frontier*, by Susan G. Butru (women's history).
Tips: "We look for authors who want to actively participate in the marketing of their books."

TECHNICAL ANALYSIS OF STOCKS & COMMODITIES, Technical Analysis, Inc., 4757 California Ave. SW, Seattle WA 98116-4499. (206)938-0570. Editor: Thom Hartle. Technical Editor: John Sweeney. Estab. 1982. Publishes trade paperback originals and reprints. Makes outright purchase. No advance. Reports in 6 months.
Nonfiction: Publishes business and economics books and software about using charts and computers to trade stocks, options, mutual funds or commodity futures. Query with SASE. Recent nonfiction title: *Charting the Stock Market*, by Hutson, Weis, Schroeder (technical analysis).
Tips: "Only traders and technical analysts really understand the industry."

TECHNICAL BOOKS FOR THE LAYPERSON, INC., P.O. Box 391, Lake Grove NY 11755. (540)877-1477. Contact: Mary Lewis. Publishes trade paperback originals. Publishes 3 titles/year. Pays 10-40% royalty on actual earnings. No advance. Reports in 2 months on mss. Book catalog and ms guidelines free on request.
Nonfiction: How-to, reference, self-help, technical, textbook. "Our primary goal is consumer-friendliness ('Books by consumers for consumers'). All topics are considered." Submit 1 sample chapter. Recent nonfiction title: *Common Blood Tests*, by Gifford (medical reference).
Tips: "Our audience is the consumer who needs very explicit information to aid in making good purchasing decisions." Format chapter for camera-ready copy, with text enclosed in $4\frac{1}{2} \times 7$ area (including headers and footers).

‡**THUNDER DOG PRESS**, 1624 Williams Hwy., #33, Grants Pass OR 97527. (541)471-0658. Publisher: Kathleen Doyle. Publishes trade paperback originals. Publishes 3 titles/year. Pays 8-10% royalty on wholesale price. Reports in 3 months on queries and proposals. Book catalog and ms guidelines for #10 SASE.
Nonfiction: How-to, humor. Subjects include agriculture/horticulture, animals, gardening, nature/environment, women's issues/studies. "We welcome all queries on cutting edge environmental and social issues." Query with writing sample and SASE. Recent nonfiction title: *Give Me Shelter: An Action Guide for Abused Women*, by Kathleen Doyle (6×9 trade paperback).
Fiction: Environmental issues. "Our focus is environmental and social issues. All fiction must somehow address one of these issues." Query with SASE.
Tips: "Research and prove that your proposed book is different from all similar books."

TIA CHUCHA PRESS, A Project of The Guild Complex, P.O. Box 476969, Chicago IL 60647. (312)252-5321. Fax: (312)252-5388. Director: Luis Rodriguez. Publishes trade paperback originals. Publishes 2-4 titles/year. Receives 60-70 queries and 25-30 mss/year. Pays 10% royalty on wholesale price. Publishes book 1 year after acceptance. Book catalog and ms guidelines free on request.
Poetry: "We are a cross-cultural poetry press—not limited to style." Submit complete ms. Recent poetry title: *Love's Instruments*, by Melvin Dixon.
Tips: Audience is "those interested in strong, multicultural, urban poetry—the best of bar-cafe poetry."

UMBRELLA BOOKS, Imprint of Epicenter Press Inc., P.O. Box 82368, Kenmore WA 98028-0368. (206)485-6822. Fax: (206)481-8253. E-mail: epibooks@aol.com. President: Kent Sturgis. Associate Editor: Christine Ummel. Estab. 1988. Publishes 3-4 titles/year. Pays royalty on net receipts. Publishes book 1 year after acceptance. Query for electronic submissions. Reports in 3 months on queries. Manuscript guidelines for #10 SASE.
• Umbrella welcomes marketing and promotion ideas.
Nonfiction: Travel (West Coast and Alaska). Query. Do *not* send original photos or slides.
Recent Nonfiction Title: *Umbrella Guide to Interior Alaska*, by B.G. Olson (travel guide).

‡**UNIVERSITY OF NEW HAVEN PRESS**, 300 Orange Ave., West Haven CT 06516. (203)932-7118. Editor: Dr. Thomas Katsaros. Publishes trade paperback originals. Publishes 3 titles/year. Pays 10-15% royalty on wholesale price. No advance.
Nonfiction: Textbook. Subjects include business and economics, history. Concentration is on college texts and manuals. Query.
Tips: Audience is college, general public.

VALIANT PRESS, INC., P.O. Box 330568, Miami FL 33233. (305)665-1889. President: Charity Johnson. Estab. 1991. Publishes hardcover and trade paperback originals. Publishes 1-3 titles/year. Pays royalty on wholesale price. Offers minimal advance. Reports in 1 month on queries. *Writer's Market* recommends allowing 2 months for reply.
Nonfiction: "We are interested in nonfiction books on Florida subjects." Submit proposal package, including outline, 2-3 sample chapters, author's background, marketing info with SASE. Recent nonfiction title: *Frost in Florida, A Memoir*, by Helen Muir.

‡**VISUAL ASSAULT COMICS PRESS**, Murray Hill Station, P.O. Box 1122, New York NY 10156. President: Rhyan Scorpio-Rhys. Publishes mass market paperback originals. Publishes 3 titles/year. Pays flat rate, payable 60 days after publication. Reports in 1 month on queries. *Writer's Market* recommends allowing 2 months for reply. Book catalog and manuscript guidelines for #10 SASE.
Fiction: Adventure, erotica, ethnic, experimental, fantasy, horror, mystery, occult and science fiction. "We're a small press comic book company. Writers should be familiar with comic book script format or at least familiar with screenplay/script writing." Query. Submit synopsis and a sample chapter with SASE. Recent fiction title: *The Revenue Man*, by Rhyan Scorpio-Rhys and Winston Pascual (science fiction).
Tips: Audience varies from all-ages to the mature reader.

WAYFINDER PRESS, P.O. Box 217, Ridgway CO 81432-0217. (303)626-5452. Owner: Marcus E. Wilson. Estab. 1980. Publishes trade paperback originals. Publishes 3 titles/year. Pays 8-12% royalty on retail price. Accepts simultaneous submissions. Reports in 2 weeks on queries with SASE. *Writer's Market* recommends allowing 2 months for reply.
• Wayfinder Press no longer accepts fiction or children manuscripts.
Nonfiction: Illustrated book, reference. Subjects include Americana, government/politics, history, nature/environment, photography, recreation, regional, travel. "We are looking for books on western Colorado: history, nature, recreation, photo, and travel. No books on subjects outside our geographical area of specialization." Query or submit outline/synopsis, sample chapters and SASE. Reviews artwork/photos as part of ms package. Recent nonfiction title: *Hiking the Gunnison Basin*, by Bloomquist (hiking guide).
Tips: "Writers have the best chance selling us tourist-oriented books. The local population and tourists comprise our audience."

‡**WHITE-BOUCKE PUBLISHING**, P.O. Box 400, Lafayette CO 80026. (303)604-0661. Partner: Laurie Boucke. Publishes trade paperback originals. Publishes 2-3 titles/year. Pays 8-15% royalty on retail price. Reports in 1 month on queries and proposals, 2 months on mss.
Nonfiction: Biography, humor, reference, self-help. Subjects include anthropology/archaeology, child guidance/parenting, music/dance, sports. "Topical, lively works, preferably containing a strong element of humor." Query with outline, 3 sample chapters and SASE. Recent nonfiction title: *Strike Four*, by Jeff Archer (sports/humor).

WHITEHORSE PRESS, 3424 N. Main St., P.O. Box 60, North Conway NH 03860-0060. (603)356-6556. Fax: (603)356-6590. Publisher: Dan Kennedy. Estab. 1988. Publishes trade paperback originals. Publishes 3-4 titles/year. Pays 10% maximum royalty on wholesale price. No advance. Reports in 1 month on queries. *Writer's Market* recommends allowing 2 months for reply.
Nonfiction: "We are actively seeking nonfiction books to aid motorcyclists in topics such as motorcycle safety, restoration, repair and touring. We are especially interested in technical subjects related to motorcycling." Query. Recent nonfiction title: *How to Set Up Your Motorcycle Workshop*, by Charlie Masi (trade paperback).
Tips: "We like to discuss project ideas at an early stage and work with authors to develop those ideas to fit our market."

WOODBINE HOUSE, 6510 Bells Mill Rd., Bethesda MD 20817. Fax: (301)897-5838. Editor: Susan Stokes. Estab. 1985. Publishes hardcover and trade paperback books. Publishes 3 titles/year. 90% of books from unagented writers. Pays royalty. Publishes book 18 months after acceptance. Accepts simultaneous submissions. Reports in 2 months. Book catalog and ms guidelines for 6×9 SAE with 3 first-class stamps.
Nonfiction: Primarily publishes books for and about children with disabilities, but will consider other nonfiction books that would appeal to a clearly defined audience. No personal accounts or general parenting guides. Submit outline and sample chapters. Reviews artwork/photos as part of ms package. Recent nonfiction title: *Uncommon Fathers*, by Donald Meyer, ed. (essays).
Tips: "Before querying, familiarize yourself with the types of books we publish and put some thought into how your book could be marketed (aside from in bookstores). Keep cover letters concise and to the point; if it's a subject that interests us, we'll ask to see more."

YMAA PUBLICATION CENTER, 38 Hyde Park Ave., Jamaica Plain MA 02130. (617)524-9235. Fax: (617)524-4184. Acquisitions Editor: Andrew D. Murray. Estab. 1982. Publishes hardcover and trade paperback originals. Publishes 3 titles/year. Pays royalty on retail price. No advance. Reports in 2 months on proposals.
Nonfiction: "We publish exclusively Chinese philosophy, health, meditation, massage, martial arts. We no longer publish or solicit works for children. We also produce instructional videos to accompany our books on traditional Chinese martial arts, meditation, massage and Chi Kung." Query with outline, 1 sample chapter and SASE. Recent nonfiction title: *Professional Budo*, by George A. Katmer, Jr. (business ethics-East/West synthesis).
Fiction: No children's books. Must have Asian, particularly Chinese focus or theme. This is a *new* focus. Submit outline, 1 sample chapter and SASE.
Tips: "We are expanding our publication focus. YMAA is well established as a publisher of books on Qigong (Chi Kung) and traditional Chinese martial arts. We are actively soliciting works on closely related subjects."

ZEPHYR PRESS, 13 Robinson St., Somerville MA 02145. Co-director: Ed Hogan. Publishes hardcover originals and trade paperback originals and reprints. Publishes 3 titles/year. Pays 6-10% royalty on retail price. Offers $0-2,000 advance. Publishes book 18 months after acceptance. "We focus on books concerning Russia: fiction, poetry, scholarly/general audience nonfiction and travel. We very rarely publish unsolicited proposals. It's essential that writers and translators be familiar with our books before considering making a proposal."
Nonfiction: Illustrated book, travel guides. Subjects include language/literature, translation, travel. Query with SASE. Recent nonfiction title: *An Explorer's Guide to Russia*, by Robert Greenall (travel).
Fiction: "We have some need of literary translators of Russian prose. We have no current plans to publish further English-language original fiction." Query with a sample of a published translation and SASE. Recent fiction title: *From Three Worlds: New Ukrainian Writing* (anthology). We also publish the Moscow-based journal, *Glas: New Russian Writing* in North America.

PUBLISHERS THAT WERE listed in the 1996 edition of *Writer's Market* but do not appear this year are listed in the General Index with a notation explaining why they were omitted.

Book Producers

Book producers provide services for book publishers, ranging from hiring writers to editing and delivering finished books. Most book producers possess expertise in certain areas and will specialize in producing books related to those subjects. They provide books to publishers who don't have the time or expertise to produce the books themselves (many produced books are highly illustrated and require intensive design and color-separation work). Some work with on-staff writers, but most contract writers on a per-project basis.

Most often a book producer starts with a proposal; contacts writers, editors and illustrators; assembles the book; and sends it back to the publisher. The level of involvement and the amount of work to be done on a book by the producer is negotiated in individual cases. A book publisher may simply require the specialized skill of a particular writer or editor, or a producer could put together the entire book, depending on the terms of the agreement.

Writers have a similar working relationship with book producers. Their involvement depends on how much writing the producer has been asked to provide. Writers are typically paid by the hour, by the word, or in some manner other than on a royalty basis. Writers working for book producers usually earn flat fees. Writers may not receive credit (a byline in the book, for example) for their work, either. Most of the contracts require work for hire, and writers must realize they do not own the rights to writing published under this arrangement.

The opportunities are good, though, especially for writing-related work, such as fact checking, research and editing. Writers don't have to worry about good sales. Their pay is secured under contract. Finally, writing for a book producer is a good way to broaden experience in publishing. Every book to be produced is different, and the chance to work on a range of books in a number of capacities may be the most interesting aspect of all.

Book producers most often want to see a query detailing writing experience. They keep this information on file and occasionally even share it with other producers. When they are contracted to develop a book that requires a particular writer's experience, they contact the writer. There are well over 100 book producers, but most prefer to seek writers on their own. The book producers listed in this section have expressed interest in being contacted by writers. For a list of more producers, contact the American Book Producers Association, 160 Fifth Ave., Suite 604, New York NY 10010, or look in *Literary Market Place* (R.R. Bowker).

For a list of publishers according to their subjects of interest, see the nonfiction and fiction sections of the Book Publishers Subject Index. Information on some book publishers and producers not included in this edition of *Writer's Market* can be found in the General Index.

B&B PUBLISHING, INC., P.O. Box 96, Walworth WI 53184-0096. (414)275-9474. Fax: (414)275-9530. President: William Turner. Managing Director: Katy O'Shea. Produces supplementary educational materials for grades K-12. Produces 5-10 titles/year. 10% of books from first-time authors, 90% from unagented writers. Payment varies, mostly "work-for-hire" contracts. Reports in 3 months. Book catalog and ms guidelines for SASE.
   • This company is also listed in Book Publishers.

Nonfiction: Query. Reviews artwork/photos as part of ms package.
Recent Nonfiction Title: *Awesome Almanac Georgia,* by Suzanna Martin (reference).

THE BENJAMIN COMPANY, INC., 21 Dupont Ave., White Plains NY 10605-3537. (914)997-0111. Fax: (914)997-7214. E-mail: ssmb77a@prodigy.com. President: Ted Benjamin. Estab. 1953. Produces custom-published hardcover and paperback originals. Produces 5-10 titles/year. 90-100% of books from un-agented writers. "Usually commissions author to write specific book; seldom accepts proffered manuscripts." Publishes book 1 year after acceptance. Makes outright purchase. Offers advance. Accepts simultaneous submissions. Reports in 1 month. *Writer's Market* recommends allowing 2 months for reply.
Nonfiction: Business/economics, cookbooks, cooking/foods, health, hobbies, how-to, self-help, sports, consumerism. Query only. "Ours is a very specialized kind of publishing—for clients (industrial and association) to use in promotional, PR, or educational programs. If an author has an idea for a book and close connections with a company that might be interested in using that book, we will be very interested in working together with the author to 'sell' the program and the idea of a special book for that company. Once published, our books often get trade distribution through a distributing publisher, so the author generally sees the book in regular book outlets as well as in the special programs undertaken by the sponsoring company. *We do not encourage submission of manuscripts.* We usually commission an author to write for us. The most helpful thing an author can do is to let us know what he or she has written, or what subjects he or she feels competent to write about. We will contact the author when our needs indicate that the author might be the right person to produce a needed manuscript."
Recent Nonfiction Title: *Golfing Birds You Know,* by Roy Benjamin (golf humor).

BLACKBIRCH GRAPHICS, INC., 26 Amity Rd., Woodbridge CT 06525. Fax: (203)389-1596. Editor-in-Chief: Bruce Glassman. Estab. 1979. Produces hardcover originals. Produces 70 titles/year. 20% of books from first-time authors; 85% from unagented writers. Pays 5-10% on net receipts. Makes outright purchase of $1,000-5,000. Offers $1,500 average advance. Does *not* return submissions, even those accompanied by SASE. Reports in 2 months. No phone calls, please.
Nonfiction: Only. Biography, how-to, illustrated books, juvenile, reference, self-help. Subjects include women, African-Americans, Native Americans, and nature/environment. Nonfiction only. Submit proposal. Reviews artwork/photos as part of ms package.
Tips: "Young adult publishing offers *series* work quite often. This means small advances and tight budgets on a *per book* basis, but can allow authors to get commitments on 4-8 titles at a time." Do not send fiction proposals or those not appropriate for young readers.

‡BOOK CREATIONS INC., Schillings Crossing Rd., Canaan NY 12029. (518)781-4171. Fax: (518)781-4170. Editorial Director: Elizabeth Tinsley. Estab. 1973. Produces trade paperback and mass market paperback originals, primarily historical fiction. Produces 10-15 titles/year. 75% of books from unagented writers. Pays royalty on net receipts or makes outright purchase. Advance varies with project. Reports in up to 8 months.
Fiction: Historicals, frontier, contemporary action/adventure, mystery. Submit proposal and 30 pages of the work in progress.
Recent Fiction Title: *Mix-Up at the O.K. Corral,* by Preston Lewis.

‡ALLEN D. BRAGDON PUBLISHERS INC., 252 Great Western Rd., South Yarmouth MA 02664. (508)398-4440. Fax: (508)760-2397. Contact: Allen D. Bragdon. Produces hardcover originals. Produces 0-20 titles/year. 100% from unagented writers. Makes outright purchase of $15/hour-$300/article. Reports in 3 weeks.
Nonfiction: How-to, self-help; puzzles, mind-benders, mazes, brain-teasers. Submit résumé, publishing history and clips.
Tips: Send samples of original puzzles: verbal, math, graphic, logic."

ALISON BROWN CERIER BOOK DEVELOPMENT, INC., 815 Brockton Lane N., Plymouth MN 55410. (612)449-9668. Fax: (612)449-9674. Produces hardcover and trade paperback originals. Produces 4 titles/year. 50% of books from first-time authors; 90% from unagented writers. Payment varies with the project. Reports in 3 weeks. *Writer's Market* recommends allowing 2 months for reply.
Nonfiction: Cookbook, how-to, reference, self-help. Subjects include business and economics, child guidance/parenting, cooking/foods/nutrition, health, psychology, sports. Query.
Recent Nonfiction Title: *The Cancer Recovery Eating Plan* (Random House hardcover).
Tips: "I often pair experts with writers and like to know about writers and journalists with co-writing experience."

COMPASS PRODUCTIONS, 211 E. Ocean Blvd., #360, Long Beach CA 90802. (310)432-7613. Fax: (310)495-0445. Vice President: Dick Dudley. Produces hardcover originals. Pays 2-8% royalty on wholesale price for total amount of books sold to publisher. Offers $2,000 advance for idea/text. Reports in 6 weeks. *Writer's Market* recommends allowing 2 months for reply.

Nonfiction: Humor, illustrated book, juvenile, ("all our books are pop-up and novelty books"). Subjects include Americana, animals, child guidance/parenting, education, recreation, regional, religion, sports, travel (concept-early age books). Query with SASE.
Recent Nonfiction Title: *Busy Beaver Pond*, by Silver (pop-up).
Fiction: Adventure, fantasy, horror, humor, juvenile, mystery, picture books, plays, religious, science fiction. Query with SASE.
Recent Fiction Title: *Counting On Angels*, by Ward (pop-up).
Tips: "Keep in mind our books are *pop-up*, *dimensional*, or novelty *only*! Short verse, couplets or short nonfiction text for 6-7 spreads per book."

‡COURSE CRAFTERS, INC., 33 Low St., 2nd Floor, Newburyport MA 01950. (508)465-2040. Fax: (508)465-5027. E-mail: ccrafters@aol.com. Vice President: Lori Jordan. Produces textbooks. Makes outright purchase. Manuscript guidelines vary based upon project-specific requirements.
Nonfiction: Textbook. Subjects include language, education (preschool-adult), and early childhood. Submit résumé, publishing history and clips. Reviews artwork/photos as part of ms package.
Tips: "Mail (or fax) résumé with list of projects related to specific experience with ESL, bilingual and/or foreign language textbook development."

‡CRACOM PUBLISHING, INC., (formerly Cracom Corporation), 27 Danbury Rd., Wilton CT 06897. (203)834-6075. Fax: (203)834-6079. Vice President and Publisher: Barbara Norwitz. Estab. 1993. Produces professional and trade originals. Produces 6-10 titles/year. 80% of books from first-time authors; 100% from unagented writers. Publishes book 2 years after acceptance. Manuscript guidelines free on request.
Nonfiction: Medical, nursing, allied health textbooks and clinical references in aging and long-term care. Subjects include nutrition, exercise, fitness, housing, rehabilitation, emergency care, delirium, Lesi dental care and resources for caregivers of older adults at home. Submit proposal package, including description of publication, intended market, outline and 2 sample chapters. Reviews artwork/photos as part of ms package. Send photocopies, transparencies or prints.
Recent Nonfiction Title: *Emergency Care of the Elder Person*, by Arthur B. Sanders.

THE CREATIVE SPARK, 26792 Calle Real, Capistrano Beach CA 92624. (714)496-0433. Fax: (714)496-0441. President: Mary Francis-Demarois. Contact: Elizabeth Sirimarco, editorial director. Produces hardcover originals. Produces 20-30 titles/year. Makes outright purchase. Assigns writers to preconceived projects. Rarely purchases finished mss.
Nonfiction: Biography, juvenile, reference, self-help. Subjects include animals, child guidance/parenting, education, ethnic, government/politics, history, sociology, sports, women's studies. Submit résumé, publishing history and clips.
Recent Nonfiction Title: *Enduring Issues in Criminology* (anthology).

J.K. ECKERT & CO., INC., 4370 S. Tamiami Tr., Suite 106, Sarasota FL 34231-3400. (941)925-0468. Fax: (941)925-0272. E-mail: jkeckert@packet.net. Website: http://www.opennet.com/webbooks/. Acquisitions Editor: William Marshall. Produces hardcover originals. Produces 12-18 titles/year. 80% of books from first-time authors; 100% from unagented writers. Pays 10-50% royalty on net receipts. Reports usually in 6 weeks. *Writer's Market* recommends allowing 2 months for reply. Manuscript guidelines free on request.
Nonfiction: Reference, software, technical, textbook. Subjects include telecommunications, circuit design, computer science and electronic engineering. Submit proposal. Reviews artwork/photos as part of ms package.
Recent Nonfiction Title: *Handbook of Parallel and Distributed Processing*, by Zomaya (professional engineering).
Tips: "1) Keep art and text separate—do not use page layout software. 2) Save any artwork as EPS or TIFF; use a real art program like Adobe Illustrator—not something built into a word processor. 3) Don't get creative with fonts—stick to Times and Helvetica. Avoid True-Type if humanly possible. 4) Send synopsis, TOC, and sample chapter (preferably not Chapter 1). Include bio if you want, but if the book is good, we don't care who you are."

ERIAKO ASSOCIATES, 1380 Morningside Way, Venice CA 90291. (310)392-9019. Fax: (310)396-4307. Director: Erika Fabian. Produces hardcover and trade paperback originals. Produces 3-4 titles/year. 100% of books from unagented writers. Pays per contract agreement per individual artist. Reports in 6 weeks. *Writer's Market* recommends allowing 2 months for reply.
Nonfiction: Coffee table book, illustrated book, juvenile. Subjects include business and economics, ethnic, photography, travel. Query with résumé, publishing history and clips with SASE. Reviews artwork/photos as part of ms package.
Recent Nonfiction Title: *The Travel Photographer's Manual*, by Albert Moldvay and Erika Fabian (photography instruction in the field).
Fiction: Young adult (multi-ethnic, educational about a particular country and its culture, through the eyes of children). Submit résumé, publishing history and clips with SASE.

Recent Fiction Title: *Adventure in Splendid China* (juvenile, ages 9-12).
Tips: "We're interested in travel writers/photographers with a proven track record in professional photojournalism, and ability to function in foreign countries under all types of circumstances."

THE K S GINIGER COMPANY INC., 250 W. 57th St., Suite 519, New York NY 10107-0599. (212)570-7499. President: Kenneth S. Giniger. Estab. 1964. Produces hardcover, trade paperback and mass paperback originals. Produces 8 titles/year. Receives 250 submissions/year. 25% of books from first-time authors; 75% from unagented writers. Pays 5-15% royalty on retail price. Offers $3,500 average advance. Publishes book 18 months after acceptance. Reports in 6 weeks on queries. *Writer's Market* recommends allowing 2 months for reply.
Nonfiction: Biography, coffee table book, illustrated book, reference, self-help. Subjects include business and economics, health, history, travel. "No religious books, cookbooks, personal histories or personal adventure." Query with SASE. All unsolicited mss returned unread (if postage is enclosed).
Recent Nonfiction Title: *Prayers and Devotions from Pope John Paul II.*
Tips: "We look for a book whose subject interests us and which we think can achieve success in the marketplace. Most of our books are based on ideas originating with us by authors we commission, but we have commissioned books from queries submitted to us."

GLEASON GROUP, INC., 12 Main St., Norwalk CT 06851. (203)854-5895. President: Gerald Gleason. Produces textbooks. Work-for-hire. No unsolicited mss.
Nonfiction: Textbook. Subjects include computer/software. Five titles in the Professional Approach series of computer application textbooks. Applications include: Word, Excel, PowerPoint, Access and PageMaker.
Recent Nonfiction Title: *Word For Windows 95: A Professional Approach*, by D. Hinkle (computer application textbook).
Tips: "We are textbook packagers who occasionally use freelance tech writers to write portions of our texts. We need more freelance writers with experience writing about computer applications such as Microsoft Word, Excel, PowerPoint, Access and PageMaker. We use freelancers familiar with Windows 95, working on IBM-compatible computers."

GRABER PRODUCTIONS INC., 60 W. 15th St., New York MI 10011. (212)929-0154. Fax: (212-929-9630. President: Eden Graber. Produces hardcover and trade paperback originals. Produces 2 books/year. 50% from agented writers. Pay varies by project or makes outright purchase.
Nonfiction: Juvenile, reference, self-help. Subjects include child guidance/parenting, gardening, health, science, sports, travel. Query.
Recent Nonfiction Titles: *Staying Healthy In A Risky Environment: The NYU Medical Center Family Guide.*

HILLER BOOK MANUFACTURING, 631 North 400 W., Salt Lake City UT 84103. (801)521-2411. Fax: (801)521-2420. President: Melvin Hiller. Produces hardcover originals. Produces 10 titles/year. 10% of books from first-time authors; 20% from unagented writers. Pays royalty on net receipts. Reports in 1 month. *Writer's Market* recommends allowing 2 months for reply. Book catalog free.
Nonfiction: Coffee table book, cookbook, illustrated book, juvenile, reference, textbook. Subjects include cooking, education, religion. Submit proposal. Reviews artwork/photos as part of ms package.
Fiction: Historical, humor, juvenile, picture books, religious.

‡**JENKINS GROUP**, 121 E. Front St., 4th Floor, Traverse City MI 49684. (616)933-0445. Fax: (616)933-0448. E-mail: jenkins.group@smallpress.com. Website: http://www.smallpress.com. Vice President: Mark Dressler. Produces hardcover, trade paperback, mass market paperback originals. Produces 50 titles/year. 50% of books from first-time authors; 75% from unagented writers. Makes outright purchase of $2,000-5,000. Reports in 1 month. *Writer's Market* recommends allowing 2 months for reply. Manuscript guidelines free on request.
Nonfiction: Biography, coffee table book, cookbook, how-to, humor, illustrated book, juvenile, self-help, corporate and premium books. Subjects include Americana, animals, business and economics, child guidance/parenting, cooking/foods/nutrition, education, gardening, government/politics, health, history, hobbies, military/war, money/finance, photography, recreation, regional, religion, sports, travel. Submit résumé, publishing history and clips. Reviews artwork/photos as part of ms package.
Recent Nonfiction Title: *Traveling Again, Dad?*, by Awesome Books (children's/travel/business).
Fiction: Adventure, ethnic, historical, horror, humor, juvenile, literary, mainstream, mystery, picture books, short stories, suspense. Submit résumé, publishing history and clips.
Recent Fiction Title: *Murder in Mackinaw*, by Agawa Press (suspense/mystery).
Tips: "We look for situation-specific experience."

JSA PUBLICATIONS, INC., 29205 Greening Blvd., Farmington Hills MI 48334-2945. (810)932-0090. Fax: (810)932-2659. E-mail: jsapub@aol.com. Director: Joseph S. Ajlouny. Editor: Gwen Foss. Imprints are Push/Pull/Press, producers of original illustrated humor books; Compositional Arts, producers of creative nonfiction; Scrivener Press, producers of history and travel. Produces trade paperback and mass market paperback originals. Produces 15-18 titles/year. Receives 400 queries and 100 mss/year. 95% of books from first-time authors; 100% from unagented writers. Negotiates fee and advance. Accepts simultaneous submissions. Reports in 1 month. Manuscript guidelines for #10 SASE.

● Formerly publishers, this group has shifted its focus to book producing.

Nonfiction: Popular culture, popular reference, humor, how-to, music, Americana, history, hobbies, sports. Submit proposal package including illustration samples (photocopies) and SASE.

Recent Nonfiction Titles: *Tell Me All That You Know: The Unofficial Grateful Dead Trivia Book*, by Brian A. Folker (Pinnacle).

Tips: "Your submissions must be clever!"

GEORGE KURIAN REFERENCE BOOKS, Box 519, Baldwin Place NY 10505. Phone/fax: (914)962-3287. President: George Kurian. Produces hardcover originals. Produces 6 titles/year. 40% of books from first-time authors; 50% from unagented writers. Pays 10-15% royalty on net receipts. Reports in 2 months. Book catalog or ms guidelines for 8½×11 SAE with 2 first-class stamps.

Nonfiction: Reference. Subjects include Americana, business and economics, education, ethnic, government/politics, history, military/war, religion, travel. Query.

Recent Nonfiction Title: *Encyclopedia of the Future* (2 vols., reference).

LAING COMMUNICATIONS INC., 16250 NE 80th St., Redmond WA 98052-3821. (206)869-6313. Fax: (206)869-6318. Vice President/Editorial Director: Christine Laing. Estab. 1985. Imprint is Laing Research Services (industry monographs). Produces hardcover and trade paperback originals. Produces 6-10 titles/year. 20% of books from first-time authors; 100% from unagented writers. Payment "varies dramatically since all work is sold to publishers as royalty-inclusive package." Reports in 1 month. *Writer's Market* recommends allowing 2 months for reply.

Nonfiction: History, biography, coffee table book, how-to, illustrated book, juvenile, reference, software, technical, textbook. Subjects include Americana, corporate histories, business and economics, computers/electronics, history. Query. Reviews artwork/photos as part of ms package. The company also manages book divisions for 3 firms, producing 8-12 titles annually in regional, technical and health care fields.

Recent Nonfiction Title: *Beyond the Mississippi: Early Westward Expansion of the United States* (Lodestar Books).

LAYLA PRODUCTIONS, INC., 340 E. 74th St., New York NY 10021. (212)879-6984. Fax: (212)879-6399. President: Lori Stein. Produces hardcover and trade paperback originals. Produces 6 titles/year. 50% of books from first-time authors; 50% from unagented writers. Pays 1-5% royalty or makes outright purchase, depending on contract with publisher. Offers $2,000-10,000 advance. Does not return submissions, even those accompanied by SASE. Reports in 6 months.

Nonfiction: Coffee table book, cookbook, how-to, humor, illustrated book, juvenile. Subjects include Americana, cooking/foods/nutrition, gardening, history, photography, recreation. Query. Reviews artwork/photos as part of ms package.

Recent Nonfiction Title: *The American Garden Guides* (Pantheon Books).

‡McCLANAHAN BOOK COMPANY INC., 23 W. 26th St., New York NY 10010. (212)725-1515. Editorial Director: Elise Donner. Produces 50-60 titles/year. 5% of books from first-time authors; 90% from unagented writers. Makes outright purchase. Reports within 3 months to submissions with SASE.

Nonfiction: Juvenile. Submit proposal. Reviews artwork/photos as part of ms package.

Recent Nonfiction Title: *Crabs Grab*, by Kees Moerbeck (pop-up).

Fiction: Juvenile, picture books. Submit complete ms, proposal, résumé, publishing history and clips. *Writer's Market* recommends sending a query with SASE first.

MARKOWSKI INTERNATIONAL PUBLISHERS, One Oakglade Circle, Hummelstown PA 17036-9525. (717)566-0468. Fax: (717)566-6423. Editor-in-Chief: Marjorie L. Markowski. Guidelines for #10 SAE with 2 first-class stamps.

Nonfiction: How-to, self-help. Subjects include business, health, aviation, model aviation, money-finance, pop-psychology, sociology, success/motivation, career, relationships, sales, marketing and Christian topics. Submit proposal with résumé, publishing history and clips.

Recent Nonfiction Title: *Amelia Earhart—Case Closed?*, by Roessler and Gomez (aviation/history).

Tips: "Our focus is on publishing bestsellers!"

MEGA-BOOKS, INC., 116 E. 19th St., New York NY 10003. (212)598-0909. Fax: (212)979-5074. President: Pat Fortunato. Produces trade paperback and mass market paperback originals and fiction and nonfiction for the educational market. Produces 95 titles/year. Works with first-time authors, established authors and unagented writers. Makes outright purchase for $3,000 and up. Offers 50% average advance. Manuscript guidelines free on request. No unsolicited mss.

Fiction: Juvenile, mystery, young adult. Submit résumé, publishing history and clips.
Recent Fiction Titles: *Nancy Drew* and *Hardy Boys* series; *Pocahontas* and *The Lion King* (Disney).
Tips: "Please be sure to obtain a current copy of our writers' guidelines before writing."

MENASHA RIDGE PRESS, INC., P.O. Box 43059, Birmingham AL 35243. (205)967-0566. Fax: (205)967-0580. Publisher: R.W. Sehlinger. Senior Acquisitions Editor: Budd Zehmer. Estab. 1982. Produces hardcover and trade paperback originals. Produces 26 titles/year. Receives 600-800 submissions/year. 40% of books from first-time authors; 85% of books from unagented writers. Average print order for a first book is 4,000. Royalty and advances vary. Publishes book 1 year after acceptance. Accepts simultaneous submissions. Reports in 2 months. Book catalog for 9×12 SAE with 4 first-class stamps.
Nonfiction: How-to, humor, outdoor recreation, travel guides, small business. Subjects include business and economics, regional, recreation, adventure sports, travel. No fiction, biography or religious copies. Submit proposal, résumé and clips. Reviews artwork/photos.
Recent Nonfiction Title: *Camping in the '90s*, by Victoria Logue (sports/recreation).
Tips: "Audience: age 25-60, 14-18 years' education, white collar and professional, $30,000 median income, 75% male, 75% east of Mississippi River."

NEW ENGLAND PUBLISHING ASSOCIATES, INC., P.O. Box 5, Chester CT 06412. (203)345-READ. Fax: (203)345-3660. President: Elizabeth Frost Knappman. Vice President/Treasurer: Edward W. Knappman. Managing Editor: Larry Hand. Editors: Victoria Harlow, Romanie Rout. Assistants: Rebecca Berardy, David Voytek. Estab. 1982. Produces hardcover and trade paperback originals. 25% of books from first-time authors. Reports in 2 months.
  ● Edward Knappman's *Great American Trials* was chosen the American Library Association, RASD, Outstanding Reference Book of the Year.
Recent Nonfiction Title: *Advertising For A Small Business Made Simple*, by Bernard Ryan (Doubleday).
Tips: "We are looking for writers in the area of women's history and political science."

‡**OTTENHEIMER PUBLISHERS, INC.**, 10 Church Lane, Baltimore MD 21208. (410)484-2100. Fax: (410)484-7591. Chairman of the Board: Allan T. Hirsh Jr. President: Allan T. Hirsh III. Publisher: Dan Wood. Contact: Laura Wallace-Smith. Estab. 1890. Produces hardcover and paperback originals and reprints. Produces 200 titles/year. Receives 500 submissions/year. 20% of books from first-time authors; 85% of books from unagented writers. Average print order for a first book is 15,000. Negotiates royalty and advance, sometimes makes outright purchase. Publishes book 9 months after acceptance. Reports in 2 months.
  ● Ottenheimer Publishers is no longer accepting fiction.
Nonfiction: Coffee table books, cookbooks, illustrated book, juvenile, reference, self-help, Subjects include animals, cooking/foods/nutrition, gardening, health, religion, alternative medicine, New Age. Submit proposal. Reviews artwork/photos as part of ms package.
Recent Nonfiction Title: *Pictorial Atlas of the World*.
Tips: "Ottenheimer Publishers is primarily a book packager. We tend to assign projects to writers based on their specialties and style, rather than accept manuscripts. We do occasionally purchase original materials. Check your proposal for accuracy and typos. We are always interested in adult health psychology and self-help books."

OWL BOOKS, 175 John St., Suite 500, Toronto, Ontario M5T 1A7 Canada. Website: http://www.owl.on.ca. Publishing Director: Sheba Meland. Estab. 1976. Produces hardcover and trade paperback originals. Produces 10 titles/year. Receives 100 queries and 500 mss/year. 15% of books from first-time authors; 80% from unagented writers. Pays royalty on retail price. Publishes book 18 months after acceptance of ms. Accepts simultaneous submissions. Reports in 3 months. Catalog and ms guidelines for #10 SAE with IRC. (No US stamps).
Nonfiction: Children's/juvenile. Subjects include animals, hobbies, nature/environment, science and science activities. "We are closely affiliated with the discovery-oriented children's magazines *Owl* and *Chickadee*, and concentrate on fresh, innovative nonfiction and picture books with nature/science themes, and quality children's craft/how-to titles." Submit proposal package, including outline, vita and 3 sample chapters. Reviews artwork/photos as part of ms package. Send photocopies or transparencies (not originals).

ALWAYS SUBMIT unsolicited manuscripts or queries with a self-addressed, stamped envelope (SASE) within your country or a self-addressed envelope with International Reply Coupons (IRC) purchased from the post office for other countries.

Recent Nonfiction Title: *CyberSurfer*, by Nyla Ahmad (kids' guide to the Internet).
Fiction: Picture books. Submit complete ms. *Writer's Market* recommends sending a query with SASE first.
Recent Fiction Title: *Wild in the City*, by Ian Thornhill (nature picture book).
Tips: "To get a feeling for our style of children's publishing, take a look at some of our recent books and at *Owl* and *Chickadee* magazines. We publish Canadian authors in the main, but will occasionally publish a work from outside Canada if it strikingly fits our list."

PUBLICOM, INC., 411 Massachusetts Ave., Acton MA 01720-3739. (508)263-5773. Fax: (508)263-7553. Vice President, Educational Materials: Patricia Moore. Produces textbooks, and produces hardcover and trade paperback originals under the imprint VanderWyk & Burnham. Produces 1-3 titles/year. 50% of books from first-time authors; 50% from unagented writers. "Work for hire" for textbooks; pays 3-10% royalty or makes variable outright purchase. Offers up to $3,000 advance for trade publishing. Reports in 6 months.
Nonfiction: Biography, how-to, illustrated book, juvenile, self-help, textbook. Subjects include business, child guidance/parenting, education, women's studies. Submit proposal, résumé, publishing history and clips.
Recent Nonfiction Title: *Bring Me the Ocean*, by Rebecca Reynolds (inspirational nonfiction).

‡PUBLISHERS RESOURCE GROUP, INC. (PRG), 307 Camp Craft Rd., Suite 100, Austin TX 78746. (512)328-7007. Fax: (512)328-9480. Editorial Project Managers: Claudia Capp and Lucia McKay. Pays per project/per page.
Nonfiction: Teacher editions, student materials—textbook and ancillary for all major educational publishing companies, all elementary and secondary subject areas. Submit résumé, publishing history and clips.
Recent Nonfiction Title: *Chemistry*, for Prentice-Hall (teacher's edition, teaching resources/student materials).
Tips: "If they have written classroom instructional materials before—have taught and/or worked for an educational publisher, they are usually the best prepared to work for PRG."

‡RESOURCE PUBLICATIONS, INC., 160 E. Virginia St., Suite #290, San Jose CA 95112. (408)286-8505. Fax: (408)287-8748. Editorial Director: Nick Wagner. Producers trade paperback originals. Produces 20 titles/year. 30% of books from first-time authors; 95% from unagented writers. Pays 8% royalty (for a first project). Offers advance of $1,000 in copies of book. Reports in 10 weeks. Catalog for 9 × 12 SAE with postage for 10 ozs. Manuscript guidelines for #10 SASE.
Nonfiction: How-to, self-help. Subjects include child guidance/parenting, education, music/dance, religion, professional ministry resources for worship, education, clergy and other leaders, for use in Roman Catholic and mainline Protestant churches. Submit proposal. Reviews artwork as part of freelance ms package.
Recent Nonfiction Title: *Writing Your Way to Wholeness* (self-help).
Fiction: Fables, anecdotes, faith sharing stories, any stories useful in preaching or teaching. Query.
Recent Fiction Title: *Nun Better* (short stories).
Tips: "We are publishers and secondarily we are book packagers. Pitch your project to us for publication first. If we can't take it on on that basis, we may be able to take it on as a packaging and production project."

SACHEM PUBLISHING ASSOCIATES, INC., P.O. Box 412, Guilford CT 06437-0412. (203)453-4328. Fax: (203)453-4320. E-mail: sachem@iconn.net. President: Stephen P. Elliott. Estab. 1974. Produces hardcover originals. Produces 3 titles/year. 25% of books from first-time authors; 100% from unagented writers. Pays royalty or makes outright purchase. Reports in 1 month. *Writer's Market* recommends allowing 2 months for reply.
Nonfiction: Reference. Subjects include Americana, government/politics, history, military/war. Submit résumé and publishing history.
Recent Nonfiction Title: *Reference Guide to U.S. Military History*, edited by Charles R. Shrader, 5 vols. (reference).

‡SETTEL ASSOCIATES INC., 11 Wimbledon Court, Jericho NY 11753. (516)681-1505. Contact: Trudy Settel. Produces hardcover, trade paperback, mass market paperback originals. Produces 3-10 titles/year. 15% of books from first-time authors; 10% from unagented writers. Pays 10-15% royalty on retail price. Reports in 1 month. *Writer's Market* recommends allowing 2 months for reply.
Nonfiction: Biography, cookbook, how-to, humor, illustrated book, juvenile, self-help. Subjects include Americana, business and economics, child guidance/parenting, cooking/foods/nutrition, health, history, hobbies, money/finance, philosophy, psychology, recreation, sociology, travel. Query.
Recent Nonfiction Title: *Low Fat Cooking*, by G. Schulman.
Fiction: Adventure, erotica, fantasy, historical, humor, juvenile, mystery, picture books, romance, suspense. Query.

SILVER MOON PRESS, 126 Fifth Ave., #803, New York NY 10011. (212)242-6499. Fax: (212)242-6799. Editor: Sarah Frampton. Produces hardcover originals. Produces 8-10 books/year. 10% of books from first-time authors; 90% from unagented writers. Book catalog free on request.

Nonfiction: Juvenile. Subjects include education, history, science, sports. Submit proposal. Reviews artwork/photos as part of ms package.
Recent Nonfiction Titles: *Techno Lab, Told Tales.*
Fiction: Historical, juvenile, mystery. Submit complete ms or proposal.
Recent Fiction Titles: *The Conspiracy of the Secret Nine.*

SOMERVILLE HOUSE BOOKS LIMITED, 3080 Yonge St., Suite 5000, Toronto Ontario M4N 3N1 Canada. Editorial Assistant: Anna Filippone. Produces trade paperback originals. Produces 6 titles/year. 5% of books from first-time authors; 0% from unagented writers. Reports in 4 months. Manuscript guidelines for #10 SASE with postage (Canadian or IRC).
Nonfiction: Subjects include technology and metaphysics. Query.
Recent Nonfiction Title: *The Skin of Culture* (media/technology).
Fiction: Literary novels and short story collections. Query.
Recent Fiction Title: *The Roaring Girl*, by Greg Hollingshead.
Tips: "Remember that we publish very few adult fiction and nonfiction a year. And all those we have published have been agented, so far. Also, we do *not* accept manuscripts for children's books."

TENTH AVENUE EDITIONS, 625 Broadway, Suite 903, New York NY 10012. (212)529-8900. Fax: (212)529-7399. Managing Editor: Clive Giboire. Submissions Editor: Matthew Moore. Estab. 1984. Produces hardcover, trade paperback and mass market paperback originals. Produces 6 titles/year. Pays advance paid by publisher less our commission. Reports in 2 months.
Nonfiction: Biography, how-to, crafts, illustrated book, juvenile, catalogs. Subjects include music/dance, photography, women's issues/studies, art, children's. *Queries only.* Reviews artwork/photos as part of ms package.
Recent Nonfiction Title: *Earth-Friendly*, by George Pfiffner (children's activity series John Wiley and Sons).
Tips: "Send query with publishing background. Return postage a must."

2M COMMUNICATIONS LTD., 121 W. 27th St., New York NY 10001. (212)741-1509. Fax: (212)691-4460. Editorial Director: Madeleine Morel. Produces hardcover, trade paperback and mass market paperback originals. Produces 15 titles/year. 50% of books from first-time authors. Reports in 2 weeks. *Writer's Market* recommends allowing 2 months for reply.
Nonfiction: Biography, cookbook, how-to, humor. Subjects include child guidance/parenting, cooking/foods/nutrition, ethnic, gay/lesbian, health, psychology, women's studies. Query or submit proposal with résumé and publishing history.

DANIEL WEISS ASSOCIATES, INC., 33 W. 17th St., 11th Floor, New York NY 10011. (212)645-3865. Fax: (212)633-1236. Editorial Assistant: Sara Algase. Estab. 1987. Produces mass market paperback originals. Produces 120 titles/year. 10% of books from first-time authors; 40% from unagented writers. Pays 1-4% royalty on retail price or makes outright purchase of $1,500-8,000 "depending on author's experience." Offers $1,500-8,000 advance. Reports in 2 months. Guidelines for #10 SASE.
Nonfiction: Adult, self-help. Submit outline, 2 sample chapters and SASE.
Fiction: Adventure, historical, horror, juvenile, romance, young adult. "All middle grade and YA. Mostly series fiction. Ask for guidelines prior to submission." Query with synopsis, 2 sample chapters and SASE.
Recent Fiction Title: Series: Love Stories, Boyfriends & Girlfriends, Bone Chillers.
Tips: "We need writers for Bone Chillers and Love Stories. Sweet Valley Kids is going to be reworked."

WIESER & WIESER, INC., 118 E. 25th St. New York NY 10010. (212)260-0860. Fax: (212)505-7186. Producer: George J. Wieser. Estab. 1976. Produces hardcover, trade paperback and mass market paperback originals. Produces 25 titles/year. 10% of books from first-time authors; 90% from unagented writers. Makes outright purchase of $5,000 or other arrangement. Offers $5,000 average advance. Reports in 2 weeks. *Writer's Market* recommends allowing 2 months for reply.
Nonfiction: Coffee table book. Subjects include Americana, cooking/foods/nutrition, gardening, health, history, hobbies, military/war, nature/environment, photography, recreation, sports, travel. Query. Reviews artwork/photos only as part of ms package.
Tips: "Have an original idea and develop it completely before contacting us."

BOOK PRODUCERS THAT APPEARED in the 1996 edition of *Writer's Market* but are not included this year are listed in the General Index with a notation explaining their absence.

Consumer Magazines

Selling your writing to consumer magazines is as much an exercise of your marketing skills as it is of your writing abilities. Editors of consumer magazines are looking not simply for good writing, but for good writing which communicates pertinent information to a specific audience—their readers. Why are editors so particular about the readers they appeal to? Because it is only by establishing a core of faithful readers with identifiable and quantifiable traits that magazines attract advertisers. And with many magazines earning up to half their income from advertising, it is in their own best interests to know their readers' tastes and provide them with articles and features that will keep them coming back.

APPROACHING THE CONSUMER MAGAZINE MARKET

Marketing skills will help you successfully discern a magazine's editorial slant and write queries and articles that prove your knowledge of the magazine's readership to the editor. The one complaint we hear from magazine editors more than any other is that many writers don't take the time to become familiar with their magazine before sending a query or manuscript. Thus, editors' desks become cluttered with inappropriate submissions—ideas or articles that simply will not be of much interest to the magazine's readers.

You can gather clues about a magazine's readership—and thus establish your credibility with the magazine's editor—in a number of ways:

• Start with a careful reading of the magazine's listing in this section of *Writer's Market*. Most listings offer very straightforward information about their magazine's slant and audience.

• Send for a magazine's writer's guidelines, if available. These are written by each particular magazine's editors and are usually quite specific about their needs and their readership.

• If possible, talk to an editor by phone. Many will not take phone queries, particularly those at the higher-profile magazines. But many editors of smaller publications will spend the time to help a writer over the phone.

• Perhaps most important, read several current issues of the target magazine. Only in this way will you see firsthand the kind of stories the magazine actually buys.

Writers who can correctly and consistently discern a publication's audience and deliver stories that speak to that target readership will win out every time over writers who simply write what they write and send it where they will.

AREAS OF CURRENT INTEREST

Today's consumer magazines reflect societal trends and interests. As baby boomers age and the so-called "Generation X" comes along behind, magazines arise to address their concerns, covering topics of interest to various subsets of both of those wide-ranging demographic groups. Some areas of special interest now popular among consumer magazines include gardening, health & fitness, family leisure, computers, multimedia and interactive technology, travel, fashion and cooking. More information about magazine trends can be found in Current Trends in Publishing, on page 22.

As in the book publishing business, magazine publishers are experimenting with a variety of approaches to marketing their publications electronically, whether on the Internet, the World Wide Web or via CD-ROM. For more information about magazines in the electronic age, see Current Trends in Publishing.

WHAT EDITORS WANT

In nonfiction, editors continue to look for short feature articles covering specialized topics. They want crisp writing and expertise. If you are not an expert in the area about which you are writing, make yourself one through research.

Always query by mail before sending your manuscript package, and do not e-mail or fax a query unless an editor specifically mentions an openness to this in the listing. Publishing, despite all the electronic advancements, is still a very paper-oriented industry. Once a piece has been accepted, however, many publishers now prefer to receive your submission via disk or modem so they can avoid re-keying the manuscript. Some magazines will even pay an additional amount for disk submission.

Fiction editors prefer to receive complete short story manuscripts. Writers must keep in mind that marketing fiction is competitive and editors receive far more material than they can publish. For this reason, they often do not respond to submissions unless they are interested in using the story. Before submitting material, check the market's listing for fiction requirements to ensure your story is appropriate for that market. More comprehensive information on fiction markets can be found in *Novel & Short Story Writer's Market* (Writer's Digest Books).

Many writers make their articles do double duty, selling first or one-time rights to one publisher and second serial or reprint rights to another noncompeting market. This year we've added a new heading, "Reprints," when a market indicates they accept previously published submissions, with submission form and payment information if available.

When considering magazine markets, be sure not to overlook opportunities with Canadian and international publications. Many such periodicals welcome submissions from U.S. writers and can offer writers an entirely new level of exposure for their work.

Regardless of the type of writing you do, keep current on trends and changes in the industry. Trade magazines such as *Folio*, *Advertising Age* and *Writer's Digest* will keep you abreast of start-ups and shut downs and other writing/business trends.

PAYMENT

Writers make their living by developing a good eye for detail. When it comes to marketing material, the one detail of interest to almost every writer is the question of payment. Most magazines listed here have indicated pay rates; some give very specific payment-per-word rates while others state a range. Any agreement you come to with a magazine, whether verbal or written, should specify the payment you are to receive and when you are to receive it. Some magazines pay writers only after the piece in question has been published. Others pay as soon as they have accepted a piece and are sure they are going to use it.

In *Writer's Market*, those magazines that pay on acceptance have been highlighted with the phrase—**"pays on acceptance"**—set in bold type. Payment from these markets should reach you faster than from those who pay "on publication." There is, however, some variance in the industry as to what constitutes payment "on acceptance"—some writers have told us of two- and three-month waits for checks from markets that supposedly pay "on acceptance." It is never out of line to ask an editor when you might expect to receive payment for an accepted article.

So what is a good pay rate? There are no standards; the principle of supply and demand operates at full throttle in the business of writing and publishing. As long as

INSIDER REPORT

The Girl With All the Questions

As a child, Sherry Von Ohlsen-Karasik was known as "The Girl With All the Questions." Her free-lance writing career has taken her all over the world for magazines such as *The Christian Science Monitor*, *The World & I* and *For the Bride* as well as for *The Star Ledger* and other newspapers and news-magazines. "What else can you do that allows you to go anywhere, meet anyone and ask questions you normally wouldn't dream of asking?," she posits.

"When I started writing, I did it all wrong—I really went about it backwards," she says. "I wrote a book. Everyone tells you to start small and local. I wrote a book-length manuscript and started sending it out. It got rejected, but the reactions I got from agents and editors were encouraging enough

Sherry Von Ohlsen-Karasik

Photography by Joe Guerriero

to keep me writing. After I'd 'cleansed my soul' by writing several more books, I realized that writing was my home, my passion. It was what I wanted to do the rest of my life and I felt by now I had paid my dues and learned the craft of writing."

At that point she started looking for regional writing opportunities. "In today's market a writer really needs to start on a local or regional level. So few magazines offer expense accounts. The writer has to absorb all sorts of expenses, travel, photos, etc., before even getting down to writing the story." Finding material close to home is the least expensive way to start out.

While honing her craft, Karasik attended several writing conferences to help keep her focused on becoming a professional writer. "At conferences like NYU and Bennington I got guidance and professional input from other writers. I learned what were my strengths and weaknesses. With my confidence boosted, I believed I could have the career in writing I was determined to have. I understood I had a voice, something to say, a mind full of questions and a world full of answers waiting for me." She finds that the hardest part of writing is dealing with rejection. "It's tough on the spirit; you've got to be an optimist, not lose heart. I read somewhere that it takes ten years to become a professional writer, which was ultimately true for me."

Karasik has found that ideas are not hard to come by, if you are open to what's around you. "I'm an observer of life, of people. There is a difference between hearing and listening, and as a writer I learned to listen. Watching and listening generate so many stories I couldn't possibly write them all." Before traveling to Iceland, for example, Karasik researched what had already been written to get an idea of what had not been done. In Iceland she kept her eyes open and came away with a number of stories. "A writer must always see something for the first

INSIDER REPORT, *continued*

time—even in your own backyard. A writer must experience a story on all levels—intellectual, emotional and sensual."

With a wide variety of articles to her credit, from essays, poetry, human interest pieces, relationship articles, to travel and profiles, Karasik can see benefits to specializing in a particular topic, but prefers to follow her diverse interests. "I've written a number of health articles, but I don't want to specialize. As a freelancer I have the privilege of following up on a wide variety of stories. I don't have to narrow the focus, as I write for a wide variety of publications." Freelancers shouldn't limit themselves, she believes. If you do decide to become an expert in one area, she advises, be sure to choose an area such as computers that is big enough to provide plenty of markets for you and the competition.

The undercurrent running through all the different types of stories is her interest in stories that heal. "I'm known for interesting, postive human stories, as a writer that sees below the surface of people and places." She recounts a call she received from a woman who had read a piece on international adoption published over a year before. The woman said that she and her husband had just about given up on having a child when she read the article, which gave them renewed hope. She called to let Karasik know that she was leaving that day for Russia to pick up their new baby, which confirmed what Karasik always believed, that writing makes a difference.

Developing ongoing relationships with editors is the only way to go, she says. Once she was published and had established a name for herself in terms of quality and reliability, editors began calling her to commission pieces. Her close working relationship with the editor of *For the Bride*, for example, enabled her to place articles in every issue for four years. Frequent editorial turnover hurts freelancers, though. When the editor changed, Karasik called to introduce herself to the new editor, who asked her to send her résumé and clips.

"Sometimes editors are arrogant and a freelancer can feel pretty powerless. To work well with an editor you must have a 'teachable' attitude. Editors have something to teach a writer. Sometimes an article needs revisions, sometimes questions that need to be answered weren't addressed. A writer must be professional, a listener, and accommodating. If you're not, an editor doesn't need to waste time with someone who is difficult to work with; she'll just move on to the next writer. Sometimes it's tempting to give editors a piece of your mind, but everybody teaches something. When I get galleys I go over them word for word to find out what the editor changed and analyze how it makes the piece better."

Karasik firmly believes in not burning your bridges. "Once I was asked to do a story for free. I said I could do it once. A year later that editor came back to me and asked me to do a story for them, for money." Early on in a career you shouldn't turn down anything, even if it only pays in copies. "It takes years to establish yourself as a writer, but at least you'll get the clips. Once you do break in, it does become easier. Once you are published and can legitimately call yourself a writer, the assignments come."

Karasik's work has appeared in books, magazines and newspapers. Writing for high-profile magazines can give you a real boost, she recognizes. "It's exhilirating when you get published by a major market. As a writer you live for those moments, but they can't happen all the time. With magazines you can place a

INSIDER REPORT, *Von Ohlsen-Karasik*

few stories a year. They pay well, but you can't live off them. Weigh that against newspapers, which publish more frequently and are more reliable in terms of opportunity to sell stories regularly."

Repurposing articles for different markets is something that Karasik has avoided for the most part. "I have so many assignments I rarely have time to do that. I should. It's something writers should do. But when you write for the creative aspect, write because you love writing, the business end is hard. You really have to force yourself to go out and market, to sell yourself." Adding skills increases your chances of winning assignments. "I'd encourage writers to learn what they can about photography. If an editor knows that he can depend on one person for both the article and the photos, it makes that writer more marketable."

In some way, Karasik feels, it's a better market than ever for freelancers. With smaller staffs, many magazines are finding that freelancers are most cost effective, since they are paid by the piece and don't receive benefits. "It's a crowded market, though, and you have to be better than the competition. There are always writers out there who will do it for less. To be better a writer must be very focused on craft, commitment and discipline."

—Kirsten Holm

there are more writers than there are opportunities for publication, wages for freelancers will never skyrocket. Rates vary widely from one market to the next, however, and the news is not entirely bleak. One magazine industry source puts the average pay rate for consumer magazine feature writing at $1.25 a word, with "stories that require extensive reporting . . . more likely to be priced at $2.50 a word." In our opinion, those estimates are on the high side of current pay standards. Smaller circulation magazines and some departments of the larger magazines will pay a lower rate. As your reputation grows (along with your clip file), you may be able to command higher rates.

For more information on getting started in the consumer magazine market, see Writer to Writer: Emergency Roadside Service on page 28.

Information on some publications not included in *Writer's Market* may be found in the General Index.

ANIMAL

The publications in this section deal with pets, racing and show horses, and other pleasure animals and wildlife. Magazines about animals bred and raised for the market are classified in the Farm category of Trade, Technical and Professional Journals. Publications about horse racing can be found in the Sports section.

AKC GAZETTE, American Kennel Club, 51 Madison Ave., New York NY 10010-1603. (212)696-8333. Fax: (212)696-8272. Website: http://www.akc.org/akc/. Editor-in-Chief: Diane Vasey. 50% freelance written. Monthly association publication on purebred dogs. "Material is slanted to interests of fanciers of purebred dogs as opposed to commercial interests or pet owners." Estab. 1889. Circ. 58,000. **Pays on acceptance of final ms.** Publishes ms an average of 6 months after acceptance. Byline given. Buys first North American serial rights. Submit seasonal/holiday material 6 months in advance. Reports in up to 2 months. Writer's guidelines for #10 SASE.
• *AKC Gazette* plans to publish more short fillers and "featurettes" in future issues.

Nonfiction: General interest, historical, how-to, humor, photo feature, profiles, dog art, travel. No poetry, tributes to individual dogs, or fiction. Buys about 75 mss/year. Query with or without published clips. Length: 1,000-2,000 words. Pays $200-350.

Photos: State availability of photos with submission. Reviews transparencies and prints. Offers $25-150/photo. Captions required. Buys one-time rights. Photo contest guidelines for #10 SASE.

Fiction: Annual short fiction contest only. Guidelines for #10 SASE.

Tips: "Contributors should be involved in the dog fancy or be expert in the area they write about (veterinary, showing, field trialing, obedience, training, dogs in legislation, dog art or history or literature). All submissions are welcome but the author must be a credible expert or be able to interview and quote the experts. Veterinary articles must be written by or with veterinarians. Humorous features are personal experiences relative to purebred dogs that have broader applications. For features generally, know the subject thoroughly and be conversant with jargon peculiar to the sport of dogs."

ANIMALS, Massachusetts Society for the Prevention of Cruelty to Animals, 350 S. Huntington Ave., Boston MA 02130. (617)522-7400. Fax: (617)522-4885. Editor: Joni Praded. Managing Editor: Paula Abend. 90% freelance written. Bimonthly magazine publishing "articles on wildlife (American and international), domestic animals, balanced treatments of controversies involving animals, conservation, animal welfare issues, pet health and pet care." Estab. 1868. Circ. 100,000. **Pays on acceptance.** Publishes ms an average of 5 months after acceptance. Byline given. Offers negotiable kill fee. Buys one-time rights or makes work-for-hire assignments. Submit seasonal/holiday material 6 months in advance. Reports in 6 weeks. Sample copy for $2.95 and 9×12 SAE with 4 first-class stamps. Writer's guidelines for #10 SASE.

Nonfiction: Exposé, general interest, how-to, opinion and photo feature on animal and environmental issues and controversies, plus practical pet-care topics. "*Animals* does not publish breed-specific domestic pet articles or 'favorite pet' stories. Poetry and fiction are also not used." Buys 50 mss/year. Query with published clips. Length: 2,200 words maximum. "Payment for features usually starts at $350." Sometimes pays the expenses of writers on assignment.

Photos: State availability of photos with submission, if applicable. Reviews contact sheets, 35mm transparencies and 5×7 or 8×10 prints. Payment depends on usage size and quality. Captions, model releases and identification of subjects required. Buys one-time rights.

Columns/Departments: Books (book reviews of books on animals and animal-related subjects), 300 words. Buys 18 mss/year. Query with published clips. Length: 300 words maximum. "Payment usually starts at $75."

Tips: "Present a well-researched proposal. Be sure to include clips that demonstrate the quality of your writing. Stick to categories mentioned in *Animals'* editorial description. Combine well-researched facts with a lively, informative writing style. Feature stories are written almost exclusively by freelancers. We continue to seek proposals and articles that take a humane approach. Articles should concentrate on how issues affect animals, rather than humans."

THE ANIMALS' AGENDA, Helping People Help Animals, P.O. Box 25881, Baltimore MD 21224. (410)675-4566. Fax: (410)675-0066. E-mail: 75543.3331@compuserve.com. Website: http://www.envirolink .org/arrs/aa/. Editor: K.W. Stallwood. 80% freelance written. Bimonthly magazine covering animals, cruelty-free living, vegetarianism. "Dedicated to informing people about animal rights and cruelty-free living for the purpose of inspiring action for animals. We serve a combined audience of animal advocates, interested individuals and the entire animal rights movement." Estab. 1979. Circ. 20,000. Pays on publication. Publishes ms an average of 6 months after acceptance. Byline given. Offers 10% kill fee. Buys first North American serial rights. Editorial lead time 3 months. Submit seasonal material 8 months in advance. Accepts simultaneous submissions. Reports in 2 months. Sample copy for $3. Writer's guidelines for #10 SASE.

Nonfiction: Book excerpts, exposé, general interest, interview/profile, opinion. Buys 1-10 mss/year. Query. Length: 1,000-3,000 words. Pays $100. Sometimes pays expenses of writers on assignment.

Reprints: Send photocopy of article. Does not pay for reprints.

Photos: State availability of photos with submission. Reviews contact sheets. Offers no additional payment for photos accepted with ms. Captions required. Buys one-time rights.

Columns/Departments: News (investigative news on animal abuse), 1,000-1,500 words; articles (in-depth writing/treatment), 1,000-3,000 words; News & Notes (news shorts, reports, updates) 500-750 words. Buys 1-10 mss/year. Query. Pays 10¢/word.

Tips: "Please read the magazine and understand how it is structured and organized and its focus. No phone calls. Every article must be accompanied by practical action you can take. Please remember we are an Animal Rights not-for-profit publication."

CAT FANCY, Fancy Publications, Inc., Box 6050, Mission Viejo CA 92690. (714)855-8822. Editor: Debbie Phillips-Donaldson. 80-90% freelance written. Monthly magazine mainly for women ages 25-54 interested in all phases of cat ownership. Estab. 1965. Circ. 303,000. Pays on publication. Publishes ms an average of 6 months after acceptance. Buys first North American serial rights. Byline given. Absolutely no simultaneous submissions. Submit seasonal/holiday material 4 months in advance. Reports in 3 months. Sample copy for $5.50. Writer's guidelines for SASE.

Nonfiction: Historical, medical, how-to, humor, informational, personal experience, photo feature, technical; must be cat oriented. Buys 5-7 mss/issue. *Query first.* Length: 500-3,000 words. Pays $35-400; special rates for photo/story packages.

Photos: Photos purchased with or without accompanying ms. Pays $35 minimum for 8 × 10 b&w glossy and $50 minimum for color prints; $50-200 for 35mm or 2¼ × 2¼ color transparencies; occasionally pays more for particularly outstanding or unusual work. Send SASE for photo guidelines. Then send prints and transparencies. Model release required.

Fiction: Adventure, fantasy, historical, humorous. Nothing written with cats speaking or from cat's point of view. Buys 3-5 mss/year. *Query first.* Length: 500-3,000 words. Pays $50-400.

Fillers: Newsworthy or unusual; items with photos. Query first. Buys 5/year. Length: 500-1,000 words. Pays $35-100.

Tips: "Most of the articles we receive are profiles of the writers' own cats or profiles of cats that have recently died. We reject almost all of these stories. What we need are well-researched articles that will give our readers the information they need to better care for their cats or to help them fully enjoy cats. Please review past issues and notice the informative nature of articles before querying us with an idea. *Please query first.*"

CATS MAGAZINE, Cats Magazine Inc., P.O. Box 290037, Port Orange FL 32129-0037. (904)788-2770. Fax: (904)788-2710. Editor: Tracey Copeland. 85% freelance written. Monthly magazine for owners and lovers of cats. Estab. 1945. Circ. 123,000. Pays on publication. Byline given. Offers 30% kill fee. Buys one-time rights. Submit seasonal/holiday material at least 1 year in advance. Reports in 6 months. Sample copy and writer's guidelines for $3 and 9 × 12 SAE.

Nonfiction: General interest (concerning cats); how-to (care, etc. for cats); health-related; personal experience; travel. Buys 50 mss/year. Query with published clips. Length 1,500-2,000 words. Pays $25-450.

Photos: State availability of photos with submissions. Reviews color slides, 2¼ × 2¼ transparencies or glossy prints no smaller than 5 × 7. Identification of subjects required. Buys one-time rights.

Columns/Departments: Tails & Tales (true and fictional cat-theme short stories), 250-1,000 words; Few Lines 'Bout Felines (cat-theme poetry), 4-64 lines. Buys 36 mss/year. Pays $5-50.

Fiction: Humorous, mainstream. No science fiction elements, written from a cat's perspective, or talking cats, please. Send complete ms. Buys 12 mss/year. Length: 250-1,000 words. Pays $20-50.

Poetry: Free verse, light verse, traditional. Length: 4-64 lines. Buys 12 poems/year. Pays $5-30.

Tips: "Writer must show an affinity for cats. Extremely well-written, thoroughly researched, carefully thought out articles have the best chance of being accepted. Innovative topics or a new twist on an old subject are always welcomed."

THE CHRONICLE OF THE HORSE, P.O. Box 46, Middleburg VA 22117-0046. (540)687-6341. Fax: (540)687-3937. Editor: John Strassburger. Managing Editor: Nancy Comer. Contact: Patricia Booker. 80% freelance written. Weekly magazine about horses. "We cover English riding sports, including horse showing, grand prix jumping competitions, steeplechase racing, foxhunting, dressage, endurance riding, handicapped riding and combined training. We are the official publication for the national governing bodies of many of the above sports. We feature news, how-to articles on equitation and horse care and interviews with leaders in the various fields." Estab. 1937. Circ. 23,000. **Pays for features on acceptance**; news and other items on publication. Publishes ms an average of 4 months after acceptance. Byline given. Buys first North American rights and makes work-for-hire assignments. Submit seasonal/holiday material 3 months in advance. Reports in 6 weeks. Sample copy for $2 and 9 × 12 SAE. Writer's guidelines for #10 SASE.

Nonfiction: General interest; historical/nostalgic (history of breeds, use of horses in other countries and times, art, etc.); how-to (trailer, train, design a course, save money, etc.); humor (centered on living with horses or horse people); interview/profile (of nationally known horsemen or the very unusual); technical (horse care, articles on feeding, injuries, care of foals, shoeing, etc.); news (of major competitions, clear assignment with us first). Special issues: Steeplechasing, Grand Prix Jumping, Combined Training, Dressage, Hunt Roster, Junior and Pony, Christmas. No Q&A interviews, clinic reports, Western riding articles, personal experience or wild horses. Buys 300 mss/year. Query or send complete ms. Length: 300-1,225 words. Pays $25-200.

Photos: State availability of photos. Accepts prints or color slides. Accepts color for b&w reproduction. Pays $15-30. Identification of subjects required. Buys one-time rights.

Columns/Departments: Dressage, Combined Training, Horse Show, Horse Care, Racing over Fences, Young Entry (about young riders, geared for youth), Horses and Humanities, Hunting. Query or send complete ms. Length: 300-1,225 words. Pays $25-200.

Poetry: Light verse, traditional. No free verse. Buys 30/year. Length: 5-25 lines. Pays $15.

Fillers: Anecdotes, short humor, newsbreaks, cartoons. Buys 300/year. Length: 50-175 lines. Pays $10-25.

Tips: "Get our guidelines. Our readers are sophisticated, competitive horsemen. Articles need to go beyond common knowledge. Freelancers often attempt too broad or too basic a subject. We welcome well-written news stories on major events, but clear the assignment with us."

DOG FANCY, Fancy Publications, Inc., P.O. Box 6050, Mission Viejo CA 92690-6050. (714)855-8822. Editor: Kim Thornton. 75% freelance written. "We'd like to see a balance of both new and established writers." Monthly magazine for men and women of all ages interested in all phases of dog ownership. Estab. 1970. Circ. 290,000. Pays on publication. Publishes ms an average of 1 year after acceptance. Buys one-time rights. Byline given. Submit seasonal/holiday material 6 months in advance. Reports in 2 months. Writer's guidelines for #10 SASE.
Nonfiction: Historical, medical, how-to, humor, informational, interview, personal experience, photo feature, profile, technical. "We'll be looking for (and paying more for) high quality writing/photo packages. Interested writers should query with topics." Buys 5 mss/issue. Query. Length: 750-3,000 words. Payment depends on ms quality, whether photos or other art are included, and the quality of the photos/art.
Photos: For photos purchased *without* accompanying ms, pays $50-200 for 35mm or 2¼×2¼ color transparencies. Send prints or transparencies. Model release required.
Tips: "We're looking for the unique experience that communicates something about the dog/owner relationship—with the dog as the focus of the story, not the owner. Medical articles are assigned to veterinarians. Note that we write for a lay audience (non-technical), but we do assume a certain level of intelligence: no talking down to people. If you've never seen the type of article you're writing in *Dog Fancy*, don't expect to. No 'talking dog' articles."

‡**THE EQUINE IMAGE**, (formerly *Equine Images*), Reflections of the Equestrian Lifestyle, Heartland Communications, P.O. Box 916, 1003 Central Ave., Ft. Dodge IA 50501. (800)247-2000. Fax: (515)574-2213. E-mail: hli1@dodgenet.com. Editor: Diane Nodurft. 45% freelance written. Bimonthly magazine covering horses and the equestrian lifestyle. "*The Equine Image* is aimed at horse owners and enthusiasts, equine art lovers and those equestrians with an appreciation for the horse in their lifestyle. Specific topics covered include celebrity and artist profiles, travel features, equestrian-styled clothing, accessories or home decor, equestrian literature and more." Estab. 1986. Circ. 12,500. Pays on publication. Publishes ms an average of 3 months after acceptance. Byline given. Buys first North American serial rights. Editorial lead time 3 months. Submit seasonal material 6 months in advance. Accepts simultaneous submissions. Reports in 6 weeks on queries; 2 months on mss. Sample copy for $6.95. Writer's guidelines free.
Nonfiction: Book excerpts, essays, general interest, historical/nostalgic, interview/profile, photo feature, travel, art; all articles must have an equestrian tie. Buys 25-40 mss/year. Query with published clips. Length: 500-2,000 words. Pays $100-500. Pays in contributor copies on individual arrangements.
Reprints: Accepts previously published submissions.
Photos: State availability of photos with submissions. Reviews contact sheets, 4×5 transparencies, 3×5 prints. Offers no additional payment for photos. Identification of subjects required. Buys one-time rights.
Columns/Departments: Style Column (equestrian-styled fashion or home decor), 1,200 words. "Most columnists are regular contributors arranged on individual basis." Query with published clips. Pays $100-500.
Fiction: Mainstream, novel excerpts, slice-of-life vignettes, western; all must have an equestrian tie. "This new section will publish only equestrian or horse-related fiction; short, general interest pieces are best; no children's fiction." Send complete ms. Pays $0-300.
Poetry: Free verse, light verse, traditional; all must have an equestrian tie. Buys 6-18 poems/year. Submit maximum 5 poems at a time. Length: 5-40 lines. Pays $0-200.
Tips: "Send complete queries with details on headlines, interviews and available visuals. Direct specific questions on editorial submissions to the editor *in writing*. Notify the editorial department with as much advance notice as possible of any specific trips. Freelance assignments are often made on basis of events and locations."

THE GREYHOUND REVIEW, P.O. Box 543, Abilene KS 67410. (913)263-4660. Fax: (913)263-4689. Editor: Gary Guccione. Managing Editor: Tim Horan. 20% freelance written. Monthly magazine covering greyhound breeding, training and racing. Estab. 1911. Circ. 5,000. **Pays on acceptance.** Byline given. Buys first rights. Submit seasonal/holiday material 2 months in advance. Reports in 2 weeks on queries; 1 month on mss. Sample copy for $3. Free writer's guidelines.
Nonfiction: How-to, interview/profile, personal experience. "Articles must be targeted at the greyhound industry: from hard news, special events at racetracks to the latest medical discoveries. Do not submit gambling systems." Buys 24 mss/year. Query. Length: 1,000-10,000 words. Pays $85-150. Sometimes pays the expenses of writers on assignment.
Reprints: Accepts previously published material. Send photocopy of article. Pays 100% of the amount paid for an original article.
Photos: State availability of photos with submission. Reviews 35mm transparencies and 8×10 prints. Offers $10-50/photo. Identification of subjects required. Buys one-time rights.

HOOF PRINT, The Northeast's Equestrian Newspaper, Glens Falls Newspapers, Inc., P.O. Box 2157, Glens Falls NY 12801-2157. (518)792-3131, ext. 3257. E-mail: jobryant@global1.net. Editor: Jennifer O. Bryant. 80% freelance written. Monthly tabloid covering equestrian (horse) news and features in the Northeast. "*Hoof Print* is an all-breed, all-discipline paper for Northeastern horse owners and horse lovers.

We try to offer something for everyone at every experience level and produce an information-filled, colorful, easy-to-read paper." Estab. 1992. Circ. 15,000. Pays on publication. Publishes ms an average of 4 months after acceptance. Buys first North American serial or second serial (reprint) rights. Editorial lead time 2 months. Submit seasonal material 3 months in advance. Accepts simultaneous submissions. Reports in 1 month on queries; 2 months on mss. Sample copy for $2. Writer's guidelines free for SASE.

● *Hoof Print*'s geographic area of coverage has expanded to include Pennsylvania.

Nonfiction: How-to, humor, personal experience (all must relate to horses). "No articles not pertinent to Northeast horse people." Buys 100 mss/year. Query or send complete ms. Length: 500-1,500 words. Pays $25 minimum.

Reprints: Accepts previously published submissions.

Photos: Send photos with submission. Reviews transparencies and prints. Offers $15/photo. Captions and identification of subjects required. Buys one-time rights.

Poetry: Light verse. Buys 5 poems/year. Length: 5-20 lines. Pays $15-25.

Fillers: Facts, tips, short humor. Pays $5.

Tips: "Articles about events, people, horses, farms, etc., *in our area* and of interest to our readers are always needed. Knowledge of horses is necessary. We offer practical advice, how-to articles, plus news, information, and a variety of features in each issue. Send for writers' guidelines and study each month's theme. Query with ideas for theme-related articles. Cover photos that reflect monthly themes are needed as well."

‡HORSE AND HORSEMAN, 34249 Camino Capistrano, Capistrano Beach CA 92629. (714)493-2101. Fax: (714)240-8680. Editor: Jack Lewis. Managing Editor: Claudia Dano. 65-70% freelance written. Monthly magazine. Estab. 1972. Circ. 89,000. **Pays on acceptance**. Publishes ms an average of 4 months after acceptance. Byline given. Buys first North American serial rights and all rights. Editorial lead time 1 year. Submit seasonal material 6 months in advance. Reports in 3 weeks on queries; 1 month on mss. Sample copy for $3. Writer's guidelines for #10 SASE.

Nonfiction: Historical/nostalgic, how-to, humor, personal experience. Buys 60-70 mss/year. Query. Length: 1,500-2,500 words. Pays $50-250.

Photos: Send photos with submission. Reviews contact sheets, negatives, transparencies. Offers no additional payment for photos accepted with ms. Captions, model releases and identification of subjects required. Buys one-time rights. Needs more black and white stories.

‡HORSE ILLUSTRATED, The Magazine for Responsible Horse Owners, Fancy Publications, Inc., P.O. Box 6050, Mission Viejo CA 92690-6050. (714)855-8822. E-mail: horseillus@aol.com. Editor: Moira C. Harris. 90% freelance written. Prefers to work with published/established writers but will work with new/unpublished writers. Monthly magazine covering all aspects of horse ownership. "Our readers are adults, mostly women, between the ages of 18 and 40; stories should be geared to that age group and reflect responsible horse care." Estab. 1976. Circ. 182,000. Pays on publication. Publishes ms an average of 8 months after acceptance. Byline given. Buys one-time rights; requires first North American rights among equine publications. Submit seasonal/holiday material 6 months in advance. Reports in 3 months. Sample copy for $3.50. Writer's guidelines for #10 SASE.

Nonfiction: How-to (horse care, training, veterinary care), photo feature. No "little girl" horse stories, "cowboy and Indian" stories or anything not *directly* relating to horses. "We are looking for longer, more authoritative, in-depth features on trends and issues in the horse industry. Such articles must be queried first with a detailed outline of the article and clips. We rarely have a need for fiction." Buys 20 mss/year. Query or send complete ms. Length: 1,000-2,000 words. Pays $100-300 for assigned articles; $50-300 for unsolicited articles.

Photos: Send photos with submission. Reviews 35mm transparencies, medium format transparencies and 5×7 prints. Occasionally offers additional payment for photos accepted with ms.

Tips: "Freelancers can break in at this publication with feature articles on Western and English training methods and trainer profiles (including training tips); veterinary and general care how-to articles; and horse sports articles. We rarely use personal experience articles. Submit photos with training and how-to articles whenever possible. We have a very good record of developing new freelancers into regular contributors/columnists. We are always looking for fresh talent, but certainly enjoy working with established writers who 'know the ropes' as well. We are accepting less freelance work—much of our material is now assigned and contracted."

‡HORSES ALL, 4000-19 St. NE, Calgary, Alberta T2E 6P8 Canada. (403)250-6633. Fax: (403)291-0703. Editor: Cindy Dickson. 30% freelance written. Eager to work with new/unpublished writers. Monthly tabloid for horse owners, 75% rural, 25% urban. Circ. 11,200. Pays on publication. Buys one-time rights. Submit seasonal material 3 months in advance. Accepts simultaneous submissions. Sample copy $2 for 9×12 SAE.

Nonfiction: Interview, humor and personal experience. Query. Phone queries OK. Pays $20-100.
Reprints: Accepts previously published submissions.
Photos: State availability of photos. Captions required.
Columns/Departments: Open to suggestions for new columns/departments. Query. Length: 1-2 columns.
Fiction: Historical and western. Query. Pays $20-100.
Tips: "We use more short articles. The most frequent mistakes made by writers in completing an article assignment for us are poor research, wrong terminology and poor (terrible) writing style."

I LOVE CATS, I Love Cats Publishing, 950 Third Ave., 16th Floor, New York NY 10022-2705. (212)888-1855. Fax: (212)838-8420. Editor: Lisa Sheets. 85% freelance written. Bimonthly magazine covering cats. "*I Love Cats* is a general interest cat magazine for the entire family. It caters to cat lovers of all ages. The stories in the magazine include fiction, nonfiction, how-to, humorous and columns for the cat lover." Estab. 1989. Circ. 200,000. Pays on publication. Publishes ms an average of 2 years after acceptance. Byline given. No kill fee. Buys all rights. Must sign copyright consent form. Submit seasonal material 9 months in advance. Reports in 2 months. Sample copy for $4. Writer's guidelines for #10 SASE.
Nonfiction: Essays, how-to, humor, inspirational, interview/profile, opinion, personal experience, photo feature. No poetry. Buys 200 mss/year. Send complete ms. Length: 100-1,000 words. Pays $40-250, contributor copies or other premiums "if requested." Sometimes pays expenses of writers on assignment. Send photos with submission. Offers no additional payment for photos accepted with ms. Identification of subjects required. Buys all rights.
Fiction: Adventure, fantasy, historical, humorous, mainstream, mystery, novel excerpts, slice-of-life vignettes, suspense. "This is a family magazine. No graphic violence, pornography or other inappropriate material. *I Love Cats* is strictly 'G-rated.' " Buys 50 mss/year. Send complete ms. Length: 500-1,200 words. Pays $40-250.
Fillers: Quizzes and short humor. Buys 20/year. Pays $10-35.
Tips: "Please keep stories short and concise. Send complete ms with photos, if possible. I buy lots of first-time authors. Nonfiction pieces w/color photos are always in short supply. With the exception of the standing columns, the rest of the magazine is open to freelancers. Be witty, humorous or take a different approach to writing."

‡ICELANDIC HORSE MAGAZINE OF NORTH AMERICA, 507 N. Sullivan Rd., Suite A-3, Veradale WA 99037. (509)928-8389. Fax: (509)928-2398. E-mail: icemag@icehorse.com. Editor: Karen Hood. Contact: Rhonda Hart, managing editor. 80% freelance written. Bimonthly magazine covering Icelandic horses and travel to and around Iceland. "The IHMNA is devoted to Icelandic horses, their heritage and the land of origin. Our readers are interested in these rare horses both on an investment and an emotional level. They read to learn more about them and understand Iceland and the culture the horses evolved in." Estab. 1995. Circ. 5,000. Pays on publication. Publishes ms an average of 4 months after acceptance. Byline given. Buys first North American serial or second serial (reprint) rights. Editorial lead time 10 months. Submit seasonal material 4 months in advance. Accepts simultaneous submissions. Reports in 1 month on queries; 2 months on mss. Sample copy for $5, $7 internationally. Writer's guidelines for #10 SASE.
Nonfiction: Historical/nostalgic, how-to (training, riding), interview/profile, personal experience, photo feature, travel, Icelandic culture, arts, etc. Special issue: Landsmot 1998 in Iceland. Buys 25 mss/year. Query or send complete ms. Length: 600-2,000 words. Pays $100 minimum for assigned articles plus contributors copies.
Reprints: Accepts previously published submissions.
Photos: Send photos with submission. Reviews 3×5 or larger prints.
Columns/Departments: Equine Law (legal responsibilities); Travel Guide (destinations in Iceland); both 300 words. Buys 10 mss/year. Query. Pays $20-50.
Fiction: "We do not currently publish fiction, but will consider short stories revolving around Icelandic horses, travel or history."
Poetry: Light verse, traditional. Buys 12 poems/year. Submit maximum 6 poems at one time. Length: 4-36 lines. Pays $10.
Fillers: Anecdotes, facts, gags to be illustrated by cartoonist, newsbreaks, short humor. Buys 16/year. Length: 10-30 words. Pays $10.
Tips: "The mission of the magazine is to reveal the wonders of Iceland and specifically the time-honored legacy of the horses to North American readers. We are published internationally so the focus on Iceland is from a 'world view.' Anything new and interesting about Iceland and the horses interests us."

MUSHING, Stellar Communications, Inc., P.O. Box 149, Ester AK 99725-0149. (907)479-0454. Fax: (907)479-3137. E-mail: mushing@polarnet.com (for contributor guidelines and queries, not submissions). Website: http://www.polarnet.com/users/mushing. Publisher: Todd Hoener. Managing Editor: Diane Herrmann. Bimonthly magazine on "all aspects of dog driving activities. We include information (how-to), nonfiction (entertaining), health, ethics, news and history stories." Estab. 1987. Circ. 7,000. Pays on publication. Publishes ms an average of 4 months after acceptance. Byline given. Buys first serial and second serial (reprint) rights. Submit seasonal/holiday material 4 months in advance. Reports in 8 months. Sample copy for $5. Writer's guidelines free. Call for information.

Nonfiction: Historical, how-to, humor, interview/profile, new product, personal experience, photo feature, technical, innovations, travel. Themes: Iditarod and long-distance racing (January/February); Expeditions (March/April); health and nutrition (May/June); musher and dog profiles, summer activities (July/August); equipment, fall training (September/October); races and places (November/December). Query with or without published clips, or send complete ms. Length: 500-3,000 words. Pays $50-250 for articles. Payment depends on quality, deadlines, experience. Sometimes pays expenses of writers on assignment.

Photos: Send photos with submission. Reviews contact sheets, transparencies, prints. Offers $20-150/photo. Captions, model releases, identification of subjects required. Buys one-time and second reprint rights. We look for good b&w and quality color for covers and specials.

Fillers: Anecdotes, facts, cartoons, newsbreaks, short humor, puzzles. Length: 100-250 words. Pays $20-35.

Tips: "Read our magazine. Know something about dog-driven, dog-powered sports."

THE QUARTER HORSE JOURNAL, P.O. Box 32470, Amarillo TX 79120. (806)376-4811. Fax: (806)376-8364. Website: http://www.aqha.com. Editor-in-Chief: Jim Jennings. Editor: Lesli Groves. 20% freelance written. Prefers to work with published/established writers. Monthly official publication of the American Quarter Horse Association. Estab. 1948. Circ. 75,000. **Pays on acceptance.** Publishes ms an average of 3 months after acceptance. Buys first North American serial rights. Submit seasonal/holiday material 2 months in advance. Reports in 2 months. Free sample copy and writer's guidelines.

Nonfiction: Historical ("those that retain our western heritage"); how-to (fitting, grooming, showing, or anything that relates to owning, showing, or breeding); informational (educational clinics, current news); interview (feature-type stories—must be about established horses or people who have made a contribution to the business); personal opinion; and technical (equine updates, new surgery procedures, etc.). Buys 20 mss/year. Length: 800-2,500 words. Pays $150-300.

Photos: Purchased with accompanying ms. Captions required. Send prints or transparencies. Uses 5×7 or 8×10 b&w glossy prints, 2¼×2¼, 4×5 or 35 mm color transparencies. Offers no additional payment for photos accepted with accompanying ms.

Tips: "Writers must have a knowledge of the horse business."

REPTILE & AMPHIBIAN MAGAZINE, RD3, Box 3709A, Pottsville PA 17901-9219. (717)622-6050. Fax: (717)622-5858. E-mail: eramus@postoffice.ptd.net. Website: http://petstation.com/repamp.html. Editor: Erica Ramus. 80% freelance written. Full-color digest-size bimonthly magazine covering reptiles and amphibians. Devoted to the amateur herpetologist who is generally college-educated and familiar with the basics of herpetology. Estab. 1989. Circ. 15,000. **Pays on acceptance.** Publishes ms an average of 6 months after acceptance. Byline given. Buys first North American serial, one-time and (occasionally) second serial (reprint) rights. Reports in 2 weeks. Sample copy for $4. Writer's guidelines for #10 SASE.

Nonfiction: General interest, photo feature, technical. Publishes articles on life cycles of various reptiles and amphibians, natural history, captive care and breeding. No first-person narrative, "me-and-Joe" stories or articles by writers unfamiliar with the subject matter. "Readers are already familiar with the basics of herpetology and are usually advanced amateur hobbyists." Buys 50 mss/year. Query or send complete ms. Length: 1,500-2,000 words. Pays $100. Sometimes pays expenses of familiar or regular writer on assignment.

Reprints: Send photocopy of article and information about when and where the article previously appeared. Pays 100% of amount paid for an original article.

Photos: Send photos with submission whenever possible. Reviews 35mm slide transparencies, 4×6, 5×7 and 8×10 glossy prints. Offers $10 for b&w, $25 for color photos. Captions, model releases and identification of subjects required. Animals should be identified by common and/or scientific name. Buys one-time rights.

Columns/Departments: Photo Dept./Herp•Art Dept., 500-750 words; Book Review, 500-750 words. Buys 12 mss/year. Send complete ms. Pays $50-75.

Tips: "Note your personal qualifications, such as experience in the field or advanced education. Writers have the best chance selling us feature articles—know your subject and supply high quality color photos."

WEST COAST HORSE REVIEW, Skies America International Publishing, Inc., 9560 SW Nimbus, Beaverton OR 97080. Fax: (503)520-1275. Contact: Barb Crabbe, DVM, editor. Managing Editor: Jacque Werner. 40% freelance written. Monthly magazine containing material of interest to West Coast horsemen. Estab. 1964. Circ. 9,000. Pays on publication. Publishes ms an average of 6-8 months after acceptance. Byline sometimes given. Offers variable kill fee. Buys first North American serial rights. Editorial lead time 3 months. Submit seasonal material 6 months in advance. Reports in 2 months. Sample copy for #10 SASE. Writer's guidelines for #10 SASE.

Nonfiction: How-to, interview/profile, technical, news/event reports. Buys 30 mss/year. Query with published clips. Length: 1,000-2,500 words. Pays $200 for assigned articles; $125 for unsolicited articles. Sometimes pays expenses of writers on assignment.

Photos: State availability of photos with submission. Reviews transparencies. Negotiates payment individually. Identification of subjects required. Buys one-time rights.

Tips: "Query with specific article ideas that would be of interest to horsemen on the West Coast."

ART AND ARCHITECTURE

Listed here are publications about art, art history, specific art forms and architecture written for art patrons, architects, artists and art enthusiasts. Publications addressing the business and management side of the art industry are listed in the Art, Design and Collectibles category of the Trade section. Trade publications for architecture can be found in Building Interiors, and Construction and Contracting sections.

THE AMERICAN ART JOURNAL, Kennedy Galleries, Inc. 730 Fifth Ave., New York NY 10019. (212)541-9600. Fax: (212)977-3833. Editor-in-Chief: Jayne A. Kuchna. Prefers to work with published/established writers; works with a small number of new/unpublished writers each year. Semiannual scholarly magazine of American art history of the 17th, 18th, 19th and 20th centuries, including painting, sculpture, architecture, photography, cultural history, etc., for people with a serious interest in American art, and who are already knowledgeable about the subject. Readers are scholars, curators, collectors, students of American art, or persons with a strong interest in Americana. Circ. 2,000. **Pays on acceptance.** Publishes ms an average of 6 months after acceptance. Buys all rights, but will reassign rights to writer. Byline given. Reports in 2 months. Sample copy for $18.
Nonfiction: "All articles are about some phase or aspect of American art history." No how-to articles or reviews of exhibitions. No book reviews or opinion pieces. No human interest approaches to artists' lives. No articles written in a casual or "folksy" style. *Writing style must be formal and serious.* Buys 10-15 mss/year. Submit complete ms "with good cover letter." No queries. Length: 2,500-8,000 words. Pays $400-600.
Photos: Purchased with accompanying ms. Captions required. Uses b&w only. Offers no additional payment for photos accepted with accompanying ms.
Tips: "Articles *must be* scholarly, thoroughly documented, well-researched, well-written and illustrated. Whenever possible, all manuscripts must be accompanied by b&w photographs, which have been integrated into the text by the use of numbers."

AMERICAN INDIAN ART MAGAZINE, American Indian Art, Inc., 7314 E. Osborn Dr., Scottsdale AZ 85251-6417. (602)994-5445. Editor: Roanne P. Goldfein. 97% freelance written. Works with a small number of new/unpublished writers each year. Quarterly magazine covering Native American art, historic and contemporary, including new research on any aspect of Native American art north of the US/Mexico border. Estab. 1975. Circ. 30,000. Pays on publication. Publishes ms an average of 3 months after acceptance. Byline given. Buys one-time and first rights. Reports in 3 weeks on queries; 3 months on mss. Writer's guidelines for #10 SASE.
Nonfiction: New research on any aspect of Native American art. No previously published work or personal interviews with artists. Buys 12-18 mss/year. Query. Length: 1,000-2,500 words. Pays $75-300.
Tips: "The magazine is devoted to all aspects of Native American art. Some of our readers are knowledgeable about the field and some know very little. We seek articles that offer something to both groups. Articles reflecting original research are preferred to those summarizing previously published information."

ARCHITECTURAL DIGEST, Condé Nast Publications, Inc., 350 Madison Ave., New York NY 10017. (212)880-8800. Publisher: Thomas P. Losee Jr. Monthly magazine covering architectural and interior design. "*Architectural Digest, The International Magazine of Fine Interior Design*, is a chronicle of aesthetic excellence. It showcases the work of some of today's most gifted interior designers and architects, with text by noted experts in the field of architecutre and interior design; and also encompasses topics such as art, travel and home electronics." Estab. 1920. Circ. 879,000. This magazine did not respond to our request for information. Query before submitting.

ART PAPERS, Atlanta Art Papers, Inc., P.O. Box 77348, Atlanta GA 30357. (404)588-1837. Fax: (404)588-1836. E-mail: cdowney@pd.org. Editor: Glenn Harper. 75% freelance written. Bimonthly magazine covering contemporary art and artists. "*Art Papers*, a bimonthly magazine about regional and national contemporary art and artists, features a variety of perspectives on current art concerns. Each issue presents topical articles, interviews, reviews from across the US, and an extensive and informative artists' classified listings section. Our writers and the artists they cover represent the scope and diversity of the country's art scene." Estab. 1977. Circ. 4,000. Pays on publication. Publishes ms an average of 3 months after acceptance. Byline given. Buys all rights. Editorial lead time 2 months. Submit seasonal material 2 months in advance. Accepts simultaneous and previously published submissions. Query for electronic submissions. "Writers should contact us regarding manuscript status." Sample copy for $1.24. Writer's guidelines for #10 SASE.
Nonfiction: Interview/profile. See our editorial schedule. Buys 300 mss/year. "We rely on the initiatives of our writers for review coverage." Pays $35-100.

Photos: Send photos with submission. Reviews color slides, b&w prints. Offers no additional payment for photos accepted with ms. Identification of subjects required.

Columns/Departments: Contact: Barbara Schrieber, associate editor. Newsbriefs (current art concerns and news—call for scope). Buys 18-24 mss/year. Query. Pays $35.

Tips: "Write for a copy of our writer's guidelines and request a sample copy of *Art Papers*. Interested writers should call Glenn Harper to discuss intents."

ART REVUE MAGAZINE, 302 W. 13th St., Loveland CO 80537. (303)669-0625. Fax: (970)669-0625. Editor: Jan McNutt. 100% freelance written. Quarterly magazine covering fine art of sculpture and painting. "Articles are focused on fine art: how to, business of art, profiles on artists, museums, galleries, art businesses, art shows and exhibitions." Estab. 1990. Circ. 7,000. Pays on publication. Publishes ms an average of 3 months after acceptance. Byline given. Offers 25% kill fee or $25. Buys first rights. Editorial lead time 3 months. Submit seasonal material 6 months in advance. Accepts simultaneous submissions. Sample copy for $3. Writer's guidelines for #10 SASE.

Nonfiction: Essays, how-to, humor, interview/profile, new product, opinion, personal experience, photo feature, technical, travel. Does not want crafts, pottery, doll-making, inspirational, religious, tie-dying. Special issue: Sculpture issue (August). Buys 12-20 mss/year. Query. Length: 1,000-2,500 words. Pays $100 and up.

Photos: Send photos with submission. Reviews 4×5 prints. Offers no additional payment for photos accepted with ms. Captions, identification of subjects required.

Columns/Departments: Art Matters (interesting art happenings), 100-200 words; Profiles (features) (famous, non-famous artists), 1,000-2,500 words; Profiles on Businesses (bronze foundries, art schools, etc.), 1,000-2,500 words; Covert (short profile on totally unknown artist), 50-150 words. Buys 12-20 mss/year. Query. Pays $100-200.

Fillers: Anecdotes, facts, gags to be illustrated by cartoonist, newsbreaks, short humor. Buys 10-12/year. Length: 50-250 words. Pays $25-100.

Tips: "Write a letter of inquiry to Jan McNutt. Present some ideas for articles."

ART TIMES, A Literary Journal and Resource for All the Arts, P.O. Box 730, Mount Marion NY 12456-0730. Phone/fax: (914)246-6944. E-mail: arttimes@mhv.net. Website: http://www.rain.org/sculptura/arttimes/arttimes.html. Editor: Raymond J. Steiner. 10% freelance written. Prefers to work with published/established writers; works with a small number of new/unpublished writers each year. Monthly tabloid covering the arts (visual, theatre, dance, etc.). "*Art Times* covers the art fields and is distributed in locations most frequented by those enjoying the arts. Our copies are sold at newsstands and are distributed throughout upstate New York counties as well as in most of the galleries in Soho, 57th Street and Madison Avenue in the metropolitan area; locations include theaters, galleries, museums, cultural centers and the like. Our readers are mostly over 40, affluent, art-conscious and sophisticated. Subscribers are located across US and abroad (Italy, France, Germany, Greece, Russia, etc.)." Estab. 1984. Circ. 15,000. Pays on publication. Publishes ms an average of 1 year after acceptance. Byline given. Buys first serial rights. Submit seasonal/holiday material 8 months in advance. Accepts simultaneous submissions. Reports in 3 months on queries; 6 months on mss. Sample copy for 9×12 SAE with 6 first-class stamps. Writer's guidelines for #10 SASE.

Fiction: Raymond J. Steiner, fiction editor. "We're looking for short fiction that aspires to be *literary*. No excessive violence, sexist, off-beat, erotic, sports, or juvenile fiction." Buys 8-10 mss/year. Send complete ms. Length: 1,500 words maximum. Pays $25 maximum (honorarium) and 1 year's free subscription.

Poetry: Cheryl A. Rice, poetry editor. Poet's Niche. Avant-garde, free verse, haiku, light verse, traditional. "We prefer well-crafted 'literary' poems. No excessively sentimental poetry." Buys 30-35 poems/year. Submit maximum 6 poems. Length: 20 lines maximum. Offers contributor copies and 1 year's free subscription.

Tips: "Be advised that we are presently on an approximate two-year lead. We are now receiving 300-400 poems and 40-50 short stories per month. We only publish two to three poems and one story each issue. Be familiar with *Art Times* and its special audience. *Art Times* has literary leanings with articles written by a staff of scholars knowledgeable in their respective fields. Although an 'arts' publication, we observe no restrictions (other than noted) in accepting fiction/poetry other than a concern for quality writing—subjects can cover anything and not specifically arts."

THE ARTIST'S MAGAZINE, F&W Publications, Inc., 1507 Dana Ave., Cincinnati OH 45207-1005. (513)531-2690, ext. 386. Fax: (513)531-2902. Editor: Sandy Carpenter. 80% freelance written. Works with a small number of new/unpublished writers each year. Monthly magazine covering primarily two-dimensional art instruction for working artists. "Ours is a highly visual approach to teaching the serious amateur artist techniques that will help him improve his skills and market his work. The style should be crisp and immediately engaging." Circ. 250,000. **Pays on acceptance.** Publishes ms an average of 6 months after acceptance. Bionote given for feature material. Offers 20% kill fee. Buys first North American serial and second serial (reprint) rights. Accepts previously published articles "as long as noted as such." Reports in 2 months. Sample copy for $3 and 9×12 SAE with 3 first-class stamps. Writer's guidelines for #10 SASE.

● Writers must have working knowledge of art techniques. This magazine's most consistent need is for instructional articles written in the artist's voice.

Nonfiction: Instructional only—how an artist uses a particular technique, how he handles a particular subject or medium, or how he markets his work. "The emphasis must be on how the reader can learn some method of improving his artwork, or the marketing of it." No unillustrated articles; no seasonal/holiday material; no travel articles; no profiles of artists. Buys 60 mss/year. Query first; all queries must be accompanied by slides, transparencies, prints or tearsheets of the artist's work as well as the artist's bio, and the writer's bio and clips. Length: 1,000-2,500 words. Pays $200-350 and up. Sometimes pays the expenses of writers on assignment.

Photos: "Transparencies are required with every accepted article since these are essential for our instructional format. Full captions must accompany these." Buys one-time rights.

Departments: Two departments are open to freelance writers. Strictly Business (articles dealing with the business and legal end of selling art; taxes, recordkeeping, copyright, contracts, etc.). Query first. Length: 1,800 word limit. Pays $200 and up. P.S. (a humorous look at art from the artist's point of view, or at least sympathetic to the artist; also art-related games, puzzles and poetry). Send complete ms. Pays $50 and up.

Tips: "Look at several current issues and read the author's guidelines carefully. Remember that our readers are fine and graphic artists. We plan to introduce a mini-feature called *Artist Highlight* that will offer a short profile of artists who've had unusual experiences or use unusual materials. Word limit: 800. Submission must include art samples."

‡**ART-TALK**, Box 8508, Scottsdale AZ 85252. (602)948-1799. Fax: (602)994-9284. Editor: Bill Macomber. Contact: Thom Romeo. 30% freelance written. Newspaper published 9 times/year covering fine art. "*Art-Talk* deals strictly with fine art, the emphasis being on the Southwest. National and international news is also covered. All editorial is of current interest/activities and written for the art collector." Estab. 1981. Circ. 40,000. **Pays on acceptance.** Publishes ms an average of 2 months after acceptance. Byline given. Buys first North American serial rights and makes work-for-hire assignments. Editorial lead time 3 months. Submit seasonal material 4 months in advance. Accepts simultaneous and previously published submissions. Reports in 2 weeks on queries; 1 month on mss. Sample copy free on request.

Nonfiction: Exposé, general interest, humor, interview/profile, opinion, personal experience, photo feature. No articles on non-professional artists (e.g., Sunday Painters) or about a single commercial art gallery. Buys 12-15 mss/year. Query with published clips. Length: 500-4,000 words. Pays $75-800 for assigned articles; $50-750 for unsolicited articles. Sometimes pays expenses of writers on assignment.

Photos: State availability of photos with submission. Reviews transparencies, prints. Offers no additional payment for photos accepted with ms. Captions, identification of subjects required. Buys one-time rights.

Columns/Departments: Maintains 9 freelance columnists in different cities. Buys 38 mss/year. Query with published clips. Pays $100-175.

Tips: "Good working knowledge of the art gallery/auction/artist interconnections. Should be a part of the 'art scene' in an area known for art."

‡**METROPOLIS, The Magazine of Architecture and Design**, Bellerophon Publications, 177 E. 87th St., New York NY 10128. (212)722-5050. Fax: (212)427-1938. E-mail: metropol@interport.net. Website: http://www.internet.net~metropol. Editor: Susan S. Szenasy. 75% freelance written. Monthly magazine (combined issues January/February and July/August) for consumers interested in architecture and design. Estab. 1981. Circ. 40,000. **Pays on acceptance.** Publishes ms an average of 3 months after acceptance. Byline given. Buys first rights or makes work-for-hire assignments. Submit calendar material 6 weeks in advance. Reports in 8 months. Sample copy for $4.95.

Nonfiction: Essays (design, architecture, urban planning issues and ideas), profiles (on multi-disciplinary designers/architects). No profiles on individual architectural practices, information from public relations firms, or fine arts. Buys approximately 30 mss/year. Query with published clips. Length: 500-2,000 words. Pays $100-1,000.

Photos: State availability of or send photos with submission. Reviews contact sheets, 35mm or 4×5 transparencies, or 8×10 b&w prints. Payment offered for certain photos. Captions required. Buys one-time rights.

Columns/Departments: Insites (short takes on design and architecture), 100-600 words; pays $50-150; In Print (book review essays), 1,000-2,000 words; The Metropolis Observed (architecture and city planning news features and opinion), 750-1,500 words; pays $200-500; Visible City (historical aspects of cities), 1,500-2,500 words; pays $600-800; By Design (product design), 1,000-2,000 words; pays $600-800. Buys approximately 40 mss/year. Query with published clips.

Tips: "We're looking for ideas, what's new, the obscure or the wonderful. Keep in mind that we are interested *only* in the consumer end of architecture and design. Send query with examples of photos explaining how you see illustrations working with article. Also, be patient and don't expect an immediate answer after submission of query."

SOUTHWEST ART, CBH Publishing, P.O. Box 460535, Houston TX 77256-8535. (713)850-0990. Fax: (713)850-1314. Editor-in-Chief: Susan H. McGarry. 60% freelance written. Monthly fine arts magazine "directed to art collectors interested in artists, market trends and art history of the American West." Estab. 1971. Circ. 60,000. **Pays on acceptance.** Publishes ms an average of 1 year after acceptance. Byline given.

Offers $125 kill fee. Submit seasonal/holiday material 8 months in advance. Reports in 6 months. Free writer's guidelines.

Nonfiction: Book excerpts, interview/profile, opinion. No fiction or poetry. Buys 70 mss/year. Query with published clips. Length 1,400-1,600 words. Pays $500 for assigned articles. Send photos with submission.
Photos: Reviews 35mm, 2¼, 4×5 transparencies and 8×10 prints. Captions and identification of subjects required. Negotiates rights.

THEDAMU, The Black Arts Magazine, Detroit Black Arts Alliance, 13217 Livernois, Detroit MI 48238-3162. (313)931-3427. Editor: David Rambeau. Managing Editor: Titilaya Akanke. Art Director: Charles Allen. 20% freelance written. Quarterly literary magazine on the arts. "We publish Afro-American feature articles on local artists." Estab. 1965. Circ. 4,000. Pays on publication. Publishes 4 months after acceptance. Byline given. Buys one-time rights. Submit seasonal/holiday material 4 months in advance. Accepts simultaneous submissions. Reports in 1 month on queries; 3 months on mss. Sample copy for $2 in U.S. postage stamps (no checks or money orders) and 6×9 SAE with 4 first-class stamps. Writer's guidelines for #10 SASE.

Nonfiction: Essays, interview/profile. Buys 20 mss/year. Send complete ms. Length: 500-1,500 words. Pays $10-25 for unsolicited articles. Pays with contributor copies or other premiums if writer agrees.
Reprints: Send photocopy of article and information about when and where the article previously appeared.
Photos: State availability of photos with submission. Reviews 5×7 prints. Offers no additional payment for photos accepted with ms. Captions, model releases and identification of subjects required. Buys one-time rights.
Tips: "Send a résumé and sample manuscript. Query for fiction, poetry, plays and film/video scenarios. Especially interested in Afro-centric cartoonists for special editions and exhibitions."

U.S. ART: All the News That Fits Prints, MSP Communications, 220 S. Sixth St., Suite 500, Minneapolis MN 55402. (612)339-7571. Fax: (612)339-5806. Editor/Publisher: Frank Sisser. Managing Editor: Sara Gilbert. 50% freelance written. Monthly magazine. Two artist profiles per issue; service articles to inform limited-edition print collectors of trends and options in the market; round-up features spotlighting a particular genre (wildlife, western, fantasy art, etc.) All artists featured must be active in the market for limited-edition prints. Circ. 55,000. Distributed primarily through galleries as a free service to their customers. Writer byline given. Pays $450 for features. Offers 25% kill fee. Departments/columns are staff-written.

WESTART, P.O. Box 6868, Auburn CA 95604. (916)885-0969. Editor-in-Chief: Martha Garcia. Semimonthly 12-page tabloid emphasizing art for practicing artists and artists/craftsmen; students of art and art patrons. Estab. 1961. Circ. 4,000. Pays on publication. Buys all rights. Byline given. Phone queries OK. Free sample copy and writer's guidelines.
Nonfiction: Informational, photo feature, profile. No hobbies. Buys 6-8 mss/year. Query or submit complete ms with SASE for reply or return. Length: 700-800 words. Pays 50¢/column inch.
Photos: Purchased with or without accompanying ms. Send b&w prints. Pays 50¢/column inch.
Tips: "We publish information which is current—that is, we will use a review of an exhibition only if exhibition is still open on the date of publication. Therefore, reviewer must be familiar with our printing and news deadlines."

‡**WILDLIFE ART, The Art Journal of the Natural World**, Pothole Publications, Inc. 4725 Hwy. 7, P.O. Box 16246, St. Louis Park MN 55416-0246. (612)927-9056. Fax: (612)927-9353. Editor-in-Chief: Robert Koenke. Editor: Rebecca Hakala Rowland. 80% freelance written. Bimonthly magazine of wildlife art and conservation. "*Wildlife Art* is the world's largest wildlife art magazine. Features cover interviews on living artists as well as wildlife art masters, illustrators and conservation organizations. Audience is publishers, collectors, galleries, museums, show promoters worldwide." Estab. 1982. Circ. 55,000. **Pays on acceptance.** Publishes ms an average of 6 months after acceptance. Byline given. Negotiable kill fee. Buys second serial (reprint) rights. Reports in 4-6 months. Sample copy for 9×12 SAE with 10 first-class stamps. Writer's guidelines for #10 SASE.
Nonfiction: Buys 40 mss/year. Query with published clips. Length: 800-5,000 words. Pays $150-1,000 for assigned articles.
Columns/Departments: Buys up to 6 mss/year. Pays $100-300.

ASSOCIATIONS

Association publications allow writers to write for national audiences while covering local stories. If your town has a Kiwanis, Lions or Rotary Club chapter, one of its projects might merit a story in the club's magazine. If you are a member of the organization, find out before you write an article if the publication pays members for stories; some associations do not. In addition, some association publications gather their own club information and rely on freelancers solely for outside features. Be sure to find out what these policies are before you submit a manuscript. Club-financed magazines that carry material not directly related to the group's activities are classified by their subject matter in the Consumer and Trade sections.

THE ELKS MAGAZINE, 425 W. Diversey, Chicago IL 60614-6196. E-mail: elksmag@aol.com. Website: http://www.elksmag.com. Editor: Fred D. Oakes. Managing Editor: Judith L. Keogh. 50% freelance written. Prefers to work with published/established writers. Magazine published 10 times/year emphasizing general interest with family appeal. Estab. 1922. Circ. 1,500,000. **Pays on acceptance.** Buys first North American serial rights. Reports in 2 months. Sample copy and writer's guidelines for 9×12 SAE with 4 first-class stamps.
Nonfiction: Articles of information, business, contemporary life problems and situations, nostalgia, or just interesting topics, ranging from medicine, science and history to sports. "The articles should not just be a rehash of existing material. They must be fresh, thought-provoking, well-researched and documented." No fiction, political articles, travel, fillers or verse. Buys 2-3 mss/issue. Query; no phone queries. Length: 1,500-3,000 words. Pays from $150.
Tips: "Requirements are clearly stated in our guidelines. Loose, wordy pieces are not accepted. A submission, following a query letter go-ahead, should include several prints if the piece lends itself to illustration. We offer no additional payment for photos accepted with manuscripts."

KIWANIS, 3636 Woodview Trace, Indianapolis IN 46268-3196. Fax: (317)879-0204. Website: http://www.kiwanis.org. Managing Editor: Chuck Jonak. 85% of feature articles freelance written. Buys about 40 mss/year. Magazine published 10 times/year for business and professional persons and their families. Estab. 1917. Circ. 276,500. **Pays on acceptance.** Buys first serial rights. Offers 40% kill fee. Publishes ms an average of 6 months after acceptance. Byline given. Reports within 2 months. Sample copy and writer's guidelines for 9×12 SAE with 5 first-class stamps.
• Ranked as one of the best markets for freelance writers in *Writer's Yearbook*'s annual "Top 100 Markets," January 1996.
Nonfiction: Articles about social and civic betterment, small-business concerns, science, education, religion, family, youth, health, recreation, etc. Emphasis on objectivity, intelligent analysis and thorough research of contemporary issues. Positive tone preferred. Concise, lively writing, absence of clichés, and impartial presentation of controversy required. When applicable, include information and quotations from international sources. Avoid writing strictly to a US audience. "We have a continuing need for articles of international interest. In addition, we are very interested in proposals that concern helping youth, particularly prenatal through age five: day care, developmentally appropriate education, early intervention for at-risk children, parent education, safety and health." Length: 2,000-2,500 words. Pays $600-1,000. "No fiction, personal essays, profiles, travel pieces, fillers or verse of any kind. A light or humorous approach is welcomed where the subject is appropriate and all other requirements are observed." Usually pays the expenses of writers on assignment. Query first. Must include SASE for response.
Photos: "We accept photos submitted with manuscripts. Our rate for a manuscript with good photos is higher than for one without." Model release and identification of subjects required. Buys one-time rights.
Tips: "We will work with any writer who presents a strong feature article idea applicable to our magazine's audience and who will prove he or she knows the craft of writing. First, obtain writer's guidelines and a sample copy. Study for general style and content. When querying, present detailed outline of proposed manuscript's focus, direction, and editorial intent. Indicate expert sources to be used for attribution, as well as article's tone and length. Present a well-researched, smoothly written manuscript that contains a 'human quality' with the use of anecdotes, practical examples, quotations, etc."

THE LION, 300 22nd St., Oak Brook IL 60521-8842. (708)571-5466. Fax: (703)571-8890. Senior Editor: Robert Kleinfelder. 35% freelance written. Works with a small number of new/unpublished writers each year. Monthly magazine covering service club organization for Lions Club members and their families. Estab. 1918. Circ. 600,000. **Pays on acceptance.** Publishes ms an average of 5 months after acceptance. Buys all rights. Byline given. Phone queries OK. Reports in 6 weeks. Free sample copy and writer's guidelines.
Nonfiction: Informational (issues of interest to civic-minded individuals) and photo feature (must be of a Lions Club service project). No travel, biography or personal experiences. Welcomes humor, if sophisticated but clean; no sensationalism. Prefers anecdotes in articles. Buys 4 mss/issue. Query. Length: 500-2,200. Pays $100-750. Sometimes pays the expenses of writers on assignment.
Photos: Purchased with or without accompanying ms or on assignment. Captions required. Query for photos. Black and white and color glossies at least 5×7 or 35mm color slides. Total purchase price for ms includes payment for photos accepted with ms. "Be sure photos are clear and as candid as possible."
Tips: "Incomplete details on how the Lions involved actually carried out a project and poor quality photos are the most frequent mistakes made by writers in completing an article assignment for us. We are geared increasingly to an international audience. Writers who travel internationally could query for possible assignments, although only locally-related expenses could be paid."

THE OPTIMIST, Optimist International, 4494 Lindell Blvd., St. Louis MO 63108. (314)371-6000. Fax: (314)371-6006. Editor: Dennis R. Osterwisch. 10% freelance written. Bimonthly magazine about the work of Optimist clubs and members for members of the Optimist clubs in the United States and Canada. Circ. 154,000. **Pays on acceptance.** Publishes ms an average of 4 months after acceptance. Buys first North American serial rights. Submit seasonal material 3 months in advance. Reports in 1 week. Sample copy and writer's guidelines for 9×12 SAE with 4 first-class stamps.
Nonfiction: "We want articles about the activities of local Optimist clubs. These volunteer community-service clubs are constantly involved in projects, aimed primarily at helping young people. With over 4,000 Optimist clubs in the US and Canada, writers should have ample resources. Some large metropolitan areas boast several dozen clubs. We are also interested in feature articles on individual club members who have in some way distinguished themselves, either in their club work or their personal lives. Good photos for all articles are a plus and can mean a bigger check." Will also consider short (200-400 word) articles that deal with self-improvement or a philosophy of optimism. Buys 1-2 mss/issue. Query. "Submit a letter that conveys your ability to turn out a well-written article and tells exactly what the scope of the article will be." Length: up to 1,000 words. Pays $300 and up.
Reprints: Send photocopy of article and information about when and where the article previously appeared. Pays 50% of amount paid for an original article.
Photos: State availability of photos. Payment negotiated. Captions preferred. Buys all rights. "No mug shots or people lined up against the wall shaking hands."
Tips: "Find out what the Optimist clubs in your area are doing, then find out if we'd be interested in an article on a specific club project. All of our clubs are eager to talk about what they're doing. Just ask them and you'll probably have an article idea. We would like to see short pieces on the positive affect an optimistic outlook on life can have on an individual. Examples of famous people who overcame adversity because of their positive attitude are welcome."

PERSPECTIVE, Pioneer Clubs, P.O. Box 788, Wheaton IL 60189-0788. (630)293-1600. Fax: (630)293-3053. Editor: Rebecca Powell Parat. 15% freelance written. Works with a number of new/unpublished writers each year. Triannual magazine for "volunteer leaders of clubs for girls and boys ages 2-grade 12. Clubs are sponsored by local churches throughout North America." Estab. 1967. Circ. 24,000. **Pays on acceptance.** Publishes ms an average of 6 months after acceptance. Buys full rights for assigned articles, first North American serial rights for unsolicited mss, and second serial (reprint) rights. Submit seasonal/holiday material 9 months in advance. Reports in 6 weeks. Writer's guidelines and sample copy for $1.75 and 9×12 SAE with 6 first-class stamps.
Nonfiction: Informational (relationship skills, leadership skills); inspirational (stories of leaders and children in Pioneer Clubs); interview (Christian education leaders, club leaders); personal experience (of club leaders). Buys 2-3 mss/year. Byline given. Length: 500-1,500 words. Pays $25-100.
Reprints: Send photocopy of article or typed ms with rights for sale noted.
Columns/Departments: Storehouse (game, activity, outdoor activity, service project suggestions—all related to club projects for ages 2 through grade 12). Buys 2-3 mss/year. Submit complete ms. Length: 150-250 words. Pays $8-15.
Tips: "Submit articles directly related to club work, practical in nature, i.e., ideas for leader training in communication, discipline, teaching skills. However, most of our articles are assigned. Writers who have contact with a Pioneer Club program in their area and who are interested in working on assignment are welcome to contact us."

RECREATION NEWS, Official Publication of the League of Federal Recreation Associations, Inc., Icarus Publishers, Inc., P.O. Box 32335, Calvert Station, Washington DC 20007-0635. (202)965-6960. E-mail: recreation_news@mcimail.com. Editor: Rebecca Heaton. 85% freelance written. Monthly guide to leisure-time activities for federal workers covering outdoor recreation, travel, fitness and indoor pastimes. Estab. 1979. Circ. 104,000. Pays on publication. Publishes ms an average of 8 months after acceptance. Byline given. Buys first rights and second serial (reprint) rights. Submit seasonal/holiday material 10 months in advance. Accepts simultaneous submissions. Reports in 2 months. Sample copy and writer's guidelines for 9×12 SAE with 4 first-class stamps.
Nonfiction: Articles Editor. Leisure travel (no international travel); sports; hobbies; historical/nostalgic (Washington-related); personal experience (with recreation, life in Washington). Special issues: skiing (December); education (August). Query with clips of published work. Length: 800-2,000 words. Pays from $50-300.
Reprints: Send tearsheet or photocopy of article, typed ms with rights for sale noted, with information about where and when it previously appeared. Pays $50.
Photos: Photo editor. State availability of photos with query letter or ms. Uses b&w prints. Pays $25. Uses color transparency on cover only. Pays $50-125 for transparency. Captions and identification of subjects required.
Tips: "Our writers generally have a few years of professional writing experience and their work runs to the lively and conversational. We like more manuscripts in a wide range of recreational topics, including the off-beat. The areas of our publication most open to freelancers are general articles on travel and sports, both

participational and spectator, also historic in the DC area. In general, stories on sites visits need to include info on nearby places of interest and places to stop for lunch, to shop, etc."

THE ROTARIAN, Rotary International, 1560 Sherman Ave., Evanston IL 60201-1461. (847)866-3000. Fax: (847)866-9732. E-mail: 75457.3577@compuserve.com. Website: http://www.rotary.org. Editor: Willmon L. White. Managing Editor: Charles W. Pratt. 40% freelance written. Monthly magazine for Rotarian business and professional men and women and their families, schools, libraries, hospitals, etc. "Articles should appeal to an international audience and in some way help Rotarians help other people. The organization's rationale is one of hope, encouragement and belief in the power of individuals talking and working together." Estab. 1911. Circ. 520,430. **Pays on acceptance**. Byline sometimes given. Kill fee negotiable. Buys one-time or all rights. Reports in 2 weeks. Sample copy for 9×12 SAE with 6 first-class stamps. Writer's guidelines for #10 SASE.
  • Ranked as one of the best markets for freelance writers in *Writer's Yearbook's* annual "Top 100 Markets," January 1996.
Nonfiction: Essays, general interest, humor, inspirational, photo feature, travel, business, environment. No fiction, religious or political articles. Query with published clips. Negotiates payment.
Reprints: Send tearsheet or photocopy of article or typed ms with rights for sale noted and information about when and where the article previously appeared.
Photos: State availability of photos with submission. Reviews contact sheets and transparencies. Usually buys one-time rights.
Columns/Departments: Manager's Memo (business), Executive Health, Executive Lifestyle, Earth Diary, Travel Tips, Trends. Length: 800 words. Query.
Tips: "Study issues, then query with SASE."

SCOUTING, Boy Scouts of America, 1325 W. Walnut Hill Lane, P.O. Box 75015, Irving TX 75015-2079. (214)580-2367. Fax: (214)580-2079. E-mail: 103064.3363@compuserve.com. Editor: Jon C. Halter. Executive Editor: Scott Daniels. 90% freelance written. Bimonthly magazine on Scouting activities for adult leaders of the Boy Scouts and Cub Scouts. Estab. 1913. Circ. 1,000,000. **Pays on acceptance**. Publishes ms an average of 6 months after acceptance. Byline given. Buys first North American serial rights. Submit seasonal/holiday material 6 months in advance. Reports in 2 weeks. Sample copy for $1 and #10 SAE with 4 first-class stamps. Writer's guidelines for #10 SASE.
  • *Scouting* is looking for more articles about scouting families involved in interesting/unusual family-together activities/hobbies, i.e., caving, bicycle touring, (two that they've done) and profiles of urban/inner-city scout leaders and packs or troop with successful histories.
Nonfiction: Buys 60 mss/year. Query with published clips. Length: 1,000-1,500 words. Pays $500-800 for assigned articles; $200-500 for unsolicited articles. Pays expenses of writers on assignment.
Reprints: Send photocopy of article and information about where and when the article previously appeared.
Photos: State availability of photos with submission. Reviews contact sheets and transparencies. Identification of subjects required. Buys one-time rights.
Columns/Departments: Family Quiz (quiz and puzzles on topics of family interest), 1,000 words; Way it Was (Scouting history), 1,200 words; Family Talk (family—raising kids, etc.), 1,200 words. Buys 6 mss/year. Query. Pays $200-400.

THE TOASTMASTER, Toastmasters International, 23182 Arroyo Vista, Rancho Santa Margarita CA 92688 or P.O. Box 9052, Mission Viejo, CA 92690-7052. (714)858-8255. Fax: (714)858-1207. Website: http://www.toastmasters.org. Editor: Suzanne Frey. Associate Editor: Beth Curtis. 50% freelance written. Monthly magazine on public speaking, leadership and club concerns. "This magazine is sent to members of Toastmasters International, a nonprofit educational association of men and women throughout the world who are interested in developing their communication and leadership skills. Members range from novice speakers to professional orators and come from a wide variety of backgrounds." Estab. 1932. Circ. 170,000. **Pays on acceptance**. Publishes ms an average of 10 months after acceptance. Byline given. Buys second serial (reprint), first-time or all rights. Submit seasonal/holiday material 3 months in advance. Accepts simultaneous submissions. Reports in 6 weeks on queries; 1 month on mss. Sample copy for 9×12 SAE with 4 first-class stamps. Writer's guidelines for #10 SASE.
Nonfiction: Book excerpts, how-to (communications related), humor (only if informative; humor cannot be off-color or derogatory), interview/profile (only if of a very prominent member or former member of Toastmasters International or someone who has a valuable perspective on communication and leadership). Buys 50 mss/year. Query. Length: 1,000-2,500 words. Pays $75-250. Sometimes pays expenses of writers on assignment. "Toastmasters members are requested to view their submissions as contributions to the organization. Sometimes asks for book excerpts and reprints without payment, but original contribution from individuals outside Toastmasters will be paid for at stated rates."
Reprints: Accepts previously published submissions.
Photos: Reviews b&w prints. Offers no additional payment for photos accepted with ms. Captions are required. Buys all rights.

Tips: "We are looking primarily for 'how-to' articles on subjects from the broad fields of communications and leadership which can be directly applied by our readers in their self-improvement and club programming efforts. Concrete examples are useful. Avoid sexist or nationalist language."

VFW MAGAZINE, Veterans of Foreign Wars of the United States, 406 W. 34th St., Kansas City MO 64111. (816)756-3390. Fax: (816)968-1169. Editor: Rich Kolb. 40% freelance written. Monthly magazine on veterans' affairs, military history, patriotism, defense and current events. "*VFW Magazine* goes to its members worldwide, all having served honorably in the armed forces overseas from World War II through Bosnia." Circ. 2,100,000. **Pays on acceptance.** Offers 50% kill fee on commissioned articles. Buys first rights. Submit seasonal/holiday material 6 months in advance. Submit detailed query letter, résumé and sample clips. Reports in 2 months. Sample copy for 9×12 SAE with 5 first-class stamps.
  • *VFW Magazine* is becoming more current-events oriented.
Nonfiction: Veterans' and defense affairs. Buys 25-30 mss/year. Query. Length: 1,500 words. Pays up to $500 maximum unless otherwise negotiated.
Photos: Send photos with submission. Reviews contact sheets, negatives, transparencies and prints. Captions, model releases and identification of subjects required. Buys first North American rights.

‡**THE WAR CRY**, The Salvation Army, 615 Slaters Lane, Alexandria VA 22313. Fax: (703)684-5539. Editor: Lt. Colonel Marlene Chase. Managing Editor: Jeff McDonald. 5% freelance written. Biweekly magazine covering army news and Christian devotional writing. Estab. 1881. Circ. 500,000. **Pays on acceptance.** Publishes ms an average of 1 year after acceptance. Byline given. Buys one-time rights. Editorial lead time 1 month. Submit seasonal material 1 year in advance. Reports in 1 month. Sample copy free on request. Writer's guidelines free on request.
Nonfiction: Humor, inspirational, interview/profile, personal experience, religious. No missionary stories, confessions. Buys 40 mss/year. Send complete ms. Pays 20¢/word minimum for assigned articles; 10-20¢ for unsolicited articles. Sometimes pays expenses of writers on assignment.
Photos: Offers $35-150/photo. Identification of subjects required. Buys one-time rights Buys all rights.
Fiction: Religious. Buys 2-4 mss/year. Send complete ms. Length: 1,200 words maximum. Pays 20¢/words.
Poetry: Free verse. Inspirational only. Buys 6-10 poems/year. Submit maximum 5 poems. Length: 16 lines maximum. Pays $20-50.
Fillers: Anecdotes (inspirational). Buys 6-8/year. Length: 200-500 words. Pays 20¢/word.
Tips: "We're soliciting more short fictional, inspirational articles and poetry, interviews with Christian athletes, evangelical leaders and celebrities, and theme-focused articles." Editorial calendar and writers' guidelines available upon request with SASE.

ASTROLOGY, METAPHYSICAL AND NEW AGE

Magazines in this section carry articles ranging from shamanism to extraterrestrial phenomena. With the coming millennium, there is increased interest in spirituality, angels, near death experiences, mind/body healing and other New Age concepts and figures. The following publications regard astrology, psychic phenomena, metaphysical experiences and related subjects as sciences or as objects of serious study. Each has an individual personality and approach to these phenomena. If you want to write for these publications, be sure to read them carefully before submitting.

FATE, Llewellyn Worldwide, Ltd., P.O. Box 64383, St. Paul MN 55164-0383. Fax: (612)291-1908. 70% freelance written. Estab. 1901. Buys all rights. Byline given. Pays after publication. Sample copy and writer's guidelines for $3 and 9×12 SAE with 5 first-class stamps. Reports in 3 months.
Nonfiction and Fillers: Personal psychic and mystical experiences, 350-500 words. Pays $25. Articles on parapsychology, Fortean phenomena, cryptozoology, parapsychology, spiritual healing, flying saucers, new frontiers of science, and mystical aspects of ancient civilizations, 500-3,000 words. Must include complete authenticating details. Prefers interesting accounts of single events rather than roundups. "We very frequently accept manuscripts from new writers; the majority are individual's first-person accounts of their own psychic/mystical/spiritual experiences. We do need to have all details, where, when, why, who and what, included

for complete documentation. We ask for a notarized statement attesting to truth of the article." Query or submit completed ms. Pays 10¢/word. Fillers must be be fully authenticated also, and on similar topics. Length: 50-300 words.

Photos: Buys slides or prints with mss. Pays $10.

Tips: "We would like more stories about *current* paranormal or unusual events."

GNOSIS, A Journal of the Western Inner Traditions, Lumen Foundation, P.O. Box 14217, San Francisco CA 94114. (415)974-0600. E-mail: smoley@well.com. Editor: Richard Smoley. 75% freelance written. Quarterly magazine covering esoteric spirituality. "*Gnosis* is a journal covering the esoteric, mystical, and occult traditions of Western civilization, including Judaism, Christianity, Islam, and Paganism." Estab. 1985. Circ. 16,000. Pays on publication. Publishes ms an average of 3 months after acceptance. Byline given. Buys first North American serial rights. Editorial lead time 5 months. Submit seasonal material 5 months in advance. Reports in 1 month on queries; 4 months on mss. Sample copy for $9. Writer's guidelines for #10 SASE.

Nonfiction: Book excerpts, essays, religious. Special issues: Love: Sacred & Profane (deadline November 1, 1996); Freemasonry (deadline February 1, 1997). Buys 32 mss/year. Query with published clips. Length: 1,000-5,000 words. Pays $100-300 for assigned articles; $50-200 for unsolicited articles. All contributors receive 4 contributor's copies plus a year's subscription in addition to payment.

Photos: State availability of photos with submissions. Reviews contact sheets, prints. Offers $50-125/photo. Captions, identification of subjects required. Buys one-time rights.

Columns/Departments: News & Notes (items of current interest in esoteric spirituality), 1,000 words; Book Reviews (reviews of new books in the field), 250-1,000 words. Buys 45 mss/year. Query with published clips. Pays $40-100.

Tips: "We give strong preference to articles related to our issue themes (available with writer's guidelines)."

‡MAGICAL BLEND MAGAZINE, A Primer for the 21st Century, Magical Blend Unlimited, P.O. Box 600, Chico CA 95927. (916)893-9037. Contact: Jerry Swider, managing editor. 50% freelance written. Quarterly magazine covering lifestyles of change. "*Magical Blend* accepts the premise that society is undergoing a fundamental transformation. A new world view is being born, and whether this birth is to be an easy or difficult one will depend largely upon the individual. It is our aim to chart the course this transformation is taking and to assist the individual to cope with and contribute to the birthing process. We believe that people's thoughts influence their reality; if this is true then the world we live in is a combination of our highest hopes, our deepest fears, and the whole range of experience that falls between. Our goal is to embrace the hopes, transform the fears, and discover the magical behind the mundane. In this way, we hope to act as a catalyst to encourage the individual to achieve his or her highest level of spiritual awareness. We endorse no one pathway to spiritual growth, but attempt to explore many alternative possibilities to help transform the planet." Estab. 1980. Circ. 65,000. Pays on publication. Publishes ms an average of 2 months after acceptance. Byline given. Buys all rights. Editorial lead time 8 months. Reports in 2 months. Sample copy free on request. Writer's guidelines for #10 SASE.

Nonfiction: Book excerpts, essays, general interest, inspirational, interview/profile, religious. "We don't want badly written articles from people who haven't seen our magazine." Buys 24 mss/year. Send complete ms. Length: 1,000-5,000 words. Pays $200. Pays writers with contributor copies.

Photos: State availability of photos with submission. Reviews transparencies. Negotiates payment individually. Model releases, identification of subjects required. Buys all rights.

Fillers: Newsbreaks. Buys 12-20/year. Length: 300-450 words. Pays $25.

PARABOLA, The Magazine of Myth and Tradition, The Society for the Study of Myth and Tradition, 656 Broadway, New York NY 10012-2317. (212)505-9037. Fax: (212)979-7325. E-mail: parabola@panix. com. Website: http://members.aol.com/parabmag/ParabolaWWW/. Quarterly magazine on mythology, tradition and comparative religion. "*Parabola* is devoted to the exploration of the quest for meaning as expressed in the myths, symbols, and tales of the religious traditions. Particular emphasis is on the relationship between this wisdom and contemporary life." Estab. 1976. Circ. 40,000. Pays on publication. Publishes ms 3 months after acceptance. Byline given. Offers kill fee for assigned articles only (usually $100). Buys first North American serial, first, one-time or second serial (reprint) rights. Editorial lead time 4 months. Accepts simultaneous submissions. Reports in 3 weeks on queries; on mss "variable—for articles directed to a particular theme, we usually respond the month of or the month after the deadline (so for an April 15 deadline, we are likely to respond in April or May). Articles not directed to themes may wait four months or more!" Sample copy for $6 current issue; $8 back issue. Writers guidelines and list of themes for SASE.

Nonfiction: Book excerpts, essays, photo feature. Send for current list of themes. No articles not related to specific themes. Special issues: Work and Play (November 1996); Ways of Knowing (February 1997); The Shadow (May 1997). Buys 4-8 mss/year. Query. Length: 2,000-4,000 words. Pays $100 minimum. Sometimes pays expenses of writers on assignment.

Reprints: Send photocopy of article or short story (must include copy of copyright page) and information about when and where the article previously appeared. Publishes novel excerpts.

Photos: State availability of photos with submission. Reviews contact sheets, any transparencies and prints. Identification of subjects required. Buys one-time rights.

Columns/Departments: Natalie Baan, managing editor. Tangents (reviews of film, exhibits, dance, theater, video, music relating to theme of issue), 2,000-4,000 words; Book Reviews (reviews of current books in religion, spirituality, mythology and tradition), 500 words; Epicycles (retellings of myths and folk tales of all cultures—no fiction or made-up mythology!), under 2,000 words. Buys 2-6 unsolicited mss/year. Query. Pays $75-300.

Fiction: "We *very* rarely publish fiction; must relate to upcoming theme. Query recommended." Query.

Poetry: Free verse, traditional. *No* concrete or experimental poetry (must relate to theme). Buys 2-4 poems/year. Pays $50-75.

THE SANTA FE SUN, New Mexico's Alternative Paper, Le Soleil de Santa Fe, Inc., P.O. Box 23168, Santa Fe NM 87502. (505)989-8381. Fax: (505)989-4767. E-mail: sfsunnm@aol.com. Editor: Shawn Townsend. 80% freelance written. Monthly newspaper covering alternative/New Age, with a preference to articles with a northern New Mexico slant. Estab. 1988. Circ. 23,000. Pays on publication. Publishes ms an average of 2 months after acceptance. Byline given. Not copyrighted. Buys first rights. Editorial lead time 2 months. Submit seasonal material 1 month in advance. Accepts simultaneous submissions. Reports in 1 month on queries. Sample copy for $3. Writer's guidelines for #10 SASE.

Nonfiction: Book excerpts, essays, inspirational, interview/profile, opinion, personal experience, photo feature, religious, travel. Special issues: Men's Issue (September), Angels (December). Buys 11 mss/year. Query with published clips. Length: 600-2,200 words. Pays $50-200 for assigned articles; $42-176 for unsolicited articles. Sometimes pays expenses of writers on assignment.

Reprints: Accepts previously published submissions.

Photos: State availability of photos with submission. Reviews contact sheets. Negotiates payment individually. Identification of subjects required. Buys one-time rights.

Columns/Departments: Pays 7¢/word.

Poetry: John Graham. Avant-garde, free verse, haiku, light verse, traditional.

SHAMAN'S DRUM, A Journal of Experiential Shamanism, Cross-Cultural Shamanism Network, P.O. Box 97, Ashland OR 97520. (541)552-0839. Editor: Timothy White. 75% freelance written. Quarterly educational magazine of cross-cultural shamanism. "*Shaman's Drum* seeks contributions directed toward a general but well-informed audience. Our intent is to expand, challenge, and refine our readers' and our understanding of shamanism in practice. Topics include indigenous medicineway practices, contemporary shamanic healing practices, ecstatic spiritual practices, and contemporary shamanic psychotherapies. Our overall focus is cross-cultural, but our editorial approach is culture-specific—we prefer that authors focus on specific ethnic traditions or personal practices about which they have significant firsthand experience. We are looking for examples of not only how shamanism has transformed individual lives but also practical ways it can help ensure survival of life on the planet. We want material that captures the heart and feeling of shamanism and that can inspire people to direct action and participation, and to explore shamanism in greater depth." Estab. 1985. Circ. 17,000. Publishes ms 6 months after acceptance. Buys first North American serial and first rights. Editorial lead time 1 year. Reports in 3 months. Sample copy for $5. Writer's guidelines for #10 SASE.

Nonfiction: Book excerpts, essays, interview/profile (please query), opinion, personal experience, photo feature. *No fiction, poetry or fillers.* Buys 16 mss/year. Send complete ms. Length: 5,000-8,000. "We pay 5-10¢/word, depending on how much we have to edit. We also send two copies and tearsheets in addition to cash payment."

Reprints: Accept occasionally. Send typed ms with rights for sale noted and information about when and where the article previously appeared. Pays 50% of amount paid for an original article.

Photos: Send photos with submission. Reviews contact sheets, transparencies and all sizes prints. Offers $40-50/photo. Identification of subjects required. Buys one-time rights.

Columns/Departments: Contact: Judy Wells, Earth Circles Editor. Earth Circles (news format, concerned with issues, events, organizations related to shamanism, indigenous peoples and caretaking Earth. Relevant clippings also sought. Clippings paid with copies and credit line), 500-1,500 words. Buys 8 mss/year. Send complete ms. Pays 5-10¢/word. Reviews: contact Timothy White, Editor (in-depth reviews of books about shamanism or closely related subjects such as indigenous lifestyles, ethnobotany, transpersonal healing and ecstatic spirituality), 500-1,500 words. "Please query us first and we will send *Reviewer's Guidelines*." Pays 5-10¢/word.

Tips: "All articles must have a clear relationship to shamanism, but may be on topics which have not traditionally been defined as shamanic. We prefer original material that is based on, or illustrated with, firsthand knowledge and personal experience. Articles should be well documented with descriptive examples and pertinent background information. Photographs and illustrations of high quality are always welcome and can help sell articles."

‡**THE SPIRIT (OF WOMAN IN THE MOON)**, P.O. Box 2087, Cupertino CA 95015-2087. (408)864-8212. Fax: (408)738-4623. E-mail: sb02701@mercury.fhda.edu. Editor: Phillip Lynch. Managing Editor: Dr.

SDiane Bogus. 90% freelance written. Semiannual news magazine covering New Age, African American, feminist, gay/lesbian. "*The Spirit* wants work that heals and guides. It wants insight and joy, new views, uncommon ideas. It wants to hear from enlightened people who know it. New stories, new approaches. Dream a world." Estab. 1990. Circ. 2,000. Pays on publication. Publishes ms an average of 6 after acceptance (depending on submission date). Byline given. Offers $10-25 kill fee. Buys first North American serial, first, one-time, second serial (reprint) rights, and makes work-for-hire assignments. Editorial lead time 3 months. Submit seasonal material 3 months in advance. Accepts simultaneous submissions, if so noted. Reports in 3 weeks on queries; 6 weeks on mss. "We write full editorial responses because we charge small fee to submit on specific contests." Sample copy for $4 and SAE with $1.01 postage. Writer's guidelines for $2 and SAE with 78¢ postage.

Nonfiction: Book excerpts, essays, exposé, how-to, humor, inspirational, interview/profile, opinion, personal experience, religious, travel, book reviews. "We have prose prizes—The Audre Lorde Memorial Prize (fiction and new fiction) opens September 1—closes December 30. Winner gets published in *Spirit*." Health, healing, Angel encounters, past life connections, writing stories, business ideas, narratives and biography. Buys 4-18 mss/year. Query with résumé, photo of self and complete ms. Length: 500-3,000 words. Pays $10-100.

Reprints: Accepts previously published submissions, if so noted.

Photos: Send photos with submission. Offers no additional payment for photos accepted with ms. Model releases, identification of subjects required. Buys one-time rights.

Columns/Departments: Omen (visions/dreams/prophesies), 50-500 words; Subject (essay feature on DCM topics), 500-3,000 words; Book Review (writers/New Age/gay/lesbian/black/business/women), 1,500 words. Query or send complete ms. Pays $10-100.

Fiction: Ethnic, experimental, historical, novel excerpts, religious, science fiction, slice-of-life vignettes, New Age. Does not want things slanted for only Anglo Saxon-European lineage audiences. Buys 4-18 mss/ year. Send complete ms. Length: 500-3,000 words. Pays $10-100.

Poetry: Wants free verse, haiku, narrative. "No bitter bombastics, unkind, explicitly sexual, pieces that refer to the white race ("her skin like milk") specifically. Diversity is the key here." Length: 5-50 lines. "We have a poetry contest—T. Nelson Gilbert Award $100, $75, $50, $25 and certificate and publication. We also have a poetry lottery, $20 plus T-shirt and publication."

Fillers: Wants the following fillers: anecdotes, facts, gags to be illustrated by cartoonist, newsbreaks, short humor, things having to do with the moon. Buys 1 filler/year. "We're looking for a regular artist whose work can appear each issue."

Tips: "We like our writers and poets to feel connected to the moon. If they can communicate their spirit, we will feel it and generally respond."

WHOLE LIFE TIMES, 21225 Pacific Coast Highway, Suite B, Malibu CA 90265. (310)317-4200. Contact: Editor. Monthly consumer tabloid covering holistic thinking. Estab. 1979. Circ. 55,000. Pays on publication. Buys first North American serial rights. Sample copy for $3. Writer's guidelines for #10 SASE.

Nonfiction: Exposé, general interest, how-to, humor, inspirational, interview/profile, spiritual, technical, travel, leading-edge information, book excerpts. Special issues: Travel (June), Women's Issue (July), Men's Issue (August), Healing Arts (September), Relationships (February). Buys 25 mss/year. Query with published clips or send complete ms. Length: 1,600-2,000 words. Pays 5¢/word.

Reprints: Send photocopy of article and information about when and where the article previously appeared. Pays 50% of amount paid for an original article.

Tips: "Queries should show an awareness of current topics of interest in our subject area. We welcome investigative reporting and are happy to see queries that address topics in a political context. We are especially looking for articles on health and nutrition."

AUTOMOTIVE AND MOTORCYCLE

Publications in this section detail the maintenance, operation, performance, racing and judging of automobiles and recreational vehicles. Publications that treat vehicles as means of shelter instead of as a hobby or sport are classified in the Travel, Camping and Trailer category. Journals for service station operators and auto and motorcycle dealers are located in the Trade Auto and Truck section.

AMERICAN IRON MAGAZINE, TAM Communications Inc., 1010 Summer St., Stamford CT 06905. (203)425-8777. Fax: (203)425-8775. Editor: Jonathan Gourlay. 80% freelance written. Monthly family-oriented magazine covering Harley-Davidson and other US brands with a definite emphasis on Harleys. Circ. 80,000. Pays on publication. Publishes ms an average of 6 months after acceptance. Byline given. Reports in 1 month on queries with SASE. Sample copy for $3.

Nonfiction: "Clean and non-offensive. Stories include bike features, touring stories, how-to tech stories with step-by-step photos, historical pieces, profiles, events, opinion and various topics of interest to the people who ride Harley-Davidsons." No fiction. Buys 60 mss/year. Pays $250 for touring articles with slides to first-time writers. Payment for other articles varies.

Photos: Submit color slides or large transparencies. No prints. Send SASE for return of photos.

Tips: "We're not looking for stories about the top ten biker bars or do-it-yourself tattoos. We're looking for articles about motorcycling, the people and the lifestyle. If you understand the Harley mystique and can write well, you've got a good chance of being published."

AMERICAN MOTORCYCLIST, American Motorcyclist Association, 33 Collegeview Rd, Westerville OH 43081-6114. (614)891-2425. Executive Editor: Greg Harrison. Monthly magazine for "enthusiastic motorcyclists, investing considerable time and money in the sport. We emphasize the motorcyclist, not the vehicle." Estab. 1942. Circ. 190,000. Pays on publication. Rights purchased vary with author and material. Pays 25-50% kill fee. Byline given. Query with SASE. Submit seasonal/holiday material 4 months in advance. Reports in 1 month. Writer's guidelines for SASE.

Nonfiction: How-to (different and/or unusual ways to use a motorcycle or have fun on one); historical (the heritage of motorcycling, particularly as it relates to the AMA); interviews (with interesting personalities in the world of motorcycling); photo feature (quality work on any aspect of motorcycling); technical articles. No product evaluations or stories on motorcycling events not sanctioned by the AMA. Buys 20-25 mss/year. Query. Length: 500 words minimum. Pays minimum $7/published column inch.

Photos: Purchased with or without accompanying ms or on assignment. Captions required. Query. Pays $40/photo minimum.

Tips: "Accuracy and reliability are prime factors in our work with freelancers. We emphasize the rider, not the motorcycle itself. It's always best to query us first and the further in advance the better to allow for scheduling."

AMERICAN WOMAN MOTORSCENE, American Woman Motorscene, 1510 11th St., Suite 201B, Santa Monica CA 90401. (310)260-0192. Fax: (310)260-0175. Publisher: Courtney Caldwell. Editor: BJ Kineen. 80% freelance written. Bimonthly magazine on women in automotive. "We are an automotive/ adventure lifestyle magazine for women. Estab. 1988. Circ. 100,000. Pays on publication an average of 2 months after acceptance. Byline always given. Buys first rights and second serial (reprint) rights or makes work-for-hire assignments. Submit seasonal/holiday material 4 months in advance. Reports in 2 months. Free sample copy.

Nonfiction: Humor, inspirational, interview/profile, new product, photo feature, travel, lifestyle. No articles depicting women in motorsports or professions that are degrading, negative or not upscale. Buys 30 mss/ year. Send complete ms. Length 250-1,000 words. Pays 10¢/word for assigned articles; 7¢ for unsolicited articles. Sometimes pays expenses of writers on assignment.

Reprints: Send tearsheet or photocopy of article and information about when and where the article previously appeared.

Photos: Send photos with submission. Reviews contact sheets. Black and white or Kodachrome 64 preferred. Offers $10-50/photo. Captions, model releases and identification of subjects required. Buys all rights.

Columns/Departments: Lipservice (from readers); Tech Talk: (The Mall) new products; Tale End (News); 100-150 words.

Fillers: Anecdotes, facts, gags to be illustrated by cartoonist, newsbreaks, short humor. Buys 12/year. Length: 25-100 words. Negotiable.

Tips: "It helps if the writer is into cars, trucks or motorcycles. It is a special sport. If he/she is not involved in motorsports, he/she should have a positive point of view of motorsports and be willing to learn more about the subject. We are a lifestyle type of publication more than a technical magazine. Positive attitudes wanted."

AUTOMOBILE QUARTERLY, The Connoisseur's Magazine of Motoring Today, Yesterday, and Tomorrow, Kutztown Publishing Co., P.O. Box 348, 15076 Kutztown Rd., Kutztown PA 19530-0348. (610)683-3169. Fax: (610)683-3287. Publishing Director: Jonathan Stein. Assistant Editor: Stuart Wells. Contact: Karla Rosenbusch, managing editor. 85% freelance written. Quarterly magazine covering "automotive history, hardcover, excellent photography." Estab. 1962. Circ. 13,000. **Pays on acceptance.** Publishes ms an average of 1 year after acceptance. Byline given. Buys first international serial rights. Editorial lead time 9 months. Reports in 2 weeks on queries; 2 months on mss. Sample copy for $19.95.

Nonfiction: Essays, historical/nostalgic, photo feature, technical. Buys 25 mss/year. Query. Length: typically 3,500-8,000 words. Pays approximately 30¢/word. Sometimes pays expenses of writers on assignment.

Photos: State availability of photos with submission. Reviews 4×5, 35mm and 120 transparencies and historical prints. Buys one-time rights.

Tips: "Study the publication, and stress original research."

BRITISH CAR, 343 Second St., Suite H, Los Altos CA 94022-3639. (415)949-9680. Fax: (415)949-9685. Editor: Dave Destler. 50% freelance written. Bimonthly magazine covering British cars. "We focus upon the cars built in Britain, the people who buy them, drive them, collect them, love them. Writers must be among the aforementioned. Written by enthusiasts for enthusiasts." Estab. 1985. Circ. 30,000. Pays on publication. Publishes ms an average of 3 months after acceptance. Byline given. Buys all rights, unless other arrangements made. Submit seasonal/holiday material 4 months in advance. Reports in 1 month. Sample copy for $5. Writer's guidelines for #10 SASE.

• The editor is looking for more technical and restoration articles by knowledgeable enthusiasts and professionals.

Nonfiction: Historical/nostalgic; how-to (repair or restoration of a specific model or range of models, new technique or process); humor (based upon a realistic nonfiction situation); interview/profile (famous racer, designer, engineer, etc.); photo feature; technical. Buys 30 mss/year. Send complete ms. "Include SASE if submission is to be returned." Length: 750-4,500 words. Pays $2-5/column inch for assigned articles; $2-3/column inch for unsolicited articles.

Photos: Send photos with submission. Reviews transparencies and prints. Offers $15-75/photo. Captions and identification of subjects required. Buys all rights, unless otherwise arranged.

Columns/Departments: Update (newsworthy briefs of interest, not too timely for bimonthly publication), approximately 50-175 words. Buys 20 mss/year. Send complete ms.

Tips: "Thorough familiarity of subject is essential. *British Car* is read by experts and enthusiasts who can see right through superficial research. Facts are important, and must be accurate. Writers should ask themselves 'I know I'm interested in this story, but will most of *British Car's* readers appreciate it?' "

CANADIAN BIKER MAGAZINE, P.O. Box 4122, Victoria British Columbia V8X 3X4 Canada. (604)384-0333. Fax: (604)384-1832. Editor: Len Creed. 65% freelance written. Magazine covers motorcycling. "A family-oriented motorcycle magazine whose purpose is to unite Canadian motorcyclists from coast to coast through the dissemination of information in a non-biased, open forum. The magazine reports on new product, events, touring, racing, vintage and custom motorcycling as well as new industry information." Estab. 1980. Circ. 20,000. Publishes non-time sensitive mss an average of 1 year after acceptance. Byline given. Buys first rights and second serial (reprint) rights. Editorial lead time 3 months. Submit seasonal material 1 year in advance. Accepts simultaneous submissions. Reports in 6 weeks on queries; 6 months on mss. Sample copy for $5. Writer's guidelines free on request.

Nonfiction: General interest, historical/nostalgic, how-to, interview/profile (Canadian personalities preferred), new product, technical, travel. Buys 12 mss/year. All nonfiction must include photos and/or illustrations. Query with or without published clips, or send complete ms. Length: 500-1,500 words. Pays $100-200 (Canadian) for assigned article; $80-150 (Canadian) for unsolicited articles. Sometimes pays expenses of writers on assignment.

Reprints: Accepts previously published submissions.

Photos: State availability of or send photos with submission. Reviews 4×4 transparencies, 3×5 prints. Negotiates payment individually. Captions, model releases, identification of subjects required. Buys one-time rights.

Columns/Departments: The Ladies Chronicle (women), 750-1,000 words; Fastlines (roadracing), 1,300-1,800 words; Dragracing, 1,000 words. Query with published clips.

Tips: Writers should be involved in the motorcycle industry and be intimately familiar with some aspect of the industry which would be of interest to readers. Observations of the industry should be current, timely and informative.

CAR AND DRIVER, Hachette Filipacchi Magazines, Inc., 2002 Hogback Rd., Ann Arbor MI 48105-9736. (313)971-3600. Fax: (313)971-9188. E-mail: editors@caranddriver.com. Website: http://www.caranddriver.com. Editor-in-Chief: Csaba Csere. Monthly magazine for auto enthusiasts; college-educated, professional, median 24-35 years of age. Estab. 1956. Circ. 1,100,000. **Pays on acceptance.** Rights purchased vary with author and material. Buys all rights or first North American serial rights. Reports in 2 months.

• Ranked as one of the best markets for freelance writers in *Writer's Yearbook*'s annual "Top 100 Markets," January 1996.

Nonfiction: Non-anecdotal articles about automobiles, new and old. Automotive road tests, informational articles on cars and equipment, some satire and humor and personalities, past and present, in the automotive industry and automotive sports. "Treat readers as intellectual equals. Emphasis on people as well as hardware." Informational, humor, historical, think articles and nostalgia. All road tests are staff-written. "Unsolicited manuscripts are not accepted. Query letters must be addressed to the Managing Editor. Rates are generous, but few manuscripts are purchased from outside."

Photos: Color slides and b&w photos sometimes purchased with accompanying mss.

Tips: "It is best to start off with an interesting query and to stay away from nuts-and-bolts ideas because that will be handled in-house or by an acknowledged expert. Our goal is to be absolutely without flaw in our presentation of automotive facts, but we strive to be every bit as entertaining as we are informative."

CAR CRAFT, Petersen Publishing Co., 6420 Wilshire Blvd., Los Angeles CA 90048. (213)782-2320. Fax: (213)782-2263. Editor: Chuck Schifsky. Monthly magazine for men and women, 18-34, "enthusiastic owners of 1949 and newer muscle cars and street machines." Circ. 400,000. Study past issues before making submissions or story suggestions. Pays generally on publication, on acceptance under special circumstances. Buys all rights. Buys 2-10 mss/year. Query.

Nonfiction: How-to articles ranging from the basics to fairly sophisticated automotive modifications. Drag racing feature stories and some general car features on modified late model automobiles. Especially interested in do-it-yourself automotive tips, suspension modifications, mileage improvers and even shop tips and home-made tools. Length: open. Pays $100-200/page.

Photos: Photos purchased with or without accompanying text. Captions suggested, but optional. Reviews 8×10 b&w glossy prints, 35mm or 2¼×2¼ color. Pays $30 for b&w, color negotiable. "Pay rate higher for complete story, i.e., photos, captions, headline, subtitle: the works, ready to go."

CHEVY HIGH PERFORMANCE, Petersen Publishing Co., 6420 Wilshire Blvd., Los Angeles CA 90048. (213)782-2000. Editor: Mike Magda. Managing Editor: Stephanie Rechtshaid. 20% freelance written. Monthly magazine covering "all aspects of street, racing, restored high-performance Chevrolet vehicles with heavy emphasis on technical modifications and quality photography." Estab. 1985. Circ. 150,000. **Pays on acceptance.** Byline given. No kill fee. Buys all rights. Submit seasonal/holiday material 6 months in advance. Reports in 1 month. Sample copy for 9×12 SAE with 5 first-class stamps.
Nonfiction: How-to, new product, photo feature, technical. "We need well-researched and photographed technical articles. Tell us how to make horse-power on a budget." Buys 30 mss/year. Query. Length: 500-2,000 words. Pays $500-1,000. Sometimes pays expenses of writers on assignment.
Photos: Send photos with submission. Reviews contact sheets, any transparencies and any prints. Offers no additional payment for photos accepted with ms. Model releases required. Buys all rights.
Columns/Departments: Buys 24 mss/year. Query. Length: 100-1,500. Pays $150-500.
Tips: "Writers must be aware of the 'street scene.' Please read the magazine closely before query. We need well-photographed step-by-step how-to technical articles. No personality profiles, fluffy features and especially personal experiences. If you don't know the difference between Z/28 and Z28 Camaros, camel-hump and 18-degree heads or what COPO and RPO stand for, there's a good chance your background isn't what we're looking for."

CLASSIC AUTO RESTORER, Fancy Publishing, Inc., P.O. Box 6050, Mission Viejo CA 92690-6050. (714)855-8822. Fax: (714)855-3045. Editor: Dan Burger. Managing Editor: Ted Kade. 85% freelance written. Monthly magazine on auto restoration. "Our readers own old cars and they work on them. We help our readers by providing as much practical, how-to information as we can about restoration and old cars." Estab. 1988. Pays on publication. Publishes ms an average of 3 months after acceptance. Offers $50 kill fee. Buys first North American serial or one-time rights. Submit seasonal/holiday material 4 months in advance. Reports in 2 months. Sample copy for $5.50. Free writer's guidelines.
Nonfiction: How-to (auto restoration), new product, photo feature, technical, product evaluation. Buys 120 mss/year. Query with or without published clips. Length: 200-2,500 words. Pays $100-500 for assigned articles; $75-500 for unsolicited articles.
Photos: Send photos with submission. Reviews contact sheets, transparencies and 5×7 prints. Offers no additional payment for photos accepted with ms.
Columns/Departments: Buys 12 mss/year. Send complete ms. Length: 400-1,000 words. Pays $75-200.
Tips: "Query first. Interview the owner of a restored car. Present advice to others on how to do a similar restoration. Seek advice from experts. Go light on history and non-specific details. Make it something that the magazine regularly uses. Do automotive how-tos."

FOUR WHEELER MAGAZINE, 3330 Ocean Park Blvd., Santa Monica CA 90405. (310)392-2998. Fax: (310)392-1171. Editor: John Stewart. 20% freelance written. Works with a small number of new/unpublished writers each year. Monthly magazine covering four-wheel-drive vehicles, competition and travel/adventure. Estab. 1963. Circ. 355,466. Pays on publication. Publishes ms an average of 4 months after acceptance. Buys all rights. Submit seasonal/holiday material at least 4 months in advance. Writer's guidelines for #10 SASE.
Nonfiction: 4WD competition and travel/adventure articles, technical, how-tos, and vehicle features about unique four-wheel drives. "We like the adventure stories that bring four wheeling to life in word and photo: mud-running deserted logging roads, exploring remote, isolated trails, or hunting/fishing where the 4×4 is a necessity for success." See features by Gary Wescott and Matt Conrad for examples. Query with photos before sending complete ms. Length: 1,200-2,000 words; average 4-5 pages when published. Pays $100/page minimum for complete package.
Photos: Requires professional quality color slides and b&w prints for every article. Captions required. Prefers Kodachrome 64 or Fujichrome 50 in 35mm or 2¼ formats. "Action shots a must for all vehicle features and travel articles."
Tips: "Show us you know how to use a camera as well as the written word. The easiest way for a new writer/photographer to break in to our magazine is to read several issues of the magazine, then query with a short vehicle feature that will show his or her potential as a creative writer/photographer."

‡4-WHEEL DRIVE & SPORT UTILITY, McMullen-Argus, 774 S. Placentia Ave., Placentia CA 92670. Fax: (714)572-1864. Editor: Phil Howell. 40% freelance written. Monthly magazine covering outdoor auto-motive adventure travel for the enthusiast. Estab. 1985. Circ. 96,000. Pays on publication. Byline given.

Buys all rights. Editorial lead time 4 months. Submit seasonal material 6 months in advance. Sample copy for $3.50. Writer's guidelines free on request.

Nonfiction: General interest, how-to, humor, new product, personal experience, photo feature, travel. No "How I Built My Truck," etc. Buys 40 mss/year. Query. Pays $100-600.

Photos: Send photos with submission. Reviews contact sheets, transparencies. Offers no additional payment for photos accepted with ms. Captions, model releases, identification of subjects required. Buys all rights.

‡**IN THE WIND**, Paisano Publications, P.O. Box 3000, Agoura Hills CA 91376-3000. (818)889-8740. Fax: (818)889-1252. Editor: Kim Peterson. Managing Editor: Lisa Pedicini. 50% freelance written. Bimonthly magazine covering Harley-Davidson motorcycle owners' lifestyle. "Aimed at Harley-Davidson motorcycle riders and motorcycling enthusiasts, *In the Wind* is mainly a pictorial—action photos of bikes being ridden, and events, with a monthly travel piece—Travelin' Trails." Estab. 1978. Circ. 90,000. Pays on publication. Publishes ms an average of 6-9 months after acceptance. Byline given. Buys all rights. Editorial lead time 6 months. Submit seasonal material 8 months in advance. Reports in 2 weeks on queries; 2 months on mss. Writer's guidelines free on request.

Nonfiction: Photo feature, travel. No long-winded tech articles. Buys 6 mss/year. Query. Length: 1,000-1,500 words. Pays $250-600. Sometimes pays expenses of writers on assignment.

Photos: Send photos with submission. Reviews transparencies. Offers $35-100/photo. Model releases, identification of subjects required. Buys all rights.

Columns/Departments: Travelin' Trails (good spots to ride to, places to stay, things to do, history), 1,200 words. Buys 6 mss/year. Query. Pays $250-600.

Poetry: Free verse. Does not want to see graphic violence. Buys 10 poems/year. Submit maximum 3 poems. Length: 10-100 lines. Pays $20-100.

Tips: "Know the subject. Looking for submissions from people who ride their own bikes."

‡**MOTOMAG**, Motomag Corp., P.O. Box 1046, Nyack NY 10960. (914)353-MOTO. Fax: (914)353-5240. E-mail: motomag@magpie.com. Editor: Mark Kalan. 95% freelance written. Monthly magazine covering motorcycles. "Positive coverage of motorcycling in America—riding, travel, racing and tech." Estab. 1989 (as *CC Motorcycle Magazine*). Circ. 30,000. Pays on publication. Publishes ms an average of 2 months after acceptance. Byline given. Buys one-time rights. Editorial lead time 3 months. Submit seasonal material 3 months in advance. Accepts simultaneous submissions. Reports in 1 month. Sample copy for $3. Writer's guidelines for #10 SASE.

Nonfiction: Essays, general interest, historical/nostalgic, how-to, humor, inspirational, interview/profile, new product, personal experience, photo feature, technical, travel. Special issues: *MotoMag* Annual Motorsports Edition. Buys 2 mss/year. Query with published clips. Length: 1,000-2,000 words. Pays $50-250 for assigned articles; $25-125 for unsolicited articles. Sometimes pays expenses of writers on assignment.

Reprints: Accepts previously published submissions.

Photos: State availability of photos with submission. Reviews contact sheets, transparencies. Negotiates payment individually. Captions, model releases, identification of subjects required. Buys one-time rights.

Fiction: Adventure, fantasy, historical, romance, slice-of-life vignettes. All fiction must be motorcycle related. Buys 2 mss/year. Query with published clips. Length: 1,500-2,500 words. Pays $50-250.

Poetry: Avant-garde, free verse, haiku, light verse, traditional. Must be motorcycle related. Buys 6 poems/year. Submit 12 maximum poems. Length: open. Pays $10-50.

Fillers: Anecdotes, cartoons. Buys 12/year. Length: 100-200 words. Pays $10-50.

Tips: "Ride a motorcycle and be able to construct a readable sentence!"

‡**MOTOR TREND**, Petersen Publishing Co., 6420 Wilshire Blvd., Los Angeles CA 90048. (213)782-2220. Editorial Director: Leonard Emanuelson. 5-10% freelance written. Prefers to work with published/established writers. Monthly magazine for automotive enthusiasts and general interest consumers. Circ. 900,000. Publishes ms an average of 3 months after acceptance. Buys all rights. "Fact-filled query suggested for all freelancers." Reports in 1 month.

Nonfiction: Automotive and related subjects that have national appeal. Emphasis on domestic and imported cars, road tests, driving impressions, auto classics, auto, travel, racing, and high-performance features for the enthusiast. Packed with facts. Freelancers should confine queries to photo-illustrated exotic drives and other feature material; road tests and related activity are handled inhouse.

Photos: Buys photos, particularly of prototype cars and assorted automotive matter. Pays $25-500 for transparencies.

‡**NASCAR SUPERTRUCK RACING**, McMullen Argus Publishing Corp., 774 S. Placentia Ave., Placentia CA 92670. Editor: Steve Stillwell. Contact: Randall Jachmann, editor at large. 50% freelance written. Bimonthly magazing covering NASCAR Craftsman Truck Series. "The *NASCAR SuperTruck Racing* magazine audience is largely race enthusiasts looking for a more personal glimpse of their 'heroes.' Articles should not be statistics, rather family-oriented slice-of-life type memoirs, personal histories." Estab. 1995. Circ. 127,000. Pays on publication. Publishes ms an average of 4 months after acceptance. Byline given. Offers

50% kill fee. Buys all rights. Editorial lead time 3 months. Accepts simultaneous submissions. Reports in 1 month. Writer's guidelines free on request.

Nonfiction: Interview/profile, photo feature, SuperTruck driver/team related articles. Technical articles must be approved by editors. Buys 35 mss/year. Query. Length: 500-2,000 words. Pays $75-150/page. Sometimes pays expenses of writers on assignment.

Reprints: Accepts previously published submissions.

Photos: Send photos with submission. Reviews contact sheets, transparencies, 3×5 prints. Negotiates payment individually. Captions, model releases, identification of subjects required.

Fillers: Newsbreaks. Buys 5-10/year. Length: 100-500 words. Pay negotiable.

Tips: "At *NASCAR SuperTruck Racing* magazine, we prefer queries, as all information must meet the guidelines of NASCAR. The book is interview-heavy, with an emphasis placed on personal rather than professional backgrounds, information, etc., for each interviewee."

‡OFF-ROAD, McMullen & Yee Publishing, Inc., 774 S. Placentia Ave., Placentia CA 92670-6846. Editor: Duane Elliott. 40% freelance written. Monthly magazine covering off-road vehicles, racing, travel. "Written to hard-core off-road truck enthusiasts." Estab. 1969. Circ. 100,000. Pays on publication. Publishes ms an average of 6 after acceptance. Byline given. Buys first North American rights. Editorial lead time 4 months. Submit seasonal material 6 months in advance. Accepts simultaneous submissions. Reports in 2 weeks on queries.

Nonfiction: How-to, interview/profile, photo feature, technical, travel. Buys 36 mss/year. Send complete ms. Length: 550-650 words. Pays $150/published page. Sometimes pays expenses of writers on assignment.

Photos: Send photos with submission. Reviews contact sheets, negatives, transparencies, prints. Offers no additional payment for photos accepted with ms. Captions, model releases, identification of subjects required. Buys one-time rights.

Fiction: Adventure, historical, humorous. Buys 1-2 mss/year. Send complete ms. Length: 500-2,000 words. Pays $150/page.

Fillers: Facts, newsbreaks. Buys 10/year. Length: 50-500 words. Pays $15/page.

Tips: "Study mag for style!"

RIDER, TL Enterprises, Inc., 2575 Vista Del Mar Dr., Ventura CA 93001. (805)667-4100. Editor: Mark Tuttle Jr.. Managing Editor: Donya Carlson. Contact: Mark Tuttle, Jr., Editor. 50% freelance written. Monthly magazine on motorcycling. "*Rider* serves owners and enthusiasts of road and street motorcycling, focusing on touring, commuting, camping and general sport street riding." Estab. 1974. Circ. 140,000. Pays on publication. Publishes ms an average of 6-12 months after acceptance. Byline given. Offers 25% kill fee. Buys first North American serial rights. Editorial lead time 4 months. Submit seasonal material 6 months in advance. Reports in 2 months. Sample copy for $2.95. Writer's guidelines for #10 SASE.

Nonfiction: General interest, historical/nostalgic, how-to (re: motorcycling), humor, interview/profile, personal experience. Does not want to see "fiction or articles on 'How I Began Motorcycling.' " Buys 30 mss/year. Query. Length: 500-1,500 words. Pays $100 minimum for unsolicited articles. Sometimes pays expenses of writers on assignment.

Photos: Send photos with submission. Reviews contact sheets, transparencies and 5×7 prints (b&w only). Offers no additional payment for photos accepted with ms. Captions required. Buys one-time rights.

Columns/Departments: Rides, Rallies & Clubs (favorite ride or rally), 800-1,000 words. Buys 15 mss/year. Query. Pays $150.

Tips: "We rarely accept manuscripts without photos (slides or b&w prints). Query first. Follow guidelines available on request. We are most open to feature stories (must include excellent photography) and material for 'Rides, Rallies and Clubs.' Include information on routes, local attractions, restaurants and scenery in favorite ride submissions."

ROAD & TRACK, Hachette Filipacchi Magazines Inc., 1499 Monrovia Ave., Newport Beach CA 92663. (714)720-5300. Editor: Thomas L. Bryant. Contact: Ellida Maki. 25% freelance written. Monthly magazine covering automotive. Estab. 1947. Circ. 740,000. Pays on publication. Publishes ms an average of 6 months after acceptance. Kill fee varies. Buys first rights. Editorial lead time 3 months. Reports in 1 month on queries; 2 months on mss.

Nonfiction: Automotive interest. No how-to. Query. Length: 2,000 words. Pay varies. Pays expenses of writers on assignment.

Photos: State availability of photos with submissions. Reviews transparencies, prints. Negotiates payment individually. Model releases required. Buys one-time rights.

Columns/Department: Reviews (automotive), 500 words. Query. Pay varies.

Fiction: Automotive. Query. Length: 2,000 words. Pay varies.

Tips: "Because mostly written by staff or assignment, we rarely purchase unsolicited manuscripts—but it can and does happen! Writers must be knowledgeable about enthusiast cars."

TRUCKIN', World's Leading Sport Truck Publication, McMullen & Yee Publishing, 774 S. Placentia Ave., Placentia CA 92670. (714)572-2255. Editor: Steve Stillwell. 15% freelance written. Monthly magazine covering customized sport trucks. "Materials we purchase are events coverage, technical articles and truck features, all having to be associated with customized —½ ton pickups and mini-trucks." Estab. 1975. Circ. 200,000. Pays on publication. Buys all rights unless previously agreed upon. Editorial lead time 3 months. Submit seasonal material 6 months in advance. Reports in 2 weeks on queries; 1 month on mss. Sample copy for $4.50. Writer's guidelines free on request.

Nonfiction: How-to, new product, photo feature, technical, events coverage. Buys 50 mss/year. Query. Length: 1,000 words minimum. Pay negotiable. Sometimes pays expenses of writers on assignment.

Photos: Send photos with submission. Reviews contact sheets and transparencies. Captions, model releases and identification of subjects required. Buys all rights unless previously agreed upon.

Columns/Departments: Bill Blankenship. Insider (latest automotive/truck news), 2,000 words. Buys 70 mss/year. Send complete ms. Pays $25 minimum.

Fillers: Bill Blankenship. Anecdotes, facts, newsbreaks. Buys 50/year. Length: 600-1,000 words. Pay negotiable.

Tips: "Send all queries and submissions in envelopes larger than letter size to avoid being detained with a mass of reader mail. Send complete packages with transparencies and contact sheets (with negatives). Submit hard copy and a computer disc when possible. Editors purchase the materials that are the least complicated to turn into magazine pages! All materials have to be fresh/new and primarily outside of California."

‡TRUCKIN' CLASSIC TRUCKS, McMullen Argus Publishing Corp., 774 S. Placentia Ave., Placentia CA 92670. Editor: Steve Stillwell. Contact: Bill Turner, project editor. 40% freelance written. Bimonthly magazine covering pickup trucks. "*Truckin' Classic Trucks* is geared toward the custom light pickup enthusiasts, years 1928-1972. The book is comprised of color features on pickups, hard-core technical how-to articles and classic truck event coverage." Estab. 1992. Circ. 175,000. Pays on publication. Publishes ms an average of 3 months after acceptance. Byline given. Offers 50% kill fee. Buys all rights. Editorial lead time 3 months minimum. Reports in 6 weeks on queries; 1 month on mss. Writer's guidelines free on request.

Nonfiction: Historical/nostalgic, how-to, new product, photo feature, technical, events. "Articles must include professional quality photos." Buys 35 mss/year. Length: 500 words minimum. Pays $75-150/page. Sometimes pays expenses of writers on assignment.

Reprints: Accepts previously published submissions.

Photos: Send photos with submission. Reviews contact sheets, transparencies, 3×5 prints. Negotiates payment individually. Captions, model releases, identification of subjects required. Buys all rights.

Columns/Departments: Garage Scene (home-built pickups), 500-750 words. Buys 10 mss/year. Query. Pays $75-150/page.

Fillers: Bill Blankenship, senior editor. Buys 20/year. Length: 300-500 words. Pay negotiable.

Tips: "Read the publication and take note of events and custom pickups in your geographical area. When submitting material, make certain it is complete (i.e. photos, copy) and be sure to include address and phone number."

AVIATION

Professional and private pilots and aviation enthusiasts read the publications in this section. Editors want material for audiences knowledgeable about commercial aviation. Magazines for passengers of commercial airlines are grouped in the Inflight category. Technical aviation and space journals and publications for airport operators, aircraft dealers and others in aviation businesses are listed under Aviation and Space in the Trade section.

AIR & SPACE/SMITHSONIAN MAGAZINE, 370 L'Enfant Promenade SW, 10th Floor, Washington DC 20024-2518. (202)287-3733. Fax: (202)287-3163. E-mail: airspacedt@aol.com. Website: http://www.airs pacemag.com. Editor: George Larson. Managing Editor: Tom Huntington. 80% freelance written. Prefers to work with published/established writers. Bimonthly magazine covering aviation and aerospace for a non-technical audience. "Features are slanted to a technically curious, but not necessarily technically knowledgeable audience. We are looking for unique angles to aviation/aerospace stories, history, events, personalities, current and future technologies, that emphasize the human-interest aspect." Estab. 1985. Circ. 310,000. **Pays on acceptance.** Byline given. Offers kill fee. Buys first North American serial rights. Adapts from previously published or soon to be published books. Reports in 3 months. Sample copy for $5. Free writer's guidelines.

• Ranked as one of the best markets for freelance writers in *Writer's Yearbook*'s annual "Top 100 Markets," January 1996.

Nonfiction: Book excerpts, essays, general interest (on aviation/aerospace), historical/nostalgic, humor, photo feature, technical. Buys 50 mss/year. Query with published clips. Length: 1,500-3,000 words. Pays $2,000 average. Pays expenses of writers on assignment.

• The editors are actively seeking stories covering space and aviation during the Cold War.

Photos: State availability of illustrations with submission. Reviews 35mm transparencies. Refuses unsolicited material.

Columns/Departments: Above and Beyond (first person), 1,500-2,000 words; Flights and Fancy (whimsy), approximately 1,200 words; From the Field (science or engineering in the trenches), 1,200 words; Collections (profiles of unique museums), 1,200 words. Buys 25 mss/year. Query with published clips. Pays $1,000 maximum. Soundings (brief items, timely but not breaking news), 500-700 words. Pays $300.

Tips: "Soundings is the section most open to freelancers. We hope to begin a series on military aviation during the Vietnam War. We are looking for articles to mark the 50th anniversary of the US Air Force in summer 1997. We continue to be interested in stories about space exploration."

AIR LINE PILOT, Air Line Pilots Association, 535 Herndon Parkway, P.O. Box 1169, Herndon VA 22070. (703)481-4460. Fax: (703)689-4370. E-mail: 73741.14@compuserve.com. Editor: Gary DiNunno. 10% freelance written. Prefers to work with published/established writers; works with a small number of new/unpublished writers each year. Monthly magazine for airline pilots covering commercial aviation industry information—economics, avionics, equipment, systems, safety—that affects a pilot's life in professional sense. Also includes information about management/labor relations trends, contract negotiations, etc. Estab. 1931. Circ. 62,000. **Pays on acceptance.** Publishes ms an average of 6 months after acceptance. Offers 50% kill fee. Buys all rights except book rights. Submit seasonal/holiday material 6 months in advance. Query for electronic submissions. Reports in 2 months. Sample copy for $2. Writer's guidelines for #10 SASE.

Nonfiction: Humor, inspirational, photo feature, technical. "We do not often use nonfiction." Buys 20 mss/year. Query with or without published clips, or send complete ms. Length: 700-3,000 words. Pays $200-600 for assigned articles; pays $50-600 for unsolicited articles.

Photos: Send photos with submission. Reviews contact sheets, 35mm transparencies and 8×10 prints. Offers $10-35/b&w photo, $20-50 for color used inside and $350 for color used as cover. For cover photography, shoot vertical rather than horizontal. Identification of subjects required.

Tips: "For our feature section, we seek aviation industry information that affects the life of a professional airline pilot from a career standpoint. We also seek material that affects a pilot's life from a job security and work environment standpoint. Any airline pilot featured in an article must be an Air Line Pilot Association member in good standing. Our readers are very experienced and require a high level of technical accuracy in both written material and photographs."

BALLOON LIFE, Balloon Life Magazine, Inc., 2145 Dale Ave., Sacramento CA 95815-3632. (916)922-9648. Fax: (916)922-4730. E-mail: blnlife@scn.org. Website: http://www.aero.com. Editor: Tom Hamilton. 75% freelance written. Monthly magazine for sport of hot air ballooning. Estab. 1986. Circ. 4,000. Pays on publication. Byline given. Offers 50-100% kill fee. Buys non-exclusive all rights. Submit seasonal/holiday material 4 months in advance. Reports in 3 weeks on queries; 1 month on mss. Sample copy for 9×12 SAE with $2 postage. Writer's guidelines for #10 SASE.

Nonfiction: Book excerpts, general interest, how-to (flying hot air balloons, equipment techniques), interview/profile, new product, letters to the editor, technical. Buys 150 mss/year. Query with or without published clips, or send complete ms. Length: 800-5,000 words. Pays $50-75 for assigned articles; $25-50 for unsolicited articles. Sometimes pays expenses of writers on assignment.

Reprints: Send photocopy of article or short story and information about when and where the article previously appeared. For reprints, pays 100% of amount paid for original article.

Photos: Send photos with submission. Reviews transparencies, prints. Offers $15-50/photo. Identification of subjects required. Buys non-exclusive all rights.

Columns/Departments: Hangar Flying (real life flying experience that others can learn from), 800-1,500 words; Preflight (a news and information column), 100-500 words; Logbook (recent balloon events—events that have taken place in last 3-4 months), 300-500 words. Buys 60 mss/year. Send complete ms. Pays $15-50.

Fiction: Humorous. Buys 3-5 mss/year. Send complete ms. Length: 800-1,500 words. Pays $50.

Tips: "This magazine slants toward the technical side of ballooning. We are interested in articles that help to educate and provide safety information. Also stories with manufacturers, important individuals and/or of historic events and technological advances important to ballooning. The magazine attempts to present articles that show 'how-to' (fly, business opportunities, weather, equipment). Both our Feature Stories section and Logbook section are where most manuscripts are purchased."

‡**CAREER PILOT**, FAPA, 4959 Massachusetts Blvd., Atlanta GA 30337-6607. (404)997-8097. Fax: (770)997-8111. Assistant Editor: David Jones. 80% freelance written. Monthly magazine covering aviation. "A career advisory magazine as a service to FAPA members. Readers largely are career pilots who are working toward their professional goals. Articles cover topics such as recent developments in aviation law and medicine, changes in the industry, job interview techniques and how to get pilot jobs." Estab. 1983. Circ. 13,500. Pays on publication. Publishes ms an average of 4 months after acceptance. Byline given. Offers 50% kill fee. Buys all rights. Accepts simultaneous submissions. Reports in 3 months.

Nonfiction: How-to (get hired by an airline), interview/profile (aviation related), personal experience (aviation related). Special issue: Corporate Aviation (September). Buys 60 mss/year. Query with clips. Length: 2,500 words. "Pays 18¢/word with $50 bonus for meeting deadlines."

Reprints: Send tearsheet or photocopy of article, typed ms with rights for sale noted and information about when and where the article previously appeared. Pays 50% of amount paid for an original article. ·

Photos: State availability of photos with submission. Reviews prints. Offers no additional payment for photos accepted with ms. Captions and identification of subjects required.

Tips: "Send articles and clips that are aviation/business related. Express your interest in writing for our publication on a semi-regular basis."

GENERAL AVIATION NEWS & FLYER, N.W. Flyer, Inc., P.O. Box 39099, Tacoma WA 98439-0099. (206)471-9888. Fax: (206)471-9911. E-mail: comments@ganflyer.com. Website: http://www.ganflyer.com. Editor: Dave Sclair. 30% freelance written. Prefers to work with published/established writers. Biweekly tabloid covering general aviation. Provides "coverage of aviation news, activities, regulations and politics of general and sport aviation with emphasis on timely features of interest to pilots and aircraft owners." Estab. 1949. Circ. 35,000. Pays 1 month after publication. Publishes ms an average of 3 months after acceptance. Byline given. Buys one-time and first North American serial rights; on occasion second serial (reprint) rights. Submit seasonal/holiday material 2 months in advance. Reports in 2 months. Sample copy for $3.50. Writer's and style guidelines for #10 SASE.

Nonfiction: Features of current interest about aviation businesses, developments at airports, new products and services, safety, flying technique and maintenance. "Good medium-length reports on current events—controversies at airports, problems with air traffic control, FAA, etc. We want solid news coverage of breaking stories. We don't cover airlines and military" Query first on historical, nostalgic features and profiles/interviews. Many special sections throughout the year; send SASE for list. Buys 100 mss/year. Query or send complete ms. Length: 500-2,000 words. Pays up to $3/printed col. in. maximum. Rarely pays the expenses of writers on assignment.

Reprints: Accepts previously published submissions from noncompetitive publications, if so noted.

Photos: "Good pics a must." Send photos (b&w or color prints preferred, no slides) with ms. Captions and photographer's ID required. Pays $10/b&w photo used.

Tips: "We always are looking for features about people and businesses using airplanes in unusual ways. Travel features must include information on what to do once you've arrived, with addresses from which readers can get more information. Get direct quotations from the principals involved in the story. We want current, first-hand information."

PROFESSIONAL PILOT, Queensmith Communications, 3014 Colvin St., Alexandria VA 22314. (703)370-0606. Fax: (703)370-7082. Editor: Mary F. Silitch. 75% freelance written. Monthly magazine on regional airline, corporate and various other types of professional aviation. "Our readers are professional pilots with highest ratings and the editorial content reflects their knowledge and experience." Estab. 1967. Circ. 32,000. **Pays on acceptance.** Publishes ms an average of 3 months after acceptance. Byline given. Kill fee negotiable. Buys all rights.

Nonfiction: How-to (avionics and aircraft flight checks), interview/profile, personal experience (if a lesson for professional pilots), photo feature, technical (avionics, weather, engines, aircraft). All issues have a theme such as regional airline operations, maintenance, jet aircraft, helicopters, etc. Buys 40 mss/year. Query. Length: 750-1,500. Pays $200-1,000. Sometimes pays expenses of writers on assignment.

Photos: Send photos with submission. Prefers transparencies. Offers no additional payment for photos accepted with ms. Captions and identification of subjects required. Buys all rights.

Tips: Query first. "Freelancer should be a professional pilot or have background in aviation. We place a greater emphasis on corporate operations and pilot concerns."

‡WOMAN PILOT, Aviatrix Publishing, Inc., P.O. Box 485, Arlington Heights IL 60006-0485. Editor: Danielle Clarneaux. 80% freelance written. Bimonthly magazine covering women who fly all types of aircraft. Personal profiles, history careers in all areas of aviation. Estab. 1993. Circ. 5,000. Pays on publication. Publishes ms an average of 10 months after acceptance. Byline given. Buys first North American serial rights. Editorial lead time 4 months. Sample copy for $3. Writer's guidelines for #10 SASE.

Nonfiction: Book excerpts, historical/nostalgic, humor, interview/profile, new product, personal experience, photo feature. Buys 35 mss/year. Query with published clips or send complete ms. Length: 500-3,000 words. Pays $ 20-55 for assigned articles; $20-40 for unsolicited articles; and contributor copies.

Photos: State availability of or send photos/photocopies with submission. Negotiates payment individually. Captions, model releases, identification of subjects required. Buys one-time rights.

Fiction: Adventure, historical, humorous, slice-of-life vignettes. Buys 4 mss/year. Query with or without published clips. Length: 500-2,000 words. Pays $20-35.

Poetry: Buys 4 poems/year. Submit maximum 3 poems. Length: short. Pays $10.

Fillers: Cartoons. Buys 6/year. Pays $10-20.

Tips: "If a writer is interested in writing articles from our leads, she/he should send writing samples and explanation of any aviation background. Include any writing background."

BUSINESS AND FINANCE

Business publications give executives and consumers a range of information from local business news and trends to national overviews and laws that affect them. National and regional publications are listed below in separate categories. Magazines that have a technical slant are in the Trade section under Business Management, Finance or Management and Supervision categories.

National

‡BUSINESS FRONT, The Publisher's Group, P.O. Box 510366, Salt Lake City UT 84151-0366. Fax: (801)322-1098. Editor: Vicki Andersen. Contact: Anne E. Zombro, publisher. 50% freelance written. Quarterly magazine covering business management. "Focuses on meeting the ever-changing needs of the businessperson. Offers company and entrepreneurial profiles, trends in finance, technology and the Internet." Estab. 1996. Circ. 10,000. Pays on publication. Publishes ms an average of 6 months after acceptance. Byline given. Buys first North American serial and second serial (reprint) rights. Editorial lead time 2 months. Submit seasonal material 4 months in advance. Accepts simultaneous submissions. Reports in 1 month on queries; 2 months on mss. Sample copy for $2 and 9×12 SAE. Writer's guidelines for #10 SASE.

Nonfiction: Book excerpts, interview/profile, new product, technical, quality control (TQM). Buys 6 mss/year. Query with published clips. Length: 1,000-1,300 words. Pays $125-800.

Reprints: Accepts previously published submissions.

Photos: Send photos with submission. Reviews 4×5 transparencies (preferred), any size prints. Negotiates payment individually. Captions, model releases, identification of subjects required. Buys one-time or all rights.

Columns/Departments: Small Business (tips for small business owners), TQM (use of quality measures in business), both 500 words. Buys 8 mss/year. Query with published clips. Pays $50-125.

BUSINESS START-UPS, Entrepreneur Group, Inc., 2392 Morse Ave., Irvine CA 92714. (714)261-2325. E-mail: bsumag@aol.com. Editor: Donna Clapp. 20-25% freelance written. Monthly magazine on small business. "Provides how-to information for starting a small business, running a small business during the 'early' years and profiles of entrepreneurs who have started successful small businesses." Estab. 1989. Circ. 210,000. **Pays on acceptance.** Byline given. Offers 20% kill fee. Buys first time international rights. Submit seasonal/holiday material 6 months in advance. Reports in 2 months on queries. Sample copy for $3. Writer's guidelines for SASE (please write: Attn: Writer's Guidelines" on envelope).

Nonfiction: "We are especially seeking how-to articles for starting a small business. Please read the magazine and writer's guidelines before querying." Interview/profiles on entrepreneurs. Query. Length: 1,800 words. Pays $300.

Photos: Markas Platt, art director. State availability of photos with submission. Identification of subjects required.

BUSINESS WEEK, The McGraw Hill Companies, 1221 Avenue of the Americas, New York NY 10020. Weekly publication covering news and trends in the worlds of business. "*Business Week* is edited to keep readers informed of important news that affects the business community in the U.S. and abroad, and to interpret, analyze and evaluate these news events for business management." Estab. 1929. Circ. 877,700. This magazine did not respond to our request for information. Query before submitting.

BUSINESS97, Success Strategies For Small Business, Group IV Communications, Inc., 125 Auburn Ct., #100, Thousand Oaks CA 91362-3617. (805)496-6156. Editor: Daniel Kehrer. Editorial Director: Don Phillipson. 75% freelance written. Bimonthly magazine for small and independent business. "We publish only practical articles of interest to small business owners all across America; also some small business owner profiles." Estab. 1993. Circ. 610,000. **Pays on acceptance.** Publishes ms an average of 4 months after acceptance. Byline given. Offers 25% kill fee. First and non-exclusive reprint rights. Reports in 6 months. Sample copy for $4. Writer's guidelines for #10 SASE.

• The editor notes that all submissions will also be considered for *Independent Business*, also published by Group IV.

Nonfiction: How-to articles for operating a small business. No "generic" business articles, articles on big business, articles on how to start a business or general articles on economic theory. Buys 80-100 mss/year. Query with résumé and published clips; do not send ms. Length: 1,000-2,000 words. Pays $500-1,500 for assigned articles. Pays expenses of writers on assignment.

Columns/Departments: Tax Tactics, Small Business Computing, Marketing Moves, Ad-visor, Banking & Finance, Business Cost-Savers, all 1,000-2,000 words. Buys 40-50 mss/year. Query with résumé and published clips. Pays $500-1,500.

Tips: "Talk to small business owners anywhere in America about what they want to read, what concerns or interests them in running a business. All areas open, but we use primarily professional business writers with top credentials in the field."

ENTREPRENEUR MAGAZINE, 2392 Morse Ave., Irvine CA 92714. Fax: (714)755-4211. Editor: Rieva Lesonsky. 40% freelance written. "Readers are small business owners seeking information on running a better business." Circ. 410,000. **Pays on acceptance.** Publishes ms an average of 5 months after acceptance. Buys first international rights. Byline given. Submit seasonal/holiday material 6 months in advance of issue date. Reports in 2 months. Sample copy for $3. Writer's guidelines for #10 SASE (please write "Attn: Writer's Guidelines" on envelope).

● The editors have recently started a new publication—*Entrepreneur International*—which covers the latest in U.S. trends and franchising for an international audience. (This is not written for a U.S. audience.) They encourage writers with expertise in this area to please query with ideas.

Nonfiction: How-to (information on running a business, dealing with the psychological aspects of running a business, profiles of unique entrepreneurs). Buys 10-20 mss/year. Query with clips of published work and SASE. Length: 2,000 words. Payment varies. Columns not open to freelancers.

Photos: "We use color transparencies to illustrate articles. Please state availability with query." Uses standard color transparencies. Buys first rights.

Tips: "Read several issues of the magazine! Study the feature articles versus the columns. Probably 75 percent of our freelance rejections are for article ideas covered in one of our regular columns. It's so exciting when a writer goes beyond the typical, flat 'business magazine query'—how to write a press release, how to negotiate with vendors, etc.—and instead investigates a current trend and then develops a story on how that trend affects small business."

EXECUTIVE FEMALE, NAFE, 30 Irving Place, 5th Floor, New York NY 10003. (212)477-2200. Fax: (212)477-8215. E-mail: nafe@nafe.com. Website: http://www.nafe.com. Editor-in-Chief: Gay Bryant. Executive Editor: Patti Watts. Managing Editor: Dorian Burden. 60% freelance written. Bimonthly magazine emphasizing "useful career, business and financial information for the upwardly mobile career woman." Prefers to work with published/established writers. Estab. 1975. Circ. 200,000. Byline given. **Pays on acceptance.** Publishes ms an average of 3 months after acceptance. Submit seasonal/holiday material 6 months in advance. Buys first rights, second serial (reprint) rights to material originally published elsewhere. Reports in 2 months. Sample copy for $2.50. Writer's guidelines for #10 SASE.

Nonfiction: "Articles on any aspect of career advancement and financial planning are welcomed." Needs how-tos for managers and articles about coping on the job, trends in the workplace, financial planning, trouble shooting, business communication, time and stress management, career goal-setting and get-ahead strategies. Written queries only. Submit photos with ms (b&w prints or transparencies) or include suggestions for artwork. Length: 800-2,000 words. Pays 50-75¢/word.

Reprints: Send photocopy of article or typed ms with rights for sale noted and information about when and where the article previously appeared. Pays 25% of amount paid for an original article.

Columns/Departments: Your Money (savings, financial advice, economic trends, interesting tips); Managing Smart (tips on managing people, getting ahead); Your Business (entrepreneurial stories); Careers (how to move ahead); Technology and Cyberspace (taking advantage of the latest workplace tools). Buys 20 mss/year. Query with published clips or send complete ms. Length: 250-1,000 words. Pays 50-75¢/word.

Tips: Plans more short book reviews, book summaries.

MONEY, Time & Life Bldg., Rockefeller Center, New York NY 10020. (212)522-3263. Managing Editor: Frank Lalli. Monthly publication covering all aspects of personal finance. "In addition to presenting solid stategies for intelligent investing and saving, *Money* offers advice relating to retirement, spending for maximum value, travel planning, consumer awareness, tax preparation and education." Estab. 1972. Circ. 1,923,000. Query before submitting.

Tips: "Know the magazine and know the readers. *Money Magazine* provides services for its readers—know how to do this."

‡THE NETWORK JOURNAL, Black Professional and Small Business News, The Network Journal Communication, 333 Nostrand Ave., Brooklyn NY 11216. (718)857-8773. Fax: (718)399-9027. E-mail: aziz@tnj.com. Editor: Tania Padgett. Managing Editor: Njeru Waithaka, Contact: Akinshijn C. Ola, editor. 25% freelance written. Monthly tabloid covering business and career articles. *The Network Journal* caters to Black professionals and small-business owners, providing quality coverage on business, financial, technology and career news germane to the Black community. Estab. 1993. Circ. 11,000. Pays on publication. Byline given. Buys all rights. Editorial lead time 2 months. Submit seasonal material 3 months in advance. Accepts simultaneous submissions. Sample copy for $1. Writer's guidelines free on request.

Nonfiction: How-to, interview/profile. Send complete ms. Length: 1,200-1,500 words. Pays $40. Sometimes pays expenses of writers on assignment.

Reprints: Accepts previously published submissions.

Photos: Send photos with submission. Offers $20/photo. Identification of subjects required. Buys one-time rights.

Columns/Departments: Book reviews, 700-800 words; career management and small business development, 800 words. Pays $25.

Tips: "We are looking for vigorous writing and reporting for our cover stories and feature articles. Pieces should have gripping leads, quotes that actually say something and that come from several sources. Unless it is a column, please do not submit a one-source story. Always remember that your article must contain a nutgraph—that's usually the third paragraph telling the reader what the story is about and why you are telling it now. Editorializing should be kept to a minimum. If you're writing a column, make sure your opinions are well-supported."

‡**PROFIT, The Magazine for Canadian Entrepreneurs**, CB Media Limited, 5th Floor, 777 Bay St., Toronto, Ontario Canada M5W 1A7. (416)596-5999. Editor: Rick Spence. 80% freelance written. Bimonthly magazine covering small and medium business. "We specialize in specific, useful information that helps our readers manage their businesses better. We want Canadian stories only." Estab. 1982. Circ. 110,000. **Pays on acceptance.** Publishes ms an average of 2 months after acceptance. Byline given. Kill fee varies. Buys first North American serial rights and database rights. Submit seasonal/holiday material 6 months in advance. Reports in 1 month on queries; 6 weeks on mss. Sample copy for 9 × 12 SAE with 84¢ postage (Canadian). Free writer's guidelines.

Nonfiction: How-to (business management tips), strategies and Canadian business profiles. Buys 50 mss/year. Query with published clips. Length: 800-2,000 words. Pays $500-2,000 (Canadian). Pays expenses of writers on assignment. State availability of photos with submission.

Columns/Departments: Finance (info on raising capital in Canada), 700 words; Marketing (marketing strategies for independent business), 700 words. Buys 80 mss/year. Query with published clips. Length: 200-800 words. Pays $150-600 (Canadian).

Tips: "We're wide open to freelancers with good ideas and some knowledge of business. Read the magazine and understand it before submitting your ideas."

TECHNICAL ANALYSIS OF STOCKS & COMMODITIES, The Trader's Magazine, Technical Analysis, Inc., 4757 California Ave. SW, Seattle WA 98116-4499. (206)938-0570. Fax: (206)938-1307. E-mail: traders.com. Website: http://www.traders.com. Publisher: Jack K. Hutson. Editor: Thomas R. Hartle. 75% freelance written. Eager to work with new/unpublished writers. Magazine covers methods of investing and trading stocks, bonds and commodities (futures), options, mutual funds and precious metals. Estab. 1982. Circ. 45,000. Pays on publication. Publishes ms an average of 3 months after acceptance. Byline given. Offers 50% kill fee. Buys all rights; however, second serial (reprint) rights revert to the author, provided copyright credit is given. Reports in 3 weeks on queries; 1 month on mss. Sample copy for $5. Writer's guidelines for #10 SASE.

Nonfiction: Thomas R. Hartle, editor. Reviews (new software or hardware that can make a trader's life easier, comparative reviews of software books, services, etc.); how-to (trade); technical (trading and software aids to trading); utilities (charting or computer programs, surveys, statistics or information to help the trader study or interpret market movements); humor (unusual incidents of market occurrences, cartoons). "No newsletter-type, buy-sell recommendations. The article subject must relate to trading psychology, technical analysis, charting or a numerical technique used to trade securities or futures. Virtually requires graphics with every article." Buys 150 mss/year. Query with published clips if available or send complete ms. Length: 1,000-4,000 words. Pays $100-500. (Applies per inch base rate and premium rate—write for information). Sometimes pays expenses of writers on assignment.

Reprints: Send tearsheet or photocopy of article or typed ms with rights for sale noted and information about when and where the article appeared.

Photos: Christine M. Morrison, art coordinator. State availability of art or photos. Pays $60-350 for b&w or color negatives with prints or positive slides. Captions, model releases and identification of subjects required. Buys one-time and reprint rights.

Columns/Departments: Buys 100 mss/year. Query. Length: 800-1,600 words. Pays $50-300.

Fillers: Karen Webb, fillers editor. Jokes and cartoons on investment humor. Must relate to trading stocks, bonds, options, mutual funds or commodities. Buys 20/year. Length: 500 words. Pays $20-50.

Tips: "Describe how to use technical analysis, charting or computer work in day-to-day trading of stocks, bonds, mutual funds, options or commodities. A blow-by-blow account of how a trade was made, including the trader's thought processes, is, to our subscribers, the very best received story. One of our prime considerations is to instruct in a manner that the lay person can comprehend. We are not hyper-critical of writing style."

The completeness and accuracy of submitted material are of the utmost consideration. Write for detailed writer's guidelines."

‡**WORLDBUSINESS, The Global Perspective**, 767 Fifth Ave., 47th Floor, New York NY 10153. (212)909-5100. Editor-in-Chief: John Van Doorn. Managing Editor: Ruth Langfelder. Contact: Charles Wilbanks. 90% freelance written. Bimonthly magazine. "We want stories of interest to business leaders. All material is analytical—puts business in perspective. All writers must be experts in global business world-around." Estab. 1995. Circ. 225,000. **Pays on acceptance**. Publishes ms an average of 6 months after acceptance. Byline given. Offers 25% kill fee. Buys all rights (negotiable). Editorial lead time 3 months. Submit seasonal material 6 months in advance. Sample copy for $2. Writer's guidelines free on request.
Nonfiction: Essays, general interest, interview/profile, opinion. Buys 20-25 mss/year. Query with published clips. Length: 300-4,800 words. Pays $250-5,000 minimum for assigned articles. Sometimes pays expenses of writers on assignment.
Photos: State availability of photos with submission. Reviews contact sheets, transparencies, prints. Negotiates payment individually. Model releases and identification of subjects required. Buys all rights.
Columns/Departments: Business/economics from experts in Asia/Pacific, Europe, the Americas. Length: 900 words. Buys 25 mss/year. Pays up to $1,200.
Tips: "Call editor-in-chief. Know his name. This is his number: (212)909-5041."

YOUR MONEY, Consumers Digest Inc., 5705 N. Lincoln Ave., Chicago IL 60659. (312)275-3590. Editor: Dennis Fertig. 75% freelance written. Bimonthly magazine on personal finance. "We cover the broad range of topics associated with personal finance—spending, saving, investing earning, etc." Estab. 1979. Circ. 500,000. **Pays on acceptance.** Publishes ms an average of 2 months after acceptance. Byline given. Offers 50% kill fee. Buys first rights and second serial (reprint) rights. Reports in 3 months (or longer) on queries. Do not send computer disks. Sample copy and writer's guidelines for 9×12 SAE with 4 first-class stamps. Writer's guidelines for #10 SASE.
  • *Your Money* has been receiving more submissions and has less time to deal with them. Accordingly, they often need more than three months reporting time.
Nonfiction: How-to. "No first-person success stories or profiles of one company." Buys 25 mss/year. Send complete ms or query and clips. Include stamped, self-addressed postcard for more prompt response. Length: 1,500-2,500 words. Pays 50¢/word for assigned articles. Pays expenses of writers on assignment.
Tips: "Know the subject matter. Develop real sources in the investment community. Demonstrate a reader-friendly style that will help make the sometimes complicated subject of investing more accessible to the average person. Fill manuscripts with real-life examples of people who actually have done the kinds of things discussed—people we can later photograph."

Regional

‡**THE ADCOM NET**, (formerly *Adcom Magazine*), P.O. Box 840, Sherborn MA 01170-1840. E-mail: publisher@adcom.net. Website: http://www.adcom.net. Editor: Carl Shedd. 10% freelance written. "*The Adcom Net* provides information and features on advertising, marketing, media, PR and related fields within New England. Primary freelance need: case studies and strategies. Readership: ad agencies, corporate advertising staff." Pays 30 days after publication. Publishes ms an average of 2 days after acceptance. Byline given. No kill fee. Reports in 1 month.
Nonfiction: How-to, opinion, strategies, case studies, industry overviews. Query with published clips. Length: 500-3,000 words. Pays $50 for assigned articles; $25 for unsolicited articles.
Reprints: E-mail copy of article and information about when and where the article previously appeared.
Photos: State availability of photos with submission. Reviews contact sheets, transparencies and 5×7 prints. Offers $10/photo. Captions, model releases and identification of subjects required. Buys one-time rights.
Columns/Departments: Case Study (case study of a company's advertising/marketing program; must be a New England company), 1,200-3,000 words; Strategies ("how-to" or explanatory articles that relate to advertising, PR, marketing, direct marketing or media), 400-700 words; Industry Overview (an overview of marketing/advertising within specific industries in New England), 700-2,500 words. Query with published clips. Length: 400-3,000 words. Pays $50.
Tips: "Our magazine is now all electronic with a private network 'The Adcom Net.' We are also developing a site on the Internet."

---

‡ **THE DOUBLE DAGGER** before a listing indicates that the listing is new in this edition. New markets are often more receptive to freelance submissions.

ARIZONA BUSINESS MAGAZINE, 3111 N. Central Ave., Suite 230, Phoenix AZ 85012. (602)277-6045. Editor: Jessica McCann. 35% freelance written. Bimonthly magazine covering business topics specific to Arizona: health care, banking, finance, legal issues, the environment, real estate and development, international, etc. "Our readers are primarily high-level executives and business owners. The magazine is recognized for our well-balanced articles and high-quality photography. We strive to offer readers well-researched, objective articles on the business issues facing our state." Estab. 1984. Circ. 90,000. Pays on completion of final draft for publication. Publishes ms an average of 3 months after acceptance. Byline given. Offers 100% kill fee. Buys first rights and makes work-for-hire assignments. Editorial lead time 2 months. Submit seasonal material 1 year in advance. Reports in 2 months on queries; 4 months on mss. Sample copy for 9 × 12 SAE with 6 first-class stamps. Writer's guidelines for #10 SASE.

• *Arizona Business* has increased their issues from quarterly to bimonthly.

Nonfiction: General interest, historical/nostalgic, interview/profile, new product, opinion, photo feature. No how-to articles. Buys 20-24 mss/year. Query with published clips. Length: 1,500-2,200 words. Pays $100-250. All articles are assigned. Sometimes pays expenses of writers on assignment.

Photos: State availability of photos with submissions. Reviews transparencies or slides. Negotiates payment individually. Captions, identification of subjects required. Buys one-time rights.

Columns/Departments: HealthWatch, High Finance, Power of Attorney, Environomics, Corporate Lifestyle, Executive Homes (all are general interest stories focusing on the industries mentioned), 1,500-2,000 words. Query with published clips. Pays $100-250.

Fillers: Personality profiles. Buys 8-12/year. Length: 400-600 words. Pays $25-100.

Tips: "Always begin with a one-page query letter/outline of the story idea and include one or two samples of your work. We rarely accept manuscripts. More often, we are impressed with the writer's presentation and respect for our time than with the story proposal. Grab us with one powerful point, fact or idea and you'll have your foot in the door for future assignments. The most important key is to be brief and to the point."

‡BC BUSINESS, Canada Wide Magazines & Communications Ltd., 4th Floor, 4180 Lougheed Highway, Burnaby, British Columbia V5C 6A7 Canada. (604)299-7311. Fax: (604)299-9188. Editor: Bonnie Irving. 80% freelance written. Monthly magazine covering business. "*BC Business* reports on the significant issues and trends shaping the province's business environment. Stories are lively, topical and extensively researched." Circ. 26,000. Pays 2 weeks prior to publication. Publishes ms an average of 2 months after acceptance. Byline given. Kill fee varies. Buys first Canadian rights. Editorial lead time 4 months. Submit seasonal material 4 months in advance. Accepts simultaneous submissions. Reports in 6 weeks on queries. Writer's guidelines free on request.

Nonfiction: Query with published clips. Length: 800-3,000 words. Pays 40-60¢/word, depending on length of story (and complexity). Sometimes pays expenses of writers on assignment.

Reprints: Accepts previously published submissions.

Photos: State availability of photos with submission.

‡BIRMINGHAM BUSINESS JOURNAL, 2101 Magnolia Ave. S., Birmingham AL 35205. (205)322-0000. Fax: (205)322-0040. E-mail: bham.biz.journal@the.matrix.com. Editor: Dick Gentry. 1-2% freelance written. Weekly tabloid covering health care, banking, commercial real estate, general business. "Writer should have expertise in subject covered." Estab. 1983. Circ. 9,000. Pays on publication. Byline given. Offers 10% kill fee. Buys all rights. Editorial lead time 2 weeks. Submit seasonal material 1 month in advance. Reports in 3 weeks on queries. Sample copy and writer's guidelines free on request.

Nonfiction: Exposé, interview/profile, new product, technical. Special issues: Economic Forecast (January). Buys 5 mss/year. Query. Pays $80-500. Sometimes pays expenses of writers on assignment.

Photos: State availability of photos with submission. Reviews 5 × 7 prints. Negotiates payment individually. Identification of subjects required. Buys one-time rights.

Tips: "Writers should submit specific story ideas and explain their expertise in the subject matter. If the idea is worth consideration, we would also like to know if the writer is experienced enough to expedite it."

BOULDER COUNTY BUSINESS REPORT, 4865 Sterling Dr., Suite 200, Boulder CO 80301-2349. (303)440-4950. Fax: (303)440-8954. E-mail: jwlewis@bcbr.com. Website: http://www.bcbr.com. Editor: Jerry W. Lewis. 75% freelance written. Prefers to work with published/established writers; works with a small number of new/unpublished writers each year. Monthly newspaper covering Boulder County business issues. Offers "news tailored to a monthly theme and read primarily by Colorado businesspeople and by some investors nationwide. Philosophy: Descriptive, well-written articles that reach behind the scene to examine area's business activity." Estab. 1982. Circ. 18,000. Pays on publication. Publishes ms an average of 1 month after acceptance. Byline given. Buys one-time rights and second serial (reprint) rights. Reports in 1 month on queries; 2 weeks on mss. *Writer's Market* recommends allowing 2 months for reply. Sample copy for $1.44.

Nonfiction: Interview/profile, new product, examination of competition in a particular line of business. "All our issues are written around one or two monthly themes. No articles are accepted in which the subject has not been pursued in depth and both sides of an issue presented in a writing style with flair." Buys 120 mss/year. Query with published clips. Length: 250-2,000 words. Pays $50-300.

Photos: State availability of photos with query letter. Reviews b&w contact sheets. Pays $10 maximum for b&w contact sheet. Identification of subjects required. Buys one-time rights and reprint rights.

Tips: "Must be able to localize a subject. In-depth articles are written by assignment. The freelancer located in the Colorado area has an excellent chance here."

‡**BUSINESS JOURNAL OF CENTRAL NY**, CNY Business Review, Inc., 231 Wallton St., Syracuse NY 13202. (315)472-3104. Fax: (315)472-3644. E-mail: blrbmeistr@aol.com. Editor: Gray Weaver. 35% freelance written. Biweekly newspaper covering business in Central New York. "*The Business Journal* covers business news in a 16-county area surrounding Syracuse. The audience consists of owners and managers of businesses." Estab. 1985. Circ. 8,500. Pays on publication. Publishes ms an average of 2 months after acceptance. Byline given. Kill fee negotiable. Buys first rights. Editorial lead time 1 month. Accepts previously published submissions. Sample copy and writer's guidelines free on request.

Nonfiction: Humor, opinion. Buys 100 mss/year. Query. Length: 750-2,000 words. Pays $75-500. Sometimes pays in copies. Sometimes pays expenses of writers on assignment.

Photos: State availability of photos with submission. Reviews contact sheets. Negotiates payment individually. Captions, model releases, identification of subjects required.

Columns/Departments: Buys 20 mss/year. Query with published clips.

Fillers: Facts, newsbreaks, short humor. Buys 10/year. Length: 300-600 words. Pays $50-150.

Tips: "The audience is comprised of owners and managers. Focus on their needs. Call or send associate editor story ideas: be sure to have a Central New York 'hook.' "

‡**BUSINESS NH MAGAZINE**, 404 Chestnut St., Suite 201, Manchester NH 03101-1831. Editor: Holly Babin. 50% freelance written. Monthly magazine with focus on business, politics and people of New Hampshire. "Our audience consists of the owners and top managers of New Hampshire businesses." Estab. 1983. Circ. 13,000. Pays on publication. Publishes ms an average of 2 months after acceptance. Byline given.

Nonfiction: Features—how-to, interview/profile. Buys 24 mss/year. Query with published clips and résumé. "No unsolicited manuscripts; interested in local writers only." Length: 750-2,500 words. $75-250 for assigned articles.

Photos: Both b&w and color photos used. Pays $40-80. Buys one-time rights.

Tips: "I *always* want clips and résumé with queries. Freelance stories are almost always assigned. Stories *must* be local to New Hampshire."

THE BUSINESS TIMES, Blackburn Magazine Group, 231 Dundas St., Suite 203, London, Ontario N6A 1H1 Canada. (519)679-4901. Fax: (519)434-7842. E-mail: editor@businesstimes.com. Editor: Nadia H. Shousher. 75% freelance written. Monthly tabloid covering local business news, events and trends. "Local angle a must—aimed at business owners and executives." Estab. 1993. Circ. 11,000. **Pays on acceptance.** Byline given. Offers $25 kill fee. Buys all rights. Editorial lead time 1 month. Submit seasonal material 2 months in advance. Accepts simultaneous submissions. Reports in 1 month on queries; 2 months on mss. Sample copy and writer's guidelines free.

Nonfiction: Interview/profile, new product, technical. No advertorial, non-local news. Query with published clips. Length: 250-700 words. Pays $50-200. Sometimes pays expenses of writers on assignment.

Photos: State availability of photos with submission. Offers $25-75/photo. Negotiates payment individually. Identification of subjects required. Buys one-time rights.

Tips: "Need local industry contacts to break news; need to know local sources, trends, events. Query by letter with sample news clips."

‡**COAST BUSINESS**, Ship Island Holding Co., P.O. Box 1209, Gulfport MS 39502. Fax: (601)867-2986. Editor: Lisa Monti. 10% freelance written. Biweekly tabloid covering business. "*Coast Business* covers local and national business news and issues. Our readers represent the business community of the Mississippi Gulf Coast." Estab. 1984. Circ. 8,000. Pays on publication. Publishes ms an average of 1 month after acceptance. Byline given. Buys first North American serial rights. Editorial lead time 3 months. Submit seasonal material 3 months in advance. Reports in 2 weeks on queries; 1 month on mss. Sample copy for $1.

Nonfiction: How-to, interview/profile, new product, opinion. All articles must be business related. Buys 26 mss/year. Query with published clips. Length: 700-1,500 words. Pays $50-150. Sometimes pays expenses of writers on assignment.

Reprints: Accepts previously published submissions.

Photos: Send photos with submission. Reviews prints. Negotiates payment individually. Captions, identification of subjects required. Buys one-time rights.

Columns/Departments: Computers (product reviews, tips); Finance (personal or business); Insurance (business); all 700-750 words. Query with published clips. Pays $50-75.

Tips: "Our audience is the business community of the Mississippi Gulf Coast. We cover local news as well as national issues that affect the way the Coast does business."

COLORADO BUSINESS, Wiesner Inc., 7009 S. Potomac St., Englewood CO 80112. (303)397-7600. Fax: (303)397-7619. Website: http://www.cobizmag.com. Editor: Cynthia Evans. Managing Editor: Bruce Goldberg. 75% freelance written. Monthly magazine covering Colorado-based businesses. Estab. 1973. Circ. 18,000. Pays on publication. Publishes ms an average of 3 months after acceptance. Byline given. Offers 50% kill fee. Buys first rights. Editorial lead time 4 months. Submit seasonal material 6 months in advance. Reports in 1 month on queries.
Nonfiction: Business, general interest, historical/nostalgic, how-to, interview/profile, new product, personal experience, photo feature, technical. Buys 40 mss/year. Query with published clips. Length: 1,500-1,800 words. Pays $350 for assigned articles. Sometimes pays expenses of writers on assignment.
Photos: State availability of photos with submission. Reviews contact sheets, transparencies. Negotiates payment individually. Captions, identification of subjects required. Buys one-time rights.
Columns/Departments: Buys 24 mss/year. Query with published clips. Pays $200.
Tips: "Know the magazine before you pitch me. Solid story ideas specifically geared to Colorado audience. No boring stories. No corporatese."

CRAIN'S DETROIT BUSINESS, Crain Communications Inc., 1400 Woodbridge Ave., Detroit MI 48207. (313)446-6000. Fax: (313)446-1687. E-mail: 75147.372@compuserve.com. Website: http://bizserve.com/crains/. Editor: Mary Kramer. Executive Editor: Cindy Goodaker. Contact: Philip Nussel, managing editor. 5% freelance written. Weekly tabloid covering business in the Detroit metropolitan area—specifically Wayne, Oakland, Macomb, Washtenaw and Livingston counties. Estab. 1985. Circ. 143,500. Pays on publication. Publishes ms an average of 1 month after acceptance. Byline given. Offers $150 kill fee. Buys all rights and all electronic rights. Sample copy for $1.
Nonfiction: New product, technical, business. Buys 100 mss/year. Query with published clips. Length: 20-40 words/column inch. Pays $10/column inch. Pays expenses of writers on assignment.
Photos: State availability of photos with submissions.
Tips: "Contact special sections editor in writing with background and, if possible, specific story ideas relating to our type of coverage and coverage area."

FLORIDA TREND, Magazine of Florida Business and Finance, Box 611, St. Petersburg FL 33731. (813)821-5800. Editor: John F. Berry. Monthly magazine covering business economics and public policy for Florida business people and investors. Circ. 50,000. Pays on publication. Byline given. Buys first North American serial rights. Reports in 2 months. Sample copy for $2.95 plus tax and postage.
Nonfiction: Business, finance and public policy. Buys 20-25 mss/year. Query with or without published clips. Length: 1,200-2,500 words. Manuscripts not returned.

‡INGRAM'S, Ingram Media LLC, 306 E. 12th St., Suite 1014, Kansas City MO 64106. (816)842-9994. Fax: (816)474-1111. E-mail: ingrams@ingramsmag.com. Website: http://www.ingramsmag.com. Editor: Robin Silverman. 75% freelance written. Monthly magazine covering Kansas City business/executive lifestyle. "Upscale, affluent audience. Business executives and professionals. Looking for sophisticated writing with style and humor when appropriate. All articles must have a Kansas City angle." Estab. 1989. Circ. 24,000. **Pays on acceptance.** Publishes ms an average of 2 months after acceptance. Byline given. Offers 50% kill fee. Buys first rights. Editorial lead time 2 months. Submit seasonal material 3 months in advance. "We don't accept unsolicited manuscripts except for opinion column." Reports in 6 weeks on queries. Sample copy for $3 current, $5 back and writer's guidelines free on request.
Nonfiction: How-to (businesses and personal finance related), interview/profile (KC execs and politicians, celebrities), opinion. Buys 30 mss/year. Query with published clips. Length: 500-3,000 words. Pays $175-1,500 maximum for assigned articles. Sometimes pays expenses of writers on assignment.
Columns/Departments: Say-So (opinion), 1,500 words. Buys 12 mms/year. Pays $175 maximum.
Tips: "Writers must understand the publication and the audience—knowing what appeals to a business executive, entrepreneur, or professional in Kansas City."

‡LONDON BUSINESS MAGAZINE, Bowes Publishers, Box 7400, London, Ontario N5Y 4X3 Canada. (519)472-7601. Editor: Janine Foster. 60% freelance written. Monthly magazine covering business stories in London and area. "Our audience is primarily small and medium businesses and entrepreneurs. Focus is on success stories and how to better operate your business." Estab. 1987. Circ. 13,000. Pays on publication. Publishes ms an average of 2 months after acceptance. Byline given. Offers 50% kill fee. Buys first rights. Editorial lead time 3 months. Reports in 10 weeks on queries. Sample copy for #10 SASE. Writer's guidelines free on request.
Nonfiction: How-to (business topics), humor, interview/profile, new product (local only), personal experience. Must have a London connection. Buys 24 mss/year. Query with published clips. Length: 250-1,500 words. Pays $25-800.
Photos: Send photos with submission. Reviews contact sheets, transparencies. Negotiates payment individually. Identification of subjects required. Buys one-time rights.
Tips: "Phone with a great idea. The most valuable thing a writer owns is ideas. We'll take a chance on an unknown if the idea is good enough."

MONEY SAVING IDEAS, The National Research Bureau, P.O. Box 1, Burlington IA 52601-0001. (319)752-5415. Fax: (319)752-3421. Editor: Nancy Heinzel. 75% freelance written. Quarterly magazine that features money saving strategies. "We are interested in money saving tips on various subjects (insurance, travel, heating/cooling, buying a house, ways to cut costs and balance checkbooks). Our audience is mainly industrial and office workers." Estab. 1948. Pays on publication. Publishes ms an average of 1 year after acceptance. Byline given. Buys all rights. Sample copy and writers guidelines for #10 SAE with 2 first-class stamps. Writer's guidelines for #10 SASE.
Nonfiction: How-to (save on grocery bills, heating/cooling bills, car expenses, insurance, travel). Query with or without published clips, or send complete ms. Length: 500-700 words. Pays 4¢/word.
Tips: "Follow our guidelines. Keep articles to stated length, double-spaced, neatly typed. If writer wishes rejected manuscript returned include SASE. Name, address and word length should appear on first page."

‡NEW MEXICO BUSINESS JOURNAL, Sierra Publishing Group, Inc., 2323 Aztec NE, Albuquerque NM 87107. (505)889-2911. Fax: (505)889-0822. E-mail: sierrapq@ix.netcom.com. Editor: Bob Lochnar. Contact: Kathryn Matousek, assistant editor. 85% freelance written. Monthly magazine covering general business in New Mexico and Southwest. "*The Business Journal* tries to provide indepth analytical coverage of subjects that are of particular interest to people doing business in New Mexico and west Texas." Estab. 1976. Circ. 22,000. Pays on the 15th of the month of publication. Publishes ms 2-3 months after acceptance. Byline given. Offers 25% kill fee. Buys one-time rights. Editorial lead time 2 months. Submit seasonal material 3 months in advance. Accepts simultaneous submissions. Reports in 2 weeks on queries; 1 month on mss. Sample copy for 9×12 SAE with 3 first-class stamps. Writer's guidelines free on request.
Nonfiction: Book excerpts, interview/profile, business subjects. Buys 50-75 mss/year. Query. Length: 900-3,000 words. Pays $200-750 for assigned articles; $150-400 for unsolicited articles. Sometimes pays expenses of writers on assignment.
Photos: State availability of photos with submission. Reviews contact sheets, transparencies. Negotiates payment individually. Captions, identification of subjects required. Buys one-time rights.
Columns/Departments: Pays $100-250.

ROCHESTER BUSINESS MAGAZINE, Rochester Business, Inc., 1600 Lyell Ave., Rochester NY 14606-2395. (716)458-8280. Fax: (716)458-9831. Editor: Kristina Hutch. 25% freelance written. Monthly magazine. "*RBM* is a colorful tutorial business publication targeted specifically toward business owners and upper-level managers in the Rochester metropolitan area. Our audience is comprised of upscale decision-makers with keen interest in the 'how-to' of business. Some features deal with lifestyle, golf, cultural focus, etc." Estab. 1984. Circ. 11,000. Pays on publication. Publishes ms an average of 6 months after acceptance. Byline given. Buys all rights. Reports in 1 month. Sample copy and writer's guidelines for SAE with 6 first-class stamps.
Nonfiction: Essays, historical/nostalgic, how-to, humor, interview/profile, personal experience, all with business slant. Buys 12-24 mss/year. Query with published clips. Length: 1,500 words maximum. Pays $50-100.
Reprints: Send tearsheet of article or typed ms with rights for sale noted and information about when and where the article previously appeared. For reprints pays 100% of the amount paid for an original article.
Photos: State availability of photos with submission. Offers no additional payment for photos accepted with ms. Captions required.

VERMONT BUSINESS MAGAZINE, Lake Iroquois Publications, 2 Church St., Burlington VT 05401. (802)863-8038. Fax: (802)863-8069. E-mail: vtbizmag@together.net. Editor: Timothy McQuiston. 80% freelance written. Monthly tabloid covering business in Vermont. Circ. 8,000. Pays on publication. Publishes ms an average of 1 month after acceptance. Byline given. Offers kill fee. Accepts simultaneous submissions. Not copyrighted. Buys one-time rights. Query for electronic submissions. Reports in 2 months. Sample copy for 11×14 SAE with 7 first-class stamps.
Nonfiction: Business trends and issues. Buys 200 mss/year. Query with published clips. Length: 800-1,800 words. Pays $100-200. Pays the expenses of writers on assignment.
Reprints: Send tearsheet of article and information about when and where the article previously appeared.
Photos: Send photos with submission. Reviews contact sheets. Offers $10-35/photo. Identification of subjects required.
Tips: "Read daily papers and look for business angles for a follow-up article. We look for issue and trend articles rather than company or businessman profiles. Note: magazine accepts Vermont-specific material *only*. The articles *must* be about Vermont."

‡VICTORIA'S BUSINESS REPORT, Monday Publications, 1609 Blanshard St., Victoria, British Columbia V8W 2J5 Canada. (604)382-7777. Fax: (604)381-2662. E-mail: nachtjag@islandnet.com. Editor: Lyle Jenish. 45% freelance written. Monthly magazine covering business. Audience is conservative, both business and politically. Estab. 1986. Circ. 20,000. Pays on publication. Publishes ms an average of 2 months after acceptance. Byline given. Buys first rights. Editorial lead time 1 month. Submit seasonal material 1 month in advance. Sample copy for $5 and postage. Writer's guidelines free on request.

Nonfiction: Exposé, interview/profile, new product. Buys 10 mss/year. Query. Length: 500-2,500 words. Pays $10-150. Sometimes pays expenses of writers on assignment.

Photos: State availability of photos with submission. Offers no additional payment for photos accepted with ms.

Columns/Departments: Pays $20.

‡**VIRGINIA BUSINESS**, Media General Business Communications Inc., 411 E. Franklin St., Suite 105, Richmond VA 23219. (804)649-6999. Fax: (804)649-6811. Executive Editor: Karl Rhodes. Contact: Leigh Anne Larance, managing editor. 95% freelance written. Monthly magazine covering business and finance in Virginia. "Virginia business and economic development. The audience is top business executives and decision-makers in government and industry." Estab. 1986. Circ. 35,500. **Pays on acceptance**. Publishes ms an average of 2 months after acceptance. Byline given. Buys all rights. Sample copy for $3.50.

Nonfiction: Business articles—insurance, health care, travel, real estate, economic development, banking, personal finance, etc. Buys 150 mss/year. Query with published clips. Length: Brights, 500 words; short articles, 1,000 words; features, 2,300 words. Pays $50-350 (depending on length). Pays $50 for "Minding Your Business" short features. Prices on longer features vary. Pays documented expenses up to $75 on assigned full-length features.

Photos: State availability of photos with submission. Negotiates payment individually. Buys one-time rights.

Tips: "Most articles are assigned, but the magazine is always looking for talented new writers, particularly Virginia-based freelancers. Most writers start on short business features. Successful writers move on to longer trend stories."

CAREER, COLLEGE AND ALUMNI

Three types of magazines are listed in this section: university publications written for students, alumni and friends of a specific institution; publications about college life for students; and publications on career and job opportunities. Literary magazines published by colleges and universities are listed in the Literary and "Little" section.

AMERICAN CAREERS, Career Communications, Inc., 6701 W. 64th St., Overland Park KS 66202. Editorial Consultant: Mary Pitchford. 50% freelance written. Middle school and high school student publication published 3 times during school year covering careers, career statistics, skills needed to get jobs. Most stories are provided at no charge by authors in business, education and government. Estab. 1990. Circ. 500,000. Byline sometimes given. Buys all rights and makes work-for-hire assignments. Reports in 1 month. Sample copy and writer's guidelines free on request.

Nonfiction: Career and education features. Buys 10 mss/year. Query with published clips. Length: 350-750 words. Negotiates payment. Pays expenses of writers on assignment.

Photos: State availability of photos with submission. Reviews contact sheets. Negotiates payment individually. Captions, model releases and identification of subjects required. Buys one-time rights.

Columns/Departments: Reality Check (brief career-related facts), 25-100 words; Career Profile, 250-300 words. Some reviewing of current related books. Buys 6 mss/year. Negotiates payment.

Tips: "Letters of introduction or query letters with samples are ways we get to know writers. Samples should include how-to articles or career articles. Articles written for publication for teenagers also would make good samples. Short feature articles on careers, career-related how-to articles and self-assessment tools (10-20 point quizzes with scoring information) are primarily what we publish. We are interested in writers for children in early elementary grades K-4, and we are interested in writers who do classroom activity books and teacher's guides for this age group."

THE BLACK COLLEGIAN, The Career & Self Development Magazine for African American Students, Black Collegiate Services, Inc., 140 Carondelet St., New Orleans LA 70130. (504)523-0154. Fax: (504)523-0271. Editor: Sonya Stinson. 25% freelance written. Magazine published biannually (October and February) during school year for African-American college students and recent graduates with an interest in career and job information, African-American cultural awareness, personalities, history, trends and current events. Estab. 1970. Circ. 109,000. Buys one-time rights. Byline given. Pays on publication. Submit seasonal and special interest material 2 months in advance of issue date. Reports in 6 months. Sample copy for $4 and 9×12 SAE. Writer's guidelines for #10 SASE.

Nonfiction: Material on careers, sports, black history, news analysis. Articles on problems and opportunities confronting African-American college students and recent graduates. Book excerpts, exposé, general interest, historical/nostalgic, how-to (develop employability), opinion, personal experience, profile, inspirational. Buys 40 mss/year (6 unsolicited). Query with published clips or send complete ms. Length: 500-1,500 words. Pays $100-500.

Photos: State availability of or send photos with query or ms. Black and white photos or color transparencies purchased with or without ms. 8×10 prints preferred. Captions, model releases and identification of subjects required. Pays $35/b&w; $50/color.

CAMPUS CANADA, Canadian Controlled Media Communications, 287 MacPherson Ave., Toronto Ontario M4V 1A4 Canada. (416)928-2909. Managing Editor: Sarah Moore. 75% freelance written. Quarterly magazine covering student (university) life. "*Campus Canada* is written for the Canadian university student. Stories range in topic from current issues (date rape, etc.) to entertainment to collegiate sports." Estab. 1984. Circ. 125,000. Pays on publication. Byline given. Offers 50% kill fee. Buys first North American serial rights. Editorial lead time 3 months. Submit seasonal material 2 months in advance. Accepts simultaneous submissions. Reports in 2 months on queries. Sample copy on request.

Nonfiction: General interest, humor, interview/profile, opinion, personal experience, travel. Buys 15 mss/year. Query with published clips. Length: 1,000 words maximum. Pays $50-300.

Photos: State availability of photos with submissions. Identification of subjects required. Buys one-time rights.

Columns/Departments: Movies (upcoming releases), 800 words; Sports (Canadian university), 800 words; Music (Canadian pop/alternative), 500 words.

CAREER FOCUS, For Today's Rising Professional, Communications Publishing Group, Inc., 250 Mark Twain Tower, 106 W. 11th St., Kansas City MO 64105-1806. (816)221-4404. Editor: Neoshia Michelle Paige. 80% freelance written. Bimonthly magazine "devoted to providing positive insight, information, guidance and motivation to assist Blacks and Hispanics (ages 21-40) in their career development and attainment of goals." Estab. 1988. Circ. 250,000. Pays on publication. Byline often given. Buys second serial (reprint) rights and makes work-for-hire assignments. Submit seasonal/holiday material 6 months in advance. Accepts simultaneous submissions. Reports in 2 months. Sample copy for 9×12 SAE with 4 first-class stamps. Writer's guidelines for #10 SASE.

   ● The editor notes that if the writer can provide the manuscript on 3.25 disk, saved in generic ASCII, pay is $10 higher and chance of acceptance is greater.

Nonfiction: Book excerpts, general interest, historical, how-to, humor, inspirational, interview/profile, personal experience, photo feature, technical, travel. Length: 750-2,000 words. Pays $150-400 for assigned articles; 10¢/word for unsolicited articles. Sometimes pays expenses of writers on assignment.

Reprints: Send tearsheet of article and information about when and where the article previously appeared. Pays 50% of amount paid for an original article.

Photos: State availability of photos with submission. Reviews transparencies. Pays $20-25/photo. Captions, model releases and identification of subjects required. Buys all rights.

Columns/Departments: Profiles (striving and successful Black and Hispanic young adult, ages 21-40). Buys 15 mss/year. Send complete ms. Length: 500-1,000 words. Pays $50-250.

Fiction: Adventure, ethnic, historical, humorous, mainstream, slice-of-life vignettes. Buys 3 mss/year. Send complete ms. Length: 500-2,000 words. Pay varies.

Fillers: Anecdotes, facts, gags to be illustrated by cartoonist, newsbreaks, short humor. Buys 10/year. Length: 25-250 words. Pays $25-100.

Tips: For new writers: Submit full ms that is double-spaced; clean copy only. If available, send clips of previously published works and résumé. Should state when available to write. Most open to freelancers are profiles of successful and striving persons including photos. Profile must be of a Black or Hispanic adult living in the US. Include on first page of ms name, address, phone number, Social Security number and number of words in article.

CAREERS & COLLEGES MAGAZINE, E.M. Guild, Inc., 989 Avenue of Americas, 6th Floor, New York NY 10018. (212)563-4688. Fax: (212)967-2531. Editor-in-Chief/Publisher: June Rogoznica. Senior Editor: Don Rauf. 85-95% freelance written. Biannual magazine for education, careers and life choices for high school students. "*Careers & Colleges* is a magazine that believes in young people. It believes that they have the power—and responsibility—to shape their own futures. That is why each issue provides high school juniors and seniors with useful, thought-provoking reading on career choices, life values, higher education and other topics that will help them enjoy profitable and self-respecting work. Delivered free to students in 1,750 high schools." Estab. 1980. Circ. 500,000. **Pays on acceptance.** Publishes ms an average of 3 months after acceptance. Byline given. Offers 20% kill fee. Buys first North American serial rights. Editorial lead time 6 months. Submit seasonal material 6 months in advance. Reports in 1 month on queries. Sample copy for $2.50 and 9×12 SAE with 5 first-class stamps. Writer's guidelines for #10 SASE.

   ● Ranked as one of the best markets for freelance writers in *Writer's Yearbook*'s annual "Top 100 Markets," January 1996.

Nonfiction: Book excerpts, how-to (job or college related), interview/profile (teen role models). May publish a Spring issue on summer jobs and other employment opportunities for young adults. "No personal essays, life experiences or fiction." Buys 36-52 mss/year. Query with published clips. Length: 600-1,500 words. Pays $150 minimum. Sometimes pays expenses of writers on assignment (limit agreed upon in advance).

Reprints: Send photocopy of article.

Photos: State availability of photos with submission. Negotiates payment individually. Buys one-time rights.

Columns/Departments: MoneyWise (strategies and resources for financing education beyond high school), 600-800 words; Career Watch (profiles of growth careers/interview plus statistics), 800 words.

College Hotline; Tech Talk; Teen Spotlight. Buys 18-24 mss/year. Query with or without published clips. Pays $150-350.
Tips: "Be sure to request writer's guidelines. Follow guidelines specifically. No unsolicited manuscripts are accepted. Send a one-page query and clips. Examine other teen magazines for current topic ideas. Many opportunities exist in our career profile section—pay is low, but it is a good testing ground for us to gauge a writer's ability—strong performance here can lead to bigger articles. Query about growth careers that we have not covered in the past (consult magazine's Career Watch Index)."

CAREERS & MAJORS (for College Students), Oxendine Publishing, Inc., P.O. Box 14081, Gainesville FL 32604-2081. (904)373-6907. E-mail: 75143.2043@compuserve.com. Editor: W.H. "Butch" Oxendine Jr. Managing Editor: Kay Quinn King. Assistant Editor: Sarah Beavers. 35% freelance written. Quarterly magazine for college careers and job opportunities. Estab. 1983. Circ. 17,000. Pays on publication. Publishes ms an average of 3 months after acceptance. Byline given. Buys all rights. Submit seasonal/holiday material 4 months in advance. Accepts simultaneous submissions. Reports in 1 month on queries. Sample copy for 8×11 SAE with 3 first-class stamps. For query/response and/or writer's guidelines send SASE.
Nonfiction: How-to, humor, new product, opinion. "No lengthy individual profiles or articles without primary and secondary sources of attribution." Buys 10 mss/year. Query with published clips. Length: 250-1,000 words. Pays $35 maximum. Pays contributor copies to students or first-time writers.
Reprints: Send tearsheet or photocopy of article or typed ms with rights for sale noted and information about when and where the article previously appeared.
Photos: State availability of photos with submission. Reviews contact sheets, negatives and transparencies; size "doesn't matter." Offers $50/photo maximum. Captions, model releases and identification of subjects required. Buys all rights.
Fiction: Publishes novel excerpts.
Columns/Departments: College Living (various aspects of college life, general short humor oriented to high school or college students), 250-1,000 words; Buys 10 mss/year. Query. Length: 250-1,000 words. Pays $35 maximum.
Fillers: Facts, newsbreaks, short humor. Buys 10/year. Length: 100-500 words. Pays $35 maximum.
Tips: "Read other high school and college publications for current issues, interests. Send manuscripts or outlines for review. All sections open to freelance work. Always looking for lighter, humorous articles, as well as features on Florida colleges and universities, careers, jobs. Multi-sourced (5-10) articles best."

CARNEGIE MELLON MAGAZINE, Carnegie Mellon University, Bramer House, Pittsburgh PA 15213-3890. (412)268-2132. Fax: (412)268-6929. Editor: Ann Curran. Estab. 1914. Quarterly alumni publication covering university activities, alumni profiles, etc. Circ, 60,000. **Pays on acceptance.** Byline given. Copyrighted. Reports in 1 month.
Nonfiction: Book reviews (faculty alumni), general interest, humor, interview/profile, photo feature. "We use general interest stories linked to Carnegie Mellon activities and research." No unsolicited mss. Buys 5 features and 5-10 alumni profiles/year. Query with published clips. Length: 800-2,000 words. Pays $100-400 or negotiable rate. Sample copy for $2 and 9×12 SAE.
Poetry: Avant-garde, traditional. No previously published poetry. No payment.

CIRCLE K MAGAZINE, 3636 Woodview Trace, Indianapolis IN 46268-3196. Fax: (317)879-0204. Executive Editor: Nicholas K. Drake. 60% freelance written. "Our readership consists almost entirely of above-average college students interested in voluntary community service and leadership development. They are politically and socially aware and have a wide range of interests." Published 5 times/year. Circ. 15,000. **Pays on acceptance.** Buys first North American serial rights. Byline given. Submit seasonal/holiday material 6 months in advance. Reports in 2 months. Sample copy and writer's guidelines for large SAE with 3 first-class stamps.
Nonfiction: Articles published in *Circle K* are of 2 types—serious and light nonfiction. "We are interested in general interest articles on topics concerning college students and their lifestyles, as well as articles dealing with careers, community concerns and leadership development. No first person confessions, family histories or travel pieces." Query. Length: 800-1,900 words. Pays $150-400.
Photos: Purchased with accompanying ms. Captions required. Total purchase price for ms includes payment for photos.
Tips: "Query should indicate author's familiarity with the field and sources. Subject treatment must be objective and in-depth, and articles should include illustrative examples and quotes from persons involved in the subject or qualified to speak on it. We are open to working with new writers who present a good article idea and demonstrate that they've done their homework concerning the article subject itself, as well as concerning our magazine's style. We're interested in college-oriented trends, for example, entrepreneur schooling is now a major shift; rising censorship on campus; high-tech classrooms; virtual reality; music; leisure; and health issues."

‡**COLLEGE BOUND**, Ramholtz Publishing Inc., 2110 Clove Rd., Staten Island NY 10306. (718)273-5700. Editor: Sara Fiedelholtz. Managing Editor: Roseann Blake. Contact: Daniel Ford, assistant editor. 85%

freelance written. Bimonthly magazine covering the transition from high school to college. "*College Bound* is written by college students for high school students." Estab. 1987. Circ. 95,000. Pays on publication. Publishes ms an average of 2 months after acceptance. Byline given. Offers 100% kill fee or $100. Buys first rights. Editorial lead time 4 months. Submit seasonal material 4 months in advance. Accepts simultaneous submissions and previously published submissions. Reports in 3 weeks on queries; 1 month on mss. Sample copy and writer's guidelines free on request.

Nonfiction: How-to (apply for college, prepare for the interview, etc.), personal experience (college experiences). Buys 30 mss/year. Query with published clips. Length: 750-2,000 words. Pays $50-150. Sometimes pays expenses of writers on assignment.

Photos: Send photos with submission. Reviews negatives, prints. Offers no additional payment for photos accepted with ms. Buys one time rights.

Columns/Departments: Campus Traditions (unique traditions from different colleges), 100-150 words. Buys 20-25 mss/year. Query with published clips. Pays $25-100.

COLLEGE MONTHLY, The Student Point-of-View, 23 E. Tenth St., #706, New York NY 10003. Phone/fax: (212)529-1519. Editor: Sara Fiedelholtz. 85% freelance written. Bimonthly magazine covering college life. "*College Monthly* is written by college students for college students." Estab. 1984. Circ. 375,000. Pays on publication. Publishes ms an average of 3 months after acceptance. Byline given. Offers 100% kill fee or $100. Buys all first rights. Editorial lead time 4 months. Submit seasonal material 4 months in advance. Accepts simultaneous submissions. Reports in 3 weeks on queries; 1 month on mss. Sample copy and writer's guidelines free on request.

Nonfiction: Interview/profile (college athletics, volunteers), personal experience, travel (spring break, study abroad). Buys 30 mss/year. Query with published clips. Length: 750-2,000 words. Pays $50-150.

Reprints: Accepts previously published submissions.

Photos: Send photos with submission. Reviews negatives, prints. Offers no additional payment for photos accepted with ms. Buys one-time rights.

Columns/Departments: Sports (profiles of college athletes), 1,000 words; Viewpoint (profiles of student volunteers), 1,000 words. Buys 10-12 mss/year. Query with pubished clips. Pays $50-150.

COLLEGE PREVIEW, A Guide for College-Bound Students, Communications Publishing Group, 250 Mark Twain Tower, 106 W. 11th St., Kansas City MO 64105-1806. (816)221-4404. Fax: (816)221-1112. Editor: Neoshia Michelle Paige. 80% freelance written. Quarterly educational and career source guide. "Contemporary guide designed to inform and motivate Black and Hispanic young adults, ages 16-21 years old about college preparation, career planning and life survival skills." Estab. 1985. Circ. 600,000. Pays on publication. Byline often given. Buys first serial and second serial (reprint) rights or makes work-for-hire assignments. Submit seasonal/holiday material 6 months in advance. Accepts simultaneous submissions. Reports in 2 months. Sample copy for 9×12 SAE with 4 first-class stamps. Writer's guidelines for #10 SASE.

 • The editor notes that if the writer can provide the manuscript on 3.25 disk, saved in generic ASCII, pay is $10 higher and chance of acceptance is greater.

Nonfiction: Book excerpts or reviews, general interest, how-to (dealing with careers or education), humor, inspirational, interview/profile (celebrity or "up and coming" young adult), new product (as it relates to young adult market), personal experience, photo feature, technical, travel. Send complete ms. Length: 750-2,000 words. Pays $150-400 for assigned articles; 10¢/word for unsolicited articles. Sometimes pays expenses of writers on assignment.

Reprints: Send tearsheet or photocopy of article or short story or typed ms with rights for sale noted and information about when and where the article previously appeared. Pays 50% of the amount paid for an original article.

Photos: State availability of photos with submission. Reviews transparencies. Offers $20-$25/photo. Captions, model releases and identification of subjects required. Will return photos—send SASE.

Columns/Departments: Profiles of Achievement (striving and successful minority young adults ages 16-35 in various careers). Buys 30 mss/year. Send complete ms. Length: 500-1,500. Pays 10¢/word.

Fiction: Adventure, ethnic, historical, humorous, mainstream, slice-of-life vignettes. Buys 3 mss/year. Send complete ms. Length: 500-2,000 words. Pay varies.

Fillers: Anecdotes, facts, gags to be illustrated by cartoonist, newsbreaks, short humor. Buys 10/year. Length: 25-250 words. Pays $25-100.

Tips: For new writers—send complete ms that is double spaced; clean copy only. If available, send clips of previously published works and résumé. Should state when available to write. Include on first page of ms name, address, phone, Social Security number, word count and SASE.

DIRECT AIM, For Today's Career Strategies, Communications Publishing Group, #250, 106 W. 11th St., Kansas City MO 64105-1806. (816)221-4404. Editor: Neoshia Michelle Paige. 80% freelance written. Quarterly educational and career source guide for Black and Hispanic college students at traditional, nontraditional, vocational and technical institutions. "This magazine informs students about college survival skills and planning for a future in the professional world." Buys second serial (reprint) rights or makes work-for-hire assignments. Submit seasonal/holiday material 6 months in advance. Accepts simultaneous submissions. Reports in 2 months. Sample copy for 9×12 SAE with 4 first-class stamps. Writer's guidelines for #10 SASE.

● The editor notes that if the writer can provide the manuscript on 3.25 disk, saved in generic ASCII, pay is $10 higher and chance of acceptance is greater.

Nonfiction: Book excerpts or reviews, general interest, how-to (dealing with careers or education), humor, inspirational, interview/profile (celebrity or "up and coming" young adult), new product (as it relates to young adult market), personal experience, photo feature, technical, travel. Query or send complete ms. Length: 750-2,000 words. Pays $150-400 for assigned articles; 10¢/word for unsolicited articles. Sometimes pays expenses of writers on assignment.

Reprints: Send tearsheet of article or short story or typed ms with rights for sale noted and information about when and where the article previously appeared. Pays 50% of amount paid for an original article.

Photos: State availability of photos with submission. Reviews transparencies. Offers $20-25/photo. Captions, model releases and identification of subjects required. Will return photos.

Columns/Departments: Profiles of Achievement (striving and successful minority young adult age 18-35 in various technical careers). Buys 25 mss/year. Send complete ms. Length: 500-1,500. Pays $50-250.

Fiction: Publishes novel excerpts. Adventure, ethnic, historical, humorous, mainstream, slice-of-life vignettes. Buys 3 mss/year. Send complete ms. Length: 500-2,000 words. Pay varies.

Fillers: Anecdotes, facts, gags to be illustrated by cartoonist, newsbreaks, short humor. Buys 30/year. Length: 25-250 words. Pays $25-100.

Tips: For new writers—send complete ms that is double spaced; clean copy only. If available, send clips of previously published works and résumé. Should state when available to write. Include on first page of ms name, address, phone, Social Security number and word count. Photo availability is important."

EEO BIMONTHLY, Equal Employment Opportunity Career Journal, CASS Communications, Inc., 1800 Sherman Place, Suite 300, Evanston IL 60201-3769. (847)475-8800. Fax: (847)475-8807. E-mail: eeobimonth@aol.com. Senior Editor: Robert Shannon. 85% freelance written. Bimonthly magazine covering career management, specifically for women, minorities and persons with disabilities. "Although our audience is specifically female and minority, much of our content applies to all white-collar professionals—career management tips, industry overviews and trends, and job search techniques. Anything job- or career-related (interviewing, résumé writing, relocating, communicating, automating, etc.) fits our publication." Estab. 1969. Circ. 7,500. **Pays on acceptance.** Publishes ms an average of 4 months after acceptance. Byline given. Buys first North American serial rights. Editorial lead time 3 months. Accepts simultaneous submissions. Reports in 3 weeks on queries; 1 month on mss. Sample copy for 10×12 SAE with 6 first-class stamps.

Nonfiction: General interest (career/workplace related), how-to (career planning related), interview/profile. Buys 24-30 mss/year. Query with published clips. Length: 1,800-3,000 words. Pays $350-600 for assigned articles; $250-500 for unsolicited articles.

Photos: State availability of photos with submissions. Reviews contact sheets, transparencies, prints. Negotiates payment individually. Captions, model releases, identification of subjects required. Buys one-time rights.

Columns/Departments: Industry Focus (trends, rising players, etc. of various industries), 2,000 words; Success Stories (profiles of successful individuals either female, minority or disabled), 2,000 words. Buys 10-12 mss/year. Query with published clips. Pays $250-600.

Tips: "Your queries can be informal outlines; just show us that you can write and that you know your subject."

EQUAL OPPORTUNITY, The Nation's Only Multi-Ethnic Recruitment Magazine for Black, Hispanic, Native American & Asian American College Grads, Equal Opportunity Publications, Inc., 1160 E. Jericho Turnpike, Suite 200, Huntington NY 11743. (516)421-9421. Fax: (516)421-0359. Editor: James Schneider. 50% freelance written. Prefers to work with published/established writers. Triannual magazine covering career guidance for minorities. "Our audience is 90% college juniors and seniors; 10% working graduates. An understanding of educational and career problems of minorities is essential." Estab. 1967. Circ. 15,000. Controlled circulation, distributed through college guidance and placement offices. Pays on publication. Publishes ms an average of 6 months after acceptance. Byline given. Buys first rights. Deadline dates: Fall (June 10); Winter (September 15); Spring (January 1). Accepts simultaneous queries. Sample copy and writer's guidelines for 9×12 SAE with 5 first-class stamps.

Nonfiction: Book excerpts and articles (job search techniques, role models); general interest (specific minority concerns); how-to (job-hunting skills, personal finance, better living, coping with discrimination); humor (student or career related); interview/profile (minority role models); opinion (problems of minorities); personal experience (professional and student study and career experiences); technical (on career fields offering opportunities for minorities); travel (on overseas job opportunities); and coverage of Black, Hispanic, Native American and Asian American interests. Special issues include career opportunities for minorities in industry and government in fields such as banking, insurance, finance, communications, sales, marketing, engineering, computers, military and defense. Query or send complete ms. Length: 1,000-1,500 words. Sometimes pays expenses of writers on assignment. Pays 10¢/word.

Reprints: Accepts previously published submissions.

Photos: Prefers 35mm color slides and b&w. Captions and identification of subjects required. Buys all rights. Pays $15/photo use.

Tips: "Articles must be geared toward questions and answers faced by minority and women students."

FIRST OPPORTUNITY, Today's Career Options, Communications Publishing Group, 250 Mark Twain Tower, 106 W. 11th St., Kansas City MO 64105-1806. (816)221-4404. Editor: Neoshia Michelle Paige. 80% freelance written. Resource publication focusing on advanced vocational/technical educational opportunities and career preparation for Black and Hispanic young adults, ages 16-21. Circ. 500,000. Pays on publication. Byline sometimes given. Buys second serial (reprint) rights or makes work-for-hire assignments. Submit seasonal/holiday material 6 months in advance. Accepts simultaneous submissions. Reports in 2 months. Sample copy for 9 × 12 SAE with 4 first-class stamps. Writer's guidelines for #10 SASE.

● The editor notes that if the writer can provide the manuscript on 3.25 disk, saved in generic ASCII, pay is $10 higher and chance of acceptance is greater.

Nonfiction: Book excerpts or reviews, general interest, how-to (dealing with careers or education), humor, inspirational, interview/profile (celebrity or "up and coming" young adult), new product (as it relates to young adult market), personal experience, photo feature, technical, travel. Length: 750-2,000 words. Pays $150-400 for assigned articles; 10¢/word for unsolicited articles. Sometimes pays expenses of writers on assignment.

Reprints: Send tearsheet of article or typed ms with rights for sale noted and information about when and where the article previously appeared. Pays 50% of the amount paid for an original article.

Photos: State availability of photos with submission. Prefers transparencies. Offers $20-25/photo. Captions, model releases, identification of subjects required. Buys all rights.

Columns/Departments: Profiles of Achievement (striving and successful minority young adult, age 16-35 in various vocational or technical careers). Buys 15 mss/year. Send complete ms. Length: 500-1,500. Pays $50-250.

Fiction: Adventure, ethnic, historical, humorous, mainstream, slice-of-life vignettes. Buys 3 mss/year. Send complete ms. Length: 500-5,000 words. Pay varies.

Fillers: Anecdotes, facts, gags to be illustrated by cartoonist, newsbreaks, short humor. Buys 10/year. Length: 25-250 words. Pays $25-100.

Tips: For new writers—send complete ms that is double spaced; clean copy only. If available, send clip of previously published works and résumé. Should state when available to write. Include on first page of ms name, address, phone, Social Security number and word count. Photo availability is important.

FLORIDA LEADER (for college students), P.O. Box 14081, Gainesville FL 32604. (904)373-6907. Fax: (904)373-8120. E-mail: 75143.2043@compuserve.com. Publisher: W.H. "Butch" Oxendine, Jr. Managing Editor: Kay Quinn King. Assistant Editor: Sarah Beavers. 10% freelance written. Quarterly "college magazine, feature-oriented, especially activities, events, interests and issues pertaining to college students." Estab. 1981. Circ. 27,000. Publishes ms an average of 2 months after acceptance. Byline given. Submit seasonal/holiday material 6 months in advance. Reports in 2 months on queries. Sample copy and writer's guidelines for 9 × 12 SAE with 5 first-class stamps.

Nonfiction: How-to, humor, interview/profile, feature—all multi-sourced and Florida college related. Special issues: Careers and Majors (January, June); Florida Leader high school edition (August, January, May); Transfer (for community college transfers, November, July); Returning Student (for nontraditional-age students, July); Back to School (September); Student Leader (October, March—pays double). Query with SASE. Length: 500 words or less. Payment varies. Sometimes pays expenses of writers on assignment.

Reprints: Send tearsheet or photocopy of article or typed ms with rights for sale noted and information about when and where the article previously appeared.

Photos: State availability of photos with submission. Reviews negatives and transparencies. Captions, model releases, identification of subjects requested.

Fiction: Publishes novel excerpts.

‡THE JOB SOURCE SERIES, 1708 Surrey Lane NW, Washington DC 20007. (202)337-7800. Fax: (202)337-3121. Editor: Donna Caroline Hicks. Managing Editor: Ben Psillas. 50% freelance written. Annual career/job guide covering careers/where to live in Baltimore, Pittsburgh, Miami & Washington, DC. "The JOB Source Series focuses on how and where to find internships, entry-level or middle management jobs in metropolitan areas across the country. Our job guides also help people find places to live, shop and dine in their respective metro area." Estab. 1992. Circ. 15,000. **Pays on acceptance.** Publishes ms an average of 9 months after acceptance. Byline given. Offers 50% kill fee. Buys all rights. Editorial lead time 3 months. Submit seasonal material 9 months in advance. Sample copy $7.50. Writer's guidelines free on request.

Nonfiction: How-to, careers/jobs. Special issues: Future Books: New Jersey, New York, LA, Connecticut, Jacksonville, Orlando Job Sources. September-November 96. Buys 5 mss/year. Query with published clips. Length: 500-2,000 words. Pays $350-750 for assigned articles. Sometimes pays expenses of writers on assignment.

LINK MAGAZINE, The College Magazine, Creative Media Generations, Inc., 110 Greene St., #407, New York NY 10012. (212)966-1100. Website: http://www.linkmag.com. Editor-in-Chief: Ty Wenger. 95% of mss are solicited. Rarely accepts unsolicited materials. Quarterly magazine covering college news, issues and lifestyle. Estab. 1993. Circ. 1,000,000. Pays on publication. Publishes ms an average of 6 months after acceptance. Byline given. Offers 25% kill fee. Buys first or one-time rights. Editorial lead time 4 months. Submit seasonal material 4 months in advance. Accepts simultaneous submissions. Reports in 2 months on queries, 3 months on mss. Writer's guidelines for #10 SASE.
Nonfiction: Book excerpts, essays, exposé, general interest, how-to (educational, financial, lifestyle, etc.), interview/profile, photo feature, travel. Special issues: Environmental, Job Hunting, Computers. Buys 5 mss/year. Query with published clips. Length: 400-3,000. Pays $150-500 for assigned articles; $100-200 for unsolicited articles. Pays expenses of writers on assignment.
Photos: Send photos with submission. Reviews contact sheets, transparencies, prints. Negotiates payment individually. Captions required. Buys one-time rights.
Columns/Departments: Get A Job (how-to job hunting), 700-800 words; It's Your Life (lifestyle articles), 700-800 words; Interview (national politicians and writers), 700-1,500 words. Buys 5 mss/year. Query with published clips. Pays $200-250.
Tips: "Research very informative, insightful or how-to articles and present completed ideas with clips in a query. Keep everything geared only to what college students would appreciate."

‡**NATIONAL BUSINESS EMPLOYMENT WEEKLY**, Dow Jones & Co., P.O. Box 300, Princeton NJ 08543. (609)520-4306. Editor: Tony Lee. Senior Editor: Perri Capell. 60% freelance written. Weekly magazine covering career-guidance and job-search issues. Estab. 1981. Circ. 30,000. Pays on publication. Publishes ms an average of 2 months after acceptance. Byline given. Offers 50% kill fee. Buys first North American serial, second serial (reprint), all rights or makes work-for-hire assignments. Editorial lead time 3 months. Submit seasonal material 3 months in advance. Reports in 3 weeks on queries; 1 month on mss. Writer's guidelines free on request.
Nonfiction: Book excerpts, how-to (job search), opinion, personal experience. No generic job-search advice. Buys 50 mss/year. Query with published clips. Length: 1,200-1,800 words. Pays $100-250 for assigned articles; $50-200 for unsolicited articles. Sometimes pays expenses of writers on assignment.
Reprints: Accepts previously published submissions.
Columns/Departments: From My Perspective (opinion/personal experience on job hunting/career advancement), 800-1,000 words. Buys 50 mss/year. Send complete ms. Pays $50.
Tips: "We are aimed at middle- to senior-level executives who are attempting to change jobs or advance their careers. All submissions must be targeted to that audience."

NOTRE DAME MAGAZINE, University of Notre Dame, Administration Bldg., Room 415, Notre Dame IN 46556-0775. (219)631-5335. Fax: (219)631-6767. E-mail: ndmag.1@nd.edu. Editor: Kerry Temple. Managing Editor: Carol Schaal. 75% freelance written. Quarterly magazine covering news of Notre Dame and education and issues affecting contemporary society. "We are interested in the moral, ethical and spiritual issues of the day and how Christians live in today's world. We are universal in scope, Catholic in viewpoint and serve Notre Dame alumni, friends and other constituencies." Estab. 1972. Circ. 135,000. **Pays on acceptance.** Publishes ms an average of 1 year after acceptance. Byline given. Kill fee negotiable. Buys first rights. Reports in 1 month. Free sample copy.
Nonfiction: Opinion, personal experience, religion. Buys 35 mss/year. Query with clips of published work. Length: 600-3,000 words. Pays $250-1,500. Sometimes pays expenses of writers on assignment.
Photos: State availability of photos. Reviews b&w contact sheets, transparencies and 8×10 prints. Model releases and identification of subjects required. Buys one-time rights.

OREGON QUARTERLY, The Magazine of the University of Oregon, 5228 University of Oregon, Eugene OR 97403-5228. (541)346-5048. Fax: (541)346-2220. E-mail: gmaynard@oregon.uoregon.edu. Website: http://www.uoregon.edu/~oqrtly/oq.html. Editor: Guy Maynard. Assistant Editor: Kathleen Holt. 50% freelance written. Quarterly university magazine of people and ideas at the University of Oregon and the Northwest. Estab. 1919. Circ. 95,000. Pays on publication. Publishes ms an average of 3 months after acceptance. Byline given. Offers 20% kill fee. Buys first North American serial rights. Reports in 2 months. Sample copy for 9×12 SAE with 4 first-class stamps.
Nonfiction: Northwest issues and culture from the perspective of UO alumni and faculty. Buys 30 mss/year. Query with published clips. Length: 250-2,500 words. Pays $50-500. Sometimes pays expenses of writers on assignment.
Reprints: Send photocopy of article and information about when and where the article previously appeared. Pays 50% of the amount paid for an original article.
Photos: State availability of photos with submission. Reviews 8×10 prints. Offers $10-25/photo. Identification of subjects required. Buys one-time rights.
Fiction: Publishes novel excerpts.
Tips: "Query with strong, colorful lead; clips."

‡**THE PENN STATER**, Penn State Alumni Association, 105 Old Main, University Park PA 16802. (814)865-2709. Fax: (814)863-5690. E-mail: penn-stater@psu.edu. Website: http://www.alumni.alu.psu.edu. Editor: Tina Hay. 75% freelance written. Bimonthly magazine covering Penn State and Penn Staters. "All of our readers are members of the Penn State Alumni Association. They are highly educated, but view our publication as 'easy reading' and a link back to their alma mater. There is a lot of pride in knowing that one out of every 750 Americans went to Penn State." Estab. 1910. Circ. 120,000. **Pays on acceptance.** Publishes ms an average of 4 months after acceptance. Byline given. Offers 50% kill fee. Buys first North American serial rights or second serial (reprint) rights. Editorial lead time 3 months. Submit seasonal material 4-5 months in advance. Accepts simultaneous and previously published submissions. Query for electronic submissions. Reports in 1 month on queries; 2 months on mss. Sample copy and writer's guidelines free on request.

Nonfiction: Book excerpts (by Penn Staters), general interest, historical/nostalgic, humor, interview/profile, personal experience (sometimes), photo feature, science/research. Buys 20 mss/year. Query with published clips. Length: 750-3,000 words. Pays $150-300. Sometimes pays expenses of writers on assignment.

Photos: Send photos with submission. Reviews transparencies and prints. Negotiates payment individually. Captions required. Buys one-time rights.

Tips: "We're always looking for stories from out of state. Stories that have some national slant, that consider a national view of an issue, and somehow involve a Penn Stater are desirable. Profiles of unusual or successful alumni are an 'easy in.' We accept freelance articles almost exclusively for our features section. Generally we run three to four features per issue, plus a photo feature and nostalgia/history piece."

PORTLAND MAGAZINE, The University of Portland Quarterly, 5000 N. Willamette Blvd., Portland OR 97203. Editor: Brian Doyle. 70% freelance written. Quarterly magazine covering University of Portland news, issues, concerns. Generally features are about spirituality (especially Catholicism), the Northwest, higher education, or the University itself. Estab. 1984. Circ. 25,000. Pays on publication. Publishes ms an average of 6 months after acceptance. Byline given. Buys first North American serial rights. Editorial lead time 8 months. Submit seasonal material 8 months in advance. Reports in 1 month on queries. Sample copy and writer's guidelines free on request.

Nonfiction: Book excerpts, essays, general interest, interview/profile, opinion, personal experience, religious. Buys 6 mss/year. Query with published clips or send complete ms. Length: 1,000-3,000 words. Pays $100-500. Sometimes pays expenses of writers on assignment.

THE PURDUE ALUMNUS, Purdue Alumni Association, Purdue Memorial Union 160, 101 N. Grant St., West Lafayette IN 47906-6212. (317)494-5184. Fax: (317)494-9179. Editor: Tim Newton. 75% freelance written. Prefers to work with published/established writers; works with small number of new/unpublished writers each year. Bimonthly magazine covering subjects of interest to Purdue University alumni. Estab. 1912. Circ. 65,000. Pays on publication. Publishes ms an average of 2 months after acceptance. Byline given. Buys first rights and makes work-for-hire assignments. Submit seasonal/holiday material 6 months in advance. Accepts simultaneous submissions. Reports in 2 weeks on queries; 1 month on mss. Sample copy for 9×12 SAE with 2 first-class stamps.

Nonfiction: Book excerpts, general interest, historical/nostalgic, humor, interview/profile, personal experience. Focus is on alumni, campus news, issues and opinions of interest to 65,000 members of the Alumni Association. Feature style, primarily university-oriented. Issues relevant to education. Buys 12-20 mss/year. Length: 1,500-2,500 words. Pays $250-500. Pays expenses of writers on assignment.

Reprints: Accepts previously published submissions.

Photos: State availability of photos. Reviews b&w contact sheet or 5×7 prints.

Tips: "We have 280,000 living, breathing Purdue alumni. If you can find a good story about one of them, we're interested. We use local freelancers to do campus pieces."

RIPON COLLEGE MAGAZINE, P.O. Box 248, Ripon WI 54971-0248. (414)748-8364. Fax: (414)748-9262. E-mail: booneL@mac.ripon.edu. Website: http://www.ripon.edu. Editor: Loren J. Boone. 15% freelance written. Quarterly magazine that "contains information relating to Ripon College and is mailed to alumni and friends of the college." Estab. 1851. Circ. 14,000. Pays on publication. Publishes ms an average of 3 months after acceptance. Byline given. Not copyrighted. Makes work-for-hire assignments. Reports in 2 weeks.

Nonfiction: Historical/nostalgic, interview/profile. Buys 4 mss/year. Query with or without published clips, or send complete ms. Length: 250-1,000 words. Pays $25-350.

Photos: State availability of photos with submission. Reviews contact sheets. Offers additional payment for photos accepted with ms. Captions and model releases are required. Buys one-time rights.

Tips: "Story ideas must have a direct connection to Ripon College."

RUTGERS MAGAZINE, Rutgers University, Alexander Johnston Hall, New Brunswick NJ 08903. (908)932-7315. Fax: (908)932-8412. E-mail: lchambe@communications.rutgers.edu. Website: http://www.rutgers.edu. Editor: Lori Chambers. 50% freelance written. Quarterly university magazine of "general interest, but articles must have a Rutgers university or alumni tie-in." Circ. 134,000. **Pays on acceptance.** Publishes ms an average of 4 months after acceptance. Byline given. Pays 30-35% kill fee. Buys first North American serial rights. Submit seasonal/holiday material 8 months in advance. Reports in 1 month. Sample copy for $3 and 9×12 SAE with 5 first-class stamps.

Nonfiction: Book excerpts, essays, general interest, historical/nostalgic, science/research, interview/profile, arts/humanities, and photo feature. No articles without a Rutgers connection. Buys 15-20 mss/year. Query with published clips. Pays competitively. Pays expenses of writers on assignment.

Photos: State availability of photos with submission. Payment varies. Identification of subjects required. Buys one-time rights.

Columns/Departments: Business, Opinion, Sports, Alumni Profiles (related to Rutgers), 1,200-1,800 words. Buys 6-8 mss/year. Query with published clips. Pays competitively.

Tips: "Send ideas. We'll evaluate clips and topic for most appropriate use."

THE STUDENT, 127 Ninth Ave. N., Nashville TN 37234. Fax: (615)251-3953. Editor: Gina Howard. 10% freelance written. Works with a small number of new/unpublished writers each year. Publication of National Student Ministry of The Sunday School Board of the Southern Baptist Convention. Monthly magazine for college students. Estab. 1922. Circ. 40,000. Buys all rights. **Pays on acceptance.** Publishes ms an average of 10 months after acceptance. Manuscripts should be double-spaced on white paper with 50-space line, 25 lines/page. Sources for quotes and statistics should be given for verification. Reports usually within 2 months. Sample copy and guidelines for 9×12 SAE with 3 first-class stamps.

Nonfiction: Contemporary questions, problems, and issues facing college students viewed from a Christian perspective to develop high moral and ethical values. Cultivating interpersonal relationships, developing self-esteem, dealing with the academic struggle, coping with rejection, learning how to love and developing a personal relationship with Jesus Christ. Prefers complete ms rather than query. Length: 1,000 words maximum. Pays 5½¢/word after editing with reserved right to edit accepted material.

Fiction: Satire and parody on college life, humorous episodes; emphasize clean fun and the ability to grow and be uplifted through humor. Contemporary fiction involving student life, on campus as well as off. Length: 1,000 words. Pays 5½¢/word.

STUDENT LEADER (for college students), Oxendine Publishing Inc., P.O. Box 14081, Gainesville FL 32604-2081. (904)373-6907. E-mail: 75143.2043@compuserve.com. Editor: W.H. "Butch" Oxendine Jr.. Managing Editor: Kay Quinn King. 30% freelance written. Semiannual magazine covering student government, leadership. Estab. 1993. Circ. 200,000. Pays on publication. Byline given. Buys all rights. Submit seasonal material 4 months in advance. Reports in 1 month on queries. Sample copy for #10 SAE with 3 first-class stamps. For query response and/or writer's guidelines send #10 SASE.

Nonfiction: How-to, humor, new product, opinion. "No lengthy individual profiles or articles without primary or secondary sources of attribution." Buys 10 mss/year. Query. Length: 250-1,000 words. Pays $100 maximum. Pays contributor copies to students or first-time writers.

Photos: State availability of or send photos with submission. Reviews contact sheets, negatives, transparencies. Offers $50 photo/maximum. Captions, model releases, identification of subjects required. Buys all rights.

Columns/Departments: Buys 10 mss/year. Query. Length: 250-1,000 words. Pays $100 maximum.

Fillers: Facts, newsbreaks, short humor. Buys 10/year. Length: 100 words minimum. Pays $35 maximum.

Tips: "Read other high school and college publications for current ideas, interests. Send outlines or manuscripts for review. All sections open to freelance work. Always looking for lighter, humorous articles, as well as features on colleges and universities, careers, jobs. Multi-sourced (5-10) articles are best."

‡SUCCEED, The Magazine for Continuing Education, Ramholtz Publishing Inc., 2110 Clove Rd., Staten Island NY 10305. (718)273-5700. Editor: Sara Fiedelholtz. Managing Editor: Roseann Blake. Contact: Daniel Ford, assistant editor. 85% freelance written. Semiannual magazine covering continuing education. "*Succeed*'s readers are interested in continuing education, whether it be for changing careers or enhancing their current career." Estab. 1994. Circ. 155,000. Pays on publication. Publishes ms an average of 2 months after acceptance. Byline given. Offers 100% kill fee or $100. Buys first rights. Editorial lead time 4 months. Submit seasonal material 4 months in advance. Accepts simultaneous submissions. Reports in 3 weeks on queries; 1 month on mss. Sample copy and writer's guidelines free on request.

Nonfiction: How-to (change careers), interview/profile (interesting careers). Buys 15 mss/year. Query with published clips. Length: 750-2,000 words. Pays $50-150. Sometimes pays expenses of writers on assignment.

Reprints: Accepts previously published submissions.

Photos: Send photos with submission. Reviews negatives, prints. Offers no additional payment for photos accepted with ms. Buys one-time rights.

Columns/Departments: Query with published clips. Pays $50-150.

WHAT MAKES PEOPLE SUCCESSFUL, The National Research Bureau, Inc., P.O. Box 1, Burlington IA 52601-0001. (319)752-5415. Fax: (319)752-3421. Editor: Nancy Heinzel. 75% freelance written. Eager to work with new/unpublished writers and works with a small number each year. Quarterly magazine. Estab. 1948. Pays on publication. Publishes ms an average of 1 year after acceptance. Buys all rights. Submit seasonal/holiday material 8 months in advance of issue date. Sample copy and writer's guidelines for #10 SAE with 2 first-class stamps.

Nonfiction: How-to (be successful); general interest (personality, employee morale, guides to successful living, biographies of successful persons, etc.); experience; opinion. No material on health. Buys 3-4 mss/issue. Query with outline. Length: 500-700 words. Pays 4¢/word.

Tips: Short articles (rather than major features) have a better chance of acceptance because all articles are short.

CHILD CARE AND PARENTAL GUIDANCE

Magazines in this section address the needs and interests of families with children. Some publications are national in scope, others such as *Bay Area Baby* are geographically specific. Some offer general advice for parents of all ages, while magazines such as *Black Child Magazine* or *Catholic Parent* answer the concerns of smaller demographic groups. Other markets that buy articles about child care and the family are included in the Religious and Women's sections and in the Trade Education sections. Publications for children can be found in the Juvenile and Teen section.

‡**AMERICAN BABY MAGAZINE, For Expectant and New Parents**, K-III Communications, 249 W. 17th St., New York NY 10011. (212)463-4608. Editor: Judith Nolte. 90% freelance written. Prefers to work with published/established writers; works with a small number of new/unpublished writers each year. Monthly magazine covering pregnancy, baby care and parenting. "Our readership is composed of women in late pregnancy and early new motherhood. Most readers are first-time parents; some have older children. A simple, straightforward, clear approach is mandatory." Estab. 1938. Circ. 1,600,000. **Pays on acceptance.** Publishes ms an average of 6 months after acceptance. Byline given. Buys first North American serial rights. Submit seasonal holiday material 6 months in advance. Simultaneous and previously published submissions OK. Reports in 4 weeks on queries; 2 months on mss. Sample copy for 9×12 SAE with 6 first-class stamps. Writer's guidelines for #10 SASE.

• Ranked as one of the best markets for freelance writers in *Writer's Yearbook*'s annual "Top 100 Markets," January 1996.

Nonfiction: Book excerpts, how-to (some aspect of pregnancy or baby care), humor and personal experience. "No 'hearts and flowers' or fantasy pieces." Buys 60 mss/year. Query with published clips or send complete ms. Length: 1,000-2,500 words. Pays $500-1,000 for assigned articles; $500-750 for unsolicited articles. Pays the expenses of writers on assignment.

Reprints: Send tearsheet, photocopy of article or typed ms with rights for sale noted and information about when and where the article previously appeared. Pays 75% of amount paid for an original article.

Photos: State availability of photos with submission. Reviews transparencies and prints. Model release and identification of subjects required. Buys one-time rights.

Tips: "Articles should either give 'how to' information on some aspect of pregnancy or baby care, cover some common problem of child raising, along with solutions, give advice to the mother on some psychological or practical subject, or share an experience with some universal aspect of new parenthood."

ATLANTA PARENT/ATLANTA BABY, Suite 506, 4330 Georgetown Square II, Atlanta GA 30338-6217. (770)454-7599. Editor: Liz White. Managing Editor: Peggy Middendorf. 50% freelance written. *Atlanta Parent* is a monthly tabloid covering parenting of children from birth-16 years old. Offers "down-to-earth help for parents." Estab. 1983. Circ. 65,000. *Atlanta Baby* is a quarterly magazine for expectant and new parents. Circ. 35,000. Pays on publication. Publishes ms 3 months after acceptance. Byline given. Buys one-time rights. Submit seasonal material 6 months in advance. Reports in 4 months. Sample copy for $2.

Nonfiction: General interest, how-to, humor, interview/profile, travel. Special issues: Private school (January); Birthday parties (February); Camp (March/April); Maternity and Mothering (May); Child care (July); Back-to-school (August); Drugs (October); Holidays (November/December). No first-person accounts or philosophical discussions. Buys 60 mss/year. Query with or without published clips, or send complete ms. Length: 700-2,100 words. Pays $15-30. Sometimes pays expenses of writers on assignment.

Reprints: Send photocopy of article or typed ms with rights for sale noted and information about when and where the article previously appeared. Pays $15-30.

Photos: State availability of photos with submission and send photocopies. Reviews 3×5 photos "b&w preferably." Offers $10/photo. Buys one-time rights.

Columns/Departments: Pack up and go (travel). Buys 8-10 mss/year. Send complete ms. Length: 700-1,500 words. Pays $15-30.

Tips: "Articles should be geared to problems or situations of families and parents. Should include down-to-earth tips and clearly written. No philosophical discussions or first person narratives."

BABY, Cradle Publishing, 52 Vanderbilt Ave., New York NY 10017. (212)986-1422. Fax: (212)986-0816. E-mail: thebabymag@aol.com. Contact: Jeanne Muchnick. 20% freelance written. Bimonthly magazine covering birth, first year of baby's life. "*Baby* is distributed by diaper services, doctor's offices and retail outlets to national circulation of 750,000. The primary recipients are women in the last trimester of pregnancy and new parents." Estab. 1994. Circ. 750,000. **Pays on acceptance.** Publishes ms an average of 2 months after acceptance. Byline given. Buys first North American serial rights. Editorial lead time 4 months. Submit seasonal material 4 months in advance. Reports in 1 month. Sample copy for SAE with 3 first-class stamps.
  • With a new editor and a new look, *Baby* is aiming for a more "mom-friendly" feel to the contents.
Nonfiction: Essays (e.g. first-time dad), how-to (any topics of interest to new parents, e.g. baby care, photography, siblings, traveling, choosing doctor, breast feeding, etc.), personal experience, photo feature, professional or expert articles on baby care, family issues. Buys 18 mss/year. Send complete ms. Length: 900-2,000 words.
Reprints: Accepts previously published submissions.

‡**BAY AREA BABY**, 401 Alberto Way, Suite A, Los Gatos CA 95032. (408)358-1414. Editor: Lynn Berardo. Contact: Many Brence Martin, managing editor. Semiannual magazine covering pregnancy and new parenthood (usually first-time). "*Bay Area Baby* targets pregnant couples and new (usually first-time) parents. We provide local, up-to-the-minute information on pregnancy and babies." Estab. 1986. Circ. 60,000. Pays on publication. Publishes ms an average of 6 months after acceptance. Byline given. Buys first rights. Editorial lead time 4 months. Submit seasonal material 6 months in advance. Accepts simultaneous submissions. Reports in 2 months. Sample copy for 8½ × 11½ SAE with 4 first-class stamps. Writer's guidelines for #10 SASE.
Nonfiction: Book excerpts, essays, interview/profile, personal experience (must be related to pregnancy or new parenthood). Buys 9 mss/year. Send complete ms. Length: 600-1,400 words. Pays 6¢/word. Sometimes pays expenses of writers on assignment.
Reprints: Accepts previously published submissions.
Photos: State availability of photos with submission. Reviews contact sheets, transparencies, prints. Offers $10-15/photo. Buys one-time rights.

BAY AREA PARENT MAGAZINE, Bay Area Publishing Group Inc., 401 Alberto Way, Suite A, Los Gatos CA 95032-5404. Fax: (408)356-4903. Editor: Lynn Berardo. Contact: Mary Brence Martin, managing editor. 80% freelance written. Works with locally-based published/established writers and some non-local writers. Monthly tabloid of resource information for parents and teachers. Circ 77,000. Pays on publication. Publishes ms an average of 6 months after acceptance. Byline given. Buys one-time rights. Submit seasonal/holiday material 4 months in advance. Accepts simultaneous submissions. Sample copy for 9 × 12 SAE with 7 first-class stamps. Writer's guidelines for #10 SASE.
Nonfiction: Book excerpts (related to our interest group); exposé (health, psychology); historical/nostalgic ("History of Diapers"); how-to (related to kids/parenting); humor; interview/profile; photo feature; travel (with kids, family). Special issues: Music (March); Art and Kid's Birthdays (April); Summer Camps and Vacations (May); Family Fun and Health and Medicine (June); Working Parents (July); Fashion and Sports (August); Back-to-School (September). No opinion or religious articles. Buys 45-60 mss/year. Query or send complete ms. Length: 150-1,500 words. Pays 6¢/word. Sometimes pays expenses of writers on assignment.
Reprints: Send typed ms with rights for sale noted and information about when and where the article previously appeared.
Photos: State availability of photos. Prefers b&w contact sheets and/or 3 × 5 b&w prints. Pays $5-25. Model release required. Buys one-time rights.
Columns/Departments: Child Care, Family Travel, Birthday Party Ideas, Baby Page, Toddler Page, Adolescent Kids. Buys 36 mss/year. Send complete ms. Length: 400-1,200 words. Pays 6-9¢/word.
Tips: "Submit new, fresh information concisely written and accurately researched. We also produce *Bay Area Baby Magazine*, a semiannual publication and *Valley Parent* Magazine, which focuses on central Contra Costa County and southern Alameda County."

BIG APPLE PARENTS' PAPER, Family Communications, Inc., 36 E. 12th St., New York NY 10003. (212)533-2277. Fax: (212)475-6186. Managing Editor: Helen Freedman. 99% freelance written. Monthly tabloid covering New York City family life. Estab. 1985. Circ. 62,000. Pays on publication. Byline given.

● **A BULLET** introduces comments by the editors of *Writer's Market* indicating special information about the listing.

Offers 50% kill fee. Buys first New York City rights. Submit seasonal material 3 months in advance. Accepts simultaneous submissions. Reports immediately; however, request no submissions during the summer months. Sample copy and writer's guidelines free on request.

Nonfiction: Essays, exposé, general interest, how-to, humor, inspirational, interview/profile, opinion, personal experience, photo feature, travel. Buys 60-70 mss/year. Send complete ms. Length: 600-1,000 words. Pays $35-50. Sometimes pays expenses of writers on assignment.

Reprints: Accepts previously published submissions.

Photos: State availability of or send photos with submission. Reviews contact sheets, prints. Offers $20/photo. Captions required. Buys one-time rights.

Columns/Departments: Dads; Education; Family Finance; Travel. Buys 50-60 mss/year. Send complete ms.

Tips: "Mostly looking for pieces targeted to New York City parents, or which can be localized. Always looking for the news angle. Controversy welcomed!"

‡**BLACK CHILD MAGAZINE**, Interrace Publications, P.O. Box 12048, Atlanta GA 30355. (404)364-9195. Fax: (404)364-9965. Contact: Candy Mills, editor. 80% freelance written. Bimonthly magazine covering parenting of black children. "Covers all concerns/issues relating to healthy parenting of African-American children from birth to early teens.!" Estab. 1995. Circ. 50,000. Pays on publication. Publishes ms an average of 3 months after acceptance. Byline given. Buys first, one- or second serial (reprint) rights. Submit seasonal material 4 months in advance. Reports in 1 month on queries; 2 months on mss. Sample copy for $2 and 9 × 12 SAE with 4 first-class stamps. Writer's guidelines for #10 SASE.

Nonfiction: Book excerpts, essays, exposé, general interest, historical/nostalgic, how-to, humor, inspirational, interview/profile, new product, opinion, personal experience, photo feature. Buys 30 mss/year. Send complete ms. Length: 200-3,000 words. Pays $35-50 for feature articles. Sometimes pays expenses of writers on assignment.

Reprints: Accepts previously published submissions.

Photos: State availability of or send photos with submissions. Reviews contact sheets, negatives, transparencies, prints. Offers $25-50/photo. Model releases, identification of subjects required. Buys one-time rights.

Columns/Departments: Health/Fitness, Education, Discipline; all 700-1,400 words. Buys 10 mss/year. Query. Pays $25-50 for featured articles.

Tips: "Unique parental articles with hard hitting, no-nonsense approach always preferred. Empowering the parents to raise happy healthy African-American children is our goal!"

‡**CATHOLIC PARENT**, Our Sunday Visitor, 200 Noll Plaza, Huntington IN 46750. (219)356-8400. Editor: Woodeene Koenig-Bricker. 95% freelance written. Bimonthly magazine covering parenting with a Catholic emphasis. "We look for practical, realistic parenting articles written with a primarily Roman Catholic audience. They key is practical, not pious." Estab. 1993. Circ. 32,000. **Pays on acceptance.** Publishes ms an average of 6 months after acceptance. Byline given. Kill fee varies. Buys first North American serial rights. Editorial lead time 6 months. Submit seasonal material 6 months in advance. Accepts simultaneous submissions. Reports in 2 months. Sample copy for $3.

Nonfiction: Essays, how-to, humor, inspirational, personal experience, religious. Buys 50 mss/year. Send complete ms. Length: 850-1,200 words. Pay varies. Sometimes pays expenses of writers on assignment.

Photos: State availability of photos with submissions.

Columns/Departments: This Works (parenting tips), 200 words. Buys 50 mss/year. Send complete ms. Pays $15-25.

CHILD, Gruner & Jahr, 110 Fifth Ave., New York NY 10011. (212)463-1000. Editor: Pamela Abrams. Executive Editor: Miriam Arond. 95% freelance written. Monthly magazine for parenting. Estab. 1986. Circ. 775,000. **Pays on acceptance.** Byline given. Offers 25% kill fee. Buys first North American serial, first, one-time and second serial (reprint) rights. Editorial lead time 3 months. Submit seasonal material 6 months in advance. Reports in 2 months. Sample copy for $3.95. Writer's guidelines free on request.

● Ranked as one of the best markets for freelance writers in *Writer's Yearbook's* annual "Top 100 Markets," January 1996.

Nonfiction: Book excerpts, general interest, interview/profile, new product, photo feature. No poetry. Query with published clips. Length: 250 words minimum. Payment negotiable. Pays expenses of writers on assignment.

Photos: State availability of photos with submission. Reviews transparencies. Negotiates payment individually. Buys one-time rights.

Columns/Departments: Nancy Kalish, articles editor. Love, Dad (fathers' perspective); Child of Mine (mothers' or fathers' perspective). Query with published clips.

CHILDBIRTH, Cahners Publishing Co., 249 W. 17th St., New York NY 10011. (212)645-0067. Fax: (212)463-6407. Editor: Marsha Rehns. Biannual magazine covering maternity and early months of life. "*Childbirth* answers the questions of couples approaching the birth of their child." The magazine is divided into four sections: 'The Last Three Months of Pregnancy' (including nutrition, intimacy, prenatal test, and childbirth preparation). 'Getting Ready for Baby' (nursery and layette, infant feeding decisions, circumcision and car safety). 'Labor and Birth' (delivery, bonding, and first hours of life). 'Life with Baby' (bathing, playing, problems and solutions)." Estab. 1984. Circ. 2,008,000. This magazine did not respond to our request for information. Query before submitting.

CHRISTIAN PARENTING TODAY, Good Family Magazines, 4050 Lee Vance View, Colorado Springs CO 80918. (719)531-7776. Fax: (719)535-0172. Editor: Brad Lewis. Associate Editor: Erin Healy. 90% freelance written. Bimonthly magazine covering parenting today's children. "*CPT* encourages and informs parents of children ages birth to 12 who want to build strong families and raise their children from a positive, authoritative Christian perspective. *CPT* strives to give parents practical tools in four areas: 1) encouraging the spiritual and moral growth of their children; 2) guiding the physical, emotional, social and intellectual development of their children; 3) enriching the reader's marriage; and 4) strengthening the reader's family relationships." Estab. 1988. Circ. 250,000. Pays on acceptance or publication. Byline given. Buys first North American serial or second serial (reprint) rights. Submit seasonal/holiday material 6 months in advance. Reports in 2 months. Sample copy for 9×12 SAE with 7 first-class stamps. Writer's guidelines for #10 SASE.

Nonfiction: Book excerpts, how-to, humor, inspirational, religious. Feature topics of greatest interest: practical guidance in spiritual/moral development and values transfer; practical solutions to everyday parenting issues; tips on how to enrich readers' marriages; ideas for nurturing healthy family ties; family activities that focus on parent/child interaction; humorous pieces about everyday family life. Buys 50 mss/year. Query. Length: 750-2,000 words. Pays 15-25¢/word. Sometimes pays expenses of writers on assignment.

Reprints: Send tearsheet or photocopy of article, or typed ms with rights for sale noted and information about when and where the article previously appeared. Pays 7¢/word.

Photos: State availability of photos with submission. Do not submit photos without permission. Reviews transparencies. Model release required. Buys one-time rights.

Columns/Departments: Parent Exchange (family-tested parenting ideas from our readers), 25-100 words; Life In Our House (entertaining, true, humorous stories about your family), 25-100 words; Your Child Today (specifics of emotional, physical, social and intellectual development of children in five age brackets: Babies, Toddlers, Preschoolers, Early Elementary and Late Elementary), 300-400 words (pays $50-75); Train Them Up (spiritual development topics from a Christian perspective); Healthy & Safe (practical how-to articles that speak to parents' desire to provide their children with an emotionally and physically safe environment both at home and away), 300-400 words (pays $50-75). Buys 120 mss/year. Send complete ms. Pays $25-40. Submissions become property of *CPT*.

Tips: Tell it like it is. Readers have a "get real" attitude that demands a down-to-earth, pragmatic take on topics. Don't sugar-coat things. Give direction without waffling. If you've "been there," tell us. Don't distance yourself from readers. They trust people who have walked in their shoes. Get reader friendly. Fill your article with nuts and bolts: developmental information, age-specific angles, multiple resources, soundbite sidebars, real-life people and anecdotes and realistic, vividly explained suggestions.

FAMILY LIFE, Hachette-Filipacchi Magazines, Inc., 1633 Broadway, New York NY 10019. E-mail: family life@aol.com. Editor-in-Chief: Peter Herbst. Contact: Jennifer Cook. 90% freelance written. Bimonthly magazine for parents of children ages 3-12. Estab. 1993. Circ. 400,000. Pays on publication. Publishes ms an average of 4 months after acceptance. Byline given. Offers 25% kill fee. Buys first North American rights. Editorial lead time 5 months. Submit seasonal material 8 months in advance. Accepts simultaneous submissions. Reports in 6 weeks on queries. Sample copy for $3, call (908)367-2900. Writer's guidelines for #10 SASE.

Nonfiction: Book excerpts, essays, general interest, new product, photo feature, travel. Does not want to see articles about children under 3 or childbirth. Query with published clips. Pays $1/word. Pays expenses of writers on assignment.

Photos: State availability of photos with submission. Reviews transparencies. Negotiates payment individually. Buys one-time rights.

FAMILY TIMES, Family Times, Inc., 1900 Superfine Lane, Wilmington DE 19802. (302)575-0935. Fax: (302)575-0933. Editor: Denise Yearian. 50% freelance written. Monthly tabloid for parenting. "Our targeted distribution is to parents via a controlled network of area schools, daycares, pediatricians and places where families congregate. We only want articles related to parenting, children's issues and enhancing family life." Estab. 1990. Circ. 35,000. Pays on publication. Publishes ms an average of 2 months after acceptance. Byline given. Buys one-time or second serial (reprint) rights. Editorial lead time 2 months. Submit seasonal material 2 months in advance. Accepts simultaneous submissions. Reports in 3 months on mss. Sample copy for 3 first-class stamps.

Nonfiction: Book excerpts, how-to parenting, inspirational, interview/profile, new product, opinion, personal experience, photo feature, travel, children, parenting. Special issues: Schools (October); Camps (February); Maternity (July); Holiday (December); Fitness (March); Birthday (May); Back to School (August). Buys 60 mss/year. Send complete ms. Length: 350-1,200 words. Pays $30 minimum for assigned articles; $25 for unsolicited articles. Sometimes pays expenses of writers on assignment.

Reprints: Accepts previously published submissions.

Photos: State availability of photos with submission. Negotiates payment individually. Identification of subjects required. Buys one-time rights.

Columns/Departments: Pays $25-50.

Tips: "Work with other members of PPA (Parenting Publications of America). Since we all share our writers and watch others' work. We pay little but you can sell the same story to 30 other publications in different markets. Online use (Internet) offers additional author credit and additional payment based on accesses. We are most open to general features."

FAMILYFUN, Disney Magazine Publishing Inc., 244 Main St., Northampton MA 01060. Editor: Susan Clare Ellis. Contact: Ann Hallock. Magazine published 10 times/year covering activities for families with kids ages 3-12. "*Family Fun* is about all the great things families can do together. Our writers are either parents or professionals in education." Estab. 1991. Circ. 800,000. **Pays on acceptance.** Publishes ms an average of 4 months after acceptance. Byline sometimes given. Offers 25% kill fee. Buys simultaneous rights or makes work-for-hire assignments. Editorial lead time 4 months. Submit seasonal material 6 months in advance. Accepts simultaneous submissions. Reports in 2 months on queries. Sample copies or back issues and writer's guidelines for $3 (call (800)289-4849).

Nonfiction: Book excerpts, essays, general interest, how-to (crafts, cooking, educational activities), humor, interview/profile, personal experience, photo feature, travel. Special issues: Crafts, Holidays, Back to School, Summer Vacations. Buys hundreds mss/year. Query with published clips. Length: 75-3,000 words. Pays 50¢-$1/word. Sometimes pays expenses of writers on assignment.

Photos: State availability of photos with submissions. Reviews contact sheets, negatives, transparencies. Offers $75-500/photo. Model releases, identification of subjects required. Buys all rights (simultaneous).

Columns/Departments: Family Ties (essay on family relationships and traditions), 1,500 words; My Great Idea (essay on a simple idea [usually a tradition] that is wonderful for families and is a proven hit with author's family), 600-800 words. Buys 20-25 mss/year. Query with published clips or send complete ms. Pays 75¢-$1/word.

Tips: "Many of our writers break into *FF* by writing for either *Family Almanac* (front-of-book department with 75-300 word pieces on crafts, food, games, etc.) or *Family Traveler* (also a front-of-the-book department, but with 75-800 word pieces)."

GROWING PARENT, Dunn & Hargitt, Inc., P.O. Box 620, Lafayette IN 47902-0620. (317)423-2624. Fax: (317)423-4495. Editor: Nancy Kleckner. 40-50% freelance written. Works with a small number of new/unpublished writers each year. "We do receive a lot of unsolicited submissions but have had excellent results in working with some unpublished writers. So, we're always happy to look at material and hope to find one or two jewels each year." Monthly newsletter which focuses on parents—the issues, problems, and choices they face as their children grow. "We want to look at the parent as an adult and help encourage his or her growth not only as a parent but as an individual." Estab. 1973. **Pays on acceptance.** Publishes ms an average of 6 months after acceptance. Byline given. Buys first North American serial rights; maintains exclusive rights for three months. Submit seasonal/holiday material 6 months in advance. Reports in 2 weeks. Sample copy and writer's guidelines for 5×8 SAE with 2 first-class stamps.

Nonfiction: "We are looking for informational articles written in an easy-to-read, concise style. We would like to see articles that help parents deal with the stresses they face in everyday life—positive, upbeat, how-to-cope suggestions. We rarely use humorous pieces, fiction or personal experience articles. Writers should keep in mind that most of our readers have children under three years of age." Buys 15-20 mss/year. Query. Length: 1,000-1,500 words; will look at shorter pieces. Pays 10-15¢/word (depends on article).

Reprints: Send photocopy of article and information about when and where it previously appeared.

Tips: "Submit a very specific query letter with samples."

HEALTHY KIDS, K-III Publishing, 249 W. 17th St., New York NY 10011. (212)463-6578. Fax: (212)463-6410. Managing Editor: Laura Broadwell. 90% freelance written. Bimonthly magazine covering children's health. Estab. 1989. Circ. 1.5 million. **Pays on acceptance.** Byline given. Buys first rights. Submit seasonal/holiday material at least 6 months in advance. Reports in 1 month on queries. Writer's guidelines for #10 SASE.

Nonfiction: How-to help your child develop as a person, keep safe, keep healthy. No poetry, fiction, travel or product endorsement. Buys 30 mss/year. Query. Length: 1,500-2,000 words. Pays $500-1,000. Pays expenses of writers on assignment. No unsolicited mss.

Columns/Departments: Buys 30 mss/year. Query. Length: 1,500-2,000 words. Pays $750.

‡HIP MAMA, The Parenting Zine, P.O. Box 9097, Oakland CA 94613. (510)658-4508. Editor: Arieli Gore. 75% freelance written. Quarterly magazine covering progressive parenting. "*Hip Mama* is a progressive, liberal, feminist parenting/mothering zine. Our readers are smart, young(ish), diverse, politically aware, often urban and sometimes poor." Estab. 1993. Circ. 5,000. Pays on publication. Publishes ms an average of 6 months after acceptance. Byline given. Buys one-time or second serial (reprint) rights. Editorial lead time 6 months. Submit seasonal material 6 months in advance. Accepts simultaneous submissions. Reports in 6 months on mss; 1 month on queries. Sample copy for $4.

Nonfiction: Book excerpts, essays, exposé, humor, inspirational, interview/profile, opinion, personal experience, photo feature, news, ethnic issues. Buys 50-60 mss/year. Send complete ms. Length: 500-2,000 words. Pays $5-100.

Reprints: Accepts previously published material, if so noted.

Photos: Send photos with submission. Reviews 3×5 prints. Offers $0-10/photo. Identification of subjects required. Buys one-time rights. "We always need more photos of children of color with or without story!"

Columns/Departments: Up for Review (book review [adult book for parents]); Beyond Whirled Peas (recipes); Loose Grip (humor); all 400 words. Buys 20 mss/year. Pays from copies to $30.

Fiction: Ethnic, experimental, humorous, mainstream, slice-of-life vignettes (only related to parenting). Buys 4 mss/year. Send complete ms. Length: 500-1,500 words. Pays $5-25.

Poetry: Lara Candland, poetry editor. Avant-garde, free verse, haiku, light verse, traditional. Buys 25 poems/year. Submit maximum 10 poems. Length: 60 lines maximum. Pays from copies to $5.

Fillers: Anecdotes, facts, newsbreaks, short humor. Buys 20/year. Length: 400 words maximum. Pays from copies to $5.

Tips: "Read the zine, be a parent, go out on a limb, be creative, do your research, just send it."

HOME EDUCATION MAGAZINE, P.O. Box 1083, Tonasket WA 98855-1083. Fax: (509)486-2628. E-mail: homeedmag@aol.com. Website: http://www.home-ed-press.com. Editors: Mark J. Hegener, Helen E. Hegener. 80% freelance written. Eager to work with new/unpublished writers each year. Bimonthly magazine covering home-based education. "We feature articles which address the concerns of parents who want to take a direct involvement in the education of their children—concerns such as socialization, how to find curriculums and materials, testing and evaluation, how to tell when your child is ready to begin reading, what to do when homeschooling is difficult, teaching advanced subjects, etc." Estab. 1983. Circ. 20,000. **Pays on acceptance.** Publishes ms an average of 2 months after acceptance. Byline given. ("Please include a 30-50 word credit with your article.") Buys first North American serial, first, one-time rights. Submit seasonal/holiday material 6 months in advance. Reports in 2 months. Sample copy for $4.50. Writer's guidelines for #10 SASE.

Nonfiction: Essays, how-to (related to home schooling), humor, interview/profile, personal experience, photo features, technical. Buys 40-50 mss/year. Query with or without published clips, or send complete ms. Length: 750-2,500 words. Pays $25-50. Sometimes pays expenses of writers on assignment.

Photos: Send photos with submission. Reviews enlargements, 35mm prints, b&w snapshots, CD-ROMs. Color transparencies for covers $50 each; inside b&w $10 each. Identification of subjects preferred. Buys one-time rights.

Tips: SASE. "We would like to see how-to articles (that don't preach, just present options); articles on testing, accountability, working with the public schools, socialization, learning disabilities, resources, support groups, legislation and humor. We need answers to the questions that homeschoolers ask."

HOME LIFE, Sunday School Board, 127 9th Ave. N., Nashville TN 37234. Fax: (615)251-5008. Editor-in-Chief: Charlie Warren. Managing Editor: Leigh Neely. 50% freelance written. Prefers to work with published/established writers, but will work with new/unpublished writers. Monthly magazine emphasizing Christian marriage and family life for married adults of all ages, but especially newlyweds and middle-aged marrieds. Estab. 1947. Circ. 550,000. **Pays on acceptance.** Publishes ms an average of 15 months after acceptance. Buys first North American serial and all rights. Byline given. Query. Submit seasonal/holiday material 1 year in advance. Reports in 2 weeks on queries; 3 months on mss. Sample copy for $1. Writer's guidelines for #10 SASE.

Nonfiction: How-to (good articles on marriage and family life); informational (about some current family-related issue of national significance such as "Television and the Christian Family" or "Whatever Happened to Family Worship?"); personal experience (informed articles by people who have solved marriage and family problems in healthy, constructive ways). "No column material. We are not interested in material that will not in some way enrich Christian marriage or family life. We are interested in articles on fun family activities for a new department called Family Time." Buys 100-150 mss/year. Query only. "After query is accepted, send disk copy." Pays $75-275.

Reprints: Send typed ms with rights for sale noted. Pays 75% of amount paid for an original article.

Fiction: "Fiction should be family-related and should show a strong moral about how families face and solve problems constructively." Buys 12-20 mss/year. Submit complete ms. Length: 1,500-1,800 words. Pays from $150.

Tips: "Study the magazine to see our unique slant on Christian family life. We prefer a life-centered case study approach, rather than theoretical essays on family life. Our top priority is marriage enrichment material."

‡**INDY'S CHILD**, 8900 Keystone Crossing, Suite 538, Indianapolis IN 46240. Fax: (317)574-3233. Editor: Pamela Fettig. 100% freelance written. Monthly magazine covering parenting. "*Indy's Child* is a parenting magazine circulated throughout Central Indiana. We cover topics ranging from maternity, camps, birthday

parties, mental health, enrichment, education and discipline to finances and computers. Ninety-five percent of our readers are college-educated, middle to upperclass women ages 25-45." Estab. 1984. Circ. 70,000. Pays on publication. Publishes ms an average of 3 months after acceptance. Byline given. Buys first rights or second serial (reprint) rights. Editorial lead time 3 months. Submit seasonal material 3 months in advance. Reports in 2 months. Sample copy for 9×12 SAE with 4 first-class stamps. Writer's guidelines for #10 SASE.

Nonfiction: Essays, general interest, how-to (anything that deals with parenting. humor, inspirational, personal experience, travel. Nothing political or one sided. Special issue: Baby Guide. Buys 36 mss/year. Send complte ms. Length: 1,000-2,500 words. Pays $50-175 for assigned articles; $25-135 for unsolicited articles. Sometimes pays expenses of writers on assignment.

Reprints: Accepts previously published submissions.

Photos: State availability of photos with submission. Reviews 3×5 prints. Negotiates payment individually. Identification of subjects required. Negotiates rights purchased.

Fiction: Humorous, life lesson. Buys 2 mss/year. Send complete ms. Length: 1,000-1,500 words. Pays $50-150.

Tips: "We tend to accept articles that are not only serious issues to parents but that also have great solutions or specific places to turn to for help. Everything needs a local slant."

L.A. PARENT, The Magazine for Parents in Southern California, P.O. Box 3204, Burbank CA 91504. (818)846-0400. Fax: (818)841-4964. E-mail: 73311.514@compuserve.com. Editor: Jack Bierman. Article Editor: David Jamieson. 80% freelance written. Prefers to work with published/established writers, but works with a small number of new/unpublished writers each year. Monthly tabloid covering parenting. Estab. 1980. Circ. 200,000. **Pays on acceptance.** Publishes ms an average of 4 months after acceptance. Byline given. Buys first and reprint rights. Submit seasonal/holiday material 3 months in advance. Accepts simultaneous queries. Reports in 2 months. Sample copy and writer's guidelines for $2 and 11×14 SAE with 5 first-class stamps.

• *L.A. Parent* is looking for more articles pertaining to infants and early childhood. They have increased their reprint payment from 35 to 50% of the amount paid for the original article.

Nonfiction: David Jamieson, articles editor. General interest, how-to. "We focus on generic parenting for ages 0-10 and southern California activities for families, and do round-up pieces, i.e., a guide to private schools, art opportunities." Buys 60-75 mss/year. Query with clips of published work. Length: 700-1,200 words. Pays $200-300 plus expenses.

Reprints: Send tearsheet of article and information about when and where the article previously appeared. Pays 50% of amount paid for an original article.

Tips: "We will be using more contemporary articles on parenting's challenges. If you can write for a 'city magazine' in tone and accuracy, you may write for us. The 'Baby Boom' has created a need for more generic parenting material. We look for a sophisticated tone in covering the joys and demands of being a mom or dad in the 90s."

LONG ISLAND PARENTING NEWS, RDM Publishing, P.O. Box 214, Island Park NY 11558. (516)889-5510. Fax: (516)889-5513. Editor: Pat Simms-Elias. Director: Andrew Elias. 70% freelance written. Free community newspaper published monthly covering parenting, children and family issues. "A publication for concerned parents with active families and young children. Our slogan is: 'For parents who care to know.' " Estab. 1989. Circ. 50,000. Pays on publication. Publishes ms an average of 3 months after acceptance. Byline given (also 1-3 line bio, if appropriate). Buys one-time rights. Accepts simultaneous submissions. Reports in 3 months. Sample copy for $3 and 9×12 SAE with 5 first-class stamps. Free writer's guidelines.

Nonfiction: Essays, general interest, humor, interview/profile, travel. Needs articles covering childcare, childbirth/maternity, schools, camps and back-to-school. Special issues: Maternity & Birthing (June), Music Education (September). Buys 30-50 mss/year. Query with or without published clips, or send complete ms. Length: 350-2,000 words. Pays $25-150. "Sometimes trade article for advertising space." Sometimes pays expenses of writers on assignment.

Reprints: Send photocopy of article or typed ms with rights for sale noted and information about when and where the article previously appeared. Negotiates fee.

Photos: Send photos with submission. Reviews 4×5 prints. Offers $5-50/photo. Captions required. Buys one-time rights.

Columns/Departments: Off The Shelf (book reviews); Fun & Games (toy and game reviews); KidVid (reviews of kids' video); The Beat (reviews of kids' music); Monitor (reviews of computer hardware and software for kids); Big Screen (reviews of kids' films); Soon Come (for expectant parents); Educaring (parenting info and advice); Something Special (for parents of kids with special needs); Growing Up (family health issues); On the Ball (sports for kids); Perspectives (essays on family life); Words Worth (storytelling); Getaway (family travel). Buys 20-30 mss/year. Send complete ms. Length: 500-1,000 words. Pays 25-150.

Fillers: Facts and newsbreaks. Buys 1-10/year. Length: 200-500. Pays $10-25.

‡**METRO PARENT MAGAZINE**, All Kids Considered, Ltd., 24567 Northwestern Hwy., Suite 150, Southfield MI 48075. (810)352-0990. Fax: (810)352-5066. Editor: Jody Densmore. 80% freelance written. Monthly tabloid covering parenting/family issues. "*Metro Parent* is a local parenting publication geared toward parents with children under the age of 12. We look for sound, pertinent information for our readers." Estab. 1986. Circ. 70,000. Pays on publication. Publishes ms an average of 2 months after acceptance. Byline given. Buys one-time rights. Editorial lead time 3 months. Submit seasonal material 4 months in advance. Accepts simultaneous submissions. Sample copy and writer's guidelines free on request.

Nonfiction: Book excerpts, general interest, how-to, humor, inspirational, interview/profile, new product, travel. Special issues: Metro Baby Magazine (geared for expectant parents). Buys 25 mss/year. Query with published clips. Length: 600-2,000 words. Pays $40-150 for assigned articles; $25-50 for unsolicited articles..

Reprints: Accepts previously published submissions.

Photos: State availability of photos with submission. Reviews 4×6 prints. Negotiates payment individually. Captions, model releases, identification of subjects required. Buys one-time rights.

Columns/Departments: Bits'n' Pieces (new products) 100 words; Health Beat (health news for parents/kids), 700 words; Mixed Media (video, movie, books, audio, software), 700 (total) words. Buys 35 mss/year. Query with published clips. Pays $40-50.

METROKIDS MAGAZINE, The Resource for Delaware Valley Families, Kidstuff Publications, Inc., Riverview Plaza, 1080 N. Delaware Ave., #702, Philadelphia PA 19125-4330. (215)291-5560. Fax: (215)291-5563. E-mail: metrokids@family.com. Editor: Nancy Lisagor. 70% freelance written. Monthly tabloid providing information for parents and kids in Philadelphia and surrounding counties. Estab. 1990. Circ. 75,000. Pays on publication. Byline given. Buys one-time rights. Submit seasonal material 4 months in advance. Reports in up to 8 months on queries. Sample copy for 9×12 SAE with 4 first-class stamps. Writer's guidelines for #10 SASE.

● *MetroKids* welcomes query letters or faxes. They especially want to hear from writers in their area.

Nonfiction: General interest, how-to, humor, new product, travel. "Each issue has a focus (for example: finance, extra-curricular lessons for kids, health and nutrition, new babies, birthdays, child care, etc.)." Buys 20 mss/year. Query with or without published clips. Length: 1,000 words maximum. Pays $1-50. Sometimes pays expenses of writers on assignment.

Reprints: Send tearsheet of article and information about when and where the article previously appeared. Pays 75-80% of amount paid for an original article.

Photos: State availability of photos with submission. Captions required. Buys one-time rights.

Columns/Departments: Away We Go (travel), 500 words; On Call (medical), 500 words; Book Beat (book reviews), 500 words; Bytesize, 500 words. Buys 25 mss/year. Query. Pays $1-50.

Tips: "Send a query letter several months before a scheduled topical issue; then follow-up with a telephone call. We are interested in receiving feature articles (on specified topics) or material for our regular columns (which should have a regional/seasonal base). 1997 editorial calendar available on request. We are also interested in finding local writers for assignments."

‡**NEW JERSEY FAMILY NEW MAGAZINE**, 104 La Barre Ave., Trenton NJ 08618. (609)695-5646. Fax: (609)695-5612. Editor: Barbara M. Gaeta. 90% freelance written. Monthly newspaper covering family oriented topics for parents and kids. "We publish an information-based newsmagazine where articles should provide information specifically for New Jersey families." Estab. 1993. Circ. 30,000. Pays 30 days after publication. Publishes ms an average of 6 months after acceptance. Byline given. Buys first, one-time, second serial (reprint) rights or makes work-for-hire assignments. Editorial lead time 6 months. Submit seasonal material 3 months in advance. Accepts simultaneous submissions. Only responds when interested in publishing material. Sample copy and writer's guidelines free on request.

Nonfiction: Books excerpts, essays, general interest, historical/nostalgic, how-to, interview/profile, new product, photo feature, travel. No first person narratives about potty-training littly Johnny or other "cute" stories. Buys 40-60 mss/year. Send complete ms. Length: 500-1,500 words. Pays $30-75 for assigned articles; $10-75 for unsolicited articles. Sometimes pays expenses of writers on assignment.

Reprints: Accepts previously published submissions.

Photos: Send photos with submission. Reviews prints. Offers no additional payment for photos accepted with ms. Identification of subjects required. Buys one-time rights.

Columns/Departments: "We expect to include reviews (books, video, movie and software) within the year." Query with published clips. Pays $10-35.

Poetry: Free verse, light verse, traditional. Buys 1-2 poems/year. Length: open. Pays $10.

Fillers: Anecdotes, facts, gags to be illustrated by cartoonist, newsbreaks, short humor. Length: 75-200 words. Pays $5-10.

Tips: "Send well written, informational articles with facts or resources documented, on any topics relevant to today's family environment."

PARENTING MAGAZINE, 301 Howard, 17th Floor, San Francisco CA 94105. (415)546-7575. Fax: (415)546-0578. Editor-in-Chief: Anne Krueger. Managing Editor: Bruce Raskin. Contact: Articles Editor. Magazine published 10 times/year "for parents of children from birth to ten years old, with the most emphasis put on the under-sixes." Estab. 1987. **Pays on acceptance.** Byline given. Offers 25% kill fee. Buys first rights. Reports in 1 month. Sample copy for $1.95 and 9×12 SAE with 5 first-class stamps. Writer's guidelines for #10 SASE.

● Ranked as one of the best markets for freelance writers in *Writer's Yearbook*'s annual "Top 100 Markets," January 1996.

Nonfiction: Articles editor. Book excerpts, humor, investigative reports, personal experience, photo feature. Buys 20-30 features/year. Query with or without published clips, or send complete ms. Length: 1,000-3,500 words. Pays $500-2,000. Sometimes pays expenses of writers on assignment.

Columns/Departments: News and Views (news items relating to children/family), 100-400 words; Ages and Stages (health, nutrition, new products and service stories), 100-500 words. Buys 50-60 mss/year. Pays $50-500.

PARENTING'S BABYTALK, Time Inc. Ventures, 25 W. 43rd St., 20th Floor, New York NY 10036. (212)840-4200. Fax: (212)827-0019. Editor-in-Chief: Susan Strecker. Magazine published 10 times/year covering parenting. "*Parenting's BabyTalk* offers an array of baby and child care experts who guide parents with up-to-date medical and developmental information and hands-on baby care articles." Estab. 1935. Circ. 1,006,000. This magazine did not respond to our request for information. Query before submitting.

PARENTLIFE, Baptist Sunday School Board, 127 Ninth Ave. N., Nashville TN 37234. (615)251-2229. Fax: (615)251-5008. Managing Editor: Michelle Hicks. Contact: Ellen Oldacre, editor. 30% freelance written. Works with a small number of new/unpublished writers each year. Monthly magazine covering parenting issues for parents of infants through 12-year-olds, "written and designed from a Christian perspective." Estab. 1994. Circ. 120,000. **Pays on acceptance.** Byline given. "We generally buy all rights to manuscripts. First and reprint rights may be negotiated." Submit seasonal/holiday material 1 year in advance. Résumés and queries only. Reports in 1 month on queries; 2 months on mss. Sample copy for 9×12 SASE. Free writer's guidelines.

PARENTS MAGAZINE, 685 Third Ave., New York NY 10017. Fax: (212)867-4583. Editor-in-Chief: Ann Pleshette Murphy. 25% freelance written. Monthly. Estab. 1926. Circ. 1,825,000. **Pays on acceptance.** Publishes ms an average of 8 months after acceptance. Usually buys first serial or first North American serial rights; sometimes buys all rights. Pays 25% kill fee. Reports in approximately 2 months. Sample copy for $2. Writer's guidelines for #10 SASE.

Nonfiction: "We are interested in well-documented articles on the development and behavior of infants, preschool, school-age and pre-teen children and their parents; good, practical guides to the routines of baby care; articles that offer professional insights into family and marriage relationships; reports of new trends and significant research findings in education and in mental and physical health; articles encouraging informed citizen action on matters of social concern; and first-person true stories on aspects of parenthood. Especially need articles on women's issues, pregnancy, birth, baby care and early childhood. We prefer a warm, colloquial style of writing, one that avoids the extremes of either slang or technical jargon. Anecdotes and examples should be used to illustrate points which can then be summed up by straight exposition." Query. Length: 2,500 words maximum. Payment varies. Pays the expenses of writers on assignment up to an agreed-upon limit.

PARENTS' PRESS, The Monthly Newspaper for Bay Area Parents, 1454 Sixth St., Berkeley CA 94710. (510)524-1602. Editor: Dixie M. Jordan. Contact: Patrick Totty, managing editor. 50% freelance written. Monthly tabloid for parents. Estab. 1980. Circ. 75,000. Pays within 60 days of publication. Publishes ms an average of 6 months after acceptance. Kill fee varies (individually negotiated). Buys first rights, second serial (reprint) and almost always Northern California Exclusive rights. Submit seasonal material 6 months in advance. Reports in 2 months. Sample copy for $3. Writer's guidelines for #10 SASE.

Nonfiction: Book excerpts (family, children), how-to (parent, raise children, nutrition, health, etc.), humor (family life, children), interview/profile (of Bay Area residents, focus on their roles as parents), travel (family), family resources and activities. "Annual issues include Pregnancy and Birth, Travel, Back-to-School, Children's Health. Write for planned topic or suggest one. We require a strong Bay Area focus where appropriate. Please don't send 'generic' stories. While we publish researched articles which spring from personal experience, we do not publish strictly personal essays. Please, no birth stories." Buys 30-50 mss/year. Query with or without published clips, or send complete ms. Length: 300-3,000 words; 1,500-2,000 average. Pays $50-500 for assigned articles; $25-125 for unsolicited articles. Will negotiate fees for special projects written by Bay Area journalists.

Reprints: Send photocopy of article with rights for sale noted and information about when and where the article previously appeared. For reprints pays 10-25% of amount paid for an original article.

Photos: State availability of photos with submission. Reviews prints, any size, b&w only. Offers $10-15/ photo. Model release and identification of subject required. Buys one-time rights.

Columns/Departments: "In My Life" column pays $150 for first-person essays or reminiscences relating to parenthood. "Sole criterion for acceptance: The manuscript must be superlatively written. 'Cute' doesn't make it."

Tips: "All sections of Parents' Press are open to freelancers, but we are protective of our regular columnists' turf (children's health, women's health, infant and child behavior), so we ask writers to query whether a topic has been addressed in the last three years. Best bets to break in are family activities, education, nutrition, family dynamics and issues. While we prefer articles written by experts, we welcome well-researched journalism."

SAN DIEGO FAMILY PRESS, San Diego County's Leading Resource for Parents & Educators Who Care!, P.O. Box 23960, San Diego CA 92193-3960. Editor: Sharon Bay. 75% freelance written. Monthly magazine for parenting and family issues. "*SDFP* strives to provide informative, educational articles emphasizing positive parenting for our typical readership of educated mothers, ages 25-45, with an upper-level income. Most articles are factual and practical, some are humor and personal experience. Editorial emphasis is uplifting and positive." Estab. 1982. Circ. 74,000. Pays on publication. Byline given. Buys first, one-time or second serial (reprint) rights. Editorial lead time 2 months. Submit seasonal material 3 months in advance. Reports in 2 months on queries; 3 months on mss. Sample copy and writer's guidelines for $3.50 with 9×12 SAE.

Nonfiction: How-to, parenting, new baby help, enhancing education, family activities, interview/profile (influential or noted persons or experts included in parenting or the welfare of children) and articles of specific interest to or regarding San Diego (for California) families/children/parents/educators. "No rambling, personal experience pieces." Buys 75 mss/year. Send complete ms. Length: 1,000 maximum words. Pays $1.25/column inch. "Byline and contributor copies if writer prefers."

Photos: State availability of photos with submission. Reviews contact sheets and 3½×5 or 5×7 prints. Negotiates payment individually. Identification of subjects preferred. Buys one-time rights.

Columns/Departments: Kids' Books (topical book reviews), 800 words. Buys 12 mss/year. Query with published clips. Pays $1.25/column inch minimum.

Fillers: Facts and newsbreaks (specific to the family market). Buys 10/year. Length: 50-200 words. Pays $1.25/column inch minimum.

SAN FRANCISCO PENINSULA PARENT, Peninsula Parent Newspaper Inc., 1480 Rollins Rd., Burlingame CA 94010. (415)342-9203. Fax: (415)342-9276. E-mail: sfpp@aol.com. Website: http://family.com. Editor: Lisa Rosenthal. 25% freelance written. Monthly newsprint magazine geared to parents of children from birth to age 12. "We provide articles that empower parents with the essential parenting skills they need. We provide parents with local resource information." Estab. 1984. Circ. 60,000. Pays on publication. Publishes ms 3 months after acceptance. Byline given. Offers 50% kill fee. Buys first and second serial (reprint) rights. Editorial lead time 5 months. Submit seasonal material 4 months in advance. Reports in 2 months on queries; 3 months on mss. Sample copy and writer's guidelines free.

Nonfiction: Humor, interview/profile, travel (family-related). No articles that preach to parents, no first-person memories. Buys 8 mss/year. Query with or without published clips. Length: 800-1,200 words. Pays $100-200 for assigned articles; $25-100 for unsolicited articles. Sometimes pays expenses of writers on assignment.

Reprints: Accepts previously published submissions.

Photos: State availability of photos with submission. Offers $25-$50/photo; negotiates payment individually. Captions and model releases required. Buys one-time rights.

Columns/Departments: Upclose (profile), 1,000 words; Healthbeat (health news for families), 1,000 words. Buys 2 mss/year. Query with or without published clips. Pays $25-100.

SESAME STREET PARENTS, Children's Television Workshop, 1 Lincoln Plaza, New York NY 10023. (212)595-3456. Fax: (212)875-6105. Editor-in-Chief: Ira Wolfman. 80% freelance written. Magazine published 10 times/year for parents of preschoolers that accompanies every issue of Sesame Street Magazine. Circ. 1,000,000. **Pays on acceptance.** Byline given. Offers 33% kill fee. Buys varying rights. Submit seasonal/holiday material 7 months in advance. Reports in 1 month on queries. Sample copy for 9×12 SAE with 6 first-class stamps. Writer's guidelines for #10 SASE.

• Ranked as one of the best markets for freelance writers in *Writer's Yearbook*'s annual "Top 100 Markets," January 1996.

Nonfiction: Child development/parenting, how-to (practical tips for parents of preschoolers), interview/profile, personal experience, book excerpts, essays, photo feature, travel (with children). Buys 100 mss/year. Query with published clips or send complete ms. Length: 500-2,000 words. Pays $300-2,000 for articles.

Reprints: Send typed ms with rights for sale noted and information about when and where the article previously appeared. Negotiates payment.

Photos: State availability of photos with submission. Model releases, identification of subjects required. Buys one-time or all rights.

‡**SOUTH FLORIDA PARENTING**, 4200 Aurora St., Suite R, Coral Gables FL 33146. (305)448-6003. Fax: (305)448-6290. Managing Editor: KiKi Bochi. 90% freelance written. Monthly magazine covering parenting, family. Estab. 1989. Circ. 100,000. Pays on publication. Publishes ms an average of 3 months after acceptance. Byline given. Buys one-time rights or second serial (reprint) rights. Editorial lead time 4

months. Submit seasonal material 4 months in advance. Accepts simultaneous submissions. Prefers submission of actual ms. Response to queries only if SASE enclosed. Will rarely contract with a writer without sample of work. Writer's guidelines for SASE.

Nonfiction: General interest, how-to, humor, interview/profile, new product, personal experience. Special issues: Education Issue/Winter Health Issue (January); Birthday Party Issue (February); Spring Catalog/Summer Camp Issue (March); Maternity Issue (April); Florida/Vacation Guide (May); Sports and Your Child (June); Healthy, from Head to Toe (July); Back to School Catalog (August); Getting To Know You (September); Kid Crown Awards (October); Family Restaurant Guide, All About Kids Show (November); Holiday Catalog (December); Annual Survival Guide. Buys 30-40 mss/year. Send complete ms. Length: 600-1,800 words. Pays $75-350 for articles; $25 for reprints. Sometimes pays expenses of writers on assignment.

Reprints: Accepts previously published submissions "if not published in our circulation area."

Photos: State availability of photos with submission. Sometimes offers additional payment for photos accepted with ms.

Tips: "A unique approach to a universal parenting concern will be considered for publication. Profiles or interviews of courageous parents, unparalleled parents are sought. Opinion pieces on child rearing should be supported by experts and research should be listed. First person stories should be fresh and insightful. All writing should be clear and concise. Submissions can be typewritten, double-spaced, but the preferred format is on diskette."

‡SUCCESSFUL BLACK PARENTING MAGAZINE, KLS Communications, P.O. Box 6359, Philadelphia PA 19139. (215)476-7660. Fax: (215)476-8266. E-mail: jrobinsonl@com.aol. Acting Editor: Marta Sanchez-Speer. 90% freelance written. Bimonthly magazine covering black parenting/black family. "*Successful Black Parenting* is designed to portray the unique characteristics of black family; to offer information on child development, parenting and other family issues important to adults working with and or raising black children; to provide a forum for black parents to share their experiences in support of one another." Estab. 1993. Circ. 35,000. Pays on publication. Publishes ms an average of 3 months after acceptance. Byline given. Buys one-time rights. Editorial lead time 3 months. Submit seasonal material 2 months in advance. Accepts simultaneous submissions. Sample copy for $2.50 and SAE with $1.10 postage. Writer's guidelines free on request.

Nonfiction: How-to, humor, inspirational, interview/profile, new product, opinion, personal experience, photo feature, travel. No articles that are negative towards the black family. Buys 12 mss/year. Query with published clips. Length: 800-1,000 words. Pays $50. Sometimes pays expenses of writers on assignment.

Photos: Send photos with submission. Reviews 2×2 transparencies. Offers no additional payment for photos accepted with ms. Captions, model releases, identification of subjects required. Buys one-time rights.

Columns/Departments: Rites of Passage (adolescent issues), Nubian Dad (Dad's point of view on parenting), On My Own (single parenting issues); all 800 words. Buys 10 mss/year. Query with published clips. Pays $50.

Poetry: Avant-garde, free verse, haiku, light verse, traditional. Buys 4 poems/year. Length: 20-30 lines. Pays $50.

Fillers: Anecdotes, facts, gags to be illustrated by cartoonist, short humor. Buys 4/year. Length: 200-300 words. Pays $50.

Tips: "Articles should be parent friendly. Audience ages 18-34, majority women readers. If you include an activity that parents can do with their children, that is related to the theme of your article, it will get our attention."

‡TOLEDO AREA PARENT NEWS, Toledo Area Parent News, Inc., P.O. Box 8037, Sylvania OH 43560. (419)531-0726. Fax: (419)531-0728. E-mail: tolparent@aol.com. Editor: Veronica Hughes. 50% freelance written. Monthly tabloid covering parenting issues. "We are a publication for Northwest Ohio/Southeast Michigan parents. We accept queries and opinion pieces only, from local writers only. Send cover letter and clips to be considered for assignments." Estab. 1992. Circ. 40,000. Pays on publication. Publishes ms an average of 1 month after acceptance. Byline given. Makes work-for-hire assignments. Editorial lead time 6 months. Reports in 1 month. Sample copy for $1.50. Writer's guidelines free on request (we use only local writers, by assignment only).

Nonfiction: General interest, interview/profile, opinion. Buys 30 mss/year. Query with published clips. Length: 1,000-2,500 words. Pays $75-125 for assigned articles.

Photos: State availability of photos with submission. Negotiates payment individually. Identification of subjects required. Buys all rights.

TWINS, The Magazine for Parents of Multiples, P.O. Box 12045, Overland Park KS 66282-2045. (913)722-1090. Fax: (913)722-1767. Website: http://www.twinsmagazine.com. Editorial Director: Barbara C. Unell. Contact: Jean Cerne, editor-in-chief. 90% freelance written. Eager to work with new/unpublished writers. Bimonthly national magazine designed to give professional guidance to help multiples, their parents and those professionals who care for them learn about twin facts and research. Estab. 1984. Circ. 57,000. Pays on publication. Publishes ms an average of 6 months after acceptance. Byline given. Buys all rights.

Submit seasonal/holiday material 10 months in advance. Reports in 6 weeks on queries; 2 months on mss. Sample copy for $5. Writer's guidelines for #10 SASE.

   • *Twins* is no longer in the market for fillers.

Nonfiction: General interest, how-to, humor, interview/profile, personal experience, photo feature. "No articles that substitute the word 'twin' for 'child'—those that simply apply the same research to twins that applies to singletons without any facts backing up the reason to do so." Buys 150 mss/year. Query with or without published clips, or send complete ms. Length: 1,250-3,000 words. Payment varies.

Photos: Send photos with submission. Reviews contact sheets, 4×5 transparencies, all size prints. Captions, model releases, identification of subjects required. Buys all rights.

Columns/Departments: Resources, Supertwins, Family Health, Twice as Funny, Double Focus (series from pregnancy through adolescence), Personal Perspective (first-person accounts of beliefs about a certain aspect of parenting multiples), Over the Back Fence (specific tips that have worked for the writer in raising multiples), Research, On Being Twins (first-person accounts of growing up as a twin), On Being Parents of Twins (first-person accounts of the experience of parenting twins), Double Takes (fun photographs of twins), Education Matters, Special Miracles (first-person accounts of life with physically, mentally or emotionally challenged twins). Buys 70 mss/year. Query with published clips. Length: 1,250-2,000 words. Payment varies.

Tips: "Features and columns are both open to freelancers. Columnists write for *Twins* on a continuous basis, so the column becomes their own. We are looking for a wide variety of the latest, well-researched practical information. There is no other magazine of this type directed to this market. We are interested in personal interviews with celebrity twins or celebrity parents of twins, tips on rearing twins from experienced parents and/or twins themselves and reports on national and international research studies involving twins."

‡**VALLEY PARENT MAGAZINE**, Bay Area Publishing Group, Inc., 401 Alberto Way, Suite A, Los Gatos CA 95032. (408)358-1414. Editor: Lynn Berardo. Contact: Mary Brence Martin, managing editor. 43% freelance written. Monthly magazine covering parenting children ages birth through early teens. "The information we are most likely to use is local, well-researched and geared to our readers, who are primarily parents of children ages birth to early teens." Estab. 1992. Circ. 55,000. Pays on publication. Publishes ms an average of 6 months after acceptance. Byline given. Buys first rights. Editorial lead time 4 months. Submit seasonal material 4 months in advance. Accepts simultaneous submissions. Reports in 2 weeks on queries; 2 months on mss. Sample copy for 8½×12 SAE with 5 first-class stamps. Writer's guidelines for #10 SASE.

Nonfiction: Book excerpts, interview/profile, opinion, personal experience (all must be parenting-related). Buys 22 mss/year. Length: 900-2,000 words. Pays 6-9¢/word. Sometimes pays expenses of writers on assignment.

Reprints: Accepts previously published submissions.

Photos: State availability of photos with submission. Reviews contact sheets, negatives, transparencies, prints. Offers $10-15/photo. Buys one-time rights.

Columns/Departments: Way to Go! (local and state outings); Little Kids' (children ages 2-5) 950-1,000 words. Query with published clips or send complete ms. Pays $6-9¢/word.

WORKING MOTHER MAGAZINE, MacDonald Communications, 230 Park Ave., New York NY 10169. (212)551-9500. Editor: Judsen Culbreth. Executive Editor: Mary McLaughlin. Articles Editor: Linda Hamilton. 90% freelance written. Prefers to work with published/established writers; works with a small number of new/unpublished writers each year. Monthly magazine for women who balance a career with the concerns of parenting. Circ. 925,000. **Pays on acceptance.** Publishes ms an average of 4 months after acceptance. Byline given. Buys all rights. Pays 20% kill fee. Submit seasonal/holiday material 6 months in advance. Reports in 6 weeks. Sample copy for $2.95. Writer's guidelines for SASE.

   • *Working Mother* was recently purchased by MacDonald Communications.

Nonfiction: Service, humor, child development, material pertinent to the working mother's predicament. Send query to attention of *Working Mother Magazine*. Buys 9-10 mss/issue. Length: 750-2,000 words. Pays $700-2,000. "We pay more to people who write for us regularly." Pays the expenses of writers on assignment.

   • Ranked as one of the best markets for freelance writers in *Writer's Yearbook*'s annual "Top 100 Markets," January 1996.

Tips: "We are looking for pieces that help the reader. In other words, we don't simply report on a trend without discussing how it specifically affects our readers' lives and how they can handle the effects. Where can they look for help if necessary?"

COMIC BOOKS

Comic books aren't just for kids. Today, this medium also attracts a reader who is older and wants stories presented visually on a wide variety of topics. In addition, some instruction manuals, classics and other stories are being produced in a comic book format.

This doesn't mean you have to be an artist to write for comic books. Most of these publishers want to see a synopsis of one to two double-spaced pages. Be concise. Comics use few words and rely on graphics as well as words to forward the plot.

Once your synopsis is accepted, either an artist will draw the story from your plot, returning these pages to you for dialogue and captions, or you will be expected to write a script. Scripts run approximately 23 typewritten pages and include suggestions for artwork as well as dialogue. Try to imagine your story on actual comic book pages and divide your script accordingly. The average comic has six panels per page, with a maximum of 35 words per panel.

If you're submitting a proposal to Marvel, your story should center on an already established character. If you're dealing with an independent publisher, characters are often the property of their creators. Your proposal should be for a new series. Include a background sheet for main characters who will appear regularly, listing origins, weaknesses, powers or other information that will make your character unique. Indicate an overall theme or direction for your series. Submit story ideas for the first three issues. If you're really ambitious, you may also include a script for your first issue. As with all markets, read a sample copy before making a submission. The best markets may be those you currently read, so consider submitting to them even if they aren't listed in this section.

MARVEL COMICS, 387 Park Ave. S., New York NY 10016. (212)696-0808. Submissions Editor/New Talent Manager: John Lewandowski. 80% freelance written. Publishes 75 comics and magazines/month, specials, paperbacks and industrials. Over 9 million copies sold/month. Pays a flat fee for most projects, plus a royalty type incentive based upon sales. Also works on advance/royalty basis on certain projects. **Pays on acceptance.** Publishes ms an average of 4 months after acceptance. Byline given. Offers variable kill fee. Rights purchased depend upon format and material. Submit seasonal/holiday material 1 year in advance. Accepts simultaneous submissions. Reports in 6 months. Writer's guidelines for #10 SASE. Additional guidelines on request.
  • Since Marvel has been cutting their line of books, there are more professional writers looking for work, making it a much tougher market for a newcomer to break in.
Fiction: Super hero, action-adventure, science fiction, fantasy and other material. Only comics. Buys 600-800 mss/year. Query with brief plot synopses only. Do not send scripts, short stories or long outlines. A plot synopsis should be less than two typed pages; send two synopses at most. Pays expenses of writers on assignment.

CONSUMER SERVICE AND BUSINESS OPPORTUNITY

Some of these magazines are geared to investing earnings or starting a new business; others show how to make economical purchases. Publications for business executives and consumers interested in business topics are listed under Business and Finance. Those on how to run specific businesses are classified by category in the Trade section.

ECONOMIC FACTS, The National Research Bureau, Inc., P.O. Box 1, Burlington IA 52601-0001. (319)752-5415. Fax: (319)752-3421. Editor: Nancy Heinzel. 75% freelance written. Eager to work with new/unpublished writers; works with a small number of new/unpublished writers each year. Published 4 times/year. Estab. 1948. Pays on publication. Publishes ms an average of 1 year after acceptance. Buys all rights. Byline given. Sample copy and writer's guidelines for #10 SAE with 2 first-class stamps.
Nonfiction: General interest (private enterprise, government data, graphs, taxes and health care). Buys 10 mss/year. Query with outline of article. Length: 500-700 words. Pays 4¢/word.

KIPLINGER'S PERSONAL FINANCE, 1729 H St. NW, Washington DC 20006. (202)887-6400. Editor: Ted Miller. Less than 10% freelance written. Prefers to work with published/established writers. Monthly magazine for general, adult audience interested in personal finance and consumer information. Estab. 1947. Circ. 1,000,000. **Pays on acceptance.** Publishes ms an average of 2 months after acceptance. Buys all rights. Reports in 1 month. Thorough documentation required for fact-checking.

Nonfiction: "Most material is staff-written, but we accept some freelance." Query with clips of published work. Pays expenses of writers on assignment.
Tips: "We are looking for a heavy emphasis on personal finance topics."

LIVING SAFETY, A Canada Safety Council publication for safety in the home, traffic and recreational environments, 1020 Thomas Spratt Place, Ottawa, Ontario K1G 5L5 Canada. (613)739-1535. Fax (613)739-1566. E-mail: csc@safety-council.org. Website: http://www.safety-council.org. Editor: Jack Smith. 65% freelance written. Quarterly magazine covering off-the-job safety. "Off-the job health and safety magazine covering topics in the home, traffic and recreational environments. Audience is the Canadian employee and his/her family." Estab. 1983. Circ. 100,000. **Pays on acceptance.** Publishes ms an average of 2 months after acceptance. Byline given. Buys all rights. Editorial lead time 4 months. Submit seasonal material 6 months in advance. Accepts simultaneous submissions. Reports in 1 month on queries. Sample copy and writer's guidelines free on request.
Nonfiction: General interest, how-to (safety tips, health tips), personal experience. Buys 24 mss/year. Query with published clips. Length: 1,000-2,500 words. Pays $500 maximum. Sometimes pays expenses of writers on assignment.
Reprints: Accepts previously published submissions.
Photos: State availability of photos with submission. Reviews contact sheet, negatives, transparencies, prints. Offers no additional payment for photos accepted with ms. Identification of subjects required.
Tips: "Send intro letter, query, résumé and published clips (magazine preferable). Wait for a phone call from editor."

OPPORTUNITY MAGAZINE, (formerly *Income Plus Magazine*), 18 E. 41st St., New York NY 10017. Fax: (212)376-7723. Editor: Ingrid Eisenstadter. 75% freelance written. Monthly magazine on small business and money-making ideas. Provides "hands-on service to help small-business owners, home office workers and entrepreneurs successfully start up and run their enterprises." Estab. 1989. Circ. 150,000. Pays on publication. Byline given. Offers 10% kill fee. Buys first North American serial or second serial rights. Sample copy for $2.50. Writer's guidelines for #10 SASE.
Nonfiction: Articles should be fact-filled: book excerpts, how-to (business, finance, home office, technical, start-up), interview/profile. Buys 48 mss/year. Query. Length: 900-2,000 words. Pays $400-600 for assigned articles; $100-200 for unsolicited articles. Pays expenses of writers on assignment.
Photos: State availability of photos with submission. Offers no additional payment for photos accepted with ms.
Columns/Departments: Small-Biz; Finance & Law; Trends; Publicity; Success Stories, 750-900 words. Pays $100-150.
Tips: Write for editorial calendar as well as ms guidelines.

CONTEMPORARY CULTURE

These magazines often combine politics, current events and cultural elements such as art, literature, film and music, to examine contemporary society. Their approach to institutions is typically irreverant and investigative. Some, like *Strength* or *Might*, report on alternative culture and appeal to a young adult "Generation X" audience. Others, such as *Mother Jones* or *Rolling Stone*, treat mainstream culture for a baby boomer generation audience as well as younger readers.

‡**BOSTON REVIEW**, E53-407, 30 Wadsworth St., M.I.T., Cambridge MA 02139. (617)253-3642. Fax: (617)252-1549. E-mail: bostonreview@mit.edu. Website: http://polisci-mac-2.mit.edu/BostonReview/Boston Review.html. Editor: Josh Cohen. Contact: Betsy Reed, managing editor. 100% freelance written. Works with a small number of new/unpublished writers each year. Bimonthly magazine of the arts, politics and culture. Estab. 1975. Circ. 20,000. **Pays on acceptance.** Publishes ms an average of 3 months after acceptance. Buys first American serial rights. Byline given. Accepts simultaneous submissions. Reports in 6 months. Sample copy $4.50. Writer's guidelines for #10 SASE.
Nonfiction: Critical essays and reviews, natural and social sciences, literature, music, painting, film and photography. Uses 20 unsolicited mss/year. Length: 1,500-4,000 words. Pays $100 average. Sometimes pays expenses of writers on assignment.
Fiction: Length: 2,000-4,000 words. Pays $100 average. Publishes novel excerpts.
Poetry: Pays according to length and author.
Tips: "Generally, we look for in-depth knowledge of an area, an original view of the material, and a presentation which makes these accessible to a sophisticated reader who will be looking for more and better articles which anticipate ideas and trends on the intellectual and cultural frontier."

BRUTARIAN, The Magazine That Dares To Be Lame, Box 25222, Arlington VA 22202. Editor: Dominick Salemi. 100% freelance written. Quarterly magazine covering popular and unpopular culture. "A healthy knowledge of the great works of antiquity and an equally healthy contempt for most of what passes today as culture." Estab. 1991. Circ. 3,000. Pays on publication. Publishes ms an average of 3 months after acceptance. Byline given. Buys first or one-time rights. Editorial lead time 2 months. Submit seasonal material 6 months in advance. Reports in 1 week on queries; 2 months on mss. Sample copy for $5. Writer's guidelines free on request with SASE.

Nonfiction: Book excerpts, essays, exposé, general interest, humor, interview/profile, reviews of books, film and music. Buys 10-20 feature articles/year. Send complete ms. Length: 1,000-10,000 words. Pays $100-400, depending on length. Sometimes pays expenses of writers on assignment.

Reprints: Send typed ms with rights for sale noted and information about when and where the article previously appeared. Pays 100% of amount paid for an original article.

Photos: State availability of photos with submission. Reviews contact sheets. Offers no additional payment for photos accepted with ms. Caption, model releases, identification of subjects required. Buys one-time rights.

Columns/Departments: Celluloid Void (critiques of cult and obscure films), 500-1,000 words; Brut Library (critiques of books), 500-1,000 words; Audio Depravation (short critiques of odd, R&B, jazz and R&R music), 50-100 words. Buys "hundreds" of mss/year. Send complete ms. Pays $5-25.

Fiction: Adventure, confession, erotica, experimental, fantasy, horror, humorous, mystery, novel excerpts, science fiction, slice-of-life vignettes, suspense. Buys 4-10 mss/year. Send complete ms. Length: 1,000-10,000 words. Pays $100-500. 10¢/word for established writers. Publishes novel excerpts.

Poetry: Avant-garde, free verse, traditional. Buys 10-15 poems/year. Submit maximum 10 poems. Length: 25-1,000. Pays $20-200.

Tips: "Send résumé with completed manuscript. Avoid dry tone and excessive scholasticism. Do not cover topics or issues which have been done to death unless you have a fresh approach or new insights on the subject."

HIGH TIMES, Trans High Corp., 235 Park Ave. S., 5th Floor, New York NY 10003-1405. (212)387-0500. Fax: (212)475-7684. E-mail: hteditor@hightimes.com. Editor: Steve Hager. News Editor: Bill Weinberg. 30% freelance written. Monthly magazine covering marijuana and the counterculture. Estab. 1974. Circ. 250,000. Pays on publication. Byline given. Offers 20% kill fee. Buys one-time or all rights or makes work-for-hire assignments. Submit seasonal/holiday material 6 months in advance. Accepts previously published submissions. Reports in 1 month on queries; 4 months on mss. Sample copy for $5 and #10 SASE. Writer's guidelines for SASE.

● No longer accepts fiction or poetry. Staff now writes more for each issue than freelancers.

Nonfiction: Book excerpts, exposé, humor, interview/profile, new product, personal experience, photo feature, travel. Buys 30 mss/year. Send complete ms. Length: 1,000-10,000 words. Pays $150-1,000. Sometimes pays in trade for advertisements. Sometimes pays expenses of writers on assignment.

Reprints: Send tearsheet of article or typed ms with rights for sale noted. Pays in ad trade.

Photos: Chris Eudaley, photo editor. Send photos with submission. Pays $50-500. Captions, model release, identification of subjects required. Buys all rights or one-time use.

Columns/Departments: Steve Bloom, music editor. Chris Simunek, cultivation editor. Peter Gorman, views editor. Drug related books; drug related news. Buys 10 mss/year. Query with published clips. Length: 100-2,000 words. Pays $25-300.

Fillers: Gags to be illustrated by cartoonist, newsbreaks, short humor. Buys 10 mss/year. Length: 100-500 words. Pays $10-50. Cartoon Editor: John Holmstrom.

Tips: "All sections are open to good, professional writers."

‡MIGHT, Issues/Irony/Insolence, 150 Fourth St., Suite 650, San Francisco CA 94103. (415)896-1528. Fax: (415)974-1216. E-mail: mightmag@aol.com. Editor: David Eggers. Contact: Zev Borow, associate editor. Bimonthly magazine. "*Might* covers cultural and political issues with a mix of investigative grit and irreverent wit." Estab. 1994. Circ. 30,000. Publishes ms 3 months after acceptance. Byline given. Buys first North American serial rights. Editorial lead time 1 month. Submit seasonal material 1 month in advance. Sample copy for $5 and 9×12 SAE and 6 first-class stamps. Writer's guidelines for #10 SASE.

Nonfiction: Book excerpts, essays, exposé, general interest, humor, interview/profile, opinion, personal experience, photo feature, religious. Does not want to see celebrity profiles, articles about dogs. Buys 10 mss/year. Query with published clips or send complete ms. Length: 50-7,000 words. Pays $25 minimum. Pays contributor copies "if there's no cash." Sometimes pays expenses of writers on assignment.

Photos: State availability of photos with submission.

Fiction: Paul Tullis, senior editor. Condensed novels, confession, erotica, ethnic, experimental, historical, humorous, mainstream, novel excerpts, religious, science fiction, serialized novels, slice-of-life vignettes, suspense, western. No flowery prose. Buys 2 mss/year. Query with published clips. Send complete ms.

MOTHER JONES, Foundation for National Progress, 731 Market St., Suite 600, San Francisco CA 94103. (415)665-6637. Website: http://www.motherjones.com. Editor: Jeffrey Klein. Contact: Chris Orr, Sarah Pollock, senior editors. 80% freelance written. Bimonthly national magazine covering politics, investigative reporting. "*Mother Jones* is a 'progressive' magazine—but the core of its editorial well is reporting (i.e., fact-based). No slant required." Estab. 1976. Circ. 120,000. Pays on publication. Publishes ms an average of 4 months after acceptance. Byline given. Offers 33% kill fee. Buys first North American serial rights, first rights, one-time rights or online rights (limited). Editorial lead time 4 months. Submit seasonal material 6 months in advance. Query only with SASE. Reports in 2 months. Sample copy for 9×12 SAE with 4 first-class stamps. Writer's guidelines for #10 SASE.

Nonfiction: Book excerpts, essays, exposé, humor, interview/profile, opinion, personal experience, photo feature, current issues, policy. Buys 70-100 mss/year. Length: 2,000-5,000 words. Pays 80¢/word. Sometimes pays expenses of writers on assignment.

Columns/Departments: Kerry Lauerman. Outfront (short, newsy and/or outrageous and/or humorous items), 200-500 words; Profiles of "Hellraisers," "Visionaries" (short interviews), 250 words. Pays 80¢/word.

Tips: "Send a great, short query and establish your credibility as a reporter."

‡**NEW HAVEN ADVOCATE, New Haven's News & Arts Weekly,** New Mass Media Inc., 1 Long Wharf Dr., New Haven CT 06571. (203)789-0010. Fax: (203)787-1418. E-mail: newhadvo@pcnet.com. Editor: Joshua Mamis. 10% freelance written. Alternative weekly tabloid. "Alternative, investigative, cultural reporting with a strong voice. We like to shake things up." Estab. 1975. Circ. 55,000. Pays on publication. Byline given. Buys on speculation. Buys one-time rights. Editorial lead time 1 month. Submit seasonal material 2 months in advance. Accepts simultaneous submissions. Reports in 1 month on queries.

Nonfiction: Book excerpts, essays, exposé, general interest, humor, interview/profile. Buys 15-20 mss/year. Query with published clips. Length: 750-2,000 words. Pays $50-150. Sometimes pays expenses of writers on assignment.

Photos: Freelancers should state availability of photos with submission. Captions, model releases, identification of subjects required. Buys one-time rights.

Tips: "Strong local focus; strong literary voice, controversial, easy-reading, contemporary, etc."

ROLLING STONE, Wenner Media Inc., 1290 Avenue of the Americas, New York NY 10104. (212)484-1616. Fax: (212)767-8205. Editor: Jann S. Wenner. Magazine published 24 times/year covering popular culture. "*Rolling Stone* is a magazine edited for young adults who have a special interest in popular culture, particularly music, film and politics." Estab. 1967. Circ. 1,176,000. This magazine did not respond to our request for information. Query before submitting.

SHEPHERD EXPRESS, Alternative Publications, Inc., 1123 N. Water St., Milwaukee WI 53202. Website: http://www.shepherd-express.com. Contact: Scott Kerr, editor. 50% freelance written. Weekly tabloid covering "news and arts with a progressive news edge and a hip entertainment perspective." Estab. 1982. Circ. 55,000. Pays on publication. Publishes ms an average of 2 weeks after acceptance. Byline given. No kill fee. Buys first, one-time or all rights or makes work-for-hire assignments. Editorial lead time 2 weeks. Submit seasonal material 1 month in advance. Accepts simultaneous submissions. Reports in 2 weeks on queries; 1 month on mss. Sample copy for $3.

Nonfiction: Book excerpts, essays, exposé, opinion. Buys 300 mss/year. Query with published clips or send complete ms. Length: 600-3,500 words. Pays $25-350 for assigned articles; $10-200 for unsolicited articles. Sometimes pays expenses of writers on assignment.

Reprints: Accepts previously published submissions.

Photos: State availability of photos with submissions. Reviews prints. Negotiates payment individually. Captions, model releases, identification of subjects required. Buys one-time rights.

Columns/Departments: Opinions (social trends, politics, from progressive slant), 800-1,200 words; Books Reviewed (new books only: Social trends, environment, politics), 600-1,200 words. Buys 10 mss/year. Send complete ms.

Tips: "Include solid analysis with point of view in tight but lively writing. Nothing cute. Do not tell us that something is important, tell us why."

‡**STRENGTH MAGAZINE, Quality Boards and Noize since 1995,** Delinquent Publishing, 5050 Section Ave., Cincinnati OH 45212. (513)531-0202. E-mail: strength@iglov.com. Editor: Christian Strike. 50% freelance written. Bimonthly magazine covering music, surfing, snow boarding, skating. "*Strength* is a core music and board sports magazine." Estab. 1995. Circ. 30,000. **Pays on acceptance.** Publishes ms an average of 2 months after acceptance. Byline given. Offers 20% kill fee. Buys all rights. Editorial lead time

---

FOR EXPLANATION of symbols, see the Key to Symbols and Abbreviations. For unfamiliar words, see the Glossary.

2 months. Submit seasonal material 3 months in advance. Accepts simultaneous submissions. Reports in 2 weeks on queries; 2 months on mss. Sample copy for $5. Writer's guidelines free on request.

Nonfiction: General interest, humor, interview/profile, new product, opinion, personal experience, photo feature, travel. Query. Length: 200-1,500 words. Pays $300-600 for assigned articles; $100-400 for unsolicited articles. Pays expenses of writers on assignment.

Photos: State availability of photos with submission. Reviews contact sheets, transparencies. Negotiates payment individually. Identification of subjects required. Buys one-time rights.

Columns/Departments: Music Interviews, Board Sports Location Stories and Board Sports Interviews (no holds barred, in your face), 500-2,000 words. Buys over 50 mss/year. Query. Pays $500-1,000.

Fiction: Adventure, humorous. Buys 5-10 mss/year. Query. Length: 500-2,000 words. Pays $300-500.

Poetry: Free verse, haiku. Length: 10-100 lines. Pays $20-100.

Fillers: Anecdotes, facts, gags to be illustrated by cartoonist, newsbreaks, short humor. Buys 500/year. Length: 20-500 words. Pays $20-200.

Tips: "We're very accessible. Just give us a call."

TIKKUN MAGAZINE, A Bimonthly Jewish Critique of Politics, Culture and Society, 251 W. 100th St., New York NY 10025. (212)864-4110. Editor: Michael Lerner. Contact: Alice Chasan, executive editor. 95% freelance written. Bimonthly magazine covering politics, culture, society. Estab. 1986. Circ. 25,000. Pays on publication. Publishes ms an average of 6 months after acceptance. Byline given. Kill fee varies. Buys first North American serial rights. Editorial lead time 2 months. Submit seasonal material 4 months in advance. Reports in 6 months. Sample copy for $8.

Nonfiction: Book excerpts, essays, general interest, historical/nostalgic, humor, opinion, personal experience, photo feature, religious, political analysis media and cultural analysis. Buys 25 mss/year. Send complete ms. Length: 2,000 words maximum. Pays $150.

Photos: State availability of photos with submissions. Reviews contact sheets or prints. Negotiates payment individually. Buys one-time rights.

Fiction: Contact: Melvin Jules Bukiet, fiction editor. Ethnic, historical, humorous, mystery, novel excerpts, religious, romance, slice-of-life vignettes. Buys 6 mss/year. Send complete ms.

Poetry: Contact: Marge Piercy, poetry editor. Avant-garde, free verse, Haiku, light verse traditional. We specifically reserve *Tikkun* for poetry with Jewish themes since there are so few places where such work can find a home. Submit maximum 5 poems. Long poems cannot be considered. Does not pay for poetry.

Tips: "Internships are available. Write to *Tikkun* for information. Enclose a résumé and self-revealing letter."

UTNE READER, 1624 Harmon Place, Suite 330, Minneapolis MN 55403. Fax: (612)338-6043. E-mail: editor@utnereader.com. Website: http://www.utne.com. Managing Editor: Craig Cox. No unsolicited mss.

Reprints: Accepts previously published submissions only. Send tearsheet or photocopy of article or typed ms with rights for sale noted and information about when and where the article previously appeared.

‡XSESS LIVING, CDZeene, Proving Ground Publications. 3932 Wilshire Blvd., #212, Los Angeles CA 90010. Fax: (213)383-1093. E-mail: xsesscdzne@aol.com. Website: http://www.pureartmkt.com. Editor: Sean Perkin. 80% freelance written. Bimonthly lifestyles publication covering fashion, business, politics, music, entertainment, etc. Estab. 1992. Circ. 30,000. Pays within 2 weeks after publication. Publishes ms an average of 1 month after acceptance. Byline given. Buys one-time rights, makes work-for-hire assignments. Editorial lead time 3 months. Submit seasonal material 4 months in advance. Accepts simultaneous submissions. Sample copy for $8.95 plus $1 postage. Writer's guidelines free on request.

Nonfiction: Exposé, interview/profile, new product, travel.

Reprints: Accepts previously published submissions.

DETECTIVE AND CRIME

Fans of detective stories want to read accounts of actual criminal cases, detective work and espionage. Markets specializing in crime fiction are listed under Mystery publications.

P. I. MAGAZINE, America's Private Investigation Journal, 755 Bronx, Toledo OH 43609. (419)382-0967. Fax: (419)382-0967. Website: http://www.PIMALL.com/pimag/pimag1.html. Editor: Bob Mackowiak. 75% freelance written. "Audience includes professional investigators and mystery/private eye fans. Estab. 1988. Circ. 4,000. Pays on publication. Publishes ms an average of 3 months after acceptance. Buys one-time rights. Submit seasonal/holiday material 3 months in advance. Accepts simultaneous submissions. Reports in 3 months on queries; 4 months on mss. Sample copy for $6.75.

• *P.I. Magazine* has just increased its number of pages by 20%, so even more good profiles and true cases are needed.

Nonfiction: Interview/profile, personal experience and accounts of real cases. Buys 4-10 mss/year. Send complete ms. Length: 1,500 words. Pays $50 minimum for unsolicited articles.
Photos: Send photos with submission. May offer additional payment for photos accepted with ms. Model releases and identification of subjects required. Buys one-time rights.
Tips: "The best way to get published in *P.I.* is to write a detailed story about a professional private investigator's true-life case."

DISABILITIES

These magazines are geared toward disabled persons and those who care for or teach them. A knowledge of disabilities and lifestyles is important for writers trying to break in to this field; editors regularly discard material that does not have a realistic focus. Some of these magazines will accept manuscripts only from disabled persons or those with a background in caring for disabled persons.

ACCENT ON LIVING, P.O. Box 700, Bloomington IL 61702-0700. (309)378-2961. Fax: (309)378-4420. Editor: Betty Garee. 75% freelance written. Eager to work with new/unpublished writers. Quarterly magazine for physically disabled persons and rehabilitation professionals. Estab. 1956. Circ. 20,000. Buys first and second (reprint) rights. Byline usually given. Buys 50-60 unsolicited mss/year. Pays on publication. Publishes ms an average of 6 months after acceptance. Reports in 1 month. Sample copy and writer's guidelines $3.50 for #10 SAE with 7 first-class stamps. Writer's guidelines for #10 SASE.
Nonfiction: Articles about new devices that would make a disabled person with limited physical mobility more independent; should include description, availability and photos. Medical breakthroughs for disabled people. Intelligent discussion articles on acceptance of physically disabled persons in normal living situations; topics may be architectural barriers, housing, transportation, educational or job opportunities, organizations, or other areas. How-to articles concerning everyday living, giving specific, helpful information so the reader can carry out the idea himself/herself. News articles about active disabled persons or groups. Good strong interviews. Vacations, accessible places to go, sports, organizations, humorous incidents, self improvement and sexual or personal adjustment—all related to physically handicapped persons. No religious-type articles. "We are looking for upbeat material." Query. Length: 250-1,000 words. Pays 10¢/word for article as it appears in magazine (after editing and/or condensing by staff).
Reprints: Send tearsheet or photocopy of article and information about when and where the article previously appeared.
Photos: Pays $10 minimum for b&w photos purchased with accompanying captions. Amount will depend on quality of photos and subject matter. Pays $50 and up for four-color slides used on cover. "We need good-quality transparencies or slides with submissions—or b&w photos."
Tips: "Ask a friend who is disabled to read your article before sending it to *Accent*. Make sure that he/she understands your major points and the sequence or procedure."

ARTHRITIS TODAY, Arthritis Foundation. 1314 Spring St. NW, Atlanta GA 30309. (404)872-7100. Fax: (404)872-9559. E-mail: smorrow@arthritis.org. Website: http://www.arthritis.org. Editor: Cindy T. McDaniel. Managing Editor: Tracy Ballew. 70% freelance written. Bimonthly magazine about living with arthritis; latest in research/treatment. "*Arthritis Today* is written for the nearly 40 million Americans who have arthritis and for the millions of others whose lives are touched by an arthritis-related disease. The editorial content is designed to help the person with arthritis live a more productive, independent and painfree life. The articles are upbeat and provide practical advice, information and inspiration." Estab. 1987. Circ. 600,000. Buys first North American serial rights but requires unlimited reprint rights in any Arthritis Foundation affiliated endeavor. Submit seasonal/holiday material 6 months in advance. Will consider simultaneous submissions. Reports in 1 month on queries; 2 months on mss. Sample copy for 9×11 SAE with 4 first-class stamps. Writer's guidelines for #10 SASE.
  • Ranked as one of the best markets for freelance writers in *Writer's Yearbook*'s annual "Top 100 Markets," January 1996.
Nonfiction: General interest, how-to (tips on any aspect of living with arthritis), service, inspirational, opinion, personal experience, photo feature, technical, nutrition, general health and lifestyle. Buys 45 mss/year. Query with published clips. Length: 750-3,500. Pays $450-1,800. Pays expenses of writers on assignment.
Reprints: Send photocopy of article with rights for sale noted and information about when and where the article previously appeared. Pays 25-50% of amount paid for an original article.
Photos: Submit slides, tearsheets or prints for consideration. Reprints $50. Captions, model releases, identification of subjects required. Buy one-time North American serial rights.
Columns/Departments: Quick Takes (general news and information); Scientific Frontier (research news about arthritis), 200-600 words. Buys 16-20 mss/year. Query with published clips. Pays $150-400.

Tips: "In addition to articles specifically about living with arthritis, we look for articles to appeal to an older audience on subjects such as hobbies, general health, lifestyle, etc."

DIABETES SELF-MANAGEMENT, R.A. Rapaport Publishing, Inc., 150 W. 22nd St., Suite 800, New York NY 10011-2421. (212)989-0200. Fax: (212)989-4786. Editor: James Hazlett. 20% freelance written. Bimonthly magazine about diabetes. "We publish how-to health care articles for motivated, intelligent readers who have diabetes and who are actively involved in their own health care management. All articles must have immediate application to their daily living." Estab. 1983. Circ. 285,000. Pays on publication. Publishes ms an average of 3 months after acceptance. Byline given. Offers 20% kill fee. Buys all rights. Submit seasonal/holiday material 6 months in advance. Reports in 1 month. Sample copy for $3.50 and 9 × 12 SAE with 6 first-class stamps. Writer's guidelines for #10 SASE.
Nonfiction: How-to (exercise, nutrition, diabetes self-care, product surveys), technical (reviews of products available, foods sold by brand name), travel (considerations and prep for people with diabetes). Buys 10-12 mss/year. Query with published clips. Length: 2,000-4,000 words. Pays $400-600 for assigned articles; $200-600 for unsolicited articles.
Tips: "The rule of thumb for any article we publish is that it must be clear, concise, useful and instructive, and it must have immediate application to the lives of our readers."

‡DIALOGUE, Blindskills, Inc., P.O. Box 5181, Salem OR 97301-0181. (800)860-4224; (503)581-4224. Fax: (503)581-0178. E-mail: blindskl@teleport.com. Editor: Carol M. McCarl. 85% freelance written. Quarterly journal covering the visually impaired. Estab. 1961. Circ. 1,100. Pays on publication. Publishes ms an average of 6-8 months after acceptance. Byline given. Buys first rights. Editorial lead time 3 months. Submit seasonal material 3 months in advance. Sample copy $6. Writer's guidelines free on request.
Nonfiction: Essays, general interest, historical/nostalgic, how-to, humor, interview/profile, new product, personal experience. Prefer material by visually impaired writers. No controversial, explicit sex. No religious or political. Buys 20 mss/year. Query with complete ms. Length: 500-1,200 words. Pays $10-35 for assigned articles; $10-25 for unsolicited articles.
Columns/Departments: All material should be relative to blind and visually impaired readers. Careers, 1,000 words; What's New & Where to Get It (resources, new product), 2,500 words; What Do You Do When . . . ? (dealing with sight loss), 1,000 words. Buys 40 mss/year. Query with complete ms. Pays $10-25.
Fiction: Adventure, humorous, science fiction, slice-of-life vignettes, first person experiences. Prefer material by visually impaired writers. No controversial, explicit sex. No religious or political. Buys 6-8 mss/year. Query with complete ms. Length: 800-1,200 words. Pays $15-25.
Poetry: Free verse, light verse, traditional. Prefer material by visually impaired writers. No controversial, explicit sex. No religious or political. Buys 15-20 poems/year. Submit maximum 5 poems. Length: 20 lines maximum. Pays $10-15.
Fillers: Anecdotes, facts, newsbreaks, short humor. Length: 50-150 words. No payment.
Tips: Send SASE for free writers guidelines, $6 for sample in Braille, cassette or large print.

THE DISABILITY RAG & RESOURCE, The Advocado Press, P.O. Box 145, Louisville KY 40201. E-mail: therag@ntr.net. Editor: Eric Francis. Bimonthly magazine covering disability-related rights issues. "*The Rag* is a forum for discussion of issues related to living with a disability in American society today. It is interested in exploring and exposing the roots of discrimination, supporting positive change and developing disability community and culture. Its readers tend to be active, involved and informed, and want to be better informed." Estab. 1980. Circ. 3,200. Pays on publication. Publishes ms an average of 8 months after acceptance. Byline given. Buys first North American serial rights. Editorial lead time 2 months. Submit seasonal material 6 months in advance. Accepts electronic submissions by disk. Reports in 1 month on queries; 3 months on mss. Sample copy for $4.50. Writer's guidelines for #10 SASE.
Nonfiction: Book excerpts, essays, exposé, humor, opinion, reportage, analysis. Does not want to see inspirational, profile, personal experience except as part of or sidebar to broader piece. Buys 30 mss/year. Query. Length: 500-3,500 words. Pays $25-150 ($25 per printed page). Sometimes pays expenses of writers on assignment.
Photos: State availability of photos with submissions. Reviews contact sheets, prints. Offers $25/photo. Model releases, identification of subjects required. Buys one-time rights.
Columns/Departments: Reading (book reviews on disability, rights issues), 500-1,200 words; Myth and Media (film, TV, other media images of disability), 500-1,500 words; Views of Ourselves (disability identity), 500-1,500 words. Buys 12 mss/year. Query with published clips. Pays $25-75.
Fiction: Anne Finger, poetry/fiction editor. Erotica, ethnic, experimental, humorous, mainstream, novel excerpts, science fiction, slice-of-life vignettes, interested in work by writers with disabilities or treating disability themes. Buys 2 mss/year (but would like to use more). Send complete ms. Length: 500-3,500 words. Pays $25-150 ($25 for printed page).
Poetry: Anne Finger, poetry/fiction editor. Any contemporary form, by writers with disabilities or dealing with aspects of the disability experience. Buys 18 poems/year. Submit maximum 5 poems. Pays $25/poem (unless exceptionally long, multi-part).
Tips: "Be familiar with the disability rights movement and the issues that concern it."

DISABILITY TODAY, Disability Today Publishing Group, Inc., P.O. Box 237, Grimsby, Ontario L3M 3C4 Canada. Fax: (905)338-1836. Editor: Hilda Hoch. 70% freelance written. Quarterly magazine covering disability issues/profiles. "An awareness magazine for and about people with physical disabilities." Estab. 1990. Circ. 45,000. Pays on publication. Publishes ms an average of 3 months after acceptance. Byline given. Offers 75% kill fee. Buys one-time or second serial (reprint) rights. Editorial lead time 3 months. Submit seasonal material 6 months in advance. Sample copy $5.50. Writer's guidelines for #10 SAE and IRC.
Nonfiction: Publisher: Jeffrey Tiessen. Book excerpts, general interest, humor, inspirational, interview/profile, new product, opinion, personal experience, photo feature, travel. Annual features: Acquired Brain Injury (August); Kids & Disability (November). Buys 12 mss/year. Query. Length: 1,000-2,500 words. Pays $100-400. Sometimes pays expenses of writers on assignment.
Reprints: Accepts previously published submissions.
Photos: Send photos with submission. Reviews 4×6 prints. Offers no additional payment for photos accepted with ms. Model releases and identification of subjects required. Buys one-time rights.
Columns/Departments: Injury Prevention, 800 words; Newspage ("what's new"), 400 words; Sports (disabled sports), 800 words. Buys 24 mss/year. Query. Pays $50-200.
Tips: "Provide outline for a series of contributions; identify experience in field of disability."

‡HEARING HEALTH, Voice International Publications, Inc., P.O. Drawer V, Ingleside TX 78362-0500. Fax: (512)776-3278. Editor: Paula Bonillas. 20% freelance written. Bimonthly magazine covering issues and concerns pertaining to hearing and hearing loss. Estab. 1984. Circ. 20,000. Pays on publication. Byline given. Buys one-time rights. Editorial lead time 2 months. Submit seasonal material 4 months in advance. Accepts simultaneous submissions. Reports in 6 weeks on queries; 2 months on mss. Sample copy for $2. Writer's guidelines for #10 SASE.
Nonfiction: Books excerpts, essays, exposé, general interest, historical/nostalgic, humor, inspirational, interview/profile, new product, opinion, personal experience, photo feature, technical, travel. No self-pitying over loss of hearing. Query with published clips. Length: 500-2,000 words. Sometimes pays expenses of writers on assignment.
Reprints: Accepts previously published submissions, if so noted.
Photos: State availability of photos with submission. Reviews contact sheets. Negotiates payment individually. Captions, model releases, identification of subjects required. Buys one-time rights.
Columns/Departments: Kidink (written by kids with hearing loss), 300 words; People (shares stories of successful, everyday people who have loss of hearing), 300-400 words. Buys 2 mss/year. Query with published clips.
Fiction: Fantasy, historical, humorous, novel excerpts, science fiction. Nothing inappropriate for children 10 or younger. Buys 2 mss/year. Query with published clips. Length: 400-1,500 words.
Poetry: Avant-garde, free verse, light verse, traditional. Buys 2 poems/year. Submit maximum 2 poems. Length: 4-50 lines.
Fillers: Anecdotes, facts, gags to be illustrated by cartoonist, newsbreaks, short humor. Buys 6/year. Length: 25-1,500 words.
Tips: "We look for fresh stories, usually factual but occasionally fictitious, about coping with hearing loss. A positive attitude is a must for *Hearing Health*. Unless one has some experience with deafness or hearing loss—whether their own or a loved one's—it's very difficult to 'break in' to our publication. Experience brings the empathy and understanding—the sensitivity—and the freedom to write humorously about any handicap or disability."

KALEIDOSCOPE: International Magazine of Literature, Fine Arts, and Disability, Kaleidoscope Press, 326 Locust St., Akron OH 44302-1876. (330)762-9755. Fax: (330)762-0912. Editor-in-Chief: Dr. Darshan Perusek. Contact: Gail Willmott, senior editor. Subscribers include individuals, agencies and organizations that assist people with disabilities and many university and public libraries. Estab. 1979. Circ. 1,500. 75% freelance written. Eager to work with new/unpublished writers. Byline given. Rights return to author upon publication. Appreciate work by established writers as well. Especially interested in work by writers with a disability. Features writers both with and without disabilities. Writers without a disability must limit themselves to our focus, while those with a disability may explore any topic (although we prefer original perspectives about experiences with disability). Submit photocopies with SASE for return of work. Please type submissions. All submissions should be accompanied by an autobiographical sketch. May include art or photos that enhance works, prefer b&w with high contrast. Reports in 3 weeks, acceptance or rejection may take 6 months. Sample copy for $4 prepaid. Guidelines free for SASE.
Nonfiction: Special issues: Disability: The Lighter Side (deadline August, publication January); Disability and Visual Arts (deadline March, publication July). Publishes 8-14 mss/year. Maximum 5,000 words. Pays $10-125 plus 2 copies. Personal experience essays, book reviews and articles related to disability.
Reprints: Send typed ms with rights for sale noted and information about when and where the article previously appeared. Publishes novel excerpts.
Fiction: Short stories, excerpts. Traditional and experimental styles. Works should explore experiences with disability. Use people-first language.

Poetry: Limit 5 poems/submission. Publishes 12-20 poems/year. Do not get caught up in rhyme scheme. High quality with strong imagery and evocative language. Will review any style.

Tips: Inquire about future themes of upcoming issues. Sample copy very helpful. Works should not use stereotyping, patronizing or offending language about disability. We seek fresh imagery and thought-provoking language.

MAINSTREAM, Magazine of the Able-Disabled, Exploding Myths, Inc., 2973 Beech St., San Diego CA 92102. (619)234-3138. Fax: (619)234-3155. E-mail: wstothers@aol.com. Website: http://www.mainstream-mag.com. Editor: Cyndi Jones. Managing Editor: William Stothers. 100% freelance written. Eager to develop writers who have a disability. Magazine published 10 times/year (monthly except January and June) covering disability-related topics, written for active and upscale disabled consumers. Estab. 1975. Circ. 19,400. Pays on publication. Publishes ms an average of 3 months after acceptance. Byline given. Buys all rights. Submit seasonal/holiday material 4 months in advance. Payment varies. Reports in 4 months. Sample copy for $5, or 9×12 SAE and $4 with 6 first-class stamps. Writer's guidelines for #10 SASE.

Nonfiction: Book excerpts, exposé, how-to (daily independent living tips), humor, interview/profile, personal experience (dealing with problems/solutions), photo feature, technology, computers, travel, politics and legislation. "All must be disability-related, directed to disabled consumers." *NO* articles on " 'my favorite disabled character', 'my most inspirational disabled person', 'poster child stories.' " Buys 65 mss/year. Query with or without published clips and send complete ms. Length: 8-12 pages. Pays $100-150. May pay subscription if writer requests.

Photos: State availability of photos with submission. Reviews contact sheets, 1½×¾ transparencies and 5×7 or larger prints. Offers $20-25/b&w photo. Captions and identification of subjects required. Buys all rights.

Columns/Departments: Creative Solutions (unusual solutions to common aggravating problems); Personal Page (deals with personal relations: dating, meeting people). Buys 10 mss/year. Send complete ms. Length: 500-800 words. Pays $75. "We also are looking for disability rights cartoons."

Tips: "It seems that politics and disability are becoming more important. Please include your phone number on cover page. We accept 5.25 or 3.5 floppy disks—ASCII, Wordperfect, IBM."

NEW MOBILITY, P.O. Box 8987, Malibu CA 90265-8987. (310)317-4522. Fax: (310)317-9644. E-mail: jean@miramar.com. Website: http://www.newmobility.com. Managing Editor: Jean Dobbs. 60% freelance written. Monthly full color magazine for people who use wheelchairs. "*New Mobility* covers the lifestyles of *active* wheelchair users with articles on health and medicine; sports, recreation and travel; equipment and technology; relationships, family and sexual issues; personalities; civil rights and legal issues. Writers should address issues with solid reporting and strong voice." Estab. 1989. Circ. 30,000. Pays 30 days after publication. Publishes ms an average of 6 months after acceptance. Byline given. Offers 50% kill fee. Buys first North American serial rights. Editorial lead time 6 months. Accepts simultaneous submissions. Reports in 3 months. Sample copy $5. Writer's guidelines for #10 SASE.

Nonfiction: Essays, exposé, humor, interview/profile, new product, opinion, photo feature, travel and medical feature. "No inspirational tear-jerkers." Buys 30 mss/year. Query with 1-2 published clips. Length: 700-2,000 words. Pays 15¢/word. Sometimes pays expenses of writers on assignment.

Reprints: Accepts previously published submissions only if material does not appear in other disability publications and is rewritten. Send photocopy of article with rights for sale noted, information about when and where the article previously appeared. Pays 100% of amount paid for an original article "because we require additional work."

Photos: State availability of photos with submission. Reviews contact sheets, transparencies and prints. Negotiates payment individually. Identification of subjects required. Buys one-time rights.

Columns/Departments: My Spin (opinion piece on disability-related topic), 700 words; Media (reviews of books, videos on disability), 300-400 words; People (personality profiles of people w/disabilities), 300-700 words. Buys 20 mss/year. Query with published clips. Send complete ms.

Tips: "Avoid 'courageous' or 'inspiring' tales of people who 'overcome' their disability. Writers don't have to be disabled to write for this magazine, but they should be familiar with the issues people with disabilities face. Most of our readers have disabilities, so write for this audience. We are most open to personality profiles, either for our short People department or as feature articles. In all of our departments, we like to see adventurous people, irreverent opinions and lively writing. Don't be afraid to let your *voice* come through."

ENTERTAINMENT

This category's publications cover live, filmed or videotaped entertainment, including home video, TV, dance, theater and adult entertainment. In addition to celebrity interviews, most publications want solid reporting on trends and upcoming productions. Magazines in the Contemporary Culture and General Interest sections also use articles on entertainment. For those publications with an emphasis on music and musicians, see the Music section.

ANGLOFILE, British Entertainment & Pop Culture, The Goody Press, P.O. Box 33515, Decatur GA 30033. (404)633-5587. Fax: (404)321-3109. Contact: William P. King, editor. Managing Editor: Leslie T. King. 15% freelance written. Monthly newsletter. "News and interviews on British entertainment, past and present, from an American point of view." Circ. 3,000. Pays on publication. Publishes ms an average of 6 months after acceptance. Byline given. Buys all rights. Reports in 2 months. Free sample copy.
Nonfiction: Justin Stonehouse articles editor. Book excerpts, essays, historical/nostalgic, interview/profile, opinion, personal experience, photo feature, and travel. "No articles written for general audience." Buys 5 mss/year. Send complete ms. Length: 1,500 words. Pays $25-250.
Reprints: Accepts previously published submissions. Send information about when and where the article previously appeared.
Photos: Send photos with submission. Reviews prints. Offers $10-25/photo. Identification of subjects required. Buys all rights.

CINEFANTASTIQUE MAGAZINE, The Review of Horror, Fantasy and Science Fiction Films, P.O. Box 270, Oak Park IL 60303. (708)366-5566. Editor: Frederick S. Clarke. 100% freelance written. Willing to work with new/unpublished writers. Bimonthly magazine covering horror, fantasy and science fiction films. Estab. 1970. Circ. 60,000. Pays on publication. Publishes ms an average of 6 months after acceptance. Byline given. Buys all magazine rights. Reports in 2 months or longer. Sample copy for $7 and 9 × 12 SAE. "Enclose SASE if you want your manuscript back."
Nonfiction: Historical/nostalgic (retrospects of film classics); interview/profile (film personalities); new product (new film projects); opinion (film reviews, critical essays); technical (how films are made). Buys 100-125 mss/year. Query with published clips and SASE. Length: 1,000-10,000 words. Pays expenses of writers on assignment.
Photos: State availability of photos with query letter or ms.
Tips: "Study the magazine to see the kinds of stories we publish. Develop original story suggestions; develop access to film industry personnel; submit reviews that show a perceptive point of view."

COUNTRY AMERICA, Meredith Corporation, 1716 Locust, Des Moines IA 50309-3023. (515)284-3787. Fax: (515)284-3035. Editor: Richard Krumme. Contact: Bill Eftink, managing editor. Magazine published 10 times/year covering country entertainment/lifestyle. Estab. 1989. Circ. 900,000. **Pays on acceptance.** Buys all rights (lifetime). Submit seasonal/holiday material 8 months or more in advance. Reports in 3 months. Free writer's guidelines.
Nonfiction: Food, general interest, historical/nostalgic, how-to, interview/profile (country music entertainers), photo feature, travel. Special issues: Christmas, travel, country music. Buys 130 mss/year. Query. Pays $100-1,000 for assigned articles. Sometimes pays expenses of writers on assignment.
Photos: State availability of photos with submission. Reviews contact sheets, negatives, 35mm transparencies. Offers $50-500/photo. Captions and identification of subjects required. Buys all rights.
Fillers: Country curiosities that deal with animals, people, etc.
Tips: "Think visually. Our publication will be light on text and heavy on photos. Be general; this is a general interest publication meant to be read by every member of the family. We are a service-oriented publication; please stress how-to sidebars and include addresses and phone numbers to help readers find out more."

‡DANCE INTERNATIONAL, Vancouver Ballet Society, 1415 Barclay St., Vancouver, British Columbia V6G 1J6 Canada. (604)681-1525. Fax: (604)681-7732. Editor: Maureen Riches. Contact: Deborah Meyers, contributing editor. 100% freelance written. Quarterly magazine covering dance arts. "Articles and reviews on current activities in world dance, with occasional historical essays (generally on Canadian issues); reviews of dance films, video and books." Estab. 1973. Circ. 850. Pays on publication. Publishes ms an average of 3 months after acceptance. Byline given. Offers 50% kill fee. Buys one-time rights. Editorial lead time 3 months. Submit seasonal material 2 months in advance. Reports in 2 weeks on queries; 1 month on mss. Sample copy and writer's guidelines free on request.
Nonfiction: Book excerpts, essays, historical/nostalgic, interview/profile, personal experience, photo feature. Buys 100 mss/year. Query. Length: 1,200-2,200 words. Pays $40-150.
Reprints: Accepts previously published submissions.
Photos: Send photos with submission. Reviews prints. Offers no additional payment for photos accepted with ms. Identification of subjects required.
Columns/Departments: Leland Windreich, copy editor. Dance Bookshelf (recent books reviewed), 1,200 words; Regional Reports (events in each region), 1,200-2,000 words. Buys 100 mss/year. Query. Pays $60-70.
Tips: "Send résumé and samples of recent writings."

THE DISNEY MAGAZINE, Walt Disney's Magic Kingdom Club, P.O. Box 4489, 1313 Harbor Blvd., Anaheim, CA 92803-4489. (714)520-2535. Fax: (714)520-2501. Quarterly magazine covering entertainment.

"*The Disney Magazine* includes behind the scenes reports on the progress of new projects such as attractions, resorts and films; nostalgia pieces on Walt Disney, early animators, and the beginning years of Disneyland; development of new business entities; dialogues with Disney executives; information for Disney collectors; and Theme Park current events, trivia pursuits and general interest stories." Estab. 1965. Circ. 394,000. This magazine did not respond to our request for information. Query before submitting.

DRAMATICS MAGAZINE, Educational Theatre Association, 3368 Central Pkwy., Cincinnati OH 45225-2392. (513)559-1996. Editor-in-Chief: Donald Corathers. 70% freelance written. Works with small number of new/unpublished writers. For theater arts students, teachers and others interested in theater arts education. Magazine published monthly, September-May. Estab. 1929. Circ. 35,000. **Pays on acceptance.** Publishes ms an average of 3 months after acceptance. Buys first North American serial rights. Byline given. Submit seasonal/holiday material 3 months in advance. Accepts simultaneous submissions. Reports in 3 months; may be longer on unsolicited mss. Sample copy for 9×12 SAE with 5 first-class stamps. Free writer's guidelines.
Nonfiction: How-to (technical theater, directing, acting, etc.), informational, interview, photo feature, humorous, profile, technical. Buys 30 mss/year. Submit complete ms. Length: 750-3,000 words. Pays $50-300. Rarely pays expenses of writers on assignment.
Reprints: Send tearsheet or photocopy of article or play, or typed ms with rights for sale noted and information about when and where the article previously appeared. Pays 50% of amount paid for an original article.
Photos: Purchased with accompanying ms. Uses b&w photos and transparencies. Query. Total purchase price for ms usually includes payment for photos.
Fiction: Drama (one-act and full-length plays). "No plays for children, Christmas plays or plays written with no attention paid to the conventions of theater." Prefers unpublished scripts that have been produced at least once. Buys 5-9 mss/year. Send complete ms. Pays $100-400.
Tips: "The best way to break in is to know our audience—drama students, teachers and others interested in theater—and to write for them. Writers who have some practical experience in theater, especially in technical areas, have a leg-up here, but we'll work with anybody who has a good idea. Some freelancers have become regular contributors. Others ignore style suggestions included in our writer's guidelines."

EAST END LIGHTS, The Quarterly Magazine for Elton John Fans, Voice Communications Corp., P.O. Box 760, New Baltimore MI 48047. (810)949-7900. Fax: (810)949-2217. Editor: Tom Stanton. 70% freelance written. Quarterly magazine covering British rock star Elton John. "In one way or another, a story must relate to Elton John, his activities or associates (past and present). We appeal to discriminating Elton fans. No gushing fanzine material. No current concert reviews." Estab. 1990. Circ. 1,400. Pays 3 weeks after publication. Publishes ms an average of 3 months after acceptance. Byline given. Offers 100% kill fee. Buys first rights and second serial (reprint) rights. Submit seasonal material 3 months in advance. Reports in 2 months. Sample copy for $2.
Nonfiction: Book excerpts, essays, exposé, general interest, historical/nostalgic, humor and interview/profile. Buys 20 mss/year. Query with or without published clips or send complete ms. Length: 400-1,000 words. Pays $50-200 for assigned articles; $40-150 for unsolicited articles. Pays with contributor copies only if the writer requests.
Reprints: Send information about when and where the article previously appeared. Pays 50% of amount paid for an original article.
Photos: State availability of photos with submission. Reviews negatives and 5×7 prints. Offers $40-75/ photo. Buys one-time rights and all rights.
Columns/Departments: Clippings (non-wire references to Elton John in other publications), maximum 200 words. Buys 12 mss/year. Send complete ms. Length: 50-200 words. Pays $10-20.
Tips: "Approach with a well-thought-out story idea. We'll provide direction. All areas equally open. We prefer interviews with Elton-related personalities—past or present. We are particularly interested in music/ memorabilia collecting of Elton material."

EMMY MAGAZINE, Academy of Television Arts & Sciences, 5220 Lankershim Blvd., North Hollywood CA 91601-3109. (818)754-2800. Fax: (818)761-2827. Website: http://www.emmys.org/. Editor/Publisher: Hank Rieger. Managing Editor: Gail Polevoi. 100% freelance written. Prefers to work with published established writers. Bimonthly magazine on television for TV professionals and enthusiasts. Circ. 12,000. Pays on publication or within 6 months. Publishes ms an average of 4 months after acceptance. Byline given. Offers 25% kill fee. Buys first North American serial rights. Reports in 1 month. Sample copy for 9×12 SAE with 6 first-class stamps.
Nonfiction: Articles on issues, trends, and VIPs (especially those behind the scenes) in broadcast and cable TV; programming; new technology; and important international developments. "We require TV industry expertise and clear, lively writing." Query with published clips. Length: 2,000 words. Pay $750-950. Pays some expenses of writers on assignment.
Columns/Departments: Most written by regulars, but newcomers can break into CloseUps, Viewpoint or Innerviews. Query with published clips. Length: 500-1,500 words, depending on department. Pays $250-700.

Tips: Study publication. No fanzine or academic approaches, please.

ENTERTAINMENT WEEKLY, Time Inc. Magazine Co., 1675 Broadway, New York NY 10016. (212)522-5600. (212)522-0074. Publisher: Michael J. Klingensmith. Weekly magazine covering popular entertainment. *"Entertainment Weekly* provides both a critical guide to popular culture and an informative inside look at the people, motives and ideas that shape the increasingly influential world of entertainment." Estab. 1990. Circ. 1,201,000. This magazine did not respond to our request for information. Query before submitting.

EROTIC X-FILM GUIDE, 1701 N. Orange Grove Ave., Hollywood CA 90046. Editorial Director: William Mann. 25% freelance written. Monthly magazine covering erotic entertainment. "We cover all aspects of the adult entertainment/sex industry." Estab. 1984. Circ. 150,000. **Pays on acceptance.** Publishes ms an average of 3 months after acceptance. Byline given. Offers 25% kill fee. Buys first North American serial rights. Editorial lead time 3 months. Submit seasonal material 3 months in advance. Accepts simultaneous submissions. Reports in 1 month on queries; 2 months on mss. Sample copy and writer's guidelines for 10×13 SAE with $3.90 in postage.
Nonfiction: Book excerpts, essays, exposé, general interest, historical/nostalgic, how-to, humor, interview/profile, new product, personal experience, photo feature, travel. Buys 6 mss/year. Query with published clips. Length: 500-4,000 words. Pays $50-750. Sometimes pays expenses of writers on assignment.
Reprints: Accepts previously published submissions.
Photos: Send photos with submission. Reviews transparencies, prints. Negotiates payment individually. Captions, model releases, identification of subjects required. Buys one-time rights.
Columns/Departments: Video Reviews (porn films), 50-300 words; Q&A (porn stars), 300 words. Buys 6 mss/year. Query with published clips. Pays $50-750.
Fiction: Adventure, confession, erotica, fantasy, horror, humorous, romance, science fiction, suspense. Buys 6 mss/year. Query with published clips. Length: 250-3,000 words. Pays $100-600.

‡ET AL., The Publisher's Group, P.O. Box 510366, Salt Lake City UT 84151-0366. Fax: (801)322-1098. Editor: Vicki Andersen. Contact: Anne E. Zombro, publisher. 80% freelance written. Quarterly magazine covering entertainment. "Entertainment and fine arts are the major thrusts of *Et Al.* Includes articles on celebrities, Q&As and stories of everyday folks who have made a difference." Estab. 1996. Circ. 15,000. Pays on publication. Publishes ms an average of 4 months after acceptance. Byline given. Buys first North American serial and second serial (reprint) rights. Editorial lead time 2 months. Submit seasonal material 4 months in advance. Accepts simultaneous submissions. Reports in 1 month on queries; 2 months on mss. Sample copy for $2 and 9×12 SAE. Writer's guidelines for #10 SASE.
Nonfiction: Essays, general interest, humor, inspirational, interview/profile. Nothing controversial. Buys 6-8 mss/year. Query with published clips. Length: 1,000-1,300 words. Pays $125-800.
Reprints: Accepts previously published submissions.
Photos: Send photos with submission. Reviews 4×5 transparencies (preferred), any size prints. Negotiates payment individually. Captions, model releases, identification of subjects required. Buys one-time or all rights.

‡FANGORIA: Horror in Entertainment, Starlog Communications, Inc., 475 Park Ave. S., 8th Floor, New York NY 10016. (212)689-2830. Fax: (212)889-7933. Editor: Anthony Timpone. 95% freelance written. Works with a small number of new/unpublished writers each year. Magazine published 10 times/year covering horror films, TV projects, comics, videos and literature and those who create them. Estab. 1979. Pays on publication. Publishes ms an average of 3 months after acceptance. Byline given. Buys all rights. Submit seasonal/holiday material 6 months in advance. Reports in 6 weeks. "We provide an assignment sheet (deadlines, info) to writers, thus authorizing queried stories that we're buying." Sample copy for $5.99 and 10×13 SAE with 4 first-class stamps. Writer's guidelines for #10 SASE.
  • *Fangoria* is looking for more articles on independent filmmakers and video game companies.
Nonfiction: Book excerpts, interview/profile of movie directors, makeup FX artists, screenwriters, producers, actors, noted horror novelists and others—with genre credits. No "think" pieces, opinion pieces, reviews (excluding books), or sub-theme overviews (i.e., vampire in the cinema). Buys 100 mss/year. Query with published clips. Length: 1,000-3,000 words. Pays $100-225. Rarely pays the expenses of writers on assignment. Avoids articles on science fiction films—see listing for sister magazine *Starlog* in *Writer's Market* science fiction magazine section.
Photos: State availability of photos. Reviews b&w and color prints and transparencies. "No separate payment for photos provided by film studios." Captions and identification of subjects required. Photo credit given. Buys all rights.
Columns/Departments: Monster Invasion (news about new film productions; must be exclusive, early information; also mini-interviews with filmmakers and novelists). Query with published clips. Length: 300-500 words. Pays $45-75.

Fiction: "We do *not* publish any fiction or poetry. *Don't* send any."

Tips: "Other than recommending that you study one or several copies of *Fangoria*, we can only describe it as a horror film magazine consisting primarily of interviews with technicians and filmmakers in the field. Be sure to stress the interview subjects' words—not your own opinions as much. We're very interested in small, independent filmmakers working outside of Hollywood. These people are usually more accessible to writers, and more cooperative. *Fangoria* is also sort of a *de facto* bible for youngsters interested in movie makeup careers and for young filmmakers. We are devoted only to *reel* horrors—the fakery of films, the imagery of the horror fiction of a Stephen King or a Clive Barker—*we do not* want nor would we *ever* publish articles on real-life horrors, murders, etc. A writer must *like* and *enjoy* horror films and horror fiction to work for us. If the photos in *Fangoria* disgust you, if the sight of (*stage*) blood repels you, if you feel 'superior' to horror (and its fans), you aren't a writer for us and we certainly aren't the market for you."

FILM COMMENT, Film Society of Lincoln Center, 70 Lincoln Center Plaza, New York NY 10023. (212)875-5610. Fax: (212)875-5636. E-mail: rtjfc@aol.com. Editor: Richard T. Jameson. 100% freelance written. Bimonthly magazine covering film criticism and film history. "*FC* publishes authoritative, personal writing (not journalism) reflecting experience of and involvement with film as an art form." Estab. 1962. Circ. 30,000. Pays on publication. Publishes ms an average of 2 months after acceptance. Byline given. Offers 50% kill fee (assigned articles only). Editorial lead time 6 weeks. Accepts simultaneous submissions. Reports in 2 weeks on queries. Writer's guidelines free on request.

Nonfiction: Essays, historical/nostalgic, interview/profile, opinion, personal experience. Buys 100 mss/year. Send complete ms. "We respond to queries, but rarely *assign* a writer we don't know." Length: 800-8,000 words. "We don't use a separate pay scale for solicited or unsolicited. There is no fixed rate, but roughly based on 3 words/$1."

Reprints: Rarely accepts previously published submissions. Send typed ms with information about when and where the article previously appeared. Pays 50% of amount paid for an original article.

Photos: State availability of photos with submission. Offers no additional payment for photos accepted with ms. Buys one-time rights.

Columns/Departments: Life With Video (impact of video on availability and experience of films; video as new imaginative dimension), 1,000-2,000 words. Pays $250 and up.

Tips: "Demonstrate ability and inclination to write *FC*-worthy articles. We read and consider everything we get, and we do print unknowns and first-timers. Probably the writer with a shorter submission (1,000-2,000 words) has a better chance than with an epic article that would fill half the issue."

‡HOME THEATER, Curt Co./Freedom Group, 29160 Heathecliff Rd., Malibu CA 90265. (310)589-3100. Fax: (310)589-3133. E-mail: hometheater@curtco.com. Contact: Brent Butterworth, editor. Managing Editor: Christy Grosz. 30% freelance written. Monthly magazine covering audio/video hardware and software. Estab. 1994. Circ. 100,000. Pays on publication. Publishes ms an average of 1 month after acceptance. Byline given. Offers 25% kill fee. Buys first North American serial, second serial and electronic rights. Editorial lead time 3 months. Reports in 2 months. Sample copy for $4.95.

Nonfiction: Interview/profile, new product, technical. Publishes quarterly buyer's guides. No general interest, non-technical articles. Buys 50 mss/year. Query with published clips. Length: 150-2,500 words. Pays $100-1,000 for assigned articles. Sometimes pays expenses of writers on assignment.

Photos: State availability of photos with submission. Reviews contact sheets, negatives, transparencies, prints. Negotiates payment individually. Captions required. Buys all rights.

Columns/Departments: Disk Head (satellite TV), 1,500 words; Howdaya (technical how-to), Tech Talk, all 1,000 words. Buys 20 mss/year. Query. Pays $500-1,000.

Tips: "You must be highly experienced with audio and/or video gear, and preferably a published writer."

KPBS ON AIR MAGAZINE, San Diego's Guide to Public Broadcasting, KPBS-TV/FM, 5200 Campanile Dr., San Diego CA 92182-5400. Mailing address: KPBS Radio/TV, San Diego CA 92182-5400. (619)594-3766. Fax: (619)265-6417. Editor: Michael Good. 15% freelance written. Monthly magazine on public broadcasting programming and San Diego arts. "Our readers are very intelligent, sophisticated and rather mature. Your writing should be, too." Estab. 1970. Circ. 63,000. Pays on publication. Publishes ms an average of 1 month after acceptance. Byline given. Offers 50% kill fee. Not copyrighted. Buys first North American serial rights. Submit seasonal/holiday material 3 months in advance. Reports in 3 months. Sample copy for 9×12 SAE with 4 first-class stamps.

Nonfiction: Interview/profile of PBS personalities and/or artists performing in San Diego, opinion, profiles of public TV and radio personalities, backgrounds on upcoming programs. Nothing over 1,500 words. Buys 60 mss/year. Query with published clips. Length: 300-1,500 words. Pays 20¢/word; 25¢/word if the article is received via modem or computer disk. Sometimes pays expenses of writers on assignment.

Reprints: Send tearsheet of article with rights for sale noted and information about when and where the article previously appeared. Pays 25¢/word.

Photos: State availability of photos with submission. Reviews transparencies and 5×7 prints. Offers $30-300/photo. Identification of subjects required. Buys one-time rights.

Columns/Departments: On the Town (upcoming arts events in San Diego), 800 words; Short Takes (backgrounds on public TV shows), 500 words; Radio Notes (backgrounders on public radio shows), 500 words. Buys 35 mss/year. Query or query with published clips. Length: 300-800 words. Pays 20¢/word; 25¢/word if the article is received via modem or computer disk.

Tips: "Feature stories for national writers are most open to freelancers. Arts stories for San Diego writers are most open. Read the magazine, then talk to me."

LONG ISLAND UPDATE, (formerly *New York/Long Island Update*), 990 Motor Pkwy., Central Islip NY 11722. (516)435-8890. Fax: (516)435-8925. Contact: Cheryl Ann Meglio, editor. Managing Editor: Allison A. Whitney. 50% freelance written. Monthly magazine covering "regional entertainment interests as well as national interests." Estab. 1980. Circ. 60,000. Pays on publication. Publishes ms an average of 4 months after acceptance. Byline given. Buys all rights. Submit seasonal/holiday material 3 months in advance. Reports in 5 weeks on queries.

Nonfiction: General interest, humor, interview/profile, new product, travel. Special issue: Bridal Guide (September). Query with published clips. Length: 250-1,500 words. Pays $25-125.

Columns/Departments: Nightcap (humor piece), 700 words. Query with published clips. Pays $50.

Fiction: Humorous. Buys 8 mss/year. Length: 700 maximum words. Pays $50 maximum.

‡THE NEWFOUNDLAND HERALD, Sunday Herald Ltd., Box 2015, St. John's, Newfoundland A1C 5R7 Canada. (709)726-7060. Fax: (709)726-8227/6971. Editor-in-Chief: Greg Stirling. Contact: Karen Dawe, acting managing editor. 25% freelance written. Weekly entertainment magazine. "We prefer Newfoundland and Labrador-related items." Estab. 1946. Circ. 45,000. Pays on publication. Publishes ms an average of 2 months after acceptance. Byline given. Buys first North American serial, one-time or all rights. Editorial lead time 4 months. Submit seasonal material 3 months in advance. Sample copy and writer's guidelines free on request.

Nonfiction: General interest, how-to, interview/profile, travel. No opinion, humor, poetry, fiction, satire. Buys 500 mss/year. Query with published clips. Length: 700-2,500 words. Pays $50 minimum. Sometimes pays expenses of writers on assignment.

Reprints: Accepts previously published submissions.

Photos: Send photos with submission. Offers $7.50-25/photo. Captions required. Buys one-time rights.

Columns/Departments: Music (current artists), Video/Movies (recent releases/themes), TV shows (Top 20); all 1,500-2,500 words. Buys 500 mss/year. Query with published clips.

Tips: "Know something about Newfoundlanders and Labradorians—for example, travel writers should know where we like to travel."

PALMER VIDEO MAGAZINE, 1767 Morris Ave., Union NJ 07083. (908)686-3030. Fax: (908)686-2151. Editor: Susan Haney. 15% freelance written. Monthly magazine covering video and film related topics. "The *Palmer Video Magazine* is a 24-page magazine designed exclusively for Palmer Video members. It is both entertaining and informative as it pertains to film and video." Estab. 1983. Circ. 200,000. Pays 30 days after receipt of article. Publishes ms 1 month after acceptance. Makes work-for-hire assignments. Submit seasonal/holiday material 2 months in advance. Accepts simultaneous submissions. Reports in 2 months. Free sample copy and writer's guidelines.

Nonfiction: How-to (video related), interview/profile (film related), technical (video related). Special issues: Horror Films (October); Holiday Films (December); Year in Review films (January); Romance Films (February); Academy Awards (March). Buys 40 mss/year. Query with published clips. Length: 500-2,000 words. Pays $50-200 for assigned articles.

Reprints: Send typed ms with rights for sale noted and information about when and where the article previously appeared.

Photos: State availability of photos with submission. Offers no additional payment for photos accepted with ms.

Columns/Departments: Profile (interviews of profiles on actors/directors, etc.), 1,000 words; Cinemascope (article pertaining to film genre), 1,000-2,000 words. Buys 40 mss/year. Query with published clips. Pays $50-200.

PEOPLE, Time Inc. Magazine Co., Time & Life Bldg., Rockefeller Center, New York NY 10020. (212)522-1212. Fax: (212)522-0536. Publisher: Nora McAniff. Weekly magazine covering celebrities and other interesting people. "*People* is a guide to who and what is hot in the arts, science, business, politics, television, movies, books, records and sports." Estab. 1984. Circ. 2,284,000. This magazine did not respond to our request for information. Query before submitting.

PREMIERE, Hachette Filipacchi Magazines, 1633 Broadway, New York NY 10019. (212)767-5400. Fax: (212)767-5444. Publisher: Mark Furlong. Monthly magazine covering movies. "*Premiere* is a magazine for young adults that goes behind the scenes of movies in release and production. Feature articles include interviews, profiles plus film commentary and analysis. Monthly departments provide coverage of the movie business, video technology and hardware, home video, film and video reviews/releases, movie music/scoring and books." Estab. 1987. Circ. 617,000. This magazine did not respond to our request for information. Query before submitting.

‡PRE-VUE ENTERTAINMENT MAGAZINE, National Pre-Vue Network, 7825 Fay Ave., La Jolla CA 92037. (619)456-5577. Editor: Penny Langford. 100% freelance written. Bimonthly magazine covering movies, music celebrities. Estab. 1990. Circ. 200,000. Sometimes pays on acceptance, sometimes up to 30 days after publication. Byline given. Offers 10% kill fee. Buys one-time rights. Editorial lead time 1 month. Submit seasonal material 2 months in advance. Accepts simultaneous submissions. Reports in 2 weeks on queries. Sample copy for 6×9 SAE with 55¢ postage. Writer's guidelines free on request.
Nonfiction: General interest, interview/profile, photo feature. Buys 30 mss/year. Query with published clips. Length: 225-1,200 words. Pays $100-300 for assigned articles; $75-200 for unsolicited articles. Sometimes pays expenses of writers on assignment.
Photos: State availability of photos with submission. Reviews transparencies. Negotiates payment individually. Captions, model releases, identification of subjects required. Buys one-time rights.
Columns/Departments: Interviews (personal lifestyles) 225-1,200 words. Buys 6-12 mss/year. Query with published clips. Pays $25-75.
Fillers: Facts, gags to be illustrated by cartoonist, newsbreaks, short humor. Buys 6/year. Length: 25-75 words. Pays $25-50.
Tips: "If writers have an appealing writing style which shows personality as well as well-thought-out and well researched text, I tend to request more from them or give them assignments."

RIGHT ON!, Sterling's Magazines, 233 Park Ave. S., New York NY 10003. (212)780-3519. Editor: Cynthia Horner. 10% freelance written. Monthly black entertainment magazine for teenagers and young adults. Circ. 250,000. Pays on publication. Publishes ms an average of 3 months after acceptance. Byline given. Buys all rights. Submit seasonal/holiday material 4 months in advance. Reports in 1 month on queries.
Nonfiction: Interview/profile. "We only publish entertainment-oriented stories or celebrity interviews." Buys 15-20 mss/year. Query with or without published clips, or send ms. Length: 500-4,000 words. Pays $50-200. Sometimes pays the expenses of writers on assignment.
Photos: State availability of photos with submission. Reviews transparencies and 8×10 b&w prints. Offers no additional payment for photos accepted with ms. Identification of subjects required. Buys one-time rights or all rights.

SOAP OPERA DIGEST, K-III Magazines, 45 W. 25 St., New York NY 10010. Editor: Lynn Leahey. Deputy Editor: Jason Bonderoff. Managing Editor: Roberta Caploe. 5% freelance written. Bimonthly magazine covering soap operas. "Extensive knowledge of daytime and prime time soap operas is required." Estab. 1975. Circ. 1,400,000. **Pays on acceptance.** Publishes ms an average of 3 months after acceptance. Byline given. Offers 30% kill fee. Buys first North American serial and second serial (reprint) rights. Submit seasonal/holiday material 4 months in advance. Reports in 1 month.
Nonfiction: Interview/profile. No essays. Buys 10 mss/year. Query with published clips. Length: 1,000-2,000 words. Pays $250-500 for assigned articles; $150-250 for unsolicited articles. Pays meal expenses of writers on assignment.
Photos: Offers no additional payment for photos accepted with ms. Buys all rights.

‡SPORTSCASTER, The Complete Guide to Televised Sports, Liberty/Fox Sports, 2080 N. Hwy. 360, Suite 200, Grand Prairie TX 75050. (800)766-9763. Fax: (214)988-1088. Editor: Richard M. Hill. Contact: Bruce Wernick, production manager. 65-70% freelance written. Monthly magazine covering sports and entertainment television. "We produce television entertainment guides and include insightful editorial on current television entertainment and what will be shown." Estab. 1992. Circ. 25,000. Byline given. Makes work-for-hire assignments. Editorial lead time 2 months. Submit seasonal material 3 months in advance. Accepts simultaneous submissions. Sample copy and writer's guidelines free on request.
Nonfiction: Exposé, general interest, humor, inspirational, opinion, photo feature. No commentary. Buys 12-16 mss/year. Query. Length: 500-3,000 words. Pays $300-1,000 for assigned articles. Sometimes pays expenses of writers on assignment.
Photos: State availability of photos with submission. Reviews negatives. Negotiates payment individually. Identification of subjects required. Buys one-time rights.
Columns/Departments: John Nagle, senior writer. Pay-Per-View (on all these we would need); Movies (editorial written highlights); Specials (the events the upcoming months); all 500-1,000 words. Buys 12 mss/year. Query. Pays $200-1,000.
Tips: "Call Bruce Wernick at (214)868-1400 and sell yourself to him."

TDR; The Drama Review: The Journal of Performance Studies, New York University, 721 Broadway, 6th Floor, New York NY 10003. (212)998-1626. Fax: (212)995-4571. E-mail: tdr@nyu.edu. Managing Editor: Marta Ulvaeus. Editor: Richard Schechner. Contact: Mariellen R. Sandford, associate editor. 95% freelance written. Works with a small number of new/unpublished writers each year. Quarterly magazine with "emphasis not only on theater but also dance, ritual, musical performance, performance art and other facets of performative behavior. For the theater and art community, students and professors of anthropology, performance studies and related fields. Political material is welcome." Estab. 1955. Circ. 5,000. Pays on publication. Submit material 1 year in advance. Reports in 3 months. Publishes ms an average of 6 months after acceptance. Sample copy for $10 (from MIT Press). Free writer's guidelines.

Nonfiction: Buys 10 mss/issue. Query by letter only. Pay determined by page count. Submit both hard copy and disk (Word or WordPerfect).

Reprints: Accepts previously published submissions (if published in another language).

Photos: State availability of photos and artwork with submission. Prefers 5×7 b&w photos. Captions required.

Tips: "*TDR* is a place where contrasting ideas and opinions meet. A forum for writing about performances and the social, economic and political contexts in which performances happen. The editors want interdisciplinary, intercultural, multivocal, eclectic submissions."

TV GUIDE, 1211 Avenue of the Americas, New York NY 10036. Contact: Editor (National Section). 50% freelance written. Prefers to work with published/established writers but works with a small number of new/unpublished writers each year. Weekly. Estab. 1953. Circ. 13,000,000.

Nonfiction: "The national editorial section looks at the shows, the stars and covers the medium's impact on news, sports, politics, literature, the arts, science and social issues through reports, profiles, features and commentaries.

VIDEO, Hachette Filipacchi, 1633 Broadway, New York NY 10019. (212)767-6000. Fax: (212)767-5615. Editor-in-Chief: Bill Wolfe. 50% freelance written. Prefers to work with published/established writers; works with a small number of new/unpublished writers each year. Monthly magazine covering home video equipment, technology, CD-ROM, laser discs and prerecorded tapes. Circ. 350,000. **Pays on acceptance.** Publishes ms an average of 3 months after acceptance. Byline given. Buys first North American serial rights. Query for electronic submissions. Reports in 3 weeks on queries; 1 month on mss.

Nonfiction: Buys 50 mss/year. Query with published clips. Pays $300-1,000. Sometimes pays the expenses of writers on assignment.

Tips: "The entire feature area is open to freelancers. Write a brilliant query and send samples of published articles."

ETHNIC/MINORITY

Ideas and concerns of interest to specific nationalities and religions are covered by publications in this category. General interest lifestyle magazines for these groups are also included. Many ethnic publications are locally-oriented or highly specialized and do not wish to be listed in a national publication such as *Writer's Market*. Query the editor of an ethnic publication with which you're familiar before submitting a manuscript, but do not consider these markets closed because they are not listed in this section. Additional markets for writing with an ethnic orientation are located in the following sections: Career, College and Alumni; Juvenile; Literary and "Little"; Men's; Women's; and Teen and Young Adult.

AIM MAGAZINE, AIM Publishing Company, 7308 S. Eberhart Ave., Chicago IL 60620-0554. (312)874-6184. Editor: Ruth Apilado. Managing Editor: Dr. Myron Apilado. Estab. 1975. 75% freelance written. Works with a small number of new/unpublished writers each year. Quarterly magazine on social betterment that promotes racial harmony and peace for high school, college and general audience. Circ. 10,000. Pays on publication. Publishes ms an average of 3 months after acceptance. Offers 60% kill fee. Not copyrighted. Buys one-time rights. Submit seasonal/holiday material 6 months in advance. Accepts simultaneous submissions. Reports in 2 months on queries. Sample copy and writer's guidelines for $4 and 9×12 SAE with $1.70 postage.

Nonfiction: Exposé (education); general interest (social significance); historical/nostalgic (Black or Indian); how-to (create a more equitable society); profile (one who is making social contributions to community); book reviews and reviews of plays "that reflect our ethnic/minority orientation." No religious material. Buys 16 mss/year. Send complete ms. Length: 500-800 words. Pays $25-35.

Photos: Reviews b&w prints. Captions, identification of subjects required.

Fiction: Ethnic, historical, mainstream, suspense. "Fiction that teaches the brotherhood of man." Buys 20 mss/year. Send complete ms. Length: 1,000-1,500 words. Pays $25-35.

Poetry: Avant-garde, free verse, light verse. No "preachy" poetry. Buys 20 poems/year. Submit maximum 5 poems. Length: 15-30 lines. Pays $3-5.

Fillers: Jokes, anecdotes, newsbreaks. Buys 30/year. Length: 50-100 words. Pays $5.
Tips: "Interview anyone of any age who unselfishly is making an unusual contribution to the lives of less fortunate individuals. Include photo and background of person. We look at the nations of the world as part of one family. Short stories and historical pieces about Blacks and Indians are the areas most open to freelancers. Subject matter of submission is of paramount concern for us rather than writing style. Articles and stories showing the similarity in the lives of people with different racial backgrounds are desired."

ALBERTA SWEETGRASS, Aboriginal Multi-Media Society of Alberta, 15001 112th Ave., Edmonton, Alberta T5M 2V6 Canada. (403)455-2945. Contact: R. John Hayes, editor. Monthly tabloid newspaper. 75% freelance written. Pays 10th of month following publication. Editorial lead time 2 months. Sample copy free. Writer's guidelines and production schedule for #10 SASE.
Nonfiction: Features, profiles, community-based stories, all with an Alberta angle (no exceptions). Usually runs 2-3 focus sections/month. Query with SASE. Length: 200-1,000 words (most often 500-800 words). Pays $3/published inch for one-source stories; $3.60 for multiple sources (reduced rate for excess editorial work). Pays expenses of writers by prior arrangement.
Photos: Reviews color or b&w prints, slides or negatives. Offers $15/b&w photo used; $50/color cover photo; $25/photo for inside color.
Tips: "We are moving from profiles to more news-hook-oriented items. Don't let our Alberta angle requirement scare you off. We've had stories from Alaska, Minnesota, the Vatican and all across Canada in the last year."

AMERICAN VISIONS, The Magazine of Afro-American Culture, 1156 15th St. NW, Suite 615, Washington DC 20005. (202)496-9593. Fax: (202)496-9851. E-mail: 72662.2631@compuserve.com. or Amvisions@i x.netcom.com. Editor: Joanne Harris. Contact: Articles Editor. 75% freelance written. Bimonthly magazine on African-American art, culture and history. "Editorial is reportorial, current, objective, 'pop-scholarly'. Audience is ages 25-54, mostly black, college educated." Estab. 1986. Circ. 125,000. Pays 30 days after publication. Publishes ms an average of 2 months after acceptance. Byline given. Offers 25% kill fee. Buys all and second serial (reprint) rights. Submit seasonal/holiday material 5 months in advance. Accepts simultaneous submissions. Reports in 2-3 months. Free sample copy and writer's guidelines with SASE.
Nonfiction: Book excerpts, general interest, historical, interview/profile literature, photo feature, travel. Publishes travel supplements—domestic, Africa, Europe, Canada, Mexico. No fiction, poetry, personal experience or opinion. Buys about 60-70 mss/year. Query with or without published clips, or send complete ms. Length: 500-2,500 words. Pays $100-600 for assigned articles; $100-400 for unsolicited articles. Sometimes pays expenses of writers on assignment.
Reprints: Accepts previously published submissions.
Photos: State availability of photos with submission. Reviews contact sheets, 3×5 transparencies, and 3×5 or 8×10 prints. Offers $15 minimum. Identification of subjects required. Buys one-time rights.
Columns/Departments: Books, Cuisine, Film, Music, Profile, Geneology, Computer Technology, Travel, 750-1,750 words. Buys about 40 mss/year. Query or send complete ms. Pays $100-400.
Tips: "Little-known but terribly interesting information about black history and culture is desired. Aim at an upscale audience. Send ms with credentials." Looking for writers who are enthusiastic about their topics.

ARMENIAN INTERNATIONAL MAGAZINE, 207 S. Brand Blvd., Suite 205, Glendale CA 91204. (818)246-7979. Fax: (818)246-0088. E-mail: aim4m@aol.com. Editor: Salpi H. Ghazarian. 50% freelance written. Monthly magazine about the Causasus and the global Armenian diaspora. "Special reports and features about politics, business, education, culture, interviews and profiles." Estab. 1989. Circ. 10,000. Pays on publication. Publishes ms an average of 3 months after acceptance. Byline given. Buys all rights. Reports in 2 weeks on queries; 6 weeks on mss.
Nonfiction: General interest, historical, interview/profile, photo feature and travel. Special issue: Armenian restaurants around the world. Buys 60 mss/year. Query with published clips. Length: 600-1,200 words. Pays $50-400 for assigned articles; $50-200 for unsolicited articles. Sometimes pays expenses of writers on assignment.
Photos: State availability of photos with submission. Reviews negatives, transparencies and prints. Offers $10-50/photo. Captions and identification of subjects required.

BLACK DIASPORA MAGAZINE, (formerly *Class* magazine), Black Diaspora Communications Ltd., 900 Broadway, 8th Floor, New York NY 10003. (212)477-1440. Fax: (212)477-3649. Executive Editor: Denolyn Carroll. Contact: Brennon Marcano and Michelle Phipps, associate editors. 25% freelance written. Monthly "general interest publication geared toward the entire Black Diaspora between ages 18-49." Estab. 1979. Circ. 250,000. Pays 45 days after publication. Byline given. Buys first North American serial and second serial (reprint) rights. Submit seasonal/holiday material 3 months in advance. Reports in 6 weeks. Sample copy for 9×12 SAE with 4 first-class stamps. Writer's guidelines for #10 SASE.
Nonfiction: Exposé, general interest, historical/nostalgic, interview/profile, religious, travel, international, In Focus. Query with published clips. Length: 500-1,300 words. Pays 10¢/word maximum. Sometimes pays expenses of writers on assignment.

Photos: Send photos with submission. Offers no additional payment for photos accepted with ms. Captions, model releases and identification of subjects required. Buys all rights.
Columns/Departments: Length: 500-1,300 words. Pays 10¢/word maximum.
Poetry: Buys 10-20 poems/year. Submit maximum 5 poems. Pays $10 maximum.

THE B'NAI B'RITH INTERNATIONAL, JEWISH MONTHLY, 1640 Rhode Island Ave. NW, Washington DC 20036. (202)857-6645. Fax: (202)296-1092. E-mail: jrubin@bnaibrith.org. Website: http://bnaibrith.org/ijm. Editor: Jeff Rubin. 50% freelance written. Magazine published 8 times/year covering Jewish affairs. Estab. 1886. Circ. 200,000. **Pays on acceptance.** Publishes ms an average of 3 months after acceptance. Byline given. Kill fee depends on rate of payment. Buys first North American serial rights. Submit seasonal/holiday material 6 months in advance. Reports in 1 month. Sample copy for $2 and 9×13 SAE with 2 first-class stamps. Free writer's guidelines.
Nonfiction: Book excerpts, essay, exposé, general interest, historical, interview/profile, photo feature. Buys 20-30 mss/year. Query with published clips. Length: 750-3,000 words. Pays $50-750 for assigned articles; $50-500 for unsolicited articles. Sometimes pays expenses of writers on assignment.
Photos: State availability of photos with submission. Reviews contact sheets, 2×3 transparencies and prints. Payment depends on quality and type of photograph. Identification of subjects required. Buys one-time rights.
Tips: "Writers should submit clips with their queries. The best way to break in to the *Jewish Monthly* is to submit a range of good story ideas accompanied by clips. We aim to establish relationships with writers and we tend to be loyal. All sections are equally open."

CONGRESS MONTHLY, American Jewish Congress, 15 E. 84th St., New York NY 10028. (212)879-4500. Editor: Maier Deshell. 90% freelance written. Bimonthly magazine covering topics of concern to the American Jewish community representing a wide range of views. Distributed mainly to the members of the American Jewish Congress. "Readers are intellectual, Jewish, involved." Estab. 1933. Circ. 35,000. Pays on publication. Publishes ms an average of 3 months after acceptance. Byline given. Buys one-time rights. Submit seasonal/holiday material 2 months in advance. Reports in 2 months.
Nonfiction: General interest ("current topical issues geared toward our audience"). No technical material. Send complete ms. Length: 2,000 words maximum. Pays $100-150/article.
Photos: State availability of photos. Reviews b&w prints. "Photos are paid for with payment for ms."
Columns/Departments: Book, film, art and music reviews. Send complete ms. Length: 1,000 words maximum. Pays $100-150/article.

EBONY MAGAZINE, 820 S. Michigan Ave., Chicago IL 60605. (312)322-9200. Publisher: John H. Johnson. Executive Editor: Lerone Bennett, Jr. Monthly magazine. "*Ebony* is a black-oriented, general, picture magazine dealing primarily with contemporary topics." Estab. 1945. Circ. 1,928,000. *Ebony* is completely staff-written.

‡EMERGE, Black America's Newsmagazine, Emerge Communications, Inc., 1 BET Plaza, 1900 W Place NE, Washington DC 20018. (202)608-2093. Fax: (202)608-2598. Editor: George E. Curry. Managing Editor: Florestine Purnell. 80% freelance written. African-American news monthly. "*Emerge* is a general interest publication reporting on a wide variety of issues from health to sports to politics, almost anything that affects Black Americans. Our audience is comprised primarily of African-Americans 25-49, individual income of $35,000, professional and college educated." Estab. 1989. Circ. 200,000. **Pays on acceptance.** Publishes ms an average of 3 months after acceptance. Byline given. Offers 25% kill fee. Buys first North American serial rights. Submit seasonal material 6 months in advance. Query for electronic submissions. Reports in 5 weeks. Sample copy for $3 and 9×12 SAE. Writer's guidelines for #10 SAE with 2 first-class stamps.
 • Ranked as one of the best markets for freelance writers in *Writer's Yearbook*'s annual "Top 100 Markets," January 1996.
Nonfiction: Essays, exposé, general interest, historical/nostalgic, humor, interview/profile, technical, travel. "We are not interested in standard celebrity pieces that lack indepth reporting as well as analysis, or pieces dealing with interpersonal relationships." Query with published clips. Length: 600-2,000 words. Pays 60-75¢/word.
Photos: State availability of photos with submission. Reviews contact sheets. Negotiated payment. Captions, model releases, and indentification of subjects required. Buys one-time rights.

ALWAYS SUBMIT unsolicited manuscripts or queries with a self-addressed, stamped envelope (SASE) within your country or a self-addressed envelope with International Reply Coupons (IRC) purchased from the post office for other countries.

Columns/Departments: Query.

Tips: "If a writer doesn't have a completed manuscript, then he should mail a query letter with clips. No phone calls. First-time authors should be extremely sensitive to the *Emerge* style and fit within these guidelines as closely as possible. We do not like to re-write or re-edit pieces. We are a news monthly so articles must be written with a three month lead time in mind. If an assignment is given and another one is desired, writers must assist our research department during fact checking process and closing. Read at least six issues of the publication before submitting ideas."

FILIPINAS, A magazine for all Filipinos, Filipinas Publishing, Inc., 655 Sutter St., Suite 333, San Francisco CA 94102. (415)563-5878. Fax: (415)292-5993. E-mail: filmagazin@aol.com. Website: http://www.filipinas.com. Editor: Rene Ciria-Cruz. Monthly magazine focused on Filipino American affairs. "*Filipinas* answers the lack of mainstream media coverage of Filipinos in America. It targets both Filipino immigrants and American-born Filipinos, gives in-depth coverage of political, social, cultural events in The Philippines and in the Filipino American community. Features role models, history, travel, food and leisure, issues and controversies." Estab. 1992. Circ. 25,000. Pays on publication. Publishes ms an average of 3 months after acceptance. Byline given. Offers $10 kill fee. Buys first rights or all rights. Editorial lead time 2 months. Submit seasonal material 4 months in advance. Reports in 5 weeks on queries; 18 months on mss. Sample copy for $5. Writer's guidelines for 9½×4 SAE with 1 first-class stamp.
Nonfiction: Exposé, general interest, historical/nostalgic, how-to, humor, interview/profile, personal experience, travel. No academic papers. Buys 80-100 mss/year. Query with published clips. Length: 800-1,500 words. Pays $50-100. Sometimes pays writers other than cash payment "per specific agreement with writer."
Photos: State availability of photos with submission. Reviews 2¼×2¼ and 4×5 transparencies. Offers $15-35/photo. Captions and model releases required. Buys one-time rights.
Columns/Departments: Entree (reviews of Filipino restaurants), 1,200 words; Cultural Currents (Filipino traditions, beliefs), 1,500 words. Query with published clips. Pays $50-75.

‡GERMAN LIFE, Zeitgeist Publishing, 1 Corporate Dr., Grantsville MD 21536. (301)895-3859. Fax: (301)895-5029. E-mail: gwwc14a@prodigy.com. Website: http://langlab.uta.edu/germ/German_Life/. Editor: Heidi L. Whitesell. 50% freelance written. Bimonthly magazine covering Germany. "*German Life* is for all interested in the diversity of German culture, past and present, and in the various ways that the United States (and North America in general) has been shaped by its German element. The magazine is dedicated to solid reporting on cultural, historical, social and political events." Estab. 1994. Circ. 50,000. Pays on publication. Publishes ms an average of 3 months after acceptance. Byline given. Buys first North American serial rights. Editorial lead time 4 months. Submit seasonal material 4 months in advance. Reports in 6 weeks on queries; 3 months on mss. Sample copy for $3.95 and SAE with 4 first-class stamps. Writer's guidelines free on request.
Nonfiction: Exposé, general interest, historical/nostalgic, how-to (German crafts, recipes, gardening), interview/profile, opinion (only for final column), photo feature, travel. Special issues: Oktoberfest-related (October); seasonal/holiday relative to Germany (December); travel to German-speaking Europe (April). Buys 60 mss/year. Query with published clips. Length: 1,000-2,500 words. Pays $200-500 for assigned articles; $200-350 for unsolicited articles. Sometimes pays expenses of writers on assignment.
Photos: State availability of photos with submission. Reviews color transparencies, 5×7 color or b&w prints. Offers no additional payment for photos accepted with ms. Identification of subjects required. Buys one-time rights.
Columns/Departments: German-Americana (regards specific German-American communities, organizations and/or events past or present), 1,500 words; Profile (portrays prominent Germans, Americans, or German-Americans), 800 words; At Home (cuisine, home design, gardening, crafts, etc. relating to Germany), 800 words; Library (reviews of books, videos, CDs, etc.), 300 words. Buys 30 mss/year. Query with published clips. Pays $130-300.
Fillers: Anecdotes, facts, newsbreaks, short humor. Length: 100-300 words. Pays $50-150.
Tips: "The best queries include several informative proposals. Ideally, clips show a background in a German-related topic, but more importantly, a flair for 'telling stories.' Majority of articles present a human interest angle. Even though *German Life* is a special interest magazine, writers should avoid overemphasizing autobiographical experiences/stories."

HADASSAH MAGAZINE, 50 W. 58th St., New York NY 10019. Executive Editor: Alan M. Tigay. 90% freelance written. Works with small number of new/unpublished writers each year. Monthly (except combined issues June/July and August/September). Circ. 334,000. Buys first rights (with travel and family articles, buys all rights). Sample copy and writer's guidelines for SASE.
Nonfiction: Primarily concerned with Israel, Jewish communities around the world and American civic affairs as relates to the Jewish community. "We are also open to art stories that explore trends in Jewish art, literature, theater, etc. Will not assign/commission a story to a first-time writer for Hadassah." Buys 10 unsolicited mss/year. No phone queries. Send query and writing samples. Length: 1,500-2,000 words. Pays minimum $350, $75 for reviews. Sometimes pays the expenses of writers on assignment.

Photos: "We buy photos only to illustrate articles, with the exception of outstanding color from Israel which we use on our covers. We pay $175 and up for a suitable cover photo." Offers $50 for first photo; $35 for each additional. "Always interested in striking cover (color) photos, especially of Israel and Jerusalem."
Columns/Departments: "We have a Family column and a Travel column, but a query for topic or destination should be submitted first to make sure the area is of interest and the story follows our format."
Fiction: Joan Michel. Short stories with strong plots and positive Jewish values. No personal memoirs, "schmaltzy" or women's magazine fiction. "We continue to buy very little fiction because of a backlog." Length: 3,000 words maximum. Pays $300 minimum. "Require proper size SASE."
Tips: "We are interested in reading articles that offer an American perspective on Jewish affairs (1,500 words). For example, a look at the presidential candidates from a Jewish perspective. Send query of topic first."

THE HIGHLANDER, Angus J. Ray Associates, Inc., P.O. Box 397, Barrington IL 60011-0397. (847)382-1035. Editor: Angus J. Ray. 50% freelance written. Works with a small number of new/unpublished writers each year. Bimonthly magazine covering Scottish history, clans, genealogy, travel/history, and Scottish/American activities. Estab. 1961. Circ. 40,000. **Pays on acceptance.** Publishes ms an average of 6 months after acceptance. Byline given. Buys first North American serial and second serial (reprint) rights. Submit seasonal/holiday material 6 months in advance. Reports in 1 month. Sample copy for $3. Free writer's guidelines.
Nonfiction: Historical/nostalgic. "No fiction; no articles unrelated to Scotland." Buys 50 mss/year. Query. Length: 750-2,000 words. Pays $75-150.
Reprints: Send tearsheet or photocopy of article. Pays 50% of amount paid for an original article.
Photos: State availability of photos. Pays $5-10 for 8×10 b&w prints or transparencies. Reviews b&w contact sheets. Identification of subjects required. Buys one-time rights.
Tips: "Submit something that has appeared elsewhere."

HISPANIC, 98 San Jacinto Blvd., Suite 1150, Austin TX 78701. (512)476-5599. Fax: (512)320-1943. E-mail: editor@hisp.com. Publisher: Alfredo J. Estrada. Contact: Managing Editor. 80% freelance written. Monthly English magazine for the US-Hispanic community. "*Hispanic* is a general interest publication emphasizing political issues, business news and cultural affairs." Estab. 1987. Circ. 250,000. Pays on publication. Publishes ms an average of 4 months after acceptance. Byline given. Offers 25% kill fee. Buys all rights, puts some features on the Internet (*Hispanic Online*).
Nonfiction: General interest, business news, career strategies, investigative pieces, opinion, personal essays. Buys 200 mss/year. Query in writing or submit ms on spec. Length: 1,500-3,000 words. Pays $300-500. Pays phone expenses, "but these must be cleared with editors first."
Photos: State availability of photos with submission. Reviews transparencies. Offers $25-500/photo. Captions, model releases, identification of subjects required. Buys one-time rights.
Columns/Departments: Forum (opinion and analysis), reviews, money, cars, destinations, culture, politics, business. Pays $50-175.

INSIDE, The Jewish Exponent Magazine, Jewish Federation of Greater Philadelphia, 226 S. 16th St., Philadelphia PA 19102. (215)893-5700. Fax: (215)546-3957. E-mail: expent@netaxs.com. Contact: Jane Biberman, editor. Managing Editor: Martha Ledger. 95% freelance written (by assignment). Works with published/established writers and a small number of new/unpublished writers each year. Quarterly Jewish regional magazine for a sophisticated and upscale Jewish readership 25 years of age and older. Estab. 1979. Circ. 75,000. Pays on publication. Offers 20% kill fee. Publishes ms an average of 2 months after acceptance. Byline given. Buys first rights. Submit seasonal/holiday material 3 months in advance. Reports in 2 weeks on queries; 1 month on mss. Sample copy for $5 and 9×12 SAE. Writer's guidelines for #10 SASE.
Nonfiction: Book excerpts, general interest, historical/nostalgic, humor, interview/profile, personal experience, religious. Philadelphia angle desirable. Buys 12 unsolicited mss/year. Query. Length: 1,000-3,500 words. Pays $100-1,000.
Reprints: Send photocopy of article or short story. Pays $50-100. Publishes novel excerpts.
Photos: State availability of photos with submission. Identification of subjects required. Buys first rights.
Fiction: Short stories.
Tips: "Personalities—very well known—and serious issues of concern to Jewish community needed."

‡**ISRAEL HORIZONS, Progressive Zionist Quarterly**, Hashomer Hatzair, 224 W. 35th St., Suite 403, New York NY 10001. (212)868-0377. Fax: (212)868-0364. Editor: Don Goldstein. 15% freelance written. Quarterly magazine covering Israel and the American Jewish community. "We have an educated and intellectual readership. We cover political, social and economic issues concerning Israel and the American Jewish community from a progressive viewpoint. Our major concern is the peace process. We are also very interested in the Kibbutz movement." Estab. 1952. Circ. 3,000. Pays on publication. Publishes ms an average of 3 months after acceptance. Byline given. Buys one-time or second serial (reprint) rights. Editorial lead time 2 months. Submit seasonal material 3 months in advance. Reports in 3 weeks on queries; 1 month on mss.

Nonfiction: Essays, historical/nostalgic, interview/profile, opinion, personal experience. Buys 8 mss/year. Send complete ms. Length: 800-3,000 words. Pays $25-50.
Reprints: Accepts previously published submissions.
Photos: State availability of photos with submission. Offers no additional payment for photos accepted with ms. Identification of subjects required.
Columns/Departments: Book, Film Reviews (Jewish, Israeli, progressive political), 1,000 words. Buys 3 mss/year. Pays $25-50.
Poetry: Rochelle Ratner, Jonathan Shevin, poetry consultants. Free verse, light verse, traditional. Buys 6 poems/year. Submit maximum 2 poems. Length: 12-50 lines. Pays $10-20.

JEWISH ACTION, Union of Orthodox Jewish Congregations of America, 333 Seventh Ave., 18th Floor, New York NY 10001-5072. (212)563-4000, ext. 146, 147. Fax: (212)564-9058. Editor: Charlotte Friedland. Assistant Editor: Elissa Feldman. 80% freelance written. "Quarterly magazine offering a vibrant approach to Jewish issues, Orthodox lifestyle and values." Circ. 30,000. Pays 4-6 weeks after publication. Byline given. Submit seasonal/holiday material 4 months in advance. Reports in 3 months. Sample copy and guidelines for 9×12 SAE with 5 first-class stamps.
Nonfiction: Current Jewish issues, history, biography, art, inspirational, humor, book reviews. Query with published clips. Length: 1,500-2,500 words. Pays $100-300 for assigned articles; $75-150 for unsolicited articles. Buys 30-40 mss/year.
Fiction: Must have relevance to Orthodox reader. Length: 1,000-2,000 words.
Poetry: Limited number accepted. Pays $25-75.
Columns/Departments: Student Voice (about Jewish life on campus), 1,000 words. Buys 4 mss/year. Just Between Us (personal opinion on current Jewish life and issues), 1,000 words. Buys 4 mss/year. Jewish Living (section pertaining to holidays, contemporary Jewish practices), 1,000-1,500 words. Buys 10 mss/year.
Photos: Send photos with submission. Identification of subjects required.
Tips: "Remember that your reader is well-educated and has a strong commitment to Orthodox Judaism. Articles on the Holocaust, holidays, Israel and other common topics should offer a fresh insight."

‡JEWISH AFFAIRS, P.O. Box 87557, Houghton 872041 South Africa. Fax: 27 + 11 + 646 + 4940. E-mail: 071jos@muse.arts.wits.ac.za. Editor: Joseph Sherman. 95% freelance written. Quarterly magazine covering Jewish issues throughout the world, especially in South Africa. "*JA* is an intellectual quarterly devoted to issues that affect the Jewish community in South Africa and elsewhere. It is non-political and aims to promote an awareness of Jewish cultural, intellectual and social achievements past and present, and critically to examine the role Jews are playing in the world today." Estab. 1941. Circ. 2,000. **Pays on acceptance.** Publishes ms an average of 1 year after acceptance. Byline given. Buys first rights. Editorial lead time 1 year. Submit seasonal material 6 months in advance. Accepts simultaneous submissions. Reports in 1 month on mss. Sample copy for $10.
Nonfiction: Book excerpts, essays, historical/nostalgic, interview/profile, opinion, personal experience, religious. Buys 100 mss/year. Send complete ms. Length: 2,000-6,000 words. Pays $ 50. Pays writers with contributor copies.
Fiction: Ethnic, historical, humorous, mainstream, novel excerpts, religious. Buys 6-20 mss/year. Send complete ms. Length: 1,500-6,000 words. Pays $50 maximum.
Poetry: Accepts the following types of poetry: avant-garde, free verse, light verse, traditional. Buys 25-35 poems/year. Submit no more than 5 poems at one time. Pays $5-10.
Tips: "Research papers should show evidence of scholarly preparation and make a fresh contribution to the subject. Unusual or little known areas of Jewish cultural life, history, thought or current affairs will be especially favored. Welcomes potential articles and top quality fiction and poetry. *JA* has published Nadine Gordimer, Lionel Abrahams, Don Mattera and many leading scholars, so we're looking for the best."

‡MANGAJIN, Japanese Pop Culture and Language Learning, Mangajin, Inc., 200 N. Cobb Pkwy, Suite 421, Marietta GA 30062. Fax: (770)590-0890. Website: http://www.mangajin.com. Editor: V.P. Simmons. 10-20% freelance written. Magazine published 10 times/year. "Japanese pop culture provides a window on Japanese society and language. We look at contemporary Japanese culture as accessible, understandable, and entertaining. No inscrutable Orient here." Estab. 1990. Circ. 28,000. Pays on publication. Byline given. Offers $50-100 kill fee. Buys all rights or makes work-for-hire assignments. Editorial lead time 3 months. Submit seasonal material 3 months in advance. Reports in 2 weeks on queries; 1 month on mss.
Nonfiction: General interest, humor, interview/profile, new product. No "My experience in Japan" articles. Buys 15 mss/year. Query. Length: 500-2,000 words. Pays $150-850 for assigned articles; $150-500 for unsolicited articles. Sometimes pays expenses of writers on assignment.
Reprints: Accepts previously published submissions.
Photos: State availability of photos with submission. Netotiates payment individually. Buys all rights.
Columns/Departments: Virginia Murray, associate editor. Book Reviews (Japan-related books), 750 words; Computer Corner (Japan-oriented software), 750 words. Buys 15 mss/year. Query. Pays $125-250.

‡**MOMENT, The Magazine of Jewish Culture & Opinion**, Jewish Educational Ventures & Biblical Archaeology Society, 4710 41st St. NW, Washington DC 20016. (202)364-3300. E-mail: basmom@clark.net. Publisher/Editor: Hershel Shanks. Managing Editor: Suzanne Singer. Contact: Andrew Silow-Carrol, senior editor. 90% freelance written. Bimonthly magazine covering Jewish culture and opinion (US and abroad). "*Moment* is an independent Jewish bimonthly magazine. We print cultural, political, historical, religious and 'lifestyle' articles relating to the North American Jewish community and Israel." Estab. 1975. Circ. 70,000. Pays on publication. Publishes ms an average of 6 months after acceptance. Byline given. Buys first North American serial rights. Editorial lead time 3 months. Submit seasonal material 3-6 months in advance. Accepts simultaneous submissions. Reports in 1 month on queries; 2 months on mss. Sample copy for $4.50 and SAE. Writer's guidelines free on request.

Nonfiction: Book excerpts, essays, interview/profile, opinion, religious. Buys 60-80 mss/year. Query with published clips. Length: 800 words. Pays $40-1,100 for assigned articles; $40-500 for unsolicited articles. Sometimes pays expenses of writers on assignment.

Photos: Freelancers should state availability of photos with submission. Negotiates payment individually. Identification of subjects required. Buys one-time rights.

Columns/Departments: Stacy Freed, assistant editor. Guest Column (personal/opinion), 850-1,000 words; Holiday (seasonal celebrations), 850-1,500 words; Responsa (rabbinic response to a query), 850-1,000 words. Buys 15 mss/year. Query with published clips. Pays $150-250.

NA'AMAT WOMAN, Magazine of NA'AMAT USA, the Women's Labor Zionist Organization of America, NA'AMAT USA, 200 Madison Ave., New York NY 10016. (212)725-8010. Editor: Judith A. Sokoloff. 80% freelance written. Magazine published 5 times/year covering Jewish themes and issues; Israel; women's issues; and social, political and economic issues. Estab. 1926. Circ. 25,000. Pays on publication. Byline given. Not copyrighted. Buys first North American serial, one-time, first serial and second serial (reprint) rights to book excerpts and makes work-for-hire assignments. Reports in 3 months. Writer's guidelines for SASE.

Nonfiction: Exposé, general interest (Jewish), historical/nostalgic, interview/profile, opinion, personal experience, photo feature, travel, art and music. "All articles must be of particular interest to the Jewish community." Buys 35 mss/year. Query with clips of published work or send complete ms. Pays 10¢/word.

Photos: State availability of photos. Pays $10-30 for 4×5 or 5×7 prints. Captions, identification of subjects required. Buys one-time rights.

Columns/Departments: Film and book reviews with Jewish themes. Buys 20-25 mss/year. Query with clips of published work or send complete ms. Pays 10¢/word.

Fiction: Historical/nostalgic, humorous, women-oriented and novel excerpts. "Good intelligent fiction with Jewish slant. No maudlin nostalgia or trite humor." Buys 3 mss/year. Send complete ms. Length: 1,200-3,000 words. Pays 10¢/word.

NATIVE PEOPLES MAGAZINE, The Arts and Lifeways, 5333 N. Seventh St., Suite C-224, Phoenix AZ 85014-2804. (602)252-2236. Fax: (602)265-3113. E-mail: native_peoples@amcolor.com. Website: http://www.atiin.com/native_peoples/. Contact: Rebeca Withers, managing editor. Editor: Gary Avey. Quarterly full-color magazine on Native Americans. "The primary purpose of this magazine is to offer a sensitive portrayal of the arts and lifeways of native peoples of the Americas." Estab. 1987. Circ. 120,000. Pays on publication. Byline given. Buys one-time rights. Reports in 1 month on queries; 2 months on mss. Sample copy for 9×12 SAE with 6 first-class stamps. Free writer's guidelines and sample copy. "Extremely high quality reproduction with full-color throughout."

Nonfiction: Book excerpts, historical/nostalgic, interview/profile, personal experience, photo feature. Buys 45 mss/year. Query with published clips. Length: 1,800-2,200 words. Pays 25¢/word. Publishes nonfiction book excerpts.

Photos: State availability of photos with submission. Reviews transparencies (all formats). Offers $45-150 per page rates. Identification of subjects required. Buys one-time rights.

THIRD FORCE MAGAZINE, Issues & Actions in Communities of Color, Center for Third World Organizing, 1218 E. 21st St., Oakland CA 94606. (510)533-7583. Fax: (510)533-0923. E-mail: ctwo@igc.apc .org. Editor/Publisher: John Anner. Contact: Andrea Lewis, senior editor. 65% freelance written. Bimonthly magazine covering communities of color, grassroots organizing, low-income communities. "Must reflect knowledge and understanding of issues in various communities of color. Writers of color are especially encouraged to submit queries. Approximately 70% of articles are written by authors of color." Estab. 1984. Circ. 3,000. Pays on publication. Publishes ms an average of 3 months after acceptance. Byline given. Offers 40% kill fee. Buys first North American serial rights. Editorial lead time 3 months. Submit seasonal material 4 months in advance. Reports in 6 weeks on queries; 2 months on mss. Sample copy and writer's guidelines free on request.

Nonfiction: Essays, exposé, general interest, historical, interview/profile, opinion, photo feature. Special issues: 2 each year. Buys 40 mss/year. Query with published clips or writing samples. Length: 700-3,500 words. Pays $150 minimum plus 1 year subscription. Sometimes pays expenses of writers on assignment.

Reprints: Accepts previously published submissions.

Photos: State availability of photos with submissions. Negotiates payment individually. Captions, identification of subjects required. Buys one-time rights.

Columns/Departments: Editorial/Commentary (political, cultural, social), 800 words; Historical (histories of organizing or other issues in communities of color), 1,000 words. Buys 6 mss/year. Query with published clips or send complete ms. Pay negotiable.

Fillers: Timely political/social cartoons (strip or single panel) or illustrations. Buys 6/year. Pay negotiable.

Tips: "The best way for writers to break in is to write or propose a short feature about a particular political struggle or grassroots campaign that the writer is familiar with. Authors of short features are often assigned longer features. Queries should be concise and clear and should include information on the writer's experience and expertise."

THE UKRAINIAN WEEKLY, Ukrainian National Association, 30 Montgomery St., Jersey City NJ 07302-3821. (201)434-0237. Website: http://world.std.com/~sabre/UKRAINE.html. Editor-in-Chief: Roma Hadzewycz. 30% freelance written (mostly by a corps of regular contributors). Weekly tabloid covering news and issues of concern to Ukrainian community, primarily in North America but also around the world, and events in Ukraine. "We have news bureaus in Kyiv, capital of Ukraine, and in Toronto." Estab. 1933. Circ. 11,000. Pays on publication. Publishes ms an average of 2 months after acceptance. Byline given. Buys first North American serial and second serial (reprint) rights or makes work-for-hire assignments. Submit seasonal/holiday material 1 month in advance. Reports in 1 month. Free sample copy for 9×12 SAE with 3 first-class stamps.

Nonfiction: Book excerpts, essays, exposé, general interest, historical/nostalgic, interview/profile, opinion, personal experience, photo feature, news events. Special issues: Easter, Christmas, anniversary of Ukraine's independence (August 24, 1991) (proclamation), student scholarships, anniversary of Chornobyl nuclear accident and year-end review of news. Buys 80 mss/year. Query with published clips. Length: 500-2,000 words. Pays $45-100 for assigned articles. Pays $25-100 for unsolicited articles. Sometimes pays the expenses of writers on assignment.

Reprints: Send typed ms with rights for sale noted and information about when and where the article previously appeared. Pays 25-50% of amount paid for an original article.

Photos: Send photos with submission. Reviews contact sheets, negatives and 3×5, 5×7 or 8×10 prints. Offers no additional payment for photos accepted with ms.

Columns/Departments: News & Views (commentary on news events), 500-1,000 words. Buys 10 mss/year. Query. Pays $25-50.

Tips: "Become acquainted with the Ukrainian community in the US and Canada. The area of our publication most open to freelancers is community news—coverage of local events. We put more emphasis on events in Ukraine now that it has re-established its independence."

UPSCALE MAGAZINE, The Successful Black Magazine, Upscale Communications, Inc., 600 Bronner Brothers Way SW, Atlanta, GA 30310. (404)758-7467. Fax: (404)755-9892. Editor-in-Chief: Sheila Bronner. Contact: Kimberly Nesbit, associate editor. 75-80% freelance written. Monthly magazine covering topics that inspire, inform or entertain African-Americans. "*Upscale* is a general interest publication featuring a variety of topics—beauty, health and fitness, business news, travel, arts, relationships, entertainment and other issues that affect day to day lives of African-Americans." Estab. 1989. Circ. 242,000. Byline given. Offers 25% kill fee. Buys all rights in published form. Editorial lead time 3 months. Submit seasonal material 4 months in advance. Accepts simultaneous submissions. Sample copy for $2. Writer's guidelines free on request.

Nonfiction: Book excerpts/reviews, general interest, historical/nostalgic, inspirational, interview/profile, personal experience, religious, travel. Buys 135 mss/year. Query. Length varies. Pays $150 minimum. Sometimes pays expenses of writers.

Photos: State availability of photos with submission. Reviews contact sheets, transparencies, prints. Negotiates payment individually. Captions, model releases, identification of subjects required. Buys one-time or reprint rights.

Columns/Departments: Lee Bliss, senior editor. Positively You, Viewpoint, Perspective (personal inspiration/perspective). Buys 50 mss/year. Query. Pays $75.

Tips: "*Upscale* does not accept unsolicited fiction, poetry or essays. Unsolicited nonfiction is accepted for our Perspective, Positively You, and Viewpoint sections. Query letters for exciting and informative nonfiction story ideas are welcomed."

WINDSPEAKER, Aboriginal Multi-Media Society of Alberta, 15001-112 Ave., Edmonton Alberta T5M 2V6 Canada. (403)455-2700. Editor: Debora Lockyer. 75% freelance written. Monthly tabloid covering native issues. "Focus on events and issues that affect and interest native peoples." Estab. 1983. Circ. 12,500. Pays on publication. Publishes ms an average of 1 month after acceptance. Byline given. Offers $25 kill fee. Buys first rights. Editorial lead time 1 month. Submit seasonal material 2 months in advance. Accepts simultaneous submissions. Query for electronic submissions. Sample copy and writer's guidelines free on request.

Nonfiction: Humor, interview/profile, opinion, personal experience, photo feature, travel, reviews: books, music, movies. Special issues: Powwow (June); Travel supplement (May). Buys 200 mss/year. Query with published clips. Length: 300-1,000 words. Pays $3-3.60/published inch. Sometimes pays expenses of writers on assignment. "Query editor by phone with story ideas."

Photos: Send photos with submission. Reviews negatives, prints. Offers $15-50/photo. Identification of subjects required. Buys one-time rights.

Columns/Departments: Arts reviews (Aboriginal artists), 500-800 words. Buys 25 mss/year. Query with published clips. Pays $3-3.60/inch.

FOOD AND DRINK

Magazines appealing to gourmets, health-conscious consumers and vegetarians are classified here. Publications such as *Bon Appetit*, *Fine Cooking* and *Food & Wine* emphasize "the art and craft" of cooking for food enthusiasts who enjoy developing these skills as a leisure activity. Another popular trend stresses healthy eating and food choices, and is represented by such magazines as *Eating Well*, *Fast and Healthy* and *Delicious!* Many magazines in the Health and Fitness category present a holistic approach to well-being through nutrition and fitness for healthful living. Magazines in General Interest and Women's categories also buy articles on food topics. Journals aimed at food processing, manufacturing and retailing are in the Trade section.

‡**ALL ABOUT BEER MAGAZINE**, Chautauqua, Inc., 1627 Marion Ave., Durham NC 27705. (919)490-0589. Fax: (919)490-0865. E-mail: allabtbeer@aol.com. Editor: Daniel Bradford. Managing Editor: Nick Sholley. Contact: Mary Matthews, editor. 15% freelance written. Bimonthly magazine covering specialty beer. Estab. 1979. Circ. 40,000. Pays on publication. Byline given. Offers 50% kill fee. Buys first North American serial rights. Editorial lead time 4 months. Submit seasonal material 4 months in advance. Reports in 6 weeks on queries; 2 months on mss. Sample copy for $3.50. Writer's guidelines for #10 SASE.

Nonfiction: Essays, historical/nostalgic, humor, interview/profile, new product, travel. Buys 7-10 mss/year. Query with published clips. Length: 500-3,000 words. Pays $100-350 for assigned articles; $50-250 for unsolicited articles.

Photos: State availability of photos with submissions. Reviews contact sheets, transparencies. Offers $25-50/photo. Captions, identification of subjects required. Buys one-time rights.

Columns/Departments: Stylistically Speaking (a look at a specific beer style) 700-900 words; Small Beers (news items) 200-500 words. Buys 28 mss/year. Query with published clips. Pays $100-250.

Fillers: Wants these fillers: anecdotes, facts, newsbreaks. Buys 14/year. Length: 50-150 words. Pays $25.

‡**BEER ACROSS AMERICA**, GulfStream Communications, P.O. Box 1794, Mt. Pleasant SC 29465. (803)971-9811. Editor-in-Chief: Billy Sims. Editor: Kathleen W. Kranking. 85% freelance written. Quarterly magazine covering microbrewed beer and the microbrew movement. "*Beer Across America* is a lifestyle magazine for educated, affluent readers who have an appreciation for microbrewed beer." Estab. 1995. Circ. 150,000. Pays on publication. Publishes ms an average of 6 months after acceptance. Byline given. Offers 25% kill fee. Buys first North American serial rights. Editorial lead time 3 months. Submit seasonal material 3 months in advance. Reports in 6 weeks. Sample copy for $2 and 9×12 SAE with 5 first-class stamps. Writer's guidelines for #10 SASE.

Nonfiction: General interest, historical/nostalgic, humor, interview/profile, travel, music (all with a microbrew tie-in). No articles on big national breweries. Buys 10 mss/year. Query with published clips. Length: 750-2,000 words. Pays $100-550 for assigned articles; $100-450 for unsolicited articles. Sometimes pays expenses of writers on assignment.

Photos: State availability of photos with submission. Reviews transparencies. Negotiates payment individually. Identification of subjects required. Buys one-time rights.

Columns/Departments: Beer Nuts (people with an out of the ordinary dedication to beer, i.e., a brew pub poet's society); Affordable Luxuries (any indulgence that would appeal, i.e., steins, gourmet coffee); both 900 words. Buys fewer than 10 mss/year. Query with published clips. Pays $100-350.

Tips: "Query first with published clips. We're looking for light, clever writing covering fresh angles. No beer-party stories or beer festival reviews. Look for original ways to cover beer; for example, we recently did an article called 'A Beer Drinker's Guide to the Olympics.' "

BON APPETIT, America's Food and Entertaining Magazine, Condé Nast Publications, Inc., 6300 Wilshire Blvd., Los Angeles CA 90048. (213)965-3600. Fax: (213)937-1206. Executive Editor: Barbara Fairchild. Editor-in-Chief: William J. Garry. 10% freelance written. Monthly magazine that covers fine food, restaurants and home entertaining. "*Bon Appetit* readers are upscale food enthusiasts and sophisticated travelers. They eat out often and entertain four to six times a month." Estab. 1975. Circ. 1,331,853. **Pays**

on acceptance. Byline given. Negotiates rights. Submit seasonal/holiday material 1 year in advance. Reports in 6 weeks on queries. Writer's guidelines for #10 SASE.

Nonfiction: Travel (restaurant or food-related), food feature, dessert feature. "No cartoons, quizzes, poetry, historic food features or obscure food subjects." Buys 45 mss/year. Query with published clips. Length: 750-2,000 words. Pays $500-1,800. Pays expenses of writers on assignment.

Photos: Never send photos.

Tips: "We are most interested in receiving travel stories from freelancers. They must have a good knowledge of food (as shown in accompanying clips) and a light, lively style with humor. Nothing long and pedantic please."

CHILE PEPPER, The Magazine of Spicy Foods, Out West Publishing Company, 5106 Grand NE, P.O. Box 80780, Albuquerque NM 87198-0780. (505)266-8322. Fax: (505)266-2127. Managing Editor: Melissa Stock. Contact: Kellye Hunter, assistant editor. 25-30% freelance written. Bimonthly magazine on spicy foods. "The magazine is devoted to spicy foods, and most articles include recipes. We have a very devoted readership who love their food hot!" Estab. 1986. Circ. 80,000. Pays on publication. Offers 50% kill fee. Buys first and second rights. Submit seasonal/holiday material 6 months in advance. Reports in 2 months. Sample copy for 9×12 SAE with 5 first-class stamps. Writer's guidelines for #10 SASE.

Nonfiction: Book excerpts (cookbooks), how-to (cooking and gardening with spicy foods), humor (having to do with spicy foods), new product (hot products), travel (having to do with spicy foods). Buys 20 mss/year. Query. Length: 1,000-3,000 words. Pays $300 minimum for feature article. Sometimes pays expenses of writers on assignment.

Reprints: Accepts previously published submissions. Send tearsheet or photocopy of article and information about when and where the article previously appeared. Pays 25% of the amount paid for an original article.

Photos: State availability of photos with submission. Reviews contact sheets, negatives, transparencies and prints. Offers $25 minimum/photo. Captions and identification of subjects required. Buys one-time rights.

Tips: "We're always interested in queries from *food* writers. Articles about spicy foods with six to eight recipes are just right. No fillers. Need exotic location travel/food pieces."

COOKING LIGHT, The Magazine of Food and Fitness, Southern Living, Inc. P.O. Box 1748, Birmingham AL 35201-1681. (205)877-6000. Editor: Douglas Crichton. Managing Editor: Nathalie Dearing. 75% freelance written. Magazine published 9 times/year on healthy recipes and fitness information. "*Cooking Light* is a positive approach to a healthier lifestyle. It's written for healthy people on regular diets who are counting calories or trying to make calories count toward better nutrition. Moderation, balance and variety are emphasized. The writing style is fresh, upbeat and encouraging, emphasizing that eating a balanced, varied, lower-calorie diet and exercising regularly do not have to be boring." Estab. 1987. Circ. 1,300,000. **Pays on acceptance.** Publishes ms an average of 1 year after acceptance. Byline sometimes given. Offers 25% of original contract fee as kill fee. Submit seasonal/holiday material 1 year in advance. Reports in 1 year.

● Ranked as one of the best markets for freelance writers in *Writer's Yearbook*'s annual "Top 100 Markets," January 1996.

Nonfiction: Personal experience on nutrition, healthy recipes, fitness/exercise. Back up material a must. Buys 150 mss/year. Query with published clips. Length: 400-2,000 words. Pays $250-2,000 for assigned articles. Pays expenses of writers on assignment.

Columns/Departments: Try On a Sport (introducing readers to new sports as well as new ways to view old sports), 1,000 words; Attitudes (on the human mind at work; psychology, changing attitudes, trends and other issues involving the mind), 1,000 words; Health Matters (focuses on wide range of health issues), 1,000 words; Walk Talk (ways to make the most of our readers number one exercise), 1,000 words; Food for Thought (collection of food-related articles on the following topics—mini profile on a chef, restaurant and eating-out trends, food products and equipment, cooking tips and diet concerns) 250-350 words, short, 400-500 words, long. Buys 30 mss/year. Query. Pays $50-2,000.

Tips: "Emphasis should be on achieving a healthier lifestyle through food, nutrition, fitness, exercise information. In submitting queries, include information on professional background. Food writers should include examples of healthy recipes which meet the guidelines of *Cooking Light*."

‡DELICIOUS!, Your Magazine of Natural Living, New Hope Communications, 1301 Spruce St., Boulder CO 80302. Website: http://www.newhope.com/delicious. Editor: Kathryn Arnold. Contact: Laurel Kallenbach, senior editor. 65% freelance written. Monthly magazine covering natural products, nutrition, herbal medicines. "*Delicious!* magazine empowers natural foods store shoppers to make health-conscious choices in their lives. Our goal is to improve consumers' perception of the value of natural methods in achieving health. To do this, we educate consumers on nutrition, disease prevention, botanical medicines and natural personal care products." Estab. 1985. Circ. 340,000. **Pays on acceptance.** Publishes ms an average of 6 months after acceptance. Byline given. Offers 10% kill fee. Buys first North American serial rights. Editorial lead time 4 months. Submit seasonal material 6 months in advance. Accepts simultaneous submissions. Reports in 6 weeks on queries; 2 months on mss. Sample copy and writer's guidelines free on request.

Nonfiction: Book excerpts, how-to, personal experience (regarding natural or alternative health), health nutrition, herbal medicines, alternative medicine. Buys 150 mss/year. Query with published clips. Length: 700-1,500 words. Pays $50-350 for assigned articles; $25-100 for unsolicited articles.

Photos: State availability of photos with submission. Reviews 3×5 prints. Offers no additional payment for photos accepted with ms. Identification of subjects required. Buys one-time rights.

Columns/Departments: Herbal Kingdom (scientific evidence supporting herbal medicines) 1,200 words; Nutrition (new research on diet for good health) 1,000 words; Dietary Supplements (new research on vitamins/minerals, etc.) 1,000 words. Query with published clips. Pays $50-250.

Tips: "Highlight any previous health/nutrition/medical writing experience. Demonstrate a knowledge of natural medicine, nutrition, or natural products. Health practitioners who demonstrate writing ability are ideal freelancers."

EATING WELL, The Magazine of Food and Health, Telemedia Communications (US) Inc., P.O. Box 1001, Charlotte VT 05445-1001. (802)425-3961. Fax: (802)425-3307. Editor: Marcelle DiFalco. Food Editor: Susan Stuck. 90% freelance written. Bimonthly magazine covering food, health. Estab. 1989. Circ. 640,000. Pays 45 days after acceptance. Publishes ms an average of 6 months after acceptance. Byline given. Buys first North American serial rights. Submit seasonal/holiday material 1 year in advance. Reports in 2 months.
  ● Ranked as one of the best markets for freelance writers in *Writer's Yearbook*'s annual "Top 100 Markets," January 1996.

Nonfiction: Book excerpts, nutrition, cooking, interview/profile, food, travel. Query with published clips. Length: 2,000-4,000 words. Pays $1,500-3,500. Pays expenses of writers on assignment.

Columns/Departments: Mary Nowlan. Nutrition Report (timely nutrition research news), 150-400 words; Marketplace (current news in the food world), 150-400 words. Buys 60 mss/year. Query. Pays $200-500.

Tips: "We invite experienced, published science writers to do a broad range of in-depth, innovative food-health-nutrition features. Read the magazine first."

FAST AND HEALTHY MAGAZINE, Pillsbury Co., 200 S. Sixth St., M.S. 28M7, Minneapolis MN 55402. Fax: (612)330-4875. Editor: Betsy Wray. 50% freelance written. Bimonthly digest covering food. "*Fast and Healthy* is a family-oriented food magazine with healthful recipes for active people. All recipes can be prepared in 30 minutes or less and meet the U.S. Dietary guidelines for healthful eating. The magazine's emphasis is on Monday through Friday cooking. Our readers are busy people who are looking for information and recipes that help them prepare healthy meals quickly." Estab. 1992. Circ. 200,000. **Pays on acceptance.** Publishes ms an average of 8 months after acceptance. Byline given. Offers 20% kill fee. Buys all rights. Editorial lead time 1 year. Submit seasonal material 18 months in advance. Reports in 6 weeks on queries. Sample copy for $3. Writer's guidelines for #10 SASE.

Nonfiction: Food topics related to health, nutrition, convenience. Buys 6 mss/year. Query with published clips. Length: 100-1,500 words. Pays $50-500.

Columns/Departments: Living Better (health, nutrition, healthy lifestyle news), 25-200 words. Buys 25 mss/year. Query with published clips. Pays $25-200.

FINE COOKING, The Taunton Press, P.O. Box 5506, 63 S. Main St., Newtown CT 06470. (203)426-8171. Editor: Martha Holmberg. Managing Editor: Jan Newberry. Bimonthly magazine focusing exclusively on cooking. "*Fine Cooking* is a magazine for people who are passionate about the craft of cooking. Most readers are avid home cooks, though many are professionals. Our writers are not necessarily professional writers. It is more important to us that they are experienced cooks with first-hand knowledge and information to share." Estab. 1993. Circ. 120,000. Pays on receiving corrected galleys. Byline given. Offers $150 kill fee or page rate. Buys magazine, promo, reprint, electronic rights. Author retains reuse rights. Editorial lead time 6-9 months. Submit seasonal material 9 months in advance. Reports in 6 weeks on queries. Sample copy for $4.95. Writer's guidelines free on request.

Nonfiction: Cooking, how-to, humor, personal experience. Buys approximately 40 mss/year. Query. Pays $150/page minimum. Sometimes pays expenses of writers on assignment.

Columns/Departments: Tidbits (humor), 500-600 words; Tips (shortcuts), 100 words. Does not accept unsolicited pieces for other departments.

Tips: "Our entire magazine is written by experienced cooks. We welcome submissions in all these areas. Unless you have first-hand experience, we're not the right magazine for you."

FOOD & WINE, American Express Publishing Corp., 1120 Avenue of the Americas, New York NY 10036. (212)382-5618. Editor-in-Chief: Dana Cowin. Managing Editor: Mary Ellen Ward. Executive Editor: Denise Martin. Food Editor: Tina Ujlaki. Monthly magazine for "active people for whom eating, drinking, entertaining, dining out and travel are central to their lifestyle." Estab. 1978. Circ. 750,000. **Pays on acceptance.** Byline given. Offers 25% kill fee. Buys first world rights. Submit seasonal/holiday material 9 months in advance. Reports in 3 weeks on queries; 2 weeks on mss. Sample copy for $5. Writer's guidelines for #10 SASE.

Nonfiction: Food trends and news, how-to, kitchen and dining room design, travel. Query with published clips. Buys 125 mss/year. Length: 1,000-3,000 words. Pays $800-2,000. Pays expenses of writers on assignment.
Photos: State availability of photos with submission. No unsolicited photos or art. Offers $100-450/photo. Model releases and identification of subjects required. Buys one-time rights.
Columns/Departments: Restaurants, Travel, Style, Selects-Food, Selects-Design, Health, Low-fat Cooking, Dinner in Under an Hour, Experts. Buys 120 mss/year. Query with published clips. Length: 800-3,000 words. Pays $800-2,000.
Tips: "Good service, good writing, up-to-date information, interesting article approach and appropriate point of view for *F&W*'s audience are important elements to keep in mind. Look over several recent issues before writing query."

GOURMET, Condé Nast Publications, Inc., 560 Lexington Ave., New York NY 10022. (212)880-2712. Publisher: Peter K. Hunsinger. Editor: Zanne Zakroff. Monthly magazine covering the affluent lifestyle, with an emphasis on fine dining. "*Gourmet, The Magazine of Good Taste*, encompasses world travel, cooking, fine dining and entertaining, including elegant table settings, wines and spirits, shopping, culture and history, art and antiques." Estab. 1940. Circ. 893,000. This magazine did not respond to our request for information. Query before submitting.

KASHRUS MAGAZINE, The Bimonthly for the Kosher Consumer and the Trade, Yeshiva Birkas Reuven, P.O. Box 204, Parkville Station, Brooklyn NY 11204. (718)336-8544. Editor: Rabbi Yosef Wikler. 25% freelance written. Prefers to work with published/established writers, but will work with new/unpublished writers. Bimonthly magazine covering kosher food industry and food production. Estab. 1980. Circ. 10,000. Pays on publication. Publishes ms an average of 2 months after acceptance. Byline given. Offers 50% kill fee. Buys first or second serial (reprint) rights. Submit seasonal/holiday material 2 months in advance. Accepts simultaneous and previously published submissions. Send tearsheet or photocopy of article. Pays 25% of amount paid for an original article. Prefers submissions in major word processing programs on disk with accompanying hard copy. Reports in 1 week on queries, 2 weeks on mss. *Writer's Market* recommends allowing 2 months for reply. Sample copy for $3. Professional discount on subscription: $18/10 issues (regularly $33).
Nonfiction: General interest, interview/profile, new product, personal experience, photo feature, religious, technical and travel. Special issues feature; International Kosher Travel (October) and Passover (March). Buys 8-12 mss/year. Query with published clips. Length: 1,000-1,500 words. Pays $100-250 for assigned articles; pays up to $100 for unsolicited articles. Sometimes pays the expenses of writers on assignment.
Photos: State availability of photos with submission. Offers no additional payment for photos accepted with ms. Buys one-time rights.
Columns/Departments: Book Review (cook books, food technology, kosher food), 250-500 words; People in the News (interviews with kosher personalities), 1,000-1,500 words; Regional Kosher Supervision (report on kosher supervision in a city or community), 1,000-1,500 words; Food Technology (new technology or current technology with accompanying pictures), 1,000-1,500 words; Travel (international, national), must include Kosher information and Jewish communities, 1,000-1,500 words; Regional Kosher Cooking, 1,000-1,500 words. Buys 8-12 mss/year. Query with published clips. Pays $50-250.
Tips: "*Kashrus Magazine* will do more writing on general food technology, production, and merchandising as well as human interest travelogs and regional writing in 1997 than we have done in the past. Areas most open to freelancers are interviews, food technology, cooking and food preparation, dining, regional reporting and travel. We welcome stories on the availability and quality of Kosher foods and services in communities across the US and throughout the world. Some of our best stories have been by non-Jewish writers about kosher observance in their region. We also enjoy humorous articles. Just send a query with clips and we'll try to find a storyline that's right for you."

RISTORANTE, Foley Publishing, P.O. Box 73, Liberty Corner NJ 07938. (908)766-6006. Editor: Jaclyn Foley. 75% freelance written. Bimonthly magazine covering "Italian anything! *Ristorante—The magazine for the Italian Connoisseur*. For Italian restaurants and those who love Italian food, travel, wine and all things Italian!" Estab. 1994. Circ. 40,000. Pays on publication. Publishes ms an average of 3 months after acceptance. Byline sometimes given. Buys first North American and one-time rights. Editorial lead time 3 months. Submit seasonal material 3 months in advance. Accepts previously published submissions. Reports in 1 month on queries; 2 months on mss. Sample copy and writer's guidelines for 9 × 12 SAE and 4 first-class stamps.
Nonfiction: Book excerpts, general interest, historical/nostalgic, how-to (prepare Italian foods), humor, new product, opinion, personal experience, travel. Buys 25 mss/year. Send complete ms. Length: 100-1,000 words. Pays $100-350 for assigned articles; $75-300 for unsolicited articles. Sometimes pays expenses of writers on assignment.
Photos: Send photos with submission. Reviews 3 × 5 prints. Negotiates payment individually. Captions, model releases required. Buys one-time rights.

Columns/Departments: Send complete ms. Pays $50-200.
Fillers: Anecdotes, facts, short humor. Buys 10/year. Pays $10-50.

SAVEUR, Mether Communications, 100 Avenue of the Americas, New York NY 10013. (212)334-2400. Fax: (212)334-1257. Publisher: Joe Armstrong. Bimonthly magazine covering fine dining. *"Saveur* is for people who are interested in the subject of food. It covers the world of food to make the cooking, the eating, the reading about food more satisfying. Special features include *'Saveur* Fare,' with informative news about the food world and an agenda of culinary events, and 'The *Saveur* Kitchen,' with tips, techniques and discoveries from the food editor." Estab. 1994. Circ. 114,000. This magazine did not respond to our request for information. Query before submitting.

‡SIMPLY SEAFOOD, Waterfront Press Co., 5305 Shilshole Ave. NW, Seattle WA 98107. (206)789-6506. Fax: (206)789-9193. Editor: Peter Redmayne. Contact: Lawrence W. Cheek, managing editor. 50% freelance written. Quarterly magazine covering seafood. "We are a consumer food magazine aimed at amateur cooks who enjoy seafood or would like to learn more about it. Contributors must be able to write knowledgeably and provide excellent, tested recipes." Estab. 1991. Circ. 105,000. **Pays on acceptance.** Publishes ms an average of 3 months after acceptance. Byline given. Buys first North American serial rights and makes work-for-hire assignments. Editorial lead time 3 months. Submit seasonal queries 6 months in advance. Reports in 1 month on queries. Sample copy for 9×12 SASE and 7 first-class stamps. Writer's guidelines for #10 SASE.
Nonfiction: How-to (cooking), interview/profile (chefs, celebrities), travel. Buys 16 mss/year. Length: 1,000-2,000 words. Pays $100-600 for assigned articles. Sometimes pays expenses of writers on assignment.
Photos: State availability of photos with submission. Reviews transparencies (any format). Negotiates payment individually. Captions, identification of subjects required. Buys one-time rights.
Columns/Departments: Seafood City (tour of a city's great seafood restaurants), 700 words. Buys 4 mss/year. Pays $100.
Tips: "Read our magazine and writer's guidelines first. Then imagine a story idea that would compel a grocery shopper passing by the seafood counter to buy our magazine. Write from a standpoint of knowledge—you need to be skilled with seafood in your own kitchen."

VEGETARIAN TIMES, P.O. Box 570, Oak Park IL 60303. (708)848-8100. Fax: (708)848-8175. Editorial Director: Toni Apgar. 50% freelance written. Prefers to work with published/established writers; works with small number of new/unpublished writers each year. Monthly magazine. Circ. 320,000. Buys first serial or all rights. Byline given unless extensive revisions are required or material is incorporated into a larger article. **Pays on acceptance.** Publishes ms an average of 4 months after acceptance. Submit seasonal material 6 months in advance. Reports in 3 months. Query. Writer's guidelines for #10 SASE.
Nonfiction: Features articles that inform readers about how vegetarianism relates to diet, cooking, lifestyle, health, consumer choices, natural foods, environmental concerns and animal welfare. "All material should be well-documented and researched, and written in a sophisticated and lively style." Informational, how-to, personal experience, interview, profile, investigative. Length: average 2,000 words. Pays flat rate of $100-1,000, sometimes higher, depending on length and difficulty of piece. Also uses 200-500-word items for news department. Sometimes pays expenses of writers on assignment.
Photos: Payment negotiated/photo.
Tips: "You don't have to be a vegetarian to write for *Vegetarian Times*, but it is vital that your article have a vegetarian perspective. The best way to pick up that slant is to read several issues of the magazine (no doubt a tip you've heard over and over). We are looking for stories that go beyond the obvious 'Why I Became a Vegetarian.' A well-written provocative query plus samples of your best writing will increase your chances of publication."

VEGGIE LIFE, Growing Green, Cooking Lean, Feeling Good, EGW Publishing, 1041 Shary Circle, Concord CA 94518. (510)671-9852. E-mail: veggieed@aol.com. Website: http://www.vegilife.com. Editor: Sharon Mikkelson. 90% freelance written. Bimonthly magazine covering vegetarian cooking, natural health and organic gardening. Estab. 1992. Circ. 280,000. **Pays on acceptance.** Publishes ms an average of 6 months after acceptance. Byline given. Offers 25% kill fee. Buys simultaneous rights or makes work-for-hire assignments. Editorial lead time 4 months. Submit seasonal material 4 months in advance. Reports in 2 months. Writer's guidelines for #10 SASE.
Nonfiction: Vegetarian cooking/recipes, gardening how-to, natural health, herbal healing, nutrition. No animal rights issues/advocacy or religious/philosophical. Buys 30-50 mss/year. Query with published clips. Length: 1,000-2,000 words. Pays 25-35¢/word.
Photos: State availability of photos with submission. Negotiates payment individually. Captions, model releases and identification of subjects required. Buys one-time rights.
Columns/Departments: Pays $200-600.
Tips: "Research back issues; be authoritative; no 'Why I Became a Vegetarian . . . ' stories. Please state why you are qualified to write particular subject matter—a *must* on health/herbal mss."

WINE SPECTATOR, M. Shanken Communications, Inc., 387 Park Ave. S., New York NY 10016. (212)684-4224. Fax: (212)684-5424. Managing Editor: Jim Gordon. 20% freelance written. Prefers to work with published/established writers. Biweekly consumer news magazine covering wine. Estab. 1976. Circ. 150,000. Pays within 30 days of publication. Publishes ms an average of 2 months after acceptance. Byline given. Buys all rights and makes work-for-hire assignments. Submit seasonal/holiday material 4 months in advance. Reports in 3 months. Sample copy for $5. Free writer's guidelines.
Nonfiction: General interest (news about wine or wine events); interview/profile (of wine, vintners, wineries); opinion; travel, dining and other lifestyle pieces; photo feature. No "winery promotional pieces or articles by writers who lack sufficient knowledge to write below just surface data." Query. Length: 100-2,000 words average. Pays $50-500.
Photos: Send photos with ms. Pays $75 minimum for color transparencies. Captions, model releases and identification of subjects required. Buys all rights.
Tips: "A solid knowledge of wine is a must. Query letters essential, detailing the story idea. New, refreshing ideas which have not been covered before stand a good chance of acceptance. *Wine Spectator* is a consumer-oriented *news magazine*, but we are interested in some trade stories; brevity is essential."

GAMES AND PUZZLES

These publications are written by and for game enthusiasts interested in both traditional games and word puzzles and newer role-playing adventure, computer and video games. Other puzzle markets may be found in the Juvenile section.

‡THE ADULT GAMER, The Role-Playing Aid for Adults, Lost Coast Publishing, P.O. Box 2074, Trinidad CA 95570. Managing Editor: Alesia Chamness-Matson. 90% freelance written. Quarterly newspaper covering role playing games. "*TAG* is written for the mature, well-educated gamer. Articles submitted should reflect a well-researched topic, presented with good vocabulary and grammar. If the right word or phrase has 20 syllables, go ahead and use it! You don't need to "write down" to our audience." Estab. 1994. Circ. 100. **Pays on acceptance**. Publishes ms an average of 6 months after acceptance. Byline given. Offers 10% kill fee. Buys first or second world-wide serial rights. Editorial lead time 6 months. Accepts simultaneous and previously published submissions. 2 Reports in weeks on queries; 2 months on mss. Sample copy $3 and 6×9 SAE and 3 first-class stamps. Writer's guidelines for #10 SASE.
Nonfiction: How-to (game mechanics, design, campaign maintenance, etc.), humor, new product, personal experience, tips and advice on game-related topics. Buys 15-20 mss/year. Send complete ms. No word length limits. Pays $10-50. Pays in contributor's copies upon request.
Photos: State availability of photos with submissionnn. Reviews 4× b&w prints. Offers $5-25/photo. Captions, model releases, identification of subjects required.
Columns/Departments: The Goody Bag ("Drop-in" Campaign material—NPC's, places, etc.); Voices from Beyond (explain fantasy phenomena from scientific principles); At the Hearth ("Drop-in" myths, legends, stories, etc.). Buys 3-12 mss/year. Pays $5-25.
Fillers: Anecdotes, short humor. Buys 4-12/year. Length: 25-150 words. Pays in contributor copies.
Tips: "We're eager to work with writers—there's a wealth of untapped talent in the gaming community that we'd be happy to publish. Just be sure to use your dictionaries, spell-checkers, and grammar lexicons—the more literate and well-written your piece, the better the chance we'll like it. Adult gamers have little time to enjoy this hobby—we want to give our readers new and exciting things to add to their campaigns."

bePUZZLED, Mystery Jigsaw Puzzles, 22 E. Newberry Rd., Bloomfield CT 06002. (203)769-5700. Fax: (203)286-8710. E-mail: malbepuzzd@aol.com. CEO: Mary Ann Lombard. Creative Director: Richard DeZinno. 100% freelance written. Mystery jigsaw puzzle using short mystery stories published 2-4 times/year. Covers mystery, suspense, adventure for children and adults. Estab. 1987. Pays on completion. Publishes ms an average of 9 months after acceptance. Byline given (sometimes pen name required). Buys all rights. Submit seasonal/holiday material 9 months in advance. Accepts simultaneous submissions. Reports in 2 weeks on queries, 3 months on mss. Writer's guidelines for SASE.
Reprints: Send photocopy of article or typed ms with rights for sale noted and information about when and where the article previously appeared.
Fiction: Adventure, humorous, mainstream, mystery, suspense (*exact* subject within genre above is released to writers as available.) Buys 10 mss/year. Query. Length: 3,500-5,500 words. Pays $250-2,000.
Fillers: "Writers must follow submission format as outlined in writer's guidelines. We incorporate short mystery stories and jigsaw puzzles into a game where the clues to solve the mystery are cleverly hidden in both the short story and the puzzle picture. Writer must be able to integrate the clues in the written piece to these to appear in puzzle picture. Playing one of our games helps to clarify how we like to 'marry' the story clues and the visual clues in the puzzle."

CHESS LIFE, United States Chess Federation, 186 Route 9W, New Windsor NY 12553-7698. (914)562-8350. Fax: (914)561-2437. Editor: Glenn Petersen. 15% freelance written. Works with a small number of new/unpublished writers each year. Monthly magazine covering the chess world. Estab. 1939. Circ. 70,000. Pays variable fee. Publishes ms an average of 5 months after acceptance. Byline given. Offers kill fee. Buys first or negotiable rights. Submit seasonal/holiday material 8 months in advance. Accepts simultaneous submissions. Reports in 3 months. Sample copy and writer's guidelines for 9×11 SAE with 5 first-class stamps.

Nonfiction: General interest, historical, interview/profile, technical—all must have some relation to chess. No "stories about personal experiences with chess." Buys 30-40 mss/year. Query with samples "if new to publication." Length: 3,000 words maximum. Sometimes pays the expenses of writers on assignment.

Reprints: Send typed ms with rights for sale noted and information about when and where the article previously appeared.

Photos: Reviews b&w contact sheets and prints, and color prints and slides. Captions, model releases and identification of subjects required. Buys all or negotiable rights.

Fiction: "Chess-related, high quality." Buys 2-3 mss/year. Pays variable fee.

Tips: "Articles must be written from an informed point of view—not from view of the curious amateur. Most of our writers are specialized in that they have sound credentials as chessplayers. Freelancers in major population areas (except New York and Los Angeles, which we already have covered) who are interested in short personality profiles and perhaps news reporting have the best opportunities. We're looking for more personality pieces on chessplayers around the country; not just the stars, but local masters, talented youths, and dedicated volunteers. Freelancers interested in such pieces might let us know of their interest and their range. Could be we know of an interesting story in their territory that needs covering."

DRAGON MAGAZINE, TSR, Inc., 201 Sheridan Springs Rd., Lake Geneva WI 53147-0111. (414)248-3625. Fax: (414)248-0389. Editor: Anthony J. Bryant. Monthly magazine of fantasy and science-fiction role-playing games. 90% freelance written. Eager to work with published/established writers as well as new/unpublished writers. "Most of our readers are intelligent, imaginative teenage males." Estab. 1976. Circ. 100,000, primarily across the US, Canada and Great Britain. Byline given. Offers kill fee. Submit seasonal/holiday material 8 months in advance. Pays on publication for articles to which all rights are purchased; pays on acceptance for articles to which first/worldwide rights in English are purchased. Publishing dates vary from 1-24 months after acceptance. Reports in 3 months. Sample copy $4.50. Writer's guidelines for #10 SAE with 1 first-class stamp.

Nonfiction: Articles on the hobby of science fiction and fantasy role-playing. No general articles on gaming hobby. "Our article needs are *very* specialized. Writers should be experienced in gaming hobby and role-playing. No strong sexual overtones or graphic depictions of violence." Buys 120 mss/year. Query. Length: 1,000-8,000 words. Pays $50-500 for assigned articles; $5-400 for unsolicited articles.

Fiction: Michelle Vuckovich, fiction editor. Fantasy only. "No strong sexual overtones or graphic depictions of violence." Buys 12 mss/year. Send complete ms. Length: 2,000-8,000 words. Pays 6-8¢/word.

Tips: "*Dragon Magazine* is *not* a periodical that the 'average reader' appreciates or understands. A writer must *be* a reader and must share the serious interest in gaming our readers possess."

‡FANTASY BASEBALL INDEX, DFL Publishing, 18247 66th Ave. NE Seattle WA 98155. (206)487-9000. Fax: (206)485-3699. E-mail: ffmag@netcom.com. Editor: Bruce Taylor. 5-10% freelance written. Annual magazine covering fantasy sports games. "*Fantasy Baseball Index* and its sister publications are study guides for participants in fantasy sports leagues. All articles are written from a fantasy perspective. We are not interested in articles on handicapping." Estab. 1987. Circ. 210,000. Pays on publication. Publishes ms an average of 2 months after acceptance. Byline given. Buys all rights. Editorial lead time 2 months. Submit seasonal material 2 months in advance. Sample copy $3. Writer's guidelines free on request.

Nonfiction: How-to (general interest to fantasy coaches), opinion, technical. Special issues: Football (March); Baseball (November); Basketball (June). Nothing pertaining to handicapping or gambling. Buys 2 mss/year. Query. Length: 1,000-4,000 words. Pays $100-300.

Photos: State availability of photos with submission. Reviews 35mm transparencies, 5×7 prints. Negotiates payment individually. Identification of subjects required.

Columns/Departments: Pays $100-300

Tips: "Please contact us several months in advance if you have an idea for a story. We will want to see a brief outline along with samples of your work. We are interested only in articles focusing on fantasy sports— please, no general interest."

‡FANTASY BASKETBALL INDEX, DFL Publishing, 18247 66th Ave. NE Seattle WA 98155. (206)487-9000. Fax: (206)485-3699. E-mail: ffmag@netcom.com. Editor: Bruce Taylor. 5-10% freelance written. Annual magazine covering fantasy sports games. "*Fantasy Basketball Index* and its sister publications are study guides for participants in fantasy sports leagues. All articles are written from a fantasy perspective. We are not interested in articles on handicapping." Estab. 1987. Circ. 150,000. Pays on publication. Publishes ms an average of 2 months after acceptance. Byline given. Buys all rights. Editorial lead time 2 months. Submit seasonal material 2 months in advance. Sample copy $3. Writer's guidelines free on request.

Nonfiction: How-to (general interest to fantasy coaches), opinion, technical. Special issues: Football (March); Baseball (November); Basketball (June). Nothing pertaining to handicapping or gambling. Buys 2 mss/year. Query. Length: 1,000-4,000 words. Pays $100-300.

Photos: State availability of photos with submission. Reviews 35mm transparencies, 5×7 prints. Negotiates payment individually. Identification of subjects required.

Columns/Departments: Pays $100-300

Tips: "Please contact us several months in advance if you have an idea for a story. We will want to see a brief outline along with samples of your work. We are interested only in articles focusing on fantasy sports—please, no general interest."

‡**FANTASY FOOTBALL INDEX**, DFL Publishing, 18247 66th Ave. NE Seattle WA 98155. (206)487-9000. Fax: (206)485-3699. E-mail: ffmag@netcom.com. Editor: Bruce Taylor. 5-10% freelance written. Annual magazine covering fantasy sports games. "*Fantasy Football Index* and its sister publications are study guides for participants in fantasy sports leagues. All articles are written from a fantasy perspective. We are not interested in articles on handicapping." Estab. 1987. Circ. 210,000. Pays on publication. Publishes ms an average of 2 months after acceptance. Byline given. Buys all rights. Editorial lead time 2 months. Submit seasonal material 2 months in advance. Sample copy $3. Writer's guidelines free on request.

Nonfiction: How-to (general interest to fantasy coaches), opinion, technical. Special issues: Football (March); Baseball (November); Basketball (June). Nothing pertaining to handicapping or gambling. Buys 2 mss/year. Query. Length: 1,000-4,000 words. Pays $100-300.

Photos: State availability of photos with submission. Reviews 35mm transparencies, 5×7 prints. Negotiates payment individually. Identification of subjects required.

Columns/Departments: Pays $100-300

Tips: "Please contact us several months in advance if you have an idea for a story. We will want to see a brief outline along with samples of your work. We are interested only in articles focusing on fantasy sports—please no general interest."

GIANT CROSSWORDS, Scrambl-Gram, Inc., Puzzle Buffs International, 1772 State Rd., Cuyahoga Falls OH 44223-1200. (216)923-2397. Editor: C.R. Elum. Submissions Editor: S. Bowers. 40% freelance written. Eager to work with new/unpublished writers. Quarterly crossword puzzle and word game magazine. Estab. 1970. **Pays on acceptance.** Publishes ms an average of 1 month after acceptance. No byline given. Buys all rights. Reports in 1 month. "We offer constructors' kits, master grids, clue sheets and a 'how-to-make-crosswords' book for $37.50 postpaid." Send #10 SASE for details.

Nonfiction: Crosswords and word games only. Query. Pays according to size of puzzle and/or clues.

Reprints: Send information about when and where the article previously appeared.

Tips: "We are expanding our syndication of original crosswords and our publishing schedule to include new titles and extra issues of current puzzle books."

PC GAMES, The Complete Guide to Computer Gaming, (formerly *Electronic Entertainment*), IDG Communications, 951 Mariners Island Blvd., #700, San Mateo CA 94404. (415)349-4300. Fax: (415)349-7482. E-mail: cgrech@iftw.com. Features Editor: Christine Grech Wendin. 40% freelance written. Monthly magazine covering PC and Mac games, virtual reality, interactive TV, entertainment. Estab. 1993. Circ. 150,000. **Pays on acceptance.** Publishes ms an average of 3 months after acceptance. Byline given. Buys all rights. Editorial lead time 3-4 months. Submit seasonal material 6 months in advance.

● No longer publishing fiction.

Nonfiction: Exposé, how-to, humor, interview/profile, new product, opinion, personal experience, photo feature, technical (games or gaming experiences). Query with published clips. Length: 100-4,000 words. Pays $50-1,000.

Photos: Send photos with submission. Reviews negatives, transparencies or computer files. Offers no additional payment for photos accepted with ms. Captions required. Buys all rights.

Columns/Departments: Game reviews, 400-600 words. Buys 12 mss/year. Query with published clips. Pays $50-150.

Fillers: Contact: Steve Klett. Anecdotes, facts, short humor. Length: 25-100 words. Pays $25.

Tips: "Read the magazine, know something about the field, have proven writing skills, and propose ideas with fresh angles."

SCHOOL MATES, United States Chess Federation, 186 Route 9W, New Windsor NY 12553-5794. (914)562-8350 ext. 152. Fax: (914)561-CHES (2437). E-mail: uscf@delphi.com. Editor: Brian Bugbee. Contact: Judy Levine, assistant editor. 10% freelance written. Bimonthly magazine of chess for the beginning (some intermediate) player. Includes instruction, player profiles, chess tournament coverage, listings. Estab. 1987. Circ. 30,000. Pays on publication. Publishes ms an average of 6 months after acceptance. Byline given. Publication copyrighted "but not filed with Library of Congress." Buys first rights. Editorial lead time 2 months. Submit seasonal material 3 months in advance. Accepts simultaneous submissions. Reports in 6 months. Sample copy and writer's guidelines free on request.

Nonfiction: How-to, humor, personal experience (chess, but not "my first tournament"), photo feature, technical, travel and any other chess related item. Poetry. Fiction. Buys 10-20 mss/year. Query. Length: 250-1,000 words. Pays $50/1,000 words, $20 minimum). "We are not-for-profit; we try to make up for low $ rate with complimentary copies." Sometimes pays expenses of writers on assignment.

Reprints: Send tearsheet, photocopy of article or typed ms with rights for sale noted and information about when and where the article previously appeared. Pays 100% of amount paid for an original article.

Photos: Send photos with submission. Reviews prints. Offers $25/photo for first time rights. Captions and identification of subjects required. Buys one-time rights, pays $15 for subsequent use.

Columns/Departments: Test Your Tactics/Winning Chess Tactics (explanation, with diagrams, of chess tactics; 8 diagrammed chess problems, e.g. "white to play and win in 2 moves"); Basic Chess (chess instruction for beginners). Query with published clips. Pays $50/1,000 words ($20 minimum).

Tips: "Know your subject; chess is a technical subject, and you can't fake it. Human interest stories on famous chess players or young chess players can be 'softer,' but always remember you are writing for children, and make it lively. We use the Frye readability scale (3rd-6th grade reading level), and items written on the appropriate reading level do stand out immediately! We are most open to human interest stories, puzzles, cartoons, photos. We are always looking for an unusual angle, e.g. (wild example) a kid who plays chess while surfing, or (more likely) a blind kid and how she plays chess with her specially-made chess pieces and board, etc."

GAY AND LESBIAN INTEREST

The magazines listed here cover a wide range of politics, culture, news, art, literature and issues of general interest to gay and lesbian communities. Magazines of a strictly sexual content are listed in the new Sex section.

BAY WINDOWS, New England's Largest Gay and Lesbian Newspaper, Bay Windows, Inc., 1523 Washington St., Boston MA 02118-2034. (617)266-6670. Fax: (617)266-5973. E-mail: news@baywindows.com. Editor: Jeff Epperly. Arts Editor: Rudy Kikel. Contact: Loren King, assistant editor. 30-40% freelance written. Weekly newspaper of gay news and concerns. "*Bay Windows* covers predominantly news of New England, but will print non-local news and features depending on the newsworthiness of the story. We feature hard news, opinion, news analysis, arts reviews and interviews." Estab. 1983. Publishes ms within 2 months of acceptance, pays within 2 months of publication. Byline given. Offers 50% kill fee. Rights obtained varies, usually first serial rights. Simultaneous submissions accepted if other submissions are outside of New England. Submit seasonal material 3 months in advance. Reports in 3 months. Sample copy for $5. Writer's guidelines for #10 SASE.

Nonfiction: Hard news, general interest with a gay slant, interview/profile, opinion, photo features. Publishes 200 mss/year. Query with published clips or send complete ms. Length: 500-1,500 words. Pay varies: $25-100 news; $10-60 arts.

Reprints: Send typed ms with rights for sale noted and information about when and where the article previously appeared. Pays 75% of amount paid for an original article.

Photos: Pays $25/published photo. Model releases and identification of subjects required.

Columns/Departments: Film, music, dance, books, art. Length: 500-1,500 words. Buys 200 mss/year. Pays $10-100. Letters, opinion to Jeff Epperly, editor; news, features to Loren King, assistant editor; arts, reviews to Rudy Kikel, arts editor.

Poetry: All varieties. Publishes 50 poems/year. Length: 10-30 lines. No payment.

Tips: "Too much gay-oriented writing is laden with the clichés and catch phrases of the movement. Writers must have intimate knowledge of gay community; however, this should not mean that standard English usage is not required. We look for writers with new—even controversial perspectives on the lives of gay men and lesbians. While we assume gay is good, we will print stories which examine problems within the community and movement. No pornography or erotica."

EVERGREEN CHRONICLES, A Journal of Gay And Lesbian Arts And Cultures, P.O. Box 8939, Minneapolis MN 55408. (612)649-4982. Editor: Jim Berg. Contact: Susan Raffo, managing editor. 75% freelance written. Triannual magazine covering gay, lesbian and bisexual communities. "*The Evergreen Chronicles* is a semi-annual journal dedicated to exploring gay and lesbian arts and cultures. We are interested in work that challenges and explores the meaning of 'gay' or 'lesbian,' especially as related to race, class, sexuality and gender." Estab. 1984. Circ. 2,000. Pays on publication. Publishes ms an average of 3 months after acceptance. Byline given. Buys first rights. Submit seasonal material 2 months in advance. Reports in 2 weeks on queries; 3 months on mss. Sample copy for $8. Writer's guidelines for #10 SASE.

Nonfiction: Book excerpts, essays, historical/nostalgic, interview/profile, opinion, personal experience. Buys 6 mss/year. Query or send complete ms. Length: up to 4,000 words. Pays $25.

Photos: State availability of photos with submissions. Reviews contact sheets. Captions required. Buys one-time rights.

Fiction: Erotica, ethnic, experimental, fantasy, historical, novel excerpts. Buys 20 mss/year. Send 4 copies of ms. Length: up to 4,000 words. Pays $25.
Poetry: All types. Buys 40 poems/year. Submit maximum 4 poems. Pays $25.

‡GENRE, Genre Publishing, 7080 Hollywood Blvd., #1104, Hollywood CA 90028. (213)896-9778. E-mail: genre@aol.com. Editor: Ronald Mark Kraft. Contact: John Polly, associate editor. 90% freelance written. Magazine published 10 times/year. "*Genre*, America's best-selling gay men's lifestyle magazine, covers entertainment, fashion, travel and relationships in a hip, upbeat, upscale voice. The award-winning publication's mission is best summarized by its tagline—'How We Live.' " Estab. 1991. Circ. 50,000. Pays on publication. Publishes ms an average of 2 months after acceptance. Byline given. Offers 25% kill fee. Buys first North American serial rights and all rights. Editorial lead time 3 months. Submit seasonal material 3 months in advance. Sample copy for $7.95 ($5 plus $2.95 postage). Writer's guidelines for #10 SASE.
Nonfiction: Book excerpts, exposé, general interest, interview/profile, photo feature, travel, relationships, fashion. Query with published clips. Length: 1,500-3,500 words. Pays 10-50¢/word. Pays writer with contributor copies or other premiums rather than a cash payment if so negotiated.
Photos: State availability of photos with submission. Negotiates payment individually. Model releases and identification of subjects required.
Columns/Departments: Tweaked (short, punchy, celeb Q&As), 500 words. Buys 20 mss/year. Query with published clips. Pays $25-150.
Fiction: Adventure, experimental, horror, humorous, mainstream, mystery, novel excerpts, religious, romance, science fiction, slice-of-life vignettes, suspense. Buys 10 mss/year. Send complete ms. Length: 2,000-4,000 words.

GIRLFRIENDS MAGAZINE, America's fastest-growing lesbian magazine, 3415 Cesar Chavez, Suite 101, San Francisco CA 94110. (415)648-9464. Fax: (415)648-4705. E-mail: staff@g.friends.com. Website: http://www.gfriends.com. Editor: Heather Findlay. Contact: Diane Anderson, managing editor. Bimonthly lesbian magazine. *Girlfriends* provides its readers with intelligent, entertaining and visually-pleasing coverage of culture, politics and sexuality—all from an informed and critical lesbian perspective. Estab. 1994. Circ. 60,000. Pays on publication. Publishes ms an average of 6 months after acceptance. Byline given. Offers 25% kill fee. Buys first rights, use for advertising/promoting *Girlfriends*. Editorial lead time 3 months. Submit seasonal material 6 months in advance. Accepts simultaneous submissions. Reports in 3 weeks on queries; 3 months on mss. Sample copy for $4.95 plus $1.50 shipping and handling. Writer's guidelines for #10 SASE.
Nonfiction: Book excerpts, essays, exposé, humor, interview/profile, personal experience, photo feature, travel. Special features: lesbians related to famous historical figures; best lesbian restaurants in the US; exposé on Scientology and its followers. Buys 20-25 mss/year. Query with published clips. Length: 1,000-3,500 words. Pays 10¢/word.
  • This magazine was recently redesigned and has expanded its editorial pages. It is doing more profiles (celebrities, political leaders) and more investigative features.
Photos: Send photos with submissions. Reviews contact sheets, 4×5 or $2\frac{1}{4} \times 2\frac{1}{4}$ transparencies, prints. Offers $30-250/photo. Captions, model releases, identification of subjects required. Buys one-time rights, use for advertising/promoting *GF*.
Columns/Departments: Crib Notes (lesbian parenting), 600 words; Out of Bounds (sports), 800 words; Playgrounds (travel), 800 words; Health, 600 words; Spirituality, 600 words. Buys 50 mss/year. Query with published clips. Pays 10¢/word.
Fiction: Erotica, ethnic, experimental, fantasy, historical, humorous, mystery, novel concepts, science fiction. Buys 6-10 mss/year. Query with complete ms. Length: 800-2,500 words. Pays 10¢/word.
Poetry: Avant-garde, free verse, Haiku, light verse, traditional. Buys 6-10 poems/year. Submit maximum 5 poems. Length: 3-75 lines. Pays $50.
Fillers: Gags to be illustrated by cartoonist, short humor. Buys 6-10/year. Length: 500-800 words. Pays $50.
Tips: "Be unafraid of controversy—articles should focus on problems and debates raised around lesbian culture, politics, and sexuality. Fiction should be innovative and eyebrow-raising. Avoid being 'politically correct.' Photographers should aim for the suggestive, not the explicit. We don't want just to know what's happening in the lesbian world, we want to know how what's happening in the world affects lesbians."

THE GUIDE, To Gay Travel, Entertainment, Politics and Sex, Fidelity Publishing, P.O. Box 593, Boston MA 02199-0593. (617)266-8557. Fax: (617)266-1125. E-mail: theguide@guidemag.com. Website: http://www.guidemag.com. Editor: French Wall. 25% freelance written. Monthly magazine on the gay and lesbian community. Estab. 1981. Circ. 31,000. **Pays on acceptance.** Publishes ms an average of 2 months after acceptance. Kill fee negotiable. Buys first-time rights. Submit seasonal material 2 months in advance. Accepts simultaneous submissions. Reports in 3 months. Sample copy for 9×12 SAE with 8 first-class stamps. Writer's guidelines for #10 SASE.
Nonfiction: Book excerpts (if yet unpublished), essays, exposé, general interest, historical/nostalgic, humor, interview/profile, opinion, personal experience, photo feature, religious. Buys 24 mss/year. Query with or without published clips or send complete ms. Length: 500-5,000 words. Pays $60-200.

Photos: Send photos with submission. Reviews contact sheets. Offers no additional payment for photos accepted with ms (although sometimes negotiable). Captions, model releases, identification of subjects prefered; releases required sometimes. Buys one-time rights.
Tips: "Brevity, humor and militancy appreciated."

‡**HX MAGAZINE**, Two Queens, Inc., 19 W. 21 St., #504, New York NY 10010. (212)627-0747. Fax: (212)627-5280. E-mail: editor@hx.com. Editor: Timothy Murphy. 25% freelance written. Weekly magazine covering gay New York City nightlife and entertainment. "We publish a magazine for gay men and lesbians who are interested in New York City nightlife and entertainment." Estab. 1991. Circ. 27,708. **Pays on acceptance**. Publishes ms an average of 1 month after acceptance. Byline given. Offers 50% kill fee. Buys first North American serial, second serial (reprint) and electronic reprint rights. Editorial lead time 3 months. Submit seasonal material 3 months in advance. "We must be exclusive publisher to accept." Only responds if interested. Sample copy free on request.
Nonfiction: Essays, exposé, general interest, humor, personal experience, reviews. Buys 200 mss/year. Query with published clips. Length: 500-3,000 words. Pays $50-300 for assigned articles; $25-300 for unsolicited articles. Sometimes pays expenses of writers on assignment.
Photos: State availability of photos with submission. Reviews contact sheets, negatives, 8×10 prints. Negotiates payment individually. Captions, model releases, identification of subjects required. Buys one-time, reprint and electronic reprint rights.
Columns/Departments: Buys 200 mss/year. Query with published clips. Pays $25-125.

LAMBDA BOOK REPORT, A Review of Contemporary Gay and Lesbian Literature, Lambda Rising, Inc., 1625 Connecticut Ave. NW, Washington DC 20009-1013. (202)462-7924. Fax: (202)462-7257. E-mail: lbreditor@aol.com. Contact: Jim Marks, senior editor. Assistant Editor: Kanani Kauka. 90% freelance written. Monthly magazine that covers gay/lesbian literature. "*Lambda Book Report* devotes its entire contents to the discussion of gay and lesbian books and authors. Any other submissions would be inappropriate." Estab. 1987. Circ. 11,000. Pays 30 days after publication. Byline given. Buys first rights. Reports in 2 months. Sample copy for $3.95 and 9×12 SAE with 5 first-class stamps. Free writer's guidelines.
  • This editor sees an increasing need for writers familiar with economic and science/medical-related topics.
Nonfiction: Book excerpts, essays (on gay literature), interview/profile (of authors), book reviews. "No historical essays, fiction or poetry." Query with published clips. Length: 200-2,000 words. Pays $15-125 for assigned articles; $5-25 for unsolicited articles.
Photos: Send photos with submission. Reviews contact sheets. Offers $10-25/photo. Model releases required. Buys one-time rights.
Tips: "Assignments go to writers who query with 2-3 published book reviews and/or interviews. It is helpful if the writer is familiar with gay and lesbian literature and can write intelligently and objectively on the field. Review section is most open. Writers should demonstrate with clips their scope of knowledge, ability and interest in reviewing gay books."

MOM GUESS WHAT NEWSPAPER, 1725 L St., Sacramento CA 95814. (916)441-6397. Editor: Linda Birner. 80% freelance written. Works with small number of new/unpublished writers each year. Biweekly tabloid covering gay rights and gay lifestyles. Estab. 1977. Circ. 21,000. Publishes ms an average of 3 months after acceptance. Byline given. Buys all rights. Submit seasonal material 3 months in advance. Reports in 2 months. Sample copy for $1. Writer's guidelines for 10×13 SAE with 4 first-class stamps.
Nonfiction: Interview/profile and photo feature of international, national or local scope. Buys 8 mss/year. Query. Length: 200-1,500 words. Payment depends on article. Pays expenses of writers on special assignment.
Photos: Send photos with submission. Reviews 5×7 prints. Offers no additional payment for photos accepted with ms. Captions and identification of subjects required. Buys one-time rights.
Columns/Departments: News, Restaurants, Political, Health, Film, Video, Book Reviews. Buys 12 mss/year. Query. Payment depends on article.

OUT, 110 Greene St., Suite 600, New York NY 10012. (212)334-9119. Editor: Sarah Pettit. 80% freelance written. Monthly "national gay and lesbian general-interest magazine. Our subjects range from current affairs to culture, from fitness to finance. Stories may be anywhere from 50-word items to 8,000-word investigative features." Estab. 1992. Circ. 120,000. Pays on publication. Publishes ms an average of 3 months after acceptance. Byline given. Offers 25% kill fee. Buys first North American serial rights, second serial (reprint) rights for anthologies (additional fee paid) and 30-day reprint rights (additional fee paid if applicable). Editorial lead time 3 months. Submit seasonal material 5 months in advance. Accepts simultaneous submissions. Reports in 6 weeks on queries; 2 months on mss. Sample copy for $6. Writer's guidelines. for #10 SASE.
Nonfiction: Book excerpts, essays, exposé, general interest, historical/nostalgic, humor, interview/profile, new product, opinion, personal experience, photo feature, travel, fashion/lifestyle. Buys 200 mss/year. Query with published clips. Length: 50-10,000 words. Pays 50¢/word. Sometimes pays expenses of writers on assignment.

Photos: State availability of photos with submission. Reviews contact sheets, transparencies, prints. Negotiates payment individually. Captions, model releases, identification of subjects required. Buys one-time rights.

Tips: "*Out's* contributors include editors and writers from the country's top consumer titles: skilled reporters, columnists, and writers with distinctive voices and specific expertise in the fields they cover. But while published clips and relevant experience are a must, the magazine also seeks out fresh, young voices. The best guide to the kind of stories we publish is to review our recent issues—is there a place for the story you have in mind? Be aware of our long lead time."

OUTSMART, Up & Out Communications, 3406 Audubon Place, Houston TX 77006. (713)520-7237. Editor: Eric Roland. Contact: Greg Jeu, publisher. 70% freelance written. Monthly magazine covering gay and lesbian issues. "*OutSmart* provides positive information to gay men, lesbians and their associates to enhance and improve the quality of our lives." Estab. 1994. Circ. 15,000. Pays on publication. Publishes ms an average of 2 months after acceptance. Byline given. Buys one-time rights and simultaneous rights. Editorial lead time 2 months. Submit seasonal material 2 months in advance. Accepts simultaneous submissions. Reports in 6 weeks on queries; 2 months on mss. Sample copy and writer's guidelines for SASE.

Nonfiction: Historical/nostalgic, interview/profile, opinion, personal experience, photo feature, travel. Special issues: Communicating Through Computers (September 1996); Arts & Entertainment (October 1996); Mental Health (November 1996). Buys 10 mss/year. Send complete ms. Length: 700-4,000 words. Pays $20-60.

Reprints: Accepts previously published submissions.

Photos: State availability of photos with submission. Reviews 4×6 prints. Negotiates payment individually. Identification of subjects required. Buys one-time rights.

Tips: Using fewer personal experience stories, more hard-hitting feature articles.

TEN PERCENT, Crane Communications, 54 Mint St., Suite 200, San Francisco CA 94103. (415)905-8590. 75% freelance written. Bimonthly magazine covering gay men. Estab. 1992. Circ. 75,000. Pays on publication. Publishes ms an average of 3 months after acceptance. Byline given. Offers 25% kill fee. Buys first North American serical rights. Editorial lead time 4 months. Submit seasonal material 6 months in advance. Accepts simultaneous submissions. Query for electronic submissions. Reports in 2 weeks on queries; 1 month on mss. Writer's guidelines for SASE.

THE JAMES WHITE REVIEW, A Gay Men's Literary Quarterly, P.O. Box 3356, Butler Quarter, Minneapolis MN 55403. (612)339-8317. E-mail: jwrmail@aol.com. Publisher: Phil Willkie. Fiction Editor: David Rolfing. Poetry Editors: Clif Mayhood and William Reichard. 100% freelance written. Quarterly tabloid covering gay men. Estab. 1983. Circ. 4,500. Byilne given. Buys first North American serial rights. Editorial lead time 3 months. Submit seasonal material 3 months in advance. Reports in 3 months on queries. Sample copy for $3. Writer's guidelines for #10 SASE.

Nonfiction: Book excerpts and essays. Buys 4 mss/year. Send complete ms. Length: 2,000 words maximum. Pays $50 minimum.

Photos: Send photos with submission. Reviews prints. Negotiates payment individually. Buys one-time rights.

Fiction: Confession, erotica, experimental, fantasy, historical, novel excerpts and serialized novels. Buys 20 mss/year. Send complete ms. Length: 2,000 words maximum. Pays $50 maximum.

Poetry: Clif Mayhood, poetry editor. Avant-garde, free verse and traditional. Buys 80 poems/year. Submit no more than 8 poems, or no more than 250 lines of verse (whichever is less). Pays $20.

GENERAL INTEREST

General interest magazines need writers who can appeal to a broad audience—teens and senior citizens, wealthy readers and the unemployed. Each magazine still has a personality that suits its audience—one that a writer should study before sending material to an editor. Other markets for general interest material are in these Consumer categories: Contemporary Culture, Ethnic/Minority, Inflight, Men's, Regional and Women's.

THE AMERICAN LEGION MAGAZINE, P.O. Box 1055, Indianapolis IN 46206-1055. (317)630-1200. Executive Editor of Operations: Miles Z. Epstein. Monthly. 70% freelance written. Prefers to work with published/established writers, but works with a small number of new/unpublished writers each year. Estab. 1919. Circ. 2,850,000. Buys first North American serial rights. Reports on submissions "promptly." **Pays on acceptance.** Publishes ms an average of 6 months after acceptance. Byline given. Reports in 2 months. Sample copy for 9×12 SAE with 6 first-class stamps. Writer's guidelines for #10 SASE.

Nonfiction: Query first, considers unsolicited mss only from veterans concerning their wartime experiences. Query should explain the subject or issue, article's angle and organization, writer's qualifications and experts to be interviewed. Well-reported articles or expert commentaries cover issues/trends in world/national affairs, contemporary problems, general interest, sharply-focused feature subjects. Monthly Q&A with national figures/experts. Few personality profiles. No regional topics. Buys 50-60 mss/year. Length: 1,000-2,000 words. Pays negotiable rates. Pays phone expenses of writers on assignment.

Photos: On assignment.

Tips: "Queries by new writers should include clips/background/expertise; no longer than 1½ pages. Submit suitable material showing you have read several issues. *The American Legion Magazine* considers itself '*the* magazine for a strong America.' Reflect this theme (which includes economy, educational system, moral fiber, social issues, infrastructure, technology and national defense/security). We are a general interest, national magazine, not a strictly military magazine. No unsolicited jokes."

THE AMERICAN SCHOLAR, The Phi Beta Kappa Society, 1811 Q Street NW, Washington DC 20009-9974. (202)265-3808. Editor: Joseph Epstein. Managing Editor: Jean Stipicevic. 100% freelance written. Intellectual quarterly. "Our writers are specialists writing for the college-educated public." Estab. 1932. Circ. 26,000. Pays after author has seen edited piece in galleys. Byline given. Offers 50% kill fee. Buys first rights. Submit seasonal/holiday material 6 months in advance. Reports in 2 weeks on queries; 2 months on ms. Sample copy for $6.95. Writer's guidelines for #10 SASE.

Nonfiction: Book excerpts (prior to publication only), essays, historical/nostalgic, humor. Buys 40 mss/year. Query. Length: 3,000-5,000 words. Pays $500.

Columns/Departments: Buys 16 mss/year. Query. Length: 3,000-5,000 words. Pays $500.

Poetry: Sandra Costich, poetry editor. Buys 20/year. Submit maximum 3 poems. Length: 34-75 lines. Pays $50. "Write for guidelines."

Tips: "The section most open to freelancers is the book review section. Query and send samples of reviews written."

THE ATLANTIC, 745 Boylston St., Boston MA 02116. (617)536-9500. Editor: William Whitworth. Managing Editor: Cullen Murphy. Monthly magazine of arts and public affairs. Circ. 500,000. Pays on acceptance. Byline given. Buys first North American serial rights. Simultaneous submissions discouraged. Reporting time varies. All unsolicited mss must be accompanied by SASE.

● Writers should be aware that this is not a market for beginner's work (nonfiction and fiction), nor is it truly for intermediate work. Study this magazine before sending only your best, most professional work.

Nonfiction: Book excerpts, essays, general interest, humor, personal experience, religious, travel. Query with or without published clips or send complete ms. Length: 1,000-6,000 words. Payment varies. Sometimes pays expenses of writers on assignment.

Fiction: C. Michael Curtis, fiction editor. Buys 12-15 mss/year. Send complete ms. Length: 2,000-6,000 words preferred. Payment $2,500.

● Ranked as one of the best markets for fiction writers in *Writer's Digest*'s annual "Fiction 50," June 1996.

Poetry: Peter Davison, poetry editor. Buys 40-60 poems/year.

CAPPER'S, Stauffer Communications, Inc., 1503 SW 42nd St., Topeka KS 66609-1265. (913)274-4346. Fax: (913)274-4305. Contact: Nancy Peavler, editor. Associate Editors: Cheryl Ptacek, Ann Crahan, Rosemary Rebek. 25% freelance written. Works with a small number of new/unpublished writers each year. Biweekly tabloid emphasizing home and family for readers who live in small towns and on farms. Estab. 1879. Circ. 325,000. **Pays for poetry and fiction on acceptance;** articles on publication. Publishes ms an average of 6 months after acceptance. Buys first serial rights only. Submit seasonal/holiday material at least 3 months in advance. Reports in 4 months; 10 months for serialized novels. Sample copy for $1.50. Writer's guidelines for #10 SASE.

Nonfiction: Historical (local museums, etc.), inspirational, nostalgia, budget travel (Midwest slants), people stories (accomplishments, collections, etc.). Special issues: Health issue (September); Holiday/Entertaining (November). Buys 50 mss/year. Submit complete ms. Length: 700 words maximum. Pays $2/inch.

Reprints: Send typed ms with rights for sale noted and information about when and where the article previously appeared. Pays $1.50/column inch as printed.

Photos: Purchased with accompanying ms. Submit prints. Pays $10-15 for 8×10 or 5×7 b&w glossy prints. Total purchase price for ms includes payment for photos. Limited market for color photos (35mm color slides); pays $35-40 each.

FOR INFORMATION on setting your freelance fees, see How Much Should I Charge?

Columns/Departments: Heart of the Home (homemakers' letters, recipes, hints); Community Heartbeat (volunteerism). Submit complete ms. Length: 300 words maximum. Pays $1 gift certificate-$20.
Fiction: "We buy very few fiction pieces—longer than short stories, shorter than novels." Adventure and romance mss. No explicit sex, violence or profanity. Buys 4-5 mss/year. Query. Pays $75-400 for 7,500-60,000 words.
Poetry: Free verse, haiku, light verse, traditional, nature, inspiration. "The poems that appear in *Capper's* are not too difficult to read. They're easy to grasp. We're looking for everyday events and down-to-earth themes." Buys 4-5/issue. Limit submissions to batches of 5-6. Length: 4-16 lines. Pays $5-15.
Tips: "Study a few issues of our publication. Most rejections are for material that is too long, unsuitable or out of character for our magazine (too sexy, too much profanity, wrong kind of topic, etc.). On occasion, we must cut material to fit column space."

THE CHRISTIAN SCIENCE MONITOR, 1 Norway St., Boston MA 02115. (617)450-2000. Contact: Submissions. International newspaper issued daily except Saturdays, Sundays and holidays in North America; weekly international edition. Estab. 1908. Circ. 95,000. Buys all newspaper rights worldwide for 3 months following publication. Buys limited number of mss, "top quality only." Publishes original (exclusive) material only. Pays on publication. Reports in 1 month. Submit complete original ms or letter of inquiry. Writer's guidelines for #10 SASE.
Nonfiction: Jane Lampmann, feature editor. In-depth features and essays. "Style should be bright but not cute, concise but thoroughly researched. Try to humanize news or feature writing so reader identifies with it. Avoid sensationalism, crime and disaster. Accent constructive, solution-oriented treatment of subjects." Home Forum page buys essays of 400-900 words. Pays $150 average. Education, arts, environment, food, science and technology pages will consider articles not usually more than 800 words appropriate to respective subjects. No medical stories." *Writer's Market* recommends sending a query with SASE first. Pays $150-200.
Poetry: Traditional, blank and free verse. Seeks non-religious poetry of high quality and of all lengths up to 75 lines. Pays $35-75 average.
Tips: "We prefer neatly typed originals. No handwritten copy. Enclosing an SAE and postage with ms is a must."

CIVILIZATION, L.O.C. Associates, 475 Park Ave. S., 7th Floor, New York NY 10016. (212)532-6400. (212)532-9770. Publisher: Quentin Walz. Bimonthly magazine. "*Civilization* is the membership magazine of the Library of Congress covering contemporary culture. Well-known writers contribute articles on the arts, travel, government, history, education, biography and social issues." Estab. 1994. Circ. 200,000. This magazine did not respond to our request for information. Query before submitting.

‡DIVERSION, Hearst Business Publishing, 1790 Broadway, New York NY 10019. (212)969-7500. Fax: (212)969-7563. Editor-in-Chief: Tom Passavant. Monthly magazine covering travel and lifestyle, edited for physicians. "*Diversion* offers an eclectic mix of interests beyond medicine. Regular features include stories on domestic and foreign travel destinations, discussions of food and wine, sports columns, guidance on gardening and photography, and information on investments and finance. The editorial reflects its readers' affluent lifestyles and diverse personal interests. Although *Diversion* doesn't cover health subjects, it does feature profiles of doctors who excel at nonmedical pursuits." Estab. 1973. Circ. 176,000. Pays 3 months after acceptance. Offers 25% kill fee. Editorial lead time 4 months.
  • Ranked as one of the best markets for freelance writers in *Writer's Yearbook*'s annual "Top 100 Markets," January 1996.
Nonfiction: Length: 2,200 words. Pays $750-1,000. Query with proposal, published clips and author's credentials.
Columns/Departments: Travel, food & wine, photography, gardening, finance. Length: 1,200 words. Pays $650-750. Query with proposal, published clips and author's credentials.

EQUINOX: Canada's Magazine of Discovery, Telemedia Communications, Inc., 25 Sheppard Ave. W., Suite 100, North York, Ontario M2N 6S7 Canada. (416)733-7600. E-mail: letters@equinox.ca. Website: http://www.equinox.ca. Editor: Jim Cormier. Bimonthly magazine "encompassing the worlds of human cultures and communities, the natural world and science and technology." Estab. 1982. Circ. 175,000. **Pays on acceptance.** Byline given. Offers 50% kill fee. Buys first North American serial rights only. Submit seasonal queries 1 year in advance. Reports in 2 months. Sample copy for $5. Writer's guidelines for #10 SASE (U.S. writers must send IRCs, not American stamps).
Nonfiction: Book excerpts (occasionally). No travel articles. Should have Canadian focus. Query. Length: 1,500-5,000 words. Pays $1,750-3,000 negotiated.
Photos: Send photos with ms. Reviews color transparencies—must be of professional quality; no prints or negatives. Captions and identification of subjects required.
Columns/Departments: Nexus (current science that isn't covered by daily media); Scope (reviews). Query with clips of published work. Length: 200-800 words. Pays $250-500.
Tips: "Submit ideas for short photo essays as well as longer features."

FRIENDLY EXCHANGE, The Aegis Group: Publishers, Friendly Exchange Business Office, P.O. Box 2120, Warren MI 48090-2120. Publication Office: (810)558-7226. Editor: (702)786-7419. Editor: Adele Malott. 80% freelance written. Works with a small number of new/unpublished writers each year. Quarterly magazine for policyholders of Farmers Insurance Group of Companies exploring travel, lifestyle and leisure topics of interest to active families. "These are traditional families (median adult age 39) who live primarily in the area bounded by Ohio on the east and the Pacific Ocean on the west, along with Tennessee, Alabama, and Virginia." Estab. 1981. Circ. 5,700,000. **Pays on acceptance.** Publishes ms an average of 5 months after acceptance. Offers 25% kill fee. Buys all rights. Submit seasonal/holiday material 1 year in advance. Accepts simultaneous queries. Reports in 2 months. Sample copy for 9×12 SAE with 5 first-class stamps. Writer's guidelines for #10 SASE.

• Ranked as one of the best markets for freelance writers in *Writer's Yearbook*'s annual "Top 100 Markets," January 1996.

Nonfiction: "Domestic travel and leisure topics of interest to the family can be addressed from many different perspectives, including health and safety, consumerism, heritage and education. Articles offer a service to readers and encourage them to take some positive action such as taking a trip. Style is colorful, warm and inviting, making liberal use of anecdotes and quotes. The only first-person articles used are those assigned; all others in third person. Only domestic travel locations are considered. Buys 8 mss/issue. Query. Length: 600-1,500 words. Pays $500-1,000/article, plus agreed-upon expenses.

Photos: Art director. Pays $150-250 for 35mm color transparencies; $50 for b&w prints. Cover photo payment negotiable. Pays on publication.

Columns/Departments: All columns and departments rely on reader-generated materials; none used from professional writers.

Tips: "We concentrate exclusively on the travel and leisure hours of our readers. Do not use destination approach in travel pieces—instead, for example, tell us about the people, activities, or events that make the location special. We prefer to go for a small slice rather than the whole pie, and we are just as interested in the cook who made it or the person who will be eating it as we are in the pie itself. Concentrate on what families can do together."

GRIT: American Life and Traditions, Stauffer Magazine Group, 1503 SW 42nd St., Topeka KS 66609-1265. (913)274-4300. Editor-in-Chief: Michael Scheibach. 60% freelance written. Open to new writers. "*Grit* is Good News. As a wholesome, family-oriented magazine published for more than a century and distributed nationally, *Grit* is characterized by old-fashioned friendliness. *Grit* features articles about family lifestyles, family traditions, our American heritage, social themes and family values. In short, *Grit* accents the best of American life and traditions—past and present. Our readers cherish family values and appreciate practical and innovative ideas. Many of them live in small towns and rural areas across the country; others live in cities but share many of the values typical of small-town America." Estab. 1882. Circ. 200,000. Pays on publication. Publishes ms an average of 2 months after acceptance. Byline given. Buys first rights. Occasionally buys reprint rights if first publication was to extremely local or regional audience. Submit seasonal material 8 months in advance. Reports in 2 months on queries. Sample copy and writer's guidelines for $4 and 11×14 SAE with 4 first-class stamps.

Nonfiction: Most in need of cover stories (timely, newsworthy, but with a *Grit* angle); Profile, Americana and human interest features, Home, and Health stories. Also need touching, humorous or off-beat shorts with art (color or b&w). Writers will best be able to successfully sell their work by becoming familiar with the publication. Pays minimum of 22¢/word for assigned articles (average $150-500 for a feature, more with photos), less for unsolicited mss or reprints. Main features run 1,200 to 1,500 words, sidebars often additional; department features average 800-1,000 words.

Reprints: Send typed ms with rights for sale noted and information about when and where article previously appeared.

Fiction: Short stories, 1,500-2,000 words; may also purchase accompanying art if of high quality and appropriate occasionally publishes shorter or longer work also. Send complete ms with SASE. Note Fiction Dept. on envelope!

Photos: Professional quality photos (b&w prints or color slides) increase acceptability of articles. Black and white prints *required* with Profile submissions. Photos: $35-200 each, dependent on quality, placement and color/b&w.

Tips: "With the exception of Profile submissions, articles should be nationalized with several sources identified fully. Third-person accounts are preferred. Information in sidebar or graphic form is appropriate for many stories. *Grit* readers enjoy lists of tips, resources, or questions that help them understand the topic. *Grit* stories should be helpful and conversational with an upbeat approach. Preferred to queries: Submit a list of several brief but developed story ideas by department/feature along with a brief bio and examples of your published work."

HARPER'S MAGAZINE, 666 Broadway, 11th Floor, New York NY 10012. (212)614-6500. Fax: (212)228-5889. Editor: Lewis H. Lapham. 90% freelance written. Monthly magazine for well-educated, socially concerned, widely read men and women who value ideas and good writing. Estab. 1850. Circ. 205,000. Rights purchased vary with author and material. Pays negotiable kill fee. **Pays on acceptance.** Reports in 2 weeks.

Publishes ms an average of 3 months after acceptance. Sample copy for $3.95.

• Ranked as one of the best markets for freelance writers in *Writer's Yearbook*'s annual "Top 100 Markets," January 1996.

Nonfiction: "For writers working with agents or who will query first only, our requirements are: public affairs, literary, international and local reporting and humor." No interviews; no profiles. Complete ms and query must include SASE. No unsolicited poems will be accepted. Publishes one major report per issue. Length: 4,000-6,000 words. Publishes one major essay/issue. Length: 4,000-6,000 words. "These should be construed as topical essays on all manner of subjects (politics, the arts, crime, business, etc.) to which the author can bring the force of passionately informed statement."

• *Harper's Magazine* is the first national magazine to announce a policy of splitting past and future revenues from new-media and online sources with the material's original writers.

Reprints: Accepts previously published submissions for its "Readings" section. Send tearsheet or photocopy of article, or typed ms with rights for sale noted and information about when and where the article previously appeared.

Fiction: Publishes one short story/month. Generally pays 50¢-$1/word.

Photos: Contact: Angela Riechers, art director. Occasionally purchased with mss; others by assignment. Pays $50-500.

‡**HOPE MAGAZINE, Humanity Making A Difference**, Hope Publishing, Inc., P.O. Box 160, Brooklin ME 04616. (207)359-4651. Fax: (207)359-8920. E-mail: editor@hopemag.com. Editor: Jon Wilson. Contact: Kimberly Ridley, associate editor. 90% freelance written. Bimonthly magazine covering humanity at its best and worst. "We strive to evoke empathy among readers." Estab. 1996. Circ. 50,000. **Pays on acceptance**. Publishes ms an average of 6 months after acceptance. Byline given. Offers 20% kill fee. Buys first, one-time or second serial (reprint) rights. Editorial lead time 4 months. Submit seasonal material 6 months in advance. Accepts simultaneous submissions. Reports in 1 month on queries; 2 months on mss. Sample copy for $5. Writer's guidelines for #10 SASE.

Nonfiction: Book excerpts, essays, general interest, historical/nostalgic, humor, inspirational, interview/profile, opinion, personal experience, photo feature. Nothing explicitly religious, political or New Age. Buys 50-75 mss/year. Query with published clips. Length: 250-6,000 words. Pays $50-3,000. Sometimes pays expenses of writers on assignment.

Reprints: Accepts previously published submissions.

Photos: State availability of or send photos with submission. Reviews contact sheets and 5×7 prints. Negotiates payment individually. Captions and identification of subjects required. Buys one-time rights.

Columns/Departments: Signs of Hope (inspiring dispatches/news) 250-1,000 words. Buys 50-60 mss/year. Query with published clips. Send complete ms. Pays $50-300.

Tips: "Write very personally, and very deeply. We're not looking for shallow 'feel-good' pieces. Approach uncommon subjects. Cover the ordinary in extraordinary ways. Go to the heart."

‡**IDEALS MAGAZINE**, Ideals Publications Inc., P.O. Box 305300, Nashville TN 37230. (615)333-0478. Publisher: Patricia Pingry. Editor: Lisa Ragan. 95% freelance written. Bimonthly magazine. "Our readers are generally conservative, educated women over 50. The magazine is mainly light poetry and short articles with a nostalgic theme. Issues are seasonally oriented and thematic." Circ. 180,000. Pays on publication. Publishes ms an average of 1 year after acceptance. Byline given. Buys one-time, worldwide serial and subsidiary rights. Submit seasonal/holiday material 8 months in advance. Accepts simultaneous submissions. Reports in 3 months. Sample copy for $4. Writer's guidelines for #10 SASE.

Nonfiction: Essays, historical/nostalgic, humor, inspirational, personal experience. "No depressing articles." Buys 20 mss/year. Send complete ms. Length: 800-1,000 words. Pays 10¢/word.

Reprints: Send tearsheet or photocopy of article or short story and information about when and where the article previously appeared. Pays 100% of amount paid for an original article.

Photos: Guidelines for SASE. Reviews tearsheets. Offers no additional payment for photos accepted with ms. Captions, model releases, identification of subjects required. Buys one-time rights. Payment varies.

Fiction: Slice-of-life vignettes. Buys 10 mss/year. Length: 800-1,000 words. Pays 10¢/word.

Poetry: Light verse, traditional. "No erotica or depressing poetry." Buys 250 poems/year. Submit maximum 15 poems, 20-30 lines. Pays $10/poem.

Tips: "Poetry is the area of our publication most open to freelancers. It must be oriented around a season or theme. Nostalgia is an underlying theme of every issue. Poetry must be optimistic."

LEFTHANDER MAGAZINE, Lefthander International, P.O. Box 8249, Topeka KS 66608-0249. (913)234-2177. Managing Editor: Kim Kipers. 80% freelance written. Eager to work with new/unpublished writers. Bimonthly magazine for "lefthanded people of all ages and interests in 50 US states and 12 foreign countries. The one thing they have in common is an interest in lefthandedness." Estab. 1975. Circ. 26,000. Pays on publication. Publishes ms an average of 4 months after acceptance. Byline usually given. Offers 25% kill fee. Rights negotiable. Reports on queries in 2 months. Sample copy for $2 and 9×12 SAE. Writer's guidelines for #10 SASE.

Nonfiction: Interviews with famous lefthanders; features about lefthanders with interesting talents and occupations; how-to features (sports, crafts, hobbies for lefties); research on handedness and brain dominance; exposé on discrimination against lefthanders in the work world; features on occupations and careers attracting lefties; education features relating to ambidextrous right brain teaching methods. Buys 50-60 mss/year. Length: 1,500-2,000 words for features. Pays $85-100. Buys 6 personal experience shorts/year. Pays $25. Pays expenses of writer on assignment. Query with SASE.

Photos: State availability of photos for features. Pays $10-15 for good contrast color glossies, slides, transparencies. Rights negotiable.

Tips: "All material must have a lefthanded hook. We prefer practical, self-help and self-awareness types of editorial content of general interest."

LIFE, Time & Life Bldg., Rockefeller Center, New York NY 10020. (212)522-1212. Managing Editor: Daniel Okrent. Articles: Jay D. Lovinger, executive editor: 10% freelance written. Prefers to work with published/established writers; rarely works with new/unpublished writers. (*Life* used no previously unpublished writers in 1994.) Monthly general interest picture magazine for people of all ages, backgrounds and interests. Estab. 1936. Circ. 1,500,000. **Pays on acceptance.** Publishes ms an average of 3 months after acceptance. Byline given. Buys first North American serial rights. Submit seasonal material 4 months in advance. Accepts simultaneous submissions. Reports in 2 months.

Nonfiction: "We've done articles on anything in the world of interest to the general reader and on people of importance. It's extremely difficult to break in since we buy so few articles. Most of the magazine is pictures. We're looking for very high quality writing. We select writers whom we think match the subject they are writing about." Query with clips of previously published work. Length: 1,000-4,000 words.

NATIONAL GEOGRAPHIC MAGAZINE, 1145 17th St. NW, Washington DC 20036. (202)857-7000. Fax: (202)828-6667. Editor: William Allen. 50% freelance written. Prefers to work with published/established writers. Monthly magazine for members of the National Geographic Society. Estab. 1888. Circ. 9,500,000.

Nonfiction: *National Geographic* publishes general interest, illustrated articles on science, natural history, exploration, politics and geographical regions. Almost half of the articles are staff-written. Of the freelance writers assigned, some are experts in their fields; the remainder are established professionals. Fewer than 1% of unsolicited queries result in assignments. Query (500 words) by letter, not by phone, to Associate Editor Robert Poole. Do not send mss. Before querying, study recent issues and check a *Geographic Index* at a library since the magazine seldom returns to regions or subjects covered within the past 10 years. Pays expenses of writers on assignment.

Photos: Photographers should query in care of the Photographic Division.

NEW YORK TIMES MAGAZINE, New York Times Co., Magazine Group, 229 W. 43rd St., New York NY 10036. (212)556-7777. Fax: (212)556-5845. Weekly supplement to Sunday New York Times newspaper. "*The New York Times Magazine* editorial is devoted to helping its readers understand a changing world. It contains articles and photographs on a wide range of subjects: foreign affairs, politics, medicine, the arts, science, religion and business. There are features on fashion, design, food, beauty, health, collecting and the New York Times Magazine puzzles." Estab. 1851. Circ. 1,800,000. This magazine did not respond to our request for information. Query before submitting.

THE NEW YORKER, ~~20 W. 43rd St., New York NY 10036-7441~~. 4 Times Square NY NY (212)~~536-5400~~. 286-5400. Editor: ~~Tina Brown~~ David Remnick. Weekly. Estab. 1925. Circ. 600,000. *The New Yorker* is one of today's premier markets for top-notch nonfiction, fiction and poetry. Query before submitting. To submit material, please direct your ms to the appropriate editor, (i.e., fact, fiction, poetry or humor) and enclose SASE. The editors deal with a tremendous number of submissions every week; writers hoping to crack this market should be prepared to wait at least 2 or 3 months for a reply.

NEWSWEEK, 251 W. 57th St., New York NY 10019. (212)445-4000. Circ. 3,180,000. Contact: My Turn Editor. Accepts unsolicited mss for My Turn, a column of personal opinion. The 1,000- to 1,100-word essays for the column must be original, not published elsewhere and contain verifiable facts. Payment is $1,000, on publication. Buys non-exclusive world-wide rights. Reports in 2 months only on submissions with SASE.

‡THE NORTHERN CENTINEL, The Centinel Company, 115 E. 82 St., Suite 8-B, New York 10028. Managing Editor: Peter J. Gardner. 75% freelance written. Bimonthly tabloid. Estab. 1788. Circ. 20,000. Pays on publication. Publishes ms an average of 4 months after acceptance. Byline given. Buys first rights. Editorial lead time 3 months. Submit seasonal material 4 months in advance. Accepts simultaneous submissions. Reports in 1 month on queries; 3 months on mss. Sample copy for $2.50. Writer's guidelines for #10 SASE.

Nonfiction: Essays, exposé, general interest, humor, interview/profile, opinion (does not mean letters to the editor), photo feature, travel, political. Buys 40 mss/year. Send complete ms. Length: 800-1,200 words. Pays $40 minimum.

Photos: State availability of photos with submission. Offers $40/photo. Captions, identification of subjects required. Buys one-time rights.

Columns/Departments: Buys 60-70 mss/year. Send complete ms. Pays $40 minimum.

Fiction: Adventure, humorous, mystery, science fiction, suspense, western. Send complete ms. Length: 1,200-2,400 words. Pays $40 minimum.

Poetry: Ellen Rachlin, Lucie Aidinoff, poetry editors. Avant-garde, free verse, haiku, light verse, traditional. Buys 12-18 poems/year. Length: 50 lines. Pays $40 minimum.

PARADE, Parade Publications, Inc., 711 Third Ave., New York NY 10017. (212)450-7000. Editor: Walter Anderson. Contact: Articles Editor. Weekly magazine for a general interest audience. 90% freelance written. Circ. 37,000,000. **Pays on acceptance.** Publishes ms an average of 3 months after acceptance. Kill fee varies in amount. Buys first North American serial rights. Reports in 6 weeks on queries. Writer's guidelines for #10 SASE.

Nonfiction: General interest (on health, trends, social issues or anything of interest to a broad general audience); interview/profile (of news figures, celebrities and people of national significance); and "provocative topical pieces of news value." Spot news events are not accepted, as *Parade* has a 6-week lead time. No fiction, fashion, travel, poetry, cartoons, nostalgia, regular columns, quizzes or fillers. Unsolicited queries concerning celebrities, politicians, sports figures, or technical are rarely assigned. Address single-page queries to Articles Correspondent; include SASE. Length of published articles: 800-1,500 words. Pays $2,500 minimum. Pays expenses of writers on assignment.

Tips: "Send a well-researched, well-written three-paragraph query targeted to our national market. Please, no phone or fax queries. Keep subject tightly focused—a writer should be able to state the point or theme of the query in three or four sentences."

PRIME TIMES, Grote Publishing, 634 W. Main St., Suite 207, Madison WI 53703-2634. Managing Editor: Barbara Walsh. 75% freelance written. Quarterly membership magazine for the National Association for Retired Credit Union People (NARCUP). "*Prime Times* is a topical magazine of broad appeal to a general adult audience, emphasizing issues relevant to people over age 50. It offers timely articles on health, fitness, finance, travel, outdoor sports, consumer issues, lifestyle, home arts and family relationships. Estab. 1979. Circ. 76,000. May share a core of editorial material with sister magazine *American Times* (est. 1993), sent to financial institutions' older adult customers. Pays on publication. Publishes ms an average of 9 months after acceptance. Byline given. Buys first North American serial rights, one-time rights and second serial (reprint) rights. Editorial lead time 7 months. Submit seasonal material 8 months in advance. Reports in 6 weeks on queries; 2 months on mss. Sample copy for $3 and 9 × 12 SAE with 4 first-class stamps. Writer's guidelines for #10 SASE.

Nonfiction: Book excerpts, general interest, health/fitness, travel, historical, humor, photo features. "No nostalgia pieces, medical or financial pieces based solely on personal anecdotes, personal opinion essays, fiction or poetry." Buys 10-20 mss/year. Prefers to see complete ms. Length: 1,000-2,000 words. Pays $250 minimum for full-length assigned articles; $100 minimum for unsolicited full-length articles; $50 for "American Short Tales."

Reprints: Send photocopy of article or typed ms with rights for sale noted and information about when and where the article previously appeared. Pays $50-125, depending on length, quality and number of times published.

Photos: Needs professional-quality photos. State availability of or send photos with submission. Welcomes text-photo packages. Reviews contact sheets, transparencies and prints. Negotiates payment individually. Model releases and identification of subjects required. Buys one-time rights.

Tips: "Articles that contain useful, well-documented, up-to-date information have the best chance of publication. Don't send personal essays, or articles that repeat information readily available in mainstream media. Articles on health and medical issues *must* be founded in sound scientific method and include current data. You must be able to document your research. Make it easy for us to make a decision on your submission. If the article is written, submit the entire thing—manuscript with professional-quality photos. If you query, be specific. Write part of it in the style in which you would write the article. Be sure to enclose clips. With every article we publish, something about the story must lend itself to strong graphic representation."

RANDOM LENGTHS, Harbor Independent News, P.O. Box 731, San Pedro CA 90733-0731. (310)519-1016. Editor: James Elmendorf. 30% freelance written. Biweekly tabloid covering alternative news/features. "*Random Lengths* follows Twain's dictum of printing news 'to make people mad enough to do something about it.' Our writers do exposés, scientific, environmental, political reporting and fun, goofy, insightful, arts and entertainment coverage, for a lefty, labor-oriented, youngish crowd." Estab. 1979. Circ. 30,000. Pays in 60 days. Byline given. Offers 50% kill fee. Buys all rights. Editorial lead time 1 month. Submit seasonal material 2 months in advance. Accepts simultaneous submissions. Reports in 6 weeks on queries. Sample copy for 9 × 13 SAE with 3 first-class stamps. Writer's guidelines free on request.

Nonfiction: Exposé, general interest, historical/nostalgic, interview/profile, opinion. Special issues: Labor Day, triannual book edition; women and black history months. Buys 150 mss/year. Query. Length: 300-2,000 words. Pays 5¢/word. Sometimes pays expenses of writers on assignment.

Reprints: Accepts previously published submissions.

Photos: State availability of photos with submissions. Reviews prints. Offers $10/photo. Captions, identification of subjects required. Buys all rights.

Columns/Departments: Community News (local angle), 300-600 words; Commentary (national/world/opinion), 600-800 words; Feature (books/music/local events), 300-600 words. Buys 75 mss/year. Query. Pays 5¢/word.

Tips: "We use mostly local material and local writers, but we are open to current-event, boffo entertaining writing. Read other alternative weeklies for reference. We need local news most. Next, entertainment stuff with a local pitch."

READER'S DIGEST, Reader's Digest Rd., Pleasantville NY 10570-7000. E-mail: readersdigest@notes.co mpuserve.com. Monthly general interest magazine. "We are looking for contemporary stories of lasting interest that give the magazine variety, freshness and originality." Estab. 1922. Circ. 15,000,000. Byline given. Buys exclusive world periodical rights, electronic rights, among others. Editorial lead time 3 months. Submit seasonal material 6 months in advance. Reports in 6 weeks on queries. Does not read or return unsolicited mss. Address article queries and tearsheets of published articles to the editors.

• Ranked as one of the best markets for freelance writers in *Writer's Yearbook*'s annual "Top 100 Markets," January 1996.

Nonfiction: Book excerpts, essays, exposé, general interest, historical/nostalgic, humor, inspirational, interview/profile, opinion, personal experience. Buys 100 mss/year. Query with published clips. Length: 2,500-4,000 words. Original article rates begin at $3,000.

Reprints: Send tearsheet of article or typed ms with rights for sale noted and information about where and when the article appeared. Pays $1,200/*Reader's Digest* page for World Digest rights (usually split 50/50 between original publisher and writer).

Columns/Departments: "Original contributions become the property of *Reader's Digest* upon acceptance and payment. Life-in-These-United States contributions must be true, unpublished stories from one's own experience, revealing adult human nature, and providing appealing or humorous sidelights on the American scene." Length: 300 words maximum. Pays $400 on publication. True, unpublished stories are also solicited for Humor in Uniform, Campus Comedy, Tales Out of School and All in a Day's Work. Length: 300 words maximum. Pays $400 on publication. Towards More Picturesque Speech—the first contributor of each item used in this department is paid $50 for original material, $35 for reprints. For items used in Laughter, the Best Medicine, Personal Glimpses, Quotable Quotes, Notes From All Over, Points to Ponder and elsewhere in the magazine payment is as follows; to the *first* contributor of each from a published source, $35. For original material, $30/*Reader's Digest* two-column line. Previously published material must have source's name, date and page number. Please address your submission to the appropriate feature editor. Send complete anecdotes to *Reader's Digest*, Box LL, Pleasantville NY 10570, or fax to (914)238-6390. CompuServe address is notes:readersdigest or use readersdigest@notes.compuserve.com from other online services and the Internet."

READER'S DIGEST (CANADA), 215 Redfern, Westmount, Quebec H3Z 2V9 Canada. (514)934-0751. Fax: (514)935-4463. Editor-in-Chief: Alexander Farrell. Associate Editor: Ron Starr. 10-25% freelance written. Monthly magazine of general interest articles and subjects. Estab. 1948. Circ. 1.3 million. **Pays on acceptance** for original works. Pays on publication for "pickups." Byline given. Offers $500 (Canadian) kill fee. Buys one-time rights (for reprints), all rights (for original articles). Submit seasonal/holiday material 5 months in advance. Reports in 5 weeks on queries. Writer's guidelines for #10 SASE with Canadian postage or #10 SAE with 1 IRC.

Nonfiction: General interest, how-to (general interest), inspirational, personal experience. "No fiction, poetry or articles too specialized, technical or esoteric—read *Reader's Digest* to see what kind of articles we want." Query with published clips to Associate Editor: Ron Starr. Length: 3,000-5,000 words. Pays a minimum of $2,700 for assigned articles. Pays expenses of writers on assignment.

Reprints: Send photocopy of article. Reprint payment is negotiable.

Photos: State availability of photos with submission.

Tips: "*Reader's Digest* usually finds its freelance writers through other well-known publications in which they have previously been published. There are guidelines available and writers should read *Reader's Digest* to see what kind of stories we look for and how they are written. We do not accept unsolicited manuscripts."

‡**READERS REVIEW**, The National Research Bureau, Inc., P.O. Box 1, Burlington IA 52601-0001. (319)752-5415. Fax: (319)752-3421. Editor: Nancy Heinzel. 75% freelance written. Works with a small number of new/unpublished writers each year, and is eager to work with new/unpublished writers. Quarterly magazine. Estab. 1948. Pays on publication. Publishes ms an average of 1 year after acceptance. Buys all rights. Submit seasonal/holiday material 7 months in advance of issue date. Sample copy and writers guidelines for #10 SAE with 2 first-class stamps.

Nonfiction: General interest (steps to better health, attitudes on the job); how-to (perform better on the job, do home repairs, car maintenance); travel. Buys 10-12 mss/year. Query with outline or submit complete ms. Length: 500-700 words. Pays 4¢/word.

Tips: "Writers have a better chance of breaking in at our publication with short articles."

REAL PEOPLE, The Magazine of Celebrities and Interesting People, Main Street Publishing Co., Inc., 950 Third Ave. 16th Floor, New York NY 10022-2705. (212)371-4932. Fax: (212)838-8420. Editor: Alex Polner. 75% freelance written. Bimonthly magazine for ages 35 and up focusing on celebs and show business, but also interesting people who might appeal to a national audience. Estab. 1988. Circ. 100,000. Pays on publication. Byline given. Pays 33% kill fee. Buys all rights. Submit seasonal/holiday material 6 months in advance. Reports within 1 month. Sample copy for $4 and 8 × 11 SAE with 3 first-class stamps. Writer's guidelines for #10 SASE.
Nonfiction: Interview/profile. Buys 80 mss/year. Query with published clips and SAE. Length: 500-2,000 words. Pays $200-500 for assigned articles; $100-250 for unsolicited articles.
Columns/Departments: Newsworthy shorts—up to 200 words. "We are doing more shorter (75-250 word) pieces for our 'Real Shorts' column." Pays $25-50. Submit to Brad Hamilton, editor.
Photos: State availability of photos with submissions. Reviews 5 × 7 prints and/or slides. Offers no additional payment for photos accepted with ms. Captions, model releases and identification of subjects required. Buys one-time rights.

REMEMBER, The People And News We Can't Forget, Kapro Publishing, 7002 West Butler Pike, Ambler PA 19002. (215)675-0616. Editor: Craig Peters. 75% freelance written. Bimonthly magazine covering events and people of 1920s-1980s. "We focus on reminiscences and reappraisals of past people and events in America. We concentrate on entertainment, sports and politics from 1920-1985." Estab. 1994. Circ. 100,000. Pays on publication. Publishes ms an average of 5 months after acceptance. Byline given. Buys first North American serial and second serial (reprint) rights. Editorial lead time 5 months. Submit seasonal material 6 months in advance. Accepts simultaneous submissions. Sample copy for $3.50. Writer's guidelines for #10 SASE.
Nonfiction: Book excerpts, general interest, historical/nostalgic, interview/profile, personal experience (remembrances of famous figures if writer had personal contact), photo feature. No personal nostalgic essays. Buys 50-60 mss/year. Query with published clips. Length: 400-2,500 words. Pays $75-300.
Photos: State availability of photos with submissions.
Columns/Departments: I Remember (remembrance of celebrity), 500 words; Where Are They Now? (what former stars are doing now), 500 words; Goofs & Gaffes (famous blunders in entertainment and society), 500 words; Souvenirs (covering a unique corner of the collecting world; photos required), 250 words. Buys 20-25 mss/year. Query with published clips. Pays $75-150.
Tips: "Be aware of anniversaries of big events that are at least six months down the road. Explain why you are the best person to write this story."

REUNIONS MAGAZINE, P.O. Box 11727, Milwaukee WI 53211-0727. (414)263-4567. Fax: (414)263-6331; (query first by fax). E-mail: reunions@execpc.com. Website: http://www.execpc.com/~reunions. Publisher: Edith Wagner. 75% freelance written. Quarterly magazine covering reunions—all aspects, all types. "*Reunions Magazine* is primarily for people actively involved with class, family and military reunions or ongoing adoptive or genealogical searchers. We want easy, practical ideas about organizing, planning, researching/searching, attending or promoting reunions." Estab. 1990. Circ. 7,000. Pays on publication. Publishes ms an average of 9 months after acceptance. Byline given. Buys one-time rights. Editorial lead time minimum 6 months. Submit seasonal material 1 year in advance. Appreciates e-mail submissions. Reports in 3 months on queries. Sample copy free. Writer's guidelines for #10 SASE.
Nonfiction: Historical/nostalgic, how-to, humor, interview/profile, new product, personal experience, photo feature, travel, reunion recipes with reunion anecdote—all must be reunion-related. Needs reviewers for books, videos, software (include your requirements). Special issues: African-American family reunions (December); Kids Stuff (March); Golf at Reunions (June); reunions in various sections of the US; ethnic reunions. Buys 18 mss/year. Query with published clips. Length: 500-3,000 words. Pays $25 minimum. Often rewards with generous copies. May pay some expenses of writers on assignment.
Reprints: Send tearsheet or photocopy of article or typed ms with rights for sale noted and information about when and where the article previously appeared.
Photos: State availability of photos with submission. Reviews contact sheets, negatives, 35mm transparencies and prints. Offers no additional payment for photos accepted with ms. Captions, model releases and identification of subjects required. Buys one-time rights. Always looking for cover photos.
Fillers: Anecdotes, facts, newsbreaks, short humor—must be reunion-related. Buys 20/year. Length: 50-250 words. Pays $5.
Tips: "Write a lively account of an interesting or unusual reunion, either upcoming or soon afterward while it's hot. Tell readers why reunion is special, what went into planning it and how attendees reacted. Our *Masterplan* section is a great place for a freelancer to start. Send us how-tos or tips on any aspect of reunion organizing. Open your minds to different types of reunions—they're all around!"

ROBB REPORT, The Magazine for the Affluent Lifestyle, 1 Acton Place, Acton MA 01720. (508)263-7749. Fax: (508)263-0722. Contact: Robert Feeman, editor. Managing Editor: Janice Stillman. 60% freelance written. Monthly magazine. "We are a lifestyle magazine geared toward active, affluent readers. Addresses upscale autos, luxury travel, boating, technology, lifestyles, watches, fashion, sports, investments, collectibles." Estab. 1975. Circ. 80,000. Pays on publication. Byline given. Offers 50% kill fee. Buys all rights or first North American serial rights. Submit seasonal/holiday material 5 months in advance. Reports in 2 months on queries; 1 month on mss. Sample copy for $10.95. Writer's guidelines for #10 SASE.

Nonfiction: General interest (autos, lifestyle, etc.), interview/profile (business), new product (autos, boats, consumer electronics), travel (international and domestic). No essays, personal travel experiences, bargain travel. Special issues: Home issue (September); Watch issue (November). Buys 60 mss/year. Query with published clips if available. Length: 500-3,500 words. Pays $100-900. Sometimes pays expenses of writers on assignment.

Photos: State availability of photos with submission. Payment depends on article. Buys one-time rights.

Tips: "Always need profiles of affluent individuals focusing on the luxury lifestyle. Also, we're increasing our coverage on watches, fashion and home interiors. There are opportunities for new writers to break into departments. Study the magazine carefully. We have very specific needs for articles on the luxury lifestyle and many queries are off base."

THE SATURDAY EVENING POST, The Saturday Evening Post Society, 1100 Waterway Blvd., Indianapolis IN 46202. (317)636-8881. Editor: Cory SerVaas, M.D. Managing Editor: Ted Kreiter. 30% freelance written. Bimonthly general interest, "family-oriented magazine focusing on physical fitness, preventive medicine." Estab. 1728. Circ. 500,000. Pays on publication. Publishes ms an average of 3 months after acceptance. Byline given. Buys second serial (reprint) and all rights. Submit seasonal/holiday material 4 months in advance. Accepts simultaneous submissions. Reports in 1 month on queries; 6 weeks on mss. Writer's guidelines for #10 SASE.

Nonfiction: Book excerpts, general interest, how-to (gardening, home improvement), humor, interview/profile, travel. "No political articles or articles containing sexual innuendo or hypersophistication." Buys 50 mss/year. Query with or without published clips, or send complete ms. Length: 750-2,500 words. Pays $200 minimum, negotiable maximum for assigned articles. Sometimes pays expenses of writers on assignment.

Photos: State availability of photos with submission. Reviews negatives and transparencies. Offers $50 minimum, negotiable maxmium per photo. Model release, identification required. Buys one-time or all rights.

Columns/Departments: Travel (destinations). Buys 16 mss/year. Query with published clips or send complete ms. Length: 750-1,500 words. Pays $200 minimum, negotiable maximum.

Fiction: Jack Gramling, fiction editor. Historical, humorous, mainstream, mystery, science fiction, western. "No sexual innuendo or profane expletives." Send complete ms. Length: 1,000-2,500 words. Pays $150 minimum, negotiable maximum.

Poetry: Light verse.

Fillers: PostScripts Editor: Steve Pettinga. Anecdotes, short humor. Buys 200/year. Length: 300 words. Pays $15.

Tips: "Areas most open to freelancers are Health, PostScripts and Travel. For travel we like text-photo packages, pragmatic tips, side bars and safe rather than exotic destinations. Query by mail, not phone. Send clips."

‡SATURDAY NIGHT, Saturday Night Magazine Ltd., 184 Front St. E, Suite 400, Toronto, Ontario M5A 4N3 Canada. Phone/fax: (416)368-7237. Editor: Kenneth Whyte. Contact: Kiran Ahluwalia, editorial manager. 95% freelance written. Monthly magazine. Readership is urban concentrated. Well-educated, with a high disposable income. Average age is 43. Estab. 1887. Circ. 410,000. Pays on receipt of a publishable ms. Byline sometimes given. Offer 50% kill fee. Buys first North American serial rights. Editorial lead time 3-4 months. Submit seasonal material 3-4 months in advance. Accepts simultaneous submissions. Sample copy for $3.50. Writer's guidelines free on request.

Nonfiction: Book excerpts, essays, general interest, interview/profile, opinion, personal experience, photo feature. Buys 100 mss/year. Query. Length: 200-5,000 words. Pays $1/word.

Photos: State availability of photos with submission. Negotiates payment individually. Model releases and identification of subjects required. Buys one-time rights.

Columns/Departments: Findings (short, interesting stories), Flavor of the Month, both 200-500 words. Query. Pays $1/word.

Fiction: Robert Weaver, fiction editor. Adventure, confession, ethnic, experimental, fantasy, historical, horror, humorous, mainstream, mystery, religious, science fiction, slice-of-life vignettes, suspense, western. Send complete ms. Length: 2,000-5,000 words. Pays $1/word.

SILVER CIRCLE, Home Savings of America, 4900 Rivergrade Rd., Irwindale CA 91706. Editor: Jay A. Binkly. 80% freelance written. Triannual magazine. "Despite the magazine's title, editorial is *not* the stereotypical senior fare. Articles that are aimed solely at *seniors* are rejected 99% of the time. Articles should have broad demographic appeal. Along with gardening and financial planning, subjects that have appeared in the magazine include computer software, heli-hiking tours, home fitness centers, high-tech new-car options, video cameras, investment scams, party planning, etc. Our editorial mission is to provide our readers with practical, relevant, upbeat consumer service information." Estab. 1974. Circ. 575,000. **Pays on acceptance.**

Byline given. Offers 20% kill fee. Buys first North American serial rights. Editorial lead time 5 months. Submit seasonal material 5 months in advance. Accepts simultaneous submissions. Reports in 3 weeks on queries; 1 month on mss. Sample copy for 8½×11 SASE. Writer's guidelines for #10 SASE.

Nonfiction: How-to, new product, travel. Buys 15 mss/year. Query with published clips. Length: 800-3,000 words. Pays $150-2,000. Pays expenses of writers on assignment.

Reprints: Send tearsheet of article.

Photos: Send photos with submissions. Offers $35-500/photo. Captions required. Buys one-time rights.

Columns/Departments: To Your Health (practical health items); Minding Your Money (practical money items); Travel Notes (practical travel items); all 100-300 words. Pays $25.

SMITHSONIAN MAGAZINE, 900 Jefferson Dr., Washington DC 20560. E-mail: siarticles@aol.com. Articles Editor: Marlane A. Liddell. 90% freelance written. Prefers to work with published/established writers. Monthly magazine for "associate members of the Smithsonian Institution; 85% with college education." Circ. 2,300,000. Buys first North American serial rights. "Payment for each article to be negotiated depending on our needs and the article's length and excellence." **Pays on acceptance.** Publishes ms an average of 3-6 months after acceptance. Submit seasonal material 3 months in advance. Reports in 2 months. Sample copy for $3, % Judy Smith. Writer's guidelines for #10 SASE.

 • Ranked as one of the best markets for freelance writers in *Writer's Yearbook*'s annual "Top 100 Markets," January 1996.

Nonfiction: "Our mandate from the Smithsonian Institution says we are to be interested in the same things which now interest or should interest the Institution: cultural and fine arts, history, natural sciences, hard sciences, etc." Query. Back Page humor: 1,000 words; full length article 3,500-4,500 words. Payment negotiable. Pays expenses of writers on assignment.

Photos: Purchased with or without ms and on assignment. Captions required. Pays $400/full color page.

‡**THE SOURCE**, Source Publishing, 19 Cumberland St., Edinburgh EH3 6RT United Kingdom. (011)44 131 556 8673. Co-Editors: Corene Lemaitre and Andrew Kelly. Quarterly literary magazine covering fiction, journalism and art. "*The Source* aims to broaden both the range and appeal of the literary magazine. The emphasis is on cutting-edge fiction and provocative reportage. We target readers interested in the international political and cultural scene." Estab. 1995. Pays on publication. Publishes ms an average of 2 months after acceptance. Byline given. Buys first or first British serial rights. Reports in 1 month on queries; 2 months on mss. Sample copy for $10 cash or £5 sterling. Writer's guidelines for #10 SAE and 2 IRCs.

Nonfiction: Opinion; arts controversies; literary debate; analysis and critical overviews of topical events (international). Buys 12 mss/year. Send complete ms. Length: 2,000 words maximum. Pays $20 plus 2 contributor's copies.

Photos: Send photos with submission. Reviews any size b&w prints only. Buys one-time rights.

Columns/Departments: Real Life (metropolitan life from a personal point of view), 2,000 words. Buys 4 mss/year. Send complete ms. Pays $20 plus 2 contributor's copies.

Fiction: Literary. No genre fiction. Buys 30 mss/year. Send complete ms. Length: 3,000 words maximum. Pays $20 plus 2 contributor's copies.

Poetry: Buys 12 poems/year. Submit maximum 6 poems. Pays $20 plus 2 contributor's copies.

Tips: "Study the magazine. More material is rejected because it is unsuitable than for any other reason. Dynamic, imaginative fiction is sought, not safe, careful, conventional fiction. Short shorts are encouraged. *The Source* reaches editors, agents and critics in both the US and the UK; submit your strongest work. Include sufficient IRCs."

THE STAR, 660 White Plains Rd., Tarrytown NY 10591. (914)332-5000. Fax: (914)332-5043. Editor: Richard Kaplan. Executive Editor: Steve LeGrice. 40% freelance written. Prefers to work with published/established writers. Weekly magazine "for every family; all the family—kids, teenagers, young parents and grandparents." Estab. 1974. Circ. 2,800,000. Publishes ms an average of 1 month after acceptance. Buys first North American serial, occasionally second serial book rights. Reports in 2 months. Pays expenses of writers on assignment.

Nonfiction: Exposé (government waste, consumer, education, anything affecting family); general interest (human interest, consumerism, informational, family and women's interest); how-to (psychological, practical on all subjects affecting readers); interview (celebrity or human interest); new product; photo feature; profile (celebrity or national figure); health; medical; diet. No first-person articles. Query or submit complete ms. Length: 500-1,000 words. Pays $50-1,500.

Photos: Contact: Alistair Duncan, photo editor. State availability of photos with query or ms. Pays $25-100 for 8×10 b&w glossy prints, contact sheets or negatives; $150-1,000 for 35mm color transparencies. Captions required. Buys one-time or all rights.

THE SUN, A Magazine of Ideas, The Sun Publishing Company, 107 N. Roberson St., Chapel Hill NC 27516. (919)942-5282. Editor: Sy Safransky. 90% freelance written. Monthly general interest magazine. "We are open to all kinds of writing, though we favor work of a personal nature." Estab. 1974. Circ. 27,000. Pays on publication. Publishes ms an average of 6 months after acceptance. Byline given. Buys first or one-time rights. Reports in 1 month on queries; 3 months on mss. Sample copy for $3.50. Send SASE for writer's guidelines.

• *The Sun* no longer accepts simultaneous submissions.

Nonfiction: Book excerpts, essays, general interest, interview, opinion, personal experience, spiritual. Buys 24 mss/year. Send complete ms. Length: 7,000 words maximum. Pays $300-750. "Complimentary subscription is given in addition to payment (applies to payment for *all* works, not just nonfiction)."

Reprints: Send photocopy of article or short story and information about when and where the article previously appeared. Pays 50% of amount paid for an original article.

Photos: Send b&w photos with submission. Offers $50-200/photo. Model releases preferred. Buys one-time rights.

Fiction: Experimental, humorous, literary, mainstream, novel excerpts. "We avoid stereotypical genre pieces like sci-fi, romance, western and horror. Read an issue before submitting." Buys 30 mss/year. Send complete ms. Length: 7,000 words maximum. Pays $300-500 for original fiction.

• Ranked as one of the best markets for fiction writers in *Writer's Digest*'s annual "Fiction 50," June 1996.

Poetry: Free verse, prose poems, short and long poems. Buys 24 poems/year. Submit 6 poems maximum. Pays $50-200.

TIME, Time Inc. Magazine, Time & Life Bldg., 1271 Avenue of the Americas, New York NY 10020. (212)522-1212. Fax: (212)522-0536. Contact: Jim Gaines. Weekly magazine. "*Time* covers the full range of information that is important to people today—breaking news, national and world afairs, business news, societal and lifestyle issues, culture and entertainment news and reviews." Estab. 1923. Circ. 4,096,000. This magazine did not respond to our request for information. Query before submitting.

TOWN & COUNTRY, The Hearst Corp., 1700 Broadway, New York NY 10019. (212)903-5000. Fax: (212)765-8308. Publisher: Molly Schaefer. Monthly lifestyle magazine. "*Town & Country* is a lifestyle guide for the affluent market. Features focus on fashion, beauty, travel, design and architecture, as well as individuals' accomplishments and contributions to society." Estab. 1846. Circ. 488,000. **Pays on acceptance.**

Nonfiction: "We're looking for engaging service articles for a high income, well-educated audience." Length: 1,500-2,000 words. Pay varies. Also buys shorter pieces; pay varies. Query before submitting.

‡TROIKA, Wit, Wisdom & Wherewithal, Lone Tout Publications, Inc., 125 Main St., Suite 360, Westport CT 06880. (203)227-5377. Editor: Celia Meadow. 80% freelance written. Quarterly magazine covering general interest, lifestyle. "A new magazine for men and women seeking a balanced, three-dimensional lifestyle: personal achievement, family commitment, community involvement. Readers are upscale, educated, 30-50 age bracket." Estab. 1993. Circ. 100,000. Pays on publication. Publishes ms an average of 6 months after acceptance. Byline given. Buys first North American serial rights. Editorial lead time 3 months. Submit seasonal material 6 months in advance. Accepts simultaneous submissions. Reports in 1 month. Sample copy for $5. Writer's guidelines for #10 SASE.

• See the interview with Editor Celia Meadow in this edition of *Writer's Market*.

Nonfiction: Essays, exposé, general interest, historical/nostalgic, how-to (leisure activities, pro bono, finance), humor, inspirational, interview/profile (non-celebrity), opinion, personal experience, travel (exotic or unusual only). No celebrity profiles. Buys 60-80 mss/year. Send complete ms. Length:1,800-3,000 words. Pays $250-1,000 for assigned articles; $250-400 for first appearance of unsolicited articles.

Reprints: Accepts previously published submissions (depending on locale and circulation).

Photos: State availability of photos with submission. Reviews negatives, transparencies. Offers no additional payment for photos accepted with ms. Captions, model releases, identification of subjects required.

Columns/Departments: Literati; Pub Performances (literary, theater, arts, culture); Blueprints (architecture, interior design, fashion); Body of Facts (science); Hippocratic Horizons (health); Home Technology; Capital Commitments (personal finance); all 750-1,200 words. Buys 40-60 mss/year. Send complete ms. Pays $250 maximum.

Fiction: Lawrence Crowe. Adventure, confession, experimental, fantasy, historical, mainstream, mystery, romance, science fiction, slice-of-life vignettes, suspense. Buys 4-8 mss/year. Send complete ms. Length: 3,000 words maximum. Pays $400 maximum.

‡UNION PLUS, Cadmus Custom Publishing, 375 Boylston St., Boston MA 02116-3812. (617)424-7700. Fax: (617)437-7714. Editor: Michael Ruller. Quarterly magazine. "*Union Plus* is a lifestyle magazine for working people. Articles have a strong 'how-to' orientation. Features focus on money, family, home, health and leisure. Each issue also includes information on consumer products and profiles of people engaged in exciting and extraordinary activities." Estab. 1993. Circ. 2,000,000.

Nonfiction: Consumer health, financial issues (for novices) real estate. Buys 8-10 mss/year. Pays $1/word-$2,000. Query.

Columns/Departments: Labor issues. Buys 3-4 mss/year. Pays $1/word-$750. Query.

USA WEEKEND, Gannett Co., Inc., 1000 Wilson Blvd., Arlington VA 22229. Editor: Marcia Bullard. Contact: Richard Vega. 70% freelance written. Weekly Friday-Sunday newspaper magazine. Estab. 1985. Circ. 17,500,000. **Pays on acceptance.** Publishes ms an average of 3 months after acceptance. Byline given. Offers 25% kill fee. Buys first worldwide serial rights. Submit seasonal material 5 months in advance. Query for electronic submissions. Reports in 5 weeks.

Nonfiction: Food and Family Issues; Trends and Entertainment (contact: Gayle Carter); Recreation; Cover Stories (contact: Dan Olmsted). Also looking for book excerpts, general interest articles, how-to, interview/profile, travel, food, recreation. No first-person essays, historic pieces or retrospective pieces. Buys 200 mss/year. Query with published clips. No unsolicited mss accepted. Length: 50-2,000 words. Pays $75-2,000. Sometimes pays expenses of writers on assignment.

Photos: State availability of photos with submission.

Columns/Departments: Food, Travel, Entertainment, Books, Recreation. "All stories must be pegged to an upcoming event, must report new and refreshing trends in the field and must include high profile people." Length: 50-1,000 words. Query with published clips. Pays $250-500.

Tips: "We are looking for authoritative, lively articles that blend the author's expertise with our style. All articles must have a broad, timely appeal. One-page query should include peg or timeliness of the subject matter. We generally look for sidebar material to accompany each article."

VANITY FAIR, Condé Nast Publications, Inc., 350 Madison Ave., New York NY 10017. (212)880-8800. Publisher: Mitchell B. Fox. Monthly magazine. "*Vanity Fair* presents the issues, events and people that define our times. This chronicle of contemporary culture features art, entertainment, politics, business, and the media." Estab. 1983. Circ. 1,200,000. This magazine did not respond to our request for information. Query before submitting.

THE WORLD & I, A Chronicle of Our Changing Era, News World Communications, Inc., 3600 New York Ave. NE, Washington DC 20002. (202)635-4000. Fax: (202)269-9353. Editor: Morton A. Kaplan. Executive Editor: Michael Marshall. Contact: Gary Rowe. 90% freelance written. Publishing more than 40 articles each month, this is a broad interest magazine for the thinking person. Estab. 1986. Circ. 30,000. Pays on publication. Publishes ms an average of 6 months after acceptance. Byline given. Offers 20% kill fee. Buys all rights. Submit seasonal material 5 months in advance. Reports in 6 weeks on queries; 10 weeks on mss. Sample copy for $5 and 9×12 SASE. Writer's guidelines for #10 SASE.

Nonfiction: "Description of Sections: Current Issues: Politics, economics and strategic trends covered in a variety of approaches, including special report, analysis, commentary and photo essay. The Arts: International coverage of music, dance, theater, film, television, design, architecture, photography, poetry, painting and sculpture—through reviews, features, essays and a 10-page Gallery of full-color reproductions. Life: Articles on well-known and respected people, cultural trends, adventure, travel, family and youth issues, education, consumer issues, gardens, home, health and food. Natural Science: Covers the latest in science and technology, relating it to the social and historical context, under these headings: At the Edge, Impacts, Nature Walk, Science and Spirit, Science and Values, Scientists: Past and Present, Crucibles of Science and Science Essay. Book World: Excerpts from important, timely books (followed by commentaries) and 10-12 scholarly reviews of significant new books each month, including untranslated works from abroad. Covers current affairs, intellectual issues, contemporary fiction, history, moral/religious issues and the social sciences. Currents in Modern Thought: Examines scholarly research and theoretical debate across the wide range of disciplines in the humanities and social sciences. Featured themes are explored by several contributors. Investigates theoretical issues raised by certain current events, and offers contemporary reflection on issues drawn from the whole history of human thought. Culture: Surveys the world's people in these subsections: Peoples (their unique characteristics and cultural symbols), Crossroads (changes brought by the meeting of cultures), Patterns (photo essay depicting the daily life of a distinct culture), Folk Wisdom (folklore and practical wisdom and their present forms), and Heritage (multicultural backgrounds of the American people and how they are bound to the world. Photo Essay: The 10-page Life and Ideals dramatizes a human story of obstacles overcome in the pursuit of an ideal. Three other photo essays appear each month: Focus (Current Issues), Gallery (The Arts), and Patterns (Culture). 'No *National Enquirer*-type articles.' " Buys 1,200 mss/year. Query with published clips. Length: 1,000-5,000 words. Pays 10-20¢/word. Sometimes pays expenses of writers on assignment. First-person work is discouraged.

Reprints: Send tearsheet or photocopy of article, typed ms with rights for sale noted and information about when and where the article previously appeared.

Poetry: Contact: Arts Editor. Avant-garde, free verse, haiku, light verse, traditional. Buys 6-12 poems/year. Query with maximum 5 poems. Pays $25-50.

Photos: State availability of photos with submission. Reivews contact sheets, transparencies and prints. Payment negotiable. Model releases and identification of subjects required. Buys one-time rights.

Tips: "Send a short query letter with a viable story idea (no unsolicited manuscripts, please!) for a specific section and/or subsection."

HEALTH AND FITNESS

The magazines listed here specialize in covering health and fitness topics for a general audience. Health and fitness magazines have experienced a real boom lately. Most emphasize developing healthy lifestyle choices in exercise, nutrition and general fitness. Many magazines offer alternative healing and therapies that are becoming more mainstream, such as medicinal herbs, health foods and a holistic mind/body approach to well-being. As wellness is a concern to all demographic groups, publishers have developed editorial geared to specific audiences. *Men's Fitness* is aimed at men's concerns. *Shape* addresses women's issues, while *Heart & Soul* presents information expressly for African-American women. Older readers find their needs dealt with in titles such as ℞*emedy* and *New Choices*. Also see the Sports/Miscellaneous section where publications dealing with health and particular sports may be listed. For magazines that cover healthy eating, refer to the Food and Drink section. Many general interest publications are also potential markets for health or fitness articles. Magazines covering health topics from a medical perspective are listed in the Medical category of Trade.

AMERICAN FITNESS, 15250 Ventura Blvd., Suite 200, Sherman Oaks CA 91403. (818)905-0040. Fax: (818)990-5468. Editor-at-Large: Peg Jordan, R.N. Managing Editor: Rhonda J. Wilson. 75% freelance written. Eager to work with new/unpublished writers. Bimonthly magazine covering exercise and fitness, health and nutrition. "We need timely, in-depth, informative articles on health, fitness, aerobic exercise, sports nutrition, age-specific fitness and outdoor activity." Circ. 33,000. Pays 6 weeks after publication. Publishes ms an average of 6 months after acceptance. Byline given. Buys all rights. Submit seasonal material 4 months in advance. Accepts simultaneous submissions. Reports in 6 weeks. Sample copy for $1 and SAE with 6 first-class stamps. Writer's guidelines for SAE.
Nonfiction: Women's health and fitness issues (pregnancy, family, pre- and post-natal, menopause and eating disorders); exposé (on nutritional gimmickry); historical/nostalgic (history of various athletic events); inspirational (sports leader's motivational pieces); interview/profile (fitness figures); new product (plus equipment review); personal experience (successful fitness story); photo feature (on exercise, fitness, new sport); youth and senior fitness; travel (spas that cater to fitness industry). No articles on unsound nutritional practices, popular trends or unsafe exercise gimmicks. Buys 18-25 mss/year. Query. Length: 800-1,500 words. Pays $140-160. Sometimes pays expenses of writers on assignment.
Reprints: Accepts previously published submissions.
Photos: Sports, action, fitness, aquatic aerobics, aerobic competitions and exercise classes. "We are especially interested in photos of high-adrenalin sports like rock climbing and mountain biking." Pays $10 for b&w prints; $35 for transparencies. Captions, model release and identification of subjects required. Usually buys all rights; other rights purchased depend on use of photo.
Columns/Departments: Alternative paths (non-mainstream approaches to health, wellness and fitness); strength (the latest breakthroughs in weight training); research (latest exercise and fitness findings); clubscene (profiles and highlights of the fitness club industry). Query with published clips or send complete ms. Length: 800-1,000 words. Pays $120-140.
Fillers: Cartoons, clippings, jokes, short humor, newsbreaks. Buys 12/year. Length: 75-200 words. Pays $35.
Tips: "Cover a unique aerobics or fitness angle, provide accurate and interesting findings, and write in a lively, intelligent manner. We are looking for new health and fitness reporters and writers. *AF* is a good place for first-time authors or for regularly published authors who want to sell spin-offs or reprints."

AMERICAN HEALTH MAGAZINE, Fitness of Body and Mind, Reader's Digest Corp., 28 W. 23rd St., New York NY 10010. (212)366-8900. Fax: (212)366-8760. Editor: Carey Winfrey. Executive Editor: Judith Groch. Contact: Cindy Shute. 70% freelance written. General interest health magazine published 10 times/year covering both scientific and "lifestyle" aspects of health, including medicine, fitness, nutrition and psychology. Estab. 1982. Circ. 800,000. **Pays on acceptance.** Publishes ms an average of 6 months after acceptance. Byline or tagline given. Offers 25% kill fee. Buys first North American serial rights. Reports in 6 weeks. Sample copy for $3. Writer's guidelines for #10 SASE.
  ● Ranked as one of the best markets for freelance writers in *Writer's Yearbook*'s annual "Top 100 Markets," January 1996.
Nonfiction: Mail to Editorial/Features. News-based articles usually with a service angle; well-written pieces with an investigative or unusual slant; profiles (health or fitness related). No mechanical research reports,

quick weight-loss plans or unproven treatments. "Stories should be written clearly, without jargon. Information should be new, authoritative and helpful to readers." Buys 60-70 mss/year (plus many more news items). Query with 2 clips of published work. Length: 1,000-3,000 words. Payment varies. Pays expenses of writers on assignment.

Photos: Pays $100-600 for 35mm transparencies and 8×10 prints, "depending on use." Captions and identification of subjects required. Buys one-time rights.

Columns/Departments: Mail to Editorial/News, Medicine, Fitness, Nutrition, The Mind, Environment, Family, Dental, Looking Good, First Person, Second Opinion. Other news sections included from time to time. Buys about 300 mss/year. Query with clips of published work. Pays $150-250 upon acceptance.

Tips: "*American Health* has no full-time staff writers; we rely on outside contributors for most of our articles. The magazine needs good ideas and good articles from experienced journalists and writers. Feature queries should be short (no longer than a page) and to the point. Give us a good angle and a paragraph of background. Queries only. We are not responsible for material not accompanied by a SASE."

‡BETTER HEALTH, Better Health Press, 1450 Chapel St., New Haven CT 06511-4440. (203)789-3972. Fax: (203)789-4053. Publishing Director: Magaly Olivero. 90% freelance written. Prefers to work with published/established writers; will consider new/unpublished writers. Bimonthly magazine devoted to health, wellness and medical issues. Estab. 1979. Circ. 450,000. **Pays on acceptance.** Byline given. Offers $75 kill fee. Buys first rights. Query first; do not send article. Sample copy for $2.50. Writer's guidelines for #10 SASE.

Nonfiction: Wellness/prevention issues are of prime interest. New medical techniques or nonmainstream practices are not considered. No fillers, poems, quizzes, seasonal, heavy humor, inspirational or personal experience. Length: 2,500-3,000 words. Pays $500.

COMMON GROUND MAGAZINE, Ontario's Quarterly Guide to Natural Foods & Lifestyles, New Age Times Ink, 356 Dupont St., Toronto, Ontario M5R 1V9 Canada. Editor: Julia Woodford. 50% freelance written. Quarterly magazine covering holistic health, nutritional medicine. "We give top priority to well-researched articles on nutritional medicine, healing properties of foods and herbs, environmental health issues, natural lifestyles, alternative healing for cancer, arthritis, heart disease, etc. Organic foods and issues. Estab. 1985. Circ. 50,000. Pays on publication. Publishes ms 3 months after acceptance. Byline given. Buys first rights, one-time rights or second serial (reprint) rights. Editorial lead time 3 months. Submit seasonal material 3 months in advance. Accepts simultaneous submissions. Reports "when we have time." Sample copy for $2. Writer's guidelines free on request by phone.

Nonfiction: Book excerpts, exposé, how-to (on self-health care), inspirational, personal experience. "Nothing endorsing drugs, surgery, pharmaceuticals. No submissions from public relations firms." Buys 8-12 mss/ year. Query with ms. Length 1,000-1,800 words. Pays 10¢ (Canadian)/word. Sometimes pays expenses of writers on assignment.

Reprints: Accepts previously published submissions.

Photos: Send photos with submission. Offers $25-30 (Canadian)/photo. Identification of subjects required. Buys one-time rights.

Fillers: Facts, newsbreaks.

Tips: "Must have a good working knowledge of subject area and be patient if not responded to immediately. Features are most open to freelancers. Write well, give me the facts, but do it in layman's terms. A sense of humor doesn't hurt. All material must be relevant to our *Canadian* readership audience. If you're doing a critical piece on products in the marketplace, give me brand names."

COUNTDOWN, Juvenile Diabetes Foundation, 120 Wall St., New York NY 10005-4001. (212)785-9500. Fax: (212)785-9595. Website: http://www.jdfcure.com. Editor: Julie Mettenburg. 75% freelance written. Quarterly magazine focusing on medical research. "*Countdown* is published for people interested in diabetes research. Written for a lay audience. Often, stories are interpretation of highly technical biomedical research." Estab. 1970. Circ. 150,000. **Pays on acceptance.** Byline given. Buys first rights. Editorial lead time 3 months. Submit seasonal material 3 months in advance. Accepts simultaneous submissions. Reports in 1 month. Sample copy free on request.

Nonfiction: Essays, general interest, how-to, interview/profile, new product and personal experience. "All articles must relate to diabetes. 95% published freelance stories are assigned." Buys 15 mss/year. Query with published clips. Length: 500-2,500 words. Pays $500 minimum for assigned articles. Pays expenses of writers on assignment.

Reprints: Send photocopy of article. Pays 50% of amount paid for an original article.

Photos: Send photos with submission. Reviews transparencies and prints. Negotiates payment individually. Captions, model releases and identification of subjects required. Buys one-time rights.

Tips: "Knowledge of biomedical research, specifically immunology and genetics, is helpful. We are most open to feature stories and profiles."

ENERGY TIMES, Enhancing Your Life Through Proper Nutrition, 548 Broadhollow Rd., Melville NY 11747. (516)777-7773. Editor: Gerard McIntee. Contact: Mike Finnegan. 90% freelance written. Magazine published 10 times/year covering nutrition, health and beauty aids, alternative medicinal, herbs (medicinal and culinary), natural foods. Estab. 1991. Circ. 575,000. **Pays on acceptance**. Publishes ms an average of 1 month after acceptance. Byline given. Offers 10% kill fee or $100. Buys all rights. Editorial lead time 2 months. Submit seasonal material 6 months in advance. Accepts simultaneous submissions. Reports in 1 month on queries, 2 months on mss. Sample copy for $2.50. Writer's guidelines for #10 SASE.

Nonfiction: Book excerpts, how-to (food, natural beauty aids, homemade products), humor, inspirational, interview/profile, new product, photo feature, technical (science related to nutrition and alternative medicines), travel. Buys 36 mss/year. Query. Length: 1,500-2,500 words. Pays $300. Sometimes pays expenses of writers on assignment.

Reprints: Accepts previously published submissions.

Photos: State availability of photos with submissions. Reviews negatives, transparencies, prints. Negotiates payment individually. Identification of subjects required. Buys one-time rights.

Columns/Departments: Nutritional news (current information on nutrition foods/supplements/vitamins), 850 words; university update (current research on nutrition, health related topics, herbs, vitamins), 850 words. Send complete ms. Pays $50.

Fillers: Crossword puzzles, word games. Buys 10/year. Puzzles should fit on ½ page 4 × 5¼. Pays $75.

Tips: "Although we hire lay freelancers and professional journalists, we prefer to maintain an active group of professional medical/healthcare practitioners with accredited degrees. Queries should be brief (one page) and to the point. Show us why your article needs to be in our magazine."

FDA CONSUMER, 5600 Fishers Lane, Rockville MD 20857. (301)443-3220. Website: http://www.fda.gov. Editor: Judith Levine Willis. 30% freelance written. Prefers to work with experienced health and medical writers. Monthly magazine (January/February and July/August issues combined) for general public interested in health issues. A federal government publication (Food and Drug Administration). Circ. 20,000. Pays after acceptance. Publishes ms an average of 3 months after acceptance. Byline given. Not copyrighted. Pays 50% kill fee. "All rights must be assigned to the USA so that the articles may be reprinted without permission." Query with résumé and clips only. Buys 15-20 freelance mss/year. "We cannot be responsible for any work by writer not agreed upon by prior contract." Free sample copy.

Nonfiction: "Upbeat feature articles of an educational nature about FDA regulated products and specific FDA programs and actions to protect the consumer's health and pocketbook. Articles based on health topics connected to food, drugs, medical devices, and other products regulated by FDA. All articles subject to clearance by the appropriate FDA experts as well as acceptance by the editor. All articles based on prior arrangement by contract." Length: 2,000-2,500 words. Pays $800-950 for "first-timers," $1,200 for those who have previously published in *FDA Consumer*. Pays phone and mailing expenses.

Photos: Black and white photos are purchased on assignment only.

Tips: "Besides reading the feature articles in *FDA Consumer*, a writer can best determine whether his/her style and expertise suit our needs by submitting a résumé and clips; story suggestions are unnecessary as most are internally generated."

FIT, GCR Publishing Group, Inc., 1700 Broadway, 34th Floor, New York NY 10019. (212)541-7100. Editor: Lisa Goldstein. Managing Editor: Sandra Kosherick. 50% freelance written. Works with a small number of new/unpublished writers each year. Bimonthly magazine covering fitness and health for active young, middle-class women. Circ. 125,000. Pays on publication. Publishes ms an average of 5 months after acceptance. Byline given. Offers 20% kill fee. Buys all rights. Submit seasonal/holiday material 6 months in advance. Reports in 1 month if rejecting ms, longer if considering for publication.

Nonfiction: Health, fitness, sports, beauty, psychology, relationships, celebrities, and nutrition. Please no telephone queries. No first-person articles. Buys 60 mss/year. Query with published clips. Length: variable. Pays $100-300 for assigned articles; $50-150 for unsolicited articles.

Photos: Reviews contact sheets, transparencies, prints. Model releases and identification of subjects required. Buys all rights.

Columns/Departments: Finally Fit! Contest. Readers can submit "before and after" success stories along with color slides or photos. Pays $100.

Tips: "We are moving toward more general interest women's material on relationships, emotional health, etc. We look for a fresh angle—a new way to present the material. Health, nutrition, psychology and lifestyles are good topics to consider. Make a clean statement of what your article is about, what it would cover—not why the article is important. We're interested in new ideas, new trends or new ways of looking at old topics."

HEALTH, Time Publishing Ventures, 301 Howard St., 18th Floor, San Francisco CA 94105. (415)512-9100. Editor: Barbara Paulsen. Send submissions to: Amanda Uhry, editorial assistant. Magazine published 7 times/year on health, fitness and nutrition. "Our readers are predominantly college-educated women in their 30s and 40s. Edited to focus not on illness, but on events, ideas and people." Estab. 1987. Circ. 900,000. **Pays on acceptance**. Byline given. Offers 25% kill fee. Buys first North American serial rights. Accepts simultaneous submissions. Reports in 2 months on queries. Sample copy for $5 to "Back Issues." Writer's guidelines for #10 SASE. "No phone calls, please."

• *Health* stresses that writers must send for guidelines before sending a query, and that only queries that closely follow the guidelines get passed on to editors.

Nonfiction: Buys 25 mss/year. No unsolicited mss. Query with published clips and SASE. Length: 1,200 words. Pays $1,800 for assigned articles. Pays the expenses of writers on assignment.

Columns/Departments: Food, Mind, Vanities, Fitness, Family, Money.

Tips: "We look for well-articulated ideas with a narrow focus and broad appeal. A query that starts with an unusual local event and hooks it legitimately to some national trend or concern is bound to get our attention. Use quotes, examples and statistics to show why the topic is important and why the approach is workable. We need to see clear evidence of credible research findings pointing to meaningful options for our readers. Stories should offer practical advice and give clear explanations."

‡HEALTH STYLES, The Publisher's Group, P.O. Box 510366, Salt Lake City UT 84151-0366. Fax: (801)322-1098. Editor: Vicki Andersen. Contact: Anne E. Zombro, publisher. 50% freelance written. Quarterly magazine covering health and fitness. "The slant is towards fitness, mental wellness and nutrition. Also features inspirational profiles and people in the health-care profession." Estab. 1996. Circ. 15,000. Pays on publication. Publishes ms an average of 6 months after acceptance. Byline given. Buys first North American serial and second serial (reprint) rights. Editorial lead time 2 months. Submit seasonal material 4 months in advance. Accepts simultaneous submissions. Reports in 1 month on queries; 2 months on mss. Sample copy for $2 and 9×12 SAE. Writer's guidelines for #10 SASE.

Nonfiction: Book excerpts, inspirational, interview/profile, new product, personal experience, fitness. No medical treatments or diseases. Buys 6-8 mss/year. Query with published clips. Length: 1,000-1,300 words. Pays $125-800.

Reprints: Accepts previously published submissions.

Photos: Send photos with submission. Reviews 4×5 transparencies (preferred), any size prints. Negotiates payment individually. Captions, model releases, identification of subjects required. Buys one-time or all rights.

Columns/Departments: Nutrition (eating well), Fitness (new trends in exercise), both 500 words. Buys 8-10 mss/year. Query with published clips. Pays $50-125.

HEART & SOUL, Health and Fitness for African-American Women, Rodale Press, 733 Third Ave., New York NY 10017. Editor-in-Chief: Stephanie Stokes Oliver. Managing Editor: Teresa L. Ridley. Contact: Claire McIntosh, senior editor. Bimonthly magazine covering how-to health, fitness, nutrition, beauty, healthy travel, weight loss, parenting, relationships; information researched and edited specifically for African-Americans. Estab. 1993. Circ. 200,000. **Pays on acceptance.** Publishes ms an average of 4 months after acceptance. Byline given. Offers 25% kill fee. Buys all rights or first North American serial rights. Editorial lead time 6-9 months. Submit seasonal material 6 months in advance. Reports in 6 weeks. Sample copy for 9×12 SAE with $1.93 postage. Writer's guidelines for #10 SASE.

• Ranked as one of the best markets for freelance writers in *Writer's Yearbook*'s annual "Top 100 Markets," January 1996.

Nonfiction: Book excerpts, how-to (health, fitness), relationships, interview/profile (champions of the community), humor, spiritual health. Buys 30 mss/year. Query with published clips. Length: 1,200-2,000 words. Pays 75¢-$1/word for assigned articles; 75¢/word for unsolicited articles. Pays itemized expenses of writers on assignment.

Reprints: Accepts previously published submissions.

Columns/Departments: My Body (personal experience, makeovers); Healthy Smile (dental health); Health Front (health news); Weight Loss (how-to); Mind and Spirit (inspiration); Body (illness prevention); Healthy Vacations; Healthy Kids. Length: 1,000-1,500 words. Buys 60 mss/year. Query with published clips. Pays 75¢-$1.

Tips: "Writers should be experienced in health and service writing and knowledgeable about issues important to African-American women. We do not accept unsolicited manuscripts; queries only."

LET'S LIVE MAGAZINE, Franklin Publications, Inc., 320 N. Larchmont Blvd., P.O. Box 74908, Los Angeles CA 90004-3030. (213)469-3901. Fax: (213)469-9597. E-mail: letslive@caprica.com. Editor-in-Chief: Beth Salmon. Monthly magazine emphasizing nutrition. 15% freelance written. Works with a small number of new/unpublished writers each year; expertise in health field helpful. Estab. 1933. Circ. 1,700,000. Pays on publication. Publishes ms an average of 4 months after acceptance. Buys all rights. Byline given. Submit seasonal/holiday material 6 months in advance. Reports in 2 months on queries; 3 months on mss. Sample copy for $3 for 10×13 SAE with 6 first-class stamps. Writer's guidelines for #10 SASE.

• The editors are looking for more interactive-style writing (i.e., reader-friendly copy, interesting sidebars, quizzes).

Nonfiction: General interest (effects of vitamins, minerals and nutrients in improvement of health or afflictions); historical (documentation of experiments or treatment establishing value of nutrients as boon to health); how-to (enhance natural beauty, exercise/bodybuilding, acquire strength and vitality, improve health of adults and/or children and prepare tasty, healthy meals); interview (benefits of research in establishing prevention as key to good health); personal opinion (views of orthomolecular doctors or their patients on value of health foods toward maintaining good health); profile (background and/or medical history of preventive medicine, M.D.s or Ph.D.s, in advancement of nutrition). Manuscripts must be well-researched, reliably documented and written in a clear, readable style. Buys 2-4 mss/issue. Query with published clips. Length: 1,200-1,400 words. Pays $250. Sometimes pays expenses of writers on assignment.

Photos: Send photos with ms. Pays $50 for 8 × 10 color prints and 35mm transparencies. Captions and model releases required.

Tips: "We want writers with experience in researching nonsurgical medical subjects and interviewing experts with the ability to simplify technical and clinical information for the layman. A captivating lead and structural flow are essential. The most frequent mistakes made by writers are in writing articles that are too technical; in poor style; written for the wrong audience (publication not thoroughly studied), or have unreliable documentation or overzealous faith in the topic reflected by flimsy research and inappropriate tone."

MASSAGE MAGAZINE, Keeping Those Who Touch—In Touch, 1315 W. Mallon Ave., Spokane WA 99201. (509)324-8117. Fax: (509)324-8606. E-mail: massagemag@aol.com. Publisher: Robert Calvert. Contact: Karen Menehan, managing editor. Southwest Editor: Melissa B. Mower. 80% freelance written. Prefers to work with published/established writers, but works with a number of new/unpublished writers each year. Bimonthly magazine on massage-bodywork and related healing arts. Estab. 1985. Circ. 25,000. Pays 30 days after publication. Publishes ms an average of 6 months after acceptance. Byline given. Buys first North American rights. Reports in 1 month on queries; 2 months on mss. Free sample copy and writer's guidelines.

Nonfiction: General interest, historical/nostalgic, how-to, experiential, inspirational, interview/profile, new product, photo feature, technical, travel. Length: 600-2,000 words. Pays $25-250 for articles.

Reprints: Send photocopy of article or typed ms with rights for sale noted. Pays 50-75% of amount paid for an original article.

Photos: Send photos with submission. Offers $10-25/photo. Identification of subjects required. Buys one-time rights.

Columns/Departments: Touching Tales (experiential); Profiles, Insurance; Table Talk (news briefs); Practice Building (business); In Touch with Associations (convention highlights); In Review/On Video (product, book, and video reviews); Technique; Body/mind; Convention Calendar (association convention listings). Length: 800-1,200 words. Pays $60-150 for most of these columns.

Fillers: Facts, news briefs. Length: 100 words. Pays $25 maximum.

MEN'S FITNESS, Men's Fitness, Inc., 21100 Erwin St., Woodland Hills CA 91367-3712. (818)884-6800. Fax: (818)704-5734. Editor-in-Chief: Peter Sikowitz. Editorial Assistant: Kevin Foley. 95% freelance written. Works with small number of new/unpublished writers each year. Monthly magazine for health-conscious men ages 18-45. Provides reliable, entertaining guidance for the active male in all areas of lifestyle. Estab. 1984. Circ. 306,500. Pays 1 month after acceptance. Publishes ms an average of 4 months after acceptance. Offers 33% kill fee. Buys all rights. Submit seasonal material 4 months in advance. Reports in 2 months. Writer's guidelines for 9 × 12 SAE. Query before sending ms.

Nonfiction: Service, informative, inspirational and scientific studies written for men. Few interviews or regional news unless extraordinary. Query with published clips. Length: 1,200-1,800 words. Pays $500-1,000.

Columns/Departments: Nutrition, Mind, Appearance, Sexuality, Health. Length: 1,200-1,500 words. Pays $400-500.

Tips: "Be sure to know the magazine before sending in queries."

‡**MUSCLE & FITNESS**, The Science of Living Super-Fit, Weider Health & Fitness, 21100 Erwin St., Woodland Hills, CA 91367. (818)884-6800. Fax: (818)704-5734. Editors: Bill Geiger, Bob Wolff. Contact: Mary Ann Mucica, executive editor. 50% freelance written. Monthly magazine covering fitness, health, bodybuilding. Estab. 1950. Circ. 500,000. Pays on publication. Publishes ms an average of 2 months after acceptance. Offers 25-40% kill fee. Buys all rights and second serial (reprint) rights. Editorial lead time 3 months. Submit seasonal material 3 months in advance. Accepts simultaneous submissions. Reports in 2 weeks on queries; 1 month on mss. Sample copy free.

Nonfiction: Bill Geiger. Book excerpts, how-to (training), humor, interview/profile, photo feature. Buys 120 mss/year. Query with published clips. Length: 800-2,000 words. Pays $250-800. Pays expenses of writers on assignment.

ALWAYS CHECK the most recent copy of a magazine for the address and editor's name before you send in a query or manuscript.

Photos: State availability of photos with submission.
Tips: "Have a knowledge of weight-training (especially in gyms); know the 'culture'; know nutrition."

‡**MUSCLE MAG INTERNATIONAL**, 6465 Airport Rd., Mississauga, Ontario L4V 1E4 Canada. Editor: Johnny Fitness. 80% freelance written. "We do not care if a writer is known or unknown; published or unpublished. We simply want good instructional articles on bodybuilding." Monthly magazine for 16- to 60-year-old men and women interested in physical fitness and overall body improvement. Estab. 1972. Circ. 300,000. Buys all rights. **Pays on acceptance.** Publishes ms an average of 4 months after acceptance. Byline given. Buys 200 mss/year. Sample copy for $5 and 9×12 SAE. Reports in 2 months. Submit complete ms with IRCs.
Nonfiction: Articles on ideal physical proportions and importance of supplements in the diet, training for muscle size. Should be helpful and instructional and appeal to young men and women who want to live life in a vigorous and healthy style. "We would like to see articles for the physical culturist on new muscle building techniques or an article on fitness testing." Informational, how-to, personal experience, interview, profile, inspirational, humor, historical, expose, nostalgia, personal opinion, photo, spot news, new product, merchandising technique. "Also now actively looking for good instructional articles on Hardcore Fitness." Length: 1,200-1,600 words. Pays 20¢/word. Sometimes pays the expenses of writers on assignment.
Columns/Departments: Nutrition Talk (eating for top results) Shaping Up (improving fitness and stamina). Length: 1,300 words. Pays 20¢/word.
Photos: Color and b&w photos are purchased with or without ms. Pays $25 for 8×10 glossy exercise photos; $20 for 8×10 b&w posing shots. Pays $200-500 for color cover and $30 for color used inside magazine (transparencies). More for "special" or "outstanding" work.
Fillers: Newsbreaks, puzzles, quotes of the champs. Length: open. Pays $5 minimum.
Tips: "The best way to break in is to seek out the muscle-building 'stars' and do in-depth interviews with biography in mind. Color training picture support essential. Writers have to make their articles informative in that readers can apply them to help gain bodybuilding success. Specific fitness articles should quote experts and/or use scientific studies to strengthen their theories."

‡**NEW CHOICES FOR RETIREMENT LIVING**, RD. Publications, Inc., 28 W. 23rd St., New York NY 10010. (212)366-8600. Fax: (212)366-8617. Contact: JoAnn Tomback, editorial administrative assistant. Magazine published 10 times/year covering retirement lifestyle. "*New Choices for Retirement Living* is a lifestyle magazine for adults 50 and over. Editorial focuses on travel, health, fitness, investments, food and home." Estab. 1960. Circ. 604,000.
Nonfiction: Planning for retirement, personal health and fitness, financial strategies, housing options, travel, profiles/interviews (celebrities and newsmakers), relationships, leisure pursuits, various lifestyle/service subjects. Buys 60 mss/year. Length: 750-2,000 words. Pay varies. Query with 2-3 published clips.
Columns/Departments: Personal essays, humor, manners/etiquette, news of interest to over-50s, single lifestyle, travel, style. Buys 84 mss/year. Pay varies. Query with 2-3 published clips.

‡**NOURISH, Nutrition & Health for Body & Mind**, EGW Publishing, 1041 Shary Circle, Concord CA 94518. (510)671-9852. Fax: (510)671-0692. Editor: John Westerdahl. Managing Editor: Carol Polson. 100% freelance written. Bimonthly newsletter covering nutrition and health. Estab. 1995. Circ. 60,000. Pays on publication. Publishes ms an average of 6 months after acceptance. Byline given. Offers 25% kill fee. Buys first, one-time, all rights and makes work-for-hire assignments. Editorial lead time 6 months. Submit seasonal material 8 months in advance. Reports in 2 months. Sample copy for $3.50. Writer's guidelines for #10 SASE.
Nonfiction: General interest, humor, inspirational, interview/profile, new product, opinion, personal experience, photo feature. Buys 50 mss/year. Query with published clips. Length: 1,000-3,000 words. Pays $200-1,000.
Photos: Send photos with submission. Reviews transparencies, prints. Negotiates payment individually. Buys all rights.
Columns/Departments: Best Choices (nutritious foods) 500-1,000 words; Healthy Paths (eating for good health) 500-1,000 words; Personally Speaking (interview with food expert) 500-1,000 words. Buys 25 mss/year. Query with published clips. Pays $200-750.
Tips: Bimonthly 4-color newsletter for vegetarians or people with reduced meat diets who want to stay abreast of reliable nutrition information and current scientific research in order to eat healthfully. We emphasize practical suggestions as to how to apply this information to one's everyday life.

PREVENTION, Rodale Press, Inc., 33 E. Minor St., Emmaus, PA 18098. (610)967-5171. Fax: (610)967-7723. Editor: Mark Bricklin. Monthly magazine covering health and fitness. "*Prevention* is for readers who take an active role in achieving and maintaining good health and fitness for themselves and their families. Stressing health promotion and disease prevention, *Prevention* features practical guidance on nutrition, diet and food preparation, medical care, exercise, weight control, skin care and personal psychology." Estab. 1950. Circ. 3,519,000. This magazine did not respond to our request for information. Query before submitting.

℞EMEDY MAGAZINE, Prescriptions for a Healthy Life, ℞emedy, Inc., 120 Post Rd., W., Westport CT 06880. Editor: Valorie G. Weaver. 95% freelance written. Bimonthly magazine covering health for people age 55 and over. "℞EMEDY covers everything that affects and improves the health of people 55 and up—nutrition and exercise, medicine and medications, mainstream and alternative approaches, agism in health care, hormones and hair loss, you name it—and does it in an in-depth but reader-friendly way." Estab. 1992. Circ. 2,000,000 households. **Pays on acceptance**. Publishes ms an average of 4 months after acceptance. Byline given. Offers 20% kill fee. Buys first North American serial rights. Editorial lead time 3 months. Submit seasonal material 6 months in advance. Accepts simultaneous submissions. Reports in 6 weeks on queries; 2 months on mss. Samples for $3 and SAE with 4 first-class stamps. Writer's guidelines free on request.

● Ranked as one of the best markets for freelance writers in *Writer's Yearbook*'s annual "Top 100 Markets," January 1996.

Nonfiction: Book excerpts, exposé (medical), how-to (exercise and nutrition for people age 55 and over), interview/profile (health); medical journalism/reporting for lay readers. Buys 30 mss/year. Query with published clips. Length: 600-2,500 words. Pays $1-1.25/word for assigned articles; 50¢-$1.25/word for unsolicited articles. Pays pre-approved expenses of writers on assignment.

Photos: State availability of photos with submission. Negotiates payment individually. Model releases, identification of subjects required. Buys one-time rights.

Columns/Departments: The Nutrition Prescription (how-to research), The Fitness Prescription (how-to research), Housecall (interviews with top specialists), Mediview (overviews of topical subjects, e.g., "endless" menopause, see-better surgery), all 600-900 words. Buys 15 mss/year. Query. Pays $1-1.25/word.

Tips: "Query should include specific doctors/practitioners likely to be interviewed for piece, and at least one clip showing writing/reporting familiarity with topic of query. Also, an ability to write in a casual, friendly way about often complex material is essential."

‡RHYTHM OF THE DRUM, The Wholistic Health Magazine for Black Folk, P.O. Box 470379, Los Angeles CA 90047-0379. (800)324-DRUM. Fax: (310)323-0634. E-mail: thedrum@earthlink.net. Publisher: J.Y. Parhams. 75% freelance written. Quarterly magazine covering wholistic health (health and fitness). "*Rhythm of the Drum* deals with all aspects of our health—the physical, mental, emotional, spiritual, financial, political, etc., health. *The Drum* covers issues and solutions facing Africans all over the globe with respect to the whole health of individuals, the family and the community." Estab. 1994. Circ. 15,000. Pays on publication. Publishes ms an average 6 months after acceptance. Byline given. Offers 15% kill fee. Buys one-time and second serial (reprint) rights. Editorial lead time 4 months. Submit seasonal material 6 months in advance. Accepts simultaneous submissions. Reports in 6 weeks on queries. Please request guidelines before querying. Sample copy for 9×12 SASE and 4 first-class stamps or $2.50. Writer's guidelines for #10 SASE.

Nonfiction: Book excerpts, essays, exposé, historical/nostalgic, how-to, inspirational, interview/profile, new product, opinion, personal experience, photo feature, religious, technical, travel, cartoons, puzzles, political. Special issue: Black History Month/Anniversary Issue (February). Buys 36 mss/year. Query with published clips if available. Length: 25-2,000 words. Pays $10-500 for assigned articles; $3-240 for unsolicited articles. Sometimes pays expenses of writers on assignment.

Reprints: Send tearsheet or photocopy of article with rights for sale noted and information about when and where it previously appeared.

Photos: Send photos with submission. Reviews 8½×11 transparencies and 3×5 or larger prints. Offers no additional payment for photos accepted with ms. Negotiates payment individually. Model releases and identification of subjects required.

Columns/Departments: The Political Skinny (political); Tree of Life (physical health); Ourstory (our history); Safety First (being careful in- and outdoors); The Dollars & $ense of It (economics and finance); Spiritually Speaking (spiritual health and growth). Buys 44 mss/year. Query with published clips if available. Pays $3-500.

Fiction: Lamaur, creative director/editor. Adventure, condensed novels, ethnic, historical, novel excerpts, religious, science fiction, slice-of-life vignettes, suspense, African/American African culture. Buys 8 mss/year. Query. Length: 25-750 words. Pays $15-150.

Poetry: Avant-garde, free verse, haiku, light verse, traditional. Buys no more than 20 poems/year. Submit maximum 2 poems. Length: 1-50 lines. Pays $5-100.

Fillers: Anecdotes, facts, newsbreaks. Buys 8/year. Length: 5-50 words. Pays 50¢-$5.

Tips: "*Rhythm of the Drum* is a magazine of enlightenment and uplifting. No articles will be accepted that lift up people of African descent at the expense of others. We do not need to tear down others to build ourselves up. Articles that denigrate other peoples will be rejected. Photos and other photo-ready artwork are encouraged but not required; many articles are published without photos."

SHAPE MAGAZINE, Weider Health & Fitness, 21100 Erwin St., Woodland Hills CA 91367. (818)595-0593. Fax: (818)704-5734. Editor-in-Chief: Barbara Harris. Contact: Peg Moline, editorial director. 70% freelance written. Prefers to work with published/established writers. Monthly magazine covering women's health and fitness. Estab. 1981. Circ. 900,000. **Pays on acceptance**. Offers 33% kill fee. Buys all rights and reprint rights. Submit seasonal/holiday material 8 months in advance. Reports in 2 months. Sample copy for 9×12 SAE and 4 first-class stamps.

• Weider Health Fitness also publishes *Living Fit*, covering women's health and fitness for women over 35.

Nonfiction: Book excerpts; exposé (health, fitness, nutrition related); how-to (get fit); interview/profile (of fit women); health/fitness. "We use some health and fitness articles written by professionals in their specific fields. No articles that haven't been queried first." Query with clips of published work. Length: 500-2,000 words. Pays negotiable fee. Pays expenses of writers on assignment.

VIBRANT LIFE, A Magazine for Healthful Living, Review and Herald Publishing Assn., 55 W. Oak Ridge Dr., Hagerstown MD 21740-7390. (301)791-7000. Fax: (301)790-9734. Contact: Larry Becker, editor. 80% freelance written. Enjoys working with published/established writers; works with a small number of new/unpublished writers each year. Bimonthly magazine covering health articles (especially from a prevention angle and with a Christian slant). Estab. 1845. Circ. 50,000. **Pays on acceptance.** "The average length of time between acceptance of a freelance-written manuscript and publication of the material depends upon the topics: some immediately used; others up to 2 years." Byline always given. Buys first serial, first world serial, or sometimes second serial (reprint) rights. Submit seasonal/holiday material 9 months in advance. Reports in 2 months. Sample copy for $1. Writer's guidelines for #10 SASE.

• Ranked as one of the best markets for freelance writers in *Writer's Yearbook*'s annual "Top 100 Markets," January 1996.

Nonfiction: Interview/profile (with personalities on health). "We seek practical articles promoting better health and a more fulfilled life. We especially like features on breakthroughs in medicine, and most aspects of health. We need articles on how to integrate a person's spiritual life with their health. We'd like more in the areas of exercise, nutrition, water, avoiding addictions of all types and rest—all done from a wellness perspective." Buys 20-25 mss/year. Send complete ms. Length: 500-1,500 words. Pays $75-250.

Reprints: Send tearsheet of article and information about when and where the article previously appeared. Pays 50% of amount paid for an original article.

Photos: Send photos with ms. Needs 35mm transparencies. Not interested in b&w photos.

Tips: "*Vibrant Life* is published for baby boomers, particularly young professionals, age 30-45. Articles must be written in an interesting, easy-to-read style. Information must be reliable; no faddism. We are more conservative than other magazines in our field. Request a sample copy, and study the magazine and writer's guidelines."

VIM & VIGOR, America's Family Health Magazine, 1010 E. Missouri Ave., Phoenix AZ 85014-2601. (602)395-5850. Fax: (602)395-5853. Editor: Jake Poinier. 75% freelance written. Quarterly magazine covering health and healthcare. Estab. 1985. Circ. 900,000. **Pays on acceptance.** Publishes ms an average of 3 months after acceptance. Byline given. Buys all rights. Reports in 2 weeks on queries. Sample copy for 9×12 SAE with 8 first-class stamps. Writer's guidelines for #10 SASE.

Nonfiction: Health, diseases and healthcare. "Absolutely no complete manuscripts will be accepted. All articles are assigned to freelance writers. Send samples of your style." Buys 4 mss/year. Query with published clips. Length: 2,000 words. Pays $500. Pays expenses of writers on assignment.

Photos: Send photos with submission. Reviews contact sheets and any size transparencies. Offers no additional payment for photos accepted with ms. Captions, model releases, identification of subjects required. Buys one-time rights.

Tips: "We rarely accept suggested story ideas."

WALKING MAGAZINE, The, Walking Inc., 9-11 Harcourt St., Boston MA 02116. (617)266-3322. Fax: (617)266-7373. Publisher: Kevin Weaver. Bimonthly magazine covering health and fitness. "*The Walking Magazine* is written for healthy, active adults who are committed to fitness walking as an integral part of their lifestyle. Each issue offers advice on exercise techniques, diet, nutrition, personal care and contemporary health issues. It also covers information on gear and equipment, competition and travel, including foreign and domestic destinations for walkers." Estab. 1986. Circ. 510,200. This magazine did not respond to our request for information. Query before submitting.

WEIGHT WATCHERS MAGAZINE, 360 Lexington Ave., 11th Floor, New York NY 10017. (212)370-0644. Fax: (212)687-4398. Editor-in-Chief: Nancy Gagliardi. Health Editor: Randi Rose. Food Editor: Regina Ragone. Beauty & Fitness Editor: Geri Anne Fennessey. Features Editor: Laurie Saloman. Approximately 80% freelance written. Monthly magazine for women interested in healthy lifestyle/behavior information/advice, including news on health, nutrition, fitness, psychology and food/recipes. Success and before-and-after stories also welcome. Estab. 1968. Circ. 1,000,000. Buys first North American rights. **Pays on acceptance.** Sample copy and writer's guidelines $1.95 for 9×12 SASE.

• Ranked as one of the best markets for freelance writers in *Writer's Yearbook*'s annual "Top 100 Markets," January 1996.

Nonfiction: "We are interested in general health, nutrition and behavorial/psychological articles (stories with a strong weight loss angle always a plus). Some fitness—everything from beginner to advanced ideas—

freelanced out. Personal triumph/success stories of individuals who lost weight on the Weight Watchers plan also of interest. Back page a humorous look at some aspect of getting/staying in shape or achieving better health. Our articles have an authoritative yet friendly tone. How-to and service information crucial for all stories. To expedite fact-checking, we require a second, annotated manuscript including names, phone numbers, journal/newsletter citations of sources." Send detailed queries with published clips and SASE. Average article length: 700-1,200 words. Pay: $350-800.

Tips: "Well developed, tightly written queries always a plus, as are ideas that have a strong news peg. Trend pieces welcome and we're always on the lookout for a fresh angle on an old topic. Sources must be reputable; we prefer subjects to be medical professionals with university affiliations who are published in their field of expertise."

THE YOGA JOURNAL, California Yoga Teachers Association, 2054 University Ave., Berkeley CA 94704. (510)841-9200. Editor: Rick Fields. 75% freelance written. Bimonthly magazine covering yoga, holistic health, conscious living, spiritual practices and nutrition. "We reach a middle-class, educated audience interested in self-improvement and higher consciousness." Estab. 1975. Circ. 85,000. Pays on publication. Publishes ms an average of 10 months after acceptance. Byline given. Offers $50 kill fee. Buys first North American serial rights only. Submit seasonal/holiday material 4 months in advance. Reports in 3 months. Sample copy for $3.50. Free writer's guidelines.

Nonfiction: Book excerpts; how-to (exercise, yoga, massage, etc.); inspirational (yoga or related); interview/ profile; opinion; photo feature; and travel (if about yoga). "Yoga is our main concern, but our principal features in each issue highlight other New Age personalities and endeavors. Nothing too far-out and mystical. Prefer stories about Americans incorporating yoga, meditation, etc., into their normal lives." Buys 40 mss/ year. Query. Length: 750-3,500 words. Pays $150-1,000.

Reprints: Submit tearsheet or photocopy of article and information about when and where the article previously appeared.

Photos: Jonathan Wieder, art director. Send photos with ms. Pays $200-600 for cover transparencies; $25-100 for 8 × 10 b&w prints. Model release (for cover only) and identification of subjects required. Buys one-time rights.

Columns/Departments: Forum; Cooking; Nutrition; Natural Body Care; Bodywork; Meditation; Well-Being; Psychology; Profiles; Music (reviews of New Age music); and Book Reviews. Buys 12-15 mss/year. Pays $150-400 for columns; $50-100 for book reviews.

Tips: "We always read submissions. We are very open to freelance material and want to encourage writers to submit to our magazine. We're looking for out-of-state contributors, particularly in the Midwest and East Coast."

YOUR HEALTH, Globe Communications Corp., 5401 NW Broken Sound Blvd., Boca Raton FL 33487. (407)997-7733. E-mail: yhealth@aol.com. Editor: Susan Gregg. Associate Editor: Lisa Rappa. 70% freelance written. Semimonthly magazine on health and fitness. "*Your Health* is a lay-person magazine covering the entire gamut of health, fitness and medicine." Estab. 1962. Circ. 50,000. Pays on publication. Byline given. Buys first North American serial and second serial (reprint) rights. Submit seasonal/holiday material 3 months in advance. Reports in 1 month on queries; 6 weeks on mss. Free sample copy and writer's guidelines.

Nonfiction: Book excerpts, general interest, how-to (on general health and fitness topics), inspirational, interview/profile, medical breakthroughs, natural healing and alternative medicine, new products. "Give us something new and different." Buys 75-100 mss/year. Query with published clips or send complete ms. Length: 300-2,000 words. Pays $25-200.

Reprints: Send photocopy of article and information about when and where the article previously appeared. Pays $150-200.

Photos: Send photos with submission. Reviews contact sheets, negatives, transparencies, prints. Offers $50-100/photo. Captions, model releases, identification of subjects required. Buys one-time rights.

Tips: "Freelancers can best break in by offering us stories of national interest that we won't find through other channels, such as wire services. Well-written self-help articles, especially ones that focus on natural prevention and cures are always welcome. We're looking for more natural health and alternative therapy stories."

YOUR HEALTH & FITNESS, General Learning Communications, 60 Revere Dr., Northbrook IL 60062-1574. (847)205-3000. Executive Editor: Carol Lezak. 90-95% freelance written. Prefers to work with published/established writers. Quarterly magazine covering health and fitness. Needs "general, educational material on health, fitness and safety that can be read and understood easily by the layman." Estab. 1969. Circ. 1,000,000. Pays after publication. Publishes ms an average of 6 months after acceptance. No byline given (contributing editor status given in masthead). Offers 50% kill fee. Buys all rights. Reports in 1 year.

Nonfiction: General interest. "All article topics assigned. No queries; if you're interested in writing for the magazine, send a cover letter, résumé, curriculum vitae and writing samples. All topics are determined a year in advance of publication by editors; no unsolicited manuscripts." Buys approximately 65 mss/year. Length: 350-850 words. Pays $100-400 for assigned articles.

Tips: "Write to a general audience that has only a surface knowledge of health and fitness topics. Possible subjects include exercise and fitness, psychology, nutrition, safety, disease, drug data, and health concerns."

HISTORY

There has been an increasing interest in history in recent years. The popularity of historical documentaries, such as "The Civil War" and "Baseball," The History Channel debut in 1995, and the approach of the year 2000 may all play a part in this trend. Listed here are magazines and other periodicals written for historical collectors, genealogy enthusiasts, historic preservationists and researchers. Editors of history magazines look for fresh accounts of past events in a readable style. Some publications cover an era, such as the Civil War, or a region, while others specialize in historic preservation.

AMERICAN HISTORY, P.O. Box 8200, Harrisburg PA 17105-8200. (717)657-9555. Fax: (717)657-9526. Editor: Peggy Fortier. 60% freelance written. Bimonthly magazine of cultural, social, military and political history published for a general audience. Estab. 1966. Circ. 120,000. **Pays on acceptance.** Byline given. Buys all rights. Reports in 10 weeks on queries. Writer's guidelines for #10 SASE. Sample copy and guidelines for $4.50 (includes 3rd class postage) or $4 and 9×12 SAE with 4 first-class stamps.
Nonfiction: Features biographies of noteworthy historical figures and accounts of important events in American history. Also includes pictorial features on artists, photographers and graphic subjects. "Material is presented on a popular rather than a scholarly level." Query. "Query letters should be limited to a concise 1-2 page proposal defining your article with an emphasis on its unique qualities." Buys 10-15 mss/year. Length: 1,000-5,000 words depending on type of article. Pays $200-1,000. Occasionally pays the expenses of writers on assignment.
Photos: Welcomes suggestions for illustrations. Pays for the reproduced color illustrations that the author provides.
Tips: "Key prerequisites for publication are thorough research and accurate presentation, precise English usage and sound organization, a lively style, and a high level of human interest. Submissions received without return postage will not be considered or returned. Inappropriate materials include: fiction, book reviews, travelogues, personal/family narratives not of national significance, articles about collectibles/antiques, living artists, local/individual historic buildings/landmarks and articles of a current editorial nature. Currently seeking articles on significant Civil War subjects."

AMERICA'S CIVIL WAR, Cowles History Group, 741 Miller Dr., SE, Suite D-2, Leesburg VA 22075. (703)771-9400. Fax: (703)779-8345. Editor: Roy Morris, Jr. Managing Editor: Carl Von Wodtke. Contact: Cheryl Stringer. 95% freelance written. Bimonthly magazine of "popular history and straight historical narrative for both the general reader and the Civil War buff." Estab. 1988. Circ. 125,000. Pays on publication. Publishes ms up to 2 years after acceptance. Byline given. Buys all rights. Reports in 3 months on queries; 6 months on mss. Sample copy for $3.95. Writer's guidelines for #10 SASE.
Nonfiction: Book excerpts, historical, travel. No fiction or poetry. Buys 24 mss/year. Query. Length: 4,000 words maximum. Pays $300 maximum.
Photos: Send photos with submission or cite sources. "We'll order." Captions and identification of subjects required.
Columns/Departments: Personality (probes); Ordnance (about weapons used); Commands (about units); Travel (about appropriate historical sites). Buys 24 mss/year. Query. Length: 2,000 words. Pays up to $150.
Tips: "Include suggested readings in a standard format at the end of your piece. Manuscript must be typed, double-spaced on one side of standard white 8½×11, 16 to 30 pound paper—no onion skin paper or dot matrix printouts. All submissions are on speculation. Prefer subjects to be on disk (floppy or hard). Choose stories with strong art possibilities."

THE ARTILLERYMAN, Historical Publications, Inc., RR 1 Box 36, Tunbridge VT 05077. (802)889-3500. Fax: (802)889-5627. Editor: C. Peter Jorgensen. 60% freelance written. Quarterly magazine covering antique artillery, fortifications and crew-served weapons 1750-1900 for competition shooters, collectors and living history reenactors using artillery. "Emphasis on Revolutionary War and Civil War but includes everyone interested in pre-1900 artillery and fortifications, preservation, construction of replicas, etc." Estab. 1979. Circ. 2,200. Pays on publication. Publishes ms an average of 6 months after acceptance. Byline given. Not copyrighted. Buys one-time rights. Accepts simultaneous submissions. Reports in 3 weeks. Sample copy and writer's guidelines for 9×12 SAE with 4 first-class stamps.
Nonfiction: Historical; how-to (reproduce ordnance equipment/sights/implements/tools/accessories, etc.); interview/profile; new product; opinion (must be accompanied by detailed background of writer and include references); personal experience; photo feature; technical (must have footnotes); travel (where to find interesting antique cannon). Interested in "artillery *only*, for sophisticated readers. Not interested in other weapons,

battles in general." Buys 24-30 mss/year. Send complete ms. Length: 300 words minimum. Pays $20-60. Sometimes pays the expenses of writers on assignment.

Reprints: Send tearsheet or photocopy of article and information about when and where the article previously appeared.

Photos: Send photos with ms. Pays $5 for 5×7 and larger b&w prints. Captions, identification of subjects required.

Tips: "We regularly use freelance contributions for Places-to-Visit, Cannon Safety, The Workshop and Unit Profiles departments. Also need pieces on unusual cannon or cannon with a known and unique history. To judge whether writing style and/or expertise will suit our needs, writers should ask themselves if they could knowledgeably talk *artillery* with an expert. Subject matter is of more concern than writer's background."

‡AVIATION HISTORY, Cowles History Group, 741 Miller Dr., SE, Suite D-2, Leesburg VA 22075. (703)771-9400. Fax: (703)779-8345. Editor: Arthur Sanfelici. Managing Editor: Carl von Wodtke. Contact: Cheryl Stringer. 95% freelance written. Bimonthly magazine that aims to make aeronautical history not only factually accurate and complete, but also enjoyable to varied subscriber and newsstand audience. Estab. 1990. Circ. 80,000. Pays on publication. Publishes ms up to 2 years after acceptance. Byline given. Buys all rights. Editorial lead time 6 months. Submit seasonal material 1 year in advance. Accepts simultaneous submissions. Reports in 3 months on queries; 6 months on mss. Sample copy for $3.95. Writers guidelines for #10 SASE.

Nonfiction: Book excerpts, historical/nostalgic, interview/profile, personal experience, travel. Buys 24 mss/year. Query. Length: Feature articles should be 3,500-4,000 words, each with a 500-word sidebar, author's biography and book suggestions for further reading. Pays $300.

Photos: State availability of art and photos with submission, cite sources. "We'll order." Reviews contact sheets, negatives, transparencies. Identification of subjects required. Buys one-time rights.

Columns/Departments: People and Planes, Enduring Heritage, Aerial Oddities, Art of Flight; all 2,000 words. Pays $150. Book reviews, 300-750 words; payment by the word.

Tips: "Manuscripts must be typed, double-spaced on one side of standard white 8½×11, 16 to 30 pound paper—no onion skin paper or dot-matrix printouts. All submissions are on speculation. Prefer subjects to be on disk (floppy or hard). Our computer system is compatible to most computer systems. Submit a query letter. Choose stories with strong art possibilities."

CHICAGO HISTORY, The Magazine of the Chicago Historical Society, Chicago Historical Society, Clark St. at North Ave., Chicago IL 60614-6099. (312)642-4600. Fax: (312)266-2077. E-mail: adams@chicag ohs.org. Website: http://www.chicagohs.org. Editor: Rosemary Adams. 100% freelance written. Works with a small number of new/unpublished writers each year. Triannual magazine covering Chicago history: cultural, political, economic, social and architectural. Estab. 1945. Circ. 9,500. Pays on publication. Publishes ms an average of 1 year after acceptance. Byline given. Buys all rights. Submit seasonal/holiday material 9 months in advance. Reports in 4 months. Sample copy for $3.50 and 9×12 SAE with 3 first-class stamps. Free writer's guidelines.

● Writer's guidelines for *Chicago History* are also available on its website.

Nonfiction: Book excerpts, essays, historical, photo feature. Articles should be "analytical, informative, and directed at a popular audience with a special interest in history." No "cute" articles, no biographies. Buys 8-12 mss/year. Query or send complete ms. Length: approximately 4,500 words. Pays $150-250.

Photos: Send photocopies with submission. Would prefer no originals. Offers no additional payment for photos accepted with ms. Identification of subjects required.

Tips: "A freelancer can best break in by 1) calling to discuss an article idea with editor; and 2) submitting a detailed outline of proposed article. All sections of *Chicago History* are open to freelancers, but we suggest that authors do not undertake to write articles for the magazine unless they have considerable knowledge of the subject and are willing to research it in some detail. We require a footnoted manuscript, although we do not publish the notes."

‡GATEWAY HERITAGE, Missouri Historical Society, P.O. Box 11940, St. Louis MO 63112-0040. (314)746-4557. Fax: (314)746-4548. Editor: David Miles. 75% freelance written. Quarterly magazine covering Missouri history. "*Gateway Heritage* is a popular history magazine which is sent to members of the Missouri Historical Society. Thus, we have a general audience with an interest in history." Estab. 1980. Circ. 6,200. Pays on publication. Publishes ms an average of 6 months after acceptance. Byline given. Offers $75 kill fee. Buys first North American serial rights. Editorial lead time 6 months. Submit seasonal material 1 year in advance. Reports in 2 weeks on queries; 2 months on mss. Sample copy for 9×12 SAE with 7 first-class stamps. Writer's guidelines for #10 SASE.

Nonfiction: Book excerpts, historical/nostalgic, interview/profile, personal experience, photo feature. No genealogies. Buys 12-15 mss/year. Query with published clips. Length: 3,500-5,000 words. Pays $200.

Photos: State availability of photos with submission.

Columns/Departments: Literary Landmarks (biographical sketches and interviews of famous Missouri literary figures) 1,500-2,500 words; Missouri Biographies (biographical sketches of famous and interesting

Missourians) 1,500-2,500 words; Gateway Album (excerpts from diaries and journals) 1,500-2,500 words. Buys 6-8 mss/year. Query with published clips. Pays $100.

Tips: "Ideas for submissions to our departments are a good way to break into *Gateway Heritage*."

GOOD OLD DAYS, America's Premier Nostalgia Magazine, House of White Birches, 306 E. Parr Rd., Berne IN 46711. (219)589-8741. Editor: Ken Tate. 75% freelance written. Monthly magazine of first person nostalgia, 1900-1955. "We look for strong narratives showing life as it was in the first half of this century. Our readership is comprised of nostalgia buffs, history enthusiasts and the people who actually lived and grew up in this era." Pays on publication. Publishes ms an average of 8 months after acceptance. Byline given. Buys all, first North American serial or one-time rights. Submit seasonal/holiday material 10 months in advance. Reports in 2 months. Sample copy for $2. Writer's guidelines for #10 SASE.

Nonfiction: Historical/nostalgic, humor, interview/profile, personal experience, favorite food/recipes and photo features. Buys 350 mss/year. Query or send complete ms. Length: 1,000-1,800 words maximum. Pays 2-4¢/word or more, depending on quality and photos. No fiction accepted.

Reprints: Reprints rarely accepted.

Photos: Send photos or photocopies of photos with submission. Offers $5/photo. Identification of subjects required. Buys one-time or all rights.

MILITARY HISTORY, Cowles History Group, 741 Miller Dr., SE, Suite D-2, Leesburg VA 22075. (703)771-9400. Fax: (703)779-8345. Editor: Jon Guttman. Managing Editor: Carl Von Wodtke. 95% freelance written. Circ. 150,000. "We'll work with anyone, established or not, who can provide the goods and convince us as to its accuracy." Bimonthly magazine covering all military history of the world. "We strive to give the general reader accurate, highly readable, often narrative popular history, richly accompanied by period art." Pays on publication. Publishes ms 2 years after acceptance. Byline given. Buys all rights. Submit anniversary material at least 1 year in advance. Reports in 3 months on queries; 6 months on mss. Sample copy for $3.95. Writer's guidelines for #10 SASE.

Nonfiction: Historical; interview (military figures of commanding interest); personal experience (only occasionally). Buys 18 mss, plus 6 interviews/year. Query with published clips. "To propose an article, submit a short, self-explanatory query summarizing the story proposed, its highlights and/or significance. State also your own expertise, access to sources or proposed means of developing the pertinent information." Length: 4,000 words. Pays $400.

Columns/Departments: Intrigue, Weaponry, Perspectives, Personality and review of books, video, CD-ROMs, software—all relating to military history. Buys 24 mss/year. Query with published clips. Length: 2,000 words. Pays $200.

Tips: "We would like journalistically 'pure' submissions that adhere to basics, such as full name at first reference, same with rank, and definition of prior or related events, issues cited as context or obscure military 'hardware.' Read the magazine, discover our style, and avoid subjects already covered. Pick stories with strong art possibilities (*real* art and photos), send photocopies, tell us where to order the art. Avoid historical overview, focus upon an event with appropriate and accurate context. Provide bibliography. Tell the story in popular but elegant style."

PERSIMMON HILL, 1700 NE 63rd St., Oklahoma City OK 73111. Fax: (405)478-4714. Editor: M.J. Van Deventer. 70% freelance written. Prefers to work with published/established writers; works with a small number of new/unpublished writers each year. Quarterly magazine for an audience interested in Western art, Western history, ranching and rodeo, including historians, artists, ranchers, art galleries, schools, and libraries. Publication of the National Cowboy Hall of Fame and Western Heritage Center. Estab. 1970. Circ. 15,000. Buys first rights. Byline given. Pays on publication. Publishes ms an average of 6-24 months after acceptance. Reports in 3 months. Sample copy for $8 and 10 first-class stamps. Writer's guidelines for #10 SASE.

Nonfiction: Historical and contemporary articles on famous Western figures connected with pioneering the American West, Western art, rodeo, cowboys, etc. (or biographies of such people), stories of Western flora and animal life and environmental subjects. "We want thoroughly researched and historically authentic material written in a popular style. May have a humorous approach to subject. No broad, sweeping, superficial pieces; i.e., the California Gold Rush or rehashed pieces on Billy the Kid, etc." Length: 1,500 words. Buys 35-50 mss/year. Query with clips. Pays $100-250; special work negotiated.

Photos: Glossy b&w prints or color transparencies purchased with ms, or on assignment. Pays according to quality and importance for b&w and color photos. Suggested captions required.

Tips: "Excellent illustrations for articles are essential! No telephone queries."

PRESERVATION MAGAZINE, (formerly *Historic Preservation*), National Trust for Historic Preservation, 1785 Massachusetts Ave. NW, Washington DC 20036. (202)673-4075. Editor: Robert Wilson. 75% freelance written. Prefers to work with published/established writers. Bimonthly tabloid covering preservation of historic buildings in the US. "We cover subjects related in some way to place. Most entries are features, department or opinion pieces." Circ. 250,000. Pays on publication. Publishes ms an average of 1 month after acceptance. Byline given. Offers variable kill fee. Buys one-time rights. Reports in 2 months on queries.

• *Preservation Magazine* recently underwent a redesign, and has considerably expanded its scope and number of freelance pieces accepted.

Nonfiction: Features, news, profiles, opinion, photo feature, travel. Buys 30 mss/year. Query with published clips. Length: 500-3,500 words. Sometimes pays expenses of writers on assignment, but not long-distance travel.

Tips: "Do not send or propose histories of buildings, descriptive accounts of cities or towns or long-winded treatises on any subjects."

TIMELINE, Ohio Historical Society, 1982 Velma Ave., Columbus OH 43211-2497. (614)297-2360. Fax: (614)297-2367. Editor: Christopher S. Duckworth. 90% freelance written. Works with a small number of new/unpublished writers each year. Bimonthly magazine covering history, natural history, archaeology and fine and decorative arts. Estab. 1885. Circ. 19,000. **Pays on acceptance.** Publishes ms an average of 1 year after acceptance. Byline given. Offers $75 minimum kill fee. Buys first North American serial or all rights. Submit seasonal/holiday material 6 months in advance. Reports in 3 weeks on queries; 6 weeks on mss. Sample copy for $6 and 9 × 12 SAE. Writer's guidelines for #10 SASE.

Nonfiction: Book excerpts, essays, historical, profile (of individuals), photo feature. Buys 22 mss/year. Query. Length: 500-6,000 words. Pays $100-900.

Photos: Send photos with submission. Will not consider submissions without ideas for illustration. Reviews contact sheets, transparencies, 8 × 10 prints. Captions, model releases, and identification of subjects required. Buys one-time rights.

Tips: "We want crisply written, authoritative narratives for the intelligent lay reader. An Ohio slant may strengthen a submission, but it is not indispensable. Contributors must know enough about their subject to explain it clearly and in an interesting fashion. We use high-quality illustration with all features. If appropriate illustration is unavailable, we can't use the feature. The writer who sends illustration ideas with a manuscript has an advantage, but an often-published illustration won't attract us."

TRACES OF INDIANA AND MIDWESTERN HISTORY, Indiana Historical Society, 315 W Ohio St., Indianapolis IN 46202-3299. (317)232-1884. Fax: (317)233-3109. Website: http://www.ihs1830.org. Executive Editor: Thomas A. Mason. Managing Editor: J. Kent Calder. 80% freelance written. Quarterly magazine on Indiana and Midwestern history. Estab. 1989. Circ. 11,000. **Pays on acceptance.** Publishes ms an average of 6 months after acceptance. Byline given. Buys one-time rights. Submit seasonal/holiday material 1 year in advance. Reports in 3 months on mss. Sample copy for $5 and 9 × 12 SAE with 6 first-class stamps. Writer's guidelines for #10 SASE.

• This publication was awarded with certificates of Design Excellence from *Print Magazine.*

Nonfiction: Book excerpts, historical essays, historical photographic features. Buys 20 mss/year. Send complete ms. Length: 2,000-4,000 words. Pays $100-500.

Photos: Send photos with submission. Reviews contact sheets, photocopies, transparencies and prints. Pays "reasonable photographic expenses." Captions, permissions and identification of subjects required. Buys one-time rights.

Tips: "Freelancers should be aware of prerequisites for writing history for a broad audience. Should have some awareness of this magazine and other magazines of this type published by midwestern and western historical societies. Preference is given to subjects with an Indiana connection and authors who are familiar with *Traces.* Quality of potential illustration is also important."

TRUE WEST, Western Periodicals, Inc., P.O. Box 2107, Stillwater OK 74076-2107. (405)743-3370. Fax: (405)743-3374. E-mail: western@cowboy.net. Website: http://www.cowboy.net/western.html. Editor: John Joerschke. 100% freelance written. Works with a small number of new/unpublished writers each year. Magazine on Western American history before 1940. "We want reliable research on significant historical topics written in lively prose for an informed general audience." Estab. 1953. Circ. 30,000. **Pays on acceptance.** Publishes ms an average of 4 months after acceptance. Byline given. Buys first North American serial rights. Submit seasonal/holiday material 6 months in advance. Reports in 1 month on queries; 2 months on mss. Sample copy for $2 and 9 × 12 SAE. Writer's guidelines for #10 SASE.

Nonfiction: Historical/nostalgic, how-to, photo feature, travel. "We do not want rehashes of worn-out stories, historical fiction or history written in a fictional style." Buys 150 mss/year. Query. Length: 500-4,500 words. Pays 3-6¢/word.

Photos: Send photos with accompanying query or ms. Pays $10 for b&w prints. Identification of subjects required. Buys one-time rights.

Columns/Departments: Western Roundup—200-300-word short articles on historically oriented places to go and things to do in the West. Should include one b&w print. Buys 12-16 mss/year. Send complete ms. Pays $35.

Tips: "Do original research on fresh topics. Stay away from controversial subjects unless you are truly knowledgable in the field. Read our magazines and follow our guidelines. A freelancer is most likely to break in with us by submitting thoroughly researched, lively prose on relatively obscure topics. First person accounts rarely fill our needs."

VIETNAM, Cowles History Group, 741 Miller Dr. SE, #D-2, Leesburg VA 22075-8920. (703)771-9400. Editor: Colonel Harry G. Summers, Jr. Managing Editor: Carl Von Wodtke. Contact: Cheryl Stringer. 80-90% freelance written. Bimonthly magazine that "provides in-depth and authoritative accounts of the many complexities that made the war in Vietnam unique, including the people, battles, strategies, perspectives, analysis and weaponry." Estab. 1988. Circ. 115,000. Pays on publication. Publishes ms up to 2 years after acceptance. Byline given. Buys all rights. Reports in 3 months on queries; 6 months on mss. Sample copy for $3.95. Writer's guidelines for #10 SASE.

Nonfiction: Book excerpts (if original), historical, interview, personal/experience, military history. "Absolutely no fiction or poetry; we want straight history, as much personal narrative as possible, but not the gung-ho, shoot-em-up variety, either." Buys 24 mss/year. Query. Length: 4,000 words maximum. Pays $300 for features, sidebar 500 words.

Photos: Send photos with submission or state availability and cite sources. "We'll order." Identification of subjects required.

Columns/Departments: Arsenal (about weapons used, all sides); Personality (profiles of the players, all sides); Fighting Forces (about various units or types of units: air, sea, rescue); Perspectives. Query. Length: 2,000 words. Pays $150.

Tips: "Manuscripts must be typed, double-spaced on one side of standard white 8½×11, 16 to 30 pound paper—no onion skin paper or dot matrix printouts. All submissions are on speculation. Prefer subjects to be on disk (floppy or hard). Choose stories with strong art possibilities.

‡WESTERN TALES, P.O. Box 33842, Granada Hills CA 91394. Editor: Mariann Kumke. Contact: Dorman Nelson, publisher. 100% freelance written. Quarterly magazine covering "Western fiction genre—prose and poetry—westward expansion, Native Americans, pioneers, cowboys, wildlife, romance, adventure, mystery, intrigue. Primarily historical fiction and tales, but modern and future western subjects considered." Estab. 1993. Circ. 3,000. **Pays on acceptance.** Publishes ms an average of 4 months after acceptance. Byline given. Buys first North American serial rights. Editorial lead time 4 months. Submit seasonal material 4 months in advance. Accepts simultaneous submissions. Reports in 1 month on queries; 4 months on mss. Sample copy for $6. Writer's guidelines for #10 SASE.

Nonfiction: Book excerpts, essays, general interest (western fiction), how-to (western-oriented), humor, inspirational, new product (for advertising and information section), opinion, personal experience (fictionalized). Special issues: Edgar Rice Burroughs edition (he did write western genre fiction as well as his Tarzan and Carter of Mars.) Also—a women's edition created and written by women authors. Send complete ms. Pays $100 for unsolicited articles and 1 copy.

Reprints: Accepts previously published submissions.

Photos: Send photos with submission. Negotiates payment individually. Buys one-time rights.

Columns/Departments: Book review (Western fiction genre), 1,200-2,000 words. Buys 4-10 mss/year. Send complete ms. Pay negotiable.

Fiction: Adventure, historical, horror, humorous, mainstream, mystery, novel excerpts, romance, slice-of-life vignettes, suspense, western. Buys 80-100 mss/year. Send complete ms. Pays $100 maximum.

Poetry: Avant-garde, free verse, haiku, light verse, traditional (all Western oriented). Buys 60 poems/year. Submit maximum 4 poems. Pays $25.

Fillers: Mariann Kumke, editor. Anecdotes, facts, gags to be illustrated by cartoonist, short humor. Buys 25/year. Length: 50 words maximum. Pays $5-25.

Tips: "Send in a good tale!"

WILD WEST, Cowles History Group, 741 Miller Dr., SE, Suite D-2, Leesburg VA 22075-8920. (703)771-9400. Fax: (703)779-8345. Editor: Gregory Lalire. Managing Editor: Carl Von Wodtke. Contact: Cheryl Stringer. 95% freelance written. Bimonthly magazine on history of the American West. "*Wild West* covers the popular (narrative) history of the American West—events, trends, personalities, anything of general interest." Estab. 1988. Circ. 175,000. Pays on publication. Byline given. Buys all rights. Submit seasonal/holiday material 1 year in advance. Sample copy for $3.95. Writer's guidelines for #10 SASE.

Nonfiction: Historical/nostalgic, humor, travel. No fiction or poetry—nothing current. Buys 24 mss/year. Query. Length: 4,000 words with a 500-word sidebar. Pays $300.

Photos: Send photos with submission; cite sources. "We'll order." Captions, identification of subjects required.

Columns/Departments: Travel; Gun Fighters & Lawmen; Personalities; Warriors & Chiefs; Artist West; Books Reviews. Buys 16 mss/year. Length: 2,000. Pays $150 for departments, by the word for book reviews.

Tips: "Manuscripts must be typed, double-spaced on one side of standard white 8½×11, 16 to 30 pound paper—no onion skin paper or dot matrix printouts. All submissions are on speculation. Prefer subjects to be on disk (floppy or hard). Submit a query letter. Choose stories with strong art possibilities."

WORLD WAR II, Cowles History Group, 741 Miller Dr., SE, Suite D-2, Leesburg VA 22075-8920. (703)771-9400. Fax: (703)779-8345. Editor: Michael Haskew. Managing Editor: Carl Von Wodtke. Contact: Cheryl Stringer. 95% freelance written. Prefers to work with published/established writers. Bimonthly magazine covering "military operations in World War II—events, personalities, strategy, national policy, etc."

Estab. 1986. Circ. 200,000. Pays on publication. Publishes ms an average of 2 years after acceptance. Byline given. Buys all rights. Submit anniversary-related material 1 year in advance. Reports in 3 months on queries; 6 months or more on mss. Sample copy for $4. Writer's guidelines for #10 SASE.
Nonfiction: World War II military history. No fiction. Buys 24 mss/year. Query. Length: 4,000 words with a 500-word sidebar. Pays $200.
Photos: State availability of art and photos with submission. For photos and other art, send photocopies and cite sources. "We'll order." Captions and identification of subjects required.
Columns/Department: Undercover (espionage, resistance, sabotage, intelligence gathering, behind the lines, etc.); Personalities (WW II personalities of interest); Armaments (weapons, their use and development), all 2,000 words. Pays $100. Book reviews, 300-750 words. Buys 18 mss/year (plus book reviews). Query.
Tips: "List your sources and suggest further readings in standard format at the end of your piece—as a bibliography for our files in case of factual challenge or dispute. All submissions are on speculation."

HOBBY AND CRAFT

Magazines in this category range from home video to cross stitch. Craftspeople and hobbyists who read these magazines want new ideas while collectors need to know what is most valuable and why. Collectors, do-it-yourselfers and craftspeople look to these magazines for inspiration and information. Publications covering antiques and miniatures are also listed here. Publications covering the business side of antiques and collectibles are listed in the Trade Art, Design and Collectibles section.

THE AMERICAN MATCHCOVER COLLECTORS CLUB, The Retskin Report, P.O. Box 18481, Asheville NC 28814-0481. (704)254-4487. Fax: (704)254-1066. Editor: Bill Retskin. 50% freelance written. Quarterly newsletter for matchcover collectors and historical enthusiasts. Estab. 1986. Circ. 750. Pays on publication. Publishes ms an average of 3 months after acceptance. Byline given. Offers 20% kill fee. Buys first North American serial rights. Submit seasonal material 6 months in advance. Sample copy for 9×12 SAE with 2 first-class stamps. Writer's guidelines for #10 SASE.
Nonfiction: General interest, historical/nostalgic, how-to (collecting techniques), humor, personal experience, photo feature; all relating to match industry, matchcover collecting hobby or ephemera. Buys 2 mss/year. Query with published clips. Length: 200-1,200 words. Pays $25-50 for assigned articles; $10-25 for unsolicited articles.
Photos: Send photos with submission. Reviews b&w contact sheets and 5×7 prints. Offers $2-5/photo. Captions and identification of subjects required.
Fiction: Historical (match cover related only). Buys 2 mss/year. Query with published clips. Length: 200-1,200 words. Pays $25-50.
Tips: "We are interested in clean, direct style with the collector audience in mind."

AMERICAN WOODWORKER, Rodale Press, Inc., 33 E. Minor St., Emmaus PA 18098-0099. (610)967-5171. Fax: (610)967-7692. Editor/Publisher: David Sloan. Executive Editor: Ellis Wallentine. Managing Editor: Tim Snyder. 70% freelance written. Magazine published 7 times/year. "*American Woodworker* is a how-to magazine edited for the woodworking enthusiast who wants to improve his/her skills. We strive to motivate, challenge and entertain." Estab. 1985. Circ. 300,000. Pays on publication. Publishes ms an average of 6 months after acceptance. Byline given. Buys one-time and second serial (reprint) rights. Submit seasonal material 8 months in advance. Reports in 1 month. Free sample copy and writer's guidelines.
Nonfiction: Essays, historical/nostalgic, how-to (woodworking projects and techniques), humor, inspirational, interview/profile, new product, personal experience, photo feature, technical. ("All articles must have woodworking theme.") Buys 30 mss/year. Query. Length: up to 2,500 words. Pays new authors base rate of $150/published page. Sometimes pays expenses of writers on assignment.
Reprints: Send photocopy of article or typed ms with rights for sale noted.
Photos: Send photos with submission. Reviews 35mm or larger transparencies. Offers no additional payment for photos accepted with ms. Model releases required. Buys one-time rights.
Columns/Departments: Offcuts (woodworking news and nonsense, 1,000 word max). Buys 10 mss/year. Send complete ms. Pays $100-300.
Poetry: Avant-garde, free verse, Haiku, light verse, traditional. "All poetry must have woodworking or craftsmanship theme." Buys 1 poem/year. Submit maximum 5 poems. Pays $50-100.
Tips: "Reading the publication is the only real way to get a feel for the niche market *American Woodworker* represents and the needs and interests of our readers. Magazine editorial targets the serious woodworking enthusiast who wishes to improve his/her skills. Feature stories and articles most accessible for freelancers. Articles should be technically accurate, well organized and reflect the needs and interests of the amateur and small-shop professional woodworking enthusiast."

ANTIQUE REVIEW, P.O. Box 538, Worthington OH 43085-0538. Editor: Charles Muller. (614)885-9757. Fax: (614)885-9762. 60% freelance written. Eager to work with new/unpublished writers. Monthly tabloid for an antique-oriented readership, "generally well-educated, interested in Early American furniture and decorative arts, as well as folk art." Estab. 1975. Circ. 10,000. Pays on publication date assigned at time of purchase. Publishes ms an average of 2 months after acceptance. Buys first North American serial and second (reprint) rights to material originally published in dissimilar publications. Byline given. Phone queries OK. Reports in 3 months. Free sample copy and writer's guidelines for #10 SASE.
Nonfiction: "The articles we desire concern history and production of furniture, pottery, china, and other quality Americana. In some cases, contemporary folk art items are acceptable. We are also interested in reporting on antiques shows and auctions with statements on conditions and prices. We do not want articles on contemporary collectibles." Buys 5-8 mss/issue. Query with clips of published work. Query should show "author's familiarity with antiques, an interest in the historical development of artifacts relating to early America and an awareness of antiques market." Length: 200-2,000 words. Pays $100-200. Sometimes pays the expenses of writers on assignment.
Reprints: Accepts previously published submissions if not first printed in competitive publications. Send tearsheet or photocopy of article or typed ms with rights for sale noted and information about when and where the article previously appeared. Pays 100% of amount paid for an original article.
Photos: Send photos with query. Payment included in ms price. Uses 3×5 or larger glossy b&w or color prints. Captions required. Articles with photographs receive preference.
Tips: "Give us a call and let us know of specific interests. We are more concerned with the background in antiques than in writing abilities. The writing can be edited, but the knowledge imparted is of primary interest. A frequent mistake is being too general, not becoming deeply involved in the topic and its research. We are interested in primary research into America's historic material culture."

THE ANTIQUE TRADER WEEKLY, P.O. Box 1050, Dubuque IA 52004-1050. (800)531-0880. Fax: (319)588-0888. E-mail: traderpubs@aol.com. Editor: Juli Hoppensteadt. Contact: Jon Brecka, executive editor. 50% freelance written. Works with a small number of new/unpublished writers each year. Weekly newspaper for collectors and dealers in antiques and collectibles. Estab. 1957. Circ. 60,000. Publishes ms an average of 1 year after acceptance. Buys all rights. Payment at beginning of month following publication. Accepts simultaneous submissions. Submit seasonal/holiday material 4 months in advance. Sample copy for $1 and #10 SASE. Free writer's guidelines.
Nonfiction: "We invite authoritative and well-researched articles on all types of antiques and collectors' items and in-depth stories on specific types of antiques and collectibles. No human interest stories. We do not pay for brief information on new shops opening or other material printed as a service to the antiques hobby." Buys about 60 mss/year. Query or submit complete ms. Pays $25-100 for feature articles; $100-250 for feature cover stories.
Photos: Submit a liberal number of good b&w photos to accompany article. Uses 35mm slides for cover. Offers no additional payment for photos accompanying mss.
Tips: "Send concise, polite letter stating the topic to be covered in the story and the writer's qualifications. No 'cute' letters rambling on about some 'imaginative' story idea. Writers who have a concise yet readable style and know their topic are always appreciated. I am most interested in those who have personal collecting experience or can put together a knowledgable and informative feature after interviewing a serious collector/authority."

BECKETT BASEBALL CARD MONTHLY, Statabase, Inc., 15850 Dallas Pkwy., Dallas TX 75248. (214)991-6657. Fax: (214)991-8930. Website: http://www.beckett.com. Editor: Dr. James Beckett. Editorial Director: Pepper Hastings. Contact: Mike Pagel, assistant editor. 85% freelance written. Monthly magazine on baseball card and sports memorabilia collecting. "Our readers expect our publication to be entertaining and informative. Our slant is that hobbies are fun and rewarding. Especially wanted are how-to-collect articles." Estab. 1984. Circ. 620,341. **Pays on acceptance.** Publishes ms an average of 4 months after acceptance. Byline given. Pays $50 kill fee. Buys all rights. Submit seasonal/holiday material 6 months in advance. Reports in 1 month. Sample copy for $2.95. Writer's guidelines free.
Nonfiction: Book excerpts, historical/nostalgic, how-to, humor, interview/profile, new product, opinion, personal experience, photo feature, technical. Special issues: Spring training (February); season preview (April); All-Star game (July); stay in school (August); World Series (October). No articles that emphasize speculative prices and investments. Buys 145 mss/year. Send complete ms. Length: 300-1,500 words. Pays $100-400 for assigned articles; $50-200 for unsolicited articles. Sometimes pays expenses of writers on assignment.
Photos: Send photos with submission. Reviews 35mm transparencies, 5×7 or larger prints. Offers $10-300/photo. Captions, model releases and identification of subjects required. Buys one-time rights.
Fiction: Humorous only.
Tips: "A writer for *Beckett Baseball Card Monthly* should be an avid sports fan and/or a collector with an enthusiasm for sharing his/her interests with others. Articles must be factual, but not overly statistic-laden. First person (not research) articles presenting the writer's personal experiences told with wit and humor, and emphasizing the stars of the game, are *always* wanted. Acceptable articles must be of interest to our two

basic reader segments: teenaged boys and their middle-aged fathers who are re-experiencing a nostalgic renaissance of their own childhoods. Prospective writers should write down to neither group!"

BECKETT BASKETBALL MONTHLY, Statabase, Inc., 15850 Dallas Pkwy., Dallas TX 75248. (214)991-6657. Fax: (214)991-8930. Website: http://www.beckett.com. Publisher: Dr. James Beckett. Editorial Director: Pepper Hastings. Contact: Mike Payne, managing editor. 85% freelance written. Monthly magazine on basketball card and sports memorabilia collecting. "Our readers expect our publication to be entertaining and informative. Our slant is that hobbies are fun and rewarding. Especially wanted are articles dealing directly with the hobby of basketball card collecting." Estab. 1990. Circ. 392,854. **Pays on acceptance.** Publishes ms an average of 4 months after acceptance. Byline given. Pays $50 kill fee. Buys first North American serial rights. Submit seasonal/holiday material 6 months in advance. Reports in 1 month. Sample copy for $2.95. Writer's guidelines free.
Nonfiction: Book excerpts, historical/nostalgic, how-to, humor, interview/profile, new product, opinion, personal experience, photo feature, technical. Special issues: All Star game, stay in school (February); playoffs (June); new card sets (September). No articles that emphasize speculative prices and investments. Buys 145 mss/year. Send complete ms. Length: 300-1,500 words. Pays $100-400 for assigned articles; $100-200 for unsolicited articles. Sometimes pays expenses of writers on assignment.
Photos: Send photos with submission. Reviews 35mm transparencies, 5×7 or larger prints. Offers $10-300/photo. Captions, model releases and identification of subjects required. Buys one-time rights.
Fiction: Humorous only.
Tips: "A writer for *Beckett Basketball Monthly* should be an avid sports fan and/or a collector with an enthusiasm for sharing his/her interests with others. Articles must be factual, but not overly statistic-laden. First person (not research) articles presenting the writer's personal experiences told with wit and humor, and emphasizing the stars of the game, are *always* wanted. Acceptable articles must be of interest to our two basic reader segments: late teenaged boys and their fathers who are re-experiencing a nostalgic renaissance of their own childhoods. Prospective writers should write down to neither group!"

BECKETT FOCUS ON FUTURE STARS, Statabase, Inc., 15850 Dallas Pkwy., Dallas TX 75248. (214)991-6657. Fax: (214)991-8930. Website: http://www.beckett.com. Editor: Dr. James Beckett. Editorial Director: Pepper Hastings. Contact: Mike Pagel, assistant editor. 85% freelance written. Monthly magazine offering superstar coverage of young, outstanding players in baseball (major-league rookies, minor league stars and college), basketball (college), football (college) and hockey (juniors and college), with an emphasis on collecting sports cards and memorabilia. "Our readers expect our publication to be entertaining and informative. Our slant is that hobbies are fun and rewarding. Especially wanted are how-to-collect articles." Estab. 1991. Circ. 73,128. **Pays on acceptance.** Publishes ms an average of 4 months after acceptance. Byline given. Pays $50 kill fee. Buys all rights. Submit seasonal/holiday material 8 months in advance. Reports in 1 month. Sample copy for $2.95. Writer's guidelines free.
Nonfiction: Book excerpts, historical/nostalgic, how-to, humor, interview/profile, new product, opinion, personal experience, photo feature, technical. Special issues: card sets in review (January); stay in school (February); draft special (June). No articles that emphasize speculative prices and investments on cards. Buys 145 mss/year. Send complete ms. Length: 300-1,500 words. Pays $100-400 for assigned articles; $50-200 for unsolicited articles. Sometimes pays expenses of writers on assignment.
Photos: Send photos with submission. Reviews 35mm transparencies, 5×7 or larger prints. Offers $25-300/photo. Captions, model releases and identification of subjects required. Buys one-time rights.
Fiction: Humorous only
Tips: "A writer for *Beckett Focus on Future Stars* should be an avid sports fan and/or a collector with an enthusiasm for sharing his/her interests with others. Articles must be factual, but not overly statistic-laden. First person (not research) articles presenting the writer's personal experiences told with wit and humor, and emphasizing the stars of the game, are *always* wanted. Acceptable articles must be of interest to our two basic reader segments: teenaged boys and their middle-aged fathers who are re-experiencing a nostalgic renaissance of their own childhoods. Prospective writers should write down to neither group!"

BECKETT FOOTBALL CARD MONTHLY, Statabase, Inc., 15850 Dallas Pkwy., Dallas TX 75248. (214)991-6657. Fax: (214)991-8930. Website: http://www.beckett.com. Editor: Dr. James Beckett. Editorial Director: Pepper Hastings. Contact: Mike Pagel, assistant editor. 85% freelance written. Monthly magazine on football card and sports memorabilia collecting. "Our readers expect our publication to be entertaining and informative. Our slant is that hobbies are fun and rewarding. Especially wanted are how-to collect articles." Estab. 1989. Circ. 206,194. **Pays on acceptance.** Publishes ms an average of 4 months after acceptance. Byline given. Pays $50 kill fee. Buys all rights. Submit seasonal/holiday material 6 months in advance. Reports in 1 month. Sample copy for $2.95. Writer's guidelines free.
Nonfiction: Book excerpts, historical/nostalgic, how-to, humor, interview/profile, new product, opinion, personal experience, photo feature, technical. Special issues: Super Bowl (January); Pro Bowl (February); NFL draft (April); stay in school (August) preview (September). No articles that emphasize speculative prices and investments. Buys 145 mss/year. Send complete ms. Length: 300-1,500 words. Pays $100-400 for assigned articles; $50-200 for unsolicited articles. Sometimes pays expenses of writers on assignment.

Photos: Send photos with submission. Reviews 35mm transparencies, 5×7 or larger prints. Offers $10-300/photo. Captions, model releases and identification of subjects required. Buys one-time rights.
Fiction: Humorous only.
Tips: "A writer for *Beckett Football Card Monthly* should be an avid sports fan and/or a collector with an enthusiasm for sharing his/her interests with others. Articles must be factual, but not overly statistic-laden. Acceptable articles must be of interest to our two basic reader segments: teenaged boys and their middle-aged fathers who are re-experiencing a nostalgic renaissance of their own childhoods. Prospective writers should write down to neither group!"

BECKETT HOCKEY MONTHLY, Statabase, Inc., 15850 Dallas Pkwy., Dallas TX 75248. (214)991-6657. Fax: (214)991-8930. Website: http://www.beckett.com. Editor: Dr. James Beckett. Editorial Director: Pepper Hastings. Contact: Mike Pagel, assistant editor. 85% freelance written. Monthly magazine on hockey, hockey card and memorabilia collecting. "Our readers expect our publication to be entertaining and informative. Our slant is that hobbies are for fun and rewarding. Especially wanted are how-to collect articles." Estab. 1990. Circ. 159,346. **Pays on acceptance.** Publishes ms an average of 3 months after acceptance. Byline given. Pays $50 kill fee. Buys all rights. Submit seasonal/holiday material 6 months in advance. Reports in 1 month. Sample copy for $2.95. Writer's guidelines free.
Nonfiction: Book excerpts, historical/nostalgic, how-to, humor, interview/profile, new product, opinion, personal experience, photo feature, technical. Special issues: All-Star game (February); Stanley Cup preview (April); draft (June); season preview (October). No articles that emphasize speculative prices and investments. Buys 145 mss/year. Send complete ms. Length: 300-1,500 words. Pays $100-400 for assigned articles; $50-200 for unsolicited articles. Sometimes pays expenses of writers on assignment.
Photos: Send photos with submission. Reviews 35mm transparencies, 5×7 or larger prints. Offers $10-300/photo. Captions, model releases and identification of subjects required. Buys one-time rights.
Fiction: Humorous only.
Tips: "A writer for *Beckett Hockey Monthly* should be an avid sports fan and/or a collector with an enthusiasm for sharing his/her interests with others. Articles must be factual, but not overly statistic-laden. Acceptable articles must be of interest to our two basic reader segments: teenaged boys and their middle-aged fathers who are re-experiencing a nostalgic renaissance of their own childhoods. Prospective writers should write down to neither group!"

BECKETT RACING MONTHLY, Statabase, Inc., 15850 Dallas Pkwy., Dallas TX 75248. (214)991-6657. Fax: (214)991-8930. Website: http://www.beckett.com. Editor: Dr. James Beckett. Editorial Director: Pepper Hastings. Contact: Mike Pagel, assistant editor. 85% freelance written. Monthly magazine on racing card, die cast and sports memorabilia collecting. "Our readers expect our publication to be entertaining and informative. Our slant is that hobbies are fun and rewarding. Especially wanted are articles dealing directly with the hobby of card collecting." Estab. 1994. Circ. 100,000 **Pays on acceptance.** Publishes ms an average of 4 months after acceptance. Byline given. Pays $50 kill fee. Buys all rights. Submit seasonal/holiday material 6 months in advance. Reports in 1 month Sample copy for $3.95. Writer's guidelines free.
Nonfiction: Book excerpts, historical/nostalgic, how-to, humor, interview/profile, new product, opinion, personal experience, photo feature, technical. No articles that emphasize speculative prices and investments. Send complete ms. Length: 300-1,500 words. Pays $100-400 for assigned articles; $100-200 for unsolicited articles. Sometimes pays expenses of writer on assignment.
Photos: Send photos with submission. Reviews 35mm transparencies, 5×7 or larger prints. Offers $10-300/photo. Captions, model releases and identification of subjects required. Buys one-time rights.
Fiction: Humorous only.
Tips: "A writer for *Beckett Racing Monthly* should be an avid sports fan and/or a collector with an enthusiasm for sharing his/her interests with others. Articles must be factual, but not overly statistic-laden. First person (not research) articles presenting the writer's personal experiences told with wit and humor, and emphasizing the stars of the sport, are always wanted."

THE BLADE MAGAZINE, Krause Publications, 700 E. State St., Iola WI 54945. (715)445-2214. Fax: (715)445-4087. Editor: Steve Shackleford. 90% freelance written. Magazine published 12 times/year for knife enthusiasts who want to know as much as possible about quality knives and edged weapons. Estab. 1973. Pays on publication. Publishes ms an average of 6 months after acceptance. Buys all rights. Submit seasonal/holiday material 6 months in advance. Reports in 2 months. Sample copy for $3.25. Writer's guidelines for #10 SASE.
   • *Blade Magazine* is putting more emphasis on new products, knife accessories, knife steels, knife handles, knives and celebrities, knives in the movies.
Nonfiction: How-to; historical (on knives and weapons); adventure on a knife theme; celebrities who own knives; knives featured in movies with shots from the movie, etc.; new product; nostalgia; personal experience; photo feature; technical. "We would also like to receive articles on knives in adventuresome life-saving situations." No poetry. Buys 75 unsolicited mss/year. "We evaluate complete manuscripts and make our decision on that basis." Length: 500-1,000 words, longer if content warrants it. Pays $200/story minimum;

more for "better" writers. "We will pay top dollar in the knife market." Sometimes pays the expenses of writers on assignment.

Reprints: Accepts previously published submissions if not run in other knife publications. Send photocopy of article or typed ms with rights for sale noted and information about when and where the article previously appeared. Pays 90% of the amount paid for an original article.

Photos: Send photos with ms. Pays $5 for 8 × 10 b&w glossy prints, $25-75 for 35mm color transparencies. Captions required. "Photos are critical for story acceptance."

Fiction: Publishes novel excerpts.

Tips: "We are always willing to read submissions from anyone who has read a few copies and studied the market. The ideal article for us is a piece bringing out the romance, legend, and love of man's oldest tool— the knife. We like articles that place knives in peoples' hands—in life saving situations, adventure modes, etc. (Nothing gory or with the knife as the villain.) People and knives are good copy. We are getting more and better written articles from writers who are reading the publication beforehand. That makes for a harder sell for the quickie writer not willing to do his homework."

CLASSIC TOY TRAINS, Kalmbach Publishing Co., 21027 Crossroads Circle, Waukesha WI 53187. (414)796-8776. Editor: Roger Carp. 75-80% freelance written. Magazine published 8 times/year covering collectible toy trains (O, S, Standard, G scale, etc.) like Lionel, American Flyer, Marx, Dorfan, etc. "For the collector and operator of toy trains, *CTT* offers full-color photos of layouts and collections of toy trains, restoration tips, operating information, new product reviews and information, and insights into the history of toy trains." Estab. 1987. Circ. 77,000. **Pays on acceptance**. Publishes ms an average of 1 year after acceptance. Byline given. Buys all rights. Editorial lead time 2 months. Submit seasonal material 6 months in advance. Reports in 2 weeks on queries; 3 months on mss. Sample copy for $3.95 plus s&h. Writer's guidelines for #10 SASE.

Nonfiction: General interest, historical/nostalgic, how-to (restore toy trains; designing a layout; build accessories; fix broken toy trains), interview/profile, personal experience, photo feature, technical. Buys 90 mss/ year. Query. Length: 500-5,000 words. Pays $75-500. Sometimes pays expenses of writers on assignment.

Photos: Send photos with submission. Reviews 4 × 5 transparencies; 5 × 7 prints preferred. Offers no additional payment for photos accepted with ms or $15-75/photo. Captions required. Buys all rights.

Fillers: Uses cartoons. Buys 6 fillers/year. Pays $30.

Tips: "It's important to have a thorough understanding of the toy train hobby; most of our freelancers are hobbyists themselves. One-half to two-thirds of *CTT*'s editorial space is devoted to photographs; superior photography is critical."

COLLECTORS NEWS & THE ANTIQUE REPORTER, P.O. Box 156, Grundy Center IA 50638-0156. (319)824-6981. Fax: (319)824-3414. Editor: Linda Kruger. 20% freelance written. Estab. 1959. Works with a small number of new/unpublished writers each year. Monthly magazine-size publication on newsprint covering antiques, collectibles and nostalgic memorabilia. Circ. 13,000. Byline given. Pays on publication. Publishes ms an average of 1 year after acceptance. Buys first rights and makes work-for-hire assignments. Submit seasonal/holiday material 3 months in advance. Reports in 2 weeks on queries; 6 weeks on mss. Sample copy for $4 for 9 × 12 SAE. Free writer's guidelines.

Nonfiction: General interest (any subject re: collectibles, antique to modern); historical/nostalgic (relating to collections or collectors); how-to (display your collection, care for, restore, appraise, locate, add to, etc.); interview/profile (covering individual collectors and their hobbies, unique or extensive; celebrity collectors, and limited edition artists); technical (in-depth analysis of a particular antique, collectible or collecting field); and travel (coverage of special interest or regional shows, seminars, conventions—or major antique shows, flea markets; places collectors can visit, tours they can take, museums, etc.). Special issues: show/flea market (January, June) and usual seasonal emphasis. Buys 70 mss/year. Query with sample of writing. Length: 800-1,000 words. Pays $1/column inch.

Photos: Reviews color or b&w prints. Payment for photos included in payment for ms. Captions required. Buys first rights.

Tips: Articles most open to freelancers are on farm/country/rural collectibles; celebrity collectors; collectors with unique and/or extensive collections; music collectibles; transportation collectibles; advertising collectibles; bottles; glass, china and silver; primitives; furniture; toys; black memorabilia; political collectibles; and movie memorabilia.

‡CRAFTS 'N' THINGS, Clapper Communications Companies, 2400 Deven, Suite 375, Des Plaines IL 60018-4618. (847)635-5800. Fax: (847)635-6311. Editor: Julie Stephani. 80% freelance written. How-to and craft project magazine published 10 times/year. "We publish instruction for craft projects for beginners to intermediate level hobbyists." Estab. 1975. Circ. 300,000. Pays on publication. Publishes ms an average of 4 months after acceptance. Byline given. Offers $50 kill fee. Buys first, second serial (reprint) or all rights. Submit seasonal material 6 months in advance. Free sample copy and writer's guidelines.

Nonfiction: How-to (craft projects), new product (for product review column). Send SASE for list of issue themes. Buys 240 mss/year. Send complete ms with photos and instructions. Pays $50-250. Offers listing exchange as a product source instead of payment in some cases.

Reprints: Send photocopy of article and information about when and where the article previously appeared.

Columns/Departments: Bright Ideas (original ideas for working better with crafts—hints and tips). Buys 30 mss/year. Send complete ms. Length: 25-50 words. Pays $20.

Tips: "Query for guidelines and list of themes and deadlines. How-to articles are the best bet for freelancers."

CROCHET WORLD, House of White Birches, P.O. Box 776, Henniker NH 03242. Editor: Susan Hankins. 100% freelance written. Bimonthly magazine covering crochet patterns. "Crochet World is a pattern magazine devoted to the art of crochet. We also feature a Q&A column, letters (swap shop) column and occasionally non-pattern manuscripts, but it must be devoted to crochet." Estab. 1978. Circ. 75,000. Pays on publication. Byline given. Buys all rights. Editorial lead time 4 months. Submit seasonal material 6 months in advance. Reports in 1 month. Sample copy for $2. Writer's guidelines free on request.

Nonfiction: How-to (crochet). Buys 0-2 mss/year. Send complete ms. Length: 500-1,500 words. Pays $50.

Columns/Departments: Touch of Style (crocheted clothing); It's a Snap! (quick one-night simple patterns); Pattern of the Month, first and second prize each issue. Buys dozens of mss/year. Send complete pattern. Pays $40-300.

Poetry: Strictly crochet-related. Buys 0-10 poems/year. Submit maximum 2 poems. Length: 6-20 lines. Pays $10-20.

Fillers: Anecdotes, facts, gags to be illustrated by cartoonist, short humor. Buys 0-10/year. Length: 25-200 words. Pays $5-30.

Tips: "Be aware that this is a pattern generated magazine for crochet designs. I prefer the actual item sent along with the complete directions/graphs etc. over queries. In some cases a photo submission or good sketch will do. Crocheted designs must be well-made and original and directions must be complete. Write for my Designer's Guidelines which details how to submit designs. Non-crochet items, such as fillers, poetry *must* be crochet related, not knit, not sewing, etc."

DECORATIVE ARTIST'S WORKBOOK, F&W Publications, Inc., 1507 Dana Ave., Cincinnati OH 45207-1005. (513)531-2690, ext. 257. Fax: (513)531-2902. Editor: Anne Hevener. Estab. 1987. 50% freelance written. Bimonthly magazine covering decorative painting projects and products of all sorts. Offers "straightforward, personal instruction in the techniques of decorative painting." Circ. 90,000. **Pays on acceptance.** Byline given. Offers 20% kill fee. Buys first North American serial rights. Submit seasonal/holiday material 8 months in advance. Reports in 1 month. Sample copy for $4.65 and 9×12 SAE with 5 first-class stamps.

Nonfiction: How-to (related to decorative painting projects), new products, techniques, artist profiles. Buys 30 mss/year. Query with slides or photos. Length: 1,200-1,800 words. Pays 10-12¢/word.

Photos: State availability of or send photos with submission. Reviews 35mm, 4×5 transparencies and quality photos. Offers no additional payment for photos accepted with ms. Captions required. Buys one-time rights.

Fillers: Anecdotes, facts, short humor. Buys 10/year. Length: 50-200 words. Pays $10-25.

Tips: "The more you know—and can prove you know—about decorative painting the better your chances. I'm looking for experts in the field who, through their own experience, can artfully describe the techniques involved. How-to articles are most open to freelancers. Be sure to query with slides or transparencies, and show that you understand the extensive graphic requirements for these pieces and are able to provide progressives—slides or illustrations that show works in progress."

FIBERARTS, The Magazine of Textiles, Altamont Press, 50 College St., Asheville NC 28801. (704)253-0467. Fax: (704)253-7952. Editor: Ann Batchelder. 100% freelance written. Eager to work with new writers. Magazine published 5 times/year covering textiles as art and craft (weaving, quilting, surface design, stitchery, knitting, fashion, crochet, etc.) for textile artists, craftspeople, hobbyists, teachers, museum and gallery staffs, collectors and enthusiasts. Estab. 1975. Circ. 25,250. Pays 60 days after publication. Publishes ms an average of 4 months after acceptance. Byline given. Buys first rights. Editorial guidelines and style sheet available. Sample copy for $4.95 and 10×12 SAE with 2 first-class stamps. Writer's guidelines for #10 SAE with 2 first-class stamps.

Nonfiction: Historical, artist interview/profile, opinion, photo feature, technical, education, trends, exhibition reviews, textile news. Query. "Please be very specific about your proposal. Also an important consideration in accepting an article is the kind of photos—35mm slides and/or b&w glossies—that you can provide as illustration. We like to see photos in advance." Length: 250-2,000 words. Pays $75-400, depending on article. Rarely pays the expenses of writers on assignment or for photos.

Tips: "Our writers are very familiar with the textile field, and this is what we look for in a new writer. Familiarity with textile techniques, history or events determines clarity of an article more than a particular style of writing. The writer should also be familiar with *Fiberarts*, the magazine."

FINE WOODWORKING, The Taunton Press, P.O. Box 5506, Newtown CT 06470-5506. (203)426-8171. Fax: (203)426-3434. Editor: Scott Gibson. Bimonthly magazine on woodworking in the small shop. "All writers are also skilled woodworkers. It's more important that a contributor be a woodworker than a writer. Our editors (also woodworkers) will fix the words." Estab. 1975. Circ. 292,000. Pays on publication. Byline given. Kill fee varies; "editorial discretion." Buys first rights and rights to republish in anthologies and use in promo pieces. Submit seasonal/holiday material 6 months in advance. Accepts simultaneous submissions. Reports in 2 months. Sample copy for $5.50 and 10 first-class stamps. Free writer's guidelines.

Nonfiction: How-to (woodworking). Buys 120 mss/year. "No specs—our editors would rather see more than less." Pays $150/magazine page. Sometimes pays expenses of writers on assignment.

Photos: Send photos with submission. Reviews contact sheets, negatives, transparencies and prints. Captions, model releases and identification of subjects required. Buys one-time rights.

Columns/Departments: Notes & Comment (topics of interest to woodworkers); Question & Answer (woodworking Q & A); Follow-Up (information on past articles/readers' comments); Methods of Work (shop tips); Tool Forum (short reviews of new tools). Buys 400 items/year. Length varies. Pays $10-150/published page.

Tips: "Send for authors guidelines and follow them. Stories about woodworking reported by non-woodworkers *not* used. Our magazine is essentially reader-written by woodworkers."

GOLD AND TREASURE HUNTER, 27 Davis Rd., P.O. Box 47, Happy Camp CA 96039-0047. (916)493-2062. Fax: (916)493-2095. E-mail: goldgold@snowcrest.net. Editor: Dave McCracken. Managing Editor: Marcie Stumpf. Bimonthly magazine on small-scale gold mining and treasure hunting. "We want interesting fact and fiction stories and articles about small-scale mining, treasure hunting, camping and the great outdoors." Estab. 1987. Circ. 50,000. Pays on publication. Buys all rights. Submit seasonal/holiday material 4 months in advance. Reports in 1 month. Sample copy for 9×12 SAE with 5 first-class stamps. Writer's guidelines free.

Nonfiction: How-to, humor, inspirational, interview/profile, new product, personal experience, photo feature, travel. "No promotional articles concerning industry products." Buys 125 mss/year. Send complete ms. Length: 1,500-2,000 words. Pays 3¢/word.

Reprints: Send tearsheet, photocopy of article or typed ms with rights for sale noted and information about when and where the article previously appeared. Pays 50% of amount paid for an original article.

Photos: Send photos with submission. Reviews any size transparencies and prints. Pays $10-50/photo. Captions are required. Buys all rights.

Fiction: Adventure, experimental, historical, horror, humorous, mystery, suspense, western—all related to gold mining/treasure hunting.

Tips: "Our general readership is comprised mostly of individuals who are actively involved in gold mining and treasure hunting, or people who are interested in reading about others who are active and successful in the field. True stories of actual discoveries, along with good color photos—particularly of gold—are preferred. Also, valuable how-to information on new and workable field techniques, preferably accompanied by supporting illustrations and/or photos."

HOME MECHANIX, 2 Park Ave., New York NY 10016. (212)779-5000. Fax: (212)725-3281. Website: http://www.homideas.com. Editor: Michael Chotiner. Contact: Alan Kearney. 50% freelance written. Prefers to work with published/established writers. "If it's good, and it fits the type of material we're currently publishing, we're interested, whether writer is new or experienced." Magazine published 10 times/year for the active home and car owner. "Articles emphasize an active, home-oriented lifestyle. Includes information useful for maintenance, repair and renovation to the home and family car. Information on how to buy, how to select products useful to homeowners/car owners. Emphasis in home-oriented articles is on good design, inventive solutions to styling and space problems, useful home-workshop projects." Estab. 1928. Circ. 1,000,000. **Pays on acceptance.** Publishes ms an average of 6 months after acceptance. Byline given. Buys first North American serial rights. Reports in 3 months. Query.

• Ranked as one of the best markets for freelance writers in *Writer's Yearbook*'s annual "Top 100 Markets," January 1996.

Nonfiction: Feature articles relating to homeowner/car owner, 1,500-2,500 words. "This may include personal home-renovation projects, professional advice on interior design, reports on different or unusual construction methods, energy-related subjects, outdoor/backyard projects, etc. No high-tech subjects such as aerospace, electronics, photography or military hardware. Most of our automotive features are written by experts in the field, but fillers, tips, how-to repair, or modification articles on the family car are welcome. Articles on construction, tool use, refinishing techniques, etc., are also sought. Pays $300 minimum for features; fees based on number of printed pages, photos accompanying mss., etc." Pays expenses of writers on assignment.

Photos: Photos should accompany mss. Pays $600 and up for transparencies for cover. Inside color: $300/1 page, $500/2, $700/3, etc. Captions and model releases required.

Tips: "The most frequent mistake made by writers in completing an article assignment for *Home Mechanix* is not taking the time to understand its editorial focus and special needs."

THE HOME SHOP MACHINIST, 2779 Aero Park Dr., P.O. Box 1810, Traverse City MI 49685. (616)946-3712. Fax: (616)946-3289. Editor: Joe D. Rice. 95% freelance written. Bimonthly magazine covering machining and metalworking for the hobbyist. Circ. 29,400. Pays on publication. Publishes ms an average of 2 years after acceptance. Byline given. Buys first North American serial rights only. Reports in 2 months. Free sample copy and writer's guidelines for 9×12 SASE.

Nonfiction: How-to (projects designed to upgrade present shop equipment or hobby model projects that require machining), technical (should pertain to metalworking, machining, drafting, layout, welding or foundry work for the hobbyist). No fiction or "people" features. Buys 40 mss/year. Query or send complete ms. Length: open—"whatever it takes to do a thorough job." Pays $40/published page, plus $9/published photo.

Photos: Send photos with ms. Pays $9-40 for 5×7 b&w prints; $70/page for camera-ready art; $40 for b&w cover photo. Captions and identification of subjects required.

Columns/Departments: Book Reviews; New Product Reviews; Micro-Machining; Foundry. "Writer should become familiar with our magazine before submitting." Query first. Buys 25-30 mss/year. Length: 600-1,500 words. Pays $40-70/page.

Fillers: Machining tips/shortcuts. No news clippings. Buys 12-15/year. Length: 100-300 words. Pays $30-48.

Tips: "The writer should be experienced in the area of metalworking and machining; should be extremely thorough in explanations of methods, processes—always with an eye to safety; and should provide good quality b&w photos and/or clear dimensioned drawings to aid in description. Visuals are of increasing importance to our readers. Carefully planned photos, drawings and charts will carry a submission to our magazine much farther along the path to publication."

KITPLANES, For designers, builders and pilots of experimental aircraft, Fancy Publications, P.O. Box 6050, Mission Viejo CA 92690. (714)855-8822. Fax: (714)855-3045. Editor: Dave Martin. Managing Editor: Keith Beveridge. 70% freelance written. Eager to work with new/unpublished writers. Monthly magazine covering self-construction of private aircraft for pilots and builders. Estab. 1972. Circ. 85,000. Pays on publication. Publishes ms an average of 3 months after acceptance. Byline given. Offers negotiable kill fee. Buys first North American serial rights. Submit seasonal/holiday material 6 months in advance. Reports in 2 weeks on queries; 6 weeks on mss. Sample copy for $3. Free writer's guidelines.

Nonfiction: How-to, interview/profile, new product, personal experience, photo feature, technical, general interest. "We are looking for articles on specific construction techniques, the use of tools, both hand and power, in aircraft building, the relative merits of various materials, conversions of engines from automobiles for aviation use, installation of instruments and electronics." No general-interest aviation articles, or "My First Solo" type of articles. Buys 80 mss/year. Query. Length: 500-5,000 words. Pays $100-400, including story photos.

Photos: State availability of or send photos with query or ms. Pays $250 for cover photos. Captions and identification of subjects required. Buys one-time rights.

Tips: "*Kitplanes* contains very specific information—a writer must be extremely knowledgeable in the field. Major features are entrusted only to known writers. I cannot emphasize enough that articles must be directed at the individual aircraft builder. We need more 'how-to' photo features in all areas of homebuilt aircraft."

‡KNITTING DIGEST, House of White Birches, 306 E. Parr Rd., Berne IN 46711. Fax: (219)589-8093. Managing Editor: Vicki Steensma. 100% freelance written. Bimonthly magazine covering knitting designs and patterns. "We print only occasional articles, but are always open to knitting designs and proposals." Estab. 1993. Circ. 50,000. Pays within 2 months of acceptance. Publishes ms an average of 6 months after acceptance. Byline given. Offers 100% kill fee. Buys all rights. Accepts simultaneous submissions. Reports in 2 months on queries; 6 months on mss. Writer's guidelines free on request.

Nonfiction: How-to (knitting skills); humor, technical (knitting field). Buys 6-8 mss/year. Send complete ms. Length: 500 words maximum. Pay varies. Also pays in contributor copies.

Fillers: Anecdotes, facts, gags to be illustrated by cartoonist, short humor. Buys 24-36/year. Length: 50 words maximum. Pays $15-25.

Tips: "Clear concise writing. Humor is appreciated in this field, as much as technical tips. The magazine is a digest, so space is limited. All submissions must be typed and double-spaced."

‡KNIVES ILLUSTRATED, The Premier Cutlery Magazine, McMullen-Argus Publishing, Inc., 774 S. Placentia Ave., Placentia CA 92670. (714)572-6887. Fax: (714)572-4265. Editor: Bud Lang. 40-50% freelance written. Bimonthly magazine covering high-quality factory and custom knives. "We publish articles on different types of factory and custom knives, how-to make knives, technical articles, shop tours, articles on knife makers and artists. Must have knowledge about knives and the people who use and make them. Estab. 1987. Circ. 35,000. Pays on publication. Byline given. Editorial lead time 3 months. Reports in 2 weeks on queries. Sample copy and writer's guidelines for #10 SASE.

Nonfiction: How-to, interview/profile, photo features, technical. Buys 35-40 mss/year. Query first. Length: 400-2,000 words. Pays $100-500 minimum for assigned articles. Sometimes pays expenses of writers on assignment.

Photos: Send photos with submission. Reviews 35mm, 2¼×2¼, 4×5 transparencies, 5×7 prints. Negotiates payment individually. Captions, model releases, identification of subjects required.

Tips: "Most of our contributors are involved with knives, either as collectors, makers, engravers, etc. To write about this subject requires knowledge. A 'good' writer can do OK if they study some recent issues."

‡**LAPIDARY JOURNAL**, 60 Chestnut Ave., Suite 201, Devon PA 19333-1312. (610)293-1112. Fax: (610)293-1717. E-mail: ljmagazine@aol.com. Editor: Merle White. Contact: Hazel Wheaton, managing editor. 70% freelance written. Monthly magazine covering gem, mineral and jewelry arts. "Our audience is hobbyists who usually know something about the subject before they start reading. Our style is conversational and informative. There are how-to projects and profiles of artists and materials." Estab. 1947. Circ. 59,800. Pays on publication. Publishes ms an average of 4 months after acceptance. Byline given. Buys one-time and worldwide rights. Editorial lead time 3 months.
Nonfiction: How-to jewelry/craft, interview/profile, new product, personal experience, technical, travel. Buys 50-100 mss/year. Query. Sometimes pays expenses of writers on assignment.
Reprints: Accepts previously published submissions.

THE LEATHER CRAFTERS & SADDLERS JOURNAL, 331 Annette Court, Rhinelander WI 54501-2902. (715)362-5393. Fax: (715)362-5391. Contact: William R. Reis, editor-in-chief. Managing Editor: Dorothea Reis. 100% freelance written. Bimonthly magazine. "Aid to craftsmen using leather as the base medium. All age groups and skill levels from beginners to master carvers and artisans." Estab. 1990. Circ. 7,000. Pays on publication. Publishes ms an average of 2 months after acceptance. Byline given. "All assigned articles subject to review for acceptance by editor." Buys first North American serial and second serial (reprint) rights. Submit seasonal/holiday material 6 months in advance. Accepts simultaneous submissions. Reports in 1 month. Sample copy for $5. Writer's guidelines for #10 SASE.
Nonfiction: How-to (crafts and arts and any other projects using leather). "I want only articles that include hands-on, step-by-step, how-to information." Buys 75 mss/year. Send complete ms. Length: 500-2,500 words. Pays $20-200 for assigned articles; $20-150 for unsolicited articles. Send good contrast color print photos and full size patterns and/or full-size photo-carve patterns with submission. Lack of these reduces payment amount. Captions required.
Reprints: Send tearsheet or photocopy of article. Pays 50% of amount paid for original article.
Columns/Departments: Beginners, Intermediate, Artists, Western Design, Saddlemakers, International Design and Letters (the open exchange of information between all peoples). Length: 500-2,500 on all. Buys 75 mss/year. Send complete ms. Pays 5¢/word.
Fillers: Anecdotes, facts, gags illustrated by cartoonist, newsbreaks. Length: 25-200 words. Pays $3-10.
Tips: "We want to work with people who understand and know leathercraft and are interested in passing on their knowledge to others. We would prefer to interview people who have achieved a high level in leathercraft skill."

LINN'S STAMP NEWS, Amos Press, 911 Vandemark Rd., P.O. Box 29, Sidney OH 45365. (513)498-0801. Fax: (513)498-0814. E-mail: linns@bright.net. Website: http://www.best.com/~linns. Editor: Michael Laurence. Managing Editor: Elaine Boughner. 50% freelance written. Weekly tabloid on the stamp collecting hobby. "All articles must be about philatelic collectibles." Estab. 1928. Circ. 70,000. Pays on publication. Publishes ms an average of 1 month after acceptance. Byline given. Buys first North American serial rights. Submit seasonal/holiday material 2 months in advance. Reports in 2 weeks on mss. Free sample copy. Writer's guidelines for #10 SAE with 2 first-class stamps.
Nonfiction: General interest, historical/nostalgic, how-to, interview/profile, technical. "No articles merely giving information on background of stamp subject. Must have philatelic information included." Buys 300 mss/year. Send complete ms. Length: 500 words maximum. Pays $10-50. Rarely pays expenses of writers on assignment.
Photos: Send photos with submission. Prefers glossy b&w prints. Offers no additional payment for photos accepted with ms. Captions required. Buys all rights.

LIVE STEAM, Live Steam, Inc., 2779 Aero Park Dr., Box 629, Traverse City MI 49685. (616)946-3712. Fax: (616)946-3289. E-mail: steambook@aol.com. Editor: Joe D. Rice. 90% freelance written. Eager to work with new/unpublished writers. Bimonthly magazine covering steam-powered models and full-size engines (i.e., locomotives, traction, cars, boats, stationary, etc.) "Our readers are hobbyists, many of whom are building their engines from scratch. We are interested in anything that has to do with the world of live steam-powered machinery." Circ. 12,000. Pays on publication. Publishes ms an average of 2 years after acceptance. Byline given. Buys first North American serial rights only. Reports in 1 month. Free sample copy and SASE for writer's guidelines.
Nonfiction: Historical/nostalgic, how-to (build projects powered by steam), new product, personal experience, photo feature, technical (must be within the context of steam-powered machinery or on machining techniques). No fiction. Buys 50 mss/year. Query or send complete ms. No photocopies. Length: 500-3,000 words. Pays $30-500/published page.
Photos: Send photos with ms. Pays $50/page of finished art. Pays $8 for 5×7 b&w prints; $40 for color cover. Captions and identification of subjects required.

Columns/Departments: Steam traction engines, steamboats, stationary steam, steam autos. Buys 6-8 mss/year. Query. Length: 1,000-3,000 words. Pays $20-50.

Tips: "At least half of all our material is from the freelancer. Requesting a sample copy and author's guide will be a good place to start. The writer must be well-versed in the nature of live steam equipment and the hobby of scale modeling such equipment. Technical and historical accuracy is an absolute must. Often, good articles are weakened or spoiled by mediocre to poor quality photos. Freelancers must learn to take a *good* photograph."

LOST TREASURE, INC., P.O. Box 1589, Grove OK 74344. Fax: (918)786-2192. Managing Editor: Patsy Beyel. 75% freelance written. Monthly and annual magazines covering lost treasure. Estab. 1966. Circ. 55,000. Buys all rights. Byline given. Buys 225 mss/year. Pays on publication. Reports in 2 months. Writers guidelines for #10 SASE. Sample copies (2 magazines) and guidelines for 10×13 SAE with $1.47 postage each magazine.

Nonfiction: 1) *Lost Treasure*, a monthly publication, is composed of lost treasure stories, legends, folklore, and how-to articles. 2) *Treasure Facts*, a monthly publication, consists of how-to information for treasure hunters, treasure hunting club news, who's who in treasure hunting, tips, etc. 3) *Treasure Cache*, an annual publication, contains stories about documented treasure caches with a sidebar from the author telling the reader how-to search for the cache highlighted in the story. Length: 1,200-1,500 words. Pays 4¢/word.

Photos: Black and white or color prints with mss help sell your story. Pays $5/published photo. Cover photos pay $100/published photo; must be 35mm color slides, vertical. Captions required.

Tips: "We are only interested in treasures that can be found with metal detectors. Queries welcome but not required. If you write about famous treasures and lost mines, be sure we haven't used your selected topic recently and story must have a new slant or new information. Source documentation required. How-To's should cover some aspect of treasure hunting and how-to steps should be clearly defined. If you have a *Treasure Cache* story we will, if necessary, help the author with the sidebar telling how to search for the cache in the story."

MINIATURE QUILTS, Chitra Publications, 2 Public Ave., Montrose PA 18801. (717)278-1984. Fax: (717)278-2223. Contact: Editorial Team. 40% freelance written. Bimonthly magazine on miniature quilts. "We seek articles of an instructional nature (all techniques), profiles of talented quiltmakers and informational articles on all aspects of miniature quilts. Miniature is defined as quilts made up of blocks smaller than five inches." Estab. 1990. Circ. 50,000. Pays on publication. Publishes ms an average of 6 months after acceptance. Byline given. Buys second serial (reprint) rights. Submit seasonal/holiday material 8 months in advance. Reports in 2 months on queries and mss. Writer's guidelines for SASE.

Photos: Send photos with submission. Reviews 35mm slides and larger transparencies. Offers $20/photo. Captions, model releases and identification of subjects required. Buys all rights, unless rented from a museum.

Tips: "Publication hinges on good photo quality. Query with ideas; send samples of prior work."

MODEL RAILROADER, P.O. Box 1612, Waukesha WI 53187. Editor: Andy Sperandeo. Monthly for hobbyists interested in scale model railroading. Buys exclusive rights. "Study publication before submitting material." Reports on submissions within 60 days.

Nonfiction: Wants construction articles on specific model railroad projects (structures, cars, locomotives, scenery, benchwork, etc.). Also photo stories showing model railroads. Query. First-hand knowledge of subject almost always necessary for acceptable slant. Pays base rate of $90/page.

Photos: Buys photos with detailed descriptive captions only. Pays $10 and up, depending on size and use. Pays double b&w rate for color; full color cover earns $200.

MONITORING TIMES, Grove Enterprises Inc., P.O. Box 98, Brasstown NC 28902-0098. (704)837-9200. Fax: (704)837-2216. E-mail: mteditor@grove.net. Website: www.grove.net/hmpgmt.html. Managing Editor: Rachel Baughn. Publisher: Robert Grove. 20% freelance written. Monthly magazine for radio hobbyists. Estab. 1982. Circ. 30,000. Pays 30-60 days before date of publication. Publishes ms an average of 4 months after acceptance. Byline given. Buys first North American serial rights and limited reprint rights. Submit seasonal/holiday material 4 months in advance. Reports in 1 month. Sample copy and writer's guidelines for 9×12 SAE and 9 first-class stamps.

Nonfiction: General interest, how-to, humor, interview/profile, personal experience, photo feature, technical. Buys 72 mss/year. Query. Length: 1,000-2,500 words. Pays $150-200.

Reprints: Send photocopy of article and information about when and where the article previously appeared. Pays 25% of amount paid for an original article.

Photos: Send photos with submission. Captions required. Buys one-time rights.

Columns/Departments: "Query managing editor."

Tips: "Need articles explaining new wireless technology and trunked systems; are accepting more technical projects.

‡**PACK-O-FUN, Projects For Kids & Families**, Clapper Communications, 2400 Devon Ave., Des Plaines IL 60018-4618. (847)635-5800. E-mail: 72567.1066@compuserve.com. Editor: Bill Stephani. Con-

tact: Janice Brandon, associate editor. 85% freelance written. Bimonthly magazine covering crafts and activities for kids and those working with kids. "We request quick and easy, inexpensive crafts and activities. Projects must be original, and complete instructions are required upon acceptance." Estab. 1951. Circ. 102,000. Pays 30 days after signed contract. Byline given. Buys all rights. Editorial lead time 8 months. Submit seasonal material 8 months in advance. Accepts simultaneous submissions. Reports in 1 month. Sample copy for $2.95.

Photos: Photos of project may be submitted in place of project at query stage.

Fillers: Facts, gags to be illustrated by cartoonist. Buys 20/year. Length: 25-50 words.

Tips: "*Pack-O-Fun* is looking for original how-to projects for kids and those working with kids. We're looking for recyclable ideas for throwaways. It would be helpful to check out our magazine before submitting."

‡PAPERWEIGHT NEWS, 761 Chestnut St., Santa Cruz CA 95060. (408)427-0111. E-mail: iselman@got. net. Editor: Lawrence Selman. Managing Editor: Ron Rosenberg. Contact: Ron Rosenberg. 80% freelance written. Quarterly magazine covering glass paperweights. "We accept fiction, technical and inspriational stories that revolve around glass paperweights. Contributors range from museum creators to housewives." Estab. 1975. Circ. 10,000. Pays on publication. Publishes ms an average of 6 months after acceptance. Byline given. Buys first North American serial rights. Editorial lead time 6 months. Submit seasonal material 6 months in advance. Accepts simultaneous submissions. Reports in 10 weeks on queries; 2 months on mss. Sample copy for $15.

Nonfiction: Book excerpts, essays, exposé, general interest, historical/nostalgic, how-to, humor, inspirational, interview/profile, new paperweight, personal experience, photo feature, technical, travel, puzzles/cartoons. "All stories must focus on paperweights." Buys 18 mss/year. Query. Length: 1,000-5,000 words. Pays $25-200 for assigned articles; $25-100 for unsolicited articles.

Photos: State availability of photos with submission. Send photos with submission. Reviews negatives, 4×transparencies, 4×6 prints. Offers no additional payment for photos accepted with ms. Negotiates payment individually. Captions, model releases, identification of subjects required.

Columns/Departments: Technically Speaking . . . (paperweight legends). Query.

Fiction: Adventure, condensed novels, confessions, ethnic, experimental, fantasy, historical, horror, humorous, mainstream, mystery, novel excerpts, romance, science fiction, serialized novels, slice-of-life vignettes, suspense, western. Length: 1,000-5,000 words. Pays $25-200.

Poetry: Avant-garde, free verse, haiku, light verse, traditional, limericks. Buys 5-10 poems/year. Pays $25-100.

Fillers: Anecdotes, facts, gags to be illustrated by cartoonist, newsbreaks, short humor. Buys 20/year. Length: 80-500 words. Pays $25-100.

Tips: "Do not send a submission that shows ignorance about the art form."

POPULAR ELECTRONICS, Gernsback Publications, Inc., 500 Bi-County Blvd., Farmingdale NY 11735-3931. (516)293-3000. Fax: (516)293-3115. Editor: Carl Laron. 80% freelance written. Monthly magazine covering hobby electronics—"features, projects, ideas related to audio, radio, experimenting, test equipment, computers, antique radio, communications, consumer electronics, state-of-the-art, etc." Circ. 78,000. **Pays on acceptance.** Byline given. Buys all rights. Submit seasonal/holiday material 9 months in advance. Reports in 1 month. Free sample copy, "include mailing label." Writer's guidelines for #10 SASE.

Nonfiction: General interest, how-to, photo feature, technical. Buys 200 mss/year. Query or send complete ms. Length: 1,000-3,500 words. Pays $100-500.

Photos: Send photos with submission. Wants b&w glossy photos. Offers no additional payment for photos accepted with ms. Captions required. Buys all rights.

Tips: "All areas are open to freelancers. Project-type articles and other 'how-to' articles have best success."

POPULAR ELECTRONICS HOBBYISTS HANDBOOK, Gernsback Publications, Inc., 500 Bi-County Blvd., Farmingdale NY 11735. (516)293-3000. Fax: (516)293. Editor: Julian S. Martin. 95% freelance written. Semiannual magazine on hobby electronics. Estab. 1989. Circ. 125,000. **Pays on acceptance.** Byline given. Buys all rights. Submit seasonal/holiday material 6 months in advance. Reports in 2 weeks.

Nonfiction: General interest, historical/nostalgic, how-to (build projects, fix consumer products, etc., all of which must be electronics oriented), photo feature, technical. "No product reviews!" Buys 20-30 mss/year. Send complete ms. Length: 1,000-5,000 words. Pays $100-500.

Photos: Send photos with submission. "We want b&w glossy photos." Reviews 5×7 or 8×10 b&w prints. Offers no additional payment for photos accepted with ms. Captions and model releases are required. Buys all rights.

Tips: "Read the magazine. Know and understand the subject matter. Write it. Submit it."

POPULAR MECHANICS, Hearst Corp., 224 W. 57th St., 3rd Floor, New York NY 10019. (212)649-2000. Editor: Joe Oldham. Managing Editor: Deborah Frank. 50% freelance written. Monthly magazine on automotive, home improvement, science, boating, outdoors, electronics. "We are a men's service magazine that tries to address the diverse interests of today's male, providing him with information to improve the way he lives. We cover stories from do-it-yourself projects to technological advances in aerospace, military, automotive and so on." Estab. 1902. Circ. 1,400,000. **Pays on acceptance**. Publishes ms an average of 6 months after acceptance. Byline given. Offers 25% kill fee. Buys all rights. Submit seasonal/holiday material 6 months in advance. Query. Reports in 2 weeks on queries; 1 month on mss. Sample copy and writer's guidelines for 9×12 SASE.

Nonfiction: General interest, how-to (shop projects, car fix-its), new product, technical. Special issues: Design and Engineering Awards (January); Boating Guide (February); Home Improvement Guide (April); Car Care Guide (May); Automotive Parts & Accessories Guide (October); Woodworking Guide (November). No historical, editorial or critique pieces. Buys 24 mss/year. Query with or without published clips or send complete ms. Length: 500-3,000 words. Pays $500-1,500 for assigned articles; $150-1,000 for unsolicited articles. Sometimes pays expenses of writers on assignment.

Photos: Send photos with submission. Reviews 5×7 transparencies and prints. Offers no additional payment for photos accepted with ms. Captions, model releases and identification of subjects required. Buys first and exclusive publication rights in the US during on-sale period of issue in which photos appear plus 90 days after.

Columns/Departments: New Cars (latest and hottest cars out of Detroit and Europe), Car Care (Maintenance basics, How It Works, Fix-Its and New products: send to Don Chaikin. Electronics, Audio, Home Video, Computers, Photography: send to Brian Fenton. Boating (new equipment, how-tos, fishing tips), Outdoors (gear, vehicles, outdoor adventures): send to Rick Taylor. Home & Shop Journal: send to Steve Willson. Science (latest developments), Tech Update (breakthroughs) and Aviation (sport aviation, homebuilt aircraft, new commercial aircraft, civil aeronautics): send to Jim Wilson. All columns are about 1,000 words.

POPULAR WOODWORKING, F&W Publications, 1507 Dana Ave., Cincinnati OH 45207. (513)531-2690, ext 238. Fax: (513)531-1843. E-mail: wudworker@aol.com. Editor: Steve Shanesy. Contact: Cristine Antolik, managing editor. 60% freelance written. Eager to work with new/unpublished writers. Bimonthly magazine covering woodworking. "Our readers are the woodworking hobbyist and small woodshop owner. Writers should have a knowledge of woodworking, or be able to communicate information gained from woodworkers." Estab. 1981. Circ. 284,000. **Pays on acceptance**. Publishes ms an average of 10 months after acceptance. Byline given. Buys first North American serial rights. Submit seasonal/holiday material 6 months in advance. Reports in 2 months. Sample copy and writer's guidelines for $4.50 and 9×12 SAE with 6 first-class stamps.

● Ranked as one of the best markets for freelance writers in *Writer's Yearbook*'s annual "Top 100 Markets," January 1996.

Nonfiction: How-to (on woodworking projects, with plans); humor (woodworking anecdotes); technical (woodworking techniques). Special issues: Shop issue, Finishing issue, "Cutting Edge" issue (on sharpening tools); Hand Tools issue, Alternative Materials issue and Holiday Projects issue. Buys 75 mss/year. Query with or without published clips or send complete ms. Pays up to $125/published page. "The project must be well-designed, well constructed, well built and well finished. Technique pieces must have practical application."

Reprints: Send photocopy of article or typed ms with rights for sale noted and information about when and where the article previously appeared. Pays 100% of amount paid for an original article.

Photos: Send photos with submission. Reviews color only, slides and transparencies, 3×5 glossies acceptable. Offers no additional payment for photos accepted with ms. Photographic quality may affect acceptance. Need sharp close-up color photos of step-by-step construction process. Captions and identification of subjects required.

Columns/Departments: Tricks of the Trade (helpful techniques), Out of the Woodwook (thoughts on woodworking as a profession or hobby, can be humorous or serious), 500-1,500 words. Buys 6 mss/year. Query.

Fillers: Anecdotes, facts, short humor, shop tips. Buys 15/year. Length: 50-500 words.

Tips: "Submissions should include materials list, complete diagrams (blue prints not necessary), and discussion of the step-by-step process. We have become more selective on accepting only practical, attractive projects with quality construction. We are also looking for more original topics for our other articles."

QST, American Radio Relay League, Inc., 225 Main St., Newington CT 06111-1494. (860)594-0200. Fax: (860)594-0259. E-mail: qst@arrl.org. Website: http://www.arrl.org. Editor: Mark Wilson. Contact: Steve Ford, managing editor. 40% freelance written. Monthly magazine covering amateur radio interests and technology. "Ours are topics of interest to radio amateurs and persons in the electronics and communications fields." Estab. 1914. Circ. 175,000. Pays on publication. Publishes ms an average of 4 months after acceptance. Byline given. Usually buys all rights. Submit seasonal/holiday material 5 months in advance. Reports in 3 weeks on queries. Free sample copy and writer's guidelines for 10×13 SAE with 5 first-class stamps.

Nonfiction: General interest, how-to, humor, new products, personal experience, photo feature, technical (anything to do with amateur radio). Buys 50 mss/year. Query with or without published clips, or send complete ms. Length: open. Pays $65/published page. Sometimes pays expenses of writers on assignment.

Photos: Send photos with submission. Sometimes offers additional payment for photos accepted with ms or for cover. Captions, model releases and identification of subjects required. Usually buys all rights.

Columns/Departments: Hints and Kinks (hints/time saving procedures/circuits/associated with amateur radio), 50-200 words. Buys 100 mss/year. Send complete ms. Pays $20.

Tips: "Write with an idea, ask for sample copy and writer's guide. Technical and general interest to amateur operators, communications and electronics are most open."

QUILTER'S NEWSLETTER MAGAZINE, 741 Corporate Circle, Suite A, Golden CO 80401-5622. Fax: (303)277-0370. Editor: Bonnie Leman. Senior Features Editor: Jeannie Spears. Magazine published 10 times/year. Estab. 1969. Circ. 200,000. Buys first North American serial rights or second rights. Buys about 15 mss/year. Pays on publication, sometimes on acceptance. Reports in 2 months. Free sample copy.

Nonfiction: "We are interested in articles on the subject of quilts and quiltmakers *only*. We are not interested in anything relating to 'Grandma's Scrap Quilts' but could use fresh material." Submit complete ms. Pays 10¢/word minimum, usually more.

Reprints: Send tearsheet of article or typed ms with rights for sale noted and information about when and where the article previously appeared.

Photos: Additional payment for photos depends on quality.

Fillers: Related to quilts and quiltmakers only.

Tips: "Be specific, brief, and professional in tone. Study our magazine to learn the kind of thing we like. Send us material which fits into our format but which is different enough to be interesting. Realize that we think we're the best quilt magazine on the market and that we're aspiring to be even better, then send us the cream off the top of your quilt material."

QUILTING TODAY MAGAZINE, Chitra Publications, 2 Public Ave., Montrose PA 18801. (717)278-1984. Fax: (717)278-2223. Contact: Editorial Team. 80% freelance written. Bimonthly magazine on quilting, traditional and contemporary. "We seek articles that will cover one or two full pages (800 words each); informative to the general quilting public, present new ideas, interviews, instructional, etc." Estab. 1986. Circ. 90,000. Pays on publication. Publishes ms an average of 6 months after acceptance. Byline given. Buys second serial (reprint) rights. Submit seasonal/holiday material 8 months in advance. Reports in 1 month on queries; 2 months on mss. Writer's guidelines for SASE.

● *Quilting Today Magazine* has a new department appearing occasionally—"History Lessons," featuring a particular historical style or period in quiltmaking history.

Nonfiction: Book excerpts, essays, how-to (for various quilting techniques), humor, interview/profile, new product, opinion, personal experience, photo feature. "No articles about family history related to a quilt or quilts unless the quilt is a masterpiece of color and design, impeccable workmanship." Buys 20-30 mss/ year. Query with or without published clips, or send complete ms. Length: 800-1,600 words. Pays $50-75/ page.

Reprints: Occasionally accepts previously published submissions. Send photocopy of article or typed ms with rights for sale noted and information about when and where the article previously appeared. Pays $75/ published page.

Photos: Send photos with submission. Reviews 35mm slides and larger transparencies. Offers $20/photo. Captions, identification of subjects required. Buys all rights unless rented from a museum.

Columns/Departments: Quilters Lesson Book (instructional), 800-1,600 words. Buys 10-12 mss/year. Send complete ms. Pays up to $75/column.

Tips: "Query with ideas; send samples of prior work so that we can assess and suggest assignment. Our publications appeal to traditional quilters (generally middle-aged) who use the patterns in each issue. Must have excellent photos."

‡RUG HOOKING MAGAZINE, Stackpole Magazines, 500 Vaughn St., Harrisburg PA 17110-2220. Fax: (717)234-1359. Editor: Patrice Crowley. 25% freelance written. Magazine published 5 times/year covering the craft of rug hooking. "This is the only magazine in the world devoted exclusively to rug hooking. Our readers are both novices and experts. They seek how-to pieces, features on fellow artisans and stories on beautiful rugs new and old." Estab. 1989. Circ. 10,000. **Pays on acceptance.** Publishes ms an average of 1 year after acceptance. Byline given. Buys all rights. Editorial lead time 6 months. Submit seasonal material 6 months in advance. Reports in 2 months. Sample copy for $5.

Nonfiction: How-to (hook a rug or a specific aspect of hooking), personal experience. Buys 30 mss/year. Query with published clips. Length: 825-2,475 words. Pays $74.25-222.75. Sometimes pays expenses of writers on assignment.

Photos: Send photos with submission. Reviews 2×2 transparencies, 3×5 prints. Negotiates payment individually. Identification of subjects required. Buys all rights.

SEW NEWS, The Fashion Magazine for People Who Sew, PJS Publications, Inc., News Plaza, P.O. Box 1790, Peoria IL 61656. (309)682-6626. Fax: (309)682-7394. E-mail: sewnews@aol.com. Editor: Linda Turner Griepentrog. 90% freelance written. Works with a small number of new/unpublished writers each year. Monthly magazine covering fashion-sewing. "Our magazine is for the beginning home sewer to the professional dressmaker. It expresses the fun, creativity and excitement of sewing." Estab. 1980. Circ. 261,000. **Pays on acceptance.** Publishes ms an average of 6 months after acceptance. Byline given. Buys all rights. Submit seasonal/holiday material 6 months in advance. Reports in 2 months. Sample copy for $3.95. Writer's guidelines for #10 SAE with 2 first-class stamps.

• All stories submitted to *Sew News* must be on disk.

Nonfiction: How-to (sewing techniques), interview/profile (interesting personalities in home-sewing field). Buys 200-240 ms/year. Query with published clips if available. Length: 500-2,000 words. Pays $25-500. Rarely pays expenses of writers on assignment.

Photos: Send photos. Prefers b&w, color photographs or slides. Payment included in ms price. Identification of subjects required. Buys all rights.

Tips: "Query first with writing sample and outline of proposed story. Areas most open to freelancers are how-to and sewing techniques; give explicit, step-by-step instructions plus rough art. We're using more home decorating editorial content."

SPORTS COLLECTORS DIGEST, Krause Publications, 700 E. State St., Iola WI 54990. (715)445-2214. Fax: (715)445-4087. Editor: Tom Mortenson. Estab. 1952. 50% freelance written. Works with a small number of new/unpublished writers each year. Weekly sports memorabilia magazine. "We serve collectors of sports memorabilia—baseball cards, yearbooks, programs, autographs, jerseys, bats, balls, books, magazines, ticket stubs, etc." Circ. 52,000. Pays after publication. Publishes ms an average of 3 months after acceptance. Byline given. Buys first North American serial rights only. Submit seasonal/holiday material 3 months in advance. Reports in 5 weeks on queries; 2 months on mss. Free sample copy. Writer's guidelines for #10 SASE.

Nonfiction: General interest (new card issues, research on older sets); historical/nostalgic (old stadiums, old collectibles, etc.); how-to (buy cards, sell cards and other collectibles, display collectibles, ways to get autographs, jerseys and other memorabilia); interview/profile (well-known collectors, ball players—but must focus on collectibles); new product (new card sets); personal experience ("what I collect and why"-type stories). No sports stories. "We are not competing with *The Sporting News*, *Sports Illustrated* or your daily paper. Sports collectibles only." Buys 100-200 mss/year. Query. Length: 300-3,000 words; prefers 1,000 words. Pays $50-125.

Reprints: Send tearsheet of article. Pays 100% of amount paid for an original article.

Photos: Unusual collectibles. Send photos. Pays $5-15 for b&w prints. Identification of subjects required. Buys all rights.

Columns/Departments: "We have all the columnists we need but welcome ideas for new columns." Buys 100-150 mss/year. Query. Length: 600-3,000 words. Pays $90-125.

Tips: "If you are a collector, you know what collectors are interested in. Write about it. No shallow, puff pieces; our readers are too smart for that. Only well-researched articles about sports memorabilia and collecting. Some sports nostalgia pieces are OK. Write only about the areas you know about."

SUNSHINE ARTIST, America's Premier Show & Festival Publication, Palm House Publishing Inc., 2600 Temple Dr., Winter Park FL 32789. (407)539-1399. Fax: (407)539-1499. Publisher: David F. Cook. Editor: Amy Detwiler. Monthly magazine covering art shows in the United States. "We are the premier marketing/reference magazine for artists and crafts professionals who earn their living through art shows nationwide. We list more than 4,000 shows annually, critique many of them and publish articles on marketing, selling and other issues of concern to professional show circuit artists." Estab. 1972. Circ. 12,000. Pays on publication. Publishes ms an average of 3 months after acceptance. Byline given. Buys first North American serial rights. Reports within 2 months. Sample copy for $5.

Nonfiction: "We publish articles of interest to artists and crafts professionals who travel the art show circuit. Current topics include marketing, computers and RV living." No how-to. Buys 5-10 freelance mss/year. Query or ms. Length: 1,000-2,000 words. Pays $50-150 for accepted articles.

Photos: Send photos with submission. Offers no additional payment for photos accepted with ms. Captions, model releases and identification of subjects required.

‡**TRADING CARDS MAGAZINE**, L.F.P., Inc. 8484 Wilshire Blvd., Suite 900, Beverly Hills CA 90211. (213)651-5400. Fax: (213)655-2339. E-mail: tradingc. Editor: Steve Ryan. 65% freelance written. Monthly magazine covering sports cards and collectibles. "*Trading Cards Magazine* describes and features new card sets in all sports, investigate various subjects in the hobby." Estab. 1991. Circ. 135,000. Pays on publication. Publishes ms an average of 1 month after acceptance. Byline given. Offers $100 kill fee. Not copyrighted. Buys one-time rights. Editorial lead time 2 months. Submit seasonal material 3 months in advance. Accepts simultaneous submissions. Reports in 1 month. Sample copy and writer's guidelines free on request.

• *Trading Cards Magazine* is looking for shorter pieces, more sidebars, more interviews.

Nonfiction: Book excerpts, general interest, how-to, interview/profile, personal experience, photo feature. Special issues: Football (November 1996); Basketball (January 1997). Buys 75 mss/year. Query with published clips. Length: 1,500-2,500 words. Pays $200-350 for assigned articles. Sometimes pays expenses of writers on assignment.

Photos: State availability of photos with submission. Negotiates payment individually. Captions required. Buys one-time rights.

Columns/Departments: Investment Tips (best cards to invest in), 1,000 words; Batter's Box, Slap Shots, etc. (reporting on industry), 1,250-1,750 words. Buys 25 mss/year. Query with published clips. Pays $150-250.

‡TRADITIONAL QUILTER, The Leading Teaching Magazine for Creative Quilters, All American Crafts, Inc., 243 Newton-Sparta Rd., Newton NJ 07860. (201)383-8080. Fax: (201)383-8133. E-mail: tqphyllis@aol.com. Editor: Phyllis Barbieri. 45% freelance written. Bimonthly magazine on quilting. Estab. 1988. Pays on publication. Byline given. Buys first or all rights. Submit seasonal/holiday 6 months in advance. Reports in 2 months. Sample copy for 9 × 12 SAE with 4 first-class stamps. Writer's guidelines for #10 SASE.

Nonfiction: Quilts and quilt patterns with instructions, quilt-related projects, historical/nostalgic, humor, interview/profile, opinion, personal experience, photo feature, travel—all quilt related. Query with published clips. Length: 350-1,000 words. Pays 7-10¢/word.

Photos: Send photos with submission. Reviews all size transparencies and prints. Offers $10-15/photo. Captions and identification of subjects required. Buys one-time or all rights.

Columns/Departments: Feature Teacher (qualified quilt teachers with teaching involved—with slides); Remnants (reports on conventions, history—humor); Profile (award-winning and interesting quilters); The Guilded Newsletter (reports on quilting guild activities, shows, workshops, and retreats). Length: 1,000 words maximum. Pays 7-10¢/word.

TRADITIONAL QUILTWORKS, The Pattern Magazine for Creative Quilters, Chitra Publications, 2 Public Ave., Montrose PA 18801. (717)278-1984. Fax: (717)278-2223. Contact: Editorial Team. 50% freelance written. Bimonthly magazine on quilting. "We seek articles of an instructional nature, profiles of talented teachers, articles on the history of specific areas of quiltmaking (patterns, fiber, regional, etc.)." Estab. 1988. Circ. 90,000. Pays on publication. Publishes ms an average of 6 months after acceptance. Byline given. Buys second serial (reprint) rights. Submit seasonal/holiday material 8 months in advance. Reports in 2 months. Writer's guidelines for SASE.

Nonfiction: Historical, instructional, quilting education. "No light-hearted entertainment." Buys 12-18 mss/year. Query with or without published clips, or send complete ms. Length: 1,600 words maximum. Pays $75/page.

Reprints: Occasionally buys previously published submissions. Send photocopy of article or typed ms with rights for sale noted and information about when and where the article previously appeared. Pays $75/published page.

Photos: Send photos with submission. Reviews 35mm slides and larger transparencies (color). Offers $20/photo. Captions, model releases and identification of subjects required. Buys all rights.

Tips: "Query with ideas; send samples of prior work so that we can assess and suggest assignment. Our publications appeal to traditional quilters, generally middle-aged and mostly who use the patterns in the magazine. Publication hinges on good photo quality."

TREASURE CHEST, The Information Source & Marketplace for Collectors and Dealers of Antiques and Collectibles, Venture Publishing Co., 2112 Broadway, Suite 414, New York NY 10023. (212)496-2234. Editor: Howard E. Fischer. 100% freelance written. Monthly newspaper on antiques and collectibles. Estab. 1988. Circ. 50,000. Pays on publication. Publishes ms an average of 3 months after acceptance. Byline given. Buys first rights and second serial (reprint) rights. Reports in 2 months on mss. Sample copy for 9 × 12 SAE with $2. Writer's guidelines for #10 SASE.

Nonfiction: Primarily interested in feature articles on a specific field of antiques or collectibles which includes a general overview of that field. Buys 35 mss/year. Send complete ms. Length: 1,000 words. Pays $30 with photos. Payment in contributor copies or other premiums negotiable.

Reprints: Send tearsheet or photocopy of article and information about when and where the article previously appeared. Pays 60% of amount paid for original article.

Fillers: Anecdotes, facts, gags to be illustrated by cartoonist, short humor. Buys 12/year. Length: 100-350 words. Pays $10.

Tips: "Learn about your subject by interviewing experts—appraisers, curators, dealers."

VIDEOMAKER, Camcorders, Editing, Desktop Video, Audio and Video Production, Videomaker Inc., P.O. Box 4591, Chico CA 95927. (916)891-8410. Fax: (916)891-8443. E-mail: editor@videomaker.com. Website: http://www.videomaker.com. Editor: Stephen Muratore. Managing Editor: Don Keller. 75% freelance written. Monthly magazine on video production. "Our audience encompasses video camera users ranging from broadcast and cable TV producers to special-event videographers to video hobbyists . . . labeled professional, industrial, 'prosumer' and consumer. Editorial emphasis is on video*making* (production and exposure), *not* reviews of commercial videos. Personal video phenomenon is a young 'movement'; readership is encouraged to participate—get in on the act, join the fun." Estab. 1986. Circ. 90,000. Pays on publication. Publishes ms an average of 4-6 months after acceptance. Byline given. Buys all rights. Submit seasonal/holiday material 6 months in advance. Accepts simultaneous submissions. Reports in 3 months. Sample copy for 9 × 12 SAE with 9 first-class stamps. Free writer's guidelines.

Nonfiction: How-to (tools, tips, techniques for better videomaking); interview/profile (notable videomakers); product probe (review of latest and greatest or innovative); personal experience (lessons to benefit other videomakers); technical (state-of-the-art audio/video). Articles with comprehensive coverage of product line or aspect of videomaking preferred. Buys 70 mss/year. Query with or without published clips, or send complete ms. Length: open. Pays 10¢/word.

Reprints: Send information about when and where the article previously appeared. Payment negotiable.

Photos: Send photos and/or other artwork with submissions. Reviews contact sheets, transparencies and prints. Captions required. Payment for photos accepted with ms included as package compensation. Buys one-time rights.

Columns/Departments: Sound Track (audio information); Getting Started (beginner's column); Quick Focus (brief reviews of current works pertaining to video production); Camera Work (tools and tips for beginning videomakers); Video Entrepreneur (money-making opportunities); Edit Points (tools and techniques for successful video editions). Buys 40 mss/year. Pays 10¢/word.

Tips: "Comprehensiveness a must. Article on shooting tips covers *all* angles. Buyer's guide to special-effect generators cites *all* models available. Magazine strives for an 'all-or-none' approach. Most topics covered once (twice tops) per year, so we must be thorough. Manuscript/photo package submissions helpful. *Videomaker* wants videomaking to be fulfilling and fun."

‡VINTAGE RAILS, Pentrex, P.O. Box 379, Waukesha WI 53187. (414)542-4900. Editor: John Gruber. 80% freelance written. Quarterly magazine covering railroading, 1930s to 1970s. Estab. 1995. Circ. 30,000. Pays on publication. Publishes ms an average of 6 months after acceptance. Byline given. Buys first North American serial rights. Editorial lead time 4 months. Submit seasonal material 1 year in advance. Reports in 1 month. Sample copy and writer's guidelines free on request.

Nonfiction: Historical/nostalgic, personal experience, photo feature. Buys 25 mss/year. Query with published clips. Length: 1,500-4,500 words. Pays $150-400. Pays with contributor copies if author requests.

Photos: State availability of photos with submission. Reviews transparencies and prints. Offers $20-50/photo. Captions required. Buys one-time rights.

Columns/Departments: Readers Recall (remembrances of railroads) up to 500 words. Buys 20 mss/year. Send complete ms. Pays $50.

VOGUE KNITTING, Butterick Company, 161 Sixth Ave., New York NY 10013-1205. Fax: (212)620-2731. Editor: Gay Bryant. Managing Editors: Ruth Tobacco, Lillian Esposito. 100% freelance written. Quarterly magazine that covers knitting. "High fashion magazine with projects for knitters of all levels. In-depth features on techniques, knitting around the world, interviews, bios and other articles of interest to well-informed readers." Estab. 1982. Circ. 200,000. **Pays on acceptance**. Publishes ms an average of 4 months after acceptance. Buys all rights. Editorial lead time 6 months. Submit seasonal material 6 months in advance. Accepts simultaneous submissions. Writer's guidelines free on request.

Nonfiction: Essays, general interest, historical/nostalgic, how-to, interview/profile, personal experience, photo feature, technical, travel. Buys 25 mss/year. Query. Length: 600-1,200 words. Pays $250 minimum.

Photos: Send photos with submission. Reviews 3×5 transparencies. Negotiates payment individually. Captions, model releases and identification of subjects required. Buys all rights.

WOODSHOP NEWS, Soundings Publications Inc., 35 Pratt St., Essex CT 06426-1185. (860)767-8227. Fax: (860)767-1048. E-mail: riptides@ix.netcom.com. Website: http://www.woodweb.com. Editor: Ian C. Bowen. Senior Editor: Thomas Clark. 20% freelance written. Monthly tabloid "covering woodworking for professionals and hobbyists. Solid business news and features about woodworking companies. Feature stories about interesting amateur woodworkers. Some how-to articles." Estab. 1986. Circ. 100,000. Pays on publication. Publishes ms an average of 3 months after acceptance. Byline given. Offers 25% kill fee. Buys first North American serial rights. Submit seasonal/holiday material 4 months in advance. Reports in 3 weeks on queries; 1 month on mss. Free sample copy and writer's guidelines.

● *Woodshop News* needs writers in major cities in all regions except the Northeast. Also looking for more editorial opinion pieces.

Nonfiction: How-to (query first), interview/profile, new product, opinion, personal experience, photo feature. No general interest profiles of "folksy" woodworkers. Buys 50-75 mss/year. Query with published clips. Length: 100-1,800 words. Pays $50-400 for assigned articles; $40-250 for unsolicited articles; $40-100 for workshop tips. Pays expenses of writers on assignment.

Reprints: Accepts previously published submissions.

Photos: Send photos with submission. Reviews contact sheets and prints. Offers $20-35/photo. Captions and identification of subjects required. Buys one-time rights.

Columns/Departments: Pro Shop (business advice, marketing, employee relations, taxes etc. for the professional written by an established professional in the field). Length: 1,200-1,500 words. Buys 12 mss/year. Query. Pays $250-350.

Tips: "The best way to start is a profile of a business or hobbyist woodworker in your area. Find a unique angle about the person or business and stress this as the theme of your article. Avoid a broad, general-interest theme that would be more appropriate to a daily newspaper. Our readers are woodworkers who want more depth and more specifics than would a general readership. If you are profiling a business, we need standard business information such as gross annual earnings/sales, customer base, product line and prices, marketing strategy, etc. Black and white 35 mm photos are a must. We need more freelance writers from the Mid-Atlantic, Midwest and West Coast."

WOODWORK, A magazine for all woodworkers, Ross Periodicals, P.O. Box 1529, Ross CA 94957-1529. (415)382-0580. Fax: (415)382-0587. Editor: John McDonald. Publisher: Tom Toldrian. 90% freelance written. Bimonthly magazine covering woodworking. "We are aiming at a broad audience of woodworkers, from the home enthusiast/hobbyist to more advanced." Estab. 1986. Circ. 80,000. Pays on publication. Byline given. Buys first North American serial and second serial (reprint) rights. Sample copy for $3 and 9 × 12 SAE with 6 first-class stamps. Writer's guidelines for #10 SASE.
Nonfiction: How-to (simple or complex, making attractive furniture), interview/profile (of established woodworkers that make attractive furniture), photo feature (of interest to woodworkers), technical (tools, techniques). "Do not send a how-to unless you are a woodworker." Query first. Length: 1,500-2,000 words. Pays $150/published page.
Photos: Send photos with submission. Reviews 35mm slides. Offers no additional payment for photos accepted with ms. Captions and identification of subjects required. Buys one-time rights.
Columns/Departments: Feature articles 1,500-3,000 words. From non-woodworking freelancers, we use interview/profiles of established woodworkers. Bring out woodworker's philosophy about the craft, opinions about what is happening currently. Good photos of attractive furniture a must. Section on how-to desirable. Query with published clips. Pays $150/published page.
Tips: "If you are not a woodworker, the interview/profile is your best, really only chance. Good writing is essential as are good photos. The interview must be entertaining, but informative and pertinent to woodworkers' interests."

WORKBENCH, 700 W. 47th St., Suite 310, Kansas City MO 64112. (816)531-5730. Fax: (816)531-3873. Executive Editor: A. Robert Gould. 75% freelance written. Prefers to work with published/established writers; but works with a small number of new/unpublished writers each year. For woodworkers and home improvement do-it-yourselfers. Estab. 1957. Circ. 750,000. **Pays on acceptance.** Publishes ms an average of 1 year after acceptance. Byline given. Buys all rights. Reports in 3 months. Sample copy for 9 × 12 SAE with 6 first-class stamps. Free writer's guidelines.
Nonfiction: "We have continued emphasis on do-it-yourself woodworking, home improvement and home maintenance projects. We provide in-progress photos, technical drawings and how-to text for all projects. We are very strong in woodworking, cabinetmaking and classic furniture construction. Projects range from simple toys to reproductions of furniture now in museums. We would like to receive woodworking projects that can be duplicated by both beginning do-it-yourselfers and advanced woodworkers." Query. Pays $175/published page or more depending on quality of submission. Additional payment for good color photos. "If you can consistently provide good material, including photos, your rates will go up and you will get assignments."
Columns/Departments: Shop Tips bring $25 with a line drawing and/or b&w photo.
Tips: "Our magazine focuses on woodworking, covering all levels of ability, and home improvement projects from the do-it-yourselfer's viewpoint, emphasizing the most up-to-date materials and procedures. We would like to receive articles on home improvements and remodeling, and/or simple contemporary furniture. We place a heavy emphasis on projects that are both functional and classic in design. We can photograph projects worthy for publication, so feel free to send snapshots."

HOME AND GARDEN

The baby boomers' turn inward, or "cocooning," has caused an explosion of publications in this category. Gardening magazines in particular have blossomed, as more people are developing leisure interests at home. *American Homestyle* added *Gardening* to the title and *Organic Gardening* led to the semiannual *Organic Flower Gardening*. Some magazines here concentrate on gardens; others on the how-to of interior design. Still others focus on homes and gardens in specific regions of the country. Be sure to read the publication to determine its focus before submitting a manuscript or query.

THE ALMANAC FOR FARMERS & CITY FOLK, Greentree Publishing, Inc., 850 S. Rancho, #2319, Las Vegas NV 89106. (702)387-6777. Editor: Lucas McFadden. Managing Editor: Thomas Alexander. 40% freelance written. Annual almanac of farm, garden, animal, anecdotes, etc. "Down-home, folksy material pertaining to farming, gardening, animals, etc." Estab. 1983. Circ. 1,000,000. Pays on publication. Publishes ms 6 months after acceptance. Byline given. Buys first North American serial rights. Deadline: January 31. Reports in 2 weeks on queries; 1 month on mss. Sample copy for $2.95.

Nonfiction: Essays, general interest, how-to, humor. No fiction or controversial topics. Buys 30 mss/year. Send complete ms. Length: 350-1,400 words. Pays $45/page.
Poetry: Buys 1 poem/year. Pays $45.
Fillers: Anecdotes, facts, short humor. Buys 60/year. Length 125 words maximum. Pays $10-45.
Tips: "Typed submissions essential as we scan in manuscript before editing. Short, succinct material is preferred. Material should appeal to a wide range of people and should be on the 'folksy' side, preferably with a thread of humor woven in."

THE AMERICAN GARDENER, Publication of the American Horticultural Society, (formerly *American Horticulturalist*), 7931 E. Blvd. Dr., Alexandria VA 22308-1300. (703)768-5700. E-mail: garden@ahs.org. Website: http://eMall.com. Editor: Kathleen Fisher. 90% freelance written. Bimonthly magazine covering gardening. Estab. 1922. Circ. 25,000. Pays on publication. Publishes ms an average of 6 months after acceptance. Byline given. Buys first North American serial rights. Reports in 3 months on queries if SASE included. Sample copy for $3. Writer's for SASE.
• *The American Gardener* stresses environmentally-responsible gardening, conservation, use of natives.
Nonfiction: Book excerpts, historical, children and nature, plants and health, city gardening, humor, interview/profile, personal experience, technical (explain science of horticulture to lay audience). Buys 30-40 mss/year. Query with published clips. Length: 1,000-2,500 words. Pays $100-400. Pays with contributor copies or other premiums when other horticultural organizations contribute articles.
Photos: Send photos with query. Pays $50-75/photo. Captions required. Buys one-time rights.
Tips: "We are read by sophisticated gardeners, but also want to interest beginning gardeners. Subjects should be unusual plants, recent breakthroughs in breeding, experts in the field, translated for lay readers. We are particularly interested in creative landscape solutions."

‡**AMERICAN HOMESTYLE & GARDENING MAGAZINE**, Gruner & Jahr USA Publishing, 110 Fifth Ave., New York NY 10011. (212)463-1574. Fax: (212)463-1608. Editor-in-Chief: Karen Sales. Bimonthly magazine for individuals interested in improving their homes. "*American Homestyle & Gardening* is a guide to complete home design. It is edited for buyers of decorating, building and remodeling products. It focuses on an actionable approach to home design." Estab. 1986. Circ. 707,000. **Pays on acceptance.** Byline given. Offers 20% kill fee. Buys first North American serial rights with additional fee for electronic rights. Reports in 1 month on queries. Sample copy and writer's guidelines for #10 SASE.
• Ranked as one of the best markets for freelance writers in *Writer's Yearbook*'s annual "Top 100 Markets," January 1996.
Nonfiction: Writers with expertise in design, decorating, building or gardening. Buys 60 mss/year. Query. Length: 750-1,250 words. Pays $750-1,500. Pays expenses of writers on assignment.
Tips: "Knowledge of design, building and gardening, and ability to entertain."

ATLANTA HOMES AND LIFESTYLES, 5775-B Glenridge Dr., Suite 580, Atlanta GA 30328. (404)252-6670. Fax: (404)252-6673. Editor: Barbara S. Tapp. 65% freelance written. Bimonthly magazine on shelter design, lifestyle in the home. "*Atlanta Homes and Lifestyles* is designed for the action-oriented, well-educated reader who enjoys his/her shelter, its design and construction, its environment, and living and entertaining in it." Estab. 1983. Pays on publication. Byline given. Publishes ms an average of 6 months after acceptance. Pays 25% kill fee. Buys all rights. Reports in 3 months. Sample copy for $2.95.
Nonfiction: Historical, interview/profile, new products, well-designed homes, antiques (then and now), photo features, gardens, local art, remodeling, food, preservation, entertaining. "We do not want articles outside respective market area, not written for magazine format, or that are excessively controversial, investigative or that cannot be appropriately illustrated with attractive photography." Buys 35 mss/year. Query with published clips. Length: 500-750 words. Pays $350 for features. Sometimes pays expenses of writers on assignment "if agreed upon in advance of assignment."
Reprints: Send tearsheet or photocopy of article and information about where and when it previously appeared. Pays 50% of amount paid for original article.
Photos: Send photos with submission; most photography is assigned. Reviews transparencies. Offers $40-50/photo. Captions, model releases, and identification of subjects required. Buys one-time rights.
Columns/Departments: Short Takes (newsy items on home and garden topics); Quick Fix (simple remodeling ideas); Cheap Chic (stylish decorating that is easy on the wallet); Digging In (outdoor solutions from Atlanta's gardeners); Big Fix (more extensive remodeling projects); Real Estate News; Interior Elements (hot new furnishings on the market); Weekender (long or short weekend getaway subjects). Query with published clips. Buys 25-30 mss/year. Length: 350-500 words. Pays $50-200.

BACKHOME: Hands On & Down to Earth, Wordsworth Communications, Inc., P.O. Box 70, Hendersonville NC 28792. (704)696-3838. Fax: (704)696-0700. E-mail: backhome@mailbox.ioa.com. Website: http://www.magamall.com. Editor: Lorna K. Loveless. 80% freelance written. Quarterly magazine covering self-sufficiency in home, garden, shop and community. "*BackHome* encourages readers to take more control over their lives by doing more for themselves: productive organic gardening; building and repairing their homes; utilizing alternative energy systems; raising crops and livestock; building furniture; toys and games and other projects; creative cooking. *BackHome* promotes respect for family activities, community programs and the environment." Estab. 1990. Circ. 23,000. Pays on publication. Publishes ms 3-12 months after acceptance. Byline given. Offers $25 kill fee at publisher's discretion. Buys first North American serial rights. Editorial lead time 3 months. Submit seasonal material 3-6 months in advance. Reports in 6 weeks on queries; 2 months on mss. Sample copy for $5. Writer's guidelines with SASE.

• *The Millennium Whole Earth Catalog*, 1995, stated that *BackHome* contains "the most effective, practical, and appropriate tools and ideas for thinking and acting independently for the 21st century."

Nonfiction: How-to (gardening, construction, energy, home business), interview/profile, personal experience, technical, self-sufficiency. Buys 80 mss/year. Query. Length: 750-5,000 words. Pays $25 (approximately) for printed page.

Reprints: Send tearsheet or photocopy of article or typed ms with rights for sale noted and information about when and where the article previously appeared. Pays 100% of amount paid for an original article.

Photos: Send photos with submission: 35mm slides, color and b&w prints. Offers additional payment for photos published. Identification of subjects required. Buys one-time rights.

Columns/Departments: FeedBack (new products; book, tape and video reviews), 250 words. Buys 4 mss/year. Query. Pays $25-50.

Tips: "Very specific in relating personal experiences in the areas of gardening, energy, and homebuilding how-to. Third-person approaches to others' experiences are also acceptable but somewhat less desireable. Clear b&w or color photo prints help immensely when deciding upon what is accepted, especially those in which people are prominent."

BETTER HOMES AND GARDENS, 1716 Locust St., Des Moines IA 50309-3023. (515)284-3000. Editor-in-Chief: Jean LemMon. Editor (Building): Joan McCloskey. Editor (Foods): Nancy Byal. Editor (Garden/Outdoor Living): Mark Kane. Editor (Health & Education): Martha Miller. Editor (Money Management, Automotive, Electronics): Lamont Olson. Editor (Features & Travel): Martha Long. Editor (Interior Design): Sandy Soria. 10-15% freelance written. "*Better Homes and Gardens* provides home service information for people who have a serious interest in their homes." Estab. 1922. Circ. 7,605,000. **Pays on acceptance.** Buys all rights. "We read all freelance articles, but much prefer to see a letter of query rather than a finished manuscript."

Nonfiction: Travel, education, health, cars, money management, home entertainment. "We do not deal with political subjects or with areas not connected with the home, community, and family." Pays rates "based on estimate of length, quality and importance." No poetry.

• Most stories published by this magazine go through a lengthy process of development involving both editor and writer. Some editors will consider *only* query letters, not unsolicited manuscripts.

Tips: Direct queries to the department that best suits your story line.

CANADIAN GARDENING, Camar Communications, 130 Spy Court, Markham, Ontario L3R 0W5 Canada. (905)475-8440. Fax: (905)475-9560. Editor: Liz Primeau. Contact: Rebecca Fox, managing editor. 99% freelance written. Magazine published 7 times/year covering home gardening. "We cover garden design, growing, projects for the garden, products, regional information (pests, growing, etc.) for the Canadian gardener. Fundamental plants are the focus, but each issue contains at least one vegetable piece, usually with recipes." Estab. 1990. Circ. 140,000. **Pays on acceptance.** Publishes ms 18 months after acceptance. Byline given. Offers 25-50% kill fee. Buys first North American serial rights. Editorial lead time 3 months. Submit seasonal material 5 months in advance. Reports in 3 months. Sample copy and writer's guidelines free.

Nonfiction: Book excerpts, how-to (gardening, garden projects, pruning, pest control, etc.), personal experience and photo feature (as they relate to gardening). No US gardens or growing; no *public* gardens. Buys about 70 mss/year. Query with published clips. Length: 300-2,000 words. Pays $50-700. Sometimes pays expenses of writers on assignment.

Photos: State availability of photos with submission. Offers $50-250/photo. Identification of subjects required. Buys one-time rights.

Columns/Departments: Gardeners' Journal (garden facts, how-tos—homemade pest sprays, e.g.—and personal experience), 300-500 words; Techniques (gardening techniques), 500-800 words. Buys 50 mss/year. Query. Pays $50-200.

Tips: "We prefer to use untried (to us) writers on small items for Gardeners' Journal, the upfront section. Short outlines that are already well-focused receive the most attention."

COLONIAL HOMES, Hearst Magazines, 1790 Broadway, 14th Floor, New York NY 10019. Fax: (212)586-3455. Editor: Annette Stramesi. Contact: Roberta Dell'Aquilo, chief copy editor. 40% freelance written. Bimonthly magazine. "*Colonial Homes* is a shelter book that celebrates 17th, 18th and 19th century design, architecture, decorative arts and decorating." Estab. 1975. Circ. 600,000. Pays on publication. Byline given. Offers 20% kill fee. Buys all rights. Editorial lead time 3 months. Submit seasonal material 6 months in advance. Accepts simultaneous submissions. Reports in 2 weeks on queries; 1 month on mss. Sample copy for #10 SASE. Writer's guidelines free on request.

Nonfiction: Contact individual department editors. General interest, historical/nostalgic, new product, travel. Buys 2 mss/year. Query with pubished clips. Length: 500-1,500 words. Pays $500-1,000. Pays expenses of writers on assignment.

Photos: Send photos with submission. Negotiates payment individually. Identification of subjects required. Buys all rights.

Columns/Departments: Masterworks (craftsperson), 750 words; Genealogy (colonial-era) 750 words. Buys 4 mss/year. Query. Pays $500-800.

Tips: "As we accept few unsolicited story ideas, the best way to propose an idea is with an outline and snapshots."

COLORADO HOMES & LIFESTYLES, 7009 S. Potomac St., Englewood CO 80112-4029. (303)397-7600. Fax: (303)397-7619. Editor: Evalyn McGraw. Assistant Editor: Heather Prowty. Publisher: Pat Cooley. 50% freelance written. Bimonthly magazine covering Colorado homes and lifestyles for upper-middle-class and high income households as well as designers, decorators and architects. Circ. 30,000. **Pays on acceptance.** Publishes ms an average of 4 months after acceptance. Byline given. Buys all rights. Submit seasonal/holiday material 6 months in advance. Reports in 3 months.

• The editor reports that *Colorado Homes & Lifestyles* is doing many more lifestyle articles and needs more unusual and interesting stories. A recent addition has been profiles of Colorado artisans and craftspeople.

Nonfiction: Fine homes and furnishings, regional interior design trends, interesting personalities and lifestyles, gardening and plants—all with a Colorado slant. Special issues: Rustic Mountain Homes and Lifestyles (people, etc.) (January/February); Great Bathrooms (September/October); Great Kitchens (March/April). Buys 30 mss/year. Send complete ms. Length: 1,000-1,500 words. "For unique, well-researched feature stories, pay is $150-200. For regular departments, $125-140." Sometimes pays the expenses of writers on assignment.

Photos: Send photos with ms. Reviews 35mm, 4×5 and 2¼ color transparencies and b&w glossy prints. Identification of subjects required. Please include photographic credits.

Tips: "The more interesting and unique the subject the better. A frequent mistake made by writers is failure to provide material with a style and slant appropriate for the magazine, due to poor understanding of the focus of the magazine."

COTTAGE LIFE, Quarto Communications, 111 Queen St. E., Suite 408, Toronto, Ontario M5C 1S2 Canada. (416)360-6880. Fax: (416)360-6814. E-mail: cottage_life@magic.ca. Contact: Ann Vanderhoof, editor. Managing Editor: David Zimmer. 80% freelance written. Bimonthly magazine covering waterfront cottaging. "*Cottage Life* is written and designed for the people who own and spend time at cottages throughout Canada and bordering U.S. states." Estab. 1988. Circ. 70,000. **Pays on acceptance.** Publishes ms an average of 2 months after acceptance. Byline given. Buys first North American serial rights.

Nonfiction: Book excerpts, exposé, historical/nostalgic, how-to, humor, interview/profile, personal experience, photo feature, technical. Buys 90 mss/year. Query with published clips. Length: 150-3,500 words. Pays $100-2,200 for assigned articles. Pays $50-1,000 for unsolicited articles. Sometimes pays expenses of writers on assignment. Query first.

Columns/Departments: Cooking, Real Estate, Fishing, Nature, Watersports, Personal Experience and Issues. Length: 150-1200 words. Query with published clips. Pays $100-750.

COUNTRY HOME, Meredith Corp., 1716 Locust St., Des Moines IA 50309-3023. (515)284-5000. Fax: (515)284-3684. Editor-in-Chief: Molly Culbertson. Managing Editor: Beverly Hawkins. Bimonthly magazine "for people interested in the country way of life." Circ. 1,000,000. "Although the majority of articles are staff written, approximately two or three full-length features per issue are assigned to freelance writers. *Country Home* magazine is a lifestyle publication created for readers who share passions for American history, style, craftsmanship, tradition, and cuisine. These people, with a desire to find a simpler, more meaningful lifestyle, live their lives and design their living spaces in ways that reflect those passions." Reports in 4-6 weeks. Sample copy for $4.95 (includes postage); make check payable to Kathy Stevens.

Nonfiction: Architecture and Design, Families at Home, Travel, Food and Entertaining, Art and Antiques, Gardens and Outdoor Living, Personal Reflections. Query with writing samples and SASE. "We are not responsible for unsolicited manuscripts, and we do not encourage telephone queries." Length: features, 750-1,500 words; columns or departments, 500-750 words. Pays $500-1,500 for features, $300-500 for columns or departments. Pays on completion of assignment.

‡**COUNTRY LIVING**, The Hearst Corp., 224 W. 57th St., New York NY 10019. (212)649-3192. Features Editor: Marjorie Gage. Monthly magazine covering home design and interior decorating with an emphasis on 'country' style. "*Country Living* is a lifestyle magazine for today's families who appreciate the warmth and tradition of American home and family life. Each monthly issue embraces American country decorating and includes features on furnishings, cooking, antiques, home building, real estate and travel." Estab. 1978. Circ. 1,816,000.

Nonfiction: Most open to freelancers: antiques articles from authorities, personal essay. Buys 20-30 mss/year. Pay varies. Send complete ms. *Writer's Market* recommends sending a query before submitting.
Columns/Departments: Most open to freelancers: Kids in the Country, Readers Corner. Pay varies. Send complete ms. *Writer's Market* recommends sending a query before submitting.

DESIGN TIMES, Beautiful Interiors of the Northeast, Regis Publishing Co., Inc., 1 Design Center Place, Suite 615, Boston MA 02210. (617)443-0636. E-mail: dtimes@aol.com. Website: http://www.architect sonline.com. Managing Editor: Leeann Boyer. 75% freelance written. Bimonthly magazine covering high-end residential interior design in Northeast. "Show, don't tell. Readers want to look over the shoulders of professional interior designers. Avoid cliché. Love design." Estab. 1988. Circ. 20,000. Pays on publication. Publishes ms an average of 4 months after acceptance. Byline given. Offers 10% kill fee. Buys all rights. Editorial lead time 3 months. Submit seasonal material 6 months in advance. Accepts simultaneous submissions. Reports in 1 month. Sample copy for 10×13 SAE with 10 first-class stamps.
Nonfiction: Residential interiors (Northeast only). Buys 25 mss/year. Query with published clips. Length: 1,200-3,000 words. Pay varies. Sometimes pays the expenses of writers on assignment.
Photos: State availability of photos with submission. Reviews 4×5 transparencies, 9×10 prints. Negotiates payment individually. Caption, model releases, identification of subject required. Buys one-time rights.
Columns/Departments: Pays $100-150.
Tips: "A Northeast home owned by a well-known personality or designer would be a good feature query."

EARLY AMERICAN HOMES, (formerly *Early American Life*), Cowles Magazines, Inc., P.O. Box 8200, Harrisburg PA 17105-8200. Fax: (717)657-9552. Editor: Mimi Handler. 20% freelance written. Bimonthly magazine for "people who are interested in capturing the warmth and beauty of the 1600 to 1840 period and using it in their homes and lives today. They are interested in antiques, traditional crafts, travel, restoration and collecting." Estab. 1970. Circ. 150,000. Buys worldwide rights. Buys 40 mss/year. **Pays on acceptance.** Publishes ms an average of 1 year after acceptance. Reports in 3 months. Sample copy and writer's guidelines for 9×12 SAE with 4 first-class stamps. Query or submit complete ms with SASE.
● The editor of this publication is looking for more on architecture, gardens and antiques.
Nonfiction: "Social history (the story of the people, not epic heroes and battles), travel to historic sites, country inns, antiques and reproductions, refinishing and restoration, architecture and decorating. We try to entertain as we inform. While we're always on the lookout for good pieces on any of our subjects. Would like to see more on how real people did something great to their homes." Buys 40 mss/year. Query or submit complete ms. Length: 750-3,000 words. Pays $100-600. Pays expenses of writers on assignment.
Photos: Pays $10 for 5×7 (and up) b&w photos used with mss, minimum of $25 for color. Prefers 2¼×2¼ and up, but can work from 35mm.
Tips: "Our readers are eager for ideas on how to bring early America into their lives. Conceive a new approach to satisfy their related interests in arts, crafts, travel to historic sites, and especially in houses decorated in the early American style. Write to entertain and inform at the same time, be prepared to help us with sources for illustrations."

FINE GARDENING, Taunton Press, 63 S. Main St., P.O. Box 5506, Newtown CT 06470-5506. (203)426-8171. Fax: (203)426-3434. Editor: Suzanne LaRosa. Bimonthly magazine on gardening. "Focus is a high-value technical magazine on landscape and ornamental gardening. Articles written by avid gardeners—first person, hands-on-gardening experiences." Estab. 1988. Circ. 200,000. **Pays on acceptance.** Publishes ms an average of 6 months after acceptance. Byline given. Buys all rights. Editorial lead time 1 year. Submit seasonal material 1 year in advance. Free writer's guidelines.
Nonfiction: Book review, essays, how-to, opinion, personal experience, photo feature. Buys 60 mss/year. Query. Length: 1,000-3,000 words. Pays 300-1,000. Sometimes pays expenses of writers on assignment.
Photos: Send photos with submission. Reviews 35mm transparencies. Buys serial rights.
Columns/Department: Book, video and software reviews (on gardening); Last Word (essays/serious, humorous, fact or fiction). Query. Length: 250-1,000 words. Buys 30 mss/year. Pays $50-200.
Tips: "It's most important to have solid first-hand experience as a gardener. Tell us what you've done with your own landscape and plants."

FLOWER AND GARDEN MAGAZINE, 700 W. 47th St., Suite 310, Kansas City MO 64112. (816)531-5730. Fax: (816)531-3873. Editor: Kay Melchisedech Olson. 50% freelance written. Works with a small number of new/unpublished writers each year. Bimonthly picture magazine for home gardeners. Estab. 1957. Circ. 750,000. Buys first time nonexclusive reprint rights. Byline given. **Pays on acceptance.** Publishes ms an average of 1 year after acceptance. Reports in 2 months. Sample copy for $2.95 and 10×13 SAE. Writer's guidelines for #10 SASE.
● The editor tells us good quality photos accompanying articles are more important than ever.
Nonfiction: Interested in illustrated articles on how to do certain types of gardening and descriptive articles about individual plants. Flower arranging, landscape design, house plants and patio gardening are other aspects covered. "The approach we stress is practical (how-to-do-it, what-to-do-it-with). We emphasize plain talk, clarity and economy of words. An article should be tailored for a national audience." Buys 20-30 mss/

year. Query. Length: 500-1,500 words. Rates vary depending on quality and kind of material.
Reprints: Sometimes accepts previously published articles. Send typed ms with rights for sale noted, including information about when and where the article previously appeared.
Photos: Buys transparencies, 35mm and larger. Photos are paid for on publication.
Tips: "The prospective author needs good grounding in gardening practice and literature. Offer well-researched and well-written material appropriate to the experience level of our audience. Use botanical names as well as common. Photographs help sell the story. Describe special qualifications for writing the particular proposed subject."

‡**FOREMOST LIVING TRENDS**, 2001 Killebrew Dr., Suite 105, Bloomington MN 55425. (612)854-0155. Editor: Mary Lou Brooks. Quarterly magazine for residents of mobile homes. "*Foremost Living Trends* portrays mobile home living in a positive light and centers around enhancing the mobile home lifestyle." Pays within 2 months of acceptance. Byline given. Buys first North American serial rights. Sample copy for SAE with 4 first-class stamps. Writer's guidelines for #10 SASE.
Nonfiction: How-to, lifestyle articles on living in mobile homes. Buys 16 mss/year. Query with clips. Length: 1,400-1,800 words. Pays $325-500.
Columns/Departments: Ask the Experts, What's Cookin'?, Savvy Consumer. Length: 500-1,400 words. Buys 8 mss/year. Query with published clips. Pays $200-350.

‡**GARDEN DESIGN**, 4401 Connecticut Ave. NW, Suite 500, Washington DC 20008. (202)686-2752. Fax: (202)334-1260. E-mail: grdndsgn@aol.com. Executive Editor: Deborah Papier. Contact: Jenny Krause. 90% freelance written. Eager to work with new writers. Bimonthly magazine devoted to the fine art of garden design. Circ. 100,000. Pays 2 months after acceptance. Byline given. Offers 20-30% kill fee. Buys first North American rights. Submit seasonal/holiday material 6 months in advance. Reports in 2 months. Sample copy for $5. Writer's guidelines for #10 SASE.
Nonfiction: "We look for literate writing on a wide variety of garden-related topics—art, architecture, food, furniture, decorating, travel, shopping, personalities." Buys 100-120 mss/year. Query with published clips. Length: 800-2,000 words. Pays 50¢/word. Sometimes pays expenses of writer or photographer on assignment.
Photos: Submit scouting photos when proposing article on a specific garden. Offers $75-150/photo or day rate for assigned shoot. Buys one-time rights.
Tips: "Our greatest need is for extraordinary private gardens. Scouting locations is a valuable service freelancers can perform, by contacting designers and garden clubs in the area, visiting gardens and taking snapshots for our review. All departments of the magazine are open to freelancers. Writing should be as stylish as the gardens we feature."

THE HERB COMPANION, Interweave Press, 201 E. Fourth St., Loveland CO 80537-5655. (970)669-7672. Fax: (970)667-8317. Editor: Kathleen Halloran. Contact: Trish Faubion, managing editor. 80% freelance written. Bimonthly magazine about herbs: culture, history, culinary use, crafts and some medicinal. Audience includes a wide range of herb enthusiasts. Circ. 110,000. Pays on publication. Byline given. Buys first North American serial rights. Reports in 2 months. Query in writing. Length: 6-12 pages. Typical payment is $125/published page. Sample copy for $4. Writer's guidelines for #10 SASE.
Photos: Send photos.
Tips: "Articles must show depth and working knowledge of the subject, though tone should be informal and accessible."

HERB QUARTERLY, P.O. Box 689, San Anselmo CA 94960-0689. Fax: (415)455-9541. E-mail: herbquart @aol.com. Publisher: James Keough. 80% freelance written. Quarterly magazine for herb enthusiasts. Estab. 1979. Circ. 35,000. Pays on publication. Publishes ms an average of 6 months after acceptance. Buys first North American serial and second (reprint) rights. Query letters recommended. Reports in 2 months. Sample copy for $5 and 9×12 SASE. Writer's guidelines for #10 SASE.
Nonfiction: Gardening (landscaping, herb garden design, propagation, harvesting); medicinal and cosmetic use of herbs; crafts; cooking; historical (folklore, focused piece on particular period—*not* general survey); interview of a famous person involved with herbs or folksy herbalist; personal experience; photo essay ("cover quality" 8×10 b&w or color prints). "We are particularly interested in herb garden design, contemporary or historical." No fiction. Query. Length: 1,000-3,500 words. Pays $75-250.
Tips: "Our best submissions are narrowly focused on herbs with much practical information on cultivation and use for the experienced gardener."

‡**HOME FRONT**, The Publisher's Group, P.O. Box 510366, Salt Lake City UT 84151-0366. Fax: (801)322-1098. Editor: Vicki Andersen. Contact: Anne E. Zombro, publisher. 30% freelance written. Quarterly magazine. "*Home Front* features mid-income approaches to home decorating, do-it-yourself projects, gardening, remodeling and cooking." Estab. 1996. Circ. 15,000. Pays on publication. Publishes ms an average of 4 months after acceptance. Byline given. Buys first North American serial and second serial (reprint) rights. Editorial lead time 2 months. Submit seasonal material 4 months in advance. Accepts simultaneous submis-

sions. Reports in 1 month on queries; 2 months on mss. Sample copy for $2 and 9×12 SAE. Writer's guidelines for #10 SASE.
Nonfiction: How-to (decorating, crafts), new product, remodeling. Buys 8 mss/year. Query with published clips. Length: 1,000-1,300 words. Pays $125-800.
Reprints: Accepts previously published submissions.
Photos: Send photos with submission. Reviews 4×5 transparencies (preferred), any size prints. Negotiates payment individually. Captions, model releases, identification of subjects required. Buys one-time or all rights.
Columns/Departments: Gardening, Remodeling, Decorating, all with a do-it-yourself slant, all 500 words. Buys 6-10 mss/year. Query with published clips. Pays $50-125.

HOME MAGAZINE, The Magazine of Remodeling and Decorating, 1633 Broadway, 44th Floor, New York NY 10019. Fax: (212)489-4576. E-mail: homell@aol.com. Editor-in-Chief: Gale C. Steves. Contact: Linda Lentz, articles editor. 80% freelance written. Monthly magazine covering remodeling, decorating, architecture, entertaining, building and gardens. Estab. 1981. Circ. 1,000,000. **Pays on acceptance.** Publishes ms an average of 6 months after acceptance. Offers kill fee. Buys all rights, including electronic. Submit seasonal/holiday material 13 months in advance. Reports immediately. Free sample copy and writer's guidelines.
  • *Home* is online with America Online and is currently using about half of its monthly articles in this media extension of the magazine.
Nonfiction: Environmental, financial, personal experience, technical. Buys 100-120 mss/year. Query with published clips. Length: 1,500-2,000 words. Special issues: Kitchen & Bath (April); Decorating (May); Building (February).

HOMES & COTTAGES, The In-Home Show Ltd., 6557 Mississauga Rd., Suite D, Mississauga, Ontario L5N 1A6 Canada. (905)567-1440. Fax: (905)567-1442. E-mail: janhvc@pathcom.com. Editor: Janice Naisby. Contact: Lisa Gardiner, editorial assistant. 80% freelance written. Magazine published 8 times/year covering building and renovating; "technically comprehensible articles." Estab. 1989. Circ. 54,000 Pays on publication. Publishes mss average of 2 months after acceptance. Byline given. Offers $100 kill fee. Buys first North American serial rights. Editorial lead time 3 months. Submit seasonal material 3 months in advance. Sample copy for SAE. Writer's guidelines free on request.
Nonfiction: Humor (building and renovation related), new product, technical. Buys 32 mss/year. Query. Length: 1,500-2,000 words. Pays $600-750. Sometimes pays expenses of writers on assignment.
Photos: State availability of photos with submission. Reviews transparencies. Negotiates payment individually. Captions and identification of subjects required. Buys one-time rights.

HOUSE BEAUTIFUL, The Hearst Corp., 1700 Broadway, New York NY 10019-5905. (212)903-5100. Fax: (212)586-3439. Publisher: Jeffrey I. Burch. Monthly magazine covering home design and interior decorating. "*House Beautiful*'s editorial encompasses the world of decorating and design. Editorial includes architecture, remodeling, travel, food, entertaining and gardening features." Estab. 1896. Circ. 973,000. This magazine did not respond to our request for information. Query before submitting.

ISLAND HOME MAGAZINE, The Showcase of Island Architecture, Design & Lifestyle, Island Productions, Inc., 6490 South McCarran Blvd., Suite 30, Reno NV 89509. (702)826-2044. Fax: (702)826-1971. Contact: Editorial Department. 30% freelance written. Bimonthly magazine. "We have lavishly illustrated articles about architecture and interior design of island homes around the world from Hawaii and the South Pacific to Caribbean, Mediterranean, etc. Also travel features about international world-class destinations, island dining around the world, art and culture (both islands and other places), plus designer fashions, fine wines, expensive yachts, automobiles, planes, etc. Our readership is decidedly upscale, with about half of our readership in Hawaii, a large share on the West Coast of the U.S. mainland and the rest scattered across the U.S. and in several foreign countries." Estab. 1990. Circ. 30,000. Pays within 30 days after publication. Byline given. Kill fee negotiable. Buys one-time rights. Editorial lead time 4 months. Submit seasonal material 6 months in advance. Reports in 2 months. Sample copy for 10×13 SAE with 10 first-class stamps. Writer's guidelines for #10 SASE.
Nonfiction: Travel, island dining features, island home features (focus on architecture and design as well as location), island artist features. "Our annual golf issue is every March/April, in which we feature homes, restaurants and travel destinations with a golf or golf course focus. No articles that do not fall into our categories, which are Private Places, Interiors, Dining, Travel and Art/Collectibles. Nothing else will be considered as our categories do not change." Buys 3-4 mss/year from new freelancers; the rest are from existing pool of Hawaii freelance writers. Query with published clips. Length: 1,200-1,700 words. Pays 20¢/word.
Reprints: Accepts previously published submissions.
Photos: State availability of photos or send photos with submission—preferable. No additional payment for photos with articles. Reviews contact sheets, 2¼×2¼ and 4×5 transparencies and 8×10 prints. Captions required—after acceptance only. Buys one-time rights.

‡**KITCHEN GARDEN: The Art of Growing Fine Food**, The Taunton Press, 63 S. Main St., Newtown CT 06801. (203)426-8171. Fax: (203)426-3434. Editor: Suzanne Roman. 90% freelance written. Bimonthly magazine covering vegetable gardening. Estab. 1996. Circ. 100,000. **Pays on acceptance.** Publishes ms an average of 6 months after acceptance. Byline given. Kill fee negotiated. Buys all rights. Editorial lead time 1 year. Submit seasonal material 1 year in advance. Reports in 1 month. Writer's guidelines free.
Nonfiction: How-to (vegetable gardening). Buys 60 mss/year. Query with published clips. Length: 1,000-3,000 words. Pays $300-1,000. Sometimes pays expenses of writer on assignment.
Photos: Send photos with submission. Reviews contact sheets, negatives, transparencies, prints. Negotiates payment individually. Identification of subjects required. Buys all rights.
Columns/Departments: Reviews (books, software), 500 words. Buys 30 mss/year. Query with published clips. Pays $50-200.

LOG HOME LIVING, Home Buyer Publications Inc., 4200-T Lafayette Center Dr., Chantilly VA 22022. (703)222-9411. Fax: (703)222-3209. Editor: John Kupferer. Contact: Janice Brewster, executive editor. 50% freelance written. Bimonthly magazine for enthusiasts who are dreaming of, planning for, or actively building a log home. Estab. 1989. Circ. 132,000. **Pays on acceptance.** Publishes ms an average of 6 months after acceptance. Byline given. Buys first or second serial (reprint) rights. Editorial lead time 6 months. Submit seasonal/holiday material 6 months in advance. Reports in 6 weeks. Sample copy for $3.50. Writer's guidelines for #10 SASE.
Nonfiction: Book excerpts, how-to (build or maintain log home), interview/profile (log home owners), personal experience, photo feature (log homes), technical (design/decor topics), travel. "We do not want historical/nostalgic material." Buys 6 mss/year. Query. Length: 800-2,000 words. Pays $350-600. Pays expenses of writers on assignment.
Reprints: Send photocopy of article. Pays 50% of amount paid for an original article.
Photos: State availability of photos with submission. Reviews contact sheets, 4×5 transparencies and 4×6 prints. Negotiates payment individually. Buys one-time rights.

‡**LOG HOMES DESIGN IDEAS**, H+S Media, 1620 S. Lawe St., Suite 2, Appleton WI 54915. Editor-in-Chief: Bettyann Kowalski. Less than 20% freelance written. Bimonthly magazine covering log homes. "We are a full-color, slick publication devoted to log homes, their design, decoration and the delight log home owners have for their lifestyle. Our readers are couples 30-35 years of age who either own a log home or dream of owning a modern manufactured or handcrafted log home." Estab. 1994. Circ. 150,000. Pays on publication. Publishes ms an average of 6-12 months after acceptance. Byline given. Buys first rights. Editorial lead time 9 months. Submit seasonal material year in advance. Reports in 6 months. Sample copy not available. Writer's guidelines for #10 SASE.
Nonfiction: Essays, how-to, interview/profile, personal experience, photo feature, technical. Limited historical and nostalgic. Busy 2-6 mss/year. Send complete ms. Length: 500-1,200 words. Pays $100-500. Sometimes pays expenses of writers on assignment.
Photos: Send photos with submission. Reviews contact sheets, negatives, 2½×2½ and 4×5 transparencies—only color. Negotiates payment individually. Captions, model releases, identification of subjects required. Buys one-time rights.
Columns/Departments: "We will consider well-written columns on interior decor, how-to/technical, 'folksy' essays. Show us what you can do, it may become a regular feature." Length: 250-600 words. Buys 6 mss/year. Send complete ms. Pays $50-300.
Tips: "Concentrate on satisfied log home owners and their experiences while planning, building and decorating their homes. We're also looking for new columns with a laid-back, folksy bent that will appeal to log home owners who have discovered the good life. The right columns could become regular features."

‡**METROPOLITAN HOME**, Hachette Filipacchi Inc., 1633 Broadway, New York NY 10019. (212)767-5522. Fax: (212)767-5600. Articles Director: Michael Lassell. Monthly magazine covering "home design, home furnishings, fashion, food, wines and spirits, entertaining, electronics and travel with an editorial focus on the art of living well. It is edited for quality-conscious young adults and contains news and guidance toward achieving personal style." Estab. 1969. Circ. 632,000. **Pays on acceptance.** Byline given. Offers 25% kill fee. Buy first North American serial rights with additional fee for electronic rights. Reports in 2 months on queries.
  • Ranked as one of the best markets for freelance writers in *Writer's Yearbook*'s annual "Top 100 Markets," January 1996.
Nonfiction: Needs home-related lifestyle stories for sophisticated audience; full of accessible ideas; written from expert view. No how-to stories. Buys 8-12 mss/year. Query with published clips. Length: 1,000-2,000 words. Pays $1,000-2,000. Pays expenses of writers on assignment.
Columns/Departments: 800-1,500 words. Buys 10-20 mss/year. Query with published clips. Pays $750-1,800.
Tips: "We use only experienced writers or experts who know their subject—interior design and home style. We're on the cutting edge of home style."

MIDWEST LIVING, Meredith Corp., 1912 Grand Ave., Des Moines IA 50309-3379. (515)284-3062. Fax: (515)284-2832. Publisher: Matt Petersen. Bimonthly magazine covering Midwestern lifestyle. "*Midwest Living* is a regional service magazine that celebrates the interests, values and lifestyles of Midwestern families. It provides region-specific information on travel and events, food and dining, and home and garden." Estab. 1986. Circ. 841,000.
Nonfiction: Query with outline and SASE; explain why article would be suitable for *Midwest Living*.

NATIONAL GARDENING, National Gardening Association, 180 Flynn Ave., Burlington VT 05401. (802)863-1308. Fax: (802)863-5962. Editor: Michael MacCaskey. Managing Editor: Dan Hickey. 80% freelance written. Willing to work with new/unpublished writers. Bimonthly magazine covering all aspects of food gardening and ornamentals. "We publish not only how-to garden techniques, but also news that affects home gardeners, like breeding advancements and new variety releases. Detailed, experienced-based articles with carefully worked-out techniques for planting, growing, harvesting and using garden fruits and vegetables sought as well as profiles of expert gardeners in this country's many growing regions. Our material is for both experienced and beginning gardeners." Estab. 1979. Circ. 250,000. **Pays on acceptance.** Publishes ms an average of 9 months after acceptance. Byline given. Buys first serial and occasionally second (reprint) rights. Reports in 2 months. Sample copy for $3. Writer's guidelines for #10 SASE.
Nonfiction: How-to, humor, interview/profile, pest profiles, opinion, personal experience, recipes. Buys 50-60 mss/year. Query first. Length: 500-2,500 words. Pays 25¢/word. Sometimes pays expenses of writers on assignment with prior approval.
Photos: Dan Hickey, managing editor. Send photos with ms. Pays $20-40 for b&w photos; $50 for color slides. Captions, model releases and identification of subjects required.
Tips: "Take the time to study the style of the magazine—the focus of the features and the various departments. Keep in mind that you'll be addressing a national audience."

‡**NEW HOME LIFE**, 179 Wells Rd., Orange Park FL 32073. (904)264-6372. Fax: (904)269-9149. Editor: Lani Barna. 100% freelance written. Bimonthly magazine covering new home buyers, move up buyers, general lifestyle. Estab. 1990. Circ. 30,000. Pays on publication. Byline given. Buys one-time rights. Editorial lead time 6 months. Submit seasonal material 3 months in advance. Sample copy and writer's guidelines free.
Nonfiction: How-to, new product, personal experience, travel, lifestyle. No technical articles. Buys 20-30 mss/year. Query. Length: 1,000-2,000 words. Pays $50-150.
Photos: Send photos with submission. Reviews 2×2 transparencies. Offers no additional payment for photos accepted with ms. Captions, model releases, identification of subjects required. Buys one-time rights.
Columns/Departments: Upfront (local builder properties), 1000 words; Question & Answer (homebuying questions), 800 words; Tips From a Pro (any homeowning-related topic), 800 words. Buys 10 mss/year. Query.

ORGANIC GARDENING, Rodale Press, 33 E. Minor, Emmaus PA 18098. (610)967-5171. Managing Editor: Vicki Mattern. 30% freelance written. Magazine published 9 times/year. "*Organic Gardening* is for gardeners who enjoy gardening as an integral part of a healthy lifestyle. Editorial shows readers how to grow anything they choose without chemicals. Editorial details vegetable and fruit care, soil building, pest control, regional tips and outdoor power equipment use; and includes includes regular features on flowers, ornamental and lawn care, food preparation and building projects." Pays between acceptance and publication. Buys all rights. Reports in 2 months on queries; 1 month on mss.
Nonfiction: "Our title says it all. We seem to put more emphasis on the gardening aspect." Query with published clips and outline. Pays 50¢/word.

PLANT & GARDEN, Canada's Practical Gardening Magazine, Gardenvale Publishing Co. Ltd., 1 Pacifique, Ste. Anne de Bellevue, Quebec H9X 1C5 Canada. Phone/fax: (514)457-2744. E-mail: p&gmag@la nzen.net. Editor: Robert H. Paul. 95% freelance written. Magazine published 5 times/year covering gardening in Canada. "*Plant & Garden* is a *practical* gardening magazine focusing on how-to, step-by-step type articles on all aspects of garden and houseplant care. Readers are both novice and experienced Canadian gardeners." Estab. 1988. Circ. 36,000. Pays on publication. Publishes ms 4 months after acceptance. Byline given. Offers 50% kill fee. Buys first North American serial rights. Editorial lead time 4 months. Submit seasonal material 4 months in advance. Accepts simultaneous submissions. Reports in 2 months. Sample copy for $4 and 9×12 SAE. Writer's guidelines for SAE and IRC or, preferably, SAE with sufficient Canadian postage affixed.
Nonfiction: Historical/nostalgic, how-to, humor, interview/profile, new product, personal experience—garden-related topics only. Buys 60 mss/year. Query with published clips. Length: 600-1,800 words. Pays $75 minimum (600 words). Sometimes pays expenses of writers on assignment.
Photos: Send photos with submission. Reviews negatives and 4×5 transparencies. Offers no additional payment for photos accepted with ms. Captions required. Buys one-time rights. Illustrations are usually commissioned.

Columns/Departments: Profile (profiles of gardens and/or gardeners); Hydroponics (how-to for home gardener); Environment; Down to Earth (humor/essay on gardening); Herb Garden (herb profiles). Length: 600-800 words. Buys 16 mss/year. Query with published clips. Pays $75-150.

Tips: "Please be knowledgeable about gardening—not just a freelance writer. Be accurate and focus on plants/techniques that are appropriate to Canada. Be as down to earth as possible. We want good quality writing and interesting subject matter. Areas most open to freelancers are Down to Earth, Profile and Environment. We are especially looking for garden profiles from outside Ontario and Quebec. All submitted materials must be accompanied by a SAE with sufficient Canadian postage affixed to ensure return."

‡**RESIDENTIAL LIVING**, The Publisher's Group, P.O. Box 510366, Salt Lake City UT 84151-0366. Fax: (801)322-1098. Editor: Vicki Andersen. Contact: Anne E. Zombro, publisher. 30% freelance written. Quarterly magazine. "The spotlight is on upscale living. A gracious home environment comes to life through the advice of experts in the areas of entertaining, interior and exterior design, and landscaping." Estab. 1996. Circ. 50,000. Pays on publication. Publishes ms an average of 4 months after acceptance. Byline given. Buys first North American serial and second serial (reprint) rights. Editorial lead time 2 months. Submit seasonal material 4 months in advance. Accepts simultaneous submissions. Reports in 1 month on queries; 2 months on mss. Sample copy for $2 and 9×12 SAE. Writer's guidelines for #10 SASE.

Nonfiction: Interview/profile, new product, photo feature, interior design trends. No how-to. Buys 8 mss/year. Query with published clips. Length: 1,000-1,300 words. Pays $125-800.

Reprints: Accepts previously published submissions.

Photos: Send photos with submission. Reviews 4×5 transparencies (preferred), any size prints. Negotiates payment individually. Captions, model releases, identification of subjects required. Buys one-time or all rights.

Columns/Departments: Accents (selecting the right accents for the home), Design Trends (new decorating techniques), both 500 words. Buys 6-12 mss/year. Query with published clips. Pays $50-125.

‡**SAN DIEGO HOME/GARDEN LIFESTYLES**, Mckinnon Enterprises, Box 719001, San Diego CA 92171-9001. (714)233-4567. Fax: (619)233-1004. Editor: Wayne Carlson. Senior Editor: Phyllis Van Doren. 50% freelance written. Works with a small number of new/unpublished writers each year. Monthly magazine covering homes, gardens, food, intriguing people, business and real estate, art, culture, and local travel for residents of San Diego city and county. Estab. 1979. Circ. 45,000. **Pays on acceptance.** Publishes ms an average of 3 months after acceptance. Byline given. Buys first North American serial rights only. Submit seasonal material 3 months in advance. Reports in 3 months. Sample copy for $4.

Nonfiction: Residential architecture and interior design (San Diego-area homes only); remodeling (must be well-designed—little do-it-yourself); residential landscape design; furniture; other features oriented towards upscale readers interested in living the cultured good life in San Diego. Articles must have local angle. Buys up to 5 unsolicited mss/year. Query with published clips. Length: 700-2,000 words. Pays $50-350.

Tips: "No out-of-town, out-of-state subject material. Most freelance work is accepted from local writers. Gear stories to the unique quality of San Diego. We try to offer only information unique to San Diego—people, places, shops, resources, etc. We plan more food and entertaining-at-home articles and more articles on garden products. We also need more in-depth reports on major architecture, environmental, and social aspects of life in San Diego and the border area."

MARTHA STEWART LIVING, Time Inc. Ventures Magazine Co., 11 W. 42nd St., 25th Floor, New York NY 10036. (212)522-7800. Fax: (212)522-1499. Editor: Susan Wyland. Magazine published 10 times/year covering lifestyle and home. "*Martha Stewart Living* is a lifestyle magazine featuring information for people who are actively involved in making their homes more beautiful and comfortable, who enjoy entertaining and 'living well.' Each issue includes features on decorating, restoring, cooking, gardening, entertaining, homekeeping, traveling and working." Estab. 1990. Circ. 1,215,000. This magazine did not respond to our request for information. Query before submitting.

TEXAS GARDENER, The Magazine for Texas Gardeners, by Texas Gardeners, Suntex Communications, Inc., P.O. Box 9005, Waco TX 76714-9005. (817)772-1270. Editor: Chris S. Corby. Managing Editor: Ashley Blythe. 80% freelance written. Works with a small number of new/unpublished writers each year. Bimonthly magazine covering vegetable and fruit production, ornamentals and home landscape information for home gardeners in Texas. Estab. 1981. Circ. 30,000. Pays on publication. Publishes ms an average of 4 months after acceptance. Byline given. Buys first North American serial and all rights. Submit seasonal/holiday material 6 months in advance. Reports in 2 months. Sample copy for $2.75 and SAE with 5 first-class stamps. Writer's guidelines for #10 SASE.

Nonfiction: How-to, humor, interview/profile, photo feature. "We use feature articles that relate to Texas gardeners. We also like personality profiles on hobby gardeners and professional horticulturists who are doing something unique." Buys 50-100 mss/year. Query with clips of published work. Length: 800-2,400 words. Pays $50-200.

Photos: "We prefer superb color and b&w photos; 90% of photos used are color." Send photos. Pays negotiable rates for 2¼ or 35mm color transparencies and 8×10 b&w prints and contact sheets. Model release and identification of subjects required.

Tips: "First, be a Texan. Then come up with a good idea of interest to home gardeners in this state. Be specific. Stick to feature topics like 'How Alley Gardening Became a Texas Tradition.' Leave topics like 'How to Control Fire Blight' to the experts. High quality photos could make the difference. We would like to add several writers to our group of regular contributors and would make assignments on a regular basis. Fillers are easy to come up with in-house. We want good writers who can produce accurate and interesting copy. Frequent mistakes made by writers in completing an article assignment for us are that articles are not slanted toward Texas gardening, show inaccurate or too little gardening information or lack good writing style. We will be doing more 'people' features and articles on ornamentals."

TRADITIONAL HOME, Meredith Corp., 1716 Locust St., Des Moines IA 50309-3023. (515)284-2267. Fax: (515)284-2877. Publisher: Deborah Jones Barrow. Bimonthly magazine covering home design and interior decorating. "*Traditional Home* focuses on a classic, refined and gracious way of living. Interiors, architecture, renovation, gardening, collecting, cuisine, table settings, travel and new products are featured." Estab. 1978. Circ. 801,000. This magazine did not respond to our request for information. Query before submitting.

HUMOR

Publications listed here specialize in gaglines or prose humor, some for readers and others for performers or speakers. Other publications that use humor can be found in nearly every category in this book. Some have special needs for major humor pieces; some use humor as fillers; many others are interested in material that meets their ordinary fiction or nonfiction requirements but also has a humorous slant. The majority of humor articles must be submitted as complete manuscripts on speculation because editors usually can't know from a query whether or not the piece will be right for them.

‡FLATTER!, The Journal of Oblate Puffery, Around & Around Publications, P.O. Box 40923, San Francisco CA 94140-0923. E-mail: jainabee@aol.com. Editor: Jaina A. Davis. 100% freelance written. Semiannual magazine covering office supplies, avant garde. "Unique, quirky magazine with a humorous bent. No ads, pays well. How can it be?! Insane editor." Estab. 1992. Circ. 3,000. Pays on publication. Publishes ms an average of 6 months after acceptance. Byline given. Buys one-time rights. Editorial lead time 2 months. Reports in 1 month on queries. Sample copy for $4.

Nonfiction: Humor, new product (office supplies), photo feature, comics. Special issues: "Chickens & Barrymores." Must pertain to office supplies. Buys 5 mss/year. Query. Length: 12-100 words. Pays $20-80. Pays in copies for letters to editor, news clippings.

Photos: State availability of photos with submission. Reviews contact sheets. Negotiates payment individually.

Columns/Departments: Not Allowed (disgusting words); Last Disc on Earth (disgusting music). Buys 8 mss/year. Query. Pays in contributor copies-$10.

Fiction: Experimental, humorous, serialized novels. Must be office supply related. Buys 2 mss/year. Query. Length: 12-100 words. Pays $20-80.

Poetry: Avant-garde, free verse, haiku, light verse, traditional, unique. Wants poetry about office supplies. "Very specific theme." Buys 10 poems/year. Length: 1-44 lines maximum. Pays $10-20.

Fillers: Anecdotes, facts, gags to be illustrated by cartoonist, newsbreaks, short humor. Buys 20/year. Pays $10-30.

Tips: "This is a silly, irreverent, humor magazine. Personal notes with submissions a plus. Be very strange. I will pay you."

FUNNY TIMES, A Monthly Humor Review, Funny Times, Inc., P.O. Box 18530, Cleveland Heights OH 44118. (216)371-8600. Fax: (216)371-8696. E-mail: ft@funnytimes.com. Website: http://www.funnytimes.com. Editors: Raymond Lesser, Susan Wolpert. 10% freelance written. Monthly tabloid for humor. "*Funny Times* is a monthly review of America's funniest cartoonists and writers. We are the *Reader's Digest* of modern American humor with a progressive/peace-oriented/environmental/politically activist slant." Estab. 1985. Circ. 43,000. Pays on publication. Publishes ms an average of 3 months after acceptance. Byline given. Buys one-time or second serial (reprint) rights. Editorial lead time 2 months. Accepts simultaneous submissions. Reports in 3 months on mss. Sample copy for $3 or 9×12 SAE with 4 first-class stamps. Writer's guidelines for #10 SASE.

Nonfiction: Essays (funny), humor, interview/profile, opinion (humorous), personal experience (absolutely funny). "We only publish humor or interviews with funny people (comedians, comic actors, cartoonists, etc.). Everything we publish is very funny. If your piece isn't extremely funny then don't bother to send it. Don't send us anything that's not outrageously funny. Don't send anything that other people haven't already read and told you they laughed so hard they peed their pants." Buys 36 mss/year. Send complete ms. Length: 1,000 words. Pays $50 minimum for unsolicited articles.

Reprints: Accepts previously published submissions.

Fiction: Humorous. Buys 6 mss/year. Query with published clips. Length: 500 words. Pays $50-150.

Fillers: Short humor. Buys 6/year. Pays $20.

Tips: "Send us a small packet (1-3 items) of only your very funniest stuff. If this makes us laugh we'll be glad to ask for more. We particularly welcome previously published material that has been well-received elsewhere."

LAF!, Scher Maihem Publishing, Ltd., P.O. Box 313, Avilla IN 46710-0313. Fax: (219)897-2674. E-mail: scherlaf@igc.apc.org. Submissions Editor: Fran Glass. 100% freelance written. Bimonthly tabloid that features modern life cooperative humor. Estab. 1991. Circ. 1,000. Pays within 30 days of publication. Buys first or second serial (reprint) rights. Submit seasonal/holiday material 6 months in advance. Limit 3 simultaneous submissions. Reports in 3 months. Sample copy for 9×12 SASE with 3 first-class stamps. Writer's guidelines for #10 SASE.

  ● *Laf!* also sponsors the Loudest Laf! Laurel contest. See the Contests and Awards section for information.

Fiction: Humor, cartoons. "No religious, political, sexually or racially offensive humor. No poems." Buys 100 mss/year; 70 cartoons/year. Send complete ms. Length: 250-600 words. Pays $5-15. No series.

Tips: "If your humor writing appeals to people ages 45 and younger and spoofs modern living, send it. Our audience is broad, so the writing and subject must have wide appeal. We highly suggest writers take a look at the tabloid and guidelines first. Also indicate if submission is disposable."

LATEST JOKES, P.O. Box 23304, Brooklyn NY 11202-0066. (718)855-5057. Editor: Robert Makinson. Estab. 1974. 20% freelance written. Bimonthly newsletter of humor for TV and radio personalities, comedians and professional speakers. **Pays on acceptance.** Byline given. Buys all rights. Submit seasonal/holiday material 3 months in advance. Reports in 2 months. Sample copy for $3 and SASE.

Nonfiction: Humor (short jokes). "No stupid, obvious, non-funny vulgar humor. Jokes about human tragedy also unwelcome." Send up to 20 jokes with SASE. Pays $1-3/joke.

Tips: "No famous personality jokes. Clever statements are not enough. Be original and surprising. Our emphasis is on jokes for professional speakers."

MAD MAGAZINE, 1700 Broadway, New York NY 10019. (212)506-4850. Editors: Nick Meglin, John Ficarra. 100% freelance written. Monthly magazine. Estab. 1952. Circ. 1,000,000. **Pays on acceptance.** Publishes ms an average of 6 months after acceptance. Byline given. Buys all rights. Submit seasonal/holiday material 6 months in advance. Reports in 10 weeks. Writer's guidelines for #10 SASE.

Nonfiction: Satire, parody. "We're always on the lookout for new ways to spoof and to poke fun at hot trends. We're *not* interested in formats we're already doing or have done to death like 'what they say and what they really mean.' " Buys 400 mss/year. "Submit a premise with three or four examples of how you intend to carry it through, describing the action and visual content. Rough sketches not necessary. One-page gags: two to eight panel cartoon continuities at minimum very funny, maximum hilarious!" Pays minimum of $400/*MAD* page. "*Don't* send riddles, advice columns, TV or movie satires, book manuscripts, top ten lists, articles about Alfred E. Neuman, poetry, essays, short stories or other text pieces."

Tips: "Have fun! Remember to think visually! Surprise us! Freelancers can best break in with nontopical material. Include SASE with each submission. Originality is prized. We like outrageous, silly and/or satirical humor."

‡NATIONAL LAMPOON, National Lampoon Inc., 10850 Wilshire Blvd., Suite 1000, Los Angeles CA 90029. (310)474-5252. Editor-in-Chief: Duncan Murray. 50% freelance written. Works with small number of new/unpublished writers each year. Quarterly magazine of "offbeat, irreverent satire." Circ. 250,000. **Pays on acceptance.** Publishes ms an average of 4 months after acceptance. Byline given. Offers 20% kill fee. Buys first North American serial rights. Accepts simultaneous submissions. Reports in 3 months. Sample copy for $4.95 with SAE.

Nonfiction: Humor. Buys 60 mss/year. Query with published clips. Length: approximately 2,000 words maximum. Payment negotiable. Pays expenses of writers on assignment.

Columns/Departments: True Facts (weird true-life photos or clippings). Buys 240/year. Send complete ms. Length: 100 words maximum.

Tips: "We welcome freelancer's submissions." True Facts section is most open to freelancers.

‡NEW HUMOR MAGAZINE, Savaria Jr./Tschanz Publishers, P.O. Box 216, Lafayette Hill PA 19444. Fax: (215)487-2640. E-mail: newhumor@aol.com. Contact: Edward Savaria Jr., editor-in-chief. Managing Editor: Suzanne Tschanz. 90% freelance written. Quarterly magazine covering humor. "Tasteful, intelligent and funny. Looking for clean humor in a sense that funny stories, jokes, poems and cartoons do not have to sink to sexist, bathroom or ethnic subjects to be humorous." Estab. 1994. Circ. 9,500. **Pays on acceptance**. Publishes ms an average of 4 months after acceptance. Byline given. "If accepted, will pay published or not." Buys first North American serial, second serial (reprint) or simultaneous rights. Editorial lead time 4 months. Submit seasonal material 4 months in advance. Accepts simultaneous submissions. Reports in 1 month on queries. Sample copy for $4.50. Writer's guidelines for #10 SASE.

Nonfiction: Book excerpts, essays, humor, interview/profile, new product (humorous), travel. Buys 6 mss/year. Send complete ms. Length: 250-1,500 words. Pays $25-200.

Reprints: Accepts previously published submissions.

Columns/Departments: Open to Column Ideas, 250-750 words. Pays $25-100.

Fiction: Humorous. Buys 40 mss/year. Send complete ms. Length: 25-1,500 words. Pays $25-200.

Poetry: Avant-garde, free verse, haiku, light verse. Buys 30 poems/year. Submit maximum 10 poems. Length: 1-50 lines. Pays $7-30.

Fillers: Anecdotes, short humor. Buys 20/year. Length: 25-300 words. Pays $15-65.

Tips: "If you think it's funny—it might be. Test stories on friends, see if they laugh. Don't be afraid to send odd humor—something completely different."

INFLIGHT

Most major inflight magazines cater to business travelers and vacationers who will be reading, during the flight, about the airline's destinations and other items of general interest.

ABOARD MAGAZINE, 100 Almeria, Suite 220, Coral Gables FL 33134. Fax: (305)441-9739. Editor: Robert Casin. Contact: Estrella Bibas. 40% freelance written. Bimonthly bilingual inflight magazine designed to reach travelers to and from Latin America, carried on 11 major Latin-American airlines. Estab. 1976. Circ. 140,000. Pays on publication. Byline given. Buys one-time or simultaneous rights or makes work-for-hire assignments. Accepts simultaneous submissions. Reports in 1 month. "SASE please."

Nonfiction: General interest, new product, business, science, art, fashion, photo feature, technical, travel. "No controversial or political material." Buys 50 mss/year. Length: 1,200-1,500 words. Pays $100-150. Sometimes pays expenses of writers on assignment.

Reprints: Send photocopy of article. Pays 100% of amount paid for an original article.

Photos: Send photos with submission, 35mm slides or transparencies only. Reviews transparencies. Offers no additional payment for photos accepted with ms. Offers $20/photo minimum. Identification of subjects required. Buys one-time rights.

Fillers: Facts. Buys 6/year. Length: 800-1,200 words. Pays $100.

Tips: "Send article with photos. We need lots of travel material on Chile, Ecuador, Bolivia, El Salvador, Honduras, Guatemala, Dominican Republic, Uruguay, Nicaragua, Paraguay."

AMERICA WEST AIRLINES MAGAZINE, Skyword Marketing, Inc., 4636 E. Elwood St., Suite 5, Phoenix AZ 85040-1963. (602)997-7200. Editor: Michael Derr. 60% freelance written. Works with small number of new/unpublished writers each year. Monthly general interest inflight magazine covering destinations served by the airline. We look for unconventional, newsworthy, compelling subject matter." Estab. 1986. Pays on publication. Publishes ms an average of 4 months after acceptance. Byline given. Offers 15% kill fee. Buys first North American rights. Submit seasonal/holiday material 8 months in advance. Accepts simultaneous submissions, if so noted. Reports in 1 month on queries; 5 weeks on mss. Sample copy for $3. Writer's guidelines for 9×12 SAE with 3 first-class stamps.

   • This publication is not accepting unsolicited queries or manuscripts at this time.

Nonfiction: General interest, adventure, profile, photo feature, science, sports, business, entrepreneurs, nature, arts, travel, trends. Also considers essays and humor. No puzzles, reviews or highly controversial features. Buys 130-140 mss/year. Length: 300-2,200. Pays $150-900. Pays some expenses.

Photos: State availability of original photography. Offers $50-250/photo. Captions, model releases and identification of subjects required. Buys one-time rights.

AMERICAN WAY, P.O. Box 619640, Dallas/Fort Worth Airport TX 75261-9640. (817)967-1804. Fax: (817)967-1571. Editor-in-Chief: John H. Ostdick. Managing Editor: Elaine Srnka. 98% freelance written. Prefers to work with published/established writers. Biweekly inflight magazine for passengers flying with American Airlines. Estab. 1966. **Pays on acceptance.** Publishes ms an average of 4 months after acceptance. Buys first serial rights. Reports in 5 months.

   • *American Way* is only accepting fiction queries now.

Fiction: Chuck Thompson, associate editor. Length: 2,500 words maximum. Payment varies.

‡FANTASTIC FLYER MAGAZINE, Two Roads Publishing for Delta Air Line, 3060 Peachtree St. NW, Suite 500, Atlanta GA 30305. (404)364-8684. Fax: (404)262-0300. Editor: Leah M. Hughes. 50% freelance written. Quarterly magazine covering travel for children. "Children want to read about children. We educate and entertain interactively." Estab. 1990. Circ. 1,200,000. **Pays on acceptance**. Publishes ms an average of 2 months after acceptance. Byline sometimes given. Offers $100 kill fee. Buys all rights. Editorial lead time varies. Submit seasonal material 9 months in advance. Reports in 3 months on queries. Sample copy for 8½×11 SAE with 3 first-class stamps. Writer's guidelines for #10 SASE.

Nonfiction: Historical/nostalgic, how-to, humor, interview/profile, photo feature, travel, educational. Buys 6 mss/year. Query. Length: 200-700 words. Pays $300-450 for assigned articles. Pay in contributor copies for activities.

Photos: Send photos with submission. Negotiates payment individually. Captions, model releases, identification of subjects required. Buys all rights.

Columns/Departments: Geography, Games. Buys 12 mss/year. Query. Pays $250-400.

Fiction: Adventure, historical, humorous, mainstream, slice-of-life vignettes. Buys 4 mss/year. Query. Length: 300-700 words. Pays $200-400.

Poetry: Traditional (children like form). Buys 1 poem/year. Submit maximum 4 poems. Length: 10-30 lines. Pay negotiated.

Tips: "Contact us with great idea; write for an 8½ year old."

GOLDEN FALCON, Fortune Promoseven, P.O. Box 5989, Manama, Bahrain. (973)225148 ext. 535. Fax: (973)224375. E-mail: fpromo7@batelco.com.bb. Managing Editor: Kamilia Ahmed. Contact: Roberta Collier-Wright. 60% freelance written. Monthly magazine covering travel, general interest for Gulf Air. Estab. 1988 (relaunched January 1993). Circ. 50,000. Pays on publication. Publishes ms an average of 4 months after acceptance. Byline given. Offers 50% kill fee. Buys first, one-time, or Arabic language rights. Editorial lead time 4 months. Submit seasonal material 5 months in advance. Reports in 1 month. Sample copy for 8½×12 SAE with 2 IRCs. Writer's guidelines free on request.

Nonfiction: General interest, historical/nostalgic, interview/profile, photo feature, travel. "No humor, politics, sex or religion. Humor translates poorly, the other three are unusable. Special issues: We are interested in seeing articles on Gulf states and in particular on the four owner states of Gulf Air to be featured during months of respective national days." Qatar (September); Oman (November); United Arab Emirates and Bahrain (December). Buys 50 mss/year. Query with published clips. Length: 800-1,300 words. Pays $250-500. Sometimes pays the expenses of writers on assignment.

Reprints: Send typed ms with rights for sale noted and information about when and where the article previously appeared. Pays 50% of amount paid for an original article.

Photos: State availability of photos with submission. Reviews contact sheets, transparencies and prints (5×7 minimum). Offers $50-200/photo. Captions required. Buys one-time rights.

Columns/Departments: Technology (popular science, new gadgets), 300-500 words and photos; Business (no bad news—upbeat and optimistic), 300-500 words and photos; The Arts/Music/Show Biz (personalities, history, mini-articles), 300-500 words and photos. Buys 48 mss/year. Query with published clips. Pays $110-150.

Tips: "Read contributor notes carefully. Remember where we are published. National and religious sensibilities must be observed. The articles will be read by non-Americans, so avoid Americanisms and slang. Write internationally, appeal individually. Stories which are complete with captioned photos and computer disk go to the head of the queue. Send for destination list and produce stories from places where travel companies do *not* send writers for 'familiarization trips.' Short columns, easily researched, complete with one picture, can be produced quickly. We have a prodigious appetite for them and they can be assembled from assorted manufacturers' and companies' press releases. Motoring, Business, Fashion, etc., columns must refrain from mention of a single company. Prefer three or more."

HEMISPHERES, Pace Communications for United Airlines, 1301 Carolina St., Greensboro NC 27401. (910)378-6065. Editor: Kate Greer. 95% freelance written. Monthly magazine for inflight passengers covering travel and business—a global perspective with information for the professional who travels frequently. Estab. 1992. Circ. 500,000. **Pays on acceptance**. Publishes ms 1 year after acceptance. Byline given. Offers 20% kill fee. Buys first, worldwide rights. Editorial lead time 8 months. Submit seasonal material 8 months in advance. Reports in 10 weeks on queries; 4 months on mss. Sample copy for $5. Writer's guidelines for #10 SASE.

 • Ranked as one of the best markets for freelance writers in *Writer's Yearbook*'s annual "Top 100 Markets," January 1996.

Nonfiction: Book excerpts, general interest, humor, personal experience. No "What I did (or am going to do) on a trip to . . ." Query with published clips. Length: 500-3,000 words. Negotiates payment individually.

Photo: State availability of photos with submission. Reviews transparencies "only when we request them." Negotiates payment individually. Captions, model releases and identification of subjects required. Buys one-time rights.

Columns/Departments: Making a Difference (Q&A interview with world leaders, movers and shakers); On Location (1-sentence "25 Fun Facts" about a city, state, country or destination); Executive Secrets (things that top executives know—e.g., business strategies); Case Study (business strategies of international companies or organizations); Weekend Breakaway (physically active getaway—hiking, windsurfing, etc.—

just outside a major city); Roving Gourmet (insider's guide to interesting eating in major city, resort area, or region; Collecting (photo with lengthy caption or occasional 800-word story on collections and collecting with emphasis on travel); Eye on Sports (global look at anything of interest in sports); Vintage Traveler (options for mature, experienced travelers); Savvy Shopper (insider's tour of best places in the world to shop); Science and Technology alternates with Computers (substantive, insightful story); Aviation Journal (for those fascinated with aviation); Of Grape And Grain (wine and spirits with emphasis on education); Show Business (films, music and entertainment); Musings (humor or just curious musings); Quick Quiz (tests to amuse and educate); Travel News (brief, practical, invaluable, trend-oriented tips). Length: 800-1,400 words. Query with published clips.

Fiction: Adventure, humorous, mainstream, slice-of-life vignettes. Buys 4 mss/year. Query. Length: 500-2,000 words. Negotiates payment individually.

Tips: "We increasingly require writers of 'destination' pieces or departments to 'live whereof they write.' Increasingly want to hear from U.S., U.K. or other English speaking/writing journalists (business & travel) who reside outside the U.S. in Europe, South America, Central America and the Pacific Rim—all areas that United flies."

LATITUDES, (formerly *Latitudes South Magazine*), Caribbean Travel & Life, Inc., 8403 Colesville Rd., Suite 830, Silver Spring MD 20910. (301)588-2300. E-mail: affcarib@aol.com. Editor: Mike Harms. 50% freelance written. Quarterly magazine covering travel in Florida, the Caribbean, Northeast US and Canada. Estab. 1991. Circ. 80,000. Pays on publication. Publishes ms 6-12 months after acceptance. Byline given. Buys first North American serial rights. Submit seasonal material 9 months in advance. Accepts simultaneous submissions. Reports in 1 month on queries; 2 months on mss. Sample copy for 9×12 SAE with 5 first-class stamps. Writer's guidelines for #10 SASE.

Nonfiction: Travel. Query with published clips. Length: 2,000-3,000. Pays $250 minimum. Sometimes pays expenses of writers on assignment.

Reprints: Accepts previously published submissions.

Photos: State availability of photos with submission. Reviews slides. Offers $75-250/photo. Buys one-time rights.

Columns/Departments: Tropical Pantry (food/dining in the Caribbean and Florida, i.e., "St. Thomas Dining"); Island Buys (i.e., "Palm Beach Shopping"); all 1,000-1,500 words; Taking Off (short destination pieces focusing on attractions/events), 500 words. Buys 1-2 mss/year. Query. Pays $150.

Fillers: Brief descriptions of new or interesting attractions and festivals in Florida, the Caribbean, Northeast US and Canada. Buys 10-12/year. Length 300-800 words. Pays $75 minimum.

Tips: "We've expanded our coverage to include those destinations served by American Eagle's New York City (JFK) hub. Whereas we used to cover the Caribbean and Florida only, we now additionally cover the Northeastern U.S. and Canada."

MIDWEST EXPRESS MAGAZINE, Paradigm Communications Group, 2701 First Ave., Suite 250, Seattle WA 98121. Editor: Eric Lucas. 90% freelance written. Bimonthly magazine for Midwest Express Airlines. "Positive depiction of the changing economy and culture of the US, plus travel and leisure features." Estab. 1993. Circ. 32,000. Pays on publication. Byline given. Buys first North American serial rights. Editorial lead time 9 months. Reports in 6 weeks on queries. Do not phone or fax. Sample copy for 9×12 SASE. Writer's guidelines free on request.

    ● *Midwest Express* continues to look for *sophisticated* travel and golf writing.

Nonfiction: Business, travel, sports and leisure. No humor or how-to. "Need good ideas for golf articles in spring." Buys 20-25 mss/year. Query with published clips and résumé. Length: 250-3,000 words. Pays $100 minimum. Sometimes pays expenses of writers on assignment.

Columns/Department: Contact: Heidi Schuessler, associate editor. Preview (arts and events), 200-400 words; Portfolio (business-queries to Eric Lucas), 200-500 words. Buys 12-15 mss/year. Query with published clips. Pays $100-150.

Tips: "Article ideas *must* encompass areas within the airline's route system. We buy quality writing from reliable writers. Editorial philosophy emphasizes innovation and positive outlook. Do not send manuscripts unless you have no clips."

USAIR MAGAZINE, NYT Custom Publishing, 122 E. 42nd St., New York NY 10168. (212)499-3500. Editor: Catherine Sabino. Contact: Justin D. McCarthy, assistant editor. 95% freelance written. Monthly magazine covering travel/lifestyle. Estab. 1979. Circ. 450,000. **Pays on acceptance**. Publishes ms an average of 6 months after acceptance. Byline given. Offer 25% kill fee. Editorial lead time 3 months. No simultaneous submissions. Reports in 3 weeks on queries. Sample copy for $5. Writer's guidelines for #10 SASE.

Nonfiction: General interest, interview/profile, travel, lifestyle, essays. Buys 120-150 mss/year. Query with published clips. Length: 850-2,200. Pays approximately $1/word. Sometimes pays expenses of writers on assignment.

Photos: State availability of photos with submission. Reviews contact sheets, negatives, transparencies. Negotiates payment individually. Model releases, identification of subjects required. Buys one-time rights.

Columns/Departments: Buys 80-100 mss/year. Query with published clips. Pays approximately $1/word. **Tips:** "Study the magazine—offer a clear, intelligent writing style. Queries for story ideas should be short and well-thought out. Any correspondence should include SASE."

JUVENILE

Just as children change and grow, so do juvenile magazines. Children's magazine editors stress that writers must read recent issues. A wide variety of issues are addressed in the numerous magazines for the baby boomlet. Respecting nature, developing girls' self-esteem and establishing good healthy habits all find an editorial niche. This section lists publications for children up to age 12. *Babybug* is for infants as young as 6 months. Magazines for young people 13-19 appear in the Teen and Young Adult category. Many of the following publications are produced by religious groups and, where possible, the specific denomination is given. A directory for juvenile markets, *Children's Writer's and Illustrator's Market*, is available from Writer's Digest Books.

‡**AMERICAN GIRL**, Pleasant Company Publications, 8400 Fairway Place, Middleton WI 53562. Editor: Judith Woodburn. Managing Editor: Julie Finlay. Contact: Magazine Department Assistant. 5% freelance written. Bimonthly magazine covering hobbies, crafts, profiles and history of interest to girls ages 8-12. "*American Girl* is a bimonthly 4-color magazine for girls. Our mission is to celebrate girls yesterday and today." Estab. 1992. Circ. 600,000. **Pays on acceptance.** Byline given for larger features, not departments. Offers 50% kill fee. Buys all rights, occasionally first North American serial rights. Editorial lead time 6 months. Submit seasonal material 6 months in advance. Accepts simultaneous submissions. Reports in 3 months on queries. Sample copy for 9 × 12 SAE with $1.93 postage. Writer's guidelines for #10 SASE.
Nonfiction: General interest, historical/nostalgic, how-to. No historical profiles about obvious female heroines—Annie Oakley, Amelia Earhart; no romance or dating. Buys 1 ms/year. Query with published clips. Length: 100-800 words, depending on whether its a feature or for a specific department. Pay varies. Pays expenses of writers on assignment.
Photos: State availability of photos with submission. "We prefer to shoot." Buys all rights.
Fiction: Adventure, condensed novels, ethnic, historical, humorous, slice-of-life vignettes. No romance, science fiction, fantasy. Buys 1 ms/year. Query with published clips. Length: 2,300 words maximum. Pay varies.

‡**BABYBUG**, Carus Corporation, P.O. Box 300, Peru IL 61354. (815)224-6656. Editor-in-Chief: Marianne Carus. Contact: Paula Morrow, editor. 50% freelance written. Board-book magazine published every 6 weeks. "*Babybug* is 'the listening and looking magazine for infants and toddlers,' intended to be read aloud by a loving adult to foster a love of books and reading in young children ages 6 months-2 years." Estab. 1994. Circ. 35,000. Pays on publication. Publishes ms an average of 18 months after acceptance. Byline given. Buys first, second serial (reprint) or all rights. Editorial lead time 8-10 months. Submit seasonal material 1 year in advance. Accepts simultaneous submissions. Sample copy for $5. Writer's guidelines for #10 SASE.
Nonfiction: General interest and "World Around You" for infants and toddlers. Buys 5-10 mss/year. Send complete ms. Length: 1-10 words. Pays $25.
Fiction: Adventure, humorous and anything for infants and toddlers. Buys 5-10 mss/year. Send complete ms. Pays $25.
Poetry: Buys 8-10 poems/year. Submit maximum 5 poems. Length: 2-3 lines. Pays $25.
Tips: "Imagine having to read your story or poem—out loud—50 times or more! That's what parents will have to do. Babies and toddlers demand, 'Read it again!' Your material must hold up under repetition."

BOYS' LIFE, Boy Scouts of America, P.O. Box 152079, Irving TX 75015-2079. Managing Editor: J.D. Owen. 75% freelance written. Prefers to work with published/established writers; works with small number of new/unpublished writers each year. Monthly magazine covering activities of interest to all boys ages 8-18. Most readers are Scouts or Cub Scouts. Estab. 1911. Circ. 1,300,000. **Pays on acceptance.** Publishes ms an average of 1 year after acceptance. Buys one-time rights. Reports in 2 months. Sample copy for $2.50 and 9 × 12 SAE. Writer's guidelines for #10 SASE.
● Ranked as one of the best markets for freelance writers in *Writer's Yearbook's* annual "Top 100 Markets," January 1996.
Nonfiction: Major articles run 750-1,500 words; preferred length is about 1,000 words including sidebars and boxes. Pays $500 minimum for major article text. Uses strong photo features with about 500 words of text. Separate payment or assignment for photos. "Much better rates if you really know how to write for our market." Buys 60 major articles/year. Also needs how-to features and hobby and crafts ideas. Query in

writing with SASE. No phone queries. Pays expenses of writers on assignment. Also buys freelance comics pages and scripts.

Columns: "Food, Health, Pets, Bicycling, Sports, Electronics, Space and Aviation, Science, Entertainment, Music, History, Cars and Magic are some of the columns for which we use 400-600 words of text. This is a good place to show us what you can do." Query first in writing. Pays $150-350. Buys 75-80 columns/year.

Fiction: Short stories 1,000-1,400 words; rarely longer. Send complete ms with SASE. Pays $500 minimum. Buys 12-15 short stories/year.

Tips: "We strongly recommend reading at least 12 issues of the magazine before you submit queries. We are a good market for any writer willing to do the necessary homework."

‡**BOYS QUEST**, Bluffton News Publishing, 103 N. Main, P.O. Box 227, Bluffton OH 45817. (419)358-4610. Editor: Marilyn Edwards. 100% freelance written. Bimonthly magazine covering boys ages 6-12, inspiring boys to read, with a mission to maintain traditional family values, and emphasize wholesome, innocent childhood interests. Estab. 1995. Circ. 3,000. Pays on publication. Byline given. Buys first North American serial rights. Editorial lead time 9 months. Submit seasonal material 9 months in advance. Accepts simultaneous submissions. Reports in 1 month on queries; 2 months on mss. Sample copy for $3. Writer's guidelines for #10 SASE.

Nonfiction: General interest, historical/nostalgic, how-to (building), humor, interview/profile, personal experience. Send complete ms. Length: 300-700 words with photos. Pays 5¢/word.

Photos: State availability of or send photos with submission. Offers $10/photo. Model releases required. Buys one-time rights.

Columns/Departments: Send complete ms. Pays 5¢/word.

Fiction: Adventure, historical, humorous. Send complete ms. Length: 300-700 words. Pays 5¢/word.

Poetry: Traditional. Buys 25-30 poems/year. Length: 10-30 lines. Pays $10-15.

CALLIOPE: The World History Magazine for Young People, Cobblestone Publishing, Inc., 7 School St., Peterborough NH 03458-1454. (603)924-7209. Fax: (603)924-7380. Editors: Rosalie and Charles Baker. 50% freelance written. Prefers to work with published/established writers. Magazine published 5 times/year covering world history through 1800 AD for 8- to 14-year-olds. Articles must relate to the issue's theme. Pays on publication. Byline given. Buys all rights. Accepts simultaneous submissions. Previously published submissions rarely accepted. Sample copy for $4.50 and 7½×10½ SASE with 4 first-class stamps. Writer's guidelines for SASE.

Nonfiction: Essays, general interest, historical/nostalgic, how-to (activities), recipes, humor, interview/profile, personal experience, photo feature, technical, travel. Articles must relate to the theme. No religious, pornographic, biased or sophisticated submissions. Buys approximately 30-40 mss/year. Query with published clips. Feature articles 700-800 words. Pays 20-25¢/printed word. Supplemental nonfiction 300-600 words. Pays 20-25¢/printed word.

Photos: State availability of photos with submission. Reviews contact sheets, color slides and b&w prints. Buys one-time rights. Pays $15-100 for b&w (color cover negotiated).
  • Ranked as one of the best markets for freelance writers in *Writer's Yearbook*'s annual "Top 100 Markets," January 1996.

Fiction: All fiction must be theme-related. Buys 10 mss/year. Query with published clips. Length: up to 800 words. Pays 20-25¢/word.
  • Ranked as one of the best markets for fiction writers in *Writer's Digest*'s annual "Fiction 50," June 1996.

Poetry: Light verse, traditional. No religious or pornographic poetry or poetry not related to the theme. Submit maximum 1 poem. Pays on individual basis. Poetry, up to 100 lines.

Columns/Departments: Puzzles and Games (no word finds); crossword and other word puzzles using the vocabulary of the issue's themes; mazes and picture puzzles that relate to the theme. Pays on an individual basis.

Tips: "Writers must have an appreciation and understanding of world history. Writers must not condescend to our readers."

CHICKADEE MAGAZINE, For Young Children from *OWL*, Owl Communications, 179 John St., Suite 500, Toronto, Ontario M5T 3G5 Canada. (416)971-5275. Managing Editor: Catherine Jane Wren. 25% freelance written. Magazine published 10 times/year (except July and August) for 3 to 8 year-olds. "We aim to interest young children in the world around them in an entertaining and lively way." Estab. 1979. Circ. 110,000 Canada and US. Pays on publication. Byline given. Buys all rights. Reports in 2 months. Sample copy for $4 and SAE ($2 money order or IRCs). Writer's guidelines for SAE.

Nonfiction: How-to (easy and unusual arts and crafts); personal experience (real children in real situations). No articles for older children; no religious or moralistic features.

Photos: Send photos with ms. Reviews 35mm transparencies. Identification of subjects required.

Fiction: Adventure (relating to the 3-8-year-old), humor. No talking animal stories or religious articles. Send complete ms with $1 money order for handling and return postage. Pays $210 (US).

Tips: "A frequent mistake made by writers is trying to teach too much—not enough entertainment and fun."

CHILD LIFE, Children's Better Health Institute, P.O. Box 567, Indianapolis IN 46206-0567. (317)636-8881. Fax: (317)684-8094. Editor: Lise Hoffman. 40% freelance written. Magazine (published 8 times/year) covering "general topics of interest to children—emphasis on health preferred." Pays on publication. Byline given. Buys all rights. Submit seasonal/holiday material 8 months in advance. Reports in 3 months. Sample copy for $1.25. Writer's guidelines for #10 SASE.

• *Child Life* has recently changed its editorial focus, and features nostalgia items from its past and nonfiction profiles and articles, mostly health-related in nature. It no longer buys fiction or poetry.

Nonfiction: Profiles of child and adult athletes or those with active hobbies, accompanied by professional quality slides suitable for the cover, how-to (simple crafts), anything children might like—health topics preferred. Buys 20 mss/year. Send complete ms. Length: 400-800. Pays up to 12¢/word.

Photos: Send photos only with accompanying editorial material. Reviews transparencies. Offers $20-30 for inside color photo. Please, no snapshots; professional-quality slides or photos only. Captions, model releases and identification of subjects required. Buys one-time rights.

Columns/Departments: "Pencil Pages" is a regular column especially hospitable to freelancers. Needs simple, unusual games that do not use words. Please see sample issues!

Fillers: "Constant, ongoing demand for puzzles, games, mazes, etc." Variable pay.

Tips: "Present health-related items in an interesting, non-textbook manner."

CHILDREN'S DIGEST, Children's Better Health Institute, P.O. Box 567, Indianapolis IN 46206-0567. (317)636-8881. Fax: (317)684-8094. Editor: Layne Cameron. 85% freelance written. Works with a small number of new/unpublished writers each year. Magazine published 8 times/year covering children's health for preteen children. Estab. 1950. Pays on publication. Publishes ms an average of 1 year after acceptance. Byline given. Buys all rights. Submit seasonal/holiday material 8 months in advance. Submit *only* complete mss. "No queries, please." Reports in 2 months. Sample copy for $1.25. Writer's guidelines for #10 SASE.

• *Children's Digest* would like to see more photo stories about environmental topics and concerns and more nonfiction in general.

Nonfiction: Historical, interview/profile (biographical), craft ideas, health, nutrition, fitness and sports. "We're especially interested in factual features that teach readers about fitness and sports or encourage them to develop better health habits. We are *not* interested in material that is simply rewritten from encyclopedias. We try to present our health material in a way that instructs *and* entertains the reader." Buys 15-20 mss/year. Send complete ms. Length: 500-1,000 words. Pays up to 12¢/word. Sometimes pays the expenses of writers on assignment.

Photos: State availability of full color or b&w photos. Payment varies. Model releases and identification of subjects required. Buys one-time rights.

Fiction: Adventure, humorous, mainstream, mystery. Stories should appeal to both boys and girls. "We need some stories that incorporate a health theme. However, we don't want stories that preach, preferring instead stories with implied morals. We like a light or humorous approach." Buys 15-20 mss/year. Length: 500-1,500 words. Pays up to 12¢/word.

Poetry: Pays $20 minimum.

Tips: "Many of our readers have working mothers and/or come from single-parent homes. We need more stories that reflect these changing times while communicating good values."

CHILDREN'S PLAYMATE, Children's Better Health Institute, P.O. Box 567, Indianapolis IN 46206-0567. (317)636-8881. Editor: (Ms.) Terry Harshman. 75% freelance written. Eager to work with new/unpublished writers. Magazine published 8 times/year for children ages 6-8. "We are looking for articles, stories, and activities with a health, sports, fitness or nutritionally oriented theme. We also publish general interest fiction and nonfiction. We try to present our material in a positive light, and we try to incorporate humor and a light approach wherever possible without minimizing the seriousness of what we are saying." Estab. 1928. Buys all rights. Byline given. Pays on publication. Publishes ms an average of 1 year after acceptance. Submit seasonal material 8 months in advance. Reports in 3 months. Sometimes may hold mss for up to 1 year, with author's permission. Sample copy for $1.25. Writer's guidelines for #10 SASE.

Nonfiction: 500 words maximum. "A feature may be an interesting presentation on animals, people, events, objects or places, especially about good health, exercise, proper nutrition and safety. Include word count. Buys 40 mss/year. "We would very much like to see more nonfiction features on nature and gardening. We do not consider outlines. Reading the whole manuscript is the only way to give fair consideration. Material will not be returned unless accompanied by a SASE." No queries. Pays up to 17¢/word.

Fiction: Short stories for beginning readers, not over 700 words. Seasonal stories with holiday themes. Humorous stories, unusual plots. "We are interested in stories about children in different cultures and stories about lesser-known holidays (not just Christmas, Thanksgiving, Halloween, Hanukkah)." Vocabulary suitable for ages 6-8. Submit complete ms. Pays up to 17¢/word. Include word count with stories.

Fillers: Recipes, puzzles, dot-to-dots, color-ins, hidden pictures, mazes. Buys 30 fillers/year. Payment varies. Prefers camera-ready activities. Activity guidelines for #10 SASE.

Tips: Especially interested in features, stories, poems and articles about special holidays.

COBBLESTONE: The History Magazine for Young People, Cobblestone Publishing, Inc., 7 School St., Peterborough NH 03458-1457. (603)924-7209. Fax: (603)924-7380. Editor: Meg Chorlian. 100% (except letters and departments) freelance written (approximately 1 issue/year is by assignment only). Prefers to work with published/established writers. Monthly magazine (September-May) covering American history for children ages 8-14. "Each issue presents a particular theme, from different angles, making it exciting as well as informative. Half of all subscriptions are for schools." Circ. 36,000. Pays on publication. Publishes ms an average of 4 months after acceptance. Byline given. Offers 50% kill fee. Buys all rights. All material must relate to monthly theme. Editorial lead time 9 months. Accepts simultaneous submissions. Reports in 4 months. Sample copy for $4.50 and 7½ × 10½ SAE with 4 first-class stamps. Writer's guidelines and query deadlines for SASE.

Nonfiction: Historical, interview, plays, biography, recipes, activities, personal experience. "Request a copy of the writer's guidelines to find out specific issue themes in upcoming months." No material that editorializes rather than reports. Buys 80 mss/year. Query with published clips, outline and bibliography. Length: Feature articles 600-800 words. Supplemental nonfiction 300-500 words.

Reprints: Accepts previously published submissions.

Photos: State availability of photos with submission. Reviews contact sheets, transparencies, prints. Offers $15 for non-professional quality, $100 for professional quality. Captions, identification of subjects required. Buys one-time rights. Photos must relate to theme.

Fiction: Adventure, ethnic, historical, biographical fiction. "Has to be very strong and accurate." Buys 5 mss/year. Length: 500-800 words. Query with published clips. Pays 20-25¢/printed word.

Poetry: Free verse, light verse, traditional. Buys 5 poems/year. Length: up to 100 lines. Pays on an individual basis. Must relate to theme.

Columns/Departments: Puzzles and Games (no word finds); crossword and other word puzzles using the vocabulary of the issue's theme.

Tips: "All material is considered on the basis of merit and appropriateness to theme. Query should state idea for material simply, with rationale for why material is applicable to theme. Request writer's guidelines (includes themes and query deadlines) before submitting a query. Include SASE. In general, please keep in mind that we are a magazine for children ages 8-14. We want the subject to be interesting and historically accurate, but not condescending to our readers. We are looking for articles from social science teachers and educators in the middle school grades. Queries should include a detailed outline and a bibliography."

COUNSELOR, Scripture Press Publications, Inc., 1825 College Ave., Wheaton IL 60187. Editor: Janice K. Burton. 60% freelance written. Quarterly Sunday School take-home paper with 13 weekly parts. "Our readers are 8-12 years old. All materials attempt to show God's working in the lives of children. Must have a true Christian slant, not just a moral implication." **Pays on acceptance.** Publishes ms an average of 2 years after acceptance. Byline given. Buys first North American serial rights, first rights, one-time rights, second serial (reprint) rights or all rights. Editorial lead time 1 year. Submit seasonal material 1 year in advance. Reports in 2 months on mss. Sample copy and writer's guidelines for #10 SASE.

Nonfiction: Inspirational (stories), Interview/profile, personal experience, religious. All stories, etc., must have a spiritual perspective. Show God at work in a child's life. Buys 10-20 mss/year. Send complete ms. Length: 900-1,100 words. Pays 7-10¢/word.

Reprints: Accepts previously published submissions.

Columns/Departments: God's Wonders (seeing God through creation and the wonders of science), Kids in Action (kids doing unusual activities to benefit others), World Series (missions stories from child's perspective), all 300-500 words. Send complete ms. Pays 7-10¢/word.

Fiction: Adventure, ethnic, religious. Buys 10-15 mss/year. Send complete ms. Length: 900-1,100 words. Pays 7-10¢/word.

Fillers: Buys 8-12 puzzles, games, fun activities/year. Length: 150 words maximum. Pays 7-10¢/word.

Tips: "Show a real feel for the age level. Know your readers and what is age appropriate in terms of concepts and vocabulary. Submit only best quality manuscripts."

‡CRAYOLA KIDS MAGAZINE, Co-published by Meredith Corporation and Binney & Smith Properties, Inc., 1912 Grand Ave., Des Moines IA 50309-3379. (515)284-2390. Fax: (515)284-2064. E-mail: mlheaton@ aol.com. Editor: Deborah Gore Ohrn. Managing Editor: Mary L. Heaton. Contact: Lavonne Simon, administrative assistant. 25% freelance written. Bimonthly magazine covering children (ages 3-8). "Our mission is to excite young children about the magic of reading and the wonder of creativity and, in so doing, help lay a solid foundation for a lifetime of special learning. We do that by reprinting a children's trade book (in for a lifetime of special learning. We do that by reprinting a children's trade book (in its entirety) and by presenting open-ended crafts and fun puzzles and activities related to a particular theme." Estab. 1994. Circ. 350,000 subscribers plus newsstand. **Pays on acceptance.** Publishes ms an average of 4 months after acceptance. Byline sometimes given. Buys second serial (reprint) and all rights, makes work-for-hire assignments. Editorial lead time 8 months. Submit seasonal material anytime. Accepts simultaneous submissions. 3 Reports in weeks on queries; 2 months on mss. Sample copy for $2.95 and writer's guidelines for #10 SASE.

Nonfiction: How-to/kids' crafts—seasonal and theme-related, interview/profile, puzzles. Buys 30-40 mss/ year. Query. Length: 250 words maximum. Pays $50-300 for assigned articles; $30-150 for unsolicited articles.

Photos: "It would be very rare for us to buy a photo. We usually assign a freelance photographer for off-site shoots."

Fiction: "We buy only prepublished fiction from major publishing houses."

Fillers: For fillers we want ideas for visual puzzles that are fresh and fun will be reviewed. Do not send art except as a rough indicator of how the puzzle works."

Tips: "Send a sample with crafts—they should be made from easy-to-find materials, be fun to make and then play with and should be kid-tested. Send for list of themes before submitting crafts or puzzles or activities that are not seasonal."

CRICKET, Carus Publishing Co., P.O. Box 300, Peru IL 61354-0300. (815)224-6656. Editor-in-Chief: Marianne Carus. Monthly magazine. Estab. 1973. Circ. 100,000. Pays on publication. Byline given. Buys first publication rights in the English language. Submit seasonal/holiday material 1 year in advance. Reports in 3 months. Sample copy and writer's guidelines for $4 and 9×12 SAE. Writer's guidelines only for #10 SASE.

• *Cricket* is looking for more fiction and nonfiction for the older end of its age range.

Nonfiction: Adventure, biography, foreign culture, geography, history, science, social science, sports, technology, travel. (A short bibliography is required for *all* nonfiction articles.) Send complete ms. Length: 200-1,200 words. Pays up to 25¢/word.

Reprints: Send typed ms with rights for sale noted and information about when and where the article previously appeared. Pays 50% of amount paid for an original article.

Fiction: Adventure, ethnic, fairy tales, fantasy, historical, humorous, mystery, novel excerpts, science fiction, suspense, western. No didactic, sex, religious or horror stories. Buys 24-36 mss/year. Send complete ms. Length: 200-1,500 words. Pays up to 25¢/word.

• Ranked as one of the best markets for fiction writers in *Writer's Digest*'s annual "Fiction 50," June 1996.

Poetry: Buys 8-10 poems/year. Length: 50 lines maximum. Pays up to $3/line on publication.

CRUSADER MAGAZINE, P.O. Box 7259, Grand Rapids MI 49510-7259. Fax: (616)241-5558. E-mail: cadets@aol.com. Editor: G. Richard Broene. 40% freelance written. Works with a small number of new/ unpublished writers each year. Magazine published 7 times/year. "*Crusader Magazine* shows boys 9-14 how God is at work in their lives and in the world around them." Estab. 1958. Circ. 14,000. **Pays on acceptance.** Byline given. Publishes ms an average of 8 months after acceptance. Rights purchased vary with author and material; buys first serial, one-time, second serial (reprint) and simultaneous rights. Submit seasonal material (Christmas, Easter) at least 5 months in advance. Accepts simultaneous submissions. Reports in 2 months. Sample copy and writer's guidelines for 9×12 SAE with 3 first-class stamps.

Nonfiction: Articles about young boys' interests: sports, outdoor activities, bike riding, science, crafts, etc., and problems. Emphasis is on a Christian multi-racial perspective, but no simplistic moralisms. Informational, how-to, personal experience, interview, profile, inspirational, humor. Buys 20-25 mss/year. Submit complete ms. Length: 500-1,500 words. Pays 2-5¢/word.

Photos: Pays $4-25 for b&w photos purchased with mss.

Fiction: "Considerable fiction is used. Fast-moving stories that appeal to a boy's sense of adventure or sense of humor are welcome. Avoid preachiness. Avoid simplistic answers to complicated problems. Avoid long dialogue and little action." Length: 900-1,500 words. Pays 2¢/word minimum.

Fillers: Uses short humor and any type of puzzles as fillers.

‡CURIOCITY for Kids, Thomson Newspapers, 730 N. Franklin, Suite 706, Chicago IL 60610. Editor: Jessica Solomon. 85% freelance written. Monthly kids magazine. "*Curiocity* is a monthly kid-driven magazine that uses humor and a light-hearted, inquisitive approach to inform and entertain kids 7-12 about people, places and things around the country and around the town." Estab. 1994. Circ. 20,000. Pays on publication. Publishes ms an average of 2 months after after acceptance. Offers 50% kill fee. Buys all rights. Editorial lead time 2 months. Submit seasonal material 5 months in advance. Reports in 1 month.

Nonfiction: General interest, how-to, humor, interview/profile, travel, kid sports. Buys 60 mss/year. Length: 150-800 words. Pays $100-450.

• Ranked as one of the best markets for freelance writers in *Writer's Yearbook*'s annual "Top 100 Markets," January 1996.

Photos: State availability of photos with submission. Reviews contact sheets and prints. Offers no additional payment for photos accepted with ms. Identification of subjects required.

Columns/Departments: Good Sports (sports for kids), 500 words; Profile (profiles of adults with interesting jobs), 500 words. Query with published clips. Pays $100-450.

Fiction: Adventure, fantasy, humorous, mystery, science fiction, suspense, western. Buys 12 mss/year. Query with published clips. Length: 600 words. Pays $150-300.

‡**DISNEY ADVENTURES**, Walt Disney Magazine Publishing Group, 114 Fifth Ave., 16th Floor, New York NY 10011. Senior Editor: Sean Plottner. Monthly magazine for kids ages 7-14, emphasizing fun and action-packed adventure. It covers the worlds of entertainment, real-life adventures, comics, sports, technology, and weird and wacky science." Estab. 1990. Circ. 962,000. **Pays on acceptance.** Byline given. Offers 25% kill fee. Buys all rights and first North American serial rights for fiction. Accepts simultaneous submissions. Reports in 1-2 months on queries. Sample copy for SASE and $2.99. Writer's guidelines available.
   • Ranked as one of the best markets for freelance writers in *Writer's Yearbook's* annual "Top 100 Markets," January 1996.
Nonfiction: Adventure, science, sports. Buys 25 mss/year. Query with published clips. Length: 150-500 words. Pays $1/word. Pays expenses of writers on assignment.
Columns/Departments: 100-150 words. Buys 50 mss/year. Pays $1/word.
Fiction: Suzanne Harper, executive editor. Adventure. Query with published clips. Pays $1/word.
Tips: "We'll consider almost anything. Surprise us!" Would like to see "a subject fascinating to kids that presents new information in a fresh way. We strive for articles that are fun, entertaining and adventurous—not educational."

FACES, The Magazine About People, Cobblestone Publishing Co. Inc., 7 School St., Peterborough NH 03458. (603)924-7209. Editor: Carolyn P. Yoder. 90-100% freelance written. Monthly magazine published during school year. "*Faces* stands apart from other children's magazines by offering a solid look at one subject and stressing strong editorial content and black-and-white photographs and original illustrations. *Faces* offers an equal balance of feature articles and activities, as well as folktales and legends." Estab. 1984. Circ. 15,000. Pays on publication. Publishes ms an average of 4 months after acceptance. Byline given. Offers 50% kill fee. Buys all rights. Editorial lead time 1 year. Accepts simultaneous submissions. Sample copy for $4.50 and 7½ × 10½ SAE with 4 first-class stamps. Writer's guidelines for #10 SASE.
Nonfiction: Historical/nostalgic, humor, interview/profile, personal experience, photo feature, travel, recipes, activities (puzzles, mazes). All must relate to theme. Buys 45-50 mss/year. Query with published clips. Length: 300-1,000. Pays 20-25¢/word.
Photos: State availability of photos with submission or send copies of related images for photo researcher. Reviews contact sheets, transparencies, prints. Offers $15-100 (for professional). Negotiates payment individually (for non-professional). Captions, model releases, identification of subjects required. Buys one-time rights.
Fiction: Ethnic, historical, retold legends or folktales. Depends on theme. Query with published clips. Length: 500-1,000 words. Pays 20-25¢/word.
Poetry: Avant-garde, free verse, haiku, light verse, traditional. Length: 100 words maximum. Pays on individual basis.
Tips: "Freelancers should send for a sample copy of magazine and a list of upcoming themes and writer's guidelines. The magazine is based on a monthly theme (upcoming themes include Insects and Spiders, Mali, Argentina, Gypsies). We appreciate professional queries that follow our detailed writer's guidelines."

THE FRIEND, 50 E. North Temple, Salt Lake City UT 84150. Managing Editor: Vivian Paulsen. 50% freelance written. Eager to work with new/unpublished writers as well as established writers. Monthly publication of The Church of Jesus Christ of Latter-Day Saints for children ages 3-11. Circ. 350,000. **Pays on acceptance.** Buys all rights. Submit seasonal material 8 months in advance. Sample copy and writer's guidelines for $1.50 and 9 × 12 SAE with 4 first-class stamps.
Nonfiction: Subjects of current interest, science, nature, pets, sports, foreign countries, things to make and do. Special issues: Christmas, Easter. "Submit only complete manuscript—no queries, please." Length: 1,000 words maximum. Pays 9¢/word minimum.
Fiction: Seasonal and holiday stories, stories about other countries and their children. Wholesome and optimistic; high motive, plot and action. Character-building stories preferred. Length: 1,200 words maximum. Stories for younger children should not exceed 250 words. Pays 9¢/word minimum.
Poetry: Serious, humorous, holiday. Any form with child appeal. Pays $25.
Tips: "Do you remember how it feels to be a child? Can you write stories that appeal to children ages 3-11 in today's world? We're interested in stories with an international flavor and those that focus on present-day problems. Send material of high literary quality slanted to our editorial requirements. Let the child solve the problem—not some helpful, all-wise adult. No overt moralizing. Nonfiction should be creatively presented—not an array of facts strung together. Beware of being cutesy."

GIRL'S LIFE, Monarch Publishing, 4517 Harford Rd., Baltimore MD 21214. Fax: (410)254-0991. Editor: Karen Bokram. Contact: Kelly A. White, senior editor. Bimonthly magazine covering girls ages 7-14. Estab. 1994. Circ. 200,000. Pays on publication. Publishes ms an average of 3 months after acceptance. Byline given. Buys first North American serial rights. Editorial lead time 4 months. Submit seasonal material 6 months in advance. Reports in 3 months. Sample copy for $5. Writer's guidelines for #10 SASE.
Nonfiction: Book excerpts, essays, general interest, how-to (crafts), humor, inspirational, interview/profile, new product, personal experience, photo feature, travel. Buys 20 mss/year. Query with published clips. Submit complete mss on spec only. Length: 700-2,000 words. Pays $150-800 for assigned articles.

Photos: State availability of photos with submission. Reviews contact sheets, negatives, transparencies. Negotiates payment individually. Captions, model releases, identification of subjects required.
Columns/Departments: Outta Here! (travel information); Crafts (how-to, cheap); Try It! (new stuff to try); all 1,200 words. Buys 12 mss/year. Query with published clips. Pays $150-450.
Fillers: Gags to be illustrated by cartoonist, short humor. Buys 12/year. Pays $25-100.
Tips: Send queries with published writing samples and detailed résumé.

GUIDEPOSTS FOR KIDS, P.O. Box 538A, Chesterton IN 46304. Website: http://guideposts.org. Editor: Mary Lou Carney. Contact: Sailor Metts, associate editor. 30% freelance written. Bimonthly magazine. "Value centered—fun to read kids magazine for 7- to 12-year-olds (emphasis on upper end of age bracket). Issue oriented, thought provoking. No preachy stories." Estab. 1990. Circ. 200,000. **Pays on acceptance.** Byline given. Offers 25% kill fee. Buys all rights. Editorial lead time 6 months. Submit seasonal material 6 months in advance. Reports in 6 weeks. Sample copy for $3.25. Writer's guidelines for #10 SASE.
Nonfiction: Issue-oriented features, general interest, humor, inspirational, interview/profile, technical (technology), travel. Does not want articles with adult voice/frame of reference. No Sunday-School-type articles. Buys 12 mss/year. Query. (Send complete ms if under 300 words.) Length: 300-1,500 words. Pays $100-400. Sometimes pays expenses of writers on assignment.
Photos: State availability of or send photos with submission. Negotiates payment individually. Identification of subjects required. Buys one-time rights.
Columns/Departments: Tips from the Top (Christian celebrities), 650 words; Featuring Kids (profiles of interesting kids), 300 words. Buys 8 mss/year. Query. Send complete ms. Pays $100-350.
Fiction: Adventure, fantasy, historical, humorous, mystery, suspense, western. Buys 8 mss/year. Send complete ms. Length: 700-1,300 words. Pays $200-400.
Fillers: Facts, newsbreaks, short humor. Buys 8-10/year. Length: 250 words maximum. Pays $25-175.
Tips: "Before you submit to one of our departments, study the magazine. In most of our pieces, we look for a strong kid voice/viewpoint. We do not want preachy or overtly religious material. Looking for value-driven stories and profiles. In the fiction arena, we are very interested in historical and mysteries. In nonfiction, we welcome tough themes and current issues."

‡HIGH ADVENTURE, Gospel Publishing House, 1445 Boonville, Springfield MO 65802-1894. (417)862-2781, ext. 4178. Fax: (417)862-0416. Editor: Marshall Bruner. Willing to work with new/unpublished writers. Quarterly magazine "designed to provide boys with worthwhile, enjoyable, leisure reading; to challenge them in narrative form to higher ideals and greater spiritual dedication; and to perpetuate the spirit of the Royal Rangers program through stories, ideas and illustrations." Estab. 1971. Circ. 86,000. **Pays on acceptance.** Byline given. Buys one-time rights. Submit seasonal/holiday material 9 months in advance. Accepts simultaneous submissions. Reports in 2 months. Sample copy for 9×12 SAE with 3 first-class stamps. Free writer's guidelines.
Nonfiction: Historical/nostalgic, how-to, humor, inspirational, sports, nature, current events and outdoor activities. Buys 25-50 mss/year. Query or send complete ms. Length: 800-1,200 words. Pays 3¢/word.
Reprints: Send typed ms with rights for sale noted.
Photos: Reviews b&w negatives, color transparencies and prints. Identification of subjects required. Buys one-time rights.
Fiction: Adventure, historical, humorous, religious and western. Buys 25-50 mss/year. Send complete ms. Length: 1,000 words maximum. Pays 3¢/word.
Fillers: Jokes, gags and short humor. Pays $2-4 for jokes; $12-20 for cartoons; others vary.

HIGHLIGHTS FOR CHILDREN, 803 Church St., Honesdale PA 18431-1824. Fax: (717)253-0179. Editor: Kent L. Brown Jr. Managing Editor: Christine French Clark. Manuscript Coordinator: Beth Troop. 80% freelance written. Monthly magazine for children ages 2-12. Estab. 1946. Circ. 2,800,000. **Pays on acceptance.** Buys all rights. Reports in about 2 months. Free sample copy. Writer's guidelines for #10 SASE.
Nonfiction: "We need articles on science, technology and nature written by persons with strong backgrounds in those fields. Contributions always welcomed from new writers, especially engineers, scientists, historians, teachers, etc., who can make useful, interesting facts accessible to children. Also writers who have lived abroad and can interpret the ways of life, especially of children, in other countries in ways that will foster world brotherhood. Sports material, biographies and articles of general interest to children. Direct, original approach, simple style, interesting content, not rewritten from encyclopedias. State background and qualifications for writing factual articles submitted. Include references or sources of information." Length: 900 words maximum. Pays $125 minimum. Also buys original party plans for children ages 7-12, clearly described in 300-600 words, including drawings or samples of items to be illustrated. Also, novel but tested ideas in crafts, with clear directions and made-up models. Projects must require only free or inexpensive, easy-to-obtain materials. Especially desirable if easy enough for early primary grades. Also, fingerplays with lots of action, easy for very young children to grasp and to dramatize. Avoid wordiness. We need creative-thinking puzzles that can be illustrated, optical illusions, brain teasers, games of physical agility and other 'fun' activities." Pays minimum $35 for party plans; $20 for crafts ideas; $25 for fingerplays.

Fiction: Unusual, meaningful stories appealing to both girls and boys, ages 2-12. "Vivid, full of action. Engaging plot, strong characterization, lively language." Prefers stories in which a child protagonist solves a dilemma through his or her own resources. Seeks stories that the child ages 8-12 will eagerly read, and the child ages 2-7 will begin to read and/or will like to hear when read aloud (400-900 words). "We publish stories in the suspense/adventure/mystery, fantasy and humor category, all requiring interesting plot and a number of illustration possiblities. Also need rebuses (picture stories 125 words or under), stories with urban settings, stories for beginning readers (100-400 words), sports and horse stories and retold folk tales. We also would like to see more material of 1-page length (300-500 words), both fiction and factual. War, crime and violence are taboo." Pays $120 minimum.

● Ranked as one of the best markets for fiction writers in *Writer's Digest*'s annual "Fiction 50," June 1996.

Tips: "We are pleased that many authors of children's literature report that their first published work was in the pages of *Highlights*. It is not our policy to consider fiction on the strength of the reputation of the author. We judge each submission on its own merits. With factual material, however, we do prefer that writers be authorities in their field or people with first-hand experience. In this manner we can avoid the encyclopedic article that merely restates information readily available elsewhere. We don't make assignments. Query with simple letter to establish whether the nonfiction *subject* is likely to be of interest. A beginning writer should first become familiar with the type of material that *Highlights* publishes. Include special qualifications, if any, of author. Write for the child, not the editor."

HOPSCOTCH, The Magazine for Girls, Bluffton News Publishing & Printing Co., P.O. Box 164, Bluffton OH 45817-0164. (419)358-4610. Fax: (419)358-5027. Editor: Marilyn B. Edwards. Contact: Becky Jackman, editorial assistant. 90% freelance written. Bimonthly magazine on basic subjects of interest to young girls. "*Hopscotch* is a digest-size magazine with a four-color cover and two-color format inside. It is designed for girls ages 6-12 and features pets, crafts, hobbies, games, science, fiction, history, puzzles, careers, etc." Estab. 1989. Pays on publication. Byline given. Buys first or second rights. Submit seasonal/holiday material 8 months in advance. Accepts simultaneous submissions. Reports in 3 weeks on queries; 2 months on mss. Sample copy for $3. Writer's guidelines, current theme list and needs for #10 SASE.

● *Hopscotch* has a new magazine, *Boys' Quest*, for ages 6-13. It has the same old-fashioned principles that *Hopscotch* has and is a good market for freelance writers. Send $3 for copy and guidelines.

Nonfiction: Book excerpts, general interest, historical/nostalgic, how-to (crafts), humor, inspirational, interview/profile, personal experience, pets, games, fiction, careers, sports, cooking. "No fashion, hairstyles, sex or dating articles." Buys 60 mss/year. Send complete ms. Length: 400-1,000 words. Pays 5¢/word.

Reprints: Send tearsheet or photocopy of article or typed ms with rights for sale noted. Pays 100% of amount paid for original article.

Photos: Send photos with submission. Prefers b&w photos, but color photos accepted. Offers $5-10/photo. Captions, model releases and identification of subjects required. Buys one-time rights.

Columns/Departments: Science—nature, crafts, pets, cooking (basic), 400-1,000 words. Send complete ms. Pays $10-35/column.

Fiction: Adventure, historical, humorous, mainstream, mystery, suspense. Buys 15 mss/year. Send complete ms. Length: 600-1,000 words. Pays 5¢/word.

Poetry: Free verse, light verse, traditional. "No experimental or obscure poetry." Submit maximum 6 poems. Pays $10-30.

Tips: "Almost all sections are open to freelancers. Freelancers should remember that *HOPSCOTCH* is a bit old-fashioned, appealing to *young* girls (6-12). We cherish nonfiction pieces that have a young girl or young girls directly involved in unusual and/or worthwhile activities. Any piece accompanied by decent photos stands an even better chance of being accepted."

HUMPTY DUMPTY'S MAGAZINE, Children's Better Health Institute, P.O. Box 567, Indianapolis IN 46206-0567. Editor: Sandy Grieshop. 90% freelance written. "We try not to be overly influenced by an author's credits, preferring instead to judge each submission on its own merit." Bimonthly magazine (monthly March, June, September, December) covering health, nutrition, hygiene, exercise and safety for children ages 4-6. Pays on publication. Publishes ms at least 8 months after acceptance. Buys all rights (but will return one-time book rights if author has name of interested publisher and tentative date of publication). Submit seasonal material 8 months in advance. Reports in 3 months. Sample copy for $1.25. Writer's guidelines for #10 SASE.

Nonfiction: "We are open to nonfiction on almost any age-appropriate subject, but we especially need material with a health theme—nutrition, safety, exercise, hygiene. We're looking for articles that encourage readers to develop better health habits without preaching. Very simple factual articles that creatively teach readers about their bodies. We use simple crafts, some with holiday themes. We also use several puzzles and activities in each issue—dot-to-dot, hidden pictures and other activities that promote following instructions, developing finger dexterity and working with numbers and letters." Submit complete ms with word count. Length: 500 words maximum. Pays up to 22¢/word.

Fiction: "We use some stories in rhyme and a few easy-to-read stories for the beginning reader. All stories should work well as read alouds. Currently we need sports/fitness stories and seasonal stories with holiday themes. We use contemporary stories and fantasy, some employing a health theme. We try to present our health material in a positive light, incorporating humor and a light approach wherever possible. Avoid stereotyping. Characters in contemporary stories should be realistic and up-to-date. Remember, many of our readers have working mothers and/or come from single-parent homes. We need more stories that reflect these changing times but at the same time communicate good, wholesome values." Submit complete ms with word count. Length: 500 words maximum. Pays up to 22¢/word.

Poetry: Short, simple poems. Pays $20 minimum.

Tips: "Writing for *Humpty Dumpty* is similar to writing picture book manuscripts. There must be a great economy of words. We strive for at least 50% art per page (in stories and articles), so space for text is limited. Because the illustrations are so important, stories should lend themselves well to visual imagery. We are always looking for cute, funny stories that lend well to illustration, especially those with a health theme. We are also looking for nonfiction articles, particularly those about nature, animals, the environment—those things kids find outside their back doors."

JACK AND JILL, Children's Better Health Institute, P.O. Box 567, Indianapolis IN 46206-0567. (317)636-8881. Editor: Daniel Lee. 70% freelance written. Magazine published 8 times/year for children ages 7-10. Pays on publication. Publishes ms an average of 8 months after acceptance. Buys all rights. Byline given. Submit seasonal material 8 months in advance. Reports in 10 weeks. May hold material being seriously considered for up to 1 year. "Material will not be returned unless accompanied by SASE with sufficient postage." Sample copy for $1.25. Writer's guidelines for #10 SASE.

Nonfiction: "Because we want to encourage youngsters to read for pleasure and for information, we are interested in material that will challenge a young child's intelligence *and* be enjoyable reading. Our emphasis is on good health, and we are in particular need of articles, stories, and activities with health, safety, exercise and nutrition themes. We try to present our health material in a positive light—incorporating humor and a light approach wherever possible without minimizing the seriousness of what we are saying." Straight factual articles are OK if they are short and interestingly written. "We would rather see, however, more creative alternatives to the straight factual article. We'd like to see articles about interesting kids involved in out-of-the-ordinary activities. We're also interested in articles about people with unusual hobbies for our Hobby Shop department." Buys 10-15 nonfiction mss/year. Length: 500-800 words. Pays a minimum of 15¢/word.

Photos: When appropriate, photos should accompany ms. Reviews sharp, contrasting b&w glossy prints. Sometimes uses color slides, transparencies or good color prints. Pays $20 for b&w, $35 for color, minimum of $50 for cover. Buys one-time rights.

Fiction: May include, but is not limited to, realistic stories, fantasy adventure—set in past, present or future. "All stories need a well-developed plot, action and incident. Humor is highly desirable. Stories that deal with a health theme need not have health as the primary subject." Length: 500-800 words (short stories). Pays 15¢/word minimum. Buys 20-25 mss/year.

Fillers: Puzzles (including various kinds of word and crossword puzzles), poems, games, science projects, and creative craft projects. We get a lot of these. To be selected, an item needs a little extra spark and originality. Instructions for activities should be clearly and simply written and accompanied by models or diagram sketches. "We also have a need for recipes. Ingredients should be healthful; avoid sugar, salt, chocolate, red meat and fats as much as possible. In all material, avoid references to eating sugary foods, such as candy, cakes, cookies and soft drinks."

Tips: "We are constantly looking for new writers who can tell good stories with interesting slants—stories that are not full of out-dated and time-worn expressions. We like to see stories about kids who are smart and capable, but not sarcastic or smug. Problem-solving skills, personal responsibility and integrity are good topics for us. Obtain *current* issues of the magazines and *study* them to determine our present needs and editorial style."

LADYBUG, the Magazine for Young Children, Carus Publishing Co., P.O. Box 300, Peru IL 61354-0300. (815)224-6656. Editor-in-Chief: Marianne Carus. Editor: Paula Morrow. Monthly general interest magazine for children (ages 2-6). "We look for quality writing—quality literature, no matter the subject." Estab. 1990. Circ. 130,000. Pays on publication. Byline given. All accepted mss are published. Buys first publication rights in the English language. Submit seasonal/holiday material 1 year in advance. Do not query; send completed ms. Reports in 3 months. Sample copy and guidelines for $4 and 9×12 SAE. Guidelines only for #10 SASE.

● *Ladybug* needs even more activities based on concepts (size, color, sequence, comparison, etc.) and interesting, appropriate nonfiction. Also needs articles and parent-child activities for its parents' section. See sample issues for what they like.

Columns/Departments: Can You Do This?, 2-3 pages; The World Around You, 2-4 pages; activities based on concepts (size, color, sequence, comparison, etc.), 1-2 pages. Buys 35 mss/year. Send complete ms. "Most *Ladybug* nonfiction is in the form of illustration. We'd like more simple science, how-things-work and behind-the-scenes on a preschool level. Maximum length 250-300 words."

Fiction: Adventure, ethnic, fantasy, folklore, humorous, mainstream, mystery. Buys 30 mss/year. Send complete ms. Length: 850 maximum words. Pays up to 25¢/word.

• Ranked as one of the best markets for fiction writers in *Writer's Digest*'s annual "Fiction 50," June 1996.

Poetry: Light verse, traditional, humorous. Buys 20 poems/year. Submit *maximum* 5 poems. Length: 20 lines maximum. Pays up to $3/line.

Fillers: Anecdotes, facts, short humor. Buys 10/year. Length: 250 (approximately) maximum words. Pays up to 25¢/word. We welcome interactive activities: rebuses, up to 100 words; *original* fingerplays and action rhymes (up to 8 lines).

Tips: "Reread a manuscript *before* sending it in. Be sure to keep within specified word limits. Study back issues before submitting to learn about the types of material we're looking for. Writing style is paramount. We look for rich, evocative language and a sense of joy or wonder. Remember that you're writing for preschoolers—be age-appropriate but not condescending. A story must hold enjoyment for both parent and child through repeated read-aloud sessions. Remember that we live in a multicultural world. People come in all colors, sizes, physical conditions and have special needs. Be inclusive!"

‡MY FRIEND, The Catholic Magazine for Kids, Pauline Books & Media/Daughters of St. Paul, 50 St. Paul's Ave., Jamaica Plan, Boston MA 02130-3491. (617)522-8911. Website: http://www.pauline.org. Editor: Sister Mary Mark Wickenhiser, FSP. Managing Editor: Sister Anne Joan Flanagan, FSP. 50% freelance written. Magazine published 10 times/year. Christian entertainment and formation for young people ages 6-12. Estab. 1979. Circ. 12,000. **Pays on acceptance**. Publishes ms an average of 1 year after acceptance. Byline given. Buys first or all rights. Editorial lead time 1 year. Submit seasonal material 1 year in advance. Reports in 2 months on queries. Sample copy for $2, SAE and 5 first-class stamps. Writer's guidelines for #10 SASE.

Nonfiction: How-to, religious, technical, scientific, crafts, picture-based puzzles, media-related articles, real life features about kids doing something interesting or overcoming difficulties, seasonal and media literacy. Buys 15 mss/year. Send complete ms. Length: 150-600 words. Pays $35-100. Pays writers with contributor copies if prior agreement with author who wishes to write as a form of sharing our ministry.

Photos: Send photos with submission.

Fiction: Adventure, ethnic, experimental, fantasy, historical, humorous, mystery, religious, science fiction. Buys 23 mss/year. Send complete ms. Length: 150-600 words. Pays $35-100.

Fillers: Bible facts. Buys 5/year. Length: 10-30 words. Pays $5.

NEW MOON: THE MAGAZINE FOR GIRLS & THEIR DREAMS, New Moon Publishing, Inc., P.O. Box 3620, Duluth MN 55803. Website: http://newmoon.duluth.mn.us/~newmoon. Managing Editor: Joe Kelly. 10% freelance written. Bimonthly magazine covering girls ages 8-14, edited by girls aged 8-14. "In general, all material should be pro-girl and feature girls and women as the primary focus. *New Moon* is for every girl who wants her voice heard and her dreams taken seriously." Estab. 1992. Circ. 25,000. Pays on publication. Publishes ms 6 months after acceptance. Byline given. Buys first rights and second serial (reprint) rights. Editorial lead time 6 months. Submit seasonal material 10 months in advance. Accepts simultaneous submissions. Reports in 2 months on queries; 3 months on mss. Sample copy for $6.50. Writer's guidelines free on request.

Nonfiction: General interest, humor, inspirational, interview/profile, opinion, personal experience, photo feature, religious, technical, travel, multicultural/girls from other countries. Buys 6 mss/year. Query. Length: 300-900 words. Pays 4-8¢/word.

Reprints: Accepts previously published submissions.

Photos: State availability of photos with submission. Reviews 4×5 prints. Negotiates payment individually. Captions, model releases, identification of subjects required. Buys one-time rights.

Columns/Departments: Global Village (girl's life in another country), 900 words; Women's Work (profile of a woman's career), 600-900 words; She Did It (real girls doing real things), 300-600 words. Buys 3 mss/ year. Query. Pays 4-8¢/word.

Fiction: Adventure, experimental, fantasy, historical, humorous, mystery, religious, romance, science fiction, serialized novels (on occasion), slice-of-life vignettes, suspense, girl centered. Buys 3 mss/year. Query. Send complete ms. Length: 300-900 words. Pays 4-8¢/word.

Poetry: Avant-garde, free verse, haiku, light verse. Buys 1 poem/year. Does not pay for poetry.

Tips: "Writers and artists who comprehend our goals have the best chance of publication. Refer to our guidelines and upcoming themes."

ON THE LINE, Mennonite Publishing House, 616 Walnut Ave., Scottdale PA 15683-1999. (412)887-8500. Fax: (412)887-3111. Editor: Mary Clemens Meyer. 90% freelance written. Works with a small number of new/unpublished writers each year. Monthly magazine for children ages 10-14. Estab. 1908. Circ. 6,500. **Pays on acceptance.** Publishes ms an average of 1 year after acceptance. Byline given. Buys one-time rights. Submit seasonal/holiday material 6 months in advance. Accepts simultaneous submissions. Reports in 1 month. Sample copy for 9×12 SAE with 2 first-class stamps.

Nonfiction: How-to (things to make with easy-to-get materials including food recipes); informational (350-500 word articles on wonders of nature, people who have made outstanding contributions also puzzles and activities). Buys 95 unsolicited mss/year. Send complete ms. Pays $10-30.

Reprints: Accepts previously published submissions.

Photos: Photos purchased with or without ms. Pays $25-50 for 8×10 b&w photos. Total purchase price for ms includes payment for photos.

Fiction: Adventure, humorous, religious. Buys 50 mss/year. Send complete ms. Length: 1,000-1,500 words. Pays 2-4¢/word.

Poetry: Light verse, religious. Length: 3-12 lines. Pays $5-15.

Tips: "Study the publication first. We need short well-written how-to and craft articles. Don't send query; we prefer to see the complete manuscript."

OWL MAGAZINE, The Discovery Magazine for Children, Owl Communications, 179 John St., Suite 500, Toronto, Ontario M5T 3G5 Canada. (416)971-5275. Editor: Nyla Ahmad. Managing Editor: Keltie Thomas. 25% freelance written. Works with small number of new writers each year. Magazine published 10 times/year (no July or August issues) covering science and nature. Aims to interest children in their environment through accurate, factual information about the world presented in an easy, lively style. Estab. 1976. Circ. 160,000. Pays on publication. Publishes ms an average of 3 months after acceptance. Byline given. Buys all rights. Submit seasonal/holiday material 1 year in advance. Reports in 10 weeks. Sample copy for $4.28. Writer's guidelines for SAE (large envelope if requesting sample copy) and money order for $1 postage (no stamps please).

Nonfiction: Personal experience (real life children in real situations); photo feature (natural science, international wildlife, and outdoor features); science and environmental features. No problem stories with drugs, sex or moralistic views, or talking animal stories. Query with clips of published work.

Photos: State availability of photos. Reviews 35mm transparencies. Identification of subjects required. Send for photo package before submitting material.

Tips: "Write for editorial guidelines first. Review back issues of the magazine for content and style. Know your topic and approach it from an unusual perspective. Our magazine never talks down to children. We would like to see more articles about science and technology that aren't too academic."

POCKETS, The Upper Room, P.O. Box 189, Nashville TN 37202-0189. (615)340-7333. Fax: (615)340-7006. Editor: Janet R. Knight. Contact: Lynn Gilliam, associate editor. 60% freelance written. Eager to work with new/unpublished writers. Monthly magazine (except January/February) covering children's and families' spiritual formation. "We are a Christian, non-denominational publication for children 6-12 years of age." Estab. 1981. Circ. 99,000. **Pays on acceptance.** Byline given. Offers 4¢/word kill fee. Buys first North American serial rights. Submit seasonal/holiday material 1 year in advance. Reports in 10 weeks on mss. Sample copy for $7\frac{1}{2} \times 10\frac{1}{2}$ SAE with 4 first-class stamps. Writer's guidelines and themes for #10 SASE.
- *Pockets* has expanded to 48 pages and needs more fiction and poetry, as well as short, short stories (500-750 words) for children 4-7. We publish one of these stories per issue.

Nonfiction: Interview/profile, religious (retold scripture stories), personal experience. List of themes for special issues available with SASE. No violence or romance. Buys 5 mss/year. Send complete ms. Length: 600-1,500 words. Pays 12¢/word.

Reprints: Accepts one-time previously published submissions. Send typed ms with rights for sale noted and information about when and where the article previously appeared. Pays 100% of amount paid for an original article.

Photos: Send photos with submission. Prefer no photos unless they accompany an article. Reviews contact sheets, transparencies and prints. Offers $25-50/photo. Buys one-time rights.

Columns Departments: Refrigerator Door (poetry and prayer related to themes), 25 lines; Pocketsful of Love (family communications activities), 300 words; Activities/Games ($25 and up); Peacemakers at Work (profiles of people, particularly children, working for peace, justice and ecological concerns), 300-800 words. Buys 20 mss/year. Send complete ms. Pays 12¢/word; recipes $25.

Fiction: Adventure, ethnic, slice-of-life. "Stories should reflect the child's everyday experiences through a Christian approach. This is often more acceptable when stories are not preachy or overtly Christian." Buys 44 mss/year. Send complete ms. Length: 750-1,600 words. Pays 12¢/word and up.
- Ranked as one of the best markets for fiction writers in *Writer's Digest*'s annual "Fiction 50," June 1996.

Poetry: Buys 22 poems/year. Length: 4-25 lines. Pays $25-50.

Tips: "Theme stories, role models and retold scripture stories are most open to freelancers. We are also looking for nonfiction stories about children involved in peace/justic/ecology efforts. Poetry is also open. It's very helpful if writers send for our themes. These are *not* the same as writer's guidelines. We also have an annual $1,000 Fiction Writing Contest. Guidelines available with SASE."

POWER AND LIGHT, 6401 The Paseo, Kansas City MO 64131. Fax: (816)333-4439. E-mail: mhammer@ nazarene.org. Editor: Beula Postlewait. Associate Editor: Melissa Hammer. Mostly freelance written. Weekly magazine for boys and girls ages 11-12 using WordAction Sunday School curriculum. Estab. 1992. Publishes ms an average of 1 year after acceptance. Buys multiple use rights. "Minimal comments on pre-printed form are made on rejected material." Reports in 3 months. Sample copy and guidelines for SASE.

Fiction: Stories with Christian emphasis on high ideals, wholesome social relationships and activities and right choices. Informal style. Submit complete ms. Length: 500-700 words. Pays 5¢/word.

Reprints: Send tearsheet or photocopy of article or article ms with rights for sale noted and information about when and where article previously appeared. Pays 3½¢/word.

Tips: "All themes and outcomes should conform to the theology and practices of the Church of the Nazarene."

PRIMARY DAYS, Scripture Press Publications, Inc., 1825 College Ave., Wheaton IL 60187. Editor: Janice K. Burton. 75% freelance written. Quarterly Sunday School take-home paper with 13 weekly parts. "Our readers are 6-8 years old. All materials attempt to show God's working in the lives of children. Must have a true Christian slant, not just a moral implication." **Pays on acceptance.** Publishes ms an average of 2 years after acceptance. Byline given. Buys first North American serial rights, first rights, one-time rights, second serial (reprint) rights and all rights. Editorial lead time 1 year. Submit seasonal material 1 year in advance. Reports in 2 months on mss. Sample copy and writer's guidelines for #10 SASE.

Nonfiction: Inspirational (stories), interview/profile. "All stories, etc. must have a spiritual perspective. Show God at work in a child's life. Buys 10-20 mss/year. Send complete ms. Length: 300-350 words. Pays 7-10¢/word.

Reprints: Accepts previously published submissions.

Fiction: Adventure, ethnic, religious. Buys 10-15 mss/year. Send complete ms. Length: 300-350 words. Pays 7-10¢/word.

Fillers: Buys 8-12 puzzles, games, fun activities/year. Length: 150 words maximum. Pays 7-10¢/word.

Tips: "Show a real feel for the age level. Know your readers and what is age-appropriate in terms of concepts and vocabulary. Submit only best quality manuscripts."

R-A-D-A-R, 8121 Hamilton Ave., Cincinnati OH 45231. (513)931-4050. Editor: Elaina Meyers. 75% freelance written. Weekly for children in grades 3-6 in Christian Sunday schools. Estab. 1866 (publishing house). Rights purchased varies with author and material; prefers buying first serial rights, but will buy second (reprint) rights. Occasionally overstocked. **Pays on acceptance.** Publishes ms an average of 1 year after acceptance. Reports in 2 months. Free sample copy and writer's guidelines for #10 SASE.

Nonfiction: Articles on hobbies and handicrafts, nature, famous people, seasonal subjects, etc., written from a Christian viewpoint. No articles about historical figures with an absence of religious implication. Length: 500 words. Pays 3-7¢/word.

Reprints: Send tearsheet or photocopy of article or short story or typed ms with rights for sale noted and information about when and where article previously appeared.

Fiction: Short stories of heroism, adventure, travel, mystery, animals, biography. "True or possible plots stressing clean, wholesome, Christian character-building ideas, but not preachy. Make prayer, church attendance and Christian living a natural part of the story. We correlate our fiction and other features with a definite Bible lesson. Writers who want to meet our needs should send a #10 SASE for a theme list." No talking animal stories, science fiction, Halloween stories or first-person stories from an adult's viewpoint. Length: up to 1,000 words. Pays 3-7¢/word.

- Ranked as one of the best markets for fiction writers in *Writer's Digest*'s annual "Fiction 50," June 1996.

RANGER RICK, National Wildlife Federation, 1400 16th St. NW, Washington DC 20036. (703)790-4274. Editor: Gerald Bishop. 40% freelance written. Works with a small number of new/unpublished writers each year. Monthly magazine for children from ages 6-12, with the greatest concentration in the 7-10 age bracket. Buys all world rights unless other arrangements made. Byline given "but occasionally, for very brief pieces, we will identify author by name at the end. Contributions to regular columns usually are not bylined." Estab. 1967. **Pays on acceptance.** Publishes ms an average of 18 months after acceptance. Reports in 6 weeks. "Anything written with a specific month in mind should be in our hands at least 10 months before that issue date." Writer's guidelines for #10 SASE.

Nonfiction: "Articles may be written on anything related to nature, conservation, the outdoors, environmental problems or natural science. Please avoid articles about animal rehabilitation, unless the species are endangered." Buys 25-35 unsolicited mss/year. Query. Pays from $50-575, depending on length, quality and content (maximum length, 900 words). Unless you are an expert in the field or are writing from direct personal experience, all factual information must be footnoted and backed up with current, reliable references.

Fiction: "Same categories as nonfiction plus fantasy and science fiction. The attributing of human qualities to animals is limited to our regular feature, 'The Adventures of Ranger Rick,' so please do not humanize wildlife. We discourage keeping wildlife as pets."

Photos: "Photographs, when used, are paid for separately. It is not necessary that illustrations accompany material."

Tips: "In your query letter, include details of what the manuscript will cover; sample lead; evidence that you can write playfully and with great enthusiasm, conviction and excitement (formal, serious, dull queries indicate otherwise). Think of an exciting subject we haven't done recently, sell it effectively with query, and produce a manuscript of highest quality. Read past issues to learn successful styles and unique approaches to subjects.

SHOFAR MAGAZINE, 43 Northcote Dr., Melville NY 11747-3924. (516)643-4598. Fax: (516)643-4598. Managing Editor: Gerald H. Grayson. 80-90% freelance written. Monthly children's magazine on Jewish subjects. Estab. 1984. Circ. 17,000. Pays on publication. Byline given. Buys one-time rights. Submit seasonal/holiday material 6 months in advance. Accepts simultaneous submissions. Reports in 2 months. Sample copy and writer's guidelines for 9×12 SAE and $1.01 postage.
Nonfiction: Historical/nostalgic, humor, inspirational, interview/profile, personal experience, photo feature, religious, travel. Buys 15 mss/year. Send complete ms. Length: 750-1,000 words. Pays 7-10¢/word. Sometimes pays the expenses of writers on assignment.
Photos: State availability of or send photos with submission. Offers $10-50/photo. Identification of subjects required. Buys one-time rights.
Fiction: Adventure, historical, humorous, religious. Buys 15 mss/year. Send complete ms. Length: 750-1,000 words. Pays 7-10¢/word.
Poetry: Free verse, light verse, traditional. Buys 4-5 poems/year. Length: 8-50 words. Pays 7-10¢/word.
Tips: "Submissions *must* be on a Jewish theme and should be geared to readers who are 8 to 12 years old."

‡SPIDER, The Magazine for Children, The Cricket Magazine Group, P.O. Box 300, Peru IL 61354. (815)224-6656. Fax: (815)224-6675. Editor-in-Chief: Marianne Carus. Associate Editor: Christine Walske. Contact: Submissions Editor. 80% freelance written. Monthly magazine covering literary, general interest. "*Spider* introduces 6- to 9-year-old children to the highest quality stories, poems, illustrations, articles and activities. It was created to foster in beginning readers a love of reading and discovery that will last a lifetime. We're looking for writers who respect children's intelligence." Estab. 1994. Circ. 100,000. Pays on publication. Publishes ms an average of 1 year after acceptance. Byline given. Buys first North American serial rights (for stories, poems, articles), second serial (reprint) rights or all rights (for crafts, recipes, puzzles). Editorial lead time 9 months. Submit seasonal material 1 year in advance. Accepts simultaneous submissions. Reports in 4 months on mss. Sample copy for $4. Writer's guidelines for #10 SASE.
Nonfiction: Adventure, biography, geography, history, science, social science, sports, technology, travel. A bibliography is required with all nonfiction submissions. Buys 12-15 mss/year. Send complete ms. Length: 300-800 words. Pays 25¢/word.
Reprints: Note rights for sale and information about when and where article previously appeared.
Photos: Send photos with submission (prints or slide dupes OK). Reviews contact sheets, 35mm to 4×4 transparencies, 8×10 maximum prints. Offers $50-200/photo. Captions, model releases, identification of subjects required. Buys one-time rights.
Fiction: Adventure, ethnic, fantasy, historical, humorous, mystery, science fiction, suspense, realistic fiction, folk tales, fairy tales. No romance, horror, religious. Buys 30-40 mss/year. Send complete ms. Length: 300-1,000 words. Pays 25¢/word.
Poetry: Free verse, traditional, nonsense, humorous, serious. No forced rhymes, didactic. Buys 20-30 poems/year. Submit maximum 5 poems. Length: 20 lines maximum. Pays $3 per line maximum.
Fillers: Puzzles, mazes, hidden pictures, games, brainteasers, math and word activities. Buys 15-20/year. Payment depends on type of filler.
Tips: "Most importantly, do not write down to children. We'd like to see more of the following: multicultural fiction and nonfiction, strong female protagonists, stories about people who are physically or mentally challenged, fantasy, science fiction, environmental articles, hard science (e.g., physics, chemistry, cosmology, microbiology, science biography and history)."

SPORTS ILLUSTRATED FOR KIDS, Time-Warner, Time & Life Building, 1271 Sixth Ave., New York NY 10020. (212)522-5437. Fax: (212)522-0120. Managing Editor: Neil Cohen. Contact: Erin Egan, associate editor. 20% freelance written. Monthly magazine on sports for children 8 years old and up. Content is divided 50/50 between sports as played by kids, and sports as played by professionals. Estab. 1989. **Pays on acceptance.** Publishes ms an average of 3 months after acceptance. Byline given. Offers 25% kill fee. Buys all rights. For sample copy call (800)992-0196. Writer's guidelines for #10 SASE.
Nonfiction: Games, general interest, how-to, humor, inspirational, interview/profile, photo feature, puzzles. Buys 15 mss/year. Query with published clips. Length: 100-1,500 words. Pays $75-1,000 for assigned articles; $75-800 for unsolicited articles. Pays expenses of writers on assignment.
Photos: State availability of photos with submission. Buys one-time rights.
Columns/Departments: The Worst Day I Ever Had (tells about day in pro athlete's life when all seemed hopeless), 500-600 words; Sports Shorts (short, fresh news about kids doing awaiting things, on and off the field), 100-250 words. Buys 10-15 mss/year. Query with published clips. Pays $75-600.

STONE SOUP, The Magazine by Young Writers and Artists, Children's Art Foundation, P.O. Box 83, Santa Cruz CA 95063-0083. (408)426-5557. Fax: (408)426-1161. E-mail: editor@stonesoup.com. Website: http://www.stonesoup.com. Editor: Ms. Gerry Mandel. 100% freelance written. Bimonthly magazine of writing and art by children, including fiction, poetry, book reviews, and art by children through age 13.

Estab. 1973. Audience is children, teachers, parents, writers, artists. "We have a preference for writing and art based on real-life experiences; no formula stories or poems." Pays on publication. Publishes ms an average of 3 months after acceptance. Buys all rights. Submit seasonal/holiday material 6 months in advance. Reports in 1 month. Sample copy for $4. Writer's guidelines with SASE.

Nonfiction: Book reviews. Buys 10 mss/year. Query. Pays $15 for assigned articles.

Reprints: Send photocopy of article or story and information about when and where the article or story previously appeared.

Fiction: Adventure, ethnic, experimental, fantasy, historical, humorous, mystery, science fiction, slice-of-life vignettes, suspense. "We do not like assignments or formula stories of any kind." Accepts 55 mss/year. Send complete ms. Pays $10 for stories. Authors also receive 2 copies and discounts on additional copies and on subscriptions.

Poetry: Avant-garde, free verse. Accepts 20 poems/year. Pays $10/poem. (Same discounts apply.)

Tips: "All writing we publish is by young people ages 13 and under. We do not publish any writing by adults. We can't emphasize enough how important it is to read a couple of issues of the magazine. We have a strong preference for writing on subjects that mean a lot to the author. If you feel strongly about something that happened to you or something you observed, use that feeling as the basis for your story or poem. Stories should have good descriptions, realistic dialogue and a point to make. In a poem, each word must be chosen carefully. Your poem should present a view of your subject and a way of using words that are special and all your own."

STORY FRIENDS, Mennonite Publishing House, 616 Walnut Ave., Scottdale PA 15683-1999. (412)887-8500. Fax: (412)887-3111. Editor: Rose Mary Stutzman. 80% freelance written. Monthly story paper in weekly parts for children ages 4-9. "*Story Friends* is planned to provide wholesome Christian reading for the 4-9-year-old. Practical life stories are included to teach moral values and remind the children that God is at work today. Activities introduce children to the Bible and its message for them." Estab. 1905. Circ. 7,000. **Pays on acceptance.** Publishes ms an average of 1 year after acceptance. Byline given. Publication not copyrighted. Buys one-time and second serial (reprint) rights. Submit seasonal/holiday material 6 months in advance. Accepts simultaneous submissions. Reports in 1 month. Sample copy for 9×12 SAE with 2 first-class stamps. Writer's guidelines for #10 SASE.

Nonfiction: How-to (craft ideas for young children), photo feature. Buys 20 mss/year. Send complete ms. Length: 300-500 words. Pays 3-5¢/word.

Reprints: Send photocopy or typed ms with rights for sale noted and information about when and where the article previously appeared. Pays 50% of amount paid for an original article.

Photos: Send photos with submission. Reviews $8\frac{1}{2} \times 11$ b&w prints. Offers $20-25/photo. Model releases required. Buys one-time rights.

Fiction: See writer's guidelines for *Story Friends*. Buys 50 mss/year. Send complete ms. Length: 300-800 words. Pays 3-5¢/word.

Poetry: Traditional. Buys 20 poems/year. Length: 4-16 lines. Pays $5-10/poem.

Tips: "Send stories that children from a variety of ethnic backgrounds can relate to; stories that deal with experiences similar to all children. For example, all children have fears but their fears may vary depending on where they live. I want to include more humor. I hope to choose stories with a humorous twist."

TOUCH, P.O. Box 7259, Grand Rapids MI 49510. Editor: Jan Boone. Publications Coordinator: Carol Smith. 80% freelance written. Prefers to work with published/established writers. Monthly magazine "to show girls ages 7-14 how God is at work in their lives and in the world around them. The May/June issue annually features material written by our readers." Estab. 1972. Circ. 15,500. **Pays on acceptance.** Publishes ms an average of 1 year after acceptance. Byline given. Buys second serial (reprint) and first North American serial rights. Submit seasonal/holiday material 9 months in advance. Accepts simultaneous submissions. Reports in 2 months. Sample copy and writer's guidelines for 9×12 SAE with 3 first-class stamps.

Nonfiction: How-to (crafts girls can make easily and inexpensively); informational (write for issue themes); humor (need much more); inspirational (seasonal and holiday); interview; multicultural materials; travel; personal experience (avoid the testimony approach); photo feature (query first). "Because our magazine is published around a monthly theme, requesting the letter we send out twice a year to our established freelancers would be most helpful. We do not want easy solutions or quick character changes from bad to good. No pietistic characters. Constant mention of God is not necessary if the moral tone of the story is positive. We do not want stories that always have a good ending." Buys 36-45 unsolicited mss/year. Submit complete ms. Length: 100-1,000 words. Pays 2½-5¢/word, depending on the amount of editing.

Reprints: Send typed ms with rights for sale noted.

Photos: Purchased with or without ms. Reviews 5×7 or 8×10 clear color glossy prints. Appreciate multicultural subjects. Pays $20-50 on publication.

Fiction: Adventure (that girls could experience in their hometowns or places they might realistically visit); humorous; mystery (believable only); romance (stories that deal with awakening awareness of boys are appreciated); suspense (can be serialized); religious (nothing preachy). Buys 30 mss/year. Submit complete ms. Length: 300-1,000 words. Pays 2½-5¢/word.

Poetry: Free verse, haiku, light verse, traditional. Buys 10/year. Length: 30 lines maximum. Pays $5-15 minimum.

Fillers: Puzzles, short humor, cartoons. Buys 3/issue. Pays $7-15.

Tips: "Prefers not to see anything on the adult level, secular material or violence. Writers frequently oversimplify the articles and often write with a Pollyanna attitude. An author should be able to see his/her writing style as exciting and appealing to girls ages 7-14. The style can be fun, but also teach a truth. The subject should be current and important to *Touch* readers. We would like to receive material that features a multicultural slant."

‡**TOY FARMER**, Toy Farmer Publications, 7496-106 A Ave. SE, LaMoune ND 58458. (701)883-5206. Fax: (701)883-5209. Editor: Claire D. Scheibe. Contact: Cathy Scheibe, assistant editor. 65% freelance written. Monthly magazine covering farm toys. Must slant toward youth involvement. Estab. 1978. Circ. 27,000. Pays on publication. Publishes ms an average of 1 month after acceptance. Byline given. Buys first North American serial rights. Editorial lead time 3 months. Submit seasonal material 3 months in advance. Accepts previously published submissions. Reports in 1 month on queries; 2 months on mss. Sample copy for $4. Writer's guidelines free on request.

Nonfiction: General interest, historical/nostalgic, humor, new product, technical. Buys 100 mss/year. Query with published clips. 800-1,500 words. Pays $50-150 for assigned articles. Sometimes pays expenses of writers on assignment.

Photos: State availability of photos with submission. Reviews transparencies. Offers no additional payment for photos accepted with ms. Buys one-time rights.

Columns/Departments: Buys 36 mss/year. Query with published clips. Pays $50-150.

TURTLE MAGAZINE FOR PRESCHOOL KIDS, Children's Better Health Institute, P.O. Box 567, Indianapolis IN 46206-0567. (317)636-8881. Editor: Nancy S. Alelrad. 90% freelance written. Bimonthly magazine (monthly March, June, September, December). General interest, interactive magazine with the purpose of helping preschoolers develop healthy minds and bodies. Pays on publication. May hold mss for up to 1 year before acceptance/publication. Byline given. Buys all rights. Submit seasonal/holiday material 8 months in advance. Reports in 3 months. Sample copy for $1.25. Writer's guidelines for #10 SASE.

Nonfiction: "Uses very simple science experiments. These should be pretested. Also publish simple, healthful recipes."

Fiction: All should have single-focus story lines and work well as read-alouds. "Most of the stories we use have a character-building bent, but are not preachy or overly moralistic. We are in constant need of stories to help a preschooler appreciate his/her body and what it can do; stories encouraging active, vigorous play; stories about good health. We no longer buy stories about 'generic' turtles because we now have PokeyToes, our own trade-marked turtle character. All should 'move along' and lend themselves well to illustration. Writing should be energetic, enthusiastic and creative—like preschoolers themselves."

Poetry: "We're especially looking for action rhymes to foster creative movement in preschoolers. We also use short verse on our back cover."

Tips: "We are trying to include more material for our youngest readers. Stories must be age-appropriate for two- to five-year-olds, entertaining and written from a healthy lifestyle perspective."

VENTURE, Christian Service Brigade, P.O. Box 150, Wheaton IL 60189-0150. (708)665-0630. Fax: (708)665-0372. E-mail: brigadecsb@aol.com. Website: http://infoweb.magi.com/~hbcsb/csb.htm. Editor: Deborah Christensen. 30% freelance written. Works with a small number of new/unpublished writers each year. Magazine published 5 times/year to support and compliment CSB's Stockade program. We aim to provide wholesome, entertaining reading for boys ages 8-11." Estab. 1959. Circ. 21,000. Pays on publication. Publishes ms an average of 6 months after acceptance, sometimes longer. Byline given. Offers $35 kill fee. Buys first North American serial, one-time and second serial (reprint) rights. Submit seasonal/holiday material 6 months in advance. Reports in 1 week. Sample copy for $1.85 and 9×12 SAE with 4 first-class stamps. Writer's guidelines for #10 SASE.

Nonfiction: General interest, humor, inspirational, interview/profile, personal experience, photo feature, religious. Buys 18-20 mss/year. Send complete ms. Length: 500-1,000 words. Pays $75-150 for assigned articles; $40-100 for unsolicited articles. Sometimes pays expenses of writers on assignment.

Reprints: Send typed ms with rights for sale noted. Pays 75% of amount paid for an original article.

Photos: Send photos with submission. Reviews color slides. Offers $50/photo. Buys one-time rights.

Fiction: Adventure, humorous, mystery, religious. Buys 10-12 mss/year. Send complete ms. Length: 500-1,000 words. Pays $40-100.

Tips: "Talk to young boys. Find out the things that interest them and write about those things. We are looking for material relating to our theme: Building Men to Serve Christ. We prefer shorter (1,000 words) pieces. Writers *must* weave Christianity throughout the story in a natural way, without preaching or token prayers. How does a boy's faith in Christ influence the way he responds to a situation. We want to see humor, humor, humor! Will accept disks or e-mail submissions only after we decide to publish piece. Don't send disks or e-mail submissions unsolicited."

WONDER TIME, 6401 The Paseo, Kansas City MO 64131. (816)333-7000. Fax: (816)333-4439. Editor: Lois Perrigo. 75% freelance written. "Willing to read and consider appropriate freelance submissions." Published weekly by WordAction for children ages 6-8. Correlates to the Bible Truth in the weekly Sunday School lesson. Pays on publication. Publishes ms an average of 1 year after acceptance. Byline given. Buys rights to reuse and all rights for curriculum assignments. Reports in 1 month. Sample copy and writer's guidelines for 9 × 12 SAE with 2 first-class stamps.

Fiction: Buys stories portraying Christian attitudes without being preachy. Uses stories for special days—stories teaching honesty, truthfulness, kindness, helpfulness or other important spiritual truths, and avoiding symbolism. Also, stories about real life problems children face today. "God should be spoken of as our Father who loves and cares for us; Jesus, as our Lord and Savior." Buys 52 mss/year. Length: 250-350 words. Pays $25 on publication.

Tips: "Any stories that allude to church doctrine must be in keeping with Wesleyan beliefs. Any type of fantasy must be in good taste and easily recognizable."

LITERARY AND "LITTLE"

Fiction, poetry, essays, book reviews and scholarly criticism comprise the content of the magazines listed in this section. Some are published by colleges and universities, and many are regional in focus.

Everything about "little" literary magazines is different than other consumer magazines. Most carry few or no ads, and many do not even seek them. Circulations under 1,000 are common. And sales often come more from the purchase of sample copies than from the newsstand.

The magazines listed in this section cannot compete with the pay rates and exposure of the high-circulation general interest magazines also publishing fiction and poetry. But most "little" literary magazines don't try. They are more apt to specialize in publishing certain kinds of fiction or poetry: traditional, experimental, works with a regional sensibility, or the fiction and poetry of new and younger writers. For that reason, and because fiction and poetry vary so widely in style, writers should *always* invest in the most recent copies of the magazines they aspire to publish in.

Many "little" literary magazines pay contributors only in copies of the issues in which their works appear. *Writer's Market* lists only those that pay their contributors in cash. However, *Novel & Short Story Writer's Market* includes nonpaying fiction markets, and has in-depth information about fiction techniques and markets. The same is true of *Poet's Market* for nonpaying poetry markets (both books are published by Writer's Digest Books). Many literary agents and book editors regularly read these magazines in search of literary voices not found in mainstream writing. There are also more literary opportunities listed in the Contests and Awards section.

‡**AFRICAN AMERICAN REVIEW**, Indiana State University, Department of English, ISU, Terre Haute IN 47809. (812)237-2968. Fax: (812)237-4382. E-mail: aschoal@amber.indstate.edu. Contact: Joe Weixlmann, editor. Managing Editor: Keith Byerman. 65% freelance written. Quarterly magazine covering African-American literature and culture. "Essays on African-American literature, theater, film, art and culture generally; interviews; poetry and fiction by African-American authors; book reviews." Estab. 1967. Circ. 3,976. Pays on publication. Publishes ms an average of 1 year after acceptance. Byline given. Buys first North American serial rights. Editorial lead time 1 year. Reports in 1 month on queries; 3 months on mss. Sample copy for $5. Writer's guidelines for #10 SASE.

Nonfiction: Essays, interview/profile. Buys 30 mss/year. Query. Length: 3,500-6,000 words. Pays $50-150. Pays in contributor copies upon request.

Photos: State availability of photos with submission. Offers no additional payment for photos accepted with ms. Captions required.

Fiction: Ethnic. Buys 4 mss/year. Send complete ms. Length: 2,500-5,000 words. Pays $50-150.

Poetry: Avant-garde, free verse, haiku, traditional. No light verse. Buys 20 poems/year. Submit maximum 6 poems. Pays $25-75.

ALASKA QUARTERLY REVIEW, College of Arts & Sciences, University of Alaska Anchorage, 3211 Providence Dr., Anchorage AK 99508. (907)786-4775. Executive Editor: Ronald Spatz. 95% freelance written. Prefers to work with published/established writers; eager to work with new/unpublished writers. Semiannual magazine publishing fiction, poetry, literary nonfiction and short plays in traditional and experimental styles. Estab. 1982. Circ. 1,500. Pays honorariums on publication when funding permits. Publishes ms an average of 6 months after acceptance. Byline given. Buys first North American serial rights. Upon request, rights will be transferred back to author after publication. Reports in 4 months. Sample copy for $5. Writer's guidelines for SASE.

Nonfiction: Literary nonfiction: essays and memoirs. Buys 0-5 mss/year. Query. Length: 1,000-20,000 words. Pays $50-200 subject to funding; pays in copies and subscriptions when funding is limited.

Fiction: Experimental and traditional literary forms. No romance, children's or inspirational/religious. Publishes novel excerpts. Buys 20-26 mss/year. Send complete ms. Length: Up to 20,000 words. Pays $50-200 subject to funding; pays in contributor's copies and subscriptions when funding is limited.

Drama: Experimental and traditional one-act plays. Buys 0-2 mss/year. Query. Length: Up to 20,000 words but prefers short plays. Pays $50-200 subject to funding; contributor's copies and subscriptions when funding is limited.

Poetry: Avant-garde, free verse, traditional. No light verse. Buys 10-30 poems/year. Submit maximum 10 poems. Pays $10-50 subject to availability of funds; pays in contributor's copies and subscriptions when funding is limited.

Tips: "All sections are open to freelancers. We rely almost exclusively on unsolicited manuscripts. *AQR* is a nonprofit literary magazine and does not always have funds to pay authors."

AMELIA MAGAZINE, Amelia Press, 329 E St., Bakersfield CA 93304. (805)323-4064. Editor: Frederick A. Raborg Jr. Estab. 1983. 100% freelance written. Eager to work with new/unpublished writers. "*Amelia* is a quarterly international magazine publishing the finest poetry and fiction available, along with expert criticism and reviews intended for all interested in contemporary literature. *Amelia* also publishes three supplements each year: *Cicada*, which publishes only high quality traditional or experimental haiku and senryu plus fiction, essays and cartoons pertaining to Japan; *SPSM&H*, which publishes the highest quality traditional and experimental sonnets available plus romantic fiction and essays pertaining to the sonnet; and the annual winner of the Charles William Duke long poem contest." Circ. 1,500. **Pays on acceptance.** Publishes ms an average of 6 months after acceptance. Byline given. Offers 50% kill fee. Buys first North American serial rights. Submit seasonal/holiday material 2 months in advance. Reports in 3 months on mss. Sample copy for $8.95 (includes postage). Sample copy of any supplement for $4.95. Writer's guidelines for #10 SASE.

● An eclectic magazine, open to greater variety of styles—especially genre and mainstream stories unsuitable for other literary magazines. Receptive to new writers.

Nonfiction: Historical/nostalgic (in the form of belles lettres); humor (in fiction or belles lettres); interview/profile (poets and fiction writers); opinion (on poetry and fiction only); personal experience (as it pertains to poetry or fiction in the form of belles lettres); travel (in the form of belles lettres only); criticism and book reviews of poetry and small press fiction titles. "Nothing overtly slick in approach. Criticism pieces must have depth; belles lettres must offer important insights into the human scene." Buys 8 mss/year. Send complete ms. Length: 1,000-2,000 words. Pays $25 or by arrangement. Sometimes pays the expenses of writers on assignment.

Fiction: Adventure, book excerpts (original novel excerpts only), erotica (of a quality seen in Anais Nin or Henry Miller only), ethnic, experimental, fantasy, historical, horror, humorous, mainstream, mystery, novel excerpts, science fiction, suspense, western. "We would consider slick fiction of the quality seen in *Esquire* or *Vanity Fair* and more excellent submissions in the genres—science fiction, wit, Gothic horror, traditional romance, stories with complex *raisons d'être*; avant-garde ought to be truly avant-garde." No pornography ("good erotica is not the same thing"). Buys 24-36 mss/year. Send complete ms. Length: 1,000-5,000 words. Pays $35 or by arrangement for exceptional work.

● Ranked as one of the best markets for fiction writers in *Writer's Digest*'s annual "Fiction 50," June 1996.

Poetry: Avant-garde, free verse, haiku, light verse, traditional. "No patently religious or stereotypical newspaper poetry." Buys 100-160 poems/year depending on lengths. Prefers submission of at least 3 poems. Length: 3-100 lines. Pays $2-25; additional payment for exceptional work, usually by established professionals. *Cicada* pays $10 each to 3 "best of issue" poets; *SPSM&H* pays $14 to 2 "best of issue" sonnets; winner of the long poem contest receives $100 plus copies and publication.

Tips: "*Have something to say* and say it well. If you insist on waving flags or pushing your religion, then do it with subtlety and class. We enjoy a good cry from time to time, too, but sentimentality does not mean we want to see mush. Read our fiction carefully for depth of plot and characterization, then try very hard to improve on it. With the growth of quality in short fiction, we expect to find stories of lasting merit. I also hope to begin seeing more critical essays which, without sacrificing research, demonstrate a more entertaining obliqueness to the style sheets, more 'new journalism' than MLA. In poetry, we also often look for a good 'storyline' so to speak. Above all we want to feel a sense of honesty and value in every piece."

AMERICAN SHORT FICTION, University of Texas Press, University of Texas at Austin, Dept. of English, Austin TX 78712-1164. (512)471-1772. Editor: Joseph Kruppa. 100% freelance written. Quarterly fiction magazine. "*American Short Fiction* carries fiction of all lengths up to and including the novella, and is aimed at a general readership. No special slant or philosophy is required in writing for our readers." Estab. 1990. **Pays on acceptance.** Publishes ms an average of 1 year after acceptance. Buys first serial rights. Reports in 4 months. Sample copy for $9.95 and $2 for foreign postage if necessary.

Fiction: "Stories are selected for their originality and craftsmanship. No condensed novels or slice-of-life vignettes, please." Publishes novel excerpts. Buys 20-30 mss/year. Send complete ms. Pays $400.

• Ranked as one of the best markets for fiction writers in *Writer's Digest*'s annual "Fiction 50," June 1996.

Tips: "Manuscripts are only accepted September 1-May 31."

ANTIETAM REVIEW, 7 W. Franklin St., Hagerstown MD 21740-4804. (301)791-3132. Contact: Susanne Kass, editor Editor: Ann Knox. 100% freelance written. Annual magazine of fiction (short stories), poetry and b&w photography. Estab. 1982. Circ. 1,500. Pays on publication. Byline given. Reports in 2 months. Sample copy for $3.15 (back issue), $5.25 (current issue). Writer's guidelines for SASE.

Fiction: Novel excerpts (if work as independent pieces), short stories of a literary quality. No religious, romance, erotica, confession, horror or condensed novels. Buys 9 mss/year. Query or send complete ms. Length: 5,000 words. Pays $50-100.

Poetry: Crystal Brown. Avant-garde, free verse, traditional. Does not want to see haiku, religious and most rhyme. Buys 15-20 poems/year. Submit 5 poems maximum. Pays $20.

Tips: "Spring 97 annual issue will need fiction, poetry and b&w photography not previously published. Still seeking high quality work from both published and emerging writers. Writers must live in or be native of, Maryland, Pennsylvania, Delaware, Virginia, West Virginia or District of Columbia. Also we now have a Literary Contest. We consider materials from September 1-February 1."

ANTIOCH REVIEW, P.O. Box 148, Yellow Springs OH 45387-0148. Editor: Robert S. Fogarty. Quarterly magazine for general, literary and academic audience. Estab. 1941. Copyright held by *Antioch Review*; reverts to author upon publication. Byline given. Pays on publication. Publishes ms an average of 10 months after acceptance. Reports in 2 months. Sample copy for $6. Writer's guidelines for #10 SASE.

Nonfiction: "Contemporary articles in the humanities and social sciences, politics, economics, literature and all areas of broad intellectual concern. Somewhat scholarly, but never pedantic in style, eschewing all professional jargon. Lively, distinctive prose insisted upon." Length: 2,000-8,000 words. Pays $10/published page.

Fiction: Quality fiction only, distinctive in style with fresh insights into the human condition. No science fiction, fantasy or confessions. Pays $10/published page.

Poetry: No light or inspirational verse. Contributors should be familiar with the magazine before submitting. "We do not read poetry May 15-September 1."

THE ATLANTEAN, (formerly *The Atlantean Press Review*), P.O. Box 7336, Golden CO 80403. Fax: (303)604-0788. Publisher: Patricia LeChevalier. 95% freelance written. Bimonthly magazine. "The Roman-tic-Realist school of literature and art is our primary focus. The essence of this kind of writing is choice—in fiction, the characters have free will and there is no sense that they are predestined; choice is also reflected in the fact that the writer exercises great selectivity in details, themes and characters." Estab. 1993. Circ. 500. Pays 50% on acceptance, 50% on publication. Byline given. Offers 50% kill fee. "We are now also looking for articles on 'real-life heroes'—achievers and innovators and their achievements." Buys one-time rights. Editorial lead time 3 months. Submit seasonal material at least 4 months in advance. Accepts simultaneous submissions. Reports in 2 months on queries, within 10 weeks on mss. Sample copies available. Writer's guidelines for SAE with 1 first-class stamp.

Nonfiction: Essays, interview/profile, photo feature. Buys 12 mss/year. Query. Length: 1,500-25,000 words. Pays $15 and up. Sometimes pays expenses of writers on assignment.

• *The Atlantean* reports an increased need for more nonfiction—essays, reviews and profiles.

Reprints: Accepts previously published submissions.

Photos: Send photos with submissions. Reviews contact sheets and prints. Negotiates payment individually. Model releases required. Buys one-time rights.

Columns/Departments: Reviews of books, films, music, visual art, 250 words (can be much longer). Buys 12 mss/year. Query. Pays $10-50.

Fiction: Adventure, fantasy (alternate world OK, but no supernaturalism), historical, mystery, novel excerpts, science fiction, suspense, western. "No erotica, confession, horror, religious, slice of life." Buys 20 mss/ year. Send complete ms. Length: 1,000-25,000 words. Pays $15-125.

Poetry: "Please study a sample issue. We rarely publish poems that don't rhyme." Especially interested in translations of 19th century Romantic works (e.g., Victor Hugo). "No work that depends on the appearance of the poem rather than its sound; nothing obscene, vulgar or malevolent." Buys 15 poems/year. Submit maximum 10 poems. Length: 4-300 lines. Pays $15-75.

Tips: "Our focus is on the Romantic school of art, so the best way to break in is to learn about this school. The best introduction is Ayn Rand's book *The Romantic Manifesto*, available at most bookstores or from us. If you've studied and understand the Romantic school, we'll be very interested in your work. If you haven't, it's unlikely your work would be right for us. For nonfiction writers, reviews of of articles about little known Romantic works or writers and artists would be welcome."

AUTHORS, 501 Cambridge St. SE, Medicine Hat, Alberta T1A 0T3 Canada. Fax: (403)526-8020. E-mail: authmag@aol.com. Website: http://public.navisoft.com/a/u/authors/index.htm. Editor: Philip Murphy. 100% freelance written. Monthly magazine providing a competitive platform that will both enhance professional skills as well as develop the novice. Estab. 1992. Circ. 300. Pays for assignments on publication. Byline given. Offer 50% kill fee. Buys one-time rights. Editorial lead time 2 months. Submit seasonal material 3 months in advance. Accepts simultaneous submissions. Reports in 2 weeks on queries; 1 month on mss. Sample copy and writer's guidelines free on request.
Nonfiction: Book excerpts, essays, general interet, historical/nostalgic, humor, inspirational, interview/profile, opinion, personal experience, religious, travel. Buys 6 mss/year. Query. Length: 1,500-10,000 words. Pays $150-250 for assigned articles and 1 free copy; $100 for unsolicited articles. Sometimes pays expenses of writers on assignment.
Reprints: Accepts previously published submissions.
Fiction: Adventure, condensed novel, confession, ethnic, experimental, fantasy, historical, horror, humorous, mainstream, mystery, novel excerpts, religious, romance, science fiction, serialized novels, slice-of-life vignettes, suspense, western. Buys 12 mss/year. Query. Length: 300-10,000 words. Pays $100.
Poetry: Avant-garde, free verse, haiku, light verse, traditional. Buys 12 poems/year. Length: 1-1,000 lines. Pays $100.
Fillers: Anecdotes, facts, short humor. Pays free copy.
Tips: "*Authors* is reluctant to send out rejection slips. Since its purpose is to provide a platform for both novice and professional writers, it will endeavour to publish all serious noncontroversial inquiries, either on a nonmonetary or monetary basis, affording them both exposure and feedback, limited only by the subscriber base."

BLACK WARRIOR REVIEW, P.O. Box 2936, Tuscaloosa AL 35486-2936. (205)348-4518. Contact: Mindy Wilson, editor. Managing Editor: Christopher Chambers. 95% freelance written. Semiannual magazine of fiction, poetry, essays and reviews. Estab. 1974. Circ. 2,000. Pays on publication. Publishes ms an average of 6 months after acceptance. Byline given. Buys first rights. Reports in 2 weeks on queries; 3 months on mss. Sample copy for $6. Writer's guidelines for #10 SASE.
   ● Consistently excellent magazine. Placed stories and poems in recent *Best American Short Stories*, *Best American Poetry* and *Pushcart Prize* anthologies.
Nonfiction: Interview/profile, book reviews and literary/personal essays. Buys 5 mss/year. Query or send complete ms. No limit on length. Payment varies.
Photos: State availability of photos with submission. Offers no additional payment for photos accepted with ms. Identification of subjects required. Buys one-time rights.
Fiction: Jim Hilgartner. Buys 10 mss/year. Publishes novel excerpts. One story/chapter per envelope, please.
Poetry: Anthony Caleshu. Submit 3-6 poems. Long poems encouraged. Buys 50 poems/year.
Tips: "Read the *BWR* before submitting; editor changes each year. Send us your best work. Submissions of photos and/or artwork is encouraged. We sometimes choose unsolicited photos/artwork for the cover. Address all submissions to the appropriate genre editor."

BOHEMIAN CHRONICLE, Bohemian Enterprises, P.O. Box 387, Largo FL 34649. Publisher: Emily Skinner. 90% freelance written. Monthly literary magazine/newsletter. "*Bohemian Chronicle* is an international publication dedicated to promoting sensitivity in the arts." Estab. 1991. Pays on publication. Publishes ms an average of 1 year after acceptance. Byline given. Buys first rights or all rights. Editorial lead time 4 months. Submit seasonal material 6 months in advance. Reports in 1 month on queries; 3 months on mss. Sample copy for $1 and #10 SASE. Writer's guidelines for #10 SASE.
Nonfiction: Essays, humor, inspirational, interview/profile, opinion, personal experience, photo feature, experimental. Would like to see more alternative nonfiction articles. Awards "Bohos" each year (the "best of . . ." the previous year's published works. Buys 10-20 mss/year. Send complete ms. Length: 1,500 words maximum. Pays $5 plus 5 copies.
Photos: Send photos with submission. (No slides.) Offers no additional payment for photos accepted with ms. Identification of subjects required. Buys one-time or all rights.
Fiction: Adventure, ethnic, experimental, historical, humorous, mystery, slice-of-life vignettes, suspense. Buys 60 mss/year. Send complete ms. Length: 500-1,500 words. Pays $5 plus 5 copies.
Poetry: Avant-garde, free verse. Buys 20 poems/year. Submit maximum 3 poems. Length: 1 page maximum. Pays $2 plus 2 copies.

BOULEVARD, Opojaz, Inc., P.O. Box 30386, Philadelphia PA 19103-4326. Editor: Richard Burgin. 100% freelance written. Triannual literary magazine covering fiction, poetry and essays. "*Boulevard* is a diverse triquarterly literary magazine presenting original creative work by well-known authors, as well as by writers of exciting promise." Estab. 1985. Circ. 3,000. Pays on publication. Publishes ms an average of 1 year after acceptance. Byline given. No kill fee. Buys first North American serial rights. Accepts simultaneous submissions. Reports in 2 weeks on queries; 2 months on mss. Sample copy for $7. Writer's guidelines for #10 SASE.

Nonfiction: Book excerpts, essays, interview/profile. "No pornography, science fiction, children's stories or westerns." Buys 8 mss/year. Send complete ms. Length: 8,000 words maximum. Pays $50-150 (sometimes higher).

Fiction: Confession, experimental, mainstream, novel excerpts. "We do not want erotica, science fiction, romance, western or children's stories." Buys 20 mss/year. Send complete ms. Length: 8,000 words maximum. Pays $50-150 (sometimes higher).

Poetry: Avant-garde, free verse, haiku, traditional. "Do not send us light verse." Buys 80 poems/year. Submit maximum 5 poems. Length: up to 200 lines. Pays $25-150 (sometimes higher).

Tips: "Read the magazine first. The work *Boulevard* publishes is generally recognized as among the finest in the country. We continue to seek more good literary or cultural essays. Send only your best work."

THE CAPILANO REVIEW, The Capilano Press Society, 2055 Purcell Way, North Vancouver, British Columbia V7J 3H5 Canada. Website: http://www.capcollege.bc.ca. Editor: Robert Sherrin. 100% freelance written. Triannual journal of fresh, original writing. Estab. 1972. Circ. 1,000. Pays on publication. Publishes ms 2 months after acceptance. Byline given. Buys first North American serial rights. Reports in 1 month on queries; 4 months on mss. Sample copy for $9. Writer's guidelines for #10 SASE.

• *The Capilano Review* is seeking more stories focusing on experiences in British Columbia or other areas of Canada, and more stories that reflect multiculturalism.

Nonfiction: Essays, interview/profile, personal experience, creative nonfiction. Buys 1-2 mss/year. Query. Pays $50-200 plus 2 copies and 1 year subscription. Sometimes pays expenses of writers on assignment.

Fiction: Literary. Buys 10-15 mss/year. Send complete ms. Pays $50-200.

Poetry: Avant-garde, free verse. Buys 40 poems/year. Submit maximum 10 poems. Pays $50-200.

THE CHARITON REVIEW, Northeast Missouri State University, Kirksville MO 63501-9915. (816)785-4499. Fax: (816)785-7486. Editor: Jim Barnes. 100% freelance written. Semiannual (fall and spring) magazine covering contemporary fiction, poetry, translation and book reviews. Circ. 600. Pays on publication. Publishes ms an average of 6 months after acceptance. Byline given. Buys first North American serial rights. Reports in 1 week on queries; 1 month on mss. Sample copy for $2.50 and 7×10 SAE with 4 first-class stamps.

Nonfiction: Essays, essay reviews of books. Buys 2-5 mss/year. Send complete ms. Length: 1,000-5,000. Pays $15.

Fiction: Ethnic, experimental, mainstream, novel excerpts, traditional. Publishes novel excerpts if they can stand alone. "We are not interested in slick material." Buys 6-10 mss/year. Send complete ms. Length: 1,000-6,000 words. Pays $5/page.

Poetry: Avant-garde, free verse, traditional. Buys 50-55 poems/year. Submit maximum 5 poems. Length: open. Pays $5/page.

Tips: "Read *Chariton*. Know the difference between good literature and bad. Know what magazine might be interested in your work. We are not a trendy magazine. We publish only the best. All sections are open to freelancers. Know your market or you are wasting your time—and mine. Do *not* write for guidelines; the only guideline is excellence in all matters."

CHELSEA, Chelsea Associates, P.O. Box 773, Cooper Station, New York NY 10276. Editor: Richard Foerster. 70% freelance written. Semiannual literary magazine. "We stress style, variety, originality. No special biases or requirements. Flexible attitudes, eclectic material. We take an active interest, as always, in cross-cultural exchanges, superior translations, and are leaning toward cosmopolitan, interdisciplinary techniques, but maintain no strictures against traditional modes." Estab. 1958. Circ. 1,500. Pays on publication. Publishes ms an average of 6 months after acceptance. Byline given. Buys first North American serial rights. Reports in 3 months on mss. Include SASE. Sample copy for $6.

• *Chelsea* also sponsors fiction and poetry contests. Send SASE for guidelines.

Nonfiction: Essays, book reviews (query first with sample). Buys 6 mss/year. Send complete ms. Length: 6,000 words. Pays $15/page.

Fiction: Mainstream, literary. Buys 12 mss/year. Send complete ms. Length: 5-6,000 words. Pays $15/page.

Poetry: Avant-garde, free verse, traditional. Buys 60-75 poems/year. Pays $15/page.

Tips: "We are looking for more super translations, first-rate fiction and work by writers of color."

CICADA, *Amelia Magazine*, 329 E St., Bakersfield CA 93304. (805)323-4064. Editor: Frederick A. Raborg, Jr. 100% freelance written. Quarterly magazine covering Oriental fiction and poetry (haiku, etc.). "Our readers expect the best haiku and related poetry forms we can find. Our readers circle the globe and know their subjects. We include fiction, book reviews and articles related to the forms or to the Orient." Estab. 1984. Circ. 600. Pays on publication. Publishes ms an average of 6 months after acceptance. Byline given. Offers 50% kill fee. Buys first North American serial rights. Editorial lead time 2 months. Submit seasonal material 3 months in advance. Accepts simultaneous submissions. Reports in 2 weeks on queries, 3 months on mss. Sample copy for $4.95. Writer's guidelines for #10 SASE.

Nonfiction: Essays, general interest, historical/nostalgic, humor, interview/profile, opinion, personal experience, travel. Buys 1-3 mss/year. Send complete ms. Length: 500-2,500 words. Pays $10.
Photos: Send photos with submission. Reviews 5×7 or 8×10 prints. Offers $10-25/photo. Model releases required. Buys one-time rights.
Fiction: Adventure, erotica, ethnic, experimental, fantasy, historical, horror, humorous, mainstream, mystery, romance, science fiction, slice-of-life vignettes, suspense. Buys 4 mss/year. Send complete ms. Length: 500-2,500 words. Pays $10-20.
Poetry: Buys 400 poems/year. Submit maximum 12 poems. Length: 1-50 lines. Pays 3 "best of issue" poets $10.
Fillers: Anecdotes, short humor. Buys 1-4/year. Length: 25-500 words. No payment for fillers.
Tips: "Writers should understand the limitations of contemporary Japanese forms particularly. We also use poetry based on other Asian ethnicities and on the South Seas ethnicities. Don't be afraid to experiment within the forms. Be professional in approach and presentation."

CIMARRON REVIEW, Oklahoma State University, 205 Morrill Hall, OSU, Stillwater OK 74078-0135. (405)744-9476. Editor: E.P. Walkiewicz. 85% freelance written. Quarterly literary magazine. "We publish short fiction, poetry, and essays of serious literary quality by writers often published, seldom published and previously unpublished. We have no bias with respect to subject matter, form (traditional or experimental) or theme. Though we appeal to a general audience, many of our readers are writers themselves or members of a university community." Estab. 1967. Circ. 500. Pays on publication. Published ms an average of 1 year after acceptance. Byline given. Buys all rights (reprint permission freely granted on request). Reports in 1 week on queries; 3 months on mss. Sample copy for $3 and 7×10 SASE. Writer's guidelines for #10 SASE.
Nonfiction: Essays, general interest, historical, interview/profile, opinion, personal experience, travel, literature and arts. "We are not interested in highly subjective personal reminiscences, obscure or arcane articles, or short, light 'human interest' pieces." Special issues: flash fiction; Native American writers; Irish writers. Buys 9-12 mss/year. Send complete ms. Length: 1,000-7,500 words. Pays $50 plus 1 year's subscription.
Fiction: Mainstream, literary. No juvenile or genre fiction. Buys 12-17 mss/year. Send complete ms. Length: 1,250-7,000 words. Pays $50.
Poetry: Free verse, traditional. No haiku, light verse or experimental poems. Buys 55-70 poems/year. Submit maximum 6 poems. Pays $15/poem.
Tips: "For prose, submit legible, double-spaced typescript with name and address on manuscript. Enclose SASE and brief cover letter. For poetry, same standards apply, but single-spaced is conventional. Be familiar with high quality, contemporary mainstream writing. Evaluate your own work carefully."

CLOCKWATCH REVIEW, (a journal of the arts), Dept. of English, Illinois Wesleyan University, Bloomington IL 61702-2900. (309)556-3352. Editor: James Plath. 85% freelance written. Semiannual literary magazine. Estab. 1983. Circ. 1,400. **Pays on acceptance.** Byline given. Buys first North American serial rights. Submit seasonal/holiday material 6 months in advance. Reports in 6 months. Sample copy for $4. Writer's guidelines for #10 SASE.
Nonfiction: Literary essays, criticism (MLA style), interviews with writers, musicians, artists. Buys 4-8 mss/year. Query with or without published clips. Length: 1,500-4,000 words. Pays up to $25.
Photos: State availability of photos with submission. Reviews contact sheets, negatives, transparencies. Offers no additional payment for photos accepted with ms. Buys one-time rights.
Fiction: Experimental, humorous, mainstream, novel excerpts. "Also literary quality genre stories that break the mold. No straight mystery, fantasy, science fiction, romance or western." Buys 8-10 mss/year. Send complete ms. Length: 1,500-4,000 words. Pays up to $25.
Poetry: Avant-garde, free verse, light verse, traditional. Buys 30-40 poems/year. Submit maximum 6 poems. Length: 32 lines maximum. Pays $5.

CONFRONTATION, A Literary Journal, Long Island University, Brookville NY 11548. (516)299-2391. Fax: (516)299-2735. Editor: Martin Tucker. Assistant to Editor: Emily Berkowitz. 75% freelance written. Semiannual literary magazine. "We are eclectic in our taste. Excellence of style is our dominant concern." Estab. 1968. Circ. 2,000. Pays on publication. Publishes ms an average of 1 year after acceptance. Byline given. "We rarely offer kill fee." Buys first North American serial, first, one-time or all rights. Accepts simultaneous submissions. Reports in 3 weeks on queries; 2 months on mss. Sample copy for $3.
Nonfiction: Essays, personal experience. Buys 15 mss/year. Send complete ms. Length: 1,500-5,000 words. Pays $100-300 for assigned articles; $15-300 for unsolicited articles.
Photos: State availability of photos with submission. Offers no additional payment for photos accepted with ms. Buys one-time rights.
Fiction: Katherine Hill-Miller. Experimental, mainstream, science fiction, slice-of-life vignettes, novel excerpts (if they are self-contained stories). "We judge on quality, so genre is open." Buys 60-75 mss/year. Send complete ms. Length 6,000 words maximum. Pays $25-250.
Poetry: Joseph Cosenza. Avant-garde, free verse, haiku, light verse, traditional. Buys 60-75 poems/year. Submit maximum 6 poems. Length open. Pays $10-100.
Tips: "Most open to fiction and poetry."

CRAZYHORSE, Crazyhorse Association at UALR, English Dept., University of Arkansas, Little Rock AR 72204. (501)569-3161. Contact: Zabelle Stodola, business manager. Editor: Ralph Burns. 100% freelance written. Semiannual magazine of short fiction and poetry. "*Crazyhorse* publishes quality poetry and short fiction; no special slant." Estab. 1960. Circ. 1,000. Pays on publication. Publishes ms 1 year after acceptance. Buys first North American serial rights. Editorial lead time 18 months. Reports in 3 weeks on queries; 6 months on mss. Sample copy for $5 and #10 SASE.

Nonfiction: Dennis Vannatta: criticism editor. Interview/profile, reviews of contemporary poetry and short fiction. Buys 3 mss/year. Send complete ms. Length 1,000-6,000 words. Pays $10/printed page and 2 contributor's copies.

Fiction: Judy Troy, fiction editor. Mainstream; short fiction only. Buys 10 mss/year. Send complete ms. Length: 500-10,000 words. Pays $10/printed page and 2 contributor's copies.

Poetry: Ralph Burns: poetry editor. Traditional. Buys 50-60 poems/year. Submit maximum 6 poems. Pays $10/printed page and 2 contributor's copies.

Tips: "Buy a sample copy to see the kind of work we publish. We do not have any guidelines for poetry or short fiction."

‡CURRICULUM VITAE, Curriculum Vitae, Rd. #1 Box 226A, Polk PA 16342-9204. Editor: Michael Dittman. Managing Editor: Mark McClusky. 50% freelance written. Quarterly magazine covering pop culture with a Generation-X intellectual edge. "We cater to an audience of highly-educated with young readers who are concerned with social and philosophical issues." Estab. 1995. Circ. 2,500. Pays on publication. Publishes ms an average of 3 months after acceptance. Byline given. Offers 10% kill fee. Editorial lead time 3 months. Submit seasonal material 3 months in advance. Accepts simultaneous submissions. Reports in 3 weeks on queries; 1 month on mss. Sample copy for $4. Writer's guidelines for #10 SASE.

Nonfiction: Book excerpts, essays, exposé, general interest, interview/profile, new product, opinion (does not mean letters to the editor), personal experience, photo feature, travel. No overly sentimental articles. Buys 6 mss/year. Pays $15-100. Sometimes pays writers with contributor's copies. Sometimes pays expenses of writers on assignment.

Reprints: Accepts previously published submissions.

Photos: Send photos with submission. Reviews contact sheets. Offers no additional payment for photos accepted with ms. Captions, model releases and identification of subjects required.

Columns/Departments: Reviews (film, book, product) 100 words. Buys 12 mss/year. Query. Send complete ms. Pays $5-25.

Fiction: Erotica, ethnic, experimental, novel excerpts, serialized novels. "Must be top-notch cutting edge, no sentimentality." Buys 3 mss/year. Query. Send complete ms. Pays $5-100.

Poetry: Avant-garde, free verse, haiku, traditional. "Moon, June, croon stuff is a big no." Buys 2 poems/year. Submit maximum 5 poems. Pays $5-25.

Tips: "*Curriculum Vitae* is committed to giving breaks to new writers. We want edgy work. We want new writing. We want to reshape American culture. We especially want to work with hungry new artists. All of our issues have themes. Artists should query ahead of time for the theme. We make exceptions for great work."

DANDELION, Dandelion Magazine Society, 922 Ninth Ave. SE, Calgary, Alberta T2G 0S4 Canada. (403)265-0524. Managing Editor: Bonnie Bennoit. 90% freelance written. Semiannual magazine. "*Dandelion* is a literary and visual arts journal with an international audience. There is no restriction on subject matter or form, be it poetry, fiction, visual art or review." Reviews Canadian book authors—showcases Canadian visual artists. Estab. 1975. Circ. 1,000. Pays on publication. Publishes ms an average of 3 months after acceptance. Byline given. Buys one-time rights. Editorial lead time 3 months. Reports in 3 weeks on queries; 4 months on mss. Sample copy for $5. Writer's guidelines for #10 SAE and IRC.

Nonfiction: Margo Laing, reviews editor. Buys 4-6 mss/year. Query with published clips. Length: 750 words.

Photos: Alice Simmons. Send photos with submission. Reviews contact sheets. Negotiates payment individually. Captions required. Buys one-time rights.

Fiction: Elizabeth Haynes and Adele Megann, fiction editors. Adventure, ethnic, experimental, historical, humorous, mainstream, novel excerpts. Buys 6-8 mss/year. Send complete ms. Length: approx. 3,500 words maximum. Pays $125.

ALWAYS SUBMIT unsolicited manuscripts or queries with a self-addressed, stamped envelope (SASE) within your country or a self-addressed envelope with International Reply Coupons (IRC) purchased from the post office for other countries.

Poetry: Gordon Pengilly, Janeen Werner-King, Bob Stallworthy, poetry editors. Avant-garde, free verse, haiku, traditional, long poem. Buys 50 poems/year. Submit maximum 10 poems. Pays $15/poem; payment negotiated for long poems.

Tips: "The mandate is so large and general, only a familiarity with literary journals and reviews will help. Almost all our material comes unsolicited; thus, find out what we publish and you'll have a means of 'breaking in.' "

DESCANT, Descant Arts & Letters Foundation, P.O. Box 314, Station P, Toronto, Ontario M5S 2S8. (416)593-2557. Editor: Karen Mulhallen. Managing Editor: Tracy Jenkins. Quarterly literary journal. Estab. 1970. Circ. 1,200. Pays on publication. Publishes ms 16 months after acceptance. Editorial lead time 4 months. Submit seasonal material 4 months in advance. Sample copy for $8. Writer's guidelines for SASE.

Nonfiction: Book excerpts, essays, historical/nostalgic, interview/profile, personal experience, photo feature, travel. Special issues: Former Yugoslavia (fall 1996). Query or send complete ms. Pays $100 honorarium plus 1 year's subscription.

Photos: State availability of photos with submission. Reviews contact sheets and prints. Offers no additional payment for photos accepted with ms. Buys one-time rights.

Fiction: Send complete ms. Pays $100.

Poetry: Free verse, light verse, traditional. Submit maximum 10 poems. Pays $100.

Tips: "Familiarize yourself with our magazine before submitting."

EAGLE'S FLIGHT, P.O. Box 465, Granite OK 73547. (405)535-2452. Editor: Shyamkant Kulkarni. 60% freelance written. Quarterly literary tabloid "read by young and new writers with talent for writing. They should understand networking." Estab. 1989. Circ. 300. Pays on publication. Publishes ms an average of 1 year after acceptance. Buys first North American serial, first or one-time rights. Editorial lead time 3 months. Submit seasonal material 3 months in advance. Accepts simultaneous submissions. Reports in 6 weeks on queries; 6 months on mss. Sample copy for $1.25 and #10 SASE. Writer's guidelines for #10 SASE.

Fiction: Contact: Rekha Kulkarni. Adventure, condensed novels, humorous, mainstream, mystery, romance, slice-of-life vignettes, suspense. Buys 4-8 mss/year. Send complete ms. Length: 500-2,500 words. Pays $5-20.

Poetry: Avant-garde, free verse, haiku, light verse, traditional. Buys 8-10 poems/year. Submit maximum 10 poems. Length: 5-30. Pays $5 maximum (mostly contributor's copies or 1 year subscription).

Tips: "A writer should be ready to read and appreciate other writers as well. One needs to read and read successful writers, develop his own style and form, search his heart and try to reach the truth."

FIELD MAGAZINE, Contemporary Poetry & Poetics, Rice Hall, Oberlin College, Oberlin OH 44074-1095. (216)775-8407/8. Fax: (216)775-8124. Editors: Stuart Friebert, David Young, David Walker, Alberta Turner. Managing Editor: Dolorus Nevels. 60% freelance written. Semiannual magazine of poetry, poetry in translation, and essays on contemporary poetry by poets. Estab. 1969. Circ. 2,300. Pays on publication. Byline given. Buys first rights. Editorial lead time 4 months. Reports in 1 month on mss. Sample copy for $7.

Poetry: Buys 100 poems/year. Submit maximum 10 poems. Pays $15-25 minimum/page.

‡FIRST WORD BULLETIN, Amick Associates Magazines, Box 500, Calle Domingo Fernandez 5, 28036 Madrid Spain. (34)1-359-64-18. Fax: (34)1-320-8961. E-mail: george.washington@mad.servicom.es. Editor: G.W. Amick. 60-80% freelance written. Quarterly magazine. "Our audience is the general public, but the magazine is specifically aimed at writers who wish to get published for credits. We welcome unpublished writers; since our audience is mainly writers we expect high-quality work. We like writers who have enough self-confidence to be willing to pay the postage to get to us. They should write for guidelines first and then follow them to the letter." Estab. 1995. Pays on publication. Publishes ms an average of 6 months after acceptance. Byline given. Offers 10% kill fee or $5. Buys first world or second serial (reprint) rights. Editorial lead time 3 months. Submit seasonal material 5 months in advance. Accepts simultaneous submissions. Reports in 3 weeks on queries; 2 months on mss. Sample copy for $3.50 and SAE with $3 postage or 3 IRCs. Writer's guidelines free on request for SAE with $2 postage or 2 IRCs.

Nonfiction: General interest, how-to, humor, personal experience, environment, self-help. Buys 40 mss/year. Send complete ms. Length: 500-4,000 words. Pays 25¢/word to $50. Pays in contributor copies for fillers, bullets, pieces less than 50 words.

Reprints: Accepts previously published submissions.

Fiction: Adventure, environment, experiment, humorous, mainstream, self-help. No smut, pornographic, science fiction, romance/love stories or horror. Buys 10-30 mss/year. Send complete ms. Length: 500-4,000 words. Pays 25¢/word to $50.

Poetry: Free verse, light verse. "We are not interested in poetry per se, but will accept poetry as a sidebar or filler." Buys 4-8 poems/year. Submit maximum 1 poem. Length: 14 lines for filler; 24 lines for sidebar. Pays 25¢/word.

Fillers: Anecdotes, facts, gags to be illustrated by cartoonist, short humor. Buys 32/year. Length: 10-80 words. Pays 25¢/word.

Tips: "Write for guidelines. Pay close attention to the market study. Follow directions to the letter. Get the editor's name correct. Don't request return of manuscript, ask for the first page only to save postage. If you submit a self-help article, don't let God do all the work. For an environmental article, study the subject carefully and get your facts correct. Use positive thinking at all times. Last year was heavy on ecology and I still feel strong about it but this year I would like to see something on alternative medicine, homeopathy, perhaps some exotic stories on medicines from herbs in Brazil and Venezuela. I need crossword puzzles also."

‡FORKROADS, A Journal of Ethnic American Literature, Forkroads Press, Box 150, Spencertown NY 12165. (518)392-9607. Editor: David Kherdian. Contact: Nonny Hogrogian, associate editor. 100% freelance written. Quarterly magazine covering ethnic American literature only. Prefers first person memoirs, and stories, poems, plays that come out of one's experience as an ethnic American. Estab. 1995. Circ. 5,000. Pays on publication. Publishes ms an average of 4 months after acceptance. Buys first North American serial and rights for inhouse publications and resale to other mags and anthologies, etc. Editorial lead time 3 months. Accepts simultaneous submissions. Reports in 2 weeks on queries; 2 months on mss. Sample copy for $6. Writer's guidelines for #10 SASE.
Nonfiction: Book excerpts, essays, interview/profile, personal experience. Buys 20 mss/year. Send complete ms. Length: 1,000-7,000 words. Pays $50-200. Sometimes pays expenses of writers on assignment.
Photos: Send photos with submission. Offers no additional payment for photos accepted with ms. Identification of subjects required. Buys one-time rights.
Columns/Departments: Studies of literature of separate ethnic groups (personal, intimate), 6,000 words; Storytelling (working method, personal stance, etc. of storytellers), 2,000 words; Growing up ethnic in America (personal, intimate first person memoir), 6,000 words. Buys 16 mss/year. Query. Pays $100-200.
Fiction: Ethnic, novel excerpts, short stories, memoirs, one act plays, poetry (all must be ethnic) book reviews. Buys 8 mss/year. Send complete ms. Length: 500-6,000 words. Pays $50-200.
Poetry: Buys free verse and traditional poetry. Buys 40 poems/year. Submit maximum of 6 poems. Pays $25-50.

‡FRANK, An International Journal of Contemporary Writing & Art, The Association Frank, 32 rue Edouard Vaillant, Montreuil France. (33)(1)48596658. E-mail: david@paris-anglo.com. Website: http://www.paris-anglo.com/frank. Editor: David Applefield. 80% freelance written. Bilingual magazine covering contemporary writing of all genres. "Writing that takes risks and isn't ethnocentric is looked upon favorably." Estab. 1983. Circ. 4,000. Pays on publication. Publishes ms an average of 1 year after acceptance. Byline given. Buys one-time rights. Editorial lead time 6 months. Reports in 1 month on queries; 2 months on mss. Sample copy for $10. Writer's guidelines free on request.
Nonfiction: Interview/profile, travel. Buys 2 mss/year. Query. Pays $100. Pays in contributor copies by agreement.
Photos: State availability of photos with submission. Negotiates payment individually. Buys one-time rights.
Fiction: Experimental, international. Buys 8 mss/year. Send complete ms. Length: 1-3,000 words. Pays $100.
Poetry: Avant-garde, translations. Buys 20 poems/year. Submit maximum 10 poems. Pays $20.
Tips: "Suggest what you do or know best. Avoid query form letters—we won't read the manuscript."

THE GETTYSBURG REVIEW, Gettysburg College, Gettysburg PA 17325. (717)337-6770. Editor: Peter Stitt. Managing Editor: Emily Ruark Clarke. Quarterly literary magazine. "Our concern is quality. Manuscripts submitted here should be extremely well-written." Estab. 1988. Circ. 4,000. Pays on publication. Byline given. Buys first North American serial rights. Editorial lead time 1 year. Submit seasonal material 9 months in advance. Reports in 1 month on queries; 3 months on mss. Sample copy for $7. Writer's guidelines for #10 SASE. Reading period September-May.
Nonfiction: Essays. Buys 20/year. Send complete ms. Length: 3,000-7,000. Pays $25/page.
Fiction: High quality, literary. Publishes novel excerpts. Buys 20 ms/year. Send complete ms. Length: 2,000-7,000. Pays $25/page.
Poetry: Buys 50 poems/year. Submit maximum 3 poems. Pays $2/line.

GLIMMER TRAIN STORIES, Glimmer Train Press, Inc., 710 SW Madison St., #504, Portland OR 97205. (503)221-0836. Fax: (503)221-0837. Contact: Linda Davies, co-editor. Co-editor: Susan Burmeister-Brown. 90% freelance written. Quarterly magazine covering short fiction. "We are interested in well-written, emotionally-moving short stories published by unknown, as well as known, writers." Estab. 1991. Circ. 16,000. Pays on acceptance. Byline given. Buys first rights. Accepts simultaneous submissions. Reports in 3 months on mss. Sample copy for $9. Writer's guidelines for #10 SASE.
Fiction: "We are not restricted to any types (other than erotica or condensed novels)." Buys 32 mss/year. Send complete ms. Length: 1,200-8,000 words. Pays $500.
  • Ranked as one of the best markets for fiction writers in *Writer's Digest*'s annual "Fiction 50," June 1996.

Tips: "Manuscripts should be sent to us in the months of January, April, July and October. Be sure to include a sufficiently-stamped SASE. We are particularly interested in receiving work from new writers." See *Glimmer Train*'s Short Story Award for New Writers' listing in Contest and Awards section.

GRAIN LITERARY MAGAZINE, Saskatchewan Writers Guild, P.O. Box 1154, Regina, Saskatchewan S7K 2Z4 Canada. Fax: (306)665-7707. E-mail: grain@bailey2.unibase.com. Website: http://www.sasknet. com/corporate/skwriter. Contact: J. Jill Robinson, editor. Business Manager: Steven Smith. 100% freelance written. Quarterly literary magazine covering poetry, fiction, creative nonfiction, drama. "*Grain* publishes writing of the highest quality, both traditional and nontraditional in nature. *The Grain* editors' aim: To publish work that challenges its readers; to encourage promising new writers; and to produce a well-designed, visually exciting magazine." Estab. 1971. Circ. 1,800. Pays on publication. Publishes ms an average of 11 months after acceptance. Byline given. Buys first, Canadian, serial rights. Editorial lead time 6 months. Reports in 1 month on queries; 3 months on mss. Sample copy for $6.95. Writer's guidelines free on request.
Nonfiction: Interested in creative nonfiction.
Fiction: Literary fiction of all types. "No romance, confession, science fiction, vignettes, mystery." Buys 40 mss/year. Query or send complete ms. Pays $30-100. Publishes novel excerpts.
Poetry: Avant-garde, free verse, haiku, traditional. "High quality, imaginative, well-crafted poetry. No sentimental, end-line rhyme, mundane." Buys 78 poems/year. Submit maximum 10 poems. Pays $30-100.
Tips: "Submit your best unpublished work."

‡GRAND TOUR, The Journal of Travel Literature, P.O. Box 66, Thorofare NJ 08086. Editor: Jason Wilson. Contact: Jennifer Fisher, managing editor. 100% freelance written. Quarterly magazine covering the genre of travel reportage. Estab. 1996. Circ. 3,000. Pays on publication. Publishes ms an average of 6 months after acceptance. Byline given. Buys first North American or second serial (reprint) rights. Editorial lead time 3 months. Submit seasonal material 6 months in advance. Reports in 2 months on mss. Sample copy for $8.95. Writer's guidelines for #10 SASE.
Nonfiction: Book excerpts, essays, historical/nostalgic, humor, personal experience, travel. "We do not want traditional travel magazine pieces, how-to, etc." Buys 40-50 mss/year. Send complete ms. Length: 1,000-7,000 words. Pays $50-200 for unsolicited articles. Sometimes pays expenses of writers on assignment.
Reprints: Accepts previously published submissions.
Poetry: "We do not want any poetry that does not deal specifically with **place**." Buys 8 poems/year. Submit maximum 4 poems. Pays $10-50.
Tips: "Read Paul Theroux, V.S. Naipaul, Annie Dillard, Joan Didion, John McPhee, Ted Conover, etc."

HIGH PLAINS LITERARY REVIEW, 180 Adams St., Suite 250, Denver CO 80206. (303)320-6828. Contact: Robert O. Greer, Jr., editor-in-chief. Managing Editor: Phyllis A. Harwell. 80% freelance written. Triannual literary magazine. "The *High Plains Literary Review* publishes short stories, essays, poetry, reviews and interviews, bridging the gap between commercial quarterlies and academic reviews." Estab. 1986. Circ. 1,200. Pays on publication. Byline given. Buys first North American serial rights. Accepts simultaneous submissions. Reports in 3 months. Sample copy for $4. Writer's guidelines for #10 SASE.
  ● Its unique editorial format—between commercial and academic—makes for lively reading. Could be good market for that "in between" story.
Nonfiction: Essays, reviews. Buys 20 mss/year. Send complete ms. Length: 10,000 words maximum. Pays $5/page.
Fiction: Ethnic, historical, humorous, mainstream. Buys 12 mss/year. Send complete ms. Length: 10,000 words maximum. Pays $5/page.
Poetry: Buys 45 poems/year. Pays $10/page.

THE HOLLINS CRITIC, P.O. Box 9538, Hollins College, Roanoke VA 24019. Contact: Ara W. Morgan, associate editor. 18% freelance written. "Non-specialist periodical published 5 times/year with artist's cover sketch and an essay on work of a contemporary poet, fiction writer or dramatist. Brief book review section and a few poems. *The Hollins Critic* owns the copyright." Estab. 1964. Circ. 488. Pays on publication. Buys all rights. Sample copy for $1.25. Writer's guidelines for #10 SASE.
Nonfiction: Essays. Buys 3 mss/year. Query with published clips and SASE. Length: 4,500-5,000 words. Pays $200 for feature essay.

INDIANA REVIEW, Indiana University, 316 N. Jordan, Bloomington IN 47405. (812)855-3439. Editor: Shirley Stephenson. Associate Editor: Geoffry Pollock. 100% freelance written. Semiannual magazine. "We publish innovative fiction and poetry. We're interested in energy, originality and careful attention to craft. While we publish many well-known writers, we also welcome new and emerging poets and fiction writers." Estab. 1982. **Pays on acceptance.** Byline given. Buys first North American serial rights. Reports within 4 months. Sample copy for $7. Free writer's guidelines.
Nonfiction: Essays. No strictly academic articles dealing with the traditional canon. Buys 8 mss/year. Query. Length: 7,500 maximum. Pays $25-200.

Fiction: Experimental, mainstream. Buys 18 mss/year. Send complete ms. Length: 250-15,000. Pays $5/page.

Poetry: Avant-garde, free verse. Looks for inventive and skillful writing. Buys 80 mss/year. Submit up to 5 poems at one time only. Length: 5 lines minimum. Pays $5/page.

Tips: "Read us before you submit. Often reading is slower in summer months."

THE IOWA REVIEW, 369 EPB, The University of Iowa, Iowa City IA 52242. (319)335-0462. Fax: (319)335-2535. Website: http://www.uiowa.edu/english/iareview.html. Editor: David Hamilton. Contact: Mary Hussmann, associate editor. Triannual magazine. Estab. 1970. Buys first serial rights. Reports in 3 months. Sample copy for $6.

Nonfiction, Fiction and Poetry: "We publish essays, reviews, stories and poems and would like for our essays not always to be works of academic criticism." Buys 65-85 unsolicited mss/year. Submit complete ms with SASE. Pays $1/line for verse; $10/page for prose.

• This magazine uses the help of colleagues and graduate assistants. Its reading period is September-April.

IOWA WOMAN, Iowa Woman Endeavors, Inc., P.O. Box 680, Iowa City IA 52244-0680. Contact: Joan Taylor, editor. Managing Editor: Kristen Hanlon. Quarterly magazine of "award-winning fiction, poetry, essays, reviews, interviews and visual art by women everywhere. For readers of fine literature anywhere. As the publication of a nonprofit educational organization, we steer away from rhetoric and polemics." Estab. 1979. Circ. 2,500. Pays on publication. Publishes ms an average of 8 months after acceptance. Byline given. Buys first North American serial rights. Submit seasonal material 1 year in advance. Reports in 2 weeks on queries, 3 months on mss. Sample copy for $6.95. Writer's guidelines for #10 SASE.

Nonfiction: Essays, historical, humor, interview/profile articles, personal experience. "No rhetorical slant on current political or environmental causes." Buys 16 mss/year. Query or send complete ms. Length: 2,000-6,000. Pays $5/page and 2 copies. Sometimes pays expenses of writers on assignment.

Photos: State availability of or send photos with submission. Reviews contact sheets. Offers no additional payment for photos accepted with ms. Captions, model releases and identification of subjects required. Buys one time rights.

Fiction: Adventure, ethnic, experimental, fantasy, historical, humorous, mystery, science fiction, slice-of-life vignettes, women, novel excerpts. "Nothing raunchy or maudlin." Buys 12 mss/year. Send complete ms. Length: 6,500 words maximum. Pays $5/page.

Poetry: Debra Marquart, poetry editor. Free verse, traditional. "No greeting card types or predictable rhymes or rhythms." Buys 25-40 poems/year. Submit maximum 5 poems. Pays $5/poem.

Tips: "We publish many writers and artists each year for their first time and welcome new and emerging writers who submit quality work in any sector of the magazine. Submissions have a better chance through the year; don't necessarily wait for the annual writing contest which is quite competitive."

JAPANOPHILE, P.O. Box 223, Okemos MI 48864-0223. E-mail: japanlove@aol.com. or xtxp326@prodig y.com. Website: http://www.voyager.net/japanophile. Editor: Earl Snodgrass. 80% freelance written. Works with a small number of new/unpublished writers each year. Quarterly magazine for literate people who are interested in Japanese culture anywhere in the world. Estab. 1974. Pays on publication. Publishes ms an average of 3 months after acceptance. Buys first North American serial rights. Reports in 3 months. Sample copy for $4, postpaid. Writer's guidelines for #10 SASE.

• *Japanophile* would like to receive more haiku and more humorous articles and fillers. It needs more book reviews. It would also like to find one or more columnists to cover: California, Hawaii, New York. This column would probably be like "Tokyo Topics."

Nonfiction: "We want material on Japanese culture in *North America or anywhere in the world*, even Japan. We want articles, preferably with pictures, about persons engaged in arts of Japanese origin: a Michigan naturalist who is a haiku poet, a potter who learned raku in Japan, a vivid 'I was there' account of a Go tournament in California. We would like to hear more about what it's like to be a Japanese in the U.S. Our particular slant is a certain kind of culture wherever it is in the world: Canada, the U.S., Europe, Japan. The culture includes flower arranging, haiku, sports, religion, travel, art, photography, fiction, etc. It is important to study the magazine." Buys 8 mss/issue. Query preferred but not required. Length: 1,600 words maximum. Pays $8-20.

Reprints: Send information about when and where the article was previously published. Pays up to 100% of amount paid for original article.

Photos: Pays $10-20 for glossy prints. "We prefer b&w people pictures."

Fiction: Experimental, mainstream, mystery, adventure, humorous, romance, historical. Themes should relate to Japan or Japanese culture. Length: 1,000-4,000 words. Annual contest pays $100 to best short story (contest reading fee $5). Should include 1 or more Japanese and non-Japanese characters in each story.

Columns/Departments: Regular columns and features are Tokyo Topics and Japan in North America. "We also need columns about Japanese culture in various American cities." Query. Length: 1,000 words. Pays $20 maximum.

Poetry: Traditional, avant-garde and light verse related to Japanese culture or any subject in a Japanese form such as haiku. Length: 3-50 lines. Pays $1-20.

Fillers: Newsbreaks, clippings and short humor of up to 200 words. Pays $1-5.

Tips: "We prefer to see more articles about Japanese culture in the U.S., Canada and Europe. Lack of convincing fact and detail is a frequent mistake."

THE JOURNAL, Ohio State University, 421 Denney Hall, 164 W. 17th Ave., Columbus OH 43210. (614)292-4076. Editors: Kathy Fagan, Michelle Herman. 100% freelance written. Semiannual literary magazine. "We're open to all forms; we tend to favor work that gives evidence of a mature and sophisticated sense of the language." Estab. 1972. Circ. 1,500. Pays on publication. Byline given. Buys first North American serial rights. Reports in 2 weeks on queries; 2 months on mss. Sample copy for $5. Writer's guidelines for #10 SASE.

Nonfiction: Essays, interview/profile. Buys 2 mss/year. Query. Length: 2,000-4,000 words. Pays $25 maximum and contributor's copies.

Columns/Departments: Reviews of contemporary poetry, 2,000-4,000 words. Buys 2 mss/year. Query. Pays $25.

Fiction: Novel excerpts, literary short stories. Pays $25 minimum.

Poetry: Avant-garde, free verse, traditional. Buys 100 poems/year. Submit maximum 5 poems/year. Pays $25.

‡JUS WRITE, Nu' People, Z-Publication, P.O. Box 574, South Bend IN 46624. Contact: Kalishia Naté, editor. Publisher: Izola Bird. 60% freelance written. Quarterly literary magazine. Estab. 1993. Circ. 250. Publishes ms 4 months after acceptance. Buys first rights, second serial (reprint) rights. Submit seasonal material 4 months in advance. Accepts simultaneous submissions. Reports in 1 month on queries. Sample copy for $2.50, 5% sales tax and SASE. Writer's guidelines for #10 SASE.

Nonfiction: General interest, how-to, humor, interview/profile, personal experience, photo feature, religious, entertainment, poetry, movie review illustration. Query with published clips. Send complete ms. Length: 300-400 words. Pays $50 minimum.

Reprints: Accepts previously published submissions.

Photos: State availability of photos with submission. Reviews prints. Negotiates payment individually.

Columns/Departments: Profiles, 200 words; Articles (inspirational, educational), 300 words; Reviews, (movies), 150 words. Buys 3 mss/year. Send complete ms. Pays $50-75.

Fiction: Adventure, fantasy, horror, humorous, mainstream, mystery, religious, romance, science fiction. Buys 3 mss/year. Query. Send complete ms. Length: 200 words minimum. Pays $50 minimum.

Poetry: Traditional, humorous, strong. Buys 8 poems/year. Submit maximum 4 poems. Pays $10-15.

Fillers: Anecdotes, facts, gags to be illustrated by cartoonist, short humor. Buys 10/year. Length: 10 words minimum. Pays $3 minimum.

Tips: "It's best to order the magazine. Write nice letters, nothing phony, be yourself, be honest. African-American writers welcome."

KALLIOPE, a journal of women's art, Florida Community College at Jacksonville, 3939 Roosevelt Blvd., Jacksonville FL 32205. (904)381-3511. Editor: Mary Sue Koeppel. 100% freelance written. Triannual magazine. "*Kalliope* publishes poetry, short fiction, reviews, and b&w art, usually by women artists. We look for artistic excellence." Estab. 1978. Circ. 1,600. Pays on publication. Publishes ms an average of 3 months after acceptance. Buys first rights. Reports in 1 week on queries. Sample copy for $7 (recent issue) or $4 (back copy). Writer's guidelines for #10 SASE.

Nonfiction: Interview/profile, reviews of new works of poetry and fiction. Buys 6 mss/year. Send complete ms. Length: 500-2,000 words. Pays $10 honorarium.

Fiction: Ethnic, experimental, fantasy, humorous, mainstream, slice-of-life vignettes, suspense. Buys 12 mss/year or more. Send complete ms. Length: 100-3,000 words. Pays $10 honorarium.

Poetry: Avant-garde, free verse, haiku, light verse, traditional. Buys 75 poems/year. Submit maximum 6 poems. Length 2-120 lines. Pays $10 honorarium.

Tips: "We publish the best of the material submitted to us each issue. (We don't build a huge backlog and then publish from that backlog for years.) Although we look for new writers and usually publish several with each issue alongside already established writers, we love it when established writers send us their work. We've recently published Tess Gallagher, Enid Shomer and works of Colette published in English for the first time. Send a bio with all submissions."

THE KENYON REVIEW, Kenyon College, Gambier OH 43022. (614)427-5208. Fax: (614)427-5417. E-mail: kenyonreview@kenyon.edu. Editor: David H. Lynn. 100% freelance written. Triannual magazine covering contemporary literature and criticism. "An international journal of literature, culture and the arts dedicated to an inclusive representation of the best in new writing, interviews and criticism from established and emerging writers." Estab. 1939. Circ. 4,500. Pays on publication. Publishes ms 1 year after acceptance. Byline given. Buys first, one-time rights. Editorial lead time 1 year. Submit seasonal material 1 year in advance. Reports in 2 weeks on queries; 3 months on mss. Sample copy for $8. Writer's guidelines for 4×9 SASE.

Nonfiction: Book excerpts (before publication), essays, interview/profile (query first), translations. Buys 12 mss/year. Query. Length: 7,500 words maximum. Pays $10/published page.

Fiction: Experimental, humorous, mainstream, novel excerpts (before publication), science fiction, slice-of-life vignettes. Buys 30 mss/year. Send complete ms. Length: 7,500 words maximum. Pays $10/published page.

Poetry: Avant-garde, free verse, haiku, light verse, traditional. Buys 60 poems/year. Submit maximum 6 poems. Pays $15/published page.

MAGIC REALISM, Pyx Press, P.O. Box 922648, Sylmar CA 91392-2648. Editor: C. Darren Butler. Managing Editor: Julie Thomas. 75% freelance written. Quarterly literary magazine of magic realism, literary fantasy and related fiction. Estab. 1990. Circ. 1,200. **Pays on acceptance.** Publishes ms an average of 6-18 months after acceptance. Buys first North American serial or one-time rights, non-exclusive (reprint) rights or Spanish language rights (optional). Editorial lead time 4 months. Accepts simultaneous submissions. Reports in 1 month on queries, 6 months on mss. Sample copy for $4.95 (back issue); $5.95 (current issue). Writer's guidelines for #10 SASE.

• *Magic Realism* also offers a short fiction contest. See the Contest and Awards section.

Nonfiction: Book excerpts, essays, interview/profile, translations. Buys 2 mss/year. Query. Length: 8,000 words maximum. Pays ¼¢/word.

Reprints: Accepts previously published submissions.

Photos: State availability of photos with submission. Reviews contact sheets, prints. Offers $2-100/photo. Model releases preferred. Buys one-time rights.

Fiction: Experimental, fantasy, magic realism. Buys 70-80 mss/year. Send complete ms. Length: 8,000 words. Pays ¼¢/word.

• Ranked as one of the best markets for fiction writers in *Writer's Digest*'s annual "Fiction 50," June 1996.

Poetry: All styles considered. Buys 25 poems/year. Submit maximum 8 poems. Pays $3/magazine page.

Tips: "We prefer a short cover letter with bio and/or credits. We especially need short-short fiction of 200-2,000 words."

THE MALAHAT REVIEW, The University of Victoria, P.O. Box 1700, Victoria, British Columbia V8W 2Y2 Canada. Contact: Editor. 100% freelance written. Eager to work with new/unpublished writers. Quarterly covering poetry, fiction, drama and reviews. Estab. 1967. Circ. 1,700. **Pays on acceptance.** Publishes ms up to 1 year after acceptance. Byline given. Offers 100% kill fee. Buys first serial rights. Reports in 2 weeks on queries; 3 months on mss. Sample copy for $7.

Nonfiction: Interview/profile (literary/artistic). Buys 2 mss/year. Query first. Length: 1,000-8,000. Pays $35-175.

Photos: Pays $25 for b&w prints. Captions required. Pays $100 for color print used as cover.

Fiction: Buys 20 mss/year. Send complete ms. Length: no restriction. Pays $25/magazine page.

• Ranked as one of the best markets for fiction writers in *Writer's Digest*'s annual "Fiction 50," June 1996.

Poetry: Avant-garde, free verse, traditional. Buys 100/year. Pays $25/magazine page.

MANOA, A Pacific Journal of International Writing, University of Hawaii Press, 1733 Donaghho Rd., Honolulu HI 96822. (808)956-3070. Fax: (808)956-3083. Website: http://wwwz/hawaii.edu/uhpress/Journals/MA/MAHome.html. Editor: Frank Stewart. Associate Editor: Charlene Gilmore. Managing Editor: Patricia Matsueda. Semiannual literary magazine. "No special slant. Just high quality literary fiction, poetry, essays, personal narrative, reviews. About half of each issue devoted to U.S. writing, and half translations of new work from Pacific and Asian nations. Our audience is primarily in the U.S., although expanding in Pacific countries. U.S. writing need not be confined to Pacific settings or subjects." Estab. 1989. Circ. 2,500. Pays on publication. Byline given. Buys first North American serial or non-exclusive, one-time reprint rights. Editorial lead time 6 months. Submit seasonal material 8 months in advance. Reports in 3 weeks on queries; 2 months on poetry mss, 4 months on fiction. Sample copy for $10. Writer's guidelines free on request.

Nonfiction: Frank Stewart, editor. Book excerpts, essays, interview/profile, creative nonfiction or personal narrative related to literature or nature. No Pacific exotica. Charlene Gilmore, reviews editor. Buys 3-4 mss/year, excluding reviews. Query or send complete ms. Length: 1,000-5,000 words. Pays $25/printed page, plus contributor copies.

Fiction: Ian MacMillan, fiction editor. "We're potentially open to anything of literary quality, though usually not genre fiction as such." Publishes novel excerpts. No Pacific exotica. Buys 12-18 mss/year in the US (excluding translation). Send complete ms. Length: 1,000-7,500. Pays $100-500 normally ($25/printed page).

Poetry: Frank Stewart, editor. No light verse. Buys 40-50 poems/year. Pays $25.

Tips: "Although we are a Pacific journal, we are a general interest U.S. literary journal, not limited to Pacific settings or subjects. Translations are least open to freelancers, since these are usually solicited by a special guest editor for a special feature."

THE MASSACHUSETTS REVIEW, Memorial Hall, University of Massachusetts, Amherst MA 01003-9934. (413)545-2689. Editors: Mary Heath, Jules Chametzky, Paul Jenkins. Quarterly magazine. Estab. 1959. Pays on publication. Publishes ms 6-18 months after acceptance. Buys first North American serial rights. Reports in 3 months. Does not return mss without SASE. Sample copy for $5 with 3 first-class stamps.
Nonfiction: Articles on literary criticism, women, public affairs, art, philosophy, music and dance. Length: 6,500 words average. Pays $50.
Fiction: Short stories. Length: 25-30 pages maximum. Pays $50.
Poetry: Pays 35¢/line or $10 minimum.
Tips: "No manuscripts are considered June-October."

MICHIGAN QUARTERLY REVIEW, 3032 Rackham Bldg., University of Michigan, Ann Arbor MI 48109-1070. Editor: Laurence Goldstein. 75% freelance written. Prefers to work with published/established writers. Quarterly. Estab. 1962. Circ. 1,500. Publishes ms an average of 1 year after acceptance. Pays on publication. Buys first serial rights. Reports in 2 months. Sample copy for $2.50 with 2 first-class stamps.
Nonfiction: "*MQR* is open to general articles directed at an intellectual audience. Essays ought to have a personal voice and engage a significant subject. Scholarship must be present as a foundation, but we are not interested in specialized essays directed only at professionals in the field. We prefer ruminative essays, written in a fresh style and which reach interesting conclusions. We also like memoirs and interviews with significant historical or cultural resonance." Length: 2,000-5,000 words. Pays $100-150.
Fiction and Poetry: No restrictions on subject matter or language. "We publish about ten stories a year and are very selective. We like stories which are unusual in tone and structure, and innovative in language." Send complete ms. Pays $10/published page.
Tips: "Read the journal and assess the range of contents and the level of writing. We have no guidelines to offer or set expectations; every manuscript is judged on its unique qualities. On essays—query with a very thorough description of the argument and a copy of the first page. Watch for announcements of special issues, which are usually expanded issues and draw upon a lot of freelance writing. Be aware that this is a university quarterly that publishes a limited amount of fiction and poetry; that it is directed at an educated audience, one that has done a great deal of reading in all types of literature."

MID-AMERICAN REVIEW, Dept. of English, Bowling Green State University, Bowling Green OH 43403. (419)372-2725. Editor-in-Chief: George Looney. Willing to work with new/unpublished writers. Semiannual literary magazine of "the highest quality fiction, poetry and translations of contemporary poetry and fiction." Also publishes critical articles and book reviews of contemporary literature. Estab. 1972. Pays on publication. Publishes ms an average of 6 months after acceptance. Byline given. Buys one-time rights. Reports in 4 months. Sample copy for $7 (current issue), $5 (back issue); rare back issues $10.
Fiction: Contact: Rebecca Meachem, fiction editor. Character-oriented, literary. Buys 12 mss/year. Send complete ms; do not query. Pays $10/page up to $50, pending funding.
Poetry: Contact: Tony Gardner, poetry editor. Strong imagery, strong sense of vision. Buys 60 poems/year. Pays $10/page up to $50.
Tips: "We are seeking translations of contemporary authors from all languages into English; submissions must include the original."

THE MISSOURI REVIEW, 1507 Hillcrest Hall, University of Missouri, Columbia MO 65211. (573)882-4474. Website: http://www.missouri.edu/~moreview. Editor: Speer Morgan. Managing Editor: Greg Michalson. 100% freelance written. Triannual literary magazine. "We publish contemporary fiction, poetry, interviews, personal essays, cartoons, special features—such as 'History as Literature' series and 'Found Text' series—for the literary and the general reader interested in a wide range of subjects." Estab. 1978. Circ. 6,500. Pays on signed contract. Byline given. Buys first rights or one-time rights. Editorial lead time 6 months. Reports in 2 weeks on queries; 3 months on mss. Sample copy for $7. Writer's guidelines for #10 SASE.
Nonfiction: Evelyn Somers, associate editor. Book excerpts, essays. No literary criticism. Buys 10 mss/year. Send complete ms. Pays approximately $15-20/printed page up to $750.
Fiction: Mainstream, literary. Buys 25 mss/year. Send complete ms. Pays $15-20 per printed page up to $750.
  ● Ranked as one of the best markets for fiction writers in *Writer's Digest*'s annual "Fiction 50," June 1996.
Poetry: Greg Michalson, poetry editor. Publishes 3-5 poetry features of 6-12 pages each per issue. "Please familiarize yourself with the magazine before submitting poetry." Buys 50 poems/year. Pays $125-250.

‡NEW ENGLAND REVIEW, University Press of New England, 23 S. Main St., Hanover NH 03755. (603)643-7112. E-mail: nereview@middlebury.edu. Editor: Stephen Donadio. Managing Editor: Jessica Dineen. Contact on envelope: Poetry, Fiction, or Nonfiction Editor; on letter: Stephen Donadio. Literary quarterly magazine. Serious literary only. Estab. 1978. Pays on publication. Publishes ms an average of 6 months after acceptance. Byline given. Buys first North American serial rights. Editorial lead time 6 months. Submit seasonal material 6 months in advance. Accepts simultaneous submissions. Reports in 2 weeks on queries; 3 months on mss. Sample copy for $7. Writer's guidelines for #10 SASE.

Nonfiction: Serious literary only. Buys 20-25 mss/year. Send complete ms. Length: 7,500 words maximum, though exceptions may be made. Pays $20 minimum for assigned articles; $10/page; plus 2 copies.

Reprints: Rarely accepts previously published submissions, (only if out of print or previously published abroad only).

Fiction: Pays $20 and 2 copies of issue work appears. Serious literary only. Buys 20 mss/year. Send complete ms. Length: 7,500 words, through exceptions may be made. Pays $10/page or $20.

Poetry: Serious literary only. Buys 75-90 poems/year. Submit maximum 6 poems. Pays $10/page or $20.

Tips: "We consider short fiction, including shorts, short-shorts, novellas, and self-contained extracts from novels. We consider a variety of general and literary, but not narrowly scholarly, nonfiction: long and short poems; speculative, interpretive, and personal essays; book reviews; screenplays; graphics; translations; critical reassessments; statements by artists working in various media; interviews; testimonies; and letters from abroad. We are committed to exploration of all forms of contemporary cultural expression in the United States and abroad. With few exceptions, we print only work not published previously elsewhere."

‡**NEW LETTERS**, University of Missouri-Kansas City, University House, 5101 Rockhill Rd., Kansas City MO 64110-2499. (816)235-1168. Fax: (816)235-2611. Contact: James McKinley, editor. Managing Editor: Robert Stewart. 100% freelance written. Quarterly magazine. "*New Letters* is intended for the general literate reader. We publish literary fiction, nonfiction, essays, poetry. We also publish art." Estab. 1934. Circ. 1,800. Pays on publication. Publishes ms an average of 5 months after acceptance. Byline given. Buys first North American serial rights. Editorial lead time 6 months. Submit seasonal material 6 months in advance. Accepts simultaneous submissions. Reports in 1 month on queries; 3 months on mss. Sample copy for $2.50. Writer's guidelines free on request.

Nonfiction: Essays. No self-help, how-to or non-literary work. Buys 6-8 mss/year. Send complete ms. Length: 5,000 words maximum. Pays $40-100.

Photos: Send photos with submission. Reviews contact sheets, 2×4 transparencies, prints. Offers $10-40/photo. Buys one-time rights.

Fiction: No genre fiction. Buys 12 mss/year. Send complete ms. Length: 5,000 words maximum. Pays $30-75.

Poetry: Avant-garde, free verse, haiku, traditional. No light verse. Buys 40 poems/year. Submit maximum 3 poems. Length: open. Pays $10-25.

THE NORTH AMERICAN REVIEW, University of Northern Iowa, Cedar Falls IA 50614-0516. (319)273-6455. Editor: Robley Wilson. 50% freelance written. Bimonthly. Circ. 5,000. Buys first rights. Pays on publication. Publishes ms an average of 1 year after acceptance. Reports in 10 weeks. Sample copy for $4.

● This is one of the oldest and most prestigious literary magazines in the country. Also one of the most entertaining—and a tough market for the young writer.

Nonfiction: No restrictions, but most nonfiction is commissioned. Query. Rate of payment arranged.

Fiction: No restrictions; highest quality only. Length: open. Pays minimum $15/published page. Fiction department closed (no mss read) from April 1-December 31.

Poetry: Peter Cooley. No restrictions; highest quality only. Length: open. Pays 50¢/line; $20 minimum/poem.

NORTH CAROLINA LITERARY REVIEW: A Magazine of Literature, Culture, and History, English Dept., East Carolina University, Greenville NC 27858-4353. (919)328-4876. Fax: (919)328-4889. Editor: Tom Douglas. 80% freelance written. Annual literary magazine published in spring covering North Carolina/Southern writers, literature, culture, history. "Articles should have North Carolina/Southern slant; essays by writers associated with North Carolina may address any subject. First consideration is always for quality of work. Although we treat academic and scholarly subjects, we do not wish to see jargon-laden prose; our readers, we hope, are found as often in bookstores and libraries as in academia. We seek to combine best elements of magazine for serious readers with best of scholarly journal." Estab. 1992. Circ. 1,500. Pays on publication. Publishes ms 9 months after acceptance. Byline given. Offers 25% kill fee. Buys first North American serial rights. (Rights returned to writer on request.) Editorial lead time 6 months. Reports in 10 weeks on queries, 2 months on mss, 8 months on unsolicited mss. Sample copy for $10. Writer's guidelines free on request.

Nonfiction: Book excerpts, essays, exposé, general interest, historical/nostalgic, humor, interview/profile, opinion, personal experience, photo feature, travel, reviews, short narratives; surveys of archives. "No reviews that treat single books by contemporary authors or jargon-laden academic articles." Buys 25-35 mss/year. Query with published clips. Length: 500-5,000 words. Pays $50 minimum. (Pay usually is in $100-300 range, sometimes higher, depending on article.)

Photos: State availability of photos with query. Reviews 5×7 or 8×10 prints; snapshot size or photocopy OK. Negotiates payment individually. Captions and identification of subjects required. (Releases when appropriate.) Buys one-time rights.

Columns/Departments: Archives (survey of North Carolina-writer archives), 500-1,500 words; Thomas Wolfe (Wolfe-related articles/essays), 1,000-2,000 words; Readers/Writers Places (bookstores or libraries, or other places readers and writers gather), 500-1,500; Black Mountain College, 1,000-2,000 words; Reviews (essay reviews of North Carolina-related literature (fiction, creative nonfiction, poetry). Buys 10 mss/year. Send complete ms. Pays $50-150.

Fiction: "No unsolicited manuscripts; fiction and poetry are published in thematic sections or by invitation." Adventure, ethnic, experimental, fantasy, historical, horror, humorous, mainstream, mystery, novel excerpts, romance, science fiction,slice-of-life vignettes, suspense, western. Buys 3-4 mss/year. Query. Length: 5,000 words maximum. Pays $100-300.

Poetry: Solicited by editor only; *no unsolicited submissions, please.* Buys 8-10 poems/year. Length: 30-150 lines. Pays $30-150.

Fillers: Buys 2-10/year. Length: 50-300 words. Pays $10-25.

Tips: "By far the easiest way to break in is with departments; we are especially interested in reports on conferences, readings, meetings that involve North Carolina writers; and personal essays or short narratives with strong sense of place to use in loosely defined Readers/Writers Places department. We are more interested in essays that use creative nonfiction approaches than in straight articles of informational nature. See back issues for other departments. These are the only areas in which we encourage unsolicited manuscripts; but we welcome queries and proposals for all others. Interviews are probably the other easiest place to break in; no discussions of poetics/theory, etc., except in reader-friendly (accessible) language; interviews should be personal, more like conversations, that explore connections between a writer's life and his/her work."

THE NORTHWOODS JOURNAL, A Magazine for Writers, Conservatory of American Letters, P.O. Box 298, Thomaston ME 04861. (207)354-0998. Fax: (207)354-8953. E-mail: tzyhzia@prodigy.com. Managing Editor: Robert Olmsted. 70% freelance written. Quarterly literary magazine. Estab. 1993. Circ. 500. **Pays on acceptance.** Byline given. Buys first American serial rights. Editorial lead time 6 months. Submit seasonal material 9 months in advance. Sample copy for $5 for next issue, $7.75 for current issue. Writer's guidelines for #10 SASE.

Nonfiction: Essays, writing-related, exposé, historical/nostalgic, opinion. "No porn or evangelical material." Send complete ms. Length: 480-2,000 or so. Pays $4/page and up for unsolicited articles. "Do not submit anything until you've read our guidelines."

Photos: Offers $5. Model releases required. Buys one-time rights.

Columns/Departments: Reviews, 800 words; Contest, 800-1,000 words. Buys 8 mss/year. Query with clips. Pays $4 and up.

Fiction: Adventure, erotica, experimental, fantasy, historical, horror, humorous, mainstream, mystery, science fiction, slice-of-life vignettes, suspense, western. "No brilliantly written stuff without a plot." Buys 10 mss/year. Send complete ms. Length: 400-2,500 words. Pays $5-25.

Poetry: Avant-garde, free verse, haiku, light verse, traditional. "No religious poetry."Buys 30-40 poems. Pays $2.50-25.

Fillers: Anecdotes, facts, newsbreaks, short humor. Anything of interest to writers. Pays $2-5.

Tips: "Keep in mind that we are a magazine for writers, We consider it a showcase not a 'how-to.' We're not interested in sloppy writing or writing for information. We seek writing as art. Be nit picky. You have lots of competition, especially in fiction."

NOSTALGIA, A Sentimental State of Mind, Nostalgia Publications, P.O. Box 2224, Orangeburg SC 29116. Editor: Connie L. Martin. 100% freelance written. Semiannual magazine for poetry and true short stories. "True, personal experiences that relate faith, struggle, hope, success, failure and rising above problems common to all." Estab. 1986. Circ. 1,000. Pays on publication. Publishes ms an average of 1 year after acceptance. Byline given. Buys one-time rights. Submit seasonal material 6 months in advance. Reports in 6 weeks on queries. Sample copy for $5. Writer's guidelines for #10 SASE.

Nonfiction: General interest, historical/nostalgic, humor, inspirational, opinion, personal experience, photo feature, religious and travel. Does not want to see anything with profanity or sexual references. Buys 10 or more stories/year. Send complete ms. Length: 1,500 words. Pays $25 minimum. Pays contributor copies "if copies are preferred." Short Story Award $150 plus publication.

Photos: State availability of photos with submission. Offers no additional payment for photos with ms.

Poetry: Free verse, haiku, light verse, traditional and modern prose. "No ballads—no profanity—no sexual references." Submit 3 poems maximum. Length: no longer than 45-50 lines preferably. Pays $150 (/semiannual Nostalgia Poetry Award).

Tips: Write for guidelines before entering contests. Short Story Award (deadlines March 31 and August 31); Poetry Award (deadlines June 30 and December 31). Entry fees reserve future edition.

THE OHIO REVIEW, 209C Ellis Hall, Ohio University, Athens OH 45701-2979. (614)593-1900. Editor: Wayne Dodd. 40% freelance written. Semiannual magazine. "A balanced, informed engagement of contemporary American letters, with special emphasis on poetics." Circ. 3,500. Publishes ms an average of 8 months after acceptance. Rights acquired vary with author and material; usually buys first serial or first North American serial rights. Unsolicited material will be read September-May only. Reports in 10 weeks.

Nonfiction, Fiction and Poetry: Buys essays of general intellectual and special literary appeal. Not interested in narrowly focused scholarly articles. Seeks writing that is marked by clarity, liveliness and perspective. Interested in the best fiction and poetry. Submit complete ms. Buys 75 unsolicited mss/year. Pays minimum $5/page, plus copies.
Tips: "Make your query very brief, not gabby—one that describes some publishing history, but no extensive bibliographies. We publish mostly poetry—essays, short fiction, some book reviews."

THE PARIS REVIEW, 45-39 171st Place, Flushing NY 11358. Submit mss to 541 E. 72nd St., New York NY 10021. (212)861-0016. Editor: George A. Plimpton. Quarterly magazine. Buys all rights. Pays on publication. Reporting time varies. Address submissions to proper department. Sample copy for $10. Writer's guidelines for #10 SASE (from Flushing Office). Reporting time often 6 months or longer.
Fiction: Study the publication. No length limit. Pays up to $600. Makes award of $1,000 in annual Aga Khan Fiction Contest.
Poetry: Richard Howard, poetry editor. Study the publication. Pay varies according to length, $35 minimum. Awards $1,000 in Bernard F. Conners Poetry Prize contest.

‡PARNASSUS, Poetry in Review, Poetry in Review Foundation, 205 W. 89th St., #8-F, New York NY 10024. (212)362-3492. Fax: (212)875-0148. Editor: Herbert Leibowitz. Managing Editor: Ben Downing. Semiannual trade paperback-size magazine covering poetry and criticism. Estab. 1972. Circ. 1,500. Pays on publication. Publishes ms an average of 5 months after acceptance. Byline given. Buys one-time rights. Sample copy for $15.
Nonfiction: Essays. Buys 30 mss/year. Query with published clips. Length: 1,500-7,500 words. Pays $50-300. Sometimes pays writers in contributor copies or other premiums rather than a cash payment upon request.
Poetry: Accepts most types of poetry including avant-garde, free verse, traditional. Buys 3-4 unsolicited poems/year.

‡PIG IRON SERIES, Pig Iron Press, P.O. Box 237, Youngstown OH 44501-0237. (330)747-6932. Editor-in-Chief: Jim Villani. 95% freelance written. Annual magazine emphasizing literature/art for writers, artists and intelligent lay audience interested in popular culture. Circ. 1,000. Buys one-time rights. Pays on publication. Publishes ms an average of 18 months after acceptance. Byline given. Reports in 3 months. Sample copy $4. Writer's guidelines and current theme list for #10 SASE. Theme for 1998: Years of Rage: 1960s; reading dates August 1996-December 1997.
Nonfiction: General interest, personal opinion, criticism, new journalism and lifestyle. Buys 5-10 mss/year. Query. Length: 6,000 words maximum. Pays $5/page minimum.
Reprints: Accepts previously published submissions.
Photos: Submit photo material with query. Pays $5 minimum for 5×7 or 8×10 b&w glossy prints. Buys one-time rights.
Fiction: Narrative fiction, psychological fiction, environment, avant-garde, experimental, metafiction, satire and parody. Buys 4-12 mss/issue. Submit complete ms. Length: 6,000 words maximum. Pays $5 minimum.
Poetry: Avant-garde and free verse. Buys 25-50/issue. Submit in batches of 5 or less. Length: open. Pays $5 minimum.
Tips: "Looking for fiction and poetry that is sophisticated, elegant, mature and polished. Interested in literary works that are consistent with the fundamental characteristics of modern and contemporary literature, including works that address alienation, the unconscious, loss, despair and historical discontinuity."

‡A PLACE TO ENTER, Showcasing Writers of African Descent, Drayton-Iton Communications, Inc., 1328 Broadway, Suite 1054, New York NY 10001. (212)714-7032. Editor: Brian Iton. Quarterly literary magazine covering fiction by writers of African descent. Audience is primarily patrons of black bookstores throughout the country and Canada. Estab. 1994. Circ. 1,000. Pays 90 days after publication. Publishes ms 3 months after acceptance. Byline given. Buys first North American serial rights. Reports in 4 months on manuscripts. Sample copy for $4. Writer's guidelines free on request.
Nonfiction: Book excerpts. Pays $100 and 1 copy.
Fiction: Adventure, condensed novels, confession, erotica, ethnic, experimental, fantasy, historical, horror, humorous, mainstream, mystery, novel excerpts, religious, romance, science fiction, serialized novels, slice-of-life vignettes, suspense, Western. Buys 16-20 mss/year. Send complete ms. Length: 1,000-10,000 words. Pays $100.

PLOUGHSHARES, Emerson College, Dept. M, 100 Beacon St., Boston MA 02116. Editor: Don Lee. Triquarterly magazine for "readers of serious contemporary literature." Circ. 6,000. Pays on publication, $50 minimum/title, $250/author maximum, with 2 copies and 1-year subscription. Publishes ms an average of 6 months after acceptance. Buys first North American serial rights. Reports in 5 months. Sample copy for $6 (back issue). Writer's guidelines for SASE. Reading period: August 1-March 31.
  ● A competitive and highly prestigious market. Rotating and guest editors make cracking the line-up even tougher, since it's difficult to know what is appropriate to send.

Nonfiction: Personal and literary essays (accepted only occasionally). Length: 5,000 words maximum. Pays $25/printed page. Reviews (assigned). Length: 500 words maximum. Pays $50/printed page, $250 maximum.
Fiction: Literary and mainstream. Buys 25-35 unsolicited mss/year. Length: 300-6,000 words. Pays $25/printed page, $50 minimum, $250 maximum.
• Ranked as one of the best markets for fiction writers in *Writer's Digest*'s annual "Fiction 50," June 1996.
Poetry: Traditional forms, blank verse, free verse and avant-garde. Length: open. Pays $25/printed page, $50 minimum, $250 maximum.
Tips: "We no longer structure issues around preconceived themes. If you believe your work is in keeping with our general standards of literary quality and value, submit at any time during our reading period."

‡**THE PRAIRIE JOURNAL of Canadian Literature**, P.O. Box 61203, Brentwood Postal Services, 217K-3630 Brentwood Rd. NW, Calgary, Alberta T2L 2K6 Canada. Editor: A. Burke. 100% freelance written. Semiannual magazine of Canadian literature. Estab. 1983. Circ. 600. Pays on publication; "honorarium depends on grant." Byline given. Buys first North American serial rights. Reports 6 months. Sample copy for $6 and IRC or payment for postage.
Nonfiction: Interview/profile, scholarly, literary. Buys 5 mss/year. Query first. Include IRCs. Pays $25-100 depending on length. Pays contributor copies or honoraria for literary work.
Photos: Send photocopies of photos with submission. Offers additional payment for photos accepted with ms. Identification of subjects required. Buys first North American rights.
Fiction: Literary. Buys 10 mss/year. Send complete ms.
Poetry: Avant-garde, free verse. Buys 10 poems/year. Submit maximum 6-10 poems.
Tips: "Commercial writers are advised to submit elsewhere. Art needed, b&w pen and ink drawings or good-quality photocopy. Do not send originals. We are strictly small press editors interested in highly talented, serious artists. We are oversupplied with fiction but seek more high-quality poetry, especially the contemporary long poem or sequences from longer works."

PRISM INTERNATIONAL, Department of Creative Writing, Buch E462, 1866 Main Mall, University of British Columbia, Vancouver, British Columbia V6T 1Z1 Canada. Fax: (604)822-3616. E-mail: prism@unixg.ubc.ca. Website: http://www.arts/ubc.ca/crwr/prism/prism.html. Contact: Sara O'Leary, editor-in-chief. Executive Editor: Tim Mitchell. 100% freelance written. Eager to work with new/unpublished writers. Quarterly magazine emphasizing contemporary literature, including translations, for university and public libraries, and private subscribers. Estab. 1959. Circ. 1,200. Pays on publication. Publishes ms an average of 4 months after acceptance. Buys first North American serial rights. Reports in 3 months. Sample copy for $5. Writer's guidelines for #10 SAE with 1 first-class Canadian stamp (Canadian entries) or 1 IRC (US entries).
Nonfiction: "*Creative* nonfiction that reads like fiction." No reviews, tracts or scholarly essays.
Fiction: Rick Maddocks, fiction editor. Experimental, traditional, novel excerpts. Buys 3-5 mss/issue. Send complete ms. Length: 5,000 words maximum. Pays $20/printed page and 1-year subscription. Publishes novel excerpts, maximum length: 25 double-spaced pages.
Poetry: Regina Weaver, poetry editor. Avant-garde, traditional. Buys 20 poems/issue. Submit maximum 6 poems. Pays $20/printed page and 1-year subscription.
Drama: One-acts preferred. Pays $20/printed page and 1-year subscription.
Tips: "We are looking for new and exciting fiction. Excellence is still our number one criterion. As well as poetry, imaginative nonfiction and fiction, we are especially open to translations of all kinds, very short fiction pieces and drama which work well on the page. Translations must come with a copy of the original language work. Work may be submitted through e-mail or our website. We pay an additional $10/printed page to selected authors whose work we place on our on-line version of *Prism*."

QUEEN'S QUARTERLY, A Canadian Review, Queen's University, Kingston, Ontario K7L 3N6 Canada. (613)545-2667. Fax: (613)545-6822. E-mail: qquartly@qucdn.bitnet. Editor: Boris Castel. Estab. 1893. Quarterly magazine covering a wide variety of subjects, including science, humanities, arts and letters, politics and history for the educated reader. 15% freelance written. Circ. 3,000. Pays on publication. Publishes ms an average of 3 months after acceptance. Byline given. Buys first North American serial rights. Requires 1 double-spaced hard copy and 1 copy on disk in WordPerfect. Reports in 1 month on mss. *Writer's Market* recommends allowing 2 months for reply. Sample copy $6.50.
• No longer accepting fantasy fiction.
Fiction: Historical, humorous, mainstream and science fiction. Buys 8-12 mss/year. Send complete ms. Length: 4,000 words maximum. Pays $150-250.
Poetry: Avant-garde, free verse, haiku, light verse, traditional. No "sentimental, religious, or first efforts by unpublished writers." Buys 25/year. Submit maximum 6 poems. Length: open. Pays $100-200.
Tips: "Poetry and fiction are most open to freelancers. Don't send less than the best. No multiple submissions. No more than six poems or two stories per submission. We buy very few freelance submissions."

ROOM OF ONE'S OWN, A Canadian Feminist Quarterly of Literary Criticism, West Coast Feminist Literary Magazine Society, P.O. Box 46160, Station D, Vancouver, British Columbia V6J 5G5

Canada. Contact: Growing Room Collective. 100% freelance written. Quarterly literary journal of feminist literature. Estab. 1975. Circ. 1,000. Pays on publication. Publishes ms an average of 8 months after acceptance. Byline given. Buys first North American serial rights. Editorial lead time 9 months. Reports in 3 months on queries; 6 months on mss. Sample copy for $7. Writer's guidelines for #10 SAE with 2 IRCs (US postage not valid in Canada).

Nonfiction: Essays, interview/profile, reviews. Buys 1-2 mss/year. Send complete ms. Length: 1,000-2,500 words. Pays $25 (Canadian) and 1-year subscription.

Photos: Send photos with submission. Reviews prints. Offers no additional payment for photos accepted with ms. Buys one-time rights.

Fiction: Adventure, ethnic, experimental, fantasy, humorous, mainstream, slice-of-life vignettes, science fiction, feminist literature. Buys 80 mss/year. Length: 2,000-3,500 words. Pays $25 (Canadian).

Poetry: Avant-garde, free verse. "Nothing light, undeveloped." Buys 20 poems/year. Submit maximum 8 poems. Length: 3-80 lines. Pays $25 (Canadian).

ROSEBUD, For People Who Enjoy Writing, Rosebud, Inc., P.O. Box 459, Cambridge WI 53523. (608)423-9609. Editor: Rod Clark. 100% freelance written. Quarterly magazine "for people who love to read and write. Our readers like good storytelling, real emotion, a sense of place and authentic voice." Estab. 1993. Circ. 6,500. Pays on publication. Publishes ms an average of 2 months after acceptance. Byline given. Buys one-time or second serial (reprint) rights. Editorial lead time 3 months. Submit seasonal material 3 months in advance. Accepts simultaneous submissions. Reports in 2 months. Sample copy for $5.95. Writer's guidelines for SASE.

Nonfiction: Book excerpt, essays, general interest, historical/nostalgic, humor, interview/profile, personal experience, travel. "No editorializing." Buys 6 mss/year. Send complete ms. Length: 1,200-1,800 words. Pays $45-195 and 2 contributor's copies.

Reprints: Accepts previously published submissions.

Photos: State availability of photos with submission. Offers no additional payment for photos accepted with ms. Captions, model releases and identification of subjects required. Buys one-time rights.

Fiction: Ethnic, experimental, historical, humorous, mainstream, novel excerpts, slice-of-life vignettes, suspense. "No contrived formula pieces." Buys 80 mss/year. Send complete ms. Length: 1,200-1,800 words. Pays $45-195.

Poetry: Avant-garde, free verse, traditional. No inspirational poetry. Buys 36 poems/year. Submit maximum 5 poems. Length: open. Pays $45-195.

Tips: "Something has to 'happen' in the pieces we choose, but what happens inside characters is much more intereting to us than plot manipulation."

‡SAN FRANCISCO REVIEW, Santa Fe Ventures, 582 Market St., San Francisco CA 94104. Fax: (415)403-1339. E-mail: SFReview@aol.com. Editor: Matthew T. Humphrey. Contact: Emily E. Lundberg, assistant editor. 100% freelance written. Bimonthly magazine covering books. "We publish book reviews, interviews with authors, commentary on the book publishing industry, short fiction, and pieces concerning the process of writing. Circ. 10,000. Pays on publication. Publishes ms an average of 6 weeks after acceptance. Byline given. Buys one-time rights. Editorial lead time 2 months. Submit seasonal material 2 months in advance. Reports in 2 months. Sample copy for $2.95. Writer's guidelines for #10 SASE.

Nonfiction: Essays, expose, humor, inspirational, interview/profile, opinion, book reviews (prefer short). Buys 400 mss/year. Query with published clips. Length: 200-1,900 words. Pays 5¢/word.

Columns/Departments: Short Cuts (short book reviews), 300-600 words.

Fiction: Curtis Bonney, fiction editor. Buys 12 mss/year. Send complete ms. *Writer's Market* recommends sending a query letter first.

Tips: "We are most concerned with the quality of writing we publish. Please send published clips. We review books right when they are pubilshed. Reviewers must receive galleys from publishers. Interviews can take place directly after publication of the book."

‡SHENANDOAH, The Washington and Lee University Review, Washington and Lee University, Troubadour Theater, 2nd Floor, Lexington VA 24450. (540)463-8765. Contact: R.T. Smith, editor. Managing Editor: Lynn Leech. Literary quarterly magazine. Estab. 1950. Circ. 2,000. Pays on publication. Publishes ms an average of 10 months after acceptance. Byline given. Buys first North American serial and one-time rights. Reports in 2 months on mss. Sample copy for $3.50.

Nonfiction: Book excerpts, essays. Buys 6 mss/year. Send complete ms. Pays $25/page.

Fiction: Mainstream, novel excerpts. No sloppy, hasty, slight fiction. Buys 15 mss/year. Send complete ms. Pays $25/page.

Poetry: No inspirational, confessional poetry. Buys 70 poems/year. Submit maximum 6 poems. Length open. Pays $2.50/line.

SHORT STUFF, for Grown-ups, Bowman Publications, P.O. Box 7057, Loveland CO 80537. (970)669-9139. Editor: Donna Bowman. 98% freelance written. Monthly magazine. "We are perhaps an enigma in that we publish only clean stories in any genre. We'll tackle any subject, but don't allow obscene language or pornographic description. Our magazine is for grown-ups, *not* X-rated 'adult' fare." Estab. 1989. Circ. 5,400. Pays on publication. Publishes ms an average of 6 months after acceptance. Byline given. Buys first North American serial rights. Editorial lead time 3 months. Submit seasonal material 3 months in advance. Reports in 6 months on mss. Sample copy for $1.50 and 11 × 14 SAE with 5 first-class stamps. Writer's guidelines for #10 SASE.

Nonfiction: Humor. Special issues: Celebrate February Valentine Issue (deadline November). Buys 20 mss/ year. Most nonfiction is staff written. Send complete ms. Length: 500-1,800 words. Pays $10-50.

Photos: Send photos with submission. Offers no additional payment for photos accepted with ms. Identification of subjects required. Buys one-time rights.

Fiction: Adventure, historical, humorous, mainstream, mystery, romance, science fiction (seldom), suspense, western. Buys 144 mss/year. Send complete ms. Length: 500-1,800 words. Pays $10-50.

Fillers: Anecdotes, short humor. Buys 200/year. Length: 20-500 words. Pays $1-5.

Tips: "We are holiday-oriented and like writers to mark on *outside* of envelope if story is for Easter, Mother's Day, etc. We receive 300 manuscripts each month. This is up about 200%. Because of this, I implore writers to send one manuscript at a time. I would not use stories from the same author more than once an issue and this means I might keep the others too long."

SING HEAVENLY MUSE!, Women's Poetry and Prose, Sing Heavenly Muse! Inc., Box 13320, Minneapolis MN 55414. Contact: Editorial Circle. 100% freelance written. Annual journal of women's literature. Circ. 1,000. Pays on publication. Publishes ms an average of 1 year after acceptance. Byline given. Buys first North American serial rights. Reports in 3 months. Sample copy for $4. Writer's guidelines for #10 SASE.

● Manuscripts that pass the first screening may be held longer.

Fiction: Women's literature, journal pieces, memoir and novel excerpts. Buys 15-20 mss/year. Length: 10,000 words maximum. Pays $15-25; contributors receive 2 free copies. Publishes novel excerpts.

Poetry: Avant-garde, free verse, haiku, light verse, traditional. Accepts 75-100 poems/year. No limit on length. Pays $15-25.

Tips: "To meet our needs, writing must be feminist and women-centered. Reading periods vary. Issues are often related to a specific theme; writers should always query for guidelines and upcoming themes and reading periods before submitting manuscripts."

THE SOUTHERN REVIEW, 43 Allen Hall, Louisiana State University, Baton Rouge LA 70803-5001. (504)388-5108. Fax: (504)388-5098. Editors: James Olney and Dave Smith. 75% freelance written. Works with a moderate number of new/unpublished writers each year. Quarterly magazine for academic, professional, literary, intellectual audience. Estab. 1935. Circ. 3,100. Buys first serial rights only. Byline given. Pays on publication. Publishes ms an average of 6 months after acceptance. No queries. Reports in 2 months. Sample copy for $6. Writer's guidelines for #10 SASE.

Nonfiction: Essays with careful attention to craftsmanship, technique and seriousness of subject matter. "Willing to publish experimental writing if it has a valid artistic purpose. Avoid extremism and sensationalism. Essays should exhibit thoughtful and sometimes severe awareness of the necessity of literary standards in our time." Emphasis on contemporary literature, especially southern culture and history. No footnotes. Buys 25 mss/year. Length: 4,000-10,000 words. Pays $12/page for prose.

Fiction and Poetry: Short stories of lasting literary merit, with emphasis on style and technique. Length: 4,000-8,000 words. Pays $12/page for prose; $20/page for poetry.

SPARROW, Sparrow Press, 103 Waldron St., West Lafayette IN 47906. Editor: Felix Stefanile. 60% freelance written. Annual magazine covering poetry, the sonnet, articles on craft, criticism. "Writers who admire and are loyal to the lyric tradition of the English language enjoy our magazine. We are not affiliated with any group or ideology, and encourage poetry that uses meter, rhyme and structured verse, mainly the sonnet. We are not a 'school of resentment' publication." Estab. 1954. Circ. 1,000. Pays on publication. Publishes ms 8 months after acceptance. Byline given. Offers 100% kill fee. Buys first North American serial rights and second serial (reprint) rights. Editorial lead time up to 6 months. Reports in 6 weeks. Sample copy for $5 for back issue, $6 for current issue. Writer's guidelines for #10 SASE.

● *Sparrow* does not read manuscripts from October-December.

Poetry: Traditional, 90% sonnets. No free verse. Submit maximum 5 poems. Length: 14 lines. Pays $3/ poem; $25 prize, best of the issue.

Tips: "We are interested in seeing material from poets and critics with a serious commitment to the lyric tradition of the English language, with emphasis on the formal sonnet of a contemporary accent. Our yearbook is used in classes, an audience we aim for. We are not for 'poets' who think the sonnet is passé. Neither do we consider ourselves part of any creative writing program network."

SPSM&H, *Amelia Magazine*, 329 E St., Bakersfield CA 93304. (805)323-4064. Editor: Frederick A. Raborg, Jr., 100% freelance written. Quarterly magazine featuring fiction and poetry with Romantic or Gothic theme. "SPSM&H (Shakespeare, Petrarch, Sidney, Milton and Hopkins) uses one short story in each issue and 20-36 sonnets, plus reviews of books and anthologies containing the sonnet forms and occasional articles about the sonnet form or about some romantic or Gothic figure or movement. We look for contemporary aspects of the sonnet form." Estab. 1984. Circ. 600. Pays on publication. Publishes ms an average of 6 months after acceptance. Byline given. Offers 50% kill fee. Buys first North American serial rights. Editorial lead time 2 months. Submit seasonal material 3 months in advance. Accepts simultaneous submissions. Reports in 2 weeks on queries; 3 months on mss. Sample copy for $4.95. Writer's guidelines for #10 SASE.

Nonfiction: Essays, general interest, historical/nostalgic, humor, interview/profile, opinion and anything related to sonnets or to romance. Buys 1-4 mss/year. Send complete ms. Length: 500-2,000 words. Pays $10.

Photos: Send photos with submission. Reviews 8×10 or 5×7 prints. Offers $10-25/photo. Model releases required. Buys one-time rights.

Fiction: Confession, erotica, experimental, fantasy, historical, humor, humorous, mainstream, mystery, romance, slice-of-life vignettes. Buys 4 mss/year. Send complete ms. Length: 500-2,500 words. Pays $10-20.

Poetry: Sonnets, sonnet sequences. Buys 140 poems/year. Submit maximum 10 poems. Length: 14 lines. Two "best of issue" poets each receive $14.

Fillers: Anecdotes, short humor. Buys 2-4/year. Length: 25-500 words. No payment for fillers.

Tips: "Read a copy certainly. Understand the limitations of the sonnet form and, in the case of fiction, the requirements of the romantic or Gothic genres. Be professional in presentation, and realize that neatness does count. Be contemporary and avoid Victorian verse forms and techniques. Avoid convolution and forced rhyme. Idiomatics ought to be contemporary. Don't be afraid to experiment. We consider John Updike's 'Love Sonnet' to be the extreme to which poets may experiment."

STAND MAGAZINE, 179 Wingrove Rd., Newcastle Upon Tyne NE4 9DA United Kingdom. Phone/fax: (091)273-3280. Editors: Jon Silkin, Lorna Tracy, Rodney Pybus, Peter Bennet. Managing Editor: Philip Bomford. 99% freelance written. Quarterly magazine covering short fiction, poetry, criticism and reviews. "*Stand Magazine* was given this name because it was begun as a stand against apathy towards new writing and in social relations." Estab. 1952. Circ. 4,500 worldwide. Pays on publication. Publishes ms an average of 2 years after acceptance. Byline given. Buys first world rights. Editorial lead time 2 months. Reports in 1 week on queries, 2 months on mss. Sample copy for $7. Writer's guidelines for sufficient number of IRCs.

Nonfiction: Essays, interview/profile, reviews of poetry/fiction. "Reviews are commissioned from known freelancers." Buys 8 mss/year. Query. Length: 200-5,000 words. Pays $30.

Fiction: "No genre fiction." Buys 8-10 mss/year. Send complete ms. Length: 8,000 words maximum. Pays $37.50/1,000 words.

Poetry: Avant-garde, free verse, traditional. Buys 30-40 poems/year. Submit maximum 6 poems. Pays $37.50/poem.

Tips: "Poetry/fiction areas are most open to freelancers. Buy a sample copy first (suggestion)." Submissions should be accompanied by UK SAE or sufficient IRCs.

STORY, F&W Publications, Inc., 1507 Dana Ave., Cincinnati OH 45207-1005. (513)531-2222. Fax: (513)531-1843. Editor: Lois Rosenthal. 100% freelance written. Quarterly literary magazine of short fiction. "We want short stories and self-inclusive novel excerpts that are extremely well written. Our audience is sophisticated and accustomed to the finest imaginative writing by new and established writers." Estab. 1931. Circ. 34,000. **Pays on acceptance.** Byline given. Buys first North American serial rights. Reports in 1 month. Sample copy for $6.95 and $7\frac{1}{2} \times 10\frac{1}{2}$ SAE with 5 first-class stamps. Writer's guidelines for #10 SASE.

 • *Story* won the National Magazine Award for Fiction in 1992 and 1995, was nominated in 1994 and 1996.

Fiction: No genre fiction. Buys 50-60 mss/year. Send complete ms. Length: up to 8,000 words. Pays $1,000 for short stories and $750 for short shorts.

Tips: "No replies without SASE."

SULFUR, A Literary Biannual of the Whole Art, 210 Washtenaw Ave., Ypsilanti MI 48197. (313)483-9787. Editor: Clayton Eshleman. Managing Editor: Caryl Eshleman. 75% freelance written. Semiannual literary magazine covering poetry and criticism plus art and reviews. Estab. 1981. Circ. 2,000. Pays on publication. Publishes ms an average of 4 months after acceptance. Byline given. Editorial lead time 6 months. Sample copy for $6.

Nonfiction: Essays, interview/profile. Query. Pays $40.

Poetry: Avant-garde, free verse. Buys 150 poems/year. Pays $40-50.

Tips: Book reviews are most open to freelancers.

TAMPA REVIEW, University of Tampa Press, 401 W. Kennedy Blvd., Tampa FL 33606. (813)253-3333. Editor: Richard B. Mathews. Semiannual literary magazine. An international literary journal publishing art and literature from Florida and Tampa Bay as well as new work and translations from throughout the world. Estab. 1988. Circ. 500. Pays on publication. Publishes ms an average of 10 months after acceptance. Byline given. Buys first North American serial rights. Editorial lead time 6-18 months. Reports in 5 months on mss. Sample copy for $5. Writer's guidelines free on request.

Nonfiction: Paul Linnehan, nonfiction editor. Essays, general interest, interview/profile, personal experience. No "how-to" articles; fads; journalistic reprise etc. Buys 6 mss/year. Send complete ms. Length: 250-7,500 words. Pays $10/printed page upon publication.

Photos: State availability of photos with submission. Reviews contact sheets, negatives, transparencies, prints. Offers $10/photo. Caption identification of subjects required. Buys one-time rights.

Fiction: Andy Solomon, fiction editor. Ethnic, experimental, fantasy, horror, humorous, mainstream, science fiction, literary fiction. Buys 6 mss/year. Send complete ms. Length: 200-10,000 words. Pays $10/printed page upon publication.

Poetry: Don Morrill, Kathryn Van Spanckeven, poetry editors. Avant-garde, free verse, haiku, light verse, traditional, visual/experimental. No greeting card verse; hackneyed, sing-song, rhyme-for-the-sake-of-rhyme. Buys 45 poems/year. Submit up to 10 poems at one time. Length: 2-225 lines.

Tips: "Send a clear cover letter stating previous experience or background."

‡**THEATER MAGAZINE**, Yale School of Drama, Yale University, 222 York St., New Haven CT 06511. (203)432-8336. E-mail: theater.magazine@quickmail.yale.edu. Editor: Erika Munk. Managing Editors: Tom Sellar, Samantha Rabetz. University journal published 3 times/year covering theater—US and Abroad. Estab. 1968. Circ. 2,600. Pays on publication. Publishes ms an average of 4 months after acceptance. Byline given. Editorial lead time 4 months. Sample copy and writer's guidelines free on request.

Nonfiction: Essays, general interest, interview/profile, reviews. Buys 3 mss/year. Query. Pays $75-200. Sometimes pays expenses of writers on assignment.

Photos: Send photos with submission. Negotiates payment individually. Captions required. Photographer retains photo rights.

Columns/Departments: Book Reviews, Performance Reviews, Symposia. Buys 3 mss/year. Query.

Fiction: Buys 2 mss/year. Query. Pays $150 minimum.

Tips: "We want critical writing and polemics on modern and contemporary theater in the U.S. and abroad; new plays, translations, adaptations; book and production reviews."

THEMA, Box 74109, Metairie LA 70033-4109. (504)887-1263. Editor: Virginia Howard. 100% freelance written. Triannual literary magazine covering a different theme for each issue. "*Thema* is designed to stimulate creative thinking by challenging writers with unusual themes, such as 'laughter on the steps' and 'jogging on ice.' Appeals to writers, teachers of creative writing and general reading audience." Estab. 1988. Circ. 350. **Pays on acceptance.** Byline given. Buys one-time rights. Reports in 4 months on mss (after deadline for particular issue). Sample copy for $8. Writer's guidelines for #10 SASE. Query with SASE for upcoming themes.

Fiction: Adventure, ethnic, experimental, fantasy, historical, humorous, mainstream, mystery, religious, science fiction, slice-of-life vignettes, suspense, western, novel excerpts. "No alternate lifestyle or erotica." Special issues: Too proud to ask (November '96); Scrawled in a library book (March '97); Eureka! (July '97). Buys 33 mss/year. Send complete ms and *specify theme* for which it is intended. Pays $10-25.

● Ranked as one of the best markets for fiction writers in *Writer's Digest*'s annual "Fiction 50," June 1996.

Poetry: Avant-garde, free verse, haiku, light verse, traditional. No erotica. Buys 27 poems/year. Submit maximum 3 poems. Length: 4-50 lines. Pays $10.

Tips: "Be familiar with the themes. *Don't submit* unless you have an upcoming theme in mind. Specify the target theme on the first page of your manuscript or in a cover letter. Put your name on *first* page of manuscript only. (All submissions are judged in blind review after the deadline for a specified issue.) Most open to fiction and poetry. Don't be hasty when you consider a theme—mull it over and let it ferment in your mind. We appreciate interpretations that are carefully constructed, clever, subtle, well thought out."

360 DEGREES, Art & Literary Review, Hunting Creek Publishing, 980 Bush St., Suite 404, San Francisco CA 94109. Fax: (415)346-2514. E-mail: phwu@aol.com. City Managing Editor: Karen Kinnison. 100% freelance written. Quarterly literary magazine covering the arts—literature and artwork. "We are interested in writing and art which we feel contributes to civilization, that moves us forward. More like a museum than a magazine, we want to preserve the best from our times so readers in the future will seek us as a rare source." Estab. 1993. Circ. 1,000. Pays on publication. Publishes ms an average of 3 months after acceptance. Buys one-time rights and second serial (reprint) rights. Editorial lead time 6 months. Submit seasonal material 3 months in advance. Accepts simultaneous submissions. Reports in 2 weeks on queries, 1 month on mss. Sample copy for $5. Writer's guidelines free on request.

● The editor reports a need for more short stories.

Nonfiction: Book excerpts, essays, personal experience. "No technical or religious submissions." Buys 2 mss/year. Send complete ms. Length: open. Pays $10.

Photos: Send photos with submission. Reviews contact sheets, negatives, 3×5 prints. Offers no additional payment for photos accepted with ms. Identification of subjects required. Buys one-time rights with secondary reprint rights.

Fiction: Experimental, historical, mainstream, novel excerpts, stories by children or young writers. No religious or erotica. Buys 4 mss/year. Send complete ms. Pays $10-20.

Poetry: Avant-garde, free verse, haiku, traditional, poetry by children or young writers. No light verse. Buys 40 poems/year. Pays $5-10.
Tips: "For writers, write well. For artists, send clear photographs of artwork. The poetry department is most open to freelancers. Most of the poems we accept not only show mastery of words, but present new ideas. The mastery of language is something we expect from freelancers, but the content of the idea being presented is the selling point."

THE THREEPENNY REVIEW, P.O. Box 9131, Berkeley CA 94709. (510)849-4545. Editor: Wendy Lesser. 100% freelance written. Works with small number of new/unpublished writers each year. Quarterly literary tabloid. "We are a general interest, national literary magazine with coverage of politics, the visual arts and the performing arts as well." Estab. 1980. Circ. 9,000. **Pays on acceptance.** Publishes ms an average of 1 year after acceptance. Byline given. Buys first North American serial rights. Reports in 1 month on queries; 2 months on mss. Does *not* read mss in summer months. No simultaneous submissions. Sample copy for $6 and 10×13 SAE with 5 first-class stamps. Writer's guidelines for SASE.
Nonfiction: Essays, exposé, historical, personal experience, book, film, theater, dance, music and art reviews. Buys 40 mss/year. Query with or without published clips, or send complete ms. Length: 1,500-4,000 words. Pays $200.
Fiction: No fragmentary, sentimental fiction. Buys 10 mss/year. Send complete ms. Length: 800-4,000 words. Pays $200.
  ● Ranked as one of the best markets for fiction writers in *Writer's Digest*'s annual "Fiction 50," June 1996.
Poetry: Free verse, traditional. No poems "without capital letters or poems without a discernible subject." Buys 30 poems/year. Submit maximum 5 poems. Pays $100.
Tips: "Nonfiction (political articles, memoirs, reviews) is most open to freelancers."

‡TRAFIKA, Trafika Press, Inc., Janovskébo 14, Prague 7, the Czech Republic 17000. Editors: Jeffrey Young, Dorsey Dunn. Contact: Scott Lewis. Triannual. "*Trafika* is a magazine of current international literature." Estab. 1993. Circ. 6,000. Pays on publication. Publishes ms an average of 3 months after acceptance. Byline given. Offers 50% kill fee. Buys first international rights. Reports 4 months on queries. Sample copy for cost $10. Writer's guidelines for #10 SASE with IRC coupon.
Fiction: Buys 30 mss/year. Query with published clips. Send complete ms. Length: 10,000 words maximum. Pays $15/printed page.
Poetry: Donna Stonecipher, editorial assistant. Avant-garde, free verse. Buys 75 poems/year. Pays $15/printed page.

TRIQUARTERLY, 2020 Ridge Ave., Northwestern University, Evanston IL 60208-4302. (312)491-3490. Editors: Reginald Gibbons, Susan Hahn. 70% freelance written. Eager to work with new/unpublished writers. Triannual magazine of fiction, poetry and essays, as well as artwork. Estab. 1964. Pays on publication. Publishes ms an average of 1 year after acceptance. Buys first serial and nonexclusive reprint rights. Reports in 3 months. Study magazine before submitting. Sample copy for $5. Writer's guidelines for #10 SASE.
  ● *TriQuarterly* has had several stories published in the *O. Henry Prize* anthology and *Best American Short Stories* as well as poetry in *Best American Poetry*.
Nonfiction: Query before sending essays (no scholarly or critical essays except in special issues).
Fiction and Poetry: No prejudice against style or length of work; only seriousness and excellence are required. Buys 20-50 unsolicited mss/year. Pays $20/printed page.

VIRGINIA QUARTERLY REVIEW, University of Virginia, One West Range, Charlottesville VA 22903. (804)924-3124. Fax: (804)924-1397. E-mail: jco7e@virginia.edu. Contact: Staige D. Blackford, editor. Managing Editor: Janna Olson Gies. Quarterly magazine. "A national journal of literature and thought." Estab. 1925. Circ. 4,000. Pays on publication. Publishes ms an average of 1 year after acceptance. Byline given. Buys first rights. Editorial lead time 6 months. Submit seasonal material 6 months in advance. Reports in 2 weeks on queries; 2 months on mss. Sample copy $5. Writer's guidelines for #10 SASE.
Nonfiction: Book excerpts, essays, general interest, historical/nostalgic, humor, inspirational, personal experience, travel. Send complete ms. Length: 2,000-4,000 words. Pays $10/page maximum.
Fiction: Adventure, ethnic, historical, humorous, mainstream, mystery, novel excerpts, romance. Send complete ms. Length: 2,000-4,000 words. Pays $10/page maximum.
Poetry: Gregory Orr, poetry editor. All types. Submit maximum 5 poems. Pays $1/line.

‡WASCANA REVIEW OF CONTEMPORARY POETRY AND SHORT FICTION, University of Regina, Department of English, Regina, Sasketchewan S4T 1V9 Canada. Editor: Kathleen Wall. 100% freelance written. Semiannual magazine covering contemporary poetry and short fiction. "We seek poetry and short fiction that combines craft with risks, pressure with grace. Critical articles should articulate a theoretical approach and also explore either poetry or short fiction. While we frequently publish established writers, we also welcome—and seek to foster—new voices." Estab. 1966. Circ. 200. Pays on publication. Publishes ms an average of 4 months after acceptance. Buys first North American rights. Editorial lead time

4 months. Reports in 1 week on queries; 2 months on mss. Writer's guidelines free on request.

Columns/Departments: Reviews of contemporary poetry and short fiction (ask for guidelines), 1,000-1,500 words. Buys 8 mss/year. Query. Pays $3/printed page.

Fiction: No genre-bound fiction, or stories with sentimental or predictable endings. Buys 8-10 mss/year. Send complete ms. Pays $3/printed page plus 2 contributor's copies.

Poetry: Troni Grande. Avant-garde, free verse. No sentimental, fee-good verse, no predictable rhyme and meter. Buys 40 poems/year. Submit maximum 5 poems. Pays $10/printed page plus contributor's copies.

Tips: "The best advice I can give is to read back issues."

WEST COAST LINE, A Journal of Contemporary Writing & Criticism, West Coast Review Publishing Society, 2027 EAA. Simon Fraser University, Burnaby, British Columbia V5A 1S6 Canada. (604)291-4287. Fax: (604)291-5737. Website: http://www.sfu.ca/west-coast-line/WCL.html. Managing Editor: Jacqueline Larson. Triannual magazine of contemporary literature and criticism. Estab. 1990. Circ. 500. Pays on publication. Buys one-time rights. Editorial lead time 4 months. Submit seasonal material 4 months in advance. Reports in 2 weeks on queries; 3 months on mss. Sample copy for $10. Writer's guidelines free on request, only with SASE (US must include IRC).

Nonfiction: Essays (literary/scholarly), experimental prose. "No journalistic articles or articles dealing with nonliterary material." Buys 8-10 mss/year. Send complete ms. Length: 1,000-5,000 words. Pays $8/page and a year's free subscription.

Fiction: Experimental, novel excerpts. Buys 3-6 mss/year. Send complete ms. Length: 1,000-7,000 words. Pays $8/page.

Poetry: Avant-garde. "No light verse, traditional." Buys 10-15 poems/year. Length: 5-6 pages maximum. Pays $8/page.

Tips: "Submissions must be either scholarly or formally innovative. Contributors should be familiar with current literary trends in Canada and the US. Scholars should be aware of current schools of theory. All submissions should be accompanied by a brief cover letter; essays should be formatted according to the MLA guide. The publication is not divided into departments. We accept poetry, fiction, experimental prose and scholarly essays."

WINDSOR REVIEW, Windsor, Ontario N9B 3P4 Canada. (519)253-4232. ext. 2332. Fax: (519)973-7050. Website: http://www.CS.uwindsor.ca/units/english/pub.htm. Contact: Editor. Biannual comprising original poetry, fiction and art. Estab. 1965. Circ. 300. Buys first North American serial rights. Reports in 2 months. Sample copy for $5 and postage. Enclose SAE with Canadian postage or IRCs only.

Fiction: Alistair MacLeod. Mainstream prose with open attitude toward themes. Length: 2,000-6,000 words. Pays $50.

Poetry: John Ditsky. Accepts traditional forms, blank verse, free verse, avant-garde. No epics. Pays $15.

WITNESS, Oakland Community College, 27055 Orchard Lake Rd., Farmington Hills MI 48334. (313)471-7740. Editor: Peter Stine. 100% freelance written. Semiannual literary magazine. "*Witness* highlights the role of writer as witness." Estab. 1987. Circ. 2,800. Pays on publication. Publishes ms an average of 1 year after acceptance. Byline given. Buys first North American serial rights. Editorial lead time 6 months. Accepts simultaneous submissions. Reports in 3 months. Sample copy for $7. Writer's guidelines for #10 SASE.

• A rising and energetic magazine. The frequent theme issues require more work from the writer in studying this market.

Nonfiction: Essays, interview/profile. Buys 10 mss/year. Send complete ms. Length: 1,000-6,000 words. Pays $6/page.

Fiction: Ethnic, experimental, mainstream, literary. Buys 20 mss/year. Send complete ms. Length: 1,000-6,000 words. Pays $6/page.

Poetry: Avant-garde, free verse, traditional. Buys 20 poems/year. Submit maximum 4 poems. Pays $10/page.

THE YALE REVIEW, Yale University, P.O. Box 208243, New Haven CT 06520-8243. (203)432-0499. Editor: J.D. McClatchy. Managing Editor: Susan Bianconi. 20% freelance written. Buys first North American serial rights. Estab. 1911. Pays prior to publication. Responds in 2 months. Publishes in 5-12 months. "No writer's guidelines available. Consult back issues."

• *The Yale Review* has published work chosen for the Pushcart anthology, *The Best American Poetry*, and the O. Henry Award.

Nonfiction and Fiction: Authoritative discussions of politics, literature and the arts. Buys quality fiction. Length: 3,000-5,000 words. Pays $100-500.

YELLOW SILK: Journal of Erotic Arts, verygraphics, Box 6374, Albany CA 94706. (510)644-4188. E-mail: shebert@well.com. Editor: Lily Pond. 90% freelance written. Prefers to work with published/established writers. International journal of erotic literature and visual arts. "Editorial policy: All persuasions; no brutality. Our publication is artistic and literary, not pornographic or pandering. Humans are involved: heads, hearts and bodies—not just bodies alone; and the quality of the literature is as important as the erotic content though erotic content is important too." Pays on publication. Byline given. Buys all publication rights for 1 year following publication, at which time they revert to author, non-active and reprint electronic and anthology rights for duration of copyright. Reports in 3 months on mss. Sample copy for $7.50.

Nonfiction: Book excerpts, essays, humor, reviews. "We often have theme issues, but non-regularly and usually not announced in advance. No pornography, romance-novel type writing, sex fantasies. No first-person accounts or blow-by-blow descriptions. No articles. No novels." Buys 5-10 mss/year. Send complete ms. All submissions should be typed, double-spaced, with name, address and phone number on each page; always enclose SASE. No specified length requirements.

Photos: Photos may be submitted independently, not as illustration for submission. Reviews photocopies, contact sheets, transparencies and prints. "We accept 4-color and b&w artwork." Offers varying payment for series of 8-20 used, plus copies. Buys one-time rights and reprint rights.

Columns/Departments: Reviews (book, movie, art, dance, food, music, anything). "Erotic content and how it's handled is focus of importance. Old or new does not matter. We want to bring readers information of what's out there." Buys 8-10 mss/year. Send complete ms or query.

Fiction: Erotic literature, including ethnic, experimental, fantasy, humorous, mainstream, novel excerpts, science fiction. See "Nonfiction." Buys 12-16 mss/year. Send complete ms.

Poetry: Avant-garde, free verse, haiku, light verse, traditional. "No greeting-card poetry." Buys 40-60 poems/year. No limit on number of poems submitted, "but don't send book-length manuscripts."

Tips: "The best way to get into *Yellow Silk* is produce excellent, well-crafted work that includes eros freshly, with strength of voice, beauty of language, and insight into character. I'll tell you what I'm sick of and have, unfortunately, been seeing more of lately: the products of 'How to Write Erotica' classes. This is not brilliant fiction; it is poorly written fantasy and not what I'm looking for."

ZYZZYVA, The Last Word: West Coast Writers & Artists, 41 Sutter St., Suite 1400, San Francisco CA 94104-4987. (415)752-4393. Fax: (415)752-4391. E-mail: zyzzyvainc@aol.com. Editor: Howard Junker. 100% freelance written. Works with a small number of new/unpublished writers each year. "We feature work by West Coast writers only. We are essentially a literary magazine, but of wide-ranging interests and a strong commitment to nonfiction." Estab. 1985. Circ. 3,500. **Pays on acceptance.** Publishes ms an average of 3 months after acceptance. Byline given. Buys first North American serial rights and one-time anthology rights. Reports in 1 week on queries; 1 month on mss. Sample copy for $10.

Nonfiction: Book excerpts, general interest, historical/nostalgic, humor, personal experience. Buys 15 mss/year. Query. Length: open. Pays $50-250.

Fiction: Ethnic, experimental, humorous, mainstream. Buys 20 mss/year. Send complete ms. Length: open. Pays $50-250.

  • Ranked as one of the best markets for fiction writers in *Writer's Digest*'s annual "Fiction 50," June 1996.

Poetry: Buys 20 poems/year. Submit maximum 5 poems. Length: 3-200 lines. Pays $50-250.

MEN'S

Magazines in this section offer features on topics of general interest primarily to men. Magazines that also use material slanted toward men can be found in Business and Finance, Child Care and Parental Guidance, Ethnic/Minority, Gay & Lesbian Interest, General Interest, Health and Fitness, Military, Relationships and Sports sections. Magazines featuring pictorial layouts accompanied by stories and articles of a sexual nature, both gay and straight, appear in the Sex section.

‡DETAILS, Condé Nast Publications, Inc., 632 Broadway, New York NY 10012. Monthly magazine for men ages 18-34 interested in style, sex, pop cultures, new and sports. *Details* is edited as a lifestyle magazine for today's generation of young adults who are rapidly assuming their places as leaders in American society. Articles are written from the standpoint of a peer—in contemporary language that readers can relate to, within an intelligent, sophisticated perspective on the world. From culture to sports to entertaining to relationships—fashion, careers, music, clubs and technology, *Details* covers the various aspects of its readers' lives." Estab. 1982. Circ. 473,000. **Pays on acceptance.** Byline given. Offers 25-50% kill fee. Accepts simultaneous submissions. Reports in 2 months on queries.

  • Ranked as one of the best markets for freelance writers in *Writer's Yearbook*'s annual "Top 100 Markets," January 1996.

Nonfiction: News stories of interest to young men; personal essays and service features on lifestyle topics from shops to booze, sports, travel, relationships, courtship, automotive. Buys 60 mss/year. Query with published clips. Length: 3,000-5,000 words. Pays 75¢-$1/word.

Columns/Departments: 800-1,500 words. Buys 120 mss/year. Query with published clips. Pays 75¢-$1/word.

Fillers: Buys 60/year. Length: 500-800 words. Pays 75¢-$1/word.

Tips: "Topical news stories that affect or interest men in their 20s. Timely subject, stylishly written that makes people laugh and cry. *Details* maintains a high standard of modern journalism and encourages a creative, stylish, confessional, personal emotional writing style. We include all kinds of people with all kinds of interest and beliefs. We speak to our readers in a contemporary manner, with a unique tone that touches the heart and mind and tickles that funny bone."

ESQUIRE, 250 W. 55th St., New York NY 10019. (212)649-4020. Editor-in-Chief: Edward Kosner. Articles Editor: Bill Tonelli. Men's monthly. Estab. 1933. General readership is college educated and sophisticated, between ages 30 and 45. Written mostly by contributing editors on contract. Rarely accepts unsolicited mss. **Pays on acceptance**. Publishes ms an average of 2 months after acceptance. Retains first worldwide periodical publication rights for 90 days from cover date. Queries must be sent by letter.

• Ranked as one of the best markets for freelance writers in *Writer's Yearbook*'s annual "Top 100 Markets," January 1996.

Nonfiction: Columns average 1,500 words; features average 6,000 words; short front-of-book pieces average 200-400 words. Focus is on the ever-changing trends in American culture. Topics include current events and politics, social criticism, sports, celebrity profiles, the media, art and music, men's fashion.

Photos: Marianne Butler, photo editor. Uses mostly commissioned photography. Payment depends on size and number of photos.

Fiction: Will Blythe, literary editor. "Literary excellence is our only criterion." Accepts work chiefly from literary agencies. Publishes short stories, some poetry, and excerpts from novels, memoirs and plays.

Tips: "A writer has the best chance of breaking in at *Esquire* by querying with a specific idea that requires special contacts and expertise. Ideas must be timely and national in scope."

GENTLEMEN'S QUARTERLY, Condé Nast, 350 Madison Ave., New York NY 10017. (212)880-8800. Editor-in-Chief: Arthur Cooper. Managing Editor: Martin Beiser. 60% freelance written. Circ. 650,000. Monthly magazine emphasizing fashion, general interest and service features for men ages 25-45 with a large discretionary income. **Pays on acceptance.** Byline given. Pays 25% kill fee. Submit seasonal/holiday material 6 months in advance. Reports in 1 month.

Nonfiction: Politics, personality profiles, lifestyles, trends, grooming, nutrition, health and fitness, sports, travel, money, investment and business matters. Buys 4-6 mss/issue. Query with published clips. Length: 1,500-4,000 words. Pay varies.

Columns/Departments: Martin Beiser, managing editor. Query with published clips. Length: 1,000-2,500 words. Pay varies.

Tips: "Major features are usually assigned to well-established, known writers. Pieces are almost always solicited. The best way to break in is through the columns, especially Contraria, Enthusiasms or First Person."

HEARTLAND USA, UST Publishing, 1 Sound Shore Dr., Suite 3, Greenwich CT 06830-7251. (203)632-3456. Fax: (203)863-5893. E-mail: husaedit@aol.com. Editor: Brad Pearson. 50% freelance written. Bimonthly magazine for working people. "*Heartland USA* is a general interest, lifestyle magazine for working people 18 to 53. It covers spectator sports (primarily motor sports, football, baseball and basketball, hunting, fishing, how-to, travel, music, gardening, the environment, human interest, etc.), emphasizing the upbeat or humorous." Estab. 1991. Circ. 1,000,000. **Pays on acceptance**. Byline given. Offers 20% kill fee. Buys first North American serial and second serial (reprint) rights. Submit seasonal material 1 year in advance. Accepts simultaneous submissions. Reports in 1 month on queries. Sample copy on request. Free writer's guidelines.

Nonfiction: Book excerpts, general interest, historical/nostalgic, how-to, humor, inspirational, interview/profile, new product, personal experience, photo feature, technical, travel. "No fiction or dry expository pieces." Buys 30 mss/year. Query with or without published clips or send complete ms. Length: 350-1,200 words. Pays 50-80¢/word for assigned articles; 25-80¢/word for unsolicited articles. Sometimes pays expenses of writers on assignment.

Reprints: Accepts previously published submissions. Send photocopy of article and information about when and where the article previously appeared. Pays $200.

Photos: Send photos with submission. Reviews transparencies. Identification of subjects required. Buys one-time rights.

Tips: "Features with the possibility of strong photographic support are open to freelancers, as are our shorter departments. We look for a relaxed, jocular, easy-to-read style, and look favorably on the liberal use of anecdote or interesting quotations."

MEN'S JOURNAL, Wenner Media Inc., 1290 Avenue of the Americas, New York NY 10104. (212)484-1616. Fax: (212)767-8205. Editor: John Rasmus. Monthly magazine covering general lifestyle for men. "*Men's Journal* is for active men with an interest in participatory sports, travel, fitness and adventure. It provides practical, informative articles on how to spend quality leisure time." Estab. 1992. Circ. 334,000. This magazine did not respond to our request for information. Query before submitting.

‡**NEW MAN**, Strang Communications Co., 600 Rinehart Rd., Lake Mary FL 32746. (407)333-0600. Fax: (407)333-7133. Website: http://www.strang.com. Editor: Brian Peterson. Magazine published 8 times a year covering Christian men with Christ-centered lives. Estab. 1994. Circ. 300,000. Pays on publication. Publishes ms an average of 4 months after acceptance. Byline given. Buys first or simultaneous rights. Editorial lead time 8 months. Submit seasonal material 8 months in advance. Accepts simultaneous submissions. Reports in 4 months. Sample copy for $3. Writer's guidelines free on request.

Nonfiction: Book excerpts, humor, interview/profile, personal experience, photo feature. Buys 50 mss/year. Length: 2,000 words maximum. Pays 10-35¢/word. Sometimes pays expenses of writers on assignment.

Columns/Departments: Women (written to men about women) 1,000 words; Health (men's health concerns) 1,000 words; Finances 1,000 words. Buys 15 mss/year. Send complete ms. Pays $100-300.

Fillers: Anecdotes, facts, newsbreaks. Length: 250 words maximum. Pays 10-35¢/word.

MILITARY

These publications emphasize military or paramilitary subjects or other aspects of military life. Technical and semitechnical publications for military commanders, personnel and planners, as well as those for military families and civilians interested in Armed Forces activities are listed here. Publications covering military history can be found in the History section.

AMERICAN SURVIVAL GUIDE, McMullen Argus Publishing, Inc., 774 S. Placentia Ave., Placentia CA 92670-6832. (714)572-6887, ext.219, 216. Fax: (714)572-1864. Editor: Jim Benson. Managing Editor: Scott Stoddard. 50% freelance written. Monthly magazine covering "self-reliance, defense, meeting day-to-day and possible future threats—survivalism for survivalists." Circ. 48,000. Pays on publication. Publishes ms up to 1 year after acceptance. Byline given. Submit seasonal material 5 months in advance. Sample copy for $3.50. Writer's guidelines for SASE.

- This staff is always looking for more good material with quality artwork (photos). They want articles on recent events and new techniques, etc. giving the latest available information to their readers.

Nonfiction: Exposé (political); how-to; interview/profile; personal experience (how I survived); photo feature (equipment and techniques related to survival in all possible situations); emergency medical; health and fitness; communications; transportation; food preservation; water purification; self-defense; terrorism; nuclear dangers; nutrition; tools; shelter; etc. "No general articles about how to survive. We want specifics and single subjects." Buys 60-100 mss/year. Query or send complete ms. Length: 1,500-2,000 words. Pays $140-350. Sometimes pays some expenses of writers on assignment.

Photos: Send photos with ms. "One of the most frequent mistakes made by writers in completing an article assignment for us is sending photo submissions that are inadequate." Captions, model releases and identification of subjects mandatory. Buys all rights.

Tips: "Prepare material of value to individuals who wish to sustain human life no matter what the circumstance. This magazine is a text and reference."

ARMY MAGAZINE, Box 1560, Arlington VA 22210. (703)841-4300. Fax: (703)525-9039. E-mail: ausaar mag@aol.com. Editor: Mary Blake French. 70% freelance written. Prefers to work with published/established writers. Monthly magazine emphasizing military interests. Estab. 1904. Circ. 130,000. Pays on publication. Publishes ms an average of 5 months after acceptance. Buys all rights. Byline given except for back-up research. Submit seasonal/holiday material 3 months in advance. Sample copy and writer's guidelines for 9×12 SAE with $1 postage.

- *Army Magazine* is now looking for shorter articles.

Nonfiction: Historical (military and original); humor (military feature-length articles and anecdotes); interview; new product; nostalgia; personal experience dealing especially with the most recent conflicts in which the US Army has been involved (Desert Storm, Panama, Grenada); photo feature; profile; technical. No rehashed history. "We would like to see more pieces about little-known episodes involving interesting military personalities. We especially want material lending itself to heavy, contributor-supplied photographic treatment. The first thing a contributor should recognize is that our readership is very savvy militarily. 'Gee-whiz' personal reminiscences get short shrift, unless they hold their own in a company in which long military service, heroism and unusual experiences are commonplace. At the same time, Army readers like a well-written story with a fresh slant, whether it is about an experience in a foxhole or the fortunes of a corps in battle." Buys 8 mss/issue. Submit complete ms. Length: 1,500 words, but shorter items, especially in 1,000 to 1,500 range, often have better chance of getting published. Pays 12-18¢/word. No unsolicited book reviews.

Photos: Submit photo material with accompanying ms. Pays $25-50 for 8×10 b&w glossy prints; $50-350 for 8×10 color glossy prints or 2¼×2¼ transparencies; will also accept 35mm. Captions preferred. Buys all rights. Pays $35-50 for cartoon with strong military slant.

Columns/Departments: Military news, books, comment (*New Yorker*-type "Talk of the Town" items). Buys 8/issue. Submit complete ms. Length: 1,000 words. Pays $40-150.

‡**ARMY/NAVY/AIR FORCE TIMES**, Army Times Publishing Co., 6883 Commerce Dr., Springfield VA 22159. Weeklies edited separately for Army, Navy, Marine, Coast Guard, and Air Force military personnel and their families. They contain career information such as pay raises, promotions, news of legislation affecting the military, housing, base activities and features of interest to military families. Estab. 1940. Circ. 286,800. **Pays on acceptance**. Byline given. Offers kill fee. Buys first rights. Accepts simultaneous submissions. Reports in 1 month on queries. Sample copy and writer's guidelines free on request.
  • Ranked as one of the best markets for freelance writers in *Writer's Yearbook*'s annual "Top 100 Markets," January 1996.
Nonfiction: Features of interest to career military personnel and their families. No advice pieces. Buys 150-175 mss/year. Length: 750-2,000 words. Pays $100-250 for assigned articles.
Columns/Departments: Length: 500-900 words. Buys 75 mss/year. Pays $100-150.
Fillers: Buys 5-10/year. Length: 250-500 words. Pays $25-75.
Tips: Looking for "travel pieces with a military connection. Stories on successful civilian careers after military service, and about military authors. Understand the special demands of military life."

FAMILY MAGAZINE, The Magazine for Military Wives, PABCO, 169 Lexington Ave., New York NY 10016. Editor: Stacy P. Brassington. 90% freelance written. Monthly magazine covering military family lifestyle. "*Family* contains features on military family life: relocating, decorating, cooking, travel, education, children, careers, marriage and family health." Estab. 1973. Circ. 500,000. Pays on publication. Byline given. Buys one-time rights. Editorial lead time 3 months. Submit seasonal material 6 months in advance. Accepts simultaneous submissions. Reports in 2 months on queries. Sample copy for $1.25. Writer's guidelines for #10 SASE.
Nonfiction: General interest, how-to, travel, food/recipe. Buys 100 mss/year. Send complete ms. Length: 1,000-1,500 words. Pays $50-200.
Photos: State availability of photos with submission. Offers $25-50/photo. Buys one-time rights.
Columns/Departments: Send complete ms. Pays $75-150.

NAVAL HISTORY, US Naval Institute, 118 Maryland Ave., Annapolis MD 21402-5035. (410)268-6110. Contact: Fred L. Schultz, editor. Associate Editor: Bruce Gibson. 90% freelance written. Bimonthly magazine covering naval and maritime history, worldwide. "We are committed, as a publication of the 121-year-old US Naval Institute, to presenting the best and most accurate short works in international naval and maritime history. We do find a place for academicians, but they should be advised that a good story generally wins against a dull topic, no matter how well-researched." Estab. 1988. Circ. 34,000. **Pays on acceptance**. Publishes ms an average of 2 years after acceptance. Byline given. Buys first North American serial rights; occasionally allows rights to revert to authors. Editorial lead time 6 months. Submit seasonal material 6 months in advance. Reports in 1 month on queries; 2 months on mss. Sample copy for $3.50 and SASE. Writer's guidelines free on request.
Nonfiction: Book excerpts, essays, historical/nostalgic, humor, inspirational, interview/profile, personal experience, photo feature, technical. Buys 80-100 mss/year. Query. Length: 1,000-3,000 words. Pays $300-500 for assigned articles; $75-400 for unsolicited articles.
Photos: State availability of photos with submission. Reviews contact sheets, transparencies, 4 × 6 or larger prints. Offers $10 minimum. Captions, model releases, identification of subjects required. Buys one-time rights.
Fillers: Anecdotes, news breaks (naval-related), short humor. Buys 40-50/year. Length: 50-1,000 words. Pays $10-50.
Tips: "A good way to break in is to write a good, concise, exciting story supported by primary sources and substantial illustrations. Naval history-related news items (ship decommissionings, underwater archaeology, etc.) are also welcome. We currently have a glut of first-person pieces on World War II and are also still well-supplied with Civil War-era manuscripts. We are in need of Korean and Vietnam War-era material."

NAVY TIMES, Times Journal, 6883 Commercial Dr., Springfield VA 22159. (703)750-8636. Fax: (703)750-8622. Editor: Tobias Naegele. Managing Editor: Jean Reid Norman. Weekly newspaper covering sea services. News and features of men and women in the Navy, Coast Guard and Marine Corps. Estab. 1950. Circ. 90,000. **Pays on acceptance.** Byline given. Buys first North American serial or second serial (reprint) rights. Submit seasonal material 2 months in advance. Reports in 2 months. Free writer's guidelines.
Nonfiction: Historical/nostalgic, opinion. No poetry. Buys 100 mss/year. Query. Length: 500-1,000 words. Pays $50-500. Sometimes pays expenses of writers on assignment.
Photos: Send photos with submission. Offers $20-100/photo. Captions and identification of subjects required. Buys one-time rights.

OFF DUTY MAGAZINE, 3303 Harbor Blvd., Suite C-2, Costa Mesa CA 92626-1500. (714)549-7172. Fax: (714)549-4222. E-mail: odutyedit@aol.com. Editorial Director: Jim Shaw. Contact: Gary Burch, managing editor. 30% freelance written. Monthly magazine covering the leisure-time activities and interests of the military community. "Our audience is solely military members and their families; many of our articles could appear in other consumer magazines, but we always slant them toward the military; i.e. where to get a military discount when traveling." Estab. 1970. Circ. 507,000. **Pays on acceptance.** Publishes ms an average of 3 months after acceptance. Byline given. Buys one-time rights. Submit seasonal material at least 4 months in advance. Accepts simultaneous submissions. Reports in 2 months on queries. Sample copy for 9×12 SAE with 6 first class stamps. Writer's guidelines for SASE.

Nonfiction: Travel, finance, lifestyle (with a military angle), interview/profile (music and entertainment). "Must be familiar with *Off Duty* and its needs." Buys 30-40 mss/year. Query. Length: 800-2,100 words. Pays $160-420 for assigned articles.

• Editor is not interested in seeing World War II reminiscences. He reports they are buying fewer articles due to slimmer issues and fewer magazines per year.

Reprints: Send photocopy of article and information about when and where the article previously appeared. Pays 50% of amount paid for an original article.

Photos: Send photos with submission. Reviews contact sheets and 35mm transparencies. Offers $50-300/photo (cover). Captions and identification of subjects required. Buys one-time rights. Unsolicited photos not returned without SASE.

Tips: "Get to know the military community and its interests beyond the stereotypes. Travel—query with the idea of getting on our next year's editorial calendar. We choose our primary topics at least six months in advance."

PARAMETERS: U.S. Army War College Quarterly, U.S. Army War College, Carlisle Barracks PA 17013-5050. (717)245-4943. Editor: Col. John J. Madigan, U.S. Army Retired. 100% freelance written. Prefers to work with published/established writers or experts in the field. Readership consists of senior leadership of US defense establishment, both uniformed and civilian, plus members of the media, government, industry and academia interested in national and international security affairs, military strategy, military leadership and management, art and science of warfare, and military history (provided it has contemporary relevance). Most readers possess a graduate degree. Estab. 1971. Circ. 12,000. Not copyrighted; unless copyrighted by author, articles may be reprinted with appropriate credits. Buys first serial rights. Byline given. Pays on publication. Publishes ms an average of 6 months after acceptance. Reports in 6 weeks. Free sample copy and writer's guidelines.

Nonfiction: Articles are preferred that deal with current security issues, employ critical analysis and provide solutions or recommendations. Liveliness and verve, consistent with scholarly integrity, appreciated. Theses, studies and academic course papers should be adapted to article form prior to submission. Documentation in complete endnotes. Submit complete ms. Length: 4,500 words average, preferably less. Pays $150 average (including visuals).

Tips: "Make it short; keep it interesting; get criticism and revise accordingly. Tackle a subject only if you are an authority."

‡**THE RETIRED OFFICER MAGAZINE**, 201 N. Washington St., Alexandria VA 22314-2539. (800)245-8762. Fax: (703)838-8179. E-mail: editor@troa.org. Website: http://www.troa.org. Editor: Col. Charles D. Cooper, USAF-Ret. Managing Editor: Julia Leigh. Contact: Lisa Frantz, associate editor. 60% freelance written. Prefers to work with published/established writers. Monthly magazine for officers of the 7 uniformed services and their families. Estab. 1945. Circ. 395,000. **Pays on acceptance.** Publishes ms an average of 9-12 months after acceptance. Byline given. Buys first serial rights. Submit seasonal material (holiday stories with a military theme) at least 9-12 months in advance. Reports on material accepted for publication within 3 months. Sample copy and writer's guidelines for 9×12 SAE with 6 first-class stamps.

• Ranked as one of the best markets for freelance writers in *Writer's Yearbook*'s annual "Top 100 Markets," January 1996.

Nonfiction: Current military/political affairs, health and wellness, recent military history, travel, second-career job opportunities, military family lifestyle. Emphasis now on current military and defense issues. "We rarely accept unsolicited manuscripts. We look for detailed query letters with résumé and sample clips attached. We do not publish poetry or fillers." Buys 48 mss/year. Length: 800-2,000 words. Pays up to $1,000.

Photos: Query with list of stock photo subjects. Reviews 8×10 b&w photos (normal halftone). Original slides or transparencies must be suitable for color separation. Pays up to $125 for inside color; up to $200 for cover.

SOLDIER OF FORTUNE, The Journal of Professional Adventurers, Omega Group, Ltd., P.O. Box 693, Boulder CO 80306-0693. (303)449-3750. Fax: (303)444-5617. Managing Editor: Dwight Swift. Deputy Editor: Tom Reisinger. 50% freelance written. Monthly magazine covering military, paramilitary, police, combat subjects and action/adventure. "We are an action-oriented magazine; we cover combat hot spots around the world such as Afghanistan, El Salvador, Angola, etc. We also provide timely features on state-of-the-art weapons and equipment; elite military and police units; and historical military operations. Readership is primarily active-duty military, veterans and law enforcement." Estab. 1975. Circ. 175,000. Byline given. Offers 25% kill fee. Buys all rights; will negotiate. Submit seasonal material 5 months in advance. Reports in 3 weeks on queries; 1 month on mss. Sample copy for $5. Writer's guidelines for #10 SASE. Send mss to articles editor; queries to managing editor.

Nonfiction: Exposé; general interest; historical/nostalgic; how-to (on weapons and their skilled use); humor; profile; new product; personal experience; novel excerpts; photo feature ("number one on our list"); technical; travel; combat reports; military unit reports and solid Vietnam and Operation Desert Storm articles. "No 'How I won the war' pieces; no op-ed pieces *unless* they are fully and factually backgrounded; no knife articles (staff assignments only). *All* submitted articles should have good art; art will sell us on an article." Buys 75 mss/year. Query with or without published clips or send complete ms. Length: 2,000-3,000 words. Pays $150-250/page. Sometimes pays the expenses of writers on assignment.

Reprints: Send photocopy of article and information about when and where the article previously appeared. Pays 25% of amount paid for an original article.

Photos: Send photos with submission (copies only, no originals). Reviews contact sheets and transparencies. Offers no additional payment for photos accepted with ms. Pays $500 for cover photo. Captions and identification of subjects required. Buys one-time rights.

Columns/Departments: Combat craft (how-to military and police survival skills) and I Was There (first-person accounts of the arcane or unusual based in a combat or law enforcement environment), both 600-800 words. Buys 16 mss/year. Send complete ms. Length: 600-800 words. Combat craft pays $200; I was There $100.

Fillers: Bulletin Board editor. Newsbreaks; military/paramilitary related, "*has* to be documented." Length: 100-250 words. Pays $25.

Tips: "Submit a professionally prepared, complete package. All artwork with cutlines, double-spaced typed manuscript with 5.25 or 3.5 IBM-compatible disc, if available, cover letter including synopsis of article, supporting documentation where applicable, etc. Manuscript must be factual; writers have to do their homework and get all their facts straight. One error means rejection. We will work with authors over the phone or by letter, tell them if their ideas have merit for an acceptable article, and help them fine-tune their work. I Was There is a good place for freelancers to start. Vietnam features, if carefully researched and art heavy, will always get a careful look. Combat reports, again, with good art, are number one in our book and stand the best chance of being accepted. Military unit reports from around the world are well received as are law enforcement articles (units, police in action). If you write for us, be complete and factual; pros read *Soldier of Fortune*, and are *very* quick to let us know if we (and the author) err. We will be Operation Desert Storm-oriented for years to come, in terms of first-person accounts and incisive combat reports. Read a current issue to see where we're taking the magazine in the 1990s."

TIMES NEWS SERVICE, Army Times Publishing Co., 6883 Springfield Dr., Springfield VA 22159-0200. (703)750-8125. Fax: (703)750-8781. E-mail: mconews@aol.com. Website: http://www.armytimes.com. Special Sections Editor: Margaret Roth. Features Editor: Maureen Rhea. 15% freelance written. Willing to work with new/unpublished writers. Manages weekly lifestyle section of Army, Navy and Air Force Times covering current lifestyles and problems of career military families around the world. Circ. 300,000. **Pays on acceptance.** Publishes ms an average of 2 months after acceptance. Byline given. Buys first worldwide rights. Submit seasonal material 3 months in advance. Reports in about 1 month. Writer's guidelines for #10 SASE.

- *Times News Service* accepts few exposé-type articles from freelancers but it is always interested in seeing queries. If you have news, they will accept it from a freelancer, but staff writers generally get the news before any freelancers can.

Nonfiction: Exposé (current military); interview/profile (military); personal experience (military only); travel (of military interest). Buys about 200 mss/year. Query with published clips. Length: 500-2,000 words. Pays $75-300. Sometimes pays the expenses of writers on assignment.

Photos: Send photos or send photos with ms. Reviews 35mm color contact sheets and prints. Captions, model releases and identification of subjects required.

Tips: "In your query write a detailed description of story and how it will be told. A tentative lead is nice. A military angle is crucial. Just one good story 'breaks in' a freelancer. Follow the outline you propose in your query letter and humanize articles with quotes and examples."

MUSIC

Music fans follow the latest industry news in these publications that range from opera to hip hop. Types of music and musicians or specific instruments are the sole focus of some magazines. Publications geared to the music industry and professionals can be found in the Trade Music section. Additional music and dance markets are found in the Contemporary Culture and Entertainment section.

BLUEGRASS UNLIMITED, Bluegrass Unlimited, Inc., P.O. Box 111, Broad Run VA 20137-0111. (540)349-8181 or (800)BLU-GRAS. Fax: (540)341-0011. Editor: Peter V. Kuykendall. Contact: Sharon

Watts, managing editor. 80% freelance written. Prefers to work with published/established writers. Monthly magazine on bluegrass and old-time country music. Estab. 1966. Circ. 24,500. Pays on publication. Publishes ms an average of 4 months after acceptance. Byline given. Kill fee negotiated. Buys first North American serial, one-time, all rights and second serial (reprint) rights. Submit seasonal material 4 months in advance. Reports in 2 weeks on queries; 2 months on mss. Free sample copy and writer's guidelines for #10 SASE.
Nonfiction: General interest, historical/nostalgic, how-to, interview/profile, personal experience, photo feature, travel. No "fan"-style articles. Buys 75-80 mss/year. Query with or without published clips. No set word length. Pays 8-10¢/word.
Reprints: Send photocopy or typed ms with rights for sale noted and information about when and where the article previously appeared. Payment is negotiated.
Photos: State availability of or send photos with query. Reviews 35mm transparencies and 3×5, 5×7 and 8×10 b&w and color prints. Pays $50-150 for transparencies; $25-50 for b&w prints; $50-250 for color prints. Identification of subjects required. Buys one-time and all rights.
Fiction: Ethnic, humorous. Buys 3-5 mss/year. Query. No set word length. Pays 8-10¢/word.
Tips: "We would prefer that articles be informational, based on personal experience or an interview with lots of quotes from subject, profile, humor, etc."

‡**CHAMBER MUSIC**, Chamber Music America, 545 Eighth Ave., New York NY 10018-4385. (212)244-2772. Fax: (212)244-2776. Editor: Gwendolyn Freed. Bimonthly magazine covering chamber music. Estab. 1977. Circ. 13,000. Pays on publication. Publishes ms an average of 8 months after acceptance. Byline given. Offers $200 kill fee. Buys all rights. Editorial lead time 4 months. Submit seasonal material 4 months in advance.
Nonfiction: General interest, humor, interview/profile, travel as related to chamber music. Buys 100 mss/year. Query. Length: 2,500-3,500 words. Pays $500 minimum for assigned articles. Sometimes pays expenses of writers on assignment.
Photos: State availability of photos with submission. Offers no additional payment for photos accepted with ms.

HIT PARADER, 210 Route 4 E., Suite 401, Paramus NJ 07652. (201)843-4004. Editor: Andy Secher. Managing Editor: Mary Anne Cassata. 5% freelance written. Monthly magazine covering heavy metal music. "We look for writers who have access to the biggest names in heavy metal music." Estab. 1943. Circ. 200,000. Pays on publication. Publishes ms an average of 4 months after acceptance. Byline given. Buys all rights. Submit seasonal material 5 months in advance. Sample copy for 9×12 SAE with 5 first-class stamps.
Nonfiction: General interest, interview/profile. Buys 3-5 mss/year. Query with published clips. Length: 600-800 words. Pays $75-140. Lifestyle-oriented and hardball pieces. "Study and really know the bands to get new angles on story ideas."
Photos: Reviews transparencies, 5×7 and 8×10 b&w prints and Kodachrome 64 slides. Offers $25-200/photo. Buys one-time rights. "We don't work with new photographers."
Tips: "Interview big names in metal, get published in other publications. We don't take chances on new writers."

ILLINOIS ENTERTAINER, 124 W. Polk, Suite 103, Chicago IL 60605. (312)922-9333. Fax: (312)922-9369. E-mail: ieeditors@aol.com. Editor: Michael C. Harris. 95% freelance written. Prefers to work with published/established writers but open to new writers with "style." Monthly tabloid covering music and entertainment for consumers within 100-mile radius of Chicago. Estab. 1974. Circ. 80,000. Pays on publication. Publishes ms an average of 2 months after acceptance. Byline given. Offers 10% kill fee. Buys one-time rights. Reports in 2 months. Sample copy for $5.
Nonfiction: Interview/profile (of entertainment figures). Special issues: Chicago Club Guide (October); Local Band Directory (January); Local Studio Directory (February); National Guitar Month (April); Local Indie Label Guide (May); Record Collecting (July); Sound Reinforcement (August). Buys 75 mss/year. Query with published clips. Length: 500-2,000 words. Pays $15-100. Sometimes pays expenses of writers on assignment.
Reprints: Send tearsheet or photocopy of article and information about when and where the article previously appeared. Pays 100% of amount paid for an original article.
Photos: Send photos. Pays $20-30 for 5×7 or 8×10 b&w prints; $125 for color cover photo, both on publication only. Captions and identification of subjects required.
Columns/Departments: Spins (record reviews stress record over band or genre). Buys 200 mss/year. Query with published clips. Length: 250 words. Pays $10-40.
Tips: "Send clips (published or unpublished) with phone number, and be patient. Full staff has seniority, but if you know the ins and outs of the entertainment biz, and can balance that knowledge with a broad sense of humor, then you'll have a chance. Also, *IE* is more interested in alternative music than the pop-pap you can hear/read about everywhere else."

‡**JAM MAGAZINE**, P.O. Box 1867, Pinellas Park FL 34664. (813)578-1400. Fax: (813)578-1414. E-mail: jam-west@digital.net. Contact: Curtis Hayes, editor. Managing Editor: Bill Templeton. 95% freelance written.

Consumer publication. Biweekly free magazine for music. "Intelligent news, reviews and interviews about music and the people who make it." Estab. 1990. Circ. 30,000. Pays on publication. Byline given. Buys one-time, second serial (reprint) rights (not within market), simultaneous rights (not within market) or other rights (exclusive within market only). Submit seasonal material 6 weeks in advance. Accepts simultaneous submissions. Sample copy for $2. Call for writer's guidelines.

Nonfiction: Exposé, interview/profile and music. Special issues: Guitar Month (April). Buys 150 mss/year. Query with published clips or send complete ms. Length: 200-2,500 words. Pays $20-50. Sometimes pays expenses of writers on assignment.

Reprints: Accepts previously published submissions.

Photos: Send photos with submission. Reviews prints. Offers $10-15/photo. Captions and identification of subjects required. Buys one-time rights (exclusive within market only).

MODERN DRUMMER, 12 Old Bridge Rd., Cedar Grove NJ 07009. (201)239-4140. Fax: (201)239-7139. Editor-in-Chief: Ronald Spagnardi. Features Editor: William F. Miller. Managing Editor: Rick Van Horn. Monthly magazine for "student, semi-pro and professional drummers at all ages and levels of playing ability, with varied specialized interests within the field." 60% freelance written. Circ. 98,000. Pays on publication. Publishes ms an average of 3 months after acceptance. Buys all rights. Reports in 2 weeks. Sample copy for $3.95. Free writer's guidelines.

Nonfiction: How-to, informational, interview, new product, personal experience, technical. "All submissions must appeal to the specialized interests of drummers." Buys 20-30 mss/year. Query or submit complete ms. Length: 5,000-8,000 words. Pays $200-500.

Reprints: Accepts previously published submissions.

Photos: Purchased with accompanying ms. Reviews 8×10 b&w prints and color transparencies.

Columns/Departments: Jazz Drummers Workshop, Rock Perspectives, In The Studio, Show Drummers Seminar, Teachers Forum, Drum Soloist, The Jobbing Drummer, Strictly Technique, Book Reviews, Record Reviews, Video Reviews, Shop Talk. "Technical knowledge of area required for most columns." Buys 40-50 mss/year. Query or submit complete ms. Length: 500-1,000 words. Pays $25-150.

MUSICIAN, Billboard Publications, 11th Floor, 1515 Broadway, New York NY 10036. (212)536-5208. Editor: Robert Doerschuk. Senior Editors: Mark Rowland, Mac Randall. 85% freelance written. Monthly magazine covering contemporary music, especially rock, pop and jazz. Estab. 1976. Circ. 170,000. Pays on publication. Byline given. Offers 25-33% kill fee. Buys first world serial rights. Submit seasonal material 3 months in advance.

Nonfiction: All music-related: book excerpts, exposé, historical, how-to (recording and performing), humor, interview/profile, new product, technical. Buys 150 mss/year. Query with published clips. Length: 300-10,000 words. Payment negotiable. Pays expenses of writers on assignment.

Photos: Assigns photo shoots. Uses some stock. Offers $50-300/photo.

Columns/Departments: Jazz (jazz artists or works), 1,000-5,000 words; Reviews (record reviews), 300-500 words; Rough Mix (short, newsy stories), 300 words; Fast Forward (technical "trade" angles on musicians), 1,000-3,000 words. Query with published clips. Length 300-1,500 words.

Tips: "Be aware of special music writers' style; don't gush, be somewhat skeptical; get the best quotes you can and save the arcane criticism for reviews; know and apply Strunk and White; be interesting. Please send *published* clips; we don't want to be anyone's first publication. Our writing is considered excellent (in all modesty), even though we don't pay as much as we'd like. We recognize National Writers Union."

‡ON THE DOWNLOW, Underground Hip-Hop Zine, Myriad Publication, 1201 Jordan St., Longview TX 75602. (903)753-4933. Editor: LaTosha Stanfield-Addison. 90% freelance written. Monthly magazine covering underground hip-hop music news. "The writers must live and breathe hip-hop music. It is for the purist, the outspoken, and the romantic lovers of the art of hip-hop and rap." Estab. 1993. Pays on publication. Publishes ms an average of 3 months after acceptance. Byline given. Buys all rights. Editorial lead time 2 months. Submit seasonal material 2 months in advance. Accepts simultaneous submissions. Sample copy and writer's guidelines free on request.

Nonfiction: Book excerpts, exposé, historical/nostalgic, humor, inspirational, interview/profile, opinion, photo feature, religious. Buys 200 mss/year. Send complete ms. Length: 800-2,000 words. Pays $75-100 for assigned articles; $25-50 for unsolicited articles. Also pays in concert tickets, backstage passes, new unreleased music from new and professional artists. Sometimes pays expenses of writers on assignment.

Photos: Send photos with submission. Reviews 8×10 maximum prints. Offers no additional payment for photos accepted with ms. Captions, model releases, identification of subjects required. Buys all rights.

FOR INFORMATION on setting your freelance fees, see How Much Should I Charge?

Columns/Departments: Record Album Review (open minded objectivity), 50 words; Honies (beautiful women with a hip-hop edge), 25 words; For the Love of (a passionate review of a pioneering hip-hop artist), 800 words. Buys 175 mss/year. Send complete ms. Pays $30-75.

Fiction: Erotica, ethnic, experimental, humorous, slice-of-life vignettes, futuristic, psychedelic, inner city superheroes. "It has to be an overwhelming 'live and die hip-hop' attitude in every sentence." Buys 15 mss/year. Send complete ms. Length: 800-2,000 words. Pays $60-80.

Poetry: Avant-garde, free verse, traditional, deep psychedelic thoughts on paper. "Go light on the traditional." Buys 175 poems/year. Submit maximum 2 poems. Length: 20-80 lines. Pays $35-50.

Fillers: Facts, newsbreaks. Buys 350/year. Length: 25-150 words. Pays $10-25.

Tips: "You must express a genuine love for hip-hop in everything you write. No one-hit wonder stories or flash in the pan artists. We need writers who cover artists who have an agenda of long standing career goals of becoming part of this institution we call hip-hop."

OPERA NEWS, Metropolitan Opera Guild, Inc., 70 Lincoln Center Plaza, New York NY 10023-6593. (212)769-7080. Fax: (212)769-7007. Editor: Patrick J. Smith. Managing Editor: Brian Kellow. Contact: Kitty Marsh. 75% freelance written. Monthly magazine (May-November, biweekly December-April), for people interested in opera; the opera professional as well as the opera audience. Estab. 1936. Circ. 130,778. Pays on publication. Publishes ms an average of 4 months after acceptance. Byline given. Buys first serial rights only. Sample copy for $4.

Nonfiction: Most articles are commissioned in advance. Monthly issues feature articles on various aspects of opera worldwide; biweekly issues contain articles related to the broadcasts from the Metropolitan Opera. Emphasis is on high quality writing and an intellectual interest to the opera-oriented public. Informational, personal experience, interview, profile, historical, think pieces, personal opinion, opera reviews. "Also willing to consider quality fiction and poetry on opera-related themes though acceptance is rare." Query by mail. Length: 1,500-2,800 words. Pays $450-1,000. Sometimes pays expenses of writers on assignment.

Photos: State availability of photos with submission. Buys one-time rights.

Columns/Departments: Buys 24 mss/year.

PULSE!, MTS Inc./Tower Records/Video, 2500 Del Monte St., Sacramento CA 95691. (916)373-2450. Fax: (916)373-2480. Editor/Publisher: Michael Farrace. Monthly magazine covering music and popular culture. "*Pulse!* is for young adults with a specific focus on pre-recorded entertainment—music, film, video, multimedia CD-ROM. Focusing on the progressive new music culture, it currently covers over 40 musical styles." Estab. 1983. Circ. 335,000. This magazine did not respond to our request for information. Query before submitting.

‡RAP SHEET, Jeff Stern & Associates, 2601 Ocean Park #200, Santa Monica CA 90405. Fax: (310)399-1590. E-mail: sheetrap@aol.com. Editor: Darryl James. Contact: Billy Johnson, Jr., managing editor. Monthly newspaper covering hip hop artists, music and culture. Estab. 1992. Circ. 100,000. Pays on publication. Byline given. Editorial lead time 2 months. Accepts simultaneous submissions.

Nonfiction: Exposé, general interest, historical/nostalgic, interview/profile, photo feature, technical. Query with published clips. Length: 500-3,500. Pays $50-300. Sometimes pays expenses of writers on assignment.

Photos: Send photos with submission. Negotiates payment individually.

Columns/Departments: Check the Wax, Trax (album and single reviews), albums (200-300 words) singles (100 words); Back in the Day (profile on old school hip hop artist) 500-800 words; On the set (hip hop related film news) 1,000 words. Buys 50 mss/year. Query with published clips. Pays $50-300.

Tips: "Submit writing samples consistent with our style and format. Explain specifically how you would like to contribute and offer ideas."

RELIX MAGAZINE, Music for the Mind, P.O. Box 94, Brooklyn NY 11229. Fax: (718)692-4345. E-mail: relixedit@aol.com. Editor: Toni A. Brown. 60% freelance written. Eager to work with new/unpublished writers. Bimonthly magazine covering rock 'n' roll music and specializing in Grateful Dead and other San Francisco and 60s related groups for readers ages 15-65. Estab. 1974. Circ. 70,000. Pays on publication. Publishes ms an average of 6 months after acceptance. Byline given. Buys all rights. Reports in 1 year. Sample copy for $4.

Nonfiction: Historical/nostalgic, interview/profile, new product, personal experience, photo feature, technical. Special issue: year-end special. Query with published clips if available or send complete ms. Length open. Pays $1.75/column inch.

Reprints: Send photocopy of article and information about when and where the article previously appeared.

Fiction: Publishes novel excerpts.

Columns/Departments: Query with published clips, if available, or send complete ms. Pays variable rates.

Tips: "The most rewarding aspects of working with freelance writers are fresh writing and new outlooks."

SOUNDTRACK, The Journal of the Independent Music Association, SoundTrack Publishing, P.O. Box 609, Ringwood NJ 07456. (201)818-6789. Fax: (201)818-6996. Editor: Don Kulak. 60% freelance written. Bimonthly music and business magazine. Estab. 1988. Circ. 10,000. Pays on publication. Publishes ms an average of 3 months after acceptance. Byline sometimes given. Buys first rights and second serial (reprint) rights. Submit seasonal/holiday material 4 months in advance. Accepts simultaneous submissions. Reports in 1 week on queries; 3 weeks on mss. Free sample copy and writer's guidelines for 9×12 SAE with $2 postage.

• *Soundtrack* now has an investigative reporting section on political, social, economic and environmental topics.

Nonfiction: Book excerpts, exposé, how-to, interview/profile, opinion, technical. Buys 36 mss/year. Query with published clips. Length: 1,000-2,000 words. Pays $50-200 for assigned articles. No unsolicited mss. Sometimes pays writers with contributor copies or other premiums rather than cash by "mutually beneficial agreement." Sometimes pays expenses of writers on assignment.

Reprints: Send photocopy of article. Pays 50% of amount paid for an original article.

Photos: Send photos with submissions. Offers $10-20/photo. Buys all rights.

Columns/Departments: The Business of Music (promotion, distribution, forming a record label; alternative markets—film scores, jingles, etc.; how-to's on generating more income from own music). Buys 24 mss/year. Query with published clips. Length: 1,000-2,000 words.

Tips: "Write a letter explaining background, interests, and areas of special study and what you hope to get out of writing for our publication. All sections are open to freelancers. Writing should be fluid and direct. We especially need more how-to information on record marketing and distribution."

THE SOURCE, Source Publications, Inc. 594 Broadway, Suite 510, New York NY 10012-3233. (212)274-0464. Fax: (212)274-9253. Publisher: David Mays. Monthly magazine covering music and popular culture. "*The Source* covers hip-hop music, culture and politics. It is a lifestyle magazine for the hip-hop generation covering the music, styles, trends, people and places that comprise this musical and cultural movement." Estab. 1988. Circ. 159,000. This magazine did not respond to our request for information. Query before submitting.

‡SPIN, 6 W. 18th St., 8th Floor, New York NY 10011-4608. (212)633-8200. Publisher: Bob Guccione, Jr. Contact: Craig Marks, executive editor. Monthly magazine covering music and popular culture. "*Spin* covers progressive rock as well as investigative reporting on issues from politics, to pop culture. Editorial includes reviews, essays, profiles and interviews on a wide range of music from rock to jazz. It also covers sports, movies, politics, humor, fashion and issues—from AIDS research to the environment. The editorial focuses on the progressive new music scene and young adult culture more from an 'alternative' perspective as opposed to mainstream pop music. The magazine discovers new bands as well as angles for the familiar stars." Estab. 1985. Circ. 413,000.

Nonfiction: Cultural, political or social issues. New writers: submit complete ms with SASE. Established writers: query specific editor with published clips. Features not assigned to writers who have not established a prior relationship with *Spin*.

Columns/Departments: Most open to freelancers: Exposure (short articles on music and popular culture), 300-600 words, query Lee Smith, associate editor; Spins (record reviews), 150 or 400 words, queries/mss to Eric Weisbard, senior editor. Query before submitting.

Tips: "The best way to break into the magazine is the Exposure and Spin sections. We primarily work with seasoned, professional writers who have extensive national magazine experience and very rarely make assignments based on unsolicited queries."

VIBE, Quincy Jones/David Salzman Entertainment, 205 Lexington Ave., 3rd Floor, New York NY 10016. (212)522-7092. (212)522-4578. Publisher: John Rollins. Magazine published 10 times/year covering music and popular culture. "*Vibe* chronicles the many forms of urban music—rap, dancehall, reggae, new jack swing, rhythm and blues—as well as the culture that inspires and absorbs it. From a multicultural vantage point *Vibe* covers politics, fashion, media, the arts, technology and sports with reporting, photography, essays and criticism." Estab. 1993. Circ. 301,000. This magazine did not respond to our request for information. Query before submitting.

MYSTERY

These magazines buy fictional accounts of crime, detective work, mystery and suspense. Skim through other sections to identify markets for fiction; some will consider mysteries. Markets for true crime accounts are listed under Detective and Crime. Also see the second edition of *Mystery Writer's Sourcebook* (Writer's Digest Books).

HARDBOILED, Gryphon Publications, P.O. Box 209, Brooklyn NY 11228. Editor: Gary Lovisi. 100% freelance written. Quarterly magazine covering crime/mystery fiction and nonfiction. "Hard-hitting crime fiction and columns/articles and reviews on hardboiled crime writing and private-eye stories—the newest and most cutting-edge work and classic reprints." Estab. 1988. Circ. 1,000. Pays on publication. Publishes ms an average of 18 months after acceptance. Byline given. Offers 100% kill fee. Buys one-time rights. Editorial lead time 2 months. Submit seasonal material 6 months in advance. Accepts simultaneous submissions. Reports in 2 weeks on queries; 2 months on mss. Sample copy for $7. Writer's guidelines for #10 SASE.

Nonfiction: Book excerpts, essays, exposé. Query first. Buys 8-10 mss/year. Length: 500-3,000 words. Pays 1 copy for nonfiction.

Reprints: Query first.

Photos: State availability of photos with submission.

Columns/Departments: "Various review columns/articles on hardboiled writers—query first." Buys 16-24 mss/year. Query.

Fiction: Mystery, hardboiled crime and private-eye stories *all* on the cutting-edge. Buys 60 mss/year. Send complete ms. Length: 500-3,000 words. Pays $5-50, depending on length and quality.

ALFRED HITCHCOCK MYSTERY MAGAZINE, Dell Magazine Fiction Group, 1270 Avenue of the Americas, New York NY 10022. (212)698-6400. E-mail: 71154.662@compuserve.com. Editor: Cathleen Jordan. Monthly magazine featuring new mystery short stories. Circ. 215,000 paid; 615,000 readers. **Pays on acceptance.** Byline given. Buys first, first anthology and foreign rights. Submit seasonal/holiday material 7 months in advance. Reports in 2 months. Writer's guidelines for SASE.

● Alfred Hitchcock Mystery Magazine was recently sold to Penny Marketing.

Fiction: Original and well-written mystery and crime fiction. Length: up to 14,000 words. Pays 8¢/word.

● Ranked as one of the best markets for fiction writers in *Writer's Digest*'s annual "Fiction 50," June 1996.

‡MURDEROUS INTENT, A Magazine of Mystery & Suspense, Madison Publishing Co., P.O. Box 5947, Vancouver WA 98668-5947. E-mail: madison@teleport.com. Website: http://www.teleport.com/~madison. Editor: Margo Power. 90% freelance written. Quarterly magazine covering mystery. "Everything in *Murderous Intent* is mystery/suspense-related. We bring you quality nonfiction articles, columns, interviews and 10-12 (or more) pieces of short mystery fiction per issue. You'll find stories and interviews by Carolyn Hart, Ed Gorman, Barbara Paul, Jerimiah Healy and many more excellent authors." Estab. 1994. Circ. 5,000. **Pays on acceptance**. Publishes ms an average of 12-18 months after acceptance. Byline given. Offers 100% kill fee or $10. Buys first North American serial rights. Submit seasonal material 6 months in advance. Accepts simultaneous submissions, if so noted. Reports in 1 month on queries; 4 months on mss. Sample copy for $5, 9×12 SAE and 4 first-class stamps. Writer's guidelines for #10 SASE.

Nonfiction: Humor (mystery), interview/profile (mystery authors), mystery-related nonfiction. Buys 8-12 mss/year. Query with published clips. Length: 2,000-4,000 words. Pays $10. Sometimes pays expenses of writers on assignment.

Photos: State availability of photos and artwork with submission. Offers no additional payment for photos accepted with ms or negotiates payment individually. Captions, model releases, identification of subjects required. Buys one-time rights.

Fiction: Humorous (mystery), mystery. "Please don't send anything that is not mystery/suspense-related in some way." Buys 48-52 mss/year. Send complete ms. Length: 200-6,000 words. Pays $10.

● Ranked as one of the best markets for fiction writers in *Writer's Digest*'s annual "Fiction 50," June 1996.

Poetry Free verse, haiku, light verse, traditional. Nothing that is not mystery/suspense-related. Buys 12-36 poems/year. Length: 4-16 lines. Pays $2-5.

Fillers: Anecdotes, facts. All fillers must be mystery related. Length: 25-50 words. Pays $2-5.

Tips: "Mail all submissions flat in 9×12 envelopes. Follow the guidelines. Submit only one story or article at a time. Do include a typed cover letter. Be prepared to submit accepted material on 3½" floppy. We don't publish material that is not on disk. We also seek permission to include select stories and articles on the Website. There is no additional payment at this time."

THE MYSTERY REVIEW, A Quarterly Publication for Mystery Readers, C. von Hessert & Associates, P.O. Box 233, Colborne, Ontario K0K 1S0 Canada. (613)475-4440. Fax: (613)475-3400. E-mail: 71554.551@compuserve.com. Editor: Barbara Davey. 80% freelance written. Quarterly magazine covering mystery and suspense. "Our readers are interested in mystery and suspense books, films. All topics related to mystery—including real life unsolved mysteries." Estab. 1992. Circ. 4,500 (70% of distribution is in US). Pays on publication. Publishes ms an average of 6 months after acceptance. Byline given. Buys first North American serial rights or second serial (reprint) rights. Editorial lead time 6 months. Submit seasonal material 6 months in advance. Reports in 6 weeks on queries; 1 month on mss. Sample copy for $5. Writer's guidelines free on request.

Nonfiction: Interview/profile. Query. Length: 2,000-5,000 words. Pays $50 maximum for assigned articles.

Photos: Send photos with submission. Reviews 5×7 b&w prints. Offers no additional payment for photos accepted with ms. Model releases, identification of subjects required. Buys all rights.

Columns/Departments: Book reviews (mystery/suspense titles only), 500-700 words; True "unsolved" mysteries (less generally known cases), 2,000-5,000 words; Bookstore profiles (mystery bookstores only), 500 words. Buys 50 mss/year. Query with published clips. Pays $10-30.
Poetry: Only poems with a mystery theme. Buys 3 poems/year. Submit maximum 2 poems. Pays $10-20.
Fillers: Puzzles, items related to mystery/suspense. Buys 4/year. Length: 100-500 words. Pays $10-20.

ELLERY QUEEN'S MYSTERY MAGAZINE, Dell Magazine Fiction Group, 1270 Avenue of the Americas, New York NY 10022. (212)698-6400. E-mail: 71154.662@compuserve.com. Editor: Janet Hutchings. 100% freelance written. Magazine published 13 times/year featuring mystery fiction. Estab. 1941. Circ. 279,000 readers. **Pays on acceptance.** Publishes ms an average of 6 months after acceptance. Byline given. Buys first serial or second serial (reprint) rights. Accepts simultaneous submissions. Reports in 3 months. Writer's guidelines for #10 SASE.
● Ellery Queen's Mystery Magazine was recently sold to Penny Marketing.
Fiction: Special consideration given to "anything timely and original. We publish every type of mystery: the suspense story, the psychological study, the private-eye story, the deductive puzzle—the gamut of crime and detection from the realistic (including stories of police procedure) to the more imaginative (including 'locked rooms' and impossible crimes). We always need detective stories. No sex, sadism or sensationalism-for-the-sake-of-sensationalism, no gore or horror. Seldom publishes parodies or pastiches. Buys up to 13 mss/issue. Length: 6,000 words maximum; occasionally higher but not often. Also buys 2-3 short novels/year of up to 17,000 words, by established authors and minute mysteries of 250 words. Pays 3-8¢/word.
● Ranked as one of the best markets for fiction writers in *Writer's Digest*'s annual "Fiction 50," June 1996.
Poetry: Short mystery verses, limericks. Length: 1 page, double-spaced maximum.
Tips: "We have a Department of First Stories to encourage writers whose fiction has never before been in print. We publish an average of 13 first stories every year."

NATURE, CONSERVATION AND ECOLOGY

These publications promote reader awareness of the natural environment, wildlife, nature preserves and ecosystems. Many of these "green magazines" also concentrate on recycling and related issues, and a few focus on environmentally-conscious sustainable living. They do not publish recreation or travel articles except as they relate to conservation or nature. Other markets for this kind of material can be found in the Regional; Sports (Hiking and Backpacking in particular); and Travel, Camping and Trailer categories, although magazines listed there require that nature or conservation articles be slanted to their specialized subject matter and audience. Some publications listed in Juvenile and Teen, such as *Ranger Rick* or *Owl*, focus on nature-related material for young audiences, while others occasionally purchase such material. For more information on recycling publications, turn to the Resources and Waste Reduction section in Trade.

AMC OUTDOORS, The Magazine of the Appalachian Mountain Club, Appalachian Mountain Club, 5 Joy St., Boston MA 02108. (617)523-0655 ext. 312. Fax: (617)523-0722. E-mail: ancontdoors@mcim ail.com. Editor/Publisher: Catherine K. Buni. 90% freelance written. Monthly magazine covering outdoor recreation and conservation issues. Estab. 1907. Circ. 66,000. Pays on publication. Publishes ms an average of 3 months after acceptance. Byline given. Offers 25% kill fee. Buys all rights. Editorial lead time 3 months. Submit seasonal material 4 months in advance. Reports in 1 month on queries; 2 months on mss. Sample copy for 9 × 12 SASE. Writer's guidelines free on request.
Nonfiction: Book excerpts, essays, exposé, general interest, historical/nostalgic, how-to, interview/profile, opinion, personal experience, photo feature, technical, travel. Special issues: Northern Forest Report (April) featuring the northern areas of New York, New Hampshire, Vermont, and Maine, and protection efforts for these areas. Buys 10 mss/year. Query with or without published clips. Length: 500-3,000 words. Sometimes pays expenses of writers on assignment.
Photos: State availability of photos with submission. Reviews contact sheets, transparencies and prints. Model releases and identification of subjects required.
Columns/Departments: Jane Bamberg. News (environmental/outdoor recreation coverage of Northeast), 1,300 words. Buys 20 mss/year. Query. Pays $50-500.

AMERICAN FORESTS, American Forests, 1516 P St. NW, Washington DC 20005. (202)667-3300. Fax: (202)667-2407. E-mail: mrobbins@amfor.org. Website: member@amfor.org. Editor: Michelle Robbins. 70% freelance written. Quarterly magazine "of trees and forests, published by a nonprofit citizens' organization for the advancement of intelligent management and use of our forests, soil, water, wildlife and all other natural resources necessary for an environment of high quality." Estab. 1895. Circ. 30,000. **Pays on acceptance.** Publishes ms an average of 8 months after acceptance. Byline given. Buys one-time rights. Written queries preferred. Submit seasonal material 5 months in advance. Reports in 2 months. Sample copy for $2. Writer's guidelines for SASE.

• This magazine is looking for more urban and suburban-oriented pieces.

Nonfiction: General interest, historical, how-to, humor, inspirational. All articles should emphasize trees, forests, forestry and related issues. Buys 7-10 mss/issue. Query. Length: 2,000 words. Pays $300-800.

Reprints: Send tearsheet of article or typed ms with rights for sale noted and information about when and where the article previously appeared. Pays 50% of amount paid for an original article.

Photos: Send photos. Offers no additional payment for photos accompanying ms. Uses 8×10 b&w glossy prints; 35mm or larger transparencies, originals only. Captions required. Buys one-time rights.

Tips: "Query should have honesty and information on photo support."

THE AMICUS JOURNAL, Natural Resources Defense Council, 40 W. 20th St., New York NY 10011. (212)727-2700. Fax: (212)727-1773. E-mail: amicus@nrdc.org. Website: http:///www.nrdc.org/nrdc. Editor: Kathrin Day Lassila. 80% freelance written. Quarterly magazine covering national and international environmental issues. "*The Amicus Journal* is intended to provide the general public with a journal of thought and opinion on environmental affairs, particularly those relating to policies of national and international significance." Estab. 1979. Estab. 175,000. Pays on publication. Publishes ms an average of 6 months after acceptance. Offers 25% kill fee. Buys first North American serial rights (and print/electronic reprint rights). Submit seasonal material 6 months in advance. Reports in 3 months on queries. Sample copy for $4 with 9×12 SAE. Writer's guidelines for SASE.

• This publication is now accepting occasional literary (personal) essays on environmental issues or with environmental themes. The editor stresses that submissions must be of the highest quality only and must be grounded in thorough knowledge of subject.

Nonfiction: Exposé, interview/profile, essays, reviews. Query with published clips. Length: 200-3,500 words. Pay negotiable. Sometimes pays expenses of writers on assignment. Buys 35 mss/year.

Photos: State availability of photos with submission. Reviews contact sheets, color transparencies, 8×10 b&w prints. Negotiates payment individually. Captions, model releases, identification of subjects required. Buys one-time rights.

Columns/Departments: News & Comment (summary reporting of environmental issues, usually tied to topical items), 700-2,000 words; International Notebook (new or unusual international environmental stories), 700-2,000 words; People, 2,000 words; Reviews (in-depth reporting on issues and personalities, well-informed essays on books of general interest to environmentalists interested in policy and history), 500-1,000 words. Query with published clips. Pay negotiable.

Poetry: Brian Swann. Avant-garde, free verse, haiku, others. All poetry should be rooted in nature. Must submit with SASE. Buys 16 poems/year. Pays $50 plus a year's subscription.

Tips: "Please stay up to date on environmental issues, and review *The Amicus Journal* before submitting queries. Except for editorials all departments are open to freelance writers. Queries should precede manuscripts, and manuscripts should conform to the Chicago Manual of Style."

APPALACHIAN TRAILWAY NEWS, Appalachian Trail Conference, P.O. Box 807, Harpers Ferry WV 25425-0807. (304)535-6331. Fax: (304)535-2667. Editor: Judith Jenner. 50% freelance written. Bimonthly magazine. Estab. 1925. Circ. 26,000. **Pays on acceptance.** Byline given. Buys first North American serial or second serial (reprint) rights. Reports in 2 months. Sample copy for $2.50 includes guidelines. Writer's guidelines only for SASE.

• Articles must relate to Appalachian Trail.

Nonfiction: Essays, general interest, historical/nostalgic, how-to, humor, inspirational, interview/profile, photo feature, technical, travel. No poetry or religious materials. Buys 15-20 mss/year. Query with or without published clips, or send complete ms. Length: 250-3,000 words. Pays $25-300. Pays expenses of writers on assignment. Publishes, but does not pay for "hiking reflections."

Reprints: Send photocopy of article or typed ms with rights for sale noted and information about when and where the article previously appeared.

Photos: State availability of b&w photos with submission. Reviews contact sheets, negatives, 5×7 prints. Offers $25-125/photo. Identification of subjects required. Negotiates future use by Appalachian Trail Conference.

Tips: "Contributors should display an obvious knowledge of or interest in the Appalachian Trail. Those who live in the vicinity of the Trail may opt for an assigned story and should present credentials and subject of interest to the editor."

THE ATLANTIC SALMON JOURNAL, The Atlantic Salmon Federation, P.O. Box 429, St. Andrews, New Brunswick E0G 2X0 Canada. Fax: (506)529-4985. E-mail: asfpub@nbnet.nb.ca. Website: http://www.fl yfishing.com/flyfishing/asf/. Editor: Harry Bruce. 50-68% freelance written. Quarterly magazine covering conservation efforts for the Atlantic salmon, catering to "affluent and responsive audience—the dedicated angler and conservationist." Circ. 10,000. Pays on publication. Publishes ms an average of 6 months after acceptance. Byline given. Buys first serial rights to articles and one-time rights to photos. Submit seasonal material 3 months in advance. Accepts simultaneous submissions. Reports in 2 months. Sample copy for 9×12 SAE with $1 (Canadian), or IRC. Free writer's guidelines.

Nonfiction: Exposé, historical/nostalgic, how-to, humor, interview/profile, new product, opinion, personal experience, photo feature, technical, travel, conservation, science, research and management. "We are seeking articles that are pertinent to the focus and purpose of our magazine, which is to inform and entertain our membership on all aspects of the Atlantic salmon and its environment, preservation and conservation." Buys 15-20 mss/year. Query with published clips and state availability of photos. Length: 1,500-2,500 words. Pays $200-400. Sometimes pays the expenses of writers on assignment.

Photos: Send photos with query. Pays $50 for 3×5 or 5×7 b&w prints; $50-100 for 2¼×3¼ or 35mm color slides. Captions and identification of subjects required.

Tips: "Articles must reflect informed and up-to-date knowledge of Atlantic salmon. Writers need not be authorities, but research must be impeccable. Clear, concise writing is essential, and submissions must be typed. The odds are that a writer without a background in outdoor writing and wildlife reporting will not have the 'informed' angle I'm looking for. Our readership is well-read and critical of simplification and generalization."

AUDUBON, The Magazine of the National Audubon Society, National Audubon Society, 700 Broadway, New York NY 10003-9501. Fax: (212)477-9069. Website: http://audubon/.org/audubon. Editor: Michael W. Robbins. 85% freelance written. Bimonthly magazine. Estab. 1887. Circ. 430,000. **Pays on acceptance.** Byline given. Buys first North American serial rights, second serial (reprint) rights on occasion. Reports in 3 months. Sample copy for $4 and 9×12 SAE with 10 first-class stamps or $5 for magazine and postage. Writer's guidelines for #10 SASE.
- Ranked as one of the best markets for freelance writers in *Writer's Yearbook*'s annual "Top 100 Markets," January 1996.

Nonfiction: Essays, investigative, historical, humor, interview/profile, opinion, photo feature, book excerpts (well in advance of publication). Query before submission. Length: 250-4,000 words. Pays $250-4,000. Pays expenses of writers on assignment.

Photos: Query with photographic idea before submitting slides. Reviews 35mm transparencies. Offers page rates per photo on publication. Captions and identification of subjects required. Write for photo guidelines.

BIRD WATCHER'S DIGEST, Pardson Corp., P.O. Box 110, Marietta OH 45750. Editor: William H. Thompson III. 60% freelance written. Works with a small number of new/unpublished writers each year. Bimonthly magazine covering natural history—birds and bird watching. "*BWD* is a nontechnical magazine interpreting ornithological material for amateur observers, including the knowledgeable birder, the serious novice and the backyard bird watcher; we strive to provide good reading and good ornithology." Estab. 1978. Circ. 85,000. Pays on publication. Publishes ms an average of 1 year after acceptance. Byline given. Buys one-time, first serial and second serial (reprint) rights. Submit seasonal material 6 months in advance. Reports in 2 months. Sample copy for $3. Writer's guidelines for #10 SASE.

Nonfiction: Book excerpts, how-to (relating to birds, feeding and attracting, etc.), humor, personal experience, travel (limited—we get many). "We are especially interested in fresh, lively accounts of closely observed bird behavior and displays and of bird watching experiences and expeditions. We often need material on less common species or on unusual or previously unreported behavior of common species." No articles on pet or caged birds; none on raising a baby bird. Buys 75-90 mss/year. Send complete ms. All submissions must be accompanied by SASE. Length: 600-3,500 words. Pays from $50.

Reprints: Accepts previously published submissions.

Photos: Send photos with ms. Pays $10 minimum for b&w prints; $50 minimum for transparencies. Buys one-time rights.
- *Bird Watcher's Digest* no longer accepts poetry.

Tips: "We are aimed at an audience ranging from the backyard bird watcher to the very knowledgeable birder; we include in each issue material that will appeal at various levels. We always strive for a good geographical spread, with material from every section of the country. We leave very technical matters to others, but we want facts and accuracy, depth and quality, directed at the veteran bird watcher and at the enthusiastic novice. We stress the joys and pleasures of bird watching, its environmental contribution, and its value for the individual and society."

E THE ENVIRONMENTAL MAGAZINE, Earth Action Network, P.O. Box 5098, Westport CT 06881-5098. (203)854-5559. Fax: (203)866-0602. E-mail: emagazine@prodigy.com. Editor: Doug Moss. Contact: Jim Motavalli, managing editor. 80% freelance written. Bimonthly magazine on environmentalism. "*E Magazine* was formed for the purpose of acting as a clearinghouse of information, news and commentary on environmental issues." Estab. 1990. Circ. 70,000. Pays on publication. Byline given. Offers 50% kill fee. Buys first North American serial rights. Editorial lead time 3 months. Submit seasonal material 6 months in advance. Accepts simultaneous submissions. Query for all submissions. Sample copy for $5. Writer's guidelines for #10 SASE.

Nonfiction: Exposé (environmental), how-to (the "Green Living" section), interview/profile, new product, opinion. No fiction or poetry. Buys 100 mss/year. Query with published clips. Length: 100-5,000 words. Pays 20¢/word, negotiable. On spec or free contributions welcome. Sometimes pays telephone expenses of writers on assignment.

Reprints: Occasionally accepts previously published articles. Send tearsheet or photocopy of article or typed ms with rights for sale noted and information about when and where the article previously appeared.

Photos: Mention photo availability, but send only when requested. Reviews printed samples, e.g., magazine tearsheet, postcards, etc. to be kept on file. Negotiates payment individually. Identification of subjects required. Buys one-time rights.

Columns/Departments: In Brief/Currents (environmental news stories/trends), 400-1,000 words; Interviews (environmental leaders), 2,000 words; Green Living; Your Health; Going Green (travel); Eco-home; Green Business; Consumer News; New & Different Products (each 700-1,200 words). Query with published clips. Pays 20¢/word, negotiable. On spec or free contributions welcome.

Tips: "Contact us to obtain writer's guidelines and back issues of our magazine. Tailor your query according to the department/section you feel it would be best suited for. Articles must be lively, well-researched, and relevant to a mainstream, national readership."

‡ENVIRONMENT, Heldref Publications, 1319 18th St. NW, Washington DC 20036-1802. Managing Editor: Barbara T. Richman. 2% freelance written. Magazine published 10 times/year for high school and college students and teachers, scientists, business and government executives, teachers, citizens interested in environment or effects of technology and science in public affairs. Estab. 1958. Circ. 12,500. Buys all rights. Byline given. Pays on publication to professional writers. Publishes ms an average of 4 months after acceptance. Reports in 3 months. Sample copy for $7.

Nonfiction: Scientific and environmental material, effects of technology on society. Preferred length: 4,000 words for full-length article. Pays $100-300, depending on material. Query or submit 3 double-spaced copies of complete ms. "All full-length articles must offer readers authoritative analyses of key environmental problems. Articles must be annotated (referenced), and all conclusions must follow logically from the facts and arguments presented." Prefers articles centering around policy-oriented, public decision-making, scientific and technological issues.

Columns/Departments: 1,000-1,700/words. Pays $100.

HIGH COUNTRY NEWS, High Country Foundation, P.O. Box 1090, Paonia CO 81428-1090. (303)527-4898. Website: http://www.infosphere.comHCN. Editor: Betsy Marston. 80% freelance written. Works with a small number of new/unpublished writers each year. Biweekly tabloid covering environment and natural resource issues in 10 western states for environmentalists, politicians, companies, college classes, government agencies, etc. Estab. 1970. Circ. 18,000. Pays on publication. Publishes ms an average of 2 months after acceptance. Byline given. Buys one-time rights. Reports in 1 month. Free sample copy and writer's guidelines.

Nonfiction: Reporting (local issues with regional importance); exposé (government, corporate); interview/profile; opinion; personal experience; centerspread photo feature. Special issues include those on states in the region. Buys 100 mss/year. Query. Pays 20¢/word minimum. Sometimes pays expenses of writers on assignment for lead stories.

Reprints: Send tearsheet of article.

Photos: Send photos with ms. Prefers b&w prints. Captions and identification of subjects required.

Tips: "We use a lot of freelance material, though very little from outside the Rockies. Familiarity with the newspaper is a must. Start by writing a query letter."

INTERNATIONAL WILDLIFE, National Wildlife Federation, 8925 Leesburg Pike, Vienna VA 22184-0001. (703)790-4000. Editor: Jonathan Fisher. 85% freelance written. Prefers to work with published/established writers. Bimonthly magazine for persons interested in natural history and the environment in countries outside the US. Estab. 1971. Circ. 350,000. **Pays on acceptance.** Publishes ms an average of 4 months after acceptance. Usually buys all rights. "We are now assigning most articles but will consider detailed proposals for quality feature material of interest to a broad audience." Reports in 6 weeks. Writer's guidelines for #10 SASE.

• Ranked as one of the best markets for freelance writers in *Writer's Yearbook*'s annual "Top 100 Markets," January 1996.

Nonfiction: Focuses on world wildlife, environmental problems and peoples' relationship to the natural world as reflected in such issues as population control, pollution, resource utilization, food production, etc. Stories deal with non-US subjects. Especially interested in articles on animal behavior and other natural history, first-person experiences by scientists in the field, well-reported coverage of wildlife-status case studies which also raise broader themes about international conservation and timely issues. Query. Length: 2,000 words. Also in the market for short, 750-word "one-pagers." Examine past issues for style and subject matter. Pays $1,500 minimum for long features. Sometimes pays expenses of writers on assignment.

Photos: Purchases top-quality color photos; prefers packages of related photos and text, but single shots of exceptional interest and sequences also considered. Prefers Kodachrome or Fujichrome transparencies. Buys one-time rights.

NATIONAL PARKS, 1776 Massachusetts Ave. NW, Washington DC 20036. (202)223-6722. Fax: (202)659-0650. E-mail: editornp@aol.com. Editor: Sue Dodge. Associate Editor: Linda Rancourt. 85% freelance written. Prefers to work with published/established writers. Bimonthly magazine for a highly educated audience interested in preservation of National Park System units, natural areas, and protection of wildlife habitat. Estab. 1919. Circ. 450,000. **Pays on acceptance.** Publishes ms an average of 5 months after acceptance. Buys first North American serial and second serial (reprint) rights. Send query. Reports in 3 months. Sample copy for $3 and 9 × 12 SAE. Writer's guidelines for #10 SASE.
  • Ranked as one of the best markets for freelance writers in *Writer's Yearbook*'s annual "Top 100 Markets," January 1996.
Nonfiction: Exposé (on threats, wildlife problems in national parks); descriptive articles about new or proposed national parks and wilderness parks; natural history pieces describing park geology wildlife, or plants. All material must relate to national parks. No poetry, philosophical essays or first person narratives. "Queries are welcome, but unsolicited manuscripts are not accepted." Length: 2,000-2,500 words. Pays $1,000 for full-length features; $350 for serial articles.
Photos: Pays $100-250 for transparencies. Captions required. Buys first North American serial rights.

NATIONAL WILDLIFE, National Wildlife Federation, 8925 Leesburg Pike, Vienna VA 22184-0001. (703)790-4524. Editor-in-Chief: Bob Strohm. Editor: Mark Wexler. 75% freelance written, "but assigns almost all material based on staff ideas. Assigns few unsolicited queries." Bimonthly magazine on wildlife, natural history and environment. "Our purpose is to promote wise use of the nation's natural resources and to conserve and protect wildlife and its habitat. We reach a broad audience that is largely interested in wildlife conservation and nature photography. We avoid too much scientific detail and prefer anecdotal, natural history material." Estab. 1963. Circ. 660,000. **Pays on acceptance.** Publishes ms an average of 1 year after acceptance. Offers 25% kill fee. Buys all rights. Submit seasonal material 8 months in advance. Reports in 6 weeks. Writer's guidelines for #10 SASE.
  • Ranked as one of the best markets for freelance writers in *Writer's Yearbook*'s annual "Top 100 Markets," January 1996.
Nonfiction: General interest (2,500-word features on wildlife, new discoveries, behavior, or the environment); how-to (an outdoor or nature related activity); personal experience (outdoor adventure); photo feature (wildlife); short 700-word features on an unusual individual or new scientific discovery relating to nature. Buys 50 mss/year. Query with or without published clips. Length: 750-2,500 words. Pays $500-2,000. Sometimes pays expenses of writers on assignment.
Photos: John Nuhn, photo editor. Send photos or send photos with query. Prefers Kodachrome or Fujichrome transparencies. Buys one-time rights.
Tips: "Writers can break in with us more readily by proposing subjects (initially) that will take only one or two pages in the magazine (short features)."

NATURAL HISTORY, Natural History Magazine, Central Park W. at 79th St., New York NY 10024. (212)769-5500. Editor: Bruce Stutz. 15% freelance written. Monthly magazine for well-educated, ecologically aware audience: professional people, scientists and scholars. Circ. 500,000. Pays on publication. Publishes ms an average of 3 months after acceptance. Byline given. Buys first serial rights and becomes agent for second serial (reprint) rights. Submit seasonal material at least 6 months in advance.
  • *Natural History* recently underwent a top-to-bottom redesign. Obtaining a recent sample copy is strongly recommended.
Nonfiction: Uses all types of scientific articles except chemistry and physics—emphasis is on the biological sciences and anthropology. "We always want to see new research findings in almost all the branches of the natural sciences—anthropology, archeology, zoology and ornithology. We find that it is particularly difficult to get something new in herpetology (amphibians and reptiles) or entomology (insects), and we would like to see material in those fields. We expect high standards of writing and research. We favor an ecological slant in most of our pieces, but do not generally lobby for causes, environmental or other. The writer should have a deep knowledge of his subject, then submit original ideas either in query or by manuscript. Acceptance is more likely if article is accompanied by high-quality photographs." Buys 60 mss/year. Query or submit complete ms. Length: 1,500-3,000 words. Pay varies, additional payment for photos used.
Photos: Rarely uses 8 × 10 b&w glossy prints; pays $125/page maximum. Much color is used; pays $300 for inside and up to $600 for cover. Buys one-time rights.
Tips: "Learn about something in depth before you bother writing about it."

‡**NATURAL LIFE**, The Alternate Press, RR1, St. George, Ontario N0E 1N0 Canada. Fax: (519)448-4001. E-mail: natlife@netroute.net. Website: http://www.netroute.net/~altpress. Editor: Wendy Priesnitz. 25% freelance written. Bimonthly tabloid covering self-reliant living. "Access to news about self-reliance and sustainability. How-to and inspiration for people living an environmentally aware lifestyle. Includes gardening, natural foods, health, home business, renewal energy." Estb. 1976. Circ. 25,000. Pays on publication. Publishes ms an average of 3 months after acceptance. Byline given. Offers 50% kill fee. Buys first North American serial and electronic rights. Editorial lead time 4 months. Submit seasonal material 4 months in

advance. Reports in 3 weeks on queries. Sample copy for $3.50. Writer's guidelines for #10 SASE (Canadian stamps please).

Nonfiction: How-to. Buys 30 mss/year. Query with published clips. Length: 800-1,000 words. Pays 10¢/word to $100 maximum.

Photos: State availability of photos with query. Reviews prints. Offers no additional payment for photos accepted with ms. Captions, identification of subjects required. Buys all rights.

NATURE CANADA, Canadian Nature Federation, 1 Nicholas St., Suite 520, Ottawa, Ontario KIN 7B7 Canada. Fax: (613)562-3371. E-mail: 72233.3536@compuserve.com. Website: http://www.web.apc.org/~C NF. Editor: Barbara Stevenson. Quarterly membership magazine covering conservation, natural history and environmental/naturalist community. "*Nature Canada* is written for an audience interested in nature. Its content supports the Canadian Nature Federation's philosophy that all species have a right to exist regardless of their usefulness to humans. We promote the awareness, understanding and enjoyment of nature." Estab. 1971. Circ. 20,000. Pays on publication. Publishes ms an average of 3 months after acceptance. Byline given. Offers $100 kill fee. Buys one-time rights. Editorial lead time 3 months. Submit seasonal material 6 months in advance. Reports in 3 months on mss. Sample copy for $5. Writer's guidelines free on request.

Nonfiction: Canadian environmental issues and natural history. Buys 20 mss/year. Query with published clips. Length: 2,000-4,000 words. Pays 25¢/word (Canadian).

Photos: State availability of photos with submission. Offers $40-100/photo (Canadian). Identification of subjects required. Buys one-time rights.

Columns/Departments: The Green Gardener (naturalizing your backyard), 1,200 words; Small Wonder (on less well-known species such as invertebrates, nonvascular plants, etc.), 800-1,500 words; Connections (Canadians making a difference for the environment), 1,000-1,500 words. Buys 16 mss/year. Query with published clips. Pays 25¢/word (Canadian).

Tips: "Our readers are knowledgeable about nature and the environment so contributors should have a good understanding of the subject. We also deal exclusively with Canadian issues and species."

‡SEASONS, Ontario's Nature and Environment Magazine, Federation of Ontario Naturalists, 355 Lesmill Rd., Don Mills, Ontario M3B 2W8 Canada. (416)652-6556. Website: http://www.web.net.fon. Editor: Gail Muir. 75% freelance written. Quarterly magazine covering natural history and the environment. "*Seasons* focuses on Ontario natural history, parks and environmental issues, with appeal for general readers as well as naturalists." Estab. 1963 (published as *Ontario Naturalist* 1963-1980). Circ. 16,000. Pays on publication. Publishes ms an average of 6 months after acceptance. Byline given. Offers 50% kill fee. Buys first Canadian serial rights. Editorial lead time 6 months. Submit seasonal material 1 year in advance. Reports in 2-3 months. Sample copy for $7.20. Writer's guidelines for #10 SASE.

Nonfiction: Essays, general interest, how-to (identify species, be a better birder, etc.), opinion, personal experience, photo feature, travel. No cute articles about cute animals or biology articles cribbed from reference books. Buys 16-20 mss/year. Query with published clips. Length: 1,500-3,000 words. Pays $350-700. Sometimes pays expenses of writers on assignment.

Photos: State availability of photos with submission. Reviews 35mm transparencies. Negotiates payment individually. Model releases, identification of subjects required. Buys one-time rights.

Columns/Departments: Birder's Notebook (bird behavior, biology, identification, conservation), 1,500 words. Buys 4 mss/year. Query with published clips. Pays $300-400.

SIERRA, 730 Polk St., San Francisco CA 94109-7813. (415)923-5656. Fax: (415)776-4868. E-mail: sierra.let ters@sierraclub.org. Website: http://www.sierraclub.org. Editor-in-Chief: Joan Hamilton. Senior Editors: Reed McManus, Paul Rauber. Contact: Marc Lecard, managing editor. Works with a small number of new/unpublished writers each year. Bimonthly magazine emphasizing conservation and environmental politics for people who are well educated, activist, outdoor-oriented and politically well informed with a dedication to conservation. Estab. 1893. Circ. 500,000. **Pays on acceptance.** Publishes ms an average of 4 months after acceptance. Byline given. Buys first North American serial rights. Reports in 2 months.

● Ranked as one of the best markets for freelance writers in *Writer's Yearbook*'s annual "Top 100 Markets," January 1996.

Nonfiction: Exposé (well-documented on environmental issues of national importance such as energy, wilderness, forests, etc.); general interest (well-researched nontechnical pieces on areas of particular environmental concern); photo feature (photo essays on threatened or scenic areas); journalistic treatments of semi-technical topics (energy sources, wildlife management, land use, waste management, etc.). No "My trip to . . . " or "why we must save wildlife/nature" articles; no poetry or general superficial essays on environmentalism; no reporting on purely local environmental issues. Buys 5-6 mss/issue. Query with published clips. Length: 800-3,000 words. Pays $450-2,000. Pays limited expenses of writers on assignment.

● A new department, "Food For Thought," has been launched and is open to freelancers. The travel column, "Good Going" is again open to freelancers. "Whereabouts" department has been discontinued.

Reprints: Send typed ms with rights for sale noted and information about when and where the article previously appeared.

Photos: Naomi Williams, art and production manager. Send photos. Pays $300 maximum for transparencies; more for cover photos. Buys one-time rights.

Tips: "Queries should include an outline of how the topic would be covered and a mention of the political appropriateness and timeliness of the article. Statements of the writer's qualifications should be included."

‡**WATERFOWL & WETLANDS**, South Carolina Waterfowl Association, 434 King St., Charleston SC 29403. (803)722-0942. Editor: Tim Jaskiewicz. Managing Editor: David Wielicki. 35% freelance written. Quarterly company publication of South Carolina Waterfowl Association covering waterfowl and wetland issues. "We are a 5,000 member nonprofit association. Our quarterly magazine includes feature articles on waterfowl and current issues affecting duck and goose populations, hunting and behavior." Estab. 1987. Circ. 6,500. **Pays on acceptance.** Publishes ms an average of 6 months after acceptance. Byline given. Not copyrighted. Buys one-time or second serial (reprint) rights. Editorial lead time 4 months. Submit seasonal material 4 months in advance. Accepts simultaneous and previously published submissions. Reports in 3 weeks on queries. Sample copy and writer's guidelines free on request.

Nonfiction: Book excerpts, general interest, historical/nostalgic, how-to, humor, interview/profile, new product, opinion, personal experience, photo feature, travel. Buys 6 mss/year. Query. Length: 1,000-3,000 words. Pays $150-500 for unsolicited articles. Offer work barter arrangements with different groups.

Photos: State availability of photos with submission. Reviews 3×5 prints. Offers no additional payment for photos accepted with ms. Captions, identification of subjects required. Buys one-time rights.

Columns/Departments: Going Places (hunting/fishing trips) 1,200 words. Buys 2 mss/year. Query. Pays $50-200.

Poetry: Avant-garde, free verse, traditional.

Tips: "We are interested in national waterfowl issues and also articles which address the waterfowler and waterfowling tradition. A query letter to the editor will be responded to in a timely fashion."

WILDLIFE CONSERVATION MAGAZINE, Wildlife Conservation Society, 185th St. and Southern Blvd., Bronx NY 10460-1068. (212)220-5121. Editor: Joan Downs. 50% freelance written. Bimonthly magazine covering wildlife. Estab. 1895. Circ. 167,000. **Pays on acceptance.** Publishes ms an average of 1 year or more after acceptance. Byline given. Buys first North American serial rights. Submit seasonal material 1 year in advance. Accepts simultaneous submissions. Reports in 2 months on queries; 3 months on mss. Sample copy for $3.95 and 9×12 SAE with 7 first-class stamps. Writer's guidelines for SASE.

• Ranked as one of the best markets for freelance writers in *Writer's Yearbook*'s annual "Top 100 Markets," January 1996.

Nonfiction: Nancy Simmons, senior editor. Essays, personal experience, wildlife articles. No pet or domestic animal stories. Buys 12 mss/year. Query. Length 1,500 words. Pays $500-1,500 for assigned articles; $500-750 for unsolicited articles.

Photos: Send photos with submission. Reviews transparencies. Buys one-time rights.

PERSONAL COMPUTERS

Personal computer magazines continue to evolve. The most successful have a strong focus on a particular family of computers or widely-used applications and carefully target a specific type of computer use, although as technology evolves, some computers and applications fall by the wayside. Be sure you see the most recent issue of a magazine before submitting material.

BYTE MAGAZINE, 1 Phoenix Mill Lane, Peterborough NH 03458-0809. (603)924-9281. Fax: (603)924-2550. E-mail: jmontgomery@bix.com. Website: ftp://www.byte.com. Editor: Rafe Needleman. Contact: John Montgomery, features editor. Monthly magazine covering personal computers for professional users of computers. 50% freelance written. Estab. 1975. Circ. 515,000. **Pays on acceptance.** Byline given. Buys all rights. Reports on rejections in 6 weeks; 3 months if accepted. Writer's guidelines for #10 SASE.

Nonfiction: News, reviews, in-depth discussions of topics related to microcomputers or technology. Buys 160 mss/year. Query. Length: 1,500-5,000 words. Pays $350-1,000 for assigned articles; $500-750 for unassigned.

Tips: "Always interested in hearing from freelancers who are technically astute users of personal computers. Especially interested in stories on new computing technologies, from anywhere in the world. Read several issues of *Byte* to see what we cover, and how we cover it. Read technical journals to stay on the cutting edge of new technology and trends. Send us a proposal with a short outline of an article explaining some new technology, software trend, and the relevance to advanced business users of personal computers. Our readers want accurate, useful, technical information; not fluff and not meaningless data presented without insight or analysis."

‡**COMPUTER CURRENTS, Computing in the Real World**, Computer Currents Publishing, 5720 Hollis St., Emeryville CA 94608. Fax: (510)547-4613. E-mail: rluhn@aol.com. Website: www.currents.net.

Editor: Robert Luhn. 85% freelance written. Biweekly magazine covering personal computing (PC and Mac). "For fairly experienced PC and Mac users. We provide where to buy, how to buy and how to use information. That includes buyers guides, reviews, tutorials and more." Estab. 1984. Circ. 650,000. **Pays on acceptance**. Byline given. Offers 25% kill fee. Buys first North American serial and nonexclusive reprint rights. Editorial lead time 2 months. Submit seasonal material 2 months in advance. Reports in 2 weeks on queries; 2 months on mss. Sample copy for 10×12 SAE with $3 postage. Writer's guidelines for #10 SASE.

Nonfiction: Book excerpts, exposé, how-to (using PC or Mac products), new product, opinion, technical. Buys 40 mss/year. Query with published clips. Length: 2,000-3,000 words. Pays $75-1,500. Sometimes pays expenses of writers on assignment.

Photos: State availability of photos with submission. Reviews 35mm transparencies, 8×10 prints. Offers no additional payment for photos accepted with ms. Buys first North American and nonexclusive reprint rights.

Columns/Departments: Multimedia in Review (new multimedia CDs and hardware; web sites; books), 300 words. Buys 60 mss/year. Query with published clips. Pays $50-75.

Tips: "Know PC or Mac technology; know product category; query with relevant clips; read the magazine. We're using more short reviews of CD-ROMs, books and websites; and doing more investigative features."

‡**COMPUTER LIFE**, Ziff-Davis Publishing, 135 Main St., San Francisco CA 94105. (415)357-5200. Fax: (415)357-5216. E-mail: ceditors@zd.com. Editor: John Dickinson. Contact: Michael Penwarden, executive editor. 90% freelance written. Monthly magazine covering personal computers. "*Computer Life* is aimed at computer enthusiasts who are looking for new and interesting ways to use PCs in their personal (nonwork) lives." Estab. 1994. Circ. 400,000. **Pays on acceptance**. Publishes ms an average of 3 months after acceptance. Byline given. Offers 25-50% kill fee. Buys all rights. Editorial lead time 3 months. Submit seasonal material 5 months in advance. Reports in 6 weeks on queries. Writer's guidelines free on request.

Nonfiction: How-to, new product, technical. Buys 50-100 mss/year. Query with published clips. Length: 500-3,000 words. Pays $100 minimum for assigned articles. Sometimes pays expenses of writers on assignment.

Photos: State availability of photos with submissions. Negotiates payment individually. Captions, model releases, identification of subjects required. Buys one-time rights.

COMPUTOREDGE, San Diego's Computer Magazine, The Byte Buyer, Inc., P.O. Box 83086, San Diego CA 92138. (619)573-0315. Fax: (619)573-0205. E-mail: editor@computoredge.com. Website: http://www.computoredge.com. Executive Editor: Leah Steward. Editor: John San Filippo. 90% freelance written. Weekly magazine on computers. "We cater to the novice/beginner/first-time computer buyer. Humor is welcome." Estab. 1983. Circ. 90,000. Pays on publication. Net 30 day payment after publication. Byline given. Offers $15 kill fee. Buys first North American serial rights. Submit seasonal material 2 months in advance. Query for electronic submissions. Reports in 2 months. Writer's guidelines and an editorial calendar for #10 SASE "or call (619)573-1675 with your modem and download writer's guidelines. Read sample issue on-line." Sample issue for SAE with 7 first-class stamps.

• *ComputorEdge* has added another regional publication in the Denver area.

Nonfiction: General interest (computer), how-to, humor, personal experience. Buys 80 mss/year. Send complete ms. Length: 900-1,200 words. Pays $100-150.

Columns/Departments: Beyond Personal Computing (a reader's personal experience). Buys 80 mss/year. Send complete ms. Length: 500-1,000 words. Pays $50-75.

Fiction: Confession, fantasy, slice-of-life vignettes. No poetry. Buys 20 mss/year. Send complete ms. Length: 900-1,200 words. Pays $100-150.

Tips: "Be relentless. Convey technical information in an understandable, interesting way. We like light material, but not fluff. Write as if you're speaking with a friend. Avoid the typical 'Love at First Byte' article. Avoid the 'How My Grandmother Loves Her New Computer' article. We do not accept poetry. Avoid sexual innuendoes/metaphors. Reading a sample issue is advised."

‡**FAMILYPC**, 244 Main St., Northampton MA 01060. (413)582-9200. Editor: Dan Muse. 60% freelance written. Monthly magazine covering personal computing for families. Estab. 1994. Circ. 239,233. Pays on publication. Publishes ms an average of 4 months after acceptance. "*FamilyPC* is written and edited for parents who want to integrate a personal computer into their family life. Our goal is to provide information on the best hardware and software products for families and inspiration on how to use those products. Our readers rely on *FamilyPC* to help them enhance their children's education, create fun and functional projects (birthday cards, decorations, family yearbooks, and so on), take control of their family finances, increase work-at-home productivity (i.e., work taken home from the office, volunteer or hobby work, or small business), solve their technical problems, think of other fun, creative, educational, and productive ways to use the family computer." Sometimes offers byline. Offers 25% kill fee. Buys all rights. Editorial lead time 4 months. Reports in 2 weeks on queries.

Nonfiction: Interview/profile, technical, projects and crafts with computer product reviews. Length: 100-5,000 words. Pay varies. Pays expenses of writers on assignment.

Photos: State availability of photos with submission. Negotiates payment individually. Captions, identification of subjects required. Buys all rights.

Columns/Departments: Family Shopper (consumer issue for computer, family) 500 words; What's On (online issues) 500 words.

HOME OFFICE COMPUTING/SMALL BUSINESS COMPUTING, Scholastic Inc., 411 Layfayette, New York NY 10003. (212)505-4220. Fax: (212)505-4260. E-mail: 76703.2025@compuserve.com. Editorial Director: Bernadette Gray. Editor-in-Chief: Dennis Eskow. Executive Editor: Cathy Grayson Bowen. Managing Editor: Gail Gabriel. 75% freelance written. Monthly magazine on home/small business and computing. Estab. 1983. Circ. 440,000. **Pays on acceptance.** Publishes ms an average of 3 months after acceptance. Byline given. Offers 25% kill fee. Buys all rights or makes work-for-hire assignments. Submit seasonal/holiday material 6 months in advance. Accepts simultaneous submissions. Sample copy and writer's guidelines for 9×12 SAE.

Nonfiction: How-to, interview/profile, new product, technical, reviews. "No fiction, humor, opinion." Buys 30 mss/year. Query with published clips. Length: 200-4,000 words. Pays $100-2,000. Sometimes pays the expenses of writers on assignment.

Photos: Send photos with submission.

Columns/Departments: Sales & Marketing, Desktop Publishing, Office Design, Communications, Legal Matters, Money, Hardware/Software Reviews. Length: 800-1,200 words. Pays $100-2,000.

Tips: "Submission must be on disk or telecommunicated."

LINK-UP, The Newsmagazine for Users of Online Services, CD-ROM and the Internet, Information Today, Inc., 2222 River Dr., King George VA 22485. E-mail: 72105.1753@compuserve.com. Website: http://www.iworld.com/info2day/lu.htm. Editor: Loraine Page. 70% freelance written. Bimonthly tabloid covering online communications and electronic information. "Our readers have modems or CD-ROM drives. We need articles on what they can do with them. Our primary audience is business users. What databases can they log onto to gain a business edge? What new CD-ROM titles are worthy of investing in? We also cover personal and educational use." Estab. 1980. Circ. 10,000. Pays on publication. Publishes ms an average of 2 months after acceptance. Byline given. Offers 50% kill fee. Buys first rights. Editorial lead time 2 months. Query by e-mail preferred. Reports in 3 months. Sample copy for $2. "Study a few issues to determine types of articles used."

• *Link-up* has an Education Link section. It is looking for stories dealing with the educational aspects of online services, the Internet and CD-ROM.

Nonfiction: Features, how-to, humor, personal experience. Buys 40 mss/year. Query with published clips. Length: 500-1,500 words. Pays $90-220. Sometimes pays half the phone expenses of writers on assignment, but only by special arrangment.

Fillers: "Would love cartoons having to do with going online."

Tips: "Be on target. Please, no 'How I bought my first computer' stories! Our readers are way beyond that."

MACPOWER MAGAZINE, The Magazine for the Macintosh PowerBook and Newton, Hollow Earth Publishing, P.O. Box 1355, Boston MA 02205-1355. Editor: Heilan Yvette Grimes. 95% freelance written. Monthly magazine covering PowerBooks and Newton. "We offer helpful information about the PowerBook and Newton." Estab. 1994. Circ. 35,000. **Pays on acceptance**. Byline given. Buys all rights or makes work-for-hire assignments. Editorial lead time 2 months. Submit seasonal material 5 months in advance. Reports in 2 weeks on queries; 1 months on mss. Sample copy for 9×12 SAE with 3 first-class stamps. Writer's guidelines for #10 SASE.

Nonfiction: Book excerpts, general interest, historical/nostalgic, how-to, humor, interview/profile, new product, personal experience, technical. Query. Length: 300 or more words. Pays per page, negotiated. Sometimes pays expenses of writers on assignment.

Photos: Send photos with submission. Reviews transparencies. (Prefers electronic PICT of TIFF files.) Negotiates payment individually. Captions, model releases and identification of subjects required. Buys all rights.

Columns/Departments: "We are interested in Help columns on individual topics. Check the magazine for an idea of what we publish." Buys 60 mss/year. Query with published clips.

Fillers: Anecdotes, facts, gags to be illustrated by cartoonist, newsbreaks, short humor. Length: 20-50 words.

Tips: "Contact us in writing first. Know your subject and have something interesting to say. Reviews and new ideas are most open to freelancers."

MACWEEK, Ziff-Davis, 301 Howard St., 15th Floor, San Francisco CA 94105. (415)243-3500. Fax: (415)243-3651. E-mail: macweek@macweek.com. Website: http://www.zdnet.com/macweek/. Editor-in-Chief: Mark Hall. Managing Editor: Brenda Benner. Contact: Catherine LaCroux, senior editor. 35% freelance written. Weekly tabloid covering Macintosh market and products. "Reaches sophisticated buyers of Macintosh-related products for large organizations." Estab. 1986. Circ. 100,000. **Pays on acceptance.** Publishes ms an average of 1 month after acceptance. Byline given. Offers 25% kill fee. Buys all worldwide rights.

Editorial lead time: news, 10 days; reviews; 2 months; features, 1 month. Submit seasonal material 2 months in advance. Reports in 1 month on mss. Writer's guidelines free on request.

• Ranked as one of the best markets for freelance writers in *Writer's Yearbook*'s annual "Top 100 Markets," January 1996.

Columns/Departments: Andrew Gore (news); Stephen Howard (reviews); Anita Malnig (features). Reviews (new product testing), 500-1,200 words; Solutions (case histories), 1,000 words. Buys 30 mss/year. Query with published clips. Pays 65 cents-$1/word.

Tips: "Knowledge of the Macintosh market is essential. Know which section you would like to write for and submit to the appropriate editor."

PC WORLD, PCW Communications, Inc., 501 2nd St., San Francisco CA 94107. (415)243-0500. Editor-in-Chief: Phil Lemmons. 60% freelance written. Monthly magazine covering IBM Personal Computers and compatibles. Circ. 1,020,000. **Pays on acceptance.** Byline given. Offers negotiable kill fee. Buys all rights. Free writer's guidelines.

Nonfiction: "*PC World* is composed of four departments: News, How-tos, Review and Features. Reviews critically and objectively analyzes new hardware and software. How-tos gives readers instructions for improving their PC productivity. Features help readers understand the impact of PC technology on their business lives. News keeps readers apprised of new products, trends and industry events." Articles must focus on the IBM PC or compatibles. Query with or without published clips, or send complete ms. Buys 50 mss/year. Length: 1,500-2,500 words. Pays $50-2,000. Does not accept unsolicited mss.

Tips: "Familiarity with the IBM PC or technical knowledge about its operations—coupled with a solid understanding of business needs—often determines whether we accept a query. Send all queries to the attention of Proposals—Editorial Department. Writers should be able to write for a mass audience. *PC World* requires real consumer journalism skills as well as familiarity with PC technology."

PC/COMPUTING, Ziff-Davis Publishing Co., 950 Tower Lane, 19th Floor, Foster City CA 94404-2121. (415)578-7000. Fax: (415)578-7029. Vice President/Editor-in-Chief: Paul Somerson. Monthly magazine for business users of desktop computers. Estab. 1988. Circ. 1,000,000. **Pays on acceptance.** Byline given. Offers negotiable kill fee. Makes work-for-hire assignments. Reports in 1 month. Sample copy for $2.95. Writer's guidelines for #10 SASE.

• Ziff-Davis Publishing Company has created an electronic information service called the Interchange Online Network that draws on the contents of its various computer magazines. It includes *PC Magazine*, *PC Computing*, *PC Week*, *Mac User*, *Mac Week*, *Computer Shopper* and *Computer Gaming World*.

Nonfiction: Book excerpts, how-to, new product, technical. Query with published clips. Payment negotiable. Sometimes pays expenses of writers on assignment.

Tips: "We're looking for helpful, specific information that appeals to advanced users of PCs. No novice material. Writers must be knowledgeable about personal computers."

‡**PUBLISH, The Art and Technology of Electronic Publishing**, 501 Second St., San Francisco CA 94107. (415)243-0600. Website: http://www.publish.com. Editor: Jake Widman. 50% freelance written. Monthly magazine on desktop publishing and presentations. Estab. 1986. Circ. 95,000. Pays on publication. Publishes ms an average of 4-5 months after acceptance. Byline given. Buys first international rights. Reports in 3 weeks. Writer's guidelines for #10 SASE.

Nonfiction: Book excerpts, product reviews, how-to (publishing topics), news, new products, technical tips. Buys 120 mss/year. Query with published clips. Length: 400-2,300 words. No unsolicited mss.

Photos: Send photos with submission. Reviews contact sheets. Captions and identification of subjects required.

‡**WINDOWS MAGAZINE**, CMP Publications, Inc., 1 Jericho Plaza, Jericho NY 10465. Senior Editor: Donna Tapelli. Monthly magazine for business users of Windows hardware and software. "*Windows* contains information on how to evaluate, select, acquire, implement, use, and master Windows-related software and hardware." Estab. 1990. Circ. 570,000. **Pays on acceptance.** Byline given. Offers 25% kill fee. Buys first worldwide and electronic rights. Reports in 1-2 months on queries. Sample copy and writer's guidelines available.

• Ranked as one of the best markets for freelance writers in *Writer's Yearbook*'s annual "Top 100 Markets," January 1996.

Nonfiction: How-to, technical. Buys 30 mss/year. Query with published clips. Length: 1,500-4,000 words. Pays $1,200-3,000 for assigned articles.

Columns/Departments: 1,500 words. Buys 12 mss/year. Query with published clips. Pays $1,000-1,500.

Tips: Needs "clear, entertaining, technical features on Windows hardware and software." Wants to see "how-to and how-to-buy articles, and insider's look at new products." Should be well-written, entertaining and technically accurate. "We concentrate on hands-on tips and how-to information."

WIRED MAGAZINE, 520 Third St., 4th Floor, San Francisco CA 94107-1815. (415)222-6200. Editor/Publisher: Louis Rossetto. Contact: Editorial Department. 95% freelance written. Monthly magazine covering technology and digital culture. "We cover the digital revolution and related advances in computers, communications and lifestyles." Estab. 1993. Circ. 180,000. Pays on publication. Publishes ms an average of 3 months after acceptance. Byline given. Offers 25% kill fee. Buys first North American serial rights, global rights with 25% payment. Editorial lead time 3 months. Query for electronic submissions. Reports in 3 weeks on queries. Sample copy for $4.95. Writer's guidelines for #10 SASE or e-mail to guidelines@wired.com.
Nonfiction: Essays, interview/profile, opinion. "No poetry or trade articles." Buys 85 features, 130 short pieces, 200 reviews, 36 essays and 50 other mss/year. Query. Pays expenses of writers on assignment.

WORDPERFECT DOS MAGAZINE, WordPerfect Publishing Corp., 270 W. Center St., Orem UT 84057-4683. (801)226-5555. Fax: (801)226-8804. E-mail: wpmag@wpmag.com. Website: http://www.wpmag.com. Editorial Director: Clair F. Rees. Contact: Lisa Bearnson, editor-in-chief. 70% freelance written. Monthly magazine of "how-to" articles for users of various WordPerfect computer software. Estab. 1988. Circ. 275,000. **Pays on acceptance.** Publishes ms an average of 6-8 months after acceptance. Byline given. Negotiable kill fee. Buys first and secondary world rights. Submit seasonal/holiday material 8 months in advance. Query for electronic submissions only. Reports in 2 months. Sample copy for 9×12 SAE with 7 first-class stamps. Free writer's guidelines.
  ● Articles should cover both WordPerfect 5.1 for DOS and WordPerfect 6.0 for DOS. When discussing a feature, keystrokes should be provided for both versions.
Nonfiction: How-to, step-by-step applications (with keystrokes), humor, interview/company profile, new product, technical. "Easy-to-understand articles written with *minimum* jargon. Articles should provide readers good, useful information about word processing and other computer functions." Buys 120-160 mss/year. Query with or without published clips. Length: 800-1,800 words.
Photos: Send photos with submission. Reviews transparencies (35mm or larger). Offers no additional payment for photos accepted with ms. Captions and identification of subjects required. Buys one-time rights.
Columns/Departments: Advanced Macro (WordPerfect macros), 1,000-1,400 words; Basics (tips for beginners), 1,000-1,400 words; Home Office, 1,000-1,400 words; Desktop Publishing, 1,000-1,400 words; Final Keystrokes (humor), 800 words. Buys 90-120 mss/year. Query with published clips. Pays $400-700.
Tips: "Studying publication provides best information. We're looking for writers who can both inform *and* entertain our specialized group of readers."

WORDPERFECT FOR WINDOWS MAGAZINE, Ivy International Communications, 270 W. Center St., Orem UT 84057-4683. (801)226-5555. Fax: (801)226-8804. Editorial Director: Jeff Hadfield. 60% freelance written. Monthly magazine of "how-to" articles for users of WordPerfect for Windows and compatible software. Estab. 1991. Circ. 200,000. **Pays on acceptance.** Publishes ms an average of 8 months after acceptance. Byline given. Pays negotiable kill fee. Buys first and secondary world rights. Submit seasonal material 8 months in advance. Reports in 2 months. Sample copy for 9×12 SAE with 7 first-class stamps. Free writers guidelines.
Nonfiction: How-to, step-by-step applications (with keystrokes and screenshots in PCX format), interview/company profile, new product, technical. "Easy-to-understand articles written with *minimum* jargon. Articles should provide readers good, useful information about word processing and other computer functions." Buys 120-160 mss/year. Query with or without published clips. Length: 800-1,800 words.
Columns/Departments: Desktop Publishing, Printing; Basics (tips for beginners); Advanced Macros, Help, all 1,000-1,400 words. Buys 90-120 mss/year. Query with published clips. Pays $400-700.
Tips: "Studying publication provides best information. We're looking for writers who can both inform *and* entertain our specialized group of readers."

PHOTOGRAPHY

Readers of these magazines use their cameras as a hobby and for weekend assignments. To write for these publications, you should have expertise in photography. Magazines geared to the professional photographer can be found in the Professional Photography section.

ALWAYS CHECK the most recent copy of a magazine for the address and editor's name before you send in a query or manuscript.

NATURE PHOTOGRAPHER, Nature Photographer Publishing Co., Inc., P.O. Box 2037, West Palm Beach FL 33402-2037. (407)586-3491. Fax: (407)586-9521. Editor: Evamarie Mathaey. 65% freelance written. Bimonthly magazine "emphasizing nature photography that uses low-impact and local less-known locations, techniques and ethics. Articles include how-to, travel to world-wide wilderness locations and how nature photography can be used to benefit the environment and environmental education of the public." Estab. 1990. Circ. 20,000. Pays on publication. Buys one-time rights. Submit seasonal material 8 months in advance. Accepts simultaneous submissions. Reports in 2 months. Sample copy for 9 × 12 SAE with 6 first-class stamps. Writer's guidelines for #10 SASE.
Nonfiction: How-to (underwater, exposure, creative techniques, techniques to make photography easier, low-impact techniques, macro photography, large-format, wildlife), photo feature, technical, travel. No articles about photographing in zoos or on game farms. Buys 12-18 mss/year. Query with published clips or writing samples. Length: 750-2,500 words. Pays $75-150.
Reprints: Send photocopy of article and information about when and where the article previously appeared. Pays 75% of amount paid for an original article.
Photos: Send photos upon request. Do not send with submission. Reviews 35mm, 2¼ × 2¼ and 4 × 5 transparencies. Offers no additional payment for photos accepted with ms. Identification of subjects required. Buys one-time rights.
Tips: "Query with original, well-thought-out ideas and good writing samples. Make sure you send SASE. Areas most open to freelancers are travel, how-to and conservation. Must have good, solid research and knowledge of subject. Be sure to obtain guidelines by sending SASE with request before submitting query. If you have not requested guidelines within the last year, request an updated version of guidelines."

‡PHOTO TECHNIQUES, Preston Publications, Inc., P.O. Box 48312, Niles IL 60714. (847)965-0566. Fax: (847)965-7639. E-mail: 70007.3477@compuserve.com. Publisher: S. Tinsley Preston III. Contact: Mike Johnston, editor. 50% freelance written. Bimonthly publication covering photochemistry, lighting, optics, processing and printing, Zone System, special effects, sensitometry, etc. Aimed at advanced workers. Prefers to work with experienced photographer-writers; happy to work with excellent photographers whose writing skills are lacking. "Article conclusions often require experimental support." Estab. 1979. Circ. 35,000. Pays within 2 weeks of publication. Publishes an average of 8 months after acceptance. Byline given. Buys one-time rights. Sample copy for $5. Writer's guidelines with #10 SASE.
Nonfiction: Special interest articles within above listed topics; how-to, technical product reviews, photo features. Query or send complete ms. Length open, but most features run approximately 2,500 words or 3-4 magazine pages. Pays $100/published page for well-researched technical articles.
Photos: Photographers have a much better chance of having their photos published if the photos accompany a written article. Manuscript payment includes payment for photos. Prefers transparencies and 8 × 10 b&w prints. Captions, model releases (where appropriate) and technical information required. Buys one-time rights.
Tips: "Study the magazine! We are now more receptive than ever to articles about photographers, history, aesthetics and informative backgrounders about specific areas of the photo industry or specific techniques. Successful writers for our magazine are doing what they write about."

‡PICTURE PERFECT, Aquino International, Box 15760, Stamford CT 06901-0760. (203)967-9952. Fax: (203)353-9661. E-mail: aaquinoint@aol.com. Contact: Elaine Hallgren, editor. Managing Editor: Andres Aquino. 50% freelance written. Bimonthly magazine covering photography in all its facets: fashion, commercial, travel, stock, creative, beauty. Estab. 1989. Circ. 100,000. Pays on publication. Publishes an average of 3 months after acceptance. Offers 50% kill fee. Buys first North American serial rights or all rights. Submit seasonal/holiday material 4 months in advance. Accepts simultaneous submissions. Reports in 3 weeks on queries; 6 weeks on mss. Sample copy for $4. Writer's guidelines for SAE and 2 first-class stamps.
Nonfiction: Book excerpts, how-to, interview/profile, new product, personal experience, photo feature, travel. Buys 36-48 mss/year. Send complete ms. Length 250-1,500 words. Pays 10¢/word for assigned articles; 10¢/word for unsolicited articles.
Photos: Send photos with submission. Reviews b&w prints, 35mm slides, 2¼ × 2¼ transparencies. Offers $25/photo. Captions, model releases and identification of subjects required. Buys one-time rights or first North American rights.

POPULAR PHOTOGRAPHY, 1633 Broadway, New York NY 10019. Editor: Jason Schneider. Query with SASE. All articles must include photographs. Looking for specialty; different, unusual photos. Do not send originals—dupes or prints. Most articles are written by staff.

SHUTTERBUG MAGAZINE, Patch Communications, 5211 S. Washington Ave., Titusville FL 32780. (407)268-5010. Editor: Bob Shell. Editorial Director: Bonnie Paulk. Contact: Bob Shell. 100% freelance written. Monthly magazine covering photography. "Provides how-to articles for advanced amateur to professional photographers." Estab. 1970. Circ. 100,000. Byline given. Buys first rights and second serial (reprint) rights. Editorial lead time 6 months. Submit seasonal material at least 6 months in advance. Accepts previously published submissions. Reports in 6-8 weeks on queries. Sample copy free on request. Writer's guidelines for #10 SASE.

Nonfiction: Historical/nostalgic (photography), how-to (photography), humor, interview/profile, new product, photo feature, technical. "All photo related." *No unsolicited articles.* Buys 60 mss/year. Query. Pays $300 minimum for assigned articles; $200 minimum for unsolicited articles. Pays expenses of writers on assignment.
Photos: Send photos with submission. Reviews any transparencies, 8×10 prints. Offers no additional payment for photos accepted with ms. Captions and model releases required. Buys one-time rights.
Tips: "Submit only material similar in style to that in our magazine. All sections open to freelancers."

POLITICS AND WORLD AFFAIRS

These publications cover politics for the reader interested in current events. Other publications that will consider articles about politics and world affairs are listed under Business and Finance, Contemporary Culture, Regional and General Interest. For listings of publications geared toward the professional, see Government and Public Service in the Trade section.

CALIFORNIA JOURNAL, 2101 K St., Sacramento CA 95816. (916)444-2840. E-mail: editor@statenet.c om. Executive Editor: Richard Zeiger. Contact: A.G. Block, editor. 20% freelance written. Prefers to work with published/established writers. Monthly magazine that emphasizes analysis of California politics and government. Estab. 1970. Circ. 20,000. Pays on publication. Publishes ms an average of 2 months after acceptance. Byline given. Buys all rights. Writer's guidelines for #10 SASE.
Nonfiction: Profiles of state and local government and political analysis. No outright advocacy pieces. Buys 25 unsolicited mss/year. Query. Length: 900-3,000 words. Pays $150-1,000. Sometimes pays the expenses of writers on assignment.

COMMONWEAL, A Review of Public Affairs, Religion, Literature and the Arts, Commonweal Foundation, 15 Dutch St., New York NY 10038. (212)732-0800. Contact: Patrick Jordan, managing editor. Editor: Margaret O'Brien Steinfels. Biweekly magazine. Estab. 1924. Circ. 19,000. **Pays on acceptance** or publication. Byline given. Buys all rights. Submit seasonal material 2 months in advance. Reports in 2 months. Free sample copy.
Nonfiction: Essays, general interest, interview/profile, personal experience, religious. Buys 20 mss/year. Query with published clips. Length: 1,200-3,000 words. Pays $75-100.
Poetry: Rosemary Deen, poetry editor. Free verse, traditional. Buys 25-30 poems/year. Pays 75¢/line.

EMPIRE STATE REPORT, The Magazine of Politics and Public Policy in New York State, 4 Central Ave., 3rd Floor, Albany NY 12210. (518)465-5502. Fax: (518)465-9822. Editor: Victor Schaffner. 50% freelance written. Monthly magazine providing "timely political and public policy features for local and statewide public officials in New York State. Anything that would be of interest to them is of interest to us." Estab. 1983. Circ. 10,000. Pays 2 months after publication. Byline given. Buys first North American serial rights. Reports in 1 month on queries; 2 months on mss. Sample copy for $3.95 with 9×12 SASE.
Nonfiction: Essays, exposé, interview/profile and opinion. "Writers should send for our editorial calendar." Buys 48 mss/year. Query with published clips. Length: 500-3,000 words. Pays $50-400 for assigned articles. Sometimes pays expenses of writers on assignment.
Photos: Send photos with submission. Reviews any size prints. Offers $50-100/photo. Identification of subjects required. Buys one-time rights.
Columns/Departments: New York Digest (short news stories about state politics), 300-900 words; Perspective (opinion pieces), 750-800 words. Buys 24 mss/year. Query. Length: 750-1,000 words. Pays $50-100.
Tips: "Send us a query. If we are not already working on the idea, and if the query is well written, we might work something out with the writer. Writers have the best chance selling something for New York Digest."

EUROPE, 2300 M St. NW, 3rd Floor, Washington DC 20037. (202)862-9555. Fax: (202)429-1766. Editor: Robert Guttman. Managing Editor: Peter Gwin. 75% freelance written. Magazine published 10 times/year for anyone with a professional or personal interest in Europe and European/US relations. Estab. 1963. Circ. 75,000. Pays on publication. Publishes ms an average of 3 months after acceptance. Buys first serial and all rights. Submit seasonal material 3 months in advance. Reports in 6 months.
Nonfiction: Interested in current affairs (with emphasis on economics, business and politics), the Single Market and Europe's relations with the rest of the world. Publishes monthly cultural travel pieces, with European angle. "High quality writing a must. We publish articles that might be useful to people with a professional interest in Europe." Query or submit complete ms or article outline. Include résumé of author's background and qualifications. Length: 500-2,000 words. Pays $150-500.
Photos: Photos purchased with or without accompanying mss. Buys b&w and color. Pays $25-35 for b&w print, any size; $100 for inside use of transparencies; $450 for color used on cover; per job negotiable.

THE FREEMAN, 30 S. Broadway, Irvington-on-Hudson NY 10533. (914)591-7230. Fax: (914)591-8910. Managing Editor: Beth Hoffman. 85% freelance written. Eager to work with new/unpublished writers. Monthly for "the layman and fairly advanced students of liberty." Buys all rights, including reprint rights. Estab. 1946. Pays on publication. Byline given. Publishes ms an average of 5 months after acceptance. Sample copy for 7½×10½ SASE with 4 first-class stamps.
Nonfiction: "We want nonfiction clearly analyzing and explaining various aspects of the free market, private enterprise, limited government philosophy. Though a necessary part of the literature of freedom is the exposure of collectivistic cliches and fallacies, our aim is to emphasize and explain the positive case for individual responsibility and choice in a free economy. Especially important, we believe, is the methodology of freedom—self-improvement, offered to others who are interested. We try to avoid name-calling and personality clashes and find satire of little use as an educational device. Ours is a scholarly analysis of the principles underlying a free market economy. No political strategy or tactics." Buys 100 mss/year. Length: 3,500 words maximum. Pays 10¢/word. Sometimes pays expenses of writers on assignment.
Reprints: Send tearsheet or photocopy of article and information about when and where the article previously appeared. Pays 50% of amount paid for an original article.
Tips: "It's most rewarding to find freelancers with new insights, fresh points of view. Facts, figures and quotations cited should be fully documented, to their original source, if possible."

GEORGE, Hachette Filippacchi Magazines, 1633 Broadway, 41st Floor, New York NY 10019. (212)767-6100. Publisher: Elinor Carmody. "*George* is edited to spotlight the personalities who shape public issues; from elected officials to media moguls to Hollywood stars. It contains insightful reporting, commentary, cartoons, photos and charts. It covers the points where politics and popular culture converge. *George* demystifies the political process and shows readers how to get the most from their government while staying abreast of the issues that matter." Estab. 1995. This magazine did not respond to our request for information. Query before submitting.

‡NACLA REPORT ON THE AMERICAS, North American Congress on Latin America, 475 Riverside Dr., Room 454, New York NY 10115. (212)870-3146. E-mail: nacla@igc.apc.org. Editor: Deidre McFadyen. Associate Editor: Jo-Marie Burt. 50% freelance written. Bimonthly magazine on Latin America, the Caribbean and US foreign policy. Estab. 1966. Circ. 8,000. Pays on publication. Byline given. Offers 25% kill fee. Buys one-time rights. Accepts simultaneous submissions. Reports in 2 months. Sample copy for $5.75.
Nonfiction: Exposé and features emphasizing analysis. Also short newsbriefs on current events from the region. Buys 25 mss/year. Query with published clips or send complete ms. Length: 2,000-3,000 words. Pays 12¢/published word.
Reprints: Send photocopy of article and information about when and where the article previously appeared. Pays negotiable rate.
Photos: Send photos with submission. Reviews contact sheets and prints (5×7). Pays $25 minimum. Identification of subjects required. Buys one-time rights.

THE NATION, 72 Fifth Ave., New York NY 10011-8046. (212)242-8400. Fax: (212)463-9712. Editor: Katrina Vanden Heuvel. Assistant to Editor: Dennis Selby. 75% freelance written. Estab. 1865. Works with a small number of new/unpublished writers each year. Weekly. Buys first serial rights. Free sample copy and writer's guidelines for 6×9 SASE.
Nonfiction: "We welcome all articles dealing with the social scene, from an independent perspective." Queries encouraged. Buys 100 mss/year. Length: 2,500 words maximum. Modest rates. Sometimes pays expenses of writers on assignment.
Tips: "We are firmly committed to reporting on the issues of labor, national politics, business, consumer affairs, environmental politics, civil liberties and foreign affairs."

THE NEIGHBORHOOD WORKS, Building Alternative Visions for the City, Center for Neighborhood Technology, 2125 W. North Ave., Chicago, IL 60647. (312)278-4800 ext. 113. Fax: (312)278-3840. E-mail: tnwedit@cnt.org. Website: http://www.mcs.com/~cnt/tnw.html. Editor: Carl Vogel. Contact: Mary Abowd, associate editor. 50% freelance written. Bimonthly magazine covering community organizing, urban environmentalism. "We write to, for and about community organizers in low- and middle-income neighborhoods specifically areas of environmentalism, energy, transportation, housing and economic development." Estab. 1978. Circ. 2,000. Pays on publication. Publishes ms an average of 4 months after acceptance. Byline given. Kill fee negotiable. Buys all rights. Editorial lead time 2 months. Submit seasonal material 4 months in advance. Accepts simultaneous submissions. Reports in 2 months. Sample copy for 8½×11 SAE with 4 first-class stamps. Writer's guidelines free on request.
Nonfiction: Exposé, general interest, how-to (related to organizing and technical assistance to urban communities), interview/profile. Buys 10-20 mss/year. Query with published clips. Length: 800-2,000 words. Pays $250-500 for assigned articles; $150-300 for unsolicited articles. "We don't pay students and policy people for writing articles, but will give them a subscription." Sometimes pays expenses of writers on assignment.

Reprints: Accepts previously published submissions.
Photos: State availability of photos with submission. Reviews contact sheets, 5×7 prints. Negotiates payment individually. Identification of subjects required. Buys one-time rights.
Columns/Departments: Reproducible feature (how-to), 1,400 words. Buys 4 mss/year. Query with published clips. Pay varies.

NEW JERSEY REPORTER, A Journal of Public Issues, The Center for Analysis of Public Issues, 16 Vandeventer Ave., Princeton NJ 08542. (609)924-9750. Fax: (609)924-0363. E-mail: njreporter@aol.com. Website: http://njreporter.org. Managing Editor: Bob Narus. 90% freelance written. Prefers to work with published/established writers but will consider proposals from others. Bimonthly magazine covering New Jersey politics, public affairs and public issues. "*New Jersey Reporter* is a hard-hitting and highly respected magazine published for people who take an active interest in New Jersey politics and public affairs, and who want to know more about what's going on than what newspapers and television newscasts are able to tell them. We publish a great variety of stories ranging from analysis to exposé." Estab. 1970. Circ. 2,200. Pays on publication. Byline given. Buys all rights. Reports in 1 month. Sample copy available on request.
 • This magazine continues to increase its use of freelance writing.
Nonfiction: Book excerpts, exposé, interview/profile, opinion. "We like articles from specialists (in planning, politics, economics, corruption, etc.)—particularly if written by professional journalists—but we reject stories that do not read well because of jargon or too little attention to the actual writing of the piece. Our magazine is interesting as well as informative." Buys 18-25 mss/year. Query with published clips. Length: 1,000-4,000 words. Pays $100-600.
Tips: "Queries should be specific about how the prospective story is an issue that affects or will affect the people of New Jersey and its government. The writer's résumé should be included. Stories—unless they are specifically meant to be opinion—should come to a conclusion but avoid a 'holier than thou' or preachy tone. Allegations should be scrupulously substantiated. Our magazine represents a good opportunity for freelancers to acquire great clips. Our publication specializes in longer, more detailed, analytical features. The most frequent mistake made by writers in completing an article for us is too much personal opinion versus reasoned advocacy. We are less interested in opinion than in analysis based on sound reasoning and fact. *New Jersey Reporter* is a well-respected publication, and many of our writers go on to nationally respected newspapers and magazines."

THE NEW REPUBLIC, 1220 19th St. NW, Washington DC 20036. (202)331-7494. Fax: (202)331-0275. Editor-in-Chief: Martin Peretz. Weekly newsmagazine. "*The New Republic* is a journal of opinion with an emphasis on politics and domestic and international affairs. It carries feature articles by staff and contributing editors. The second half of each issue is devoted to books and the arts." Estab. 1914. Circ. 101,200. This magazine did not respond to our request for information. Query before submitting.

POLICY REVIEW: The Journal of American Citizenship, The Heritage Foundation, 214 Massachusetts Ave. NE, Washington DC 20002. (202)546-4400. Editor: Adam Meyerson. Managing Editor: D.W. Miller. Deputy Editor: Joe Loconte. Bimonthly magazine for conservative ideas about politics and policy. "We have been described as 'the most thoughtful, the most influential and the most provocative publication of the intellectual right.' *Policy Review* illuminates the families, communities, voluntary associations, churches and other religious organizations, business enterprises, public and private schools, and local governments that are solving problems more effectively than large, centralized, bureaucratic government." Estab. 1977. Circ. 30,000. Pays on publication. Byline given.
Nonfiction: "We are looking especially for articles on private and local institutions that are putting the family back together, cutting crime, improving education and repairing the bankruptcy of government." Buys 4 mss/year. Send complete ms. Length: 2,000-6,000 words. Pays average $500 per article.

THE PROGRESSIVE, 409 E. Main St., Madison WI 53703-2899. (608)257-4626. Fax: (608)257-3373. E-mail: progressive@peacenet.org. Editor: Matthew Rothschild. 75% freelance written. Monthly. Estab. 1909. Pays on publication. Publishes ms an average of 6 weeks after acceptance. Byline given. Buys all rights. Reports in 1 month. Sample copy for 9×12 SAE with 4 first-class stamps. Writer's guidelines for #10 SASE.
Nonfiction: Primarily interested in articles which interpret, from a progressive point of view, domestic and world affairs. Occasional lighter features. "*The Progressive* is a *political* publication. General-interest material is inappropriate." Query. Length: 3,000 words maximum. Pays $100-300.
Tips: "Display some familiarity with our magazine, its interests and concerns, its format and style. We want query letters that fully describe the proposed article without attempting to sell it—and that give an indication of the writer's competence to deal with the subject."

RISING TIDE, Republican National Committee, 310 E. First St. SE, Washington DC 20003. (202)863-8885. Fax: (202)863-8773. Director of Publishing: Lisa McCormack. Bimonthly magazine covering political issues. "*Rising Tide* covers the political issues of the day through in-depth features and departments. Its emphasis is conservative, its focus informational." Estab. 1993. Circ. 544,000. This magazine did not respond to our request for information. Query before submitting.

TOWARD FREEDOM, A progressive perspective on world events, Toward Freedom Inc., 209 College St., Burlington VT 05401. (802)658-2523. Fax: (802)658-3738. Editor: Greg Guma. 75% freelance written. Political magazine published 8 times/year covering politics/culture, focus on Third World, Europe and global trends. "*Toward Freedom* is an internationalist journal with a progressive perspective on political, cultural, human rights and environmental issues around the world. Also covers the United Nations, the post-nationalist movements and U.S. foreign policy." Estab. 1952. Byline given. Circ. 3,500. Pays on publication. Kill fee "rare–negotiable." Buys first North American serial and one-time rights. Editorial lead time 1 month. Reports in 1 month on queries and mss. Sample copy for $3. Writer's guidelines free on request.

Nonfiction: Features, essays, book reviews, interview/profile, opinion, personal experience, travel, foreign, political analysis. Special issues: Global Media (an annual theme issue for *TF*, December '96/January '97). No how-to, fiction. Buys 80-100 mss/year. Query. Length: 700-2,500 words. Pays 10¢/word for all used.

Photos: Send photos with submission, if available. Reviews any prints. Offers $35 maximum/photo. Identification of subjects required. Buys one-time rights.

Columns/Departments: *TF* Reports (from foreign correspondents), UN, Population, Art and Book Reviews, 800-1,200 words. Buys 20-30 mss/year. Query. Pays 10¢/word. Last Word (creative commentary), 900 words. Buys 8/year. Pays $100.

Tips: "Except for book or other reviews, writers should have first-hand knowledge of country, political situation, foreign policy, etc., on which they are writing. Occasional cultural 'travelogues' accepted, especially those that would enlighten our readers about a different way of life. Writing must be professional."

‡WASHINGTON MONTHLY, The Washington Monthly Company, 1611 Connecticut Ave. NW, Washington DC 20009. (202)462-0128. Contact: Attn Submissions. Editor: Charles Peters. 80% freelance written. Monthly magazine covering political commentary, Washington news. Estab. 1969. Circ. 35,000. Pays on publication. Publishes ms an average of 5 months after acceptance. Byline given. Buys all rights. Editorial lead time 2 months. Submit seasonal material 2 months in advance. Reports in 1 week on queries; 1 month on mss. *Writer's Market* recommends allowing 2 months for reply. Sample copy for $3.95 and SASE. Writer's guidelines free on request.

Nonfiction: Book excerpts, essays, exposé, historical/nostalgic, interview/profile, opinion, personal experience, "anything exposing frauds of government—interesting memos—government foibles." Buys 30 mss/year. Query. Length: 1,500-5,000 words. Pays 10¢/word.

Photos: Send photos with submission. Negotiates payment individually. Captions, model releases and identification of subjects required.

Fillers: R. Carey Jones. Anecdotes, facts, gags to be illustrated by cartoonist, newsbreaks, short humor. Accepted de gratis. Length: 15-100 words.

Tips: "Freelancers should read previous issues and articles of *The Washington Monthly* to gain an understanding of its journalistic purpose and intent."

WORLD POLICY JOURNAL, World Policy Institute, Suite 413, 65 Fifth Ave., New York NY 10003. (212)229-5808. Fax: (212)229-5579. Fax: (206)815-3445. E-mail: @mary.wvus.org. Editor: James Chace. Estab. 1983. 10% freelance written. "We are eager to work with new or unpublished writers as well as more established writers." A quarterly journal covering international politics, economics, and security issues, as well as historical and cultural essays, book reviews, profiles, and first-person reporting from regions not covered in the general media. "We hope to bring a new sense of imagination, principle and proportion, as well as a restored sense of reality and direction to America's discussion of its role in the world." Circ. 8,000. Pays on publication. Publishes ms an average of 3 months after acceptance. Byline given. Offers variable kill fee. Buys all rights. Reports in 2 months. Sample copy for $7.50 and 9×12 SAE with 10 first-class stamps.

Nonfiction: Articles that "define policies that reflect the shared needs and interests of all nations of the world." Query. Length: 20-30 pages (8,000 words maximum). Pays variable commission rate.

Tips: "By providing a forum for many younger or previously unheard voices, including those from Europe, Asia, Africa and Latin America, we hope to replace lingering illusions and fears with new priorities and aspirations. Articles submitted on speculation very rarely suit our particular needs."

WORLD VISION, World Vision, Inc., 919 W. Huntington Blvd., Monrovia CA 91016. Fax: (206)815-3445. E-mail: @mary.wvus.org. Editor: Terry Madison. Contact: Bruce Brander, managing editor. Up to 50%

ALWAYS ENCLOSE a self-addressed, stamped envelope (SASE) with all your queries and correspondence.

freelance written. "*World Vision*, a Christian humanitarian relief and development agency working in 100 countries." Bimonthly magazine covering world humanitarian issues for opinion leaders. Estab. 1955. Circ. 80,000. **Pays on acceptance.** Byline given. Kill fee varies. Buys multiple-use international rights and makes work-for-hire assignments. Editorial lead time 6 months. Submit seasonal material 6 months in advance. Reports in 3 weeks on queries; 2 weeks on mss. Sample copy and writer's guidelines free on request.

Nonfiction: Essays, general interest, inspirational, interview/profile, photo feature, religious, global issues. Buys 8 mss/year. Query with published clips. Send complete ms. Length: 700-3,000. Pays $1,500 maximum for assigned articles; $850 maximum for unsolicited articles. Sometimes pays expenses of writers on assignment.

Photos: State availability of photos with submissions. Reviews contact sheets, transparencies, 3×5 prints. Offers no additional payment for photos accepted with ms. Captions, identification of subjects required. Negotiable rights bought.

Tips: "As a nonprofit humanitarian agency aiding the poor worldwide, we give assignments to accomplished journalistic writers and photographers who travel the globe. We cover world issues with a humanitarian slant, such as: 'Are We Trashing Our Third-World Neighbors?' 'Homeless With Children,' and 'The Human Cost of the Small Arms Trade.' We invite traveling journalists to check with us for pick-a-back assignments."

PSYCHOLOGY AND SELF-IMPROVEMENT

These publications focus on psychological topics, how and why readers can improve their own outlooks, and how to understand people in general. Many General Interest, Men's and Women's publications also publish articles in these areas. Magazines treating spiritual development appear in the Astrology, Metaphysical and New Age section, as well as in Religion, while markets for holistic mind/body healing strategies are listed in Health and Fitness.

THE HEALING WOMAN, The Monthly Newsletter for Women Survivors of Childhood Sexual Abuse, P.O. Box 3038, Moss Beach CA 94038. (415)728-0339. Fax: (415)728-1324. E-mail: healingw@aol.com. Website: http://www.cs.utk.edu/~bartley/other/healingWoman.html. Contact: Brenda Anderson, editor. Publisher/Editorial Director: Margot Silk Forrest. 70% freelance written. Monthly newsletter covering recovery from childhood sexual abuse. "Submissions accepted only from writers with personal or professional experience with childhood sexual abuse. We are looking for intelligent, honest and compassionate articles on topics of interest to survivors. We also publish first-person stories, poetry, interviews and book reviews." Estab. 1992. Circ. 11,000. **Pays on acceptance.** Publishes ms an average of 1 year after acceptance. Byline given. Offers 50% kill fee. Buys first North American serial rights. Submit seasonal material 4 months in advance. Submit no more than 3 pieces at a time. Reports in 1 month on queries. Writer's guidelines for #10 SASE. "No fax or e-mail submissions please."

Nonfiction: Book excerpts, essays, general interest, interview/profile, opinion, personal experience. "No articles on topics with which the writer has not had first-hand experience. If you've been there, you can write about it for us. If not, don't write about it." Buys 30 mss/year. Query with published clips. Length: 300-1,500 words. Pays $25-50. "Pays in copies for poems, short first-person pieces."

Reprints: Send photocopy of article and information about when and where the article previously appeared. Pays 100% of amount paid for an original article.

Photos: Send photos with submission. Negotiates payment for photos individually. Identification of subjects required. Buys one-time rights.

Columns/Departments: Book Reviews (books or accounts of incest survivors, therapy for incest survivors), 500-600 words; and Survivors Speak Out (first-person stories of recovery), 200-400 words.

Poetry: No poems preoccupied with painful aspects of sexual abuse. 40 line limit. Buys 25 poems/year, but pays only in copies.

Tips: "Although our subject matter is painful, *The Healing Woman* is not about suffering—it's about healing. Our department called 'Survivors Speak Out' features short, honest, insightful first-person essays with a conversational tone. We are happy to work with unpublished writers in this department."

SCIENCE OF MIND MAGAZINE, 3251 W. Sixth St., P.O. Box 75127, Los Angeles CA 90075. (213)388-2181. Fax: (213)388-1926. Contact: Jim Shea, assistant editor. Editor: Sandra Sarr. 30% freelance written. Monthly magazine that features articles on spirituality, self-help and inspiration. "Our publication centers on oneness of all life and spiritual empowerment through the application of Science of Mind principles." Pays on publication. Publishes ms an average of 5 months after acceptance. Byline given. Buys first North American serial rights. Submit seasonal material 6 months in advance. Reports in 6 weeks on queries; 3 months on mss. Free writer's guidelines.

Nonfiction: Book excerpts, inspirational, personal experience of Science of Mind, spiritual. Buys 35-45 mss/year. Query or send complete ms. Length: 750-2,000 words. Pays $25/printed page. Pays in contributors copies for some special features written by readers.

Photos: Reviews 35mm transparencies and 5×7 or 8×10 b&w prints. Buys one-time rights.
Poetry: Inspirational and Science of Mind oriented. "We are not interested in poetry not related to Science of Mind principles." Buys 10-15 poems/year. Length: 7-25 lines. Pays $25.
Tips: "We are interested in first person experiences of a spiritual nature having to do with the Science of Mind."

REGIONAL

Many regional publications rely on staff-written material, but others accept work from freelance writers who live in or know the region. The best regional publication to target with your submissions is usually the one in your hometown, whether it's a city or state magazine or a Sunday supplement in a newspaper. Since you are familiar with the region, it is easier to propose suitable story ideas.

Listed first are general interest magazines slanted toward residents of and visitors to a particular region. Next, regional publications are categorized alphabetically by state, followed by Canada. Publications that report on the business climate of a region are grouped in the regional division of the Business and Finance category. Recreation and travel publications specific to a geographical area are listed in the Travel, Camping and Trailer section. Keep in mind also that many regional publications specialize in specific areas, and are listed according to those sections. Regional publications are not listed if they only accept material from a select group of freelancers in their area or if they did not want to receive the number of queries and manuscripts a national listing would attract. If you know of a regional magazine that is not listed, approach it by asking for writer's guidelines before you send unsolicited material.

General

BLUE RIDGE COUNTRY, Leisure Publishing, P.O. Box 21535, Roanoke VA 24018-9900. (703)989-6138. Fax: (703)989-7603. E-mail: leisure@infi.net. Editor: Kurt Rheinheimer. 75% freelance written. Bimonthly magazine on the Blue Ridge region from Maryland to Georgia. "The magazine is designed to celebrate the history, heritage and beauty of the Blue Ridge region. It is aimed at the adult, upscale readers who enjoy living or traveling in the mountain regions of Virginia, North Carolina, West Virginia, Maryland, Kentucky, Tennessee, South Carolina and Georgia." Estab. 1988. Circ. 75,000. Pays on publication. Publishes ms an average of 8 months after acceptance. Byline given. Offers $50 kill fee for commissioned pieces only. Buys first and second serial (reprint) rights. Submit seasonal material 6 months in advance. Reports in 2 months. Sample copy for 9×12 SAE with 6 first-class stamps. Writer's guidelines for #10 SASE.
Nonfiction: General interest, historical/nostalgic, personal experience, photo feature, travel, history. Buys 25-30 mss/year. Query with or without published clips or send complete ms. Length: 500-1,800 words. Pays $50-250 for assigned articles; $25-250 for unsolicited articles.
   • This magazine is looking for more travel pieces.
Photos: Send photos with submission. Prefers transparencies. Offers $10-25/photo and $100 for cover photo. Identification of subjects required. Buys all rights.
Columns/Departments: Country Roads (stories on people, events, travel, ecology, history, antiques, books). Buys 12-24 mss/year. Query. Pays $10-40.
Tips: "Freelancers needed for regional departmental shorts and 'macro' issues affecting whole region. Need field reporters from all areas of Blue Ridge region. Also, we need updates on the Blue Ridge Parkway, Appalachian Trail, national forests, ecological issues, preservation movements."

NORTHWEST TRAVEL, Northwest Regional Magazines, 1525 12th St., P.O. Box 18000, Florence OR 97439. (541)997-8401. (800)348-8401. Website: http://www.presys.com/highway. Contact: Judy Fleagle, co-editor. Co-editor: Jim Forst. 60% freelance written. Bimonthly consumer magazine covering the Pacific Northwest. "We like energetic writing about popular activities and destinations in the Northwest. *Northwest Travel* aims to give readers practical ideas on where to go in the region. Magazine covers Oregon, Washington, Idaho, B.C.; occasionally Alaska." Estab. 1991. Circ. 50,000. Pays after publication. Publishes ms an average of 8 months after acceptance. Offers 33% kill fee. Buys first North American serial rights. Submit seasonal material 6 months in advance. Reports in 1 month on queries; 3 months on mss. Sample copy for $4.50. Writer's guidelines for #10 SASE.
   • *Northwest Travel* now emphasizes day trips in the Pacific Northwest area.

Nonfiction: Book excerpts, general interest, historical/nostalgic, interview/profile (rarely), photo feature, travel (only in Northwest region). "No cliche-ridden pieces on places that everyone covers." Buys 40 mss/year. Query with or without published clips. Length: 300-2,500 words. Pays $75-350 for feature articles and 2-5 contributor copies.

Photos: State availability of photos with submission. Reviews transparencies (prefers dupes) and prints ("for good color we need reproduction negatives with prints"). Captions, model releases (cover photos), credits and identification of subjects required. Buys one-time rights.

Columns/Departments: Restaurant Features, 1,000 words. Pays $125. Worth a Stop (brief items describing places "worth a stop"), 300-500 words. Buys 25-30 mss/year. Send complete ms. Pays $50. Back Page (photo and text package keyed to a specific activity, season or festival with some technical photo info), 80-100 words and 1 photo. Pays $75.

Tips: "Write fresh, lively copy (avoid clichés) and cover exciting travel topics in the region that haven't been covered in other magazines. A story with stunning photos will get serious consideration. Areas most open to freelancers are Worth a Stop and the Restaurant Feature. Take us to fascinating and interesting places we might not otherwise discover."

SOUTHERN EXPOSURE, A Journal of Politics and Culture, Institute for Southern Studies, P.O. Box 531, Durham NC 27702. (919)419-8311. Editor: Pat Arnow. 80% freelance written. Quarterly magazine covering Southern politics and culture. "With special focus sections, investigative journalism, features, fiction, interviews, and news, *Southern Exposure* covers the wide range of Southern life today—and puts events and trends in perspective. Our goal is to provide information, ideas, and historical understanding of Southern social struggles that will help bring about progressive change." Estab. 1973. Circ. 4,000. Pays on publication. Publishes ms an average of 6 months after acceptance. Byline given. Buys first rights, one-time rights, second serial (reprint) rights or all rights. Editorial lead time 6 months. Accepts simultaneous submissions. Reports in 3 months on queries; 6 months on mss. Sample copy for $5. Writer's guidelines for #10 SASE.

Nonfiction: Book excerpts, essays, exposé, how-to (build a grass roots organization, how-to conduct a citizen's campaign), humor, interview/profile, personal experience, photo feature. "Everything we publish has to have something to do with the South." Special issues: Women & Health, Timber, building community—community breakdown. Buys 50 mss/year. Query with published clips. Length: 250-3,500 words. Pays $50-250. Sometimes pays expenses of writers on assignment.

Photos: Send photos with submission. Reviews contact sheets, transparencies, prints. Offers $50 maximum/photo. Negotiates payment individually. Captions, identification of subjects required. Buys one-time rights.

Columns/Departments: Blueprint (how to change the South—from a person or organization's experience), 1,400 words; Voices (stories by or about people who have developed a point of view, strong feelings, actions), 2,100 words; Roundup (anecdotes and news from the region), 250-700 words; Still the South (information and statistics on some aspect of Southern life), 650 words; Reviews (essay on one or more related books and/or other media), 2,100 words. Buys 15 mss/year. Query with published clips or send complete ms. Pays $50-100.

Fiction: Erotica, ethnic, experimental, historical, horror, humorous, novel excerpts. Buys 4 mss/year. Send complete ms. Length: 3,500 words maximum. Pays $100-250.

Tips: "Lively writing and original thinking are what we're after, new ways to look at events, people, places. Give a new perspective on arts, politics, local struggles, corruption, movements. We like in-depth reporting, plenty of specific information—quotes!—and everything we publish must pertain to the South in some way."

THE SOUTHERN JOURNAL/THE APPALACHIAN LOG, Appalachian Log Publishing Company, P.O. Box 20297, Charleston WV 25362-1297. (304)342-5789. Editor: Ron Gregory. 50% freelance written. Works with new/unpublished writers. Monthly magazine covering Southern mountain region. "We are dedicated to promoting the people and places of the Southern mountains. We publish only 'positive' articles concerning our region. We are *not* interested in religious or political material." Estab. 1992. Circ. 5,000. Pays 60 days from publication. Publishes ms an average of 9 months after acceptance. Byline given. Offers 10% kill fee or $10. Not copyrighted. Buys first, one-time, second serial (reprint) or simultaneous rights. Editorial lead time 2 months. Submit seasonal material 2 months in advance. Accepts simultaneous submissions. Reports in 6 weeks on queries; 6 months on mss. Sample copy for $1.50. Writer's guidelines for #10 SASE.

Nonfiction: Book excerpts, essays, historical/nostalgic, humor, inspirational, interview/profile, personal experience, photo feature, travel, genealogy. Special issues include snow skiing in the South, festivals in the South, whitewater rafting in the South. "No religious, exposé or opinion pieces. (We are no longer interested in political/opinion articles.)" Buys 20 mss/year. Send complete ms. Length: 300 words minimum. Pays $50 minimum for assigned articles; $10 minimum for unsolicited articles. Sometimes pays expenses of writers on assignment.

Reprints: Accepts previously published submissions.

Photos: Send photos with submission. Reviews contact sheets. Captions required. Buys one-time rights.

Columns/Departments: Betty Gregory, publisher. Family History (genealogy), 1,000-2,000 words. Buys 4 mss/year. Query. Pays $20-50.

Fiction: Condensed novels, historical, humorous, mainstream, slice-of-life vignettes. No religious or erotic material. Buys 5 mss/year. Send complete ms. Length: 500-5,000 words. Pays $25-200.

Poetry: Betty Gregory, publisher. Avant-garde, free verse, light verse, traditional. Buys 20 poems/year. Length: 10-80 lines. Pays $7.50-30.

Fillers: Anecdotes, facts, short humor. Buys 15/year. Length: 25-250 words. Pays $5-50.

Tips: "Cover letters that give some indication of the author's knowledge of our region are helpful. All articles and submissions should, likewise, display the author's familiarity with the Southern mountains. Details—particularly nostalgic ones—must be authentic and correct. Fiction and nonfiction short stories or longer works that can be serialized appeal to us. Writers in this area should be clear in their storyline (no 'hidden' meanings) and should keep in mind that our magazine loves the South and its people."

SOUTHERN LIVING, Southern Progress Corp., 2100 Lakeshore Dr., Birmingham AL 35209. (205)877-6000. Editor: John A. Floyd, Jr. Managing Editor: Clay Nordan. Contact: Dianne Young. Monthly magazine covers travel, foods, homes, gardens, Southern lifestyle. Estab. 1966. Circ. 2,461,416. **Pays on acceptance.** Publishes ms an average of 1 year after acceptance. 25% kill fee. Buys all rights or other negotiated rights. Editorial lead time 6 months. Submit seasonal material 1 year in advance. Reports in 1 month on queries, 2 months on mss. Writer's guidelines free on request.

Nonfiction: Essays, humor. Accepts unsolicited freelance only for personal, nonfiction essays about Southern life. Buys 45-50 mss/year. Query with or without published clips, but prefers completed mss. Length: 800 words minimum. Payment negotiated individually. Sometimes pays expenses of writers on assignment.

Photos: State availability of photos with submissions. Reviews 4×5 transparencies. Negotiates payment individually. Captions, model releases, identification of subjects required. Buys one-time rights.

Columns/Departments: Southern Journal (Southern lifestyle and subjects), 800 words. Buys 12 mss/year. Query with published clips.

SUNSET MAGAZINE, Sunset Publishing Corp., 80 Willow Rd., Menlo Park CA 94025-3691. (415)321-3600. Fax: (415)321-8193. Executive Editor: Melissa Houtte. Monthly magazine covering the lifestyle of the Western states. "*Sunset* is a Western lifestyle publication for educated, active consumers. Editorial provides localized information on gardening and travel, food and entertainment, home building and remodeling." Freelance articles should be timely and only about the 13 Western states. Pays on acceptance. Byline given. Guidelines for freelance travel items for #10 SASE addressed to Editorial Services.

Nonfiction: Travel in the West. Buys 50-75 mss/year. Length: 550-750 words. Pays $1/word. Query before submitting.

Columns/Departments: Departments open to freelancers are: Building & Crafts, Food, Garden, Travel. *Travel Guide* length: 300-350 words. Direct queries to the specific editorial department.

Tips: "Here are some subjects regularly treated in *Sunset*'s stories and Travel Guide items: outdoor recreation (i.e., bike tours, bird-watching spots, walking or driving tours of historic districts); indoor adventures (i.e., new museums and displays, hand-on science programs at aquariums or planetariums, specialty shopping); special events (i.e., festivals that celebrate a region's unique social, cultural, or agricultural heritage). Also looking for great weekend getaways, backroad drives, urban adventures and culinary discoveries such as ethnic dining enclaves."

YANKEE, Yankee Publishing Inc., P.O. Box 520, Dublin NH 03444-0520. (603)563-8111. Fax: (603)563-8252. Editor: Judson D. Hale, Sr. Managing Editor: Tim Clark. Assistant Editor: Don Weafer. 50% freelance written. Monthly magazine that features articles on New England. "Our mission is to express and perhaps, indirectly, preserve the New England culture—and to do so in an entertaining way. Our audience is national, and has one thing in common—they love New England." Estab. 1935. Circ. 700,000. Pays within 30 days of acceptance. Byline given. Offers 33% kill fee. Buys first rights. Submit seasonal material 5 months in advance. Accepts simultaneous submissions. Send tearsheet, photocopy of article or short story, typed ms with rights for sale noted and information about when and where the material previously appeared. For reprints, pays 100% of the amount paid for an original article. Query for electronic submissions." Reports in 2 months on queries. Writer's guidelines for #10 SASE.

• *Yankee* won two White Awards for Public Affairs Reporting from the William Allen White School of Journalism, in 1994, four in 1995 and seven in 1996. In addition, it was a finalist for General Excellence in the National Magazine Awards in 1995 and 1996.

Nonfiction: Don Weafer, assistant editor. Essays, general interest, historical/nostalgic, humor, interview/profile, personal experience. "No 'good old days' pieces, no dialect humor and nothing outside New England!" Buys 30 mss/year. Query with published clips. Length: 250-2,500 words. Pays $50-2,000 for assigned articles; $50-500 for unsolicited articles. Sometimes pays expenses of writers on assignment.

Photos: Send photos with submission. Reviews contact sheets and transparencies. Offers $50-150/photo. Identification of subjects required. Buys one-time rights.

Columns/Departments: New England Sampler (short bits on interesting people, anecdotes, lost and found), 100-400 words; Yankee's Home Companion (short pieces about home-related items), 100-400 words; I Remember (nostalgia focused on specific incidents), 400-500 words. Buys 80 mss/year. Query with published clips. Pays $50-400.

Fiction: Edie Clark, fiction editor. "We publish high-quality literary fiction that explores human issues and concerns in a specific place—New England." Publishes novel excerpts. Buys 6 mss/year. Send complete ms. Length: 500-2,500 words. Pays $1,000.
   • Ranked as one of the best markets for fiction writers in *Writer's Digest*'s annual "Fiction 50," June 1996.
Poetry: Jean Burden, poetry editor. "We don't choose poetry by type. We look for the best. No inspirational, holiday-oriented, epic, limericks, etc." Buys 40 poems/year. Submit maximum 3 poems. Length: 2-20 lines. Pays $50.
Tips: "Submit lots of ideas. Don't censor yourself—let *us* decide whether an idea is good or bad. We might surprise you. Remember we've been publishing for 60 years, so chances are we've already done every 'classic' New England subject. Try to surprise us—it isn't easy. These departments are most open to freelancers: New England Sampler; Home Companion; I Remember. Study the ones we publish—the format should be apparent. Surprise us!"

Alaska

ALASKA, The Magazine of Life on the Last Frontier, 4220 B St., Suite 210, Anchorage AK 99503. (907)561-4772. Fax: (907)561-5669. General Manager: David C. Foster. Contact: Ken Marsh, managing editor. Editorial Assistant: Donna Rae Thompson. 80% freelance written. Eager to work with new/unpublished writers. Monthly magazine covering topics "uniquely Alaskan." Estab. 1935. Circ. 235,000. Pays on publication. Publishes ms an average of 6 months after acceptance. Byline given. Buys first or one-time rights. Submit seasonal material 1 year in advance. Reports in 2 months. Sample copy for $3 and 9×12 SAE with 7 first-class stamps. Writer's guidelines for #10 SASE.
Nonfiction: Historical/nostalgic, adventure, how-to (on anything Alaskan), outdoor recreation (including hunting, fishing), humor, interview/profile, personal experience, photo feature. Also travel articles and Alaska destination stories. No fiction or poetry. Buys 60 mss/year. Query. Length: 100-2,500 words. Pays $100-1,250 depending upon length. Pays expenses of writers on assignment.
Photos: Send photos with submission. Reviews 35mm or larger transparencies. Captions and identification of subjects required.
Tips: "We're looking for top-notch writing—original, well-researched, lively. Subjects must be distinctly Alaskan."

Arizona

ARIZONA HIGHWAYS, 2039 W. Lewis Ave., Phoenix AZ 85009-9988. (602)258-6641. Fax: (602)254-4505. Website: http://www.ARIZHWAYS.com/. Managing Editor: Richard G. Stahl. 90% freelance written. Prefers to work with published/established writers. State-owned magazine designed to help attract tourists into and through the state. Estab. 1925. **Pays on acceptance.** Reports in up to 3 months. Writer's guidelines for SASE.
Nonfiction: Feature subjects include narratives and exposition dealing with history, anthropology, nature, wildlife, armchair travel, out of the way places, small towns, old west history, Indian arts and crafts, travel, etc. Travel articles are experience-based. All must be oriented toward Arizona and the Southwest. Buys 6 mss/issue. Buys first serial rights. Query with a lead paragraph and brief outline of story. "We deal with professionals only, so include list of current credits." Length: 600-2,000 words. Pays 35-55¢/word. Sometimes pays expenses of writers on assignment.
Photos: "We will use transparencies of 2¼×2¼, 4×5 or larger, and 35mm when they display exceptional quality or content. We prefer 35mm Kodachrome. Each transparency *must* be accompanied by information attached to each photograph: where, when, what. No photography will be reviewed by the editors unless the photographer's name appears on *each* and *every* transparency." Pays $80-350 for "selected" transparencies. Buys one-time rights.
Columns/Departments: Departments include Focus on Nature, Along the Way, Back-Road Adventure, Legends of the Lost, Hike of the Month and Arizona Humor. "Back Road and Hikes also must be experience-based."
Tips: "Writing must be of professional quality, warm, sincere, in-depth, well-peopled and accurate. Avoid themes that describe first trips to Arizona, the Grand Canyon, the desert, Colorado River running, etc. Emphasis is to be on Arizona adventure and romance as well as flora and fauna, when appropriate, and themes that can be photographed. Double check your manuscript for accuracy."

‡**TUCSON LIFESTYLE**, Citizen Publishing Company of Wisconsin, Inc., dba Old Pueblo Press, Suite 12, 7000 E. Tanque Verde Rd., Tucson AZ 85715-5318. (602)721-2929. Fax: (602)721-8665. Editor-in-Chief: Sue Giles. 90% freelance written. Prefers to work with published/established writers. Monthly maga-

zine covering city-related events and topics. Estab. 1982. Circ. 27,000. **Pays on acceptance.** Publishes ms an average of 6 months after acceptance. Byline given. Buys first rights and second serial (reprint) rights. Submit seasonal material 1 year in advance. Reports in 6 months. Sample copy for $3.20. Free writer's guidelines.

Nonfiction: All stories need a Tucson angle. Historical/nostalgic, humor, interview/profile, personal experience, travel, local stories. Special issue: Christmas (December). "We do not accept *anything* that does not pertain to Tucson or Arizona." Buys 100 mss/year. Query. Pays $50-300. Sometimes pays expenses of writers on assignment.

Reprints: Accepts previously published submissions. Send typed ms with rights for sale noted and information about when and where the article previously appeared. Pays 25-50% of amount paid for an original article.

Photos: Reviews contact sheets, $2\frac{1}{4} \times 2\frac{1}{4}$ transparencies and 5×7 prints. Offers $25-100/photo. Identification of subjects required. Buys one-time rights.

Columns/Departments: In Business (articles on Tucson businesses and business people); Southwest Homes (environmental living in Tucson: homes, offices). Buys 36 mss/year. Query. Pays $100-200.

Tips: Features are most open to freelancers. " 'Style' is not of paramount importance; good, clean copy with interesting lead is a 'must.' "

California

BUZZ, The Talk of Los Angeles, 11835 W. Olympic Blvd., Suite 450, Los Angeles CA 90064-5000. (310)473-2721. E-mail: queries@buzzmag.com.Website: http://www.buzzmag.com. Editor-in-Chief: Allan Mayer. Deputy Editor: Marilyn Bethany. Contact: Ned Zeman, features editor. 80% freelance written. Monthly magazine for Los Angeles. "We are looking for lively, provocative, insightful journalism, essays and fiction that reflect L.A. sensibility." Estab. 1990. Circ. 110,000. Pays within 45 days of acceptance. Byline given. Offers 25% kill fee. Buys first North American serial rights. Submit seasonal material 4 months in advance. Reports in 3 months. Sample copy for $3 and 10×13 SAE with 10 first-class stamps.

• Ranked as one of the best markets for freelance writers in *Writer's Yearbook*'s annual "Top 100 Markets," January 1996.

Nonfiction: Ned Zeman, features editor. Book excerpts, essays, general interest, interview/profile. "No satirical essays, book/movie/theater reviews or personal memoirs." Buys 30 mss/year. Query with published clips. Length: 2,500-4,000 words. Pays $2,000-5,000. Sometimes pays expenses of writers on assignment.

Photos: Send photos with submission. Photos are assigned separately. Model releases and identification of subjects required. Buys one-time rights.

Columns/Departments: Susan Gordon, senior editor. "What's the Buzz" (witty, "Talk of the Town"-like pieces on personalities, trends and events in L.A.), 300-1,000 words. Buys 20 mss/year. Query with published clips. Pays $200-1,000.

Fiction: Renee Vogel, fiction editor. "We are interested in any type fiction by L.A. writers, and in fiction relevant to L.A. by non-L.A.-based writers. No unagented submissions, no fiction that has no connection with L.A." Publishes novel excerpts. Buys 5 mss/year. Send complete ms. Length: 1,500-4,000 words. Pays $1,000-2,500.

• Ranked as one of the best markets for fiction writers in *Writer's Digest*'s annual "Fiction 50," June 1996.

Tips: "The 'What's the Buzz' section is the best place to break into *Buzz*. Freelancers should keep in mind that we're looking for national-quality works."

THE EAST BAY MONTHLY, The Berkeley Monthly, Inc., 1301 59th St., Emeryville CA 94608. (510)658-9811. Editor: Tim Devaney. 95% freelance written. Monthly tabloid. "We like stories about local people and issues, but we also accept ideas for articles about topics that range beyond the East Bay's borders or have little or nothing to do with the region." Estab. 1970. Circ. 75,000. Pays on publication. Byline given. Offers 25% kill fee. Buys first rights or second serial (reprint) rights. Editorial lead time 2 months. Submit seasonal material 2 months in advance. Accepts simultaneous submissions. Reports in 1 month. Sample copy for $1. Writer's guidelines for #10 SASE.

Nonfiction: Essays, exposé, general interest, historical/nostalgic, humor, interview/profile, opinion, personal experience, photo feature, travel. Buys 55 mss/year. Query with published clips. Length: 1,500-3,000 words. Pays 10¢/word.

Reprints: Accepts previously published submissions.

Photos: State availability of photos with submission. Reviews contact sheets, 4×5 transparencies, 8×10 prints. Negotiates payment individually. Identification of subjects required. Buys one-time rights.

Columns/Departments: Shopping Around (local retail news), 2,000 words; Food for Thought (local food news), 2,000 words; First Person, 2,000 words. Buys 15 mss/year. Query with published clips. Pays 10¢/word.

LOS ANGELES MAGAZINE, ABC, 11100 Santa Monica Blvd., 7th Floor, Los Angeles CA 90025. Phone/fax: (310)996-6885. Executive Editor: Bob Roe. Editor: Michael Caruso. 98% freelance written. Monthly magazine about southern California. "The primary editorial role of the magazine is to aid a literate, upscale audience in getting the most out of life in the Los Angeles area." Estab. 1963. Circ. 174,000. Pays on publication. Publishes ms an average of 4 months after acceptance. Byline given. Offers 30% kill fee. Buys first North American serial rights. Submit seasonal material 6 months in advance. Reports in 3 months. Sample copy for $5. Writer's guidelines for #10 SASE.
   ● *Los Angeles Magazine* continues to do stories with local angles but it is expanding its coverage to include topics of interest on a national level.
Nonfiction: Book excerpts (about L.A. or by famous L.A. author); exposé (any local issue); general interest; historical/nostalgic (about L.A. or Hollywood); interview/profile (about L.A. person). Buys up to 100 mss/year. Query with published clips. Length: 250-3,500 words. Pays $50-2,000. Sometimes pays expenses of writers on assignment.
Photos: Amy Osburn, photo editor. Send photos.
Columns/Departments: Buys 170 mss/year. Query with published clips. Length: 250-1,200 words. Pays $50-600.

LOS ANGELES READER, 5550 Wilshire Blvd., Suite 301, Los Angeles CA 90036-3389. (213)965-7430. Fax: (213)933-0281. Editor: James Vowell. Contact: Erik Himmelsbach, managing editor. 85% freelance written. Weekly magazine of features and reviews for "intelligent young Los Angelenos interested in politics, the arts and popular culture." Estab. 1978. Circ. 100,000. Pays on publication. Publishes ms an average of 60 days after acceptance. Byline given. Buys first North American serial rights. Submit seasonal material 3 months in advance. Accepts simultaneous submissions. Reports in 2 months. Sample copy and writer's guidelines free.
Nonfiction: General interest, journalism, interview/profile, personal experience, photo features—all with strong local slant. Buys "scores" of mss/year. Query, send complete ms. Length: 200-3,500 words. Pays $25-500.
Tips: "Break in with submissions for our Cityside pages which use short (400-800 words) news items on Los Angeles happenings, personalities and trends. Try to have some conflict in submissions: 'x exists' is not as good a story as 'x is struggling with y over z.' Stories must have Los Angeles angle. We much prefer submissions in electronic form."

LOS ANGELES TIMES MAGAZINE, *Los Angeles Times*, Times Mirror Sq., Los Angeles CA 90053. (213)237-7000. Fax: (213)237-7386. Editor: John Lindsay. 50% freelance written. Weekly magazine of regional general interest. Circ. 1,164,388. Payment schedule varies. Publishes ms an average of 2 months after acceptance. Byline given. Buys first North American serial rights. Submit seasonal material 3 months in advance. Accepts simultaneous submissions. Reports in 2 months. Sample copy and writer's guidelines are free.
Nonfiction: General interest, investigative and narrative journalism, interview/profiles and reported essays. Covers California, the West, the nation and the world. Query with published clips only. Length: 2,500-4,500 words. Pays agreed upon expenses.
Photos: Query first; prefers to assign photos. Reviews color transparencies and b&w prints. Payment varies. Captions, model releases and identification of subjects required. Buys one-time rights.
Tips: "Prospective contributors should know their subject well and be able to explain why a story merits publication. Previous national magazine writing experience preferred."

‡**METRO**, Metro Newspapers, 550 S. 1st St., San Jose CA 95113-2806. (408)298-8000. Website: http://www.metroactive.com. Editor: Dan Pulcrano. Managing Editor: Corinne Asturias. 20-40% freelance written. Weekly alternative newspaper. "*Metro* is for a sophisticated urban audience—stories must be more in-depth with an unusual slant not covered in daily newspapers." Estab. 1985. Circ. 85,000. Pays on publication from one week to two months. Publishes ms after acceptance. Byline given. Offers kill fee only with assignment memorandum signed by editor. Buys first North American serial and second serial (reprint) rights—nonexclusive. Submit seasonal material 3 months in advance. Reports in 2 months on queries; 4 months on mss. Sample copy for $3. Writer's guidelines for #10 SASE.
Nonfiction: Book excerpt, exposé and interview/profile (particularly entertainment oriented). Some sort of local angle needed. Buys 75 mss/year. Query with published clips. Length: 500-4,000 words. Pays $50-500 for articles. Sometimes pays expenses of writers on assignment.
Reprints: Send photocopy of article including information about when and where the article previously appeared. Pays $25-200.
Photos: Send photos with submission. Reviews contact sheets, negatives, any size transparencies and prints. Offers $25-50/photo, more if used on cover. Captions, model releases and identification of subjects required. Buys one-time rights.
Columns/Departments: MetroMenu (copy related to food, dining out), 500-1,000 words; and MetroGuide (entertainment features, interviews), 500-1,500 words. Buys 100 mss/year. Query with published clips. Pays $25-150.

Tips: "Seasonal features are most likely to be published, but we take only the best stuff. Stories on local news events or national news events with a local angle will also be considered. Preferred submission format is Macintosh disk with accompanying printout."

ORANGE COAST MAGAZINE, The Magazine of Orange County, Orange Coast Kommunications Inc., 245-D Fischer Ave., Suite 8, Costa Mesa CA 92626-4514. (714)545-1900. Fax: (714)545-1900. E-mail: ocmag@aol.com. Website: http://orangecoast.com. Contact: Martin J. Smith, editor. Managing Editor: Allison Joyce. 95% freelance written. Monthly magazine "designed to inform and enlighten the educated, upscale residents of Orange County, California; highly graphic and well-researched." Estab. 1974. Circ. 40,000. **Pays on acceptance.** Publishes ms an average of 4 months after acceptance. Byline given. Buys first serial rights. Submit seasonal material at least 6 months in advance. Accepts simultaneous submissions. Reports in 2 months. Sample copy for $2.95 and 10×12 SAE with 8 first-class stamps. Writer's guidelines for SASE.
● Ranked as one of the best markets for freelance writers in *Writer's Yearbook*'s annual "Top 100 Markets," January 1996.
Nonfiction: Exposé (Orange County government, politics, business, crime), general interest (with Orange County focus); historical/nostalgic, guides to activities and services, interview/profile (prominent Orange County citizens), local sports, travel. Special issues: Dining and Entertainment (March); Health and Fitness (January); Resort Guide (November); Home and Garden (June); Holiday (December). Buys 100 mss/year. Query or send complete ms. Absolutely no phone queries. Length: 1,000-3,000 words. Pays $400-800.
Reprints: Accepts previously published submissions. Send tearsheet or photocopy of article or typed ms with rights for sale noted and information about when and where the article previously appeared.
Columns/Departments: Business statistics. Most departments are not open to freelancers. Buys 200 mss/year. Query or send complete ms. Length: 1,000-2,000 words. Pays $200 maximum.
Fiction: Buys only under rare circumstances. Send complete ms. Length: 1,000-5,000 words. Pays $250.
Tips: "Most features are assigned to writers we've worked with before. Don't try to sell us 'generic' journalism. *Orange Coast* prefers articles with specific and unusual angles focused on Orange County. A lot of freelance writers ignore our Orange County focus. We get far too many generalized manuscripts."

‡PALM SPRINGS LIFE, The Town & Club Magazine, Desert Publications, Inc., 303 N. Indian Canyon, Palm Springs CA 92262. (619)325-2333. Fax: (619)325-7008. Editor: Stewart Weiner. Contact: Sarah Hagerty, senior editor. Estab. 1958. 100% freelance written. Monthly magazine covering "affluent resort/southern California/Palm Springs desert resorts. *Palm Springs Life* is a luxurious magazine aimed at the 'affluence' market." Circ. 16,000. Pays on publication. Publishes ms an average of 3 months after acceptance. Byline given. Offers 25% kill fee. Buys all rights (negotiable). Submit seasonal material 6 months in advance. Reports in 3 weeks on queries. Sample copy for $3.95.
Nonfiction: Book excerpts, essays, interview/profile. Query with published clips. Length: 500-2,500 words. Pays $50-750 for assigned articles; $25-500 for unsolicited articles. Sometimes pays the expenses of writers on assignment.
● Increased focus on desert region and business writing opportunities.
Photos: State availability of photos with submissions. Reviews contact sheets. Offers $5-125/photo. Captions, model releases, identification of subjects required. Buys all rights.
Columns/Departments: Around Town (local news), 50-250 words. Buys 12 mss/year. Query with or without published clips. Pays $5-200.

PALO ALTO WEEKLY, Embarcadero Publishing Co., 703 High St., P.O. Box 1610, Palo Alto CA 94302. (415)326-8210. Fax: (415)326-3928. Website: http://www.paweekly.com/paw/home.html. Editor: Paul Gullixson. 5% freelance written. Semiweekly tabloid focusing on local issues and local sources. Estab. 1979. Circ. 48,000. Pays on publication. Publishes ms an average of 1 month after acceptance. Byline given. Offers 50% kill fee. Buys first rights. Submit seasonal/holiday material 2 months in advance. Reports in 2 weeks. Sample copy for 9×12 SAE with 2 first-class stamps.
● *Palo Alto Weekly* covers sports and has expanded its arts and entertainment coverage. It is still looking for stories in Palo Alto/Stanford area or features on people from the area.
Nonfiction: General interest, historical/nostalgic, interview/profile, photo feature. Special issues: Together (weddings—mid February); Interiors (May, October). Nothing that is not local; no travel. Buys 25 mss/year. Query with published clips. Length: 700-1,000 words. Pays $35-60.
Reprints: Accepts previously published submissions. Payment is negotiable.
Photos: Send photos with submission. Reviews contact sheets and 5×7 prints. Offers $10 minimum/photo. Captions, model releases and identification of subjects required. Buys one-time rights.
Tips: "Writers have the best chance if they live within circulation area and know publication and area well. DON'T send generic, broad-based pieces. The most open sections are food, interiors and sports. Longer 'cover story' submissions may be accepted, but very rare. Keep it LOCAL."

SAN FRANCISCO BAY GUARDIAN, 520 Hampshire St., San Francisco CA 94110-1417. (415)255-3100. Fax: (415)255-8762. Website: http://www.sfbayguardian.com. Editor/Publisher: Bruce Brugmann. 40% freelance written. Works with a small number of new/unpublished writers each year. Weekly news magazine specializing in investigative, consumer and lifestyle reporting for a sophisticated, urban audience. Estab. 1966. Circ. 140,000. Pays 2 weeks after publication. Publishes ms an average of 1 month after acceptance. Byline given. Buys 200 mss/year. Buys first rights. No simultaneous or multiple submissions. Query for electronic submissions. Reports in 2 months.

Nonfiction: Ron Curren, news editor; Tommy Tompkins, arts editor; Miriam Wolf, features editor. Publishes "incisive local news stories, investigative reports, features, analysis and interpretation, how-to, consumer and entertainment reviews. Most stories have a Bay Area angle." Freelance material should have a "public interest advocacy journalism approach." Sometimes pays the expenses of writers on assignment.

Photos: Ondine Kilker, art director. Purchased with or without mss.

Tips: "Work with our volunteer and intern projects in investigative, political and consumer reporting. We teach the techniques and send interns out to do investigative research. We like to talk to writers in our office before they begin doing a story."

SAN FRANCISCO FOCUS, The City Magazine for the San Francisco Bay Area, 2601 Mariposa St., San Francisco CA 94110-1400. (415)553-2800. Fax: (415)553-2470. Editor: Amy Rennert. Managing Editor: Rick Clogher. 80% freelance written. Prefers to work with published/established writers. Monthly city/regional magazine. Estab. 1968. Circ. 180,000. Pays on publication. Publishes ms an average of 2 months after acceptance. Byline given. Offers 25% kill fee. Submit seasonal material 5 months in advance. Reports in 2 months. Sample copy for $2.50. Free writer's guidelines with SASE.

Nonfiction: Exposé, interview/profile, the arts, politics, public issues, sports, consumer affairs and travel. All stories should relate in some way to the San Francisco Bay Area (travel excepted). Query with published clips. Length: 750-4,000 words. Pays $75-2,000 plus some expenses.

VENTURA COUNTY & COAST REPORTER, VCR Inc., 1567 Spinnaker Dr., Suite 202, Ventura CA 93001. (805)658-2244. Fax: (805)658-7803. Editor: Nancy Cloutier. 12% freelance written. Works with a small number of new/unpublished writers each year. Weekly tabloid covering local news. Circ. 35,000. Pays on publication. Publishes ms an average of 2 weeks after acceptance. Byline given. Buys first North American serial rights. Reports in 3 weeks.

Nonfiction: General interest (local slant), humor, interview/profile, travel (local—within 500 miles). Local (Ventura County) slant predominates. Length: 2-5 double-spaced typewritten pages. Pays $10-25.

Photos: Send photos with ms. Reviews b&w contact sheet.

Columns/Departments: Entertainment, Sports, Dining News, Real Estate, Boating Experience (Southern California). Send complete ms. Pays $10-25.

Tips: "As long as topics are up-beat with local slant, we'll consider them."

Colorado

ASPEN MAGAZINE, Ridge Publications, P.O. Box G-3, Aspen CO 81612. (303)920-4040. Fax: (303)920-4044. Editor: Janet C. O'Grady. Senior Editor: Jeff Gremillion. 85% freelance written. "We rarely accept submissions by new freelance writers." Bimonthly magazine covering Aspen and the Roaring Fork Valley. Estab. 1974. Circ. 16,000. Pays within 30 days of publication. Byline given. Kill fee varies. Buys first North American serial rights. Reports in 6 months. Sample copy for 9×12 SAE with 10 first-class stamps. Writer's guidelines for #10 SASE.

Nonfiction: Essay, historical, interview/profile, photo feature, enrivonmental and local issues, architecture and design, sports and outdoors, arts. "We do not publish general interest articles without a strong Aspen hook. We do not publish 'theme' (skiing in Aspen) or anniversary (40th year of Aspen Music Festival)." Buys 30-60 mss/year. Query with published clips. Length: 50-4,000 words. Pays $50-1,000.

Photos: Send photos with submission. Reviews contact sheets, negatives, transparencies, prints. Model release and identification of subjects required.

Columns/Departments: Town and mountain news, sports, business, travel, health, beauty, fitness, art news. "We rarely accept freelance travel stories. Virtually all travel is written inhouse." Query with published clips. Length: 200-1,500. Pays $50-150.

FLATIRONS MAGAZINE, Mac Media LLC, 5775 Flatiron Pkwy., Suite 205, Boulder CO 80301-5730. (303)449-1847. Fax: (303)440-5421. E-mail: flatirons@mtnmags.com. Website: http://www.boulderdenverweb.com. Contact: Leland Rucker, managing editor. 80% freelance written. Quarterly magazine covering Colorado's Front Range region, including Boulder, Denver, Ft. Collins and Colorado Springs, showcasing the people, events, lifestyles, interests and history." Our readers are generally well-educated, well-traveled, active people in the area or visiting the region from all 50 states and many foreign countries. Writing should be fresh, entertaining and informative." Estab. 1993. Circ. 15,000. Pays on publication. Publishes ms an average of 6 months after acceptance. Byline given. Offers 100% kill fee. Buys one-time rights. Editorial lead time 1 year. Submit seasonal material 1 year in advance. Accepts simultaneous submissions. Reports in 1 month on queries; 2 months on mss. Sample copy for $5.95 and SASE. Writer's guidelines free on request.

Nonfiction: Essays, general interest, historical/nostalgic, humor, interview/profile, personal experience, photo feature. "No poetry." Buys 15-20 mss/year. Query with published clips. Length: 500-3,000 words. Pays $100-500 for assigned articles; $50-300 for unsolicited articles. Sometimes pays expenses of writers on assignment.

Reprints: Send photocopy of article with information about when and where the article previously appeared.

Photos: State availability of photos with submission. Reviews transparencies. Offers $50-250/photo. Captions, model releases and identification of subjects required. Buys one-time rights.

Tips: "(1) It is essential for writers to study current and past issues of our magazine to become familiar with type and balance of subject matter and angles. (2) It is also helpful for writers to have visited our region to capture the unique 'sense of place' aspects we try to share with readers. (3) We try to make subjects and treatments 'timeless' in nature because the magazine is a 'keeper' with a multi-year shelf life. Western lifestyles and regional history are very popular topics for our readers. So are nature (including environmental subjects), sports and recreation. Please query first with ideas to make sure subjects are fresh and appropriate."

STEAMBOAT MAGAZINE, Mac Media LLC, 2955 Village Dr., P.O. Box 4328, Steamboat Springs CO 80477. (303)879-5250 ext. 12. Fax: (970)879-4650. E-mail: rollywahl@m&nmags.com. Website: http://www.steamboatweb.com. Editor: Rolly Wahl. 80% freelance written. Semiannual magazine covering Steamboat Springs and Northwest Colorado region. "Steamboat Magazine showcases the history, people, lifestyles and interests of Northwest Colorado. Our readers are generally well-educated, well-traveled, active people visiting our region to ski in winter and recreate in summer. They come from all 50 states and many foreign countries. Writing should be fresh, entertaining and informative." Estab. 1978. Circ. 20,000. Pays on publication. Publishes ms an average of 6 months after acceptance. Byline given. Offers 100% kill fee. Buys one-time and electronic reprint rights. Editorial lead time 1 year. Submit seasonal material 1 year in advance. Accepts simultaneous submissions. Reports in 1 month on queries; 2 months on mss. Sample copy for $5.95 and SAE with 10 first-class stamps. Writer's guidelines free on request.

Nonfiction: Essays, general interest, historical/nostalgic, humor, interview/profile, personal experience, photo feature. Buys 10-15 mss/year. Query with published clips. Length: 500-3,000 words. Pays $100-500 for assigned articles; $50-300 for unsolicited articles. Sometimes pays expenses of writers on assignment.

Reprints: Send tearsheet or photocopy of article. Pays 50% of the amount paid for an original article.

Photos: State availability of photos with submission. Reviews transparencies. Offers $50-250/photo. Captions, model releases, identification of subjects required. Buys one-time rights.

Tips: "Western lifestyles and regional history are very popular topics for our readers. So is nature (including environmental subjects) and sports and recreation. Please query first with ideas to make sure subjects are fresh and appropriate. We try to make subjects and treatments "timeless" in nature, because our magazine is a "keeper" with a multi-year shelf life."

VAIL/BEAVER CREEK MAGAZINE, Flatirons/Vail L.L.C., P.O. Box 4328, Steamboat Springs CO 80477. (970)476-6600. Editor: Don Berger. 80% freelance written. Semiannual magazine covering Vail, Central Rocky Mountains, and mountain living. "*Vail/Beaver Creek Magazine* showcases the lifestyles and history of the Vail Valley. We are particularly interested in personality profiles, home and design features, the arts, winter and summer recreation and adventure stories, and environmental articles." Estab. 1975. Circ. 30,000. Pays on publication. Publishes ms an average of 6 months after acceptance. Byline given. Offers 100% kill fee. Buys one-time rights. Editorial lead time 1 year. Submit seasonal material 1 year in advance. Accepts simultaneous submissions. Reports in 1 month on queries; 2 months on mss. Sample copy for $5.95 and SAE with 10 first-class stamps. Writer's guidelines free on request.

Nonfiction: Essays, general interest, historical/nostalgic, humor, interview/profile, personal experience, photo feature. Buys 20-25 mss/year. Query with published clips. Length: 500-3,000 words. Pays $100-500 for assigned articles; $50-300 for unsolicited articles. Sometimes pays expenses of writers on assignment.

Photos: State availability of photos with submission. Reviews transparencies. Offers $50-250/photo. Captions, model releases and identification of subjects required. Buys one-time rights.

Tips: "Be familiar with the Vail Valley and its 'personality.' Approach a story that will be relevant for several years to come. We produce a magazine that is a 'keeper.' "

Connecticut

NORTHEAST MAGAZINE, *The Hartford Courant*, 285 Broad St., Hartford CT 06115-2510. (203)241-3700. Website: http://www.courant.com. Contact: Donna Winzler, editorial assistant. Editor: Lary Bloom. 10% freelance written. Eager to work with new/unpublished writers. Weekly magazine for a Connecticut audience. Estab. 1982. Circ. 320,000. **Pays on acceptance.** Publishes ms an average of 5 months after acceptance. Byline given. Buys one-time rights. Reports in 3 months.

Nonfiction: General interest (has to have strong Connecticut tie-in); in-depth investigation of stories behind news (has to have strong Connecticut tie-in); historical/nostalgic; interview/profile (of famous or important people with Connecticut ties); personal essays (humorous or anecdotal). No poetry. Buys 50 mss/year. Length: 750-2,500 words. Pays $200-1,500.

Photos: Most assigned; state availability of photos. "Do not send originals."

Fiction: Well-written, original short stories and (rarely) novel excerpts. Length: 750-1,500 words.

● Ranked as one of the best markets for fiction writers in *Writer's Digest*'s annual "Fiction 50," June 1996.

Tips: "Less space available for all types of writing means our standards for acceptance will be much higher. We can only print three to four short stories a year."

District of Columbia

‡**WASHINGTON CITY PAPER**, 2390 Champlain St., Washington DC. (202)232-2100. Fax: (202)462-8323. E-mail: dcarr@washcp.com. Editor: David Carr. 50% freelance written. Weekly tabloid covering Washington DC news, arts. "Relentlessly local alternative weekly in nation's capitol. City politics, media and arts. No national stories." Estab. 1981. Circ. 90,000. Pays on publication. Publishes ms an average of 1 month after acceptance. Byline given. Offers 10% kill fee. Buys all rights. Editorial lead time 1 week. Accepts simultaneous submissions. Reports in 1 month. Writer's guidelines for #10 SASE.

Nonfiction: Exposé, general interest. No national politics. Buys 100 mss/year. Length: 1,000-10,000 words. Pays 10-20¢/word. Sometimes pays expenses of writers on assignment.

Columns/Departments: Glenn Dixon. Music Writing (eclectic), 1,200 words. Buys 30 mss/year. Query with published clips. Pays 10-20¢/word.

Tips: "Send local stories that describe the city in new ways. A great idea is the best leverage. We will work with anyone who has a strong idea, regardless of vita."

THE WASHINGTON POST, 1150 15th St. NW, Washington DC 20071. (202)334-7750. Travel Editor: Linda L. Halsey. 60% freelance written. Prefers to work with published/established writers. Weekly newspaper travel section (Sunday). Pays on publication. Publishes ms an average of 6 months after acceptance. Byline given. "We are now emphasizing staff-written articles as well as quality writing from other sources. Stories are rarely assigned; all material comes in on speculation; there is no fixed kill fee." Buys only first North American serial rights. Travel must not be subsidized in any way. Usually reports in 1 month.

Nonfiction: Emphasis is on travel writing with a strong sense of place, color, anecdote and history. Query with published clips. Length: 1,500-2,500 words, plus sidebar for practical information.

Photos: State availability of photos with ms.

Florida

BOCA RATON MAGAZINE, JES Publishing, 6413 Congress Ave., Suite 100, Boca Raton FL 33487. (407)997-8683. Fax: (407)997-8909. E-mail: bocamag@aol.com. Editor: Marie Speed. 70% freelance written. Bimonthly magazine covering Boca Raton lifestyles. "Ours is a lifestyle magazine devoted to the residents of South Florida, featuring fashion, interior design, food, people, places and issues that shape the affluent South Florida market." Estab. 1981. Circ. 20,000. **Pays on acceptance.** Publishes ms an average of 3 months after acceptance. Byline given. Offers $50 kill fee. Buys second serial (reprint) rights. Submit seasonal material 7 months in advance. Accepts simultaneous submissions. Reports in 1 month. Sample copy for $3.95 for 10×13 SAE with 10 first-class stamps. Writer's guidelines for #10 SASE.

Nonfiction: General interest, historical/nostalgic, humor, interview/profile, photo feature, travel. Special issues: Interior Design (September-October); Bridal (January-February); Health (March-April). Query with or without published clips, or send complete ms. Length: 800-2,500 words. Pays $50-600 for assigned articles; $50-300 for unsolicited articles.

Reprints: Send tearsheet of article. Pays 50% of amount paid for an original article.

Photos: Send photos with submission.

Columns/Departments: Body & Soul (health, fitness and beauty column, general interest), 1,000 words; Hitting Home (family and social interactions), 1,000 words. Buys 6 mss/year. Query with published clips or send complete ms. Length: 600-1,500 words. Pays $50-250.

Tips: "We prefer shorter manuscripts, highly localized articles, excellent art/photography."

FLORIDA KEYS MAGAZINE, Gibbons Publishing, Inc., P.O. Box 6524, Key West FL 33041-6524. (800)273-1026. Fax: (305)296-7414. Contact: Vanessa Richards, editorial assistant. Editor: Gibbons D. Cline. 75% freelance written. Bimonthly magazine for lifestyle in the Florida Keys. "*FKM* caters to full-time residents of the Florida Keys. These are people with a unique lifestyle and a rich, colorful history." Estab. 1978. Circ. 10,000. Pays on publication. Publishes ms an average of 4-6 months after acceptance. Byline given. Buys first North American serial, first or all rights. Editorial lead time 4-6 months. Submit seasonal material at least 6 months in advance. Reports in 1 month on queries; 2 months on mss. Sample copy for $2.50. Writer's guidelines free on request.

Nonfiction: General interest, historical/nostalgic, how-to (water sports, home improvement, gardening, crafts), humor, interview/profile (Keys residents *only*), travel. Special issues: Gourmet (January); Home & Garden (March); Weddings and Travel (May); Fantasy Fest-Key West (September); The Holidays (November). "No erotica or personal experiences in the Keys . . . please do not send Hemingway-related stories or stories regarding your Keys vacation!" Buys 20-30 mss/year. Query with published clips. Length: 500-2,000 words. Pays $2/column inch, $100 maximum per story.

Photos: Send photos with submissions. Reviews transparencies (any size), prints, slides. Offers no additional payment for photos accepted with ms. Model releases and identification of subjects required. Buys all rights.

Columns/Departments: Dining Guide (Keys recipes, restaurant reviews), 1,200 words; Keys Travel (short getaways); FKM Highlights (profiles of interesting residents); Conch Republic Update (current goings-on of this tiny island nation); Keys Currents (tidbits of interesting information); Nature of the Keys (environmental issues); Fact or Fishin'? (fishing tales, tips, tournaments and recipes); History of the Keys.

Tips: "It is difficult to write about Keys unless writer is resident of Monroe County, Florida, or frequent visitor. Must be familiar with unique atmosphere and lifestyle of Florida Keys. Request résumé to be submitted with query and/or manuscript. If author is unfamiliar with Keys, massive research is suggested (strongly). We are most open to new and unusual angles on fishing, boating, diving, snorkeling, sailing, shelling, sunbathing and Keys special events."

FLORIDA LIVING MAGAZINE, North Florida Publishing Co. Inc., 102 NE Tenth Ave., Suite 6, Gainesville FL 32601-2322. Fax: (904)372-3453. E-mail: magflliv@aol.com. Editor: E. Douglas Cifers. Monthly lifestyle magazine covering Florida travel, food and dining, heritage, homes and gardens and all aspects of Florida lifestyle. Full calendar of events each month. Estab. 1981. Circ. 125,000. Publishes ms an average of 6 months after acceptance. Byline given. No kill fee. Buys first rights only. Submit seasonal/holiday material 1 year in advance. Reports in 2 months. Writer's guidelines sent on request with SASE.

Nonfiction: General Florida interest, historical/nostalgic, interview/profile, personal experience, travel, out-of-the-way Florida places. Buys 50-60 mss/year. Query. Length: 500-1,500 words. Pays $25-200 for assigned articles; $25-100 for unsolicited articles.

Photos: Send photos with submission. Reviews 3 × 5 color prints. Offers up to $10/photo. Captions required. Buys first rights only.

Fiction: Historical. Buys 2-3 mss/year. Send complete ms. Length: 1,000-3,000 words. Publishes novel excerpts. Pays $50-200.

GULFSHORE LIFE, 2975 S. Horseshoe Dr., Suite 100, Naples FL 33942. (941)643-3933. Fax: (941)643-5017. Editor: Amy Bennett. 75% freelance written. Lifestyle magazine published 11 times/year for southwest Florida. Estab. 1970. Circ. 26,000. Pays on publication. Publishes ms an average of 4 months after acceptance. Byline given. Offers 25-33% kill fee. Buys first North American serial rights. Submit seasonal/holiday material 8 months in advance. Accepts simultaneous submissions. Sample copy for 9 × 12 SAE with 10 first-class stamps.

Nonfiction: Historical/nostalgic (SW Florida), interview/profile (SW Florida), issue/trend (SW Florida). All articles must be related to SW Florida. Buys 100 mss/year. Query with published clips. Length: 500-3,000 words. Pays $100-1,000 for assigned articles.

Reprints: Send photocopy of article or tearsheet and information about when and where the article previously appeared. Fee negotiated.

Photos: Send photos with submission, if available. Reviews 35mm transparencies and 5 × 7 prints. Pays $25-50. Model releases and identification of subjects required. Buys one-time rights.

Tips: "We buy superbly written stories that illuminate southwest Florida personalities, places and issues. Surprise us!"

‡ISLAND LIFE, The Enchanting Barrier Islands of Florida's Southwest Gulf Coast, Island Life Publications, P.O. Box 929, Sanibel FL 33957. Contact: Van B. Hooper, publisher. Editor: Joan Hooper. Editorial Associate: Susan Shores. 40% freelance written. Prefers to work with published/established writers, but works with a small number of new/unpublished writers each year. Quarterly magazine of the Barrier Islands Sanibel, Captiva, Marco, for upper-income residents and vacationers of Florida's Gulf Coast area. Estab. 1980. Circ. 20,000. Pays on publication. Publishes ms an average of 1 year after acceptance. Byline given. Buys first serial and second serial (reprint) rights. Accepts simultaneous submissions. Reports in 1 month on queries; 3 months on mss.

Nonfiction: General interest, historical. "Travel and interview/profile done by staff. Our past use of freelance work has been heavily on Florida wildlife (plant and animal) and sports, Florida cuisine, and Florida parks and conservancies. We are a regional magazine. No fiction or first-person experiences. No poetry. Our editorial emphasis is on the history, culture, wildlife, art, scenic, sports, social and leisure activities of the area." Buys 10-20 mss/year. Query with ms, photos and SASE. Length: 500-1,500 words. Pays 3-8¢/word.

Reprints: Send information about when and where the article previously appeared.

Photos: Send photos (color only) with ms. No additional payment. Captions, model releases, identification of subjects required.

Tips: "Submissions are rejected, most often, when writer sends other than SW Florida focus."

JACKSONVILLE, White Publishing Co., 1032 Hendricks Ave., Jacksonville FL 32207. (904)396-8666. Editor-in-Chief: Larry Marscheck. 80% freelance written. Consumer magazine published 10 times/year covering life and business in northeast Florida. "City/regional magazine for Jacksonville and the Beaches, Orange Park, St. Augustine and Amelia Island, Florida." Targets upwardly mobile residents. Estab. 1985. Circ. 25,000. Pays on publication. Byline given. Offers 25-33% kill fee to writers on assignment. Buys first North American serial rights or second serial (reprint) rights. Editorial lead time 3 months. Submit seasonal 4 months in advance. Reports in 6 weeks on queries; 1 month on mss. Sample copy for $5 (includes postage). Writer's guidelines free on request.

Nonfiction: Book excerpts, exposé, general interest, historical, how-to (service articles), humor, interview/ profile, personal experience, commentary, photo feature, travel, local business successes, trends, personalities, community issues, how institutions work. All articles *must* have relevance to Jacksonville and Florida's First Coast (Duval, Clay, St. Johns, Nassau, Baker counties). Buys 50 mss/year. Query with published clips. Length: 1,200-3,000 words. Pays $50-500 for feature-length pieces. Sometimes pays expenses of writers on assignment.

Photos: State availability of photos with submission. Reviews contact sheets, transparencies. Negotiates payment individually. Captions, model releases required. Buys one-time rights.

Columns/Departments: Business (trends, success stories, personalities), 1,000-1,200 words; Health (trends, emphasis on people, hopeful outlooks), 1,000-1,200 words; Smart Money (practical personal financial/advice using local people, anecdotes and examples), 1,000-1,200 words; Real Estate/Home (service, trends, home photo features), 1,000-1,200 words; Technology (local people and trends concerning electronics and computers), 1,000-1,200 words; Travel (weekends; daytrips; excursions locally, regionally and internationally), 1,000-1,200 words; occasional departments and columns covering local history, sports, family issues, etc; Last Word (commentary on local topic or issue), 600-750 words. Buys 40 mss/year. Pays $150-250.

Fiction: Any submission *must* have Jacksonville or northeast Florida setting and/or characters. Buys 1 or more mss/year. Send complete ms. Length: 1,000-2,500 words. Pays $150-500. "It should be noted that we have bought only a few fiction pieces since publication began. We are open to buying more, if they are well-written and relevant to our area."

Tips: "We are a writer's magazine, therefore we demand writing that tells a story with flair. While the whole magazine is open to freelancers, new writers can break in via 'The Insider'—50-300 word stories about trends, phenomena, products, services, offbeat lists, trivia, events, significant historical anniversaries, gossip and people in the First Coast area."

ORLANDO MAGAZINE, Abarto Metro Publishing, 260 Maitland Ave., Suite 2000, P.O. Box 2207, Altamonte Springs FL 32701. (407)767-8338. Fax: (407)767-8348. E-mail: orlandomag@aol.com. Editor: Brooke Lange. 90% freelance written. Monthly magazine covering the greater Orlando area and its people; features include profiles, business, food, interiors, travel. Estab. 1946. Circ. 33,000. Pays on publication. Publishes ms an average of 4 months after acceptance. Byline given. Offers kill fee. Submit seasonal/holiday material 8 months in advance. Accepts simultaneous submissions. Reports in 2 months. Sample copy for $5. Writer's guidelines for #10 SASE..

Nonfiction: Buys 24-30 mss/year. Send complete ms. Length: 1,500-2,500 words. Pays $100-450 for articles. "Looking for insightful and entertaining articles that create a sense of community pride by informing readers about people, issues and businesses that impact their lives. Publishes 6-10 issue-oriented stories per year."

Photos: Send photos with submission. Reviews transparencies. Offers $5/photo. Captions and identification of subjects required. Buys one-time rights.

Columns/Departments: Food, Interiors, City Life, In the Neighborhood. All submissions should have local slant. Length: 1,200 words. Buys 12 mss/year. Pays $200-300.

PENSACOLA MAGAZINE, PEC Printing and Publishing, 2101 W. Government St., Pensacola FL 32501. (904)438-5421. Fax: (904)434-2785. Editor: Donna Peoples. 100% freelance written. Magazine published 11 times/year for news about city of Pensacola. Estab. 1983. Pays on publication. Publishes ms an average of 2 months after acceptance. Byline given. Buys one-time or second serial (reprint) rights or makes work-for-hire assignments. Editorial lead time 2 months. Submit seasonal material 4 months in advance. Accepts simultaneous submissions. Reports in 3 weeks on queries; 1 month on mss. *Writer's Market* recommends allowing 2 months for reply. Sample copy for $3.

Nonfiction: General interest, historical/nostalgic, how-to, humor, interview/profile (of Pensacola residents), photo feature, travel. Rarely runs stories that don't relate to Pensacola other than travel articles. Buys 80 mss/year. Query with published clips. Length: 800-1,500 words. Pays 7¢/word.

Reprints: Send photocopy of article and information about when and where the article previously appeared. Pays 100% of amount paid for an original article.

Photos: Send photos with submission. Reviews contact sheets, transparencies and prints. Offers $35/photo minimum. Negotiates payment individually. Captions, model releases and identification of subjects required. Buys one-time rights.

SENIOR VOICE OF FLORIDA, Florida's Leading Newspaper for Active Mature Adults, Suncoast Publishing Group, 18860 US Hwy. 19N, Suite 151, Clearwater FL 34624-3106. Publisher: Donna Castellanos. Contact: Nancy Yost, editor. 25% freelance written. Prefers to work with published/established writers. Monthly newspaper for mature adults 50 years of age and over. Estab. 1981. Circ. 70,000. Pays on publication. Publishes ms an average of 3 months after acceptance. Byline given. Buys one-time rights. Submit seasonal material 6 months in advance. Accepts simultaneous submissions. Reports in 2 months. Sample copy for $1 and 10×13 SAE with 6 first-class stamps.

Nonfiction: General interest, historical, how-to, humor, inspirational, interview/profile, opinion, photo feature, travel, health, finance, all slanted to a senior audience. Buys 10 mss/year. Query or send complete ms. Length: 300-600 words. Pays $5-15.

Reprints: Send typed ms with rights for sale noted. Pays flat fee.

Photos: Send photos with submission. Reviews 3×5 color and 5×7 b&w prints. Identification of subjects required.

Columns/Departments: Travel (senior slant) and V.I.P. Profiles (mature adults). Buys 3 mss/year. Send complete ms. Length: 300-600 words. Pays $5-15.

Fillers: Anecdotes, facts, cartoons, short humor. Buys 3/year. Length: 150-250 words. Pays $5.

Tips: "Our service area is the Florida Gulf Coast, an area with a high population of resident retirees and repeat visitors who are 50 plus. We are interested primarily in serving their needs. In writing for that readership, keep their interests in mind. What they are interested in, we are interested in. We like a clean, concise writing style. Photos are important."

SUNSHINE: THE MAGAZINE OF SOUTH FLORIDA, The Sun-Sentinel Co., 200 E. Las Olas Blvd., Fort Lauderdale FL 33301-2293. (305)356-4685. 60% freelance written. Prefers to work with published/established writers, but works with a small number of new/unpublished writers each year. General interest Sunday magazine for the *Sun-Sentinel*'s 800,000 readers in south Florida. Circ. 360,000. Pays within 1 month of acceptance. Publishes ms an average of 2 months after acceptance. Byline given. Offers 25% kill fee for assigned material. Buys first serial rights or one-time rights in the state of Florida. Submit seasonal/holiday material 2 months in advance. Accepts simultaneous submissions. Reports in 1 month on queries; 2 months on mss. Free sample copy and writer's guidelines.

Nonfiction: General interest, interview/profile, travel. "Articles must be relevant to the interests of adults living in south Florida." Buys about 150 mss/year. Query with published clips. Length: 1,000-3,000 words; preferred length 2,000-2,500 words. Pays 25-30¢/word to $1,000 maximum.

Reprints: Send tearsheet or photocopy of article or typed ms with rights for sale noted and information about when and where the article previously appeared.

Photos: Send photos. Pays negotiable rate for 35mm and 2¼×2¼ color slides. Captions and identification of subjects required; model releases required for sensitive material. Buys one-time rights for the state of Florida.

Tips: "Do not phone, but do include your phone number on query letter. Keep your writing tight and concise—south Florida readers don't have the time to wade through masses of prose. We are always in the market for first-rate profiles, human-interest stories, travel stories and contributions to our regular 1,000-word features, 'First Person' and 'Weekenders.' "

TROPIC MAGAZINE, Sunday Magazine of the Miami Herald, Knight Ridder, 1 Herald Plaza, Miami FL 33132-1693. (305)376-3432. Editor: Bill Rose. Executive Editor: Tom Shroder. 20% freelance written. Works with small number of new/unpublished writers each year. Weekly magazine covering general interest, locally oriented topics for local readers. Circ. 500,000. Pays on publication. Publishes ms an average of 2 months after acceptance. Byline given. Buys first serial rights. Submit seasonal material 2 months in advance. Reports in 3 months. Sample copy for 11×14 SAE.

Nonfiction: General interest, interview/profile (first person), personal experience. No fiction or poetry. Buys 20 mss/year. Query with published clips or send complete ms with SASE. Length: 1,500-3,000 words. Pays $200-1,000/article.

Reprints: Send photocopy of article and information about when and where the article previously appeared. Pays 50% of the amount paid for an original article.

Photos: Janet Santelices, art director. Send photos.

‡**WATERFRONT NEWS**, Ziegler Publishing Co., Inc., 1523 S. Andrews Ave., Ft. Lauderdale FL 33316-2507. (305)524-9450. Fax: (305)524-9464. Editor: Jennifer Heit. 40% freelance written. Monthly tabloid covering marine and boating topics for the Greater Ft. Lauderdale waterfront community. Estab. 1984. Circ. 36,000. Pays on publication. Publishes ms an average of 2 months after acceptance. Byline given. Buys first

serial, second serial (reprint) rights or simultaneous rights in certain circumstances. Submit seasonal material 3 months in advance. Reports in 1 month on queries. Sample copy for 9×12 SAE with 4 first-class stamps.
Nonfiction: Regional articles on south Florida's waterfront issues; marine communities; personality profiles on people important in boating, i.e., racers, boat builders, designers, etc. (does not have to be from south Florida); trends in boating and the waterfront lifestyle; some how-to (how-to find a good marina, boat mechanic, how to teach kids about sailing, etc.); humor with an eye toward boating topics. Buys 50 mss/year. Query with published clips. Length: 500-1,000 words. Pays $50-125 for assigned articles; $25-125 for unsolicited articles. Sometimes pays the expenses of established writers on assignment.
Photos: Send photos or send photos with submission. Reviews contact sheets and 3×5 or larger prints. Offers $15/photo. Buys one-time rights.
Columns/Departments: Query with published clips. Length 500 words. Pays $25-100.
Fillers: Anecdotes, facts, nautical one-liners to be illustrated by cartoonist, newsbriefs, short humor. Buys 12/year. Length 100-500 words. Pays $10-200.
Tips: "Nonfiction marine, nautical or south Florida stories only. No fiction or poetry. Keep it under 1,000 words. Photos or illustrations help. Send for a sample copy of *Waterfront News* so you can acquaint yourself with our publication and our unique audience. Although we're not necessarily looking for technical articles, it helps if the writer has sailing or powerboating experience."

Georgia

GEORGIA JOURNAL, The Indispensable Atlanta Co., Inc., P.O. Box 1604, Decatur GA 30031-1604. (404)377-4275. Fax: (404)377-1820. E-mail: 74467.1243@compuserve.com. Editor: David R. Osier. 90% freelance written. Works with a small number of new/unpublished writers each year. Bimonthly magazine covering the state of Georgia. Estab. 1980. Circ. 20,000. Please query first. Pays on publication. Publishes ms an average of 1 year after acceptance. Byline given. Buys first serial rights. Submit seasonal material 6 months in advance. Reports in 6 months. Sample copy for #10 SASE. Writer's guidelines for #10 SASE.
Nonfiction: "*Georgia Journal* primarily is interested in *authoritative* nonfiction articles with a *well-defined point of view* on any aspect of Georgia's human and natural history. Included among these are articles on the roles historic personalities played in shaping our state, important yet sometimes overlooked historical/political events, archaeological discoveries, unsolved mysteries (both natural and human), flora and fauna, and historic preservation. Sidebars are encouraged, such as interesting marginalia and bibliographies. We also are looking for adventures that explore the Georgia landscape. These can range from weekend antique hunting, camping, walking tours, arts & crafts festivals, and auto trips to more strenuous activities such as biking, boating, rafting, back-packing, rock climbing and caving. Adventures should also have a well-defined point of view, and be told through the author's personal experience. Articles should be accompanied by detailed map data and other pertinent location information, such as tips on access, lodging and camping. *Georgia Journal* has a place for authoritative topical articles as well, ranging from those about Georgia's environment, mysteries and trends in Georgia living to profiles of Georgia authors, adventurers, artisans, artists, sports figures and other personalities." Buys 30-40 mss/year. Query. Length: 200-5,000 words. Pays 10¢/word.
Columns/Departments: Books and writers; interesting or historic houses/buildings for sale; Commentary section; Pure Georgia—uses shorter pieces; Calendar of events; reviews of restaurants, B&Bs and historic inns.
Fiction: See submission guidelines. *Georgia Journal* does publish a limited amount of fiction, but while it encourages promising new writers, it is not looking for first-time or unpublished authors. Optimum length is 4,000 words. Stories must have a Georgia theme or Georgia setting. Payment varies, depending on publishing history. Unless mss are submitted with a return envelope with sufficient postage, they will not be returned.
Poetry: Janice Moore. Free verse, haiku, light verse, traditional. Uses poetry from or dealing with Georgia which is suitable for a general audience. Uses 20 poems/year. Submit maximum 4 poems. Length: 25 lines. Pays in copies.

‡**GEORGIA MAGAZINE**, Georgia Electric Membership Corp., P.O. Box 1707, Tucker GA 30085. (770)270-6950. Fax: (770)270-6995. E-mail: ann.elstad@opc.com. Editor: Ann Elstad. 50% freelance written. Monthly magazine covering Georgia people and places. "We are a magazine for Georgians, about Georgians, with a friendly, conversational tone and human interest topics." Estab. 1945. Circ. 280,000. Pays on publication. Publishes ms an average of 4 months after acceptance. Byline given. Offers 50% kill fee. Buys first North American serial rights. Editorial lead time 2 months. Submit seasonal material 6 months in advance. Accepts simultaneous submissions. Reports in 3 weeks on queries; 1 month on mss. Sample copy for $2 each. Writer's guidelines free on request.
Nonfiction: General interest, historical/nostalgic, how-to (in the home and garden), humor, inspirational, interview/profile, photo feature, travel. Buys 8 mss/year. Query with published clips. Length: 500-1,000 words. Pays $200-500 for assigned articles. Pays contributor copies upon negotiation. Sometimes pays expenses of writers on assignment.

Photos: State availability of photos with submission. Reviews contact sheets, transparencies, prints. Negotiates payment individually. Model releases, identification of subjects required. Buy one-time rights.

NORTH GEORGIA JOURNAL, Legacy Communications, Inc., P.O. Box 127, Roswell GA 30077. Editor: Olin Jackson. 70% freelance written. Quarterly magazine covering travel and history, "designed for readers interested in travel, history, and mountain lifestyles of the North Georgia region." Estab. 1987. Circ. 17,000. Pays on publication. Publishes ms an average of 5 months after acceptance. Byline given. Offers 25% kill fee. Buys first and all rights. Editorial lead time 6 months. Submit seasonal material 6 months in advance. Sample copy for 9×12 SAE and 8 first-class stamps. Writer's guidelines for #10 SASE.
Nonfiction: Historical/nostalgic, how-to (survival techniques; mountain living; do-it-yourself home construction and repairs, etc.), interview/profile (celebrity), personal experience (anything unique or unusual pertaining to north Georgia mountains), photo feature (any subject of a historic nature which can be photographed in a seasonal context, i.e.—old mill with brilliant yellow jonquils in foreground), travel (subjects highlighting travel opportunities in North Georgia). Query with published clips. Pays $75-350 for assigned articles.
Photos: Send photos with submission. Reviews contact sheets, transparencies. Negotiates payment individually. Captions, model releases, identification of subjects required. Buys all rights.
Tips: "Good photography is crucial to the acceptance of all articles. Send written queries then *wait* for a response. *No telephone calls please.* The most useful material involves a first person experience of an individual who has explored a historic site or scenic locale and *interviewed* a person or persons who were involved with or have first-hand knowledge of a historic site/event. Interviews and quotations are crucial to acceptance. Articles should be told in the writer's own words."

Hawaii

ALOHA, THE MAGAZINE OF HAWAII AND THE PACIFIC, Davick Publications, P.O. Box 3260, Honolulu HI 96801. (808)593-1191. Fax: (808)593-1327. Editorial Director: Cheryl Tsutsumi. 50% freelance written. Bimonthly regional magazine of international interest. "Most of our readers do not live in Hawaii, although most readers have been to the Islands at least once. The magazine is directed primarily to residents of Hawaii in the belief that presenting material to an immediate critical audience will result in a true and accurate presentation that can be appreciated by everyone. Travelers to Hawaii will find *Aloha* shares vignettes of the real Hawaii. Estab. 1977. Circ. 95,000. Pays on publication. Publishes ms an average of 6 months after acceptance; unsolicited mss can take a year or more. Byline given. Offers variable kill fee. Buys first rights. Submit seasonal material 1 year in advance. Reports in 2 months. Sample copy for $2.95 with SAE and 10 first-class stamps. Free writer's guidelines.
Nonfiction: Book excerpts, historical/nostalgic (historical articles must be researched with bibliography), interview/profile, photo features. Subjects include the arts, business, flora and fauna, people, sports, destinations, food, interiors, history of Hawaii. "We don't want stories of a tourist's experiences in Waikiki or odes to beautiful scenery." Buys 24 mss/year. Query with published clips. Length: 1,000-4,000 words. Pay ranges from $200-500. Sometimes pays expenses of writers on assignment.
Photos: Send photos with query. Pays $25 for b&w prints; prefers negatives and contact sheets. Pays $75 for 35mm (minimum size) color transparencies used inside; $100 for full page; $125 for double-page bleeds; $250 for color transparencies used as cover art. "*ALOHA* features Beautiful Hawaii, a collection of photographs illustrating that theme, in every issue. A second photo essay by a sole photographer on a theme of his/her own choosing is also published occasionally. Queries are essential for the sole photographer essay." Model releases, identification of subjects are required. Buys one-time rights.
Fiction: Ethnic, historical. "Fiction depicting a tourist's adventures in Waikiki is not what we're looking for. As a general statement, we welcome material reflecting the true Hawaiian experience." Buys 2 mss/year. Send complete ms. Length: 1,000-2,500 words. Pays $300.
Poetry: Haiku, light verse, traditional. No seasonal poetry or poetry related to other areas of the world. Buys 6 poems/year. Submit maximum 6 poems. Prefers "shorter poetry"—20 lines or less. Pays $30.
Tips: "Read *Aloha*. Be meticulous in your research and have good illustrative material available to accompany your text."

HAWAII MAGAZINE, Fancy Publications, Inc., 1400 Kapiolani Blvd., A-25, Honolulu HI 96814. (808)942-2556. Fax: (808)947-0924. Editor: Jim Borg. Managing Editor: Julie Applebaum. 60% freelance written. Bimonthly magazine covering The Islands of Hawaii. "*Hawaii Magazine* is written for residents and frequent visitors who enjoy the culture, people and places of the Hawaiian Islands." Estab. 1984. Circ. 71,000. Pays on publication. Byline given. Buys first North American serial rights. Submit seasonal material 6 months in advance. Reports in 1 month on queries; 6 weeks on mss. Sample copy for $3.95. Free writer's guidelines.
Nonfiction: General interest, historical/nostalgic, how-to, interview/profile, personal experience, photo feature, travel. "No articles on the following: first trip to Hawaii—How I discovered the Islands, the Hula, Poi,

or Luaus." Buys 66 mss/year. Query with or without published clips, or send complete ms. Length: 4,000 words maximum. Pays $100-500 for assigned articles.

Photos: Send photos with submission. Reviews contact sheets and transparencies. Offers $35-250/photo. Identification of subjects preferred. Buys one-time rights.

Columns/Departments: Backdoor Hawaii (a light or nostalgic look at culture or history), 800-1,200 words; Hopping the Islands (news, general interest items), 100-200 words. Buys 6-12 mss/year. Query. Length: 800-1,500 words. Pays $100-200. New department, WeatherWatch, focuses on Hawaii weather phenomena (450 words). Pays $50.

Tips: "Freelancers must be knowledgeable about Island subjects, virtual authorities on them. We see far too many first-person, wonderful-experience types of gushing articles. We buy articles only from people who are thoroughly grounded in the subject on which they are writing."

HONOLULU, Honolulu Publishing Co., Ltd., 36 Merchant St., Honolulu HI 96813. (808)524-7400. Fax: (808)531-2306. E-mail: honmag@pixi.com. Publisher: John Alves. Contact: John Heckathorn, editor. Managing Editor: Janice Otaguro. 50% freelance written. Prefers to work with published/established writers. Monthly magazine covering general interest topics relating to Hawaii. Estab. 1888. Circ. 30,000. **Pays on acceptance.** Publishes ms an average of 4 months after acceptance. Byline given. Buys first-time rights. Submit seasonal material 5 months in advance. Accepts simultaneous submissions. Reports in 2 months. Sample copy for $2 and 9×12 SAE with 8 first-class stamps. Free writer's guidelines.

Nonfiction: Exposé, general interest, historical/nostalgic, photo feature—all Hawaii-related. "We write for Hawaii residents, so travel articles about Hawaii are not appropriate." Buys 30 mss/year. Query with published clips if available. Length: 2,000-4,000 words. Pays $100-700. Sometimes pays expenses of writers on assignment.

Photos: Teresa Black, art director. Send photos. Pays $75-175 for single image inside; $500 maximum for cover. Captions and identification of subjects required as well as model release. Buys one-time rights.

Columns/Departments: Calabash ("newsy," timely, humorous department on any Hawaii-related subject). Buys 15 mss/year. Query with published clips or send complete ms. Length: 50-750 words. Pays $35-100. First Person (personal experience or humor). Buys 10 mss/year. Length: 1,500 words. Pays $200-300.

Idaho

‡SUN VALLEY MAGAZINE, Wood River Publishing, Drawer 697, Hailey ID 83333. (208)788-0770. Fax: (208)788-3881. E-mail: 103057.201@compuserve.com. Contact: Colleen Daly, editor. Editor-in-Chief: Celeste Earls. 95% freelance written. Triannual magazine covering lifestyle of Sun Valley area (recreation, history, profiles). Estab. 1973. Circ. 15,000. Pays on publication. Publishes ms an average of 4 months after acceptance. Byline given. Buys all rights. Editorial lead time 4 months. Submit seasonal material 6 months in advance. Accepts simultaneous submissions. Reports in 10 weeks on queries; 3 months on mss. Sample copy for $3.95 and $3 postage.

Nonfiction: General interest, historical/nostalgic, how-to, humor, interview/profile, photo feature, travel. Special issues: Sun Valley Home Design (fall). Query with published clips. Length varies. Pays $40-450 for assigned articles. Sometimes pays expenses of writers on assignment.

Reprints: Occasionally accepts previously published submissions.

Photos: State availability of photos with submission. Reviews transparencies. Offers $60-250/photo. Model releases, identification of subjects required. Buys one-time rights.

Columns/Departments: History, Home Music Reviews, Book Review, Adventure Travel Food, (all must have local slant). Query with published clips. Pays $40-250.

Fiction: No religious, erotic, ethnic, romance. Buys 2 mss/year. Query with published clips. Length: 1,200-2,000 words. Pays $200-300.

Tips: "Most of our writers are locally based. Also, we rarely take submissions that are not specifically assigned, with the exception of fiction. However, we always appreciate queries."

Illinois

CHICAGO LIFE, P.O. Box 11311, Chicago IL 60611-0311. E-mail: chgolife@mcs.com. Publisher: Pam Berns. Editor: Paula Lyon. 95% freelance written. Bimonthly magazine on Chicago life. Estab. 1984. Circ. 60,000. Pays on publication. Byline given. Kill fee varies. Submit seasonal/holiday material 8 months in advance. Accepts simultaneous submissions. Reports in 3 months. Sample copy for 9×12 SAE with 7 first-class stamps.

Nonfiction: Book excerpts, essays, exposé, how-to, photo feature, travel. Buys 50 mss/year. Send complete ms. Length: 400-1,200 words. Pays $30 for unsolicited articles. Sometimes pays the expenses of writers on assignment.

Reprints: Send photocopy of article and information about when and where the article previously appeared. Pays 100% of amount paid for an original article.

Photos: Send photos with submission. Reviews contact sheets, negatives, transparencies, prints. Offers $15-30/photo. Buys one-time rights.

Columns/Departments: Law, Book Reviews, Travel. Send complete ms. Length: 500 words. Pays $30.

Fillers: Facts. Pays $15-30.

Tips: "Please send finished work with visuals (photos, if possible). Topics open include travel, self improvement, how-to-do almost anything, entrepreneurs, how to get rich, beautiful, more well-informed."

CHICAGO MAGAZINE, 500 N. Dearborn, Suite 1200, Chicago IL 60610-4901. Fax: (312)222-0699. Managing Editor: Shane Tritsch. 40% freelance written. Prefers to work with published/established writers. Monthly magazine for an audience which is "95% from Chicago area; 90% college educated; upper income, overriding interests in the arts, politics, dining, good life in the city and suburbs. Most are in 25-50 age bracket, well-read and articulate." Estab. 1968. Circ. 165,000. Buys first serial rights. **Pays on acceptance.** Publishes ms an average of 6 months after acceptance. Submit seasonal material 4 months in advance. Reports in 1 month. For sample copy, send $3 to Circulation Dept. Writer's guidelines for #10 SASE.

Nonfiction: "On themes relating to the quality of life in Chicago: past, present, and future." Writers should have "a general awareness that the readers will be concerned, influential longtime Chicagoans reading what the writer has to say about their city. We generally publish material too comprehensive for daily newspapers." Personal experience and think pieces, profiles, humor, spot news, historical articles, exposés. Buys about 50 mss/year. Query; indicate "specifics, knowledge of city and market, and demonstrable access to sources." Length: 500-6,000 words. Pays $100-$2,500. Pays expenses of writers on assignment.

Photos: Reviews b&w glossy prints, 35mm color transparencies or color prints. Usually assigned separately, not acquired from writers.

Tips: "Submit detailed queries, be business-like and avoid clichéd ideas."

THE CHICAGO TRIBUNE MAGAZINE, Chicago Tribune Newspaper, 435 N. Michigan Ave., Chicago IL 60611. (312)222-3573. Editor: Denis Gosselin. Managing Editor: Douglas Balz. 50% freelance written. Weekly Sunday magazine. "We look for unique, compelling, all-researched, elequently written articles on subjects of general interest." Circ. 1,300,000. Pays on publication. Publishes ms an average of 2 months after acceptance. Offers $250 kill fee. Buys one-time rights. Submit seasonal/holiday material 6 months in advance. Reports in 1 month on queries; 6 weeks on mss.

Nonfiction: Book excerpts, exposé, general interest, interview/profile, photo feature, technical, travel. Buys 35 mss/year. Query or send complete ms. Length: 2,500-5,000 words. Pays $750-1,000. Sometimes pays the expenses of writers on assignment.

Photos: Send photos with submission. Payment varies for photos. Captions and identification of subjects required. Buys one-time rights.

Columns/Departments: First Person (Chicago area subjects only, talking about their occupations), 1,000 words; Chicago Voices (present or former high-profile Chicago area residents with their observations on or reminiscences of the city of Chicago), 1,000 words. Buys 40 mss/year. Query. pays $250. Buys 52 mss/year. Query. Pays $250.

Fiction: Length: 1,500-2,000 words. Pays $750-1,000.

NEAR WEST GAZETTE, Near West Gazette Publishing Co., 1335 W. Harrison St., Suite 301, Chicago IL 60607. (312)243-4288. Editor: Mark J. Valentino. Associate Editor: William S. Bike. 50% freelance written. Work with new/unpublished writers. Monthly neighborhood newspaper covering Near West Side of Chicago and South Loop/Dearborn Park community. News and issues for residents, students and faculty of the neighborhood west of the University of Illinois of Chicago. Estab. 1983. Circ. 10,000. Pays on publication. Publishes ms an average of 1 month after acceptance. Byline given. Not copyrighted. Buys one-time or simultaneous rights. Submit seasonal material 2 months in advance. Reports in 5 weeks. Accepts simultaneous submissions. Sample copy for 11 × 14 SAE with 4 first-class stamps.

Nonfiction: Essays, exposé, general interest, historical/nostalgic, humor, inspirational, interview/profile, opinion, personal experience, religious or sports (must be related to Near West Side/South Loop communities). Publishes a special Christmas issue. Doesn't want to see product promotions. Buys 60 mss/year. Length: 300-1,800 words. Pays $40. Sometimes pays the expenses of writers on assignment.

Reprints: Send photocopy of article and information about when and where the article previously appeared. Pays $40.

Photos: Send photos with submission. Reviews 5×7 prints. Offers no additional payment for photos accepted with ms. Identification of subjects required. Buys one-time rights.

Columns/Departments: To Your Health (health/exercise tips), 600 words; Forum (opinion), 750 words; Streets (Near West Side/South Loop history), 500 words. Buys 12 mss/year. Query. Pays $40.

NEW CITY, Chicago's News and Arts Weekly, New City Communications, Inc., 770 N. Halsted, Suite 208, Chicago IL 60622. (312)243-8786. Fax: (312)243-8802. Website: http://www.suba.com/~newcity. Contact: Frank Sennett, managing editor. Editor: Brian Hieggelke. 30% freelance written. Weekly magazine.

Estab. 1986. Circ. 65,000. Pays 30 days after publication. Publishes ms an average of 1 month after acceptance. Byline given. Offers 20% kill fee in certain cases. Buys first rights and non-exclusive electronic rights. Editorial lead time 2 months. Submit seasonal material 2 months in advance. Reports in 1 month. Sample copy for $3. Writer's guidelines for #10 SASE.

Nonfiction: Book excerpts, essays, exposé, general interest, historical/nostalgic, humor, interview/profile, personal experience. Buys 20 mss/year. Query with published clips. Length: 100-4,000 words. Pays $10-300. Sometimes pays expenses of writers on assignment.

Photos: State availability of photos with submissions. Reviews contact sheets. Captions, model releases, identification of subjects required. Buys one-time rights.

Columns/Departments: Lit (literary supplement), 300-2,000 words; Music, Film, Arts (arts criticism), 150-800 words; Chow (food writing), 300-2,000 words. Buys 50 mss/year. Query with published clips. Pays $10-300.

NORTH SHORE, The Magazine of Chicago's North and Northwest Suburbs, PB Communications, 874 Green Bay Rd., Winnetka IL 60093. (847)441-7892. Publisher: Asher Birnbaum. Senior Editor: Craig Keller. Managing Editor: Jon Birnbaum. 75% freelance written. Monthly magazine. "Our readers are a diverse lot, from middle-class communities to some of the country's wealthiest zip codes. But they all have one thing in common—our proximity to Chicago." Pays on publication. Publishes ms an average of 3 months after acceptance. Byline given. Offers 50% kill fee. Buys first North American serial rights. Submit seasonal material 5 months in advance. Reports in 3 months. Free writer's guidelines for #10 SASE.

Nonfiction: Book excerpts, exposé, general interest, how-to, interview/profile, photo feature, travel. Special issues: Weddings (January, July); Fitness (February); Homes/Gardens (March, June, September, December); Weekend Travel (May); Nursing/Retirement Homes (August); Dining and Nightlife (October). Buys 50 mss/year. Query with published clips. Length: 500-4,000 words. Pays $100-800. Sometimes pays expenses of writers on assignment.

Reprints: Accepts previously published submissions.

Photos: Send photos with submission. Reviews contact sheets, negatives, transparencies, prints. Offers $25-100/photo. Identification of subjects required. Buys one-time rights.

Fiction: Publishes novel excerpts.

Columns/Departments: "Prelude" (shorter items of local interest), 250 words. Buys 12 mss/year. Query with published clips. Pays $50.

Tips: "We're always looking for something of local interest that's fresh and hasn't been reported elsewhere. Look for local angle. Offer us a story that's exclusive in the crowded Chicago-area media marketplace. Well-written feature stories have the best chance of being published. We cover all of Chicago's north and northwest suburbs together with some Chicago material, not just the North Shore."

‡WINDY CITY SPORTS MAGAZINE, Chicago Sports Resources, 1450 W. Randolph, Chicago IL 60607. (312)421-1551. Fax: (312)421-2060. E-mail: wcpublish@aol.com. Editor: Jeff Banowetz. 75% freelance written. Monthly magazine covering amateur, participatory sports. "*Windy City Sports Magazine* is a 70-130 page monthly magazine covering amateur, participatory, endurance sports in the Chicago metropolitan area. We cover running, cycling, in-line skating, outdoor sports; we do not cover professional football, basketball, etc." Estab. 1987. Circ. 100,000. "We pay on publication." Byline given. Offers 25% kill fee. Buys one-time rights. Editorial lead time 2 months. Submit seasonal material at least 2 months in advance. Accepts simultaneous submissions. Reports in 1 month. Sample copy for $2 or SAE (manila) with $2 postage. Writer's guidelines free on request.

Nonfiction: Book excerpts, essays, general interest, historical/nostalgic, how-to, humor, inspirational, interview/profile, new product, opinion, personal experience, technical, travel. "No articles on professional sports." Query with published clips. Length: 700-1,200 words. Pays $75-150. Sometimes pays expenses of writers on assignment.

Reprints: Send photocopy of article or typed ms with rights for sale noted and information about when and where the article previously appeared. Payment varies.

Photos: Freelancers should state availability of photos with submission. Send photos with submission. Reviews b&w photos. Negotiates payment individually. Captions, identification of subject required. Buys one-time rights.

Columns/Departments: Running, women's, nutrition, cycling, road trip, sports medicine, fitness centers. 800-1,000 words for all columns. Buys 70 mss/year. Query with published clips. Send complete ms. Pays $75-125.

Poetry: Anything. "Must be sports-related."

Fillers: Anecdotes, facts, cartoons, short humor. Buys 25/year. Length: 50-250 words. Pays $25-100.

Tips: "It helps to be active in the sport you choose to write about. Being a runner when writing a running article gives extra credentials. The columns/departments are most open to freelancers. I must fill these columns every month, 11 times per year. Also, be aware of the season when pitching ideas."

Indiana

ARTS INDIANA, Arts Indiana, Inc. 47 S. Pennsylvania, Suite 701, Indianapolis IN 46204-3622. (317)632-7894. Contact: Lou Harry, editor-in-chief. 90% freelance written. Monthly (September-June) magazine on artists, writers, performers and arts organizations working in Indiana—literary, visual and performing. Estab. 1978. Circ. 11,000. **Pays on acceptance.** Publishes ms an average of 3 months after acceptance. Byline given. Offers 10% kill fee. Buys first North American serial rights. Submit seasonal material 5 months in advance. Reports in 5 weeks. Sample copy available for $3.50 plus postage

Nonfiction: Indiana-linked essays, historical/nostalgic, interview/profile, opinion, photo feature, interviews. Query with published clips. Length: 1,000-3,000 words. Pays $50-300 for articles. Sometimes pays expenses of writer on assignment.

Photos: Send b&w photos with submission. Reviews 5×7 or larger prints. Sometimes offers additional payment for photos accepted with ms. Captions and identification of subjects required. Buys one-time rights.

Fiction: Publishes novel excerpts (if by an Indiana author).

Tips: "We are looking for interesting, insightful features that go beyond the press release and open doors to the arts for our readers. We also publish short stories, poetry and novel excerpts from *established*, published writers as part of our 'Writer's Block' column. Best to read a copy of the magazine (we redesigned in February of '96 with new departments)."

INDIANAPOLIS MONTHLY, Emmis Publishing Corp., 950 N. Meridian St., Suite 1200, Indianapolis IN 46204. (317)237-9288. Fax: (317)237-9496. E-mail: im-input@iquest.net. Website: http://www.iquest.net/indymonthly. Editor-in-Chief: Deborah Paul. Contact: Sam Stall, editor. 50% freelance written. Prefers to work with published/established writers. Monthly magazine of "upbeat material reflecting current trends. Heavy on lifestyle, homes and fashion. Material must be regional (Indianapolis and/or Indiana) in appeal." Estab. 1977. Circ. 42,000. Pays on publication. Publishes ms an average of 2 months after acceptance. Byline given. Offers 50% kill fee in some cases. Buys first North American serial rights and one-time rights. Submit seasonal material 3 months in advance. Reports in 2 months. Sample copy for $6.10. Writers' guidelines for #10 SASE.

Nonfiction: General interest, interview/profile, photo feature, but only with a strong Indianapolis or Indiana angle. No poetry, fiction or domestic humor; no "How Indy Has Changed Since I Left Town" or "An Outsider's View of the 500" stories. Buys 50 mss/year. Query with published clips or send complete ms. Length: 200-6,000 words. Pays $50-500.

● This magazine is using more first-person essays, but they must have a strong Indianapolis or Indiana tie. It will consider nonfiction book excerpts of material relevant to its readers.

Reprints: Accepts previously published submissions if published in a non-competing market. Send photocopy of article or typed ms with rights for sale noted and information about when and where the article previously appeared. Pays 100% of the amount paid for an original article.

Columns/Departments: Around the Circle; 9 to 5 (profile of person with intriguing job); Sport (star athletes and trendy activities); Health (new technology; local sources); Controversy; Hoosiers at Large; Coping (overcoming adversity). "Again, a local angle is the key." Query with published clips or send complete mss. Pays $150-300.

Tips: "Tell us something we didn't know about Indianapolis. Find a trendy subject with a strong Indianapolis (or Indiana) angle and sell it with a punchy query and a few of your best clips. Don't confuse 'general interest' with 'generic interest'—all material must focus sharply on Indianapolis and/or Indiana. Topics, however, can vary from serious to wacky: Recent issues have included everything from a feature story about Indiana Pacers star Rik Smits to a two-paragraph piece on an Indiana gardening supply house that sells insects by mail. Another good bet is to pitch us an inside piece on a national celeb with Hoosier ties; a recent hot-selling cover story was titled 'Oprah's Indiana home.' Best breaking-in topics for freelancers are Around the Circle (short takes on trendy local topics); Hoosiers at Large (Indiana natives relate first-person experiences); and First Person (self-explanatory, relating to Indiana). Fax and e-mail queries OK; no phone queries please."

Kansas

KANSAS!, Kansas Department of Commerce and Housing, 700 SW Harrison, Suite 1300, Topeka KS 66603-3957. (913)296-3479. Editor: Andrea Glenn. 90% freelance written. Quarterly magazine emphasizing Kansas "people and places for all ages, occupations and interests." Estab. 1945. Circ. 52,000. **Pays on acceptance.** Publishes ms an average of 1 year after acceptance. Byline given. Buys one-time rights. Submit seasonal material 8 months in advance. Reports in 2 months. Sample copy and writer's guidelines available.

Nonfiction: General interest, photo feature, travel. "Material must be Kansas-oriented and have good potential for color photographs. The focus is on travel with articles about places and events that can be enjoyed by the general public. In other words, events must be open to the public, places also. Query letter

should clearly outline story in mind. I'm especially interested in Kansas freelancers who can supply their own photos." Length: 750-1,250 words. Pays $150-250. Sometimes pays expenses of writers on assignment.
Photos: "We are a full-color photo/manuscript publication." Send photos (original transparencies only) with query. Pays $50-75 (generally included in ms rate) for 35mm or larger format transparencies. Captions required.
Tips: "History and nostalgia stories do not fit into our format because they can't be illustrated well with color photography."

‡KANSAS CITY MAGAZINE, ABARTA Metro Publishing, 7007 College Blvd., Suite 430, Overland Park KS 66211. Fax: (913)338-1148. Editor: Doug Worgul. 75% freelance written. Bimonthly magazine covering Kansas City. Our mission is to celebrate living in Kansas City. We are a consumer lifestyle/general interest magazine focused on Kansas City, its people and places. Estab. 1994. Circ. 31,000. **Pays on acceptance.** Publishes ms an average of 3 months after acceptance. Byline given. Offers 10% kill fee. Buys first North American serial rights. Editorial lead time 4 months. Submit seasonal material 6 months in advance. Accepts simultaneous submissions. Sample copy for #10 SASE.
Nonfiction: Exposé, general interest, interview/profile, photo feature. Buys 30-50 mss/year. Query with published clips. Length: 250-2,500 words. Pays 50¢/word minimum for assigned articles. Sometimes pays expenses of writers on assignment.
Photos: Negotiates payment individually. Buys one-time rights.
Columns/Departments: Entertainment (Kansas City entertainment only), 1,000 words; Food (Kansas City food and restaurants only), 1,000 words. Buys 10 mss/year. Query with published clips. Pays $200-500.

Kentucky

BACK HOME IN KENTUCKY, Greysmith Publishing Inc., P.O. Box 681629, Franklin TN 37068-1629. (615)794-4338. Fax: (615)790-6188. Managing Editor: Nanci P. Gregg. 50% freelance written. Bimonthly magazine covering Kentucky heritage, people, places, events. We reach Kentuckians and "displaced" Kentuckians living outside the state. Estab. 1977. Pays on publication. Publishes ms an average of 8 months after acceptance. Byline given. Buys first North American serial rights. Submit seasonal material 8 months in advance. Reports in 2 months. Sample copy for $3 and 9×12 SAE with 5 first-class stamps. Writer's guidelines for #10 SASE.
  ● This magazine is increasing its emphasis on the "Back Home." It is interested in profiles of Kentucky gardeners, Kentucky cooks, Kentucky craftspeople.
Nonfiction: Historical (Kentucky related eras or profiles), profiles (Kentucky cooks, gardeners and craftspersons), photo feature (Kentucky places and events), travel (unusual/little known Kentucky places). No inspirational or religion—all must be Kentucky related. Buys 25 mss/year. Query with or without published clips, or send complete ms. Length: 500-2,000 words. Pays $50-150 for assigned articles; $15-75 for unsolicited articles. "In addition to normal payment, writers receive 4 copies of issue containing their article." Sometimes pays expenses of writers on assignment.
Reprints: Occasionally accepts previously published submissions. Send photocopy of article, typed ms with rights for sale noted and information about when and where the article previously appeared. Pays 25% of amount paid for an original article.
Photos: Send photos with submission. Reviews transparencies and 4×6 prints. Offers no additional payment for photos accepted with ms. Model releases and identification of subjects required. Rights purchased depends on situation. Also looking for color transparencies for covers. Vertical format. Pays $50-150.
Columns/Departments: Kentucky travel, Kentucky crafts, Kentucky gardeners. Buys 10-12 mss/year. Query with published clips. Length: 500-750 words. Pays $15-40.
Tips: "We work mostly with unpublished writers who have a feel for Kentucky—its people, places, events, etc. The areas most open to freelancers are little known places in Kentucky, unusual history, and profiles of interesting, unusual Kentuckians."

Louisiana

SUNDAY ADVOCATE MAGAZINE, P.O. Box 588, Baton Rouge LA 70821-0588. (504)383-1111, ext. 350. Fax: (504)388-0351. Website: HTTP://www.TheAdvocate.com. Newsfeatures Editor: Freda Yarbrough. 5% freelance written. "We are backlogged but still welcome submissions." Byline given. Estab. 1925. Pays on publication. Publishes ms up to 3 months after acceptance.
Nonfiction and Photos: Well-illustrated, short articles; must have local, area or Louisiana angle, in that order of preference. Also interested in travel pieces. Photos purchased with mss. Pays $100-200.
Reprints: Send tearsheet or typed ms with rights for sale noted and information about when and where the article previously appeared.

Tips: "Styles and subject matter may vary. Local interest is most important. No more than 4-5 typed, double-spaced pages."

Maryland

BALTIMORE MAGAZINE, 16 S. Calvert St., Suite 1000, Baltimore MD 21202. (410)752-7375. Fax: (410)625-0280. Website: http://www.softaid.net/baltimoremag. Editor: Ramsey Flynn. Managing Editor: Ken Iglehart. 10-20% freelance written. Monthly magazine covering the Baltimore area. "Pieces must address an educated, active, affluent reader and must have a very strong Baltimore angle." Estab. 1907. Circ. 57,000. Pays within 60 days of acceptance. Byline given. Offers 30% kill fee. Buys first rights. Submit seasonal/holiday material 4 months in advance. Reports in 2 months on queries; 2 weeks on assigned mss; 3 months on unsolicited mss. Sample copy for $2.95 and 9×12 SAE with 10 first-class stamps. Writer's guidelines for a business-sized SASE.

• Ranked as one of the best markets for freelance writers in *Writer's Yearbook*'s annual "Top 100 Markets," January 1996.

Nonfiction: Contact: Ken Iglehart. Book excerpt (Baltimore subject or Baltimore author), essays (Baltimore subject), exposé (Baltimore subject), humor (Baltimore focus), interview/profile (w/Baltimorean), personal experience (Baltimore focus), photo feature, travel (local and regional to Maryland *only*). "Nothing that lacks a strong Baltimore focus or angle." Query with published clips or send complete ms. Length: 200-4,500 words. Pays $25-2,500 for assigned articles; $25-500 for unsolicited articles. Sometimes pays expenses of writers on assignment.

Tips: "Writers who live in the Baltimore area can send résumé and published clips to be considered for first assignment. Must show an understanding of writing that is suitable to an educated magazine reader and show ability to write with authority, describe scenes, help reader experience the subject. Too many writers send us newspaper-style articles, instead. We are seeking: 1) *Human interest features*—strong, even dramatic profiles of Baltimoreans of interest to our readers. 2) *First-person accounts* of experience in Baltimore, or experiences of a Baltimore resident. 3) *Consumer*—according to our editorial needs, and with Baltimore sources." Writers new to us have most success with small humorous stories and 1,000-word personal essays that exhibit risky, original thought.

Massachusetts

BOSTON GLOBE MAGAZINE, *Boston Globe*, P.O. Box 2378, Boston MA 02107. (617)929-2955. Editor-in-Chief: Evelynne Kramer. Assistant Editors: Paul Hemp, Louise Kennedy. 50% freelance written. Weekly magazine. Circ. 805,099. **Pays on acceptance**. Publishes ms an average of 2 months after acceptance. Buys first serial rights. Submit seasonal material 3 months in advance. Reports in 1 month. Sample copy for 9×12 SAE with 2 first-class stamps.

Nonfiction: Exposé (variety of issues including political, economic, scientific, medical and the arts), interview (not Q&A), profile, book excerpts (first serial rights only). No travelogs or poetry. Buys up to 100 mss/year. Query; SASE must be included with ms or queries for return. Length: 2,500-5,000 words. Payment negotiable.

Photos: Purchased with accompanying ms or on assignment. Reviews contact sheets. Pays standard rates according to size used. Captions required.

BOSTON MAGAZINE, Metrocorp, 300 Massachusetts Ave., Boston MA 02115. (617)262-9700. Fax: (617)267-1774. E-mail: bosmag@aol.com. Contact: Kerry Nugent-Wells. Editor: Craig Unger. 15% freelance written. Monthly magazine covering the city of Boston. Estab. 1972. Circ. 114,476. Pays on publication. Publishes ms an average of 3 months after acceptance. Byline given. Offers 20% kill fee. Buys first North American serial rights. Editorial lead time 2 months. Submit seasonal material 4 months in advance. Reports in 2 weeks on queries; 1 month on mss. Writer's guidelines free on request with SASE.

Nonfiction: Book excerpts, exposé, general interest, how-to, interview/profile, new product. Buys 20 mss/year. Query. Length: 1,200-5,000 words. Pays $400-5,000. Sometimes pays expenses of writers on assignment.

Photos: State availability of photos with submissions. Negotiates payment individually. Buys one-time rights.

Columns/Departments: Sports, Dining, Finance, City Life, Personal Style, Politics. Query. Pays $400-1,200.

CAPE COD LIFE, Including Martha's Vineyard and Nantucket, Cape Cod Life, Inc., P.O. Box 1385, Pocasset MA 02559-1385. (508)564-4466. Fax: (508)564-4470. E-mail: capecod@capecodlife.com. Website: www.capecodlife.com. Editor: Brian F. Shortsleeve. 80% freelance written. Bimonthly magazine focusing on "area lifestyle, history and culture, people and places, business and industry, and issues and answers." Readers are "year-round and summer residents of Cape Cod as well as non-residents who spend their leisure time on the Cape." Circ. 35,000. Pays 30 days after publication. Byline given. Offers 20% kill fee. Buys first North American serial rights or makes work-for-hire assignments. Submit seasonal/holiday material 6 months in advance. Reports in 6 months on queries and ms. Sample copy for $5. Writer's guidelines for #10 SASE.

Nonfiction: General interest, historical, gardening, interview/profile, photo feature, travel, marine, nautical, nature, arts, antiques. Buys 20 mss/year. Query with or without published clips. Length: 1,000-3,000 words. Pays $100-400.Address queries to Laura Reckford, Managing Editor.

Photos: Pays $25-225 for photos. Captions and identification of subjects required. Buys first rights with right to reprint. Photo guidelines for #10 SASE.

Tips: "Freelancers submitting *quality* spec articles with a Cape Cod angle have a good chance at publication. We do like to see a wide selection of writer's clips before giving assignments. We accept more spec work written about Cape and Islands history than any other subject. We are planning an additional issue 'Cape Cod Home, Living and Gardening on the Cape and Islands' covering architecture, landscape design and interior design with a Cape and Islands focus."

PROVINCETOWN ARTS, Provincetown Arts, Inc., 650 Commercial St., Provincetown MA 02657. (508)487-3167. Fax: (508)487-8634. Editor: Christopher Busa. 90% freelance written. Annual magazine for contemporary art and writing. "*Provincetown Arts* focuses broadly on the artists and writers who inhabit or visit the Lower Cape, and seeks to stimulate creative activity and enhance public awareness of the cultural life of the nation's oldest continuous art colony. Drawing upon a 75-year tradition rich in visual art, literature, and theater, *Provincetown Arts* offers a unique blend of interviews, fiction, visual features, reporting, and poetry." Estab. 1985. Circ. 8,000. Pays on publication. Publishes ms an average of 4 months after acceptance. Offers 50% kill fee. Buys one-time and second serial (reprint) rights. Editorial lead time 6 months. Submit seasonal material 6 months in advance. Reports in 3 weeks on queries; 2 months on mss. Sample copy for $10. Writer's guidelines for #10 SASE.

Nonfiction: Book excerpts, essays, humor, interview/profile. Buys 40 mss/year. Send complete ms. Length: 1,500-4,000 words. Pays $150 minimum for assigned articles; $125 minimum for unsolicited articles. Sometimes pays expenses of writers on assignment.

Photos: Send photos with submission. Reviews 8×10 prints. Offers $20-100/photo. Identification of subjects required. Buys one-time rights.

Fiction: Mainstream. Also publishes novel excerpts. Buys 7 mss/year. Send complete ms. Length: 500-5,000 words. Pays $75-300.

Poetry: Buys 25 poems/year. Submit maximum 3 poems. Pays $25-150.

WORCESTER MAGAZINE, 172 Shrewsbury St., Worcester MA 01604-4636. Senior Editor: Martha M. Akstin. 10% freelance written. Weekly tabloid emphasizing the central Massachusetts region. Estab. 1976. Circ. 40,000. Pays on publication. Publishes ms an average of 3 weeks after acceptance. Byline given. Buys all rights. Submit seasonal material 2 months in advance. Does not report on unsolicited material.

Nonfiction: Exposé (area government, corporate), how-to (concerning the area, homes, vacations), interview (local), personal experience, opinion (local), photo feature. "We are interested in any piece with a local angle." Buys 75 mss/year. Length: 500-1,500 words. Pays $35-250.

Photos: Send photos with query. Pays $10 for b&w photos. Captions preferred; model release required. Buys all rights.

Michigan

ABOVE THE BRIDGE MAGAZINE, P.O. Box 41, Marquette MI 49855. Editor: Mikel B. Classen. 100% freelance written. Quarterly magazine on the Upper Peninsula of Michigan. "All material, including fiction, has an Upper Peninsula of Michigan slant. Our readership is past and present Upper Peninsula residents." Circ. 2,500. Pays on publication. Publishes ms an average of 1 year after acceptance. Byline given. Buys one-time rights. Submit seasonal/holiday material 6 months in advance. Reports in 1 year. Sample copy for $3.50. Writer's guidelines for #10 SASE.

Nonfiction: Book excerpts (books on Upper Peninsula or UP writer), essays, historical/nostalgic (UP), interview/profile (UP personality or business), personal experience, photo feature (UP). Note: Travel by assignment only. "This is a family magazine; therefore, no material in poor taste." Buys 60 mss/year. Send complete ms. Length: 1,000-2,000 words. Pays 2¢/word.

Reprints: Send typed ms with rights for sale noted and information about when and where the article previously appeared.

Photos: Send photos with submission. Reviews prints (5×7 or larger). Offers $5. Captions, model releases, identification of subjects required. Buys one-time rights.

Fiction: Ethnic (UP heritage), humorous, mainstream, mystery. No horror or erotica. "Material set in UP has preference for publication." Buys 12 mss/year. Send complete ms. Length: 1,000-2,000 words. Pays 2¢/word.

Poetry: Free verse, haiku, light verse, traditional. No erotica. Buys 20 poems/year. Shorter poetry preferred. Pays $5.

Fillers: Anecdotes, short humor. Buys 25/year. Length: 100-500 words. Pays 2¢/word maximum.

Tips: "Material on the shorter end of our requirements has a better chance for publication. We're very well-stocked at the moment. We can't use material by out-of-state writers with content not tied to Upper Peninsula of Michigan. Know the area and people, read the magazine. Most material received is too long. Stick to our guidelines. We love to publish well written material by previously unpublished writers."

ANN ARBOR OBSERVER, Ann Arbor Observer Company, 201 E. Catherine, Ann Arbor MI 48104. Fax: (313)769-3375. Editor: John Hilton. 50% freelance written. Works with a small number of new/unpublished writers each year. Monthly magazine featuring stories about people and events in Ann Arbor. Estab. 1976. Circ. 60,000. Pays on publication. Publishes ms an average of 2 months after acceptance. Byline given. Reports in 3 weeks on queries; several months on mss. Sample copy for 12½×15 SAE with $3 postage. Free writer's guidelines.

Nonfiction: Historical, investigative features, profiles, brief vignettes. Must pertain to Ann Arbor. Buys 75 mss/year. Length: 100-7,000 words. Pays up to $1,000/article. Sometimes pays expenses of writers on assignment.

Tips: "If you have an idea for a story, write a 100-200-word description telling us why the story is interesting. We are most open to intelligent, insightful features of up to 5,000 words about interesting aspects of life in Ann Arbor."

TRAVERSE, Northern Michigan's Magazine, Prism Publications, Inc., 121 S. Union St., Traverse City MI 49684. (616)941-8174. Contact: Carolyn Faught. Editor: Deborah W. Fellows. 40% freelance written. Monthly magazine covering Northern Michigan. Estab. 1981. Circ. 15,000. Pays on publication. Publishes ms an average of 6 months after acceptance. Offers 25% kill fee. Buys first North American serial rights. Editorial lead time 6 months. Submit seasonal material 1 year in advance. Accepts simultaneous submissions. Reports in 3 weeks on queries; 1 months on mss. Sample copy for $3.50 and SAE. Writer's guidelines for #10 SASE.

Nonfiction: Book excerpts, essays, exposé, general interest, historical/nostalgic, how-to, humor, interview/profile, personal experience. Buys 25-35 mss/year. Query with published clips or send complete ms. Length: 700-3,500 words. Pays $75-500 for assigned articles; $50-400 for unsolicited articles. Sometimes pays expenses of writers on assignment.

Columns/Departments: Up in Michigan (profiles, or first person accounts of elements of life in Northern Michigan), 750 words; Your Environment (what *you* can do to help the Northern environment—i.e., from land use to nature preservation, etc. Also can detail a hike or other natural experience as a destination.), 750 words. Buys 9-12 mss/year. Query with published clips or send complete ms. Pays $50-175.

Fiction: Adventure, historical, humorous, novel excerpts, slice-of-life vignettes. Buys 5 mss/year. Query with published clips or send complete ms. Length: 1,000-3,500 words. Pays $150-350.

Tips: "We're very writer-friendly! We encourage submissions on spec. We will review and accept, or return with comments/suggestions where applicable."

Minnesota

LAKE SUPERIOR MAGAZINE, Lake Superior Port Cities, Inc., P.O. Box 16417, Duluth MN 55816-0417. (218)722-5002. Fax: (218)722-4096. E-mail: edit@lakesuperior.com. Editor: Paul L. Hayden. Contact: Hugh Bishop, managing editor. 60% freelance written. Works with a small number of new/unpublished writers each year. Bimonthly regional magazine covering contemporary and historic people, places and current events around Lake Superior. Estab. 1979. Circ. 20,000. Pays on publication. Publishes ms an average of 10 months after acceptance. Byline given. Offers $25 kill fee. Buys first North American serial and some second rights. Submit seasonal material 1 year in advance. Reports in 2 months. Sample copy for $3.95 and 5 first-class stamps. Writer's guidelines for #10 SASE.

Nonfiction: Book excerpts, general interest, historic/nostalgic, humor, interview/profile (local), personal experience, photo feature (local), travel (local), city profiles, regional business, some investigative. Buys 45 mss/year. Query with published clips. Length 300-2,200 words. Pays $80-400. Sometimes pays the expenses of writers on assignment.

Photos: Quality photography is our hallmark. Send photos with submission. Reviews contact sheets, 2×2 transparencies, 4×5 prints. Offers $20 for b&w and $35 for color. $75 for covers. Captions, model releases, identification of subjects required.

Columns/Departments: Current events and things to do (for Events Calendar section), short, less than 300 words; Around The Circle (media reviews and short pieces on Lake Superior or Great Lakes environmental issues and themes and letters and short pieces on events and highlights of the Lake Superior Region); I Remember (nostalgic lake-specific pieces), up to 1,100 words; Life Lines (single personality profile with photography), up to 900 words. Other headings include Destinations, Nature, Wilderness Living, Heritage, Shipwreck, Chronicle, Lake Superior's Own, House for Sale. Buys 20 mss/year. Query with published clips. Pays $90.

Fiction: Ethnic, historic, humorous, mainstream, novel excerpts, slice-of-life vignettes, ghost stories. Must be regionally targeted in nature. Buys only 2-3 mss/year. Query with published clips. Length: 300-2,500 words. Pays $1-125.

Tips: "Well-researched queries are attended to. We actively seek queries from writers in Lake Superior communities. We prefer manuscripts to queries. Provide enough information on why the subject is important to the region and our readers, or why and how something is unique. We want details. The writer must have a thorough knowledge of the subject and how it relates to our region. We prefer a fresh, unused approach to the subject which provides the reader with an emotional involvement. Almost all of our articles feature quality photography, color or black and white. It is a prerequisite of all nonfiction. All submissions should include a *short* biography of author/photographer; mug shot sometimes used. Blanket submissions need not apply."

‡**MPLS. ST. PAUL MAGAZINE**, 220 S. Sixth St., Suite 500, Pillsbury Center-South Tower, Minneapolis MN 55402-4507. (612)339-7571. Fax: (612)339-5806. Editor: Brian Anderson. Contact: Bonnie Blodgett, executive editor. Managing Editor: Debbie Mazzollo. 70% freelance written. Monthly general interest magazine covering the metropolitan area of Minneapolis/St. Paul and aimed at college-educated professionals who enjoy living in the area and taking advantage of the cultural, entertainment and dining out opportunities. Reports on people and issues of importance to the community. Estab. 1978. Circ. 64,335. **Pays on acceptance.** Publishes ms an average of 3 months after acceptance. Byline given. Offers 25% kill fee. Buys first North American serial rights. Submit seasonal material 5 months in advance. Reports in 1 month. Sample copy for $4.18.

Nonfiction: Book excerpts, general interest, historical/nostalgic, interview/profile (local), new product, photo feature (local), travel (regional). Buys 200 mss/year. Query with published clips. Length: 1,000-4,000 words. Pays $100-1,500. Sometimes pays expenses of writers on assignment.

Photos: Jim Nelson, photo editor.

Columns/Departments: Nostalgia (Minnesota historical); Home (interior design, local). Query with published clips. Length: 750-2,000 words. Pays $100-500.

Mississippi

‡**COAST MAGAZINE**, Ship Island Holding Co., P.O. Box 1209, Gulfport MS 39502. (601)868-1182. Fax: (601)867-2986. Editor: Michelle Roberts. 30% freelance written. Bimonthly magazine. "We describe ourselves as a 'lifestyle magazine'—our slant is positive and upbeat, but we aren't afraid to tackle tough or sensitive issues." Estab. 1993. Circ. 25,000. Pays on publication. Publishes ms an average of 4 months after acceptance. Byline given. Offers $25 kill fee. Buys first North American serial rights. Editorial lead time 4 months. Submit seasonal material 4 months in advance. Reports in 1 month on queries. Sample copy for $3. Writer's guidelines for #10 SASE.

Nonfiction: General interest, historical/nostalgic, humor, inspirational, interview/profile, new product, photo feature, travel. Buys 6 mss/year. Query with published clips. Pays $25-500. Sometimes pays expenses of writers on assignment.

Photos: Send photos with submission. Reviews 3×5 transparencies. Negotiates payment individually. Captions, model releases, identification of subjects required. Buys all rights.

Columns/Departments: Kathy O'Brien, assistant editor. Hot Shots (interesting people), 400 words; Art Scene (local artists), 1,000 words; Reflections (historical), 2,000 words. Buys 6 mss/year. Query with published clips. Pays $25-150.

Fiction: Buys 1 ms/year. Query with published clips. Length: 3,000 words maximum.

Tips: "Being familiar with *Coast Magazine* and its readership is a must. Freelancers should send the editor a cover letter that is indicative of his or her writing style along with strong writing samples."

Missouri

PITCH WEEKLY, Pitch Publishing, Inc., 3535 Broadway, Suite 400, Kansas City MO 64111-2826. (816)561-6061. Fax: (816)756-0502. E-mail: pitchwee@qni.com. Editor: Bruce Rodgers. 75% freelance written. Weekly alternative newspaper that covers arts, entertainment, politics and social and cultural awareness in the Kansas City metro region. Estab. 1980. Circ. 85,000. Pays 1 month from publication. Buys first or one-time rights or makes work-for-hire assignments. Editorial lead time 1 month. Submit seasonal material 2 months in advance. *Query first!* Reports in 2 months on queries.

Nonfiction: Exposé, humor, interview/profile, opinion, news, photo feature. Buys 40-50 mss/year. Query with published clips. Length: 500-5,000 words. Pays $25-250. Sometimes pays expenses of writers on assignment. Prefer nonfiction with local hook.

Reprints: Send photocopy of article or typed ms with rights for sale noted and information about when and where the article previously appeared. Pays 50% of amount paid for an original article.

Photos: Send photos with submission. Reviews contact sheets. Pays for photos with ms: $15-50. Captions and identification of subjects required. Buys one-time rights.

Fiction: Holiday-theme fiction published on Christmas, Thanksgiving, Valentine's Day, Halloween, April Fool's (humor/satire). "Must be slightly off-beat and good." Length: 1,500-2,500 words. Payment $75-125.

Tips: "Approach us with unusual angles on current political/social topics. Send well-written, clear, concise query with identifiable direction of proposed piece and SASE for reply or return. Previous publication in AAN paper a plus. We're looking for features and secondary features: current events in visual and performing arts (include new trends, etc.); social issues (OK to have an opinion as long as facts are well-documented); liberal politics."

RIVER HILLS TRAVELER, Todd Publishing, Route 4 Box 4396, Piedmont MO 63957. (314)223-7143. Editor: Bob Todd. 60% freelance written. Monthly consumer tabloid covering fishing, hunting, camping and southern Missouri. "We are about outdoor sports and nature in the southeast quarter of Missouri. Topics like those in *Field & Stream* and *National Geographic*." Estab. 1973. Circ. 7,500. Pays on publication. Publishes ms an average of 2 months after acceptance. Byline given. Buys one-time rights. Editorial lead time 2 months. Submit seasonal material 1 year in advance. Accepts simultaneous submissions. Reports in 1 month. Sample copy and writer's guidelines free on request.

Nonfiction: Historical/nostalgic, how-to, humor, opinion, personal experience. photo feature, technical, travel. "No stories about other geographic areas." Buys 80 mss/year. Query with writing samples. Length: 1,500 maximum words. Pays $25. Sometimes pays expenses of writers on assignment.

Reprints: Send typed ms with rights for sale noted and information about when and where the article previously appeared.

Photos: Send photos with submission. Reviews contact sheets and prints. Negotiates payment individually. Identification of subjects required. Buys one-time rights.

Fillers: Gags. Pays $10.

Tips: "We are a 'poor man's version' of *Field & Stream* and *National Geographic*—about the eastern Missouri Ozarks."

SPRINGFIELD! MAGAZINE, Springfield Communications Inc., P.O. Box 4749, Springfield MO 65808-4749. (417)882-4917. Editor: Robert C. Glazier. 85% freelance written. Works with a small number of new/unpublished writers each year; eager to work with new/unpublished writers. Monthly magazine. "This is an extremely local and provincial magazine. No *general* interest articles." Estab. 1979. Circ. 10,000. Pays on publication. Publishes ms an average of 6 months after acceptance. Byline given. Buys first serial rights. Submit seasonal/holiday material 1 year in advance. Reports in 3 months on queries; 6 months on mss. Sample copy for $5 and 9½×12½ SAE.

Nonfiction: Book excerpts (by Springfield authors only), exposé (local topics only), historical/nostalgic (top priority but must be local history), how-to (local interest only), humor (if local angle), interview/profile (needs more on females than on males), personal experience (local angle), photo feature (local photos), travel (1 page/month). No material that could appeal to any other magazine anywhere else. Buys 150 mss/year. Query with published clips or send complete ms with SASE. Length: 500-5,000 words. Pays $25-250. Sometimes pays expenses of writers on assignment.

Photos: Send photos or send photos with query or ms. Reviews b&w and color contact sheets, 4×5 color transparencies, 5×7 b&w prints. Pays $5-35 for b&w, $10-50 for color. Captions, model releases, identification of subjects required. Buys one-time rights.

● *Springfield! Magazine* needs more photo features of a nostalgic bent.

Columns/Departments: Buys 250 mss/year. Query or send complete ms. Length varies widely but usually 500-2,500 words.

Tips: "We prefer that a writer read eight or ten copies of our magazine prior to submitting any material for our consideration. The magazine's greatest need is for features which comment on these times in Springfield. We are overstocked with nostalgic pieces right now. We also are much in need of profiles about young women and men of distinction."

Montana

MONTANA MAGAZINE, American Geographic Publishing, P.O. Box 5630, Helena MT 59604-5630. (406)443-2842. Fax: (406)443-5480. Editor: Beverly R. Magley. 90% freelance written. Bimonthly "strictly

Montana-oriented magazine that features community and personality profiles, contemporary issues, travel pieces." Estab. 1970. Circ. 45,000. Publishes ms an average of 1 year after acceptance. Byline given. Offers $50-100 kill fee on assigned stories only. Buys one-time rights. Submit seasonal material at least 6 months in advance. Accepts simultaneous submissions. Reports in 2 months. Sample copy for $3. Writer's guidelines for #10 SASE.

Nonfiction: Essays, general interest, interview/profile, photo feature, travel. Special features on summer and winter destination points. Query by January for summer material; July for winter material. No 'me and Joe' hiking and hunting tales; no blood-and-guts hunting stories; no poetry; no fiction; no sentimental essays. Buys 30 mss/year. Query. Length: 300-4,500 words. Pays 15¢/word for articles. Sometimes pays the expenses of writers on assignment.

Reprints: Send information about when and where the article previously appeared. Pays 50% of amount paid for an original article.

Photos: Send photos with submission. Reviews contact sheets, 35mm or larger format transparencies, 5×7 prints. Offers additional payment for photos accepted with ms. Captions, model releases, identification of subjects required. Buys one-time rights.

Columns/Departments: Memories (reminisces of early-day Montana life) 800-1,000 words; Small Towns (profiles of communities) 1,500 words; Over the Weekend (destination points of interest to travelers, family weekends and exploring trips to take), 500-1,000 words plus b&w or color photo; Food and Lodging (great places to eat; interesting hotels, resorts, etc.), 700-1,000 words plus b&w or color photo; Made in MT (successful cottage industries), 700-1,000 words plus b&w or color photo. Humor 800-1,000 words. Query.

Nevada

NEVADA MAGAZINE, 1800 E. Hwy. 50, Carson City NV 89710-0005. (702)687-5416. Fax: (702)687-6159. Publisher: Rich Moreno. Editor: David Moore. Associate Editor: Carolyn Graham. 50% freelance written. Works with a small number of new/unpublished writers each year. Bimonthly magazine published by the state of Nevada to promote tourism in the state. Estab. 1936. Circ. 90,000. Pays on publication. Publishes ms an average of 6 months after acceptance. Byline given. Buys first North American serial rights. Submit seasonal material at least 6 months in advance. Reports in 1 month. Sample copy for $1. Free writer's guidelines.

Nonfiction: Nevada topics only. Historical, nostalgia, photo feature, people profile, recreational, travel, think pieces. "We welcome stories and photos on speculation." Publishes nonfiction book excerpts. Buys 40 unsolicited mss/year. Submit complete ms or queries to Associate Editor, Carolyn Graham. Accepts phone queries. Length: 500-2,000 words. Pays $75-300.

Photos: Denise Barr, art director. Send photo material with accompanying ms. Pays $15-100 for color transparencies and glossy prints. Name, address and caption should appear on each photo or slide. Buys one-time rights.

Tips: "Keep in mind that the magazine's purpose is to promote tourism in Nevada. Keys to higher payments are quality and editing effort (more than length). Send cover letter; no photocopies. We look for a light, enthusiastic tone of voice without being too cute; articles bolstered by amazing facts and thorough research; and unique angles on Nevada subjects."

New Jersey

ATLANTIC CITY MAGAZINE, P.O. Box 2100, Pleasantville NJ 08232-1924. (609)272-7912. Fax: (609)272-7910. Editor: Paula Rackow. 80% freelance written. Works with small number of new/unpublished writers each year. Monthly regional magazine covering issues pertinent to the Jersey Shore area. Estab. 1978. Circ. 50,000. Pays on publication. Publishes ms an average of 4 months after acceptance. Byline given. Buys one-time rights. Offers variable kill fee. Submit seasonal material 6 months in advance. Reports in 6 weeks. Sample copy for $3 and 9×12 SAE with 6 first-class stamps. Writer's guidelines for SASE.

Nonfiction: Entertainment, general interest, recreation, history, lifestyle, interview/profile, photo feature, trends. "No hard news or investigative pieces. No travel pieces or any article without a South Jersey shore area/Atlantic City slant." Query. Length: 100-3,000 words. Pays $50-700 for assigned articles; $50-500 for unsolicited articles. Sometimes pays the expenses of writers on assignment.

Photos: Send photos. Reviews contact sheets, negatives, 2¼×2¼ transparencies, 8×10 prints. Pay varies. Captions, model releases, identification of subjects required. Buys one-time rights.

Columns/Departments: Art, Business, Entertainment, Sports, Dining, History, Style, Real Estate. Query with published clips. Length: 500-2,000 words. Pays $150-400.

Tips: "Our readers are a broad base of local residents and visiting tourists. We need stories that will appeal to both audiences."

NEW JERSEY MONTHLY, P.O. Box 920, Morristown NJ 07963-0920. (201)539-8230. Editor: Jenny De Monte. 50% freelance written. Monthly magazine covering "almost anything that's New Jersey-related." Estab. 1976. Circ. 94,000. Pays on completion of fact-checking. Byline given. Offers 10-30% kill fee. Buys first rights. Submit seasonal material 6 months in advance. Reports in 3 months. Sample copy for $5.95 (% Back Issue Dept.); writer's guidelines for #10 SASE.
- This magazine continues to look for strong investigative reporters with novelistic style and solid knowledge of New Jersey issues.

Nonfiction: Book excerpts, essays, exposé, general interest, historical, humor, interview/profile, opinion, personal experience, travel. Special issues: Dining Out (February, August); Real Estate (March); Home & Garden (April); Great Weekends (May); Shore Guide (June); Fall Getaways (October); Holiday Shopping & Entertaining (November). "No experience pieces from people who used to live in New Jersey or general pieces that have no New Jersey angle." Buys 96 mss/year. Query with published magazine clips and SASE. Length: 200-3,000 words. Pays 30¢/word and up. Pays reasonable expenses of writers on assignment with prior approval.
- Ranked as one of the best markets for freelance writers in *Writer's Yearbook*'s annual "Top 100 Markets," January 1996.

Photos: Send photos with submission. Payment negotiated. Identification of subjects and return postage required. "Submit dupes only. Drop off for portfolios on Wednesdays only. The magazine accepts no responsibility for unsolicited photography, artwork or cartoons." Buys exclusive first serial or one-time rights.
Columns/Departments: Business (company profile, trends, individual profiles); Health & Fitness (trends, personal experience, service); Home & Garden (homes, gardens, trends, profiles, etc.); Travel (in and out-of-state). Buys 36 mss/year. Query with published clips. Length: 750-1,500 words. Pays 30¢ and up/word.
Tips: "To break in, we suggest contributing briefs to our front-of-the-book section, 'Garden Variety' (light, off-beat items, trends, people, things; short service items, such as the 10 best NJ-made ice creams; short issue-oriented items; gossip; media notes). We pay a flat fee, from $50-150."

‡**NEW JERSEY OUTDOORS**, New Jersey Department of Environmental Protection, CN 402, Trenton NJ 08625. (609)777-4182. Fax: (609)984-0583. Editor: Beth Kuhles. 50% freelance written. Quarterly consumer magazine covering outdoor activities, history and culture in N.J. "*New Jersey Outdoors* celebrates the natural and historic resources of New Jersey with articles and photography on wildlife, nature, historic treasures, recreation, fishing, hunting, conservation and environmental protection." Estab. 1950. Circ. 20,000. Pays on publication. Byline given. Buys one-time rights. Editorial lead time 6 months. Submit seasonal material 6 months in advance. Accepts simultaneous submissions. Reports in 3 months on queries. Sample copy free on request. Writer's guidelines for #10 SASE.
Nonfiction: General interest, historical/nostalgic, how-to, interview/profile, personal experience, photo feature. "*New Jersey Outdoors* is not interested in articles showing disregard for the environment or in items demonstrating unskilled persons taking extraordinary risks." Buys 30-40 mss/year. Query with published clips. Length: 600-2,000 words. Pays $100-500. Sometimes pays expenses of writers on assignment.
Reprints: Accepts previously published submissions.
Photos: State availability of photos with submission. Reviews contact sheets, negatives, transparencies. Offers $20-125/photo. Captions and identification of subjects required. Buys one-time rights.
Columns/Departments: Afield (first person outdoor activities); Cityscape (environmental activities in cities or suburbs); Gardens (gardens or gardening tips); Outings (trips to specific N.J. locations); Profile (people who make a difference in environment); Volunteers (volunteers for environment). Buys 25 mss/year. Query with published clips. Pays $100-500.
Tips: "*New Jersey Outdoors* generally publishes season-specific articles, which are planned six months in advance. Stories should be accompanied by *great* photography. Articles *must* relate to New Jersey."

THE SANDPAPER, Newsmagazine of the Jersey Shore, The SandPaper, Inc., 1816 Long Beach Blvd., Surf City NJ 08008-5461. (609)494-2034. Fax: (609)494-1437. Managing Editor: Jay Mann. Freelance Submissions Editor: Gail Travers. 10% freelance written. Weekly tabloid covering subjects of interest to Jersey shore residents and visitors. "*The SandPaper* publishes two editions covering many of the Jersey Shore's finest resort communities including Long Beach Island and Ocean City, New Jersey. Each issue includes a mix of news, human interest features, opinion columns and entertainment/calendar listings." Estab. 1976. Circ. 60,000. Pays on publication. Publishes ms an average of 1 month after acceptance. Byline given. Offers 100% kill fee. Buys first or all rights. Submit seasonal material 3 months in advance. Accepts simultaneous submissions. Reports in 1 month. Sample copy for 9 × 12 SAE with 8 first-class stamps.
Nonfiction: Essays, general interest, historical/nostalgic, humor, opinion, environmental submissions relating to the ocean, wetlands and pinelands. Must pertain to New Jersey shore locale. Also, arts, entertainment news, reviews if they have a Jersey shore angle. Buys 10 mss/year. Send complete ms. Length: 200-2,000 words. Pays $25-200. Sometimes pays the expenses of writers on assignment.
Reprints: Send photocopy of article and information about when and where the article previously appeared. Pays 25-50% of amount paid for an original article.

Photos: Send photos with submission. Offers $8-25/photo. Buys one-time or all rights.

Columns/Departments: SpeakEasy (opinion and slice-of-life; often humorous); Commentary (forum for social science perspectives); both 1,000-1,500 words, preferably with local or Jersey shore angle. Buys 50 mss/year. Send complete ms. Pays $30.

Tips: "Anything of interest to sun worshippers, beach walkers, nature watchers, water sports lovers is of potential interest to us. There is an increasing coverage of environmental issues. The opinion page and columns are most open to freelancers. We are steadily increasing the amount of entertainment-related material in our publication. Articles on history of the shore area are always in demand."

New Mexico

NEW MEXICO MAGAZINE, Lew Wallace Bldg., 495 Old Santa Fe Trail, Santa Fe NM 87503. (505)827-7447. Editor-in-Chief: Emily Drabanski. Editor: Jon Bowman. Associate Editors: Walter K. Lopez, Camille Flores-Turney. 80% freelance written. Monthly magazine emphasizing New Mexico for a college-educated readership, above average income, interested in the Southwest. Estab. 1922. Circ. 125,000. **Pays on acceptance.** Publishes ms an average of 6 months to a year after acceptance. Buys first North American serial rights. Submit seasonal material 1 year in advance. Reports in 2 months. Sample copy for $2.95. Free writer's guidelines.

• Ranked as one of the best markets for freelance writers in *Writer's Yearbook*'s annual "Top 100 Markets," January 1996.

Nonfiction: New Mexico subjects of interest to travelers. Historical, cultural, informational articles. "We are looking for more short, light and bright stories for the 'Asi Es Nuevo Mexico' section." No columns, cartoons, poetry or non-New Mexico subjects. Buys 5-7 mss/issue. Query with 3 published writing samples. No phone or fax queries. Length: 250-1,500 words. Pays $100-500.

Reprints: Rarely publishes reprints but sometimes publishes excerpts from novels and nonfiction books.

Photos: Purchased with accompanying ms or on assignment. Query or send contact sheet or transparencies. Pays $50-80 for 8 × 10 b&w glossy prints; $50-150 for 35mm—prefers Kodachrome. Photos should be in plastic-pocketed viewing sheets. Captions and model releases required. Mail photos to Art Director John Vaughan. Buys one-time rights.

Tips: "Send a superb short (300 words) manuscript on a little-known person, event, aspect of history or place to see in New Mexico. Faulty research will ruin a writer's chances for the future. Good style, good grammar. No generalized odes to the state or the Southwest. No sentimentalized, paternalistic views of Indians or Hispanics. No glib, gimmicky 'travel brochure' writing. No first-person vacation stories. We're always looking for well-researched pieces on unusual aspects of New Mexico history. Lively writing."

New York

ADIRONDACK LIFE, P.O. Box 97, Jay NY 12941-0097. Fax: (518)946-7461. Editor: Elizabeth Folwell. 70% freelance written. Prefers to work with published/established writers. Emphasizes the Adirondack region and the North Country of New York State in articles concerning outdoor activities, history, and natural history directly related to the Adirondacks. Publishes 7 issues/year, including special Annual Outdoor Guide. Estab. 1970. Circ. 50,000. Pays 45 days after acceptance. Publishes ms an average of 6 months after acceptance. Buys one-time rights. Byline given. Submit seasonal material 1 year in advance. Reports in 1 month. Sample copy for 9 × 12 SAE with 8 first-class stamps. Writer's guidelines for #10 SASE.

Nonfiction: "*Adirondack Life* attempts to capture the unique flavor and ethos of the Adirondack mountains and North Country region through feature articles directly pertaining to the qualities of the area and through department articles examining specific aspects. Example: Barkeater: personal essay; Special Places: unique spots in the Adirondack Park; Working: careers in the Adirondacks and Wilderness: environmental issues, personal experiences." Buys 20-25 unsolicited mss/year. Query. Length: for features, 5,000 words maximum; for departments, 2,200 words. Pays up to 25¢/word. Sometimes pays expenses of writers on assignment.

• Also considers first-serial novel excerpts in its subject matter and region.

Photos: All photos must have been taken in the Adirondacks. Each issue contains a photo feature. Purchased with or without ms or on assignment. All photos must be individually identified as to subject or locale and must bear photographer's name. Submit color transparencies or b&w prints. Pays $100 for full page, b&w or color; $300 for cover (color only, vertical in format). Credit line given.

Tips: "We are looking for clear, concise, well-organized manuscripts, that are strictly Adirondack in subject. Check back issues to be sure we haven't already covered your topic."

‡AVENUE, 950 Third Ave., New York NY 10022. Fax: (212)758-7395. Editor-in-Chief: Laura Fisher. Managing Editor: Quinn Halford. Contact: Elena Kornbluth, associate editor. 50% freelance written. Monthly magazine covering New York art, fashion, restaurants; business, design travel. "As *Avenue* is intended for

Estab. 1989. Circ. 72,000. Pays on publication. Publishes ms an average of 10 months after acceptance. Byline given. Offers 5% kill fee. Buys first North American serial rights. Editorial lead time 2 months. Submit seasonal material 3 months in advance. Sample copy and writer's guidelines free on request.

Nonfiction: Book excerpts, humor, interview/profile, opinion, personal experience, photo feature, travel. Special issue: Women's (March). Query with published clips. Length: 200 words minimum. Pays $25 for assigned articles. Sometimes pays expenses of writers on assignment.

Reprints: Accepts previously published submissions.

Photos: Send photos with submission. Reviews contact sheets. Offers no additional payment for photos accepted with ms. Captions, identification of subjects required. Buys all rights.

Columns/Departments: Around Urban NY (events) 200 words; Health (mind and body) 200 words; New Reads/Books (literary) 200 words. Buys mss/year. Query with published clips. Pays $25-55

Poetry: Accepts avant-garde, free verse, traditional poetry. Buys 20 poems/year. Pays $15-25.

Fillers: Anecdotes, facts, newsbreaks. Buys 25/year.

Tips: "Just call or fax–It's simple, easy and positive!"

NEWSDAY, Melville NY 11747-4250. Viewpoints Editor: Noel Rubinton. Opinion section of daily newspaper. Byline given. Estab. 1940.

Nonfiction: Seeks "opinion on current events, trends, issues—whether national or local, government or lifestyle. Must be timely, pertinent, articulate and opinionated. Preference for authors within the circulation area including New York City." Length: 700-800 words. Pays $150-200.

Tips: "It helps for prospective authors to be familiar with our paper and section."

SPOTLIGHT MAGAZINE, Meadow Publications Inc., 126 Library Lane, Mamaroneck NY 10543. (914)381-4740. Fax: (914)381-4641. Editor-in-Chief: Dana B. Asher. 50% freelance written. Monthly magazine of general interest. Audience is "upscale, educated, 30-60, in the NY-NJ-CT tri-state area. We try to appeal to a broad audience throughout our publication area." Estab. 1977. Circ. 73,000. Pays on publication. Byline given. Editorial lead time 3 months. Submit seasonal material 5 months in advance. Reports in 1 month. Sample copy for $3.

  ● *Spotlight* is looking for human interest articles and issue-related features woven around New York, New Jersey and Connecticut.

Nonfiction: Book excerpts, essays, exposé, general human interest, historical/nostalgic, how-to, humor, inspirational, interview/profile, new product, photo feature, travel, illustrations. Annual special-interest guides: Wedding (February, June, September); Dining (December); Home Design (March, April, October); Home Technology (May); Travel (June); Health (July, January); Education (January, August); Holiday Gifts (November); Corporate (March, July, October). No fiction or poetry. Buys 25 mss/year. Query. Pays $150 minimum.

Photos: State availability of or send photos with submission. Reviews transparencies and prints. Negotiates payment individually. Captions, model releases, identification of subjects required (when appropriate). Buys one-time rights.

SYRACUSE NEW TIMES, A. Zimmer Ltd., 1415 W. Genesee St., Syracuse NY 13204. Fax: (315)422-1721. E-mail: newtimes@ras.com. Website: http://www.rway.com/newtimes/. Editor: Mike Greenstein. 50% freelance written. Weekly tabloid covering news, sports, arts and entertainment. "*Syracuse New Times* is an alternative weekly that can be topical, provocative, irreverent and intensely local." Estab. 1969. Circ. 43,000. Pays on publication. Publishes ms an average of 1 month after acceptance. Byline given. Buys one-time rights. Editorial lead time 3 months. Submit seasonal material 3 months in advance. Accepts simultaneous submissions. Reports in 2 weeks on queries; 1 month on mss. Sample copy for 9 × 11 SAE with 2 first-class stamps. Writer's guidelines for #10 SASE.

Nonfiction: Essays, general interest. Buys 200 mss/year. Query with published clips. Length: 250-2,500 words. Pays $25-200.

Reprints: Accepts previously published submissions.

Photos: State availability of photos or send photos with submission. Reviews 8 × 10 prints and color slides. Offers $10-25/photo or negotiates payment individually. Identification of subjects required. Buys one-time rights.

Tips: "Move to Syracuse and query with strong idea."

‡UPSTATE NEW YORKER, JRH Communications, 401 N. Salina St., Syracuse NY 13203. (315)422-0194. Fax: (315)422-0197. Editor: Stephanie DeJoseph. 75% freelance written. Bimonthly magazine. Estab. 1994. Circ. 100,000. Pays on publication. Byline given. Offers $50 kill fee. Buys first rights. Editorial lead time 2 months. Submit seasonal material 6 months in advance. Accepts simultaneous submissions. Reports in 3 months on queries; 6 months on mss. Sample copy 9 × 12 SAE and $1.60. Writer's guidelines for #10 SASE.

Nonfiction: General interest, historical/nostalgic, humor, inspirational, interview/profile, new product, opinion, photo feature, travel. No erotic or inappropriate subject matter that is not mainstream. Buys 6-10 mss/

year. Send complete ms. Length: 750-1,500 words. Pays 25-75¢/word and contributor's copies. Sometimes pays expenses of writers on assignment.

Photos: State availability of photos with submission. Reviews 3×5 transparencies. Negotiates payment individually. Identification of subjects required. Buys one-time rights.

Columns/Departments: Barth Myers, senior editor. Political, Education, Home, Arts, Money, Sports, Travel, Law (contemporary issues relevant issues, profiles, events and ideas, must be relevant to Upstate NY market) 750. Buys 36 mss/year. Send complete ms. Pays from contributor copies to 75¢-$1/word.

Fiction: Adventure, historical, humorous, mainstream, mystery, romance, suspense. Buys 2 mss/year. Send completel ms. Length: 1,000-2,200 words.

Poetry: Accepts free verse, light verse and traditional poetry. Buys 3 poems/year. Submit maximum 5 poems.

Fillers: Stephanie DeJoseph, editor. Buys facts and newsbreaks, fillers. Buys 5/year. Length: 50-300 words. Pays contributor copies-75¢/word.

Tips: "Send query and a follow-up phone call. Submit an interesting, unusual, unique idea pertinent to the upstate reader."

North Carolina

CAROLINA COUNTRY, North Carolina Association of Electric Cooperatives, 3400 Summer Blvd,, Raleigh NC 27604. Editor: Michael E.C. Gery. 30% freelance written. Monthly magazine for members of North Carolina's electric cooperatives. General interest material concerning North Carolina's culture, business, history, people. Estab. 1952. Circ. 340,000. **Pays on acceptance.** Publishes ms an average of 3 months after acceptance. Byline given. Offers 50% kill fee. Buys all rights. Editorial lead time 3 months. Submit seasonal material 3 months in advance. Accepts simultaneous and previously published submissions (if outside North Carolina). Reports in 1 month on queries; 2 months on mss.

Nonfiction: General interest, historical/nostalgic, humor, photo feature. Buys 12 mss/year. Send complete ms. Length: 600-1,500 words. Pays $100-400.

Photos: Send photos with submission. Reviews transparencies, prints. Negotiates payment individually. Captions, identification of subjects required. Buys one-time rights.

Columns/Departments: Focus (useful resource news in North Carolina), 100 words. Buys 10 mss/year. Send complete ms. Pays $20-100.

Tips: "Interested in North Carolina information that would not likely appear in local newspapers. Our readers are rural and suburban residents."

‡**RALEIGH MAGAZINE,** 5 West Hargett St., Suite 809, Raleigh NC 27601. (919)755-9200. Fax: (919)755-9201. Publisher: Bob Dill. 90% freelance written. Bimonthly magazine for Raleigh and regional NC lifestyles. "Though expanding, our current readership is largely female, 25-50. Our audience as a whole is urban, upscale, well-educated, and an ad mixture of native Raleigh or North Carolinians and young, mobile professionals making a warmer life in the sunbelt." Estab. 1978. Circ. 20,000. Pays on publication. Publishes ms an average of 2 months after acceptance. Byline given. Buys first North American serial rights. Editorial lead time 2 months. Submit seasonal material 4 months in advance. Accepts simultaneous submissions. Reports in 2 weeks on queries. Sample copy for $3 with 9×12 SASE. Writer's guidelines for #10 SASE.

Nonfiction: Essays, exposé, general interest, historical/nostalgic, how-to, humor, interview/profile, personal experience, photo feature, travel. "No generic how-to, pieces with no Raleigh or regional connection, humor with no Raleigh connection or syndicated (self or otherwise) material." Buys 30 mss/year. Query with published clips. Length: 750-2,500 words. Pays 12¢/word. Sometimes pays expenses of writers on assignment.

Reprints: Accepts previously published submissions.

Photos: Send photos with submission. Reviews transparencies and prints. Negotiates payment individually. Model releases and identification of subjects required. Buys one-time rights.

Columns/Departments: Essays (well written, humorous short essays on topics of interest to people who live in Raleigh), 750-1,000 words. Pays 12¢/word minimum; negotiable.

Fiction: "We run fiction once a year in our summer reading issue." Buys 1-2 mss/year. Query.

Tips: "For us, a strong feature idea is the best way to break in. New or interesting Raleigh or NC slants on travel, fashion, personalities, are sought constantly here."

---

‡ **THE DOUBLE DAGGER** before a listing indicates that the listing is new in this edition. New markets are often more receptive to freelance submissions.

THE STATE: Down Home in North Carolina, 128 S. Tryon St., Suite 2200, Charlotte NC 28202. Fax: (704)375-8129. Managing Editor: Scott Smith. 80% freelance written. Monthly. Estab. 1933. Circ. 25,000. Publishes ms an average of 1 year after acceptance. Byline given. No kill fee. Buys first serial rights. Pays on publication. Submit seasonal material 1 year in advance. Reports in 2 months. Sample copy for $2.75.
Nonfiction: General articles about places, people, events, history, nostalgia, general interest in North Carolina. Emphasis on travel in North Carolina. Will use humor if related to region. Length: 700-2,000 words average. Pays $125-150 for assigned articles; $75-125 for unsolicited articles.
Photos: Send photos with submission if possible. Reviews contact sheets and transparencies. Offers additional payment for photos. Captions and identification of subjects required. Buys one-time rights.
Columns/Departments: The State We're In (newsbriefs about current events in NC; most have travel, historic or environmental slant), 150-500 words. Also: Tar Heel History ($125); Tar Heel Memories ($75); Tar Heel Profile (profiles of newsworthy North Carolinians). Buys 10 mss/year. Pays $25.

Ohio

CINCINNATI MAGAZINE, 409 Broadway, Cincinnati OH 45202-3340. (513)421-4300. Fax: (513)421-0105. Contact: Emily Foster, editor. Homes Editor: Linda Vaccariello. Food Editor: Lilia F. Brady. Monthly magazine emphasizing Cincinnati living. Circ. 32,000. Pays on publication. Byline given. Buys all rights.
Nonfiction: Articles on personalities, business, sports, lifestyles, history relating to Cincinnati. Query. Length: 1,500-3,500 words. Pays $150-500.
Columns/Departments: Cincinnati dining, media, arts and entertainment, people, politics, sports. Buys 2 mss/issue. Query. Length: 750-1,500 words. Pays $75-150. "We do special features each month. January (Homes); February (Dining out, restaurants); March (Health, Personal finance); April (Home and Fashion); May (Environment and Golf); June (Health); July (Food and Homes); August (Fashion); September (Homes); October (Best and Worst); November (Automotive Guide and Fashion); December (City guide). We also have a special issue in August where we feature a local fiction contest."
Tips: "Freelancers may find a market in quarterly Homes section (January, April, July, September), special sections on varying topics from golf to cardiac care. Always query in writing, with clips. All articles have a Cincinnati base. No generics, please. Also: no movie, book, theater reviews, poetry or fiction."

CLEVELAND MAGAZINE, City Magazines, Inc., 1422 Euclid Ave., #730Q, Cleveland OH 44115. Editor: Liz Ludlow. 70% freelance written, mostly by assignment. Monthly magazine with a strong Cleveland/NE Ohio angle. Estab. 1972. Circ. 45,000. Pays on publication. Publishes ms an average of 3 months after acceptance. Byline given. Offers 50% kill fee. Buys first rights and second serial (reprint) rights. Editorial lead time 6 months. Submit seasonal material 8 months in advance. Accepts simultaneous submissions. Reports in 2 months.
Nonfiction: Book excerpts, general interest, historical/nostalgic, humor, interview/profile. Buys 1 ms/year. Query with published clips. Length: 800-5,000 words. Pays $200-800. Sometimes pays expenses of writers on assignment.
Columns/Departments: City Life (Cleveland trivia/humor/info briefs), 200 words. Buys 2 mss/year. Query with published clips. Pays $50.

‡COLUMBUS MONTHLY, P.O. Box 29913, Columbus OH 43229-7513. (614)888-4567. Editor: Lenore E. Brown. 20-40% freelance written. Prefers to work with published/established writers. Monthly magazine emphasizing subjects specifically related to Columbus and central Ohio. Pays on publication. Publishes ms an average of 2 months after acceptance. Byline given. Buys all rights. Reports in 1 month. Sample copy for $4.89.
Nonfiction: No humor, essays or first person material. "I like query letters which are well-written, indicate the author has some familiarity with *Columbus Monthly*, give me enough detail to make a decision and include at least a basic biography of the writer." Buys 4-5 unsolicited mss/year. Query. Length: 400-4,500 words. Pays $50-400. Sometimes pays the expenses of writers on assignment.
Photos: Send photos. Pay varies for b&w or color prints. Model release required.
Columns/Departments: Art, business, food and drink, politics, sports and theatre. Buys 2-3 columns/issue. Query. Length: 1,000-2,000 words. Pays $100-175.
Tips: "It makes sense to start small—something for our City Journal section, perhaps. Stories for that section run between 400-1,000 words."

NORTHERN OHIO LIVE, LIVE Publishing Co., 11320 Juniper Rd., Cleveland OH 44106. (216)721-1800. Fax: (216)721-2525. E-mail: nohiolive@aol.com. Managing Editor: Anton Zuiker. 70% freelance written. Monthly magazine covering Northern Ohio's arts, entertainment, education and dining. "*LIVE*'s reader demographic is mid-30s to 50s, though we're working to bring in the late 20s. Our readers are well-educated, many with advanced degrees. They're interested in Northern Ohio's cultural scene and support it." Estab. 1980. Circ. 32,000. Pays 20th of publication month. Publishes ms an average of 1 month after acceptance. Byline given. Offers 50% kill fee. Buys first North American serial rights. Editorial lead time 2 months. Submit seasonal material 4 months in advance. Reports in 3 weeks on queries; 2 months on mss. Sample copy for $3.

Nonfiction: Essays, exposé, general interest, humor, interview/profile, photo feature, travel. All should have a Northern Ohio slant and preferably an arts focus. Special issues: Gourmet Guide (restaurants), (May); Gallery Tour (May, October); After 5 (nightlife) (November). "No business/corporate articles, stories outside Northern Ohio." Buys 100 mss/year. Query with published clips. Length: 1,000-3,500 words. Pays $100-350. Sometimes pays expenses of writers on assignment.

Photos: State availability of photos with submission. Reviews contact sheets, 4×5 transparencies and 3×5 prints. Negotiates payment individually. Identification of subjects required. Buys one-time rights.

Columns/Departments: News & Reviews (arts previews, personality profiles, general interest), 800-1,800 words. Buys 60-70 mss/year. Query with published clips. Pays $100-150.

OHIO MAGAZINE, Ohio Magazine, Inc., Subsidiary of Dispatch Printing Co., 62 E. Broad St., Columbus OH 43215-3522. (614)461-5083. Editor: Jean P. Kelly. 70% freelance written. Works with a small number of new/unpublished writers each year. Monthly magazine emphasizing news and feature material of Ohio for an educated, urban and urbane readership. Estab. 1978. Circ. 100,000. Pays on publication. Publishes ms an average of 6 months after acceptance. Buys all, second serial (reprint), one-time, first North American serial or first serial rights. Byline given except on short articles appearing in sections. Submit seasonal material minimum 6 months in advance. Reports in 3 months. Sample copy for $3 and 9×12 SAE. Writer's guidelines for #10 SASE.

Nonfiction: Features: 2,000-8,000 words. Pays $800-1,400. Cover pieces $650-1,200. Sometimes pays expenses of writers on assignment.

Columns/Departments: Ohioans (should be offbeat with solid news interest; 1,000-2,000 words, pays $300-500); Business (covering business related news items, profiles of prominent people in business community—all Ohio angle; 1,000 words and up, pays $300-500); Environment (issues related to Ohio and Ohioans, 1,000-2,000 words, pays $400-700). Buys minimum 20 unsolicited mss/year.

Reprints: Accepts previously published submissions. Send tearsheet or photocopy of article and information about when and where it previously appeared. Pays 50% of amount paid for an original article.

Photos: Brooke Wenstrup, art director. Rate negotiable.

Tips: "Freelancers should send all queries in writing, not by telephone or fax. Subject matter should be global enough to appeal to readers outside of Ohio, but regional enough to call our own."

OVER THE BACK FENCE, Southern Ohio's Own Magazine, Back Fence Publishing, Inc., P.O. Box 756, Chillicothe OH 45601. (614)772-2165. Editor-in-Chief: Ann Zalek. Quarterly magazine covering regional history, people, events, etc. "We are a regional magazine serving 18 counties in Southern Ohio. *Over The Back Fence* has a wholesome, neighborly style. It appeals to readers from young adults to seniors, often encouraging reader participation through replies." Estab. 1994. Circ. 15,000. Pays on publication. Byline given. Buys one-time North American print publication rights, making some work-for-hire assignments. Editorial lead time 1 year. Submit seasonal material 1 year in advance. Accepts simultaneous submissions, if so noted. Reports in 3 months. Sample copy for $4. Writer's guidelines for #10 SASE.

Nonfiction: General interest, historical/nostalgic, humor, inspirational, interview/profile, personal exprience, photo feature, travel. Buys 9-12 mss/year. Query with or without published clips or send complete ms. Length: 750-2,000 words. Pays 10¢/word minimum, negotiable depending on experience.

Reprints: Accepts previously published submissions.

Photos: State availability of photos with submission or send photos with submission. Reviews transparencies (35mm or larger), 3⅓×5 prints and b&w contact sheets. Offers $25-100/photo. Captions, model releases and identification of subjects required. Buys one-time usage rights. "Our format changed from black and white to color. If photos are sent as part of a text/photo package, please request our new photo guidelines and submit color transparencies."

Columns/Departments: The Arts, 750-2,000 words; History (relevant to a designated county), 750-2,000 words; Inspirational (poetry or short story), minimum for poetry 4 lines, short story 600-850 words; Recipes, 750-2,000 words; Profiles From Our Past, approx. 300-600 words; Sport & Hobby, 750-2,000 words; Our Neighbors (i.e. people helping others), 750-2,000 words. All must be relevant to Southern Ohio. Buys 24 mss/year. Query with or without published clips or send complete ms. Pays 10¢/word minimum, negotiable depending on experience; 10¢/word or minimum $25 whichever is greater for poetry.

Fiction: Humorous. Buys 4 mss/year. Query with published clips. Length: 300-850 words. Pays 10¢/word minimum, negotiable depending on experience.

Poetry: Wholesome, traditional free verse, light verse and rhyming. Buys 4 poems/year. Submit maximum 4 poems. Length: 4-32 lines preferred. Pays 10¢/word or a $25 minimum.

Fillers: Anecdotes, short humor. Buys 0-8/year. Length: 100 words maximum. Pays 10¢/word or a $25 minimum.

Tips: "Our approach can be equated to a friendly and informative conversation with a neighbor about interesting people, places and events in Southern Ohio (counties: Adams, Athens, Clinton, Fayette, Fairfield,

Gallia, Greene, Highland, Hocking, Jackson, Lawrence, Meigs, Pickaway, Pike, Ross, Scioto, Vinton and Washington)."

PLAIN DEALER MAGAZINE, Plain Dealer Publishing Co., 1801 Superior Ave., Cleveland OH 44114. (216)344-4546. Fax: (216)999-6354. Editor: Anne Gordon. 30% freelance written. Sunday weekly/general interest newspaper magazine focusing on Cleveland and northeastern Ohio. Circ. 550,000. Pays on publication. Publishes ms an average of 3 months after acceptance. Byline given. Buys first or one-time rights. Submit seasonal/holiday material 3 months in advance. Reports in 1 month on queries; 2 months on mss. Sample copy for $1.
Nonfiction: Profiles, in-depth features, essays, exposé, historical/nostalgic, humor, personal experience. Must focus on northeast Ohio, people, places and issues of the area. Buys 20 mss/year. Query with published clips or send complete ms. Manuscripts must be double-spaced and should include a daytime telephone number. Length: 800-3,000 words. Pays $150-500.
Reprints: Occasionally accepts previously published submissions. Send typed ms with rights for sale noted and information about when and where the article previously appeared.
Photos: Send photos with submission. Buys one-time rights.
Tips: "We're always looking for good writers and good stories."

Oklahoma

OKLAHOMA TODAY, P.O. Box 53384, Oklahoma City OK 73152-9971. Fax: (405)521-3992. Editor: Jeanne M. Devlin. 80% freelance written. Works with a small number of new/unpublished writers each year. Bimonthly magazine covering people, places and things Oklahoman. "We are interested in showing off the best Oklahoma has to offer; we're pretty serious about our travel slant but regularly run history, nature and personality profiles." Estab. 1956. Circ. 45,000. **Pays on final acceptance.** Publishes ms an average of 6 months after acceptance. Byline given. Buys first serial rights. Submit seasonal material 1 year in advance "depending on photographic requirements." Reports in 4 months. Sample copy for $2.50 and 9×12 SASE. Writer's guidelines for #10 SASE.
   ● *Oklahoma Today* has won Magazine of the Year, awarded by the International Regional Magazine Association, three out of the last five years.
Nonfiction: Book excerpts (on Oklahoma topics); photo feature and travel (in Oklahoma). Buys 40-60 mss/year. Query with published clips; no phone queries. Length: 1,000-3,000 words. Pays $25-750.
Reprints: Send tearsheet of article or typed ms with rights for sale noted and information about when and where the article previously appeared. Pay varies.
Photos: High-quality transparencies, b&w prints. "We are especially interested in developing contacts with photographers who either live in Oklahoma or have shot here. Send samples and price range." Free photo guidelines with SASE. Pays $50-100 for b&w and $50-750 for color; reviews 2¼ and 35mm color transparencies. Model releases, identification of subjects, other information for captions required. Buys one-time rights plus right to use photos for promotional purposes.
Tips: "The best way to become a regular contributor to *Oklahoma Today* is to query us with one or more story ideas, each developed to give us an idea of your proposed slant. We're looking for *lively*, concise, well-researched and reported stories, stories that don't need to be heavily edited and are not newspaper style. We have a two-person editorial staff, and freelancers who can write and have done their homework get called again and again."

Oregon

CASCADES EAST, P.O. Box 5784, Bend OR 97708-5784. (541)382-0127. Fax: (541)382-7057. Publisher: Geoff Hill. Associate publisher/Editor: Kim Hogue. 90% freelance written. Prefers to work with published/established writers. Quarterly magazine for "all ages as long as they are interested in outdoor recreation in central Oregon: fishing, hunting, sight-seeing, golf, tennis, hiking, bicycling, mountain climbing, backpacking, rockhounding, skiing, snowmobiling, etc." Estab. 1972. Circ. 10,000 (distributed throughout area resorts and motels and to subscribers). Pays on publication. Publishes ms an average of 6 months after acceptance. Buys all rights. Byline given. Submit seasonal material 6 months in advance. Reports in 3 months. Sample copy and writer's guidelines for $5 and 9×12 SAE.
   ● *Cascades East* now accepts and prefers manuscripts along with a 3.5 disk. They can translate most word processing programs.
Nonfiction: General interest (first person experiences in outdoor central Oregon—with photos, can be dramatic, humorous or factual), historical (for feature, "Little Known Tales from Oregon History," with b&w photos), personal experience (needed on outdoor subjects: dramatic, humorous or factual). "No articles that are too general, sight-seeing articles that come from a travel folder, or outdoor articles without the first-

person approach." Buys 20-30 unsolicited mss/year. Query. Length: 1,000-3,000 words. Pays 5-10¢/word.
Reprints: Send information about when and where the article previously appeared.
Photos: "Old photos will greatly enhance chances of selling a historical feature. First-person articles need b&w photos, also." Pays $10-25 for b&w; $15-100 for transparencies. Captions preferred. Buys one-time rights.
Tips: "Submit stories a year or so in advance of publication. We are seasonal and must plan editorials for summer '97 in the spring of '96, etc., in case seasonal photos are needed."

OREGON COAST, P.O. Box 18000, 1525 12st St., Florence OR 97439-0130. (541)997-8401 or (800)348-8401. Website: http://www.Oregon-Coast.com. Editors: Judy Fleagle and Jim Forst. 65% freelance written. Bimonthly magazine covering the Oregon Coast. Estab. 1982. Circ. 65,000. Pays after publication. Publishes ms an average of 1 year after acceptance. Byline given. Offers 33% kill fee. Buys first North American serial rights. Submit seasonal material 6 months in advance. Reports in 1 month on queries; 3 months on mss. Sample copy for $4.50. Writer's guidelines for #10 SASE.
 • This magazine is using fewer freelancers because its staff is doing more writing inhouse.
Nonfiction: "A true regional with general interest, historical/nostalgic, humor, interview/profile, personal experience, photo feature, travel and nature as pertains to Oregon Coast." Buys 55 mss/year. Query with published clips. Length: 500-2,000 words. Pays $75-350 plus 2-5 contributor copies.
Reprints: Sometimes accepts previously published submissions. Enclose clips. Send tearsheet or photocopy of article and information about when and where the articles previously appeared.
Photos: Send photos with submission. Reviews 35mm or larger transparencies and 3×5 or larger prints (with negatives for color). Photo submissions with no ms for stand alone or cover photos. Captions, model releases (for covers), photo credits, identification of subjects required. Buys one-time rights.
Fillers: Newsbreaks (no-fee basis).
Tips: "Slant article for readers who do not live at the Oregon Coast. At least one historical article is used in each issue. Manuscript/photo packages are preferred over mss with no photos. List photo credits and captions for each print or slide. Check all facts, proper names and numbers carefully in photo/ms packages. Need stories with great color photos—could be photo essays. Must pertain to Oregon Coast somehow."

WILLAMETTE WEEK, Portland's Newsweekly, City of Roses Co., 822 SW Tenth Ave., Portland OR 97205. (503)243-2122. Fax: (503)243-1115. E-mail: ngollogly@wweek.com. Website: http://www.wweek.com. Editor: Mark Zusman. 50% freelance written. Weekly alternative newsweekly focusing on local news. Estab. 1974. Circ. 75,000. Pays on publication. Byline given. Offers 25% kill fee. Buys first North American serial rights. Editorial lead time 2 months. Submit seasonal material 2 months in advance. Accepts simultaneous submissions. Reports in 1 month. Sample copy and writer's guidelines for #10 SASE.
Nonfiction: Exposé, interview/profile. Special issues: Summer Guide, Best of Portland, Fall Arts, 21st Anniversary. Buys 30 mss/year. Query. Length: 400-3,000 words. Pays 10-30¢/word. Sometimes pays expenses of writers on assignment.
Reprints: Accepts previously published submissions.
Photos: State availability of photos with submission. Reviews contact sheets. Negotiates payment individually. Model releases, identification of subjects required. Buys one-time rights.

Pennsylvania

PENNSYLVANIA, Pennsylvania Magazine Co., P.O. Box 576, Camp Hill PA 17001-0576. (717)761-6620. Publisher: Albert E. Holliday. Managing Editor: Matt Holliday. 90% freelance written. Bimonthly magazine. Estab. 1981. Circ. 40,000. Pays on acceptance except for articles (by authors unknown to us) sent on speculation. Publishes ms an average of 1 year after acceptance. Byline given. Offers 25% kill fee for assigned articles. Buys first North American serial or one-time rights. Reports in 1 month. Sample copy for $2.95. Writer's guidelines for #10 SASE.
Nonfiction: General interest, historical/nostalgic, photo feature, travel—all dealing with or related to Pennsylvania. Nothing on Amish topics, hunting or skiing. Buys 75-120 mss/year. Query. Length: 250-2,500 words. Pays $50-400. Sometimes pays the expenses of writers on assignment. All articles must be illustrated; send photocopies of possible illustrations with query or mss. *Will not consider without illustrations.*
Reprints: Send photocopy of article, typed ms with rights for sale noted and information about when and where the article previously appeared. Pays 50% of amount paid for an original article.
Photos: Reviews 35mm and 2¼ color transparencies (no originals) and 5×7 to 8×10 color and b&w prints. Do not send original slides. Pays $15-25 for inside photos; up to $100 for covers. Captions required. Buys one-time rights.
Columns/Departments: Panorama (short items about people, unusual events, family and individually owned consumer-related businesses); Almanac (short historical items). All must be illustrated.
Tips: "Our publication depends upon freelance work—send queries."

PENNSYLVANIA HERITAGE, Pennsylvania Historical and Museum Commission, P.O. Box 1026, Harrisburg PA 17108-1026. (717)787-7522. Fax: (717)787-8312. Website: http://www.state.pa.us. Editor: Michael J. O'Malley III. 90% freelance written. Prefers to work with published/established writers. Quarterly magazine. "*Pennsylvania Heritage* introduces readers to Pennsylvania's rich culture and historic legacy, educates and sensitizes them to the value of preserving that heritage and entertains and involves them in such as way as to ensure that Pennsylvania's past has a future. The magazine is intended for intelligent lay readers." Estab. 1974. Circ. 10,000. **Pays on acceptance.** Publishes ms an average of 1 year after acceptance. Byline given. Buys all rights. Accepts simultaneous queries and submissions. Reports in 6 weeks on queries; 6 months on mss. Sample copy for $4.50 and 9×12 SAE; writer's guidelines for #10 SASE.

• *Pennsylvania Heritage* is now considering freelance submissions that are shorter in length (2,000 to 3,000 words), pictorial/photographic essays, biographies of famous (and not-so-famous Pennsylvanians) and interviews with individuals who have helped shape, make, preserve the Keystone State's history and heritage.

Nonfiction: Art, science, biographies, industry, business, politics, transportation, military, historic preservation, archaeology, photography, etc. No articles which in no way relate to Pennsylvania history or culture. "Our format requires feature-length articles. Manuscripts with illustrations are especially sought for publication. We are now looking for shorter (2,000 words) manuscripts that are heavily illustrated with *publication-quality* photographs or artwork." Buys 20-24 mss/year. Prefers to see mss with suggested illustrations. Length: 2,000-3,500 words. Pays $100-500.

Photos: State availability of, or send photos with ms. Pays $25-100 for transparencies; $5-10 for b&w photos. Captions and identification of subjects required. Buys one-time rights.

Tips: "We are looking for well-written, interesting material that pertains to any aspect of Pennsylvania history or culture. Potential contributors should realize that, although our articles are popularly styled, they are not light, puffy or breezy; in fact they demand strident documentation and substantiation (sans footnotes). The most frequent mistake made by writers in completing articles for us is making them either too scholarly or too nostalgic. We want material which educates, but also entertains. Authors should make history readable and enjoyable."

PITTSBURGH MAGAZINE, WQED Pittsburgh, 4802 5th Ave., Pittsburgh PA 15213. (412)622-1360. Fax: (412)622-7066. Contact: Michelle Pilecki, managing editor. 60% freelance written. Prefers to work with published/established writers. The magazine is purchased on newsstands and by subscription and is given to those who contribute $40 or more a year to public TV in western Pennsylvania. Estab. 1970. Circ. 65,000. Pays on publication. Publishes ms an average of 2 months after acceptance. Buys first North American serial rights and second serial (reprint) rights. Offers kill fee. Byline given. Submit seasonal material 6 months in advance. Reports in 2 months. Sample copy for $2 (old back issues).

• Editor reports a need for more hard news and more stories geared to young readers.

Nonfiction: Exposé, lifestyle, sports, informational, service, business, medical, profile. Must have regional angle. Query in writing with outline. Length: 3,500 words or less. Pays $100-1,200.

Photos: Query for photos. Model releases required. Pays pre-negotiated expenses of writers on assignment.

Tips: "Less need for soft stories, e.g. feature profiles and historical pieces. Expanded need for service pieces geared to our region. More hard news."

SEVEN ARTS, Penn Communications Group, 260 S. Broad St., 3rd Floor, Philadelphia PA 19102. E-mail: editorial@sevenarts.voicenet.com. Website: http://sevenarts.voicenet.com. Editor: Virginia Moles. Executive Editor: Judith West. 25% freelance written. Monthly magazine covering arts and culture. "*Seven Arts* magazine aims to stimulate interest in the arts in the Philadelphia region." Estab. 1993. Circ. 135,000. Pays on publication. Publishes ms an average of 3 months after acceptance. Byline given. Offers 20% kill fee. Buys first North American serial rights. Editorial lead time 2 months. Submit seasonal material 6 months in advance. Accepts simultaneous submissions. Reports in 3 months. Sample copy free.

Nonfiction: Book excerpts, interview/profile, events-related. No non-arts related material. Buys 25 mss/year. Query with published clips. Length: 800-2,000 words. Pays $200-700. Sometimes pays expenses of writers on assignment.

Reprints: Accepts previously published submissions.

Photos: State availability of photos with submission. Reviews contact sheets. Negotiates payment individually. Captions, model releases and identification of subjects required. Buys one-time rights.

Columns/Departments: Theater, Music, Dance, Art, Film, Literature; 500 words. Buys 25 mss/year. Query with published clips. Pays $200.

Tips: "Consider breaking in with small, front-of-the-book pieces; pitch ideas for specific sections of the magazine; hook to specific cultural events."

Rhode Island

NEWPORT LIFE, 174 Bellevue Ave., Suite 207, Newport RI 02840. Fax: (401)847-5267. Editor: Susan Ryan. 90% freelance written. Quarterly magazine covering Newport County's people, history and general interest. "*Newport Life* is a community magazine focusing on the people, issues, history and events that make Newport County unique." Estab. 1993. Circ. 10,000. Pays on publication. Publishes ms an average of 3 months after acceptance. Byline given. Offers 20% kill fee. Buys one-time rights. Editorial lead time 1 year. Submit seasonal material 6 months in advance. Accepts simultaneous submissions. Reports in 1 month. Writer's guidelines for #10 SASE.

Nonfiction: General interest, historical/nostalgic, interview/profile, opinion, photo feature. Buys 20 mss/ year. Query with published clips. Length: 650-3,000 words. Pays $65-300 for assigned articles. Sometimes pays expenses of writers on assignment.

Reprints: Accepts previously published submissions.

Photos: State availability of photos with submission. Reviews 3×5 prints. Negotiates payment individually. Captions, model releases, identification of subjects required. Buys one-time rights.

Columns/Departments: Historical Newport (person or aspect of Newport County's history), 750-1,000 words; In Our Midst (local individuals who've made contribution to community), 650 words; At The Helm (significant person in the boating industry), 500 words; Arts Marquee (local artisans), 650 words. Buys 24 mss/year. Query with published clips. Pays $65-100.

Tips: "Articles should be specific, informative and thoroughly researched. Historical information and quotes are encouraged. New/unpublished writers welcome. Query with lead paragraph and outline of story."

South Carolina

CHARLESTON MAGAZINE, P.O. Box 1794, Mt. Pleasant SC 29465-1794. (803)971-9811. Fax: (803)971-0121. E-mail: gulfstream@awod.com. Contact: Patrick Sharbaugh, editor. Assistant Editor: Jennifer MacKenzie. 80% freelance written. Bimonthly magazine covering current issues, events, arts and culture, leisure pursuits, personalities as they pertain to the city of Charleston. "Consumer magazine with a general focus on the city and her residents; each issue reflects an essential element of Charleston life and Lowcountry living." Estab. 1986. Circ. 20,000. Pays 30 days after publication. Publishes ms an average of 3 months after acceptance. Byline given. Buys one-time rights. Submit seasonal material 4 months in advance. Reports in 1 month. Sample copies for 9×12 SAE with 5 first-class stamps. Free writer's guidelines.

Nonfiction: General interest, humor, food, architecture, sports, interview/profile, opinion, photo feature, travel, current events/issues, art. "Not interested in 'Southern nostalgia' articles or gratuitous history pieces. Must pertain to the Charleston area and its present culture." Buys 50 mss/year. Query with published clips. Length: 150-1,500 words. Pays 15¢/published word. Sometimes pays expenses of writers on assignment.

Photos: Send photos with submission if available. Reviews contact sheets, transparencies, slides. Offers $35/photo maximum. Identification of subjects required. Buys one-time rights.

Columns/Departments: Channel Markers (general local interest), 200-400 words; Spotlight (profile of local interest), 300-400 words; The Home Front (interiors, renovations and gardens), 1,000 words; Sporting Life (humorous, adventurous tales of life outdoors), 1,000-1,200 words; Dining (restaurants and culinary trends in the city), 1,000-1,200 words; On the Road (travel opportunities near Charleston), 1,000-1,200 words.

Tips: "Charleston, although a city with a 300-year history, is a vibrant, modern community with a tremendous dedication to the arts and no shortage of newsworthy subjects. Don't bother submitting coffee-table magazine-style pieces. Areas most open to freelancers are Columns/Departments and features. Should be of local interest. We're looking for the freshest stories about Charleston—and those don't always come from insiders, but outsiders who are keenly observant."

SANDLAPPER, The Magazine of South Carolina, The Sandlapper Society, Inc., P.O. Box 1108, Lexington SC 29071-1108. (803)359-9954. Fax: (803)957-8226. Contact: Dolly Patton, executive director. Editor: Robert P. Wilkins. Managing Editor: Daniel E. Harmon. 35% freelance written. Quarterly feature magazine focusing on the positive aspects of South Carolina. Estab. 1989. Circ. 5,000. Pays during the dateline period. Publishes ms an average of 4 months after acceptance. Byline given. Buys first North American serial rights and the right to reprint. Submit seasonal material 6 months in advance. Query for electronic submissions. Free writer's guidelines.

Nonfiction: Feature articles and photo essays about South Carolina's interesting people, places, cuisine, things to do. Occasional history articles. Query. Length: 600-5,000 words. Pays $50-500. Sometimes pays the expenses of writers on assignment.

Tips: "We're not interested in articles about topical issues, politics, crime or commercial ventures. Humorous angles are encouraged. Avoid first-person nostalgia and remembrances of places that no longer exist."

South Dakota

DAKOTA OUTDOORS, South Dakota, Hipple Publishing Co., P.O. Box 669, 333 W. Dakota Ave., Pierre SD 57501-0669. (605)224-7301. Fax: (605)224-9210. E-mail: 73613.3456. Editor: Kevin Hipple.

Contact: Rachel Engbrecht, managing editor. 50% freelance written. Monthly magazine on Dakota outdoor life. Estab. 1975. Circ. 6,500. Pays on publication. Publishes ms an average of 2 months after acceptance. Byline given. Submit seasonal material 3 months in advance. Accepts simultaneous submissions. Reports in 3 months. Sample copy for 9×12 SAE with 3 first-class stamps.

Nonfiction: General interest, how-to, humor, interview/profile, new product, opinion, personal experience, photo feature, technical (all on outdoor topics—prefer in Dakotas). Buys 50 mss/year. Query with or without published clips, or send complete ms. Length: 200-1,000 words. Pays $5-50 for assigned articles; $40 maximum for unsolicited articles. Sometimes pays in contributor copies or other premiums (inquire).

Reprints: Send typed ms with rights for sale noted and information about when and where the article previously appeared. Pays 50% of amount paid for an original article.

Photos: Send photos with submission. Reviews 5×7 prints. Offers no additional payment for photos accepted with ms. Identification of subjects preferred. Buys one-time rights.

Fiction: Occasionally publishes novel excerpts.

Fillers: Anecdotes, facts, gags to be illustrated by cartoonist, newsbreaks, short humor. Buys 10/year. Also publishes line drawings of fish and game. Prefers 5×7 prints.

Tips: "Submit samples of manuscript or previous works for consideration; photos or illustrations with manuscript are helpful."

Tennessee

MEMPHIS, Contemporary Media, P.O. Box 256, Memphis TN 38101-0256. (901)521-9000. Fax: (901)521-0129. Editor: Tim Sampson. Contact: Michael Finger, senior editor. 60% freelance written. Works with a small number of new/unpublished writers. Estab. 1976. Circ. 21,917. Pays on publication. Publishes ms an average of 3 months after acceptance. Byline given. Buys first North American serial rights. Offers 20% kill fee. Accepts simultaneous submissions. Reports in 2 months. Sample copy for 9×12 SAE with 9 first-class stamps. Writer's guidelines for SASE.

Nonfiction: Exposé, general interest, historical, how-to, humor, interview, profile. "Virtually all of our material has strong Memphis area connections." Buys 25 freelance mss/year. Query or submit complete ms or published clips. Length: 500-5,000 words. Pays $50-500. Sometimes pays expenses of writers on assignment.

Tips: "The kinds of manuscripts we most need have a sense of story (i.e., plot, suspense, character), an abundance of evocative images to bring that story alive, and a sensitivity to issues at work in Memphis. The most frequent mistakes made by writers in completing an article for us are lack of focus, lack of organization, factual gaps and failure to capture the magazine's style. Tough investigative pieces would be especially welcomed."

Texas

TEXAS HIGHWAYS, Official Travel Magazine of Texas, Texas Department of Transportation, Box 141009, Austin TX 78714-1009. (512)483-3675. Fax: (512)483-3672. Editor: Jack Lowry. Managing Editor: Jill Lawless. 70% freelance written. Prefers to work with published/established writers. Monthly tourist magazine covering travel and history for Texas only. **Pays on acceptance.** Publishes ms an average of 10 months after acceptance. Byline given. Offers $100 kill fee. Buys one-time rights. Submit seasonal/holiday material 1 year in advance. Reports in 1 month on queries. Sample copy and writer's guidelines for 9×12 SAE with 3 first-class stamps.

Nonfiction: Historical/nostalgic, photo feature and travel. Must be concerned with travel in Texas. Send material on "what to see, what to do, where to go in *Texas*." Material must be tourist-oriented. "No disaster features." Buys 75 mss/year. Query with published clips. Length: 1,000-2,000 words. Pays $400-1,000. Sometimes pays expenses of writers on assignment "after we have worked with them awhile."

Photos: Michael A. Murphy, photo editor. Send photos with query or ms. Pays upon publication $80 for less than half a page, $120 for half page, $170 for a full page, $400 for front cover, $300 for back cover. Accepts 35mm and large original color transparencies. Captions and identification of subjects required. Buys one-time rights.

TEXAS PARKS & WILDLIFE, 3000 South I.H. 35, Suite 120, Austin TX 78704. (512)912-7000. Fax: (512)707-1913. E-mail: jim.cox@tpwd.state.tx.us. Website: http://www.state.tx.us. Editor: David Baxter. Managing Editor: Mary-Love Bigony. Contact: Jim Cox, senior editor. 80% freelance written. Monthly magazine featuring articles about Texas hunting, fishing, outdoor recreation, game and nongame wildlife, state parks, environmental issues. All articles must be about Texas. Estab. 1942. Circ. 180,000. **Pays on acceptance.** Publishes ms an average of 6 months after acceptance. Byline given. Kill fee determined by editor, usually $200-250. Buys first rights. Submit seasonal material 6 months in advance. Reports in 1 month on queries; 3 months on mss. Free sample copy and writer's guidelines.

● *Texas Parks & Wildlife* needs more hunting and fishing material.

Nonfiction: Jim Cox, articles editor. General interest (Texas only), historical/nostalgic, how-to (outdoor activities), interview/profile, photo feature, travel (state parks). Buys 60 mss/year. Query with published clips. Length: 250-2,500 words. Pays $600 maximum.

Photos: Send photos with submission. Reviews transparencies. Offers $65-350/photo. Captions and identification of subjects required. Buys one-time rights.

Columns/Departments: Buys 6 mss/year. Query with published clips. Pays $100-300. Monthly departments: hunting and fishing, the environment, photo column, places to go. Maximum 1,000 words.

Tips: "Read outdoor pages of statewide newspapers to keep abreast of news items that can lead to story ideas. Feel free to include more than one story idea in one query letter. All areas are open to freelancers. All articles must have a Texas focus."

UPTOWN EXPRESS, Up & Out Communications, 3406 Audubon Place, Houston TX 77006. (713)520-7237. Contact: Greg Jeu, publisher. 70% freelance written. Bimonthly magazine covering holistic community. "*Uptown Express* provides information for personal growth and awareness; information on Houston's holistic community, human potential, spirituality and creativity." Estab. 1985. Circ. 32,000. Pays on publication. Publishes ms an average of 2 months after acceptance. Byline given. Buys one-time rights and simultaneous rights. Editorial lead time 2 months. Submit seasonal material 2 months in advance. Accepts simultaneous submissions. Reports in 6 weeks on queries, 2 months on mss. Sample copy and writer's guidelines for SASE.

Nonfiction: Book excerpts, inspirational, interview/profile, new product. Buys 10 mss/year. Send complete ms. Length: 700-4,000 words. Pays $20-60.

Reprints: Accepts previously published submissions.

Photos: State availability of photos with submission. Reviews 4×6 prints. Negotiates payment individually. Identification of subjects required. Buys one-time rights.

Utah

SALT LAKE CITY, 1270 West 2320 S., Suite A, Salt Lake City UT 84119-1449. (801)975-1927. Fax: (801)975-1982. E-mail: slmagazine@aol.com. Editor: Michael Phillips. Contact: Barry Scholl, associate editor. Art Director: Scott Perry. 60% freelance written. Bimonthly magazine. "Ours is a lifestyle magazine, focusing on the people, issues and places that make Utah and the Intermountain West unique. Our audience is mainly educated, affluent, ages 25-55. Again, we focus heavily on people." Estab. 1989. Circ. 18,000. Pays on publication. Publishes ms an average of 6 months after acceptance. Byline given. Offers $25 kill fee. Buys first North American serial or second serial (reprint) rights. Submit seasonal material 6 months in advance. Accepts simultaneous submissions. Reports in 3 months on mss. Free sample copy and writer's guidelines.

Nonfiction: Essays (health, family matters, financial), general interest, historical/nostalgic (pertaining to Utah and Intermountain West), humor, interview/profile (famous or powerful people associated with Utah business, politics, media), personal experience, photo feature, travel. "No movie reviews or current news subjects, please." Even essays need a tight local angle. Buys 5 mss/year. Query with published clips or send complete ms. Follows Chicago style. Length: 800-2,000 words. Pays $75-400 for assigned articles; $75-250 for unsolicited articles. "A major feature is negotiable."

Reprints: Send photocopy or typed ms with rights for sale noted and information about when and where the article previously appeared.

Photos: Send photos with submission. Reviews transparencies (size not important). Captions, model releases, identification of subjects required. Payment and rights negotiable. Don't send original negs/transparencies unless requested.

Columns/Departments: Up Close (standard personality profile), 1,200-1,500 words; Q & A of famous person, 1,200-1,500 words; Executive Signature (profile, business slant of major Utah entrepeneur); and Food (recipes must be included), 1,000-1,500 words. Buys 5-10 mss/year. Query with published clips or send complete ms. Pays $75-250.

● No longer accepting fiction and poetry. Also, more articles are being produced in-house. They are overstocked on general travel pieces and are focusing on travel pieces on the intermountain West.

Tips: "We are looking for well-written, well-researched, complete manuscripts. Writers are advised to refer to a sample issue before submitting work. *Salt Lake City* magazine is most interested in unique, people-oriented profiles, historical pieces and stories of local interest. For instance, the magazine has covered local recreation, child abuse, education, air pollution, health care issues, wilderness, militias and local personalities. The majority of our stories are focused on Utah and the West. Please write for a free sample issue if you have never read our magazine."

Vermont

VERMONT LIFE MAGAZINE, 6 Baldwin St., Montpelier VT 05602-2109. (802)828-3241. E-mail: vtlife mag@aol.com. Website: http://www.state.vt.us/rtlife. Editor-in-Chief: Thomas K. Slayton. 90% freelance written. Prefers to work with published/established writers. Quarterly magazine. Estab. 1946. Circ. 90,000. Publishes an average of 9 months after acceptance. Byline given. Offers kill fee. Buys first serial rights. Submit seasonal material 1 year in advance. Reports in 1 month. Writer's guidelines for #10 SASE.
  • Ranked as one of the best markets for freelance writers in *Writer's Yearbook*'s annual "Top 100 Markets," January 1996.
Nonfiction: Wants articles on today's Vermont, those which portray a typical or, if possible, unique aspect of the state or its people. Style should be literate, clear and concise. Subtle humor favored. No "Vermont clichés"—maple syrup, town meetings or stereotyped natives. Buys 60 mss/year. Query by letter essential. Length: 1,500 words average. Pays 20¢/word. Seldom pays expenses of writers on assignment.
Photos: Buys photographs with mss; buys seasonal photographs alone. Prefers b&w contact sheets to look at first on assigned material. Color submissions must be 4×5 or 35mm transparencies. Pays $75-150 inside color; $200 for cover. Gives assignments but only with experienced photographers. Query in writing. Captions, model releases, identification of subjects required. Buys one-time rights, but often negotiates for reuse rights.
Fiction: Publishes novel excerpts.
Tips: "Writers who read our magazine are given more consideration because they understand that we want authentic articles about Vermont. If a writer has a genuine working knowledge of Vermont, his or her work usually shows it. Vermont is changing and there is much concern here about what this state will be like in years ahead. It is a beautiful, environmentally sound place now and the vast majority of residents want to keep it so. Articles reflecting such concerns in an intelligent, authoritative, non-hysterical way will be given very careful consideration. The growth of tourism makes *Vermont Life* interested in intelligent articles about specific places in Vermont, their history and attractions to the traveling public."

VERMONT MAGAZINE, 2 Maple St., Suite 400, Middlebury VT 05753. (802)388-8480. Managing Editor: Julie Kirgo. Bimonthly magazine about Vermont. Estab. 1989. Buys first North American serial rights. Editorial lead time 6 months. Reports in 2 weeks. Writer's guidelines for #10 SASE.
Nonfiction: Journalism and reporting, book excerpts (pre- or post-book publication), essays, exposé, general interest, how-to, humor, interview/profile, photo feature, calendar. All material must be about contemporary Vermont. Buys 30 mss/year but most are assigned by the editor. Query with published clips. Length: 900-3,500 words. Pays $200-800. Sometimes pays expenses of writers on assignment. Rarely publishes reprints.
Photos: Vermont subjects a must. Send photos and illustrations to Carolyn Brown, art director. Reviews contact sheets, 35mm transparencies, 8×10 b&w prints. Captions, model releases (if possible), identification of subjects required. Buys one-time rights.
Fiction: Publishes novel excerpts and stories about Vermont (1-2/year, maximum).
Tips: "Our readers *know* their state well, and they know the 'real' Vermont can't be slipped inside a glib and glossy brochure. We're interested in serious journalism on major issues, plus coverage of arts, outdoors, living, nature, architecture."

Virginia

THE ROANOKER, Leisure Publishing Co., 3424 Brambleton Ave., P.O. Box 21535, Roanoke VA 24018-9900. (703)989-6138. Fax: (703)989-7603. Editor: Kurt Rheinheimer. 75% freelance written. Works with a small number of new/unpublished writers each year. Magazine published 10 times/year covering people and events of Western Virginia. "*The Roanoker* is a general interest city magazine edited for the people of Roanoke, Virginia and the surrounding area. Our readers are primarily upper-income, well-educated professionals between the ages of 35 and 60. Coverage ranges from hard news and consumer information to restaurant reviews and local history." Estab. 1974. Circ. 14,000. Pays on publication. Publishes ms an average of 4 months after acceptance. Byline given. Buys all rights; makes work-for-hire assignments. Submit seasonal material 4 months in advance. Reports in 2 months. Sample copy for $2 and 9×12 SAE with 5 first-class stamps.
Nonfiction: Exposé, historical/nostalgic, how-to (live better in western Virginia), interview/profile (of well-known area personalities), photo feature, travel (Virginia and surrounding states). "Were looking for more photo feature stories based in western Virginia. We place special emphasis on investigative and exposé articles." Periodic special sections on fashion, real estate, media, banking, investing. Buys 60 mss/year. Query with published clips or send complete ms. Length: 1,400 words maximum. Pays $35-200.
Photos: Send photos with ms. Reviews color transparencies. Pays $5-10 for 5×7 or 8×10 b&w prints; $10 maximum for 5×7 or 8×10 color prints. Captions and model releases required. Rights purchased vary.
Tips: "It helps if freelancer lives in the area. The most frequent mistake made by writers in completing an article for us is not having enough Roanoke-area focus: use of area experts, sources, slants, etc."

Washington

SEATTLE, The Magazine for the Pacific Northwest, Adams Publishing of the Pacific Northwest, 701 Dexter Ave. N, Suite 101, Seattle WA 98109. (206)284-1750. Fax: (206)284-2550. Editor: Giselle Smith. 90% freelance written. Monthly magazine serving the Seattle area and the Pacific Northwest. Articles for the magazine should be written with our readers in mind. They are interested in the arts, social issues, their homes, gardens, travel and in maintaining the region's high quality of life. Estab. 1992. Circ. 70,000. Pays on publication. Publishes ms an average of 4 months after acceptance. Byline given. Offers 33% kill fee. Buys first rights or second serial (reprint) rights. Editorial lead time 3 months. Submit seasonal material 6 months in advance. Reports in 6 weeks on queries; 2 months on mss. Sample copy and writer's guidelines for #10 SASE.
Nonfiction: Book excerpts, general interest, interview/profile, photo feature, local interest. Buys 60-75 mss/year. Query with published clips. Length: 200-2,500 words. Pays $75 minimum for assigned articles; $50 minimum for unsolicited articles. Sometimes pays expenses of writers on assignment.
Photos: State availability of photos with submission. Negotiates payment individually. Buys one-time rights.
Columns/Departments: Northwest Portrait, At Issue, Weekends, Nightlife, Dining, Style, Neighborhood, Private Eye. Query with published clips. Pays $150-300.

SEATTLE WEEKLY, Sasquatch Publishing, 1008 Western Ave., Suite 300, Seattle WA 98104. (206)623-0500. Fax: (206)467-4377. Editor: David Brewster. 20% freelance written. Eager to work with writers in the region. Weekly tabloid covering arts, politics, food, business and books with local and regional emphasis. Estab. 1976. Circ. 70,000. Pays 1 week after publication. Publishes ms an average of 1 month after acceptance. Byline given. Offers variable kill fee. Buys first North American serial rights. Submit seasonal material minimum 2 months in advance. Reports in 1 month. *Writer's Market* recommends allowing 2 months for reply. Sample copy for $2. Writer's guidelines for #10 SASE.
Nonfiction: Book excerpts, exposé, general interest, historical/nostalgic (Northwest), humor, interview/profile, opinion, arts-related essays. Buys 6-8 cover stories/year. Query with résumé and published clips. Length: 700-4,000 words. Pays $75-800. Sometimes pays the expenses of writers on assignment.
Reprints: Send tearsheet of article. Pay varies.
Tips: "The *Seattle Weekly* publishes stories on Northwest politics and art, usually written by regional and local writers, for a mostly upscale, urban audience; writing is high-quality magazine style."

Wisconsin

MILWAUKEE MAGAZINE, 312 E. Buffalo St., Milwaukee WI 53202. (414)273-1101. Fax: (414)273-0016. E-mail: milmag@qgraph.com@inet#. Editor: John Fennell. 40% freelance written. Monthly magazine covering Milwaukee and surrounding region. "We publish stories about Milwaukee, of service to Milwaukee-area residents and exploring the area's changing lifestyle, business, arts, politics and dining." Circ. 40,000. Pays on publication. Publishes ms an average of 2 months after acceptance. Byline given. Offers 20% kill fee. Buys first rights. Submit seasonal material 6 months in advance. Reports in 6 weeks on queries. Sample copy for $4.
Nonfiction: Essays, exposé, general interest, historical, interview/profile, photo feature, travel, food and dining and other services. "No articles without a strong Milwaukee or Wisconsin angle." Buys 30-50 mss/year. Query with published clips. Length: 1,500-5,000 words. Pays $600-1,000. Sometimes pays expenses of writers on assignment.
Photos: Send photos with submission. Reviews contact sheets, negatives, any transparencies and any prints. Offers no set rate per photo. Identification of subjects required. Buys one-time rights.
Columns/Departments: Steve Filmanowicz, departments editor. Insider (inside information on Milwaukee), 200-700 words. Buys 60 mss/year. Query with published clips. Pays $30-125.
Tips: "Pitch something for the Insider, or suggest a compelling profile we haven't already done and submit clips that prove you can do the job. The department most open is Insider. Think short, lively, offbeat, fresh, people-oriented."

‡WISCONSIN TRAILS, P.O. Box 5650, Madison WI 53705-1056. (608)231-2444. Fax: (608)231-1557. Associate Editor: Lucy J. Rhodes. 40% freelance written. Prefers to work with published/established writers. Bimonthly magazine for readers interested in Wisconsin; its contemporary issues, personalities, recreation, history, natural beauty and the arts. Estab. 1959. Circ. 55,000. Buys first serial rights, one-time rights occasionally. Pays on publication. Submit seasonal material at least 1 year in advance. Publishes ms an average of 6 months after acceptance. Byline given. Reports in 2 months. Sample copy for 9 × 12 SAE with 10 first-class stamps. Writer's guidelines for #10 SASE.
Nonfiction: "Our articles focus on some aspect of Wisconsin life; an interesting town or event, a person or industry, history or the arts and especially outdoor recreation. We do not use first-person essays or

biographies about people who were born in Wisconsin but made their fortunes elsewhere. No poetry. No articles that are too local for our regional audience, or articles about obvious places to visit in Wisconsin. We need more articles about the new and little-known." Buys 3 unsolicited mss/year. Query or send outline. Length: 1,000-3,000 words. Pays $150-500 (negotiable), depending on assignment length and quality. Sometimes pays expenses of writers on assignment.

Photos: Purchased with or without mss or on assignment. Uses 35mm transparencies; larger format OK. Color photos usually illustrate an activity, event, region or striking scenery. Prefer photos with people in scenery. Black and white photos usually illustrate a given article. Pays $50 each for b&w on publication. Pays $50-75 for inside color; $100-200 for covers. Captions preferred.

Tips: "We're looking for active articles about people, places, events and outdoor adventures in Wisconsin. We want to publish one in-depth article of state-wide interest or concern per issue, and several short (600-1,500 words) articles about short trips, recreational opportunities, restaurants, inns and cultural activities. We're looking for more articles about out-of-the-way Wisconsin places that are exceptional in some way."

Canada

CANADIAN GEOGRAPHIC, 39 McArthur Ave., Ottawa, Ontario K1L 8L7 Canada. (613)745-4629. Fax: (613)744-0947. E-mail: editorial@cangeo.ca. Website: http://www.cangeo.ca/. Contact: Rick Boychuk, editor. Managing Editor: Eric Harris. 90% freelance written. Works with a small number of new/unpublished writers each year. Estab. 1930. Circ. 246,000. Bimonthly magazine. **Pays on acceptance.** Publishes ms an average of 3 months after acceptance. Buys first Canadian rights; interested only in first-time publication. Reports in 1 month. Sample copy for $4.25 (Canada.) and 9×12 SAE. Free writer's guidelines.

Nonfiction: Buys authoritative geographical articles, in the broad geographical sense, written for the average person, not for a scientific audience. Predominantly Canadian subjects by Canadian authors. Buys 30-45 mss/year. *Always query first in writing and enclose SASE.* Cannot reply personally to all unsolicited proposals. Length: 1,500-3,000 words. Pays 80¢/word minimum. Usual payment for articles ranges between $1,000-3,000. Higher fees reserved for commissioned articles. Sometimes pays the expenses of writers on assignment.
  • They need articles on earth sciences.

Photos: Pays $75-400 for color photos, depending on published size.

THE COTTAGE MAGAZINE, Country Living in B.C. and Alberta, Harrison House Publishing, 4611 William Head Rd., Victoria, British Columbia V9B 5T7 Canada. (604)478-9209. Editor: Peter Chetteburgh. 60% freelance written. Bimonthly magazine covering recreational property in British Columbia and Alberta. Estab. 1992. Circ. 10,000. Pays on publication. Publishes ms an average of 1 month after publication. Byline given. Offers 50% kill fee. Not copyrighted. Buys first North American serial rights. Editorial lead time 2 months. Submit seasonal material 3 months in advance. Accepts simultaneous submissions. Reports in 1 month on queries; 2 months on mss. Sample copy for $2. Writer's guidelines free on request.

Nonfiction: General interest, historical/nostalgic, how-to, humor, interview/profile, new product, personal experience, technical. Buys 30 mss/year. Query. Length: 200-2,000 words. Pays $50-500. Sometimes pays expenses of writers on assignment (telephone expenses mostly).

Photos: State availability of photos with submission. Reviews contact sheets, transparencies and prints. Offers no additional payment for photos accepted with ms. Buys one-time rights.

Columns/Departments: Utilities (solar and/or wind power), 650-700 words; Cabin Wit (humor), 650 words. Buys 10 mss/year. Query. Pays $100-200.

Fillers: Anecdotes, facts, gags to be illustrated by cartoonist, newsbreaks. Buys 12/year. Length: 50-200 words. Pays 20¢/word.

‡LONDON MAGAZINE, Blackburn Magazine Group, 231 Dundas St., Suite 203, London, Ontario N6A 1H1 Canada. (519)679-4901. Fax: (519)434-7842. Editor: Jackie Skender. 90% freelance written. Magazine published 7 times/year covering city of London, Canada. Estab. 1982. Circ. 35,000. **Pays on acceptance**. Publishes ms an average of 2 months after acceptance. Byline given. Offers 50% kill fee. Editorial lead time 4 months. Submit seasonal material 2 months in advance. Reports in 2 weeks on queries. Sample copy and writer's guidelines free on request.

Nonfiction: General interest, interview/profile, personal experience, photo feature. Buys 40-60 mss/year. Query with or without published clips. Length: 250-3,000 words. Pays $50-500. Sometimes pays expenses of writers on assignment.

Columns/Departments: Query with or without published clips. Pays $350 maximum.

OUTDOOR CANADA MAGAZINE, 703 Evans Ave., Suite 202, Toronto Ontario M9C 5E9 Canada. (416)695-0311. Fax: (416)695-0381. Editor-in-Chief: James Little. 90% freelance written. Works with a small number of new/unpublished writers each year. Magazine published 8 times/year emphasizing noncompetitive outdoor recreation in Canada *only*. Estab. 1972. Circ. 95,000. Pays on publication. Publishes ms an average of 8 months after acceptance. Buys first rights. Submit seasonal/holiday material 1 year in advance of issue date. Byline given. *Enclose SASE or IRCs or material will not be returned.* Reports in 1 month. *Writer's Market* recommends allowing 2 months for reply. Mention *Writer's Market* in request for editorial guidelines.

Nonfiction: Fishing, hiking, canoeing, hunting, adventure, outdoor issues, exploring, outdoor destinations in Canada, some how-to. Buys 35-40 mss/year, usually with photos. Length: 1,000-2,500 words. Pays $100 and up.

Photos: Emphasize people in the outdoors. Pays $35-225 for 35mm transparencies; and $400/cover. Captions and model releases required.

Fillers: Short news pieces. Buys 70-80/year. Length: 200-500 words. Pays $6/printed inch.

REGINA MAGAZINE, (formerly *Uptown, Regina's City Magazine*), Concept Media Ltd., 3030 Victoria Ave., Regina, Saskatchewan S4T 1K9 Canada. Fax: (306)522-5988. Editor: Pat Rediger. 50% freelance written. Monthly tabloid covering issues, events, and people of downtown Regina. *"Regina* profiles the people, places and events of Regina's Market Square. It is intended to showcase all the things that are good within the city. We place a special emphasis on the downtown." Estab. 1992. Circ. 35,000. Pays on publication. Publishes ms an average of 3 months after acceptance. Byline given. Offers 10% kill fee. Buys first rights. Editorial lead time 3 months. Submit seasonal material 3 months in advance. Reports in 2 weeks on queries. Sample copy and writer's guidelines for #10 SASE.

Nonfiction: General interest, historical/nostalgic, how-to, humor, interview/profile, personal experience, photo feature. Special issues: The Financial Times of Regina (February), Fiction (September). Buys 15-20 mss/year. Query with published clips. Length: 1,000-2,500 words. Pays $125-150 for assigned articles; $75-100 for unsolicited articles. Pays expenses of writers on assignment.

Photos: Send photos with submission. Reviews contact sheets. Negotiates payment individually. Identification of subjects required. Buys one-time rights.

Columns/Departments: Upfront (off-beat stories), 300 words; After Five (entertainment), 300 words; Lunch Hour (humor), 100 words. Buys 10 mss/year. Query with published clips. Pays $50-75.

Fiction: "We only accept fiction as part of our literary issue." Buys 3 mss/year. Send complete ms. Length: 500-1,000 words. Pays $25-100.

Fillers: Anecdotes, gags to be illustrated by cartoonist, short humor. Buys 25/year. Length: 50-200 words. Pays $5-10.

Tips: "The magazine mainly profiles people and issues that pertain specifically to Regina. Very little freelance material from outside the city is required. However, we do purchase fillers, cartoons and jokes. We're also open to new ideas. If you think you've got a good one, let us know."

TORONTO LIFE, 59 Front St. E., Toronto, Ontario M5E 1B3 Canada. (416)364-3333. Editor: John Macfarlane. 95% freelance written. Prefers to work with published/established writers. Monthly magazine emphasizing local issues and social trends, short humor/satire, and service features for upper income, well educated and, for the most part, young Torontonians. **Pays on acceptance.** Publishes ms an average of 4 months after acceptance. Byline given. Buys first North American serial rights. Pays 50% kill fee for commissioned articles only. Reports in 3 weeks. Sample copy for $3.50 with SAE and IRCs.

Nonfiction: Uses most types of articles. Buys 17 mss/issue. Query with published clips. Phone queries OK. Buys about 40 unsolicited mss/year. Length: 1,000-5,000 words. Pays $800-3,000.

Photos: Send photos with query. Uses good color transparencies and clear, crisp b&w prints. Seldom uses submitted photos. Captions and model release required.

Columns/Departments: "We run about five columns an issue. They are all freelanced, though most are from regular contributors. They are mostly local in concern and cover politics, money, fine art, performing arts, movies and sports." Length: 1,800 words. Pays $1,500.

UP HERE, Life in Canada's North, OUTCROP The Northern Publishers, Box 1350, Yellowknife, Northwest Territories X1A 2N9 Canada. (403)920-4652. Fax: (403)873-2844. Editorial Assistant: Chris Fournier. 50% freelance written. Bimonthly magazine covering general interest about Canada's North. "We publish features, columns and shorts about people, wildlife, native cultures, travel and adventure in Northern Canada, with an occasional swing into Alaska. Be informative, but entertaining." Estab. 1984. Circ. 37,500. Pays on publication. Publishes ms an average of 4 months after acceptance. Buys first North American serial rights. Editorial lead time 4 months. Submit seasonal material 6 months in advance. Reports in 4 months. Sample copy for $3 (Canadian). Writer's guidelines free on request.

• This publication was a finalist for Best Editorial Package, National Magazine Awards.

Nonfiction: Historical/nostalgic, interview/profile, personal experience, photo feature, travel. Buys 40 mss/year. Send complete ms. Length: 750-3,000 words. Pays $150-750 (Canadian).

Photos: Send photos with submission. Reviews transparencies and prints. Offers $35-150/photo (Canadian). Captions required. Buys one-time rights.

Columns/Departments: Photography (how-to for amateurs), 1,250 words; Natural North (wildlife—the land, environment), 1,250-1,800 words; On the Road (driving in Northern regions, RV, etc.), 750-1,800 words. Buys 12 mss/year. Send complete ms. Pays $150-350.

Tips: "You must have lived in or visited Canada's North (the Northwest Territories, Yukon, the extreme north of British Columbia, Alberta, etc.). We like well-researched, concrete adventure pieces, insights about

Northern people and lifestyles, readable natural history. Features are most open to freelancers—travel, adventure and so on. Top-quality photos can sell a piece better than any other factor."

‡**WESTERN PEOPLE, Supplement to the Western Producer**, Western Producer Publications, Box 2500, Saskatoon, Saskatchewan S7K 2C4 Canada. (306)665-3500. E-mail: people@producer.com. Website: http://www.producer.com. Managing Editor: Michael Gillgannon. Weekly farm newspaper supplement covering rural Western Canada. "Our magazine reflects the life and people of rural Western Canada both in the present and historically." Estab. 1978. Circ. 100,000. **Pays on acceptance.** Publishes ms an average of 6 months after acceptance. Byline given. Buys first rights. Submit seasonal material 3 months in advance. Reports in 3 weeks. Sample copy for 9×12 SAE and 3 IRCs. Writer's guidelines for #10 SAE and 2 IRCs.
Nonfiction: General interest, historical/nostalgic, humor, interview/profile, personal experience, photo feature. Buys 225 mss/year. Send complete ms. Length: 500-2,500 words. Pays $100-300.
Photos: Send photos with submission. Reviews transparencies and prints. Captions and identification of subjects required. No stand-alone photos.
Fiction: Adventure, historical, humorous, mainstream, mystery, romance, suspense, western stories reflecting life in rural western Canada. Buys 25 mss/year. Send complete ms. Length: 1,000-2,000 words. Pays $150-250.
Poetry: Free verse, traditional, haiku, light verse. Buys 75 poems/year. Submit maximum 3 poems. Length: 4-50 lines. Pays $15-50.
Tips: "Western Canada is geographically very large. The approach for writing about an interesting individual is to introduce that person *neighbor-to-neighbor* to our readers."

WESTWORLD MAGAZINE, Canada Wide Magazines and Communications, 4180 Lougheed Hwy., 4th floor, Burnaby, British Columbia V5C 6A7 Canada. Fax: (604)299-9188. Editor: (Ms.) Robin Roberts. 30% freelance written. Quarterly association magazine. "Magazine is distributed to members of The Canadian Automobile Association, so we require automotive and travel-related topics of interest to members." Estab. 1983. Circ. 500,000. Pays on publication. Byline given. Offers 50% kill fee. Buys first North American serial rights; second serial (reprint) rights at reduced rate. Editorial lead time 6 months. Submit seasonal material 1 year in advance. Accepts simultaneous submissions. Reports in 1 month on queries; 4 months on mss. Writer's guidelines for #10 SASE.
Nonfiction: Automotive. "No purple prose." Buys 6 mss/year. Query with published clips. Length: 1,000-1,500 words. Pays 35-50¢/word.
Reprints: Accepts previously published submissions.
Photos: State availability of photos with submission. Reviews transparencies and prints. Offers $35-75/photo. Captions, model releases and identification of subjects required. Buys one-time rights.
Columns/Departments: Buys 6 mss/year. Query with published clips. Pays 35-50¢/word.
Tips: "Don't send gushy, travelogue articles. We prefer stories that are informative with practical, useful tips that are well written and researched. Approach an old topic/destination in a fresh/original way."

RELATIONSHIPS

These publications focus on lifestyles and relationships of single adults. Other markets for this type of material can be found in the Women's category. Magazines of a primarily sexual nature, gay or straight, are listed under the Sex category. Gay and Lesbian Interest contains general interest editorial targeted to that audience.

ATLANTA SINGLES MAGAZINE, Hudson Brooke Publishing, Inc., 180 Allen Rd., Suite 304N, Atlanta GA 30328. (404)256-9411. Fax: (404)256-9719. Editor: Shannon V. McClintock. 10% freelance written. Works with a small number of new/unpublished writers each year. Bimonthly magazine for single, widowed or divorced adults, medium to high income level, many business and professionally oriented; single parents, ages 25-55. Estab. 1977. Circ. 15,000. Pays on publication. Publishes ms an average of 6 months after acceptance. Byline given. Buys one-time, second serial (reprint) and simultaneous rights. Submit seasonal material 6 months in advance. Accepts simultaneous submissions. Reports in 1 month. Sample copy for $2 and 8×10 SAE with 7 first-class stamps. Writer's guidelines for #10 SASE.
Nonfiction: General interest, humor, personal experience, photo feature, travel. No fiction or pornography. Buys 5 mss/year. Send complete ms. Length: 600-1,200 words. Pays $50-150 for unsolicited articles; sometimes trades for personal ad.
Reprints: Send tearsheet or photocopy of article and information about when and where the article previously appeared. Pays 50% of amount paid for an original article.
Photos: Send photos with submission. Cover photos also considered. Reviews prints. Offers no additional payment for photos accepted with ms. Model releases and identification of subjects required. Buys one-time rights.

Columns/Departments: Will consider ideas. Query. Length: 600-800 words. Pays $25-150/column or department.

Tips: "We are open to articles on *any* subject that would be of interest to singles. For example, travel, autos, movies, love stories, fashion, investments, real estate, etc. Although singles are interested in topics like self-awareness, being single again, and dating, they are also interested in many of the same subjects that married people are, such as those listed."

CHRISTIAN SINGLE, Baptist Sunday School Board, 127 9th Ave. N., Nashville TN 37234-0140. (615)251-5721. Fax: (615)251-5008. Editor-in-Chief: Stephen Felts. 30% freelance written. Prefers to work with published/established writers. Monthly "current events magazine that addresses day to day issues from a Christian perspective. Seeks to be constructive and creative in approach." Estab. 1979. Circ. 73,000. **Pays on acceptance.** Byline given. Buys first rights or makes work-for-hire assignments. Submit seasonal material 6 months in advance. Reports in 2 months. Sample copy and writer's guidelines for 9×12 SAE with 4 first-class stamps.

  ● *Christian Single* reports they want more humor and articles dealing with current news events.

Nonfiction: Humor (good, clean humor that applies to Christian singles), how-to (specific subjects which apply to singles), inspirational (of the personal experience type), high adventure personal experience (of single adults), photo feature (on outstanding Christian singles), financial articles targeted to single adults. Buys 60-75 unsolicited mss/year. Query with published clips. Length: 600-1,200 words. Payment negotiable.

Reprints: Send photocopy of article and typed ms and disk with rights for sale noted and information about when and where article previously appeared. Pays 75% of amount paid for an original article.

Fiction: "We are also looking for fiction suitable for our target audience." Publishes novel excerpts.

Tips: "We are looking for people who experience single living from a positive, Christian perspective."

‡ON THE SCENE MAGAZINE, 3507 Wyoming NE, Albuquerque NM 87111-4427. (505)299-4401. Fax: (505)299-4403. Editor: Gail Skinner. 60% freelance written. Eager to work with new/unpublished writers. Monthly tabloid covering lifestyles for all ages. Estab. 1979. Pays on publication. Publishes ms within 12 months after acceptance. Byline given. Submit seasonal material 3 months in advance. Reports in 3 months. Sample copy for 9×12 SAE with 5 first-class stamps. Writer's guidelines for #10 SASE.

Nonfiction: General interest, how-to, humor, inspirational, opinion, personal experience, relationships, consumer guide, travel, finance, real estate, parenting, astrology. No suggestive or pornographic material. Buys 60 mss/year. Send complete ms. "Manuscripts returned only if adequate SASE included. Also publishes some fiction. Length: 500-1,200 words. Pays $20-60.

Reprints: Send photocopy of article or typed ms with rights for sale noted.

Photos: Send photos with ms. Captions, model releases, identification of subjects required. Photo returned only if adequate SASE is included.

Tips: "We are looking for articles that deal with every aspect of living—whether on a local or national level. Our readers are of above-average intelligence, income and education. The majority of our articles are chosen from 'relationships,' 'humor' and seasonal submissions."

RELIGIOUS

Religious magazines focus on a variety of subjects, styles and beliefs. Most are sectarian, but a number approach topics such as public policy, international affairs and contemporary society from a non-denominational perspective. Fewer religious publications are considering poems and personal experience articles, but many emphasize special ministries to singles, seniors or other special interest groups. Such diversity makes reading each magazine essential for the writer hoping to break in. Educational and inspirational material of interest to church members, workers and leaders within a denomination or religion is needed by the publications in this category. Religious magazines for children and teenagers can be found in the Juvenile and Teen and Young Adult classifications. Other religious publications can be found in the Contemporary Culture and Ethnic/Minority sections as well. Spiritual topics are also addressed in Astrology, Metaphysical and New Age as well as Health and Fitness. Publications intended to assist professional religious workers in teaching and managing church affairs are classified in Church Administration and Ministry in the Trade section.

‡AMERICA, 106 W. 56th St., New York NY 10019. (212)581-4640. Editor: Rev. George W. Hunt. Published weekly for adult, educated, largely Roman Catholic audience. Estab. 1909. **Pays on acceptance.** Byline given. Usually buys all rights. Reports in 3 weeks. Free writer's guidelines.

Nonfiction: "We publish a wide variety of material on politics, economics, ecology, and so forth. We are not a parochial publication, but almost all pieces make some moral or religious point. We are not interested in purely informational pieces or personal narratives which are self-contained and have no larger moral interest." Articles on literature, current political, social events. Length: 1,500-2,000 words. Pays $50-100.
Poetry: Patrick Samway, S.J., poetry editor. Length: 15-30 lines.

AREOPAGUS, A Living Encounter with Today's Religious World, Tao Fong Shan Christian Centre, P.O. Box 33, Shatin, New Territories, Hong Kong. (852)691-1904. Fax: (852)265-9885. E-mail: areos@asiaon line.com. Website: www.areopagus.org.hk. Managing Editor: Eric Bosell. Contact: John G. Lemond, editor. 75% freelance written. Quarterly magazine for interreligious dialogue. "*Areopagus* is a Christian periodical that seeks to engage its readers in a living encounter with today's religious world. Respecting the integrity of religious communities, *Areopagus* provides a forum for dialog between the good news of Jesus Christ and people of faith both in major world religious and new religious movements." Estab. 1987. Circ. 1,000. Pays on publication. Publishes ms an average of 6 months after acceptance. Offers 50% kill fee. Buys first-time rights. Editorial lead time 6 months. Submit seasonal material 6 months in advance. Accepts simultaneous submissions. Reports in 6 weeks on queries; 3 months on mss. Sample copy for $4. Writer's guidelines free on request.

● *Areopagus* no longer solicits poetry.
Nonfiction: Book excerpts, essays and exposé (all on religious themes), humor (of a religious nature), inspirational (interreligious encounter), interview/profile (w/religious figures), opinion (on religious subjects), personal experience (of spiritual journey), photo feature and religious. Issue themes under consideration: birth rites, death, family, sex, aging, suffering, war, hope, healing. "We are not interested in articles that seek to prove the superiority or inferiority of a particular religious tradition." Buys 40 mss/year. Send complete ms. Length: 1,000-5,000 words. Pays $100 minimum.
Reprints: Send typed ms with rights for sale noted and information about when and where the article previously appeared.
Photos: Send photos with submission. Offers $50-100/photo. Identification of subjects required. Buys one-time rights.
Columns/Departments: Getting to Know (objective description of major world religions), 4,000 words; Pilgrimage (stories of personal faith journies), 3,000 words; and People and Communities (description of faith communities), 3,000 words. Buys 10 mss/year. Send complete ms. Pays $50-100.
Fillers: Facts, newsbreaks. Buys 5/year. Length: 100-400 words. Pays $10-25.
Tips: "Articles that reflect a balanced approach to interreligious dialogue are the most likely candidates. Followers of all faiths are encouraged to write about personal experience. Articles about religious conspiracy and arcane religious conjecture are of little interest. Virtually all of our departments are open to freelancers. In general, we look for compassionate, direct and unself-conscious prose that reflects a writer firmly rooted in his or her own tradition but unafraid to encounter other traditions."

CATHOLIC DIGEST, University of St. Thomas, P.O. Box 64090, St. Paul MN 55164. (612)962-6739. Editor: Richard J. Reece. Managing Editor: Kathleen Stauffer. Contact: Articles Editor. 15% freelance written. Monthly magazine covering Catholic and spiritual living. Estab. 1936. Circ. 540,000. **Pays on acceptance** for articles. Publishes ms an average of 4 months after acceptance. Byline given. Buys first rights, one-time rights or second serial (reprint) rights. Editorial lead time 4 months. Submit seasonal material 5 months in advance. Reports in 2 months on mss. Sample copy and writer's guidelines free on request.
Nonfiction: Book excerpts, essays, general interest, historical/nostalgic, how-to, humor, inspirational, interview/profile, personal experience, religious, travel. Buys 60 mss/year. Send complete ms. Length: 500-3,000 words. Pays $150-400.
Reprints: Accepts previously published submissions.
Photos: State availability of photos with submission. Reviews contact sheets, transparencies, prints. Negotiates payment individually. Captions, model releases, identification of subjects required.
Columns/Departments: Buys 75 mss/year. Send complete ms. Pays $4-50.
Fillers: Contact: Susan Schaefer, filler editor. Anecdotes, short humor. Buys 200/year. Length: 1 line minimum, 500 words maximum. Pays $2-50 on publication.
Tips: "We're a lot more aggressive with inspirational/pop psychology/how-to articles these days. Spiritual and all other wellness self help is a good bet for us."

CATHOLIC HERITAGE, Our Sunday Visitor, Inc., 200 Noll Plaza, Huntington IN 46750. (219)356-8400. Fax: (219)359-9117. E-mail: 76440.3571@compuserve.com. Editor: Bill Dodds. 75% freelance written. Bimonthly magazine covering the Catholic faith. "Explores the history and heritage of the Catholic faith with special emphasis on its impact on culture." Estab. 1991. Circ. 25,000. **Pays on acceptance.** Publishes ms an average of 1 year after acceptance. Byline given. Buys first North American serial rights. Editorial lead time 6 months. Submit seasonal material 6 months in advance. Reports in 3 weeks on queries; 1 month on mss. Send SASE for guidelines.
● This editor prefers manuscript on computer disks or submitted through CompuServe.

Nonfiction: Book excerpts, general interest, interview/profile, photo feature, religious, travel, Church history. "No nostalgia pieces about what it was like growing up Catholic or about life in the Church prior to Vatican II." Buys 30 mss/year. Query. Length: 900 words. Pays $200. Sometimes pays expenses of writers on assignment.

Reprints: Send tearsheet and information about when and where the article previously appeared. Payment is negotiated.

Photos: State availability of photos with submission. Reviews prints. Negotiates payment individually. Captions required. Buys one-time rights.

Tips: "Write solid queries that take an aspect of the Catholic heritage and apply it to developments today. Show a good knowledge of the Church and a flair for historical writing. General features are most open to freelancers."

CATHOLIC NEAR EAST MAGAZINE, Catholic Near East Welfare Association, 1011 First Ave., New York NY 10022-4195. (212)826-1480. Fax: (212)826-8979. Editor: Michael La Città. 50% freelance written. Bimonthly magazine for a Catholic audience with interest in the Near East, particularly its current religious, cultural and political aspects. Estab. 1974. Circ. 110,000. **Pays on acceptance.** Publishes ms an average of 6 months after acceptance. Byline given. Buys all rights. Reports in 2 months. Sample copy and writer's guidelines for 7½×10½ SAE with 2 first-class stamps.

Nonfiction: "Cultural, devotional, political, historical material on the Near East, with an emphasis on the Eastern Christian churches. Style should be simple, factual, concise. Articles must stem from personal acquaintance with subject matter, or thorough up-to-date research." Length: 1,200-1,800 words. Pays 20¢/edited word.

Photos: "Photographs to accompany manuscript are welcome; they should illustrate the people, places, ceremonies, etc. which are described in the article. We prefer color transparencies but occasionally use b&w. Pay varies depending on use—scale from $50-300."

Tips: "We are interested in current events in the regions listed above as they affect the cultural, political and religious lives of the people."

THE CHRISTIAN CENTURY, 407 S. Dearborn St., Chicago IL 60605-1150. (312)427-5380. Editor: James M. Wall. Senior Editors: Martin E. Marty and Dean Peerman. Managing Editor: David Heim. 50% freelance written. Eager to work with new/unpublished writers. Weekly magazine for ecumenically-minded, progressive church people, both clergy and lay. Circ. 37,000. Pays on publication. Publishes ms an average of 2 months after acceptance. Usually buys all rights. Reports in 2 months. Sample copy available for $2. All queries, mss should be accompanied by SASE.

Nonfiction: "We use articles dealing with social problems, ethical dilemmas, political issues, international affairs and the arts, as well as with theological and ecclesiastical matters. We focus on concerns that arise at the juncture between church and society, or church and culture." Query appreciated, but not essential. Length: 2,500 words maximum. Payment varies, but averages $50/page.

CHRISTIAN COURIER, Calvinist Contact Publishing, 4-261 Martindale Rd., St. Catharines, Ontario L2W 1A1 Canada. (905)682-8311. Fax: (905)682-8313. Editor: Bert Witvoet. 20% freelance written. Weekly newspaper covering news of importance to Christians, comments and features. "We assume a Christian perspective which acknowledges that this world belongs to God and that human beings are invited to serve God in every area of society." Estab. 1945. Circ. 5,000. Pays 30 days after publication. Publishes ms an average of 2 months after acceptance. Byline given. Offers 50% kill fee. Editorial lead time 1 month. Submit seasonal material 6 months in advance. Accepts simultaneous submissions. Reports back only if material accepted.

Nonfiction: Interview/profile, opinion. Buys 40 mss/year. Send complete ms. Length: 500-1,200 words. Pays $35-60 for assigned articles; $25-50 for unsolicited articles. Sometimes pays expenses of writers on assignment.

Reprints: Accepts previously published submissions.

Photos: State availability of photos with submission.

CHRISTIAN HOME & SCHOOL, Christian Schools International, 3350 East Paris Ave. SE, Grand Rapids MI 49512. (616)957-1070, ext. 234. Executive Editor: Gordon L. Bordewyk. Contact: Roger Schmurr, senior editor. 30% freelance written. Works with a small number of new/unpublished writers each year. Bimonthly magazine covering family life and Christian education. "For parents who support Christian education. We feature material on a wide range of topics of interest to parents." Estab. 1922. Pays on publication. Publishes ms an average of 4 months after acceptance. Byline given. Buys first North American serial rights. Submit seasonal material 4 months in advance. Reports in 1 month. Sample copy for 9×12 SAE with 4 first-class stamps. Writer's guidelines for #10 SASE.

Nonfiction: Book excerpts, interview/profile, opinion, personal experience, articles on parenting and school life. "We publish features on issues which affect the home and school and profiles on interesting individuals, providing that the profile appeals to our readers and is not a tribute or eulogy of that person." Buys 40 mss/

year. Send complete ms. Length: 500-2,000 words. Pays $75-150. Sometimes pays the expenses of writers on assignment.

Photos: "If you have any color photos appropriate for your article, send them along."

Tips: "Features are the area most open to freelancers. We are publishing articles that deal with contemporary issues that affect parents. Use an informal easy-to-read style rather than a philosophical, academic tone. Try to incorporate vivid imagery and concrete, practical examples from real life."

‡**CHRISTIAN READER, A Digest of the Best in Christian Reading**, Christianity Today, 465 Gundersen Dr., Carol Stream IL 60188. (708)260-6200. Fax: (708)260-0114. Editor: Bonne Steffen. 60% freelance written. Bimonthly magazine for adult evangelical Christian audience. Estab. 1963. Circ. 225,000. **Pays on acceptance for first rights**; on publication for reprints. Byline given. Editorial lead time 6 months. Submit seasonal material 9 months in advance. Reports in 3 weeks. Sample copy for 5×8 SAE with 4 first-class stamps. Writer's guidelines for #10 SASE.

Nonfiction: Humor, inspirational, personal experience, religious. Buys 50 mss/year. Query. Length: 500-1,500 words. Pays $100-250 depending on length. Pays expenses of writers on assignment.

Reprints: Send tearsheet or photocopy of article or typed manuscript with rights for sale noted and information about when and where the article previously appeared. Pays $50-100.

Photos: State availability of photos with submission. Negotiates payment individually. Buys one-time rights.

Columns/Departments: Contact: Cynthia Thomas, editorial coordinator. Lite Fare (adult church humor), 50-200 words; Kids of the Kingdom (kids say and do funny things), 50-200 words; Rolling Down the Aisle (humorous wedding tales), 50-200 words. Buys 150 mss/year. Send complete ms. Pays $25-35.

‡**CHRISTIAN SOCIAL ACTION**, 100 Maryland Ave. NE, Washington DC 20002. (202)488-5621. Fax: (202)488-5619. Editor: Lee Ranck. 2% freelance written. Works with a small number of new/unpublished writers each year. Monthly for "United Methodist clergy and lay people interested in in-depth analysis of social issues, with emphasis on the church's role or involvement in these issues." Circ. 2,500. May buy all rights. Pays on publication. Publishes ms an average of 2 months after acceptance. Rights purchased vary with author and material. Returns rejected material in 5 weeks. Reports on material accepted for publication in a month. Free sample copy and writer's guidelines for #10 SASE.

Nonfiction: "This is the social action publication of The United Methodist Church published by the denomination's General Board of Church and Society. Our publication tries to relate social issues to the church—what the church can do, is doing; why the church should be involved. We only accept articles relating to social issues, e.g., war, draft, peace, race relations, welfare, police/community relations, labor, population problems, drug and alcohol problems. No devotional, 'religious,' superficial material, highly technical articles, personal experiences or poetry." Buys 25-30 mss/year. "Query to show that writer has expertise on a particular social issue, give credentials, and reflect a readable writing style." Query or submit complete ms. Length: 2,000 words maximum. Pays $75-125. Sometimes pays the expenses of writers on assignment.

Tips: "Write on social issues, but not superficially; we're more interested in finding an expert who can write (e.g., on human rights, alcohol problems, peace issues) than a writer who attempts to research a complex issue."

‡**CHRISTIANITY TODAY**, 465 Gundersen Dr., Carol Stream IL 60188-2498. Fax: (708)260-0114. Administrative Editor: Carol Thiessen. 80% freelance written. Works with a small number of new/unpublished writers each year. Semimonthly magazine emphasizing orthodox, evangelical religion. Estab. 1956. Circ. 180,000. Publishes ms an average of 6 months after acceptance. Usually buys first serial rights. Submit seasonal material at least 8 months in advance. Reports in 3 months. Sample copy and writer's guidelines for 9×12 SAE with 3 first-class stamps.

Nonfiction: Theological, ethical, historical, informational (not merely inspirational). Buys 4 mss/issue. *Query only.* Unsolicited mss not accepted and not returned. Length: 1,000-4,000 words. Pays negotiable rates. Sometimes pays the expenses of writers on assignment.

Reprints: Send typed ms with rights for sale noted and information about when and where the article previously appeared. Pays 25% of amount paid for an original article.

Columns/Departments: Church in Action (profiles of not-so-well-known Christians involved in significant or offbeat services). Buys 7 mss/year. Query only. Length: 900-1,000 words.

Tips: "We are developing more of our own manuscripts and requiring a much more professional quality from others. Queries without SASE will not be answered and manuscripts not containing SASE will not be returned."

FOR INFORMATION on setting your freelance fees, see How Much Should I Charge?

CHRYSALIS READER, P.O. Box 549, West Chester PA 19381-0549. Fax: (804)983-1074. E-mail: lawson @aba.org. Send inquiries and mss directly to the editorial office: Route 1, Box 184, Dillwyn VA 23936-9616. Contact: Carol S. Lawson, editor. Managing Editor: Susanna van Rensselaer. 50% freelance written. Biannual literary magazine on spiritually related topics. "*It is very important to send for writer's guidelines and sample copies before submitting.* Content of fiction, articles, reviews, poetry, etc., should be directly focused on that issue's theme and directed to the educated, intellectually curious reader." Estab. 1985. Circ. 3,000. Pays at page-proof stage. Publishes ms an average of 9 months after acceptance. Byline given. Buys first rights and makes work-for-hire assignments. Reports in 1 month on queries; 3 months on mss. Sample copy for $10 and 9×12 SAE. Writer's guidelines and copy deadlines for SASE.
Nonfiction: Essays and interview/profile. Upcoming themes: Play (Autumn 1996); The Good Life (Spring 1997); Symbols (Autumn 1997). Buys 30 mss/year. Query. Length: 2,500-3,500 words. Pays $50-250 for assigned articles; $50-150 for unsolicited articles.
Photos and Illustrations: Send suggestions for illustrations with submission. Offers no additional payment for photos accepted with ms. Captions and identification of subjects required. Buys original artwork for cover and inside copy; b&w illustrations related to theme; pays $25-150. Buys one-time rights.
Fiction: Phoebe Loughrey, fiction editor. Adventure, experimental, historical, mainstream, mystery, science fiction, related to theme of issue. Buys 6 mss/year. Query. Length: 2,500-3,500 words. Short fiction more likely to be published. Pays $50-150.
Poetry: Rob Lawson, poetry editor. Avant-garde and traditional *but not religious.* Buys 15 poems/year. Pays $25. Submit maximum 6.

COLUMBIA, 1 Columbus Plaza, New Haven CT 06507. (203)772-2130. Editor: Richard McMunn. Monthly magazine for Catholic families. Caters particularly to members of the Knights of Columbus. Estab. 1921. Circ. 1,500,000. **Pays on acceptance.** Buys first serial rights. Free sample copy and writer's guidelines.
Nonfiction and Photos: Fact articles directed to the Catholic layman and his family dealing with current events, social problems, Catholic apostolic activities, education, ecumenism, rearing a family, literature, science, arts, sports and leisure. Color glossy prints, transparencies or contact prints with negatives are required for illustration. Articles without ample illustrative material are not given consideration. Pays up to $500, including photos. Buys 30 mss/year. Query. Length: 1,000-1,500 words.

COMPASS: A JESUIT JOURNAL, Jesuit Fathers of Upper Canada, Box 400, Stn. F., 50 Charles St., East, Toronto, Ontario M4Y 2L8 Canada.(416)921-0653. Fax: (416)921-1864. E-mail: 74163.247@comp userve.com. Website: http://www.io.org/~gvanv/. Editor: Robert Chodos. 80% freelance written. Bimonthly magazine covering religious affairs, "directed at an informed general audience, made up primarily but by no means exclusively of Canadian Catholics. It provides an ethical perspective on contemporary social and religious affairs." Estab. 1983. Circ. 3,500. Pays on publication. Byline given. Offers 50% kill fee. Buys first rights. Editorial lead time 4 months. Submit seasonal material 4 months in advance. Reports in 3 months. Sample copy and writer's guidelines for $2.
Nonfiction: Essays, general interest, opinion, personal experience, religious. Query for special issues. Buys 50 mss/year. Query with published clips. Length: 750-2,000 words. Pays $100.
Photos: State availability of photos with submission. Offers no additional payment for photos accepted with ms. Identification of subjects required. Buys one-time rights.
Columns/Departments: Testament (commentary on Scripture); Colloquy (relationship between theology and daily life); Disputation (comment on articles previously appearing in *Compass*). Length: 750 words. Buys 18 mss/year. Query. Pays $50-150.
Fiction: Mainstream, religious. Buys 2 mss/year. Send complete ms. Length: 1,000-2,500 words. Pays $100-350.
Poetry: Free verse, traditional. Buys 1 poem/year. Submit maximum 10 poems. Length: 50 lines maximum. Pays $50-100.
Fillers: Jack Costello, SJ, Points editor. Anecdotes, short humor. Buys 12/year. Length: 20-100 words. Pays 1 year subscription to *Compass*.
Tips: "*Compass* publishes theme issues. The best chance of being published is to get a list of upcoming themes and gear proposals to them. All sections are open to freelancers."

CONSCIENCE, A Newsjournal of Prochoice Catholic Opinion, Catholics for a Free Choice, 1436 U St. NW, Suite 301, Washington DC 20009-3997. (202)986-6093. Editor: Maggie Hume. 80% freelance written. Sometimes works with new/unpublished writers. Quarterly newsjournal covering reproductive health and rights, including but not limited to abortion rights in the church, and church-state issues in US and worldwide. "A feminist, pro-choice perspective is a must, and knowledge of Christianity and specifically Catholicism is helpful." Estab. 1980. Circ. 12,000. Pays on publication. Publishes ms an average of 4 months after acceptance. Byline given. Buys first North American serial rights or makes work-for-hire assignments. Reports in 4 months. Sample copy for 9×12 SAE with 4 first-class stamps. Writer's guidelines for #10 SASE.
Nonfiction: Book excerpts, interview/profile, opinion, issue anaylsis, a small amount of personal experience. Especially needs material that recognizes the complexity of reproductive issues and decisions, and offers

original, honest insight. Buys 8-12 mss/year. Query with published clips or send complete ms. Length: 1,000-3,500 words. Pays $25-150. "Writers should be aware that we are a nonprofit organization."

Reprints: Sometimes accepts previously published submissions. Send tearsheet or photocopy of article or typed ms with rights for sale noted and information about when and where the article previously appeared. Pays 20-30% of amount paid for an original article.

Photos: State availability of photos with query or ms. Prefers b&w prints. Identification of subjects required.

Columns/Departments: Book reviews. Buys 6-10 mss/year. Length: 600-1,200 words. Pays $25-50.

Fillers: Newsbreaks. Uses 6/year. Length: 100-300 words. $25-35.

Tips: "Say something new on the issue of abortion, or sexuality, or the role of religion or the Catholic church, or women's status in the church. Thoughtful, well-researched and well-argued articles needed. The most frequent mistakes made by writers in submitting an article to us are lack of originality and wordiness."

CORNERSTONE, Cornerstone Communications, Inc., 939 W. Wilson, Chicago IL 60640-5718. Editor: Dawn Mortimer. Submissions Editor: Misty Files. 10% freelance written. Eager to work with new/unpublished writers. Quarterly magazine covering contemporary issues in the light of Evangelical Christianity. Estab. 1972. Pays after publication. Byline given. Buys first serial rights. Submit seasonal material 6 months in advance. Accepts simultaneous submissions. Does not return mss. "We will contact you *only* if your work is accepted for possible publication. Manuscripts not accepted will be discarded. We *encourage* simultaneous submissions because we take so long to get back to people! We prefer actual manuscripts to queries." Sample copy and writer's guidelines for 8½×11 envelope with 5 first-class stamps.

Nonfiction: Essays, personal experience, religious. Buys 1-2 mss/year. Query with SASE or send complete ms. 2,700 words maximum. Pays 8-10¢/word. Sometimes pays expenses of writers on assignment.

Reprints: Accepts previously published submissions.

Columns/Departments: Music (interview with artists, mainly rock, focusing on artist's world view and value system as expressed in his/her music), Current Events, Personalities, Film and Book Reviews (focuses on meaning as compared and contrasted to biblical values). Buys 1-4 mss/year. Query. Length: 100-2,500 words (negotiable). Pays 8-10¢/word.

Fiction: "Articles may express Christian world view but should not be unrealistic or 'syrupy.' Other than porn, the sky's the limit. We want fiction as creative as the Creator." Buys 1-4 mss/year. Send complete ms. Length: 250-2,500 words (negotiable). Pays negotiable rate, 8-10¢/word.

Poetry: Tammy Boyd, poetry editor. Avant-garde, free verse, haiku, light verse, traditional. No limits *except* for epic poetry ("We've not the room!"). Buys 10-50 poems/year. Submit maximum 5 poems. Payment negotiated. 1-15 lines: $10. Over 15 lines: $25.

Tips: "A display of creativity which expresses a biblical world view without clichés or cheap shots at non-Christians is the ideal. We are known as one of the most avant-garde magazines in the Christian market, yet attempt to express orthodox beliefs in language of the '90s. *Any* writer who does this may well be published by *Cornerstone*. Creative fiction is begging for more Christian participation. We anticipate such contributions gladly. Interviews where well-known personalities respond to the gospel are also strong publication possibilities."

THE COVENANT COMPANION, Covenant Publications of the Evangelical Covenant Church, 5101 N. Francisco Ave., Chicago IL 60625. (312)784-3000. Fax: (312)784-1540. E-mail: 73430.3316@compuserve.com. Website: http://www.npcts.edu/cov/. Editor: John E. Phelan, Jr. 10-15% freelance written. "As the official monthly organ of The Evangelical Covenant Church, we seek to inform, stimulate and gather the denomination we serve by putting members in touch with each other and assisting them in interpreting contemporary issues. We also seek to inform them on events in the church. Our background is evangelical and our emphasis is on Christian commitment and life." Circ. 22,000. Publishes an average of 2 months after acceptance. Byline given. Buys first or all rights. Submit seasonal material 4 months in advance. Accepts simultaneous submissions. Sample copy for $2.25 and 9×12 SASE. Writer's guidelines for #10 SASE.

Nonfiction: Humor, inspirational, religious. Buys 20-25 mss/year. Send complete ms. Unused mss returned only if accompanied by SASE. Length: 500-2,000 words. Pays $15-50 for assigned articles; pays $15-35 for unsolicited articles.

Reprints: Send tearsheet, photocopy of article or typed ms with rights for sale noted.

Photos: Send photos with submissions. Reviews prints. Offers no additonal payment for photos accepted with ms. Identification of subjects required. Buys one-time rights.

Poetry: Traditional. Buys 10-15 poems/year. Submit maximum 10 poems. Pays $10-15.

Tips: "Seasonal articles related to church year and on national holidays are welcome."

DECISION, Billy Graham Evangelistic Association, 1300 Harmon Place, Minneapolis MN 55403-1988. (612)338-0500. Fax: (612)335-1299. E-mail: 103115.2747@compuserve.com. Editor: Roger C. Palms. 25-40% freelance written. Works each year with small number of new/unpublished writers, as well as a solid stable of experienced writers. Monthly magazine with a mission "to set forth to every reader the Good News of salvation in Jesus Christ with such vividness and clarity that he or she will be drawn to make a commitment to Christ; to encourage, teach and strengthen Christians." Estab. 1960. Circ. 1,700,000. Pays on publication. Byline given. Buys first rights and assigns work-for-hire manuscripts, articles, projects. Include telephone number with submission. Submit seasonal material 10 months in advance; other mss published up to 18 months after acceptance. Reports in 3 months on mss. Sample copy for 9×12 SAE with 4 first-class stamps. Writer's guidelines for #10 SASE.

Nonfiction: How-to, motivational, personal experience and religious. "No personality-centered articles or articles that are issue-oriented or critical of denominations." Buys approximately 75 mss/year. Send complete ms. Length: 400-1,800 words. Pays $30-250. Pays expenses of writers on assignment.

Photos: State availability of photos with submission. Reviews prints. Captions, model releases and identification of subjects required. Buys one-time rights.

Poetry: Accepting submissions. No queries.

Tips: "We are seeking personal conversion testimonies and personal experience articles that show how God intervened in a person's daily life and the way in which Scripture was applied to the experience in helping to solve the problem. The conversion testimonies describe in first person what author's life was like before he/she became a Christian, how he/she committed his/her life to Christ and what difference He has made since that decision. We also are looking for vignettes on various aspects of personal evangelism. SASE required with submissions."

THE DOOR, P.O. Box 1444, Waco TX 76703-1444. E-mail: 103361.23@compuserve.com. Contact: Robert Darden. 50% freelance written. Works with a small number of new/unpublished writers each year. Bimonthly magazine for men and women connected with the church. Circ. 14,000. Pays on publication. Publishes ms an average of 1 year after acceptance. Buys first rights. Reports in 3 months. Sample copy for $4.50. Writer's guidelines for SASE.

Nonfiction: Humorous/satirical articles on church renewal, Christianity and organized religion. No book reviews. Buys about 30 mss/year. Submit complete ms. Length: 1,500 words maximum, 750-1,000 preferred. Pays $60-200. Sometimes pays expenses of writers on assignments.

Reprints: Send typed ms with rights for sale noted and information about when and where the article previously appeared.

Tips: "We look for someone who is clever, on our wave length, and has some savvy about the evangelical church. We are very picky and highly selective. The writer has a better chance of breaking in with our publication with short articles since we are a bimonthly publication with numerous regular features and the magazine is only 44 pages. The most frequent mistake made by writers is that they do not understand satire. They see we are a humor magazine and consequently come off funny/cute (like *Reader's Digest*) rather than funny/satirical (like *National Lampoon*)." *No* poetry.

EVANGEL, Free Methodist Publishing House, P.O. Box 535002, Indianapolis IN 46253-5002. (317)244-3660. Editor: Julie Innes. 100% freelance written. Weekly take-home paper for adults. Estab. 1897. Circ. 22,000. Pays on publication. Publishes ms an average of 1 year after acceptance. Buys simultaneous, second serial (reprint) or one-time rights. Submit seasonal material 9 months in advance. Reports in 1 month. Sample copy and writer's guidelines for #10 SASE.

Nonfiction: Interview (with ordinary person who is doing something extraordinary in his community, in service to others), profile (of missionary or one from similar service profession who is contributing significantly to society), personal experience (finding a solution to a problem common to young adults; coping with handicapped child, for instance, or with a neighborhood problem. Story of how God-given strength or insight saved a situation). Buys 100 mss/year. Submit complete ms. Length: 300-1,000 words. Pays 4¢/word.

Reprints: Send photocopy of article and information about when and where the article previously appeared.

Photos: Purchased with accompanying ms. Captions required. Send prints. Pays $10 for 8×10 b&w glossy prints.

Fiction: Religious themes dealing with contemporary issues dealt with from a Christian frame of reference. Story must "go somewhere." Buys 50 mss/year. Submit complete ms.

Poetry: Free verse, haiku, light verse, traditional, religious. Buys 20 poems/year. Submit maximum 6 poems. Length: 4-24 lines. Pays $10.

Tips: "Seasonal material will get a second look (won't be rejected so easily). Write an attention grabbing lead followed by an article that says something worthwhile. Relate the lead to some of the universal needs of the reader—promise in that lead to help the reader in some way. Lack of SASE brands author as a nonprofessional; I seldom even bother to read the script."

EVANGELIZING TODAY'S CHILD, Child Evangelism Fellowship Inc., Box 348, Warrenton MO 63383-0348. (314)456-4321. Editor: Elsie Lippy. 50% freelance written. Prefers to work with published/established writers. Bimonthly magazine. "Our purpose is to equip Christians to win the world's children to Christ and disciple them. Our readership is Sunday school teachers, Christian education leaders and children's workers in every phase of Christian ministry to children up to 12 years old." Estab. 1942. Circ. 18,000. Pays within 90 days of acceptance. Publishes ms an average of 6 months after acceptance. Byline given. Offers kill fee if assigned. Buys first serial rights. Submit seasonal material 6 months in advance. Reports in 2 months. Sample copy for $2. Writer's guidelines for SASE.

Nonfiction: Unsolicited articles welcomed from writers with Christian education training or current experience in working with children. Buys 35 mss/year. Query. Length: 1,200. Pays 10-12¢/word.

Reprints: Send photocopy of article and information about when and where the article previously appeared. Pays 35% of amount paid for an original article.

Photos: Submissions of photos on speculation accepted. Needs photos of children or related subjects. Pays $45 for inside color prints or transparencies, $125 for cover transparencies.

FAITH TODAY, Canada's Evangelical News/Feature Magazine, Evangelical Fellowship of Canada, MIP Box 3745, Markham, Ontario L3R 0Y4 Canada. (905)479-5885. Fax: (905)479-4742. E-mail: ft@nrzone .com. Editor: Brian C. Stiller. Contact: Marianne Meed Ward, interim managing editor. Bimonthly magazine covering evangelical Christianity. *"FT* is an interdenominational, evangelical news/feature magazine that informs Canadian Christians on issues facing church and society, and on events within the church community. It focuses on corporate faith interacting with society rather than on personal spiritual life. Writers should have a thorough understanding of the *Canadian evangelical* community." Estab. 1983. Circ. 18,000. Pays on publication. Publishes ms an average of 6 months after acceptance. Byline given. Offers 30-50% kill fee. Buys first rights. Editorial lead time 4 months. Reports in 6 weeks. Sample copy and writer's guidelines free on request.

Nonfiction: Religious, news feature. Buys 75 mss/year. Query. Length: 1,000-2,000 words. Pays $250-600. Sometimes pays expenses of writers on assignment.

Photos: State availability of photos with submission. Reviews contact sheets, prints. Identification of subjects required. Buys one-time rights.

Tips: "Query should include brief outline and names of the sources you plan to interview in your research. Use Canadian postage on SASE."

THE FAMILY DIGEST, P.O. Box 40137, Fort Wayne IN 46804. Editor: Corine B. Erlandson. 95% freelance written. Bimonthly digest-sized magazine. *"The Family Digest* is dedicated to the joy and fulfillment of the Catholic family, and its relationship to the Catholic parish." Estab. 1945. Circ. 150,000. Pays within 6 weeks of acceptance. Publishes ms usually within 1 year after acceptance. Byline given. Buys first North American rights. Submit seasonal material 7 months in advance. Reports in 2 months. Sample copy and writer's guidelines for 6×9 SAE with 2 first-class stamps.

Nonfiction: Family life, parish life, how-to, seasonal, inspirational, prayer life, Catholic traditions. Send ms with SASE. No poetry or fiction. Buys 60 unsolicited mss/year. Length: 750-1,200 words. Pays 5¢/word.

Reprints: Prefers to publish previously unpublished articles. Send typed ms with rights for sale noted and information about when and where the article previously appeared. Pays 5¢/word.

Fillers: Anecdotes, tasteful humor based on personal experience. Buys 5/issue. Length: 25-125 words maximum. Cartoons: Publishes 5-8 cartoons/issue, related to family and Catholic parish life. Pays $20/cartoon, on acceptance.

Tips: "Prospective freelance contributors should be familiar with the publication, and the types of articles we accept and publish. We are especially looking for upbeat articles which affirm the simple ways in which the Catholic faith is expressed in our daily life. Articles on family and parish life, including seasonal articles, how-to pieces, inspirational prayer, spiritual life and Church traditions, will be gladly reviewed for possible publication."

GROUP MAGAZINE, P.O. Box 481, Loveland CO 80538. (303)669-3836. Fax: (303)669-3269. E-mail: rick_lawrence@ministrynet.usa.net. Contact: Rick Lawrence, editor. Publisher: Rocky Gilmore. Departments Editor: Barbara Beach. 60% freelance written. Bimonthly magazine covering youth ministry. "Writers must be actively involved in youth ministry. Articles we accept are practical, not theoretical, and focused for local church youth workers." Estab. 1974. Circ. 57,000. **Pays on acceptance.** Publishes ms an average of 6 months after acceptance. Byline given. Offers $20 kill fee. Buys all rights. Submit seasonal material 7 months in advance. Reports in 2 months. Sample copy for $2 and 9×12 SAE. Writer's guidelines for SASE.

Nonfiction: How-to (youth ministry issues). No personal testimony, theological or lecture-style articles. Buys 50-60 mss/year. Query. Length: 250-2,200 words. Pays $35-250. Sometimes pays for phone calls on agreement.

Photos: State availability of photos with submission. Model releases and identification of subjects required. Buys all rights.

Tips: "Need more 'mini-articles' of 250 words or less in the following areas: youth outreach ideas; working with parents; working with youth; working with adult volunteers; tips on managing your personal life."

GUIDEPOSTS MAGAZINE, 16 E. 34th St., New York NY 10016-4397. Website: http://www.guideposts. org. Editor: Fulton Oursler, Jr. 30% freelance written. "Works with a small number of new/unpublished writers each year. *Guideposts* is an inspirational monthly magazine for people of all faiths, in which men and women from all walks of life tell in first-person narrative how they overcame obstacles, rose above failures, handled sorrow, learned to master themselves and became more effective people through faith in God." Estab. 1945. Publishes ms an "indefinite" number of months after acceptance. Pays 25% kill fee for assigned articles. "Most of our stories are ghosted articles, so the writer would not get a byline unless it was his/her own story." Buys all rights and second serial (reprint) rights. Reports in 2 months.

Nonfiction and Fillers: Articles and features should be written in simple, anecdotal style with an emphasis on human interest. Short mss of approximately 250-750 words (pays $50-200) considered for such features as "Angels Among Us," "The Divine Touch" and general one-page stories. Address short items to Celeste McCauley. For full-length mss, 750-1,500 words, pays $200-400. All mss should be typed, double-spaced and accompanied by SASE. Annually awards scholarships to high school juniors and seniors in writing contest. Buys 40-60 unsolicited mss/year. Pays expenses of writers on assignment.

Tips: "Study the magazine before you try to write for it. Each story must make a single spiritual point. The freelancer would have the best chance of breaking in by aiming for a one- or two-page article. Sensitively written anecdotes are extremely useful. And it is much easier to just sit down and write them than to have to go through the process of preparing a query. They should be warm, well written, intelligent and upbeat. We like personal narratives that are true and have some universal relevance, but the religious element does not have to be driven home with a sledge hammer. A writer succeeds with us if he or she can write a true article in short-story form with scenes, drama, tension and a resolution of the problem presented. We are over-stocked with medical-type, personal experience stories, but we're in need of stories in which faith in God helps people succeed in business or with other life challenges."

HOME TIMES, A Good Little Newspaper, Neighbor News, Inc., 3676 Collin Dr., #12, West Palm Beach FL 33406. (407)439-3509. Editor: Dennis Lombard. 80% freelance written. Monthly tabloid of conservative, pro-Christian news and views. "*Home Times* is a conservative newspaper written for the general public but with a pro-Christian, family-values slant. It is not religious or preachy." Estab. 1988. Circ. 5,000. Pays on publication. Publishes ms an average of 3 months after acceptance. Byline given. No kill fee. Buys one-time rights or makes work-for-hire assignments. Editorial lead time 1 month. Submit seasonal material 1 month in advance. Accepts simultaneous submissions. Reports in 1 month. Sample copy for $3 and 9×12 SASE with 4 first-class stamps. Writer's guidelines for #10 SASE.

  • *Home Times* wants material for Human Heroes, Fatherhood, The Children and People Features with photos. The editor notes the magazine will become a weekly later this year, tripling freelance needs.

Nonfiction: Current events, essays, general interest, historical/nostalgic, how-to, humor, inspirational, interview/profile, opinion, personal experience, photo feature, religious, travel. "Nothing preachy, moralistic or with churchy slant." Buys 50 mss/year. Send complete ms. Length 900 maximum words. Pays $5 minimum. Pays contributor's copies on mutual agreement. Sometimes pays expenses of writers on assignment.

Reprints: Send tearsheet or photocopy of article or short story and information about when and where the material previously appeared. Pays up to 50% of amount paid for an original article.

Photos: Send photos with submission. Reviews 4×5 prints. Offers $5-10/photo used. Captions, model releases, identification of subjects required. Buys one-time rights.

Columns/Departments: Buys 50 mss/year. Send complete ms. Pays $5-15.

Fiction: Historical, humorous, mainstream, religious, issue-oriented contemporary. "Nothing preachy, moralistic." Buys 10 mss/year. Send complete ms. Length: 500-1,000 words. Pays $5-15.

Poetry: Free verse, light verse, traditional. Buys 12 poems/year. Submit maximum 3 poems. Lines: 2-24 lines. Pays $5.

Fillers: Anecdotes, facts, newsbreaks, short humor. Uses 25/year. Length: to 100 words. Pays 6 issues.

Tips: "We encourage new writers. We are different from ordinary news or religious publications. We strongly suggest you read guidelines and sample issues. (2 issues for $3 and 9×12 SASE with 4 stamps; writer's subscription 12 issues for $9.) We are most open to material for new columns; journalists covering hard news in major news centers—with Conservative slant. Also, lots of letters and op-eds though we don't always pay for them."

‡THE JEWISH NEWS, (formerly *Jewish Weekly News*), Or V'Shalom, Inc., P.O. Box 269, Northampton MA 01061. (413)582-9870. Editor: Kenneth G. White. 25% freelance written. Jewish news and features, secular and non-secular; World Judaism; arts (New England based). Estab. 1945. Circ. 5,000. Pays on publication. Publishes ms an average of 2 months after acceptance. Byline given. Not copyrighted. Buys first North American serial rights and second serial (reprint) rights. Submit seasonal material 2 months in advance. Accepts simultaneous submissions. Reports in 3 months. Sample copy for 9×12 SAE with 5 first-class stamps.

Nonfiction: Interview/profile, religious, travel. Special issues: Jewish New Year (September); Chanukah (December); Bridal (Winter/Fall); Bar/Bat Mitzvahs (May). Buys 20 mss/year. Query with published clips. Length: 300-1,000 words. Pays $15-25/article.

Reprints: Send photocopy of article or typed ms with rights for sale noted and information about when and where the article previously appeared. Pays 100% of amount paid for an original article.

Photos: Send photos with submission. Reviews 5×7 prints. Offers no additional payment for photos accepted with ms. Identification of subjects required.

Columns/Departments: Jewish Kitchen (Kosher recipes), 300-500 words. Buys 10 mss/year. Query with published clips. Length: 300-1,000 words. Pays $15-25/article.

KALEIDOSCOPE, A Magazine About Today's Christians, P.O. Box 2103, Ellicott City MD 21041. (410)203-2577. Fax: (410)992-9118. E-mail: kaleidomin@aol.com. Editor: J. E. Skillington. 95% freelance written. Bimonthly magazine covering United Methodists and other mainstream Christians. "*Kaleidoscope* is a lifestyle magazine about today's United Methodists facing challenges and together building a church for future generations. It includes inspiring articles and photos about mission work, faith in action, new ideas for personal ministries, and the history of our church." Estab. 1993. Circ. 110,000. Pays on publication. Publishes ms 6 months after acceptance. Byline given. Offers $75 kill fee. Buys first North American serial rights. Editorial lead time 6 months. Submit seasonal material 9 months in advance. Reports in 6 weeks on queries; 2 months on mss. Sample copy for 9×12 SAE. Writer's guidelines free.

Nonfiction: General interest, historical/nostalgic, interview/profile, personal experience, photo feature, religious. Special issues: Christmas and Easter. No poetry, no general articles without any Christian angle. Buys 75 mss/year. Query with published clips. Length: 1,500-2,300 words. Pays $125-300. Pays expenses of writers on assignment.

Photos: Send photos with submission. Reviews transparencies. Offers $75-150/article. Captions, model releases and identification of subjects required. Buys all rights.

Columns/Departments: Query. Pays $75-100.

‡THE LIVING CHURCH, Living Church Foundation, 816 E. Juneau Ave., P.O. Box 92936, Milwaukee WI 53202. (414)276-5420. Fax: (414)276-7483. E-mail: livngchrch@aol.com. Editor: David Kalvelage. Managing Editor: John Schuessler. 50% freelance written. Weekly religious magazine on the Episcopal church. News or articles of interest to members of the Episcopal church. Estab. 1878. Circ. 8,000. Does not pay unless article is requested. Publishes ms an average of 3 months after acceptance. Byline given. Buys one-time rights. Editorial lead time 3 weeks. Submit seasonal material 1 month in advance. Reports in 2 weeks on queries; 1 month on mss. Sample copy free on request.

Nonfiction: Opinion, personal experience, photo feature, religious. Buys 10 mss/year. Send complete ms. Length: 1,000 words. Pays $25-100 for assigned articles. Sometimes pays expenses of writers on assignment.

Photos: Send photos with submission. Reviews any size prints. Offers $15-50/photo. Buys one-time rights.

Columns/Departments: Benediction (devotional) 250 words; Viewpoint (opinion) under 1,000 words. Send complete ms. Pays $50 maximum.

Poetry: Light verse, traditional.

LIVING WITH TEENAGERS, Baptist Sunday School Board, 127 Ninth Ave. N., Nashville TN 37234. (615)251-2229. Fax: (615)251-5008. Editor: Ellen Oldacre. 30% freelance written. Works with a number of new/unpublished writers each year. Monthly magazine about teenagers for parents of teenagers. Estab. 1978. Circ. 50,000. Pays within 2 months of acceptance. Publishes ms an average of 10 months after acceptance. Buys all or first rights. Submit seasonal material 1 year in advance. Reports in 2 months. Sample copy for 9×12 SAE with 4 first-class stamps. Writer's guidelines for #10 SASE. Résumés and queries only.

THE LOOKOUT, 8121 Hamilton Ave., Cincinnati OH 45231-9981. (513)931-4050. Fax: (513)931-0904. Assistant Editor: Andrea C. Ritze. 50-60% freelance written. Often works with new/unpublished writers. Weekly magazine for Christian adults, with emphasis on spiritual growth, family life, and topical issues. Audience is mainly conservative Christians. Estab. 1894. **Pays on acceptance.** Publishes ms an average of 6 months after acceptance. Byline given. Buys first serial, one-time, second serial (reprint) or simultaneous rights. Accepts simultaneous submissions. Reports in 4 months, sometimes longer. Sample copy and writer's guidelines for 50¢. "We now work from a theme list, which is available on request with our guidelines." Guidelines only for #10 SASE.

Nonfiction: "Seeks stories about real people; items that are helpful in practical Christian living (how-to's); items that shed Biblical light on matters of contemporary controversy; and items that motivate, that lead the reader to ask, 'Why shouldn't I try that?' Articles should tell how real people are involved for Christ. In choosing topics, *The Lookout* considers timeliness, the church and national calendar, and the ability of the material to fit the above guidelines. Remember to aim at laymen." Submit complete ms. Length: 400-2,000 words. Pays 5-12¢/word. We also use inspirational short pieces. "About 400-700 words is a good length for these. Relate an incident that illustrates a point without preaching."

Reprints: Send typed ms with rights for sale noted and information about when and where the article previously appeared. Pays 60% of amount paid for an original article.

Fiction: "A short story is printed in many issues; it is usually between 1,200-2,000 words long and should be as true to life as possible while remaining inspirational and helpful. Use familiar settings and situations. Most often we use stories with a Christian slant." Pays 5-12¢/word.

Photos: Reviews b&w prints, 4×6 or larger. Pays $25-50. Pays $75-200 for color transparencies for covers and inside use. Needs photos of people, especially adults in a variety of settings. Send to Photo Editor, Standard Publishing, at the above address.

Tips: "We have tightened the focus of *The Lookout*, to concentrate on three areas: (1) personal Christian growth; (2) home and family life; (3) social issues from a Christian perspective."

THE LUTHERAN, Magazine of the Evangelical Lutheran Church in America, Evangelical Lutheran Church in America, 8765 W. Higgins Rd., Chicago IL 60631-4183. (312)380-2540. Fax: (312)380-2751. E-mail: lutheran.parti@ecunet.org. Editor: Edgar R. Trexler. Managing Editor: Roger R. Kahle. 30%

freelance written. Monthly magazine for "lay people in church. News and activities of the Evangelical Lutheran Church in America, news of the world of religion, ethical reflections on issues in society, personal Christian experience." Estab. 1988. Circ. 800,000. **Pays on acceptance.** Publishes ms an average of 3 months after acceptance. Byline given. Offers 50% kill fee. Buys first rights. Submit seasonal/holiday material 4 months in advance. Query required. Reports in 3 weeks. Free sample copy and writer's guidelines.

Nonfiction: David L. Miller. Inspirational, interview/profile, personal experience, photo feature, religious. "No articles unrelated to the world of religion." Buys 40 mss/year. Query with published clips. Length: 1,000-1,500 words. Pays $400-1,000 for assigned articles; $100-500 for unsolicited articles. Pays expenses of writers on assignment.

Photos: Send photos with submission. Reviews contact sheets, transparencies, prints. Offers $50-175/photo. Captions and identification of subjects required. Buys one-time rights.

Columns/Departments: Lite Side (humor—church, religious), In Focus, Living the Faith, Values & Society, In Our Churches, Our Church at Work, 25-100 words. Send complete ms. Length: 25-100 words. Pays $10.

Tips: "Writers have the best chance selling us feature articles."

THE LUTHERAN JOURNAL, 7317 Cahill Rd., Edina MN 55439-2081. Publisher: Michael L. Beard. Editor: Rev. Armin U. Deye. Quarterly family magazine for Lutheran Church members, middle age and older. Estab. 1938. Circ. 125,000. Pays on publication. Byline given. Accepts simultaneous submissions. Reports in 4 months. Sample copy for 9×12 SAE with 2 first-class stamps.

Nonfiction: Inspirational, religious, human interest, historical articles. Interesting or unusual church projects. Informational, how-to, personal experience, interview, humor, think articles. Buys 25-30 mss/year. Submit complete ms. Length: 1,500 words maximum; occasionally 2,000 words. Pays 1-4¢/word.

Reprints: Send tearsheet or photocopy of article typed ms with rights for sale noted and information about when and where the article previously appeared. Pays 50% of amount paid for an original article.

Photos: Send b&w and color photos with accompanying ms. Captions required.

Fiction: Mainstream, religious, historical. Must be suitable for church distribution. Length: 2,000 words maximum. Pays 1-2¢/word.

THE LUTHERAN WITNESS, The Lutheran Church—Missouri Synod, 1333 S. Kirkwood Rd., St. Louis MO 63122. (314)965-9000. Editor: Rev. David Mahsman. Contact: David Strand. 50% freelance written. Monthly magazine. "*The Lutheran Witness* provides Missouri Synod laypeople with stories and information that complement congregational life, foster personal growth in faith, and help interpret the contemporary world from a Christian perspective." Estab. 1882. Circ. 325,000. **Pays on acceptance.** Publishes ms an average of 6 months after acceptance. Byline given. Offers 50% kill fee. Buys first rights. Editorial lead time 4 months. Submit seasonal material 6 months in advance. Accepts simultaneous submissions. Reports in 2 months. Sample copy and writer's guidelines free on request.

Nonfiction: General interest, humor, inspirational, interview/profile, opinion, personal experience, religious. Buys 40-50 mss/year. Send complete ms. Length: 250-1,600. Pays $100-300. Pays expenses of writers on assignment.

Reprints: Accepts previously published submissions.

Photos: Send photos with submission. Offers $50-200/photo. Captions required. Buys one-time rights.

Columns/Departments: Humor, Opinion, Bible Studies. Buys 60 mss/year. Send complete ms. Pays $50-100.

THE MESSENGER OF THE SACRED HEART, Apostleship of Prayer, 661 Greenwood Ave., Toronto, Ontario M4J 4B3 Canada. (416)466-1195. Editor: Rev. F.J. Power, S.J. Monthly magazine for "Canadian and US Catholics interested in developing a life of prayer and spirituality; stresses the great value of our ordinary actions and lives." 20% freelance written. Estab. 1891. Circ. 16,000. Buys first rights only. Byline given. **Pays on acceptance.** Submit seasonal material 5 months in advance. Reports in 1 month. Sample copy for $1 and 7½×10½ SAE. Writer's guidelines for #10 SASE.

Fiction: Religious/inspirational. Stories about people, adventure, heroism, humor, drama. Buys 12 mss/year. Send complete ms with SAE and IRCs. Does not return unsolicited mss without SASE. Length: 750-1,500 words. Pays 4¢/word.

Tips: "Develop a story that sustains interest to the end. Do not preach, but use plot and characters to convey the message or theme. Aim to move the heart as well as the mind. Before sending, cut out unnecessary or unrelated words or sentences. If you can, add a light touch or a sense of humor to the story. Your ending should have impact, leaving a moral or faith message for the reader."

‡**THE MIRACULOUS MEDAL,** 475 E. Chelten Ave., Philadelphia PA 19144-5785. (215)848-1010. Fax: (215)848-1014. Editorial Director: Rev. John W. Gouldrick, C.M. 40% freelance written. Quarterly. Estab. 1915. **Pays on acceptance.** Publishes ms an average of 2 years after acceptance. Buys first North American serial rights. Buys articles only on special assignment. Reports in 3 months. Sample copy for 6×9 SAE with 2 first-class stamps.

Fiction: Should not be pious or sermon-like. Wants good general fiction—not necessarily religious, but if religion is basic to the story, the writer should be sure of his facts. Only restriction is that subject matter and treatment must not conflict with Catholic teaching and practice. Can use seasonal material, Christmas stories. Length: 2,000 words maximum. Occasionally uses short-shorts from 750-1,250 words. Pays 2¢/word minimum.

Poetry: Maximum of 20 lines, preferably about the Virgin Mary or at least with religious slant. Pays 50¢/line minimum.

‡THE MONTANA CATHOLIC, Diocese of Helena, P.O. Box 1729, Helena MT 59624. (406)442-5820. Fax: (406)442-5191. Editor: Gerald M. Korson. 5-10% freelance written. Tabloid published 16 times/year. "We publish news and features from a Catholic perspective, particularly as they pertain to the church in western Montana." Estab. 1932. Circ. 8,800. **Pays on acceptance.** Publishes ms an average of 1 year after acceptance. Byline sometimes given. Offers 35% kill fee. Buys first North American serial, first, one-time, second serial (reprint) or simultaneous rights. Editorial lead time 1 month. Submit seasonal material 3 months in advance. Accepts simultaneous submissions. Reports in 1 month on queries; 2 months on mss. Sample copy for $1. Writer's guidelines for #10 SASE.

Nonfiction: Humor, inspirational, interview/profile, religious. Special issues: Marriage (February); Vocations (Spring and Fall); Easter, Lent, Christmas, Advent; Health; Older Persons; Death and Dying (Fall). Buys 10 mss/year. Send complete ms. Length: 400-1,200 words. Pays $10-100 for assigned articles; $10-50 for unsolicited articles. Sometimes pays expenses of writers on assignment.

Reprints: Accepts previously published submissions.

Photos: Reviews contact sheets, 5×7 prints. Offers $5-20/photo. Identification of subjects required. Buys one time rights.

Poetry: Free verse, light verse, traditional. Buys 2 poems/year. Submit maximum 3 poems. Length: 6-40 lines. Pays $5-10..

Tips: "Best bet is seasonal pieces, topics related to our special supplements and features with a tie-in to western Montana—always with a Catholic angle."

MOODY MAGAZINE, Moody Bible Institute, 820 N. LaSalle Blvd., Chicago IL 60610. (312)329-2164. Fax: (312)329-2149. E-mail: moodyltrs.@aol.com. Website: http://moody.edu. Managing Editor: Andrew Scheer. 62% freelance written. Bimonthly magazine for evangelical Christianity (6 issues/year). "Our readers are conservative, evangelical Christians highly active in their churches and concerned about applying their faith in daily living." Estab. 1900. Circ. 115,000. **Pays on acceptance.** Publishes ms an average of 9 months after acceptance. Byline given. Buys first North American serial rights. Submit seasonal material 9 months in advance. Query for all submissions. Unsolicited mss will be returned unread. Reports in 2 months. Sample copy for 9×12 SASE with $2 first-class postage. Writer's guidelines for #10 SASE.

  ● Ranked as one of the best markets for freelance writers in *Writer's Yearbook*'s annual "Top 100 Markets," January 1996.

Nonfiction: Personal narratives (on living the Christian life), a few reporting articles. Buys 55 mss/year. Query. Length: 750-2,000 words. Pays 15¢/word for queried articles; 20¢/word for assigned articles. Sometimes pays the expenses of writers on assignment.

Columns/Departments: First Person (the only article written for non-Christians; a personal conversion testimony written by the author [will accept 'as told to's']; the objective is to tell a person's testimony in such a way that the reader will understand the gospel and want to receive Christ as Savior), 800-1,000 words; and Just for Parents (provides practical anecdotal guidance for parents, solidly based on biblical principles), 1,500-1,600 words. Buys 12 mss/year. Query. Pays 15¢/word.

Tips: "We have moved to bimonthly publication, with a larger editorial well in each issue. We want articles that cover a broad range of topics, but with one common goal: to foster application by a broad readership of specific biblical principles. By publishing accounts of people's spiritual struggles, growth and discipleship, our aim is to encourage readers in their own obedience to Christ. While *Moody* continues to look for many authors to use a personal narrative style, we're also looking for some pieces that use an anecdotal reporting approach."

MY DAILY VISITOR, Our Sunday Visitor, Inc., 200 Noll Plaza, Huntington IN 46750. (219)356-8400. Editors: Catherine and William Odell. 99% freelance written. Bimonthly magazine of Scripture meditations based on the day's Catholic mass readings. Circ. 30,000. **Pays on acceptance.** Publishes ms an average of 6 months after acceptance. Byline given. Not copyrighted. Buys one-time rights. Reports in 2 months. Sample copy and writer's guidelines for #10 SAE with 2 first-class stamps. "Guest editors write on assignment basis only."

Nonfiction: Inspirational, personal experience, religious. Buys 12 mss/year. Query with published clips. Length: 150-160 words times number of days in month. Pays $500 for 1 month (28-31) of meditations. Pays writers 25 gratis copies.

NEW WORLD OUTLOOK, The Mission Magazine of The United Methodist Church, General Board of Global Ministries, 475 Riverside Dr., Room 1333, New York NY 10115. Editor: Alma Graham.

Contact: Christie R. House. 20% freelance written. Bimonthly magazine covering United Methodist mission programs, projects, and personnel. "As the mission magazine of The United Methodist Church, we publish articles on or related to the mission programs, projects, institutions, and personnel of the General Board of Global Ministries, both in the United States and around the world." Estab. 1911. Circ. 30,000. Pays on publication. Publishes ms an average of 4 months after acceptance. Byline given. Offers 50% kill fee or $100. Buys all rights. Editorial lead time 4 months. Submit seasonal material 4 months in advance. No simultaneous or previously published submissions. Sample copy for $2.50.

Nonfiction: Photo features, mission reports, mission studies. Special issues: Brazil; Christians Living in a Violent World. Buys 24 mss/year. Query. Length: 500-2,000 words. Pays $50-300. Sometimes pays expenses of writers on assignment.

Photos: State availability of photos with submission. Reviews transparencies, prints. Offers $25-150/photo. Captions, identification of subjects required.

Tips: "Write for a list of United Methodist mission institutions, projects, or personnel in the writer's geographic area or in an area of the country or the world to which the writer plans to travel (at writer's own expense). Photojournalists have a decided advantage."

OBLATES, Missionary Association of Mary Immaculate, 15 S. 59th St., Belleville IL 62223-4694. (618)233-2238. Managing Editor: Christine Portell. Contact: Mary Mohrman, manuscripts editor. 30-50% freelance written. Prefers to work with published writers. Bimonthly inspirational magazine for Christians; audience mainly older adults. Circ. 500,000. **Pays on acceptance.** Usually publishes ms within 2 years after acceptance. Byline given. Buys first North American serial rights. Submit seasonal material 8 months in advance. Reports in 6 months. Sample copy and writer's guidelines for 6×9 or larger SAE with 2 first-class stamps.

Nonfiction: Inspirational and personal experience with positive spiritual insights. No preachy, theological or research articles. Avoid current events and controversial topics. Send complete ms. Length: 500 words. Pays $80.

Poetry: Light verse—reverent, well written, perceptive, with traditional rhythm and rhyme. "Emphasis should be on inspiration, insight and relationship with God." Submit maximum 2 poems. Length: 8-16 lines. Pays $30.

Tips: "Our readership is made up mostly of mature Americans who are looking for comfort, encouragement, and a positive sense of applicable Christian direction to their lives. Focus on sharing of personal insight to problem (i.e. death or change), but must be positive, uplifting. We have well-defined needs for an established market, but are always on the lookout for exceptional work."

‡ORTHODOX MISSION, AXIOS Publishing, Inc., 30-32 Macaw Ave., P.O. Box 279, Belmopan, Belize. (011)501-823284. Fax: (011)501-823633. E-mail: danielg@btl.net. Editor: Father Daniel. 20% freelance written. Quarterly newsletter. "We cover the mission activities of the Orthodox Church in Belize, as well as cover all items of interest concerning Belize so the world in general may get to know the country better." Estab. 1990. Circ. 15,487. **Pays on acceptance**. Publishes ms an average of 4 months after acceptance. Byline given. Buys first rights. Editorial lead time 4 months. Submit seasonal material 5 months in advance. Accepts simultaneous submissions. Reports in 1 month on queries; 4 months on mss. Sample copy for $2. No American stamps please. Belize has its own post office.

Nonfiction: Book excerpts, essays, general interest, historical/nostalgic, interview/profile, religious, travel. Buys 10-20 mss/year. Query. Length: open. Pays $50-1,000.

Reprints: Accepts previously published submissions.

Fillers: Anecdotes, facts, gags to be illustrated by cartoonist, short humor. Buys 10-15/year. Length: open. Pays $10-100.

OUR FAMILY, Oblate Fathers of St. Mary's Province, P.O. Box 249, Battleford, Saskatchewan S0M 0E0 Canada. (306)937-7771. Fax: (306)937-7644. Editor: Nestor Gregoire. 60% freelance written. Prefers to work with published/established writers. Monthly magazine for average family men and women with high school and early college education. Estab. 1949. Circ. 14,265. **Pays on acceptance.** Publishes ms an average of 6 months after acceptance. Byline given. Offers 100% kill fee. Generally purchases first North American serial rights; also buys all, simultaneous, second serial (reprint) or one-time rights. Submit seasonal material 4 months in advance. Accepts simultaneous submissions. Reports in 1 month. *Writer's Market* recommends allowing 2 months for reply. Sample copy for 9×12 SAE with $2.50 postage. Only Canadian postage or IRC useful in Canada. Writer's guidelines.

Nonfiction: Humor (related to family life or husband/wife relations), inspirational (anything that depicts people responding to adverse conditions with courage, hope and love), personal experience (with religious dimensions), photo feature (particularly in search of photo essays on human/religious themes and on persons whose lives are an inspiration to others). Accepts phone queries. Buys 72-88 unsolicited mss/year. Pays expenses of writers on assignment.

Reprints: Send tearsheet or photocopy of article or typed ms with rights for sale noted and information about when and where the article previously appeared.

Photos: Photos purchased with or without accompanying ms. Pays $35 for 5×7 or larger b&w glossy prints and color photos (which are converted into b&w). Offers additional payment for photos accepted with ms (payment for these photos varies according to their quality). Free photo spec sheet for SASE.

Poetry: Avant-garde, free verse, haiku, light verse, traditional. Buys 4-10 poems/issue. Length: 3-30 lines. Pays 75¢-$1/line. Must have a religious dimension.

Fillers: Jokes, gags, anecdotes, short humor. Buys 2-10/issue.

Tips: "Writers should ask themselves whether this is the kind of an article, poem, etc. that a busy housewife would pick up and read when she has a few moments of leisure. We are particularly looking for articles on the spirituality of marriage. We will be concentrating more on recent movements and developments in the church to help make people aware of the new church of which they are a part."

‡PENTECOSTAL EVANGEL, The General Council of the Assemblies of God, 1445 Boonville, Springfield MO 65802-1894. (417)862-2781. Fax: (417)862-0416. E-mail: pevangel@ag.org. Editor: Hal Donaldson. Contact: Ann Floyd, technical editor. 20% freelance written. Works with a small number of new/unpublished writers each year. Weekly magazine emphasizing news of the Assemblies of God for members of the Assemblies and other Pentecostal and charismatic Christians. Estab. 1913. Circ. 245,000. **Pays on acceptance.** Publishes ms an average of 6 months after acceptance. Byline given. Buys first serial rights, a few second serial (reprint) or one-time rights. Submit seasonal material 6 months in advance. Reports in 3 months. Free sample copy and writer's guidelines.

Nonfiction: Informational (articles on homelife that convey Christian teachings), inspirational, personal experience. Buys 3 mss/issue. Send complete ms. Length: 500-1,200 words. Pays $25-100. Sometimes pays expenses of writers on assignment.

Photos: Photos purchased without accompanying ms. Pays $30 for 8×10 b&w glossy prints; $50 for 35mm or larger color transparencies. Total purchase price for ms includes payment for photos.

Tips: "We publish first-person articles concerning spiritual experiences; that is, answers to prayer for help in a particular situation, of unusual conversions or healings through faith in Christ. All articles submitted to us should be related to religious life. We are Protestant, evangelical, Pentecostal, and any doctrines or practices portrayed should be in harmony with the official position of our denomination (Assemblies of God)."

THE PENTECOSTAL MESSENGER, Messenger Publishing House, P.O. Box 850, Joplin MO 64802-0850. (417)624-7050. Fax: (417)624-7102. Editor: Aaron Wilson. Managing Editor: Peggy Lee Allen. 10% or less freelance written. Works with small number of new/unpublished writers each year. Monthly magazine covering Pentecostal Christianity. "*The Pentecostal Messenger* is the official organ of the Pentecostal Church of God. It goes to ministers and church members." Estab. 1919. Circ. 6,000. Pays on publication. Publishes ms an average of 6 months after acceptance. Byline given. Buys second serial (reprint) or simultaneous rights. Submit seasonal material 4 months in advance. Accepts simultaneous submissions. Reports in 2 months. Sample copy for 9×12 SAE with 4 first-class stamps. Free writer's guidelines.

Nonfiction: Inspirational, personal experience, religious. Send complete ms. Length: 1,800 words. Pays 1½¢/word.

Reprints: Send tearsheet or photocopy of article or typed ms with rights for sale noted and information about when and where the article previously appeared. Pays 100% of amount paid for an original article.

Photos: Send photos with submission. Reviews 2¼×2¼ transparencies and prints. Offers $10-25/photo. Captions and model releases required. Buys one-time rights.

Tips: "Articles need to be inspirational, informative, written from a positive viewpoint, and not extremely controversial."

PIME WORLD, 17330 Quincy St., Detroit MI 48221-2765. (313)342-4066. Managing Editor: Paul Witte. 10% freelance written. Monthly (except July and August) magazine emphasizing foreign missionary activities of the Catholic Church in Burma, India, Bangladesh, the Philippines, Hong Kong, Africa, etc., for an adult audience, interested in current issues in the missions. Audience is largely high school educated, conservative in both religion and politics." Estab. 1954. Circ. 30,000. Pays on publication. Publishes ms an average of 3 months after acceptance. Buys all rights. Byline given. Submit seasonal material 4 months in advance. Accepts simultaneous submissions. Reports in 2 months.

Nonfiction: Informational and inspirational foreign missionary activities of the Catholic Church. Buys 5-10 unsolicited mss/year. Query or send complete ms. Length: 800-1,200 words. Pays 6¢/word.

Photos: Pays $10/color photo.

Tips: "Submit articles dealing with current issues of social justice, evangelization and pastoral work in Third World countries. Interviews of missionaries accepted. Good quality color photos greatly appreciated."

POWER FOR LIVING, Scripture Press Publications Inc., 1825 College Ave., Wheaton IL 60187. Editor: Donald H. Alban, Jr. 100% freelance written. Quarterly Sunday School take-home paper with 13 weekly parts. **Pays on acceptance.** Publishes ms an average of 1 year after acceptance. Byline given. Buys one-time rights and second serial (reprint) rights. Editorial lead time 1 year. Submit seasonal material 1 year in advance. Accepts simultaneous submissions. Sample copy and writer's guidelines for #10 SASE.

Nonfiction: Inspirational, personal experience. Buys 150 mss/year. Send complete ms. Length: 1,500 words. Pays to 15¢/word for assigned articles.

Reprints: Pays up to 10¢/word.

Photos: State availability of photos with submission. Negotiates payment individually. Model releases, identification of subjects required. Buys one-time rights.

PRAIRIE MESSENGER, Catholic Journal, Benedictine Monks of St. Peter's Abbey, P.O. Box 190, Muenster, Saskatchewan S0K 2Y0 Canada. (306)682-1772. Fax: (306)682-5285. Editor: Rev. Andrew Britz, OSB. Associate Editor: Marian Noll and Maureen Weber. 10% freelance written. Weekly Catholic journal with strong emphasis on social justice, Third World and ecumenism. Estab. 1904. Circ. 7,800. Pays on publication. Publishes ms an average of 4 months after acceptance. Byline given. Not copyrighted. Buys first North American serial, first, one-time, second serial (reprint) or simultaneous rights. Submit seasonal material 3 months in advance. Reports in 2 months. Sample copy and writers guidelines for 9×12 SAE with $1 Canadian postage or IRCs.

Nonfiction: Interview/profile, opinion, religious. "No articles on abortion or homosexuality." Buys 15 mss/year. Send complete ms. Length: 250-600 words. Pays $40-60. Sometimes pays expenses of writers on assignment.

Photos: Send photos with submission. Reviews 3×5 prints. Offers $15/photo. Captions required. Buys all rights.

PRESBYTERIAN RECORD, 50 Wynford Dr., North York, Ontario M3C 1J7 Canada. (416)444-1111. Fax: (416)441-2825. E-mail: perecord@web.ape.org. Website: http://www.presbycan.ca/. Editor: Rev. John Congram. 50% freelance written. Eager to work with new/unpublished writers. Monthly magazine for a church-oriented, family audience. Circ. 60,000. Pays on publication. Publishes ms an average of 4 months after acceptance. Buys first serial, one-time or simultaneous rights. Submit seasonal material 3 months in advance. Reports on accepted ms in 2 months. Returns rejected material in 3 months. Sample copy and writer's guidelines for 9×12 SAE with $1 Canadian postage or IRCs.

Nonfiction: Material on religious themes. Check a copy of the magazine for style. Also personal experience, interview, inspirational material. No material solely or mainly American in context. When possible, photos should accompany manuscript; e.g., current events, historical events and biographies. Buys 15-20 unsolicited mss/year. Query. Length: 1,000-2,000 words. Pays $40-60 (Canadian). Sometimes pays expenses of writers on assignment.

Photos: Pays $15-20 for b&w glossy photos. Uses positive transparencies for cover. Pays $50 plus. Captions required.

Tips: "There is a trend away from maudlin, first-person pieces redolent with tragedy and dripping with simplistic, pietistic conclusions."

PURPOSE, 616 Walnut Ave., Scottdale PA 15683-1999. (412)887-8500. Editor: James E. Horsch. 95% freelance written. Weekly magazine "for adults, young and old, general audience with varied interests. My readership is interested in seeing how Christianity works in difficult situations." Estab. 1968. Circ. 15,000. **Pays on acceptance.** Publishes ms an average of 8 months after acceptance. Byline given, including city, state/province. Buys one-time rights. Submit seasonal material 6 months in advance. Accepts simultaneous submissions. Reports in 2 months. Sample copy and writer's guidelines for 6×9 SAE with 2 first-class stamps.

Nonfiction: Inspirational stories from a Christian perspective. "I want upbeat stories that go to the core of human problems in family, business, politics, religion, gender and any other areas—and show how the Christian faith resolves them. *Purpose* is a magazine which conveys truth either through quality fiction or through articles that use the best story techniques. Our magazine accents Christian discipleship. Christianity affects all of life, and we expect our material to demonstrate this. I would like to see story-type articles about individuals, groups and organizations who are intelligently and effectively working at such human problems as hunger, poverty, international understanding, peace, justice, etc., because of their faith." Buys 130 mss/year. Submit complete ms. Length: 900 words maximum. Pays 5¢/word maximum. Buys one-time rights only.

Reprints: Send tearsheet or photocopy of article or short story or typed ms with rights for sale noted and information about when and where the material previously appeared.

Photos: Photos purchased with ms. Pays $5-15 for b&w (less for color), depending on quality. Must be sharp enough for reproduction; requires prints in all cases. Captions desired.

Fiction: Humorous, religious, historical fiction related to discipleship theme. "Produce the story with specificity so that it appears to take place somewhere and with real people. Essays and how-to-do-it pieces must include a lot of anecdotal, life exposure examples."

• Ranked as one of the best markets for fiction writers in *Writer's Digest*'s annual "Fiction 50," June 1996.

Poetry: Traditional poetry, blank verse, free verse, light verse. Buys 130 poems/year. Length: 12 lines maximum. Pays $7.50-15/poem depending on length and quality. Buys one-time rights only.

Fillers: Anecdotal items from 200-599 words. Pays 4¢/word maximum.

Tips: "We are looking for articles which show the Christian faith working at issues where people hurt; stories need to be told and presented professionally. Good photographs help place material with us."

‡QUEEN OF ALL HEARTS, Montfort Missionaries, 26 S. Saxon Ave., Bay Shore NY 11706-8993. (516)665-0726. Fax: (516)665-4349. Managing Editor: Roger Charest, S.M.M. 50% freelance written. Bimonthly magazine covering Marian doctrine and devotion. "Subject: Mary, Mother of Jesus, as seen in the sacred scriptures, tradition, history of the church, the early Christian writers, lives of the saints, poetry, art, music, spiritual writers, apparitions, shrines, ecumenism, etc." Estab. 1950. Circ. 4,000. **Pays on acceptance.** Publishes ms an average of 6 months after acceptance. Byline given. Not copyrighted. Submit seasonal material 6 months in advance. Reports in 2 months. Sample copy for $2.50.

Nonfiction: Essays, inspirational, personal experience, religious. Buys 25 ms/year. Send complete ms. Length: 750-2,500 words. Pays $40-60. Sometimes pays writers in contributor copies or other premiums "by mutual agreement."

Photos: Send photos with submission. Reviews transparencies, prints. Pay varies. Buys one-time rights.

Fiction: Religious. Buys 6 mss/year. Send complete ms. Length: 1,500-2,500 words. Pays $40-60.

Poetry: Joseph Tusiani, poetry editor. Free verse. Buys approximately 10 poems/year. Submit maximum of 2 poems at one time. Pays in contributor copies.

‡THE REPORTER, Women's American ORT, Inc., 315 Park Ave. S., New York NY 10010. (212)505-7700. Fax: (212)674-3057. Editor: Terese Loeb Kreuzer. 85% freelance written. Nonprofit journal published by Jewish women's organization. Quarterly magazine covering "Jewish topics, social issues, education, Mideast and women." Estab. 1966. Circ. 80,000. Payment time varies. Publishes ms ASAP after acceptance. Byline given. Buys first North American serial rights. Submit seasonal material 6 months in advance. Reports in 3 months. Free sample copy for 9×12 SAE with 3 first-class stamps.

Nonfiction: Book excerpts, essays, general interest, opinion. Buys approximately 30 mss/year. Send complete ms. Length: 1,800 words. Pay varies.

Photos: Send photos with submission. Identification of subjects required.

Columns/Departments: Books. Buys 4-10 mss/year. Send complete ms. Length: 200-1,000 words. Pay varies.

Tips: "Simply send manuscript; do not call. Open Forum (opinion section) is most open to freelancers, although all are open. Looking for well-written, substantive essays on relevant topics that evoke a response from the reader."

REVIEW FOR RELIGIOUS, 3601 Lindell Blvd., Room 428, St. Louis MO 63108-3393. (314)977-7363. Fax: (314)977-7362. Editor: David L. Fleming, S.J. 100% freelance written. Bimonthly magazine for Roman Catholic priests, brothers and sisters. Estab. 1942. Pays on publication. Publishes ms an average of 9 months after acceptance. Byline given. Buys first North American serial rights; rarely buys second serial (reprint) rights. Reports in 2 months.

Nonfiction: Articles on spiritual, liturgical, canonical matters only; not for general audience. Length: 2,000-8,000 words. Pays $6/page.

Tips: "The writer must know about religious life in the Catholic Church and be familiar with prayer, vows, community life and ministry."

ST. ANTHONY MESSENGER, 1615 Republic St., Cincinnati OH 45210-1298. Fax: (513)241-0399. Editor-in-Chief: Norman Perry. 55% freelance written. "Willing to work with new/unpublished writers if their writing is of a professional caliber." Monthly magazine for a national readership of Catholic families, most of which have children in grade school, high school or college. Circ. 325,000. **Pays on acceptance.** Publishes ms an average of 9 months after acceptance. Byline given. Buys first North American serial rights. Submit seasonal material 6 months in advance. Reports in 2 months. Sample copy and writer's guidelines for 9×12 SAE with 4 first-class stamps.

● The editor says he is short on seasonal, special occasion pieces. He also informs us that *St. Anthony Messenger* won four first place, two second place, two third place and four honorable mention awards in Catholic Press Association competition in 1995.

Nonfiction: How-to (on psychological and spiritual growth, problems of parenting/better parenting, marriage problems/marriage enrichment), humor, informational, inspirational, interview, personal experience (if pertinent to our purpose), personal opinion (limited use; writer must have special qualifications for topic), profile. Buys 35-50 mss/year. Length: 1,500-3,000 words. Pays 14¢/word. Sometimes pays the expenses of writers on assignment.

Fiction: Mainstream, religious. Buys 12 mss/year. Submit complete ms. Length: 2,000-3,000 words. Pays 14¢/word.

Tips: "The freelancer should ask why his or her proposed article would be appropriate for us, rather than for *Redbook* or *Saturday Review*. We treat human problems of all kinds, but from a religious perspective. Articles should reflect Catholic theology, spirituality and employ a Catholic terminology and vocabulary. We need more articles on prayer, scripture, Catholic worship. Get authoritative information (not merely library research); we want interviews with experts. Write in popular style; use lots of examples, stories and personal quotes. Word length is an important consideration."

ST. JOSEPH'S MESSENGER & ADVOCATE OF THE BLIND, Sisters of St. Joseph of Peace, St. Joseph's Home, P.O. Box 288, Jersey City NJ 07303-0288. Editor-in-Chief: Sister Ursula Maphet. 30% freelance written. Eager to work with new/unpublished writers. Semi annual magazine. Estab. 1898. Circ. 20,000. **Pays on acceptance.** Publishes ms an average of 3 months after acceptance. Buys first serial and second serial (reprint) rights; reassigns rights back to author after publication in return for credit line in next publication. Submit seasonal material 3 months in advance (no Christmas issue). Accepts simultaneous submissions. Reports in 1 month. Sample copy and writer's guidelines for 9×12 SAE with 2 first-class stamps.

Nonfiction: Humor, inspirational, nostalgia, personal opinion, personal experience. Buys 24 mss/year. Submit complete ms. Length: 300-1,500 words. Pays $3-15.

Reprints: Send typed ms with rights for sale noted and information about when and where the article previously appeared. Pays 100% of amount paid for an original article.

Fiction: Romance, suspense, mainstream, religious. Buys 30 mss/year. Submit complete ms. Length: 600-1,600 words. Pays $6-25.

Poetry: Light verse, traditional. Buys 25 poems/year. Submit maximum 10 poems. Length: 50-300 words. Pays $5-20.

Tips: "It's rewarding to know that someone is waiting to see freelancers' efforts rewarded by 'print'. It's annoying, however, to receive poor copy, shallow material or inane submissions. Human interest fiction, touching on current happenings, is what is most needed. We look for social issues woven into story form. We also seek non-preaching articles that carry a message that is positive."

SCP JOURNAL and SCP NEWSLETTER, Spiritual Counterfeits Project, P.O. Box 4308, Berkeley CA 94704-4308. (510)540-0300. Fax: (510)540-1107. Editor: Tal Brooke. Co-editor: Brooks Alexander. 5-10% freelance written. Prefers to work with published/established writers. "The *SCP Journal* and *SCP Newsletter* are quarterly publications geared to reach demanding non-believers while giving Christians authentic insight into the very latest spiritual and cultural trends." Their targeted audience is the educated lay reader. Estab. 1975. Circ. 18,000. Pays on publication. Publishes ms an average of 6 months after acceptance. Byline given. Rights negotiable. Accepts simultaneous submissions. Reports in 3 months. Sample copy for $8.75. Writer's guidelines for SASE.

Nonfiction: Book excerpts, essays, exposé, interview/profile, opinion, personal experience, religious. Query by telephone. Length: 2,500-3,500 words. Pay negotiated by phone.

• Less emphasis on book reviews and more focus on specialized "single issue" topics.

Reprints: Accepts previously published submissions after telephone inquiry. Send photocopy of article. Payment is negotiated.

Photos: State available photos. Reviews contact sheets and prints or slides. Offers no additional payment for photos accepted with ms. Captions, model releases, identification of subjects required. Buys one-time rights.

Tips: "The area of our publication most open to freelancers is specialized topics covered by *SCP*. Do not send unsolicited samples of your work until you have checked with us by phone to see it it fits *SCP*'s area of interest and publication schedule. The usual profile of contributors is that they are published within the field, have advanced degrees from top ranked universities, as well as experience that makes their work uniquely credible."

SIGNS OF THE TIMES, Pacific Press Publishing Association, P.O. Box 5353, Nampa ID 83653-5353. (208)465-2500. Fax: (208)465-2531. Editor: Marvin Moore. 40% freelance written. Works with a small number of new/unpublished writers each year. Monthly magazine on religion. "We are a Seventh-day Adventist publication encouraging the general public to practice the principles of the Bible." Estab. 1874. Circ. 245,000. Pays on publication. Publishes ms an average of 8 months after acceptance. Byline given. Offers kill fee. Buys first North American serial rights. Submit seasonal material 8 months in advance. Reports in 1 month on queries; 2 months on mss. *Writer's Market* recommends allowing 2 months for reply. Sample copy and writer's guidelines for 9×12 SAE with 3 first-class stamps.

Nonfiction: General interest, how-to, inspirational, interview/profile. "We want writers with a desire to share the good news of reconciliation with God. Articles should be people-oriented, well-researched and should have a sharp focus." Buys 75 mss/year. Query with or without published clips or send complete ms. Length: 650-2,500 words. Pays $100-400. Sometimes pays the expenses of writers on assignment.

Reprints: Send tearsheet or photocopy of article or typed ms with rights for sale noted and information about when and where the article previously appeared. Pays 50% of amount paid for an original article.

Photos: Merwin Stewart, photo editor. Send photos with query or ms. Reviews b&w contact sheets, 35mm color transparencies, 5×7 or 8×10 b&w prints. Pays $35-300 for transparencies; $20-50 for prints. Model releases and identification of subjects required (captions helpful). Buys one-time rights.

Tips: "Don't write for us unless you've read us and are familiar with Adventist beliefs."

‡**SISTERS TODAY**, The Liturgical Press, St. John's Abbey, Collegeville MN 56321-2099. Fax: (612)363-7130. E-mail: mwagner@csbsju.edu. Editor-in-Chief: Sister Mary Anthony Wagner, O.S.B. Associate Editor: Sister Mary Elizabeth Mason, O.S.B. Review Editor: Sister Stefanie Weisgram, O.S.B. Poetry Editor: Sister Mary Virginia Micka, C.S.J. 80% freelance written. Prefers to work with published/established writers. Bimonthly magazine exploring the role of women and the Church, primarily. Circ. 8,000. Pays on publication. Publishes ms several months after acceptance. Byline given. Buys first rights. Submit seasonal material 4 months in advance. Sample copy for $3.50.

Nonfiction: How-to (pray, live in a religious community, exercise faith, hope, charity etc.), informational, inspirational. Also articles concerning religious renewal, community life, worship, the role of women in the Church and in the world today. Buys 50-60 unsolicited mss/year. Query. Length: 500-2,500 words. Pays $5/printed page.

Poetry: Free verse, haiku, light verse, traditional. Buys 5-6 poems/issue. Submit maximum 4 poems. Pays $10.

Tips: "Some of the freelance material evidences the lack of familiarity with *Sisters Today*. We would prefer submitted articles not to exceed eight or nine pages."

‡**SOCIAL JUSTICE REVIEW**, 3835 Westminster Place, St. Louis MO 63108-3472. (314)371-1653. Contact: Rev. John H. Miller, C.S.C. 25% freelance written. Works with a small number of new/unpublished writers each year. Bimonthly. Estab. 1908. Publishes ms an average of 1 year after acceptance. Not copyrighted; "however special articles within the magazine may be copyrighted, or an occasional special issue has been copyrighted due to author's request." Buys first serial rights. Sample copy for 9 × 12 SAE with 3 first-class stamps.

Nonfiction: Scholarly articles on society's economic, religious, social, intellectual, political problems with the aim of bringing Catholic social thinking to bear upon these problems. Query with SASE. Length: 2,500-3,000 words. Pays about 2¢/word.

Reprints: Send typed ms with rights for sale noted and information about when and where the article previously appeared.

SPIRITUAL LIFE, 2131 Lincoln Rd. NE, Washington DC 20002-1199. (202)832-8489. Fax: (202)832-8967. E-mail: edodonnell@aol.com. Website: http://www.ocd.or.at/. Editor: Br. Edward O'Donnell, O.C.D. 80% freelance written. Prefers to work with published/established writers. Quarterly magazine for "largely Catholic, well-educated, serious readers. A few are non-Catholic or non-Christian." Circ. 12,000. **Pays on acceptance.** Publishes ms an average of 1 year after acceptance. Buys first North American serial rights. Reports in 2 months. Sample copy and writer's guidelines for 7 × 10 or larger SASE with 5 first-class stamps.

Nonfiction: Serious articles of contemporary spirituality. High quality articles about our encounter with God in the present day world. Language of articles should be college level. Technical terminology, if used, should be clearly explained. Material should be presented in a positive manner. Sentimental articles or those dealing with specific devotional practices not accepted. Buys inspirational and think pieces. "Brief autobiographical information (present occupation, past occupations, books and articles published, etc.) should accompany article." No fiction or poetry. Buys 20 mss/year. Length: 3,000-5,000 words. Pays $50 minimum and 5 contributor's copies. Book reviews should be sent to Br. Edward O'Donnell, O.C.D.

STANDARD, Nazarene International Headquarters, 6401 The Paseo, Kansas City MO 64131. (816)333-7000. Editor: Everett Leadingham. 100% freelance written. Works with a small number of new/unpublished writers each year. Weekly inspirational paper with Christian reading for adults. Estab. 1936. Circ. 160,000. **Pays on acceptance.** Publishes ms an average of 15-18 months after acceptance. Byline given. Buys one-time rights and second serial (reprint) rights. Submit seasonal material 6 months in advance. Reports in 10 weeks. Free sample copy. Writer's guidelines for SAE with 2 first-class stamps.

• *Standard* no longer publishes nonfiction but prefers fiction or fiction-type stories. Does not want how-to, inspiration/devotionals or social issues pieces.

Reprints: Send tearsheet of short story.

Fiction: Prefers fiction-type stories *showing* Christianity in action. Send complete ms; no queries. Length: 500-1,500 words. Pays 3½¢/word for first rights; 2¢/word for reprint rights.

Poetry: Free verse, haiku, light verse, traditional. Buys 50 poems/year. Submit maximum 5 poems. Length: 50 lines maximum. Pays 25¢/line.

Tips: "Stories should express Christian principles without being preachy. Setting, plot and characterization must be realistic. Fiction articles should be labeled 'Fiction' on the manuscript. True experience articles may be first person, 'as told to,' or third person."

ALWAYS CHECK the most recent copy of a magazine for the address and editor's name before you send in a query or manuscript.

TEACHERS INTERACTION, Concordia Publishing House, 3558 S. Jefferson Ave., St. Louis MO 63118-3968. Fax: (314)268-1329. Editor: Jane Haas. 20% freelance written. Quarterly magazine of practical, inspirational, theological articles for volunteer church school teachers. Material must be true to the doctrines of the Lutheran Church—Missouri Synod. Estab. 1960. Circ. 20,400. Pays on publication. Publishes ms an average of 1 year after acceptance. Byline given. Buys all rights. Submit seasonal material 1 year in advance. Reports in 3 months on mss. Sample copy for $2.75. Writer's guidelines for #10 SASE.

Nonfiction: How-to (practical help/ideas used successfully in own classroom), inspirational (to the church school worker—must be in accordance with LCMS doctrine), personal experience (of a Sunday school classroom nature—growth). No theological articles. Buys 6 mss/year. Send complete ms. Length: 750-1,500 words.

Fillers: "*Teachers Interaction* buys short Interchange items—activities and ideas planned and used successfully in a church school classroom." Buys 48/year. Length: 200 words maximum. Pays $20.

Tips: "Practical, or 'it happened to me' experiences articles would have the best chance. Also short items—ideas used in classrooms; seasonal and in conjunction with our Sunday school material, Our Life in Christ. Our format includes *all* volunteer church school teachers, Sunday school teachers, Vacation Bible School, and midweek teachers, as well as teachers of adult Bible studies."

THE UNITED CHURCH OBSERVER, 478 Huron St., Toronto, Ontario M5R 2R3 Canada. (416)960-8500. Fax: (416)960-8477. Editor: Muriel Duncan. 20% freelance written. Prefers to work with published/established writers. Monthly newsmagazine for people associated with The United Church of Canada. Deals primarily with events, trends and policies having religious significance. Most coverage is Canadian, but reports on international or world concerns will be considered. Pays on publication. Publishes ms an average of 4 months after acceptance. Byline usually given. Buys first serial rights and occasionally all rights.

Nonfiction: Occasional opinion features only. Extended coverage of major issues usually assigned to known writers. No opinion pieces or poetry. Submissions should be written as news, no more than 1,200 words length, accurate and well-researched. Queries preferred. Rates depend on subject, author and work involved. Pays expenses of writers on assignment "as negotiated."

Photos: Buys photographs with mss. Black & white should be 5×7 minimum; color 35mm or larger format. Payment varies.

Tips: "The writer has a better chance of breaking in at our publication with short articles; this also allows us to try more freelancers. Include samples of previous *news* writing with query. Indicate ability and willingness to do research, and to evaluate that research. The most frequent mistakes made by writers in completing an article for us are organizational problems, lack of polished style, short on research, and a lack of inclusive language."

UNITY MAGAZINE, Unity School of Christianity, 1901 NW Blue Parkway, Unity Village MO 64065. Editor: Philip White. Contact: Janet McNamara, associate editor. 25% freelance written. Interested in working with authors who are skilled at writing in the metaphysical Christian/New Thought/spiritual development persuasion. Estab. 1889. Circ. 120,000. **Pays on acceptance.** Publishes ms an average of 6-12 months after acceptance. Byline given. Buys first North American serial rights. Submit seasonal material 9 months in advance. Reports in 2 months on queries; 3 months on mss. Free sample copy and writer's guidelines upon request.

Nonfiction: *Spiritual* self-help and personal experience, holistic health, prosperity, biblical interpretation, religious, inspirational. Buys 200 mss/year. Send complete ms. Length: 1,000-1,800 words. Pays 20¢/word.

Reprints: Sometimes publishes reprints of previously published articles. Send photocopy of article and information about when and where the article previously appeared.

Photos: State availability of photos with submission. Reviews transparencies and prints. Offers $35-220/photo. Model releases and identification of subjects required. Buys one-time rights.

Poetry: Inspirational, religious and seasonal. Buys 25 poems/year. Submit maximum 5 poems. Length: 30 lines maximum. Pays $50 minimum.

THE UPPER ROOM, Daily Devotional Guide, P.O. Box 189, Nashville TN 37202-0189. (615)340-7252. Fax: (615)340-7006. Editor and Publisher: Janice T. Grana. Managing Editor: Mary Lou Redding. 95% freelance written. Eager to work with new/unpublished writers. Bimonthly magazine "offering a daily inspirational message which includes a Bible reading, text, prayer, 'Thought for the Day,' and suggestion for further prayer. Each day's meditation is written by a different person and is usually a personal witness about discovering meaning and power for Christian living through scripture study which illuminates daily life." Circ. 2.2 million (US); 385,000 outside US Pays on publication. Publishes ms an average of 1 year after acceptance. Byline given. Buys first North American serial rights and translation rights. Submit seasonal material 14 months in advance. Manuscripts are not returned. If writers include a stamped, self addressed postcard, we will notify them that their writing has reached us. This does not imply acceptance or interest in purchase. Sample copy and writer's guidelines with a 4× SAE and 2 first-class stamps.

• This market does not respond unless material is accepted for publication.

Nonfiction: Inspirational, personal experience, Bible-study insights. No poetry, lengthy "spiritual journey" stories. Buys 365 unsolicited mss/year. Send complete ms. Length: 250 words maximum. Pays $20.

Tips: "The best way to break into our magazine is to send a well-written manuscript that looks at the Christian faith in a fresh way. Standard stories and sermon illustrations are immediately rejected. We very much want to find new writers and welcome good material. We are particularly interested in meditations based on Old Testament characters and stories. Good repeat meditations can lead to work on longer assignments for our other publications, which pay more. A writer who can deal concretely with everyday situations, relate them to the Bible and spiritual truths, and write clear, direct prose should be able to write for *The Upper Room*. We want material that provides for more interaction on the part of the reader—meditation suggestions, journaling suggestions, space to reflect and link personal experience with the meditation for the day."

VIRTUE, The Christian Magazine for Women, 4050 Lee Vance View, Colorado Springs CO 80918-7102. (719)531-7776. Fax: (719)535-0172. Editor-at-Large: Nancie Carmichael. Contact: Jeanette Thomason, editor. 75% freelance written. Works with small number of new/unpublished writers each year. Bimonthly magazine that "shows through features and columns the depth and variety of expression that can be given to women and faith." Estab. 1978. Circ. 111,000. Pays on acceptance or publication. Publishes ms an average of 4 months after acceptance. Byline given. Buys first North American serial rights. Submit seasonal material 9 months in advance. Reports in 2 months. Sample copy for 9×12 SAE with 7 first-class stamps. Writer's guidelines for #10 SASE.

Nonfiction: Book excerpts, how-to, humor, inspirational, interview/profile, opinion, personal experience, religious. Buys 60 mss/year. Query. Length: 600-1,800 words. Pays 15-25¢/word.

Reprints: Accepts previously published submissions from a non-competing market. Send photocopy of article or short story or typed ms with rights for sale noted and information about when and where the article previously appeared.

Photos: State availability of photos with submission.

Columns/Departments: In My Opinion (reader editorial); One Woman's Journal (personal experience); Equipped for Ministry (Christian service potpourri). Buys 25 mss/year. Query. Length: 1,000-1,500. Pays 15-25¢/word.

Fiction: Humorous, religious. Buys 4-6 mss/year. Send complete ms. Length: 1,500-1,800 words. Pays 15-25¢/word.

Poetry: Free verse, traditional. Buys 7-10 poems/year. Submit maximum 3 poems. Length: 3-30 lines. Pays $15-50.

VITAL CHRISTIANITY, Warner Press, Inc., P.O. Box 2499, Anderson IN 46018-2499. (317)644-7721. E-mail: sb128@aol.com. or vchristmag@aol.com. Website: http://www.warnerpress.org. Editor-in-Chief: David C. Shultz. Contact: Steven A. Beverly, managing editor. 20-25% freelance written. Prefers to work with published/established writers. Monthly magazine covering Christian living for people attending local Church of God congregations. Estab. 1881. Circ. 26,000. **Pays on acceptance.** Byline given. Buys one-time rights. Submit seasonal material 6 months in advance. Reports in 6 weeks. Sample copy and writer's guidelines for 9×12 SASE with 7 first-class stamps.

Nonfiction: Humor (with religious point); inspirational (religious—not preachy); personal experience (related to putting one's faith into practice). Buys 125 mss/year. Length: 900 words maximum. Pays $10-140.

Reprints: Send typed ms with rights for sale noted and information about when and where the article previously appeared. Pays 100% of amount paid for an original article.

Tips: "Fillers, personal experience and good holiday articles are areas of our magazine open to freelancers. Writers should request our guidelines and list of upcoming topics of interest to determine if they have interest or expertise in writing for us. Always send SASE."

WHEREVER, In The World For Jesus' Sake, The Evangelical Alliance Mission, P.O. Box 969, Wheaton IL 60189. Editor: Jack Kilgore. Contact: Dana Felmly. 70% freelance written. Triannual magazine covering missionary activities. *"Wherever* is a thematic magazine which helps people decide if overseas missions is for them. Our audience is mostly college students, grad and seminary students, young professionals." Estab. 1976. Circ. 7,700. Pays on publication. Publishes ms an average of 8 months after acceptance. Byline given. Buys all rights unless other arrangements are made. Editorial lead time 9 months. No simultaneous submissions. Reports in 1 month on queries. Sample copy for 9×12 SAE with 3 first-class stamps. Writer's guidelines for #10 SASE.

Nonfiction: Book excerpts, humor, inspirational, interview/profile, personal experience. Buys 13 mss/year. Write for guidelines. Length: 500-1,000 words. Pays $75-125. Sometimes pays expenses of writers on assignment.

Photos: Send photos with submission. Reviews transparencies, prints. Offers no additional payment for photos accepted with ms. Captions, identification of subjects required. Buys first and reprint rights.

Fiction: *Only* if piece addresses the theme of a particular issue. Buys 1 mss/year. Write for guidelines. Length: 500-1,000 words. Pays $75-125.

Poetry: Avant-garde, free verse, Haiku, light verse, traditional considered. Buys up to 3 poems/year. Submit maximum 1 poem. Pays $75.

Tips: "Because of our focus, we have very specific needs. Write to us to get on our author mail list. Three times a year, we will send guidelines, story ideas, and the theme for the particular issue. After reading the guidelines, query us with your proposals. Authors are encouraged to go beyond our guides, suggesting more creative approaches to the theme."

THE WITNESS, Episcopal Church Publishing Co., 1249 Washington Blvd., #3115, Detroit MI 48226. (313)962-2650. Fax: (313)962-1012. E-mail: thewitness@ecunet.org. Editor: Jeanie Wylie-Kellermann. Managing Editor: Julie A. Wortman. Contact: Marianne Arbogast. 20% freelance written. Monthly magazine covering religion and politics from a left perspective. "Our readers are people of faith who are interested in wrestling with scripture and current events with the goal of serving God and effecting change that diminishes the privilege of the rich." Estab. 1917. Circ. 4,000. Pays on publication. Publishes ms an average of 3 months after acceptance. Byline given. Offers 50% kill fee. Buys first rights. Editorial lead time 6 weeks. Submit seasonal material 3 months in advance. Responds only to material accepted for publication. Sample copy and writer's guidelines free on request.

Nonfiction: Exposé, general interest, historical/nostalgic, humor, interview/profile, personal experience, photo feature, religious. Buys 10 mss/year. Query with or without published clips, or send complete ms. Length: 250-1,800 words. Pays $50-250 for assigned articles; $50-100 for unsolicited articles; and 1-year subscription. Sometimes pays expenses of writers on assignment.

Reprints: Accepts simultaneous submissions.

Photos: State availability of photos with submissions. Reviews prints. Offers $0-30/photo. Captions, identification of subjects required. Buys one-time rights.

Poetry: Buys 10 poems/year. Submit maximum 5 poems. Pays $0-30.

Tips: "We're eager for *short* news pieces that relate to racial-, gender- and eco-justice. Our issues are thematic which makes queries advisable. We don't publish material written in a dry academic style, we like stories that allow marginalized people to speak in their own words."

WOMAN'S TOUCH, Assemblies of God Women's Ministries Department (GPH), 1445 Boonville, Springfield MO 65802-1894. (417)862-2781. Fax: (417)862-0503. Editor: Peggy Musgrove. Associate Editor: Aleda Swartzendruber. 50% freelance written. Willing to work with new/unpublished writers. Bimonthly inspirational magazine for women. "Articles and contents of the magazine should be compatible with Christian teachings as well as human interests. The audience is women, both homemakers and those who are career-oriented." Estab. 1977. Circ. 21,000. **Pays on acceptance.** Byline given. Buys one-time rights. Submit seasonal/holiday material 8 months in advance. Reports in 3 months. Sample copy for 9½×11 SAE with 3 first-class stamps. Writer's guidelines for #10 SASE.

Nonfiction: General interest, how-to, inspirational, personal experience, religious, travel. Buys 30 mss/year. Send complete ms. Length: 500-800 words. Pays $10-35 for unsolicited articles.

Reprints: Send photocopy of article and information about when and where the article previously appeared.

Photos: State availability of photos with submission. Reviews negatives, transparencies, 4×6 prints. Offers no additional payment for photos accepted with ms. Identification of subjects required. Buys one-time rights.

Columns/Departments: 'A Final Touch' for short human interest articles—home and family or career-oriented." Length: 80-500 words. Pays $20-35. "A Better You" (health, wellness, beauty). Length: 200-500 words. Pays $15-25. "A Lighter Touch" (true, unpublished anecdotes). Length: 100 words. Pays $10.

Fillers: Facts. Buys 5/year. Length: 50-200. Pays $5-15.

THE WORLD, Unitarian Universalist Association, 25 Beacon St., Boston MA 02108-2800. (617)742-2100. Fax: (617)367-3237. E-mail: worldmag@uua.org. Editor-in-Chief: Linda Beyer McHugh. 50% freelance written. Bimonthly magazine covering religious education, spirituality, social consciousness, UUA projects and news, church communities, and personal philosophies of interesting people. "Purpose: to promote and inspire denominational self-reflection; to inform readers about the wide range of UU values, purposes, activities, aesthetics, and spiritual attitudes, and to educate readers about the history, personalities, and congregations that comprise UUism; to enhance its dual role of leadership and service to member congregations." Estab. 1987. Circ. 115,000. **Pays on acceptance.** Publishes ms an average of 1 year after acceptance. Byline given. Buys one-time rights. Editorial lead time 3 months. Submit seasonal material 3 months in advance. Pay varies. Reports in 2 months on queries; 3 months on mss. Sample copy and writer's guidelines for 9×12 SASE.

Nonfiction: All articles must have a UU angle. Essays, historical/nostalgic (Unitarian or Universalist focus), inspirational, interview/profile (with UU individual or congregation), commentary, photo feature (of UU congregation or project), religious and travel. No unsolicited poetry or fiction. Buys 10 mss/year. Query with published clips. Length: 1,500-3,500 words. Pays $400 minimum for assigned feature articles. Sometimes pays expenses of writers on assignment.

Photos: State availability of photos with submission. Reviews contact sheets. Offers no additional payment for photos accepted with ms. Captions, model releases and identification of subjects required. Buys one-time rights.

Columns/Departments: Among Ourselves (news, profiles, inspirational reports), 300-700 words; Book Reviews (liberal religion, social issues, politics), 600-800 words. Buys 15 mss/year. Query (profiles, book reviews) or send complete mss (news). Pays $75-250 for assigned articles and book reviews.

Tips: "Get to know your local congregation, find its uniqueness, tell its story. We don't have enough congregational profiles."

RETIREMENT

January 1, 1996 the first baby boomer turned 50. With peak earning power and increased leisure time, this generation is able to pursue varied interests while maintaining active lives. More people are retiring in their 50s, while others are starting a business or traveling and pursuing hobbies. These publications give readers specialized information on health and fitness, medical research, finances and other topics of interest, as well as general articles on travel destinations and recreational activities.

ACTIVE TIMES MAGAZINE, 417 Main St., Carbondale CO 81623. Editor: Chris Kelly. 80% freelance written. Quarterly magazine covering over-50 market. "We target active, adults over-50. We emphasize the positive, enjoyable aspects of aging." Estab. 1992. Circ. 7 million. **Pays on acceptance.** Publishes ms an average of 6 months after acceptance. Byline given. Offers 50% kill fee. Buys first North American serial rights. Editorial lead time 3 months. Submit seasonal material 6-9 months in advance. Reports in 3 weeks on queries. Sample copy for 9×12 SAE and 5 first-class stamps. Writer's guidelines for #10 SASE.

Nonfiction: General interest, historical/nostalgic, interview/profile, travel. Buys 50 mss/year. Query with published clips. Length: 500-2,000 words. Pays $75-1,000 for assigned articles; $50-250 for unsolicited articles. Sometimes pays expenses of writers on assignment.

Photos: State availability of photos with submission. Reviews contact sheets, 35mm transparencies, prints. Negotiates payment individually. Identification of subjects required. Buys one-time rights.

Columns/Departments: Profile (interesting over-50), 700 words. Buys 4-8 mss/year. Query with published clips. Pays $150-400.

Tips: "Write a detailed query, with substantiating clips. Query should show how story will appeal to active over-50 reader."

‡ALIVE! A Magazine for Christian Senior Adults, Christian Seniors Fellowship, P.O. Box 46464, Cincinnati OH 45246-0464. (513)825-3681. Editor: J. David Lang. Office Editor: A. June Lang. 60% freelance written. Quarterly magazine for senior adults ages 55 and older. "We need timely articles about Christian seniors in vital, productive lifestyles, travels or ministries." Estab. 1988. Pays on publication. Byline given. Buys first or second serial (reprint) rights. Submit seasonal material 6 months in advance. Reports in 6 weeks. Membership $10/year. Sample copy for 9×12 SAE with 3 first-class stamps. Writer's guidelines for #10 SASE.

Nonfiction: General interest, humor, inspirational, interview/profile, photo feature, religious, travel. Buys 25 mss/year. Send complete ms. Length: 600-1,200 words. Pays $18-75. Organization membership may be deducted from payment at writer's request.

Reprints: Send tearsheet or information about when and where the article previously appeared. Pays 60-75% of amount paid for an original article.

Photos: State availability of photos with submission. Offers $10-25. Model releases and identification of subjects required. Buys one-time rights.

Columns/Departments: Heart Medicine (humorous personal anecdotes; prefer grandparent/grandchild stories or anecdotes re: over 55 persons), 10-100 words; Games n' Stuff (word games, puzzles, word search), 200-500 words. Buys 50 mss/year. Send complete ms. Pays $2-25.

Fiction: Adventure, humorous, religious, romance (if it fits age group), slice-of-life vignettes, motivational/inspirational. Buys 12 mss/year. Send complete ms. Length: 600-1,500 words. Pays $20-60.

Fillers: Anecdotes, facts, gags to be illustrated by cartoonist, short humor. Buys 15/year. Length: 50-500 words. Pays $2-15.

Tips: "Include SASE. If second rights, list where article has appeared and whether manuscript is to be returned or tossed."

‡50 AND FORWARD MAGAZINE, D&D Communications, Inc., 160 Mayo Rd., Suite 100, Edgewater MD 21037. Editor: Debra Asberry. 85% freelance written. Monthly magazine covering editorial for active adults over 50. "Our editorial informs, educates and entertains the active adult over 50. The editorial is diverse, ranging from funny to serious subjects." Estab. 1993. Circ. 50,000. **Pays on acceptance**. Publishes ms an average of 6 months after acceptance. Byline given. Not copyrighted. Buys first rights. Editorial lead time 3 months. Submit seasonal material 6 months in advance. Accepts simultaneous submissions. Reports in 6 weeks on queries; 2 months on mss. Sample copy for 9×13 SAE and 4 first-class stamps.

Nonfiction: General interest, historical/nostalgic, interview/profile, photo feature, technical, travel. No opinion, religious or controversial. Buys 24-50 mss/year. Query or send complete ms. Length: 1,000-2,000 words. Pays $50-300 for assigned articles; $50-200 for unsolicited articles. Sometimes pays expenses of writers on assignment.

Photos: Send photos with submission. Reviews 3×5 prints. Offers no additional payment for photos accepted with ms. Captions required. Buys one-time rights.

Columns/Departments: Caregiver (issues for caring for others), 800-1,200 words; Book Reviews (interest to 50+ reader), 800-1,200. Buys 10 mss/year. Query or send complete ms. Pays $25-100.

Fiction: Adventure, historical, humorous, mystery, slice-of-life vignettes, suspense. No religious or horror. Buys 4 mss/year. Send complete ms. Length: 3,000-6,000 words. Pays $150-600.

Fillers: Facts, gags to be illustrated by cartoonist. Buys 6/year. Length: 100-500 words. Pays $25-100.

Tips: "Include a cover letter which summarizes your submission and suggest other topics you could write on."

‡FIFTY-SOMETHING MAGAZINE, For the Fifty-or-Better Mature Adult, Media Trends Publications, 1168 Beachview, Willoughby OH 44094. (216)951-2468. Editor: Linda L. Lindeman. 40% freelance written. Bimonthly magazine on aging, travel, relationships, money, health, hobbies. "We are looking for a positive and upbeat attitude on aging. Proving that 50 years old is *not* over-the-hill but instead a prime time of life." Estab. 1989. Circ. 25,000. Pays on publication. Byline given. Buys all rights. Submit seasonal material 4 months in advance. Accepts simultaneous submissions. Reports in 8 months. Sample copy for 9×12 SASE with 4 first-class stamps; writer's guidelines for #10 SASE.

Nonfiction: Book excerpts, essays, exposé, general interest, historical/nostalgic, how-to (sports), humor, inspirational, opinion, personal experience, photo feature, religious, travel, health, employment. Buys 6 mss/year. Query with published clips, or send complete ms. Length: 100-1,000 words. Pays $25-100. Sometimes pays expenses of writers on assignment.

• This magazine is overstocked with manuscripts.

Reprints: Send typed ms with rights for sale noted and information about when and where the material previously appeared. Pays 20% of amount paid for an original article.

Photos: Send photos with submission. Reviews contact sheets, negatives, transparencies, 5×7 prints. Offers $25-100/photo. Captions, model releases, identification of subjects required. Buys one-time or all rights.

Columns/Departments: Book Review (50 and over market); Movie/Play Review (new releases); Sports (for the mature adult); Travel (for the mature adult). Buys 50 mss/year. Send complete ms. Length: 100-1,000 words. Pays $25-100.

Fiction: Adventure, condensed novels, ethnic, experimental, fantasy, historical, humorous, mainstream, mystery, religious, romance, slice-of-life vignettes, suspense. Buys 25 mss/year. Send complete ms. Length: 100-1,000 words. Pays $25-100.

Poetry: Avant-garde, free verse, light verse, traditional. Buys 15 poems/year. Length: 25-150 lines. Pays $25-100.

Fillers: Anecdotes, facts, gags to be illustrated by cartoonist, newsbreaks, short humor. Buys 100/year. Length: 25-150 words. Pays $25-100.

Tips: "We are a regional publication in northeast Ohio. All areas are open. If you are 50 or more, write as if you are addressing your peers. If you are younger, take a generic approach to age. You don't have to be 50 to address this market."

FLORIDA RETIREMENT LIFESTYLES, Housing • Travel • Leisure, Gidder House Publishing, Inc., P.O. Box 66, Mount Dora FL 32757-0066. E-mail: retiretofl@aol.com. Website: http://www.inetgate.com/frl/. Editor: Kerry Smith. 20% freelance written. Monthly magazine directed toward Florida or Florida-bound retirees in an upbeat manner—unusual as well as typical Florida places, people, etc. Estab. 1946. Circ. 35,000. Pays on publication. Publishes ms an average of 3 months after acceptance. No kill fee. Buys first North American serial, first, one-time, second serial (reprint), simultaneous rights, all rights and/or makes work-for-hire assignments. Submit seasonal material 3 months in advance. Reports in 3 weeks on queries. Free writer's guidelines. Sample copy for $2.

Nonfiction: Hobbies, new careers, transition how to's, how-to (learn new skill as senior), humor, inspirational, interview/profile, new product, personal experience, photo feature, travel. Editorial calendar available on request. No negative or health related articles. Buys 30 mss/year. Query with or without published clips or send complete ms. Length: 800-1,500 words. Pays 10¢/word up to $100. Sometimes pays expenses of writers on assignment.

Reprints: Send tearsheet or photocopy of article and information about when and where the article previously appeared. Pays 50% of amount paid for an original article.

Photos: Send photos with submissions. Reviews transparencies and prints. Offers $5-25/photo. Model releases and identification of subjects required. Buys one-time rights or all rights.
Tips: "Look for the unusual, little known but interesting aspects of Florida living that seniors want or need to know about. Housing, finance and real estate are of primary interest."

‡**GRAND TIMES, Exclusively for Active Retirees**, 403 Village Dr., El Cerrito CA 94530. (510)527-4337. E-mail: mags@grandtimes.com. Website: http://www.grandtimes.com. Managing Editor: Kira Albin. 10% freelance written. Bimonthly magazine designed for active retirees (60+). *"Grand Times* is a magazine for active retirees in the San Francisco Bay Area. *Grand Times* also publishes an online edition for active retirees worldwide (see website). Controversial, entertaining and informative, *Grand Times* celebrates life's opportunities and examines life's challenges." Estab. 1992. Circ. 30,000. **Pays on acceptance.** Publishes ms an average of 2 months after acceptance. Byline given. Buys one-time rights. Editorial lead time 3 months. Accepts simultaneous submissions. Reports in 2 months on mss. Sample copy for $2 or 9×12 SAE and 4 first-class stamps (or $1.24 in postage stamps). Writer's guidelines for #10 SASE.
Nonfiction: Book excerpts, general interest, historical/nostalgic, humor, inspirational, interview/profile, personal experience, travel. Buys 6-10 mss/year. Send complete ms. Length: 600-1,700 words. Pays $10-35 for unsolicited articles.
Reprints: Accepts previously published submissions.
Photos: State availability of photos with submission. Negotiates payment individually. Buys one-time rights.
Columns/Departments: Grand Travel (travel for older adults) 1,500 words; Grand Kids (things to do with grand kids, issues of grandparenting, etc.) 800-900 words; Making Sense (alternates between legal issues and finance) 800-900 words. Buys 4-6 mss/year. Send complete ms. Pays $10-35.
Fiction: Adventure, ethnic, historical, humorous, mainstream, mystery, romance, slice-of-life vignettes. Buys 4-6 mss/year. Send complete ms. Length: 600-1,700 words. Pays $10-35.
Tips: "Writers should first read guidelines then submit manuscripts that meet those guidelines Articles should have a cohesive theme. We are not interested in meandering 'I remember when . . .'' articles. Do not stereotype characters as weak, forgetful, rigid, etc. It's okay to discuss disabilities and acknowledge issues of aging if done with humor or compassion."

MATURE LIVING, A Christian Magazine for Senior Adults, Sunday School Board of the Southern Baptist Convention, 127 Ninth Ave. N., Nashville TN 37234. (615)251-2274. Editor: Al Shackleford. 70% freelance written. Monthly leisure reading magazine for senior adults 50 and older. Estab. 1977. Circ. 350,000. **Pays on acceptance.** Byline given. Buys one-time rights. Submit seasonal material 1 year in advance. Reports in 3 months. Sample copy for 9×12 SAE with 4 first-class stamps. Writer's guidelines for #10 SASE.
Nonfiction: General interest, historical/nostalgic, how-to, humor, inspirational, interview/profile, personal experience, photo feature, crafts, travel. No pornography, profanity, occult, liquor, dancing, drugs, gambling. No book reviews. Buys 100 mss/year. Send complete ms. Length: 1,200 words maximum; prefers 950 words. Pays 5½¢/word (accepted); $75 minimum.
Photos: State availability of photos with submission. Offers $10-25/photo. Pays on publication. Buys one-time rights.
Fiction: Humorous, mainstream, slice-of-life vignettes. No reference to liquor, dancing, drugs, gambling; no pornography, profanity or occult. Buys 12 mss/year. Send complete ms. Length: 900-1,200 words. Pays 5½¢/word; $75 minimum.
Poetry: Light verse, traditional. Buys 30 poems/year. Submit maximum 5 poems. Length: open. Pays $13-20.

MATURE OUTLOOK, Meredith Corp., 1912 Grand Ave., Des Moines IA 50309-3379. Associate Editor: Peggy Person. 80% freelance written. Bimonthly magazine on travel, health, nutrition, money and people for over-50 audience. They may or may *not* be retired. Circ. 925,000. **Pays on acceptance.** Publishes ms an average 7 months after acceptance. Byline given. Offers 20% kill fee. Buys all rights or makes work-for-hire assignments. Submit all material 9 months in advance. Reports in 2 weeks. Sample copy for $1. Writer's guidelines for #10 SASE.
Nonfiction: How-to, travel, health, fitness, financial, people profiles. No poetry. Buys 50-60 mss/year. Query with published clips. Length: 150-1,500 words. Pays $100-1,000 for assigned articles. Pays telephone expenses of writers on assignment.
Photos: State availability of photos with submission.
Tips: "Please query. Please don't call."

MATURE YEARS, The United Methodist Publishing House, 201 Eighth Ave. S., Nashville TN 37202-0801. Fax: (615)749-6512. Editor: Marvin W. Cropsey. 50% freelance written. Prefers to work with published/established writers. Quarterly magazine covering interests of older adults and Bible study. *"Mature Years* is designed to help persons in and nearing the retirement years understand and appropriate the resources of the Christian faith in dealing with specific problems and opportunities related to aging. Estab. 1954. Circ. 70,000. **Pays on acceptance.** Publishes ms an average of 1 year after acceptance. Buys first North American serial rights. Submit seasonal material 14 months in advance. Reports in 2 weeks on queries; 2 months for mss.

Sample copy for $3.95 and 9×12 SAE. Writer's guidelines for #10 SASE.

Nonfiction: How-to (hobbies), inspirational, religious, travel (special guidelines), older adult health, finance issues. Buys 75-80 mss/year. Send complete ms. Length: 900-2,500 words. Pays $45-125. Sometimes pays expenses of writers on assignments.

Reprints: Send photocopy or typed ms with rights for sale noted and information about when and where the article previously appeared.

Photos: Send photos with submission. Negotiates payment individually. Captions, model releases required. Buys one-time rights.

Columns/Departments: Health Hints (retirement, health), 900-1,200 words; Going Places (travel, pilgrimmage), 1,000-1,500 words; Fragments of Life (personal inspiration), 250-600 words; Modern Revelations (religious/inspirational), 900-1,100 words; Money Matters (personal finance), 1,200-1,800 words; Puzzle Time (religioius puzzles, crosswords). Buys 4 mss/year each. Send complete ms. Pays $45-125.

Fiction: Religious, slice-of-life vignettes, retirement years. Buys 4 mss/year. Send complete ms. Length: 1,000-2,500 words. Pays $60-125.

Poetry: Free verse, haiku, light verse, traditional. Buys 24 poems/year. Submit 6 poems maximum. Length: 3-16 lines. Pays $5-20.

MODERN MATURITY, American Association of Retired Persons, 3200 E. Carson St., Lakewood CA 90712. (310)496-2277. Editor: J. Henry Fenwick. 50% freelance written. Prefers to work with published/established writers. Bimonthly magazine for readership of persons 50 years of age and over. Circ. 22,600,000. **Pays on acceptance.** Publishes ms an average of 6 months after acceptance. Byline given. Buys first North American serial rights. Submit seasonal material 6 months in advance. Reports in 3 months. Free sample copy and writer's guidelines.

Nonfiction: Careers, workplace, practical information in living, financial and legal matters, personal relationships, consumerism. Query first. *No unsolicited mss.* Length: up to 2,000 words. Pays up to $3,000. Sometimes pays expenses of writers on assignment.

Photos: Photos purchased with or without accompanying ms. Pays $250 and up for color; $150 and up for b&w.

Fiction: Very occasional short fiction.

Tips: "The most frequent mistake made by writers in completing an article for us is poor follow-through with basic research. The outline is often more interesting than the finished piece. We do not accept unsolicited manuscripts."

SENIOR MAGAZINE, 3565 S. Higuera St., San Luis Obispo CA 93401. (805)544-8711. Fax: (805)544-4450. Editor/Publisher: Gary D. Suggs. 90% freelance written. Monthly magazine covering seniors to inform and entertain the "over-50" audience. Estab. 1981. Circ. 240,000. Pays on publication. Byline given. Publishes ms an average of 1 month after acceptance. Not copyrighted. Buys first or second rights. Submit seasonal material 2 months in advance. Reports in 1 month. Sample copy for 9×12 SAE with 6 first-class stamps. Writer's guidelines for SASE.

Nonfiction: Historical/nostalgic, humor, inspirational, personal experience, travel. Special issues: War Years (November); Christmas (December); Travel (October, March). Buys 30-75 mss/year. Query. Length: 300-900 words. Pays $1.50/inch.

Photos: Send photos with submission. Reviews 8×10 b&w prints only. Offers $10-25/photo. Captions and identification of subjects required. Buys one-time rights. Uses mostly well known personalities.

Columns/Departments: Finance (investment), Taxes, Auto, Health. Length: 300-900 words. Pays $1.50/inch.

SENIOR WORLD NEWSMAGAZINE, Kendell Communications, Inc., 1000 Pioneer Way, P.O. Box 1565, El Cajon CA 92020-1565. (619)593-2910. Executive Editor: Laura Impastato. Travel Editor: Jerry Goodrum. Entertainment Editor: Wendy Worrall. Health Editor: Carolyn Pantier. Feature Editor: Carolyn Pantier. 2% freelance written. Prefers to work with published/established writers. Monthly tabloid newspaper for active older adults living in San Diego, Orange, Los Angeles, Riverside and San Bernardino counties. Estab. 1973. Circ. 450,000. Pays on publication. Buys first serial rights. Accepts simultaneous submissions. Reports in 2 months. Sample copy for $4. Free writer's guidelines.

• *Senior World* is using little freelance material right now.

Nonfiction: "We are looking for stories on health, stressing wellness and prevention; travel—international, domestic and how-to; profiles of senior celebrities and remarkable seniors; finance and investment tips for seniors; and interesting hobbies." Send query or complete ms. Length: 500-1,000 words. Pays $50-100.

Photos: State availability of photos with submission. Needs b&w with model release.

Columns/Departments: Most of our columns are local or staff-written. We will consider a query on a column idea accompanied by a sample column.

Tips: "No 'pity the poor seniors' material. Remember that we are primarily a news publication and that our content and style reflect that. Our readers are active, vital adults 55 years of age and older." No telephone or fax queries.

SUCCESSFUL RETIREMENT, Grass Roots Publishing, 950 Third Ave., 16th Floor, New York NY 10022. Editor: Marcia Vickers. 90% freelance written. Bimonthly magazine covering retirement. "Fun, upbeat, a youthful approach to retirement. No fuddy-duddyness. Our audience consists of "pretirees and retirees— average age 65. (No 'little old lady from Pasadena' stories)." Estab. 1993. Circ. 100,000. Pays on publication. Publishes an average of 6 months after acceptance. Byline given. Buys all rights. Editorial lead time 6 months. Submit seasonal material 6 months in advance. Reports in 3 months. Sample copy for $3.50 (plus postage and handling). Writer's guidelines free on request.

• Circulation of *Successful Retirement* has increased from 20,000 to 100,000.

Nonfiction: Health, how-to, humor, motivational, interview/profile, older celebrity profiles, relationships, travel, retirement locales, second careers, profiles of retirees doing unusual, interesting things and retirement life. "No lengthy, essay-type pieces, memoirs or opinion pieces. Nothing negative or drab. Must pertain to retirement or aging." Buys 60 mss/year. Query with published clips. For humor pieces, send entire ms. Length: 500-1,000 words. Pays $75 minimum.

Reprints: Occasionally accepts previously published submissions. Send tearsheet of article and information about when and where the article previously appeared with rights for sale noted.

Photos: State availability of photos with submission or send photos with submission. Identification of subjects required.

Columns/Departments: "Columns are written by staff writers. Query *only* if you have new column idea." Query with published clips. Pays $150-300.

‡**WESTCOAST REFLECTIONS**, RAND Communications, 2604 Quadra St., Victoria, British Columbia V8T 4E4 Canada. Website: http://www.islandnet.com/~magazine. Contact: Jane Kezar, associate editor. Editor: Jim Bisakowski. 30% freelance written. Monthly magazine covering lifestyle for seniors. "We publish upbeat, humorous, positive articles on travel, recreation, health & fitness, hobbies, home & garden, cooking, finance and continuing education. While the majority of the articles we publish are light-hearted in nature, periodically, we do accept material dealing with important societal concerns as it relates to housing, finances and health. The articles we do publish are not necessarily about people over fifty, but for them." Estab. 1993. Circ. 30,000. Byline given. Buys all rights. Editorial lead time 2 months. Submit seasonal material 4 months in advance. Accepts simultaneous and previously published submissions. Reports in 1 month on queries; 2 months on mss. Sample copy and writer's guidelines for SAE with IRCs.

Nonfiction: General interest, historical/nostalgic, how-to, interview/profile, photo feature, travel. Buys 10 mss/year. Length: 700-950 words. Pays 10¢/word.

Reprints: Accepts previously published submissions.

Photos: Reviews contact sheets, negatives. Negotiates payment individually. Buys one-time rights.

ROMANCE AND CONFESSION

Listed here are publications that need stories of romance ranging from ethnic and adventure to romantic intrigue and confession. Each magazine has a particular slant; some are written for young adults, others to family-oriented women. Some magazines also are interested in general interest nonfiction on related subjects.

‡**AFFAIRE DE COEUR,**, 3976 Oak Hill Rd., Oakland CA 94605. Editor: Louise Snead. 56% freelance written. Monthly magazine of book reviews, articles and information on publishing for romance readers and writers. Circ. 115,000. Pays on publication. Publishes ms an average of 1 year after acceptance. Byline given. Buys one-time rights. Submit seasonal/holiday material 3 months in advance. Accepts simultaneous submissions. Reports in 4 months. Sample copy for $5.

Nonfiction: Book excerpts, essays, general interest, historical/nostalgic, how-to, interview/profile, personal experience, photo feature. Buys 2 mss/year. Query. Length: 500-2,200 words. Pays $25-35. Sometimes pays writers with contributor copies or other premiums.

Reprints: Accepts previously published submissions.

Photos: State availability of photos with submission. Review prints. Identification of subjects required. Buys one-time rights.

Columns/Departments: Reviews (book reviews), bios, articles, 2,000 word or less.

Fiction: Historical, mainstream, romance. Pays $25.

Fillers: Newsbreaks. Buys 2/year. Length: 50-100 words. Does not pay.

Tips: "Please send clean copy. Do not send material without SASE. Do not expect a return for 2-3 months. Type all information. Send some sample of your work."

BLACK SECRETS, Sterling/McFadden Partnership, 233 Park Ave. S., 7th Floor, New York NY 10003. (212)780-3500. Fax: (212)979-7342. Editor: Marcia Mahan. See *Intimacy/Black Romance*.

Fiction: "This is our most romantic magazine of the five. We use one longer story between 20-24 pages for this book, and sometimes we feature it on the cover. Save your harsh, sleazy stories for another magazine.

Give us your softest, dreamiest, most imaginative, most amorous story with a male love interest we can't help but fall in love with. Make sure your story has body and not just bodies. Our readers love romance, but they also require substance."

Reprints: Send short story or typed ms with rights for sale noted and information about when and where story previously appeared.

Tips: "Please request a sample and guidelines before submitting. Enclose a 9×12 SASE with 5 first-class stamps."

INTIMACY/BLACK ROMANCE, Sterling/McFadden Partnership, 233 Park Ave. S., 7th Floor, New York NY 10003. (212)780-3500. Fax: (212)979-7342. Editor: Marcia Mahan. 100% freelance written. Eager to work with new/unpublished writers. Bimonthly magazine of romance and love. Estab. 1982. Circ. 100,000. Pays on publication. Publishes ms an average of 2 months after acceptance. Byline given on articles only. Buys all rights. Submit seasonal material 6 months in advance. Reports in 2 months. Sample copy for 9×12 SAE with 5 first-class stamps. Writer's guidelines for #10 SASE.

Nonfiction: How-to (relating to romance and love) and feature articles on any aspect of relationships. Buys 100 mss/year. Query with published clips or send complete ms. Length: 3-5 pages. Pays $100.

Photos: Send photos with submission. Reviews contact sheets, negatives, transparencies.

Fiction: Confession and romance. "Stories that are too graphic in content and lack romance are unacceptable." Buys 300 mss/year. Accepts stories which are a bit more romantic than those written for *Jive, Black Confessions* or *Bronze Thrills*. Send complete ms (4,000-5,000 words). Pays $75-100.

Tips: "I still get excited when I read a ms by an unpublished writer whose use of language is magical and fresh. I'm always looking for that diamond in the fire. Send us your *best* shot. Writers who are careless, sloppy and ungrammatical are an immediate turn-off for me. Please do your homework first. Is it the type of story we buy? Is it written in ms format? Does it make one want to read it?"

INTIMACY/BRONZE THRILLS, Sterling/McFadden, 233 Park Ave. S., 5th Floor, New York NY 10003. (212)780-3500. Fax: (212)979-7342. Editor: Marcia Mahan. Estab. 1982. See *Intimacy/Black Romance*.

Fiction: "Stories can be a bit more extraordinary and uninhibited than in the other magazines but still they have to be romantic. For example, we might buy a story about a woman who finds out her husband is a transsexual in *Bronze Thrills*, but not for *Jive* (our younger magazine). The stories for this magazine tend to have a harder, more adult edge of reality than the others."

JIVE, Sterling/McFadden Partnership, 233 Park Ave. S., 7th Floor, New York NY 10003. (212)780-3500. Fax: (212)979-7342. Editor: Marcia Mahan. 100% freelance written. Eager to work with new/unpublished writers. Bimonthly magazine of romance and love. Estab. 1982. Circ. 100,000. Pays on publication. Publishes ms an average of 2 months after acceptance. Byline given on articles only. Buys all rights. Submit seasonal material 6 months in advance. Reports in 2 months on queries; 6 months on mss. Sample copy for 9×12 SASE with 5 first-class stamps. Free writer's guidelines.

Nonfiction: How-to (relating to romance and love) and feature articles on any aspect of relationships. "We like our articles to have a down-to-earth flavor. They should be written in the spirit of sisterhood, fun and creativity. Come up with an original idea our readers may not have thought of but will be dying to try out." Buys 100 mss/year. Query with published clips or send complete ms. Length: 3-5 typed pages. Pays $100.

Columns/Departments: Fashion, health, beauty articles accepted. Length: 3-5 pages.

Fiction: Confession and romance. "Stories that are too graphic and lack romance are unacceptable. However, all stories must contain one or two love scenes. Love scenes should allude to sex—romantic, not lewd." Buys 300 mss/year. Send complete ms (4,000-5,000 words). Pays $75-100.

Tips: "We are leaning toward more romantic writing styles as opposed to the more graphic stories of the past. Our audience is largely black teenagers. The stories should reinforce Black pride and should be geared toward teenage issues. Our philosophy is to show our experiences in as positive a light as possible without promoting any of the common stereotypes that are associated with Black men, lovemaking prowess, penile size, etc. Stereotypes of any kind are totally unacceptable. The fiction section which accepts romance stories and confession stories is most open to freelancers. Also, our special features section is very open. We would also like to see stories that are set outside the US (perhaps they could be set in the Caribbean, Europe, Africa, etc.) and themes that are reflective of things happening around us in the 90s—abortion, AIDS, alienation, surrogate mothers, etc. But we also like to see stories that transcend our contemporary problems and can give us a moment of pleasure, warmth, joy and relief. The characters should be anywhere from teenage to 30s but not the typical 'country bumpkin girl who was turned out by a big city pimp' type story. Please, writers who are not Black, research your story to be sure that it depicts Black people in a positive manner. Do not make a Black character a caricature of a non-Black character. Read contemporary Black fiction to ensure that your dialogue and speech idioms are natural to the Black vernacular."

MODERN ROMANCES, Sterling/Macfadden Partnership, 233 Park Ave. S., New York NY 10003. (212)979-4800. Fax: (212)979-7342. Editor: Eileen Fitzmaurice. 100% freelance written. Monthly magazine for family-oriented working women, ages 18-65 years old. Circ. 200,000. Pays the last week of the month of issue. Buys all rights. Submit seasonal material at least 6 months in advance. Reports in 11 months. Writer's guidelines for #10 SASE.

● This editor is especially in need of short, well-written stories (approximately 3,000-5,000 words).

Nonfiction: Confession stories with reader identification and a strong emotional tone; a strong emphasis on characterization and well-defined plots. Should be realistic and compelling. No third-person material. Buys 10 mss/issue. No query letters; submit complete ms. Length: 2,500-10,000 words. Pays 5¢/word. Buys all rights.

Poetry: Light, romantic poetry and seasonal/holiday subjects. Length: 24 lines maximum. Pays $2/line. Look at poetry published in previous issues before submitting.

TRUE CONFESSIONS, Macfadden Women's Group, 233 Park Ave. S., New York NY 10003. (212)979-4800. Editor: Pat Byrdsong. 100% freelance written. Eager to work with new/unpublished writers. Monthly magazine for high-school-educated, blue-collar women, teens through maturity. Circ. 280,000. Buys all rights. Byline given on featured columns: My Man, Woman to Woman, Incredible But True, My Moment With God, and Family Zoo. Pays during the last week of month of issue. Publishes ms an average of 4 months after acceptance. Submit seasonal material 6 months in advance. Reports in 6 months.

Nonfiction: Timely, exciting, true emotional first-person stories on the problems that face today's women. The narrators should be sympathetic, and the situations they find themselves in should be intriguing, yet realistic. Many stories may have a strong romantic interest and a high moral tone; however, personal accounts or "confessions," no matter how controversial the topic, are encouraged and accepted. Careful study of a current issue is suggested. Length: 4,000-7,000 words; also book lengths of 8,000-10,000 words. Pays 5¢/word. Also publishes humor, poetry and mini-stories (3,000 words maximum). Submit complete ms. No simultaneous submissions. SASE required. Buys all rights.

● Asian, Latina and African-American stories are encouraged.

TRUE EXPERIENCE, The Sterling/MacFadden Partnership, 233 Park Ave. S., New York NY 10003. (212)979-4800. Editor: Rose Bernstein. Associate Editor: Heather Young. 100% freelance written. Monthly magazine covering women's confession stories. "*True Experience* is a women's confession magazine which publishes first-person short stories on actual occurrences. Our stories cover such topics as love, romance, crime, family problems and social issues. The magazine's primary audience consists of working-class women in the South, Midwest and rural West. Our stories aim to portray the lives and problems of 'real women.' " Estab. 1928. Circ. 100,000. Pays on publication. Publishes ms an average of 4 months after acceptance. No byline. Buys all rights. Editorial lead time 4 months. Submit seasonal material 6 months in advance. Reports in 2 weeks on queries; 4 months on mss. Sample copy for $1.69. Writer's guidelines for #10 SASE.

Nonfiction: Confession, humorous, mystery, romance, slice-of-life vignettes. Buys 125 mss/year. Send complete ms. Length: 1,000-10,000 words. Pays 3¢/word.

Columns/Departments: Woman Talk (brief stories covering rites of passage in women's lives), 500-1,500 words; How We Met (anecdotes describing a couple's first meeting), 300-1,000 words. Buys 24 mss/year. Send complete ms. Pays $50-75.

Poetry: Light verse, traditional. Buys 5 poems/year. Submit maximum 10 poems. Length: 4-50 lines. Pays $2/line.

Tips: "The best way to break into our publication is to send us a well-written, interesting story with sympathetic characters. Stories focusing on topical subjects like sexual harassment, crime, AIDS, or natural disasters are most likely to receive serious considerations. No special submission methods are called for. All stories must be written in first person."

TRUE LOVE, Macfadden Women's Group, 233 Park Ave. S., New York NY 10003. (212)979-4800. Fax: (212)979-7342. Editor: Kristina Kracht. 100% freelance written. Monthly magazine for young, blue-collar women, 22-55. Confession stories based on true happenings, with reader identification and a strong emotional tone. Circ. 200,000. Pays the last week of the month of the issue. Buys all rights. Submit seasonal material 6 months in advance. Reports in 8 months. Sample copy for $2 and 9 × 12 SAE. Writer's guidelines for #10 SASE.

● *True Love* needs more romance stories.

Nonfiction: Confessions, true love stories, problems and solutions, health problems, marital and child-rearing difficulties. Avoid graphic sex. Stories dealing with reality, current problems, everyday events, with emphasis on emotional impact. No stories written in third person. Buys 10 stories/issue. Buy all rights. No query letters; submit complete ms; returned only with SAE and sufficient postage. Length: 2,000-10,000 words. Pays 3¢/word.

Columns/Departments: The Life I Live, $100; How I Know I'm In Love, 700 words or less; $75; Pet Shop, $50; Kids Will Be Kids, $50; Here Comes The Bride, $50.

Poetry: Light romantic poetry or holiday-related poems. Length: 24 lines maximum. Pay $2/line.

Tips: "The story must appeal to the average blue-collar woman. It must deal with her problems and interests. Characters—especially the narrator—must be sympathetic. Focus is especially on young working women."

TRUE ROMANCE, Sterling/Macfadden Partnership, 233 Park Ave. S., New York NY 10003. (212)979-4800. Fax: (212)979-7342. Editor: Pat Vitucci. 100% freelance written. Monthly magazine for young, working class women, teens through retired, offering confession stories based on true happenings, with reader identification and strong emotional tone. No third-person material. Estab. 1923. Circ. 225,000. Pays 1 month after publication. Buys all rights. Submit seasonal/holiday material at least 6 months in advance. Reports in 5 months.
Nonfiction: Confessions, true love stories; problems and solutions; dating and marital and child-rearing difficulties. Realistic stories dealing with current problems, everyday events, with strong emotional appeal. Buys 12 stories/issue. Submit complete ms. Length 1,500-7,500 words. Pays 3¢/word; slightly higher rates for short-shorts.
Poetry: Light romantic poetry. Buys 100/year. Length: 24 lines maximum. Pay depends on merit.
Tips: "A timely, well-written story that is told by a sympathetic narrator who sees the central problem through to a satisfying resolution is *all* important to break into *True Romance*. We are always looking for good emotional, identifiable stories."

TRUE STORY, Sterling/Macfadden Partnership, 233 Park Ave. S., New York NY 10003. (212)979-4800. Editor: Lisa Rabidoux Finn. 80% freelance written. Monthly magazine for young married, blue-collar women, 20-35; high school education; increasingly broad interests; home-oriented, but looking beyond the home for personal fulfillment. Circ. 1,700,000. Buys all rights. Byline given "on articles only." Pays 1 month after publication. Submit seasonal material 1 year in advance. Reports in 1 year.
Nonfiction: "First-person stories covering all aspects of women's interests: love, marriage, family life, careers, social problems, etc. The best direction a new writer can be given is to carefully study several issues of the magazine; then submit a fresh, exciting, well-written true story. We have no taboos. It's the handling and believability that make the difference between a rejection and an acceptance." Buys about 125 full-length mss/year. Submit only complete mss for stories. Length: 1,500-10,000 words. Pays 5¢/word; $150 minimum. Pays a flat rate for columns or departments, as announced in the magazine. Query for fact articles.

RURAL

These publications draw readers interested in rural lifestyles. Surprisingly, many readers are from urban centers who dream of or plan to build a house in the country. Magazines featuring design, construction, log homes and "country" style interior decorating appear in Home and Garden.

THE COUNTRY CONNECTION, The Magazine for Country Folk, Pinecone Publishing, P.O. Box 100, Boulter, Ontario K0L 1G0 Canada. (613)332-3651. Editor: Gus Zylstra. 75% freelance written. Semiannual magazine covering country life and tourism. "*The Country Connection* is a magazine for country folk and those who wish they were. Building on our commitment to heritage, cultural, artistic, and outdoor themes, we continually add new topics to illuminate the country experience of people living within nature. Our goal is to chronicle rural life in its many aspects, giving 'voice' to the countryside." Estab. 1989. Circ. 15,000. Pays on publication. Publishes ms an average of 6 months after acceptance. Byline given. Buys first rights. Editorial lead time 4 months. Submit seasonal material 4 months in advance. Sample copy $3.95. Writer's guidelines for #10 SAE and IRC.
Nonfiction: General interest, historical/nostalgic, humor, personal experience, photo feature, travel. No hunting and fishing articles. Buys 20 mss/year. Send complete ms. Length: 500-2,000 words. Pays 7-10¢/word. Sometimes pays expenses of writers on assignment.
Photos: Send photos with submission. Reviews transparencies and prints. Offers $10-50/photo. Captions required. Buys one-time rights.
Columns/Departments: Pays 7-10¢/word.
Fiction: Adventure, fantasy, historical, humorous, slice-of-life vignettes, country living. Buys 4 mss/year. Send complete ms. Length: 500-1,500 words. Pays 7-10¢/word.
Tips: "Send (original content) manuscript with appropriate support material such as photos, illustrations, maps, etc. We are getting a lot us SASE from the US with US stamps which are unusable here in Canada."

FARM & RANCH LIVING, Reiman Publications, 5400 S. 60th St., Greendale WI 53129. (414)423-0100. E-mail: 76150.162@compuserve.com. Editor: Nick Pabst. 80% freelance written. Eager to work with new/unpublished writers. Bimonthly lifestyle magazine aimed at families that farm or ranch full time. "*F&RL* is *not* a 'how-to' magazine—it focuses on people rather than products and profits." Estab. 1968. Circ. 380,000.
Pays on acceptance. Publishes ms an average of 6 months after acceptance. Byline given. Buys first serial rights and one-time rights. Submit seasonal material 6 months in advance. Reports in 6 weeks. Sample copy for $2. Writer's guidelines for #10 SASE.
Nonfiction: Interview/profile, photo feature, nostalgia, humor, inspirational, personal experience. No how-to articles or stories about "hobby farmers" (doctors or lawyers with weekend farms); no issue-oriented

stories (pollution, animal rights, etc.). Buys 30 mss/year. Submit query or finished ms. Length: 600-1,200 words. Pays $150-300 for text-and-photos package.

Reprints: Send tearsheet of article or typed ms with rights for sale noted.

Photos: Scenic. State availability of photos with query. Pays $75-200 for 35mm color slides. Buys one-time rights.

Fillers: Jokes, anecdotes, short humor with farm or ranch slant. Buys 50/year. Length: 50-150 words. Pays $20.

Tips: "Our readers enjoy stories and features that are upbeat and positive. A freelancer must see *F&RL* to fully appreciate how different it is from other farm publications—ordering a sample is strongly advised (not available on newsstands). Photo features (about interesting farm or ranch families) and personality profiles are most open to freelancers. We can make separate arrangements for photography if writer is unable to provide photos."

FARM FAMILY AMERICA, Fieldhagen Publishing, Inc., 190 Fifth St. E., Suite 121, St. Paul MN 55101. (612)292-1747. Editor: George Ashfield. 75% freelance written. Five issues per year. Published by American Cyanamid and written to the non-farm related lifestyle, activities and travel interests of American farm families. Circ. 300,000. **Pays on acceptance.** Publishes ms an average of 2 months after acceptance. Byline given. Offers 25% kill fee. Buys first rights or second serial (reprint) rights. Submit seasonal material 6 months in advance. Accepts simultaneous submissions. Reports in 6 weeks. Writer's guidelines for #10 SASE.

Nonfiction: General interest and travel. Buys 30 mss/year. Query with published clips. Length: 1,000-1,800 words. Pays $400-650.

Photos: State availability of photos with submission. Reviews 35mm transparencies and prints. Offers $160-700/photo. Model releases and identification of subjects required. Buys one-time rights.

FARM TIMES, P.O. Box 158, Rupert ID 83350. (208)436-1111. Fax: (208)436-9455. E-mail: farmpub@cyberhighway.net. Editor: Eric Goodell. 50% freelance written. Monthly tabloid for agriculture-farming/ranching. "*Farm Times* is 'dedicated to rural living.' Stories related to farming and ranching in the states of Idaho, Nevada, Utah, Wyoming and Oregon are our mainstay, but farmers and ranchers do more than just work. General, or human interest articles that appeal to rural readers, are used on occasion." Estab. 1987. Pays on publication. Byline given. Editorial lead time 1 month. Submit seasonal material 3 months in advance. Reports in 2 months on queries. Writer's guidelines free on request. Send $1 for sample copy.

Nonfiction: Farm or ranch issues, exposé, general interest, how-to, interview/profile, new product (few), opinion, late breaking ag news. No humor, inspirational, essay, first person, personal experience or book excerpts. Special issue: Dairy Farming (June). Buys 200 mss/year. Query with published clips. Send complete ms. Length: 600-800 words. Pays $1.25/column inch.

Reprints: Send information about when and where the article previously appeared. Pays 100% of amount paid for an original article.

Photos: Send photos with submission. Reviews contact sheets with negatives, 35mm or larger transparencies and 5×7 or larger prints. Offers $5/b&w inside, $35/color cover. Captions, model releases, identification of subjects required. Buys one-time rights.

Column/Departments: Hoof Beats (horse care/technical), 500-600 words; Rural Religion (interesting churches/missions/religious activities) 600-800 words; Dairy (articles of interest to dairy farmers) 600-800 words. Buys 12 mss/year. Query. Send complete ms. Pays $1.25/column inch.

Tips: "Query with a well-thought-out idea that will appeal to rural readers. Of special interest is how environmental issues will affect farmers/ranchers, endangered species act, EPA, etc. We are always looking for well-written articles on subjects that affect western farmers and ranchers."

HARROWSMITH COUNTRY LIFE MAGAZINE, Telemedia Communications, Inc., 25 Sheppard Ave. W, North York Ontario M2N 6S7 Canada. (416)733-7600. Fax: (416)733-7981. Editor: Peter Carter. 75% freelance written. Published 6 times/year "for those interested in country living, organic gardening, family, food and country homes." Estab. 1976. Circ. 360,000. **Pays on acceptance.** Publishes ms an average of 4 months after acceptance. Byline given. Buys first North American serial rights. Submit seasonal material 6 months in advance. Reports in 6 weeks. Sample copy for $5. Free writer's guidelines.

Nonfiction: Country living, how-to, general interest, gardening, homes, country famiy activities, environmental, profile. "We are always in need of quality gardening articles geared to northern conditions. No how-to articles written by people who are not totally familiar with their subject. We feel that in this field simple research does not compensate for lack of long-time personal experience." Buys 10 mss/issue. Query. Length: 500-2,000 words. Pays $150-2,000.

Photos: State availability of photos with query. Captions required. Buys one-time rights.

Tips: "We have high standards of excellence. We welcome and give thorough consideration to all freelance submissions. Our magazine is read by Canadians who live in rural areas or who hope to make the urban to rural transition. They want to know about the realities of country life as well as the dreams."

THE MOTHER EARTH NEWS, 49 E. 21st St., 11th Floor, New York NY 10010. (212)260-7210. Fax: (212)260-7445. E-mail: mearthnews@aol.com. Contact: Molly Miller, associate editor. Editor: Matthew Scanlon. Managing Editor: Christine Canchon Summer. Mostly freelance written. Bimonthly magazine emphasizing "country living and country skills, for both long-time and would-be ruralites." Circ. 450,000. Pays on publication. Byline given. Submit seasonal material 5 months in advance. No handwritten mss. Reports within 3 months. Publishes ms an average of 6 months after acceptance. Sample copy for $5. Writer's guidelines for #10 SASE with 2 first-class stamps.

Nonfiction: How-to, home business, alternative energy systems, home building, home retrofit and home maintenance, energy-efficient structures, seasonal cooking, gardening, crafts. Buys 100-150 mss/year. Query. "A short, to-the-point paragraph is often enough. If it's a subject we don't need at all, we can answer immediately. If it tickles our imagination, we'll ask to take a look at the whole piece. No phone queries, please." Length: 300-3,000 words. Publishes nonfiction book excerpts.

Reprints: Rarely accepts previously published submissions. Send information about when and where the article previously appeared.

Photos: Purchased with accompanying ms. Send prints or transparencies. Uses 8×10 b&w glossies or any size color transparencies. Include type of film, speed and lighting used. Total purchase price for ms includes payment for photos. Captions and credits required.

Tips: "Probably the best way to break in is to study our magazine, digest our writer's guidelines, and send us a concise article illustrated with color transparencies that we can't resist. When folks query and we give a go-ahead on speculation, we often offer some suggestions. Failure to follow those suggestions can lose the sale for the author. We want articles that tell what real people are doing to take charge of their own lives. Articles should be well-documented and tightly written treatments of topics we haven't already covered. The critical thing is length, and our payment is by space, not word count. *No phone queries.*"

RURAL HERITAGE, 281 Dean Ridge Lane, Gainesboro TN 38562-5039. (615)268-0655. Editor: Gail Damerow. Publisher: Allan Damerow. 98% freelance written. Willing to work with a small number of new/unpublished writers. Bimonthly magazine devoted to the training and care of draft animals, and other traditional country skills. Estab. 1975. Circ. 3,000. Pays on publication. Publishes ms an average of 6 months after acceptance. Byline given. Buys first English language rights. Submit seasonal material 6 months in advance. Reports in 3 months. Sample copy for $6. Writer's guidelines #10 SASE.

Nonfiction: How-to (crafting and farming); interview/profile (people using draft animals); photo feature. No articles on *mechanized* farming. Buys 100 mss/year. Query or send complete ms. Length: 750-1,500 words. Pays 5¢/word.

Reprints: Accepts previously published submissions, but only if previous publication had limited or regional circulation. Send tearsheet or photocopy of article, typed ms with rights for sale noted and information about when and where the article previously appeared. Pays 100% of amount paid for an original article.

Photos: Send photos with ms. Pays $10. Captions and identification of subjects required. Buys one-time rights. Six covers/year (color transparency or 5×7 vertical print), animals in harness $50; back covers, humorous rural scene (same size, horizontal format) $25. Photo guidelines for #10 SASE.

Columns/Departments: Self-sufficiency (modern people preserving traditional American lifestyle), 750-1,500 words; Drafter's Features (draft animals used for farming, shows and pulls—their care), 750-1,500 words; Crafting (implement designs and patterns), 750-1,500 words; Country Kids (descriptions of rural youngsters who have done [or are doing] remarkable things), 750 words; Humor, 750-900 words. Pays 5¢/word.

Poetry: Traditional. Pays $5-25.

Tips: "Always welcome are: 1) Detailed descriptions and photos of horse-drawn implements 2) Prices and other details of draft animal and implement auctions and sales."

RURALITE, P.O. Box 558, Forest Grove OR 97116-0558. (503)357-2105. Fax: (503)357-8615. Editor-in-Chief: Curtis Condon. Associate Editor: Walt Wentz. 80% freelance written. Works with new, unpublished writers "who have mastered the basics of good writing." Monthly magazine aimed at members of consumer-owned electric utilities throughout 9 western states, including Alaska. Publishes 50 regional editions. Estab. 1954. Circ. 265,000. Buys first rights, sometimes reprint rights. Rights may be reassigned. Byline given. **Pays on acceptance.** Query first; unsolicited manuscripts submitted without request rarely read by editors. Reports in 1 month. Sample copy and writer's guidelines for 10×13 SAE with 4 first-class stamps.

Nonfiction: Looking for well-written nonfiction, (occasional fiction piece) dealing primarily with human interest topics. Must have strong Northwest perspective and be sensitive to Northwest issues and attitudes. Wide range of topics possible, from energy-related subjects to little-known travel destinations to unusual businesses located in areas served by consumer-owned electric utilities. "About half of our readers are rural and small town residents; others are urban and suburban. Topics with an obvious 'big-city' focus not accepted. Family-related issues, Northwest history (no encyclopedia rewrites), people and events, unusual tidbits that tell the Northwest experience are best chances for a sale. Nostalgic, dripping sentimental pieces rejected out of hand." Buys 50-60 mss/yr. Length 800-2,000 words. Pays $140-400, quality photos may increase upper pay limit for "polished stories with impact."

Reprints: Send photocopy of article or typed ms with rights for sale noted and information about when and where the article previously appeared. For reprints, pays 50% of "*our* regular freelance rates."
Photos: "Illustrated stories are the key to a sale. Stories without art rarely make it, with the exception of humor pieces. Black and white prints, color slides, all formats, accepted with 'razor-sharp' focus. Fuzzy, low-contrast photos may lose the sale."
Tips: "Study recent issues. Follow directions when given an assignment. Be able to deliver a complete package (story and photos). We're looking for regular contributors to whom we can assign topics from our story list after they've proven their ability to deliver quality mss."

SCIENCE

These publications are published for laymen interested in technical and scientific developments and discoveries, applied science and technical or scientific hobbies. Publications of interest to the personal computer owner/user are listed in the Personal Computers section. Journals for scientists and engineers are listed in Trade in various sections.

‡**AD ASTRA**, 922 Pennsylvania Ave. SE, Washington DC 20003-2140. (202)543-3991. Fax: (202)546-4189. E-mail: adastra@ari.net. Website: http://www.nss.org. Editor-in-Chief: Pat Dasch. 80% freelance written. Bimonthly magazine covering the space program. "We publish non-technical, lively articles about all aspects of international space programs, from shuttle missions to planetary probes to plans for the future." Estab. 1989. Circ. 25,000. Pays on publication. Byline given. Buys first North American serial rights. Reports on queries when interested. Sample copy for 9×12 SASE. Writer's guidelines for #10 SASE.
Nonfiction: Book excerpts, essays, expose, general interest, interview/profile, opinion, photo feature, technical. No science fiction or UFO stories. Query with published clips. Length: 1,200-3,000 words. Pays $100-250 for features.
Photos: State availability of photos with submission. Reviews 3×5 color transparencies and b&w prints. Negotiates payment. Identification of subjects required. Buys one-time rights.
Columns/Departments: Touchdown (opinion pieces). Query.
Tips: "Strongly prefer manuscripts to be accompanied by ASCII Word or Word Perfect 6.0 floppy disk."

ARCHAEOLOGY, Archaeological Institute of America, 135 William St., New York NY 10038. (212)732-5154. Fax: (212)732-5707. Editor-in-Chief: Peter A. Young. 5% freelance written. "We generally commission articles from professional archaeologists." Bimonthly magazine on archaeology. "The only magazine of its kind to bring worldwide archaeology to the attention of the general public." Estab. 1948. Circ. 200,000. Pays on publication. Byline given. Offers 25% kill fee. Buys first North American serial rights. Submit seasonal material 6 months in advance. Accepts simultaneous submissions. Query preferred. Free sample copy and writer's guidelines.
Nonfiction: Essays, general interest. Buys 6 mss/year. Length: 1,000-3,000 words. Pays $750 maximum. Sometimes pays expenses of writers on assignment.
  ● Ranked as one of the best markets for freelance writers in *Writer's Yearbook*'s annual "Top 100 Markets," January 1996.
Photos: Send photos with submission.

DISCOVER, Walt Disney Magazine Publishing Group, 114 Fifth Ave., New York NY 10011. (212)633-4400. Fax: (212)633-4809. "*Discover* magazine chronicles the evolution of the brightest ideas and newest developments in science and technology. It is edited for men and women interested in keeping pace with progress." Circ. 1,321,000. This magazine did not respond to our request for information. Query before submitting.

THE ELECTRON, CIE Publishing, 1776 E. 17th St., Cleveland OH 44114-3679. (216)781-9400. Fax: (216)781-0331. Managing Editor: Michael Manning. 80% freelance written. Quarterly tabloid on electronics and high technology. Estab. 1934. Circ. 25,000. Pays on publication. Publishes ms an average of 2 months after acceptance. Byline given. Buys all rights. Reports as soon as possible. Sample copy and writer's guidelines for 8½×11 SASE.
Nonfiction: Technical (tutorial and how-to), technology news and feature, photo feature, career/educational. All submissions must be electronics/technology-related. Query with letter/proposal and published clips. Pays $50-500.
Reprints: Accepts previously published submissions.
Photos: State availability of photos. Reviews 8×10 and 5×7 b&w prints. Captions and identification of subjects required.
Tips: "We would like to receive educational electronics/technical articles. They must be written in a manner understandable to the beginning-intermediate electronics student. We are also seeking news/feature-type articles covering timely developments in high technology."

‡**FINAL FRONTIER**, 1017 S. Mountain Ave., Monrovia CA 91016. Editor: George Hague. Bimonthly magazine covering space exploration. "*Final Frontier* is about space technology, commerce and exploration. The missions and machines. People and politics. The pure adventures of space travel and astronomical discovery. Plus behind-the-scenes coverage of the international arena of space, commerce and exploration." Estab. 1988. Circ. 100,200. **Pays on acceptance**. Byline given. Buys first North American serial rights. Reports in 2 weeks on queries. Sample copy free on request.
  • Ranked as one of the best markets for freelance writers in *Writer's Yearbook*'s annual "Top 100 Markets," January 1996.
Nonfiction: Interview/profile, human interest. Buys 20 mss/year. Query with published clips. Length:1,240-2,400 words. Pays 40¢/word. Sometimes pays expenses of writers on assignment.
Reprints: Accepts previously published submissions from non-competing markets.
Columns/Departments: Buys 30 mss/year. Pays 40¢/word.
Fillers: Buys 30/year. Length: 150-450 words. Pays 40¢/word.

OMNI, Omni International, Ltd., 277 Park Ave., Fourth Floor, New York NY 10172-0003. This magazine of science and science fiction has moved to an online format only. Query before submitting.
  • Ranked as one of the best markets for freelance writers in *Writer's Yearbook*'s annual "Top 100 Markets," January 1996 and one of the best markets for fiction writers in *Writer's Digest*'s annual "Fiction 50," June 1996.

‡**SCIENCE SPECTRA, The Intl. Magazine of Contemporary Scientific Thought**, Gordon and Breach, 820 Town Center Dr., Langhorne PA 19047. Editor: Herhart Friedlander. Contact: Heather Wagner, managing editor. 25% freelance written. Quarterly magazine covering science. "Our magazine's audience is composed primarily of scientists and the 'scientifically literate.' Writers must have experience writing for a scientific audience." Estab. 1995. Circ. 10,000. Pays on publication. Byline given. Buys all rights. Editorial lead time 3 months. Reports in 1 month on queries. Writer's guidelines for SAE and 1 first-class stamp.
Nonfiction: Interview/profile, science and technology. Buys 10-15 mss/year. Length: approximately 2,000 words. Pays 25¢/word for assigned articles.
Photos: Offers no additional payment for photos accepted with ms. Captions required. Buys all time rights.
Columns/Departments: From the Front Lines (cutting edge research/technology) 2,000 words; Portrait (profile of leading scientific figure) 2,000 words; Controversy Corner (presents both sides of current scientific debate) 2,000 words. Buys 5-10 mss/year. Query with published clips. Pays 25¢/word.
Tips: "Writers should include clips that demonstrate their knowledge of and/or experience in the scientific area about which they are writing. Do not send complete manuscripts; query letter with clips only."

SCIENTIFIC AMERICAN, 415 Madison Ave., New York NY 10017. Fax: (212)755-1976. Contact: Marguerite Holloway, news editor. Monthly publication covering developments and topics of interest in the world of science. Query before submitting. Freelance opportunities limited to news and analysis section.

‡**WEATHERWISE, The Magazine About the Weather**, Heldref Publications, 1319 18th St. NW, Washington DC 20036. (202)296-6267. Managing Editor: Jeff Rosenfeld. 75% freelance written. Bimonthly magazine covering weather and meteorology. "*Weatherwise* is America's only popular magazine about the weather. Our readers' range from professional weathercasters and scientists to basement-bound hobbyists, but all share a common craving for information about weather as it relates to technology, history, culture, society, art, etc." Estab. 1948. Circ. 12,500. Pays on publication. Publishes ms an average of 6 months after acceptance. Byline given. Offers 25% kill fee. Buys all rights or first North American serial or second (reprint) serial rights. Editorial lead time 6 months. Submit seasonal material 6 months in advance. Reports in 2 months on queries. Sample copy free on request. Writer's guidelines for #10 SASE.
Nonfiction: Book excerpts, essays, general interest, historical/nostalgic, how-to, humor, interview/profile, new product, opinion, personal experience, photo feature, technical, travel. Special issue: Photo Contest (August/September deadline May 31). Special issue: 1996 Weather in Review (February/March 97). "No blow-by-blow accounts of the biggest storm to ever hit your backyard." Buys 15-18 mss/year. Query with published clips. Length: 1,500-2,500 words. Pays $200-500 for assigned articles; $0-200 for unsolicited articles. Sometimes pays expenses of writers on assignment.
Reprints: Accepts previously published submissions.
Photos: State availability of or send photos with submission. Reviews contact sheets, negatives, transparencies, prints. Negotiates payment individually. Captions, identification of subjects required. Buys one-time rights.
Columns/Departments: Front & Center (news, trends, opinion), 300-400 words; Weather Talk (folklore and humor), 1,000 words; The Lee Word (first person accounts of adventures with weather), 1,000 words. Buys 12-15 mss/year. Query with published clips. Pays $0-200.
Tips: "Don't query us wanting to write about broad types like the Greenhouse Effect, the Ozone Hole, El Niño, etc. If it's capitalized, you can bet you won't be able to cover it all in 2,000 words. With these topics and all others, find the story within the story. And whether you're writing about a historical storm or

new technology, be sure to focus on the human element—the struggles, triumphs, and other anecdotes of individuals.''

SCIENCE FICTION, FANTASY AND HORROR

These publications often publish experimental fiction and many are open to new writers. More information on these markets can be found in the Contests and Awards section under the Fiction heading.

ABERRATIONS, Sirius Fiction, P.O. Box 460430, San Francisco CA 94146-0430. (415) 777-3909. Editor: Richard Blair. Monthly magazine of science fiction, fantasy, and horror aimed at a mature audience. "We're looking for speculative stories that run the gamut from the pulp-era SF/F/H of the 30s and 40s to the experimental and literary work of today." Estab. 1992. Circ. 1,500. Pays on publication. Publishes ms an average of 1 year after acceptance. Byline given. Buys first English language serial and one-time rights. Submit seasonal material 8 months in advance. Reports in 4 months. Sample copy for $4.50 postpaid. Writer's guidelines for #10 SASE.

Nonfiction: Anything with a SF/F/H tie-in. "However, please keep in mind that we're not interested in the paranormal, UFOs, nor are we looking for 'how to write science fiction' pieces." Send complete ms. Length: 3,000 words (query for longer). Pays ¼¢/word.

Fiction: Science fiction, fantasy, and horror. "We use a variety of 'types' of stories within the speculative genres. Whether it's humorous horror or cerebral sci-fi, we want character-driven, plot intensive storylines. From sword-&-sorcery to space opera to psychological horror, however and whatever your muse is trying to beat out of you send it our way." Buys 120 mss/year. Send complete ms. Length: 8,000 words max. Pays ¼¢/word.

Tips: "While there are still no restrictions on language and subject matter, we're seeking to expand the scope of stories within the magazine, and are therefore no longer looking exclusively for shock or splatter SF/F/H fiction. Stories that do possess graphically violent/sexual scenes should have these aspects be crucial to the plot. Under *no* circumstances are we interested in stories dealing with the violent/sexual abuse of children. All that said, we're very open to stories that take chances (whether this be through characterization, plotting, or structuring) as well as those that take more traditional approaches to science fiction, fantasy and horror. Both fiction and nonfiction are wide open."

‡ABORIGINAL SCIENCE FICTION, The 2nd Renaissance Foundation Inc., P.O. Box 2449, Woburn MA 01888-0849. Editor: Charles C. Ryan. 99% freelance written. Quarterly science fiction magazine. "We publish short, lively and entertaining science fiction short stories and poems, accompanied by b&w illustrations." Estab. 1986. Circ. 12,000. Pays on publication. Publishes ms an average of 18 months after acceptance. Byline given. Buys first North American serial rights, non-exclusive options on other rights. Reports in 3 months. Sample copy for $5.95 and 9 × 12 SAE with 4 first-class stamps. Writer's guidelines for #10 SASE.

Fiction: Science fiction of all types. "We do not use fantasy, horror, sword and sorcery or *Twilight Zone*-type stories." Buys 40-48 mss/year. Send complete ms. Length: 2,000-6,500 words. Pays $200. Send photocopy of short story. Publishes novel excerpts only if they can stand by themselves as a short story.

  ● Ranked as one of the best markets for fiction writers in *Writer's Digest*'s annual "Fiction 50," June 1996.

Poetry: Science and science fiction. Buys 8-12 poems/year. Length: 1-2 pages, typewritten.

Tips: "Read science fiction novels and all the science fiction magazines. Do not rely on science fiction movies or TV. We are open to new fiction writers who are making a sincere effort. We are now looking at short articles on cutting-edge science, 1,000-1,500 words. Pays $100 on publication."

ABSOLUTE MAGNITUDE, Science Fiction Adventures, DNA Publications, P.O. Box 13, Greenfield MA 01302. Editor: Warren Lapine. 95% freelance written. Quarterly science fiction magazine covering science fiction short stories. "We specialize in action/adventure science fiction with an emphasis on hard science. Interested in tightly-plotted, character-driven stories." Estab. 1993. Circ. 6,000. Pays on publication. Publishes ms an average of 6 months after acceptance. Byline given. Buys first North American serial rights, first rights and second serial (reprint) rights. Editorial lead time 1 month. Accepts simultaneous submissions. Reports in 2 weeks on queries; 1 month on mss. Sample copy for $5. Writer's guidelines for #10 SASE.

  ● This editor is still looking for tightly plotted stories that are character driven. He is now purchasing more short stories than before.

Reprints: Send typed ms with rights for sale noted and information about when and where the article previously appeared. Pays 33% of amount paid for an original article.

Fiction: Science fiction. Buys 30 mss/year. Send complete ms. Length: 1,000-25,000 words. Pays 3-5¢/word.

  ● Ranked as one of the best markets for fiction writers in *Writer's Digest*'s annual "Fiction 50," June 1996.

Poetry: Any form. Buys 4 poems/year. Submit maximum 3 poems. Length: up to 25,000 words. Pays 1½¢/word.

Tips: "We are not interested in 'drawer-cleaning' exercises. There is no point in sending less than your best effort if you are interested in a career in writing."

ANALOG SCIENCE FICTION & FACT, Dell Magazine Fiction Group, 1270 Avenue of the Americas, New York NY 10020. (212)698-1313. Editor: Dr. Stanley Schmidt. 100% freelance written. Eager to work with new/unpublished writers. For general future-minded audience. Monthly. Estab. 1930. Buys first North American serial and nonexclusive foreign serial rights. **Pays on acceptance.** Publishes ms an average of 10 months after acceptance. Byline given. Reports in 1 month. Sample copy for $3 and 6×9 SASE with 5 first-class stamps. Writer's guidelines for #10 SASE.

● *Analog* was recently sold to Penny Marketing.

Nonfiction: Illustrated technical articles dealing with subjects of not only current but future interest, i.e., topics at the present frontiers of research whose likely future developments have implications of wide interest. Buys about 12 mss/year. Query. Length: 5,000 words. Pays 6¢/word.

Fiction: "Basically, we publish science fiction stories. That is, stories in which some aspect of future science or technology is so integral to the plot that, if that aspect were removed, the story would collapse. The science can be physical, sociological or psychological. The technology can be anything from electronic engineering to biogenetic engineering. But the stories must be strong and realistic, with believable people doing believable things—no matter how fantastic the background might be." Buys 60-100 unsolicited mss/year. Send complete ms of short fiction; query about serials. "We don't publish novel excerpts as such, though we occasionally do one that can stand on its own as an independent story." Length: 2,000-80,000 words. Pays 4¢/word for novels; 5-6¢/word for novelettes; 6-8¢/word for shorts under 7,500 words; $450-600 for intermediate lengths.

● Ranked as one of the best markets for fiction writers in *Writer's Digest*'s annual "Fiction 50," June 1996.

Tips: "In query give clear indication of central ideas and themes and general nature of story line—and what is distinctive or unusual about it. We have no hard-and-fast editorial guidelines, because science fiction is such a broad field that I don't want to inhibit a new writer's thinking by imposing 'Thou Shalt Not's.' Besides, a really good story can make an editor swallow his preconceived taboos. I want the best work I can get, regardless of who wrote it—and I need new writers. So I work closely with new writers who show definite promise, but of course it's impossible to do this with *every* new writer. No occult or fantasy."

ASIMOV'S SCIENCE FICTION, Dell Magazine Fiction Group, 1270 Avenue of the Americas, New York NY 10020. (212)698-1313. (212)856-6400. Fax: (212)782-8309 (for correspondence only, no submissions). E-mail: 71154.662@compuserve.com. Editor: Gardner Dozois. Executive Editor: Sheila Williams. 98% freelance written. Works with a small number of new/unpublished writers each year. Published 11 times a year, including 1 double issue. Estab. 1977. Circ. 100,000. **Pays on acceptance.** Buys first North American serial and nonexclusive foreign serial rights; reprint rights occasionally. No simultaneous submissions. Reports in 2 months. Sample copy for $3 and 6½×9½ SAE. Writer's guidelines for #10 SASE.

● *Asimov's* was recently sold to Penny Marketing.

Fiction: Science fiction primarily. Some fantasy and poetry. "It's best to read a great deal of material in the genre to avoid the use of some *very* old ideas." Buys 10 mss/issue. Submit complete ms and SASE with *all* submissions. Length: 100-20,000 words. Pays 5-8¢/word except for novel serializations at 4¢/word.

● Ranked as one of the best markets for fiction writers in *Writer's Digest*'s annual "Fiction 50," June 1996.

Tips: "We prefer stories which contain good character development."

MARION ZIMMER BRADLEY'S FANTASY MAGAZINE, P.O. Box 249, Berkeley CA 94701-0249. Editor: Mrs. Marion Z. Bradley. 100% freelance written. Quarterly magazine of fantasy fiction. Estab. 1988. **Pays on acceptance.** Publishes ms an average of 1 year after acceptance. Byline given. Buys first North American serial rights. Reports in 3 months. Sample copy for $4.

Fiction: Fantasy. No science fiction, very little horror. Buys 55-60 mss/year. Send complete ms. Length: 300-5,500 words. Pays 3-10¢/word.

● Ranked as one of the best markets for fiction writers in *Writer's Digest*'s annual "Fiction 50," June 1996.

Tips: "Do not submit without first reading guidelines."

CENTURY, Century Publishing, Inc., P.O. Box 150510, Brooklyn NY 11215. E-mail: robkill@aol.com. Website: http://www.supranet.com/century/. Editor: Robert K.J. Killheffer. 100% freelance written. Bimonthly 6×9 magazine covering speculative fiction (science fiction, fantasy, horror). "We're looking for speculative fiction with a high degree of literary accomplishment—ambitious work which can appeal not only to the genre's regular audience but to readers outside the genre as well." Estab. 1994. Circ. 5,000. **Pays on acceptance.** Publishes ms an average of 6 months after acceptance. Byline given. Buys first world English

rights, non-exclusive reprint rights. Reports in 3 months on mss. Sample copy for $5.95. Writer's guidelines for #10 SASE.
Fiction: Experimental, fantasy, horror, science fiction. Buys 65 mss/year. Send complete ms. Length: 1,000-20,000 words. Pays 4-6¢/word.

DEAD OF NIGHT MAGAZINE, Dead of Night Publications, P.O. Box 60730, Longmeadow MA 01116-0730. Editor: Lin Stein. 90% freelance written. Annual magazine (October). "Our readers enjoy horror, mystery, fantasy and sci-fi, and they also don't mind an 'old-fashioned' vampire or ghost story on occasion. Because of the genre mix in our magazine, we appeal to a wide readership." Estab. 1989. Circ. 3,200. Pays on publication. Publishes ms an average of 18 months after acceptance. Byline given. Offers 10% kill fee. Buys 1st North American serial rights or one-time rights. Reports in 3 weeks on queries; 2 months on mss. Sample copy for $5 (current issue); $2.50 (back issue subject to availability). Writer's guidelines for #10 SASE.
Nonfiction: Book excerpts, interview/profile, book/film reviews. Buys 8-10 mss/year. Send complete ms. Length: 350-3,000 words. Pays 2¢/word minimum.
Fiction: Fantasy, horror, mystery, novel excerpts, science fiction. Nothing non-genre. Buys 10-15 mss/year. Send complete ms. Length: 500-3,000 words (occasionally longer, to 4,500 words). Pays 4-7¢/word. Publishes novel excerpts.
Poetry: Used occasionally. Pays $7/poem.
Tips: "We are most open to fiction. (Most of our reviews are written by our contributing editors—on a regular basis, but freelancers may query.) We are featuring *longer* works (both fiction and non) in *more* of the 'dark genres' (to clarify: we've recently begun using suspense fiction, for example). For tips or hints, the best, of course, is to read the magazine! The second best is to at least read our guidelines, and the last tip is to try to present us with a horror/mystery/fantasy or science fiction story that is fresh, original, and entertaining. If the story entertains the editors here, we'll buy it so our *readers* can enjoy it and be entertained by it as well."

‡FANTASTIC WORLDS, Science Fiction ● Fantasy ● Horror, 1644 s. 11th West, Missoula MT 59801. Editor: Scott Becker. 90% freelance written. Science fiction, fantasy, horror magazine published 4-6 times a year. Estab. 1995. Circ. 1,000. Pays on publication. Publishes ms an average of 1 year after acceptance. Byline given. Offers 50% kill fee. Buys first North American serial rights and option to reprint story if it is subsequently chosen for a *Fantastic Worlds* "Best of" Anthology. Editorial lead time 3 months. Submit seasonal material 3 months in advance. Accepts simultaneous submissions. Reports in 2 months on queries; 3 months on mss. Sample copy for $5 (add $1 for foreign orders). Writer's guidelines for #10 SASE.
Nonfiction: Book excerpts, essays, exposé, general interest, humor, interview/profile, opinion. Buys 8-12 mss/year. Query with published clips. Length: 1,000-2,500 words. Pays 1¢/word ($25-100) and contributor copy.
Photos: State availability of photos with submission. Reviews contact sheets, up to 8×10 prints. Offers $5-30/photo. Negotiates payment individually. Buys one-time rights.
Columns/Departments: Interviews, Unique Features. Buys 6-18 mss/year. Query with published clips. Pays 1¢/word ($25-100) and contributor copy.
Fiction: Adventure, erotica, fantasy, horror, mystery, science fiction, serialized novels, suspense. No pornography or work that depicts children being brutalized. Buys 40-60 mss/year. Send complete ms. Pays 1¢/word ($25-100) and contributor copy.
Poetry: Avant-garde, free verse, haiku, light verse, traditional. Buys 40-60 poems/year. Submit maximum 3 poems. Pays $5-15 and contributor copy.

‡GASLIGHT, Tales of the Unsane, Strait-Jacket Publications, P.O. Box 21, Cleveland MN 56017-0021. Editor: Melissa Gish. Estab. 1992. 90% freelance written. Triannual literary magazine covering science fiction, fantasy and horror. "We are a digest of highly imaginative fiction, poetry and artwork borne out of the darkest recesses of the creator's mind." Estab. 1992. Circ. 300. **Pays on acceptance**. Publishes ms an average of 4 months after acceptance. Byline given. Offers 100% kill fee. Buys first North American serial rights or one-time rights on reprints. Submit seasonal material 4 months in advance. Accepts simultaneous submissions. Reports in 2 weeks on queries; 1 month on mss. Sample copy for $4.25. Back issues (subject to availability) $3 ppd. Writer's guidelines for #10 SASE.
Nonfiction: Interview/profile, critical essays, of SF/F/H subjects, book and film reviews. "We don't want anything not directly related to sci-fi, fantasy or horror." Buys 9 mss/year. Query. Length: up to 2,000 words. Pays $3-15. "Must query first."
Reprints: Send typed ms with rights for sale noted and information about when and where the article previously appeared. Pays 60% of amount paid for an original article.
Fiction: Experimental, horror, science fiction, suspense. "Nothing not related to sci-fi or horror. No re-hashed monster movie plots. No sexism, racism, specism or degradation. Would like to see more 'nuts & bolts' science fiction." Buys 35 mss/year. Send complete ms. Length: up to 2,500 words. Pays ¼¢-1¢/word.
Poetry: Avant-garde, free verse, light verse, traditional. Buys 45 poems/year. Submit maximum 5 poems. Length: 50 lines maximum. Pays up to $5. Pays in contributors copies for short poetry.

Tips: "Consider the graphic horror of Clive Barker and character-driven 'sf' of Philip K. Dick and Orson Scott Card. Be creative and imaginative. Nothing is too strange to be believable. Prefer horror from character's perspective, not an observer's. Make us feel your terror and know your pain. We are most open to short short fiction (to 1,000 words). If you can tell a clear and believable tale in less than 1,000 words, you've got a better chance at getting in. We are eager to work with fledgling writers." Query for details.

HOBSON'S CHOICE, The Starwind Press, P.O. Box 98, Ripley OH 45167-0098. (513)392-4549. Editors: David F. Powell and Susannah C. West. Contact: Susannah C. West. 75% freelance written. Eager to work with new/unpublished writers. Bimonthly magazine "for older teenagers and adults who have an interest in science and technology, and who also enjoy reading well-crafted science fiction and fantasy." Estab. 1974. Circ. 2,500. Pays on publication. Publishes ms an average of 1 year after acceptance. Byline given. Rights vary with author and material; negotiated with author. Usually first serial rights and second serial reprint rights (nonfiction). "We encourage disposable submissions; easier for us and easier for the author. Just enclose SASE for our response." Prefers non-simultaneous submissions. Reports in 3 months. Sample copy for $2.25 and 9×12 SAE. Writer's guidelines for #10 SASE. "Tipsheet package for $1.50; contains all guidelines, tipsheets on science fiction writing, nonfiction science writing and submission etiquette."

• *Hobson's Choice* is often overstocked with fiction; their needs for nonfiction are greater than for fiction.

Nonfiction: How-to (technological interest, e.g., how to build a robot eye, building your own radio receiver, etc.), interview/profile (of leaders in science and technology fields), technical ("did you know" articles dealing with development of current technology). "No speculative articles, dealing with topics such as the Abominable Snowman, Bermuda Triangle, etc." Query. Length: 1,000-7,000 words. Pays 1-4¢/word.

Reprints: Send photocopy of article or short story and information about when and where material previously appeared. Pays 30% of amount paid for an original article.

Photos: Send photos with accompanying query or ms. Reviews b&w contact sheets and prints. Model releases and identification of subjects required. "If photos are available, we prefer to purchase them as part of the written piece." Buys negotiable rights.

Fiction: Fantasy, science fiction. "No stories whose characters were created by others (e.g. Lovecraft, *Star Trek*, *Star Wars* characters, etc.)." Buys 15-20 mss/year. Send complete ms. Length: 2,000-10,000 words. Pays 1-4¢/word. "We prefer previously unpublished fiction. No query necessary. We don't publish horror, poetry, novel excerpts or serialized novels."

Tips: "Almost all our fiction and nonfiction is unsolicited. We rarely ask for rewrites, because we've found that rewrites are often disappointing; although the writer may have rewritten it to fix problems, he/she frequently changes parts we liked, too."

‡**INTERZONE, Science Fiction and Fantasy**, 217 Preston Drove, Brighton England BN1 6FL United Kingdom. 01273-504710. E-mail: interzone@cix. compulink.co.uk. Editor: David Pringle. Mostly freelance written. Monthly magazine covering science fiction and fantasy. Estab. 1981. Circ. 10,000. Pays on publication. Publishes ms an average of 3 months after acceptance. Byline given. Buys first or one-time rights. Editorial lead time 3 months. Reports in 3 months on mss. Sample copy for $5.50. Writer's guidelines free on request.

Nonfiction: Essays, interview/profile, opinion. Send complete ms. Length: 1,000-5,000 words. Pays by agreement.

Photos: State availability of photos with submissions. Offers no additional payment for photos accepted with ms.

Fiction: Science fiction and fantasy. Buys 75mss/year. Send complete ms. Length: 2,000-6,000 words. Pays £30/1,000 words.

‡**INTO THE DARKNESS, The Magazine of Extreme Horror**, Necro Publications, P.O. Box 540298, Orlando FL 32854-0298. E-mail: necrodave@aol.com. Editor: David G. Barnett. 100% freelance written. Quarterly magazine covering "Extreme horror for mature readers. No taboos and all fiction must push the limit of what traditional horror has ignored. Violent, sexy, gay, harsh, disturbing horror with a modern narrative." Estab. 1993. Circ. 2,000. Pays on publication. Publishes ms an average of 1 year after acceptance. Byline given. Buys first North American serial rights. Accepts simultaneous submissions. Reports in 1 week on queries; 2 months on mss. Sample copy for $5. Writer's guidelines for #10 SASE.

Nonfiction: Interview/profile. Buys 4 mss/year. Query. Length: 1,000-3,000 words. Pays ¼¢/word to $25 for assigned articles.

Fiction: Horror. Buys 24 mss/year. Query for longer pieces. Send complete ms for shorter pieces. Length: 2,000-10,000 words. Pays ¼¢/word to $25.

Tips: "Push the envelope. Harsh, disturbing horror with complex plots and characters laced with violence, sex and gore. We take the term 'extreme horror' seriously. Avoid gothic horror and stick with a modern narrative voice and tone."

‡**THE MAGAZINE OF FANTASY & SCIENCE FICTION**, Mercury Press, P.O. Box 420, Lincoln City OR 97367. Editor: Kristine Kathryn Rusch. 100% freelance written. Monthly fantasy fiction and science

fiction magazine. Estab. 1949. Circ. 80,000. **Pays on acceptance.** Byline given. Buys first North American and foreign serial rights. Submit seasonal material 8 months in advance. Reports in 2 months. Writer's guidelines for #10 SASE.

Fiction: Fantasy, horror, science fiction. Send complete ms. Length: 2,000-20,000 words. Pays 5-7¢/word.
  ● Ranked as one of the best markets for fiction writers in *Writer's Digest*'s annual "Fiction 50," June 1996.

Tips: "We need more hard science fiction and humor."

‡NIGHTCRY, Illustrated Magazine of Horror, CFD Productions, 360-A W. Merrick Rd., Suite 350, Valley Stream NY 11580. E-mail: cfdprod@aol.com. Contact: Pamela Hazelton, editor. Managing Editor and Publisher: Joseph M. Monks. 100% freelance written. Illustrated magazine of horror. "Our readers like twisted, horrific stories. No 'things that go bump in the night.' Psychological horror also is enjoyed." Estab. 1994. Circ. 15,000. Pays one month after publication. Publishes ms an average of 8 months after acceptance. Byline given. Buys first North American serial rights. Editorial lead time 4 months. Accepts simultaneous submissions. Reports in 2 months. Copy for $3.50. Writer's guidelines for #10 SASE.

Fiction: Horror, humorous, mystery, science fiction. Buys 10-30 mss/year. Send complete ms, comic script and/or panel to panel art. Pays $20-100.

Reprints: Accepts previously published submissions.

Tips: "Follow comic script format guidelines—they are different from standard scripts. Many writers adapt their short stories to comics fairly well."

‡ON SPEC, The Canadian Magazine of Speculative Writing, The Copper Pig Writers Society, P.O. Box 4727, Edmonton, Alberta T6E 5G6 Canada. Website: http://www.greenwoods.com/onspec/. Editorial Collective: Barry Hammond, Susan MacGregor, Jena Snyder, Diane L. Walton. 95% freelance written. Quarterly literary magazine covering Canadian science fiction and fantasy. "*On Spec* is Canada's premier speculative fiction magazine. We publish Canadian writers only." Estab. 1989. Circ. 2,000. **Pays on acceptance.** Publishes ms an average of 1 year after acceptance. Byline given. Buys first North American serial rights. Editorial lead time 6 months. Reports in 5 months on queries. Sample copy for $6. Writer's guidelines for #10 SASE with Canadian stamp or IRC.
  ● *On Spec* is a 3-time Aurora winner.

Nonfiction: Commissioned only. Yearly theme issue. 1997 theme is "Canadian Geographic"; all stories should feature a Canadian place name or region or Canadian setting. "Each year we offer $100 prize to best story by a young and upcoming author published in *On Spec*."

Fiction: Science fiction, fantasy, horror. No media tie-in or shaggy-alien stories. Buys 35 mss/year. Send complete ms only. Length: 6,000 words maximum. Pays $25-150 (Canadian) 2½¢/word.

Poetry: Barry Hammond, poetry editor. Avant-garde, free verse. "We rarely buy rhyming or religious material." Buys 6 poems/year. Submit maximum 6 poems. Length: 2-100 lines. Pays $15.

Tips: "Send for guidelines! We have specific (i.e. competition) format requiqrements. Please note that we accept submissions from Canadian writers only."

SCIENCE FICTION AGE, Sovereign Media, P.O. Box 369, Damascus MD 20872-0369. Editor: Scott Edelman. 100% freelance written. Bimonthly magazine of hard, soft science fiction, new wave, old guard, magic, cyberpunk, literary science fiction. Estab. 1992. Circ. 68,000. **Pays on acceptance.** Publishes ms an average of 4 months after acceptance. Byline given. Offers 10% kill fee. Buys first North American serial rights, with an option on first world rights. Editorial lead time 3 months. Submit seasonal material 3 months in advance. Reports in 2 months. Sample copy for $5. Writer's guidelines for #10 SASE.

Nonfiction: Essays, interview/profile, new product, opinion. Buys 24 mss/year. Query with published clips. Length: 200-2,500 words. Pays 5-10¢/word. Sometimes pays expenses of writers on assignment.

Photos: State availability of photos with submission. Reviews contact sheets. Offers no additional payment for photos accepted with ms. Identification of subjects required. Buys one-time rights.

Columns/Departments: Book Reviews, 800-1,200 words; Game Reviews, 1,750 words; Comics Review, 300 words; Essay, 2,000 words. Science, 2,500 words. Buys 30 mss/year. Query with published clips. Pays 5-10¢/word.

Fiction: Fantasy, science fiction. Buys 42 mss/year. Send complete ms. Length: 1,000-21,000 words. Pays 10¢/word.
  ● Ranked as one of the best markets for fiction writers in *Writer's Digest*'s annual "Fiction 50," June 1996.

THE SCREAM FACTORY, The Magazine of Horrors, Past, Present, and Future, Deadline Press, P.O. Box 2808, Apache Junction AZ 85217. E-mail: lordbuck@aol.com. Contact: Bob Morrish (16473 Redwood Lodge Rd., Los Gatos CA 95030). Editors: Peter Enfantino, Bob Morrish and John Scoleri. 75% freelance written. Quarterly literary magazine about horror in films and literature. Estab. 1988. Circ. 2,500. Pays on publication. Publishes ms an average of 6 months after acceptance. Buys first North American serial rights. Submit seasonal material 6 months in advance. Reports in 2 weeks on queries, 1 month on ms. Sample copy for $7 (please make checks payable to *The Scream Factory*). Writer's guidelines for #10 SASE.

Nonfiction: Essays, historical/nostalgic, interview/profile, new product, personal experience. Buys 35-50 mss/year. Query or send complete ms. Pays ½¢/word.

Photos: Send photos with submission. Reviews prints. Offers no additional payment for photos accepted with ms. Captions required. Buys one-time rights.

Columns/Departments: Book reviews of horror novels/collections; Writer's Writing (what horror authors are currently working on).

Fillers: Facts, newsbreaks. Pays ½¢/word. Also small reviews (150-200 words). "Please query on these."

Tips: "Looking for reviews of horror fiction, especially the lesser known authors. News on the horror genre, interviews with horror authors and strong opinion pieces. No unsolicited fiction accepted."

THE SILVER WEB, A Magazine of the Surreal, Buzzcity Press, P.O. Box 38190, Tallahassee FL 32315. (904)385-8948. E-mail: annk@freenet.fsu.edu. Publisher/Editor: Ann Kennedy. 100% freelance written. Semiannual literary magazine that features science fiction, dark fantasy and horror. Estab. 1988. Circ. 1,000. **Pays on acceptance.** Byline given. Buys first North American serial, or one-time or second serial (reprint) rights. Accepts simultaneous submissions. Reports in 2 months. Sample copy for $5.95. Writer's guidelines for #10 SASE.

Nonfiction: Essays, interview/profile, opinion. Buys 4-8 mss/year. Query. Length: 500-8,000 words. Pays 2-3¢/word.

Reprints: Send information before submitting ms about when and where material previously appeared. For reprints, pays 100% of amount paid for an original article.

Photos: State availability of photos with submission. Reviews prints. Offers no additional payment for photos accepted with ms. Identification of subjects required. Buys one-time rights.

Fiction: Experimental, horror, science fiction. "We do not want to see typical storylines, endings or predictable revenge stories." Buys 20-25 mss/year. Send complete ms. Length: 500-8,000 words. Pays 2-3¢/word. Publishes novel excerpts but query first.

Poetry: Avant-garde, free verse, haiku. Buys 10-15/year. Submit maximum 5 poems. Pays $5-20.

Fillers: Art fillers. Buys 10/year. Pays $5-10.

Tips: "Give us an unusual unpredictable story with strong, believable characters we care about. Surprise us with something unique. We do look for interviews with people in the field (writers, artists, filmmakers)."

SPACE AND TIME, 138 W. 70th St., 4B, New York NY 10023-4468. Editor-in-chief: Gordon Linzner. 100% freelance written. Biannual magazine of science fiction and fantasy. "We feature a mix of fiction and poetry in all aspects of the fantasy genre—science fiction, supernatural horror, sword & sorcery, mixed genre, unclassifiable. Its variety makes it stand out from more narrowly focused magazines. Our readers enjoy quality material that surprises and provokes." Estab. 1966. Circ. 2,000. **Pays on acceptance.** Publishes ms an average of 6 months after acceptance. Byline given. Buys first North American serial rights. Editorial lead time 6 months. Reports in 1 month on mss. Sample copy $5 plus $1.25 handling charge. Writer's guidelines for #10 SASE.

Nonfiction: Essays on fantasy, science fiction, science, etc. "No so-called 'true' paranormal." Buys 1-2 mss/year. Send complete ms. Length: 1,000 words maximum. Pays 1¢/word plus 2 contributor copies.

Photos/Artwork: Claudia Carlson, art director. Artwork (could include photos). Send nonreturnable photocopies. Reviews prints. Pays $10 for interior illustration, $25 for cover, plus 2 contributor copies. Model releases required. Buys one-time rights.

Fiction: Tom Piccirilli, fiction editor. Fantasy, horror, science fiction, mixed genre (i.e., science-fiction-mystery, western-horror, etc.) and unclassifiable; "Do not want anything that falls outside of fantasy/science fiction (but that leaves a lot)." Buys 15-20 mss/year. Send complete ms. Length: 10,000 words maximum. Pays 1¢/word plus 2 contributor copies.

Poetry: Lawrence Greenberg, poetry editor. Avant-garde, free verse, haiku, light verse, traditional; "anything that cannot conceivably fit into fantasy/science fiction/horror." Buys 10-15 poems/year. Submit maximum 3 poems. Length: no limits. Pays 1¢/word ($5 minimum) plus 2 contributor copies.

Tips: "Avoid clichés and standard plots unless you have something new to add."

STARLOG MAGAZINE, The Science Fiction Universe, Starlog Group, 475 Park Ave. S., 8th Floor, New York NY 10016-1689. Fax: (212)889-7933. E-mail: communications@starloggroup.com. Editor: David McDonnell. 90% freelance written. Eager to work with new/unpublished writers. Monthly magazine covering "the science fiction-fantasy genre: its films, TV, books, art and personalities." Estab. 1976. "We concentrate on interviews with actors, directors, writers, producers, special effects technicians and others. Be aware that 'sci-fi' and 'Trekkie' are seen as derogatory terms by our readers and by us." Pays on publication. Publishes ms an average of 4 months after acceptance. Byline given. Offers kill fee "only to manuscripts *written* or interviews *done for us.*" Buys all rights. No simultaneous submissions. Reports in 6 weeks or less. "We provide an assignment sheet and contract to *all* writers with deadline and other info, authorizing a queried piece." Sample copy for $5. Writer's guidelines for #10 SASE.

Nonfiction: Interview/profile (actors, directors, screenwriters who've made science fiction films and science fiction novelists); photo features; retrospectives of famous science fiction films and TV series; coverage of science fiction fandom, etc. "We also sometimes cover science fiction/fantasy animation and comics." No personal opinion think pieces/essays. *No* first person. Avoids articles on horror films/creators. "We prefer article format as opposed to Q&A interviews." Buys 175 mss/year. Query first with published clips. "We accept queries by mail *only*, by fax if there's a critical time factor. No phone calls. Ever! Unsolicited phone calls *cannot* be returned." Length: 500-3,000 words. Pays $35 (500-word or less items); $50-75 (sidebars); $150-275 (1,000-4,000 word pieces).

Reprints: Pays $50 for *each* reprint in online magazine version, foreign edition or such.

Photos: State availability of photos. Pays $10-25 for slide transparencies and 8×10 b&w prints depending on quality. "No separate payment for photos provided by film studios." Captions, model releases, identification of subjects and credit line on photos required. Photo credit given. Buys all rights.

Columns/Departments: Loglines (mini interviews or stray quotes from celebrities, 25-200 words each, $25-35); Booklog (book reviews, $15 each, by assignment only); Medialog (news of upcoming science fiction films and TV projects); Videolog (videocassette and disk releases of genre interest, staff-written); Gamelog (video, computer, role-playing games). Buys 100-125 reviews/year. Query with published clips. Book review, 150 words maximum; mini-article, 300-500 words. No kill fee.

Tips: "Absolutely *no fiction*. We do *not* publish it and we throw away fiction manuscripts from writers who also *can't* be bothered to include SASE. Nonfiction only please! A writer can best break into *Starlog* by getting an unusual interview or by *out-thinking* us and coming up with something *new* on a current film or book. We are always looking for *new* angles on *Star Trek: The Next Generation, Voyager, Deep Space Nine, Star Wars*, the original *Star Trek, Doctor Who, Starman, Beauty & the Beast, Lost in Space, Space: 1999, Battlestar Galactica, The Twilight Zone, The Outer Limits.* Know your subject before you try us. Most full-length major assignments go to freelancers with whom we're already dealing. But if we like your clips and ideas, we'll be happy to give *you* a chance. We are looking for new freelancers who act professional—and they are *harder* to find. No calls! If a letter isn't good enough to pitch your story, we don't *need* that story. I'd rather see how you write (in a letter), than listen to your chit-chatty powers of persuasion on the phone."

‡STARSHIP EARTH, Black Moon Publishing, P.O. Box 484, Bellaire OH 43906. Phone/fax: (614)671-3253. Editor: Silver Shadowhorse. Contact: Kirin Lee, managing editor. 50% freelance written. Bimonthly magazine featuring science fiction. "*Starship Earth* is geared toward science fiction fans of all ages. We do mostly nonfiction, but do print short stories. Our nonfiction focus: profiles of actors and industry people, conventions, behind the scenes articles on films and TV shows. We do cover action/adventure films and TV as well. Heavy Star Trek focus. We cover classic science fiction, too." Estab. 1996. Pays on publication. Publishes ms an average of 6 months after acceptance. Byline sometimes given. Buys first or one-time rights. Editorial lead time 6 months. Submit seasonal material 6 months in advance. Accepts simultaneous submissions. Reports in 3 weeks on queries; 2 months on mss. Sample copy for $5. Writer's guidelines for #10 SASE.

Nonfiction: General interest, how-to (relating to science fiction, writing, model building, crafts, etc.), humor (cartoons), interview/profile, new product (relating to science or science fiction), nostalgia, personal experience, photo feature, travel (relating to attending conventions), behind the scenes of film/TV science fiction). Buys variable number of mss/year. Query. Length: 500-2,000 words. Pays ½-3¢/word. Pays in copies for book or film reviews. Sometimes pays expenses of writers on assignment.

Reprints: Accepts previously published submissions.

Photos: State availability of photos with submission. Reviews transparencies, prints. Negotiates payment individually. Captions, model releases, identification of subjects required. Buys one-time rights.

Columns/Departments: Contact: Jenna Dawson, assistant editor. Costumes, conventions/events, science fiction music, upcoming book, film, TV releases, film reviews, book reviews, new products; all up to 700 words. Buys variable number of mss/year. Query. Pays ½-3¢/word.

Fiction: Contact: Silver Shadowhorse, editor. Adventure, fantasy, historical (with a science fiction twist), science fiction. No erotic content or horror. Buys variable number of mss/year. Query. Length: 500-3,000 words. Pays ½-3¢/word.

Fillers: Contact: Jenna Dawson, assistant editor. Anecdotes, facts, newsbreaks, short humor. Buys variable number of mss/year. Length: 50-250 words. Pays ½-3¢/word.

Tips: "We are willing to work with new and unpublished writers in most areas. All manuscripts must be in standard format. We are always looking for new or unusual angles on old science fiction shows/films, conventions, costumes, fx and people in the business. Articles from interviews must have sparkle and be interesting to a variety of readers. Absolutely no gossip or fluff. No story submissions with erotic content."

‡TERMINAL FRIGHT, The Journal of Traditional Haunts and Horrors, Terminal Fright Publications, P.O. Box 100, Black River NY 13612. Fax: (315)779-8310. Editor: Ken Abner. 100% freelance written. Quarterly magazine covering horror. Estab. 1993. Circ. 3,000. **Pays on acceptance**. Byline given. Editorial lead time 6 months. Submit seasonal material 9 months in advance. Accepts simultaneous submissions, if so noted. Reports in 2 months on queries. Sample copy for $5.

Fiction: Horror. No slasher. Buys 40 mss/year. Send complete ms. Length: 1,500-10,000 words. Pays $7.50-200 (½-2¢/word)

Tips: "Develop likable characters in intriguing situations. Lots of atmosphere and imagery."

‡A THEATER OF BLOOD, Pyx Press, P.O. Box 922648, Sylmar CA 91392-2648. Editor: C. Darren Butler. Associate Editor: Lisa S. Laurencot. 50% freelance written. Annual serial anthology of dark fantasy and literary horror. "We try to publish intelligent horror and dark fantasy." Estab. 1990. Circ. 500. Pays on publication. Publishes ms an average of 18 months after acceptance. Byline given. Buys limited-edition first rights. Editorial lead time 6 months. Accepts simultaneous submissions. Reports in 1 month on queries; 6 months on mss (occasionally larger). Sample copy for $6.50. Writer's guidelines available for #10 SASE.
  • Open to submissions from September 1-November 30 only.
Nonfiction: Interviews, essays. Buys 0-4/year. Send complete ms. Length: up to 8,000 words. Pays $2-10.
Fiction: Horror, dark fantasy. Buys 10-20 mss/year. Send complete ms. Length: 2,500-20,000 words (query for works over 8,000 words). Pays $2-30.
Tips: "*A Theater of Blood* has been published for several years as a little magazine of horrific short-short fiction and poetry. Since 1996 it is published as a serial book-anthology of fiction. All types of literary horror and dark fantasy are needed, including cosmic, supernatural and quiet horror. All stories should contain a fantasy element. We no longer consider poetry."

THE URBANITE, Surreal & Lively & Bizarre, Urban Legend Press, P.O. Box 4737, Davenport IA 52808. Editor: Mark McLaughlin. 95% freelance written. Triannual magazine covering surreal fiction and poetry. "We look for quality fiction in an urban setting with a surrealistic tone. . . We prefer character-driven storylines. Our audience is urbane, culture-oriented, and hard to please!" Estab. 1991. Circ. 500. **Pays on acceptance.** Contributors to recent issues include Thomas Ligotti, Poppy Z. Brite, Hugh B. Cave and Joel Lane. Publishes ms an average of 6 months after acceptance. Byline given. Offers 100% kill fee. Buys first North American serial rights and non-exclusive rights for public readings (we hold readings of the magazine at various venues—like libraries). Reports in 1 month on queries; 5 months on mss. Sample copy for $5. Writer's guidelines for #10 SASE.
Fiction: Experimental, fantasy (contemporary), slipstream/cross genre, horror, humorous, science fiction (but not "high-tech"), surrealism of all sorts. Buys 45 mss/year. Send complete ms. Length: 500-3,000 words. Pays $10-90 (2-3¢/word).
  • Ranked as one of the best markets for fiction writers in *Writer's Digest*'s annual "Fiction 50," June 1996.
Reprints: Accepts previously published submissions (but query first).
Poetry: Avant-garde, free verse, traditional, narrative poetry. Buys 15 poems/year. Submit maximum 3 poems. No length limits. Pays $10/poem.
Tips: "Writers should familiarize themselves with surrealism in literature: too often, we receive stories filled with genre clichés. Also: we prefer character-driven stories.We're looking to add nonfiction (at the same pay rate—2-3¢/word—as fiction). Reviews, articles, cultural commentary . . . the more unusual, the better."

SEX

Magazines featuring pictorial layouts accompanied by stories and articles of a sexual nature, both gay and straight, are listed in this section. Dating and single lifestyle magazines appear in the Relationships section. Other markets for articles relating to sex can be found in the Men's and Women's sections.

‡DRUMMER, Desmodus, Inc., P.O. Box 410390, San Francisco CA 94141-0390. (415)252-1195. Fax: (415)252-9574. Managing Editor: Wickie Stamps. 50% freelance written. Gay male leather and related fetish erotica/news. Monthly magazine of "erotic aspects of leather and other masculine fetishes for gay men." Estab. 1976. Circ. 45,000. Pays 30 days after publication. Publishes ms an average of 3 months after acceptance. Byline given. Buys first North American serial rights or makes work-for-hire assignments. Submit seasonal/holiday material 9 months in advance. Reports in 1 month on queries; 3 months on mss. Sample copy for $6. Writer's guidelines for #10 SASE.
Nonfiction: Book excerpts, essays, historical/nostalgic, how-to, humor, interview/profile, new product, opinion, personal experience, photo feature, technical, travel. No feminine-slanted or heterosexual pieces. Buys 25 mss/year. Query with or without published clips, or send complete ms. Length: 1,000-15,000 words. Pays $50-200 for assigned articles; $50-100 for unsolicited articles. Rarely pays expenses of writers on assignment.
Reprints: Accepts previously published submissions.
Photos: Send photocopies with submission. Reviews contact sheets and transparencies. Offers $25-50/photo. Model releases, identification of subjects required. Buys one-time rights or all rights.
Fiction: Adventure, erotica, ethnic, fantasy, historical, horror, humorous, mystery, novel excerpts, science fiction, slice-of-life vignettes, suspense, western. Must have gay "macho" erotic elements. Buys 60-75 mss/year. Send complete ms. Length: 1,000-20,000 words. Occasionally serializes stories. Pays $100.
Fillers: Anecdotes, facts, gags, cartoons, newsbreaks. Manuscript must be scannable. Buys 50/year. Length: 10-100 words. Pays $10-50.

Tips: "All they have to do is write—but they must be knowledgeable about some aspect of the scene. While the magazine is aimed at gay men, we welcome contributions from straight men and from straight, bisexual and gay women who understand leather, SM and kinky erotic fetishes. Fiction is most open to freelancers."

FIRST HAND, Experiences For Loving Men, Firsthand, Ltd., 310 Cedar Lane, Teaneck NJ 07666. (201)836-9177. Fax: (201)836-5055. E-mail: firsthand3@aol.com. Contact: Bob Harris, editor. Publisher: Jackie Lewis. 75% freelance written. Eager to work with new/unpublished writers. Monthly magazine of homosexual erotica. Estab. 1980. Circ. 70,000. Pays 6 months after acceptance or on publication, whichever comes first. Publishes ms an average of 8 months after acceptance. Byline given. Buys all rights (exceptions made) and second serial (reprint) rights. Submit seasonal material 10 months in advance. Reports in 4 months. Sample copy for $5. Writer's guidelines for #10 SASE.
Reprints: Send photocopy of previously published article. Pays 50% of amount paid for original articles.
Columns/Departments: Survival Kit (short nonfiction articles, up to 1,000 words, featuring practical information on safe sex practices, health, travel, psychology, law, fashion, and other advice/consumer/lifestyle topics of interest to gay or single men). "For this section, we sometimes also buy reprint rights to appropriate articles previously published in local gay newspapers around the country." Infotainment (short reviews up to 1,000 words on books, film, TV, video, theater, performance art, museums, etc.). Reviews must have a gay slant. Query. Pays $35-70, depending on length.
Fiction: Erotic fiction up to 5,000 words, average 2,000-3,000 words. "We prefer fiction in the first person which is believable—stories based on the writer's actual experience have the best chance. We're not interested in stories which involve underage characters in sexual situations. Other taboos include bestiality, rape—except in prison stories, as rape is an unavoidable reality in prison—and heavy drug use. Writers with questions about what we can and cannot depict should write for our guidelines, which go into this in more detail. We print mostly self-contained stories; we will look at novel excerpts, but only if they stand on their own."
Poetry: Free verse and light verse. Buys 12/year. Submit maximum 5 poems. Length: 10-30 lines. Pays $25.
Tips: "*First Hand* is a very reader-oriented publication for gay men. Half of each issue is made up of letters from our readers describing their personal experiences, fantasies and feelings. Our readers are from all walks of life, all races and ethnic backgrounds, all classes, all religious and political affiliations, and so on. They are very diverse, and many live in far-flung rural areas or small towns; for some of them, our magazines are the primary source of contact with gay life, in some cases the only support for their gay identity. Our readers are very loyal and save every issue. We return that loyalty by trying to reflect their interests—for instance, by striving to avoid the exclusively big-city bias so common to national gay publications. So bear in mind the diversity of the audience when you write."

GALLERY MAGAZINE, Montcalm Publishing Corp., 401 Park Ave. S., New York NY 10016-8802. (212)779-8900. Fax: (212)725-7215. Editorial Director: Barry Janoff. Managing Editor: Rich Friedman. 50% freelance written. Prefers to work with published/established writers. Monthly magazine "focusing on features of interest to the young American man." Estab. 1972. Circ. 500,000. Pays 50% on acceptance, 50% on publication. Byline given. Pays 25% kill fee. Buys first North American serial rights or makes work-for-hire assignments. Submit seasonal/holiday material 6 months in advance. Reports in 1 month on queries; 2 months on mss. Sample copy for $7.95 (add $2 for Canadian and foreign orders). Writer's guidelines for SASE.
  • *Gallery* works on Macintosh Performa 475, so it accepts material on Mac or compatible disks if accompanied by hard copy.
Nonfiction: Investigative pieces, general interest, how-to, humor, interview, new products, profile. "We *do not* want to see pornographic articles." Buys 4-5 mss/issue. Query or send complete mss. Length: 1,000-3,000 words. Pays $300-1,500. "Special prices negotiated." Sometimes pays expenses of writers on assignment.
Photos: Send photos with accompanying mss. Pay varies for b&w or color contact sheets and negatives. Buys one-time rights. Captions preferred; model release required.
Fiction: Adventure, erotica (special guidelines available), experimental, humorous, mainstream, mystery, suspense. Buys 1 ms/issue. Send complete ms. Length: 1,000-3,000 words. Pays $350-500.

GENT, "Home of the D-Cups," Dugent Publishing Corp., 14411 Commerce Way, Suite 420, Miami Lakes FL 33016. Managing Editor: Steve Dorfman. 80% freelance written. Monthly men's sophisticate magazine with emphasis on big breasts. Estab. 1960. Circ. 150,000. Pays on publication. Byline given. Buys first North American serial or second serial (reprint) rights. Editorial lead time 4 months. Submit seasonal material 6 months in advance. Reports in 2 weeks on queries; 3 months on mss. Sample copy for $7. Writer's guidelines for #10 SASE.
Nonfiction: How-to ("anything sexually related"), personal experience ("any and all sexually related matters"). Buys 13-26 mss/year. Query. Length: 2,000-3,500 words. Pays $250.
Reprints: Accepts previously published submissions.
Photos: Send photos with submission. Reviews 35mm transparencies. Negotiates payment individually. Model releases and identification of subjects required. Buys first North American with reprint rights.

Fiction: Erotica, fantasy. Buys 26 mss/year. Send complete ms. Length: 2,000-3,500 words. Pays $200-250.

GUYS, First Hand Ltd., P.O. Box 1314, Teaneck NJ 07666-3441. (201)836-9177. Fax: (201)836-5055. E-mail: firsthand3@aol.com. Editor: William Spencer. 80% freelance written. Monthly magazine of erotica for gay men. "A positive, romantic approach to gay sex." Estab. 1988. Circ. 100,000. Pays on publication. Publishes ms an average of 1 year after acceptance. Byline given. Buys first North American serial or all rights. Reports in 6 months. Sample copy for $5.50. Writer's guidelines for #10 SASE.
Fiction: Erotica. Buys 72 mss/year. Send complete ms. Length: 1,000-10,000 words. Pays $75-250.

‡HIGH SOCIETY MAGAZINE, Crescent Publishers, 801 Second Ave., New York NY 10017. (212)661-7878. Fax: (212)692-9297. Editor: Vincent Stevens. Contact: Rick S. Hall, managing editor. 50% freelance written. Men's sophisticate magazine emphasizing men's entertainment. "Everything of interest to the American male." Estab. 1976. Circ. 400,000. **Pays on acceptance.** Byline given. Offers 20% kill fee. Buys first North American serial rights. Submit seasonal material 6 months in advance. Accepts simultaneous submissions. Reports in 2 weeks on queries. Sample copy for $2 and 9×12 SAE.
Nonfiction: Exposé, general interest, interview/profile, photo feature. Buys 12 mss/year. Query with or without published clips, or send complete ms. Length: 1,500-3,000 words. Pays $300-800 for assigned articles; $200-500 for unsolicited articles. Sometimes pays expenses of writers on assignment.
Photos: Send photos with submission. Reviews 35mm slides, 2¼×2¼ transparencies, 8×10 prints. Offers $100-200/photo. Captions, model releases and photo identification of proof of age of subjects required. Buys one-time rights. Any photos of celebrity nudes entertained. Negotiates payment individually.
Columns/Departments: Private Passions (first person sexual accounts), 3,000 words; Bad Guys (crime-related exposes), 1,800 words; Sex & Music (biographies of female celebs in music business), 1,000 words. Buys 30 mss/year. Query with published clips. Pays $150-800.

HUSTLER, HG Inc., 8484 Wilshire Blvd., Suite 900, Beverly Hills CA 90211. Fax: (213)651-2741. Editor: Allan MacDonell. Contact: Dylan Ford, articles editor. 60% freelance written. Magazine published 13 times/year. "*Hustler* is the no-nonsense men's magazine. Our audience does not need to be told whether to wear their trousers cuffed or plain. The *Hustler* reader expects honest, unflinching looks at hard topics—sexual, social, political, personality profile, true crime." Estab. 1974. Circ. 750,000. Pays as boards ship to printer. Publishes ms an average of 3 months after acceptance. Byline given. Offers 20% kill fee. Buys all rights. Editorial lead time 4 months. Submit seasonal material 6 months in advance. Reports in 2 weeks on queries; 1 month on mss. Writer's guidelines for #10 SASE.
  • *Hustler* is most interested in profiles of dynamic ground-breaking, indomitable individuals who don't mind "flipping a bird" at the world in general.
Nonfiction: Book excerpts, exposé, general interest, how-to, interview/profile, personal experience, trends. Buys 30 mss/yer. Query. Length: 3,500-4,000 words. Pays $1,500. Sometimes pays expenses of writers on assignment.
Columns/Departments: Sex Play (some aspect of sex that can be encapsulated in a limited space), 2,500 words. Buys 13 mss/year. Send complete ms. Pays $750.
Fiction: "Difficult fiction market. Must have two sex scenes; yet not be rote or boring." Buys 2 mss/year. Send complete ms. Length: 3,000-3,500. Pays $1,000.
Fillers: Pays $50-100. Jokes and "Graffilthy," bathroom-wall humor.
Tips: "Don't try and mimic the *Hustler* style. If a writer needs to be molded into our voice, we'll do a better job of it than he or she will."

IN TOUCH/INDULGE FOR MEN, In Touch International, Inc., 13122 Saticoy St., North Hollywood CA 91605-3402. (818)764-2288. Fax: (818)764-2307. Editor: Alan W. Mills. 80% freelance written. Works with a small number of new/unpublished writers each year. Monthly magazine covering the gay male lifestyle, gay male humor and erotica. Estab. 1973. Circ. 70,000. Pays on publication. Byline given, pseudonym OK. Buys one-time rights. Accepts simultaneous submissions. Reports in 2 months. Sample copy for $5.95. Writer's guidelines for #10 SASE.
Nonfiction: Rarely buys nonfiction. Send complete ms. Length: 3,000-3,500 words. Pays $25-75.
Photos: Send photos with submission. Reviews contact sheets, transparencies, prints. Offers $35/photo. Captions, model releases, identification of subjects required. Buys one-time rights.
Fiction: Gay male erotica. Buys 54 mss/year. Send complete ms. Length: 3,000-3,500 words. Pays $75 maximum.
Fillers: Short humor. Buys 12/year. Length: 1,500-3,500 words. Pays $50-75.
Tips: "Our publication features male nude photos plus three fiction pieces, several articles, cartoons, humorous comments on items from the media, photo features. We try to present the positive aspects of the gay lifestyle, with an emphasis on humor. Humorous pieces may be erotic in nature. We are open to all submissions that fit our gay male format; the emphasis, however, is on humor and the upbeat. We receive many fiction manuscripts but not nearly enough humor."

LIBIDO, The Journal of Sex & Sensibility, Libido, Inc., 5318 N. Paulina St., Chicago IL 60640, Fax: (312)275-0752. E-mail: rune@mcs.com. Website: www.indra.com\libido. Co-editors: Marianna Beck and Jack Hafferkamp. Submissions Editor: J.L. Beck. 50% freelance written. Quarterly magazine covering literate erotica. "*Libido* is about sexuality. Orientation is not an issue, writing ability is. The aim is to enlighten as often as it is to arouse. Humor—sharp and smart—is important, so are safer sex contexts." Estab. 1988. Circ. 9,000. Pays on publication. Byline given. Kill fee "rare, but negotiable." Buys one-time or second serial (reprint) rights. Editorial lead time 3 months. Submit seasonal material 4 months in advance. Payment negotiable. Reports in 6 months. Sample copy for $8. Writer's guidelines for #10 SASE.

Nonfiction: Book excerpts, essays, historical/nostalgic, humor, photo feature, travel. "No violence, sexism or misty memoirs." Buys 10-20 mss/year. Send complete ms. Length: 300-2,500 words. Pays $50 minimum for assigned articles; $15 minimum for unsolicited articles. Pays contributor copies "when money isn't an issue and copies or other considerations have equal or higher value." Sometimes pays expenses of writers on assignment.

Reprints: Send tearsheet of article or short story and information about when and where the material previously appeared.

Photos: Reviews contact sheets and 5×7 and 8×10 prints. Negotiates payment individually. Model releases required. Buys one-time rights.

Fiction: Erotica, novel excerpts. Buys 10 mss/year. Send complete ms. Length: 800-2,500 words. Pays $20-50.

Poetry: Uses humorous short erotic poetry. No limericks. Buys 10 poems/year. Submit maximum 3 poems. Pays $15.

Tips: "Send us a manuscript—make it short, sharp and with a lead that makes us want to read. If we're not hooked by paragraph three, we reject the manuscript."

NUGGET, Dugent Publishing Corp., 14411 Commerce Way, Suite 420, Miami Lakes FL 33016-1598. Fax: (305)557-6005. E-mail: editor-nugget@dngent.com. Website: http://www.dugent.com/nug/. Managing Editor: Nye Willden. Contact: Christopher James, editor-in-chief. 100% freelance written. Men's/adult magazine published 10 times a year covering fetish and kink. "*Nugget* is a one-of-a-kind publication which appeals to daring, open-minded adults who enjoy all forms of both kinky, alternative sex (catfighting, transvestism, fetishism, bi-sexuality, etc.) and conventional sex." Estab. 1960. Circ. 30,448. Pays on publication. Publishes ms an average of 1 year after acceptance. Byline given. Buys first North American serial rights. Editorial lead time 5 months. Submit seasonal material 1 year in advance. Accepts simultaneous submissions. Reports in 2 weeks on queries; 2 months on mss. Sample copy for $3.50. Writer's guidelines free on request.

Nonfiction: Interview/profile, sexual matters/trends (fetish and kink angle). Buys 8 mss/year. Query. Length: 2,000-3,000 words. Pays $200 minimum.

Photos: Send photos with submission. Reviews transparencies. Offers no additional payment for photos accepted with ms. Model releases required. Buys one-time second rights.

Fiction: Erotica, fantasy. Buys 20 mss/year. Send complete ms. Length: 2,000-3,000 words. Pays $200-250.

Tips: Most open to fiction submissions. (Follow readers guidelines for suitable topics.)

OPTIONS, AJA Publishing, P.O. Box 470, Port Chester NY 10573. (914)939-2111. E-mail: dianaeditor@aol.com. Editor: Don Stone. Contact: Diana Sheridan, associate editor. Mostly freelance written. Sexually explicit magazine for and about bisexuals and homosexuals, published 10 times/year. "Articles, stories and letters about bisexuality. Positive approach. Safe-sex encounters unless the story clearly pre-dates the AIDS situation." Estab. 1977. Circ. 100,000. Pays on publication. Publishes mss an average of 10 months after acceptance. Byline given, usually pseudonymous. Buys all rights. Submit seasonal material 8 months in advance; buys very little seasonal material. Reports in 3 weeks. Sample copy for $2.95 and 6×9 SAE with 5 first-class stamps. Writer's guidelines for SASE.

Nonfiction: Essays (occasional), how-to, humor, interview/profile, opinion, personal experience (especially). All must be bisexually or gay related. Does not want "anything not bisexually/gay related, anything negative, anything opposed to safe sex, anything dry/boring/ponderous/pedantic. Write even serious topics informally if not lightly." Buys 10 nonfiction mss/year. Send complete ms. Length: 2,000-3,000. Pays $100.

Photos: Reviews transparencies and prints. Pays $20 for b&w photos; $200 for full color. Color or b&w sets $150. Previously published photos acceptable.

Fiction: "We don't usually get enough true first-person stories and need to buy some from writers. They must be bisexual, usually man/man, hot and believable. They must not read like fiction." Buys 70 fiction mss/year. Send complete ms. Length: 2,000-3,000. Pays $100.

Tips: "We use many more male/male pieces than female/female. Use only one serious article per issue. A serious/humorous approach is good here, but only if it's natural to you; don't make an effort for it. No longer buying 'letters'. We get enough real ones."

PENTHOUSE, General Media, 277 Park Ave., 4th Floor, New York NY 10172-0033. (212)702-6000. Fax: (212)702-6279. Contact: Editorial Department. Monthly magazine. "*Penthouse* is for the sophisticted male. Its editorial scope ranges from outspoken contemporary comment to photography essays of beautiful women. *Penthouse* features interviews with personalities, sociological studies, humor, travel, food and wines, and fashion and grooming for men." Estab. 1969. Circ. 1,100,000. Query before submitting. This magazine did not respond to our request for information. Query before submitting.

PLAYBOY, 680 N. Lakeshore Dr., Chicago, IL 60611. Contact: Articles Editor or Fiction Editor. Monthly magazine. "*Playboy* is a general interest, lifestyle magazine for men. Editorial covers all the interests in men's lives: movies, music, sports, cars, fashion and sophisticated entertaining. In addition, *Playboy*'s 'Interview' and '20 Questions' present profiles of politicians, athletes and today's hottest personalities." Estab. 1953. Circ. 3,283,000. Writer's guidelines for SASE. This magazine did not respond to our request for information. Query before submitting.

‡SCORE, Score Publishing Group, 13360 SW 128 St., Miami FL 33133. Fax: (305)238-6716. E-mail: quad@netrunner.net. Editor: John C. Fox. Contact: Keli Townsend, assistant to editor. 20% freelance written. Monthly magazine covering men's sophisticate-big bust niche. Top flight men's sophisticate, specializing in the big bust area. Models of the slim-stacked. Estab. 1991. Circ. 187,000. Pays on publication. Publishes ms an average of 3 months after acceptance. Byline given. Buys first rights. Editorial lead time 4 months. Submit seasonal material 5 months in advance. Reports in 1 month on queries; 2 months on mss. Sample copy for 10×12 SAE and $2 postage or SASE. Writer's guidelines for #10 SASE.
Nonfiction: Erotic. Buys 20-30 mss/year. Send complete ms. Length: 2,000-5,000 words. Pays $350-500. Sometimes pays expenses of writers on assignment.
Photos: Send photos with submission. Negotiates payment individually. Model releases required. Buys one-time rights.
Fiction: Buys 48 mss/year. Send complete ms. Length: 2,000-5,000 words. Pays $350-500.
Tips: Send for writer's guidelines.

SWANK, Swank Publications, 210 Route 4 E., Suite 401, Paramus NJ 07652. (201)843-4004. Fax: (201)843-8636. Editor: Paul Gambino. Assistant Editor: Rob Ruvo. 75% freelance written. Works with new/unpublished writers. Monthly magazine on "sex and sensationalism, lurid. High quality adult erotic entertainment." Audience of men ages 18-38, high school and some college education, medium income, skilled blue-collar professionals, union men, some white-collar. Estab. 1954. Circ. 400,000. Pays on publication. Publishes ms an average of 4 months after acceptance. Byline given, pseudonym if wanted. Buys first North American serial rights. Submit seasonal material 6 months in advance. Reports in 3 weeks on queries; 1 month on mss. Sample copy for $5.95. Writer's guidelines for SASE.
• *Swank* reports a need for more nonfiction, non-sex-related articles.
Nonfiction: Exposé (researched), adventure must be accompanied by color photographs. "We buy articles on sex-related topics, which don't need to be accompanied by photos." Interested in unusual lifestyle pieces. Buys photo pieces on autos, action, adventure. Buys 34 mss/year. Query with or without published clips. Pays $350-500. Sometimes pays the expenses of writers on assignment. "It is strongly recommended that a sample copy is reviewed before submitting material."
Photos: Bruce Perez, photo editor. Send photos. "If you have good photographs of an interesting adventure/lifestyle subject, the writing that accompanies is bought almost automatically." Model releases required.

SPORTS

A variety of sports magazines, from general interest to sports medicine, are covered in this section. For the convenience of writers who specialize in one or two areas of sport and outdoor writing, the publications are subcategorized by the sport or subject matter they emphasize. Publications in related categories (for example, Hunting and Fishing; Archery and Bowhunting) often buy similar material. Writers should read through this entire section to become familiar with the subcategories. Publications on horse breeding and hunting dogs are classified in the Animal section, while horse racing is listed here. Publications dealing with automobile or motorcycle racing can be found in the Automotive and Motorcycle category. Markets interested in articles on exercise and fitness are listed in the Health and Fitness section. Outdoor publications that promote the preservation of nature, placing only secondary emphasis on nature as a setting for sport, are in the Nature, Conservation and Ecology category. Regional magazines are frequently interested in sports material with a local angle. Camping publications are classified in the Travel, Camping and Trailer category.

Archery and Bowhunting

BOWHUNTER, The Number One Bowhunting Magazine, Cowles Enthusiast Media, 6405 Flank Dr., Harrisburg PA 17112-8200. (717)657-9555. Fax: (717)657-9552. Contact: Richard Cochran, editorial director. Editor/Founder: M.R. James. Publisher: David Canfield. 50% freelance written. Bimonthly magazine (with two special issues) on hunting big and small game with bow and arrow. "We are a special interest publication, produced by bowhunters for bowhunters, covering all aspects of the sport. Material included in each issue is designed to entertain and inform readers, making them better bowhunters." Estab. 1971. Circ. 180,000. **Pays on acceptance.** Publishes ms an average of 1 year after acceptance. Byline given. Kill fee varies. Buys first North American serial and one-time rights. Submit seasonal material 8 months in advance. Reports in 1 month on queries; 5 weeks on mss. Sample copy for $2. Free writer's guidelines.
Nonfiction: General interest, how-to, interview/profile, opinion, personal experience, photo feature. "We publish a special 'Big Game' issue each Fall (September) but need all material by mid-March. Our other annual publication, *Whitetail Bowhunter*, is staff written or by assignment only. We don't want articles that graphically deal with an animal's death. And, please, no articles written from the animal's viewpoint." Buys 60 plus mss/year. Query. Length: 250-2,000 words. Pays $500 maximum for assigned articles; $100-400 for unsolicited articles. Sometimes pays expenses of writers on assignment.
Photos: Send photos with submission. Reviews 35mm and 2¼×2¼ transparencies and 5×7 and 8×10 prints. Offers $75-250/photo. Captions required. Buys one-time rights.
Tips: "A writer must know bowhunting and be willing to share that knowledge. Writers should anticipate *all* questions a reader might ask, then answer them in the article itself or in an appropriate sidebar. Articles should be written with the reader foremost in mind; we won't be impressed by writers seeking to prove how good they are—either as writers or bowhunters. We care about the reader and don't need writers with 'I' trouble. Features are a good bet because most of our material comes from freelancers. The best advice is: Be yourself. Tell your story the same as if sharing the experience around a campfire. Don't try to write like you think a writer writes."

‡BOWHUNTING WORLD, Ehlert Publishing Group, Suite 600, 601 Lakeshore Parkway, Minnetonka MN 55305-5215. (612)476-2200. Fax: (612)476-8065. Editor: Mike Strandlund. 70% freelance written. Monthly magazine for bowhunting and archery enthusiasts who participate in the sport year-round. Estab. 1951. Circ. 130,000. **Pays on acceptance.** Publishes ms an average of 5 months after acceptance. Byline given. Buys first rights and reprint rights. Reports in 3 weeks on queries, 6 weeks on mss. Sample copy for $3 and 9×12 SAE with 10 first-class stamps. Writer's and photographers guidelines for SASE.
Nonfiction: How-to articles with creative slants on knowledgeable selection and use of bowhunting equipment and bowhunting methods. Articles must emphasize knowledgeable use of archery or hunting equipment, and/or specific bowhunting techniques. Straight hunting adventure narratives and other types of articles now appear only in special issues. Equipment-oriented articles must demonstrate wise and insightful selection and use of archery equipment and other gear related to the archery sports. Some product-review, field-test, equipment how-to and technical pieces will be purchased. We are not interested in articles that rely on random mentioning of brands. Technique-oriented articles most sought are those that briefly cover fundamentals and delve into leading-edge bowhunting or recreational archery methods. Purchase a few narrative bowhunting articles describing particular hunts. "We are also looking for professional-quality articles and photos for our *Archery Business* and *3-D & Target Archery* titles. Primarily focusing on retail archery and tournament coverage." Buys 60 mss/year. Query or send complete ms. Length: 1,500-3,000 words. Pays $350 to over $500.
Photos: "We are seeking cover photos that depict specific behavioral traits of the more common big game animals (scraping whitetails, bugling elk, etc.) and well-equipped bowhunters in action. Must include return postage."
Tips: "Writers are strongly advised to adhere to guidelines and become familiar with our new format, as our needs are very specific. Because our needs have changed so dramatically, writers are urged to query before sending packages. We prefer detailed outlines of up to six article ideas per query. Assignments are made for the next 18 months."

PETERSEN'S BOWHUNTING, Petersen Publishing Company, 6420 Wilshire Blvd., Los Angeles CA 90048-5515. (213)782-2000. Editor: Greg Tinsley. 70% freelance written. Magazine published 8 times/year covering bowhunting. "Very equipment oriented. Our readers are 'superenthusiasts,' therefore our writers must have an advanced knowledge of hunting archery." Circ. 135,000. **Pays on acceptance.** Byline given. Buys all rights. Editorial lead time 6 months. Submit seasonal material 6 months in advance. Reports in 1 month. Sample copy for #10 SASE. Writer's guidelines free on request.
Nonfiction: How-to, humor, interview/profile, new product, opinion, personal experience, photo feature. Buys 40 mss/year. Send complete ms. Length: 2,000 words. Pays $300.
Photos: Send photos with submission. Reviews contact sheets, 35mm transparencies, 5×7 prints. Offers $35-250/photo. Captions and model releases required. Buys one-time rights.

Columns/Departments: Query. Pays $200-300.
Fillers: Facts, newsbreaks. Buys 12/year. Length: 150-400 words. Pays $25-75.
Tips: Feature articles must be supplied to *Petersen's Bowhunting* in either 5.25 IBM (or compatible) or 3.50 MacIntosh floppy disks.

Bicycling

ADVENTURE CYCLIST, Adventure Cycling Assn., Box 8308, Missoula MT 59807. (406)721-1776. Fax: (406)721-8754. Editor: Daniel D'Ambrosio. 75% freelance written. Bicycle touring magazine for Adventure Cycling members published 9 times/year. Circ. 30,000. Pays on publication. Byline given. Buys first serial rights. Submit seasonal/holiday material 3 months in advance. Sample copy and guidelines for 9×12 SAE with 4 first-class stamps.
Nonfiction: How-to; humor; interview/profile; personal experience; photo feature; technical; travel. Buys 20-25 mss/year. Query with published clips or send complete ms; include short bio with ms. Length: 800-2,500 words. Pay negotiable.
Photos: Bicycle, scenery, portraits. State availability of photos. Model releases, identification of subjects required.

BICYCLING, Rodale Press, Inc., 33 E. Minor St., Emmaus PA 18098. (610)967-5171. Fax: (610)967-8960. Publisher: Mike Greehan. Executive Editor: Edward Pavelka. 20-25% freelance written. Prefers to work with published/established writers. Magazine published 10 times/year covering topics of interest to committed cyclists. Estab. 1961. Circ. 330,000. **Pays on acceptance**. Byline given. Buys all rights. Submit seasonal/holiday material 6 months in advance. Reports in 2 months. Sample copy for $2.50. Writer's guidelines for #10 SASE.
Nonfiction: How-to (on all phases of bicycle touring, repair, maintenance, commuting, new products, clothing, riding technique, nutrition for cyclists, conditioning); fitness is more important than ever; also travel (bicycling must be central here); photo feature (on cycling events of national significance); and technical (component review—query). "We are strictly a bicycling magazine. We seek readable, clear, well-informed pieces. We sometimes run articles that are pure humor or inspiration and some of each might flavor even our most technical pieces. No poetry or fiction." Buys 1-2 unsolicited mss/issue. Send complete ms. Length: 1,500 words average. Pays $25-1,200. Sometimes pays expenses of writers on assignment.
Photos: State availability of photos with query letter or send photo material with ms. Pays $15-50 for b&w prints and $35-250 for transparencies. Captions preferred; model release required.
Fillers: Anecdotes and news items for Bike Shorts section.
Tips: "We're alway seeking interesting accounts of cycling as a lifestyle."

CRANKMAIL, Cycling in Northern Ohio, P.O. Box 110236, Cleveland OH 44111-0236. Editor: James Guilford. Magazine published 10 times/year covering bicycling in all aspects. "Our publication serves the interests of bicycle enthusiasts . . . established, accomplished adult cyclists. These individuals are interested in reading about the sport of cycling, bicycles as transportation, ecological tie-ins, sports nutrition, the history and future of bicycles and bicycling." Estab. 1977. Circ. 1,000. Pays on publication. Byline given. Not copyrighted. Buys one-time or second serial (reprint) rights. Editorial lead time 1 month. Submit seasonal material 3 months in advance. Sample copy for $1. Writer's guidelines for #10 SASE.
Reprints: Accepts previously published submissions.
Nonfiction: Essays, historical/nostalgic, how-to, humor, interview/profile, personal experience, technical. "No articles encouraging folks to start or get involved in bicycling—our readers are already cyclists." Send complete ms; No queries." Length: 2,500 words maximum. Pays $10 minimum for unsolicited articles.
Fillers: Cartoons. Pays $5-10.

CYCLING USA, The Official Publication of the U.S. Cycling Federation, One Olympic Plaza, Colorado Springs CO 80909. (719)578-4581. Fax: (719)578-4596. E-mail: usacycling@aol.com. Website: www.usacycling.com. Editor: Frank Stanley. 25% freelance written. Monthly magazine covering reportage and commentary on American bicycle racing, personalities and sports physiology, for USCF licensed cyclists. Circ. 35,000. Pays on publication. Publishes ms an average of 2 months after acceptance. Byline given. Reports in 2 weeks. Sample copy for 10×12 SAE with 2 first-class stamps.
   • *Cycling USA* is looking for longer, more in-depth features (1,000-1,500 words).
Nonfiction: How-to (train, prepare for a bike race), interview/profile, opinion, personal experience, photo feature, technical and race commentary on major cycling events. No comparative product evaluations. Buys 15 mss/year. Query with published clips. Length: 800-1,200 words. Pays 10¢/word.
Reprints: Send photocopy of article. Pays 100% of amount paid for an original article.
Photos: State availability of photos. Pays $15-50 for 5×7 b&w prints; $100 for transparencies used as cover. Captions required. Buys one-time rights.

Tips: "A background in bicycle racing is important because the sport is somewhat insular, technical and complex. Most major articles are generated inhouse. Race reports are most open to freelancers. Be concise, informative and anecdotal. Our format is more compatible with 800-1,200 word articles than longer features."

‡DIRT RAG, A.K.A. Productions, 181 Saxonburg Rd., Pittsburgh PA 15238. (412)767-9910. Fax: (412)767-9920. Publisher: Maurice Tierney. Contact: Elaine Tierney, editor. 75% freelance written. Mountain biking magazine published 7 times/year. "*Dirt Rag*'s style is much looser, fun and down to earth than mainstream (glossy) magazines on the same subject. We appeal to hard-core (serious) mountain bikers, and these people make our finest contributions. Avant-garde, humorous, off-beat, alternative." Estab. 1989. Circ. 20,000. Pays on publication. Byline given. No kill fee. Buys one-time rights. Accepts simultaneous submissions. Sample copy for 5 first-class stamps. Writer's guidelines for SASE.
Nonfiction: Book excerpts, essays, exposé, general interest, historical/nostalgic, how-to (bike maintenance, bike technique), humor, interview/profile, opinion, personal experience, photo feature, technical, travel (places to ride). Anything with mountain biking. Buys 24 mss/year. Query. Pays $25-100.
Reprints: Send typed ms with rights for sale noted and information about when and where the material previously appeared. Pays 75% of amount paid for original material.
Photos: Send art or photos with or without submission. Reviews contact sheets and/or prints. Offers additional payment for photos accepted with ms. $200 for color cover. $25 inside (b&w preferred, color OK). Captions preferred. Buys one-time rights. Always looking for good photography and art regardless of subject.
Columns/Departments: Place to Ride (must have map!), 500-2,000 words; Trials In (coverage of the sport), 50-500 words; Race Reports (coverage of race events), 50-250 words. Buys 14 mss/year. Query. Pays $10-50.
Fiction: Adventure, fantasy, historical, humorous, mainstream, slice-of-life vignettes. Buys 1-10 mss/year. Query. Pays $25-100.
Poetry: Avant-garde, free verse, light verse, traditional. Pays $20-100.
Fillers: Anecdotes, facts, gags, newsbreaks, short humor. Buys 20/year. Pays $0-50.

VELONEWS, The Journal of Competitive Cycling, 1830 55th St., Boulder CO 80301-2700. (303)440-0601. Fax: (303)444-6788. Website: http://www.VeloNews.com/VeloNews. Senior Editor: John Rezell. 60% freelance written. Monthly tabloid September-February, biweekly March-August covering bicycle racing. Estab. 1972. Circ. 48,000. Pays on publication. Publishes ms an average of 1 month after acceptance. Byline given. Buys one-time rights. Accepts simultaneous submissions. Reports in 3 weeks. Sample copy for 9 × 12 SAE with 7 first-class stamps.
Nonfiction: Freelance opportunities include race coverage, reviews (book and videos), health-and-fitness departments. Buys 100 mss/year. Query. Length: 300-1,200 words. Pays 10¢/word minimum.
Photos: State availability of photos. Pays $16.50-50 for b&w prints. Pays $150 for color used on cover. Captions and identification of subjects required. Buys one-time rights.

Boating

CURRENTS, Voice of the National Organization for Rivers, 212 W. Cheyenne Mountain Blvd., Colorado Springs CO 80906. (719)579-8759. Fax: (719)576-6238. Editors: Greg Moore, Eric Leaper. 25% freelance written. Quarterly magazine covering river running (kayaking, rafting, river canoeing). Estab. 1979. Circ. 5,000. Pays on publication. Publishes ms an average of 6 months after acceptance. Byline given. Offers 25% kill fee. Buys first North American serial, first and one-time rights. Submit seasonal/holiday material 4 months in advance. Accepts simultaneous submissions. Reports in 2 weeks on queries; 1 month on mss. Sample copy for $1 and 9 × 12 SAE with 3 first-class stamps. Writer's guidelines for #10 SASE.
Nonfiction: How-to (run rivers and fix equipment), in-depth reporting on river conservation and access issues and problems, humor (related to rivers), interview/profile (any interesting river runner), opinion, personal experience, technical, travel (rivers in other countries). "We tell river runners about river conservation, river access, river equipment, how to do it, when, where, etc." No trip accounts without originality; no stories about "my first river trip." Buys 20 mss/year. Query with or without clips. Length: 500-2,500 words. Pays $35-150.
Reprints: Accepts previously published submissions, if so noted.
Photos: State availability of photos. Pays $35-50. Reviews b&w or color prints or slides; b&w preferred. Captions and identification of subjects (if racing) required. Buys one-time rights. Captions must include names of the river and rapid.
Columns/Departments: Book and film reviews (river-related). Buys 5 mss/year. Query with or without clips, or send complete ms. Length: 100-500 words. Pays $25.
Fiction: Adventure (river). Buys 2 mss/year. Query. Length: 1,000-2,500 words. Pays $35-75. "Must be well-written, on well-known river and beyond the realm of possibility."
Fillers: Clippings, jokes, gags, anecdotes, short humor, newsbreaks. Buys 5/year. Length: 25-100 words. Pays $5-10.

Tips: "We need more material on river news—proposed dams, wild and scenic river studies, accidents, etc. If you can provide brief (300-500 words) on these subjects, you will have a good chance of being published. Material must be on rivers. Go to a famous river and investigate it; find out something we don't know— especially about rivers that are *not* in Colorado or adjacent states—we already know about those."

‡48° NORTH, Boundless Enterprises, 6327 Seaview Ave. NW, Seattle WA 98107. Fax: (206)789-6392. Editor: Richard Hazelton. Contact: C. Streatch, R. Hazelton, publishers. Monthly magazine covering sailing. "Must be sailing (as in boats with sails). No faking it. Our readers are pros. Would like fiction or humor with a hook." Estab. 1981. Circ. 27,000. Pays on publication. Publishes ms an average of 5 months after acceptance. Byline given. Not copyrighted. Buys one-time rights. Editorial lead time 1 month minimum.
Nonfiction: Exposé, general interest, how-to, humor, personal experience, photo feature, technical, travel. All must deal with sailing. Buys 50 mss/year. Send complete ms. Length: 2-3 pages. Payment negotiable.
Photos: Send photos with submission. Negotiates payment individually. Identification of subjects required. Buys one-time rights.
Columns/Departments: Pays $75-150.
Fiction: Adventure, erotica (mild), fantasy, historical, horror, humorous, mystery, science fiction, slice-of-life vignettes, suspense. Buys 25-35 mss/year. Send complete ms. Length: 2-3 pages. Payment negotiable.
Tips: Send SASE with manuscripts.

HEARTLAND BOATING, Inland Publications, Inc., P.O. Box 1067, Martin TN 38237-1067. (901)587-6791. Fax: (901)587-6893. Website: http://www.gsn.com/heartland_boating.htm. Editor: Molly Lightfoot Blom. Estab. 1988. 50% freelance written. Magazine published 7 times/year during boating season "devoted to both power and sail boating enthusiasts throughout middle America; houseboats are included. The focus is on the freshwater inland rivers and lakes of the Heartland; primarily the Tennessee, Cumberland, Ohio and Mississippi rivers and the Tennessee-Tombigbee Waterway. No Great Lakes or salt water material will be considered unless it applies to our area." Circ. 20,000. Pays on publication. Publishes ms an average of 3 months after acceptance. Byline given. Buys first North American serial and sometimes second serial (reprint) rights. Submit seasonal/holiday material 6 months in advance. Accepts simultaneous submissions. Reports in 4 months. Sample copy for $5. Free writer's guidelines.
Nonfiction: General interest, historical/nostalgic, how-to, humor, interview/profile, new product, personal experience, photo feature, technical, travel. Special issue: Houseboats (May). Buys 20-40 mss/year. Prefers queries to unsolicited mss with or without published clips. Length: 800-2,000 words. Negotiates payment.
Reprints: Send tearsheet or photocopy of article and information about where and when it previously appeared. Pays 50% of amount paid for an original article.
Photos: Send photos with query. Reviews contact sheets, transparencies. Buys one-time rights.
Columns/Departments: Buys 50 mss/year. Query. Negotiates payment.

HOT BOAT, LFP Publishing, 8484 Wilshire Blvd., Suite 900, Beverly Hills CA 90211. (213)651-5400. Fax: (310)274-7985. E-mail: hbmail@aol.com. Contact: Kevin Spaise, executive editor. Senior Editor: Brett Bayne. 50% freelance written. Monthly magazine on performance boating (16-35 feet), water skiing and water sports in general. "We're looking for concise, technically oriented 'how-to' articles on performance modifications; personality features on interesting boating-oriented personalities, and occasional event coverage." Circ. 90,000. Pays upon publication. Publishes ms an average of 2 months after acceptance. Byline given. Offers 40% kill fee. Buys all rights; also reprint rights occasionally. Submit seasonal/holiday material 3 months in advance. Reports in 3 weeks on queries; 1 month on mss. Sample copy for $3 and 9 × 12 SAE with $1.35 postage.
Nonfiction: How-to (increase horsepower, perform simple boat related maintenance), humor, interview/profile (racers and manufacturers), new product, personal experience, photo feature, technical. "Absolutely no sailing—we deal strictly in powerboating." Buys 30 mss/year. Query with published clips. Length: 500-2,000 words. Pays $75-450. Sometimes pays expenses of writers on assignment.
Photos: Send photos with submission. Reviews transparencies. Captions, model releases, identification of subjects required. Buys all rights.
Tips: "We're always open to new writers. If you query with published clips and we like your writing, we can keep you on file even if we reject the particular query. It may be more important to simply establish contact. Once we work together there will be much more work to follow."

LAKELAND BOATING, The Magazine for Great Lakes Boaters, O'Meara-Brown Publications, 1560 Sherman Ave., Suite 1220, Evanston IL 60201-4802. (847)869-5400. Fax: (847)869-5989. E-mail: lbonline@aol.com. Contact: Randy Hess, editor. Associate Editor: Chad Schegel. 50% freelance written. Monthly magazine covering Great Lakes boating. Estab. 1946. Circ. 60,000. Pays on publication. Byline given. Buys first North American serial rights. Reports in 4 months. Sample copy for $5.50 and 9 × 12 SAE with 6 first-class stamps. Writer's guidelines for #10 SASE.
Nonfiction: Book excerpts, historical/nostalgic, how-to, interview/profile, personal experience, photo feature, technical, travel. No inspirational, religious, expose or poetry. Must relate to boating in Great Lakes. Buys 20-30 mss/year. Query. Length: 800-3,500 words. Pays $100-600 for assigned articles.

Photos: State availability of photos. Reviews transparencies; prefers 35mm. Captions required. Buys one-time rights.
Columns/Departments: Bosun's Locker (technical or how-to pieces on boating), 100-1,000 words. Buys 40 mss/year. Query. Pays $30-100.

NOR'WESTING, Nor'westing Publications, Inc., 6044 Seaview Ave. NW, Seattle WA 98107. (206)783-8939. Fax: (206)783-9011. Editor: Gloria Kruzner. 75% freelance written. Monthly magazine covering Pacific Northwest boating, cruising destinations. "We want to pack our pages with cruising articles, special Northwest destinations, local boating personalities, practical boat maintenance tips." Estab. 1965. Circ. 9,000. Pays 1 month after publication. Publishes timely ms an average of 2 months after acceptance. Byline given. Buys first North American serial rights. Editorial lead time 3 months. Submit seasonal material 3 months in advance. Accepts simultaneous submissions; note where else it's being submitted. Reports in 2 months. Sample copy and writer's guidelines for large SASE.
Nonfiction: How-to (boat outfitting, electronics, fish, galley), interview/profile (boater personalities), new product, personal experience (cruising), photo feature, technical, travel (local destinations). Special issues: Seattle boat shows (January/February); Spring outfitting (March/April); Cruising destinations (June/August); Winter boating (November/December). Buys 35-40 mss/year. Send complete ms. Length: 900-2,000 words. Pays $100-150.
Photos: Send photos with submission. Reviews transparencies, 3×5 prints. Negotiates payment individually. Identification of subjects required. Normally buys one-time rights.
Columns/Departments: Trailerboating (small craft boating—tech/destination), 900 words; Galley Ideas (cooking afloat—recipes/ideas), 900 words; Hardwired (Boating Electronics), 1,000 words; Cruising Fisherman (Fishing tips, destinations), 1,000 words. Buys 36-40 mss/year. Query with published clips. Pays $50-100.
Tips: "Include specific information on destination—how many moorage buoys, cost for showers, best time to visit. Any hazards to watch for while approaching? Why bother going if excitement for area/boating doesn't shine through in piece?"

POWER BOATING CANADA, 2585 Skymark Ave., Unit 306, Mississauga, Ontario L4W 4L5 Canada. (905)624-8218. Fax: (905)624-6764. Editor: Pam Cottrell. 40% freelance written. Bimonthly magazine covering power boating. Estab. 1984. Circ. 50,000. Pays on publication. Publishes ms an average of 3 months after acceptance. Byline given. Not copyrighted. Buys first North American serial rights in English and French or second serial (reprint) rights. Accepts simultaneous submissions.
Nonfiction: "Any articles related to the sport of power boating, especially boat tests." Travel (boating destinations). No personal anecdotes. Buys 20 mss/year. Query. Length: 1,000-2,500 words. Pays $150-300.
Reprints: Send photocopy of article or typed ms with rights for sale noted and information about when and where the article previously appeared.
Photos: State availability of photos with submission. Send photos with submission. Reviews contact sheets, negatives, transparencies, prints. Offers no additional payment for photos accepted with ms. Identification of subjects required. Buys one-time rights.
Fiction: Publishes novel excerpts.

SAIL, 84 State St., Boston MA 02109-2262. (617)720-8600. Fax: (617)723-0911. Editor: Patience Wales. Managing Editor: Amy Ullrich. 50% freelance written. Works with a small number of new/unpublished writers each year. Monthly magazine for audience that is "strictly sailors, average age 42, above average education." Estab. 1970. **Pays on acceptance.** Publishes ms an average of 10 months after acceptance. Buys first North American rights. Submit seasonal or special material at least 6 months in advance. Reports in 10 weeks. Writer's guidelines for 1 first-class stamp.
Nonfiction: Amy Ullrich, managing editor. Wants "articles on sailing: technical, techniques and feature stories." Interested in how-to, personal experience, distance cruising, destinations, technical aspects of boat construction, systems. "Generally emphasize the excitement of sail and the human, personal aspect. No logs." Special issues: "Cruising, chartering, fitting-out, special race (e.g., America's Cup), boat show." Buys 100 mss/year (freelance and commissioned). Length: 1,000-2,800 words. Pays $200-800. Sometimes pays the expenses of writers on assignment.
Photos: Offers additional payment for photos. Uses 50-100 ASA transparencies. Pays $600 if photo is used on the cover.
Tips: "Request an articles specification sheet."

SAILING MAGAZINE, 125 E. Main St., Port Washington WI 53074-0249. (414)284-3494. Fax: (414)284-7764. E-mail: 75553.3666@compuserv.com. Website: http://www.sailnet.com. Contact: Micca Leffingwell Hutchins, editor. Publisher: William F. Schanen, III. Monthly magazine. Estab. 1966. Circ. 52,000. Pays on publication. Reports in 2 months.
Nonfiction: "Experiences of sailing—cruising, racing or learning." Must be written to AP Stylebook. Buys 8 mss/year. Length: 750-1,500 words. Must be accompanied by photos, and maps if applicable. Payment dependent length of article and use in the magazine.

Photos: Color photos (transparencies) purchased with or without accompanying text. Captions are required.
Tips: Prefers text in Word on disk for Mac or to e-mail address.

‡**SAILING WORLD**, N.Y. Times Magazine Group, 5 John Clarke Rd., Box 3400, Newport RI 02840-0992. Fax: (401)848-5048. E-mail: 70672.2725@compuserve.com. Editor: John Burnham. Contact: Kristan McClintock, managing editor. 40% freelance written. Monthly magazine. Estab. 1962. Circ. 68,089. Pays on publication. Publishes ms an average of 4 months after acceptance. Buys first North American and world serial rights. Byline given. Reports in 3 months. Sample copy for $5.
Nonfiction: How-to for racing and performance-oriented sailors, photo feature, profile, regatta reports and charter. No travelogs. Buys 5-10 unsolicited mss/year. Query. Length: 500-1,500 words. Pays $150-200/page text.
Tips: "Send query with outline and include your experience. The writer may have a better chance of breaking in with short articles and fillers such as regatta news reports from his or her own area."

SEA KAYAKER, Sea Kayaker, Inc., P.O. Box 17170, Seattle WA 98107-0870. (206)789-1326. Fax: (206)781-1141. Managing Editor: Christopher Cunningham. Contact: Karen Reed, editor. 80% freelance written. Works frequently with new/unpublished writers each year. Bimonthly magazine on the sport of sea kayaking. Estab. 1984. Circ. 20,000. Pays on publication. Publishes ms an average of 6 months after acceptance. Byline given. Offers 10% kill fee. Buys first North American serial or second serial (reprint) rights. Submit seasonal material 6 months in advance. Reports in 2 months. Sample copy for $5.30. Writer's guidelines for SASE.
Nonfiction: Essays, historical, how-to (on making equipment), humor, profile, opinion, personal experience, technical, travel. Buys 40 mss/year. Query with or without published clips, or send complete ms. Length: 750-4,000 words. Pays about 12¢/word. Sometimes pays the expenses of writers on assignment.
Photos: Send photos with submission. Reviews contact sheets. Offers $25-100/photo. Captions requested. Buys one-time rights.
Columns/Departments: History, Safety, Environment, Journey. Length: 750-4,000 words. Pays 10¢/word, minimum.
Fiction: Kayak related adventure, fantasy, historical, humorous, mainstream, slice-of-life vignettes. Send complete ms. Length: 750-4,000 words. Pays about 12¢/word.
Tips: "We consider unsolicited manuscripts that include a SASE, but we give greater priority to brief descriptions (several paragraphs) of proposed articles accompanied by at least two samples—published or unpublished—of your writing. Enclose a statement as to why you're qualified to write the piece and indicate whether photographs or illustrations are available to accompany the piece."

TRAILER BOATS MAGAZINE, Poole Publications, Inc., 20700 Belshaw Ave., Carson CA 90746-3510. (310)537-6322. Fax: (310)537-8735. Editor: Randy Scott. 30-40% freelance written. Works with a small number of new/unpublished writers each year. Monthly magazine (November/December issue combined) covering legally trailerable boats and related powerboating activities. Circ. 85,000. **Pays on acceptance.** Publishes ms 6 months after acceptance. Byline given. Buys all rights. Submit seasonal/holiday material 5 months in advance. Reports in 1 month. Sample copy $1.25; writer's guidelines for #10 SASE.
Nonfiction: General interest (trailer boating activities); historical (places, events, boats); how-to (repair boats, installation, etc.); humor (almost any boating-related subject); nostalgia (same as historical); personal experience; photo feature; profile; technical; and travel (boating travel on water or highways). No "How I Spent My Summer Vacation" stories, or stories not even remotely connected to trailerable boats and related activities. Buys 18-30 unsolicited mss/year. Query or send complete ms. Length: 500-2,000 words. Pays expenses of writers on assignment.
Photos: Send photos with ms. Pays $10-75 for 8 × 10 b&w prints; $25-350 for color transparencies. Captions required.
Columns/Departments: Boaters Bookshelf (boating book reviews); Over the Transom (funny or strange boating photos). Buys 2/issue. Query. Length: 100-500 words. Watersports (boat-related), 750-1,000 words. Pays $350. Open to suggestions for new columns/departments.
Tips: "Query should contain short general outline of the intended material; what kind of photos; how the photos illustrate the piece. Write with authority, covering the subject like an expert. Frequent mistakes are not knowing the subject matter or the audience. Use basic information rather than prose, particularly in travel stories. The writer may have a better chance of breaking in at our publication with short articles and fillers if they are typically hard to find articles. We do most major features inhouse."

WATERFRONT NEWS, SOUTHERN CALIFORNIA, Your Local Boating News, Duncan McIntosh Co., Inc., 17782 Cowan, 2nd Floor, Suite C, Irvine CA 92714. (714)660-6150. Fax: (714)660-6172. Associate Editor: Erin McNiff. 10% freelance written. Monthly news magazine covering recreational boating, sailing, sportfishing and lifestyles in Southern California. Articles are aimed at owners of pleasureboats with an emphasis on where to go, what to do with their vessel, locally. Est. 1993. Circ. 40,000. Pays on publication. Publishes ms an average of 2 months after submission. Byline given. Buys first North American rights. Reports in 1 month on queries. Sample copy and writer's guidelines for SASE.

Nonfiction: Sportfishing how-to, cruising destinations, spot news of interest to boaters. Length: 150-1,000 words. Query. Pays $25-150. No fiction. Some shipping expenses covered if requested in advance, in writing.
Photos: State availability of photos with query. Reviews any size prints and transparencies, color or b&w. Offers $15-50/photo. Identification of subjects required. Buys one-time rights.
Columns/Departments: News (including changes, developments in state and federal law that affect local boaters, personality profile on a local boater who cruises somewhere outside Southern California, or a how-to piece on a Southern California port of call, or an interview/profile about a unique cruiser who is visiting Southern California during a long-range voyage aboard his own boat); Racing (covers major regattas in Southern California, both power and sail, and local racers who travel to compete at the highest levels around the world); Sportfishing (short how-to articles for catching fish in Southern California with your own boat); Business (new developments in boating accessories and services of interest to Southern California boat owners.) Query with published clips.

WATERWAY GUIDE, Argus Inc., a division of Intertec Publishing Corp., 6151 Powers Ferry Rd. NW, Atlanta GA 30339-2941. (404)618-0313. Fax: (404)618-0349. Associate Publisher: Judith Powers. 90% freelance written. Quarterly magazine on intracoastal waterway travel for recreational boats. "Writer must be knowledgeable about navigation and the areas covered by the guide." Estab. 1947. Circ. 45,000. Pays on publication. Publishes ms an average of 3 months after acceptance. Byline given sometimes. Kill fee varies. Buys all rights. Reports in 3 months on queries; 4 months on mss. Sample copy for $33.95 with $3 postage.
Nonfiction: Historical/nostalgic, how-to, photo feature, technical, travel. "No personal boating experiences." Buys 25 mss/year. Query with or without published clips, or send complete ms. Length: 200 words minimum. Pays $50-3,000 for assigned articles. Pays in contributor copies or other premiums for helpful tips and useful information.
Photos: Send photos with submission. Reviews 3×5 prints. Offers $25/b&w photo, $600/color photos used on the cover. Identification of subjects required. Buys one-time rights.
Fillers: Facts. Buys 6/year. Length: 250-1,000 words. Pays $50-150.
Tips: "Must have on-the-water experience and be able to provide new and accurate information on geographic areas covered by *Waterway Guide*."

WOODENBOAT MAGAZINE, The Magazine for Wooden Boat Owners, Builders, and Designers, WoodenBoat Publications, Inc., P.O. Box 78, Brooklin ME 04616. (207)359-4651. Fax: (207)359-8920. Editor-in-Chief: Jonathan A. Wilson. Contact: Matthew P. Murphy, editor. Senior Editor: Mike O'Brien. Managing Editor: Jenny Bennett. 50% freelance written. Works with a small number of new/unpublished writers each year. Bimonthly magazine for wooden boat owners, builders and designers. "We are devoted exclusively to the design, building, care, preservation, and use of wooden boats, both commercial and pleasure, old and new, sail and power. We work to convey quality, integrity and involvement in the creation and care of these craft, to entertain, inform, inspire, and to provide our varied readers with access to individuals who are deeply experienced in the world of wooden boats." Estab. 1974. Circ. 106,000. Pays on publication. Publishes ms an average of 1 year after acceptance. Byline given. Offers variable kill fee. Buys first North American serial rights. Accepts simultaneous submissions. Reports in 3 weeks on queries; 2 months on mss. Sample copy for $4.50. Writer's guidelines for SASE.
Nonfiction: Technical (repair, restoration, maintenance, use, design and building wooden boats). No poetry, fiction. Buys 50 mss/year. Query with published clips. Length: 1,500-5,000 words. Pays $150-200/1,000 words. Sometimes pays expenses of writers on assignment.
Reprints: Send tearsheet or photocopy of article or typed ms with rights for sale noted with information about when and where the article previously appeared.
Photos: Send photos with query. Negatives must be available. Pays $15-75 for b&w; $25-350 for color. Identification of subjects required. Buys one-time rights.
Columns/Departments: On the Waterfront pays for information on wooden boat-related events, projects, boatshop activities, etc. Buys 25/year. "We use the same columnists for each issue." Send complete information. Length: 250-1,000 words. Pays $5-50 for information.
Tips: "We appreciate a detailed, articulate query letter, accompanied by photos, that will give us a clear idea of what the author is proposing. We appreciate samples of previously published work. It is important for a prospective author to become familiar with our magazine first. It is extremely rare for us to make an assignment with a writer with whom we have not worked before. Most work is submitted on speculation. The most common failure is not exploring the subject material in enough depth."

YACHTING, Times Mirror Magazines Inc., 2 Park Ave., 5th Floor, New York NY 10016-5695. (212)779-5300. Fax: (212)725-1035. Associate Publisher: Linda Lindquist. Editor-in-Chief: Charles Barthold. 50% freelance written. "The magazine is written and edited for experienced, knowledgeable yachtsmen." Estab. 1907. Circ. 130,000. Pays on publication. Byline given. Buys first rights. Submit seasonal/holiday material 6 months in advance. Reports in 1 month.
Nonfiction: Book excerpts, personal experience, photo feature, travel. No cartoons, fiction, poetry. Query with published clips. Length: 250-2,000 words. Pays $250-1,000 for assigned articles. Pays expenses of writers on assignment.

• Ranked as one of the best markets for freelance writers in *Writer's Yearbook*'s annual "Top 100 Markets," January 1996.

Photos: Send photos with submission. Reviews 35mm transparencies. Offers some additional payment for photos accepted with ms. Captions, model releases and identification of subjects required.

Columns/Departments: Cruising Yachtsman (stories on cruising; contact Cynthia Taylor, senior editor); Racing Yachtsman (stories about sail or power racing; contact Lisa Ken Wooten); Yacht Yard (how-to and technical pieces on yachts and their systems; contact Dennis Caprio, Senior editor). Buys 30 mss/year. Send complete ms. Length: 750 words maximum. Pays $250-500.

Tips: "We require considerable expertise in our writing because our audience is experienced and knowledgeable. Vivid descriptions of quaint anchorages and quainter natives are fine, but our readers want to know how the yachtsmen got there, too. They also want to know how their boats work."

Bowling

BOWLING, Dept. WM, 5301 S. 76th St., Greendale WI 53129. (414)421-6400, ext. 230. Editor: Bill Vint. 15% freelance written. Bimonthly, official publication of the American Bowling Congress. Estab. 1934. Circ. 135,000. **Pays on acceptance.** Publishes ms an average of 2 months after acceptance. Byline given. Rights purchased vary with author and material; usually buys all rights. Reports in 1 month. Sample copy for $2.50.

Nonfiction: "This is a specialized field and the average writer attempting the subject of bowling should be well-informed. However, anyone is free to submit material for approval." Wants articles about unusual ABC sanctioned leagues and tournaments, personalities, etc., featuring male bowlers. Nostalgia articles also considered. No first-person articles or material on history of bowling. Length: 500-1,200 words. Pays $100-300. No poems, songs or fiction.

Photos: Pays $10-15/photo.

Tips: "Submit feature material on bowlers, generally amateurs competing in local leagues, or special events involving the game of bowling. Should have connection with ABC membership. Queries should be as detailed as possible so that we may get a clear idea of what the proposed story would be all about. It saves us time and the writer time. Samples of previously published material in the bowling or general sports field would help. Once we find a talented writer in a given area, we're likely to go back to him in the future. We're looking for good writers who can handle assignments professionally and promptly." No articles on professionals.

Gambling

‡BLACKJACK FORUM, RGE Publishing, 414 Santa Clara Ave., Oakland CA 94610. (510)465-6452. Fax: (510)465-4330. Editor: Arnold Synder. 40% freelance written. Quarterly magazine covering casino blackjack. "For sophisticated and knowledgeable casino gamblers interested in legal issues, mathematical analyses, computer simulations, commonplace techniques. This is *not* a get-rich-quick type mag." Estab. 1981. Circ. 2,500. Pays on publication. Publishes ms an average of 6 months after acceptance. Byline given. Buys first and second serial (reprint) rights. Editorial lead time 6 months. Submit seasonal material 6 months in advance. Reports in 4 months on queries. Sample copy for $12.50.

Nonfiction: Exposé, how-to, personal experience, technical, travel. Buys 10-12 mss/year. Query or send complete ms. Length: 200-3,000 words. Pays $35/page. Sometimes pays expenses of writers on assignment.

Photos: State availability of or send photos with submission. Reviews contact sheets, prints. Negotiates payment individually. Buys one-time rights.

Columns/Departments: Around The States (reports on blackjack conditions in US casinos); Around The World (ditto for foreign casinos); both 200-1,500 words. Buys 25 mss/year. Query or send complete ms. Pays in contributor's copies—$35.

Tips: "Be very knowledgeable about casino blackjack, especially familiar with all noted authors—Thorp, Revere, Uston, Wong, Griffin, Carlson, etc."

CASINO REVIEW, Hyde Park Media, 635 Chicago Ave., #250, Evanston IL 60202. Contact: Articles Editor. 80% freelance written. Bimonthly covering casino and other legal gambling. Estab. 1994. Circ. 50,000. Pays on publication. Publishes ms an average of 4 months after acceptance. Byline given. Buys first rights, one-time rights, second serial (reprint) rights, simultaneous rights and all rights. Editorial lead time 4 months. Submit seasonal material 4 months in advance. Accepts simultaneous submissions. Reports in 1 month on queries; 2 months on mss. Sample copy for $4 and 10×13 SAE.

Nonfiction: Book excerpts, historical/nostalgic, how-to, humor, inspirational, interview/profile, opinion, personal experience, photo feature, travel (all with a gambling hook). Buys 100-150 mss/year. Query or send complete ms. Length: 800-2,000 words. Pays $50-250 for assigned articles; $25-100 for unsolicited articles.

Reprints: Accepts previously published submissions.

Photos: State availability of photos with submission. Reviews 5×7 prints. Negotiates payment individually. Captions, model releases, identification of subjects required. Buys all rights.

Tips: "Detailed queries and having quality art to go along with any proposed articles. We're always looking for highly stylized, quality art, i.e., photos and line art."

‡LOTTOWORLD MAGAZINE, Dynamic World Distributors, Inc., Suite 200, 2150 Goodlette Rd., Naples FL 33940. (813)643-1677. Editor-in-Chief: Rich Holman. Managing Editor: Barry Miller. 60% freelance written. Monthly magazine covering lottery-related news. "LottoWorld Magazine is a national lottery news magazine targeted to the 100 million U.S. lottery players. Each issue is devoted to systems, tips, strategies, techniques and research 40%; human interest stories 30%; winning pick forecasting 20%; software, astrology, miscellaneous 10%." Estab. 1993. Pays 30 days after publication. Byline given. Buys exclusive serial rights. Editorial lead time 2 months. Sample copy or writers guidelines for 8 × 11 SAE with 87¢ postage.
Nonfiction: General interest, how-to, humor, interview/profile, photo feature. Buys 36-72 mss/year. Query. Length: 400-1,200 words. Pay negotiated. Sometimes pays expenses of writers on assignment.
Photos: Freelancers should send photos with submission. Reviews prints. Additional payment for photos accepted with ms.

WIN, Gambling Times Incorporated, 120 S. San Fernando Blvd., Suite 439, Burbank CA 91502. Fax: (818)845-0325 (9-5 p.m. weekdays, Pacific Time). E-mail: ag497@1afn.org. Website: http://gamblingtimes.com. No voice calls. Editor: Joey Sinatra. Monthly magazine for gambling, entertainment, computers. Estab. 1979. Circ. 56,000. Pays on publication. Publishes ms an average of 3 months after acceptance. Byline given. Buys first North American serial rights. Editorial lead time 3 months. Submit seasonal material 3 months in advance. Accepts simultaneous submissions. Reports in 6 weeks on queries, 2 months on mss. Writer's guidelines with SASE.
Nonfiction: Book excerpts, essays, historical/nostalgic, how-to (casino games), interview/profile, new product, photo feature, technical. Buys 10 mss/year. Send complete ms. Length: 1,600-2,000 words. Pays $75 minimum for assigned articles. Sometimes "pays" contributors with travel, hotel rooms.
Photos: Send photos with submission. Reviews 4 × 5 transparencies and prints. Negotiates payment individually. Captions, model releases and identification of subjects required. Buys all rights.
Fiction: Gambling subplots. No previously published fiction. Buys 12 mss/year. Send complete ms. Length: 1,200-2,500 words. Pay negotiable.
Fillers: Facts, newsbreaks. Buys 30/year. Length: 250-600 words. Pays $25 minimum.

General Interest

EXPLORE, Canada's Outdoor Adventure Magazine, Thompson & Gordon Publishing Co. Ltd., 301-14 St. NW, Suite 420, Calgary, Alberta T2N 2A1 Canada. (403)270-8890. Editor: Marion Harrison. 30% freelance written. Bimonthly magazine covering outdoor recreation "for those who seek some form of adventure in their travels. The magazine covers popular activities such as backpacking, bicycling, canoeing, and backcountry skiing featuring Canadian and international destinations. Other topics covered include ecotourism, the environment, outdoor photography, sports medicine, equipment, and new products for the outdoor recreationist." Estab. 1981. Circ. 35,000. Pays on publication. Byline given. Offers 50% kill fee on assigned stories. Buys first North American serial rights. Editorial lead time 1 year. Submit seasonal material 6 months in advance. Accepts simultaneous submissions. Reports in 2 months. Sample copy for $5. Writer's guidelines for #10 SASE—IRCs required from outside Canada.
Nonfiction: Personal experience, travel. Query with published clips. Length: 1,500-2,500 words. Pays $250-500 (Canadian).
Photos: Send photos with submission. Reviews contact sheets, transparencies and prints. Offers no additional payment for photos accepted with ms. Captions required. Buys one-time rights.
Columns/Departments: Gearing Up (clothing, equipment for outdoor recreation). 1,800; Photography (outdoor photography tips), 1,200. Buys 5 mss/year. Query. Pays $275.
Tips: "Remember *Explore* is a *Canadian* magazine with 95% Canadian readership that wants to read about Canada! We buy three articles *per year* which feature U.S. destinations. Submit manuscript and photos for fastest response. Feature articles are required more often than departments. Features are first-person narratives that are exciting and interesting. We are using fewer travel pieces, more researched issue-oriented articles. Quality photos are a must."

---

‡ THE DOUBLE DAGGER before a listing indicates that the listing is new in this edition. New markets are often more receptive to freelance submissions.

‡**THE FRONT ROW**, The Publisher's Group, P.O. Box 510366, Salt Lake City UT 84151-0366. Fax: (801)322-1098. Editor: Vicki Andersen. Contact: Anne E. Zombro, publisher. 60% freelance written. Quarterly magazine covering sports. "*The Front Row* covers the biggest names, the best games and everything in between. Emphasis is on professional sports. Also includes trivia, nostalgia, new equipment and outdoor sports." Estab. 1996. Circ. 20,000. Pays on publication. Publishes ms an average of 4 months after acceptance. Byline given. Buys first North American serial and second serial (reprint) rights. Editorial lead time 2 months. Submit seasonal material 4 months in advance. Accepts simultaneous submissions. Reports in 1 month on queries; 2 months on mss. Sample copy for $2 and 9 × 12 SAE. Writer's guidelines for #10 SASE.
Nonfiction: Book excerpts, humor, inspirational, interview/profile (of pro athletes). Buys 6 mss/year. Query with published clips. Length: 1,000-1,300 words. Pays $125-800.
Reprints: Accepts previously published submissions.
Photos: Send photos with submission. Reviews 4 × 5 transparencies, any size prints. Negotiates payment individually. Captions, model releases, identification of subjects required. Buys one-time or all rights.
Columns/Departments: Famous Moments (nostalgia), Rules (updates), Personal Experiences (outdoor adventures) all 500 words. Buys 6-8 mss/year. Query with published clips. Pays $50-125.

‡**INSIDE SPORTS**, Century Publishing Co., 990 Grove St., Evanston IL 60201. (847)491-6440. Editor: Ken Leiker. 90% freelance written. Monthly magazine. Circ. 675,000. Pays on publication. Publishes ms an average of 4 months after acceptance. Offers 100% kill fee. Rights are negotiated individually. Reports on queries and mss in 6 weeks.
Nonfiction: Query with or without published clips, or send complete ms. Length of article and payment vary with each article and writer. "Please include a SASE with query/article."

NEW YORK OUTDOORS, 51 Atlantic Ave., Floral Park NY 11001. Fax: (516)437-6841. Fax: (516)487-6841. E-mail: nyomag@aol.com. Editor: John Tsaousis. 100% freelance written. Estab. 1992. Buys first North American serial rights. Publishes ms an average of 6 months after acceptance. Reports in 1 month on queries. Writer's guidelines for #10 SASE.
Nonfiction: "*New York Outdoors* is dedicated to providing information to its readers about all outdoor participatory activities in New York and its surrounding states. Paddlesports, camping, hiking, cycling, 'adventure' sports, etc." Query. Length: 1,500-2,000 words. A good selection of transparencies must accompany mss. Pays $250. Lead time 4 months. "Aside from accurate and interesting writing, provide source material for our readers who may wish to try the activity. We also use shorter pieces (to 500 words) on the same type of topics, but focusing on a single event, person, place or occurrence. Query. Pays up to $100."
Reprints: Send photocopy of article and information about where and when article previously appeared. Pays 35% of amount paid for an original article.
Tips: Would like to see more queries on camping, hiking, in line, climbing, mountain biking topic areas with destination focus.

‡**CHRISTIAN OKOYE'S SPORTS IMAGE**, Sports Image Publishing Inc., 940 E. Alosta Ave., Azusa CA 91702. E-mail: images05@ibm.net. Editor: Phil Barber. Managing Editor: Chip Boughner. Contact: Eric Smith, administrative assistant. 100% freelance written. Bimonthly magazine covering sports. "*Sports Image* portrays the humanitarian side of the athlete. We feature the athlete on and off the field with exclusive interviews. There is very little concentration on statistics. The focus is on personalities—the good things athletes do (charities, etc.)." Estab. 1995. Circ. 105,000. Pays on publication. Publishes ms an average of 3 months after acceptance. Byline sometimes given. Offers $250 kill fee. Buys first North American serial rights. Editorial lead time 2 months. Submit seasonal material 3 months in advance. Reports in 2 weeks on queries; 2 months on mss. Sample copy for 9 × 12 SAE with 5 first-class stamps. Writer's guidelines free on request.
Nonfiction: General interest, interview/profile, photo feature, technical. Length: 1,500-3,500 words. Pays $500-600 for assigned articles; $400-500 for unsolicited articles. Sometimes pays expenses of writers on assignment.
Photos: Send photos with submission. Reviews transparencies. Negotiates payment individually. Identification of subjects required. Buys one-time rights.
Columns/Departments: Warm-Ups (short human interest stories), 300 words; The Athlete at Work (pro athletes on fitness), 2,000 words; Flash Forward ("where are they now"), 2,000 words. Buys 10 mss/year. Pays $400-600.

‡**OUTDOOR**, All Weather Publishing Co., P.O. Box 305, Stowe VT 05672. (802)253-8282. Fax: (802)253-6236. E-mail: outdoormag@aol.com. Managing Editor: Kim Fredericks. 90% freelance written. Quarterly magazine covering outdoor sports—hiking, mountain biking, in-line skating, etc. "A magazine for outdoor enthusiasts who participate in a variety of outdoor sports." Estab. 1990. Circ. 410,000. Pays on publication. Publishes ms 3 months after acceptance. Byline given. Buys first North American serial rights. Editorial lead time 3 months. Submit seasonal material 3 months in advance. Reports in 3 weeks on queries; 3 months on mss. Sample copy for 8½ × 11 SAE with 4 first-class stamps. Writer's guidelines for #10 SASE.

Nonfiction: Exposé, general interest, historical/nostalgic, how-to, humor, interview/profile, new product, opinion, personal experience, technical, travel. Buys 20 mss/year. Query with published clips. Length: 500-2,500 words. Pays 15-20¢/word. Sometimes pays expenses of writers on assignment.

Photos: Send photos with submission. Negotiates payment individually. Identification of subjects required. Buys one-time rights.

Columns/Departments: Techniques (how-to improve your in-line and/or mountain bike techniques) 500-1,500 words. Buys 6mss/year. Query with published clips. Pays 15-20¢/word.

Fillers: Facts, newsbreaks, short humor. Length: 500-1,200 words. Pays 15-20¢/word.

Tips: "Be an expert on what you are writing about. We want our articles to capture the 'feel' of the sport they are reading about and to be excited about getting out and participating in the sport. Content should not be too technical or too basic."

‡**OUTDOOR ACTION MAGAZINE,** McMullen-Argus Publishers, 774 S. Placentia Ave., Placentia CA 52670-6846. (714)572-2255. Fax: (714)572-1864. E-mail: odamag@aol.com. Editor: Dan Sanchez. Contact: Marie Loggia, managing editor. 75% freelance written. Monthly magazine covering outdoor-adventure sports. Estab. 1995. Circ. 40,000. Pays on publication. Publishes ms an average of 4 months after acceptance. Byline given. Buys first North American serial and one-time rights. Editorial lead time 4 months. Submit seasonal material 4 months in advance. Accepts simultaneous submissions. Writer's guidelines for SASE.

Nonfiction: How-to, humor, personal experience, photo feature. Query. Pays $250-750 for assigned articles; $350 maximum for unsolicited articles. Sometimes pays expenses of writers on assignment.

Photos: State availability of photos with submission. Reviews contact sheets, transparencies. Negotiates payment individually. Captions, identification of subjects required. Buys one-time rights.

Columns/Departments: Query.

Fillers: Buys 10-15/year. Length: 200-500 words. Pays $350.

Tips: "Best way to break in are '50 tips' articles, trivia articles, locations of where to go mountain biking, rockclimbing, kayaking, hiking in U.S."

ROCKY MOUNTAIN SPORTS MAGAZINE, Sports & Fitness Publishing, 2025 Pearl St., Boulder CO 80302. (303)440-5111. Publisher: Scot Harris. Editor: Don Silver. 50% freelance written. Monthly magazine of sports in the Rocky Mountain States and Canada. "*Rocky* is a magazine for sports-related lifestyles and activities. Our mission is to reflect and inspire the active lifestyle of Rocky Mountain residents." Estab. 1987. Circ. 45,000. Pays on publication. Publishes ms an average of 2 months after acceptance. Byline given. Offers 25% kill fee. Buys second serial (reprint) rights. Editorial lead time 1½ months. Submit seasonal material 2 months in advance. Reports in 3 weeks on queries; 2 months on mss. Sample copy and writer's guidelines for #10 SASE.

• The editor of this publication says he wants to see mountain outdoor sports writing **only**. No ball sports, no hunting, no fishing.

Nonfiction: Book excerpts, essays, exposé, how-to: (no specific sports, trips, adventures), humor, inspirational, interview/profile, new product, opinion, personal experience, photo feature, travel. Special issues: Snowboarding (December); Alpine and Nordic (January and February); Mountain Biking (April). No articles on football, baseball, basketball or other sports covered in-depth by newspapers. Buys 24 mss/year. Query with published clips. Length: 2,500 words maximum. Pays $150 minimum for assigned articles. Sometimes pays expenses of writers on assignment.

Reprints: Send photocopy of article or short story. Pays 20-50% of amount paid for an original article.

Photos: State availability of photos with submission. Reviews transparencies and prints. Offers $25-250/ photo. Captions and identification of subjects required. Buys one-time rights.

Columns/Departments: Scree (short newsy items), 50-800 words; High Altitude (essay on quirky topics related to Rockies). Buys 20 mss/year. Query. Pays $25-200.

Fiction: Adventure, experimental, humorous. "Nothing that isn't sport-related." Buys 5 mss/year. Query. Length: 250-1,500 words. Pays $50-200. Publishes novel excerpts.

Fillers: Anecdotes, facts, gags to be illustrated by cartoonist, newsbreaks, short humor. Buys 20/year. Length: 10-200 words. Pays $25-75.

Tips: "Submit stories for the Scree section first."

SILENT SPORTS, Waupaca Publishing Co., P.O. Box 152, Waupaca WI 54981-9990. (715)258-5546. Fax: (715)258-8162. Editor: Greg Marr. 75% freelance written. Eager to work with new/unpublished writers. Monthly magazine on running, cycling, cross-country skiing, canoeing, in-line skating, camping, backpacking and hiking aimed at people in Wisconsin, Minnesota, northern Illinois and portions of Michigan and Iowa. "Not a coffee table magazine. Our readers are participants from rank amateur weekend athletes to highly competitive racers." Estab. 1984. Circ. 10,000. Pays on publication. Publishes ms an average of 3 months after acceptance. Byline given. Offers 20% kill fee. Buys one-time rights. Submit seasonal/holiday material 4 months in advance. Reports in 3 months. Sample copy and writer's guidelines for 10×13 SAE with 6 first-class stamps.

• The editor needs local angles on in-line skating, recreation bicycling and snowshoeing.

Nonfiction: General interest, how-to, interview/profile, opinion, technical, travel. All stories/articles must focus on the Upper Midwest. First-person articles discouraged. Buys 25 mss/year. Query. Length: 2,500 words maximum. Pays $15-100. Sometimes pays expenses of writers on assignment.

Reprints: Send typed ms with rights for sale noted and information about when and where the article previously appeared. Pay negotiated.

Tips: "Where-to-go and personality profiles are areas most open to freelancers. Writers should keep in mind that this is a regional, Midwest-based publication. We want only stories/articles with a focus on our region."

SPORT, Petersen Publishing Co., 6420 Wilshire Blvd., Los Angeles CA 90048-5515. (213)782-2828. Editor: Cam Benty. 80% freelance written. Monthly magazine "for the active adult sports fan. *Sport* offers profiles of the players and the people behind the scenes in the world of sports." Estab. 1946. Circ. 721,500. **Pays on acceptance.** Publishes ms an average of 3 months after acceptance. Offers 25% kill fee. Buys first North American serial or all rights. Reports in 2 months.

Nonfiction: "Prefers to see articles on professional, big-time sports: basketball, football, baseball, with some boxing. The articles we buy must be contemporary pieces, not a history of sports or a particular sport." Query with published clips. Length: News briefs, 200-300 words; Departments, 1,400 words; Features, 1,500-3,000 words. Averages 50¢/word for articles.

SPORTS ILLUSTRATED, Time Inc. Magazine Co., Time & Life Bldg., Rockefeller Center, New York NY 10020. (212)522-1212. Fax: 9212)522-0536. Editorial Project Director: Larry Keith. Weekly magazine covering sports. "*Sports Illustrated* reports and interprets the world of sport, recreation and active leisure. It previews, analyzes and comments upon major games and events, as well as those noteworthy for character and spirit alone. It features individuals connected to sport and evaluates trends concerning the part sport plays in contemporary life. In addition, the magazine has articles on such subjects as fashion, physical fitness and conservation. Special departments deal with sports equipment, books and statistics." Estab. 1954. Circ. 3,339,000. This magazine did not respond to our request for information. Query before submitting.

‡SPORTS TRAVELER, Sports Traveler, 167 Madison Ave., New York NY 10016. (212)686-6480. Fax: (212)685-6240. Editor: Carol Cooper Garey. 90% freelance written. Quarterly magazine covering adventure travel—sports travel. "Our emphasis is on all types of sports with travel as an important part of the experience. We concentrate mainly on participating in the sport (beginner-experienced) rather than being a spectator. Other important areas of interest are the great outdoors, personal challenges, ecology, animals, sport fashion, reader service, training, gear, nutrition and profiles. We look for first person as well as reported articles about any one of these topics." Estab. 1995. Circ. 250,000. **Pays on acceptance.** Publishes ms an average of 3 months after acceptance. Byline given. Offers 25% kill fee. Buys first North American serial rights. Editorial lead time 3 months. Submit seasonal material 1 year in advance. Accepts simultaneous submissions. Reports in 3 months on queries and mss. Sample copy for $2.95 with SAE and $2.30 postage. Writer's guidelines for #10 SASE.

Nonfiction: Humor, inspirational, interview/profile, new product, personal experience, photo feature, technical, travel. No fiction or poetry. Query with published clips. Length: 400-2,000 words. Pays $100-1,000 for assigned articles; $100-750 for unsolicited articles. Sometimes pays expenses of writers on assignment.

Photos: State availability of photos with submission. Reviews transparencies. Negotiates payment individually. Model releases, identification of subjects required.

Columns/Departments: Sidelines (behind scenes reporting), 750-1,250 words; Rookie (1st time at a new sport), 750-1,250 words; Weekend Warrior (profile of celeb doing sport), 750-1,250 words. Query with published clips. Pays $200-750.

Fillers: Facts, newsbreaks, short humor. Length: 50-400 words. Pays $25-250.

Tips: "Send really focused query letter combining travel and sports, especially to remote or exotic locations."

WINDY CITY SPORTS MAGAZINE, Chicago Sports Resources, 1450 W. Randolph, Chicago IL 60607. (312)421-1551. Fax: (312)421-1454. E-mail: wcpublish@aol.com. Editor: Jeff Banowetz. 75% freelance written. Monthly magazine covering amateur, participatory sports. Estab. 1987. Circ. 100,000 (Chicago and suburbs). **Pays on acceptance**; pays on publication for blind submissions. Offers 25% kill fee. Buys one-time rights. Editorial lead time 2 months. Submit seasonal material 2-12 months in advance. Accepts simultaneous submissions. Reports in 1 month on queries. Sample copy for $2 or SASE. Writer's guidelines free on request.

Nonfiction: Essays (re: sports controversial issues), how-to (do sports), inspirational (profiles of accomplished athletes), interview/profile, new product, opinion, personal experience, photo feature (in Chicago), travel. No articles on professional sports. Buys 120 mss/year. Query with clips. Length: 500-1,200 words. Pays 10¢/word. Sometimes pays expenses of writers on assignment.

Reprints: Accepts previously published submissions.

Photos: State availability or send photos with submission. Reviews contact sheets and prints. Negotiates payment individually. Captions and identification of subjects required. Buys one-time rights.

Columns/Departments: "We run the following columns every month: running, cycling, fitness centers, nutrition, sports medicine, women's, road trip (adventure travel) and in-line skating, all 750-900 words." Buys 70 mss/year. Query with published clips. Pays $75-125.

Fillers: Anecdotes, facts, gags to be illustrated by cartoonist, short humor. Buys 10/year. Length: 20-500 words. Pays $25-100.

Tips: "Best way to get assignment: ask for writer's guidelines, editor's schedule and sample copy ($2 SASE). *Read magazine!* Query me with story ideas for a column (I run columns every month and am always looking for ideas) or query on features using editorial schedule. Always try to target Chicago looking Midwest."

WOMEN'S SPORTS + FITNESS MAGAZINE, Women's Sports & Fitness, Inc., 2025 Pearl St., Boulder CO 80302-5323. (303)440-5111. Fax: (303)440-3313. E-mail: janetllee@aol.com. Senior Editors: Daryn Eller and Lisa Peters O'Brien. Contact: Janet Lee, assistant editor. 90% freelance written. Works with a small number of new/unpublished writers each year. Magazine published 8 times/year emphasizing women's sports, fitness and health. Estab. 1974. Circ. 200,000. Pays on publication. Publishes ms an average of 3 months after acceptance. Buys first North American serial rights. Submit seasonal/holiday material 3 months in advance. Reports in 3 months. Sample copy for $5 and 9×12 SAE. Writer's guidelines for #10 SASE.

Nonfiction: Profile, service piece, interview, how-to, historical, personal experience, new product. "All articles should have the latest information from knowledgeable sources. All must be of national interest to athletic women." Buys 4 mss/issue. Length: 500-1,500 words. Query with published clips. Pays $500-2,000 for features, including expenses.

Reprints: Sometimes accepts previously published submissions. Send photocopy of article or typed ms with rights for sale noted and information about when and where the article previously appeared. Payment varies.

Photos: State availability of photos. Pays about $50-300 for b&w prints; $50-500 for 35mm color transparencies. Buys one-time rights.

Columns/Departments: Buys 5-8/issue. Query with published clips. Length: 200-750 words. Pays $100-400.

Tips: "If the writer doesn't have published clips, best advice for breaking in is to concentrate on columns and departments (News & Views and Health & Fitness) first. Query letters should tell why our readers— active women (with an average age in the mid-thirties) who partake in sports or fitness activities six times a week—would want to read the article. We're especially attracted to articles with a new angle, fresh or difficult-to-get information. We go after the latest in health, nutrition and fitness research, or reports about lesser-known women in sports who are on the threshold of greatness. We also present profiles of the best athletes and teams. We want the profiles to give insight into the person as well as the athlete. We have a cadre of writers whom we've worked with regularly, but we are always looking for new writers."

Golf

‡GOLF GEORGIA, Moorhead Publications, 121 Village Pkwy., Bldg. 3, Marietta GA 30067. Editor: Bill Gregory. 25% freelance written. Bimonthly magazine covering "golf-related stories or features with some connection to the state of Georgia or members of the state association." Estab. 1986. Circ. 72,500. Pays on publication. Publishes ms an average of 3 months after acceptance. Byline given. Not copyrighted. Buys first North American serial rights. Editorial lead time 6 months. Submit seasonal material 3 months in advance.

Nonfiction: Historical/nostalgic, inspirational, interview/profile, new product, personal experience, photo feature, travel. Buys 6-9 mss/year. Query with published clips. Length: 800-2,500 words. Pays $200-600 for assigned articles; $100-250 for unsolicited articles. Sometimes pays expenses of writers on assignment.

Photos: State availability of photos with submission. Reviews contact sheets. Negotiates payment individually. Model releases, identification of subjects required. Buys all rights.

‡GOLF ILLUSTRATED, Kachina Publications, Suite 250, 5050 N. 40th St., Phoenix AZ 85018. (602)955-0611. Editor: Mike Corcoran. Managing Editor: John Poinier. Contact: John Poinier. 15% freelance written. Monthly magazine for golf. "We cover everything and anything to do with golf, but we're not into the *politics* of the game. Humor, history, profiles of influential figures in golf, are the primary focus." Estab. 1983. Circ. 500,000. **Pays 30 days after acceptance.** Publishes ms an average of 3 months after acceptance. Byline given. Offers 20% kill fee. Buys first North American serial rights. Editorial lead time 10 weeks. Submit seasonal material 6 months in advance. Reports in 2 months on queries. Writer's guidelines free on request.

Nonfiction: Historical/nostalgic, how-to (golf instruction), humor, interview/profile (golf figures), technical, travel (focus on golf) and golf equipment. "No opinion or politics." Buys 20 mss/year. Query. Length: 1,500-2,000 words. Pays $1/word minimum. Sometimes pays expenses of writers on assignment.

Photos: Negotiates payment individually. Identification of subjects required. Buys one-time rights.

Columns/Departments: Gallery Shots (humorous short pieces), 200-400 words. Buys 40 mss/year. Query. Pays $50-400.

Fiction: Humorous and slice-of-life vignettes. Buys 10 mss/year. Query. Length: 1,000-1,500 words. Pays $1/word minimum.

Poetry: Light verse. Buys 8 poems/year. Submit maximum 5 poems. Length: 10-20 lines. Pays $50-100.

Fillers: Anecdotes and short humor. Buys 20/year. Length: 50-200 words. Pays $50-200.

Tips: "Offer a unique perspective; short and sweet queries with SASE are appreciated. *Don't* call up every two weeks to find out when your story is going to be published. Be patient, we get lots of submissions and try our best to respond promptly. We are most open to humorous pieces—anything genuinely well-written."

‡**THE GOLFER**, Heather & Pine Publishing, 42 W. 38th St., New York NY 10024. (212)768-8360. Fax: (212)768-8365. Editor: H.K. Pickens. Managing Editor: Matthew Tolan. Contact: Evan Rothman, features editor. 40% freelance written. Bimonthly magazine covering golf. "A sophisticated, controversational tone for a lifestyle-oriented magazine." Estab. 1994. Circ. 253,000. Pays on publication. Publishes ms an average of 2 months after acceptance. Byline given. Offers negotiable kill fee. Buys all rights. Editorial lead time 2 months. Submit seasonal material 4 months in advance. Accepts simultaneous submissions. Sample copy free on request.

Nonfiction: Book excerpts, essays, general interest, historical/nostalgic, how-to, humor, inspirational, interview/profile, new product, opinion, personal experience, photo feature, technical, travel. Send complete ms. Length: 300-2,000 words.

Reprints: Accepts previously published submissions.

Photos: Send photos with submission. Reviews any size transparencies. Buys one-time rights.

‡**THE LEADER BOARD**, The Publisher's Group, P.O. Box 510366, Salt Lake City UT 84151-0366. Fax: (801)322-1098. Editor: Vicki Andersen. Contact: Anne E. Zombro, publisher. 80% freelance written. Quarterly magazine. "Drive the fairway with Nicklaus, putt the green with Faldo, visit Pebble Beach. This magazine brings you all of this and more—tips from the pros, new equipment, rules and tour updates." Estab. 1996. Circ. 15,000. Pays on publication. Publishes ms an average of 6 months after acceptance. Byline given. Buys first North American serial and second serial (reprint) rights. Editorial lead time 2 months. Submit seasonal material 4 months in advance. Accepts simultaneous submissions. Reports in 1 month on queries; 2 months on mss. Sample copy for $2 and 9×12 SAE. Writer's guidelines for #10 SASE.

Nonfiction: Historical/nostalgic, interview/profile, personal experience, technical, golf. Buys 8-10 mss/year. Query with published clips. Length: 1,000-1,300 words. Pays $125-800.

Reprints: Accepts previously published submissions.

Photos: Send photos with submission. Reviews 4×5 transparencies (preferred), any size prints. Negotiates payment individually. Captions, model releases, identification of subjects required. Buys one-time or all rights.

Columns/Departments: Golf Tips (for the weekend golfer), Personal Experiences/Nostalgia (for the average golfer), both 500 words. Buys 8-10 mss/year. Query with published clips. Pays $50-125.

‡**LINKS MAGAZINE**, Southern Links Magazine Publishing Assoc., Box 7628, Hilton Head SC 29938. Editor: George Fuller. Magazine published 7 times/year for avid, affluent golfers. "*Links Magazine* is edited for club-level golfers interested in travel and real estate opportunities. Other areas of editorial focus include history and traditions of golf, golf equipment updates, and interviews with golf's leaders and legends." Pays within 60 days of acceptance. Byline given. Offers 50% kill fee. Buys all rights. Accepts simultaneous submissions. Reports in 2 months on queries. Sample copy for $3. Writer's guidelines available.

• Ranked as one of the best markets for freelance writers in *Writer's Yearbook*'s annual "Top 100 Markets," January 1996.

Nonfiction: Historical/nostalgic, interview/profile, travel. "No instruction; we're 'where-to' not 'how-to.' " Buys 10-15 mss/year. Query with published clips. Length: 1,500 words minimum. Pays $800-1,200. Sometimes pays expenses of writers on assignment.

Reprints: Accepts previously published submissions.

Columns/Departments: Buys 15-20 mss/year. Query with published clips. Pays $800-1,200.

Fillers: Buys 10-15/year. Length: 300-1,000 words. Pays $300-500.

‡**PACIFIC GOLF**, Canada Wide Magazine & Communications Ltd., 4180 Lougheed Hwy., 4th Floor, Burnaby, British Columbia V5C 6A7 Canada. (604)299-7311. Fax: (604)299-9188. Editor: Bonnie Irving. 80% freelance written. Magazine published 7 times/year covering golf in the Pacific Northwest. "*Pacific Golf* provides business professionals with a dynamic, informative and inclusive publication about golf and the business of golf. It concentrates on the new, the influential, the players, the financial aspects and the challenges and successes of those involved in the golf business." Circ. 16,000. Pays on publication. Publishes ms an average of 2 months after acceptance. Byline given. Kill fee varies. Buys first Canadian rights. Editorial lead time 4 months. Submit seasonal material 4 months in advance. Reports in 6 weeks on queries.

Nonfiction: Query with published clips. Length: 500-2,500 words. Pays 40-60¢/word, depending on length of story and complexity. Sometimes pays expenses of writers on assignment.

Photos: State availability of photos with submission.

SCORE, Canada's Golf Magazine, Canadian Controlled Media Communications, 287 MacPherson Ave., Toronto, Ontario M4V 1A4 Canada. (416)928-2909. Fax: (416)928-1357. E-mail: weeksy@idirect.com. Website: http://www.scoregolf.com. Publisher: (Mr.) Kim Locke. Managing Editor: Bob Weeks. 70% freelance written. Works with a small number of new/unpublished writers each year. Magazine published 7 times/year covering golf. "*Score* magazine provides seasonal coverage of the Canadian golf scene, professional, amateur, senior and junior golf for men and women golfers in Canada, the US and Europe through profiles, history, travel, editorial comment and instruction." Estab. 1982. Circ. 130,000 audited. **Pays on acceptance.** Byline given. Offers negotiable kill fee. Buys all rights and second serial (reprint) rights. Submit seasonal/holiday material 8 months in advance. Reports in 8 months. Sample copy for $2.50 (Canadian) and 9×12 SAE with IRCs. Writer's guidelines for #10 SAE and IRC.

Nonfiction: Book excerpts (golf); historical/nostalgic (golf and golf characters); interview/profile (prominent golf professionals); photo feature (golf); travel (golf destinations only). The yearly April/May issue includes tournament results from Canada, the US, Europe, Asia, Australia, etc., history, profile, and regular features. No personal experience, technical, opinion or general-interest material. Most articles are by assignment only. Buys 25-30 mss/year. Query with published clips. Length: 700-3,500 words. Pays $200-1,500.

Photos: Send photos with query or ms. Pays $50-100 for 35mm color transparencies (positives) or $30 for 8×10 or 5×7 b&w prints. Captions, model release (if necessary), identification of subjects required. Buys all rights.

Columns/Departments: Profile (historical or current golf personalities or characters); Great Moments ("Great Moments in Canadian Golf"—description of great single moments, usually game triumphs); New Equipment (Canadian availability only); Travel (golf destinations, including "hard" information such as greens fees, hotel accommodations, etc.); Instruction (by special assignment only; usually from teaching golf professionals); The Mental Game (psychology of the game, by special assignment only); History (golf equipment collections and collectors, development of the game, legendary figures and events). Buys 17-20 mss/year. Query with published clips or send complete ms. Length: 700-1,700 words. Pays $140-400.

Tips: "Only writers with an extensive knowledge of golf and familiarity with the Canadian golf scene should query or submit in-depth work to *Score*. Many of our features are written by professional people who play the game for a living or work in the industry. All areas mentioned under Columns/Departments are open to freelancers. Most of our *major* features are done on assignment only."

Guns

GUN DIGEST, DBI Books, Inc., 4092 Commercial Ave., Northbrook IL 60062. (847)272-6310. Editor-in-Chief: Ken Warner. 50% freelance written. Prefers to work with published/established writers but works with a small number of new/unpublished writers each year. Annual journal covering guns and shooting. Estab. 1944. **Pays on acceptance.** Publishes ms an average of 20 months after acceptance. Byline given. Buys all rights. Reports in 1 month.

Nonfiction: Buys 50 mss/issue. Query. Length: 500-5,000 words. Pays $100-600; includes photos or illustration package from author.

Photos: State availability of photos with query letter. Reviews 8×10 b&w prints. Payment for photos included in payment for ms. Captions required.

Tips: Award of $1,000 to author of best article (juried) in each issue.

‡**GUN WORLD**, 34249 Camino Capistrano, Box HH, Capistrano Beach CA 92624. Editorial Director: Jack Lewis. Managing Editor: Steve Comus. 50% freelance written. Monthly magazine for ages that "range from mid-teens to mid-60s; many professional types who are interested in relaxation of hunting and shooting." Estab. 1960. Circ. 128,000. Buys 80-100 unsolicited mss/year. **Pays on acceptance.** Publishes ms an average of 6 months after acceptance. Buys first rights and sometimes all rights, but rights reassigned on request. Byline given. Submit seasonal material 6 months in advance. Reports in 6 weeks. Editorial requirements for #10 SASE.

Nonfiction: General subject matter consists of "well-rounded articles—not by amateurs—on shooting techniques, with anecdotes; hunting stories with tips and knowledge integrated. No poems or fiction. We like broad humor in our articles, so long as it does not reflect upon firearms safety. Most arms magazines are pretty deadly, and we feel shooting can be fun. Too much material aimed at pro-gun people. Most of this is staff-written and most shooters don't have to be told of their rights under the Constitution. We want articles on new developments; off-track inventions, novel military uses of arms; police armament and training techniques; do-it-yourself projects in this field." Buys informational, how-to, personal experience, nostalgia articles. Pays up to $300, sometimes more. Prefers electronic submissions.

Photos: Purchases photos with mss. Captions required. Wants 5×7 b&w photos. Occasionally pays expenses of writers on assignment.

Tips: "The most frequent mistake made by writers in completing an article for us is surface writing with no real knowledge of the subject. To break in, offer an anecdote having to do with proposed copy."

GUNS & AMMO, Petersen Publishing Co., 6420 Wilshire Blvd., Los Angeles CA 90048. (213)782-2160. Fax: (213)782-2477. Editor: Kevin E. Steele. Managing Editor: Christine Skaglund. 10% freelance written. Monthly magazine covering firearms. "Our readers are enthusiasts of handguns, rifles, shotguns and accessories." Circ. 600,000. **Pays on acceptance.** Publishes ms 6 months after acceptance. Byline given. Buys all rights. Submit seasonal material 6 months in advance. Writer's guidelines for #10 SASE.
Nonfiction: Opinion. Buys 24 mss/year. Send complete ms. Length: 800-2,500 words. Pays $125-500.
Reprints: Send typed ms with rights for sale noted along with information about when and where the article previously appeared.
Photos: Send photos with submissions. Review 7×9 prints. Offers no additional payment for photos accepted with ms. Captions, model releases, identification of subjects required. Buys all rights.
Columns/Departments: RKBA (opinion column on right to keep and bear arms). Send complete ms. Length: 800-1,200 words. Pays $300.

GUNS & AMMO ANNUAL, Petersen Publishing Co., 6420 Wilshire Blvd., Los Angeles CA 90048. (213)782-2160. Fax: (213)782-2477. Contact: Jerry Lee, editor. Managing Editor: Joy Whittemore. 50% freelance written. Annual magazine covering firearms. "Our audience consists of enthusiasts of firearms, shooting sports and accessories." **Pays on acceptance.** Publishes ms an average of 1 year after acceptance. Byline given. Buys all rights. Reports in 1 month.
Nonfiction: Buys 15 mss/year. Send complete ms. Length: 2,000-4,000 words. Pays $300-600.
Photos: Send photos with submission. Reviews 8×10 prints. Offers no additional payment for photos accepted with ms. Captions, model releases, identification of subjects required. Buys all rights.
Fiction: Publishes novel excerpts.
Tips: "We need feature articles on firearms and accessories. See current issue for examples."

HANDGUNS, Petersen Publishing Co., 6420 Wilshire Blvd., Los Angeles CA 90048. (213)782-2868. Fax: (213)782-2477. Contact: (Mr.) Jan M. Libourel, editor. Managing Editor: Chris Skaglund. 60% freelance written. Monthly magazine covering handguns and handgun accessories. Estab. 1986. Circ. 150,000. **Pays on acceptance.** Byline given. No kill fee. Buys all rights. Reporting time varies. Free sample copy and writer's guidelines.
Nonfiction: General interest, historical, how-to, profile, new product and technical. "No articles not germane to established topics of magazine." Buys 50 mss/year. Send complete ms. Pays $300-500.
Photos: Send photos with submission. Reviews contact sheets, color transparencies, 5×7 prints. No additional payment for photos. Captions, model releases and identification of subjects required. Buys all rights.
Tips: "Send manuscript after querying editor by telephone and establishing acceptability. We are most open to feature stories. Be guided by published examples appearing in the magazine."

Hiking/Backpacking

AMERICAN HIKER, American Hiking Society, P.O. Box 20160, Washington DC 20041-2160. (301)565-6704. Editor: Laura Loftus. 25% freelance written. Bimonthly magazine. "*American Hiker* covers the recreation opportunities on America's trails and focuses on the people who work to protect them." Estab. 1988. Circ. 10,000. Pays on publication. Publishes ms 3 months after acceptance. Byline given. Buys first rights. Editorial lead time 3 months. Submit seasonal material 6 months in advance. Accepts simultaneous submissions. Reports in 2 weeks on queries; 2 months on mss. Sample copy for $1. Writer's guidelines for #10 SASE.
Nonfiction: Book excerpts, essays, interview/profile, travel. Special issue: National Trails Day issue (June 1997). Buys 18 mss/year. Query with published clips. Length: 250-1,400 words. Pays $25-150 for assigned articles; $25-75 for unsolicited articles.
Reprints: Accepts previously published submissions.
Photos: State availability of photos with submission. Reviews transparencies. Offers $25/photo. Buys one-time rights.
Columns/Departments: Hiking Family (family tips); Club Profile on AHS affiliate club; Soft Wear (low-impact camping); Hiker's Access (book reviews); all 800 words. Buys 12 mss/year. Query with published clips. Pays $75-125.
Tips: "Focus on people who are building and protecting trails—not accounts of travel."

BACKPACKER, Rodale Press, Inc., 33 E. Minor St., Emmaus PA 18098-0099. (610)967-8296. Fax: (610)967-8181. E-mail: bpeditor@aol.com. Editor: John Viehman. Managing Editor: Tom Shealey. Contact: Jim Gorman, Michele Morris, senior editors. 50% freelance written. Magazine published 9 times/year covering wilderness travel. Estab. 1973. Circ. 230,000. **Pays on acceptance.** Byline given. Offers 25% kill fee. Buys one-time rights or all rights. Reports in 2 months. Writer's guidelines for #10 SASE.
  • *Backpacker* tells us better writers are applying; competition is getting *tougher.*

Nonfiction: Essays, exposé, historical/nostalgic, how-to (expedition planner), humor, inspirational, interview/profile, new product, opinion, personal experience, technical, travel. No step-by-step accounts of what you did on your summer vacation—stories that chronicle every rest stop and gulp of water. Query with published clips and SASE. Length: 750-3,000 words. Pays $400-2,000. Sometimes pays (pre-determined) expenses of writers on assignment. "What we want are features that let us and the readers 'feel' the place, and experience your wonderment, excitement, disappointment or other emotions encountered 'out there.' If we feel like we've been there after reading your story, you've succeeded."
 • Ranked as one of the best markets for freelance writers in *Writer's Yearbook*'s annual "Top 100 Markets," January 1996.
Photos: State availability of photos with submission. Amount varies—depends on size of photo used. Buys one-time rights.
Columns/Departments: Signpost, "News From All Over" (adventure, environment, wildlife, trails, techniques, organizations, special interests—well-written, entertaining, short, newsy item), 50-500 words; Body Language (in-the-field column), 750-1,200 words; Moveable Feast (food-related aspects of wilderness: nutrition, cooking techniques, recipes, products and gear), 500-750 words; Weekend Wilderness (brief but detailed guides to wilderness areas, providing thorough trip-planning information, only enough anecdote to give a hint, then the where/when/hows), 500-750 words; Technique (ranging from beginner to expert focus, written by people with solid expertise, details ways to improve performance, how-to-do-it instructions, information on equipment manufacturers and places readers can go), 750-1,500 words; and Backcountry (personal perspectives, quirky and idiosyncratic, humorous critiques, manifestos and misadventures, interesting angle, lesson, revelation or moral), 750-1,200 words. Buys 50-75 mss/year. Query with published clips. Pays $200-600. No phone calls regarding story ideas. Written queries only.
Tips: "Our best advice is to read the publication—most freelancers don't know the magazine at all. The best way to break in is with an article for the Backcountry, Weekend Wilderness or Signpost Department."

SIGNPOST FOR NORTHWEST TRAILS MAGAZINE, 1305 Fourth Ave., Suite 512, Seattle WA 98101-2401. E-mail: dnelson024@aol.com. Website: http://pasko.physiol.washington.edu/wt~/. Publisher: Washington Trails Association. Executive Editor: Dan A. Nelson. 30% freelance written. "We will consider working with both previously published and unpublished freelancers." Monthly magazine about hiking, backpacking and similar trail-related activities, strictly from a Pacific Northwest viewpoint. Estab. 1966. Will consider any rights offered by author. Publishes ms an average of 6 months after acceptance. Reports in 2 months. Query or submit complete ms. Writer's guidelines for #10 SASE.
Nonfiction: "Most material is donated by subscribers or is staff-written. Payment for purchased material is low, but a good way to break in to print and share your outdoor experiences."
Reprints: Include information about when and where the article previously appeared.
Tips: "We cover only *self-propelled* backcountry sports and won't consider manuscripts about trail bikes, snowmobiles or power boats. We *are* interested in articles about modified and customized equipment, food and nutrition, and personal experiences in the Pacific Northwest backcountry."

‡SOUTHERN HIKER, The South's Guide to the Great Outdoors, Treks & Journeys Press, 715 Canyon Rd., Tuscaloosa AL 35406.(205)348-8247. (205)348-2780. E-mail: GFrangou@sa.ua.edu. Editor: George Frangoulis. 75% freelance written. Quarterly magazine covering hiking and camping. "*Southern Hiker* is the South's guide to the finest camping, hiking, canoeing and biking. It takes a comprehensive look at top camping sites, hiking and biking trails, and waterways. Mostly for the states of AL, GA, KY, NC, SC, AK, TN and VA, the magazine offers advice and tips for beginners to experts. It is for the serious hiker and outdoorsperson." Estab. 1996. Circ. 56,000. **Pays on acceptance.** Byline given. Offers 50% kill fee. Buys first North American serial rights. Editorial lead time 6 months. Submit seasonal material 6 months in advance. Reports in 2 months on queries; 3 months on mss. Sample copy and writer's guidelines free.
Nonfiction Book excerpts, essays, general interest, historical/nostalgic, how-to, humor, inspirational, interview/profile, new product, opinion, personal experience, photo feature, travel. Buys 15-20 mss/year. Query. Length: 500-3,500 words. Pays $50-350 for asigned articles; $25-250 for unsolicited articles.
Reprints: Accepts previously published submissions.
Photos: State availability of photos with submission. Reviews contact sheets, transparencies, 5×7 prints. Offers $5-25/photo. Captions, model releases, identification of subjects required.
Tips: "*Southern Hiker* is particularly interested in how-to articles, such as how to make the outdoors experience more enjoyable and easier. Examples of recent features include: Getting the Best Boot For Your Money, Packing Your Backpack Properly, Campsite Cuisine—Blueberry Pancakes and Chicken Burritos and How to Cope With Allergies On the Trail."

Hockey

‡HOCKEY PLAYER MAGAZINE, Hockey Player L.P., P.O. Box 312, Okemos MI 48805-0312. Fax: (517)347-0686. E-mail: hockeymag@aol.com. Website: http://www.hockeyplayer.com. Editor: Alex Carswell. 90% freelance written. Monthly tabloid covering hockey for recreational players. "*Hockey Player* is written for players of recreational ice, roller and street hockey. It is not just a pro hockey fan magazine." Estab. 1991. Circ. 18,000. Pays on publication. Publishes ms an average of 2 months after acceptance. Byline given. Buys first North American serial and electronic rights. Editorial lead time 3 months. Submit seasonal material 4 months in advance. Accepts simultaneous submissions. Reports in 1 month. Sample copy and writer's guidelines free on request.

Nonfiction: How-to, interview/profile, new product, personal experience, photo feature. technical. Buys 50 mss/year. Query with published clips. Length: 1,500-2,500 words. Pays $75-100.

Tips: "Writing 'how-to' article about playing the game is the easiest way to break in. We don't need a profile on some minor league player."

Horse Racing

THE BACKSTRETCH, United Thoroughbred Trainers of America, Inc., P.O. Box 7065, Louisville KY 40257-0065. (502)893-0025. Fax: (502)893-0026. Managing Editor: Barrett Shaw. 90% freelance written. Estab. 1962. Circ. 10,000. Uses mostly established turf writers, but works with a few less experienced writers each year. Bimonthly magazine directed chiefly to Thoroughbred trainers but also to owners, fans and others working in or involved with the racing industry. Publishes ms 3 months after acceptance, sometimes longer. Sample copy $3.

Nonfiction: Profiles of trainers, owners, jockeys, horses and other personalities who make up the world of racing; analysis of industry issues; articles on particular tracks or races, veterinary topics; information on legal or business aspects of owning, training or racing horses; and historical perspectives. Opinions should be informed by expertise on the subject treated. Non-commissioned articles are accepted on a speculation basis. Pays on publication. If not suitable, articles are returned only if a SASE is included. Length: 1,500-2,500 words.

Reprints: Occasionally accepts previously published material, especially if it has appeared only in a regional or specialized publication. Pays about 50% of amount paid for an original article.

Photos: It is advisable to include photo illustrations when possible, or these can be arranged for separately.

Tips: "If an article is a simultaneous submission, this must be stated and we must be advised if it is accepted elsewhere. Articles should be double spaced and may be submitted by mail, fax or on 3½-inch disk saved in text or in program compatible with Quark XPress for Macintosh."

HOOF BEATS, United States Trotting Association, 750 Michigan Ave., Columbus OH 43215. (614)224-2291. Fax: (614)228-1385. Editor: Dean A. Hoffman. 35% freelance written. Works with a small number of new/unpublished writers each year. Monthly magazine covering harness racing for the participants of the sport of harness racing. "We cover all aspects of the sport—racing, breeding, selling, etc." Estab. 1933. Circ. 17,000. Pays on publication. Publishes ms an average of 3 months after acceptance. Byline given. Buys negotiable rights. Submit seasonal/holiday material 3 months in advance. Reports in 1 month. Free sample copy, postpaid.

Nonfiction: General interest, historical/nostalgic, humor, inspirational, interview/profile, new product, personal experience, photo feature. Buys 15-20 mss/year. Query. Length: open. Pays $100-400. Pays the expenses of writers on assignment with approval.

Reprints: Send photocopy of article or short story. Pay is negotiable.

Photos: State availability of photos. Pays variable rates for 35mm transparencies and prints. Identification of subjects required. Buys one-time rights.

Fiction: Historical, humorous, novel excerpts, interesting fiction with a harness racing theme. Buys 2-3 mss/year. Query. Length: open. Pays $100-400.

THE QUARTER RACING JOURNAL, American Quarter Horse Association, P.O. Box 32470, Amarillo TX 79120. (806)376-4811. Fax: (806)376-8364. Website: http://www.aqha.com. Contact: Amy Owens, editor. Executive Editor: Jim Jennings. 10% freelance written. Monthly magazine. "The official racing voice of The American Quarter Horse Association. We promote quarter horse racing. Articles include training, breeding, nutrition, sports medicine, health, history, etc." Estab. 1988. Circ. 10,000. **Pays on acceptance.** Publishes ms an average of 3 months after acceptance. Buys first North American serial rights. Submit seasonal/holiday material 3 months in advance. Reports in 1 month on queries. Free sample copy and writer's guidelines.

Nonfiction: Historical (must be on quarter horses or people associated with them), how-to (training), nutrition, health, breeding and opinion. "We welcome submissions year-round. No fiction." Query. Length: 700-2,500 words. Pays $150-300.

Photos: Send photos with submission. Offers no additional payment for photos accepted with ms. Captions and identification of subjects required.

Tips: "Query first—must be familiar with quarter horse racing and be knowledgeable of the sport. If writing on nutrition, it must be applicable. Most open to features covering nutrition, health care. Use a knowledgeable source with credentials."

Hunting and Fishing

ALABAMA GAME & FISH, Game & Fish Publications, Inc., P.O. Box 741, Marietta GA 30061. Editor: Jimmy Jacobs. See *Game & Fish Publications*.

AMERICAN HUNTER, 11250 Waples Mill Rd., Fairfax VA 22030-7400. Fax: (703)267-3971. Website: http://www.nra.org. Editor: Tom Fulgham. Contact: John Zent, managing editor. For hunters who are members of the National Rifle Association. Circ. 1,500,000. Buys first North American serial rights. Byline given. Writer's guidelines for #10 SASE.
Nonfiction: Factual material on all phases of hunting. Not interested in material on fishing or camping. Prefers queries. Length: 1,000-2,000 words. Pays $250-450.
Photos: No additional payment made for photos used with mss. Pays $25 for b&w photos purchased without accompanying mss. Pays $50-300 for color.

ARKANSAS SPORTSMAN, Game & Fish Publications, Inc., P.O. Box 741, Marietta GA 30061. (404)953-9222. Editor: Bob Borgwat. See *Game & Fish Publications*.

BASSMASTER MAGAZINE, B.A.S.S. Publications, 5845 Carmichael Pkwy., Montgomery AL 36141-0900. (205)272-9530. Fax: (205)279-9530. Editor: Dave Precht. 80% freelance written. Prefers to work with published/established writers. Magazine published 10 issues/year about largemouth, smallmouth and spotted bass for dedicated beginning and advanced bass fishermen. Circ. 550,000. **Pays on acceptance.** Publication date of ms after acceptance "varies—seasonal material could take years"; average time is 8 months. Byline given. Buys all rights. Submit seasonal material 6 months in advance. Reports in 2 months. Sample copy for $2. Writer's guidelines for #10 SASE.
Nonfiction: Historical, interview (of knowledgeable people in the sport), profile (outstanding fishermen), travel (where to go to fish for bass), how-to (catch bass and enjoy the outdoors), new product (reels, rods and bass boats), conservation related to bass fishing. "No 'Me and Joe go fishing' type articles." Query. Length: 400-2,100 words. Pays 25¢/word.
  • Needs destination stories (how to fish a certain area) for the Northwest and Northeast.
Columns/Departments: Short Cast/News & Views (upfront regular feature covering news-related events such as new state bass records, unusual bass fishing happenings, conservation, new products and editorial viewpoints); 250-400 words.
Photos: "We want only color photos." Pays $600 for color cover transparencies. Captions required; model releases preferred. Buys all rights.
Fillers: Anecdotes, short humor, newsbreaks. Buys 4-5 mss/issue. Length: 250-500 words. Pays $50-100.
Tips: "Editorial direction continues in the short, more direct how-to article. Compact, easy-to-read information is our objective. Shorter articles with good graphics, such as how-to diagrams, step-by-step instruction, etc., will enhance a writer's articles submitted to *Bassmaster Magazine*. The most frequent mistakes made by writers in completing an article for us are poor grammar, poor writing, poor organization and superficial research."

BC OUTDOORS, OP Publishing, 202-1132 Hamilton St., Vancouver, British Columbia V6B 2S2 Canada. (604)687-1581. Fax: (604)687-1925. E-mail: op@mindlink.bc.ca. Editor: Karl Bruhn. 80% freelance written. Works with a small number of new/unpublished writers each year. Magazine published 8 times/year covering fishing, camping, hunting and the environment of outdoor recreation. Estab. 1946. Circ. 42,000. Pays on publication. Publishes ms an average of 3 months after acceptance. Byline given. Offers negotiable kill fee. Buys first North American serial rights. Reports in 1 month. Sample copy and writer's guidelines for 8×10 SAE with 7 first-class stamps.
Nonfiction: How-to (new or innovative articles on outdoor subjects), personal experience (outdoor adventure), outdoor topics specific to British Columbia. "We would like to receive how-to, where-to features dealing with hunting and fishing in British Columbia." Buys 80-90 mss/year. Query. Length: 1,500-2,000 words. Pays $300-500. Sometimes pays the expenses of writers on assignment.
  • Wants in-depth, informative, professional writing only.
Photos: State availability of photos with query. Pays $25-75 on publication for 5×7 b&w prints; $35-150 for color contact sheets and 35mm transparencies. Captions and identification of subjects required. Buys one-time rights.
Tips: "Emphasis on environmental issues. Those pieces with a conservation component have a better chance of being published. Subject must be specific to British Columbia. We receive many manuscripts written by people who obviously do not know the magazine or market. The writer has a better chance of breaking in at our publication with short, lesser-paying articles and fillers, because we have a stable of regular writers in constant touch who produce most main features."

BUGLE, Journal of Elk and the Hunt, Rocky Mountain Elk Foundation, 2291 W. Broadway, Missoula MT 59802. (406)523-4568. Editor: Dan Crockett. Contact: Jan Brocci, assistant editor. 50% freelance written.

Quarterly magazine covering conservation and hunting. "*Bugle* is the membership publication of the Rocky Mountain Elk Foundation, a nonprofit wildlife conservation group; it also sells on newsstands. Our readers are predominantly hunters, many of them naturalists who care deeply about protecting wildlife habitat. Hunting stories and essays should celebrate the hunting experience, demonstrating respect for wildlife, the land and the hunt. Articles on elk behavior or elk habitat should include personal observations and entertain as well as educate." Estab. 1984. Circ. 150,000. **Pays on acceptance**. Publishes ms 9 months after acceptance. Byline given. Offers variable kill fee. Buys one-time rights. Editorial lead time 6 months. Submit seasonal material 6 months in advance. Reports in 1 month on queries; 2 months on mss. Sample copy $5. Writer's guidelines for #10 SASE.

Nonfiction: Book excerpts, essays, general interest (elk related), historical/nostalgic, humor, opinion, personal experience, photo feature. No how-to, where-to. Buys 20 mss/year. Query with or without published clips, or send complete ms. Length: 1,500-4,500 words. Pays 20¢/word and 3 contributor copies; more issues at cost.

Reprints: Accepts previously published submissions.

Columns/Departments: Situation Ethics, 1,000-2,000 words; Thoughts & Theories, 1,500-4,000 words; Women in the Outdoors, 1,000-3,000 words. Buys 12 mss/year. Query with or without published clips or send complete ms. Pays 20¢/word.

Fiction: Adventure, historical, humorous, slice-of-life vignettes, western. No fiction that doesn't pertain to elk or elk hunting. Buys 4 mss/year. Query with or without published clips or send complete ms. Length: 1,500-4,500 words. Pays 20¢/word.

Poetry: Free verse, haiku, light verse, traditional. Buys 1-2 poems/year. Submit maximum 6 poems.

Tips: "Creative queries (250-500 words) that showcase your concept and your style remain the most effective approach. We're hungry for submissions for two specific columns: Situation Ethics and Women in the Outdoors. Send a SASE for guidelines. We also welcome strong well-reasoned opinion pieces on topics pertinent to hunting and wildlife conservation, and humorous pieces about elk behavior or encounters with elk (hunting or otherwise)."

CALIFORNIA GAME & FISH, Game & Fish Publications, Inc., Box 741, Marietta GA 30061. Editor: Burt Carey. See *Game & Fish Publications*.

‡DISCOVERING AND EXPLORING NEW JERSEY'S FISHING STREAMS AND THE DELAWARE RIVER, New Jersey Sportsmen's Guides, P.O. Box 100, Somerdale NJ 08083. (609)783-1271. (609)665-8350. Fax: (609)665-8656. Editor: Steve Perrone. 60-70% freelance written. Annual magazine covering freshwater stream and river fishing. Estab. 1993. Circ. 2,500. **Pays on acceptance**. Publishes ms an average of 6 months after acceptance. Byline given. Buys first rights and makes work-for-hire assignments. Editorial lead time 6 months. Sample copy for $12.50 postage paid.

Nonfiction: How-to fishing and freshwater fishing. Buys 6-8 mss/year. Query with published clips. Length: 500-2,000 words. Pays $75-250 for assigned articles.

Photos: State availability of photos with submission. Reviews 4×5 transparencies and prints. Negotiates payment individually. Captions, model releases, identification of subjects required. Buys one-time rights.

Tips: "We want queries with published clips of articles describing fishing experiences on New Jersey streams and the Delaware River."

FIELD & STREAM, 2 Park Ave., New York NY 10016-5695. Editor: Duncan Barnes. Contact: David E. Petzal, executive editor. 50% freelance written. Eager to work with new/unpublished writers. Monthly. "Broad-based service magazine for the hunter and fisherman. Editorial content ranges from very basic how-to stories detailing a useful technique or a device that sportsmen can make, to articles of penetrating depth about national hunting, fishing, and related activities. Also humor and personal essays, nostalgia and 'mood pieces' on the hunting or fishing experience and profiles on outdoor people." Estab. 1895. **Pays on acceptance**. Buys first rights. Byline given. Reports in 2 months. Query. Writer's guidelines for #10 SASE.

● Ranked as one of the best markets for freelance writers in *Writer's Yearbook*'s annual "Top 100 Markets," January 1996.

Nonfiction: Length: 1,500-2,000 words for features. Payment varies depending on the quality of work, importance of the article. Pays $800 and up to $1,500 and more on a sliding scale for major features. *Field & Stream* also publishes regional sections with feature articles on hunting and fishing in specific areas of the country. The sections are geographically divided into East, Midwest, West and South, and appear 12 months/year.

Reprints: Occasionally accepts previously published submissions if suitable. Send photocopy of article and information about when and where it previously appeared.

Photos: Prefers color slides to b&w. Query first with photos. When photos purchased separately, pays $450 minimum for color. Buys first rights to photos.

Fillers: Buys short "how it's done" fillers, 75 to 150 words, on unusual or helpful subjects. Also buys short (up to 500 words) pieces on tactics or techniques for specific hunting or fishing situations; short "Field Guide" pieces on natural phenomena as related to hunting and fishing; "Myths and Misconceptions," short pieces debunking a commonly held belief about hunting and fishing, and short "Outdoor Basics" and

"Sportsman's Project" articles. In addition, welcomes queries on "Health and Safety" categories likely to affect outdoor sportsmen; hunting, fishing and natural history items of interest to young sportsmen; and odd or noteworthy items with hunting or fishing themes. Pays $75-400.

FLORIDA GAME & FISH, Game & Fish Publications, Inc., Box 741, Marietta GA 30061. (404)953-9222. Editor: Jimmy Jacobs. See *Game & Fish Publications*.

FLORIDA SPORTSMAN, Wickstrom Publishers Inc., 5901 SW 74 St., Miami FL 33143. (305)661-4222. Fax: (305)284-0277. E-mail: editor@flsportsman.com. Website: www.flsportsman.com. Editor: Glenn Law. 70% freelance written. Works with new/unpublished writers. Monthly magazine covering fishing, boating and related sports—Florida and Caribbean only. Circ. 110,000. **Pays on acceptance**. Publishes ms an average of 6 months after acceptance. Byline given. Offers 50% kill fee. Buys first North American serial rights. Submit seasonal/holiday material 6 months in advance. Reports in 1 week on queries; 1 month on mss. Free sample copy. Writer's guidelines for #10 SASE.
Nonfiction: Essays (environment or nature), how-to (fishing, hunting, boating), humor (outdoors angle), personal experience (in fishing, etc.), technical (boats, tackle, etc., as particularly suitable for Florida specialties). "We use reader service pieces almost entirely—how-to, where-to, etc. One or two environmental pieces per issue as well. Writers *must* be Florida based, or have lengthy experience in Florida outdoors. All articles must have strong Florida emphasis. We do not want to see general how-to-fish-or-boat pieces which might well appear in a national or wide-regional magazine." Buys 40-60 mss/year. Query. Length: 2,000-3,000 words. Pays $300-400. Sometimes pays expenses of writers on assignment.
Photos: Send photos with submission. Reviews 35mm transparencies and 4×5 and larger prints. Offers no additional payment for photos accepted with ms. Buys one-time rights.
Tips: "Feature articles are most open to freelancers; however there is little chance of acceptance unless contributor is an accomplished and avid outdoorsman *and* a competent writer-photographer with considerable experience in Florida."

FLORIDA WILDLIFE, Florida Game & Fresh Water Fish Commission, 620 S. Meridian St., Tallahassee FL 32399-1600. (904)488-5563. Fax: (904)488-6988. Website: http://www.state.fl.us/gfc/gfchome.html. Editor: Dick Sublette. Contact: Frank Adams, associate editor. About 40% freelance written. Bimonthly 4-color state magazine covering hunting, natural history, fishing, endangered species and wildlife conservation. "In outdoor sporting articles we seek themes of wholesome recreation. In nature articles we seek accuracy and conservation purpose." Estab. 1947. Circ. 26,000. Pays on publication. Byline given. Buys first North American serial and occasionally second serial (reprint) rights. Submit seasonal/holiday material 6 months in advance. Accepts simultaneous submissions. Reports in 2 months (acknowledgement of receipt of materials); up to 2 years for acceptance, usually less for rejections. Prefers photo/ms packages. Sample copy for $2.95. Writer's/photographer's guidelines for SASE.
Nonfiction: General interest (bird watching, hiking, camping, boating), how-to (hunting and fishing), humor (wildlife related; no anthropomorphism), inspirational (conservation oriented), personal experience (wildlife, hunting, fishing, outdoors), photo feature (Florida species: game, nongame, botany), technical (rarely purchased, but open to experts). "We buy general interest hunting, fishing and nature stories. No stories that humanize animals, or opinionated stories not based on confirmable facts." Special issues: 50th Anniversary edition (May/June 1997); Fishing edition (March/April 1997); Hunting season (September/October 1996, November/December 1996). Buys 30-40 mss/year. Send slides/ms. Length: 500-1,500 words. Generally pays $50/published page plus a per-photo disbursement.
Reprints: Accepts previously published submissions, if so noted. Send tearsheet of article or typed ms with rights for sale noted.
Photos: State availability of photos with story query. Accepts transparencies only (slides) of hunting, fishing, and natural science series of Florida wildlife species. Pays $25-75 for inside photos; $100 for front cover photos, $75 for back cover. "We like short, specific captions." Buys one-time rights.
Fiction: "We rarely buy fiction, and then only if it is true to life and directly related to good sportsmanship and conservation. No fairy tales, erotica, profanity or obscenity." Buys 2-3 mss/year. Send complete mss and label "fiction." Length: 500-1,200 words. Generally pays $50/published page.
Tips: "Read and study recent issues for subject matter, style and examples of our viewpoint, philosophy and treatment. We look for wholesome recreation, ethics, safety, and good outdoor experience more than bagging the game in our stories. We usually need well-written hunting and freshwater fishing articles that are entertaining and informative and that describe places to hunt and fish in Florida. We do not publish articles that feature a commercial interest or a specific brand name product."

FLY FISHING IN SALT WATERS, Hook and Release Publications, Inc., 2001 Western Ave., Suite 210, Seattle WA 98121. (206)443-3273. Fax: (206)443-3293. Editor: R.P. Van Gytenbeek. 90% freelance written. Bimonthly magazine covering fly fishing in salt waters. Estab. 1994. Circ. 44,000. **Pays on acceptance**. Publishes ms an average of 1 year after acceptance. Byline given. Kill fee negotiable. Buys first North American serial rights and electronic rights. Editorial lead time 2 months. Submit seasonal material at least

2 months in advance. Reports in 1 month on queries; 2 months on mss. Sample copy for $6. Writer's guidelines for #10 SASE.

Nonfiction: Book excerpts, essays, historical/nostalgic, how-to, interview/profile, new product, personal experience, photo feature, technical, travel, resource issues (conservation). Buys 40-50 mss/year. Query. Length: 1,500-2,500 words. Pays $400-500.

Photos: Send photos with submission. Reviews transparencies (35mm color only). Negotiates payment individually. Captions, identification of subjects required. Buys one-time rights.

Columns/Departments: Legends/Reminiscences (history-profiles-nostalgia), 2,000-2,500 words; Resource (conservation issues), 1,500 words; Fly Tier's Bench (how to tie saltwater flies), 1,000-1,200 words, photos critical; Tackle & Technique (technical how-to), 1,500 words, photos or illustrations critical; Boating (technical how-to), 2,000-2,500 words. (Other departments are mostly staff written or by assignment only.) Buys 25-30 mss/year. Query. Pays $400-500.

Fiction: Adventure, humorous, mainstream. Send complete ms. Length: 2,000-3,000 words. Pays $500.

Fillers: Most fillers are staff-written.

FUR-FISH-GAME, 2878 E. Main, Columbus OH 43209-9947. Editor: Mitch Cox. 65% freelance written. Works with a small number of new/unpublished writers each year. Monthly magazine for outdoorsmen of all ages who are interested in hunting, fishing, trapping, dogs, camping, conservation and related topics. Estab. 1900. Circ. 105,000. **Pays on acceptance.** Publishes ms an average of 7 months after acceptance. Byline given. Buys first serial rights or all rights. Reports in 2 months. Query. Sample copy for $1 and 9 × 12 with SAE. Writer's guidelines for #10 SASE.

Nonfiction: "We are looking for informative, down-to-earth stories about hunting, fishing, trapping, dogs, camping, boating, conservation and related subjects. Nostalgic articles are also used. Many of our stories are 'how-to' and should appeal to small-town and rural readers who are true outdoorsmen. Some recent articles have told how to train a gun dog, catch big-water catfish, outfit a bowhunter and trap late-season muskrat. We also use personal experience stories and an occasional profile, such as an article about an old-time trapper. 'Where-to' stories are used occasionally if they have broad appeal." Length: 500-3,000 words. Pays $75-150 depending upon quality, photo support, and importance to magazine. Short filler stories pay $35-80.

Photos: Send photos with ms. Photos are part of ms package and receive no additional payment. Prefers color prints or transparencies. Prints can be 5 × 7 or 8 × 10. Captions required.

Tips: "We are always looking for quality articles that tell how to hunt or fish for game animals or birds that are popular with everyday outdoorsmen but often overlooked in other publications, such as catfish, bluegill, crappie, squirrel, rabbit, crows, etc. We also use articles on standard seasonal subjects such as deer and pheasant, but like to see a fresh approach or new technique. Trapping articles, especially instructional ones based on personal experience, are useful all year. Articles on gun dogs, ginseng and do-it-yourself projects are also popular with our readers. An assortment of photos and/or sketches greatly enhances any manuscript, and sidebars, where applicable, can also help."

GAME & FISH PUBLICATIONS, INC., 2250 Newmarket Pkwy., Suite 110, Marietta GA 30067. (770)953-9222. Fax: (770)933-9510. Editorial Director: Ken Dunwoody. Publishes 30 different monthly outdoor magazines, each one covering the fishing and hunting opportunities in a particular state or region (see individual titles and editors). 90% freelance written. Estab. 1975. Circ. 507,000. Pays 75 days prior to cover date of issue. Publishes ms an average of 7 months after acceptance. Byline given. Offers negotiable kill fee. Buys first North American serial rights. Submit seasonal material at least 8 months in advance. Editors prefer to hold queries until that season's material is assigned. Reports in 3 months on mss. Sample copy for $2.50 and 9 × 12 SASE. Writer's guidelines for #10 SASE.

Nonfiction: Prefer queries over unsolicited ms. Article lengths either 1,500 or 2,500 words. Pays separately for articles and accompanying photos. Manuscripts pay $125-300, cover photos $250, inside color $75 and b&w $25. Reviews transparencies and b&w prints. Prefers captions and identification of species/subjects. Buys one-time rights to photos.

Fiction: Buys some humor and nostalgia stories pertaining to hunting and fishing. Pays $125-250. Length 1,500-2,500 words.

Tips: "Our readers are experienced anglers and hunters, and we try to provide them with useful, entertaining articles about where, when and how to enjoy the best hunting and fishing in their state or region. We also cover topics concerning game and fish management, conservation and environmental issues. Most articles should be aimed at outdoorsmen in one particular state. After familiarizing themselves with our magazine(s), writers should query the appropriate state editor (see individual listings) or send to Ken Dunwoody."

GEORGIA SPORTSMAN, Game & Fish Publications, Box 741, Marietta GA 30061. (404)953-9222. Editor: Jimmy Jacobs. See *Game & Fish Publications.*

GREAT PLAINS GAME & FISH, Game & Fish Publications, Box 741, Marietta GA 30061. (404)953-9222. Editor: Nick Gilmore. See *Game & Fish Publications.*

ILLINOIS GAME & FISH, Game & Fish Publications, Inc., Box 741, Marietta GA 30061. (404)953-9222. Editor: Bill Hartlage. See *Game & Fish Publications.*

INDIANA GAME & FISH, Game & Fish Publications, Inc., Box 741, Marietta GA 30061. (404)953-9222. Editor: Ken Freel. See *Game & Fish Publications*.

‡IN-FISHERMAN, 2 In-Fisherman Dr., Brainerd MN 56401. Editor-in-Chief: Doug Stange. Magazine published 7 times/year for "freshwater anglers from beginners to professionals. Most articles focus on bass, walleyes, catfish, panfish, pike, muskies, trout and salmon. Maps, charts, photos, graphs illustrations and cartoons accompany each article. Regular features, include trip tips to fishing hot spots; peak daily and monthly fishing times; a Master Angler award program; editorial commentary; fishery science, industry issues; alternative fish species; reader feedback, a tested recipe; a time for reflection and a humorous offering." Estab. 1975. Circ. 334,000. **Pays on acceptance**. Byline given. Offers 50% kill fee. Buys first rights. Accepts simultaneous submissions. Reports in 2 months on queries.
  • Ranked as one of the best markets for freelance writers in *Writer's Yearbook*'s annual "Top 100 Markets," January 1996.
Nonfiction: How-to, personal experience. Buys 20 mss/year. Query with published clips. Length: 1,500-4,500 words. Pay varies.
Columns/Departments: Length 1,000-1,500 words. Buys 14 mss/year. Query with published clips. Pay varies.
Tips: Need "new information on freshwater fishing techniques. Species-specific presentations that haven't appeared elsewhere." Would like to see "well-written, informative and entertaining treatment of a breakthrough presentation."

IOWA GAME & FISH, Game & Fish Publications, Inc., Box 741, Marietta GA 30061. (404)953-9222. Editor: Bill Hartlage. See *Game & Fish Publications*.

KENTUCKY GAME & FISH, Game & Fish Publications, Inc., Box 741, Marietta GA 30061. (404)953-9222. Editor: Bill Hartlage. See *Game & Fish Publications*.

LOUISIANA GAME & FISH, Game & Fish Publications, Inc., Box 741, Marietta GA 30061. (404)953-9222. Editor: Bob Borgwat. See *Game & Fish Publications*.

THE MAINE SPORTSMAN, P.O. Box 365, Augusta ME 04330. Editor: Harry Vanderweide. 80% freelance written. "Eager to work with new/unpublished writers, but because we run over 30 regular columns, it's hard to get into *The Maine Sportsman* as a beginner." Monthly tabloid. Estab. 1972. Circ. 30,000. Pays during month of publication. Buys first rights. Publishes ms an average of 3 months after acceptance. Byline given. Reports in 2 weeks.
Nonfiction: "We publish only articles about Maine hunting and fishing activities. Any well-written, researched, knowledgeable article about that subject area is likely to be accepted by us." Mostly wants Maine-specific where-to-go articles. Buys 25-40 mss/issue. Submit complete ms. Length: 200-2,000 words. Pays $20-300. Sometimes pays the expenses of writers on assignment.
Reprints: Send typed ms with rights for sale. Pays 100% of amount paid for an original article.
Photos: "We can have illustrations drawn, but prefer 1-3 b&w photos." Submit photos with accompanying ms. Pays $5-50 for b&w print.
Tips: "It's rewarding finding a writer who has a fresh way of looking at ordinary events. Specific where-to-go about Maine is needed."

MICHIGAN OUT-OF-DOORS, P.O. Box 30235, Lansing MI 48909. (517)371-1041. Fax: (517)371-1505. Editor: Kenneth S. Lowe. 50% freelance written. Works with a small number of new/unpublished writers each year. Monthly magazine emphasizing outdoor recreation, especially hunting and fishing, conservation and environmental affairs. Estab. 1947. Circ. 130,000. **Pays on acceptance.** Publishes ms an average of 6 months after acceptance. Byline given. Buys first North American serial rights. Phone queries OK. Submit seasonal/holiday material 6 months in advance. Reports in 1 month. Sample copy for $2. Free writer's guidelines.
Nonfiction: Exposé, historical, how-to, informational, interview, nostalgia, personal experience, personal opinion, photo feature, profile. No humor or poetry. "Stories *must* have a Michigan slant unless they treat a subject of universal interest to our readers." Buys 8 mss/issue. Send complete ms. Length: 1,000-3,000 words. Pays $75 minimum for feature stories. Pays expenses of writers on assignment.

MARKET CONDITIONS are constantly changing! If this is 1998 or later, buy the newest edition of *Writer's Market* at your favorite bookstore or order directly from Writer's Digest Books.

Photos: Purchased with or without accompanying ms. Pays $15 minimum for any size b&w glossy prints; $150 maximum for color (for cover). Offers no additional payment for photos accepted with accompanying ms. Buys one-time rights. Captions preferred.

Tips: "Top priority is placed on true accounts of personal adventures in the out-of-doors—well-written tales of very unusual incidents encountered while hunting, fishing, camping, hiking, etc. The most rewarding aspect of working with freelancers is realizing we had a part in their development. But it's annoying to respond to queries that never produce a manuscript."

MICHIGAN SPORTSMAN, Game & Fish Publications, Inc., Box 741, Marietta GA 30061. (404)953-9222. Editor: Dennis Schmidt. See *Game & Fish Publications*.

MID WEST OUTDOORS, Mid West Outdoors, Ltd., 111 Shore Drive, Hinsdale (Burr Ridge) IL 60521-5885. (708)887-7722. Fax: (708)887-1958. Editor: Gene Laulunen. Monthly tabloid emphasizing fishing, hunting, camping and boating. 100% freelance written. Estab. 1967. Circ. 50,000. Pays on publication. Buys simultaneous rights. Byline given. Submit seasonal material 2 months in advance. Accepts simultaneous submissions. Reports in 3 weeks. Publishes ms an average of 3 months after acceptance. Sample copy for $1. Writer's guidelines for #10 SASE.

Nonfiction: How-to (fishing, hunting, camping in the Midwest) and where-to-go (fishing, hunting, camping within 500 miles of Chicago). "We do not want to see any articles on 'my first fishing, hunting or camping experiences,' 'cleaning my tackle box,' 'tackle tune-up,' or 'catch and release.' " Buys 1,800 unsolicited mss/year. Send complete ms and 1 or 2 photos on 3.5 diskette with ms included. Length: 1,000-1,500 words. Pays $15-30.

Reprints: Send tearsheet of article.

Photos: Offers no additional payment for photos accompanying ms unless used as covers; uses slides and b&w prints. Buys all rights. Captions required.

Columns/Departments: Fishing, Hunting. Open to suggestions for columns/departments. Send complete ms. Pays $25.

Tips: "Break in with a great unknown fishing hole or new technique within 500 miles of Chicago. Where, how, when and why. Know the type of publication you are sending material to."

MID-ATLANTIC GAME & FISH, Game & Fish Publications, Inc., Box 741, Marietta GA 30061. (404)953-9222. Editor: Ken Freel. See *Game & Fish Publications*.

MINNESOTA SPORTSMAN, Game & Fish Publications, Inc., Box 741, Marietta GA 30061. (404)953-9222. Editor: Dennis Schmidt. See *Game & Fish Publications*.

MISSISSIPPI GAME & FISH, Game & Fish Publications, Inc., Box 741, Marietta GA 30061. (404)953-9222. Editor: Bob Borgwat. See *Game & Fish Publications*.

MISSOURI GAME & FISH, Game & Fish Publications, Inc., Box 741, Marietta GA 30061. (404)953-9222. Editor: Bob Borgwat. See *Game & Fish Publications*.

MUSKY HUNTER MAGAZINE, Willow Creek Press, P.O. Box 147, Minocqua WI 54548. (715)356-6301. Fax: (715)358-2807. Editor: Jim Saric. 90% freelance written. Bimonthly magazine on musky fishing. "Serves the vertical market of musky fishing enthusiasts. We're interested in how-to where-to articles." Estab. 1988. Circ. 25,000. Pays on publication. Publishes ms an average of 4 months after acceptance. Byline given. Buys first or one-time rights. Submit seasonal/holiday material 4 months in advance. Reports in 2 months. Sample copy for 9×12 SAE with $1.93 postage. Writer's guidelines for #10 SASE.

Nonfiction: Historical/nostalgic (related only to musky fishing), how-to (modify lures, boats and tackle for musky fishing), personal experience (must be musky fishing experience), technical (fishing equipment), travel (to lakes and areas for musky fishing). Buys 50 mss/year. Send complete ms. Length: 1,000-2,000 words. Pays $100-200 for assigned articles; $50-200 for unsolicited articles. Payment of contributor copies or other premiums negotiable.

Photos: Send photos with submission. Reviews 35mm transparencies and 3×5 prints. Offers no additional payment for photos accepted with ms. Identification of subjects required. Buys one-time rights.

NEW ENGLAND GAME & FISH, Game & Fish Publications, Inc., Box 741, Marietta GA 30061. (404)953-9222. Editor: Steve Carpenteri. See *Game & Fish Publications*.

‡**NEW JERSEY LAKE SURVEY FISHING MAPS GUIDE**, New Jersey Sportsmen's Guides, P.O. Box 100, Somerdale NJ 08083. (609)783-1271. (609)665-8350. Fax: (609)665-8656. Editor: Steve Perrone.30-40% freelance written. Annual magazine covering freshwater lake fishing. "*New Jersey Survey Fishing Maps Guide* is edited for freshwater fishing for trout, bass, perch, catfish and other species. It contains 128 pages and approximately 112 full page maps of the surveyed lakes that illustrate contours, depths, bottom characteristics, shorelines and vegetation present at each location. The guide includes a 10-page chart which describes over

250 fishing lakes in New Jersey. It also covers trout stocked lakes, fishing tips and 'Bass'n Notes.' " Estab. 1989. Circ. 4,500. **Pays on acceptance**. Publishes ms an average of 6 months after acceptance. Byline given. Buys first rights and makes work-for-hire assignments. Editorial lead time 6 months. Sample copy for $11.50 postage paid.

Nonfiction: How-to fishing, freshwater fishing. Length: 500-2,000 words. Pays $75-250 for assigned articles.

Photos: State availability of photos with submission. Reviews transparencies 4×5 slides or 4× prints. Captions, model releases, identification of subjects required. Buys one-time rights.

Tips: "We want queries with published clips of articles describing fishing experiences on New Jersey lakes and ponds."

NEW YORK GAME & FISH, Game & Fish Publications, Inc., Box 741, Marietta GA 30061. (404)953-9222. Editor: Steve Carpenteri. See *Game & Fish Publications*.

NORTH AMERICAN FISHERMAN, Official Publication of North American Fishing Club, 12301 Whitewater Dr., Suite 260, Minnetonka MN 55343. (612)936-0555. Publisher: Rich Sundberg. Editor: Steve Pennaz. 75% freelance written. Magazine published 7 times a year on fresh and saltwater fishing across North America. Estab. 1987. Circ. 475,000. **Pays on acceptance.** Publishes ms an average of 4 months after acceptance. Offers $150 kill fee. Buys first North American serial, one-time and all rights. Submit seasonal/holiday material 6 months in advance. Reports in 1 month. Sample copy for $5 and 9×12 SAE with 6 first-class stamps.

Nonfiction: How-to (species-specific information on how-to catch fish), news briefs on fishing from various state agencies, travel (where to information on first class fishing lodges). Buys 35-40 mss/year. Query by mail. Length: 700-2,100. Pays $100-500.

Photos: Send photos with submission. Additional payment made for photos accepted with ms. Captions and identification of subjects required. Buys one-time rights. Pays up to $200 for inside art, $500 for cover.

Fillers: Facts, newsbreaks. Buys 60/year. Length: 50-100. Pays $35-50.

Tips: "We are looking for news briefs on important law changes, new lakes, etc. Areas most open for freelancers are: full-length features, cover photos and news briefs. Know what subject you are writing about. Our audience of avid fresh and saltwater anglers know how to fish and will see through weak or dated fishing information. Must be on cutting edge for material to be considered."

NORTH AMERICAN WHITETAIL, The Magazine Devoted to the Serious Trophy Deer Hunter, Game & Fish Publications, Inc., 2250 Newmarket Pkwy., Suite 110, Marietta GA 30067. (404)953-9222. Fax: (404)933-9510. Editor: Gordon Whittington. 70% freelance written. Magazine published 8 times/year about hunting trophy-class white-tailed deer in North America, primarily the US. "We provide the serious hunter with highly sophisticated information about trophy-class whitetails and how, when and where to hunt them. We are not a general hunting magazine or a magazine for the very occasional deer hunter." Estab. 1982. Circ. 170,000. Pays 75 days prior to cover date of issue. Publishes ms an average of 6 months after acceptance. Byline given. Offers negotiable kill fee. Buys first North American serial rights. Submit seasonal/holiday material 10 months in advance. Reports in 3 months on mss. Editor prefers to keep queries on file, without notification, until the article can be assigned or author informs of prior sale. Sample copy for $3 and 9×12 SAE with 7 first-class stamps. Writer's guidelines for #10 SASE.

Nonfiction: How-to interview/profile. Buys 50 mss/year. Query. Length: 1,000-3,000 words. Pays $150-400.

Photos: Send photos with submission. Reviews 2×2 transparencies and 8×10 prints. Offers no additional payment for photos accepted with ms. Captions and identification of subjects required. Buys one-time rights.

Columns/Departments: Trails and Tails (nostalgic, humorous or other entertaining styles of deer-hunting material, fictional or nonfictional), 1,400 words. Buys 8 mss/year. Send complete ms. Pays $150.

Tips: "Our articles are written by persons who are deer hunters first, writers second. Our hard-core hunting audience can see through material produced by non-hunters or those with only marginal deer-hunting expertise. We have a continual need for expert profiles/interviews. Study the magazine to see what type of hunting expert it takes to qualify for our use, and look at how those articles have been directed by the writers. Good photography of the interviewee and his hunting results must accompany such pieces."

NORTH CAROLINA GAME & FISH, Game & Fish Publications, Inc., Box 741, Marietta GA 30061. (404)953-9222. Fax: (419)394-7405. Editor: Jeff Samsel. See *Game & Fish Publications*.

OHIO GAME & FISH, Game & Fish Publications, Inc., Box 741, Marietta GA 30061. (404)953-9222. Editor: Steve Carpenteri. See *Game & Fish Publications*.

OKLAHOMA GAME & FISH, Game & Fish Publications, Box 741, Marietta GA 30061. (404)953-9222. Fax: (404)933-9510. Editor: Nick Gilmore. See *Game & Fish Publications*.

‡**OUTDOOR LIFE**, Times Mirror Magazines, Inc., 2 Park Ave., New York NY 10016. (212)779-5000. Fax: (212)686-6877. E-mail: olmagazine@aol.com. Editor: Stephen Byers. Executive Editor: Will Bourne. 95% freelance written. Monthly magazine covering hunting and fishing. Estab. 1890. Circ. 1,500,000. **Pays on acceptance.** Publishes ms an average of 1 year after acceptance. Byline given. Buys first North American serial rights. Submit seasonal/holiday material 1 year in advance. Reports in 1 month on queries; 2 months on mss. Writer's guidelines for #10 SASE.

Nonfiction: Book excerpts, essays, how-to (must cover hunting, fishing or related outdoor activities), interview/profile, new product, personal experience, photo feature, technical, travel. No articles that are too general in scope—need to write specifically. Buys 400 mss/year. "Query first; photos are *very important.*" Length: 800-3,000 words. Pays $350-600 for 1,000-word features and regionals; $900-1,200 for 2,000-word or longer national features.

Reprints: Accepts previously published submissions on occasion.

Photos: Send photos with submission. Reviews 35mm transparencies and 8×10 b&w prints. Offers variable payment. Captions and identification of subjects required. Buys one-time rights. "May offer to buy photos after first use if considered good and have potential to be used with other articles in the future (file photos)." Pays $100 for ¼ page color to $800 for 2-page spread in color; $1,000 for covers. All photos must be stamped with name and address.

Columns/Departments: This Happened to Me (true-to-life, personal outdoor adventure, harrowing experience), approximately 300 words. Buys 12 mss/year. Pays $50. Only those published will be notified.

Fillers: National and International newsbreaks (200 words maximum). Newsbreaks and do-it-yourself for hunters and fishermen. Buys unlimited number/year. Length: 1,000 words maximum. Payment varies.

Tips: "It is best for freelancers to break in by writing features for one of the regional sections—East, Midwest, South, West. These are where-to-go oriented and run from 800-1,500 words. Writers must send one-page query with photos."

‡**PENNSYLVANIA ANGLER**, Pennsylvania Fish and Boat Commission, P.O. Box 67000, Harrisburg PA 17106-7000. (717)657-4518. E-mail: 76247.624.@compuserve.com. Editor: Art Michaels. 80% freelance written. Prefers to work with published/established writers but works with a few unpublished writers every year. Monthly magazine covering fishing and related conservation topics in Pennsylvania. Circ. 40,000. Pays 2 months after acceptance. Publishes ms an average of 8 months after acceptance. Byline given. Rights purchased vary. Submit seasonal/holiday material 8 months in advance. Query. Reports in 2 weeks on queries; 2 months on mss. Sample copy for 9×12 SAE with 4 first-class stamps. Writer's guidelines for #10 SASE.

Nonfiction: How-to, where-to, technical. No saltwater or hunting material. Buys 120 mss/year. Query. Length: 500-3,000 words. Pays $25-300.

Photos: Send photos with submission. Reviews 35mm and larger transparencies and 8×10 b&w prints. Offers no additional payment for photos accepted with ms. Captions, model releases and identification of subjects required. Also reviews photos separately. Rights purchased and rates vary.

Tips: "Our mainstays are how-tos, where-tos and conservation pieces."

PENNSYLVANIA GAME & FISH, Game & Fish Publications, Inc., Box 741, Marietta GA 30061. (404)953-9222. Editor: Steve Carpenteri. See *Game & Fish Publications.*

PETERSEN'S HUNTING, Petersen Publishing Co., 6420 Wilshire Blvd., Los Angeles CA 90048. (213)782-2184. Editor: Todd Smith. Managing Editor: Duke Anderson. 40% freelance written. Works with a small number of new/unpublished writers each year. Monthly magazine covering sport hunting. "We are a 'how-to' magazine devoted to all facets of sport hunting, with the intent to make our readers more knowledgeable, more successful and safer hunters." Circ. 325,000. **Pays on acceptance.** Publishes ms an average of 9 months after acceptance. Byline given. Offers $50 kill fee. Buys all rights. Submit seasonal/holiday queries 9 months in advance. Reports in 2 weeks. Free sample copy and writer's guidelines covering format, sidebars and computer disks available on request.

Nonfiction: General interest, historical/nostalgic, how-to (on hunting techniques), travel. Special issues: Hunting Annual (August). Buys 30 mss/year. Query. Length: 2,000 words. Pays $350 minimum.

Photos: Send photos with submission. Reviews 35mm transparencies and 8×10 b&w prints. Offers no additional payment for b&w photos accepted with ms; offers $50-250/color photo. Captions, model releases, identification of subjects required. Buys one-time rights.

ROCKY MOUNTAIN GAME & FISH, Game & Fish Publications, Inc., Box 741, Marietta GA 30061. Editor: Burt Carey. See *Game & Fish Publications.*

SAFARI MAGAZINE, The Journal of Big Game Hunting, Safari Club International, 4800 W. Gates Pass Rd., Tucson AZ 85745. (520)620-1220. Fax: (520)617-0233. Director of Publications/Editor: William R. Quimby. Contact: Elaine Cummings, manuscripts editor. 90% freelance written. Bimonthly club journal covering international big game hunting and wildlife conservation. Circ. 30,000. Pays on publication. Publishes ms an average of 18 months after acceptance. Byline given. Offers $100 kill fee. Buys all rights.

Submit seasonal/holiday material 1 year in advance. Reports in 2 weeks on queries; 6 weeks on mss. Sample copy for $4. Writer's guidelines for SASE.

Nonfiction: Photo feature (wildlife), technical (firearms, hunting techniques, etc.). Buys 72 mss/year. Query or send complete ms. Length: 1,500-2,500 words. Pays $200 for professional writers, lower rates if not professional.

Photos: State availability of photos with query or ms, or send photos with query or ms. Payment depends on size in magazine. Pays $45 for b&w; $50-150 color. Captions, model releases, identification of subjects required. Buys one-time rights.

Tips: "Study the magazine. Send manuscripts and photo packages with query. Make it appeal to knowledgeable, world-traveled big game hunters. Features on conservation contributions from big game hunters around the world are open to freelancers. We have enough stories on first-time African safaris and North American hunting. We need South American and Asian hunting stories, plus stories dealing with hunting and conservation, especially as it applies to our organization and members."

SALT WATER SPORTSMAN MAGAZINE, 77 Franklin St., Boston MA 02110. (617)338-2300. Fax: (617)338-2309. Website: Waterway/http://www.iwol.com/show.me/SWS. Editor: Barry Gibson. Emphasizes saltwater fishing. 85% freelance written. Works with a small number of new/unpublished writers each year. Monthly magazine. Circ. 150,000. **Pays on acceptance.** Publishes ms an average of 5 months after acceptance. Byline given. Buys first North American serial rights. Offers 100% kill fee. Submit seasonal material 8 months in advance. Reports in 1 month. Sample copy and writer's guidelines for 9×12 SAE with 10 first-class stamps.
   ● Ranked as one of the best markets for freelance writers in *Writer's Yearbook*'s annual "Top 100 Markets," January 1996.

Nonfiction: How-to, personal experience, technical, travel (to fishing areas). "Readers want solid how-to, where-to information written in an enjoyable, easy-to-read style. Personal anecdotes help the reader identify with the writer." Prefers new slants and specific information. Query. "It is helpful if the writer states experience in salt water fishing and any previous related articles. We want one, possibly two well-explained ideas per query letter—not merely a listing. Good pictures with query often help sell the idea." Buys 100 mss/year. Length: 1,200-1,500 words. Pays $350 and up. Sometimes pays the expenses of writers on assignment.

Reprints: Send tearsheet of article and information about when and where the article previously appeared. Pay negotiable.

Photos: Purchased with or without accompanying ms. Captions required. Uses color slides. Pays $1,000 minimum for 35mm, 2¼×2¼ or 8×10 transparencies for cover. Offers additional payment for photos accepted with accompanying ms.

Columns/Departments: Sportsman's Workbench (how to make fishing or fishing-related boating equipment), 100 or more words.

Tips: "There are a lot of knowledgeable fishermen/budding writers out there who could be valuable to us with a little coaching. Many don't think they can write a story for us, but they'd be surprised. We work with writers. Shorter articles that get to the point which are accompanied by good, sharp photos are hard for us to turn down. Having to delete unnecessary wordage—conversation, clichés, etc.—that writers feel is mandatory is annoying. Often they don't devote enough attention to specific fishing information."

SOUTH CAROLINA GAME & FISH, Game & Fish Publications, Inc., Box 741, Marietta GA 30061. (404)953-9222. Editor: Jeff Samsel. See *Game & Fish Publications*.

SOUTH CAROLINA WILDLIFE, P.O. Box 167, Rembert Dennis Bldg., Columbia SC 29202-0167. (803)734-3972. Editor: John Davis. Managing Editor: Linda Renshaw. Bimonthly magazine for South Carolinians interested in wildlife and outdoor activities. 75% freelance written. Estab. 1954. Circ. 60,000. Byline given. **Pays on acceptance.** Publishes ms an average of 6 months after acceptance. Buys first rights. Free sample copy. Reports in 2 months.

Nonfiction: Articles on outdoor South Carolina with an emphasis on preserving and protecting our natural resources. "Realize that the topic must be of interest to South Carolinians and that we must be able to justify using it in a publication published by the state department of natural resources—so if it isn't directly about outdoor recreation, a certain plant or animal, it must be somehow related to the environment and conservation. Readers prefer a broad mix of outdoor related topics (articles that illustrate the beauty of South Carolina's outdoors and those that help the reader get more for his/her time, effort, and money spent in outdoor recreation). These two general areas are the ones we most need. Subjects vary a great deal in topic, area and style, but must all have a common ground in the outdoor resources and heritage of South Carolina. Review back issues and query with a one-page outline citing sources, giving ideas for photographs, explaining justification and giving an example of the first two paragraphs." Does not need any column material. Generally does not seek photographs. The publisher assumes no responsibility for unsolicited material. Buys 25-30 mss/year. Length: 1,000-3,000 words. Pays an average of $200-400/article depending upon length and subject matter.

Tips: "We need more writers in the outdoor field who take pride in the craft of writing and put a real effort toward originality and preciseness in their work. Query on a topic we haven't recently done. Frequent mistakes made by writers in completing an article are failure to check details and go in-depth on a subject."

‡**SPORT FISHING, The Magazine of Saltwater Fishing**, 330 W. Canton Ave., Winter Park FL 32789-7061. (407)628-4802. Fax: (407)628-7061. E-mail: sportfish@worldzine.com. Contact: Doug Olander, editor-in-chief. Managing Editor: Dave Ferrell. 60% freelance written. Magazine covering offshore sport fishing. Estab. 1986. Circ. 150,000. Pays within 6 weeks of acceptance. Byline given. Offers $100 kill fee. Buys first North American serial or one-time rights. Submit seasonal/holiday material 3 months in advance. Accepts simultaneous submission. Reports in 2 months. Sample copy and writer's guidelines for SASE.
Nonfiction: How-to, humor, new product, personal experience, photo feature, technical, travel (all on sport fishing). Buys 32-40 mss/year. Query with or without clips, or send complete ms. Length: 1,500-4,500 words. Pays $150-600 for assigned articles.
Photos: Send photos with submission. Reviews transparencies. Offers $50-500/photo. Identification of subjects required. Buys one-time rights.
Columns/Departments: Fish Tales (humorous sport fishing anecdotes), 800-1,500 words; Rigging (how-to rigging for sport fishing), 800-1,500 words; Technique (how-to technique for sport fishing), 800-1,500 words. Buys 8-24 mss/year. Send complete ms. Pays $200.

SPORTS AFIELD, 250 W. 55th St., New York NY 10019-5201. (212)649-4000. Editor-in-Chief: Terry McDonell. Executive Editor: Fred Kesting. 20% freelance written. Magazine for the outdoor enthusiast with special interest in fishing and hunting. Covers a wide range of outdoor interests such as: boating, off-road, archery, survival, conservation, tackle, new gear, shooting sports, camping. Published 10 times/year. Estab. 1887. Circ. 450,000. Buys first North American serial rights for features. **Pays on acceptance.** Publishes ms an average of 6 months after acceptance. Byline given. "Our magazine is seasonal and material submitted should be in accordance. Fishing in spring and summer; hunting in the fall." Submit seasonal material 9 months in advance. Reports in 2 months. Query or submit complete ms. SASE for reply or writer's guidelines.
Nonfiction: "Informative how-to articles with emphasis on product and service and personal experiences with good photos on hunting, fishing, camping, conservation, and environmental issues (limited where-to-go) related to hunting and fishing. We want first-class writing and reporting." Buys 15-17 unsolicited mss/year. Length: 500-2,500 words.
Photos: "For photos without ms, duplicates of 35mm color transparencies preferred."
Fiction: Adventure, humor, nostalgia (if related to hunting and fishing).
Fillers: Send to *Almanac* editor. For outdoor tips specifically for hunters, fishermen and campers, unusual, how-to and nature items. Payment on publication. Buys all rights.
Tips: "Read a recent copy of *Sports Afield* so you know the market you're writing for. Manuscript *must* be available on disk."

TENNESSEE SPORTSMAN, Game & Fish Publications, Box 741, Marietta GA 30061. (404)953-9222. Editor: Jeff Samsel. See *Game & Fish Publications*.

TEXAS SPORTSMAN, Game & Fish Publications, Inc., Box 741, Marietta GA 30061. (404)953-9222. Editor: Nick Gilmore. See *Game & Fish Publications*.

TIDE MAGAZINE, Coastal Conservation Association, 220W, 4801 Woodway, Houston TX 77056. (713)626-4222. Fax: (713)961-3801. Editor: Doug Pike. Bimonthly magazine on saltwater fishing and conservation of marine resources. Estab. 1977. Circ. 40,000. Pays on publication. Byline given. Buys one-time rights. Submit seasonal material 6 months in advance. Reports in 1 month.
Nonfiction: Essays, exposé, general interest, historical/nostalgic, humor, opinion, personal experience and travel. Buys 30 mss/year. Query with published clips. Length: 1,200-1,500 words. Pays $300 for ms/photo package.
Photos: Reviews 35mm transparencies and 8×10 b&w prints. Offers no additional payment for photos accepted with ms. Captions required. Buys one-time rights. Pays $25 for b&w, $50 for color inside.

TRAPPER & PREDATOR CALLER, Krause Publications Inc., 700 E. State St., Iola WI 54990. (715)445-2214. Fax: (715)445-4087. Editor: Gordy Krahn. 90% freelance written. Monthly tabloid covers trapping, predator calling and muzzleloading. "Our editorial goal is to entertain and educate our readers with national and regional articles that promote trapping." Estab. 1975. Circ. 35,000. Pays on publication. Offers $50 kill fee. Buys first North American serial rights. Submit seasonal material 6 months in advance. Reports in 2 weeks. *Writer's Market* recommends allowing 2 months for reply. Free sample copy and writer's guidelines.
Nonfiction: How-to, humor, interview/profile, new product, opinion and personal experience. Buys 60 mss/year. Query with or without published clips, or send complete ms. Length: 1,200-2,500 words. Pays $80-250 for assigned articles; $40-200 for unsolicited articles.
Photos: Send photos with submission. Reviews prints. Offers no additional payment for photos accepted with ms. Captions and identification of subjects required. Buys one-time rights.
Fillers: Facts, gags to be illustrated by cartoonist, newsbreaks and short humor. Buys 60/year. Length: 200-800 words. Pays $25-80.
Tips: "We are always looking for new ideas and fresh material on trapping, predator calling and black powder hunting."

TURKEY CALL, Wild Turkey Center, P.O. Box 530, Edgefield SC 29824-0530. (803)637-3106. Fax: (803)637-0034. Editor: Jay Langston. Contact: Camille Roberegé-Myers, publishing assistant. 50-60% freelance written. Eager to work with new/unpublished writers and photographers. Bimonthly educational magazine for members of the National Wild Turkey Federation. Estab. 1973. Circ. 120,000. Buys one-time rights. Byline given. **Pays on acceptance.** Publishes ms an average of 6 months after acceptance. Reports in 1 month. Queries required. Submit complete package. Wants original mss only. Sample copy for $3 and 9×12 SAE. Writer's guidelines for #10 SASE.

Nonfiction: Feature articles dealing with the hunting and management of the American wild turkey. Must be accurate information and must appeal to national readership of turkey hunters and wildlife management experts. No poetry or first-person accounts of unremarkable hunting trips. May use some fiction that educates or entertains in a special way. Length: up 2,500 words. Pays $100 for short fillers of 600-700 words, $200-500 for illustrated features.

Photos: "We want quality photos submitted with features." Art illustrations also acceptable. "We are using more and more inside color illustrations." For b&w, prefer 8×10 glossies, but 5×7 OK. Transparencies of any size are acceptable. No typical hunter-holding-dead-turkey photos or setups using mounted birds or domestic turkeys. Photos with how-to stories must make the techniques clear (example: how to make a turkey call; how to sculpt or carve a bird in wood). Pays $35 minimum for one-time rights on b&w photos and simple art illustrations; up to $100 for inside color, reproduced any size; $200-400 for covers.

Tips: "The writer should simply keep in mind that the audience is 'expert' on wild turkey management, hunting, life history and restoration/conservation history. He/she *must know the subject*. We are buying more third-person, more fiction, more humor—in an attempt to avoid the 'predictability trap' of a single subject magazine."

VIRGINIA GAME & FISH, Game & Fish Publications, Inc., Box 741, Marietta GA 30061. (404)953-9222. Editor: Jeff Samsel. See *Game & Fish Publications*.

WASHINGTON-OREGON GAME & FISH, Game & Fish Publications, Inc., Box 741, Marietta GA 30061. Editor: Burt Carey. See *Game & Fish Publications*.

WEST VIRGINIA GAME & FISH, Game & Fish Publications, Inc., Box 741, Marietta GA 30061. (404)953-9222. Editor: Ken Freel. See *Game & Fish Publications*.

WESTERN OUTDOORS, 3197-E Airport Loop, Costa Mesa CA 92626. (714)546-4370. E-mail: woutdoors@aol.com. Editor: Jack Brown. 60% freelance written. Works with a small number of new/unpublished writers each year. Emphasizes fishing, boating for California, Oregon, Washington, Baja California, and Alaska. Publishes 9 issues/year. Estab. 1961. Circ. 100,000. **Pays on acceptance.** Publishes ms an average of 6 months after acceptance. Buys first North American serial rights. Submit seasonal material 6 months in advance. Reports in 2 weeks. Sample copy for $2, OWAA members, $1. Writer's guidelines for #10 SASE.
   • *Western Outdoors* now emphasizes freshwater and saltwater fishing and boating exclusively. Area of coverage is limited to far west states and Baja California.

Nonfiction: Where-to (catch more fish, improve equipment, etc.), how-to informational, photo feature. "We do not accept fiction, poetry." Buys 45-55 assigned mss/year. Query in writing. Length: 1,000-1,500 words. Pays average $450.

Photos: Purchased with accompanying ms. Captions required. Prefers professional quality 35mm slides. Offers no additional payment for photos accepted with accompanying ms. Pays $250 for covers.

Tips: "Provide a complete package of photos, map, trip facts and manuscript written according to our news feature format. Excellence of color photo selections make a sale more likely. Include sketches of fishing patterns and techniques to guide our illustrators. Graphics are important. The most frequent mistake made by writers in completing an article for us is that they don't follow our style. Our guidelines are quite clear."

WESTERN SPORTSMAN, 140 Avenue F North, Saskatoon, Saskatchewan S7L 1V8 Canada. (306)665-6302. Fax: (306)244-8859. E-mail: copi@sasknet.sk.ca. Editor: George Gruenefeld. 90% freelance written. Bimonthly magazine for fishermen, hunters, campers and others interested in outdoor recreation. "Note that our coverage area is Alberta, Saskatchewan and Manitoba." Estab. 1968. Circ. 29,000. Rights purchased vary with author and material. Usually buys first North American serial or second serial (reprint) rights. Byline given. Pays on publication. "We try to include as much information as possible on all subjects in each edition. Therefore, we often publish fishing articles in our winter issues along with a variety of winter stories." Reports in 1 month. Sample copy for $4 and 9×12 SAE with 4 IRCs (US). Free writer's guidelines with SASE.
   • *Western Sportsman* now accepts articles and news items relating to British Columbia, Yukon and Northwest Territories hunting and fishing.

Nonfiction: "It is necessary that all articles can identify with our coverage area. We are interested in manuscripts from writers who have experienced an interesting fishing or hunting experience. We also publish other informational pieces as long as they relate to our coverage area. We are more interested in articles which tell about the average guy living on beans, guiding his own boat, stalking his game and generally doing his own thing in our part of Western Canada than a story describing a well-to-do outdoorsman traveling by motorhome, staying at an expensive lodge with guides doing everything for him except catching the fish or shooting the big game animal. The articles that are submitted to us need to be prepared in a knowledgeable way and include more information than the actual fish catch or animal or bird kill. Discuss the terrain, the people involved on the trip, the water or weather conditions, the costs, the planning that went into the trip, the equipment and other data closely associated with the particular event. We're always looking for new writers." Buys 60 mss/year. Submit complete ms and SASE or IRCs. Length: 1,500-2,000 words.

Reprints: Send typed ms with rights for sale noted and information about when and where the article previously appeared.

Photos: Photos purchased with ms with no additional payment. Also purchased without ms. Pays $150 for 35mm or larger transparency for front cover.

WISCONSIN SPORTSMAN, Game & Fish Publications, Inc., Box 741, Marietta GA 30061. Editor: Dennis Schmidt. See *Game & Fish Publications*.

Martial Arts

BLACK BELT, Rainbow Publications, Inc., 24715 Ave. Rockefeller, Valencia CA 91355. (805)257-4066. Fax: (805)257-3028. Executive Editor: Jim Coleman. 80-90% freelance written. Works with a small number of new/unpublished writers each year. Monthly magazine emphasizing martial arts for both practitioner and layman. Estab. 1961. Circ. 100,000. Pays on publication. Publishes ms an average of 5 months after acceptance. Buys first North American serial rights, retains right to republish. Submit seasonal/holiday material 6 months in advance. Reports in 3 weeks.

Nonfiction: Exposé, how-to, informational, interview, new product, personal experience, profile, technical, travel. Buys 8-9 mss/issue. Query or send complete ms. Length: 1,200 words minimum. Pays $100-300.

Photos: Very seldom buys photos without accompanying mss. Captions required. Total purchase price for ms includes payment for photos. Model releases required.

Fiction: Historical, modern day. Buys 1-2 mss/year. Query. Pays $100-150.

Tips: "We also publish an annual yearbook and special issues periodically. The yearbook includes our annual 'Black Belt Hall of Fame' inductees."

INSIDE KUNG-FU, The Ultimate In Martial Arts Coverage!, Unique Publications, 4201 Vanowen Place, Burbank CA 91505. (818)845-2656. Fax: (818)845-7761. Editor: Dave Cater. 75% freelance written. Monthly magazine covering martial arts for those with "traditional, modern, athletic and intellectual tastes. The magazine slants toward little-known martial arts, and little-known aspects of established martial arts." Estab. 1973. Circ. 100,000. Pays on publication date on magazine cover. Publishes ms an average of 6 months after acceptance. Byline given. Buys first North American serial rights. Submit seasonal/holiday material 4 months in advance. Accepts simultaneous submissions. Reports in 1 month on queries; 2 months on mss. Sample copy for $2.95 and 9×12 SAE with 5 first-class stamps. Writer's guidelines for #10 SASE.

● *Inside Kung-Fu* is looking for external-type articles (fighting, weapons, multiple hackers).

Nonfiction: Exposé (topics relating to the martial arts), historical/nostalgic, how-to (primarily technical materials), cultural/philosophical, interview/profile, personal experience, photo feature, technical. "Articles must be technically or historically accurate." No "sports coverage, first-person articles or articles which constitute personal aggrandizement." Buys 120 mss/year. Query or send complete ms. Length: 8-10 pages, typewritten and double-spaced.

Reprints: Send tearsheet of article or short story or typed ms with rights for sale noted and information about when and where the article previously appeared. No payment.

Photos: Send photos with accompanying ms. Reviews b&w contact sheets, b&w negatives, 5×7 or 8×10 b&w prints. Offers no additional payment for photos. Captions and model release required.

Fiction: Adventure, historical, humorous, mystery, suspense. "Fiction must be short (1,000-2,000 words) and relate to the martial arts. We buy very few fiction pieces." Publishes novel excerpts. Buys 2-3 mss/year.

Tips: "The writer may have a better chance of breaking in at our publication with short articles and fillers since smaller pieces allow us to gauge individual ability, but we're flexible—quality writers get published, period. The most frequent mistakes made by writers in completing an article for us are ignoring photo requirements and model releases (always number one—and who knows why? All requirements are spelled out in writer's guidelines)."

JOURNAL OF ASIAN MARTIAL ARTS, Via Media Publishing Co., 821 W. 24th St., Erie PA 16502-2523. (814)455-9517. Fax: (814)838-7811. Editor: Michael A. DeMarco. 90% freelance written. Quarterly magazine covering "all historical and cultural aspects related to Asian martial arts, offering a mature, well-rounded view of this uniquely fascinating subject. Although the journal treats the subject with academic accuracy (references at end), writing need not lose the reader!" Estab. 1991. Pays on publication. Publishes ms an average of 1 year after acceptance. Byline given. Buys first rights and second serial (reprint) rights.

Submit seasonal/holiday material 6 months in advance. Reports in 1 month on queries; 2 months on mss. Sample copy for $10. Writer's guidelines for #10 SASE.

Nonfiction: Essays, exposé, historical/nostalgic, how-to (martial art techniques and materials, e.g., weapons, symbols), interview/profile, personal experience, photo feature (place or person), religious, technical, travel. "All articles should be backed with solid, reliable reference material. No articles overburdened with technical/foreign/scholarly vocabulary, or material slanted as indirect advertising or for personal aggrandizement." Buys 30 mss/year. Query. Length: 2,000-10,000 words. Pays $150-500 for unsolicited articles.

Photos: State availability of photos with submission. Reviews contact sheets, negatives, transparencies, prints. Offers no additional payment for photos accepted with ms. Model releases and identification of subjects required. Buys one-time and reprint rights.

Columns/Departments: Location (city, area, specific site, Asian or Non-Asian, showing value for martial arts, researchers, history); Media Review (film, book, video, museum for aspects of academic and artistic interest). Buys 16 mss/year. Query. Length: 1,000-2,500 words. Pays $50-200.

Fiction: Adventure, historical, humorous, slice-of-life vignettes, translation. "We are not interested in material that does not focus on martial arts culture." Buys 2 mss/year. Query. Length: 1,000-10,000 words. Pays $50-500 or in copies.

Poetry: Avant-garde, free verse, haiku, light verse, traditional, translation. "No poetry that does not focus on martial art culture." Buys 4 poems/year. Submit maximum 10 poems. Pays $10-100 or in copies.

Fillers: Anecdotes, facts, gags to be illustrated by cartoonist, newsbreaks, short humor. Buys 10/year. Length: 25-500 words. Pays $1-50 in copies.

Tips: "Always query before sending a manuscript. We are open to varied types of articles; most however require a strong academic grasp of Asian culture. For those not having this background, we suggest trying a museum review, or interview, where authorities can be questioned, quoted and provide supportive illustrations. We especially desire articles/reports from Asia, with photo illustrations, particularly of a martial art style, so readers can visually understand the unique attributes of that style, its applications, evolution, etc. 'Location' and media reports are special areas that writers may consider, especially if they live in a location of martial art significance."

KARATE/KUNG FU ILLUSTRATED, Rainbow Publications, Inc., P.O. Box 918, Santa Clarita CA 91380. (805)257-4066. Fax: (805)257-3028. Website: http://www.blackbeltmag.com. Executive Editor: Robert Young. 70% freelance written. Bimonthly consumer magazine covering martial arts. "KKI presents factual historical accounts of the development of the martial arts, along with technical pieces on self-defense. We use only material from which readers can learn." Estab. 1969. Circ. 35,000. Pays on publication. Publishes ms an average of 6 months after acceptance. Byline given. Buys all rights. Editorial lead time 3 months. Submit seasonal material 4 months in advance. Accepts simultaneous submissions. Reports in 2 weeks on queries; 1 month on mss. Sample copy for 9×12 SAE and 5 first-class stamps. Writer's guidelines free on request.

  • *Karate/Kung Fu Illustrated* now publishes "Black Belt for Kids," a separate section currently attached to the main magazine. Query with article ideas for young martial artists.

Nonfiction: Book excerpts, general interest (martial arts), historical/nostalgic (martial arts development), how-to (technical articles on specific kicks, punches, etc.), interview/profile (only with *major* martial artist), new products (for annual product review), travel (to Asian countries for martial arts training/research), comparisons of various styles and techniques. "No fiction or self-promotional pieces." Buys 30 mss/year. Query. Length: 1,000-3,000 words. Pays $100-150.

Photos: Freelancers should send photos with submission. Reviews contact sheets, negatives and 5×7 prints. Offers no additional payment for photos accepted with ms. Captions, model releases and identification of subjects required.

Columns/Departments: Bushido (essays explaining martial arts philosophy), 1,000-1,500 words; Counterkicks (letters to the editor). Buys 12 mss/year. Query. Pays $0-75.

Tips: "You need not be an expert in a specific martial art to write about it. But if you are not an expert, find one and use his knowledge to support your statements. Also, references to well-known books can help lend credence to the work of unknown writers. Inexperienced writers should begin by writing about a subject they know well. For example, if you study karate, start by writing about karate. Don't study karate for one year, then try to break in to a martial arts magazine by writing about Kung fu, because we already have Kung fu practitioners who write about that."

MARTIAL ARTS TRAINING, Rainbow Publications, P.O. Box 918, Santa Clarita CA 91380-9018. (805)257-4066. Fax: (805)257-3028. E-mail: iczer1@anime-central.com. Website: http://www.blackbeltmag.com. Executive Editor: Douglas Jeffrey. 75% freelance written. Works with many new/unpublished writers each year. Bimonthly magazine about martial arts training. Estab. 1973. Circ. 35,000. Pays on publication. Publishes ms an average of 6 months after acceptance. Buys all rights. Submit seasonal material 4 months in advance. Reports in 1 month. Writer's guidelines for #10 SASE.

Nonfiction: How-to (training related features). Buys 30-40 unsolicited mss/year. Query. Length: 1,500-2,500 words. Pays $100-175.

Photos: "While we accept b&w photos, we prefer color prints. Please include the negatives." Model releases required. Buys all rights.

Tips: "I'm looking for how-to, nuts-and-bolts training stories that are martial arts related. Weight training, plyometrics, speed drills, cardiovascular workouts, agility drills, etc. Our magazine covers fitness and conditioning, not the martial arts techniques themselves."

T'AI CHI, Leading International Magazine of T'ai Chi Ch'uan, Wayfarer Publications, P.O. Box 26156, Los Angeles CA 90026. (213)665-7773. Fax: (213)665-1627. E-mail: taichi@tai-chi.com. Website: http://www.tai-chi.com. Editor/Publisher: Marvin Smalheiser. 90% freelance written. Bimonthly consumer magazine covering T'ai Chi Ch'uan as a martial art and for Health & Fitness. "Covers T'ai Chi Ch'uan and other internal martials, plus qigong and Chinese health, nutrition and philosophical disciplines. Readers are practitioners or laymen interested in developing skills and insight for self-defense, health and self-improvement." Estab. 1977. Circ. 30,000. Pays on publication. Publishes ms an average of 5 months after acceptance. Byline given. Buys first North American serial rights. Editorial lead time 3 months. Submit seasonal material 6 months in advance. Reports in 3 weeks on queries; 3 months on mss. Sample copy for $3.50. Writer's guidelines for #10 SASE.

   • This publication needs more material but it must be related to the needs of its readers.

Nonfiction: Book excerpts, essays, how-to (on T'ai Chi Ch'uan, qigong and related Chinese disciplines), interview/profile, personal experience. "Do not want articles promoting an individual, system or school." Buys 50-60 mss/year. Query or send complete ms. Length: 1,200-4,500 words. Pays $75-500. Sometimes pays expenses of writers on assignment.

Photos: Send photos with submission. Reviews color transparencies and color or b&w 3×5 prints. Offers no additional payment for photos accepted with mss but overall payment takes into consideration the number and quality of photos. Captions, model releases and identification of subjects required. Buys one-time and reprint rights.

Poetry: Free verse, light verse, traditional. "No poetry unrelated to our content." Buys 6 poems/year. Submit maximum 3 poems. Length: 12-30 lines. Pays $25-50.

Tips: "Think and write for practitioners and laymen who want information and insight and who are trying to work through problems to improve skills and their health. No promotional material."

Miscellaneous

‡**COLLEGE SPORTS MAGAZINE,** CS Communications Sports Group, 1 Salem Square, Suite 201E, Whitehouse Station NJ 08889. (908)534-5390. Fax: (908)534-5308. E-mail: fansforum@aol.com. Editor: Norb Garrett. Contact: John Roach, managing editor. 60% freelance written. Monthly magazine covering college sports. "*College Sports* is intended to entertain, educate and satisfy the fan of intercollegiate sports. We want our stories to be so interesting that a die-hard Kentucky fan will be as interested in a story on the Wildcats as one on a kid from UCLA." Estab. 1992. Circ. 200,000. Pays on publication. Publishes ms an average of 2 months after acceptance. Byline given. Offers 33% kill fee. Buys first North American serial second serial (reprint) rights. Editorial lead time 6 weeks. Submit seasonal material 6 months in advance. Sample copy and writer's guidelines free on request.

Nonfiction: Interview/profile. Special issues include football and basketball previews, NFL Draft and NBA Draft previews. Buys 80 mss/year. Query with published clips. Length: 800-2,400 words. Pays 30¢/word. Sometimes pays expenses of writers on assignment.

Photos: State availability of photos with submission. Reviews transparencies, prints. Negotiates payment individually. Captions required. Buys one-time rights.

Tips: "Fax us the unusual story—not one we might already know is reported in the national media. Small school human-interest stories are most likely to be used."

‡**POLO,** Polo Publications, Inc., 3500 Fairlane Farms Rd., Suite 9, Wellington FL 33414. (407)793-9524. Fax: (407)793-9576. Editor: Peter Rizzo. Contact: Gwen Rizzo, managing editor. Magazine published 10 times/year on polo—the sport and lifestyle. "Our readers are an affluent group. Most are well-educated, well-read and highly sophisticated." Circ. 6,500. **Pays on acceptance.** Publishes ms an average 4 months after acceptance. Kill fee varies. Buys first North American serial rights and makes work-for-hire assignments. Submit seasonal/holiday material 3 months in advance. Accepts simultaneous submissions. Reports in 3 months. Writer's guidelines for #10 SAE with 2 first-class stamps.

Nonfiction: Gwen Rizzo, senior editor. Historical/nostalgic, interview/profile, personal experience, photo feature, technical, travel. Buys 20 mss/year. Query with published clips or send complete ms. Length: 800-3,000 words. Pays $150-400 for assigned articles; $100-300 for unsolicited articles. Sometimes pays expenses of writers on assignment.

Reprints: Send tearsheet of article and information about when and where the article previously appeared. Pays 50% of amount paid for an original article.

Photos: State availability of photos or send photos with submission. Reviews contact sheets, transparencies, prints. Offers $20-150/photo. Captions required. Buys one-time rights.

Columns/Departments: Yesteryears (historical pieces), 500 words; Profiles (clubs and players), 800-1,000 words. Buys 15 mss/year. Query with published clips. Pays $100-300.

Tips: "Query us on a personality or club profile or historic piece or, if you know the game, state availability to cover a tournament. Keep in mind that ours is a sophisticated, well-educated audience."

PRIME TIME SPORTS & FITNESS, GND Prime Time Publishing, P.O. Box 6097, Evanston IL 60204. Fax: (847)864-1206. Editor: Dennis A. Dorner. Managing Editor: Steven Ury. 80% freelance written. Eager to work with new/unpublished writers. Monthly magazine covering seasonal pro sports and racquet and health club sports and fitness. Estab. 1974. Circ. 35,000. Pays on publication. Publishes ms an average of 6 months after acceptance. Byline given. Buys all rights; will assign back to author in 85% of cases. Submit seasonal/holiday material 6 months in advance. Accepts simultaneous submissions. Reports in 6 months. Sample copy on request.

Nonfiction: Book excerpts (fitness and health), exposé (in tennis, fitness, racquetball, health clubs, diets), adult (slightly risqué and racy fitness), how-to (expert instructional pieces on any area of coverage), humor (large market for funny pieces on health clubs and fitness), inspirational (on how diet and exercise combine to bring you a better body, self), interview/profile, new product, opinion (only from recognized sources who know what they are talking about), personal experience (definitely—humor), photo feature (on related subjects); technical (on exercise and sport), travel (related to fitness, tennis camps, etc.), news reports (on racquetball, handball, tennis, running events). Special issues: Swimsuit and Resort Issue (March); Baseball Preview (April); Summer Fashion (July); Pro Football Preview (August); Fall Fashion (October); Ski Issue (November); Christmas Gifts and related articles (December). "We love short articles that get to the point. Nationally oriented big events and national championships. No articles on local only tennis and racquetball tournaments without national appeal." Buys 150 mss/year. Length: 2,000 words maximum. Pays $20-150. Sometimes pays the expenses of writers on assignment.

Reprints: Send photocopy of article or short story or typed ms with rights for sale noted and information about when and where the article previously appeared. Pays 20% of amount paid for an original article.

Photos: Nancy Thomas, photo editor. Specifically looking for fashion photo features. Send photos with ms. Pays $5-75 for b&w prints. Captions, model releases, identification of subjects required. Buys all rights, "but returns 75% of photos to submitter."

Columns/Departments: George Thomas, column/department editor. New Products; Fitness Newsletter; Handball Newsletter; Racquetball Newsletter; Tennis Newsletter; News & Capsule Summaries; Fashion Spot (photos of new fitness and bathing suits and ski equipment); related subjects. Buys 100 mss/year. Send complete ms. Length: 50-250 words ("more if author has good handle to cover complete columns"). "We want more articles with photos and we are searching for 3 women columnists." Pays $5-25.

Fiction: Judy Johnson, fiction editor. Erotica (if related to fitness club), fantasy (related to subjects), humorous (definite market), religious ("no God-is-my shepherd, but Body-is-God's-temple OK"), romance (related subjects). "Upbeat stories are needed." Buys 20 mss/year. Send complete ms. Length: 500-2,500 words maximum. Pays $20-150.

Poetry: Free verse, haiku, light verse, traditional on related subjects. Length: up to 150 words. Pays $10-25.

Tips: "Send us articles dealing with court club sports, exercise and nutrition that exemplify an upbeat 'you can do it' attitude. Pro sports previews 3-4 months ahead of their seasons are also needed. Good short fiction or humorous articles can break in. Expert knowledge of any related subject can bring assignments; any area is open. We consider everything as a potential article, but are turned off by credits, past work and degrees. We have a constant demand for well-written articles on instruction, health and trends in both. Other articles needed are professional sports training techniques, fad diets, tennis and fitness resorts, photo features with aerobic routines. A frequent mistake made by writers is length—articles are too long. When we assign an article, we want it newsy if it's news and opinion if opinion."

RACQUETBALL MAGAZINE, American Amateur Racquetball Association, 1685 W. Uintah, Colorado Springs CO 80904. (719)635-5396. Fax: (719)635-0685. Director of Communications: Linda Mojer. 20-30% freelance written. Bimonthly magazine "geared toward a readership of informed, active enthusiasts who seek entertainment, instruction and accurate reporting of events." Estab. 1990. Circ. 45,000. Pays on publication. Publishes ms an average of 2 months after acceptance. Buys one-time rights. Editorial lead time 3 months. Submit seasonal material 3 months in advance. Accepts simultaneous submissions. Reports in 2 months. Sample copy for $4. Writer's guidelines free on request.

Nonfiction: How-to (instructional racquetball tips), humor, interview/profile (personalities who play racquetball). Buys 2-3 mss/year. Send complete ms. Length: 1,500-3,000 words. Pays $100. Sometimes pays expenses of writers on assignment.

Reprints: Send typed ms with rights for sale noted and information about when and where the article previously appeared.

Photos: Send photos with submission. Reviews 3×5 prints. Negotiates payment individually. Model releases, identification of subjects required. Buys one-time rights.

Fiction: Humorous (racquetball related). Buys 1-2 mss/year. Send complete ms. Length: 1,500-3,000 words. Pays $100-250.

REFEREE, Referee Enterprises, Inc., P.O. Box 161, Franksville WI 53126-9987. (414)632-8855. Fax: (414)632-5460. Editor: Scott Ehret. 20-25% freelance written. Works with a small number of new/unpublished writers each year. Monthly magazine for well-educated, mostly 26- to 50-year-old male sports officials. Estab. 1975. Circ. 35,000. **Pays on acceptance** of completed ms. Publishes ms an average of 4 months after acceptance. Rights purchased varies. Submit seasonal/holiday material 6 months in advance. Reports in 2 weeks. Sample copy for 10×13 SAE with 7 first-class stamps. Writer's guidelines for #10 SASE.
Nonfiction: How-to, informational, humor, interview, profile, personal experience, photo feature, technical. Buys 54 mss/year. Query. Length: 700-3,000 words. Pays 4-10¢/word. "No general sports articles."
Reprints: Send tearsheet or photocopy of article or typed ms with rights for sale noted and information about when and where it previously appeared. Pays 50% of amount paid for an original article.
Photos: Purchased with or without accompanying ms or on assignment. Captions preferred. Send contact sheet, prints, negatives or transparencies. Pays $20 for each b&w used; $35 for each color used; $100 for color cover; $75 for b&w cover.
Columns/Departments: Law (legal aspects); Between the Lines (anecdotes); Heads Up (psychology). Buys 24 mss/year. Query. Length: 200-800 words. Pays 4¢/word up to $100 maximum for regular columns.
Fillers: Jokes, gags, anecdotes, puzzles, referee shorts. Query. Length: 50-200 words. Pays 4¢/word in some cases; others offer only author credit lines.
Tips: "Queries with a specific idea appeal most to readers. Generally, we are looking more for feature writers, as we usually do our own shorter/filler-type material. It is helpful to obtain suitable photos to augment a story. Don't send fluff—we need hard-hitting, incisive material tailored just for our audience. Anything smacking of public relations is a no sale. Don't gloss over the material too lightly or fail to go in-depth looking for a quick sale (taking the avenue of least resistance)."

SKYDIVING, 1725 N. Lexington Ave., DeLand FL 32724. (904)736-4793. Fax: (904)736-9786. Editor: Michael Truffer. 25% freelance written. Works with a small number of new/unpublished writers each year. Monthly tabloid featuring skydiving for sport parachutists, worldwide dealers and equipment manufacturers. Circ. 12,600. Average issue includes 3 feature articles and 3 columns of technical information. Pays on publication. Publishes ms an average of 3 months after acceptance. Byline given. Buys one-time rights. Accepts simultaneous submissions, if so noted. Reports in 1 month. Sample copy for $2. Writer's guidelines for 9×12 SAE with 4 first-class stamps.
Nonfiction: "Send us news and information on equipment, techniques, events and outstanding personalities who skydive. We want articles written by people who have a solid knowledge of parachuting." No personal experience or human-interest articles. Query. Length: 500-1,000 words. Pays $25-100. Sometimes pays the expenses of writers on assignment.
Reprints: Accepts previously published submissions.
Photos: State availability of photos. Reviews 5×7 and larger b&w glossy prints. Offers no additional payment for photos accepted with ms. Captions required.
Fillers: Newsbreaks. Length: 100-200 words. Pays $25 minimum.
Tips: "The most frequent mistake made by writers in completing articles for us is that the writer isn't knowledgeable about the sport of parachuting."

‡STROKES, Sportsurf and Sportsreader, Sports Support Syndicate, Inc. 108 S. 12th St., Pittsburgh PA 15203. (412)481-2497. Fax: (412)481-2540. E-mail: mrauterkus@pittsburgh.net. Website: http://www.sportsreader.com. Publisher: Mark Rauterkus. 75% freelance written. Monthly electronic magazine covering sports participation and cyberspace sports. "We are a cutting-edge sports magazine for athletes, coaches and administrators an any sport." Estab. 1989. Circ. 15,000. Pays on publication. Publishes ms an average of 6 months after acceptance. Byline given. Buys all rights. Editorial lead time 2 months. Submit seasonal material anytime in advance. Accepts simultaneous submissions. Reports in 2 weeks on queries; 2 months on mss. Sample copy and writer's guidelines for $3.
Nonfiction: Book excerpts, essays, exposé, general interest, historical/nostalgic, how-to, humor, inspirational, interview/profile, new product, opinion, personal experience, photo feature, religious, technical, travel. Buys 15 mss/year. Send complete ms. Length: 2,000 words minimum. Pays $150-400 for assigned articles. Pays writers with contributor copies or other premiums rather than a cash payment. Sometimes pays expenses of writers on assignment.

Reprints: Accepts previously published submissions.
Photos: State availability of photos with submissiion. Captions, model releases, identification of subjects required. Buys one-time rights.
Tips: "Send e-mail to: sss@sendit.com. and visit our website."

VOLLEYBALL MAGAZINE, Avcom Publishing, Ltd., 21700 Oxnard St., Suite 1600, Woodland Hills CA 91367. (818)593-3900. Fax: (818)593-2274. Contact: Rick Hazeltine, editor. Executive Editor: Don Patterson. 50% freelance written. Monthly magazine covering the sport of volleyball. Estab. 1990. Circ. 85,000. Pays on publication. Publishes ms an average of 3 months after acceptance. Byline given. Offers 50% kill fee. Buys first North American serial rights. Editorial lead time 3 months. Submit seasonal material 3 months in advance.
  • The editor notes that he is particularly interested in short features (600-900 words) on individuals who are doing exceptional things in volleyball—such as a player overcoming tragedy or illness; someone who works to build the sport locally; special people; doing special things for the game. Pays $100-150.
Nonfiction: Historical/nostalgic, how-to (skills instruction, nutrition strategy, fitness), humor, interview/profile, technical. No event coverage. Buys 72 mss/year. Query with published clips. Length: 250-3,000 words. Pays $100. Pays expenses of writers on assignment.
Photos: Send photos with submission. Reviews transparencies—no duplicates. Offers $40-225/photo. Captions, model releases and identification of subjects requried. Buys one-time rights.
Columns/Departments: Fitness (must relate specifically to volleyball); Nutrition (for athletes); both 1,000-1,200 words. Buys 36 mss/year. Query with published clips. Pays $200-250.

Olympic Sports

INTERNATIONAL OLYMPIC LIFTER, IOL Publications, 3602 Eagle Rock, P.O. Box 65855, Los Angeles CA 90065. (213)257-8762. Editor: Bob Hise. 20% freelance written. Bimonthly magazine covering the Olympic sport of weightlifting. Estab. 1973. Circ. 10,000. Pays on publication. Publishes ms an average of 3 months after acceptance. Byline given. Offers $25 kill fee. Buys one-time rights or negotiable rights. Submit seasonal/holiday material 5 months in advance. Reports in 3 months. Sample copy for $4. Writer's guidelines for 9×12 SAE with 5 first-class stamps.
  • *International Olympic Lifter* needs more biographies and training routines on the *Olympic* weightlifting top names.
Nonfiction: Training articles, contest reports, diet—all related to Olympic weightlifting. Buys 4 mss/year. Query. Length: 250-2,000 words. Pays $25-100.
Reprints: Send photocopy of article and information about when and where the article previously appeared. Payment is negotiated.
Photos: Action (competition and training). State availability of photos. Pays $1-5 for 5×7 b&w prints. Identification of subjects required.
Poetry: Dale Rhoades, poetry editor. Light verse, traditional—related to Olympic lifting. Buys 6-10 poems/year. Submit maximum 3 poems. Length: 12-24 lines. Pays $10-20.
Tips: "A writer must be acquainted with Olympic-style weightlifting. Since we are an international publication we do not tolerate ethnic, cultural, religious or political inclusions. Articles relating to AWA are readily accepted."

OLYMPIAN MAGAZINE, US Olympic Committee, One Olympic Plaza, Colorado Springs CO 80909. (719)578-4529. Fax: (719)578-4677. Managing Editor: Frank Zang. 50% freelance written. Bimonthly magazine covering olympic sports and athletes. Estab. 1974. Circ. 120,000. Pays on publication. Byline given. Offers 100% kill fee. Free writer's guidelines.
Nonfiction: Photo feature, feature/profiles of athletes in Olympic sports. Query. Length: 1,200-2,000 words. Pays $300 for assigned articles.
Reprints: Send photocopy of article. Pay 50% of amount paid for an original article.
Photos: State availability of photos with submission. Reviews transparencies and prints. Offers $50-250/photo. Captions, model releases and identification of subjects required. Buys one-time rights.

Running

NEW YORK RUNNING NEWS, New York Road Runners Club, 9 E. 89th St., New York NY 10128. (212)860-2280. Fax: (212)860-9754. Editor: Raleigh Mayer. Managing Editor: Don Mogelefsky. 75% freelance written. Bimonthly regional sports magazine covering running, racewalking, nutrition and fitness. Material should be of interest to members of the New York Road Runners Club. Estab. 1958. Circ. 45,000.

Pays on publication. Time to publication varies. Byline given. Offers 33% kill fee. Buys first North American serial rights. Submit seasonal/holiday material 4 months in advance. Accepts simultaneous submissions. Reports in 2 months. Sample copy for $3. Writer's guidelines for #10 SASE.

Nonfiction: Running and marathon articles. Special issues: N.Y.C. Marathon (submissions in by August 1). No non-running stories. Buys 25 mss/year. Query. Length: 750-1,750 words. Pays $50-250. Pays documented expenses of writers on assignment.

Reprints: Send photocopy of article with information about when and where it previously appeared. Pays 25-50% of amount paid for an original article.

Photos: Send photos with submission. Reviews 8×10 b&w prints. Offers $35-300/photo. Captions, model releases, identification of subjects required. Buys one-time rights.

Columns/Departments: Essay (running-related topics). Query. Length: 750 words. Pays $50-125.

Tips: "Be knowledgeable about the sport of running. Write like a runner."

RUNNER'S WORLD, Rodale Press, 33 E. Minor St., Emmaus PA 18098. (215)967-5171. Senior Editor: Bob Wischnia. 10% freelance written. Monthly magazine on running, mainly long-distance running. "The magazine for and about distance running, training, health and fitness, injury precaution, race coverage, personalties of the sport." Estab. 1966. Circ. 450,000. Pays on publication. Publishes ms an average of 6 months after acceptance. Byline given. Buys one-time rights. Submit seasonal/holiday material 6 months in advance. Reports in 2 months. Writer's guideline requests to Pat Erickson for #10 SASE.

Nonfiction: How-to (train, prevent injuries), interview/profile, personal experience. No "my first marathon" stories. No poetry. Buys 10 mss/year. Query. Pays expenses of writers on assignment.

Photos: State availability of photos with submission. Identification of subjects required. Buys one-time rights.

Columns/Departments: Christina Negron. Finish Line (personal experience—humor); Training Log (training of well-known runner). Buys 15 mss/year. Query.

Skiing and Snow Sports

AMERICAN SKATING WORLD, Independent Publication of the American Ice Skating Community, Business Communications Inc., 1816 Brownsville Rd., Pittsburgh PA 15210-3908. (412)885-7600. Fax: (412)885-7617. Editor: Robert A. Mock. Contact: H. Kermit Jackson, managing editor. 70% freelance written. Eager to work with new/unpublished writers. Monthly tabloid on figure skating. Estab. 1979. Circ. 15,000. Pays following publication. Publishes ms an average of 3 months after acceptance. Byline given. Buys first North American serial rights and occasionally second serial (reprint) rights. Submit seasonal/holiday material 3 months in advance. Reports in 3 months. Sample copy and writer's guidelines for $3.50.

● The increased activity and interest in figure skating have increased demands on *American Skating World*'s contributor network. New writers from nontraditional areas (i.e., outside of East Coast, Upper Midwest, California) are particularly welcome.

Nonfiction: Exposé, historical/nostalgic, how-to (technique in figure skating), humor, inspirational, interview/profile, new product, opinion, personal experience, photo feature, technical, travel. Special issues: annual fashion issue (September); Industry (May). Rarely accepts fiction. AP Style Guidelines are the basic style source, but we are not bound by that convention. Short, snappy paragraphs desired. Buys 150 mss/year. Send complete ms. "Include phone number; response time longer without it." Length: 600-1,000 words. Pays $25-100.

Reprints: Occasionally accepts previously published submissions. Send tearsheet of article. Payment is negotiated.

Photos: Send photos with query or ms. Reviews transparencies and b&w prints. Pays $5 for b&w; $15 for color. Identification of subjects required. Buys all rights for b&w; one-time rights for color.

Columns/Departments: Buys 30 mss/year. Send complete ms. Length: 500-750 words. Pays $25-50.

Fillers: Clippings, anecdotes. No payment for fillers.

Tips: "Event coverage is most open to freelancers; confirm with managing editor to ensure event has not been assigned. We are drawing more extensively from non-U.S. based writers. Questions are welcome; call managing editor EST, 10-4, Monday-Friday."

SKATING, United States Figure Skating Association, 20 First St., Colorado Springs CO 80906-3697. (719)635-5200. Fax: (719)635-9548. E-mail: skatemag@aol.com. Editor: Jay Miller. Monthly magazine official publication of the USFSA. Estab. 1923. Circ. 40,000. Pays on publication. Publishes ms an average of 3 months after acceptance. Buys all rights. Byline given.

Nonfiction: Historical, informational, interview, photo feature, historical biographies, profile (background and interests of national-caliber amateur skaters), technical and competition reports. Buys 4 mss/issue. All work by assignment. Length: 400-800 words. Pay varies.

Reprints: Send photocopy of article and information about when and where the article previously appeared. Pay varies.

Photos: Photos purchased with or without accompanying ms. Pays $15 for 8×10 or 5×7 b&w glossy prints and $35 for color prints or transparencies. Query.

Columns/Departments: Ice Breaker (news briefs), Foreign National Reports, Center Ice (guest), Letters to Editor, People. Buys 4 mss/issue. All work by assignment. Length: 500-2,000 words.

Tips: "We want writing by experienced persons knowledgeable in the technical and artistic aspects of figure skating with a new outlook on the development of the sport. Knowledge and background in technical aspects of figure skating are essential to the quality of writing expected. We would also like to receive articles on former competitive skaters. No professional skater material."

‡SKI MAGAZINE, 2 Park Ave., New York NY 10016. (212)779-5000. Fax: (212)481-9261. Website: skinet.com. Editor-in-Chief: Ed Pitoniak. Contact: Lisa Gosselin, executive editor. 15% freelance written. Monthly magazine on snow skiing. "*Ski* is a ski-lifestyle publication written and edited for recreational skiers. Its content is intended to help them ski better (technique), buy better (equipment and skiwear), and introduce them to new experiences, people and adventures." Estab. 1936. Circ. 430,000. **Pays on acceptance.** Publishes ms an average of 3 months after acceptance. Byline given. Offers 15% kill fee. Buys first North American serial rights. Submit seasonal/holiday material 8 months in advance. Reports in 1 month. Sample copy for 9×12 SAE with 5 first-class stamps.

Nonfiction: Essays, historical/nostalgic, how-to, humor, interview/profile and personal experience. Buys 5-10 mss/year. Send complete ms. Length: 1,000-3,500 words. Pays $500-1,000 for assigned articles; $300-700 for unsolicited articles. Pays the expenses of writers on assignment.

Photos: Send photos with submission. Offers $75-300/photo. Captions, model releases and identification of subjects required. Buys one-time rights.

Columns/Departments: Ski Life (interesting people, events, oddities in skiing), 150-300 words; Going Places (items on new or unique places, deals or services available to skiers); and Take It From Us (special products or services available to skiers that are real values or out of the ordinary), 25-50 words.

Fillers: Facts and short humor. Buys 10/year. Length: 60-75 words. Pays $50-75.

Tips: "Writers must have an extensive familiarity with the sport and know what concerns, interests and amuses skiers. Columns are most open to freelancers."

SKI TRIPPER, P.O. Box 20305, Roanoke VA 24018. (540)772-7644. Editor: Tom Gibson. 60% freelance written. Newsletter published monthly November-March covering snow skiing in mid-Atlantic and southeast regions. "Need reports on trips taken to regional ski resorts and to long-distance resorts (western U.S./ Canada, Europe, New Zealand, South America) from the region. Trip reports are written from an unbiased viewpoint and tell good and bad things other people making the trip in the future should look out for. Also need informational pieces on resorts, skiers and skiing-related activities." Estab. 1993. Circ. 1,000. **Pays on acceptance.** Publishes ms an average of 3 months after acceptance. Buys first North American serial rights. Editorial lead time 1 month. Submit seasonal material 2 months in advance. Reports in 3 weeks on queries and mss. Sample copy and writer's guidelines free on request.

Nonfiction: Personal experience, travel. "No articles on ski shops and ski equipment." Buys 12 mss/year. Query. Length: 500-1,700 words. Pays $75-225.

Tips: "If you're going on a ski trip, let us know—it may be one we'd like to cover."

‡SKIER, All Weather Publishing Co., P.O. Box 305, Stowe VT 05672. (802)253-8282. Fax: (802)253-6236. E-mail: skiermagaz@aol.com. Managing Editor: Kim Fredericks. 90% freelance written. Quarterly magazine covering Alpine skiing and snowboarding and other winter sports. "A magazine for active people who pursue various outdoor sports, especially skiing." Estab. 1992. Circ. 410,000. Pays on publication. Publishes ms an average of 3 months after acceptance. Byline given. Buys first North American serial rights. Editorial lead time 3 months. Submit seasonal material 3 months in advance. Reports in 3 weeks on queries; 3 months on mss. Sample copy for 8½×11 SAE with 4 first-class stamps. Writer's guidelines for #10 SASE.

Nonfiction: General interest, how-to (skiing, snowboarding, X-C, snowshoe, mountaineering), humor, interview/profile, new product, opinion, personal experience, photo feature, technical (skis, boots), travel (ski resorts). Buys 20 mss/year. Query with published clips. Length: 500-2,500 words (depending on subject). Pays 15-20¢/word. Sometimes pays expenses of writers on assignment.

Photos: State availability of or send photos with submission. Identification of subjects required. Buys one-time rights.

Columns/Departments: Techniques (how-to improve your skiing or snowboarding technique), 250-500 words. Buys 6 mss/year. Query with published clips. Pays 15-20¢/word.

Fillers: Facts, newsbreaks, short humor. Length: 250-1,000 words. Pays 15-20¢/word.

Tips: "Most of our writers have been working in the ski industry as either technicians or competitive athletes. They are experts in their field."

SKIING, Times Mirror Magazines, Inc., 2 Park Ave., New York NY 10016. Website: http://www.skinet.com/skiing. Editor-in-Chief: Rick Kahl. Contact: Josh Lerman, executive editor. Magazine published 7 times/year for the active skier who is interested in learning about skiing, travel, adventure, instruction, equipment, fashion and news. Estab. 1948. Circ. 440,000. Query before submitting. No personal stories, previously published articles or poetry.

Soccer

SOCCER NOW, Official Publication of the American Youth Soccer Organization, American Youth Soccer Organization, 5403 W. 138th St., Hawthorne CA 90250. (800)USA-AYSO. Editor: Sean Hilferty. 15% freelance written. Quarterly magazine covering soccer (AYSO and professional). "For AYSO members, both players (age 5-18) and their parents. We want to focus mostly on the 6-12 age group. Human interest about AYSO players and adult volunteers, or professional players (especially if they played in AYSO as kids)." Estab. 1976. Circ. 425,000. Pays on publication. Publishes ms an average of 3 months after acceptance. Byline given. Makes work-for-hire assignments. Editorial lead time 3 months. Reports in 1 month on queries. Sample copy free on request.
Nonfiction: General interest (soccer), historical/nostalgic, how-to (playing tips subject to approval by Director of Coaching), interview/profile, personal experience, photo feature. Query. Length: 400-2,000 words. Pays $50-200. Sometimes pays expenses of writers on assignment.
Photos: Send photos with submission. Reviews contact sheets, transparencies, prints. Offers $0-50/photo. Identification of subjects required. Buys one-time rights.
Columns/Departments: Hot Shots (profile of AYSO player who is a standout in something *other* than soccer), 750 words; On The Spot (interview (Q&A format) with pro player), 1,300 words; Ask the Experts (soccer experts answer questions); You Call It (reference feature). Query. Pays $100-200.

Tennis

‡RACQUET, Heather & Pine, Inc., 42 W. 38th, #1202, New York NY 10018. (212)768-8360. Fax: (212)768-8365. Senior Editor: Matthew Tolan. Contact: Allison Roarty, associate editor. 30% freelance written. Bimonthly tennis/lifestyle magazine. "*Racquet* celebrates the lifestyle of tennis." Estab. 1978. Circ. 145,000. Pays on publication. Publishes ms an average of 3 months after acceptance. Byline given. Offers negotiable kill fee. Rights purchased negotiable. Submit seasonal/holiday material 5 months in advance. Accepts simultaneous submissions. Reports in 1 month. Sample copy for $4.
Nonfiction: Essays, exposé, historical/nostalgic, humor, interview/profile, opinion, personal experience, travel. "No instruction or poetry." Buys 15-20 mss/year. Query. Length: 1,000-4,000 words. Pays $200-750 for assigned articles; $100-300 for unsolicited articles. Pays in contributor copies or other negotiable premiums. Sometime pays expenses of writers on assignment.
Reprints: Send tearsheet or photocopy of article.
Photos: State availability of photos with submission. Offers no additional payment for photos accepted with ms. Rights negotiable.
Columns/Departments: "Courtside" (personal experience—fun facts), 500-2,000 words; "Business of Tennis" (financial side of tennis and related industries), 2,000-2,500 words. Buys 5-10 mss/year. Query. Pays $100-300.
Fillers: Anecdotes, short humor. Buys 5/year. Length: 250-750 words. Pays $50-150.
Tips: "Get a copy, understand how we approach tennis, submit article written to style and follow-up. We are always looking for innovative or humorous ideas."

TENNIS WEEK, Tennis News, Inc., 341 Madison Ave., 6th Floor, New York NY 10017. (212)808-4750. Fax: (212)983-6302. Managing Editors: Heather H. Holland, Kim Kodl. 10% freelance written. Biweekly magazine covering tennis. "For readers who are either tennis fanatics or involved in the business of tennis." Estab. 1974. Circ. 80,000. Pays on publication. Byline given. Buys all rights. Editorial lead time 1 month. Submit seasonal material 1 month in advance. Reports in 1 month on queries. Sample copy for $3.
Nonfiction: Buys 15 mss/year. Query with or without published clips. Length: 1,000-2,000 words. Pays $300.

Water Sports

DIVER, Seagraphic Publications, Ltd., 11780 Hammersmith Way, Richmond, British Columbia V7A 5E3 Canada. (604)274-4333. Fax: (604)274-4366. E-mail: divermag@axionnet.com. Website: http://medianetcom .com/divermag/. Editor/Publisher: Peter Vassilopoulos. Contact: Stephanie Bold, assistant editor. Magazine published 9 times/year emphasizing scuba diving, ocean science and technology (commercial and military diving) for a well-educated, outdoor-oriented readership. Circ. 17,500. Payment "follows publication." Buys first North American serial rights. Byline given. Submit seasonal/holiday material July-September for consideration for following year. Send SAE with IRCs. Reports in up to 3 months. Publishes ms up to 1 year after acceptance. "Articles are subject to being accepted for use in supplement issues on tabloid."

Nonfiction: How-to (underwater activities such as photography, etc.), general interest (underwater oriented), humor, historical (shipwrecks, treasure artifacts, archeological), interview (underwater personalities in all spheres—military, sports, scientific or commercial), personal experience (related to diving), photo feature (marine life), technical (related to oceanography, commercial/military diving, etc.), travel (dive resorts). No subjective product reports. Buys 25 mss/year. Travel features considered only in September/October for use following year. Buys only 6 freelance travel items a year. Submit complete ms. Length: 800-1,500 words. Pays $2.50/column inch.

Photos: "Features are mostly those describing dive sites, experiences, etc. Photo features are reserved more as specials, while almost all articles must be well illustrated with color or b&w prints supplemented by color transparencies." Submit original photo material with accompanying ms. Pays $7 minimum for 5×7 or 8×10 b&w glossy prints; $15 minimum for 35mm color transparencies. Captions and model releases required. Buys one-time rights.

Columns/Departments: Book reviews. Submit complete ms. Length: 200 words maximum. No payment.
Fillers: Anecdotes, newsbreaks, short humor. Buys 8-10/year. Length: 50-150 words. No payment for news items.
Tips: "No phone calls inquiring about status of manuscript. Write if no response within reasonable time. Only brief, to-the-point correspondence will be answered. Lengthy communications will probably result in return of work unused. Publisher assumes no liability to use material even after lengthy waiting period. Acceptances only subject to final and actual use."

‡THE DIVER, 6772 Colony Dr., S., Saint Petersburg FL 33705-5905. (813)866-9856. Editor: Bob Taylor. 50% freelance written. Magazine published 6 times/year for divers, coaches and officials. Estab. 1978. Circ. 1,500. Pays on publication. Byline given. Submit material at least 2 months in advance. Accepts simultaneous submissions. Reports in 2 weeks on queries; 1 month on mss. Sample copy for 9×12 SAE with 3 first-class stamps.
Nonfiction: Interview/profile (of divers, coaches, officials), results, tournament coverage, any stories connected with platform and springboard diving, photo features, technical. Buys 35 mss/year. Query. Length: 500-2,500 words. Pays $25-50.
Reprints: Accepts previously published submissions.
Photos: Pays $5-10 for b&w prints. Captions and identification of subjects required. Buys one-time rights.
Tips: "We're very receptive to new writers."

‡HOT WATER, Taylor Publishing Group, 2585 Skymark Ave., Unit 306, Mississauga, Ontario L4W 4L5 Canada. (905)624-8218. Fax: (905)624-6764. Editor: P. Cottrell. 50% freelance written. Quarterly magazine covering personal watercraft market (jet skis sea-doo's). "Focused on fun-loving watersports enthusiasts, *Hot Water* contains features on new personal watercraft and accessories, places to ride, racing, and profiles on people in the industry. Technical and handling tips are also included." Estab. 1993. Circ. 18,000. Pays on publication. Publishes ms an average of 2 months after acceptance. Byline given. Offers 100% kill fee. Buys first North American serial rights. Editorial lead time 2 months. Submit seasonal material 3 months in advance. Sample copy and writer's guidelines free on request.
Nonfiction: Historical/nostalgic, how-to (anything technical or handling etc.), humor, interview/profile, personal experience, photo feature, technical, travel. Send complete ms. Length: 1,000-3,000 words. Pays $300 maximum. Sometimes pays expenses of writers on assignment.
Photos: Send photos with submission. Reviews transparencies, 4×6 prints. Offers no additional payment for photos accepted with ms. Captions, model releases, identification of subjects required.
Columns/Departments: Klipboard (a racer's viewpoint); Workbench (technical tips); Hot Waterways (riding adventures); all 1,000 words. Buys 6 mss/year. Send complete ms. Pays $200 maximum.
Fillers: Facts, newsbreaks. Length: 500-1,000 words. Pays $150 maximum.
Tips: "If you have a story idea you feel is appropriate, feel free to contact the editor to discuss. Or, if you're familiar with watercraft but need some direction, call the editor who will gladly assign a feature."

SCUBA TIMES, The Active Diver's Magazine, GBP, Inc., 14110 Perdido Key Dr., Pensacola FL 32507. (904)492-7805. Fax: (904)492-7805. Website: http://www.scubatimes.com. Managing Editor: Fred D. Garth. Contact: Christopher Grant, editor. 90% freelance written. Bimonthly magazine on scuba diving. Estab. 1979. Circ. 43,000. Pays on publication. Publishes ms an average of 6 months after acceptance. Byline given. Buys first North American serial rights. Submit seasonal material 1 year in advance. Reports in 6 weeks. Sample copy for $3. Writer's guidelines for #10 SASE.
Nonfiction: How-to (advanced diving techniques such as technical, very deep, mixed gases, cave diving, wreck diving); humor; interview/profile (colorful characters in diving); personal experience (only if it is astounding); photo feature (creatures, places to dive); technical (physics, biology, medicine as it relates to diving); travel (dive destinations). No beginner-level dive material. Buys 75 mss/year. Query with published

clips or send complete ms. Length: 1,500 for major destination features, 150 words for sidebars. Pays $75/published page. Sometimes pays expenses of writers on assignment.

Reprints: Send information about when and where the article previously appeared. Pays 100% of amount paid for an original article.

Photos: Send photos with submission. Reviews transparencies. Offers $25-75/page; $150/ cover photo. Captions, identification of subjects required. Buys one-time rights.

Columns/Departments: What a Wreck (informative guide to any wreck, old or new), 750 words; Creature Feature (one knock-out photo of a mysterious sea creature plus story of life cycle and circumstances that led to photo), 500 words; Last Watering Hole, (great photos, usually topside, and story about a dive site so remote most divers will never go), 500 words; Dive America (informative article on local, fresh water dive sites, with photo), 300 words; Advanced Diving (how-to and advanced techniques for expanding dive adventure), 750 words. Buys 60 mss/year. Query with published clips. Length; 500-1,000 words. Pays $25-75/page.

Fillers: " 'Free Flowing' sections allows writers to be creative, thought provoking as they contemplate diver's relationship to the marine world." Anecdotes, short humor. Buys 10/year. Length: 300-900 words. Pays $25-75/page.

Tips: "Be a diver. Everyone tries for the glamorous destination assignments, but it is easier to break into the columns, especially, 'Last Watering Hole,' 'What a Wreck,' 'Dive America' and 'Creature Feature.' Outstanding photos are a must. We will coax a good article out of a great photographer whose writing skills are not developed. Very little is written inhouse. Diving freelancers are the heart and soul of *STM*. Unknowns receive as much consideration as the big names. Know what you are talking about and present it with a creative flair. Divers are often technical or scientific by profession or disposition and their writing lacks flow, power and grace. Make us *feel* those currents and *smell* the diesel from the yacht."

‡SPLASH MAGAZINE, The Complete Personal Watercraft Magazine, McMullen/Argus Publishing, 774 S. Placentia Ave., Placentia CA 92670. (714)572-2255. Fax: (714)572-1864. E-mail: splashmag@aol.com. Editor: Jeff Ames. 20% freelance written. Monthly magazine covering personal watercraft, riding spots, technical and racing. "From month to month, *Splash Magazine* provides extensive coverage of personal watercraft, equipment, accessories and personalities. Stunning color photography highlights all makes and models and showcases the best in custom craft, watersport events and races." Estab. 1987. Circ. 55,000. Pays on publication. Byline given. Buys first North American serial rights. Editorial lead time 3 months. Submit seasonal material 5 months in advance. Reports in 1 month. Sample copy free on request. Writer's guidelines for #10 SASE.

Nonfiction: General interest, how-to, humor, inspirational, interview/profile, new product, opinion, photo feature, technical, travel, race and new product test features. Buys 15-20 mss/year. Query with published clips. Length varies. Pays $100-150/page. Sometimes pays expenses of writers on assignment.

Photos: Send photos with submission. Reviews 35mm transparencies. Negotiates payment individually. Captions, model releases, identification of subjects required.

Columns/Departments: Free Ridin' (recreational and racer experiences), 250 words; Races Report (PWC racers articles), 1,000-2,000 words. Buys 60 mss/year. Pays $75-150/page.

Tips: "Submit query or completed editorial/photography with cover letter. Editorial may be submitted on disk. Photography should be captioned and numbered. Be knowledgeable of the sport."

SURFER, Surfer Publications, P.O. Box 1028, Dana Point CA 92629. (714)496-5922. Fax: (714)496-7849. E-mail: surferedit@aol.com. Website: http://www.surfermag.com. Editor: Steve Hawk. Assistant Editor: Lisa Boelter. Contact: Sam George, managing editor. 75% freelance written. Monthly magazine "aimed at experts and beginners with strong emphasis on action surf photography." Estab. 1960. Circ. 110,000. Pays on publication. Byline given. Buys first North American serial rights. Submit seasonal/holiday material 6 months in advance. Accepts simultaneous submissions. Reports in 2 months. Sample copy for $3.95 with 9 × 12 SASE. Writer's guidelines for #10 SASE.

Nonfiction: How-to (technique in surfing), humor, inspirational, interview/profile, opinion, personal experience (all surf-related), photo feature (action surf and surf travel), technical (surfboard design), travel (surf exploration and discovery—photos required). Buys 30-50 mss/year. Query with or without published clips, or send complete ms. Length: 500-2,500 words. Pays 20-25¢/word. Sometimes pays the expenses of writers on assignment.

Photos: Send photos with submission. Reviews 35mm negatives and transparencies. Buys 12-24 illustrations/year. Prices vary. Used for columns: Environment, Surf Docs and sometimes features. Send samples with SASE to Art Director. Offers $25-250/photo. Identification of subjects required. Buys one-time and reprint rights.

Columns/Departments: Environment (environmental concerns to surfers), 1,000-1,500 words; Surf Stories (personal experiences of surfing), 1,000-1,500 words; Reviews (surf-related movies, books), 500-1,000 words; Sections (humorous surf-related items with b&w photos), 100-500 words. Buys 25-50 mss/year. Send complete ms. Pays 20-25¢/word.

Fiction: Surf-related adventure, fantasy, horror, humorous, science fiction. Buys 10 mss/year. Send complete ms. Length: 750-2,000 words. Pays 15-20¢/word.

Tips: "All sections are open to freelancers but interview/profiles are usually assigned. 'People Who Surf' is a good way to get a foot in the door. Stories must be authoritative, oriented to the hard-core surfer."

SWIM MAGAZINE, Sports Publications, Inc., P.O. Box 2025, Sedona AZ 86339-2025. (520)282-4799. Fax: (520)282-4697. Editor: Dr. Phillip Whitten. 50% freelance written. Prefers to work with published/ selected writers. Bimonthly magazine for adults interested in swimming for fun, fitness and competition. Readers are fitness-oriented adults from varied social and professional backgrounds who share swimming as part of their lifestyle. Readers are well-educated, affluent and range in age from 20-100 with most in the 30-49 age group; about 50% female, 50% male." Estab. 1984. Circ. 44,600. Pays approximately 1 month after publication. Publishes ms an average of 4 months after acceptance. Byline given. Submit seasonal/ holiday material 4 months in advance. Reports in 1 month on queries; 3 months on mss. Sample copy for $3 (prepaid) and 9 × 12 SAE with 5 first-class stamps. Free writer's guidelines.
Nonfiction: How-to (training plans and techniques), interview/profile (people associated with fitness and competitive swimming), inspirational, general health, new product (articles describing new products for fitness and competitive training). "Articles need to be informative as well as interesting. In addition to fitness and health articles, we are interested in exploring fascinating topics dealing with swimming for the adult reader." Send complete ms. Length: 500-3,000 words. Pays 12¢/word minimum.
Reprints: Occasionally accepts previously published submissions. Send tearsheet, photocopy of article or typed ms with rights for sale noted with information about when and where the article previously appeared.
Photos: Send photos with ms. Offers no additional payment for photos accepted with ms. Captions, model releases, identification of subjects required.
Tips: "Our how-to and profile articles best typify *Swim Magazine*'s style for fitness and competitive swimmers. *Swim Magazine* accepts medical guidelines and exercise physiology articles primarily by M.D.s and Ph.Ds."

‡**THE WATER SKIER**, American Water Ski Association, 799 Overlook Dr., Winter Haven FL 33884. (813)324-4341. Editor-in-Chief: Don Cullimore. Contact: Jonathan W. Cullimore, assistant editor. 10-20% freelance written. Magazine published 7 times/year for water skiing—all aspects of the sport. "*The Water Skier* is the official publication of the American Water Ski Association (AWSA), the national governing body for organized water skiing in the United States. The magazine has a controlled circulation and is available only to AWSA's membership, which is made up of 10,000 active competitive water skiers and 20,000 members who are supporting the sport. These supporting members may participate in the sport but they don't compete. The editorial content of the magazine features distinctive and informative writing about the sport of water skiing only." Estab. 1951. Circ. 30,000. Byline given. Offers 30% kill fee. Buys all rights (no exceptions). Editorial lead time 4 months. Submit seasonal material 6 months in advance. Reports in 2 weeks on queries. Sample copy for $1.25. Writer's guidelines for #10 SASE.
Nonfiction: Historical/nostalgic (has to pertain to water skiing), interview/profile (call for assignment), new product (boating and water ski equipment), travel (water ski vacation destinations). Buys 10-15 mss/year. Query. Length: 1,500-3,000 words. Pays $125 minimum for assigned articles; $150 minimum for unsolicited articles.
Photos: State availability of photos with submission. Reviews contact sheets. Negotiates payment individually. Captions and identification of subjects required. Buys all rights.
Columns/Departments: Sports Science/Medicine (athlete conditioning, physical/mental training), 1,000-1,500 words; The Starting Dock (small news items about people and events in the sport), 400-500 words; Waterways Issues (water skier's rights of access to waterways, environmental issues), 1,000-1,500 words. Query. Pays $75-125. Pay for columns negotiated individually with each writer.
Tips: "Contact the editor through a query letter (please no phone calls) with an idea. Avoid instruction, these articles are written by professionals. Concentrate on articles about the people of the sport. We are always looking for the interesting storys about people in the sport. Also, short news features which will make a reader say to himself, 'Hey, I didn't know that.' Keep in mind that the publication is highly specialized about the sport of water skiing." Most open to material for: feature articles (query editor with your idea), Sports/Science Medicine columns (query editor with ideas, looking for unique training or conditioning and method or sports rehabilitation), and The Starting Dock (interesting and unique news slants that are about the people and events in sport of water skiing).

TEEN AND YOUNG ADULT

The publications in this category are for young people ages 13-19. Publications for college students are listed in Career, College and Alumni. Those for younger children are listed in the Juvenile category.

‡**CAMPUS LIFE**, Christianity Today, Inc., 465 Gundersen Dr., Carol Stream IL 60188. (708)260-6200. Editor: Harold Smith. Contact: Christopher Lutes, manuscripts editor. 35% freelance written. Magazine

published 10 times/year for the Christian life as it related to today's teen. "*Campus Life* is a magazine for high-school and college-age teenagers. Our editorial slant is not overtly religious. The indirect style is intended to create a safety zone with our readers and to reflect our philosophy that God is interested in all of life. Therefore, we publish 'message stories' side by side with general interest, humor, etc." Estab. 1942. Circ. 100,000. **Pays on acceptance.** Publishes ms an average of 5 months after acceptance. Byline given. Offers 50% kill fee. Buys first and one-time rights. Editorial lead time 4 months. Accepts simultaneous submissions. Reports in 5 weeks on queries; 2 months on mss. Sample copy for $2 and 8×10 SAE with 3 first-class stamps. Writer's guidelines for #10 SASE.

Nonfiction: Humor, personal experience, photo feature. The *Christian* college experience. Buys 10-20 mss/year. Query with published clips. Length: 250-2,500 words. Pays 15-20¢ minimum.

Reprints: Accepts previously published submissions.

Photos: State availability of photos with submission. Reviews contact sheets, transparencies, 5×7 prints. Negotiates payment individually. Model release required. Buys one-time rights.

Fiction: Buys 1-5 mss/year. Query. Length: 1,000-3,500 words. Pays 15-20¢/word.

Poetry: Free verse. "No material that does not 'communicate' to the average teenager." Buys 1-5 poems/year. Submit maximum 2 poems. Length: 5-20 lines. Pays $25-50.

Fillers: Anecdotes, facts, short humor. Buys 3-5/year. Length: $25-250 words. Pays $10-50.

Tips: "The best way to break in to *Campus Life* is through writing first-person or as-told-to first-person stories. But query first—with theme info, telling way this story would work for our audience. We are seeking humor: high school experiences with a 'Dave Barry' flair, first-person, capturing a teen's everyday 'life lesson' experience."

CHALLENGE, Baptist Brotherhood Commission, 1548 Poplar Ave., Memphis TN 38104-2493. (901)272-2461. Editor: Joe Conway. 5% freelance written. Monthly magazine for "boys age 12-18 who are members of a missions organization in Southern Baptist churches." Circ. 28,500. Byline given. Pays on publication. Publishes ms an average of 8 months after acceptance. Buys simultaneous rights. Submit seasonal/holiday material 8 months in advance. Accepts simultaneous submissions. Reports in 1 month. Sample copy and writer's guidelines for 9×12 SAE with 3 first-class stamps. Writer's guidelines only for #10 SASE.

Nonfiction: How-to (crafts, hobbies), informational (youth), inspirational (sports/entertainment personalities); photo feature (sports, teen subjects). No "preachy" articles, fiction or excessive dialogue. Submit complete ms. Length: 500-800 words. Pays $20-50.

Reprints: Accepts previously published submissions. Send tearsheet or photocopy of article and information about where and when the article previously appeared. Pays 90% of the amount paid for an original article.

Photos: Purchased with accompanying ms or on assignment. Captions required. Query. Pays $10 for 8×10 b&w glossy prints.

Tips: "The writer has a better chance of breaking in at our publication with youth related articles (youth issues, and sports figures). Most topics are set years in advance. The most frequent mistake made by writers is sending us preachy articles. Aim for the mid- to older-teen instead of younger teen."

‡**EDGE**, Christian Service Brigade, P.O. Box 150, Wheaton IL 60189. (708)665-0630. Fax: (708)665-0372. E-mail: brigadecsb@aol.com. Editor: Deborah Christensen. 25% freelance written. Quarterly tabloid covering teenage boys and Christian Service Brigade. Estab. 1995. Circ. 5,000. Pays on publication. Publishes ms an average of 1 year after acceptance. Byline given. Offers $35 kill fee. Buys first or second serial (reprint) rights. Editorial lead time 3 months. Submit seasonal material 6 months in advance. Reports in 2 weeks on mss. Sample copy for $1 and 9× SAE with 3 first-class stamps. Writer's guidelines for #10 SASE.

Nonfiction: Humor, interview/profile, photo feature, religious. Buys 4 mss/year. Send complete ms. Length: 250-750 words. Pays 9-10¢/word for assigned articles; 5-8¢/word for unsolicited articles. Sometimes pays expenses of writers on assignment.

Reprints: Accepts previously published submissions.

Photos: Send photos with submission. Reviews 5×7 prints. Negotiates payment individually. Buys one-time rights.

Fiction: Adventure, humorous, mystery, religious. Buys 4 mss/year. Send complete ms. Length: 250-750 words. Pays 5-10¢/word.

Fillers: Short humor. Buys 4/year. Length: 100-250 words. Pays 5-10¢/word.

Tips: "Know teenage boys and know Biblical Christianity. We're especially looking for male writers."

EXPLORING MAGAZINE, Boy Scouts of America, P.O. Box 152079, Irving TX 75015-2079. (214)580-2365. Fax: (214)580-2079. Executive Editor: Scott Daniels. 85% freelance written. Prefers to work with published/established writers. Quarterly magazine covering the co-ed teen-age Exploring program of the BSA. Estab. 1970. Circ. 350,000. **Pays on acceptance.** Publishes ms an average of 8 months after acceptance. Byline given. Buys first rights. Submit seasonal/holiday material 6 months in advance. Reports in 1 month. Sample copy for 9×12 SAE with 5 first-class stamps. Writer's guidelines and "What is Exploring?" fact sheet for #10 SASE.

Nonfiction: General interest: teenage popular culture, music, films, health, fitness, fashion, cars, computers, how-to (organize trips, meetings, etc.); interview/profile (of outstanding Explorer), travel (backpacking or canoeing with Explorers). Buys 15-20 mss/year. Query with clips. Length: 800-1,500 words. Pays $350-1,000. Pays expenses of writers on assignment.

Photos: Brian Payne, photo editor. State availability of photos. Reviews b&w contact sheets and 35mm transparencies. Captions required. Buys one-time rights.

Tips: "Contact the local Exploring Director in your area (listed in phone book white pages under Boy Scouts of America). Find out if there are some outstanding post activities going on and then query magazine editor in Irving, Texas. Strive for shorter texts, faster starts and stories that lend themselves to dramatic photographs."

FLORIDA LEADER (for high school students), Oxendine Publishing, Inc., P.O. Box 14081, Gainesville FL 32604-2081. (904)373-6907. E-mail: 75143.2043@compuserve.com. Editor: W.H. "Butch" Oxendine Jr. Managing Editor: Kay Quinn King. Contact: Sarah Beavers, assistant editor. Quarterly magazine covering high school and pre-college youth. Estab. 1983. Circ. 50,000. Pays on publication. Publishes ms an average of 3 months after acceptance. Buys all rights. Submit seasonal material 4 months in advance. Accepts simultaneous submissions. Reports in 2 months on queries. Sample copy for 8 × 11 with 3 first-class stamps. For query response and/or writer's guidelines send #10 SASE.

Nonfiction: How-to, humor, new product, opinion. "No lengthy individual profiles or articles without primary and secondary sources of attribution." Length: 250-1,000 words. Pays $35 maximum. Pays students or first-time writers with contributor's copies.

Reprints: Accepts previously published submissions.

Photos: Send photos with submission. Reviews contact sheets, negatives, transparencies. Offers $50/photo maximum. Captions, model releases, identification of subjects required. Buys all rights.

Columns/Departments: College Living (various aspects of college life, general short humor oriented to high school or college students), 250-1,000 words. Buys 10 mss/year. Query. Length: 250-1,000 words. Pays $35 maximum.

Fillers: Facts, newsbreaks, short humor. Buys 10/year. Length: 100-500 words. Pays $35 maximum.

Tips: "Read other high school and college publications for current issues, interests. Send manuscripts or outlines for review. All sections open to freelance work. Always looking for lighter, humorous articles as well as features on Florida colleges and universities, careers, jobs. Multi-sourced (5-10) articles are best."

GUIDE, 55 W. Oak Ridge Dr., Hagerstown MD 21740. Fax: (301)790-9734. Editor: Carolyn Rathbun. 50% freelance written. Works with a small number of new/unpublished writers each year. Weekly magazine journal for junior youth and early teens. "Its content reflects Christian Seventh-Day Adventist beliefs and standards." Estab. 1953. Circ. 34,000. Buys first serial, simultaneous and second serial (reprint) rights. **Pays on acceptance.** Publishes ms an average of 9 months after acceptance. Byline given. Submit seasonal/holiday material 6 months in advance. Reports in 3 weeks. Sample copy for SAE with 2 first-class stamps.

Nonfiction: We are especially interested in *true* stories that show God's involvement in 10- to 14-year-olds' lives. True adventure that illustrates a spiritual principle is high priority.

Reprints: Send typed ms with rights for sale noted and information about when and where the material previously appeared. Pays 50% of amount paid for an original article.

Fiction: Wants stories of character-building and spiritual value. Should emphasize the positive aspects of living, obedience to parents, perseverance, kindness, etc. "*We can always use Christian humor* and 'drama in real life' stories that show God's protection, and seasonal stories—Christmas, Thanksgiving, special holidays. We do not use stories of hunting, fishing, trapping or spiritualism. Many authors miss the mark by not setting forth a *clear application* of Biblical principles to everyday situations." Buys about 300 mss/year. Send complete ms (include word count and Social Security number). Length: up to 1,200 words. Pays 3-6¢/word. Length: 1,200 words maximum.

• *Guide* is still looking for sparkling humor and adventure stories, filled with mystery, action, discovery, dialogue.

Tips: "Typical topics we cover in a yearly cycle include choices (music, clothes, friends, diet); friend-making skills; school problems (cheating, peer pressure, new school); self-esteem; changes; sibling relationships; divorce; step-families; drugs; and communication. We often buy short fillers, and an author who does not fully understand our needs is more likely to sell with a short-short. Our target age is 10-14. Our most successful writers are those who present stories from the viewpoint of a young teen-ager, written in the active voice. Stories that sound like an adult's sentiments passing through a young person's lips are *not* what we're looking for. Use believable dialogue."

INSIGHT, A Spiritual Lift for Teens, The Review and Herald Publishing Association, 55 W. Oak Ridge Dr., Hagerstown MD 21740. (301)791-7000. Editor: Lori Peckham. 80% freelance written. Weekly magazine covering spiritual life of teenagers. "*INSIGHT* publishes true dramatic stories, interviews, and community and mission service features that relate directly to the lives of Christian teenagers, particularly those with a Seventh-day Adventist background." Estab. 1970. Circ. 20,000. Pays on publication. Publishes ms an average of 4 months after acceptance. Byline given. Offers 50% kill fee. Buys first rights and second serial (reprint) rights. Editorial lead time 3 months. Submit seasonal material 6 months in advance. Reports in 1 month. Sample copy for $2 and #10 SASE. Writer's guidelines free on request.

Nonfiction: How-to (teen relationships and experiences), humor, interview/profile, personal experience, photo feature, religious. Buys 120 mss/year. Send complete ms. Length: 500-2,000 words. Pays $25-150 for assigned articles; $25-125 for unsolicited articles.
Reprints: Accepts previously published submissions.
Photos: State availability of photos with submission. Reviews contact sheets, negatives, transparencies, prints. Negotiates payment individually. Model releases required. Buys one-time rights.
Columns/Departments: Interviews (Christian culture figures, esp. musicians), 2,000 words; Service With a Smile (teens contributing to community or church), 1,000 words; On the Edge (dramatic true stories about Christians), 2,000 words. Accepting reviews of contemporary Christian music and Christian books for teens. Buys 80 mss/year. Send complete ms. Pays $40-125.
Tips: "Skim two months of *INSIGHT*. Write about your teen experiences. Use informed, contemporary style and vocabulary. Become a Christian if you haven't already."

‡**JUNIOR SCHOLASTIC**, Scholastic Inc., 555 Broadway, New York NY 10017. (212)343-6565. Fax: (212)343-6620. Editor: Lee Baier. Biweekly magazine for junior high school students. "*Junior Scholastic* is a current events, world cultures and U.S. history magazine that brings students the people, places and events of our country and the world. It helps young magazine readers explore their own country, the world and our nation's history in pictures, maps and articles written expressly to relate to their lives. Contains geography, economics, profiles and fun features to supplement classroom study." Estab. 1937. Circ. 590,000.
Nonfiction: Most open to freelancers: On-the-spot reports on events and trends in foreign countries. Buys 25 mss/year. Pays $600-800. Query.

‡**KEYNOTER**, Key Club International, 3636 Woodview Trace, Indianapolis IN 46268-3196. Executive Editor: Julie A. Carson. 65% freelance written. Works with a small number of new writers each year, but is eager to work with new/unpublished writers willing to adjust their writing styles to *Keynoter*'s needs. Monthly youth magazine (December/January combined issue), distributed to members of Key Club International, a high school service organization for young men and women. Estab. 1946. Circ. 171,000. **Pays on acceptance.** Publishes ms an average of 5 months after acceptance. Byline given. Buys first North American serial rights. Submit seasonal/holiday material 7 months in advance. Accepts simultaneous submissions. Reports in 2 months. Sample copy for 9×12 SAE with 3 first-class stamps. Writer's guidelines for #10 SASE.
Nonfiction: Book excerpts (included in articles), general interest (for intelligent teen audience), historical/nostalgic (generally not accepted), how-to (advice on how teens can enhance the quality of lives or communities), humor (accepted if adds to story), interview/profile (rarely purchased, "would have to be on/with an irresistible subject"), new product (affecting teens), photo feature (if subject is right), technical (understandable and interesting to teen audience), travel (must apply to club travel schedule), subjects that entertain and inform teens on topics that relate directly to their lives. "We would also like to receive self-help and school-related nonfiction on leadership, community service, and teen issues. *Please, no first-person confessions, fiction or articles that are written down to our teen readers.*" Buys 10-15 mss/year. Query. Length: 1,500-1,800 words. Pays $150-350. Sometimes pays the expenses of writers on assignment.
Reprints: Accepts previously published submissions.
Photos: State availability of photos. Reviews color/b&w contact sheets and negatives. Identification of subjects required. Buys one-time rights. Payment for photos included in payment for ms.
Tips: "We want to see articles written with attention to style and detail that will enrich the world of teens. Articles must be thoroughly researched and must draw on interviews with nationally and internationally respected sources. Our readers are 13-18, mature and dedicated to community service. We are very committed to working with good writers, and if we see something we like in a well-written query, we'll try to work it through to publication."

LISTEN MAGAZINE, Review & Herald Publishing Association, 55 W. Oak Ridge Dr., Hagerstown MD 21740. (301)791-7000, ext. 2534. Fax: (301)790-9734. Editor: Lincoln Steed. Editorial Assistant: Anita Jacobs. 75% freelance written. Works with a small number of new/unpublished writers each year. Monthly magazine specializing in drug prevention, presenting positive alternatives to various drug dependencies. "*Listen* is used in many high school classes and by professionals: medical personnel, counselors, law enforcement officers, educators, youth workers, etc." Circ. 70,000. Buys first rights for use in *Listen*, reprints and associated material. Byline given. **Pays on acceptance.** Publishes ms an average of 6 months after acceptance. Reports in 3 months. Sample copy for $1 and 9×12 SASE. Free writer's guidelines.
Nonfiction: Seeks articles that deal with causes of drug use such as poor self-concept, family relations, social skills or peer pressure. Especially interested in youth-slanted articles or personality interviews encouraging non-alcoholic and non-drug ways of life. Teenage point of view is essential. Popularized medical, legal and educational articles. Also seeks narratives which portray teens dealing with youth conflicts, especially those related to the use of or temptation to use harmful substances. Growth of the main character should be shown. "We don't want typical alcoholic story/skid-row bum, AA stories. We are also being inundated with drunk-driving accident stories. Unless yours is unique, consider another topic." Buys 15-20 unsolicited mss/year. Query. Length: 1,200-1,500 words. Pays 5-7¢/word. Sometimes pays the expenses of writers on assignment.

Reprints: Send tearsheet or photocopy of article or typed ms with rights for sale noted and information about when and where it previously appeared. Pays 50% of amount paid for an original article.
Photos: Purchased with accompanying ms. Captions required. Color photos preferred, but b&w acceptable.
Fillers: Word square/general puzzles are also considered. Pays $15.
Tips: "True stories are good, especially if they have a unique angle. Other authoritative articles need a fresh approach. In query, briefly summarize article idea and logic of why you feel it's good. Make sure you've read the magazine to understand our approach."

THE NEW ERA, 50 E. North Temple, Salt Lake City UT 84150. (801)240-2951. Fax: (801)240-5997. Managing Editor: Richard M. Romney. 60% freelance written. "We work with both established writers and newcomers." Monthly magazine for young people of the Church of Jesus Christ of Latter-day Saints (Mormon), their church leaders and teachers. Estab. 1971. Circ. 230,000. **Pays on acceptance.** Publishes ms an average of 1 year after acceptance. Byline given. Buys all rights. Rights reassigned upon written request. Submit seasonal material 1 year in advance. Reports in 2 months. Sample copy for $1 and 9×12 SAE with 2 first-class stamps. Writer's guidelines for SASE.
Nonfiction: Material that shows how the Church of Jesus Christ of Latter-day Saints is relevant in the lives of young people today. Must capture the excitement of being a young Latter-day Saint. Special interest in the experiences of young Mormons in other countries. Special issues: Mormon Pioneers in Utah (July 97); Mormon Temples (February 97). No general library research or formula pieces without the *New Era* slant and feel. Uses informational, how-to, personal experience, interview, profile, inspirational, humor, historical, think pieces, travel, spot news. Query preferred. Length: 150-2,000 words. Pays 3-12¢/word. *For Your Information* (news of young Mormons around the world). Pays expenses of writers on assignment.
Photos: Uses b&w photos and transparencies with mss. Payment depends on use, $10-125 per photo. Individual photos used for *Photo of the Month*.
Fiction: Adventure, science fiction, humorous. Must relate to young Mormon audience. Pays minimum 3¢/word.
Poetry: Traditional forms, blank verse, free verse, light verse, all other forms. Must relate to editorial viewpoint. Pays minimum 25¢/line.
Tips: "The writer must be able to write from a Mormon point of view. We're especially looking for stories about successful family relationships. We anticipate using more staff-produced material. This means freelance quality will have to improve."

SEVENTEEN, 850 Third Ave., New York NY 10022. Fax: (212)935-4536/7. E-mail: thespin@aol.com. Editor-in-Chief: Caroline Miller. Managing Editor: Kelly Crouch. Contact: Joe Bargmann, features editor. 80% freelance written. Works with a small number of new/unpublished writers each year. Monthly. Circ. 1,900,000. Buys one-time rights for nonfiction and fiction by adult writers and work by teenagers. Pays 25% kill fee. **Pays on acceptance.** Publishes ms an average of 6 months after acceptance. Byline given. Reports in up to 3 months.
Nonfiction: Articles and features of general interest to young women who are concerned with the development of their lives and the problems of the world around them; strong emphasis on topicality and helpfulness. Send brief outline and query, including a typical lead paragraph, summing up basic idea of article. Length: 1,200-2,000 words. Pays $50-150 for articles written by teenagers but more to established adult freelancers. Articles are commissioned after outlines are submitted and approved. Fees for commissioned articles $650-1,500. Sometimes pays the expenses of writers on assignment.
Reprints: Likes to receive articles and features on spec. Query with tearsheets or copies of published articles.
Photos: Margaret Kemp, art director. Photos usually by assignment only.
Fiction: Thoughtful, well-written stories on subjects of interest to young women between the ages of 12 and 20. Avoid formula stories—"My sainted Granny," "My crush on Brad," etc.—no heavy moralizing or condescension of any sort. Humorous stories and mysteries are welcomed. Length: 1,000-3,000 words. Pays $500-1,500.
  • *Seventeen* no longer accepts poetry.
Tips: "Writers have to ask themselves whether or not they feel they can find the right tone for a *Seventeen* article—a tone which is empathetic yet never patronizing; lively yet not superficial. Not all writers feel comfortable with, understand or like teenagers. If you don't like them, *Seventeen* is the wrong market for you. The best way for beginning teenage writers to crack the *Seventeen* lineup is for them to contribute suggestions and short pieces to the Voices section, a literary format which lends itself to just about every kind of writing: profiles, essays, exposes, reportage and book reviews."

‡SPIRIT, Lectionary-based Weekly for Catholic Teens, Editorial Development Associates, 1884 Randolph Ave., St. Paul MN 55105-1700. (612)690-7005. Fax: (612)690-7039. Editor: Joan Mitchell, CSJ. Managing Editor: Therese Sherlock, CSJ. 50% freelance written. Weekly newsletter for religious education of high schoolers. "We want realistic fiction and nonfiction that raises current ethical and religious questions and conflicts in multi-racial contexts." Estab. 1988. Circ. 26,000. Pays on publication. Publishes ms an average of 6 months after acceptance. Byline given. Buys all rights. Submit seasonal material 6 months in advance. Accepts simultaneous submissions. Reports in 2 weeks on queries; 6 weeks on mss. Free sample copy and writer's guidelines.

Nonfiction: Interview/profile, personal experience, photo feature (homelessness, illiteracy), religious, Roman Catholic leaders, human interest features, social justice leaders, projects, humanitarians. "No Christian confessional pieces." Buys 12 mss/year. Query. Length: 1,100-1,200 words. Pays $135-150 for articles; $75 for one-page articles.

Photos: State availability of photos with submission. Reviews contact sheets, transparencies, prints. Offers $25-35/photo. Identification of subjects required. Buys one-time rights.

Fiction: Conflict vignettes. "We want realistic pieces for and about teens—non-pedantic, non-pious." We need good Christmas stories that show spirit of the season, and stories about teen relationship conflicts (boy/girl, parent/teen). Buys 12 mss/year. Query. Length: 1,100-1,200 words. Pays $150.

Tips: "Query to receive call for stories, spec sheet, sample issues."

STRAIGHT, Standard Publishing Co., 8121 Hamilton Ave., Cincinnati OH 45231-2323. (513)931-4050. Fax: (513)931-0904. Editor: Heather E. Wallace. 90% freelance written. Estab. 1950. Weekly magazine (published quarterly) for "teens, age 13-19, from Christian backgrounds who generally receive this publication in their Sunday School classes or through subscriptions." **Pays on acceptance.** Publishes ms an average of 1 year after acceptance. Buys first rights, second serial (reprint) rights or simultaneous rights. Byline given. Submit seasonal/holiday material 9-12 months in advance. Reports in 2 months. Sample copy free. Writer's guidelines for #10 SAE with 2 first-class stamps.

Nonfiction: Religious-oriented topics, teen interest (school, church, family, dating, sports, part-time jobs), humor, inspirational, personal experience. "We want articles that promote Christian values and ideals." No puzzles. Query or submit complete ms. Include Social Security number on ms. "We're buying more short pieces these days; 12 pages fill up much too quickly." Length: 800-1,500 words.

Reprints: Send tearsheet of article or story.

Fiction: Adventure, humorous, religious, suspense. "All fiction should have some message for the modern Christian teen. Fiction should deal with all subjects in a forthright manner, without being preachy and without talking down to teens. No tasteless manuscripts that promote anything adverse to the Bible's teachings." Submit complete ms. Length: 1,000-1,500 words. Pays 3-7¢/word.

• Ranked as one of the best markets for fiction writers in *Writer's Digest*'s annual "Fiction 50," June 1996.

Photos: May submit photos with ms. Pays $75-125 for color slides. Model releases should be available. Buys one-time rights.

Tips: "Don't be trite. Use unusual settings or problems. Use a lot of illustrations, a good balance of conversation, narration, and action. Style must be clear, fresh—no sermonettes or sickly-sweet fiction. Take a realistic approach to problems. Be willing to submit to editorial policies on doctrine; knowledge of the *Bible* a must. Also, be aware of teens today, and what they do. Language, clothing, and activities included in manuscripts should be contemporary. We are also looking for articles for a monthly feature entitled 'Straight Spotlight.' The purpose of 'Straight Spotlight' is to introduce our readers to real teens who are making a difference in their school, community or church. Articles for this feature should be approx. 900 words in length. We would also like a picture of the teen or group of teens to run with the article."

TEEN POWER, Scripture Press Publications, Inc., Box 632, Glen Ellyn IL 60138. Contact: Editor. 90% freelance written. Quarterly Sunday School take-home paper with weekly parts. "*Teen Power* is a Sunday School take-home paper for young teens (ages 11-15). Its purpose is to show readers how biblical principles for Christian living can be applied to everyday life." **Pays on acceptance.** Publishes ms an average of 2 years after acceptance. Byline given. Buys one-time rights. Editorial lead time 1 year. Submit seasonal material 6 months in advance. Accepts simultaneous submissions. Reports in 3 months on mss. Sample copy and writer's guidelines for #10 SASE.

Nonfiction: Humor, inspirational, interview/profile, personal experience, religious. Buys 75 mss/year. Send complete ms. Length: 300-1,000 words. Pays $25-120.

Reprints: Accepts previously published submissions.

Photos: State availability of photos with submissions. Negotiates payment individually. Model releases required. Buys one-time rights.

Fiction: Humorous, religious, slice-of-life vignettes. Buys 75 mss/year. Send complete ms. Length: 600-1,200 words. Pays $45-120.

Tips: "We are looking for fresh, creative true stories, true-to-life fiction, and nonfiction articles. All must show how God and the Bible are relevant in the lives of today's teens. All manuscripts *must* have a clear, spiritual emphasis or 'take away value.' We don't use stories which have a good moral. Be careful not to preach or talk down to kids. Also, be realistic. Dialogue should be natural. Resolutions should not be too easy or tacked on. We are a specialized market with a distinct niche, but we do rely heavily on freelance writers. We are open to any new writer who grasps the purpose of our publication."

'TEEN, Petersen Publishing Co., 6420 Wilshire Blvd., Los Angeles CA 90048. (213)782-2950. Editor: Roxanne Camron. 40% freelance written. Monthly magazine covering teenage girls ages 12-19. " *'Teen* is edited for high school girls. We include all topics that are of interest to females aged 12-19. Our readers want articles on heavy hitting subjects like drugs, sex, teen pregnancy, etc., and we also devote a significant number of pages each month to health, beauty and fashion." Estab. 1957. Circ. 1,143,653. **Pays on acceptance.** Byline sometimes given. Buys all rights. Editorial lead time 6 months. Submit seasonal material 6 months in advance. Accepts simultaneous submissions. Reports in 10 weeks. Sample copy for $2.50. Writer's guidelines for #10 SASE.

Nonfiction: General interest, how-to (geared for teen market), humor, inspirational, personal experience. Buys 35 mss/year. Query with or without published clips. Length: 250-750 words. Payment varies depending on length of research required.

Fiction: Roxanne Camron. Adventure, condensed novels, fantasy, horror, mainstream, mystery, romance. Buys 12 mss/year. Send complete ms. Length: 2,500-3,500 words. Pays $250.

‡WHAT! A MAGAZINE, What! Publishers Inc., 108-93 Lombard Ave., Winnipeg, Manitoba R3B 3B1 Canada. Editor: Stu Slayen. 60% freelance written. Bimonthly magazine (during school year) covering teen issues. "*What! A Magazine* is distributed to high school students across Canada. We endeavor to produce a mag that is empowering, interactive and entertaining. We always respect the reader—today's teens are smart and creative (and critical)." Estab. 1987. Circ. 200,000. Pays 30 days after publication. Publishes ms an average of 3 months after acceptance. Byline given. Offers negotiable kill fee. Buys first North American serial rights. Editorial lead time 5 months. Submit seasonal material 5 months in advance. Reports in 2 months on queries; 1 month on mss. Sample copy for 9 × 12 SASE with Canadian postage. Writer's guidelines for #10 SASE with Canadian postage.

• See the interview with Stu Slayen in this edition of *Writer's Market.*

Nonfiction: General interest, humor, interview/profile, issue-oriented features. No cliché teen material. Buys 6-10 mss/year. Query with published clips. Length: 700-1,900 words. Pays $100-500 (Canadian). Sometimes pays expenses of writers on assignment.

Photos: Send photos with submission. Reviews transparencies, 4 × 6 prints. Negotiates payment individually. Identification of subjects required.

Tips: "Because *What! A Magazine* is distributed through schools (with the consent of school officials), it's important that each issue find the delicate balance between very cool and very responsible. We target very motivated young women and men. Pitches should stray from cliché and stories should challenge readers with depth, insight and color. All stories must be meaningful to a Canadian readership."

WITH, The Magazine for Radical Christian Youth, Faith and Life Press, 722 Main St., P.O. Box 347, Newton KS 67114-0347. (316)283-5100. Coeditors: Eddy Hall, Carol Duerksen. 60% freelance written. Magazine for teenagers published 8 times/year. "We are the magazine for Mennonite, Brethren, and Mennonite Brethren Youth. Our purpose is to disciple youth within congregations." Circ. 6,100. **Pays on acceptance.** Byline given. Buys one-time rights. Submit seasonal/holiday material 6 months in advance. Accepts simultaneous submissions. Reports in 1 month on queries; 2 months on mss. Sample copy for 9 × 12 SAE with 4 first-class stamps. Writer's guidelines and theme list for #10 SASE. Additional detailed guidelines for first person stories, how-to articles and/or fiction available for #10 SASE.

Nonfiction: Humor, personal experience, religious, how-to, youth. Buys 15 mss/year. Send complete ms. Length: 400-1,800 words. Pays 5¢/word for simultaneous rights; 3¢/word for reprint rights for unsolicited articles. Higher rates for first-person stories and how-to articles written on assignment. (Query on these.)

Reprints: Send typed ms with rights for sale noted, including information about when and where the material previously appeared. Pays 60% of amount paid for an original article.

Photos: Sometimes pays the expenses of writers on assignment. Send photos with submission. Reviews 8 × 10 b&w prints. Offers $10-50/photo. Identification of subjects required. Buys one-time rights.

Fiction: Humorous, religious, youth, parables. Buys 15 mss/year. Send complete ms. Length: 500-2,000 words. Payment same as nonfiction.

Poetry: Avant-garde, free verse, haiku, light verse, traditional. Buys 4-6 poems. Pays $10-25.

Tips: "We're looking for more wholesome humor, not necessarily religious—fiction, nonfiction, cartoons, light verse. Christmas and Easter material has a good chance with us because we receive so little of it."

‡YM, Gruner & Jahr, 685 Third Ave., New York NY 10017. (212)878-8644. Editor: Sally Lee. Contact: Stephanie Dolgoff, senior editor. 25% freelance written. Magazine covering teenage girls/dating. "We are a national magazine for young women ages 15-24. They're bright, enthusiastic and inquisitive. Our goal is to guide them—in effect, to be a 'best friend' and help them through the many exciting, yet often challenging, experiences of young adulthood." Estab. 1940s. Circ. 2,000,000. **Pays on acceptance.** Byline given. Offers 25% kill fee. Buys all rights. Editorial lead time 4 months. Submit seasonal material 5 months in advance. Accepts simultaneous submissions. Sample copy for $2.50. Writer's guidelines free on request.

• Ranked as one of the best markets for freelance writers in *Writer's Yearbook*'s annual "Top 100 Markets," January 1996.

Nonfiction: How-to, interview/profile, personal experience, first-person stories. "*YM* publishes two special issues a year. One is a self-discovery issue, the other is a love issue filled with articles on relationships." Buys 20 mss/year. Query with published clips. Length: 2,000 words maximum. Pays 75¢/word for assigned articles; 50-75¢/word for unsolicited articles. Pays expenses of writers on assignment.

Tips: "Our relationship articles are loaded with advice from psychologists and real teenagers. Areas most open to freelancers are: 2,000 word first-person stories covering a personal triumph over adversity—incorporating a topical social/political problem; 2,000 word relationship stories; 1,200 word relationship articles."

YOUNG SALVATIONIST, The Salvation Army, P.O. Box 269, Alexandria VA 22313-0269. (703)684-5500. Fax: (703)684-5539. Address all correspondence to Youth Editor. 75% freelance written. Works with a small number of new/unpublished writers each year. Monthly magazine for high school teens. "Only material with a definite Christian emphasis or from a Christian perspective will be considered." Circ. 50,000. **Pays on acceptance.** Publishes ms an average of 10 months after acceptance. Byline given. Buys first North American serial, first, one-time or second serial (reprint) rights. Submit seasonal/holiday material 6 months in advance. Reports in 2 months. Sample copy for 9×12 SAE with 3 first-class stamps. Writer's guidelines and theme list for #10 SASE.

Nonfiction: Inspirational, how-to, humor, interview/profile, personal experience, photo feature, religious. "Articles should deal with issues of relevance to teens (high school students) today; avoid 'preachiness' or moralizing." Buys 60 mss/year. Send complete ms. Length: 1,000-1,500 words. Pays 10¢/word.

Reprints: Send tearsheet, photocopy of article or typed ms with rights for sale noted and information about when and where the article previously appeared. Pays 100% of amount paid for an original article.

Fiction: Adventure, fantasy, humorous, religious, romance, science fiction—all from a Christian perspective. Length: 500-1,200 words. Pays 10¢/word. Occasionally publishes novel excerpts.

Tips: "Study magazine, familiarize yourself with the unique 'Salvationist' perspective of *Young Salvationist*; learn a little about the Salvation Army; media, sports, sex and dating are strongest appeal."

YOUTH UPDATE, St. Anthony Messenger Press, 1615 Republic St., Cincinnati OH 45210-1298. (513)241-5615. Editor: Carol Ann Morrow. 90% freelance written. Monthly newsletter of faith life for teenagers, "designed to attract, instruct, guide and challenge Catholics of high school age by applying the Gospel to modern problems/situations." Circ. 26,000. **Pays on acceptance.** Publishes ms an average of 6 months after acceptance. Byline given. Reports in 3 months. Sample copy and writer's guidelines for #10 SASE.

Nonfiction: Inspirational, practical self-help, spiritual. "Adults who pay for teen subs want more church-related and curriculum-related topics." Buys 12 mss/year. Query. Length: 2,200-2,300 words. Pays $350-400. Sometimes pays expenses of writers on assignment.

Tips: "Query first!"

YSB, Young Sisters & Brothers, Black Entertainment Television, 1900 W. Place NE, Washington DC 20018. (202)608-2200. Fax: (202)608-2598. Publisher: Debra Lee. Magazine published 10 times/year. "*YSB, Young Sisters & Brothers*, is a lifestyle magazine for today's African-American young adults. Editorial focuses on building self-esteem, and cultural awareness. It contains articles on music, fashion and sports; relationships, political and social issues; money management and finance. Issues also feature Black History, Black Colleges, Black Music Month, prom, spring and fall fashions and annual car reviews. Estab. 1991. This magazine did not respond to our request for information. Query before submitting.

ZELOS, P.O. Box 632, Glen Ellyn IL 60138-0632. Contact: Editor. 50% freelance written. Eager to work with new/unpublished writers. Quarterly notebook. Estab. 1973. Prefers one-time rights but buys some reprints. Purchases 52 mss/year. Byline given. Reports on accepted material in 3 months. Publishes ms an average of 1 year after acceptance. Returns rejected material in 2 months. Sample material and writer's guidelines for SASE. Sample copies for $5.50 (1-800-323-9409).

  • *Zelos* has gone to a quarterly, spiral-bound Christian Life Notebook. The book includes monthly and weekly calendars, staff-written devotionals and journaling activities, an advice column and a freelance-written feature to correlate with each weekly section. It is trying to publish more personal experience, profile, and "as told to to" stories. All material needs to be 1,000 words or less.

Nonfiction: "*Zelos*'s greatest need is for personal experience stories showing how God has worked in teens' lives. Stories are best written in first-person, 'as told to' author. Incorporate specific details, anecdotes, and dialogue. Show, don't tell, how the subject thought and felt. Weave spiritual conflicts and prayers into entire manuscript; avoid tacked-on sermons and morals. Stories should show how God has helped the person resolve a problem or how God helped save a person from trying circumstances (1,000 words or less). Avoid stories about accident and illness; focus on events and emotions of everyday life. We also need self-help or how-to articles with practical Christian advice on daily living, and trend articles addressing secular fads from a Christian perspective. We do not use devotional material, or fictionalized Bible stories." Pays 6-10¢/word. Some poetry ($20-50).

Reprints: Send tearsheet or photocopy of article or typed ms with rights for sale noted and information about when and where the article previously appeared. Pays 100% of the amount paid for an original article.

Photos: Whenever possible, provide clear 8×10 or 5×7 b&w photos to accompany mss (or any other available photos). Payment is $5-30.

Fiction: "We use true-to-life and humorous fiction."
Tips: "Study our 'Tips to Writers' pamphlet and sample copy, then send complete ms. In your cover letter, include information about who you are, writing qualifications, and experience working with teens. Include SASE."

TRAVEL, CAMPING AND TRAILER

Travel magazines give travelers indepth information about destinations, detailing the best places to go, attractions in the area and sites to see—but they also keep them up-to-date about potential negative aspects of these destinations. Publications in this category tell tourists and campers the where-tos and how-tos of travel. This category is extremely competitive, demanding quality writing, background information and professional photography. Each has its own slant. *Eco Traveler*, for example, covers "adventure travel with an environmental conscience," while *Trailer Life* presents articles on the recreational vehicle lifestyle. Sample copies should be studied carefully before sending submissions.

ADVENTURE WEST, America's Guide to Discovering the West, Adventure Media, Inc., P.O. Box 3210, Incline Village NV 89450. (702)832-1641. Executive Editor: Brian Beffort. Managing Editor: Kristina Schreck. 80% freelance written. Bimonthly magazine covering adventure travel in the West. Estab. 1992. Circ. 155,000. Pays on publication. Publishes ms an average of 6 months after acceptance. Byline given. Offers 15% kill fee. Buys first North American serial rights. Editorial lead time 4 months. Submit seasonal material 6 months in advance. Accepts simultaneous submissions. Reports in 2 months. Sample copy for $3.50 and 10×13 SASE with 9 first-class stamps. Writer's guidelines for SASE.
Nonfiction: Historical/nostalgic, humor, interview/profile, personal experience, photo feature, travel. "We only publish adventure travel done in the West, including Alaska, Hawaii, western Canada and western Mexico." Buys 80 mss/year. Query with published clips. Length: 800-3,000 words. Pays $150-500. Sometimes pays expenses of writers on assignment.
Reprints: Occasionally accepts previously published submissions. Send tearsheet of article or short story and information about when and where the article previously appeared.
Photos: Send photos with submission. Reviews transparencies and slides. Negotiates payment individually. Captions and identification of subjects required. "We need itemized list of photos submitted." Buys one-time rights.
Columns/Departments: Buys 80 mss/year. Query with published clips. Pays $150-450.
Fiction: Humorous, western. "We publish humorous experiences in the West; that is the only fiction we accept." Buys 4 mss/year. Query with published clips. Length: 1,000-1,500 words. Pays $270-450.
Tips: "We like exciting, inspirational first-person stories on adventure. If the query or the unsolicited ms grabs us, we will use it. Our writer's guidelines are comprehensive. Follow them."

‡ARRIVING MAGAZINE, The Ultimate in Transportation, M.A.K. Publishing, 3249 Cherry Ave., Long Beach CA 90807. Managing Editor: Barbara Witz. 100% freelance written. Monthly magazine covering extremely high end buses and RVs. "We cater to the lifestyle of multi-millionaire coach owners who are 50-75 and have the disposable time and income to travel. We are open to people with ideas on extremely expensive things for these people to do in all aspects of life." Estab. 1995. Circ. 20,000. Pays on publication. Publishes ms an average of 2 months after acceptance. Byline given. Offers $25 kill fee. Buys first North American serial rights. Editorial lead time 3 months. Submit seasonal material 3 months in advance. Accepts simultaneous submissions. Reports in 1 month only if we want to purchase the piece unless you send SASE. Sample copy for #10 SASE and $3 postage.
Nonfiction: How-to (anything relating to RVs and buses), interview/profile, new product, personal experience, photo feature, technical, travel, anything and everything relating to consumer buses, RVs, transportation and the good life. Buys 150 mss/year. Length: 1,000-3,000 words. Pays $100-250. Sometimes pays expenses of writers on assignment.
Reprints: Accepts previously published submissions.
Photos: State availability of photos with submission. Reviews contact sheets, negatives, transparencies, prints. Offers $10/photo. "We use 8-14 pictures per story." Buys one-time rights.
Columns/Departments: A Day In The Life (looks at people who work in the RV business); With Design in Mind (how to decorate your bus); Road Fix (how to repair your bus); all 1,000-2,000 words. Query. Pays $100-150.
Tips: "We hire people who have good ideas and can put them across convincingly. I think it's important that people think to the future—I've had people send me really nasty notes about how little we pay, without realizing that the eager query letter that they just sent to another magazine who pays more is one that I

freelance for at night. We're a brand new magazine, and I'm a young editor. We have nowhere to go but up and we're going to take our supporters with us."

ARUBA NIGHTS, Nights Publications, 1831 Rene Levesque Blvd. West, Montreal, Quebec H3H 1R4 Canada. Fax: (514)931-6273. Contact: Stephen Trotter, editor. Managing Editor: Zelly Zuskin. 90% freelance written. Annual magazine covering the Aruban vacation lifestyle experience with an upscale touch. Estab. 1988. Circ. 200,000. **Pays on acceptance.** Publishes ms an average of 9 months after acceptance. Offers 15% kill fee. Buys first North American serial and first Caribbean rights. Editorial lead time 1 month. Reports in 2 weeks on queries; 1 months on mss. Sample copy for $5. Writer's guidelines free on request.
Nonfiction: General interest, historical/nostalgic, how-to features relative to Aruba vacationers, humor, inspirational, interview/profile, eco-tourism, opinion, personal experience, photo feature, travel, Aruban culture, art, activities, entertainment, topics relative to vacationers in Aruba. "No negative pieces or stale rewrites." Buys 5-10 mss/year. Query with published clips. Length: 250-750 words. Pays $125-350 for assigned articles; $100-250 for unsolicited articles.
Photos: State availability with submission. Offers $25-100/photo. Captions, model releases, identification of subjects required. Buys one-time rights.
Tips: "Demonstrate your voice in your query letter. Be descriptive, employ vivid metaphors. Focus on individual aspects of the Aruban lifestyle and vacation experience (e.g., art, gambling tips, windsurfing, a colorful local character, a personal experience, etc.), rather than generalized overviews. Provide an angle that will be entertaining to both vacationers and Arubans."

ASU TRAVEL GUIDE, ASU Travel Guide, Inc., 1525 Francisco Blvd. E., San Rafael CA 94901. (415)459-0300. Fax: (415)459-0494. E-mail: asuguide.com. Website: http://www.ASUguide.com. Managing Editor: Christopher Gil. 80% freelance written. Quarterly guidebook covering international travel features and travel discounts for well-traveled airline employees. Estab. 1970. Circ. 60,000. Publishes ms an average of 4 months after acceptance. Byline given. Buys first North American serial rights, first and second rights to the same material, and second serial (reprint) rights to material originally published elsewhere; also makes work-for-hire assignments. Submit seasonal/holiday material 6 months in advance. Accepts simultaneous submissions. Reports in 1 year. Sample copy available for 6×9 SAE with 5 first-class stamps. Writer's guidelines for #10 SASE.
Nonfiction: International travel articles "similar to those run in consumer magazines. Not interested in amateur efforts from inexperienced travelers or personal experience articles that don't give useful information to other travelers." Buys 16 ms/year. Destination pieces only; no "Tips On Luggage" articles. Unsolicited mss or queries without SASE will not be acknowledged. No telephone queries. Length: 1,800 words. Pays $200.
Reprints: Send tearsheet of article with information about when and where the article previously appeared. Pays 100% of amount paid for an original article.
Photos: "Interested in clear, high-contrast photos." Reviews 5×7 and 8×10 b&w or color prints. "Payment for photos is included in article price; photos from tourist offices are acceptable."
Tips: "Query with samples of travel writing and a list of places you've recently visited. We appreciate clean and simple style. Keep verbs in the active tense and involve the reader in what you write. Avoid 'cute' writing, coined words and stale cliches. The most frequent mistakes made by writers in completing an article for us are: 1) Lazy writing—using words to describe a place that could describe any destination such as 'there is so much to do in (fill in destination) that whole guidebooks have been written about it'; 2) Including fare and tour package information—our readers make arrangements through their own airline."

‡BIG WORLD, Travel: On The Cheap & Down To Earth, Big World Publishing, P.O. Box 21, Coraopolis PA 15108-0021. E-mail: bigworld@ix.netcom.com. Editor: Jim Fortney. 85% freelance written. Bimonthly magazine covering independent travel. "We're looking for casual, first-person narratives that take into account the cultural/sociological/political side of travel." Estab. 1995. Circ. 2,000. Pays on publication. Publishes ms an average of 3 months after acceptance. Byline given. Buys one-time rights. Editorial lead time 2 months. Submit seasonal material 4 months in advance. Reports in 1 months on queries; 2 months on mss. Sample copy for $3. Writer's guidelines for #10 SASE.
Nonfiction: New product, opinion, personal experience, photo feature, travel. Buys 45 mss/year. Query. Pays $10-30.
Photos: Reviews prints. Negotiates payment individually. Captions required. Buys one-time rights.
Columns/Departments: Readers Writes (book reviews by subscribers) 400-500 words. Pay varies.
Tips: "We're not looking for romantic getaway pieces or lap-of-luxury bits. Our readers are decidedly downbeat and are looking for similarly-minded on-the-cheap and down-to-earth, first-person articles. Be breezy. Be yourself. First-time writers especially encouraged."

BONAIRE NIGHTS, Nights Publications, 1831 René Lévesque Blvd. W., Montreal, Quebec H3H 1R4 Canada. Fax: (514)931-6273. Editor: Stephen Trotter. 90% freelance written. Annual magazine covering Bonaire vacation experience. "Upbeat entertaining lifestyle articles: colorful profiles of locals, eco-tourism; lively features on culture, activities (particularly scuba and snorkeling), special events, historical attractions, how-to features. Audience is North American tourist." Estab. 1993. Circ. 60,000. **Pays on acceptance.** Publishes ms an average of 9 months after acceptance. Byline given. Offers 15% kill fee. Buys first North American serial rights and first Caribbean rights. Editorial lead time 1 month. Reports in 2 weeks on queries; 1 month on mss. Sample copy for $5. Writer's guidelines for #10 SASE.

Nonfiction: Lifestyle, general interest, historical/nostalgic, how-to, humor, inspirational, interview/profile, opinion, personal experience, photo feature, travel, local culture, art, activities, especially scuba diving, snorkeling, eco-tourism. Buys 6-9 mss/year. Query with published clips. Length: 250-750 words. Pays $125-350 for assigned articles; $100-250 for unsolicited articles.

Photos: State availability of photos with submission. Reviews transparencies. Offers $25-100/slide. Captions, model releases, identification of subjects required. Buys one-time or first rights.

Tips: "Demonstrate your voice in your query letter. Focus on the Bonaire lifestyle, what sets it apart from other islands. We want personal experience, not generalized overviews. Be positive and provide an angle that will appeal to residents as well as visitors."

BUON GIORNO, The Port Magazine of Costa Cruises, Onboard Media, 777 Arthur Godfrey Rd., Suite 300, Miami Beach FL 33140. (305)673-0400. Fax: (305)674-9396. Managing Editor: Lynn Ulivieri. 95% freelance written. Annual magazine covering Caribbean region. "This trilingual (English/French/Italian) in-cabin magazine reaches French, Italian and American cruise passengers travelling to various Caribbean port destinations. Stories must appeal to a multi-national readership." Estab. 1992. Circ. 69,950. Pays half on execution of agreement, half on acceptance of material. Publishes ms an average of 4 months after acceptance. Byline given. Offers 50% kill fee. Buys first or second serial (reprint) rights. Editorial lead time 6 months. Reports in 1 month. Sample copy for 11×14 SAE with 8 first-class stamps. Writer's guidelines for #10 SASE.

Nonfiction: Book excerpts, essays, general interest, humor, interview/profile, new product, photo feature, travel. Does not want politics, sex, religion, general history, shopping information or advertorials, no personal experience. Buys 12 features/year, plus assigned editorial covering ports-of-call and numerous fillers. Query with published clips. Length: 800-2,000 words. Pays $400-1,000 and contributor's copies, negotiable per assignment. Sometimes pays expenses of writers on assignment.

Reprints: Accepts previously published submissions, if so noted.

Photos: State availability of photos with submission. Negotiates payment individually. Captions, model releases, identification of subjects required. Buys one-time and seasonal reprint rights. Photo credit and contributor copies given.

Fillers: Anecdotes, facts, newsbreaks, short humor. Buys 50/year. Length: 50-300 words. Pays $25-100 and contributor copies.

Tips: "Do not send any general overviews on port destinations or editorial on shopping or long-standing attractions that can be found in any travel guide. Focus on unique aspects of island culture, colorful local personalities, new twists on the themes of ecology/wildlife, food, folklore, festivals, etc. A first-hand knowledge of the subject matter is a must. News-oriented material is always welcomed. Demonstrate your voice in your query letter, send a selection of writing samples that reveal your range, and include a list of subjects and regions of expertise."

CAMPERS MONTHLY, Northeast Edition–Maine to New York; Mid Atlantic Edition—New York to Virginia; Mid-Central Edition—Western Pennsylvania, Western New York, West Virginia, Eastern Ohio, P.O. Box 260, Quakertown PA 18951. (215)536-6420. Fax: (215)536-6509. E-mail: werv2@aol.com. Website: http://www.channel1/com/users/brosium. Editor: Paula Finkbeiner. 50% freelance written. Monthly (except December) tabloid covering tenting and recreational vehicle camping and travel. "With the above emphasis, we want to encourage our readers to explore all forms of outdoor recreation using a tent or recreational vehicle as a 'home away from home.' Travel-places to go, things to do and see." Estab. 1991 (Mid-Atlantic), 1993 (Northeast), 1995 (Mid-Central). Circ. 35,000 (Mid-Atlantic), 25,000 (Northeast), 20,000 (Mid-Central). Pays on publication. Publishes ms an average of 2 months after acceptance. Byline given. Buys simultaneous rights. Editorial lead time 2 months. Submit seasonal material 4 months in advance. Accepts simultaneous submissions. Reports in 2 months. Sample copy and writer's guidelines free on request.

Nonfiction: Historical/nostalgic (tied into a camping trip), how-to (selection, care, maintenance of RV's, tents, accessories, etc.) humor, personal experience, travel (camping in the Mid-Atlantic or Northeast region). Special issue: Snowbird Issue (October)—geared towards campers heading South. This is generally the only time we accept articles on areas outside our coverage area. Buys 15-20 mss/year. Send complete ms. Length: 800-1,500 words. Pays $90-100 for assigned articles; $50 or more for unsolicited articles. Sometimes pays expenses of writers on assignment.

Reprints: Send photocopy of article or typed ms with rights for sale noted and information about when and where the article previously appeared. Pays 50% of amount paid for an original article.

Photos: Send photos with submission. Reviews 5×7 or 8×10 glossy b&w prints. Offers $3-5/photo. Don't send snapshots or polaroids. Avoid slides.

Columns/Departments: Campground Cook (Ideas for cooking in RV's, tents and over campfires, should include recipes), 500-1,000 words; Tales From The Road (humorous stories of "on-the-road" travel), 350-

800 words; Tech Tips (technical pieces on maintenance and enhanced usage of RV-related equipment), 350-1,800 words. Buys 15 mss/year. Send complete ms. Pays $40-60.

Fiction: Humorous, slice-of-life vignettes. Buys 10 mss/year. Query. Length: 300-1,000 words. Pays $60-75.

Fillers: Facts, short humor. Buys 8/year. Length: 30-350. Pays $20-35.

Tips: Most open to freelancers are "destination pieces focusing on a single attraction or activity or closely clustered attractions are always needed. General interest material, technical or safety ideas (for RVs and tents) is an area we're always looking for pieces on. Off the beaten track destinations always get priority.We need submissions for destination pieces for our Northeast edition."

CAMPING TODAY, Official Publication of the Family Campers & RVers, 126 Hermitage Rd., Butler PA 16001-8509. (412)283-7401. Editors: DeWayne Johnston and June Johnston. 30% freelance written. Prefers to work with published/established writers. Monthly official membership publication of the FCRV, "the largest nonprofit family camping and RV organization in the United States and Canada. Members are heavily oriented toward RV travel, both weekend and extended vacations. Concentration is on member activities in chapters. Group is also interested in conservation and wildlife. The majority of members are retired." Estab. 1983. Circ. 25,000. Pays on publication. Publishes ms an average of 6 months after acceptance. Byline given. Buys one-time rights. Submit seasonal/holiday material 3 months in advance. Accepts simultaneous submissions. Reports in 2 months. Sample copy and guidelines for 4 first-class stamps. Writer's guidelines only for #10 SASE.

Nonfiction: Travel (interesting places to visit by RV, camping), humor (camping or travel related, please, no "our first campout stories"), interview/profile (interesting campers), new products, technical (RVs related). Buys 10-15 mss/year. Send complete ms with photos. Length: 750-2,000 words. Pays $50-150.

Reprints: Send typed ms with rights for sale noted and information about when and where the article previously appeared. Pays 35-50% of amount paid for an original article.

Photos: Send photos with ms. Need b&w or sharp color prints inside (we can make prints from slides) and vertical transparencies for cover. Captions required.

Tips: "Freelance material on RV travel, RV maintenance/safety, and items of general camping interest throughout the United States and Canada will receive special attention."

CANCÚN NIGHTS, Nights Publications, 1831 Rene Levesque Blvd. West, Montreal, Quebec H3H 1R4 Canada. Fax: (514)931-6273. Editor: Stephen Trotter. Managing Editor: Zelly Zuskin. 80% freelance written. Semiannual destination lifestyle magazine covering the Cancún vacation experience. Seeking "upbeat, entertaining lifestyle articles: colorful profiles of locals; lively features on culture, activities, night life, special events, historical attractions, Mayan achievements; how-to features; humor. Our audience is the North American vacationer." Estab. 1991. Circ. 650,000. **Pays on acceptance.** Publishes ms an average of 5 months after acceptance. Offers 15% kill fee. Buys first North American serial rights and first Mexican rights. Editorial lead time 1 month. Reports 2 weeks on queries; 1 month on mss. Sample copy for $5. Writer's guidelines free on request.

Nonfiction: General interest, historical/nostalgic, how-to let vacationers get the most from their holiday, humor, inspirational, eco-tourism, interview/profile, lifestyle, opinion, personal experience, photo feature, travel, local culture, art, activities, night life, topics relative to vacationers in Cancún. No negative pieces, stale rewrites or cliché copy. Buys 8-12 mss/year. Query with published clips. Length: 250-750 words. Pays $125-350 for assigned articles; $100-250 for unsolicited articles.

Photos: State availability of photos with submission. Reviews transparencies. Offers $25-100/photo. Captions, model releases, identification of subjects required. Buys one-time rights.

Tips: "Demonstrate your voice in your query letter. Focus on individual aspects of the Cancún lifestyle and vacation experience (e.g., art, history, snorkeling, fishing, a colorful local character, a personal experience, etc.), entertaining to both vacationers and residents."

‡CAR & TRAVEL, American Automobile Association, 1000 AAA Dr., Heathrow Fl 32746-5063. (407)444-8544. Editor-in-Chief: Doug Damerst. Contact: Marianne Camas, senior editor. 20% freelance written. Magazine covering cars and travel. Short-form features and departments on automotive and travel subjects. Tightly focused, reportorial style. Audience AAA members—50+, college-educated, over $45,000 annual income. Estab. 1995. Circ. 5,000,000. Pays on publication. Byline given. Offers 25% kill fee. Buys first North American serial rights. Editorial lead time 4 months. Submit seasonal material 6 months in advance. Reports in 2 months. Sample copy and writer's guidelines free on request.

Nonfiction: Travel (automotive). No first-person travel. Buys 25 mss/year. Query with published clips. Length: 750-1,300 words. Pays $350-800 for assigned articles. Sometimes pays expenses of writers on assignment.

Photos: State availability of photos with query. Reviews tearsheets (cannot return samples). Negotiates payment individually. Captions, model releases, identification of subjects required. Buys one-time rights.

Columns/Departments: Cars (products, maintenance); Destination News (upcoming events); both 150-200 words. Buys 6 mss/year. Query with published clips. Pays $75-150.

Tips: "We're looking for tightly focused, reportorial style on caring for/buying cars and travel tips. Very few destination queries are considered."

CARIBBEAN TRAVEL AND LIFE, 8403 Colesville Rd., Suite 830, Silver Spring MD 20910. (301)588-2300. Editor-in-Chief: Veronica Gould Stoddart. 90% freelance written. Prefers to work with published/established writers. Bimonthly magazine covering travel to the Caribbean, Bahamas and Bermuda. Estab. 1985. Circ. 130,000. Pays on publication. Publishes ms an average of 3 months after acceptance. Byline given. Offers 25% kill fee. Buys first North American serial rights. Submit seasonal/holiday material 6 months in advance. Reports in 2 months. Sample copy for 9 × 12 SAE with 9 first-class stamps. Writer's guidelines for #10 SASE.
Nonfiction: General interest, how-to, interview/profile, culture, personal experience, travel. No guidebook rehashing; superficial destination pieces or critical exposes. Buys 30 mss/year. Query with published clips. Length: 2,000-2,500 words. Pays $550.
Photos: Send photos with submission. Reviews 35mm transparencies. Offers $75-400/photo. Captions and identification of subjects required. Buys one-time rights.
Columns/Departments: Resort Spotlight (in-depth review of luxury resort); Tradewinds (focus on one particular kind of water sport or sailing/cruising); Island Buys (best shopping for luxury goods, crafts, duty-free); Island Spice (best cuisine and/or restaurant reviews with recipes); Money Matters (dollar-wise travel, bargain destinations, how to save money); EcoWatch (conservation efforts and projects); all 1,000-1,500 words; Postcards from Paradise (short items on great finds in travel, culture, and special attractions), 500 words. Buys 36 mss/year. Query with published clips or send complete ms. Length: 500-1,250 words. Pays $75-200.
Tips: "We are especially looking for stories with a personal touch and lively, entertaining anecdotes, as well as strong insight into people and places being covered. Writer should demonstrate why he/she is the best person to do that story based on extensive knowledge of the subject, frequent visits to destination, residence in destination, specialty in field."

‡**CHICAGO TRIBUNE**, Travel Section, 435 N. Michigan Ave., Chicago IL 60611. (312)222-3999. Travel Editor: Randy Curwen. Weekly Sunday newspaper leisure travel section averaging 22 pages aimed at vacation travelers. Circ. 1,100,000. Pays on publication. Publishes ms an average of 6 weeks after acceptance. Byline given. Buys one-time rights (which includes microfilm, online and CD/ROM usage). Submit seasonal/holiday material 2 months in advance. Accepts simultaneous submissions. Reports in 1 month. Sample copy for large SAE with $1.50 postage. Writer's guidelines for #10 SASE.
Nonfiction: Essays, general interest, historical/nostalgic, how-to (travel, pack), humor, opinion, personal experience, photo feature, travel. "There will be 16 special issues in the next 18 months." Buys 250 mss/year. Send complete ms. Length: 500-2,000 words. Pays $100-400.
Photos: State availability of photos with submission. Reviews 35mm transparencies, 8 × 10 or 5 × 7 prints. Offers $100/color photo; $25/b&w; $100 for cover. Captions required. Buys one-time rights.
Tips: "Be professional. Use a word processor. Make the reader want to go to the area being written about. Only 1% of manuscripts make it."

‡**CLUBMEX**, 3450 Bonita Rd., Suite 101, Chula Vista CA 91910-3249. (619)585-3033. Fax: (619)420-8133. Publisher/Editor: Chuck Stein. 75% freelance written. Bimonthly newsletter on Baja California and Mexico as a travel destination. "Our readers are travelers to Mexico, and are interested in retirement, RV news and tours. They are knowledgeable but are always looking for new places to see." Estab. 1975. Circ. 5,000. Pays on publication. Publishes an average of 2 months after acceptance. Byline given. Buys first North American serial rights. Submit seasonal/holiday material 3 months in advance. Reports in 1 month. Free sample copy. Writer's guidelines for #10 SAE with 2 first-class stamps.
  ● *Clubmex* now accepts articles dealing with all of Mexico.
Nonfiction: Historical, humor, interview, personal experience, travel. Buys 36-50 mss/year. Send complete ms. Length: 900-1,500 words. Pays $65 for the cover story and $50 for other articles used.
Reprints: Send photocopy of article. Pays 100% of amount paid for an original article.
Photos: State availability of photos with submission. Reviews 3 × 5 prints. Offers no additional payment for photos accepted with ms. Captions required. Buys one-time rights.

COAST TO COAST MAGAZINE, A Publication for the Members of Coast to Coast Magazine, 2575 Vista Del Mar Dr., Ventura CA 93001-3920. Editor: Valerie Law. 80% freelance written. magazine published 8 times/year for members of Coast to Coast Resorts. Estab. 1972. Circ. 300,000. **Pays on acceptance.** Publishes ms an average of 3 months after acceptance. Byline given. Offers 33% kill fee. Buys first North American serial rights. Submit seasonal/holiday material 5 months in advance. Reports in 1 month on queries; 2 months on mss. Sample copy for $2 and 9 × 12 SASE.
Nonfiction: Book excerpts, essays, general interest, historical/nostalgic, how-to, humor, inspirational, interview/profile, new product, opinion, personal experience, photo feature, technical, travel. Buys 50 mss/year. Query with published clips or send complete ms. Length: 500-2,500 words. Pays $75-600.

Reprints: Send photocopy of article, information about when and where the article previously appeared. Pays approximately 50% of the amount paid for an original article.
Photos: Send photos with submission. Reviews transparencies. Offers $50-600/photo. Identification of subjects required. Buys one-time rights.
Tips: "Send published clips with queries, or story ideas will not be considered."

CONDÉ NAST TRAVELER, The Condé Nast Publications, 360 Madison Ave., New York NY 10017. (212)880-8800. Editor: Thomas J. Wallace. Managing Editor: Dee Aldrich. 75% freelance written. Monthly magazine covering travel. "Our motto, Truth in Travel, sums up our editorial philosophy: to present travel destinations, news and features in a candid, journalistic style. Our writers do not accept complimentary tickets, hotel rooms, gifts, or the like. While our departments present service information in a tipsheet or newsletter manner, our destination stories are literary in tone. Our readers are affluent, well-educated, and sophisticated about travel." Estab. 1987. Circ. 850,000. "Please keep in mind that we very rarely assign stories based on unsolicited queries because (1) our inventory of unused stories (features and departments) is very large, and (2) most story ideas are generated inhouse by the editors, as it is very difficult for outsiders to anticipate the needs of our inventory. To submit story ideas, send a brief (one paragraph) description of the idea(s) to the appropriate editor. Please do not send clips, resumes, photographs, itineraries, or abridged or full-length manuscripts. Due to our editorial policy, we *do not* purchase completed manuscripts. Telephone calls are not accepted."

THE COOL TRAVELER, P.O. Box 273, Selins Grove PA 17870-1813. Contact: Bob Moore, editor/publisher. Managing Editor: MaryBeth Feeney. 100% freelance written. Bimonthly publication covering travel. "We do not emphasize affluence but rather the experiences one has while traveling: romance, adventure, thrills, chills, etc. We have even published excerpts from diaries!" Estab. 1988. Circ. 750. Pays on publication. Publishes ms an average of 5 months after acceptance. Byline given. Send bio. Buys one-time rights. Submit seasonal/holiday material 4 months in advance. Accepts simultaneous submissions. Reports in 6 weeks "unless we like it—then it could be 4-6 months." Sample copy for $3. Free writer's guidelines with SASE.
   • *The Cool Traveler* would like more information-based material and would like to hear from travelers on journeys lasting over six months: on-the-scene information.
Nonfiction: Personal experience, travel, art history. Special issues: Christmas and International Festival. "We don't want a listing of names and prices but personal experiences and unusual experiences. Writers should have a sense of humor." Buys 15 mss/year. Send complete ms. Length: 800-1,200 words. Pays $5-20 for unsolicited articles.
Reprints: Send information about when and where the article previously appeared. Payment is negotiable.
Columns/Departments: News items pertaining to particular countries. ("Really need these!") Seasonal (material pertaining to a certain time of year: like a winter festival or summer carnival), 1,500 words maximum. Women travel. Pays $5-20. Big need for tidbits.
Poetry: Free verse, light verse, traditional. No poetry that is too sentimental. Buys 3 poems/year. Submit maximum 3 poems. Length: 5-75 lines. Pays $5-20.
Tips: "We would strongly like some strictly news-oriented material."

CROWN & ANCHOR, The Port Magazine of Royal Caribbean Cruise Line, Onboard Media. 777 Arthur Godfrey Rd., Suite 300, Miami Beach FL 33140. (305)673-0400. Fax: (305)674-9396. Managing Editor: Lynn Ulivieri. 95% freelance written. Annual magazine covering the Caribbean, Far East, Mexican Riviera, the Bahamas and Alaska. "This publication reaches cruise vacationers on board RCCL ships on 3-11 night Caribbean, Bahamas, Mexican Riviera, Alaska and Far East itineraries. Culture, art, architecutre, natural wonders, food, folklore, legends, lingo/idioms, festivals, literature, eco-systems, local wares of these regions. Current themes such as celebrity retreats, hit recordings and hot artists and writers are welcomed." Estab. 1992. Circ. 792,184. Pays half on execution of agreement, half on acceptance of material. Publishes ms an average of 4 months after acceptance. Offers 50% kill fee. Buys first or second serial (reprint) rights. Editorial lead time 6 months. Reports in 1 month. Sample copy for 11 × 14 SAE with 10 first-class stamps. Writer's guidelines for #10 SASE.
Nonfiction: Book excerpts, essays, general interest, humor, interview/profile, new product, photo feature, travel. Does not want politics, sex, religion, general history, shopping information or advertorials, no personal experience. Buys 25 features/year, plus assigned editorial covering ports-of-call and numerous fillers. Query with published clips. Length: 800-2,000 words. Pays $400-1,000, negotiable per assignment. Sometimes pays expenses of writers on assignment. Byline and bionote given. Contributor copies given.
Reprints: Accepts previously published submissions, if so noted.
Photos: State availability of photos with submission. Negotiates payment individually. Captions, model releases, identification of subjects required. Buys one-time and seasonal reprint rights.
Fillers: Anecdotes, facts, newsbreaks, short humor. Buys 50/year. Length: 50-200 words. Pays $25-100 or contributors copies. Byline given.
Tips: "Do not send any general overviews on port destinations or editorial on shopping or long-standing attractions that can be found in any travel guide. Focus on unique aspects of island culture, colorful local

personalities, new twists on the themes of ecology/wildlife, food, folklore, festivals, etc. A first-hand knowl-edge of the subject matter is a must. News-oriented material is always welcomed. Demonstrate your voice in your query letter, send a selection of writing samples that reveal your range, and include a list of subjects and regions of expertise."

CRUISE TRAVEL MAGAZINE, World Publishing Co., 990 Grove St., Evanston IL 60201-4370. (708)491-6440. Editor: Robert Meyers. Contact: Charles Doherty, managing editor. 95% freelance written. Bimonthly magazine on cruise travel. "This is a consumer-oriented travel publication covering the world of pleasure cruising on large cruise ships (with some coverage of smaller ships), including ports, travel tips, roundups." Estab. 1979. **Pays on acceptance.** Publishes ms an average of 6 months after acceptance. Byline given. Offers 50% kill fee. Buys first North American serial, one-time or second serial (reprint) rights. Accepts simultaneous submissions. Reports in 1 month. Sample copy for $5 and 9×12 SAE with 6 first-class stamps. Writer's guidelines for #10 SASE.
Nonfiction: General interest, historical/nostalgic, interview/profile, personal experience, photo feature, travel. "No daily cruise 'diary', My First Cruise, etc." Buys 72 mss/year. Query with or without published clips, or send complete ms. Length: 500-1,500 words. Pays $100-400.
Reprints: Send tearsheet or photocopy of article and typed ms with rights for sale noted.
Photos: Send photos with submission. Reviews transparencies and prints. "Must be color, 35m preferred (other format OK); color prints second choice." Offers no additional payment for photos accepted with ms "but pay more for well-illustrated ms." Captions and identification of subjects required. Buys one-time rights.
Fillers: Anecdotes, facts. Buys 3 mss/year. Length: 300-700 words. Pays $75-200.
Tips: "Do your homework. Know what we do and what sorts of things we publish. Know the cruise industry—we can't use novices. Good, sharp, bright color photography opens the door fast. We still need good pictures—we are not interested in developing any new contributors who cannot provide color support to manuscripts."

CRUISING IN STYLE, The Port Magazine of Crystal Cruises, Onboard Media, Inc. 777 Arthur Godfrey Rd., Suite 300, Miami Beach FL 33140. (305)673-0400. Fax: (305)674-9396. Managing Editor: Lynn Ulivieri. 95% freelance written. Annual magazine covering Caribbean, Panama Canal, Mexican Riviera. "This in-cabin magazine reaches sophisticated cruise passengers seeking a vacation/learning experience. We are looking for well-researched original material on interesting aspects of the port destination." Estab. 1992. Circ. 792,184. **Pays half on execution of agreement, half on acceptance of material.** Publishes ms an average of 4 months after acceptance. Byline given. Offers 50% kill fee. Buys first or second serial (reprint) rights. Editorial lead time 6 months. Reports in 1 month. Sample copy for 11×14 SAE with 10 first-class stamps. Writer's guidelines for #10 SASE.
Nonfiction: Book excerpts, essays, general interest, humor, interview/profile, new product, photo feature, travel. Does not want politics, sex, religion, general history, shopping information or advertorials, no personal experience. Buys 12 features/year, plus assigned editorial covering ports-of-call and numerous fillers. Query with published clips. Length: 800-2,000 words. Pays $400-1,000, negotiable per assignment. Sometimes pays expenses of writers on assignment.
Reprints: Accepts previously published submissions, if so noted.
Photos: State availability of photos with submission. Negotiates payment individually. Captions, model releases, identification of subjects required. Buys one-time and seasonal reprint rights. Photo credit and contributor copies given.
Fillers: Anecdotes, facts, newsbreaks, short humor. Buys 50/year. Length: 50-300 words. Pays $25-100 and contributor copies.
Tips: "Do not send any general overviews on port destinations or editorial on shopping or long-standing attractions that can be found in any travel guide. Focus on unique aspects of island culture, colorful local personalities, new twists on the themes of ecology/wildlife, food, folklore, festivals, etc. A first-hand knowl-edge of the subject matter is a must. News-oriented material is always welcomed. Demonstrate your voice in your query letter, send a selection of writing samples that reveal your range, and include a list of subjects and regions of expertise."

CURAÇAO NIGHTS, Nights Publications, 1831 Rene Levesque Blvd. West, Montreal, Quebec H3H 1R4 Canada. Fax: (514)931-6273. Editor: Stephen Trotter. Managing Editor: Zelly Zuskin. 90% freelance written. Annual magazine covering the Curaçao vacation experience. "We are seeking upbeat, entertaining lifestyle articles; colorful profiles of locals; lively features on culture, activities, night life, eco-tourism, special events,

ALWAYS CHECK the most recent copy of a magazine for the address and editor's name before you send in a query or manuscript.

gambling; how-to features; humor. Our audience is the North American vacationer." Estab. 1989. Circ. 155,000. **Pays on acceptance.** Publishes ms an average of 10 months after acceptance. Byline given. Offers 15% kill fee. Buys first North American serial and first Caribbean rights. Editorial lead time 1 month. Reports in 2 weeks on queries; 1 month on mss. Sample copy for $5. Writer's guidelines free on request.

Nonfiction: General interest, historical/nostalgic, how-to help a vacationer get the most from their vacation, eco-tourism, humor, inspirational, interview/profile, lifestyle, opinion, personal experience, photo feature, travel, local culture, art, activities, night life, topics relative to vacationers in Curaçao. "No negative pieces, generic copy or stale rewrites." Buys 5-10 mss/year. Query with published clips. Length: 250-750 words. Pays $125-$350 for assigned articles; $100-$250 for unsolicited articles.

Photos: State availability of photos with submission. Reviews transparencies. Offers $25-100/photo. Captions, model releases, identification of subjects required. Buys one-time rights.

Tips: "Demonstrate your voice in your query letter. Focus on individual aspects of the island lifestyle and vacation experience (e.g., art, gambling tips, windsurfing, a colorful local character, a personal experience, etc.), rather than generalized overviews. Provide an angle that will be entertaining to both vacationers and Curaçaoans."

DESTINATIONS, The Port Magazine of Celebrity Cruises, Onboard Media, 777 Arthur Godfrey Rd., Suite 300, Miami Beach FL 33140. (305)673-0400. Fax: (305)674-9396. Managing Editor: Lynn Ulivieri. 95% freelance written. Annual magazine covering Caribbean, Panama Canal, Bahamas regions. "This in-cabin magazine reaches cruise passengers traveling to various Caribbean ports of call. We are looking for original material on interesting aspects of the island destination. We are not interested in articles on cruising, per se, or anything related to the cruise ship." Estab. 1992. Circ. 792,184. **Pays half on execution of agreement, half on acceptance of material.** Publishes ms an average of 4 months after acceptance. Offers 50% kill fee. Buys first or second serial (reprint) rights. Editorial lead time 6 months. Reports in 1 month. Sample copy free on written request and 11 × 14 SAE with 10 first-class stamps. Writer's guidelines for #10 SASE.

Nonfiction: Book excerpts, essays, general interest, humor, interview/profile, new product, photo feature, travel. Does not want politics, sex, religion, general history, shopping information or advertorials, no personal experience. Buys 12 features/year, plus assigned editorial covering ports-of-call and numerous fillers. Query with published clips. Length: 800-2,000 words. Pays $400-1,000 and contributors copies, negotiable per assignment. Sometimes pays expenses of writers on assignment.

Reprints: Accepts previously published submissions, if so noted.

Photos: State availability of photos with submission. Negotiates payment individually. Captions, model releases, identification of subjects required. Buys one-time and seasonal reprint rights. Photo credit and contributor copies given.

Fillers: Anecdotes, facts, newsbreaks, short humor. Buys 50/year. Length: 50-300 words. Pays $25-100 and contributor copies.

Tips: "Do not send any general overviews on port destinations or editorial on shopping or long-standing attractions that can be found in any travel guide. Focus on unique aspects of island culture, colorful local personalities, new twists on the themes of ecology/wildlife, food, folklore, festivals, etc. A first-hand knowledge of the subject matter is a must. News-oriented material is always welcomed. Demonstrate your voice in your query letter, send a selection of writing samples that reveal your range, and include a list of subjects and regions of expertise."

‡ECOTRAVELER, EcoTraveler, Inc., 2535 NW Upshur St., Portland OR 97210. (503)224-9080. Fax: (503)224-4266. E-mail: ecotrav@aol.com. Editor: Lisa Tabb. 90% freelance written. Bimonthly magazine covering adventure travel with an environmental conscience. "Our readers are educated, affluent, conscientious adventure seekers. They are left-leaning and active. The median age is 42 years old." Estab. 1990. Circ. 100,000. Pays 30 days after date of publication. Publishes ms an average of 4 months after acceptance. Byline given. Offers 25% kill fee or $150. Buys first North American serial and one-time rights. Editorial lead time 6 months. Submit seasonal material 4 months in advance. Accepts simultaneous submissions. Sample copy for $5. Writer's guidelines for #10 SASE.

Nonfiction: Book excerpts, general interest, historical/nostalgic, how-to, humor, inspirational, interview/profile, new product, opinion, personal experience, photo feature, travel. Special issues: Adventure cruises, Eco-hotels in the Caribbean. Buys 100 mss/year. Send complete ms. Pays $50-1,000 for assigned articles; $50-600 for unsolicited articles. Sometimes pays expenses of writers on assignment.

Reprints: Accepts previously published submissions.

Photos: State availability of or send photos with submission. Negotiates payment individually. Captions, identification of subjects required. Buys one-time and CD rights.

Columns/Departments: Heatlh, General, Travel Tips, Explorations, Photo, Historical, Profiles. Buys lots of mss/year. Send complete ms. Pays $50-300.

ENDLESS VACATION, Endless Vacation, P.O. 80260, Indianapolis IN 46280-0260. (317)871-9504. Fax: (317)871-9507. Senior Editor: Jami Stall. Prefers to work with published/established writers. Bimonthly magazine covering travel destinations, activities and issues that enhance the lives of vacationers. Estab. 1974.

Circ. 1,024,287. **Pays on acceptance.** Publishes ms an average of 6 months after acceptance. Byline given. Buys first North American serial rights. Accepts simultaneous submissions. Reports in 1 month. Sample copy for $5 and 9×12 SAE with 3 first-class stamps. Writer's guidelines for #10 SASE.

• Ranked as one of the best markets for freelance writers in *Writer's Yearbook's* annual "Top 100 Markets," January 1996.

Nonfiction: Contact: Senior Editor. Buys 24 mss/year (approximately). Most are from established writers already published in *Endless Vacation. Accepts very few unsolicited pieces.* Query with published clips. Length: 1,000-2,000 words. Pays $500-1,000 for assigned articles; $250-800 for unsolicited articles. Sometimes pays the expenses of writers on assignment.

Reprints: Send photocopy of article and typed ms with rights for sale noted and information about when and where the article previously appeared. Pays 25% of amount paid for an original article.

Photos: Reviews 4×5 transparencies and 35mm slides. Offers $100-500/photo. Model releases and identification of subjects required. Buys one-time rights.

Columns/Departments: Complete Traveler (on travel news and service-related information); Weekender (on domestic weekend vacation travel). Query with published clips. Length: 800-1,000 words. Pays $150-600. Sometimes pays the expenses of writers on assignment. Also news items for Facts, Fads and Fun Stuff column on travel news, products or problems. Length: 100-200 words. Pays $100/item.

Tips: "We will continue to focus on travel trends and timeshare resort destinations. Articles must be packed with pertinent facts and applicable how-tos. Information—addresses, phone numbers, dates of events, costs—must be current and accurate. We like to see a variety of stylistic approaches, but in all cases the lead must be strong. A writer should realize that we require first-hand knowledge of the subject and plenty of practical information. For further understanding of *Endless Vacation's* direction, the writer should study the magazine and guidelines for writers."

FAMILY MOTOR COACHING, Official Publication of the Family Motor Coach Association, 8291 Clough Pike, Cincinnati OH 45244-2796. (513)474-3622. Fax: (513)474-2332. Editor: Pamela Wisby Kay. Associate Editor: Robbin Gould. 80% freelance written. "We prefer that writers be experienced RVers." Monthly magazine emphasizing travel by motorhome, motorhome mechanics, maintenance and other technical information. Estab. 1963. Circ. 99,000. **Pays on acceptance.** Publishes ms an average of 8 months after acceptance. Buys first North American serial rights. Byline given. Submit seasonal/holiday material 4 months in advance. Reports in 2 months. Sample copy for $2.50. Writer's guidelines for #10 SASE.

Nonfiction: Motorhome travel (various areas of country accessible by motor coach), how-to (do it yourself motor home projects and modifications), bus conversions, humor, interview/profile, new product, technical, nostalgia. Buys 15-20 mss/issue. Query with published clips . Length: 1,000-2,000 words. Pays $100-500.

Photos: State availability of photos with query. Offers no additional payment for b&w contact sheets, 35mm or 2¼×2¼ color transparencies. Captions, model releases required. Prefers first North American serial rights but will consider one-time rights on photos only.

Tips: "The greatest number of contributions we receive are travel; therefore, that area is the most competitive. However, it also represents the easiest way to break in to our publication. Articles should be written for those traveling by self-contained motor home. The destinations must be accessible to motor home travelers and any peculiar road conditions should be mentioned."

‡GETAWAYS, The Publisher's Group, P.O. Box 510366, Salt Lake City UT 84151-0366. Fax: (801)322-1098. Editor: Vicki Andersen. Contact: Anne E. Zombro, publisher. 80% freelance written. Quarterly magazine covering travel, "both domestic and foreign destinations. *Getaways* takes you to all the places you've always wanted to go to—from budget tours to extravagant vacations." Estab. 1996. Circ. 25,000. Pays on publication. Publishes ms an average of 6 months after acceptance. Byline given. Buys first North American serial and second serial (reprint) rights. Editorial lead time 2 months. Submit seasonal material 4 months in advance. Accepts simultaneous submissions. Reports in 1 month on queries; 2 months on mss. Sample copy for $2 and 9×12 SAE. Writer's guidelines for #10 SASE.

Nonfiction: Essays, personal experience, photo feature, travel. Buys 10-12 mss/year. Query with published clips. Length: 1,000-1,300 words. Pays $125-800.

Reprints: Accepts previously published submissions.

Photos: Send photos with submission. Reviews 4×5 transparencies (preferred), any size prints. Negotiates payment individually. Captions, model releases, identification of subjects required. Buys one-time or all rights.

Columns/Departments: Travel tips (domestic and foreign), 500 words. Buys 6 mss/year. Query with published clips. Pays $50-125.

‡GIBBONS-HUMMS GUIDE, Florida Keys-Key West, Gibbons Publishing, Inc., P.O. Box 6524, Key West FL 33041-6524. (305)296-7300 or (800)273-1026. Fax: (305)296-7414. Editor: Gibbons D. Cline. Contact: Vanessa Richards, editorial assistant. 15% freelance written. Quarterly magazine covering travel, tourism. Targeted to tourists and frequent visitors to Florida Keys (Monroe County, FL, from Key Largo to Key West). Estab. 1972. Circ. 55,000. Pays on publication. Publishes ms an average of 6 months after acceptance. Byline given. Buys all rights. Editorial lead time 6 months. Submit seasonal material at least 6 months in advance. Reports in 6 months on queries; 3 months on mss. Sample copy free on request. Writer's guidelines free on request.

Nonfiction: General interest, historical/nostalgic, how-to (water sports), humor, new product (marine related), technical (water sports), travel. Special issues: Reefs and wrecks—highlighting artificial and natural reefs offshore for fishing, diving and snorkeling enthusiasts; Vacation accommodations—condos, bed and breakfast inns, resorts, hotels, hostels, etc. "We need accurate tourist tips—tell us about the best attractions and dining spots. No more vacation stories, quizzes, trivia. Would like to see more fishing, diving and boating. No religious or erotic material." Buys 5-10 mss/year. Query with published clips. Length: 500-1,500 words. Pays $2/column inch.

Photos: State availability of photos with submission. No additional payment offered for photos with ms. Reviews any size transparencies, prints, slides. Model releases and identification of subjects required. Buys all rights.

Columns/Departments: Fishing Digest (fishing hotspots, how-to, new equipment), 1,000 words; Keys Under the Seas (diving how-to, new equipment), 1,000 words; Touring Highlights (attractions: Key West, Lower Keys, Marathon, Islamorada, Key Largo), 1,000 words. Buys 5 mss/year. Query with published clips. Pays $2/column inch to $100.

Fillers: Facts, trivia, puzzles—crossword or otherwise. Buys 3-5/year. Length: 100-800 words. Pays $2/column inch to $100.

Tips: "Please send résumé with query and/or manuscripts. It is helpful to visit Keys before trying to write about them. Get a feel for unique attitude, atmosphere and lifestyle in the Keys. Focus on things to do, like water sports. Try it, then write about it—but not from a personal experience angle. Find unique angles: strange characters, humorous anecdotes, etc. What makes *your* experience in the Keys different from everyone else's? Find a special bargain? Use new, state-of-the-art equipment? Meet a 90-year-old grandmother who windsurfs? We're looking for the unusual."

‡**HIGHWAYS, The Official Publication of the Good Sam Club**, TL Enterprises Inc., 2575 Vista Del Mar, Ventura CA 93001. (805)667-4100. Fax: (805)667-4454. E-mail: 73324.2656@compuserve.com. Website: http://www.tl.com. Editor: Ronald H. Epstein. 40% freelance written. Monthly magazine (November/December issues combined) covering recreational vehicle lifestyle. "All of our readers—since we're a membership publication—own or have a motor home, trailer, camper or van conversion. Thus, our stories include road-travel conditions and terms and information about campgrounds and locations. Estab. 1966. Circ. 912,214. **Pays on acceptance**. Publishes ms an average of 6 months after acceptance. Byline given. Offers 50% kill fee. Buys first North American serial and electronic rights. Editorial lead time 15 weeks. Submit seasonal material 5 months in advance. Accepts simultaneous submissions. Reports in 2 weeks on queries; 3 months on mss. Sample copy and writer's guidelines free on request.

Nonfiction: How-to (repair/replace something on an RV); humor; technical; travel; (all RV related). Buys 15-25 mss/year. Query or send complete ms. Length: 1,800-2,500 words. Pays $150-500 for unsolicited articles.

Photos: Send photos with submission. Reviews contact sheets, negatives, transparencies, prints. Offers no additional payment for photos accepted with ms. Captions, model releases, identification of subjects required. Buys one-time rights.

Columns/Departments: Healthy Traveler (health issues), 1,200 words; Beginners (people buying an RV for the first time), 1,200 words; View Points (issue-related, 750 words). Query. Pays $200-250.

Tips: "Understand RVs and RVing. It's a unique lifestyle and different than typical traveling. Aside from that, we welcome good writers!"

ISLANDS, An International Magazine, Islands Publishing Company, 3886 State St., Santa Barbara CA 93105-3112. Fax: (805)569-0349. E-mail: islands@islandsmag.com. Editor: Joan Tapper. Contact: Denise Iest, assistant editor. 95% freelance written. Works with established writers. Bimonthly magazine covering islands throughout the world. "We cover accessible and once-in-a-lifetime islands from many different perspectives: travel, culture, lifestyle. We ask our authors to give us the essence of the island and do it with literary flair." Estab. 1981. Circ. 190,000. **Pays on acceptance**. Publishes ms an average of 8 months after acceptance. Byline given. Buys all rights. Reports in 1 month on queries; 6 weeks on ms. Sample copy for $6. Writer's guidelines for #10 SASE.

• Ranked as one of the best markets for freelance writers in *Writer's Yearbook's* annual "Top 100 Markets," January 1996.

Nonfiction: General interest, personal experience, photo feature, any island-related material. No service stories. "Each issue contains 3-4 feature articles and 4-5 departments. Any authors who wish to be commissioned should send a detailed proposal for an article, an estimate of costs (if applicable) and samples of previously published work." Buys 25 feature mss/year. "The majority of our feature manuscripts are commissioned." Query with published clips or send complete ms. Feature length: 2,000-4,000 words. Pays $800-3,000. Pays expenses of writers on assignment.

Photos: State availability of or send photos with query or ms. Pays $75-300 for 35mm transparencies. "Fine color photography is a special attraction of *Islands*, and we look for superb composition, technical quality and editorial applicability." Label slides with name and address, include captions, and submit in protective plastic sleeves. Identification of subjects required. Buys one-time rights.

Columns/Departments: "Arts, Profiles, Nature, Sports, Lifestyle, Food, Encounters, Island Hopping featurettes—all island related. Brief Logbook items should be highly focused on some specific aspect of islands." Buys 50 mss/year. Query with published clips. Length: 750-1,500 words. Pays $100-700.

Tips: "A freelancer can best break in to our publication with short (500-1,000 word) departments or Logbooks that are highly focused on some aspect of island life, history, people, etc. Stay away from general, sweeping articles. We are always looking for topics for our Islanders and Logbook pieces. We will be using big name writers for major features; will continue to use newcomers and regulars for columns and departments."

JOURNAL OF CHRISTIAN CAMPING, Christian Camping International, P.O. Box 62189, Colorado Springs CO 80962-2189. (719)260-9400. Fax: (719)260-6398. E-mail: cciusa@aol.com. Website: http://www.gospelcom.net/cci. Editor: Dean Ridings. 75% freelance written. Prefers to work with published/established writers. Bimonthly magazine emphasizing the broad scope of organized camping with emphasis on Christian camping. "Leaders of youth camps and adult conferences read our magazine to get practical help in ways to run their operations." Estab. 1963. Circ. 6,500. Pays on publication. Publishes ms an average of 4 months after acceptance. Rights negotiable. Byline given. Reports in 1 month. Sample copy for $2.25 plus 9×12 SASE. Writer's guidelines for #10 SASE.

Nonfiction: General interest (trends in organized camping in general and Christian camping in particular); how-to (anything involved with organized camping from motivating staff, to programming, to record keeping, to camper follow-up); inspirational (limited use, but might be interested in practical applications of Scriptural principles to everyday situations in camping, no preaching); interview (with movers and shakers in camping and Christian camping in particular; submit a list of basic questions first); and opinion (write a letter to the editor). Buys 20-30 mss/year. Query required. Length: 600-1,200 words. Pays 6¢/word.

Reprints: Send photocopy of article and information about when and where the article previously appeared. Pays 50% of amount paid for an original article.

Photos: Send photos with ms. Pays $25-150 for 5×7 b&w contact sheet or print; price negotiable for 35mm color transparencies. Rights negotiable.

Tips: "The most frequent mistake made by writers is that they send articles unrelated to our readers. Ask for our publication guidelines first."

LEISURE WORLD, Ontario Motorist Publishing Company, 1253 Ouellette Ave., Box 580, Windsor, Ontario N8X 1J3 Canada. (519)971-3208. Fax: (519)977-1197. Editor: Douglas O'Neil. 30% freelance written. Bimonthly magazine distributed to members of the Canadian Automobile Association in southwestern and midwestern Ontario, the Niagara Peninsula and the maritime provinces. Editorial content is focused on travel, entertainment and leisure time pursuits of interest to CAA members." Estab. 1988. Circ. 345,000. Pays on publication. Publishes ms an average of 2 months after acceptance. Buys first rights only. Submit seasonal/holiday material 4 months in advance. Reports in 2 months. Sample copy for $2. Free writer's guidelines.

Nonfiction: Lifestyle, humor, travel. Buys 20 mss/year. Send complete ms. Length: 800-1,200 words. Pays $50-200.

Photos: Reviews slides only. Offers $60/photo. Captions, model releases required. Buys one-time rights.

Tips: "We are most interested in travel destination articles that offer a personal, subjective and positive point of view on international (including US) destinations. Good quality color slides are a must."

‡**LLOYD'S TRAVEL LETTER, Serving the Very Frequent Traveler**, Lloyd's Travel, P.O. Box 13842, Research Triangle Park NC 27709-3842. (919)361-5953. Editor: Max Lloyd. 30% freelance written. Monthly newsletter "for business travelers and the industry that serves them. Articles include: consumer reports and comparisons, frequent flyer programs, tips for travelers, industry trends." Estab. 1994. Circ. 1,000. **Pays on acceptance.** Byline given. Buys one-time rights. Sample copy $2.

Nonfiction: General interest, how-to, interview/profile, new product, opinion, personal experience, technical, travel. No vacation or leisure travel articles. Buys 14 mss/year. Length: 150-1,500 words. Pays $15-100 or in subscriptions.

THE MATURE TRAVELER, Travel Bonanzas for 49ers-Plus, GEM Publishing Group, Box 50400, Reno NV 89513-0400. (702)786-7419. E-mail: maturetrav@aol.com. Editor: Gene E. Malott. 30% freelance written. Monthly newsletter on senior citizen travel. Estab. 1984. Circ. 2,500. **Pays on acceptance.** Publishes ms an average of 3 months after acceptance. Byline given. Offers 25% kill fee. Buys one-time rights. Submit seasonal/holiday material 3 months in advance. Accepts simultaneous submissions. Reports in 1 month. Sample copy and guidelines for $1 and #10 SAE with 2 first-class stamps. Writer's guidelines only for #10 SASE.

Nonfiction: Travel for seniors. "General travel and destination pieces should be senior-specific, aimed at 49ers and older." Query. Length: 600-1,200 words. Pays $50-100.

Reprints: Send tearsheet or photocopy of article and information about when and where the article previously appeared. Pays 50% of amount paid for an original article.

Photos: State availability of photos with submission. Reviews contact sheets and b&w (only) prints. Captions required. Buys one-time rights.

Tips: "Read the guidelines and write stories to our readers' needs—not to the general public. Most articles we reject are not senior-specific."

‡**MICHIGAN LIVING**, AAA Michigan, 1 Auto Club Dr., Dearborn MI 48126-2963. (313)336-1211. Fax: (313)336-1344. Editor: Len Barnes. 50% freelance written. Monthly magazine emphasizing travel and auto use. Estab. 1922. Circ. 1,000,000. **Pays on acceptance.** Publishes ms an average of 6 months after acceptance. Buys first North American serial rights. Offers 20% kill fee. Byline given. Submit seasonal/holiday material 3 months in advance. Reports in 6 weeks. Free sample copy and writer's guidelines.

Nonfiction: Travel articles on US and Canadian topics. Buys 50-60 unsolicited mss/year. Send complete ms. Length: 200-1,000 words. Pays $88-315.

Photos: Photos purchased with accompanying ms. Captions required. Pays $350 for cover photos; $50-220 for color transparencies; total purchase price for ms includes payment for b&w photos.

Tips: "In addition to descriptions of things to see and do, articles should contain accurate, current information on costs the traveler would encounter on his trip. Items such as lodging, meal and entertainment expenses should be included, not in the form of a balance sheet but as an integral part of the piece. We want the sounds, sights, tastes, smells of a place or experience so one will feel he has been there and knows if he wants to go back."

THE MIDWEST MOTORIST, AAA Auto Club of Missouri, 12901 N. 40 Dr., St. Louis MO 63141. (314)523-7350. Fax: (314)523-7427. Editor: Michael J. Right. Managing Editor: Deborah M. Klein. 80% freelance written. Bimonthly magazine focusing on travel and auto-related topics. "We feature articles on regional and world travel, area history, auto safety, highway and transportation news." Estab. 1971. Circ. 398,173. **Pays on acceptance.** Byline given. Not copyrighted. Buys first North American serial rights, second serial (reprint) rights. Accepts simultaneous submissions. Reports in 1 month with SASE enclosed. Sample copy for 12½×9½ SAE with 3 first-class stamps. Writer's guidelines for #10 SASE.

Nonfiction: Buys 40 mss/year. Query. Length: 2,000 words maximum. Pays $350 (maximum).

Reprints: Send typed ms with rights for sale noted and information about when and where the article previously appeared. Pays 40% of amount paid for an original article.

Photos: State availability of photos with submission. Reviews transparencies. Offers no additional payment for photos accepted with ms. Captions required. Buys one-time rights.

Tips: "Editorial schedule set 18 months in advance. Request a copy. Serious writers ask for media kit to help them target their piece. Some stories available throughout the year. Travel destinations and tips are most open to freelancers; auto-related topics handled by staff. Make the story bright and quick to read. We see too many 'Here's a recount of our family vacation' manuscripts. Go easy on first-person accounts."

‡**MOTORLAND, Travel and news magazine of the West**, California State Automobile Assn., 150 Van Ness Ave., San Francisco CA 94102. (415)565-2451. Editor: Lynn Ferrin. 25% freelance written. Bimonthly magazine specializing in northern California and the West, with occasional stories on world-wide travel, especially in the September "cruise" section. Also, traffic safety and motorists' consumer issues. "Our magazine goes to members of the AAA in northern California and Nevada. Our surveys show they are an upscale audience, well-educated and widely traveled. We like our travel stories to be finely crafted, evocative and personal, but we also include nitty gritty details in arranging travel to the destinations covered." Estab. 1917. Circ. 2,400,000. **Pays on acceptance.** Byline usually given. Offers 25% kill fee. Buys first rights or makes work-for-hire assignments. Editorial lead time 2 months. Submit seasonal material 6 months in advance. Usually reports in 1 month on queries. Writer's guidelines for #10 SASE.

● Ranked as one of the best markets for freelance writers in *Writer's Yearbook*'s annual "Top 100 Markets," January 1996.

Nonfiction: Travel. Special issue: Cruise issue (September/October). Buys 15 mss/year. Prefers to see finished mss with SASE from writers new to them. Length: 500-2,000 words. Pays $150-500. Sometimes pays expenses of writers on assignment.

Photos: State availability of photos with submission. Reviews 35mm and 4×5 transparencies. Offers $50-400/photo. Model releases, identification of subjects required. Buys first-time rights.

Tips: "We are looking for beautifilly written pieces that evoke a destination. We purchase less than 1% of the material submitted. Send SASE with all queries and mss."

‡**MYSTIC TRAVELER**, Traveler Publications Inc., Suite 205, 174 Bellevue Ave., Newport RI 02840. (401)847-0226. Fax: (401)847-5267. Managing Editor: Joseph Albano. Contact: Jeff Hall, publisher. 100% freelance written. Monthly tabloid covering places of interest. "Stories that get the reader to "do, see, or act upon." Estab. 1992. Circ. 120,000 winter, 240,000 summer. Pays on publication. Byline given. Buys all rights. Editorial lead time 2 months. Submit seasonal material 2 months in advance. Accepts simultaneous submissions. Reports in 2 months on mss. Sample copy and writer's guidelines free on request.

Nonfiction: Essays, general interest, historical/nostalgic, photo feature (travel). Buys 60 mss/year. Send complete ms. Length: 700-1,200 words. Pays 5¢/word. Sometimes pays expenses of writers on assignment.

Reprints: Accepts previously published submissions.

Photos: Send photos with submission. Reviews prints. Negotiates payment individually. Buys one-time rights.

Fillers: Facts. Buys 30/year. Length: 50-200 words. Pays 5¢/word.

Tips: "We are very interested in tours that cover an entire area. It could be a tour of wineries, a certain kind of shop, golf courses, etc. Always include address, phone, hours, admission prices. Get reader to act upon an editorial."

NATIONAL GEOGRAPHIC TRAVELER, National Geographic Society, 17th & M Sts. NW, Washington DC 20036. (202)775-6700. Fax: (202)828-5658. Vice President/Operations Director: Sarita L. Moffat. Bimonthly magazine for active travelers. "*National Geographic Traveler* is filled with practical information and detailed maps that are designed to encourage readers to explore and travel the glove. Features on both domestic and foreign destinations, photography, the economics of travel, scenic drives, and weekend getaways help readers plan a variety of excursions. The Travel Wise section that accompanies each feature recommends places to stay and eat as well as things to see and do. Regional highlights list upcoming cultural events." Estab. 1984. Circ. 732,000. This magazine did not respond to our request for information. Query before submitting.

NEW YORK DAILY NEWS, Travel Section, 450 W. 33rd St., New York NY 10001. (212)210-1699. Fax: (212)210-2203. Travel Editor: Gunna Biteé Dickson. 30% freelance written. Prefers to work with published/established writers. Weekly tabloid. Circ. 1,800,000. "We are the largest circulating newspaper travel section in the country and take all types of articles ranging from experiences to service oriented pieces that tell readers how to make a certain trip." Pays on publication. Publishes ms an average of 3 months after acceptance. Byline given. Submit seasonal/holiday material 4 months in advance. Reports "as soon as possible." Writer's guidelines for #10 SASE.

Nonfiction: General interest, historical/nostalgic, humor, inspirational, personal experience, travel. "Most of our articles involve practical trips that the average family can afford—even if it's one you can't afford every year. We also run stories for the Armchair Traveler, an exotic and usually expensive trip. We are looking for professional quality work from professional writers who know what they are doing. The pieces have to give information and be entertaining at the same time. No 'How I Spent My Summer Vacation' type articles. No PR hype." Buys 60 mss/year. Query with SASE. Length: 1,000 words maximum. Pays $75-200.

Photos: "Good pictures always help sell good stories." State availability of photos with ms. Reviews contact sheets and negatives. Captions and identification of subjects required. Buys all rights.

Columns/Departments: Short Hops is based on trips to places within a 300-mile radius of New York City. Length: 700-800 words. Weekly staff columns: Dollar Wise and Business Travel Tips.

Tips: "A writer might have some luck gearing a specific destination to a news event or date: In Search of Irish Crafts in March, for example, but do it well in advance."

NEWSDAY, 235 Pinelawn Rd., Melville NY 11747. (516)843-2980. Fax: (516)843-2065. Travel Editor: Marjorie Robins. 30% freelance written. General readership of Sunday newspaper travel section. Estab. 1940. Circ. 650,000. Buys all rights for New York area only. Buys 75 mss/year. Pays on publication. Prefers typewritten mss. Simultaneous submissions considered if outside the New York area.

Nonfiction: No assignments to freelancers. No query letters. Only completed mss accepted on spec. All trips must be paid for in full by writer. Proof required. Service stories preferred. Destination pieces must be for the current year. Length: 1,200 words maximum. Pays $75-350, depending on space allotment.

Photos: Color slides and b&w photos accepted: $50-250, depending on size of photo used.

NORTHEAST OUTDOORS, Northeast Outdoors, Inc., P.O. Box 2180, Waterbury CT 06722-2180. (203)755-0158. Fax: (203)755-3480. Managing Editor: Mike Griffin. 50% freelance written. Works with a small number of new/unpublished writers each year. Monthly tabloid covering family camping in the Northeastern US. Estab. 1968. Circ. 10,000. Pays on publication. Publishes ms an average of 8 months after acceptance. Byline given. Buys first rights and regional rights. Submit seasonal/holiday material 5 months in advance. Reports in 2 weeks. Sample copy for 9×12 SAE with 6 first-class stamps. Writer's guidelines for #10 SASE.

• At this publication there is less freelance need since more is done now by staff.

Nonfiction: How-to (camping), humor, new product (company and RV releases only), recreation vehicle and camping experiences in the Northeast, features about private (only) campgrounds and places to visit in the Northeast while RVing, personal experience, photo feature, travel. "No diaries of trips, dog or fishing-only stories, or anything not camping and RV related." Length: 300-1,500 words. Pays $40-80 for articles with b&w photos; pays $30-75 for articles without art.

Reprints: Accepts previously published submissions if published outside Northeast region. Send typed ms with rights for sale noted and information about when and where the article previously appeared. Pays 50% of their fee for an original article.

Photos: Send photos with submission. Reviews contact sheets and 5×7 prints or larger. Captions and identification of subjects required. Buys one-time rights.

Columns/Departments: Mealtime (campground cooking), 300-900 words. Buys 12 mss/year. Query or send complete ms. Length: 750-1,000 words. Pays $25-50.

Tips: "We most often need material on private campgrounds and attractions in New England. We are looking for upbeat, first-person stories about where to camp, what to do or see, and how to enjoy camping."

OUTDOOR TRAVELER, Mid-Atlantic, WMS Publications, 1 Morton Dr., Suite 102, P.O. Box 2748, Charlottesville VA 22902. (804)984-0655. Fax: (804)984-0656. Editor: Marianne Marks. Associate Editor: Scott Clark. 85% freelance written. Quarterly magazine. "*Outdoor Traveler* is designed to help readers (well-educated, active adults) enjoy the Mid-Atlantic outdoors through year-round seasonal coverage of outdoor recreation, travel, adventure and nature." Estab. 1993. Circ. 35,000. Pays on publication. Byline given. Offers 25% kill fee. Buys first North American serial rights. Editorial lead time 6 months. Submit seasonal material 8 months in advance. Accepts simultaneous submissions. Reports in 2 months. Sample copy for $4. Writer's guidelines for #10 SASE.

● This publication needs more short features (1-2 pages), as well as more profiles, humor pieces and service/informational articles.

Nonfiction: Travel, nature, personal experience, humor, interview/profile, essays, book excerpts, how-to (outdoor sports technique), photo feature, historic/nostalgic (related to outdoor sports or travel). No "What I did on my vacation" articles; no golf or tennis. Buys 40 mss/year. Query with published clips. Length: 300-2,000 words. Pays 20¢/word.

Photos: Send photos with submission. Reviews transparencies. Offers $50/photo minimum. Captions, model releases and identification of subjects required. Buys one-time rights.

Columns/Departments: Base Camp (camping vacation destinations), 600 words; Destinations (brief but detailed guides to outdoor sports destinations), 600-800 words. Buys 40 mss/year. Query with published clips. Pays 20¢/word.

Tips: "Freelancers should query with clips that reveal strong writing skills, a professional style, and knowledge of our region and subject matter."

RV WEST MAGAZINE, Vernon Publications Inc., 3000 Northup Way, Suite 200, Bellevue WA 98004. (800)700-6962. Fax: (206)822-9372. Publisher: Geoffrey P. Vernon. Contact: Sandi Becker, editor. 85% freelance written. Monthly magazine for those who own or are about to purchase an RV. The magazine provides comprehensive information on where to go and what to do in the West. Estab. 1976. Circ. 75,000. Pays 1 month following publication. Byline given. Buys one-time rights and electronic/digital rights. Submit seasonal/holiday material at least 3 months in advance of best month for publication. Accepts simultaneous submissions. Submit complete ms. Send SASE for writer's guidelines.

Nonfiction: Travel (Western destinations for RVs), historical/nostalgic (if RV-related), new product, personal experience (if RV-related), events of interest to RVers. No non-RV travel articles. Query with or without published clips. Length: 750-1,750 words. Pays $1.50/inch.

Photos: Send photos with submissions. Color slides and b&w prints preferred. Offers $5 for each published photo. Identification of subjects required.

Tips: "Include all information of value to RVers, and reasons why they would want to visit the location (13 Western states). Short items of interest may also be submitted, including tips, humorous anecdotes and jokes related to RVing. Indicate best time frame for publication."

ST. MAARTEN NIGHTS, Nights Publications, 1831 Rene Levesque Blvd. West, Montreal, Quebec H3H 1R4 Canada. Fax: (514)931-6273. Editor: Stephen Trotter. Managing Editor: Zelly Zuskin. 90% freelance written. Annual magazine covering the St. Maarten/St. Martin vacation experience seeking "upbeat entertaining lifestyle articles: colorful profiles of islanders; lively features on culture, activities, night life, eco-tourism, special events, gambling; how-to features; humor. Our audience is the North American vacationer." Estab. 1981. Circ. 225,000. **Pays on acceptance.** Publishes ms an average of 9 months after acceptance. Byline given. Offers 15% kill fee. Buys first North American serial and first Caribbean rights. Editorial lead time 1 month. Reports in 2 weeks on queries; 1 month on mss. *Writer's Market* recommends allowing 2 months for reply. Sample copy for $5. Writer's guidelines free on request.

Nonfiction: Lifestyle with an upscale touch. General interest, historical/nostalgia, how-to (gamble), sail, etc., humor, inspirational, interview/profile, opinion, ecological (eco-tourism), personal experience, photo feature, travel, local culture, art, activities, entertainment, topics relative to vacationers in St. Maarten/St. Martin. "No negative pieces or stale rewrites or cliché copy." Buys 8-10 mss/year. Query with published clips. Length: 250-750 words. Pays $125-350 for assigned articles; $100-250 for unsolicited articles.

Photos: State availability of photos with submission. Reviews transparencies. Offers $25-100/photo. Captions, model releases, identification of subjects required. Buys one-time rights.

‡SPA, Travel, Well-Being and Renewal, Waterfront Press Co., 5305 Shilshole Ave. NW, #200, Seattle WA 98107. (206)789-6506. Fax: (206)789-9193. Contact: Lawrence W. Cheek, managing editor. Quarterly magazine covering spa resorts, lifestyle issues, well-being and travel. "Our readership is sophisticated, well-educated and discerning. We want reporting of real substance and writing that is clear and bright. We also want to encourage a variety of voices." Estab. 1996. Circ. 75,000. **Pays on acceptance.** Publishes ms an average of 3 months after acceptance. Byline sometimes given. Buys first North American serial, one-time, second serial (reprint) rights and makes work-for-hire assignments. Editorial lead time 6 months. Reports in 1 month on queries. Sample copy for 9×12 and 8 first-class stamps. Writer's guidelines for #10 SASE.

Nonfiction: Essays, how-to, interview/profile, personal experience, photo feature, travel, health and fitness. Buys 30 mss/year. Query with published clips. Length: 300-3,000 words. Pays $100-2,000.

Photos: State availability of photos with submission. Reviews transparencies (any format). Negotiates payment individually. Captions, identification of subjects required. Buys one-time rights.

Columns/Departments: Cuisine (spa food) 600-1,000 words; Destinations (very short travel pieces involving resort spas and day spas) 300-400 words; Guys (men's point of view) 600-1,000 words. Buys 20 mss/year. Query with published clips. Pays $100-500.

STAR SERVICE, Reed Travel Group, 500 Plaza Dr., Secaucus NJ 07096-3602. (201)902-2000. Fax: (201)319-1797. Publisher: Steven R. Gordon. "Eager to work with new/unpublished writers as well as those working from a home base abroad, planning trips that would allow time for hotel reporting, or living in major ports for cruise ships." Worldwide guide to accommodations and cruise ships founded in 1960 (as *Sloane Travel Agency Reports*) and sold to travel agencies on subscription basis. Pays 15 days after publication. Buys all rights. Query should include details on writer's experience in travel and writing, clips, specific forthcoming travel plans, and how much time would be available for hotel or ship inspections. Buys 5,000 reports/year. Pays $20/report used. Sponsored trips are acceptable. General query should precede electronic submission. Reports in 3 months. Writer's guidelines and list of available assignments for #10 SASE.

Nonfiction: Objective, critical evaluations of hotels and cruise ships suitable for international travelers, based on personal inspections. Freelance correspondents ordinarily are assigned to update an entire state or country. "Assignment involves on-site inspections of all hotels and cruise ships we review; revising and updating published reports; and reviewing new properties. Qualities needed are thoroughness, precision, perseverance and keen judgment. Solid research skills and powers of observation are crucial. Travel and travel writing experience are highly desirable. Reviews must be colorful, clear, and documented with hotel's brochure, rate sheet, etc. We accept no advertising or payment for listings, so reviews should dispense praise and criticism where deserved."

Tips: "We may require sample hotel or cruise reports on facilities near freelancer's hometown before giving the first assignment. No byline because of sensitive nature of reviews."

‡TRAILER LIFE, RVing At Its Best, TL Enterprises Inc.. 2575 Vista Del Mar Dr., Ventura CA 93001. Fax: (805)667-4100. Editor: Barbara Leonard. Managing Editor: Sherry McBride. 50% freelance written. Monthly consumer magazine covering recreational vehicle (RV) lifestyle. Estab. 1941. Circ. 290,000. **Pays on acceptance**. Byline given. Offers 33% kill fee. Buys one-time rights. Editorial lead time 4 months. Submit seasonal material 6 months in advance. Reports in 1 month on queries; 2 months on mss. Sample copy free on request. Writer's guidelines free on request.

• Ranked as one of the best markets for freelance writers in *Writer's Yearbook*'s annual "Top 100 Markets," January 1996.

Nonfiction: Historical/nostalgic, how-to, humor, personal experience, travel. No vehicle tests, product evaluations or road tests; tech material is strictly assigned. Buys 75 mss/year. Query with or without published clips, send complete ms. Length: 250-2,500 words. Pays $150-600. Sometimes pays expenses of writers on assignment.

Photos: Send photos with submission. Reviews b&w contact sheets, transparencies. Offers no additional payment for photos accepted with ms. Model releases, identification of subjects required. Buys one-time rights.

Columns/Departments: Campground Spotlight (recommended for RVers) 250 words; Bulletin Board (news, trends of interest to RVers) 100 words; Etcetera (information affecting RVers) 240 words. Buys 60 mss/year. Send complete ms. Pays $75-250.

Tips: "Prerequisite: must have RV focus. Photos must be magazine quality. These are the two biggest reasons why manuscripts are rejected. Our readers are travel enthusiasts who own all types of RVs (travel trailers, truck campers, van conversions, motorhomes, tent trailers, fifth-wheels) in which they explore North and South America, embrace the great outdoors in national, state and private parks as well as scenic roads, city sights, etc. They're very active although mature."

TRANSITIONS ABROAD, P.O. Box 1300, Amherst MA 01004-1300. E-mail: trabroad@aol.com. Editor/Publisher: Clay Hubbs. Contact: Jason Whitmarsh, managing editor. 80-90% freelance written. Eager to work with new/unpublished writers. Magazine resource for low-budget international travel with an educational or work component. Estab. 1977. Circ. 20,000. Pays on publication. Buys first rights and second (reprint) rights. Byline given. Written or e-mail queries only. Reports in 1 month. Sample copy for $6.25. Writer's guidelines and topics schedule for #10 SASE. Manuscript returned only with SASE.

Nonfiction: Lead articles (up to 2,000 words) provide first-hand practical information on independent travel to featured country or region (see topics schedule). Pays $75-150. Also, how-to find educational and specialty travel opportunities, practical information (evaluation of courses, special interest and study tours, economy travel), travel (new learning and cultural travel ideas). Foreign travel only. Few destination ("tourist") pieces.

Transitions Abroad is a resource magazine for educated and adventurous travelers, not for travel novices or armchair travelers. Emphasis on information—which must be usable by readers—and on interaction with people in host country. Buys 20 unsolicited mss/issue. Query with credentials. Length: 500-1,500 words. Pays $25-150. Include author's bio with submissions.

Photos: Send photos with ms. Pays $10-45 for prints (color acceptable, b&w preferred), $125 for covers (b&w only). Photos increase likelihood of acceptance. Buys one-time rights. Captions and ID on photos required.

Columns/Departments: Worldwide Travel Bargains (destinations, activities and accomodations for budget travelers—featured in every issue); Tour and Program Notes (new courses or travel programs); Travel Resources (new information and ideas for independent travel); Working Traveler (how to find jobs and what to expect); Activity Vacations (travel opportunities that involve action and learning, usually by direct involvement in host culture); Responsible Travel (information on community-organized tours). Buys 10/issue. Send complete ms. Length: 1,000 words maximum. Pays $20-50.

Fillers: Info Exchange (information, preferably first-hand—having to do with travel, particularly offbeat educational travel and work or study abroad). Buys 10/issue. Length: 750 words maximum. Pays $20.

Tips: "We like nuts and bolts stuff, practical information, especially on how to work, live and cut costs abroad. Our readers want usable information on planning a travel itinerary. Be specific: names, addresses, current costs. We are very interested in educational and long-stay travel and study abroad for adults and senior citizens. *Educational Travel Resource Guide* published each year in July provides best information sources on work, study, and independent travel abroad. Each bimonthly issue contains a worldwide directory of educational and specialty travel programs. (Topics schedule included with writers' guidelines.)"

TRAVEL & LEISURE, American Express Publishing Corp., 1120 Avenue of the Americas, New York NY 10036. (212)382-5600. E-mail: tlquery@amexpub.com. Editor-in-Chief: Nancy Novogrod. Executive Editor: Barbara Peck. Managing Editor: Mark Orwoll. 80% freelance written. Monthly magazine. Circ. 960,000. **Pays on acceptance.** Byline given. Offers 25% kill fee. Buys first world rights. Reports in 6 weeks. Sample copy for $5 from (800)888-8728 or P.O. Box 2094, Harlan IA 51537-4094. Writer's guidelines for #10 SASE.

• There is no single editorial contact for *Travel & Leisure.* It is best to find the name of the editor of each section, as appropriate for your submission.

Nonfiction: Travel. Buys 200 mss/year. Query by e-mail preferred. Length open. Payment varies. Pays the expenses of writers on assignment.

• Ranked as one of the best markets for freelance writers in *Writer's Yearbook*'s annual "Top 100 Markets," January 1996.

Photos: Discourages submission of unsolicited transparencies. Payment varies. Captions required. Buys one-time rights.

Tips: "Read the magazine. There are 2 regional editions: East and West. Regional sections are best places to start."

‡TRAVEL NEWS, Travel Agents International, Inc., P.O. Box 42008, St. Petersburg FL 33742-4008. (813)576-8241. Fax: (813)579-0529. Editor: Matthew Wiseman. 40% freelance written. Monthly travel tabloid. "Travel stories written to praise a particular trip. We want readers to consider taking a trip themselves." Estab. 1982. Circ. 200,000. Pays on publication. Publishes ms an average of 2 months after acceptance. Byline given. Not copyrighted. Buys simultaneous rights. Submit seasonal/holiday material 6 months in advance. Accepts simultaneous submissions. Reports in 2 months. Sample copy and writer's guidelines for 9×12 SAE with 4 first-class stamps. No phone calls, please.

Nonfiction: General interest, new product, photo feature, travel. "Each issue focuses on one travel category. We will accept submissions anytime but prefer SASE for publication calendar. No negative articles that would discourage travel. Make sure stories you submit are geared toward the traveler using a travel agent." Buys 50 mss/year. Query with or without published clips or send complete ms. Length: 1,000-1,500 words. Pays $20-200 for assigned articles; $10-125 for unsolicited articles.

Reprints: Send photocopy of article or typed ms with rights for sale noted. Pays 100% of the amount paid for an original article.

Photos: State availability of photos with submission. Buys one-time rights.

Tips: "Send SASE for publication calendar, sample copy and submission requirements. Write well in advance of a trip to see what angle we would like the story to take. We will also review outlines."

‡TRAVEL SMART, Communications House, Inc., Dobbs Ferry NY 10522. (914)693-4208. Editor/Publisher: H.J. Teison. Managing Editor: Nancy Dunnan. Covers information on "good-value travel." Monthly newsletter. Estab. 1976. Pays on publication. Buys all rights. Reports in 6 weeks. Sample copy and writer's guidelines for 9×12 SAE with 3 first-class stamps.

Nonfiction: "Interested primarily in bargains or little-known deals on transportation, lodging, food, unusual destinations that are really good values. No destination stories on major Caribbean islands, London, New York, no travelogs, 'my vacation,' poetry, fillers. No photos or illustrations. Just hard facts. We are not part of 'Rosy fingers of dawn . . .' school." Write for guidelines, then query. Length: 100-1,500 words. Pays $150 maximum."

Tips: "When you travel, check out small hotels offering good prices, little known restaurants, and send us brief rundown (with prices, phone numbers, addresses). Information must be current. Include your phone number with submission, because we sometimes make immediate assignments."

TRAVELER PUBLICATIONS, Publishers of *Sea Mass Traveler*, *Mystic Traveler* and *Newport Traveler*, 174 Bellevue Ave., Suite 207, Newport RI 02840. (401)847-0226. Fax: (401)847-5267. Managing Editor: Jeffrey Hall. 100% freelance written. Monthly regional tabloid covering places of interest in southern Massachusetts, southern Connecticut and all of Rhode Island. "Stories that get the reader to "do, see, or act upon." Estab. 1992. Circ. 120,000 winter 240,000 summer. Pays on publication. Byline given. Buys all rights. Editorial lead time 2 months. Submit seasonal material 2 months in advance. Accepts simultaneous submissions. Reports in 2 months on mss. Sample copy and writer's guidelines free on request.
  • Three magazines (above) are published by one editorial office. Send only one manuscript and it
    will be circulated among magazines.
Nonfiction: Essays, general interest, historical/nostalgic, photo feature (travel). Buys 60 mss/year. Send complete ms. Length: 700-1,200 words. Pays 5¢/word. Sometimes pays expenses of writers on assignment.
Reprints: Accepts previously published submissions.
Photos: Send photos with submission. Reviews prints. Negotiates payment individually. Buys one-time rights.
Fillers: Facts. Buys 30/year. Length: 50-200 words. Pays 5¢/word.
Tips: "We are very interested in tours that cover an entire area. It could be a tour of wineries, a certain kind of shop, golf courses, etc. Always include address, phone, hour, admissions prices."

‡TREKS & JOURNEYS, The Student International Travel Journal, Treks & Journeys Press, 715 Canyon Rd., Tuscaloosa AL 35406. (205)348-8247. Fax: (205)348-2780. E-mail: GFrangou@sa.ua.edu. Editor: George Frangoulis. 85% freelance written. Quarterly magazine covering travel. "*Treks & Journeys* is for a different kind of traveller. Directed towards students and young adults ages 20-35, it is for a person who is independent, adventurous, interested in spreading their wings and discovering new places of cultural interest and enrichment. It encompasses all aspects of travel, as well as study and working abroad." Estab. 1995. Circ. 127,000. **Pays on acceptance.** Byline given. Offers 50% kill fee. Editorial lead time 6 months. Submit seasonal material 6 months in advance. Reports in 2 weeks on queries; 3 months on mss. Sample copy and writer's guidelines free.
Nonfiction Book excerpts, essays, general interest, historical/nostalgic, how-to, humor, inspirational, interview/profile, new product, opinion, personal experience, photo feature, travel. Buys 15-20 mss/year. Query. Length: 500-3,500 words. Pays $50-350 for assigned articles; $25-250 for unsolicited articles.
Reprints: Accepts previously published submissions.
Photos: State availability of photos with submission. Reviews contact sheets, transparencies, 5×7 prints. Offers $5-25/photo. Captions, model releases, identification of subjects required.
Tips: "*Treks & Journeys* is particularly interested in articles on new destinations that are 'off the beaten path,' recreational opportunities, budget travel for both short-term and long-term stays, and environmentally responsible tourism experiences."

‡VOYAGEUR, The Magazine of Carlson Hospitality Worldwide, Pace Communications, 1301 Carolina St., Greensboro NC 27401. Editor: Jaci H. Ponzoni. 90% freelance written. In room magazine for Radisson hotels and affiliates. Quarterly magazine covering travel. All travel related stories must be in destinations where Radisson or Country Inns and Suites have hotels. Estab. 1992. Circ. 150,000. **Pays on acceptance**. Publishes ms an average of 2 months after acceptance. Offers 25% kill fee. Buys first North American serial rights. Editorial lead time 4 months. Submit seasonal material 6 months in advance. Reports in 1 month. Sample for $5. Writer's guidelines for #10 SASE.
  • *Voyageur* was recently redesigned. Obtaining a recent sample copy is strongly recommended.
Nonfiction: Humor, travel. Query with published clips. Length: 1,260 words maximum. Pays $400-900 for assigned articles. Sometimes pays expenses of writers on assignment.
Photos: State availability of photos with submission. Reviews contact sheets, transparencies, prints. Negotiates payment individually. Model releases and identification of subjects required. Buys one-time rights.
Columns/Departments: Check Out (the lighter, humorous side of international travel) 360 words; Good Earth (positive environmental piece emphasizing "win-win" business) 360 words; Business Wise (insights into conducting business internationally) 360 words. Buys 16 mss/year. Query with published clips. Pays $200-400.
Tips: "We are actively seeking writers with an authentic European, Asian, South American or Australian perspective. Travel stories should be authoritative yet personal."

WESTERN RV NEWS, 56405 Cascade View Lane, Warren OR 97053-9736. (503)222-1255. Fax: (503)222-1255. E-mail: wrvneph@aol.com. Editor: Elsie Hathaway. 75% freelance written. Monthly magazine for owners of recreational vehicles. Estab. 1966. Pays on publication. Publishes ms an average of 6 months after acceptance. Byline given. Buys first rights and second serial (reprint) rights. Accepts simultaneous submissions. Reports in 1 month. Sample copy and writer's guidelines for 9×12 SAE with 5 first-class stamps. Guidelines for #10 SASE. Request to be put on free temporary mailing list for publication.

Nonfiction: How-to (RV oriented, purchasing considerations, maintenance), humor (RV experiences), new product (with ancillary interest to RV lifestyle), personal experiences (varying or unique RV lifestyles) technical (RV systems or hardware), travel. "No articles without an RV slant." Buys 100 mss/year. Submit complete ms. Length: 250-1,200 words. Pays $15-100.

Reprints: Send photocopy of article and typed ms with rights for sale noted and information about when and where the article previously appeared. Pays 60% of amount paid for an original article.

Photos: Send photos with submission. Prefer b&w. Offers $5-10/photo. Captions, model releases, identification of subjects required. Buys one-time rights.

Fillers: Encourage anecdotes, RV related tips and short humor. Length: 50-250 words. Pays $5-25.

Tips: "Highlight the RV lifestyle! Western travel (primarily NW destinations) articles should include information about the availability of RV sites, dump stations, RV parking and accessibility. Thorough research and a pleasant, informative writing style are paramount. Technical, how-to, and new product writing is also of great interest to us. Photos definitely enhance the possibility of article acceptance."

WOMEN'S

Women have an incredible variety of publications available to them. A number of titles in this area have been redesigned to compete in the crowded marketplace. Many have stopped publishing fiction and are focusing more on short, human interest nonfiction articles. Magazines that also use material slanted to women's interests can be found in the following categories: Business and Finance; Child Care and Parental Guidance; Contemporary Culture; Food and Drink; Gay and Lesbian Interest; Health and Fitness; Hobby and Craft; Home and Garden; Relationships; Religious; Romance and Confession; and Sports.

ALLURE, Condé Nast, 360 Madison Ave., New York NY 10017. Articles Editor: Tom Prince. Monthly publication covering beauty, lifestyle and culture. "*Allure* looks at the complex role beauty plays in the culture and analyzes the trends in cosmetics, skincare, fashion, haircare, fitness, health and more." Estab. 1991. Circ. 731,500. Query before submitting. Call or write for guidelines, include SASE. Most beauty articles are written inhouse. Reflections section most open to freelancers. "Read and become *very* familiar with the magazine."

BRIDAL GUIDE, Globe Communications Corp., 3 E. 54th St., 15th Floor, New York NY 10022. (212)838-7733. Fax: (212)308-7165. Editor-in-Chief: Diane Forden. Travel Editor: Cherylann Coutts. Contact: Monica Bernstein, senior editor. 50% freelance written. Prefers to work with experienced/published writers. A bimonthly magazine covering relationships, sexuality, health and nutrition, psychology, finance, travel. Please do not send queries concerning wedding planning articles, beauty, and fashion, since we produce them inhouse. We do not accept personal wedding essays, fiction, or poetry. Reports in 3 months. Sample copy for $4.95 and SASE with 4 first-class stamps. Writer's guidelines available.

Nonfiction: We prefer queries rather than actual manuscript submissions. Also send clips. All correspondence accompanied by an SASE will be answered (response time is within 8 weeks). Length: 1,500-3,000 words. Pays on acceptance. Buys 100 mss/year.

Photos: Lisa del Altomare, art director. Stephen Wilder, associate art director. Photography and illustration submissions should be sent to the art department.

Columns/Departments: Regular columns include finance, sex and health, new products, etiquette, relationships, travel, entertaining, food. Welcome queries from men who are engaged or married for Groom with a View essay end page.

BRIDE'S, Condé Nast, 350 Madison Ave., New York NY 10017. (212)880-2518. Managing Editor: Sally Kiobridge. Editor-in-Chief: Millie Martini-Bratten. Bimonthly magazine for the first- or second-time bride, her family and friends, the groom and his family and friends. Circ. 400,000. Writer's guidelines for #10 SASE. Query before submitting.

‡**THE BUSINESS & PROFESSIONAL WOMAN**, Val Publications Ltd., 95 Leeward Glenway, Unit 121, North York, Ontario M3C 2Z6 Canada. Editor: Valerie M. Dunn. 100% freelance written. Quarterly tabloid covering working women. "Women's issues (Canadian or abroad) personal development, self-employment, corporate women, lifestyles, Most readers are members of the Canadian Federation of Business & Professional Women's Clubs." Estab. 1930. Circ. 4,500. Pays on publication. Publishes ms an average of 4 months after acceptance. Byline given. Buys simultaneous rights. Editorial lead time 4 months. Submit

seasonal material 4 months in advance. Accepts simultaneous submissions. Reports in 6 weeks on queries. Sample copy and writer's guidelines free on request.
Nonfiction: Book excerpts, how-to, humor, technical. Buys 10 mss/year. Send complete ms. Length: 800-1,500 words. Pays $25 minimum.
Reprints: Accepts previously published submissions.
Photos: Send photos with submission. Reviews prints. Offers $10 minimum. Captions required.

COMPLETE WOMAN, For All The Women You Are, Associated Publications, Inc., 875 N. Michigan Ave., Chicago IL 60611-1901. (312)266-8680. Editor: Bonnie L. Krueger. Contact: Martha Carlson, associate editor. 90% freelance written. Bimonthly magazine of general interest for women. Areas of concern are love life, health, fitness, emotions, etc. Estab. 1980. Circ. 350,000. Pays on publication. Publishes ms an average of 5 months after acceptance. Byline given. Buys first North American serial, second serial (reprint) and simultaneous rights. Submit seasonal/holiday material 5 months in advance. Accepts simultaneous submissions. Reports in 2 months. Writer's guidelines for #10 SASE.
• The editor reports a need for more relationship stories.
Nonfiction: Book excerpts, general interest, how-to, humor, inspirational, interview/profile, new product, personal experience, photo feature. "We want self-help articles written for today's woman. Articles that address dating, romance, sexuality and relationships are an integral part of our editorial mix, as well as inspirational and motivational pieces." Buys 60-100 mss/year. Query with published clips, or send complete ms. Length: 800-2,000 words. Pays $80-400. Sometimes pays expenses of writers on assignment.
Reprints: Send tearsheet or photocopy of article or short story or send typed ms with rights for sale noted and information about when and where the article previously appeared.
Photos: Send photos with submission. Reviews 2¼ or 35mm transparencies and 5×7 prints. Offers $35-75/photo. Captions, model releases, identification of subjects required. Buys one-time rights.
Poetry: Avant-garde, free verse, light verse, traditional. Nothing over 30 lines. Buys 50 poems/year. Submit maximum 5 poems. Pays $10.

COSMOPOLITAN, The Hearst Corp., 224 W. 57th St., New York NY 10019. (212)649-2000. Executive Editor: Roberta Ashley. 90% freelance written. Monthly magazine for 18- to 35-year-old single, married, divorced women—all working. Estab. 1886. Circ. 2,573,100. **Pays on acceptance.** Byline given. Offers 10-15% kill fee. Buys all magazine rights and occasionally negotiates first North American rights. Submit seasonal/holiday material 6 months in advance. Reports in 1 week on queries; 3 weeks on mss. Sample copy for $2.50. Writer's guidelines for #10 SASE.
• Ranked as one of the best markets for freelance writers in *Writer's Yearbook*'s annual "Top 100 Markets," January 1996.
Nonfiction: Book excerpts, how-to, humor, opinion, personal experience and anything of interest to young women. Buys 350 mss/year. Query with published clips or send complete ms. Length: 500-3,500 words. Pays expenses of writers on assignment.
Reprints: Accepts previously published submissions appearing in minor publications. Send tearsheet of article, typed ms with rights for sale noted and information about when and where the article previously appeared. Pays 100% of amount paid for an original article.
Fiction: Betty Kelly. Condensed novels, humorous, novel excerpts, romance. Buys 18 mss/year. Query. Length: 750-3,000 words.
• *Cosmopolitan* no longer accepts short stories.
Poetry: Free verse, light verse. Buys 30 poems/year. No maximum number. Length: 4-30 lines.
Fillers: Irene Copeland. Facts. Buys 240/year. Length: 300-1,000 words.

COUNTRY WOMAN, Reiman Publications, P.O. Box 643, Milwaukee WI 53201. (414)423-0100. Managing Editor: Kathy Pohl. 75-85% written by readers. Willing to work with new/unpublished writers. Bimonthly magazine on the interests of country women. "*Country Woman* is for contemporary rural women of all ages and backgrounds and from all over the US and Canada. It includes a sampling of the diversity that makes up rural women's lives—love of home, family, farm, ranch, community, hobbies, enduring values, humor, attaining new skills and appreciating present, past and future all within the context of the lifestyle that surrounds country living." Estab. 1970. **Pays on acceptance.** Byline given. Buys first North American serial, one-time and second serial (reprint) rights. Submit seasonal/holiday material 5 months in advance. Reports in 2 months on queries; 3 months on mss. Sample copy for $2. Writer's guidelines for #10 SASE.
Nonfiction: General interest, historical/nostalgic, how-to (crafts, community projects, decorative, antiquing, etc.), humor, inspirational, interview/profile, personal experience, photo/feature packages profiling interesting country women—all pertaining to a rural woman's interest. Articles must be written in a positive, light and entertaining manner. Query. Length: 1,000 words maximum.
Reprints: Send typed ms with rights for sale noted and information about when and where the material previously appeared. Payment varies.
Photos: Send color photos with query or ms. Reviews 35mm or 2¼ transparencies or excellent-quality color prints. Uses only excellent quality color photos. No b&w. "We pay for photo/feature packages." Captions, model releases and identification of subjects required. Buys one-time rights.

Columns/Departments: Why Farm Wives Age Fast (humor), I Remember When (nostalgia) and Country Decorating. Buys 10-12 mss/year (maximum). Query or send complete ms. Length: 500-1,000 words. Pays $50-125.

Fiction: Main character *must* be a country woman. All fiction must have a country setting. Fiction must have a positive, upbeat message. Includes fiction in every issue. Would buy more fiction if stories suitable for our audience were sent our way. Query or send complete ms. Length: 750-1,000 words. Pays $90-125.

Poetry: Traditional, light verse. "Poetry must have rhythm and rhyme! It must be country-related. Always looking for seasonal poetry." Buys 30 poems/year. Submit maximum 6 poems. Length: 5-24 lines. Pays $10-25.

Tips: "We have recently broadened our focus to include 'country' women, not just women on farms and ranches. This allows freelancers a wider scope in material. Write as clearly and with as much zest and enthusiasm as possible. We love good quotes, supporting materials (names, places, etc.) and strong leads and closings. Readers relate strongly to where they live and the lifestyle they've chosen. They want to be informed and entertained, and that's just exactly why they subscribe. Readers are busy—not too busy to read—but when they do sit down, they want good writing, reliable information and something that feels like a reward. How-to, humor, personal experience and nostalgia are areas most open to freelancers. Profiles, to a certain degree, are also open. Be accurate and fresh in approach."

DAUGHTERS OF SARAH, The Magazine for Christian Feminists, Daughters of Sarah, 2121 Sheridan Rd., Evanston IL 60201. (708)866-3882. Editor: Elizabeth Anderson. 85% freelance written. Quarterly Christian feminist magazine "published by women calling for justice, mutuality, and reconciliation in the church and the world. We are a forum for a wide variety of viewpoints that are both Christian and feminist." Estab. 1974. Circ. 5,000. Pays on publication. Publishes ms an average of 4 months after acceptance. Byline given. Buys first North American and one-time rights. Editorial lead time 3 months. Submit seasonal material 3 months in advance. Reports in 4 months. Sample copy for $6. Writer's guidelines for #10 SASE.
  • Upcoming themes include Women and Education (fall 1996), Women and Money (winter 1997), Women, Work and Welfare (spring 1997).

Nonfiction: Essays, exposé, general interest, historical/nostalgic, humor, inspirational, interview/profile, opinion, personal experience, religious. "We are a thematic magazine. Each issue focuses on a specific theme. It is essential to send for a theme list. We don't want to see anything *not* relating to women or women's issues and anything without biblical or feminist perspective." Query. Length: 500-2,100 words. Pays $15/printed page minimum plus 2 copies.

Photos: Send photos with submission. Reviews 8×10 prints. Negotiates payment individually. Identification of subjects required. Buys one-time rights. Address art submissions to Trevor Bechtel, design director.

Columns/Departments: Elizabeth Anderson, editor. Segue (feminist women in conservative/mainline churches), 800 words; Feminist Pilgrim (biblical exegesis/theological discourse), 1,000 words; Women in Ministry (clergy women and lay women in ministry tell personal stories), 1,000 words, (presently untitled) Womanist column, 1,000 words. Buys 12 mss/year. Query. Pays $15-80.

Fiction: Confession, historical, humorous, religious. Buys 2 mss/year. Query. Length: 600-2,000 words. Pays $15-80.

Poetry: Free verse, light verse. Buys 12-15/year. Submit maximum 3 poems. Length: 4-50 lines. Pays $15-45.

Tips: "Query, query, query! Our writer's guidelines are very helpful and speak to specific areas (and pet peeves) that will help you get published in *Daughters of Sarah*. Use inclusive language. Use a personal approach and avoid 'preachy' academic-ese, and issues not relating to women, feminism and Christianity. Our nonfiction area is most open. My greatest advice is to send for our guidelines and themes and then please query first before sending a manuscript. Stick to issues relating to a specific theme. We reserve our highest standards for poetry; we generally reject rhymed couplets—and *please*, no prose cut into lines and verses."

ESSENCE, 1500 Broadway, New York NY 10036. (212)642-0600. Editor-in-Chief: Susan L. Taylor. Executive Editor: Linda Villarosa. Editor-at-Large: Valerie Wilson Wesley. Monthly magazine. Estab. 1970. Circ. 1 million. **Pays on acceptance.** Makes assignments on one-time serial rights basis. 3 month lead time. Pays 25% kill fee. Byline given. Submit seasonal/holiday material 6 months in advance. Accepts previously published submissions. Send tearsheet of article, information about when and where the article previously appeared. Pays 50% of the amount paid for an original article. Reports in 2 months. Sample copy for $3.25. Free writer's guidelines.
  • Ranked as one of the best markets for freelance writers in *Writer's Yearbook*'s annual "Top 100 Markets," January 1996.

Nonfiction: Buys 200 mss/year. Query only; word length will be given upon assignment. Pays $500 minimum. Also publishes novel and nonfiction book excerpts.

Photos: Janice Wheeler, art director. State availability of photos with query. Pays $100 for b&w page; $300 for color page. Captions and model release required. "We particularly would like to see photographs for our travel section that feature Black travelers."

Columns/Departments: Query department editors: Living (home, food, lifestyle, travel, consumer information): Corliss Hill and Cara Roberts; Entertainment: Gordon Chambers; Health & Fitness: Tonya Adam; Travel: Cara Roberts. Query only, word length will be given upon assignment. Pays $100 minimum.

Tips: "Please note that *Essence* no longer accepts unsolicited mss for fiction, poetry or nonfiction, except for the Brothers, Windows, Back Talk and Interiors columns. So please only send query letters for nonfiction story ideas."

FAMILY CIRCLE MAGAZINE, 110 Fifth Ave., New York NY 10011. (212)463-1000. Fax: (212)463-1808. Editor-in-Chief: Susan Ungaro. 70% freelance written. Magazine published 17 times/year. Usually buys all print rights. Offers 20% kill fee. Byline given. **Pays on acceptance.** "We are a national women's magazine which covers many stages of a woman's life, along with her everyday concerns about social, family and health issues. Query should stress the unique aspects of an article and expert sources; we want articles that will help our readers or make a difference in how they live." Reports in 2 months.
 • Ranked as one of the best markets for freelance writers in *Writer's Yearbook*'s annual "Top 100 Markets," January 1996.

Nonfiction: Nancy Clark, deputy editor. Women's interest subjects such as family and personal relationships, children, physical and mental health, nutrition, self-improvement and profiles of ordinary women doing extraordinary things for her community or the nation for 'Women Who Make a Difference' series. "We look for well-written, well-reported stories told through interesting anecdotes and insightful writing. We want well-researched service journalism on all subjects." Query. Length: 1,000-2,500 words. Pays $1/word.

Tips: "Query letters should be concise and to the point. Also, writers should keep close tabs on *Family Circle* and other women's magazines to avoid submitting recently run subject matter."

FIRST FOR WOMEN, Bauer Publishing Co., P.O. Box 1648, 270 Sylvan Ave., Englewood Cliffs NJ 07632. (201)569-6699. Magazine published 18 times/year. Executive Editor: Teresa Hagen. "*First for Women* speaks directly to a woman about her real-life needs, concerns and interests. *First* provides an equal combination of service editorial (family, kids, health, food and home) with personal lifestyle and general interest topics (personal health, fitness, nutrition, beauty, fashion and contemporary issues) for the "30-something" woman." Query before submitting. Feature sections more open to freelancers. Estab. 1989. Circ. 1,282,600.

‡FLARE MAGAZINE, 777 Bay St., 5th Floor, Toronto, Ontario M5W 1A7 **Canada**. Fax: (416)596-5184. E-mail: editors@flare.com. Contact: Liza Finlay, managing editor. Monthly magazine for English-speaking, working women ages 18-39. **Pays on acceptance.** Byline given. Offers 50% kill fee. Buys first North American serial and electronic rights. Sample copy and writer's guidelines free on request.
 • Ranked as one of the best markets for freelance writers in *Writer's Yearbook*'s annual "Top 100 Markets," January 1996.

Nonfiction: Fashion, beauty, health and fitness, career, sex. Length: 1,200-2,000 words. Pays 50¢/word. Pays expenses of writers on assignment.

Reprints: Accepts previously published submissions.

Columns/Departments: 700 words. Pays 50¢/word.

Fillers: Length: 700 words minimum. Pays 50¢/word.

Tips: "Know our demographics."

GLAMOUR, Condé Nast, 350 Madison Ave., New York NY 10017. (212)880-8800. Fax: (212)880-6922. E-mail: glamourmag@aol.com. Editor-in-Chief: Ruth Whitney. 75% freelance written. Works with a small number of new/unpublished writers each year. Monthly magazine for college-educated women, 18-35 years old. Estab. 1939. Circ. 2,300,000. **Pays on acceptance.** Offers 20% kill fee. Publishes ms an average of 1 year after acceptance. Byline given. Reports in 3 months. Writer's guidelines for #10 SASE.

Nonfiction: Pamela Erens, articles editor. "Editorial approach is 'how-to' with articles that are relevant in the areas of careers, health, psychology, interpersonal relationships, etc. We look for queries that are fresh and include a contemporary, timely angle. Fashion, beauty, travel, food and entertainment are all staff-written. We use 1,000-word opinion essays for our Viewpoint section. Our His/Hers column features generally stylish essays on relationships or comments on current mores by male and female writers in alternate months." Pays $1,000 for His/Hers mss; $500 for Viewpoint mss. Buys first North American serial rights. Buys 10-12 mss/issue. Query "with letter that is detailed, well-focused, well-organized, and documented with surveys, statistics and research; personal essays excepted." Short articles and essays (1,500-2,000 words) pay $1,000 and up; longer mss (2,500-3,000 words) pay $1,500 minimum. Sometimes pays the expenses of writers on assignment.

Reprints: Send information about when and where the article previously appeared. Payment varies.

Tips: "We're looking for sharply focused ideas by strong writers and are constantly raising our standards. We are interested in getting new writers, and we are approachable, mainly because our range of topics is so broad. We've increased our focus on male-female relationships."

GOOD HOUSEKEEPING, Hearst Corp., 959 Eighth Ave., New York NY 10019. (212)649-2000. Editor-in-Chief: Ellen Levine. Executive Editor: Janet Chan. Deputy Editor: Diane Salvatore. Prefers to work with published/established writers. Monthly magazine. Circ. 5,000,000. **Pays on acceptance.** Buys first North American serial rights. Pays 25% kill fee. Byline given. Submit seasonal/holiday material 6 months in advance. Reports in 2 months. Sample copy for $2. Writer's guidelines for #10 SASE.

Nonfiction: Diane Salvatore, deputy editor. Health, consumer, social issues, dramatic narrative, nutrition, work. Buys 4-6 mss/issue. Query. Length: 1,500-2,500 words. Pays $1,500+ on acceptance for full articles from new writers. Pays $250-350 for local interest and travel pieces of 2,000 words. Pays expenses of writers on assignment.

Photos: Scott Yardley, art director. Maya MacMillan, photo editor. Photos purchased on assignment mostly. Pays $100-350 for b&w; $200-400 for color photos. Query. Model releases required.

Columns/Departments: The Better Way, edited by Lisa Benenson (consumer issues, how-to, shopping strategies, money savers, health). Profile, edited by Evelyn Renolds (inspirational, activist or heroic women), 300-600 words. My Problem and How I Solved It, edited by Sandy Lee (as told-to format), 2,000 words. Query. Pays $1/word for items 300-600 words.

Fiction: Lee Quarfoot, fiction editor. Uses original short fiction and condensations of novels that can appear in one issue. Looks for reader identification. "We get 1,500 unsolicited mss/month. A freelancer's odds are overwhelming, but we do look at all submissions." Send complete mss. Manuscripts will not be returned. Only responds on acceptance. Length: 1,500 words (short-shorts); novel according to merit of material; average 5,000-word short stories. Pays $1,000 minimum for fiction from new writers.

● Ranked as one of the best markets for fiction writers in *Writer's Digest*'s annual "Fiction 50," June 1996.

Tips: "Always send a SASE and clips. We prefer to see a query first. Do not send material on subjects already covered in-house by the Good Housekeeping Institute—these include food, beauty, needlework and crafts."

‡HARPER'S BAZAAR, The Hearst Corp., 1700 Broadway, New York, NY 10019. (212)903-5300. Fax: (212)265-8579. Publisher: Jeannette Chang. Monthly magazine covering fashion and beauty. "*Harper's Bazaar* is a specialist magazine for women who love fashion and beauty. It is edited for sophisticated women with exceptional taste. *Bazaar* offers ideas in fashion and beauty, and reports on issues and interests relevant to the lives of modern women." Estab. 1867. Circ. 711,000. This magazine did not respond to our request for information. Query before submitting.

HERIZONS, Women's News & Feminist Views, Herizons Inc., P.O. Box 128 Station Main, Winnipeg, Manitoba R3C 2G1 Canada. (204)779-3665. Coordinating Editor: Penni Mitchell. 50% freelance written. Quarterly magazine covering women's issues. Estab. 1991. Circ. 4,000. Pays on publication. Publishes ms an average of 3 months after acceptance. Byline given. Buys second serial (reprint) rights. Editorial lead time 3 months. Sample copy $5.50. Writer's guidelines for #10 SAE and IRC.

Nonfiction: Interview/profile, opinion, personal experience. Query. Length: 600-2,000 words. Pays $100-300.

Photos: State availability of photos with submission. Offers $25-50/photo. Captions required. Buys one-time rights.

Columns/Departments: Query. Pays $100-200.

LADIES' HOME JOURNAL, Meredith Corporation, 125 Park Ave., New York NY 10017-5516. (212)557-6600. Publishing Director/Editor-in-Chief: Myrna Blyth. 50% freelance written. Monthly magazine focusing on issues of concern to women. Circ. 5,000,000. **Pays on acceptance.** Offers 25% kill fee. Rights bought vary with submission. Reports on queries within 3 months with SASE. Writer's guidelines for #10 SASE, mark Attention: Writer's guidelines on envelope.

Nonfiction: Submissions on the following subjects should be directed to the editor listed for each: investigative reports, news-related features, psychology/relationships/sex (Pam O'Brien, features editor); medical/health (Deborah Pike, health editor); celebrities/entertainment (Melanie Gerosa, entertainment editor); travel stories (Karyn Dabaghian, associate editor). Query with published clips. Length: 1,500-3,000 words. Pay varies. Pays expenses of writers on assignment.

Photos: State availability of photos with submission. Offers variable payment for photos accepted with ms. Captions, model releases and identification of subjects required. Rights bought vary with submission. (*LHJ* arranges for its own photography almost all the time.)

Columns/Departments: Query the following editor or box for column ideas. A Woman Today (Box WT); Woman to Woman (Box WW); Parents' Journal (Mary Mohler, senior editor); Pet News (Shana Aborn, associate features editor).

Fiction: Mary Mohler, editor, books and fiction. Only short stories and novels submitted by an agent or publisher will be considered. Buys 12 mss/year. Does not accept poetry of any kind.

● Ranked as one of the best markets for fiction writers in *Writer's Digest*'s annual "Fiction 50," June 1996.

McCALL'S, 110 Fifth Ave., New York NY 10011-5603. (212)463-1000. Editor: Sally Koslow. Executive Editor: Cathy Cavender. 90% freelance written. "Study recent issues. Our publication carefully and conscientiously serves the needs of the woman reader—concentrating on matters that directly affect her life and offering information and understanding on subjects of personal importance to her." Monthly. Circ. 5 million. **Pays on acceptance.** Publishes ms an average of 6 months after acceptance. Offers 20% kill fee. Byline given. Buys exclusive or First North American rights. Reports in 2 months. Writer's guidelines for #10 SASE.

• Ranked as one of the best markets for freelance writers in *Writer's Yearbook*'s annual "Top 100 Markets," January 1996.

Nonfiction: The editors are seeking meaningful stories of personal experience, fresh slants for self-help and relationship pieces, and well-researched action-oriented articles and narratives dealing with social problems concerning readers. Topics must have broad appeal, but they must be approached in a fresh, new, you-haven't-read-this-elsewhere way. *McCall's* buys 200-300 articles/year, many in the 1,500-2,000-word length. Pays variable rates for nonfiction. These are on subjects of interest to women: health, personal narratives, celebrity biographies and autobiographies, etc. Almost all features on food, fashion, beauty and decorating are staff-written. Sometimes pays the expenses of writers on assignment.

Tips: Query first. Use the tone and format of our most recent issues as your guide. Preferred length: 1,500-2,000 words. Address submissions to executive editor unless otherwise specified.

MADEMOISELLE, Condé Nast, 350 Madison Ave., New York NY 10017. Managing Editor: Faye Haun. Contact: Katherine Brown Weissman, executive editor. 95% freelance written. Prefers to work with published/established writers. Columns are written by columnists; "sometimes we give new writers a 'chance' on shorter, less complex assignments." Monthly magazine for women age 21-31. Circ 1,200,000. Buys first North American serial rights. **Pays on acceptance**; rates vary.

Nonfiction: Particular concentration on articles of interest to the intelligent young woman, including personal relationships, health, careers, trends, and current social problems. Send health queries to Dana Points, health editor. Send entertainment queries to Jeanie Pyun, entertainment editor. Query with published clips and SAE. Length: 1,000 words.

Photos: Cindy Searight, creative director. Commissioned work assigned according to needs. Photos of fashion, beauty, travel. Payment ranges from no-charge to an agreed rate of payment per shot, job series or page rate. Buys all rights. Pays on publication for photos.

Tips: "We are looking for timely, well-researched manuscripts."

‡MARIE CLAIRE, Hearst Corp., 250 W. 55th St., New York NY 10019. (212)649-4450. Fax: (212)541-4295. E-mail: marieclaire@hearst.com. Editor: Bonnie Fuller. Executive Editor: Clare McHugh. Contact: Catherine Romano, features editor. Monthly magazine covering fashion, beauty, lifestyle. "American *Marie Claire* was launched in September, 1994. There are currently 22 other international editions. The magazine aims to provide a great read on everything from world issues to intimate advice, fashion, beauty and service." Estab. 1994. Circ. 500,000. **Pays on acceptance**. Publishes ms an average of 5 months after acceptance. Byline given. Offers 25% kill fee. Makes work-for-hire assignments. Editorial lead time 3 months. Submit seasonal material 6 months in advance. Accepts simultaneous submissions. Reports in 3 weeks on queries. Sample copy for $5. Writer's guidelines free on request.

Nonfiction: Book excerpts, exposé, general interest, humor, personal experience. Does not want to see fiction, personal essays. Buys 50 mss/year. Query with published clips. Length: 500-3,000 words. Pays $1-1.50/word. Sometimes pays expenses of writers on assignment.

Photos: State availability of photos with submission. Reviews contact sheets, negatives, prints. Negotiates payment individually. Model releases, identification of subjects required.

Columns/Departments: Women of the world (the lead feature in every edition, an issue addressing women of another country or culture, but somehow relatable to an American woman as well); first person (personal and dramatic stories, always written from the female subject's point of view); true lives (may be written in first or third person, male or female, discussing a non-traditional lifestyle or unusual experience); emotional issues (relationship/sex related stories, provocative and newsy); working (career issues women face at work, at home, or in relationships); love life (any facet of love, sex, marriage and dating); review (movies, music, books, celebrities, TV, etc.).

MODERN BRIDE, 249 W. 17th St., New York NY 10011. (212)337-7096. Editor: Cele Lalli. Executive Editor: Mary Ann Cavlin. **Pays on acceptance.** Offers 25% kill fee. Buys first periodical rights. Reports in 1 month.

Nonfiction: Book excerpts, general interest, how-to, personal experience. Buys 60 mss/year. Query with published clips. Length: 500-2,000 words. Pays $600-1,200.

Reprints: Accepts previously published submissions.

Columns/Departments: Geri Bain, editor. Travel.

Poetry: Free verse, light verse and traditional. Buys very few. Submit maximum 6 poems.

‡MS. MAGAZINE, MacDonald Communications, Inc., 230 Park Ave., 7th Floor, New York NY 10169-0799. (212)551-9595. Editor-in-Chief: Marcia Gillespie. Executive Editor: Barbara Findlen. 75% freelance written. Bimonthly magazine on women's issues and news. Estab. 1972. Circ. 200,000. Sample copy for $5. Writer's guidelines for #10 SASE.

• Ranked as one of the best markets for freelance writers in *Writer's Yearbook*'s annual "Top 100 Markets," January 1996. This magazine was recently sold to MacDonald Communications.

Nonfiction: International and national (US) news, the arts, books, popular culture, feminist theory and scholarship, ecofeminism, women's health, spirituality, political and economic affairs. Photo essays. Runs fiction and poetry but does not accept, acknowledge, or return unsolicited fiction or poetry. Query with published clips. No phone queries. Length: 300-3,000 words. Pays expenses of writers on assignment.

Photos: State availability of photos with submission. Model releases and identification of subjects required. Buys one-time rights.

NEW WOMAN MAGAZINE, K-III, 215 Lexington Ave., New York NY 10016. (212)251-1500. Editor: Betsy Carter. Contact: Sharlene Breakey, managing editor. Monthly magazine. Estab. 1970. Circ. 1,300,000. **Pays on acceptance.** Byline given. Offers variable kill fee. Buys first North American serial, first, one-time and electronic rights. Editorial lead time 5 months. Submit seasonal material 5 months in advance. Accepts simultaneous submissions. Reports in 3 months. Writer's guidelines for #10 SASE.

Nonfiction: Book excerpts, essays, exposé, general interest, humor, interview/profile, opinion, personal experience, travel. Buys over 20 mss/year. Query with published clips. Length: 500-2,500 words. Pays variable rates. Pays expenses of writers on assignment.

Columns/Departments: Contact: Jane Reilly.

PLAYGIRL, 801 Second Ave., New York NY 10017. (212)661-7878. Editor-in-Chief: Judy Cole. Contact: Patrice Baldwin, managing editor. 75% freelance written. Prefers to work with published/established writers. Monthly entertainment magazine for 18- to 55-year-old females. Circ. 500,000. Pays within 6 weeks of acceptance. Publishes ms an average of 3 months after acceptance. Byline given. Offers 20% kill fee. Buys all rights. Submit seasonal material 6 months in advance. Accepts simultaneous submissions, if so noted. Reports in 1 month on queries; 3 months on mss. Writer's guidelines for #10 SASE.

Nonfiction: Humor for the modern woman/man, exposés (related to women's issues), interview (Q&A format with major show business celebrities), articles on sexuality, medical breakthroughs, relationships, coping, careers, insightful, lively articles on current issues, investigative pieces particularly geared to *Playgirl*. Average issue 3 articles; 1 celebrity interview. Buys 6 mss/issue. Query with published clips. Length: 1,000-2,500 words. Pays $300-1,000. Sometimes pays expenses of writers on assignment.

Tips: "Best bets for first-time writers: Women's Room (humor) and Fantasy Forum. No phone calls please."

RADIANCE, The Magazine for Large Women, Box 30246, Oakland CA 94604. (510)482-0680. E-mail: radmag2@aol.com. Editor: Alice Ansfield. 95% freelance written. Quarterly magazine "that encourages and supports women *all* sizes of large to live fully now, to stop putting their lives on hold until they lose weight." Estab. 1984. Circ. 10,000. Pays on publication. Publishes ms an average of 10 months after acceptance. Byline given. Offers $25 kill fee. Buys one-time and second serial (reprint) rights. Submit seasonal/holiday material at least 8-10 months in advance. Accepts previously published submissions. Query for electronic submissions. Reports in 4 months. Sample copy for $3.50. Writer's guidelines for #10 SASE.

Nonfiction: Book excerpts (related to large women), essays, exposé, general interest, historical/nostalgic, how-to (on health/well-being/fashion/fitness, etc.), humor, inspirational, interview/profile, opinion, personal experience, photo feature, travel. "No diet successes or articles condemning people for being fat." Query with published clips. Length: 1,000-2,500 words. Pays $35-100. Sometimes pays writers with contributor copies or other premiums.

Photos: State availability of photos with submission. Offers $15-50/photo. Captions and identification of subjects preferred. Buys one-time rights.

Columns/Departments: Up Front and Personal (personal profiles of women from all areas of life); Health and Well-Being (physical/emotional well-being, self care, research); Expressions (features on artists who celebrate the full female figure); Images (designer interviews, color/style/fashion, features); Inner Journeys (spirituality, personal experiences, interviews); Perspectives (cultural and political aspects of being in a larger body); On the Move (women active in all kinds of sports, physical activities); Young Activists (bringing size awareness and esteem to the younger generation); Travel. Buys 60 mss/year. Query with published clips. Length: 1,000-3,500 words. Pays $50-100.

Fiction: Condensed novels, ethnic, fantasy, historical, humorous, mainstream, novel excerpts, romance, science fiction, serialized novels, slice-of-life vignettes relating somehow to large women. "No woman-hates-self-till-meets-man'-type fiction!" Buys 15 mss/year. Query with published clips. Length: 800-2,500 words. Pays $35-100.

Poetry: Reflective, empowering, experiential. Related to women's feelings and experience, re: their bodies, self-esteem, acceptance. Buys 30 poems/year. Length: 4-45 lines. Pays $10-30.

Tips: "We welcome talented, sensitive, responsible, open-minded writers. We profile women from all walks of life who are all sizes of large, of all ages and from all ethnic groups and lifestyles. We welcome writers' ideas on interesting large women from across the US and abroad. We're an open, light-hearted magazine that's working to help women feel good about themselves now, whatever their body size. *Radiance* is one of the major forces working for size acceptance. We want articles to address all areas of vital importance in women's lives. Please read a copy of *Radiance* before writing for us."

REDBOOK MAGAZINE, 224 W. 57th St., New York NY 10019. Senior Editors: Harriet Lyons and Toni Gerber Hope. Health Editor: Toni Gerber Hope. Fiction Editor: Dawn Raffel. Contact: Any of editorial assistants listed on masthead. 90% freelance written. Monthly magazine. Estab. 1903. Circ. 3,200,000. **Pays on acceptance.** Publishes ms an average of 6 months after acceptance. Rights purchased vary with author and material. Reports in 3 months. Writer's guidelines for #10 SASE.

• Ranked as one of the best markets for freelance writers in *Writer's Yearbook*'s annual "Top 100 Markets," January 1996.

Nonfiction: "*Redbook* addresses young mothers between the ages of 25 and 39. Most of our readers are married with children 12 and under; over 60 percent work outside the home. The articles entertain, educate and inspire our readers to confront challenging issues. Each article must be timely and relevant to *Redbook* readers' lives. Article subjects of interest: social issues, parenting, sex, marriage, news profiles, true crime, dramatic narratives, money, psychology, health. Query with published clips. Length: articles, 2,500-3,000 words; short articles, 1,000-1,500 words. "Please review at least the past six issues of *Redbook* to better understand subject matter and treatment." Enclose SASE for response.

Columns/Departments: "We are interested in stories for 'The Secret Life of Mothers' series. These are first-person essays about motherhood from the point of view of mothers. See past issues for samples. Length: 1,200-1,500 words. Manuscripts accompanied by a 9×12 SASE, must be signed and mailed to: The Secret Life of Mothers, c/o *Redbook Magazine*. Reports in 6 months.

Fiction: "Of the 20,000 unsolicited manuscripts that we receive annually, we buy about 10 or more stories/year. We also find many more stories that are not necessarily suited to our needs but are good enough to warrant our encouraging the author to send others. *Redbook* looks for fresh, well-crafted stories that reflect some aspect of the experiences and interests of our readers; it's a good idea to read several issues to get a feel for what we buy. No unsolicited novels or novellas, please." Payment begins at $1,000 for short stories. Please include SASE with all stories.

• Ranked as one of the best markets for fiction writers in *Writer's Digest*'s annual "Fiction 50," June 1996.

Tips: "Most *Redbook* articles require solid research, well-developed anecdotes from on-the-record sources, and fresh, insightful quotes from established experts in a field that pass our 'reality check' test."

REVIEW, A Publication of Woman's Life Insurance Society, 1338 Military St., P.O. Box 5020, Port Huron MI 48061-5020. (313)985-5191, ext. 29. Fax: (810)985-6970. Editor: Janice U. Whipple. Contact: Patricia J. Samar, director of communications. 30% freelance written. Works only with published/established writers. Quarterly magazine published for a primarily female-membership to help them care for themselves and their families. Estab. 1892. Circ. 36,000. Pays on publication. Publishes ms an average of 1 year after acceptance. Byline given. Not copyrighted. Buys one-time, simultaneous and second serial (reprint) rights. Submit seasonal/holiday material 6 months in advance. Accepts simultaneous submissions. Reports in 1 year (usually less). Sample copy for 9×12 SASE with 4 first-class stamps. Writer's guidelines for #10 SASE.

Nonfiction: The cover of this publication states: "Key Information Vital to Every Woman's Fiscal and Physical Health." Looking primarily for general interest stories for women aged 25-44 regarding physical, mental and emotional health and fitness; and financial/fiscal health and fitness. "We would like to see more creative financial pieces that are directed at women. Also interested in creative interesting stories about marketing life insurance and annuities to the women's market." Buys 4-10 mss/year. Send complete ms. Length: 1,000-2,000 words. Pays $150-500/ms.

Reprints: Send photocopy of article or send typed ms with rights for sale noted and information about when and where ms previously appeared. Pays 15% of amount paid for an original article.

Photos: Not interested in photos at this time, unless accompanied by a ms. Model release and identification of subjects required.

Tips: "We have begun more clearly defining the focus of our magazine. We receive FAR TOO MANY stories from people who clearly ignore the information in this listing and/or our writer's guidelines. No more stories about Tippy the Spotted Pig, please!"

‡**TODAY'S BRIDE**, Family Communications, 37 Hanna Ave., Suite #1, Toronto, Ontario M6K 1X1 Canada. (416)537-2604. Fax: (416)538-1794. Editor: Bettie Bradley. Contact: Shirley-Anne Ohannessian. Less than 10% freelance written. Semiannual magazine covering wedding fashion and planning. "The magazine is geared to engaged couples who are looking for bridal fashion and wedding planning tips. All standard planning pieces and travel are written in-house; the only freelance articles we purchase are those that look at something unique or different." Estab. 1980. Circ. 108,000. **Pays on acceptance.** Byline given. Offers kill fee. Buys all rights. Editorial lead time 6 months. Accepts simultaneous submissions. Reports in 2 months on queries. Writer's guidelines free on request.

Nonfiction: Humor, opinion, personal experience. No travel and standard planning pieces (i.e. choosing flowers, music, etc.). Query with or without published clips or send complete ms. Length: 800-1,400 words. Pays $250-300. Sometimes pays expenses of writers on assignment.

Photos: Send photos with submission. Reviews transparencies, prints. Negotiates payment individually. Identification of subjects required. Rights purchased negotiated on individual basis.

TODAY'S CHRISTIAN WOMAN, 465 Gundersen Dr., Carol Stream IL 60188-2498. (708)260-6200. Fax: (708)260-0114. E-mail: tcwedit@aol.com. Editor: Ramona Cramer Tucker. Associate Editors: Linda Piepenbrink, Jane Johnson Struck. Assistant Editor: Camerin Courtney. 25% freelance written. Works with a small number of new/unpublished writers each year. Bimonthly magazine for Christian women of all ages, single and married, homemakers and career women. Estab. 1979. Circ. 310,000. **Pays on acceptance.** Publishes ms an average of 6 months after acceptance. Byline given. Buys first rights only. Submit seasonal/holiday material 9 months in advance. Reports in 2 months. Sample copy for $5. Writer's guidelines for #10 SASE.

Nonfiction: How-to, narrative, inspirational. Query only; no unsolicited mss. "The query should include article summary, purpose and reader value, author's qualifications, suggested length and date to send." Pays 15¢/word.

Tips: "Articles focus on the following relationships: marriage, parenting, self, spiritual life and friendship. All articles should be highly anecdotal, personal in tone, and universal in appeal."

VICTORIA, The Hearst Corp., 224 W. 57th St., 4th Floor, New York NY 10019. (212)649-3700. Fax: (212)582-6792. Publisher: Cindy Sperling. Monthly magazine. "*Victoria* is a contemporary women's magazine with an intimate editorial perspective on home, fashion, beauty, food, entertaining, literature and the arts." Estab. 1987. Circ. 948,000. This magazine did not respond to our request for information. Query before submitting.

‡**VOGUE**, Condé Nast, 350 Madison Ave., New York NY 10017. (212)880-8800. E-mail: voguemail@aol. com. Features Editor: Susan Morrison. Monthly magazine. "*Vogue* mirrors the changing roles and concerns of women, covering not only evolutions in fashion, beauty and style, but the important issues and ideas of the arts, health care, politics and world affairs. Articles about European and American fashion designers suggest concepts, create new trends—and encourage ideas that keep life exciting and modern." Estab. 1892. Circ. 1,136,000. **Pays on acceptance.** Byline given. Offers 33% kill fee. Buys first North American serial rights. Reports in 2 months on queries. Writer's guidelines for #10 SASE.

● Ranked as one of the best markets for freelance writers in *Writer's Yearbook*'s annual "Top 100 Markets," January 1996.

Nonfiction: "Needs fresh voices on unexpected topics." Buys 36 mss/year. Query with published clips. Length: 2,500 words maximum. Pays $1-2/word for assigned articles. Pays expenses of writers on assignment.

Columns/Departments: 1,500-2,000 words. Buys 48 mss/year. Query with published clips.

Tips: "Sophisticated, surprising and compelling writing a must."

‡**WEDDING DAY MAGAZINE, For The Modern Bride In New England**, Wedding Day Expositions, 100 Crescent Rd., Suite 1A, Needham MA 02194. (617)455-1480. Editor: Paula Roy. 80% freelance written. Bimonthly magazine covering wedding planning, bridal showers. "Articles must relate to weddings, wedding planning, bridal fashion or female related topics (i.e. beauty, skin care, home decorating). Majority of readers are female between 18-25." Estab. 1985. Circ. 15,000. Pays on publication. Publishes ms an average of 2 months after acceptance. Byline given. Buys first and second serial (reprint) rights. Editorial lead time 2 months. Submit seasonal material 2 months in advance. Accepts simultaneous submissions. Sample copy and writer's guidelines free on request—call ahead.

Nonfiction: Historical/nostalgic (origin of wedding traditions), how-to (i.e. skin-care, nails), interview/profile (of designers of bridal or formalwear), new products, personal experience (of something related to getting married from bridegroom prospective), travel (honeymoon). Buys 12 mss/year. Query. Length: 600-2,200 words. Pays $150-250.

Reprints: Accepts previously published submissions.

Photos: State availability of photos with submission. List exactly what photo is of or for. Send a copy of what original looks like. Offers no additional payment for photos accepted with ms. Captions required. Buys all rights.

Columns/Departments: Honeymoon Hotspots (vacation sites for newlyweds) 2,000 words; Fashion (latest in formalwear, gowns, attendants wear, cruisewear) 2,000 words; Male Perspective (getting married from male point of view) 800 words. Buys 24 mss/year. Query. Pays $100-250.

Fiction: "We publish very little fiction." Buys 1 mss/year. Query.

Fillers: Wants these fillers: anecdotes, facts, gags to be illustrated by cartoonist, newsbreaks. Buys 40/year. Length: 50-600 words. Pays $50-200.

WEST COAST WOMAN, LMB Media, Inc., P.O. Box 819, Sarasota FL 34230-0819. (813)954-3300. Fax: (813)954-3300. Editor: Louise Bruderle. 50% freelance written. Monthly tabloid for women on the west coast of Florida. "*West Coast Woman* is a lifestyle publication." Estab. 1988. Circ. 30,000. Pays on publication. Byline given. Offers 50% kill fee. Buys first or one-time rights. Sample copy for $3.50. Writer's guidelines for #10 SASE.

• *West Coast Woman* is focusing less on fashion, beauty, and more on first-person stories.

Nonfiction: Real estate, gardening, how-to, health, beauty, book reviews, seniors, car care, home design, fitness, photo feature, technical, travel, sports, fashion, money/finance, nutrition, cooking, food/wine. No humor, slice-of-life, essays, poems, poetry or comics/cartoons." Buys 130 mss/year. Query with published clips. Length: 750-3,000 words. Pays $35-65 for 750 words. Also makes ad trades for promotional tie-ins.

Photos: State availability of photos with submission. Reviews contact sheets, 35mm transparencies. Model releases required. Buys one-time rights.

WOMAN'S DAY, 1633 Broadway, New York NY 10019. (212)767-6000. Fax: (212)767-5610. E-mail: maureenmcf@aol.com. Senior Features Editor: Maureen McFadden. 75% or more of articles freelance written. 17 issues/year. Circ. 6,000,000. Pays 25% kill fee. Byline given. **Pays on acceptance.** Reports in 1 month or less on queries. Submit detailed queries.

• Ranked as one of the best markets for freelance writers in *Writer's Yearbook*'s annual "Top 100 Markets," January 1996.

Nonfiction: Uses articles on all subjects of interest to women—family life, childrearing, education, homemaking, money management, careers, family health, work and leisure activities. Also interested in fresh, dramatic narratives of women's lives and concerns. "These must be lively and fascinating to read." Length: 500-2,200 words, depending on material. Payment varies depending on length, type, writer, and whether it's for regional or national use, but rates are high. Pays a bonus fee in addition to regular rate for articles based on writer's idea (as opposed to assigned story.) Bonus fee is an additional 20% of fee (up to $500). Pays the expenses of writers on confirmed assignment. "We no longer accept unsolicited manuscripts—and can not return or be responsible for those that are sent to us."

Fillers: Neighbors columns also pay $75/each for brief practical suggestions on homemaking, childrearing and relationships. Address to the editor of the section.

Tips: "Our primary need is for ideas with broad appeal that can be featured on the cover. These include diet stories, organizing tips and money saving information. We're buying more short pieces."

MAGAZINES THAT APPEARED in the 1996 edition of *Writer's Market* but are not included this year are listed in the General Index with a notation explaining their absence.

Trade, Technical and Professional Journals

Many writers who pick up a *Writer's Market* for the first time do so with the hope of selling an article or story to one of the popular, high-profile consumer magazines found on newsstands and in bookstores. Many of those writers are surprised to find an entire world of magazine publishing that exists outside the realm of commercial magazines and that they may have never known about—trade journals. Writers who *have* discovered trade journals have found a market that offers the chance to publish regularly in subject areas they find interesting, editors who are typically more accessible than their commercial counterparts and pay rates that rival those of the big-name magazines.

Trade journal is the general term for any publication focusing on a particular occupation or industry. Other terms used to describe the different types of trade publications are business, technical and professional journals. They are read by truck drivers, brick layers, farmers, commercial fishermen, heart surgeons—let's not forget butchers, bakers, and candlestick makers—and just about everyone else working in a trade or profession. Trade periodicals are sharply angled to the specifics of the professions they report on. They offer business-related news, features and service articles that will foster their readers' professional development. A teacher reads *Creative Classroom News* to keep up with developments in lesson plans and classroom management. Readers of *Beverage World* are looking for the latest news and information about the beverage industry.

Trade magazine editors tell us their readers are a knowledgeable and highly interested audience. Writers for trade magazines have to either possess knowledge about the field in question or be able to report it accurately from interviews with those who do. Writers who have or can develop a good grasp of a specialized body of knowledge will find trade magazine editors who are eager to hear from them. And since good writers with specialized knowledge are a somewhat rare commodity, trade editors tend, more than typical consumer magazine editors, to cultivate ongoing relationships with writers. If you can prove yourself as a writer who "delivers," you will be paid back with frequent assignments and regular paychecks.

An ideal way to begin your foray into trade journals is to write for those that report on your present profession. Whether you've been teaching dance, farming or working as a paralegal, begin by familiarizing yourself with the magazines that serve your occupation. After you've read enough issues to have a feel for the kinds of pieces they run, approach the editors with your own article ideas. If you don't have experience in a profession but can demonstrate an ability to understand (and write about) the intricacies and issues of a particular trade that interests you, editors will still be willing to hear from you.

Photographs help increase the value of most stories for trade journals. If you can provide photos, mention that in your query or send copies. Since selling photos with a story usually means a bigger paycheck, it is worth any freelancer's time to develop basic camera skills.

Query a trade journal as you would a consumer magazine. Most trade editors like to discuss an article with a writer first and will sometimes offer names of helpful

INSIDER REPORT

Building a Trade Magazine Career

Sometimes misfortune leads to opportunity. That's pretty much what happened to Rebecca Day. "Freelancing was a jump I couldn't make without a little push," she says. "I'd always wanted to be a freelancer but never had the guts to do it on my own until I was laid off from my fulltime staff position."

Rebecca Day

Before the layoff, Day was a staff writer for *Electronic News*, *Audio Times* and *Stereo Review*, all of which helped her gain knowledge and develop a career in consumer electronics writing. "I learned a lot about retail and business electronics and other aspects of the electronic field from my fulltime jobs. I was able to start writing for other publications while I was still employed, and by the time I was laid off I had a fairly good base of magazines I wrote for outside of my staff job."

While freelancing, Day has found her way into numerous trade and consumer publications. She's been published in *American Homestyle & Gardening*, *Home Magazine*, *Home Theater Technology*, *Popular Mechanics* and *Windows Magazine*, and she is a contributing editor to *Audio/Video Interiors*, *CD Review*, *Stereo Review* and *The Robb Report*. "I wouldn't consider myself a technical writer, but I know how to write about technical topics in a nontechnical way. I always try to think of myself as being the typical reader."

Day manages to write for both specialized trade magazines and more general consumer-oriented magazines because she keeps her audience in mind at all times, thus knowing what each magazine wants from a particular subject. "When I write for trade magazines I find out what new products are coming out and get information about trends and what's going on in the marketplace. Then I can take that information and turn it around conceptually for other markets." If, for example, Day writes about the technical aspects of installing V-chips into televisions for a trade magazine, she'll change the slant and write another article for a consumer publication in which she'll define the V-chip, what it can do for the reader, how it might alter the viewing experience, etc. "That's a much different article than something more technical or market-oriented that I'd write for a trade publication."

Those who deem trade magazine-writing inferior to writing for consumer publications need to reconsider their assumptions. "I really value writing for trade magazines," says Day. "Everyone thinks the pay is better for consumer magazines but that's not necessarily true. Some trade magazines can pay well. I find it really useful to do trade articles because it's a great way to do research and become knowledgeable about something. There's also a big misconception that all the better writers are writing for consumer magazines. I don't find that true at all."

INSIDER REPORT, *continued*

Although confident she can write about almost anything in the electronics industry, Day is cautious about assuming she knows too much about a subject. "I think ignorance is a good asset for a journalist, because the less you know the more open you are to learn about a subject. Sometimes if you go in with preconceived notions you might miss something entirely."

Contrary to that statement, though, Day enumerates the benefits to reap when specializing in a complicated area. "When you become established in a particular field it can bring steady income. In a way I feel pigeonholed, but I think the writing business requires you these days to be more specialized especially when it comes to technology, because things get so complicated. When you're an expert in a certain field, it can often lead to other things in related fields."

Payment isn't the top consideration for Day when deciding which publication she'll approach. "I would be much more willing to write for 40 cents a word for *The New York Times* than I would for a less-established magazine that pays more. You have to consider the exposure and portfolio value of the piece."

But Day will not write for just any high-circulation publication, either. "When I judge a magazine I look at the quality of the paper stock, how well the magazine is laid out, and most important, I check the editorial tone or voice to see whether the writers are allowed to have their own voices or whether the editor wants everything to sound like one voice. I like to have my own personality in my writing. If that's going to be taken out, I'd rather not write that piece."

Finding the right publications in which to publish isn't much of a problem for Day. While a lot of writers must spend countless hours generating interesting proposals to sell to editors, Day is already so well-known in the electronics industry that editors come to her. "Usually I get an assignment from an editor. Sometimes I don't like it, but I have to do it anyway. Other times something will pique my interest and I'll research it. If I learn something about consumer electronics or satellite dishes or something that I think other people will be interested in, then I might try to pitch that idea."

Granted, Day's lot in the writing life is pretty outstanding—and her flexible relationships with editors are something every writer craves—but she warns that freelancing isn't as easy as it used to be. "Editors are wanting shorter copy, and thus are paying less money, because attention spans are shorter. There's a lot of stuff to pay attention to in this world, and people want bite-sized snippets rather than lengthy tomes. So if you get paid by the word you're in trouble." What, then, is one to do, since most assignments pay by the word? "Getting a regular column is by far the best deal a writer can get because it's steady income."

Even with her success, assignments don't just fall in Day's lap. Like all freelancers, Day must force herself to find new outlets for her work. "I'm always trying to come up with ideas, of course, because you never know what's going to happen. But with new ideas you always have to weigh whether all the research time is worth it. You have to do a lot of research before you propose a piece because you have to give the editor a lot to work with. The more information you have going in with your query the more appealing it's going to be. You've got to keep selling yourself and your writing."

—*Don Prues*

sources. Mention any direct experience you may have in the industry in your cover letter. Send a resume and clips if they show you have some background or related experience in the subject area. Read each listing carefully for additional submission guidelines.

To stay abreast of new trade magazines starting up, watch for news in *Folio* and *Advertising Age* magazines. Another source for information about trade publications is the *Business Publication Advertising Source*, published by Standard Rate and Data Service (SRDS) and available in most libraries. Designed primarily for people who buy ad space, the volume provides names and addresses of thousands of trade journals, listed by subject matter.

For information on additional trade publications not listed in *Writer's Market*, see the General Index.

ADVERTISING, MARKETING AND PR

Trade journals for advertising executives, copywriters and marketing and public relations professionals are listed in this category. Those whose main focus is the advertising and marketing of specific products, such as home furnishings, are classified under individual product categories. Journals for sales personnel and general merchandisers can be found in the Selling and Merchandising category.

AMERICAN ADVERTISING, The American Advertising Federation, 1101 Vermont Ave. NW, Suite 500, Washington DC 20005. E-mail: aaf@aaf.org. Website: http://www.aaf.org/pub/aaf/. Editor: Jenny Pfalzgraf. 50% freelance written. Quarterly association magazine covering advertising and marketing issues. "*American Advertising* is a nonprofit publication of the American Advertising Federation, covering trends in marketing, advertising and media and the activities of the AAF." Estab. 1984. Circ. 50,000. **Pays on acceptance.** Publishes ms an average of 1 month after acceptance. Byline given. Buys first rights or second serial (reprint) rights. Editorial lead time 3 months. Accepts simultaneous submissions. Reports in 2 months on queries. "Do not send manuscripts cold." Sample copy for 9×12 SAE with 4 first-class stamps.
 • *American Advertising* is offering more coverage of interactive media/new technology.
Nonfiction: Book excerpts, how-to (marketing/advertising strategies), humor. "Not interested in negative stories about the ad business." Buys 4 mss/year. Query with published clips. Length: 500-2,000 words. Pays 25¢/word or negotiates rates. All articles are assigned.
Reprints: Send photocopy of article. Negotiates payment.
Photos: State availability of photos with submission. Reviews contact sheets. Negotiates payment individually. Captions required. Buys one-time rights.
Columns/Departments: Ad Club Spotlight (features unique programs of AAF-member ad clubs), 500 words; Legislative Watch (focuses on legislative developments affecting ad business), 500 words; People (profiles top dogs in advertising and media), 500 words. Buys 1 mss/year. Query with published clips. Pays 25¢/word.
Tips: "Because we are nonprofit, a lot of work is commissioned pro bono from industry experts. All stories must have some tie-in to the AAF's membership and activities. Please familiarize yourself with the magazine and the American Advertising Federation before submitting."

AMERICAN DEMOGRAPHICS, American Demographics, Inc., P.O. Box 68, Ithaca NY 14851-0068. (607)273-6343. Fax: (607)273-3196. Editor-in-Chief: Brad Edmondson. Managing Editor: Nancy Ten Kate. Contact: Diane Crispell, executive editor. 25% freelance written. Works with a small number of new/unpublished writers each year. Monthly magazine for business executives, market researchers, media and communications people, public policymakers. Estab. 1978. Circ. 35,000. Pays on publication. Publishes ms 4 months after acceptance. Buys all rights. Submit seasonal material 6 months in advance. Reports in 6 months. Include self-addressed stamped postcard for return word that ms arrived safely. Sample copy for $10 and 9×11 SAE. Writer's guidelines for #10 SASE.
Nonfiction: General interest (on demographic trends, implications of changing demographics, profile of business using demographic data); how-to (on the use of demographic techniques, psychographics, understand projections, data, apply demography to business and planning). No anecdotal material. Sometimes pays the expenses of writers on assignment.
Tips: "Writer should have clear understanding of specific population trends and their implications for business and planning. The most important thing a freelancer can do is to read the magazine and be familiar with its style and focus."

ART DIRECTION, Advertising Trade Publications, Inc., 456 Glenbrook Rd., Stamford CT 06906-1800. (203)353-1441. Fax: (203)353-1371. Editor: Dan Barron. 10% freelance written. Prefers to work with published/established writers. Monthly magazine emphasizing advertising design for art directors of ad agencies (corporate, in-plant, editorial, freelance, etc.). Circ. 9,108. Pays on publication. Buys one-time rights. Reports in 3 months. Sample copy for $4.50.
Nonfiction: How-to articles on advertising campaigns. Pays $100 minimum.

‡**DECA DIMENSIONS**, 1908 Association Dr., Reston VA 22091. (703)860-5000. Editor: Carol Lund. 30% freelance written. Bimonthly magazine covering professional development, business, vocational training. "*Deca Dimensions* is the membership magazine for the Association of Marketing Students—primarily ages 16-20 in all 50 states. The magazine is delivered through the classroom. These students are interested in developing their professional, leadership and career skills." Estab. 1947. Circ. 145,000. Pays on publication. Byline given. Buys first rights and second serial (reprint) rights. Editorial lead time 4 months. Submit seasonal material 5 months in advance. Accepts simultaneous submissions. Sample copy free on request.
Nonfiction: Essays, general interest, how-to (get jobs, start business, plan for college, etc.), interview/profile (business leads), personal experience (working). Buys 4 mss/year. Send complete ms. Length: 800-1,000 words. Pays $125 for assigned articles; $100 for unsolicited articles.
Reprints: Send photocopy of article and information about when and where the article previously appeared. Pays 85% of amount paid for an original article.
Photos: State availability of photos with submission. Reviews negatives, transparencies, prints. Offers $15-25/photo. Captions required. Buys one-time rights.
Columns/Departments: Professional Development leadership. Buys 4 mss/year. Send complete ms. Pays $75-100. Length: 200-500 words.
Fillers: Anecdotes, facts, short humor. Length: 400-600 words. Pays $25-50.

‡**FORMAT**, Decker Publications, P.O. Box 29488, Minneapolis MN 55429. (612)649-4931. E-mail: format2 @aol.com. Editor: Sheri O'Meara. 90% freelance written. Monthly magazine covering Minnesota advertising and media industry. "Articles should be of interest to those who produce or place advertising in Minnesota. We also cover retail trends, creative topics and business side of media." Estab. 1954. Circ. 3,000. Pays on publication. Byline given. Buys all rights. Editorial lead time 1 month. Submit seasonal material 2 months in advance. Accepts simultaneous submissions. Sample copy and writer's guidelines for #10 SASE.
Nonfiction: General interest, historical/nostalgic, humor, interview/profile, new product, opinion, personal experience, photo feature, technical. Query with published clips. Pays $25-150.
Reprints: Accepts previously published submissions.
Photos: State availability of photos with submission. Negotiates payment individually. Model releases, identification of subjects required. Buys all rights.
Columns/Departments: Media (business media); Advertising (advertising creative-legal-business); Technology (advertising creative/production); all 100-300 words. Buys 20 mss/year. Query. Pays $25-150.
Tips: "We should appreciate advertising and know what could be of interest to those in the industry story should have local implications/interest (Minnesota)."

‡**MARKETING TOOLS, Information-based Tactics and Techniques**, American Demographics, 127 W. State St., Ithaca NY 14850. Website: http://www.marketingtools.com. Managing Editor: Claudia Montague. 85% freelance written. Magazine published 8 times/year covering database marketing, online marketing, direct marketing. "*Marketing Tools* is a magazine for professionals who deal with customer information—consumer and business-to-business. Our focus is on the technology used to gather, analyze, and act on customer data, as opposed to the data itself." Estab. 1994. Circ. 20,000. **Pays on acceptance**. Publishes ms an average of 2 months after acceptance. Byline given. Offers 50% kill fee. Rights shared with author. Editorial lead time 5 months. Submit seasonal material 1 year in advance. Sample copy for 9×12 SAE. Writer's guidelines for #10 SASE.
Nonfiction: Book excerpts, essays, how-to, interview/profile, new product, technical. Buys 70 mss/year. Query with published clips. Length: 750-4,000 words. Pays $200-700. Sometimes pays expenses of writers on assignment.
Reprints: Accepts previously published submissions.
Photos: State availability of photos with submission. Reviews prints. Negotiates payment individually. Captions, model releases, identification of subjects required. Buys one-time rights.
Columns/Departments: Marketing Research (collecting, analyzing data); Database/Direct Marketing (collecting, managing, using data); Business-to-business (special concerns of B2B companies); all 1,500 words. Buys 40 mss/year. Query. Pays $350-400.

---

‡ **THE DOUBLE DAGGER** before a listing indicates that the listing is new in this edition. New markets are often more receptive to freelance submissions.

Tips: "Well-written queries from writers with some knowledge/experience in database or direct marketing are always welcome. Do NOT telephone to pitch a story idea. We stipulate in our writers agreement that we reserve the right to reproduce work electronically—i.e., to upload it to our website."

‡**MARKETSHARE, The Small Business Marketing Journal**, P.O. Box 194, Simpsonville SC 29681. (864)963-7478. Fax: (864)967-4882. E-mail: marketshare@marketshr.com. Website: http://www.marketshr. com. Editor: Harry B. Roemisch. 30% freelance written. Newsletter published 8 times/year covering market-ing advice for small business. "We publish a marketing publication for entrepreneurs, small business owners and managers and inhouse marketing directors. Each article is written to focus on one major idea. Articles are 350-500 words and contain practical information." Estab. 1995. Circ. 500. Pays on publication. Publishes ms an average of 2 months after acceptance. Byline given. Buys one-time rights. Editorial lead time 2 months. Submit seasonal material 6 months in advance. Sample copy and writer's guidelines free on request.
Nonfiction: Essays, how-to, humor, personal experience, technical. Buys 16 mss/year. Query with published clips or send complete ms. Length: 350-500 words. Pays $50.
Reprints: Accepts previously published submissions.
Photos: State availability of photos with submission. Reviews contact sheets, prints. No additional payment for photos accepted with ms. Model releases, identification of subjects required. Buys one-time rights.
Columns/Departments: Public Relations, Image, Advertising, Research, Personal Selling, Strategy; all 350-500 words. Pays $50.
Fillers: Anecdotes, facts, gags to be illustrated by cartoonist, newsbreaks, short humor (must be marketing related). Length: 50-100 words. Pays $25.

MEDIA INC., Pacific Northwest Media, Marketing and Creative Services News, P.O. Box 24365, Seattle WA 98124-0365. (206)382-9220. Fax: (206)382-9437. E-mail: mediaindx@aol.com. Publisher: Rich-ard K. Woltjer. Contact: Elizabeth Bye, associate editor. 20% freelance written. Monthly tabloid covering Northwest US media, advertising, marketing and creative-service industries. Audience is Northwest ad agen-cies, marketing professionals, media and creative-service professionals. Estab. 1987. Circ. 10,000. Byline given. Reports in 1 month. Sample copy for 9 × 12 SAE with 6 first-class stamps.
Tips: "It is best if writers live in the Pacific Northwest and can report on local news and events in Media Inc.'s areas of business coverage."

MORE BUSINESS, 11 Wimbledon Court, Jericho NY 11753. Editor: Trudy Settel. 50% freelance written. Monthly magazine "selling publications material to business for consumer use (incentives, communication, public relations)—look for book ideas and manuscripts." Estab. 1975. Circ. 10,000. **Pays on acceptance.** Publishes ms an average of 1 month after acceptance. Buys all rights. Reports in 3 months. Sample copy for 9 × 12 SAE with first class stamps.
Nonfiction: General interest, how-to, vocational techniques, nostalgia, photo feature, profile, travel. Reviews new computer software. Buys 10-20 mss/year. Word length varies with article. Payment negotiable. Query. Pays $4,000-7,000 for book mss.

‡**PRESENTATIONS**, Lakewood Publications, 50 South Ninth St., Minneapolis MN 55402. (612)333-0471. Fax: (612)333-6526. E-mail: presmag@aol.com. Editor: Larry Tuck. 50% freelance written. Monthly magazine covering audiovisual/presentations/multimedia. "*Presentations* magazine provides business users of visual communications media with information on the latest technology and techniques for more effective presentations." Estab. 1988. Circ. 70,000. **Pays on acceptance.** Publishes ms an average of 3 months after acceptance. Byline given. Offers 25% kill fee. Makes work-for-hire assignments. Editorial lead time 4 months. Reports in 1 month on queries; 2 months on mss. Sample copy for 9 × 12 SASE. Writer's guidelines for #10 SASE.
Nonfiction: How-to, interview/profile, new product, technical. Buys 60 mss/year. Query with published clips. Length: 1,000-3,000 words. Pays approximately 50¢/word (negotiated individually with writers). Pays in copies for guest columns.
Photos: State availability of photos with submission. Reviews 35mm transparencies. Negotiates payment individually. Identification of subjects required. Buys all rights.
Columns/Departments: Speaker's Notes (public speaking techniques), 1,000 words; Reviews (presenta-tion hardware/software), 1,000 words; Case Studies (user profiles), 1,500 words. Buys 24 mss/year. Query with published clips. Pays 50¢/word.
Tips: "Always query with published clips. We don't accept unsolicited manuscripts. We're looking for writers with proven experience in writing about technology."

RESPONSE TV, The Information Leader for the Electronic Merchandising Industry, Advanstar Communications, 201 E. Sandpointe, Suite 600, Santa Ana CA 92707. (714)513-8400. Fax: (714)513-8482. E-mail: rtvdave@aol.com. Website: http://www.advanstar.com. Editor: David Nagel. 30% freelance written. Monthly magazine covering direct response television. "We look for business writers with experience in advertising, marketing, direct marketing, telemarketing, TV production, cable TV industry and home shop-ping." Estab. 1992. Circ. 21,000. **Pays on acceptance.** Byline given. Offers 50% kill fee. Buys all rights.

Editorial lead time 2 months. Accepts previously published submissions. Reports in 2 weeks on queries, 1 month on mss. Sample copy for $6.
Nonfiction: General interest, interview/profile, opinion, technical, case studies. Buys 25 mss/year. Query with published clips. Length: 1,200-2,000 words. Pays $300-500. Sometimes pays expenses of writers on assignment.
Photos: State availability of photos with submission. Reviews contact sheets, negatives, transparencies. Negotiates payment individually. Model releases, identification of subjects required. Buys one-time rights.
Columns/Departments: New media (interactive advertising and merchandising), 200 words; International, 200 words; Legal (advertising and marketing law), 800 words. Buys 12 mss/year. Query with published clips. Pays $300.
Tips: "Familiarity with topics such as home shopping, direct response TV, interactive TV and infomercials. General interest in advertising and marketing."

SIGNCRAFT, The Magazine for the Commercial Sign Shop, SignCraft Publishing Co., Inc., P.O. Box 60031, Fort Myers FL 33906. (941)939-4644. Editor: Tom McIltrot. 10% freelance written. Bimonthly magazine of the sign industry. "Like any trade magazine, we need material of direct benefit to our readers. We can't afford space for material of marginal interest." Estab. 1980. Circ. 19,500. Pays on publication. Publishes ms an average of 9 months after acceptance. Byline given. Offers negotiable kill fee. Buys first North American serial or all rights. Reports in 1 month. Sample copy and writer's guidelines for $3.
Nonfiction: Interviews, profiles. "All articles should be directly related to quality commercial signs. If you are familiar with the sign trade, we'd like to hear from you." Buys 20 mss/year. Query with or without published clips. Length: 500-2,000 words. Pays up to $250.
Reprints: Accepts previously published submissions.

ART, DESIGN AND COLLECTIBLES

The businesses of art, art administration, architecture, environmental/package design and antiques/collectibles are covered in these listings. Art-related topics for the general public are located in the Consumer Art and Architecture category. Antiques and collectibles magazines for enthusiasts are listed in Consumer Hobby and Craft. (Listings of markets looking for freelance artists to do artwork can be found in *Artist's and Graphic Designer's Market*, Writer's Digest Books).

‡**ADOBE MAGAZINE**, Adobe Systems Inc., 411 First Ave. S., Seattle WA 98104-2871. Fax: (206)470-7106. Editor: Nicholas H. Allison. Contact: Tamis Nordling, managing editor: 60% freelance written. Bimonthly magazine covering graphic design, publishing, Adobe software. "Mission: To help users of Adobe products get their work done better and faster, and to entertain, educate, and inspire along the way." Estab. 1989. Circ. 300,000. **Pays on acceptance.** Publishes ms an average of 3 months after acceptance. Byline given. Offers 25% kill fee. Buys all rights. Editorial lead time 5 months. Sample copy free on request.
Nonfiction: How-to, humor, interview/profile, technical. Buys 60-70 mss/year. Query with published clips or send complete ms. Length: 500-2,500 words. Pays $300-1,500. Sometimes pays expenses of writers on assignment.
Columns/Departments: Well-Equipped Desktop (overviews of relevant hardware/software), 500-2,000 words. Pays $300-1,200.

ANTIQUEWEEK, Mayhill Publications Inc., P.O. Box 90, Knightstown IN 46148-0090. (317)345-5133. Fax: (800)695-8153. E-mail: antiquewk@aol.com. Central Edition Editor: Tom Hoepf. Eastern Edition Editor: Connie Swaim. Genealogy Editor: Shirley Richardson. 80% freelance written. Weekly tabloid on antiques, collectibles and genealogy with 2 editions: Eastern and Central. "*AntiqueWeek* has a wide range of readership from dealers and auctioneers to collectors, both advanced and novice. Our readers demand accurate information presented in an entertaining style." Estab. 1968. Circ. 60,000. Pays on publication. Byline given. Buys first and second serial (reprint) rights. Submit seasonal material 1 month in advance. Free sample copy. Writer's guidelines for #10 SASE.
Nonfiction: Historical/nostalgic, how-to, interview/profile, opinion, personal experience, antique show and auction reports, feature articles on particular types of antiques and collectibles. Buys 400-500 mss/year. Query with or without published clips, or send complete ms. Length: 1,000-2,000 words. Pays $50-150.
Reprints: Send typed ms with rights for sale noted and information about when and where the article previously appeared. Pays 50% of amount paid for an original article.
Photos: Send photos with submission. Identification of subjects required.
Columns/Departments: Insights (opinions on buying, selling and collecting antiques), 500-1,000 words; Your Ancestors (advice, information on locating sources for genealogists). Buys 150 mss/year. Query. Length: 500-1,500 words. Pays $25-50.

Tips: "Writers should know their topics thoroughly. Feature articles must be well-researched and clearly written. An interview and profile article with a knowledgeable collector might be the break for a first-time contributor. As we move toward the year 2000, there is much more interest in 20th-century collectibles. *Antiqueweek* also seeks articles that reflect the lasting popularity of traditional antiques."

APPLIED ARTS, 885 Don Mills Rd., Suite 324, Toronto, Ontario M3C 1V9 Canada. (416)510-0909. Fax: (416)510-0913. E-mail: app-arts@interlog.com. Website: http://www.interlog.com/~app.arts. Editor: Joanna Pachner. 70% freelance written. Magazine published 7 times/year covering graphic design, advertising, photography and illustration. Estab. 1986. Circ. 12,000. **Pays on acceptance.** Byline given. Buys first North American serial rights. Reports in 2 months on queries. Sample copy for 10×13 SAE with $1.70 Canadian postage or 4 IRCs.
Nonfiction: Portfolio/profile, technical (computers and the applied arts), trade articles about graphic design, advertising, photography and illustration. Buys 20-30 mss/year. Query with published clips. Length: 500-2,500 words. Pays 50-60¢/word (Canadian).
Photos: Offers no additional payment for photos accepted with ms. Buys one-time rights.
Tips: "It helps if writers have some familiarity with the communication arts field and graphics technology. Writers should include a solid selection of published articles. Ideas of most interest include specific recent advertising or design projects—print, video, multimedia or combined—preferably with a Canadian angle. Take time to read back issues of the magazine before querying."

THE APPRAISERS STANDARD, New England Appraisers Assocation, 5 Gill Terrace, Ludlow VT 05149-1003. (802)228-7444. Publisher/Editor: Linda L. Tucker. 50% freelance written. Works with a small number of new/unpublished writers each year. Bimonthly publication on the appraisals of antiques, art, collectibles, jewelry, coins, stamps and real estate. "The writer should be extremely knowledgeable on the subject, and the article should be written with appraisers in mind, with prices quoted for objects, good pictures and descriptions of articles being written about." Estab. 1980. Circ. 1,300. Pays on publication. Publishes ms an average of 1 year after acceptance. Byline given, with short bio to establish writer's credibility. Buys first and simultaneous rights. Submit seasonal material 2 months in advance. Accepts simultaneous submissions. Reports in 1 month on queries, 2 months on mss. Sample copy for 9×12 SAE with 78¢ postage. Writer's guidelines for #10 SASE.
Nonfiction: Interview/profile, personal experience, technical, travel. "All geared toward professional appraisers." Query with or without published clips, or send complete ms. Length: 700 words. Pays $50.
Reprints: Send typed ms with rights for sale noted and information about when and where the article previously appeared. Pays 100% of amount paid for an original article.
Photos: Send photos with submission. Reviews negatives and prints. Offers no additional payment for photos accepted with ms. Identification of subjects required. Buys one-time rights.
Tips: "Interviewing members of the association for articles, reviewing, shows and large auctions are all ways for writers who are not in the field to write articles for us."

ARTS MANAGEMENT, 110 Riverside Dr., Suite 4E, New York NY 10024. (212)245-3850. Editor: A.H. Reiss. Magazine published 5 times/year for cultural institutions. 2% freelance written. Estab. 1962. Circ. 6,000. Pays on publication. Byline given. Buys all rights. Query. Reports in 2 months. Writer's guidelines for #10 SASE.
● Mostly staff-written; uses very little outside material.
Nonfiction: Short articles, 400-900 words, tightly written, expository, explaining how art administrators solved problems in publicity, fund raising and general administration; actual case histories emphasizing the how-to. Also short articles on the economics and sociology of the arts and important trends in the nonprofit cultural field. Must be fact-filled, well-organized and without rhetoric. Pays 2-4¢/word. No photographs or pictures.

CONTEMPORARY STONE DESIGN, Business News Publishing Co., 1 Kalisa Way, Suite 205, Paramus NJ 07652. (201)599-0136. Fax: (201)599-2378. E-mail: stoneworld@aol.com. Website: http://www.stoneworld.com. Publisher: Alex Bachrach. Editor: Michael Reis. Quarterly magazine covering the full range of stone design and architecture—from classic and historic spaces to current projects. Estab. 1995. Circ. 14,000. Pays on publication. Publishes ms an average of 3 months after acceptance. Byline given. Buys first rights only. Submit seasonal material 6 months in advance. Reports in 3 weeks. Sample copy for $10.
Nonfiction: Overall features on a certain aspect of stone design or specific articles on individual architectural projects. Interview/profile of a prominent architect/designer or firm. Photo feature, technical, architectural design. Buys 8 mss/year. Query with published clips. Length: 1,500-3,000 words. Pays $6/column inch. Pays expenses of writers on assignment.
Photos: State availability of photos with submission. Reviews transparencies and prints. Pays $10/photo accepted with ms. Captions and identification of subjects required. Buys one-time rights.
Columns/Departments: Upcoming Events (for the architecture and design community); Stone Classics (featuring historic architecture); question and answer session with a prominent architect or designer. 1,500-2,000 words. Pays $6/inch.

Tips: "The visual aspect of the magazine is key, so architectural photography is a must for any story. Cover the entire project, but focus on the stonework and how it relates to the rest of the space. Architects are very helpful in describing their work and often provide excellent quotes. As a relatively new magazine, we are looking for freelance submissions and are open to new feature topics. This is a narrow subject, however, so it's a good idea to speak with an editor before submitting anything."

COREL MAGAZINE, Omray Inc., 9801 Anderson Mill Rd., Suite 207, Austin TX 78730. (512)250-1700. Fax: (512)250-1016. E-mail: scottc@jumpnet.com. Website: http://www.corelmag.com. Editor: Scott Campbell. Contact: Jennifer Campbell, managing editor. 80-90% freelance written. Monthly magazine covering computer graphic design software and hardware. "*Corel Magazine* is edited for users of CorelDraw, Photo-Paint, and other graphics software from Corel Corp. and third parties. Focus is on step-by-step tutorials, technical and product solutions, and real-world graphic design. Targeted to graphic design professionals and business presentation graphics users." Byline given. Offers $50 kill fee. Buys first North American serial rights. Editorial lead time 10 weeks. Submit seasonal material 3 months in advance. Reports in 2 weeks on queries; 1 month on mss. Sample copy free on request.
Nonfiction: How-to (step-by-step graphics and text explaining how to create image or effect using any Corel software), new product, personal experience, technical, product reviews, tips and tricks. Buys 180 mss/year. Query. Length: 500-2,500 words. Pays $150-750 for assigned articles; $50-500 for unsolicited articles. Sometimes pays expenses of writers on assignment.
Photos: Most artwork will be computer-generated. Send photos with submission. Offers no additional payment for photos accepted with ms.
Columns/Departments: In the Box (review/how-to), 1,500 words plus art. Query. Pays $150-500.

HOW, The Bottomline Design Magazine, F&W Publications, Inc., 1507 Dana Ave., Cincinnati OH 45207-1005. (513)531-2222. E-mail: howedit@aol.com. Editor: Kathleen Reinmann. 75% freelance written. Bimonthly graphic design and illustration business journal. "*HOW* gives a behind-the-scenes look at not only *how* the world's best graphic artists and illustrators conceive and create their work, but *why* they did it that way. We also focus on the *business* side of design—how to run a profitable studio." Estab. 1985. Circ. 38,000. **Pays on acceptance.** Byline given. Buys first North American serial rights. Reports in 6 weeks. Sample copy for cover price plus $1.50 (cover price varies per issue). Writer's guidelines for #10 SASE.
● Ranked as one of the best markets for freelance writers in *Writer's Yearbook*'s annual "Top 100 Markets," January 1996.
Nonfiction: Interview/profile, business tips, new products, environmental graphics, digital design. Special issues: Self-Promotion Annual (September/October); Business Annual (November/December). No how-to articles for beginning artists or fine-art-oriented articles. Buys 40 mss/year. Query with published clips and samples of subject's work (artwork or design). Length: 1,200-1,500 words. Pays $250-700. Sometimes pays expenses of writers on assignment.
Photos: State availability of artwork with submission. Reviews 35mm or larger transparencies. May reimburse mechanical photo expenses. Captions are required. Buys one-time rights.
Columns/Departments: Marketplace (focuses on lucrative fields for designers/illustrators); Production (ins, outs and tips on production); Applications (behind the scenes of electronically produced design projects); Software Review and Workspace (takes an inside look at the design of creatives' studios). Buys 20 mss/year. Query with published clips. Length: 1,000-2,000 words. Pays $150-400.
Tips: "We look for writers who can recognize graphic designers on the cutting-edge of their industry, both creatively and business-wise. Writers must have an eye for detail, and be able to relay *HOW*'s step-by-step approach in an interesting, concise manner—without omitting any details. Showing you've done your homework on a subject—and that you can go beyond asking 'those same old questions'—will give you a big advantage."

LETTER ARTS REVIEW, 1624 24th Ave. SW, Norman OK 73072. (405)364-8794. Fax: (405)364-8914. Publisher/Editor: Karyn L. Gilman. 98% freelance written. Eager to work with new/unpublished writers with calligraphic expertise and language skills. Quarterly magazine on lettering and related book arts, both historical and contemporary in nature. Estab. 1982. Circ. 5,500. Pays on publication. Publishes ms an average of 9 months after acceptance. Byline given. Offers 20% kill fee. Buys first rights. Reports in 3 months. Sample copy for 9 × 12 SAE with 7 first-class stamps. Free writer's guidelines.
Nonfiction: Interview/profile, opinion, contemporary, historical. Buys 50 mss/year. Query with or without published clips, or send complete ms. Length: 1,000-2,000 words. Pays $50-200 for assigned articles; $25-200 for unsolicited articles. Sometimes pays the expenses of writers on assignment.
Photos: State availability of photos with submission. Reviews contact sheets, negatives, transparencies and prints. Pays agreed upon cost. Captions and identification of subjects required. Buys one-time rights.
Columns/Departments: Book Reviews, Viewpoint (critical), 500-1,500 words; Ms. (discussion of manuscripts in collections), 1,000-2,000 words; Profile (contemporary calligraphic figure), 1,000-2,000 words. Query. Pays $50-200.
Tips: "*Letter Arts Review*'s primary objective is to encourage the exchange of ideas on calligraphy and the lettering arts—its past and present as well as trends for the future. Historical research, typography, graphic

design, fine press and artists' books, and other related aspects of the lettering arts are welcomed. Third person is preferred, however first person will be considered if appropriate. Writer should realize that this is a specialized audience."

THE MIDATLANTIC ANTIQUES MAGAZINE, Monthly Guide to Antiques, Art, Auctions & Collectibles, Henderson Newspapers, Inc., P.O. Box 908, Henderson NC 27536-0908. (919)492-4001. Fax: (919)430-0125. Editor: Lydia Stainback. 65% freelance written. Monthly tabloid covering antiques, art, auctions and collectibles. "The *MidAtlantic* reaches dealers, collectors, antique shows and auction houses primarily on the East Coast, but circulation includes 48 states and Europe." Estab. 1984. Circ. 14,000. Pays on publication. Byline given. Buys first rights. Submit seasonal material 6 months in advance. Reports in 1 month on queries; 2 months on mss. Sample copy and writer's guidelines for 10×13 SAE with 10 first-class stamps.
Nonfiction: Book excerpts, historical/nostalgic, how-to (choose an antique to collect; how to sell your collection; how to identify market trends), interview/profile, personal experience, photo feature, technical. Buys 60-75 mss/year. Query. Length: 800-2,000 words. Pays $50-125. Trade for advertising space. Rarely pays expenses of writers on assignment.
Photos: Send photos with submission. Offers no additional payment for photos accepted with ms. Identification of subjects required. Buys one-time rights.
Tips: "Please contact by mail first, but a writer may call with specific ideas after initial contact. Looking for writers who have extensive knowledge in specific areas of antiques. Articles should be educational in nature. We are also interested in how-to articles, i.e., how to choose antiques to collect; how to sell your collection and get the most for it; looking for articles that focus on future market trends. We want writers who are active in the antiques business and can predict good investments. (Articles with photographs are given preference.) We are looking for people who are not only knowledgeable, but can write well."

‡**TEXAS ARCHITECT,** Texas Society of Architects, 114 W. Seventh St., Suite 1400, Austin TX 78701. (512)478-7386. Editor: Vincent P. Hauser. Associate Editor: Susan Williamson. Publisher: Canan Yetmen. 30% freelance written by unpaid members of the professional society. Bimonthly trade journal of architecture and architects of Texas. "*Texas Architect* is a highly visually-oriented look at Texas architecture, design and urban planning. Articles cover varied subtopics within architecture. Readers are mostly architects and related building professionals." Estab. 1951. Circ. 10,000. Pays on publication. Publishes ms an average of 2 months after acceptance. Byline given. Buys one-time rights, all rights or makes work-for-hire assignments. Submit seasonal material 4 months in advance. Reports in 6 weeks. Free sample copy and writer's guidelines.
Nonfiction: Book reviews, interview/profile, photo feature, technical. Query with published clips. Length: 100-2,000 words. Pays $50-500 for assigned articles.
Photos: Send photos with submission. Reviews contact sheets, 35mm or 4×5 transparencies and 4×5 prints. Offers no additional payment for photos accepted with ms. Identification of subjects required. Buys one-time rights.
Columns/Departments: Contact: Susan Williamson. News (timely reports on architectural issues, projects and people); 100-500 words. Buys 10 mss/year. Query with published clips. Pays $50-100.

AUTO AND TRUCK

These publications are geared to automobile, motorcycle and truck dealers; professional truck drivers; service department personnel; or fleet operators. Publications for highway planners and traffic control experts are listed in the Government and Public Service category.

AUTOMOTIVE COOLING JOURNAL, National Automotive Radiator Service Association, P.O. Box 97, E. Greenville PA 18041. (215)541-4500. Fax: (215)679-4977. E-mail: narsa@aol.com. Editor: Wayne Juchno. Contact: Richard Krisher, managing editor. 20% freelance written. Monthly magazine covering cooling system and mobile A/C service. "The *ACJ* is targeted to the cooling system and air conditioning service shop owner and operator. Its mission is to provide these independent business people with information they need about service, management, marketing, regulation, environment and industry trends." Estab. 1956. Circ. 10,000. **Pays on acceptance.** Publishes ms an average of 3 months after acceptance. Byline given. Editorial lead time 3 months. Submit seasonal material 6 months in advance. Accepts simultaneous submissions. Reports in 2 months on mss; 1 month on queries.
Nonfiction: Interview/profile, new product, photo feature, technical. Buys 12 mss/year. Query with published clips. Length: 1,000-5,000 words. Pays $100-500 for assigned articles; $100-300 for unsolicited articles. Sometimes pays expenses of writers on assignment.
Reprints: Accepts previously published submissions.
Photos: State availability of photos with submission. Reviews contact sheets. Negotiates payment individually. Captions, model releases, identification of subjects required. Buys one-time rights.

‡**AUTOMOTIVE FLEET MAGAZINE**, Bobit Publishing Co., 2512 Artesia Blvd., Redondo Beach CA 90278. Phone/fax: (310)376-8788. E-mail: autofleet@aol.com. Editor/Publisher: Ed Bobit. Contact: Mike Antich, executive editor. 30-40% freelance written. Monthly magazine. "*Automotive Fleet* is designed and written for those who administer and manage fleets of cars, vans and trucks. Its editorial focus is to report, analyze and interpret fleet industry information, news, market research and data, developments, resources, trends and applications relating to fleet management including vehicle leasing, purchasing, remarketing, maintenance, funding, operations, costing and utilization. *Automotive Fleet* is dedicated to fostering and supporting fleet management professionalism through the achievement of cost-efficiency, productivity and resource allocation in all aspects of vehicle and asset management." Estab. 1961. Circ. 22,170. Pays on publication. Publishes ms an average of 6 months after acceptance. Byline sometimes given. Buys all rights. Editorial lead time 3 months. Submit seasonal material 8 months in advance. Accepts simultaneous submissions. Reports in 2 months. Sample copy for $5.
Nonfiction: How-to, interview/profile, new product, photo feature. Buys 20-30 mss/year. Query with published clips. Length: 500-2,000 words. Pays $100-400. Sometimes pays expenses of writers on assignment.
Photos: Send photos with submission. Reviews 3×5 transparencies, 4×6 prints. Offers no additional payment for photos accepted with ms. Captions, identification of subjects required. Buys all rights.

‡**THE BATTERY MAN**, Independent Battery Manufacturers Association, Inc., 100 Larchwood Dr., Largo FL 34640-2811. (813)586-1409. Fax: (813)586-1400. Editor: Celwyn E. Hopkins. 20% freelance written. Monthly magazine emphasizing SLIG battery manufacture, applications and new developments. Target audience: The entire, international industry that is involved in manufacturing, distributing and selling of batteries and battery-related products and technologies. Estab. 1959. Circ. 5,200. **Pays on acceptance.** Publishes ms an average of 4 months after acceptance. Submit seasonal material 2 months in advance. Accepts simultaneous submissions. Reports in 2 months.
Nonfiction: Technical articles on secondary, storage and industrial batteries; new developments in battery manufacturing; energy topics, such as Electric Vehicles, UPS, etc. are acceptable. Also publishes articles on alloys, metals, plastics, etc. and governmental and legislative concerns of the industry. Submit complete ms with SASE. Buys 15-20 unsolicited mss/year. Length: 750-2,000 words preferred. Pays 10¢/word. Photos accepted with article also, pays $10/photo.
Reprints: Accepts previously published submissions.
Tips: "Most writers are not familiar enough with this industry to be able to furnish a feature article. They try to palm off something that they wrote for a hardware store, or a dry cleaner, by calling everything a 'battery store.' We receive a lot of manuscripts on taxes and tax information (such as US income tax) and on business management in general and managing a family-owned business. Since this is an international publication, we try to stay away from such subjects. US tax information is of no use or interest to overseas readers."

‡**BUSINESS DRIVER MAGAZINE**, Bobit Publishing Co., 2512 Artesia Blvd., Redondo Beach CA 90278. (310)376-8788. Fax: (310)374-7878. E-mail: autofleet@aol.com. Editor/Publisher: Chuck Parker. Contact: Mike Antich, executive editor. 95% freelance written. Annual magazine. "*Business Driver* focuses on helping sales and servicepeople who drive and use a company car or truck to take better care of their assigned company vehicles and operate them more safely. By fostering the care, maintenance and support of the company vehicle and emphasizing safety in its operation, *Business Driver* contributes to individual driver productivity and the ultimate profitability of the company or enterprise they represent. *Business Driver* is a communication tool for fleet management to reach and educate company employees on the road and in the field." Circ. 400,000. Pays on publication. Publishes ms an average of 2 years after acceptance. Byline given. Buys all rights. Editorial lead time 1 year. Submit seasonal material 1 year in advance. Accepts simultaneous submissions. Reports in 1 year. Sample copy for $2.
Nonfiction: General interest, how-to, humor, interview/profile, personal experience, photo feature. Buys 10-15 mss/year. Query with published clips. Length: 500-1,500 words. Pays $100-300. Sometimes pays expenses of writers on assignment.
Photos: Send photos with submission. Reviews 3×5 transparencies, 4×6 prints. Offers no additional payment for photos accepted with ms. Captions, identification of subjects required. Buys all rights.

‡**BUSINESS VEHICLE MANAGEMENT**, Bobit Publishing Company, 2512 Artesia Blvd., Redondo Beach CA 90278. (310)376-8788. Fax: (310)374-7878. E-mail: autofleet@aol.com. Editor/Publisher: Ed Bobit. Contact: Mike Antich, executive editor. 85% freelance written. Quarterly magazine. "*Business Vehicle Management* is created as a quarterly directed to management decision-makers to educate, inform and provide resource knowledge in all phases of vehicle and business operations and management." Estab. 1995. Circ. 250,000. Pays on publication. Publishes ms an average of 2 months after acceptance. Byline sometimes given. Buys all rights. Editorial lead time 8 months. Submit seasonal material 10 months in advance. Accepts simultaneous submissions. Reports in 6 weeks on queries; 3 months on mss. Sample copy for $5.
Nonfiction: How-to, humor, interview/profile, photo feature. Buys 15-20 mss/year. Query with published clips. Length: 500-1,500 words. Pays $100-300. Sometimes pays expenses of writers on assignment.

Photos: Send photos with submission. Reviews 3×5 transparencies, 4×6 prints. Offers no additional payment for photos accepted with ms. Captions, identification of subjects required. Buys all rights.

‡**COLLISION REPAIR SPECIALIST**, Thomas Greco Publishing Inc., P.O. Box 4263, Clifton NJ 07110. (201)667-6965. Fax: (201)235-1963. Editor: Chris Kemp. Contact: Thomas Greco, president/publisher. 90% freelance written. Bimonthly magazine covering collision repair. "*Collision Repair Specialist* specializes in in-depth features and interviews pertaining to the collision and mechanical repair industries." Estab. 1991. Circ. 7,000. Pays on publication. Publishes ms an average of 1 month after acceptance. Byline given. Buys first rights. Editorial lead time 2 months. Submit seasonal material 2 months in advance. Sample copy for #10 SASE.
Nonfiction: Essays, exposé, interview/profile, new product, opinion, photo feature, technical. Buys 24 mss/year. Query. Length: 500-10,000 words. Pays $50-300. Sometimes pays expenses of writers on assignment.
Photos: Send photos with submission. Reviews 3×5 prints. Negotiates payment individually. Captions, identification of subjects required. Buys one-time rights.
Columns/Departments: The Paint Room; The Source; Bu$ine$$ ene; SCRS Newsfile; SCRS Affiliate News. Buys 12 mss/year. Query. Pays $50-200.

‡**FLEET FINANCIALS MAGAZINE**, Bobit Publishing Co., 2512 Artesia Blvd., Redondo Beach CA 90278. (310)376-8788. Fax: (310)374-7878. E-mail: autofleet@aol.com. Editor/Publisher: Chuck Parker. Contact: Mike Antich, executive editor. Triannual magazine. "*Fleet Financials* is an executive vehicle management magazine that gives top executives of major corporations with significant and identifiable fleets a single resource for information needed to quickly grasp the financial, operational and marketing implications of fleet and vehicle management." Estab. 1987. Circ. 16,011. Pays on publication. Publishes ms an average of 6 months after acceptance. Byline sometime given. Buys all rights. Editorial lead time 6 months. Submit seasonal material 8 months in advance. Accepts simultaneous submissions. Reports in 3 months. Sample copy for $10.
Nonfiction: Exposé, how-to, interview/profile, photo feature. Buys 10-20 mss/year. Query with published clips. Length: 500-2,000 words. Pays $100-400. Sometimes pays expenses of writers on assignment.
Photos: Send photos with submission. Reviews 3×5 transparencies, 4×6 prints. Offers no additional payment for photos accepted with ms. Captions, identification of subjects required. Buys all rights.

‡**INSIDE AUTOMOTIVES**, Ancar Publications, 314 Tribble Gap Rd., Suite B, Cumming GA 30130. (770)889-6884. Fax: (770)889-6298. E-mail: autoinfo@atlanta.com. Editor: Chris Gardner. Contact: Sandra Farrer, managing editor. 25% freelance written. Bimonthly magazine covering automotive interiors. "Our readers are OEM designers and engineers as well as material and component suppliers." Estab. 1994. Circ. 11,200. Pays on publication. Publishes ms an average of 4 months after acceptance. Byline given. Buys one-time rights. Editorial lead time 2 months. Submit seasonal material 6 months in advance. Reports in 2 weeks on queries; 1 month on mss. Sample copy and writer's guidelines free on request.
Nonfiction: Interview/profile, new product, technical. Buys 10-12 mss/year. Query. Length: 1,500 words minimum. Pays $75-300/page. Sometimes pays expenses of writers on assignment.
Photos: Send photos with submission. Reviews negatives, 3×5 transparencies and prints. Offers no additional payment for photos accepted with ms. Captions, identification of subjects required. Buys one-time rights.
Columns/Departments: Issue Spotlight (industry specific issue), 1,500-2,500 words; Material/Components Spotlight (current material), 1,500-2,500 words; Supplier Spotlight (tier one suppliers), 3,000 words. Buys 5-6 mss/year. Query. Pays $75-300/page.
Tips: "We are always looking for articles specific to automotive interiors. It's best to contact editorial department to check on current trends and issues. Fax queries work best. Contact publication for editorial calendar."

‡**NEW ENGLAND MECHANIC**, P.O. Box M, Franklin MA 02038. (508)528-6211. Managing Editor: Brad Sears. Contact: M. Zingraff. 40% freelance written. Bimonthly newspaper covering automotive repair, testing, maintenance. "Our slant on technical information is both for advanced technician and apprentice. We cover news on laws and regulations, some management information and profiles of shops and wholesales. Estab. 1996. Circ. 5,000. **Pays on acceptance**. Byline given. Offers 50% kill fee on assignments only. Buys one-time or second serial (reprint) rights. Editorial lead time 1 month. Reports in 2 months. Sample copy for 10×12 SAE with 4 first-class stamps. Writer's guidelines for #10 SASE.
Nonfiction: General interest, how-to, interview/profile, technical. Buys 18 mss/year. Query with published clips. Length: 500-1,500 words. Pays $100-200 for assigned articles; $35-100 for unsolicited articles. Sometimes pays expenses of writers on assignment.
Reprints: Accepts previously published submissions.
Photos: State availability of photos with submission. Reviews contact sheets, 3×5 or larger prints. Pays $25 for first photo, $10 for each additional photo in series purchased. Captions, identification of subjects required. Buys one-time rights.

Columns/Departments: Query.
Fillers: Facts. Buys 6 fillers/year. Length: 50-150words. Pays $25-50.

O&A MARKETING NEWS, KAL Publications Inc., 532 El Dorado St., Suite 200, Pasadena CA 91101. Fax: (818)683-0969. Editor: Kathy Laderman. 10% freelance written. Bimonthly tabloid covering petroleum marketing industry. "*O&A Marketing News* is editorially directed to people engaged in the distribution, merchandising, installation and servicing of gasoline, oil, TBA, alternative fuel and automotive aftermarket products in the 13 Western states." Estab. 1966. Circ. 8,000. Pays on publication. Publishes ms an average of 3 months after acceptance. Byline sometimes given. Not copyrighted. Buys one-time rights. Editorial lead time 1 month. Accepts simultaneous submissions. Reports in 1 month on mss. Sample copy for $3.
Nonfiction: Exposé, interview/profile, photo feature, industry news. Buys 20 mss/year. Send complete ms. Length: 100-10,000 words. Pays per column inch typeset.
Photos: State availability of photos with submission. Reviews contact sheets, prints (5×7 preferred). Offers $5/photo. Identification of subjects required. Buys one-time rights.
Fillers: Gags to be illustrated by cartoonist, short humor. Buys 7/year. Length: 1-200 words. Pays per column inch.
Tips: "Seeking Western industry news. We're always seeking more stories covering the more remote states such as Montana, Idaho, and Hawaii—but any timely, topical *news* oriented stories will be considered."

OVERDRIVE, The Magazine for the American Trucker, Randall Publishing Co./Overdrive, Inc., P.O. Box 3187, Tuscaloosa AL 35403-3187. (205)349-2990. Fax: (205)750-8070. Editorial Director: G.C. Skipper. Managing Editor: Deborah Lockridge. 15% freelance written. Monthly magazine for independent truckers. Estab. 1961. Circ. 115,800. Pays on publication. Publishes ms an average of 2 months after acceptance. Byline given. 10% kill fee. Buys all North American rights. Reports in 2 months. Sample copy and writers' guidelines for 9×12 SASE.
Nonfiction: Essays, exposé, how-to (truck maintainance and operation), interview/profile (successful independent truckers), personal experience, photo feature, technical. All must be related to independent trucker interest. Query with or without published clips, or send complete ms. Length: 500-2,000 words. Pays $100-600 for assigned articles; $50-500 for unsolicited articles.
Photos: Send photos with submission. Reviews transparencies and 5×7 prints. Offers $25-50/photo. Identification of subjects required. Buys all rights.
Tips: "Talk to independent truckers. Develop a good knowledge of their concerns as small business owners, truck drivers and individuals. We prefer articles that quote experts, people in the industry and truckers to first-person expositions on a subject. Get straight facts. Look for good material on truck safety, on effects of government regulations, and on rates and business relationships between independent truckers, brokers, carriers and shippers."

‡**REFRIGERATED TRANSPORTER**, Tunnell Publications, P.O. Box 66010, Houston TX 77266. (713)523-8124. Editor: Gary Macklin. 5% freelance written. Monthly. Byline given. Pays on publication. Reports in 1 month.
Nonfiction: "Articles on fleet management and maintenance of vehicles, especially the refrigerated van and the refrigerating unit, shop tips, loading or handling systems—especially for frozen or refrigerated cargo, new equipment specifications, conversions of equipment for better handling or more efficient operations. Prefers articles with illustrations obtained from fleets operating refrigerated trucks or trailers." Pays variable rate, $100/printed page and up.

TOW-AGE, Kruza Kaleidoscopix, Inc., P.O. Box 389, Franklin MA 02038-0389. Editor: J. Kruza. For readers who run their own towing service business. 5% freelance written. Prefers to work with published/ established writers. Published every 6 weeks. Estab. 1960. Circ. 18,000. Buys all rights; usually reassigns rights. **Pays on acceptance.** Accepts simultaneous submissions. Reports in 1 month. Sample copy for $3. Writer's guidelines for #10 SASE.
Nonfiction: Articles on business, legal and technical information for the towing industry. "Light reading material; short, with punch." Informational, how-to, personal, interview, profile. Buys about 18 mss/year. Query or submit complete ms. Length: 600-800 words. Pays $50-150. Spot news and successful business operations. Length: 300-800 words. Technical articles. Length: 400-1,000 words. Pays expenses of writers on assignment.
Photos: Black and white 8×10 photos purchased with or without mss, or on assignment. Pays $25 for first photo; $10 for each additional photo in series. Captions required.

‡**TRUCK WEST**, Southern Business Communications, 1555 Dublin Ave., #9, Winnipeg, Manitoba R3E 3M8 Canada. (416)442-2268. Fax: (416)442-2092. Editor: Patricia Cancilla. 10% freelance written. Monthly tabloid covering trucking industry. "We write for the owner/operator audience in particular, as well as cover issues concerning fleets, truck manufacturers, legislators, etc." Estab. 1989. Circ. 20,000. Pays on publication. Publishes ms an average of 1 month after acceptance. Byline given. Not copyrighted. Makes work-for-hire assignments. Editorial lead time 1 month. Submit seasonal material 3 months in advance. Accepts simultane-

ous submissions. Reports in 1 month on queries. Sample copy and writer's guidelines free on request.

Nonfiction: Exposé, how-to (i.e. maintain your truck), interview/profile, new product, opinion, personal experience, technical. No product testimonials. Buys 15 mss/year. Query with published clips. Length: 300-1,500 words. Pays 25¢/word minimum. Sometimes pays expenses of writers on assignment.

Photos: State availability of photos with submission. Reviews transparencies, prints. Negotiates payment individually. Captions, identification of subjects required. Buys one-time rights.

Columns/Departments: News Briefs (new regulations, etc.), 500-800 words; Profiles (industry leaders), 1,000-1,500 words; Features (change monthly, i.e. tires, brakes, etc.), 1,000-1,500 words. Buys 5 mss/year. Query with published clips. Pays 25¢/word minimum.

‡**WARD'S AUTO WORLD**, Intertec Publishing Corp., 3000 Town Center, Suite 2750, Southfield MI 48075. (810)357-0800. Fax: (810)357-0810. Editor-in-Chief: David C. Smith. Contact: Michael Arnholt, managing editor. 10% freelance written. Monthly magazine covering the auto industry. *"Ward's Auto World* is written for all disciplines in the auto industry, with a special slant toward engineers." Estab. 1965. Circ. 105,000. Pays 1 month after acceptance. Byline given. Kill fee varies. Buys all rights. Reports in 1 month. Sample copy and writer's guidelines for 8×10 SAE with 5 first class stamps.

Nonfiction: Essays, general interest, international automotive news, interview, new product, opinion, personal experience, photo feature, technical. Few consumer type articles. No nostalgia or personal history stories (like "My Favorite Car"). Buys 5-10 mss/year. Query. Phone queries OK. Length: 500-2,500 words. Pays $250-1,000. Sometimes pays expenses of writers on assignment.

Photos: State availability of or send photos with submission. Negotiates payment individually. Identification of subjects required. Buys one-time rights.

Columns/Departments: Drew Winter, executive editor. On assignment only. Buys 12-24 mss/year. Query. Pays $200-400.

Tips: *"Ward's Auto World* is a business newsmagazine with strong emphasis on reporting and writing. It is 90% staff-written, though uses a stable of solid freelancers."

‡**WESTERN CANADA HIGHWAY NEWS**, Craig Kelman & Associates, 3C-2020 Portage Ave., Winnipeg, Manitoba R3J 0K4 Canada. (204)885-7798. Fax: (204)889-3576. Managing Editor: Terry Ross. 30% freelance written. Quarterly magazine covering trucking. "The official magazine of the Alberta, Saskatchewan and Manitoba trucking associations." Estab. 1995 (formerly *Manitoba Highway News*). Circ. 4,000. Pays on publication. Publishes ms an average of 2 months after acceptance. Byline given. Buys one-time rights. Editorial lead time 3 months. Submit seasonal material 3 months in advance. Accepts simultaneous submissions. Reports in 2 months on queries; 4 months on mss. Sample copy for 10×13 SAE with $1 IRC. Writer's guidelines free on request.

Nonfiction: Essays, general interest, how-to (run a trucking business), interview/profile, new product, opinion, personal experience, photo feature, technical, profiles in excellence (bios of trucking or associate firms enjoying success). Buys 10-12 mss/year. Query. Length: 500-3,000 words. Pays 18-25¢/word. Sometimes pays expenses of writers on assignment.

Reprints: Accepts previously published submissions.

Photos: State availability of photos with submission. Reviews 4×6 prints. Identification of subjects required. Buys one-time rights.

Columns/Departments: Safety (new safety innovation/products), 500 words; Trade Talk (new products), 300 words. Query. Pays 18-25¢/word.

Tips: "Our publication is fairly time-sensitive re: issues affecting the trucking industry in Western Canada. Current 'hot' topics are international trucking (NAFTA-induced changes), deregulation, health and safety, alcohol and drug testing legislation/programs and national/international highway systems."

AVIATION AND SPACE

In this section are journals for aviation business executives, airport operators and aviation technicians. Publications for professional and private pilots can be found in the Consumer Aviation section.

AG-PILOT INTERNATIONAL MAGAZINE, Graphics Plus, P.O. Box 1607, Mt. Vernon WA 98273-1607. (360)336-9737. Fax: (360)336-2506. Editor/Publisher: Tom J. Wood. Contact: Tamara Pugh, editorial director. Monthly magazine emphasizing agricultural aviation, aerial firefighting, forestry spraying. 10% freelance written. Estab. 1978. Circ. 6,872. Pays on publication. Publishes ms an average of 3 months after acceptance. Buys all rights. Byline given. Reports in 2 months. Sample copy for $3 and 9×12 SAE with 7 first-class stamps. Writer's guidelines for #10 SASE.

Nonfiction: Exposé (of EPA, OSHA, FAA, NTSB or any government function concerned with this industry), general interest, historical, humor, interview (of well-known ag/aviation person), new product, personal experience, photo feature. Sometimes pays expenses of writers on assignment. Buys 20 mss/year. Send complete ms. Length: 500-10,000 words. Pays $100-200.

Photos: Send photos with submission. Reviews 4×5 transparencies, 5×7 prints. Offers no additional payment for photos accepted with ms. Captions required.

Columns/Departments: Good Old Days (ag/aviation history), 500-700 words. Buys 10 mss/year. Send complete ms. Pays $50-150.

Poetry: Interested in all ag-aviation related poetry. Buys 10 poems/issue. Submit maximum 2 at one time. Length: 24-72 lines. Pays $25-50.

Fillers: Short jokes, short humor and industry-related newsbreaks. Length: 40-100 words. Pays $15-20.

Tips: "Writers should be witty and knowledgeable about the crop dusting aviation world. Material *must* be agricultural/aviation-oriented."

MOUNTAIN PILOT, (formerly *Wings West*), 7009 S. Potomac St., Englewood CO 80112-4209. (303)397-7600. Fax: (303)397-7619. Publisher/Editor: Edward D. Huber. 50% freelance written. Bimonthly magazine on mountain flying performance, aviation and aerospace in the West. Estab. 1985. Circ. 15,000. Pays on publication. Publishes ms an average of 1 year after acceptance. Byline given. Offers $25 kill fee. Buys all rights. Submit seasonal/holiday material 6 months in advance. Sample copy available. Writing and photographic guidelines available.

Nonfiction: General interest illustrative of people, how to fly, flying experiences, mountain flying, humor, new products, opinion, opportunities, challenges, cultures, and special places. Buys 18-35 mss/year. Send cover letter with copy of ms, Mac or DOS file saved as text only, unformed ASCII, or in QuarkXPress (Mac) on 3½-inch floppy diskette (telephonic submissions (303)397-6987), author's bio and photo. Length: 800-2,000 words. Pay starts at $50/published page (includes text and photos).

Reprints: Send tearsheet or photocopy of article or short story and information about when and where the article previously appeared.

Photos: Send photos with submission (copies acceptable for evaluation). Credit line given.

Columns/Departments: Medical (aeromedical factors), legal (FARs, enforcement, legal problems), mountain flying, travel, safety, product news and reviews, industry news. *Mountain Pilot* purchases first serial rights. May consider second serial reprint rights, query.

BEAUTY AND SALON

‡AMERICAN SALON, Advanstar, 270 Madison Ave., New York NY 10016. Fax: (212)481-6562. Editor: Kathy McFarland. Contact: Amanda Hathaway, managing editor. 5% freelance written. Monthly magazine covering professional beauty industry. "Business stories that are of interest to salon owners and stylists, distributors and manufacturers of professional beauty products." Estab. 1876. Circ. 132,000. **Pays on acceptance.** Publishes ms an average of 3 months after acceptance. Byline given. Offers 50% kill fee. Buys first North American serial rights. Editorial lead time 3 months. Sample copy and writer's guidelines free on request.

Nonfiction: Query. Length: 250-1,000 words. Pays $300-500.

Reprints: Accepts previously published submissions.

COSMETICS, Canada's Business Magazine for the Cosmetics, Fragrance, Toiletry and Personal Care Industry, Maclean Hunter Publishing Ltd., 777 Bay St., 5th Floor, Toronto, Ontario M5W 1A7 Canada. (416)596-5817. Fax: (416)596-5179. Editor: Ronald A. Wood. 35% freelance written; "99.9% of freelance articles are assigned by the editor to writers whose work he is familiar with and who have a broad knowledge of this industry as well as contacts, etc." Bimonthly magazine. "Our main reader segment is the retail trade—department stores, drugstores, salons, estheticians—owners and cosmeticians/beauty advisors; plus manufacturers, distributors, agents and suppliers to the industry." Estab. 1972. Circ. 13,000. **Pays on acceptance.** Publishes ms an average of 3 months after acceptance. Byline given. Offers 50% kill fee. Buys all rights. Editorial lead time 4 months. Submit seasonal material 4 months in advance. Reports in 1 month. Sample copy for $6 (Canadian) and 8% GST.

Nonfiction: General interest, interview/profile, photo feature. Buys 60 mss/year. Query. Length: 250-1,200 words. Pays 25¢/word. Sometimes pays expenses of writers on assignment.

Photos: Send photos with submission. Reviews transparencies (2½ up to 8×10) and prints (4×6 up to 8×10). Offers no additional payment for photos accepted with ms. Captions, model releases and identification of subjects required. Buys all rights.

Columns/Departments: Behind the Scenes (brief profile of person not directly involved with major industry firms), 300 words and portrait photo. Buys 28 mss/year, "all assigned on a regular basis from correspondents and columnists that we know personally from the industry." Pays 25¢/word.

Tips: "Must have broad and intense knowledge of the Canadian cosmetics, fragrance and toiletries industry and retail business."

‡**DERMASCOPE MAGAZINE, The Encyclopedia of Aesthetics**, Geneva Corporation, 3939 E. Hwy. 80, #408, Mesquite TX 75150. Fax: (214)686-5901. E-mail: dermascope@aol.com. Editor: Naomi Stokes-Wesson. Bimonthly magazine covering aesthetics (skin care) and body and spa therapy. "Our magazine is a source of practical advice and continuing education for skin care and body and spa therapy professionals. Our main readers are salon, day spa and destination spa owners, managers or technicians." Estab. 1976. Circ. 10,000. Pays on publication. Publishes ms an average of 6 months after acceptance. Byline given. Buys all rights. Editorial lead time 6 months. Submit seasonal material 9 months in advance. Reports in 2 months. Sample copy and writer's guidelines free on request.

Nonfiction: Book excerpts, general interest, historical/nostalgic, how-to, inspirational, personal experience, photo feature, technical. Buys 6 mss/year. Query with published clips. Length: 700-2,000 words. Pays $50-250.

Photos: State availability of photos with submission. Reviews 4×5 prints. Offers no additional payment for photos accepted with ms. Captions, model releases, identification of subjects required. Buys all rights.

Tips: "Write from the practitioner's point of view. Step-by-step how to's that show the skin care and body and spa therapist practical methodology are a plus. Would like more business and finance ideas, applicable to the industry."

NAILPRO, The Magazine for Nail Professionals, Creative Age Publications, 7628 Densmore Ave., Van Nuys CA 91406. Fax: (818)782-7450. Editor: Linda Lewis. 75% freelance written. Monthly magazine "written for manicurists and nail technicians working in full-service salons or nails-only salons. It covers technical and business aspects of working in and operating a nail-care service, as well as the nail-care industry in general." Estab. 1989. Circ. 47,000. **Pays on acceptance.** Publishes ms 6 months after acceptance. Byline given. Offers 50% kill fee. Buys one-time, second serial (reprint), simultaneous or all rights. Editorial lead time 3 months. Submit seasonal material 3 months in advance. Accepts simultaneous submissions. Reports in 6 weeks. Sample copy for $2 and 8½×11 SASE.

Nonfiction Book excerpts, how-to, humor, inspirational, interview/profile, personal experience, photo feature, technical. No general interest articles or business articles not geared to the nail-care industry. Buys 50 mss/year. Query. Length: 1,000-3,000 words. Pays $150-350.

Reprints: Send typed ms with rights for sale noted and information about when and where the article previously appeared. Pays 50-75% of amount paid for an original article.

Photos: Send photos with submission. Reviews transparencies and prints. Negotiates payment individually. Model releases and identification of subjects required. Buys one-time rights.

Columns/Departments: Building Business (articles on marketing nail services/products), 1,500-3,000 words; Shop Talk (aspects of operating a nail salon), 1,500-3,000 words; Hollywood File (nails in the news, movies or TV), 1,000-1,500 words. Buys 50 mss/year. Query. Pays $200-300.

NAILS, Bobit Publishing, 2512 Artesia Blvd., Redondo Beach CA 90278-3296. (310)376-8788. Fax: (310)376-9043. E-mail: bobitpub@aol.com. Editor: Cyndy Drummey. Managing Editor: Erika Kotite. 10% freelance written. Monthly magazine for the nail care industry. "*NAILS* seeks to educate its readers on new techniques and products, nail anatomy and health, customer relations, working safely with chemicals, salon sanitation, and the business aspects of working in or running a salon." Estab. 1983. Circ. 52,000. **Pays on acceptance.** Byline given. Buys all rights. Submit seasonal material 4 months in advance. Reports in 3 months on queries. Free sample copy. No writer's guidelines available.

Nonfiction: Historical/nostalgic, how-to, inspirational, interview/profile, personal experience, photo feature, technical. "No articles on one particular product, company profiles or articles slanted towards a particular company or manufacturer." Buys 20 mss/year. Query with published clips. Length: 1,200-3,000 words. Pays $100-400. Sometimes pays expenses of writers on assignment.

Photos: State availability of photos with submission. Reviews contact sheets, transparencies and prints (any standard size acceptable). Offers $50-200/photo. Captions, model releases and identification of subjects required. Buys all rights.

Tips: "Send clips and query; *do not send unsolicited manscripts*. We would like to see ideas for articles on a unique salon or a business article that focuses on a specific aspect or problem encountered when working in a salon. The Modern Nail Salon section, which profiles nail salons and full-service salons, is most open to freelancers. Focus on an innovative business idea or unique point of view. Articles from experts on specific business issues—insurance, handling difficult employees, cultivating clients—are encouraged."

SKIN INC. MAGAZINE, The Business Magazine for Skin Care Professionals, Allured Publishing Corp., 362 S. Schmale Rd., Carol Stream IL 60188. (708)653-2155. Fax: (708)653-2192. Publisher/Editor: Marian Raney. Contact: Melinda Taschetta-Millane, managing editor. 30% freelance written. Bimonthly magazine covering the skin care industry. "Manuscripts considered for publication that contain original and new information in the general fields of skin care and makeup, dermatological, plastic and reconstructive surgical techniques. The subject may cover the science of skin, the business of skin care and makeup and plastic surgeons on healthy (i.e. non-diseased) skin. Subjects may also deal with raw materials, formulations and regulations concerning claims for products and equipment." Estab. 1988. Circ. 8,000. Pays on publication. Publishes ms an average of 6 months after acceptance. Byline given. No kill fee. Buys all rights.

Editorial lead time 6 months. Submit seasonal material 1 year in advance. Reports in 1 week on queries; 1 month on mss. Sample copy and writer's guidelines free on request.

Nonfiction: General interest, how-to, interview/profile, personal experience, technical. Buys 6 mss/year. Query with published clips. Length: 2,000 words. Pays $100-350 for assigned articles; $50-250 for unsolicited articles.

Photos: State availability of photos with submission. Reviews 3×5 prints. Offers no additional payment for photos accepted with ms. Captions, model releases, identification of subjects required. Buys one-time rights.

Columns/Departments: Dollars & Sense (tips and solutions for managing money), 2,000-2,500 words; Person to Person (managing personnel), 2,000-2,500 words; Marketing for the 90s (marketing tips for salon owners), 2,000-2,500 words. Query with published clips. Pays $50-250.

Fillers: Facts, newsbreaks. Buys 6 mss/year. Length: 250-500 words. Pays $50-100.

Tips: Have an understanding of the skin care industry.

BEVERAGES AND BOTTLING

Manufacturers, distributors and retailers of soft drinks and alcoholic beverages read these publications. Publications for bar and tavern operators and managers of restaurants are classified in the Hotels, Motels, Clubs, Resorts and Restaurants category.

AMERICAN BREWER, The Business of Beer, Box 510, Hayward CA 94543-0510. (415)538-9500 (a.m. only). Fax: (510)538-7644. Publisher: Bill Owens. 100% freelance written. Quarterly magazine covering micro-breweries. Estab. 1986. Circ. 15,000. Pays on publication. Publishes ms an average of 4 months after acceptance. Byline given. Buys one-time rights. Reports in 2 weeks on queries. Sample copy for $5.

Nonfiction: Business humor, opinion, travel. Query. Length: 1,500-2,500 words. Pays $50-250 for assigned articles.

Reprints: Send tearsheet or photocopy of article.

‡**BEVERAGE WORLD**, Strategic Business Communications, 150 Great Neck Rd., Great Neck NY 11021. (516)829-9210. Fax: (516)829-5414. Editor: Havis Dawson. Monthly magazine on the beverage industry. Estab. 1882. Circ. 35,000. **Pays on acceptance.** Publishes ms an average of 2 months after acceptance. Byline given. Buys all rights. Submit seasonal material 2 months in advance. Accepts simultaneous submissions. Free sample copy and writer's guidelines.

Nonfiction: How-to (increase profit/sales), interview/profile, technical. Buys 15 mss/year. Query with published clips. Length: 1,000-2,500 words. Pays $250/printed page. Sometimes pays expenses of writers on assignment.

Photos: State availability of photos with submission. Reviews contact sheets. Captions required. Buys one-time rights.

Columns/Departments: Buys 5 mss/year. Query with published clips. Length: 750-1,000 words. Pay varies, $150/minimum.

Tips: "Background in beverage production and marketing a real plus. Business and/or technical writing experience *a must*. Please submit on paper; do not call."

‡**THE MASSACHUSETTS BEVERAGE PRICE JOURNAL**, New Beverage Publications Inc., 55 Clarendon St., Boston MA 02116. (617)423-7200. Fax: (617)482-7163. Editor: Terry King. 100% freelance written. Monthly magazine covering beverage alcohol industry. Estab. 1934. Circ. 7,800. Pays on publication. Publishes ms an average of 2 months after acceptance. Byline given. Offers $250-350 kill fee. Buys one-time rights or makes work-for-hire assignments. Editorial lead time 2 months. Submit seasonal material 3 months in advance. Accepts simultaneous submissions.

● *The Massachusetts Beverage Price Journal* is expanding its editorial coverage to include cigars, store design, ancillary products, etc.

Nonfiction: General interest, new product, technical, travel. Buys 96 mss/year. Send complete ms. Length: 1,200-3,000 words. Pays $200-300. Sometimes pays expenses of writers on assignment.

Photos: Send photos with submission. Reviews negatives, transparencies. Offers no additional payment for photos accepted with ms. Buys one-time rights.

MID-CONTINENT BOTTLER, 8575 W. 110th, Suite 218, Overland Park KS 66210. (913)469-8611. Fax: (913)469-8626. Publisher: Floyd E. Sageser. 5% freelance written. Prefers to work with published/established writers. Bimonthly magazine for "soft drink bottlers in the 20-state Midwestern area." Estab. 1970. Not copyrighted. **Pays on acceptance.** Publishes ms an average of 2 months after acceptance. Buys first rights only. Reports immediately. Sample copy for 9×12 SAE with 10 first-class stamps. Guidelines for #10 SASE.

Nonfiction: "Items of specific soft drink bottler interest with special emphasis on sales and merchandising techniques. Feature style desired." Buys 2-3 mss/year. Length: 2,000 words. Pays $50-200. Sometimes pays the expenses of writers on assignment.
Photos: Photos purchased with mss.

TEA & COFFEE TRADE JOURNAL, Lockwood Trade Journal Co., Inc., 130 W. 42nd St., Suite 1050, New York NY 10036. (212)391-2060. Fax: (212)827-0945. E-mail: teacof@aol.com. Editor: Jane Phillips McCabe. 50% freelance written. Prefers to work with published/established writers. Monthly magazine covering the international coffee and tea market. "Tea and coffee trends are analyzed; transportation problems, new equipment for plants and packaging are featured." Estab. 1901. Circ. 10,000. Pays on publication. Publishes ms an average of 2 months after acceptance. Byline given. Makes work-for-hire assignments. Submit seasonal material 1 month in advance. Accepts simultaneous submissions. Reports in 4 months. Free sample copy.
Nonfiction: Exposé, historical/nostalgic, interview/profile, new product, photo feature, technical. Special issue includes the Coffee Market Forecast and Review (January). "No consumer-related submissions. I'm only interested in the trade." Buys 60 mss/year. Query. Length: 750-1,500 words. Pays $5.50/published inch 4 months after publication.
Photos: State availability of photos with submission. Reviews contact sheets, negatives, transparencies and prints. Pays $5.50/published inch. Captions and identification of subjects required. Buys one-time rights.
Columns/Departments: Specialties (gourmet trends); Transportation (shipping lines). Buys 36 mss/year. Query. Pays $5.50/published inch.

VINEYARD & WINERY MANAGEMENT, P.O. Box 231, Watkins Glen NY 14891-0231. (607)535-7133. Fax: (607)535-2998. E-mail: vandwm@aol.com. Editor: J. William Moffett. 80% freelance written. Bimonthly trade magazine of professional importance to grape growers, winemakers and winery sales and business people. Estab. 1975. Circ. 4,500. Pays on publication. Byline given. Buys first North American serial rights and occasionally simultaneous rights. Reports in 3 weeks on queries; 1 month on mss. Sample copy free. Writer's guidelines for #10 SASE.
Nonfiction: How-to, interview/profile, technical. Subjects are technical in nature and explore the various methods people in these career paths use to succeed, and also the equipment and techniques they use successfully. Business articles and management topics are also featured. The audience is national with western dominance. Buys 30 mss/year. Query. Length: 300-5,000 words. Pays $30-1,000. Pays some expenses of writers on some assignments.
Photos: State availability of photos with submission. Reviews contact sheets, negatives and transparencies. Identification of subjects required. "Black and white often purchased for $20 each to accompany story material; 35mm and/or 4×5 transparencies for $50 and up; 6/year of vineyard and/or winery scene related to story. Query."
Tips: "We're looking for long-term relationships with authors who know the business and write well. Electronic submissions preferred; query for formats."

‡**WINES & VINES**, 1800 Lincoln Ave., San Rafael CA 94901-1298. Fax: (415)453-2517. Editor: Philip E. Hiaring. 10-20% freelance written. Works with a small number of new/unpublished writers each year. Monthly magazine for everyone concerned with the grape and wine industry including winemakers, wine merchants, growers, suppliers, consumers, etc. Estab. 1919. Circ. 4,500. Buy first North American serial or simultaneous rights. **Pays on acceptance.** Publishes ms an average of 3 months after acceptance. Special issues: Winetech (January); Vineyard (February); State-of-the-Art (March); Brandy/Specialty Wines, (April); Export-import (May); Enological (June); Statistical (July); Merchandising (August); Marketing (September); Equipment and Supplies (November); Champagne (December). Submit special issue material 3 months in advance. Reports in 2 months. Sample copy for 11 × 14 SAE with 7 first-class stamps. Free writer's guidelines.
Nonfiction: Articles of interest to the trade. "These could be on grape growing in unusual areas; new winemaking techniques; wine marketing, retailing, etc." Interview, historical, spot news, merchandising techniques and technical. No stories with a strong consumer orientation against trade. Author should know the subject matter, i.e., know proper grape growing/winemaking terminology. Buys 3-4 ms/year. Query. Length: 1,000-2,500 words. Pays 5¢/word. Sometimes pays the expenses of writers on assignment.
Reprints: Send typed ms with rights for sale noted and information about when and where the article previously appeared.
Photos: Pays $10 for 4×5 or 8×10 b&w photos purchased with mss. Captions required.
Tips: "Ours is a trade magazine for professionals. Therefore, we do not use 'gee-whiz' wine articles."

BOOK AND BOOKSTORE

Publications for book trade professionals from publishers to bookstore operators are found in this section. Journals for professional writers are classified in the Journalism and Writing category.

BLOOMSBURY REVIEW, A Book Magazine, Dept. WM, Owaissa Communications Co., Inc., 1762 Emerson St., Denver CO 80218-1012. (303)863-0406. Fax: (303)863-0408. E-mail: bloomsb@aol.com. Publisher/Editor-in-chief: Tom Auer. Editor/Associate Publisher: Marilyn Auer. Contact: Lori Kranz, associate editor. 75% freelance written. Bimonthly tabloid covering books and book-related matters. "We publish book reviews, interviews with writers and poets, literary essays and original poetry. Our audience consists of educated, literate, *non-specialized* readers." Estab. 1980. Circ. 50,000. Pays on publication. Publishes ms an average of 4 months after acceptance. Byline given. Buys first or one-time rights. Reports in 4 months. Sample copy for $4 and 9 × 12 SASE. Writer's guidelines for #10 SASE.
Nonfiction: Essays, interview/profile, book reviews. "Summer issue features reviews, etc. about the American West. *We do not publish fiction.*" Buys 60 mss/year. Query with published clips or send complete ms. Length 800-1,500 words. Pays $10-20. Sometimes pays writers with contributor copies or other premiums "if writer agrees."
Reprints: Considered but not encouraged. Send photocopy of article and information about when and where the article previously appeared. Pays 100% of amount paid for an original article.
Photos: State availability of photos with submissions. Reviews prints. Offers no additional payment for photos accepted with ms. Buys one-time rights.
Columns/Departments: Book reviews and essays. Buys 6 mss/year. Query with published clips or send complete ms. Length: 500-1,500 words. Pays $10-20.
Poetry: Ray Gonzalez, poetry editor. Avant-garde, free verse, haiku, light verse, traditional. Buys 20 poems/year. Submit up to 5 poems at one time. Pays $5-10.
Tips: "We appreciate receiving published clips and/or completed manuscripts. Please—no rough drafts. Book reviews should be of new books (within 6 months of publication)."

THE HORN BOOK MAGAZINE, The Horn Book, Inc., 11 Beacon St., Suite 1000, Boston MA 02108. (617)227-1555. Editor: Roger Sutton. 10% freelance written. Prefers to work with published/established writers. Bimonthly magazine covering children's literature for librarians, booksellers, professors, teachers and students of children's literature. Estab. 1924. Circ. 21,500. Pays on publication. Publishes ms an average of 4 months after acceptance. Byline given. Submit seasonal material 6 months in advance. Accepts simultaneous submissions. Reports in 2 weeks on queries; 1 month on mss. Writer's guidelines available upon request.
Nonfiction: Interview/profile (children's book authors and illustrators); topics of interest to the children's bookworld. Writers should be familiar with the magazine and its contents. Buys 20 mss/year. Query or send complete ms. Length: 1,000-2,800 words. Honorarium paid upon publication.
Tips: "Writers have a better chance of breaking in to our publication with a query letter on a specific article they want to write."

‡LOS ANGELES TIMES BOOK REVIEW, Times Mirror, Times Mirror Square, Los Angeles CA 90053. (213)237-7778. Editor: Sonja Bolle. 90% freelance written. Weekly tabloid reviewing current books. Estab. 1881. Circ. 1,500,000. Pays on publication. Publishes ms an average of 3 weeks after acceptance. Byline given. Offers variable kill fee. Buys first North American serial rights. No unsolicited book reviews or requests for specific titles to review. "Query with published samples—book reviews or literary features." Buys 500 mss/year. Length: 200-1,500 words. Pay varies; approximately 35¢/word.

‡QUILL & QUIRE, Canada's Magazine of Book News & Reviews, Key Publishers, 70 The Esplanade, Suite 210, Toronto, Ontario M5E 7R2 Canada. (416)360-0044. Fax: (416)955-0794. E-mail: quill@hookup. net. Editor: Scott Anderson. Monthly tabloid covering Canadian book industry. "Our readers are primarily booksellers, librarians, publishers and writers." Estab. 1935. Circ. 7,000. **Pays on acceptance**. Publishes ms an average of 1 month after acceptance. Offers 50% kill fee. Buys all rights. Editorial lead time 2 months. Submit seasonal material 2 months in advance. Reports in 1 month on queries; 2 months on mss. Sample copy for $4.75 (Canadian).
Nonfiction: Essays, interview/profile, opinion, technical, business, book reviews. Buys hundreds of mss/year. Query. Length: 250-3,000 words. Pays $45-1,000 (Canadian). Sometimes pays writers with contributor copies or other premiums. Pays expenses of writers on assignment.
Photos: State availability of photos with submission. Reviews contact sheets. Offers $100-300/photo.
Columns/Departments: Carol Toller, news editor. Writers' Bloc (issues of interest to writers); Terms of Trade (issues relating to book trade in Canada); Calculating (issues relating to librarianship in Canada); all 850-1,000 words. Buys 36 mss/year. Query. Pays $100 (Canadian) minimum.

THE WOMEN'S REVIEW OF BOOKS, The Women's Review, Inc., Wellesley College, Wellesley MA 02181-8259. (617)283-2500. Editor: Linda Gardiner. Monthly newspaper. "Feminist review of recent trade and academic writing by and about women. Reviews recent nonfiction books, primarily." Estab. 1983. Circ. 16,000. Pays on publication. Publishes ms an average of 2 months after acceptance. Byline given. Offers $50 kill fee. Buys first North American serial rights. Editorial lead time 2 months. Reports in 2 months. Sample copy free on request.
Nonfiction: Book reviews only. No articles considered. Query. No unsolicited mss. Buys 200 mss/year. Query with published clips. Pays 12¢/word. Sometimes pays expenses of writers on assignment.

Tips: "Only experienced reviewers for national media are considered. Reviewers must have expertise in subject of book under review. Never send unsolicited manuscripts."

BRICK, GLASS AND CERAMICS

These publications are read by manufacturers, dealers and managers of brick, glass and ceramic retail businesses. Other publications related to glass and ceramics are listed in the Consumer Art and Architecture and Consumer Hobby and Craft sections.

STAINED GLASS, Stained Glass Association of America, 6 SW Second St., #7, Lee's Summit MO 64063. Fax: (816)524-9405. E-mail: sgmagaz@kcnet.com. Editor: Richard Gross. 70% freelance written. Quarterly magazine covering stained glass and glass art. "Since 1906, *Stained Glass* has been the official voice of the Stained Glass Association of America. As the oldest, most respected stained glass publication in North America, *Stained Glass* preserves the techniques of the past as well as illustrates the trends of the future. This vital information, of significant value to the professional stained glass studio, is also of interest to those for whom stained glass is an avocation or hobby." Estab. 1906. Circ. 5,000. Pays on publication. Publishes ms an average of 6 months after acceptance. Byline given. Buys one-time rights. Editorial lead time 3 months. Submit seasonal material 6 months in advance. Accepts simultaneous submissions. Reports in 3 months. Sample copy and writer's guidelines free on request.
Nonfiction: How-to, humor, interview/profile, new product, opinion, photo feature, technical. Strong need for technical and how to create architectural type stained glass. Glass etching, use of etched glass in stained glass compositions, framing. Buys 9 mss/year. Query or send complete ms but must include photos or slides—very heavy on photos. Pays $25/page. Sometimes pays expenses of writers on assignment.
Reprints: Accepts previously published submissions.
Photos: Send photos with submission. Reviews 4×5 transparencies. Negotiates payment individually. Identification of subjects required. Buys one-time rights.
Columns/Departments: Teknixs (technical, how-to, stained and glass art), word length varies by subject. Buys 4 mss/year. Query or send complete ms, but must be illustrated.
Tips: "Writers should be extremely well versed in the glass arts. Photographs are extremely important and must be of very high quality. Very sight-oriented magazine. Submissions without photographs or illustrations are seldom considered unless something special and writer states that photos are available. However, prefer to see with submission."

BUILDING INTERIORS

Owners, managers and sales personnel of floor covering, wall covering and remodeling businesses read the journals listed in this category. Interior design and architecture publications may be found in the Consumer Art, Design and Collectibles category. For journals aimed at other construction trades see the Construction and Contracting section.

‡**THE PAINT DEALER, Dedicated to the Retail Paint Market**, Mugler Publications, 10097 Manchester, #208, St. Louis MO 63122. (314)984-0800. Fax: (314)984-0866. E-mail: primecoat@aol.com. Editor: Mike Matthews. Associate Editor: Jerry Rabushka. Monthly magazine covering architectural paint and paint sundries. "For retail paint store owners and paint/sundry buyers in larger chains. Topics covered are new products and how to use them, how to sell, how to manage or operate store, laws and regulations that affect architectural paint industry." Estab. 1992. Circ. 23,000. Pays on publication. Byline sometimes given. Buys one-time rights. Editorial lead time 3 months. Reports in 3 weeks on queries; 2 months on mss. Sample copy for $3. Writer's guidelines for #10 SASE.
Nonfiction: How-to, new product, technical, store management. Query with published clips. Length: 750-2,000 words. Pays $50-250. Sometimes pays expenses of writers on assignment.
Reprints Accepts previously published submissions.
Photos: Send photos with submission. Offers no additional payment for photos accepted with ms.
Tips: "We are very specifically targeted and follow a pre-planned editorial calendar. Unsolicited manuscripts probably won't fit in. Best to check first. Frankly, we don't use a lot of freelancers but welcome inquiries."

PWC, Painting & Wallcovering Contractor, Finan Publishing Co. Inc., 8730 Big Bend Blvd., St. Louis MO 63119-3730. (314)961-6644. Fax: (314)961-4809. E-mail: jbeckner@finan.com. Website: http://www.paintstore.com. Editor: Jeffery Beckner. 90% freelance written. Bimonthly magazine for painting and wallcovering contracting. "*PWC* provides news you can use: information helpful to the painting and wallcovering contractor in the here and now." Estab. 1928. Circ. 30,000. Pays 30 days after acceptance. Publishes ms an average of 1 month after acceptance. Byline given. Kill fee determined on individual basis. Buys first North American serial rights. Editorial lead time 2 months. Submit seasonal material 2 months in advance.

Accepts simultaneous submissions. Reports in 2 weeks. Sample copy free on request.
Nonfiction: Essays, exposé, how-to (painting and wallcovering), interview/profile, new product, opinion personal experience. Buys 40 mss/year. Query with published clips. Length: 1,500-2,500 words. Pays $300 minimum. Pays expenses of writers on assignment.
Reprints: Send photocopy of article and information about when and where the article previously appeared. Negotiates payment.
Photos: State availability of or send photos with submission. Reviews contact sheets, negatives, transparencies and prints. Offers no additional payment for photos accepted with ms. Identification of subjects required. Buys one-time and all rights.
Columns/Departments: Anything of interest to the small businessman, 1,250 words. Buys 2 mss/year. Query with published clips. Pays $50-100.
Tips: "We almost always buy on an assignment basis. The way to break in is to send good clips, and I'll try and give you work."

‡**REMODELING NEWS**, SR Sound, Inc., 600C Lake St., Ramsey NJ 07446-1245. (201)327-1600. Fax: (201)327-3185. 80% freelance written. Monthly magazine covering professionally installed home remodeling, custom building and light construction. Estab. 1987. Circ. 82,000. Pays within 30 days of publication. Publishes ms an average of 3 months after acceptance. Byline given. Negotiates rights. Submit seasonal material 6 months in advance. Reports in 2 months. Free sample copy and writer's guidelines.
Nonfiction: How-to for professional remodelers, running a contracting business, remodeling products and materials. "Do not submit article for consumers or do-it-yourselfers." Query with published clips. Length: 600-3,000 words.
Reprints: Pays $50 for reprints.
Photos: State availability of photos with submission. Reviews transparencies, slides or photos. Captions, model releases and identification of subjects required. Buys all rights.
Tips: "Articles must be geared toward professional contractors/remodelers, not do-it-yourselfers."

BUSINESS MANAGEMENT

These publications cover trends, general theory and management practices for business owners and top-level business executives. Publications that use similar material but have a less technical slant are listed in the Consumer Business and Finance section. Journals for middle management, including supervisors and office managers, appear in the Management and Supervision section. Those for industrial plant managers are listed under Industrial Operations and under sections for specific industries, such as Machinery and Metal. Publications for office supply store operators are included in the Office Environment and Equipment section.

ACCOUNTING TECHNOLOGY, Faulkner & Gray (Division of Thompson Professional Publishing), 11 Penn Plaza, New York NY 10001. (212)967-7000. Fax: (212)563-3630. Website: http://www.faulknergray.com. Editor: Ted Needleman. Contact: Mike Cohn, senior editor. 40% freelance written. Magazine published 11 times/year covering hardware and software for accountants. "*Accounting Technology* is a high quality magazine dedicated to a simple editorial charter. We show our readers how to make more money by applying technology. Our writers must have a background in technology or accounting and a clear readable writing style." Estab. 1984. Circ. 30,000. Pays on publication. Publishes ms an average of 3 months after acceptance. Offers 25% kill fee. Buys first North American, second serial (reprint) rights and electronic rights. Editorial lead time 3 months. Reports in 6 weeks. Sample copy and writer's guidelines free on request.
Nonfiction: How-to, review. Buys 50 mss/year. Query with published clips; no unsolicited mss. Pays $150-3,000.
Columns/Departments: By assignment only, 2,000 words. Buys 40 mss/year. Query with published clips. Pays $400.

‡**ACCOUNTING TODAY**, Faulkner & Gray, 11 Penn Plaza, New York NY 10001. (212)967-7000. Editor: Rick Telberg. Biweekly newspaper covering accounting. "*Accounting Today* is the newspaper of record for the accounting industry." Estab. 1987. Circ. 35,000. Pays on publication. Publishes ms an average of 1 month after acceptance. Byline given. Buys all rights. Editorial lead time 2 week. Reports in 1 month. Sample copy for $5.
Nonfiction: Book excerpts, essays, exposé, how-to, interview/profile, new product, technical. Buys 35 mss/year. Query with published clips. Length: 500-1,500 words. Pays 25-50¢/word for assigned articles. Pays expenses of writers on assignment.
Photos: State availability of photos with submission. Negotiates payment individually.

ACROSS THE BOARD, The Conference Board Magazine, The Conference Board, 845 Third Ave., New York NY 10022. Editor: A.J. Vogl. 60-70% freelance written. Monthly magazine covering general management. "Our audience is primarily senior executives of large American companies." Estab. 1976. Circ. 25,000. Pays on publication. Publishes ms an average of 3 months after acceptance. Byline given. Offers 33% kill fee. Buys first North American serial rights. Editorial lead time 3 months. Accepts simultaneous submissions. Reports in 3 weeks on queries; 2 weeks on mss. Sample copy and writer's guidelines free on request.

Nonfiction: Book excerpts, essays, how-to, opinion, personal experience. Buys 40 mss/year. Query with published clips, or send complete ms. Length: 2,500-3,500 words. Pays $800-1,000. Sometimes pays expenses of writers on assignment.

Reprints: Accepts previously published submissions.

Photos: State availability of photos with submission.

Columns/Departments: Soundings (strong opinions on subjects of pertinence to our readers), 600-800 words. Pays $100-200.

BUSINESS ETHICS MAGAZINE, The Magazine of Socially Responsible Business, Mavis Publishing, 52 S. Tenth St., Suite 110, Minneapolis MN 55403-2001. (612)962-4701. Senior Editor: Mary Scott. 70% freelance written. Bimonthly magazine. "*Business Ethics* is the only magazine focused on socially responsible capitalism—the art of making money ethically, and in a socially responsible manner. It covers socially responsible investing, business news, trends and issues. We present insightful interviews with major business leaders, news features and timely analysis stories, charts tracking socially responsible businesses, and fresh perspectives on life and work. Issues covered include progressive personnel management, truth in marketing, employee ownership, environmental protection, corporate ethics, workplace diversity, philanthropy, and more." Estab. 1987. Circ. 30,000. Pays on publication. Publishes ms 3 months after acceptance. Byline given. Offers 15-20% kill fee. Buys first North American serial rights and second serial (reprint) rights. Editorial lead time 2 months. Reports in 1 month. Sample copy for 8×10 SAE with 5 first-class stamps. Writer's guidelines for #10 SASE.

Nonfiction: Essays, exposé, general interest, humor, inspirational, interview/profile, opinion, personal experience. Special issue: Year-End Annual on trends, news, "best-of." Buys 120 mss/year. Query with published clips. Length: 200-2,000 words. Pays $50-700.

Photos: State availability of photos or send photos with submission. Reviews contact sheets, negatives, transparencies, prints. Negotiates payment individually. Identification of subjects required. Buys one-time rights.

Columns/Departments: Commentary (opinion piece), Perspectives (essay on work life), Book Review Essays; 400-800 words. Query with published clips.

Fillers: Newsbreaks, short humor. Buys 60/year. Length: 100-300 words. Pays $50-100.

Tips: "Cater submissions to one of our sections, such as Trend Watch, Working Ideas, Perspectives and Commentary. Please send in published clips along with the idea."

‡CHAMBER EXECUTIVE, American Chamber of Commerce Executives, 4232 King St., Alexandria VA 22302. (703)998-0072. Fax: (703)931-5624. Managing Editor: Christina Tetreault. 10% freelance written. Monthly newsletter covering chambers of commerce. Circ. 5,000. **Pays on acceptance.** Publishes ms an average of 1 month after acceptance. Byline given. Offers 100% kill fee. Buys all rights. Editorial lead time 1 month. Submit seasonal material 2 months in advance. Accepts simultaneous submissions. Sample copy free on request.

Nonfiction: Essays, general interest, interview/profile, photo feature, technical. No personal experience, opinion, new products. Buys 0-10 mss/year. Query with published clips. Length: 100-1,000 words. Pays $25-500 for assigned articles.

Photos: State availability of photos with submission. Reviews contact sheets. Offers no additional payment for photos accepted with ms. Captions, identification of subjects required. Buys one-time rights.

Tips: "Attend local chamber functions. Follow business news with an impact on chambers."

‡COMMUNICATION BRIEFINGS, Encoders, Inc., Dept. WM, 1101 King St., Suite 110, Alexandria VA 22314. (703)548-3800. Fax: (703)684-2137. Website: http://www.cappubs.com/tpg. Editor: Jack Gillespie. Managing Editor: Susan Marshall. 15% freelance written. Prefers to work with published/established writers. Monthly newsletter covering business communication and business management. "Most readers are in middle and upper management. They comprise public relations professionals, editors of company publications, marketing and advertising managers, fund raisers, directors of associations and foundations, school and college administrators, human resources professionals, and other middle managers who want to communicate better on the job." Estab. 1980. Circ. 54,000. **Pays on acceptance.** Publishes ms an average of 3 months after acceptance. Byline given sometimes on Bonus Items and on other items if idea originates with the writer. Buys one-time rights. Submit seasonal material 2 months in advance. Reports in 1 month. Sample copy and writer's guidelines for #10 SAE and 2 first-class stamps.

Nonfiction: "Most articles we buy are 'how-to,' consisting of practical ideas, techniques and advice that readers can use to improve business communication and management. Areas covered: writing, speaking,

listening, employee communication, human relations, public relations, interpersonal communication, persuasion, conducting meetings, advertising, marketing, fund raising, telephone techniques, tele-conferencing, selling, improving publications, handling conflicts, negotiating, etc. Because half of our subscribers are in the nonprofit sector, articles that appeal to both profit and nonprofit organizations are given priority." *Short Items:* Articles with one or two brief tips that can stand alone. Length: 40-70 words. *Articles:* A collection of tips or ideas that offer a solution to a communication or management problem or that show a better way to communicate or manage. Examples: "How to produce slogans that work," "The wrong way to criticize employees," "Mistakes to avoid when leading a group discussion," and "5 ways to overcome writer's block." Length: 125-150 words. *Bonus Items:* In-depth pieces that probe one area of communication or management and cover it thoroughly. Examples: "Producing successful special events," "How to evaluate your newsletter," and "How to write to be understood." Length: 1,300 words. Buys 30-50 mss/year. Pays $20-50 for 40- to 150-word pieces; Bonus Items, $300. Pays expenses of writers on assignment.
Reprints: Previously published submissions "must be rewritten to conform to our style."
Tips: "Our readers are looking for specific, practical ideas and tips that will help them communicate better both within their organizations and with outside publics. Most ideas are rejected because they are too general or too elementary for our audience. Our style is down-to-earth and terse. We pack a lot of useful information into short articles. Our readers are busy executives and managers who want information dispatched quickly and without embroidery. We omit anecdotes, lengthy quotes and long-winded exposition. The writer has a better chance of breaking in at our publication with short articles and fillers since we buy only six major features (bonus items) a year. We require queries on longer items and bonus items. Writers may submit short tips (40-70 words) without querying. The most frequent mistakes made by writers completing an article for us are failure to master the style of our publication and to understand our readers' needs."

CONVENTION SOUTH, Covey Communications Corp., 2001 W. First St., P.O. Box 2267, Gulf Shores AL 36547-2267. (334)968-5300. Fax: (334)968-4532. Contact: Kristen McIntosh, managing editor. Editor: J.Talty O'Connor. 50% freelance written. Trade journal on planning meetings and conventions in the South. Estab. 1983. Circ. 10,000. Pays on publication. Byline given. Buys first rights or second serial (reprint) rights. Submit seasonal/holiday material 2 months in advance. Accepts simultaneous and previously published submissions. Query for electronic submissions. Reports in 2 months on queries. Free sample copy.
Nonfiction: How-to (relative to meeting planning/travel), photo feature, travel. Buys 20 mss/year. Query. Length: 1,250-3,000 words. Pays $75-150. Pays in contributor copies or other premiums if arranged in advance. Sometime pays expenses of writers on assignment.
Photos: Send photos with submission. Reviews 5×7 prints. Offers no additional payment for photos accepted with ms. Captions and identification of subjects required. Buys one-time rights.

HR MAGAZINE, Society for Human Resource Management, 606 N. Washington St., Alexandria VA 22314. (703)548-3440. Fax: (703)836-0367. Website: http://www.shrm.org. Editor: Michelle Martinez. Monthly magazine covering human resource profession "with special focus on business news that affects the workplace including court decisions, legislative actions and government regulations." Estab. 1950. Circ. 74,000. **Pays on acceptance.** Publishes ms an average of 6 months after acceptance. Byline given. Offers $200 kill fee. Buys first North American, first, one-time, all or world rights or makes work-for-hire assignments. Sample copy for $10. Writer's guidelines free on request.
Nonfiction: Interview/profile, new product, opinion, personal experience, technical. Buys 6 mss/year. Query. Length: 700-2,200 words. Pays 40¢/word. Pays expenses of writers on assignment.
Photos: State availability of photos with submission. Reviews contact sheets. Offers no additional payment for photos accepted with ms. Model releases and identification of subjects required. Buys electronic rights.

HR NEWS, Society for Human Resource Management, 606 N. Washington St., Alexandria VA 22314. (703)548-3440. Fax: (703)836-0367. Website: http://www.shrm.org. Editor: Michelle Martinez. Monthly tabloid covering human resource profession "with special focus on business news that affects the workplace including court decisions, legislative actions and government regulations." Estab. 1982. Circ. 69,000. Pays on publication. Publishes ms an average of 1 month after acceptance. Byline given. Buys first or one-time rights or makes work-for-hire assignments. Editorial lead time 2 months. Reports in 1 month on queries. Sample copy and writer's guidelines free.
Nonfiction: Interview/profile, business trends. Buys 6 mss/year. Query with published clips. Length: 300-1,000 words. Pays 40¢/word. Sometimes pays expenses of writers on assignment.
Photos: State availability of photos with submission. Reviews contact sheets, any prints. Negotiates payment individually. Captions and identification of subjects required. Buys one-time rights.
Tips: "Experienced business/news writers should send some clips and story ideas for our file of potential writers in various regions and for various subjects. Local/state business news or government actions affecting HR management of potentially national interest is an area open to freelancers."

INSIDE SELF-STORAGE, Virgo Publishing Inc., 4141 N. Scottsdale Rd., Suite 316, Scottsdale AZ 85251. (602)990-1101. Editor: Drew Whitney. 60-70% freelance written. Monthly magazine covering the self-storage industry with regard to owners and operators. "Articles must be thoroughly researched, and we prefer that the author have some experience or expertise in the industry." Estab. 1990. Circ. 15,000. Pays on publication. Publishes ms an average of 2 months after acceptance. Byline given. Buys first North American serial rights. Editorial lead time 4 months. Submit seasonal material 6 months in advance. Reports in 2 weeks on queries; 1 month on mss. Sample copy for 9×12 SASE.

Nonfiction: Book excerpts, interview/profile, new product, technical. Buys 30 mss/year. Query with or without published clips. Length: 850-3,500 words. Pays $200 maximum for assigned articles. Pays expenses of writers on assignment.

Photos: Reviews 3×5 prints. Negotiates payment individually. Model releases and identification of subjects required. Buys one-time rights.

Columns/Departments: Managers' World, Marketing, Straight Talk; 1,000 words. Buys 24 mss/year. Query with published clips. Pays $200 maximum.

Tips: "Demonstrate a knowledge and understanding of the self-storage industry. Submit story ideas in writing."

‡NATIONAL HOME CENTER NEWS, International News & Analysis for the Retail Home Improvement Industry, Lebhan-Friedman Inc., 425 Park Ave., New York NY 10022. (212)256-5107. Fax: (212)756-5295. Editor: Don Longo. Managing Editor: Susan Carlucci. Contact: John Caulfield, executive editor. 5% freelance written. Biweekly tabloid covering home improvement retail. "Articles require a broad in-depth knowledge of the retail home improvement market. Issues consist of a mix of news (company expansion, executive movement, financial developments), trends (customer service, consumer research, etc.) and merchandising (product category reports)." Estab. 1974. Circ. 53,000. Pays on publication. Publishes ms an average of 1 month after acceptance. Byline given. Kill fee negotiated. Buys all rights. Editorial lead time 3 months. Submit seasonal material 3 months in advance. Reports asap. Sample copy for 11×14 SAE with 3 first-class stamps.

Nonfiction: How-to, interview/profile, photo feature, product trends. Buys 48 mss/year. Query with or without published clips. Length: 500-1,000 words. Pays $300-500. Sometimes pays expenses of writers on assignment.

Photos: State availability of photos with submission. Reviews contact sheets, negatives, transparencies, 5×7 prints. Negotiates payment individually. Buys all rights.

RECORDS MANAGEMENT QUARTERLY, Association of Records Managers and Administrators, Inc., P.O. Box 4580, Silver Spring MD 20914-4580. Editor: Ira A. Penn, CRM, CSP. 10% freelance written. Eager to work with new/unpublished writers. Quarterly professional journal covering records and information management. Estab. 1967. Circ. 12,000. Pays on publication. Publishes ms an average of 6 months after acceptance. Byline given. Buys all rights. Accepts simultaneous submissions. Reports in 1 month on mss. Sample copy for $16. Free writer's guidelines.

Nonfiction: Professional articles covering theory, case studies, surveys, etc., on any aspect of records and information management. Buys 20-24 mss/year. Send complete ms. Length: 2,500 words minimum. Pays $50-300 "stipend"; no contract.

Photos: Send photos with ms. Offers no additional payment for photos accepted with ms. Prefers b&w prints. Captions required.

Tips: "A writer *must* know our magazine. Most work is written by practitioners in the field. We use very little freelance writing, but we have had some and it's been good. A writer must have detailed knowledge of the subject he/she is writing about. Superficiality is not acceptable."

SECURITY DEALER, PTN Publishing Co., 445 Broad Hollow Rd., Melville NY 11747. (516)845-2700. Fax: (516)845-7109. Editor: Susan A. Brady. 25% freelance written. Monthly magazine for electronic alarm dealers, burglary and fire installers, with technical, business, sales and marketing information. Circ. 25,000. Pays 3 weeks after publication. Publishes ms an average of 4 months after acceptance. Byline sometimes given. Buys first North American serial rights. Accepts simultaneous submissions.

Nonfiction: How-to, interview/profile, technical. No consumer pieces. Query or send complete ms. Length: 1,000-3,000 words. Pays $300 for assigned articles; $100-200 for unsolicited articles. Sometimes pays the expenses of writers on assignment.

Photos: State availability of photos with submission. Reviews contact sheets and transparencies. Offers $25 additional payment for photos accepted with ms. Captions and identification of subjects required.

Columns/Departments: Closed Circuit TV, Access Control (both on application, installation, new products), 500-1,000 words. Buys 25 mss/year. Query. Pays $100-150.

Tips: "The areas of our publication most open to freelancers are technical innovations, trends in the alarm industry and crime patterns as related to the business as well as business finance and management pieces."

‡SMALL BUSINESS NEWS, Cincinnati edition, Small Business News Inc., 635 W. Seventh St., Suite 410, Cincinnati OH 45203. (513)357-8500. Fax: (513)357-8506. Website: http://www.sbnpub.com. Editor: Katie Byers. Monthly tabloid covering business-to-business. "*SBN* offers advice and tips for Cincinnati business owners to help them grow." Pays 30 days after acceptance. Byline given. Offers 10% kill fee. Buys

first North American serial rights. Editorial lead time 1 month. Submit seasonal material 1 month in advance. Sample copy and writer's guidelines free on request.
Nonfiction: How-to, interview/profile. Buys 30 mss/year. Length: 500-1,000 words. Pays $100-300 for assigned articles. Sometimes pays expenses of writers on assignment.
Photos: State availability of photos with submission. Captions required.

‡**VIDEO BUSINESS**, 825 Seventh Ave., New York NY 10019-6001. Fax: (212)887-8484. E-mail: bgapar@ aol.com. Website: http://www.chilton.com. Executive Editor: Amy Wickstrom. 35% freelance written. Monthly magazine on video software retailing. "*Video Business* covers trends in marketing and videocassette programming for 40,000 retailers of all sizes. All articles should be written with the intent of providing information that a retailer can apply to his/her business immediately." Estab. 1981. Byline given. Buys first rights. Submit seasonal/holiday material 2 months in advance. Reports in 2 weeks. Free sample copy.
Nonfiction: Historical/nostalgic (movie genres), interview/profile, new product, technical. Query with published clips. Pays 25-35¢/word. Sometimes pays the expenses of writers on assignment.
Photos: State availability of photos with submission. Reviews negatives. Offers additional payment for photos accepted with ms. Buys one-time rights.

CHURCH ADMINISTRATION AND MINISTRY

Publications in this section are written for clergy members, church leaders and teachers. Magazines for lay members and the general public are listed in the Consumer Religious section.

CHILDREN'S MINISTRY, Group Publishing Inc., 2890 N. Monroe Ave., Loveland CO 80538. (303)669-3836. Editor: Christine Yount. Contact; Barbara Beach, departments editor. 73% freelance written. Bimonthly magazine of practical articles for Christian adults who work with children from birth to 6th grade. "The magazine's purpose is to supply practical ideas to help adults encourage children to grow spiritually." Estab. 1991. Circ. 50,000. **Pays on acceptance.** Byline given. Offers $25 kill fee. Buys all rights. Editorial lead time 6 months. Submit seasonal material 5 months in advance. Reports in 2 months. Sample copy for $2 and 9×12 SAE. Writer's guidelines for #10 SASE.
Nonfiction: How-to (practical, quick teaching ideas—games, crafts, devotional). No "preachy" articles. Query with or without published clips. Length: 50-1,200 words. Pays $25-100. Sometimes pays other than cash payments to reviewers. Sometimes pays expenses of writers on assignment.
Photos: State availability of photos with submission. Reviews contact sheets and prints. Offers $50-75/ photo. Buys one-time rights.
Columns/Departments: Preschool Page (hints, songs, Bible activities), 50-125 words; Group Games, 125 words; Seasonal Specials, 125 words; Nursery Notes (help for nursery workers), 125 words; 5-Minute Messages (Scripture based, fun), 125 words; For Parents Only (ideas for parent self-help, communication with children), 125 words. Buys 50 mss/year. Send complete ms. Pays $25.
Tips: "Potential authors should be familiar with children's ministry and its style. Most successful authors are ones who have experience working with children in the church. We like new ideas with 'ah-hahs.' "

CHRISTIAN EDUCATION LEADERSHIP, (formerly *Youth and Christian Education Leadership*), Pathway Press, P.O. Box 2250, Cleveland TN 37320-2250. Editor: Lance Colkmire. 15% freelance written. Quarterly magazine covering Christian education. "*Leadership* is written for teachers, youth pastors, children's pastors, and other local church Christian education leaders." Estab. 1976. Circ. 10,000. **Pays on acceptance.** Publishes ms an average of 6 months after acceptance. Not copyrighted. Buys first North American serial, first, one-time, second serial (reprint) or simultaneous rights. Editorial lead time 6 months. Submit seasonal material 6 months in advance. Accepts simultaneous submissions. Reports in 3 months on mss. Sample copy for $1. Writer's guidelines free on request.
Nonfiction: How-to (for church teachers), inspirational, interview/profile. Buys 12 mss/year. Send complete ms. Length: 400-1,200 words. Pays $25-55 for assigned articles; $25-45 for unsolicited articles.
Reprints: Accepts previously published submissions.
Photos: State availability of photos with submission. Reviews contact sheets, transparencies. Negotiates payment individually. Buys one-time rights.
Columns/Departments: Sunday School Leadership, Reaching Out (creative evangelism), The Pastor and Christian Education, Music Ministry, Singles Ministry, Children's Church; all 500 words. Send complete ms. Pays $25-40.

‡**THE CHRISTIAN MINISTRY**, The Christian Century Foundation, 407 S. Dearborn St., Suite 1405, Chicago IL 60605-1150. Editor: James M. Wall. Managing Editor: Victoria Rebeck. Attn: Manuscripts. 80% freelance written. Bimonthly magazine covering issues confronting local parish ministers in their day-to-day work. "We look for practical advice, e.g.: theological treatment of a particular issue, preparing better sermons,

church budget, congregation conflict, counseling techniques, etc." Estab. 1969. Circ. 6,400. Pays on publication. Publishes ms an average of 1 year after acceptance. Byline given. Buys all rights. Editorial lead time 5 months. Submit seasonal material 3 months in advance. Reports in 1 week on queries; 2 months on mss. Sample copy for 9×11 SAE and 3 first-class stamps. Writer's guidelines free on request.

Nonfiction: Humor, inspirational, opinion, personal experience, religious. No articles that do not demonstrate theological education. Buys 50 mss/year. Query. Send complete ms. Length: 1,000-2,500 words. Pays $60-100. Pays in contributor copies for book reviews.

Photos: State availability of photos with submission. Reviews prints. Offers $35-50/photo. Negotiates payment individually. Identification of subjects required. Buys one-time rights.

Columns/Departments: Women of the Word, Reflection on Ministry, Ministers' Workshop. Buys 50 mss/year. Query or send complete ms. Pays $75-1,100.

Fiction: Religious. Articles must relate to ministers' work. Buys 1 ms/year. Query or send complete ms. Length: 1,200-1,800 words. Pays $60-75.

Fillers: Anecdotes, facts, newsbreaks. Buys 50/year. Length: 100-200 words. Pays $10.

Tips: "1) Read the magazine to get a feel for our mainline protestant audience. 2) Ask to do a book review first. Either submit a review of a brand new book (less than 12 months old), or submit résumé and cover letter citing desire to review a book and topics of interest. We'll send a book for review when a match is available."

CREATOR MAGAZINE, Bimonthly Magazine of Balanced Music Ministries, Church Music Associates Inc., 920 S. Roundtail Place, Tucson AZ 85748. (520)885-8996. Fax: (520)885-8996. E-mail: creatormag @aol.com. Editor: Marshall Sanders. 35% freelance written. Bimonthly magazine covering music ministry and worship. "All readers are church music choir directors. Content focuses on the spectrum of worship styles from praise and worship to traditional to liturgical. All denominations subscribe. Articles on worship, choir rehearsal, handbells, children's/youth choirs, technique, relationships, etc." Estab. 1978. Circ. 6,000. Pays on publication. Publishes ms an average of 4 months after acceptance. Byline given. Buys first rights, one-time rights or second serial (reprint) rights; occasionally buys no rights. Editorial lead time 3 months. Submit seasonal material 4 months in advance. Accepts simultaneous submissions, if so noted. Sample copy for 9×12 SAE with 5 first-class stamps. Writer's guidelines free on request.

Nonfiction: Essays, how-to (be a better church musician, choir director, rehearsal technician, etc.), humor (short personal perspectives), inspirational, interview/profile (call first), new product (call first), opinion, personal experience, photo feature, religious, technical (choral technique). Special issues: July/August is directed toward adult choir members, rather than directors. Buys 20 mss/year. Query or send complete ms. Length: 1,000-10,000 words. Pays $30-75 for assigned articles; $30-60 for unsolicited articles. Pays expenses of writers on assignment.

Reprints: Accepts previously published submissions.

Photos: State availability of or send photos with submission. Reviews negatives, 8×10 prints. Offers no additional payment for photos accepted with ms. Captions appreciated. Buys one-time rights.

Columns/Departments: Hints & Humor (music ministry short ideas, anecdotes [cute] ministry experience), 75-250 words; Inspiration (motivational ministry stories), 200-500 words; Children/Youth (articles about specific choirs), 1,000-5,000 words. Buys 15 mss/year. Query or send complete ms. Pays $20-60.

Tips: "Request article guidelines and stick to it. If theme is relevant and guidelines are followed, we will probably publish."

THE JOURNAL OF ADVENTIST EDUCATION, General Conference of SDA, 12501 Old Columbia Pike, Silver Spring MD 20904-6600. (301)680-5075. Editor: Beverly J. Rumble. Bimonthly (except skips issue in summer) professional journal covering teachers and administrators in SDA school system. Estab. 1939. Circ. 7,500. Pays on publication. Publishes ms 1 year after acceptance. Byline given. Buys first rights. Editorial lead time 3 months. Reports in 6 weeks on queries; 4 months on mss. Sample copy for 10×12 SAE with 5 first-class stamps. Writer's guidelines free on request.

Nonfiction: Book excerpts, essays, how-to, personal experience, photo feature, religious, education. Theme issues have assigned authors. "No brief first-person stories about Sunday Schools." Query. Length: 1,000-1,500 words. Pays $25-100.

Reprints: Accepts previously published submissions.

Photos: State availability of photos or send photos with submission. Uses mostly b&w. Reviews prints. Negotiates payment individually. Captions required. Buys one-time rights.

LEADERSHIP, A Practical Journal for Church Leaders, Christianity Today, Inc., 465 Gundersen Dr., Carol Stream IL 60188. (708)260-6200. E-mail: LeaderJ@aol.com. Editor: Kevin A. Miller. 75% freelance written. Works with a small number of new/unpublished writers each year. Quarterly magazine covering church leadership. Writers must have a "knowledge of and sympathy for the unique expectations placed on pastors and local church leaders. Each article must support points by illustrating from real life experiences in local churches." Estab. 1980. Circ. 70,000. **Pays on acceptance.** Publishes ms an average of 6 months after acceptance. Byline given. Buys first North American serial rights. Submit seasonal material 6 months in advance. Reports in 6 weeks on queries; 2 months on mss. Sample copy for $3. Free writer's guidelines.

Nonfiction: How-to, humor, personal experience. "No articles from writers who have never read our journal." Buys 50 mss/year. Send complete ms. Length: 100-5,000 words. Pays $50-350. Sometimes pays the expenses of writers on assignment.

Reprints: Send photocopy of article and information about when and where the article previously appeared. Pays 50% of amount paid for an original article.

Photos: State availability of photos with submission. Offers no additional payment for photos accepted with ms. Identification of subjects required. Buys one-time rights.

Columns/Departments: To Illustrate (short stories or analogies that illustrate a biblical principle), 100 words. Buys 25 mss/year. Send complete ms. Pays $25-50. To Quip (clean, funny humor that makes a point), 100 words. Buys 12 mss/year. Send complete ms. Pays $25-35.

PASTORAL LIFE, Society of St. Paul, P.O. Box 595, Canfield OH 44406-0595. Fax: (216)533-1076. Editor: Anthony Chenevey, SSP. 66% freelance written. Works with new/unpublished writers. Monthly magazine emphasizing priests and those interested in pastoral ministry. Estab. 1953. Circ. 2,500. Buys first rights only. Byline given. Pays on publication. Publishes ms an average of 4 months after acceptance. Reports in 1 month. Sample copy and writer's guidelines for 6×9 SAE with 4 first-class stamps.

Nonfiction: "*Pastoral Life* is a professional review, principally designed to focus attention on current problems, needs, issues and important activities related to all phases of pastoral work and life." Query with outline before submitting ms. "New contributors are expected to include, in addition, a few lines of personal data that indicate academic and professional background." Buys 30 unsolicited mss/year. Length: 2,000-3,000 words. Pays 4¢/word minimum.

THE PREACHER'S MAGAZINE, Nazarene Publishing House, E. 10814 Broadway, Spokane WA 99206-5003. Editor: Randal E. Denny. Assistant Editor: Cindy Osso. 15% freelance written. Works with a small number of new/unpublished writers each year. Quarterly resource for ministers, Wesleyan-Arminian in theological persuasion." Circ. 18,000. Pays on publication. Publishes ms an average of 9 months after acceptance. Byline given. Buys first serial, second serial (reprint) and simultaneous rights. Submit seasonal material 9 months in advance. Writer's guidelines for #10 SASE.

Nonfiction: How-to, humor, inspirational, opinion, personal experience, all relating to aspects of ministry. No articles that present problems without also presenting answers to them or not relating to pastoral ministry. Buys 48 mss/year. Send complete ms. Length: 700-2,500 words. Pays 3½¢/word.

Reprints: Send photocopy of article or typed ms with rights for sale noted and information about when and where the article previously appeared. Pays 100% of amount paid for an original article.

Photos: Send photos with ms. Reviews 35mm transparencies, b&w prints. Model release, identification of subjects required. Buys one-time rights.

Columns/Departments: Stories Preachers Tell Each Other (humorous).

Fiction: Publishes novel excerpts.

Fillers: Anecdotes, short humor. Buys 10/year. Length: 400 words maximum. Pays 3½¢/word.

Tips: "Writers for the *Preacher's Magazine* should have insight into the pastoral ministry, or expertise in a specialized area of ministry. Our magazine is a highly specialized publication aimed at the minister. Our goal is to assist, by both scholarly and practical articles, the modern-day minister in applying Biblical theological truths."

‡VISION NEWSLETTER, Christian Educators Association International, P.O. Box 41300, Pasadena CA 91114. (818)798-1124. Fax: (818)798-2346. E-mail: ceaieduca@aol.com. Editor: Forrest Turpen. Contact: Ranelda Hunicker, managing editor. Newsletter published 9 times/year covering education and Christianity. "*Vision* is the official publication of CEAI, focusing on education issues pertinent to the Christian educator in public education. Topics include prayer in public schools, union activities, religious expression and activity in public schools and legal rights of Christian educators." Estab. 1953. Circ. 5,600. Pays on publication. Publishes ms an average of 6 months after acceptance. Byline given. Buys first rights. Editorial lead time 4 months. Submit seasonal material 6 months in advance. Accepts simultaneous submissions. Reports in 6 weeks on queries; 3 months on mss. Sample copy for 9×12 SAE and 3 first-class stamps. Writer's guidelines free on request.

Nonfiction: Humor, inspirational, interview/profile, opinion, personal experience, religious, book review, curriculum review. Buys 1-2 mss/year. Query. Length: 300-1,000 words. Pays $30-40. Pays in contributor copies for non-main features (book reviews, etc.).

Reprints: Accepts previously published submissions.

Photos: Send photos with submission. Offers no additional payment for photos accepted with ms. Identification of subjects required. Buys one-time rights.

Columns/Departments: Bible Study (for public school educators), 200-250 words.

Fiction: Ethnic, historical, humorous, religious. Buys 2-6 mss/year. Send complete ms. Length: 600-1,200 words. Pays $30-40.

Poetry: Avant-garde, free verse, haiku, light verse, traditional. Buys 1-4 poems/year. Submit maximum 1-2 poems. Pays in copies.

Fillers: Anecdotes, facts, newsbreaks, book reviews of interest to educators. Buys 1-5/year. Pays in copies..

YOUR CHURCH, Helping You With the Business of Ministry, Christianity Today, Inc., 465 Gundersen Dr., Carol Stream IL 60188. (630)260-6200. E-mail: YCEditor@aol.com. Managing Editor: Richard Doebler. 70% freelance written. Bimonthly magazine for the business of today's church. "Articles pertain to the business aspects of ministry pastors are called upon to perform: administration, purchasing, management, technology, building, etc." Estab. 1955. Circ. 200,000. **Pays on acceptance.** Publishes ms an average of 4 months after acceptance. Byline given. Buys one-time rights. Submit seasonal material 5 months in advance. Accepts simultaneous submissions. Reports in 1 month on queries; 2 months on mss. Sample copy and writer's guidelines for 9×12 SAE with 5 first-class stamps.

Nonfiction: How-to, new product, technical. Buys 25 mss/year. Send complete ms. Length: 900-1,500 words. Pays about 10¢/word.

Reprints: Send photocopy of article and information about when and where the article previously appeared. Pays 30% of the amount paid for an original article.

Photos: State availability of photos with submission. Reviews 4×5 transparencies and 5×7 or 8×10 prints. Offers no additional payment for photos accepted with ms. Captions, model releases and identification of subjects required. Buys one-time rights.

Tips: "The editorial is generally geared toward brief and helpful articles dealing with some form of church business. Concise, bulletted points from experts in the field are typical for our articles."

CLOTHING

ATI, America's Textiles International, Billian Publishing Co., 2100 Powers Ferry Rd., Atlanta GA 30339. (404)955-5656. Fax: (404)952-0669. Editor: Monte G. Plott. Associate Editor: Rolf Viertel. 10% freelance written. Monthly magazine covering "the business of textile, apparel and fiber industries with considerable technical focus on products and processes. No puff pieces pushing a particular product." Estab. 1887. Pays on publication. Byline sometimes given. Buys first North American serial rights.

Nonfiction: Technical, business. "No PR, just straight technical reports." Buys 10 mss/year. Query. Length: 500 words minimum. Pays $100/published page. Sometimes pays expenses of writers on assignment.

Photos: Send photos with submission. Reviews prints. Offers no additional payment for photos accepted with ms. Captions required. Buys one-time rights.

BOBBIN, Bobbin Blenheim Media, 1110 Shop Rd., P.O. Box 1986, Columbia SC 29202-1986. (803)771-7500. Fax: (803)799-1461. Website: http://www.bobbin.com. Editor-in-Chief: Susan Black. 25% freelance written. Monthly magazine for CEO's and top management in apparel and sewn products manufacturing companies. Circ. 9,788. Pays on publication. Byline given. Buys all rights. Reports in 6 weeks. Free sample copy and writer's guidelines.

Columns/Departments: Trade View, R&D, Information Strategies, Personnel Management, Labor Forum, NON-Apparel Highlights, Fabric Notables, West Coast Report.

Tips: "Articles should be written in a style appealing to busy top managers and should in some way foster thought or new ideas, or present solutions/alternatives to common industry problems/concerns. CEOs are most interested in quick read pieces that are also informative and substantive. Articles should not be based on opinions but should be developed through interviews with industry manufacturers, retailers or other experts, etc. Sidebars may be included to expand upon certain aspects within the article. If available, illustrations, graphs/charts, or photographs should accompany the article."

IMPRINTING BUSINESS, WFC, Inc., 3000 Hadley Rd., South Plainfield NJ 07080. (908)769-1160. Fax: (908)769-1171. Editor: Bruce Sachenski. Monthly magazine for persons in imprinted garment industry and screen printing. Circ. 23,000. Pays on publication. Publishes ms an average of 3 months after acceptance. Byline given. Buys one-time rights. Submit seasonal/holiday material 3 months in advance. Reports in 2 months. Sample copy for $10.

Nonfiction: How-to, new product, photo feature, technical, business. Buys 3 mss/year. Send complete ms. Length: 1,500-3,500 words. Pays $200-500 for assigned articles.

Reprints: Accepts previously published submissions.

Photos: Send photos with submission. Reviews contact sheets. Offers no additional payment for photos accepted with ms. Identification of subjects required.

Tips: "We need general business stories, advertising, shop management, etc."

MR MAGAZINE, The Magazine of Menswear Retailing, Business Journals, Inc., 50 Day St., Norwalk CT 06854. (203)853-6015. Editor: Karen Alberg Grossman. Contact: Katherine Grayson. 20% freelance written. Magazine published 8 times/year covering "up-to-the-minute coverage of menswear industry and retailers." Estab. 1990. Circ. 30,000. Pays on publication. Publishes ms an average of 2 months after acceptance. Byline given. Buys all rights. Editorial lead time 2 months. Submit seasonal material 2 months in advance. Reports in 1 month. Sample copy for $3.50 (if available). Writer's guidelines free on request.

Nonfiction: Humor, interview/profile, new product, opinion, personal experience (all dealing with men and menswear). Editorial calendar available. Buys 25-30 mss/year. Query with published clips or send complete ms. Length: 500-2,000 words. Pays $150-750. Sometimes pays expenses of writers on assignment.

Photos: Send photos with submission. Reviews transparencies or prints. Offers no additional payment for photos accepted with ms. Identification of subjects required. Buys all rights.

TEXTILE RENTAL, Uniform and Linen Service Management Trends, Textile Rental Services Association of America, 1130 E. Hallandale Beach Blvd., Suite B, Hallandale FL 33009. (954)457-7555. E-mail: srbiller@aol.com. Editor: Christine Seaman. Contact: Steven R. Biller, managing editor. 25% freelance written. Monthly magazine covering management and trends for uniform and linen rental executives. "*Textile Rental* covers government, environment, labor, workplace safety, regulatory compliance, computer technology, the economy, plant operations, strategic management, marketing, sales and service." Byline usually given. Offers negotiable kill fee. Editorial lead time 3 months. Submit seasonal material 4 months in advance. Reports in 1 month on queries; 2-3 months on mss. Sample copy free on request. Writer's guidelines for #10 SASE.

Nonfiction: Historical/nostalgic, how-to, inspirational, interview/profile, new product, technical. Buys 10-12 mss/year. Query with published clips. Length: 1,000-5,000 words. Pays $50-400. Pays in contributor copies at writer's request. Sometimes pays expenses of writers on assignment.

Reprints: Accepts previously published submissions.

Photos: Reviews contact sheets. Negotiates payment individually. Captions and identification of subjects preferred. Buys one-time rights.

Fillers: Anecdotes, facts, gags to be illustrated by cartoonist, newsbreaks, short humor. Buys 25-30/year. Length: 150-500 words. Pays $35-100.

‡**TEXTILE WORLD**, 4170 Ashford-Dunwoody Rd. NE, Suite 420, Atlanta GA 30319. Fax: (404)252-6150. Editorial Director: McAllister Isaacs III. Monthly magazine. Estab. 1868. **Pays on acceptance.** Buys all rights. Reports in 2 months.

Nonfiction: Uses articles covering textile management methods, manufacturing and marketing techniques, new equipment, details about new and modernized mills, etc., but avoids elementary, historical or generally well-known material.

Photos: Photos purchased with accompanying ms with no additional payment, or purchased on assignment.

CONFECTIONERY AND SNACK FOODS

These publications focus on the bakery, snack and candy industries. Journals for grocers, wholesalers and other food industry personnel are listed in Groceries and Food Products.

PACIFIC BAKERS NEWS, 180 Mendell St., San Francisco CA 94124-1740. (415)826-2664. Publisher: C.W. Soward. 30% freelance written. Eager to work with new/unpublished writers. Monthly business newsletter for commercial bakeries in the western states. Estab. 1961. Pays on publication. No byline given; uses only 1-paragraph news items.

Nonfiction: Uses bakery business reports and news about bakers. Buys only brief "boiled-down news items about bakers and bakeries operating only in Alaska, Hawaii, Pacific Coast and Rocky Mountain states. We welcome clippings. We need monthly news reports and clippings about the baking industry and the donut business. No pictures, jokes, poetry or cartoons." Length: 10-200 words. Pays 10¢/word for news and 6¢ for clips (words used).

CONSTRUCTION AND CONTRACTING

Builders, architects and contractors learn the latest industry news in these publications. Journals targeted to architects are also included in the Consumer Art and Architecture category. Those for specialists in the interior aspects of construction are listed under Building Interiors.

ABERDEEN'S CONCRETE CONSTRUCTION, The Aberdeen Group, 426 S. Westgate St., Addison IL 60101. (708)543-0870. Managing Editor: Anne Balogh. 20% freelance written. Monthly magazine covering concrete construction, "a how-to magazine for concrete contractors. It also covers job stories and new equipment in the industry." Estab. 1956. Circ. 85,000. **Pays on acceptance.** Publishes ms an average of 3 months after acceptance. Byline given. Editorial lead time 2 months. Submit seasonal material 3 months in advance. Reports in 2 weeks on queries; 1 month on mss. Sample copy free on request.

Nonfiction: How-to, new product, personal experience, photo feature, technical, job stories. Buys 7-10 mss/year. Query. Length varies. Pays $250 for assigned articles; $200 minimum for unsolicited articles. Sometimes pays expenses of writers on assignment.

Photos: State availability of photos with submission. Reviews contact sheets, negatives, transparencies, prints. Negotiates payment individually. Captions required. Buys one-time rights.
Tips: "Must have a good understanding of the concrete construction industry. How-to stories only accepted from industry experts. Job stories must cover the procedures, materials, and equipment used as well as the scope of the project."

AUTOMATED BUILDER, CMN Associates, Inc., P.O. Box 120, Carpinteria CA 93014-0120. (805)684-7659. Fax: (805)684-1765. E-mail: abmag@autbhdrmag.com. Website: http://www.autbhdrmag.com/~ab mag/. Editor-in-Chief: Don Carlson. 15% freelance written. Monthly magazine specializing in management for industrialized (manufactured) housing and volume home builders. Estab. 1964. Circ. 25,000. **Pays on acceptance.** Publishes ms an average of 3 months after acceptance. Buys first North American serial rights. Phone queries OK. Reports in 2 weeks. Free sample copy and writer's guidelines.
Nonfiction: Case history articles on successful home building companies which may be 1) production (big volume) home builders; 2) mobile home manufacturers; 4) modular home manufacturers; 4) prefabricated (panelized) home manufacturers; 5) house component manufacturers; or 6) special unit (in-plant commercial building) manufacturers. Also uses interviews, photo features and technical articles. "No architect or plan 'dreams'. Housing projects must be built or under construction." Buys 15 mss/year. Query. Length: 500-1,000 words maximum. Pays $300 minimum.
Photos: Purchased with accompanying ms. Query. No additional payment. Wants 4×5, 5×7 or 8×10 glossies or 35mm or larger color transparencies (35mm preferred). Captions required.
Tips: "Stories often are too long, too loose; we prefer 500 to 750 words. We prefer a phone query on feature articles. If accepted on query, article usually will not be rejected later."

‡BUILDING RENOVATION, Reuse, Rehabilitation & Restoration Technology, Penton Publishing, 600 Summer St., Stamford CT 06901. (203)348-7531, ext. 557. Fax: (203)348-4023. E-mail: breditor@aol.com. Editor: Derek H. Trelstad. 50% freelance written. Quarterly magazine covering renovation of commercial office structures and other buildings used in commerce (factories, etc.). "BR is distributed nationally to contractors, building owners, facility managers and architects. The editorial has a technical slant that emphasizes the technology and processes used in the renovation of existing structures, historic or otherwise. Knowledge of the basic tenets of historic preservation is helpful, but not essential. Familiarity with architectural history and construction are required." Estab. 1992. Circ. 40,000. Pays on publication. Publishes ms an average of 4 months after acceptance. Byline given. Buys first North American serial, second serial (reprint), electronic rights and makes work-for-hire assignments. Editorial lead time 1 year. Submit seasonal material 4 months in advance. Accepts simultaneous submissions. Reports in 3 weeks on queries; 2 months on mss. Sample copy and writer's guidelines free on request.
Nonfiction: Book excerpts, historical/nostalgic, how-to/processes for renovation, technical. No general interest, firm profiles or features on specific products. Buys 24 mss/year. Query with published clips. Length: 1,800-2,700 words. Pays $400-800. Sometimes pays expenses of writers on assignment.
Reprints: Accepts previously published submissions.
Photos: Send photos with submission. Reviews transparencies, prints. Negotiates payment individually. Captions, identification of subjects required. Buys one-time rights.

CAM MAGAZINE, Construction Association of Michigan, 500 Stephenson Hwy., Suite 400, Troy MI 48083. (810)585-1000. Fax: (810)583-0082. Editor: Phyllis L. Brooks. 5% freelance written. Monthly magazine covering all facets of the construction industry. "CAM Magazine is devoted to the growth and progress of individuals and companies serving and servicing the construction industry. It provides a forum on new construction industry technology and practices, current information on new construction projects, products and services, and publishes information on industry personnel changes and advancements." Estab. 1978. Circ. 4,300. Pays on publication. Byline given. Buys all rights. Editorial lead time 2 months. Submit seasonal material 3 months in advance. Sample copy free on request.
Nonfiction: Construction-related only. Buys 3 mss/year. Query with published clips. Length: 1,000-2,000 words. Pays $250-500.
Photos: Send photos with submission. Reviews contact sheets, negatives, transparencies and prints. Offers no additional payment for photos accepted with ms. Buys one-time rights.
Tips: "Anyone having *current* knowledge or expertise on some of our featured topics is welcomed to submit articles. Recent experience or information on a construction-related issue or new trends and innovations, is also helpful."

CONSTRUCTION COMMENT, Naylor Communications Ltd., 920 Yonge St., Suite 600, Toronto, Ontario M4W 3C7 Canada. (416)961-1028. Fax: (416)924-4408. E-mail: 1knowles@interlog.com. Editor: Lori Knowles. 80% freelance written. Semiannual magazine on construction industry in Ottawa. "*Construction Comment* reaches all members of the Ottawa Construction Association and most senior management of firms relating to the industry." Estab. 1970. Circ. 3,000. Byline given. Offers 33% kill fee. Buys first North American serial rights. Submit seasonal material 4 months in advance. Accepts simultaneous submissions. Reports in 6 weeks.

Nonfiction: General interest, historical, interview/profile, new product, photo feature, technical. "We publish a spring/summer issue and a fall/winter issue. Submit correspondingly or inquire four months ahead of these times." Buys 10 mss/year. Query with published clips and SASE in Canadian funds or an SAE with IRCs. Length: 500-2,500 words. Pays expenses of writers on assignment.

Reprints: Send tearsheet or photocopy of article and information about when and where the article previously appeared.

Photos: State availability of photos with submission. Reviews transparencies and prints. Offers $25-200/photo. Identification of subjects required.

Tips: "Please send copies of work and a general query. I will respond as promptly as my deadlines allow."

‡**CONSTRUCTION DIMENSIONS**, Association of the Wall and Ceiling Industries-International, 307 E. Annandale Rd., Suite 200, Falls Church VA 22042. (703)534-8300. Fax: (703)534-8307. E-mail: editorcd @ix.netcom.com. Editor: E.M. Porinchak. 25% freelance written. Monthly magazine covering wall and ceiling industry: drywall, acoustics, framing, etc. "*Construction Dimensions* is written and edited for acoustical, ceiling, drywall, EIFS, fireproofing, insulation, plaster, steel framing and stucco contractors, suppliers and distributors, manufacturers and those in allied trades. Editorial coverage focuses on general management and human resources, construction systems how-to applications, new products and techniques available to the industry, and information to help contractors increase business an operate profitably." Estab. 1972. Circ. 23,000. **Pays on acceptance**. Publishes ms an average of 2 months after acceptance. Byline given. Buys first North American serial, second serial (reprint) rights and makes work-for-hire assignments. Editorial lead time 2 months. Reports in 1 month on queries; 2 months on mss. Sample copy for $3 prepaid. Writer's guidelines not available.

Nonfiction: How-to, humor, interview/profile, new product, opinion, personal experience, photo feature, technical. No advertorials. Buys 20 mss/year. Send complete ms. Length: 800-1,200 words. Pay negotiated; no set rates. Pays 3 copies in addition to payment.

Photos: State availability of photos with submission. Negotiates payment individually. Captions required. Rights purchased are negotiable.

Columns/Departments: Time Out for Safety (construction safety advice), 500 words. Buys 3 mss/year ("would publish more if we got them"). Query. Pays $50-150.

Fiction: Humorous, slice-of-life vignettes. Buys 3 mss/year. Query. Length: 500-1,200 words. Pays $50.

Tips: The best approach—a phone call. The editor will gladly speak to freelancers about potential work."

‡**CONSTRUCTION EQUIPMENT GUIDE**, 2627 Mt. Carmel Ave., Glenside PA 19038-0156. (800)523-2200. Fax: (215)885-2910. E-mail: cegglen@aol.com. Editor: Beth Baker. 25-30% freelance written. Biweekly newspaper covering construction industry. "We are looked at as the primary source of information in the construction industry by equipment manufacturers, sellers and users. We cover the Midwest, Northeast and Southeast states with our 3 editions published biweekly. We give the latest news on current construction projects, legislative actions, political issues, mergers and acquisitions, new unique applications of equipment and indepth features." Estab. 1957. Circ. 80,000. Pays on publication. Publishes ms an average of 1 month after acceptance. Byline given. Offers 100% kill fee. Buys all rights. Editorial lead time varies. Accepts simultaneous submissions. Sample copy and writer's guidelines free on request.

Nonfiction: General interest, historical/nostalgic, how-to (winterizing construction equipment, new methods of construction applications), interview/profile, new product, personal experience, photo feature, technical. Buys 150 mss/year. Query with published clips. Length: 150-600 words. Negotiates payment individually. Pays expenses of writers on assignment.

Photos: Send photos with submission. Negotiates payment individually. Captions, identification of subjects required.

Columns/Departments: Equipment Auctions (photo coverage only with captions). Query. Pays $60 and expenses.

Tips: "Keep an eye out for commercial construction in your area. Take note of the name of the contractors on site. Then give us a call to see if you should follow up with a full story and photos. Pay attention to large and small jobs right around you. Read articles in *Construction Equipment Guide* to learn what information is important to our readers who are mostly equipment users, sellers and makers."

CONSTRUCTION MARKETING TODAY, The Aberdeen Group, 426 S. Westgate St., Addison IL 60101. (708)543-0870. Fax: (708)543-3112. E-mail: aberdeen@wocnet.com. Editor: Diana Granitto. 25% freelance written. Monthly tabloid covering marketing equipment or materials to the construction industry. "Our readers are manufacturers of construction equipment and building materials. Specifically, our readers

---

ALWAYS CHECK the most recent copy of a magazine for the address and editor's name before you send in a query or manuscript.

are marketing people and top execs at those companies. The magazine carries business news, marketing case studies and marketing how-to articles. The magazine does not have heavily technical content, so writers need not be knowledgeable of the industry. Business writing and company profile writing experience is a plus." Estab. 1990. Circ. 4,000. Pays on publication. Byline given. Buys first rights and simultaneous rights. Editorial lead time 2 months. Pay varies. Reports in 5 weeks on queries; 2 months on mss. Sample copy free on request.

Nonfiction: Exposé, how-to (marketing), interview/profile, opinion, personal experience, business news, marketing trends. "No stories aimed at contractors or stories that show no relevancy to the industry." Buys 15 mss/year. Query with published clips. Length: 800-3,000 words. Pays $250. Pays in contributor's copies if "author is an industry consultant or has a service he is trying to sell to our readers, or he works for a manufacturing company." Sometimes pays expenses of writers on assignment.

Reprints: Occasionally accepts previously published submissions. Send tearsheet, photocopy of article or typed ms with rights for sale noted and information about when and where the article previously appeared.

Photos: State availability of photos with submission. Reviews contact sheets. Negotiates payment individually. Captions and identification of subjects required. Buys all rights.

Tips: "Show that you have a grasp of what the magazine is about. We are not a technical how-to magazine geared to contractors, as most construction publications are. We have a unique niche. We are targeted to manufacturers marketing to contractors. We are looking for stories that have a fresh and intriguing look, that are entertaining to read, that are relevant to our readers, that are informative and that show an attention to detail in the reporting. Page 1 news, inside features, company profiles, industry marketing trends and marketing how-to stories are most open to freelancers. Stories should be tailored to our industry."

COST CUTS, The Enterprise Foundation, American City Bldg., 10227 Wincopin Circle, Suite 500, Columbia MD 21044-3400. (410)964-1230. Fax: (410)964-1918. Editor: Deborah Young. Quarterly newsletter. "*Cost Cuts* provides technical information on housing and related community services to low-income housing practitioners, raises awareness of the issues and approaches to housing low-income people and provides information on reducing costs in low-income housing development." Estab. 1983. Circ. 8,000. Pays on publication. Byline given. Buys one-time rights. Submit seasonal material 3 months in advance. Reports in 1 month. Sample copy for 9×12 SAE with 2 first-class stamps. Writer's guidelines for #10 SASE.

Nonfiction: How-to, interview/profile, technical. "No personal experience of do-it-yourselfers in single-family homes. We want articles concerning high production of low-income housing." Query with published clips. Length: 1,600-1,800 words. Pays $50-200 for assigned articles; $200 maximum for unsolicited articles. Sometimes pays expenses of writers on assignment.

Reprints: Send tearsheet of article, typed ms with rights for sale noted and information about when and where the article previously appeared.

Photos: Send photos with submission. Reviews contact sheets and 3×5 and 5×7 prints. Captions and identification of subjects required. Buys one-time rights.

Fillers: Facts, newsbreaks. Buys 20/year. Length: 100-500 words. Pays $25-50.

Tips: "The Foundation's mission is to see that all low-income people in the United States have the opportunity for fit and affordable housing and to move up and out of poverty into the mainstream of American life. Freelancers must be conscious of this context. Articles must include case studies of specific projects where costs have been cut. Charts of cost comparisons to show exactly where cuts were made are most helpful."

INDIANA BUILDER, Pro Tec Publishing & Printing, 500 S. Cory Lane, Bloomington IN 47403. (812)332-1639. Fax: (812)332-0117. E-mail: buildermag@aol.com. Editor: C. Dale Risch. 40% freelance written. Monthly magazine covering residential construction. "Our readers are professional builders and remodelers." Estab. 1989. Circ. 12,500. **Pays on acceptance.** Byline given. Buys one-time rights. Editorial lead time 1 month. Submit seasonal material 3 months in advance. Accepts simultaneous submissions. Sample copy free on request.

Nonfiction: How-to (construction). Buys 60 mss/year. Query with published clips. Length: 500-2,000 words. Pays 5¢/word. Sometimes pays expenses of writers on assignment.

Reprints: Accepts previously published submissions.

Photos: State availability of or send photos with submission. Reviews contact sheets. Negotiates payment individually. Captions required. Buys one-time rights.

‡JOINERS' QUARTERLY, Journal of Timber Framing & Traditional Joinery, Fox Maple Press, Inc., P.O. Box 249, Brownfield ME 04010. (207)935-3720. Managing Editor: Laurie LaMountain. Contact: Steve K. Chappell, editor. 75% freelance written. Quarterly magazine covering traditional building, timber framing, natural and sustainable construction. Estab. 1982. Circ. 10,000. Pays on publication. Publishes ms an average of 9 months after acceptance. Byline given. Buys all rights. Editorial lead time 9 months. Submit seasonal material 6 months in advance. Accepts simultaneous submissions. Reports in 1 month on queries; 2 months on mss. Sample copy for $4.50. Writer's guidelines for #10 SASE.

Nonfiction: Historical/nostalgic (building techniques), how-to (timber frame, log build, sustainable materials, straw building), inspirational (craftsmanship), new product, technical (alternative building techniques).

Buys 12 mss/year. Query. Length: 500-2,500 words. Pays $100-500. Sometimes pays expenses of writers on assignment.

Reprints: Accepts previously published submissions.

Photos: Send photos with submission. Reviews transparencies and prints. Offers no additional payment for photos accepted with ms. Identification of subjects required. Buys all rights.

Tips: "We're looking for articles on sustainable construction, especially from a timber framing aspect. Architects, builders and owner/builders are our primary readers and writers. We also like to feature natural and historical home building techniques such as straw/clay, roof thatching, sod home, etc."

MASONRY, 1550 Spring Rd., Suite 320, Oak Brook IL 60521. (708)782-6767. Fax: (708)782-6786. Editor: Gene Adams. 10% freelance written. Bimonthly magazine covering masonry contracting. "*Masonry Magazine* for masonry contractors and other members of the masonry industry, who are engaged in commercial, residential, institutional, governmental, industrial and renovation building projects. Readers include architects, engineers, specifiers, project manufacturers and others." Estab. 1961. Circ. 8,000. **Pays on acceptance.** Byline given. Buys first North American serial, first, one-time, second serial (reprint), simultaneous or all rights or makes work-for-hire assignments. Editorial lead time 2 months. Submit seasonal material 3 months in advance. Accepts simultaneous submissions. Reports in 3 weeks on queries; 8 months on mss. Sample copy and writer's guidelines free on request.

Nonfiction: Book excerpts, historical/nostalgic, how-to (contracting problems), interview/profile, new product, personal experience, photo feature, technical. Buys 12-18 mss/year. Query. Length: 500-4,000 words. Pays $150-250 for assigned articles; $25-50 for unsolicited articles.

Reprints: Send tearsheet or typed ms with rights for sale noted and information about when and where the article previously appeared. Negotiates payment.

Photos: Send photos with submission. Reviews contact sheets. Offers $10-50/photo or negotiates payment individually. Captions and identification of subjects required. Buys one-time and/or all rights.

PACIFIC BUILDER & ENGINEER, Vernon Publications Inc., 3000 Northup Way, Suite 200, Bellevue WA 98004. (206)827-9900. Fax: (206)822-9372. Editor: Carl Molesworth. Editorial Director: Michele Andrus Dill. 44% freelance written. Biweekly magazine covering non-residential construction in the Northwest and Alaska. "Our readers are construction contractors in Washington, Oregon, Idaho, Montana and Alaska. The feature stories in *PB&E* focus on ongoing construction projects in our coverage area. They address these questions: What is the most significant challenge to the general contractor? What innovative construction techniques or equipment are being used to overcome the challenges?" Estab. 1902. Circ. 14,500. Pays on publication. Publishes ms an average of 2 months after acceptance. Byline given. Buys first North American serial and second serial (reprint) rights. Editorial lead time 6 weeks. Submit seasonal material 2 months in advance. Reports in 2 months on queries; 6 weeks on mss. Sample copy for $7. Writer's guidelines for #10 SASE.

Nonfiction: How-to, new product, photo feature. "No non-construction stories; no residential construction articles; no construction stories without a Northwest or Alaska angle." Buys 18 mss/year. Query with published clips. Length: 750-2,000 words. Pays $100. Sometimes pays expenses of writers on assignment.

Photos: State availability of photos with submission. Reviews contact sheets, transparencies. Offers $15-125/photo. Captions and identification of subjects and equipment required. Buys one-time rights.

Tips: "Find an intriguing, ongoing construction project in our five-state region. Talk to the general contractor's project manager to see what he/she thinks is unusual, innovative or exciting about the project to builders. Then go ahead and query us. If we haven't already covered the project, there's a possibility that we may assign a feature. Be prepared to tour the site, put on a hard hat and get your boots dirty."

‡PERMANENT BUILDINGS & FOUNDATIONS, R.W. Nielsen Co., P.O. Box 11067, 5245 N. Kensington, Kansas City MO 64119. (816)453-0590. Fax: (816)453-0591. E-mail: pbfmag@aol.com. Managing Editor: Carolyn R. Nielsen. Contact: Roger W. Nielsen, editor. 25% freelance written. Magazine published 7 times/year. "*PBF* readers are contractors who build residential, commercial and industrial buildings. Editorial focus is on materials that last: concrete and steel—and new technologies to build solid, energy efficient structures—insulated concrete and tilt-up, waterproofing, underpinning, roofing—and the business of contracting and construction." Estab. 1989. Circ. 35,000. Pays on publication. Byline given. Buys first North American serial rights. Editorial lead time 2 months. Submit seasonal material 2 months in advance. Reports in 2 weeks on queries; 2 months on mss. Sample copy for #10 SASE. Writer's guidelines free on request.

Nonfiction: General interest, how-to (concrete construction methods, managment techniques), humor, interview/profile, new product, technical, travel. Buys 10 mss/year. Query. Length: 500-1,500 words. Pays $150-750 for assigned articles; $50-500 for unsolicited articles. Sometimes pays expenses of writers on assignment.

Photos: State availability of photos with submission. Reviews contact sheets. Offers no additional payment for photos accepted with ms. Captions, model releases, identification of subjects required. Buys one-time rights.

Columns/Departments: Shop Talk (organizational tips), 250 words; Q&A (solutions to contractor problems), 200-500 words; Off the Wall (humorous anecdotes), 200-500 words. Query. Pays $50-500.

Fillers: Anecdotes, gags to be illustrated by cartoonist, short humor. Length: 30-500 words. Pays $25-250.

PIPELINE & UTILITIES CONSTRUCTION, Oildom Publishing Co. of Texas, Inc., P.O. Box 219368, Houston TX 77218-9368. (713)558-6930. Fax: (713)558-7029. Editor: Robert Carpenter. 15% freelance written. Monthly magazine covering underground oil and gas pipeline, water and sewer pipeline, cable construction for contractors and owning companies. Circ. 31,000. Buys first North American serial rights. Publishes ms an average of 3 months after acceptance. Reports in 1 month. Sample copy for SASE.
Nonfiction: How-to, job stories. Query with published clips. Length: 1,000-2,000 words. Pays $3-500 "unless unusual expenses are incurred in getting the story." Sometimes pays the expenses of writers on assignment.
Photos: Send photos with ms. Reviews color prints and slides. Captions required. Buys one-time rights.
Tips: "We supply guidelines outlining information we need." The most frequent mistake made by writers in completing articles is unfamiliarity with the field.

ROOFER MAGAZINE, Construction Publications, Inc., 12734 Kenwood Lane, #73, Ft. Myers FL 33907. (813)489-2929. E-mail: roofmag@pagenet.com. Editor: Angela Williamson. 10% freelance written. Eager to work with new/unpublished writers. Monthly magazine covering the roofing industry for roofing contractors. Estab. 1981. Circ. 22,000. Pays on publication. Publishes ms an average of 5 months after acceptance. Byline given. Buys first and second serial (reprint) rights. Submit seasonal material 4 months in advance. Reports in 2 months. Sample copy and writer's guidelines for SAE with 6 first-class stamps.
Nonfiction: Profiles of roofing contractors (explicit guidelines available), humorous pieces; other ideas welcome. Buys 5-10 mss/year. Query in writing. Length: approximately 1,500 words. Pays $125-250 (average: $175).
Photos: Send photos with completed mss; color slides are preferred. Identification of subjects required. "We purchase photographs for specific needs, but those that accompany an article are not purchased separately. The price we pay in the article includes the use of the photos. Always searching for photos of unusual roofs or those with a humorous slant."
Tips: "Contractor profiles are our most frequent purchase from freelance writers and a favorite to our readers. Our guidelines explain exactly what we are looking for and should help freelancers select the right person to interview. We provide sample questions to ask about the topics we would like discussed the most. For those submitting queries about other articles, we prefer substantial articles (no fillers please). Slant articles toward roofing contractors. We have little use for generic articles that can appear in any business publication and give little consideration to such material submitted."

‡ST. LOUIS CONSTRUCTION NEWS & REVIEW, Finan Publishing Co., 8730 Big Bend Blvd., St. Louis MO 63119. (314)961-6644. Fax: (314)961-4809. E-mail: tfinan@finan.com. Editor: Nancy Roenfeldt. 75% freelance written. Monthly tabloid covering local construction. "A construction-related publication which focuses on projects, products, processes which affect the local industry." Estab. 1969. Circ. 6,500. Pays 30 days after acceptance. Byline given. Offers 50% kill fee. Buys first North American serial rights or makes work-for-hire assignment. Editorial lead time 2 months. Submit seasonal material 3 months in advance. Sample copy free on request.
Nonfiction: Business, insurance, finance, hazard, computers as they relate to local construction. Query with published clips. Length: 1,600-2,000 words. Pays $250-400. Pays in contributor copies for business-related or sidebar-type articles published for byline only. Sometimes pays expenses of writers on assignment.
Reprints: Accepts previously published submissions.
Photos: State availability of photos with submission. Reviews contact sheets. Negotiates payment individually. Identification of subjects required. Negotiates rights purchased.
Columns/Departments: Business, Finance, Insurance (all construction related), 800 words. Buys very few mss/year. Query with published clips. Pays $50-300.
Tips: "Anyone interested in freelance writing on an assigned basis may inquire regarding feature-length stories. All others interested in submitting business-related material which may be utilized in conjunction with a previously scheduled feature topic may do so."

DENTAL

‡DENTAL ECONOMICS, PennWell Publishing Co., P.O. Box 3408, Tulsa OK 74101-3400. (918)835-3161. Fax: (918)831-9804. Publisher: Dick Hale. Senior Editor: Penny Anderson. Associate Editor: Ron Combs. Assistant Editor: Melba Koch. 50% freelance written. Monthly dental trade journal. "Our readers are actively practicing dentists who look to us for current practice-building, practice-administrative and personal finance assistance." Estab. 1911. Circ. 110,000. **Pays on acceptance.** Publishes ms an average of 4 months after acceptance. Byline given. Buys first rights. Submit seasonal material 6 months in advance. Reports in 2 months. Free sample copy and writer's guidelines.
Nonfiction: General interest, how-to, new products. "No human interest and consumer-related stories." Buys 40 mss/year. Query. Length: 750-3,500 words. Pays $150-500 for assigned articles; $75-350 for unsolicited articles. Sometimes pays the expenses of writers on assignment.

Photos: State availability of photos with submission. Reviews contact sheets. Offers no additional payment for photos accepted with ms. Model releases and identification of subjects required. Buys one-time rights.

Columns/Departments: Ron Combs, associate editor: Tax Q&A (tax tips for dentists), 1,500 words; Office Of the Month (office design). Penny Anderson, senior editor: Capitol Gram (late legislative news—dentistry), 750 words; Dental Insurance, 750 words; User Friendly; Money Matters Staff Notebook. Buys 36 mss/year. Pays $50-300. Other monthly columns/departments are: News Digest, RX for Success, Viewpoint, Letters from Readers, Practice Productivity, Product-Profiles.

Tips: "How-to articles on specific subjects such as practice-building, newsletters and collections should be relevant to a busy, solo-practice dentist."

PROOFS, The Magazine of Dental Sales and Marketing, PennWell Publishing Co., P.O. Box 3408, Tulsa OK 74101-3400. (918)835-3161. Fax: (918)831-9804. E-mail: maryg@pennwell.com. Editor: Mary Elizabeth Good. Assistant Editor: Julie Harris. 5% freelance written. Magazine published 10 times/year covering dental trade. "*Proofs* is the only publication of the dental trade, for dental dealers, sales forces and key marketing personnel of manufacturers. It publishes news of the industry (not the profession), personnel changes and articles on how to sell dental equipment and merchandise and services that can be provided to the dentist-customer." Estab. 1917. Circ. 7,000. Pays on publication. Byline given. Buys first North American serial rights. Editorial lead time 1 month. Reports in 2 weeks on queries. Sample copy and writer's guidelines free on request.

Nonfiction: General interest, historical/nostalgic, how-to, interview/profile, opinion, personal experience. "No articles written for dentist-readers." Buys 15 mss/year. Query or send complete ms. Length: 400-1,250. Pays $100-200.

Photos: Either state availability of photos with submission or send photos with submission. Reviews minimum size $3\frac{1}{2} \times 5$ prints. Offers no additional payment for photos accepted with ms. Identification of subjects required. Buys one-time rights.

Tips: "Learn something about the dental industry and how it operates. We have no interest in manufacturers who sell only direct. We do not want information on products and how they work, but will take news items on manufacturers' promotions involving products. Most interested in stories on how to sell *in the dental industry*; industry personnel feel they are 'unique' and not like other industries. In many cases, this is true, but not entirely. We are most open to feature articles on selling, supply-house operations, providing service."

‡RDH, The National Magazine for Dental Hygiene Professionals, PennWell Publishing Co., P.O. Box 3306, Tulsa OK 74101. (918)831-9742. E-mail: markh@pennwell.com. Website: http://www.penwell. com. Editor: Mark Hartley. 30% freelance written. Monthly magazine covering information relevant to dental hygiene professionals as business-career oriented individuals. "Dental hygienists are highly trained, licensed professionals; most are women. They are concerned with ways to develop rewarding careers, give optimum service to patients and to grow both professionally and personally." Circ. 67,000. Usually pays 30 days after acceptance. Publishes ms an average of 4 months after acceptance. Byline given. Buys first serial rights. Reports in 1 month on queries and mss. Sample copies and writer's guidelines available.

Nonfiction: Essays, general interest, interview/profile, personal experience, photo feature, technical. "We are interested in any topic that offers broad reader appeal, especially in the area of personal growth (communication, managing time, balancing career and personal life). No undocumented clinical or technical articles; how-it-feels-to-be-a-patient articles; product-oriented articles (unless in generic terms); anything cutesy-unprofessional." Length: 1,500-3,000 words. Pays $200-350 for assigned articles; $50-200 for unsolicited articles. Sometimes pays expenses of writers on assignment.

Photos: Covers are shot on location across US.

Tips: "Freelancers should have a feel for the concerns of today's business-career woman—and address those interests and concerns with practical, meaningful and even motivational messages. We want to see good-quality manuscripts on both personal growth and lifestyle topics. For clinical and/or technical topics, we prefer the writers be members of the dental profession. New approaches to old problems and dilemmas will always get a close look from our editors. *RDH* is also interested in manuscripts for our feature section. Other than clinical information, dental hygienists are interested in all sorts of topics—finances, personal growth, educational opportunities, business management, staff/employer relations, communication and motivation, office rapport and career options. Other than clinical/technical articles, *RDH* maintains an informal tone. Writing style can easily be accommodated to our format."

DRUGS, HEALTH CARE AND MEDICAL PRODUCTS

‡CANADIAN PHARMACEUTICAL JOURNAL, 1785 Alta Vista Dr., Ottawa, Ontario K1G 3Y6 Canada. (613)523-7877. Fax: (613)523-0445. Editor: Andrew Reinboldt. Works with a small number of new/unpublished writers each year. Monthly journal for pharmacists. Estab. 1868. Circ. 13,038. Pays after editing. Publishes ms an average of 6 months after acceptance. Buys first serial rights. Reports in 2 months. Free sample copy and writer's guidelines.

Nonfiction: Relevant to Canadian pharmacy. Publishes continuing education, pharmacy practice, education and legislation, how-to; historical. Length: 200-400 words (for news notices); 800-1,500 words (for articles). Query. Payment is contingent on value. Sometimes pays expenses of writers on assignment.

Photos: Color and b&w 5×7 glossies purchased with mss. Captions, model releases required.

Tips: "Query with complete description of proposed article, including topic, sources (in general), length, payment requested, suggested submission date, and whether photographs will be included. It is helpful if the writer has read a *recent* copy of the journal; we are glad to send one if required. References should be included where appropriate (this is vital where medical and scientific information is included). Send 3 copies of each manuscript. Author's degree and affiliations (if any) and writing background should be listed."

PHARMACY PRACTICE, The Professional Journal for Canada's Pharmacists, Thomson Healthcare Communications, 1120 Birchmount Rd., Suite 200, Scarborough, Ontario M1K 5G4 Canada. (416)750-8900. Editor: Anne Bokma. 80% freelance written. Monthly magazine covering pharmacy. "We look for clinical and professional topics of interest to retail pharmacists. Most articles and columns are written by pharmacists." **Pays on acceptance.** Publishes ms an average of 2 months after acceptance. Byline given. Offers 50% kill fee. Buys first rights. Editorial lead time 4 months. Submit seasonal material 4 months in advance. Reports in 2 weeks on queries. Sample copy free on request.

Nonfiction: Pays telephone expenses of writers on assignment.

Photos: Reviews contact sheets, negatives, transparencies and prints. Negotiates payment individually. Buys one-time rights.

EDUCATION AND COUNSELING

Professional educators, teachers, coaches and counselors—as well as other people involved in training and education—read the journals classified here. Many journals for educators are nonprofit forums for professional advancement; writers contribute articles in return for a byline and contributor's copies. *Writer's Market* includes only educational journals that pay freelancers for articles. Education-related publications for students are included in the Consumer Career, College and Alumni; and Teen and Young Adult sections. Listings in the Childcare and Parental Guidance and Psychology and Self-Improvement sections of Consumer Magazines may also be of interest.

THE ATA MAGAZINE, The Alberta Teachers' Association, 11010 142nd St., Edmonton, Alberta T5N 2R1 Canada. (403)453-2411. Fax: (403)455-6481. Editor: Tim Johnston. Contact: Raymond Gariepy, managing editor. 50% freelance written. Quarterly magazine covering education. Estab. 1920. Circ. 39,500. Pays on publication. Publishes ms an average of 2 months after acceptance. Byline given. Offers kill fee of $75. Buys one-time rights. Editorial lead time 2 months. Submit seasonal material 2 months in advance. Accepts simultaneous submissions. Reports in 2 months. Sample copy and writer's guidelines free on request.

Nonfiction: Education-related topics. Length: 750-1,250 words. Pays $75-150. Sometimes pays expenses of writers on assignment.

Photos: Send photos with submission. Reviews 4×6 prints. Negotiates payment individually. Captions required. Negotiates rights.

CLASS ACT, Class Act, Inc., P.O. Box 802, Henderson KY 42420. Editor: Susan Thurman. 75% freelance written. Educational newsletter published 9 times/year covering English/language arts education. "Our writers must know English as a classroom subject and should be familiar with writing for teens. If you can't make your manuscript interesting to teenagers, we're not interested." Estab. 1993. Circ. 300. **Pays on acceptance.** Publishes ms an average of 6 months after acceptance. Byline given. Offers 100% kill fee. Buys all rights. Editorial lead time 2 months. Submit seasonal material 3 months in advance. Accepts simultaneous submissions. Reports in 1 month. Sample copy for $3. Writer's guidelines for #10 SASE.

Nonfiction: How-to (games, puzzles, assignments relating to English education). "NO Masters theses; no esoteric articles; no poetry; no educational theory or jargon." Buys 15 mss/year. Send complete ms. Length: 100-2,000 words. Pays $10-40.

Columns/Departments: Writing assignments (innovative, thought-provoking for teens), 500 words; puzzles, games (English education oriented), 200 words; teacher tips (bulletin boards, time-saving devices), 100 words. Send complete ms. Pays $10-40.

Fillers: Teacher tips. Pays $10.

Tips: "Please know the kind of language used by junior/senior high students. Don't speak above them. Also, it helps to know what these students *don't* know, in order to explain or emphasize the concepts. Clip art is sometimes used but is not paid extra for. We like material that's slightly humorous while still being educational. Especially open to innovative writing assignments; educational puzzles and games and instructions on basics. Again, be familiar with this age group."

‡CREATIVE CLASSROOM, Children's Television Workshop, One Lincoln Plaza, New York NY 10023. (212)595-3456. Fax: (212)875-6101. Editor: Elaine Israel. Contact: Brenda Pilson, assistant editor. 40% freelance written. Bimonthly magazine covering elementary education. Circ. 190,000. Pays on publication. Publishes ms an average of 6 months after acceptance. Byline given. Offers 33% kill fee. Makes work-for-hire assignments. Editorial lead time 5 months. Submit seasonal material 8 months in advance. Sample copy and writer's guidlines for #10 SASE.

Nonfiction: How-to (classroom strategies, teaching ideas). No articles without hands-on activities or advice for grade school teachers. Buys 40-50 mss/year. Send complete ms. Length: 800-2,400 words. Pays $150-1,600 for assigned articles; $15-500 for unsolicited articles. Pays expenses of writers on assignment.

Photos: Send photos with submission. Reviews transparencies. Negotiates payment individually. Captions, model releases, identification of subjects required. Buys all rights.

DANCE TEACHER NOW, The Practical Magazine of Dance, SMW Communications, Inc., 3101 Poplarwood Court, #310, Raleigh NC 27604-1010. Fax: (919)872-6888. E-mail: danceeditor@aol.com. Website: http://www.enews.com/magazines/dance. Editor: K.C. Patrick. 80% freelance written. Magazine published 10 times/year. "Our readers are professional dance educators, business persons and related professionals in all forms of dance. Estab. 1979. Circ. 8,000. **Pays on acceptance.** Publishes ms an average of 3 months after acceptance. Byline given. Negotiates rights and permission to reprint on request. Submit seasonal/holiday material 6 months in advance. Reports in 3 months. Sample copy for 9×12 SAE with 6 first-class stamps. Free writer's guidelines.

Nonfiction: How-tos (teach, business), interview/profile, new product, personal experience, photo feature. Special issues: Summer Programs (February); Music & More; (July/August); Costumes and Production Preview (November); College/Training Schools (December). No PR or puff pieces. All articles must be well researched. Buys at least 50 mss/year. Query first. Length: 1,500-3,500 words. Pays $100-400.

Photos: Send photos with submission. Reviews contact sheets, negatives, transparencies and prints. Limited photo budget.

Columns/Departments: Practical Tips (how-tos or updates, 100-350 words. Pays $25/published tip. Free Calendar Listings (auditions/competitions/workshops), 50 words.

Tips: "Read several issues—particularly seasonal. Stay within writers guidelines."

EDUCATION IN FOCUS, Books for All Times, Inc., Box 2, Alexandria VA 22313. (703)548-0457. Editor: Joe David. Semiannual newsletter covering educational issues. Pays on publication. Buys first, one-time and second serial (reprint) rights. Negotiates rights to include articles in books. Accepts simultaneous submissions. Reports in 1 month. Query with SASE.

Nonfiction: "We are looking for articles that expose the failures and discuss the successes of education."

‡ELECTRONIC LEARNING, Your Resource for Technology and School Change, Scholastic, 555 Broadway, New York NY 10012. (212)505-4944. Fax: (212)260-8587. Editor: Mickey Revenaugh. Contact: Jessica Siegel, managing editor. 90% freelance written. Magazine published bimonthly during school year covering education and technology. "*Electronic Learning* deals with education issues and what part technology can or does play. We believe technology can be an ingredient in reforming schools." Estab. 1987. Circ. 75,000. **Pays on acceptance.** Publishes ms an average of 2 months after acceptance. Byline given. Offers 50% kill fee. Makes work-for-hire assignments. Editorial lead time 2 months. Reports in 1 month on queries. Call to discuss writer's guidelines

Nonfiction: General interest, opinion, technical. Buys 6 mss/year. Query with published clips. Length: 650-3,000 words. Pays $250-2,000 for assigned articles. Pays expenses of writers on assignment.

Reprints: Accepts previously published submissions.

‡INSTRUCTOR MAGAZINE, Scholastic, Inc., 555 Broadway, New York NY 10012-3199. Website: http://scholastic.com/Instructor. Editor-in-Chief: Mickey Revenaugh. Publishing Coordinator: Ellen Ungaro. Eager to work with new/unpublished writers, especially teachers. Monthly magazine emphasizing elementary education. Estab. 1891. Circ. 275,000. **Pays on acceptance.** Publishes ms an average of 1 year after acceptance. Byline given. Buys all rights. Submit seasonal material 6 months in advance. Reports in 1 month on queries; 2 months on mss. Sample copy for $3. Writer's guidelines for SASE; mention *Writer's Market*.

Nonfiction: How-to articles on elementary classroom practice—practical suggestions and project reports. Occasionally publishes first-person accounts of classroom experiences. Buys 100 mss/year. Query. Length: 400-2,000 words. Pays $25-75 for short items; $125-400 for articles and features. Send all queries Attention: manuscripts editor.

Photos: Send photos with submission. Reviews 4×5 transparencies and prints. Offers no additional payment for photos accepted with ms. Model releases, identification of subjects required. Buys all rights.

Columns/Departments: Idea Notebook (quick teacher tips and ideas, seasonal activities, bulletin boards and crafts); At the End of the Day (first person essays by teachers). Buys 100 mss/year. Query with SASE. Length: 50-1,000 words. Pays $30-100.

Tips: "How-to articles should be kept practical, with concrete examples whenever possible. Writers should keep in mind that our audience is elementary teachers."

LEARNING, 1607 Battleground Ave., Greensboro NC 27408. Fax: (910)272-8020. E-mail: learning@spyde r.net. Editor/Publisher: Charlene F. Gaynor. 60% freelance written by teachers and other experts in education. Bimonthly magazine covering elementary and middle-school education topics. Estab. 1972. Circ. 207,000. **Pays on acceptance.** Buys all rights. Submit seasonal material 9 months in advance. Reports in up to 6 months. Sample copy for $4.95. Free writer's guidelines.
   ● *Learning* has become more selective; submissions must meet the format.
Nonfiction: "We publish manuscripts that describe innovative, practical teaching strategies." How-to (class-room management and hints for teaching in all curriculum areas); personal experience (from teachers in elementary and middle schools); profile (with teachers who are in unusual or innovative teaching situations). Strong interest in articles that deal with discipline, teaching strategy, motivation and working with parents. Buys 250 mss/year. Query. Length: 500-3,500 words. Pays $15-350.
Tips: "We're looking for innovative ideas and practices as well as first-hand personal accounts of dramatic successes—or failures—with a lesson to be drawn. No theoretical or academic papers. We're also interested in examples of especially creative classrooms and teachers. Emphasis on professionalism will increase: top teachers telling what they do best and how."

MEDIA PROFILES: The Health Sciences Edition, Olympic Media Information, P.O. Box 190, West Park NY 12493-0190. (914)384-6563. E-mail: omi@mhv.net. Website: http://www1.mhv.net/~omi/omi.htm. Publisher: Walt Carroll. 100% freelance written. Consists entirely of signed reviews of videos, CAI, CD-ROMs, etc. plus articles on medical and nursing sites on the Internet for health care education. Subscribers are medical and nursing libraries, colleges and universities where health sciences are taught. Journal magazine format, published quarterly. Estab. 1967. Circ. 1,000. Pays on publication. Publishes ms an average of 4 months after acceptance. Buys all rights. Buys 160 mss/year. "Sample copies and writer's guidelines sent on receipt of résumé, background, and mention of subject areas you are interested (most qualified) in review-ing. Enclose $5 for writer's guidelines and sample issue. (Refunded with first payment upon publication)." Reports in 1 month. Query.
Nonfiction: "We are the only review publication devoted exclusively to evaluation of films, videos, CAI and CD-ROMs for medical and health training. We have a highly specialized, definite format that must be followed in all cases. Samples should be seen by all means. Our writers should first have a background in health sciences; second, have some experience with audiovisuals; and third, follow our format precisely. Writers with advanced degrees and teaching affiliations with colleges and hospital education departments given preference. We are interested in reviews of media materials for nursing education, in-service education, continuing education, personnel training, patient education, patient care and medical problems. Currently seeking MDs, RNs, PhDs with clinical and technical expertise. Unsolicited mss not welcome. We will have videos sent directly to reviewers who accept the assignments." Pays $15/review.
Reprints: Send photocopy of article. Pays negotiable amount.

SCHOOL ARTS MAGAZINE, 50 Portland St., Worcester MA 01608-9959. Fax: (508)753-3834. Editor: Eldon Katter. 85% freelance written. Monthly magazine (September-May), serving arts and craft education profession, K-12, higher education and museum education programs written by and for art teachers. Estab. 1901. Pays on publication. Publishes ms an average of 3 months "if timely; if less pressing, can be 1 year or more" after acceptance. Buys all rights. Reports in 3 months. Free sample copy and writer's guidelines.
Nonfiction: Articles on art and craft activities in schools. Should include description and photos of activity in progress, as well as examples of finished artwork. Query or send complete ms. Length: 600-1,400 words. Pays $30-150.
Tips: "We prefer articles on actual art projects or techniques done by students in actual classroom situations. Philosophical and theoretical aspects of art and art education are usually handled by our contributing editors. Our articles are reviewed and accepted on merit and each is tailored to meet our needs. Keep in mind that art teachers want practical tips, above all—more hands-on information than academic theory. Write your article with the accompanying photographs in hand." The most frequent mistakes made by writers are "bad visual material (photographs, drawings) submitted with articles, or a lack of complete descriptions of art processes; and no rationale behind programs or activities. Familiarity with the field of art education is essential."

TEACHING TOLERANCE, The Southern Poverty Law Center, 400 Washington Ave., Montgomery AL 36104. (205)264-0286. Fax: (205)264-3121. Editor: Sara Bullard. 50% freelance written. Semiannual maga-zine covering education for diversity. "*Teaching Tolerance* is dedicated to helping K-12 teachers promote tolerance and understanding between widely diverse groups of students. Includes articles, teaching ideas, and reviews of other resources available to educators." Estab. 1991. Circ. 150,000. **Pays on acceptance.** Byline given. Buys all rights. Editorial lead time 6 months. Submit seasonal material 6 months in advance. Sample copy and writer's guidelines free on request.
Nonfiction: Essays, how-to (classroom techniques), interview/profile, personal experience, photo feature, multicultural education. "No jargon, rhetoric or academic analysis. No theoretical discussions on the pros/cons of multicultural education." Buys 6-8 mss/year. Query with published clips. Length: 1,000-3,000 words. Pays $500-3,000 maximum. Sometimes pays expenses of writers on assignment.

Photos: State availability of photos with submission. Reviews contact sheets and transparencies. Offers no additional payment for photos accepted with ms. Captions and identification of subjects required. Buys one-time rights.

Columns/Departments: Essays (personal reflection, how-to, school program), 400-800 words; Idea Exchange (special projects, other school activities), 100 words; Between the Lines, (using literature to teach tolerance); Interview/profile (usually features nationally known figure), 1,000-2,500 words; Student Writings (Short essays dealing with diversity, tolerance & justice), 300-500 words. Buys 8-12 mss/year. Pays $100-1,000. Query with published clips.

Tips: "We want lively, simple, concise writing. The writing style should be descriptive and reflective, showing the strength of programs dealing successfully with diversity by employing clear descriptions of real scenes and interactions, and by using quotes from teachers and students. We ask that prospective writers study previous issues of the magazine and writer's guidelines before sending a query with ideas. Most open to articles that have a strong classroom focus. We are interested in approaches to teaching tolerance and promoting understanding that really work—approaches we might not have heard of. We want to inform our readers; we also want to inspire and encourage them. We know what's happening nationally; we want to know what's happening in your neighborhood classroom."

TEACHING/K-8, The Professional Magazine, Early Years, Inc., 40 Richards Ave., 7th Floor, Norwalk CT 06854-2319. (203)855-2650. Fax: (203)855-2656. Editor: Allen Raymond. Editorial Director: Patricia Broderick. 90% freelance written. "We prefer material from classroom teachers." Monthly magazine covering teaching of K-8. Estab. 1970. Pays on publication. Publishes ms an average of 7 months after acceptance. Byline given. Buys all rights. Submit seasonal material 6 months in advance. Reports in 2 months. Sample copy for $3 and 9×12 SAE with 10 first-class stamps. Writer's guidelines for #10 SASE.

Nonfiction: Classroom curriculum material. Send complete ms. Length: 1,200 words. Pays $50 maximum.

Photos: Offers no additional payment for photos accepted with ms. Model releases and identification of subjects required.

Tips: "Manuscripts should be specifically oriented to a successful teaching strategy, idea, project or program. Broad overviews of programs or general theory manuscripts are not usually the type of material we select for publication. Because of the definitive learning level we cover (pre-school through grade eight) we try to avoid presenting general groups of unstructured ideas. We prefer classroom tested ideas and techniques."

TODAY'S CATHOLIC TEACHER, 330 Progress Rd., Dayton OH 45449-2386. (513)847-5900. Fax: (513)847-5910. Editor: Mary C. Noschang. 40% freelance written. Works with a small number of new/unpublished writers each year. For administrators and teachers concerned with Catholic schools and education in general. Estab. 1967. Circ. 50,000. Pays after publication. Publishes ms an average of 3 months after acceptance. Byline given. Buys all rights. Phone queries OK. Submit seasonal material 3 months in advance. Reports in 4 months. Sample copy for $3. Writer's guidelines for #10 SASE; mention *Writer's Market* in request.

Nonfiction: How-to (based on experience, particularly for teachers to use in the classroom to supplement curriculum, philosophy with practical applications); interview (of practicing educators, educational leaders); personal experience (classroom happenings other educators can learn from); a few profiles (of educational leaders). Buys 40-50 mss/year. Submit complete ms. Length: 800-2,000 words. Pays $150-250.

Photos: State availability of photos with ms. Possible additional payment for color or b&w glossy prints or transparencies. Buys one-time rights. Captions preferred; model releases required.

Tips: "We prefer articles that are of interest or practical help to educators—educational trends, teaching ideas, curriculum-related material, administration suggestions, articles teachers can use in classroom to teach current topics, etc."

UNIVERSITY AFFAIRS, Association of Universities and Colleges of Canada, 600-350 Albert St., Ottawa, Ontario K1R 1B1 Canada. (613)563-1236. Fax: (613)563-9745. E-mail: pberkowi@aucc.ca. Website: http://www.aucc.ca. Editor: Christine Tausig Ford. Associate Editor: Peggy Berkowitz. 25% freelance written. Tabloid published 10 times/year covering Canadian higher education. "For university faculty and administrators across Canada, *University Affairs* contains news, issues and commentary about higher education and research." Estab. 1959. Circ. 31,000. **Pays on acceptance.** Byline given. Buys first or all rights. Editorial lead time 3 months. Reports in 6 weeks on queries; 2 months on mss. Sample copy free on request.

• *University Affairs* is looking for greater analysis and more issues-oriented articles related to "hot" topics in higher education.

Nonfiction: Essays, general interest, interview/profile, opinion, photo feature. Buys 25 mss/year. Query with published clips. Length: 1,000-1,800 words. Pays $400-1,200 (Canadian).

Photos: State availability of photos with submission. Reviews contact sheets, negatives, transparencies, prints. Negotiates payment individually. Captions, model releases, identification of subjects required. Buys one-time rights.

Columns/Departments: Around the Universities (short articles about research or teaching achievements or "firsts"), 200 words. Query with published clips. Pay $50-75 (Canadian).

Tips: "Read the publication before contacting me. Have a solid understanding of both my needs and the subject matter involved. Be accurate, check facts, and make sure your writing is high quality. Look for the human interest angle. Put yourself in place of the readers—what makes your story meaningful for them."

‡VIRGINIA EDUCATOR, The Journal of Higher Education in the Commonwealth, P.O. Box 6400, Roanoke VA 24017. Executive Editor: Jamie Hendry. 90% freelance written. Bimonthly magazine covering higher education in Virginia. "*Virginia Educator* provides information and commentary on higher education in Virginia to college and university administrators, professors, and other industry professionals. These readers are interested in innovations and innovators, current events, controversial issues, and trends." Estab. 1996. Circ. 5,000. Pays on publication. Publishes ms an average of 3 months after acceptance. Byline given. Buys first North American serial rights; will consider simultaneous rights. Accepts simultaneous submissions. Reports in 1 month on queries. Sample copy and writer's guidelines free on request.
Nonfiction: Essays, exposé, general interest, interview/profile, new product, opinion. Buys 48 mss/year. Query with published clips. Length: 750-2,500 words. Pays $125-375. Sometimes pays expenses of writers on assignment.
Photos: Send photos with submission. Reviews transparencies, prints. Offers $25/photo. Captions required. Buys one-time rights.
Columns/Departments: News Briefs (news in VA higher ed), 200-300 words. Buys 36 mss/year. Send complete ms. Pays $30-60.
Fillers: Anecdotes, facts, gag to be illustrated by cartoonist, newsbreaks, short humor. Buys 24 mss/year. Length: 200-500 words. Pays $30-75.

WONDERFUL IDEAS, P.O. Box 64691, Burlington VT 05406-4691. 1-(800)92-IDEAS. Fax: (617)239-1496. E-mail: nancy@wonderful.com. Editor: Nancy Segal Janes. 40% freelance written. Newsletter published 8 times/year covering elementary and middle school mathematics. "*Wonderful Ideas* provides elementary and middle school teachers with creative and thought-provoking math activities, games, and lessons, with a focus on manipulatives and problem solving. Teacher-written and classroom-tested, these activities are designed to challenge students, while drawing strong connections between mathematical concepts and concrete problems. Book reviews and relationships of activities to NCTM Standards are also included." Estab. 1989. Circ. 1,600. Pays on publication. Publishes ms an average of 6 months after acceptance. Byline given. Buys all rights. Editorial lead time 2 months. Submit seasonal material 2 months in advance. Accepts simultaneous submissions. Reports in 1 month on queries; 3 months on mss. Sample copy and writer's guidelines free on request.
Nonfiction: Ideas for teaching elementary and middle school mathematics. Buys 10-15 mss/year. Query. Length: 900 words. Pays $20-60.
Columns/Departments: Wonderful Materials (review of new math materials and books), 700 words. Buys 3 mss/year. Query. Pays $20-60.

ELECTRONICS AND COMMUNICATION

These publications are edited for broadcast and telecommunications technicians and engineers, electrical engineers and electrical contractors. Included are journals for electronic equipment designers and operators who maintain electronic and telecommunication systems. Publications for appliance dealers can be found in Home Furnishings and Household Goods.

BROADCAST TECHNOLOGY, P.O. Box 420, Bolton, Ontario L7E 5T3 Canada. (905)857-6076. Fax: (905)857-6045. Editor-in-Chief: Doug Loney. 50% freelance written. Monthly magazine (except August, December) covering Canadian broadcasting industry. Estab. 1975. Circ. 8,000. Pays on publication. Byline given. Buys all rights.
Nonfiction: Technical articles on developments in broadcast engineering, especially pertaining to Canada. Query. Phone queries OK. Length: 500-1,500 words. Pays $100-300.
Photos: Purchased with accompanying ms. Color or b&w. Captions required.
Tips: "Most of our outside writing is by regular contributors, usually employed fulltime in broadcasting. The specialized nature of our magazine requires a specialized knowledge on the part of a writer."

‡CANADIAN ELECTRONICS, Action Communications Inc., 135 Spy Court, Markham, Ontario L3R 5H6 Canada. (905)477-3222. Fax: (905)477-4320. Editor: Tony Chisholm. 5% freelance written. Bimonthly tabloid covering electronics engineering. Estab. 1985. Circ. 25,000. Pays on publication. Publishes ms an average of 2 months after acceptance. Byline given. Buys first Canadian rights. Editorial lead time 2 months. Reports in 1 week on queries; 1 month on mss. Sample copy free on request.
Nonfiction: New product, technical. No consumer electronics. Buys 3 mss/year. Query with published clips. Length: 500-700 words. Pays $200-400. Sometimes pays expenses of writers on assignment.

Photos: Send photos with submission. Negotiates payment individually. Captions, identification of subjects required. Buys one-time rights.

COMMUNICATIONS QUARTERLY, P.O. Box 465, Barrington NH 03825-0465. Phone/Fax: (603)664-2515. E-mail: commquart@aol.com or 72127.745@compuserve.com. Publisher: Richard Ross. Editor: Terry Littlefield. 80% freelance written. Quarterly publication on theoretical and technical aspects of amateur radio and RF communication industry technology. Estab. 1990. Circ. 10,000. Pays on publication. Publishes ms an average of 6 months after acceptance. Byline given. Buys first rights. Reports in 1 month. Writer's guidelines for #10 SASE.
Nonfiction: "Interested in technical and theory pieces on all aspects of amateur radio and the RF communications industry. State-of-the-art developments are of particular interest to our readers. No human interest stories or articles related to the cable TV or broadcast industries." Query or send complete ms. Pays $40/published page.
Reprints: Sometimes accepts previously published submissions. Send photocopy of article and information about when and where the article previously appeared. Pays 100% of amount paid for an original article.
Photos: Send photos with submission. Reviews 5×7 b&w prints. Offers no additional payment for photos accepted with ms. Captions and identification of subjects required. Buys one-time rights.
Tips: "We are looking for writers with knowledge of the technical or theoretical aspects of the amateur radio and communication industries. Our readers are interested in state-of-the-art developments, high-tech construction projects and the theory behind the latest technologies."

ELECTRONIC SERVICING & TECHNOLOGY, The Professional Magazine for Electronics and Computer Servicing, CQ Communications, P.O. Box 12487, Overland Park KS 66282-2487. Phone/fax: (913)492-4857. E-mail: cpersedit@aol.com. Contact: Conrad Persson, editor. Managing Editor: Kirstie Wickham. 80% freelance written. Monthly magazine covering consumer electronics servicing. "*Electronic Servicing & Technology* is edited for service technicians, field service personnel, and avid servicing enthusiasts, who service audio, video and computer equipment." Estab. 1950. Circ. 30,000. Pays on publication. Publishes ms an average of 4 months after acceptance. Byline given. Buys one-time rights. Editorial lead time 2 months. Accepts simultaneous submissions. Reports in 1 month on queries; 2 months on mss. Sample copy and writer's guidelines free on request.
Nonfiction: How-to, new product, technical. Buys 40 mss/year. Query or send complete ms. Pays $300.
Reprints: Accepts previously published submissions.
Photos: Send photos with submission. Offers no additional payment for photos accepted with ms. Buys one-time rights.
Columns/Departments: Business Corner (business tips); Computer Corner (computer servicing tips); Video Corner(understanding/servicing TV and video); all 1,000-2,000 words. Buys 30 mss/year. Query or send complete ms. Pays $100-300.
Tips: "Writers should have a strong background in electronics, especially consumer electronics servicing."

‡**RADIO WORLD NEWSPAPER**, Industrial Marketing Advisory Services, Suite 310, 5827 Columbia Pike, Falls Church VA 22041. (703)998-7600. Fax: (703)998-2966. E-mail: 24103.7435@compuserve.com. Editor: Lucia Cobo. News Editor: Lynn Meadows. Contact: Al Peterson, technical editor. 50% freelance written. Bimonthly newspaper on radio station technology and regulatory news. "Articles should be geared toward radio station engineers, producers, technical people and managers wishing to learn more about technical subjects. The approach should be more how-to than theoretical, although emerging technology may be approached in a more abstract way." Estab. 1976. Pays on publication. Publishes ms an average of 2 months after acceptance. Byline given. Buys first North American serial rights plus right to publish in monthly international and annual directory supplements. Submit seasonal material 2 months in advance. Reports in 2 months.
Nonfiction: Exposé, historical/nostalgic, how-to (radio equipment maintenance and repair), humor, interview/profile, new product, opinion, personal experience, photo feature, technical. Length: 750-1,250 words. Pays $75-200. Pays in contributor copies or other premiums "if they request it, and for one special feature called Workbench." Sometimes pays expenses of writers on assignment.
Photos: Send photos with submission. Reviews 3×5 or larger prints. Identification of subjects required. Buys one-time rights.
Columns/Departments: Chris Nicholson, Buyers Guide editor. Buyers Guide User Reports (field reports from engineers on specific pieces of radio station equipment). Query. Length: 750-1,250 words.
Fillers: Newsbreaks, short humor. Buys 6/year. Length: 500-1,000 words. Pays $25-75.
Tips: "I frequently assign articles by phone. Sometimes just a spark of an idea can lead to a story assignment or publication. The best way is to have some radio station experience and try to think of articles other readers would benefit from reading."

ENERGY AND UTILITIES

People who supply power to homes, businesses and industry read the publications in this section. This category includes journals covering the electric power, natural gas, petroleum, solar and alternative energy industries.

ELECTRICAL APPARATUS, The Magazine of Electromechanical & Electronic Application & Maintenance, Barks Publications, Inc., 400 N. Michigan Ave., Chicago IL 60611-4198. (312)321-9440. Editorial Director: Elsie Dickson. Senior Editor: Kevin N. Jones. Managing Editor: Ann Coles. Monthly magazine for persons working in electrical and electronic maintenance, chiefly in industrial plants, who install and service electrical motors, transformers, generators, controls and related equipment. Estab. 1967. Circ. 17,000. **Pays on acceptance.** Publishes ms an average of 3 months after acceptance. Byline given. Buys all rights unless other arrangements made. Reports in 1 week on queries; 1 month on mss. Sample copy for $4.
Nonfiction: Technical. Length: 1,500-2,500. Pays $250-500 for assigned articles plus authorized expenses.
Tips: "All feature articles are assigned to staff and contributing editors and correspondents. Professionals interested in appointments as contributing editors and correspondents should submit résumé and article outlines, including illustration suggestions. Writers should be competent with a camera, which should be described in résumé. Technical expertise is absolutely necessary, preferably an E.E. degree, or practical experience. We are also book publishers and some of the material in *EA* is now in book form, bringing the authors royalties. Also publishes an annual directory, subtitled *ElectroMechanical Bench Reference.*"

NATIONAL PETROLEUM NEWS, 2101 S. Arlington Heights Rd., Suite 150, Arlington Heights IL 60005. (847)427-9512. Fax: (847)427-2041. E-mail: 102615.55@compuserve.com. Website: http://www.aip.com. Editor: Don Smith. 3% freelance written. Prefers to work with published/established writers. Monthly magazine for decision-makers in the oil marketing and convenience store industry. Estab. 1909. Circ. 14,000. Rights purchased vary with author and material; usually buys all rights. Pays on acceptance if done on assignment. Publishes ms an average of 2 months after acceptance. "The occasional freelance copy we use is done on assignment." Query.
● This magazine is particularly interested in articles on international industry-related material.
Nonfiction: Material related directly to developments and issues in the oil marketing and convenience store industry and "how-to" and "what-with" case studies. "No unsolicited copy, especially with limited attribution regarding information in story." Buys 3-4 mss/year. Length: 2,000 words maximum. Pays $50-150/printed page. Sometimes pays the expenses of writers on assignment.
Reprints: Send typed ms on disk with rights for sale noted and information about when and where the article previously appeared.
Photos: Pays $150/printed page. Payment for b&w photos "depends upon advance understanding."

RELAY MAGAZINE, Florida Municipal Electric Association, P.O. Box 10114, Tallahassee FL 32302-2114. (904)224-3314. Editor: Stephanie Wolanski. 5% freelance written. Monthly magazine. "Must be electric utility-oriented, or must address legislative issues of interest to us." Estab. 1942. Circ. 1,900. Pays on publication. Byline given. Not copyrighted. Buys first North American serial, one-time and second serial (reprint) rights. Accepts simultaneous submissions. Send photocopy of article or typed ms with rights for sale noted and information about when and where article previously appeared. Reports in 3 months.
Nonfiction: Interview/profile, technical and electric innovations. Query first; no articles that haven't been pre-approved. Length: 3-6 pages double-spaced. Pays $50.
Reprints: Accepts previously published submissions.
Photos: State availability of photos with submission. Pay and rights purchased vary. Captions and identification of subjects required.

ENGINEERING AND TECHNOLOGY

Engineers and professionals with various specialties read the publications in this section. Publications for electrical, electronics and telecommunications engineers are classified separately under Electronics and Communication. Magazines for computer professionals are in the Information Systems section.

‡AMERICAN MACHINIST, Penton Publishing, Dept. WM, 1100 Superior Ave., Cleveland OH 44114. (216)296-7000. Fax: (216)696-0177. E-mail: ameditor@penton.com. Website: http://www.penton.com. Editor: Diane Hallum. Monthly magazine about metalworking. Circ. 82,000. Publishes ms an average of 4 months after acceptance. Byline sometimes given. Makes work-for-hire assignments. Reports in 2 months on queries; 3 months on mss. Sample copy for SASE.
Nonfiction: Technical. Query with or without published clips, or send complete ms. Length: 1,500-4,000 words. Pay negotiable.
Photos: Send photos with submission. Offers no additional payment for photos accepted with ms. Buys all rights.

Tips: "Articles that are published are probably 85% engineering details. We're interested in feature articles on technology of manufacturing in the metalworking industries (automaking, aircraft, machinery, etc.). Accepting fewer submissions. Contact editor before sending in articles."

‡**HIGH TECHNOLOGY CAREERS**, %Writers Connection, P.O. Box 24770, San Jose CA 95154-4770. (408)445-3600. E-mail: writerscxn@aol.com. Managing Editor: Meera Lester. 100% freelance written. Magazine published every six weeks. "We buy three full-length feature articles (1,200 words) that examine cutting-edge or futuristic developments of high technology and their effects on life as we know it. These articles may include up to three sidebars. All material must provide a nonacademic and lively treatment of developments in computers, science, the Internet, aerospace, biotechnology, etc." Circ. 348,000. Pays on publication. Publishes ms an average of 3 months after acceptance. Byline given. Offers 25% kill fee. Buys all rights. Reports in 2 months. Sample copy for 9×12 SAE with $4 in postage. Writer's guidelines for #10 SASE.
Nonfiction: General interest (with high-tech tie-in) and technical articles. Also publishes ten 750-word (career-oriented) columns aimed at high-tech professionals: How-To, On-the Job Strategies, The Next Step, Ethics, Health & Fitness, Innovations, Lifestyle, Manager's Corner, Online Job-Search Strategies and Valley News (staff written). Buys 60-75 mss/year. Pay 17½¢/word. Sometimes pays expenses on writers on assignment.
Photos: State availability of photos with submission.

LASER FOCUS WORLD MAGAZINE, Pennwell Publishing, 10 Tara Blvd., #5FL, Nashua NH 03062-2801. (603)891-0123. Fax: (603)891-0574. Website: http://www.lfw.com. Publisher: Florence L. Oreiro. Group Editorial Director: Jeffrey N. Bairstow. Executive Editor: Heather W. Messenger. Contact: Barbara Murray, managing editor. Less than 1% freelance written. Monthly magazine for physicists, scientists and engineers involved in the research and development, design, manufacturing and applications of lasers, laser systems and all other segments of electro-optical technologies. Estab. 1968. Circ. 65,000. Publishes ms an average of 6 months after acceptance. Byline given unless anonymity requested. Retains all rights. Reports in 2 months. Free sample copy and writer's guidelines.
Nonfiction: Lasers, laser systems, fiberoptics, optics, detectors, sensors, imaging and other electro-optical materials, components, instrumentation and systems. "Each article should serve our reader's need by either stimulating ideas, increasing technical competence or improving design capabilities in the following areas: natural light and radiation sources, artificial light and radiation sources, light modulators, optical materials and components, image detectors, energy detectors, information displays, image processing, information storage and processing, subsystem and system testing, support equipment and other related areas. No flighty prose, material not written for our readership or irrelevant material. Query first with a clear statement and outline of why the article would be important to our readers."
Photos: Send photos with ms. Reviews 8×10 b&w glossies or 4×5 color transparencies. Drawings: Rough drawings acceptable, are finished by staff technical illustrator.
Tips: "The writer has a better chance of breaking in at our publication with short articles because shorter articles are easier to schedule, but must address more carefully our requirements for technical coverage. Most of our submitted materials come from technical experts in the areas we cover. The most frequent mistake made by writers in completing articles for us is that the articles are too commercial, i.e., emphasize a given product or technology from one company. Also articles are not the right technical depth, too thin or too scientific."

MINORITY ENGINEER, An Equal Opportunity Career Publication for Professional and Graduating Minority Engineers, Equal Opportunity Publications, Inc., 1160 E. Jericho Turnpike, Suite 200, Huntington NY 11743. (516)421-9421. Fax: (516)421-0359. Editor: James Schneider. 60% freelance written. Prefers to work with published/established writers. Triannual magazine covering career guidance for minority engineering students and minority professional engineers. Estab. 1969. Circ. 10,000. Pays on publication. Publishes ms an average of 6 months after acceptance. Byline given. Buys first rights. Accepts simultaneous submissions. Sample copy and writer's guidelines for 9×12 SAE with 5 first-class stamps.
Nonfiction: Book excerpts; articles (on job search techniques, role models); general interest (on specific minority engineering concerns); how-to (land a job, keep a job, etc.); interview/profile (minority engineer role models); new product (new career opportunities); opinion (problems of ethnic minorities); personal experience (student and career experiences); technical (on career fields offering opportunities for minority engineers). "We're interested in articles dealing with career guidance and job opportunities for minority engineers." Query or send complete ms. Length: 1,000-1,500 words. Sometimes pays the expenses of writers on assignment. Pays 10¢/word.
Reprints: Accepts previously published submissions.
Photos: Prefers 35mm color slides but will accept b&w. Captions and identification of subjects required. Buys all rights. Pays $15. Cartoons accepted. Pays $25.
Tips: "Articles should focus on career guidance, role model and industry prospects for minority engineers. Prefer articles related to careers, not politically or socially sensitive."

SENSORS, The Journal of Applied Sensor Technology, Helmers Publishing, Inc., 174 Concord St., Peterborough NH 03458. (603)924-9631. Fax: (603)924-2076. E-mail: editors@sensorsmag.com. Website: http://www.sensorsmag.com. Editor: Dorothy Rosa. 5% freelance written. Monthly magazine covering electrical and mechanical engineering. "To provide timely, authoritative technical information on the integration of sensors—via data acquisition hardware and software—into subassemblies, manufacturing and process control systems, and products." Estab. 1984. Circ. 65,000. **Pays on acceptance.** Publishes ms an average of 6 months after acceptance. Byline given. Buys first North American serial rights, all rights or makes work-for-hire assignments. Editorial lead time 6 months. Query for electronic submissions. Reports in 1 month on queries; 2 months on mss. Sample copy and writer's guidelines free on request.

Nonfiction: Technical, new product, opinion. Special issue: Data acquisition (June). Buys 3 mss/year. Query. Length: 800-2,400 words. Pay negotiable. Sometimes pays expenses of writers on assignment.

Photos: Send photos with submission. Reviews prints. Offers no additional payment for photos accepted with ms. Caption, model releases and identification of subjects required. Buys one-time rights.

ENTERTAINMENT AND THE ARTS

The business of the entertainment/amusement industry in arts, film, dance, theater, etc. is covered by these publications. Journals that focus on the people and equipment of various music specialties are listed in the Music section, while art and design business publications can be found in Art, Design and Collectibles. Entertainment publications for the general public can be found in the Consumer Entertainment section.

AMUSEMENT BUSINESS, Billboard Publications, Inc., P.O. Box 24970, Nashville TN 37202. (615)321-4269. Fax: (615)327-1575. Managing Editor: Linda Deckard. 25% freelance written. Works with a small number of new/unpublished writers each year. Weekly tabloid emphasizing hard news of the amusement, sports business, and mass entertainment industry for top management. Circ. 15,000. Pays on publication. Publishes ms an average of 3 weeks after acceptance. Byline sometimes given; "it depends on the quality of the individual piece." Buys all rights. Submit seasonal/holiday material 3 weeks in advance. Sample copy for 11×14 SAE with 5 first-class stamps.

● *Amusement Business* is placing an increased emphasis on international developments and looking for shorter news stories.

Nonfiction: How-to (case history of successful advertising campaigns and promotions); interviews (with leaders in the areas we cover highlighting appropriate problems and issues of today, i.e. insurance, alcohol control, etc.). Likes lots of financial support data: grosses, profits, operating budgets and per-cap spending. Also needs lots of quotes. No personality pieces or interviews with stage stars. Publishes profiles of key industry leaders, but must be well-known within the entertainment industry. Buys 500-1,000 mss/year. Query. Phone queries OK. Length: 400-700 words.

Photos: State availability of photos with query. Captions and model release required. Buys all rights.

Columns/Departments: Auditorium Arenas; Fairs; Parks & Attractions; Food Concessions; Merchandise; Promotion; Shows (carnival and circus); Talent & Touring; Management Changes; Sports; Profile; Eye On Legislation; Commentary and International News.

Tips: "There will be more and more emphasis on financial reporting of areas covered. Submission must contain the whys and whos, etc. and be strong enough that others in the same field will learn from it and not find it naive. We will be increasing story count while decreasing story length."

BOXOFFICE MAGAZINE, RLD Publishing Co., 6640 Sunset Blvd., Suite 100, Hollywood CA 90028-7159. (213)465-1186. Fax: (213)465-5049. E-mail: boxoff@earthlink.net. Website: http://www.boxoffice.c om. Editor-in-Chief: Ray Greene. 15% freelance written. Monthly business magazine about the motion picture industry for members of the film industry: theater owners, film producers, directors, financiers and allied industries. Estab. 1920. Circ. 8,000. Pays on publication. Publishes ms an average of 4 months after acceptance. Byline given. Buys all rights, including electronic publishing. Submit seasonal material 4 months in advance. Send typed ms with rights for sale noted. Sample copy for $5.50.

Nonfiction: Investigative, interview, profile, new product, photo feature, technical. "We are a general news magazine about the motion picture industry and are looking for stories about trends, developments, problems or opportunities facing the industry. Almost any story will be considered, including corporate profiles, but we don't want gossip or celebrity coverage." Query with published clips. Length: 800-2,500 words. Pays 10¢/word or set price.

Photos: State availability of photos. Pays $10 maximum for 8×10 b&w prints. Captions required.

Tips: "Request a sample copy, indicating you read about *Boxoffice* in *Writer's Market*. Write a clear, comprehensive outline of the proposed story and enclose a résumé and clip samples. We welcome new writers but don't want to be a classroom; know how to write. We look for 'investigative' articles."

CALLBOARD, Monthly Theatre Trade Magazine, Theatre Bay Area, 657 Mission St., #402, San Francisco CA 94105. (415)957-1557. Fax: (415)957-1556. E-mail: tba@well.com. Editor: Belinda Taylor.

50% freelance written. Monthly magazine for theater. "We publish news, views, essays and features on the Northern California theater industry. We also include listings, audition notices and job resources." Estab. 1976. Circ. 5,000. Pays on publication. Publishes ms an average of 4 months after acceptance. Byline given. Offers 50% kill fee. Buys first rights. Editorial lead time 1 month. Submit seasonal material 2 months in advance. Accepts simultaneous submissions. Reports in 1 month on queries. Sample copy for $4.75.

Nonfiction: Book excerpts, essays, opinion, personal experience, technical (theater topics only). *No profiles of actors.* Buys 12-15 mss/year. Query with published clips. Length: 800-2,000 words. Pays $100 minimum for assigned articles. Pays other for unsolicited articles. Sometimes pays expenses of writers on assignment (phone calls and some travel).

Reprints: Send tearsheet of article or typed ms with rights for sale noted and information about when and where the article previously appeared. Pays 50% of amount paid for an original article.

Photos: State availability of photos with submission. Reviews contact sheets or 5×7 prints. Offers no additional payment for photos accepted with ms. Identification of subjects required. Buys one-time rights.

CLUB MODÈLE, Aquino International, P.O. Box 15760, Stamford CT 06901. (203)967-9952. Fax: (203)353-9661. E-mail: aaquinoint@aol.com. Editor: Andres Aquino. 40% freelance written. Monthly magazine on fashion modeling, entertainment (video, film). "*Club Modèle* covers the business of modeling entertainment and fashion, including: performers, entertainers, dancers, actors, models, celebrities, agents, producers and managers, photographers; casting, TV, film, video, theater and show productions; fashion industries, trade shows and exhibits." Estab. 1991. Circ. 100,000. Pays on publication. Publishes ms an average of 2 months after acceptance. Byline given sometimes. Offers 50% kill fee. Buys first North American serial or all rights. Editorial lead time 3 months. Submit seasonal material 3 months in advance. Accepts simultaneous submissions. Reports in 6 weeks on queries; 2 months on mss. Sample copy for $4. Writer's guidelines for 9×12 SAE with 6 first-class stamps.

Nonfiction: General interest, how-to, interview/profile, photo feature and travel. Buys 24 mss/year. Send complete ms. Length: 250-1,500 words. Pays 10¢/word minimum for unsolicited articles.

Photos: Send photos with submission. Reviews 35 mm slides, 2×2 transparencies and 8×10 prints. Offers $10-25/photo. Captions, model release and identification of subjects required. Buys one-time or all rights.

Columns/Departments: Pays $25-50.

Tips: "Covers how-to articles: how to succeed in film, video, modeling. How to break into any aspect of the fashion and entertainment industries. Be specific. Send $4 for a sample and specific guidelines. Know the content of *Club Modèle*. We are most open to interviews with celebrities (with photos), and how-to articles."

THE HOLLYWOOD REPORTER, 5055 Wilshire Blvd., Los Angeles CA 90036-4396. (213)525-2000. Fax: (213)525-2377. Website: http://www.hollywoodreporter.com. Publisher/Editor-in-Chief: Robert J. Dowling. Editor: Alex Ben Block. Editorial Director of Special Issues: Randall Tierney. Contact: Matthew King, managing editor. Daily is 10% freelance written. Specials are 90% freelance written. Daily entertainment trade publication emphasizing indepth analysis and news coverage of creative and business aspects of film, TV, theater and music production. Estab. 1930. Circ. 23,000. Publishes ms an average of 1 week after acceptance for daily, 1 month for special issues. Query first.

Tips: "Short articles fit our format best. The most frequent mistake made by writers in completing an article for us is that they are not familiar with our publication. We are a business publication; we don't want celebrity gossip."

OPPORTUNITIES FOR ACTORS & MODELS, A Guide to Working in Cable TV-Radio-Print Advertising, Copy Group, 1900 N. Vine St., Suite 315, Hollywood CA 90068-3980. Fax: (213)464-4575. Editor: Len Miller. 50% freelance written. Works with a small number of new/unpublished writers each year. Monthly newsletter "serving the interests of those people who are (or would like to be) a part of the cable-TV, radio, and print advertising industries." Estab. 1969. Circ. 10,000. **Pays on acceptance.** Publishes ms an average of 3 months after acceptance. Byline given. Buys all rights. Reports in 1 month. Free sample copy and writer's guidelines for #10 SASE.

Nonfiction: How-to, humor, inspirational, interview/profile, local news, personal experience, photo feature, technical (within cable TV). Coverage should include the model scene, little theatre, drama groups, comedy workshops and other related events and places. "Detailed information about your local cable TV station should be an important part of your coverage. Get to know the station and its creative personnel." Buys 120 mss/year. Query. Length: 100-950 words. Pays $50 maximum.

Photos: State availability of photos. Model release and identification of subjects required. Buys one-time or all rights.

Columns/Departments: "We will consider using your material in a column format with your byline." Buys 60 mss/year. Query. Length: 150-450 words. Pays $50 maximum.

Tips: "Good first person experiences, interviews and articles, all related to modeling, acting, little theater, photography (model shots) and other interesting items are needed."

STAGE DIRECTIONS, For and About Regional Community and Academic Theater, *SMW* Communications, Inc., 3101 Poplarwood, Suite 310, Raleigh NC 27604. Fax: (919)872-6888. E-mail: stagedir@aol.com. Editor: Stephen Peithman. 25% freelance written. Magazine published 10 times/year covering theater: community, regional and academic. *"Stage Directions* covers a full range of theater—productions, design, management and marketing. Articles are based on problem-solving." Estab. 1988. Circ. 4,500. Pays on publication. Publishes ms an average of 3 months after acceptance. Byline given. Buys all rights. Editorial lead time 6 months. Submit seasonal material 6 months in advance. Accepts simultaneous submissions, if so noted. Reports in 3 weeks on queries. Sample copy for 9×12 SAE with 2 first-class stamps. Writer's guidelines free on request.

Nonfiction: How-to, new product, personal experience, photo feature, technical. Buys 24 mss/year. Special issues: Sets and Scenery (September); Costumes (January); Summer Learning (February). Query. Length: 350-1,000 words. Pays 10¢/word. Sometimes pays expenses of writers on assignment.

Reprints: Send typed ms with rights for sale noted and information about when and where the article previously appeared. Pays 50% of the amount paid for an original article.

Photos: State availability of photos with submission and describe. Reviews contact sheets, 2×2 transparencies and 5×7 prints. Offers $20/photo. Captions, model releases and identification of subjects required. Buys one-time rights.

Tips: "We are very receptive to new writers, but they must give evidence of quality writing and ability to follow through. Keep story focused and upbeat as you describe a theatrical problem-solving experience or situation. Use quotes from participants/experts."

FARM

The successful farm writer focuses on the business side of farming. For technical articles, editors feel writers should have a farm background or agricultural training, but there are opportunities for the general freelancer too. The following farm publications are divided into six categories, each specializing in a different aspect of farming: crops and soil management; dairy farming; livestock; management; miscellaneous; and regional.

Agricultural Equipment

‡CUSTOM APPLICATOR, Vance Publishing Corp., 6263 Poplar Ave., Suite 540, Memphis TN 38119. (901)767-4020. Fax: (901)767-4026. Editor: Rob Wiley. 50% freelance written. Works with a small number of new/unpublished writers each year. Magazine for firms that sell and custom apply agricultural fertilizer and chemicals. Estab. 1957. Circ. 16,100. **Pays on acceptance.** Publishes ms an average of 2 months after acceptance. Buys all rights. Free sample copy and writer's guidelines.

Nonfiction: "We need articles on spray/dry chemical delivery technology related to the agriculture industry. We are seeing an incredible jump in computer-related technology and software packages for farm and custom application management that need reviewing. And we always need 'people' stories, interviews of actual dealers & applicators." Length: 750-1500 words. Must have photos (color or b&w). Pays 20¢/word.

Reprints: Send typed ms with rights for sale noted and information about when and where the article previously appeared.

Photos: Accepts b&w glossy prints, prefers color. Color slides accepted for cover photos. Pays extra for cover shots.

Tips: "Our audience doesn't need to decipher 'computerese' or 'tech lingo' so make it readable; for a general audience. Conciseness sells here. A story without photos will not be published, so plan that into your work. Our readers are looking for methods to increase efficiency and stay abreast of new government regulations, so accuracy is important."

Crops and Soil Management

CITRUS & VEGETABLE MAGAZINE, 7402 N. 56th St., Suite 560, Tampa FL 33617-7737. (813)980-6386. Fax: (813)980-2871. Editor: Gordon Smith. Contact: Scott Emerson, managing editor. Monthly magazine on the citrus and vegetable industries. Estab. 1938. Circ. 12,000. Pays on publication. Publishes ms an average of 1 month after acceptance. Byline given. Kill fee varies. Buys exclusive first rights. Query first. Reports in 2 months on queries. Free sample copy and writer's guidelines.

Nonfiction: Book excerpts (if pertinent to relevant agricultural issues); how-to (grower interest—cultivation practices, etc.); new product (of interest to Florida citrus or vegetable growers); personal experience; photo feature. Buys 20 mss/year. Query with published clips or send complete ms. Length: approximately 1,200 words. Pays about $200.

Photos: Send photos with submission. Reviews 5×7 prints. Prefers color slides. Offers $15 minimum/photo. Captions and identification of subjects required. Buys first rights.

Columns/Departments: Citrus Summary (news to citrus industry in Florida: market trends, new product lines), Vegetable Vignettes (new cultivars, anything on trends or developments within vegetable industry of Florida). Send complete ms.

Tips: "Show initiative—don't be afraid to call whomever you need to get your information for story together—accurately and with style. Submit ideas and/or completed ms well in advance. Focus on areas that have not been widely written about elsewhere in the press. Looking for fresh copy. Have something to sell and be convinced of its value. Become familiar with the key issues, key players in the citrus industry in Florida. Have a specific idea in mind for a news or feature story and try to submit manuscript at least one month in advance of publication."

GRAIN JOURNAL, Grain Publications, Inc., 2490 N. Water St., Decatur IL 62526. (217)877-8660. Fax: (217)877-6647. Editor: Ed Zdrojewski. 10% freelance written. Bimonthly magazine covering grain handling and merchandising. "*Grain Journal* serves the North American grain industry, from the smallest country grain elevators and feed mills to major export terminals." Estab. 1972. Circ. 11,444. Pays on publication. Publishes ms an average of 2 months after acceptance. Byline sometimes given. Buys first rights. Editorial lead time 2 months. Submit seasonal material 2 months in advance. Accepts simultaneous submissions. Sample copy free on request.

Nonfiction: How-to, interview/profile, new product, technical. Query. Length: 750 words maximum. Pays $100.

Photos: Send photos with submission. Reviews contact sheets, negatives, transparencies, 3×5 prints. Offers $50-100/photo. Captions and identification of subjects required. Buys one-time rights.

Tips: "Call with your idea. We'll let you know if it is suitable for our publication."

‡ONION WORLD, Columbia Publishing, 2809A Fruitvale Blvd., P.O. Box 1467, Yakima WA 98907-1497. (509)248-2452. Fax: (509)248-4056. Editor: D. Brent Clement. 50% freelance written. Monthly magazine covering the world of onion production and marketing for onion growers and shippers. Estab. 1985. Circ. 5,500. Pays on publication. Publishes ms an average of 1 month after acceptance. Byline given. Not copyrighted. Buys first North American serial rights. Submit seasonal material 1 month in advance. Accepts simultaneous submissions. Reports in 1 month. Sample copy for 9×12 SAE with 5 first-class stamps.

Nonfiction: General interest, historical/nostalgic, interview/profile. Buys 60 mss/year. Query. Length: 1,200-1,500 words. Pays $75-150 for assigned articles.

Reprints: Send photocopy of article and information about when and where the article previously appeared. Pays 50% of amount paid for an original article.

Photos: Send photos with submission. Offers no additional payment for photos accepted with ms unless it's a cover shot. Captions, identification of subjects required. Buys all rights.

Tips: "Writers should be familiar with growing and marketing onions. We use a lot of feature stories on growers, shippers and others in the onion trade—what they are doing, their problems, solutions, marketing plans, etc."

• Columbia Publishing also produces *Fresh Cut*, *Packer/Shipper*, *Potato Country* and *Carrot Country*.

‡WESTERN HAY MAGAZINE, Idea Productions, P.O. Box 1177, Royal City WA 99357. (509)346-9456. Fax: (509)346-2808. Editor: John Yearout. 30-50% freelance written. Bimonthly magazine covering Western Hay Production, Processing and Marketing. "Writers must be knowledgeable of hay production and agriculture practices. Stories are to be educational while also being entertaining." Estab. 1993. Circ. 6,000. Pays on publication. Publishes ms an average of 3 months after acceptance. Byline given. Buys simultaneous rights. Editorial lead time 2 months. Submit seasonal material 4 months in advance. Accepts simultaneous submissions. Sample copy for $2.75 and postage. Writer's guidelines free on request.

Nonfiction: How-to (how hay is grown, processed and marketed), interview/profile, new product, personal experience, photo feature, technical. Buys 6-12 mss/year. Query with published clips. Length: 1,000-2,000 words. Sometimes pays expenses of writers on assignment.

Photos: Send photos with submission. Reviews 4×5 prints. Offers $15/photo. Captions and identification of subjects required. Buys all rights.

Columns/Departments: Hay Hauler (stories/experiences of truckers hauling hay), Barns of the West (photos & descriptive history of old barns); A Look Back (historical photos & narrative of old hay scenes); all 1,000 words maximum. Buys 6 mss/year. Query with published clips. Pays $100-150 plus photo payments.

Tips: "Sample material should be ag-oriented if possible. Must demonstrate capability to produce well composed, reproducible photos. Writer should be living in the western states or provinces of Canada so story material can be of local nature. All stories are about hay production in Western US and Canada."

Dairy Farming

DAIRY GOAT JOURNAL, P.O. Box 10, 128 E. Lake St., Lake Mills WI 53551. (414)648-8285. Fax: (414)648-3770. Editor: Dave Thompson. 50% freelance written. Monthly. "We are looking for clear and accurate articles about dairy goat owners, their herds, cheesemaking, and other ways of marketing products. Some readers own two goats; others own 1,500 and are large commercial operations." Estab. 1917. Circ. 8,000, including copies to more than 70 foreign countries. Pays on publication.
Nonfiction: Information on personalities and on public issues affecting dairy goats and their owners. How-to articles with plenty of practical information. Health and husbandry articles should be written with appropriate experience or academic credentials. Buys 100 mss/year. Query with published clips. Makes assignments. Length: 750-2,500 words. Pays $50-150. Pays expenses of writers on assignment.
Photos: Color or b&w. Vertical or horizontal for cover. Goats and/or people. Pays $100 maximum for 35mm slides for covers; $20 to $70 for inside use or for b&w. Accurate identification of all subjects acquired.
Tips: "We love good articles about dairy goats and will work with beginners, if you are cooperative."

THE WESTERN DAIRYMAN, Dept. WM, P.O. Box 819, Corona CA 91718-0819. (909)735-2730. Fax: (909)735-2460. E-mail: westdairy2@aol.com. Editor: Dennis Halladay. 10% freelance written. Prefers to work with published/established writers. Monthly magazine dealing with large herd commercial dairy industry. *Rarely* publishes information about non-Western producers or dairy groups and events. Estab. 1922. Circ. 19,000. Pays on acceptance or publication. Publishes ms an average of 3 months after acceptance. Byline given. Buys first North American serial rights. Submit seasonal material 3 months in advance. Reports in 1 month. Sample copy for 9×12 SAE with 4 first-class stamps.
Nonfiction: Interview/profile, new product, opinion, industry analysis. Special issues: Computers (February); Herd Health (August); Feeds and Feeding (May); Barns and Equipment (November). "No religion, nostalgia, politics or 'mom and pop' dairies." Query or send complete ms. Length: 300-5,000 words. Pays $100-300.
Reprints: Seldom accepts previously published submissions. Send information about when and where the article previously appeared. Pays 50% of amount paid for an original article.
Photos: Send photos with query or ms. Reviews b&w contact sheets and 35mm or $2\frac{1}{4} \times 2\frac{1}{4}$ transparencies. Pays $25 for b&w; $50-100 for color. Captions and identification of subjects required. Buys one-time rights.
• Photos are now a more critical part of story packages.
Tips: "Pretend you're an editor for a moment; would you want to buy a story without any artwork? Neither would I. Writers often don't know modern commercial dairying and they forget they're writing for an audience of *dairymen*. Publications are becoming more and more specialized. You've really got to know who you're writing for and why they're different."

Livestock

‡THE BRAHMAN JOURNAL, Sagebrush Publishing Co., Inc., P.O. Box 220, Eddy TX 76524-0220. (817)859-5451. Editor: Joe Ed Brockett. 10% freelance written. Monthly magazine covering Brahman cattle. Estab. 1971. Circ. 4,000. Pays on publication. Publishes ms an average of 2 months after acceptance. Byline given. Not copyrighted. Buys first North American serial, one-time and second serial (reprint) rights or makes work-for-hire assignments. Submit seasonal/holiday material 3 months in advance. Sample copy for 9×12 SAE with 5 first-class stamps.
Nonfiction: General interest, historical/nostalgic, interview/profile. Special issues: Herd Bull (July); Texas (October). Buys 3-4 mss/year. Query with published clips. Length: 1,200-3,000 words. Pays $100-250.
Reprints: Send typed ms with rights for sale noted. Pays 50% of amount paid for an original article.
Photos: Photos needed for article purchase. Send photos with submission. Reviews 4×5 prints. Offers no additional payment for photos accepted with ms. Captions required. Buys one-time rights.

‡CANADIAN GUERNSEY JOURNAL, Canadian Guernsey Association, 368 Woolwich St., Guelph, Ontario N1H 3W6 Canada. (519)836-2141. Fax: (519)824-9250. Editor: V.M. Macdonald. 10% freelance written. Bimonthly magazine covering diary farming and especially Guernsey cattle. Estab. 1905. Circ. 400. Pays on publication. Publishes ms an average of 3 months after acceptance. Byline given. Buys one-time rights. Editorial lead time 2 months. Sample copy for $5.

ALWAYS ENCLOSE a self-addressed, stamped envelope (SASE) with all your queries and correspondence.

Nonfiction: How-to, humor, new product, personal experience, technical. Buys 2-4 mss/year. Query. Length: 400-2,000 words. Pays $25-150.
Reprints: Accepts previously published submissions.
Photos: Send photos with submission. Negotiates payment individually. Buys one-time rights.
Columns/Departments: Buys 2 mss/year. Pays $25-150.

‡**FEED LOT MAGAZINE**, Feed Lot Limited Partnership, P.O. Box 850, Dighton KS 67839. (316)397-2838. Editor: Robert A. Strong. 40% freelance written. Quarterly magazine covering agricultural/cattle feeding. "The editorial information content fits a dual role: large feedlots and their related cow/calf, operations, and large 500+ cow/calf, stocker operations. The information covers all phases of production from breeding, genetics, animal health, nutrition, equipment design, research through finishing fat cattle. *Feed Lot* publishes a mix of new information and timely articles which directly effect the cattle industry." Estab. 1993. Circ. 12,000. Pays on publication. Publishes ms an average of 3 months after acceptance. Byline given. Offers 50% kill fee. Buys all rights. Editorial lead time 4 months. Submit seasonal material 6 months in advance. Reports in 1 month. Sample copy and writer's guidelines for $1.50.
Nonfiction: Interview/profile, new product (cattle-related). Send complete ms. Length: 100-400 words. Pays 10¢/word.
Photos: State availability of or send photos with submission. Reviews contact sheets. Negotiates payment individually. Captions, model releases required. Buys all rights.
Tips: "Know what you are writing about—have a good knowledge of the subject."

LLAMAS MAGAZINE, The International Camelid Journal, Clay Press, Inc., P.O. Box 100, Herald CA 95638. (209)223-0469. Fax: (209)223-0466. Editor: cheryl Dal Porto. Magazine published 7 times/year covering llamas, alpacas, camels, vicunas and guanacos. Estab. 1979. Circ. 6,000. Pays on publication. Publishes ms an average of 4 months after acceptance. Byline given. Buys first rights, second serial (reprint) rights and makes work-for-hire assignments. Submit seasonal material 6 months in advance. Reports in 1 month. Free sample copy. Writer's guidelines for 8½×11 SAE with $2.90 postage.
Nonfiction: How-to (on anything related to raising llamas), humor, interview/profile, opinion, personal experience, photo feature, travel (to countries where there are camelids). "All articles must have a tie-in to one of the camelid species." Buys 30 mss/year. Query with published clips. Length: 1,000-5,000 words. Pays $50-300 for assigned articles; $50-250 for unsolicited articles. May pay new writers with contributor copies. Sometimes pays the expenses of writers on assignment.
Reprints: Send tearsheet of article and information about when and where the article previously appeared.
Photos: State availability of or send duplicates photos with submission. Reviews transparencies, 5×7 prints. Offers $25-100/photo. Captions, model releases and identification of subjects required. Buys one-time rights.
Fillers: Anecdotes, gags, short humor. Buys 25/year. Length: 100-500 words. Pays $25-50.
Tips: "Get to know the llama folk in your area and query us with an idea. We are open to any and all ideas involving llamas, alpacas and the rest of the camelids. We are always looking for good photos. You must know about camelids to write for us."

‡**NATIONAL CATTLEMEN**, National Cattlemen's Beef Association, 5420 S. Quebec St., Greenwood Village CO 80111-1904. (303)694-0305. Website: http://www.cowtown.org/. Editor: Kendal Frazier. Contact: Colleen Church. Monthly trade journal on the beef-cattle industry. "We deal extensively with animal health, price outlook, consumer demand for beef, costs of production, emerging technologies, developing export markets, marketing and risk management." Estab. 1898. Circ. 40,000. Pays on publication. Byline given. "Buys one-time rights but requires non-compete agreements." Sample copy for 9×12 SAE.
Nonfiction: How-to (cut costs of production, risk management strategies), new product (emerging technologies), opinion, technical (emerging technologies, animal health, price outlook). Query with published clips. Length: 1,000-1,300 words. Sidebars encouraged. Pays $200-300 for assigned articles.
Photos: Send photos with submission. Reviews negatives, transparencies. Identification of subjects required.

SHEEP! MAGAZINE, P.O. Box 10, 128 E. Lake St., Lake Mills WI 53551. (414)648-8285. Fax: (414)648-3770. Editor: Dave Thompson. 50% freelance written. Prefers to work with published/established writers. Monthly magazine. "We're looking for clear, concise, useful information for sheep raisers who have a few sheep to a 1,000 ewe flock." Estab. 1980. Circ. 15,000. Pays on publication. Byline given. Offers $30 kill fee. Buys all rights. Makes work-for-hire assignments. Submit seasonal material 3 months in advance. Free sample copy and writer's guidelines.
Nonfiction: Book excerpts; information (on personalities and/or political, legal or environmental issues affecting the sheep industry); how-to (on innovative lamb and wool marketing and promotion techniques, efficient record-keeping systems or specific aspects of health and husbandry). Health and husbandry articles should be written by someone with extensive experience or appropriate credentials (i.e., a veterinarian or animal scientist); profiles (on experienced sheep producers who detail the economics and management of their operation); features (on small businesses that promote wool products and stories about local and regional sheep producer's groups and their activities); new products (of value to sheep producers; should be written by someone who has used them); technical (on genetics, health and nutrition); first person narratives. Buys

80 mss/year. Query with published clips or send complete ms. Length: 750-2,500 words. Pays $45-150. Pays the expenses of writers on assignment.
Reprints: Send tearsheet or photocopy of article. Pays 40% of amount paid for an original article.
Photos: Color—vertical compositions of sheep and/or people—for cover. Use only b&w inside magazine. Black and white, 35mm photos or other visuals improve chances of a sale. Pays $100 maximum for 35mm color transparencies; $20-50 for 5×7 b&w prints. Identification of subjects required. Buys all rights.
Tips: "Send us your best ideas and photos! We love good writing!"

Management

AGRI-NEWS, Western Livestock Reporter Inc., P.O. Box 30755, Billings MT 59107. (406)259-5406. Fax: (406)259-6888. E-mail: wlrpubs@imt.net. Senior Editor: Chuck Rightmire. Editor: Linda Grosskopf. 5% freelance written. Weekly newspaper covering agriculture. "*Agri-News* follows a generally conservative slant on news and features for agricultural producers and businesses in Montana and northern Wyoming. We focus on general agricultural interests—farming and ranching—in those areas." Estab. 1968. Circ. 17,000. Pays 30 days after publication. Publishes ms an average of 1 month after acceptance. Byline given. Buys first rights. Editorial lead time 1 month. Submit seasonal material 1 month in advance. Accepts simultaneous submissions. Reports in 1 week on queries; 1 month on mss.
Nonfiction: Exposé, general interest, historical/nostalgic, how-to, humor, inspirational, interview/profile, new product, personal experience, (all from agricultural and area viewpoint), photo feature. Buys 24 mss/year. Send complete ms. Length: 1,000 words maximum. Pays $50 for assigned articles; $35 for unsolicited articles. Sometimes pays expenses of writers on assignment.
Reprints: Accepts previously published submissions.
Photos: Send photos with submission. Reviews prints. Offers $7.50/photo. Identification of subjects required. Buys one-time rights.
Tips: "Contact the editor with an idea, submit a final piece, or send a résumé with clips to set up a freelance relationship. Unless assigned, all articles, etc., must be submitted on speculation."

AGWAY COOPERATOR, P.O. Box 4933, Syracuse NY 13221-4933. (315)449-6117. Editor: Sue Zarins. 2% freelance written. Bimonthly magazine for farmers. Estab. 1964. **Pays on acceptance.** Publishes ms an average of 6 months after acceptance. Time between acceptance and publication varies considerably. Usually reports in 1 month. Free sample copy.
Nonfiction: Should deal with topics of farm or rural interest in the Northeastern US. Length: 1,200 words maximum. Pays $150-300, depending on length, illustrations.
Tips: "We prefer an Agway tie-in, if possible. Fillers don't fit into our format. Occasionally assigns freelance articles. We will be acquiring more outside articles on topics of importance to progressive commercial farmers."

FARM & COUNTRY, Ontario's Commercial Farmer Trade Journal, Agricultural Publishing Co., 1 Yonge St., Suite 1504, Toronto, Ontario M5E 1E5 Canada. (416)364-5324. Managing Editor: John Muggeridge. 25% freelance written. Tabloid published 18 times/year covering agriculture. Estab. 1935. Circ. 52,000. Pays on publication. Publishes ms an average of 1 month after acceptance. Not copyrighted. Buys first rights and one-time rights. Editorial lead time 2 weeks. Submit seasonal material 1 month in advance. Reports in 1 month. Sample copy and writer's guidelines free on request.
Nonfiction: Book excerpts, essays, exposé, general interest, historical/nostalgic, how-to, humor, interview/profile, new product, opinion, personal experience, photo feature, technical, travel. Buys 200 mss/year. Query with published clips. Length: 500-1,000 words. Pays $100-400 (Canadian).
Reprints: Accepts previously published submissions.
Photos: Send photos with submission. Reviews 2¼×2¼ transparencies and 4×5 prints. Offers $10-300 (Canadian)/photo. Captions, identification of subjects required. Buys one-time rights.
Columns/Departments: Opinion, humour, how-to (all dealing with agriculture), 700 words. Buys 75 mss/year. Query with published clips. Pays $100-200 (Canadian).

FARM JOURNAL, Centre Square West, 1500 Market St., Philadelphia PA 19102-2181. (215)557-8900. Fax: (215)568-3989. Website: http://www.farmjournal.com. Editor: Earl Ainsworth. Contact: Karen Freiburg, managing editor. Magazine published 13 times/year with many regional editions. Material bought for one or more editions depending upon where it fits. Buys all rights. Byline given "except when article is too short or too heavily rewritten to justify one." **Pays on acceptance.** Payment is the same regardless of editions in which the piece is used.
Nonfiction: Timeliness and seasonableness are very important. Material must be highly practical and should be helpful to as many farmers as possible. Farmers' experiences should apply to one or more of these 8 basic commodities: corn, wheat, milo, soybeans, cotton, dairy, beef and hogs. Technical material must be accurate.

No farm nostalgia. Query to describe a new idea that farmers can use. Length: 500-1,500 words. Pays 10-20¢/published word.

Photos: Much in demand either separately or with short how-to material in picture stories and as illustrations for articles. Warm human-interest-pix for covers—activities on modern farms. For inside use, shots of home-made and handy ideas to get work done easier and faster, farm news photos, and pictures of farm people with interesting sidelines. In b&w, 8×10 glossies are preferred; color submissions should be 2¼×2¼ for the cover and 35mm for inside use. Pays $50 and up for b&w shot; $75 and up for color.

Tips: "*Farm Journal* now publishes in hundreds of editions reflecting geographic, demographic and economic sectors of the farm market."

FORD NEW HOLLAND NEWS, P.O. Box 1895, New Holland PA 17557-0903. Fax: (717)355-3600. Editor: Gary Martin. 50% freelance written. Works with a small number of new/unpublished writers each year. Magazine published 8 times/year on agriculture; designed to entertain and inform farm families. Estab. 1960. **Pays on acceptance.** Publishes ms an average of 6 months after acceptance. Byline given. Offers negotiable kill fee. Buys first North American serial, one-time and second serial (reprint) rights. Submit seasonal material 6 months in advance. Reports in 2 months. Sample copy and writer's guidelines for 9×12 SAE with 2 first-class stamps.

Nonfiction: "We need strong photo support for articles of 1,200-1,700 words on farm management and farm human interest." Buys 40 mss/year. Query. Pays $500-700. Sometimes pays the expenses of writers on assignment.

Reprints: Accepts previously published submissions.

Photos: Send photos with query when possible. Reviews color transparencies. Pays $50-300, $500 for cover shot. Captions, model release and identification of subjects required. Buys one-time rights.

Tips: "We thrive on good article ideas from knowledgeable farm writers. The writer must have an emotional understanding of agriculture and the farm family and must demonstrate in the article an understanding of the unique economics that affect farming in North America. We want to know about the exceptional farm managers, those leading the way in agriculture. We want new efficiencies and technologies presented through the real-life experiences of farmers themselves. Use anecdotes freely. Successful writers keep in touch with the editor as they develop the article."

SMALL FARM TODAY, The How-to Magazine of Alternative Crops, Livestock, and Direct Marketing, Missouri Farm Publishing, Inc., Ridge Top Ranch, 3903 W. Ridge Trail Rd., Clark MO 65243-9525. (573)687-3525. Fax: (573)687-3148. Editor: Ron Macher. Contact: Paul Berg, managing editor. Bimonthly magazine "for small farmers and small-acreage landowners interested in diversification, direct marketing, alternative crops, horses, draft animals, small livestock, exotic and minor breeds, home-based businesses, gardening, vegetable and small fruit crops." Estab. 1984 as *Missouri Farm Magazine*. Circ. 12,000. Pays 30 days after publication. Publishes ms an average of 6 months after acceptance. Byline given. Buys first serial and nonexclusive reprint rights (right to reprint article in an anthology). Submit seasonal/holiday material 4 months in advance. Reports in 3 months. Sample copy for $3. Writer's guidelines available.

Nonfiction: Practical and how-to (small farming, gardening, alternative crops/livestock). Query letters recommended. Length: 500-2,000 words. Pays 3½¢/word.

Reprints: Send information about when and where the article previously appeared. Pays 58% of amount paid for an original article.

Photos: Send photos with submission. Offers $6 for inside photos and $10 for cover photos. Captions required. Pays $4 for negatives or slides. Buys one-time rights and nonexclusive reprint rights (for anthologies).

Tips: "Topic must apply to the small farm or acreage. It helps to provide more practical and helpful information without the fluff."

Regional

‡AGRI-TIMES NORTHWEST, J/A Publishing Co., 206 SE Court, P.O. Box 189, Pendleton OR 97801. (503)276-7845. Fax: (503)276-7964. Editor: Virgil Rupp. Managing Editor: Jim Eardley. 50% freelance written. Biweekly newspaper on agriculture in western Idaho, eastern Oregon and eastern Washington. "News, features about regional farmers/agribusiness *only*." Estab. 1983. Circ. 3,000. Pays on 15th of month after publication. Publishes ms an average of 1 month after acceptance. Byline given. Buys one-time rights. Submit seasonal material 1 month in advance. Accepts simultaneous submissions. Reports in 1 month. Sample copy for 50¢ and 8×10 SAE with 4 first-class stamps. Writer's guidelines for #10 SASE.

Nonfiction: How-to (regional farming and ranching), humor (regional farming and ranching), interview/profile (regional farmers/ranchers), photo feature (regional agriculture), technical (regional farming and ranching). Buys 50 mss/year. Query with or without published clips, or send complete ms. Length: 750 words maximum. Pays 75¢/column inch.

Reprints: Send typed ms with rights for sale noted and information about when and where the article previously appeared. Pays 100% of amount paid for an original article.

Photos: Send photos with submission. Reviews contact sheets, negatives and prints. Offers $5-10/photo. Captions and identification of subjects required. Buys one-time rights.

Columns/Departments: Agri-Talk (quips, comments of farmers/ranchers). Buys 50 mss/year. Send complete ms. Length: 100 words maximum. Pays 75¢ per column inch.

Tips: "Focus on our region's agriculture. Be accurate."

ARKANSAS FARMER, 28 Fontaine Cove, Pontotoc MS 38863. Fax: (601)489-1777. E-mail: eadorris@aol.com. Editor: Eva Ann Dorris. 20% freelance written. Monthly tabloid covering agriculture, commercial farmers and ranchers doing business in Arkansas. Estab. 1985. Circ. 11,700. Pays on publication. Byline given. Negotiable kill fee. Submit seasonal/holiday material 6 weeks in advance. Reports in 3 weeks on queries; 1 month on mss. Sample copy for 9×13 SAE with 3 first class stamps.

Nonfiction: How-to (farming or ranching only), interview/profile (farmer, rancher, agribusiness or legislator), new product, technical (farm oriented products or method). No general interest pieces without relevance to farming. Buys 15-20 mss/year. Query with or without published clips, or send complete ms. Length: 500-1,000 words. Pays $75 without photos, $100 with usable color prints.

Photos: State availability of photos with submission. Reviews contact sheets and 3×5 or larger prints. Offers $5-20/photo. Captions and identification of subjects required. Buys rights to any Rural Press USA publication.

Tips: "Query with good ideas that will be of interest to Arkansas farmers and ranchers. We serve their interests *only*. Keep manuscripts short (15-25 inches maximum). Photos are helpful."

‡FARM FOCUS, Fundy Group Publications, P.O. Box 128, 2 Second St., Yarmouth, Nova Scotia B5A 4B1 Canada. (902)742-7111. Fax: (902)742-2311. Editor: Heather Jones. 50-60% freelance written. Bimonthly newspaper covering agriculture of interest in Atlantic Canada. Estab. 1972. Circ. 9,000. Pays on publication. Publishes ms an average of 1 month after acceptance. Byline given. Offers $20-25 kill fee. Buys first North American serial, first or second serial (reprint) rights. Editorial lead time 1 month. Submit seasonal material 1 month in advance. Accepts previously published submissions. Reports in 2 weeks on queries; 1 month on mss. Sample copy free on request.

Nonfiction: Humor, opinion. Buys 1 mss/year. Query. Length: 1,500 words maximum. Pays per column inch. Pays copies for special columns. Pays expenses of writers on assignment.

Photos: State availability of or send photos with submission. Reviews negatives, transparencies, prints (b&w and color). Offers $10-20/photo. Captions required. Buys one-time rights.

Fiction: Buys 1-2 mss/year. Query. Length: 1,500 words maximum. Pays per column inch.

Tips: "Call with an idea/ideas of their own. Do not ask if any work is available."

‡FARMWEEK, Mayhill Publications, Inc., P.O. Box 90, Knightstown IN 46148-1242. (317)345-5133. Fax: 1(800)318-1055. E-mail: farmwk@aol.com. Editor: Nancy Searfoss. Associate Editor: Amy McKenzie. 5% freelance written. Weekly newspaper that covers agriculture in Indiana, Ohio and Kentucky. Estab. 1955. Circ. 30,000. Pays on publication. Byline given. Buys first rights. Submit seasonal material 1 month in advance. Reporting time varies; up to 1 year. Free sample copy and writer's guidelines.

Nonfiction: General interest (agriculture), interview/profile (ag leaders), new product, photo feature (Indiana, Ohio, Kentucky agriculture). "We don't want first-person accounts or articles from states outside Indiana, Kentucky, Ohio (unless of general interest to all farmers and agribusiness)." Query with published clips. Length: 500-1,500 words. Pays $50 maximum. Sometimes pays expenses of writers on assignment.

Photos: State availability of photos with submission. Reviews contact sheets and 4×5 and 5×7 prints. Offers $10 maximum/photo. Identification of subjects required. Buys one-time rights.

Tips: "We want feature stories about farmers and agribusiness operators in Indiana, Ohio and Kentucky. How do they operate their business? Keys to success? etc. Best thing to do is call us first with idea, or write. Could also be a story about some pressing issue in agriculture nationally that affects farmers everywhere."

‡FLORIDA GROWER AND RANCHER, The Oldest Spokesman For All Aspects of Florida Agriculture, Meister Publishing Co., 1331 N. Mills Ave., Orlando FL 32803. (407)894-6522. Editor: Frank Garner. 25% freelance written. Monthly magazine covering all aspects of Florida agriculture. "The magazine is edited for the Florida farmer with commercial production interest primarily in citrus, vegetables, and other ag endeavors. Our goal is to provide articles which update and inform on such areas as production, ag financing, farm labor relations, technology, safety, education and regulation." Estab. 1907. Circ. 14,000. Pays on publication. Byline given. Buys all rights. Editorial lead time 2 months. Submit seasonal material 3 months in advance. Reports in 1 month. Sample copy for 9×12 SAE with 5 first class stamps. Writer's guidelines free on request.

Nonfiction: Interview/profile, photo feature, technical. Query with published clips. Length: 750-1,500 words. Pays 12¢/word.

Photos: Send photos with submission.

Columns/Departments: Query with published clips. Pays $150-250.

IOWA REC NEWS, 8525 Douglas, Suite 48, Urbandale IA 50322-2992. (515)276-5350. Editor: Jody Garlock. 15% freelance written. Monthly magazine emphasizing energy issues and human interest features for residents of rural Iowa. Estab. 1946. Circ. 116,000. Pays on publication. Publishes ms an average of 3 months after acceptance. Buys first serial and second serial (reprint) rights. Accepts simultaneous submissions. Reports in 2 months.

Nonfiction: General interest, historical, humor, rural lifestyle trends, energy awareness features, photo feature. Send complete ms.

Reprints: Send tearsheet of article and information about when and where the article previously appeared. Pay varies.

Tips: "The easiest way to break into our magazine is: research a particular subject well, include appropriate attributions to establish credibility, authority and include a couple paragraphs about the author. Reading and knowing about rural people is important. Stories that touch the senses or can improve the lives of the readers are highly considered, as are those with a strong Iowa angle. We're also looking for good humor articles. Freelancers have the advantage of offering subject matter that existing staff may not be able to cover. Inclusion of nice photos is also a plus. The most frequent mistakes made by writers are: story too long or too biased; no attribution to any source of info; and not relevant to electric consumers, rural living."

THE LAND, Minnesota's Ag Publication, Free Press Co., P.O. Box 3169, Mankato MN 56002-3169. E-mail: theland@ic.mankato.mn.us. Editor: Randy Frahm. 50% freelance written. Weekly tabloid covering Minnesota agriculture. "We are interested in articles on farming in Minnesota. Although we're not tightly focused on any one type of farming, our articles must be of interest to farmers. In other words, will your article topic have an impact on people who live and work in rural areas?" Estab. 1976. Circ. 40,000. **Pays on acceptance.** Publishes ms an average of 3 months after acceptance. Byline given. Buys first North American serial rights. Editorial lead time 1 month. Submit seasonal material 2 months in advance. Reports in 3 weeks on queries; 2 months on mss. Prefer to work with Minnesota writers. Writer's guidelines for #10 SASE.

Nonfiction: General interest (ag), how-to, interview/profile, personal experience, technical. Buys 15-40 mss/year. Query. Length: 500-1,500 words. Pays $25 minimum for assigned articles.

Photos: State availability of photos with submission. Reviews contact sheets. Negotiates payment individually. Buys one-time rights.

Tips: "Be enthused about rural Minnesota life and agriculture and be willing to work with our editors. We try to stress relevance." Most open to feature articles.

MAINE ORGANIC FARMER & GARDENER, Maine Organic Farmers & Gardeners Association, RR 2, Box 594, Lincolnville ME 04849. (207)763-3043. Editor: Jean English. 40% freelance written. Prefers to work with published/established local writers. Quarterly magazine covering organic farming and gardening for urban and rural farmers and gardeners and nutrition-oriented, environmentally concerned readers. "*MOF&G* promotes and encourages sustainable agriculture and environmentally sound living. Our primary focus is organic farming, gardening and forestry, but we also deal with local, national and international agriculture, food and environmental issues." Estab. 1976. Circ. 10,000. Pays on publication. Publishes ms an average of 8 months after acceptance. Byline and bio given. Buys first North American serial, one-time, first serial or second serial (reprint) rights. Submit seasonal material 1 year in advance. Accepts simultaneous submissions. Reports in 2 months. Sample copy for $2 and SAE with 7 first-class stamps. Free writer's guidelines.

Nonfiction: Book reviews; how-to based on personal experience, research reports, interviews. Profiles of farmers, gardeners, plants. Information on renewable energy, recycling, nutrition, health, non-toxic pest control, organic farm management and marketing. "We use profiles of New England organic farmers and gardeners and news reports (500-1,000 words) dealing with US/international sustainable ag research and development, rural development, recycling projects, environmental and agricultural problems and solutions, organic farms with broad impact, cooperatives and community projects." Buys 30 mss/year. Query with published clips or send complete ms. Length: 1,000-3,000 words. Pays $20-150.

Reprints: Send typed ms with rights for sale noted and information about when and where the article previously appeared. Pays 50% of amount paid for an original article.

Photos: State availability of b&w photos with query; send 3×5 b&w photos with ms. Captions, model releases, identification of subjects required. Buys one-time rights.

Tips: "We are a nonprofit organization. Our publication's primary mission is to inform and educate, but we also want readers to enjoy the articles."

OHIO FARMER, 1350 W. Fifth Ave., Columbus OH 43212. (614)486-9637. Editor: Tim White. 10% freelance written. Magazine for Ohio farmers and their families published 15 issues/year (monthly April-December; biweekly January-March). Estab. 1848. Circ. 60,000. Usually buys all rights. Pays on publication. Publishes ms an average of 2 months after acceptance. Reports in 2 months. Sample copy for $1, SAE with 4 first-class stamps. Free writer's guidelines.

• This magazine is part of Farm Progress Co. State Farm magazine group.

Nonfiction: Technical and on-the-farm stories. Buys informational, how-to and personal experience. Buys 10 mss/year. Submit complete ms. Length: 600-700 words. Pays $200.

Photos: Offers no additional payment for photos purchased with ms. Pays $5-25 for b&w; $35-100 for color. Send 4×5 b&w glossies and transparencies or 8×10 color prints.

Tips: "Freelance submissions must be of a technical agricultural nature. We are actively seeking journalists with a good understanding of production and technical aspects of ag for freelance assignments."

PENNSYLVANIA FARMER, Farm Progress Publications, P.O. Box 4475, Gettysburg PA 17325. (717)334-4300. Fax: (717)334-3120. Editor: John Vogel. 20% freelance written. Monthly farm business magazine "oriented to providing readers with ideas to help their businesses and personal lives." Estab. 1877. Circ. 57,000. Pays on publication. Publishes ms an average of 3 months after acceptance. Buys first-time rights. Submit seasonal material 3 months in advance. Accepts simultaneous submissions. Reports in 1 month. Writer's guidelines for #10 SASE.

Nonfiction: Humor, inspirational, technical. No stories without a strong tie to Mid-Atlantic farming. Buys 15 mss/year. Query. Length: 500-1,000 words. Pays $50-150. Sometimes pays the expenses of writers on assignment.

Photos: Send photos with submission. Reviews 35mm transparencies. Pays $25-300 for each color photo accepted with ms. Captions and identification of subjects required.

‡**WYOMING RURAL ELECTRIC NEWS**, P.O. Box 380, Casper WY 82602-0380. (307)234-6152. Fax: (307)234-4115. Editor: Kris Wendtland. 10% freelance written. Monthly magazine for audience of small town residents, vacation-home owners, farmers and ranchers. Estab. 1950. Circ. 31,000. Byline given. Pays on publication. Publishes ms an average of 1 month after acceptance. Buys first serial rights. Submit seasonal material 2 months in advance. Reports in 3 months. Sample copy for SAE with 3 first-class stamps.

Nonfiction and Fiction: Wants science articles with question/answer quiz at end—test your knowledge. Buys electrical appliance articles. No nostalgia. No sad stories. Articles welcome that put present and/or future in positive light. Submit complete ms. Buys 4-10 mss/year. Length: 500-800 words. Pays $25-45.

Reprints: Sometimes buys reprints. Pays 30% of amount paid for an original article.

Photos: Pays up to $40 for cover photos. Color only.

Tips: "Study an issue or two of the magazine to become familiar with our focus and the type of freelance material we're using. We're always looking for positive humor. Always looking for fresh, new writers, original perspectives. Submit entire manuscript. Don't submit a regionally set story from some other part of the country. Photos and illustrations (if appropriate) are always welcomed."

FINANCE

These magazines deal with banking, investment and financial management. Publications that use similar material but have a less technical slant are listed under the Consumer Business and Finance section.

‡**BANK MARKETING MAGAZINE**, 1120 Connecticut Ave., Washington DC 20036. (202)663-5070. Fax: (202)828-4540. E-mail: tlian@aba.com. Editor: Tanja Lian. 20-60% freelance written. Monthly magazine covering marketing financial services and related topics—customer service, batabase. "We use several approaches: how-tos; indepth discussion of a marketing philosophy or approach; case studies; interviews; and profiles." Estab. 1968. Circ. 5,000. **Pays on acceptance**. Publishes ms an average of 2 after acceptance. Byline given. Offers 20% kill fee. Buys first North American serial rights. Editorial lead time 5 months. Submit seasonal material 6 months in advance. Reports in 3 weeks on queries; 2 months on mss. Sample copy for 9×12 SAE with $1.50 postage. Writer's guidelines free on request.

Nonfiction: Book excerpts, essays, historical/nostalgic, how-to, inspirational/motivational, interview/profile, opinion, case study. Buys 20-30 mss/year. Query with published clips. Length: 2,300-3,000 words. Pays $500-750. Sometimes pays expenses of writers on assignment.

Photos: State availability of or send photos with submission. Reviews contact sheets, negatives, transparencies, prints. Negotiates payment individually. Captions, model releases, identification of subjects required. Buys one-time rights.

Tips: "Be prepared with a clear story outline to pitch (if you have an idea), complete with sources. Too many people call and say 'a recent study shows' without being able to say which study. If you want an assignment, please send clips! Also indicate if you can send manuscript on diskette—very useful."

‡**BUYSIDE, Ideas For Today's Money Managers**, Buyside, Ltd., P.O. Box 1329, Sonoma CA 95476. (707)935-9200. Fax: (707)935-9300. E-mail: mail@buyside.com. Managing Editor: Lauren Keyson. 100% freelance written. Monthly magazine covering stocks; investment ideas. Estab. 1994. Circ. 30,000. Pays on publication. Publishes ms an average of 2 months after acceptance. Byline given. Offers 50% kill fee. Buys

first rights. Editorial lead time 1 month. Submit seasonal material 3 months in advance. Accepts simultaneous submissions. Sample copy and writer's guidelines free on request.

Nonfiction: Opinion, financial (buyside, sellside). Buys 80 mss/year. Query. Length: 750-3,000 words. Pays $375-3,000. Pays expenses of writers on assignment.

Photos: Query first. Reviews contact sheets, negatives, 4×5 transparencies, 3×5 prints. Offers $50-500/photos. Negotiates payment individually. Buys one-time rights.

Columns/Departments: Take Five (financial humor), 500 words; Small Cap, 500 words. Query.

Fiction: Humorous (financial). Buys 12 mss/year. Query. Length: 450-500 words. Pays $375-500.

Tips: "Be knowledgeable about a particular industry—keep abreast of news, make contacts with analysts, heads of public companies and IR (investor relation) firms. Know the investment thesis and secular reason for writing on the industry."

THE FEDERAL CREDIT UNION, National Association of Federal Credit Unions, P.O. Box 3769, Washington DC 20007-0269. (703)522-4770. Fax: (703)524-1082. E-mail: tfcu@nafcunet.org. Website: http://www.nafcunet.org. Editor: Patrick M. Keefe. Contact: Robin Johnston, managing editor. 25% freelance written. "Looking for writers with financial, banking or credit union experience, but will work with inexperienced (unpublished) writers based on writing skill." Bimonthly magazine covering credit unions. Estab. 1967. Circ. 8,200. Pays on publication. Publishes ms an average of 3 months after acceptance. Byline given. Buys first North American serial rights. Submit seasonal material 5 months in advance. Accepts simultaneous submissions. Reports in 2 months. Sample copy for 10×13 SAE with 5 first-class stamps. Writer's guidelines for #10 SASE.

Nonfiction: Query with published clips and SASE. Length: 1,200-2,000 words. Query. Pays $200-800.

Reprints: Send ms with rights for sale noted and information about when and where the article previously appeared.

Photos: Send photos with submission. Reviews 35mm transparencies and 5×7 prints. Offers no additional payment for photos accepted with ms. Model releases and identification of subjects required. Buys all rights.

Tips: "Provide résumé or listing of experience pertinent to subject. Looking only for articles that focus on events in Congress, regulatory agencies or technological developments applicable to financial institutions."

ILLINOIS BANKER, Illinois Bankers Association, 111 N. Canal St., Suite 1111, Chicago IL 60606-7204. (312)876-9900. Fax: (312)876-3826. Editor: Kathleen Gill. "Our audience is approximately 3,000 bankers and vendors related to the banking industry. The purpose of the publication is to educate and inform readers on major public policy issues affecting banking today, as well as provide new ideas that can be applied to day-to-day operations and management. Writers may not sell or promote a product or service." Estab. 1891. Circ. 2,500. Publishes ms an average of 3 months after acceptance. Reports in 3 months. Byline given. Buys first North American serial rights. Editorial lead time 8 weeks. Accepts simultaneous submissions. Sample copy and writer's guidelines free on request.

Nonfiction: Essays, historical/nostalgic, interview/profile, new product, opinion, personal experience, financially related. "It is *IBA* policy that writers do not sell or promote a particular product, service or organization within the content of an article written for publication." Buys 3-5 mss/year. Query. Length: 1,000-1,500 words.

Reprints: Send tearsheet of article or short story or typed ms with rights for sale noted and information about when and where the article previously appeared.

Photos: State availability of photos with submission. Reviews contact sheets, negatives, transparencies and prints. Captions and identification of subjects required.

Tips: "We appreciate that authors contact the editor before submitting articles to discuss topics. Articles published in *Illinois Banker* address current issues of key importance to the banking industry in Illinois. Our intention is to keep readers informed of the latest industry news, developments and trends, as well as provide necessary technical information. We publish articles on any topic that affects the banking industry, provided the content is in agreement with Association policy and position. Because we are a trade association, most articles need to be reviewed by an advisory committee before publication; therefore, the earlier they are submitted the better. Some recent topics include: agriculture, bank architecture, commercial and consumer credit, marketing, operations/cost control, security and technology. In addition, articles are also considered on the topics of economic development and business/banking trends in Illinois and the Midwest region."

NAPFA ADVISOR, The Newsletter for Fee-Only Financial Advisors, National Association of Personal Financial Advisors, 355 West Dundee Rd., Suite 107, Buffalo Grove IL 60089. (708)537-7723. Editor: Margery Wasserman. Contact: Peter Phillips, managing editor. 60% freelance written. Monthly newsletter covering financial planning. "*NAPFA Advisor* publishes practice management and investment strategy articles targeted to fee-only financial advisors. Topics that relate to comprehensive financial planning geared to the practitioner are desired. Readers range from sole practitioners to members of larger firms." Estab. 1985. Circ. 1,000. Pays on publication. Publishes ms an average of 3 months after acceptance. Byline given. Buys first North American serial, first, one-time or second serial (reprint) rights. Editorial lead time 2 months. Submit seasonal material 3 months in advance. Accepts simultaneous submissions. Reports in 3 months on queries. Sample copy for 9×12 SAE with 4 first-class stamps.

Nonfiction: Reviews of financial planning books and software programs, financial planning issues, practice management tips. Buys 50 mss/year. Query. Length: 750-2,000 words. Pays 20¢/word up to $300.
Reprints: Send tearsheet of article.
Photos: State availability of photos with submission. Reviews 5×7 prints. Offers no additional payment for photos accepted with ms. Captions, model releases, identification of subjects required. Buys one-time rights.
Columns/Departments: Practice Profile (assigned), 1,700-2,000 words; Book Reviews (fee-only planning perspective), 750-1,500 words; Software Reviews (fee-only planning perspective), 750-1,500 words. Pays 20¢/word up to $300.
Tips: "All writing must be directed to the financial practitioner, not the consumer. Freelancers who are interested in writing for *NAPFA Advisor* will have a strong background in financial planning, investment, and practice management issues and will understand the differences between fee-only, fee-based, fee and commission, and commission-based financial planning."

FISHING

NORTHERN AQUACULTURE, Harrison House Publishers, 4611 William Head Rd., Victoria, British Columbia V9B 5T7 Canada. (604)478-9209. Fax: (604)478-1184. Editor: Peter Chettleburgh. 50% freelance written. Works with a small number of new/unpublished writers each year. Bimonthly magazine covering aquaculture in Canada and northern US. Estab. 1985. Circ. 4,000. Pays on publication. Publishes ms an average of 3 months after acceptance. Byline given. Buys first North American serial rights. Submit seasonal material 5 months in advance. Reports in 3 weeks. Sample copy for 9×12 SAE with $2 IRCs. Free writer's guidelines.
Nonfiction: How-to, interview/profile, new product, opinion, photo feature. Buys 20-24 mss/year. Query. Length: 200-1,500 words. Pays 10-20¢/word for assigned articles; 10-15¢/word for unsolicited articles. May pay writers with contributor copies if writer requests. Sometimes pays the expenses of writers on assignment.
Photos: Send photos with submission. Reviews 5×7 prints. Captions required. Buys one-time rights.

WESTCOAST FISHERMAN, Westcoast Publishing Ltd., 1496 West 72 Ave., Vancouver, British Columbia V6P 3C8 Canada. (604)266-8611. Fax: (604)266-6437. E-mail: wcoast@west-coast.com. Website: http://www.west-coast.com. Editor: David Rahn. 40% freelance written. Monthly trade journal covering commercial fishing in British Columbia. "We're a non-aligned magazine dedicated to the people in the B.C. commercial fishing industry. Our publication reflects and celebrates the individuals and communities that collectively constitute B.C. fishermen." Estab. 1986. Pays on publication. Publishes ms an average of 3 months after acceptance. Byline given. Buys first and one-time rights. Reports in 2 months.
Nonfiction: Interview/profile, photo feature, technical. Buys 30-40 mss/year. Query with or without published clips, or send complete ms. Length: 250-2,500 words. Pays $25-450.
Reprints: Send photocopy of article or typed ms with rights for sale noted and information about when and where the article previously appeared. Pays 100% of amount paid for an original article.
Photos: Send photos with submission. Reviews contact sheets, negatives, transparencies and 5×7 prints. Offers $5-100/photo. Identification of subjects required. Buys one-time rights.
Poetry: Avant-garde, free verse, haiku, light verse, traditional. "We use poetry written by or for West Coast fishermen." Buys 6 poems/year. Length: 1 page. Pays $25.

FLORISTS, NURSERIES AND LANDSCAPERS

Readers of these publications are involved in growing, selling or caring for plants, flowers and trees. Magazines geared to consumers interested in gardening are listed in the Consumer Home and Garden section.

FLORIST, The FTD Association, 29200 Northwestern Hwy., P.O. Box 2227, Southfield MI 48037-2227. (313)355-9300. Fax: (810)948-6415. Editor-in-Chief: William P. Golden. Contact: Barbara Koch, managing editor. 5% freelance written. Monthly magazine for retail flower shop owners, managers and floral designers. Other readers include floriculture growers, wholesalers, researchers and teachers. Circ. 28,000. **Pays on acceptance.** Publishes ms an average of 2 months after acceptance. Buys one-time rights. Pays 10-25% kill fee. Reports in 1 month.
Nonfiction: Articles should pertain to marketing, merchandising, financial management or personnel management in a retail flower shop. Also, giftware, floral and interior design trends. No general interest, fiction or personal experience. Buys 5 unsolicited mss/year. Query with published clips. Length: 1,200-2,500 words. Pays $200-400.
Photos: State availability of photos with query. Pays $10-25 for 5×7 b&w photos or color transparencies. Buys one-time rights.

Tips: "Business management articles must deal specifically with retail flower shops and their unique merchandise and concerns. Send samples of published work with query. Suggest several ideas in query letter."

GROWERTALKS, Ball Publishing, 335 N. River St., P.O Box 9, Batavia IL 60510. (708)208-9080. Fax: (708)208-9350. E-mail: growertalk@aol.com. Website: http://www.growertalks.com. Managing Editor: Chris Beytes. 50% freelance written. Monthly magazine covering ornamental horticulture—primarily greenhouse flower growers. "*GrowerTalks* serves the commercial greenhouse grower. Editorial emphasis is on floricultural crops: bedding plants, potted floral crops, foliage and fresh cut flowers. Our readers are growers, managers and owners. We're looking for writers who've had experience in the greenhouse industry." Estab. 1937. Circ. 10,500. Pays on publication. Publishes ms an average of 6 months after acceptance. Byline given. Buys first North American serial rights. Editorial lead time 4 months. Submit seasonal material 6 months in advance. Reports in 1 month. Sample copy and writer's guidelines free on request.
Nonfiction: How-to (time- or money-saving projects for professional flower/plant growers); interview/profile (ornamental horticulture growers); personal experience (of a grower); technical (about growing process in greenhouse setting). "No articles that promote only one product." Buys 36 mss/year. Query. Length: 1,200-1,600 words. Pays $125 minimum for assigned articles; $75 minimum for unsolicited articles. Sometimes pays in other premiums or contributor copies.
Photos: State availability of photos with submission. Reviews 2½×2½ slides and 3×5 prints. Negotiates payment individually. Captions, model releases and identification of subjects required. Buys one-time rights.
Tips: "Discuss magazine with ornamental horticulture growers to find out what topics that have or haven't appeared in the magazine interest them."

THE GROWING EDGE, New Moon Publishing Inc., 215 SW Second, Suite 201, P.O. Box 1027, Corvallis OR 97339-1027. (541)757-2511. Fax: (541)757-0028. E-mail: tcoene@peak.org. Website: http://www.teleport/com/~tomalex. Editor: Trisha Coene. 85% freelance written. Quarterly magazine signature covering indoor and outdoor high-tech gardening techniques and tips. Estab. 1980. Circ. 20,000. Pays on publication. Publishes ms an average of 3 months after acceptance. Byline given. Buys first serial and reprint rights. Submit seasonal material at least 6 months in advance. Reports in 3 months. Sample copy for $7. Writer's guidelines for #10 SASE.
Nonfiction: Book excerpts and reviews relating to high-tech gardening, general interest, how-to, interview/profile, personal experience, technical. Query first. Length: 500-2,500 words. Pays 10¢/published word.
Photos: Pays $175/color cover photos; $25-50/inside photo. Pays on publication. Credit line given. Buys first and reprint rights.
Tips: Looking for more hydroponics articles and information which will give the reader/gardener/farmer the "growing edge" in high-tech gardening and farming on topics such as high intensity grow lights, water conservation, drip irrigation, advanced organic fertilizers, new seed varieties and greenhouse cultivation.

‡**LANDSCAPE DESIGN**, Adams/Green Industry Publishing, 68860 Perez Rd., Suite J, Cathedral City CA 92234. (619)770-4370. Fax: (619)770-8019. Website: http://www.aip.com. Editor: Nancy Sappington. 35% freelance written. Monthly magazine covering landscape design and garden design. "*Landscape Design* features topics such as site amenities, plant materials, irrigation, erosion control, paving concepts and water features. Also, features large and small projects, designer profiles and problem-solving techniques and design methodologies." Estab. 1987. Circ. 14,000. Pays on publication. Publishes ms an average of 3 months after acceptance. Byline given. Buys all rights. Editorial lead time 1 month. Submit seasonal material 3 months in advance. Accepts simultaneous submissions. Sample copy and writer's guidelines free on request.
Nonfiction: Book excerpts, essays, how-to, new product, opinion, personal experience, photo feature, technical. Special issues: Trends in Land Planning (November); Planting for Color (December). No product endorsements. Buys 8 mss/year. Send complete ms. Length: 1,000-3,000 words. Pays $50-275.
Reprints: Accepts previously published submissions.
Photos: Send photos with submission. Reviews 35mm or 4×5 transparencies, prints. Offers no additional payment for photos accepted with ms. Captions required. Buys one-time rights.
Tips: "Request an editorial calendar—choose topics that might be of interest to our readers and pitch them in one or two paragraphs."

‡**LINK MAGAZINE**, Wholesale Florists and Florist Suppliers of America, P.O. Box 639, Vienna VA 22183. (703)242-7000. Fax: (703)319-1647. Editor: Lisa Mickey. 1% freelance written. Monthly magazine covering wholesale floristry. "*Link Magazine* covers floral and business issues that help WF & FSA members run their companies more effectively." Estab. 1978. Circ. 1,800. **Pays on acceptance.** Publishes ms an average of 2 months after acceptance. Byline given. Buys first North American serial rights. Editorial lead time 2 months. Submit seasonal material 4 months in advance. Accepts simultaneous submissions. Reports in 1 month. Sample copy for 8½×11 SAE with 7 first-class stamps.
Nonfiction: General interest (business, economics), technical (floriculture). Buys 5-10 mss/year. Query. Length: 1,500-2,500 words. Pays $200.

Reprints: Accepts previously published submissions.

Photos: State availability of photos with submission. Offers no additional payment for photos accepted with ms. Captions, model releases and identification of subjects required. Buys one-time rights.

Tips: Looking for "business articles centering on new laws, new management techniques, new technology or family business issues are most desirable. Learn something about *Link*'s audience. Articles that are too broad aren't accepted."

ORNAMENTAL OUTLOOK, The Professional Magazine for the Professional Grower, Meister Publishing Co., 1331 N. Mills Ave., Orlando FL 32803-2598. (407)894-6522. Fax: (407)894-6511. Editor: Kris Sweet. 50% freelance written. Bimonthly magazine covering ornamental horticulture. "*Ornamental Outlook* is written for commercial growers of ornamental plants in Florida. Our goal is to provide interesting and informative articles on such topics as production, legislation, safety, technology, pest control, water management and new varieties as they apply to Florida growers." Estab. 1991. Circ. 12,500. Pays 30 days after publication. Publishes ms an average of 4 months after acceptance. Byline given. Buys all rights. Editorial lead time 2 months. Submit seasonal material 3 months in advance. Reports in 1-3 months. Sample copy for 9×12 SAE with 5 first-class stamps. Writer's guidelines free on request.

Nonfiction: Interview/profile, photo feature, technical. "No first-person articles. No word-for-word meeting transcripts or all-quote articles." Query with published clips. Length: 750-1,000 words. Pays $250/article including photos.

Photos: Send photos with submission. Reviews contact sheets, transparencies and prints. Offers $50-100/ photo. Captions and identification of subjects required. Buys one-time rights.

Tips: "I am most impressed by written queries that address specific subjects of interest to our audience, which is the *Florida* grower of *commercial* horticulture. Our biggest demand is for features, about 1,000 words, that follow subjects listed on our editorial calendar (which is sent with guidelines). Please do not send articles of national or consumer interest."

TREE CARE INDUSTRY MAGAZINE, National Arborist Association, P.O. Box 1094, Amherst NH 03031-1094. (800)733-2622. Editor: Peter Gerstenberger. 50% freelance written. Monthly magazine covering tree care and landscape maintenance. Estab. 1990. Circ. 25,000. Pays on publication. Publishes ms an average of 3 months after acceptance. Byline given. Buys first North American serial rights. Editorial lead time 10 weeks. Submit seasonal material 3 months in advance. Reports in 2 weeks on queries; 2 months on mss. Sample copy for 9×12 SAE with 6 first-class stamps. Writer's guidelines free on request.

Nonfiction: Book excerpts, general interest, historical/nostalgic, humor, interview/profile, new product, personal expeience, technical. Buys 10 mss/year. Query with published clips Length: 900-3,500 words. Payment negotiable. Sometimes pays expenses of writers on assignment.

Photos: Send photos with submission. Reviews prints. Negotiates payment individually. Captions, identification of subjects required. Buys one-time rights.

Columns/Departments: Management Exchange (business management-related), 1,200-1,800 words; Industry Innovations (inventions), 1,200 words; From The Field (OP/ED from practioners), 1,200 words. Buys 40 mss/year. Send complete ms. Pays $100 and up.

Tips: "Preference is given to writers with background and knowledge of the tree care industry; our focus is relatively narrow. Preference is also given to photojournalists willing to work on speculation."

‡TURF MAGAZINE, P.O. Box 391, 50 Bay St., St. Johnsbury VT 05819. (802)748-8908. Fax: (802)748-1866. E-mail: turfmag@aol.com. Publishers: Francis Carlet and Dan Hurley. Managing Editor: Bob Labbance. 40% freelance written. "Our readers are professional turf grass managers: superintendents of grounds for golf courses, cemeteries, athletic fields, parks, recreation fields, lawn care companies, landscape contractors/architects." Estab. 1977. Four regional editions: North, South, Central and West; with a combined national circulation of 58,000. Pays on publication. Byline given. Buys all rights or makes work-for-hire assignments. Submit seasonal material 3 months in advance. Reports in 3 months. Sample copy for 10×13 SAE with 8 first-class stamps.

Nonfiction: How-to, interview/profile, opinion, technical. "We use on-the-job type interviews with good b&w photos that combine technical information with human interest." Buys 80 mss/year. Query with clips or send complete ms. Pays $100 for columns; $200 minimum for feature stories. Often pays expenses of writers on assignment.

Photos: Send photos with ms. Payment for photos is included in payment for articles. Reviews b&w prints. Needs a variety of photos with the story. Also seeking color transparencies for cover.

Tips: "Turf scoops and high profile articles preferred."

GOVERNMENT AND PUBLIC SERVICE

Listed here are journals for people who provide governmental services at the local, state or federal level or for those who work in franchised utilities. Journals for city managers, politicians, bureaucratic decision makers, civil servants, firefighters, police officers, public administrators, urban transit managers and utilities managers are listed in this section.

THE CALIFORNIA HIGHWAY PATROLMAN, California Association of Highway Patrolmen, 2030 V Street, Sacramento CA 95818-1730. (916)452-6751. Editor: Carol Perri. 60% freelance written. Monthly magazine covering CHP info, California history, history of vehicles and/or transportation. "Our readers are either uniformed officers or pro-law enforcement." Estab. 1937. Circ. 20,000. Pays on publication. Publishes ms an average of 9 months after acceptance. Byline given. Buys one-time rights. Submit seasonal material 6 months in advance. Accepts simultaneous submissions. Reports in 1 month on queries, up to 3 months on mss. Sample copy for 9×12 SAE with 5 first-class stamps. Writer's guidelines for #10 SASE.
Nonfiction: General interest, historical/nostalgic, humor, interview/profile, photo feature, technical, travel. "No 'how you felt when you received a ticket (or survived an accident)!' No fiction." Buys 80-100 mss/year. Query with or without published clips, or send complete ms. No telephone queries. Length: 750-3,000 words. Pays 5¢/word or $50 minimum.
Reprints: Send tearsheet or photocopy of article telling when and where the article previously appeared.
Photos: State availability of photos with submission. Send photos (or photocopies of available photos) with submission. Reviews prints. Offers $5/photo. Captions and identification of subjects required. Returns all photos. Buys one-time rights.
　● Articles with accompanying photos receive preference.

CAMPAIGNS AND ELECTIONS, 1020 1511 K St., NW, Washington DC 20005. (202)638-7788. Editor: Ron Faucheux. 30% freelance written. Magazine published 10 times/year covering US campaigns and elections; political professionals. Estab. 1980. Circ. 83,000. Publishes ms an average of 2 months after acceptance. Byline given. Offers negotiable kill fee. Buys first North American serial rights. Reports in 2 weeks on queries; 3 weeks on mss. Sample copy for 9×12 SAE with 5 first class stamps. Free writer's guidelines.
Nonfiction: Political campaign case studies, local news, how-to, humor/political, interview/profile/political, new product campaign industry, personal experience/political and technical/political-campaign industry. "Nothing unrelated to campaign industry. No policy 'issues,' i.e., abortion, health care, etc." Query with or without published clips, or send complete ms. Length: 400-2,800 words.
Reprints: Send typed ms with rights for sale noted.
Photos: Send photos with submission. Reviews contact sheets, negatives, transparencies, 5×7 prints. Offers no additional payment for photos. Captions, identification of subjects required. Buys one-time rights.
Columns/Departments: Inside Politics (tales involving political professionals—unpublished information), 400 words; From the Field (from the campaign trail-hard, fast, unpublished), 200 words. Buys 15 mss/year. Query. Length: 200-400 words.
Fillers: Anecdotes, short humor "must be political, true, unpublished." Buys 6 items/year. Length: 100-250 words.
Tips: "Call—discuss a topic. Understand we write for candidates, elected officials and the political professionals who support them, with how-to help, and case studies (always sought). Also information on corporate public affairs and grassroots lobbying."

CHIEF OF POLICE MAGAZINE, National Association of Chiefs of Police, 3801 Biscayne Blvd., Miami FL 33137. (305)573-0070. Executive Editor: Jim Gordon. Bimonthly trade journal for law enforcement commanders (command ranks). Circ. 13,500. **Pays on acceptance.** Publishes ms an average of 6 months after acceptance. Byline given. Buys first rights. Submit seasonal material 6 months in advance. Accepts simultaneous submissions. Reports in 2 weeks. Sample copy for $3 and 9×12 SAE with 5 first-class stamps. Writer's guidelines for #10 SASE.
Nonfiction: General interest, historical/nostalgic, how-to, humor, inspirational, interview/profile, new product, personal experience, photo feature, religious, technical. "We want stories about interesting police cases and stories on any law enforcement subject or program that is positive in nature. No exposé types. Nothing anti-police." Buys 50 mss/year. Send complete ms. Length: 600-2,500 words. Pays $25-75 for assigned articles; $10-50 for unsolicited articles. Sometimes (when pre-requested) pays the expenses of writers on assignment.
Reprints: Accepts previously published submissions.
Photos: Send photos with submission. Reviews 5×6 prints. Pays $5-10 for b&w; $10-25 for color. Captions required. Buys one-time rights.
Columns/Departments: New Police (police equipment shown and tests), 200-600 words. Buys 6 mss/year. Send complete ms. Pays $5-25.
Fillers: Anecdotes, short humor, law-oriented cartoons. Buys 100/year. Length: 100-1,600 words. Pays $5-25.
Tips: "Writers need only contact law enforcement officers right in their own areas and we would be delighted. We want to recognize good commanding officers from sergeant and above who are involved with the commu-

nity. Pictures of the subject or the department are essential and can be snapshots. We are looking for interviews with police chiefs and sheriffs on command level with photos."

CORRECTIONS FORUM, Partisan Publishing Inc., 320 Broadway, Bethpage NY 11714. Fax: (516)942-3606. Editor: George Abruzzese. 60% freelance written. Monthly magazine covering prison and jail management. Estab. 1992. Circ. 11,000. Pays on publication. Publishes ms an average of 2 months after acceptance. Byline given. Editorial lead time 3 months. Submit seasonal material 3 months in advance. Accepts simultaneous submissions. Reports in 1 month on queries; 6 months on unsolicited mss. Sample copy for 9×12 SAE with 5 first-class stamps.
Nonfiction: How-to (as done by peers successfully), humor, interview/profile, new product, technical. Buys 10 mss/year. Query. Length: 750-2,000 words. Pays $200-300 for assigned articles; $150-200 for unsolicited articles. Sometimes pays expenses of writers on assignment.
Reprints: Accepts previously published submissions.
Photos: Send photos with submission. Offers no additional payment for photos accepted with ms. Captions, identification of subjects required. Buys all rights.
Filler: Anecdotes, gags to be illustrated by cartoonist, newsbreaks, short humor. Buys 3/year. Length: 500-750 words. Pays $100-150.
Tips: Looking for interesting treatment of common themes, in-depth technology treatment for layman, brief, thorough coverage of complex topics.

FIRE CHIEF, Argus Inc., a division of Intertec Publishing Corp., 35 E. Wacker Dr., Suite 700, Chicago IL 60601. (312)726-7277. Fax: (312)726-0241. E-mail: firechfmag@connectinc.com. Website: http://www.argusinc.com. Editor: Scott Baltic. 90% freelance written. Monthly magazine covering fire department management and leadership. "*Fire Chief* is the management magazine of the fire service, addressing the administrative, personnel, training, prevention/education, professional development and operational issues faced by chiefs and other fire officers, whether in paid, volunteer or combination departments." Estab. 1956. Circ. 44,000. Pays on publication. Publishes ms an average of 6 months after acceptance. Byline given. Offers 50% kill fee. Buys first, one-time, second serial (reprint) or all rights. Editorial lead time 2 months. Submit seasonal material 4 months in advance. Reports in 1 month on queries; 2 months on mss. Sample copy and writer's guidelines free on request.
Nonfiction: How-to, technical. Buys 50-60 mss/year. Query with published clips. Length: 1,500-8,000 words. Pays $50-400. Sometimes pays expenses of writers on assignment.
Photos: State availability of photos with submissions. Reviews transparencies, prints. Negotiates payment individually. Captions, identification of subjects required. Buys one-time rights.
Tips: "Writers who are unfamiliar with the fire service are very unlikely to place anything with us. Many pieces that we reject are either too unfocused or too abstract. We want articles that help keep fire chiefs well informed and effective at their jobs."

FIREHOUSE MAGAZINE, PTN Publishing, 445 Broad Hollow Rd., Suite 21, Melville NY 11747. (516)845-2700. Fax: (516)845-7109. Editor-in-Chief: Harvey Eisner. 85% freelance written. Works with a small number of new/unpublished writers each year. Monthly magazine covering fire service. "*Firehouse* covers major fires nationwide, controversial issues and trends in the fire service, the latest firefighting equipment and methods of firefighting, historical fires, firefighting history and memorabilia. Fire-related books, fire safety education, hazardous materials incidents and the emergency medical services are also covered." Estab. 1976. Circ. 127,000. Pays on publication. Byline given. Exclusive submissions only. Sample copy for 9×12 SAE with 7 first-class stamps. Writer's guidelines free.
Nonfiction: Book excerpts (of recent books on fire, EMS and hazardous materials); historical/nostalgic (great fires in history, fire collectibles, the service of yesteryear); how-to (fight certain kinds of fires, buy and maintain equipment, run a fire department); technical (on almost any phase of firefighting, techniques, equipment, training, administration); trends (controversies in the fire service). No profiles of people or departments that are not unusual or innovative, reports of nonmajor fires, articles not slanted toward firefighters' interests. No poetry. Buys 100 mss/year. Query with or without published clips, or send complete ms. Length: 500-3,000 words. Pays $50-400 for assigned articles; $50-300 for unsolicited articles. Sometimes pays expenses of writers on assignment.
Photos: Send photos with query on ms. Pays $15-45 for b&w prints; $20-200 for transparencies and color prints. Cannot accept negatives. Captions and identification of subjects required.
Columns/Departments: Training (effective methods); Book Reviews; Fire Safety (how departments teach fire safety to the public); Communicating (PR, dispatching); Arson (efforts to combat it). Buys 50 mss/year. Query or send complete ms. Length: 750-1,000 words. Pays $100-300.
Tips: "Read the magazine to get a full understanding of the subject matter, the writing style and the readers before sending a query or manuscript. Send photos with manuscript or indicate sources for photos. Be sure to focus articles on firefighters."

FOREIGN SERVICE JOURNAL, Dept. WM, 2101 E St. NW, Washington DC 20037-2990. (202)338-8244. Fax: (202)338-6820. Editor: Karen Krebsbach. 75% freelance written. Monthly magazine for Foreign

Service personnel and others interested in foreign affairs and related subjects. Estab. 1924. Pays on publication. Publishes ms an average of 3 months after acceptance. Byline given. Buys first North American serial rights. Reports in 1 month. Sample copy for $3.50 and 10×12 SAE with 6 first-class stamps. Writer's guidelines for SASE.

Nonfiction: Uses articles on "diplomacy, professional concerns of the State Department and Foreign Service, diplomatic history and articles on Foreign Service experiences. Much of our material is contributed by those working in the profession. Informed outside contributions are welcomed, however." Query. Buys 15-20 unsolicited mss/year. Length: 1,000-4,000 words. Offers honoraria.

Fiction: Publishes short stories about foreign service life in the annual August fiction issue.

Tips: "We're more likely to want your article if it has something to do with diplomacy or US foreign policy."

‡**GOVERNMENT INFORMATION & IMAGING TECHNOLOGY**, GI Communications Corp., 1738 Elton Rd., Suite 304, Silver Spring MD 20903. (301)445-4405. E-mail: wminami@aol.com. Editor: Wayde R. Minami. Bimonthly tabloid covering information technology as used by government. "We prefer general interest articles with a government and imaging/information technology slant. Should be understandable by readers with little technical background." Estab. 1992. Circ. 32,000. Pays on publication. Publishes ms an average of 6 months after acceptance. Byline given. Buys first North American serial and electronic rights. Editorial lead time 2 months. Submit seasonal material 2 months in advance. Sample copy for $5. Writer's guidelines for #10 SASE.

Nonfiction: Book excerpts, general interest, how-to (imaging technology conversion and related), humor, interview/profile, opinion, personal experience, technical. No poetry, fiction, overly-technical articles. Query with published clips. Send complete ms. Length: 500-2,000 words. Pays $200.

Reprints: Accepts previously published submissions.

Photos: Send photos with submission. Reviews transparencies and prints. Offers no additional payment for photos accepted with ms. Captions required. Buys one-time rights.

Columns/Departments: Commentary (policy, management, technical issues) 1,500 words. Query with published clips. Send complete ms.

Tips: Include photos and other graphics. Include brief bio, article summary and statement that article is offered for sale in cover letter; give publication history of article if previously published. Don't get overly technical if it can be avoided.

HEADWAY, (formerly *National Minority Politics*), 13555 Bammel N. Houston, Suite 227, Houston TX 77066. (713)444-4265. Fax: (713)583-9534. Website: http://www.townhall.com/headwaymag. Editor: Gwenevere Daye Richardson. 10-15% freelance written. Monthly award-winning opinion and news magazine taking a moderate to conservative political approach. Estab. 1988. Circ. 15,000. Pays on publication. Publishes ms an average of 1 month after acceptance. Byline given. Buys one-time rights. Editorial lead time 2 months. Submit seasonal material 2 months in advance. Accepts simultaneous submissions. Reports in 1 month on queries. Sample copy and writer's guidelines on request for $2.

Nonfiction: Exposé, interview/profile, commentary and features on national political topics. "These topics can be, but are not limited to, those which are considered traditionally 'minority' concerns. But prefer those which give a broad view or analysis of national or regional political elections, trends, issues, and economic issues as well." Buys approximately 24 mss/year. Query with published clips. Length: 750-1,000 words. Pays $150-250 for assigned articles; $100 for unsolicited mss.

Columns/Departments: The Nation (commentaries on national issues), 750-1,000 words; features, 1,000-1,500 words; Speaking Out, (personal commentary), 750-1,000 words.

Fillers: Political cartoons. Pays $25.

Tips: "Submissions must be well-written, timely, have depth and take an angle not generally available in national newspapers and magazines. Since our magazine takes a moderate to conservative approach, we prefer not to receive commentaries which do not fall in either of these categories."

‡**THE JOURNAL OF SAFE MANAGEMENT OF DISRUPTIVE AND ASSAULTIVE BEHAV-IOR**, Crisis Prevention Institute, Inc., 3315-K N. 124th St., Brookfield WI 53005. Fax: (414)783-5906. E-mail: cpi@execpc.com. Editor: Diana B. Kohn. 20% freelance written. Quarterly journal covering safe management of disruptive and assaultive behavior. "Our audience is human service and business professionals concerned about workplace violence issues. *CPI* is the world leader in violence prevention training." Estab. 1992. Circ. 8,000. Estab. 1992. Pays on publication. Publishes ms an average of 6 months after acceptance. Byline given. Offers 50% kill fee. Buys one-time and second serial (reprint) rights. Editorial lead time 6 months. Submit seasonal material 3 months in advance. Reports in 1 month on queries. Sample copy and writer's guidelines free.

Nonfiction: Interview/profile, new product, opinion, personal experience, research. Inquire for editorial calendar. Buys 30-40 mss/year. Query. Length: 1,500-3,000 words. Pays $50-300 for assigned articles; $50-100 for unsolicited mss.

Reprints: Accepts previously published submissions.
Tips: "Writers can inquire more about what our company does and how our resources fit in the marketplace. We can provide them with a good background on CPI if they write or e-mail us."

LAW AND ORDER, Hendon Co., 1000 Skokie Blvd., Wilmette IL 60091. (847)256-8555. Fax: (847)256-8574. E-mail: 71171.1344@compuserve.com. Editor: Bruce W. Cameron. 90% freelance written. Prefers to work with published/established writers. Monthly magazine covering the administration and operation of law enforcement agencies, directed to police chiefs and supervisors. Estab. 1952. Circ. 38,000. Pays on publication. Publishes ms an average of 6 months after acceptance. Byline given. Buys first North American serial rights. Submit seasonal material 3 months in advance. Reports in 1 month. Sample copy for 9×12 SAE. Free writer's guidelines.
Nonfiction: General police interest; how-to (do specific police assignments); new product (how applied in police operation); technical (specific police operation). Special issues: Buyers Guide (January); Communications (February); Training (March); International (April); Administration (May); Small Departments (June); Mobile Patrol (July); Equipment (August); Weapons (September); Police Science (November); Community Relations (December). No articles dealing with courts (legal field) or convicted prisoners. No nostalgic, financial, travel or recreational material. Buys 150 mss/year. Length: 2,000-3,000 words. Query; no simultaneous queries. Pays 10¢/word for professional writers; 5¢/word for others.
Photos: Send photos with ms. Reviews transparencies and prints. Identification of subjects required. Buys all rights.
Tips: "*L&O* is a respected magazine that provides up-to-date information that chiefs can use. Writers must know their subject as it applies to this field. Case histories are well received. We are upgrading editorial quality—stories *must* show some understanding of the law enforcement field. A frequent mistake is not getting photographs to accompany article."

LAW ENFORCEMENT TECHNOLOGY, PTN Publishing Co., 445 Broad Hollow Rd., #21, Melville NY 11747. Fax: (516)845-2797. Editor: Donna Rogers. 50% freelance written. Monthly magazine covering police management and technology. Estab. 1974. Circ. 35,000. Pays on publication. Publishes ms an average of 6 months after acceptance. Byline given. Offers 25% kill fee. Buys first North American serial rights. Editorial lead time 6 months. Submit seasonal material 6 months in advance. Reports in 1 month on queries; 2 months on mss. Sample copy for SAE with 6 first-class stamps. Writer's guidelines for #10 SASE.
Nonfiction: Book excerpts, how-to, humor, interview/profile, photo feature, police management and training. Buys 15 mss/year. Query. Length: 800-1,800 words. Pays $75-300 for assigned articles.
Photos: Send photos with submission. Reviews contact sheets, transparencies, 5×7 or 8×10 prints. Offers no additional payment for photos accepted with ms. Captions required. Buys one-time rights.
Fiction: Adventure, condensed novels, historical, humorous, mystery, novel excerpts, slice-of-life vignettes, suspense, (all must be police oriented). Buys 4 mss/year. Send complete ms. Length: 1,000-2,000 words. Pays $150-300.
Tips: "Writer should have background in police work or currently work for a police agency. Most of our articles are technical or supervisory in nature. Please query first after looking at a sample copy."

9-1-1 MAGAZINE, Official Publications, Inc., 18201 Weston Place, Tustin CA 92680-2251. (714)544-7776. Fax: (714)838-9233. E-mail: magazn911@aol.com. Editor: Randall Larson. 85% freelance written. Bimonthly magazine for knowledgeable public safety communications and response personnel and those associated with those respective professions. "*9-1-1 Magazine* is published to provide information valuable to all those interested in this exciting and rewarding profession." Estab. 1947. Circ. 20,000. Pays on publication. Publishes ms an average of 2 months after acceptance. Byline given. Offers 20% kill fee. Buys one-time and second serial (reprint) rights. Submit seasonal material well in advance. Accepts simultaneous submissions. Reports in 2 months on queries; 3 months on mss. Sample copy for 9×12 SAE with 5 first-class stamps. Writer's guidelines for #10 SASE.
Nonfiction: Incident report, new product, photo feature, technical. Buys 10 mss/year. Query with SASE. "We prefer queries, but will look at manuscripts on speculation. Most positive responses to queries are considered on spec, but occasionally we will make assignments." Length: 1,000-2,500 words. Pays $100-300 for unsolicited articles.
Photos: Send photos with submission. Reviews color transparencies and prints. Offers $25-300/photo. Captions and identification of subjects required. Buys one-time rights.
Fillers: Cartoons. Buys 10/year. Pays $25-50.
Tips: "What we don't need are 'my first call' articles, or photography of a less-than-excellent quality. We seldom use poetry or fiction. *9-1-1 Magazine* is published for a knowledgeable, up-scale professional. Our primary considerations in selecting material are: quality, appropriateness of material, brevity, knowledge of our readership, accuracy, accompanying photography, originality, wit and humor, a clear direction and vision, and proper use of the language."

PLANNING, American Planning Association, 122 S. Michigan Ave., Suite 1600, Chicago IL 60603. (312)431-9100. Editor: Sylvia Lewis. 25% freelance written. Monthly magazine emphasizing urban planning for adult, college-educated readers who are regional and urban planners in city, state or federal agencies or in private business or university faculty or students. Estab. 1972. Circ. 30,000. Pays on publication. Publishes ms an average of 3 months after acceptance. Buys all rights. Byline given. Reports in 2 months. Sample copy and writer's guidelines for 9×12 SAE with 5 first-class stamps.

Nonfiction: Exposé (on government or business, but topics related to planning, housing, land use, zoning); general interest (trend stories on cities, land use, government); how-to (successful government or citizen efforts in planning, innovations, concepts that have been applied); technical (detailed articles on the nitty-gritty of planning, zoning, transportation but no footnotes or mathematical models). Also needs news stories up to 400 words. "It's best to query with a fairly detailed, one-page letter. We'll consider any article that's well written and relevant to our audience. Articles have a better chance if they are timely and related to planning and land use and if they appeal to a national audience. All articles should be written in magazine feature style." Buys 2 features and 1 news story/issue. Length: 500-2,000 words. Pays $100-900. "We pay freelance writers and photographers only, not planners."

Photos: "We prefer that authors supply their own photos, but we sometimes take our own or arrange for them in other ways." State availability of photos. Pays $25 minimum for 8×10 matte or glossy prints and $200 for 4-color cover photos. Captions required. Buys one-time rights.

POLICE, Hare Publications, 6300 Yarrow Dr., Carlsbad CA 92009-1597. (619)438-2511. Fax: (619)931-5809. Editor: Randall C. Resch. 90% freelance written. Monthly magazine covering topics related to law enforcement officers. "Our audience is primarily law enforcement personnel such as patrol officers, correction officers, detectives and security police." Estab. 1968. Circ. 58,000. **Pays on acceptance.** Publishes ms an average of 6 months after acceptance. Buys all rights (returned to author 45 days after publication). Submit theme material 6 months in advance. Reports in 3 months. Sample copy for $2. Writer's guidelines for #10 SAE with 2 first-class stamps.

Nonfiction: General interest, interview/profile, new product, personal experience, technical. Buys 30 mss/year. Query only. Length: 2,000-3,000 words. Pays $250-350.

Photos: Send photos with submission. Reviews color transparencies. Captions required. Buys all rights.

Columns/Departments: The Beat (entertainment section—humor, fiction, first-person drama, professional tips); The Arsenal (weapons, ammunition and equipment used in the line of duty); Fit For Duty (fitness, nutrition, mental health life style changes); Officer Survival (theories, skills and techniques used by officers for street survival); Behind the Wheel (traffic investigation/accident investigation); New Age (what's new in community policing). Buys 50 mss/year. Query only. Length: 1,000-2,500 words. Pays $75-250.

Tips: "You are writing for police officers—people who live a dangerous and stressful life. Study the editorial calendar—yours for the asking—and come up with an idea that fits into a specific issue. We are actively seeking talented writers."

POLICE AND SECURITY NEWS, DAYS Communications, Inc., 15 Thatcher Rd., Quakertown PA 18951-2503. (215)538-1240. Fax: (215)538-1208. Editor: James Devery. 40% freelance written. Bimonthly tabloid on public law enforcement and private security. "Our publication is designed to provide educational and entertaining information directed toward management level. Technical information written for the expert in a manner that the non-expert can understand." Estab. 1985. Circ. 20,964. Pays on publication. Publishes ms an average of 2 months after acceptance. Byline given. Buys first North American serial rights. Accepts simultaneous submissions. Sample copy and writer's guidelines for 9×12 SAE with $1.93 postage.

Nonfiction: Al Menear, articles editor. Exposé, historical/nostalgic, how-to, humor, interview/profile, opinion, personal experience, photo feature, technical. Special issue: SWAT/Tactical (November). Buys 12 mss/year. Query. Length: 200-4,000 words. Pays 10¢/word. Sometimes pays in trade-out of services.

Reprints: Accepts previously published submissions.

Photos: State availability of photos with submission. Reviews 3×5 prints. Offers $10-50/photo. Buys one-time rights.

Fillers: Facts, newsbreaks, short humor. Buys 6/year. Length: 200-2,000 words. Pays 10¢/word.

POLICE TIMES, American Federation of Police, 3801 Biscayne Blvd., Miami FL 33137. (305)573-0070. Fax: (305)573-9819. Executive Editor: Jim Gordon. 80% freelance written. Eager to work with new/unpublished writers. Bimonthly tabloid covering "law enforcement (general topics) for men and women engaged in law enforcement and private security, and citizens who are law and order concerned." Circ. 55,000. **Pays on acceptance.** Publishes ms an average of 6 months after acceptance. Byline given. Buys second serial (reprint) rights. Submit seasonal material 4 months in advance. Accepts simultaneous submissions. Sample copy for $2.50 and 9×12 SAE with 3 first-class stamps. Writer's guidelines for #10 SASE.

Nonfiction: Book excerpts; essays (on police science); exposé (police corruption); general interest; historical/nostalgic; how-to; humor; interview/profile; new product; personal experience (with police); photo feature; technical—all police-related. "We produce a special edition on police killed in the line of duty. It is mailed May 15 so copy must arrive six months in advance. Photos required." No anti-police materials. Buys 50 mss/year. Send complete ms. Length: 200-4,000 words. Pays $5-50 for assigned articles; $5-25 for unsolicited articles.

Reprints: Accepts previously published submissions.

Photos: Send photos with submission. Reviews 5×6 prints. Offers $5-25/photo. Identification of subjects required. Buys all rights.

Columns/Departments: Legal Cases (lawsuits involving police actions); New Products (new items related to police services); Awards (police heroism acts). Buys variable number of mss/year. Send complete ms. Length: 200-1,000 words. Pays $5-25.

Fillers: Anecdotes, facts, newsbreaks, cartoons, short humor. Buys 100/year. Length: 50-100 words. Pays $5-10. Fillers are usually humorous stories about police officer and citizen situations. Special stories on police cases, public corruptions, etc. are most open to freelancers.

TRANSACTION/SOCIETY, Bldg. 4051, Rutgers University, New Brunswick NJ 08903. (908)445-2280 ext. 83. Fax: (908)445-3138. E-mail: lhorowit@gandalf.rutgers.edu. Website: www/transactionpub.com. Editor: Irving Louis Horowitz. Publisher: Mary E. Curtis. 10% freelance written. Prefers to work with published/established writers. Bimonthly magazine for social scientists (policymakers with training in sociology, political issues and economics). Estab. 1962. Circ. 45,000. Buys all rights. Byline given. Pays on publication. Publishes ms an average of 6 months after acceptance. Reports in 3 months. Sample copy and writer's guidelines for 9×12 SAE with 5 first-class stamps.

Nonfiction: Brigitte M. Goldstein, managing editor. "Articles of wide interest in areas of specific interest to the social science community. Must have an awareness of problems and issues in education, population and urbanization that are not widely reported. Articles on overpopulation, terrorism, international organizations. No general think pieces." Query. Payment for assigned articles only; *no payment for unsolicited articles.*

Photos: Douglas Harper, photo editor. Pays $200 for photographic essays done on assignment or accepted for publication.

Tips: "Submit an article on a thoroughly unique subject, written with good literary quality. Present new ideas and research findings in a readable and useful manner. A frequent mistake is writing to satisfy a journal, rather than the intrinsic requirements of the story itself. Avoid posturing and editorializing."

YOUR VIRGINIA STATE TROOPER MAGAZINE, Virginia State Police Association, 6944 Forest Hill Ave., Richmond VA 23225. Editor: Rebecca V. Jackson. 40% freelance written. Triannual magazine covering police topics for troopers and special agents (state police), non-sworn members of the department and legislators. Estab. 1974. Circ. 5,000. **Pays on acceptance.** Publishes ms an average of 3 months after acceptance. Byline given. Buys first North American serial, one-time rights and all rights on assignments. Submit seasonal material 4 months in advance. Accepts simultaneous submissions. Reports in 2 months. No sample copies.

Nonfiction: Exposé (consumer or police-related); general interest; fitness/health; tourist (VA sites); historical/nostalgic; how-to; book excerpts/reports (law enforcement related); humor, interview/profile (notable police figures); technical (radar); other (recreation). Buys 55-60 mss/year. Query with clips or send complete ms. Length: 2,500 words. Pays $250 maximum/article (10¢/word). Sometimes pays expenses of writers on assignment.

Reprints: Send typed ms with rights for sale noted and information about when and where the article previously appeared.

Photos: Send photos with ms. Pays $50 maximum for several 5×7 or 8×10 b&w glossy prints to accompany ms. Cutlines and model releases required. Buys one-time rights.

Cartoons: Send copies. Pays $20. Buys one-time rights. Buys 20 cartoons/year.

Fiction: Adventure, humorous, mystery, novel excerpts, suspense. Buys 3 mss/year. Send complete ms. Length: 2,500 words minimum. Pays $250 maximum (10¢/word) on acceptance.

Tips: In addition to items of interest to the VA State Police, general interest is stressed.

GROCERIES AND FOOD PRODUCTS

In this section are publications for grocers, food wholesalers, processors, warehouse owners, caterers, institutional managers and suppliers of grocery store equipment. See the section on Confectionery and Snack Foods for bakery and candy industry magazines.

CANADIAN GROCER, Maclean-Hunter Ltd., Maclean Hunter Building, 777 Bay St., Toronto, Ontario M5W 1A7 Canada. (416)596-5772. Fax: (416)593-3162. Website: http://www.mhbizlink.com/bizlink. Editor: George H. Condon. Assistant Editor: Julie Cooper. 40% freelance written. Prefers to work with published/established writers. Monthly magazine about supermarketing and food retailing for Canadian chain and independent food store managers, owners, buyers, executives, food brokers, food processors and manufacturers. Estab. 1886. Circ 18,500. **Pays on acceptance.** Publishes an average of 2 months after acceptance.

Byline given. Buys first Canadian rights. Submit seasonal material 2 months in advance. Reports in 2 months. Sample copy for $5.

Nonfiction: Interview (Canadian trendsetters in marketing, finance or food distribution); technical (store operations, equipment and finance); news features on supermarkets. "Freelancers should be well versed on the supermarket industry. We don't want unsolicited material. Writers with business and/or finance expertise are preferred. Know the retail food industry and be able to write concisely and accurately on subjects relevant to our readers: food store managers, senior corporate executives, etc. A good example of an article would be 'How a dairy case realignment increased profits while reducing prices, inventory and stock-outs.' " Query with clips of previously published work. Phone queries OK. Pays 30¢/word. Pays the expenses of writers on assignment.

Reprints: Send typed ms with rights for sale noted and information about when and where the article previously appeared. Pays 50% of amount paid for an original article.

Photos: State availability of photos. Pays $10-25 for prints or slides. Captions preferred. Buys one-time rights.

Tips: "Suitable writers will be familiar with sales per square foot, merchandising mixes and efficient consumer response."

FDM (FOOD DISTRIBUTION MAGAZINE), Products and Promotions for Mainstream Distribution, National Food Distribution Network, 406 Water St., Warren RI 02885-0330. Fax: (401)245-4699. E-mail: nfdn@aol.com. Editor: Ty Davis. 40% freelance written. Monthly magazine covering the specialty food industry. "We are looking for pieces of interest to supermarket buyers, food distributors, and gourmet and specialty food stores. Quality writing, interesting and informative articles." Estab. 1958. Circ. 35,000. Pays on publication. Publishes ms an average of 2 months after acceptance. Byline given. Buys all rights. Editorial lead time 2-4 months. Submit seasonal material 4 months in advance. Reports in 2 months. Sample copy for $5.

● *Food Distribution* is looking to use more freelancers from across the nation, and is particularly interested in retailer profile features and indepth looks at specialty food retail operations.

Nonfiction: Humor, new product, photo feature. Buys 3-10 mss/year. Query with published clips. Length: 1,000-3,000 words. Pay negotiable. Often pays expenses of writers on assignment.

Reprints: Send information about when and where the article appeared. Pays negotiable rate.

Photos: Send color photos with submission. Reviews transparencies, prints. Negotiates payment individually. Buys one-time rights or all rights.

Tips: Query first with clips. Send color photos with story.

FLORIDA GROCER, Florida Grocer Publications, Inc., P.O. Box 430760, South Miami FL 33243-0760. (305)441-1138. Fax: (305)661-6720. Editor: Dennis Kane. 3% freelance written. "*Florida Grocer* is a 19,500-circulation monthly trade newspaper, serving members of the food industry in Florida, Georgia, Alabama, North and South Carolina. Our publication is edited for chain and independent food store owners and operators as well as members of allied industries." Estab. 1956. **Pays on acceptance.** Byline given. Buys all rights. Submit seasonal material 3 months in advance. Reports in 2 months. Sample copy for 10×14 SAE with 10 first-class stamps.

Nonfiction: Book excerpts, exposé, general interest, humor, features on supermarkets and their owners, new product, new equipment, photo feature, video. Buys variable number of mss/year. Query with or without published clips or send complete ms. Payment varies. Sometimes pays the expenses of writers on assignment.

Photos: State availability of photos with submission. Terms for payment on photos "included in terms of payment for assignment."

Tips: "We prefer feature articles on new stores (grand openings, etc.), store owners, operators; food manufacturers, brokers, wholesalers, distributors, etc. We also publish a section in Spanish and also welcome the above types of materials in Spanish (Cuban)."

THE FOOD CHANNEL, America's Source For Food Trends, Noble & Associates, 515 N. State, 29th Floor, Chicago IL 60610. (312)644-4600. E-mail: jscroggins@foodchannel.com. Editor: John Scroggins. 30% freelance written. Biweekly electronic newsletter covering food trends. "*The Food Channel* is published by Noble & Associates, a food-focused advertising, promotional marketing and new product development company. *The Food Channel* provides insight into emerging trends in the food and beverage industries and the implications for manufacturers, suppliers and consumers. Our print publication no longer exists—we are totally electronic." Estab. 1988. Circ. 2,500. Pays on publication. Publishes ms an average of 2 months after acceptance. Byline given. Editorial lead time 2 months. Reports in 1 month. Sample copy and writer's guidelines free on request.

Nonfiction: Trends in food marketing, consumer behavior, future of food. Length: 500-1,100 words. Pays 50¢/word.

Columns/Departments: Buys 15 mss/year. Query.

Tips: "We are most open to 500-1,100-word articles covering food marketing trends. Using freelancers for very focused articles on legislation, specialty foods and demographics as related to food."

‡FOODSERVICE DIRECTOR, Bill Communications, 355 Park Ave. S., New York NY 10010. (212)592-6533. Fax: (212)592-6539. Editor: Walter J. Schruntek. Managing Editor: Karen Weisberg. 20% freelance written. Monthly tabloid on non-commercial foodservice operations for operators of kitchens and dining halls in schools, colleges, hospitals/health care, office and plant cafeterias, military, airline/transportation, correctional institutions. Estab. 1988. Circ. 45,000. Pays on publication. Byline given sometimes. Offers 25% kill fee. Buys all rights. Submit seasonal material 3 months in advance. Accepts simultaneous submissions. Free sample copy.
Nonfiction: How-to, interview/profile. Buys 60-70 mss/year. Query with published clips. Length: 700-900 words. Pays $250-500. Sometimes pays the expenses of writers on assignment.
Photos: Send photos with submission. Reviews transparencies. Offers no additional payment for photos accepted with ms. Identification of subjects required. Buys all rights.
Columns/Departments: Equipment (case studies of kitchen/serving equipment in use), 700-900 words; Food (specific category studies per publication calendar), 750-900 words. Buys 20-30 mss/year. Query. Pays $150-250.

FRESH CUT MAGAZINE, The Magazine for Value-added Produce, Columbia Publishing, P.O. Box 1467, Yakima WA 98907. (509)248-2452. Fax: (509)248-4056. E-mail: columbia@wolfenet.com. Editor: Ken Hodge. 40% freelance written. Monthly magazine covering minimally processed fresh fruits and vegetables, packaged salads, etc. "We want informative articles about processing produce. We also want stories about how these products are sold at retail, in restaurants, etc." Estab. 1993. Circ. 9,500. Pays on publication. Publishes ms an average of 2 months after acceptance. Byline given. Buys all rights. Editorial lead time 2 months. Submit seasonal material 3 months in advance. Reports in 1 month on queries; 2 months on mss. Sample copy for 9 × 12 SASE. Writer's guidelines for #10 SASE.
Nonfiction: Historical/nostalgic, new product, opinion, technical. Buys 20-40 mss/year. Query with published clips. Special issues: Retail issue (May 97); Foodservice issue (August 97). Pays $125-200 for assigned articles; $75-125 for unsolicited articles.
Photos: Send photos with submission. Reviews transparencies. Offers no additional payment for photos accepted with ms. Identification of subjects required. Buys one-time rights.
Columns/Departments: Packaging; Food Safety; Processing/engineering. Buys 20 mss/year. Query. Pays $125-200.
Fillers: Facts. Length: 300 words maximum. Pays $25-50.

GOURMET NEWS, United Publications, 38 Lafayette St., Box 1056, Yarmouth ME 04096. (207)846-0600. Editor: Joanne Friedrick. 10% freelance written. Monthly tabloid covering gourmet and specialty food industry. "We are a business newspaper covering the gourmet food industry. Our readers are gourmet food retailers and distributors and articles should be written with them in mind. We do not write about gourmet restaurants." Estab. 1991. Circ. 22,000. Pays on publication. Publishes ms an average of 2 months after acceptance. Byline given. Offers $50 kill fee. Buys first rights. Editorial lead time 2 months. Reports in 4 months on queries.
Nonfiction: General interest, news articles, such as trends and issues. Buys 5-10 mss/year. Query. No unsolicited mss. Length: 800-2,000 words. Pays $100-500. Sometimes pays expenses of writers on assignment.
Photos: State availability of photos with submissions. Reviews transparencies, prints. Offers no additional payment for photos accepted with ms.
Tips: "If you are a proven writer with proven skills, I will consider assigning articles to you. If you are relatively new in journalism, be prepared to pitch a specific story with a news angle. There must be a news angle, such as a trend in gourmet foods (growth of teas, organic foods, the growing influence of men in buying food) or an issue."

THE GOURMET RETAILER, 3301 Ponce De Leon Blvd., #300, Coral Gables FL 33134-7273. (305)446-3388. Fax: (305)446-2868. Executive Editor: Michael Keighley. 30% freelance written. Monthly magazine covering specialty foods and housewares. "Our readers are owners and managers of specialty food and upscale housewares retail units. Writers must know the trade exceptionally well and be research-oriented." Estab. 1979. Circ. 21,000. Pays on publication. Publishes ms an average of 3 months after acceptance. Byline sometimes given. No kill fee. Buys all rights. Submit seasonal material 6 months in advance. Reports in 2 months on queries. Free sample copy and writer's guidelines.
Nonfiction: Interview/profile (retail stores, manufacturers). Buys 12 mss/year. Query with published clips. No unsolicited mss. Length: 1,500-2,200 words.
Photos: State availability of photos with submission. Reviews negatives, 5 × 7 transparencies, 8 × 10 prints. Offers $15-25/photo. Identification of subjects required. Buys one-time rights.
Tips: "I enjoy hearing from established business writers. I am looking for upmarket food/housewares news; and for profiles of specialty retailers. We are extremely stringent on editorial quality."

GROCERY DISTRIBUTION MAGAZINE, The Magazine for Physical Distribution and Plant Development for the Food Industry, Trend Publishing, Inc., 625 N. Michigan Ave., #2500, Chicago IL

60611. Fax: (312)654-2323. E-mail: TrayDough3@aol.com. Editor: Richard W. Mulville. 35% freelance written. Bimonthly magazine covering food distribution. "Edited for executives responsible for food warehousing/transportation functions." Estab. 1975. Circ. 15,000. **Pays on acceptance.** Publishes ms an average of 2 months after acceptance. No byline. Offers 100% kill fee. Buys all rights. Editorial lead time 1 month. Reports in 2 weeks on queries. Writer's guidelines free on request.

Nonfiction: How-to (emphasize case history articles detailing use of systems or equipment by food distributors). Buys 4-5 mss/year. Query with published clips. Length: 1,500-3,000. Pays $150-400 (more if photos submitted by writer). Sometimes pays expenses of writers on assignment (if overnight travel required).

Photos: State availability of photos with submissions. Reviews contact sheets, negatives, 3×5 transparencies or prints. "All forms acceptable, usually make agreement before hand." Negotiates payment individually. Captions, identification of subjects required. Buys all rights.

Tips: "Write advising us of availability to do articles. If indicated, we send form for freelancer to complete and return to us (gives us information on territory covered, experience, payment expected, photographic abilities, etc."

HEALTH FOODS BUSINESS, PTN Publishing Co., 2 University Plaza, Suite 11, Hackensack NJ 07601. (201)487-7800. Fax: (201)487-1061. Editor: Gina Geslewitz. 70% freelance written. Monthly magazine covering health foods. "The business magazine for natural products retailers." Estab. 1953. Circ. 12,600. Pays on publication. Publishes ms an average of 3 months after acceptance. Byline given. Buys first North American serial rights. Editorial lead time 4 months. Submit seasonal material 3 months in advance. Reports in 1 month on queries. Sample copy for $3. Writer's guidelines free on request.

Nonfiction: Store profile. Query. Pays $125-150.

Photos: State availability of photos with submissions.

Tips: "We are always looking for well-written store profiles with lots of detailed information, but new writers should always query first to receive writer's guidelines and other directions."

PACKER/SHIPPER, Columbia Publishing, P.O. Box 1467, Yakima WA 98907. (509)248-2457. Fax: (509)248-4056. E-mail: columbia@wolfenet.com. Editor: Ken Hodge. 75-100% freelance written. Magazine published 8 times/year covering packing, shipping and marketing fresh fruit and vegetables. Estab. 1992. Circ. 8,900. Pays on publication. Publishes ms an average of 2 months after acceptance. Byline given. Buys all rights. Editorial lead time 2 months. Submit seasonal material 3 months in advance. Accepts simultaneous submissions. Reports in 2 weeks on queries; 2 months on mss. Sample copy for 9×12 SASE.

Nonfiction: Historical/nostalgic, interview/profile, new product, opinion, technical. Buys 10-12 mss/year. Query. Length: 750-1,200 words. Pays $125-300 for assigned articles; $75-125 for unsolicited articles.

Photos: State availability of photos with submissions. Reviews contact sheets, transparencies, prints. Offers no additional payment for photos accepted with ms. Captions, identification of subjects required. Buys one-time rights.

Columns/Departments: Machinery; Sanitation/food safety; Marketing/packaging. Buys 70 mss/year. Query. Pays $125-200.

Fillers: Facts. Length: 100-300 words. Pays $25-50.

PRODUCE NEWS, 2185 Lemoine Ave., Fort Lee NJ 07024-6003. Fax: (201)592-0809. Editor: Gordon Hochberg. 10-15% freelance written. Works with a small number of new/unpublished writers each year. Weekly magazine for commercial growers and shippers, receivers and distributors of fresh fruits and vegetables, including chain store produce buyers and merchandisers. Estab. 1897. Pays on publication. Publishes ms an average of 2 weeks after acceptance. Deadline is 2 weeks before Thursday press day. Reports in 1 month. Sample copy and writer's guidelines for 10×13 SAE with 4 first-class stamps.

Nonfiction: News stories (about the produce industry). Buys profiles, spot news, coverage of successful business operations and articles on merchandising techniques. Query. Pays $1/column inch minimum for original material. Sometimes pays the expenses of writers on assignment.

Photos: Black and white glossies. Pays $8-10/photo.

Tips: "Stories should be trade-oriented, not consumer-oriented. As our circulation grows in the next year, we are interested in stories and news articles from all fresh fruit-growing areas of the country."

‡QUICK FROZEN FOODS INTERNATIONAL, E.W. Williams Publishing Co., Suite 305, 2125 Center Ave., Fort Lee NJ 07024-5898. (201)592-7007. Fax: (201)592-7171. Editor: John M. Saulnier. 20% freelance written. Works with a small number of new writers each year. Quarterly magazine covering frozen foods around the world—"every phase of frozen food manufacture, retailing, food service, brokerage, transport, warehousing, merchandising. Especially interested in stories from Europe, Asia and emerging nations." Circ. 13,700. Pays on publication. Publishes ms an average of 3 months after acceptance. Byline given. Offers kill fee; "if satisfactory, we will pay promised amount. If bungled, half." Buys all rights, but will relinquish any rights requested. Submit seasonal material 6 months in advance. Sample copy for $10.

Nonfiction: Book excerpts, general interest, interview/profile, new product (from overseas), personal experience, photo feature, technical, travel. No articles peripheral to frozen food industry such as taxes, insurance, government regulation, safety, etc. Buys 20-30 mss/year. Query or send complete ms. Length: 500-4,000

words. Pays 5¢/word or by arrangement. "We will reimburse postage on articles ordered from overseas."
Photos: "We prefer photos with all articles." State availability of photos or send photos with accompanying ms. Pays $10 for 5×7 color or b&w prints (contact sheet if many shots). Captions and identification of subject required. Buys all rights. Release on request.
Columns/Departments: News or analysis of frozen foods abroad. Buys 20 columns/year. Query. Length: 500-1,500 words. Pays by arrangement.
Fillers: Newsbreaks. Length: 100-500 words. Pays $5-20.
Tips: "We are primarily interested in feature materials (1,000-3,000 words with pictures). We are now devoting more space to frozen food company developments in Pacific Rim and East European countries. Stories on frozen food merchandising and retailing in foreign supermarket chains in Europe, Japan, China, Korea and Australia/New Zealand are welcome. National frozen food production profiles are also in demand worldwide. A frequent mistake is submitting general interest material instead of specific industry-related stories."

SEAFOOD LEADER, Waterfront Press Co., 5305 Shilshole Ave., NW, #200, Seattle WA 98107. (206)789-6506. Fax: (206)789-9193. Editor: Peter Redmayne. Managing Editor: Rob Lovitt. 20% freelance written. Works with a small number of new/unpublished writers each year. Bimonthly journal on the seafood business. Estab. 1980. Circ. 15,000. Pays on publication. Publishes ms an average of 3 months after acceptance. Byline given. Buys first rights and second serial (reprint) rights. Accepts simultaneous submissions. Reports in 1 month on queries; 2 months on mss. Sample copy for $4 with 9×12 SAE.
Nonfiction: General seafood interest, marketing/business, historical/nostalgic, interview/profile, opinion, photo feature. Each of *Seafood Leader's* 6 issues has a slant: Retail/Aquaculture (January/February), Buyer's Guide (March/April), International (May/June), Foodservice/Restaurant (July/August), Seafood Catalog (September/October) and Shrimp/Alaska (November/December). Each issue also includes stories outside of the particular focus, particularly shorter features and news items. No recreational fishing; no first person articles. Buys 12-15 mss/year. Query with or without published clips, or send complete ms. Length: 1,000-2,500 words. Pays 15-25¢/word published depending upon amount of editing necessary. Sometimes pays the expenses of writers on assignment.
Reprints: Send tearsheet or photocopy of article, typed ms with rights for sale noted and information about when and where the article previously appeared. Pays 50% of amount paid for an original article.
Photos: State availability of photos with submission. Reviews contact sheets and transparencies. Offers $50/inside color photo, $100 for cover. Buys one-time rights.
Fillers: Newsbreaks. Buys 10-15/year. Length: 100-250 words. Pays $50-100.
Tips: "*Seafood Leader* is steadily increasing in size and has a growing need for full-length feature stories and special sections. Articles on innovative, unique and aggressive people or companies involved in seafood are needed. Writing should be colorful, tight and fact-filled, always emphasizing the subject's formula for increased seafood sales. Readers should feel as if they have learned something applicable to their business."

HOME FURNISHINGS AND HOUSEHOLD GOODS

Readers rely on these publications to learn more about new products and trends in the home furnishings and appliance trade. Magazines for consumers interested in home furnishings are listed in the Consumer Home and Garden section.

APPLIANCE SERVICE NEWS, 110 W. Saint Charles Rd., P.O. Box 789, Lombard IL 60148-0789. Fax: (708)932-9552. Editor: William Wingstedt. Monthly "newspaper style" publication for professional service people whose main interest is repairing major and/or portable household appliances—service shop owner, service manager or service technician. Estab. 1950. Circ. 37,000. Buys all rights. Byline given. Pays on publication. Accepts simultaneous submissions. Reports in 1 month. Sample copy for $3.
Nonfiction: James Hodl, associate editor. "Our main interest is in technical articles about appliances and their repair. Material should be written in a straightforward, easy-to-understand style. It should be crisp and interesting, with high informational content. Our main interest is in the major and portable appliance repair field. We are not interested in retail sales." Query. Pays $200-300/feature.
Photos: Pays $20 for b&w photos used with ms. Captions required.

FLOORING MAGAZINE, 114 Elkton Lane, North Babylon NY 11703. (516)254-3719. Fax: (516)667-4129. Editor: Greg Valero. 20% freelance written. Prefers to work with published/established writers. Monthly magazine for floor covering retailers, wholesalers, contractors, specifiers and designers. Estab. 1931. Circ. 21,000. Pays on publication. Publishes ms an average of 3 months after acceptance. Byline given. Buys all rights. "Send letter with writing sample to be placed in our freelance contact file." Editorial calendar available for #10 SASE.
Nonfiction: "Mostly staff written. Buys a small number of manuscripts throughout the year. Needs writers with 35mm photography skills for local assignments. Study our editorial calender and send a concise query."

HAPPI, (Household and Personal Products Industry), 17 S. Franklin Turnpike, P.O. Box 555, Ramsey NJ 07446-0555. Fax: (201)825-0553. E-mail: rpubl@aol.com. Editor: Tom Branna. 5% freelance written. Magazine for "manufacturers of soaps, detergents, cosmetics and toiletries, waxes and polishes, insecticides, and aerosols." Estab. 1964. Circ. 18,000. Not copyrighted. Pays on publication. Publishes ms an average of 2 months after acceptance. Submit seasonal material 2 months in advance. Reports in 1 month.
Nonfiction: "Technical and semi-technical articles on manufacturing, distribution, marketing, new products, plant stories, etc., of the industries served. Some knowledge of the field is essential in writing for us." Buys informational interview, photo feature, spot news, coverage of successful business operations, new product articles, coverage of merchandising techniques and technical articles. No articles slanted toward consumers. Query with published clips. Buys 3-4 mss/year. Length: 500-2,000 words. Pays $25-300. Sometimes pays expenses of writers on assignment.
Photos: 4-color 5×7 or 8×10 glossies purchased with mss. Pays $10.
Tips: "The most frequent mistakes made by writers are unfamiliarity with our audience and our industry; slanting articles toward consumers rather than to industry members."

‡**HOME FURNISHINGS EXECUTIVE**, National Home Furnishings Association, P.O. Box 2396, High Point NC 27261. (910)883-1650. Editor: Michael J. Healey. 75% freelance written. Monthly magazine covering the home furnishings industry. "We hope that home furnishings retailers view our magazine as a profitability tool. We want each issue to help them make money or save money." Estab. 1927. Circ. 10,500. **Pays on acceptance**. Publishes ms an average of 6 weeks after acceptance. Byline given. Offers 20% kill fee. Buys first North American serial rights. Editorial lead time 6 weeks. Reports in 1 month on queries; 6 weels on mss. Sample copy and writer's guidelines for #10 SASE.
Nonfiction: Book excerpts, interview/profile, new product, Buys 55 mss/year. Query with published clips. Length: 300-2,000 words. Pays $50-750. Sometimes pays expenses of writers on assignment.
Photos: State availability of photos with submission. Reviews transparencies. Negotiates payment individually. Identification of subjects required. Buys one-time rights.
Columns/Departments: Executive Tipsheet (short "in box" items of interest—trend analysis, etc.) 250-300 words; On Managing Well (point-by-point articles on how retailers can manage their people better) 1,500 words; Advertising (how small retailers can create effective, low-cost advertising) 1,500 words. Query. Pays $50-500.
Fillers: Anecdotes, facts, newsbreaks, short humor. Buys about 15/year. Length: 50-200 words. Pays $10-25.
Tips: "Our readership includes owners of small 'ma and pa' furniture stores, executives of medium-sized chains (two to 10 stores), and the executives of big chains (e.g., Heilig-Meyers), which have hundreds of stores. My bias in choosing what stories to run is toward the ma's and pa's because, in today's fiercely competitive retail environment, their survival is at stake."

HOME LIGHTING & ACCESSORIES, P.O. Box 2147, Clifton NJ 07015. (201)779-1600. Fax: (201)779-3242. Editor: Linda Longo. 25% freelance written. Prefers to work with published/established writers. Monthly magazine for lighting showrooms/department stores. Estab. 1923. Circ. 10,000. Pays on publication. Publishes ms an average of 6 months after acceptance. Buys first rights. Submit seasonal material 6 months in advance. Reports in 2 months. Sample copy for 9×12 SAE with 4 first class stamps.
Nonfiction: Interview (with lighting retailers); personal experience (as a businessperson involved with lighting); profile (of a successful lighting retailer/lamp buyer); technical (concerning lighting or lighting design). Special issues: Outdoor (March); tribute to Tiffany's (August). Buys less than 6 mss/year. Query. Pays $60/published page. Sometimes pays the expenses of writers on assignment.
Reprints: Send tearsheet of article and information about when and where the article previously appeared.
Photos: State availability of photos with query. Offers no additional payment for 5×7 or 8×10 b&w glossy prints. Pays additional $90 for color transparencies used on cover. Captions required.
Tips: "We don't need fillers—only features. Deadline for all editorial is two months prior to publication."

HOSPITALS, NURSING AND NURSING HOMES

In this section are journals for medical and nonmedical nursing home personnel, clinical and hospital staffs and medical laboratory technicians and managers. Journals publishing technical material on medical research and information for physicians in private practice are listed in the Medical category.

AMERICAN JOURNAL OF NURSING, 555 W. 57th St., New York NY 10019-2961. (212)582-8820. Fax: (212)586-5462. E-mail: martin.d@ajn.org. Website: http://www.ajn.org. Editorial Director: Martin DiCarlantonio. Contact: Santa Crisall, N,C,MA, clinical director. Eager to work with new/unpublished nurse-authors. Monthly magazine covering nursing and health care. Estab. 1900. Circ. 239,000. Pays on publication.

Publishes ms an average of 8 months after acceptance. Byline given. Reports in 2 weeks on queries, 6 weeks on mss. Sample copy for $4. Writer's guidelines free.

● *American Journal of Nursing* is particularly interested in articles dealing with women's health issues and implications for nursing care.

Nonfiction: Practical, hands-on clinical articles of interest to hospital staff nurses; professional issues; personal experience. No material other than nursing care and nursing issues. Nurse-authors only accepted for publication.

Photos: Karliese Greiner, art director. Reviews b&w and color transparencies and prints. Model release and identification of subjects required. Buys variable rights.

Tips: "Everything we publish is written by nurses and edited inhouse."

JOURNAL OF CHRISTIAN NURSING, Nurses Christian Fellowship, a division of Inter-Varsity Christian Fellowship, 430 E. Plaza Dr., Westmont IL 60559. (708)887-2500. Fax: (708)887-2520. E-mail: jcn@ivpress.com. Editor: Judith Allen Shelly. Contact: Melodee Yohe, Managing Editor. 30-40% freelance written. Quarterly professional journal/magazine covering spiritual care, ethics, crosscultural issues, etc. "Our target audience is Christian nurses in the US and is nondenominational in character. We are prolife in position. We strive to help Christian nurses view nursing practice through the eyes of faith. Articles must be relevant to Christian nursing and consistent with our statement of faith." Estab. 1984. Circ. 10,000. Pays on publication. Publishes ms 2 years after acceptance. Byline given unless subject matter requires pseudonym. Offers 50% kill fee. Not copyrighted. Buys first rights; second serial (reprint) rights, rarely; all rights, only multiple-authored case studies. Editorial lead time up to 2 years. Submit seasonal material 1 year in advance. Reports in 1 month on queries; 2 months on mss. Sample copy for $5 (sub price $19.95/year) and SAE with 4 first-class stamps. Writers guidelines for #10 SASE.

Nonfiction: How-to, humor, inspirational, interview/profile, opinion, personal experience, photo feature, religious. All must be appropriate for Christian nurses. No purely academic articles, subjects not appropriate for Christian nurses, devotionals, Bible study. Buys 20-30 mss/year. Send complete ms. Length: 6-12 pages (typed, double spaced). Pays $25-80 and up to 8 complimentary copies.

Reprints: Occasionally accepts previously published submissions.

Photos: State availability of photos or send photos with submission. Reviews prints. Offers no additional payment for photos accepted with ms. Model releases and identification of subjects required. No rights purchased; all photos returned.

Columns/Departments: The Last Word (personal opinion), 750-900 words; Book Reviews (Resources). Buys 2-3 mss/year. Send complete ms. Pays $25-50 (Last Word); no payment for Book Reviews.

Tips: "Unless an author is a nurse, it will be unlikely that he/she will have an article accepted—unless they write a very interesting story about a nurse who is involved in creative ministry with a strong faith dimension."

JOURNAL OF NURSING JOCULARITY, The Humor Magazine for Nurses, JNJ Publishing, Inc., P.O. Box 40416, Mesa AZ 85274. (602)835-6165. E-mail: 73314.3032@compuserve.com. Website: http://www.jocularity.com. Editor: Fran London, RN, MS. 75% freelance written. Quarterly magazine covering nursing and medical humor. "*Journal of Nursing Jocularity* is read by health care professionals. Published manuscripts pertain to the lighter side of health care, from the perspective of the health care provider." Estab. 1990. Circ. 20,000. Pays on publication. Publishes ms an average of 1 year after acceptance. Buys one-time rights. Editorial lead time 1 year. Submit seasonal material 1 year in advance. Accepts simultaneous submissions. Reports in 2 months on queries; 3 months on mss. Sample copy for $2. Writer's guidelines for 9×10 SAE with 2 first-class stamps.

Nonfiction: Essays, historical/nostalgic, humor, interview/profile, opinion, personal experience, *current* research on therapeutic use of humor. "Our readers are primarily active nurses. Our focus is *insider humor*." Buys 4-8 mss/year. Length: 500-1,500 words. Pays $5 and up. Sometimes pays expenses of writers on assignment.

Reprints: Send typed ms with rights for sale noted and information about when and where the article previously appeared.

Photos: State availability of photos with submission. Model releases required. Buys one-time rights.

Columns/Departments: Stories from the Floor (anecdotes—true nursing experiences), 16-200 words; Call Lites (health care jokes with insider edge), 16-200 words; Student Nurse Cut-Ups (anecdotes—true student nurse experiences), 16-150 words; Liven Up (anecdotes using humor therapeutically at work), 50-200 words. Pays *JNJ* T-shirt.

Fiction: Humorous, slice-of-life vignettes. Buys 30 mss/year. Query or send complete ms. Length: 500-1,500 words. Pays $5 and up.

Poetry: Avant-garde, free verse, haiku, light verse, traditional, songs and cheers. Buys 4-6 poems/year. Submit maximum 3 poems. Pays $5.

Fillers: Anecdotes, gags to be illustrated by cartoonist, short humor. Length: 16-200 words. Pays JNJ T-shirt.

Tips: "Our readers are primarily working nurses. *JNJ*'s focus is insider humor—the kind only a health care provider understands. *Very few* non-health care providers have been able to submit material that rings true. We do not publish material written from a patient's point of view."

‡**LONG TERM CARE**, The Ontario Nursing Home Assoc., 345 Renfrew Dr., Suite 102-202, Markham, Ontario L3R 9S9 Canada. (905)470-8995. Fax: (905)470-9595. Editor: Heather Lang-Runtz. Assistant Editor: Tracey Ann Schofield. Quarterly magazine covering long term care. "Practical articles of interest to staff working in a long term care setting (nursing home, retirement home); professional issues; information must be applicable to a Canadian setting; focus should be on staff and for resident well-being." Estab. 1990. Circ. 4,800. Pays on publication. Publishes ms an average of 4 months after acceptance. Byline given. Buys one-time rights. Editorial lead time 3 months. Submit seasonal material 5 months in advance. Reports in 3 months. Sample copy and writer's guidelines free.
Nonfiction General interest, how-to (practical, of use to long term care practitioners), inspirational, interview/profile. No personal experience, product-oriented, historical articles. Query with published clips. Length: 800-1,500 words. Pays up to $1,000.
Photos: Send photos with submission. Reviews contact sheets, 5×5 prints. Offers no additional payment for photos accepted with ms. Captions, model releases required. Buys one-time rights.
Columns/Departments: Resident Health (nursing rehabilitation, food services); Resident Life (activities, volunteers, spiritual and pastoral care); Environment (housekeeping, laundry, maintenance, safety, landscape and architecture, staff health and well being); all 800 words. Query with published clips. Pays up to $1,000.
Tips: "Articles must be positive, upbeat, and contain helpful information that staff and managers working in the long term care field can use. Focus should be on staff and resident well being. Articles that highlight new ways of doing things are particularly useful. Please call the editor to discuss ideas. Must be applicable to Canadian settings."

‡**NURSEWEEK, California's Largest Newspaper and Career Guide for Nurses**, California Nursing Review, 1156-C Aster Ave., Sunnyvale CA 94086. (408)249-5877. Fax: (408)249-3756. E-mail: ed@nursewe ek.com. Website: http://www.nurseweek.com. Editor: Deanna Hodgin. 25% freelance written. Biweekly nursing newspaper for greater L.A., Orange County and S.F. areas with 6 additional statewide issues throughout year. Estab. 1989. Circ. 80,000 metro; 210,000+ statewide. Pays on publication. Byline given. Offers kill fee, which may vary. Buys all rights. Submit seasonal material 6 months in advance. Reports in 3 months. Sample copy and writer's guidelines for 9×12 SAE with 2 first class stamps.
Nonfiction: News, workplace, socio-economic, historical/nostalgic, interview/profile, personal experience, technical (continuing education articles) and travel, all nursing related. "Open to new ideas. No articles unrelated to nursing." Special issues: National Allied Health Professionals Week (October); National Nurses Week (May); Maternal Child Nursing (October). Buys 120 mss/year. Query with published clips. Length: 300-2,500 words. Pays $100-500 for assigned articles; $75-300 for unsolicited articles. Pays expenses of writers on assignment.
Photos: State availability of photos with submission. Reviews transparencies and prints. Captions, model releases and identification of subjects required; no exceptions. Buys one-time rights.
Columns/Departments: After Hours (what nurses do in their off hours); Newsmaker (profile of a distinguished nurse or health care leader), 1,500-2,000 words. Buys 40 mss/year. Query with published clips. Pays $100-500.
Tips: "Query the editor. Keep the audience in mind; we are more focused and clinically oriented than consumer health publications. Strongly urge writers to read several issues before inquiring. Features and news items relevant to registered nurses are the best areas for freelancers."

NURSING97, Springhouse Corporation, 1111 Bethlehem Pike, P.O. Box 908, Springhouse PA 19477-0908. (215)646-8700. Fax: (215)653-0826. E-mail: 73751.42@compuserve.com. Contact: Pat Wolf, Editorial Dept. Administrator. Clinical Director: Patricia Nornhold. Managing Editor: Jane Benner. 100% freelance written by nurses. Monthly magazine on the nursing field. "Our articles are written by nurses for nurses; we look for practical advice for the direct caregiver that reflects the author's experience." Estab. 1971. Circ. 430,000. Pays on publication. Publishes ms an average of 18 months after acceptance. Byline given. Offers 50% kill fee. Buys all rights. Submit seasonal material 8 months in advance. "Any form acceptable, but focus must be nursing." Prefers submissions on disk in any program. Reports in 2 weeks on queries; 3 months on mss. Sample copy for $4. Call 800-617-1717, ext. 300 for free writers' guidelines. Guidelines also available on CompuServe.

MARKET CONDITIONS are constantly changing! If this is 1998 or later, buy the newest edition of *Writer's Market* at your favorite bookstore or order directly from Writer's Digest Books.

Nonfiction: Book excerpts, exposé, how-to (specifically as applies to nursing field), inspirational, new product, opinion, personal experience, photo feature. No articles from patients' point of view, humor articles, poetry, etc. Buys 100 mss/year. Query. Length: 100 words minimum. Pays $50-400 for feature articles.
Reprints: Accepts previously published submissions.
Photos: State availability of photos with submission. Offers no additional payment for photos accepted with ms. Model releases required. Buys all rights.

HOTELS, MOTELS, CLUBS, RESORTS AND RESTAURANTS

These publications offer trade tips and advice to hotel, club, resort and restaurant managers, owners and operators. Journals for manufacturers and distributors of bar and beverage supplies are listed in the Beverages and Bottling section.

BARTENDER MAGAZINE, Foley Publishing, P.O. Box 158, Liberty Corner NJ 07938. (908)766-6006. Fax: (908)766-6607. Publisher: Raymond P. Foley. Editor: Jaclyn M. Wilson. Quarterly magazine emphasizing liquor and bartending for bartenders, tavern owners and owners of restaurants with full-service liquor licenses. 100% freelance written. Prefers to work with published/established writers; eager to work with new/unpublished writers. Circ. 147,000. Pays on publication. Publishes ms an average of 3 months after acceptance. Buys first serial, first North American serial, one-time, second serial (reprint), all or simultaneous US rights. Byline given. Submit seasonal material 3 months in advance. Accepts simultaneous submissions. Reports in 2 months. Sample copies for 9 × 12 SAE with 4 first-class stamps.
Nonfiction: General interest, historical, how-to, humor, interview (with famous bartenders or ex-bartenders), new products, nostalgia, personal experience, unique bars, opinion, new techniques, new drinking trends, photo feature, profile, travel, bar sports or bar magic tricks. Send complete ms. Length: 100-1,000 words.
Reprints: Send tearsheet of article and information about when and where the article previously appeared. Pays 60% of amount paid for an original article.
Photos: Send photos with ms. Pays $7.50-50 for 8 × 10 b&w glossy prints; $10-75 for 8 × 10 color glossy prints. Caption preferred and model release required.
Columns/Departments: Bar of the Month; Bartender of the Month; Drink of the Month; Creative Cocktails; Bar Sports; Quiz; Bar Art; Wine Cellar; Tips from the Top (from prominent figures in the liquor industry); One For The Road (travel); Collectors (bar or liquor-related items); Photo Essays. Query. Length: 200-1,000 words. Pays $50-200.
Fillers: Clippings, jokes, gags, anecdotes, short humor, newsbreaks, anything relating to bartending and the liquor industry. Length: 25-100 words. Pays $5-25.
Tips: "To break in, absolutely make sure that your work will be of interest to all bartenders across the country. Your style of writing should reflect the audience you are addressing. The most frequent mistake made by writers in completing an article for us is using the wrong subject."

BED & BREAKFAST, The Journal for Innkeepers, Virgo Publishing Inc., 4141 N. Scottsdale Rd., Suite 316, Scottsdale AZ 85251. (602)990-1101. Editor: Drew Whitney. Managing Editor: Valerie Demetros. 60-70% freelance written. Bimonthly magazine covering the bed-and-breakfast and innkeeping industries with regard to innkeepers. "Articles must be thoroughly researched, and we prefer that the author have some experience or expertise in the industry." Estab. 1994. Circ. 15,000. Pays on publication. Publishes ms 4 months after acceptance. Byline given. Buys first North American serial rights. Editorial lead time 4 months. Submit seasonal material 6 months in advance. Reports in 2 weeks on queries; 1 month on mss. Sample copy for 9 × 12 SASE.
Nonfiction: Book excerpts, interview/profile, new product, personal experience, technical. Buys 12 mss/year. Query with or without published clips. Length: 800-3,500 words. Pays $200 maximum for assigned articles. Pays expenses of writers on assignment.
Photos: Send photos, slides or transparencies with submission. Negotiates payment individually. Model releases and identification of subjects required. Buys one-time rights.
Columns/Departments: Buys 6 mss/year. Pays $200 maximum.

CULINARY TRENDS, Dedicated to the World of Culinary Arts, Culinary Publication, Inc., 6285 E. Spring St., Long Beach CA 90808. (310)496-2558. Editor: Tim Linden. 50% freelance written. Quarterly magazine covering food, restaurant, hotel industry. "Our primary audience is chefs, restaurant owners, caterers, hotel managers, and anyone interested in cooking and food!" Pays on publication. Publishes ms an average of 4 months after acceptance. Byline given. Buys first or one-time rights. Editorial lead time 4 months. Sample copy for $7.
Nonfiction: How-to (cooking techniques), humor, interview/profile, opinion, photo feature, articles on restaurants must include photos and recipes. Buys 12 mss/year. Query with published clips. Length: 700-3,000 words. Pays $100-300.

Photos: Send photos with submission. Reviews transparencies, prints. Offers no additional payment for photos accepted with ms. Captions required. Buys one-time rights.
Columns/Departments: Wine (selling wine), 700 words. Buys 4 mss/year. Query with published clips. Pays $0-100.
Tips: "We like to get stories about restaurants with the focus on the chef and the food. Quality color or transparencies or slides are essential along with recipes."

FLORIDA HOTEL & MOTEL JOURNAL, The Official Publication of the Florida Hotel & Motel Association, Accommodations, Inc., P.O. Box 1529, Tallahassee FL 32302-1529. (904)224-2888. Fax: (904)222-FHMA. Editor: Mrs. Jayleen Woods. Contact: Janet Litherland, editorial associate. 10% freelance written. Prefers to work with published/established writers. Magazine published 10 times/year for managers in the lodging industry (every licensed hotel, motel and resort in Florida). Estab. 1978. Circ. 7,000. Pays on publication. Publishes ms an average of 2 months after acceptance. Byline given. Offers $50 kill fee. Buys all rights and makes work-for-hire assignments. Submit seasonal material 2 months in advance. Reports in 6 weeks. Sample copy and writer's guidelines for 9×12 SAE with 4 first-class stamps.
Nonfiction: General interest (business, finance, taxes); historical/nostalgic (old Florida hotel reminiscences); how-to (improve management, housekeeping procedures, guest services, security and coping with common hotel problems); humor (hotel-related anecdotes); inspirational (succeeding where others have failed); interview/profile (of unusual hotel personalities); new product (industry-related and non brand preferential); photo feature (queries only); technical (emerging patterns of hotel accounting, telephone systems, etc.); travel (transportation and tourism trends only—no scenics or site visits); property renovations and maintenance techniques. "We would like to run more humorous anecdotes on hotel happenings than we're presently receiving." Buys 10-12 mss/year. Query with proposed topic and clips of published work. Length: 750-2,500 words. Pays $75-250 "depending on type of article and amount of research." Sometimes pays the expenses of writers on assignment.
Reprints: Send tearsheet of article and information about when and where the article previously appeared. Pays flat fee of $55.
Photos: Send photos with ms. Pays $25-100 for 4×5 color transparencies; $10-15 for 5×7 b&w prints. Captions, model release and identification of subjects required.
Tips: "We prefer feature stories on properties or personalities holding current membership in the Florida Hotel and Motel Association. Membership and/or leadership brochures are available (SASE) on request. We're open to articles showing how hotel management copes with energy systems, repairs, renovations, new guest needs and expectations. The writer may have a better chance of breaking in at our publication with short articles and fillers because the better a writer is at the art of condensation, the better his/her feature articles are likely to be."

FOOD & SERVICE, Texas Restaurant Association, P.O. Box 1429, Austin TX 78767-1429. (512)472-3666 (in Texas, 1-800-395-2872). Fax: (512)472-2777. Editor: Julie Stephen Sherrier. 50% freelance written. Magazine published 8 times/year providing business solutions to Texas restaurant owners and operators. Estab. 1941. Circ. 6,000. **Pays on acceptance.** Reports in 1 month. Byline given. Buys first rights. Pay varies. Sample copy and editorial calendar for 11×14 SAE with 6 first-class stamps. Free writer's guidelines.
Nonfiction: Features must provide business solutions to problems in the restaurant and food service industries. Topics vary but always have business slant; usually particular to Texas. No restaurant critiques, human interest stories or seasonal copy. Quote members of the Texas Restaurant Association; substantiate with facts and examples. Query in writing. Length: 1,500-2,500 words, features; shorter articles sometimes used; product releases, 300-word maximum. Payment rates vary.
Reprints: Send tearsheet or photocopy of article.
Photos: State availability of photos, but photos usually assigned.

‡**FOODSERVICE AND HOSPITALITY,** Kostuch Publications, 23 Lesmill Rd., Don Mills, Ontario M3B 3P6 Canada. (416)447-0888. Fax: (416)447-5333. E-mail: rcaira@foodservice.ca. Editor: Rosanna Caira. Associate Editor: Carolyn Cooper. 40-50% freelance written. Monthly magazine covering restaurant and hotel trade. Estab. 1968. Circ. 25,000. Pays on publication. Byline given. Buys first North American serial rights. Editorial lead time 3 months. Submit seasonal material 2 months in advance. Sample copy and writer's guidelines free on request.
Nonfiction: How-to, new product. No case studies. Buys 30-50 mss/year. Query with or without published clips. Length: 700-1,500 words. Pays 30-35¢ for assigned articles. Sometimes pays expenses of writers on assignment.
Photos: Send photos with submission. Offers $30-75/photo.

INNKEEPING WORLD, P.O. Box 84108, Seattle WA 98124. Fax: (206)362-7847. Editor/Publisher: Charles Nolte. 75% freelance written. Eager to work with new/unpublished writers. Magazine published 10 times/year emphasizing the hotel industry worldwide. Estab. 1979. Circ. 2,000. **Pays on acceptance.** Publishes ms an average of 2 months after acceptance. Buys all rights. No byline. Submit seasonal material 1 month in advance. Reports in 1 month. Sample copy and writer's guidelines for 9×12 SAE with 3 first-class stamps.

Nonfiction: Managing—interviews with successful hotel managers of large and/or famous hotels/resorts (600-1,200 words); Marketing—interviews with hotel marketing executives on successful promotions/case histories (300-1,000 words); Sales Promotion—innovative programs for increasing business (100-600 words); Food Service—outstanding hotel restaurants, menus and merchandising concepts (300-1,000 words); and Guest Relations—guest service programs, management philosophies relative to guests (200-800 words). Pays $100 minimum or 20¢/word (whichever is greater) for main topics. Other topics—advertising, cutting expenses, guest comfort, hospitality, ideas, reports and trends, special guestrooms, staff relations. Length: 50-500 words. Pays 20¢/word. "If a writer asks a hotel for a complimentary room, the article will not be accepted, nor will *Innkeeping World* accept future articles from the writer."

Tips: "We need more in-depth reporting on successful sales promotions—results-oriented information."

PIZZA & PASTA MAGAZINE, Talcott Communications Corp., 20 N. Wacker Dr., Suite 3230, Chicago IL 60015. (312)849-2220. Editor: Joseph Declan Moran. 5% freelance written. Monthly magazine covering Italian American foodservice in America. "*Pizza & Pasta Magazine* is the business publication for the Italian American foodservice industy. An informative, how-to magazine that helps operators of pizza and pasta restaurants improve their business." Estab. 1988. Circ. 35,000. Pays on publication. Publishes ms an average of 1 month after acceptance. Byline given. Buys one-time rights. Editorial lead time 2 months. Submit seasonal material 4 months in advance. Sample copy free on request.

Nonfiction: How-to, interview/profile, new product, technical, news briefs, promotions. "We do not accept unsolicited stories. If a writer has an idea or a suggestion for a story, please call the editor first." Special issue: National Pizza and Pasta Month (October). Buys 4 mss/year. Length: 1,000-2,000 words. Pays $150-250.

Photos: State availability of photos with submissions. Reviews transparencies. Negotiates payment individually. Captions required. Buys one-time rights.

Columns/Departments: Independent Spotlight (mom & pop pizza, pasta restaurant), 800 words; Franchise Spotlight (profile of franchise/franchisor), 800-1,000 words. Buys 2 mss/year. Query with published clips. Pays $150-250.

Fillers: Facts, newsbreaks. Buys 2/year. Length: 100-300 words. Does not pay for fillers.

Tips: "Always call me first. Everyone has a great story idea, but call and ask what we have on our editorial calendar so that we can determine if your idea will fit in with an upcoming issue. Do not call more than once a week. There are a lot of people with great story ideas, but only so much space each month. The October issue of *Pizza & Pasta Magazine* showcases national pizza & pasta month. That is really the biggest issue every year where we will need freelance pieces."

VACATION INDUSTRY REVIEW, Interval International, P.O. Box 431920, South Miami FL 33243-1920. (305)666-1861, ext. 7022. Fax: (305)667-4495. E-mail: gleposky@interval-iwtl.com. Editor: George Leposky. 30% freelance written. Prefers to work with published/established writers. Quarterly magazine covering leisure lodgings (timeshare resorts, fractionals, and other types of vacation-ownership properties). Estab. 1982. Circ. 15,000. Pays on publication. Publishes ms an average of 6 months after acceptance. Byline given. Buys all rights and makes work-for-hire assignments. Submit seasonal material at least 6 months in advance. Reports in 1 month. Writer's guidelines for #10 SASE.

Nonfiction: How-to, interview/profile, new product, opinion, personal experience, technical, travel. No consumer travel or non-vacation real-estate material. Buys 10-12 mss/year. Query with published clips. Length: 1,000-1,500 words. Pays 30¢/word. Pays expenses of writers on assignment, if previously arranged.

Photos: Send photos with submission. Reviews contact sheets, 35mm transparencies, 5×7 or larger prints. Offers no additional payment for photos accepted with ms. Captions and identification of subjects required. Buys one-time rights.

Tips: "We want articles about the business aspects of the vacation ownership industry: entrepreneurship, project financing, design and construction, sales and marketing, operations, management—anything that will help our readers plan, build, sell and run a quality vacation ownership property that satisfies the owners/guests and earns a profit for developer and marketer. Our destination pieces are trade-oriented, reporting the status of tourism and the development of various kinds of vacation-ownership facilities in a city, region, or country. You can discuss things to see and do in the context of a resort located near an attraction, but that shouldn't be the main focus or reason for the article. We're also interested in owner associations at vacation-ownership resorts (not residential condos). Prefers electronic submissions. Query for details."

‡THE WISCONSIN RESTAURATEUR, Wisconsin Restaurant Association, #300, 31 S. Henry, Madison WI 53703. (608)251-3663. Fax: (608)251-3666. Editor: Sonya Knecht Bice. 20% freelance written. Eager to work with new/unpublished writers. Bimonthly magazine emphasizing restaurant industry, particularly Wisconsin, for restaurateurs, hospitals, institutions, food service students, etc. Estab. 1933. Circ. 4,000. **Pays on acceptance** or publication, varies. Publishes ms an average of 6 months after acceptance. Buys all rights or first rights. Editorial lead time 2 months. Pays 10% kill fee or $10. Byline given. Submit seasonal/holiday material 3 months in advance. Reports in 3 weeks. Sample copy and writer's guidelines for 9×12 SASE.

Nonfiction: Historical/nostalgia, how-to, humor, inspirational interview/profile, new product, opinion, personal experience, photo feature articles. "All must relate to foodservice. Need more in-depth articles. No features on nonmember restaurants." Buys 6 mss/year. Query with "copyright clearance information and a note about the writer in general." Phone queries OK. Length: 1,000-5,000 words. Pays $100 minimum for assigned articles; $25 minimum for unsolicited articles. Pays other than cash payment when requested.
Reprints: Send tearsheet of article and information about when and where it previously appeared.

INDUSTRIAL OPERATIONS

Industrial plant managers, executives, distributors and buyers read these journals. Some industrial management journals are also listed under the names of specific industries. Publications for industrial supervisors are listed in Management and Supervision.

COMPRESSED AIR, 253 E. Washington Ave., Washington NJ 07882-2495. Fax: (908)689-5576. Editor/Publications Manager: Tom McAloon. 75% freelance written. Magazine published 8 times/year emphasizing applied technology and industrial management subjects for engineers and managers. Estab. 1896. Circ. 145,000. Buys all rights. Publishes ms an average of 6 months after acceptance. Reports in 2 months. Free sample copy; mention *Writer's Market* in request.
Nonfiction: "Articles must be reviewed by experts in the field." Buys 56 mss/year. Query with published clips. Pays negotiable fee. Sometimes pays expenses of writers on assignment.
Photos: State availability of photos in query. Payment for slides, transparencies and glossy prints is included in total purchase price. Captions required. Buys all rights.
Tips: "We are presently looking for freelancers with a track record in industrial/technology/management writing. Editorial schedule is developed in the summer before the publication year and relies heavily on article ideas from contributors. Résumé and samples help. Writers with access to authorities preferred; we prefer interviews over library research. The magazine's name doesn't reflect its contents. We suggest writers request sample copies."

INDUSTRIAL FABRIC PRODUCTS REVIEW, Industrial Fabrics Association International, 345 Cedar St., Suite 800, St. Paul MN 55101-1088. (612)222-2508. Fax: (612)225-6966. Editor: Gene Rebeck. 75% staff- and industry-written. Monthly magazine covering industrial textiles and products made from them for company owners, salespeople and researchers in a variety of industrial textile areas. Estab. 1915. Circ. 11,000. Pays on publication. Publishes ms an average of 2 months after acceptance. Byline given. Buys all rights. Reports in 1 month.
Nonfiction: Technical, marketing and other topics related to any aspect of industrial fabric industry from fiber to finished fabric product. Special issues: new products, new fabrics and equipment. No historical or apparel-oriented articles. Buys 8-10 mss/year. Query with phone number. Length: 1,200-3,000 words.
Tips: "We encourage freelancers to learn our industry and make regular, solicited contributions to the magazine. We do not buy photography."

‡QUALITY DIGEST, 40 Declaration Dr., Suite 100C, Chico CA 95973. (916)893-4095. Fax: (916)893-0395. E-mail: qualitydig@aol.com. Website: http://www.tqm.com. Editor: Scott M. Paton. 75% freelance written. Monthly trade magazine covering quality improvement. Estab. 1981. Circ. 45,000. Pays on acceptance. Byline given. Buys all rights. Submit seasonal material 4 months in advance. Accepts simultaneous submissions. Reports in 3 months. Free sample copy and writer's guidelines.
Nonfiction: Book excerpts, how-to implement quality programs, etc., interview/profile, opinion, personal experience, technical. Buys 25 mss/year. Query with or without published clips or send complete ms. Length: 2,000-3,000 words. Pays $200-600. Pays in contributor copies for unsolicited mss. Sometimes pays expenses of writers on assignment.
Reprints: Send tearsheet of article.
Photos: Send photos with submission. Reviews any size prints. Offers no additional payment for photos accepted with ms. Captions, model releases and identification of subjects required. Buys one-time rights.
Tips: "Please be specific in your articles. Explain what the problem was, how it was solved and what the benefits are. Tell the reader how the technique described will benefit him or her."

WEIGHING & MEASUREMENT, Key Markets Publishing Co., P.O. Box 5867, Rockford IL 61125. (815)636-7739. Fax: (815)636-7741. Editor: David M. Mathieu. Bimonthly magazine for users of industrial scales and meters. Estab. 1914. Circ. 15,000. Pays on acceptance. Buys all rights. Offers 20% kill fee. Byline given. Reports in 2 weeks. Sample copy for $2.
Nonfiction: Interview (with presidents of companies); personal opinion (guest editorials on government involvement in business, etc.); profile (about users of weighing and measurement equipment); technical.

Buys 25 mss/year. Query on technical articles; submit complete ms for general interest material. Length: 750-1,500 words. Pays $125-200.

INFORMATION SYSTEMS

These publications give computer professionals more data about their field. Consumer computer publications are listed under Personal Computers.

ACCESS TO WANG, The Independent Magazine for Wang System Users, New Media Publications, 10711 Burnet Rd., Suite 305, Austin TX 78758. Fax: (512)873-7782. E-mail: 75730.2465@compuserve .com. Editor: Richard Zelade. 75% freelance written. Monthly magazine covering Wang computers, providing how-to articles for users of Wang computer systems, Wang office automation software and coexistence and migration applications. Estab. 1984. Circ. 10,000. Pays 30 days after publication. Publishes ms an average of 2 months after acceptance. Byline given. Offers $25 kill fee. Buys first North American serial rights. Editorial lead time 3 months. Submit seasonal material 4 months in advance. Sample copy and writer's guidelines free on request.

Nonfiction: How-to, new product, technical, computer reviews, computer product reviews. Buys 50 mss/year. Query. Length: 1,500-2,000 words. Pays $150 for assigned articles; $100 for unsolicited articles.

Photos: Send photos with submissions. Reviews 3×5 transparencies, prints. Offers no additional payment for photos accepted with ms. Captions, model releases, identification of subjects required. Buys all rights.

Columns/Departments: Special Report (varies from month to month), 2,000-2,500. Buys 12 mss/year. Query. Pays $150.

Tips: "Writer must have computer experience specific to Wang computers. Also must have networking, Unix, programming, or similar experience. First step: call for the editorial calendar."

AS/400 SYSTEMS MANAGEMENT, (formerly *3X/400 Systems Management*), Adams/Hunter Publishing, 2101 S. Arlington Heights Rd., Suite 150, Arlington Heights IL 60005. (847)427-9512. Fax: (847)427-2006. E-mail: 71333.730@compuserve.com. Editor: Wayne Rhodes. 10% freelance written. Works with a small number of new/unpublished writers. Monthly magazine covering applications of IBM minicomputers (AS/400 and RS/6000) in business. Estab. 1973. Circ. 55,000. Pays on publication. Publishes ms an average of 3 months after acceptance. Byline given. Buys all rights. Submit seasonal material 4 months in advance. Reports in 3 months on queries. Sample copy for 9×12 SAE with 4 first-class stamps. Writer's guidelines for #10 SASE.

Nonfiction: How-to (use the computer in business), technical (organization of a data base or file system). "A writer who submits material to us should be an expert in computer applications. No material on large-scale computer equipment." No poetry. Buys 8 mss/year. Query. Length: 2,000-4,000 words. Sometimes pays expenses of writers on assignment.

Tips: "Frequent mistakes are not understanding the audience and not having read past issues of the magazine."

‡CANADIAN COMPUTER RESELLER, The news magazine for value-added reselling, Maclean Hunter, 777 Bay St., 5th Floor, Toronto, Ontario M5W 1A7 Canada. (416)596-5000. Fax: (416)593-3166. E-mail: ccr@inforamp.net. Editor: Steve McHale. 70% freelance written. Biweekly magazine covering computer reseller industry. Estab. 1988. Circ. 15,000. **Pays on acceptance**. Publishes ms an average of 1 month after acceptance. Byline given. Buys negotiable rights. Editorial lead time 2 months. Sample copy free on request.

Nonfiction: Interview/profile, new product, technical. Buys 24 mss/year. Query with published clips. Length: 800-3,000 words. Pays $400-800 for assigned articles.

Photos: State availability of photos with submission. Reviews slides or 4×6 prints. Prefers color. Negotiates payment individually. Identification of subjects required. Buys negotiable rights.

Columns/Departments: Small Business (tips for small resellers and system integratory profiles of successful small businesses), 800 words. Buys 6 mss/year. Query with published clips. Pays $400.

Tips: "Writers need familiarity with technology, specifically with issues that relate to resellers and system integrators. Call before submitting any stories."

THE C/C++ USERS JOURNAL, Miller Freeman, Inc., 1601 W. 23rd, Suite 200, Lawrence KS 66046. (913)841-1631. Fax: (913)841-2624. E-mail: marc@rdpub.com. Website: http://www.cuj.com. Editor: P.J. Plauger. Contact: Marc Briand. 90% freelance written. Monthly magazine covering C and C++ programming. "*CUJ* is written for professional C and C++ programmers. Articles are practical, advanced, and code-intensive. Authors are *always* professional C and C++ programmers." Estab. 1988. Circ. 40,000. Pays on publication. Publishes ms an average of 5 months after acceptance. Byline given. Offers $150 kill fee. Buys all rights. Editorial lead time 4 months. Reports in 1 month on queries. Sample copy and writer's guidelines free on request.

Nonfiction: Technical. Buys 90-110 mss/year. Query. Length: 500 minimum. Pay varies.
Reprints: Send electronically readable ms with rights for sale noted.

CIRCUIT CELLAR INK, The Computer Applications Journal, 4 Park St., Vernon CT 06066. (860)875-2199. Fax: (860)872-2204. E-mail: ken.davidson@circellar.com. Website: http://www.circellar.com/. Editor: Kenneth Davidson. 99% freelance written. Monthly magazine covering design of embedded controllers. "Most of our articles are written by engineers for engineers. They deal with the lower level details of computer hardware and software design. Most articles deal with dedicated, embedded processors rather than desktop computers." Estab. 1988. Circ. 45,000. Pays on publication. Publishes ms an average of 6 months after acceptance. Byline given. Offers $100 kill fee. Buys first rights. Editorial lead time 2 months. Submit seasonal material 3 months in advance. Reports in 1 month. Sample copy and writer's guideline free on request.
Nonfiction: New product, technical. Buys 40 mss/year. Send complete ms. Length: 1,000-5,000 words. Pays $50/page.
Photos: Send photos with submissions. Reviews transparencies, slides, 3×5 prints. Offers no additional payment for photos accepted with ms. Captions required. Buys one-time rights.
Tips: "Contact editor with address, phone number, fax number, e-mail address, and article subject interests. Will send an author's guide."

‡COMPUTER GRAPHICS WORLD, PennWell Publishing Company, 10 Tara Blvd., 5th Floor, Nashua NH 03062-2801. (603)891-9160. Fax: (603)891-0539. E-mail: stevep@pennwell.com. Website: www.cgw.com. Editor: Stephen Porter. Managing Editor: Audrey Doyle. 60% freelance written. Monthly magazine covering computer graphics. "*Computer Graphics World* specializes in covering computer-aided 3D modeling, animation, and visualization and their uses in engineering, science, and entertainment applications." Estab. 1978. Circ. 70,000. **Pays on acceptance.** Publishes ms an average of 4 months after acceptance. Byline given. Offers 20% kill fee. Buys all rights. Editorial lead time 4 months. Submit seasonal material 3 months in advance. Sample copy free on request.
Nonfiction: General interest, how-to (how-to create quality models and animations), interview/profile, new product, opinion, technical, user application stories. "We do not want to run articles that are geared to computer programmers. Our focus as a magazine is on users involved in specific applications." Buys 40 mss/year. Query with published clips. Length: 1,200-3,000 words. Pays $500 minimum. Sometimes pays expenses of writers on assignment.
Columns/Departments: Output (offers personal opinion on relevant issue), 700 words; Reviews (offers hands-on review of important new products), 750 words; and Application Stories (highlights unique use of the technology by a single user), 800 words. Buys 36-40 mss/year. Query with published clips. Pays $100-500.
Tips: "Freelance writers will be most successful if they have some familiarity with computers and know how to write from a user perspective. They do not need to be computer experts, but they do have to understand how to explain the impact of the technology and the applications in which a user is involved. Both our feature section and our application story section are quite open to freelancers. The trick to winning acceptance for your story is to have a well-developed idea that highlights a fascinating new trend or development in computer graphics technology or profiles a unique and fascinating use of the technology by a single user or a specific class of users."

‡DESKTOP PUBLISHERS JOURNAL, (formerly *NADTP Journal*), National Association of Desktop Publishers, 462 Boston St., Topsfield MA 01983. (508)887-7900. Fax: (508)887-6117. E-mail: nadtp@aol.com. Editor-in-Chief: Robert Runck. Contact: Marta Dils. 80% freelance written. Monthly magazine covering desktop publishing. "*The Journal* educates and informs readers on all aspects of desktop publishing technology and shows them how to get the most out of the technology on their desktops." Estab. 1987. Circ. 67,000. Pays 45 days after acceptance. Publishes ms an average of 4 months after acceptance. Byline given. Kill fee. Buys all rights. Editorial lead time 4 months. Reports in 1 month on queries. Sample copy for $4. Writer's guidelines for #10 SASE.
Nonfiction: How-to (use and apply DTP hardware, software and special techniques), interview/profile, new product, personal experience (within narrow limits), technical. Buys 75 mss/year. Query with published clips. Length: 300-5,000 words. Rates negotiated based on article length and complexity of topic.
Columns/Departments: Digital Imaging, Paper, Scanning, Color, Alternative Media, Online Publishing, Business, Type, Law, Design, Hands On (product reviews), FPO (opinion), Pre-Press and Printing, (all helping readers to understand and apply existing and emerging technologies in their work as desktop publishers), 500-1,500 words. Buys 30 mss/year. Query with published clips. Rates negotiated based on topic and complexity.
Tips: "Writers should have a clear understanding of the needs of desktop publishers and what they need to know to work faster, smarter and more professionally. Familiarity with the desktop publishing industry is essential, as is some technical knowledge of the ways DTP hardware and software are used. Departments are the easiest way to break in, although we're always looking for new writers for feature length articles."

DGFOCUS, The Official Publication of NADGUG, the Independent Data General Users Group, Turnkey Publishing, Inc., P.O. Box 200549, Austin TX 78720. (512)335-2286. Fax: (512)335-3083. E-mail: djohnson@zilker.net. Editor: Doug Johnson. 80% freelance written. Monthly trade journal covering Data General computers. Technical and practical information specific to the use of Data General computers. Estab. 1985. Circ. 8,000. Pays on publication. Publishes ms an average of 2 months after acceptance. Buys first North American serial rights. Reports in 1 month. Sample copy and writer's guidelines for 9 × 12 SAE with 6 first-class stamps.

Nonfiction: How-to (programming techniques, macros), technical. Query. Length: 1,000-3,000 words. Pays $50 minimum for assigned articles. Pays in contributor copies or other premiums if the writer works for a company that sells hardware or software to the Data General marketplace.

• *Focus* reports an increased need for articles about the commercial Unix market, applicable to Data General.

Photos: State availability of photos with submission. Reviews contact sheets, transparencies and prints. Offers no additional payment for photos accepted with ms. Model releases, identification of subjects required. Buys one-time rights.

‡**DIGITAL AGE, OpenVMS•UNIX•Windows NT**, Cardinal Business Media Inc., 1300 Virginia Dr., Suite 400, Fort Washington PA 19034. (215)643-8000. Fax: (215)643-4827. E-mail: simpsoncm@box101.cardinal.com or schwartzdr@box101.cardinal.com. Editor-in-Chief: Charlie Simpson. 30% freelance written. Monthly magazine covering Digital Equipment Corp. computers and third-pardy vendors in that market. "*Digital Age* includes information about VAX, Alpha and open systems hardware and software, specifically how Digital and related technology can be integrated in multivendor enfironments. Areas of focus include OpenVMS, UNIX, Windows NT, networking and client-server computing." Estab. 1982. Circ. 50,000. Pays on publication. Publishes ms an average of 3 months after acceptance. Byline given. Buys all rights and makes work-for-hire assignments. Editorial lead time 3 months. Sample copy and writer's guidelines free on request.

Nonfiction: Interview/profile, new product, opinion, technical. Buys 20 mss/year. Query with published clips. Length: 500-2,000 words. Pays $100-800.

Photos: State availability of photos with submission. Reviews transparencies, 3 × 5 prints. Offers no additional payment for photos accepted with ms. Captions, model releases, identification of subjects required. Buys all rights.

Columns/Departments: Industry Watch (industry news), 500 words; Case By Case (case study solutions), 800-1,000 words; Product Watch (hands-off product review), 500 words; Directions (look at corporate strategy of prominent or new companies), 500-800 words. Buys 6 mss/year. Query. Pays $0-300.

Tips: "Queries should reflect topics listed on editorial calendar. Writers should have a background in technical writing and be knowledgeable about the computer industry in general and Digital Equipment Corp. specifically."

‡**ENTERPRISE SYSTEMS JOURNAL**, Cardinal Business Media, 12225 Greenville Ave., Suite 700, Dallas TX 75243. (214)669-9000. Fax: (214)669-9909. E-mail: 76130.221@CompuServe.com. Managing Editor: Kathie Clark. Contact: Joyce Garner, assistant editor. 100% freelance written. Monthly magazine covering mainframe computing. "*Enterprise Systems Journal* is a technical publication geared to I/S professionals involved in IBM host-based enterprise-wide computing." Estab. 1985. Circ. 85,000. Pays on publication. Publishes ms an average of 6 months after acceptance. Byline given. Buys all rights and makes work-for-hire assignments. Editorial lead time 4 months. Accepts simultaneous submissions. Writer's guidelines free on request.

Nonfiction: How-to (mainframe systems-related), personal experience (mainframe user stories). No high-level overviews or basic tutorials. Buys approximately 100 mss/year. Query. Length: 1,500-2,500 words. Pays $150/page. Sometimes pays expenses of writers on assignment.

Photos: State availability of photos with submission. Offers no additional payment for photos accepted with ms. Buys one-time rights.

Tips: "*ESJ* readers are technically savvy mainframe computer professionals. Our writers must demonstrate technical knowledge at least equal to our readers."

FOXTALK, Making Microsoft FoxPro Development Easier, Pinnacle Publishing, Inc., P.O. Box 888, Kent WA 98035-0888. (206)251-1900. E-mail: foxtalk@pinpub.com. Website: http://www.pinpub.com. Editor: Whil Hentzen. Contact: Laurie Maloney, associate editor. 95% freelance written. Monthly trade newsletter covering Microsoft FoxPro development. "*FoxTalk* shows professional developers how to create more effective, more efficient software applications using Microsoft FoxPro, Visual FoxPro." Estab. 1989. Circ. 8,000. Pays on publication. Publishes ms an average of 3 months after acceptance. Byline given. Offers 25% kill fee. Buys all rights. Editorial lead time 4 months. Reports in 2 months on queries; 3 months on mss. Sample copy and writers kit free on request.

Nonfiction: Book excerpts, how-to, new product, technical, technical tips. "Please! No general interest articles about software use. Must be targeted to the product the newsletter covers." Buys 72 mss/year. Send complete ms. Length: 500-5,000 words. Pays $25-600. Sometimes pays expenses of writers on assignment.

Tips: "Use the software product the newsletter covers. Be an expert in it! Develop a specific technique that other users would want to try out and explain it thoroughly in your article. Start with tips! Figure out ways to do something easier or faster and share that in a brief write-up. We pay $25 and a pound of coffee for each tip and we use scads of them!"

‡**HP PROFESSIONAL, The Magazine For Hewlett-Packard Enterprise Computing**, Cardinal Business Media Inc., 1300 Virginia Dr., Suite 400, Fort Washington PA 19034. (215)643-8000. Fax: (215)643-4827. E-mail: simpsoncm@box101.cardinal.com or schwartzdr@box101.cardinal.com. Website: www.cardin al.com/~hppro. Editor-in-Chief: Charlie Simpson. 30% freelance written. Monthly magazine covering Hewlett-Packard computers and third-party companies in that market. "*HP Professional*'s mission is to assist managers with strategic planning and purchasing decisions by providing unbiased reporting and analysis on the use and integration of the HP9000 UNIX systems and servers, HP workstations, PCs, LANs and the HP 3000 business systems—all in multiplatform computing environments." Estab. 1987. Circ. 30,000. Pays on publication. Publishes ms an average of 3 months after acceptance. Byline given. Buys all rights and makes work-for-hire assignments. Editorial lead time 3 months. Sample copy free on request.
Nonfiction: Interview/profile, new product, opinion, technical. Buys 20 mss/year. Query with published clips. Length: 500-2,000 words. Pays $100-800.
Photos: State availability of photos with submission. Reviews negatives. Offers no additional payment for photos accepted with ms. Captions, model releases, identification of subjects required. Buys all rights.
Columns/Departments: And Another Thing . . (opinion on current computer trend or event), 800 words; INsites (case study solutions), 800-1,000 words; Product Watch (hands-off product review), 500 words; Strategic Directions (look at corporate strategy of prominent or new companies), 500 words. Buys 6 mss/year. Query. Pays $0-300.
Fillers: Newsbreaks. Buys 6/year. Length: 100-500 words. Pays $0-200.
Tips: "Queries should reflect topics listed on the editorial calendar. Writers should have a background in technical writing and be knowledgeable about the computer industry in general and Hewlett-Packard specifically."

HUM-THE GOVERNMENT COMPUTER MAGAZINE, Hum Communications Ltd., 202-557 Cambridge St. S., Ottawa Ontario K1S 4J4 Canada. (613)237-4862. Fax: (613)746-4744. E-mail: editor@hum.c om. Website: http://www.hum.com. Editor: Tim Lougheed. 60% freelance written. Monthly magazine covering use and management of computers in Canadian public sector. Estab. 1991. Circ. 13,500. Pays on publication. Publishes ms an average of 10 weeks after acceptance. Byline given. Offers 10% kill fee. Buys first rights or second serial (reprint) rights. Editorial lead time 3 months. Reports in 3 weeks on queries; 2 months on mss. Sample copy for 10×12 SASE.
Nonfiction: Book excerpts, essays, how-to, humor, interview/profile, new product, opinion, personal experience, technical. Buys 30 mss/year. Query with published clips. Length: 750-3,000 words. Pays $75-500. Sometimes pays expenses of writers on assignment.
Reprints: Accepts previously published submissions.
Photos: State availability of photos with submissions. Negotiates payment individually. Captions, identification of subjects required. Buys one-time rights.

ID SYSTEMS, The Magazine of Automated Data Collection, Helmers Publishing, Inc. 174 Concord St., Peterborough NH 03458. (603)924-9631. Fax: (603)924-7408. Managing Editor: Joe Fatton. Contact: Mary Langen, editor. 20% freelance written. Monthly magazine about automatic identification technologies. Circ. 75,000. **Pays on acceptance.** Byline given. Buys all rights. Reports in 2 months on queries. Free sample copy and writer's guidelines.
Nonfiction: Application stories, technical tutorials. "We want articles we have assigned, not spec articles." Buys 36 mss/year. Query with published clips. Length: 1,200 words. Pays $300.
Photos: Send photos with submission. Reviews contact sheets, transparencies (35mm) and prints. Offers no additional payment for photos accepted with ms. Identification of subjects required. Rights vary article to article.
Tips: "Send letter, résumé and clips. If background is appropriate, we will contact writer as needed. We give detailed instructions."

‡**INFORM, The Magazine of Information and Image Management**, Association for Information and Image Management, 1100 Wayne Ave., Silver Spring MD 20910. (301)587-8202. Fax: (301)587-5129. Editor: Bob Head. 30% freelance written. Prefers to work with writers with business/high tech experience. Monthly trade magazine on information and image processing. "Specifically we feature coverage of micrographics, electronic imaging and developments in storage and retrieval technology like optical disk, computer-assisted retrieval." Estab. 1943. Circ. 40,000. Pays on publication. Publishes ms an average of 3 months after acceptance. Byline given. Offers $50 kill fee. Buys first North American serial and second serial (reprint) rights. Accepts simultaneous submissions. Free sample copy and writer's guidelines.
Nonfiction: Interview/profile, new product, photo feature, technical. Buys 4-12 mss/year. Query. Length: 1,500 words. Pays $750. Sometimes pays expenses of writers on assignment.

Reprints: Send tearsheet, photocopy of article or typed ms with rights for sale noted.

Photos: State availability of photos with submission. Reviews negatives, 4×5 transparencies and prints. Offers no additional payment for photos accepted with ms. Captions, identification of subjects required. Buys all rights.

Columns/Departments: Trends (developments across industry segments); Technology (innovations of specific technology); Management (costs, strategies of managing information). Query. Length: 500-1,500 words. Pays $250.

Fillers: Facts, newsbreaks. Length: 150-500 words. Pays $50-250.

Tips: "We would encourage freelancers who have access to our editorial calendar to contact us regarding article ideas, inquiries, etc. Our feature section is the area where the need for quality freelance coverage of our industry is most desirable. The most likely candidate for acceptance is someone who has a proven background in business writing, and/or someone with demonstrated knowledge of high-tech industries as they relate to information management."

‡IN-HOUSE JOURNAL, Pacific Science Publishing, Inc., 2113 Wilshire Blvd., Suite 441, Santa Monica CA 90403. (310)473-9580. Fax: (310)477-1164. E-mail: pacificsci@aol.com. Managing Editor: John O'Brien. 25% freelance written. Bimonthly magazine covering desktop media—management, planning, problem solving. Estab. 1993. Circ. 17,000. Pays on publication. Publishes ms an average of 1 months after acceptance. Byline given. Buys all rights. Editorial lead time 2 months. Submit seasonal material 2 months in advance. Reports in 2 weeks on queries; 2 months on mss. Sample copy for $8\frac{1}{2} \times 11$ SAE with 4 first-class stamps. Writer's guidelines on assignment only.

Nonfiction: How-to, humor, interview/profile, new product, photo feature, technical. Buys 6 mss/year. Query with published clips. Length: 1,800-2,700 words. Pays $600-1,000. Sometimes pays expenses of writers on assignment.

Photos: Send photos with submission. Offers no additional payment for photos accepted with ms. Captions, model releases, identification of subjects required. Buys all rights.

JOURNAL OF INFORMATION ETHICS, McFarland & Co., Inc., Publishers, Box 611, Jefferson NC 28640. (910)246-4460. Fax: (910)246-5018. Editor: Robert Hauptman, LRS, 720 Fourth Ave. S., St. Cloud State University, St. Cloud MN 56301. (612)255-4822. Fax: (612)246-5018. All ms queries to Editor. 90% freelance written. Semiannual magazine covering information sciences, ethics. "Addresses ethical issues in all of the information sciences with a deliberately interdisciplinary approach. Topics range from electronic mail monitoring to library acquisition of controversial material. The journal's aim is to present thoughtful considerations of ethical dilemmas that arise in a rapidly evolving system of information exchange and dissemination." Estab. 1992. Circ. 500. Pays on publication. Publishes ms an average of 9 months after acceptance. Byline given. Buys all rights. Submit seasonal material 8 months in advance. Sample copy for $21. Writer's guidelines free on request.

Nonfiction: Essays, opinion, book reviews. Buys 10 mss/year. Send complete ms. Length: 500-3,500 words. Pays $25.

Tips: "Familiarize yourself with the many areas subsumed under the rubric of information ethics, e.g., privacy, scholarly communication, errors, peer review, confidentiality, e-mail, etc."

‡LAN MAGAZINE, The Network Solutions Magazine, Miller Freeman/United News & Media, 600 Harrison St., San Francisco CA 94107. Fax: (415)905-2587. E-mail: mmcmullen@infi.com. Website: http://www.lanmag.com. Editor: Melanie McMullen. Contact: Hanna Hurley, senior managing editor. 60% freelance written. Monthly magazine covering computer networking. Estab. 1986. Circ. 82,500. Pays on publication. Publishes ms an average of 3 months after acceptance. Byline given. Offers $500 kill fee. Buys first rights. Editorial lead time 4 months. Submit seasonal material 4 months in advance. Reports in 3 weeks on queries; 1 month on mss. Sample copy for $4.95 on newsstand. Writer's guidelines free on request.

Nonfiction: Technical. Buys 50 mss/year. Query with published clips. Length: 3,800-4,200 words. Pays $300/page.

‡MICROSTATION WORLD, Bentley Systems, 690 Pennsylvania Dr., Exton PA 19353. (610)458-2745. Editor: Jonathan Graham. Managing Editor: Peter Haapaniemi. 80% freelance written. Bentley Systems quarterly magazine covering computer-aided design. "*MicroStation World* magazine serves the information needs of managers, engineers and users of the various MicroStation software products. The magazine presents high-level user profiles, serves as the forum for the discussion of computer-aided design in the enterprise, articulates the latest executive issues, and provides in-depth profiles of Independent Software Developers. This kind of information, when balanced with clear application stories, news about the industry, and new Bentley products and services, will help executives maximize the effectiveness of technology." Estab. 1995. Circ. 60,000. Pays on publication. Publishes ms an average of 6 months after acceptance. Byline given. Offers 50% kill fee. Buys first North American serial or all rights. Editorial lead time 2 months. Accepts simultaneous submissions. Reports in 3 weeks on queries; 1 month on mss. Sample copy free on request.

Nonfiction: How-to (managing technology), new product (CAD industry), technical (companies using CAD), MicroStation CAD software-related stories. Buys 20 mss/year. Query with published clips. Length:

1,000-5,000 words. Pays $200-1,700. Sometimes pays expenses of writers on assignment.

Reprints: Accepts previously published submissions.

Photos: State availability of photos with submission. Reviews contact sheets, transparencies. Model releases, identification of subjects required.

Columns/Departments: Executive Insider (information to assist executives manage technology), 300 words. Buys 24 mss/year. Query with published clips. Pays $10-500.

Tips: "Address technology as it impacts management. *MicroStation World* helps executives understand and implement 3D CAD technology through interesting profiles and descriptions of companies and individuals using MicroStation."

NETWORK WORLD, Network World Publishing, 161 Worcester Rd., Framingham MA 01701. (508)875-6400. Fax: (508)820-3467. Website: http://www.nwfusion.com. Editor-in-Chief: John Gallant. Contact: Paul Desmond, features editor. 25% freelance written. Weekly tabloid covering data, voice and video communications networks (including news and features on communications management, hardware and software, services, education, technology and industry trends) for senior technical managers at large companies. Estab. 1986. Circ. 150,000. **Pays on acceptance.** Byline given. Offers negotiable kill fee. Buys all rights. Submit all material 2 months in advance. Reports in 5 months. Free sample copy and writer's guidelines.

Nonfiction: Exposé, general interest, how-to (build a strong communications staff, evaluate vendors, choose a value-added network service), humor, interview/profile, opinion, technical. Editorial calendar available. "Our readers are users: avoid vendor-oriented material." Buys 100-150 mss/year. Query with published clips. Length: 500-2,500 words. Pays $600 minimum.

Photos: Send photos with submission. Reviews 35mm, 2¼ and 4×5 transparencies and b&w prints (prefers 8×10 but can use 5×7). Captions, model releases and identification of subjects required. Buys one-time rights.

Tips: "We look for accessible treatments of technological, managerial or regulatory trends. It's OK to dig into technical issues as long as the article doesn't read like an engineering document. Feature section is most open to freelancers. Be informative, stimulating, controversial and technically accurate."

‡**NEWS/400**, Duke Communications International, 221 E. 29th St., Loveland CO 80538. (970)663-4700. Fax: (970)663-3285. E-mail: editors@news400.com. Website: http://www.news400.com. Editorial Director: Dale Agger. 40% freelance written. Magazine published 16 times/year covering AS/400 computer platform. "Programming, networking, IS management, technology for users of IBM AS/400 platform." Estab. 1982. Circ. 30,000 (international). Pays on publication. Publishes ms an average of 3 months after acceptance. Byline given. Offers 50% kill fee. Buys first, second serial (reprint) and all rights. Editorial lead time 4 months. Submit seasonal material 4 months in advance. Reports in 3 weeks on queries; 5 weeks on mss. Writer's guidelines free on request at http://www.news400.com.

Nonfiction: Opinion, technical. Buys 70 mss/year. Query. Length: 1,500-3,500 words. Pays 17-50¢/word. Pays in copies upon request of author. Sometimes pays expenses of writers on assignment.

Reprints: Accepts previously published submissions.

Photos: State availability of photos with submission. Offers no additional payment for photos accepted with ms.

Columns/Departments: Dialog Box (computer industry opinion), 1,500 words; Load'n'go (complete utility). Buys 24 mss/year. Query. Pays $250-1,000.

Tips: "Be familiar with IBM AS/400 computer platform."

‡**OEM MAGAZINE, For Systems & Software Builders**, CMP Publications, 600 Community Dr., Manhasset NY 11030. (516)562-5624. E-mail: rbmerrit@eet.cmp.com. Website: http://www.techwes.com/oem. Editor: Rick Boyd Merritt. Managing Editor: David Lieberman. 50% freelance written. Monthly magazine covering computer and communication system design. "Our readers are techno-business savvy managers on the lookout for trends in new technology and markets." Estab. 1993. Circ. 80,000. **Pays on acceptance.** Publishes ms an average of 2 months after acceptance. Byline given. Buys all rights. Editorial lead time 3 months. Sample copy free on request.

Nonfiction: Essays, exposé, interview/profile, opinion, technical. Buys 20-25 mss/year. Query with published clips. Length: 800-2,500 words. Pays 50¢-$1/word. Sometimes pays expenses of writers on assignment.

‡**RESELLER MANAGEMENT**, Cahners Publishing Co., 275 Washington St., Newton MA 02158. (617)558-4723. Fax: (617)558-4757. Editor: John Russell. 65% freelance written. Monthly magazine covering value added resellers, computer technology. "*Reseller Management*'s readers are managers in the Value Added Reseller Channel for computer products, charged with supervising, planning, and often executing reseller strategies. *Reseller Management*'s mission is a practical handbook for value added resellers. Virtually all editorial should be 'actionable.' Readers should generally be able to make a job-related decision or take a job-related action based on articles." Circ. 85,000. **Pays on acceptance.** Byline given. Kill fee varies. Buys all rights or makes work-for-hire assignments. Editorial lead time 5 months. Writer's guidelines free on request.

Nonfiction: How-to, interview/profile, new product, opinion, technical. Buys 60 mss/year. Query. Length: 2,000 words maximum. Pays 70¢/word. Pays expenses of writers on assignment when agreed upon in advance.
Reprints: Accepts previously published submissions.
Photos: State availability of photos. Offers no additional payment for photos accepted with ms.
Columns/Departments: Pays 70¢/word.
Tips: "Think of all assignments as a package of elements. Look for sidebar opportunities. Pull out pieces of the main text. Create lists of action items. Look for mini-case history opportunities (one per package is usually right) at 300 words. Key Questions in Approaching Assignments: How does this story topic impact a VAR's business and the VAR community? What specific opportunities and perils exist for VARs relative to the topic? What quantifiable data elements support/disprove the above questions? What do VARs say, pro and con about the issue? What advice do they offer? What do vendors and experts say and what advice do they offer. What specific how-to guidelines should VARs follow to best deal with this particular story topic and exploit the relevant opportunity? How should the assignment be broken into multiple elements to present the material in keeping with the magazine's packaging goals?"

SMART ACCESS, Solutions for Microsoft Access Developers and Power Users, Pinnacle Publishing, Inc., P.O. Box 888, Kent WA 98035-0888. (206)251-1900. Fax: (206)251-5057. E-mail: smartacc@pinpub.com. Website: http://www.pinpub.com. Editor: Paul Litwin. Contact: Laurie Maloney, associate editor. 95% freelance written. Monthly technical newsletter covering software development with Microsoft Access. "*Smart Access* provides hands-on advice, techniques, and tips for creating more effective software applications—faster—using Microsoft Access." Estab. 1993. Circ. 9,000. Pays on publication. Publishes ms an average of 3 months after acceptance. Byline given. Offers 25% kill fee. Buys all rights. Editorial lead time 4 months. Reports in 2 months on queries; 3 months on mss. Sample copy with writer's kit free on request.
Nonfiction: Book excerpts, how-to, new product, technical. "Please! No general interest articles about software use. Must be targeted to the product the newsletter covers." Buys 72 mss/year. Send complete ms. Length: 500-5,000 words. Pays $100 and up.
Tips: "Use the software product the newsletter covers. Be an expert in it! Develop a specific technique that other users would want to try out and explain it thoroughly in your article. Start with tips! Figure out ways to do something easier or faster and share that in a brief write-up. We pay $25 and a pound of coffee for each tip and we use scads of them!"

‡SOFTWARE QUARTERLY (SQ), IBM's Magazine of Software Technologies, IBM Corp. 5 W. Kirkwood Blvd., Roanoke TX 76299-0001. (817)962-6551. Fax: (817)962-7218. E-mail: hodel@vnet.ibm.com. Editor: Alan E. Hodel. 80% freelance written. Quarterly magazine covering advanced software and networking. "Requires knowledge of computer/networking industry and software technologies. *SQ* goes to top corporate and IS execs at at Fortune 500 class companies worldwide." Estab. 1994. Circ. 300,000 (in six languages). Pays on publication. Publishes ms an average of 3 months after acceptance. Byline given. Buys all rights or makes work-for-hire assignments. Editorial lead time 6 months. Sample copy free on request.
Nonfiction: How-to, interview/profile, technical. Query with published clips. Length: 2,000-3,500 words. Pays $1/word. Pays expenses of writers on assignment.

SUN WORLD ONLINE, IDG's Web Magazine for Unix Professionals, (formerly *Advanced Systems/Sun World*, IDG, 501 Second St., San Francisco CA 94107. (415)267-1725. Fax: (415)267-1732. E-mail: mark@sunworld.com. Website: http://www.sun.com/sunworldonline. (Prefers correspondence by e-mail.) Editor: Mark Cappel. 20% freelance written. Monthly web magazine covering Unix-on-Risc. "We are a product and how-to magazine for Unix professionals with an emphasis on Sun. *Sunworld Online* is written to be accessible to a semi-technical audience." Estab. 1989. Circ. 50,000. **Pays on acceptance.** Publishes ms an average of 1 month after acceptance. Byline given. Offers 50% kill fee. Buys first North American serial rights and nonexclusive all other and international rights. Editorial lead time 3 months. Submit seasonal material 3 months in advance. Query for electronic submissions. Reports in 3-4 weeks on queries; 1 month on mss.
Nonfiction: Technical, technical features, emphasis on practical issues, selections. Buys 15 mss/year. Query. Length: 1,500-5,000 words. Pays $250-2,000. Sometimes pays expenses of writers on assignment.
Photos: State availability of photos with submission. Negotiates payment individually. Captions required. Buys all rights.
Columns/Departments: Seek columnists with hands-on experience. Query. Pays $500-750.
Tips: "We need authors who have Risc workstations, work experience/expertise in a particular field relevant to the topics being discussed, who can write a well organized, readable article, meet a deadline, and know what they're talking about."

UNIFORUM'S IT SOLUTIONS, (formerly *UniForum Monthly*), UniForum Association, 2901 Tasman Dr., #205, Santa Clara CA 95054-1100. (408)986-8840. Fax: (408)986-1645. E-mail: pubs@uniforum.org. Website: http://www.uniforum.org. Publications Director: Richard Shippee. Managing Editor: Cedric Braun.

Contact: Jeff Bartlett, executive editor. 80% freelance writtten. Monthly trade journal covering UNIX and open systems. "Writers must have a sound knowledge of the UNIX operating system." Estab. 1981. Circ. 50,000. **Pays on acceptance.** Publishes ms an average of 2 months after acceptance. Byline given. Offers 30% kill fee. Buys all rights. Reports in 2 months. Free sample copy and writer's guidelines.

Nonfiction: Interview/profile, opinion, technical. Buys 35 mss/year. Query with or without published clips. Length: 1,000-3,500 words. Pays $0-1,200. Sometimes pays in other premiums or contributors copies "when article is written by industry member." Pays expenses of writers on assignment. International writers actively sought.

Photos: Send photos with submission. "Photos are required with manuscript but offers no additional payment." Buys one-time rights.

Columns/Departments: Career Corner (career tips), 700-800 words; VAR Update, 700-800 words. Federal Watch, 700-800 words. Buys 12 mss/year. Query. Pays $0-250.

‡**UNISPHERE, The Magazine for Unisys Users**, Cardinal Business Media Inc.12225 Greenville Ave., Suite 700, Dallas TX 75243. (214)669-9000. Fax: (214)669-9909. E-mail: 73430.2347@compuserve.com. Website: http://www.btb.com/cardina/uni. Managing Editor: Debby English. 30% freelance written. Monthly magazine covering computer industry as it applies to Unisys users. "*Unisphere* provides information for IS management and technical professionals in Unisys host-based enterprises. Each issue includes a cover story or comprehensive focus section on significant new products, trends and strategies in the industry. Regular features and technical articles cover client/server computing, networking, storage management, etc." Estab. 1981. Circ. 19,600. Pays on publication. Publishes ms an average of 2 months after acceptance. Byline given. Buys all rights and makes work-for-hire assignments. Editorial lead time 3 months. Reports in 2 weeks on queries; 1 month on mss (sooner if possible). Sample copy and writer's guidelines free on request.

Nonfiction: How-to (computer industry), interview/profile, new product, opinion, technical. Nothing about vendor products that is self-serving or promotional. Buys 25 mss/year. Query. Length: 800-2,500 words. Pays $120/page or as agreed in advance. Sometimes pays expenses of writers on assignment.

Photos: State availability of photos with submission. Reviews 4×5 transparencies. Offers no additional payment for photos accepted with ms. Captions, model releases, identification of subjects required.

Tips: "Stay informed about news and product releases in the Unisys market."

‡**VB TECH JOURNAL**, Oakley Publishing Company, P.O. Box 70167, Eugene OR 97401. (541)747-0800. E-mail: 76701.32@compuserve.com. Editor: J.D. Hildebrand. 95% freelance written. Monthly magazine covering Visual Basic programming. "*VB Tech* contains indepth reviews of Visual Basic programming tools and also techniques for programmers. There is also a section devoted to VB-related industry news and new product information." Estab. 1995. Circ. 30,000. Pays on publication. Publishes ms an average of 4 months after acceptance. Byline given. Kill fee is based on article length and content. Buys first North American serial rights (for fiction) or all rights. Editorial lead time 3 months. Submit seasonal material 5 months in advance. Reports in 6 weeks on queries; 1 month on mss. Sample copy and writer's guidelines free on request.

Nonfiction: How-to (VB Programming Tips and Traps), new product (VB Tools—we assign reviews; do not submit reviews), personal experience (2 per issue, 500 word editorials about: programming, computer industry), technical (Tips and Traps). "We are not a user magazine; articles must be about Visual Basic programming." Buys 130 mss/year. Query. Length: 2,500-5,000 words. Pays a minimum of $75 for articles but payment is determined by length, content.

Fiction: Dean Wesley Smith, fiction editor. Send fiction to Dean Smith P.O. Box 419, Lincoln City, OR 97367. Buys 24 mss/year. Send complete ms. Length: 1,000-5,000 words. Pays 10¢/word.

Tips: "Our magazine is a highly technical resource for Visual Basic programmers and developers. Freelancers should call for a copy of the editorial calendar and writer's guidelines. If they have an idea to fit in the editorial calendar, then query the Editor, J.D. Hildebrand via regular mail or e-mail. Please state your programming experience."

‡**WINDOWS TECH JOURNAL**, Oakley Publishing Company, P.O. Box 70167, Eugene OR 97401. (541)747-0800. E-mail: 70262.2051@compuserve.com. Editor: J.D. Hildebrand. Contact: Kevin Weeks, senior editor. 95% freelance written. Monthly magazine covering Windows computer programming. "The publication contains tools and techniques for Windows programmers; it covers component based development." Estab. 1992. Circ. 25,000. Pays on publication. Publishes ms an average of 4 months after acceptance. Byline given. Kill fee based on article length and content. Buys all rights. Editorial lead time 3 months. Submit seasonal material 5 months in advance. Reports in 6 weeks on queries; 1 month on mss. Sample copy and writer's guidelines free on request.

Nonfiction: How-to (programming how-tos in Windows environment), new product/reviews (we assign reviews; do not submit), technical (programming). "We are not a user magazine; articles must be about Windows programming." Buys 130 mss/year. Query. Length: 2,500-5,000 words. Pay determined by length and content; $75 minimum.

Tips: "Our magazine is a highly technical resource for Windows programmers and developers. Freelancers should call for a copy of our editorial calendar and writer's guidelines. If they have an idea to fit in the editorial calendar, then query the senior editor, Kevin Weeks, via regular mail or e-mail. We are interested in articles about Delphi, Visual Basic, C, C++, Access."

‡X-RAY MAGAZINE, Publishing Workgroup & Multimedia Technology for Quark Users, X-Ray Publishing Ventures International, 2700 19th St., San Francisco CA 94110. (415)861-9258. E-mail: xrayedit@aol.com. Editor: John Cruise. 90-95% freelance written. Bimonthly magazine covering Quark (Inc.) and Quark-related software/hardware. "Topics must be of interest to users of Quark software (QuarkX-Press Quark Publishing System, etc.)." Estab. 1995. Circ.250,000. Pays within 30 days of publication. Publishes ms an average of 2 months after acceptance. Byline given. Buys all rights. Editorial lead time 4 months. Accepts simultaneous submissions. Reports in 2 weeks on queries. Sample copy for 8½×11 SAE with 6 first-class stamps.
Nonfiction: General interest, how-to (Quark/Quark-related software), new product, opinion, technical. Buys 50-60 mss/year. Query with published clips, preferably by e-mail. Length: 1,200-4,000 words. Pays $300-1,250. Sometimes pays expenses of writers on assignment.
Photos: State availability of photos with submission. Reviews contact sheets, negatives, transparencies, prints. Negotiates payment individually. Identification of subjects required. Buys one-time rights.
Columns/Departments: In The Trenches/Editorial, Design & Production (hands-on, how-to articles) 1,250-1,500 words; On a Budget (being frugal), 1,250-1,500 words; Xclamation Point! (first-person/opinion) 1,100 words. Query with published clips, preferably by e-mail. Buys 25-30 mss/year. Pays $350-450.

INSURANCE

‡BUSINESS & HEALTH, Solutions in Managed Care, Medical Economics Publishing Co., 5 Paragon Dr., Montvale NJ 07645-1742. (201)358-7208. Fax: (201)573-8979. E-mail: b&h@medec.com. Editor: Richard Service. Managing Editor: Helen Lippman. 90% freelance written. Monthly magazine covering health care for employers offering benefits for workers. "*B&H* carries articles about how employers can cut their health care costs and improve the quality of care they provide to workers. We also write about health care policy at the federal, state and local levels." Estab. 1983. Circ. 50,000. **Pays on acceptance.** Publishes ms an average of 2 months after acceptance. Byline given. Offers 20% kill fee. Buys all rights. Editorial lead time 3 months. Submit seasonal material 4 months in advance. Reports in 3 months. Sample copy for 9×12 SAE with 6 first-class stamps. Writer's guidelines for #10 SASE.
Nonfiction: How-to (cut health care benefits costs, provide better care); case studies (of successful employer-led efforts); trend piece on broad issues such as 24-hour coverage or benefits for retirees. Buys approx. 50 mss/year. Query with published clips. Length: 2,000-3,500 words. Pays $1,000-1,700 for features, plus expenses of writers on assignment.
Columns/Departments: Primarily staff-written but will consider queries.
Tips: "Please be familiar with *B&H* and follow writer's guidelines. Articles should combine a business angle with a human interest approach and address both cost-containment and quality of care. Include cost-benefit analysis data and material for charts or graphs whenever possible."

FLORIDA UNDERWRITER, National Underwriter Co., 9887 Fourth St., N., Suite 230, St. Petersburg FL 33702-2488. (813)576-1101. Editor: James E. Seymour. Editorial Director: Ian Mackenzie. 20% freelance written. Monthly magazine about insurance. "*Florida Underwriter* covers insurance for Florida insurance professionals: producers, executives, risk managers, employee benefit administrators. We want material about any insurance line, Life & Health or Property & Casualty, but *must* have a Florida tag—Florida authors preferred." Estab. 1984. Circ. 10,000. Pays on publication. Publishes ms an average of 3 months after acceptance. Byline given. Buys all rights. Submit seasonal material 3 months in advance. Accepts simultaneous submissions. Reports in 1 month. Free sample copy and writer's guidelines.
Nonfiction: Essay, exposé, historical/nostalgic, how-to, interview/profile, new product, opinion, technical. "We don't want articles that aren't about insurance for insurance people or those that lack Florida angle. No puff pieces. Note: Most non-inhouse pieces are contributed gratis by industry experts." Buys 6 mss/year. Query with or without published clips, or send complete ms. Length: 500-1,500 words. Pays $50-150 for assigned articles; $25-100 for unsolicited articles. "Industry experts contribute in return for exposure." Sometimes pays expenses of writers on assignment.
Reprints: Send tearsheet or photocopy of article or typed ms with rights for sale noted and information about when and where the article previously appeared. Pays 25% of amount paid for an original article.
Photos: State availability of photos with submission. Send photos with submission. Reviews 5×7 prints. Offers no additional payment for photos accepted with ms. Identification of subjects required.

GEICO DIRECT, K.L. Publications, 2001 Killebrew Dr., Suite 105, Bloomington MN 55425-1879. Editor: Bernadette Baczynski. 60% freelance written. Semiannual magazine published for the Government Employees Insurance Company (GEICO) policyholders. Estab. 1988. Circ. 2,000,000. **Pays on acceptance.** Byline given. Buys first North American serial rights. Reports in 2 months. Writer's guidelines for #10 SASE.

Nonfiction: Americana, home and auto safety, car care, financial, lifestyle, travel. Query with published clips. Length: 1,000 words. Pays $350-500.
Photos: Reviews 35mm transparencies. Payment varies.
Columns/Departments: Moneywise, 50+, Your Car. Query with published clips. Length: 500-600 words. Pays $175-350.
Tips: "We prefer work from published/established writers, especially those with specialized knowledge of the insurance industry, safety issues and automotive topics."

‡INSURANCE JOURNAL, The Property/Casualty Magazine of the West, Wells Publishing Co., 9191 Towne Centre Dr., Suite 550, San Diego CA 92122. (619)455-7717. Fax: (619)546-1462. E-mail: ijwest@adnc.com or 74407.635@compuserve.com. Website: http://www.insurancejrnl.com. Publisher: Mark Wells. Managing Editor: Richard A. Sherer. 20% freelance written. Biweekly trade magazine covering property/casualty insurance. "Market-insurance brokers and agents in 4 western states; articles must be need-to-knows; news/trend driven; insurance savvy a must; also political know-how." Estab. 1921. Circ. 10,248. Pays on publication. Byline given. Offers 10% kill fee. Buys other negotiated rights. Editorial lead time 2 months. Submit seasonal material 3 months in advance. Reports in 2 weeks on queries. Sample copy free on request.
Nonfiction: By assignment. "Nothing personal, inspirational or not intelligently pegged to P/C insurance. Query. Length: 600-1,500 words. Sometimes pays expenses of writers on assignment.
Photos: State availability of photos with submission. Reviews contact sheets and negatives. Negotiates payment individually. Identification of subjects required. Buys one-time rights.
Tips: "Identify trend in insurance—on sales or management sides—and be able to find right sources to intelligently discuss."

THE LEADER, Fireman's Fund Insurance Co., 777 San Marin Dr., Novato CA 94998-0000. (415)899-2109. Fax: (415)899-2126. E-mail: jim_toland%ffic@notesgw.compuserve.com. Website: http://www.the-fund.com. Editor/Communications Manager: Jim Toland. 70% freelance written. Quarterly magazine on insurance. "*The Leader* contains articles and information for Fireman's Fund employees and retirees about special projects, meetings, events, employees and offices nationwide—emphasizing the business of insurance and the unique people who work for the company. Some travel and lifestyle features." Estab. 1863. **Pays on acceptance.** Publishes ms an average of 3 months after acceptance. Buys one-time rights. Accepts simultaneous submissions. Reports in 1 month or less on mss. Sample copy for SASE.
Nonfiction: Interview/profile, new products, employees involved in positive activities in the insurance industry and in the communities where company offices are located. Query with published clips. Length: 200-2,500 words. Pays $100-500.
Reprints: Send photocopy of article or typed ms with rights for sale noted. Pays 100% of amount paid for an original article.
Photos: Reviews contact sheets, prints. Sometimes buys color slides. Offers $50-100/photo for b&w, up to $250 for color. Buys one-time rights.
Tips: "It helps to work in the insurance business and/or know people at Fireman's Fund. Writers with business reporting experience are usually most successful—though we've published many first-time writers. Research the local Fireman's Fund branch office (not sales agents who are independents). Look for newsworthy topics. Strong journalism and reporting skills are greatly appreciated."

JEWELRY

THE DIAMOND REGISTRY BULLETIN, 580 Fifth Ave., #806, New York NY 10036. (212)575-0444. Fax: (212)575-0722. E-mail: diamond58@aol.com. Editor-in-Chief: Joseph Schlussel. 50% freelance written. Monthly newsletter. Estab. 1969. Pays on publication. Buys all rights. Submit seasonal material 1 month in advance. Accepts simultaneous submissions. Reports in 3 weeks. Sample copy for $5.
Nonfiction: Prevention advice (on crimes against jewelers); how-to (ways to increase sales in diamonds, improve security, etc.); interview (of interest to diamond dealers or jewelers). Submit complete ms. Length: 50-500 words. Pays $75-150.
Reprints: Accepts previously published submissions.
Tips: "We seek ideas to increase sales of diamonds. We also have interest in diamond mining."

THE ENGRAVERS JOURNAL, 26 Summit St., P.O. Box 318, Brighton MI 48116. (313)229-5725. Fax: (313)229-8320. Co-Publisher: Michael J. Davis. Managing Editor: Rosemary Farrell. 15% freelance written. "We are eager to work with published/established writers as well as new/unpublished writers." Magazine published 10 times/year covering the recognition and identification industry (engraving, marking devices, awards, jewelry, and signage.) "We provide practical information for the education and advancement of our readers, mainly retail business owners." Estab. 1975. **Pays on acceptance.** Publishes ms an average of 1 year after acceptance. Byline given "only if writer is recognized authority." Buys one-time rights and makes work-for-hire assignments. Reports in 2 weeks. Free writer's guidelines. Sample copy to "those who send writing samples with inquiry."

Nonfiction: General interest (industry-related); how-to (small business subjects, increase sales, develop new markets, use new sales techniques, etc.); technical. No general overviews of the industry. Query with writing samples "published or not, or send samples and résumé to be considered for assignments on speculation." Length: 1,000-5,000 words. Pays $100-500 for assigned articles; $50 for unsolicited articles.

Reprints: Accepts previously published submissions.

Photos: Send photos with query. Pays variable rate. Captions, model release, identification of subjects required.

Tips: "Articles should always be down to earth, practical and thoroughly cover the subject with authority. We do not want the 'textbook' writing approach, vagueness, or theory—our readers look to us for sound practical information. We use an educational slant, publishing both trade-oriented articles and general business topics of interest to a small retail-oriented readership."

JOURNALISM AND WRITING

Journalism and writing magazines cover both the business and creative sides of writing. Writing publications offer inspiration and support for professional and beginning writers. Although there are many valuable writing publications that do not pay, we list those that pay for articles.

AUTHORSHIP, National Writers Association, 1450 S. Havana, Suite 424, Aurora CO 80012. (303)751-7844. Editor: Sandy Whelchel. Bimonthly magazine covering writing articles only. "Association magazine targeted to beginning and professional writers. Covers how-to, humor, marketing issues." Estab. 1950s. Circ. 4,000. **Pays on acceptance.** Byline given. Buys first North American serial or second serial (reprint) rights. Editorial lead time 3 months. Submit seasonal material 6 months in advance. Accepts simultaneous submissions. Reports in 2 months on queries. Sample copy for #10 SASE.

Nonfiction: Writing only. Poetry (November/December). Buys 25 mss/year. Query or send complete ms. Length: 900 words. Pays $10 or discount on memberships and copies.

Photos: State availability of photos with submission. Reviews 5×7 prints. Offers no additional payment for photos accepted with ms. Model releases and identification of subjects required. Buys one-time rights.

Reprints: Accepts previously published submissions.

Tips: "Members of National Writers Association are given preference."

BOOK DEALERS WORLD, North American Bookdealers Exchange, P.O. Box 606, Cottage Grove OR 97424. Phone/fax: (541)942-7455. Editorial Director: Al Galasso. 50% freelance written. Quarterly magazine covering writing, self-publishing and marketing books by mail. Circ. 20,000. Pays on publication. Publishes ms an average of 3 months after acceptance. Byline given. Buys first serial and second serial (reprint) rights. Accepts simultaneous submissions. Reports in 1 month. Sample copy for $3.

Nonfiction: Book excerpts (writing, mail order, direct mail, publishing); how-to (home business by mail, advertising); interview/profile (of successful self-publishers). Positive articles on self-publishing, new writing angles, marketing, etc. Buys 10 mss/year. Send complete ms. Length: 1,000-1,500 words. Pays $25-50.

Reprints: Send typed ms with rights for sale noted and information about when and where the article previously appeared. Pays 80% of amount paid for an original article.

Columns/Departments: Print Perspective (about new magazines and newsletters); Self-Publisher Profile (on successful self-publishers and their marketing strategy). Buys 20 mss/year. Send complete ms. Length: 250-1,000 words. Pays $5-20.

Fillers: Fillers concerning writing, publishing or books. Buys 6/year. Length: 100-250 words. Pays $3-10.

Tips: "Query first. Get a sample copy of the magazine."

BYLINE, P.O. Box 130596, Edmond OK 73013-0001. (405)348-5591. Editor/Publisher: Marcia Preston. Managing Editor: Kathryn Fanning. 80-90% freelance written. Eager to work with new/unpublished writers. Monthly magazine for writers and poets. "We stress encouragement of beginning writers." Estab. 1981. **Pays on acceptance.** Publishes ms an average of 3 months after acceptance. Byline given. Buys first North American serial rights. Reports in 2 months or less. Sample copy for $4 postpaid. Writer's guidelines for #10 SASE.

Nonfiction: How-to, humor, inspirational, personal experience, *all* connected with writing and selling. Read magazine for special departments. Buys approximately 100 mss/year. Prefers queries; will read complete mss. Length: 1,500-1,800 words for features. Usually pays $50 for features. Needs short humor on writing (300-600 words). Pays $15-25 on acceptance.

Fiction: General fiction of high quality. Send complete ms: 2,000-4,000 words preferred. Pays $100.

Poetry: Betty Shipley, poetry editor. Any style, on a writing theme. Preferred length: 4-30 lines. Pays $5-10 on acceptance, plus free issue.

Tips: "We'd like to see more 1,500-1,800 word features on how to write better, market better, etc."

CANADIAN WRITER'S JOURNAL, Gordon M. Smart Publications, P.O. Box 6618, Depot 1, Victoria, British Columbia V8P 5N7 Canada. (604)477-8807. Editor: Gordon M. Smart. Accepts well-written articles by inexperienced writers. Quarterly magazine for writers. Estab. 1985. Circ. 350. 75% freelance written. Pays on publication. Publishes ms an average of 9 months after acceptance. Byline given. Reports in 2 months. Sample copy for $3 and $1 postage. Writer's guidelines for #10 SAE and IRC.
Nonfiction: How-to articles for writers. Buys 50-55 mss/year. Query optional. Length: 500-1,200 words. Pays about $5/published magazine page.
Reprints: Send typed ms with rights for sale noted and information about when and where the article previously appeared. Pays 100% of amount paid for an original article.
Fiction: Requirements currently being met by annual contest. SASE for rules.
Poetry: Short poems or extracts used as part of articles on the writing of poetry. Annual poetry contest. Wind Song Column uses some short poems. Consult guidelines for details.
Tips: "We prefer short, tightly written, informative how-to articles. US writers note that US postage cannot be used to mail from Canada. Obtain Canadian stamps, use IRCs or send small amounts in cash."

‡**THE COMICS JOURNAL**, Fantagraphics Book Inc., 7563 Lake City Way NE, Seattle WA 98115. (206)524-1967. Editor: Gary Groth. Contact: Tom Spurgeon, managing editor. 80% freelance written. Monthly magazine covering comics industry. "*The Comics Journal* is the comics industry's leading magazine for investigative journalism and criticism." Estab. 1976. Circ. 9,000. Pays on publication. Publishes ms an average of 2 months after acceptance. Byline given. Offers 100% kill fee. Buys first and electronic rights. Editorial lead time 1 month. Submit seasonal material 1 month in advance. Accepts simultaneous submissions. Reports in 6 weeks on queries; 1 month on mss. Sample copy for $5. Writer's guidelines free on request.
Nonfiction: Essays, historical/nostalgic, interview/profile, opinion, criticism. Buys 250 mss/year. Length: 800-6,500 words. Pays 3-5¢/word. Sometimes pays expenses of writers on assignment.
Reprints: Accepts previously published submissions.
Photos: Send photos with submission. Negotiates payment individually. Identification of subjects required. Buys one-time rights.
Columns/Departments: Objective Opinions (criticism), 2,000 words; Art and Craft (historical/aesthetic), 2,000 words. Buys 50 mss/year. Send complete ms. Pays 2-5¢/word.

EDITOR & PUBLISHER, 11 W. 19th St., New York NY 10011-4234. Fax: (212)929-1259. Website: http://www.mediainfo.com/edpub. Editor: Robert U. Brown. Managing Editor: John Consoli. Contact: Beth Hoben, editorial assistant. 10% freelance written. Weekly magazine for newspaper publishers, editors, executives, employees and others in communications, marketing, advertising, etc. Estab. 1884. Circ. 25,000. Pays on publication. Publishes ms an average of 2 months after acceptance. Buys first serial rights. Reports in 2 months. Sample copy for $2.25.
Nonfiction: Uses newspaper business articles and news items; also newspaper personality features and printing technology. Query by fax.
Tips: "Freelancer may sell electronic or print rights elsewhere after publication in *E&P*, but we reserve the right to make articles printed in *E&P* available online for research purposes."

EXCHANGE, A Newsletter for Writers Who Are Christian, Exchange Publishing, 15 Torrance Rd., #104, Scarborough, Ontario M1J 3K2 Canada. (416)439-4320 (evenings & weekends). Editor: Audrey Dorsch. 70% freelance written. Quarterly newsletter on the craft of writing. "A vehicle for Christian writers to exchange information and ideas, and receive professional development." Estab. 1991. Circ. 300. Pays on publication. Byline given. Offers 30-50% kill fee. Not copyrighted. Buys one-time rights. Editorial lead time 2 months. Reports in 1 month.
Nonfiction: How-to, humor, opinion, personal experience. All must be related to writing. Buys 20 mss/year. Send complete ms. Length: 300-500 words. Pays 8¢/word. Sometimes pays copies or other premiums to foreign contributors who cannot exchange Canadian currency. Sometimes pays expenses of writers on assignment.
Tips: "Think about what writing help you would have liked. Now that you are past that hurdle, write about it to help other writers."

‡**FACTSHEET FIVE, The Definitive Guide to the Zine Revolution**, P.O. Box 170099, San Francisco CA 94117-0099. Fax: (415)668-1781. E-mail: f5seth@sirius.com. Editor: R. Seth Friedman. Contact: Miriam

---

ALWAYS ENCLOSE a self-addressed, stamped envelope (SASE) with all your queries and correspondence.

Wolf. Magazine published 5 times/year covering 'zines. "*Factsheet Five* reviews more than 1,000 small press publications each issue. We also run features of interest to the 'zine community." Circ. 13,000. Pays on publication. Byline given. Not copyrighted. Buys first North American serial rights. Editorial lead time 2 months. Submit seasonal material 3 months in advance. Accepts simultaneous submissions. Sample copy for $6. Writer's guidelines for #10 SASE.

Nonfiction: Book excerpts, essays, exposé, general interest, historical/nostalgic, how-to, interview/profile, opinion, personal experience. Buys 10 mss/year. Send complete ms. Length: 500-3,000 words. Pays $25-100. Sometimes pays expenses of writers on assignment.

Photos: State availability of photos with submission. Negotiates payment individually. Identification of subjects required.

FICTION WRITER'S GUIDELINE, The Newsletter of Fiction Writer's Connection (FWC), P.O. Box 4065, Deerfield Beach FL 33442-4065. (954)426-4705. Editor: Blythe Camenson. 50% freelance written. Monthly newsletter covering how-to for fiction writers. "*Fiction Writer's Guideline* takes an upbeat approach to encourage writers, but doesn't shy away from the sometimes harsh realities of the publishing industry." Estab. 1993. Circ. 1,000. Pays on publication. Publishes ms an average of 3 months after acceptance. Byline given. Buys first, one-time or second serial (reprint) rights. Editorial lead time 1 month. Submit seasonal material 3 months in advance. Accepts simultaneous submissions. Reports in 2 weeks on queries; 1 month on mss. Sample copy for $3.50. Writer's guidelines for #10 SASE.

Nonfiction: General interest, how-to (the business and craft of writing fiction), interview/profile (of agents, editors, and authors), new product, personal experience (on getting published), short book reviews (how-to books for writers). Buys 30 mss/year. Query. Length: 200-1,500 words. Pays $1-25. Sometimes pays expenses of writers on assignment. Send complete ms.

Reprints: Send typed ms with rights for sale noted and information about when and where the article previously appeared.

Columns/Departments: Advice From An Agent/Editor (how to approach, what they're looking for, advice to fiction writers), 1,500 words; "Writing Tips" (specific advice on style and structure), 400 words. Buys 12 mss/year. Query. Pays $1-25.

Fillers: Anecdotes, facts, newsbreaks; all to do with the business or craft of writing fiction. Buys 50/year. Length: 20-100 words. Pays $1-10.

Tips: Looking for "interviews with agents or editors. Our guidelines include specific questions to ask. Query or call first to make sure your choice hasn't already been interviewed. We also need a monthly cover article on some aspect of writing fiction, from specific tips for different categories/genres, to handling viewpoint, characterization, dialogue etc. Also fillers. Request sample copy to see the format."

GOTTA WRITE NETWORK LITMAG, Maren Publications, 612 Cobblestone Circle, Glenview IL 60025. Fax: (847)296-7631. E-mail: netera@aol.com. Editor: Denise Fleischer. 80% freelance written. Semi-annual literary magazine covering writer's techniques, markets. "Any article should be presented as if openly speaking to the reader. It should inform from the first paragraph to the last." Estab. 1988. Circ. 200. Pays after publication. Publishes ms an average of 1 year after acceptance. Byline given. Buys first North American serial rights or makes work-for-hire assignments. Editorial lead time 6 months. Reports in 4 months. Sample copy for $5. Writer's guidelines for #10 SASE.

Nonfiction: Articles (on writing), how-to (on writing techniques), interview/profile (for Behind the Scenes section), new product (books, software, computers), photo feature (on poets/writers/editors big and small press). "Don't want to see 'My First Sale,' 'When I Can't Write,' 'Dealing With Rejection,' 'Writer's Block,' a speech from a writers convention, an article published 10 times by other editors." Buys 25 mss/year. Query with published clips or send complete ms. Accepts e-mail queries and submissions. Length: 3-5 pages. Pays $5 and contributor's copy.

Photos: State availability of photos with submission. Offers $10 (more for cover art). Captions, model releases and identification of subjects required. Buys one-time rights.

Columns/Departments: In Print (writing books—reviews), 2 pages. Buys 50 mss/year. Pays $5.

Fiction: Adventure, ethnic, experimental, fantasy, historical, horror, humorous, mainstream, mystery, romance, science fiction, slice-of-life vignettes, suspense, western. No dark fantasy. Buys 15 and up mss/year. Query with published clips. Send complete ms. Page length: 5-10. Pays $10 maximum.

Poetry: Avant-garde, free verse, haiku, beat—experimental. No poetry no one can understand or that has no meaning.

Fillers: Anecdotes, facts, newsbreaks, tips. Buys 100/year. Length: 100-250 words. Pays in contributor's copies. Open to editor's releases, feature ideas and product information from the manufacturer.

MAINE IN PRINT, Maine Writers and Publishers Alliance, 12 Pleasant St., Brunswick ME 04011. (207)729-6333. Fax: (207)725-1014. Editor: Lisa Holbrook. Monthly newsletter for writers, editors, teachers, librarians, etc. focusing on Maine literature and the craft of writing. Estab. 1975. Circ. 5,000. Pays on publication. Publishes ms an average of 2 months after acceptance. Byline given. Offers 50% kill fee. Buys one-time rights. Editorial lead time 1 month. Accepts simultaneous submissions. Reports in 2 weeks on queries; 1 month on mss. Sample copy and writer's guidelines free.

Nonfiction: Essays, how-to (writing), interview/profile, technical writing. No creative writing, fiction or poetry. Buys 20 mss/year. Query with published clips. Length: 400-1,500 words. Pays $25-75 for assigned articles.

Photos: State availability of photos with submission. Offers no additional payment for photos accepted with ms.

Columns/Departments: Front-page articles (writing related), 500-1,500 words. Buys 12 mss/year. Query. Pays $25 minimum.

Tips: "Become a member of Maine Writers & Publishers Alliance. Become familiar with Maine literary scene."

NEW WRITER'S MAGAZINE, Sarasota Bay Publishing, P.O. Box 5976, Sarasota FL 34277-5976. (941)953-7903. E-mail: newriters@aol.com. Editor: George J. Haborak. 95% freelance written. Bimonthly magazine for new writers. "*New Writer's Magazine* believes that *all* writers are *new* writers in that each of us can learn from one another. So, we reach pro and non-pro alike." Estab. 1986. Circ. 5,000. Pays on publication. Byline given. Buys first rights. Reports in 2 weeks on queries; 1 month on mss. *Writer's Market* recommends allowing 2 months for reply. Sample copy for $3. Writer's guidelines for #10 SASE.

Nonfiction: General interest, how-to (for new writers), humor, interview/profile, opinion, personal experience (with pro writer). Buys 50 mss/year. Send complete ms. Length: 700-1,000 words. Pays $10-50.

Photos: Send photos with submission. Reviews 5×7 prints. Offers no additional payment for photos accepted with ms. Captions required.

Fiction: Experimental, historical, humorous, mainstream, slice-of-life vignettes. "Again, we do *not* want anything that does not have a tie-in with the writing life or writers in general." Buys 2-6 mss/year. "We offer a special fiction contest held each year with cash prizes." Send complete ms. Length: 700-800 words. Pays $20-40.

Poetry: Free verse, light verse, traditional. Does not want anything *not* for writers. Buys 10-20 poems/year. Submit maximum 3 poems. Length: 8-20 lines. Pays $5 maximum.

Fillers: Anecdotes, facts, newsbreaks, short humor. Buys 5-15/year. Length: 20-100 words. Pays $5 maximum. Cartoons, writing lifestyle slant. Buys 20-30/year. Pays $10 maximum.

Tips: "Any article *with photos* has a good chance, especially an *up close and personal* interview with an established professional writer offering advice, etc."

OHIO WRITER, Poets League of Greater Cleveland, P.O. Box 91801, Cleveland OH 44101. Editor: Linda Rome. 75% freelance written. Bimonthly magazine covering writing and Ohio writers. Estab. 1987. Pays on publication. Publishes ms an average of 4 months after acceptance. Byline given. Buys one-time rights and second serial (reprint) rights. Editorial lead time 4 months. Submit seasonal material 4 months in advance. Reports in 1 month. Sample copy for $2. Writer's guidelines for SASE.

Nonfiction: Essays, how-to, humor, inspirational, interview/profile, opinion, personal experience—"all must relate to the writing life or Ohio writers, or Ohio publishing scene." Buys 24 mss/year. Send complete ms. Length: 1,000-2,000 words. Pays $25 minimum, up to $50 for lead article; other payment under arrangement with writer.

Reprints: Send photocopy of article or typed ms with rights for sale noted and information about when and where the article previously appeared. Pays 50% of amount paid for an original article.

Columns/Departments: Subjectively Yours (opinions, controversial stance on writing life), 1,500 words; Reviews (Ohio writers, publishers or publishing), 500 words; Focus On (Ohio publishing scene, how to write/publish certain kind of writing (e.g., travel). Buys 6 mss/year. Send complete ms. Pays $25-50; $5/book review.

Tips: "Profiles and interviews of writers who live in Ohio are always needed."

POETS & WRITERS, 72 Spring St., 3rd Floor,New York NY 10012. Editor: Darlyn Brewer. 100% freelance written. Bimonthly professional trade journal for poets and fiction writers. No poetry or fiction. Estab. 1973. Circ. 58,000. **Pays on acceptance** of finished draft. Publishes ms an average of 4 months after acceptance. Byline given. Offers 20% kill fee. Buys first North American serial and first rights or makes work-for-hire assignments. Editorial lead time 1 year. Submit seasonal material 1 year in advance. Reports in 6 weeks on mss. Sample copy for $3.95 to Circulation Dept. Writer's guidelines for #10 SASE.

Nonfiction: Personal essays about literature, how-to (craft of poetry or fiction writing), interview/profile with poets or fiction writers (no Q&A), regional reports of literary activity, reports on small presses, service pieces about publishing trends. Buys 35 mss/year. Query with published clips or send complete ms. Length: 1,500-3,600 words.

Photos: State availability of photos with submission. Reviews b&w prints. Offers no additional payment for photos accepted with ms.

Columns/Departments: Literary and publishing news, 500-600 words; profiles of emerging and established poets and fiction writers, 2,400-3,600 words; regional reports (literary activity in US), 1,800-3,600 words. Query with published clips, or send complete ms. Pays $100-300.

‡**THE PROLIFIC FREELANCER**, BSK Communications and Assoc., P.O. Box 554, Oradell NJ 07649. (201)262-3277. Editor: Brian S. Konradt. 95% freelance written. Bimonthly newsletter covering freelance writing as a part-time/full-time business. *"The Prolific Freelancer* helps freelance writers manage, market and make money successfully." Estab. 1995. Circ. 3,000. Pays on publication. Publishes ms an average of 6 months after acceptance. Byline given. Buys first North American serial or second serial (reprint) rights. Editorial lead time 2 months. Submit seasonal material 2 months in advance. Reports in 1 month on queries, 2 months on mss. Sample copy for $5. Writer's guidelines for #10 SASE.

Nonfiction: General interest, how-to, new product, technical, travel. Buys 40 mss/year. Query with published clips or send complete ms with clips. Length: 200-2,500 words. Pays $5-100 plus 1-3 contributor's copies.
Photos: State availability of photos with submission. Reviews prints. Offers $5-15/photo. Identification of subjects required. Buys one-time rights.
Columns/Departments: Second Profit Ventures (secondary sources of income through writing), 500-2,500 words; Private Eye Publicity (special insert to help self-publishers get publicity), 300-1,000 words; Sources of Outsources (listing of sources for potential clients), open length. Buys 24 mss/year. Query with published clips or send complete ms with clips. Pays $5-25.
Fillers: Facts, newsbreaks. Buys 20/year. Length: 100-500 words. Pays $5-15.
Tips: "We cover commercial freelance writing, copwriting, travel writing, technical writing, editorial free-lancing, PR, and direct mail. We want articles that show how our readers can build a freelance writing business, how to prepare promotional material, how to market their services, how to get clients, how to deal with clients, and more."

RISING STAR, 47 Byledge Rd., Manchester NH 03104. Phone/fax: (603)623-9796. Editor: Scott E. Green. 50% freelance written. Bimonthly newsletter on science fiction and fantasy markets for writers and artists. Estab. 1980. Circ. 150. Pays on publication. Publishes ms an average of 3 months after acceptance. Byline given. Not copyrighted. Buys first rights. Accepts simultaneous submissions. Reports in 1 month on queries. Sample copy for $1.50 and #10 SASE. Free writer's guidelines. Subscription $7.50 for 6 issues, payable to Scott Green.

Nonfiction: Book excerpts, essays, interview/profile, opinion. Buys 8 mss/year. Query. Length: 500-900 words. Pays $3 minimum.
Reprints: Send tearsheet or typed ms with rights for sale noted and information about when and where the article previously appeared. Pays $5.

ST. LOUIS JOURNALISM REVIEW, 8380 Olive Blvd., St. Louis MO 63132. (314)991-1699. Fax: (314)997-1898. Editor/Publisher: Charles L. Klotzer. 80% freelance written. Prefers to work with published/established writers. Monthly tabloid newspaper critiquing St. Louis media, print, broadcasting, TV and cable primarily by working journalists and others. Also covers issues not covered adequately by dailies. Occasionally buys articles on national media criticism. Estab. 1970. Circ. 4,000. Buys all rights. Byline given. Sample copy for $2.50.

Nonfiction: "We buy material which analyzes, critically, St. Louis metro area media and, less frequently, national media institutions, personalities or trends." No taboos. Pays the expenses of writers on assignment subject to prior approval.

SCAVENGER'S NEWSLETTER, 519 Ellinwood, Osage City KS 66523-1329. (913)528-3538. Editor: Janet Fox. 15% freelance written. Eager to work with new/unpublished writers. Monthly newsletter covering markets for science fiction/fantasy/horror/mystery materials especially with regard to the small press. Estab. 1984. Circ. 1,000. **Pays on acceptance**. Publishes ms an average of 8 months after acceptance. Byline given. Not copyrighted. Buys one-time rights. Accepts simultaneous submissions. Reports in 1 month if SASE included. Sample copy for $2. Writer's guidelines for #10 SASE.

Nonfiction: Essays, general interest, how-to (write, sell, publish science fiction/fantasy/horror/mystery), humor, interview/profile (writers, artists in the field), opinion. Buys 12-15 mss/year. Send complete ms. Length: 1,000 words maximum. Pays $4.
Reprints: Send information about when and where the article previously appeared. Pays 100% of amount paid for an original article.
Fiction: "Seeking a few (4-6) outstanding pieces of flash fiction to 1,200 words in the genre of SF/fantasy/horror/mystery. Eventually I plan to alternate nonfiction and fiction. Looking for work that uses the techniques of poetry to make a short piece seem like a complete story." Pays $4.
Poetry: Avant-garde, free verse, haiku, traditional. All related to science fiction/fantasy/horror/mystery genres. Buys 36 poems/year. Submit maximum 3 poems. Length: 10 lines maximum. Pays $2.
Tips: "Because this is a small publication, it has occasional overstocks. We're especially looking for science fiction/flash fiction/fantasy/horror/mystery."

SMALL PRESS REVIEW, P.O. Box 100, Paradise CA 95967. Editor: Len Fulton. Monthly for "people interested in small presses and magazines, current trends and data; many libraries." Circ. 3,500. Byline given. Reports in 2 months. Free sample copy.

Nonfiction: News, short reviews, photos, short articles on small magazines and presses. Uses how-to, personal experience, interview, profile, spot news, historical, think, photo, and coverage of merchandising techniques. Accepts 50-200 mss/year. Length: 100-200 words. "Query if you're unsure."

THE WRITER, 120 Boylston St., Boston MA 02116-4615. Editor-in-Chief/Publisher: Sylvia K. Burack. 20-25% freelance written. Prefers to buy work of published/established writers. Monthly. Estab. 1887. **Pays on acceptance.** Publishes ms an average of 8 months after acceptance. Buys first serial rights. Sample copy for $3.50.
Nonfiction: Practical articles for writers on how to write for publication, and how and where to market manuscripts in various fields. Considers all submissions promptly. No assignments. Length: 2,000 words maximum.
Tips: "New types of publications and our continually updated market listings in all fields will determine changes of focus and fact."

‡WRITERS CONNECTION, P.O. Box 24770, San Jose CA 95154-4770. Editor: Jan Stiles. 60% freelance written. Works with new/unpublished writers each year. Monthly newsletter covering writing and publishing. Estab. 1983. Circ. 1,500. Pays in services on acceptance or in cash on publication. Publishes ms an average of 8 months after acceptance for articles; much less for column updates. Byline given on articles. Buys first serial or second serial (reprint) rights. Issues are also distributed electronically. Submit seasonal material 4 months in advance. Prefers complete ms. Reports in 2 months. Sample copy for $3 postpaid. Writer's guidelines for #10 SASE.
Nonfiction: Book excerpts (on writing/publishing); how-to (write and publish, market your writing); interview/profile (editors, agents, writers and publishers with how-to or marketing slant); new product occasionally (books, videotapes, software etc., on writing and publishing); writing for business and technical fields. "All types of writing from technical to romance novels and article writing are treated." No personal experience without a strong how-to slant. Buys 25-32 mss/year. Length: 800-2,200 words. Pays $25-75 on publication, or in certificates, on acceptance, for $50 to $150 toward WC membership and/or conferences.
Reprints: Send typed ms with rights for sale noted and information about when and where the article previously appeared. Pays 50-60% of amount paid for an original article.
Columns/Departments: Markets, contests, events, etc., are staff-written. Send information or announcements 6 weeks in advance of issue date for free listings in our newsletter; space available basis.
Tips: "We are currently seeking quality articles on fiction technique—novel or short story, any genre. We always need 800-word how-to articles for our Business & Technical Writing column. Pieces should benefit writers working for business and high-tech companies. Also, find and report on new markets where freelancers can break in. Provide new techniques, ideas or perspectives for writing fiction or nonfiction; present your ideas in a lively, but practical style. No parodies or sarcasm, please. And no why-I-have-to-write or how-I-faced-writer's-block essays. We see (and return) far too many of these."

WRITER'S DIGEST, 1507 Dana Ave., Cincinnati OH 45207. (513)531-2222. Fax: (513)531-1843. E-mail: writersdig@aol.com. Submissions Editor: Amanda Boyd. 90% freelance written. Monthly magazine about writing and publishing. "Our readers write fiction, poetry, nonfiction, plays and all kinds of creative writing. They're interested in improving their writing skills, improving their ability to sell their work and finding new outlets for their talents." Estab. 1921. Circ. 225,000. **Pays on acceptance.** Publishes ms an average of 1 year after acceptance. Buys first North American serial rights for one-time editorial use, possible electronic posting, microfilm/microfiche use and magazine promotional use. Pays 20% kill fee. Byline given. Submit seasonal material 8 months in advance. Reports in 2 months. Sample copy for $3.50 ($3.70 in Ohio). Writer's guidelines for #10 SASE.
● Ranked as one of the best markets for freelance writers in *Writer's Yearbook*'s annual "Top 100 Markets," January 1996.
Nonfiction: "Our mainstay is the how-to article—that is, an article exploring some technique of how to write or sell more of what you write. For instance, how to write compelling leads and conclusions, how to improve your character descriptions, how to become more efficient and productive. We like plenty of examples, anecdotes and $$$ in our articles—so other writers can actually see what's been done successfully by the author of a particular piece. We like our articles to speak directly to the reader through the use of the first-person voice. Don't submit an article on what five book editors say about writing mysteries. Instead, submit an article on how you cracked the mystery market and how our readers can do the same. But don't limit the article to your experiences; include the opinions of those five editors to give your article increased depth and authority." General interest (about writing); how-to (writing and marketing techniques that work); inspirational; interview and profile (query first); new product; personal experience (marketing and freelancing experiences). "We can always use articles on fiction and nonfiction technique, and solid articles on poetry or scriptwriting are always welcome. No articles titled 'So You Want to Be a Writer,' and no first-person pieces that ramble without giving a lesson or something readers can learn from in the sharing of the story." Buys 90-100 mss/year. Queries are preferred, but complete mss OK. Length: 500-3,000 words. Pays 10¢/word minimum. Sometimes pays expenses of writers on assignment.

Reprints: Accepts previously published submissions from noncompeting markets. Send tearsheet or photocopy of article, noting rights for sale and when and where the article previously appeared.
Photos: Used only with interviews and profiles. State availability of photos or send contact sheet with ms. Captions required.
Columns/Departments: Chronicle (first-person narratives about the writing life; length: 1,200-1,500 words); The Writing Life (length: 50-500 words); and Tip Sheet (short items that offer solutions to writing and freelance business-related problems that writers commonly face). Humor is welcome for Chronicle and Writing Life. Buys approximately 150 articles/year for Writing Life and Tip Sheet sections. Send complete ms.
Poetry: Light verse about "the writing life"—joys and frustrations of writing. "We are also considering poetry other than short light verse—but still related to writing, publishing, other poets and authors, etc." Buys an average of 1 an issue. Submit poems in batches of 1-5. Length: 2-20 lines. Pays $10-50/poem.
Fillers: Anecdotes and short humor, primarily for use in The Writing Life column. Uses up to 4/issue. Length: 50-250 words.

WRITER'S FORUM, Writer's Digest School, 1507 Dana Ave., Cincinnati OH 45207. (513)531-2222. Editor: Amanda Boyd. 100% freelance written. Quarterly newsletter covering writing techniques, marketing and inspiration for students enrolled in fiction and nonfiction writing courses offered by Writer's Digest School. Estab. 1970. Circ. 13,000. **Pays on acceptance.** Publishes ms an average of 6 months after acceptance. Byline given. Buys first serial or second serial (reprint) rights. Submit seasonal/holiday material 4 months in advance. Accepts simultaneous submissions. Reports in 6 weeks. Free sample copy.
Nonfiction: How-to (write or market short stories, or articles, novels and nonfiction books) and inspirational articles that will motivate beginning writers. Buys 12 mss/year. Prefers complete mss to queries. "If you prefer to query, please do so by mail, not phone." Length: 500-1,000 words. Pays $10-25.
Reprints: Accepts previously published submissions.

WRITERS INFORMATION NETWORK, The Professional Association for Christian Writers, P.O. Box 11337, Bainbridge Island WA 98110. (206)842-9103. Editor: Elaine Wright Colvin. 33⅓% freelance written. Bimonthly newsletter covering religious publishing industry. Estab. 1983. Circ. 1,000. **Pays on acceptance.** Publishes ms 1 month after acceptance. Byline given. Buys first North American serial rights. Editorial lead time 2 months. Submit seasonal material 2 months in advance. Reports in 1 month. Sample copy for 9×12 SAE with 4 first-class stamps. Writer's guidelines for #10 SASE.
Nonfiction: How-to (writing), humor, inspirational, personal experience. Send complete ms. Length: 50-300 words. Pays $5-50; sometimes pays other than cash. Sometimes pays expenses of writers on assignment.
Columns/Departments: Bulletin Board, Speakers' Platform, Computer Corner. Send complete ms.

WRITERS' INTERNATIONAL FORUM, Bristol Services International, P.O. Box 516, Tracyton WA 98393-0516. Editorial Director: Sandra E. Haven. 90% freelance written. Bimonthly publication designed to publish aspiring writers' stories and to forward resulting responses from readers. Estab. 1990. Buys first rights. Byline and brief bio given. No poetry. Also offers a column of tips from readers, a markets listing, lessons on writing, Tips of the Trade, and features about the writing craft. Reports in 6 weeks. Guidelines, contest information and details on upcoming themes or special Junior editions available for SASE. Sample copy for $3.50, Juniors Edition $5; subscription $14.
Columns/Departments: Writer to Writer: tips on writing sent in by writers (maximum 300 words), pays 1 copy; Perspectives: 1 essay published per issue that offers a writer's personal, philosophic and/or humorous perspective on a non-writing topic (maximum 500 words), pays $5 and 2 contributor copies. Submit mss with SASE, cover letter, clear copies (not originals as notations may be made prior to return). Mark for intended column.
Fiction: Any genre (no slice-of-life, violence, graphic sex or experimental formats). Each issue usually includes at least one children's story, a fairy or folk tale, a mystery and humor as well as a mixture of stories in other genres and mainstream stories. "We also publish a Juniors edition of stories written for and/or by those aged 8-16 (mark manuscript accordingly)." Length: 2,000 words maximum, 600-1,200 preferred. **Pays on acceptance**, $5 minimum, plus 2 contributor's copies.
Essays: Any subject, but must make a point or offer some insight, be encouraging or upbeat. Humor especially favored. Length: 400-1,200 words (400-800 preferred). **Pays on acceptance,** $5 minimum (more for exceptional material), plus 2 contributor's copies.
Tips: "We specialize in traditional fiction with definite plots and resolutions resulting from the main character's action and/or decision. Always include a cover letter that says something about you and your manuscript's intended audience. We are a friendly magazine and we make every effort to treat writers on a personal level, however, we insist that all of our requirements be met. Please read our guidelines and follow them carefully. All submissions by subscribers will receive a complimentary critique."

WRITER'S YEARBOOK, 1507 Dana Ave., Cincinnati OH 45207. (513)531-2222. Fax: (513)531-1843. E-mail: writersdig@aol.com. Submissions Editor: Amanda Boyd. 90% freelance written. Newsstand annual for freelance writers, journalists and teachers of creative writing. "Please note that the *Yearbook* is a 'best of' format. That is, we are reprinting the best writing about writing published in the last year: articles, fiction and book excerpts. The *Yearbook* now uses little original material, so do not submit queries or original manuscripts. We will, however, consider already-published material for possible inclusion." Estab. 1929. **Pays on acceptance.** Publishes ms an average of 6 months after acceptance. Offers 20% kill fee. Byline given. Buys reprint rights. "If you don't want your manuscript returned, indicate that on the first page of the manuscript or in a cover letter."

Reprints: "In reprints, we want articles that reflect the current state of writing in America: trends, inside information, and money-saving and money-making ideas for the freelance writer. We try to touch on the various facets of writing in each issue of the *Yearbook*—from fiction to poetry to playwriting, and any other endeavor a writer can pursue. How-to articles—that is, articles that explain in detail how to do something—are very important to us. For example, you could explain how to establish mood in fiction, how to improve interviewing techniques, how to write for and sell to specialty magazines, or how to construct and market a good poem. We are also interested in the writer's spare time—what she/he does to retreat occasionally from the writing wars, where and how to refuel and replenish the writing spirit. 'How Beats the Heart of a Writer' features interest us, if written warmly, in the first person, by a writer who has had considerable success. We also want interviews or profiles of well-known bestselling authors, always with good pictures. Articles on writing techniques that are effective today are always welcome. We provide how-to features and information to help our readers become more skilled at writing and successful at selling their writing." Buys 15-20 mss (reprints only)/year. Send tearsheet or photocopy of article, noting rights for sale and when and where the article previously appeared. Length: 750-4,500 words. Pays 2½¢/word minimum.

Photos: Interviews and profiles must be accompanied by high-quality photos. Reviews b&w photos only, depending on use. Captions required.

Fillers: Interested in funny, weird, wacky or otherwise offbeat incidents for our annual "Year in Revue" roundup. Send us the clip reporting the incident, indicate date and source. Pays $20 finder's fee.

THE WRITING SELF, Journeys Into The Act of Writing, P.O. Box 245, Lenox Hill Station NY 10021. Editors: Julia Nourok, Helen Gorenstein. Contact: Scot Nourok, managing editor. 80% freelance written. Quarterly magazine covering trade/journalism and writing for nonfiction, fiction and poetry. "We're interested in a broad range of subjects that share with our readers the writing life. We look for manuscripts that will stimulate our readers to keep on writing even when the refrigerator breaks down, the computer won't save, or the book gets published. We're partial to pieces that are honestly written, intimate, or that make us laugh." Estab. 1992. Circ. 800. **Pays on acceptance.** Publishes ms an average of 3 months after acceptance. Byline given. Buys one-time rights. Editorial lead time 6 months. Accepts simultaneous submissions. Reports in 2 months on queries; 6 months on mss. Sample copy for $3. Writer's guidelines for #10 SASE.

Nonfiction: Book excerpts, essays, humor, opinion, personal experience. Buys 25-35 mss/year. Send complete ms. Length: 500-1,200 words. Pays $5-20 plus 3 copies of journal.

Columns/Departments: Book Review (writers' journals, diaries, letters, memoirs, essays), 750-1,000 words; Short Short Inner Voices (writers' personal experiences—coping with isolation), 500-1,000 words; Workshop Beat (impressions/insights gained in attending writers' conference), 750-1,000 words. Buys 15-20 mss/year. Send complete ms. Pays $10-20 plus 3 copies of journal.

Fiction: Humorous, novel excerpts, slice-of-life vignettes. Buys 1-2 mss/year. Send complete ms. Length: 500-1,000 words. Pays $10-20.

Poetry: Buys 2-3 poems/year. Submit maximum 4 poems. Length: 5-25 lines. Pays $5-10.

Fillers: Short humor, anecdotes. Buys 2-3/year. Length: 50-250 words. Pays $5.

Tips: "We're interested in pieces that examine the hazardous and uplifting experiences of the writing life in a personal way. We buy manuscripts that share your joys, conflicts, and survival techniques with other writers. No how-to articles with an instructional tone, please. Send for a sample issue and guidelines. Read the journal. We always like hearing from our readers."

LAW

While all of these publications deal with topics of interest to attorneys, each has a particular slant. Be sure that your subject is geared to a specific market—lawyers in a single region, law students, paralegals, etc. Publications for law enforcement personnel are listed under Government and Public Service.

‡**ABA JOURNAL**, American Bar Association, Dept. WM, 6th Floor, 750 N. Lake Shore Dr., Chicago IL 60611. (312)988-5000. Fax: (312)988-6014. E-mail: abajournal@attmail.com. Website: http://www.abanet. org. Editor: Gary A. Hengstler. Managing Editor: Kerry Klumpe. 35% freelance written. Prefers to work with published/established writers. Monthly magazine covering law and lawyers. "The content of the *Journal* is designed to appeal to the association's diverse membership with emphasis on the general practitioner." Circ. 400,000. **Pays on acceptance.** Publishes ms an average of 2 months after acceptance. Byline given.

"Editor works with writer until article is in acceptable form." Buys all rights. Submit seasonal material 3 months in advance. Accepts simultaneous submissions. Reports in 1 month. Free writer's guidelines. Sample copy $7.

- Ranked as one of the best markets for freelance writers in *Writer's Yearbook*'s annual "Top 100 Markets," January 1996.

Nonfiction: Book excerpts, general interest (legal), how-to (law practice techniques), interview/profile (law firms and prominent individuals), technical (legal trends). "The emphasis of the *Journal* is on the practical problems faced by lawyers in general practice and how those problems can be overcome. Articles should emphasize the practical rather than the theoretical or esoteric. Writers should avoid the style of law reviews, academic journals or legal briefs and should write in an informal, journalistic style. Short quotations from people and specific examples of your point will improve an article." Special issues have featured women and minorities in the legal profession. Buys 30 mss/year. Send complete ms. Length: 3,000 words. Pays $350-2,000. Pays expenses of writers on assignment.

Tips: "We require more sophisticated treatment of complex topics in a narrative style. Writers must provide sidebars and breakouts. Write to us with a specific idea in mind and spell out how the subject would be covered. Full-length profiles and feature articles are always needed. We look for practical information. If *The New York Times* or *Wall Street Journal* would like your style, so will we."

THE ALTMAN WEIL PENSA REPORT TO LEGAL MANAGEMENT, Altman Weil Pensa Publications, 1100 Commerce Dr., Racine WI 53406. (414)886-1304. Fax: (414)886-1139. Website: http://www.altmanweil.com. Editor: James Wilber. 15-20% freelance written. Works with a small number of new/unpublished writers each year. Monthly newsletter covering law office management, purchases (equipment, insurance services, space, etc.) and technology. Estab. 1974. Circ. 2,200. Pays on publication. Publishes ms an average of 6 months after acceptance. Byline given. Buys all rights; sometimes second serial (reprint) rights. Reports in 1 month on queries; 3 months on mss. Sample copy for #10 SASE.

Nonfiction: How-to (buy, use, repair), interview/profile, new product. "Looking especially for practical, "how-to" articles on law office management and technology." Buys 12 mss/year. Query. Submit a sample of previous writing. Length: 500-2,500 words. Pays $125/published page.

Reprints: Send photocopy of article or typed ms with rights for sale noted plus diskette, and information about when and where the article previously appeared. Pays 50% of amount paid for an original article.

BENCH & BAR OF MINNESOTA, Minnesota State Bar Association, 514 Nicollet Ave., Suite 300, Minneapolis MN 55402-1021. (612)333-1183. Fax: (612)333-4927. Editor: Judson Haverkamp. 10% freelance written. Magazine published 11 times/year covering the law/legal profession. "Audience is mostly Minnesota lawyers. *Bench & Bar* seeks reportage, analysis, and commentary on trends and issues in the law and the legal profession, especially in Minnesota. Preference to items of practical/human interest to professionals in law." Estab. 1931. Circ. 15,000. **Pays on acceptance.** Publishes ms an average of 3 months after acceptance. Byline given. Buys first North American serial rights and makes work-for-hire assignments. Reports in 1 month. Sample copy for 9×12 SAE with 4 first-class stamps. Writer's guidelines free.

Nonfiction: General interest, historical/nostalgic, how-to (how to handle particular types of legal, ethical problems in office management, representation, etc.), humor, interview/profile, technical/legal. "We do not want one-sided opinion pieces or advertorial." Buys 4-5 mss/year. Query with published clips or send complete ms. Length: 1,500-3,000 words. Pays $300-800. Sometimes pays expenses of writers on assignment.

Photos: State availability of photos with submission. Reviews 5×7 or larger prints. Offers $25-100/photo upon publication. Model releases and identification of subjects required. Buys one-time rights.

‡CORPORATE LEGAL TIMES, 3 E. Huron St., Chicago IL 60611. (312)654-3500. E-mail: cltking@aol.com. Editor: Jennifer E. King. 50% freelance written. Monthly tabloid covering corporate general counsel and inhouse attorneys. "*Corporate Legal Times* is a monthly national magazine that gives general counsel and inhouse attorneys information on legal and business issues to help them better manage corporate law departments. It routinely addresses changes and trends in law departments, litigation management, legal technology, corporate governance and in-house careers. Law areas covered monthly include: environmental, intellectual property, international, and labor and employment. All stories need to be geared toward the inhouse attorney's perspective." Estab. 1991. Circ. 40,000. Pays on publication. Publishes ms an average of 3 months after acceptance. Byline given. Buys all rights. Editorial lead time 3 months. Submit seasonal material 6 months in advance. Reports in 3 weeks on queries. Sample copy for 9×12 SAE with 8 first-class stamps. Writer's guidelines for #10 SASE.

Nonfiction: Interview/profile, technical, news about legal aspects of business issues and events. Buys 12-25 mss/year. Query with published clips. Length: 500-2,000 words. Pays $300-1,000. Freelancers should state availability of photos with submission.

Photos: Reviews color transparencies, b&w prints. Offers $25-150/photo. Identification of subjects required. Buys all rights.

Tips: "Our publication targets general counsel and in-house lawyers. All stories need to speak to them—not to the general attorney population. Query with clips and a list of potential in-house sources. Non-paid, contributed articles from law firm attorneys are accepted only if there is an inhouse attorney co-author."

THE LAWYERS WEEKLY, The Newspaper for the Legal Profession in Canada, Butterworth (Canada) Inc., 75 Clegg Rd., Markham, Ontario L6G IA1 Canada. (905)479-2665. Fax: (905)479-3758. E-mail: hw@butterworths.ca. Editor: Beverly Spencer. 30% freelance written. "We will work with any *talented* writer of whatever experience level." Tabloid published 48 times/year covering Canadian law and legal affairs for a "sophisticated up-market readership of lawyers." Estab. 1983. Circ. 7,000/week; 22,500 once per month. Pays on publication. Publishes ms within 1 month after acceptance. Byline given. Offers 50% kill fee. Usually buys all rights. Submit seasonal material 6 weeks in advance. Accepts simultaneous submissions. Reports in 1 month. Sample copy for $8 (Canadian) with 9×12 SAE.

Nonfiction: Exposé, general interest (law), how-to (professional), humor, interview/profile (Canadian lawyers and judges), opinion, technical, news, case comments. "We try to wrap up the week's legal events and issues in a snappy informal package. We especially like news stories with photos or illustrations. We are always interested in feature or newsfeature articles involving current legal issues, but contributors should keep in mind our audience is trained in *English/Canadian common law*—not US law. That means most US-focused stories will generally not be accepted. No routine court reporting or fake news stories about commercial products. Buys 200-300 mss/year. Query or send complete ms. Length: 700-1,500 words. Payment negotiable in Canadian dollars. Sometimes pays the expenses of writers on assignment.

Photos: State availability of photos with query letter or ms. Reviews b&w and color contact sheets, negatives and 5×7 prints. Identification of subjects required. Buys one-time rights.

Fillers: Clippings, newsbreaks. Length: 50-200 words. Pays $10 minimum.

Tips: "Freelancers can best break into our publication by submitting news, features, and accounts of unusual or bizarre legal events. A frequent mistake made by writers is forgetting that our audience is intelligent and learned in law. They don't need the word 'plaintiff' explained to them." No unsolicited mss returned without SASE (or IRC to US or non-Canadian destinations). "No US postage on SASEs, please!"

LEGAL ASSISTANT TODAY, James Publishing, Inc., 3520 Cadillac Ave., Suite E, Costa Mesa CA 92626. (714)755-5450. Fax: (714)751-5508. Editor-in-Chief: Niccol Kording. Executive Editor: Leanne Cazares. Bimonthly magazine covering information for paralegals/legal assistants. "Our magazine is geared toward all legal assistants/paralegals throughout the country, regardless of specialty (litigation, corporate, bankruptcy, environmental law, etc.). How-to articles to help paralegals do their jobs more effectively are most in demand, as is career and salary information, and timely news and trends pieces." Estab. 1983. Circ. 17,000. **Pays on acceptance.** Publishes ms an average of 3 months after acceptance. Byline given. Usually buys all rights. Editorial lead time 10 weeks. Submit seasonal material 3 months in advance. Accepts simultaneous submissions. Reports in 1 month on queries; 2 months on mss. Sample copy free on request. Writer's guidelines free on request.

● *Legal Assistant Today* needs much more practitioner, "how-to" articles, noting that readers want articles on how to do their jobs better and faster.

Nonfiction: How-tos for paralegals, issues affecting the paralegal profession, profiles of new products for law office, opinion on legal topics (paralegal), personal experience of paralegals on the job. "Each issue has a theme: litigation support, research and discovery, corporate services. Since ours is a national magazine, we limit regional or local stories (except for the news)." Buys 36 mss/year. Query with published clips. Length: 2,000-4,000 words. (News, profiles shorter.) Pays $100 minimum. "Pay is negotiated per assignment; pay can be *substantially* more depending on experience and length and quality of manuscript." Pays expenses of writers on assignment.

Photos: Send photos with submission. Reviews prints. Negotiates payment individually. Identification of subjects required. Buys one-time rights.

Columns/Departments: "Last Laugh"—humorous piece on legal world; 1,000-1,200 words. Pays $75-100.

Fillers: Anecdotes, facts, newsbreaks and short humor "pertaining to paralegals." Pay negotiated.

Tips: "We prefer writers with previous experience working in a law office or writing for legal publications who have some understanding of what paralegals would find interesting or useful. Writers must understand our audience. There is some opportunity for investigative journalism as well as the usual features, profiles and news. How-to articles are especially desired. If you are a great writer who can interview effectively, and really dig into the topic to grab the readers' attention, we need you! We are open to ideas (queries), but also assign selected topics: News: brief, hard news topics regarding paralegals (or trend pieces on the profession.); Profiles: paralegals who've worked on fascinating cases, etc.; Features: presents information to help paralegals advance in their careers."

‡**THE NATIONAL LAW JOURNAL**, New York Law Publishing Company, Dept. WM, 345 Park Ave. S., New York NY 10010. (212)741-8300. Fax: (212)696-1875. E-mail: nljeds@ljextra.com. Editor: Ben Gerson. Managing Editor: Joan Cheever. Contact: Adam Klein (articles), Joan Cheever (news). 25-50% freelance written. Weekly newspaper for the legal profession. Estab. 1978. Circ. 50,000. Pays on publication. Publishes ms an average of 1 month after acceptance. Byline given. Kill fee varies. Buys all rights. Reports in 3 weeks on queries; 5 weeks on mss. Sample copy for $2 and 9×12 SAE with 2 first-class stamps.

Nonfiction: News, exposé (on subjects of interest to lawyers); interview/profile (of lawyers or judges of note); nonfiction book excerpts. "The bulk of our freelance articles are short, spot-news stories on local court decisions, lawsuits and lawyers; often, these come from legal affairs writers on local newspapers. Pays $25-150. We also buy longer pieces, 1,500-2,000-word profiles of prominent lawyers or legal trend stories. No articles without a legal angle, but we like to see good, idiomatic writing, mostly free of legal jargon." Buys 50-100 mss/year. Query with published clips or send complete ms. Pays $500. Sometimes pays the expenses of writers on assignment.

Columns/Departments: "For those who are not covering legal affairs on a regular basis, a good way into *The National Law Journal* is through our Exhibit A feature. Every week we print a sort of reporter's notebook on some proceeding currently underway in a courtroom or a short profile. The feature is stylistically and thematically quite flexible—we've even run pieces about lawyers' hangouts, mini-travelogues, and television reviews. It runs about 1,800 words and pays $250. We also use op-ed pieces on subjects of legal interest, many of which come from freelancers. Writers interested in doing an op-ed piece should query first. Pays $150. We have a legal section with an alternating topic each week (i.e. Banking Law, Legal Tech etc.). The section is written by contributing attorneys, usually from firms with multiple offices and typically not paid. Articles are submitted at 2,000 words."

THE PENNSYLVANIA LAWYER, Pennsylvania Bar Association, P.O. Box 186, 100 South St., Harrisburg PA 17108-0186. (717)238-6715. Executive Editor: Marcy Carey Mallory. Contact: Donald C. Sarvey, editorial director. Managing Editor: Sherri Kimmel. 25% freelance written. Prefers to work with published/established writers. Bimonthly magazine published as a service to the legal profession. Estab. 1895. Circ. 27,000. **Pays on acceptance.** Publishes ms an average of 6 months after acceptance. Byline given. Buys generally first rights, occasionally one-time rights or second serial (reprint) rights. Submit seasonal material 6 months in advance. Simultaneous submissions discouraged. Reports in 6 weeks. Sample copy and writer's guidelines for #10 SAE with 3 first-class stamps.

Nonfiction: General interest, how-to, interview/profile, new product, law-practice management, personal experience. All features *must* relate in some way to Pennsylvania lawyers or the practice of law in Pennsylvania. Buys 10-12 mss/year. Query. Length: 600-1,500 words. Pays $75-350. Sometimes pays the expenses of writers on assignment.

STUDENT LAWYER, American Bar Association, 750 N. Lake Shore Dr., Chicago IL 60611. (312)988-6048. Fax: (312)988-6281. Website: http://www.abanet.org/lsd/stulawyer/home.html. Editor: Stephanie Johnston. 99% freelance written. Works with a small number of writers each year. Monthly magazine (September-May). Estab. 1972. Circ. 33,000. **Pays on acceptance.** Buys first serial and second serial (reprint) rights. Byline given. Submit seasonal material 4 months in advance. Reports in 6 weeks. Publishes ms an average of 3 months after acceptance. Sample copy for $4. Free writer's guidelines.

Nonfiction: Features cover legal education and careers and social/legal subjects. Also profiles (prominent persons in law-related fields); opinion (on matters of current legal interest); essays (on legal affairs); interviews. Query. Length: 3,000-4,000 words. Pays $450-900 for features. Covers some writer's expenses.

Columns/Departments: Briefly (short stories on unusual and interesting developments in the law); Legal Aids (unusual approaches and programs connected to teaching law students and lawyers); Esq. (brief profiles of people in the law); End Note (short pieces on a variety of topics; can be humorous, educational, outrageous); Pro Se (opinion slot for authors to wax eloquent on legal issues); Et Al. (column for short features that fit none of the above categories). Buys 4-8 mss/issue. Length: 1,200-1,500 words. Pays $200-350.

Tips: "*Student Lawyer* actively seeks good new reporters and writers eager to prove themselves. Legal training definitely not essential; writing talent is. The writer should not think we are a law review; we are a feature magazine with the law (in the broadest sense) as the common denominator. Find issues of national scope and interest to write about; be aware of subjects the magazine—and other media—have already covered and propose something new. Write clearly and well."

LEATHER GOODS

SHOE SERVICE, SSIA Service Corp., 5024-R Campbell Blvd., Baltimore MD 21236-5974. (410)931-8100. Fax: (410)931-8111. Editor: Mitchell Lebovic. 25% freelance written. Monthly magazine for business people who own and operate small shoe repair shops. Estab. 1921. Circ. 8,000. Pays on publication. Publishes ms an average of 3 months after acceptance. Byline given. Buys first serial, first North American serial and one-time rights. Submit seasonal material 3 months in advance. Accepts simultaneous submissions. Reports in 6 weeks. Sample copy for $2 and 9×12 SAE.

Nonfiction: How-to (run a profitable shop); interview/profile (of an outstanding or unusual person on shoe repair); business articles (particularly about small business practices in a service/retail shop). Buys 12-24 mss/year. Query with published clips or send complete ms. Length: 500-2,000 words. Pays 5¢/word.

Reprints: Accepts previously published submissions.

Photos: "Quality photos will help sell an article." State availability of photos. Pays $10-30 for 8×10 b&w prints. Uses some color photos, but mostly b&w glossies. Captions, model release and identification of subjects required.

Tips: "Visit some shoe repair shops to get an idea of the kind of person who reads *Shoe Service*. Profiles are the easiest to sell to us if you can find a repairer we think is unusual."

LIBRARY SCIENCE

Librarians read these journals for advice on promotion and management of libraries, library and book trade issues and information access and transfer. Be aware of current issues such as censorship, declines in funding and government information policies. For journals on the book trade see Book and Bookstore.

THE LIBRARY IMAGINATION PAPER, Carol Bryan Imagines, 1000 Byus Dr., Charleston WV 25311-1310. (304)345-2378. 30% freelance written. Quarterly newspaper covering public relations education for librarians. Clip art included in each issue. Estab. 1978. Circ. 3,000. Pays on publication. Publishes ms an average of 6 months after acceptance. Byline given. Buys one-time rights. Submit seasonal material 3 months in advance. Accepts simultaneous submissions. Reports in 2 months. Sample copy for $5. Writer's guidelines for SASE.
Nonfiction: How-to (on "all aspects of good library public relations—both mental tips and hands-on methods. We need how-to and tips pieces on all aspects of PR, for library subscribers—both school and public libraries. In the past we've featured pieces on taking good photos, promoting an anniversary celebration, working with printers, and producing a slide show.") No articles on "what the library means to me." Buys 4-6 mss/year. Query with or without published clips, or send complete ms. Length: 600 or 2,200 words. Pays $25 or $50.
Reprints: Send tearsheet or photocopy of article and information about when and where the article previously appeared.
Photos: Send photos with submission. Reviews 3×5, 5×7 or 8×10 prints. Offers $5/photo. Captions required. Buys one-time rights.
Tips: "Someone who has worked in the library field and has first-hand knowledge of library PR needs, methods and processes will do far better with us. Our readers are people who cannot be written down to—but their library training has not always incorporated enough preparation for handling promotion, publicity and the public."

LUMBER

SOUTHERN LUMBERMAN, Greysmith Publishing, Inc., P.O. Box 681629, Franklin TN 37068-1629. (615)791-1961. Fax: (615)790-6188. Editor: Nanci P. Gregg. 20-30% freelance written. Works with a small number of new/unpublished writers each year. Monthly trade journal for the sawmill industry. Estab. 1881. Circ. 12,000. Pays on publication. Publishes ms an average of 3 months after acceptance. Byline given. Not copyrighted. Buys first North American rights. Submit seasonal material 6 months in advance. Reports in 1 month on queries; 2 months on mss. Sample copy for $3 and 9×12 SAE with 5 first-class stamps. Writer's guidelines for #10 SASE.
Nonfiction: How to sawmill better, interview/profile, equipment analysis, technical. Sawmill features. Buys 10-15 mss/year. Query with or without published clips, or send complete ms. Length: 500-2,000 words. Pays $150-350 for assigned articles; $100-250 for unsolicited articles. Sometimes pays the expenses of writers on assignment.
Reprints: Send tearsheet or photocopy of article and information about when and where the article previously appeared. Pays 25-50% of amount paid for an original article.
Photos: Send photos with submission. Reviews transparencies, 4×5 color prints. Offers $10-25/photo. Captions and identification of subjects required. Always looking for news feature types of photos featuring forest products industry materials or people.
Tips: "Like most, we appreciate a clearly-worded query listing merits of suggested story—what it will tell our readers they need/want to know. We want quotes, we want opinions to make others discuss the article. Best hint? Find an interesting sawmill operation owner and start asking questions—I bet a story idea develops. We need color photos too. Most open is what we call the Sweethart Mill stories. We publish at least one per month, and hope to be printing two or more monthly in the immediate future. Find a sawmill operator and ask questions—what's he doing bigger, better, different. We're interested in new facilities, better marketing, improved production."

MACHINERY AND METAL

AMERICAN METAL MARKET, Chilton Publications, A Unit of the Walt Disney Co., 825 Seventh Ave., New York NY 10019. (212)887-8550. Fax: (212)887-8520. E-mail: 74521.3225@compuserve.com. Website:

www/chiltonco.com/amm. Editor: Michael G. Botta. Contact: Bob Manas, managing editor. 5% freelance written. Daily newspaper covering metals production and trade. "Bible of the metals industry. Covers production and trade of ferrous, nonferrous, and scrap metals. Read by senior executives. Focus on *breaking* news and price information." Estab. 1882. Circ. 11,000. Pays on publication per inch used in publication. Publishes ms an average of 1 month after acceptance. Byline given. Buys all rights and electronic rights. Editorial lead time 1 month. Reports in 2 weeks on queries. Sample copy and writer's guidelines free on request.

Nonfiction: Publishes roughly 45 special issues/year. Query. Pays $7/in.

Photos: Send photos with submission. Reviews 5×7 prints. Negotiates payment individually. Identification of subjects required. Buys all rights.

Tips: "Contact Bob Manas, managing editor, directly with story ideas. Primarily we are interested in purchasing *breaking* news items. Clear all stories with news desk (Manas) in advance. Unsolicited articles submitted at writer's risk. Contact Chuck Berry, senior editor, special issues, to discuss upcoming topics."

FABRICATOR, Ornamental & Miscellaneous Metal, National Ornamental & Miscellaneous Metals Association, 804-10 Main St., #E, Forest Park GA 30050. Editor: Todd Daniel. 20% freelance written. Bimonthly magazine covering ornamental metalwork. "Any business stories published must contain an angle specific to our industry." Estab. 1959. Circ. 10,000. **Pays on acceptance.** Byline given. Not copyrighted. Buys one-time rights. Editorial lead time 2 months. Accepts simultaneous submissions. Reports in 6 weeks on queries. Sample copy for SASE. Writer's guidelines for $1.

Nonfiction: How-to, humor, interview/profile, personal experience, photo feature, technical. Nothing in a Q&A format. Buys 10-12 mss/year. Query. Length: 1,200-2,000 words. Pays $200 minimum for assigned articles; $125 minimum for unsolicited articles. "Many write for publicity." Pays expenses of writers on assignment.

Reprints: Send typed ms with rights for sale noted.

Photos: State availability of photos with submission. Reviews contact sheets, negatives, transparencies and prints. Buys photos of metalwork-related subjects. Model releases required. Buys one-time rights.

Tips: "Don't write articles in passive voice."

‡MANUFACTURING SYSTEMS, Chilton Publications, 191 S. Gary Ave., Carol Stream IL 60188. (708)665-1000. Fax: (708)462-2225. Editor: Kevin Parker. Monthly magazine covering manufacturing/information technology. "*Manufacturing Systems* is about the use of information technology to improve productivity in discrete manufacturing and process industries." Estab. 1984. Circ. 105,000. Pays on publication. Publishes ms an average of 3 months after acceptance. Byline sometime given. Buys first North American serial rights. Editorial lead time 2 months. Submit seasonal material 4 months in advance. Sample copy and writer's guidelines free on request.

Nonfiction: Interview/profile, new product, technical. Buys 9 mss/year. Send complete ms. Length: 1,200-2,000 words. Pays $1,200-1,500. Pays expenses of writers on assignment.

Photos: Send photos with submission. No additional payment for photos. Captions required.

MODERN MACHINE SHOP, 6600 Clough Pike, Cincinnati OH 45244-4090. (513)231-8020. Fax: (513)231-2818. E-mail: malbert@gardnerweb.com. Website: http://www. gardnerweb.com. Executive Editor: Mark Albert. 25% freelance written. Monthly. Estab. 1928. Pays 1 month following acceptance. Publishes ms an average of 6 months after acceptance. Byline given. Reports in 1 month. Call for sample copy. Writer's guidelines for #10 SASE.

Nonfiction: Uses articles dealing with all phases of metalworking, manufacturing and machine shop work, with photos. No general articles. "Ours is an industrial publication, and contributing authors should have a working knowledge of the metalworking industry. We regularly use contributions from machine shop owners, engineers, other technical experts, and suppliers to the metalworking industry. Almost all of these contributors pursue these projects to promote their own commercial interests." Buys 10 unsolicited mss/year. Query. Length: 1,000-3,500 words. Pays current market rate.

Tips: "Articles that review basic metalworking/machining processes, especially if they include a rethinking or re-evaluation of these processes in light of today's technical trends, are always welcome."

33 METALPRODUCING, Penton Publishing Inc., 1100 Superior Ave., Cleveland OH 44114. (216)696-7000. Fax: (216)696-7658. E-mail: 74512.3437@compuserve.com. Editor: Wallace D. Huskonen. 50% freelance written. Monthly magazine covering producing metal mill products from ore/scrap. "The mission of *33 Metalproducing* is to provide timely, authoritative and useful information on domestic and global trends in the metalproducing industry (SIC 33) for operating management engineers, and other management personnel." Estab. 1962. Circ. 18,000. Pays on publication. Publishes ms an average of 1 month after acceptance. Byline given. Editorial lead time 2 months. Reports in 2 weeks on queries; 1 month on mss. Sample copy and writer's guidelines free on request.

Nonfiction: Book excerpts, interview/profile, technical. Buys 20 mss/year. Query with published clips. Length: 750-3,000 words. Pays $100-1,000.

Photos: State availability of photos with submissions. Reviews contact sheets, negatives, transparencies, prints. Offers no additional payment for photos accepted with ms. Captions, identification of subjects required. Buys all rights.
Tips: "A freelance writer should demonstrate ability to use the language of metal producing in producing features for *33MP.*"

MAINTENANCE AND SAFETY

BRUSHWARE, Centaur, Inc., Route 3, Box 165, Huddleston VA 24104. (540)297-1517. Editor: Leslie W. Neff. Publisher: Carl H. Wurzer. 100% freelance written. Bimonthly magazine covering brush, applicator, mop industry. "General management articles are what we look for. Writers who can do plant profiles of our industry." Estab. 1898. Circ. 1,200. **Pays on acceptance.** Publishes ms an average of 4 months after acceptance. Byline given. Offers 100% kill fee. Buys second serial (reprint) rights or makes work-for-hire assignments. Editorial lead time 4 months. Accepts simultaneous submissions.
Nonfiction General interest, plant profiles with photos. Buys 20 mss/year. Query with or without published clips. Length: 800-2,000 words. Pays $500-1,000 for assigned articles; $25-100 for unsolicited articles. Pays expenses of writers on assignment.
Reprints: Accepts previously published submissions.
Photos: State availability of photos with submissions. Reviews 4×6 prints. Negotiates payment individually. Captions, identification of subjects required. Buys one-time rights.

CLEANING AND MAINTENANCE MANAGEMENT, The Magazine for Today's Building Cleaning Maintenance/Housekeeping Executive, National Trade Publications, Inc., 13 Century Hill Dr., Latham NY 12110-2197. (518)783-1281. Fax: (518)783-1386. E-mail: anne@cleannet.com. Website: http://cleannet.com. Managing Editor: Anne Dantz. Monthly national trade magazine covering building cleaning maintenance/housekeeping operations in larger institutions such as hotels, schools, hospitals, office buildings, industrial plants, recreational and religious buildings, shopping centers, airports, etc. Articles must be aimed at managers of on-site building/facility cleaning staffs or owners/managers of contract cleaning companies. Estab. 1963. Circ. 42,000. Pays on publication, with invoice. Byline given. Buys all rights. Reports in 2 weeks. Sample copy and writer's guidelines for 9×12 SAE with 8 first-class stamps.
Nonfiction: Articles on: discussions of facility-wide systems for custodial operations/cleaning tasks; system-wide analysis of custodial task cost-effectiveness and staffing levels; the organization of cleaning tasks on an institution-wide basis; recruitment, training, motivation and supervision of building cleaning employees; the cleaning of buildings or facilities of unusual size, type, design, construction or notoriety; interesting case studies; or advice for the successful operation of a contract cleaning business. Buys 6-12 mss/year. Length: 500-1,500 words. Pays $50-200. Please query.
Photos: State availability of photos. Prefer color or b&w prints, rates negotiable. Captions, model releases and identification of subjects required.
Tips: Chances of acceptance are directly proportional to the article's relevance to the professional, on-the-job needs and interests of facility/custodial managers or contract building cleaners.

CLEANING BUSINESS, P.O. Box 1273, Seattle WA 98111. (206)622-4241. Fax: (206)622-6876. Publisher: William R. Griffin. Associate Editor: Jim Saunders. 80% freelance written. Quarterly magazine covering technical and management information relating to cleaning and self-employment. "We cater to those who are self-employed in any facet of the cleaning and maintenance industry and seek to be top professionals in their field. *Cleaning Business* is published for self-employed cleaning professionals, specifically carpet, upholstery and drapery cleaners; janitorial and maid services; window washers; odor, water and fire damage restoration contractors. Our readership is small but select. We seek concise, factual articles, realistic but definitely upbeat." Circ. 6,000. Pays 1 month after publication. Publishes ms an average of 3 months after acceptance. Byline given. Buys first serial, second serial (reprint) and all rights or makes work-for-hire assignments. Submit seasonal material 6 months in advance. Reports in 3 months. Sample copy for $3 and 8×10 SAE with 3 first-class stamps. Writer's guidelines for #10 SASE.
Nonfiction: Exposé (safety/health business practices); how-to (on cleaning, maintenance, small business management); humor (clean jokes, cartoons); interview/profile; new product (must be unusual to rate full article—mostly obtained from manufacturers); opinion; personal experience; technical. Special issues: "What's New?" (February). No "wordy articles written off the top of the head, obviously without research, and needing more editing time than was spent on writing." Buys 40 mss/year. Query with or without published clips. Length: 500-3,000 words. Pays $5-80. ("Pay depends on amount of work, research and polishing put into article much more than on length.") Pays expenses of writers on assignment with prior approval only.
Photos: State availability of photos or send photos with ms. Pays $5-25 for "smallish" b&w prints. Captions, model release and identification of subjects required. Buys one-time rights and reprint rights. "Magazine size is 8½×11—photos need to be proportionate. Also seeks full-color photos of relevant subjects for cover."
Columns/Departments: "Ten regular columnists now sell four columns per year to us. We are interested in adding Safety & Health and Fire Restoration columns (related to cleaning and maintenance industry). We

are also open to other suggestions—send query." Buys 36 columns/year; department information obtained at no cost. Query with or without published clips. Length: 500-1,500 words. Pays $15-85.

Fillers: Jokes, gags, anecdotes, short humor, newsbreaks, cartoons. Buys 40/year. Length: 3-200 words. Pays $1-20.

Tips: "We are constantly seeking quality freelancers from all parts of the country. A freelancer can best break in to our publication with fairly technical articles on how to do specific cleaning/maintenance jobs; interviews with top professionals covering this and how they manage their business; and personal experience. Our readers demand concise, accurate information. Don't ramble. Write only about what you know and/or have researched. Editors don't have time to rewrite your rough draft. Organize and polish before submitting."

‡INTERACTIVE TECHNOLOGIES, INC., 2266 N. Second St., North St. Paul MN 55109. (612)777-2690. Fax: (612)779-4879. Managing Editor: Joe Moses. 30% freelance written. Monthly magazines covering wireless security installations. "Applications of wireless security systems, written for dealers and installers." **Pays on acceptance.** Publishes ms an average of 4 months after acceptance. Byline sometimes given. Buys first rights or makes work-for-hire assignments. Editorial lead time varies. Submit seasonal material 6 months in advance. Writer's guidelines for #10 SASE.

● This listing differs from others. Interactive technologies, Inc. is a wireless security company seeking articles on their products which they then place in appropriate trade journals. "We pay for the article ($300-400) and we worry about getting it published."

Nonfiction: Exposé, how-to, interview/profile, new product, photo feature, technical. No unsolicited ms. No non-wireless installations. Buys 8-12 mss/year. Query with published clips. Length: 1,200-2,500 words. Pays $300-400. Sometimes pays expenses of writers on assignment.

Photos: State availability of photos with submission. Reviews 4×6 prints. Negotiates payment individually. Model releases, identification of subjects required. Buys one-time rights.

Tips: "We're looking for technical articles and profiles of dealers who install our wireless security products. Go through the Yellow Pages and find an ITI security dealer and tell him/her you want to write a story on a noteworthy wireless installation they've done. Then send a query."

PEST CONTROL MAGAZINE, 7500 Old Oak Blvd., Cleveland OH 44130. (216)243-8100. Fax: (216)891-2675. Editor: Jerry Mix. Monthly magazine for professional pest control operators and sanitarians. Estab. 1933. Circ. 20,000. Buys all rights. Buys 12 mss/year. Pays on publication. Submit seasonal material 2 months in advance. Reports in 1 month. Query or submit complete ms.

Nonfiction: Business tips, unique control situations, personal experience (stories about pest control operations and their problems). Must have trade or business orientation. No general information type of articles desired. Buys 3 unsolicited mss/year. Length: 1,000 words. Pays $150-500 minimum.

Columns/Departments: Regular columns use material oriented to this profession. Length: 2,000 words.

Photos: No additional payment for photos used with mss. Pays $50-150 for 8×10 color or transparencies.

SAFETY COMPLIANCE LETTER, with OSHA Highlights, Bureau of Business Practice, 24 Rope Ferry Rd., Waterford CT 06386. (203)442-4365. Fax: (203)434-3078. Editor: Michele Rubin. Publisher; James O'Shea. 80% freelance written. Bimonthly newsletter covering occupational safety and health. Publishes interview-based how-to and success stories for personnel in charge of safety and health in manufacturing/industrial environments. Circ. 15,000. Pays on acceptance after editing. Publishes ms an average of 6 months after acceptance. No byline given. Buys all rights. Submit seasonal material 4 months in advance. Reports in 1 month. Sample copy and writer's guidelines for SASE.

Nonfiction: How-to implement a particular occupational safety/health program, changes in OSHA regulations, and examples of exceptional safety/health programs. Only accepts articles that are based on an interview with a safety manager, safety consultant, occupational physician, or OSHA expert. Buys 48 mss/year. Query. Length: 750-1,200 words. Pays 12-17¢/word.

SECURITY SALES, Management Resource for the Professional Installing Dealer, Bobit Publishing, 2512 Artesia Blvd., Redondo Beach CA 90278-3296. (310)376-8788. Fax: (310)376-9043. E-mail: bobitpub@aol.com. Editor/Associate Publisher: Jason Knott. Associate Editor: Vi Pangelinan. Contact: Amy Jones, managing editor. 5% freelance written. Monthly magazine that covers the security industry. "Editorial covers technology, management and marketing designed to help installing security dealers improve their businesses. Closed-circuit TV, burglary and fire equipment, and access control systems are main topics." Estab. 1979. Circ. 23,940. Pays on publication. Publishes ms an average of 6 months after acceptance. Byline sometimes given. Buys all rights or one-time rights. Editorial lead time 2 months. Submit seasonal material 4 months in advance. Accepts simultaneous submissions. Sample copy free on request.

Nonfiction: How-to, technical. "No generic business operations articles. Submissions must be specific to security and contain interviews with installing dealers." Buys 6-10 mss/year. Send complete ms. Length: 800-1,500 words. Pays $50 minimum.

Photos: Send photos with submission. Reviews prints. Offers no additional payment for photos accepted with ms. Captions, model releases, identification of subjects required.

Tips: "Case studies of specific security installations with photos and diagrams are needed. Interview dealers who installed system and ask how they solved specific problems, why they chose certain equipment, cost of job, etc."

MANAGEMENT AND SUPERVISION

This category includes trade journals for middle management business and industrial managers, including supervisors and office managers. Journals for business executives and owners are classified under Business Management. Those for industrial plant managers are listed in Industrial Operations.

HR BRIEFING, Bureau of Business Practice, 24 Rope Ferry Rd., Waterford CT 06386. (860)442-4365, ext. 798. Editor: Mary-Lou Devine. 75% freelance written. Eager to work with new/unpublished writers. Semimonthly newsletter emphasizing all aspects of personnel practices for HR managers in all types and sizes of companies, both white collar and industrial. **Pays on acceptance.** Publishes ms an average of 5 months after acceptance. Buys all rights. Submit seasonal material 4 months in advance. Reports in 1 month. Sample copy and writer's guidelines for 10×13 SAE with 2 first class stamps.
Nonfiction: Interviews with personnel managers or human resource professionals on topics of current interest in the personnel field. Buys 30 mss/year. Query with brief, specific outline. Length: 800-1,500 words.
Tips: "We're looking for concrete, practical material on how to solve problems. We're providing information about trends and developments in the field. We don't want filler copy. It's very easy to break in. Include your phone number with your query so we can discuss the topic. Send for guidelines first, though, so we can have a coherent conversation."

HUMAN RESOURCE EXECUTIVE, LRP Publications Magazine Group, 747 Dresher Rd., P.O. Box 980, Dept. 500, Dresher PA 19044. (215)784-0910. E-mail: 75372.436@compuserve.com. Editor: David Shadovitz. 30% freelance written. Monthly magazine serving the information needs of chief human resource professionals/executives in companies, government agencies and nonprofit institutions with 500 or more employees." Estab. 1987. Circ. 45,000. **Pays on acceptance.** Publishes ms an average of 2 months after acceptance. Byline given. Offers 50% kill fee on assigned stories. Buys first and all rights including reprint rights. Reports in 1 month. Sample copy for 10×13 SAE with 2 first-class stamps. Writer's guidelines for #10 SAE with 1 first-class stamp.
Nonfiction: Book excerpts, interview/profile. Buys 16 mss/year. Query with published clips. Length: 1,700-2,000 words. Pays $200-850. Sometimes pays expenses of writers on assignment.
Photos: State availability of photos with submission. Reviews contact sheets. Offers no additional payment for photos accepted with ms. Identification of subjects required. Buys first and repeat rights.

‡**INDUSTRY WEEK, The Management Magazine for Industry**, Penton Publishing Inc., Dept. WM, 1100 Superior Ave., Cleveland OH 44114-2543. (216)696-7000. Fax: (216)696-7670. E-mail: 74777.3671@ compuserve.com. Assitant Managing Editor: Patricia Panchak. 15% freelance written. Biweekly industrial management magazine. "*Industry Week* is designed to help its audience—mid- and upper-level managers in industry—manage and lead their organizations better. Every article should address this editorial mission." Estab. 1921. Circ. 233,000. **Pays on acceptance.** Publishes ms an average of 4 months after acceptance. Byline given. Reports in 1 month. Free sample copy and writer's guidelines. "An SAE speeds replies."
Nonfiction: Interview/profile. "Any article submitted to *Industry Week* should be consistent with its mission. We suggest authors contact us before submitting anything." Buys 15-20 mss/year. Query with or without published clips, or send complete ms, with SASE. Length: 750-2,500 words. Pays $350 minimum. "We pay *routine* expenses; we do *not* pay for travel unless arranged in advance."
Photos: State availability of photos with submission or send photo with submission. Reviews contact sheets, transparencies, prints. Payment arranged individually. Captions, identification of subjects required.
Tips: "Become familiar with *Industry Week*. We're after articles about managing in industry, period. While we do not use freelancers too often, we do use some. The stories we accept are written with an understanding of our audience, and mission. We prefer multi-source stories that offer lessons for all managers in industry."

‡**MANAGE**, 2210 Arbor Blvd., Dayton OH 45439. (513)294-0421. Fax: (513)294-2374. Website: http:// www.cris.com/~nma1/index.html. Editor-in-Chief: Douglas E. Shaw. 60% freelance written. Works with a small number of new/unpublished writers each year. Quarterly magazine for first-line and middle management and scientific/technical managers. Estab. 1925. Circ. 40,000. **Pays on acceptance.** Publishes ms an average of 6 months after acceptance. Buys North American magazine rights with reprint privileges; book rights remain with the author. Reports in 3 months. Sample copy and writer's guidelines for 9×12 SAE with 3 first-class stamps.
Nonfiction: "All material published by *Manage* is in some way management-oriented. Most articles concern one or more of the following categories: communications, executive abilities, human relations, job status,

leadership, motivation and productivity and professionalism. Articles should be specific and tell the manager how to apply the information to his job immediately. Be sure to include pertinent examples, and back up statements with facts. *Manage* does not want essays or academic reports, but interesting, well-written and practical articles for and about management." Buys 6 mss/issue. Phone queries OK. Submit complete ms. Length: 600-1,000 words. Pays 5¢/word.

Tips: "Keep current on management subjects; submit timely work. Include word count on first page of ms."

QUALITY MANAGEMENT, (formerly *Quality Assurance Bulletin*), Bureau of Business Practice, 24 Rope Ferry Rd., Waterford CT 06386-0001. (800)243-0876. Fax: (203)434-3078. Contact: Editor. 80% freelance written. Biweekly newsletter for quality assurance supervisors and managers and general middle to top management. **Pays on acceptance.** No byline given. Buys all rights. Reports in 2 weeks on queries; 1 month on mss. *Writer's Market* recommends allowing 2 months for reply. Free sample copy and writer's guidelines.
Nonfiction: Interview and articles with a strong how-to slant that make use of direct quotes whenever possible. Query before writing your article. Length: 800-1,500 words. Pays 10-15¢/word.
Tips: "Write for freelance guidelines and follow them closely."

SALES MANAGER'S BULLETIN, The Bureau of Business Practice, 24 Rope Ferry Rd., Waterford CT 06386-0001. Fax: (203)434-3078. Editor: Paulette S. Kitchens. 33% freelance written. Prefers to work with published/established writers. Semimonthly newsletter for sales managers and salespeople interested in getting into sales management. Estab. 1917. **Pays on acceptance.** Publishes ms an average of 6 months after acceptance. Submit seasonal material 6 months in advance. Original interview-based material only. No byline. Buys all rights. Reports in 1 month. Sample copy and writer's guidelines for SAE with 2 first-class stamps.
Nonfiction: How-to (motivate salespeople, cut costs, create territories, etc.); interview (with working sales managers who use innovative techniques); technical (marketing stories based on interviews with experts). "No articles on territory management, saving fuel in the field, or public speaking skills. Break into this publication by reading the guidelines and sample issue. Follow the directions closely and chances for acceptance go up dramatically. One easy way to start is with an interview article ('Here's what sales executives have to say about . . .') Query is vital to acceptance. Send a simple note explaining briefly the subject matter, the interviewees, slant, length, and date of expected completion, accompanied by a SASE." No unqueried mss. Length: 800-1,000 words. Pays 12-15¢/word.
Tips: "Freelancers should always request samples and writer's guidelines, accompanied by SASE. Requests without SASE are discarded immediately. Examine the sample, and don't try to improve on our style. Write as we write. Don't 'jump around' from point to point and don't submit articles that are too chatty and with not enough real information. The more time a writer can save the editors, the greater his or her chance of a sale and repeated sales, when queries may no longer be necessary. We will focus more on selling more product, meeting intense competition, customer relations/partnerships, and sales forecasting."

SECURITY MANAGEMENT BULLETIN: Protecting People, Property & Assets, Bureau of Business Practice, 24 Rope Ferry Rd., Waterford CT 06386. Editor: Alex Vaughn. 75% freelance written. Eager to work with new/unpublished writers. Biweekly newsletter emphasizing security for industry. "All material should be slanted toward security directors, primarily industrial, retail and service businesses, but others as well." Circ. 3,000. Pays when article assigned to future issue. Buys all rights. Free sample copy and writer's guidelines.
Nonfiction: Interview (with security professionals only). "Articles should be tight and specific. They should deal with new security techniques or new twists on old ones." Buys 2-5 mss/issue. Query. Phone queries OK. Length: 750-1,000 words. Pays 15¢/word and up.

‡SUPERVISION, P.O. Box 1, Burlington IA 52601-0001. Fax: (319)752-3421. Publisher: Michael S. Darnall. Editor: Barbara Boeding. 95% freelance written. Monthly magazine for first-line foremen, supervisors and office managers. Estab. 1939. Circ. 2,620. Pays on publication. Publishes ms an average of 6 months after acceptance. Buys all rights. Reports in 1 month. Sample copy and writer's guidelines for 9 × 12 SAE with 4 first-class stamps; mention *Writer's Market* in request.
Nonfiction: How-to (cope with supervisory problems, discipline, absenteeism, safety, productivity, goal setting, etc.); personal experience (unusual success story of foreman or supervisor). No sexist material written from only a male viewpoint. Include biography and/or byline with ms submissions. Author photos requested. Buys 12 mss/issue. Query. Length: 1,500-1,800 words. Pays 4¢/word.
Tips: "Following AP stylebook would be helpful." Uses no advertising. Send correspondence to Editor.

TRAINING MAGAZINE, The Human Side of Business, Lakewood Publications, 50 S. Ninth St., Minneapolis MN 55402. (612)333-0471. Fax: (612)333-6526. Editor: Jack Gordon. Contact: Chris Lee, managing editor. 10% freelance written. Monthly magazine covering training and employee development in the business world. "Our core readers are managers and professionals who specialize in employee training and development (e.g., corporate training directors, VP-human resource development, etc.). We have a large secondary readership among managers of all sorts who are concerned with improving human performance in their organizations. We take a businesslike approach to training and employee education." Estab. 1964.

Circ. 56,000. **Pays on acceptance.** Publishes ms an average of 3 months after acceptance. Byline given. Buys first North American serial and second serial (reprint) rights. Reports in 2 weeks on queries; 2 months on mss. Sample copy for 10×13 SAE with 4 first-class stamps. Writer's guidelines for #10 SASE.

Nonfiction: Essays; exposé; how-to (on training, management, sales, productivity improvement, etc.); humor; interview/profile; new product; opinion; photo feature; technical (use of audiovisual aids, computers, etc.). "No puff, no 'testimonials' or disguised ads in any form." Buys 15 mss/year. Query. Length: 200-3,000 words. Pays $50-900.

Photos: State availability of photos with submission. Reviews transparencies, prints. Negotiates payment individually. Identification of subjects required. Buys first rights and limited reprint rights.

Columns/Departments: Training Today (news briefs, how-to tips, reports on pertinent research, trend analysis, etc.), 400 words. Buys 4 mss/year. Query. Pays $50-125.

Tips: "Send an intriguing query that demonstrates writing ability, as well as some insight into the topic you propose to cover. Then be willing to submit the piece on spec."

MARINE AND MARITIME INDUSTRIES

MARINE BUSINESS JOURNAL, The Voice of the Marine Industries Nationwide, 1766 Bay Rd., Miami Beach FL 33139. (305)538-0700. Fax: (305)532-8657. Editorial Director: David Strickland. Contact: Dru J. Murray. 25% freelance written. Bimonthly magazine that covers the recreational boating industry. "*The Marine Business Journal* is aimed at boating dealers, distributors and manufacturers, naval architects, yacht brokers, marina owners and builders, marine electronics dealers, distributors and manufacturers, and anyone involved in the US marine industry. Articles cover news, new product technology and public affairs affecting the industry." Estab. 1986. Circ. 26,000. Pays on publication. Publishes ms an average of 1 month after acceptance. Byline given. Buys first North American serial, one-time or second serial (reprint rights). Reports in 2 weeks on queries. Sample copy for $2.50 and 9×12 SAE with 7 first-class stamps. Writer's guidelines for #10 SASE.

Nonfiction: Buys 20 mss/year. Query with published clips. Length: 500-2,000 words. Pays $100-200 for assigned articles. Sometimes pays expenses of writers on assignment.

Photos: State availability of photos with submission. Reviews 35mm or larger transparencies, 5×7 prints. Offers $25-50/photo. Captions, model releases, identification of subjects required. Buys one-time rights.

Tips: "Query with clips. It's a highly specialized field, written for professionals by professionals, almost all on assignment or by staff."

‡**MARINE MECHANIC**, Middle Coast Publishing, Inc., P.O. Box 2522, Iowa City IA 52244. (319)339-1877. Editor: Tim Banse. 50% freelance written. Bimonthly magazine covering marine engine repair. Estab. 1995. Circ. 10,000. Pays on publication. Byline given. Editorial lead time 6 months.

Nonfiction: How-to, new product, technical. Buys 10 mss/year. Query with published clips. Length: 500-2,000 words. Pays $50-1,000. Sometimes pays expenses of writers on assignment.

Reprints: Accepts previously published submissions.

Photos: State availability of photos with submission. Negotiates payment individually.

Columns/Departments: Pays $100-500.

OCEAN NAVIGATOR, Marine Navigation & Ocean Voyaging, Navigator Publishing Corp., 18 Danforth St., Portland ME 04101. (207)772-2466. Editor: Tim Queeney. Bimonthly magazine covering marine navigation and ocean voyaging. Estab. 1985. Circ. 40,600. Pays on publication. Byline given. Accepts simultaneous submissions. Writer's guidelines available on request.

Nonfiction: How-to, personal experience (voyaging stories), technical. No racing (except navigational challenges); no travel logs/diaries. Query or send complete ms. Pays 15¢/word.

Reprints: Send typed ms with rights for sale noted and information about when and where the article previously appeared.

Photos: Send photos with submission. Offers $50-75/photo; $400 for cover photo.

MEDICAL

Through these journals physicians, therapists and mental health professionals learn how other professionals help their patients and manage their medical practices. Publications for nurses, laboratory technicians and other medical personnel are listed in the Hospitals, Nursing and Nursing Home section. Publications for drug store managers and drug wholesalers and retailers, as well as hospital equipment suppliers, are listed with Drugs, Health Care and Medical Products. Publications for consumers that report trends in the medical field are found in the Consumer Health and Fitness categories.

ALTERNATIVE THERAPIES IN HEALTH AND MEDICINE, InnoVision Communications, 101 Columbia, Aliso Viejo CA 92656. (800)899-1712. Fax: (714)362-2020. E-mail: alttherapy@aol.com. Publisher: Bonnie Horrigan. Managing Editor: Michael Villaire. Contact: Editorial Assistant. 10% freelance written. Bimonthly magazine covering alternative/complementary health care for the practitioner. "*AT* is a forum for sharing information concerning the practical use of alternative therapies in preventing and treating disease, healing illness and promoting health. We publish a variety of disciplined inquiry methods, including high quality scientific research. We encourage the integration of alternative therapies with conventional medical practices. Our audience is primary care physicians and nurses, and alternative health care practitioners. Stories should provide useful information for them." Estab. 1994. Circ. 20,000. **Pays on acceptance.** Publishes ms an average of 3 months after acceptance. Offers 50% kill fee. Buys first North american serial and second serial (reprint) rights. Editorial lead time 3 months. Submit seasonal material 6 months in advance. Reports in 1 month on queries; 2 months on mss. Sample copy for $10. Writer's guidelines for #10 SASE.

Nonfiction: News of interest to practitioner. No consumer-oriented articles, weight-loss plans, personal experiences. Buys 6 mss/year. Query with published clips. Length: 500-1,200 words. Pays $500-750.

Photos: State availability of photos with submissions. Reviews contact sheets. Negotiates payment individually. Model releases, identification of subjects required. Buys one-time and reprint rights.

Fillers: Newsbreaks, short humor. Buys 6-12/year. Length: 100-250 words. Pays $25-100.

Tips: "Remember who our audience is—health care practitioners. Spot and report thoroughly and responsibly on trends in the field that would interest our audience. A recent issue had stories on insurance programs that cover alternative therapies and medical schools that teach courses on alternative medicine to students."

AMA ALLIANCE TODAY, (formerly *Facets* magazine), American Medical Association Alliance, Inc., 515 N. State St., Chicago IL 60610. (312)464-4470. Fax: (312)464-5020. Editor: Sarah E. Bisbee. 10% freelance written. Work with both established and new writers. Bimonthly magazine for physicians' spouses. Estab. 1965. Circ. 60,000. **Pays on acceptance.** Publishes ms an average of 6 months after acceptance. Buys first rights. Accepts simultaneous submissions. Reports in 2 months. Sample copy for 9×12 SAE with 2 first-class stamps.

Nonfiction: All articles must be related to the experiences of physicians' spouses. Current health issues; financial topics, physicians' family circumstances, business management and volunteer leadership how-to's. Query with clear outline of article—what points will be made, what conclusions drawn, what sources will be used. No personal experience or personality stories. Length: 1,000 words. Pays $300-800. Pays expenses of writers on assignment.

Reprints: Accepts previously published submissions.

Photos: State availability of photos with query. Uses all color visuals.

Tips: "This is a new publication—*AMA Alliance Today.* The writing will be more mass appeal. Yet, the magazine will still focus on public health issues and report on the events of state and county alliances which are made up of physician's spouses."

CARDIOLOGY WORLD NEWS, Medical Publishing Enterprises, P.O. Box 1548, Marco Island FL 33969. (813)394-0400. Fax: (813)394-0400. Editor: John H. Lavin. 75% freelance written. Prefers to work with published/established writers. Quarterly magazine covering cardiology and the cardiovascular system. "We need short news articles *for doctors* on any aspect of our field—diagnosis, treatment, risk factors, etc." Estab. 1985. **Pays on acceptance.** Publishes ms an average of 2 months after acceptance. Byline given "for special reports and feature-length articles." Offers 20% kill fee. Buys first North American serial rights. Reports in 2 months. Sample copy for $1. Free writer's guidelines with #10 SASE.

Nonfiction: New product and technical (clinical). No fiction, fillers, profiles of doctors or poetry. Query with published clips. Length: 250-1,200 words. Pays $50-300; $50/column for news articles. Pays expenses of writers on assignment.

Photos: State availability of photos with query. Pays $50/photo. Rough captions, model release and identification of subjects required. Buys one-time rights.

Tips: "Submit written news articles of 250-500 words on speculation with basic source material (not interview notes) for fact-checking. We demand clinical or writing expertise for full-length feature. Clinical cardiology conventions/symposia are the best source of news and feature articles."

CINCINNATI MEDICINE, Academy of Medicine, 320 Broadway, Cincinnati OH 45234-9506. (513)421-7010. Fax: (513)721-4378. Associate Editor: Shawna Geist. Editor: Pamela G. Fairbanks. One freelance article/issue. Works with a small number of new/unpublished writers each year. Monthly membership newspaper for the Academy of Medicine of Cincinnati covering socio-economic and political factors that affect the practice of medicine in Cincinnati. For example: Effects of Medicare changes on local physicians and patients. (99% of readers are Cincinnati physicians.) Estab. 1978. Circ. 3,000. **Pays on acceptance.** Publishes ms an average of 1 month after acceptance. Byline given. Makes work-for-hire assignments. Reports in 6 weeks on queries; 3 months on mss. Sample copy for $3 and 9×12 SAE with 9 first-class stamps.

● *Cincinnati Medicine* reports that in January 1995 they switched to a tabloid newspaper format, making stories shorter and newsier.

Nonfiction: Historical/nostalgic (history of, or reminiscences about, medicine in Cincinnati); interview/profile (of medical leaders in Cincinnati); opinion (opinion pieces on controversial medico-legal and medico-ethical issues). "We do not accept scientific/research articles." Buys 12 mss/year. Query with published clips. Length: 500 words. Pays $125-400.
Photos: State availability of photos with query or ms. Captions and identification of subjects required. Buys one-time rights.
Tips: Send published clips. "We emphasize solid reporting and accurate, well-balanced analysis."

EMERGENCY, The Journal of Emergency Services, 6300 Yarrow Dr., Carlsbad CA 92009-1597. (619)438-2511. Fax: (619)931-5809. E-mail: emergency@aol.com. Editor: Doug Fiske. 100% freelance written. Works with a small number of new/unpublished writers each year. Monthly magazine covering prehospital emergency care. "Our readership is primarily composed of EMTs, paramedics and other EMS personnel. We prefer a professional, semi-technical approach to prehospital subjects." Estab. 1969. Circ. 30,000. **Pays on acceptance.** Publishes ms an average of 4 months after acceptance. Byline given. Buys all rights (revert to author after 3 months). Submit seasonal material 6 months in advance. Reports in 2 months. Sample copy for $3. Writer's guidelines for #10 SASE.
Nonfiction: Semi-technical how-to (on treating prehospital emergency patients), interview/profile, new techniques, opinion, photo feature. "We do not publish cartoons, term papers, product promotions disguised as articles or overly technical manuscripts." Buys 60 mss/year. Query with published clips. Length 1,500-3,000 words. Pays $100-400.
Photos: If possible, send photos with submission. Reviews color transparencies and b&w prints. Photos accepted with mss increase payment. Offers $30/photo without ms; $100 for cover photos. Captions and identification of subjects required. All medics pictured must be using universal precautions (gloves, etc.).
Columns/Departments: Open Forum (opinion page for EMS professionals), 750-800 words; Skills Primer (basic skills, how-to, with photos), 1,000-2,000 words; Rescue Call (covers a specific rescue or technique); Drug Watch (focuses on one particular drug a month). Buys 10 mss/year. Query first. Pays $50-300.
Fillers: Facts, newsbreaks. Buys 10/year. Length: 500 words maximum. Pays $0-75.
Tips: "Writing style for features and departments should be knowledgeable and lively with a clear theme or story line to maintain reader interest and enhance comprehension. The biggest problem we encounter is dull, lifeless term-paper-style writing with nothing to pique reader interest. Keep in mind we are not a textbook, but all technical articles must be well referenced with footnotes within the text. We follow AP style. Accompanying photos are a plus. We appreciate a short, one paragraph biography on the author."

HEALTHPLAN, American Association of Health Plans, (formerly *HMO*), 1129 20th St. NW, Suite 600, Washington DC 20036. (202)778-3250. Fax: (202)331-7487. E-mail: jcook@ghaa.org. Website: www//http:GHAA.org. Editor: Susan Pisano. Contact: Diana Madden, managing editor. 35% freelance written. Bimonthly magazine for news and analysis. "*Healthplan* magazine is geared toward senior administrative and medical managers in Healthplans. Articles must ask 'why' and 'how' and answer with examples. Articles should inform and generate interest and discussion about topics on anything from medical management to regulatory issues." Estab. 1990. Circ. 7,000. Pays within 30 days of acceptance of article in final form. Publishes ms an average of 2 months after acceptance. Byline given. Offers 30% kill fee. Buys all rights. Editorial lead time 2 months. Submit seasonal material 2 months in advance. Accepts simultaneous submissions. Reports in 1 month on queries. Sample copy and writer's guidelines free on request.
Nonfiction: How-to (how industry professionals can better operate their health plans), opinion. "We do not accept stories that promote products." Buys 20 mss/year. Query. Length: 1,800-2,500 words. Pays 40¢/word minimum. Pays phone expenses of writers on assignment.
Photos: State availability of photos with submission. Reviews contact sheets. Offers no additional payment for photos accepted with ms. Buys all rights.
Columns/Departments: Washington File (health policy issues relating to managed health care), 1,800 words; Preventive Care (case study or discussion of public health), 1,800 words; The Market (market niches for HMOs—with examples), 1,800 words. Buys 6 mss/year. Query with published clips. Pays 35-50¢/word.
Tips: "Follow the current health care debate. Look for health plan success stories in your community; we like to include case studies on everything from medical management to regulatory issues so that our readers can learn from their colleagues. Our readers are members of our trade association and look for advice and news. Topics relating to the quality of health plans are the ones most frequently assigned to writers, whether a feature or department."

JEMS, The Journal of Emergency Medical Services, Jems Communications, Suite 200, 1947 Camino Vida Roble, Carlsbad CA 92008-2789. (619)431-9797. Fax: (619)431-8176. Website: http://www.jems.com.

 A BULLET introduces comments by the editors of *Writer's Market* indicating special information about the listing.

Executive Editor: Keith Griffiths. Contact: Lauren Simon Ostrow, senior editor. 80% freelance written. Monthly magazine for emergency medical services—all phases. The journal is directed to personnel who serve the pre-hospital emergency medicine industry: paramedics, EMTs, emergency physicians and nurses, administrators, EMS consultants, etc. Estab. 1980. Circ. 45,000. Pays on publication. Publishes ms an average of 6 months after acceptance. Byline given. Buys all North American serial rights. Submit seasonal material 6 months in advance. Free sample copy and writer's guidelines.

Nonfiction: Essays, general interest, how-to, continuing education, humor, interview/profile, new product, opinion, photo feature, technical. Buys 50 mss/year. Query. Length: 750-3,000 words. Pays $125-500.

Photos: State availability of photos with submission. Buys one-time rights.

Columns/Departments: Teacher Talk (directed toward EMS instructors), 1,000 words; Management Perspective (EMS administrators), 1,000 words; First Person (personal accounts of life in EMS); Commentary, 750 words. No payment for First Person or Commentary.

Tips: "Looking for authors with clinical and technical expertise who can present sophisticated topics in a lively and readable way."

MANAGED CARE, A Guide for Physicians, Stezzi Communications, Inc., 301 Oxford Valley Rd., Suite 1105A, Yardley PA 19067. (215)321-5480. Fax: (215)321-6670. E-mail: stezzicomm@aol.com. Editor: Patrick Mullen. Contact: Timothy Kelley, managing editor. 75% freelance written. Monthly magazine serving primary care physicians who are involved in managed care as well as decision-makers in managed care organizations. "We emphasize practical, usable information that helps the family physician, internist or other physician cope with the ever more complex array of options, challenges and hazards that accompanies the rapidly changing health care industry. Our regular readers understand that 'health care reform' isn't a piece of legislation; it's an evolutionary process that's already well under way. But we hope to help our readers also keep the faith that led them to medicine in the first place." Estab. 1992. Circ. 80,000. **Pays on acceptance.** Publishes ms an average of 1 month after acceptance. Byline given. Offers 20% kill fee. Buys all rights. Editorial lead time 3 months. Submit seasonal material 4 months in advance. Reports in 3 weeks on queries; 2 months on mss. Sample copy free.

Nonfiction: Book excerpts, general interest, how-to (deal with requisites of managed care, such as contracts with health plans, affiliation arrangements, relationships with staffers, computer needs, etc.), humor, interview/profile, opinion, personal experience, technical. Buys 35 mss/year. Query. Length: 1,000-3,000 words. Pays $1,000-1,500 for assigned articles; $100-1,000 for unsolicited articles. Pays expenses of writers on assignment.

Photos: State availability of photos with submissions. Reviews contact sheets, negatives, transparencies, prints. Negotiates payment individually. Buys one-time rights.

Columns/Departments: Paul Wynn. News/Commentary (usually staff-written, but regional editions, may increase needs in 95). 100-300 words. Pays $50-100.

Tips: "We're looking for reliable freelancers who can write for our audience with our approach, so 'breaking in' may yield assignments. Do this by writing impeccably and with flair, and try to reflect the practicing physician's interests and perspective. (Cardinal rule: That physician is busy, with many things vying for his/her reading time. Be sprightly, but don't waste our readers' time.)"

‡**MEDICAL ECONOMICS**, 5 Paragon Dr., Montvale NJ 07645. (201)358-7500. Fax: (201)573-0867. E-mail: nancy_meehan@medec.com. Contact: Nancy J. Meehan, outside copy chief. Biweekly magazine. Circ. 192,000. **Pays on acceptance.** Byline given. Offers 25% kill fee. Buys first world publication rights. Reports in 1 month on queries. Sample copy free on request.

• Ranked as one of the best markets for freelance writers in *Writer's Yearbook*'s annual "Top 100 Markets," January 1996.

Nonfiction: Articles about private physicians in innovative, pioneering and/or controversial situations affecting medical care delivery, patient relations or malpractice prevention/litigation; personal finance topics. Buys 40-50 mss/year. Query with published clips. Length: 1,500-3,000 words. Pays $1,200-2,500 for assigned articles. Pays expenses of writers on assignment.

Tips: "We look at health care issues from the perspective of practicing physicians."

MEDICAL IMAGING, The Business Magazine for Technology Management, 10 Risho Ave, East Providence RI 02916. (401)434-1050. Fax: (401)434-1090. E-mail: sspubs@tiac.net. Website: http://www.ssp ubs.com. Editor: Jack Spears. Contact: Mark Gordon, associate editor. 5% freelance written. Monthly magazine covering diagnostic imaging equipment. Estab. 1986. Circ. 18,000. Pays on publication. Publishes ms an average of 2 months after acceptance. Byline given. Offers 50% kill fee. Buys all rights. Editorial lead time 2 months. Responds to query letters "as soon as possible." Sample copy for $10 prepaid. Writer's guidelines for #10 SASE.

Nonfiction: Interview/profile, technical. "No general interest/human interest stories about healthcare. Articles *must* deal with our industry, diagnostic imaging." Buys 6 mss/year. Query with published clips. Length: 1,500-2,500 words. Pays approximately 25¢/word. Sometimes pays expenses of writers on assignment.

Photos: State availability of photos with submission. Reviews negatives. Offers no additional payment for photos accepted with ms "unless assigned separately." Model releases, identification of subjects required. Buys all rights.

Tips: "Send a letter with an interesting story idea that is applicable to our industry, diagnostic imaging. Then follow up with a phone call. Areas most open to freelancers are features and technology profiles. You don't have to be an engineer or doctor but you have to know how to talk and listen to them."

OPTICAL PRISM, VezCom Inc., 31 Hastings Dr., Unionville Ontario L3R 4Y5 Canada. (905)475-9343. Fax: (905)477-2821. E-mail: vezina@hookup.net. Editor: Allan K. Vezina. 50% freelance written. Magazine published 9 times/year covering a wide variety of material including contact lens fitting, eyeglass and contact lens dispensing, practice management, marketing and merchandising articles, as well as wholesale and retail 'success stories.' " Estab. 1983. Circ. 7,883. **Pays on acceptance.** Publishes ms an average of 4 months after acceptance. Offers 100% kill fee. Buys first, one-time and second serial (reprint) rights. Editorial lead time 4 months. Submit seasonal material 5 months in advance. Accepts simultaneous submissions. Reports in 2 weeks on story outlines; 1 month on mss. Sample copy free on request.

Nonfiction: Essays, exposé, general interest, historical/nostalgic, how-to (fit contact lens types, fit eyeglasses, grind lenses, etc.), humor, inspirational, interview/profile, new product (full article only), personal experience, photo feature, technical. Buys 15-20 mss/year. Send complete ms, story outline. Length: 1,500-10,000 words. Pays 10¢/word to a maximum of $500 (Canadian).

Reprints: Pays 3¢/word to a maximum of $200 (Canadian).

Photos: Send photos with submission. Reviews transparencies. Offers no additional payment for photos accepted with ms. Captions, model releases, identification of subjects required. Buys one-time rights.

Tips: "Writers should remember they are writing for doctors of optometry and doctors of medicine—therefore, standards should be very high to reflect the educational backgrounds of the readers."

PHYSICIAN'S MANAGEMENT, Advanstar Communications, 7500 Old Oak Blvd., Cleveland OH 44130. (216)243-8100. Fax: (216)891-2683. Editor-in-Chief: Bob Feigenbaum. Prefers to work with published/established writers. Monthly magazine emphasizing finances, investments, malpractice, socioeconomic issues, estate and retirement planning, small office administration, practice management, computers and taxes for primary care physicians in private practice. Estab. 1960. Circ. 120,000. **Pays on acceptance.** Publishes ms an average of 6 months after acceptance. Submit seasonal material 5 months in advance. Reports in 1 month. Sample copy for $10. Writer's guidelines for #10 SASE.

Nonfiction: *"Physician's Management* is a practice management/economic publication, not a clinical one." Publishes how-to articles (limited to medical practice management); informational (when relevant to audience); personal experience articles (if written by a physician). No fiction; clinical material or satire that portrays MD in an unfavorable light; or soap opera, "real-life" articles. Length: 2,000-2,500 words. Query with SASE. Pays $125/3-column printed page. Use of charts, tables, graphs, sidebars and photos strongly encouraged. Sometimes pays expenses of writers on assignment.

Tips: "Talk to doctors first about their practices, financial interests, and day-to-day nonclinical problems and then query us. Also, the ability to write a concise, well-structured and well-researched magazine article is essential. Freelancers who think like patients fail with us. Those who can think like MDs are successful."

PHYSICIAN'S PRACTICE DIGEST, 100 S. Charles St., 13th Floor, Baltimore MD 21201. (410)539-3100. Fax: (410)539-3188. E-mail: ppd@clark.net. Website: http://www.rothnet.com/ppd. Editor: Cathy Canning. 75% freelance written. Bimonthly magazine covering the business side of medical practice. "Magazine is about physician practice management, the business of medicine and health care. Readers are primarily in solo practice or small groups. Not a clinical publication." Estab. 1990. Circ. 60,000. Pays 1 month after publication. Publishes ms an average of 2 months after acceptance. Byline given. Offers 25% kill fee. Buys one-time rights. Editorial lead time 3 months. Submit seasonal material 6 months in advance. Sample copy and writer's guidelines free on request.

● *Physician's Practice Digest* reports a need for local news stories from the following states: TN, SC, NC, GA, MD, VA, DC. Articles should cover topics such as physician networks, merger activity between doctors, between hospitals, etc.

Nonfiction: How-to, interview/profile, opinion. "Anything related to health reform is hot now—managed care, reimbursement. No clinical articles." Buys 40 mss/year. Query with published clips. Length: 500-2,500 words. Pays 25¢/word minimum for assigned articles. Sometimes pays expenses of writers on assignment.

Reprints: Send typed ms with rights for sale noted and information about when and where the article previously appeared.

Photos: State availability of photos with submission. Reviews transparencies. Negotiates payment individually. Captions, model releases and identification of subjects required. Buys one-time rights.

Columns/Departments: Office Technology (computers, software, simulators, etc.), 500 words; Malpractice (reform, arbitration, etc.), 500 words; Managed Care (contracting, UR, guidelines, Marketing, Law, Insurance, etc.), 500 words. Query with published clips. Pays 25-50¢/word.

Tips: "It's absolutely essential to read the magazine. We *do not* run clinical articles. We're trying to help our readers cope while the health care industry undergoes radical transformation. We welcome ideas and information that will help the physician better manage the practice. Read the magazine! Think about what the reader *needs to know*. Look for health care trends and find the angle that affects physicians."

PODIATRY MANAGEMENT, P.O. Box 750129, Forest Hills NY 11375. (718)897-9700. Fax: (718)896-5747. E-mail: gcfg37a@prodigy.com. Website: http://www.podiatrymanagement.com. Publisher: Scott C. Borowsky. Editor: Barry Block, DPM, J.D. Managing Editor: Martin Kruth. Magazine published 9 times/year for practicing podiatrists. "Aims to help the doctor of podiatric medicine to build a bigger, more successful practice, to conserve and invest his money, to keep him posted on the economic, legal and sociological changes that affect him." Estab. 1982. Circ. 13,000. Pays on publication. Byline given. Buys first North American serial and second serial (reprint) rights. Submit seasonal material 4 months in advance. Accepts simultaneous submissions. Reports in 2 weeks. Sample copy for $3 and 9×12 SAE. Writer's guidelines for #10 SASE.
Nonfiction: General interest (taxes, investments, estate planning, recreation, hobbies); how-to (establish and collect fees, practice management, organize office routines, supervise office assistants, handle patient relations); interview/profile about interesting or well-known podiatrists; and personal experience. "These subjects are the mainstay of the magazine, but offbeat articles and humor are always welcome." Send tax and financial articles to Martin Kruth, 5 Wagon Hill Lane, Avon, CT 06001. Buys 25 mss/year. Query. Length: 1,000-2,500 words. Pays $150-600.
Reprints: Send photocopy of article. Pays 33% of amount paid for an original article.
Photos: State availability of photos. Pays $15 for b&w contact sheet. Buys one-time rights.

STITCHES, The Journal of Medical Humour, 16787 Warden Ave., R.R. #3, Newmarket, Ontario L3Y 4W1 Canada. Editor: Simon Hally. 90% freelance written. Magazine published 11 times/year covering humor for physicians. "*Stitches* is read primarily by physicians in Canada. Stories with a medical slant are particularly welcome, but we also run a lot of non-medical material. It must be funny and, of course, brevity is the soul of wit." Estab. 1990. Circ. 43,000. Pays on publication. Publishes ms 6 months after acceptance. Byline given. Offers 50% kill fee. Buys first North American serial rights. Editorial lead time 2 months. Submit seasonal material 3 months in advance. Reports in 6 weeks on queries; 2 months on mss. Sample copy free on request.
Nonfiction: Humor, personal experience. Buys 20 mss/year. Send complete ms. Length: 100-2,000 words. Pays $35-750 (Canadian).
Fiction: Humorous. Buys 30 mss/year. Send complete ms. Length: 100-2,000 words. Pays $35-750 (Canadian).
Poetry: Humorous. Buys 5 poems/year. Submit maximum 5 poems. Length: 2-20 lines. Pays $20-100.
Fillers: Gags to be illustrated by cartoonist, short humor. Pay negotiable.
Tips: "Due to the nature of humorous writing, we have to see a completed manuscript, rather than a query, to determine if it is suitable for us. Along with a short cover letter, that's all we require."

STRATEGIC HEALTH CARE MARKETING, Health Care Communications, 11 Heritage Lane, P.O. Box 594, Rye NY 10580. (914)967-6741. Editor: Michele von Dambrowski. 75% freelance written. Prefers to work with published/established writers. "Will only work with unpublished writer on a 'stringer' basis initially." Monthly newsletter covering health care marketing and management in a wide range of settings including hospitals and medical group practices, home health services and managed care organizations. Emphasis is on strategies and techniques employed within the health care field and relevant applications from other service industries. Estab. 1984. Pays on publication. Publishes ms an average of 2 months after acceptance. Byline given. Offers 25% kill fee. Buys first North American serial rights. Reports in 1 month. Sample copy for 9×12 SAE with 3 first-class stamps. Guidelines sent with sample copy only.
  • *Strategic Health Care Marketing* is specifically seeking writers with expertise/contacts in managed care, integrated delivery systems and demand management.
Nonfiction: How-to, interview/profile, new product, technical. Buys 45 mss/year. Query with published clips. No unsolicited mss. Length: 700-3,000 words. Pays $100-450. Sometimes pays the expenses of writers on assignment with prior authorization.
Photos: State availability of photos with submissions. (Photos, unless necessary for subject explanation, are rarely used.) Reviews contact sheets. Offers $10-30/photo. Captions and model releases required. Buys one-time rights.
Tips: "Writers with prior experience on business beat for newspaper or newsletter will do well. We require a sophisticated, indepth knowledge of health care reform issues and impact. This is not a consumer publication—the writer with knowledge of both health care and marketing will excel. Interviews or profiles are most open to freelancers. Absolutely no unsolicited manuscripts; any received will be returned or discarded unread."

UNIQUE OPPORTUNITIES, The Physician's Resource, U O Inc., Suite 1236, 455 S. Fourth Ave., Louisville KY 40202. Fax: (502)587-0848. E-mail: bettuo@aol.com. Editor: Mollie Vento Hudson. Contact: Bett Coffman, assistant editor. 45% freelance written. Bimonthly magazine covering physician relocation "published for physicians interested in a new career opportunity. It offers physicians useful information and first-hand experiences to guide them in making informed decisions concerning their first or next career opportunity. It provides regular features and columns about specific aspects of the search process." Estab. 1991. Circ. 80,000 physicians. **Pays on acceptance.** Publishes ms an average of 2 months after acceptance. Byline given. Offers 33% kill fee. Buys first North American serial rights. Editorial lead time 3 months. Submit seasonal material 6 months in advance. Reports in 2 months on queries. Sample copy for 9 × 12 SAE with 6 first-class stamps. Writer's guidelines for #10 SASE.

Nonfiction: Opinion (on issues relating to physician recruitment), practice options and information of interest to relocating physicians. Buys 12 mss/year. Query with published clips. Length: 1,500-3,500 words. Pays $750-1,500. Sometimes pays expenses of writers on assignment.

Photos: State availability of photos with submission. Negotiates payment individually. Model releases and identification of subjects required. Buys one-time rights.

Columns/Departments: Remarks (opinion from industry experts on physician career issues), 500 words; Physician Profiles (doctors with unusual or interesting careers), 500 words. Pays $200. Buys up to 6 mss/ year. Query with published clips. Pays $250-500.

Tips: "Submit queries via letter with ideas for articles that directly pertain to physician career issues, such as specific or unusual practice opportunities, relocation or practice establishment subjects, etc. Feature articles are most open to freelancers. Physician sources are most important, with tips and advice from both the physicians and business experts. Physicians like to know what other physicians think and are doing, but also appreciate the suggestions of other business people."

MUSIC

Publications for musicians and for the recording industry are listed in this section. Other professional performing arts publications are classified under Entertainment and the Arts. Magazines featuring music industry news for the general public are listed in the Consumer Entertainment and Music sections. (Markets for songwriters can be found in *Songwriter's Market*, Writer's Digest Books.)

THE CHURCH MUSICIAN, 127 Ninth Ave. N., Nashville TN 37234. (615)251-2961. Fax: (615)251-2614 or 5951. Editor: Jere Adams. Estab. 1950. 20% freelance written. Works with a small number of new/ unpublished writers each year; eager to work with new/unpublished writers. Quarterly publication for South ern Baptist church music leaders. Estab. 1950. Circ. 16,000. Buys all rights. **Pays on acceptance.** Publishes ms an average of 1 year after acceptance. Reports in 2 months. Sample copy for 9 × 12 SAE with 3 first-class stamps.

Nonfiction: Leadership and how-to features, success stories and articles on Protestant church music. "We reject material when the subject of an article doesn't meet our needs. And they are often poorly written, or contain too many 'glittering generalities' or lack creativity. We're interested in success stories; a 'this-worked-for-me' type of story." Length: maximum 1,300 words. Pays up to 5½¢/word, 6¢ on diskette.

Reprints: Send photocopy of article or typed ms with rights for sale noted and information about when and where the article previously appeared.

Photos: Purchased with mss; related to mss content only. "We can use color photos."

Fiction: Inspiration, guidance, motivation and morality with Protestant church music slant. Length: to 1,300 words. Pays up to 5½¢/word, 6¢ on diskette.

Poetry: Church music slant, inspirational. Uses very little. Length: 8-24 lines. Pays $5-15.

Fillers: Short humor. Church music slant. No clippings. Pays $5-15.

Tips: "I'd advise a beginning writer to write about his or her experience with some aspect of church music; the social, musical and spiritual benefits from singing in a choir; a success story about their instrumental group; a testimonial about how they were enlisted in a choir—especially if they were not inclined at first. A writer might speak to hymn singers—what turns them on and what doesn't. Some might include how music has helped them to talk about Jesus as well as sing about Him. We prefer most of these experiences be related to the church, of course, although we include many articles by writers whose affiliation is other than Baptist. A writer might relate his experience with a choir of blind or deaf members. Some people receive benefits from working with unusual children—retarded, or culturally deprived, emotionally unstable, and so forth. First choice for material will relate to music and worship and music administration."

MIX MAGAZINE, Cardinal Business Media Inc., 6400 Hollis St., Suite 12, Emeryville CA 94608. Fax: (510)693-5143. E-mail: 74673.3872@compuserve.com. Website: http://www.mixmag.com. Editor: George Petersen. Contact: Blair Jackson, executive editor. 50% freelance written. Monthly magazine covering pro audio. "*Mix* is a trade publication geared toward professionals in the music/sound production recording and post-production industries. We include stories about music production, sound for picture, live sound, etc. We prefer in-depth technical pieces that are applications-oriented." Estab. 1977. Circ. 50,000. Pays on publication. Publishes ms an average of 3 months after acceptance. Byline given. Offers 50% kill fee. Buys first North American serial rights. Editorial lead time 10 weeks. Submit seasonal material 3 months in advance.

Reports in 2 weeks on queries; 1 month on mss. Sample copy for $6. Writer's guidelines free on request.

Nonfiction: How-to, interview/profile, new product, technical, project/studio spotlights. Special issues: Sound for picture supplement (April, September), Design issue (August). Buys 60 mss/year. Query. Length 500-2,000 words. Pays $100-400 for assigned articles; $100-300 for unsolicited articles.

Photos: State availability of photos with submissions. Reviews 4×5 transparencies, prints. Negotiates payment individually. Captions, identification of subjects required. Buys one-time rights.

Tips: "Send Blair Jackson a letter outlining the article, including a description of the topic, information sources, what qualifies writers for the story, and mention of available graphics. A writing sample is also helpful."

‡**RECORDING, The Magazine for the Recording Musician**, Music Maker Publications, 7318 Topanga Canyon Blvd., Suite 200, Canoga Park CA 91303-1242. (818)346-3404. Fax: (818)346-3597. E-mail: recordi n@haven.ios.com. Editor: Nicholas Batzdorf. 90% freelance written. Monthly magazine covering technical and practical information to help musicians make better recordings. Estab. 1987. Circ. 30,000. Pays on publication. Publishes ms an average of 4 months after acceptance. Byline given. Kill fee negotiable. Buys all rights. Editorial lead time 3 months. Accepts simultaneous submissions. Reports in 2 weeks on queries. Writer's guidelines free on request.

Nonfiction: Book excerpts, how-to (record, or get the most from your recording equipment), opinion, technical. No personality interviews. Buys 65 mss/year. Query. Length: 1,000-4,500 words. Pays $100 and up. Sometimes pays expenses of writers on assignment.

Photos: State availability of photos with submission. Reviews transparencies, prints. Negotiates payment individually. Buys one-time rights.

Columns/Departments: Fade Out (guest editorial), 1,000 words; Digital Diary (digital recording tips), 2,000 words. Buys 36 mss/year. Query. Pays $100 and up.

Tips: Query by phone or mail.

THE WOODWIND QUARTERLY, 1513 Old CC Rd., Colville WA 99114-9526. (509)935-4875. Fax: (509)935-6835. E-mail: wq@iv.netcom.com. Editor: Scott Hirsch. 90% freelance written. Quarterly journal covering making and repairing woodwind instruments. "A 124-page soft-bound journal covering a wide variety of topics directed at repair technicians and makers of woodwind instruments, both historical instruments and modern. Articles can be about the history of woodwinds, tools used, or other how-to articles on construction methods and repair techniques." Estab. 1993. Circ. 1,500. **Pays on acceptance.** Publishes ms an average of 3 months after acceptance. Byline given. Offers 100% kill fee. Buys all rights. Editorial lead time 3 months. Accepts simultaneous submissions. Reports in 1 week on queries. Sample copy for $4. Writer's guidelines free on request.

Nonfiction: Book excerpts, essays, exposé, general interest, historical/nostalgic, how-to, humor, inspirational, interview/profile, new product, opinion, personal experience, photo feature, technical. Articles should not be directed to players but makers and repair technicians. Buys 75-100 mss/year. Query. Length: open. Pays $10/page (about 400 words).

Reprints: Accepts previously published submissions.

Photos: State availability of photos with submission. Reviews 5×3½ prints. Some articles consist of captioned photos only.

Columns/Departments: Laws Column (how to make a small business succeed), 4,000-6,000 words. Buys 12 mss/year. Query. Pays $10/page.

Fillers: Anecdotes, facts, gags to be illustrated by cartoonist, newsbreaks, short humor. Buys 25/year. Length: 50-500 words. Pays $20-100.

Tips: "Freelancers are invited to speak to the editor and discuss ideas for how to tailor articles to the readership. The Woodwind Quarterly would be happy to suggest articles that are in the Writer's backyard. (There are dozens of instrument makers spread out through North America and around the globe)."

OFFICE ENVIRONMENT AND EQUIPMENT

MODERN OFFICE TECHNOLOGY, Penton Publishing, Dept. WM, 1100 Superior Ave., Cleveland OH 44114-2501. (216)696-7000. Fax: (216)696-2891. E-mail: luraromei@aol.com. Contact: Lura K. Romei, editor. Production Manager: Gina Runyon-McKenna. 10-20% freelance written. Monthly magazine covering office automation for corporate management and personnel, financial management, administrative and operating management, systems and information management, managers and supervisors of support personnel and purchasing. Estab. 1956. Circ. 110,000. **Pays on acceptance.** Publishes ms an average of 6 months after acceptance. Byline given. Buys first and one-time rights. Reports in 3 months. Sample copy and writer's guidelines for 9×12 SAE with 4 first-class stamps.

Nonfiction: New product, opinion, technical. Query with or without published clips or send complete ms. Length: open. Pays $300-600 for assigned articles; $250-400 for unsolicited articles. Pays expenses of writers on assignment.

Reprints: Send photocopy of article and information about when and where the article previously appeared.
Photos: Send photos with submission. Reviews contact sheets, 4×5 transparencies and prints. Consult editor. Captions, identification of subjects required. Buys one-time rights.
Tips: "Submitted material should alway present topics and ideas, on issues that are clearly and concisely defined. Material should describe problems and solution. Writer should describe benefits to reader in tangible results whenever possible."

PAPER

‡BOXBOARD CONTAINERS, Maclean Hunter Publishing Co., Dept. WM, 29 N. Wacker Dr., Chicago IL 60606-3298. (312)726-2802. Fax: (312)726-2574. Editor: Greg Kishbaugh. Managing Editor: Robin Litwin. Monthly magazine covering box and carton manufacturing for corrugated box, folding carton, setup box manufacturers internationally emphasizing technology and management. Circ. 15,000. Pays on publication. Byline given. Buys first North American serial rights. Submit seasonal material 2 months in advance. Reports in 1 month. Free sample copy.
Nonfiction: How-to, interview/profile, new product, opinion, personal experience, photo feature, technical. Buys 10 mss/year. Query. Length: 2,000-6,000 words. Pays $75-350 for assigned articles; $75-250 for unsolicited articles. Sometimes pays expenses of writers on assignment.
Photos: Send photos with submission. Reviews 35mm, 4×5 and 6×6 transparencies and 8×10 prints. Offers no additional payment for photos accepted with ms. Captions, model releases, identification of subjects required. Buys one-time rights.
Tips: Features are most open to freelancers.

PULP & PAPER CANADA, Southam Inc., Suite 410, 3300 Côte Vertu, St. Laurent, Quebec H4R 2B7 Canada. (514)339-1399. Fax: (514)339-1396. Publisher: Mark Yerbary. Contact: Graeme Rodden, editor. 5% freelance written. Prefers to work with published/established writers. Monthly magazine. Estab. 1903. Circ. 10,361. **Pays on acceptance.** Publishes ms "as soon as possible" after acceptance. Byline given. Negotiates kill fee. Buys first North American serial rights. Reports in 1 month. Free sample copy.
Nonfiction: How-to (related to processes and procedures in the industry); interview/profile (of Canadian leaders in pulp and paper industry); technical (relevant to modern pulp and/or paper industry). No fillers, short industry news items, or product news items. Buys 10 mss/year. Query first with published clips or send complete ms. Articles with photographs (b&w glossy) or other good quality illustrations will get priority review. Length: 1,500 words maximum (with photos). Pays $160 (Canadian)/published page including photos, graphics, charts, etc.
Tips: "Any return postage must be in either Canadian stamps or International Reply Coupons *only*."

PETS

Listed here are publications for professionals in the pet industry—pet product wholesalers, manufacturers, suppliers, and retailers, and owners of pet specialty stores, grooming businesses, aquarium retailers and those interested in the pet fish industry. Publications for pet owners are listed in the Consumer Animal section.

‡GROOM & BOARD H.H. Backer Associates Inc., 20 E. Jackson Blvd., Suite 200, Chicago IL 60604-2383. (312)663-4040. Fax: (312)663-5676. E-mail: petage@aol.com. Editor: Karen Long MacLeod. 75-90% freelance written. Magazine published 9 times/year about grooming and boarding pets. "*Groom & Board* is the only national trade publication for pet-care professionals, including pet groomers, boarding kennel operators and service-oriented veterinarians. Features emphasize professional development, including progressive business management, animal handling procedures, emerging business opportunities and profiles of successful pet-care operations. Estab. 1980. Circ. 16,431. **Pays on acceptance.** Publishes ms an average of 6 months after acceptance. Byline given. Buys first North American serial, one-time, or exclusive to industry. Sample copy for $6 ($2.50 plus $3.50 shipping and handling).
Nonfiction: How-to (groom specific breeds of pets, run business, etc.), interview/profile (successful grooming and/or kennel operations), technical. No consumer-oriented articles or stories about a single animal (animal heroes, grief, etc.). Buys 40 mss/year. Query by phone after 3 pm CST. Length: 1,000-2,000 words. Pays $100-400 for assigned articles; $70-125 for unsolicited articles. Sometimes pays expenses of writers on assignment.
Photos: Reviews slides, transparencies, 5×7 color glossy prints. Offers $10/photo (negotiable). Captions, identification of subjects required. Buys one-time rights.

‡PET AGE, The Magazine for the Professional Retailer, H.H. Backer Associates, Inc., 20 E. Jackson Blvd., Suite 200, Chicago IL 60604-2383. (312)663-4040. Fax: (312)663-5676. E-mail: petage@aol.com.

Editor: Karen Long MacLeod. 75-90% freelance written. Prefers to work with published/established writers. Monthly magazine for pet/pet supplies retailers, covering the complete pet industry. Estab. 1971. Circ. 21,029. **Pays on acceptance.** Publishes ms an average of 6 months after acceptance. Byline given. Buys first North American serial, one-time, or exclusive industry rights. Submit seasonal material 6 months in advance. Sample copy for $6 ($2.50 plus $3.50 shipping and handling).

Nonfiction: Profile (of a successful, well-run pet retail operation), how-to, business management, technical—all trade-related. Query by phone after 3 pm CST. Query with the name and location of a pet operation you wish to profile and why it would make a good feature. No general retailing articles or consumer-oriented pet articles. Buys 120 mss/year. Length: 1,000-2,500 words. Pays $100-500 for assigned articles; $70-150 for unsolicited articles. Sometimes pays the expenses of writers on assignment.

Photos: Reviews slides, transparencies, 5×7 color glossy prints. Captions, identification of subjects required. Offers $10/photo (negotiable). Buys one-time rights.

Tips: "This is a business publication for busy people, and must be very informative in easy-to-read, concise style. Articles about animal care or business practices should have the pet-retail angle or cover issues specific to this industry."

PET BUSINESS, 7-L Dundas Circle, Greensboro NC 27407. (910)292-4047. Executive Editor: Rita Davis. 30% freelance written. "Our monthly news magazine reaches retailers, distributors and manufacturers of pet products. Groomers, veterinarians and serious hobbyists are also represented." Estab. 1973. Circ. 18,000. Pays on publication. Publishes ms an average of 2 months after acceptance. Byline given. Buys first rights. Submit seasonal/holiday material 3 months in advance. Reports in 4 months. Sample copy for $3. Writer's guidelines for SASE.

Nonfiction: "Articles must be well-researched and pertain to major business trends in the pet industry. Research, legislative and animal behavior reports are of interest. All data must be attributed. Articles should be business-oriented, not intended for the pet owner market. Send query or complete ms." Length: 250-2,000 words. Pays 12¢/word.

Photos: Send color slides, transparencies or prints with submission. Offers $20/photo. Buys one-time rights.

Tips: "We are open to national and international news of the pet industry written in standard news format, or well-researched, business- or trend-oriented feature articles."

THE PET DEALER, PTN Publishing Co., 445 Broad Hollow Rd., Melville NY 11747. (516)845-2700. Fax: (201)487-1061. Managing Editor: Jean Miller, (201)487-7800/Hackensack, NJ office. 70% freelance written. Prefers to work with published/established writers, but works with new/published writers. "We want writers who are good reporters and clear communicators with a good command of the English language." Monthly magazine emphasizing merchandising, marketing and management for owners and managers of pet specialty stores, departments, and pet groomers and their suppliers. Estab. 1949. Circ. 20,500. Pays on publication. Byline given. Submit seasonal material 4 months in advance. Reports in 3 months. Sample copy for $5 and 8×10 SAE with 10 first-class stamps.

Nonfiction: How-to (store operations, administration, merchandising, marketing, promotion and purchasing). Consumer pet articles—lost pets, best pets, humane themes—*not* welcome. Emphasis is on *trade* merchandising and marketing of pets and supplies. Buys 2-4 unsolicited mss/year. Query; queries without SASE will not be answered. Length: 1,000-2,000 words. Pays $50-125.

Reprints: Send typed ms with rights for sale noted and information about when and where the article previously appeared. Pays 1-10% of amount paid for an original article.

Photos: Submit undeveloped color photo material with ms. No additional payment for 5×7 b&w glossy prints. Buys one-time rights. Will give photo credit for photography students. Also seeking cover art: original illustrated animal portraits (paid).

Fillers: Publishes cartoons (unpaid).

Tips: "We're interested in store profiles outside the New York, New Jersey, Connecticut and Pennsylvania metro areas. Photos are of key importance and should include a storefront shot. Articles focus on new techniques in merchandising or promotion, and overall trends in the Pet Industry. Want to see more articles from retailers and veterinarians with retail operations. Submit query letter first, with writing background summarized; include samples. We seek one-to-one, interview-type features on retail pet store merchandising. Indicate the availability of the proposed article, and your willingness to submit on exclusive or first-in-the-trade-field basis."

PET PRODUCT NEWS, Fancy Publications, P.O. Box 6050, Mission Viejo CA 92690. (714)855-8822. Fax: (714)855-3045. Editor: Stacy N. Hackett. 70% freelance written. Monthly magazine for retail pet stores. "*Pet Product News* covers business/legal and economic issues of importance to pet product retailers, suppliers and distributors, as well as product information and animal care issues. We're looking for straightforward articles on the proper care of dogs, cats, birds, fish and exotics (reptiles, hamsters, etc.) as information the retailers can pass on to new pet owners." Estab. 1947. Circ. 25,000. Pays on publication. Byline given. Offers $50 kill fee. Buys first North American serial rights. Editorial lead time 3 months. Submit seasonal material 4 months in advance. No multiple submissions. Reports in 2 weeks on queries. Sample copy for $4.50. Writer's guidelines free on request.

● *Pet Product News* stories are taking a more news-oriented approach; fewer profiles and "how-tos" for Mom & Pop retailers and more coverage of business developments at multi-store chains and mass merchants.

Nonfiction: General interest, interview/profile, new product, photo feature, technical. "No cute animal stories or those directed at the pet owner." Buys 150 mss/year. Query. Length: 500-1,500 words. Pays $175-350.

Columns/Departments: "Retail News" (timely news stories about business issues affecting pet retailers), 800-1,000 words; "Industry News" (news articles representing coverage of pet product suppliers, manufacturers, distributors and associations), 800-1,000 words; Dog & Cat (products and care of), 1,000-1,500 words; Fish & Bird (products and care of) 1,000-1,500 words; Exotics (products and care of), 1,000-1,500 words. Buys 120 mss/year. Query first. Pays $150-300.

Tips: "Be more than just an animal lover. You have to know about health, nutrition and care. Product and business articles are told in both an informative and entertaining style. Go into pet stores, talk to the owners and see what they need to know to be better business people in general, who have to deal with everything from balancing the books and free trade agreements to animal right activists. All sections are open, but you have to be extremely knowledgeable on the topic, be it taxes, management, profit building, products, nutrition, animal care or marketing."

PROFESSIONAL PHOTOGRAPHY

Journals for professional photographers are listed in this section. Magazines for the general public interested in photography techniques are in the Consumer Photography section. (For listings of markets for freelance photography use *Photographer's Market*, Writer's Digest Books.)

‡**AMERICAN CINEMATOGRAPHER**, A.S.C. Holding Corp., P.O. Box 2230, Hollywood CA 90078-2230. (213)969-4333. Fax: (213)876-4973. E-mail: ascmag@aol.com. Executive Editor: Stephen Pizzello. 50% freelance written. Monthly international journal of film and video production techniques "addressed to creative, managerial and technical people in all aspects of production. Its function is to disseminate practical information about the creative use of film and video equipment, and it strives to maintain a balance between technical sophistication and accessibility." Estab. 1919. Circ. 30,000. Pays on publication. Buys all rights. Submit one-page proposal. Writer's guidelines for #10 SASE.

Nonfiction: David E. Williams, associate editor. Descriptions of new equipment and techniques or accounts of specific productions involving unique problems or techniques; historical articles detailing the production of a classic film, the work of a pioneer or legendary cinematographer or the development of a significant technique or type of equipment. Also discussions of the aesthetic principles involved in production techniques. Special issues: Digital Postproduction (September); Teleproduction (October 96); Working Relationships (November 96); Special Effects (December 96); Documentaries (January 97); Shooting On Location (February 97); Indie Films (March 97); Digital Post (April 97); Postproduction (May 97); Special Venue Productions (August 97). Pays according to position and worth. Negotiable.

Photos: Color and b&w purchased with mss. No additional payment.

Tips: "No unsolicited articles. Do not call. Doesn't matter whether you are published or new. Queries must describe writer's qualifications and include writing samples."

THE COMMERCIAL IMAGE, PTN Publishing Co., 445 Broad Hollow Rd., Melville NY 11747. (516)845-2700. Editor: Steven Shaw. Contact: Jennifer Gidman. 50% freelance written. Monthly tabloid covering commercial photography. Pays on publication. Byline given. Buys one-time rights. Editorial lead time 3 months. Submit seasonal material 3 months in advance. Sample copy and writer's guidelines free on request.

Nonfiction: Interview/profile, technical. Buys 10 mss/year. Query with published clips. Length: 1,000-2,000 words. Pays $75/printed page.

Photos: Send photos with submission. Reviews 8 × 10 transparencies and prints. Offers no additional payment for photos accepted with ms. Captions, model releases, identification of subjects required. Buys one-time rights.

PHOTO EDITORS REVIEW, Photo Editors International, 1201 Montego #4, Walnut Creek CA 94598-2819. Phone/fax: (510)935-7406. Publisher/Photo Editor: Bob Shepherd. Bimonthly newsletter for photo editors. Audience is mostly professional photo editors and magazine photographers. Estab. 1994. Circ. 5,000. **Pays on acceptance.** Byline given. Offers 25% kill fee. Buys first North American serial, first, one-time or simultaneous rights. Editorial lead time 3 months. Submit seasonal material 4 months in advance. Accepts simultaneous submissions. Reports in 1 month on queries; 2 months on mss. Sample copy for $3 and 9 × 12 SAE with 4 first-class stamps. Writer's guidelines for #10 SASE on request.

Nonfiction: Photo critiques from the editor's point of view and how-to photo features; legal and photo editing advice from professional photo editors. Buys 12-18 mss/year. Query. Length: 750-1,500 words. Pays up to $200 for assigned articles; up to $100 for unsolicited articles.
Reprints: Accepts previously published submissions.
Photos: Send photos with submission. Reviews contact sheets, 3½×5 to 8×10 prints. Offers $50/photo. Captions, model releases, identification of subjects required. Buys one-time rights.
Columns/Departments: Photo critiques, 750-1,500 words; legal (the photo editor and the law), 750-1,500 words; how-to photo features, 750-1,500 words. Buys 12-18 mss/year. Query. Pays $100-200.
Tips: "We are a trade publication that caters to the needs of professional photo editors; therefore, marketable photos that exhibit universal themes will be given top priority. We look for five characteristics by which we judge photographic materials: Sharp exposure (unless the image was intended as a soft-focus shot), impact, easily identifiable theme or subject, emphasis of the theme or subject, and simplicity."

‡**PHOTO LAB MANAGEMENT**, PLM Publishing, Inc., 1312 Lincoln Blvd., Santa Monica CA 90401. (310)451-1344. Fax: (310)395-9058. Contact: Carolyn Ryan, editor. Associate Editor: Karre Marino. 75% freelance written. Monthly magazine covering process chemistries and equipment, digital imaging, and marketing/administration for photo lab owners, managers and management personnel. Estab. 1979. Circ. 21,000. Pays on publication. Publishes ms an average of 3 months after acceptance. Byline and brief bio given. Buys first North American serial rights. Reports on queries in 6 weeks.
Nonfiction: Personal experience (lab manager); technical; management or administration. Buys 40-50 mss/year. Query with brief bio. Length: 1,200-1,800 words. Payment negotiable.
Photos: Reviews 35mm color transparencies and 4-color prints suitable for cover. "We're looking for outstanding cover shots of photofinishing images."
Tips: "Our departments are written inhouse and we don't use 'fillers'. Send a query if you have some background in the industry or have a specific news story relating to photo processing or digital imaging. This industry is changing quickly due to computer technology, so articles must be cutting edge. Business management articles must focus on a photo lab approach and not be generic. Writers must have photofinishing knowledge."

THE PHOTO REVIEW, 301 Hill Ave., Langhorne PA 19047-2819. (215)757-8921. Fax: (215)757-6421. Editor: Stephen Perloff. 50% freelance written. Quarterly magazine on photography with reviews, interviews and articles on art photography. Estab. 1976. Circ. 2,500. Pays on publication. Publishes ms an average of 3 months after acceptance. Byline given. Buys one-time rights. Accepts simultaneous submissions. Reports in 1 month on queries; 2 months on mss. Sample copy for 9×12 SAE with 6 first-class stamps. Writer's guidelines for #10 SASE.
Nonfiction: Essays, historical/nostalgic, interview/profile, opinion. No how-to articles. Buys 10-15 mss/year. Query. Pays $25-200.
Reprints: Accepts previously published submissions.
Photos: Send photos with submission. Reviews 8×10 prints. Offers no additional payment for photos accepted with ms. Captions and identification of subjects required. Buys one-time rights.

PHOTOGRAPHIC PROCESSING, PTN Publishing Co., 445 Broad Hollow Rd., Melville NY 11747. (516)845-2700. Fax: (516)845-2797. Editor: Bill Schiffner. 30-40% freelance written. Monthly magazine covering photographic (commercial/minilab) and electronic processing markets. Estab. 1965. Circ. 23,000. Pays on publication. Publishes ms an average of 4 months after acceptance. Byline given. Offers $75 kill fee. Editorial lead time 3 months. Submit seasonal material 3 months in advance. Accepts simultaneous submissions. Sample copy and writer's guidelines free on request.
Nonfiction: How-to, interview/profile, new product, photo processing/digital imaging features. Buys 30-40 mss/year. Query with published clips. Length: 1,500-2,200 words. Pays $250-325 for assigned articles; $200-250 for unsolicited articles.
Photos: Send photos with submission. Reviews 4×5 transparencies, 4×6 prints. Offers no additional payment for photos accepted with ms. Captions required. Buys one-time rights.
Columns/Departments: Surviving in the 90s (business articles offering tips to labs on how make their businesses run better), 1,500-1,800 words; Productivity Focus (getting more productivity out of your lab). Buys 10 mss/year. Query with published clips. Pays $150-200.

THE RANGEFINDER, 1312 Lincoln Blvd., Santa Monica CA 90401. (310)451-8506. Fax: (310)395-9058. Contact: Karre Marino, editor. Associate Editor: Marquita Thomas. Monthly magazine emphasizing professional photography. Circ. 50,000. Pays on publication. Publishes ms an average of 9 months after acceptance. Byline given. Buys first North American serial rights. Submit seasonal material 4 months in advance. Reports in 6 weeks. Sample copy for $3.50. Writer's guidelines for SASE.
Nonfiction: How-to (solve a photographic problem, such as new techniques in lighting, new poses or set-ups), profile, technical. "Articles should contain practical, solid information. Issues should be covered in-depth. Look thoroughly into the topic." Buys 5-7 mss/issue. Query with outline. Length: 800-1,200 words. Pays $100/published page.

Photos: State availability of photos with query. Captions preferred; model release required.

Tips: "Exhibit knowledge of photography. Introduce yourself with a well-written letter and a great story idea."

PLUMBING, HEATING, AIR CONDITIONING AND REFRIGERATION

HEATING, PLUMBING, AIR CONDITIONING, 1370 Don Mills Rd., Suite 300, Don Mills, Ontario M3B 3N7 Canada. (416)759-2500. Fax: (416)759-6979. Publisher: Bruce Meacock. Contact: Lynne Erskine Cheld, editor. 20% freelance written. Monthly magazine for mechanical contractors; plumbers; warm air and hydronic heating, refrigeration, ventilation, air conditioning and insulation contractors; wholesalers; architects; consulting and mechanical engineers who are in key management or specifying positions in the plumbing, heating, air conditioning and refrigeration industries in Canada. Estab. 1923. Circ. 16,500. Pays on publication. Publishes ms an average of 3 months after acceptance. Reports in 2 months. For a prompt reply, "enclose a sheet on which is typed a statement either approving or rejecting the suggested article which can either be checked off, or a quick answer written in and signed and returned." Sample copy free.

Nonfiction: News, technical, business management and "how-to" articles that will inform, educate, motivate and help readers to be more efficient and profitable who design, manufacture, install, sell, service, maintain or supply all mechanical components and systems in residential, commercial, institutional and industrial installations across Canada. Length: 1,000-1,500 words. Pays 25¢/word. Sometimes pays expenses of writers on assignment.

Reprints: Send tearsheet or photocopy of article or typed ms with rights for sale noted and information about when and where article appeared.

Photos: Photos purchased with ms. Prefers 4×5 or 5×7 glossies.

Tips: "Topics must relate directly to the day-to-day activities of *HPAC* readers in Canada. Must be detailed, with specific examples, quotes from specific people or authorities—show depth. We specifically want material from other parts of Canada besides southern Ontario. Not really interested in material from US unless specifically related to Canadian readers' concerns. We primarily want articles that show *HPAC* readers how they can increase their sales and business step-by-step based on specific examples of what others have done."

SNIPS MAGAZINE, 1949 N. Cornell Ave., Melrose Park IL 60160. (708)544-3870. Fax: (708)544-3884. Editor: Nick Carter. 2% freelance written. Monthly magazine for sheet metal, warm air heating, ventilating, air conditioning and roofing contractors. Estab. 1932. Publishes an average of 3 months after acceptance. Buys all rights. "Write for detailed list of requirements before submitting any work."

Nonfiction: Material should deal with information about contractors who do sheet metal, warm air heating, air conditioning, ventilation and metal roofing work; also about successful advertising campaigns conducted by these contractors and the results. Length: under 1,000 words unless on special assignment. Pays 5¢/word for first 500 words, 2¢/word thereafter.

Photos: Pays $5 each for small snapshot pictures, $10 each for usable 8×10 pictures.

PRINTING

PERSPECTIVES, In-Plant Management Association (IPMA), 1205 W. College St., Liberty MO 64068-3733. (816)781-1111. Fax: (816)781-2790. E-mail: laaron@ipma.org. Website: http://www.ipma.org. Editor: Jon Ratliff. 40% freelance written. Monthly trade newsletter covering inhouse print and mail operations. "Inhouse print/mail departments are faced with competition from commercial printers and facilities management companies. Writers must be pro-insourcing and reflect that this industry is a profitable profession." Estab. 1986. Circ. 2,300; twice a year it reaches 5,000. Pays on publication. Publishes an average of 2 months after acceptance. Byline given. Buys all rights. Editorial lead time 2 months. Reports in 1 month. Sample copy for 9×12 SAE.

Nonfiction: Interview/profile, new product, technical, general management. Payment negotiated individually. Sometimes pays expenses of writers on assignment.

Reprints: Send photocopy of article and information about when and where the article previously appeared.

Photos: State availability of photos with submission. Reviews contact sheets, 5×7 prints. Offers no additional payment for photos accepted with ms. Captions required. Buys one-time rights.

Columns/Departments: Executive Insight (management, personnel how-tos, employment law), 650-1,500 words. Buys 12 mss/year. Query with published clips.

Tips: "A knowledge of the printing industry is helpful. Articles with concrete examples or company/individual profiles work best."

PRINT & GRAPHICS, 30 E. Padonia Rd., Suite 504, Timonium MD 21093. (410)628-7826. Fax: (410)628-7829. E-mail: spencecom1@aol.com. Publisher: Kaj Spencer. Contact: Henry Mortimer, editor. 10% freelance written. Eager to work with new/unpublished writers. Monthly tabloid of the commercial printing industry for owners and executives of graphic arts firms. Estab. 1980. Circ. 20,000. **Pays on acceptance.** Publishes ms an average of 2 months after acceptance. Byline given. Buys one-time rights. Accepts simultaneous submissions. Reports in 2 months. Sample copy for $2.
Nonfiction: Book excerpts, historical/nostalgic, how-to, interview/profile, new product, opinion, personal experience, photo feature, technical. "All articles should relate to graphic arts management or production." Buys 20 mss/year. Query with published clips. Length: 750-2,000 words. Pays $100-250.
Reprints: Send photocopy of article and information about when and where the article previously appeared. Pays $150 flat fee. Publishes trade book excerpts.
Photos: State availability of photos. Pays $25-75 for 5×7 b&w prints. Captions, identification of subjects required.

‡PRINTING JOURNAL, Spencer Communications, Inc., 30 E. Padonia Rd., Suite 504, Timonium MD 21093. (410)628-7826. Fax: (410)628-7829. E-mail: spencecom1@aol.com. Editor: Henry Mortimer. 10% freelance written. Monthly tabloid of the western commercial printing industry for owners and executives of graphics arts firms. Estab. 1974. Circ. 19,000. **Pays on acceptance**. Byline given. Buys one-time rights. Submit seasonal material 2 months in advance. Accepts simultaneous submissions. Reports in 1 month on queries; 2 months on mss.
Nonfiction: How-to, interview/profile, new product, opinion, technical. Buys 15-20 mss/year. Query with published clips. Length: 1,000-2,000 words. Pays $150. Sometimes pays expenses of writers on assignment.
Photos: Send photos with submission. Reviews transparencies. Buys one-time rights.

‡QUICK PRINTING, PTN Publishing, 445 Broadhollow Rd., Melville NY 11747. (516)845-2700. Fax: (516)249-5774. E-mail: ptngrafnet@aol.com. Publisher: William Lewis. Assistant Editor: Jean Scott. Contact: Gerald Walsh, editor. 50% freelance written. Monthly magazine covering the quick printing industry. "Our articles tell quick printers how they can be more profitable. We want figures to illustrate points made." Estab. 1977. Circ. 69,000. Pays on publication. Publishes ms an average of 4 months after acceptance. Byline given. Buys first North American serial or all rights. Submit seasonal material 6 months in advance. Reports in 1 month. Sample copy for $5 and 9×12 SAE with 7 first-class stamps. Writer's guidelines for #10 SASE.
Nonfiction: How-to (on marketing products better or accomplishing more with equipment); new product; opinion (on the quick printing industry); personal experience (from which others can learn); technical (on printing). No generic business articles, or articles on larger printing applications. Buys 75 mss/year. Send complete ms. Length: 1,500-3,000 words. Pays $150 and up.
Photos: State availability of photos with submission. Reviews transparencies, prints. Offers no additional payment for photos accepted with ms. Captions and identification of subjects required.
Columns/Departments: Viewpoint/Counterpoint (opinion on the industry); QP Profile (shop profiles with a marketing slant); Management (how to handle employees and/or business strategies); Marketing Impressions, all 500-1,500 words. Buys 10 mss/year. Send complete ms. Pays $75.
Tips: "The use of electronic publishing systems by quick printers is of increasing interest. Show a knowledge of the industry. Try visiting your local quick printer for an afternoon to get to know about us. When your articles make a point, back it up with examples, statistics, and dollar figures. We need good material in all areas, but avoid the shop profile. Technical articles are most needed, but they must be accurate. No puff pieces for a certain industry supplier."

SCREEN PRINTING, 407 Gilbert Ave., Cincinnati OH 45202-2285. (513)421-2050. Fax: (513)421-5144. Editor: Steve Duccilli. 30% freelance written. Works with a small number of new/unpublished writers each year. Monthly magazine for the screen printing industry, including screen printers (commercial, industrial and captive shops), suppliers and manufacturers, ad agencies and allied professions. Estab. 1953. Circ. 15,000. Pays on publication. Publishes ms an average of 4 months after acceptance. Byline given. Buys all rights. Reporting time varies. Sample copy available. Writer's guidelines for SAE.
Nonfiction: "Because the screen printing industry is a specialized but diverse trade, we do not publish general interest articles with no pertinence to our readers. Subject matter is open, but should fall into one of four categories—technology, management, profile, or news. Features in all categories must identify the relevance of the subject matter to our readership. Technology articles must be informative, thorough, and objective—no promotional or 'advertorial' pieces accepted. Management articles may cover broader business or industry specific issues, but they must address the screen printer's unique needs. Profiles may cover serigraphers, outstanding shops, unique jobs and projects, or industry personalities; they should be in-depth features, not PR puff pieces, that clearly show the human interest or business relevance of the subject. News pieces should be timely (reprints from non-industry publications will be considered) and must cover an event or topic of industry concern." Buys 6-10 mss/year. Query. Unsolicited mss not returned. Length: 1,500-3,500 words. Pays $200 minimum for major features. Sometimes pays the expenses of writers on assignment.

Photos: Cover photos negotiable; b&w or color. Published material becomes the property of the magazine.
Tips: "If the author has a working knowledge of screen printing, assignments are more readily available. General management articles are rarely used."

REAL ESTATE

‡**AFFORDABLE HOUSING FINANCE**, Business Communication Services, 220 Montgomery St., Suite 2601, San Francisco CA 94104. (415)546-7255. Fax: (415)546-0954. E-mail: 102367.3011@compuserve. com. Editor: Andre Shashaty. 20% freelance written. Bimonthly magazine covering financing for affordable apartments. "We are a nuts-and-bolts magazine written for developers of affordable apartments. Not generally interested in articles aimed at realtors or home buyers." Estab. 1992. Circ. 5,000. **Pays on acceptance**. Publishes ms an average of 3 months after acceptance. Byline given. Offers 50% kill fee. Buys all rights including electronic rights. Accepts simultaneous submissions. Reports in 3 weeks on queries; 1 month on mss. Sample copy for 9×12 SAE with $2.16 postage. Writer's guidelines free on request.
Nonfiction: How-to, interview/profile (developer or financier), new product (new financing services). Special issues: Rehab, Renovation and Repositioning. "We have a very knowledgeable reader base in terms of housing finance—articles need to have hard news angle and skip the basics." Buys 10-20 mss/year. Query with published clips. Length: 500-2,000. Pays 25-45¢/word. Sometimes pays expenses of writers on assignment.
Reprints: Accepts previously published submissions.
Photos: State availability of photos with submission. Reviews prints. Offers no additional payment for photos accepted with ms. Captions required. Buys all rights.
Tips: "Best to see sample copy before submitting."

‡**AREA DEVELOPMENT MAGAZINE, Sites and Facility Planning**, Halcyon Business Publications, Inc., 400 Post Ave., Westbury NY 11590. (516)338-0900. Fax: (516)338-0100. Managing Editor: Pam Karr. Contact: Geraldine Gambala, editor. 80% freelance written. Prefers to work with published/established writers. Monthly magazine covering corporate facility planning and site selection for industrial chief executives worldwide. Estab. 1965. Circ. 42,000. Pays on publication. Publishes ms an average of 2 months after acceptance. Byline given. Buys all rights. Reports in 3 months. Free sample copy. Writer's guidelines for #10 SASE.
Nonfiction: How-to (experiences in site selection and all other aspects of corporate facility planning); historical (if it deals with corporate facility planning); interview (corporate executives and industrial developers); and related areas of site selection and facility planning such as taxes, labor, government, energy, architecture and finance. Buys 60 mss/year. Query. Length: 800-1,200 words. Pays 25¢/word. Sometimes pays expenses of writers on assignment.
Photos: State availability of photos with query. Reviews transparencies. Captions, identification preferred. Negotiates payment individually.

BUSINESS FACILITIES, Group C Communications, Inc., 121 Monmouth St., P.O. Box 2060, Red Bank NJ 07701. (908)842-7433. Fax: (908)758-6634. E-mail: 74723.376@compuserve.com. Website: http://www. busfac.com. Contact: Eric Peterson, editor. Managing Editor: Mary Ellen McCandless. 20% freelance written. Prefers to work with published/established writers. Monthly magazine covering corporate expansion, economic development and commercial and industrial real estate. "Our audience consists of corporate site selectors and real estate people; our editorial coverage is aimed at providing news and trends on the plant location and corporate expansion field." Estab. 1967. Circ. 40,000. Pays on publication. Publishes ms an average of 2 months after acceptance. Byline given. Buys all rights. Reports in 2 weeks. Sample copy and writer's guidelines for SASE.
 • Magazine is currently overstocked, and will be accepting fewer pieces for the near future.
Nonfiction: General interest, how-to, interview/profile, personal experience. No news shorts or clippings; feature material only. Buys 12-15 mss/year. Query. Length: 1,000-3,000 words. Pays $200-1,000 for assigned articles; $200-600 for unsolicited articles. Sometimes pays the expenses of writers on assignment.
Photos: State availability of photos with submission. Reviews contact sheets, transparencies, 8×10 prints. Payment negotiable. Captions, identification of subjects required. Buys one-time rights.
Tips: "First, remember that our reader is a corporate executive responsible for his company's expansion and/or relocation decisions and our writers have to get inside that person's head in order to provide him with something that's helpful in his decision-making process. And second, the biggest turnoff is a telephone query. We're too busy to accept them and must require that all queries be put in writing. Submit major feature articles only; all news departments, fillers, etc., are staff-prepared. A writer should be aware that our style is not necessarily dry and business-like. We tend to be more casual and a writer should look for that aspect of our approach."

‡**CANADIAN PROPERTY MANAGEMENT**, Mediaedge Communications Inc., 33 Fraser Ave., Suite 208, Toronto, Ontario M6K 3J9 Canada. (416)588-6220. Managing Editor: Kim Morningstar. 10% freelance

written. Magazine published 8 times/year covering Canadian commercial, industrial, institutional (medical and educational), residential properties. *"Canadian Property Management* magazine is a trade journal supplying building owners and property managers with Canadian industry news, case law reviews, technical updates for building operations and events listings. Feature building and professional profile articles are regular features." Estab. 1985. Circ. 14,500. Pays on publication. Publishes ms an average of 3 months after acceptance. Byline given. Buys all rights. Editorial lead time 2 months. Submit seasonal material 2 months in advance. Accepts simultaneous submissions, if so noted. Reports in 3 weeks on queries; 2 months on mss. Sample copy for $5, subject to availability. Writer's guidelines free on request.

Nonfiction: Interview/profile, technical. No promotional articles (eg. marketing a product or service geared to this industry)! Query with published clips. Length: 700-1,200 words. Pays an average of 35¢/word.

Reprints: Accepts previously published submissions.

Photos: State availability of photos with submission. Reviews transparencies, 3×5 prints. Offers no additional payment for photos accepted with ms. Captions, model releases, identification of subjects required.

Tips: "We do not accept promotional articles serving companies or their products. Freelance articles that are strong, information-based pieces that serve the interests and needs of property managers and building owners stand a better chance of being published. Proposals and inquiries with article ideas are appreciated the most. A good understanding of the real estate (management structure) is also helpful for the writer."

‡COMMERCIAL INVESTMENT REAL ESTATE JOURNAL, Commercial Investment Real Estate Institute, 430 N. Michigan Ave., Suite 600, Chicago IL 60611-4092. (312)321-4460. Fax: (312)321-4530. E-mail: csimpson@cirei.mhs.compuserve.com. Editor: Catherine Simpson. 10% freelance written. Bimonthly magazine covering commercial investment real estate. *"CIERJ* offers practical articles on current trends and business development ideas for commercial investment real estate practitioners." Estab. 1982. Circ. 10,000. **Pays on acceptance.** Publishes ms an average of 4 months after acceptance. Byline given. Offers 25% kill fee. Buys all rights. Editorial lead time 4 months. Submit seasonal material 4 months in advance. Reports in 2 weeks on queries; 1 month on mss. Sample copy for 9×12 SAE with 5 first-class stamps. Writer's guidelines for #10 SASE.

Nonfiction: Book excerpts, how-to, personal experience, technical. Buys 4 mss/year. Query with published clips. Length: 2,000-3,500 words. Pays $1,000-2,000. Sometimes pays expenses of writers on assignment.

Photos: Send photos with submission. Reviews prints. Offers no additional payment for photos accepted with ms. Buys all rights.

Tips: "Always query first with a detailed outline and published clips. Authors whould have a background in writing on real estate or business subjects."

‡CONDO MANAGEMENT MAGAZINE, Papers Inc., 866 Waverly St., Framingham MA 01701. (508)879-4744. Fax: (508)879-0816. Editor: L Charles F. Bennett. 90% freelance written. Monthly magazine covering condminium management in New England, Florida and California. "We are particularly interested in articles on the dynamics between condo board members and property managers concerning condo law, finance, roofing, painting, siding, landscaping, maintenance, construction, security, insurance, pool care. Features must be educational, informative, non-promotional." Estab. 1983. Circ. 42,000. Pays on publication. Publishes ms an average of 2 months after acceptance. Byline given. Buys first North American serial rights. Editorial lead time 4 months. Reports in 2 weeks on queries; 1 month on mss. Sample copy for 9×12 SAE with 5 first-class stamps. Writer's guidelines for #10 SASE.

Nonfiction: How-to, humor, interview/profile, new product, opinion, personal experience, all on condo industry topics of national interest including related fields. Buys 40 mss/year. Query with published clips. Length: 1,000-4,000 words. Pays $125.

Photos: Send photos with submission. Reviews prints. Offers no additional payment for photos accepted with ms. Captions, identification of subjects required. Buys one-time rights.

Columns/Departments: Patrick McLaughlin, Florida editor; Danielle Belanger, California editor; David Hannon, New England editor. Unique condo board experiences in: Florida (Orlando, Tampa, West Palm Beach, Miami), California (San Diego, Los Angeles, Orange County), New England (Massachusetts, Rhode Island, Northern New England); all 1,000 words. Query. Pays $125.

Tips: "Understand condo living and relationships between their board of directors, the property managers and vendors who do business with the $1 billion condo industry. Experiences on how a specific problem was solved. Ability to identify and write about unique condo management issues common to all regions."

FINANCIAL FREEDOM REPORT QUARTERLY, 4505 S. Wasatch Blvd., Salt Lake City UT 84124. (801)273-5301. Fax: (801)273-5422. E-mail: carolyn@homebusiness.com. Website: http://www.homebusiness.com. Chairman of the Board: Mark O. Haroldsen. Managing Editor: Carolyn Tice. 25% freelance written. Eager to work with new/unpublished writers. Quarterly magazine for "professional and nonprofessional investors and would-be investors in real estate—real estate brokers, insurance companies, investment planners, truck drivers, housewives, doctors, architects, contractors, etc. The magazine's content is presently expanding to interest and inform the readers about other ways to put their money to work for them." Estab. 1976. Pays on publication. Publishes ms an average of 3 months after acceptance. Buys all rights. Accepts simultaneous submissions. Reports in 3 months. Sample copy for $5.

Nonfiction: How-to (find real estate bargains, finance property, use of leverage, managing property, developing market trends, goal setting, motivational); interviews (success stories of those who have relied on own initiative and determination in real estate market or related fields). Buys 10 unsolicited mss/year. Query with clips of published work or submit complete ms. Phone queries OK. Length: 1,500-3,000 words. Pays 5-10¢/word. Sometimes pays the expenses of writers on assignment.

Photos: Send photos with ms. Uses 8×10 b&w or color matte prints. Captions required.

Tips: "We would like to find several specialized writers in our field of real estate investments. A writer must have had some hands-on experience in the real estate field."

JOURNAL OF PROPERTY MANAGEMENT, Institute of Real Estate Management, P.O. Box 109025, Chicago IL 60610-9025. (312)329-6058. Fax: (312)661-0217. E-mail: mevans@irem.org. Website: http://www.irem.org. Executive Editor: Mariwyn Evans. 30% freelance written. Bimonthly magazine covering real estate management. "The *Journal* has a feature/information slant designed to educate readers in the application of new techniques and to keep them abreast of current industry trends." Circ. 23,000. **Pays on acceptance.** Publishes ms an average of 3 months after acceptance. Byline given. Buys all rights. Reports in 6 weeks on queries; 1 month on mss. Free sample copy and writer's guidelines.

Nonfiction: How-to, interview, technical (building systems/computers), demographic shifts in business employment and buying patterns, marketing. "No non-real estate subjects, personality or company, humor." Buys 8-12 mss/year. Query with published clips. Length: 1,200-1,500 words. Sometimes pays the expenses of writers on assignment.

Photos: State availability of photos with submission. Reviews contact sheets. May offer additional payment for photos accepted with ms. Model releases, identification of subjects required. Buys one-time rights.

Columns/Departments: Katherine Anderson, associate editor. Insurance Insights, Tax Issues, Investment and Finance Insights, Legal Issues. Buys 6-8 mss/year. Query. Length: 500-750 words.

‡MANAGERS REPORT: The Only National Trade Journal Serving Condominiums and Property Management, Ivor Thomas and Associates, 1700 Southern Blvd., West Palm Beach FL 33406. (407)687-4700. Fax: (407)687-9654. Editor: Ivor Thomas. Business Manager: Marcia Thomas. Contact: Lisa Pinder, managing editor. 40% freelance written. Monthly magazine covering condominiums and property management. Estab. 1987. Circ. 20,000. **Pays on acceptance.** Buys second serial (reprint) rights. Editorial lead time 3 months. Submit seasonal material 4 months in advance. Accepts simultaneous submissions. Sample copy and writers guidelines free on request.

Nonfiction: How-to, interview/profile, new product, opinion, personal experience, photo feature, technical. Buys 120 mss/year. Query. Length: 50-3,000 words. Pays 10¢/word.

Reprints: Accepts previously published submissions.

Photos: Send photos with submission. Reviews contact sheets, negatives, prints. Offers $5-50/photo. Identification of subjects required. Buys all rights.

Poetry: Light verse, humorous relating to condominiums. Buys 12 poems/year. Submit maximum 12 poems at one time. Pays $10-50.

Fillers: Anecdotes, facts, gags to be illustrated by cartoonist, newsbreaks, short humor. Buys 60/year. Length: 6-50 words. Pays $10-50.

Tips: "We want to get more technical information. We need a layman's description of: e.g., how an air conditioner really cools air. We would like maintenance remedies: e.g., what is the best thing to be done for cracked pavement in a parking lot. Consult the reader response in the magazine for maintenance categories. We ask that our advertisers be used exclusively for research. Our readers are extremmly interested in knowing such things as the difference between latex and acrylic paint and when you use one or the other. We find that the more specific and technical the better. This also applies to interviews. Interviews are to gather good technical information. Legal, administrative maintenance. See our guidelines for primer questions. We would like interviews with pictures of individuals and/or associations. 95% of our interviews are done by phone. We would like to have regular correspondents in different areas of the country."

RESOURCES AND WASTE REDUCTION

EROSION CONTROL, The Journal for Erosion and Sediment Control Professionals, Forester Communications, Inc., 5638 Hollister Ave., Suite 301, Santa Barbara CA 93117. (805)681-1300. Fax: (805)681-1312. E-mail: erosion@ix.netcom.com. Editor: John Trotti. 60% freelance written. Bimonthly magazine covering all aspects of erosion prevention and sediment control. "*Erosion Control* is a practical, hands-on, 'how-to' professional journal. Our readers are civil engineers, landscape architects, builders, developers, public works officials, road and highway construction officials and engineers, soils specialists, farmers, landscape contractors and others involved with any activity that disturbs significant areas of surface vegetation." Estab. 1994. Circ. 17,000. Pays on publication. Publishes ms an average of 3 months after acceptance. Byline given. Buys all rights. Editorial lead time 3 months. Submit seasonal material 3 months in advance. Reports in 2 weeks. Accepts simultaneous submissions. Sample copy and writer's guidelines free on request.

Nonfiction: Photo feature. Buys 20 mss/year. Query with published clips. Length: 3,000-4,000 words. Pays $350-600. Sometimes pays expenses of writers on assignment.

Photos: Send photos with submission. Reviews transparencies, prints. Negotiates payment individually. Captions, model releases, identification of subjects required. Buys all rights.

MSW MANAGEMENT, The Journal for Municipal Solid Waste Professionals, Forester Communications, Inc., 5638 Hollister Ave., Suite 301, Santa Barbara CA 93117. (805)681-1300. Fax: (805)681-1312. E-mail: erosion@ix.netcom.com. Editor: John Trotti. 70% freelance written. Bimonthly magazine covering solid waste management—landfilling, composting, recycling, incineration. "*MSW Management* is written for *public sector* solid waste professionals—the people working for the local counties, cities, towns, boroughs and provinces. They run the landfills, recycling programs, composting, incineration. They are responsible for all aspects of garbage collection and disposal; buying and maintaining the associated equipment; and designing, engineering and building the waste processing facilities, transfer stations and landfills." Estab. 1991. Circ. 24,000. Pays on publication. Byline given. Offers 10% or $100 kill fee. Buys all rights. Editorial lead time 3 months. Submit seasonal material 4 months in advance. Reports in 6 weeks on queries; 2 months on mss. Sample copy free on request.

Nonfiction: Book excerpts, interview/profile, personal experience, photo feature, technical. *Elements of Integral Solid Waste Management*, published every October, includes articles and essays on *all* aspects of solid waste management. "No rudimentary, basic articles written for the average person on the street. Our readers are experienced professionals with years of practical, in-the-field experience. Any material submitted that we judge as too fundamental will be rejected." Buys 27 mss/year. Query. Length: 1,800-3,500 words. Pays $400. Sometimes pays expenses of writers on assignment.

Photos: Send photos with submission. Reviews transparencies, 5×7 or 8×10 prints. Negotiates payment individually. Captions, model releases, identification of subjects required. Buys all rights.

Columns/Departments: Field Report (news from the readers), 2,000 words; Washington Watch (news from DC), 1,500 words; Contracting (negotiating with the private sector). Buys 18 mss/year. Query. Pays $50-250.

Tips: "We're a small company, easy to reach. We're open to any and all ideas as to possible editorial topics. We endeavor to provide the reader with usable material, and present it in full color with graphic embellishment whenever possible. Dry, highly technical material is edited to make it more palatable and concise. Most of our feature articles come from freelancers. Interviews and quotes should be from public sector solid waste managers and engineers—*not* PR people, *not* manufacturers. Strive to write material that is 'over the heads' of our readers. If anything, attempt to make them 'reach.' Anything submitted that is too basic, elementary, fundamental, rudimentary, etc. cannot be accepted for publication."

PUMPER, COLE Publishing Inc., P.O. Box 220, Three Lakes WI 54562-0220. (715)546-3347. President: Robert J. Kendall. Editor: Ken Lowther. 50% freelance written. Eager to work with new/unpublished writers. Monthly tabloid covering the liquid waste hauling industry (portable toilet renters, septic tank pumpers, industrial waste haulers, chemical waste haulers, oil field haulers, and hazardous waste haulers). "Our publication is read by companies that handle liquid waste and manufacturers of equipment." Estab. 1979. Circ. 20,000. Pays on publication. Publishes ms an average of 1 month after acceptance. Byline given. Buys first serial rights. Free sample copy and writer's guidelines.

Nonfiction: Exposé (government regulations, industry problems, trends, public attitudes, etc.); general interest (state association meetings, conventions, etc.); how-to (related to industry, e.g., how to incorporate septage or municipal waste into farm fields, how to process waste, etc.); humor (related to industry, especially septic tank pumpers or portable toilet renters); interview/profile (including descriptions of business statistics, type of equipment, etc.); new product; personal experience; photo feature; technical (especially reports on research projects related to disposal). "We are looking for quality articles that will be of interest to our readers; length is not important. We publish trade journals. We need articles that deal with the trade. Studies on land application of sanitary waste are of great interest." Query or send complete ms. Pays 7½¢/word.

Photos: Send photos with query or ms. Pays $15 for b&w and color prints that are used. No negatives. "We need good contrast." Captions, model release required. Buys one-time rights.

Tips: "Material must pertain to liquid waste-related industries listed above. We hope to expand the editorial content of our monthly publications. We also have a publication for sewer and drain cleaners with the same format as *Pumper*; however, *Cleaner* has a circulation of 22,000. We are looking for the same type of articles and pay is the same."

RESOURCE RECYCLING, North America's Recycling Journal, Resource Recycling, Inc., Dept. WM, P.O. Box 10540, Portland OR 97210-0540. (503)227-1319. Fax: (503)227-6135. E-mail: resrecycle@ aol.com. Editor-in-Chief: Jerry Powell. Contact: Meg Lynch, editor. 5% freelance written. Eager to work with new/unpublished writers. Monthly trade journal covering post-consumer recycling of paper, plastics, metals, glass and other materials. Estab. 1982. Circ. 16,000. Pays on publication. Publishes ms an average of 9 months after acceptance. Byline given. Buys first rights. Accepts simultaneous submissions. Reports in 3 months on queries. Sample copy and writer's guidelines for 9×12 SAE with 7 first-class stamps.

Nonfiction: "No non-technical pieces." Buys 2-4 mss/year. Query with published clips. Length: 1,200-1,800 words. Pays $300-350. Pays with contributor copies "if writers are more interested in professional recognition than financial compensation." Sometimes pays the expenses of writers on assignment.
Reprints: Send photocopy of article and information about when and where the article previously appeared. Pays 100% of amount paid for an original article.
Photos: State availability of photos with submission. Reviews contact sheets, negatives, prints. Offers $5-50. Identification of subjects required. Buys one-time rights.
Tips: "Overviews of one recycling aspect in one state (e.g., oil recycling in Alabama) will receive attention. We will increase coverage of source reduction and yard waste composting."

SELLING AND MERCHANDISING

Sales personnel and merchandisers interested in how to sell and market products successfully consult these journals. Publications in nearly every category of Trade also buy sales-related materials if they are slanted to the product or industry with which they deal.

‡**THE AMERICAN SALESMAN**, P.O. Box 1, Burlington IA 52601-0001. Fax: (319)752-3421. Publisher: Michael S. Darnall. Editor: Barbara Boeding. Monthly magazine for distribution through company sales representatives. Estab. 1955. Circ. 1,500. Publishes ms an average of 4 months after acceptance. Sample copy and writer's guidelines for 6×9 SAE with 3 first-class stamps; mention *Writer's Market* in request.
Nonfiction: Sales seminars, customer service and follow-up, closing sales, sales presentations, handling objections, competition, telephone usage and correspondence, managing territory, new innovative sales concepts. No sexist material. Written from a salesperson's viewpoint. Public relations articles or case histories reviewed. Length: 900-1,200 words. Uses no advertising. Follow AP Stylebook. Include biography and/or byline with ms submissions. Author photos used. Send correspondence to Editor.

ANSOM, Army Navy Store and Outdoor Merchandiser, PTN Publishing Co., 2 University Plaza, Suite 204, Hackensack NJ 07601. (201)487-7800. Fax: (201)487-1061. Editor: Paul Bubny. 10% freelance written. Monthly tabloid covering army/navy and outdoor product retailing (camping, hunting, fishing and related outdoor sports). Estab. 1949. Circ. 12,300. Pays on publication. Publishes ms an average of 2 months after acceptance. Byline given. Buys one-time rights. Editorial lead time 6 weeks. Submit seasonal material 3 months in advance. Reports in 1 week on queries; 1 month on mss. Writer's guidelines free on request.
Nonfiction: Book excerpts, how-to (merchandise various products, manage a retail operation), interview/profile, new product, technical. Buys 6-9 mss/year. Send complete ms. Length: 800-4,000 words. Pays $125-200 for assigned articles; $75-125 for unsolicited articles. Sometimes pays expenses of writers on assignment.
Reprints: Accepts previously published submissions, if non-competing market.
Photos: Send photos with submission. Reviews 5×8 prints, color slides. Negotiates payment individually. Captions, identification of subjects required. Buys one-time rights.
Columns/Departments: Legal Advisor (legal issues for small business owners), 1,000-1,200 words; Business Insights (general management topics of interest to small business owners), 1,000-1,500 words. Buys 12-18 mss/year. Send complete ms. Pays $75-175.
Tips: "Approach the editor either with subject matter that fits in with the magazine's specific area of concern, or with willingness to take on assignments that fit magazine's editorial scope."

‡**ART MATERIALS TODAY, The Retailer's Guide to Success**, F&W Publications, 1507 Dana Ave., Cincinnati OH 45207. (513)531-2690 ext. 422. Fax: (513)531-2902. E-mail: fwpub@aol.com. Editor: Lisa Baggerman. Contact: Todd Tedesco, assistant editor. 60-70% freelance written. Bimonthly magazine covering art material retail trade. "*Art Materials Today* is written for art material retailers. Offers practical business advice, industry news and information, general art tips, techniques and new products." Estab. 1993. Circ. 10,500. **Pays on acceptance.** Publishes ms an average of 4 months after acceptance. Byline given. Offers 20% kill fee. Buys first North American serial rights. Editorial lead time 5 months. Submit seasonal material 4 months in advance. Accepts simultaneous submissions. Reports in 1 month. Sample copy for 10×13 SAE with 5 first-class stamps. Writer's guidelines free on request.
Nonfiction: Essays, how-to, humor, interview/profile, new product, opinion. Buys 30 mss/year. Query with published clips or send complete ms. Length: 1,000-2,000 words. Pays $150-350. Sometimes pays expenses of writers on assignment.

FOR EXPLANATION of symbols, see the Key to Symbols and Abbreviations.
For unfamiliar words, see the Glossary.

Reprints: Accepts previously published submissions.
Photos: Send photos with submission. Reviews 4×5 transparencies, 3½×5 prints. Offers no additional payment for photos accepted with ms. Captions required. Buys one-time rights.
Columns/Departments: Art Technique (how-to for particular art method), 1,500 words; Etc. (inspirational/humorous tidbits about business/industry), 1,000 words; Marketing Magic (marketing tips for retailers), 2,000 words. Buys 20 mss/year. Query with published clips or send complete ms. Pays $75-350.
Tips: "Know the retail industry in general. Some art knowledge is helpful."

BALLOONS AND PARTIES MAGAZINE, Festivities Publications, 1205 W. Forsyth St., Jacksonville FL 32204. (904)634-1902. Fax: (904)633-8764. Publisher: Debra Paulk. 10% freelance written. Monthly international trade journal for professional party decorators and for gift delivery businesses. Estab. 1986. Circ. 7,000. Pays on publication. Publishes ms an average of 3 months after acceptance. Byline given. Buys all rights. Submit seasonal material 6 months in advance. Reports in 6 weeks. Sample copy for 9×12 SAE.
Nonfiction: Interview/profile, photo feature, technical, craft. Buys 12 mss/year. Query with or without published clips, or send complete ms. Length: 500-1,500 words. Pays $100-300 for assigned articles; $50-200 for unsolicited articles. Sometimes pays expenses of writers on assignment.
Photos: Send photos with submission. Reviews 2×2 transparencies, 3×5 prints. Captions, model releases, identification of subjects required. Buys all rights.
Columns/Departments: Great Ideas (craft projects using balloons, large scale decorations), 200-500 words. Send complete ms with photos.
Tips: "Show unusual, lavish, and outstanding examples of balloon sculpture, design and decorating and other craft projects. Offer specific how-to information. Be positive and motivational in style."

CHRISTIAN RETAILING, Strang Communications, 600 Rinehart Road, Lake Mary FL 32746. (407)333-0600. Fax: (407)333-7133. Website: http://www.strang.com. Managing Editor: Carol Chapman Stertzer. 60% freelance written. Magazine published 20 times/year covering issues and products of interest to Christian vendors and retail stores. "Our editorial is geared to help retailers run a successful business. We do this with product information, industry news and feature articles." Estab. 1958. Circ. 9,500. Pays on publication. Publishes ms an average of 5 months after acceptance. Bylines sometimes given. Kill fee varies. Buys all rights. Submit seasonal material 5 months in advance. Reports in 2 months. Sample copy for $3. Writer's guidelines for #10 SASE.
Nonfiction: How-to (any articles on running a retail business—books, gifts, music, video, clothing of interest to Christians), new product, religious, technical. Buys 36 mss/year. Send complete ms. Length: 700-2,000 words. Pays $200-340. Sometimes pays expenses of writers on assignment.
Reprints: Send photocopy of article and information about when and where the article previously appeared.
Photos: State availability of photos with submission. Reviews contact sheets, transparencies, prints. Usually offers no additional payment for photos accepted with ms. Captions required. Buys one-time rights.
Columns/Departments: Industry News; Book News; Music News; Video Update; Product Spectrum; Gift News.
Fillers: Cartoon, illustrations, graphs/charts.
Tips: "Visit Christian bookstores and see what they're doing—the products they carry, the issues that concern them. Then write about it!"

COLLEGE STORE, National Association of College Stores, 500 E. Lorain, Oberlin OH 44074. (216)775-7777. E-mail: rstevens@nacs.org. Website: www.nacs.org. Editor: Ronald D. Stevens. 50% freelance written. Bimonthly association magazine covering college bookstore operations (retailing). "*College Store* is the journal of record for the National Association of College Stores and serves its members by publishing information and expert opinion on all phases of college store retailing." Estab. 1928. Circ. 7,200. Pays on publication or special arrangement. Byline given. Buys first rights. Editorial lead time 2 months. Submit seasonal material 6 months in advance. Accepts simultaneous submissions. Reports in 1 month. Sample copy free on request. Writer's guidelines not available.
Nonfiction: Historical/nostalgic, how-to, interview/profile, personal experience, technical (unique attributes of college stores/personnel). "Articles must have clearly defined connection to college stores and collegiate retailing." Buys 24 mss/year. Query with published clips. Length: 1,500-3,000 words. Pays $400 minimum for assigned articles; $200 minimum for unsolicited articles. Sometimes pays expenses of writers on assignment.
Photos: Send photos with submission. Reviews 2¼×2¼ transparencies, 5×7 prints. Negotiates payment individually. Captions, identification of subjects required. Buys one-time rights.
Columns/Departments: Buys 12 mss/year. Query with published clips. Pays $200-400.
Tips: "It's best if writers work (or have worked) in a college store. Articles on specific retailing successes are most open to freelancers—they should include information on how well an approach worked and the reasons for it, whether they are specific to a campus or region, etc."

‡**THE CRAFTS REPORT, The Business Journal for the Crafts Industry**, 300 Water St., P.O. Box 1992, Wilmington DE 19899. (302)656-2209. Fax: (302)656-4894. E-mail: tcrmag@aol.com. Website: http://

www.craftsreport.com/. Editor: Bernadette Smedile Finnerty. 50% freelance written. Monthly magazine covering the entire craft industry. "Our readers are professional craft artists, retailers, show promoters, from beginners to established professionals. We publish articles that help them market and sell their work, keep track of finances, inspire their creativity or anything else that will help them enhance their livelihood in craft." Estab. 1975. Circ. 20,000. Pays on publication. Publishes ms an average of 4 months after acceptance. Byline given. Offers $50 kill fee. Buys first North American serial rights. Editorial lead time 4 months. Sample copy for $5. Writer's guidelines for #10 SASE.

Nonfiction: Inspirational, interview/profile, new product (no pay), opinion, personal experience, photo feature. Special issues: Shows and Fairs (April); Bridal (May). No how-to or fluff. Buys 36 mss/year. Query with published clips. Length: 1,500-3,000 words. Pays 20¢/word maximum for assigned articles; 13¢/word maximum for unsolicited articles. Sometimes pays expenses of writers on assignment.

Photos: Send photos with submission. Reviews transparencies, 3×5 prints. Offers no additional payment for photos accepted with ms. Identification of subjects required.

Columns/Departments: Noelle Backer, associate editor. Craft Show Reviews (for the benefit of buyers and craft artists to choose shows to participate in), 700-900 words; Profiles (unusual crafts/success stories), 900 words; Crafting Your Business (business/management how-to), 900 words. Buys 6 mss/year. Query with published clips. Pays $75-200.

Tips: "First person articles and point of view articles are a good way to break in. For others, such as columns and features, we're looking for well-researched in-depth material. Research plans must be outlined in the query letter. Well-researched articles are a must. Know what you're asking to write about and prove it in your query letter. Queries are considered more seriously than unsolicited manuscripts. Also, we're looking for more coverage of craft shows in the Midwest."

‡EDUCATIONAL DEALER, Fahy-Williams Publishing, Inc., 171 Reed St., P.O. Box 1080, Geneva NY 14456-8080. (315)789-0458. Fax: (315)781-6820. Editor: J. Kevin Fahy. 50% freelance written. Magazine published 5 times/year covering the educational supply industry. "Slant should be toward educational supply *dealers*, not teachers or educators, as most commonly happens." Estab. 1973. Circ. 12,500. Pays on publication. Byline given. Buys one-time rights. Accepts simultaneous submissions. Reports in 3 weeks on queries; 3 months on mss. Sample copy for $3.

Nonfiction: Practical how-tos on merchandising, marketing, retailing, customer service, managing people, etc. Buys 10 mss/year. Query. Length: 1,500 words minimum. Pays $50 minimum.

Reprints: Send photocopy of article.

Photos: Send photos with submission. Reviews contact sheets. Offers no additional payment for photos accepted with ms. Identification of subjects required. Buys one-time rights.

Tips: "Our special features section is most open to freelancers. Become familiar with the educational supply industry, which is growing quickly. While the industry is a large one in terms of dollars spent on school supply products, it's a 'small' one in terms of its players and what they're doing. Everyone knows everyone else; they belong to the same organizations: NSSEA and EDSA. We are accepting more freelance material."

ELECTRONIC RETAILING, The Magazine for the New Age of Marketing, Creative Age Publications, 7628 Densmore Ave., Van Nuys CA 91406-2088. (818)782-7328. Fax: (818)782-7450. E-mail: eretailing@aol.com. Editor: Brett Bush. 80% freelance written. Bimonthly magazine covering electronic retailing applications for marketers. "Writing for our readers requires knowledge of basic marketing (advertising principles), familiarity with emerging fields of computer-based selling (online shopping, CD-ROM, CDi), direct response television, television shopping, cable television industry." Estab. 1994. Circ. 21,500. **Pays on acceptance**. Publishes ms 2 months after acceptance. Byline given. Offers 50% kill fee. Buys first rights and one-time rights. Editorial lead time 2 months. Submit seasonal material 6 months in advance. Accepts simultaneous submissions. Sample copy free.

Nonfiction: How-to (market or sell product or service using new electronic media), interview/profile, opinion. Buys 20-30 mss/year. Query with published clips. Length: 500-2,000 words. Pays $150-400 for assigned articles; $100-300 for unsolicited articles. Sometimes pays expenses of writers on assignment.

Photos: Send photos with submission. Offers no additional payment for photos accepted with ms. Identification of subjects required. Buys one-time rights.

Columns/Departments: On the Air (new TV advertising), 500 words; Channel News (new cable TV channels), 500 words; New Media (new marketing applications in CD-ROM, on-line services, interactive TV, kiosks), 500-750 words; Book Review (new-age marketing related), 500-750 words. Buys 20 mss/year. Query with published clips. Pays $50-100.

Tips: "Provide summary of similar writing experience, business background, areas of expertise. Fax or mail, then follow up with phone call to discuss with editor."

EVENTS BUSINESS NEWS, S.E.N. Inc., 523 Route 38, Suite 207, Cherry Hill NJ 08002. (609)488-5255. Fax: (609)488-8324. Contact: Jake O'Brien. 20% freelance written. Bimonthly glossy magazine covering special events across North America, including festivals, fairs, auto shows, home shows, trade shows, etc. Covers 15 categories of shows/events. Byline given. Buys first rights. Submit seasonal material 3 months in advance. Sample copy and writers guidelines free.

Nonfiction: How-to, interview/profile, event review, new product. Special issues: annual special event directory, covering over 38,000 events. No submissions unrelated to selling at events. Query. Length: 400-750 words. Pays $2.50/column inch.

Reprints: Send photocopy of article and information about when and where the article previously appeared.

Photos: Send photos with submission. Reviews contact sheets. Offers $20/photo. Captions required. Buys one-time rights.

Columns/Departments: Five columns monthly (dealing with background of event, vendors or unique facets of industry in North America). Query with published clips. Length: 400-700 words. Pays $3/col. in.

‡**EXHIBITOR TIMES, The Exhibitor's Journal for Trade Show Marketing**, Virgo Publishing Inc., 4141 N. Scottsdale Rd., Suite 316, Scottsdale AZ 85251. (602)990-1101. Fax: (602)990-0819. E-mail: etmag @vpico.com. Editor: Valerie A.M. Demetros. Managing Editor: Drew Whitney. 60-70% freelance written. Monthly magazine covering the trade show industry with regard to exhibit managers. Estab. 1993. Circ. 15,000. Pays 30 days after publication. Publishes ms an average of 2 months after acceptance. Byline given. Buys first North American serial rights. Editorial lead time 4 months. Submit seasonal material 6 months in advance. Reports in 2 weeks on queries; 1 month on mss. Sample copy for 9×12 SAE.

Nonfiction: Book excerpts, interview/profile, new product, technical. No lighthearted trade show articles, just informative, interesting material. Buys 4-5 mss/year. Query with published clips. Length: 850-3,500 words. Pays $50-200. Pays expenses of writers on assignment.

Photos: Send photos with submission. Reviews 3×5 prints. Offers no additional payment for photos accepted with ms. Negotiates payment individually. Model releases, identification of subjects required. Buys one-time rights.

Columns/Departments: Damon Gross, associate editor. Trends (trends in trade shows/marketing), 1,000 words; Marketing (marketing news/ideas), 1,000 words. Query with published clips. Pays $50-200.

Tips: "Talk to trade show managers about their interests, attend trade shows for a closer look at booth construction and the industry itself. Research the industry and call with valid ideas. Request a copy and plan ahead. Articles must be thoroughly researched and we prefer that writers have some expertise or experience in the industry. Most of the freelance articles in *Exhibitor Times* are written by field experts. The goal of the magazine is to help exhibit managers succeed in the exhibit industry through relevant information on marketing, management and design and production."

‡**GIFT BASKET REVIEW**, Festivities Publications, 1205 W. Forsyth St., Jacksonville FL 32204. (904)634-1902. Fax: (904)633-8764. Publisher: Debra Paulk. Editor: Kathy Horak. 25% freelance written. Monthly magazine for gourmet food and gift basket retailers. "Our readers are creative small business entrepreneurs. Many are women who start their business out of their homes and eventually branch into retail." Estab. 1990. Circ. 15,000. Pays on publication. Publishes ms an average of 3 months after acceptance. Byline given. Buys all rights. Submit seasonal material 9 months in advance. Accepts simultaneous submissions. Reports in 2 months.

Nonfiction: How-to (how to give a corporate presentation, negotiate a lease, etc.), photo feature, technical. "No personal profiles or general experience." Buys 6-8 mss/year. Send complete ms. Length: 500-2,000 words. Pays 10¢/word. Sometimes pays expenses of writers on assignment.

Reprints: Accepts previously published submissions.

Photos: Send photos with submission. Reviews contact sheets, negatives, 2×2 transparencies, 3×5 prints. Model releases, identification of subjects required. Buys all rights.

Columns/Departments: Corporate Talk (deals with obtaining corporate clients), 1,500 words; In the Storefront (emphasis on small business owners with a retail storefront), 1,500 words; On the Homefront (specifically for home-based entrepreneurs), 1,500 words. Buys 12 mss/year. Send complete ms. Pays 10¢/word.

Fillers: Anecdotes, facts, newsbreaks, short humor. Length: 300 words maximum. Pays 10¢/word.

PARTY & PAPER RETAILER, 4Ward Corp, 70 New Canaan Ave., Norwalk CT 06850. (203)845-8020. Editor: Trisha McMahon Drain. 90% freelance written. Monthly magazine for party goods and fine stationery industry covering "every aspect of how to do business better for owners of party and fine stationery shops. Tips and how-tos on display, marketing, success stories, advertising, operating costs, etc." Estab. 1986. Circ. 25,000. Pays on publication. Offers 15% kill fee. Buys first North American serial rights. Editorial lead time 2 months. Submit seasonal material 6 months in advance. Reports in 2 months. Sample copy for $5

Nonfiction: Book excerpts, how-to (retailing related). No articles written in the first person. Buys 100 mss/ year. Query with published clips. Length: 800-1,800 words. Pay "depends on topic, word count expertise, deadline." Pays telephone expenses of writers on assignment.

Reprints: Send tearsheet or photocopy of article and information about when and where the article previously appeared.

Photos: State availability of photos with submission. Reviews transparencies. Negotiates payment individually. Captions, identification of subjects required. Buys one-time rights.

Columns/Departments: Shop Talk (successful party/stationery store profile), 1,800 words; Storekeeping (selling, employees, market, running store), 800 words; Cash Flow (anything finance related), 800 words;

On Display (display ideas and how-to). Buys 30 mss/year. Query with published clips. Pay varies.

PROFESSIONAL SELLING, 24 Rope Ferry Rd., Waterford CT 06386-0001. (203)442-4365. Fax: (203)434-3078. Editor: Paulette S. Kitchens. 33% freelance written. Prefers to work with published/established writers. Bimonthly newsletter in 2 sections for sales professionals covering industrial, wholesale, high-tech and financial services sales. "*Professional Selling* provides field sales personnel with both the basics and current information that can help them better perform the sales function." Estab. 1917. **Pays on acceptance.** Publishes ms an average of 6 months after acceptance. No byline given. Buys all rights. Submit seasonal material 6 months in advance. Reports in 1 month. Sample copy and writer's guidelines for #10 SAE with 2 first-class stamps.
Nonfiction: How-to (successful sales techniques); interview/profile (interview-based articles). "We buy only interview-based material." Buys 12-15 mss/year. Written queries only; no unsolicited mss. Length: 800-1,000 words. Pays 12-15¢/word.
Tips: "*Professional Selling* includes a four-page (Sales Spotlight) devoted to a single topic of major importance to sales professionals. Only the lead article for each section is open to freelancers. Lead article must be based on an interview with an actual sales professional. Freelancers may occasionally interview sales managers, but the slant must be toward field sales, *not* management."

SALES AND MARKETING STRATEGIES & NEWS, Hughes Communications, 211 W. State St., Rockford IL 61101. Fax: (815)963-7773. Managing Editor: Bruce Ericson. Contact: Kristi Nelson, senior editor. Tabloid published 8 times/year covering brand marketing, promotion, incentives, sales automation, sales training, integrated marketing, meetings, p.o.p., trade shows. Estab. 1991. Circ. 72,000. Pays on publication. Publishes ms 3 months after acceptance. Byline given. Offers 15% kill fee. Buys first North American serial rights. Editorial lead time 4 months. Sample copy and writer's guidelines free on request.
Nonfiction: How-to, technical. Buys 120 mss/year. Query. Length: 500-900 words. Pays $150-300 for assigned articles. Expert writers are given a bio at end of story. Sometimes pays expenses of writers on assignment.
Photos: Send photos with submission. Reviews transparencies and prints. Offers no additional payment for photos accepted with ms. Identification of subjects required.

SPORT TRADE

Retailers and wholesalers of sports equipment and operators of recreation programs read these journals. Magazines about general and specific sports are classified in the Consumer Sports section.

AMERICAN FIREARMS INDUSTRY, AFI Communications Group, Inc., 2455 E. Sunrise Blvd., 9th Floor, Ft. Lauderdale FL 33304-3118. Fax: (954)561-4129. Articles Editor: R.A. Legmeister. 10% freelance written. Works with writers specifically in the firearms trade. Monthly magazine specializing in the sporting arms trade. Estab. 1973. Circ. 32,000. Pays on publication. Publishes ms an average of 1 month after acceptance. Buys all rights. Reports in 2 weeks.
Nonfiction: Publishes informational, technical and new product articles. No general firearms subjects. Query. Length: 900-1,500 words. Pays $150-300. Sometimes pays expenses of writers on assignment.
Photos: Reviews 8×10 color glossy prints. Manuscript price includes payment for photos.

FITNESS MANAGEMENT, Issues and Solutions in Fitness Services, Leisure Publications, Inc., 215 S. Highway 101, Suite 110, P.O. Box 1198, Solana Beach CA 92075-0910. (619)481-4155. Fax: (619)481-4228. E-mail: fitmgt@cts.com. Website: http://www.fitnessworld.com. Editor: Edward H. Pitts. Managing Editor: Ronale Tucker. 50% freelance written. Monthly magazine covering commercial, corporate and community fitness centers. "Readers are owners, managers and program directors of physical fitness facilities. *FM* helps them run their enterprises safely, efficiently and profitably. Ethical and professional positions in health, nutrition, sports medicine, management, etc., are consistent with those of established national bodies." Estab. 1985. Circ. 26,000. Pays on publication. Publishes ms an average of 5 months after acceptance. Byline given. Pays 50% kill fee. Buys all rights (all articles published in *FM* are also published and archived on its website). Submit seasonal material 6 months in advance. Reports in 3 months. Sample copy for $5. Writer's guidelines for #10 SASE.
Nonfiction: Book excerpts (prepublication); how-to (manage fitness center and program); new product (no pay); photo feature (facilities/programs); technical; other (news of fitness research and major happenings in fitness industry). No exercise instructions or general ideas without examples of fitness businesses that have used them successfully. Buys 50 mss/year. Query. Length: 750-2,000 words. Pays $60-300 for assigned articles. Pays expenses of writers on assignment.
Photos: Send photos with submission. Reviews contact sheets, 2×2 and 4×5 transparencies; prefers glossy prints, 5×7 to 8×10. Offers $10-25/photo. Captions, model releases required.

Tips: "We seek writers who are expert in a business or science field related to the fitness-service industry or who are experienced in the industry. Be current with the state of the art/science in business and fitness and communicate it in human terms (avoid intimidating academic language; tell the story of how this was learned and/or cite examples or quotes of people who have applied the knowledge successfully)."

GOLF COURSE NEWS, The Newspaper for the Golf Course Industry, United Publications Inc., P.O. Box 997, 38 Lafayette St., Yarmouth ME 04096. (207)846-0600. Fax: (207)846-0657. Managing Editor: Mark Leslie. 15% freelance written. Monthly tabloid covering golf course maintenance, design, construction and management. "Articles should be written with the golf course superintendent in mind. Our readers are superintendents, course architects and builders, owners and general managers." Estab. 1989. Circ. 25,000. **Pays on acceptance.** Publishes ms an average of 2 months after acceptance. Byline given. Buys first North American serial rights. Editorial lead time 1 month. Submit seasonal material 2 months in advance. Reports in 2 weeks on queries; 2 months on mss. Free sample copy and writer's guidelines.
Nonfiction: Book excerpts, general interest, interview/profile, new product, opinion, photo feature. "No how-to articles." Buys 24 mss/year. Query with published clips. Length: 500-1,000 words. Pays $200. Sometimes pays expenses of writers on assignment.
Photos: Send photos with submission. Reviews negatives, transparencies, prints. Offers no additional payment for photos accepted with ms. Identification of subjects required. Buys one-time rights.
Columns/Departments: On the Green (innovative ideas on the golf course), 1,000 words; Shop Talk (in the maintenance facility). Buys 4 mss/year. Query with published clips. Pays $200-500.
Tips: "Keep your eye out for news affecting the golf industry. Then contact us with your story ideas. We are a national paper and accept both national and regional interest articles. We are interested in receiving features on development of golf projects. We also have an edition covering the golf industry in the Asia-Pacific retion—aptly called *Golf Course News Asia-Pacific* published four times per year—April, June, September and November. Contact person is Editor Hal Phillips."

INLINE RETAILER & INDUSTRY NEWS, Sports & Fitness Publishing, 2025 Pearl St., Boulder CO 80302. (303)440-5111. Fax: (303)440-3313. E-mail: MShafran@aol.com. Website: http://www.s2.com/inli ne. Editor: Michael W. Shafran. 15% freelance written. Monthly tabloid covering the in-line skating industry. "*InLine Retailer* is a business magazine dedicated to spotting new trends, products and procedures that will help in-line retailers and manufacturers keep a competitive edge." Estab. 1992. Circ. 8,000. Pays on publication. Publishes ms an average of 1 month after acceptance. Byline given. Offers 30% kill fee. Buys first North American serial rights. Editorial lead time 2 months. Submit seasonal material 4 months in advance. Reports in 2 weeks on queries. Sample copy for $5.
  ● *Inline Retailer* reports that it is looking for more writers with a background in business, particularly sporting goods, to help write news pieces providing insight or analysis into the in-line industry.
Nonfiction: How-to, interview/profile, new product, technical. Buys 30 mss/year. Query with published clips. Length: 500-2,000 words. Pays 15¢/word minimum for assigned articles; 10¢/word for unsolicited articles. Sometimes pays expenses of writers on assignment.
Columns/Departments: Retailer Corner (tips for running an in-line retail store), 1,000-1,200 words; First Person (insights from high-level industry figures), 1,200-1,500 words. Buys 20 mss/year. Query with published clips or send complete ms. Pays 15-20¢/word.
Tips: "It's best to write us and explain your background in either the sporting goods business or in-line skating. Mail several clips and also send some ideas that you think would be suitable for our readers. The features and Retailer Corner sections are the ones we typically assign to freelancers. Writers should have solid reporting skills, particularly when it comes to getting subjects to disclose technology, news or tips that they may be willing to do without some prodding."

POOL & SPA NEWS, Leisure Publications, 3923 W. Sixth St., Los Angeles CA 90020-4290. (213)385-3926. Fax: (213)383-1152. E-mail: psn@poolspanews.com. Editor-in-Chief: Anne Blakey. 15-20% freelance written. Semimonthly magazine emphasizing news of the swimming pool and spa industry for pool builders, pool retail stores and pool service firms. Estab. 1960. Circ. 17,000. Pays on publication. Publishes ms an average of 2 months after acceptance. Buys all rights. Reports in 2 weeks. Sample copy for $5 and 9×12 SAE with 10 first-class stamps.
Nonfiction: Interview, profile, technical. Phone queries OK. Length: 500-2,000 words. Pays 5-14¢/word. Pays expenses of writers on assignment.
Photos: Pays $10/b&w photo used.

THOROUGHBRED TIMES, Thoroughbred Times Company, Inc., 496 Southland Dr., P.O. Box 8237, Lexington KY 40533. (606)260-9800. Editor: Mark Simon. 10% freelance written. Weekly tabloid covering thoroughbred racing and breeding. "Articles are written for professionals who breed and/or race thoroughbreds at tracks in the US. Articles must help owners and breeders understand racing to help them realize a profit." Estab. 1985. Circ. 22,000. Pays on publication. Publishes ms an average of 1 month after acceptance. Byline given. Offers 50% kill fee. Buys all rights. Submit seasonal material 2 months in advance. Reports in 2 weeks.

Nonfiction: General interest, historical/nostalgic, interview/profile, technical. Buys 52 mss/year. Query. Length: 500-2,500 words. Pays 10-20¢/word. Sometimes pays expenses of writers on assignment.
Photos: State availability of photos with submission. Reviews prints. Offers $25/photo. Identification of subjects required. Buys one-time rights.
Tips: "We are looking for farm stories and profiles of owners, breeders, jockeys and trainers."

WOODALL'S CAMPGROUND MANAGEMENT, Woodall Publications Corp., 13975 W. Polo Trail Dr., Lake Forest IL 60045. (847)362-6700. Editor: Mike Byrnes. 10% freelance written. Monthly tabloid covering campground management and operation for managers of private and public campgrounds throughout the US. Estab. 1970. Circ. 10,000. Pays after publication. Publishes ms an average of 8 months after acceptance. Byline given. Buys all rights. Reassigns rights to author upon written request. Submit seasonal material 4 months in advance. Reports in 1 month on queries; 2 months on mss. Free sample copy and writer's guidelines.
Nonfiction: How-to, interview/profile, technical. "Our articles tell our readers how to maintain their resources, manage personnel and guests, market, develop new campground areas and activities, and interrelate with the major tourism organizations within their areas. 'Improvement' and 'profit' are the two key words." Buys 14 mss/year. Query. Length: 500 words minimum. Pays $50-200.
Photos: Send contact sheets, negatives. "We pay for each photo used."
Tips: "The best type of story to break in with is a case history approach about how a campground improved its maintenance, physical plant or profitability."

STONE, QUARRY AND MINING

COAL PEOPLE MAGAZINE, Al Skinner Inc., Dept. WM, 629 Virginia St. W., P.O. Box 6247, Charleston WV 25362. (304)342-4129. Fax: (304)343-3124. Editor/Publisher: Al Skinner. Contact: Christina Karawan, managing editor. 50% freelance written. Monthly magazine with stories about coal people, towns and history. "Most stories are about people or historical—either narrative or biographical on all levels of coal people, past and present—from coal execs down to grass roots miners. Most stories are upbeat—showing warmth of family or success from underground up!" Estab. 1976. Circ. 11,000. Pays on publication. Publishes ms an average of 3 months after acceptance. Byline given. Buys first rights, second serial (reprint) rights and makes work-for-hire assignments. Submit seasonal material 2 months in advance. Reports in 3 months. Sample copy for 9 × 12 SAE with 10 first-class stamps.
Nonfiction: Book excerpts (and film if related to coal), historical/nostalgic (coal towns, people, lifestyles), humor (including anecdotes and cartoons), interview/profile (for coal personalities), personal experience (as relates to coal mining), photo feature (on old coal towns, people, past and present). Special issues: calendar issue for more than 300 annual coal shows, association meetings, etc. (January); surface mining/reclamation award (July); Christmas in Coal Country (December). No poetry, fiction or environmental attacks on the coal industry. Buys 32 mss/year. Query with published clips. Length: 5,000 words. Pays $75.
Reprints: Send photocopy of article and information about when and where the article previously appeared.
Photos: Send photos with submission. Reviews contact sheets, transparencies, 5 × 7 prints. Captions, identification of subjects required. Buys one-time reprint rights.
Columns/Departments: Editorials—anything to do with current coal issues (non-paid); Mine'ing Our Business (bull pen column—gossip—humorous anecdotes), Coal Show Coverage (freelance photojournalist coverage of any coal function across the US). Buys 10 mss/year. Query. Length: 300-500 words. Pays $15.
Fillers: Anecdotes. Buys 10/year. Length: 300 words. Pays $15.
Tips: "We are looking for good feature articles on coal people, towns, companies—past and present, color slides (for possible cover use) and b&w photos to complement stories. Could also use a few news writers to take photos and do journalistic coverage on coal events across the country. Slant stories more toward people and less on historical. More faces and names than old town, company store photos. Include more quotes from people who lived these moments!" The following geographical areas are covered: Eastern Canada; Mexico; Europe; China; Russia; Poland; Australia; as well as US states Alabama, Tennessee, Virginia, Washington, Oregon, North and South Dakota, Arizona, Colorado, Alaska and Wyoming.

‡**DIMENSIONAL STONE**, Dimensional Stone Institute, Inc., Suite I, 6300 Variel Ave., Woodland Hills CA 91367. Fax: (818)704-6500. E-mail: wilcampbel@aol.com. Website: http://www.infotile.com.au. Editor: William Campbell. 25% freelance written. Monthly international magazine covering dimensional stone use for managers of producers, importers, contractors, fabricators and specifiers of dimensional stone. Estab. 1985. Circ. 15,849. Pays on publication. Publishes ms an average of 2 months after acceptance. Byline given. Buys first rights or second serial (reprint) rights. Reports in 1 month. Sample copy for 9 × 12 SAE with 11 first-class stamps.
Nonfiction: Interview/profile, technical, only on users of dimensional stone. Special issues: Technology (September); Remodeling and Renovation (November). Buys 6-7 mss/year. Send complete ms. Length: 1,000-3,000 words. Pays $100 maximum. Sometimes pays expenses of writers on assignment.

Reprints: Send tearsheet of article and information about when and where the article previously appeared.
Photos: Send photos with submission. Reviews transparencies, slides, prints. Publication produced using desktop publishing with scanning capabilities. Offers no additional payment for photos accepted with ms. Identification of subjects required.
Tips: "Articles on outstanding commercial and residential uses of dimensional stone are most open to freelancers. For queries, fax editor. Editors work in Microsoft Word on Macintosh system, so copy delivered on disk is appreciated."

STONE REVIEW, National Stone Association, 1415 Elliot Place NW, Washington DC 20007. (202)342-1100. Fax: (202)342-0702. E-mail: fatlee@cais.com. Editor: Frank Atlee. Bimonthly magazine covering quarrying and supplying of crushed stone, "designed to be a communications forum for the crushed stone industry. Publishes information on industry technology, trends, developments and concerns. Audience is quarry operations/management, and manufacturers of equipment, suppliers of services to the industry." Estab. 1985. Circ. 4,000. Pays on publication. Publishes ms an average of 3 months after acceptance. Byline given. Negotiable kill fee. Buys one-time rights. Accepts simultaneous submissions. Reports in 1 month. Sample copy for 9×12 SAE with 3 first-class stamps.
Nonfiction: Technical. Query with or without published clips, or send complete ms. Length: 1,000-2,500 words. "Note: We have no budget for freelance material, but I'm willing to secure payment for right material."
Reprints: Send tearsheet, photocopy or typed ms with information about when and where the article previously appeared. Payment negotiable.
Photos: State availability of photos with query, then send photos with submission. Reviews contact sheets, negatives, transparencies, prints. Offers no additional payment for photos accepted with ms. Identification of subjects required. Buys one-time rights.
Tips: "At this point, most features are written by contributors in the industry, but I'd like to open it up. Articles on unique equipment, applications, etc. are good, as are those reporting on trends (e.g., there is a strong push on now for environmentally sound operations). Also interested in stories on family-run operations involving three or more generations."

STONE WORLD, Business News Publishing Company, 1 Kalisa Way, Suite 205, Paramus NJ 07652. (201)599-0136. Fax: (201)599-2378. E-mail: stoneworld@aol.com. Website: http://www.stoneworld.com. Publisher: John Sailer. Contact: Michael Reis, editor. Monthly magazine on natural building stone for producers and users of granite, marble, limestone, slate, sandstone, onyx and other natural stone products. Estab. 1984. Circ. 18,000. Pays on publication. Publishes ms an average of 6 months after acceptance. Byline given. Buys first rights or second serial (reprint) rights. Submit seasonal material 6 months in advance. Publishes technical book excerpts. Reports in 2 months. Sample copy for $10.
Nonfiction: How-to (fabricate and/or install natural building stone), interview/profile, photo feature, technical, architectural design, artistic stone uses, statistics, factory profile, equipment profile, trade show review. Buys 10 mss/year. Query with or without published clips, or send complete ms. Length: 600-3,000 words. Pays $4/column inch. Pays expenses of writers on assignment.
Reprints: Send photocopy of article or typed ms with rights for sale noted and information about when and where the article previously appeared. Pays 50% of amount paid for an original article.
Photos: State availability of photos with submission. Reviews transparencies, prints. Pays $10/photo accepted with ms. Captions, identification of subjects required. Buys one-time rights.
Columns/Departments: News (pertaining to stone or design community); New Literature (brochures, catalogs, books, videos, etc. about stone); New Products (stone products); New Equipment (equipment and machinery for working with stone); Calendar (dates and locations of events in stone and design communities). Query or send complete ms. Length: 300-600 words. Pays $4/inch.
Tips: "Articles about architectural stone design accompanied by professional color photographs and quotes from designing firms are often published, especially when one unique aspect of the stone selection or installation is highlighted. We are also interested in articles about new techniques of quarrying and/or fabricating natural building stone."

TRANSPORTATION

These publications are for professional movers and people involved in transportation of goods. For magazines focusing on trucking see also Auto and Truck.

BUS WORLD, Magazine of Buses and Bus Systems, Stauss Publications, P.O. Box 39, Woodland Hills CA 91365-0039. (818)710-0208. E-mail: mgpg68a@prodigy.com. Editor: Ed Stauss. 25% freelance written. Quarterly trade journal covering the transit and intercity bus industries. Estab. 1978. Circ. 5,000. Pays on publication. Reports in 2 months. Sample copy with writer's guidelines for $2.
Photos: Buys photos with mss.
Fillers: Cartoons. Buys 4-6/year. Pays $10.
Tips: "No tourist or travelog viewpoints. Be employed in or have a good understanding of the bus industry. Be enthusiastic about buses—their history and future. Acceptable material will be held until used and will

not be returned unless requested by sender. Unacceptable and excess material will be returned only if accompanied by suitable SASE."

DISTRIBUTION, The Transportation & Business Logistics Magazine, Chilton Co., One Chilton Way, Radnor PA 19089. (610)964-4244. E-mail: distmag@aol.com. Editor: Jim Thomas. Contact: Jodi Melbin, managing editor. 50% or more freelance written. Monthly magazine covering transportation and logistics. "Our audience is the companies that require transportation professionals. Stories revolve around ways—or programs—that improve distribution logistics processes within industries, as well as the use of carriers, forwarders and third-party companies." Estab. 1901. Circ. 70,000. **Pays on acceptance.** Publishes ms an average of 3 months after acceptance. Buys one-time rights. Editorial lead time 2 months. Sample copy for #10 SASE.
Nonfiction: General interest, how-to, interview/profile, technical, travel (to see departments). Buys 36 mss/year. Query with published clips. Length: 1,200-1,500 words. Pays $300-650.
Photos: Send photos with submissions. Reviews contact sheets, transparencies, prints. Negotiates payment individually. Identification of subjects required.
Columns/Departments: Global Report (global ports, DCs etc.), 500-750 words. Buys 12-20 mss/year. Query. Pays $300-650.
Tips: "Query letter with background and already published articles related to field. Most articles are assigned, so we are interested in getting writers experienced in business writing. We are developing writer's guidelines."

NATIONAL BUS TRADER, The Magazine of Bus Equipment for the United States and Canada, 9698 W. Judson Rd., Polo IL 61064-9015. (815)946-2341. Fax: (815)946-2347. Editor: Larry Plachno. 25% freelance written. Eager to work with new/unpublished writers. Monthly magazine for manufacturers, dealers and owners of buses and motor coaches. Estab. 1977. Circ. 5,800. Pays either on acceptance or publication. Publishes ms an average of 3 months after acceptance. Byline given. Not copyrighted. Buys rights "as required by writer." Accepts simultaneous submissions. Reports in 1 month. Sample copy for 9×12 SAE.
Nonfiction: Historical/nostalgic (on old buses); how-to (maintenance repair); new products; photo feature; technical (aspects of mechanical operation of buses). "We are finding that more and more firms and agencies are hiring freelancers to write articles to our specifications. We are more likely to run them if someone else pays." No material that does *not* pertain to bus tours or bus equipment. Buys 3-5 unsolicited mss/year. Query. Length varies. Pays variable rate. Sometimes pays expenses of writers on assignment.
Columns/Departments: Bus Maintenance; Buses and the Law; Regulations; Bus of the Month. Query. Length: 250-400 words. Pays variable rate.
Tips: "We are a very technical publication. Submit qualifications showing extensive background in bus vehicles. We're very interested in well-researched articles on older bus models and manufacturers or current converted coaches. We would like to receive history of individual bus models prior to 1953 and history of GMC 'new look' models. Write or phone editors with article concept or outline for comments and approval."

‡THE PRIVATE CARRIER, Private Carrier Conference, Inc., 66 Canal Center Plaza, #600, Alexandria VA 22314-1649. (703)683-1300. Fax: (703)683-1217. Editor: Jim Galligan. 20% freelance written. Monthly magazine on freight transportation. *"The Private Carrier* is the national publication for private fleet managers. Its goal is to help them manage their private fleets and their other transportation activities as efficiently and cost-effectively as possible." Circ. 16,000. Pays on publication. Publishes ms an average of 2 months after acceptance. Byline given. Offers $100 maximum kill fee. "We buy first rights and retain right to reprint. However, after publication, writer may use/sell article as he/she sees fit." Submit seasonal material 3 months in advance. Reports in 3 months. Sample copy for 9×12 SAE with 4 first class stamps.
Nonfiction: Expose, interview/profile, opinion, photo feature. Buys 2 mss/year. Query. Length: 1,000-3,000 words. Pays $100-250. Sometimes pays expenses of writers on assignment.
Reprints: Send photocopy of article and typed manuscript with rights for sale noted. Pays 50% of amount paid for an original article.
Photos: Send photos with submission. Reviews 35mm transparencies, 5×7 or 8×10 prints. Offers no additional payment for photos accepted with ms. Model releases, identification of subjects required. Buys one-time rights.
Columns/Departments: Verbatim (editorial opinions); ITS (transportation technology). Send complete ms. Length: 600 words. Pays $10-50.
Tips: "Tailor articles to our readers. Writing style is less important than clean, well-written copy. We love good photos or articles that lend themselves to good illustrations. We like the slightly off-beat, unconventional or novel way to look at subjects. Articles for whatever department that profile how a private fleet solved a problem (i.e., computers, drivers, maintenance, etc.). The structure is: 1) company identifies a problem, 2) evaluates options, 3) selects a solution, and 4) evaluates its choice."

‡TAXI NEWS, Chedmount Investments Ltd., 38 Fairmount Crescent, Toronto, Ontario M4L 2H4 Canada. (416)466-2328. Fax: (416)466-4220. Editor: Bill M'Ouat. 100% freelance written. Monthly tabloid covering taxicab industry. "We don't care about your biases/philosophy, but they must be clear to the reader. You must know what you are writing about and be able to back up opinions with facts. We are an independent newspaper covering news and views of a specific industry so you will be writing for a knowledgeable audience, while we also require stories, news items to be understandable to a wider, general audience." Estab. 1985. Circ. 10,300. Pays on publication. Publishes ms an average of 2 months after acceptance. Byline given. Offers 50% kill fee or $50 (Canadian). Buys all rights. Editorial lead time 2 months. Submit seasonal material 3 months in advance. Accepts simultaneous submissions. Reports in 2 weeks on queries; 1 month on mss. Sample copy for #10 SASE and Canadian stamp.

Nonfiction: Exposé, general interest, historical/nostalgic, how-to, humor, interview/profile, opinion, personal experience, photo feature. Buys 50 mss/year. Query or send complete ms. Length: 50-800 words. Pays $25-200 (Canadian).

Reprints: Accepts previously published submissions.

Photos: Send photos with submission. Reviews 3×5 prints. Offers $10-25/photo (Canadian). Captions, identification of subjects required. Buys all rights.

Columns/Departments: Have regular columnists, but will publish guest columns. Buys 36 mss/year. Query or send complete ms. Pays $100 (Canadian).

Tips: "We cover Toronto very well. Occasionally we'll use out-of-town material if it is A) well-written and/ or B) of direct applicability to our readers' working lives e.g. tips (new) on avoiding robberies/violence— how to save money, new regulatory approaches, cab drivers helping people (gratuitous dec...), etc. Don't get us sued."

TRAVEL

Travel professionals read these publications to keep up with trends, tours and changes in transportation. Magazines about vacations and travel for the general public are listed in the Consumer Travel section.

CORPORATE MEETINGS & INCENTIVES, Adams/Laux Publishing, 60 Main St., Maynard MA 01754. (508)897-5552. Editor: Connie Goldstein. Contact: Barbara Scofidio. 75% freelance written. Monthly magazine covering meetings and incentive travel. "Our cover stories focus on issues of interest to senior execs—from building a horizontal organization to encouraging innovation—and the integral role meetings play in achieving these goals." Circ. 36,000. Pays 30 days after acceptance. Offers 33% kill fee. Buys first North American serial rights and electronic rights. Editorial lead time 3 months. Submit seasonal material 4 months in advance. Sample copy for SAE with $1.50 postage. Writer's guidelines for #10 SASE.

Nonfiction: Interview/profile, travel with a meetings angle. Special issue: Golf (April). Buys 30 mss/year. Query with published clips. Length: 2,000-4,000 words. Pays 50¢/word. Sometimes pays expenses of writers on assignment.

Reprints: Accepts simultaneous submissions.

Photos: State availability of photos with submissions. Reviews contact sheets, transparencies, prints. Negotiates payment individually. Identification of subjects required. Buys one-time rights.

Columns/Departments: Buys 24 mss/year. Query. Pays $250-500.

Tips: "Looking for strong business writers with experience writing about employee motivation, quality programs, incentive programs—ways that companies improve productivity. Best to send relevant clips with a letter after taking a look at the magazine."

THE ROAD EXPLORER, Naylor Communications Ltd., 920 Yonge St., Suite 600, Toronto, Ontario M4W 3C7 Canada. (416)961-1028. Fax: (416)924-4408. Editor: Lori Knowles. 80% freelance written. "*Explorer* is published biannually (spring and fall) for the Ontario Motor Coach Association (OMCA). The magazine reviews events and issues of the OMCA, and serves as a destination guide for motor coach (bus) tour operators." Accepts simultaneous submissions.

Nonfiction: Looking for material directed at bus tours in the following areas: Canadian and US destinations (including provinces, states, cities, and towns), auto routes, road tours, major events, attractions, sporting attractions and historical sites. Query with published clips and SASE in Canadian funds or supply IRCs. Length: 500-2,500 words. Byline given. Pay Rate negotiated. Offers 33% kill fee. Reports in 6 weeks.

Reprints: Accepts previously published submissions.

Photos: State availability of photos with submission. Reviews transparencies, prints. Offers $25-200/photo. Identification of subjects required.

Tips: "This is a publication for bus tour operators. We do not accept submissions directed at RV owners. Please query with copy of work and SASE in Canadian funds or supply IRCs. We will respond as promptly as deadlines allow."

RV BUSINESS, TL Enterprises, Inc., P.O. Box 8550, Ventura CA 93002. (805)667-4100. Fax: (805)667-4484. Editor-in-Chief: Sherman Goldenberg. Editor: Stephen Boilon. 60% freelance written. Prefers to work with published/established writers. Monthly magazine covering the recreational vehicle and allied industries for people in the RV industry—dealers, manufacturers, suppliers and finance experts. Estab. 1950. Circ.

14,000. **Pays on acceptance.** Publishes ms an average of 2 months after acceptance. Byline given. Offers 50% kill fee. Buys first North American serial rights. Submit seasonal material 6 months in advance. Query for electronic submissions. Reports in 2 months. Sample copy for 9×12 SAE with 5 first-class stamps.

Nonfiction: Technical, financial, legal or marketing issues; how-to (deal with any specific aspect of the RV business); specifics and verification of statistics required—must be factual; technical (photos required, 4-color preferred). Buys 15 long features and 200 news items/year. Query with published clips. Send complete ms—"but only read on speculation." Length: 150-1,500 words. Pays variable rate up to $500. Sometimes pays expenses of writers on assignment.

Photos: State availability of photos with query or send photos with ms. Reviews 35mm transparencies and 8×10 b&w prints. Captions, model release, and identification of subjects required. Buys one-time or all rights; unused photos returned.

Columns/Departments: Guest editorial; News (50-500 words maximum, b&w photos appreciated); RV People (color photos/4-color transparencies; this section lends itself to fun, upbeat copy). Buys 100-120 mss/year. Query or send complete ms. Pays $25-200 "depending on where used and importance."

Tips: "Query. Phone OK; letter preferable. Send one or several ideas and a few lines letting us know how you plan to treat it/them. We are always looking for good authors knowledgeable in the RV industry or related industries. Change of editorial focus requires more articles that are brief, factual, hard hitting and business oriented. Will work with promising writers."

SPECIALTY TRAVEL INDEX, Alpine Hansen, 305 San Anselmo Ave., #313, San Anselmo CA 94960. (415)459-4900. Fax: (415)459-4974. E-mail: spectrav@ix.netcom.com. Website: http://www.spectrav.com. Editor: C. Steen Hansen. Contact: Risa Winreb, editor. 90% freelance written. Semiannual magazine covering adventure and special interest travel. Estab. 1980. Circ. 45,000. Pays on publication. Byline given. Buys one-time rights. Editorial lead time 3 months. Submit seasonal material 3 months in advance. Writer's guidelines on request.

Nonfiction: How-to, new product, personal experience, photo feature, travel. Buys 15 mss/year. Query. Length: 1,000 words. Pays $200 minimum.

Reprints: Send tearsheet of article. Pays 100% of amount paid for an original article.

Photos: State availability of photos with submission. Reviews 35mm transparencies, 5×7 prints. Negotiates payment individually. Captions, identification of subjects required.

MAGAZINES THAT APPEARED in the 1996 edition of *Writer's Market* but are not included this year are listed in the General Index with a notation explaining their absence.

Scriptwriting

Everyone has a story to tell, something to say. In telling that story as a play, movie, TV show or educational video you have selected that form over other possibilities. Scriptwriting makes some particular demands, but one thing remains the same for authors of novels, nonfiction books and scripts: you'll learn to write by rewriting. Draft after draft your skills improve until, hopefully, someone likes your work enough to hire you.

Whether you are writing a video to train doctors in a new surgical technique, alternative theater for an Off-Broadway company or you want to see you name on the credits of the next Arnold Schwarzenegger movie, you must perfect both writing and marketing skills. A successful scriptwriter is a talented artist and a savvy business person. But marketing must always be secondary to writing. A mediocre pitch for a great script will still get you farther than a brilliant pitch for a mediocre script. The art and craft of scriptwiting lies in successfully executing inspiration.

Writing a script is a private act. Polishing it may involve more people as you ask friends and fellow writers to take a look at it. Marketing takes your script public in an effort to find the person willing to give the most of what you want, whether it's money, exposure or control, in return for your work.

There are accepted ground rules to presenting and marketing scripts. Following those guidelines will maximize your chances of getting your work before an audience.

Presenting your script professionally earns a serious consideration of its content. Certain types of scripts have a definite format and structure. An educational video written in a one-column format, a feature film much longer than 120 pages or an hour-long TV show that peaks during the first 20 minutes indicates an amateur writer. There are several sources for correct formats, including *The Writer's Digest Book of Manuscript Formats*, by Buchman and Groves and *The Complete Guide to Script Formats*, by Cole and Haig.

Submission guidelines are similar to those for other types of writing. The initial contact is a one-page query letter, with a brief synopsis and a few lines as to your credits or experience relevant to the subject of your script. Never send a complete manuscript until it is requested. Almost every script sent to a producer, studio, or agent must be accompanied by a release form. Ask the producer or agent for his form when invited to submit the complete script. Always include a self-addressed stamped envelope if you want your work returned; a self-addressed stamped postcard will do for acknowledgement or reply if you do not need your script returned.

Most writers break in with spec scripts, written "for free," which serve as calling cards to show what they can do. These scripts plant the seeds of your professional reputation by making the rounds of influential people looking to hire writers, from advertising executives to movie moguls. Good writing is more important than a specific plot. Make sure you are sending out your best work; a first draft is not a finished product. Have several spec scripts completed, as a producer will often decide that a story is not right for him, or a similar work is already in production, but want to know what else you have. Be ready for that invitation.

Writing a script is a matter of learning how to refine your writing so that the work reads as a journey, not a technical manual. The best scripts have concise, visceral scenes that demand to be presented in a specific order and accomplish definite goals.

Educational videos have a message that must be expressed economically and directly, engaging the audience in an entertaining way while maintaining interest in the topic. Theatrical plays are driven by character and dialogue that expose a thematic core and engender enthusiasm or involvement in the conflict. Cinematic screenplays, while more visually-oriented, are a series of discontinuous scenes stacked to illuminate the characters, the obstacles confronting them and the resolution they reach.

A script is a difficult medium—written words that sound natural when spoken, characters that are original yet resonate with the audience, believable conflicts and obstacles in tune with the end result. One theater added to their listing the following tip: "Don't write plays. Write novels, short stories, anything but plays. But if you *must* write plays. . . ." If you are compelled to present your story visually, be aware of the intense competition it will face. Hone it, refine it, keep working on it until it can be no better, then look for the best home you can find. That's success.

BUSINESS AND EDUCATIONAL WRITING

"It's no longer the plankton of the filmmaking food chain," says Kirby Timmons, creative director of the video production company CRM Films. Scripts for corporate training, business management and education videos have become as sophisticated as those designed for TV and film, and they carry the additional requirement of conveying specific content. With an audience that is increasingly media literate, anything that looks and feels like a "training film" will be dead in the water. The trick is to produce a script that engages, compels *and* informs about the topic, whether it's customer relations, listening skills or effective employee management, while staying on a tight budget.

This can create its own challenges, but is an excellent way to increase your skills and exercise your craft. Good scriptwriters are in demand in this field. There is a strong emphasis on producing a polished complete script before filming begins, and a writer's involvement doesn't end until the film is "in the can."

A remarkably diverse industry, educational and corporate video is a $18-25 billion business, compared to theatrical films and TV, estimated at $5 billion. And there is the added advantage that opportunities are widespread, from large local corporations to small video production houses in your area. Larger companies often have inhouse video production companies, but others rely on freelance writers. Your best bet would be to find work with companies that specialize in making educational and corporate video while at the same time making yourself known to the creative directors of inhouse video staffs in large corporations. Advertising agencies are also a good source of work, as they often are asked by their clients for help in creating films and use freelance writers and producers.

Business and educational video is a market-driven industry, with material created either in response to a general need or a specific demand. The production company usually identifies a subject and finds the writer. As such, there is a perception that a spec script will not work in this media. While it is true that, as in TV and theatrical films, a writer's spec script is rarely produced, it is a good résumé of qualifications and sample of skills. It can get you other work even though it isn't produced. Your spec script should demonstrate a knowledge of this industry's specific format. For the most part video scripts are written in two-columns, video on the left, audio on the right. Computer software is available to format the action and dialogue; *The Writer's Digest Guide to Manuscript Formats* also covers the basics of video script format.

Aside from the original script, another opportunity for the writer is the user's guide that often accompanies a video. If you are hired to create the auxiliary material you'll receive a copy of the finished video and write a concurrent text for the teacher or implementor to use.

Networking is very important. There is no substitute for calling companies and finding out what is in your area. Contact local training and development companies and find out who they serve and what they need. It pays to join professional organizations such as the Association of Visual Communicators and the Association for Training and Development, which offer seminars and conventions. Making the rounds at a business convention of video producers with your business card could earn you a few calls and invitations to submit writing samples.

Budgets are tighter for educational or corporate videos than for theatrical films. You'll want to work closely with the producer to make sure your ideas can be realized within the budget. Your fee will vary with each job, but generally a script written for a production house such as CRM in a subject area with broad marketability will pay $5,000-7,000. A custom-produced video for a specific company will usually pay less. The pay does not increase exponentially with your experience; large increases come if you choose to direct and produce as well as write.

With the expansion of cable TV-based home shopping opportunities, direct response TV (informercials) is an area with increasing need for writers to create the scripts that sell the products. Production companies are located across the country, and more are popping up as the business grows. Pay can range from $5,000-18,000, depending on the type, length and success of the program. *The Hollywood Scriptwriter* (1625 N. Wilcox, #385, Hollywood CA 90028; (805)495-5447) published a three-part series on direct response scriptwriting, discussing structure, format and marketing, which is available for $8.

The future of business and educational video lies in interactive media or multimedia. Interactive media combines computer and video technology to create a product that doesn't have to progress along a linear path. Videos that offer the viewer the opportunity to direct the course of events hold exciting possibilities for corporate training and educational applications. Writers will be in high demand as stories offer dozens of choices in storylines. Interactive video will literally eat up pages of script as quickly as a good writer produces them. A training session may last only 20 minutes, but the potential untapped story lines could add up to hours worth of script that must be written, realized and made available. From training salespeople to doctors, or teaching traffic rules to issues in urbanization, corporate and educational video is about to undergo a tremendous revolution.

For information on some business and educational scriptwriting markets not listed in *Writer's Market*, see the General Index.

☐**ABS ENTERPRISES**, P.O. Box 5127, Evanston IL 60204-5127. (708)982-1414. Fax: (708)982-1418. President: Alan Soell. "We produce material for all levels of corporate, medical, cable and educational institutions for the purposes of training and development, marketing and meeting presentations. We also are developing programming for the broadcast areas." 75% freelance written. "We work with a core of three to five freelance writers from development to final drafts." All scripts published are unagented submissions. Buys all rights. Accepts previously produced material. Reports in 2 weeks on queries.
Needs: Videotape, multimedia, realia, slides, tapes and cassettes, television shows/series. Currently interested in "sports instructional series that could be produced for the consumer market on tennis, gymnastics, bowling, golf, aerobics, health and fitness, cross-country skiing and cycling. Also motivational and self-improvement type videos and film ideas to be produced. These could cover all ages '6-60' and from professional to blue collar jobs. These two areas should be 30 minutes and be timeless in approach for long shelf life. Sports audience, age 25-45; home improvement, 25-65. Cable TV needs include the two groups of programming detailed here. We are also looking for documentary work on current issues, nuclear power, solar power, urban development, senior citizens—but with a new approach." Query or submit synopsis/outline and résumé. Pays by contractual agreement.
Tips: "I am looking for innovative approaches to old problems that just don't go away. The approach should be simple and direct so there is immediate audience identification with the presentation. I also like to see

a sense of humor used. Trends in the audiovisual field include interactive video with disk—for training purposes."

ADVANTAGE MEDIA INC., 22226 Devonshire St., Chatsworth CA 91311. (818)700-0504. Fax: (818)700-0612. Vice President: Susan Cherno. Estab. 1983. Audience is "all employees, including supervisory and management staff; generic audiences; medium-large companies, educational institutions, government, healthcare, insurance, financial." Works with 1-2 writers/year. Buys exclusive rights for distribution. Accepts previously produced material (exclusive distribution only). Reports in 1 month on queries. Catalog free. Submit synopsis/outline, completed script or résumé. Usually pays flat fee for writing; negotiable by project.
Needs: Videotapes. "Generic settings, rainbow mix of characters. Topics: change, motivation, diversity, quality, safety, customer service. 20 minutes maximum. Documentary if points are clear or skill-building 'how to'. Must make a point for teaching purposes."
Tips: "Training programs must appeal to a diverse audience but be 'TV quality'. They must teach, as well as be somewhat entertaining. Must hold interest. Should present the problem, but solve it and not leave the audience hanging or to solve it themsvles. Must stay realistic, believable and be fast-paced. I think there will be a need for even more types of video-based materials for a growing need for training within organizations."

A/V CONCEPTS CORP., 30 Montauk Blvd., Oakdale NY 11769-1399. (516)567-7227. Fax: (516)567-8745. Contact: P. Solimene or L. Solimene. Produces material for elementary-high school students, either on grade level or in remedial situations. Estab. 1971. 100% freelance written. Buys 25 scripts/year from unpublished/unproduced writers. Employs video, book and personal computer media. Reports in 1 month on outline, 6 weeks on final scripts. Buys all rights. Sample copy for 9×12 SAE with 5 first-class stamps.
Needs: Interested in original educational computer (disk-based) software programs for Apple II family, IBM, Macintosh. Main concentration in language arts, mathematics and reading. "Manuscripts must be written using our lists of vocabulary words and meet our readability formula requirements. Specific guidelines are devised for each level. Length of manuscript and subjects will vary according to grade level for which material is prepared. Basically, we want material that will motivate people to read." Pays $300 and up.
Tips: "Writers must be highly creative and highly disciplined. We are interested in high interest/low readability materials."

SAM BLATE ASSOCIATES, 10331 Watkins Mill Dr., Gaithersburg MD 20879-2935. (301)840-2248. Fax: (301)990-0707. E-mail: samblate@aol.com. President: Sam Blate. Produces audiovisual and educational material for business, education, institutions, state and federal governments. "We work with 2 *local* writers per year on a per project basis—it varies as to business conditions and demand." Buys first rights when possible. Reports in 1 month. SASE for return.
Needs: Scripts on technical and outdoor subjects. Query with samples and SASE for return. Payment "depends on type of contract with principal client." Pays some expenses of writers on assignment.
Tips: "Writers must have a strong track record of technical and aesthetic excellence. Clarity and accuracy are not next to divinity—they are above it."

BOSUSTOW MEDIA GROUP, 20326 Ruston Rd., Woodland Hills CA 91364-6208. (818)999-5929. Owner: Tee Bosustow. Estab. 1983. Produces material for corporate, TV and home video clients. Reports in 2 weeks on queries.
Needs: Tapes, cassettes, videotapes. "Unfortunately, no one style, etc., exists. We produce a variety of products, a good deal of it children's programming." Submit synopsis/outline and résumé only. Pays agreed-upon fee.

CAMBRIDGE EDUCATIONAL, 90 MacCorkle Ave. SW, South Charleston WV 25303. Production Staff: Charlotte Angel. Estab. 1983. Audience is junior high/high schools, vocational schools, libraries, guidance centers. Buys 18-24 scripts/year. Works with 12-18 writers/year. Buys all rights. "Samples are kept for file reference." Reports only if interested. Free catalog. Query with synopsis, résumé or writing sample ("excerpt from a previous script, preferably"). Makes outright purchase of $2,000-4,000.
Needs: Videotapes. Educational programming suitable for junior high and high school age groups (classroom viewing and library reference). "Programs range from 20-35-minutes in length. Each should have a fresh approach for how-tos, awareness, and introductions to various subject matters. Subjects range from guidance, home economics, parenting, health, and vocational to social studies, science and business."
Tips: "We are looking for a new slant on some standard educational topics, as well as more contemporary issues. Currently focusing on science and social studies. We have also started producing CD-ROM and may need script developers for these projects."

‡THE CARRONADE GROUP, P.O. Box 36157, Los Angeles CA 90036. Also: 2355 Francisco St., Suite 6, San Francisco CA 91436. Fax: (213)939-6705. E-mail: samsel@infomedia.com. Website: http://www.carronade.com. Editor/Publisher: Jon Samsel.Estab. 1993. Produces books and online episodic serials in the fields of interactive multimedia, entertainment industry, digital media, computer software and sci-fi.

Works with 5-10 writers/year. Buys first rights, all rights and book rights. Accepts previously produced material. Reports in 1 month on queries; 2 months on submissions. Catalog for #10 SASE. Query with résumé. Royalty varies on project-to-project basis.

Needs: "Looking for unpublished manuscripts profiling the interactive multimedia field, entertainment industry. Also 'How-To' books on same subject."

CONTINENTAL FILM PRODUCTIONS CORPORATION, P.O. Box 5126, 4220 Amnicola Hwy., Chattanooga TN 37406. (423)622-1193. Fax: (423)629-0853. President: James L. Webster. Estab. 1951. Produces "AV and video presentations for businesses and nonprofit organizations for sales, training, public relations, documentation, motivation, etc." Works with many writers annually. Buys all rights. Unsolicited submissions not returned. Reports in 1 week.

Needs: "We do need new writers of various types. Please contact us by mail with samples and résumé." Produces slides, motion pictures, multi-image presentations, interactive programs and videos. Query with samples and résumé. Makes outright purchase of $250 minimum.

Tips: Looks for writers whose work shows technical understanding, humor, common sense, practicality, simplicity, creativity, etc. Important for writers to adapt script to available production budget. Suggests writers increase use of humor in training films. Also seeking scripts on human behavior in industry.

CRM FILMS, 1801 Avenue of the Stars, #715, Los Angeles CA 90067-5802. Fax: (310)789-5392. E-mail: 70206.454@compuserve.com. Creative Director: Kirby Timmons. Estab. 1960. Material for business and organizational training departments. Buys 2-4 scripts/year. Works with 6-8 writers/year. Buys all rights and interactive training rights. No previously produced material. Reports in 1 month. Catalog for 10×13 SAE with 4 first-class stamps. Query with résumé and script sample of writer's work in informational or training media. Makes outright purchase of $4,000-7,000, or in accordance with Writers Guild standard. "We accept WGA standard one-page informational/interactive agreement which stipulates *no* minimum but qualifies writer for pension and health coverage."

Needs: Videotapes, multimedia kits. "CRM is looking for short (10-20 minute) scripts on management topics such as communication, decision making, team building and customer service. No 'talking heads,' prefer drama-based, awareness approach as opposed to 'how-to' style, but will on occasion produce either."

Tips: "Know the *specific* training need which your idea or script fulfills! Total quality management will influence product line for forseeable future—learn about 'TQM' before submitting. Recent successes relate real-life events as basis for organizational or team learning—The Challenger incident to illustrate how group-think can negatively impact team decisions, for example. Other titles document the challenges of the 'New Workplace,' change and empowerment."

EFFECTIVE COMMUNICATION ARTS, INC., P.O. Box 250, Wilton CT 06897-0250. (203)761-8787. (203)761-0568. President: David Jacobson. Estab. 1965. Produces films, videotapes and interactive materials. Has produced more than 75 video based interactive multimedia programs for physician, nurse and health care audiences. In addition, produces corporate training and marketing materials. Prefers to work with writers. 80% freelance written. Buys approximately 12 scripts/year. Buys all rights. Reports in 1 month.

Needs: Multimedia kits, television shows/series, videotape presentations, interactive CD-ROM MPEG multimedia. Currently producing both custom and generic interactive programs. Submit interactive design, script and résumé. Makes outright purchase. Pays expenses of writers on assignment.

Tips: "Interactive design skills are increasingly important."

THE FILM HOUSE INC., 130 E. Sixth St., Cincinnati OH 45202. (513)381-2211. President: Ken Williamson. Estab. 1973. Audience is corporate communications and television commercials. Buys 5 scripts/year. Works with 3 writers/year. Buys all rights. No previously published material. Reoprts in 1 month on queries. Query with résumé.

Needs: Films, videotapes. Corporate, training and new product video. Writing assignments on a project basis only.

Tips: "We hire only seasonal, experienced writers on a freelance, per project basis. If interested send only a résumé."

HAYES SCHOOL PUBLISHING CO., INC., 321 Pennwood Ave., Wilkinsburg PA 15221-3398. (412)371-2373. Fax: (412)371-6408. President: Clair N. Hayes III. Estab. 1940. Produces material for school teachers and principals, elementary through high school. Also produces charts, workbooks, teacher's handbooks, posters, bulletin board material and reproducible blackline masters (grades K-12). 25% freelance written. Prefers to work with published/established writers. Buys 5-10 scripts/year from unpublished/unproduced writers. 100% of scripts produced are unagented submissions. Buys all rights. Reports in 3 months. Catalog for SAE with 3 first-class stamps. Writer's guidelines for #10 SAE with 2 first-class stamps.

Needs: Educational material only. Particularly interested in foreign language material and educational material for elementary school level. Query. Pays $25 minimum.

INFORMEDIA®, P.O. Box 13287, Austin TX 78711-3287. Contact: M. Sidoric. Estab. 1970. Audience is corporate sales/marketing meetings, general professional audiences, client-specific presentations. Buys 3-4 scripts/year. Works with 5-6 writers/year. Buys all rights, but will negotiate. No previously published material. Reports in 1 month. Query with résumé and samples. Makes outright purchase of $1,500.

Needs: Videotapes, multimedia kits, slides. AV modules 5-10 minutes in length; usually client specific in nature. Show openers—grand—bold. Topics: innovation/technology/teamwork.

Tips: Sees less emphasis on staid productions. Solid, selling information in memorable format. Has need for strong communication skills—in AV-writing for the *Ear & Imagination*; Innovative solutions for putting inspiration into staid sales presentations.

JIST WORKS, INC., 720 N. Park Ave., Indianapolis IN 46202. (317)264-3767. Fax: (317)264-3709. E-mail: jist@iquest.net. Video Production Manager: Jeff Heck. Estab. 1981. Produces career counseling, motivational materials (youth to adult) that encourage good planning and decision making for a successful future. Buys 7-10 scripts/year. Works with 2-3 writers/year. Buys all rights. Accepts previously produced material. Reports in 2 months. Catalog free. Query with synopsis. Makes outright purchase of $500 minimum.

Needs: Videotapes, multimedia kits. 15-30 minute video VHS tapes on job search materials and related markets.

Reprints: "We pay a royalty on finished video productions. We repackage, market, duplicate and take care of all other expenses when we acquire existing programs. Average sell price is $139. Producer gets a percentage of this and is not charged for any costs. Contact us, in writing, for details."

‡MIRIMAR ENTERPRISES, P.O. Box 4621, North Hollywood CA 91617-4621. (818)784-4177. Fax: (818)990-3439. CEO: Mirk Mirkin. Estab. 1967. "Audience is varied, sophisticated and intelligent." Buys 2-3 scripts/year. Buys all rights or first rights (in some cases). Accepts previously published material (in rare cases). Reports in 1 month on queries; 2 months on submissions.

Needs: Slides, tapes and cassettes, videotapes. "We are seeking travel topics—particularly exotic, rarely visited places. First person, indepth experiences, with some visuals to show them *in situ*." Query with synopsis and résumé. Pays in accordance with Writers Guild standards.

Tips: "Be honest in your approach. Don't be over-flowery in language unless you can back it up. Writers should express themselves in a down-to-earth manner. Not raw or crude, but in graphic terms that are real."

MOTIVATION MEDIA, INC., 1245 Milwaukee Ave., Glenview IL 60025-2499. (847)297-4740. Fax: (847)297-6829. Website: http://www.motivationmedia.com. Senior Creative Director: Kevin Kivikko. Produces customized meeting, training and marketing material for presentation to salespeople, customers, shareholders, corporate/industrial employees and distributors. 90% freelance written. Buys 50 scripts/year. Prefers to work with published/established writers. All scripts produced are unagented submissions. Buys all rights. Reports in 1 month.

Needs: Material for all audiovisual media—particularly marketing-oriented (sales training, sales promotional, sales motivational) material. Produces sales meeting programs, videotapes, print collateral, audio programs and interactive multimedia. Software should be AV oriented. Query with samples and résumé. Pays $150-5,000. Pays the expenses of writers on assignment.

OMNI PRODUCTIONS, P.O. Box 302, Carmel IN 46032-0302. (317)844-6664. Vice President: Dr. Sandra M. Long. Estab. 1976. Produces commercial, training, educational and documentary material. Buys all rights.

Needs: Educational, documentary, commercial, training, motivational. Produces slides, video shows, multi-image, videotapes. Query. Makes outright purchase.

Tips: "Must have experience as writer and have examples of work. Examples need to include print copy and finished copy of videotape if possible. A résumé with educational background, general work experience and experience as a writer must be included. Especially interested in documentary-style writing. Writers' payment varies, depending on amount of research needed, complexity of project, length of production and other factors."

‡ONE ON ONE COMPUTER TRAINING, Division of Mosaic Media, Inc., 2055 Army Trail Rd., Suite 100, Addison IL 60101-9961. (708)628-0500. Fax: (708)628-0550. Publisher: F. Lee McFadden. Contact: Natalie Young. Estab. 1976. Produces training courses for microcomputers and business software. Works with a small number of new/unpublished writers each year. 90% freelance written. Buys 3-5 courses/year. 100% of courses published are unagented submissions. Works with 3-7 writers/year. Buys all rights. Reports in 3 weeks. Free product literature. Sample copy for 9×12 SAE.

Needs: Training courses on how to use personal computers/software, primarily audio geared to the adult student in a business setting and usually to the beginning/intermediate user; also some courses at advanced levels. Primarily audio, also some reference manuals, other training formats for personal computers considered. Query with résumé and samples if available. Pays negotiable royalty or makes outright purchase.

Tips: "We prefer to work with Chicago-area writers with strong teaching/training backgrounds and experience with microcomputers. Writers from other regions are also welcome."

PALARDO PRODUCTIONS, 1807 Taft Ave., Suite 4, Hollywood CA 90028. Phone/fax: (213)469-8991. Director: Paul Ardolino. Estab. 1971. Produces material for youth ages 13-35. Buys 3-4 scripts/year. Buys all rights. Reports in 2 weeks on queries; 1 month on scripts.
Needs: Multimedia kits, tapes and cassettes, videotapes. "We are seeking ideas relating to virtual reality, comedy scripts involving technology and coming of age; rock'n'roll bios." Submit synopsis/outline and résumé. Pays in accordance with Writers Guild standards.
Tips: "Do not send a complete script—only synopsis of four pages or less *first.*"

PHOTO COMMUNICATION SERVICES, INC., 6055 Robert Dr., Traverse City MI 49684. (616)943-8800. President: M'Lynn Hartwell. Produces commercial, industrial, sales, training material etc. 95% freelance written. No scripts from unpublished/unproduced writers. 100% of scripts produced are unagented submissions. Buys all rights and first serial rights. Reports in 1 month.
Needs: Multimedia kits, slides, tapes and cassettes, video presentations. Primarily interested in 35mm multimedia and video. Query with samples or submit completed script and résumé. Pays by agreement.

‡CHARLES RAPP ENTERPRISES, INC., 1650 Broadway, New York NY 10019. (212)247-6646. President: Howard Rapp. Estab. 1954. Produces materials for firms and buyers. Works with 5 writers/year. "Work as personal manager/agent in sales." Accepts previously produced material. Reports in 1 month on queries; 2 months on submissions. Submit résumé or sample of writing. Pays in accordance with Writers Guild standards.
Needs: Videotapes, treatments, scripts.

ROUSER COMPANY PRESENTATION RESOURCES, 208 W. Magnolia Ave., Knoxville TN 37917. General Manager: Martin Rouser. Estab. 1932. Audience is corporate dealer network, end users. Buys 3 scripts/year. Works with 2 writers/year. Buys first rights. Accepts previously produced material. Reports in 1 month on queries and submissions. Query. Makes outright purchase.
Needs: Charts, videotapes, filmstrips (silent and sound), overhead transparencies, slides, tapes and cassettes. Corporate meeting opener multi-image module for the marine industry.

PATRICIA RUST PRODUCTIONS, 12021 Wilshire Blvd., Suite 924, Los Angeles CA 90025. President: Patricia Rust. Estab. 1984. "Company spans poetry publication to children's to humor. While it encompasses a wide range, it is highly selective and tries to be visionary and ahead of the pack in scope, originality and execution." Buys variable rights depending on the situation and goals. Reports in 2 months on queries. Query. "Our production includes publishing, audio-video and theatrical and each project is carefully conceived and executed to influence and entertain in a meaningful way. Our standards are extremely high with regard to quality, message and meaning."
Needs: Film loops, films, videotapes, tapes and cassettes.
Tips: "While we are in the business of entertainment, we look for projects that provide answers and elevate thinking. We work with only top industry professionals and strive to represent quality and commerciality."

SPENCER PRODUCTIONS, INC., 234 Fifth Ave., New York NY 10001. (212)865-8829. General Manager: Bruce Spencer. Executive Producer: Alan Abel. Produces material for high school students, college students and adults. Occasionally uses freelance writers with considerable talent. Reports in 1 month.
Needs: Prerecorded tapes and cassettes. Satirical material only. Query. Pay is negotiable.

STIEGLER GROUP, INC., 148 Patty Bowker, Tabernacle NJ 08088. Fax: (609)268-2255. President: Gary Stiegler. Estab. 1991. Audience is corporate/broadcast. Buys 6-8 scripts/year. Works with 2-3 writers/year. Buys all rights. No previously produced material. Makes outright purchase of $500-5,000.
Needs: Videotapes. Aviation, travel, environmental, corporate promotions.

TALCO PRODUCTIONS, 279 E. 44th St., New York NY 10017-4354. (212)697-4015. Fax: (212)697-4827. President: Alan Lawrence. Vice President: Marty Holberton. Estab. 1968. Produces variety of material for TV, radio, business, trade associations, nonprofit organizations, public relations (chiefly political and current events), etc. Audiences range from young children to senior citizens. 20-40% freelance written. Buys scripts from published/produced writers only. Buys all rights. No previously published material. Reports in 3 weeks on queries. *Does not accept unsolicited mss.*
• Talco reports that it is doing more public relations oriented work: print, videotape and radio.
Needs: Films (16, 35mm), slides, radio tapes and cassettes, videotape. "We maintain a file of writers and call on those with experience in the same general category as the project in production. We do not accept unsolicited manuscripts. We prefer to receive a writer's résumé listing credits. If his/her background merits, we will be in touch when a project seems right." Makes outright purchase/project and in accordance with Writers Guild standards (when appropriate). Sometimes pays the expenses of writers on assignment.
Tips: "Concentration is now in TV productions. Production budgets will be tighter."

ED TAR ASSOCIATES, INC., 230 Venice Way, Venice CA 90291. (310)306-2195. Fax: (310)306-0654. Estab. 1972. Audience is dealers, salespeople, public. Buys all rights. No previously produced material. Makes outright purchase.
Needs: Films (16, 35mm), videotapes, slides, tapes, business theater and live shows, TV infomercials. "We are constantly looking for *experienced* writers of corporate, product and live show scripts. Send résumé and samples."

TEL-AIR INTERESTS, INC., 1755 NE 149th St., Miami FL 33181. (305)944-3268. Fax: (305)944-1143. President: Grant H. Gravitt. Produces material for groups and theatrical and TV audiences. Buys all rights. Submit résumé.
Needs: Documentary films on education, travel and sports. Produces films and videotape. Makes outright purchase.

‡TROLL ASSOCIATES, 100 Corporate Dr., Mahwah NJ 07430. (201)529-4000. Contact: M. Schecter. Produces material for elementary and high school students. Buys approximately 200 scripts/year. Buys all rights. Reports in 3 weeks. Free catalog.
Needs: Produces multimedia kits, tapes and cassettes, and (mainly) books. Query or submit outline/synopsis. Pays royalty or makes outright purchase.

ULTITECH, INC., Foot of Broad St., Stratford CT 06497. (203)375-7300. Fax/BBS: (203)375-6699. E-mail: comcowic@meds.com. Website: http://www.meds.com. Estab. 1993. Designs, develops and produces online services and interactive communications programs including video, multimedia, expert systems, software tools, computer-based training and audience response meetings. Specializes in medicine, science and technology. Prefers to work with published/established writers with video, multimedia and medical experience. 90% freelance written. Buys writing for approximately 15-20 programs/year. Electronic submissions onto BBS. Buys all rights. Reports in 1 month.
Needs: Currently producing about 10 interactive programs for medical audiences. Submit résumé and complete script. Makes outright purchase. Pays expenses of writers on assignment.
Tips: "Interactive media for learning and entertainment is a growing outlet for writers—acquiring skills for interactive design and development will pay back in assignments."

VISUAL HORIZONS, 180 Metro Park, Rochester NY 14623. (716)424-5300. Fax: (716)424-5313. E-mail: 73730.2512@compuserve.com. President: Stanley Feingold. Produces material for general audiences. Buys 5 programs/year. Reports in 5 months. Free 64-page catalog.
Needs: Business, medical and general subjects. Produces silent and sound filmstrips, multimedia kits, slide sets, videotapes. Query with samples. Payment negotiable.

WILLOW ASSOCIATES, 4061 Glendenning Rd., Downers Grove IL 60515-2228. (708)969-1982. Principal: William H. Holt, Jr. Estab. 1988. Audience is corporate communications. Buys 1 script/year. Works with 4 writers/year. Submissions not returned. Reports in 2 months on queries and submissions. Query.
Needs: Films (16mm), videotapes, slides, tapes and cassettes. Short, corporate communications, training topics.

PLAYWRITING

TV and movies are visual media where the words are often less important than the images. Writing plays uses different muscles, different techniques. Plays are built on character and dialogue—words put together to explore and examine characters.

The written word is respected in the theater by producer, cast, director and even audience, to a degree unparalleled in other formats. While any work involving so many people to reach its final form is in essence a collaboration, it is presided over by the playwright and changes can be made only with her approval, a power many screenwriters can only envy. If a play is worth producing, it will be produced "as is."

Counterbalancing the greater freedom of expression are the physical limitations inherent in live performance: a single stage, smaller cast, limited sets and lighting and, most importantly, a strict, smaller budget. These conditions affect not only what but also how you write.

Start writing your play by reading. Your local library has play anthologies. Check the listings in this section for play publishers such as Aran Press, Baker's Plays and Samuel French. Reading gives you a feel for how characters are built, layer by layer, word by word, how each interaction presents another facet of a character. Exposition must mean something to the character, and the story must be worth telling for a play to be successful.

There are plenty of books, seminars and workshops to help you with the writing of your play. The development of character, setting, dialogue and plot are skills that will improve with each draft. The specific play format is demonstrated in *The Complete Book of Script Formats*, by Cole and Haig and *The Writer's Digest Book of Manuscript Formats*, by Buchman and Groves.

Once the final draft of your play is finished you begin marketing it, which can take as long (or longer) than writing it. Before you begin you must have your script bound (three brads and a cover are fine) and copyrighted at the Copyright Office of the Library of Congress or registered with the Writers Guild of America. Write either agency and ask for information and an application.

Your first goal will be to get at least a reading of your play. You might be lucky and get a small production. Community theaters or smaller regional houses are good places to start. Volunteer at a local theater. As prop mistress or spotlight operator you will get a sense of how a theater operates, the various elements of presenting a play and what can and cannot be done, physically as well as dramatically. Personal contacts are important. Get to know the literary manager or artistic director of local theaters, which is the best way to get your script considered for production. Find out about any playwrights' groups in your area through local theaters or the drama departments of nearby colleges and universities. Use your creativity to connect with people that might be able to push your work higher.

Contests can be a good way to get noticed. Many playwriting contests offer as a prize at least a staged reading and often a full production. Once you've had a reading or workshop production, set your sights on a small production. Use this as a learning experience. Seeing your play on stage can help you view it more objectively and give you the chance to correct any flaws or inconsistencies. Incorporate any comments and ideas from the actors, director or even audience that you feel are on the mark into revisions of your script.

Use a small production also as a marketing tool. Keep track of all the press reviews, any interviews with you, members of the cast or production and put together a "press kit" for your play that can make the rounds with the script.

After you've been produced you have several directions to take your play. You can aim for a larger commercial production; you can try to get it published; you can seek artistic grants. After you have successfully pursued at least one of those avenues you can look for an agent. Choosing one direction does not rule out pursuing others at the same time. *The Dramatists Sourcebook*, published annually by Theatre Communications Group (355 Lexington Ave., New York NY 10017) lists opportunities in all these areas. The Dramatists Guild (234 W. 45th St., New York NY 10036) has three helpful publications: a bimonthly newsletter with articles, news and up-to-date information and opportunities, a quarterly journal, and an annual directory, a resource book for playwrights listing theaters, agents, workshops, grants, contests, etc.

Good reviews in a smaller production can get you noticed by larger theaters paying higher royalties and doing more ambitious productions. To submit your play to larger theaters you'll put together a submission package. This will include a one-page query letter to the literary manager or dramaturg briefly describing the play. Mention any reviews and give the number of cast members and sets. You will also send a two- to three-page synopsis, a ten-page sample of the most interesting section of your play, your résumé and the press kit you've assembled. Do not send your complete manuscript until it is requested.

You can also explore publishing your play. *Writer's Market* lists many play publishers. When your script is published your play will make money while someone else does the marketing. You'll be listed in a catalog that is sent out to hundreds or thousands of potential performance spaces—high schools, experimental companies, regional and community theaters—for possible production. You'll receive royalty checks for both performance fees and book sales. In contacting publishers you'll want to send your query letter with the synopsis and reviews.

There are several sources for grants. Some are federal or state, but don't overlook sources closer to home. The category "Arts Councils and Foundations" in Contests and Awards in this book lists a number of sources. On the national level contact the NEA Theater Program Fellowship for Playwrights (1100 Pennsylvania Ave. NW, Washington DC 20506). State arts commissions are another possible source, and also offer opportunities for involvement in programs where you can meet fellow playwrights. Some cities have arts and cultural commissions that offer grants for local artists. PEN publishes a comprehensive annual book, *Grants and Awards Available to American Writers* that also includes a section for Canadian writers. The latest edition is available from the PEN American Center (568 Broadway, New York NY 10012).

Once you have been produced on a commercial level, your play has been published or you have won an important grant, you can start pursuing an agent. This is not always easy. Fewer agents represent playwrights alone—there's more money in movies and TV. No agent will represent an unknown playwright. Having an agent does *not* mean you can sit back and enjoy the ride. You will still need to get out there and network, establishing ties with theaters, directors, literary managers, other writers, producers, state art agencies and publishers, trying to get your work noticed. What it does mean is that you'll have some help. A good agent will have personal contacts that can place your work for consideration at a higher level than your efforts alone might.

There is always the possibility of moving from plays to TV and movies. There is a certain cachet in Hollywood surrounding successful playwrights. The writing style will be different—more visually oriented, less dependent on your words. The money is better, but you will have less command over the work once you've sold that copyright. It seems to be easier for a playwright to cross over to movies than for a screenwriter to cross over to plays.

Writing a script can make you feel isolated, even when your characters are so real to you they seem to be in the room as you write. Sometimes the experience and companionship of other playwrights is what you need to get you over a particular hurdle in your play. Membership and service organizations such as The Dramatists Guild, The International Women's Writing Guild and local groups such as the Playwright's Center in Minneapolis and the Northwest Playwright's Guild in Seattle can help you feel still a part of this world as you are off creating your own.

For information on some playwriting markets not listed in *Writer's Market*, see the General Index.

ACTORS' STOCK COMPANY, 3884 Van Ness Lane, Dallas TX 75220. (214)353-9916. Artistic Director: Keith Oncale. Estab. 1988. Produces 3-4 plays/year. "We stage semi-professional productions to a young adult to middle-aged general audience." Query with synopsis. Reports in 3 months. Purchases reading privileges. Pays royalty.
  • Actors Stock Company reports that two scripts by *Writer's Market* readers have received staged readings, one of which also had a full production.
Needs: Two- and three-act plays, covering a wide variety of styles, but with fewer than 12 cast members. Average staging facilities are 100-seat houses or smaller.
Tips: "Trends today reflect a return to comic realism that comments on our society without commenting on the play itself."

ACTORS THEATRE OF LOUISVILLE, 316 W. Main St., Louisville KY 40202-4218. (502)584-1265. Producing Director: Jon Jory. Estab. 1964. Produces approximately 20 new plays of varying lengths/year.

Professional productions are performed for subscription audience from diverse backgrounds. Agented submissions only for full-length plays; open submissions to National Ten-Minute Play Contest (plays 10 pages or less). Reports in 9 months on submissions, mostly in the fall. Buys variable rights. Offers variable royalty.
Needs: "We are interested in full-length, one-act and ten-minute plays and in plays of ideas, language, humor, experiment and passion."

ALABAMA SHAKESPEARE FESTIVAL, 1 Festival Dr., Montgomery AL 36117-4605. Website: http://www.wsnet.com/~pr4bard/asf.html. Artistic Director: Kent Thompson. Produces 14 plays/year. Inhouse productions, general audience, children audience. Reports in 10 months. Pays royalty.
Needs: "ASF develops works by Southern writers, works that deal with the South and/or African-American themes, works that deal with Southern and/or African-American history."

ALLEYWAY THEATRE, 1 Curtain Up Alley, Buffalo NY 14202-1911. Dramaturg: Joyce Stilson. Estab. 1980, competition 1990. Produces 4 full-length, 10-15 short plays/year. Submit complete ms. Reports in 6 months. Buys first production, credit rights. Pays 7% royalty plus travel and accommodations for opening.
• Alleyway Theatre also sponsors the Maxim Mazumdar New Play Competition. See the Contest & Awards section for more information.
Needs: "Theatrical" work as opposed to mainstream TV.
Tips: Sees a trend toward social issue-oriented works.

‡ALLIANCE THEATRE COMPANY, 1280 Peachtree St. NE, Atlanta GA 30309. (404)733-4650. Artistic Director: Kenny Leon. Estab. 1969. Produces 10 plays/year. Professional production for local audience. Query with synopsis or submit through agent. Reports in 6 months.
Needs: Full-length scripts only.

AMELIA MAGAZINE, 329 "E" St., Bakersfield CA 93304. (805)323-4064. Editor: Frederick A. Raborg, Jr. Estab. 1983. Publishes 1 play/year. Submit complete ms. Reports in 2 months. Buys first North American serial rights only. Pays $150 plus publication as winner of annual Frank McClure One-Act Play Award.
Needs: "Plays with virtually any theme or concept. We look for excellence within the one-act, 45 minutes running time format. We welcome the avant-garde and experimental. We do not object to the erotic, though not pornographic. Fewer plays are being produced on Broadway, but the regionals seem to be picking up the slack. That means fewer equity stages and more equity waivers."

‡AMERICAN STAGE FESTIVAL, P.O. Box 225, Milford NH 03055-0225. Fax: (603)889-2330. Website: http://www.americanstagefestival.com. Producing Director: Matthew Parent. Estab. 1975. "The ASF is a central New England LORT theater (professional equity company) with a 10-month season (March-December) for an audience of all ages, interests, education and sophistication levels." Query with synopsis. Produces 20% musicals, 80% nonmusicals. Nine are mainstage and ten are children's productions; 40% are originals. Royalty option and subsequent amount of gross: optional.
• This theater is looking for more comedies and musicals—works with broad appeal.
Needs: "The Festival can do comedies, musicals and dramas. However, the most frequent problems are bolder language and action than a general mixed audience will accept. Prefer not to produce plays with strictly urban themes. We have a 40-foot proscenium stage with 30-foot wings, but no fly system and a thrust, black-box theater. Length: mainstage: 2-3 acts; children's productions: 50 minutes. Cast: 8 or fewer.
Tips: "We've just opened a second performance space, a 277-seat thrust theater and expanded our season from a summer series only, to year-round theatre in 2 spaces."

AN CLAIDHEAMH SOLUIS/CELTIC ARTS CENTER, P.O. Box 861778, Los Angeles CA 90086-1778. (213)462-6844. Artistic Director: Sean Walsh. Estab. 1985. Produces 6 plays/year. Equity 99-seat plan. Query with synopsis. Reports in 6 months. Rights acquired vary. Pays $25-50.
Needs: Scripts of Celtic interest (Scottish, Welsh, Irish, Cornish, Manx, Breton). "This can apply to writer's background or subject matter. We are particularly concerned with works that relate to the survival of ethnic cultures and traditions, especially those in danger of extinction."

ARAN PRESS, 1320 S. Third St., Louisville KY 40208-2306. (502)636-0115. Fax: (502)634-8001. Editor/Publisher: Tom Eagan. Estab. 1983. Audience is professional, community, college, university, summer stock and dinner theaters. Query. Reports in 2 weeks on submissions. Contracts for publication and production rights. Pays 10% book royalty and 50% production royalty.
• Aran Press would like to see more comedies.
Tips: No children's plays. "Tip to writers of plays: don't. Write novels, nonfiction, whatever, but don't write plays. If you *must* write plays, and you can't get published by one of the other publishers, send us an inquiry. If you care for what we have to offer, welcome aboard."

ARDEN THEATRE COMPANY, 40 N. 2nd St., Philadelphia PA 19106. (215)829-8900. Website: http://www.libertynet.org/~arden. Artistic Directors: Terrence J. Arden, Aaron Pogner. Estab. 1988. Produces 5 plays/year. Query with synopsis. Reports in 6 months. Pays 5% royalty.

Needs: Full-length, adaptations and musicals. Flexible in terms of cast size.

ART CRAFT PUBLISHING CO., 233 Dows Bldg., Box 1058, Cedar Rapids IA 52406-1058. (319)364-6311. Fax: (319)364-1771. Publisher: C. Emmett McMullen. Estab. 1928. Publishes plays and musicals for the junior and senior high school market. Query with synopsis or submit complete script. Reports in 2 months. Purchases amateur rights only. Makes outright purchase or pays royalty.
Needs: "Our current need is for full-length productions, two- and three-act plays and musicals, preferably comedy or mystery-comedy with a large number of characters. We sell almost exclusively to junior and smaller senior high school groups, thus we are unable to publish material that may contain controversial or offensive subject matter."

ARTREACH TOURING THEATRE, 3074 Madison Rd., Cincinnati OH 45209. (513)871-2300. Fax: (513)871-2501. Director: Kathryn Schultz Miller. Produces 6 plays/year to be performed nationally in theaters and schools. "We are a professional company. Our audience is primarily young people in schools and their families." Submit complete ms. Reports in 5 months. Buys exclusive right to produce for 9 months. Pays $10/show (approximately 1,000 total performances through the year).
Needs: Plays for children and adolescents. Serious, intelligent plays about contemporary life or history/legend. "Limited sets and props. Scripts must use only 3 actors, 45 minutes long. Should be appropriate for touring." No clichéd approaches, camp or musicals.
Tips: "We look for opportunities to create innovative stage effects using few props, and we like scripts with good acting opportunities."

BAILIWICK REPERTORY, 1229 W. Belmont Ave., Chicago IL 60657-3205. (312)883-1090. Contact: Cecilia D. Keenan, artistic director. Executive Director: David Zak. Estab. 1982. Produces 5 mainstage plays (classic and newly commissioned) each year (submit by November 1); 5 new full-length in New Directions series; 50 1-acts in annual Directors Festival (submit by December 1); pride performance series (gay and lesbian plays, poetry), includes one acts, poetry, workshops, and staged adaptations of prose. Submit year-round. "Our audience is a typical Chicago market. Our plays are highly theatrical and politically aware." One acts should be submitted *before* April 1. (One-act play fest runs August-September). Reports in 3 months. Pays 6% royalty.
Needs: We need daring scripts that break the mold. Large cast or musicals are OK. Creative staging solutions are a must.
Tips: "Know the rules, then break them creatively and *boldly*! *Please send SASE for manuscript submission guidelines before you submit.*"

BARTER THEATRE, P.O. Box 867, Abingdon VA 24212-0867. (540)628-2281. Fax: (540)628-4551. Artistic Director: Richard Rose. Estab. 1933. Produces 14 plays/year. Play performed in residency at 2 facilities, a 500-seat proscenium theater and a smaller 150-seat flexible theater. "Our plays are intended for diversified audiences of all ages." Submit synopsis and dialogue sample only to: Richard Rose, artistic director. Reports in 6 months. Royalty negotiable.
  ● Barter Theatre has premiered eight new works over the past several years. One of the premieres was optioned for Broadway for the 1995-96 season. (Also looking for freelance publication and PR writers for feature articles.)
Needs: "We are looking for good plays, comedies and dramas, that entertain and are relevant; plays that comment on the times and mankind; plays are universal. We prefer casts of 4-12, single or unit set. Hard language can be a factor."

‡**BAY STREET THEATRE**, P.O. Box 810, Sag Harbor NY 11963. (516)725-0818. Co-Artistic Directors: Sybil Christopher, Emma Walton. Estab. 1991. Produces 4 plays/year. Performances held at the Bay Street Theatre—a 299-seat LORT-D/LOA professional theater in Sag Harbor, New York. The audience is a combination of year-round residents and New Yorkers with weekend/vacation homes. (Adults only). Agented submissions only.
Needs: Wants full-length new and contemporary classics and small musicals—comedies and dramas. Eight member casts maximum—one set preferred.

BILINGUAL FOUNDATION OF THE ARTS, 421 North Ave., #19, Los Angeles CA 90031. (213)225-4044. Fax: (213)225-1250. Artistic Director: Margarita Galban. Dramaturg/Literary Manager: Guillermo Reyes. Estab. 1973. Produces 3-5 plays plus 9-10 staged readings/year. "Productions are presented at home theater in Los Angeles, California. Our audiences are largely Hispanic and all productions are performed in English and Spanish. The Bilingual Foundation of the Arts produces plays in order to promote the rich heritage of Hispanic history and culture. Though our plays must be Hispanic in theme, we reach out to the entire community." Submit complete script. Reports in 6 months. Rights negotiable. Pays royalty.
Needs: "Plays must be Hispanic in theme. Comedy, drama, light musical, children's theater, etc., are accepted for consideration. More plays in Spanish are needed. Theater is 99-seater, no flies."

BOARSHEAD THEATER, 425 S. Grand Ave., Lansing MI 48933. (517)484-7800. Artistic Director: John Peakes. Estab. 1966. Produces 8 plays/year (6 mainstage, 2 young peoples theater productions inhouse). Mainstage Actors' Equity Association company; also Youth Theater—touring to schools by our intern company. Query with synopsis, cast list (with descriptions), 5-10 pages of representative dialogue, SASE. Reports on query and synopsis in 1 week. Full scripts (when requested) in 8 months. Pays royalty.
Needs: Thrust stage. Cast usually 8 or less; ocassionally up to 12-14. Prefer staging which depends on theatricality rather than multiple sets. Send plays re Young People's Theater % Education Director. No musicals considered. One acts only for Young People's Theater.

CALIFORNIA THEATER CENTER, P.O. Box 2007, Sunnyvale CA 94087. (408)245-2978. Fax: (408)245-0235. Literary Manager: Will Huddleston. Estab. 1976. Produces 15 plays/year. "Plays are for young audiences in both our home theater and for tour." Query with synopsis. Reports in 6 months. Negotiates set fee.
Needs: All plays must be suitable for young audiences, must be around 1 hour in length. Cast sizes vary. Many shows require touring sets.

CENTER STAGE, 700 N. Calvert St., Baltimore MD 21202-3686. (410)685-3200. Resident Dramaturg: James Magruder. Estab. 1963. Produces 6-8 plays/year. "LORT 'B' and LORT 'C' theaters; audience is both subscription and single-ticket. Wide-ranging audience profile." Query with synopsis, 10 sample pages and résumé, or submit through agent. Reports in 3 months. Rights and payment negotiated.
Needs: Produces dramas, comedies, musical theater works. No one-act plays. "Casts over 12 would give us pause. Be inventive, theatrical, not precious; we like plays with vigorous language and stage image. Domestic naturalism is discouraged; strong political or social interests are encouraged. Plays about bourgeois adultery, life in the suburbs, Amelia Earhart, Alzheimer's, midlife crises, 'wacky southerners', fear of intimacy, Hemingway, Bible stories, backstage life, are not acceptable, as are spoofs and mysteries."
Tips: "We are interested in reading adaptations and translations as well as original work."

CHARLOTTE REPERTORY THEATRE, 2040 Charlotte Plaza, Charlotte NC 28244. (704)375-4796. Fax: (704)375-9462. Literary Manager: Claudia Carter Covington. Literary Associate: Carol Bellamy. Estab. 1976. Produces 13 plays/year. "We are a not-for-profit regional theater." Submit complete script with SASE. Reports in 3 months. Writers receive free plane fare and housing for festival.
Needs: "Need full-length scripts not previously produced professionally. No limitations in cast, props, staging, etc. No children's plays or musicals"

CHICAGO PLAYS, 2632 N. Lincoln, Chicago IL 60614. (312)348-4658. President: Jill Murray. Publishes 35 titles/year. 75% of books from unagented writers. Pays royalty on retail price. No advance. Publishes book 6 months after acceptance of ms. Accepts simultaneous submissions. Reports in 6 months. Book catalog and ms guidelines free on request.
Needs: Humor. "We specialize in Chicago theater." Query.

CHILDREN'S STORY SCRIPTS, Baymax Productions, 2219 W. Olive Ave., Suite 130, Burbank CA 91506-2648. (818)563-6105. Fax: (818)563-2968. Editor: Deedra Bebout. Estab. 1990. "Our audience consists of children, grades K-8 (5-13-year-olds)." Send complete script with SASE. Reports in 1 month. Licenses all rights to story; author retains copyright. Pays graduated royalty based on sales.
Needs: "We are adding new titles now and will continue to do so as we find appropriate stories. We look for stories which are fun for kids to read, involve a number of readers throughout, and dovetail with school subjects."
Tips: "The scripts are not like theatrical scripts. They combine dialogue and prose narration, à la Readers Theatre. If a writer shows promise, we'll work with him. Our most important goal is to benefit children. We want stories that bring alive subjects studied in classrooms. Facts must be worked unobtrusively into the story—the story has to be fun for the kids to read. Send #10 SASE for guidelines with samples. We do not respond to submissions without SASE."

‡CHILDSPLAY, INC., P.O. Box 517, Tempe AZ 85280. (602)350-8101. Fax: (602)350-8584. Artistic Director: David P. Saar. Estab. 1978. Produces 5-6 plays/year. "Professional: Touring and in-house productions for youth and family audiences." Submit complete script. Reports in 6 months. "On commissioned work we hold a small percentage of royalties for 3-5 years." Pays royalty of $20-35/performance (touring) or pays $3,000-8,000 commission.
Needs: Seeking *theatrical* plays on a wide range of contemporary topics. Touring shows: 5-6 actors; van-size. Inhouse: 6-10 actors; no technical limitations.
Tips: No traditionally-handled fairy tales. "Theater for young people is growing up and is able to speak to youth and adults. The material *must* respect the artistry of the theater and the intelligence of our audience. Our most important goal is to benefit children. If you wish your manuscript returned send SASE."

CINCINNATI PLAYHOUSE IN THE PARK, Dept. WM, P.O. Box 6537, Cincinnati OH 45206-0537. (513)345-2242. Fax: (513)345-2254. E-mail: theater1@tso.cin.ix.net. Website: http://www.cincyplay.com.

Contact: Edward Stern, producing artistic director. Estab. 1960. Produces original works and previously produced plays. Nonprofit LORT theater, producing 11 plays/year in two spaces—a 629-seat thrust stage and a 220-seat three/sided arena. "The audience is a broad cross-section of people from all over the Ohio, Kentucky and Indiana areas, from varied educational and financial bases." Write for guidelines for Lois and Richard Rosenthal New Play Prize to submit previously unproduced, new plays for consideration.

CIRCUIT PLAYHOUSE/PLAYHOUSE ON THE SQUARE, 51 S. Cooper, Memphis TN 38104. (901)725-0776. Artistic Director: Jackie Nichols. Produces 16 plays/year. 100% freelance written. Professional plays performed for the Memphis/Mid-South area. Member of the Theatre Communications Group. 100% of scripts unagented submissions. Works with 1 unpublished/unproduced writer/year. Contest held each fall. Submit complete script. Reports in 6 months. Buys percentage of royalty rights for 2 years. Pays $500.

Needs: All types; limited to single or unit sets. Cast of 20 or fewer.

Tips: "Each play is read by three readers through the extended length of time a script is kept. Preference is given to scripts for the southeastern region of the US."

CITY THEATRE COMPANY, 57 S. 13th St., Pittsburgh PA 15203. Fax: (412)431-5535. Producing Director: Marc Masterson. Literary Manager: Gwen Orel. Produces 5 full productions/year. "We are a small professional theater, operating under an Equity contract, and committed to plays of ideas and substance relevant to contemporary American values and cultures. Our seasons are innovative and challenging, both artistically and socially. We perform in a 225-seat thrust or proscenium stage, playing usually seven times a week, each production running one month or more. We have a committed audience following." Query with synopsis or submit through agent. Obtains no rights. Pays 5-6% royalty. Reports in 6 months.

Needs: "No limits on style or subject, but we are most interested in theatrical plays that have something to say about the way we live. No light comedies or TV-issue dramas." Normal cast limit is 7. Plays must be appropriate for small space without flies.

Tips: "Our emphasis is on new and recent American plays."

I.E. CLARK PUBLICATIONS, P.O. Box 246, Schulenburg TX 78956-0246. (409)743-3232. Contact: Donna Cozzaglio. Estab. 1956. Publishes 15 plays/year for educational theater, children's theater, religious theater, regional professional theater and amateur community theater. 20% freelance written. Publishes 3-4 scripts/year, unagented submissions. Submit complete script, 1 at a time with SASE. Reports in 6 months. Buys all available rights; "We serve as an agency as well as a publisher." Pays standard book and performance royalty, amount and percentages dependent upon type and marketability of play. Catalog for $3. Writer's guidelines for #10 SASE.

Needs: "We are interested in plays of all types—short or long. Audiotapes of music or videotapes of a performance are requested with submissions of musicals. We require that a play has been produced (directed by someone other than the author); photos, videos, and reviews of the production are helpful. No limitations in cast, props, staging, etc. Plays with only one or two characters are difficult to sell. We insist on literary quality. We like plays that give new interpretations and understanding of human nature. Correct spelling, punctuation and grammar (befitting the characters, of course) impress our editors."

Tips: Publishes plays only. "Entertainment value and a sense of moral responsibility seem to be returning as essential qualities of a good play script. The era of glorifying the negative elements of society seems to be fading rapidly. Literary quality, entertainment value and good craftsmanship rank in that order as the characteristics of a good script in our opinion. 'Literary quality' means that the play must—in beautiful, distinctive, and un-trite language—say something; preferably something new and important concerning man's relations with his fellow man or God; and these 'lessons in living' must be presented in an intelligent, believable and creative manner. Plays for children's theater are tending more toward realism and childhood problems, but fantasy and dramatization of fairy tales are also needed."

COAST TO COAST THEATER COMPANY, P.O. Box 3855, Hollywood CA 90078. (818)782-1212. Fax: (818)782-1931. Artistic Director: Bryan W. Simon. Contact: Douglas Coler. Estab. 1989. Produces 2-3 plays/year. Equity and equity waiver theater. Query with synopsis. Responds if interested. Buys West Coast, Midwest or East Coast rights, depending on location of production. Pays 5% royalty, makes outright purchase of $100-250, or pays per performance.

Needs: Full-length off-beat comedies or dramas with small casts, simple sets.

MARKET CONDITIONS are constantly changing! If this is 1998 or later, buy the newest edition of *Writer's Market* at your favorite bookstore or order directly from Writer's Digest Books.

COLONY STUDIO THEATRE, 1944 Riverside Dr., Los Angeles CA 90039. New play selection committee: Judith Goldstein. Produces 4 mainstage productions, 4 workshop productions/year. Professional 99-seat theater with thrust stage. Casts from resident company of professional actors. No unsolicited scripts. Submission guidelines for SASE. Reports in up to 1 year. Negotiated rights. Pays royalties for each performance.
Needs: Full length (90-120 minutes) with a cast of 4-12. No musicals or experimental works.
Tips: "A polished script is the mark of a skilled writer. Submissions should be in professional (centered) format."

CONTEMPORARY DRAMA SERVICE, Meriwether Publishing Ltd., P.O. Box 7710, Colorado Springs CO 80933. (303)594-4422. Editor-in-Chief: Arthur Zapel. Associate Editors: Theodore Zapel, Rhonda Wray. Estab. 1969. Publishes 50-60 plays/year. "We publish for the secondary school market and colleges. We also publish for mainline liturgical churches—drama activities for church holidays, youth activities and fundraising entertainments. These may be plays or drama-related books." Query with synopsis or submit complete script. Reports in 6 weeks. Obtains either amateur or all rights. Pays 10% royalty or negotiates purchase.
Needs: "Most of the plays we publish are one acts, 15-45 minutes in length. We also publish full-length two-act or three-act plays. We prefer comedies. Musical plays must have name appeal either by prestige author, prestige title adaptation or performance on Broadway or TV. Comedy sketches, monologues and 2-character plays are welcomed. We prefer simple staging appropriate to high school, college or church performance. We like playwrights who see the world positively and with a sense of humor. Offbeat themes and treatments are accepted if the playwright can sustain a light touch and not take himself or herself too seriously. In documentary or religious plays we look for good research and authenticity. We are publishing many scenebooks on special themes and speech and theatrical arts textbooks. We are especially interested in authority-books on a variety of theater-related subjects."
Tips: Contemporary Drama Service is looking for creative books on: comedy writing, staging amateur theatricals and Christian youth activities.

THE COTERIE, 2450 Grand Ave., Kansas City MO 64108-2520. (816)474-6785. Fax: (816)474-7112. Artistic Director: Jeff Church. Estab. 1979. Produces 7-8 plays/year. "Plays produced at Hallmark's Crown Center in downtown Kansas City in the Coterie's resident theater (capacity 240). A typical performance run is one month in length." Query with synopsis, résumé, sample scene; submit complete script only if an established playwright in youth theater field. Reports in 6 months. "We retain some rights on commissioned plays." Pays royalty per performance and flat fee.
Needs: "We produce plays which are universal in appeal; they may be original or adaptations of classic or contemporary literature. Typically, not more than 12 in a cast—prefer 5-9 in size. No fly space or wing space."
Tips: "No couch plays. Prefer plays by seasoned writers who have established reputations. Groundbreaking and exciting scripts from the youth theater field welcome. It's prefectly fine if your play is a little off-center." Trends in the field that writers should be mindful of: "Make certain your submitted play to us is *very* theatrical and not cinematic. Writers need to see how far the field of youth and family theater has come—the interesting new areas we're going—before sending us your query or manuscript."

CREATIVE PRODUCTIONS, INC., 2 Beaver Place, Aberdeen NJ 07747. (908)566-6985. Artistic Director: Walter L. Born. Produces 2 musicals/year. Non-equity, year-round productions. "We use musicals with folks with disabilities and older performers in addition to 'normal' performers, for the broad spectrum of viewers." Query with synopsis. Reports in 2 weeks. Buys rights to perform play for specified number of performances. Pay negotiable.
Needs: Original musicals with upbeat themes adaptable to integrated company of traditional and non-traditional performers. Maximum cast of 12, sets can't fly, facilities are schools, no mammoth sets and multiple scene changes, 90 minutes maximum run time.
Tips: No blue material, pornographic, obscene language. Submit info on any performances. Demo tape (musicals) plus vocal/piano score list of references on users of their material to confirm bio info.

CREEDE REPERTORY THEATRE, P.O. Box 269, Creede CO 81130-0269. (719)658-2541. Director: Richard Baxter. Estab. 1966. Produces 6 plays/year. Plays performed for a summer audience. Query with synopsis. Reports in 1 year. Royalties negotiated with each author—paid on a per performance basis.
Needs: One-act children's scripts. Special consideration given to plays focusing on the cultures and history of the American West and Southwest.
Tips: "We seek new adaptations of classical or older works as well as original scripts."

CROSSLEY THEATRES/ACTORS CO-OP, 1760 N. Gower, Hollywood CA 90028. (213)462-8460. Artistic Director: Robin Strand. Main Stage: AEA 99 seat theater plan; September-June, 5-6 plays; Second Stage: AEA 99 seat theater plan, primarily for developing new material including full-length plays, one acts, readings, musical revues. Query with synopsis. Reports in 10 weeks. Pays per performance.
Needs: "We seek material with large themes written with intelligence. No abuse stories (substance, family, etc.) unless moral or philosophical dilemma is investigated (i.e., Equus); no family dramas unless dramatic

conflict transcends mere venting of hurt feelings (i.e., 1918)." Prefer casts of 12 or less (doubling is OK). Prefer minimum set changes.

Tips: "The Crossley Theatre and the Crossley Terrace Theatre are located on church grounds so there are some language restrictions. The Actors Co-op has received much critical acclaim including 58 Drama-Logue Awards and three Drama Critics Circle Awards in the last five years."

DELAWARE THEATRE COMPANY, 200 Water St., Wilmington DE 19801-5030. (302)594-1104. Artistic Director: Cleveland Morris. Estab. 1978. Produces 5 plays/year. 10% freelance written. "Plays are performed as part of a five-play subscription season in a 300-seat auditorium. Professional actors, directors and designers are engaged. The season is intended for a general audience." 10% of scripts are unagented submissions. Works with 1 unpublished/unproduced writer every 2 years. Query with synopsis and 5-10 page excerpt. Reports in 6 months. Buys variable rights. Pays 5% (variable) royalty.

Needs: "We present comedies, dramas, tragedies and musicals. All works must be full length and fit in with a season composed of standards and classics. All works have a strong literary element. Plays showing a flair for language and a strong involvement with the interests of classical humanism are of greatest interest. Single-set, small-cast works are likeliest for consideration." Recent trend toward more economical productions.

‡DINER THEATRE, 2015 S. 60th St., Omaha NE 68106. (402)553-4715. Artistic Director: Doug Marr. Estab. 1983. Produces 5 plays/year. Professional productions, general audience. Query with synopsis. Reports in 2 months on submissions. Pays $15-30/performance.

Needs: Comedies, dramas, musicals—original unproduced works. Full length, all styles/topics.

‡DRAMATIC PUBLISHING, 311 Washington, Woodstock IL 60098. (815)338-7170. Editor: Sara Clark. Publishes mass market paperback original plays. Publishes 50-70 titles/year. Receives 500-1,000 queries and 500-1,000 mss/year. Pays 10% royalty on scripts; performance royalty varies. Publishes play 6 months after acceptance of ms. Accepts simultaneous submissions. Reports in 1 month on queries, 2 months on proposals, 6 months on mss. Catalog and ms guidelines free on request.

Fiction: Interested in playscripts appropriate for children, middle and high schools, colleges, community and professional theaters. Send full ms.

Recent Fiction Title: *Never Come Morning*, by Paul Peditto (playscript adaptation).

‡EAST WEST PLAYERS, 4424 Santa Monica Blvd., Los Angeles CA 90029. (213)666-1929. Contact: Ken Narasaki, literary manager. Artistic Director: Tim Dang. Estab. 1965. Produces 5 plays/year. Professional theater performing under Equity 99-seat contract, presenting plays which explore the Asian or Asian-American experience. Query with synopsis. Reports in 3 months on submissions. Pays royalty against percentage of box office.

Needs: "Whether dramas, comedies or performance art or musicals, all plays must either address the Asian-American experience or have a special resonance when cast with Asian-American actors."

ELDRIDGE PUBLISHING CO., P.O. Box 1595, Venice FL 34284. (941)496-4679. Fax: (941)493-9680. Editor: Nancy Vorhis. Estab. 1906. Publishes 50-60 new plays/year for middle school, junior high, senior high, church and community audience. Query with synopsis (acceptable) or submit complete ms (preferred). Please send cassette tapes with any musicals. Reports in 2 months. Buys all rights. Pays 50% royalties and 10% copy sales. Makes outright purchase of $200-500. Writer's guidelines for #10 SASE.

Needs: "We are most interested in full-length plays and musicals for our school and community theater market. Nothing lower than junior high level, please. We always love comedies but also look for serious, high caliber plays reflective of today's sophisticated students. We also need one-acts and plays for children's theater. In addition, in our religious market we're always searching for holiday or any time plays."

Tips: "Submissions are welcomed at any time but during our fall season; response will definitely take 2 months. Authors are paid royalties twice a year. They receive complimentary copies of their published plays, the annual catalog and 50% discount if buying additional copies."

ENCORE PERFORMANCE PUBLISHING, P.O. Box 692, Orem UT 84059-4554. (801)225-0605. Editor: Michael C. Perry. Estab. 1979. Publishes 20-50 plays/year. "Our audience consists of all ages with emphasis on the family; educational institutions from elementary through college/university, community theaters and professional theaters." No unsolicited mss. Query with synopsis. Reports in 1 month on queries; 3 months on scripts. Pays 50% performance royalty; 10% book royalty. Submit from May-August.

Needs: "We are looking for plays with strong message about or for families, plays with young actors among cast, any length, all genres. We prefer scripts with at least close or equal male/female roles, could lean to more female roles." Plays must have had at least 2 fully staged productions. Unproduced plays can be read with letter of recommendation accompanying the query.

Tips: "No performance art pieces or plays with overtly sexual themes or language. Looking for adaptations of Twain and other American authors."

‡ENCORE THEATRE CO., 30 Grant, 6th Floor, San Francisco CA 94108. (415)346-7671. Artistic Director: Lisa Steindler. Estab. 1986. Professional productions in 70-seat black box theater for San Francisco and Bay Area audience, some tourists. Query with synopsis. Reports in 6 months. Buys variable rights. Pays variable royalty.
Needs: Full-length, contemporary, strong actor roles. Limitations in cost.
Tips: Wants to see contemporary issues but not polemic; strong acting ensemble required. No light material, musicals, "fluff."

‡ENSEMBLE THEATRE OF CINCINNATI, 1127 Vine St., Cincinnati OH 45248. (513)421-3555. Contact: D. Lynn Meyers, producing artistic director. Produces 8 plays/year. Professional-year round theater. Query and sysnopsis, submit complete ms or submit through agent. Reports in 5 months. Pays 5-10% royalty.
Needs: Dedicated to good writing, any style.

EUREKA THEATRE COMPANY, 330 Townsend, Suite 210, San Francisco CA 94107. (415)243-9899. Fax: (415)243-0789. Literary Manager: Nicole Galland. Estab. 1972. Produces 3-5 fully-staged plays/year. Plays performed in professional-AEA, year-round for socially involved adult audiences. Query with synopsis. Reports in 3 months. Rights negotiated. Pays negotiable royalty/commission.
 • The *Eureka* no longer accepts unsolicited scripts. Send letter of inquiry, synopsis, scene sample (15 pages maximum) and résumé.
Needs: "The mission of the Eureka Theatre Company continues to be to present productions of plays of honesty and integrity which address the concerns and realities of the time and place in which we live. We want to continue the Eureka tradition of entertaining and provoking our audiences as we present them with the urgency of dealing with the diversity and the opportunities of the society in which we live and work. In these final years of the twentieth century, we see it as an imperative to sum up this waning millenium even as we examine and question the next."
Tips: "No one-acts (although we would consider a collection and short works by a single writer or collective); no light-hearted musicals. We are tired of being told 'this is the next *Angels in America*.' We want plays which reflect the cultural diversity of the area in which we live and work. Remember, you are writing for the live stage, *not* for film or TV."

EXTRA VIRGIN PERFORMANCE COOPERATIVE, P.O. Box 224832, Dallas TX 75222. (214)941-3664. Fax: (214)942-8538. E-mail: exvirgin@aol.com. Artistic Director: Gretchen Sween. Estab. 1992. Produces 3 plays/year. "Plays are professional, low-tech productions for largely adult, intellectual audiences with more experimental tastes." Submit complete ms with synopsis. Reports in 2 months. Pays writer's travel expenses and board for attending production and/or an honorarium.
Needs: "Previously unproduced, low-tech, experimental plays that are intellectually challenging, socially conscious, and which resonate with the Western literary tradition." Prefers single set and small casts.
Tips: No old-fashioned "well-made plays," sitcoms, or those which are exceedingly technologically demanding. "We see a trend toward the resurgence of poetic language and a deemphasis on spectacle."

FLORIDA STUDIO THEATRE, 1241 N. Palm Ave., Sarasota FL 34236. (813)366-9017. Fax: (941)955-4137. Associate Director: Chris Angermann. Produces 7 established and 6 new plays/year. "FST is a professional not-for-profit theater." Plays are produced in 170-seat mainstage and 100-seat cabaret theater for subscription audiences (primarily). FST operates under a small professional theater contract of Actor's Equity. Query with synopsis. Reports in 2 months on queries; 6 months on mss. Pays $200 for workshop production of new script.
Needs: Contemporary plays, musical reviews, character plays. Prefer casts of no more than 8 and single sets on mainstage, 3-4 in cabaret.

THE FOOTHILL THEATRE COMPANY, P.O. Box 1812, Nevada City CA 95959. (916)265-9320. Artistic Director: Philip Charles Sneed. Estab. 1977. Produces 7-9 plays/year. "We are a professional theater company operating under an Actors' Equity Association contract for part of the year, and performing in the historic 246-seat Nevada Theatre (built in 1865) and in a converted space in the nearby town of Grass Valley (88-seat proscenium). The audience is a mix of locals and tourists." Query with synopsis or submit complete script. Reports in 6 months or less. Buys negotiable rights. Pay varies.
Needs: "We are most interested in plays which speak to the region and its history, as well as to its current concerns. No melodramas. Theatrical, above all." No limitations.
Tips: "Avoid the cliché at all costs, and don't be derivative; we're interested in a unique and unassailable vision."

FOUNTAIN THEATRE, 5060 Fountain Ave., Los Angeles CA 90029. (213)663-2235. Fax: (213)663-1629. Artistic Directors: Deborah Lawlor, Stephen Sachs. Estab. 1990. Produces both a theater and dance season. Produced at Fountain Theatre (99-seat equity plan). Query through agent or recommendation of theater professional. Query with synopsis to: Simon Levy, producing director/dramaturg. Reports in 6 months. Rights acquired vary. Pays royalty.

Needs: Original plays, adaptations of American literature, "material that incorporates dance or language into text with unique use and vision."

THE FREELANCE PRESS, P.O. Box 548, Dover MA 02030-2207. (508)785-1260. Managing Editor: Narcissa Campion. Estab. 1984. Publishes 4 plays/year for children/young adults. Submit complete ms with SASE. Reports in 4 months. Pays 2-3% royalty. Pays 10% of the price of each script and score.
Needs: "We publish original musical theater for young people, dealing with issues of importance to them. Also adapt 'classics' into musicals for 8-16-year-old age groups to perform." Large cast; flexible, simple staging and props.

SAMUEL FRENCH, INC., 45 W. 25th St., New York NY 10010. (212)206-8990. Fax: (212)206-1429. Editor: William Talbot. Estab. 1830. Subsidiaries include Samuel French Ltd. (London); Samuel French (Canada) Ltd. (Toronto); Samuel French, Inc. (Hollywood); Baker's Plays (Boston). Publishes paperback acting editions of plays. Averages 50-70 titles/year. Receives 1,500 submissions/year, mostly from unagented playwrights. 10% of publications are from first-time authors; 20% from unagented writers. Pays 10% royalty on retail price. Publishes play an average of 6 months after acceptance. Accepts simultaneous submissions. Allow *minimum* of 4 months for reply. Catalog set $4.50. Manuscript submission guidelines $4.
Nonfiction: Acting editions of plays.
Tips: "Broadway and Off-Broadway hit plays, light comedies and mysteries have the best chance of selling to our firm. Our market is comprised of theater producers—both professional and amateur—actors and students. Read as many plays as possible of recent vintage to keep apprised of today's market; write plays with good female roles; and be one hundred percent professional in approaching publishers and producers."

GEORGE STREET PLAYHOUSE, 9 Livingston Ave., New Brunswick NJ 08901. (908)846-2895. Producing Artistic Director: Gregory Hurst. Literary Manager: Tricia Roche. Produces 7 plays/year. Professional regional theater (LORT C). No unsolicited scripts. Professional recommendation only. Reports on scripts in 6-8 months. We also accept synopsis, dialogue sample and demo tape.
Needs: Full-length dramas, comedies and musicals that present a fresh perspective on society and challenge expectations of theatricality. Prefers cast size under 9. Also presents 40-minute social issue-plays appropriate for touring to school-age children; cast size limited to 4 actors.
Tips: "We produce up to four new plays and one new musical each season. We have a strong interest in receiving work from minority writers whose voices are not traditionally heard on America's main stages."

‡GEVA THEATRE, 75 Woodbury Blvd., Rochester NY 14610. (716)232-1366. Artistic Director: Mark Cuddy. Produces 6 plays/year. Professional theater, modified thrust, 552 seats. Subscription and single-ticket sales; no children's shows. Query with synopsis. Reports in 2 months.
Needs: Full-length plays.
Tips: No one acts, one person shows, musicals.

THE GOODMAN THEATRE, 200 S. Columbus Ave., Chicago IL 60603. (312)443-3811. Fax: (312)263-6004. E-mail: staff@goodman-theatre.org. Artistic Director: Robert Falls. Literary Manager: Susan V. Booth. Estab. 1925. Produces 9 plays/year. "The Goodman is a professional, not-for-profit theater producing both a mainstage and studio series for its subscription-based audience. The Goodman does not accept unsolicited scripts from playwrights or agents, nor will it respond to synopses of plays submitted by playwrights, unless accompanied by a stamped, self-addressed postcard. The Goodman may request plays to be submitted for production consideration after receiving a letter of inquiry or telephone call from recognized literary agents or producing organizations." Reports in 6 months. Buys variable rights. Pay is variable.
Needs: Full-length plays, translations, musicals; special interest in social or political themes.

‡GRIMPENMIRE PRESS, 162 N. 17th St., Springfield OR 97477. E-mail: grimpenmire@aol.com. Associate Editor: Toni Rakestraw. Publishes 20 titles/year. Receives 30-40 queries and 30 mss/year. 80% of plays from first-time authors; 90% unagented writers. Pays 50% royalty on retail script sales, 70% royalty on production. No advances. Publishes book 1 year after acceptance of ms. Accepts simultaneous submissions. Reports in 2 months on queries and 4 months on mss. Book catalog and ms guidelines free on request.
Fiction: Plays. "We want material suitable for community and regional theater, nothing too offensive (strong language and content must be an integral part of plot/story). Submit synopsis with SASE.
Recent Fiction Title: *In Escher's Garden*, by James L. Schempp (play).
Tips: Audiences are community and regional theater goers composed of wide variety of ages and levels of sophistication. "We're a good starting point for playwrights. We're small, personal, and have a fast turn around. We want authors who are willing to work with us for the benefit of all of us."

HARTFORD STAGE COMPANY, 50 Church St., Hartford CT 06103. (203)525-5601. Artistic Director: Mark Lamos. Estab. 1963. Produces 6 plays/year. Regional theater productions with a wide range in audience. Agented submissions only; for unsolicited scripts send synopsis and 10-page dialogue sample with SASE. Reports in 1 month for synopsis; 6 months for ms. Rights bought varies. Pays royalty.

Needs: Classics, new plays, musicals, "open to almost anything. Looking more for small to medium casts (1-12) but larger casts are also looked at."
Tips: No typical Broadway fare, i.e., Phantom of the Opera, Cats.

HEUER PUBLISHING CO., 233 Dows Bldg., Box 248, Cedar Rapids IA 52406-0248. (319)364-6311. Fax: (319)364-1771. Owner/Editor: C. Emmett McMullen. Estab. 1928. Publishes plays and musicals for junior and senior high school and church groups. Query with synopsis or submit complete script. Reports in 2 months. Purchases amateur rights only. Pays royalty or makes outright purchase.
Needs: "One- and three-act plays suitable for school production. Preferably comedy or mystery/comedy. All material should be of the capabilities of high school actors. We prefer material with one set. No special day material or material with controversial subject matter."

‡HOLVOE BOOKS, LTD., P.O. Box 62, Hewlett NY 11557-0062. (800)536-0099. E-mail: dlonstage@aol .com. Assistant Editor: Steven Fisch. Imprints are Luminaries, Voices of the Drama. Publishes hardcover and trade paperback originals. Publishes 4-8 titles/year. Receives 50 queries and 300 mss/year. 25% of plays from first-time authors; 60% unagented writers. Pays royalty and/or makes outright purchase. Advance varies. Publishes play 1-2 years after acceptance of ms. Accepts simultaneous submissions. Reports in 1 month on queries, 1-2 years on mss. Manuscript guidelines for #10 SASE.
Needs: Any length, any style, but should read well on the stage. Submit entire ms with SASE.
Recent Title: *Florida Bound*, by William S. Leavengood.
Tips: Audience is educators, theater professionals and theater lovers. "If accepted, playwright must be able to send manuscripts via electronic (disk, e-mail) form."

‡HORIZON THEATRE COMPANY, P.O. Box 5376, Station E, Atlanta GA 30307. (404)523-1477. Artistic Director: Lisa Adler. Estab. 1983. Produces 4 plays/year. Professional productions. Query with synopsis and résumé. Reports in 1-2 years. Buys rights to produce in Atlanta area. Pays 6-8% royalty or $50-75/performance.
Needs: "We produce contemporary plays with realistic base, but which utilize heightened visual or language elements. Interested in comedy, satire, plays that are entertaining and topical, but also thought provoking. Also particular interest in plays by women or with Southern themes." No more than 10 in cast.
Tips: "No plays about being in theater or film; no plays without hope; no plays that include playwrights as leading characters; no all-male casts; no plays with all older (50 plus) characters."

‡ILLINOIS THEATRE CENTRE, 400A Lakewood Blvd., Park Forest IL 60466. (708)481-3510. Fax: (708)481-3693. Artistic Director: Steve S. Billig. Literary Manager: Barbara Mitchell. Estab. 1976. Produces 8 plays/year. Professional Resident Theatre Company in our own space for a subscription-based audience. Query with synopsis or agented submission. Reports in 2 months. Buys casting and directing and designer selection rights. Pays 7-10% royalty.
Needs: Wants all types of 2-act plays, musicals, dramas. Prefers cast size of 6-10.
Tips: Always looking for mysteries and comedies.

INTIMAN THEATRE, P.O. Box 19760, Seattle WA 98109. (206)269-1901. Fax: (206)269-1928. Artistic Director: Warner Shook. Estab. 1972. Produces 6 plays/year. LORT C Regional Theater in Seattle. Query with synopsis and sample pages. Reports in 4 months.
Needs: Well-crafted dramas and comedies by playwrights who fully utilize the power of language and character relationships to explore enduring themes.
Needs: Prefers character-driven plays.
Tips: "Our play development prpogram conducts 4-6 readings per year of previously unproduced plays. Submission requirements are the same as those for the mainstage. Recent works include plays by Robert Schenkkan, William Mastrosimone, Leslie Ayvazian, Chay Yew, Jeffrey Hatcher and Jamie Baker."

JD PRODUCTIONS, 104 Forest Court, Louisville KY 40207. (502)894-8986. Artistic Director: Jolene DeLory. Estab. 1994. Produces 6-8 plays/year for community, semiprofessional, professional, dinner theater, possible traveling troupe. All audiences, including children. Query with synopsis or submit complete ms. Reports in 6 weeks. Obtains all rights. Pays negotiable royalty, 50% minimum, depending on type of material.
Needs: Plays, musical revues, full-length, (2 hours and short). Open to all subjects at this time, directed toward all audiences, including children.
Tips: "Audiences are gravitating back toward classics, or plays that resemble classics. They like the older plays, especially mystery and comedy and older musicals (or shows with that tone). I am also looking for short plays and musical revues for a particular theater group with the third oldest continuous running theater in the country. I am the director of the group."

JEWEL BOX THEATRE, 3700 N. Walker, Oklahoma City OK 73118-7099. (405)521-1786. Fax: (405)525-6562. Artistic Director: Charles Tweed. Estab. 1986. Produces 6 plays/year. Amateur productions.

For 3,000 season subscribers and general public. Submit complete script. Reports in 4 months. Pays $500 contest prize.

Needs: Send SASE for entry form during September-October. We produce dramas, comedies and musicals. Only two- or three-act plays can be accepted. Our theater is in-the-round, so we adapt plays accordingly." Deadline: mid-January.

JEWISH REPERTORY THEATRE, 1395 Lexington Ave., New York NY 10128. (212)415-5550. Artistic Director: Ran Avni. Estab. 1974. Produces 4 plays, 15 readings/year. New York City professional off-Broadway production. Submit complete script with SASE. Reports in 1 month. First production/option to move to Broadway or off-Broadway. Pays royalty.

Needs: Full-length only. Straight plays, musicals. Must have some connection to Jewish life, characters, history. Maximum 7 characters. Limited technical facilities.

Tips: No biblical plays.

KUMU KAHUA, 46 Merchant St., Honolulu HI 96813. (808)536-4222. Fax: (808)536-4226. Artistic Director: Dennis Carroll. Estab. 1971. Produces 5 productions, 3-4 public readings/year. "Plays performed at new Kumu Kahua Theatre, flexible 120-seat theater, for community audiences." Submit complete script. Reports in 4 months. Pays royalty of $35/performance; usually 14 performances of each production.

Needs: "Plays must have some interest for local audiences, preferably by being set in Hawaii or dealing with some aspect of the Hawaiian experience. Prefer small cast, with simple staging demands."

Tips: "We need time to evaluate scripts (our response time is four months)."

LAGUNA PLAYHOUSE, P.O. Box 1747, Laguna Beach CA 92652-1747. (714)497-5900, ext. 206. Fax: (714)497-6948. Artistic Director: Andrew Barnicle. Estab. 1920. Produces 10 plays/year. Equity Letter of Agreement: 5 mainstage (9,000 subscribers); Amateur: 5 youth theater (1,500 subscribers). Submit complete script, no synopses. Reports in 1 year. Royalty negotiable.

Needs: Seeking full-length plays: comedy, drama, classical, musical, youth theater.

Recent Production: *Teachers' Lounge*, by John Twomey, (world premiere, full production); world premiere, "Labors of Hercules" by David Drummond (March, 1996).

Tips: "We are committed to one full production of an original play every other season. However, limited staff to read and process original works can mean a long response time."

LILLENAS PUBLISHING CO., P.O. Box 419527, Kansas City MO 64141-6527. (816)931-1900. Fax: (816)753-4071. Editor: Paul M. Miller. Estab. 1926. "We publish on two levels: (1) Program Builders—seasonal and topical collections of recitations, sketches, dialogues and short plays; (2) Drama Resources. These assume more than one format: (a) full-length scripts, (b) one-acts, shorter plays and sketches all by one author, (c) collection of short plays and sketches by various authors. All program and play resources are produced with local church and Christian school in mind. Therefore there are taboos." Queries are encouraged, but synopses and complete scripts are read. "First rights are purchased for Program Builder scripts. For our line of Drama Resources, we purchase all print rights, but this is negotiable." Writer's guidelines for #10 SASE. Reports in 3 months.

● This publisher is more interested in one-act and full-length scripts—both religious and secular. Monologs are of lesser interest than previously. There is more interest in Readers' Theatre.

Needs: 98% of Program Builder materials are freelance written. Scripts selected for these publications are outright purchases; verse is minimum of 25¢/line, prose (play scripts) are minimum of $5/double-spaced page. "Lillenas Drama Resources is a line of play scripts that are, for the most part, written by professionals with experience in production as well as writing. However, while we do read unsolicited scripts, more than half of what we publish is written by experienced authors whom we have already published." Drama Resources (whether full-length scripts, one-acts, or sketches) are paid on a 10% royalty. There are no advances.

Tips: "All plays need to be presented in standard play script format. We welcome a summary statement of each play. Purpose statements are always desirable. Approximate playing time, cast and prop lists, etc. are important to include. We are interested in fully scripted traditional plays, reader's theater scripts, choral speaking pieces. Contemporary settings generally have it over Biblical settings. Christmas and Easter scripts must have a bit of a twist. Secular approaches to these seasons (Santas, Easter bunnies, and so on), are not considered. We sell our product in 10,000 Christian bookstores and by catalog. We are probably in the forefront as a publisher of religious drama resources." Request a copy of our newsletter and/or catalog.

LIVE OAK THEATRE, 200 Colorado St., Austin TX 78701. (512)472-5143. Fax: (512)472-7199. Contact: Michael Hankin. Estab. 1982. Professional theater produces 6 plays/season. "Strong commitment to and a history of producing new work." Pays royalty. Reports in late summer. Guidelines for #10 SASE.

Needs: Full length, translations, adaptations, musicals.

Tips: Also sponsors annual new play awards.

‡THE LOFT PRODUCTION COMPANY, 1441 E. Fletcher Ave., #413, Tampa FL 33612. (813)972-1200. Fax: (813)977-8485. Artistic Director: Mr. Kelly Smith. Estab. 1987. Produces 6 plays/year. Amateur/

professional productions. Performed at the Off-Center Theater-Tampa Bay Performing Arts Center. Diverse adult audiences. Query with synopsis or submit complete ms. Reports in 6 months. Buys performance rights. Pays $500-1,000 royalty.

Needs: All genres, topics, styles and lengths. Prefers small cast (2-8) with minimal technical requirements.

Tips: "We look for cutting edge or alternative pieces. Nothing is taboo with us."

‡**MAGIC THEATRE, INC.**, Bldg. D, Fort Mason, San Francisco CA 94123. (415)441-8001. Artistic Director: Mame Hunt. Estab. 1967. Produces 6 plays/year plus numerous co-productions. Regional theater. Query with synopsis. Reports in 4 months. Pays royalty or per performance fee.

Needs: "Plays that are innovative in theme and/or craft, cutting-edge political concerns, intelligent comedy. Full-length only, strong commitment to multicultural work

Tips: "Not interested in classics, conventional approaches and cannot produce large-cast plays."

MANHATTAN THEATRE CLUB, 453 W. 16th St., New York NY 10011-5896. Director of Play Development: Kate Loewald. Produces 8 plays/year. Two-theater performing arts complex classified as off-Broadway, using professional actors. No unsolicited scripts. No queries. Reports in 6 months.

Needs: "We present a wide range of new work, from this country and abroad, to a subscription audience. We want plays about contemporary problems and people. Comedies are welcome. Multiple set shows are discouraged. Average cast is 8."

MERIWETHER PUBLISHING LTD. (Contemporary Drama Service), Dept. WM, 885 Elkton Dr., Colorado Springs CO 80907-3557. President: Mark Zapel. Executive Editor: Arthur L. Zapel. Estab. 1969. "We publish how-to materials in book and video formats. We are interested in materials for high-school and college level students only. Our Contemporary Drama Service division publishes 60-70 plays/year." 80% written by unpublished writers. Buys 40-60 scripts/year from unpublished/unproduced writers. 90% of scripts are unagented submissions. Reports in 1 month on queries; 2 months on full-length mss. Query with synopsis/outline, résumé of credits, sample of style and SASE. Catalog available for $2 postage. Offers 10% royalty or makes outright purchase.

Needs: Book mss on theatrical arts subjects, especially books of short scenes for amateur and professional actors. "We are now looking for scenebooks with special themes: 'scenes for young women,' 'comedy scenes for two actors', etc. These need not be original, provided the compiler can get letters of permission from the original copyright owner. We are interested in all textbook candidates for theater arts subjects. Christian children's activity book mss also accepted. We will consider elementary level religious materials and plays, but no elementary level children's secular plays. Query. Pays royalty; sometimes makes outright purchase.

Tips: "We publish a wide variety of speech contest materials for high-school students. We are publishing more full length play scripts and musicals based on classic literature or popular TV shows, provided the writer includes letter of clearance from the copyright owner. Our educational books are sold to teachers and students at college and high-school levels. Our religious books are sold to youth activity directors, pastors and choir directors. Our trade books are directed at the public with a sense of humor. Another group of buyers is the professional theater, radio and TV category. We will be especially interested in full length (two- or three-act) plays with name recognition, either the playwright or the adaptation source. We are not interested in unknown playwrights for full length plays but will consider their works in one-act formats."

MERRIMACK REPERTORY THEATRE, Dept. WM, 50 E. Merrimack St., Lowell MA 01852-1205. (508)454-6324. Fax: (508)934-0166. Artistic Director: David G. Kent. Contact: Emma Fried. Estab. 1979. Produces 7 plays/year. Professional LORT D. Agented submissions and letters of inquiry only. Reports in 6 months.

Needs: All styles and genres. "We are a small 386-seat theater—with a modest budget. Plays should be good stories, with strong dialogue, real situations and human concerns. Especially interested in plays about American life and culture."

‡**MILL MOUNTAIN THEATRE**, Market Square, Center in Square, Roanoke VA 24011-1437. (703)342-5730. Fax: (540)342-5745. Executive Director: Jere Lee Hodgin. Literary Manager: Jo Weinstein. Produces 8 established plays, 10 new one-acts and 2 new full-length plays/year. "Some of the professional productions will be on the main stage and some in our alternative Theater B. We no longer accept full-length unsolicited scripts." Send letter, synopsis and 10 pages of sample dialogue. Reports in 8 months. Payment negotiable on individual play. Send SASE for guidelines; cast limit 15 for play and 24 for musicals. Do not include loose stamps or money.

 THE DOUBLE DAGGER before a listing indicates that the listing is new in this edition. New markets are often more receptive to freelance submissions.

Needs: "We are interested in plays with racially mixed casts, but not to the exclusion of others. We are constantly seeking one-act plays for 'Centerpieces', our lunch time program of script-in-hand productions. Playing time should be between 25-35 minutes. Cast limit 6."

Tips: "Subject matter and character variations are open, but gratuitous language and acts are not acceptable. A play based on large amounts of topical reference or humor has a very short life. Be sure you have written a play and not a film script."

MUSICAL THEATRE WORKS, INC., 440 Lafayette St., 4th Floor, New York NY 10003-6919. (212)677-0040. Fax: (212)598-0105. Artistic Director: Anthony Stimac. Estab. 1983. "MTW develops scripts from informal to staged readings. When the project is deemed ready for the public, a showcase is set up for commercial interest. MTW musicals are professionally produced and presented in an off-Broadway New York City theater and intended for a well-rounded, sophisticated, theater-going audience. Additionally, 50% of all MTW MainStage productions have gone on to engagements on Broadway and in 12 states across the country." Submit complete script with audiotape. Reports in 6 months. Buys 1% future gross; on fully-produced works. Pays negotiable royalty. SASE required to return script and tape.

Needs: "MTW only produces full-length works of musical theater and is interested not only in those classically written, but has a keen interest in works which expand the boundaries and subject matter of the artform. MTW is a small, but prolific, organization with a limited budget. It is, therefore, necessary to limit production costs."

Tips: "The dramatic stage of recent years has successfully interpreted social problems of the day, while the musical theater has grown in spectacle and foregone substance. Since the musical theater traditionally incorporated large themes and issues it is imperative that we now marry these two ideas—large themes and current issues—to the form. Send a neat, clean, typewritten script with a well marked, clear audiotape, produced as professionally as possible, to the attention of the Literary Manager."

THE NATIONAL PLAYWRIGHTS CONFERENCE/NEW DRAMA FOR MEDIA PROJECT AT THE EUGENE O'NEILL THEATER CENTER, 234 W. 44th St., Suite 901, New York NY 10036-3909. (212)382-2790. Fax: (212)921-5538. Artistic Director: Lloyd Richards. Estab. 1965. Develops staged readings of 9-12 stage plays, 2-3 screenplays or teleplays/year. "We accept unsolicited scripts with no prejudice toward either represented or unrepresented writers. Our theater is located in Waterford, Connecticut, and we operate under an Equity LORT contract. We have three theaters: Barn—250 seats, Amphitheater—300 seats, Instant Theater—150 seats. Submission guidelines for #10 SASE in the fall. Complete bound, professionally unproduced, original plays are eligible (no adaptations). Decision by late April. Pays stipend plus room, board and transportation. We accept script submissions September 15-December 1 of each year. Conference takes place during July each summer."

● Scripts are selected on the basis of talent, not commercial potential.

Needs: "We use modular sets for all plays, minimal lighting, minimal props and no costumes. We do script-in-hand readings with professional actors and directors. Our focus is on new play/playwright development."

THE NEW CONSERVATORY CHILDREN'S THEATRE COMPANY AND SCHOOL, New Conservatory Theatre Center, 25 Van Ness, Lower Level, San Francisco CA 94102. (415)861-4814. Fax: (415)861-6988. Artistic Director: Ed Decker. Produces 4-5 plays/year. "The New Conservatory is a children's theater school (ages 4-19) and operates year-round. Each year we produce several plays, for which the older students (usually 10 and up) audition. These are presented to the general public at the New Conservatory Theatre Center in San Francisco (50-150 seats). Our audience is approximately age 5-adult." Query with synopsis. Reports in 3 months. Royalty negotiable.

Needs: Children's theatre: family audience scripts, 6 characters maximum, non-musical, preferably with at least 1 or 2 childrens roles. Topical touring programs, non-musical, 4 characters or less. "We emphasize works in which children play *children*, and prefer relevant and controversial subjects, although we also do musicals. We have a commitment to new plays. Examples of our shows are: Mary Gail's *Nobody Home* (world premiere; about latchkey kids); Brian Kral's *Special Class* (about disabled kids); and *The Inner Circle*, by Patricia Loughrey (commissioned scripts about AIDS prevention for kids). "Gay and Lesbian Pride Season:" gay and lesbian themes/plays, 4 characters or less, non-musical. "As we are a nonprofit group on limited budget, we tend not to have elaborate staging; however, our staff is inventive—includes choreographer and composer. Write innovative theater that explores topics of concern/interest to young people, that takes risks. We concentrate more on ensemble than individual roles, too. We do *not* want to see fairy tales or trite rehashings of things children have seen/heard since the age of two. See theater as education, rather than 'children being cute.' "

Tips: "It is important for young people and their families to explore and confront issues relevant to growing up in the 90s. Theater is a marvelous teaching tool that can educate while it entertains." The New Conservatory Theatre Center is a tri-theatre complex with venues ranging in size from 50-130 seats located in the performing arts district of San Francisco. The New Conservatory Theatre Center does not currently accept unsolicited manuscripts. Playwrights are welcome to submit letters of inquiry with a synopsis and character breakdown of the proposed submission to the attention of Ed Decker, Executive Producer (include SASE response card). No phone calls please.

NEW PLAYWRIGHTS' PROGRAM, The University of Alabama, P.O. Box 870239, Tuscaloosa AL 35487-0239. (205)348-9032. Fax: (205)348-9048. E-mail: pcastagn@rojo.as.ua.edu. Director/Dramaturg: Dr. Paul C. Castagno. Endowed by Gallaway Fund, estab. 1982. Produces at least 1 new play/year. Mainstage and second stage, University Theatre, The University of Alabama. Submit synopsis or complete ms. Playwrights may submit potential workshop ideas for consideration. Reports in 6 months. Accepts scripts in various forms: new dramaturgy to traditional. Recent MFA playwriting graduates (within 1 year) may be given consideration for ACTF productions. Send SASE. Stipends competitive with or exceed most contests.
Needs: Southern themes; dramas with dance.

NEW STAGE THEATRE, 1100 Carlisle, Jackson MS 39202. (601)948-0143. Fax: (601)948-3538. Artistic Director: John Maxwell. Estab. 1965. Produces 9 plays/year. "Professional productions, 8 mainstage, 1 in our 'second space.' We play to an audience comprised of Jackson, the state of Mississippi and the Southeast." Query with synopsis. Reports in 6 weeks. Exclusive premiere contract upon acceptance of play for mainstage production. Pays royalty of 5-8% or $25-60/performance.
Needs: Southern themes, contemporary issues, small casts (5-8), single set plays and children's theater are desirable.
Tips: No historical dramas, one-acts or melodramas.

NEW TUNERS THEATRE, 1225 W. Belmont Ave., Chicago IL 60657. (312)929-7287, ext. 17. Artistic Director: Allan Chambers. Produces up to 3 new musicals/year. Mostly developed in our New Tuners workshop. "Some scripts produced are unagented submissions. Plays performed in 3 small off-Loop theaters seating 148 for a general theater audience, urban/suburban mix. Submit synopsis, cover letter and cassette selections of the score, if available. Reports in 3 months. Next step is script and score (reports in 6 months). Pays 10% of gross. "Authors are given a stipend and housing to cover a residency of at least two weeks."
Needs: "We're interested in all forms of musical theater including more innovative styles. Our production capabilities are limited by the lack of space, but we're very creative and authors should submit anyway. The smaller the cast, the better. We are especially interested in scripts using a younger (35 and under) ensemble of actors. We mostly look for authors who are interested in developing their script through workshops, reading rehearsals and production. No casts over 12. No one-man shows."
Tips: "We would like to see the musical theater articulating something about the world around us, as well as diverting an audience's attention from that world." Script Consultancy—A new program designed to assist authors and composers in developing new musicals through private feedback sessions with professional dramaturgs and musical directors. For further info contact (312)929-7367, ext. 17.

‡NEW YORK STATE THEATRE INSTITUTE, 155 River St., Troy NY 12180. (518)274-3200. Fax: (518)274-3815. Producing Artistic Director: Patricia B. Snyder. Produces 4-5 plays/year. Professional regional productions for adult and family audiences. Submit query with synopsis or complete ms. Reports in 1 month on synopsis, 4 months on complete ms. Pay varies.

NEW YORK THEATRE WORKSHOP, 79 E. Fourth St., New York NY 10003. (212)780-9037. Fax: (212)460-8996. Artistic Director: James C. Nicola. Literary Manager: Mandy Mishell. Estab. 1979. Produces 3-4 full productions; approximately 50 readings/year. Plays are performed off-Broadway, Equity LOA contract theater. Audience is New York theater-going audience and theater professionals. Query with synopsis and 10-page sample scene. Reports in 5 months. Option to produce commercially; percentage of box office gross from commercial and percentage of author's net subsidiary rights within specified time limit from our original production. Pays fee because of limited run, with additional royalty payments; for extensions; $1,500-2,000 fee range.
Needs: Full-length plays, one acts, translations/adaptations, music theater pieces; proposals for performance projects. Large issues, socially relevant issues, innovative form and language, minority issues. Plays utilizing more than 8 actors usually require outside funding.
Tips: No overtly commercial, traditional, Broadway-type musicals.

NINE O'CLOCK PLAYERS, 1367 N. St. Andrews Place, Los Angeles CA 90028. (213)469-1973. Estab. 1928. Contact: Artistic Director. Produces 2 plays/year. "Plays produced at Assistance League Playhouse by resident amateur and semi-professional company. All plays are musical adaptations of classical children's literature. Plays must be appropriate for children ages 4-12." Query with synopsis. Reports in 1 month. Pays negotiable royalty or per performance.
Needs: "Plays must have at least 9-15 characters and be 75 minutes long. Productions are done on a proscenium stage in classical theater style. All plays must have humor, music and good moral values. No audience participation improvisational plays."

THE NORTH CAROLINA BLACK REPERTORY COMPANY, Dept. WM, P.O. Box 95, Winston-Salem NC 27102. (910)723-2266. Fax: (910)723-2223. Artistic Director: Larry Leon Hamlin. Estab. 1979. Produces 4-6 plays/year. Plays produced primarily in North Carolina, New York City, the North and Southeast. Submit complete ms. Reports in 5 months. Obtains negotiable rights. Negotiable payment.

Needs: "Full-length plays and musicals: mostly African-American with special interest in historical or contemporary *statement* genre. A cast of 10 would be a comfortable limit; we discourage multiple sets."
Tips: "The best time to submit manuscripts is between September and February."

ODYSSEY THEATRE ENSEMBLE, 2055 S. Sepulveda Blvd., Los Angeles CA 90025. (310)477-2055. Fax: (310)444-0455. Director of Literary Programs: Jan Lewis. Estab. 1965. Produces 9 plays/year. Plays performed in a 3-theater facility. "All three theaters are Equity 99-seat theater plan. We have a subscription audience of 4,000 for a nine-play main season, and they are offered a discount on our rentals and co-productions. Remaining seats are sold to the general public." Query with résumé, synopsis, cast breakdown and 8-10 pages of sample dialogue and cassette if a musical. Scripts must be securely bound. Reports in 1 month on queries; 6 months on scripts. Buys negotiable rights. Pays 5-7% royalty. Does *not* return scripts without SASE.
Needs: "Full-length plays only with either an innovative form and/or provocative subject matter. We desire highly theatrical pieces that explore possibilities of the live theater experience. We are seeking full-length musicals and some plays with smaller casts (2-4). We are not reading one-act plays or light situation comedies. We are seeking Hispanic material for our resident Hispanic unit as well as plays from all cultures and ethnicities."

OLDCASTLE THEATRE COMPANY, Box 1555, Bennington VT 05201-1555. (802)447-0564. Artistic Director: Eric Peterson. Produces 7 plays/year. Plays are performed in the new Bennington Center for the Arts, by a professional Equity theater company (in a April-October season) for general audiences, including residents of a three-state area and tourists during the vacation season. Submit complete ms. Reports in 6 months. Pays by negotiation with the playwright. A not-for-profit theater company.
Needs: Produces classics, musicals, comedy, drama, most frequently American works. Usual performance time is 2 hours.

THE OPEN EYE THEATER, P.O. Box 204, Denver NY 12421. Phone/fax: (607)326-4986. Producing Artistic Director: Amie Brockway. The Open Eye is a not-for-profit professional theater company working in New York City since 1972, in the rural villages of Delaware County, NY since 1991, and on tour. The theater specializes in the development of new plays for multi-generational audiences (children ages 8 and up, and adults of all ages). Ensemble plays with music and dance, culturally diverse and historical material, myth, folklore, and stories with universal themes are of interest. Program includes readings, developmental workshops, and fully staged productions.
Tips: Send one-page letter with one-paragraph plot synopsis, cast breakdown and setting, résumé and SAE. "We will provide the stamp and contact you *if we want to see the script.*"

OREGON SHAKESPEARE FESTIVAL ASSOCIATION, P.O. Box 158, Ashland OR 97520. (541)482-2111. Fax: (541)482-0446. Associate Director/Play Development: Cynthia White. Estab. 1935. Produces 11 plays/year. The Angus Bowmer Theater has a thrust stage and seats 600. The Black Swan is an experimental space and seats 150. The Elizabethan Outdoor Theatre seats 1,200 (stages almost exclusively Shakespearean productions there, mid-June-September). Query with synopsis, résumé and 10 pages of dialogue from unsolicited sources. Complete scripts from agents only. Reports in 18 months. Negotiates individually for rights with the playwright's agent. "Most plays run within our ten-month season for 6-10 months, so royalties are paid accordingly."
Needs: "A broad range of classic and contemporary scripts. One or two fairly new scripts/season. Also a play readings series which focuses on new work. Plays must fit into our ten-month rotating repertory season. Black Swan shows usually limited to ten actors." No one-acts or musicals. Submissions from women and minority writers are strongly encouraged.
Tips: "Send your work through an agent if possible. Send the best examples of your work rather than all of it. Don't become impatient or discouraged if it takes six months or more for a response. Don't expect detailed critiques with rejections. I want to see plays with heart and soul, intelligence, humor and wit. We're seeking plays with characters that *live*—that exist as living beings, not simply mouthpieces for particular positions. Try to avoid TV writing (i.e., cliché situations, dialogue, characters), unless it's specifically for broad comic purposes. I also think theater is a place for the *word*. So, the word first, then spectacle and high-tech effects."

ORGANIC THEATER COMPANY, 3319 N. Clark, Chicago IL 60657. (312)327-2427. Fax: (312)327-8947. Artistic Director: Paul Frellick. Contact: Jeff Carey. Estab. 1969. AEA, CAT and non-equity productions and workshops. Query with synopsis and 10-page sample. Reports in 1 month on queries. Negotiable royalty. Send inquiries to Literary Manager.
Needs: "We are seeking full-length or long one-acts—challenging plays that fully explore the theatrical medium; strong visual and physical potential (unproduced works only)."

JOSEPH PAPP PUBLIC THEATER, 425 Lafayette St., New York NY 10003. (212) 539-8500. Artistic Director: George C. Wolfe. Estab. 1964. Produces 12 plays/year. Professional productions. Query with synop-

sis and 10-page sample. Reports in 1 month on query; 6 months on scripts. Pays flat fee.
Needs: All genres.

THE PASSAGE THEATRE COMPANY, P.O. Box 967, Trenton NJ 08605-0967. Artistic Director: Stephen Stout. Estab. 1985. Produces 3 plays/year. "Passage is a professional theater celebrating the new American play." Please submit synopsis and ten page sample only. Reports in 3 months. Pays royalty.
Needs: "We consider 1-3-act plays dealing with social, cultural and artistic issues. We also do workshops and readings of plays. We work actively with the writers in developing their work. Passage Theatre has a strong propensity towards plays with multi-ethnic themes and utilizing inter-racial casting."

PEOPLE'S LIGHT & THEATRE COMPANY, 39 Conestoga Rd., Malvern PA 19355. (610)647-1900. Co-Artistic Directors: Abigail Adams, Stephen Novelli. Estab. 1974. Produces 5-6 plays/year. LORT theater, general audience. Query with synopsis with 10 page dialogue sample. Reports in 6 months. Pays negotiable royalty.
Needs: Full length, sometime one acts, no musicals. Cast of 8-10 maximum. Prefers single set.

PIER ONE THEATRE, P.O. Box 894, Homer AK 99603. (907)235-7333. Artistic Director: Lance Petersen. Estab. 1973. Produces 5-8 plays/year. "Plays to various audiences for various plays—e.g. children's, senior citizens, adult, family, etc. Plays are produced on Kemai Peninsula." Submit complete script. Reports in 3 months. Pays $25-125/performance.
Needs: "No restrictions—willing to read *all* genres. However, for the near future, our New Works program will present work by Alaskan playwrights and work of specific Alaskan interest."
Tips: "We prefer to have the whole script to evaluate."

PIONEER DRAMA SERVICE, INC., P.O. Box 4267, Englewood CO 80155-4267. (303)779-4035. Fax: (303)779-4315. E-mail: piodrama@aol.com. Publisher: Steven Fendrich. Submissions Editor: Lynne Zborowski. Estab. 1963. Publishes approximately 30 new plays/year. Plays are performed by schools, colleges, community theaters, recreation programs, churches and professional children's theaters for audiences of all ages. Query preferred; unsolicited scripts with proof of production accepted. Reports in 2 weeks on queries, in 3 months on scripts. Retains all rights. Pays on royalty basis. All submissions automatically entered in Shubert Fendrich Memorial Playwriting Contest. Guidelines for SASE.
Needs: "We have a new Social Awareness section, and are looking for submissions in this area." Also musicals, comedies, mysteries, dramas, melodramas and children's theater (plays to be done by adult actors for children). Two-acts up to 90 minutes; children's theater, 1 hour. Prefer many female roles, simple sets. Plays need to be appropriate for amateur groups. Prefer secular plays..

‡**PITTSBURGH PUBLIC THEATER**, Allegheny Square, Pittsburgh PA 15212. (412)323-8200. Artistic Director: Edward Gilbert. Contact: Rob Zellers. Estab. 1974. Produces 6 plays/year. Theodore L. Hazelett Theatre, 457 seats, thrust or arena seating. Query with synopsis or agented submissions. Reports in 6 months.
Needs: Full-length plays, adaptations, musicals.

□**PLAYERS PRESS, INC.**, P.O. Box 1132, Studio City CA 91614-0132. Senior Editor: Robert W. Gordon. "We deal in all entertainment areas and handle publishable works for film and television as well as theater. Performing arts books, plays and musicals. All plays must be in stage format for publication." Also produces scripts for video and material for cable television. 80% freelance written. 20-30 scripts/year unagented submissions; 5-15 books also unagented. Works with 1-10 unpublished/unproduced writers annually. Query. "Include #10 SASE, reviews and proof of production. All play submissions must have been produced and should include a flier and/or program with dates of performance." Reports in 1 month on queries; 1 year on mss. Buys negotiable rights. "We prefer all area rights." Pays variable royalty according to area; approximately 10-75% of gross receipts. Also makes outright purchase of $100-25,000 or $5-5,000/performance.
Needs: "We prefer comedies, musicals and children's theater, but are open to all genres. We will rework the script after acceptance. We are interested in the quality, not the format. Performing Arts Books that deal with theater how-to are of strong interest."
Tips: "Send only material requested. Do not telephone."

PLAYS, The Drama Magazine for Young People, 120 Boylston St., Boston MA 02116-4615. Editor: Sylvia K. Burack. Contact: Elizabeth Preston, managing editor. Estab. 1941. Publishes approximately 75 one-act plays and dramatic program material each school year to be performed by junior and senior high, middle grades, lower grades. "Scripts should follow the general style of *Plays*. Stage directions should not be typed in capital letters or underlined. No incorrect grammar or dialect." Desired lengths are: junior and senior high—15-20 double-spaced pages (20-30 minutes playing time); middle grades—10-15 pages (15-20 minutes playing time); lower grades—6-10 pages (8-15 minutes playing time). Buys all rights. Pays "good rates on acceptance." Query first for adaptations. Reports in 2-3 weeks. Sample copy $3.50. Send SASE for specification sheet.

Needs: "Can use comedies, farces, melodramas, skits, mysteries and dramas, plays for holidays and other special occasions, such as Book Week; adaptations of classic stories and fables; historical plays; plays about black history and heroes; puppet plays; folk and fairy tales; creative dramatics; and plays for conservation, ecology or human rights programs."

‡THE PLAYWRIGHTS' CENTER'S PLAYLABS, 2301 Franklin Ave. E., Minneapolis MN 55406. (612)332-7481. Lab Director: Elissa Adams. Estab. 1971. "Playlabs is a 2-week developmental workshop for new plays. The program is held in Minneapolis and is open by script competition. It is an intensive two-week workshop focusing on the development of a script and the playwright. Four to six new plays are given rehearsed public readings at the site of the workshop." Announcements of playwrights by May 1, 1997. Playwrights receive honoraria, travel expenses, room and board.
Needs: "We are interested in playwrights with talent, ambitions for a sustained career in theater and scripts which could benefit from an intensive developmental process involving professional dramaturgs, directors and actors. US citizens or permanent residents, only. Participants must attend all or part of conference, depending on the length of their workshop. No previously produced or published materials. Send SASE after October 15, 1996 for application. Submission deadline: December 16, 1996.
Tips: "We do not buy scripts or produce them. We are a service organization that provides programs for developmental work on scripts for members."

‡PLAYWRIGHTS PREVIEW PRODUCTIONS, 17 E. 47th St., New York NY 10017. (212)421-1380. Fax: (212)421-1387. Artistic Director: Frances Hill. Literary Manager: David Sheppard. Estab. 1983. Produces 2-3 plays/year. Professional productions off or off off-Broadway—throughout the year. General audience. Submit complete script. Reports in 4 months. If produced, option for 6 months. Pays royalty.
Needs: Both one-act and full-length; generally 1 set or styled playing dual. Good imaginative, creative writing. Cast limited to 3-7.
Tips: "We tend to reject 'living-room' plays. We look for imaginative settings. Be creative and interesting with intellectual content. All submissions should be bound. Send SASE. We are looking for plays with ethnic backgrounds."

PLAYWRIGHTS THEATRE OF NEW JERSEY, 33 Green Village Rd., Madison NJ 07940. (201)514-1787. Artistic Director: John Pietrowski. Associate Artistic Director: Joseph Megel. Literary Associate: Kate McAteer. Estab. 1986. Produces 1-3 productions, 8 staged readings and sit-down readings/year. "We operate under a letter of agreement (LOA with LORT Rules) with Actors' Equity Association for all productions. Readings are held under a staged reading code." Submit complete ms. Short bio and production history required. Reports in 6 months. "For productions we ask the playwright to sign an agreement that gives us exclusive rights to the play for the production period and for 30 days following. After the 30 days we give the rights back with no strings attached, except for commercial productions. We ask that our developmental work be acknowledged in any other professional productions." Pays $500 for productions, $150 for staged readings. Scripts accepted September 1-April 30 only.
Needs: Any style or length; full length, one acts, musicals.
Tips: "We are looking for plays in the early stages of development—plays that take on important personal and social issues in a theatrical manner."

POPE THEATRE COMPANY, 262 S. Ocean Blvd., Manalapan FL 33462. (407)585-3404. Fax: (407)588-4708. Producing Artistic Director: Louis Tyrrell. Estab. 1987. Produces 7 plays/year (5 during the regular season, 2 in the summer). "We are a fully professional (LOA) theater. We attract an audience comprised of both local residents and seasonal visitors. Many, but by no means all, of our subscribers are retirees." Agented submissions only. Reports in 6 months. Buys production rights only. Pays 6-10% royalty. "A SASE is required if a playwright wants a script returned."
Needs: "We produce new American plays. We prefer to do Florida premieres of thought-provoking, socially-conscious, challenging plays. Our stage is relatively small, which prevents us from producing works with a large cast."

THE PURPLE ROSE THEATRE CO., P.O. Box 220, Chelsea MI 48118. (313)475-5817. Fax: (313)475-0802. Artistic Director: Guy Sanville. Estab. 1990. Produces 4 plays/year. PRTC is a regional theater with an S.P.T. Equity contract which produces plays intended for Midwest/Middle American audience. Query with synopsis, character breakdown, and 10-page dialogue sample. Expect replies in 3-4 months. Pays 5-10% royalty.
Needs: Modern, topical 2 acts, 90-120 minutes. Will also accept 1 acts and children's plays. Prefer scripts that use comedy to deal with serious subjects. 8 cast maximum. No fly space, unit set preferable but not required. Intimate 119 seat ¾ thrust house.

THE QUARTZ THEATRE, 392 Taylor, Ashland OR 97520-3058. (503)482-8119. Artistic Director: Dr. Robert Spira. Estab. 1973. Produces several video films/year. Send 3 pages of dialogue and personal bio. Reports in 2 weeks. Pays 5% royalty after expenses.

Needs: "Any length, any subject, with or without music. We seek playwrights with a flair for language and theatrical imagination."

Tips: "We look at anything. We do not do second productions unless substantial rewriting is involved. Our theater is a stepping stone to further production. Our playwrights are usually well-read in comparative religion, philosophy, psychology, and have a comprehensive grasp of human problems. We seek the 'self-indulgent' playwright who pleases him/herself first of all."

‡THE REP STAGE COMPANY, H.C.C., 10901 Little Patuxent Pkwy., Columbia MD 21044. (410)964-4940. Artistic Director: Valerie Costantini. Dramaturg: John Morogiello. Estab. 1993. Produces 5 plays/year. Equity small professional theater. Smith Theatre (350 seats), Theatre Outback (150 seats). Annual reading series in the Spring. General audiences. Submit complete with $5 submission fee. Reports in 4 months. Buys one-time performance rights only. Rep Stage must be acknowledged in programs of future productions. $50 for a reading, $300-500 for a production.

Needs: Wants unpublished one-acts, full-lengths, original, adaptations, not professionally produced. Open to all genres. Playwrights residing in Mid-Atlantic states only (southern PA, DE, MD, DC northern VA).

Tips: No translations, musicals, children's plays.

‡SACRAMENTO THEATRE COMPANY, 1419 H St., Sacramento CA 95814. (916)446-7501. Artistic Director: Stephen Rothman. Estab. 1941. Produces 8 plays/year. Professional 300 seat house and 90 seat house (LORT D) for subscribers and walk-ins. Query and synopsis only. Reports in 5½ weeks.

Needs: Strong characters, strong social commentary, life affirming plays. Plays for young actors (15-25) would be nice.

Tips: No serio-comic dramatic.

SAN JOSÉ REPERTORY THEATRE, P.O. Box 2399, San Jose CA 95109. (408)291-2266. Artistic Director: Ms. Timothy Near. Contact: J.R. Orlando, artistic assistant. Estab. 1980. Produces 6 plays/year. Professional Lort C theater. Query with synopsis. Reports in 6 months. Pays royalty.

Needs: Small cast musicals (no more than 8 including musicians) multicultural plays.

SEATTLE CHILDREN'S THEATRE, P.O. Box 9640, Seattle WA 98109. (206)443-0807. Artistic Director: Linda Hartzell. Queries to: Deborah L. Frockt, literary manager/dramaturg. Produces 6 plays/year. Professional (adult actors) performing for young audiences, families and school groups. Resident company—not touring. Query with synopsis, 10 pages of sample dialogue, résumé or bio. Reports on query in 6 months; mss in 1 year. Pay varies.

Needs: Challenging, imaginative, sophisticated full-length work for young audiences—both adapted and original material. We produce one musical/year. No turntable, no traps.

Tips: "We welcome queries by all populations and encourage queries by women and minorities. We prefer sophisticated material (we have many adults in our audience). All shows produced by SCT are multiracially cast."

SEATTLE REPERTORY THEATRE, 155 Mercer St., Seattle WA 98109. (206)443-2210. Artistic Director: Dan Sullivan. Estab. 1963. Produces 9 plays/year: 6 mainstage, 3 second stage. Plays performed in Seattle, with occasional transfers elsewhere. Agented submissions only. Reports in 4 months. Buys percentage of future royalties. Pays royalty.

Needs: "The Seattle Repertory Theatre produces eclectic programming. We rarely produce plays with more than 15 people in the cast! We welcome a wide variety of writing."

SHENANDOAH INTERNATIONAL PLAYWRIGHTS RETREAT, Rt. 5, Box 167F, Staunton VA 24401. (703)248-1868. Fax: (540)248-7728. Program Director: Robert Graham Small. Estab. 1976. Produces in workshop 11 plays/year. Submit complete script. Obtains no rights. Writers are provided fellowships, room and board to Shenandoah.

Tips: "We are looking for *good* material, not derivative from writers who enjoy exploration with dedicated theater professionals. Live theater *must* be theatrical! Consider global issues. Look beyond and explore connections that will lift characters/conflicts to a universal plane."

AUDREY SKIRBALL-KENIS THEATRE, 9478 W. Olympic Blvd., Suite 304, Beverly Hills CA 90212. (310)284-8965. Fax: (310)203-8067. E-mail: askplay@primenet.com. Website: http://www.primenet.com/~askplay. Director of Literary Programs: Mead Hunter. Estab. 1989. Produces 18-22 stage readings and 3-4 workshop productions/year. "We utilize three theater facilities in the Los Angeles area with professional directors and casts. Our rehearsed readings and workshop productions are offered year-round. Our audience is the general public *and* theater professionals." Query with synopsis and sample pages. Reports in 4 months. Obtains no rights. Pays $150 for staged readings; $500 for workshop productions. Workshops are selected from plays previously presented in the reading series.

● ASK now publishes a biannual magazine, *Parabasis*, which focuses on news and issues surrounding the art, business and craft of contemporary playwriting. Playwrights are asked to query about proposed articles.

Needs: "We need full-length original plays that have not yet had full productions, and which would benefit from a rehearsed reading as a means of further developing the play."

Tips: "We are a nonprofit organization dedicated to new plays and playwrights. We do not produce plays for commercial runs, nor do we request any future commitment from the playwright should their play find a production through our reading or workshop programs."

SOUTH COAST REPERTORY, P.O. Box 2197, Costa Mesa CA 92628-1197. (714)957-2602. Fax: (714)545-0391. Website: http://www.ocartsnet.org/scr/. Dramaturg: Jerry Patch. Literary Manager: John Glore. Estab. 1964. Produces 6 plays/year on mainstage, 5 on second stage. Professional nonprofit theater; a member of LORT and TCG. "We operate in our own facility which houses a 507-seat mainstage theater and a 161-seat second stage theater. We have a combined subscription audience of 21,000." Query with synopsis; scripts considered if submitted by agent. Reports in 4 months. Acquires negotiable rights. Pays negotiable royalty.

Needs: "We produce full lengths. We prefer well-written plays that address contemporary concerns and are dramaturgically innovative. A play whose cast is larger than 15-20 will need to be extremely compelling and its cast size must be justifiable."

Tips: "We don't look for a writer to write for us—he or she should write for him or herself. We look for honesty and a fresh voice. We're not likely to be interested in writers who are mindful of *any* trends. Originality and craftsmanship are the most important qualities we look for."

SOUTHERN APPALACHIAN REPERTORY THEATRE (SART), Mars Hill College, P.O. Box 620, Mars Hill NC 28754-0620. (704)689-1384. E-mail: sart@mhc.edu. Artistic Director: James W. Thomas. Asst. Managing Director: Gaynelle Caldwell. Estab. 1975. Produces 6 plays/year. "Since 1975 the Southern Appalachian Repertory Theatre has produced 35 world premieres in the 152-seat Owen Theatre on the Mars Hill College campus. The theater's goals are quality, adventurous programming and integrity, both in artistic form and in the treatment of various aspects of the human condition. SART is a professional summer theater company whose audiences range from students to senior citizens." Reports in 1 year. Also conducts an annual Southern Appalachian Playwrights' Conference in which 5 playwrights are invited for informal readings of their new scripts. Deadline for submission is October 1 and conference is held the first weekend in April. If script is selected for production during the summer season, an honorarium is paid to the playwright. Enclose SASE for return of script.

Needs: Since 1975, one of SART's goals has been to produce at least one original play each summer season. To date, 35 original scripts have been produced. Plays by southern Appalachian playwrights or about southern Appalachia are preferred, but by no means exclusively. Complete new scripts welcomed.

STAGE ONE: The Louisville Children's Theatre, 425 W. Market St., Louisville KY 40202-3300. (502)589-5946. Fax: (502)588-5910. E-mail: kystage@aol.com. Producing Director: Moses Goldberg. Estab. 1946. Produces 6-7 plays/year. 20% freelance written; 15-20% unagented submissions (excluding work of playwright-in-residence). Plays performed by an Equity company for young audiences ages 4-18; usually does different plays for different age groups within that range. Submit complete script. Reports in 4 months. Pays negotiable royalty or $25-75/performance.

Needs: "Good plays for young audiences of all types: adventure, fantasy, realism, serious problem plays about growing up or family entertainment. Cast: ideally, ten or less. Honest, visual potentiality, worthwhile story and characters are necessary. An awareness of children and their schooling is a plus. No campy material or anything condescending to children. No musicals unless they are fairly limited in orchestration."

STAGE WEST, P.O. Box 2587, Fort Worth TX 76113. (817)924-9454. Fax: (817)926-8650. Artistic Director: Jerry Russell. Estab. 1979. Produces 8 plays/year. "We stage professional productions at our own theater for a mixed general audience." Query with synopsis. Reports in 6 months. Rights are negotiable. Pays 7% royalty.

Needs: "We want full-length plays that are accessible to a mainstream audience but possess traits that are highly theatrical. Cast size of ten or less and single or unit set are desired."

‡STEPPENWOLF THEATRE COMPANY, 1650 N. Halsted, Chicago IL 60614. (312)335-1888. Artistic Director: Martha Lavey. Dramaturg/Literary Manager: Michele Volansky. Estab. 1976. Produces 9 plays/year. 500 + 300 seat subscriber audience. Many plays produced by Steppenwolf have gone to Broadway. "We currently have 18,000 savvy subscribers." Query with synopsis. Agented submissions only or letter of recommendation from theater professional. Reports in 6 months. Buys first, second class and regional rights. Pays 6-8% royalty.

Needs: Wants all sorts of full-lengths. "However, we've not done a musical in 20 years and probably won't. Also, we've rarely produced one-acts and a 28-character play may be pushing it."

Tips: No overwrought family dramas or musicals. Look to our history to know if your play is "Steppenwolf material."

‡STUDIO ARENA THEATRE, 710 Main St., Buffalo NY 14201. (716)856-8025. Artistic Director: Gavin Cameron-Webb. Estab. 1965. Produces 8 plays/year. Professional productions. Agented submissions only. Reports in 6 months.
Needs: Full-length plays. No fly space.

SYRACUSE STAGE, 820 E. Genesee, Syracuse NY 13210. (315)443-4008. Fax: (315)443-9648. Contact: Artistic Director. Estab. 1974. Produces 7 plays/year, plus one children's play. Professional LORT productions. Query with synopsis, résumé, character breakdown and an excerpt of 10 pages (cassette for musicals). Reports in 2 months on queries. Rights defined in contracts.
Needs: Full-length plays—one-person shows. Translations and adaptations accepted. All styles of theater.
Tips: No sitcom-like plays.

TADA!, 120 W. 28th St., New York NY 10001. (212)627-1732. Fax: (212)243-6736. Artistic Director: Janine Nina Trevens. Estab. 1984. Produces 2-4 plays/year. "TADA! produces original musicals and plays performed by children at our 95-seat theater. Productions are for family audiences." Submit complete script and tape, if musical. Reports in 6 months. Pays 5% royalty or commission fee (varies).
 • TADA! also sponsors a one-act play competition for their Spring Staged Reading Series. Works must be original, unproduced and unpublished one-acts. Plays may be geared toward teen audiences. Call for deadlines.
Needs: "Generally pieces run from 45-70 minutes. Must be enjoyed by children and adults and performed by a cast of children ages 6-17."
Tips: "No redone fairy tales or pieces where children are expected to play adults. Be careful not to condescend when writing for children's theater."

THE TEN-MINUTE MUSICALS PROJECT, P.O. Box 461194, West Hollywood CA 90046. (213)656-8751. Producer: Michael Koppy. Estab. 1987. Produces 1-10 plays/year. "Plays performed in Equity regional theaters in the US and Canada." Submit complete script, lead sheets and cassette. Deadline August 31; notification by December 15. Buys performance rights. Pays $250 royalty advance upon selection, against equal share of performance royalties when produced. Submission guidelines for #10 SASE.
Needs: Looking for complete short stage musicals playing between 7-14 minutes. Limit cast to 10 (5 women, 5 men).

THEATER ARTISTS OF MARIN, P.O. Box 150473, San Rafael CA 94915. (415)454-2380. Artistic Director: Charles Brousse. Estab. 1980. Produces 3 plays/year. Professional showcase productions for a general adult audience. Submit complete script. Reports in 6 months. Assists in marketing to other theaters and offers script development assistance.
Needs: All types of scripts: comedy, drama, farce. Prefers contemporary setting, with some relevance to current issues in American society. Will also consider "small musicals," reviews or plays with music. No children's shows, domestic sitcoms, one-man shows or commercial thrillers.

THEATER OF THE FIRST AMENDMENT, George Mason University MS 3E6, Fairfax VA 22030. (703)993-1122. Contact: Rick Davis. Estab. 1990. Produces 3 plays/year. Professional productions performed in an Equity LOA 150-seat theater. Query with synopsis. Reports in 3 months. Pays combination of percentage of box office gross against a guaranteed minimum royalty.

THEATRE & COMPANY, 20 Queen St. N., Kitchener, Ontario N2H 2G8 Canada. Fax: (519)579-4683. Website: http://www.cyg.net/~stamp. Artistic Director: Stuart Scadron-Wattles. Literary Manager: Wes Wikkerink. Estab. 1988. Produces 5 plays/year. Professional (non-equity) productions for a general audience. Query with synopsis and SAE with IRCs. Reports in 3 months. Pays $50-100/performance.
Needs: "One act or full length; comedy or drama; musical or straight; written from or compatible with a biblical world view." No cast above 10; prefers unit staging. Looking for small cast (less than 8) ensemble comedies.
Tips: Looks for "non-religious writing from a biblical world view for an audience which loves the theater. Avoid current trends toward shorter scenes. Playwrights should be aware that they are writing for the stage— not television. We encourage audience interaction, using an acting ensemble trained in improvisation."

THEATRE AT LIME KILN, P.O. Box 663, Lexington VA 24450. (540)463-7088. Fax: (540)463-1082. E-mail: limekiln@cfw.com. Artistic Director: Barry Mines. Estab. 1983. Produces 7 plays/year. Professional outdoor summer theater. Audience is family oriented. Query with synopsis or submit complete ms. Reports in 4 months. Rights vary. Pay varies.
Needs: Full length, musical or straight. Material should reflect culture/issues/concerns of Appalachian region. Outdoor theater, limited sets. Cast of 9 or less preferred.
Tips: No urban angst. Smaller cast shows have a better chance of being produced.

THEATRE WEST, 3333 Cahuenga W., Los Angeles CA 90068-1365. Contact: Arden Lewis or Doug Haverty. Estab. 1962. Produces 6 plays or one acts/year. "99-seat waiver productions in our theater. Audiences are primarily young urban professionals." Submit script, résumé and letter requesting membership. Reports in 4 months. Contracts a percentage of writer's share to another media. Pays royalty "based on gross box office—equal to all other participants."
Needs: Uses minimalistic scenery.
Tips: "TW is a dues-paying membership company. Only members can submit plays for production. So you must seek membership prior to action for a production."

‡THEATREVIRGINIA, 2800 Grove Ave., Richmond VA 23221-2466. Artistic Director: George Black. Estab. 1955. Produces 5-8, publishes 0-1 new play/year. Query with synopsis and 15 page sample. Accepts agented submissions. Solicitations in 1 month for initial query, 3-8 months for script. Rights negotiated. Payment negotiated.
Needs: No one-acts; no children's theater.

THEATREWORKS, University of Colorado, P.O. Box 7150, Colorado Springs CO 80933-7150. (719)593-3232. Fax: (719)593-3582. Producing Director: Ronnie Storey. Estab. 1975. Produces 4 full-length plays/year and 2 new one-acts. "New full-length plays produced on an irregular basis. Casts are semi-professional and plays are produced at the university." Query with synopsis. No unsolicited scripts. One-act plays are accepted as Playwrights' Forum competition entries. Submit complete script. Deadline: December 1; winners announced March 1. Two one-act competition winners receive full production, cash awards and travel allowances. Acquires exclusive regional option for duration of production. Full rights revert to author upon closing. Pays $200 prize plus travel and accommodations.
Needs: Full-lengths and one-acts—no restrictions on subject. "Cast size should not exceed 20; stage area is small with limited wing and fly space. Theatreworks is interested in the exploration of new and inventive theatrical work. Points are scored by imaginative use of visual image and bold approach to subject." No melodrama or children's plays.
Tips: "Too often, new plays seem far too derivative of television and film writing. We think theater is a medium which an author must specifically attack. The standard three-act form would appear to be obsolete. Economy, brevity and innovation are favorably received."

‡VIGILANTE THEATRE CO., P.O. Box 507, Bozeman MT 59771-0507. (406)586-3897. Artistic Director: Brian V. Massman. Estab. 1982. Produces 3-4 plays/year. Plays by professional touring company that does productions by or about people and themes of the Northwest. "Past productions were concerned with homeless people, agriculture, literature by Northwest writers, one-company towns and spouse abuse in rural areas." Submit complete ms. Reports in 6 months. Pays $10-50/performance.
Needs: Produces full-length plays and some one-acts. "Staging suitable for a small touring company and cast limited to four actors (two men, two women). Double casting actors for more play characters is also an option."
Tips: "No musicals requiring orchestras and a chorus line. Although we prefer a script of some thematic substance, the company is very adept at comedy and would prefer the topic to include humor."

VIRGINIA STAGE COMPANY, P.O. Box 3770, Norfolk VA 23514-3770. (804)627-6988. Fax: (804)628-5958. E-mail: jhlind@visi.net. Website: http://www.whro.org/cl/rsc/. Literary Manager: Jefferson H. Lindquist. Estab. 1979. VSC is a LORT C-1 theatre serving southeastern Virginia audiences. Performing spaces are mainstage (700-seat) theatre with proscenium stage and a 99-seat second stage. Produces 4-6 plays/year. Send letter, synopsis, SASE, and sample pages only. Submission time: January-April. Responds in 6 months. Scripts returned to author or agent only if postage is included.
Needs: Full-length plays, and musicals with tapes only.

WALNUT STREET THEATRE, Ninth and Walnut Streets, Philadelphia PA 19107. (215)574-3550. Executive Director: Bernard Havard. Literary Manager: Beverly Elliott. Estab. 1809. Produces 5 mainstage and 5 studio plays/year. "Our plays are performed in our own space. WST has 3 theaters—a proscenium (mainstage), 1,052 seats; 2 studios, 79-99 seats. We have a subscription audience, second largest in the nation." Query with synopsis and 10 pages. Writer's must be members of the Dramatists' Guild. Reports in 5 months. Rights negotiated per project. Pays royalty (negotiated per project) or outright purchase.
Needs: "Full-length dramas and comedies, musicals, translations, adaptations and revues. The studio plays must have a cast of no more than four, simple sets."
Tips: "Bear in mind that on the mainstage we look for plays with mass appeal, Broadway-style. The studio spaces are our off-Broadway. No children's plays. Our mainstage audience goes for work that is entertaining and light. Our studio season is where we look for plays that have bite and are more provocative." Include SASE for return of materials.

WATERLOO COMMUNITY PLAYHOUSE, P.O. Box 433, Waterloo IA 50704-0433. (319)235-0367. Charles Stilwill, managing artistic director. Estab. 1917. Plays performed by Waterloo Community Playhouse with a volunteer cast. Produces 11 plays (7 adult, 4 children's); 1-2 musicals and 9-10 nonmusicals/year; 1-3 originals. 17% freelance written; most unagented submissions. Works with 1-3 unpublished/unproduced writers annually. "We are one of few community theaters with a commitment to new scripts. We do at least one and have done as many as four a year. We have 4,300 season members. Average attendance is 3,300. We do a wide variety of plays. Our public isn't going to accept nudity, too much sex, too much strong language. We don't have enough Black actors to do all-Black shows. Theater has done plays with as few as 2 characters, and as many as 98. On the main stage, we usually pay between $400 and $500. We also produce children's theater. Submit complete script. Please, no loose pages. Reports negatively within 1 year, but acceptance sometimes takes longer because we try to fit a wanted script into the balanced season. We sometimes hold a script longer than a year if we like it but cannot immediately find the right slot for it. In 1994 we did the world premiere of *The Ninth Step* which was written in 1989 and the year before we did the world premiere of *Grace Under Pressure*, written in 1984. We just did the world premiere of *A Tradition of Service* written in 1990."

Needs: "For our Children's Theater and our Adult Biannual Holiday (Christmas) show, we are looking for good adaptations of name children's stories or very good shows that don't necessarily have a name. We produce children's theater with both adult and child actors."

WEST COAST ENSEMBLE, P.O. Box 38728, Los Angeles CA 90038. (213)871-8673. Artistic Director: Les Hanson. Estab. 1982. Produces 6 plays/year. Plays performed in 1 of 2 theaters in Hollywood. Submit complete script. Reports in 6-9 months. Obtains exclusive rights in southern California to present the play for the period specified. All ownership and rights remain with the playwright. Pays $25-45/performance. Writers guidelines for #10 SASE.

Needs: Prefers a cast of 6-12.

Tips: "Submit the script in acceptable dramatic script format."

‡**WESTBETH THEATRE CENTER, INC.**, 151 Bank St., New York NY 10014-2049. (212)691-2272. Fax: (212)924-7185. Producing Director: Arnold Engelman. Literary Manager: Steven Bloom. Estab. 1977. Produces 10 readings and 6 productions/year. Professional off-Broadway theater. Submit complete ms with SASE. Responds in 4 months. Obtains rights to produce as showcase with option to enter into full option agreement.

Needs: "Contemporary full-length plays. Production values (i.e., set, costumes, etc.) should be kept to a minimum." No period pieces. Limit 10 actors; doubling explained.

THE WOMEN'S PROJECT AND PRODUCTIONS, 55 West End Ave., New York NY 10033. (212)765-1706. Fax: (212)765-2024. Artistic Director: Julia Miles. Estab. 1978. Produces 3 plays/year. Professional Off-Broadway productions. Query with synopsis and 10 sample pages of dialogue. Reports in 1 month on queries.

Needs: "We are looking for full-length plays, written by women."

WOOLLY MAMMOTH THEATRE COMPANY, 1401 Church St. NW, Washington DC 20005-1903. (202)393-3939. Fax: (202)667-0904. E-mail: wollymamm@aol.com. Artistic Director: Howard Shalwitz. Literary Manager: Jim Byrnes. Produces 5 plays/year. 50% freelance written. Produces professional productions for the general public in Washington DC. 2-3 scripts/year unagented submissions. Works with 1-2 unpublished/unproduced writers/year. Accepts unsolicited scripts. Reports in 3 months on scripts; very interesting scripts often take much longer. Buys first- and second- class production rights. Pays 5% royalty.

Needs: "We look only for plays that are highly unusual in some way. Also interested in multicultural projects. Apart from an innovative approach, there is no formula. One-acts are not used." Cast limit of 8.

WORCESTER FOOTHILLS THEATRE COMPANY, 100 Front St., Suite 137, Worcester MA 01608. (508)754-3314. Fax: (508)767-0676. Artistic Director: Marc P. Smith. Estab. 1974. Produces 7 plays/year. Full time professional theater, general audience. Query with synopsis. Reports in 3 weeks. Pays royalty.

Needs: "Produce plays for general audience. No gratuitous violence, sex or language. Prefer cast under 10 and single set. 30' proscenium with apron but no fly space."

SCREENWRITING

Practically everyone you meet in Los Angeles, from your airport cabbie on, is writing a script. It might be a feature film, movie of the week, TV series or documentary, but the sheer amount of competition can seem overwhelming. Some will never make a sale, while others make a decent living on sales and options without ever having any of their work produced. But there are those writers who make a living doing what they love and see their names roll by on the credits. How do they get there? How do *you* get there?

First, work on your writing. You'll improve with each script, so there is no way of getting around the need to write and write some more. It's a good idea to read as many scripts as you can get your hands on. Check your local bookstores and libraries. Script City (8033 Sunset Blvd., Suite 1500, Hollywood CA 90046, (800)676-2522) carries thousands of movie and TV scripts, classics to current releases, as well as books, audio/video seminars and software in their $2 catalog. Book City (Dept. 101, 308 N. San Fernando Blvd., Burbank CA 91502, (800)4-CINEMA) has film and TV scripts in all genres and a large selection of movie books in their $2.50 catalog.

There are lots of books that will give you the "rules" of format and structure for writing for TV or film. Samuel French (7623 Sunset Blvd., Hollywood CA 90046 (213)876-0570) carries a number of how-to books and reference materials on these subjects. The correct format marks your script as a professional submission. Most successful scriptwriters will tell you to learn the correct structure, internalize those rules—and then throw them away and write intuitively.

Writing for TV

To break into TV you must have spec scripts—work written for free that serves as a calling card and gets you in the door. A spec script showcases your writing abilities and gets your name in front of influential people. Whether a network has invited you in to pitch some ideas, or a movie producer has contacted you to write a first draft for a feature film, the quality of writing in your spec script got their attention and that may get you the job.

It's a good idea to have several spec scripts, perhaps one each for three of the top five shows in the format you prefer to work in, whether it's sitcom (half-hour comedies), episodic (one hour series) or movie of the week (two hour dramatic movies). Perhaps you want to showcase the breadth of your writing ability; some writers have a portfolio of a few eight o'clock type shows (i.e., *Friends*, *Mad About You*, *Home Improvement*), a few nine-o'clock shows (i.e., *Ellen*, *Seinfeld*, *The X Files*) and one or two episodics (i.e., *Homicide*, *Law and Order*, *NYPD Blue*). These are all "hot" shows for writers and can demonstrate your abilities to create believable dialogue for characters already familiar to your intended readers. For TV and cable movies you should have completed original scripts (not sequels to existing movies) and you might also have a few for episodic TV shows.

In choosing the shows you write spec scripts for you must remember one thing: don't write a script for a show you want to work on. If you want to write for *NYPD Blue*, for example, you'll send a *Law and Order* script and vice versa. It may seem contradictory, but it is standard practice. It reduces the chances of lawsuits, and writers and producers can feel very proprietary about their show and their stories. They may not be objective enough to fairly evaluate your writing. In submitting another similar type of show you'll avoid those problems while demonstrating comparable skills.

In writing your TV script you must get *inside* the show and understand the characters' internal motivations. You must immerse yourself in how the characters speak, think and interact. Don't introduce new characters in a spec script for an existing show—write believable dialogue for the characters as they are portrayed. Be sure to choose a show that you like—you'll be better able to demonstrate your writing ability through characters you respond to.

You must also understand the external factors. How the show is filmed bears on how you write. Most sitcoms are shot on videotape with three cameras, on a sound stage with a studio audience. Episodics are often shot on film with one camera and include on-location shots. *Mad About You* has a flat, evenly-lit look and takes place in a limited number of locations. *Law and Order* has a gritty realism with varying lighting and a variety of settings from McCord's office to outside a bodega on East 135th.

Another important external influence in writing for TV is the timing of commercials in conjunction with the act structure. There are lots of sources detailing the suggested content and length of acts, but generally a sitcom has a teaser (short opening scene), two acts and a tag (short closing scene), and an episodic has a teaser, four acts and a tag. Each act closes with a turning point. Watching TV analytically and keeping a log of events will reveal some elements of basic structure. *Successful Scriptwriting*, by Wolff & Cox (Writer's Digest Books), offers detailed discussions of various types of shows.

Writing for the movies

With feature films you may feel at once more liberated and more bound by structure. An original movie script contains characters you have created, with storylines you design, allowing you more freedom than you have in TV. However, your writing must still convey believable dialogue and realistic characters, with a plausible plot and high-quality writing carried through the roughly 120 pages. The characters must have a problem that involves the audience. When you go to a movie you don't want to spend time watching the *second* worst night of a character's life. You're looking for the big issue that crystallizes a character, that portrays a journey with important consequences.

At the same time you are creating, you should also be constructing. Be aware of the basic three act structure for feature films. Scenes can be of varying lengths, but are usually no longer than three to three and a half pages. Some writers list scenes that must occur, then flesh them out from beginning to end, writing with the structure of events in mind. The beginning and climactic scenes are the easiest; it's how they get there from here that's difficult.

Many novice screenwriters tend to write too many visual cues and camera directions into their scripts. Your goal should be to write something readable, like a "compressed novella." Write succinct resonant scenes and leave the camera technique to the director and producer. In action/adventure movies, however, there needs to be a balance since the script demands more visual direction.

It seems to be easier for TV writers to cross over to movies. Cable movies bridge the two, and are generally less derivative and more willing to take chances with a higher quality show designed to attract an audience not interested in network offerings. Cable is also less susceptible to advertiser pullout, which means it can tackle more controversial topics.

Feature films and TV are very different and writers occupy different positions. TV is a medium for writers and producers; directors work for them. Many TV writers are also producers. In feature films the writers and producers work for the director and often have little or no say about what happens to the work once the script has been sold. For TV the writer pitches the idea; for feature films generally the producer pitches the idea and then finds a writer.

Marketing your scripts

If you intend to make writing your profession you must act professionally. Accepted submission practices should become second nature.

- The initial pitch is made through a query letter, which is no longer than one page with a one paragraph synopsis and brief summary of your credits if they are relevant to the subject of your script.
- Never send a complete manuscript until it is requested.
- Almost every script sent to a producer, studio or agent must be accompanied by a release form. Ask for that company's form when you receive an invitation to

INSIDER REPORT

Getting a Little Help From a *Friends* Writer

You envy the faces. You detest the song. Yet you still watch the show. Why? Is it because Courtney Cox did some dancing in the dark with Springsteen, or that Matthew Perry once yanked Julia Roberts from the depths of Lyle Lovett's hair? Small chance.

Mike Sikowitz

Look instead to little known figures who spend endless hours composing stories and injecting lines into the mouths of television's favorite nonbiological family. Like their wit or leave it, you can't deny the *Friends* writing team has created and sustained one of the nation's most compelling assembly of sitcom characters since *Cheers*. A crucial voice in this crack-pack is senior writer Mike Sikowitz.

Sikowitz humorously credits much of what he's learned to the University of Pennsylvania. "I think I learned what I'm doing now from my years at Penn," says the degreed history major. But he's not talking academics. "College helped most in that I shared a house with nine friends who had very good senses of humor, which created a competitive atmosphere where everyone was constantly making quips and witty insults. You were always trying to come up with the best joke—that's what it's like to be on a sitcom staff."

Sikowitz and partner Jeff Astrof had two things in mind when they wrote their first spec script for *Cheers* in 1989. "First, we wanted to see what the process of writing a script is like, and second, we thought, 'who knows, maybe we could become TV writers.' We wrote the script not knowing if it was worth anything."

Fortunately it had worth. Just as fortunately Sikowitz had a contact—his father's old army buddy was a movie producer. Sikowitz sent him the script and he forwarded it to an agency. It impressed someone there, and before long Sikowitz and Astrof became clients. They moved to L.A. but immediate employment eluded them. "We weren't getting any work because our agent wasn't doing anything for us. So we found another agent who also coincidentally went to Penn—another connection—and he's been working hard for us ever since."

A rare opportunity arose when their new agent enrolled Sikowitz and Astrof into the ten-week Warner Brothers Writing Program. "That program really helped us," says Sikowitz. "You're taken through a simulated process of what it's like to be a TV writer, from pitching ideas and writing an outline to actually writing a draft and hearing it read by actors. You ultimately develop a polished script. Because it's staffed with Warner Brothers producers and others in the industry, you get to meet several producers and executives. After the program these people really go to bat for you to staff Warner Brothers projects."

The seminar proved significantly useful for Sikowitz and Astrof. The two became writers on *Hangin' with Mr. Cooper* until they moved to the animated *Duckman*. After a season they left *Duckman* and went to *Friends*.

So how did they land a job with the ever-popular *Friends*? TV powerhouses Kaufman and Crane developed the initial television deal with NBC and needed writers. Says Sikowitz, "Agents are always up on industry needs and keep their writers aware of what's out there. Our agent thought we should go for it, so we did. After reading our past scripts and spec scripts, Kaufman and Crane picked us. When we began writing for the show we had no idea it would catch on like this."

Sikowitz claims that without his agent's nudge he wouldn't be writing for *Friends* today. "We left *Duckman* because our agent wanted us on a more visible show. We liked *Duckman* and were doing this petulant artist thing ('We don't care if nobody's watching; we like what we're writing.') because even though *Duckman* wasn't commercially successful, we were working successfully as a writing team. But we weren't getting exposure, so we decided to move on and take a risk with *Friends*. It was a great move."

So great that it's led Sikowitz and Astrof to projects outside of *Friends*. Most notable is an upcoming project with DreamWorks, the Spielberg, Geffen, Katzenberg titan *Premiere* called "the hottest movie-TV-music factory in Hollywood." Katzenberg saw an episode of *Friends* and loved it, so he called Sikowitz and Astrof in for a meeting. Now they're working on a development deal with the Dream Team.

When asked whether his success is an aberration or common affair in TV Land, Sikowitz explains it's a combination. "We're atypical in that we've only been here four and a half years and we've achieved much. Many people go through so many steps and odd jobs to land a writing position. We didn't do that. But we're typical because we had a contact, which really helps. With no contact you're just sending cold submissions to people who don't know you, and there's a slim chance they'll read something when they don't recognize the return address. At first a good contact is just as important as the writing."

Now don't stop writing to divert all energies to making contacts. Your primary concern should be to improve your writing while broadening your knowledge of topics to write about. "Don't just write a spec script and sit back for the phone to ring," says Sikowitz. "Your next script will only get better. And soak in as much information as you can. Writers should know what's going on in the world and watch things they might not normally watch, to understand the language of different kinds of television. The more things you can draw from, the better writer you'll become. Watch a cooking show and study how these people talk or learn the lingo of weather forecasters and sports announcers."

Also remember to analyze shows in a vein similar to what you're writing. "With cable everything is available now, so you have access to all the best shows. Even watch shows that aren't that great. Think about why some shows work and others don't. How differently would you handle them?"

Speaking of the varying voices in television, Sikowitz says, "The language of

INSIDER REPORT, *continued*

a sitcom is jokes." Yet jokes alone won't make a successful show; compelling characters and an interesting story are also essential, especially the latter. "In sitcoms everything revolves around a story. You can tell a really interesting story with okay characters much better than you can take great characters and have them in an episode with no story. Story is king. Still I'd also say developed characters separate a great show from just a good show. But you need good jokes, too. You've got to keep the audience entertained."

Given the show's enormous popularity, it seems *Friends* succeeds in the entertainment department. And maybe its writers are to thank. Or it could be just those pretty faces.

—*Don Prues*

submit the whole script. Mark your envelope "release form enclosed" to prevent it being returned unread.

- Always include a self-addressed stamped envelope (SASE) if you want your work returned; a disposable copy may be accompanied by a self-addressed stamped postcard for reply.
- Allow four to six weeks from receipt of your manuscript before writing a follow-up letter.

When your script is requested, be sure it's written in the appropriate format. Unusual binding, fancy covers or illustrations mark an amateur. Three brass brads with a plain or black cover indicate a pro.

There are a limited number of ideas in the world, so it's inevitable that similar ideas occur to more than one person. Hollywood is a buyer's market and a release form states that pretty clearly. An idea is not copyrightable, so be careful about sharing premises. The written expression of that idea, however, can be protected and it's a good idea to do so. The Writers Guild of America can register scripts for television and theatrical motion pictures, series formats, storylines and step outlines. You need not be a member of the WGA to use this service. Copyrighting your work with the Copyright Office of the Library of Congress also protects your work from infringement. Contact either agency for more information and an application form.

If you are a writer, you should write—all the time. When you're not writing, read. There are numerous books on the art, craft and business of screenwriting. See the Publications of Interest at the end of *Writer's Market* for a few or check the catalogs of companies previously mentioned. The different trade papers of the industry such as *Daily Variety* and *Hollywood Reporter* can keep you in touch with the day to day doings and upcoming events. Specialty newsletters such as *Hollywood Scriptwriter*, *Creative Screenwriting* and *New York Scriptwriter* offer tips from successful scriptwriters and agents. The *Hollywood Creative Directory* is an extensive list of production companies, studios and networks that also lists companies and talent with studio deals.

Computer services, such as America Online, have various bulletin boards and chat hours for scriptwriters that provide contact with other writers and a chance to share information and encouragement.

It may take years of work before you come up with a script someone is willing to take a chance on. Those years need to be spent learning your craft and understanding the business. Polishing scripts, writing new material, keeping current with the industry and networking constantly will keep you busy. When you do get that call you'll be confident in your abilities and know that your hard work is beginning to pay off.

For information on some screenwriting markets not listed in *Writer's Market*, see the General Index.

‡□**ALL AMERICAN COMMUNICATIONS**, 808 Wilshire, Santa Monica CA 90401. (310)656-1100. E-mail: allamcom@aol.com. Website: http://baywatch.compuserve.com. Contact: Dan Watanabe. Estab. 1974. Produces *Baywatch*, *Baywatch Nights* and *Sinbad*. Looking for television programs—syndicated, network, cable original. Works with 10 writers/year. Buys all rights. Reports in 1 month. Query with synopsis. Pay varies depending on project.
Needs: Looking for one-hour dramatic TV series proposals or movies of the week.

□**ALLIED ARTISTS, INC.**, 859 N. Hollywood Way, Suite 377, Burbank CA 91505. (818)594-4089. Vice President, Development: John Nichols. Estab. 1990. Produces material for broadcast and cable television, home video and film. Buys 3-5 scripts/year. Works with 10-20 writers/year. Buys first rights or all rights. Accepts previously produced material. Reports in 2 months on queries; 3 months on scripts. Submit synopsis/outline. Pays in accordance with Writers Guild standards (amount and method negotiable). Written queries only—*no phone pitches*.
Needs: Films, videotapes. Social issue TV special (30-60 minutes); special interest home video topics; instruction and entertainment; positive values feature screenplays.
Tips: "We are looking for positive, up-lifting dramatic stories involving real people situations. Future trend is for more reality-based programming, as well as interactive television programs for viewer participation."

ANGEL FILMS, 967 Highway 40, New Franklin MO 65274-9778. (573)698-3900. Fax: (573)698-3900. E-mail: euttland@aol.com. Vice President Production: Matthew Eastman. Estab. 1980. Produces material for feature films, television. Buys 10 scripts/year. Works with 20 writers/year. Buys all rights. Accepts previously published material (if rights available). Reports in 1 months on queries; 1-2 months on scripts. Query with synopsis. Makes outright purchase "depending upon budget for project. Our company is a low-budget producer which means people get paid fairly, but don't get rich."
● This company is looking for writers for a new science fiction television series, *The Chronicles of Erick Uttland*.
Needs: Films (35mm), videotapes. "We are looking for projects that can be used to produce feature film and television feature film and series work. These would be in the areas of action adventure, comedy, horror, thriller, science fiction, animation for children." Also looking for direct to video materials.
Tips: "Don't copy others. Try to be original. Don't overwork your idea. As far as trends are concerned, don't pay attention to what is 'in.' By the time it gets to us it will most likely be on the way 'out.' And if you can't let your own grandmother read it, don't send it. If you wish material returned, enclose proper postage with all submissions. Send SASE for response to queries and return of scripts."

ANGEL'S TOUCH PRODUCTIONS, 1055 Allen Ave., Suite B, Glendale CA 91201-1654. Director of Development: Phil Nemy. Estab. 1986. Professional screenplays and teleplays. Send synopsis. Reports in 6 months. Rights negotiated between production company and author. Payment negotiated.
Needs: All types, all genres, only full-length teleplays and screenplays—no one-acts.
Tips: "We are now only seeking feature film screenplays, television screenplays, and episodic teleplays. No phone calls!"

‡**BANDEIRA ENTERTAINMENT**, 176 N. Swall Dr., Beverly Hills CA 90212. Contact: Jane Gurtiza. Estab. 1991. Audience is 15 years and up—drama. Buys 10-12 scripts/year. Works with 8 writers/year. Buys all rights. Accepts previously produced material. Accepts scripts with major agents only. Reports in 2 months. Free catalog. Query with synopsis and completed script.
Needs: Film (35mm). All comedies, dramas, romance, etc. (90-150 minutes).

BARNSTORM FILMS, 73 Market St., Venice CA 90291. (310)396-5937. Contact: Josh Deighton. Estab. 1969. Produces feature films. Buys 2-3 scripts/year. Works with 4-5 writers/year. No query letters accepted; submissions by WGA signatory agents only.
Tips: Looking for strong, character-based commercial scripts. Not interested in science fiction or fantasy. Must send SASE with query letter. Query first, do not send script unless we request it!"

□**BIG STAR MOTION PICTURES LTD.**, 13025 Yonge St., #201, Richmond Hill, Ontario L4E 1Z5 Canada. (416)720-9825. Contact: Frank A. Deluca. Estab. 1991. Buys 5 scripts/year. Works with 5-10 writers/year. Reports in 1 month on queries; 3 months on scripts. Submit synopsis first. Scripts should be submitted by agent or lawyer.

Needs: Films (35mm). "We are very active in all medias, but are primarily looking for television projects, cable, network, etc. True life situations are of special interest for MOW."

‡BOZ PRODUCTIONS, 7612 Fountain Ave., Los Angeles CA 90046. (213)876-3232. Fax: (213)876-3231. E-mail: boz51@aol.com. Estab. 1987. All audiences. Buys 3-5 scripts/year. Works with several writers/year. Buys all rights. Accepts previously produced material. Reports in 1 month on queries; 1-2 months on scripts. Query with synopsis and résumé. Pay varies.
Needs: Films (35mm). Feature-length film scripts or rights to real stories for MOW's.

CANVAS HOUSE FILMS, 3671 Bear St., #E, Santa Ana CA 92704. (714)850-1964. Producer: Mitch Teemley. Estab. 1994. General audience. Buys 2-3 scripts/year. Works with 10-15 writers/year. Buys first rights, all rights. Accepts previously produced material. Reports in 1 month on queries; 4 months on submissions. Query with detailed (2-4 page) synopsis and résumé. Pays in accordance with Writers Guild standards.
Needs: Films (35mm). "Quality feature-length filmscripts—all types, but no lurid, 'hard-R'-rated material."
Tips: "Know proper formatting and story structure. There is a need for 'family' material that can appeal to *grown-ups* as well as children."

CINE/DESIGN FILMS, INC., P.O. Box 6495, Denver CO 80206. (303)777-4222. Producer/Director: Jon Husband. Produces educational material for general, sales-training and theatrical audiences. 75% freelance written; 90% unagented submissions. "Original, solid ideas are encouraged." Rights purchased vary.
Needs: Films (16, 35mm). "Motion picture outlines in the theatrical and documentary areas. We are seeking theatrical scripts in the low-budget area that are possible to produce for under $1 million. We seek flexibility and personalities who can work well with our clients." Send 8-10-page outline before submitting ms. Pays $100-200/screen minute on 16mm productions. Theatrical scripts negotiable.
Tips: "Understand the marketing needs of film production today. Materials will not be returned."

CLARK FILM PRODUCTION CHARITY, INC., P.O. Box 773, Balboa CA 92661. President: Mr. Clark. Estab. 1987. General audience. Buys 1 script/year. Works with 4 writers/year. Buys first rights. Accepts previously produced material. Reports in 6 months. Submit synopsis/outline. Pays in accordance with Writers Guild of America west standards.
Needs: Family-oriented, general audience materials.
Recent Production: "Currently working with King Kigel V, His Majesty the King of Rwanda, Africa, on a public service announcement through United Nations UNICEF for His Majesty's children and orphans with relief. Although now accepting general audience material, as always."

‡CPC ENTERTAINMENT, 840 N. Larrabee St., #2322, Los Angeles CA 90069. (310)652-8194. Development Manager: Shannon Richardson. Feature and TV. Buys 15 scripts/year. Works with 24 writer/year. Buys all rights. No previously produced material. Reports in 1 months on queries; 2-3 months on submissions. Query with 1 page synopsis, 1 sentence premise and résumé. Outright purchase WGA minimum; and up.
Needs: Film (35mm), videotapes. Needs feature and TV movie screenplays.

☐CRONUS INTERNATIONAL ENTERTAINMENT, INC., 5110 Tujunga Ave., #2, North Hollywood CA 91601-4924. (818)763-1977. Producing Director: Herb Rodgers. "The company was formed in 1990 for the purpose of selecting screenplays and developing them for production, either as movies of the week for network/cable, or for production for feature length films for distribution internationally. All scripts should follow professional format and be 95-110 pages in length. Authors of selected scripts will be contacted about options to produce. Only scripts with SASE will be returned."
Tips: Submit query letter only with a 1-page synopsis stating the protagonist, his/her goal and the "payoff." Unsolicited scripts will be returned.

EARTH TRACKS PRODUCTIONS, 4809 Avenue N, Suite 286, Brooklyn NY 11234. Contact: David Krinsky. Estab. 1985. Produces material for independent studios. Buys 1-3 scripts/year. Buys all rights. No books, no treatments, no plays, no articles. *Only* completed movie and TV movie scripts. Reports in 6 weeks on queries.
   ● This producer notes a high rate of inappropriate submissions. Please read and follow guidelines carefully.
Needs: Commercial, well-written, low budget, high concept scripts in the drama, comedy, action and thriller genres. No other genre scripts. Query with 1-page synopsis and SASE. No treatments. *Do not send any scripts unless requested.*
Tips: "Writers should be flexible and open to suggestions. Material with interest (in writing) from a known actor/director is a *major plus* in the consideration of the material. We also need sexy thrillers. Any submissions of more than two pages will *not* be read or returned. We have recently reorganized and are only seeking quality, *low budget* scripts for inhouse production. Controversial, with strong lead characters (dialogue), are preferred." (Examples: 'Natural Born Killers,' 'From Dusk Till Dawn,' 'Pulp Fiction.')

ENTERTAINMENT PRODUCTIONS, INC., 2118 Wilshire Blvd., Suite 744, Santa Monica CA 90403. (310)456-3143. Producer: Edward Coe. Contact: Story Editor. Estab. 1971. Produces films for theatrical and television (worldwide) distribution. Reports in 1 month only if SASE enclosed.
Needs: Screenplay originals. Query with synopsis and SASE. Price negotiated on a project-by-project basis. Writer's release in any form will be acceptable.
Tips: "State why script has great potential."

‡**FORTIS ENTERTAINMENT**, 9000 Sunset Blvd., Suite 405, Los Angeles CA 90069. (310)226-7114. Contact: Jane Austen. Estab. 1990. Audience is TV-motion picture and theater. Buys 2 scripts/year. Works with 8 writers/year. Buys all rights. Accepts produced theater material. Reports in 2 months on queries; 1 month on submissions. Query with synopsis, résumé and SAE. Pays in accordance with Writer's Guild standards if writer is WGA, if not, whatever the market will pay.
Needs: Film (35mm). "Tight, intelligent thrillers/action/adventure. In the mold of 'Three Days of the Condor,' 'No Way Out,' 'Cliff Hanger.' No comedies.
Tips: "Within the above genres people are always looking for something new they haven't seen. Research. Don't try to copy other writers. Don't write for yourself, but to entertain an audience."

GAMARA PICTURES, 6943 Hazeltine, #14, Van Nuys CA 91405. Producer/Director: Dali Moyzes. Intended for all audiences. Buys 4 scripts/year. Works with 4-8 writers/year. Buys all rights. Reports in 2 months. Query with complete script, résumé and SASE. Pays in accordance with WGA standards.
Needs: Films (35mm). Feature film screenplays and TV sitcoms—any subject—for future possible production.
Tips: "Please send by special 4th class mail (printed matter)—about $1.50. Copy script on both sides of the paper; be environmentally friendly, save trees."

GOLDEN QUILL, GQ-NY, 65 Bleeker St., 12th Floor, New York NY 10012; GQ-LA, 8899 Beverly Blvd., Suite 702, Los Angeles CA 90048. Executive Vice President: Hassan Ildari. Estab. 1991. Buys 3 scripts/year. Works with 6 writers/year. Accepts previously produced material. Reports in 3 weeks. Query with synopsis. Makes outright purchase.
Needs: Films (35mm).

‡**GOTHAM ENTERTAINMENT GROUP**, 99 Hudson St., Suite 200, New York NY 10013. (212)376-6063. Director of Development: Noah Baylin. Estab. 1995. Theatrical features. Buys 5-10 scripts/year. Works with 10-25 writers/year. Buys all rights. Accepts previously produced material on occasion. Reports in 2 weeks. Query with completed script. *Writer's Market* recommends sending a query first. Makes outright purchase.
Needs: Film (35mm). "We produce only feature films. We need big action scripts. We have a deal with Miramax films on our productions. Call us."
Tips: Trends in the business include less and less sex and exploitation in features.

‡**EDWARD D. HANSEN, INC.**, 437 Harvard Dr., Arcadia CA 91006-2639. Phone/fax: (818)447-3168. President: Ed Hansen. Supervisor, Literary Development: Buck Flower. Estab. 1973. Theatrical, TV and home video markets comprise our audience. Optioned, purchased, marketed and/or produced 10 screenplays in 1993. Reports in 3 months.
Needs: Looking for scripts for feature films, movies of the week and home videos: all genres. Query with synopsis and SASE for release form. Pays in accordance with Writers Guild standards. Professional assistance available for novel or play adaptations, concept development and certain properties not "ready to shoot" that contain unique characters or an extremely marketable storyline.
Tips: "Don't try to tap into a trend. By the time you get it done, it's gone. What comes around goes around. In the last year, we've seen script needs at the highest end ($20 million +) and at the lowest end ($300,000-$2 million). Very few requests for film productions between $2-20 million. More important than ever to have some money or an actor *attached* to a spec script."

INTERNATIONAL HOME ENTERTAINMENT, 1440 Veteran Ave., Suite 650, Los Angeles CA 90024. (213)460-4545. Assistant to the President: Jed Leland, Jr. Estab. 1976. Buys first rights. Reports in 2 months. Query. Pays in accordance with Writers Guild standards. *No unsolicited scripts.*
   • Looking for material that is international in scope.
Tips: "Our response time is faster on average now (3-6 weeks), but no replies without a SASE. We do not respond to unsolicited phone calls."

THE JEWISH TELEVISION COMMISSION, 1 South Franklin St., Chicago IL 60606-4694. (312)444-2896. Fax: (312)855-3757. Director of Programming and Syndication: Mindy Soble. "Television scripts are requested for *The Magic Door*, a children's program produced in conjunction with CBS's WBBM-TV in Chicago." Four scripts/TV season. Buys all rights. Reports in 1 month. Writers guidelines for #10 SASE.

Needs: "*Magic Door Television Theatre* is an anthology series of 4 specials/year designed for broadcast on weekends around the 12:00-3:00 p.m. hours. The target audience is 12 years of age, however the material should be viable for the whole family to enjoy. It is Jewish in content, yet universal in scope. Each episode should be built on an idea anchored in a Jewish value. While the perspective is Jewish, such topics as family, education, adversity, tradition, etc., are obviously not exclusive to the Jewish purview. We seek material rooted in Jewish thought, yet characterized by a 'pro-social' message. This anthology series is television theater. It is designed to look like theater and we hope to capitalize on the elements characteristic of theater such as focused use of language, interior space, condensed time and vivid characterizations. The series is produced on videotape in a TV studio which lends itself to this style. We want scripts that are highly stylized and expressionistic. For the young target audience humor is an important element in each script. Each half hour episode stands on its own and is wholly unrelated to other episodes in the series." Submit synopsis/outline, résumé or a complete ms with the right to reject. Makes outright purchase of $1,000.
Tips: "A Judaic background is helpful, yet not critical. Writing for children is key. We prefer to use Chicago writers, as script rewrites are paramount and routine."

KJD TELEPRODUCTIONS, 30 Whyte Dr., Voorhees NJ 08043. (609)751-3500. Fax: (609)751-7729. E-mail: mactoday@ios.com. President: Larry Scott. Estab. 1989. Broadcast audience. Buys 6 scripts/year. Works with 3 writers/year. Buys all rights. No previously produced material. Reports in 1 month. Catalog free. Query. Makes outright purchase.
Needs: Films, videotapes, multimedia kits.

LAKE-DAYS ENTERTAINMENT, 7060 Hollywood Blvd., #1025, Los Angeles CA 90028. Contact: George Bailey. Estab. 1992. Film and television production; family-oriented subject matter and good thrillers. Buys 25-50 scripts/year. Buys all rights. No previously produced material. Reports in 5 days on queries; 2 months on submissions. Query with synopsis or complete script. Pays in accordance with WGA stardards.
Needs: Films. Looking for feature length scripts dealing with family subject matter. Must have story, interesting characters.
Tips: "Interested in beautiful, unusual scripts of all types. Must have a great story line and interesting characters. No thrillers."

RON LEVINSON PRODUCTIONS, 7201 Raintree Circle, Culver City CA 90230. (310)559-2470. Fax: (310)559-7244. TV and film material. Buys first and all rights. Submissions through agents or with release.

LIGHTVIEW ENTERTAINMENT, 11901 Santa Monica Blvd., Suite 571, Los Angeles CA 90025. Fax: (310)820-3670. E-mail: lightview@aol.com. Producer: Laura McCorkindale. Estab. 1991. Options 20 scripts/year. Purchase price negotiable. Send 1-2 page detailed synopsis with SASE to the attention of Dana Shelbourne. "We will respond via mail within 1 month to let you know if we want to see your screenplay. If we request your screenplay after reading synopsis, please allow 3 months for a second response."
Needs: Feature film screenplays. "Our films range from smaller budget intelligent, artistic independent films to big budget commercial studio films. All genres."
Tips: "Take time writing your synopses and be detailed! Synopses should be as well written as your screenplay. Be sure it is at least one page—but not more than two! Although we are looking for all types of screenplays, we are especially drawn to inspirational stories that enlighten and entertain. *We do not accept unsolicited phone calls*, so please correspond only through the mail."

LOCKWOOD FILMS (LONDON) INC., 365 Ontario St., London, Ontario N5W 3W6 Canada. (519)434-6006. Fax: (519)645-0507. President: Nancy Johnson. Estab. 1974. Audience is entertainment and general broadcast for kids 9-12 and family viewing. Works with 5-6 writers/year. No previously produced material. Reports in 2 months on queries. Submit query with synopsis, résumé or sample scripts. "Submissions will not be considered unless a proposal submission agreement is signed. We will send one upon receiving submissions." Negotiated fee.
Needs: Family entertainment: series, seasonal specials, mini-series, and movies of the week. Also feature films.
Tips: "Potential contributors should have a fax machine and should be prepared to sign a 'proposal submission agreement.' "

‡**LONGFELLOW PICTURES**, 145 Hudson St., 12th Floor, New York NY 10013. (212)431-5550. E-mail: longpics@aol.com. Story Editor: Kathleen Thomas. All audiences. Buys 4-8 scripts/year. Works with 4-6 writers/year. Buys all rights. Accepts previously produced material. Reports in 1 month on queries, 8 months on submissions. Query with synopsis.
Needs: Films.

MARS PRODUCTIONS CORPORATION, 10215 Riverside Dr., Toluca Lake CA 91602. (818)980-8011. Fax: (818)980-1900. Producer: Mark Delo. Estab. 1969. Produces family and action films. Buys 3 scripts/year. Works with 5 writers/year. Buys all rights, options. No previously produced material. Reports

in 3 months. Query with synopsis/outline and SASE. Makes outright purchase "depending on the project." **Needs:** Film (35mm).
Tips: "Follow the standard script format. I do not like too much detail of action or camera angles."

☐MEDIACOM DEVELOPMENT CORP., P.O. Box 6331, Burbank CA 91510-6331. (818)594-4089. Director/Program Development: Felix Girard. Estab. 1978. 80% freelance written. Buys 8-12 scripts/year from unpublished/unproduced writers. 50% of scripts produced are unagented submissions. Query with samples. Reports in 1 month. Buys all rights or first rights. Written query only. Please do not call.
Needs: Produces films, multimedia kits, tapes and cassettes, slides and videotape with programmed instructional print materials, broadcast and cable television programs. Publishes software ("programmed instruction training courses"). Negotiates payment depending on project. Looking for new ideas for CD-ROM titles.
Tips: "Send short samples of work. Especially interested in flexibility to meet clients' demands, creativity in treatment of precise subject matter. We are looking for good, fresh projects (both special and series) for cable and pay television markets. A trend in the audiovisual field that freelance writers should be aware of is the move toward more interactive video disc/computer CRT delivery of training materials for corporate markets."

THE MERRYWOOD STUDIO, 85 Putnam Ave., Hamden CT 06517-2827. Phone/fax: (203)407-1834. E-mail: 03242.732@compuserve.com. Website: http://ourworld.compuserve.com/homepages/Merrywood. Creative Director: Raul daSilva. Estab. 1984. Produces animated motion pictures for entertainment audiences. "We are planning to severely limit but not close out freelance input. Will be taking roughly 5-7%. We will accept only material which we request from agent. Cannot return material or respond to direct queries."
● The Merrywood Studio is no longer producing children's animation of any kind.
Needs: Proprietary material only. Human potential themes woven into highly entertaining drama, high adventure, comedy. This is a new market for animation with only precedent in the illustrated novels published in France and Japan. Cannot handle unsolicited mail/scripts and will not return mail. Open to *agented* submissions of credit sheets, concepts and synopses only. Profit sharing depending upon value of concept and writer's following. Pays at least Writers Guild levels or better, plus expenses.
Tips: "This is *not a market for beginning writers*. Established, professional work with highly unusual and original themes is sought. If you love writing, it will show and we will recognize it and reward it in every way you can imagine. We are not a 'factory' and work on a very high level of excellence."

MILWAUKEE FILMWORKS, 4218 Whitsett Ave., Suite 4, Studio City CA 91604. (818)762-9080. Contact: Douglas. Estab. 1991. Film and TV audience. Buys 2 scripts/year. Works with 3 writers/year. Buys screenplays-option. Accepts previously produced material. Returns submissions on a case to case basis. Reports in 3 months. Query with complete script. Pay varies in accordance with Writers Guild standards.

MONAREX HOLLYWOOD CORPORATION, 9421½ W. Pico Blvd., Los Angeles CA 90035. (310)552-1069. Fax: (310)552-1724. President: Chris D. Nebe. Estab. 1978. Producers of theatrical and television motion pictures and miniseries; also international distributors. Buys 5-6 scripts/year. Buys all rights. Reports in 2 months.
Needs: "We are seeking action, adventure, comedy and character-oriented love stories, dance, horror and dramatic screenplays." First submit synopsis/outline with SASE. After review of the synopsis/outline, the screenplay will be requested. Pays in accordance with Writers Guild standards.
Tips: "We look for exciting visuals with strong characters and a unique plot."

MONTIVAGUS PRODUCTIONS, 13930 Burbank Blvd., Suite 100, Sherman Oaks CA 91401-5003. (818)782-1212. Fax: (818)782-1931. Contact: Douglas Coler, VP Creative Affairs. Estab. 1990. Buys 3 scripts/year. Works with 3-4 writers/year. Buys all rights. Query with synopsis only. Responds if interested in synopsis; 1 month on scripts. Encourages submissions from new and emerging writers. Also interested in novels, short stories and plays for adaptation to the big screen. Pays in accordance with Writers Guild standards. Also accepts plays for theatrical staging under it's stageWorks! program.
Needs: Films (35mm).
Tips: Looking for character-driven scripts; no big budget action films. Keep query short and to the point. Synopsis should be a half to three-quarters of a page. No longer. "Please don't tell me how funny, or how good or how exciting your script is. I'll find out. It's the story I want to know first." Unsolicited scripts will be returned unread. Proper script format a must. Coverage will be shared with the writer.

‡MOXIE PICTURES INC., 1040 N. Sycamore Ave., Hollywood CA 90038. (213)957-5420. Artistic Director: Gary Rose. Estab. 1989. Looking for films and MOWs. Query with synopsis. Reports in 2 months on submissions. Pay varies.
Tips: No animation projects. True stories.

MUSE OF FIRE PRODUCTIONS, 1277 Barry Ave., #5, Los Angeles CA 90025. E-mail: musofire@leonardo.net. Website: http://www.leonardo.net/musofire. Contact: Alex Epstein. Estab. 1992. Film audience.

Works with 5 writers/year. Buys all rights. No previously produced material. Reports in 1 week on queries, 1 month on submissions. Query with synopsis. Prefers queries by e-mail. Pay negotiable per industry standards.
Needs: Films. "Scripts with great hooks and decent writing; scripts without hooks with awesome roles actors will kill to play; no gangster/lowlife/world-is-horrible downers."
Tips: "Don't write for a low budget. Write what you'd pay money to see with someone you love! I'm very tired of scripts involving guns, action violence, gangsters or other lowlifes as major elements."

‡NEVER A DULL MOMENT PRODUCTIONS, 1406 N. Topanga Canyon Blvd., Topanga CA 90290. (310)455-1651. Contact: Lisa Hallas Gottlieb. Estab. 1986. General audience. Buys 3 scripts/year. Works with 10 writers/year. Buys all rights. Reports in 2 months on queries; 3 months on submissions. Query with synopsis. Buys minimal option with agreement; if script is sold will pay at least WGA minimum.
Needs: Films (35mm), videotapes. Full-length scripts for TV movies and features. Prefer dramas, romantic comedies and science fiction.

NEW & UNIQUE VIDEOS, 2336 Sumac Dr., San Diego CA 92105. (619)282-6126. Creative Director: Candace Love. Estab. 1982. General TV and videotape audiences. Buys 10-15 scripts/year. Buys first rights, all rights. No previously produced material. Reports in 1-2 months. Catalog for #10 SASE. Query with synopsis. Makes outright purchase, negotiable.
Needs: Videotapes.
Tips: "We are seeking unique slants on interesting topics in 60-90 minute special-interest videotape format, preferably already produced, packaged and ready for distribution. Imagination and passion, not to mention humor, are pluses. Titles produced include 'Massage for Relaxation'; 'Ultimate Mountain Biking' and 'Full Cycle: World Odyssey.' No theatrical titles. We concentrate on sports, health and other educational home-video titles. Please study the genre and get an understanding of what 'special interest' means. We are heading towards moving pictures (i.e. video, computers, CD-ROM, etc.) in a big way as book sales diminish. If writers can adapt to the changes, their work will always be in demand."

OCEAN PARK PICTURES, 220 Main St., Venice CA 90291. (310)450-1220. Executive Producer: Tim Goldberg. Estab. 1989. All audiences. Buys 5 scripts/year. Works with 10 writers/year. Buys first or all rights. Accepts previously produced material. Reports in 1 month on queries; 2 months on scripts. Query with synopsis, complete script and résumé. Pay varies.
Needs: Film (35mm).
Tips: Less demand for heavy violence.

‡OK PRODUCTIONS, 1727 N. Fairfax Ave., Los Angeles CA 90046. Producer: A.B. (Buddy) Cooper, Jr.. Estab. 1982. Mainstream theatrical feature and TV MOW audience. Buys 1 script/year (options 2-3). Works with 3-4 writers/year. Buys all rights. Reports in 1 month. Query or query with synopsis and signed standard release. Pays in accordance with Writer's Guild standards when appropriate or a percentage of production budget with stated minimum and maximum.
Needs: Film (35mm). Full-length feature films of all types except pornography and slasher. Salute the human spirit. Observe man's struggle. Good stories, great characters.
Tips: "Inquire only about your best work. Finished screenplays only. Get form, format, grammar, spelling and punctuation as perfect as you can. Be entertaining."

‡PACHYDERM ENTERTAINMENT, 3000 W. Olympic Blvd., Santa Monica CA 90404. Contact: Ron Parker. Estab. 1984. Audience is film, TV, theater. Buys 5 scripts/year. Works with 20 writers/year. Payment depends on project—all deals are different. Accepts previously produced plays, published books. Reports in 1 month on queries; 6 weeks on mss. Query with synopsis. Pays in accordance with Writer's Guild standards.
Needs: Feature film, TV movies, Broadway stage.
Tips: "Be specific in your query. Do your homework. We produce mainstream commercial entertainment."

☐ TOM PARKER MOTION PICTURES, 3941 S. Bristol, #285, Santa Ana CA 92704. (714)545-2887. Fax: (714)545-9775. President: Tom Parker. Contact: Jennifer Phelps, script/development. Produces and distributes feature-length motion pictures worldwide for theatrical, home video, pay and free TV. Also produces short subject special interest films (30, 45, 60 minutes). Works with 5-10 scripts/year. Previously produced and distributed "Amazing Love Secret" (R), "Amorous Adventures of Ricky D." (R), and "The Sturgis Story" (R). Reports in 6 months. "Follow the instructions herein and do not phone for info or to inquire about your script."
Needs: "Complete script *only* for low budget (under $1 million) "R" or "PG" rated action/thriller, action/adventure, comedy, adult romance (R), sex comedy (R), family action/adventure to be filmed in 35mm film for the theatrical and home video market. (Do not send TV movie scripts, series, teleplays, stage plays). *Very limited dialogue.* Scripts should be action-oriented and fully described. Screen stories or scripts OK, but no camera angles please. No heavy drama, documentaries, social commentaries, dope stories, weird or horror. Violence or sex OK, but must be well motivated with strong story line." Submit synopsis and description

of characters with finished scripts. Makes outright purchase: $5,000-25,000. Will consider participation, co-production.

Tips: "Absolutely will not return scripts or report on rejected scripts unless accompanied by SASE."

‡POP/ART FILM FACTORY, 513 Wilshire Blvd., #215, Santa Monica CA 90401. Contact: Daniel Zirilli. Estab. 1990. Produces material for "all audiences/features films." Reports in 2 months. Query with synopsis. Pays on per project basis.
Needs: Film (35mm), multimedia kits. "We are interested in producing 1 feature length film—$2 million budget or less. Hard-edged, independent."
Tips: "Be original. Do not play it safe."

‡□PROMARK ENTERTAINMENT GROUP, 3599 Cahuenga Blvd. W., Los Angeles CA 90026. (213)878-0404. Director of Development: Gil Adrienne Wishnick. Promark is a foreign sales company, producing theatrical films for the foreign market, domestic theatrical and cable as well as for video. Buys 8-10 scripts/year. Works with 8-10 writers/year. Buys all rights. Reports in 1 month on queries, 2 months on submissions. Query with synopsis. Makes outright purchase.
Needs: Film (35mm). "We are looking for screenplays in the action, action-adventure, thriller and science fiction/action genres. Our aim is to produce lower budget (3 million and under) films that have a solid, novel premise—a smart but smaller scale independent film."
Tips: "Check on the genres any potential production company accepts and slant your submissions accordingly. Do your homework before you send a query or call. Find out who to contact, what their title is and what the production company tends to make in terms of genre, budget and style. Find the address yourself—don't ask the production executive for it, for example. It's insulting to the executive to have to inform a caller of the company name or address."

THE PUPPETOON STUDIOS, P.O. Box 80141, Las Vegas NV 89180. Producer/Director: Arnold Leibovit. Estab. 1987. "Broad audience." Works with 5 writers/year. Reports in 1 month on queries; 2 months on scripts. Query with synopsis. Submit complete script. A Submission Release *must* be included with all queries. Produced and directed "The Puppetoon Movie." SASE required for return of all materials. Pays in accordance with Writers Guild standards. No novels, plays, poems, treatments; no submissions on computer disk. No unsolicited unagented material. Must include release form.
Needs: Films (35mm). "We are seeking animation properties including presentation drawings and character designs. The more detailed drawings with animation scripts the better."

RED HOTS ENTERTAINMENT, 634 N. Glen Oaks Blvd., #374, Burbank CA 91502-1024. Director of Development: Chip Miller. Contact: Dan Pomeroy, Vice President Development. Estab. 1990. Buys 1 script/year. Works with 3-5 writers/year. Buys first rights, all rights, "short and long term options, as well." No previously produced material. Reports in 3 weeks on queries; 2 months on mss. Query with synopsis or submit complete ms. Pays in accordance with Writer's Guild standards. "Negotiable on writer's previous credits, etc."
Needs: Film loops (16mm), films (35mm), videotapes. "We are a feature film and television production company and have no audiovisual material needs."
Tips: "Best advice possible: originality, uniqueness, write from your instincts and *don't* follow trends."

‡□ROSEMONT PRODUCTIONS, 11812 San Vicente Blvd., Suite 510, Los Angeles CA 90049. (310)447-3688. Executive Vice President: Susan Zachary. Buys 12 scripts/year. Works with 50 writers/year. Buys all rights. Accepts previously produced material. Reports in 2 months. Query with synopsis and résumé. Pays royalty or makes outright purchase in accordance with Writer's Guild standards.
Needs: Films, videotapes, multimedia kits. Network and cable movies.

‡□ROUGH DIAMOND PRODUCTIONS, 1424 N. Kings Rd., Los Angeles CA 90069. (213)848-2900. Producers: Julia Verdin, Brent Morris. Estab. 1995. Audience is general-adult; feature and cable films. Buys 1-2 scripts/year. Works with 6-7 writers/year. Buys film, video rights. Accepts previously produced material. Reports ASAP on queries; 2 months on submissions. Query with synopsis or completed script and résumé.

ROBERT SCHAFFEL/SHARON ROESLER, (formerly Eclectic Films, Inc.), 5750 Wilshire Blvd., Suite 580, Los Angeles CA 90036. Producers: Robert Schaffel/Sharon Roesler. Feature film audience—worldwide. Reports in 2 months on script. Call or write to request permission to submit completed screenplays.

THE SHELDON/POST COMPANY, 1437 Rising Glen Rd., Los Angeles CA 90069. Producers: David Sheldon, Ira Post. Estab. 1989. Produces theatrical motion pictures, movies and series for television. Options and acquires all rights. Reports in 2 months. Query with 1-3 page synopsis, 2-3 sample pages and SASE. "Do not send scripts or books. If the synopsis is of interest, you will be sent a release form to send with your manuscript." Pays in accordance with Writers Guild standards. No advance payments.

● The Sheldon/Post Company reports that it is expanding into children's and family stories.

Needs: "We look for all types of material, including women's stories, suspense dramas, family stories, horror, sci-fi, thrillers, action-adventure." True stories should include news articles or other documentation.

Tips: "A synopsis should tell the entire story with all of the plot—including a beginning, a middle and an end. During the past three years, the producers have been in business with 20th Century Fox, Paramount Pictures, Columbia Pictures and currently have contracts with Cosgrove-Meurer Productions ("Unsolved Mysteries"), Finnegan-Pinchuk ("Fabulous Baker Boys") and Davis Entertainment."

SHORELINE PICTURES, 1901 Avenue of the Stars, #1800, Los Angeles CA 90067. (310)551-2060. Fax: (310)201-0729. E-mail: shoreline@shorelineentertainment.com. Website: http://www.directnet.com/pictures/. Contact: Brooke Estab. 1993. Mass audience. Buys 8 scripts/year. Works with 8 writers/year. Buys all rights. Reports in 1 month on submissions. Query.

Needs: Films (35, 70mm). Looking for "character-driven films that are commercial as well as independent. No exploitation or horror. Comedies and dramas, yes. Completed screenplays only. We are especially keen to find a comedy. Also looking for television movies. True stories with leading ladies are nice. Note, there is an audience for adult films as reflected in films like *The Piano*, *The Player*, *Crying Game*, *Joy Luck Club*, etc. Principal of our company co-produced *Glengarry Glen Ross*."

SKYLARK FILMS, 1123 Pacific St., Santa Monica CA 90405. (310)396-5753. Contact: Brad Pollack. Estab. 1990. Buys 6 scripts/year. Buys first or all rights. Accepts previously produced material. Reports in 2-4 weeks on queries; 1-2 months on submissions. Query with synopsis. Option or other structures depending on circumstances. Pays in accordance with Writer's Guild standards.

Needs: Films (TV, cable, feature).

Tips: "Generally, we look for the best material we can find, other than the horror genre. Particular new areas of focus are romantic comedy, true stories for TV mow's and low-budget quicky material. No response without SASE unless we want to see material. Will also look at material for ½ weekly television syndication possibilities."

SNOWBIRD ENTERTAINMENT, P.O. Box 1172, Burbank CA 91507. Producer: Peter Jackson. Audience is all ages. G, PG, PG-13 and R. Buys 1-2 scripts/year. Works with 1-2 writers/year. Buys all rights. Query with complete script and résumé. Makes outright purchase or in accordance with Writer's Guild standards, depending on the script and budget.

Needs: Films (35mm). "Snowbird Entertainment is looking for feature length screenplays in the following genres: action, action-adventure, mystery thriller, political thriller, suspense thriller or docu-dramas (true-life stories)."

Tips: "Writers need their scripts to have excellent storytelling and good, complex characters. There are no trends in feature films (trends is a Hollywood word). It's all about stories. Is it a story the film audience wants to see. When it's all said and done it all comes down to what your 'gut' tells you. To quote Harry Cohn of Columbia Pictures 'If my ass moves, it's a winner.' Due to two feature films back to back in 1995 and a heavy response to submissions we currently have a backlog of 3-6 months. We apologize for the delay."

SOUTH FORK PRODUCTIONS, P.O. Box 1935, Santa Monica CA 90406-1935. Producer: Jim Sullivan. Estab. 1980. Produces material for TV and film. Buys 2 scripts/year. Works with 4 writers/year. Buys all rights. No previously produced material. Send synopsis/outline and motion picture treatments, plus previous credits, with SASE. No complete scripts. Pays in accordance with Writers Guild Standards.

Needs: Films (16, 35mm), videotapes.

Tips: "Follow established formats for treatments. SASE for return."

‡□STARLIGHT PICTURES, 3655 S. Decatur Blvd., Suite 14-159, Las Vegas NV 89103. E-mail: ideamaster@aol.com. Development Executive: Brian McNeal. Estab. 1989. Mass audiences, all audiences, movie-going public, international. Buys 0-2 scripts/year. Works with 1-10 writers/year. Options 0-5 scripts/year. Rights purchased according to WGA signatory regulations; rights optioned and/or purchased are motion picture/television rights. No previously produced material. Reports in 1 year on queries; 18 months on mss. Query with synopsis and self-addressed stamped postcard. Do not send a script unless requested. Submission material MUST BE represented/agented by WGA signatory agent. All submissions claiming to be properly represented will be verified. No freelance material will be considered. Freelance material will promptly be returned unread (if accompanied by proper postage), or disposed of otherwise. Pays in accordance with Writer's Guild standards.

Needs: Motion pictures for worldwide theatrical, television, cable and video release. "Production slate for next 18 months is currently at its limits. We are not actively seeking new properties. After this 18-month period, it is probable we will seek outside literary material. All submitted WGA-agented queries will be kept on file, and under consideration."

Tips: "A good script will get our attention. Horror, mystery, adventure, melodrama, comedy, etc. These are all really sub-genres. If it's not a good script first, the sub-genres become incidental. Furthermore, writers should never write with budget in mind. All too often, writers tend to downplay their stories, substituting dramatic and seemingly-expensive elements with less-expensive locations and effects. This takes away from the true story, and makes the script less appealing. Writers forget producers are in the business of make-believe. Seemingly expensive elements don't always have to be expensive. Let us, the producers, worry about the budget. Whether the ultimate finances of the movie are $500,000 or $20 million, the logistics and planning of the film are our concern. Writers should dictate the script as they would like to see it on the screen. Their only concern should be the story, and they should write it as vigorously and dramatic as possible." Contact WGA for proper format and guidelines.

☐**STONEROAD PRODUCTIONS, INC.**, 11288 Ventura Blvd., #909, Studio City CA 91604. Contact: Story Department. Estab. 1992. Produces feature films for theaters, cable TV and home video. PG, R, and G-rated films. Buys/options 15-25 scripts/year. Works with 10 writers/year. Buys all rights; if published material, subsidiary rights. Accepts previously produced material. Reports in 1 month on queries if interested; 2 months requested on submissions. Query with synopsis. Pay varies greatly: option, outright purchase, wide range.
Needs: Films (35mm). All genres. Looking for good material from writers who have taken the time to learn the unique and difficult craft of scriptwriting.
Tips: "Interesting query letters intrigue us—and tell us something about the writer. Query letter should include a short 'log line' or 'pitch' encapsulating 'what this story is about' and the genre in just a few sentences. We look for strong stories and strong characters. We make movies that we would like to see. Producers are known for encouraging new (e.g. unproduced) screenwriters and giving real consideration to their scripts."

TALKING RINGS ENTERTAINMENT, P.O. Box 80141, Las Vegas NV 89180. President and Artistic Director: Arnold Leibovit. Estab. 1988. "Produces material for motion pictures and television. Works with 5 writers/year. Reports on submissions in 2 months. Only send complete scripts. No treatments, novels, poems or plays, no submissions on computer disk. Query with synopsis. A Submission Release *must* be included with all queries. Produced and directed "The Fantasy Film Worlds of George Pal," "The Puppetoon Movie." Currently producing "The Time Machine Returns," a remake of "The Seven Faces of Dr. Lao," "Off The Funny Pages" and "Darkside of the Moon." SASE required for return of all materials. Pays in accordance with Writers Guild Standards.
Needs: Films (35mm), videotapes. No unsolicited unagented material. Must include release form.

‡☐**TEOCALLI ENTERTAINMENT, INC.**, P.O. Box 2767, Crested Butte CO 81224. President: Robert A. Nowotny. Estab. 1991. Theatrical motion pictures (all ratings except X), made-for-TV Movies (network and cable). Buys 1 script/year. Works with 5 writers/year. Buys first or all rights. Reports in 1 month on queries; 2 months on submissions. Query with résumé. Please: No inquiries unless a completed screenplay exists. Pays in accordance with Writer's Guild standards.
Needs: Films (35mm). Interested only in completed feature length screenplays suitable for motion picture/MOW distribution.

UNIFILMS, INC., 22931 Sycamore Creek Dr., Valencia CA 91354-2050. (805)297-2000. Vice President, Development: Jack Adams. Estab. 1984. Buys 0-5 scripts/year. Reports in 2 weeks on queries.
Needs: Feature films *only*. Looking for feature film screenplays, current format, 100-120 pages long; commercial but not stupid, dramatic but not "artsy," funny but not puerile. Query with synopsis and SASE. "If you don't include a SASE, we won't reply. We do not accept unsolicited scripts. Save your postage; if you send us a script we'll return it unopened."
Tips: "If you've taken classes, read books, attended seminars and writers' workshops all concerned with scriptwriting and read hundreds of produced studio screenplays *prior* to seeing the film and you're still convinced you've got a wonderful script, we might want to see it. But desire and enthusiasm are not enough; you have to have independent corroboration that your work is as good as you think it is. If you've got someone else in the entertainment industry to recommend your script, we might be more interested in seeing it. But if you waste our time with a project that's not yet ready to be seen, we're not going to react well. Your first draft is not usually the draft you're going to show to the industry. *Get a professional opinion first*, then rewrite before you submit to us. Very few people care about synopses, outlines or treatments for sales consideration. THE SCRIPT is the basic blueprint, and everyone in the country is working on a script. Ideas are a dime a dozen. If you can *execute* that idea well and get people *excited* about that idea, you've got something. But most writers are wanna-bes, who submit scripts that need a lot more work just to get to the 'promising' stage. Scripts are *always* rewritten. If you can't convince us you're a *writer*, we don't care. But if you *can* write and you've got a *second* wonderful script we might talk. But don't send a 'laundry list' of your scripts; pick the best one and pitch it to us. If it's not for us, then maybe come back with project number two. More than one project at a time confuses Hollywood; make it easy for us and you'll make it easy for yourself. And if you do it in a professional manner, you'll convince us sooner. Good luck, and keep writing (rewriting)."

‡**U.S. FILM CORP.**, 2029 Century Park E., #1260, Los Angeles CA 90067. (310)475-4547. President: Robert Nau. Estab. 1993. Action audience. Buys 5 scripts/year. Works with 10 writers/year. Buys all rights. Reports in 1 month. Query with synopsis. Pays per negotiation.
Needs Films (35mm). Action adventure, thrillers—feature length.

VANGUARD PRODUCTIONS, 12111 Beatrice St., Culver City CA 90230. Contact: Terence M. O'Keefe. Estab. 1985. Buys 1 script/year. Buys all rights or options rights. Accepts previously produced material. Reports in 3 months on queries; 6 months on scripts. Query with synopsis, résumé and SASE. Pays in accordance with Writers Guild standards or negotiated option.
Needs: Films (35mm), videotapes.

‡**WATER STREET PICTURES**, 2656 29th St., #208, Santa Monica CA 90405. Vice President, Development: Charles Freericks. Estab. 1994. General entertainment, television and feature. Buys 5 scripts/year. Works with 5 writers/year. Buys all rights. Reports in 6 months on queries; 1 year on submissions. Query with synopsis. Unsolicited scripts will be thrown away. Pays in accordance with Writer's Guild standards.
Needs: Films (35mm). "We are not interested in the ordinary, even if it's a wonderfully written script. Your concept must be surprising enough to capture our eye by the first sentence of your synopsis."
Tips: "Never pester overworked development executives. Write only from your own experience or research and always look to be different then what's in theaters now."

WONDERLAND ENTERTAINMENT GROUP, (formerly Papillon Productions), 1712 Anacapa St., Santa Barbara CA 93101. Phone/fax: (805)569-0733. Head of Acquisitions: Diane Itier. Estab. 1989. Produces material for any audience. Buys 5 scripts/year. Works with 4 writers/year. Buys all rights. Accepts previously produced material. Reports in 1 month. Submit complete script and résumé. Pays in accordance with Writers Guild standards.
Needs: Films. "We are seeking any screenplay for full-length motion pictures."
Tips: "Be patient but aggressive enough to keep people interested in your screenplay."

THE ZVEJNIEKS GROUP, INC., 187 Cocohatchee St., Naples FL 33963. Contact: Ingrida Sylvia. Estab. 1983. "Emphasis is placed on quality of original written work for major motion picture production. Good writing creates its own audience." Limited to 15 projects in development at any given time. Rights negotiated on an individual basis. Accepts previously produced material. Reports in 1-2 months. Submit 1-page synopsis of story and characters. Pay negotiated on individual basis.
Needs: "As a producer of major motion pictures, our primary goal is to entertain audiences with quality movies. We are always looking for fresh, interesting, well-written stories with good character development. The script should elicit some sort of emotion from the reader/audience."
Tips: "According to Chairman Eric S. Zvejnieks, a serious problem facing the industry is a lack of genuine original creative material which would allow for greater diversity in films. Writing talent is often overlooked, an unfortunate reality partially attributable to the system within which writers work. The underlying philosophy of the company is that every great movie starts with a great story, a simple yet often forgotten concept."

COMPANIES THAT APPEARED in the 1996 edition of *Writer's Market* but are not included this year are listed in the General Index with a notation explaining their absence.

Syndicates

Newspaper syndicates distribute columns, cartoons and other written material to newspapers around the country—and sometimes around the world. Competition for syndication slots is stiff. The number and readership of newspapers is dropping. With paper costs rising, there are fewer pages and less money to spend in filling them. Coveted spots in general interest, humor and political commentary are held by big-name columnists such as Ellen Goodman, Bob Herbert and Cal Thomas. And multitudes of aspiring writers wait in the wings, hoping one of these heavy hitters will move on to something else and leave the spotlight open.

Although this may seem discouraging, there are in fact many areas in which less-known writers are syndicated. Syndicates are not looking for general interest or essay columns. What they are looking for are fresh voices that will attract readers. As consumer interests and lifestyles change, new doors are being opened for innovative writers capable of covering emerging trends.

Most syndicates distribute a variety of columns, cartoons and features. Although the larger ones are usually only interested in running ongoing material, smaller ones often accept short features and one-shots in addition to continuous columns. Specialized syndicates—those that deal with a single area such as business—often sell to magazines, trade journals and other business publications as well as to newspapers.

THE WINNING COMBINATION

In presenting yourself and your work, note that most syndicated columnists start out writing for local newspapers. Many begin as staff writers, develop a following in a particular area, and are then picked up by a syndicate. Before approaching a syndicate, write for a paper in your area. Develop a good collection of clips that you feel is representative of your best writing.

New ideas are paramount to syndication. Sure, you'll want to study the popular columnists to see how their pieces are structured (most are short—from 500-750 words—and really pack a punch), but don't make the mistake of imitating a well-known columnist. Syndicates are looking for original material that is timely, saleable and original. Do not submit a column to a syndicate on a subject it already covers. The more unique the topic, the greater your chances of having it picked up. Most importantly, be sure to choose a topic that interests you and one you know well.

APPROACHING MARKETS

Request a copy of a syndicate's writer's guidelines. It will give you information on current needs, submission standards and response times. Most syndicates prefer a query letter and about six sample columns or writing samples and a SASE. You may also want to include a client list and business card if available. If you have a particular area of expertise pertinent to your submission, mention this in your letter and back it up by sending related material. For highly specialized or technical matter, provide credentials to show you are qualified to handle the topic.

In essence, syndicates act as agents or brokers for the material they handle. Writing material is usually sold as a package. The syndicate will promote and market the work to newspapers (and sometimes to magazines) and keep careful records of sales. Writers usually receive 40-60% of gross receipts. Some syndicates may also pay a small salary or flat fee for one-shot items.

Syndicates usually acquire all rights to accepted material, although a few are now offering writers and artists the option of retaining ownership. In selling all rights, writers give up ownership and future use of their creations. Consequently, sale of all rights is not the best deal for writers, and has been the reason many choose to work with syndicates that buy less restrictive rights. Before signing a contract with a syndicate, you may want to go over the terms with an attorney or with an agent who has a background in law. The best contracts will usually offer the writer a percentage of gross receipts (as opposed to net receipts) and will not bind the writer for longer than five years.

THE SELF-SYNDICATION OPTION

Many writers choose to self-syndicate. This route allows you to retain all rights, and gives you the freedom of a business owner. But as a self-syndicated writer, you must also act as your own manager, marketing team and sales force. You must develop mailing lists, and a pricing, billing and collections structure.

Payment is usually negotiated on a case-by-case basis. Small newspapers may offer only $10-20 per column, but larger papers may pay much more (for more information on pay rates, see How Much Should I Charge? on page 49). The number of papers you deal with is only limited by your marketing budget and your tenacity.

If you self-syndicate, be aware that some newspapers are not copyrighted, so you should copyright your own material. It's less expensive to copyright columns as a collection than individually. For more information on copyright procedures, see Copyrighting Your Writing in the Business of Writing section.

Additional information on newspaper markets can be found in *The Gale Directory of Publications* (available in most libraries). The *Editor & Publisher Syndicate Directory* (11 W. 19th St., New York NY 10011) has a list of syndicates, contact names and features; the weekly magazine, *Editor & Publisher*, also has news articles about syndicates and can provide you with information about changes and events in the industry.

For information on some syndicates not listed in *Writer's Market*, see the General Index.

ADVENTURE FEATURE SYNDICATE, 329 Harvery Dr., Glendale CA 91206. (818)551-0077. Editor: Vicky D. Letcher. Estab. 1976. Reports in 1 month. Buys all rights, first North American serial rights and second serial (reprint) rights.
Needs: Funny panel and daily comic strips; also action/adventure strips, comic book (graphic novels). Submit 2 weeks of strips for consideration.

AMERICAN CROSSWORD FEDERATION, P.O. Box 69, Massapequa Park NY 11762. Contact: Stanley Newman. Estab. 1983. 100% freelance written by writers on a one-time basis. Buys 400 features/year. Works with 50 writers/year. Works with 20 new previously unpublished writers/year. Syndicates to magazines, newspapers. Reports in 2 months. Buys all rights. Writer's guidelines for #10 SASE. Submit complete ms.
Needs: Crosswords. Pays $40-300. Currently syndicates *Newsday Crossword* and *Tough Cryptics*, by Stanley Newman.
Tips: Send for style sheet *first*.

AMPERSAND COMMUNICATIONS, 2311 S. Bayshore Dr., Miami FL 33133-4728. (305)285-2200. Editor: George Leposky. Estab. 1982. 100% written by writers on contract. "We syndicate only our own material at present, but we will consider working with others whose material is exceptionally good. Novices need not contact us." Syndicates to magazines and newspapers. Reports in up to 4 months. Buys all rights. Writer's guidelines for $2 and SASE.
Needs: Newspaper columns, travel, business, science and health, senior lifestyle, regional cuisine, natural foods, environment; typically 500-750 words, rarely up to 1,500 words. Material from other writers must complement, not compete with, our own columns. Query with clips of published work and complete ms—samples of proposed columns. Pays 50% of net after production. "Note: For columns requiring photos, the

writer must supply to us the required number of images and quantity of each image at his/her expense. We are not in the photo duplication business and will not provide this service." Currently syndicates Traveling the South, by George and Rosalie Leposky (travel); Business Insights, by Lincoln Avery (business); Food for Thought, by Rosalie Leposky (cooking); HealthScan, by George Leposky (health); EnviroScan, by George Leposky (environment); Golden Years, by George Leposky (senior lifestyle); House and Home, by Rosalie Leposky (home improvement).

Tips: "Be an *excruciatingly* good writer; good alone isn't enough. Find a niche that doesn't seem to be covered. Do research to cover your topics in-depth, but in few words. The reader's attention span is shriveling, and so are ad lineage and column inches available for syndicated features. Increasingly we operate in a paperless, electronic world, receiving material from writers and transmitting material to editors via e-mail. That works well for established contacts, but introductory queries with manuscripts and published samples still need to happen the old-fashioned way."

ARKIN MAGAZINE SYNDICATE INC., 500 Bayview Dr., Suite F, N. Miami Beach FL 33160-4747. Editorial Director: Joseph Arkin. Estab. 1958. 20% freelance written by writers on contract; 80% freelance written on a one-time basis. "We regularly purchase articles from several freelancers for syndication in trade and professional magazines." Accepts previously published submissions, "if all rights haven't been sold." Reports in 3 weeks. Buys all North American magazine and newspaper rights.

Needs: Magazine articles (nonfiction, 750-2,200 words), directly relating to business problems common to several different types of businesses and photos (purchased with written material). "We are in dire need of the 'how-to' business article." Will not consider article series or columns. Submit complete ms; "SASE required with all submissions." Pays 3-10¢/word; $5-10 for photos; "actually, line drawings are preferred instead of photos." **Pays on acceptance.**

Tips: "Study a representative group of trade magazines to learn style, needs and other facets of the field."

ARTHUR'S INTERNATIONAL, 2613 High Range Dr., Las Vegas NV 89134. (702)228-3731. Editor: Marvin C. Arthur. Syndicates to newspapers and magazines. Reports in 1 week. "SASE must be enclosed." Buys all rights.

Needs: Fillers, magazine columns, magazine features, newspaper columns, newspaper features and news items. "We specialize in timely nonfiction and historical stories, and columns, preferably the unusual. We utilize humor. Travel stories utilized in 'World Traveler.'" Buys one-shot features and article series. "Since the majority of what we utilize is column or short story length, it is better to submit the article so as to expedite consideration and reply. Do not send any lengthy manuscripts." Pays 50% of net sales, salary on some contracted work and flat rate on commissioned work. Currently syndicates "Marv," by Marvin C. Arthur (informative, humorous, commentary); "Humoresque," by Don Alexander (humorous); and "World Spotlight," by Don Kampel (commentary).

Tips: "We do not use cartoons but we are open for fine illustrators."

BUDDY BASCH FEATURE SYNDICATE, 771 West End Ave., New York NY 10025-5572. (212)666-2300. Editor/Publisher: Buddy Basch. Estab. 1965. 10% written on contract; 2% freelance written by writers on a one-time basis. Buys 10 features/year. Works with 3-4 previously unpublished writers/year. Syndicates to print media: newspapers, magazines, giveaways, house organs, etc. Reports in 3 weeks. Buys first North American serial rights.

• Most stories are done inhouse.

Needs: Magazine features, newspaper features, and one-shot ideas that are really different. "Try to make them unusual, unique, real 'stoppers,' not the usual stuff." Will consider one-shots on article series on human interest—"a wide umbrella that makes people stop and read the piece. Different, unusual and unique are the key words, not what the *writer* thinks is, but which have been done nine million times before." Query. Pays 20-50% commission. Additional payment for photos $10-50. Currently syndicates It Takes a Woman, by Frances Scott (woman's feature), Travel Whirl, Scramble Steps (puzzle) and others.

Tips: "Never mind what your mother, fiancé or friend thinks is good. If it has been done before and is old hat, it has no chance. Do some research and see if there are a number of similar items in the press. Don't just try a 'switch' on them. You don't fool anyone with this. There are fewer and fewer newspapers and magazines, with more and more people vying for the available space. But there's usually room for a really good, *different* feature or story. Trouble is few writers (amateurs especially) know a good piece, I'm sorry to say. Read *Writer's Market* carefully, noting which syndicate might be interested in the type of feature you are submitting. That will save you and the publication time and money and get you better results."

BLACK PRESS SERVICE, INC., 166 Madison Ave., New York NY 10016. (212)686-6850. Editor: Roy Thompson. Estab. 1966. 10% written on contract; 10% freelance written on a one-time basis. Buys hundreds of features/year. Works with hundreds of writers/year. Syndicates to magazines, newspapers and radio. Reports in 2 months. Buys all rights. Submit complete ms.

Needs: Magazine and newspaper columns; news items; magazine and newspaper features; radio broadcast material. Purchases single (one shot) features and articles series (current events oriented). Pays variable flat rate. Currently syndicates Bimonthly Report, by staff (roundup of minority-oriented news).

BOOTSTRAPS, 249 W. 21st St., New York NY 10011. Editor: William Neal. Estab. 1979. 100% freelance written by writers on a one-time basis. Buys 12 features/year. Works with 3 writers/year. Works with 3 new previously unpublished writers/year. Syndicates to newspapers. Reports in 1 month. Buys first North American serial rights. Writer's guidelines for #10 SASE. Query only.
Needs: Newspaper columns. Purchase single (one shot) features. Pays author's percentage 50%.

CHICAGO SUN-TIMES FEATURES SYNDICATE, 401 N. Wabash, Suite 532A, Chicago IL 60611. (312)321-2890. Fax: (312)321-2336. E-mail: elschiele@aol.com. Contact: Elizabeth Owens-Schiele. 20% written by writers on contract. Works with 10 writers/year. Works with 10 new previously unpublished writers/year. Syndicates to newspapers. Reports in 6 weeks. Buys all rights. Writer's guidelines for #10 SASE. Submit complete ms or query with clips of published work.
Needs: Newspaper columns and features, comics, editorial cartoons, "unique" columns. Does not purchase either single (one shot) features or articles series. Pays 50% author's percentage. Currently syndicates All That Zazz, by Jeffrey Zaslow (advice column); sports columns by various authors (sports features); Gaming, by John Grochowski (gambling advice). Sportswriter: Rick Telander.
Tips: "The market is highly competitive. Before you pursue syndication, check the E&P syndicate directory for the number of similar columns. Send complete packages of published/unpublished clips to syndicates and explain what makes your idea a marketable syndication product. Recognize that newsprint costs are up almost 40% and sales are down. Remember money in syndication is made in volume. We are not picking up features that are duplicated in subject manners by other syndicates. For example, a workplace Q&A column is not a "unique" column idea since every synicate offers one. However, one of our new columnists writes a column along the lines of the title of his book, 'Interior Design for Idiots'—a sarcastic, humorous yet informative look at interior design that's unique."

‡CHRONICLE FEATURES, Dept. WM, Suite 1011, 870 Market St., San Francisco CA 94102. (415)777-7212. General Manager: Stuart Dodds. Contact: Susan Peters. Buys 3 features/year. Syndicates to daily newspapers in the US and Canada with representation overseas. Reports in 2 months.
Needs: Newspaper columns and features. "In choosing a column subject, the writer should be guided by the concerns and aspirations of today's newspaper reader. We look for originality of expression and, in special fields of interest, exceptional expertise." Preferred length: 600 words. Submit complete ms. Pays 50% revenue from syndication. Offers no additional payment for photos or artwork accompanying ms. Currently syndicates Latino Spectrum by Roberto Rodriguez and Patrisia Gonazles (op-ed column); Earthweek by Steve Newman (planetary diary); Home Entertainment by Harry Somerfield (audiovisual equipment advice and reviews); and Working Life by Deborah L. Jacobs.
Tips: "We are seeking features that will be ongoing, not single articles or news releases. Examples of a proposed feature are more welcome than a query letter describing it. Please conduct all correspondence by mail rather than by telephone."

CLEAR CREEK FEATURES, Box 3303, Grass Valley CA 95945. Editor: Mike Drummond. Estab. 1988. 50% written on contract; no one shots. Buys 0 features/year. Works with 5 writers/year. Works with 2 previously unpublished writers/year. Syndicates to magazines and newspapers. Reports in 1 month. Buys first North American serial, all and second serial (reprint) rights. Submit clips of published work.
Needs: Fiction, magazine and newspaper columns, magazine features. Pays 50% author's percentage. Currently syndicates Coping in the Country, by Mike Drummond (humor); The Voice of Experience, by various (humor/commentary), This Old Klutz, by various (humor).
Tips: "Identify a niche and dig in! We seem to be moving toward the boomer/senior market, with a smaller trend in the conservative gen-X area."

COMMUNITY PRESS SERVICE, 117 W. Second St., P.O. Box 639, Frankfort KY 40602. (502)223-1736. Fax: (502)223-2679. Contact: Phyllis Cornett. Estab. 1990. 30% written by writers on contract. Buys 600 features/year. Works with 10-15 writers/year. Syndicates to newspapers. Reports in 2 months. Buys all rights. Writer's guidelines for free. Query with clips of published work.
Needs: Fillers, newspaper columns and features. Purchases single panel cartoons. Pays flat rate depending on length of article. Currently syndicates P.C. Primer, by Roger Creighton (computer column); The Bible Speaks, by Rev. Lawrence Althouse (religious); Calling Colleen, by Linette Wheeler (advice); Buddy's Workshop, by Linette Wheeler.

COMPUTERUSER MAGAZINE, 220 S. Sixth St., Suite 500, Minneapolis MN 55402. (612)336-9286. E-mail: cueditor@usinternet.com. Contact: Rachel Hankin. Estab. 1982. 100% written by writers on contract. Buys 150 features/year. Works with 40 writers/year. Syndicates to magazines, newspapers. Reports in 4 months. Buys all rights. No writer's guidelines. Submit complete ms or query with clips of published work.
Needs: Magazine features (high technology/computing only, business end-user orientation). Pays 10% author's percentage or minimum guarantee of $50-300. Currently syndicates Computer Pursuits, by Nelson King (industry observation and predictions); Down to Business, by Steve Deyo (industry and Human-factors observations); CD-ROM, by various authors (CD-ROM reviews).

Tips: "We cover the whole computer industry, all platforms from a business user perspective. We take 80% of our material from a longstanding board of contributing editors. Spots are limited and often winnowed for contributing writers. We are journalists, not technical writers or PC hacks. Send samples or finished piece with SASE. We will respond."

CONTINENTAL FEATURES/CONTINENTAL NEWS SERVICE, 341 W. Broadway, Suite 265, San Diego CA 92101-3802. (619)492-8696. Editor-in-Chief: Gary Salamone. Estab. 1981. 100% written on contract. "Writers offering the kind and quality of writing we seek stand an equal chance regardless of experience." Syndicates to print media. Reports in 1 month with SASE. Writer's guidelines for #10 SASE.
Needs: Magazine and newspaper features. "Feature material should fit the equivalent of one-quarter to one-half standard newspaper page, and Continental News considers an ultra-liberal or ultra-conservative slant inappropriate." Query with SASE. Pays 70% author's percentage. Currently syndicates News and Comment, by Charles Hampton Savage (general news commentary/analysis); Continental Viewpoint, by staff; Portfolio, (cartoon/caricature art); Travelers Checks, by Ann Hattes; Middle East Cable, by Mike Maggio; and OnVideo, by Harley Lond; over 50 features in all.
  • This syndicate is considering fewer proposals for one-time projects. Virtually all of their new feature creators are signed to work on a continuing basis.
Tips: "CF/CNS is working to develop a feature package of greater interest and value to an English-speaking international audience. That is those writers who can accompany their economic-social-political analyses (of foreign countries) with photo(s) of the key public figure(s) involved are particularly in demand. Official photos (8×10 down to 3×5) of key government leaders available from the information ministry/press office/embassy will be acceptable. CF/CNS emphasizes analytical/explanatory articles, but muckraking articles (where official-photos requests are inopportune) are also encouraged."

COPLEY NEWS SERVICE, P.O. Box 190, San Diego CA 92112. (619)293-1818. Fax: (619)293-2322. Editorial Manager: Glenda Winders. 85% written by stringers on contract; 15% freelance written on a one-time basis. Offers 200 features/week. Sells to newspapers and online services. Reports in 6 months. Buys first rights.
Needs: Fillers, newspaper columns and features. Looking for food, travel, opinion, computer technology, new ideas. Subjects include interior design, outdoor recreation, fashion, antiques, real estate, pets, gardening. Query with clips of published work. Pays $100 flat rate/story or negotiated monthly salary.
Tips: "Interested in columns and stories about new technology."

CREATE-A-CRAFT, P.O. Box 330008, Ft. Worth TX 76163. Contact: Editor. Estab. 1967. 5% written by writers on contract; 50% freelance written. Buys 5 features/year. Works with 3 writers/year. Works with 3 previously unpublished writers/year. Syndicates to magazines and newspapers. Reports in 4 months. Submissions will not be returned. Buys all rights. Writer's guidelines $2.50 for #10 SASE. Prefers agented submissions only (submit complete ms).
Needs: Magazine and newspaper columns and features. "Looking for material on appraising, art, decorative arts, politics (how politics affect art only); 400-2,000 words. Comics must be in strip form only." Pays $6-10 flat hourly rate (depending on project). All work is work-for-hire. Currently syndicates Appraisals, by Abramson (appraisal column); Those Characters from Cowtown (cartoon); Rojo (cartoon); Golden Gourmets (cartoon); Gallant Gators (cartoon). Author is always listed as Create-A-Craft (no byline given).
Tips: "Know the market you are writing for."

CREATIVE SYNDICATION SERVICES, P.O. Box 40, Eureka MO 63025-0040. (314)587-7126. Editor: Debra Holly. Estab. 1977. 10% written on contract; 50% freelance written on a one-time basis. Syndicates to magazines, newspapers and radio. Reports in 1 month. Buys all rights. Currently syndicates The Weekend Workshop, by Ed Baldwin; Woodcrafting, by Ed Baldwin; and Classified Clippers, a feature exclusive for the Classified Section of newspapers.
Tips: "We are looking for writers who do crafts, woodworking, needle-crafts and sewing."

‡**CREATORS SYNDICATE, INC.**, Suite 700, 5777 W. Century Blvd., Los Angeles CA 90045. (310)337-7003. Vice President/General Manager: Anita Tobias. Estab. 1987. Syndicates to newspapers. Reports in 1-2 months. Buys negotiable rights. Writer's guidelines for #10 SASE.
Needs: Newspaper columns and features. Query with clips of published work or submit complete ms. Author's percentage: approximately 50%. Currently syndicates Ann Landers (advice), Harris Poll, Walter E. Williams, Mona Charen, Percy Ross and Thomas Sowell (columns), B.C. and Wizard of Id (comic strips) and Herblock (editorial cartoon).
Tips: "Syndication is very competitive. Writing regularly for your local newspaper is a good start."

CRICKET COMMUNICATIONS, INC., P.O. Box 527, Ardmore PA 19003-0527. (610)789-2480 or (215)747-6684. Fax: (215)747-7082. Editor: J.D. Krickett. Estab. 1975. 10% written on contract; 10% freelance written on a one-time basis. Works with 2-3 previously unpublished writers/year. Syndicates to trade magazines and newspapers. Reports in 1 month. Buys all rights.

Needs: Magazine and newspaper columns and features, news items—all tax and financial-oriented (700-1,500 words); also newspaper columns, features and news items directed to small business. Query with clips of published work. Pays $50-500. Currently syndicates Hobby/Business, by Mark E. Battersby (tax and financial); Farm Taxes, by various authors; and Small Business Taxes, by Mark E. Battersby.

‡**CROWN SYNDICATE, INC.**, P.O. Box 99126, Seattle WA 98199. President: L.M. Boyd. Estab. 1967. Buys countless trivia items. Syndicates to newspapers, radio. Reports in 1 month. Buys first North American serial rights. Free writer's guidelines.
Needs: Filler material used weekly, items for trivia column (format guidelines sent on request). Pays $1-5/item, depending on how it's used, i.e., trivia or filler service. Offers no additional payment for photos accompanying ms. Currently syndicates columns and puzzle panels.

DANY NEWS SERVICE, 22 Lesley Dr., Syosset NY 11791. Editor: David Nydick. Estab. 1966. Buys 10% from freelancers. Buys 30 features/year (from freelancers). Syndicates to newspapers. Reports in 1 month. Buys all rights. Submit complete ms.
Needs: Newspaper columns and features, how-to (help your child). Pays $50 minimum guarantee. Currently syndicates You, Your Child and School; You, Your Child and Sports; and You, Your Child and Entertainment, (how to help your child).

EDITORIAL CONSULTANT SERVICE, P.O. Box 524, West Hempstead NY 11552-1206. (516)481-5487. Editorial Director: Arthur A. Ingoglia. Estab. 1964. 40% written on contract; 25% freelance written on a one-time basis. "We work with 75 writers in the US and Canada." Adds about 10 new columnists/year. Syndicates material to an average of 60 newspapers, magazines, automotive trade and consumer publications, and radio stations with circulation of 50,000-575,000. Buys all rights. Writer's guidelines for #10 SASE. Reports in 1-2 months.
Needs: Magazine and newspaper columns and features, news items, radio broadcast material. Prefers carefully documented material with automotive slant. Also considers automotive trade features. Will consider article series. No horoscope, child care, lovelorn or pet care. Query. Author's percentage varies; usually averages 50%. Additional payment for 8×10 b&w and color photos accepted with ms. Submit 2-3 columns. Currently syndicates Let's Talk About Your Car, by R. Hite.
Tips: "Emphasis is placed on articles and columns with an automotive slant. We prefer consumer-oriented features, how to save money on your car, what every woman should know about her car, how to get more miles per gallon, etc."

EUROPA PRESS NEWS SERVICE, Clasificador 5, Tajamar Providencia, Santiago, Chile. (562)235-2902 or (562)235-1584. Fax: (562)235-1731. Editor: Maria Marta Raggio. Estab. 1963. 50% freelance written by writers on a one-time basis. Syndicates to magazines and newspapers. Reports in 3 months. Buys second serial rights for Latin America and other customers in Europe, Far East.
Needs: Magazine features (science, technology, celebrities: interviews with candid shots), newspaper features, recipes, handiworks, etc., with color photos. Buys one-shot features and article series. "Travel, adventure, human-interest stories with pictures. Query with clips of published work or submit complete ms. Pays 50% author's percentage. Currently syndicates Moda al dia, by Claudia Moda (color photo with captions); Household Advice, by Penny Orchard (column with illustrations); and The World Today, by London Express (articles with b&w pictures).
Reprints: Send tearsheet of article. Pays 50% of amount paid for an original article.
Tips: "We are seeking good, up-to-date articles about technology, science, medicine, business, marketing; also, interviews with celebrities in show business, politics, sports preferably with color photos. Do not submit travel articles unless with color transparencies."

‡**FARM MARKETS REPORT**, 237 S. Clark Ave., St. Louis MO 63135. (314)522-1300. Fax: (314)521-1016. Editor: Michael J. Olds. Estab. 1985. "Farm Markets Report acts as the local news bureau for newspapers that are too small to operate their own state capital bureau." Buys all rights and makes work-for-hire assignments. Call for information.
Needs: Independent farm market reporters on long-term contract to open new state capital bureaus. Must be experienced news reporters to write stories with hard news emphasis. Query with clips of published work. Negotiates with writers under contract. "Farm Markets Report is interested in contracting with reporters in all states not now served, and all Canadian provinces."
Tips: "We are interested in offering a series of farm and agri-business columns to weekly rural newspapers in addition to the farm markets prices we now supply."

FEATUREPINK!, (formerly M Group Features Syndicate), P.O. Box 12486, San Antonio TX 78212-0486. E-mail: featurepink@aol.com. Website: http://users.aol.com/featurepink/. Contact: Randall Sherman. Estab. 1994. Syndicates to electronic and print media in lesbian, bisexual, gay and transgendered communities. Reports in 2 months. Buys all rights, second serial (reprint) rights. Guidelines for SASE or by e-mail.

Needs: Continuing works and filler—magazine and newspaper columns and features; cartoon strips and panels. Pays 25-50% of gross receipts for all rights, 10-25% of gross receipts for second serial rights to one-shot works.

Tips: "Writing about the positive aspects of alternative lifestyles is most important, because raising the consciousness of the lesbian, bisexual, gay and transgendered communities will promote a higher level of self-respect." Prefers continuing projects over one-shots.

FOTOPRESS, INDEPENDENT NEWS SERVICE INTERNATIONAL, Box 1268, Station Q, Toronto, Ontario M4T 2P4 Canada. (416)445-3594. Fax: (416)445-4953. E-mail: fotopres@enterprise.ca. Website: http://WWW.ENTERPRISE.CA/~fotopres. Executive Editor: John Milan Kubik. Estab. 1983. 50% written on contract; 25% freelance written on a one-time basis. Works with 30% previously unpublished writers. Syndicates to domestic and international magazines, newspapers, radio, TV stations and motion picture industry. Reports in 2 months. Buys variable rights. Writer's guidelines for $3.50 US money order, no checks.

Needs: Fillers, magazine and newspaper columns and features, news items, radio broadcast material, documentary, the environment, travel and art. Buys one-shot and article series for international politics, scientists, celebrities and religious leaders. Query or submit complete ms. Pays 50-75% author's percentage. Offers $5-150 for accompanying ms.

Tips: "We need all subjects from 500-3,000 words. Photos are purchased with or without features. All writers are regarded respectfully—their success is our success."

HISPANIC LINK NEWS SERVICE, 1420 N St. NW, Washington DC 20005. (202)234-0280. Fax: (202)234-4090. E-mail: zapoteco@aol.com. Publisher: Charles A. Ericksen. Editor: Patricia Guadalupe. Estab. 1980. 50% freelance written on contract; 50% freelance written on a one-time basis. Buys 156 columns and features/year. Works with 50 writers/year; 5 previously unpublished writers. Syndicates to 100 newspapers and magazines with circulations ranging from 5,000 to 300,000. Reports in up to 1 month. Buys second serial (reprint) or negotiable rights. For reprints, send photocopy of article. Pays 100% of the amount paid for an original article ($25 for guest columns). Free writer's guidelines.

Needs: Newspaper columns and features. One-shot features and article series. "We prefer 650-700 word op/ed analysis or new features geared to a general national audience, but focus on issue or subject of particular interest to Hispanics. Some longer pieces accepted occasionally." Query or submit complete ms. Pays $25-100. Currently syndicates Hispanic Link, by various authors (opinion and/or feature columns). Syndicated through: Los Angeles Times Syndicate.

Tips: "We would especially like to get topical material and vignettes relating to Hispanic presence and progress in the United States and Puerto Rico. Provide insights on Hispanic experience geared to a general audience. Of the columns we accept, 85 to 90% are authored by Hispanics; the Link presents Hispanic viewpoints and showcases Hispanic writing talent through its subscribing newspapers and magazines. Copy can be submitted in English or Spanish. We syndicate in both languages."

HOLLYWOOD INSIDE SYNDICATE, P.O. Box 49957, Los Angeles CA 90049-0957. (909)678-6237. Fax: (909)672-8459. E-mail: holywood@inland.net. Editor: John Austin. Estab. 1968. 30% written on contract; 40% freelance written on a one-time basis. Purchases entertainment-oriented mss for syndication to newspapers in San Francisco, Philadelphia, Detroit, Montreal, London, Sydney, Manila, South Africa, etc. Accepts previously published submissions, if published in the US and Canada only. Reports in 3 months.

Needs: News items (column items concerning entertainment—motion picture—personalities and jet setters for syndicated column; 750-800 words). Also considers series of 1,500-word articles; "suggest descriptive query first. We are also looking for off-beat travel pieces but not on areas covered extensively in the Sunday supplements; not luxury cruise liners but lower cost cruises. We also syndicate nonfiction book subjects—sex, travel, etc., to overseas markets." Also require 1,500-word celebrity profiles on internationally-recognized celebrities. We stress *internationally*." Query or submit complete ms. Currently syndicates Books of the Week column and "Celebri-Quotes," "Movie Trivia Quiz," "Hollywood Inside," "Hollywood ★ Features".

Tips: "Study the entertainment pages of Sunday (and daily) newspapers to see the type of specialized material we deal in. Perhaps we are different from other syndicates, but we deal with celebrities. No 'I' journalism such as 'when I spoke to Cloris Leachman.' Many freelancers submit material from the 'dinner theater' and summer stock circuit of 'gossip type' items from what they have observed about the 'stars' or featured players in these productions—how they act off stage, who they romance, etc. We use this material."

HYDE PARK MEDIA, Chicago Metro News Services, 1310 Howard St., Suite 3, Chicago IL 60626-1425. 10% freelance written by writers on a one-time basis. Syndicates to midwestern newspapers and magazines. Reports in 1 month. Buys first and second serial rights.

Needs: Unusual, off-beat magazine features about casino gambling (1,500-3,000 words) and newspaper features with a Midwestern gambling hook (750-1,500 words). Buys single (one-shot) features only. Send SASE with query. Pays 50% commission on sale.

Tips: "Please read 'Needs' paragraph above before sending material. Why waste anyone's time?"

INTERNATIONAL PHOTO NEWS, 226 South B St., Lake Worth FL 33400. (407)793-3424. Editor: Jay Kravetz. Estab. 1974. 10% written by freelance writers under contract. Buys 52 features/year. Works with 25 previously unpublished writers/year. Syndicates to newspapers. Reports in up to 3 months. Buys second serial (reprint) rights. Writer's guidelines for SASE.

Needs: Magazine columns and features (celebrity), newspaper columns and features (political or celebrity), news items (political). Buys one-shot features. Query with clips of published work. Pays 50% author's percentage. Pays $5 for photos accepted with ms. Currently syndicates Celebrity Interview, by Jay and Elliott Kravetz.

Tips: "Go after celebrities who are on the cover on major magazines."

INTERNATIONAL PUZZLE FEATURES, 740 Van Rensselaer Ave., Niagara Falls NY 14305. Website: http://www.ag.net/~patb/ipf.html. Contact: Pat Battaglia. Estab. 1990. 0% written on contract; 5-10% freelance written on a one-time basis. Buys 10 features/year. Works with 0 writers/year. Works with all new previously unpublished writers. Syndicates to newspapers. Reports in 1 month. Writer's guidelines for #10 SASE. Submit complete ms.

Needs: Concisely written, entertaining word puzzles. Pays $5 flat rate/puzzle. Currently syndicates If You're So Smart . . ., by Pat Battaglia (word puzzles).

Tips: "We are not interested in crossword, word search, cryptogram, mathematical or trivia puzzles."

‡**INTERSTATE NEWS SERVICE**, 237 S. Clark Ave., St. Louis MO 63135. (314)522-1300. Fax: (314)521-1016. Editor: Michael J. Olds. Estab. 1985. "Interstate acts as the local news bureau for newspapers that are too small to operate their own state capital bureau." Buys all rights and makes work-for-hire assignments. Call for information.

Needs: Independent news reporters on long-term contract to open new state capital bureaus. Must be experienced news reporters to write stories with hard news emphasis, concentrating on local delegations, tax money and local issues. Query with clips of published work. Negotiates with writers under contract. "Interstate News is interested in contracting with reporters in all states not now served, and all Canadian provinces."

Tips: "We do not buy unsolicited manuscripts."

‡**LANDMARK DESIGNS, INC.**, P.O. Box 2307, Eugene OR 97402. (503)345-3429. President: Jim McAlexander. Estab. 1977. 99% written on contract; 1% freelance written on a one-time basis. Buys 60 features/year. Works with 3 writers/year. Works with 2 previously unpublished writers/year. Syndicates to newspapers. Reports in 3 months. Buys all rights. Writer's guidelines for #10 SASE. Query with clips of published work.

Needs: Newspaper features. Purchases one shot features and article series. Pays flat rate. Currently syndicates Landmark Designs, Designer Homes and Today's Homes.

‡**LOS ANGELES FEATURES SYNDICATE**, 650 Winnetka Mews #110, Winnetka IL 60093. (708)446-4082. Managing Editor: Alice O'Neill. Estab. 1986. 75% written by writers on contract; 10% freelance written on a one-time basis. Buys 100 features/year. Works with 5 new previously unpublished writers/year. Syndicates to magazines, newspapers. Reports in 1 month. Buys all rights. Query only with SASE.

Needs: True celebrity stories of controversial nature. Must submit proof of authenticity (taped interview with sources). Pays 50% author's percentage. Pays $50 minimum for photos.

‡**LOS ANGELES TIMES SYNDICATE**, Times Mirror Square, Los Angeles CA 90053. (213)237-7987. Special Articles Editor: Beth Barber. Syndicates to US and worldwide markets. Reports in 2 months. Usually buys first North American serial rights and world rights, but rights purchased can vary. Submit seasonal material 6 weeks in advance. Material ranges from 800-2,000 words.

Needs: Reviews continuing columns and comic strips for US and foreign markets. Send comics to Cathryn Irvine, promotion manager, columns to Tim Lange, managing editor. Also reviews single articles, series, magazine reprints, and book serials; send these submissions to Beth Barber. Send complete ms. Pays 50% commission. Currently syndicates Art Buchwald, Dr. Henry Kissinger, Dr. Jeane Kirkpatrick, William Pfaff and Paul Conrad.

JERRY D. MEAD ENTERPRISES, P.O. Box 2796, Carson City NV 89702. (702)884-2648. Fax: (702)884-2484. E-mail: winetrader@aol.com. Website: http://www.wines.com/winetrader/.Contact: Jerry D. Mead. Estab. 1969. 70% written on contract; 30% freelance written on a one-time basis. Syndicates to magazines and newspapers. Reports immediately or not at all. Buys first North American serial rights or second serial (reprint) rights. Query only.

Needs: Magazine and newspaper columns and features; single features. Pays 50% author's percentage. Currently syndicates Mead on Wine, by Jerry D. Mead (weekly/newspaper); The Travel Trader, by E. Edward Boyd (monthly/travel); The Lodging Report, by Sandra Wechsler (monthly/travel).

MIDWEST FEATURES INC., P.O. Box 259907, Madison WI 53725-9907. Contact: Mary Bergin. Estab. 1991. 80% written on contract; 20% freelance written on a one-time basis. Buys 1-2 features/year. Works with 6-8 writers/year. Syndicates to newspapers. Reports in 2 months. Buys second serial (reprint) rights. Query with clips of published work.

Needs: Newspaper columns and story packages. Material *must* have a Wisconsin emphasis and already appear in a Wisconsin publication. Length: 500-1,000 words. Series in past have been book excerpts ("Nathan's Christmas") and seasonal material (spring gardening, Milwaukee Brewer spring training). Pays authors 50% when reprints of previously published work are sold. Currently syndicates: Cross Country, by John Oncken (farming); Midwest Gardening, by Jan Riggenbach (gardening); Beyond Hooks & Bullets, by Pat Durkin (outdoor sports); Images, by Barbara Quirk (aging and older adults); George Hesselberg, by George Hesselberg (humor, slice-of-life); Consumer Watch, by Bob Richards (consumer complaints).
Tips: We do not consider 'generic' copy—what you write must have a specific Wisconsin emphasis."

‡NATIONAL NEWS BUREAU, P.O. Box 43039, Philadelphia PA 19129-0628. (215)546-8088. Editor: Harry Jay Katz. "We work with more than 200 writers and buy over 1,000 stories/year." Syndicates to more than 500 publications. Reports in 2 weeks. Buys all rights. Writer's guidelines for 9×12 SAE with 3 first-class stamps.
Needs: Newspaper features; "we do many reviews and celebrity interviews. Only original, assigned material." One-shot features and article series; film reviews, etc. Query with clips. Pays $5-200 flat rate. Offers $5-200 additional payment for photos accompanying ms.

NEW LIVING, P.O. Box 1519, Stony Brook NY 11790. (516)981-7232. Publisher: Christine Lynn Harvey. Estab. 1991. 20% written under contract; 5% freelance written on one-time basis. Buys 20 features/year. Works with 20 writers/year. Works with 5 previously unpublished writers/year. Syndicates to magazines, newspapers, radio, 900 phone lines. Reports in 6 months. Buys all rights. Query with clips of published work. Writer's guidelines for #10 SASE.
Needs: Magazine and newspaper columns and features, news items, fillers, radio broadcast material. Purchases single (one shot) features and articles series. "Looking for articles on health and fitness (nutrition, healthy recipes, sports medicine, exercise tips, running, tennis, golf, bowling, aerobics, cycling, swimming, cross-training, watersports, travel, medical advice)." Also offers to list author's business affiliation, address, and phone number in article.
Photos: Offers $25-100 for photos accepted with ms.
Tips: "Be highly qualified in the area that you are writing about. If you are going to write a medical column, you must be a doctor, or at least affiliated with a nationally recognized medical organization."

‡ROYAL FEATURES, P.O. Box 58174, Houston TX 77258. (713)532-2145. Executive Director: Fay W. Henry. Estab. 1984. 80% written on contract or by staff; 10% freelance written on one-time basis. Syndicates to magazines and newspapers. Reports in 2 months. Buys all rights or first North American serial rights.
Needs: Magazine and newspaper columns and features. Buys one-shot features and article series. No fiction and/or cartoons. No previously published material. Query with or without published clips. Send SASE with all unsolicited queries or materials.

SENIOR WIRE, Clear Mountain Communications, 2377 Elm St., Denver CO 80207. (303)355-3882. Fax: (303)355-2720. E-mail: 72370.3520@compuserve.com. Editor/Publisher: Allison St. Claire. Estab. 1988. 100% freelance written. Monthly news, information and feature syndication service to various senior publications, and companies interested in senior market. Circulation nationwide, in Canada and India, varies per article depending on which articles are bought for publication. Pays 50% of fee for each use of ms (fees range from $5-30). Pays on publication. Buys first North American serial and simultaneous rights. Submit seasonal/holiday material 3 months in advance. Prefers mss; queries only with SASE. No payment for photos but they help increase sales. Reports in up to 3 months. Writer's guidelines $1 with SASE.
Needs: Does not want "anything aimed at less than age 55-plus market; anything patronizing or condescending to seniors." Manuscripts requested include: seasonal features, especially those with a nostalgic angle (750-800 words); travel tips (no more than 500-750 words); personal travel experiences as a mature traveler (700-1,000 words); personal essays and commentary (500-750 words). The following topics currently are covered by assigned columnists and similar material has little chance of immediate acceptance: national legislation; psychological, financial and legal advice; golf; internet; automotive; fitness; food; collectibles; and Q&A on relationships, pets, and beauty tips after 50. Accepts 12 mss in each category/year.
Tips: "That quintessential sweet little old lady in the rocking chair, Whistler's mother, was just 50 years old when she posed for that painting. Today, the average age of the Rolling Stones is 55. Most of our client papers like to emphasize active, thoughtful, concerned seniors and are currently picking up material that shows seniors living in the 'real,' i.e., contemporary, world. For example, do you have your own personal fax yet; how has a computer changed your life; what kind of new cars are you looking at? What adventures have you been involved in? What impact are you/seniors having on the world around them—and vice versa? Currently overloaded with humor. Seeking regular columnists in following: senior sexuality, gardening, psychology, health (both allopathic and alternative) and RV travel tips."

THE SPORTS NETWORK, 701 Masons Mill, Huntingdon Valley PA 19006. (215)947-2400. Fax: (215)938-8466. E-mail: tsnwire@aol.com. Contact: Rosalind Tucker. Estab. 1980. 30% written on contract; 10-15% freelance written on one-time basis; balance by in-house personnel. Buys 200-250 features/year.

Works with 50-60 writers/year and 10-15 new previously unpublished writers/year. Syndicates to magazines, newspapers, radio and has the additional benefit of being an international sports wire service with established awareness globally furnishing exposure world-wide for its writers/clients. Reports immediately. Buys all rights. Free writer's guidelines. Query with clips of published and/or sample works and SASE.

Needs: Fillers, magazine and newspaper columns and features, news items, radio and broadcast material, single features (timely sports pieces, from 300-2,000 words). Seeking ongoing coverage pieces of teams (professional) leagues (professional), conferences (college) and sports, 1-2 times weekly. Payments variable. Currently syndicates NHL Update, by Anthony Gargano (NHL); Olympic Update, by Steve Abbott (Olympics); College Football and Basketball Analysis, by Mark Narducci; Opinion and Commentary, by Jack Whitaker; Analysis and Trends, by JR Clarke; Sports Reporter, by Richard Bomze.

Tips: "The competition for sports is fast and furious, so right time and place, with a pinch of luck, are ingredients that complement talent. Making inroads to one syndicate for even one feature is an amazing door opener. Focus on the needs of that syndicate or wire service (as is the case with TSN) and use that as a springboard to establish a proven track record with quality work that suits specific needs. Don't give up and don't abandon the day job. This takes commitment, desire, knowledge of the topic and willingness to work at it while being able to handle rejection. No one who reads submissions really 'knows' and the history of great rejections would fill volumes, from 'Gone With The Wind' to Snoopy and Garfield. We are different in that we are looking for specific items and not a magical cartoon (although sports cartoons will work), feature or story. Give us your best in sports and make certain that it is in tune with what is happening right now or is able to stand the test of time, be an evergreen and everlasting if it is a special feature."

‡**TEENAGE CORNER, INC.**, 70-540 Gardenia Ct., Rancho Mirage CA 92270. President: Mrs. David J. Lavin. Buys 122 items/year for newspaper use. Submit complete ms. Reports in 1 week. Not copyrighted.
Needs: 500-word newspaper features. Pays $25.

‡**TRIBUNE MEDIA SERVICES**, 64 E. Concord St., Orlando FL 32801. (800)245-6536. President: David D. Williams. Editor: Mark Mathes. Syndicates to newspapers. Reports in 1 month. Buys all rights, first North American serial rights or second serial (reprint) rights.
Needs: Newspaper columns, comic strips. Query with published clips. Currently syndicates the columns of Mike Royko, Bob Greene, Andy Rooney and Marilyn Beck; and cartoons of Jeff MacNelly and Don Wright.

‡**UNIVERSAL PRESS SYNDICATE**, Dept. WM, 4900 Main St., Kansas City MO 64112. (816)932-6600. Website: http://www.uexpress.com. Contact: Syndicate editorial. Estab. 1970. Buys syndication rights. Reports normally in 1 month. Return postage required.
Nonfiction: Looking for features and columns for daily and weekly newspapers. Distributes one-shot articles (profiles, lifestyle pieces, etc.). "Any material suitable for syndication in daily newspapers." Currently handling James J. Kilpatrick, Dear Abby, Erma Bombeck and others. Payment varies according to contract.

WHITEGATE FEATURES SYNDICATE, 71 Faunce Dr., Providence RI 02906. (401)274-2149. Contact: Eve Green. Editor: Ed Isaac. Estab. 1987. Buys 100% of material from freelance writers. Syndicates to newspapers; planning to begin selling to magazines and radio. Reports in 3 months. Buys all rights.
Needs: Fiction for Sunday news magazines; magazine and newspaper columns and features, cartoon strips. Buys one-shots, article series. Query with published clips. For cartoon strips, submit samples. Pays 50% author's percentage on columns. Additional payment for photos accepted with ms. Currently syndicates Indoor Gardening, by Jane Adler; Looking Great, by Gloria Lintermans; Strong Style, by Hope Strong.
● Whitegate Features is looking for more gardening, travel, medical and food text columns.
Tips: "Please aim for a topic that is fresh. Newspapers seem to want short text pieces, 400-800 words. We do *not* return materials. We like to know a little about author's or cartoonist's background. We prefer people who have already been published. Please send material to Eve Green."

WORLD NEWS SYNDICATE, LTD., P.O. Box 419, Hollywood CA 90078-0419. Phone/fax: (213)469-2333. Managing Editor: Laurie Williams. Estab. 1965. Syndicates to newspapers. Reports in 1 month. Buys first North American serial rights. Query with *published* clips. "We're looking for short columns, featurettes, home, medical, entertainment-interest, music, TV, films. Nothing over 500-600 words."
● The managing editor says they only accept material already published regularly in writer's own living area. They accept no "new" ideas.
Needs: Fillers and newspaper columns. Pays 45-50% author's percentage.

COMPANIES THAT APPEARED in the 1996 edition of *Writer's Market* but are not included this year are listed in the General Index with a notation explaining their absence.

Greeting Cards & Gift Ideas

How many greeting cards did you buy last year? Americans bought nearly seven and a half billion cards last year. That's according to figures published by The Greeting Card Association, a national trade organization representing the multi-billion dollar greeting card industry.

In fact, nearly 50% of all first class mail now consists of greeting cards. And, of course, card manufacturers rely on writers to supply them with enough skillfully crafted sentiments to meet the demand. The perfect greeting card verse is one that will appeal to a large audience, yet will make each buyer feel that the card was written exclusively for him or her.

Three greeting card companies dominate this industry; together, American Greetings, Hallmark and Gibson Greetings supply 85% of all cards sold. The other 15% are published by approximately 1,500 companies who have found success mainly by not competing head to head with the big three but by choosing instead to pursue niche markets—regional and special-interest markets that the big three either cannot or do not supply.

A PROFESSIONAL APPROACH TO MARKETS

As markets become more focused, it's important to keep current on specific company needs. Familiarize yourself with the differences among lines of cards by visiting card racks. Ask retailers which lines are selling best. You may also find it helpful to read trade magazines such as *Greetings* and *Party and Paper Retailer*. These publications will keep you apprised of changes and events within the field, including seminars and trade shows.

Once you find a card line that appeals to you, write to the company and request its market list, catalog or submission guidelines (usually available for a SASE or a small fee). This information will help you determine whether or not your ideas are appropriate for that market.

Submission procedures vary among greeting card publishers, depending on the size and nature of the company. Keep in mind that many companies (especially the large ones) will not review your writing samples until you've signed and returned their disclosure contract or submission agreement, assuring them that your material is original and has not been submitted elsewhere.

Some editors prefer to see individual card ideas on 3×5 cards, while others prefer to receive a number of complete ideas on $8\frac{1}{2} \times 11$ bond paper. Be sure to put your best pieces at the top of the stack. Most editors do not want to see artwork unless it is professional, but they do appreciate conceptual suggestions for design elements. If your verse depends on an illustration to make its point or if you have an idea for a unique card shape or foldout, include a dummy card with your writing samples.

The usual submission includes from 5 to 15 card ideas and an accompanying cover letter, plus mechanical dummy cards, if necessary. Some editors also like to receive a résumé, client list and business card. Some do not. Be sure to check the listings and the company's writer's guidelines for such specifications before submitting material.

Payment for greeting card verse varies, but most firms pay per card or per idea; a handful pay small royalties. Some companies prefer to test a card first and will pay a small fee for a test card idea. In some instances, a company may even purchase an idea and never use it.

Greeting card companies will also buy ideas for gift products and may plan to use card material for a number of subsequent items. Licensing—the sale of rights to a particular character for a variety of products from mugs to T-shirts—is a growing part of the greetings industry. Because of this, however, note that most card companies buy all rights. We now include in this section markets for licensed product lines such as mugs, bumper stickers, buttons, posters and the like.

Information of interest to writers wishing to know more about working with the greeting card industry is available from the Greeting Card Creative Network. Write to them at 1200 G Street NW, Suite 760, Washington, DC 20005.

MANAGING YOUR SUBMISSIONS

Because you will be sending out many samples, you may want to label each sample. Establish a master card for each verse idea and record where and when each was sent and whether it was rejected or purchased. Keep all cards sent to one company in a batch and give each batch a number. Write this number on the back of your return SASE to help you match up your verses as they are returned.

For information on some greeting card companies not listed in *Writer's Market*, see the General Index.

AMBERLEY GREETING CARD CO., 11510 Goldcoast Dr., Cincinnati OH 45249-1695. (513)489-2775. Editor: Dave McPeek. Estab. 1966. 90% freelance written. Bought 200 freelance ideas/samples last year. Reports in 1 month. Material copyrighted. Buys all rights. **Pays on acceptance.** Writer's guidelines for #10 SASE. Market list regularly revised.
 • This company is now accepting alternative humor.
Needs: "Original, easy to understand, belly-laugh or outrageous humor. We sell to the 'masses, not the classes,' so keep it simple and to the point. Humor accepted in all captions, including general birthday, family birthday, get well, anniversary, thank you, friendship, etc. No non-humorous material needed or considered this year. Pays $150/card idea." Submit maximum 10 ideas/batch.
Tips: "Send SASE for our writer's guidelines before submitting. Amberley publishes humorous specialty lines in addition to a complete conventional line that is accented with humor. Since humor is our specialty, we are highly selective. Be sure that a SASE with the correct US postage is included with your material. Otherwise it will not be returned."

ARGUS COMMUNICATIONS, 200 E. Bethany, Allen TX 75002-3804. (214)390-6300. Editorial Coordinator: Beth Davis. 90% freelance written. Primarily interested in material for posters. Reports in 2 months. **Pays on acceptance.** Send for submission guidelines (send a #10 SASE) before submitting material.
 • Argus Communications has expanded its markets and is focusing on three specific groups: education, general and Christian. By describing more clearly its specific targets, freelance writers should be able to select and write for the market(s) where they feel their strengths are. In return, Argus hopes it will be able to get better use out of the submissions it receives.
Needs: "We have three specific markets for which we buy editorial: (1) Education market: poster editorial for teachers to place in their classrooms that is positive, motivational, inspirational, thought-provoking and success-oriented. Also, poster editorial that encourages teamwork and conflict resolution, and editorial that reflects basic values such as honesty, integrity, kindness, trust, etc. (2) General market: poster editorial for teenagers through adults that is bright, timely and funny. The editorial should reflect current trends, lifestyles and attitudes. Humor and light sarcasm are the emphasis for this market. (3) Christian market: poster editorial for teenagers through adults that is positive, inspirational, motivational, encouraging or even humorous. The editorial should express basic Christian faith, beliefs and values.
Other Product Lines: Postcards, calendars (for the Christian market).
Tips: "Poster editorial is an at-a-glance, brief message that makes an impression, whether it is thought-provoking, humorous or inspirational. Our posters capture your attention with a creative mixture of humorous, dynamic and motivational editorial. We do not need any long poetry. Postcard editorial should express a simple 'me to you' message. Think of a new way to express a friendly hi, thinking of you, miss you, thank you or what's new."

BLUE MOUNTAIN ARTS, INC., Dept. WM, P.O. Box 1007, Boulder CO 80306-1007. E-mail: bma@rmi i.com. Contact: Editorial Staff. Estab. 1971. Buys 100 items/year. Reports in 10 weeks. Pays on publication. Writer's guidelines for #10 SASE. Enclose SASE with submission.

Needs: "We are interested in reviewing poetry and writings that would be appropriate for greeting cards, which means that they should reflect a message, feeling, or sentiment that one person would want to share with another. We'd like to receive sensitive, original submissions about love relationships, family members, friendships, philosophies, and any other aspect of life. Poems and writings for specific holidays (Christmas, Valentine's Day, etc.) and special occasions, such as graduation, birthdays, anniversary, and get well are also considered." Submit seasonal material at least 4 months in advance. Buys worldwide, exclusive rights, $200/poem; anthology rights $25.

Other Product Lines: Calendars, gift books, prints, mugs.

Tips: "We strongly suggest that you familiarize yourself with our products before submitting material, although we caution you not to study them too hard. We do *not* need more poems that sound like something we've already published. We're looking for poetry that expresses real emotions and feelings, so we suggest that you have someone specific in mind (a friend, relative, etc.) as you write. The majority of the poetry we publish *does not* rhyme. We do not wish to receive books, unless you are interested in having portions excerpted for greeting cards; nor do we wish to receive artwork or photography. We prefer that submissions be typewritten, one poem per page. Only a small portion of the freelance material we receive is selected each year, either for publication on a notecard or in a gift anthology, and the review process can also be lengthy, but please be assured that every manuscript is given serious consideration."

BRILLIANT ENTERPRISES, 117 W. Valerio St., Santa Barbara CA 93101-2927. President: Ashleigh Brilliant. Estab. 1967. Buys all rights. Submit words and art in black on 3½×3½ horizontal, thin white paper in batches of no more than 15. Reports "usually in 2 weeks." Catalog and sample set for $2.

Needs: Postcards. Messages should be "of a highly original nature, emphasizing subtlety, simplicity, insight, wit, profundity, beauty and felicity of expression. Accompanying art should be in the nature of oblique commentary or decoration rather than direct illustration. Messages should be of universal appeal, capable of being appreciated by all types of people and of being easily translated into other languages. Because our line of cards is highly unconventional, it is essential that freelancers study it before submitting. No topical references or subjects limited to American culture or puns." Limit of 17 words/card. Pays $50 for "complete ready-to-print word and picture design."

THE CALLIGRAPHY COLLECTION INC., 2604 NW 74th Place, Gainesville FL 32653. (904)375-8530. Fax: (904)374-9957. Editor: Katy Fischer. Reports in 6 months. Buys all rights. Pays on publication.

Needs: "Ours is a line of framed prints of watercolors with calligraphy." Conventional, humorous, inspirational, sensitivity, soft line. Prefers unrhymed verse, but will consider rhymed. Submit 3 ideas/batch. Pays $75-150/framed print idea.

Other Product Lines: Gift books, plaques, musical picture frames.

Tips: "Sayings for friendship are difficult to get. Bestsellers are humorous, sentimental and inspirational ideas—such as for wedding and family and friends. Our audience is women 20 to 50 years of age. Write something they would like to give or receive as a lasting gift. The most popular size has room for about 35 words. Our gift item is for everyday use rather than just a special occasion so we do not mention birthdays or mother's day for example. It is a gift to tell someone how much they mean to you. How important their friendship is or what is special about knowing them. We need to keep sayings below 60 words. Below 35 words for the most popular size."

‡COLORS BY DESIGN, 7723 Densmore Ave., Van Nuys CA 91436. (818)376-1226. Creative Director: Jane Daly. Estab. 1985. 20% of material freelance written. Receives 500 submissions/year; bought 200 ideas/samples last year. Does not return submissions accompanied by SASE. Buys all rights. Pays on publication. Writer's guidelines/market list free. Market list regularly revised and available to writer on mailing list basis.

Needs: Announcements, informal, juvenile, conventional, humorous, invitations, soft line.

COMSTOCK CARDS, 600 S. Rock, Suite 15, Reno NV 89502-4115. Fax: (702)856-9406. Owner: Patti P. Wolf. Production Manager: David Delacroix. Estab. 1986. 35% freelance written. Receives 500 submissions/year; bought 150 freelance ideas/samples last year. Submit seasonal/holiday material 1 year in advance. Reports in 5 weeks. Buys all rights. **Pays on acceptance.** Writer's guidelines/market list for SASE. Market list issued one time only.

Needs: Humorous, informal, invitations, "puns, put-downs, put-ons, outrageous humor aimed at a sophisticated, adult female audience. Also risqué cartoon cards. No conventional, soft line or sensitivity hearts and flowers, etc." Pays $50-75/card idea, cartoons negotiable.

Other Product Lines: Notepads, cartoon cards, invitations.

Tips: "Always keep holiday occasions in mind and personal me-to-you expressions that relate to today's occurrences. Ideas must be simple and concisely delivered. A combination of strong image and strong gag line make a successful greeting card. Consumers relate to themes of work, sex and friendship combined with current social, political and economic issues."

CONTEMPORARY DESIGNS, 213 Main St., Gilbert IA 50105. (515)232-5188. Fax: (515)232-3380. Editor: Sallie Abelson. Estab. 1977. 90% freelance written. Submit seasonal/holiday material 1 year in advance. Reports in 1-2 months. Buys all rights. **Pays on acceptance.**
Needs: Short positive humorous copy for memo pads, mugs, etc. Themes: music, sports, age, diet, the working world, camp and Judaica.
Other Product Lines: Quote and gift books, mugs, tote bags, aprons and pillow cases, memo pads.

CREATE-A-CRAFT, P.O. Box 330008, Fort Worth TX 76163-0008. Estab. 1967. 5% freelance written. Receives 300 submissions/year; bought 2 freelance ideas/samples last year. Submit seasonal/holiday material 1 year in advance. "No phone calls from freelancers accepted. We deal through agents only. Submissions not returned even if accompanied by SASE—not enough staff to take time to package up returns." Buys all rights. Sample greeting cards $2.50 for #10 SASE.
Needs: Announcements, conventional, humorous, juvenile, studio. "Payment depends upon the assignment, amount of work involved, and production costs involved in project."
Tips: No unsolicited material. "Send letter of inquiry describing education and experience, or résumé with one sample first. We will screen applicants and request samples from those who interest us."

‡**DAY SPRING CARDS**, P.O. Box 1010, Siloam Springs AR 72761. Phone/fax: (501)549-9303. E-mail: annw@outreach.mhs.compuserve.com. Freelance Editor: Ann Woodruff. Estab. 1971. Submit seasonal/holiday material 1 year in advance. Reports in 2 months. **Pays on acceptance.** Guidelines for #10 SASE.
Needs: Announcements, invitations, all major seasonal and special days, all major everyday cards—birthday, anniversary, get well, friendship, etc. Material must be usable for the Christian market.
Tips: "Study our line before submitting. We are looking for sentiments with relational, inspirational messages that minister love and encouragement to the receiver." Prefer unrhymed verse.

DISKOTECH INC., 7930 State Line, Suite 210, Prairie Village KS 66208. (913)432-8606. Fax: (913)432-8606*51. E-mail: 74472.2263@compuserve.com. Publisher/Editor: John Slegman. Estab. 1989. Publishes PCcards™ which are multimedia greeting cards that come on computer diskettes and run on PCs. PCcards™ are for all seasons, ages and tastes. Looking for short, exciting computer animations, better if they include music or sound effects. Also looking for funny (not sadistic) short video clips. Enclose SASE with submissions. Reports in 2 months. Recent PCcards™ include 3-D, interactive 4-D and virtual reality.

DUCK AND COVER PRODUCTIONS, P.O. Box 21640, Oakland CA 94620. Contact: Jim Buser. Estab. 1990. 50% freelance written. Receives 1,000 submissions/year. Bought 80 ideas/samples last year. Reports in 3 weeks. Buys all rights on novelty products. Pays on publication. Guidelines for #10 SAE with 2 first-class stamps.
Other Product Lines: Novelty buttons and magnets *only.* Pays $25/idea.
Tips: "We do best with original, intelligent statements that make fun of life in the neurotic '90s. Our target audience would be educated, aware, yet skeptical and anxious young adults; however, anyone with an offbeat sense of humor can enjoy our line. We sell to novelty stores, head shops, record stores, bookstores, sex shops, comic stores, etc. There are no taboos for our writers; we encourage them to be as weird and/or rude as possible. We feel buttons and magnets are commercial cousins to graffiti and there is a definite psychological spin to our line. Cerebral material that makes use of contemporary pop vocabulary is a plus. We do *not* want to see old cliches or slogans already in the market."

EPCONCEPTS, P.O. Box 363, Piermont NY 10968. (914)359-7137. Contact: Steve Epstein. Estab. 1983. 95% freelance written. Receives 1,200 submissions/year; bought 25 ideas/samples last year. Submit seasonal/holiday material 2 months in advance. Reports in 3 months. Buys one-time greeting card rights. Pays ½ on acceptance; ½ on publication. Writer's guidelines for #10 SASE.
Needs: Announcements, conventional, humorous, informal, inspirational, invitations, juvenile, studio, all holidays. Prefers unrhymed verse ideas. Submit 20 ideas/batch on 8½×11 paper; no index cards.
Other Product Lines: Post cards, buttons, mugs, work (jotting down ideas) pads.
Tips: "Humorous sells best; especially birthdays, anniversaries, friendship/love and light risqué. Target audience is ages 20-50, upscale and appreciative of photography, antiques, illustrations and cartoons. Trends can always include certain social and political phenomenons, e.g., Presidents, first ladies, etc."

EPHEMERA, INC., P.O. Box 490, Phoenix OR 97535. E-mail: ephem@aol.com. Contact: Editor. Estab. 1979. 90% freelance written. Receives 2,000 submissions/year; bought 200 slogans for novelty buttons and magnets last year. Reports in 5 weeks. Buys all rights. Pays on publication. Writer's guidelines for SASE. Complete full color catalog available for $2.
Needs: Novelty buttons and magnets. Provocative, irreverent and outrageously funny slogans. "We want concise, high impact gems of wit that would sell in trendy card and gift shops, bookstores, record shops, political and gay shops, adult stores, amusement parks, etc! We've been in business for over 17 years and we have a reputation as *the* publisher of the wackiest slogans." Pays $25/slogan.

Tips: We're looking for satirical slogans about current events, pop culture, political causes, the president, job attitudes, coffee, booze, pot, drugs, sexual come-ons and put-downs, aging, slacker angst, gays and lesbians. But please don't limit yourself to these topics! Make us laugh out loud!

FOTOFOLIO, INC., 536 Broadway, New York NY 10012. (212)226-0923. Fax: (212)226-0072. Editors: Julie Galant, JoAnne Seador. Estab. 1976. Submit seasonal/holiday material 1 year in advance (visuals only). Reports in 1 month. Pays on publication.
Other Product Lines: Postcards, notecards, posters.
Tips: "We specialize in high quality fine art photography."

GIBSON GREETINGS, INC., P.O. Box 371804, Cincinnati OH 45222-1804. Contact: Editorial Department. Estab. 1850. "We make every effort to return material." Reports in 2 months. Buys all rights. **Pays on acceptance**. Guidelines available for #10 SAE and 1 first class stamp. Market list is regularly revised and available to writer on mailing list basis.
Needs: Will review all types of cards. Send for needs list.
Tips: "All information is provided in guidelines, which must be requested prior to submitting material."

KATE HARPER DESIGNS, P.O. Box 2112, Berkeley CA 94702. Contact: Art Director. Estab. 1993. Submit seasonal/holiday material 1 year in advance. Reports in 1 month. Pays flat fee for usage, not exclusive, $25 plus author's name on front of card. **Pays on acceptance**. Writer's guidelines/market list for SASE.
Needs: Humorous, informal, inspirational, everyday cards. "Quotes needed about work, family, love, kids, career, technology and marriage with a twist of humor. Something a working mom would laugh at and/or tips on how to have it all and still live to tell about it. Be adventurous and say what you really think in first person. Nothing cute or sweet, please. Avoid quotes about women and weight, PMS, diet, sex. Avoid traditional ideas of card quotes. Serious quotes also considered. Quotes must be 20 words or less. For front of card only." Prefers unrhymed verse ideas. Submit 10 ideas/batch.

INFINITY COLLECTIONS, P.O. Box 41201, Washington DC 20018. Contact: Karmen A. Booker. Estab. 1990. 10% freelance written. Submit material 2 months in advance. Reports in 2 months. Purchases exclusive rights to sentiment, a flat fee with no further royalties. Pays on publication. Writer's guidelines/market list for $2.
Needs: Inspirational. Submit 5-8 ideas/batch.
Tips: "Cards that sell best are Happy Birthday, Friendship, Thank You, Graduation and Mother's Day, Christmas cards. Card buyers look for a personal touch in verse. Therefore, please have someone in mind (a friend, relative, etc.) as you write."

‡IT TAKES TWO, INC., 100 Minnesota Ave., LeSueur MN 56058. Owner/Creator: Kimberly Rinehart. Estab. 1984. 1% of material freelance written. Receives 30 submissions/year; bought 10 ideas/samples last year. Submit seasonal/holiday material 10 months in advance. Reports in 1 month. Buys all rights. Pays on publication. Writer's guidelines/market list for #10 SAE. Market list issued one time only.
Needs: Humorous, not sarcastic, not off-color. Prefers unrhymed verse ideas. Submit 12 ideas/batch.

KIMBERLEY ENTERPRISES, INC., 13639 Cimarron, Gardena CA 90249-2461. (310)538-1331. Fax: (310)538-2045. Vice President: M. Hernandez. Estab. 1979. 15% freelance written. Receives less than 100 submissions/year; bought 12 ideas/samples last year. Submit seasonal material 9 months in advance. Reports in up to 3 months. Material not copyrighted. Pays on acceptance. Market list available on mailing list basis.
Needs: Announcements, conventional, inspirational, invitations. Send 12 ideas maximum.
Other Product Lines: Plaques. Pays $10-250.
Tips: "The primary future interest for the company is in the plaque line, with an emphasis on inspirational or conventional appeal."

KOGLE CARDS, INC., 1498 S. Lipan St., Denver CO 80223. (303)698-9007. President: Patricia Koller. Please send submissions Attn: Art Director. Estab. 1982. 40% freelance written. Receives 100 submissions/year; bought 80 ideas/samples last year. Submit seasonal/holiday material 18 months in advance. Reports in 1 month. Buys all rights. Pays on publication.
Needs: Humorous, business related. Rhymed or unrhymed verse ideas.
Tips: "We produce cards designed for the business community, in particular salespeople, real estate, travel, hairdresser, insurance and chiropractic."

L&H MAHAR ART PUBLISHERS, 945 Murray Rd., Middle Grove NY 12850. Contact: Larry Mahar. Estab. 1982. 5% freelance written. Receives 20 submissions/year; bought 4 ideas/samples last year. No seasonal material. Reports in 1 week. Our use only; writer retains ownership. Pays on publication. Writer's guidelines/market list for #10 SASE. Market list issued one time only.
Needs: "Verses averaging 8 lines non-rhyming prose—poem style of type that could be put on a plaque (mother, love, family, friendship). No humor. Basically serious social expression."

LOVE GREETING CARDS, INC., 1717 Opa Loca Blvd., Opa-Locka FL 33054. (305)685-5683. Fax: (305)685-8473. Contact: Norman Drittel. Estab. 1984. 75% freelance written. Receives 200-300 submissions/year; bought 400 ideas/samples last year. Submit seasonal/holiday material 6 months in advance. Reports in 1 month. Buys all rights. **Pays on acceptance**. Market list regularly revised.
Needs: Informal, juvenile, humorous, general.
Other Product Lines: Greeting cards, posters, books ($100-300), posters ($200-500).
Tips: "There's a great demand for animal cards, flowers and computer art for greeting cards."

‡MADISON PARK GREETINGS, 1407 11th Ave., Seattle WA 98105. (206)324-5711. Copywriting Coordinator: Renée Capps. Estab. 1984. 50% of material freelance written. Receives 100 submissions/year. Submit seasonal/holiday material 10 months in advance. Reports in 2 months. Pays on publication. Writer's guidelines/market list free. Market list is issued one time only.
Needs: Announcements, informal, studio, conventional, inspirational, sensitivity, humorous, invitations, soft line.

‡MILLIDAY GREETINGS, P.O. Box 708, Berea OH 44017-0708. Owner: Robert Stein. Estab. 1991. 85% of material freelance written. We do not wish to see seasonal/holiday material which is not related to our trademarks. We publish Milliday Twins ™ cards for famous persons and events. Reports in 2 months with SASE. Buys all rights. **Pays on acceptance**. Will send guidelines, song, Milliday Calculator ™, traditions list, and samples for $5 and a mailing label. Market list revised regularly. "We are looking for cards that promote our Milliday, Milleversary, and Milliday Twins trademarks and which support the celebration of Milliday or Milleversary personal holidays. (A couple would celebrate their first Wedding Milleversary on the one thousandth day of their marriage, their second Milleversary at 2,000 days etc.)" Millidays or Milleversaries are celebrated for any notable event." Prefers unrhymed verse. Submit 10 cards/batch. "We are interested in reviewing personal and business greeting cards and postcards. We especially need 'professional to client' Milliday ™ and Milleversary ™ cards both general and specific as to profession. We pay $30 to $150 for cards, buttons, t-shirts and other flat designs. A Milliday celebration is often a surprise to the celebrant since it is not annual. Have the age and point of view of the celebrant(s) in mind as you write."

‡NOVO CARD PUBLISHERS, INC., 4513 N. Lincoln Ave., Chicago IL 60625. Art Director: Maria Moleterno. 95% of material freelance written. Submit seasonal/holiday material 6 months in advance. Reports in 2 months. Pays on publication. Writer's guidelines/market list. Market list for SASE.
Needs: Announcements, conventional, humorous, informal, inspirational, invitations, juvenile, sensitivity, soft line, studio.

OATMEAL STUDIOS, P.O. Box 138W3, Rochester VT 05767. (802)767-3171. Creative Director: Helene Lehrer. Estab. 1979. 85% freelance written. Buys 200-300 greeting card lines/year. **Pays on acceptance.** Reports within 6 weeks. Current market list for #10 SASE.
Needs: Birthday, friendship, anniversary, get well cards, etc. Also Christmas, Chanukah, Mother's Day, Father's Day, Easter, Valentine's Day, etc. Will review concepts. Humorous material (clever and *very* funny) year-round. "Humor, conversational in tone and format, sells best for us." Prefers unrhymed contemporary humor. Current pay schedule available with guidelines.
Other Product Lines: Notepads, stick-on notes.
Tips: "The greeting card market has become more competitive with a greater need for creative and original ideas. We are looking for writers who can communicate situations, thoughts, and relationships in a funny way and apply them to a birthday, get well, etc., greeting and we are willing to work with them in targeting our style. We will be looking for material that says something funny about life in a new way."

PAINTED HEARTS & FRIENDS, 1222 N. Fair Oaks Ave., Pasadena CA 91103. Fax: (818)798-7385. Creative Director: Elizabeth Rush. 20% freelance written. Receives 500-1,000 submissions/year. Submit seasonal/holiday material 3 months in advance. Pays on publication. Writer's guidelines/market list for 4 × 9 SASE. Market list regularly revised.
Needs: Announcements, conventional, humorous, inspirational, realistic, invitations, juvenile. Submit 12 ideas/batch.
Other Product Lines: Invitations, post cards, poster.
Tips: Watercolor cards sell best for this company. No poetry or lengthy verse.

PALM PROJECTS INC., P.O. Box 1770, Canal St., Station, New York NY 10013-1770. (718)788-8296. Fax: (718)789-8296. E-mail: 102742.1170@compuserve.com. Contact: Paul Ketley. Estab. 1989. 25% freelance written. Bought 3 ideas/samples last year. Submit seasonal/holiday material 1 year in advance. Reports in 1-2 months. Material copyrighted. Pays on publication.
Needs: Humorous.
Other Product Lines: Calendars, post cards, posters.
Tips: "We currently only offer contemporary humorous cards of an environmental nature under the Revenge Cards Trademark."

PANDA INK GREETING CARDS, P.O. Box 5129, West Hills CA 91308-5129. (818)340-8061. Fax: (818)883-6193. Contact: Ruth Ann or Irwin Epstein. Estab. 1981. 10-20% freelance written. Receives 100 submissions/year; bought 50 ideas/samples last year. Submit seasonal/holiday material 6 months in advance. Reports in 1 month. Buys first rights. **Pays on acceptance**. Writer's guidelines free.
Needs: Conventional, humorous, juvenile, soft line, Judaic, ethnic. Prefers rhymed and unrhymed verse ideas. Submit 10 ideas/batch.
Tips: "No risqué, sarcasm, insulting. Need Jewish/Yiddish language in most cases. We now have a metaphysical line of cards."

‡**THE PAPER MAGIC GROUP, INC.**, 401 Adams Ave., Scranton PA 18510. (800) 278-4085. Director of Marketing: Richard Myles. Estab. 1907. 5-10% freelance written. Receives 20-30 submissions/year. Buys 12 ideas/samples last year. Submit seasonal/holiday material 6 months in advance. Reports in 1 month. **Pays on acceptance**. No market list.
Nonfiction: Christmas boxed cards only. No relative titles, no juvenile. Submit 6-12 ideas/batch.

‡**PAPER MOON GRAPHICS**, P.O. Box 34672, Los Angeles CA 90034. (310)645-8700. Contact: Creative Director. Estab. 1978. 90% freelance written. Receives 2,000 submissions/year; bought 500 ideas/samples last year. Submit seasonal/holiday material 7 months in advance. Reports in 2 months. Buys card, stationery, advertising rights. **Pays on acceptance.**
Needs: Humorous, alternative humor/risqué. Prefers unrhymed verse ideas. Submit 12-18 ideas/batch. No original work. Send transparencies, photocopies, etc. Enclose SASE for return of work.
Other Product Lines: Stationery.
Tips: "Humor cards sell best for female audience 19-45. Trends are changing daily—humor always sells."

C.M. PAULA COMPANY, 6049 Hi-Tek Court, Mason OH 45040. Contact: Editorial Supervisor. Estab. 1958. 10% freelance written. "Looking for humor *only* from previously published social-expression writers. Seasoned writers should submit published writing samples. If there is a match in style, we will then contact writers with assignments." Reports in 2-3 months. Buys all rights. **Pays on acceptance**.
Product Lines: Coffee mugs, key rings, stationery pads, magnets, dimensional statues and awards.
Tips: "Our needs are light humor—nothing risqué. A writer can get a quick idea of the copy we use by looking over our store displays. Please note—we do not publish greeting cards."

PLUM GRAPHICS INC., P.O. Box 136, Prince Station, New York NY 10012. (212)337-0999. President: Yvette Cohen. Estab. 1983. 100% freelance written. Bought 21 samples last year. Does not return samples unless accompanied by SASE. Reports in 3-4 months. Buys greeting card and stationery rights. Pays on publication. Guidelines sheet for SASE. "Sent out about twice a year in conjunction with the development of new cards."
Needs: Humorous. "We don't want general submissions. We want them to relate to our next line." Prefers unrhymed verse. Greeting cards pay $40.
Tips: "Sell to all ages. Humor is always appreciated. We want short, to-the-point lines."

QUALITY ARTWORKS, 2262 N. Penn Rd., P.O. Box 369, Hatfield PA 19440-0369. Creative Director: Linda Tomezsko Morris. Estab. 1985. 10% freelance written. Reports in 2 months. Buys all rights. **Pays on acceptance**. Writer's guidelines/market list for #10 SASE.
Needs: Conventional, inspirational, sensitivity, soft line. Prefers unrhymed verse.
Other Product Lines: Bookmarks, scrolls, stationery, blank books. Payment is negotiable.
Tips: "We are looking for sophisticated yet inspirational verse (directed toward women). The main emphasis of our business is bookmarks."

‡**RED FARM STUDIO**, 1135 Roosevelt Ave., P.O. Box 347, Pawtucket RI 02862-0347. Fax: (401)728-0350. Contact: Creative Director. Estab. 1955. 100% freelance written. Receives 200 submissions/year; buys 100 ideas/samples per year. Reports in 2 months. Buys exclusive publishing rights. **Pays on acceptance; within 1 month.** For verse guidelines send #10 SASE.
Needs: Everyday occasion, conservative humor and Christmas cards (including religious). "We are looking for heartfelt, sincere sentiments, often with a conversational tone, both serious and humorous. Religious verse is generally more formal, often incorporating Bible verse. No family headings (such as sister's birthday, etc.). Usually no longer than 4 lines." Submit any number of ideas/samples per batch. Pays $4/line of copy. Prose, short and sweet.
Tips: "We pride ourselves on a premier nautical line of everyday greeting cards and Christmas boxed cards as well as our traditional lines. We are buying less 'flowery' verse that is typical of greeting cards, and opting for more down-to-earth, conversational writing—things a sender would actually *say* to the recipient."

‡**RITE LITE LTD.**, 260 47th St., Brooklyn NY 11220. (718)439-6900. Contact: Rochelle Stern. Estab 1949. Receives 20 submissions/year; bought 6 ideas/samples last year. Submit seasonal/holiday material 6 months

in advance. Reports in 1 month. Buys reproduction rights. Pays royalties. Writer's guidelines/market list free. Market list regularly revised.

Needs: Conventional. Rhymed or unrhymed verse. Submit 12 ideas/batch.

Other Product Lines: Gift books, posters.

Tips: "Jewish. Should know Hebrew alphabet and Yiddish sayings. Should know correct translations.

ROCKSHOTS, INC., 632 Broadway, New York NY 10012. (212)420-1400. Fax: (212)353-8756. Editor: Bob Vesce. Estab. 1979. Buys 75 greeting card verse (or gag) lines/year. Reports in 2 months. Buys rights for greeting-card use. Writer's guidelines for SASE.

Needs: Humorous ("should be off-the-wall, as outrageous as possible, preferably for sophisticated buyer"); soft line; combination of sexy and humorous come-on type greeting ("sentimental is not our style"); and insult cards ("looking for cute insults"). No sentimental or conventional material. "Card gag can adopt a sentimental style, then take an ironic twist and end on an off-beat note." Submit no more than 10 card ideas/ samples per batch. Send to attention: Submissions. Pays $50/gagline. Prefers gag lines on 8×11 paper with name, address, and phone and social security numbers in right corner, or individually on 3×5 cards.

Tips: "Think of a concept that would normally be too outrageous to use, give it a cute and clever wording to make it drop-dead funny and you will have commercialized a non-commercial message. It's always good to mix sex and humor. Our emphasis is definitely on the erotic. Hard-core eroticism is difficult for the general public to handle on greeting cards. The trend is toward 'light' sexy humor, even cute sexy humor. 'Cute' has always sold cards, and it's a good word to think of even with the most sophisticated, crazy ideas. 80% of our audience is female. Remember that your gag line will be illustrated by a photographer. So try to think visually. If no visual is needed, the gag line *can* stand alone, but we generally prefer some visual representation. It is a very good idea to preview our cards at your local store if this is possible to give you a feeling of our style."

RUSS BERRIE & COMPANY, INC., 111 Bauer Dr., Oakland NJ 07436. Contact: Angelica Berrie. Estab. 1963. 50% freelance written. Receives thousands of submissions/year; bought hundreds of ideas last year. Submit seasonal/holiday material 2 years in advance. Reports in 2-4 months. **Pays on acceptance.** Writer's guidelines/market list for #10 SAE with 2 first-class stamps. Market list regularly revised.

Needs: Conventional, humorous, inspirational, juvenile, sensitivity, soft line. Submit 10-25 ideas/batch.

Other Product Lines: Payment varies according to each product and length of copy, as well as the number of pieces purchased, but ranges between $25-100/piece. Calendars (undated-perpetual), gift books, greeting books, plaques, post cards, promotions, bookmarks, pocket cards, magnets, mugs, key rings.

Tips: "Humorous cards for women, florals, inspirational—but we are always looking for new concepts that can also be adapted to gift products and other paper products."

SANGAMON, INC., P.O. Box 410, Taylorville IL 62568. (217)824-2261. Fax: (217)824-2300. Contact: Editorial Department. Estab. 1931. 90% freelance written. Reports in 3 months. Buys all rights. **Pays on acceptance.** Writer's guidelines for SASE.

Needs: Conventional, humorous, inspirational, juvenile, sensitivity, studio. "We offer a balance of many styles. We'd like to see more conversational prose styles for the conventional lines." Submit 15 ideas maximum/batch.

Other Product Lines: Calendars, promotions.

Tips: "We only request submissions based on background and writing experience. We work 12-18 months ahead of a season and only accept material on assignment."

‡SCANDECOR INC., 430 Pike Rd., Southampton PA 18966. (215)355-2410. Fax: (215)364-8737. Creative Director: Lauren Karp. Estab. 1970. 40% freelance written. Receives 1,000 submissions/year; bought 50 freelance ideas/samples last year. Reports in 2 months. Buys poster rights only.

Needs: Posters: Humorous, inspirational, juvenile, sensitivity, soft line, studio. Rhymed or unrhymed OK. Pays $100.

Tips: "Our posters are our main product in the US. Our target audience is mother-child, 0-8, teen market, 8-22 and adult."

‡SECOND NATURE LTD., 10 Malton Rd., London W10 5UP England. 011-44-181-960-0212. E-mail: sales@secondnature.co.uk. Website: http://secondnature.co.uk. Editor: Rod Shrager. Estab. 1980. Submit seasonal/holiday material 18 months in advance. Reports in 6 weeks. **Pays on acceptance.** Market list is regularly revised.

Needs: Humorous, informal, inspirational and soft line. Rhymed and unrhymed verse OK.

‡SNAFU DESIGNS, Box 16643, St. Paul MN 55116. (612)698-8581. Editor: Scott F. Austin. Estab. 1985. Reports in 6 weeks. Buys all rights. **Pays on acceptance.** "Before we send you our guidelines, please send us something that is representative of your sense of humor (include a SASE). We will send you our guidelines if we feel your humor is consistent with ours."

Needs: Humorous, informal, birthday, friendship, thank you, anniversary, congratulations, get well, new baby, Christmas, Valentine's Day. Prefers unrhymed verse. Submit no more than 10 ideas/batch. Pays $75/idea.

Tips: "We use clever ideas that are simple and concisely delivered and are aimed at a sophisticated adult audience. Off-the-wall humor that pokes fun at the human condition. Please do not submit anything cute."

‡SUNRISE PUBLICATIONS, INC., P.O. Box 4699, Bloomington IN 47402-4699. (812)336-9900. Contact: Text Editor. Estab. 1974. 5% freelance written. Receives 2,000 submissions/year. Reports in 3 months. Buys worldwide exclusive license in all commercial formats. **Pays on acceptance.** Writer's guidelines for SASE. Market list regularly revised.

Needs: Contemporary, humorous, informal, soft line. No "off-color humor or lengthy poetry. Generally, we like short one- or two-line captions, sincere or clever. Our customers prefer this to lengthy rhymed verse. Longer copy is used but should be conversational. Submit ideas for birthday, get well, friendship, wedding, baby congrats, sympathy, thinking of you, anniversary, belated birthday, thank you, fun and love. We also have strong seasonal lines that use traditional, humorous and inspirational verses. These seasons include Christmas, Valentine's Day, Easter, Mother's Day, Father's Day, Graduation, Halloween and Thanksgiving." Payment varies.

Tips: "Think always of the sending situation and both the person buying the card and its intended recipient. Most of our traditional versing is done inhouse. We continue to look for exceptionally fresh and lively or emotionally-compelling ideas. We avoid any put-downs or age slams, anything mean-spirited or lewd."

‡SYNCHRONICITY GREETING CARDS, 122 E. Texas Ave., #1016, Baytown TX 77520. (713)422-6326. Contact: Submissions. Receives 600 submissions/year; bought 50 ideas/samples last year. Reports in 1 month. Pays by royalty agreement only (10% of net). Writer's guidelines/market list for SAE and $1.

Needs: Sweet, sexy and sassy greeting cards. Submit 10 ideas/batch.

Other Product Lines: Fine art post cards, posters, current events, T-shirts, mugs, political buttons.

Tips: "We specialize in cards that make you laugh and cry. Send those ideas to us and we will buy them."

UNIQUE GREETINGS, INC., P.O. Box 5783, Manchester NH 03108. (603)647-6777. Contact: Michael Normand. Estab. 1988. 10% freelance written. Receives 15 submissions/year. Submit seasonal/holiday material 1 year in advance. Reports in 6 weeks. Buys all rights. Writer's guidelines/market list for SASE. Market list regularly revised.

Needs: Watercolors, cute animals, flower scenes, etc. Prefers unrhymed verse. Submit 12 ideas/batch.

Tips: "General and Happy Birthday sell the best."

VAGABOND CREATIONS, INC., 2560 Lance Dr., Dayton OH 45409. (513)298-1124. Editor: George F. Stanley, Jr. 10% freelance written. Bought 10-15 ideas/samples last year. Submit seasonal/holiday material 6 months in advance. Reports in 1 week. Buys all rights. Ideas sometimes copyrighted. **Pays on acceptance.** Writer's guidelines for #10 SASE. Market list issued one time only.

Needs: Cute, humorous greeting cards (illustrations and copy) often with animated animals or objects in people-situations with short, subtle tie-in message on inside page only. No poetry. Pays $15-25/card idea.

WARNER PRESS, PUBLISHERS, 1200 E. Fifth St., P.O. Box 2499, Anderson IN 46018-9988. Product Editorial Supervisor: Robin Fogle. Estab. 1880. 50% freelance written. Reports in 2 months. Buys all rights. **Pays on acceptance.** Must send #10 SASE for guidelines before submitting.

Needs: Religious themes; sensitive prose and inspirational verse for boxed cards, posters, calendars. Pays $20-35. Also accepts ideas for coloring and activity books.

WEST GRAPHICS, 385 Oyster Point Blvd., #7, South San Francisco CA 94080. (800)648-9378. Contact: Production Department. Estab. 1980. 80% freelance written. Receives 20,000 submissions/year; bought 200 freelance ideas/samples last year. Reports in 6 weeks. Buys greeting card rights. Pays 30 days after publication. Writer's guidelines/market list for #10 SASE.

Needs: "We are looking for outrageous contemporary humor that is on the cutting edge." Prefers unrhymed verse. Submit 10-30 ideas/batch. Pays $100.

Tips: "West Graphics is an alternative greeting card company which offers a diversity of humor from 'off the wall' to 'tastefully tasteless'. Our goal is to publish cards that challenge the limits of taste and keep people laughing. The majority of our audience is women in their 30s and 40s, ideas should be targeted to issues they care about: relationships, sex, aging, success, money, crime, etc."

COMPANIES THAT APPEARED in the 1996 edition of *Writer's Market* but are not included this year are listed in the General Index with a notation explaining their absence.

Contests and Awards

The contests and awards listed in this section are arranged by subject. Nonfiction writers can turn immediately to nonfiction awards listed alphabetically by the name of the contest or award. The same is true for fiction writers, poets, playwrights and screenwriters, journalists, children's writers and translators. You'll also find general book awards, miscellaneous awards, arts council and foundation fellowships, and multiple category contests.

New contests and awards are announced in various writer's publications nearly every day. However, many lose their funding or fold—and sponsoring magazines go out of business just as often. We have contacted the organizations whose contests and awards are listed here with the understanding that they are valid through 1997. If you are using this section in 1998 or later, keep in mind that much of the contest information listed here will not be current. Requirements such as entry fees change, as do deadlines, addresses and contact names.

To make sure you have all the information you need about a particular contest, always send a self-addressed, stamped, business-sized envelope (#10 SASE) to the contact person in the listing before entering a contest. The listings in this section are brief, and many contests have lengthy, specific rules and requirements that we could not include in our limited space. Often a specific entry form must accompany your submission. A response with rules and guidelines will not only provide specific instructions, it will also confirm that the award is still being offered.

When you receive a set of guidelines, you will see that some contests are not for some writers. The writer's age, previous publication, geographic location and the length of the work are common matters of eligibility. Read the requirements carefully to ensure you don't enter a contest for which you are not qualified. You should also be aware that every year, more and more contests, especially those sponsored by "little" literary magazines, are charging entry fees.

Contest and award competition is very strong. While a literary magazine may publish ten short stories in an issue, only one will win the prize in a contest. Give yourself the best chance of winning by sending only your best work. There is always a percentage of manuscripts a contest judge or award director casts off immediately as unpolished, amateurish or wholly unsuitable for the competition.

To avoid first-round rejection, make certain that you and your work qualify in every way for the award. Some contests are more specific than others. There are many contests and awards for a "best poem," but some award only the best lyric poem, sonnet or haiku.

Winning a contest or award can launch a successful writing career. Take a professional approach by doing a little extra research. Find out who the previous winner of the award was by investing in a sample copy of the magazine in which the prize-winning article, poem or short story appeared. Attend the staged reading of an award-winning play. Your extra effort will be to your advantage in competing with writers who simply submit blindly.

If a contest or award requires nomination by your publisher, ask your publisher to nominate you. Many welcome the opportunity to promote a work (beyond their own, conventional means) they've published. Just be sure the publisher has plenty of time before the deadline to nominate your work.

INSIDER REPORT

The Heekin Group Foundation: Three Sisters Supporting Writers

Sarah Heekin Redfield

While vacationing with her sisters in Italy in 1992, Sarah Heekin Redfield experienced "a moment of inspiration, a sort of crossroads in my life where I realized I wanted to combine doing something with my sisters and doing something for the literary arts community." Redfield, a journalist turned fiction writer, had no problem enlisting the support of sisters Deirdre Heekin who was working on a screenplay, and Anne Heekin-Canedy who was working toward a master's degree in creative writing.

Once back to their respective homes—Sarah in Oregon, Deirdre in Vermont and Anne in Connecticut—the sisters had The Heekin Group Foundation Fellowship Program up and running in three weeks. "We had our judge lined up for the '92-'93 writing fellowships program and we had our ads made up and that was that," says Redfield. The role they defined for themselves was "to help new and emerging writers launch their careers by providing financial support that would enable them to finish their projects and make their writing the best it can be."

For the first three years, the foundation was self-financed and awards included the $10,000 James Fellowship for the Novel in Progress and the $5,000 Tara Fellowship for Short Fiction. In 1996 the program was restructured to offer more fellowships with lower cash awards. "We didn't make this change just by a decision from our board," explains Redfield. "It was the applicants who felt they would rather have more, smaller awards so their chances of winning would be greater." The Heekin Group Foundation now offers two $3,000 James Fellowships and two $1,500 Tara Fellowships. Both fiction categories are directed by Sarah. In addition, the Foundation has added the $2,000 Mary Molloy Fellowship in Children's Working Fiction, directed by Deirdre, and the $2,000 Siobhan Fellowship for Nonfiction Essay, directed by Anne. There also is a new fund-raising program with plans to launch an anthology of the works of fellowship recipients, and goals to get involved with elementary educational programs.

The sisters' writing backgrounds help them understand and work with those applicants. "We're not high profile writers. We're in the trenches ourselves and in that respect feel compassion toward our applicants. We really do try to give writers as much as we possibly can through our grants but also through feedback and in the way we deal with them. We treat our applicants with respect."

The Heekin Group Foundation receives 1,200-1,300 applications annually in the fiction division, 200 in the children's division, and 100 in the nonfiction

INSIDER REPORT, *continued*

division. The selection process begins with three disqualifying rounds judged by a team of readers, "everybody from booksellers to writers to teachers—people connected to the literary arts," says Redfield. The preliminary elimination rounds are followed by the semifinalist, finalist and publishers' finalist rounds. Those selected from the publishers' finalists are forwarded to a judge in the respective category. For instance, the publisher of a literary journal judges short fiction and a book publisher judges the novel in progress.

The only application criterion is writers must be unpublished in the genre to which they are applying. Redfield says most who submit "are very close to having everything open up to them. We're seeing that the fellowships really give them a big push in the right direction and that's very exciting for us." Max Garland's story "Chiromancy," winner of the first Tara Fellowship in 1993, was subsequently published in *The New England Review* and *The Best American Short Stories 1995*. Winning the 1995 James Fellowship enabled novelist Adria Bernardi to travel to Italy where she conducted research. Barbara Branscomb, 1994 James Fellow for her novel *Father and Daughter*—then in progress, now completed—is quoted as saying, "I don't know that I would be pursuing my writing . . . if not for the acknowledgement by HGF."

As director of the fiction division, Redfield sees first-hand what works and does not. "These manuscripts that surround me in my office are like living and breathing organisms. I live with them for six months. They go out to readers and they come back. I feel like I'm part of them and they're part of me. Maybe that's good and maybe it's not, but I can become passionate about what I feel is good in them or what is a problem."

Redfield advises applicants that presentation, creativity, and excellent language and writing skills push a manuscript through the various selection stages. "Writers should be as professional as they can in their presentations. A clean manuscript that is well formatted with a cover page and a letter always stands out. This shows that writers respect their work and are serious and committed about what they are doing." When reading novels in progress, Redfield says judges are not looking for "a slick, finished piece of work" but are judging the work for its essence. "By essence," says Redfield, "I mean creativity, the skillful use of language and the writer's understanding of fiction." For short fiction, judges look for "short stories that are in fact stories." Redfield notes that, although a good deal of the work they receive can be called "experimental," winning stories are "traditional in the sense that they do have a beginning, a middle and an end."

In discussing the concept of the story, Redfield says too many writers unsuccessfully try to turn real life experiences into fiction. "Certainly we take nuggets of our lives and put them into our fiction. But our experience is not a whole story within itself." She finds recurring mistakes with language and grammar. "I see problems with tense, sentence structure, with failing to use the word that truly defines what the writer wants to say, and with the repetition of the same word too many times, even in the same sentence or paragraph."

Redfield suggests a two-year self-help regime to strengthen weaknesses and become a better writer. "For one year, read everything you can get your hands on: nonfiction, B-grade fiction and excellent fiction. The second year, reread

GET YOUR WORK INTO THE RIGHT BUYERS' HANDS!

You work hard...and your hard work deserves to be seen by the right buyers. But in a constantly changing industry, it's not easy to know who those buyers are. That's why you need to keep up-to-date and on top with the most current edition of this indispensable market guide.

Keep ahead of these changes by ordering *1998 Writer's Market* today. You'll save the frustration of getting manuscripts returned in the mail. And of NOT submitting your work to new listings that you don't know exist. To order the upcoming 1998 edition, just complete the attached order card and return it with your payment or credit card information. Order now and you'll get the 1998 edition at the 1997 price—just $27.99—no matter how much the regular price may increase! *1998 Writer's Market* will be published and ready for shipment in September 1997.

Keep on top of the fast-changing industry and get a jump on selling your work with help from the *1998 Writer's Market*. Order today! You deserve it!

And NOW, keeping up is even easier — with the **NEW Electronic Edition of** *Writer's Market*! Turn over for more information

---

☐ **Yes!** I want to get my work into the right buyers' hands right now! Please send me the following *1997 Writer's Market* edition...

☐ The *1997 Writer's Market Electronic Edition* (CD-ROM only) for only $39.99 (#10492)
☐ The *1997 Writer's Market Combination Package* (book and CD-ROM) for only $49.99 (#45148)

...and please reserve my updated *1998 Writer's Market* at the 1997 price! I've selected the following version...

☐ The *1998 Writer's Market* for only $27.99 (#10512)
☐ The *1998 Writer's Market Electronic Edition* (CD-ROM only) for only $39.99 (#10517)
☐ The *1998 Writer's Market Combination Package* (book and CD-ROM) for only $49.99 (#45149)

I also want:

Book # _____ Price $_____

Book # _____ Price $_____

Book # _____ Price $_____

Subtotal $_____

*Add $3.50 postage and handling for one book; $1.00 for each additional book.

Postage and handling $_____

Payment must accompany order.
Ohioans add 6% sales tax.

Total $_____

VISA/MasterCard orders call
TOLL-FREE 1-800-289-0963

☐ Payment enclosed $_____ (or)

Charge my: ☐ Visa ☐ MasterCard Exp._____

Account # _____

Signature_____

Name_____

Address _____

City_____ State _____ Zip _____

Phone Number _____
(will be used only if we must contact you regarding this order.)

☐ FREE CATALOG. Ask your bookstore about other fine Writer's Digest Books, or mail this card today for a complete catalog.

30-Day Money Back Guarantee on every book you buy!

W Mail to:
Writer's Digest Books
1507 Dana Avenue
Cincinnati, OH 45207

6893

NOW AVAILABLE! Writer's Market on CD-ROM!
The fastest, easiest way to locate your most promising markets!

Now you can get the same vital Writer's Market resources in a compact, searchable, electronic CD-ROM format. It's easier than ever to locate the information you need...when you need it. And, this electronic edition is expanded to offer you even more:

- Customize searches - set any parameters (by pay range, subject, state, or any other set of criteria)
- Submission Tracker - create and call up submissions records to see which publishers are past due answering your queries, or are late in paying
- *Writer's Encyclopedia, Third Edition* - also on the CD you'll have access to another handy reference tool — at no additional cost! (A $22.99 value, but yours FREE!)
- Writer's guidelines - some of the listings will now include ALL the data you need to submit your work. No more writing for guidelines!

Order your CD today, or the combination book and CD package. And, don't forget to reserve your 1998 editions at the 1997 prices! Just complete the order card on the reverse and keep up with the publishing industry (and technology!) Order Today!

CD-ROM is designed to work with:
- Windows: 486DX/66 or higher; 8MB RAM; 256-color display; mouse; Windows 3.1 or later; MS-DOS 3.1 or later; 15MB available hard disk space; double-speed CD- ROM drive.
- Macintosh: 16MHz 68040 or higher; 8MB RAM with System 7 or later; 8-bit monitor; 15MB available hard disk space; double-speed CD-ROM drive.

More Great Books to Help You Sell Your Work!

Latest Edition!
1997 Novel & Short Story Writer's Market
If you're serious about selling your fiction, you need this directory! Listed are nearly 2,000 fiction buyers hungry for your work—plus, loads of helpful articles and informative interviews with professionals who know what it takes to get published! #10493/$22.99/672 pages/available 2-97

Totally Updated!
1997 Guide to Literary Agents
Literary agents can open doors for you in the publishing industry. This invaluable directory (now in its 6th year) gives you 500 listings and answers the most-often-asked questions about working with reps! #10493/$21.99/288 pages/available 2-97

Revised and Updated!
The Writer's Essential Desk Reference
by the editors of Writer's Digest magazine
Discover the answers to your important business questions, including information on the World Wide Web! This companion to Writer's Market covers the business side of writing including desktop publishing, book contracts and self-publishing, taxes and health insurance and much more! #10485/$24.99/384 pages/available September 1996

New Edition!
Writer's Encyclopedia
by the editors of Writer's Digest magazine
Present a professional image using this best-selling writer's reference— now with information about electronic resources, plus more than 100 new entries. You'll find facts, figures, definitions and examples designed to answer your questions about every discipline connected with writing. #10464/$22.99/560 pages/62 b&w illus.

Order these helpful references today from your local bookstore, or use the handy order card on the reverse.

INSIDER REPORT, *Redfield*

some of those books, but this time analyze them—take them apart to see how writers put stories together, how they use language and point of view and how they manage their time lines." Redfield also advises writers to read books on the craft of writing, including those with differing opinions.

To become more disciplined, Redfield encourages writers to apply to contests and awards programs for the experience that meeting deadlines provides. "By giving yourself these deadlines, you get used to writing every day." And, insists Redfield, it is writing that makes writers. "People who are really writers will not worry that they need a fresh head of lettuce for dinner because they would rather write for an extra 45 minutes. To them, it is the act of writing that is important. And, chances are, with that commitment and with that obsession, a writer is going to get somewhere."

—*Barbara Kuroff*

Further information on funding for writers is available at most large public libraries. See the *Annual Register of Grant Support* (National Register Publishing Co., 3004 Glenview Rd., Wilmette IL 60091); *Foundations and Grants to Individuals* (Foundation Center, 79 Fifth Ave., New York NY 10003) and *Grants and Awards Available to American Writers* (PEN American Center, 568 Broadway, New York NY 10012). For more listings of contests and awards for fiction writers, see *Novel & Short Story Writer's Market* (Writer's Digest Books). *Poet's Market* (Writer's Digest Books) lists contests and awards available to poets. *Children's Writer's & Illustrator's Market* (Writer's Digest Books) has a section of contests and awards, as well. Two more good sources for literary contests are *Poets & Writers* (72 Spring St., New York NY 10012), and the *Associated Writing Programs Newsletter* (Old Dominion University, Norfolk VA 23529). Journalists should look into the annual Journalism Awards Issue of *Editor & Publisher* magazine (11 W. 19th St., New York NY 10011), published in the last week of December. Playwrights should be aware of the newsletter put out by The Dramatists Guild, (234 W. 44th St., New York NY 10036).

For information on some contests and awards not listed in *Writer's Market*, see the General Index.

GENERAL

‡BUNTING FELLOWSHIP, Radcliffe College, 34 Concord Ave., Cambridge MA 02138. (617)495-8212. Fax:(617)495-8136. E-mail: bunting_fellowships@radcliffe.harvard.edu. Contact: Fellowships Coordinator. "To support women of exceptional promise and demonstrated accomplishment who wish to pursue independent work in academic and professional fields and in the creative arts. Projects with public policy applications are especially encouraged. Applications will be judged on the quality and significance of the proposed project, the applicant's record of accomplishment, and on the difference the fellowship might make in advancing the applicant's career." Deadline varies. Call or write for application. Award is $33,000 stipend, plus office space and access to most resources at Harvard University and Radcliffe College. "The competition for writers is very high. We discourage writers who have not had publications or demonstrated level of accomplishment."

‡MARGARET A. EDWARDS AWARD, American Library Association, 50 E. Huron St., Chicago IL 60611. Offered annually to "an author whose book or books have provided young adults with a window through which they can view their world and which will help them to grow and to understand themselves and their role in society." Guidelines for SASE. Citation and $1,000.

‡**FRIENDS OF THE DALLAS PUBLIC LIBRARY AWARD**, The Texas Institute of Letters, P.O. Box 298300, Fort Worth TX 76129. (817)921-7822. Fax: (817)921-7333. Award Director: Judy Alter. Offered annually for submissions published January 1-December 31 of previous year to recognize the writer of the book making the most important contribution to knowledge. Deadline: January 2. Guidelines for SASE. Award: $1,000. Writer must have been born in Texas, or have lived in the state at least 2 consecutive years at some time, or the subject matter of the book should be associated with the state.

‡**GENESIS AWARD**, American Library Association, 50 E. Huron St., Chicago IL 60611. (800)545-2433. Offered annually to recognize the talents of African-American authors and illustrators at the beginning of their careers with no more than 3 published books. Guidelines for SASE. Award: plaque.

HOOSIER HORIZON WRITING CONTEST, Write-On, Hoosiers, Inc., P.O. Box 51, Crown Point IN 46307. (219)663-7307. Fax: (219)662-4097. Contact: Sharon Palmeri. Offered annually for unpublished fiction, nonfiction and poetry to build an awareness of Indiana talent. Two categories: young adults 12-18 and adults 18 and older. Deadline: July. Guidelines for SASE. Charges $2 registration fee and $1 for each additional entry. Prize: 1st-1-year W.O.H. membership, publication, complimentary copy, plaque and invitation to awards night; 2nd-6-month membership, certificate, ribbon and invitation; 3rd-3-month membership, certificate, ribbon and invitation; honorable mentions certificate, ribbon and invitation. Open to all Indiana writers.

‡**CORETTA SCOTT KING AWARDS**, American Library Association, 50 E. Huron St., Chicago IL 60611. (800)545-2433. Offered annually to an African-American author and illustrator to promote understanding and appreciation of culture and contributions of all people. Guidelines for SASE. Award: $250 and set of encyclopedias.

LOUISIANA LITERARY AWARD, Louisana Library Association, P.O. Box 3058, Baton Rouge LA 70821. (504)342-4928. Fax: (504)342-3547. E-mail: LLA@pelican.state.lib.la.us. Contact: Literary Award Committee. Estab. 1909. Offered annually for work published during the preceding year related to Louisiana. Guidelines for SASE.

MATURE WOMEN'S GRANTS, The National League of American Pen Women, 1300 17th St., Washington DC 20036. (202)785-1997. Contact: National Scholarship Chairman. Offered every 2 years to further the 35 + age woman and her creative purposes in art, music and letters. Deadline: January 15, even numbered years. Award announced by July 15. Send letter stating age, background and purpose for the monetary award. Send SASE after August 1 in odd-numbered years for information. Charges $8 fee. Prize: $1,000 in each category—art, letters and music.

MINNESOTA VOICES PROJECT COMPETITION, New Rivers Press, 420 N. Fifth St., #910, Minneapolis MN 55401. (612)339-7114. Editor/Publisher: C.W. Truesdale. Offered annually for new and emerging writers of poetry, prose, essays, and memoirs (as well as other forms of creative prose) from Wisconsin, Minnesota, Iowa and the Dakotas, to be published in book form for the first time. Deadline: April 1. Guidelines for SASE.

MODERN LANGUAGE ASSOCIATION PRIZE FOR A FIRST BOOK, Modern Language Association, 10 Astor Place, New York NY 10003-6981. (212)475-9500. Fax: (212)477-9863. Contact: Richard Brod. Offered annually for the first book-length scholarly publication by a current member of the association. To qualify, a book must be a literary or linguistic study, a critical edition of an important work, or a critical biography. Studies dealing with literary theory, media, cultural history and interdisciplinary topics are eligible. Deadline: May 1. Guidelines for SASE. Prize: $1,000 and certificate.

NATIONAL BOOK AWARDS, National Book Foundation, Attn: National Book Awards, 260 Fifth Ave., Room 904, New York NY 10001. (212)685-0261. Fax: (212)213-6570. E-mail: natbkfdn@interramp.com. Executive Director: Neil Baldwin. Awards Coordinator: Kevin La Follette. Fiction, nonfiction and poetry—books by American authors nominated by publishers.

NEW WRITING AWARD, New Writing, Box 1812, Amherst NY 14226-7812. E-mail: thebookdoc@aol.com. Contact: Sam Meade. Offered annually for unpublished work "to award the best of *new* writing. We accept short stories, poems, plays, novels, essays, films and emerging forms. All entries are considered for the award based on originality." Charges $10 reading fee for first entry; $5 + 10¢ per page per additional entry—no limit. Guidelines and form for SASE. Prize: Monetary award (up to $3,000 in cash and prizes) and possible publication. Judged by editors. "We are looking for new, interesting, experimental work."

‡JOHN NEWBERY MEDAL, American Library Association, 50 E. Huron St., Chicago IL 60611. (800)545-2433. Offered annually to a US author for the most distinguished contribution to American literature for children published in the United States in the preceding year. Guidelines for SASE. Award: medal.

OHIOANA BOOK AWARDS, Ohioana Library Association, 65 S. Front St., Room 1105, Columbus OH 43215. (614)466-3831. Fax: (614)728-6974. E-mail: ohioana@winslo.ohio.gov. Editor: Barbara Maslekoff. Estab. 1929. Books published within the past year by Ohioans or about Ohio and Ohioans, articles about Ohio writers, artists, museums, reviews of Ohio books. Submit 2 copies of book on publication.

PULITZER PRIZES, The Pulitzer Prize Board, 702 Journalism, Columbia University, New York NY 10027. (212)854-3841. Website: http://www.pulitzer.org/. Estab. 1917. Journalism in US newspapers (published daily or weekly), and in letters, drama and music by Americans. Deadline: February 1 (journalism); March 1 (music and drama); July 1 and November 1 (letters).

ROCKY MOUNTAIN ARTIST'S/ECCENTRIC BOOK COMPETITION, Hemingway Western Studies Center, Boise State University, 1910 University Dr., Boise ID 83725. (208)385-1999. Fax: (208)385-4373. E-mail: rentrusk@idbsu.idbsu.edu. Contest Director: Tom Trusky. Offered annually "to publish multiple edition artist's or eccentric books of special interest to Rocky Mountain readers. Topics must be public issues (race, gender, environment, etc.). Authors may hail from Topeka or Ulan Bator, but their books must initially have regional appeal." Deadline: September 1-December 1. Guidelines for SASE. Prize: $500, publication, standard royalties. First rights to Hemingway Center. Open to any writer.

SOCIETY OF MIDLAND AUTHORS AWARD, Society of Midland Authors, % P.O. Box 10419, Chicago IL 60610-0419. Offered annually for work published between January 1 and December 31. "Award for best work by writers of the 12 Midwestern states: IL, IN, IA, KS, MI, MN, MO, NE, ND, SD, WI and OH, and the stimulation of creative literary effort. Seven categories: poetry, adult fiction, adult nonfiction, biography, juvenile fiction, juvenile nonfiction." Deadline: January 15, 1997. Guidelines for SASE. Money and plaque given at annual dinner in Chicago, in May.

TOWSON STATE UNIVERSITY PRIZE FOR LITERATURE, College of Liberal Arts, Towson State University, Towson MD 21204-7097. (410)830-2128. Award Director: Dean, College of Liberal Arts. Estab. 1979. Book or book-length ms that has been accepted for publication, written by a Maryland author of no more than 40 years of age. Deadline: May 15.

SAUL VIENER PRIZE, American Jewish Historical Society, 2 Thornton Rd., Waltham MA 02154. Editor: Marc Lee Raphael. Estab. 1985. Offered every 2 years for work published within previous 2 years. "Award for outstanding scholarly work in American Jewish history." Deadline: February 15. Write/call Marc Lee Raphael. Prize: $500. Open to any writer.

WESTERN STATES BOOK AWARDS, Western States Arts Federation, 236 Montezuma Ave., Santa Fe NM 87501. (505)988-1166. Estab. 1984. Unpublished fiction, poetry or creative nonfiction, that has been accepted for publication in the award year, by a press in a Western States Arts Federation member state: Alaska, Arizona, California, Colorado, Idaho, Montana, Nevada, New Mexico, Oregon, Utah, Washington, and Wyoming. Manuscript duplication and return postage fee of $10. Send #10 SASE for deadline. Prize: $5,000.

WHITING WRITERS' AWARDS, Mrs. Giles Whiting Foundation, 1133 Avenue of the Americas, New York NY 10036. Director: Gerald Freund. "The Foundation gives annually $30,000 each to up to ten writers of poetry, fiction, nonfiction and plays. The awards place special emphasis on exceptionally promising emerging talent." Direct applications and informal nominations are not accepted by the Foundation.

‡H.W. WILSON LIBRARY PERIODICAL AWARD, donated by H.W. Wilson Company, administered by the American Library Association, Awards Committee, 50 E. Huron, Chicago IL 60611. (312)280-3247. Annual award presented to a periodical published by a local, state or regional library, library group, or library association in US or Canada which has made an outstanding contribution to librarianship. (This excludes publications of ALA, CLA and their divisions.) All issues for the calendar year prior to the presentation of the award will be judged on the basis of sustained excellence in both content and format, with consideration being given to both purpose and budget. Deadline for nominations is December 1. Prize: $1,000, certificate.

WORLD FANTASY AWARDS ASSOCIATION, 5 Winding Brook Dr., #1B, Guilderland NY 12084-9719. President: Peter Dennis Pautz. Estab. 1975. Previously published work recommended by previous convention attendees in several categories, including life achievement, novel, novella, short story, anthology, collection, artist, special award-pro and special award non-pro. Deadline: July 1. Works are recommended by attendees of current and previous 2 years' conventions, and a panel of judges. Winners determined by vote of panel.

‡**YOUNG COMMUNICATORS FELLOWSHIPS**, Institute for Humane Studies, 4084 University Dr., Fairfax VA 22030-6812. 703)934-6920. Fax: (703)352-7535. Contact: Paul Feine. Fellowships are awarded to candidates to help them take advantage of strategic short term opportunities that can enhance their abilities and credentials to pursue careers that involve the communication of ideas. Deadline: March 15 for summer positions, 10 weeks in advance for others. Guidelines for SASE. Award: up to stipend of $2,500 for 12-week period plus up to $2,500 housing/travel assistance. Must be college junior, senior, graduate student or recent graduate; clearly demonstrated interest in the "classical liberal" tradition of individual rights and market economies; intent on career in fiction writing, film, journalism, publishing or market-oriented public policy; must have arranged for an internship, training program or other short-term opportunity related to applicant's chosen career.

NONFICTION

‡**ABC-CLIO AMERICA: HISTORY AND LIFE AWARD**, Organization of American Historians, 112 N. Bryan St., Bloomington IN 47408-4199. (812)855-9852. Fax: (812)855-0696. E-mail: awards@oah.indian a.edu. Website: http://www.indiana.edu/~oah. Contact: Award and Prize Committee Coordinator. Offered every two years for a previously published article to recognize and encourage scholarship in American history in the journal literature advancing new perspectives on accepted interpretations or previously unconsidered topics. Deadline: November 15 of even-numbered years. Guidelines for SASE. Prize: $750 and certificate.

AIP SCIENCE WRITING AWARDS IN PHYSICS & ASTRONOMY, American Institute of Physics, One Physics Ellipse, College Park MD 20740. (301)209-3090. Fax: (301)209-0846. Contact: Joan Wrather. Offered annually for previously published work "to recognize and stimulate distinguished writing that improves the general public's understanding and appreciation of physics and astronomy." Deadlines: articles, booklets or books by professional journalists published between January 1-December 31 due February 6; articles, booklets or books intended for children up to 15 years published between July 1-June 30 due July 24; articles, booklets or books by physicists or astronomers published between May 1-April 30 due May 19. Guidelines for SASE. Prize: $3,000, inscribed Windsor chair, certificate and certificate to publisher.

ANTHEM ESSAY CONTEST, Ayn Rand Institute, Contact: Dr. Michael S. Berliner. Website: http://www.aynrand.org. Offered annually. Purpose of award is to encourage analytical thinking and excellence in writing, and to introduce students to the philosophic ideas of Ayn Rand. Deadline: April 1. Contact your English teacher or guidance counselor, or visit the website. Prizes: 1st-$1,000, 2nd-$200 (10) and 3rd-$100 (20). Open to 9th and 10th graders.

‡**ASCAP-DEEMS TAYLOR AWARD**, American Society of Composers, Authors & Publishers, One Lincoln Plaza, New York NY 10023. (212)621-6323. Director: Esther San Saurus. Offered annually for previously published work in the preceding year to authors and journalists having books and articles on the subject of music. Subject matter may be biographical or critical, repertorial or historical—any form of nonfiction prose about music and/or its creators—not an instructional textbook, how-to guide or work of fiction. Reprints or translations of works previously published outside the US are eligible. Program notes or liner notes are eligible. Deadline: April 30. Guidelines for SASE. Prize: $500 for the best book; $250 for the best newspaper, journal or magazine article; and a plaque to author or journalist and respective publisher.

VINCENT ASTOR MEMORIAL LEADERSHIP ESSAY CONTEST, US Naval Institute, 118 Maryl and Ave., Annapolis MD 21402-5035. (410)268-6110. Fax: (410)269-7940. Contact: Valry Fetrow. Essays on the topic of leadership in the sea services (junior officers and officer trainees). Deadline: February 15.

MRS. SIMON BARUCH UNIVERSITY AWARD, United Daughters of the Confederacy, 328 N. Boulev ard, Richmond VA 23220-4057. (804)355-1636. Fax: (804)353-1396. . Offered biannially in even-numbered years for unpublished work for the purpose of encouraging research in Southern history, the United Daughters of the Confederacy offers as a grant-aid of publication the Mrs. Simon Baruch University Award of $2,000. Deadline: May 1. Authors and publishers interested in the Baruch Award contest should ask for a copy of these rules. All inquiries should be addressed to the Chairman of the Mrs. Simon Baruch University Award Committee at the above address. Award: $2,000 and $500 author's award. Invitation to participate in the contest is extended (1) to anyone who has received a Master's, Doctoral, or other advanced degree within the past fifteen years, from a university in the United States; and (2) to any graduate student whose thesis or dissertation has been accepted by such an institution. Manuscripts must be accompanied by a statement from the registrar giving dates of attendance, and by full biographical data together with passport photograph of the authors.

‡**RAY ALLEN BILLINGTON PRIZE**, Organization of American Historians, 112 N. Bryan St., Blooming ton IN 47408-4199. (812)855-9852. Fax: (812)855-0696. Contact: Award and Prize Committee Coordinator.

E-mail: awards@oah.indiana.edu. Website: http://www.indiana.edu/~oah. Offered every two years for the best book in American frontier history, defined broadly so as to include the pioneer periods of all geographical areas and comparisons between American frontiers and others. Deadline: October 1 of even-numbered years. Guidelines for SASE. Prize: $1,000, certificate and medal.
frontier history, defined broadly so as to include the pioneer periods of all geographical areas and comparisons between American frontiers and others. Deadline: October 1 of even-numbered years. Guidelines for SASE. Prize: $1,000, certificate and medal.

‡**BREWER PRIZE**, American Society of Church History, P.O. Box 8517, Red Bank NJ 07701. Director: H.W. Bowden. Offered annually for unpublished quality fiction to encourage research in church history. Deadline: Nov. 1st. Guidelines for SASE. Prize: $1,000 to publisher as subvention fund. Limited to books.

THE BROSS PRIZE, Lake Forest College, 555 N. Sheridan, Lake Forest IL 60045. (847)735-5169. Fax: (847)735-6291. Contact: Professor Ron Miller. Offered every 10 years for unpublished work "to award the best book or treatise on the relation between any discipline or topic of investigation and the Christian religion." Deadline: September 1, 2000. Guidelines for SASE. Prize: Award varies depending on interest earned. Manuscripts awarded prizes become property of the college. Open to any writer.

ARLEIGH BURKE ESSAY CONTEST, US Naval Institute, 118 Maryland Ave., Annapolis MD 21402-5035. (410)268-6110. Fax: (410)269-7940. Contact: Valry Fetrow. Estab. 1873. Essay that advances professional, literary or scientific knowledge of the naval and maritime services. Deadline: December 1.

‡**JOHN BURROUGHS ASSOCIATION BRONZE MEDAL AWARD**, John Burroughs Association, 15 West 77th St., New York NY 10024. (212)769-5169. Secretary: Lesa Breslof. Offered annually for previously published quality fiction within 3 years of the award year. Burroughs Award Medal is awarded annually to the author of a book that contains outstanding nature writing. Deadline: October 1. Guidelines for SASE. Prize: Bronze Medal. Open to any writer.

CLIFFORD PRIZE, American Society for 18th Century Studies, Computer Center 108, Utah State University, Logan UT 84322-3730. Phone/fax: (801)797-4065. E-mail: uthomp@email.unc.edu. Website: http://www.usu.edu/~english/asecs.html. Executive Secretary: Dr. Jeffrey Smitten. Contact: James Thompson, Mary Sheriff (UNC-Chapel Hill). Offered annually for previously published work, "the best nominated article, an outstanding study of some aspect of 18th-century culture, interesting to any 18th-century specialist, regardless of discipline." Guidelines for SASE. Must submit 8 copies of the article. Prize: $500, certificate from ASECS. Judged by committee of distinguished members. Winners must be society members ($25-65 dues).

COAST GUARD ESSAY CONTEST, Naval Institute Essay and Photo Contests, 118 Maryland Ave., Annapolis MD 21402-5035. (410)268-6110. Fax: (410)269-7940. Contact: Valry Fatrow. Offered annually for original, analytical and/or interpretative, unpublished essays; maximum 3,000 words. Essays must discuss current issues and new directions for the Coast Guard. Deadline: June 1. Guidelines available. Prizes: $1,000, $750 and $500. Winning essays are published in December *Proceedings*. Open to anyone.

MORTON N. COHEN AWARD, Modern Language Association of America, 10 Astor Place, New York NY 10003-6981. (212)475-9500. Fax: (212)477-9863. Contact: Richard Brod. Estab. 1989. Awarded in odd-numbered years for a previously published distinguished edition of letters. At least 1 volume of the edition must have been published during the previous 2 years. Prize: $1,000. Guidelines for #10 SASE. Deadline: May 1.

‡**CARR P. COLLINS AWARD**, The Texas Institute of Letters, P.O. Box 298300, Fort Worth TX 76129. (817)921-7822. Fax: (817)921-7333. Secretary-Treasurer: Judy Alter. Offered annually for work published January 1-December 31 of previous year to recognize the best nonfiction book by a writer who was born in Texas or who has lived in the state for at least 2 consecutive years at some point or whose work has some notable connection with Texas. Deadline: January 2. Guidelines for SASE. Prize: $5,000.

‡**AVERY O. CRAVEN AWARD**, Organization of American Historians, 112 N. Bryan St., Bloomington IN 47408-4199. (812)855-9852. Fax: (812)855-0696. E-mail: awards@oah.indiana.edu. Website: http://www.indiana.edu/~oah. Contact: Award and Prize Committee Coordinator. Offered annually for the most original book on the coming of the Civil War, the Civil War years, or the Era of Reconstruction, with the exception of works of purely military history. Deadline: October 1. Guidelines for SASE. Prize: $500 and certificate.

‡**MERLE CURTI AWARD**, Organization of American Historians, 112 N. Bryan St., Bloomington IN 47408-4199. (812)855-9852. Fax: (812)855-0696. E-mail: awards@oah.indiana.edu. Website: http://www.indiana.edu/~oah. Contact: Award and Prize Committee Coordinator. Offered annually for books in the field

of American social history (even-numbered years) and intellectual history (odd-numbered years). Deadline: October 1. Guidelines for SASE. Prize: $1,000, certificate and medal.

DEXTER PRIZE, Society for the History of Technology, History Dept., Auburn University, 310 Hatch Hall, Auburn AL 36849. (334)844-6645. Fax: (334)844-6673. Contact: Society Secretary. Estab. 1968. For work published in the previous 3 years: for 1996—1993 to 1995. "Award given to the best book in the history of technology." Deadline: April 15. Guidelines for SASE. Prize: $2,000 and a plaque from the Dexter Chemical Company.

GORDON W. DILLON/RICHARD C. PETERSON MEMORIAL ESSAY PRIZE, American Orchid Society, Inc., 6000 S. Olive Ave., West Palm Beach FL 33405-9974. (407)585-8666. Fax: (407)585-0654. E-mail: 71726.1741@compuserve.com. Website: http:/www.pathfinder.com/vg/Gardens/AOS. Contact: Jane Mengel. Estab. 1985. "To honor the memory of two outstanding former editors of the *American Orchid Society Bulletin*. Annual themes of the essay competitions are announced by the Editor of the *A.O.S. Bulletin* in the May issue. Themes in past years have included Orchid Culture, Orchids in Nature and Orchids in Use. The contest is open to all individuals with the exception of A.O.S. employees and their immediate families."

‡EDUCATOR'S AWARD, The Delta Kappa Gamma Society, P.O. Box 1589, Austin TX 78767. (512)478-5748. Fax: (512)478-3961. Executive Coordinator: Dr. Theresa Fechek. Offered annually for quality fiction published January-December of previous year. This award recognizes educational research and writings of women authors whose book may influence the direction of thought and action necessary to meet the needs to today's complex society. Deadline: February 1. Guidelines for SASE. Prize: $2,000. The book must be written by one woman or by two women who are citizens of any country in which The Delta Kappa Gamma Society International is organized: Canada, Costa Rica, El Salvador, Finland, Germany Great Britain, Guatemala, Iceland, Mexico, The Netherlands, Norway, Puerto Rico, Sweden, United States.

‡EVERETT EDWARDS AWARD, Agricultural History Society, ERS, 1301 New York Ave. NW, Washington DC 20005. (202)219-0786. Fax: (202)219-0391. Contact: Douglas Hurt, Dept. of History, Iowa State University, Ames, Iowa 50011. Offered annually for best ms submitted by a graduate student. Deadline: December 31. Guidelines for SASE. Prize: $100. Judged by committees composed of member of the Society. Open to any writer. Nominations can be made by authors or publishers or anyone else.

‡WILFRED EGGLESTON AWARD FOR NONFICTION, Writers Guild of Alberta, 11759 Great Rd., Edmonton Alberta T5M 3K6 **Canada**. (403)422-8174. Fax: (403)422-2663. Director: Darlene Diver. Nonfiction book published in current year. Must be an Alberta author.

DAVID W. AND BEATRICE C. EVANS BIOGRAPHY AWARD, Mountain West Center for Regional Studies, Utah State University, University Hill, Logan UT 84322-0735. (801)750-3630. Fax: (801)797-3899. E-mail: frp@cc.usu.edu. Contact: F. Ross Peterson, Shannon R. Hoskins. Estab. 1983. Offered to encourage the writing of biography about people who have played a role in Mormon Country. (Not the religion, the country: Intermountain West with parts of Southwestern Canada and Northwestern Mexico.) Deadline: December 31, 1995. Prize: in excess of $5,000. Publishers or author may nominate book. Criteria for consideration: Work must be a biography or autobiography on "Mormon Country"; must be submitted for consideration for publication year's award; new editions or reprints are not eligible; mss are accepted. Submit 6 copies.

‡FOREIGN LANGUAGE BOOK AND FOREIGN LANGUAGE ARTICLE PRIZES, Organization of American Historians, 112 N. Bryan St., Bloomington IN 47408-4199. (812)855-9852. Fax: (812)855-0696. E-mail: awards@oah.indiana.edu. Website: http://www.indiana.edu/~oah. Contact: Award and Prize Committee Coordinator. Offered annually for the best book and the best article on American history that have been published in languages other than English. Eligible books or articles should be concerned with the past (recent or distant) or with issues of continuity and change. Entries should also be concerned with events or processes that began, developed, or ended in what is now the United States. Deadline: April 1. Guidelines for SASE. Prize: English translation and publication. Winning article will be printed in the *Journal of American History* and its author awarded a certificate and a $500 subvention for refining the article's English translation; winning book will be translated and published by Cambridge University Press, and its author will receive a certificate.

‡GEORGE FREEDLEY MEMORIAL AWARD, Theatre Library Association, Benjamin Rosenthal Library, Queens College, C.U.N.Y., 65-30 Kissena Blvd., Flushing NY 11367. (718)997-3799. Fax: (718)997-3753. Contact: Richard Wall, Book Awards Committee Chair. Estab. 1968. Book published in the United States within the previous calendar year on a subject related to live theatrical performance (including cabaret, circus, pantomime, puppetry, vaudeville, etc.). Eligible books may include biography, history, theory, criticism, reference or related fields. Prize: $250 and certificate to the winner; $100 and certificate for Honorable Mention. Submissions and deadline: Nominated books are requested from publishers; one copy should be received by each of three award jurors as well as the Chairperson by February 15 of the year following eligibility.

THE CHRISTIAN GAUSS AWARD, The Phi Beta Kappa Society, 1811 Q St. NW, Washington DC 20009-1696. (202)265-3808. Fax: (202)986-1601. Contact: Administrator, Phi Beta Kappa Book Awards. Estab. 1950. Works of literary criticism or scholarship published in the US during the 12-month period preceding the entry deadline, and submitted by the publisher. Books must have been published May 1, 1995-April 30, 1996. Deadline: April 30. Author must be a US citizen or resident.

‡LIONEL GELBER PRIZE, Lionel Gelber Foundation, 398 Adelaide St., W, Suite 1007, Toronto ON M5V 1S7 Canada. (416)504-7200. Fax: (416)504-5647. E-mail: applause@idirect.com. Manager: Marcia McClung. Offered annually for quality nonfiction published October 1-September 30, 1996. Designed to stimulate authors who write in clear language about international affairs and to encourage excellence in debate in this field, the Prize is awarded to the winning author writing in the field of foreign relations. Deadline: July 1. Guidelines for SASE; however, the publisher must submit the title on behalf of the author. Prize: $50,000 (Canadian).

LOUIS GOTTSCHALK PRIZE 1997, American Society for 18th Century Studies, Computer Center 108, Utah State University, Logan UT 84322-3730. Phone/fax: (801)797-4065. E-mail: uthomp@email.unc.edu. Website: http://www.usu.edu/~english/asecs.html. Executive Secretary: Jeffrey Smitten. Contact: James Thompson, Mary Sheriff (UNC-Chapel Hill). Offered annually for previously published (between Jan. 1995 and Dec. 1996) work. Purpose is to award outstanding historical or critical study on the 18th century. Deadline: November 15, 1996. Guidelines and form available for SASE. Publisher must send 5 copies for contest. Prize: $1,000 and certificate from ASECS. Judged by committee of distinguished members. Winners must be society members ($25-65 dues).

‡THE ILLINOIS-NWSA MANUSCRIPT AWARD, National Women's Studies Association, 7100 Baltimore Ave., #301, College Park MD 20715. (301)403-0525. Fax: (301)403-4137. Offered annually for unpublished quality fiction. Presented for the best book-length manuscript in women's studies. Deadline: January 31. Guidelines for SASE. Prize: $1,000 and publication by University of Illinois Press. Anthologies, essay collections, fiction, poetry and unrevised doctoral dissertations are ineligible.

‡THE KIRIYAMA PACIFIC RIM BOOK PRIZE, Kiriyama Pacific Rim Foundation and University of San Francisco Center for the Pacific Rim, University of San Francisco Center for the Pacific Rim, 2130 Fulton St., San Francisco CA 94117-1080. (415)666-5984. Fax: (415)666-5933. Contest Director: Dr. Barbara Bundy. Offered for work published November 1-October 31 of the previous year to promote books that will contribute to better understanding and increased cooperation throughout all areas of the Pacific Rim. Deadline: July 1. Prize: $30,000 to be divided equally between the publisher and author. Books must be submitted for entry by the publisher. Proper entry forms must be submitted including a publicity/promotion plan.

KATHERINE SINGER KOVACS PRIZE, Modern Language Association of America, 10 Astor Place, New York NY 10003-6981. (212)475-9500. Contact: Richard Brod. Estab. 1990. Offered annually for book in English on Latin American or Spanish literatures or cultures published in previous year. Authors need not be members of the MLA. Guidelines for #10 SASE. Prize: $1,000. Deadline: May 1.

‡RICHARD W. LEOPOLD PRIZE, Organization of American Historians, 112 N. Bryan St., Bloomington IN 47408-4199. (812)855-9852. Fax: (812)855-0696. E-mail: awards@oah.indiana.edu. Website: http://www. indiana.edu/~oah. Contact: Award and Prize Committee Coordinator. Offered every 2 years for the best book written by a historian connected with federal, state, or municipal government, in the areas of foreign policy, military affairs broadly construed, the historical activities of the federal government, or biography in one of the foregoing areas. The winner must have been employed in a government position for at least 5 years, and the publisher should include verification of this fact when a book is submitted. Deadline: September 1 of odd-numbered years. Prize: $1,500 and certificate.

‡LERNER-SCOTT PRIZE, Organization of American Historians, 112 N. Bryan St., Bloomington IN 47408-4199. (812)855-9852. Fax: (812)855-0696. E-mail: awards@oah.indiana.edu. Website: http://www.in diana.edu/~oah. Contact: Award and Prize Committee Coordinator. Offered annually for the best doctoral dissertation in US women's history. Each application must contain a letter of support from a faculty member at the degree-granting institution, along with an abstract, table of contents, and sample chapter from the dissertation. Finalists will be asked to submit a complete copy of the dissertation to each committee member at a later date. Deadline: November 1. Prize: $1,000 and certificate.

JAMES RUSSELL LOWELL PRIZE, Modern Language Association of America, 10 Astor Place, New York NY 10003-6981. (212)475-9500. Fax: (212)477-9863. Contact: Richard Brod. Offered annually for literary or linguistic study, or critical edition or biography published in previous year. Open to MLA members only. Guidelines for #10 SASE. Prize: $1,000. Deadline: March 1.

McLEMORE PRIZE, Mississippi Historical Society, P.O. Box 571, Jackson MS 39205-0571. (601)359-6850. Fax: (601)359-6975. Managing Editor: Christine Wilson. Estab. 1902. Scholarly book on a topic in Mississippi history/biography published in the year of competition (year previous to January 1 deadline). Deadline: January 1.

MARINE CORPS ESSAY CONTEST, Naval Institute Essay and Photo Contests, 118 Maryland Ave., Annapolis MD 21402-5035. (410)268-6110. Fax: (410)269-7940. Contact: Valry Fetrow. Offered annually for original, analytical and/or interpretative, unpublished essays; maximum 3,000 words. Essays must discuss current issues and new directions for the Marine Corps. Deadline: May 1. Guidelines available. Prizes: $1,000, $750 and $500. Winning essays published in November *Proceedings*. Open to anyone.

HOWARD R. MARRARO PRIZE and SCAGLIONE PRIZE FOR ITALIAN LITERARY STUD-IES, Modern Language Association of America, 10 Astor Place, New York NY 10003-6981. (212)475-9500. Fax: (212)477-9863. Contact: Richard Brod. Joint prize offered in even-numbered years for books or essays on any phase of Italian literature or comparative literature involving Italian, published in previous 2 years. Open to MLA members only. Guidelines for #10 SASE. Prize: $1,000. Deadline: May 1.

THE MAYFLOWER SOCIETY CUP COMPETITION, North Carolina Literary and Historical Association, 109 E. Jones St., Raleigh NC 27601-2807. (919)733-7305. Contact: Barbara Mann, awards coordinator. Previously published nonfiction by a North Carolina resident. Deadline: July 15.

MELCHER BOOK AWARD, Unitarian Universalist Association, 25 Beacon St., Boston MA 02108-2800. Fax: (617)367-3237. Staff Liaison: Patricia Frevert. Estab. 1964. Previously published book on religious liberalism. Deadline: December 31.

MID-LIST PRESS FIRST SERIES AWARD FOR CREATIVE NONFICTION, Mid-List Press, 4324 12th Ave. S., Minneapolis MN 55407-3218. Open to any writer who has never published a book of creative nonfiction. Submit either a collection of essays or a single book-length work; minimum length 50,000 words. Charges $15 fee. Submit entire ms beginning after March 31; must be postmarked by July 1. No ms returned without SASE. Manuscripts without SASE *must* include #10 SASE for notification. Will acknowledge receipt of ms only if self-addressed stamped postcard enclosed. Accepts simultaneous submissions. Guidelines and entry form for SASE. Awards include publication and an advance against royalties.

KENNETH W. MILDENBERGER PRIZE, Modern Language Association of America, 10 Astor Place, New York NY 10003-6981. (212)475-9500. Fax: (212)477-9863. Contact: Richard Brod. Offered annually for a research publication from the previous year in the field of teaching foreign languages and literatures. Guidelines for #10 SASE. Prize: $500 and a year's membership in the MLA. Deadline: May 1.

‡MLA PRIZE FOR A DISTINGUISHED SCHOLARLY EDITION, Modern Language Association of America, 10 Astor Place, New York NY 10003-6981. (212)614-6406. Director of Special Projects: Richard Brod. Offered in odd-numbered years for work published between 1995 and 1996. To qualify for the award, an edition should be based on an examination of all available relevant textual sources; the source texts and the edited text's deviations from them should be fully described; the edition should employ editorial principles appropriate to the materials edited, and those principles should be clearly articulated in the volume; the text should be accompanied by appropriate textual and other historical contextual information; the edition should exhibit the highest standards of accuracy in the presentation of its text and apparatus; and the text and apparatus should be presented as accessibly and elegantly as possible. Deadline: May 1, 1997. Guidelines for SASE. Prize: $1,000 and certificate. Editor need not be a member of the MLA.

MLA PRIZE FOR INDEPENDENT SCHOLARS, Modern Language Association of America, 10 Astor Place, New York NY 10003-6981. (212)475-9500. Fax: (212)477-9863. Contact: Richard Brod. Offered annually for book in the field of English or another modern language or literature published in previous year. Authors who hold tenure or tenure-track positions in higher education are not eligible. Guidelines and application form for SASE. Prize: $1,000 and a year's membership in the MLA. Deadline: May 1.

GEORGE JEAN NATHAN AWARD FOR DRAMATIC CRITICISM, Cornell University, Department of English, Goldwin Smith Hall, Ithaca NY 14853. (607)255-6801. Fax: (607)255-6661. E-mail: ww22@corn ell.edu. Contact: Chair, Dept. of English. Offered annually to the American "who has written the best piece of drama criticism during the theatrical year (July 1-June 30), whether it is an article, an essay, treatise or book." Guidelines for SASE. Prize: $5,000 and a silver medallion. Only published work may be submitted, and the author must be an American citizen.

NATIONAL JEWISH BOOK AWARD—AUTOBIOGRAPHY/MEMOIR, Sandra Brand and Arik Weintraub Award, Jewish Book Council, 15 E. 26th St., New York NY 10010. (212)532-4949. Director: Carolyn Starman Hessel. Offered annually to an author of an autobiography or a memoir of the life of a Jewish person.

NATIONAL JEWISH BOOK AWARD—CONTEMPORARY JEWISH LIFE, The Jewish Book Council, 15 E. 26th St., New York NY 10010. (212)532-4949. Contact: Carolyn Starman Hessel. Offered annually for a nonfiction work dealing with the sociology of modern Jewish life.

NATIONAL JEWISH BOOK AWARD—HOLOCAUST, Leon Jolson Award, Jewish Book Council, 15 E. 26th St., New York NY 10010. (212)532-4949. Contact: Carolyn Starman Hessel. Offered annually for a nonfiction book concerning the Holocaust. Deadline: September 1.

NATIONAL JEWISH BOOK AWARD—ISRAEL, Morris J. and Betty Kaplun Memorial Award, Jewish Book Council, 15 E. 26th St., New York NY 10010. (212)532-4949 ext. 297. President: Arthur Kurzweil. Executive Director: Carolyn Starman Hessel. Offered annually for a nonfiction work about Zionism and/or the State of Israel. Deadline: September.

NATIONAL JEWISH BOOK AWARD—JEWISH THOUGHT, Jewish Book Council, 15 E. 26th St., New York NY 10010. (212)532-4949. Director: Carolyn Starman Hessel. Offered annually for a book dealing with some aspect of Jewish thought, past or present. Deadline: September 1.

NATIONAL JEWISH BOOK AWARD—SCHOLARSHIP, Sarah H. and Julius Kushner Memorial Award, Jewish Book Council, 15 E. 26th St., New York NY 10010. (212)532-4949. Director: Carolyn Starman Hessel. Offered annually for a book which makes an original contribution to Jewish learning. Deadline: September 1.

NATIONAL JEWISH BOOK AWARD—VISUAL ARTS, Anonymous Award, Jewish Book Council, 15 E. 26th St., New York NY 10010. (212)532-4949. Director: Carolyn Starman Hessel. Offered annually for a book about Jewish art. Deadline: September 1.

‡NATIONAL WRITERS ASSOCIATION NONFICTION CONTEST, (formerly National Writers Association Articles and Essays Contest), The National Writers Association, Suite 424, 1450 S. Havana, Aurora CO 80012. (303)751-7844. Fax: (303)751-8593. Director: Sandy Whelchel. Annual contest "to encourage writers in this creative form and to recognize those who excel in nonfiction writing." Charges $18 fee. Deadline: December 31. Prizes: $200, $100, $50. Guidelines for #10 SASE.

THE FREDERIC W. NESS BOOK AWARD, Association of American Colleges and Universities, 1818 R St. NW, Washington DC 20009. (202)387-3760. Fax: (202)265-9532. Director for Membership: Peggy Neal. Offered annually for work previously published July 1-June 30 of the year in which it is being considered. "Each year the Frederic W. Ness Book Award Committee of the Association of American Colleges and Universities recognizes books which contribute to the understanding and improvement of liberal education." Deadline: August 15. Guidelines and entry forms for SASE. "Writers may nominate their own work; however, we send letters of invitation to publishers to nominate qualified books." Prize: Presentation at the association's annual meeting and $1,000. Transportation and one night hotel for meeting are also provided.

ALLAN NEVINS PRIZE, Society of American Historians, 2 Butler Library, Columbia University, New York NY 10027. Fax: (212)854-2883. Executive Secretary: Professor Mark Carnes. Offered for American history (nominated doctoral dissertations on arts, literature, science and American biographies). Deadline: January 15. Prize: $1,000, certificate and publication.

NEW JERSEY COUNCIL FOR THE HUMANITIES BOOK AWARD, New Jersey Council for the Humanities (NJCH), 28 W. State St., 6th Floor, New Brunswick NJ 08608. (609)695-4838. Fax: (609)695-4929. Coordinator: Erica Mosner. Offered annually for work previously published January 1-December 31 to honor a New Jersey author by virtue of birth, residence, or occupation, and to bring more exposure to humanities books that stimulate curiosity and enrich the general public's understanding of their world. Deadline: June 1. Guidelines for SASE. "Publisher only must nominate the book, but author can call us and we will send the information directly to their publisher." Prize: $1,000 for the author, and title distributed to up to 100 libraries throughout New Jersey. Judged by NJCH's Book Award Committee.

NORTH AMERICAN INDIAN PROSE AWARD, University of Nebraska Press, 327 Nebraska Hall, Lincoln NE 68588-0520. Fax: (402)472-0308. E-mail: gdunham@unlinfo.unl.edu. Contact: Award Director. Offered for the best new work by an American Indian writer. Prize: publication by the University of Nebraska Press with $1,000 advance. Guidelines for #10 SASE. Deadline: July 1.

‡NWSA GRADUATE SCHOLARSHIP IN LESBIAN STUDIES, National Women's Studies Association, 7100 Baltimore Ave., #301, College Park MD 20715. (301)403-0525. Fax: (301)403-4137. Offered annually for unpublished quality fiction awarded to a student who will be doing research for or writing a Master's thesis or Ph.D. dissertation in Lesbian Studies. Guidelines for SASE. Prize: $500.

ELI M. OBOLER MEMORIAL AWARD, American Library Association's Intellectual Freedom Round Table, 50 E. Huron St., Chicago IL 60611. (312)280-4224. Contact: Chairman. Offered every 2 years "to the author of an article (including a review), a series of thematically connected articles, a book, or a manual published on the local, state or national level, in English or in English translation. The works to be considered must have as their central concern one or more issues, events, questions or controversies in the area of intellectual freedom, including matters of ethical, political, or social concern related to intellectual freedom. The work for which the award is granted must have been published within the *two-year* period ending the December prior to the ALA Annual Conference at which it is granted." Deadline: December 1, 1997.

FRANK LAWRENCE AND HARRIET CHAPPELL OWSLEY AWARD, Southern Historical Association, Department of History, University of Georgia, Athens GA 30602-1602. (706)542-8848. Fax: (706)542-2455. Managing Editor: John B. Boles. Contact: Secretary-Treasurer. Estab. 1934. Offered in odd-numbered years for recognition of a distinguished book in Southern history published in even-numbered years. Publishers usually submit the books. Deadline: March 1.

‡LOUIS PELZER MEMORIAL AWARD, Organization of American Historians, 112 N. Bryan St., Bloomington IN 47408-4199. (812)855-9852. Fax: (812)855-0696. E-mail: awards@oah.indiana.edu. Website: http://www.indiana.edu/~oah. Contact: Award and Prize Committee Coordinator. Offered annually for the best essay in American history by a graduate student. The essay may be about any period or topic in the history of the United States, and the author must be enrolled in a graduate program at any level, in any field. Entries should not exceed 7,000 words and should be mailed to the office of the *Journal of American History*, 1125 E. Atwater, Indiana University, Bloomington, IN 47401. Deadline: November 30. Guidelines for SASE. Prize: $500, medal, certificate and publication in the *Journal of American History*.

PEN/JERARD FUND, PEN American Center, 568 Broadway, New York NY 10012. (212)334-1660. Fax: (212)334-2181. Contact: John Morrone. Estab. 1986. Biennial grant of $4,000 for American woman writer of nonfiction for a booklength work in progress in odd-numbered years. Guidelines for #10 SASE. Next award: 1997. Deadline: January 2.

PEN/MARTHA ALBRAND AWARD FOR FIRST NONFICTION, PEN American Center, 568 Broadway, New York NY 10012. (212)334-1660. Fax: (212)334-2181. E-mail: pen@echo.nyc.com. Coordinator: John Morrone. Offered annually for a first-published book of general nonfiction distinguished by qualities of literary and stylistic excellence. Eligible books must have been published in the calendar year under consideration. Authors must be American citizens or permanent residents. Although there are no restrictions on the subject matter of titles submitted, non-literary books will not be considered. Books should be of adult nonfiction for the general or academic reader. Deadline: December 15. Publishers, agents and authors themselves must submit *3* copies of each eligible title. Prize: $1,000, and a residence at the Johnson Studio Center, Johnson, Vermont.

PEN/SPIELVOGEL-DIAMONSTEIN AWARD, PEN American Center, 568 Broadway, New York NY 10012. (212)334-1660. Fax: (212)334-2181. E-mail: pen@echo.nyc.com. Coordinator: John Morrone. Offered for the best previously unpublished collection of essays on any subject by an American writer. "The $5,000 prize is awarded to preserve the dignity and esteem that the essay form imparts to literature." Authors must be American citizens or permanent residents. The essays included in books submitted may have been previously published in magazines, journals or anthologies, but must not have collectively appeared before in book form. Books will be judged on literary character and distinction of the writing. Publishers, agents, or the authors must submit 4 copies of each eligible title. Deadline: December 15.

‡PERGAMON-NWSA GRADUATE SCHOLARSHIP IN WOMEN'S STUDIES, National Women's Studies Association, 7100 Baltimore Ave., #301, College Park MD 20715. (301)403-0525. Fax: (301)403-4137. Offered annually for unpublished quality fiction to award a student who will be doing research for or writing a Master's thesis or Ph.D. dissertation in the interdisciplinary field of women's studies. Guidelines for SASE. Prize: 1st-$1,000, 2nd-$500. Special preference given to NWSA members and to those whose research projects on women examine color or class.

PHI BETA KAPPA BOOK AWARDS, The Phi Beta Kappa Society, 1811 Q St. NW, Washington DC 20009-1696. (202)265-3808. Fax: (202)986-1601. Contact: Book Awards Administrator. Estab. 1776. Offered annually to recognize and honor outstanding scholarly books published in the US May 1, 1995-April 30, 1996 in the fields of the humanities, the social sciences, and the natural sciences and mathematics. Deadline:

April 30. "Authors may request information, however books must be submitted by the publisher." Entries must be the works of authors who are US citizens or residents.

COLIN L. POWELL JOINT WARFIGHTING ESSAY CONTEST, Naval Institute Essay and Photo Contests, 118 Maryland Ave., Annapolis MD 21402-5035. (410)268-6110. Fax: (410)269-7940. Contact: Valry Faltrow. Offered annually for original, analytical and/or interpretative, unpublished essays; maximum 3,000 words. Essays must discuss combat readiness in a joint context (key issues involving two or more services). Essays may be heavy in uni-service detail, but must have joint application in terms of tactics, strategy, weaponry, combat training, force structure, doctrine, operations, organization for combat, or interoperability of hardware, software and procedures. Deadline: April 1. Guidelines available. Prizes: $2,500, $2,000 and $1,000. Winning essays published in July *Proceedings*. Open to military professionals and civilians.

‡**JAMES A. RAWLEY PRIZE**, Organization of American Historians, 112 N. Bryan St., Bloomington IN 47408-4199. (812)855-9852. Fax: (812)855-0696. E-mail: awards@oah.indiana.edu. Website: http://www.in diana.edu/~oah. Contact: Award and Prize Committee Coordinator. Offered annually for a book dealing with the history of race relations in the US. Deadline: October 1. Guidelines for SASE. Prize: $750, certificate.

‡**RESEARCH AND WRITING GRANTS FOR INDIVIDUALS**, John D. and Catherine T. MacArthur Foundation, 140 S. Dearborn St., Chicago IL 60603. Offered semi-annually to broaden and strengthen the community of writers and scholars engaged in policy-oriented work on international peace and security; to encourage the reconceptualization of security issues in light of the fluidity of international events, and to encourage attention to new developments that have not been adequately understood as peace and security issues; to foster integrated consideration of emerging relationships among economic, social, political, technological, and environmental aspects of global change. Deadline: February 1 and August 1. Write for guidelines. Prize: Grants range from $10,000-65,000 for individual applicants, with $100,000 the maximum for a two-person project. The program is open to individuals and two-person teams, including scholars, journalists, policy analysts, or others, of any nationality, who have a proven ability to do creative work. Younger persons and non-U.S. citizens are especially encouraged to apply.

‡**ELLIOTT RUDWICK PRIZE**, Organization of American Historians, 112 N. Bryan St., Bloomington IN 47408-4199. (812)855-9852. Fax: (812)855-0696. E-mail: awards@oah.indiana.edu. Website: http://www.in diana.edu/~oah. Contact: Award and Prize Committee Coordinator. Offered every two years for a book on the experience of racial and ethnic minorities in the United States. Books on interactions between two or more minority groups, or comparing the experience of two or more minority groups, would be especially welcome. Deadline: September 1 of even-numbered years. Guidelines for SASE. Prize: $2,000 and certificate. No book that has won the James A. Rawley Prize will be eligible for the Elliott Rudwick Prize.

‡**THE CORNELIUS RYAN AWARD**, The Overseas Press Club of America, 320 East 42 St., New York NY 10017. (212)983-4655. Fax: (212)983-4692. Manager: Sonya Fay. Offered annually for excellence in a nonfiction book on foreign affairs. Deadline: January 31. Guidelines for SASE. Generally publishers nominate the work, but writers may also submit in their own name. Charges $100 fee. Prize: certificate and $1,000. The work must be published and on the subject of foreign affairs.

‡**THEODORE SALOUTOS AWARD**, Agricultural History Society, ERS, 1301 New York Ave. NW, Washington DC 20005. (202)219-0786. Fax: (202)219-0391. Contact: R. Douglas Hurt, Dept. of History, Iowa State University, Ames, Iowa, 50011. Offered annually for best book published in American agricultural history during the calendar year. Deadline: December 31. Guidelines for SASE. Prize: $500. Judged by committees composed of members of the Society. Open to any writer. Nominations can be made by authors or publishers or anyone else.

THE BARBARA SAVAGE "MILES FROM NOWHERE" MEMORIAL AWARD, The Mountaineers Books, 1001 SW Klickitat Way, Suite 201, Seattle WA 98134. (206)223-6303. Award Director: Margaret Foster. Offered in even-numbered years for previously unpublished book-length nonfiction personal adventure narrative. Narrative must be based on an outdoor adventure involving hiking, mountain climbing, bicycling, paddle sports, skiing, snowshoeing, nature, conservation, ecology, or adventure travel not dependent upon motorized transport. Subjects *not* acceptable include hunting, fishing, or motorized or competitive sports. Guidelines for 9×12 SASE. Prize: $3,000 cash award, a $12,000 guaranteed advance against royalties

---

‡ **THE DOUBLE DAGGER** before a listing indicates that the listing is new in this edition. New markets are often more receptive to freelance submissions.

and publication by The Mountaineers. Next submission deadline is October 1, 1998.
- More regional and conservation-oriented titles are preferred.

ALDO AND JEANNE SCAGLIONE PRIZE FOR STUDIES IN GERMANIC LANGUAGES, Modern Language Association of America, 10 Astor Place, New York NY 10003-6981. (212)475-9500. Fax: (212)477-9863. Contact: Richard Brod. Offered in even-numbered years for outstanding scholarly work appearing in print in the previous two years and written by a member of the MLA, on the linguistics or literatures of the Germanic languages. Deadline: May 1. Guidelines for SASE. Prize: $1,000 and certificate presented at association's annual convention in December. Works of literary history, literary criticism, and literary theory are eligible. Books that are primarily translations are not.

ALDO AND JEANNE SCAGLIONE PRIZE FOR STUDIES IN SLAVIC LANGUAGES AND LITERATURES, Modern Language Association, 10 Astor Place, New York NY 10003-6981. (212)475-9500. Fax: (212)477-9863. Contact: Richard Brod. Offered biannually for books published in the previous 2 years. Books published in 1995 or 1996 are eligible for the 1997 award. Membership in the MLA is not required. Works of literary history, literary criticism, philology and literary theory are eligible for the 1997 award. Deadline: May 1, 1997. Guidelines for SASE. Prize: $1,000 and a certificate.

ALDO AND JEANNE SCAGLIONE PRIZE IN COMPARATIVE LITERARY STUDIES, Modern Language Association of America, 10 Astor Place, New York NY 10003-6981. (212)614-6406. Contact: Richard Brod. Offered annually for outstanding scholarly work published in the preceding year in the field of comparative literary studies involving at least 2 literatures. Deadline: May 1. Prize: $1,000 and certificate. Judged by committee of the MLA. Writer must be a member of the MLA. Works of scholarship, literary history, literary criticism and literary theory are eligible. Books that are primarily translations are not.

ALDO AND JEANNE SCAGLIONE PRIZE IN FRENCH AND FRANCOPHONE STUDIES, 10 Astor Place, New York NY 10003-6981. (212)614-6406. Contact: Richard Brod. Offered annually for work published in the preceding year that is an outstanding scholarly work in the field of French or francophone linguistic or literary studies. Prize: $1,000 and certificate. Judged by a committee of the MLA. Writer must be a member of the MLA. Works of scholarship, literary history, literary criticism and literary theory are eligible; books that are primarily translations are not. Deadline: May 1.

SCIENCE IN SOCIETY BOOK AWARDS, Canadian Science Writers' Association, P.O. Box 75, Station A, Toronto, Ontario M5W 1A2 Canada. (416)928-0624. Fax: (416)960-0528. E-mail: cswa@interlog.com. Website: http://www.interlog.com/~cswa. Director: Andy F. Visser-deVries. Offered annually for work published January 1-December 31 of previous year. Two awards: Children's Book Award and General Science Book Award, available for and to the general public with value in promoting greater understanding of science. Deadline: December 15. Guidelines for SASE. Prize: $1,000 and a plaque. Works entered become property of CSWA. Open to Canadian citizens or residents of Canada. Material published in Canada.

SERGEANT KIRKLAND'S PRIZE IN CONFEDERATE HISTORY, Sergeant Kirkland's Museum and Historical Society, Inc., 912 Lafayette Blvd., Fredericksburg VA 22401-5617. (540)899-5565. Fax: (540)899-7643. E-mail: civil-war@msn.com. Offered annually for the best research work focusing on an individual Confederate soldier or regimental unit. Text must have been in publication during the 12 months prior to the June 1 deadline. Studies should be in scholarly form and based, in part, on primary sources, with the usual documentation and bibliography. Must be at least 65,000 words. Prize: $500 and engraved plaque.

MINA P. SHAUGHNESSY PRIZE, Modern Language Association of America, 10 Astor Place, New York NY 10003-6981. (212)475-9500. Fax: (212)477-9863. Contact: Richard Brod. Offered annually for research publication (book or article) in the field of teaching English language, literature, rhetoric and composition published during preceding year. Guidelines for #10 SASE. Prize: $500 and a year's membership in the MLA. Deadline: May 1.

FRANCIS B. SIMKINS AWARD, Southern Historical Association, Department of History, University of Georgia, Athens GA 30602-1602. (706)542-8848. Fax: (706)542-2455. Managing Editor: John B. Boles. Contact: Secretary-Treasurer. Estab. 1934. Offered in odd-numbered years for recognition of the best first book by an author in the field of Southern history over a 2-year period. The award is sponsored jointly with Longwood College. Longwood College supplies the cash amount and the certificate to the author(s) for this award. The SHA furnishes a certificate to the publisher. Deadline: March 1.

‡**SIOBHAN FELLOWSHIP FOR NONFICTION ESSAY**, The Heekin Group Foundation, Nonfiction Division, P.O. Box 3385, Stamford CT 06905. (203)324-3430. Director: Anne Heekin-Canedy. Offered annually for unpublished quality fiction. "Our writing fellowships program is designed to support the community of new and emerging writers." Deadline: December 1. Guidelines for SASE. Charges $25 fee. Prize: $2,000. Judged by Reading panels—finalist judges are always publishers; past judges: Gray Wolf Press,

Soho Press, Dalkey Archive Press, The Echo Press, Riverhead Books, Browndeer Press, Hyperion Books for Children. 1996-97 publisher judges to be announced.

‡**THE JOHN BEN SNOW PRIZE**, Syracuse University Press, 1600 Jamesville Ave., Syracuse NY 13244. (315)443-5541. Fax: (315)443-5545. Contact: Director. Offered annually for unpublished submissions. The John Ben Snow Prize, inaugurated in 1978, is given annually by Syracuse University Press to the author of a nonfiction manuscript dealing with some aspect of New York State. The purpose of the award is to encourage the writing of books of genuine significance and literary distinction that will augment knowledge of New York State and appreciation for its unique physical, historical and cultural characteristics. A manuscript based on direct, personal experience will receive the same consideration as one relying on scholarly research. The criteria are authenticity, accuracy, readability and importance. Deadline: December 31. Prize: $1,500 to the author as advance against royalties and publication by Syracuse University Press. Guidelines for SASE.

C.L. SONNICHSEN BOOK AWARD, Texas Western Press of the University of Texas at El Paso, El Paso TX 79968-0633. (915)747-5688. Fax: (915)747-7515. Press Director: John Bristol. Contact: Marcia Daudistel, associate director. Estab. 1952. Offered for previously unpublished nonfiction ms dealing with the history, literature or cultures of the Southwest. Deadline: March 1.

BRYANT SPANN MEMORIAL PRIZE, History Department, Indiana State University, Terre Haute IN 47809. Estab. 1980. Social criticism in the tradition of Eugene V. Debs. Deadline: April 30. Guidelines for SASE. SASE also required with submissions. Prize: $1,000.

‡**AMAURY TALBOT PRIZE FUND FOR AFRICAN ANTHROPOLOGY**, Barclays Bank Trust Limited, Trust Management Office, 66 Group, Osborne Court, Gadbrook Park, Rudheath, Northwich Cheshire CW9 7UE England. Annual award for previously published nonfiction on anthropological research relating to Africa. Only works published in 1996 eligible. Preference given to those relating to Nigeria and then West Africa. Send 2 copies of book or article. Please quote reference #66/61/888. Entries will not be returned. Deadline: March 31. Guidelines for #10 SAE with 1 IRC.

‡**THE THEATRE LIBRARY ASSOCIATION AWARD**, Theatre Library Association, Benjamin Rosenthal Library, Queens College, C.U.N.Y., 65-30 Kissena Blvd., Flushing NY 11367. (718)997-3799. Fax: (718)997-3753. Contact: Richard Wall, book awards committee chair. Estab. 1973. Book published in the United States within the previous calendar year on a subject related to recorded or broadcast performance (including motion pictures, television and radio). Eligible books may include biography, history, theory, criticism, reference or related fields. Prize: $250 and certificate to the winner; $100 and certificate for Honorable Mention. Submissions and deadline: Nominated books are requested from publishers; one copy should be received by each of three award jurors as well as the Chairperson by February 15 of the year following eligibility.

‡**WESTERN HISTORY ASSOCIATION AWARDS**, Western History Association, Mesa Vista 1080, University of New Mexico, Albuquerque NM 87131-1181. (505)277-5234. Fax: (505)277-6023. Director: Patricia Campbell. Eleven awards in various aspects of the American West. Guidelines for SASE.

‡**JON WHYTE ESSAY COMPETITION**, Writers Guild of Alberta, 11759 Groat Rd., Edmonton, Alberta T5M 3K6 Canada. (403)422-8174. Fax: (403)422-2663. Director: Darlene Diver. Offered annually for unpublished work. Essay competition on announced theme. Theme is announced May 1. Winner announced October 15. 2,800 words. Deadline: September 1. Guidelines for SASE. Charges $10 fee Canadian. Prize: $2,000 plus publication in 2 newspapers and radio readings. Must be Alberta resident.

‡**GENERAL L. KEMPER WILLIAMS PRIZES**, The Historic New Orleans Collection and Louisiana Historical Association, 533 Royal St., New Orleans LA 70130-2179. Website: http://www.hnoc.org. Director: Dr. Jon Kukla. Offered annually for previously or unpublished best work on Louisiana history. Deadline: February 1. Prize: best published work-$1,000 and a plaque; best unpublished ms-$500 and a plaque. Judged by a panel of 3 judges appointed by the Louisiana Historical Association.

‡**WORD IS ART**, Austin Writers' League, 1501 West Fifth St., Suite E-2, Austin TX 78703. (512)499-8914. Fax: (512)499-0441. Director: Angela Smith. Offered annually for previously published work between January 1 and December 31 to recognize the six best submissions on the subject of writing published in the *Austin Writer*. Entries are all published articles and poetry which appear over a calendar year in the *Austin Writer*. Prize: 6 $100 prizes. Judged by non-AWL members who are representatives of the literary community. Open to any writer published in the *Austin Writer*.

FICTION

AIM MAGAZINE SHORT STORY CONTEST, P.O. Box 20554, Chicago IL 60620-0554. (312)874-6184. Managing Editor: Dr. Myron Apilado. Estab. 1974. Unpublished short stories (4,000 words maximum) "promoting brotherhood among people and cultures." Deadline: August 15.
   ● *Aim* is a nonprofit publication; its staff is volunteer.

ANVIL PRESS INTERNATIONAL 3-DAY NOVEL WRITING CONTEST, Anvil Press, 204-A 175 E. Broadway, Vancouver, British Columbia V5T 1W2 Canada. (604)876-8710. Fax: (604)879-2667. E-mail: subter@pinc.com. Website: http://www.bc.books.ca. Contact: Brian Kaufman. Estab. 1988. Offered annually for the best novel written in 3 days (Labor Day weekend). Entrants return finished novels to Anvil Press for judging. Registration deadline: Friday before Labor Day weekend. Send SASE (IRC if from the US) for details. Charges $25 fee.

‡BRAZOS BOOKSTORE (HOUSTON) SHORT STORY AWARD, The Texas Institute of Letters, P.O. Box 298300, Fort Worth TX 76129. (817)921-7822. Fax: (817)921-7333. Director: Judy Alter. Offered annually for previously published work between January 1 and December 31 of year before award is given to recognize the best short story submitted to the competition. The story submitted must have appeared in print for the first time to be eligible. Deadline: January 2. Guidelines for SASE. Prize: $500. To be eligible, the writer must have been born in Texas or must have lived in the state for at least two consecutive years or the subject matter of the work must be associated with the state.

‡GEORGES BUGNET AWARD FOR FICTION (NOVEL), Writers Guild of Alberta, 11759 Groat Rd., Edmonton Alberta T5M 3K6 Canada. (403)422-8179. Fax: (403)422-2663. Director: Darlene Diver. Offered annually for work previously published January 1-December 31 of the past year. Deadline: December 31. Guidelines for SASE. Prize: $500 and leatherbound copy of book. Must be an Alberta author.

‡DAVID DORNSTEIN MEMORIAL CREATIVE WRITING CONTEST FOR YOUNG ADULT WRITERS, The Coalition for the Advancement of Jewish Education, 261 W. 35th St., Floor 12A, New York NY 10001. (212)268-4210. Fax: (212)268-4214. E-mail: 5008447@mcimail.com. Website: http://shamash.nyserver.org/caje. Executive Director: Eliot Spack. Contest offered annually for unpublished short story based on a Jewish theme or topic. Deadline: December 31. Guidelines for SASE. Prize: $1,000 and publication in the *Jewish Education News*. Writer must prove age of 18-35 years old. Story must be based on Jewish theme, topic. Submit only 1 story each year.

THE WILLIAM FAULKNER CREATIVE WRITING COMPETITION, The Pirate's Alley Faulkner Society, 632 Pirate's Alley, New Orleans LA 70116-3254. (504)586-1609. Contest Director: Joseph J. DeSalvo, Jr. Contact: Rosemary James, editor. Offered annually for unpublished mss to encourage publisher interest in a promising writer's novel, novella, short story or short story by a Louisiana high school student. Deadline: April 15. Guidelines for SASE. Charges entry fee: novel $35, novella $30, short story $25, high school short story $10. Prize: novel-$7,500; novella-$2,500; short story-$1,500; personal essay, $1,000 (new category this year); high school-$1,000; and expenses for trip to New Orleans for Faulkner Celebration. Excerpts published in Society's Literary Quarterly, *The Double Dealer Redux*. The Society retains the right to publish excerpts of longer fiction; short stories in toto. Judges are well known authors. Open to all US residents.

FC2/ILLINOIS STATE UNIVERSITY, National Fiction Competition, PC2- Unit for Contemporary Literature, Illinois State University, Normal IL 61790-4242. (309)438-3582. Fax: (309)438-3523. Contact: Curtis White. Offered annually for unpublished book-length work of fiction chosen by a nationally distinguished judge. Deadline: November 15. Guidelines for SASE. Charges $15 fee. Prize: Publication and $500 advance. Open to any writer.

ROBERT L. FISH MEMORIAL AWARD, Mystery Writers of America, Inc., 17 E. 47th St., 6th Floor, New York NY 10017. (212)888-8171. Fax: (212)888-8107. Contact: Priscilla Ridgway. Offered annually for the best first mystery or suspense short story published during the previous year. Deadline: December 1.

‡H.E. FRANCIS SHORT STORY AWARD, University of Alabama in Huntsville & Ruth Hindman Foundation, 2007 Gallatin St., Huntsville AL 35801. (205)539-3320. Fax: (205)533-6893. E-mail: htp@aol.com. Director: Patricia Sammon. Offered annually for unpublished work. Deadline: December 31. Guidelines for SASE. Charges $15 reading fee. Prize: $1,000 and possible publication in *Hometown Press* magazine, an award-winning regional publication. Acquires first time publication rights.

GLIMMER TRAIN'S SHORT STORY AWARD FOR NEW WRITERS, Glimmer Train Press, Inc., 710 SW Madison St., Suite 504, Portland OR 97205. (503)221-0836. Fax: (503)221-0837. Contest Director:

Linda Davies. Offered 2 times/year for any writer whose fiction hasn't appeared in a nationally-distributed publication with a circulation over 5,000. "Send original, unpublished short (1,200-8,000 words) story with $11 reading fee (covers up to two stories sent together in same envelope) during the months of February/March and August/September. Title page must include name, address, phone, and 'Short-Story Award for New Writers' must be written on outside of envelope. No need for SASE as materials will not be returned. We cannot acknowledge receipt or provide status of any particular manuscript. Winners notified by July 1 (for February/March entrants) and January 1 (for August/September entrants). Winner receives $1,200 and publication in *Glimmer Train Stories*. First/second runners-up receive $500/$300, respectively, and honorable mention. All applicants receive a copy of the issue in which winning entry is published and runners-up announced."

THE JANET HEIDINGER KAFKA PRIZE, English Department, Susan B. Anthony Institute for Women's Studies, 538 Lattimore Hall, University of Rochester, Rochester NY 14627. Attention: Director SBA Center. Book-length fiction (novel, short story or experimental writing) by US woman citizen. Publishers must submit 4 copies. Deadline: February 28.

DRUE HEINZ LITERATURE PRIZE, University of Pittsburgh Press, 127 N. Bellefield Ave., Pittsburgh PA 15260. Series Editor: Ed Ochester. Estab. 1936. Collection of short fiction. Offered annually to writers who have published a book-length collection of fiction or a minimum of 3 short stories or novellas in commercial magazines or literary journals of national distribution. Does not return manuscripts. Guidelines for SASE (essential). Submit: July-August. Prize: $10,000.

HEMINGWAY DAYS FIRST NOVEL CONTEST, Hemingway Days Festival, P.O. Box 4045, Key West FL 33041. (305)294-4440. Contact: Hilary Hemingway. Offered annually for unpublished work to help an aspiring novelist get his or her book in print. Deadline: May 1. Guidelines for SASE. Charges $20 fee. Prize: $1,000 plus literary representation. Restricted to writers who have not had a novel published. Novel entries must be addressed to Hemingway Days First Novel Contest, 2323 Del Prado Blvd., Suite 13, Cape Coral, FL 33990.

ERNEST HEMINGWAY FOUNDATION PEN AWARD FOR FIRST FICTION, PEN American Center, 568 Broadway, New York NY 10012. E-mail: pen@echo.nyc. Contact: John Morrone. First-published novel or short story collection by an American author. Submit 3 copies. Deadline: December 15.

HEMINGWAY SHORT STORY COMPETITION, Hemingway Days Festival, P.O. Box 4045, Key West FL 33041-4045. (305)294-4440. Coordinator: Lorian Hemingway. Estab. 1981. Unpublished short stories. Deadline: June 1. Charges $10 fee. Guidelines for SASE. Prize: 1st-$1,000; 2nd and 3rd-$500 runner-up awards.

L. RON HUBBARD'S WRITERS OF THE FUTURE CONTEST, P.O. Box 1630C, Los Angeles CA 90078. (213)466-3310. Fax: (213)466-6474. Website: http://www.theta.com/asi. Contest Administrator: Leslie Potter. Unpublished science fiction, fantasy and horror. Guidelines for #10 SASE. Prize: $2,250 quarterly prizes; $4,000 annual Grand Prize, with 5-day workshop and publication in major anthology. Authors retain all rights.

INTERNATIONAL IMITATION HEMINGWAY COMPETITION, PEN Center West, 672 S. La Fayette Park Place, Suite 41, Los Angeles CA 90057. (213)365-8500. Fax: (213)365-9616. Contact: Rachel Hall. Offered annually for unpublished one-page (500 words) parody of Hemingway. Must mention Harry's Bar and must be funny. Deadline: March 1. Winner receives round trip transportation for 2 to Florence, Italy and dinner at Harry's Bar & American Grill in Florence.

‡**JAMES FELLOWSHIP FOR THE NOVEL IN PROGRESS**, The Heekin Group Foundation, P.O. Box 97759, Sisters OR 97759. Phone/fax: (541)548-4147. Director: Sarah Heekin Redfield. Offered annually for unpublished work. "Our writing fellowships program is designed to support the community of new and emerging writers." Deadline: December. Guidelines for SASE. Charges $25 fee. Prize: 2 for James Fellowship, $3,000. Judged by Reading panels—finalist judges are always publishers, past judges Gray Wolf Press, Soho Press, Dalkey Archive Press, The Ecco Press, Riverhead Books, Browndeer Press, Hyperion Books for Children. 1996-97 publisher judges to be announced.

‡**JAPANOPHILE ANNUAL SHORT STORY CONTEST**, *Japanophile*, Box 223, Okemos MI 48864. (517)669-2109. E-mail: japanlove@aol.com. Website: http://www.voyager.net/japanophile. Director: Earl Snodgrass. Offered annually for unpublished work to encourage good fiction-writing that contributes to understanding of Japan and Japanese culture. Deadline: December 31. Guidelines for SASE. Charges $5 fee. Prize: $100, a certificate, and usually publication. Judged by staff of *Japanophile*. Open to any writer.

‡**JESSE H. JONES AWARD**, The Texas Institute of Letters, P.O. Box 298300, Fort Worth TX 76129. (817)921-7822. Fax: (817)921-7333. Director: Judy Alter. Offered annually for work previously published

January 1-December 31 of year before award is given to recognize the writer of the best book of fiction entered in the competition. Deadline: January 2. Guidelines for SASE. Prize: $6,000. Judged by a panel selected by the TIL Council. To be eligible, a writer must have been born in Texas, or have lived in the state for at least two consecutive years at some time, or the subject matter of the work should be associated with the state.

LIBIDO SHORT FICTION CONTEST, *Libido*, 5318 N. Paulina St., Chicago IL 60640. Erotic short fiction, 1,000-4,000 words. Deadline: Entries must be postmarked by no later than September 1. Only entries with SASE will be returned. Entries must clearly say "contest" on the envelope. Charges $15 fee. Prizes: 1st-$1,000 and publication in *Libido*; 2nd-$200; 3rd through 5th-l-year subscriptions to *Libido*. Winners chosen by *Libido* editors. "Open to all sexual orientations, but winning stories will fit the general tone and style of *Libido*. Bonus points are awarded for accuracy of characterization, sense of style and humor, particularly the darker side."

LINES IN THE SAND SHORT FICTION CONTEST, LeSand Publications, 1252 Terra Nova Blvd., Pacifica CA 94044. (415)355-9069. Associate Editor: Barbara J. Less. Estab. 1992. Offered annually to encourage the writing of good, short fiction. Deadline: October 31. Guidelines for #10 SASE. Charges $5 fee. Prizes: 1st-$50; 2nd-$25; 3rd-$10; plus publication in January/February Awards edition.

LONG FICTION CONTEST, White Eagle Coffee Store Press, P.O. Box 383, Fox River Grove IL 60021. (708)639-9200. Offered annually since 1993 for unpublished work to recognize long short stories of 8,000-14,000 words (about 30-50 pages). Deadline: December 15. Guidelines for SASE. Charges $10 fee. A.E. Coppard Prize: $200 and publication plus 25 copies of chapbook. Open to any writer, no restrictions on materials.

MAGIC-REALISM-MAGAZINE SHORT-FICTION AWARD, Pyx Press, P.O. Box 922648, Sylmar CA 91392-2648. Award for works published in 1996. Entries must be original works of magic realism in English of less than 20,000 words. Only stories which first appeared in the 1996 calendar year can be considered. Reprint rights must be available. Submit tearsheets/photocopies or published material; nothing in ms format will be considered. Entries cannot be acknowledged or returned. Deadline: February 15, 1997. No entry fee. Winning entry will be announced in fall 1997 issue of *Magic Realism*. No limit on number of entries per author or publisher. Winning story will be published in chapbook form by Pyx Press. Winning author and publisher each receive $50. Any individual may nominate their own or another's published work.

‡**MALICE DOMESTIC AWARD**, Malice Domestic, % Pam Reed Bookstore, etc., 27 W. Washington St., Hagerstown MD 21740. (201)797-8896. Fax: (301)797-9453. Director: Pam Reed. Offered annually for unpublished work. MALICE will award two grants to unpublished writers in the Malice Domestic genre at MALICE VIII in April '96. The competition is designed to help the next generation of Malice authors get their first work published and to foster quality Malice literature. Deadline: December 15. Guidelines for SASE. Prize: $500. Judged by Malice Domestic Board of Directors or their designated representatives. Writers must not have published a book in any field. Members of the Malice Domestic Board of Directors and their families are ineligible to apply. MALICE encourages applications from minority candidates.

MID-LIST PRESS FIRST SERIES AWARD FOR SHORT FICTION, Mid-List Press, 4324 12th Ave. S., Minneapolis MN 55407-3218. Open to any writer who has never published a book-length collection of short fiction (short stories, novellas); minimum 50,000 words. Submit entire ms beginning *after* March 31, and must be postmarked by July 1. Accepts simultaneous submissions. Charges $15 fee. No ms returned without SASE. Mss submitted without return envelope *must* include #10 SASE for notification. Will acknowledge receipt of ms only if self-addressed stamped postcard enclosed. Guidelines and entry form for SASE. Awards include publication and an advance against royalties.

MID-LIST PRESS FIRST SERIES AWARD FOR THE NOVEL, Mid-List Press, 4324-12th Ave. S., Minneapolis MN 55407-3218. Offered annually for unpublished novels to locate and publish quality manuscripts by first-time writers, particularly those mid-list titles that major publishers may be rejecting. Deadline: February 1. Guidelines for SASE. *Applicants should write, not call, for guidelines.* Charges $15 fee. Prize: $1,000 advance against royalties, plus publication. Judged by ms readers and editors of Mid-List Press; editors and publishers make final decisions. Open to any writer who has never published a *novel*.

‡**MILKWEED NATIONAL FICTION PRIZE**, Milkweed Editions, 430 First Ave. N., Suite 400, Minneapolis MN 55401. (612)332-3192. Fax: (612)332-6248. Publisher: Emilie Buchwald. Estab. 1986. Annual award for unpublished works. "Milkweed is looking for a novel, novella, or a collection of short stories. Manuscripts should be of high literary quality and must be double-spaced and between 150-400 pages in length." *Must* request contest guidelines, send SASE. Prize: Publication by Milkweed Editions and a cash advance of $2,000 over and above any advances, royalties or other payment agreed upon in the contractual arrangement negotiated at the time of acceptance. Winner will be chosen from the manuscripts Milkweek

accepts for publication each year. All manuscripts submitted to Milkweed will automatically be considered for the prize. Submission directly to the contest is no longer necessary. "Manuscript must be written in English. Writers should have previously published a book of fiction or three short stories (or novellas) in magazines/journals with national distribution." Catalog available on request for $1.

NATIONAL JEWISH BOOK AWARD—JEWISH-CHRISTIAN RELATIONS, Chas. H. Reuson Foundation Award, Jewish Book Council, 15 E. 26th St., New York NY 10010. (212)532-4949, ext. 297. Fax: (212)481-4174. President Arthur Kurzweil. Executive Director: Carolyn Starman Hessel. Offered for Jewish fiction (novel or short story collection). Deadline: September 1.

‡NATIONAL WRITERS ASSOCIATION NOVEL WRITING CONTEST, The National Writers Association, Suite 424, 1450 S. Havana, Aurora CO 80012. (303)751-7844. Fax:(303)751-8593. Director: Sandy Whelchel. Annual contest "to help develop creative skills, to recognize and reward outstanding ability and to increase the opportunity for the marketing and subsequent publication of novel manuscripts." Deadline: April 1. Guidelines for #10 SASE. Charges $35 fee. Prizes: 1st-$500; 2nd-$300; 3rd-$200.

‡NATIONAL WRITERS ASSOCIATION SHORT STORY CONTEST, The National Writers Association, Suite 424, 1450 S. Havana, Aurora CO 80012. (303)751-7844. Fax:(303)751-8593. Director: Sandy Whelchel. Annual contest "to encourage writers in this creative form and to recognize those who excel in fiction writing." Deadline: July 1. Guidelines for #10 SASE. Charges $15 fee. Prizes: $200, $100, $50, copy of *Writer's Market*.

‡NEGATIVE CAPABILITY SHORT FICTION CONTEST, *Negative Capability*, 62 Ridgelawn Dr. E, Mobile AL 36608-6116. (205)460-6146. Fax: (334)344-8478. Contact: Sue Walker. Estab. 1981. "To recognize and support fiction writers" of previously unpublished short fiction. Deadline January 15 each year. Guidelines for #10 SASE. Reading fee $10 per story. Prize: $1,000 plus publication.

NEW RIVERS PRESS/AMERICAN FICTION CONTEST, English Department, P.O. Box 229, Moorhead State University, Moorhead MN 56563-2996. Fax: (218)236-2168. E-mail: davisa@mhdl.moorhead.ms us.edu. Contest Director: Alan Davis. Estab. 1987. Offered annually to promote established and emerging writers. Submissions cannot be previously published. Prize: $1,000, $500, $250. (20 finalists published.) All finalists also receive a free copy of publication. Submit January 1-May 1. Guidelines for #10 SASE. Charges $7.50/story fee. Multiple and simultaneous submissions acceptable. Buys first North American serial rights to winning stories.

‡CHARLES H. AND N. MILDRED NILON EXCELLENCE IN MINORITY FICTION AWARD, University of Colorado at Boulder and Fiction Collective Two, University of Colorado, Campus Box 494, Boulder CO 80309-0494. Contact: Leslee T. Alexander. Estab. 1989. Unpublished book-length fiction, 150 pages minimum. Only mss from protected racial and ethnic minority authors will be considered.

THE FLANNERY O'CONNOR AWARD FOR SHORT FICTION, The University of Georgia Press, 330 Research Dr., Athens GA 30602-4901. (706)369-6140. Fax: (706)369-6131. Series Editor: Charles East. Editorial Assistant: Jane Kobres. Estab. 1981. Submission period: June-July 31. Charges $10 fee. Does not return mss. Manuscripts must be 200-275 pages long. Authors do not have to be previously published. Guidelines for SASE. Prize: $1,000 and publication by Press under standard book contract.

‡HOWARD O'HAGER AWARD FOR SHORT FICTION, Writers Guild of Alberta, 11759 Groat Rd., Edmonton Alberta T5M 3K6 Canada. (403)422-8174. Fax: (403)422-2663. Director: Darlene Diver. Short fiction book published in current year. Must be an Alberta author.

CHRIS O'MALLEY PRIZE IN FICTION, *The Madison Review*, Dept. of English, 600 N. Park St., Madison WI 53706. (608)263-3374. Director: Ronald Kuka. Offered annually for previously unpublished work. Awarded to the best piece of fiction. Deadline: September 30. Prize: $500, plus publication in the spring issue of *The Madison Review*. All contest entries are considered as submissions to *The Madison Review*, the literary journal sponsoring the contest. No simultaneous submissions to other publications. Charges $3 fee.

‡PEN/FAULKNER AWARDS FOR FICTION, PEN/Faulkner Foundation, 201 East Capitol St., Washington DC 20003. (202)675-0345. Fax: (202)608-1719. Executive Director: Janice F. Delaney. Offered annually for published work in a calendar year for best book-length work of fiction by American citizen. Deadline: December 31. Prize: $15,000—one winner, 5,000—4 nominees. Judged by 3 writers of fiction (published); different each year.

PENNY DREADFUL SHORT STORY CONTEST, sub-TERRAIN Magazine, P.O. Box 1575, Bentall Centre, Vancouver, British Columbia V6C 2P7 Canada. (604)876-8710. Fax: (604)879-2667. Offered annually to foster new and upcoming writers. Deadline May 15. Guidelines for SASE. Charges $15 fee for first story, $5 for additional entries. Prize: $250 (Canadian), publication in summer issue and 4-issue subscription to sub-TERRAIN.

‡PLAYBOY COLLEGE FICTION CONTEST, *Playboy*, 680 N. Lake Shore Dr., Chicago IL 60611. (312)751-8000. Fiction Editor: Alice Turner. Annual award for unpublished short stories by registered students at a college or university. Deadline: January 1. Information in October issue or send SASE.

EDGAR ALLAN POE AWARD, Mystery Writers of America, Inc., 17 E. 47th St., New York NY 10017. (212)888-8171. Contact: Priscilla Ridgway. Entries must be copyrighted or produced/published in the year they are submitted. Deadline: December 1. Entries for the book categories are usually submitted by the publisher but may be submitted by the author or his agent.

PRISM INTERNATIONAL FICTION CONTEST, *Prism International*, University of British Columbia, Buch E462, 1866 Main Mall, Vancouver, British Columbia V6T 1Z1 Canada. (604)822-2514. Fax: (604)822-3616. E-mail: prism@unixg.ubc.ca. Website: http://www.arts.ubc.ca/crwr/prism/prism.html. Offered annually for previously unpublished fiction. Deadline: December 1. Maximum length: 25 pages. Story's title should appear on every page. Author's name and address must appear *only* on a separate cover page. Entry fee: $20 for one story, plus $5 for each additional story. Canadians pay in Canadian funds. Entry fee includes one year subscription. Works of translations are eligible. For complete guidelines, send #10 SASE with Canadian postage or #10 SAE with 1 IRC. Prizes: 1st-$2,000; 5 honorable mentions of $200 each, plus publication payment.

‡PROMETHEUS AWARD/HALL OF FAME, Libertarian Futurist Society, 89 Gebhardt Rd., Penfield NY 14526. (716)288-6137. Contact: Victoria Varga. Estab. 1979. Prometheus Award: pro-freedom, anti-authoritarian novel published during previous year. Hall of Fame: one classic libertarian novel at least 5 years old. Deadline: March 1.

QUARTERLY WEST NOVELLA COMPETITION, *Quarterly West*, 317 Olpin Union, University of Utah, Salt Lake City UT 84112. (801)581-3938. Estab. 1976. Offered biannually for 2 unpublished novellas. Charges $20 fee. Guidelines for SASE. Deadline: December 31 of even-numbered years. Prize: 2 winning writers receive $500 and publication in *Quarterly West*.

SIR WALTER RALEIGH AWARD, North Carolina Literary and Historical Association, 109 E. Jones St., Raleigh NC 27601-2807. (919)733-7305. Awards Coordinator: Barbara Mann. Previously published fiction by a North Carolina resident. Deadline: July 15.

HAROLD U. RIBALOW AWARD, Hadassah WZOA, 50 W. 58th St., New York NY 10019. Fax: (212)446-9521. Editor: Alan Tigay. Offered annually for an English-language book of fiction on a Jewish theme published January 1-December 31 in a calendar year. Deadline: April. Prize: $1,000. Books should be submitted by the publisher.

‡RIVER CITY WRITING AWARDS IN FICTION, The University of Memphis/Hohenberg Foundation, Dept. of English, Memphis TN 38152. (901)678-4591. Director: Paul Naylor. Offered annually for unpublished short stories. Deadline: December 7. Guidelines for SASE. Charges $12, which is put toward a one year subscription for *River City*. Prize: First place $2,000; second $500; third $300. 15 finalists are chosen by The University of Memphis Creative Writing faculty. Prize winners are chosen by a nationally-known author. Open to any writer.

SFWA NEBULA® AWARDS, Science-fiction and Fantasy Writers of America, Inc., 5 Winding Brook Dr., #1B, Guilderland NY 12084-9719. Estab. 1966. Science fiction or fantasy in the categories of novel, novella, novelette and short story recommended by members. Final ballot and awards decided by ballot of the active members for works professionally published during the previous calendar year.

JOHN SIMMONS SHORT FICTION AWARD and IOWA SHORT FICTION AWARDS, Department of English, University of Iowa. English-Philosophy Building, Iowa City IA 52242-1408. Offered annually for previously unpublished fiction. Prize: publication. Guidelines for #10 SASE. Deadline: August 1-September 30.

THE SOUTHERN REVIEW/LOUISIANA STATE UNIVERSITY SHORT FICTION AWARD, Louisiana State University, 43 Allen Hall, Baton Rouge LA 70803. (504)388-5108. Selection Committee Chairman: Dave Smith. First collection of short stories by an American published in the US during previous year. Deadline: January 31. A publisher or an author may submit an entry by mailing 2 copies of the collection.

THE STAND MAGAZINE SHORT STORY COMPETITION, *Stand Magazine*, 179 Wingrove Rd., Newcastle on Tyne, NE4 9DA United Kingdom. (0191)-2733280. Contact: Editors of *Stand Magazine*. "This biennial competition is an open international contest for unpublished writing in the English language intended to foster a wider interest in the short story as a literary form and to promote and encourage excellent writing in it." Deadline: June 30, 1997. "Please note that intending entrants enquiring from outside the UK should send International Reply Coupons, not stamps from their own countries. In lieu of an entry fee we ask for a minimum donation of £4 or $8 US per story entered." Editorial inquiries should be made with SASE to: Daniel Schenker and Amanda Kay, 122 Morris Road, Lacey's Spring AL 35754.

‡**STORY'S SHORT STORY COMPETITION**, Story, 1507 Dana Ave., Cincinnati OH 45207. (513)531-2222. Fax: (513)531-1843. Contest Director: Lois Rosenthal. Offered annually for unpublished work. Deadline: October 31. Guidelines for SASE. Charges $10 fee. Prize: 1st-$1,000; 2nd-$500; 3rd-$250. On occasion, awards merchandise prizes from additional sponsors. Entries must not be under consideration at other publications. Writers are free to market them elsewhere after winners are announced. *Story* reserves the right to publish selected winners. Buys first North American rights.

‡**TARA FELLOWSHIP FOR SHORT FICTION**, The Heekin Group Foundation, P.O. Box 1534, Sisters OR 97759. Phone/fax: (541)548-4147. Director: Sarah Heekin Redfield. Offered annually for unpublished work. "Our writing fellowships program is designed to support the community of new and emerging writers." Deadline: December 1. Guidelines for SASE. Charges $25 fee. Prize: 2 for Tara Fellowship, $1,500. Reading panels—finalists judges are always publishers. Past judges: Gray Wolf Press, Soho Press, Dalkey Archive Press, The Ecco Press, Riverhead Books, Browndeer Press, Hyperion Books for Children. 1996-97 publisher judges to be announced.

‡**STEVEN TURNER AWARD**, The Texas Institute of Letters, P.O. Box 298300, Fort Worth TX 76129. (817)921-7822. Fax: (817)921-7333. Director: Judy Alter. Offered annually for previously published work between January 1 and December 31 of year before the award is given to recognize the writer of the best first book of fiction submitted. Deadline: January 2. Guidelines for SASE. Prize: $1,000. To be eligible, a writer must have been born in Texas, or have lived in the state for at least two consecutive years at some time, or the subject matter of the work should be associated with the state.

THE VIRTUAL PRESS ANNUAL WRITER'S CONTEST, The Virtual Press, 408 Division St., Shawano WI 54166. E-mail: publisher@tvp.com. Website: http://tvp.com/. Publisher: William Stanek. Offered annually for unpublished work to promote the writing of quality short fiction, fantasy, mystery and science fiction. Deadline: November 1. Guidelines for SASE. Charges $10 fee. Prize: 12 cash awards (4 per category): 1st-$75, 2nd-$50, 3rd-$25, 4th-$10, plus publication in annual anthology.

EDWARD LEWIS WALLANT BOOK AWARD, Mrs. Irving Waltman, 3 Brighton Rd., West Hartford CT 06117. Estab. 1963. Offered for fiction with significance for the American Jew (novel or short stories) by an American writer (one who was born or educated in the United States) published during current year. Deadline: December 31.

WASHINGTON PRIZE FOR FICTION, Larry Kaltman Literary Agency, 1301 S. Scott St., # 424, Arlington VA 22204. (703)920-3771. Estab. 1989. Offered for previously unpublished fiction of at least 65,000 words. The Washington Prize For Fiction rewards writing that is imaginative, precise and economical. It does not look kindly upon the trite, the hackneyed and the cliched. Deadline: November 30. Charges $30 fee. Prizes: 1st-$5,000; 2nd-$2,500; 3rd-$1,000; and literary agency representation if desired.

WELLSPRING'S SHORT FICTION CONTEST, P.O. Box 29527, Brooklyn Center MN 55429. (612)926-3060. Contest Director: Meg Miller. Estab. 1988. Offered 2 times/year for previously unpublished short fiction to encourage the writing of well-crafted and plotted, meaningful short fiction. Deadlines: January 1, July 1. Guidelines for #10 SASE. Charges $10 fee. Prize: 1st-$100; 2nd-$75; 3rd-$25.

WINNERS' CIRCLE SHORT STORY CONTEST, Canadian Authors Association, Metropolitan Toronto Branch, 33 Springbank Ave., Scarborough, Ontario M1N 1G2 Canada. (416)698-8687. Fax: (416)698-8687. Contact: Bill Belfontaine. Contest to encourage writing of new short stories (1,500-3,500 words) which help Canadian authors to get published. Opens July 1 annually, closes November 30. Guidelines, entry form and free 24-page booklet, "How Best to Write for a Short Story Contest," for 90¢ SASE (SAE/IRC). No mss returned, but winner's list available for separate SASE (SAE/IRC). Winners announced to local and national media soon after judging, usually March of following year. Prizes: 5 cash winners (1st, $500; 4 others, $125 each). 10 or more Honorary Mentions. Winners and honorary mentions published in *Winners' Circle Anthology* and also receive official contest certificate. Entry fee $15/story, multiple submissions encouraged. All winners receive free copy of professionally published *1996 Winners' Circle Anthology*.

THOMAS WOLFE FICTION PRIZE, North Carolina Writers' Network, P.O. Box 954, Carrboro NC 27510. Fax: (919)929-0535. Offered annually for unpublished work "to recognize a notable work of fiction—

either short story or novel excerpt—while honoring one of North Carolina's best writers—Thomas Wolfe." Deadline: August 31. Guidelines for SASE. Charges $5 fee. Prize: $500 and potential publication. Past judges have included Anne Tyler, Barbara Kingsolver and C. Michael Curtis.

‡**WORLD'S BEST SHORT SHORT STORY CONTEST**, English Department, Writing Program, Florida State University, Tallahassee FL 32306. (904)644-4230. Contact: Creative Writing Program Director. Estab. 1986. Annual award for unpublished short short story (no more than 250 words). Entry fee: $1 per story. Send #10 SASE for rules. Deadline: Feb. 15. Prize $100.

WRITERS' JOURNAL, (formerly Minnesota Ink Fiction Contest), Val-Tech Publishing, P.O. Box 25376, St. Paul MN 55125. (612)730-4280. Contact: Valerie Hockert. Offered annually for previously unpublished fiction. Deadline: December 31. Charges $5 fee.

WRITERS' JOURNAL ANNUAL SHORT STORY CONTEST, Val-Tech Publishing, Inc., P.O. Box 25376, St. Paul MN 55125. (612)730-4280. Contact: Valerie Hockert. Estab. 1987. Previously unpublished short stories. Deadline: May 31. Charges $5 fee.

POETRY

‡**ANAMNESIS CHAPBOOK COMPETITION**, Anamnesis Press, P.O. Box 581153, Salt Lake City UT 84158-1153. Phone/fax: (801)583-3118. E-mail: kdaniels@ix.netcom.com. Website: http://www.iquest.net/ap/. Director: Keith Allen Daniels. Submissions accepted between January 1 and June 15. "We wish to see poems of intellectual and emotional depth that give full rein to the imagination, whether free verse or formalist." Charges $10 fee. Prize: 1st-$500 and chapbook publication plus 10 free copies of chapbook; 2nd-$200 and chapbook publication plus 10 free copies of chapbook. All contestants receive a copy of the winning chapbook. Poems are read by Keith Allen Daniels and Toni Montealegre and the winners are chosen unanimously. "Please don't send us trite, sappy, maudlin or 'inspirational' poems."

ANHINGA PRIZE FOR POETRY, Anhinga Press, P.O. Box 10595, Tallahassee FL 32302. (904)575-5592. Fax: (904)442-6323. Contact: Rick Campbell. Offered annually for a book-length collection of poetry by an author who has not published more than one book of poetry. "We use a well-known independent judge." Submit January 1-March 15. Guidelines for #10 SASE. Charges $20 fee. Prize: $2,000 and publication. Open to any writer writing in English.

ANNUAL INTERNATIONAL NARRATIVE POETRY CONTEST, Poets and Patrons, Inc., 2820 W. Birchwood, Chicago IL 60645. Contact: Robert Mills for guidelines. Unpublished poetry. Deadline: September 1. Prizes: 1st-$75; 2nd-$25.

‡**ANNUAL INTERNATIONAL POETRY CONTEST**, Poet's Study Club of Terre Haute, Indiana, 826 S. Center St., Terre Haute IN 47807. (812)234-0819. Contact: President of Poet's Study Club. Offered annually in 3 categories: Serious Poems, Light Verse, Haiku. Deadline: February 1. Guidelines for SASE. Prizes: 1st-$25 and 2nd-$15 in each category. Judged by competent writers who also often judge for our State Poetry Societies, etc. Open to any writer.

ANNUAL POETRY CONTEST, National Federation of State Poetry Societies, 1206 13th Ave., SE, St. Cloud MN 56304. Chairperson: Claire van Breemen Downes. Estab. 1959. Previously unpublished poetry. "Fifty categories. Flier lists them all." Deadline: March 15. Guidelines for #10 SASE. Charges fees. See guidelines for fees and prizes. All awards are announced in June and published the following June.

ARKANSAS POETRY AWARD, The University of Arkansas Press, 201 Ozark Ave., Fayetteville AR 72701. (501)575-3246. Fax: (501)575-6044. Award Director: Carolyn Brt. Estab. 1990. Offered for previously unpublished full-length poetry ms to recognize living US poets whose works have not been previously published or accepted for publication in book form and thus forward the Press's stated mission of "disseminating the fruits of creative activity." Deadline May 1. Charges $15 fee. Guidelines for #10 SASE. Award: publication of the collection by the University of Arkansas Press.

GEORGE BOGIN MEMORIAL AWARD, Poetry Society of America, 15 Gramercy Park S., New York NY 10003. (212) 254-9628. Contact: Award Director. Offered for a selection of 4-5 poems that reflects the encounter of the ordinary and the extraordinary, uses language in an original way, and takes a stand against oppression in any of its forms. Guidelines for #10 SASE. Guidelines subject to change. Deadline: December 22. Charges $5 fee for nonmembers. Prize: $500.

‡**BARBARA BRADLEY AWARD**, New England Poetry Club, 11 Puritan Rd., Arlington MA 02174. Contest Director: Virginia Thayer. Offered annually for a lyric poem under 21 lines, written by a woman.

Deadline: April 24. Guidelines for SASE. Charges $3 entry fee for nonmembers. Prize: $200.

BRITTINGHAM PRIZE IN POETRY, University of Wisconsin Press, 114 N. Murray St., Madison WI 53715. Contest Director: Ronald Wallace. Estab. 1985. Unpublished book-length mss of original poetry. Submissions must be *received* by the press *during* the month of September, accompanied by a SASE for contest results. Prizes: $1,000 and publication of the 2 winning mss. Guidelines for #10 SASE. Manuscripts will *not* be returned. Charges $15 fee, payable to University of Wisconsin Press. Results in February.

GERALD CABLE POETRY COMPETITION, Silverfish Review Press, P.O. Box 3541, Eugene OR 97403-0541. (503)344-5060. Series Editor: Rodger Moody. To publish a poetry book by a deserving author who has yet to publish a full-length book. Submit September. Guidelines for SASE. Charges $15 reading fee. Prize: $1,000.

‡**CHIRON REVIEW POETRY CONTEST**, Chiron Review, 522 E. South Ave., St. John KS 67576-2212. (316)549-3933. Director: Jane Hathaway. Offered annually for previously published or unpublished work. Deadline: June 20. Guidelines for SASE. Charges $4 per poet (up to 6 poems). Prize: 1st: $100 & full-page feature in *CR*; 2nd: $50 & full-page feature in *CR*. 5 third prizes: 1 year subscription; publication of winning poem in *CR*. Judged by Michael Hathaway, ed. Open to any writer.

CLEVELAND STATE UNIVERSITY POETRY CENTER PRIZE, Cleveland State University Poetry Center, Cleveland OH 44115. (216)687-3986. Fax: (216)687-6943. Contact: Editor. Estab. 1962. Offered to identify, reward and publish the best unpublished book-length poetry ms submitted. Submissions accepted only December-February. Deadline: Postmarked on or before March 1. Charges $15 fee. "Submission implies willingness to sign contract for publication if manuscript wins." $1,000 prize for best ms. One or more of the other finalist mss may be published for standard royalty (no prize). Guidelines for SASE. Manuscripts are not returned.

CONTEMPORARY POETRY SERIES, University of Georgia Press, 330 Research Dr., Athens GA 30602. (706)369-6140. Coordinator: Jane Kobres. Offered 2 times/year. Two awards: for poets who have not had a full-length book of poems published (deadline in September), and poets with at least one full-length publication (deadline in January). Guidelines for SASE. Charges $10 fee.

BILLEE MURRAY DENNY POETRY AWARD, Lincoln College, 300 Keokuk St., Lincoln IL 62656. Contest Administrator: Janet Overton. Estab. 1981. Unpublished poetry. Deadline: May 31. Prizes: $1,000, $500, $250. Charges $10/poem fee (limit 3). Entry form for SASE.

ALICE FAY DI CASTAGNOLA AWARD, Poetry Society of America, 15 Gramercy Park S., New York NY 10003. (212)254-9628. Contact: Award Director. Manuscript in progress: poetry, prose or verse-drama. Guidelines for #10 SASE. Guidelines subject to change. Deadline: December 22. Prize: $1,000. Members only.

"DISCOVERY"/THE NATION, The Joan Leiman Jacobson Poetry Prizes, The Unterberg Poetry Center of the 92nd Street YM-YWHA, 1395 Lexington Ave., New York NY 10128. Estab. 1973. Open to poets who have not published a book of poems (chapbooks, self-published books included). Deadline: early February. Write for complete competition guidelines, or call (212)415-5759 There will be an entry fee.

MILTON DORFMAN POETRY PRIZE, Rome Art & Community Center, 308 W. Bloomfield St., Rome NY 13440. (315)336-1040. Fax: (315)336-1090. Contact: Leo G. Crandall. Estab. 1990. "The purpose of the Milton Dorfman Poetry Prize is to offer poets an outlet for their craft. All submissions must be previously unpublished." Entries accepted: July 1-November 1, postmarked. Guidelines for #10 SASE. Charges $3 fee per poem entered. Prize: 1st-$500; 2nd-$200; 3rd-$100. Open to any writer.

THE EIGHTH MOUNTAIN POETRY PRIZE, The Eighth Mountain Press, 624 SE 29th Ave., Portland OR 97214-3026. (503)233-3936. Fax: (503)233-0774. E-mail: eightmt@aol.com. Contact: Ruth Gundle. Estab. 1987. "Biennial prize for a book-length manuscript by a woman writer. Poems may be considered if submission is termed 'collected' or 'selected'. Award is judged by a nationally recognized woman poet." Buys all rights. Entries must be postmarked in January of even-numbered years. Guidelines for #10 SASE. Charges $15 fee. Prize: $1,000 advance against royalties and publication in the prize series. Next reading period: January 1998.

‡**"EVE OF ST. AGNES" ANNUAL POETRY COMPETITION**, Negative Capability, 62 Ridgelawn Dr. E, Mobile AL 36608. (334)343-6163. Fax: (334)344-8478. Contact: Sue Walker. Offered annually for unpublished works to honor authors of quality poetry. Deadline Jan. 15. Guidelines for SASE. Charges $3 per poem. Prize: $1,000 plus publication. Judged by well-known poets.

NORMA FARBER FIRST BOOK AWARD, Poetry Society of America, 15 Gramercy Park S., New York NY 10003. (212)254-9628. Contact: Award Director. First book of original poetry submitted by the publisher. Deadline: December 22. Charges $10/book fee. Guidelines for #10 SASE. Guidelines subject to change. Prize: $500.

THE 49th PARALLEL POETRY AWARD, The Signpost Press Inc., M.S. 9053, Western Washington University, Bellingham WA 98225. Contest Director: Robin Hemley. Estab. 1977. Unpublished poetry. Submit October 1-December 31. Send SASE for new guidelines. Awards: 1st-$500, 2nd-$250, 3rd-$100.

GREEN LAKE CHAPBOOK PRIZE, Owl Creek Press, 1620 N. 45th St., Seattle WA 98103. Any combination of published and unpublished poems under 40 pages in length as long as the work has not previously appeared in book form (except anthologies). Guidelines for SASE. Include SASE for return of ms. Deadline: August 15. Charges $10 fee. Prize: Publication and $500 advance against royalties.

GROLIER POETRY PRIZE, Grolier Poetry Book Shop, Inc. & Ellen LaForge Memorial Poetry Foundation, Inc., 6 Plympton St., Cambridge MA 02138. (617)547-4648. Contact: Ms. Louisa Solano. Estab. 1973. For previously unpublished work to encourage and recognize developing writers. Open to all poets who have not published with either a vanity, small press, trade, or chapbook of poetry. Opens January 15; deadline: May 1. Guidelines must be followed; send SASE. Charges $6 fee. Prize: honorarium of $150 for two poets. Also poems of each winner and 4 runners-up will be published in the Grolier Poetry Prize Annual.

CECIL HEMLEY MEMORIAL AWARD, Poetry Society of America, 15 Gramercy Park S., New York NY 10003. (212)254-9628. Contact: Award Director. Unpublished lyric poem on a philosophical theme. Guidelines for #10 SASE. Deadline: December 22. Members only. Prize: $300.

‡FIRMAN HOUGHTON AWARD, New England Poetry Club, 11 Puritan Rd., Arlington MA 02174. Contest Director: Virginia Thayer. Offered annually for a lyric poem worthy of the former NEPC president. Deadline: April 24. Guidelines for SASE. Charges $3 entry fee for nonmembers. Prize: $250.

INTERNATIONAL TANKA SPLENDOR AWARDS, AHA Books, P.O. Box 1250, Gualala CA 95445-1250. (707)882-2226. E-mail: ahabooks@mcn.org. Website: http://www/Faximum.com/AHA!POETRY. Editor: Jane Reichhold. Estab. 1988. "The purpose of the contest is to acquaint writers with the Japanese poetry form, tanka and tanka sequences. By choosing 31 winners for publication in a chapbook, it is hoped that standards and examples will be set, re-evaluated, changed and enlarged. The genre is one of Japan's oldest, but the newest to English." Deadline: September 30. Guidelines for #10 SASE. Maximum 10 entries. No fee. Send SASE for winners list. 31 winning entries published in *Tanka Splendor*, which is given to the winners and then goes on sale for up to 3 years by AHA Books distribution.

IOWA POETRY PRIZES, University of Iowa Press, 119 W. Park Rd., Iowa City IA 52242. Fax: (319)335-2055. Website: http://www.uiowa.edu/~uipress. Director: Paul Zimmer. "The awards were initiated to encourage mature poets and their work." Manuscripts received in February and March. Send SASE. No reader's fee. Two $1,000 prizes are awarded annually. Final judging is performed by press editorial staff. Competition open to writers of English (whether citizens of US or not) who have published at least 1 previous book. No member of the faculty, staff or student body of University of Iowa is eligible.

RANDALL JARRELL POETRY PRIZE, North Carolina Writers' Network, 3501 Highway 54 West, Studio C, Chapel Hill NC 27516. Offered annually for unpublished work "to honor Randall Jarrell and his life at UNC-Greensboro by recognizing the best poetry submitted." Deadline: November 1. Guidelines for SASE. Charges $5 fee. Prize: $500, a public reading and reception and publication in *Parnassus: Poetry in Review*.

THE CHESTER H. JONES FOUNDATION NATIONAL POETRY COMPETITION, P.O. Box 498, Chardon OH 44024-9996. Estab. 1982. Offered annually for persons in the US, Canada and US citizens living abroad. Winning poems plus others, called "commendations," are published in a chapbook available from the foundation. Deadline: March 31. Charges $2 fee for first poem, $1 for each succeeding poem up to 10. Maximum 10 entries, no more than 32 lines each; must be unpublished. Prize: 1st-$1,000; 2nd-$750; 3rd-$500; 4th-$250; 5th-$100; several honorable mentions $50. All commendations which are printed in the winners book receive $10. Winners receive the book free.

THE JUNIPER PRIZE, University of Massachusetts, Amherst MA 01003. (413)545-2217. Fax: (413)545-1226. Contact: Chris Hammel. Estab. 1964. First book of poetry. Deadline: September 30. Charges $10 fee.

KALLIOPE'S ANNUAL SUE SANIEL ELKIND POETRY CONTEST, *Kalliope, a journal of women's art*, 3939 Roosevelt Blvd., Jacksonville FL 32205. (904)381-3511. Contact: Mary Sue Koeppel. Offered annually for unpublished work. "Poetry may be in any style and on any subject. Maximum poem length is

50 lines. Only unpublished poems and poems not submitted elsewhere are eligible." Deadline: October 30, 1996. Guidelines for SASE. Charges entry fee: $3/poem or 4 poems for $10. No limit on number of poems entered by any one poet. Prize: $1,000, publication of poem in *Kalliope*. The winning poem is published as are the finalists' poems. Copyright then returns to the authors.

LAST POEMS POETRY CONTEST, sub-TERRAIN Magazine, P.O. Box 1575, Bentall Centre, Vancouver, British Columbia V6C 2P7 Canada. (604)876-8710. Fax: (604)879-2667. Offered annually for unpublished poetry that encapsulates the North American experience at the close of the 20th Century. Deadline: January 31. Guidelines for SASE. Charges $15 fee, 4 poem maximum. Prize: $200, publication in spring issue and 4-issue subscription to sub-TERRAIN Magazine.

LEAGUE OF CANADIAN POETS AWARDS, National Poetry Contest, Gerald Lampert Award, and Pat Lowther Award, 54 Wolseley St., 3rd Floor, Toronto, Ontario M5T 1A5 Canada. (416)504-1657. Fax: (416)703-0059. E-mail: league@io.org. Website: http://www.swifty.com/lc/. Estab. 1966. Offered annually to promote new Canadian poetry/poets and also to recognize exceptional work in each category. Submissions to be published in the preceding year (awards), or previously unpublished (poetry contest). Deadline: January 31. Enquiries from publishers welcome. Charge: $6/poem fee for contest and $15 fee/title for each award. Open to Canadians living at home and abroad. The candidate must be a Canadian citizen or landed immigrant, although publisher need not be Canadian. For complete contest and awards rules, contact Edita Petrauskaite at address above.

THE RUTH LILLY POETRY PRIZE, The Modern Poetry Association, 60 W. Walton St., Chicago IL 60610-3305. Contact: Joseph Parisi. Estab. 1986. Offered annually to poet whose accomplishments in the field of poetry warrant extraordinary recognition. No applicants or nominations are accepted. Deadline varies.

LOCAL 7's ANNUAL NATIONAL POETRY COMPETITION, Santa Cruz/Monterey Local 7, National Writers Union, P.O. Box 2409, Aptos CA 95001-2409. Coordinator: Don Marsh. Offered annually for previously unpublished poetry to encourage the writing of poetry and to showcase unpublished work of high quality. Proceeds support the work of Local 7 of the National Writers Union. Deadline varies. Guidelines for #10 SASE. Charges $3/poem fee. Prize: 1st-$200; 2nd-$100; 3rd-$50.

LOUISIANA LITERATURE PRIZE FOR POETRY, *Louisiana Literature*, SLU—Box 792, Southeastern Louisiana University, Hammond LA 70402. (504)549-5022. Fax: (504)549-5021. Contest Director: Dr. David Hanson. Estab. 1984. Unpublished poetry. Deadline: February 15. Rules for SASE. Prize: $400. Entries considered for publication.

‡**LOUISE LOUIS/EMILY F. BOURNE STUDENT POETRY AWARD**, Poetry Society of America, 15 Gramercy Park NY 10003. (212)254-9628. Fax: (212)673-2352. Director: Timothy Donnelly. Offered annually for published work to promote excellence in student poetry. Deadline: December 22. Guidelines for SASE. Charges $1 per students submitting single entries. $10 per high school submitting unlimited number of their students' poems. Prize: $100. Judged by prominent established poets. Open to American high school or preparatory school students (grades 9 to 12).

‡**LYRIC POETRY AWARD**, Poetry Society of America, 15 Gramercy Park, New York NY 10003. (212)254-9628. Fax: (212)673-2352. Director: Timothy Donnelly. Offered annually for unpublished work to promote excellence in the lyric poetry field. Deadline: December 22. Guidelines for SASE. Prize: $500.

‡**THE LENORE MARSHALL PRIZE**, *The Nation* and The Academy of American Poets, 584 Broadway, #1208, New York NY 10012. Book of poems published in US during previous year and nominated by the publisher. Prize: $10,000. Deadline: June 1. Query the Academy of American Poets for details.

LUCILLE MEDWICK MEMORIAL AWARD, Poetry Society of America, 15 Gramercy Park S., New York NY 10003. (212)254-9628. Contact: Award Director. Original poem in any form or freedom on a humanitarian theme. Guidelines for #10 SASE. Guidelines subject to change. Prize: $500. Deadline: December 22. Members only.

MID-LIST PRESS FIRST SERIES AWARD FOR POETRY, Mid-List Press, 4324 12th Ave. S., Minneapolis MN 55407-3218. Estab. 1989. Offered annually for unpublished book of poetry to encourage new poets. Deadline: February 1. Guidelines for SASE. Charges $15 fee. Prize: publication and an advance against royalties. Judged by Mid-List's editors and ms readers. Winners are offered a contract at the conclusion of the judging. Contest is open to any writer who has never published a book of poetry. ("We do not consider a chapbook to be a book of poetry.")

MORSE POETRY PRIZE, Northeastern University English Deptment, 406 Holmes Hall, Boston MA 02115. (617)437-2512. Contact: Guy Rotella. Previously published poetry, book-length mss of first or second books. Charges $10/fee. Prize: Publication by Northeastern University Press and a $500 cash award.

‡**ERIKA MUMFORD PRIZE**, New England Poetry Club, 11 Puritan Rd., Arlington MA 02174. Contest Director: Virginia Thayer. Offered annually for a poem in any form about foreign culture or travel. Deadline: April 24. Guidelines for SASE. Charges $3 entry fee for nonmembers. Prize: $250.

NATIONAL LOOKING GLASS POETRY CHAPBOOK COMPETITION, *Pudding Magazine: The International Journal of Applied Poetry*, 60 N. Main St., Johnstown OH 43031. (614)967-6060. Contest Director: Jennifer Bosveld. "To publish a collection of poems that represents our magazine's editorial slant: popular culture, social justice, psychological, etc. Poems might be themed or not." Deadline: June 30. Guidelines for #10 SASE. Charges $10 fee. Prize: publication of the book and 20 copies to the author plus wholesale rights.

‡**THE NATIONAL POETRY SERIES**, The Copernicus Society of America, P.O. Box G, Hopewell NJ 08525. (609)466-9712. Fax: (609)466-4706. Director: Daniel Halpern. Offered annually for unpublished work. The National Poetry Series was established to ensure the publication of five new books of poetry in America each year. Deadline: January 1-February 15. Guidelines for SASE. Charges $25 fee. Prize: Book publication and $1,000 award. Judged by five different judges, each a poet of national reputation. Judges are different each year. Open to any writer.

‡**NATIONAL WRITERS ASSOCIATION POETRY CONTEST**, The National Writers Association, Suite 424, 1450 S. Havana, Aurora CO 80012. (303)751-7844. Fax:(303)751-8593. Director: Sandy Whelchel. Annual contest "to encourage the writing of poetry, an important form of individual expression but with a limited commercial market." Charges $10 fee. Prizes: $100, $50, $25. Guidelines for #10 SASE.

HOWARD NEMEROV SONNET AWARD, *The Formalist: A Journal of Metrical Poetry*, 320 Hunter Dr., Evansville IN 47711. Contact: Mona Baer. Offered annually for an unpublished sonnet to encourage poetic craftsmanship and to honor the memory of the late Howard Nemerov, third US Poet Laureate and a masterful writer of sonnets. Deadline: June 15. Guidelines for SASE. Entry fee: $3/sonnet. Prize: $1,000 cash and publication in *The Formalist*; 11 other finalists also published. Acquires first North American serial rights for those sonnets chosen for publication. Upon publication all rights revert to the author. Open to the international community of writers.

‡**NEW MUSE AWARD**, Broken Jaw Press/M.A.P. Productions, Box 596 Station A, Fredericton, New Brunswick E3B 5A6 Canada. Contact: Joe Blades. Offered annually for unpublished poems (individual poems may have been previously published) to encourage development of booklength mss by poets without a first book published. Deadline: March 31. Guidelines for SASE (with Canadian postage or IRC). Charges $15 fee (all entrants receive copy of winning book upon publication). Prize: book publication on trade terms.

‡**THE OHIO STATE UNIVERSITY PRESS/THE JOURNAL AWARD IN POETRY**, The Ohio State University Press and *The Journal*, 180 Pressey Hall, 1070 Carmack, Columbus OH 43210. (614)292-6930. Fax: (614)292-2065. Director: David Citino. Offered annually for unpublished work. Deadline: September 1-30. Guidelines for SASE. Charges $15 fee. Prize: $1,000 and publication royalties. Open to any writer.

‡**NATALIE ORNISH POETRY AWARD IN MEMORY OF WAYNE GARD**, The Texas Institute of Letters, P.O. Box 298300, Fort Worth TX 76129. (817)921-7822. Fax: (817)921-7333. Offered annually for previously published work between January 1 and December 31 of year before award is given to honor the writer of the best book of poems published during the previous year. Deadline: January 2. Guidelines for SASE. Prize: $1,000. Judged by a panel of three. Poet must have been born in Texas, have lived in the state at some time for at least two consecutive years, or subject matter is associated with the state.

GUY OWEN POETRY PRIZE, *Southern Poetry Review*, Advancement Studies, CPCC, Charlotte NC 28235. (704)342-6002. Award Director: Ken McLaurin. Estab. 1985. Offered annually for the best unpublished poem submitted in an open competition. Given in memory of Guy Owen, a poet, fiction writer and founder of *Southern Poetry Review*. Submit in April only—3-5 previously unpublished poems and SASE. Charges $8 fee that includes one year subscription to *SPR* to begin with the Winter issue, containing the winning poem. Prize: $500 and publication in *SPR*. All submissions considered for publication.

OWL CREEK POETRY PRIZE, Owl Creek Press, 1620 N. 45th St., Seattle WA 98103. Any combination of published and unpublished poems over 50 pages in length as long as the work has not previously appeared in book form (except anthologies). Guidelines for SASE. Include SASE for return of ms. Deadline: February 15. Charges $15 fee. Prize: Publication and $750 advance against royalties.

‡**PANHANDLER POETRY CHAPBOOK COMPETITION**, *The Panhandler Magazine*, English Dept., University of West Florida, Pensacola FL 32514-5751. (904)474-2923. Editor: Laurie O'Brien. Estab.

1979. Individual poems may have been published. To honor excellence in the writing of short collections of poetry. Two winning mss are published each year. Submit October 15-January 15. Charges $7 fee (includes copy of winning chapbooks).

‡PAT PARKER POETRY AWARD, National Women's Studies Association, 7100 Baltimore Ave., #301, College Park MD 20715. (301)403-0525. Fax: (301)403-4137. Offered annually for unpublished work. Awarded for an outstanding narrative poem or dramatic monologue by a Black, lesbian, feminist poet. Poems can be up to 50 lines and on a topic to the concerns of African American women, lesbians, and feminists, or the life and work of poet Pat Parker. Special preference will be given to poems that inspire, enlighten, or encourage. Submissions accepted May 1-July 31. Guidelines for SASE. Prize: $250.

THE RICHARD PHILLIPS POETRY PRIZE, The Phillips Publishing Co., P.O. Box 121, Watts OK 74964. Contact: Richard Phillips, Jr. Offered annually to give a modest financial reward to emerging poets who have not yet established themselves sufficiently to generate appropriate compensation for their work. Deadline: September 5. Guidelines for SASE. Charges $10 fee. Prize: $1,000 and publication. Open to all poets. "There are no anthologies to buy. No strings attached. Simply put, the poet who enters the best manuscript will win the prize of $1,000 and will receive a check in that amount within 30 days of the deadline." Winner, 1995: *Milking Time*, by Kathryn Presley of Somerville, TX.

THE POETRY CENTER BOOK AWARD, The Poetry Center, San Francisco State University, 1600 Holloway Ave., San Francisco CA 94132-9901. (415)338-2227. Fax: (415)338-2493. Award Director: Melissa Black. Estab. 1980. Offered annually for previously published books of poetry and chapbooks, appearing in year of the prize. "Prize given for an extraordinary book of American poetry." Deadline December 31. Guidelines for #10 SASE. Charges $10/book fee. Prize: $500 and an invitation to read in the Poetry Center Reading Series. Please include a cover letter noting author name, book title(s), name of person issuing check, and check number.

POETRY PUBLICATION, The PEN (Poetry Explosion Newsletter), The Poet Band Co., P.O. Box 4725, Pittsburgh PA 15206. Editor: Arthur C. Ford. Estab. 1984. Send maximum of 5 poems. Enclose $1 for reading fee. Use rhyme and non-rhyming verse. Maximum lines: 40. Prose maximum: 200-300 words. Allow 1 month for response. Sample copy $4. Send SASE for more information. Quarterly newsletter (*The Pen*) issued March, June, September and December. Subscriptions are $15 (yearly) or $28 for 2 years.

POETS CLUB OF CHICAGO INTERNATIONAL SHAKESPEAREAN/PETRARCHAN SONNET CONTEST, 130 Windsor Park Dr. C-323, Carol Stream IL 60188. Chairman: LaVone Holt. Estab. 1954. Deadline: September 1. Guidelines for SASE after March 1.

FELIX POLLAK PRIZE IN POETRY, University of Wisconsin Press, 114 N. Murray St., Madison WI 53715. Contest Director: Ronald Wallace. Estab. 1994. Unpublished book length ms of original poetry. Submissions must be received by the press during the month of September (postmark is irrelevant) and must be accompanied by SASE for contest results. Prize: $1,000 and publication to the 2 best submissions. Guidelines for #10 SASE. Does not return mss. Charges $15 fee, payable to University of Wisconsin Press. Notification in February.

QUARTERLY REVIEW OF LITERATURE POETRY SERIES, 26 Haslet Ave., Princeton NJ 08540. (609)921-6976. "QRL Poetry Series is a book publishing series chosen from an open competition." Publishes 4-6 titles/year. Prize: $1,000, publication and 100 copies to each winner for a book of miscellaneous poems, a single long poem, a poetic play or a book of translations. Guidelines for SASE. Submission May and October *only*.

THE BYRON HERBERT REECE INTERNATIONAL POETRY AWARDS, Georgia State Poetry Society, Inc., 4331 Lake Chimney Ct., Roswell GA 30075. Contact: Joan Anson-Weber. Estab. 1987. Offered annually for previously unpublished poetry to honor the late Georgia poet, Byron Herbert Reece. Deadline in January. Guidelines for #10 SASE. Charges entry fee of $5/first poem; $1/additional poem. Prize: 1st-$250; 2nd-$100; 3rd-$50.

ROANOKE-CHOWAN AWARD FOR POETRY, North Carolina Literary and Historical Association, 109 E. Jones St., Raleigh NC 27601-2807. (919)733-7305. Awards Coordinator: Barbara Mann. Previously published poetry by a resident of North Carolina. Deadline: July 15.

NICHOLAS ROERICH POETRY PRIZE, Story Line Press, Three Oaks Farm, Brownsville OR 97327-9718. (541)466-5352. Fax: (541)466-3200. E-mail: stoline@aol.com. Contact: Michele Thompson. Estab. 1988. Full-length book of poetry. Any writer who has not previously published a full-length collection of poetry (48 pages or more) in English is eligible to apply. Deadline: October 15. Charges $15 fee. Prize:

winner—$1,000, publication, a reading at the Nicholas Roerich Museum in New York. Runner-up—scholarship to Wesleyan Writers Workshop in Canada.

ANNA DAVIDSON ROSENBERG AWARD FOR POEMS ON THE JEWISH EXPERIENCE, Judah L. Magnes Museum, 2911 Russell St., Berkeley CA 94705. (510)549-6950. Contact: Paula Friedman. Offered annually for unpublished work to encourage poetry of/on/from the Jewish experience. Deadline for requesting mandatory entry forms is July 15; deadline for receipt of poems is August 31. Guidelines and entry form for SASE. Submissions must include entry form. Charges $2 fee for up to 4 poems. Prize: 1st-$100; 2nd-$50; 3rd-$25; $25-New/Emerging Poet Prize; $25-Youth Award; also, Senior Award and Honorable Mentions. All winners receive certificate, and winning poems are read in an Awards Reading here. Open to any writer.

‡SLIPSTREAM ANNUAL POETRY CHAPBOOK COMPETITION, *Slipstream*, Box 2071, Niagara Falls NY 14301. (716)282-2616 after 5 P.M. EST. Director: Dan Sicoli. Offered annually to help promote a poet whose work is often overlooked or ignored. Deadline: December 1. Guidelines for SASE. Charges $10 fee. Prize: $500 and 50 copies of published chapbook. Judged by editors of Slipstream magazine. Open to any writer. Past winners have included Gerald Locklin, David Chorlton, Serena Fusek, Robert Cooperman, Sherman Alexie, Kurt Nimmo, Katharine Harer and Richard Amidon.

‡PEREGRINE SMITH POETRY CONTEST, Gibbs Smith, Publisher, P.O. Box 667, Layton UT 84041. (801)544-2958. Fax: (801)544-5582. Poetry Editor: Gail Yngve. Offered annually for unpublished work. The purpose of this award is to recognize and publish a previously unpublished work. Deadline: April 30. "We only accept submissions during the month of April each year." Guidelines for SASE. Charges $15 fee. Prize: $500 and publication of the winning entry. Judged by Christopher Merrill. Open to any writer.

‡SNAKE NATION PRESS'S ANNUAL POETRY CONTEST, Snake Nation Press, 110 #2 W. Force St., Valdosta GA 31601. (912)219-8334. Contest Director: Roberta George. Estab. 1989. Annual contest to give a wider audience to readable, understandable poetry. Deadline: January 15. Guidelines for #10 SASE. Charges $10 fee. Prize consists of $500, 50 copies and distribution. Open to everyone.

THE SOW'S EAR CHAPBOOK PRIZE, *The Sow's Ear Poetry Review*, 19535 Pleasant View Dr., Abingdon VA 24211-6827. (540)628-2651. Contest Director: Larry K. Richman. Estab. 1988. 24-26 pages of poetry. Submit March-April. Guidelines for #10 SASE. Charges $10 fee. Prize: 1st-$500, 50 copies and distribution to subscribers; 2nd-$100; 3rd-$100.

ANN STANFORD POETRY PRIZE, The Southern California Anthology, % Master of Professional Writing Program, WPH 404, U.S.C., Los Angeles CA 90089-4034. (213)740-3252. Contest Director: James Ragan. Estab. 1988. Previously unpublished poetry to honor excellence in poetry in memory of poet and teacher Ann Stanford. Include cover sheet with name, address and titles of the 5 poems entered. Deadline: April 15. Guidelines for #10 SASE. Charges $10 fee. Prize: 1st-$750; 2nd-$250; 3rd-$100. Winning poems are published in *The Southern California Anthology* and all entrants receive a free issue.

THE AGNES LYNCH STARRETT POETRY PRIZE, University of Pittsburgh Press, 127 N. Bellefield Ave., Pittsburgh PA 15260. (412)624-4110. Fax: (412)624-7380. Series Editor: Ed Ochester. Estab. 1936. First book of poetry for poets who have not had a full-length book published. Deadline: March and April only. Guidelines for SASE (essential). Prize: $3,000.

‡STEPHEN G. STEPHANSSON AWARD FOR POETRY, Writers Guild of Alberta, 11759 Groat Rd., Edmonton Alberta T5M 3K6 Canada. (403)422-8174. Fax: (403)422-2663. Director: Darlene Diver. Poetry book published in current year. Must be an Alberta poet.

‡VASSAR MILLER PRIZE IN POETRY, English Dept., Old Dominion University, Norfolk VA 23529. Series Editor: Scott Cairns. For original book-length poetry manuscript. Manuscripts accepted during November and December. Manuscript must be accompanied by $16 handling fee payable to UNT Press and letter-sized SASE for reply. Prize: $500 and publication by University of North Texas Press.

VERVE POETRY CONTEST, *VERVE* Magazine, P.O. Box 3205, Simi Valley CA 93093. Contest Director: Ron Reichick. Estab. 1989. Offered 2 times/year for previously unpublished poetry. "Fund raiser for *VERVE* Magazine which receives no grants and has no ties with any institutions." Deadlines: April 1 and October 1. Guidelines for #10 SASE. Charges $2/poem. Prizes: 1st-$100; 2nd-$50; 3rd-$25.

‡THE ROBERT PENN WARREN POETRY PRIZE COMPETITION, Cumberland Poetry Review, P.O. Box 120128, Ackten Station, Nashville TN 37212. Contest/Award Director: Eva Touster. Offered annually for unpublished poems to encourage the writing of good poetry. Deadline: March 1. Guidelines for SASE. Charges $28 fee (includes a year's subscription to *Cumberland Party Review* which is $18 a year).

Prize: 1st-$500, 2nd-$300, 3rd-$200 and Honorable Mention. Publication in the Fall issue of *Cumberland Poetry Review*. Initial judging by the editors of *CPR*. The judge who makes the final decision is an internationally-known poet selected each year. All work submitted according to the published guidelines will be considered.

‡**THE WASHINGTON PRIZE**, The Word Works, Inc., P.O. Box 42164, Washington DC 20015. Contact: Miles David Moore. Offered annually for unpublished poetry to recognize a living American poet for an unpublished work of excellence to help further his or her life as a writer and to keep poetry alive in the United States. Contest open February 1-March 1 (postmark). Guidelines for SASE. Charges $15 fee. Prizes: $1,000 and book publication; author gets 15% of the run. Contest open to all US citizens.

‡**WICK POETRY CHAPBOOK SERIES "OPEN" COMPETITION**, Wick Poetry Program Dept. of English, Kent State University, P.O. Box 5190, Kent OH 44242-0001. (330)672-2676. Fax: (330)672-3152. E-mail: wickpoet@kentvm.kent.edu. Director: Maggie Anderson. Publication of a chapbook of poems by a poet currently living in Ohio who has not previously published a full-length book (48 or more pages, an edition of 500 or more copies). Deadline: October 31. Guidelines for SASE. Charges $5 entry fee. Prize: Publication of the chapbook by the Kent State University Press.

‡**WICK POETRY CHAPBOOK SERIES "STUDENT" COMPETITION**, Wick Poetry Program, Dept. of English, Kent State University, P.O. Box 5190, Kent OH 44242-0001. (330)672-2676. Fax: (330)672-3152. E-mail: wickpoet@kentvm.kent.edu. Director: Maggie Anderson. Publication of a chapbook of poems by a poet currently enrolled in an Ohio college or university who has not previously published a full length book (48 or more pages; edition of 500 copies or more). Deadline: October 31. Guidelines for SASE. Prize: Publication of the chapbook by the Kent State University Press.

‡**STAN AND TOM WICK POETRY PRIZE**, Wick Poetry Program, Dept. of English, Kent State University, P.O. Box 5190, Kent OH 44242-0001. (330)672-2676. Fax: (330)672-3152. E-mail: wickpoet@kentvm.k ent.edu. Director: Maggie Anderson. First Book Prize open to anyone writing in English who has not previously published a full-length book of poems (a volume of 48 pages or more published in an edition of 500 or more copies). Deadline: May 1. Guidelines for SASE. Charges $10 entry fee. Prize: $1,000 prize and book publication by the Kent State University Press.

‡**THE WILDWOOD PRIZE IN POETRY**, Harrisburg Area Community College Alumni Association, A213E, 1 HACC Dr., Harrisburg PA 17110. (717)780-2487. Fax: (717)737-6489. Director: T.H.S. Wallace. Offered annually for unpublished poems to publish the best poetry being written in America. Deadline: November 30. Charges $5 entry fee (drawn to Harrisburg Area Community College) for 3 poems. Prize: $500 cash award and publication. Acquires First North American serial rights. The works must be no more than 100 lines, in English, no translations.

ROBERT H. WINNER MEMORIAL AWARD, Poetry Society of America, 15 Gramercy Park S., New York NY 10003. (212)254-9628. Contact: Award Director. "For a poet whose first book appeared when he was almost 50, recognizing and rewarding the work of someone in midlife. Open to poets over 40, still unpublished or with one book." Guidelines for #10 SASE. Guidelines subject to change. Charges $5 fee for nonmembers. Deadline: December 22. Prize: $2,500.

WINTER POETRY COMPETITION, Still Waters Press, 459 S. Willow Ave., Galloway Township NJ 08201-4633. Contest Director: Shirley A. Warren. Estab. 1989. Guidelines for #10 SASE. Charges $10 fee. Deadline: September 30. Sample winning chapbook: $5.

WOMEN'S WORDS POETRY COMPETITION, Still Waters Press, 459 S. Willow Ave., Galloway Township NJ 08201-4633. Contest Director: Shirley A. Warren. Guidelines for #10 SASE. Charges $10 fee. Deadline: February 28.

THE WRITER MAGAZINE/EMILY DICKINSON AWARD, Poetry Society of America, 15 Gramercy Park S., New York NY 10003. (212)254-9628. Contact: Award Director. Poem inspired by Emily Dickinson, though not necessarily in her style. Guidelines for #10 SASE. Guidelines subject to change. Deadline: December 22. Members only. Prize: $100.

WRITERS' JOURNAL QUARTERLY POETRY CONTEST, Val-Tech Publishing, Inc., P.O. Box 25376, St. Paul MN 55125. (612)730-4280. Contact: Esther M. Leiper. Previously unpublished poetry. Deadlines: February 28, April 15, August 15, November 30. Charges $2 fee first poem; $1 each thereafter.

YALE SERIES OF YOUNGER POETS, Yale University Press, P.O. Box 209040, New Haven CT 06520-9040. Website: http://www.yale.edu/yup/. Contact: Richard Miller. First book of poetry by poet under the age of 40. Submit during February. Guidelines for #10 SASE. Charges $15 fee. Winning manuscript is published by Yale University Press. The author receives the usual royalties.

PHYLLIS SMART YOUNG PRIZES IN POETRY, *The Madison Review*, Dept. of English, 600 N. Park St., Madison WI 53706. (608)263-3374. Director: Ronald Kuka. Offered annually for previously unpublished work. "Awarded to the best poems submitted, out of a field of around 500 submissions yearly. The purpose of the prize is to award good poets." Submissions must consist of 3 poems. Deadline: September 30. Prize: $500; plus publication in the spring issue of *The Madison Review*. All contest entries are considered as submissions to *The Madison Review*, the literary journal sponsoring the contest. No simultaneous submissions to other publications. Charges $3 fee.

ZUZU'S PETALS POETRY CONTEST, *Zuzu's Petals Quarterly Online*, P.O. Box 156, Whitehall PA 18052. (610)821-1324. E-mail: zuzu@epix.net. Website: http://www.hway.net/zuzu/. Editor: T. Dunn. Offered 2 times/year for previously unpublished poetry. Deadline: March 1, September 1. Guidelines for #10 SASE. Charges $2 fee/poem. Prize: top 3 winners share 40% of the contest's proceeds. All entries automatically considered for publication.

PLAYWRITING AND SCRIPTWRITING

‡**ALASKA NATIVE PLAYS CONTEST**, University of Alaska Anchorage, 3211 Providence Dr., Anchorage AK 99508. (907)786-1794. Fax: (907)786-1799. Contest Director: Dr. David Edgecombe. Offered annually for unpublished works "to encourage the writing, reading and production of plays with American Native (Indian) issues, themes and characters." Deadline: March 20. Guidelines for SASE. Prize: 1st-$500; 2nd-$200; 3rd-$100. "Any writer may enter—Native American writers are strongly encouraged."

AMERICAN SHORTS, Florida Studio Theater, 1241 N. Palm Ave., Sarasota FL 34236. (941)366-9017. Fax: (941)955-4137. Offered annually for unpublished plays no more than 5 pages long on a theme that changes every year. 1996 theme was "Accepting the Other." Deadline varies. Send inquiry to above address. Prize: $500.

‡**ANNUAL KEY WEST THEATRE FESTIVAL**, P.O. Box 992, Key West FL 33041. (305)292-3725. Fax: (305)293-0845. Contact: Joan McGillis. Offered annually for unpublished submissions to develop new plays from either new or established playwrights. Deadline: April 30. Guidelines for SASE. Award: Round trip airfare to Key West and lodging in Key West for a minimum of one week. Open to any writer when submitted by agent or by professional recommendation.

‡**ANNUAL PLAYWRITING CONTEST**, Hudson River Classics, Inc., P.O. Box 940, Hudson NY 12534. (518)828-1329. Fax: (518)758-7550. Contest Director: Keith Hedrick. Offered annually for unpublished submissions. Deadline: June 1. Guidelines for SASE. Charges $5 fee. Prize: $500 and staged reading by professional actors.

‡**AUSTIN HEART OF FILM FESTIVAL FEATURE LENGTH SCREENPLAY AWARD**, 707 Rio Grande, Suite 101, Austin TX 78701. (512)478-4795. Fax: (512)478-6205. Website: http://www.awpi.com/AFF/. Award Director: Barbara Morgan. Offered annually for unpublished screenplays. The Austin Heart of Film Festival is looking for quality screenplays which will be read by industry professionals. The contest hopes to give unknown writers exposure to producers and other industry executives. Three competitions: (Adult/Mature Category, Children/Family Category) Student Short Screenplay Competition, and Best Screenplay of a Produced Film Award. Deadline: June 17th. Guidelines for SASE or call 1-800-310-3378. Charges $30 entry fee. Prize: Feature Length, both categories are $3,000 each plus airfare and accomodations to conference in Austin (October 10-13). Student Short is $750. The writer must hold the rights when submitted. It must be original work. The screenplay must be between 90 and 130 pages. It must be in standard screenplay format (industry standard).

THE MARGARET BARTLE PLAYWRITING AWARD, Community Children's Theatre of Kansas City, 8021 E. 129th Terrace, Grandview MO 64030-2114. (816)761-5775. Award Director: E. Blanche Sellens. Estab. 1951. Offered annually for unpublished plays for elementary school audiences. "Our purpose is two-fold: to award a deserving author of a good, well-written play, and to produce the play royalty-free by one of our trouping units." Deadline: January 31. Guidelines for SASE. Prize: $500.

THE BEVERLY HILLS THEATRE GUILD-JULIE HARRIS PLAYWRIGHT AWARD COMPETITION, 2815 N. Beachwood Drive, Los Angeles CA 90068. (213)465-2703. Playwright Award Coordinator: Marcella Meharg. Estab. 1978. Original full-length plays, unpublished, unproduced and not currently under option. Application required, available upon request with SASE. Submissions accepted with applications from August 1-November 1.

CALIFORNIA YOUNG PLAYWRIGHTS CONTEST, The Playwright Project, 1450 Frazee Rd., Suite 215, San Diego CA 92108. (619)298-9242. Fax: (619)298-9244. Contest Director: Deborah Salzer. Offered annually for previously unpublished plays by young writers to stimulate young people to create dramatic works, and to nurture promising young writers (under age 19). Deadline: April 1. Guidelines for 9×12 SASE. Award consists of "professional production of 3-5 winning plays at the Old Globe Theatre in San Diego, plus royalty. All entrants receive detailed evaluation letter." Judged by theater professionals in the Southern California area. Scripts must be a minimum of 10 standard typewritten pages. Writers must be California residents under age 19 as of the deadline date.

CEC JACKIE WHITE MEMORIAL NATIONAL CHILDREN'S PLAYWRITING CONTEST, Columbia Entertainment Company, 309 Parkade Blvd., Columbia MO 65202. (314)874-5628. Contact: Betsy Phillips. Estab. 1988. Offered annually for "top notch unpublished scripts for theater school use, to challenge and expand the talents of our students, ages 10-15. The entry should be a full length play with speaking roles for 20-30 characters of all ages and with at least 10 roles developed in some detail." Deadline: June 1. Production and some travel expenses for 1st and 2nd place winners, plus cash award for 1st place. Guidelines for SASE. Entrants receive written evaluation of work. Charges $10 fee.

JANE CHAMBERS PLAYWRITING AWARD, Women and Theatre Program of Association for Theatre in Higher Education (WTP/ATHE), % Tori Haring-Smith, English Department, Box 1852, Brown University, Providence RI 02912. (401)247-2911. Director: Tori Haring-Smith. Estab. 1983. "To recognize a woman playwright who has written a play with a feminist perspective, a majority of roles for women, and which experiments with the dramatic form." Deadline: February 15. Notification: May 31. Additional guidelines for #10 SASE. Prize: $1,000. Student award: $250. Synopses of both winners sent to all TCG-affiliated theatres. "Writer must be female. A recommendation from a theatre professional is helpful, but not required."

‡CHARLOTTE FESTIVAL/NEW PLAYS IN AMERICA, Charlotte Repertory Theatre, 2040 Charlotte Plaza, Charlotte NC 28244. Literary Associate: Carol Bellamy. Four plays selected for each festival. Must be full scripts—no one acts or musicals. Must not have had any previous professional production. Accepted all year. Prize: staged reading of script. Transportation to festival—small honorarium for expenses. Open to any writer. Scripts *must be bound* and include SASE if need to be returned. No cassettes or videos accepted.

CLEVELAND PUBLIC THEATRE NEW PLAYS FESTIVAL, Cleveland Public Theatre, 6415 Detroit Ave., Cleveland OH 44102. (216)631-2727. Fax: (216)631-2575. E-mail: cpt@en.com. Website: http://www.en.com/cpt. Festival Director: Terence Cranendonk. Estab. 1983. Annual festival of staged readings of 10-15 alternative, experimental, poetic, political work, and plays by women, people of color, gays/lesbians. Deadline: September 1. Guidelines for SASE. Charges $10 fee. "We accept both full-length and one-acts, but emphasize shorter works, simple set, 10 actor cast maximum. Generally, half of the works in the New Plays Festival are by Ohio playwrights."

COE COLLEGE PLAYWRITING FESTIVAL, Coe College, 1220 First Ave. NE., Cedar Rapids IA 52402-5092. (319)399-8689. Fax: (319)399-8557. Contact: Susan Wolverton. Estab. 1993. Offered 2 times/year for unpublished work to provide a venue for new works for the stage. "There is usually a theme for the festival. We are interested in full-length productions, *not* one acts or musicals." Next festival: 1996-97. Guidelines for SASE. Prize: $325, plus 1-week residency as guest artist with airfare, room and board provided. Judges are a select committee of professionals. "There are no specific criteria although a current résumé is requested."

THE CHRISTOPHER COLUMBUS SCREENPLAY DISCOVERY AWARDS, 433 N. Camden Dr., #600, Beverly Hills CA 90210. (310)288-1988. Fax: (310)288-0257. Monthly and annual contest "to discover new screenplay writers." Deadline: December 1. Charges $45 fee. Prize: options up to $10,000, plus professional development guidance and access to agents, producers, and studios. Judged by reputable industry professionals (producers, development executives, story analysts). Writer must give option to purchase if selected.

‡CORNERSTONE DRAMATURGY AND DEVELOPMENT PROJECT, Penumbra Theatre, 270 N. Kent, St. Paul MN 55102. (612)224-3180. Fax: (612)224-7074. Contest/Award Director: L. Bellamy. Annual project for "new plays addressing Pan-African and African-American experiences. Must be a full-length drama or comedy." Scripts accepted year-round. Guidelines for SASE. Selected script will receive support

---

ALWAYS ENCLOSE a self-addressed, stamped envelope (SASE) with all your queries and correspondence.

in the form of writer commissions, per diem, workshops, lodging expenses, readings and possible production in Penumbra's regular season.

CUNNINGHAM PRIZE FOR PLAYWRITING, The Theatre School, DePaul University, 2135 N. Kenmore, Chicago IL 60614. (312)325-7938. Fax: (312)325-7920. Contact: Lara Goetsch. Offered annually for published or unpublished work "to recognize and encourage the writing of dramatic works which affirm the centrality of religion, broadly defined, and the human quest for meaning, truth and community." Deadline: December 1. Guidelines for SASE. Prize: $5,000. Judged by "a panel of distinguished citizens including members of the faculty of DePaul University, representatives of the Cunningham Prize Advisory Commitee, critics and others from the theater professions, chaired by John Ransford Watts, dean of the Theatre School." Open to writers whose residence is in the Chicago area, defined as within 100 miles of the Loop.

‡DAYTON PLAYHOUSE FUTUREFEST, The Dayton Playhouse, 1301 E. Siebenthaler Ave., Dayton OH 45414-5357. (513)277-0144. Fax: (513)227-9539. Managing Director: Tina McPhearson. Estab. 1983. "Three plays selected for full productions, three for readings at July 1997 FutureFest weekend; the six authors will be given travel and lodging to attend the festival. Judges view all productions and select a winner. There is a total of $1,000 in prize money with more prize monies pending." Guidelines for SASE. Deadline: September 30.

WALT DISNEY STUDIOS FELLOWSHIP PROGRAM, Walt Disney Studios, 500 S. Buena Vista St., Burbank CA 91521-0880. (818)560-6894. Contact: Brenda Hathaway. Offering approximately 15 positions for writers to work full-time developing their craft at Disney in feature film and television writing. Deadline: April 1-26, 1996. Guidelines for SASE. "Writing samples are required, as well as a résumé, completed application form and notarized standard letter agreement (available from the Program Administrator.)" A $30,000 salary for 1 year period beginning mid-October. Fellows outside of LA area will be provided with airfare and 1 month's accommodations. Open to all writers. Members of the WGA should apply through the Guild's Employment Access Department at (213)782-4648.

DRURY COLLEGE ONE-ACT PLAY CONTEST, Drury College, 900 N. Benton Ave., Springfield MO 65802-3344. (417)873-7430. Contact: Sandy Asher. Estab. 1986. Offered in even-numbered years for unpublished and professionally unproduced plays. One play per playwright. Deadline: December 1. Guidelines for SASE.

DUBUQUE FINE ARTS PLAYERS ANNUAL ONE-ACT PLAYWRITING CONTEST, 1321 Tomahawk Dr., Dubuque IA 52003. (319)583-6748. Contest Coordinator: Jennie G. Stabenow. Annual competition since 1977 for previously unpublished, unproduced plays. Adaptations must be of playwright's own work or of a work in the public domain. No children's plays or musicals. No scripts over 35 pages or 40 minutes performance time. Two copies of ms required. Script Readers' review sheets available. "Concentrate on character, relationships, and a good story." Deadline: January 31. Guidelines for #10 SASE. Charges $10 fee. Prizes: $600, $300, $200, plus possible full production of play. Buys rights to first full-stage production and subsequent local video rights. Reports by June 30.

SAM EDWARDS DEAF PLAYWRIGHTS COMPETITION, New York Deaf Theatre, Ltd., 305 Seventh Ave., 11th Floor, New York NY 10001-6008. Voice: (212)924-9491. TTY: (212)924-9535. Offered annually for unpublished and unproduced work. "Established in 1989 to honor the memory of a founding member of the New York Deaf Theatre, the competition seeks to encourage deaf writers to create their unique stories for the stage. Keenly aware of the void which exists of plays written by deaf playwrights, the competition is the only opportunity of its kind that nurtures deaf writers in the development of their play writing skills. Unproduced scripts by deaf playwrights are accepted in two categories: full-length and one act plays." Deadline: January 31. Guidelines for SASE. Charges $10 US/Canadian and $15 foreign countries. Prize: $400 for full-length play, $200 for one-act play. "New York Deaf Theatre exercises the right to produce the winning plays, within a two-year period, as a staged reading, workshop production or full production. The competition is open to deaf writers only. It should be noted that while NYDT's mission is to create opportunities for American Sign Language Theatre for deaf theater artists and, in doing so, fosters a better understanding of Deaf Culture, the competition will accept scripts from all deaf people no matter what their primary mode of communication. However, we will only produce scripts that are in harmony with our mission."

DAVID JAMES ELLIS MEMORIAL AWARD, Theatre Americana, Box 245, Altadena CA 91003. (818)683-1740. Contact: Playreading Committee. Offered annually for previously unpublished work to produce original plays of Americana background and history or by American authors. Deadline: January 31. "No entry necessary but we will send guidelines on request with SASE." Prize: $500.

EMERGING PLAYWRIGHT AWARD, Playwrights Preview Productions, 17 E. 47th St., New York NY 10017. Phone/fax: (212)289-2168. Contact: Pamela Faith Jackson. Submissions required to be unpublished and unproduced in New York City. Send script, letter of introduction, production history, author's name résumé and SASE. Submissions accepted year-round. Plays selected in August and January for award consideration. Estab. 1983. Prize: $500 and New York showcase production.

LAWRENCE S. EPSTEIN PLAYWRITING AWARD, 115 Hatteras Rd., Barnegat NJ 08005-2814. Contact: Lawrence Epstein. Unpublished submissions. Deadline: October. Published in Dramatist's Guild and other newsletters.

SHUBERT FENDRICH MEMORIAL PLAYWRITING CONTEST, Pioneer Drama Service, Inc., P.O. Box 4267, Englewood CO 80155. (303)779-4035. Fax: (303)779-4315. E-mail: piodrama@aol.com. Contact: Editorial Staff. Offered annually for unpublished but previously produced submissions to encourage the development of quality theatrical material for educational and community theater. Deadline: March 1. Guidelines for SASE. Prize: $1,000 royalty advance, publication. Rights acquired only if published. People already published by Pioneer Drama are not eligible.

THE FESTIVAL OF EMERGING AMERICAN THEATRE, The Phoenix Theatre, 749 N. Park Ave., Indianapolis IN 46202. (317)635-7529. Contact: Bryan Fonseca. Annual playwriting competition for previously unproduced full-length and one-act works. Submit script, 1-2 page synopsis, production history of play and author's bio/résumé. Include 9 × 12 SASE for return of script; #10 SASE if judge's critique desired. Guidelines for SASE. Charges $5 entry fee. Deadline: February 28. Announcement and notification of winners in May. First prize: $750 honorarium for full-length play, $325 for one-act.

‡**FESTIVAL OF NEW WORKS**, Plays-In-Progress, 615 Fourth St., Eureka CA 95501. (707)443-3724. Contact: Susan Bigelow-Marsh. Offered fall and spring for unpublished/unproduced submissions to give playwrights an opportunity to hear their work and receive audience feedback. Deadlines: August 1 and March 1. Guidelines for SASE. Award: staged reading. Open to any writer.

‡**FMCT'S BIENNIAL PLAYWRIGHTS COMPETITION (MID-WEST)**, Fargo-Moorhead Community Theatre, P.O. Box 644, Fargo ND 58107-0644. (701)235-1901. Contact: Contest Administrator. Estab. 1988. Biennial contest (next contest will be held 1997-98). Submissions required to be unpublished, unproduced one-acts 30-50 minutes in length. Deadline: July 1, 1997.

FUND FOR NEW AMERICAN PLAYS, J.F. Kennedy Center for the Performing Arts, Washington DC 20566. (202)416-8024. Fax: (202)416-8026. Manager: Sophy Burnham. Estab. 1988. Previously unproduced work. "Program objectives: to encourage playwrights to write, and nonprofit professional theaters to produce new American plays; to ease the financial burdens of nonprofit professional theater organizations producing new plays; to provide a playwright with a better production of the play than the producing theater would normally be able to accomplish." Deadline: March 15 (date changes from year to year). "Nonprofit theater organizations can mail in name and address to be placed on the mailing list." Prize: $10,000 for playwrights plus grants to theaters based on scripts submitted by producing theaters. A few encouragement grants of $2,500 are given to promising playwrights chosen from the submitted proposals. Submissions and funding proposals only through the producing theater.

GILMAN & GONZALEZ-FALLA THEATER FOUNDATION AWARD, 109 E. 64th St., New York NY 10021. (212)734-8011. Offered annually for previously produced work to encourage the creative elements in the American musical theater. Deadline: September 15. Guidelines for SASE. Prize: $25,000. The lyricist or composer should have a work produced in the US in either a commercial theater, professional not-for-profit theater or an accredited university or college theater program.

GILMORE CREEK PLAYWRITING COMPETITION, Saint Mary's University of Minnesota, Campus Box 78, 700 Terrace Heights, Winona MN 55987-1399. (507)457-1752. Fax: (507)457-1633. Contest Director: Robert R. Pevitts. Offered every 2 years for unpublished work providing an opportunity for new works to be produced. Accept full-length plays, translations, adaptations, musicals, children's plays. Prize: $2,500 and production, plus residency fee for author.

‡**GREAT PLATTE RIVER PLAYWRIGHTS FESTIVAL**, University of Nebraska at Kearney, Theatre Department, 905 W. 25th St., Kearney NE 68849. (308)865-8406. Fax: (308)865-8157. E-mail: garrisonj@pla tte.unk.edu. Contact: Jack Garrison. Estab. 1988. Unpublished submissions. "Purpose of award is to develop original dramas and encourage playwrights to work in regional settings. There are five catagories: 1) Adult; 2) Youth (Adolescent); 3) Children's; 4) Musical Theater; 5) Native American. Entries may be drama or comedy." Deadline: March 15. Awards: 1st-$500; 2nd-$300; 3rd-$200; plus free lodging and a travel stipend. "The Festival reserves the rights to development and premiere production of the winning plays without payment of royalties." Contest open to entry by any writer "provided that the writer submits playscripts to be performed on stage—works in progress also acceptable. Works involving the Great Plains will be most favored. More than one entry may be submitted." SASE required for return of scripts. Selection announcement by May 15 only to writers who provide prepaid postcard or SASE.

‡**PAUL GREEN PLAYWRIGHTS PRIZE**, North Carolina Writers' Network, P.O. Box 954, Carrboro NC 27510. Fax: (919)929-0535. Contact: Director. Offered annually for unpublished submissions to honor a playwright, held in recognition of Paul Green, North Carolina's dramatist laureate and Pulitzer Prize-winning playwright. Deadline: September 30. Guidelines for SASE. Charges $10 ($7.50 for NCWN members). Prize: $500 and potential production of play. Open to any writer.

HENRICO THEATRE COMPANY ONE-ACT PLAYWRITING COMPETITION, Henrico Recreation & Parks, P.O. Box 27032, Richmond VA 23273. (804)672-5115. Fax: (804)672-5284. Contest/Award Director: J. Larkin Brown. Offered annually for previously unpublished plays or musicals to produce new dramatic works in 1-act form. Deadline: July 1. Guidelines for SASE. Prize: winner $250; runner-up $125; Winning entries may be produced; videotape sent to author. "Scripts with small casts and simpler sets given preference. Controversial themes should be avoided."

HIGH SCHOOL PLAYWRITING CONTEST, Baker's Plays, 100 Chauncy St., Boston MA 02111-1783. Phone/fax: (617)482-1280. Contest Director: Raymond Pape. Offered annually for previously unpublished plays. "Open to any high school student. Plays must be accompanied by the signature of a sponsoring high school drama or English teacher, and it is recommended that the play receive a production or a public reading prior to the submission." Deadline: postmarked by January 31. Guidelines for #10 SASE. Prize: 1st-$500 and the play published by Baker's Plays; 2nd-$250 and Honorable Mention; 3rd-$100 and Honorable Mention. Write for more information.

JOSEPH E. HUSTON DISTINGUISHED PLAYWRIGHTS AWARD, TORCHLIGHT PLAYERS, 215 S. Walnut, Muncie IN 47305. (317)287-0941. E-mail: gothicpoet@iquest.net or torchlight@torchlight.com. Website: http://www.torchlight.com/~gothicpoet/tpl. Contact: Tim Kowalsky. Offered annually to assist new playwrights with their unpublished work. Deadline: October 15. Guidelines for SASE. Charges $10 entry fee. Prizes: 1st $100; 2nd $50; 3rd $25; plus production of 1st place winner. Acquires rights to produce one or all of the winning plays without royalty fees.

INTERNATIONAL ONE-PAGE PLAY COMPETITION, *Lamia Ink!*, P.O. Box 202, Prince St. Station, New York NY 10012. Contact: Cortland Jessup. Offered annually to encourage and promote performance writers and to challenge all interested writers. Interested in all forms of theater and performance writing in one page format. Deadline: March 15. No phone calls. Guidelines for SASE. Charges $1/one-page play. Maximum of 3 plays per author per competition. Prize: 1st-$200. Public reading given for top 12 in NYC. Publication in *Lamia Ink!*. If play has been previously published, playwright must have retained copyright. Prize: 1st-$200.

INTERNATIONAL PLAY CONTEST, Center Theater, 1346 W. Devon, Chicago IL 60660. (312)508-0200. Contact: Dale Calandra. Offered annually for unpublished work to foster and encourage the growth of playwrights. Deadline: end of May. Guidelines for SASE. Charges $15 fee. Prize: 1st-$300 cash award and production. "No unsolicited manuscripts. We will look at a one-page synopsis/character breakdown with a cover letter and résumé. Responses only to those inquiries that include a SASE."

JEWEL BOX THEATRE PLAYWRIGHTING COMPETITION, Jewel Box Theatre, 3700 N. Walker, Oklahoma City OK 73118-7099. (405)521-1786. Contact: Charles Tweed. Estab. 1982. Two- or three-acts accepted or one-acts comprising an evening of theater. Deadline: January 15. Send SASE in November for guidelines. Prize: $500.

GEORGE R. KERNODLE ONE-ACT PLAYWRITING COMPETITION, University of Arkansas, Department of Drama, 619 Kimpel Hall, Fayetteville AR 72701. (501)575-2953. Fax: (501)575-7602. Director: Kent R. Brown. Submissions to be unpublished and unproduced (workshop productions acceptable). Deadline: June 1. Charges $3 fee per submission. Submission limit: 3. Open to all playwrights residing in the United States and Canada.

MARC A. KLEIN PLAYWRITING AWARD FOR STUDENTS, Department of Theater Arts, Case Western Reserve University, 10900 Euclid Ave., Cleveland OH 44106-7077. (216)368-2858. Fax: (216)368-5184. E-mail: jmo3@po.cwru.edu. Chair, Reading Committee: John Orlock. Estab. 1975. Unpublished, professionally unproduced full-length play, or evening of related short plays by student in American college or university. Prize: $1,000, which includes $500 to cover residency expenses; production. Deadline: May 15.

LEE KORF PLAYWRITING AWARDS, The Original Theatre Works, Cerritos College, 11110 Alondra, Norwalk CA 90650. (310)860-2451, ext. 2638. Fax: (310)467-5005. Contact: Gloria Manriquez. Estab. 1984. Previously unproduced plays. "All plays—special attention paid to plays with multicultural theme." Deadline: September 1. Send for application and guidelines. Prize: ranges from $250 for workshop production to $750 royalty award and full-scale production during summer theater.

TARGET THE MARKETS.

Order Form

☐ YES! Start my subscription to *Writer's Digest*, the magazine thousands of successful writers rely on to hit their target markets. I pay just $19.97 for 12 monthly issues...a savings of more than $15 off the newsstand price.

☐ I'm enclosing payment (or paying by credit card). Add an extra issue to my subscription FREE — 13 in all!

Charge my ☐ Visa ☐ MC

Exp. _____

Signature _____

☐ I prefer to be billed later for 12 issues.

NAME _____

ADDRESS _____

CITY_____ STATE _____ ZIP _____

Outside U.S. add $10 (includes GST in Canada) and remit in U.S. funds.
Annual newsstand rate $35.88. Allow 4-6 weeks for first issue delivery.

Writer's®
DIGEST
YOUR MONTHLY GUIDE TO GETTING PUBLISHED

SAVE MORE THAN $15!

TTWM7-WD

KUMU KAHUA/UHM THEATRE DEPARTMENT PLAYWRITING CONTEST, Kumu Kahua Theatre Inc./University of Hawaii at Manoa, Department of Theatre and Dance, 1770 East-West Rd., Honolulu HI 96822. (808)956-2588. Fax: (808)956-4234. Contact: Dennis Carroll. Offered annually for unpublished work to honor full-length and short plays, both about Hawaii (for international or local writers) or about other locations/themes (local residents only). Deadline: January 1. Guidelines available every September. Prize: $500, $250, Division I, full-length and short; $200, $100 Division II full-length and short.

L.A. DESIGNERS' THEATRE-COMMISSIONS, L.A. Designers' Theatre, P.O. Box 1883, Studio City CA 91614-0883. (213)650-9600. Fax: (818)985-9200. (818)769-9000 T.D.D. E-mail: ladesigners@mcimail.c om. Contact: Richard Niederberg. Quarterly contest "to promote new work and push it onto the conveyor belt to filmed or videotaped entertainment." All submissions must be registered with copyright office and be unpublished by "major" publishers. Material will *not* be returned. Deadline: February 15, May 15, August 15, November 15. "No rules, no fees, no entry forms. Just present an idea that can be commissioned into a full work." Prize: A production or publication of the work in the Los Angeles market. "We only want 'first refusal.' If you are picked, we negotiate royalties with the writer." Open to any writer.

LIVE OAK THEATRE'S BEST NEW AMERICAN PLAY AWARD, Live Oak Theatre, 200 Colorado St., Austin TX 78701-3923. (512)472-5143. Fax: (512)472-7199. Contact: Michael Hankin. Annual award for previously unpublished, unproduced, full-length plays. Deadline: April 1. Guidelines for SASE. Prize: $1,000, staged reading and possible production. Plays must not have had a professional (Equity) production and must be unencumbered upon submission.

LIVE OAK THEATRE'S LARRY L. KING OUTSTANDING TEXAS PLAYWRIGHT AWARD, Live Oak Theatre, 200 Colorado St., Austin TX 78701. (512)472-5143. Fax: (512)472-7199. Contact: Michael Hankin. Offered annually for unpublished work by Texas playwrights. Deadline: April 1. Guidelines for SASE. Prize: $500 and a staged reading. Production possible. Open to Texas residents. Plays must not have had a professional (Equity) production and must be unencumbered upon submission.

‡LOFT FEST—FESTIVAL OF SHORTS, The Loft Production Company, 1441 E. Fletcher Ave., #413, Tampa FL 33612. (813)972-1200. Fax: (813)977-8485. Contact: Mr. Kelly Smith. Offered annually for unpublished submissions. Six-week festival of theater. Accepting 10-minute plays, one-acts, alternative theater pieces (monologues, performance art pieces, etc.) All with simple to no set and small casts. Deadline: March 31. Send brief synopsis, character breakdown, set requirements and manuscripts. If to be returned, send SASE. Award: Production of play and possible honorarium. Open to any writer.

LOVE CREEK ANNUAL SHORT PLAY FESTIVAL, Love Creek Productions, % Granville, 79 Liberty Place, Weehawken NJ 07087-7014. Festival Manager: Cynthia Granville-Callahan. Estab. 1985. Annual festival for unpublished plays, unproduced in New York in the previous year. "We established the Festival as a playwriting competition in which scripts are judged on their merits in performance." Deadline: September 30. Guidelines for #10 SASE. All entries must specify "festival" on envelope and must include letter giving permission to produce script, if chosen and stating whether equity showcase is acceptable. Cash price awarded to winner.
  ● Love Creek is now able to produce more small cast full-length plays if they require simple sets and run under 100 minutes. Larger cast full-length are still preferred. These are not part of festival competitions.

LOVE CREEK MINI FESTIVALS, Love Creek Productions, % Granville, 79 Liberty Place, Weehawken NJ 07087-7014. Festival Literary Manager: Cynthia Granville-Callahan. "The Mini Festivals are an outgrowth of our annual Short Play Festival in which we produce scripts concerning a particular issue or theme which our artistic staff selects according to current needs, interests and concerns of our members, audiences and playwrights submitting to our Short Play Festival throughout the year." Guidelines for #10 SASE. Submissions must list name of festival on envelope and must include letter giving permission to produce script, if chosen, and stating whether equity showcase is acceptable. Finalists receive a mini-showcase production in New York City. Winner receives a cash prize. Write for upcoming themes, deadlines usually end of March, May, July, October. Fear of God: Religion in the 90s, Women Now will be presented again in 1997 along with others TBA.

McLAREN MEMORIAL COMEDY PLAYWRITING COMPETITION, Midland Community Theatre, 2000 W. Wadley, Midland TX 79705. (915)682-2544. Fax: (915)682-6136. Contact: Mary Lou Cassidy. Estab. 1990. Offered annually for unpublished work. "Entry must be a comedy. Can be one- or two-act. Number of characters or subject is not limited. Make us laugh." Deadline: January 31. Charges $5 fee. Guidelines and form for #10 SASE. Prize: $400, Reader's Theatre Performance, airfare and hotel for 1 week rehearsal and performance.

MAXIM MAZUMDAR NEW PLAY COMPETITION, Alleyway Theatre, One Curtain Up Alley, Buffalo NY 14202-1911. (716)852-2600. Dramaturg: Joyce Stilson. Estab. 1990. Annual competition. Full

Length: not less than 90 minutes, no more than 10 performers. One-Act: less than 60 minutes, no more than 6 performers. Deadline: July 1. Finalists announced January 1. "Playwrights may submit work directly. There is no entry form. Annual playwright's fee $5; may submit one in each category, but pay only one fee. Please specify if submission is to be included in competition." Prize: full length—$400, travel plus lodging, production and royalties; one-act—$100, production plus royalties. "Alleyway Theatre must receive first production credit in subsequent printings and productions."

‡**MIDWESTERN PLAYWRIGHTS FESTIVAL**, University of Toledo and Toledo Rep Theatre, University of Toledo, Toledo OH 43606. (419)530-2202. Fax: (419)530-8439. Contact: John S. Kuhn. Offered annually for unpublished submissions to celebrate regional theater. Deadline: June 1. Guidelines for SASE. Prize: The winning playwright will receive $1,000, a staged reading and full production of the winning play in the Spring at the Toledo Repertoire Theatre. A stipend will also be provided for travel, room and board for the readings and for a two-week residency during production. Two other finalists will receive $350 and $150 and staged readings. Judged by members from both sponsoring organizations. Playwright must be an Ohio, Michigan, Illinois or Indiana resident. Submission must be an unpublished, full-length, two-act play, not produced professionally. Cast limit of ten, prefer one set play which is commercially producible.

MILL MOUNTAIN THEATRE NEW PLAY COMPETITION, Mill Mountain Theatre, Center in the Square, 1 Market Square, 2nd Floor, Roanoke VA 24011-1437. (703)342-5730. Fax: (540)342-5745. Literary Manager: Jo Weinstein. Estab. 1985. Previously unpublished and unproduced plays for up to 10 cast members. Deadline: January 1. Guidelines for SASE.

MIXED BLOOD VERSUS AMERICA, Mixed Blood Theatre Company, 1501 S. Fourth St., Minneapolis MN 55454. (612)338-0984. Contact: David B. Kunz. Estab. 1983. Theater company estab. 1975. "Mixed Blood Versus America encourages and seeks out the emerging playwright. Mixed Blood is not necessarily looking for scripts that have multi-racial casts, rather good scripts that will be cast with the best actors available." Open to all playwrights who have had at least one of their works produced or workshopped (either professionally or educationally). Only unpublished, unproduced plays are eligible for contest. Limit 2 submissions per playwright. No translations or adaptations. Guidelines for SASE. Deadline: March 15.

MRTW ANNUAL RADIO SCRIPT CONTEST, Midwest Radio Theatre Workshop, 915 E. Broadway, Columbia MO 65201. (314)874-5676. Contact: Steve Donofrio. Estab. 1979. "To encourage the writing of radio scripts and showcase both established and emerging radio playwrights. Some winning works are produced for radio and all winning works are published in the annual MRTW Scriptbook, the only one of its kind in this country." Deadline: November 15. Guidelines for SASE. "A cash award of $800 is split among the top 2-4 entries, depending on recommendation of the jurors. Winners receive free workshop registration. Those who receive honorable mention, as well as award-winning plays, are included in the scriptbook; a total of 10-16 are published annually. We acquire the right to publish the script in the scriptbook, which is distributed at cost, and the right to produce the script for air; all other rights retained by the author."

NATIONAL CANADIAN ONE-ACT PLAYWRITING COMPETITION, Ottawa Little Theatre, 400 King Edward Ave., Ottawa, Ontario K1N 7M7 Canada. (613)233-8948. Fax: (613)233-8027. Director: George Stonyk. Estab. 1913. "To encourage literary and dramatic talent in Canada." Submit January-May. Guidelines for #10 SASE with Canadian postage or #10 SAE with 1 IRC. Prize: $1,000, $700, $500.

NATIONAL ONE-ACT PLAYWRITING COMPETITION, Little Theatre of Alexandria, 600 Wolfe St., Alexandria VA 22314. (703)683-5778. Contact: Chairman Playwriting Competition. Estab. 1978. To encourage original writing for theatre. Submissions must be original, unpublished, unproduced one-act stage plays. Deadline: February 28. Guidelines for SASE. Submit scripts after October 1. Charges $5 fee. Prize: 1st-$350; 2nd-$250; 3rd-$150.

NATIONAL PLAYWRIGHTS' AWARD, Unicorn Theatre, 3820 Main St., Kansas City MO 64111. (816)531-7529. Contact: Herman Wilson, literary assistant. Offered annually for previously unproduced work. "We produce contemporary original scripts, preferring scripts that deal with social concerns. However, we accept (and have produced) comedies." Guidelines for SASE. Prize: $1,000 in royalty/prize fee and mainstage production at the Unicorn as part of its regular season.

NATIONAL TEN-MINUTE PLAY CONTEST, Actors Theatre of Louisville, 316 W. Main St., Louisville KY 40202-4218. (502)584-1265. Fax: (502)561-3300. Literary Manager: Michael Bigelow Dixon. Estab. 1964. Previously unproduced (professionally) ten-minute plays (10 pages or less). "Entries must *not* have had an Equity or Equity-waiver production." Deadline: December 1. Prize: $1,000. Please write or call for submission guidelines.

‡**NATIONAL WRITERS WORKSHOP NATIONAL CONTEST**, National Writers Workshop, P.O. Box 69799, Los Angeles CA 90069. (213)933-9232. Fax: (213)933-7642. Founder/Director: Willard Rodgers.

Offered annually to discover, develop, and promote aspiring screenwriters across the United States. Submissions accepted year-round, but writers are urged to submit from September-December annually. Guidelines for SASE. Charges $25 fee; $65 for 2-page written critique. Prize: $500 for each winner, a public presentation of screenplay by professional actors before a panel of established motion picture professionals for feedback, and promotion to agents, producers, studios and directors.

NEW ENGLAND NEW PLAY COMPETITION AND SHOWCASE, The Vineyard Playhouse Co., Inc., Box 2452, Vineyard Haven MA 02568. (508)693-6450. Contact: Eileen Wilson. Offered annually for unpublished, unproduced full-length, non-musical works suitable for a cast of 10 or fewer. Deadline: June 30. Notification: September 10. Guidelines for SASE. Charges $5 fee. Prize: 4 finalists receive transportation to Martha's Vineyard from a New England location and up to 3 nights accommodation to attend staged reading and consideration for full stage production. Grand prize winner also receives $500. For New England residents or students attending a New England University only.

NEW PLAYS STAGED READING CONTEST, TADA! 120 W. 28th St., New York NY 10001, (212)627-1732. Fax: (212)243-6736. Contest Director: Janine Nina Trevens. Offered annually for unpublished and unproduced work to introduce the playwriting process to family audiences in a staged reading series featuring the winning entries. The cast must be predominantly children, the children are cast from the TADA! company and adult actors will be hired. The plays must be appropriate for children and teenage audiences. Deadline: February 1. Please send cover letter and play with SASE for return. If the play is a musical, include a tape of the music. No application form necessary. Prize: $100-500 and staged reading held in TADA!'s theater. Grand Prize is a workshopped production. Contest is open.

NEW PLAYWRIGHTS COMPETITION, The White-Willis Theatre, 5266 Gate Lake Road, Ft. Lauderdale FL 33319. (305)722-4371. Director: Ann White. Offered annually for previously unpublished full-length play scripts. Award: $500 and production by the White-Willis Theatre. Competition opens June 1. Deadline: September 15. There is a $10 reading fee.

‡NEW WOMEN PLAYWRIGHT'S FESTIVAL, Off Center Theater, P.O. Box 518, Tampa FL 33601. (813)222-1087. Fax: (813)222-1057. Contact: Karla Hartley. Offered annually for unpublished plays to encourage and produce female playwrights. Deadline: September. Charges $15 fee. Prize: 1st-$1,000 plus production; 2nd-$100 plus staged reading; 3rd-$50 plus choral reading. Judged by theatre staff. Open to women playwrights. Full-length comedies only.

‡"THE NEXT STAGE" NEW PLAY READING FESTIVAL, The Cleveland Play House, P.O. Box 1989, Cleveland OH 44106-0189. (216)795-7010. Fax: (216)795-7005. Contact: Literary Staff. Offered annually for unpublished/unproduced submissions. " 'The Next Stage' is our annual new play reading series. Up to six writers are brought to our theater for two weeks of rehearsal/development. The plays are then given public staged readings, and at least one is chosen for a full production in the upcoming season." Deadline: April 1-June 30. Send script directly during specified times. Prize: $1,000. Staged reading of play, travel and housing, consideration for full production. Writers sign a six-month option for production of script. Open to any writer.

DON AND GEE NICHOLL FELLOWSHIPS IN SCREENWRITING, Academy of Motion Picture Arts & Sciences, 8949 Wilshire Blvd., Beverly Hills CA 90211-1972. (310)247-3059. Website: http://www.oscars.org. Director: Greg Beal. Estab. 1985. Offered annually for unproduced screenplays to identify talented new screenwriters. Deadline: May 1. Charges $30 fee. Guidelines for SASE, available January 1-April 30. Prize: $25,000 fellowships (up to 5/year). Recipients announced late October. Open to writers who have not earned more than $1,000 writing for films or TV.

OFF-OFF-BROADWAY ORIGINAL SHORT PLAY FESTIVAL, 45 W. 25th St., New York NY 10010. Fax: (212)206-1429. Contact: William Talbot. Offered annually for unpublished work. "The Festival was developed in 1976 to bolster those theater companies and schools offering workshops, programs and instruction in playwriting. It proposes to encourage them by offering them and their playwrights the opportunity of having their plays seen by new audiences and critics, and of having them reviewed for publication." Deadline: late winter. Guidelines for SASE. Prize: "Presentation on NY stage before NY audiences and critics. Publication of selected plays by Samuel French Inc." "No individual writer may enter on his/her own initiative. Entries must come from theater companies, professional schools or colleges which foster playwriting by conducting classes, workshops or similar programs of assistance to playwrights."

OGLEBAY INSTITUTE TOWNGATE THEATRE PLAYWRITING CONTEST, Oglebay Institute, Stifel Fine Arts Center, 1330 National Rd., Wheeling WV 26003. (304)242-7700. Fax: (304)242-7700. Director, Performing Arts Dept. Estab. 1976. Offered annually for unpublished works. Deadline: January 1. Guidelines for SASE. Prize: $300, limited-run production of play. "All full-length *non-musical* plays that have never been professionally produced or published are eligible." Winner announced May 31.

OPUS MAGNUM DISCOVERY AWARD, Christopher Columbus Society, 433 N. Camden Dr., #600, Beverly Hills CA 90210. (310)288-1881. Fax: (310)288-0257. Contact: Carlos de Abreu. Annual award to discover new authors with books/manuscripts that can be optioned for features or TV movies. Deadline: December 1. Guidelines for SASE. Charges $75 fee. Prize: Option moneys to winner, up to $10,000. Judged by entertainment industry story analysts and producers.

MILDRED & ALBERT PANOWSKI PLAYWRITING AWARD, Forest A. Roberts Theatre, Northern Michigan University, Marquette MI 49855-5364. (906)227-2553. Fax: (906)227-2567. Award Director: Dr. James A. Panowski. Estab. 1978. Unpublished, unproduced, full-length plays. Scripts must be *received* on or before November 15. Guidelines and application for SASE.

ROBERT J. PICKERING AWARD FOR PLAYWRIGHTING EXCELLENCE, Coldwater Community Theater, % 89 Division, Coldwater MI 49036. (517)279-7963. Committee Chairperson: J. Richard Colbeck. Estab. 1982. Previously unproduced monetarily. "To encourage playwrights to submit their work, to present a previously unproduced play in full production." Deadline: end of year. Guidelines for SASE. Submit script with SASE. Prize: 1st-$200, 2nd-$100, 3rd-$50. "We reserve right to produce winning script."

‡**PILGRIM PROJECT GRANTS**, 156 Fifth, #400, New York NY 10010. (212)627-2288. Fax: (212)627-2184. Contact: Davida Goldman. Grants for a reading, workshop production or full production of plays that deal with questions of moral significance. Deadline: ongoing. Guidelines for SASE. Grants: $1,000-7,000.

‡**PLAYHOUSE ON THE SQUARE NEW PLAY COMPETITION**, Playhouse on the Square, 51 S. Cooper, Memphis TN 38104. Contact: Jackie Nichols. Submissions required to be unproduced. Deadline: April 1. Guidelines for SASE. Prize: $500 plus production.

‡**THE PLAYWORKS FESTIVAL**, University of Texas at El Paso, Theatre Arts Department, 500 W. University, El Paso TX 79968-0549. (915)747-5146. Fax: (915)747-5438. E-mail: mwright@utep.edu. Director: Michael Wright. Offered annually for 3 residencies in the program. Each writer-in-residence is expected to develop a new play during the 3-week residency through daily workshops. "We are especially interested in students of Hispanic-American or Native American origin." Deadline: January 31. Guidelines for SASE. Prize: "We pay travel and an honorarium, and provide housing." Open to undergraduate or graduate students in schools in the Southwest states from: AZ, NV, NM, TX, OK, LA, AR.

‡**PLAYWRIGHTS' CENTER JEROME PLAYWRIGHT-IN-RESIDENCE FELLOWSHIP**, The Playwrights' Center, 2301 Franklin Ave. E, Minneapolis MN 55406. (612)332-7481. Estab. 1976. To provide emerging playwrights with funds and services to aid them in the development of their craft. Deadline: September 16. Open to playwrights only—may not have had more than 2 different fully staged productions of their works by professional theaters. Must spend fellowship year in Minnesota at Playwrights' Center.

‡**PLAYWRIGHTS' CENTER McKNIGHT FELLOWSHIP**, The Playwrights' Center, 2301 Franklin Ave. E, Minneapolis MN 55406. (612)332-7481. Estab. 1982. Recognition of playwrights whose work has made a significant impact on the contemporary theater. Deadline: January 16. Open to playwrights only. Must have had a minimum of two different fully staged productions by professional theaters. Must spend 1 month at Playwrights' Center. U.S. citizens or permanent residents only.

‡**THE PLAYWRIGHTS' CENTER PLAYLABS**, The Playwrights' Center, 2301 Franklin Ave. E, Minneapolis MN 55406. (612)332-7481. Assists in the development of unproduced or unpublished new plays. Deadline: December 16. US citizen/resident playwrights only; and must be available for entire pre-conference and conference.

PLAYWRIGHTS' THEATER OF DENTON NEW PLAY COMPETITION, Playwrights' Theater of Denton, P.O. Box 732, Denton TX 76202-0732. Contact: Mark Pearce. Offered annually for stage plays of any length. Deadline: December 15. Guidelines for SASE. Charges $15 fee, payable to Sigma Corporation. Prize: $1,000, possible production. Open to any writer.

‡**PRINCESS GRACE AWARDS PLAYWRIGHT FELLOWSHIP**, Princess Grace Foundation—USA, 725 Park Avenue, New York NY 10021. (212)744-3221. Fax: (212)628-2566. Contact: Jennifer B. Reis. Offered annually for unpublished submissions to support playwright through residency program with New Dramatists, Inc. located in New York City. A ten-week residence. Deadline: March 31. Guidelines for SASE. Award: $7,500 plus ten-week residency with New Dramatists, Inc. in New York City. Foundation looks to support aspiring young artist in America. Must be a US citizen or have US status. Under ordinary circumstances the candidate should be no more than 30 years of age at time of application.

‡**GWEN PHARIS RINGWOOD AWARD FOR DRAMA**, Writers Guild of Alberta, 11759 Great Rd., Edmonton, Alberta T5M 3K6 Canada. (403)422-8174. Fax: (403)422-2663. Contact: Darlene Diver. Drama

book published in current year or script of play produced three times in current year in a community theater. Must be an Alberta playwright. Eligible plays must be registered with the WGA-APN Drama Award Production Registry. Contact either the WGA head office, or the Alberta Playwrights' Network for registry forms.

RIVERFRONT PLAYHOUSE SCRIPTWRITING COMPETITION, Riverfront Playhouse, P.O. Box 105, Palo Cedro CA 96073; Playhouse: 1620 E. Cypress, Redding, CA 96002. (916)547-4801. Contest Director: Paul Robeson. "Offered annually for unpublished scripts to broaden the appreciation, awareness, and understanding of live theater by providing the environment for local talent to act, direct and creatively express themselves in the arts of the stage.The competition is designed to encourage and stimulate artistic growth among community playwrights. It provides playwrights the unique opportunity to mount and produce an original work at the *Riverfront Playhouse*." Deadline: December 2. Guidelines for SASE. Charges $25 fee. Prize: a reading, workshop and/or a full production of the winning entry. Cash prizes, as determined by the Board of Directors of the *Riverfront Playhouse*.

‡ROCHESTER PLAYWRIGHT FESTIVAL, Midwest Theatre Network, 5031 Tongen Ave. NW, Rochester MN 55901. (507)281-1472. Executive Director: Joan Sween. Offered for unpublished submissions to support emerging playwrights. No categories, but entries are considered for production by various types of theaters: community theater, dinner theater, issues theater, satiric/new format theater, children's theater, musical theater. Entry form required. Guidelines and entry form for SASE. No fee for first entry. Subsequent entries by same author $5 fee. Prize: full production, travel stipend, accomodations, cash prize. Open to any writer.

‡RICHARD RODGERS AWARDS IN MUSICAL THEATER, American Academy of Arts and Letters, 633 W. 155th St., New York NY 10032-7599. (212)368-5900. Fax: (212)491-4615. Executive Director: Virginia Dajani. Offered annually to produce a work of musical theater in New York City. Deadline: November 1. SASE for guidelines. Prize: full production, studio production or staged reading of a musical theater piece by a nonprofit New York City theater.

THE LOIS AND RICHARD ROSENTHAL NEW PLAY PRIZE, Cincinnati Playhouse in the Park, Box 6537, Cincinnati OH 45206. (513)345-2242. Fax: (513)345-2254. E-mail: theater1@tso.cin.ix.net. Website: http://www.cincyplay.com. Contact: Madeleine Pabis, artistic associate. Unpublished full-length plays only. Complete scripts will not be accepted. Query first for guidelines. Scripts must not have received a full-scale professional production. Deadline: October 15-February 1.

‡SEARCH FOR WORLD PREMIERE, The Loft Production Company, 1441 E. Fletcher Ave., #413, Tampa FL 33612. (813)972-1200. Fax: (813)977-8485. Contact: Mr. Kelly Smith. Offered annually for unpublished full-length, original scripts for production. Simple to no sets, small casts. Accepting comedies, dramas, musicals and alternative theater pieces. Deadline: January 31. Submit only brief synopsis, character/set breakdown. No mss; will contact if interested. Award: 3-4 week production of play, $500-1,000 honorarium. Open to any writer.

‡REVA SHINER FULL-LENGTH PLAY CONTEST, Bloomington Playwrights Project, 308 S. Washington St., Bloomington IN 47401. (812)334-1188. Fax: (812)855-4704. E-mail: katfletc@indiana.edu. Contact: Literary Manager. Offered annually for unpublished, unproduced submissions. "The BPP is a script-developing organization. The winning playwright is expected to work with the director, in person or long-distance, in the development and production of the work." Scripts must be full-length (75-150 minutes), unpublished and unproduced. Deadline: January 15. Guidelines for SASE. Charges $5 fee. Prize/award: staged reading early in development process, $500, full production in following season. Open to anyone..

‡SIENA COLLEGE INTERNATIONAL PLAYWRIGHTS COMPETITION, Siena College Department of Creative Arts/Theatre Program, 515 Loudon Rd., Loudonville NY 12211-1462. (518)783-2381. Fax: (518)783-4293. Contact: Gary Maciag, director of theatre. Offered every 2 years for unpublished plays "to allow students to explore production collaboration with the playwright. In addition, it provides the playwright an important development opportunity. Plays should be previously unproduced, unpublished, full-length, non-musicals and free of copyright and royalty restrictions. Plays should require unit set or minimal changes and be suitable for a college-age cast of 3-10. There is a required 6-week residency." Deadline: June 30 even-numbered years. Guidelines for SASE. Guidelines are available after November 1 in odd-numbered years. Prize: $2,000 honorarium; up to $1,000 to cover expenses for required residency; full production of winning script. Winning playwright must agree that the Siena production will be the world premiere of the play. Open to any writer.

SOUTHEASTERN THEATRE CONFERENCE NEW PLAY PROJECT, Route 7, Box 793, Murray KY 42701-9061. (502)762-4636. Contact: James I. Schempp. Offered annually for the discovery, development and publicizing of worthy new unproduced plays and playwrights. Eligibility limited to members of 10 state SETC Region: AL, FL, GA, KY, MS, NC, SC, TN, VA, WV. Submit March 1-June 1. Bound full-length or related one acts under single cover (one submission only). Does not return scripts. Guidelines available upon request. Prize: $1,000, staged reading at SETC Convention, expenses paid trip to convention and preferred consideration for National Playwrights Conference.

‡SOUTHERN APPALACHIAN PLAYWRIGHTS' CONFERENCE, Southern Appalachian Repertory Theatre, P.O. Box 620, Mars Hill NC 28754. (704)689-1384. Fax: (704)689-1474. Director: Gaynelle M. Caldwell. Offered annually for unpublished, unproduced plays to promote the development of new plays. Deadline: September 1. Guidelines for SASE. Prize: 5 playwrights are invited for informal readings in April, room and board provided. All plays are considered for later production with honorarium provided for the playwright.

SOUTHERN PLAYWRIGHTS COMPETITION, Center for Southern Studies/Jacksonville State University, 700 Pelham Rd. N., Jacksonville AL 36265-9982. (205)782-5411. Fax: (205)782-5689. E-mail: swhitton@jsucc.jsu.edu. Contact: Steven J. Whitton. Estab. 1988. Offered annually. "The Center for Southern Studies seeks to identify and encourage the best of Southern Playwrighting." Deadline: February 15. Guidelines for SASE. Prize: $1,000 and a production of the play. Playwrights must be native to or resident of AL, AR, FL, GA, KY, LA, MS, NC, SC, TN, TX, VA or WV.

SOUTHWEST THEATRE ASSOCIATION NEW PLAY CONTEST, Southwest Theatre Association, School of Drama, University of Oklahoma, 563 Elm, Norman OK 73019. (405)325-4021. Fax: (405)325-0400. Contact: Ray Paolino. Annual contest for unpublished work to promote the writing and production of new plays in the Southwest region. Deadline: March 31. Guidelines for SASE. Charges $10. Prize: $200 honorarium, a staged reading at the annual SWTA convention, publication in *Theatre Southwest*. Judged by the New Plays Committee of the Southwest Theatre Association. Open to all writers. No musicals or children's plays. Letter of recommendation suggested.

‡STAGES, P.O. Box 214820, Dallas TX 75221. (214)630-7722. Fax: (214)630-4468. Contact: Marilyn Pyeatt. Offered annually for unpublished and unproduced submissions to encourage playwriting, develop new works and showcase talent. Deadline: March 15, 1997. Guidelines for SASE. Prize: $100 honorarium and production. Judged by a committee of play-readers. Finalists are selected for readings (public) and final decision is made by committee, Executive Director and directors. Open to any writer.

‡STANLEY DRAMA AWARD, Dept. of Humanities, Wagner College, Staten Island NY 10301. Offered for original full-length plays, musicals or one-act play sequences that have not been professionally produced or received trade book publication. Presented as a memorial to Alma Timolat Stanley (Mrs. Robert C. Stanley). Deadline: September 1. Guidelines for SASE. Award: $2,000. Stage plays only.

MARVIN TAYLOR PLAYWRITING AWARD, Sierra Repertory Theatre, P.O. Box 3030, Sonora CA 95370-3030. (209)532-3120. Producing Director: Dennis Jones. Estab. 1981. Full-length plays. Deadline: August 31.

THEATER AT LIME KILN REGIONAL PLAYWRITING CONTEST, Theater at Lime Kiln, 14 S. Randolph St., Lexington VA 24450. (540)463-7088. Fax: (540)463-1082. E-mail: linekiln@cfw.com. Contact: Eleanor Connor. Offered annually for unpublished work. "With this contest Lime Kiln seeks to encourage playwrights to create works about our region of the country. Material should be limited geographically to Appalachia (Virginia, Western North Carolina, West Virginia, Eastern Kentucky, Eastern Tennessee). Plays with music encouraged." Submit August 1-September 30. Guidelines for SASE. Prize: 1st-$1,000; 2nd-$500; possibility of staged reading. Open to all writers.

UNIVERSITY OF ALABAMA NEW PLAYWRIGHTS PROGRAM, P.O. Box 870239, Tuscaloosa AL 35487-0239. (205)348-9032. Fax: (205)348-9048. E-mail: pcastagn@woodsquad.as.ua.edu. Director/Dramaturg: Dr. Paul C. Castagno. Estab. 1982. Full-length plays for mainstage; experimental plays for B stage. Workshops and small musicals can be proposed. Queries responded to quickly. Stipends competitive with, or exceed, most contests. Development process includes readings, visitations, and possible complete productions with faculty director and dramaturg. Guidelines for SASE. Up to 6 months assessment time.

URBAN STAGES AWARD, Playwrights' Preview Productions, 17 E. 47th St., New York NY 10017. (212)289-2168. Fax: (212)380-1387. Contact: Pamela Faith Jackson. Audience development program of radio-style staged readings that tour the libraries throughout the boroughs of New York City. Ethnically diverse encouraged. Plays between 30-60 minutes. Cast maximum of 5 (doubling encouraged). Submissions must be unpublished and unproduced in New York City. Send script, letter of introduction, production or reading history, author's résumé and SASE. Submissions accepted February 1-June 15. Selections by September 15. Prize: $200; air fare for out-of-town playwrights.

VERMONT PLAYWRIGHT'S AWARD, The Valley Players, P.O. Box 441, Waitsfield VT 05673. Award Director: Jennifer Howard. Offered annually for unpublished nonmusical, full-length play suitable for product ion by a community theater group to encourage development of playwrights in Vermont, New Hampshire and Maine. Deadline: October 1. SASE. Prize: $1,000. Judged by resident professionals in theater, journalism, publishing or public relations or broadcasting. Must be a resident of VT, NH or ME.

‡VERY SPECIAL ARTS YOUNG PLAYWRIGHTS PROGRAM, Very Special Arts, Education Office, The John F. Kennedy Center for the Performing Arts, Washington DC 20566. (800)933-8721. Fax: (202)737-0725. Contact: National Programs, Young Playwrights Program. Annual contest for unpublished plays by students between the ages of 12 and 18 who may write a script that incorporates some aspect of disability. Deadline: mid-April. Write for guidelines. Selected play produced at The John F. Kennedy Center for the Performing Arts Theater Lab. "Very Special Arts retains the rights to make the script available to other organizations for educational purposes." Contestants must be 12-18 years of age.

THEODORE WARD PRIZE FOR PLAYWRITING, Columbia College Theater/Music Center, 72 E. 11th St., Chicago IL 60605-1996. Fax: (312)663-9591. E-mail: chuck.smith@mail.colum.edu. Contact: Chuck Smith. Estab. 1985. "To uncover and identify new unpublished African-American plays that are promising and produceable." Deadline: August 1. All rights for music or biographies must be secured prior to submission. All entrants must be of African-American descent and residing within the US. Only 1 complete script per playwright will be accepted.

WEST COAST ENSEMBLE FULL-PLAY COMPETITION, West Coast Ensemble, P.O. Box 38728, Los Angeles CA 90038. Artistic Director: Les Hanson. Estab. 1982. Unpublished (in Southern California) plays. No musicals or children's plays for full-play competition. No restrictions on subject matter. Deadline: December 31 for full-length plays.

‡JACKIE WHITE MEMORIAL NATIONAL CHILDREN'S PLAYWRITING CONTEST, Columbia Entertainment Co., 309 Parkade, Columbia MO 65202. (573)874-5628. Contest Director: Betsy Phillips. Offered annually for unpublished plays. "We are searching for good scripts suitable for audiences of all ages to be performed by the 35-40 students, grade 6-9, in our theater school." Deadline: June 1. Guidelines for SASE. Charges $10 entry fee. Prize: $250 and full production, plus travel expenses to come see production.

WICHITA STATE UNIVERSITY PLAYWRITING CONTEST, University Theatre, Wichita State University, Wichita KS 67260-0153. (316)689-3185. Fax: (316)689-3951. Contest Director: Professor Leroy Clark. Estab. 1974. Unpublished, unproduced full-length or 2-3 short plays of at least 90 minutes playing time. No musicals or children's plays. Deadline: February 15. Guidelines for SASE. Prize: production of winning play (ACTF) and expenses paid trip for playwright to see final rehearsals and/or performances. Contestants must be graduate or undergraduate students in a US college or university.

WOMEN'S PLAYWRITING FESTIVAL, Perishable Theatre, P.O. Box 23132, Providence RI 02903. (401)331-2695. Fax: (401)331-2867. Website: http://www.ids.net/~as220/perishable/home.html. Contact: Kathleen Jenkins. Offered annually for unpublished/unproduced one acts by women, 10-45 minutes in length, 2 submissions per author. Deadline: December 31. SASE for guidelines. Prize: 3 winners of $200 each.

Y.E.S. NEW PLAY FESTIVAL, Northern Kentucky University, 207FA, Department of Theatre, Highland Heights KY 41099-1007. (606)572-6303. Fax: (606)572-5566. E-mail: mking@nku.edu. Project Director: Michael King. Offered every 2 years for unproduced plays to encourage the development of playwrights and to bring previously unproduced works to the stage. Estab. 1981. Deadline: May 1-October 15 of even numbered years for scripts. Next festival is April 1997. Full-length plays, adaptations and musicals. Guidelines for SASE. No application fee. Prize: $400 and expense-paid visit to NKU to see play in production.

‡YOUNG PLAYWRIGHTS FESTIVAL, Young Playwrights Inc., Suite 906, 321 W. 44th St., New York NY 10036. (212)307-1140. Fax: (212)307-1454. Artistic Director: Sheri M. Goldhirsch. Offered annually. Only stage plays accepted for submission (no musicals, screenplays or adaptations). "Writers age 18 or younger are invited to send scripts for consideration in the annual Young Playwrights Festival. Winning plays will be performed in professional Off Broadway production." Deadline: October 15. Contest/award rules and entry forms available for SASE. Entrants must be 18 or younger as of the annual deadline.

JOURNALISM

AAAS SCIENCE JOURNALISM AWARDS, American Association for the Advancement of Science, 1333 H St. NW, Washington DC 20005. (202)326-6440. Fax: (202)789-0455. E-mail: rperkins@aaas.org. Website: http://cs-mac.aaas.org/aaas.html. Contact: Ellen Cooper. Offered annually for previously published work July 1, 1995-June 30, 1996 to reward excellence in reporting on science and its applications in daily newspapers with circulation over 100,000; newspapers with circulation under 100,000; general circulation magazines; radio; television." Deadline: August 1. Award: $2,500, plaque, trip to AAAS Annual Meeting. Sponsored by the Whitaker Foundation.

AMY WRITING AWARDS, The Amy Foundation, P.O. Box 16091, Lansing MI 48901. (517)323-6233. President: James Russell. Estab. 1985. Nonfiction articles containing scripture published in the secular media. Deadline: January 31, for those from previous calendar year. Prize: $10,000, $5,000, $4,000, $3,000, $2,000 and 10 prizes of $1,000.

‡ANNUAL COMMUNICATION CONTEST, National Federation of Press Women, 4510 W. 89th St., Suite 110, Prairie Village KS 66207-2282. (913)341-0165. Fax: (913)341-6912. E-mail: 71072.2356@compuserve.com. Executive Director: Priscilla Chausky. Offered annually for work published December 1-November 30 to improve professional skills by recognizing excellence in communicating. The "message"—how well it communicates, how it is directed to its target audience, how well it achieves its objectives—is the judging standard. Deadline: National entries due February 1 for books, March 1—all others. Affiliates set own fees; National fee is $10 per entry. Prize: $250 to sweepstakes winner; $150 first runner-up; $100 second runner up. Must be a member of NFPW and an affiliate (state) group.

‡THE WHITMAN BASSOW AWARD, Overseas Press Club of America and AT&T, 320 East 42 St., Mezzanine, New York NY 10017. (212)983-4655. Fax: (212)983-4692. Manager: Sonya Fry. Offered annually for previously published best reporting in any medium on international environmental issues. Deadline: January 31. Charges $100 fee. Prize: certificate and $1,000. Work must be published by US-based publications or broadcast.

‡THE ERIC AND AMY BURGER AWARD, Overseas Press Club of America, 320 East 42 St., Mezzanine, New York NY 10017. (212)983-4655. Fax: (212)983-4692. Offered annually for previously published best reporting in any medium dealing with human rights. Deadline: January 31. Charges $100 fee. Prize: certificate and $1,000. Work must be published by US-based publications or broadcast.

CANADIAN FOREST SERVICE-SAULT STE. MARIE JOURNALISM AWARD, (formerly Canadian Forest Service Ontario Journalism Award), Canadian Forest Service-Sault Ste. Marie/Natural Resources Canada, % CSWA, P.O. Box 75, Station A, Toronto, Ontario M5W 1A2 Canada. (416)928-9624. Fax: (416)960-0528. Contact: Andy F. Visser-deVries. Offered annually for work published January 1-December 31 of the previous year to recognize outstanding journalism that promotes public awareness of forests and issues surrounding forests in Ontario. Deadline: February 15. Guidelines for SASE. Prize: for 1 newspaper and for 1 magazine $750 and plaque each. Material becomes property of Canadian Forest Service. Does not return mss. Open to writers who have published in an Ontario publication.

RUSSELL L. CECIL ARTHRITIS MEDICAL JOURNALISM AWARDS, Arthritis Foundation, 1330 West Peachtree St. NW, Atlanta GA 30309-9901. (404)872-7100. Fax: (404)872-0457. E-mail: lnewbern@arthritis.org. Website: http://www.arthritis.org. Contact: Lisa M. Newbern. Estab. 1956. News stories, articles and radio/TV scripts on the subject of arthritis and the Arthritis Foundation published or broadcast for general circulation during the previous calendar year. Deadline: February 15.

HARRY CHAPIN MEDIA AWARDS, World Hunger Year, 505 Eighth Ave., 21st Floor, New York NY 10018-6582. (212)629-8850. Fax: (212)465-9274. E-mail: whyria@aol.com. Coordinator: Lucy Anderson. Estab. 1982. Critical issues of domestic and world hunger, poverty and development (newspaper, periodical, TV, radio, photojournalism, books). Prizes: $1,000-2,500. Deadline: February 15.

GREG CLARK OUTDOOR WRITING AWARD, Ontario Ministry of Natural Resources, % CSWA, P.O. Box 75, Station A, Toronto, Ontario M5W 1A2 Canada. (416)928-9624. Fax: (416)960-0528. Contact: Andy F. Visser-deVries. Offered annually for work published January 1-December 31 of the previous year to recognize outstanding journalism that increases public awareness of Ontario's natural resources. Deadline: February 15. Guidelines for SASE. Prize: $500 and plaque. Entries become property of Ontario Ministry of Natural Resources. Does not return mss. Open to writers who have published in an Ontario publication that is about natural resources of Ontario.

‡DART AWARD, Dart Foundation through Michigan State University's Victims and the Media Program, MSU School of Journalism, East Lansing MI 48824-1212. (511)432-2171. Fax: (517)355-7710. Coordinator: Bill Coté. Asst. Coord.: Bonnie Bucqueroux. Offered annually for previously published work to encourage treatment of victims and victim issues with compassion, dignity, and respect. Awarded for best newspaper feature on victim(s) of violence each year. Deadline: usually June. Guidelines for SASE. Prize: $10,000 to winning newspaper, shared with team. Open to daily and weekly newspapers.

FOURTH ESTATE AWARD, American Legion National Headquarters, 700 N. Pennsylvania, Indianapolis IN 46206. (317)630-1253. Fax: (317)630-1280. E-mail: tal@legion.org. Website: http://www.legion.org.

Contact: Lew Wood. Estab. 1919. Offered annually for excellence in journalism in a published or broadcast piece on an issue of national concern during the previous calendar year. Deadline: January 31.

THE GREAT AMERICAN TENNIS WRITING AWARDS, *Tennis Week*, 341 Madison Ave., New York NY 10017. (212)808-4750. Fax: (212)983-6302. Publisher: Eugene L. Scott. Estab. 1986. Category 1: unpublished ms by an aspiring journalist with no previous national byline. Category 2: unpublished ms by a non-tennis journalist. Category 3: unpublished ms by a tennis journalist. Categories 4-6: published tennis-related articles and one award to a book. Deadline: December 15.

‡**O. HENRY AWARD**, The Texas Institute of Letters, P.O. Box 298300, Fort Worth TX 76129. (817)921-7822. Fax: (817)921-7333. Director: Judy Alter. Offered annually for work published January 1-December 31 of previous year to recognize the best-written work of journalism appearing in a magazine or Sunday supplement. Deadline: January 2. Guidelines for SASE. Prize: $500. Judged by a panel chosen by the TIL Council. To be eligible, a writer must have been born in Texas, or have lived in the state for at least two consecutive years at some time, or the subject matter of the work should be associated with the state.

THE ROY W. HOWARD AWARDS, Scripps Howard Foundation, P.O. Box 5380, Cincinnati OH 45201-5380. (513)977-3035. Estab. 1972. Public service reporting by a daily newspaper in the US or its territories. Fact sheet available in fall of year.

INTERNATIONAL READING ASSOCIATION PRINT MEDIA AWARD, International Reading Association, P.O. Box 8139, Newark DE 19714-8139. (302)731-1600 ext. 215. Fax: (302)731-1057. Contact: Janet Butler. Estab. 1956. Recognizes outstanding reporting on reading and literacy by professional journalists. Deadline: January 15.

‡**ROBERT F. KENNEDY JOURNALISM AWARDS**, 1206 30th St., NW., Washington DC 20007. (202)333-1880. Fax: (202)333-4903. Director: Erin Scully Rush. Estab. 1968. Previously published entries on problems of the disadvantaged. Deadline: last Friday of January.

DONALD E. KEYHOE JOURNALISM AWARD, Fund for UFO Research, P.O. Box 277, Mt. Rainier MD 20712. (703)684-6032. Fax: (703)684-6032. Chairman: Richard Hall. Estab. 1979. Offered annually for the best article or story published or broadcast in a newspaper, magazine, TV or radio news outlet during the previous calendar year. Separate awards for print and broadcast media. Also makes unscheduled cash awards for published works on UFO phenomena research or public education.

LOUIS M. LYONS AWARD, Nieman Foundation at Harvard University, 1 Francis Ave., Cambridge MA 02138. (617)495-2237. Fax: (617)495-8976. Contact: Chair, Lyons Award Committee. "Annual award for previously published print or broadcast material." Previously published entries must have appeared in print January-December of the previous calendar year. "Nominees must be full-time print or broadcast journalists (domestic or foreign)." Deadline: February 1. "Nominations must be made by third parties, whether individuals or organizations. News organizations may nominate one of their own employees. Applications must contain the following: an official letter of nomination, one-page biography of the nominee, two letters of recommendation and three samples of the nominee's work. The Lyons Award carries a $1,000 honorarium."

THE EDWARD J. MEEMAN AWARDS, Scripps Howard Foundation, P.O. Box 5380, Cincinnati OH 45201-5380. (513)977-3035. Estab. 1967. Environmental reporting by a daily newspaper in the US or its territories. Fact sheet available in fall of the year.

MENCKEN AWARDS, Free Press Association, P.O. Box 63, Port Hadlock WA 98339. Fax: (360)384-3704. FPA Executive Director: Bill Bradford. Estab. 1981. Honoring defense of human rights and individual liberties, or exposés of governmental abuses of power. Categories: News Story or Investigative Report, Feature Story or Essay/Review, Editorial or Op-Ed Column, Editorial Cartoon and Book. Entries *must* have been published or broadcast during previous calendar year. Deadline: April 1 (for work from previous year). Guidelines and form for SASE. Charges $5 fee. Late deadline: June 1 with extra fee.

‡**FRANK LUTHER MOTT-KAPPA TAU ALPHA RESEARCH AWARD IN JOURNALISM**, University of Missouri, School of Journalism, Columbia MO 65211. (573)882-7685. Executive Director, Central Office: Dr. Keith Sanders. For "best researched book in journalism." Requires 6 copies. No forms required. Deadline: January 8. Award: $1,000.

NATIONAL AWARDS FOR EDUCATION REPORTING, Education Writers Association, 1331 H St. NW, #307, Washington DC 20005. (202)637-9700. Fax: (202)637-9707. Executive Director: Lisa Walker. Estab. 1960. Offered annually for submissions published during the previous year. Categories are: 1) newspapers under 100,000 circulation; 2) newspapers over 100,000 circulation; 3) magazines excluding trade and institutional journals that are circulated to the general public; 4) special interest, institutional and trade publications; 5) television; and 6) radio. Write for more information. Deadline: mid-January. Charges $35 fee.

ALICIA PATTERSON JOURNALISM FELLOWSHIP, Alicia Patterson Foundation, 1730 Pennsylvania Ave. NW, Suite 850, Washington DC 20006. (202)393-5995. Fax: (301)951-8512. E-mail: apfengel@charm.net. Website: http://www.charm.net/~apfengel/home.html. Contact: Margaret Engel. Offered annually for previously published submissions to give 5-7 print journalists a year of in-depth research and reporting. Applicants must have 5 years of professional print journalism experience and be US citizens. Fellows write 4 magazine-length pieces for the *Alicia Patterson Reporter*, a quarterly magazine, during their fellowship year. Fellows must take a year's leave from their jobs, but may do other freelance articles during the year. Deadline: October 1. Write, call or fax for applications. Prize: $30,000 stipend for calendar year.

‡**THE POPE AWARD FOR INVESTIGATIVE JOURNALISM**, The Pope Foundation, 211 W. 56 St., Suite 5H, New York NY 10019. Director: Catherine E. Pope. Offered annually to journalists who have been working for a minimum of 10 years. Deadline: November 15. Guidelines for SASE. Prize: 3 awards of $15,000 each.

‡**PRINT MEDIA AWARD**, International Reading Association, 800 Barksdale Rd., Newark DE 19714. (302)731-1600 ext. 293. Fax: (302)731-1057. Offered annually for previously published work between January 1 and December 31. Deadline: January 15. Guidelines for SASE. Prize: Announcement at annual convention, 1996. Limited to professional journalists.

ERNIE PYLE AWARD, Scripps Howard Foundation, P.O. Box 5380, Cincinnati OH 45201-5380. (513)977-3035. Estab. 1953. Human interest reporting by a newspaper man or woman for work published in a daily newspaper in the US or its territories. Fact sheet available in fall of the year.

‡**THE MADELINE DANE ROSS AWARD**, Overseas Press Club of America, 320 East 42 St., Mezzanine, New York NY 10017. (212)983-4655. Fax: (212)983-4692. Manager: Sonya Fry. Offered annually for previously published best foreign correspondent in any medium showing a concern for the human condition. Deadline: January 31. Charges $100 fee. Prize: certificate and $1,000. Work must be published by US-based publications or broadcast.

WILLIAM B. RUGGLES JOURNALISM SCHOLARSHIP, National Right to Work Committee, 8001 Braddock Rd., Suite 500, Springfield VA 22160-0999. (703)321-9820. Contact: Linda Staulcup. Estab. 1974. "To honor the late William B. Ruggles, editor emeritas of the Dallas Morning News, who coined the phrase 'Right to Work.' " Deadline: January 1-March 31. Prize: $2,000 scholarship. "We do reserve the right to reprint the material/excerpt from the essay in publicizing the award. Applicant must be a graduate or undergraduate student majoring in journalism in institutions of higher learning throughout the US."

THE CHARLES M. SCHULZ AWARD, Scripps Howard Foundation, P.O. Box 5380, Cincinnati OH 45201-5380. (513)977-3035. Estab. 1980. For a student cartoonist at a college newspaper or magazine. Fact sheet available in fall of the year.

SCIENCE IN SOCIETY JOURNALISM AWARDS, National Association of Science Writers, Box 294, Greenlawn NY 11740. (516)757-5664. Contact: Diane McGurgan. Newspaper, magazine and broadcast science writing. Deadline: (postmarked) July 1 for work published June 1-May 31 of previous year.

SCIENCE IN SOCIETY JOURNALISM AWARDS, Canadian Science Writers' Association, P.O. Box 75, Station A, Toronto, Ontario M5W 1A2 Canada. (416)960-9624. Fax: (416)928-0528. E-mail: cswa@interlog.com. Website: http://www.interlog.com/~cswa. Contact: Andy F. Visser-deVries. Offered annually for work published/aired January 1-December 31 of previous year to recognize outstanding contributions to science journalism in all media. Two newspaper, 2 magazine, 2 TV, 2 radio, 1 trade publication, 1 student science writing award. Deadline: January 31. Guidelines for SASE. Prize: $1,000 and a plaque. Material becomes property of CSWA. Does not return mss. Open to Canadian citizens or residents of Canada.

THE EDWARD WILLIS SCRIPPS AWARD, Scripps Howard Foundation, P.O. Box 5380, Cincinnati OH 45201-5380. (513)977-3035. Estab. 1976. Service to the First Amendment by a daily newspaper in the US or its territories. Fact sheet available in fall of the year.

‡**SPECIAL LIBRARIES ASSOCIATION MEDIA AWARD**, Special Libraries Association, 1700 18th St., NW, Washington DC 20009-2508. Fax: (202)265-9317. Director: Mark Serepca. Offered annually for previously published work between January 1 and December 31. Guidelines for SASE. Judged by SLA PR committee. Open to any writer.

I.F. STONE AWARD FOR STUDENT JOURNALISM, The Nation Institute, 72 Fifth Ave., New York NY 10011. (212)242-8400. Director: Peter Meyer. Offered annually to recognize excellence in student journalism. Open to undergraduate students in US colleges. Award: $1,000, plus publication. Deadline: June 30.

THE WALKER STONE AWARD, Scripps Howard Foundation, P.O. Box 5380, Cincinnati OH 45201-5380. (513)977-3035. Estab. 1973. Editorial writing by a newspaper man or woman published in a daily newspaper in the US or its territories. Fact sheet available in fall of the year.

‡STUDENT MAGAZINE CONTEST, Association for Education in Journalism and Mass Communication, 1621 College St., University of South Carolina, Columbia SC 29208-0251. (803)777-2005. Fax: (803)777-4728. Director: (1996) Carol Holstead. Offered annually for articles published or written between April 30 and April 30. Two categories: Consumer Magazine Article for nonfiction articles written for a general or special interest magazine available to the public either through newsstand sales or subscription; Trade Magazine Article (graduate category and undergraduate category) is for nonfiction articles written for a specialized business magazine covering a specific industry or occupation. "Emphasis is on useful information readers need to get ahead professionally and make their business successful; articles may also focus on trends or projections in a certain industry or profile an industry leader. For each entry: Form (1 per entry) signed by a faculty member attesting to the accuracy of the information provided; Target magazine written in the appropriate place on the entry form; Correct category checked on the entry form; (2) copies of the article manuscript or tearsheet with the author's name and school eliminated; (2) blind title pages that include article title, category and target magazine. Entries are not returned. Deadline: May 1. Guidelines for SASE. Charges $5 fee. Prize: $100. This is a contest for students in journalism and English programs. Entrants must be sponsored by a faculty member and work must be produced in a class. In other words, a student working on an internship can't enter work produced on the job."

‡LOWELL THOMAS TRAVEL JOURNALISM COMPETITION, Society of American Travel Writers Foundation, 4101 Lake Boone Trail, Suite 201, Raleigh NC 27607-6518. (919)787-5181. Award Director: Abe Peck. Offered annually for work published in last few years to recognize, encourage excellence in travel journalism. 21 categories. Deadline: January 31. Guidelines for SASE. Charges from $15 for writing and photos to $50 for newspaper, magazine travel sections, books, CD-ROM, film. Prize: $1,000 grand award, $500 for first place in most categories plus plaques, printed certificates for runners-up. All work published or broadcast in English by North American journalists. Membership in Society of American Travel Writers is not necessary.

‡STANLEY WALKER JOURNALISM AWARD, The Texas Institute of Letters, P.O. Box 298300, Fort Worth TX 76129. (817)921-7822. Fax: (817)921-7333. Director: Judy Alter. Offered annually for work published January 1-December 31 of previous year to recognize the best writing appearing in a daily newspaper. Guidelines for SASE. Prize: $500. Writer must have been born in Texas, or must have lived in the state for 2 consecutive years at some time, or the subject matter of the article must be associated with the state.

WRITING FOR CHILDREN AND YOUNG ADULTS

AMERICAN ASSOCIATION OF UNIVERSITY WOMEN AWARD, NORTH CAROLINA DIVISION, North Carolina Literary and Historical Association, 109 E. Jones St., Raleigh NC 27601-2807. (919)733-7305. Awards Coordinator: Barbara Mann. Previously published juvenile literature by a North Carolina resident. Deadline: July 15.

‡R. ROSS ANNETT AWARD FOR CHILDREN'S LITERATURE, Writers Guild of Alberta, 11759 Groat Rd., Edmonton, Alberta T5M 3K6 Canada. (403)422-8174. Fax: (403)422-2663. Director: Darlene Diver. Children's book published in current year. Must be an Alberta author.

IRMA S. AND JAMES H. BLACK AWARD, Bank Street College of Education, 610 W. 112th St., New York NY 10025. (212)875-4452. Fax: (212)875-4759. E-mail: lindag@bnk1.bnkst.edu. Website: http://www.bnkst.edu. Award Director: Linda Greengrass. Estab. 1972. Offered annually for a book for young children for excellence of both text and illustrations. Entries must have been published during the previous calendar year. Deadline for entries: January after book is published.

‡BOOK PUBLISHERS OF TEXAS AWARD FOR CHILDREN'S OR YOUNG PEOPLE'S BOOK, The Texas Institute of Letters, P.O. Box 298300 Fort Worth TX 76129. (817)921-7822. Fax: (817)921-7333. Director: Judy Alter. Offered annually for work published January 1- December 31 of previous year to recognize the best book for children or young people. Deadline: January 2. Guidelines for SASE.

Prize: $250. Writer must have been born in Texas or have lived in the state for at least 2 consecutive years at 1 time, or the subject matter is associated with the state.

BOSTON GLOBE-HORN BOOK AWARD, *The Boston Globe*, 135 Morrissey Blvd, P.O. Box 2378, Boston MA 02107. Offered annually for previously published work in children's literature. Awards for original fiction or poetry, picture book, and nonfiction. Publisher submits entry. Prize: $500 in each category.

CHILDREN'S WRITER WRITING CONTESTS, *Children's Writer* Newsletter, 95 Long Ridge Rd., West Redding CT 06896. (203)792-8600. Fax: (203)792-8406. Publisher: Prescott Kelly. Offered 3 times/ year to promote higher quality children's literature. "Each contest has its own theme. Our last 3 were (1) An animal story for ages 4-6; to 500 words. (2) A history article for ages 8-12; to 750 words. (3) A humor story for ages 8-12; to 900 words." Submissions must be unpublished. Deadline: Last Friday in February, June and October. Guidelines for SASE; put "Contest Request" in lower left of envelope. Charges $10 fee for nonsubscribers only, which is applicable against a subscription to *Children's Writer*. Prize: 1st—$100 or $1,000, a certificate and publication in *Children's Writer*; 2nd—$50 or $500, and certificate; 3rd-5th—$25 or $250 and certificates. One or two contests each year with the higher cash prizes also include $100 prizes plus certificates for 6th-12th places. Acquires first North American serial rights for grand prize winners only.

MARGUERITE DE ANGELI PRIZE, Bantam Doubleday Dell Books for Young Readers, 1540 Broadway, New York NY 10036. (212)354-6500. Fax: (212)782-9698. Offered annually for unpublished fiction manuscript suitable for readers 7-10 years of age that concerns the diversity of the American experience, either contemporary or historical. Deadline: manuscripts must be postmarked after April 1, but no later than June 30. Send manuscripts to Marguerite de Angeli Contest Bantam Doubleday Dell. Guidelines for SASE. Prize includes a book contract with a cash advance. Judged by editors at Bantam Doubleday Dell.

‡DELACORTE PRESS PRIZE FOR A FIRST YOUNG ADULT NOVEL, Delacorte Press, 1540 Broadway, New York NY 10036. (212)354-6500. Estab. 1983. Previously unpublished young adult fiction. Submissions: October 1, 1996-December 31, 1996. Guidelines for SASE. Prize: $1,500 cash, publication and $6,000 advance against royalties. Judged by editors of Delacorte.

JOAN FASSLER MEMORIAL BOOK AWARD, Association for the Care of Children's Health (ACCH), 7910 Woodmont Ave., #300, Bethesda MD 20814. (301)654-6549. Fax: (301)986-4553. Contact: Trish McClean, membership manager. Offered annually for work published in 1995 and 1996 to the author(s) of the trade book that makes the most distinguished contribution to a child's or young person's understanding of hospitalization, illness, disabling conditions, dying and death, and preventive care. Deadline: December 31. Send SASE for guidelines. Prize: $1,000 and a plaque.

HIGHLIGHTS FOR CHILDREN FICTION CONTEST, *Highlights for Children*, 803 Church St., Honesdale PA 18431-1824. Manuscript Coordinator: Beth Troop. Estab. 1946. Stories for children ages 2-12; category varies each year. Guidelines for SASE. Stories should be limited to 900 words for older readers, 500 words for younger readers. No crime or violence, please. Specify that ms is a contest entry. All entries must be postmarked January 1-February 28.

INTERNATIONAL READING ASSOCIATION CHILDREN'S BOOK AWARD, International Reading Association, P.O. Box 8139, 800 Barksdale Rd., Newark DE 19714-8139. (302)731-1600 ext. 221. Fax: (302)731-1057. E-mail: 75141.2005@compuserve.com. First or second book by an author who shows unusual promise in the children's book field. Categories: younger readers, ages 4-10; older readers, ages 10-16+, and informational book (ages 4-16+). Deadline: December 1.

‡JUVENILE LITERATURE AWARDS, Friends of American Writers, 15237 W. Redwood Ln., Libertyville IL 60048. Chairman: Kay O'Connor. Offered annually for previously published work from previous year for fiction or nonfiction. Deadline: December 31. Prize: $800. It must be the first, second or third book published by the author in the young people's categories of preschool, elementary, intermediate, or secondary school readership. The author must be a native of, or a current resident of, or have lived for five years in, or the setting of the book must be in one of these states ... Arkansas, Illinois, Indiana, Iowa, Kansas, Michigan, Minnesota, Missouri, Nebraska, North Dakota, Ohio, South Dakota, or Wisconsin.

NATIONAL JEWISH BOOK AWARD—CHILDREN'S LITERATURE, Jewish Book Council, 15 E. 26th St., New York NY 10010. (212)532-4949. Director: Carolyn Starman Hessel. Children's book on Jewish theme. Deadline: Sept.

NATIONAL JEWISH BOOK AWARD—CHILDREN'S PICTURE BOOK, Marcia and Louis Posner Award, Jewish Book Council, 15 E. 26th St., New York NY 10010. (212)532-4949, ext. 297. Director: Carolyn Starman Hessel. Author and illustrator of a children's book on a Jewish theme. Deadline: Sept. 1.

SCOTT O'DELL AWARD FOR HISTORICAL FICTION, 1700 E. 56th St., #3906, Chicago IL 60637. (312)752-7880. Director: Zena Sutherland. Estab. 1981. Historical fiction book for children set in the Americas. Entries must have been published during previous year. Deadline: December 31.
• Theodore Taylor was the 1996 winner of this award for *The Bomb*, published by Harcourt.

PEN/NORMA KLEIN AWARD, PEN American Center, 568 Broadway, New York NY 10012. (212)334-1660. Fax: (212)334-2181. E-mail: pen@echo.nyc.com. Contact: John Morrone. Offered in odd-numbered years to recognize an emerging voice of literary merit among American writers of children's fiction. *Candidates may not nominate themselves.* Next award is 1997. Deadline: December 15, 1996. Guidelines for #10 SASE. Award: $3,000.

‡PRIX ALVINE-BÉLISLE, Association pour L'avancement des sciences et des techniques de la documentation, ASTED Inc., 3414 av. Parc #202, Montreal, Quebec, Canada. (514)281-5012. Fax: (514)281-8219. E-mail: asted@ulix.net. Website: http://www.asted.org. Director: Vesna Dell'Olio. Offered annually for work published the year before the award to promote authors of French youth literature in Canada. Deadline: April 1. Prize: $500. "It is not the writers but the editors who send their books to us."

SILVER BAY AWARDS FOR CHILDREN'S LITERATURE, The Writer's Voice of the Silver Bay Association, Silver Bay NY 12874. (518)543-8833. Fax: (518)543-6733. Contact: Sharon Ofner. Offered annually for best unpublished children's ms set in the Adirondack Mountains, illustrated or non-illustrated. Deadline: February 1. Charges $25 fee. Prize: $1,000.

‡TEDDY AWARD FOR BEST CHILDREN'S BOOK, Austin Writers' League, 1501 West Fifth St., Suite E-2, Austin TX 78703. (512)499-8914. Fax: (512)499-0441. Director: Angela Smith. Offered annually for work published January 1-December 31 to honor an outstanding book for children published by a member of the Austin Writers' League. Deadline: January 31. Guidelines for SASE. Charges $10 fee. Prize: $1,000 prize and trophy. Entrants must be Austin Writers' League members. Dues may accompany entry fee.

‡TEXAS BLUEBONNET AWARD, Texas Library Association's Texas Association of School Librarians and Children's Round Table, Suite 401, 3355 Bee Cave Rd., Austin TX 78746. (512)328-1518. Fax: (512)328-8852. E-mail: crtba@tenet.edu. Website: http://www.txla.org. Contact: Patricia Smith. Published books for children recommended by librarians, teachers and students.

‡LAURA INGALLS WILDER MEDAL, American Library Association, 50 E. Huron St., Chicago IL 60611. (800)545-2433. Offered triennially to an author or illustrator whose works have made a lasting contribution to children's literature. Guidelines for SASE. Award: medal.

(ALICE WOOD MEMORIAL) OHIOANA FOR CHILDREN'S LITERATURE, Ohioana Library Association, 65 Front St., Suite 1105, Columbus OH 43215. (614)466-3831. Fax: (614)728-6974. E-mail: ohioana@winslo.ohio.gov. Contact: Linda R. Hengst. Offered "to an author whose body of work has made, and continues to make, a significant contribution to literature for children or young adults." Deadline: December 31. Nomination forms available for SASE. Recipient must have been born in Ohio or lived in Ohio at least 5 years.

WORK-IN-PROGRESS GRANT, Society of Children's Book Writers and Illustrators (SCBWI) and Judy Blume, 22736 Vanowen St., #106, West Hills CA 91307. Two grants—one designated specifically for a contemporary novel for young people—to assist SCBWI members in the completion of a specific project. Deadline: June 1. Guidelines for SASE.

TRANSLATION

AMERICAN TRANSLATORS ASSOCIATION HONORS AND AWARDS, American Translators Association, 1800 Diagonal Rd., Suite 220, Alexandria VA 22314. (703)683-6100. Fax: (703)683-6122. E-mail: 73564.2032@compuserve.com. Contact: Walter Bacak. Student award offered annually; other awards offered every 2 years. Categories: best student translation; best literary translation in German; and best literary translation in any language but German. Guidelines for SASE. Prize varies—usually $500-1,000 and a trip to annual conference.

‡SOEURETTE DIEHL FRASER TRANSLATION AWARD, The Texas Institute of Letters, P.O. Box 298300, Fort Worth TX 76129. (817)921-7822. Fax: (817)921-7333. Director: Judy Alter. Offered annually for work published January 1-December of previous year to recognize the best translation of a literary book into English. Deadline: January 2. Guidelines for SASE. Prize: $1,000. Translator must have been born in Texas or have lived in the state for at least 2 consecutive years at some time.

GERMAN PRIZE FOR LITERARY TRANSLATION, American Translators Association, 1800 Diagonal Rd., Suite 220, Alexandria VA 22314. Chair: Eric McMillen. Offered in odd-numbered years for previously published book translated from German to English. In even-numbered years, the Lewis Galentière Prize is awarded for translations other than German to English. Deadline April 15.

JOHN GLASSCO TRANSLATION PRIZE, Literary Translators' Association of Canada, Association des traducteurs et traductrices littéraires du Canada, 3492, av. Laval, Montreal, Quebec H2X 3C8 Canada. Estab. 1981. Offered annually for a translator's *first* book-length literary translation into French or English, published in Canada during the previous calendar year. The translator must be a Canadian citizen or landed immigrant. Eligible genres include fiction, creative nonfiction, poetry, published plays, children's books. Deadline: January 15. Write for application form. Award: $500.

‡JAPAN—U.S. FRIENDSHIP COMMISSION PRIZE FOR THE TRANSLATION OF JAPANESE LITERATURE, Donald Keene Center of Japanese Culture, 407 Kent Hall, New York NY 10027. (212)854-5036. Fax: (212)678-8629. Contact: Director of Donald Keene Center. Offered every two years. Previously published and unpublished book-length translations from Japanese by American translators in the categories of modern and classical Japanese. Deadline: January 31. Guidelines for SASE. Prize: $2,500 honorarium. Must be US citizen.

PEN/BOOK-OF-THE-MONTH CLUB TRANSLATION PRIZE, PEN American Center, 568 Broadway, New York NY 10012. (212)334-1660. Fax: (212)334-2181. E-mail: pen@echo.nyc.com. Contact: John Morrone. One award of $3,000 to a literary book-length translation into English published in the calendar year under consideration. (No technical, scientific or reference.) Deadline: December 15. Publishers, agents or translators may submit 3 copies of each eligible title.

PEN/RALPH MANHEIM MEDAL FOR TRANSLATION, PEN American Center, 568 Broadway, New York NY 10012. (212)334-1660. Fax: (212)334-2181. E-mail: pen@echo.nyc.com. Contact: John Morrone. Translators nominated by the PEN Translation Committee. Given every 3 years. Next award: 1997.

ALDO AND JEANNE SCAGLIONE PRIZE FOR TRANSLATION OF A LITERARY WORK, Modern Language Association of America, 10 Astor Place, New York NY 10003-6981. (212)475-9500. Fax: (212)477-9863. Director of Special Projects: Richard Brod. Offered in even-numbered years for the translation of a book-length literary work and in odd-numbered years for a book-length work of literary history, literary criticism, philology or literary theory appearing in print during the pervious two years. Deadline: May 1. Guidelines for SASE. Prize: $1,000 and a certificate presented at the association's annual convention in December. Translators need not be members of the MLA.

STUDENT TRANSLATION PRIZE, American Translators Association, % Eric McMillen, 1800 Diagonal Rd., Suite 220, Alexandria VA 22314 (703)683-6100. Support is granted for a promising project to an unpublished student enrolled in a translation program at a US college or university. Deadline: April 15. Must be sponsored by a faculty member.

MULTIPLE WRITING AREAS

AKRON MANUSCRIPT CLUB WRITER'S CONTEST, Akron Manuscript Club & Akron University, P.O. Box 1101, Cuyahoga Falls OH 44223-0101. (216)923-2094. E-mail: mmlop@aol.com. Contact: M.M. LoPiccolo. Estab. 1929. Offered annually for previously unpublished stories to provide critique, encouragement and some financial help to authors in 3 categories. Deadline is always sometime in March. Guidelines for #10 SASE. Charges $25 entry/critique fee. Prize: 1st-certificate to $50, according to funding; 2nd and 3rd-certificates.

AMELIA STUDENT AWARD, *Amelia Magazine*, 329 E St., Bakersfield CA 93304. (805)323-4064. Editor: Frederick A. Raborg, Jr. Previously unpublished poems, essays and short stories by high school students, 1 entry per student; each entry should be signed by parent, guardian *or* teacher to verify originality. Deadline: May 15. No entry fee; however, if guidelines and sample are required, please send SASE with $3 handling charge.

‡ANNUAL WRITERS CONFERENCE, Pacific Northwest Writers Conference, 2033 3rd Ave, #804, Seattle WA 98121. (206)443-3807. Fax: (206)441-8262. Director: Judy Boomer. Offered annually for unpublished work to help writers reach professional standards, to recognize and honor the best of new writing in a broad array of categories, and to provide expert evaluation for all entries. Categories: Adult Article/Essay, Adult Genre Novek, Adult Mainstream Novel, Adult Genre Short Story, Adult Mainstream Short Story, Juvenile Article or Short Story, Juvenile Novel, Picture Book For Children, Nonfiction Book, Playwriting,

Scriptwriting, Poetry. Deadline: March 15. Guidelines for SASE. Charges $20 fee for members, $30 fee for nonmembers. Prize: $7,500 cash prizes in 12 categories.

‡**ANTIETAM REVIEW LITERARY AWARD**, *Antietam Review*, 7 W. Franklin St., Hagerstown MD 21740-4804. Short fiction (up to 5,000 words) and poetry (up to 30 lines). Deadline: September 1. Guidelines for SASE. Charges $10 reading fee/short story, $3/poem. Up to 5 entries at a time are permitted. First prize for fiction $100, publication in *AR*, and 2 copies of the magazine. First prize (poetry): $50, publication plus 2 copies. ALL entries considered for publication. Open to natives or residents of MD, PA, VA, WV, DE and DC.

ARIZONA AUTHORS' ASSOCIATION ANNUAL NATIONAL LITERARY CONTEST, Arizona Authors' Association, 3509 E. Shea Blvd., #117, Phoenix AZ 85028-3339. (602)867-9001. Contact: Iva Martin. Previously unpublished poetry, short stories, essays. Deadline: July 29. Charges $5 fee for poetry; $7 fee for short stories and essays.

EMILY CLARK BALCH AWARD, *Virginia Quarterly Review*, 1 West Range, Charlottesville VA 22903. (804)924-3124. Fax:(804)924-1397. E-mail: jco7e@virginia.edu. Editor: Staige D. Blackford. Best short story/poetry accepted and published by the *Virginia Quarterly Review* during a calendar year. No deadline.

CALIFORNIA WRITERS' CLUB CONFERENCE AND CONTEST, 1090 Cambridge St., Novato CA 94947. Fax: (415)883-4546. E-mail: studio@a.crl.com. Unpublished adult fiction (short stories), adult fiction (novels), adult nonfiction, juvenile fiction, poetry and scripts. Please note: our conference and contest are biennial, offered on odd-numbered years only. Next: at Asilomar, CA, June 1997. Guidelines available to all writers with SASE only to address above.

CANADIAN AUTHORS ASSOCIATION ANNUAL CREATIVE WRITING AWARDS FOR HIGH SCHOOL, COLLEGE AND UNIVERSITY STUDENTS, (formerly Canadian Author Student Creative Writing Awards), Canadian Authors Association, Box 32219, 250 Harding Blvd. W, Richmond Hill, Ontario L4C 9R0 Canada. Fax: (905)737-2961. E-mail: bfarrar@learn.senecac.on.ca. To encourage creative writing of unpublished fiction, nonfiction and poetry at the secondary school level. Deadline: Must be postmarked by Saturday, March 22, 1997. Must be secondary school, college or university student. Prizes of $500 and 4 honorable mentions in each category (best poem, best story, best article). Send SAE and 1 IRC or SASE in Canada for guidelines.

THE CHELSEA AWARDS FOR POETRY AND SHORT FICTION, % Richard Foerster, Editor, P.O. Box 1040, York Beach ME 03910. Estab. 1958. Previously unpublished submissions. "Two prizes awarded for the best work of short fiction and for the best group of 4-6 poems selected by the editors in anonymous competitions." Deadline: June 15 for fiction; December 15 for poetry. Guidelines for SASE. Charges $10 fee (includes free subscription to *Chelsea*). Checks made payable to Chelsea Associates, Inc. Prize: $750, winning entries published in *Chelsea*. Include SASE for notification of competition results. Does not return mss. *Note:* General submissions and other business should be addressed to the editor at *Chelsea*, P.O. Box 773, Cooper Station, New York, NY 10276.

CHICANO/LATINO LITERARY CONTEST, Department of Spanish and Portuguese, University of California-Irvine, Irvine CA 92717. (714)824-5702. Contact: Alejandro Morales or Ruth M. Gratzer. Estab. 1974. "To promote the dissemination of unpublished Chicano/Latino literature, and to encourage its development. The call for entries will be genre specific, rotating through four categories: short story (1996), poetry (1997), drama (1998) and novel (1999)." Deadline: April 30. "Interested parties may write for entry procedures." The contest is open to all citizens or permanent residents of the US.

‡**CITY OF TORONTO BOOK AWARDS**, City of Toronto, City Clerk's Department, Toronto City Hall, Toronto, Ontario M5H 2N2 Canada. (416)392-0468. Fax: (416)392-7999. Offered annually for work published January 1-December 31 of previous year to honor authors of books of literary merit that are evocative of Toronto. Deadline: January 31. Guidelines for SASE. Prize: Total of $15,000 in prize money. Each finalist (usually 4-6) receives $1,000 and the winning author receives the remainder ($9,000-11,000). Fiction and nonfiction books for adults and/or children are eligible. Textbooks, reprints and mss are not eligible.

‡**CNW/FLORIDA STATE WRITING COMPETITION**, Florida Freelance Writers Association, Contest Administrator, P.O. Box A, North Stratford NH 03590. Annual contest. Deadline: March 15. Subject areas include: adult articles, adult short stories, writing for children, novels, nonfiction books, newsletters, client materials; but vary from year to year. Guidelines for #10 SASE. Entry fees vary from year to year; in 1996 were $5-10.

‡**COLORADO BOOK AWARDS**, Colorado Center for the Book, 1301 Arapahoe St., Suite 3, Golden CO 80401. (303)273-5933. Fax: (303)273-5935. E-mail: 103332.1376@compuserve.com. Website: http://

www.aclin.org/~ccftb. Director: Suzan Moore. Offered annually for work published November-December of previous year or current calendar year. The purpose is to champion all Colorado authors and in particular to honor the award winners and a reputation for Colorado as a state whose people promote and support reading, writing and literacy through books. The categories are children, young adult, fiction, nonfiction & poetry. Guidelines for SASE. Charges $30 fee. Prize: $500 cash prize in each category and an annual dinner event where winners are honored. Judged by booksellers, librarians, authors. This award is for Colorado residents (must have lived here 3 of the last 12 months).

‡VIOLET CROWN BOOK AWARDS, Austin Writers' League, 1501 West Fifth St., Suite E-2, Austin TX 78703. (512)499-8914. Fax: (512)499-0441. Director: Angela Smith. Offered annually for work published September 1-August 31 to honor three outstanding books published in fiction, nonfiction and literary categories by Austin Writers' League members. Deadline: August 31. Guidelines for SASE. Charges $10 fee. Prize: 3 $1,000 cash prizes and trophies. Entrants must be Austin Writers' League members. Membership dues may accompany entry fee.

‡CWW ANNUAL AWARDS COMPETITION, Council for Wisconsin Writers, P.O. Box 55322, Madison WI 53705. Offered annually for work published January 1-December 31 of previous year. Thirteen awards: major/life achievement, short fiction, scholarly book, short nonfiction, nonfiction book, juvenile fiction book, children's picture book, poetry book, fiction book, outdoor writing, nonfiction juvenile book, drama (produced), outstanding service to Wisconsin writers. Deadline: January 15. Guidelines for SASE. Charges entry fee: $25 for nonmembers, $10 for members. Prize: $500-1,000 and certificate. Open to Wisconsin residents.

THE DANCING JESTER PRESS "ONE NIGHT IN PARIS SHOULD BE ENOUGH" CONTEST, The Dancing Jester Press, 3411 Garth Rd., Suite 208, Baytown TX 77521. E-mail: djpress@aol.com. Contact: (Ms.) Shiloh Daniel. Offered annually for unpublished work to recognize excellence in poetics. Entry blank and guidelines for SASE. Prize: 1st-the night of 4/1/97 in Paris, France, all expenses paid; 2nd Dancing Jester Medallion; 3rd-a pair of "One Night in Paris Should Be Enough" T-shirts.

DEEP SOUTH WRITERS CONTEST, Deep South Writers Conference, P.O. Box 44691, University of Southwestern Louisiana, Lafayette LA 70504-4691. (318)482-6908. Contact: Contest Clerk. Estab. 1960. Deadline: July 15. Guidelines for SASE. Charges $15 fee for novels and full-length plays; $10 for other submissions. Does not return mss.

EDITORS' PRIZE, Missouri Review, 1507 Hillcrest Hall, University of Missouri, Columbia MO 65211. (573)882-4474. Contact: Speer Morgan, Greg Michalson. Offered annually for unpublished fiction, essays or poetry. Deadline: October 15. Guidelines for SASE. Charges $15/entry. Prize: Fiction—$1,500 and publication; Essay—$1,000 and publication; Poetry—$750 and publication. Open to any writer.

‡EMERGING LESBIAN WRITERS FUND AWARD, ASTRAEA National Lesbian Action Foundation, 116 E. 16th St., New York NY 10003. (212)529-8021. Fax: (212)982-3321. E-mail: anlaf@aol.com. Website: http://www.imageinc.com/astraea/. Contact: Program Director. Offered annually to encourage and support the work of new lesbian writers of fiction and poetry. Deadline: International Women's Day. Guidelines for SASE. Charges $5 fee. Prize: $10,000 grants. Entrants must be a lesbian writer of either fiction or poetry, a US resident, work includes some lesbian content, at least one piece of writing (in any genre) has been published in a newspaper, magazine, journal or anthology, and not more than one book. (Published work may be in any discipline. Self-published books are not included in the one book maximum.)

‡EYSTER PRIZE, *New Delta Review*, % Department of English, Louisiana State University, Baton Rouge LA 70803-5001. (504)388-4079. Contact: Fiction Editor and Poetry Editor. Estab. 1983. Semiannual award for best works of poetry and fiction in each issue. Deadlines: March 1 (spring/summer issue); September 1 (fall/winter issue).

FEMINIST WRITERS' CONTEST, Dept WM, Des Plaines/Park Ridge NOW, P.O. Box 2440, Des Plaines IL 60018. Contact: Pamela Sims. Estab. 1990. Categories: Fiction and nonfiction (5,000 or fewer words). Work should reflect feminist perspectives (should not endorse or promote sexism, racism, ageism, anti-lesbianism, etc.) Guidelines for SASE. Deadline: August 31. Charge $10 entry fee. Cash awards.

FOLIO, Department of Literature, American University, Washington DC 20016. Estab. 1984. Fiction, poetry, essays, interviews and b&w artwork. "We look for quality work and award an annual prize for best poem and best story published per year." Published twice annually. Manuscripts read September-March 15.

MILES FRANKLIN LITERARY AWARD, Arts Management Pty. Ltd., 180 Goulburn St., Darlinghurst, NSW 2010 Australia. Fax: 61-2-2648201. Offered annually for work published for the first time the year preceding award. "The award is for a novel or play which presents Australian life in any of its phases.

Biographies, collections of short stories or children's books are *not* eligible for the award." Deadline: January 31. Guidelines for #10 SAE with 1 IRC. Prize: $25,000 (Australian). "This award is open to writers of any nationality. However, the novel or play must be about Australian life."

‡**FRIENDS OF AMERICAN WRITERS AWARDS**, Friends of American Writers, 6101 N. Sheridan Rd. East, Chicago IL 60660. (312)743-7323. Contest/Award Directors: Pearl Robbins (adult) and Kay O'Connor (juvenile), 15237 W. Redwood Lane, Libertyville IL 60048. (847)362-3782. Annual award for submissions published January 1-December 31 of each year. Two categories: adult and juvenile literature, fiction or nonfiction of literary quality. Deadline: December 1. $1,600 for 1st adult award and $1,000 2nd adult award. Juvenile $1,000 1st and $600 2nd. Entry forms and guidelines for #10 SASE.

‡**GAY/LESBIAN AND BISEXUAL BOOK AWARD**, American Library Association, 50 E. Huron St., Chicago IL 60611. (800)545-2433. Offered annually to authors of fiction and nonfiction book(s) of exceptional merit relating to gay/lesbian experience. Guidelines for SASE. Prize: cash honorium.

GEORGETOWN REVIEW FICTION AND POETRY CONTEST, (formerly *Georgetown Review Short Story and Poetry Contest*), P.O. Box 6309, Southern Station, Hattiesburg MS 39406-6309. (601)583-6940. Fax: (601)545-1223. E-mail: jsfulmer@whale.st.usm.edu. Contact: Tracy Heinlein or John Fulmer. Deadline: August 1. Guidelines for SASE. Entry fee: $10/short story; $5/poem, $2 each additional poem. Prize: $1,000 for winning story; $500 for winning poem. Nine finalists receive publication and 1 year's subscription. Maximum length: 25 pages or 6,500 words. Previously published or accepted work ineligible. No mss returned.

THE GREENSBORO REVIEW LITERARY AWARD IN FICTION AND POETRY, *The Greensboro Review*, English Department, University of North Carolina-Greensboro, Greensboro NC 27412-5001. (910)334-5459. Fax: (910)334-3281. E-mail: clarkj@fagan.uncg.edu. Website: http://www.uncg.edu. Contact: Fiction or Poetry Editor. Estab. 1984. Annual award for fiction and poetry recognizing the best work published in the winter issue of *The Greensboro Review*. Deadline: September 15. Sample copy for $4.

HACKNEY LITERARY AWARDS, *Writing Today*, Box 549003/Birmingham-Southern College, Birmingham AL 35254. (205)226-4921. Fax: (205)226-3072. E-mail: bhopkins@bsc.edu. Website: http://www.bsc.edu/. Contact: Special Events Office. Estab. 1969. Offered annually for unpublished novel, short story and poetry. Deadline: September 30 (novels), December 31 (short stories and poetry). Guidelines for SASE.

‡**ROBERT F. KENNEDY BOOK AWARDS**, 1206 30th St. NW, Washington DC 20007. (202)333-1880, ext. 229. Fax: (202)333-4903. Director: Merrill Warschoff. Offered annually for work published the previous year which most faithfully and forcefully reflects Robert Kennedy's purposes—"his concern for the poor and the powerless, his struggle for honest and even-handed justice, his conviction that a decent society must assure all young people a fair chance, and his faith that a free democracy can act to remedy disparities of power and opportunity." Deadline: January 2. Charges $25 fee. Prize: $2,500.

‡**HENRY KREISEL AWARD FOR BEST FIRST BOOK**, Writers Guild of Alberta, 11759 Groat Rd., Edmonton, Alberta T5M 3K6 Canada. (403)422-8174. Fax: (403)422-2663. Director: Darlene Diver. Book can be of any genre published in current year. It must be author's first book. Must be an Alberta author.

‡**LATINO LITERATURE PRIZE**, Latin American Writers/Institute, Hostos Community College, 500 Grand Concourse, Bronx NY 10451. (718)518-4195. Fax: (718)518-4240. Director: Isaac Goldemberg. Offered annually for work published between 1995 and 1996. "There are two categories, both accept books in English or Spanish by Latino writers living in the US. The purpose is to recognize the work of Latino writers in the US." Deadline: May 28. Guidelines for SASE. Prize: $1,000 in each category.

LETRAS DE ORO SPANISH LITERARY PRIZES, Iberian Studies, University of Miami, P.O. Box 248123, Coral Gables FL 33124. (305)284-3266. Fax: (305)284-4406. Contact: Dr. Joaquin Roy. Offered annually for unpublished work. "The Spanish Literary contest Letras de Oro, now in its eleventh year, has received national and international prestige for recognizing the excellent contribution of authors who write in Spanish and reside in the US. There are prizes in five categories: novel, short story, theater, essay and poetry. The prize awards include $2,500 cash for the winning entries and the publication of the winning manuscripts in the Letras de Oro literary collection." Deadline: October 12. Guidelines available by mail, phone or fax. Contest is open to any writer who writes in Spanish and resides in the US. Poems and short stories should contain enough material to create a book. Essays require a minimum of 100 pages.

‡**LITERATURE FELLOWSHIP**, Artist Trust, 1402 Third Ave., Seattle WA 98101. (206)467-8734. Fax: (206)467-9633. Executive Director: Marshel H. Paul. Offered every two years: 1995, 1997, 1999, etc. The literature fellowship is an award to a writer (fiction/poetry) in Washington State who is a practicing professional artist. Recipient must complete a community-based "Meet the Artist" event. Deadlines are in the

summer and change depending on what creative disciplines are being awarded. Writers should send SASE two months before deadline. Recipients are chosen by a selection panel coordinated by staff. Prize: $5,000 ($4,500 upfront and $500 after the recipient completes a community event called "Meet the Artist"). Must be a resident of Washington State; must be 18 years or older; cannot be in a matriculated study program. Fiction writers and poets only.

‡**AUDRE LORDE MEMORIAL PROSE PRIZE**, National Women's Studies Association, 7100 Baltimore Ave., #301, College Park MD 20715. (301)403-0525. Fax: (301)403-4137. Offered annually for unpublished feminist writers who write fiction or prose. Submitted work should take up a topic of discourse found in the work of Lorde or seek to illustrate a condition, idea, or ideal inherent in her fiction or prose. Submissions accepted September 1-November 17. Guidelines for SASE. Prize: $250 to two winners.

MASTERS LITERARY AWARDS, Center Press, P.O. Box 16452, Encino CA 91416-6452. Contact: Gabriella Stone. Offered annually and quarterly for work published within 2 years (preferred) and unpublished work (accepted). Fiction: 15 page, maximum; Poetry: 5 pages or 150 lines, maximum; Nonfiction: 10 page, maximum. Deadlines: March 15, June 15th, August 15th, December 15. Guidelines for SASE. Charges $10 reading/administration fee. Prizes: 5 quarterly honorable mentions from which is selected one yearly Grand Prize of $1,000. "A selection of all winning entries will appear in our national literary publication" judged by "three anonymous experts chosen yearly from literary and publishing field." Center Press retains one time publishing rights to selected winners. Open to all writers.

‡**MATURE WOMEN SCHOLARSHIP AWARD**, The National League of American Pen Women, Inc., 1300 17th St. NW, Washington DC 20036. (202)785-1997. Offered every two years on even numbered years to women 35 and over. Classifications include: art, letters, music composition. Send SASE for rules (available after August). Charges $8 fee. Award is $1,000 in each classification.

THE MENTOR AWARD, *Mentor Newsletter*, P.O. Box 4382, Overland Park KS 66204-0382. Award Director: Maureen Waters. Estab. 1989. Offered annually to promote and encourage mentoring through feature articles, essays, book/movie reviews, interviews or short stories about mentoring-related subjects. Guidelines for #10 SASE. Charges $5 fee. Prize: $100. Writer must be at least 16 years old.

THE NEBRASKA REVIEW AWARDS IN FICTION AND POETRY, *The Nebraska Review*, FAB 212, University of Nebraska-Omaha, Omaha NE 68182-0324. (402)554-2771. (402)554-3436. E-mail: nereview@fa-cpacs.unomaha.edu. Contact: Susan Aizenberg (poetry), James Reed (fiction). Estab. 1973. Previously unpublished fiction and a poem or group of poems. Deadline: November 30.

‡**NEGATIVE CAPABILITY FICTION & POETRY AWARDS**, Negative Capability Press, 62 Ridgelawn Dr. E., Mobile AL 36608. (334)343-6163. Fax: (334)344-8478. Director: S. Walker. Offered annually for unpublished work to honor outstanding fiction & poetry. Deadline: January 15. Guidelines for SASE. Charges $10/fiction entry, $3/poem. Prize: $1,000 each fiction/poetry and publication.

‡**NEW MILLENNIUM WRITINGS AWARD**, New Millennium Writings Journal, P.O. Box 2463, Knoxville TN 37901. (423)428-0389. Director: Don Williams. Offered twice annually for unpublished fiction, poetry, essays, to encourage new fiction writers, poets and essayists and bring them to attention of publishing industry. Deadline: December 15, June 15. Guidelines for SASE. Charges $10 fee. Entrants receive an issue of *NMW* in which winners appear. Prize: $500 in each category & publication of winner & runner-up.

‡**NORTH AMERICAN NATIVE AUTHORS FIRST BOOK AWARDS**, The Greenfield Review Literary Center, P.O. Box 308, Greenfield Center NY 12833. (518)583-1440. Fax: (518)583-9741. Director: Joseph Bruchac. Offered annually for unpublished work in book form to recognize literary achievement in prose and in poetry by Native North American writers who have not yet published a book. Deadline: May 1. Guidelines for SASE. Prize: $500 plus publication by The Greenfield Review Press with a standard contract for royalties. Judged by a panel of established Native American writers. Only writers who are American Indian, Inuit, Aleut or Metis and who have not yet published a book.

‡**KENNETH PATCHEN COMPETITION**, Pig Iron Press, P.O. Box 237, Youngstown OH 44501. (330)747-6932. Fax: (330)747-0599. Contact: Bill Koch. Offered annually for unpublished poetry or fiction (except for individual works published in magazines/journals). Alternates annually between Poetry and Fiction. Deadline: December 31. Guidelines for SASE. Charges $10 fee. Prize: Trade Paperback publication in an edition of 1,000 copies, and $100.

PEN CENTER USA WEST ANNUAL LITERARY AWARDS, PEN Center USA West, 672 S. Lafayette Park Place, #41, Los Angeles CA 90057. (213)365-8500. Fax: (213)365-9616. Contact: Rachel Hall. Offered annually for fiction, nonfiction, poetry, children's literature, translation, drama, screenplay, teleplay published January 1-December 31 of the current year. Deadline: December 31. Guidelines for SASE. Prize: $500. Open to authors west of the Mississippi River.

‡POETRY & ART CONTEST, National Poet's Association, P.O. Box 173, Bayport MN 55003. (612)779-6952. E-mail: poim@aol.com. Director: Madia Giordana. Offered annually for published original poetry and original b&w art. Deadline: August. Guidelines for SASE. Charges $2 for first entry, $1 all others. Prize: $75—$50 & $25 plus publication of all accepted entries in full-sized anthology.

THE PRESIDIO LA BAHIA AWARD, Sons of the Republic of Texas, 1717 Eighth St., Bay City TX 77414. Fax: (409)245-6644. Offered annually "to promote suitable preservation of relics, appropriate dissemination of data, and research into our Texas heritage, with particular attention to the Spanish Colonial period." Deadline: June 1-September 30. Guidelines for SASE. Prize: $2,000 total; 1st prize a minimum of $1,200, 2nd and 3rd prizes at the discretion of the judges.

‡QSPELL LITERARY AWARDS, QSPELL-Quebec Society for the Promotion of English Language Literature, 1200 Atwater Ave., Montreal, Quebec H3Z 1X4 Canada. Fax: (514)933-0878. Offered annually for work published May 16, 1996-May 15, 1997 to honor excellence in English-language writing in Quebec. Categories—fiction, nonfiction, poetry. Deadline: May 31. Guidelines for SASE. Charges $10/title. Prize: $2,000 in each category. Author must have resided in Quebec for 3 of the past 5 years.

QUINCY WRITER'S GUILD ANNUAL CREATIVE WRITING CONTEST, Quincy Writer's Guild, c/o Rev. Michael Barrett, P.O. Box 433, Quincy IL 62306-0433. Categories include: poetry, short story, fiction. Deadline: January 1-April 15. Charges $2/poem; $4/short story or article. "No identification should appear on manuscripts, but send a separate 3×5 card attached to entry with name, address, phone number, word count, and title of work." Previously unpublished work. Cash prizes. Guidelines for SASE.

RHYME TIME CREATIVE WRITING COMPETITION, *Rhyme Time*, P.O. Box 2907, Decatur IL 62524. Award Director: Linda Hutton. Estab. 1981. Annual no-fee contest. Submit 1 typed poem, any style, any length. One winner will receive $25; one runner-up will receive a year's subscription to *Rhyme Time*. No poems will be published. Include SASE. Deadline: November 1.

SUMMERFIELD G. ROBERTS AWARD, Sons of the Republic of Texas, 1717 Eighth St., Bay City TX 77414. Fax: (409)245-6644. Offered annually for submissions published during the previous calendar year "to encourage literary effort and research about historical events and personalities during the days of the Republic of Texas, 1836-1846, and to stimulate interest in the period." Deadline: January 15. Guidelines for SASE. Prize: $2,500.

ROM/CON, 1555 Washington Ave., San Leandro CA 94577. (415)357-5665. Director: Barbara N. Keenan. Awards for previously published material in 12 categories appearing in *Affaire de Coeur* magazine. Deadline: March 15. "Rom-Con Awards are given at the annual conference and are presented for the highest quality of writing in the Romance genre."

‡BRUCE P. ROSSLEY LITERARY AWARD, 96 Inc., P.O. Box 15558, Boston MA 02215. (617) 267-0543. Fax: (617)262-3568. Director: Vera Gold. Offered annually to give greater recognition to a writer of merit. In addition to writing, accomplishments in the fields of teaching and community service are considered. Deadline: September 30. Nominations are accepted from August 1 to September 30. Guidelines for SASE. Charges $10 fee. Prize: $1,000. Any writer in New England may be nominated, but the focus is merit and those writers who have been under-recognized.

‡SHENANDOAH VALLEY WRITER'S GUILD, Lord Fairfax Community College, Middletown VA 27645. (540)869-1120. Director: Prof. F. Cogan. Offered annually for unpublished fiction, poetry, nonfiction. Deadline: March 1. Guidelines for SASE. Charges $500 fee. Prize: 1st-$25, 2nd-$15, 3rd-$10. "Winners are published in our annual magazine so should be acceptable to general readers—no sex or violence."

SONORA REVIEW ANNUAL LITERARY AWARDS, *Sonora Review*, English Department, University of Arizona, Tucson AZ 85721. $500 Fiction Award given each Spring to the best previously unpublished short story. Deadline: December 1. Charges $10 fee. $500 Poetry Award given each Fall to the best previously unpublished poem. Four poems/5 page maximum submission. Deadline: July 1. Charges $10 fee. For both awards, all entrants receive a copy of the issue in which the winning entry appears. No formal application form is required; regular submission guidelines apply. Guidelines for #10 SASE. For samples, send $6.

‡THE SOUTHERN PRIZE, *The Southern Anthology*, 2851 Johnston St., #123, Lafayette LA 70503. Director: R. Sebastian Bennett, Ph.D. Offered annually for unpublished fiction and poetry "to promote and reward outstanding fiction and poetry; to encourage both traditional and innovative forms." Deadline: May 30. Guidelines for SASE. Charges fee: $10/short fiction or novel excerpt (7,500 word limit); or $10/set of

3 poems. Prize: $600 grand prize and publication. Six finalists published; stipend for top three finalists. Contest open to all writers writing in English. No form or genre restrictions. Submissions need not address "Southern" themes. *The Southern Anthology* encourages both traditional and avant-garde writing.

SOUTHWEST REVIEW AWARDS, Southern Methodist University, 307 Fondren Library West, P.O. Box 750374, Dallas TX 75275-0374. (214)768-1036. Contact: Elizabeth Mills. Offered annually for fiction, nonfiction and poetry published in the magazine. "The $1,000 John H. McGinnis Memorial Award is given each year for fiction and nonfiction that has been published in the *Southwest Review* in the previous year. Stories or articles are not submitted directly for the award, but simply for publication in the magazine. The Elizabeth Matchett Stover Award, an annual prize of $150, is awarded to the author of the best poem or group of poems published in the magazine during the preceding year."

TENNESSEE WRITERS ALLIANCE LITERARY COMPETITION, Tennessee Writers Alliance, P.O. Box 120396, Nashville TN 37212. (615)385-3163. Contact: Literary Competition Director. Offered annually on rotating basis for unpublished short fiction, poetry, nonfiction (personal essay). Deadline varies. Guidelines for SASE. Charges $5 fee for members, $10 fee for non-member Tennessee residents. Prize: 1st-$500; 2nd-$250; 3rd-$100 and publication. Acquires right to publish once. Open to any member of Tennessee Writers Alliance and Tennessee residents. Membership open to all, regardless of residence, for $25/year, $15/year for students.

TMWC LITERARY CONTEST, Tennessee Mountain Writers' Conference, P.O. Box 4895, Oak Ridge TN 37831. (423)482-6567. Contact: Patricia Hope. Offered annually for unpublished work to give beginning writers an outlet for their work. Deadline: September 30. Guidelines for SASE. Charges $10 fee. Prize: 1st-$250; 2nd-$150; 3rd-$75.

WESTERN MAGAZINE AWARDS, Western Magazine Awards Foundation, 3898 Hillcrest Ave., North Vancouver, British Columbia V7R 4B6 Canada. (604)984-7525. Fax: (604)985-6262. Contact: Tina Baird. Offered annually for magazine work published January 1-December 31 of previous calendar year. Entry categories include business, culture, science, technology and medicine, entertainment, fiction, political issues, and much more. Write or phone for rules and entry forms. Deadline: February 1. Entry fee: $27 for work in magazines with circulation under 20,000; $35 for work in magazines with circulation over 20,000. Prize: $500. Applicant must be Canadian citizen, landed immigrant, or fulltime resident of Canada. The work must have been published in a magazine whose main editorial office is in Western Canada, the NW Territories and Yukon.

WRITERS AT WORK FELLOWSHIP COMPETITION, Writers at Work, P.O. Box 1146, Centerville UT 84014-5146. (801)292-9285. Website: http://www.ihi-env.com/w@w.html. Contact: Dawn Marano. Offered annually for unpublished short stories, novel excerpts and poetry. Deadline: March 15. Guidelines for SASE. Charges $12 fee. "Only fee is required for consideration. Short stories or novel excerpts 20 double-spaced pages maximum, one story per entry. Poetry submissions limited to 6 poems, 10 pages maximum." Prize: $1,500, publication and partial conference tuition; $500, partial conference tuition.

WRITER'S DIGEST WRITING COMPETITION, *Writer's Digest* Magazine, 1507 Dana Ave., Cincinnati OH 45207-9966. (513)531-2690, ext. 633. Fax: (513)531-1843. Contact: Kim Thompson. Contest in 65th year. Categories: Personal Essays, Feature Articles, Literary Short Stories, Mainstream/Genre Short Stories, Rhyming Poems, Non-Rhyming Poems, Stage Plays and Television/Movie Scripts. Submissions must be unpublished. For guidelines send #10 SASE. Deadline: May 31.

ARTS COUNCILS AND FOUNDATIONS

ARTIST ASSISTANCE FELLOWSHIP, Minnesota State Arts Board, Park Square Court, 400 Sibley St., Suite 200, St. Paul MN 55101-1928. (612)215-1600. Fax: (612)215-1602. E-mail: msab@maroon. tc.umn.edu. Artist Assistance Program Associate: Karen Mueller. Annual fellowships of $6,000 to be used for time, materials, living expenses. Literary categories include prose, poetry and theater arts (playwriting and screenwriting). Applicants must be Minnesota residents. Deadline: October.

‡**ARTIST FELLOWSHIP**, Alabama State Council on the Arts, One Dexter Ave., Montgomery AL 36130. (334)242-4076. Fax: (334)240-3269. Literature Programs Manager: Becky Mullen. Offered every 2 years for previously published work based on achievement and quality of work. Artists may use funds to set aside time to create their art, improve their skills, or do what they consider most advantageous to enhance their artistic careers. Deadline: May 1. Call or write to request guidelines. Prize: $5,000 (2) or $10,000 (1) (most often 2 artists are chosen). Any legal resident of Alabama who has lived in state for 2 years prior to application.

‡**ARTIST FELLOWSHIP**, Connecticut Commission on the Arts, 755 Main St., Hartford CT 06103. (860)566-4770. Fax: (860)566-6462. Director: Linda Dente. Previously published or unpublished work to assist in the development and encouragement of Connecticut writers of substantial talent. Deadline: February 1, 1988. Awards are biennial. Guidelines for SASE. Prize: $2,500 or $5,000. Must be residents of the State of Connecticut for 4 years or more. Cannot be a student.

‡**ARTIST FELLOWSHIP AWARDS**, Wisconsin Arts Board, 101 E. Wilson St. 1st Floor, Madison WI 53702. (608)267-2026. Fax: (608)267-0380. Director: Kate LaRocque. Offered every 2 years to recognize the significant contributions of professional artists in Wisconsin, and intended to support continued artistic and professional development, enabling artists to create new work, complete work in progress, and pursue activities which contribute to their artistic growth. Deadline: September 15. SASE is not necessary. Contact WAB at (608)266-0190 to receive application materials. Applicants must reside in Wisconsin a minimum of 1 year prior to application and may not be fulltime students pursuing a degree in the fine arts.

‡**ARTIST PROJECTS**, Rhode Island State Council on the Arts, Suite 103, 95 Cedar St., Providence RI 02903. (401)277-3880. Fax: (401)521-1351. Contact: Sheila Haggerty. "Artist Project grants enable an artist to create new work and/or complete works-in-progress by providing direct financial assistance. By encouraging significant development in the work of an individual artist, these grants recognize the central contribution artists make to the creative environment of Rhode Island." Deadline: October 1. Guidelines for 9 × 12 SASE. Prize: non-matching grants of $1,500-4,000. Open only to RI residents, age 18 or older. Students not eligible.

‡**ARTISTS' FELLOWSHIPS**, New York Foundation for the Arts, 155 Avenue of the Americas, New York NY 10013-1507. (212)366-6900 ext. 217. Fax: (212)366-1778. Website: http://www.tmn.com/Artswire/www/nyfa.html. Contact: Artists' Fellowships. "Artists' Fellowships are cash grants of $7,000 awarded in 15 disciplines on a biannual rotation. Nonfiction Literature and Poetry will be the literature disciplines under review in 1996-1997. Awards are based upon the recommendations of peer panels and are not project support. The fellowship may be used by each recipient as she/he sees fit. Call for application in July. Deadlines in October. Results announced in April. The New York Foundation for the Arts supports artists at all stages of their careers and from diverse backgrounds." All applicants must be 18 years of age and a New York resident for two years prior to the time of application.

ARTS RECOGNITION AND TALENT SEARCH, National Foundation for Advancement in the Arts, 800 Brickell Ave., Suite 500, Miami FL 33131. (305)377-1140 or (800)970-ARTS. Fax: (305)377-1149. E-mail: nfaa@artbank.com. Contact: Sherry Thompson, Programs Officer. Estab. 1981. For achievements in dance, music (classical, jazz and vocal), photography, theater, visual arts and writing. Students fill in and return the application, available at every public and private high school around the nation, for cash awards of up to $3,000 each and scholarship opportunities worth more than $3 million. Deadline: early—June 1, regular—October 1. Charges $25 registration fee for June; $35 for October.

GEORGE BENNETT FELLOWSHIP, Phillips Exeter Academy, 20 Main St., Exeter NH 03833-2460. Coordinator, Selection Committee: Charles Pratt. Estab. 1968. Annual award of stipend, room and board "to provide time and freedom from material considerations to a person seriously contemplating or pursuing a career as a writer. Applicants should have a manuscript in progress which they intend to complete during the fellowship period." Guidelines for SASE. Deadline: December 1. Charges $5 fee. Residence at the Academy during the Fellowship period required.

BRODY ARTS FUND FELLOWSHIP, California Community Foundation, 606 S. Olive St., Suite 2400, Los Angeles CA 90014-1526. (213)413-4042. Estab. 1985. "The Brody Arts Fund is designed to serve the needs of emerging artists and arts organizations, especially those rooted in the diverse, multicultural communities of Los Angeles. The fellowship program rotates annually between three main subsections of the arts. Literary artists will be considered in 1997; and again in 2000. Applications are available and due in the first quarter of the year. Applicants must reside in Los Angeles County. Students not eligible."

BUSH ARTIST FELLOWSHIPS, The Bush Foundation, E-900 First National Bank Bldg., 332 Minnesota St., St. Paul MN 55101. (612)227-5222. Contact: Sally F. Dixon. Estab. 1976. Award for Minnesota, North Dakota, South Dakota, and western Wisconsin residents 25 years or older "to buy 12-18 months of time for the applicant to do his/her own work." Up to 15 fellowships/year, $36,000 each. Deadline: late October.

CREATIVITY FELLOWSHIP, Northwood University, Alden B. Dow Creativity Center, Midland MI 48640-2398. (517)837-4478. Fax: (517)837-4468. Award Director: Carol B. Coppage. Estab. 1979. Eight-week summer residency for individuals in any field who wish to pursue new and creative ideas that have potential impact in their fields. No accommodations for family/pets. Deadline: December 31.

‡**FELLOWSHIP PROGRAM**, New Jersey State Council on the Arts, 20 W. State St., CN 306, Trenton NJ 08625. (609)292-6130. Fax: (609)989-1440. Director: Steven R. Runk. Offered annually. Writers may

apply in either poetry, playwriting or prose (includes both fiction and nonfiction). Fellowship awards are intended to provide support for the artist during the year to enable him or her to continue producing new work. Deadline: mid-December. Guidelines and application for SASE. Fellowship awards $5,000-12,000. Must be New Jersey residents. May *not* be undergraduate or graduate matriculating students.

‡FELLOWSHIPS (LITERATURE), RI State Council on the Arts, 95 Cedar St., Suite 103, Providence RI 02903. (401)277-3880. Fax: (401)521-1351. Director: Randall Rosenbaum. Offered every 2 years for previously published or unpublished work. Deadline: April 1, 1997. Guidelines for SASE. Prize: $5,000 fellowship; $1,000 runner-up. Judged by peer review panel for first cut; final decisions are made by out-of-state judge in Literature. Rhode Island residents only.

FELLOWSHIPS TO ASSIST RESEARCH AND ARTISTIC CREATION, John Simon Guggenheim Memorial Foundation, 90 Park Ave., New York NY 10016. (212)687-4470. Fax: (212)697-3248. E-mail: fellowships@gf.org. Website: http://www.gf.org. Offered annually to assist scholars and artists to engage in research in any field of knowledge and creation in any of the arts, under the freest possible conditions and irrespective of race, color, or creed. Application form is required. Deadline: October 1.

WILLIAM FLANAGAN MEMORIAL CREATIVE PERSONS CENTER, Edward F. Albee Foundation, 14 Harrison St., New York NY 10013. (212)226-2020. Foundation Secretary: David Briggs. Annual one-month residency at "The Barn" in Montauk, New York offers writers privacy and a peaceful atmosphere in which to work. Deadline: April 1. Prize: room only, writers pay for food and travel expenses. Judged by panel of qualified professionals.

HEEKIN GROUP FOUNDATION WRITING FELLOWSHIPS PROGRAM, The Heekin Group Foundation, P.O. Box 1534, Sisters OR 97759. (503)548-4147. Contest/Award Director: Sarah Heekin Redfield. Offered annually for unpublished works. James Fellowship for the Novel in Progress (2), Tara Fellowship for Short Fiction (2); Mary Molloy Fellowship for Children's Working Novel (1); Siobhan Fellowship for Nonfiction Essay (1). These 6 fellowships are awarded to beginning career writers for assistance in their literary pursuits. Deadline: December 1. Guidelines for SASE. Charges $25 fellowship application fee. Prize: James Fellowship: $3,000; Tara Fellowship: $1,500; Mary Molloy Fellowship: $2,000; Siobhan Fellowship: $2,000. Roster of finalist judges include Graywolf Press, SOHO Press, Dalkey Archive Press, The Ecco Press, Riverhead Books, Hyperion Books. Fellowships are available to those writers who are unpublished in the novel, short fiction and essay.

● See the interview with Sarah Heekin Redfield in this edition of *Writer's Market*.

ILLINOIS ARTS COUNCIL ARTISTS FELLOWSHIP, James R. Thompson Center, 100 W. Randolph, Suite 10-500, Chicago IL 60601. (312)814-6750. Contact: Director of Artists Services. Offered every 2 years for previously published or unpublished work. "Submitted work must have been completed no more than four years prior to deadline. Artists fellowships are awarded to Illinois artists of exceptional talent to enable them to pursue their artistic goals; fellowships are offered in poetry and prose (fiction and creative nonfiction)." Deadline: September 1 of odd-numbered years. "Interested Illinois writers should write or call for information." Prize: $500 Finalist Award; $5,000 or $10,000 Artist's Fellowship. "Writer must be Illinois resident and not a degree-seeking student. Applicants for Poetry Fellowship can submit up to 15 pages of work in manuscript; prose fellowship applicants can submit up to 30 pages of work in manuscript."

‡INDIVIDUAL ARTIST FELLOWSHIP, Oregon Arts Commission, 775 Summer St. NE, Salem OR 97310. (503)986-0086. Website: http://www.das.state.or.us/OAC/. Contact: Assistant Director. Offered in even-numbered years to reward achievement in the field of literature. Deadline: September 1. Guidelines for SASE. Prize: $3,000. "Writers must be Oregon residents 18 years and older. Degree candidate students not eligible."

‡INDIVIDUAL ARTIST FELLOWSHIP, Tennessee Arts Commission, 404 James Robertson Pkwy., Nashville TN 37243-0780. (615)741-1701. Fax: (615)741-8559. E-mail: swansona@ten-nash.ten.k12.tn.us. Director: Alice Swanson. Offered annually for recognition for emerging literary artists. Deadline: First or 2nd Monday in January. Write to above address or call—guidelines too large for SASE—we will mail. Prize: $2,000 plus some matching private funds—this year $1,000 more. Must be resident of Tennessee. 1996 entry must be poetry, 1997 prose 1998 poetry, etc. Must have publication history.

INDIVIDUAL ARTIST FELLOWSHIP AWARD, Montana Arts Council, 316 N. Park Ave., Suite 252, Helena MT 59620. (406)444-6430. Contact: Fran Morrow. Offered annually to *Montana residents only*. Deadline: August.

INDIVIDUAL ARTISTS FELLOWSHIPS, Nebraska Arts Council, 3838 Davenport St., Omaha NE 68131-2329. (402)595-2122. Fax: (402)595-2334. Contact: Suzanne Wise. Estab. 1991. Offered biannually (literature alternates with performing arts) to recognize exemplary achievements by originating artists in their fields of endeavor and supports the contributions made by Nebraska artists to the quality of life in this state. Deadline: October 1. "Generally, master awards are $3,000-4,000 and merit awards are $1,000-2,000. Funds available are announced in September prior to the deadline." Must be a resident of Nebraska for at least 2 years prior to submission date; 18 years of age; not enrolled in an undergraduate, graduate or certificate-granting program in English, creative writing, literature, or related field.

ISLAND LITERARY AWARDS, Prince Edward Island Council of the Arts, P.O. Box 2234, Charlottetown, Prince Edward Island C1A 8B9 Canada. (902)368-4410. Fax: (902)368-4418. Award Director: Judy K. MacDonald. Offers 6 awards for previously unpublished poetry, short fiction, playwriting feature article, children's literature and student writing. Deadline: February 15. Guidelines for #10 SAE with 1 IRC. Charges $6 fee. *Available to residents of PEI only.*

JOSEPH HENRY JACKSON AWARD, The San Francisco Foundation, Administered by Intersection for the Arts, 446 Valencia St., San Francisco CA 94103. (415)626-2787. Contact: Awards Coordinator. Estab. 1965. Offered annually for unpublished, work-in-progress fiction (novel or short story), nonfiction or poetry by author age 20-35, with 3-year consecutive residency in northern California or Nevada prior to submission. Deadline: November 15-January 31.

EZRA JACK KEATS MEMORIAL FELLOWSHIP, Ezra Jack Keats Foundation (funding) awarded through Kerlan Collection, University of Minnesota, 109 Walter Library, 117 Pleasant St. SE., Minneapolis MN 55455. (612)624-4576. Fax: (612)625-5525. Curator, Kerlan Collection: Karen Hoyle. "To award a talented writer and/or illustrator of children's books who wishes to use Kerlan Collection for the furtherance of his or her artistic development." Deadline: early May. Guidelines for SASE. Prize: $1,500 for travel to study at Kerlan Collection. Judged by a committee of 4-5 members from varying colleges at University of Minnesota and outside the University. "Special consideration will be given to someone who would find it difficult to finance the visit to the Kerlan Collection."

KENTUCKY ARTS COUNCILS FELLOWSHIPS IN WRITING, Kentucky Arts Council, 31 Fountain Place, Frankfort KY 40601. (502)564-3757. Fax: (502)564-2839. Contact: Irwin Pickett. Offered in even-numbered years for development/artist's work. Deadline: September 1996. Guidelines for SASE (3 months before deadline). Award: $5,000. Must be Kentucky resident.

LITERARY ARTS PROGRAMS, Arts Branch, Department of Municipalities, Culture and Housing, P.O. Box 6000, Fredericton, New Brunswick E3B 5H1 Canada. (506)453-2555. Fax: (506)453-2416. Website: http://www.gov.nb.ca/. Contact: Literary Arts Officer, Arts Branch. Grant and awards programs: Development Travel, Promotional Travel. Excellence Awards, Creation, Artist-in-Residence, Arts Scholarships and New Brunswick Arts Abroad programs. *Available to New Brunswick residents only. (Must have resided in NB 2 of past 4 years.)*

LOFT-McKNIGHT WRITERS AWARD, The Loft, Pratt Community Center, 66 Malcolm Ave. SE, Minneapolis MN 55414-3551. Website: http://www.umn.edu/n/home/m555/loft/index.html. Contact: Program Coordinator. Eight awards of $7,500 and two awards of distinction at $10,500 each for *Minnesota* writers of poetry and creative prose. Deadline: November. Guidelines for SASE.

LOFT MENTOR SERIES, The Loft, Pratt Community Center, 66 Malcolm Ave. SE, Minneapolis MN 55414-3551. Website: http://www.umn.edu/n/home/m555/loft/index.html. Contact: Program Coordinator. Estab. 1974. Opportunity to work with 4 nationally known writers and small stipend available to 8 winning poets and fiction writers. "Must live close enough to Minneapolis to participate fully in the series." Deadline: May. Guidelines for SASE.

NEW HAMPSHIRE INDIVIDUAL ARTISTS' FELLOWSHIPS, New Hampshire State Council on the Arts, 40 N. Main St., Concord NH 03301-4974. (603)271-2789. Fax: (603)271-3584. Coordinator: Audrey V. Sylvester. Estab. 1982. "To recognize artistic excellence and professional commitment." Literature is not eligible in 1996.

NEW YORK STATE WRITER IN RESIDENCE PROGRAM, New York State Council on the Arts, 915 Broadway, New York NY 10010. (212)387-7028. Fax: (212)387-7164. Website: http://www.artswire.org/artswire/nysca/nysca.html. Contact: Literature Program Director. Offered in odd-numbered years to reward writers' work and give writers a chance to work with a nonprofit organization in a community setting." Deadline: March 1, 1997. Award: $8,000 stipend for a 3 month residency. Applications are judged by a panel of writers, administrators, and translators. Applicant must be nominated by a New York state nonprofit organization.

JAMES D. PHELAN LITERARY AWARD, The San Francisco Foundation, Administered by Intersection for the Arts, 446 Valencia St., San Francisco CA 94103. (415)626-2787. Contact: Awards Coordinator. Estab.

1965. Offered annually for unpublished, work-in-progress fiction, nonfiction, short story, poetry or drama by California-born author age 20-35. Deadline: November 15-January 31.

‡**SEATTLE ARTISTS PROGRAM**, Seattle Arts Commission, 312 First Ave. N., 2nd Floor, Seattle WA 98119-4501. (206)684-7171. Fax: (206)684-7172. Seattle Artists Project Manager: Irene Gomez. Offered every 2 years. The Seattle Artists Program, commissions new works by professional artists in all disciplines. Visual artworks in 2 and 3 dimensions are commissioned each year. In alternate years, media, performing and literary artworks are commissioned. This is a biannual program, and the deadline date vary. Guidelines for SASE. Award amounts are $7,500 and $2,000. Decided through open, competitive peer-panel review process and subject to approval by the full Commission. Applicants must be residents of or maintain studio space in the city of Seattle, Washington. Established and emerging artists are eligible. Artists may not be commissioned in consecutive years through this program. Adaptations/translations are not accepted except if the content differs significantly from that of an original work.

‡**TRILLIUM BOOK AWARD/PRIX TRILLIUM**, Ontario Ministry of Citizenship, Culture and Recreation, 77 Bloor St. W., 3rd Floor, Toronto, Ontario M7A 2R9 Canada. (416)314-7611. Fax: (416)314-7635. Director: Gartly Wagner. Offered annually for work previously published between January 1 and December 31. This is the Ontario government's annual literary award. There are 2 categories—an English language category and a French language category. Deadline: mid-December. Publishers submit books on behalf of authors. Prize: the winning author in each category receives $12,000; the winning publisher is each category receives $2,500. There is an Ontario residency requirement for the authors.

UTAH ORIGINAL WRITING COMPETITION, Utah Arts Council, 617 E. S. Temple, Salt Lake City UT 84102-1177. (801)533-5895. Fax: (801)533-6196. Literary Coordinator: Guy Lebeda. Offered annually for unpublished work to recognize merits of literary writing of Utahns by national judges. Deadline: end of June. Write, phone or fax for guidelines. Prize: certificate and cash prizes of $200-1,000. Open to Utah citizens only.

‡**WEST VIRGINIA COMMISSION ON THE ARTS' FELLOWSHIP**, West Virginia Commission on the Arts, 1900 Kanawha Blvd. East, Charleston WV 25305-0300. (304)558-0220. Fax: (304)558-2779. Coordinator: Tod Ralstin. Director: Lakin Cook. Fellowships in writing are every 3 years. The 1997 Fellowships will be for artists in the writing arts. Deadline: June 1. Guidelines for SASE. Prize: 10 individual awards of $3,500 each. Any West Virginia writer who has been a legal resident of the state for at least 1 year prior to the deadline, and is over the age of 18.

‡**WRITERS FELLOWSHIPS**, NC Arts Council, Dept. of Cultural Resources, Raleigh NC 27601-2807. (919)733-2111. Literature Director: Deborah McGill. Offered every 2 years "to serve writers of fiction, poetry, literary nonfiction and literary translation in North Carolina and to recognize the contribution they make to this state's creative environment." Deadline: November 1. Guidelines for SASE. Offer 12 $8,000 grants every 2 years. Writer must have been a resident of NC for at least a year and may not be enrolled in any degree-granting program at the time of application.

WYOMING ARTS COUNCIL LITERARY FELLOWSHIPS, Wyoming Arts Council, 2320 Capitol Ave. Cheyenne WY 82002. (307)777-7742. Fax: (307)777-5499. E-mail: wyoarts@tmn.com. Literature Coordinator: Michael Shay. Estab. 1986. Fellowships to honor the most outstanding previously published or unpublished new work by Wyoming writers (all genres: poetry, fiction, nonfiction, drama). Deadline: June 1, subject to change subsequent years. Writers may call WAC office; guidelines are also printed in bimonthly *All Arts Newsletter*. Applicants must have been Wyoming residents for 2 years prior to entry deadline—and must remain so for 2 years following—and may not be fulltime students.

MISCELLANEOUS

‡**AJL JUDAICA BIBLIOGRAPHY AWARD**, Association of Jewish Libraries, 16 East 26th St., #1034, New York NY 10010. (216)381-6440. Contact: V.P., R&S Division. Offered annually for work published January 1-December 31 of year prior to AJL Convention held in June of every year. Bibliography in the field of Jewish studies. Books must contribute to the study of the field. Deadline: February-March. Prize: $500 and certificate & travel to AJL Annual Convention.

‡**AMERICAN SPEECH-LANGUAGE-HEARING ASSOCIATION (ASHA), NATIONAL MEDIA AWARDS**, 10801 Rockville Pike, Rockville MD 20852-3279. (301)897-5700. Fax: (301)897-7348. E-mail: mschreder@asha.org. Estab. 1978. Speech-language pathology and audiology (radio, TV, newspaper, magazine). Deadline: June 30.

AMWA MEDICAL BOOK AWARDS COMPETITION, American Medical Writers Association, 9650 Rockville Pike, Bethesda MD 20814. (301)493-0003. Contact: Book Awards Committee. Honors the best medical book published in the previous year in each of 3 categories: Books for Physicians, Books for Allied Health Professionals and Trade Books. Deadline April 1. Charges $20 fee.

BOWLING WRITING COMPETITION, American Bowling Congress Publications, 5301 S. 76th St., Greendale WI 53129-1127. Fax: (414)421-7977. Editor: Bill Vint. Estab. 1935. Feature, editorial and news all relating to the sport of bowling. Deadline: December 1. Prize: 1st—$300 in each category; additional awards of $225, $200, $175, $150, $75 and $50.

GOLF WRITER'S CONTEST, Golf Course Superintendents Association of America, GCSAA, 1421 Research Park Dr., Lawrence KS 66049-3859. Fax: (913)832-4433. Website: http://www.webplus.net/gcsaa/ . Contact: Scott Smith. Previously published work pertaining to golf course superintendents. Must be a member of Golf Writers Association of America.

‡LANDMARK EDITIONS NATIONAL WRITTEN & ILLUSTRATED BY AWARDS CONTEST FOR STUDENTS, Landmark Editions, Inc., P.O. Box 270169, Kansas City MO 64127. (816)241-4919. Editorial Director: Nan Thatch. Annual awards for students aged 6-19. Each ms must be written and illustrated by the same student and submitted only via the contest. Guidelines for #10 SAE with 2 first-class stamps. Charges $1 fee.

STEPHEN LEACOCK MEMORIAL AWARD FOR HUMOUR, Stephen Leacock Associates, P.O. Box 854, Orillia, Ontario L3V 6K8 Canada. (705)325-6546. Contest Director: Jean Dickson. Estab. 1947. For a book of humor published in previous year by a Canadian author. Include 10 copies of each entry and a b&w photo with bio. Deadline: December 31. Charges $25 fee. Prize: Stephen Leacock Memorial Medal and Laurentian Bank of Canada Award of $5,000.

LOUDEST LAF! LAUREL, *Laf!* Scher Maihem Publishing Ltd., P.O. Box 313, Avilla IN 46710-0313. Fax: (219)897-2674. E-mail: scherlaf@16c.apc.org. Contact: Fran Glass. "To encourage the writing of excellent short humor (600 words or less), and to develop great humorists in the tradition of Mark Twain." Deadline: June 1. Guidelines for #10 SASE. Charges $10—includes a one-year subscription to *Laf!*, a bimonthly humor tabloid. Prize: $100 grand prize. Winner and exceptional entries will be published in January/February awards edition of *Laf!*

WESTERN HERITAGE AWARD, National Cowboy Hall of Fame & Western Heritage Center, 1700 NE 63rd, Oklahoma City OK 73111. (405)478-2250 ext. 221. Fax: (405)478-4714. Contact: Dana Sullivant. Offered annually for excellence in representation of great stories of the American West published January 1-December 31 in a calendar year. Competition includes 7 literary categories: Nonfiction; Western Novel; Juvenile Book; Art Book; Short Story; Poetry Book; and Magazine Article. Deadline for entries: November 30.

CONTESTS AND AWARDS THAT APPEARED in the 1996 edition of *Writer's Market* but are not included this year are listed in the General Index with a notation explaining their absence.

Resources

Publications of Interest

In addition to newsletters and publications from local and national organizations, there are trade publications, books, and directories which offer valuable information about writing and about marketing your manuscripts and understanding the business side of publishing. Some also list employment agencies that specialize in placing publishing professionals, and some announce actual freelance opportunities.

TRADE MAGAZINES

ADVERTISING AGE, Crain Communications Inc., 740 N. Rush St., Chicago IL 60611. (312)649-5200. *Weekly magazine covering advertising in magazines, trade journals and business.*

AMERICAN JOURNALISM REVIEW, 8701 Adelphi Rd., Adelphi MD 20783. (301)431-4771. *10 issues/ year magazine for journalists and communications professionals.*

DAILY VARIETY, Daily Variety Ltd./Cahners Publishing Co., 5700 Wilshire Blvd., Los Angeles CA 90036. (213)857-6600. *Trade publication on the entertainment industry, with helpful information for screenwriters.*

EDITOR & PUBLISHER, The Editor & Publisher Co., 11 W. 19th St., New York NY 10011. (212)675-4380. *Weekly magazine covering the newspaper publishing industry.*

FOLIO, Cowles Business Media, 11 Riverbend Dr. South, P.O. Box 4949, Stamford CT 06907-0949. (203)358-9900. *Monthly magazine covering the magazine publishing industry.*

GIFTS & DECORATIVE ACCESSORIES, *Geyer-McAllister Publications, Inc., 51 Madison Ave., New YOrk NY 10010-1675. (212)689-4411. Monthly magazine covering greeting cards among other subjects, with an annual buyer's directory in September.*

HORN BOOK MAGAZINE, 11 Beacon St., Boston MA 02108. (617)227-1555. *Bimonthly magazine covering children's literature.*

PARTY & PAPER RETAILER, 4 Ward Corp., 70 New Canaan Ave., Norwalk CT 06850. (203)845-8020. *Monthly magazine covering the greeting card and gift industry.*

POETS & WRITERS INC., 72 Spring St., New York NY 10012. (212)226-3586. *Bimonthly magazine, primarily for literary writers and poets.*

PUBLISHERS WEEKLY, Bowker Magazine Group, Cahners Publishing Co., 249 W. 17th St., 6th Floor, New York NY 10011. (212)645-0067. *Weekly magazine covering the book publishing industry.*

SCIENCE FICTION CHRONICLE, P.O. Box 022730, Brooklyn NY 11202-0056. (718)643-9011. *Monthly magazine for science fiction, fantasy and horror writers.*

TRAVELWRITER MARKETLETTER, The Waldorf-Astoria, Suite 1880, New York NY 10022. *Monthly newsletter for travel writers with market listings as well as trip information.*

THE WRITER, 120 Boylston St., Boston MA 02116. (617)423-3157. *Monthly writers' magazine.*

WRITER'S DIGEST, 1507 Dana Ave., Cincinnati OH 45207. (513)531-2222. *Monthly writers' magazine.*

WRITING FOR MONEY, Blue Dolphin Communications, Inc., 83 Boston Post Rd., Sudbury MA 01776. *Bimonthly freelance market reports.*

BOOKS AND DIRECTORIES

AV MARKET PLACE, R.R. Bowker, A Reed Reference Publishing Co., 121 Chanlon Rd., New Providence NJ 07974. (908)464-6800.

THE COMPLETE BOOK OF SCRIPTWRITING, by J. Michael Straczynski, Writer's Digest Books, 1507 Dana Ave., Cincinnati OH 45207. (513)531-2222.

THE COMPLETE GUIDE TO SELF PUBLISHING, by Marilyn and Tom Ross, Writer's Digest Books, 1507 Dana Ave., Cincinnati OH 45207. (513)531-2222.

COPYRIGHT HANDBOOK, R.R. Bowker, A Reed Reference Publishing Co., 121 Chanlon Rd., New Providence NJ 07974. (908)464-6800.

DRAMATISTS SOURCEBOOK, edited by Kathy Sova, Theatre Communications Group, Inc., 355 Lexington Ave., New York NY 10017. (212)697-5230.

EDITORS ON EDITING: What Writers Need to Know About What Editors Do, edited by Gerald Gross, Grove/Atlantic Press, 841 Broadway, New York NY 10003. *Forty essays by America's most distinguished trade book editors on the art and craft of editing*

GRANTS AND AWARDS AVAILABLE TO AMERICAN WRITERS, *19th Ed., PEN American Center, 568 Broadway, New York NY 10012. (212)334-1660.*

GUIDE TO LITERARY AGENTS, edited by Kirsten Holm, Writer's Digest Books, 1507 Dana Ave., Cincinnati OH 45207. (513)531-2222.

THE GUIDE TO WRITERS CONFERENCES, ShawGuides, Inc. Educational Publishers, Box 1295, New York NY 10023. (212)799-6464.

HOW TO WRITE IRRESISTIBLE QUERY LETTERS, by Lisa Collier Cool, Writer's Digest Books, 1507 Dana Ave., Cincinnati OH 45207. (513)531-2222.

THE INSIDER'S GUIDE TO BOOK EDITORS, PUBLISHERS & LITERARY AGENTS, by Jeff Herman, Prima Publishing, Box 1260, Rocklin CA 95677-1260. (916)632-4400 .

INTERNATIONAL DIRECTORY OF LITTLE MAGAZINES & SMALL PRESSES, edited by Len Fulton, Dustbooks, P.O. Box 100, Paradise CA 95967. (916)877-6110.

LITERARY MARKET PLACE and INTERNATIONAL LITERARY MARKET PLACE, R.R. Bowker, A Reed Reference Publishing Co., 121 Chanlon Rd., New Providence NJ 07974. (908)464-6800.

MAGAZINE WRITING THAT SELLS, by Don McKinney, Writer's Digest Books, 1507 Dana Ave., Cincinnati OH 45207. (513)531-2222.

MY BIG SOURCEBOOK, 66 Canal Center Plaza, Suite 200, Alexandria VA 22314-5507. (703)683-0683.

NATIONAL WRITERS UNION GUIDE TO FREELANCE RATES & STANDARD PRACTICE, by Alexander Kopelman, distributed by Writer's Digest Books, 1507 Dana Ave., Cincinnati OH 45207, (513)531-2222.

PROFESSIONAL WRITER'S GUIDE, edited by Donald Bower and James Lee Young, National Writers Press, Suite 424, 1450 S. Havana, Aurora CO 80012. (303)751-7844.

STANDARD DIRECTORY OF ADVERTISING AGENCIES, National Register Publishing, A Reed Reference Publishing Co., 121 Chanlon Rd., New Providence NJ 07974. (908)464-6800.

SUCCESSFUL SCRIPTWRITING, by Jurgen Wolff and Kerry Cox, Writer's Digest Books, 1507 Dana Ave., Cincinnati OH 45207. (513)531-2222.

THE WRITER'S LEGAL COMPANION, by Brad Bunnin and Peter Beren, Addison-Wesley Publishing Co., 1 Jacob Way, Reading MA 01867. (617)944-3700.

WRITING TOOLS: Essential Software for Anyone Who Writes with a PC, by Hy Bender, Random House Electronic Publishing, 201 E. 50 St., New York NY 10022. (212)751-2600.

Organizations of Interest

Professional organizations, both local and national, can be very helpful in helping writers build contacts. They often provide valuable opportunities for networking, information about new developments in the industry, and guidance in business or legal matters.

The majority of organizations listed here publish newsletters and other materials that can provide you with useful information for your writing career. Some even provide opportunities such as conferences and referral services.

Keep in mind that numerous local organizations and writers' clubs also exist, and can provide occasions for networking in your own area. You can usually find information about such groups in your local library or through an area college writing program.

Some of the following national organizations have branches or chapters in different cities across the country. Write to the organization for information about its membership requirements, individual chapters and programs for writers.

American Book Producers Association
160 Fifth Ave., Suite 625
New York NY 10010-7000
(212)645-2368

American Medical Writers Association
9650 Rockville Pike
Bethesda MD 20814-3998
(301)493-0003

American Society of Journalists &
Authors, Inc.
1501 Broadway, Suite 302
New York NY 10036
(212)997-0947

American Translators Association
1800 Diagonal Rd., Suite 220
Alexandria, VA 22314-0214
(703)683-6100

Associated Writing Programs
Tallwood House MS1E3
George Mason University
Fairfax VA 22030
(703)993-4301

Association of Authors Representatives
10 Astor Pl., 3rd Floor
New York NY 10003
(212)353-3709

Association of Desk-Top Publishers
3401-A800 Adams Way
San Diego CA 92116-2429
(619)563-9714

The Authors Guild
330 W. 42nd St., 29th Floor
New York NY 10036
(212)563-5904

The Authors League of America, Inc.
330 W. 42nd St.
New York NY 10036
(212)564-8350

Copywriters Council of America, Freelance
Linick Bldg. 102, 7 Putter Lane
Middle Island NY 11953-0102
(516)924-8555

The Dramatists Guild
234 W. 44th St., 11th Floor
New York NY 10036
(212)398-9366

Editorial Freelancers Association
71 W. 23rd St., Suite 1504
New York NY 10010
(212)929-5400

Education Writers Association
1331 H. NW, Suite 307
Washington DC 20036
(202)637-9700

Freelance Editorial Association
P.O. Box 380835
Cambridge MA 02238-0835
(617)643-8626

International Association of Business
Communicators
1 Hallidie Plaza, Suite 600
San Francisco CA 94102
(415)433-3400

International Association of Crime
Writers Inc., North American Branch
JAF Box 1500
New York NY 10116
(212)243-8966

International Television Association
6311 N. O'Connor Rd., Suite 230
Irving TX 75039
(214)869-1112

International Women's Writing Guild
Box 810, Gracie Station
New York NY 10028-0082
(212)737-7536

Mystery Writers of America
17 E. 47th St., 6th Floor
New York NY 10017
(212)888-8171

National Association of Science Writers
Box 294
Greenlawn NY 11740
(516)757-5664

National Writers Association
1450 S. Havana, Suite 424
Aurora CO 80012
(303)751-7844

National Writers Union
113 University Place, 6th Floor
New York NY 10003
(212)254-0279

New Dramatists
424 W. 44th St.
New York NY 10036
(212)757-6060

PEN American Center
568 Broadway
New York NY 10012
(212)334-1660

Poetry Society of America
15 Grammercy Park
New York NY 10003
(212)254-9628

Poets & Writers
72 Spring St.
New York NY 10012
(212)226-3586

Public Relations Society of America
33 Irving Place
New York NY 10003
(212)995-2230

Romance Writers of America
13700 Veterans Memorial Dr., Suite 315
Houston TX 77014
(713)440-6885

Science-Fiction and Fantasy Writers of America
Suite 1B, 5 Winding Brook Dr.
Guilderland NY 12084
(518)869-5361

Seattle Writers Association
P.O. Box 33265
Seattle WA 98133
(206)860-5207

Society of American Business Editors & Writers
% Janine Latus-Musick
University of Missouri
School of Journalism
76 Gannett Hall
Columbia MO 65211
(314)882-7862

Society of American Travel Writers
4101 Lake Boone Trail, Suite 201
Raleigh NC 27607
(919)787-5181

Society of Children's Book Writers and Illustrators
22736 Vanowen St., Suite 106
West Hills CA 91307
(818)888-8760

Society of Professional Journalists
16 S. Jackson
Greencastle IN 46135
(317)653-3333

Volunteer Lawyers for the Arts
1 E. 53rd St., 6th Floor
New York NY 10022
(212)319-2787

Women in Communications, Inc.
Suite 417, 2101 Wilson Blvd.
Arlington VA 22201

Writers Alliance
12 Skylark Lane
Stony Brook NY 11790
(516)751-7080

Writers Guild of Alberta
11759 Groat Rd.
Edmonton, AB T5M 3K6 Canada

Writers Guild of America (East)
555 W. 57th St.
New York NY 10019
(212)767-7800

Writers Guild of America (West)
8955 Beverly Blvd.
West Hollywood CA 90048
(310)550-1000

Websites of Interest

The Internet provides a wealth of information for writers. The number of websites devoted to writing and publishing is vast and will continue to expand as the year progresses. Below is a short—and thus incomplete—list of websites that offer information and hypertext links to other pertinent sites relating to writing and publishing. Because the Internet is such an amorphous, evolving, mutable entity with website addresses launching, crashing and changing daily, some of these addresses may be obsolete by the time this book goes to print. But this list does give you a few starting points for your online journey. If, in the course of your electronic ventures, you find additional websites of interest, please let us know by e-mailing us at wdigest@aol.com.

AcqWeb: http://www.library.vanderbilt.edu/law/acqs/acqs.html
Although geared toward librarians and researchers, AcqWeb provides reference information useful to writers, such as library catalogs, bibliographic services, Books in Print, and other Web reference resources.

The Biz: http://www.bizmag.com
Entertainment information, including interviews, coverage of film, TV, and other new media.

Book Zone: http://www.bookzone.com
A catalog source for books, audio books, and more, with links to other publishing opportunities, diversions and distractions, such as news, classifieds, contests, magazines, and trade groups.

Books A to Z: http://www.booksatoz.com
Information on publications services and leads to other useful websites, including areas for book research, production services, self-publishing, bookstores, organizations, and publishers.

Books and Writing Online: http://www.clark.net/pub/iz/Books/books.html
A collection of sources directing you to other sites on the net, this is a good place to jump to other areas on the Web with information pertaining to writing, literature and publishing.

BookWeb: http://www.ambook.org
This ABA site offers books news, markets, discussions groups, events, resources and other book-related information.

Bookwire: http://www.bookwire.com
A gateway to finding information about publishers, booksellers, libraries, authors, reviews and awards. Also offers information about frequently asked publishing questions and answers, a calendar of events, a mailing list, and other helpful resources.

Children's Writing Resource Center: http://www.mindspring.com/~cbi
Presented by Children's Book Insider, The Newsletter for Children's Writers. Offers information on numerous aspects of publishing and children's literature, such as an InfoCenter, a Research Center, results of various surveys, and secrets on getting published.

Editor & Publisher: http://www.mediainfo.com:80/edpub/ep/classi.htm

The Internet source for Editor & Publisher, *this site provides up-to-date industry news, with other opportunities such as a research area and bookstore, a calendar of events and classifieds.*

E-Talent.Net.Inc.: http://www.e-talentnet.com

A writer's service covering rights, critiques, publishing and other nuts and bolts aspects of the industry, including how to network and develop projects in most creative mediums from screenplays to novels to computer programs.

Internet Entertainment Network: http://HollywoodNetwork.com

Home to Showbiz Online.com, this site covers everything in Hollywood whether its dealmaking, music, screenwriting, or profiles of agents and Hollywood executives.

Internet Road Map to Books: http://www.bookport.com/b_roadmap.html

Leads to publishers' websites, resources for writers, book reviews, online editing, and other helpful areas.

Ultimate Book List and Writer's Page: http://www.missouri.edu/~wleric/writehelp.html

Provides links and information on resources, references, authors, online writing, publishing, handouts, other websites of interest, prize winners and more.

The Write Page: http://www.writepage.com

Online newsletter for readers and writers of genre fiction, featuring information on authors, books about writing, new releases, organizations, conferences, websites, research, public service efforts writers can partake in, and writer's rights.

The Writer's Edge: http://www.nashville.net/~edge

Points you in the right direction for almost every aspect of writing, from genre fiction to agents to journalism to libraries and workshops.

Writer's Resources: http://www.interlog.com/~ohi/www/writesource.html

An elaborate site that provides information about workshops, how-to information, copyright, quotations, writing tips, resources, contests, market information, publishers, booksellers, associations, mailing lists, newsletters, conferences, and more.

U.S. Postage by the Page

Mailing costs are a growing part of a writer's expenses. One way to keep costs down is to use only the necessary amount of postage—even when the post office is closed. With the information below, you can avoid the last minute deadline need of over-stamping.

These charts can help save time as well as money by allowing you to figure the fees for sending your manuscripts to prospective publishers in your home office rather than standing in line at the post office.

Postage rates are listed by numbers of pages in 20 lb. paper according to the most commonly used envelopes and their SASEs. The cost of mailing a first-class envelope is 32¢. Increases in other areas are anticipated after further study by the post office. Watch for notices at your local post office.

First Class mail weighing more than 11 ounces is priced at the same rate as Priority Mail—up to two pounds, $3; up to three pounds, $4; up to four pounds, $5; up to five pounds, $6; over five pounds needs to be priced at the post office.

Another way to save money is on the return SASE. If the postage costs are higher than duplicating costs, a #10 stamped envelope or a postcard (20¢) can be used for the editor's reply.

For short manuscripts or long queries, use a #10 (business-size) envelope with a 32¢ stamp. Four pages is the limit for that postage, if you are including a SASE. Another option is the 6×9 envelope. For 1-3 pages, postage is 32¢; for 4-7 pages with SASE, the cost is 55¢.

Computer disks may be sent in official mailers or mid-size envelopes with stiffening for 78¢.

See page 940 for Canadian Postage by the Page.

It's where **Faulkner** and **Cheever**
submitted their early work.

It's where **Salinger, Saroyan,
McCullers** and **Mailer**
were first published.

And now it's where **today's most
exciting new writers**
come to show you their talent.

To Subscribe, mail this form in the attached envelope. You'll get 4 quarterly issues at the introductory rate of just $19.96, a savings of 28% off the newsstand price.

_____
NAME

_____
ADDRESS

_____
CITY

_____
STATE   ZIP

☐ Payment enclosed   ☐ Bill me

Charge my   ☐ Visa   ☐ MC

| | | | | | | | | | | | | | | | |
Exp. _____

Signature _____

Outside U.S. add $7 (includes GST in Canada) and remit in U.S. funds. Allow 4-6 weeks for first issue delivery. Annual newsstand rate $27.80.

TTWM7-STY

Ounces	9×12 envelope, 9×12 SASE number of pages	9×12 SASE (for return trips) number of pages	First Class Postage	Third Class ** Postage	Postage from U.S. to Canada **
under 2	...	1 to 2	$.43*	$.43*	$.63*
2	1 to 4	3 to 8	.55	.55	.72
3	5 to 10	9 to 12	.78	.78	.95
4	11 to 16	13 to 19	1.01	1.01	1.14
5	17 to 21	20 to 25	1.24	1.24	1.33
6	22 to 27	26 to 30	1.47	1.47	1.52
7	28 to 32	31 to 35	1.70	1.70	1.71
8	33 to 38	36 to 41	1.93	1.93	1.90
9	39 to 44	42 to 46	2.16	2.16	2.09
10	45 to 49	47 to 52	2.39	2.39	2.28
11	50 to 55	53 to 57	2.62	2.62	2.47
12-32	56 to 99	58 to 101	3.00	***2.90	****2.66

* This cost includes an 11¢ assessment for oversized mail that is light in weight.

** Third class mail, whose rates now are almost identical to First Class mail, is restricted to books and other printed matter that weighs less than a pound. Fourth Class Mail can be used for printed material weighing more than a pound. It is priced by weight and distance, with attached personal letters being charged at First Class rates.

*** This rate is good to 13 ounces. Between 13 ounces and a pound, the rate is $2.95.

**** This rate is good under 12 ounces. Heavier packages need to be priced at the post office.

Canadian Postage by the Page

The following chart is for the convenience of Canadian writers sending domestic mail and American writers sending a SAE with International Reply Coupons (IRCs) or Canadian stamps for return of a manuscript from a Canadian publisher.

For complete postage assistance, use in conjunction with the U.S. Postage by the Page. Remember that manuscripts returning from the U.S. to Canada will take a U.S. stamped envelope although the original manuscript was sent with Canadian postage. The reverse applies to return envelopes sent by American writers to Canada; they must be accompanied with IRCs or Canadian postage.

In a #10 envelope, you can have up to five pages for 45¢ (on manuscripts within Canada) or 52¢ (on manuscripts going to the U.S.). If you enclose a SASE, four pages is the limit. If you use 10×13 envelopes, send one page less than indicated on the chart.

IRC's are worth 45¢ Canadian postage and 60¢ U.S. postage but cost $1.05 to buy in the U.S. and $3.50 to buy in Canada. (Hint to U.S. writers: If you live near the border or have a friend in Canada, stock up on Canadian stamps. Not only are they more convenient than IRCs, they are far cheaper.)

Canada Post designations for types of mail are:

Standard Letter Mail	Minimum size: 9cm × 14cm (3⁹⁄₁₆×5½″); Maximum size: 15cm × 24.5cm (5⅞×9⅝″); Maximum thickness: 5mm (³⁄₁₆″)
Oversize Letter Mail (Exceeds any measurement for Standard)	Maximum size: 27cm ×38cm (10⅞×15″); Maximum thickness: 2cm (¹³⁄₁₆″)
International Letter Mail	Minimum size: 9cm × 14cm (3⅝×5½″); Maximum size: Length + width + depth 90cm (36″); Greatest dimension must not exceed 60cm (24″)

Insurance: To U.S.—$1 for each $100 coverage to the maximum coverage of $1,000. Within Canada—$1 for first $100 coverage; 45¢ for each additional $100 coverage to a maximum coverage of $1,000. International—$1 for each $100 coverage to the maximum coverage allowed by country of destination. (Not accepted by all countries.)

Registered Mail: $3.15 plus postage (air or surface—Canadian destination). Legal proof of mailing provided. No indemnity coverage. International destination: $5 plus postage. Fee includes fixed indemnity of $40.

Security Registered Mail: Within Canada—$5 for the first $250 indemnity (letter mail only); 45¢ for each additional $100 to a maximum of $5,000. (Plus appropriate postage.)* To U.S.—$5.60 for the first $100 indemnity; $1 for each additional $100 to a maximum of $1,000. (Plus appropriate postage.) International—$5.60 plus postage (air); fee includes fixed indemnity of $40.

---

* Acknowledgement of receipt (all destinations) 90¢ at time of mailing; $1.60 after mailing (Canadian destination only). GST (Goods and Services Tax) of 7% is charged on **all** postage and postal services.

Weight up to	9×12 envelope, 9×12 SASE number of pages*	9×12 SASE (for return trips) number of pages	Canada Standard	Canada Oversize	First Class to U.S. Standard	First Class to U.S. Oversize	International
30 g / 1.07 oz.	...	1 to 3	$ .45	$ .90	$ .52	$1.17	$ .90 (20g)
50 g / 1.78 oz.	1 to 4	4 to 7	.71	.90	.77	1.17	1.37
100 g / 3.5 oz.	5 to 14	8 to 18		.90		1.17	2.25
200 g / 7.1 oz.	15 to 46	19 to 49		1.45		2.23	5.05 (250g)
300 g / 10.7 oz.	47 to 57	50 to 61		2.05		3.80	9.90
400 g / 14.2 oz.	58 to 79	62 to 82		2.05		3.80	9.90
500 g / 17.8 oz.	80 to 101	83 to 104		2.05		3.80	9.90
1.0 kg / 2.2 lbs.	102 to 208	105 to 212	**	**			(See Small Packets, below)

*Based on 20 lb. paper and 2 adhesive labels per envelope.
**For Canadian residents mailing parcels 1 kg. and over within Canada (domestic mail), rates vary according to destination. Ask your Post Master for the chart for your area.
***Over 1 kg. rates vary by destination (country).

Small packets is a category designed to provide an alternative to Parcel Post for items weighing up to 2 kg. They may be sealed and security registered but cannot be insured (unless sent at parcel rates). An "Air Mail" sticker is required on all air mail small packets. All small packets must bear a green Customs label C1 (form no. 43-074-013). Parcels over 1 kg. to U.S. require customs label no. 43-074-076).

Small Packets to U.S.

Weight up to	Air	Surface
100g	$3.50	$2.50
250g	3.50	2.30
500g	4.85	3.55
1 kg	8.55	6.20

Small Packets—International

Weight up to	Air	Surface
100g	$ 2.20	$1.44
250g	4.10	2.60
500g	8.05	4.10
1 kg	16.10	7.20

Priority Courier: Letter—$8.55 regional, $12.70 national, $23.50 to U.S. Pack—$10.50 regional, $14.85 national, $28.65 to U.S. Overnight delivery to some major centers.
SkyPak International Courier: For rates, call 1-800-661-3434.

Glossary

Key to symbols and abbreviations is on page 70.

Advance. A sum of money a publisher pays a writer prior to the publication of a book. It is usually paid in installments, such as one-half on signing the contract; one-half on delivery of a complete and satisfactory manuscript. The advance is paid against the royalty money that will be earned by the book.

Advertorial. Advertising presented in such a way as to resemble editorial material. Information may be the same as that contained in an editorial feature, but it is paid for or supplied by an advertiser and the word "advertisement" appears at the top of the page.

All rights. See Rights and the Writer in the Minding the Details article.

Anthology A collection of selected writings by various authors or a gathering of works by one author

Assignment. Editor asks a writer to produce a specific article for an agreed-upon fee.

Auction. Publishers sometimes bid for the acquisition of a book manuscript that has excellent sales prospects. The bids are for the amount of the author's advance, advertising and promotional expenses, royalty percentage, etc. Auctions are conducted by agents.

B&W. Abbreviation for black and white photographs.

Backlist. A publisher's list of its books that were not published during the current season, but that are still in print.

Belles lettres. A term used to describe fine or literary writing—writing more to entertain than to inform or instruct.

Bimonthly. Every two months. See also *semimonthly*.

Bionote. A sentence or brief paragraph about the writer. Also called a "bio," it can appear at the bottom of the first or last page of a writer's article or short story or on a contributor's page.

Biweekly. Every two weeks.

Boilerplate. A standardized contract. When an editor says "our standard contract," he means the boilerplate with no changes. Writers should be aware that most authors and/or agents make many changes on the boilerplate.

Book packager. Draws all elements of a book together, from the initial concept to writing and marketing strategies, then sells the book package to a book publisher and/or movie producer. Also known as book producer or book developer.

Business size envelope. Also known as a #10 envelope, it is the standard size used in sending business correspondence.

Byline. Name of the author appearing with the published piece.

Category fiction. A term used to include all various labels attached to types of fiction. See also *genre*.

CD-ROM. Compact Disc-Read Only Memory. A computer information storage medium capable of holding enormous amounts of data. Information on a CD-ROM cannot be deleted. A computer user must have a CD-ROM drive to access a CD-ROM.

Chapbook. A small booklet, usually paperback, of poetry, ballads or tales.

Clean copy. A manuscript free of errors, cross-outs, wrinkles or smudges.

Clips Samples, usually from newspapers or magazines, of your *published* work.

Coffee table book. An oversize book, heavily illustrated.

Column inch. The amount of space contained in one inch of a typeset column.

Commercial novels. Novels designed to appeal to a broad audience. These are often broken down into categories such as western, mystery and romance. See also *genre*.

Commissioned work. See *assignment*.

Concept. A statement that summarizes a screenplay or teleplay—before the outline or treatment is written.

Contact sheet. A sheet of photographic paper on which negatives are transferred so you can see the entire roll of shots placed together on one sheet of paper without making separate, individual prints.

Contributor's copies. Copies of the issues of magazines sent to the author in which the author's work appears.

Cooperative publishing. See *co-publishing*.

Co-publishing. Arrangement where author and publisher share publication costs and profits of a book. Also known as *cooperative publishing*. See also *subsidy publisher*.

Copyediting. Editing a manuscript for grammar, punctuation and printing style, not subject content.

Copyright. A means to protect an author's work. See Copyright in the Minding the Details section.

Cover letter. A brief letter, accompanying a complete manuscript, especially useful if responding to an editor's request for a manuscript. A cover letter may also accompany a book proposal. A cover letter is *not* a query letter; see Targeting Your Ideas in the Getting Published section.

Derivative works. A work that has been translated, adapted, abridged, condensed, annotated or otherwise produced by altering a previously created work. Before producing a derivative work, it is necessary to secure the written permission of the copyright owner of the original piece.

Desktop publishing. A publishing system designed for a personal computer. The system is capable of typesetting, some illustration, layout, design and printing—so that the final piece can be distributed and/or sold.

Disk. A round, flat magnetic plate on which computer data may be stored.

Docudrama. A fictional film rendition of recent newsmaking events and people.

Dot-matrix. Printed type where individual characters are composed of a matrix or pattern of tiny dots. Near letter quality (see *NLQ*) dot-matrix submissions are generally acceptable to editors.

Electronic submission. A submission made by modem or on computer disk.

El-hi. Elementary to high school.

E-mail. Electronic mail. Mail generated on a computer and delivered over a computer network to a specific individual or group of individuals. To send or receive e-mail, a user must have an account with an online service, which provides an e-mail address and electronic mailbox.

Epigram. A short, witty sometimes paradoxical saying.

Erotica. Fiction or art that is sexually oriented.

Fair use. A provision of the copyright law that says short passages from copyrighted material may be used without infringing on the owner's rights.

Fax (facsimile machine). A communication system used to transmit documents over telephone lines.

Feature. An article giving the reader information of human interest rather than news. Also used by magazines to indicate a lead article or distinctive department.

Filler. A short item used by an editor to "fill" out a newspaper column or magazine page. It could be a timeless news item, a joke, an anecdote, some light verse or short humor, puzzle, etc.

First North American serial rights. See Rights and the Writer in the Minding the Details article.

Formula story. Familiar theme treated in a predictable plot structure—such as boy meets girl, boy loses girl, boy gets girl.

Frontlist. A publisher's list of its books that are new to the current season.

Galleys. The first typeset version of a manuscript that has not yet been divided into pages.

Genre. Refers either to a general classification of writing, such as the novel or the poem, or to the categories within those classifications, such as the problem novel or the sonnet. Genre fiction describes commercial novels, such as mysteries, romances and science fiction. Also called category fiction.

Ghostwriter. A writer who puts into literary form an article, speech, story or book based on another person's ideas or knowledge.

Glossy. A black and white photograph with a shiny surface as opposed to one with a non-shiny matte finish.

Gothic novel. A fiction category or genre in which the central character is usually a beautiful young girl, the setting an old mansion or castle, and there is a handsome hero and a real menace, either natural or supernatural.

Graphic novel. An adaptation of a novel in graphic form, long comic strip or heavily illustrated story, of 40 pages or more, produced in paperback form.

Hard copy. The printed copy of a computer's output.

Hardware. All the mechanically-integrated components of a computer that are not software. Circuit boards, transistors and the machines that are the actual computer are the hardware.

Home page. The first page of a World Wide Web document.

Honorarium. Token payment—small amount of money, or a byline and copies of the publication.

Hypertext. Words or groups of words in an electronic document that are linked to other text, such as a definition or a related document. Hypertext can also be linked to illustrations.

Illustrations. May be photographs, old engravings, artwork. Usually paid for separately from the manuscript. See also *package sale*.

Imprint. Name applied to a publisher's specific line or lines of books (e.g., Anchor Books is an imprint of Doubleday).

Interactive. A type of computer interface that takes user input, such as answers to computer-generated questions, and then acts upon that input.

Interactive fiction. Works of fiction in book or computer software format in which the reader determines the path the story will take. The reader chooses from several alternatives at the end of a "chapter," and thus determines the structure of the story. Interactive fiction features multiple plots and endings.

Internet. A worldwide network of computers that offers access to a wide variety of electronic resources. Originally a US Department of Defense project, begun in 1969.

Invasion of privacy. Writing about persons (even though truthfully) without their consent.

Kill fee. Fee for a complete article that was assigned but which was subsequently cancelled.

Lead time. The time between the acquisition of a manuscript by an editor and its actual publication.

Letter-quality submission Computer printout that looks typewritten.

Libel. A false accusation or any published statement or presentation that tends to expose another to public contempt, ridicule, etc. Defenses are truth; fair comment on a matter of public interest; and privileged communication—such as a report of legal proceedings or client's communication to a lawyer.

List royalty. A royalty payment based on a percentage of a book's retail (or "list") price. Compare *net royalty*.

Little magazine. Publications of limited circulation, usually on literary or political subject matter.

LORT. An acronym for League of Resident Theatres. Letters from A to D follow LORT and designate the size of the theater.

Magalog. Mail order catalog with how-to articles pertaining to the items for sale.

Mainstream fiction. Fiction that transcends popular novel categories such as mystery, romance and science fiction. Using conventional methods, this kind of fiction tells stories about people and their conflicts with greater depth of characterization, background, etc., than the more narrowly focused genre novels.

Mass market. Nonspecialized books of wide appeal directed toward a large audience. Smaller and more cheaply produced than trade paperbacks, they are found in many non-bookstore outlets, such as drug stores, supermarkets, etc.

Microcomputer A small computer system capable of performing various specific tasks with data it receives. Personal computers are microcomputers.

Midlist. Those titles on a publisher's list that are not expected to be big sellers, but are expected to have limited sales. Midlist books are mainstream, not literary, scholarly or genre, and are usually written by new or unknown writers.

Model release. A paper signed by the subject of a photograph (or the subject's guardian, if a juvenile) giving the photographer permission to use the photograph, editorially or for advertising purposes or for some specific purpose as stated.

Modem. A device used to transmit data from one computer to another via telephone lines.

Monograph. A detailed and documented scholarly study concerning a single subject.

Multimedia. Computers and software capable of integrating text, sound, photographic-quality images, animation and video.

Multiple submissions Sending more than one poem, gag or greeting card idea at the same time. This term is often used synonymously with simultaneous submission.

Net royalty. A royalty payment based on the amount of money a book publisher receives on the sale of a book after booksellers' discounts, special sales discounts and returns. Compare list royalty.

Network. A group of computers electronically linked to share information and resources.

Newsbreak. A brief, late-breaking news story added to the front page of a newspaper at press time or a magazine news item of importance to readers.

NLQ. Near letter-quality print required by some editors for computer printout submissions. See also *dot-matrix*

Novelette. A short novel, or a long short story; 7,000 to 15,000 words approximately. Also known as a novella.

Novelization. A novel created from the script of a popular movie, usually called a movie "tie-in" and published in paperback.

Offprint. Copies of an author's article taken "out of issue" before a magazine is bound and given to the author in lieu of monetary payment. An offprint could be used by the writer as a published writing sample.

On spec. An editor expresses an interest in a proposed article idea and agrees to consider the finished piece for publication "on speculation." The editor is under no obligation to buy the finished manuscript.

One-shot feature. As applies to syndicates, single feature article for syndicate to sell; as contrasted with article series or regular columns syndicated.

One-time rights. See Rights and the Writer in the Minding the Details article.

Online Service. Computer networks accessed via modem. These services provide users with various resources, such as electronic mail, news, weather, special interest groups and shopping. Examples of such providers include America Online and CompuServe.

Outline. A summary of a book's contents in five to 15 double-spaced pages; often in the form of chapter headings with a descriptive sentence or two under each one to show the scope of the book. A screenplay's or teleplay's outline is a scene-by-scene narrative description of the story (10-15 pages for a ½-hour teleplay; 15-25 pages for a 1-hour teleplay; 25-40 pages for a 90-minute teleplay; 40-60 pages for a 2-hour feature film or teleplay).

Over-the-transom. Describes the submission of unsolicited material by a freelance writer.

Package sale. The editor buys manuscript and photos as a "package" and pays for them with one check.

Page rate. Some magazines pay for material at a fixed rate per published page, rather than per word

Parallel submission. A strategy of developing several articles from one unit of research for submission to similar magazines. This strategy differs from simultaneous or multiple submission, where the same article is marketed to several magazines at the same time.

Payment on acceptance. The editor sends you a check for your article, story or poem as soon as he decides to publish it.

Payment on publication. The editor doesn't send you a check for your material until it is published.

Pen name. The use of a name other than your legal name on articles, stories or books when you wish to remain anonymous. Simply notify your post office and bank that you are using the name so that you'll receive mail and/or checks in that name. Also called a pseudonym.

Photo feature. Feature in which the emphasis is on the photographs rather than on accompanying written material.

Plagiarism. Passing off as one's own the expression of ideas and words of another writer.

Potboiler. Refers to writing projects a freelance writer does to "keep the pot boiling" while working on major articles—quick projects to bring in money with little time or effort. These may be fillers such as anecdotes or how-to tips, but could be short articles or stories.

Proofreading. Close reading and correction of a manuscript's typographical errors.

Proscenium. The area of the stage in front of the curtain

Prospectus. A preliminary written description of a book or article, usually one page in length.

Pseudonym. See *pen name*.

Public domain. Material that was either never copyrighted or whose copyright term has expired.

Query. A letter to an editor intended to raise interest in an article you propose to write.

Release. A statement that your idea is original, has never been sold to anyone else and that you are selling the negotiated rights to the idea upon payment.

Remainders. Copies of a book that are slow to sell and can be purchased from the publisher at a reduced price. Depending on the author's book contract, a reduced royalty or no royalty is paid on remainder books.

Reporting time. The time it takes for an editor to report to the author on his/her query or manuscript.

Reprint rights. See Rights and the Writer in the Minding the Details article.

Round-up article. Comments from, or interviews with, a number of celebrities or experts on a single theme.

Royalties, standard hardcover book. 10% of the retail price on the first 5,000 copies sold; 12½% on the next 5,000; 15% thereafter.

Royalties, standard mass paperback book. 4 to 8% of the retail price on the first 150,000 copies sold.

Royalties, standard trade paperback book. No less than 6% of list price on the first 20,000 copies; 7½% thereafter.

Scanning. A process through which letter-quality printed text (see *NLQ*) or artwork is read by a computer scanner and converted into workable data.

Screenplay. Script for a film intended to be shown in theaters.

Self-publishing. In this arrangement, the author keeps all income derived from the book, but he pays for its manufacturing, production and marketing.

Semimonthly. Twice per month.

Semiweekly. Twice per week.

Serial. Published periodically, such as a newspaper or magazine.

Sidebar. A feature presented as a companion to a straight news report (or main magazine article) giving sidelights on human-interest aspects or sometimes elucidating just one aspect of the story.

Similar submission. See *parallel submission*.

Simultaneous submissions. Sending the same article, story or poem to several publishers at the same time. Some publishers refuse to consider such submissions. No simultaneous submissions should be made without stating the fact in your letter.

Slant. The approach or style of a story or article that will appeal to readers of a specific magazine. For example, a magazine may always use stories with an upbeat ending.

Slice-of-life vignette. A short fiction piece intended to realistically depict an interesting moment of everyday living.

Slides. Usually called transparencies by editors looking for color photographs.

Slush pile. The stack of unsolicited or misdirected manuscripts received by an editor or book publisher.

Software. The computer programs that control computer hardware, usually run from a disk drive of some sort. Computers need software in order to run. These can be word processors, games, spreadsheets, etc.

Speculation. The editor agrees to look at the author's manuscript with no assurance that it will be bought.

Style. The way in which something is written—for example, short, punchy sentences or flowing narrative.

Subsidiary rights. All those rights, other than book publishing rights included in a book contract—such as paperback, book club, movie rights, etc.

Subsidy publisher. A book publisher who charges the author for the cost to typeset and print his book, the jacket, etc. as opposed to a royalty publisher who pays the author.

Synopsis. A brief summary of a story, novel or play. As part of a book proposal, it is a comprehensive summary condensed in a page or page and a half, single-spaced. See also *outline*.

Tabloid Newspaper format publication on about half the size of the regular newspaper page, such as the *National Enquirer*.

Tagline. A caption for a photo or a comment added to a filler.

Tearsheet. Page from a magazine or newspaper containing your printed story, article, poem or ad.

Trade. Either a hardcover or paperback book; subject matter frequently concerns a special interest. Books are directed toward the layperson rather than the professional.

Transparencies. Positive color slides; not color prints.

Treatment. Synopsis of a television or film script (40-60 pages for a 2-hour feature film or teleplay).

Unsolicited manuscript. A story, article, poem or book that an editor did not specifically ask to see.

User friendly. Easy to handle and use. Refers to computer hardware and software designed with the user in mind.

Vanity publisher. See *subsidy publisher*.

Word processor. A computer program, used in lieu of a typewriter, that allows for easy, flexible manipulation and output of printed copy.

World Wide Web (WWW). An Internet resource that utilizes hypertext to access information. It also supports formatted text, illustrations and sounds, depending on the user's computer capabilities.

Work-for-hire. See Copyright in the Minding the Details article.

YA. Young adult books.

k Publishers Subject Index

This index will help you find publishers that consider books on specific subjects—the subjects you choose to write about. Remember that a publisher may be listed here under a general subject category such as Art and Architecture, while the company publishes *only* art history or how-to books. Be sure to consult each company's detailed individual listing, its book catalog and several of its books before you send your query or proposal. The page number of the detailed listing is provided for your convenience.

FICTION

Adventure: Ariadne 265; Atheneum Books For Young Readers 87; Avanyu 88; Avon 88; Bantam Books 90; Bethel 93; Book Creations 286; Bookcraft 96; Borealis 241; Caitlin 242; Carol 103; Cave 104; Clarion 108; Comic Art 110; Compass Prods. 286; Dancing Jester 115; Davies, Robert 244; Dial Books For Young Readers 119; Fine, Donald 128; HarperCollins 136; ICS Books, Inc. 144; Jenkins Group 288; Jones Univ., Bob 152; Just Us Books 152; Kar-Ben Copies 152; Landmine 274; Little, Brown (Children's) 160; Lodestar 161; Mountaineers, The 172; New Victoria 175; PREP 192; Quintet 254; Quixote 196; Random House 197; Red Deer College 255; Settel Assoc. 291; Sierra Club 206; Sligo 208; Snowapple 257; Soho Press 209; Sunshine 257; Tudor 220; Turnstone 259; Vandamere 228; Visual Assault Comics 283; Weiss, Daniel 292; Wordstorm Prods. 262; Write Way 237; Zebra and Pinnacle 237

Confession: Carol 103; Random House 197; Sunshine 257; Dancing Jester 115; Ekstasis Editions 246; Gay Sunshine/Leyland 131; Holmes 141; New Victoria 175; Quintet 254; Settel Assoc. 291; Spectrum 210; Sunshine 257; Vandamere 228; Visual Assault Comics 283; Zebra and Pinnacle 237

Erotic: Dancing Jester 115; Ekstasis Editions 246; Gay Sunshine/Leyland 131; Holmes 141; New Victoria 175; Quintet 254; Settel Assoc. 291; Spectrum 210; Sunshine 257; Vandemere 228; Visual Assault Comics 283; Zebra and Pinnacle 237

Ethnic: Arcade 85; Arsenal Pulp 240; Atheneum Books For Young Readers 87; Aurora Editions 240; Avalon 88; Avon Flare 88; Blue Dolphin 94; Borealis 241; Branden 97; Bryant & Dillon 99; Canadian Inst. of Ukrainian Studies 242; Carolina Wren 268; Confluence 111; Coteau 244; Dancing Jester 115; Duncan & Duncan 121; Ecco 123; Fine, Donald 128; Four Walls Eight Windows 129; Gay Sunshine/Leyland 131; HarperCollins Publishers 248; Herald 139; Herald Press Canada 248; Interlink 147; Jenkins Group 288; Just Us Books 152; Kar-Ben Copies 152; Kaya Prod. 153; Lee & Low 157; Lincoln Springs 274; Little, Brown (Children's) 160; Lollipop Power 275; Mage 165; Media Bridge 168; Mercury House 168; Northland 177; Polychrome 191; Post-Apollo 279; QED 196; Quintet 254; Quixote 196; Red Deer College 255; Riverrun 200; Royal Fireworks 200; Snowapple 257; Soho Press 209; Span Press 210; Spectrum 210; Spinsters Ink 211; Stone Bridge Press 212; Third World 217; Tudor 220; Turnstone 259; Univ. of Illinois 223; Univ. of Texas 226; Visual Assault Comics 283; Ward Hill 230; White Pine 234; YMAA 284

Experimental: Arsenal Pulp 240; Atheneum Books For Young Readers 87; Aurora Editions 240; Beach Holme 240; Dancing Jester 115; Ekstasis Editions 246; Empyreal 246; Gay Sunshine/Leyland 131; Goose Lane 246; HarperCollins Publishers 248; Kaya Prod. 153; Livingston 160; McClelland & Stewart 251; Mercury House 168; Post-Apollo 279; Quarry 254; Quixote 196; Random House 197; Red Deer College 255; Riverrun 200; Ronsdale 256; Smith, The 208; Snowapple 257; Spectrum 210; Stone Bridge Press 212; Sunshine 257; Third Side 217; Turnstone 259; Univ. of Illinois 223; Visual Assault Comics 283; York Press 262

Fantasy: Atheneum Books For Young Readers 87; Avon 88; Bantam Books 90; Blue Sky Marketing, Inc. 266; Blue Star 95; Carol 103; Comic Art 110; Compass Prods. 286; Crossway 114; Davies, Robert 244; Dial Books For Young Readers 119; HarperCollins 136; HarperCollins Publishers 248; Hollow Earth 140; Humanitas 249; Just Us Books 152; Kar-Ben Copies 152; Lion Publishing 159; Little, Brown (Children's) 160; Lodestar 161; Naiad 172; New Victoria 175; Overlook 181; Random House 197; Red Deer College 255; St. Martin's 202; Settel Assoc. 291; Snowapple 257; Stone Bridge Press 212; Sunshine 257; TOR 219; Visual Assault Comics 283; Warner Books 231; Write Way 237; Zebra and Pinnacle 237

Feminist: Ariadne 265; Arsenal Pulp 240; Aurora Editions 240; Bantam Books 90; Blizzard 241; Calyx

Books 268; Carolina Wren 268; Circlet 108; Cleis 109; Coteau 244; Dancing Jester 115; Empyreal 246; Firebrand 128; Four Walls Eight Windows 129; Goose Lane 246; HarperCollins Publishers 248; Interlink 147; Kaya Prod. 153; Lincoln Springs 274; Little, Brown (Children's) 160; Mage 165; Mercury House 168; Negative Capability 174; New Victoria 175; Papier-Mache 184; Permeable Press 188; Post-Apollo 279; Quarry 254; Sligo 208; Smith, The 208; Snowapple 257; Soho Press 209; Spectrum 210; Spinsters Ink 211; Stone Bridge Press 212; Sunshine 257; Third Side 217; Third World 217; Turnstone 259

Gay/Lesbian: Alyson 81; Arsenal Pulp 240; Bantam Books 90; Blizzard 241; Brown Bear 242; Calyx Books 268; Carolina Wren 268; Champion 105; Circlet 108; Cleis 109; Dancing Jester 115; Davies, Robert 244; Empyreal 246; Firebrand 128; Gay Sunshine/Leyland 131; Kaya Prod. 153; Little, Brown (Children's) 160; Lollipop Power 275; Madwoman 275; Mercury House 168; New Victoria 175; Permeable Press 188; Post-Apollo 279; Quarry 254; Riverrun 200; Sligo 208; Spectrum 210; Spinsters Ink 211; Stone Bridge Press 212; Sunshine 257; Third Side 217

Gothic: Atheneum Books For Young Readers 87; Ekstasis Editions 246; HarperCollins 136; HarperCollins Publishers 248; Landmine 274; Lincoln Springs 274; Mercury House 168; TSR 220; Zebra and Pinnacle 237

Historical: Arcade 85; Ariadne 265; Atheneum Books For Young Readers 87; Avanyu 88; Ballantine 89; Bantam Books 90; Barbour 90; Beach Holme 240; Beacon Hill Press of Kansas City 91; Beil, Frederic 92; Berkley Publishing Group 92; Book Creations 286; Bookcraft 96; Borealis 241; Branden 97; Brassey's 97; Caitlin 242; Cave 104; Counterpoint 113; Crossway 114; Dancing Jester 115; Databooks 116; Davies, Robert 244; Dial Books For Young Readers 119; Ecco 123; Éditions La Liberté 245; Fine, Donald 128; Friends United 130; Gay Sunshine/Leyland 131; Goose Lane 246; Harlequin 247; HarperCollins 136; Harper-Collins Publishers 248; Harvest House 137; Herald Press Canada 248; Hiller Box 288; Howells House 142; Ithaca 273; Jenkins Group 288; Just Us Books 152; Kar-Ben Copies 152; Kaya Prod. 153; Kindred Prods. 250; Lincoln Springs 274; Lion Publishing 159; Little, Brown (Children's) 160; Lodestar 161; McClelland & Stewart 251; Mage 165; Nautical & Aviation 173; Negative Capability 174; New Victoria 175; Pansophic 183; Pelican 186; Permeable Press 188; Philomel 189; Pineapple 190; PREP 192; Quintet 254; Random House 197; Red Deer College 255; Riverrun 200; St. Martin's 202; Servant Publications 205; Settel Assoc. 291; Sierra Club 206; Signature Books 206; Silver Moon 291; Sligo 208; Snowapple 257; Soho Press 209; Third World 217; TOR 219; Tudor 220; Tyndale House 221; Ward Hill 230; Weiss, Daniel 292; Write Way 237; Zebra and Pinnacle 237

Horror: Atheneum Books For Young Readers 87; Bantam Books 90; Carol 103; Compass Prods. 286; Fine, Donald 128; Gryphon Pub. 134; HarperCollins Publishers 248; Jenkins Group 288; Landmine 274; Leisure Books 157; PREP 192; Random House 197; St. Martin's 202; Sunshine 257; Visual Assault Comics 283; Warner Books 231; Weiss, Daniel 292; Write Way 237; Zebra and Pinnacle 237

Humor: Acme 263; American Atheist 82; Arcade 85; Ariadne 265; Atheneum Books For Young Readers 87; Avon Flare 88; Caitlin 242; Carol 103; Catbird 103; Center Press 105; Clarion 108; Compass Prods. 286; Coteau 244; Counterpoint 113; Dancing Jester 115; Davenport, May 117; Dial Books For Young Readers 119; Dickens 269; E.M. Press, Inc. 122; HarperCollins Publishers 248; Herald Press Canada 248; Hiller Box 288; ICS Books, Inc. 144; Jenkins Group 288; Just Us Books 152; Key Porter 250; Little, Brown (Children's) 160; Lodestar 161; McClelland & Stewart 251; New Victoria 175; Orloff 181; Pelican 186; Post-Apollo 279; PREP 192; Quixote 196; Red Deer College 255; Riverrun 200; Settel Assoc. 291; Signature Books 206; SJL 207; Sligo 208; Sunshine 257; TSR 220; Tudor 220; Turnstone 259; Vandamere 228; Wordstorm Prods. 262; Zebra and Pinnacle 237

Juvenile: African American Images 79; American Diabetes 83; Archway/Minstrel 85; Atheneum Books For Young Readers 87; Bantam Books 90; Blizzard 241; Blue Sky Marketing, Inc. 266; Bookcraft 96; Borealis 241; Brown Bear 242; Camelot 101; Carolrhoda 103; Clarion 108; Cobblehill 109; Compass Prods. 286; Concordia 111; Coteau 244; Crossway 114; Dancing Jester 115; Davenport, May 117; Davies, Robert 244; Dawn 118; Dial Books For Young Readers 119; Down East 121; Dutton Children's Books 122; E.M. Press, Inc. 122; Eakin Press/Sunbelt Media 122; Éditions La Liberté 245; Editions Phidal 245; Ekstasis Editions 246; Farrar, Straus and Giroux 127; Fiesta City Publishers 271; Free Spirit 130; Friends United 130; Godine, David 132; Grapevine 132; Grosset & Dunlap 133; HarperCollins Publishers 248; Hendrick-Long 138; Herald 139; Herald Press Canada 248; Heritage House 248; Highsmith 140; Hiller Box 288; Holiday House 140; Houghton Mifflin (Children's) 141; Hyperion 144; Ideals Children's Books 144; Interlink 147; Jenkins Group 288; Jones Univ., Bob 152; Just Us Books 152; Kindred Prods. 250; Lee & Low 157; Lerner 157; Little, Brown (Children's) 160; Living the Good News 160; Lollipop Power 275; Lorimer &

Co., James 250; Lothrop, Lee & Shepard 162; McClanahan Book Co. 289; McClelland & Stewart 251; McElderry, Margaret 164; Media Bridge 168; Mega-Books 289; Milkweed 170; Morrow, William 171; Morehouse 171; Northland 177; Orca 252; Pacific Educ. 253; Pansophic 183; Pansophic 278; Pauline Books & Media 185; Peachtree 185; Pelican 186; Philomel 189; Pippin 190; Pleasant Co. 191; Polychrome 191; PREP 192; Quintet 254; Quixote 196; Random House Juvenile 197; Red Deer College 255; Ronsdale 256; Roussan 256; Royal Fireworks 200; Salina Bookshelf 202; Scholastic Canada 256; Scholastic Inc. 204; Settel Assoc. 291; Silver Moon 291; SJL 207; Soundprints 209; Speech Bin 210; Sunshine 257; Third World 217; Thistledown 258; Tidewater 218; Tudor 220; Tyndale House 221; Walker and Co. 230; Ward Hill 230; Weiss, Daniel 292; Whispering Coyote 233; Wisdom 236; Wordstorm Prods. 262

Literary: Arcade 85; Ariadne 265; Arsenal Pulp 240; Aurora Editions 240; Baker Books 89; Bantam Books 90; Beach Holme 240; Beil, Frederic 92; Blizzard 241; Blue Dolphin 94; Bookcraft 96; Borealis 241; Broadway Books 99; Broken Jaw 242; Cadmus Editions 267; Calyx Books 268; Canadian Inst. of Ukrainian Studies 242; Carol 103; Carter 268; Catbird 103; Cave 104; Center Press 105; Champion 105; Cleis 109; Coffee House 109; Confluence 111; Coteau 244; Counterpoint 113; Dancing Jester 115; Davenport, May 117; Davies, Robert 244; E.M. Press, Inc. 122; Ecco 123; Éditions La Liberté 245; Ekstasis Editions 246; Empyreal 246; Eriksson, Paul S. 125; Faber & Faber 126; Fine, Donald 128; Fjord Press 128; Four Walls Eight Windows 129; Godine, David 132; Goose Lane 246; Grove/Atlantic 134; Gutter Press 247; HarperCollins 136; HarperCollins Publishers 248; Herald Press Canada 248; Hollow Earth 140; Houghton Mifflin (Adult) 141; Hounslow 249; Howells House 142; Hyperion 144; Jenkins Group 288; Kaya Prod. 153; Knopf, Alfred 154; Landmine 274; Lincoln Springs 274; Little, Brown 160; Livingston 160; Longstreet 162; McClelland & Stewart 251; Mage 165; Mercury House 168; Mortal Press 276; Negative Capability 174; NeWest 252; Norton, W.W. 178; Orloff 181; Overlook 181; Peachtree 185; Permanent Press/Second Chance Press 188; Permeable Press 188; Pineapple 190; Post-Apollo 279; PREP 192; Puckerbrush 280; QED 196; Quarry 254; Raincoast Book Distribution 255; Red Deer College 255; Riverrun 200; Ronsdale 256; St. Martin's 202; Sand River 281; Sligo 208; Smith, The 208; Snowapple 257; Soho Press 209; Somerville House Books 292; Southern Methodist Univ. 210; Spectrum 210; Stone Bridge Press 212; Stormline 282; Summit Publishing Group 214; Sunshine 257; Third Side 217; Third World 217; Thistledown 258; Three Continents 217; Turnstone 259; Tuttle, Charles E. 259; White Pine 234; Zebra and Pinnacle 237; Zoland 238

Mainstream/Contemporary: Academy Chicago 77; Arcade 85; Ariadne 265; Atheneum Books For Young Readers 87; Avon Flare 88; Bantam Books 90; Berkley Publishing Group 92; Blue Dolphin 94; Bookcraft 96; Caitlin 242; Camelot 101; Confluence 111; Coteau 244; Crossway 114; Dancing Jester 115; Davies, Robert 244; Dickens 269; Duncan & Duncan 121; Dutton 122; E.M. Press, Inc. 122; Eakin Press/Sunbelt Media 122; Ecopress 270; Éditions La Liberté 245; Ekstasis Editions 246; Fine, Donald 128; Fjord Press 128; HarperCollins Publishers 248; Howells House 142; Hyperion 144; Ithaca 273; Jenkins Group 288; Key Porter 250; Landmine 274; Lerner 157; Lincoln Springs 274; Little, Brown 160; Lodestar 161; Longstreet 162; McClelland & Stewart 251; Mage 165; Morrow, William 171; Orloff 181; Paper Chase 183; Papier-Mache 184; Peachtree 185; Permanent Press/Second Chance Press 188; Pineapple 190; Pippin 190; PREP 192; Quarry 254; Quintet 254; Random House 197; Red Deer College 255; St. Martin's 202; Serendipity Systems 204; Seven Stories 205; Sierra Club 206; Simon & Schuster 207; Sligo 208; Snowapple 257; Soho Press 209; Spectrum 210; Sunshine 257; Third Side 217; Third World 217; Tudor 220; Turnstone 259; Univ. of Illinois 223; Univ. of Iowa 223; Univ. Press of Mississippi 227; Warner Books 231; Wordstorm Prods. 262; Zebra and Pinnacle 237

Military/War: Brassey's 97; Naval Inst. 174

Multicultural: Lerner 157; Polychrome 191

Mystery: Academy Chicago 77; Arcade 85; Atheneum Books For Young Readers 87; Avalon 88; Avon 88; Avon Flare 88; Baker Books 89; Bantam Books 90; Berkley Publishing Group 92; Book Creations 286; Bookcraft 96; Bryant & Dillon 99; Camelot 101; Carol 103; Clarion 108; Comic Art 110; Compass Prods. 286; Crossway 114; Dancing Jester 115; Davies, Robert 244; Dial Books For Young Readers 119; Doubleday 120; Duncan & Duncan 121; Fine, Donald 128; Fjord Press 128; Gay Sunshine/Leyland 131; Godine, David 132; Gryphon Pub. 134; HarperCollins 136; HarperCollins Publishers 248; Harvest House 137; Hollow Earth 140; Jenkins Group 288; Kaya Prod. 153; Landmine 274; Lincoln Springs 274; Little, Brown (Children's) 160; Lodestar 161; McClelland & Stewart 251; Mega-Books 289; Naiad 172; New Victoria 175; Orloff 181; Permanent Press/Second Chance Press 188; Pocket Books 191; PREP 192; QED 196; Raincoast Book Distribution 255; Random House 197; Royal Fireworks 200; St. Martin's 202; Scholastic Inc. 204; Settel Assoc. 291; Silver Moon 291; Sligo 208; Snowapple 257; Soho Press 209; Spinsters Ink 211; Stone Bridge Press 212; Sunshine 257; Tudor 220; Vandamere 228; Visual Assault Comics 283; Walker and Co. 230; arner

Books 231; Wordstorm Prods. 262; Write Way 237; Zebra and Pinnacle 237

Occult: Holmes 141; Llewellyn 161; Quintet 254; Sunshine 257; Visual Assault Comics 283; Write Way 237; Zebra and Pinnacle 237

Picture Books: Blizzard 241; Blue Sky Marketing, Inc. 266; Boyds Mills 97; Center Press 105; Cobblehill 109; Compass Prods. 286; Concordia 111; Dancing Jester 115; Dickens 269; Dutton Children's Books 122; Grapevine 132; Grosset & Dunlap 133; Harcourt Brace (Children's) 135; HarperCollins Publishers 248; Herald Press Canada 248; Hiller Box 288; Holiday House 140; Houghton Mifflin (Children's) 141; Ideals Children's Books 144; Interlink 147; Jenkins Group 288; Kaya Prod. 153; Key Porter 250; Little, Brown (Children's) 160; Living the Good News 160; Lodestar 161; Lothrop, Lee & Shepard 162; McClanahan Book Co. 289; Media Bridge 168; Morehouse 171; Northland 177; Orca 252; Owen, Richard 181; Owl Books 290; Pansophic 183; Pansophic 278; Philomel 189; Pippin 190; Polychrome 191; Quintet 254; Raincoast Book Distribution 255; Random House Juvenile 197; Red Deer College 255; Scholastic Inc. 204; Settel Assoc. 291; Snowapple 257; Tambourine 215; Third World 217; Whispering Coyote 233

Plays: Blizzard 241; Broken Jaw 242; Compass Prods. 286; Coteau 244; Dancing Jester 115; Drama Publishers 121; Ecco 123; Ekstasis Editions 246; Fiesta City Publishers 271; Kaya Prod. 153; Media Bridge 168; Meriwether 168; Pacific Educ. 253; Pansophic 183; Players 191; Playwrights Canada 253; Post-Apollo 279; Red Deer College 255; Riverrun 200; Spectrum 210; Third World 217

Poetry (including chapbooks): Beach Holme 240; Blue Dolphin 94; Boyds Mills 97; Broken Jaw 242; Cadmus Editions 267; Caitlin 242; Calyx Books 268; Carolina Wren 268; Center Press 105; Champion 105; Chatham 106; Cleveland State Univ. Poetry Center 268; Confluence 111; Counterpoint 113; Dante Univ. of America 116; Ecco 123; Ecrits Des Forges 245; Editions Du Noroît 245; Ekstasis Editions 246; Gaff 271; Guernica 247; High Plains 139; Hippocrene 140; Hippopotamus 248; Houghton Mifflin (Adult) 141; Humanitas 249; Intertext 273; Inverted-A 273; Jewish Pub. Soc. 151; Louisiana State Univ. 163; M.A.P. Prods. 251; Milkweed 170; Morrow, William 171; Mortal Press 276; Negative Capability 174; New Rivers 175; Northwoods 277; Nova Science 178; Oberlin College 277; Ohio State Univ. 179; Orchises 180; Owl Creek 182; Papier-Mache 184; Post-Apollo 279; Puckerbrush 280; QED 196; Quarry 254; Red Deer College 255; Ronsdale 256; Royal Fireworks 200; Salina Bookshelf 202; Signature Books 206; Smith, The 208; Sono Nis 257; Spectrum 210; Stone Bridge Press 212; Story Line 213; Third World 217; Thistledown 258; Three Continents 217; Tia Chucha 283; Turnstone 259; Tuttle, Charles E. 259; Univ. of Arkansas 222; Univ. of California 223; Univ. of Iowa 223; Univ. of Massachusetts 224; Univ. of North Texas 225; Univ. of Scranton 226; Vehicule 261; Wake Forest Univ. 230; Whispering Coyote 233; White Pine 234; Wisdom 236

Poetry in Translation: Guernica 247; Hipprocrene 140; Univ. of California 223; White Pine 234

Regional: Beach Holme 240; Blair, John 93; Borealis 241; Eakin Press/Sunbelt Media 122; Fathom 271; Hendrick-Long 138; Interlink 147; Northland 177; Pelican 186; Philomel 189; Pineapple 190; Prairie Oak 280; Signature Books 206; Southern Methodist Univ. 210; Stormline 282; Sunstone 214; Texas Christian Univ. 216; Thistledown 258; Tidewater 218; Univ. of Maine 224; Univ. of Tennessee 226; Univ. Press of Colorado 227; Univ. Press of New England 227; Wisdom 236

Religious: Barbour 90; Beacon Hill Press of Kansas City 91; Bethel 93; Blue Dolphin 94; Blue Star 95; Bookcraft 96; Branden 97; Compass Prods. 286; Concordia 111; Counterpoint 113; Crossway 114; Friends United 130; HarperCollins Publishers 248; Harvest House 137; Herald 139; Herald Press Canada 248; Hiller Box 288; Kar-Ben Copies 152; Kindred Prods. 250; Living the Good News 160; Media Bridge 168; Morehouse 171; Nelson, Thomas 174; Pansophic 183; Pauline Books & Media 185; PREP 192; Quintet 254; Resource Publications 291; Revell, Fleming 199; Signature Books 206; Summit Publishing Group 214; Tyndale House 221; Unity 221

Romance: Avon 88; Avon Flare 88; Bantam Books 90; Barbour 90; Beacon Hill Press of Kansas City 91; Berkley Publishing Group 92; Blue Dolphin 94; Bookcraft 96; Borealis 241; Bryant & Dillon 99; Dial Books For Young Readers 119; Doubleday 120; Duncan & Duncan 121; Harlequin 247; Herald Press Canada 248; Humanitas 249; Lincoln Springs 274; New Victoria 175; Pocket Books 191; PREP 192; Scholastic Inc. 204; Settel Assoc. 291; Sunshine 257; Tudor 220; Warner Books 231; Weiss, Daniel 292; Zebra and Pinnacle 237

Science Fiction: Atheneum Books For Young Readers 87; Avon 88; Bantam Books 90; Carol 103; Circlet 108; Compass Prods. 286; Doubleday 120; Ekstasis Editions 246; Gay Sunshine/Leyland 131; Gryphon Pub. 134; HarperCollins 136; Hollow Earth 140; Just Us Books 152; Kaya Prod. 153; Landmine

274; Little, Brown (Children's) 160; Lodestar 161; New Victoria 175; Permeable Press 188; Pocket Books 191; PREP 192; Quarry 254; Royal Fireworks 200; St. Martin's 202; SJL 207; Stone Bridge Press 212; Sunshine 257; Tudor 220; Visual Assault Comics 283; Warner Books 231; Write Way 237

Short Story Collections: Arcade 85; Arsenal Pulp 240; Aurora Editions 240; Bookcraft 96; Borealis 241; Broken Jaw 242; Bryant & Dillon 99; Caitlin 242; Calyx Books 268; Champion 105; Chronicle 107; Circlet 108; Confluence 111; Coteau 244; Counterpoint 113; Dancing Jester 115; E.M. Press, Inc. 122; Ecco 123; Éditions La Liberté 245; Ekstasis Editions 246; Empyreal 246; Gay Sunshine/Leyland 131; Godine, David 132; Goose Lane 246; Gryphon Pub. 134; HarperCollins Publishers 248; Herald Press Canada 248; Humanitas 249; Interlink 147; Inverted-A 273; Jenkins Group 288; Kaya Prod. 153; Lincoln Springs 274; Livingston 160; McClelland & Stewart 251; Mage 165; Mercury House 168; Naiad 172; Negative Capability 174; Orloff 181; Papier-Mache 184; Permeable Press 188; Puckerbrush 280; Quarry 254; Quixote 196; Red Deer College 255; Resource Publications 291; Riverrun 200; Ronsdale 256; Snowapple 257; Somerville House Books 292; Southern Methodist Univ. 210; Spectrum 210; Stone Bridge Press 212; Sunshine 257; Third World 217; TSR 220; Tudor 220; Turnstone 259; Univ. of Illinois 223; Univ. of Missouri 224; White Pine 234; Zebra and Pinnacle 237; Zoland 238

Suspense: Arcade 85; Atheneum Books For Young Readers 87; Avon 88; Avon Flare 88; Bantam Books 90; Berkley Publishing Group 92; Bethel 93; Bookcraft 96; Bryant & Dillon 99; Clarion 108; Comic Art 110; Dancing Jester 115; DAW 117; Dial Books For Young Readers 119; Dickens 269; Doubleday 120; Duncan & Duncan 121; Fine, Donald 128; Fjord Press 128; Gryphon Pub. 134; Harlequin 247; HarperCollins 136; Hounslow 249; Ivy League 273; Jenkins Group 288; Just Us Books 152; Kaya Prod. 153; Landmine 274; Leisure Books 157; Little, Brown (Children's) 160; Lodestar 161; Pocket Books 191; PREP 192; QED 196; Random House 197; St. Martin's 202; Settel Assoc. 291; Sligo 208; Soho Press 209; Sunshine 257; TOR 219; Tudor 220; Vandamere 228; Walker and Co. 230; Warner Books 231; Wordstorm Prods. 262; Write Way 237; Zebra and Pinnacle 237

Translation: Cleis 109; Dante Univ. of America 116; Fjord Press 128; Gay Sunshine/Leyland 131; Guernica 247; Interlink 147; Italica 150; Overlook 181; QED 196; Three Continents 217; Univ. of California 223; Univ. of Nebraska 224; Univ. of Texas 226

Western: Atheneum Books For Young Readers 87; Avanyu 88; Avon 88; Bantam Books 90; Berkley Publishing Group 92; Book Creations 286; Bookcraft 96; Comic Art 110; Crossway 114; Dancing Jester 115; Doubleday 120; Fine, Donald 128; HarperCollins 136; Leisure Books 157; Lodestar 161; New Victoria 175; Pocket Books 191; PREP 192; Red Deer College 255; St. Martin's 202; TOR 219; Tudor 220; Walker and Co. 230; Zebra and Pinnacle 237

Young Adult: Archway/Minstrel 85; Atheneum Books For Young Readers 87; Bantam Books 90; Beach Holme 240; Bethel 93; Blizzard 241; Bookcraft 96; Borealis 241; Boyds Mills 97; Caitlin 242; Cobblehill 109; Concordia 111; Coteau 244; Dancing Jester 115; Davenport, May 117; Dial Books For Young Readers 119; Dutton Children's Books 122; Éditions La Liberté 245; Eriako 287; Fawcett Juniper 127; Farrar, Straus and Giroux 127; Free Spirit 130; Harcourt Brace (Children's) 135; HarperCollins Publishers 248; Hendrick-Long 138; Herald 139; Herald Press Canada 248; Houghton Mifflin (Children's) 141; Hyperion 144; Jones Univ., Bob 152; Just Us Books 152; Lerner 157; Lion Publishing 159; Little, Brown (Children's) 160; Living the Good News 160; Lodestar 161; Lorimer & Co., James 250; McClelland & Stewart 251; McElderry, Margaret 164; Media Bridge 168; Mega-Books 289; Morehouse 171; Orca 252; Pacific Educ. 253; Philomel 189; Pippin 190; Polychrome 191; PREP 192; Random House Juvenile 197; Red Deer College 255; Roussan 256; Scholastic Canada 256; Scholastic Inc. 204; Snowapple 257; Speech Bin 210; Sunshine 257; Tambourine 215; Third World 217; Thistledown 258; TSR 220; Tudor 220; Tyndale House 221; Walker and Co. 230; Ward Hill 230; Weiss, Daniel 292; Zebra and Pinnacle 237

NONFICTION

Agriculture/Horticulture: American Press 84; Bright Mountain Books, Inc. 267; Camino 101; Counterpoint 113; Down Home 121; Ecopress 270; Hartley & Marks 136; Hoard & Sons, W.D. 272; Idyll Arbor 145; Key Porter 250; Libraries Unltd. 158; McClelland & Stewart 251; Mountain House 276; Ohio Univ. 179; Parkway 184; Pierian 189; Purich 254; Quixote 196; Stipes 212; Storey Communications/Garden Way 213; Sunshine 257; Thunder Dog 283; Univ. of Alaska 222; Univ. of Idaho 223; Univ. of Nebraska 224; Univ. of North Texas 225; Weidner & Sons 232; Windward 236; Beach Holme 240

Americana: Adams Media 78; Addicus 78; Alaska Northwest 79; Atheneum Books For Young Readers

87; Avanyu 88; B&B 90; Bantam Books 90; Berkshire House 92; Boston Mills 241; Bowling Green State Univ. Popular Press 96; Branden 97; Brevet 98; Camino 101; Carol 103; Cave 104; Charles River 268; Clear Light 108; Compass Prods. 286; Confluence 111; Cornell Maritime 112; Dancing Jester 115; Databooks 116; Davenport, May 117; Dowling 269; Down The Shore 269; Eakin Press/Sunbelt Media 122; Eastern Nat'l Park & Monument Assoc. 123; Ecco 123; Éditions La Liberté 245; Escart 246; Filter 271; General Pub. 131; Godine, David 132; Heyday 139; High Plains 139; Howells House 142; Int'l Publishers 148; J & L Lee 150; Jenkins Group 288; JSA Pub. 288; Kurian, George 289; Laing Comm. 289; Landmine 274; Layla Prods. 289; Lehigh Univ. 157; Lerner 157; Lexikos 158; Lincoln Springs 274; Lion Books 159; Longstreet 162; Lorien House 275; McDonald & Woodward 164; Meyerbooks 275; Michigan State Univ. 169; Mosaic Press Miniature Books 276; Mountain House 276; Mustang Pub. 172; Mystic Seaport Museum 276; Nova Science 178; Ohio Univ. 179; Oregon Hist. So. 278; Pacific Books 182; Parnassus 184; Pelican 186; Penguin Studio 186; Picton 189; PREP 192; Pruett 194; Quill/Driver/Word Dancer 196; Quintet 254; Quixote 196; Reference Press 198; Reference Pub. 280; Royal Fireworks 200; Sachem Publishing Assoc. 291; Scholastic Canada 256; Settel Assoc. 291; Shoreline 257; Silver Burdett 207; Spectrum 210; Storm Peak 281; Tudor 220; Univ. of Alaska 222; Univ. of Idaho 223; Univ. of Illinois 223; Univ. of North Texas 225; Univ. Press of Kentucky 227; Utah State Univ. 228; Vanderbilt Univ. 228; Voyageur 229; Wayfinder 283; Wieser & Wieser 292; Wilderness Adventure 235

Animals: Adams Media 78; Alpine 81; Atheneum Books For Young Readers 87; Ballantine 89; Barron's 91; Blackbirch 93; Carol 103; Carolrhoda 103; Cave 104; Celestial Arts 105; Compass Prods. 286; Countrysport 113; Creative Spark 287; Denlingers 119; Detselig 244; Doral 120; Ecopress 270; Éditions La Liberté 245; Epicenter 125; Heritage House 248; Hounslow 249; ICS Books, Inc. 144; Ideals Children's Books 144; Iowa State Univ. 149; Jenkins Group 288; Jones Univ., Bob 152; Kesend, Michael 153; Key Porter 250; Krieger 155; Lone Pine 250; Lyons & Burford 164; McClelland & Stewart 251; McDonald & Woodward 164; Mosaic Press Miniature Books 276; NorthWord 178; Ohio Univ. 179; Ottenheimer 290; Owl Books 290; Parrot 279; Pineapple 190; Quintet 254; Raincoast Book Distribution 255; Sandhill Crane 202; Southfarm 210; Sterling 212; Storey Communications/Garden Way 213; Sunshine 257; Thunder Dog 283; Univ. of Alaska 222; Warren 231; Weidner & Sons 232; Whitecap 262; Wilderness Adventure 235; Windward 236

Anthropology/Archaeology: American Press 84; Avanyu 88; Beacon Press 91; Blackbirch 93; Blue Dolphin 94; Broadview 241; Cave 104; Center for African-American Studies 268; Children's Press 106; Clear Light 108; Dancing Jester 115; Denali 119; Eagle's View 122; Éditions La Liberté 245; Filter 271; Heritage House 248; Horsdal & Schubart 249; Howells House 142; Humanics 142; Insight Books 146; Johnson Books 151; Kent State Univ. 153; Knowledge, Ideas & Trends 154; Learning Works 157; Lerner 157; Libraries Unltd. 158; Lone Pine 250; McDonald & Woodward 164; Mage 165; Minnesota Hist. Soc. 170; Natural Heritage 252; Nelson-Hall 174; Nova Science 178; Ohio Univ. 179; Oxford Univ. 182; Parnassus 184; Pennsylvania Historical and Museum Comm. 187; Pinter 253; Quintet 254; Red Deer College 255; Routledge, Inc. 200; Scots Plaid 281; Spectrum 210; Stanford Univ. 211; Third World 217; Univ. of Alaska 222; Univ. of Arizona 222; Univ. of Idaho 223; Univ. of Montreal 260; Univ. of Nevada 224; Univ. of New Mexico 225; Univ. of Pennsylvania 226; Univ. of Tennessee 226; Univ. of Texas 226; Vanderbilt Univ. 228; Washington State Univ. 232; Westernlore 233; White Cliffs 233; White-Boucke 284

Art/Architecture: Aberdeen 74; ACA 77; Alaska Northwest 79; Allworth 80; American Press 84; Apollo 85; Asian Humanities 87; Atheneum Books For Young Readers 87; Avanyu 88; Balcony 265; Beil, Frederic 92; Blizzard 241; Bowling Green State Univ. Popular Press 96; Branden 97; Broadview 241; Calyx Books 268; Camino 101; Carol 103; Carolrhoda 103; Celestial Arts 105; Center for African-American Studies 268; Center Press 105; Charlton 243; Children's Press 106; Chronicle 107; Clear Light 108; Comic Art 110; Consultant 112; Counterpoint 113; Crown Publishing Group 115; Dancing Jester 115; Davies, Robert 244; Detselig 244; Dundurn 245; Ecco 123; Ecopress 270; Elliott & Clark Publishing 124; Epicenter 125; Eriksson, Paul S. 125; Escart 246; Excalibur 270; Fairleigh Dickinson Univ. 126; Family Album 270; Fitzhenry & Whiteside 246; Flower Valley 271; General Pub. 131; Godine, David 132; Goose Lane 246; Guernica 247; Gutter Press 247; HarperCollins 136; HarperCollins Publishers 248; Hartley & Marks 136; High Plains 139; Hollow Earth 140; Horsdal & Schubart 249; Hounslow 249; Howells House 142; Ideals Children's Books 144; Insight Books 146; Jefferson Univ., Thomas 150; Kaya Prod. 153; Kent State Univ. 153; Lang, Peter 155; Learning Works 157; Lehigh Univ. 157; Lerner 157; Libraries Unltd. 158; Little, Brown (Children's) 160; Louisiana State Univ. 163; Loyola Press 163; Lyons & Burford 164; McClelland & Stewart 251; McFarland & Co. 164; McGraw-Hill Companies (Professional Book Group) 165; Mage 165; Mayfield 167; Meriwether 168; Minnesota Hist. Soc. 170; Morrow, William 171; Mosaic Press Miniature Books 276; Mystic Seaport Museum 276; Natural Heritage 252; Northland 177; Ohio State Univ. 179; Ohio Univ. 179; Oregon Hist. So. 278; Oxford Univ. 182; Pacific Educ. 253; Parnassus 184; Pennsylvania Historical and

Museum Comm. 187; Pogo Press 279; Post-Apollo 279; Professional Publications 193; Pruett 194; Quarry 254; Quintet 254; Raincoast Book Distribution 255; Random House 197; Reference Press 198; Scottwall Assoc. 281; Shoreline 257; Simon & Schuster 207; Sourcebooks 209; Spectrum 210; Stone Bridge Press 212; Summit Publishing Group 214; Sunstone 214; Tenth Avenue 292; Tuttle, Charles E. 259; Univ. of Alaska 222; Univ. of Alberta Press 260; Univ. of Missouri 224; Univ. of New Mexico 225; Univ. of Pennsylvania 226; Univ. of Tennessee 226; Univ. of Texas 226; Univ. Press of New England 227; Vanderbilt Univ. 228; Warren 231; Williamson Publishing 235

Astrology/Psychic/New Age: Austen Sharp 265; Bantam Books 90; Bear and Co. 91; Cassandra 103; Crossing Press 114; HarperCollins 136; Hay House 137; Huntington House 143; In Print 273; Llewellyn 161; Newcastle 176; Ottenheimer 290; Penguin Studio 186; Sterling 212; Swan-Raven 214; Thorsons 258; Weiser, Samuel 232

Audiocassettes: Schirmer 203; WalchCarolina Wren 268; Charles River 268; Pantheon 183; Scots Plaid 281; Turnstone 259; Zondervan 238

Bibliographies: Family Album 270; Klein, B. 154; Locust Hill 161; Oregon Hist. So. 278; Scarecrow 203

Biography: Aurora Editions 240; Avon 88; Balcony 265; Blackbirch Graphics 286; Bliss Publishing Co. 266; Books Beyond Borders LLC 267; Borealis 241; Borgo 96; Bright Mountain Books, Inc. 267; Caitlin 242; Cambridge Univ. 101; Cambridge Univ. 101; Canadian Plains Research Center 243; Carolina Wren 268; Charles River 268; Clarkson Potter 108; Creative Spark 287; Crown Publishing Group 115; Davidson, Harlan 117; Davies, Robert 244; Dee, Ivan 118; Detselig 244; Discipleship Resources 120; Doubleday 120; Dowling 269; Dundurn 245; Dutton Children's Books 122; Dutton Children's Books 122; Eakin Press/ Sunbelt Media 122; ECW 245; Éditions La Liberté 245; Ekstasis Editions 246; Enslow 125; Eriksson, Paul S. 125; Escart 246; Family Album 270; Fitzhenry & Whiteside 246; Giniger, K S 288; Goose Lane 246; Great Ocean 272; Guernica 247; Gutter Press 247; Hancock House 135; HarperCollins 136; HarperCollins Publishers 248; Heritage House 248; Hoard & Sons, W.D. 272; Holmes & Meier 141; Horsdal & Schubart 249; Hounslow 249; Humanitas 249; I.A.A.S. 273; Jefferson Univ., Thomas 150; Jenkins Group 288; Kent State Univ. 153; Key Porter 250; Kindred Prods. 250; Laing Comm. 289; Landmine 274; Lang, Peter 155; Lerner 157; Library of Virginia 274; Little, Brown 160; Lone Pine 250; McClelland & Stewart 251; Macmillan Canada 251; Media Forum Int'l. 275; Morrow, William 171; Mosaic Press Miniature Books 276; Mystic Seaport Museum 276; New Victoria 175; Nine Pines 252; Orca 252; Oregon Hist. So. 278; Oregon State Univ. 180; Overlook 181; Pandora 253; Pantheon 183; Partners in Publishing 279; Pennsylvania Historical and Museum Comm. 187; Pruett 194; Publicom 291; Quarry 254; Republic Of Texas 199; Rockbridge 280; Ronsdale 256; Scottwall Assoc. 281; Settel Assoc. 291; Shoreline 257; Soho Press 209; Sono Nis 257; Storm Peak 281; Taylor 215; Tenth Avenue 292; Times Books 218; Titan 258; 2M Comm. 292; Univ. of Arkansas 222; Univ. of Massachusetts 224; Univ. of Nevada 224; Univ. Press of Mississippi 227; Univ. Press of New England 227; Vanwell 260; Vehicule 261; Vital Issues 229; Warwick Publishing 261; Washington State Univ. 232; Watts, Franklin 232; Westernlore 233; White-Boucke 284; Whitecap 262; Zondervan 238

Business/Economics: Abbott, Langer 74; Adams Media 78; Adams-Blake Publishing 78; Adams-Hall 264; Addicus 78; Addison-Wesley Longman 79; Aegis 264; Allen 80; Amacom 81; America West 81; American Hospital 83; American Nurses 83; American Press 84; Atheneum Books For Young Readers 87; Autonomedia 88; Avon 88; Bantam Books 90; Barricade 91; Barron's 91; Benjamin Co. 286; Berkley Publishing Group 92; Betterway 93; Bloomberg 94; BNA 95; Bonus 95; Bookhaven 96; Bryant & Dillon 99; Business McGraw-Hill 100; Butterworth-Heinemann 100; Cambridge Univ. 101; Canadian Plains Research Center 243; Caradium 102; Carol 103; Carswell Thomson 243; Center for African-American Studies 268; Cerier, Alison Brown 286; Consultant 112; Contemporary Books 112; Cypress 115; Davies, Robert 244; Dearborn Financial 118; Detselig 244; Doubleday 120; Drama Publishers 121; Duncan & Duncan 121; Eakin Press/Sunbelt Media 122; Engineering & Management 124; Eriako 287; Eriksson, Paul S. 125; Excalibur 270; Fairleigh Dickinson Univ. 126; Free Press 130; Giniger, K S 288; Glenbridge 131; Globe Pequot 132; Great Quotations 133; HarperCollins 136; HarperCollins Publishers 248; Hastings 137; Health Comm. 137; Holmes & Meier 141; Hounslow 249; Howells House 142; I.A.A.S. 273; In Print 273; Initiatives 146; Insight Books 146; Intercultural Press 147; Int'l Found. Employee Benefit Plans 148; Int'l Publishers 148; Iowa State Univ. 149; Jain 150; Jenkins Group 288; Key Porter 250; Knowledge, Ideas & Trends 154; Kodansha America 154; Kurian, George 289; Laing Comm. 289; Lang, Peter 155; LAWCO 274; Lerner 157; Libraries Unltd. 158; Lifetime Books 158; Lorimer & Co., James 250; McClelland & Stewart 251; McFarland & Co. 164; McGraw-Hill Companies (Professional Book Group) 165; McGraw-Hill Ryerson 251; Macmillan Canada 251; Mangajin 275; Markowski Int'l Publishers 289; Maximum Press 167; Menasha

Ridge 290; Metamorphous 169; Michigan State Univ. 169; Mosaic Press Miniature Books 276; National Press 173; National Textbook 173; Neal-Schuman 174; New Lexington Press 175; New World Library 176; Nichols 176; Nova Science 178; Noyes Data 178; Ohio Univ. 179; Oxford Univ. 182; Pace Univ. 278; Pacific View 183; Pacific View 278; Paper Chase 183; Pelican 186; Pierian 189; Pinter 253; Precept 192; Prentice-Hall Canada Trade 253; PREP 192; Prima 193; Productive Pub. 254; PSI Research 195; Publicom 291; QED 196; Random House 197; Reference Press 198; Resolution Business 280; Riverrun 200; Routledge, Inc. 200; Royal Fireworks 200; Russian Information Services 201; Self-Counsel 256; Settel Assoc. 291; SJL 207; Sourcebooks 209; Steel Balls 281; Stipes 212; Stone Bridge Press 212; Success Publishing 213; Sulzburger & Graham 213; Summers Press 214; Summit Publishing Group 214; Sunshine 257; Systems Co. 215; Texas A&M Univ. 216; Third Side 217; Thompson Educ. 258; Thorsons 258; Todd 219; Tuttle, Charles E. 259; Univ. of Pennsylvania 226; Univ. of New Haven 283; Verso 261; VGM Career Horizons 229; Warwick 231; Warwick Publishing 261; Washington State Univ. 232; Weidner & Sons 232; Wiley & Sons, John 235; Wilshire 235; Ten Speed 216

Child Guidance/Parenting: Addison-Wesley Longman 79; American Diabetes 83; Ballantine 89; Bantam Books 90; Barricade 91; Barron's 91; Blue Bird 94; Bookcraft 96; Broadway Books 99; Brookline 99; Cambridge Educ. 101; Camino 101; Celestial Arts 105; Cerier, Alison Brown 286; Chicago Review 106; College Board 110; Compass Prods. 286; Consumer Press 112; Creative Spark 287; Davies, Robert 244; Detselig 244; Dickens 269; Dimi 120; Duncan & Duncan 121; Éditions La Liberté 245; Elder Books 124; Excalibur 270; Fairview 127; Focus on the Family 129; Free Spirit 130; Front Row Experience 271; Great Quotations 133; HarperCollins Publishers 248; Health Comm. 137; Heinemann 138; Herald Press Canada 248; Home Education 141; Hounslow 249; Humanics 142; I.A.A.S. 273; Ivory Tower 150; Jenkins Group 288; Learning Works 157; Lifetime Books 158; Lion Publishing 159; McBooks 275; McClelland & Stewart 251; Marlor 167; Mayfield 167; Meadowbrook 167; National Press 173; Neal-Schuman 174; New Harbinger 174; New Hope 175; Nine Pines 252; Nova Science 178; Pansophic 278; Pauline Books & Media 185; Peterson's 188; Prufrock 195; Publicom 291; Quintet 254; Resource Publications 291; Revell, Fleming 199; Royal Fireworks 200; St. John's Publishing, Inc. 281; Settel Assoc. 291; Sourcebooks 209; Student College Aid 282; Studio 4 Prod. 282; Sulzburger & Graham 213; Sunshine 257; Taylor 215; Ten Speed 216; Times Books 218; Trilobyte 258; Tudor 220; 2M Comm. 292; Vandamere 228; Walker and Co. 230; Warren 231; Weidner & Sons 232; White-Boucke 284; Wiley & Sons, John 235

Coffeetable Book: Balcony 265; Bentley, Robert 92; Bookcraft 96; Dancing Jester 115; Davies, Robert 244; Detselig 244; Dickens 269; Down The Shore 269; Dundurn 245; Ecopress 270; Eriako 287; Flower Valley 271; General Pub. 131; Giniger, K S 288; Godine, David 132; HarperCollins Publishers 248; Herald Press Canada 248; Hiller Box 288; Hounslow 249; Jenkins Group 288; Key Porter 250; Laing Comm. 289; Layla Prods. 289; McBooks 275; McClelland & Stewart 251; Mage 165; Minnesota Hist. Soc. 170; Ottenheimer 290; Quintet 254; Raincoast Book Distribution 255; Sta-Kris 281; Summit Publishing Group 214; Warwick Publishing 261; Whitecap 262; Wieser & Wieser 292

Communications: Bonus 95; Butterworth-Heinemann 100; Computer Science 111; Drama Publishers 121; Eckert, J.K. 287; Iowa State Univ. 149; Mayfield 167; Michigan State Univ. 169; Paradigm 184; Tiare 218; Wadsworth 230

Community/Public Affairs: And Books 84; Herald 139; Insight Books 146; Univ. of Nevada 224; Watts, Franklin 232

Computers/Electronics: Adams-Blake Publishing 78; Amacom 81; Branden 97; Butterworth-Heinemann 100; Carol 103; Cypress 115; Duke 121; Eckert, J.K. 287; Engineering & Management 124; Gleason Group 288; Grapevine 132; Hollow Earth 140; Index 145; Jain 150; Laing Comm. 289; Lerner 157; McGraw-Hill Companies (Professional Book Group) 165; Maximum Press 167; Neal-Schuman 174; No Starch 177; North Light 177; Nova Science 178; Noyes Data 178; One On One 180; Osborne/McGraw-Hill 181; Oxford Univ. 182; Paradigm 184; Parkway 184; PROMPT Pub. 194; PSI Research 195; Resolution Business 280; Royal Fireworks 200; SJL 207; Sulzburger & Graham 213; Sunshine 257; Systemsware 282; Teachers College 215; Tiare 218; Walch, J. Weston 230; Weidner & Sons 232; Weka 233; Wilshire 235; Wordware 236

Consumer Affairs: Almar 80; Benjamin Co. 286; Consumer Reports Books 112; Int'l Found. Employee Benefit Plans 148; Oryx 181; Silvercat Pub. 281

Contemporary Culture: Bay Press 266; Broadway Books 99; Madison 165; Thunder's Mouth 218

Cooking/Foods/Nutrition: Adams Media 78; Adams Media 78; Alaska Northwest 79; Austen

Sharp 265; Ballantine 89; Bantam Books 90; Barron's 91; Benjamin Co. 286; Berkley Publishing Group 92; Blue Dolphin 94; Bonus 95; Bright Mountain Books, Inc. 267; Broadway Books 99; Bull 99; Caitlin 242; Cambridge Educ. 101; Celestial Arts 105; Cerier, Alison Brown 286; Chatham 106; Clarkson Potter 108; Clear Light 108; Cracom 287; Crown Publishing Group 115; Dancing Jester 115; Davies, Robert 244; Dowling 269; Dowling 269; Eakin Press/Sunbelt Media 122; Ecco 123; Éditions La Liberté 245; Eriksson, Paul S. 125; Faber & Faber 126; Fiesta City Publishers 271; Filter 271; Fisher 128; Glenbridge 131; Globe Pequot 132; Godine, David 132; HarperCollins 136; HarperCollins Publishers 248; Hastings 137; Hay House 137; Herald Press Canada 248; Heritage House 248; Hiller Box 288; Hoffman Press 272; Hounslow 249; Howell Press 141; ICS Books, Inc. 144; Inner Traditions Int'l 146; Interlink 147; Interweave 149; Ivory Tower 150; Jenkins Group 288; Key Porter 250; Kodansha America 154; Landmine 274; Layla Prods. 289; Lerner 157; Lifetime Books 158; Little, Brown (Children's) 160; Longstreet 162; Lyons & Burford 164; McBooks 275; McClelland & Stewart 251; Macmillan Canada 251; Mage 165; Maverick Pub. 167; Minnesota Hist. Soc. 170; Morrow, William 171; Mosaic Press Miniature Books 276; New World Library 176; Northland 177; Nova Science 178; Ottenheimer 290; Peachtree 185; Pelican 186; Pocket Books 191; Prentice-Hall Canada Trade 253; Pruett 194; Quintet 254; Quixote 196; Ragged Mountain 197; Raincoast Book Distribution 255; Red Deer College 255; RedBrick 280; St. Martin's 202; Sandlapper 202; Settel Assoc. 291; Storey Communications/Garden Way 213; Sunshine 257; Tamarack 282; Times Books 218; Tudor 220; Tuttle, Charles E. 259; 2M Comm. 292; Univ. of North Carolina 225; Warner Books 231; Warren 231; Warwick 231; Warwick Publishing 261; Washington State Univ. 232; Whitecap 262; Wieser & Wieser 292

Counseling/Career Guidance: Almar 80; Amacom 81; Bookhaven 96; Cambridge Educ. 101; Career 102; Jist Works 151; Markowski Int'l Publishers 289; Morehouse 171; NASW 173; National Textbook 173; Pilot 190; Planning/Communications 191; PREP 192; Professional Publications 193; Student College Aid 282; Teachers College 215; Trilobyte 258; Vandamere 228; Zondervan 238

Crafts: Austen Sharp 265; Barron's 91; C&T 102; Down East 121; Flower Valley 271; Hyperion Press 249; Interweave 149; Kodansha America 154; Lark 156; Learning Works 157; Naturegraph Publishers 276; North Light 177; Owl Books 290; Quintet 254; Reference Press 198; Rutledge Hill 201; Stackpole 211; Sterling 212; Storey Communications/Garden Way 213; Tenth Avenue 292; Univ. of North Carolina 225

Educational: ABC-CLIO 74; ACA 77; Active Parenting 78; Althouse 240; Amacom 81; American Catholic 264; American Counseling 82; American Nurses 83; American Press 84; Anchorage 84; ASA 86; B&B 90; Benjamin Co. 286; Blue Bird 94; Blue Dolphin 94; Bonus 95; Bookhaven 96; Broadway Books 99; Brookline 99; Bryant & Dillon 99; Bull 99; Cambridge Educ. 101; Canadian Inst. of Ukrainian Studies 242; Carol 103; Celestial Arts 105; Chicago Review 106; Church Growth Inst. 107; College Board 110; Comic Art 110; Compass Prods. 286; Course Crafters 287; Creative Spark 287; Dancing Jester 115; Davis Pub. 117; Detselig 244; Dickens 269; Duncan & Duncan 121; Eastern Press 270; Ecopress 270; Éditions La Liberté 245; Educational Technology 123; Elder Books 124; Fitzhenry & Whiteside 246; Free Spirit 130; Front Row Experience 271; Great Ocean 272; Gutter Press 247; Harcourt Brace Jovanovich Canada 247; Hay House 137; Heinemann 138; Herald Press Canada 248; Hiller Box 288; Hi-Time 272; Howells House 142; Humanics 142; I.A.A.S. 273; Insight Books 146; Intercultural Press 147; Jenkins Group 288; Kurian, George 289; Landmine 274; Learning Works 157; Libraries Unltd. 158; Lifetime Books 158; Living the Good News 160; Love and Logic 163; McClelland & Stewart 251; Maisonneuve 166; Maupin House 275; Media Bridge 168; Meriwether 168; Metamorphous 169; Milkweed 170; MLA 170; Morehouse 171; Mountain House 276; Neal-Schuman 174; New Hope 175; Nichols 176; Nova Press 178; Nova Science 178; NTC Publishing 179; Octameron Assoc. 179; Ohio State Univ. 179; Ohio Univ. 179; Oryx 181; Pacific Educ. 253; Paideia 278; Partners in Publishing 279; Peguis 253; Pencil Point 186; Perfection Learning 279; Peterson's 188; Pierian 189; Planning/Communications 191; Prufrock 195; PSI Research 195; Publicom 291; Publishers Resource Group (PRG) 291; Quarry 254; Reference Press 198; Regnery 198; Reidmore 256; Religious Education 198; Resolution Business 280; Resource Publications 291; Riverrun 200; Routledge, Inc. 200; Royal Fireworks 200; St. Anthony Messenger 201; Shoreline 257; Silver Moon 291; Speech Bin 210; Standard 211; Sugar Hill 282; Sulzburger & Graham 213; Sunshine 257; Texas Western 217; Third World 217; Thompson Educ. 258; Trilobyte 258; Tudor 220; Univ. of Alaska 222; Univ. of Montreal 260; Univ. of Ottawa 260; Vandamere 228; Vanderbilt Univ. 228; Verso 261; Walch, J. Weston 230; Wall & Emerson 261; Warren 231; Warwick 231; Warwick Publishing 261; Weidner & Sons 232; White Cliffs 233

Entertainment/Games: Bonus 95; Borgo 96; Broadway Press 267; Cardoza 102; Devyn 119; Drama Publishers 121; Facts On File 126; Focal 128; Gambling Times 271; General Pub. 131; Index 145; McFarland & Co. 164; Speech Bin 210; Standard 211; Sterling 212; Univ. of Nevada 224

Ethnic: African American Images 79; Arsenal Pulp 240; Avanyu 88; Balcony 265; Barricade 91; Beacon

Press 91; Blackbirch Graphics 286; Blizzard 241; Books Beyond Borders LLC 267; Bowling Green State Univ. Popular Press 96; Bryant & Dillon 99; Calyx Books 268; Camino 101; Canadian Inst. of Ukrainian Studies 242; Carol 103; Carolina Wren 268; Center for African-American Studies 268; Charles River 268; Children's Press 106; Clarity 268; Clear Light 108; Commune-A-Key 110; Confluence 111; Creative Book 114; Creative Spark 287; Dancing Jester 115; David, Jonathan 117; Davidson, Harlan 117; Denali 119; Detselig 244; Discipleship Resources 120; Duncan & Duncan 121; Eagle's View 122; Eastern Press 270; Epicenter 125; Eriako 287; Evras 270; Fairleigh Dickinson Univ. 126; Filter 271; Fitzhenry & Whiteside 246; Guernica 247; Hancock House 135; HarperCollins Publishers 248; Heinemann 138; Herald 139; Herald Press Canada 248; Heyday 139; Humanics 142; Hyperion Press 249; I.A.A.S. 273; Indiana Univ. 146; Inner Traditions Int'l 146; Insight Books 146; Interlink 147; Int'l Publishers 148; Italica 150; Ivy League 273; Just Us Books 152; Kaya Prod. 153; Knowledge, Ideas & Trends 154; Kodansha America 154; Kurian, George 289; Learning Works 157; Lee & Low 157; Lerner 157; Libraries Unltd. 158; Lincoln Springs 274; Lion Books 159; Little, Brown (Children's) 160; Louisiana State Univ. 163; McDonald & Woodward 164; McFarland & Co. 164; Mage 165; Maisonneuve 166; Maverick Pub. 167; Mayfield 167; Media Bridge 168; Media Forum Int'l. 275; Michigan State Univ. 169; Middle Passage 276; Minnesota Hist. Soc. 170; Mitchell Lane 170; Natural Heritage 252; Naturegraph Publishers 276; New World Library 176; NeWest 252; Nodin 177; Ohio Univ. 179; Oregon Hist. So. 278; Pacific Educ. 253; Pacific View 183; Pacific View 278; Pansophic 278; Pelican 186; Pruett 194; Purich 254; Raincoast Book Distribution 255; Reference Pub. 280; Reference Service 198; Reidmore 256; Routledge, Inc. 200; Royal Fireworks 200; Salina Bookshelf 202; Sand River 281; Shoreline 257; South End 209; Spectrum 210; Stanford Univ. 211; Sterling 212; Stone Bridge Press 212; Summit Publishing Group 214; Texas A&M Univ. 216; Third World 217; Todd 219; 2M Comm. 292; Univ. of Alaska 222; Univ. of Arizona 222; Univ. of Idaho 223; Univ. of Manitoba 260; Univ. of Nebraska 224; Univ. of Nevada 224; Univ. of New Mexico 225; Univ. of North Texas 225; Univ. of Tennessee 226; Univ. of Texas 226; Univ. Press of Kentucky 227; Univ. Press of Mississippi 227; Warren 231; Washington State Univ. 232; White Cliffs 233; Williamson Publishing 235; YMAA 284

Feminism: Astarte Shell 265; Carolina Wren 268; Feminist Press at CUNY 127; Pandora 253; Publishers Assoc. 195; Vehicule 261; Calyx Books 268

Film/Cinema/Stage: Ardsley House 86; Betterway 93; Borgo 96; Broadway Press 267; Citadel 108; Dee, Ivan 118; Drama Publishers 121; Faber & Faber 126; Fairleigh Dickinson Univ. 126; Focal 128; Gaslight 131; Guernica 247; Heinemann 138; Indiana Univ. 146; Limelight 159; Lone Eagle 161; McFarland & Co. 164; Mayfield 167; Media Forum Int'l. 275; Meriwether 168; Meyerbooks 275; Overlook 181; Piccadilly 189; Schirmer 203; Titan 258; Univ. of Texas 226; Adams Media 78; Apollo 85; Autonomedia 88; Balcony 265; Blue Sky Marketing, Inc. 266; Camino 101; Chicago Review 106; Chronicle 107; Dowling 269; Down Home 121; Ecopress 270; Elliott & Clark Publishing 124; Fisher 128; Godine, David 132; Graber Prods. 288; HarperCollins Publishers 248; Hartley & Marks 136; Herbal Studies 272; Howell Press 141; Interweave 149; Ivory Tower 150; Jenkins Group 288; Jones Univ., Bob 152; Kodansha America 154; Lark 156; Layla Prods. 289; Lone Pine 250; Longstreet 162; Lyons & Burford 164; McClelland & Stewart 251; Naturegraph Publishers 276; Ohio Univ. 179; Ottenheimer 290; Parnassus 184; Peachtree 185; Penguin Studio 186; Peter Pauper Press 188; Pineapple 190; Quintet 254; Red Deer College 255; Red Eye 280; Reference Press 198; Richboro 199; Sasquatch 203; SJL 207; Stackpole 211; Sterling 212; Storey Communications/Garden Way 213; Summit Publishing Group 214; Sunshine 257; Ten Speed 216; Thunder Dog 283; Univ. of North Carolina 225; Warren 231; Weidner & Sons 232; Whitecap 262; Wieser & Wieser 292; Windward 236

Gay/Lesbian: American Counseling 82; Arsenal Pulp 240; Bantam Books 90; Barricade 91; Beacon Press 91; Blizzard 241; Books Beyond Borders LLC 267; Broken Jaw 242; Carol 103; Carolina Wren 268; Celestial Arts 105; Cleis 109; Companion 110; Crossing Press 114; Dancing Jester 115; Davies, Robert 244; Dowling 269; Feminist Press at CUNY 127; Gutter Press 247; HarperCollins Publishers 248; Heinemann 138; Insight Books 146; Kaya Prod. 153; Little, Brown (Children's) 160; McClelland & Stewart 251; Madwoman 275; Maisonneuve 166; Mercury House 168; Neal-Schuman 174; Oxford Univ. 182; Penguin Studio 186; Quarry 254; Riverrun 200; Routledge, Inc. 200; Sligo 208; South End 209; Spectrum 210; Sunshine 257; Third Side 217; 2M Comm. 292; Wiley & Sons, John 235

General Nonfiction: Addison-Wesley Longman 79; American Atheist 82; Arcade 85; Asian Humanities 87; B&B Publishing, Inc. 285; Brett Books, Inc. 267; Broadview 241; Charles River 268; Delancey 269; Dutton 122; Houghton Mifflin (Adult) 141; Indiana Univ. 146; Inverted-A 273; Johnston Associates, Int'l. 274; Kent State Univ. 153; Ohio State Univ. 179; Pacific Books 182; Peachtree 185; Pocket Books 191; Potentials Development 279; Quill/Driver/Word Dancer 196; Taylor 215; Univ. of Calgary 260; Verso 261

Gift Books: Adams Media 78; Andrews and McMeel 85; Blue Sky Marketing, Inc. 266; Carol 103;

Celestial Arts 105; Chronicle 107; Counterpoint 113; Databooks 116; Davies, Robert 244; Detselig 244; Dickens 269; Dowling 269; Epicenter 125; General Pub. 131; ICS Books, Inc. 144; Jain 150; Living the Good News 160; Mage 165; Marlor 167; Morehouse 171; Ohio Univ. 179; Pansophic 278; Papier-Mache 184; Peachtree 185; Penguin Studio 186; Quarry 254; Quintet 254; Raincoast Book Distribution 255; Sta-Kris 281; Sunshine 257

Government/Politics: ABC-CLIO 74; ACA 77; Adams Media 78; Addison-Wesley Longman 79; American Atheist 82; American Press 84; Arcade 85; Atheneum Books For Young Readers 87; Autonomedia 88; Avon 88; Bantam Books 90; Barricade 91; Bliss Publishing Co. 266; Blizzard 241; Borealis 241; Borgo 96; Branden 97; Brassey's 97; Broadview 241; Broadway Books 99; Brown Bear 242; Bryant & Dillon 99; Bucknell Univ. 99; Business McGraw-Hill 100; Camino 101; Canadian Inst. of Ukrainian Studies 242; Canadian Plains Research Center 243; Carol 103; Catholic Univ. of America Press 104; Cato Inst. 104; Celestial Arts 105; Center for African-American Studies 268; Cleis 109; Creative Spark 287; Crown Publishing Group 115; Dancing Jester 115; Davidson, Harlan 117; Dee, Ivan 118; Denali 119; Detselig 244; Dickens 269; Down Home 121; Duncan & Duncan 121; Dutton 122; Ecco 123; Éditions La Liberté 245; Ekstasis Editions 246; Eriksson, Paul S. 125; Fairleigh Dickinson Univ. 126; Feminist Press at CUNY 127; Foreign Policy Assoc. 129; Glenbridge 131; Guernica 247; Gutter Press 247; HarperCollins 136; HarperCollins Publishers 248; Holmes & Meier 141; Horsdal & Schubart 249; Howells House 142; I.A.A.S. 273; ICS Books, Inc. 144; Indiana Univ. 146; Insight Books 146; Int'l City/County Mgmt. Assoc. 147; Int'l Publishers 148; Jefferson Univ., Thomas 150; Jenkins Group 288; Key Porter 250; Kurian, George 289; Lake View 155; Lang, Peter 155; Lerner 157; Liberal Press, The 158; Lincoln Springs 274; Lion Books 159; Loompanics 162; Lorimer & Co., James 250; Louisiana State Univ. 163; McClelland & Stewart 251; Maisonneuve 166; Mangajin 275; Mercury House 168; Michigan State Univ. 169; Monument 170; Mountain House 276; National Press 173; Naval Inst. 174; Neal-Schuman 174; Nelson-Hall 174; New England Publishing Assoc. 290; NeWest 252; Noble Press 177; Northern Illinois Univ. 277; Nova Science 178; Ohio State Univ. 179; Oregon Hist. So. 278; Oryx 181; Oxford Univ. 182; Pantheon 183; Pelican 186; Pennsylvania Historical and Museum Comm. 187; Pierian 189; Pinter 253; Planning/Communications 191; Praeger 192; Prentice-Hall Canada Trade 253; Prima 193; Publishers Assoc. 195; Purich 254; Regnery 198; Reidmore 256; Republic Of Texas 199; Riverrun 200; Routledge, Inc. 200; Sachem Publishing Assoc. 291; Sierra Club 206; SJL 207; Sligo 208; South End 209; Spectrum 210; Stanford Univ. 211; Stone Bridge Press 212; Summit Publishing Group 214; Teachers College 215; Temple Univ. 216; Third World 217; Thompson Educ. 258; Tuttle, Charles E. 259; Univ. of Alaska 222; Univ. of Alberta Press 260; Univ. of Arkansas 222; Univ. of Illinois 223; Univ. of Massachusetts 224; Univ. of Missouri 224; Univ. of North Carolina 225; Univ. of North Texas 225; Univ. of Oklahoma 225; Univ. of Ottawa 260; Univ. Press of Mississippi 227; Univ. Press of New England 227; Utah State Univ. 228; Vanderbilt Univ. 228; Vehicule 261; Verso 229; Verso 261; Walch, J. Weston 230; Washington State Univ. 232; Watts, Franklin 232; Wayfinder 283; Wiley & Sons, John 235

Health/Medicine: Acorn 264; Adams Media 78; Adams-Blake Publishing 78; Addicus 78; Addison-Wesley Longman 79; Almar 80; American Counseling 82; American Diabetes 83; American Hospital 83; American Medical Pub. 264; American Nurses 83; American Press 84; Atheneum Books For Young Readers 87; Avon 88; Ballantine 89; Bantam Books 90; Barricade 91; Barron's 91; Benjamin Co. 286; Berkley Publishing Group 92; Blackbirch 93; Blue Dolphin 94; Blue Poppy 95; Bonus 95; Books Beyond Borders LLC 267; Branden 97; Broadview 241; Broadway Books 99; Brookline 99; Bull 99; Butterworth-Heinemann 100; Cambridge Educ. 101; Cambridge Univ. 101; Cardoza 102; Career 102; Carol 103; Cassandra 103; Cato Inst. 104; Celestial Arts 105; Cerier, Alison Brown 286; Children's Press 106; Chronicle 107; Commune-A-Key 110; Consumer Press 112; Consumer Reports Books 112; Contemporary Books 112; Cracom 287; Crown Publishing Group 115; Current Clinical Strategies 115; Dancing Jester 115; Davies, Robert 244; Detselig 244; Dimi 120; Eastland 123; Elder Books 124; Engineering & Management 124; Eriksson, Paul S. 125; Essential Medical Information Systems 270; Evans and Co. M. 125; Feminist Press at CUNY 127; Fisher 128; Free Spirit 130; Giniger, K S 288; Graber Prods. 288; Harbor 135; HarperCollins 136; HarperCollins Publishers 248; Hartley & Marks 136; Hastings 137; Hatherleigh 137; Hay House 137; Health Comm. 137; Herbal Studies 272; Hounslow 249; Human Kinetics 142; Human Services Inst. 142; Humanics 142; Hunter House 143; I.A.A.S. 273; ICS Books, Inc. 144; Idyll Arbor 145; Inner Traditions Int'l 146; Insight Books 146; Int'l Found. Employee Benefit Plans 148; Int'l Medical 148; Ivy League 273; Jain 150; Jenkins Group 288; Jones Univ., Bob 152; Kali 274; Kesend, Michael 153; Key Porter 250; Kindred Prods. 250; Krieger 155; Laing Comm. 289; Landmine 274; Lawrence, Merloyd 156; Learning Works 157; Lerner 157; Libraries Unltd. 158; Lifetime Books 158; Llewellyn 161; Love and Logic 163; McClelland & Stewart 251; McFarland & Co. 164; Macmillan Canada 251; Marketscope 166; Markowski Int'l 166; Markowski Int'l Publishers 289; Masters Press 167; Mayfield 167; Metamorphous 169; Meyerbooks 275; Monument 170;

Mosaic Press Miniature Books 276; National Press 173; Naturegraph Publishers 276; Neal-Schuman 174; Negative Capability 174; New Harbinger 174; Newcastle 176; Newjoy 277; Nova Science 178; Ohio Univ. 179; Olson & Co., C. 278; Oryx 181; Ottenheimer 290; Oxford Univ. 182; Pacific Press 182; Pacific View 183; Pacific View 278; Pandora 253; Pelican 186; Penguin Studio 186; PennWell 187; Pierian 189; Plenum 191; Pocket Books 191; Popular Medicine 279; Precept 192; Prentice-Hall Canada Trade 253; Prima 193; Productive Pub. 254; QED 196; Quest 196; Random House 197; Regnery 198; Settel Assoc. 291; Sidran Press 206; South End 209; Speech Bin 210; Sterling 212; Stillpoint 212; Storm Peak 281; Sulzburger & Graham 213; Summers Press 214; Summit Publishing Group 214; Sunshine 257; Systems Co. 215; Taylor 215; Temple Univ. 216; Ten Speed 216; Texas Western 217; Third Side 217; Third World 217; Thorsons 258; Times Books 218; Todd 219; Trilobyte 258; Tuttle, Charles 221; 2M Comm. 292; Unity 221; Univ. of Alaska 222; Univ. of Montreal 260; Univ. Press of Mississippi 227; Vanderbilt Univ. 228; VGM Career Horizons 229; Volcano 229; Walch, J. Weston 230; Walker and Co. 230; Wall & Emerson 261; Weidner & Sons 232; Weiser, Samuel 232; Wieser & Wieser 292; Wiley & Sons, John 235; Woodbine 284; YMAA 284; Zebra and Pinnacle 237

Hi-Lo: Cambridge Educ. 101; National Textbook 173; Prolingua 194

History: ABC-CLIO 74; Adams Media 78; African American Images 79; American Atheist 82; American Press 84; Appalachian Mountain Club Books 85; Arcade 85; Arden 86; Ardsley House 86; Arsenal Pulp 240; Atheneum Books For Young Readers 87; Autonomedia 88; Avanyu 88; Avon 88; Aztex 89; Balcony 265; Bandanna 266; B&B 90; Barricade 91; Beil, Frederic 92; Berkshire House 92; Blackbirch 93; Bliss Publishing Co. 266; Blizzard 241; Bookcraft 96; Books Beyond Borders LLC 267; Borealis 241; Borgo 96; Boston Mills 241; Bowling Green State Univ. Popular Press 96; Branden 97; Brassey's 97; Bright Mountain Books, Inc. 267; Broadview 241; Broadway Books 99; Broken Jaw 242; Bryant & Dillon 99; Bucknell Univ. 99; Caitlin 242; Cambridge Univ. 101; Cambridge Univ. 101; Camino 101; Canadian Inst. of Ukrainian Studies 242; Canadian Library Assoc. 243; Canadian Plains Research Center 243; Carol 103; Carolrhoda 103; Cave 104; Center for African-American Studies 268; Charles River 268; Chicago Review 106; Children's Press 106; Citadel 108; Clarion 108; Clear Light 108; Companion 110; Confluence 111; Cornell Maritime 112; Counterpoint 113; Creative Publishing 114; Creative Spark 287; Cross Cultural 114; Crown Publishing Group 115; Dante Univ. of America 116; Darlington 116; Databooks 116; Davidson, Harlan 117; Davies, Robert 244; Denali 119; Detselig 244; Dickens 269; Discipleship Resources 120; Doubleday 120; Down East 121; Down Home 121; Down The Shore 269; Drama Publishers 121; Duncan & Duncan 121; Dundurn 245; Dutton Children's Books 122; Eagle's View 122; Eakin Press/Sunbelt Media 122; Eastern Nat'l Park & Monument Assoc. 123; Ecco 123; Éditions La Liberté 245; Eerdmans, William B. 124; Elliott & Clark Publishing 124; Epicenter 125; Eriksson, Paul S. 125; Escart 246; Faber & Faber 126; Facts On File 126; Fairleigh Dickinson Univ. 126; Family Album 270; Fathom 271; Feminist Press at CUNY 127; Filter 271; Fine, Donald 128; Fitzhenry & Whiteside 246; Foreign Policy Assoc. 129; Four Walls Eight Windows 129; Gem Guides 131; Giniger, K S 288; Glenbridge 131; Golden West 132; Goose Lane 246; Guernica 247; Gutter Press 247; HarperCollins 136; HarperCollins Publishers 248; Herald Press Canada 248; Heritage House 248; Heyday 139; High Plains 139; Hippocrene 140; Holmes & Meier 141; Horsdal & Schubart 249; Hounslow 249; Howells House 142; Humanitas 249; I.A.A.S. 273; Ide House 144; Indiana Hist. So. 273; Indiana Univ. 146; Inner Traditions Int'l 146; Interlink 147; Int'l Publishers 148; Italica 150; J & L Lee 150; Jefferson Univ., Thomas 150; Jenkins Group 288; Jewish Pub. Soc. 151; Jones Univ., Bob 152; JSA Pub. 288; Kent State Univ. 153; Kesend, Michael 153; Knowledge, Ideas & Trends 154; Kodansha America 154; Krieger 155; Kurian, George 289; Laing Comm. 289; Lake View 155; Landmine 274; Lang, Peter 155; Layla Prods. 289; Learning Works 157; Lehigh Univ. 157; Lerner 157; Lexikos 158; Liberal Press, The 158; Libraries Unltd. 158; Library of Virginia 274; Lincoln Springs 274; Lion Books 159; Little, Brown (Children's) 160; Little, Brown 160; Lone Pine 250; Longstreet 162; Lorien House 275; Lorimer & Co., James 250; Louisiana State Univ. 163; Loyola Press 163; Lucent 163; M.A.P. Prods. 251; McClelland & Stewart 251; McDonald & Woodward 164; McFarland & Co. 164; McGuinn & McGuire 165; Macmillan Canada 251; Mage 165; Maisonneuve 166; Maverick Pub. 167; Meyerbooks 275; Michigan State Univ. 169; Milkweed 170; Minnesota Hist. Soc. 170; Mosaic Press Miniature Books 276; Mystic Seaport Museum 276; National Press 173; Natural Heritage 252; New England Publishing Assoc. 290; New Victoria 175; NeWest 252; Noble Press 177; Nodin 177; Northern Illinois Univ. 277; Northland 177; Norton, W.W. 178; Nova Science 178; Ohio Univ. 179; Orca 252; Oregon Hist. So. 278; Overlook 181; Oxford Univ. 182; Pacific View 183; Pansophic 183; Pansophic 278; Pantheon 183; Parnassus 184; Peachtree 185; Pelican 186; Permanent Press/Second Chance Press 188; Picton 189; Pierian 189; Pineapple 190; Pinter 253; Pogo Press 279; Praeger 192; Prairie Oak 280; Primer Publishers 280; Publishers Assoc. 195; Purich 254; QED 196; Quarry 254; Quintet 254; Raincoast Book Distribution 255; Random House 197; Rawhide Western 197; Red Deer

College 255; Regnery 198; Reidmore 256; Riverrun 200; Rockbridge 280; Ronsdale 256; Routledge, Inc. 200; Royal Fireworks 200; Sachem Publishing Assoc. 291; St. Bede's 201; Sasquatch 203; Scholastic Canada 256; Scottwall Assoc. 281; Seaside 204; Sergeant Kirkland's 205; Settel Assoc. 291; Shoreline 257; Signature Books 206; Silver Burdett 207; Silver Moon 291; Sligo 208; Social Science Education Consortium 208; Sono Nis 257; South End 209; Spectrum 210; Stackpole 211; Stanford Univ. 211; Sterling 212; Storm Peak 281; Summit Publishing Group 214; Sunstone 214; Tamarack 282; Teachers College 215; Texas State Hist. Assoc. 216; Third World 217; Three Continents 217; Times Books 218; Tudor 220; Tuttle, Charles E. 259; United Church Publishing House (UCPH) 259; Univ. of Alaska 222; Univ. of Alberta Press 260; Univ. of California 223; Univ. of Idaho 223; Univ. of Illinois 223; Univ. of Iowa 223; Univ. of Maine 224; Univ. of Manitoba 260; Univ. of Massachusetts 224; Univ. of Montreal 260; Univ. of Nebraska 224; Univ. of New Mexico 225; Univ. of North Texas 225; Univ. of Oklahoma 225; Univ. of Ottawa 260; Univ. of Pennsylvania 226; Univ. of Texas 226; Univ. Press of Kentucky 227; Univ. Press of Mississippi 227; Univ. Press of New England 227; Univ. of New Haven 283; Utah State Univ. 228; Vandamere 228; Vanderbilt Univ. 228; Vehicule 261; Verso 229; Voyageur 229; WalchWard Hill 230; Warner Books 231; Warwick 231; Warwick Publishing 261; Washington State Univ. 232; Wayfinder 283; Westernlore 233; White Mane 234; Whitecap 262; Wieser & Wieser 292; Wilderness Adventure 235; Wiley & Sons, John 235; Write Way 237; Zondervan 238

Hobby: Adams Media 78; Almar 80; Benjamin Co. 286; Berkshire House 92; Betterway 93; Blue Sky Marketing, Inc. 266; Carol 103; Charlton 243; Chicago Review 106; Children's Press 106; Comic Art 110; Countrysport 113; Crown Publishing Group 115; Cypress 115; Darlington 116; Davies, Robert 244; Dimi 120; Dowling 269; Down Home 121; Dundurn 245; E.M. Press, Inc. 122; Eagle's View 122; Éditions La Liberté 245; Eriksson, Paul S. 125; Filter 271; Gryphon Pub. 134; Index 145; Interweave 149; Ivory Tower 150; Jenkins Group 288; JSA Pub. 288; Kesend, Michael 153; Lark 156; Lifetime Books 158; Little, Brown (Children's) 160; Lyons & Burford 164; McClelland & Stewart 251; Marketscope 166; Markowski Int'l 166; Markowski Int'l Publishers 289; Maverick Pub. 167; Mosaic Press Miniature Books 276; Mustang Pub. 172; No Starch 177; Oak Knoll 179; Owl Books 290; Pansophic 183; Paper Chase 183; Parnassus 184; Productive Pub. 254; Quintet 254; Reference Press 198; Scholastic Canada 256; Settel Assoc. 291; Sligo 208; Sono Nis 257; Stackpole 211; Sterling 212; Storey Communications/Garden Way 213; Success Publishing 213; Sulzburger & Graham 213; Summit Publishing Group 214; Sunshine 257; Tudor 220; Voyageur 229; Warren 231; Weidner & Sons 232; Weka 233; Wieser & Wieser 292

House And Home: Betterway 93; Blue Sky Marketing, Inc. 266; Bonus 95; Brighton 98; Ortho 181; Pantheon 183; Sourcebooks 209; Sterling 212; Taylor 215; Warner Books 231

How-To: Accent Pub. 77; Adams Media 78; Almar 80; American Diabetes 83; Auto Book 265; Bantam Books 90; Benjamin Co. 286; Blackbirch Graphics 286; Blue Dolphin 94; Blue Sky Marketing, Inc. 266; Bookcraft 96; Bragdon, Allen D. 286; Bright Ring Publishing, Inc. 267; Bryant & Dillon 99; Camino 101; Carol 103; Celestial Arts 105; Cerier, Alison Brown 286; Chicago Review 106; Clarkson Potter 108; Concordia 111; Contemporary Books 112; Corkscrew 269; Cornell Maritime 112; Crown Publishing Group 115; Dancing Jester 115; Databooks 116; Davies, Robert 244; Detselig 244; Dickens 269; Dowling 269; Down Home 121; E.M. Press, Inc. 122; Ecopress 270; Eriksson, Paul S. 125; Fiesta City Publishers 271; Flower Valley 271; Gambling Times 271; Globe Pequot 132; Great Ocean 272; HarperCollins 136; Hastings 137; Herbal Studies 272; Heritage House 248; Hounslow 249; Humanics 142; Hyperion Press 249; I.A.A.S. 273; ICS Books, Inc. 144; In Print 273; Int'l Marine 148; Jelmar Pub. 274; Jenkins Group 288; Jist Works 151; JSA Pub. 288; Klein, B. 154; Laing Comm. 289; Landmine 274; Lark 156; Layla Prods. 289; Living the Good News 160; Lone Pine 250; Lorien House 275; McBooks 275; McClelland & Stewart 251; McDonald & Woodward 164; McGraw-Hill Ryerson 251; Markowski Int'l Publishers 289; Maupin House 275; Maverick Pub. 167; Media Bridge 168; Menasha Ridge 290; Morrow, William 171; Mountaineers, The 172; Mystic Seaport Museum 276; Naturegraph Publishers 276; Ohio Univ. 179; Olson & Co., C. 278; Owl Books 290; Pacific Press 182; Paideia 278; Paladin 183; Pansophic 278; Parrot 279; Partners in Publishing 279; Phi Delta Kappa Educ. Found. 188; PREP 192; Prima 193; Publicom 291; Quintet 254; Red Eye 280; Resource Publications 291; Revell, Fleming 199; Rocky Mountain Books 256; Royal Fireworks 200; Self-Counsel 256; Settel Assoc. 291; Sierra Club 206; Sligo 208; Sourcebooks 209; Steel Balls 281; Sterling 212; Stoeger 212; Summit Publishing Group 214; Sunshine 257; Taylor 215; Technical Books for the Layperson 282; Tenth Avenue 292; Thunder Dog 283; Tiare 218; Titan 258; Trilobyte 258; Tudor 220; Tuttle, Charles E. 259; 2M Comm. 292; Warwick 231; Warwick Publishing 261; Whitehorse 284; Williamson Publishing 235; Wilshire 235; YMAA 284; Zebra and Pinnacle 237

Humanities: Asian Humanities 87; Borgo 96; Dante Univ. of America 116; Feminist Press at CUNY 127; Free Press 130; Lang, Peter 155; Pace Univ. 278; Univ. of Arkansas 222; Zondervan 238

Humor: Adams Media 78; Arsenal Pulp 240; Atheneum Books For Young Readers 87; Bantam Books 90; Bonus 95; Bookcraft 96; Carol 103; Citadel 108; Clarion 108; Clarkson Potter 108; Clear Light 108; Compass Prods. 286; Contemporary Books 112; Corkscrew 269; Crown Publishing Group 115; Dancing Jester 115; Davenport, May 117; Davies, Robert 244; Detselig 244; Dickens 269; Dowling 269; Down Home 121; Epicenter 125; Eriksson, Paul S. 125; Fiesta City Publishers 271; General Pub. 131; Gutter Press 247; HarperCollins 136; HarperCollins Publishers 248; Hastings 137; Hoard & Sons, W.D. 272; Hounslow 249; ICS Books, Inc. 144; Ivory Tower 150; Jenkins Group 288; JSA Pub. 288; Key Porter 250; Knowledge, Ideas & Trends 154; Layla Prods. 289; Longstreet 162; McClelland & Stewart 251; Macmillan Canada 251; Marketscope 166; Meadowbrook 167; Media Forum Int'l. 275; Menasha Ridge 290; Meriwether 168; Mosaic Press Miniature Books 276; Orchises 180; Peachtree 185; Pelican 186; Piccadilly 189; PREP 192; Quarry 254; Ragged Mountain 197; Raincoast Book Distribution 255; Random House 197; Red Deer College 255; Royal Fireworks 200; Rutledge Hill 201; Sandlapper 202; Seaside 204; Settel Assoc. 291; Shoreline 257; Signature Books 206; Sound And Vision 257; Steel Balls 281; Sterling 212; Summit Publishing Group 214; Sunshine 257; Thunder Dog 283; Titan 258; Tuttle, Charles E. 259; 2M Comm. 292; Warner Books 231; White-Boucke 284; Wordstorm Prods. 262; Zebra and Pinnacle 237

Illustrated Book: Abrams, Harry 77; Adams Media 78; American & World Geographic 81; Balcony 265; Ballantine 89; Bandanna 266; Bantam Books 90; Beil, Frederic 92; Blackbirch Graphics 286; Bliss Publishing Co. 266; Boston Mills 241; Broadway Books 99; Canadian Plains Research Center 243; C&T 102; Caxton Printers 104; Celestial Arts 105; Chatham 106; Comic Art 110; Compass Prods. 286; Dancing Jester 115; Databooks 116; Davies, Robert 244; Davis Pub. 117; Detselig 244; Down The Shore 269; Eakin Press/Sunbelt Media 122; Elliott & Clark Publishing 124; Eriako 287; General Pub. 131; Giniger, K S 288; Godine, David 132; Goose Lane 246; Great Ocean 272; HarperCollins Publishers 248; Herald Press Canada 248; Heritage House 248; Hiller Box 288; Houghton Mifflin (Children's) 141; Hounslow 249; Humanics 142; I.A.A.S. 273; ICS Books, Inc. 144; Int'l Marine 148; Jefferson Univ., Thomas 150; Jenkins Group 288; Just Us Books 152; Kesend, Michael 153; Key Porter 250; Laing Comm. 289; Lark 156; Layla Prods. 289; Library of Virginia 274; Limelight 159; Living the Good News 160; Longstreet 162; Lothrop, Lee & Shepard 162; M.A.P. Prods. 251; McBooks 275; McClelland & Stewart 251; McDonald & Woodward 164; Mage 165; Minnesota Hist. Soc. 170; Mosaic Press Miniature Books 276; Mountain Automation 276; Ohio Univ. 179; Orca 252; Ottenheimer 290; Pelican 186; Penguin Studio 186; Pennsylvania Historical and Museum Comm. 187; Pogo Press 279; Publicom 291; Raincoast Book Distribution 255; Random House 197; Red Deer College 255; Royal Fireworks 200; Sandlapper 202; Scottwall Assoc. 281; Settel Assoc. 291; Shoreline 257; Soundprints 209; Sourcebooks 209; Sta-Kris 281; Sunshine 257; Tamarack 282; Tenth Avenue 292; Texas State Hist. Assoc. 216; Tidewater 218; Titan 258; Tuttle, Charles E. 259; Warren 231; Wayfinder 283; Zephyr 284

Juvenile Books: Abingdon 74; Adams Media 78; Alaska Northwest 79; Atheneum Books For Young Readers 87; Austen Sharp 265; Baker Books 89; Barbour 90; Barron's 91; Beil, Frederic 92; Blackbirch 93; Blackbirch Graphics 286; Blizzard 241; Bookcraft 96; Borealis 241; Branden 97; Bright Ring Publishing, Inc. 267; Camino 101; C&T 102; Clarion 108; Compass Prods. 286; Creative Spark 287; David, Jonathan 117; Davies, Robert 244; Down The Shore 269; Dundurn 245; Eakin Press/Sunbelt Media 122; Éditions La Liberté 245; Eerdmans, William B. 124; Eriako 287; Fiesta City Publishers 271; Fitzhenry & Whiteside 246; Friends United 130; Godine, David 132; Graber Prods. 288; Group Publishing 134; Gryphon House 134; HarperCollins Publishers 248; Hendrick-Long 138; Herald 139; Herald Press Canada 248; Hiller Box 288; Houghton Mifflin (Adult) 141; Hyperion Press 249; I.A.A.S. 273; Jain 150; Jenkins Group 288; Kali 274; Key Porter 250; Laing Comm. 289; Lark 156; Layla Prods. 289; Lerner 157; Living the Good News 160; Lone Pine 250; Lorimer & Co., James 250; McClanahan Book Co. 289; McClelland & Stewart 251; Morehouse 171; Nine Pines 252; NorthWord 178; Orca 252; Oregon Hist. So. 278; Ottenheimer 290; Owl Books 290; Pacific Educ. 253; Pacific Press 182; Pacific View 278; Pansophic 278; Peachtree 185; Pelican 186; Perfection Learning 279; Philomel 189; Publicom 291; Quarry 254; Raincoast Book Distribution 255; Red Deer College 255; Ronsdale 256; Sandlapper 202; Sasquatch 203; Scholastic Canada 256; Settel Assoc. 291; Sierra Club 206; Silver Moon 291; Speech Bin 210; Standard 211; Sterling 212; Storey Communications/Garden Way 213; Storm Peak 281; Sunshine 257; Tenth Avenue 292; Tidewater 218; Tyndale House 221; Vital Issues 229; Walker and Co. 230; Ward Hill 230; Whitecap 262; Wiley & Sons, John 235

Labor/Management: Abbott, Langer 74; BNA 95; Drama Publishers 121; Intercultural Press 147; Int'l Publishers 148; Temple Univ. 216

Language and Literature: ABC-CLIO 74; Adams Media 78; Anchorage 84; Arsenal Pulp 240; Asian Humanities 87; Bandanna 266; Bantam Books 90; Barron's 91; Beil, Frederic 92; Blizzard 241;

Borealis 241; Bowling Green State Univ. Popular Press 96; Broadview 241; Broken Jaw 242; Brookline 99; Bryant & Dillon 99; Calyx Books 268; Canadian Inst. of Ukrainian Studies 242; Carol 103; Carolina Wren 268; Center Press 105; Clarion 108; Clarkson Potter 108; College Board 110; Confluence 111; Coteau 244; Cottonwood 113; Counterpoint 113; Course Crafters 287; Dancing Jester 115; Dante Univ. of America 116; Davenport, May 117; Davidson, Harlan 117; Davies, Robert 244; Down Home 121; Dundurn 245; Eastern Press 270; Ecco 123; Éditions La Liberté 245; Facts On File 126; Family Album 270; Feminist Press at CUNY 127; Four Walls Eight Windows 129; Goose Lane 246; Gryphon Pub. 134; Guernica 247; Gutter Press 247; HarperCollins Publishers 248; Heinemann 138; Herald Press Canada 248; Highsmith 140; Hippopotamus 248; Humanitas 249; Indiana Univ. 146; Insight Books 146; Italica 150; Jefferson Univ., Thomas 150; Jewish Pub. Soc. 151; Kaya Prod. 153; Kent State Univ. 153; Kodansha America 154; Lake View 155; Landmine 274; Lang, Peter 155; Learning Works 157; Lehigh Univ. 157; Lerner 157; Libraries Unltd. 158; Lincoln Springs 274; Locust Hill 161; Longstreet 162; Louisiana State Univ. 163; M.A.P. Prods. 251; McClelland & Stewart 251; Mage 165; Maisonneuve 166; Mangajin 275; Maupin House 275; Mayfield 167; Mercury House 168; Michigan State Univ. 169; Neal-Schuman 174; Negative Capability 174; NTC Publishing 179; Ohio State Univ. 179; Ohio Univ. 179; Optima 180; Oregon State Univ. 180; Oryx 181; Oxford Univ. 182; Peguis 253; Pencil Point 186; Pinter 253; Post-Apollo 279; Prolingua 194; Puckerbrush 280; QED 196; Quarry 254; Riverrun 200; Ronsdale 256; Roxbury 200; Royal Fireworks 200; Russian Information Services 201; Sand River 281; Scots Plaid 281; Serendipity Systems 204; Sierra Club 206; Spectrum 210; Stanford Univ. 211; Stone Bridge Press 212; Stormline 282; Sunshine 257; Texas Christian Univ. 216; Texas Western 217; Third Side 217; Third World 217; Tuttle, Charles E. 259; Unfinished Monument 259; Univ. of Alaska 222; Univ. of California 223; Univ. of Idaho 223; Univ. of Illinois 223; Univ. of Montreal 260; Univ. of Nebraska 224; Univ. of Nevada 224; Univ. of North Carolina 225; Univ. of North Texas 225; Univ. of Oklahoma 225; Univ. of Ottawa 260; Univ. of Pennsylvania 226; Univ. of Scranton 226; Univ. of Tennessee 226; Univ. of Texas 226; Univ. Press of Kentucky 227; Univ. Press of Mississippi 227; Utah State Univ. 228; Vanderbilt Univ. 228; Vehicule 261; Verso 261; Wadsworth 230; WalchWarren 231; Weidner & Sons 232; White Pine 234; Wiley & Sons, John 235; York Press 262; Zephyr 284; Zoland 238

Law: Allworth 80; Almar 80; American Correctional 82; BNA 95; Carswell Thomson 243; Catbird 103; Do-It-Yourself Legal 120; Fathom 271; Graduate Group 132; Hamilton Inst., Alexander 135; Indiana Univ. 146; Inst. of Police Tech. & Mgmt. 147; LRP 163; Ohio State Univ. 179; Oxford Univ. 182; Phi Delta Kappa Educ. Found. 188; Planners Press 190; Purich 254; Self-Counsel 256; Summers Press 214; Temple Univ. 216; Tower Pub. 219; Univ. of North Carolina 225; Univ. of Pennsylvania 226

Literary Criticism: Barron's 91; Bucknell Univ. 99; Dundurn 245; ECW 245; Fairleigh Dickinson Univ. 126; Godine, David 132; Guernica 247; Gutter Press 247; Holmes & Meier 141; Lang, Peter 155; M.A.P. Prods. 251; Maisonneuve 166; NeWest 252; Northern Illinois Univ. 277; Routledge, Inc. 200; Stanford Univ. 211; Texas Christian Univ. 216; Third World 217; Three Continents 217; Univ. of Arkansas 222; Univ. of Massachusetts 224; Univ. of Missouri 224; Univ. of Tennessee 226; Univ. of Texas 226; Univ. Press of Mississippi 227; York Press 262

Marine Subjects: Gaff 271; McGraw-Hill Companies (Professional Book Group) 165; Marlor 167; Maverick Pub. 167; Mystic Seaport Museum 276; Sono Nis 257; Transportation Trails 219

Military/War: Adams Media 78; American Eagle 83; Aviation Book Co. 265; Avon 88; Blair, John 93; Brassey's 97; Canadian Inst. of Strategic Studies 242; Carol 103; Charlton 243; Crown Publishing Group 115; Darlington 116; Databooks 116; Detselig 244; Eakin Press/Sunbelt Media 122; Eastern Nat'l Park & Monument Assoc. 123; Fairleigh Dickinson Univ. 126; Fine, Donald 128; HarperCollins Publishers 248; Hippocrene 140; Howell Press 141; Howells House 142; I.A.A.S. 273; Jefferson Univ., Thomas 150; Jenkins Group 288; Key Porter 250; Kurian, George 289; Landmine 274; Libraries Unltd. 158; Lincoln Springs 274; Louisiana State Univ. 163; McClelland & Stewart 251; McGraw-Hill Ryerson 251; Macmillan Canada 251; Maisonneuve 166; Michigan State Univ. 169; Monument 170; Natural Heritage 252; Nautical & Aviation 173; Naval Inst. 174; Oxford Univ. 182; Penguin Studio 186; Praeger 192; Quintet 254; Reference Service 198; Regnery 198; Republic Of Texas 199; Rockbridge 280; Rutledge Hill 201; Sachem Publishing Assoc. 291; Sergeant Kirkland's 205; Sligo 208; Stackpole 211; Summit Publishing Group 214; Texas A&M Univ. 216; Tudor 220; Univ. of Alaska 222; Univ. of Nebraska 224; Univ. of North Carolina 225; Univ. of North Texas 225; Univ. Press of Kentucky 227; Vandamere 228; Vanwell 260; White Mane 234; Wieser & Wieser 292; Wiley & Sons, John 235; Write Way 237; Zebra and Pinnacle 237

Money/Finance: Adams Media 78; Adams-Blake Publishing 78; Adams-Hall 264; Allen 80; Almar 80; American Nurses 83; Betterway 93; Bloomberg 94; Bookhaven 96; Broadway Books 99; Bryant & Dillon 99; Business McGraw-Hill 100; Cambridge Educ. 101; Caradium 102; Carol 103; Cato Inst. 104; Center

Press 105; Charlton 243; Consumer Press 112; Consumer Reports Books 112; Contemporary Books 112; Cypress 115; Davies, Robert 244; Dearborn Financial 118; Detselig 244; Dimi 120; Duncan & Duncan 121; Elder Books 124; Focus on the Family 129; Globe Pequot 132; Harbor 135; HarperCollins Publishers 248; Hay House 137; Hensley, Virgil 138; Herald Press Canada 248; Hounslow 249; I.A.A.S. 273; Initiatives 146; Insight Books 146; Int'l Wealth 149; Jain 150; Jenkins Group 288; Key Porter 250; Lerner 157; Lifetime Books 158; McClelland & Stewart 251; McGraw-Hill Companies (Professional Book Group) 165; McGraw-Hill Ryerson 251; Macmillan Canada 251; Marketscope 166; Markowski Int'l Publishers 289; National Press 173; Neal-Schuman 174; New World Library 176; Nova Science 178; Planning/Communications 191; Prentice-Hall Canada Trade 253; PREP 192; Productive Pub. 254; PSI Research 195; Quill/Driver/Word Dancer 196; Reference Press 198; Settel Assoc. 291; Sourcebooks 209; Steel Balls 281; Success Publishing 213; Sulzburger & Graham 213; Summit Publishing Group 214; Sunshine 257; Systems Co. 215; Technical Analysis of Stocks & Commodities 282; Ten Speed 216; Todd 219; Tuttle, Charles E. 259; Warwick 231; Warwick Publishing 261; Zebra and Pinnacle 237

Multicultural: ABC-CLIO 74; Facts On File 126; Feminist Press at CUNY 127; Guernica 247; Highsmith 140; Humanics 142; Intercultural Press 147; Lerner 157; Media Bridge 168; Oryx 181; Pacific View 278; Polychrome 191; Univ. of Pennsylvania 226; Volcano 229; Ward Hill 230

Multimedia: Addison-Wesley Longman 79; Cardoza 102; Dancing Jester 115; Drama Publishers 121; Ecopress 270; Elder Book 124; Media Bridge 168; Mountain Automation 276; Paideia 278; Pansophic 183; Precept 192; Reference Press 198; Serendipity Systems 204; Sunshine 257; Trilobyte 258; Walch, J. Weston 230; Warwick 231; YMMA 284

Music/Dance: Abingdon 74; American Catholic 264; American Press 84; And Books 84; Ardsley House 86; Arsenal Pulp 240; Atheneum Books For Young Readers 87; Betterway 93; Bliss Publishing Co. 266; Branden 97; Bucknell Univ. 99; Cambridge Univ. 101; Cambridge Univ. 101; Carol 103; Carolrhoda 103; Celestial Arts 105; Center for African-American Studies 268; Children's Press 106; Dancing Jester 115; Discipleship Resources 120; Dowling 269; Drama Publishers 121; Ecco 123; Éditions La Liberté 245; Faber & Faber 126; Fairleigh Dickinson Univ. 126; Fallen Leaf 270; Feminist Press at CUNY 127; General Pub. 131; Glenbridge 131; Guernica 247; HarperCollins 136; Humanics 142; Indiana Univ. 146; Inner Traditions Int'l 146; Ivory Tower 150; JSA Pub. 288; Krieger 155; Lang, Peter 155; Lerner 157; Libraries Unltd. 158; Limelight 159; Louisiana State Univ. 163; McClelland & Stewart 251; McFarland & Co. 164; Mage 165; Mayfield 167; Media Bridge 168; Meriwether 168; Mosaic Press Miniature Books 276; Nelson-Hall 174; Norton, W.W. 178; Ohio Univ. 179; Oxford Univ. 182; Pacific Educ. 253; Pelican 186; Pencil Point 186; Penguin Studio 186; Pierian 189; Prima 193; Quarry 254; Quintet 254; Random House 197; Resource Publications 291; Riverrun 200; Scarecrow 203; Schirmer 203; Sound And Vision 257; Stipes 212; Tenth Avenue 292; Tiare 218; Titan 258; Univ. of Illinois 223; Univ. of Iowa 223; Univ. Press of Kentucky 227; Univ. Press of Mississippi 227; Univ. Press of New England 227; Vanderbilt Univ. 228; Wadsworth 230; Walch, J. Weston 230; Walker and Co. 230; Warren 231; Weiser, Samuel 232; White Cliffs 233; White-Boucke 284; Writer's Digest Books 237

Nature/Environment: ABC-CLIO 74; Adams Media 78; Appalachian Mountain Club Books 85; Arcade 85; Atheneum Books For Young Readers 87; Autonomedia 88; Bantam Books 90; Barricade 91; Beachway 266; Beacon Press 91; Bear and Co. 91; Berkshire House 92; Blackbirch 93; Blackbirch Graphics 286; Blair, John 93; Bliss Publishing Co. 266; Blue Dolphin 94; BNA 95; Broadway Books 99; Broken Jaw 242; Canadian Plains Research Center 243; Carol 103; Carolrhoda 103; Cave 104; Chatham 106; ChemTec 244; Children's Press 106; Chronicle 107; Clarion 108; Clarkson Potter 108; Clear Light 108; Confluence 111; Cornell Maritime 112; Counterpoint 113; Countrysport 113; Crown Publishing Group 115; Dancing Jester 115; Detselig 244; Dimi 120; Discipleship Resources 120; Down East 121; Down Home 121; Down The Shore 269; Dutton Children's Books 122; Eakin Press/Sunbelt Media 122; Eastern Nat'l Park & Monument Assoc. 123; Ecopress 270; Éditions La Liberté 245; Ekstasis Editions 246; Elliott & Clark Publishing 124; Epicenter 125; Eriksson, Paul S. 125; Escart 246; Faber & Faber 126; Facts On File 126; Filter 271; Fitzhenry & Whiteside 246; Four Walls Eight Windows 129; Gem Guides 131; Godine, David 132; Goose Lane 246; Great Quotations 133; Hancock House 135; HarperCollins 136; HarperCollins Publishers 248; Hartley & Marks 136; Herald Press Canada 248; Heritage House 248; Heyday 139; High Plains 139; Horsdal & Schubart 249; Houghton Mifflin (Adult) 141; ICS Books, Inc. 144; Ideals Children's Books 144; Inner Traditions Int'l 146; Insight Books 146; Johnson Books 151; Jones Univ., Bob 152; Kali 274; Kesend, Michael 153; Key Porter 250; Kodansha America 154; Lark 156; Lawrence, Merloyd 156; Learning Works 157; Lerner 157; Lexikos 158; Little, Brown (Children's) 160; Little, Brown 160; Llewellyn 161; Lone Pine 250; Longstreet 162; Lorien House 275; Lyons & Burford 164; M.A.P. Prods. 251; McClelland & Stewart

251; McDonald & Woodward 164; Marketscope 166; Maverick Pub. 167; Mercury House 168; Milkweed 170; Mosaic Press Miniature Books 276; Mountaineers, The 172; Natural Heritage 252; Naturegraph Publishers 276; New England Cartographics 277; New World Library 176; Noble Press 177; Northland 177; NorthWord 178; Nova Science 178; Noyes Data 178; Ohio Univ. 179; Olson & Co., C. 278; Orca 252; Oregon Hist. So. 278; Oregon State Univ. 180; Owen, Richard 181; Owl Books 290; Oxford Univ. 182; Pacific Educ. 253; Pacific Press 182; Parnassus 184; Pierian 189; Pineapple 190; Primer Publishers 280; Pruett 194; PSI Research 195; Quintet 254; Raincoast Book Distribution 255; Rawhide Western 197; Red Deer College 255; Reference Pub. 280; Regnery 198; Rocky Mountain Books 256; Ronsdale 256; Sandhill Crane 202; Sasquatch 203; Scholastic Canada 256; Sierra Club 206; Silver Burdett 207; Soundprints 209; South End 209; Stanford Univ. 211; Sterling 212; Stillpoint 212; Stipes 212; Storey Communications/Garden Way 213; Summit Publishing Group 214; Sunshine 257; Systems Co. 215; Ten Speed 216; Texas Western 217; Thorsons 258; Thunder Dog 283; Univ. of Alaska 222; Univ. of Alberta Press 260; Univ. of Arizona 222; Univ. of Arkansas 222; Univ. of Calgary 260; Univ. of California 223; Univ. of Idaho 223; Univ. of Iowa 223; Univ. of Massachusetts 224; Univ. of Nebraska 224; Univ. of Nevada 224; Univ. of North Carolina 225; Univ. of North Texas 225; Univ. of Oklahoma 225; Univ. of Ottawa 260; Univ. of Texas 226; Univ. Press of Colorado 227; Univ. Press of New England 227; Vanderbilt Univ. 228; Verso 261; VGM Career Horizons 229; Voyageur 229; Wadsworth 230; Walker and Co. 230; Warren 231; Washington State Univ. 232; Watts, Franklin 232; Wayfinder 283; Weidner & Sons 232; Whitecap 262; Wieser & Wieser 292; Wilderness Adventure 235; Wilderness Press 235; Williamson Publishing 235; Windward 236; Zoland 238

Philosophy: American Atheist 82; Ardsley House 86; Asian Humanities 87; Atheneum Books For Young Readers 87; Autonomedia 88; Bantam Books 90; Beacon Press 91; Books Beyond Borders LLC 267; Broadview 241; Bucknell Univ. 99; Carol 103; Cassandra 103; Catholic Univ. of America Press 104; Celestial Arts 105; Center Press 105; Clear Light 108; Counterpoint 113; Cross Cultural 114; Dancing Jester 115; Davidson, Harlan 117; Davies, Robert 244; Detselig 244; Eerdmans, William B. 124; Facts On File 126; Fairleigh Dickinson Univ. 126; Glenbridge 131; Guernica 247; Gutter Press 247; HarperCollins 136; Hay House 137; Holmes 141; Humanics 142; Humanitas 249; I.A.A.S. 273; Indiana Univ. 146; Inner Traditions Int'l 146; Institute of Psychological Research, Inc./Institut de Recherches Psychologiques, Inc. 249; International Scholars Publications 148; Int'l Publishers 148; Italica 150; Jefferson Univ., Thomas 150; Jewish Lights 150; Kaya Prod. 153; Kodansha America 154; Krieger 155; Lang, Peter 155; Lee & Low 157; Libraries Unltd. 158; Lorien House 275; Louisiana State Univ. 163; McClelland & Stewart 251; Maisonneuve 166; Maisonneuve 166; Mayfield 167; Mercury House 168; Michigan State Univ. 169; Nicolas-Hays 277; Noble Press 177; Northern Illinois Univ. 277; Nova Science 178; Ohio State Univ. 179; Ohio Univ. 179; Omega 278; Oxford Univ. 182; Paideia 278; Pansophic 183; Pansophic 278; Pierian 189; Praeger 192; PREP 192; Quest 196; Regnery 198; Riverrun 200; Routledge, Inc. 200; St. Bede's 201; Scots Plaid 281; Seaside 204; Settel Assoc. 291; Simon & Schuster 207; Somerville House Books 292; South End 209; Spectrum 210; Stone Bridge Press 212; Sunshine 257; Swedenborg Found. 214; Teachers College 215; Third World 217; Thorsons 258; Tuttle, Charles E. 259; Unfinished Monument 259; Unity 221; Univ. of Alberta Press 260; Univ. of Illinois 223; Univ. of Massachusetts 224; Univ. of Montreal 260; Univ. of Ottawa 260; Univ. of Scranton 226; Vanderbilt Univ. 228; Verso 229; Verso 261; Wadsworth 230; Wall & Emerson 261; Weiser, Samuel 232; Wisdom 236; YMAA 284

Photography: Allworth 80; Atheneum Books For Young Readers 87; Avanyu 88; Branden 97; Butterworth-Heinemann 100; Caitlin 242; Cave 104; Celestial Arts 105; Center Press 105; Chronicle 107; Clarion 108; Clarkson Potter 108; Clear Light 108; Companion 110; Consultant 112; Crown Publishing Group 115; Dancing Jester 115; Elliott & Clark Publishing 124; Epicenter 125; Eriako 287; Focal 128; General Pub. 131; Godine, David 132; HarperCollins Publishers 248; Hollow Earth 140; Hounslow 249; Howells House 142; Humanitas 249; ICS Books, Inc. 144; Jenkins Group 288; Key Porter 250; Layla Prods. 289; Lone Pine 250; Longstreet 162; Louisiana State Univ. 163; McClelland & Stewart 251; Minnesota Hist. Soc. 170; Motorbooks Int'l 172; Natural Heritage 252; Northland 177; NTC Publishing 179; Oregon Hist. So. 278; Penguin Studio 186; Quarry 254; Quintet 254; Raincoast Book Distribution 255; Random House 197; Reference Press 198; Stormline 282; Temple Univ. 216; Tenth Avenue 292; Univ. of Iowa 223; Univ. of Nebraska 224; Univ. of New Mexico 225; Univ. Press of Mississippi 227; Warner Books 231; Warwick 231; Warwick Publishing 261; Wayfinder 283; Wieser & Wieser 292; Writer's Digest Books 237; Zoland 238

Psychology: Active Parenting 78; Adams Media 78; Addicus 78; Addison-Wesley Longman 79; African American Images 79; American Counseling 82; American Diabetes 83; American Nurses 83; American Press 84; And Books 84; Aronson, Jason 86; Asian Humanities 87; Atheneum Books For Young Readers 87; Bantam Books 90; Barricade 91; Blue Dolphin 94; Books Beyond Borders LLC 267; Broadway Books 99; Brookline 99; Bucknell Univ. 99; Cambridge Univ. 101; Carol 103; Cassandra 103; Celestial Arts 105;

Center for African-American Studies 268; Cerier, Alison Brown 286; Citadel 108; Commune-A-Key 110; Contemporary Books 112; Crown Publishing Group 115; Cypress 115; Dancing Jester 115; Davies, Robert 244; Detselig 244; Dickens 269; Dimi 120; Duncan & Duncan 121; Dutton 122; Éditions La Liberté 245; Eerdmans, William B. 124; Ekstasis Editions 246; Elder Books 124; Eriksson, Paul S. 125; Essential Medical Information Systems 270; Facts On File 126; Fairleigh Dickinson Univ. 126; Fairview 127; Free Spirit 130; Glenbridge 131; Guernica 247; Harper San Francisco 136; HarperCollins 136; Hartley & Marks 136; Hastings 137; Hatherleigh 137; Hay House 137; Health Comm. 137; Herald Press Canada 248; Human Kinetics 142; Human Services Inst. 142; Humanics 142; Hyperion 144; I.A.A.S. 273; Inner Traditions Int'l 146; Insight Books 146; Institute of Psychological Research, Inc./Institut de Recherches Psychologiques, Inc. 249; Knowledge, Ideas & Trends 154; Kodansha America 154; Krieger 155; Lang, Peter 155; Lawrence, Merloyd 156; Libraries Unltd. 158; Llewellyn 161; Love and Logic 163; McClelland & Stewart 251; Maisonneuve 166; Markowski Int'l Publishers 289; Mayfield 167; Metamorphous 169; National Press 173; Nelson-Hall 174; New Harbinger 174; New Lexington Press 175; New World Library 176; Newcastle 176; Nicolas-Hays 277; Nine Pines 252; Norton, W.W. 178; Nova Science 178; Ohio Univ. 179; Ottenheimer 290; Oxford Univ. 182; Pansophic 183; Pansophic 278; Paper Chase 183; Paradigm 184; Pauline Books & Media 185; Pierian 189; Plenum 191; Praeger 192; PREP 192; Prima 193; Professional Resource 194; QED 196; Quest 196; Routledge, Inc. 200; Scots Plaid 281; Settel Assoc. 291; Sibyl 206; Sidran Press 206; Society Publishing 208; Sourcebooks 209; Stanford Univ. 211; Steel Balls 281; Stillpoint 212; Sulzburger & Graham 213; Sunshine 257; Swedenborg Found. 214; Third Side 217; Third World 217; Thorsons 258; Tudor 220; 2M Comm. 292; Unity 221; Univ. of Montreal 260; Univ. of Nebraska 224; Walch, J. Weston 230; Warner Books 231; Weidner & Sons 232; Weiser, Samuel 232; Wiley & Sons, John 235; Williamson Publishing 235; Wisdom 236

Real Estate: Contemporary Books 112; Dearborn Financial 118

Recreation: Abrams, Harry 77; Acorn 264; American & World Geographic 81; Appalachian Mountain Club Books 85; Atheneum Books For Young Readers 87; Beachway 266; Berkshire House 92; Betterway 93; Bliss Publishing Co. 266; Carol 103; Cave 104; Chatham 106; Chronicle 107; Compass Prods. 286; Crown Publishing Group 115; Dancing Jester 115; Databooks 116; Denali 119; Detselig 244; Discipleship Resources 120; Down Home 121; Ecopress 270; Enslow 125; Epicenter 125; Eriksson, Paul S. 125; Facts On File 126; Gem Guides 131; Globe Pequot 132; Golden West 132; Hay House 137; Herald Press Canada 248; Heritage House 248; Heyday 139; Horsdal & Schubart 249; Human Kinetics 142; ICS Books, Inc. 144; Idyll Arbor 145; Jenkins Group 288; Johnson Books 151; Layla Prods. 289; Lerner 157; Lion Books 159; Little, Brown (Children's) 160; Lone Pine 250; McClelland & Stewart 251; McFarland & Co. 164; Macmillan Canada 251; Marketscope 166; Masters Press 167; Maverick Pub. 167; Menasha Ridge 290; Meriwether 168; Mustang Pub. 172; Natural Heritage 252; Neal-Schuman 174; New England Cartographics 277; New York Niche 176; Nova Science 178; Ohio Univ. 179; Orca 252; Paper Chase 183; Parnassus 184; Peachtree 185; Pelican 186; Primer Publishers 280; Pruett 194; Quintet 254; Ragged Mountain 197; Raincoast Book Distribution 255; Republic Of Texas 199; Rocky Mountain Books 256; Sasquatch 203; Scholastic Canada 256; Settel Assoc. 291; Sterling 212; Stipes 212; Sulzburger & Graham 213; Summit Publishing Group 214; Ten Speed 216; Univ. of Idaho 223; Voyageur 229; Warwick 231; Warwick Publishing 261; Wayfinder 283; Whitecap 262; Wieser & Wieser 292; Windward 236

Reference: Adams Media 78; Alpine 81; American Diabetes 83; American Nurses 83; Andrews and McMeel 85; Apollo 85; Avanyu 88; Baker Books 89; Ballantine 89; Barricade 91; Beil, Frederic 92; Betterway 93; Blackbirch 93; Blackbirch Graphics 286; Bliss Publishing Co. 266; Bookcraft 96; Borealis 241; Borgo 96; Branden 97; Brassey's 97; Broadway Press 267; Cambridge Univ. 101; Canadian Library Assoc. 243; Carswell Thomson 243; Celestial Arts 105; Cerier, Alison Brown 286; Charlton 243; Christian Media 268; Christian Publications 107; Computer Science 111; Consumer Reports Books 112; Contemporary Books 112; Coteau 244; Cracom 287; Creative Spark 287; Crown Publishing Group 115; Dancing Jester 115; Dante Univ. of America 116; Databooks 116; David, Jonathan 117; Detselig 244; Dickens 269; Doral 120; Duncan & Duncan 121; Dundurn 245; Earth-Love 270; Eckert, J.K. 287; ECW 245; Enslow 125; Escart 246; Essential Medical Information Systems 270; Evans and Co. M. 125; Evras 270; Fairview 127; Fallen Leaf 270; Fathom 271; Friends United 130; Gambling Times 271; Gaslight 131; Giniger, K S 288; Graber Prods. 288; Great Ocean 272; Harper San Francisco 136; HarperCollins 136; Hastings 137; Herald Press Canada 248; Herbal Studies 272; Heritage 139; Heyday 139; Hiller Box 288; Hoard & Sons, W.D. 272; Holmes & Meier 141; Houghton Mifflin (Adult) 141; Jain 150; Jist Works 151; JSA Pub. 288; Klein, B. 154; Knowledge, Ideas & Trends 154; Kurian, George 289; Laing Comm. 289; Landmine 274; Leadership 157; Library of Virginia 274; Lifetime Books 158; Lone Eagle 161; Longstreet 162; McBooks 275; McClelland & Stewart 251; McGraw-Hill Companies (Professional Book Group) 165; McGraw-Hill Ryerson 251; Macmillan Canada

251; Madison 165; Mangajin 275; Masters Press 167; Maverick Pub. 167; Meadowbrook 167; Media Forum Int'l. 275; Meyerbooks 275; Minnesota Hist. Soc. 170; Mystic Seaport Museum 276; Nelson, Thomas 174; New England Publishing Assoc. 290; New Lexington Press 175; NTC Publishing 179; Ohio Biological Survey 277; Ohio Univ. 179; Orchises 180; Oregon Hist. So. 278; Ottenheimer 290; Oxford Univ. 182; Pacific Books 182; Pacific Educ. 253; Pacific View 183; Pandora 253; Parrot 279; Partners in Publishing 279; Peachpit 185; Pennsylvania Historical and Museum Comm. 187; PennWell 187; Phi Delta Kappa Educ. Found. 188; Philosophy Documentation Center 189; Pineapple 190; Pinter 253; Pocket Books 191; Productive Pub. 254; Purich 254; Quill/Driver/Word Dancer 196; Quintet 254; Red Eye 280; Reference Press 198; Resolution Business 280; Riverrun 200; Routledge, Inc. 200; Rutledge Hill 201; Sachem Publishing Assoc. 291; St. Martin's 202; Sandlapper 202; Scarecrow 203; Schirmer 203; Self-Counsel 256; Shoreline 257; Silver Burdett 207; SJL 207; Sono Nis 257; Sourcebooks 209; Speech Bin 210; Standard 211; Sterling 212; Technical Books for the Layperson 282; Ten Speed 216; Texas State Hist. Assoc. 216; Third World 217; Tidewater 218; Trilobyte 258; Tudor 220; Tuttle, Charles E. 259; Univ. of Montreal 260; Univ. of Ottawa 260; Univ. Press of New England 227; Vanderbilt Univ. 228; Walker and Co. 230; Wall & Emerson 261; Warner Books 231; Wayfinder 283; White-Boucke 284; Whitehorse 284; Wiley & Sons, John 235; Woodbine 284; York Press 262; Zondervan 238

Regional: Adams Media 78; Addicus 78; Alaska 264; Almar 80; American & World Geographic 81; Appalachian Mountain Club Books 85; Arsenal Pulp 240; Austen Sharp 265; Avanyu 88; Balcony 265; Berkshire House 92; Black Tooth 266; Bliss Publishing Co. 266; Blue Sky Marketing, Inc. 266; Bonus 95; Borealis 241; Boston Mills 241; Bowling Green State Univ. Popular Press 96; Bright Mountain Books, Inc. 267; Broken Jaw 242; Brown Bear 242; Caitlin 242; Camino 101; Canadian Plains Research Center 243; Carol 103; Cave 104; Caxton Printers 104; Chicago Review 106; Chronicle 107; Clear Light 108; Compass Prods. 286; Confluence 111; Cornell Maritime 112; Coteau 244; Creative Publishing 114; Databooks 116; Davidson, Harlan 117; Denali 119; Down Home 121; Down The Shore 269; Dundurn 245; Ecco 123; ECW 245; Eerdmans, William B. 124; Epicenter 125; Escart 246; Family Album 270; Fathom 271; Filter 271; Fitzhenry & Whiteside 246; Goose Lane 246; Guernica 247; Hemingway Western Studies 272; Hendrick-Long 138; Heritage House 248; Hoard & Sons, W.D. 272; Horsdal & Schubart 249; Indiana Hist. So. 273; Indiana Univ. 146; J & L Lee 150; Jenkins Group 288; Johnson Books 151; Kaya Prod. 153; Kent State Univ. 153; Kinseeker 154; Lahontan Images 274; Laing Comm. 289; Landmine 274; Lexikos 158; Library of Virginia 274; Lone Pine 250; Longstreet 162; Lorien House 275; Louisiana State Univ. 163; M.A.P. Prods. 251; McBooks 275; McGraw-Hill Ryerson 251; Marketscope 166; Maupin House 275; Menasha Ridge 290; Michigan State Univ. 169; Natural Heritage 252; New England Cartographics 277; NeWest 252; Northern Illinois Univ. 277; Northland 177; Ohio State Univ. 179; Ohio Univ. 179; Orca 252; Oregon Hist. So. 278; Oregon State Univ. 180; Overlook 181; Pacific Books 182; Pacific Educ. 253; Pacific View 183; Pacific View 278; Pansophic 183; Pansophic 278; Pelican 186; Penguin Books Canada 253; Pineapple 190; Prairie Oak 280; Prentice-Hall Canada Trade 253; PREP 192; Primer Publishers 280; Quarry 254; Quill/Driver/Word Dancer 196; Quixote 196; Raincoast Book Distribution 255; Red Deer College 255; Republic Of Texas 199; Resolution Business 280; Rockbridge 280; Rocky Mountain Books 256; Ronsdale 256; Sand River 281; Sandlapper 202; Sasquatch 203; Scottwall Assoc. 281; Shoreline 257; Signature Books 206; Sligo 208; Sono Nis 257; Southern Methodist Univ. 210; Stormline 282; Summit Publishing Group 214; Sunstone 214; Tamarack 282; Temple Univ. 216; Texas A&M Univ. 216; Texas Christian Univ. 216; Texas Western 217; Third World 217; Tidewater 218; Tudor 220; Tuttle, Charles E. 259; Umbrella 283; Univ. of Alaska 222; Univ. of Alberta Press 260; Univ. of Arizona 222; Univ. of Calgary 260; Univ. of Idaho 223; Univ. of Manitoba 260; Univ. of Missouri 224; Univ. of North Carolina 225; Univ. of North Texas 225; Univ. of Oklahoma 225; Univ. of Ottawa 260; Univ. of Scranton 226; Univ. of Tennessee 226; Univ. of Texas 226; Univ. Press of Mississippi 227; Utah State Univ. 228; Valiant Press 283; Vandamere 228; Vanderbilt Univ. 228; Vanwell 260; Vehicule 261; Voyageur 229; Walker and Co. 230; Washington State Univ. 232; Wayfinder 283; Whitecap 262; Wilderness Adventure 235; Zoland 238

Religion: American Atheist 82; American Catholic 264; American Counseling 82; And Books 84; Anima 265; Asian Humanities 87; Atheneum Books For Young Readers 87; Augsburg 88; Baker Books 89; Bantam Books 90; Barbour 90; Bear and Co. 91; Behrman House 92; Blue Dolphin 94; Blue Star 95; Bucknell Univ. 99; Canadian Inst. of Ukrainian Studies 242; Cassandra 103; Catholic Univ. of America Press 104; Celestial Arts 105; Chosen Books 107; Christian Publications 107; Compass Prods. 286; Concordia 111; Counterpoint 113; Cross Cultural 114; Dancing Jester 115; David, Jonathan 117; Davies, Robert 244; Detselig 244; Discipleship Resources 120; Duncan & Duncan 121; Elder Books 124; Facts On File 126; Friends United 130; Great Quotations 133; Greenlawn 272; Group Publishing 134; Guernica 247; Harper San Francisco 136; HarperCollins 136; HarperCollins Publishers 248; Harvest House 137; Hay House 137; Herald Press Canada

248; Hiller Box 288; Hi-Time 272; Hollow Earth 140; Holmes 141; Humanics 142; Huntington House 143; Indiana Univ. 146; Inner Traditions Int'l 146; International Scholars Publications 148; Italica 150; Jefferson Univ., Thomas 150; Jenkins Group 288; Jewish Lights 150; Jewish Pub. Soc. 151; Kindred Prods. 250; Kodansha America 154; Kregel 155; Kurian, George 289; Lang, Peter 155; Larson 156; Libraries Unltd. 158; Liguori 159; Lion Publishing 159; Living the Good News 160; Loyola Press 163; McClelland & Stewart 251; Mangajin 275; Markowski Int'l 166; Markowski Int'l Publishers 289; Mayfield 167; Media Bridge 168; Meriwether 168; Monument 170; Morrow, William 171; New Hope 175; New Leaf 175; New World Library 176; Newcastle 176; Nicolas-Hays 277; Nine Pines 252; Nova Science 178; Ohio Univ. 179; Ottenheimer 290; Oxford Univ. 182; Pacific Press 182; Pansophic 183; Pansophic 278; Pauline Books & Media 185; Pelican 186; Pierian 189; PREP 192; Publishers Assoc. 195; Quarry 254; Quest 196; Rainbow Publishers 197; Random House 197; Rawhide Western 197; Regnery 198; Religious Education 198; Resource Publica-tions 291; Revell, Fleming 199; Seaside 204; Shaw, Harold 205; Shoreline 257; Sibyl 206; Signature Books 206; Standard 211; Summit Publishing Group 214; Swedenborg Found. 214; Third World 217; Thorsons 258; Tuttle, Charles 221; Tuttle, Charles E. 259; United Church Publishing House (UCPH) 259; Unity 221; Univ. of Manitoba 260; Univ. of Montreal 260; Univ. of North Carolina 225; Univ. of Ottawa 260; Univ. of Scranton 226; Univ. of Tennessee 226; Vanderbilt Univ. 228; Wadsworth 230; Weiser, Samuel 232; Wilshire 235; Wisdom 236; Zondervan 238

Scholarly: Adams Media 78; Cambridge Univ. 101; Canadian Inst. of Ukrainian Studies 242; Canadian Plains Research Center 243; Center for African-American Studies 268; Cross Cultural 114; Dante Univ. of America 116; Eastern Press 270; Focal 128; Hemingway Western Studies 272; Johnson Books 151; Lake View 155; Lang, Peter 155; Lehigh Univ. 157; Michigan State Univ. 169; Ohio State Univ. 179; Oxford Univ. 182; Pace Univ. 278; Phi Delta Kappa Educ. Found. 188; Publishers Assoc. 195; Religious Education 198; St. Martin's 202; Schirmer 203; Scots Plaid 281; Texas Christian Univ. 216; Texas State Hist. Assoc. 216; Three Continents 217; Univ. of Alaska 222; Univ. of Alberta Press 260; Univ. of Calgary 260; Univ. of Illinois 223; Univ. of Manitoba 260; Univ. of New Mexico 225; Univ. of North Carolina 225; Univ. of Ottawa 260; Univ. of Pennsylvania 226; Univ. of Tennessee 226; Univ. Press of Kentucky 227; Univ. Press of Mississippi 227; Utah State Univ. 228; Vanderbilt Univ. 228; Verso 261; Westernlore 233; York Press 262

Science/Technology: ABC-CLIO 74; Abrams, Harry 77; Adams Media 78; Addison-Wesley Long-man 79; Aegis 264; American Eagle 83; American Nurses 83; American Press 84; Amherst Media 84; Atheneum Books For Young Readers 87; Bantam Books 90; Blackbirch 93; Cambridge Educ. 101; Cam-bridge Univ. 101; Carol 103; Cave 104; ChemTec 244; Children's Press 106; College Board 110; Counterpoint 113; Crown Publishing Group 115; Dancing Jester 115; Databooks 116; Dutton 122; Dutton Children's Books 122; Ecopress 270; Éditions La Liberté 245; Enslow 125; Faber & Faber 126; Facts On File 126; Focal 128; Four Walls Eight Windows 129; Graber Prods. 288; Grapevine 132; Grosset & Dunlap 133; HarperCollins 136; Hay House 137; Houghton Mifflin (Adult) 141; Howells House 142; Humanitas 249; Ideals Children's Books 144; Insight Books 146; Institute of Psychological Research, Inc./Institut de Recherches Psychologi-ques, Inc. 249; Johnson Books 151; Kalmbach 152; Kodansha America 154; Krieger 155; Learning Works 157; Lehigh Univ. 157; Lerner 157; Libraries Unltd. 158; Little, Brown (Children's) 160; Little, Brown 160; Lorien House 275; Lyons & Burford 164; McClelland & Stewart 251; McDonald & Woodward 164; McGraw-Hill Companies (Professional Book Group) 165; Message Co. 169; Metamorphous 169; Naturegraph Publish-ers 276; Naval Inst. 174; Nova Science 178; Oregon State Univ. 180; Owl Books 290; Oxford Univ. 182; Pacific Educ. 253; Paladin 183; Parkway 184; Pencil Point 186; Penguin Studio 186; PennWell 187; Pierian 189; Precept 192; Professional Publications 193; PROMPT Pub. 194; Quest 196; Regnery 198; Scholastic Canada 256; Silver Burdett 207; Silver Moon 291; Simon & Schuster 207; SJL 207; Somerville House Books 292; South End 209; Stanford Univ. 211; Sterling 212; Stipes 212; Sulzburger & Graham 213; Summit Publishing Group 214; Systems Co. 215; Ten Speed 216; Texas Western 217; Trilobyte 258; Tudor 220; Univ. of Alaska 222; Univ. of Arizona 222; Univ. of Maine 224; Univ. of Texas 226; Univelt 222; Verso 261; Wadsworth 230; Walch, J. Weston 230; Walker and Co. 230; Wall & Emerson 261; Warren 231; Watts, Franklin 232; Weidner & Sons 232; Wiley & Sons, John 235; Williamson Publishing 235; Windward 236

Self-Help: Accent Pub. 77; Adams Media 78; Aegis 264; Almar 80; Amacom 81; American Diabetes 83; Atheneum Books For Young Readers 87; Austen Sharp 265; Avon 88; Baker Books 89; Ballantine 89; Bantam Books 90; Barricade 91; Benjamin Co. 286; Betterway 93; Blackbirch Graphics 286; Blue Dolphin 94; Bonus 95; Bookcraft 96; Books Beyond Borders LLC 267; Bragdon, Allen D. 286; Bryant & Dillon 99; Business McGraw-Hill 100; Caradium 102; Carol 103; Cassandra 103; CCC 104; Celestial Arts 105; Cerier, Alison Brown 286; Christian Publications 107; Clarkson Potter 108; College Board 110; Commune-A-Key 110; Consumer Reports Books 112; Contemporary Books 112; Creative Spark 287; Crown Publishing Group 115; Cypress 115; Dancing Jester 115; Databooks 116; David, Jonathan 117; Davies, Robert 244; Detselig

244; Dickens 269; Dowling 269; Duncan & Duncan 121; Earth-Love 270; Elder Books 124; Eriksson, Paul S. 125; Fairview 127; Fine, Donald 128; Fisher 128; Focus on the Family 129; Giniger, K S 288; Graber Prods. 288; Great Ocean 272; Great Quotations 133; Harbor 135; Harper San Francisco 136; HarperCollins 136; HarperCollins Publishers 248; Hastings 137; Herald Press Canada 248; Herbal Studies 272; Hounslow 249; Human Kinetics 142; Humanics 142; Hyperion 144; Intercultural Press 147; Ivy League 273; Jain 150; Jist Works 151; Kesend, Michael 153; Key Porter 250; Klein, B. 154; Knowledge, Ideas & Trends 154; Landmine 274; Lifetime Books 158; Limelight 159; Living the Good News 160; Loompanics 162; McClelland & Stewart 251; McDonald & Woodward 164; McGraw-Hill Companies (Professional Book Group) 165; McGraw-Hill Ryerson 251; Macmillan Canada 251; Marketscope 166; Markowski Int'l 166; Markowski Int'l Publishers 289; Masters Press 167; Media Bridge 168; Metamorphous 169; Meyerbooks 275; Mustang Pub. 172; National Press 173; Newjoy 277; Nicolas-Hays 277; Nine Pines 252; Ohio Univ. 179; Ottenheimer 290; Pacific Press 182; Pansophic 278; Parrot 279; Partners in Publishing 279; Pauline Books & Media 185; Paulist Press 185; Peachtree 185; Pelican 186; Peter Pauper Press 188; PREP 192; Prima 193; Productive Pub. 254; Publicom 291; QED 196; Quixote 196; Random House 197; Resource Publications 291; Revell, Fleming 199; Royal Fireworks 200; Rutledge Hill 201; St. Martin's 202; Seaside 204; Self-Counsel 256; Settel Assoc. 291; Shaw, Harold 205; Sibyl 206; Silvercat Pub. 281; SJL 207; Sligo 208; Sta-Kris 281; Steel Balls 281; Studio 4 Prod. 282; Success Publishing 213; Sulzburger & Graham 213; Summit Publishing Group 214; Sunshine 257; Systems Co. 215; Technical Books for the Layperson 282; Ten Speed 216; Third World 217; Thorsons 258; Todd 219; Trilobyte 258; Trilogy 219; Tudor 220; Turtle 220; Tyndale House 221; Vital Issues 229; Walker and Co. 230; Warner Books 231; Weiss, Daniel 292; White-Boucke 284; Wiley & Sons, John 235; Williamson Publishing 235; Zondervan 238

Social Sciences: Addison-Wesley Longman 79; Borgo 96; Broadview 241; C Q Press 100; Cambridge Educ. 101; Eerdmans, William B. 124; Feminist Press at CUNY 127; Foreign Policy Assoc. 129; Indiana Univ. 146; Insight Books 146; Int'l Publishers 148; Lang, Peter 155; Nelson-Hall 174; Northern Illinois Univ. 277; Oryx 181; Pace Univ. 278; Pilgrim 189; Plenum 191; Routledge, Inc. 200; Roxbury 200; Social Science Education Consortium 208; Stanford Univ. 211; Teachers College 215; Texas Western 217; Univ. of California 223; Univ. of Missouri 224; Verso 261; Wadsworth 230; WalchAmerican Counseling 82; American Press 84; Atheneum Books For Young Readers 87; Avanyu 88; Bantam Books 90; Barricade 91; Blizzard 241; Blue Bird 94; Branden 97; Bucknell Univ. 99; Canadian Inst. of Ukrainian Studies 242; Canadian Plains Research Center 243; Cato Inst. 104; Celestial Arts 105; Center for African-American Studies 268; Cleis 109; Creative Spark 287; Cross Cultural 114; Dancing Jester 115; Davies, Robert 244; Detselig 244; Duncan & Duncan 121; Éditions La Liberté 245; Eerdmans, William B. 124; Enslow 125; Eriksson, Paul S. 125; Fairleigh Dickinson Univ. 126; Fairview 127; Feminist Press at CUNY 127; Free Spirit 130; Glenbridge 131; HarperCollins 136; Hay House 137; Howells House 142; Humanics 142; I.A.A.S. 273; Insight Books 146; Jefferson Univ., Thomas 150; Kaya Prod. 153; Knowledge, Ideas & Trends 154; Kodansha America 154; Lake View 155; Lang, Peter 155; Libraries Unltd. 158; Lincoln Springs 274; Lorimer & Co., James 250; Love and Logic 163; McClelland & Stewart 251; McFarland & Co. 164; Mage 165; Maisonneuve 166; Mangajin 275; Markowski Int'l Publishers 289; Mayfield 167; Metamorphous 169; NASW 173; Nelson-Hall 174; Noble Press 177; Nova Science 178; Ohio State Univ. 179; Ohio Univ. 179; Oxford Univ. 182; Pansophic 183; Pansophic 278; Pierian 189; Pinter 253; Planning/Communications 191; Plenum 191; Praeger 192; Random House 197; Rawhide Western 197; Regnery 198; Roxbury 200; Settel Assoc. 291; South End 209; Spectrum 210; Stanford Univ. 211; Steel Balls 281; Summit Publishing Group 214; Teachers College 215; Temple Univ. 216; Third World 217; Thompson Educ. 258; United Church Publishing House (UCPH) 259; Univ. of Alberta Press 260; Univ. of Arkansas 222; Univ. of Illinois 223; Univ. of Massachusetts 224; Univ. of Montreal 260; Univ. of North Carolina 225; Univ. of Ottawa 260; Univ. of Scranton 226; Univ. Press of New England 227; Vehicule 261; Verso 229; Verso 261; Wadsworth 230; WalchWhite Cliffs 233; Wiley & Sons, John 235; Louisiana State Univ. 163

Sociology: American Counseling 82; American Press 84; Atheneum Books For Young Readers 87; Avanyu 88; Bantam Books 90; Barricade 91; Blizzard 241; Blue Bird 94; Branden 97; Bucknell Univ. 99; Canadian Inst. of Ukranian Studies 242; Cato Inst. 104; Celestial Arts 105; Center for African-American Studies 268; Cleis 109; Cross Cultural 114; Dancing Jester 115; Davies, Robert 244; Detselig 244; Duncan & Duncan 121; Éditions La Liberté 245; Eerdmans, William B. 124; Enslow 125; Eriksson, Paul S. 125; Fairleigh Dickinson Univ. 126; Fairview 127; Feminist Press at Creative Spark 287; CUNY 127; Free Spirit 130; Glenbridge 131; HarperCollins 136; Hay House 137; Howells House 142; Humanics 142; I.A.A.S. 273; Insight Books 146; Jefferson Univ., Thomas 150; Kaya Prod. 153; Knowledge, Ideas & Trends 154; Kodansha America 154; Lake View 155; Lang, Peter 155; Libraries Unltd. 158; Lincoln Springs 274; Lorimer & Co., James 250; Louisiana State Univ. 163; Love and Logic 163; McClelland & Stewart 251; McFarland &

Co. 164; Mage 165; Maisonneuve 166; Mangajin 275; Markowski Int'l Publishers 289; Mayfield 167; Metamorphous 169; NASW 173; Nelson-Hall 174; Noble Press 177; Nova Science 178; Ohio State Univ. 179; Oxford Univ. 182; Pansophic 183, 278; Pierian 189; Planning/Communications 191; Playwrights Canada 253; Plenum 191; Praeger 192; Random House 197; Rawhide Western 197; Regnery 198; Roxbury 200; Settel Assoc. 291; South End 209; Spectrum 210; Stanford Univ. 211; Steel Balls 281; Summit Publishing Group 214; Teachers College 215; Temple Univ. 216; Third World 217; Thomposon Educ. 258; United Church Publishing House 259; Univ. of Alberta Press 260; Univ. of Arkansas 222; Univ. of Illinois 223; Univ. of Massachusettes 224; Univ. of Montreal 260; Univ. of North Carolina 225; Univ. of Ottawa 260; Univ. of Scranton 226; Univ. Press of New England 227; Vehicule 261; Verso 229, 261; Wadsworth 230; Walch, J. Weston 230; White Cliffs 223; Wiley & Sons, John 235

Software: Adams-Blake Publishing 78; Branden 97; Cardoza 102; Career 102; Cliffs Notes 109; Cypress 115; Dancing Jester 115; Eckert, J.K. 287; Family Album 270; Grapevine 132; Hollow Earth 140; Jist Works 151; Laing Comm. 289; McGraw-Hill Companies (Professional Book Group) 165; MIS 170; National Textbook 173; Neal-Schuman 174; No Starch 177; Nova Press 178; Nova Science 178; One On One 180; Paideia 278; Paradigm 184; Planning/Communications 191; Productive Pub. 254; Resolution Business 280; Richboro 199; Royal Fireworks 200; Schirmer 203; Serendipity Systems 204; Sugar Hill 282; Sulzburger & Graham 213; Summers Press 214; Sunshine 257; Systemsware 282; Technical Analysis of Stocks & Commodities 282; Wadsworth 230; Walch, J. Weston 230; Wiley & Sons, John 235

Spiritual: Acorn 264; Adams Media 78; Alaska Northwest 79; American Press 84; Atheneum Books For Young Readers 87; Avon 88; Bantam Books 90; Barron's 91; Benjamin Co. 286; Bentley, Robert 92; Betterway 93; Blackbirch 93; Blizzard 241; Bonus 95; Bowling Green State Univ. Popular Press 96; Brassey's 97; Broadway Books 99; Bull 99; Carol 103; Cave 104; Cerier, Alison Brown 286; Charlton 243; Children's Press 106; Compass Prods. 286; Contemporary Books 112; Countrysport 113; Creative Spark 287; Crown Publishing Group 115; Databooks 116; David, Jonathan 117; Devyn 119; Down Home 121; Duncan & Duncan 121; E.M. Press, Inc. 122; Eakin Press/Sunbelt Media 122; Ecopress 270; ECW 245; Eriksson, Paul S. 125; Evras 270; Facts On File 126; Fine, Donald 128; Foghorn 129; Graber Prods. 288; Great Quotations 133; HarperCollins 136; HarperCollins Publishers 248; Heritage House 248; Howell Press 141; Human Kinetics 142; ICS Books, Inc. 144; Ideals Children's Books 144; Ivory Tower 150; Jenkins Group 288; Jones Univ., Bob 152; JSA Pub. 288; Kesend, Michael 153; Key Porter 250; LAWCO 274; Learning Works 157; Lerner 157; Lion Books 159; Little, Brown (Children's) 160; Little, Brown 160; Lone Pine 250; Longstreet 162; Lyons & Burford 164; McBooks 275; McClelland & Stewart 251; McFarland & Co. 164; McGraw-Hill Companies (Professional Book Group) 165; McGraw-Hill Ryerson 251; Macmillan Canada 251; Masters Press 167; Maverick Pub. 167; Menasha Ridge 290; Mosaic Press Miniature Books 276; Motorbooks Int'l 172; Mountaineers, The 172; Mustang Pub. 172; Newcastle 176; Nodin 177; Nova Science 178; Orca 252; Paper Chase 183; Parnassus 184; Penguin Books Canada 253; Prentice-Hall Canada Trade 253; Pruett 194; Quintet 254; Ragged Mountain 197; Raincoast Book Distribution 255; Random House 197; St. Martin's 202; Sasquatch 203; Scholastic Canada 256; Silver Moon 291; SJL 207; Stackpole 211; Sterling 212; Summit Publishing Group 214; Tudor 220; Turtle 220; Tuttle, Charles E. 259; Univ. of Illinois 223; Univ. of Iowa 223; Univ. of Nebraska 224; Vital Issues 229; Walker and Co. 230; Warner Books 231; Warwick 231; Warwick Publishing 261; White-Boucke 284; Wieser & Wieser 292; Wilderness Adventure 235; Wilshire 235; Windward 236

Sports: Acorn 264; Adams Media 78; Alaska Northwest 79; American Press 84; Atheneum Books For Young Readers 87; Avon 88; Bantam Books 90; Barron's 91; Benjamin Co. 286; Bentley, Robert 92; Betterway 93; Blackbirch 93; Blizzard 241; Bonus 95; Bowling Green State Univ. Popular Press 96; Brassey's 97; Broadway Books 99; Bull 99; Carol 103; Cave 104; Cerier, Alison Brown 286; Charlton 243; Children's Press 106; Compass Prods. 286; Contemporary Books 112; Countrysport 113; Creative Spark 287; Crown Publishing Group 115; Databooks 116; David, Jonathan 117; Devyn 119; Down Home 121; Duncan & Duncan 121; E.M. Press, Inc. 122; Eakin Press/Sunbelt Media 122; Ecopress 270; ECW 245; Eriksson, Paul S. 125; Evras 270; Facts On File 126; Fine, Donald 128; Foghorn 129; Graber Prods. 288; Great Quotations 133; HarperCollins 136; HarperCollins Publishers 248; Heritage House 248; Howell Press 141; Human Kinetics 142; ICS Books, Inc. 144; Ideals Children's Books 144; Ivory Tower 150; Jenkins Group 288; Jones Univ., Bob 152; JSA Pub. 288; Kesend, Michael 153; Key Porter 250; LAWCO 274; Learning Works 157; Lerner 157; Lion Books 159; Little, Brown 160; Little, Brown (Children's) 160; Lone Pine 250; Longstreet 162; Lyons & Burford 164; McBooks 275; McClelland & Stewart 251; McFarland & Co. 164; McGraw-Hill Companies (Professional Book Group) 165; McGraw-Hill Ryerson 251; Macmillan Canada 251; Masters Press 167; Maverick Pub. 167; Menasha Ridge 290; Mosaic Press Miniature Books 276; Motorbooks Int'l 172; Mountaineers, The 172; Mustang Pub. 172; Newcastle 176; Nodin 177; Nova Science 178; Orca 252;

Paper Chase 183; Parnassus 184; Penguin Books Canada 253; Prentice-Hall Canada Trade 253; Pruett 194; Quintet 254; Ragged Mountain 197; Raincoast Book Distribution 255; Random House 197; St. Martin's 202; Sasquatch 203; Scholastic Canada 256; Silver Moon 291; SJL 207; Stackpole 211; Sterling 212; Summit Publishing Group 214; Tudor 220; Turtle 220; Tuttle, Charles E. 259; Univ. Of Illinois 223; Univ. of Iowa 223; Univ. Of Nebraska 224; Vital Issues 229; Walker and Co. 230; Warner Books 231; Warwick 231; Warwick Publishing 261; White-Boucke 284; Wieser & Wieser 292; Wilderness Adventure 235; Wilshire 235; Windward 236

Technical: Abbott, Langer 74; American Correctional 82; American Nurses 83; ASA 86; Auto Book 265; Bloomberg 94; Branden 97; Brevet 98; Broadway Press 267; Brookline 99; Business McGraw-Hill 100; Butterworth-Heinemann 100; Canadian Plains Research Center 243; ChemTec 244; Cypress 115; Darlington 116; Databooks 116; Drama Publishers 121; Duncan & Duncan 121; Eckert, J.K. 287; Evras 270; Focal 128; Graphic Arts Tech. Found. 132; Great Ocean 272; Hartley & Marks 136; Hatherleigh 137; Hoard & Sons, W.D. 272; Hollow Earth 140; Human Kinetics 142; Initiatives 146; Inst. of Police Tech. & Mgmt. 147; Jelmar Pub. 274; Laing Comm. 289; Lake View 155; Lorien House 275; McFarland & Co. 164; McGraw-Hill Companies (Professional Book Group) 165; Markowski Int'l 166; Metamorphous 169; Neal-Schuman 174; No Starch 177; Nova Press 178; Nova Science 178; Ohio Biological Survey 277; One On One 180; Orchises 180; Oxford Univ. 182; Partners in Publishing 279; Peachpit 185; Pennsylvania Historical and Museum Comm. 187; Pinter 253; Productive Pub. 254; PROMPT Pub. 194; Purich 254; Quintet 254; Reference Press 198; Royal Fireworks 200; SJL 207; Sourcebooks 209; Sterling 212; Sulzburger & Graham 213; Sunshine 257; Sybex 215; Systems Co. 215; Systemsware 282; Technical Books for the Layperson 282; Texas Western 217; Tudor 220; Univ. of Alaska 222; Univ. of Idaho 223; Weka 233; Wiley & Sons, John 235

Textbook: Amacom 81; American Correctional 82; American Hospital 83; American Nurses 83; Anima 265; Arden 86; Art Direction Inc. 86; Baker Books 89; Bandanna 266; Barron's 91; Behrman House 92; Bliss Publishing Co. 266; Blue Poppy 95; Bowling Green State Univ. Popular Press 96; Branden 97; Brassey's 97; Broadview 241; Butterworth-Heinemann 100; Cambridge Univ. 101; Canadian Plains Research Center 243; Center for African-American Studies 268; ChemTec 244; Comic Art 110; Computer Science 111; Course Crafters 287; Cracom 287; Cypress 115; Dancing Jester 115; Davidson, Harlan 117; Dearborn Financial 118; Detselig 244; Duke 121; Eckert, J.K. 287; Eerdmans, William B. 124; Engineering & Management 124; Fitzhenry & Whiteside 246; Focal 128; Friends United 130; Gleason Group 288; Grapevine 132; Graphic Arts Tech. Found. 132; Group Publishing 134; Hanser Gardner 135; Harcourt Brace Jovanovich Canada 247; Herald Press Canada 248; Hiller Box 288; Hoard & Sons, W.D. 272; Howells House 142; Human Kinetics 142; I.A.A.S. 273; Indiana Univ. 146; Inst. of Police Tech. & Mgmt. 147; Institute of Psychological Research, Inc./Institut de Recherches Psychologiques, Inc. 249; Intercultural Press 147; Int'l Found. Employee Benefit Plans 148; Int'l Publishers 148; Jain 150; Jefferson Univ., Thomas 150; Jist Works 151; Kregel 155; Krieger 155; Laing Comm. 289; Lang, Peter 155; McClelland & Stewart 251; Mangajin 275; Media Bridge 168; Meriwether 168; Metamorphous 169; Neal-Schuman 174; Nova Science 178; Ohio Biological Survey 277; Orchises 180; Oxford Univ. 182; Pacific Books 182; Pacific Educ. 253; Pacific Press 182; Pacific View 183; Paideia 278; Partners in Publishing 279; Paulist Press 185; Pencil Point 186; Pinter 253; Precept 192; Professional Publications 193; Prufrock 195; PSI Research 195; Publicom 291; Publishers Resource Group (PRG) 291; Purich 254; Reidmore 256; Royal Fireworks 200; St. Martin's 202; Sandhill Crane 202; Sandlapper 202; SAS Institute Inc. 203; Sibyl 206; Sidran Press 206; Sourcebooks 209; Speech Bin 210; Stanford Univ. 211; Sulzburger & Graham 213; Sunshine 257; Systems Co. 215; Systemsware 282; Technical Books for the Layperson 282; Third World 217; Thompson Educ. 258; Trilobyte 258; Tudor 220; Univ. of Alaska 222; Univ. of Alberta Press 260; Univ. of Idaho 223; Univ. of Montreal 260; Univ. of Ottawa 260; Univ. of New Haven 283; Utah State Univ. 228; Vanderbilt Univ. 228; Wall & Emerson 261; Weidner & Sons 232; Wiley & Sons, John 235; Wisdom 236; Wordware 236; York Press 262

Translation: Aronson, Jason 86; Aztex 89; Barron's 91; Brookline 99; Calyx Books 268; Canadian Inst. of Ukrainian Studies 242; Chatham 106; Citadel 108; Clarkson Potter 108; Cleis 109; Confluence 111; Dancing Jester 115; Dante Univ. of America 116; Davis Pub. 117; Ecco 123; Eerdmans, William B. 124; ETC 125; Evras 270; Feminist Press at CUNY 127; Free Press 130; Goose Lane 246; Guernica 247; Hartley & Marks 136; Harvard Common 136; Hippopotamus 248; Holmes & Meier 141; Hounslow 249; Howells House 142; Indiana Univ. 146; Institute of Psychological Research, Inc./Institut de Recherches Psychologiques, Inc. 249; Intercultural Press 147; Iowa State Univ. 149; Italica 150; Jefferson Univ., Thomas 150; Johnson Books 151; Kaya Prod. 153; Kodansha America 154; Landmine 274; Lang, Peter 155; M.A.P. Prods. 251; McClelland & Stewart 251; Mage 165; Maisonneuve 166; Mangajin 275; Mercury House 168; Motorbooks Int'l 172; Northern Illinois Univ. 277; Ohio Univ. 179; Pacific Books 182; Paulist Press 185;

Post-Apollo 279; Puckerbrush 280; QED 196; Riverrun 200; St. Bede's 201; Spectrum 210; Stone Bridge Press 212; Three Continents 217; Univ. of Alaska 222; Univ. of California 223; Univ. of Massachusetts 224; Univ. of Montreal 260; Univ. of Nebraska 224; Univ. of Ottawa 260; Univ. of Texas 226; Vanderbilt Univ. 228; Wake Forest Univ. 230; White Pine 234; Zephyr 284; Zoland 238

Transportation: ASA 86; Auto Book 265; Aviation Book Co. 265; Bentley, Robert 92; Boston Mills 241; Career 102; Howell Press 141; Iowa State Univ. 149; Markowski Int'l 166; Motorbooks Int'l 172; Sono Nis 257

Travel: Academy Chicago 77; Alaska Northwest 79; Almar 80; Appalachian Mountain Club Books 85; Arcade 85; Atheneum Books For Young Readers 87; Barron's 91; Beachway 266; Blair, John 93; Blue Sky Marketing, Inc. 266; Camino 101; Cardoza 102; Carol 103; Carousel 268; Cave 104; Charles River 268; Chatham 106; Chronicle 107; Compass Prods. 286; Counterpoint 113; Databooks 116; Davies, Robert 244; Dimi 120; Down Home 121; Down The Shore 269; Ecco 123; ECW 245; Ekstasis Editions 246; Epicenter 125; Eriako 287; Eriksson, Paul S. 125; Escart 246; Evras 270; Filter 271; Four Walls Eight Windows 129; Gem Guides 131; Giniger, K S 288; Golden West 132; Graber Prods. 288; HarperCollins 136; HarperCollins Publishers 248; Harvard Common 136; Hastings 137; Heyday 139; Hippocrene 140; Hollow Earth 140; Hounslow 249; Hunter Publishing 143; ICS Books, Inc. 144; Italica 150; Jain 150; Jenkins Group 288; Johnson Books 151; Johnston Associates, Int'l. 274; Kesend, Michael 153; Kodansha America 154; Kurian, George 289; Learning Works 157; Lone Pine 250; Lyons & Burford 164; McClelland & Stewart 251; McDonald & Woodward 164; Mangajin 275; Marlor 167; Maverick Pub. 167; Menasha Ridge 290; Mercury House 168; Mosaic Press Miniature Books 276; Mountain Automation 276; Mountaineers, The 172; Mustang Pub. 172; Neal-Schuman 174; Newjoy 277; Nodin 177; NTC Publishing 179; Ohio Univ. 179; Orca 252; Orca 252; Pacific View 183; Pansophic 183; Pansophic 278; Parnassus 184; Pelican 186; Pennsylvania Historical and Museum Comm. 187; Pilot 190; Prairie Oak 280; Prima 193; Primer Publishers 280; Pruett 194; Quarry 254; Quixote 196; Raincoast Book Distribution 255; Red Deer College 255; RedBrick 280; Riverrun 200; Rockbridge 280; Rocky Mountain Books 256; Rutledge Hill 201; Sasquatch 203; Seaside 204; Settel Assoc. 291; Shoreline 257; Sierra Club 206; Sligo 208; Stone Bridge Press 212; Storm Peak 281; Sulzburger & Graham 213; Tamarack 282; Todd 219; Turnstone 259; Tuttle, Charles E. 259; Umbrella 283; Verso 261; Voyageur 229; Warwick 231; Warwick Publishing 261; Wayfinder 283; Whitecap 262; Whitehorse 284; Wieser & Wieser 292; Wilderness Adventure 235; World Leisure 236; Zephyr 284; Zoland 238

True Crime: Academy Chicago 77; Addison-Wesley Longman 79; Berkley Publishing Group 92; Lifetime Books 158; St. Martin's 202

Women's Issues/Studies: ABC-CLIO 74; Adams Media 78; American Counseling 82; American Nurses 83; Arden 86; Arsenal Pulp 240; Astarte Shell 265; Aurora Editions 240; Bantam Books 90; Barricade 91; Beacon Press 91; Blackbirch 93; Blackbirch Graphics 286; Blizzard 241; Blue Dolphin 94; Bonus 95; Books Beyond Borders LLC 267; Bowling Green State Univ. Popular Press 96; Broadview 241; Broadway Books 99; Broken Jaw 242; Bryant & Dillon 99; Calyx Books 268; Carol 103; Carolina Wren 268; Celestial Arts 105; Center for African-American Studies 268; Charles River 268; Cleis 109; Commune-A-Key 110; Companion 110; Conari 111; Consumer Press 112; Contemporary Books 112; Creative Spark 287; Crossing Press 114; Dancing Jester 115; Davidson, Harlan 117; Davies, Robert 244; Detselig 244; Dowling 269; Duncan & Duncan 121; Elder Books 124; Epicenter 125; Fairleigh Dickinson Univ. 126; Feminist Press at CUNY 127; Focus on the Family 129; Goose Lane 246; Great Quotations 133; HarperCollins Publishers 248; Harvest House 137; Hay House 137; Health Comm. 137; Heinemann 138; Hensley, Virgil 138; Holmes & Meier 141; Human Services Inst. 142; Humanics 142; Hunter House 143; ICS Books, Inc. 144; Ide House 144; Indiana Univ. 146; Inner Traditions Int'l 146; Insight Books 146; Int'l Publishers 148; Ivory Tower 150; Jewish Lights 150; Jewish Pub. Soc. 151; Kaya Prod. 153; Key Porter 250; Knowledge, Ideas & Trends 154; Lake View 155; Liberal Press, The 158; Libraries Unltd. 158; Lincoln Springs 274; Llewellyn 161; Locust Hill 161; Longstreet 162; Lorimer & Co., James 250; M.A.P. Prods. 251; McClelland & Stewart 251; McFarland & Co. 164; Maisonneuve 166; Mayfield 167; Mercury House 168; Michigan State Univ. 169; Milkweed 170; Minnesota Hist. Soc. 170; Monument 170; Negative Capability 174; New Hope 175; New World Library 176; Nicolas-Hays 277; Noble Press 177; Ohio Univ. 179; Oregon Hist. So. 278; Oxford Univ. 182; Paideia 278; Pandora 253; Pansophic 278; Paper Chase 183; Penguin Studio 186; Post-Apollo 279; Praeger 192; PREP 192; Publicom 291; Publishers Assoc. 195; Reference Service 198; Routledge, Inc. 200; Royal Fireworks 200; Scarecrow 203; Shoreline 257; Sibyl 206; Signature Books 206; Sligo 208; Sourcebooks 209; South End 209; Spectrum 210; Steel Balls 281; Stone Bridge Press 212; Sulzburger & Graham 213; Sunshine 257; Swan-Raven 214; Teachers College 215; Temple Univ. 216; Tenth Avenue 292; Texas A&M Univ. 216; Third World 217; Thompson Educ. 258; Thunder Dog 283; Times Books 218; Trilogy

From the publisher of <u>Writer's</u> <u>Digest</u> and <u>Writer's</u> <u>Market</u>

Go One-On-One
With a Published Author

Are you serious about learning to write better? Getting published? Getting paid for what you write? If you're dedicated to your writing, **Writer's Digest School** can put you on the fast track to writing success.

You'll Study With A Professional

Writer's Digest School offers you more than textbooks and assignments. As a student you'll correspond <u>directly with a professional writer</u> who is currently writing **and selling** the kind of material you want to write. You'll learn from a pro who knows from personal experience what it takes to get a manuscript written and published. A writer who can guide you as you work to achieve the same thing. A true mentor.

Work On Your Novel, Short Story,
Nonfiction Book, Or Article

Writer's Digest School offers seven courses: The Novel Writing Workshop, the Nonfiction Book Workshop, Writing & Selling Short Stories, Writing & Selling Nonfiction Articles, Writing Your Personal or Family History, the Writer's Digest Criticism Service and The Secrets of Selling Your Manuscripts. Each course is described on the reverse side.

If you're serious about your writing, you owe it to yourself to check out **Writer's Digest School**. Mail the coupon below today for FREE information! Or call **1-800-759-0963**. (Outside the U.S., call (513) 531-2690 x342.) Writer's Digest School, 1507 Dana Avenue, Cincinnati, Ohio 45207-1005.

Reg. #73-0409H

Send Me Free Information!

I want to write and sell with the help of the professionals at **Writer's Digest School**. Send me free information about the course I've checked below:

☐ Novel Writing Workshop   ☐ Writing & Selling Short Stories

☐ Nonfiction Book Workshop   ☐ Writing & Selling Nonfiction Articles

☐ Writing Your Personal or Family History   ☐ Writer's Digest Criticism Service

☐ The Secrets of Selling Your Manuscripts

Name _____

Address _____

City _____ State _____ Zip + 4 _____

Phone: (Home) (____) _____ (Bus.) (_____) _____

Mail this card today! No postage needed.
Or Call **1-800-759-0963** for free information today.

IWMXX1X7

There are seven **Writer's Digest School** courses to help you write better and sell more:

Novel Writing Workshop. A professional novelist helps you iron out your plot, develop your main characters, write the background for your novel, and complete the opening scene and a summary of your novel's complete story. You'll even identify potential publishers and write a query letter.

Nonfiction Book Workshop. You'll work with your mentor to create a book proposal that you can send directly to a publisher. You'll develop and refine your book idea, write a chapter-by-chapter outline of your subject, line up your sources of information, write sample chapters, and complete your query letter.

Writing & Selling Short Stories. Learn the basics of writing/selling short stories: plotting, characterization, dialogue, theme, conflict, and other elements of a marketable short story. Course includes writing assignments and one complete short story.

Writing & Selling Nonfiction Articles. Master the fundamentals of writing/selling nonfiction articles: finding article ideas, conducting interviews, writing effective query letters and attention-getting leads, targeting your articles to the right publication. Course includes writing assignments and one complete article manuscript (and its revision).

Writing Your Personal or Family History. With the help of a professional writer you'll chronicle your life or your family's. Learn the important steps to documenting your history including researching and organizing your material, continuity, pacing and more!

Writer's Digest Criticism Service. Have your work evaluated by a professional writer before you submit it for pay. Whether you write books, articles, short stories or poetry, you'll get an objective review plus the specific writing and marketing advice that only a professional can provide.

Secrets of Selling Your Manuscripts. Discover all the best-kept secrets for mailing out strategic, targeted manuscript submissions. Learn how to "slant" your writing so you can publish the same material over and over, which publishing houses are your best bet, and much more.

Mail this card today for **FREE** information!

General Index

A double-dagger (‡) precedes listings that are new to this edition. Markets that appeared in the 1996 edition of *Writer's Market* but are not included in this edition are identified by a two-letter code explaining why the market was omitted: **(ED)**—Editorial Decision, **(NS)**—Not Accepting Submissions, **(NR)**—No (or Late) Response to Listing Request, **(OB)**—Out of Business, **(RR)**—Removed by Market's Request, **(UC)**—Unable to Contact, **(RP)**—Business Restructured or Purchased, **(NP)**—No longer Pays or Pays in Copies Only, **(SR)**—Subsidy/Royalty Publisher, **(UF)** Uncertain Future.

More Great Books for Writers!

The Writer's Essential Desk Reference—Get quick, complete, accurate answers to your important writing questions with this companion volume to *Writer's Market*. You'll cover all aspects of the business side of writing—from information on the World Wide Web and other research sites to opportunities with writers' workshops and the basics on taxes and health insurance. *#10485/$24.99/384 pages*

Writing and Selling Your Novel—Write publishable fiction from start to finish with expert advice from professional novelist Jack Bickham! You'll learn how to develop effective work habits, refine your fiction writing technique, and revise and tailor your novels for tightly targeted markets. *#10509/$17.99/208 pages*

The 30-Minute Writer—Write short, snappy articles that make editors sit up and take notice. Full-time freelancer Connie Emerson reveals the many types of quickly-written articles you can sell—from miniprofiles and one-pagers to personal essays. You'll also learn how to match your work to the market as you explore methods for expanding from short articles to columns, and even books! *#10489/$14.99/256 pages/paperback*

Writer's Encyclopedia, Third Edition—Rediscover this popular writer's reference—now with information about electronic resources, plus more than 100 new entries. You'll find facts, figures, definitions and examples designed to answer questions about every discipline connected with writing and help you convey a professional image. *#10464/$22.99/560 pages/62 b&w illus.*

The Writer's Digest Dictionary of Concise Writing—Make your work leaner, crisper and clearer! Under the guidance of professional editor Robert Hartwell Fiske, you'll learn how to rid your work of common say-nothing phrases while making it tighter and easier to read and understand. *#10482/$19.99/352 pages*

The Writer's Digest Sourcebook for Building Believable Characters—Create unforgettable characters as you "attend" a roundtable where six novelists reveal their approaches to characterization. You'll probe your characters' backgrounds, beliefs and desires with a fill-in-the-blanks questionnaire. And a thesaurus of characteristics will help you develop the many other features no character should be without. *#10463/$17.99/288 pages*

The Writer's Legal Guide, Revised Edition—Now the answer to all your legal questions is right at your fingertips! The updated version of this treasured desktop companion contains essential information on business issues, copyright protection and registration, contract negotiation, income taxation, electronic rights and much, much more. *#10478/$19.95/256 pages/paperback*

How to Write Attention-Grabbing Query & Cover Letters—Use the secrets Wood reveals to write queries perfectly tailored, too good to turn down! In this guidebook, you will discover why boldness beats blandness in queries every time, ten basics you must have in your article queries, ten query blunders that can destroy publication chances and much more. *#10462/$17.99/208 pages*

Writing to Sell—You'll discover high-quality writing and marketing counsel in this classic writing guide from well-known agent Scott Meredith. His timeless advice will guide you along the professional writing path as you get help with creating characters, plotting a novel, placing your work, formatting a manuscript, deciphering a publishing contract—even combating a slump! *#10476/$17.99/240 pages*

Discovering the Writer Within: 40 Days to More Imaginative Writing—Uncover the creative individual inside who will, with encouragement, turn secret thoughts and special moments into enduring words. You'll learn how to find something exciting in unremarkable places, write punchy first sentences for imaginary stories, give a voice to inanimate objects and much more! *#10472/$14.99/192 pages/paperback*